ISBN 978-0-428-77806-4
PIBN 11299670

1 MONTH OF FREE READING

at

www.ForgottenBooks.com

By purchasing this book you are eligible for one month membership to ForgottenBooks.com, giving you unlimited access to our entire collection of over 1,000,000 titles via our web site and mobile apps.

To claim your free month visit:

www.forgottenbooks.com/free1299670

* Offer is valid for 45 days from date of purchase. Terms and conditions apply.

U. S. DEPARTMENT OF COMMERCE
SINCLAIR WEEKS, Secretary
WEATHER BUREAU
F. W. REICHELDERFER, Chief

CLIMATOLOGICAL DATA

PENNSYLVANIA

JANUARY 1956
Volume LXI No. 1

ASHEVILLE: 1956

PENNSYLVANIA - JANUARY 1956

WEATHER SUMMARY

GENERAL

Both temperatures and precipitation were deficient again for the third consecutive month, although nearer the usual expectancy than in December. A seasonal temperature oddity occurred in the Atlantic Division which averaged about 2° warmer than last month. However, the other two divisions held to the usual seasonal trend and were slightly colder in January than in December. Precipitation was practically double that in record-dry January 1955 - actually almost triple in the Atlantic Division - but was still substantially below par, although much improved over last month which was another record-breaker for dryness.

The monthly range of temperatures was more moderate than usual, being only from 57° at Donora and Newell on the 7th to -13° at Dubois 7 E on the 26th. The highest was only 2° above the coolest maximum of record (55° in 1925) but the minimum has been excelled in both directions by considerable margins in many past Januarys. Northern and western stations experienced more days than usual when temperatures failed to rise as high as 32°, but the opposite situation prevailed in the southeastern quarter where some stations averaged above normal temperatures for the month.

Of the stations having long-term precipitation averages, all except two registered deficiencies which were mostly quite large, ranging generally from 1 to 2 inches and topped by the departure of -2.97 inches at Lehighton. Distribution of precipitation was fairly uniform over the State with the Ohio Drainage averaging a bit more than elsewhere. Monthly totals ranged from 0.75 inch at Bear Gap to 3.95 inches at Kregar 4 SE while the greatest daily amount was 1.63 inches, measured at Upper Darby on the 11th. Snowfall generally was moderately less than the long-term expectancy, however, totals of 20 inches or more occurred at several stations in the normally snowier areas of the State.

Stations in the southeastern quarter of the State recorded moderately more than usual windiness while slightly less than usual was noted in the extreme west. Available reports indicate that sunshine was slightly more than usually expected in the Philadelphia and Harrisburg areas, considerably more in the Pittsburgh area, and moderately less in the Reading and Scranton areas.

WEATHER DETAILS

The late December cold continued through the first two days of January with a reinforcing cold incursion in central and eastern portions on the 2nd. However, milder air moved into the extreme west portion on the 1st and covered all of the State during the next few days, reaching the warmest levels of the month late in the first week at many stations, particularly those in western and central counties. A fresh Canadian air mass invaded on the 7th, dropping temperatures sharply for two days, but its effects were tempered by a slow-moving disturbance offshore that circulated relatively warm, moist ocean air over the State. Interaction between the warm and cold air produced frequent light rain or snow during the 7th to 13th, and included widespread freezing rain on the 9th-10th. This warm spell produced the highest readings of the month at many stations in the eastern half at the same time as extreme western stations were barely able to maintain seasonable temperatures due to the cooler air in that section. Seasonable temperatures penetrated eastward slowly and predominated generally during the 13th to 18th although there were several air mass changes which tended to neutralize each other to prevent drastic fluctuations.

The 17th marked the beginning of another general precipitation period when a second coastal storm developed from a weak Low that moved eastward from the Great Lakes, and the situation was repeated on the 20th by the arrival of still another Low from the Gulf of Mexico. Precipitation continued with brief interruptions until the 21st, but this time fell almost entirely as snow even near the coast. Spotty light snowfall accompanied the passage of a frontal zone on the 22nd that was promptly followed by a fresh incursion of Canadian air that plunged temperatures to the lowest of the month in many areas during the 23rd to 27th, and in other instances approached the lowest readings that had been established earlier. Moderation took hold rapidly on the 29th as a low pressure area with several centers moved eastward, forcing warm moist air aloft over the colder surface air. The resulting conflict between warm and cold produced general warm rains that were rather copious in the Monongahela Basin, causing minor floods. Cold air followed the northeastward moving disturbance on the 31st, ending the month on the same chilly note with which it began.

WEATHER EFFECTS

Lack of moisture, low temperatures and bare ground much of the month were detrimental to winter grains in some areas of the State. Below average rainfall since October forced some farmers in drier sections to begin hauling water. Frozen ground permitted the hauling of manure to the fields toward the end of the month but otherwise outdoor activities were mostly limited to essential chores and maintenance work.

DESTRUCTIVE STORMS

Freezing rain covered practically all parts of the State on the 9th and 10th, resulting in considerable damage directly from the ice and from traffic accidents due to slippery roads. An unknown number of persons was injured. Local losses were not great but the area affected was so large that total damage to antennas, roofs, trees, wires, and automobiles was estimated at about $1,000,000.

FLOODS

Heavy rains on January 29 and 30, supplemented by snow melt, caused a fast rise along the Monongahela River and its tributaries. Rainfall averaged 1.50 to 1.75 inches over the basin while the water content of the snow cover was estimated to average about 1/2 inch or less, much of which was melted by the above-freezing temperatures. The Monongahela rose rapidly to exceed flood stages by 1 to 3 feet from McKeesport to Lock 5, Brownsville, during the afternoon or night of the 30th then dropped back within the following 24 hours. Estimates of flood damage were not available but were believed minor.

J. E. Stork

SUPPLEMENTAL DATA

Station	Wind direction: Prevailing	Wind direction: Percent of time from prevailing	Wind speed m. p. h.: Average	Wind speed m. p. h.: Fastest mile	Wind speed m. p. h.: Direction of fastest mile	Wind speed m. p. h.: Date of fastest mile	Relative humidity averages - percent: 1:30 a EST	Relative humidity averages - percent: 7:30 a EST	Relative humidity averages - percent: 1:30 p EST	Relative humidity averages - percent: 7:30 p EST	Number of days with precipitation: Trace	Number of days with precipitation: .01–.09	Number of days with precipitation: .10–.49	Number of days with precipitation: .50–.99	Number of days with precipitation: 1.00–1.99	Number of days with precipitation: 2.00 and over	Number of days with precipitation: Total	Percent of possible sunshine	Average sky cover sunrise to sunset
ALLENTOWN WB AIRPORT	NW	23	14.1	-	-	-	74	77	61	70	6	6	6	0	0	0	18	-	7.0
HARRISBURG WB AIRPORT	NW	24	9.2	47	W	30	62	62	53	57	9	4	6	0	0	0	19	46	7.0
PHILADELPHIA WB AIRPORT	N	27	11.3	51	NW	30	71	75	60	65	2	1	10	0	0	0	13	49	7.1
PITTSBURGH WB AIRPORT	NW	18	10.4	29*	WSW	30	84	84	73	78	8	9	7	0	0	0	24	42	7.8
READING WB CITY	-	-	14.4	49	N	8	-	-	-	-	7	3	6	0	0	0	16	39	7.2
SCRANTON WB AIRPORT	NNW	22	7.4	42	W	30	78	80	72	79	16	9	3	0	0	0	28	28	8.0
SHIPPINGPORT WB CITY	-	-	3.3	44‡	WNW	30	-	-	-	-	11	6	4	0	0	0	21	-	-
WILLIAMSPORT WB AIRPORT	-	-	-	-	-	-	-	73	61	65	7	9	5	0	0	0	21	-	7.1

* This datum is obtained by visual observation since recording equipment is not available. It is not necessarily the fastest mile occurring during the period.
‡ Peak Gust

CLIMATOLOGICAL DATA

TABLE 2

Station		Temperature: Average Maximum	Temperature: Average Minimum	Temperature: Average	Temperature: Departure From Normal	Temperature: Highest	Temperature: Date	Temperature: Lowest	Temperature: Date	Temperature: Degree Days	No. of Days Max.: 90° or Above	No. of Days Max.: 32° or Below	No. of Days Min.: 32° or Below	No. of Days Min.: 0° or Below	Precipitation: Total	Precipitation: Departure From Normal	Precipitation: Greatest Day	Precipitation: Date	Snow, Sleet: Total	Snow, Sleet: Max. Depth on Ground	Snow, Sleet: Date	No. of Days: .10 or More	No. of Days: .50 or More	No. of Days: 1.00 or More
ATLANTIC DIVISION																								
ALLENTOWN WB AP	R	36.1	22.3	29.2	.7	49	10	8	2	1103	0	9	28	0	1.68	- 1.53	.43	30	5.1	3	17	6	0	0
ALLENTOWN GAS CO	AM	36.8	22.9	29.9	.4	48	11	9	2	1083	0	6	29	0	2.04	- 1.35	.41	10	5.6	4	17	8	0	0
ALTOONA HORSESHOE CURVE		32.7	19.5	26.1	- 1.8	45	30	5	28	1197	0	15	30	0	2.28	- .69	.52	30	11.0	5	20	8	1	0
ARENDTSVILLE	AM	37.7	21.6	29.7	- .8	48	4+	10	1+	1088	0	10	28	0	1.51	- 1.36	.44	30	4.7			5	0	0
ARTEMAS 1 WNW		38.9	18.6	28.8		48	3+	4	23	1117	0	7	31	0						4	19			0
BEAVERTOWN	AM	35.4M		M		46	11				0	6		0			.33	30		3	20		0	0
BELLEFONTE 4 S	AM	34.7	19.6	27.2	- 1.8	44	16	7	26	1165	0	10	29	0	1.17	- 1.44	.38	10		3	20+	4	0	0
BERWICK		36.4	22.0	29.2		49	10	9	26	1104	0	7	29	0	.87		.26	30	4.3	2	20+	2	0	0
BETHLEHEM LEHIGH UNIV		36.3	24.0	30.2	- .5	48	10	11	2	1072	0	10	28	0	2.00	- 1.41	.43	30	4.5	4	19+	9	0	0
BURNT CABINS 2 NE		34.7	19.9	27.3		44	6	3	24	1160	0	14	30	0	1.92		.48	30		5	19+	5	0	0
CANTON 1 NW	AM	30.0	15.5	22.8		40	11	5	2	1300	0	17	30	0	1.19		.25	20	8.1	4	20+	7	0	0
CARLISLE		38.7	25.5	32.1	3.2	50	10	13	28	1015	0	5	28	0	1.72	- 1.43	.50	30	4.0	3	19+	6	1	0
CHAMBERSBURG 1 ESE		37.7	22.5	30.1	.0	47	6+	7	26	1072	0	6	28	0	1.75	- 1.10	.50	30	6.1	4	19	5	1	0
CHESTER	AM	41.1M	25.9M	33.5M		54	31			972	0	3	26	0	D 2.90		.94	30	.9	0				0
COATESVILLE 1 SW	AM	38.0	21.3	29.7	- .8	48	11+	7	28+	1088	0	7	28	0	2.34	- 1.53	.47	30	8.1	6	20	7	0	0
COLUMBIA		39.9	24.5	32.2		50	3+	10	24	1007	0	3	27	0	1.81		.45	30	5.3	3	20	7	0	0
DEVAULT 1 W		37.6		M		49	30				0	5					1.14	11		6	17		2	1
DIXON	AM	32.7M	17.0M	24.9M		47	11	0	25	1237	0	16	29	1			.29	12	5.2				0	0
DU BOIS 7 E		32.2	16.4	24.3		45	30	-13	26	1253	0	17	30	1	1.38	- 1.54	.30	30	10.5	5	23	6	0	0
EAGLES MERE	AM	28.2	14.5	21.4		40	11	5	9+	1346	0	24	31	0	1.21	- 2.56	.28	31	7.7	7	4+	5	0	0
EMPORIUM 1 E	AM	33.6	16.0	24.8	- 1.4	44	7	- 1	26	1238	0	13	29	1	1.13	- 2.23	.25	20	8.1	3	20+	5	0	0
EPHRATA		38.5	22.5	30.5	- .3	48	10	12	24+	1062	0	2	29	0	1.84	- 1.20	.53	30	4.3			8	1	0
EVERETT 1 SW		36.7	21.4	29.1	.3	50	6+	- 7	28	1105	0	10	30	1	1.88	- .96	.52	19	5.3	4	19+	6	1	0
FREDERICKSVILLE 2 SE	AM																							
FREELAND		29.8	18.8	24.3	- .3	42	11	5	26	1253	0	19	31	0						4	20+		0	0
GEORGE SCHOOL		38.3	22.8	30.6	- .8	50	30	8	28	1062	0	4	27	0	2.32	+ 1.05	.34	30	7.3	5	20+	9	0	0
GETTYSBURG	AM	38.4	24.0	31.2	.8	50	4	12	28	1040	0	8	28	0	1.42	- 1.67	.40	20+	4.0	4	20	5	0	0
GORDON																								
GRATZ 1 N	AM	35.1	21.7	28.4		48	11	11	2	1126	0	11	29	0	1.07		.34	30	2.5	3	20+	4	0	0
HANOVER	AM	38.4	21.5	30.0	- 2.7	51	4	11	28+	1075	0	7	29	0	2.07	- 1.09	.44	20+	6.0	4	20	7	0	0
HARRISBURG WB AP	R	38.0	26.0	32.0	.9	53	10	14	2	1015	0	6	27	0	1.45	- 1.17	.38	30	5.4	4	20	6	0	0
HAWLEY 1 S DAM	AM	30.5	15.2	22.9		43	10+	0	9	1300	0	17	29	3	1.63		.30	31	4.4	3	3	7	0	0
HOLTWOOD		37.1	25.5	31.3	- .7	48	30	14	28	1035	0	7	27	0	1.57	- 1.43	.34	20+	9.5	6	20	6	0	0
HUNTINGDON	AM	36.9	19.8	28.4	- .8	46	7+	7	28+	1127	0	6	29	0	1.48	- 1.60	.33	10+	5.1	4	20+	6	0	0
JIM THORPE		39.3M	22.5	30.9M	3.1	50	6	9	2	1048	0	4	27	0	1.16	- 2.45	.35	30	2.9	2	20	4	0	0

See Reference Notes Following Station Index

Station		Temperature: Average Maximum	Average Minimum	Average	Departure From Normal	Highest	Date	Lowest	Date	Degree Days	No. of Days Max. 90° or Above	Max. 32° or Below	Min. 32° or Below	Min. 0° or Below	Precipitation: Total	Departure From Normal	Greatest Day	Date	Snow, Sleet: Total	Max. Depth on Ground	Date	No. of Days .10 or More	.50 or More	1.00 or More
KEGG		35.5	19.8	27.7		50	30	4	25	1152	0	11	30	0	1.81		.50	19	13.5	5	19+	5	1	0
LANCASTER 2 NE PUMP STA		38.9	21.6	30.3	- .1	48	10	6	28	1067	0	2	29	0	1.88	- 1.28	.51	30	6.0	4	20	8	1	0
LANDISVILLE	AM	36.7	21.8	29.3		49	11	10	2	1100	0	8	29	0	1.45		.51	30	5.2	4	20	5	1	0
LAWRENCEVILLE 2 S	AM	31.1	14.1	22.6	- 2.9	41	31	- 5	25+	1304	0	15	29	5					5.8	4	23+		0	0
LEBANON 2 NW																								
LEWISTOWN	AM	37.8	22.4	30.1		48	16	11	29	1073	0	5	28	0	1.38		.43	10	4.0	3	20	5	0	0
LOCK HAVEN		36.9	22.2	29.6	1.2	47	15	5	24	1092	0	6	29	0	1.55	- 1.38	.44	10	3.8	3	20+	6	0	0
MADERA	AM	31.9	11.6	21.8		45	31	- 6	29	1332	0	17	31	4	1.70		.35	30	4.1	3	20+	6	0	0
MARCUS HOOK		39.5	27.3	33.4	- 2.3	51	30	18	8	972	0	3	23	0	2.14	- 1.31	.45	30	3.6	3	19	7	0	0
MARTINSBURG CAA AP		32.8	19.8	25.3		44	6+	6	28	1191	0	16	30	0	1.53		.56	30	8.2	4	20+	5	1	0
MIDDLETOWN OLMSTED FLD		37.1	25.3	31.2	.1	51	10	14	2+	1043	0	6	28	0	1.93	- 1.12	.47	9	4.6	4	20	7	0	0
MONTROSE 1 E	AM	27.3	15.1	21.2	- 1.9	42	11	2	2+	1350	0	22	30	0	1.48	- 1.15	.32	31	13.0	7	4	5	0	0
MORGANTOWN		36.8	21.3	29.1		48	10+	7	29	1109	0	10	28	0	2.13		.59	30	6.0	3	19+	8	1	0
MT GRETNA 2 SE		39.6	22.0	30.8		52	12	11	28	1053	0	4	28	0	1.68		.36	30	T	0		8	0	0
MT POCONO 2 N AP		30.5	16.8	23.7	.4	42	6	1	2	1276	0	17	29	0	D 1.29	- 2.08	.37	30		2	3+	5	0	0
MUHLENBURG 1 SE		32.7	17.5	25.1		45	10	5	24	1230	0	16	29	0	.92		.30	30	8.5	4	19+	2	0	0
NEWBURG 3 W		38.7	24.8	31.8		56	10	14	8+	1025	0	5	29	0	D 2.13		.47	20	5.0	5	19	7	0	0
NEWPORT	AM	38.7	21.8	30.3		49	11	10	2+	1068	0	3	27	0	1.42	- 1.55	.32	20	3.2	3	20	5	0	0
NORRISTOWN															2.80		.62	12	5.5	4	20+	8	1	0
PALMERTON		35.1	22.3	28.7M	.1	48	10	9	2	1119	0	11	28	0	.98	- 1.85	.29	30	2.5	2	20	3	0	0
PHIL DREXEL INST OF TEC		39.1	27.7	33.4		52	30	18	8+	970	0	2	22	0	2.79		.64	10	7.4	5	20	9	1	0
PHILADELPHIA WB AP	R	38.3	25.9	32.1	- 1.1	51	30	17	27	1011	0	4	25	0	2.30	- 1.07	.38	30	7.0	4	20	10	0	0
PHILADELPHIA PT BREEZE		39.0	29.3	34.2	.0	53	30	20	2	948	0	2	21	0	2.35				5.8				0	0
PHILADELPHIA SHAWMONT		39.9	25.7	32.8	.3	52	30	14	2+	989	0	3	25	0	3.30	- .03	.65	30				11	3	0
PHILADELPHIA CITY	R AM	39.4	28.7	34.1	- .8	52	30	19	2+	954	0	3	22	0	2.50	- .89	.52	11				9	1	0
PHILIPSBURG CAA AP		30.5	16.1	23.3		43	29	4	26	1285	0	21	31	0	2.25		.49	30	10.1	6	20+	6	0	0
PHOENIXVILLE 1 E		40.0	21.6	30.8	- .6	50	30	6	2+	1055	0	1	26	0	2.99	- .60	.67	11	6.0	4	20	9	2	0
PIMPLE HILL	AM	28.5	14.9	21.7		41	7	2	8	1332	0	21	30	0	1.75		.36	13	8.5	3	3+	6	0	0
PLEASANT MOUNT 1 W	AM	27.1M	13.1M	20.1M		41	11	- 8	2	1383	0	20	30	1	1.69	- 1.93	.30	31	15.0	8	3+	8	0	0
PORT CLINTON	AM	38.7	20.6	29.7	.9	51	12	10	2	1090	0	5	31	0	1.42	- 2.16	.40	30	2.0			7	0	0
QUAKERTOWN 1 E		37.3	20.5	28.9	.9	47	10	4	2	1111	0	6	29	0	D 2.85	- .61	.99	30	7.0			10	1	0
READING WB CITY	R	38.4	26.9	32.7	.5	50	10	17	2	995	0	4	27	0	1.54	- 1.61	.47	30	3.8	2	20+	6	0	0
SCRANTON	AM	33.2	19.5	26.4	- 1.8	53	11	8	2	1192	0	16	28	0	.98	- 1.28	.26	31				5	0	0
SCRANTON WB AIRPORT		31.0	19.8	25.4	- 1.5	44	10	8	2	1222	0	19	29	0	1.01	- 1.25	.27	30	4.7	3	23	3	0	0
SELINSGROVE CAA AP		36.1	21.0	28.6	- .1	47	10	8	2+	1124	0	7	28	0	1.17	- 1.84	.37	30	5.0	3	20+	4	0	0
SHIPPENSBURG		38.6	23.8	31.2	.5	48	6+	10	26	1038	0	6	28	0	1.77	- 1.32	.50	30	6.0	4	20	7	1	0
STATE COLLEGE		34.1	21.4	27.8	.7	44	15	11	8+	1149	0	14	30	0	1.39	- 1.52	.45	30		3	19+	4	0	0
STROUDSBURG	AM	36.5	20.3	28.4	1.0	48	11	5	2	1120	0	10	28	0	1.23	- 2.06	.27	10		2	20	5	0	0
TAMARACK 2 S FIRE TWR	AM	29.5	14.5	22.0		40	16	5	9+	1325	0	21	31	0	1.12		.20	20	9.4	4	20+	4	0	0
TOWANDA		33.0	18.6	25.8	- .2	44	30	1	25	1207	0	14	20	0	1.50	- .48	.33	10	7.1	3	23	6	0	0
UPPER DARBY		38.5	24.8	31.7		50	30	15	2+	1027	0	6	27	0	3.03		1.63	11	9.5	3	20+	9	3	1
WELLSBORO 3 S	AM	29.2	14.7	22.0	- 2.3	39	31	3	26	1327	0	18	31	0	1.17	- 1.18	.24	10	10.0	4	20+	4	0	0
WELLSVILLE		38.7	22.4	30.6		51	10	10	1+	1063	0	5	28	0	1.31		.36	29	4.3	3	20	5	0	0
WEST CHESTER	AM	37.4M	22.9M	30.2M	- .6	48	6	10	28	1037	0		28	0	3.07	- .69				4	20			0
WILLIAMSPORT WB AP		35.6	21.8	28.7	.2	47	10	8	25	1115	0	8	28	0	1.48	- 1.11	.35	30	6.3	4	20	5	0	0
YORK 3 SSW PUMP STA		30.7	23.1	31.4	.6	51	3	7	28	1035	0	5	27	0	1.22	- 1.86	.35	30				6	0	0
DIVISION				28.4											1.76				6.1					
OHIO DRAINAGE																								
BAKERSTOWN 3 WNW		33.1	21.5	27.3		46	6	5	23	1160	0	17	30	0			.48	29	7.0	4	19		0	0
BLAIRSVILLE 6 ENE		30.1	17.7	23.9		51	6	5	23	1266	0	24	31	0	3.21	.27	.60	29	23.4	7	19	9	2	0
BRADFORD 4 W RES		31.0	12.7	21.9	- 2.6	42	15	- 8	26	1330	0	18	31	1	1.40	- 1.79	.55	30	12.4	5	20+	4	1	0
BROOKVILLE CAA AIRPORT		32.2	17.6	24.9	- .1	44	30	- 2	26	1237	0	16	30	1	1.45	- 1.75	.39	30	10.8	5	23+	5	0	0
BURGETTSTOWN 2 W	AM	34.5	16.3	25.4		52	7	- 5	24	1220	0	12	30	3	2.01		.55	30		3	20	5	2	0
BUTLER		35.5	22.2	28.9	- 1.0	52	7	4	26	1115	0	9	28	0	1.94	- .93	.55	20	7.0	6	23+	6	1	0
CLARION 3 SW		34.2	18.0	26.1		45	6+	- 5	26	1198	0	9	30	2	1.38	- 2.12	.34	20	8.3	5	20+	5	0	0
CLAYSVILLE 3 W		37.6	17.2	27.4	- 3.6	55	6	- 3	24	1158	0	7	29	3	2.12	- 1.05	.68	30	4.4	3	20+	6	1	0
CONFLUENCE 1 SW DAM	AM	33.2	20.3	26.8		53	7	- 3	28	1179	0	15	30	1	2.68		.86	30	11.5	7	20+	5	2	0
CORRY		30.8	17.9	24.4	- .7	44	6	- 1	26	1251	0	20	30	1	1.62	- 1.76	.48	30	24.0	8	31	5	0	0
COUDERSPORT 2 NW		29.0	14.6	21.8		37	10+	0	26	1332	0	23	31	1	1.60		.39	20	17.7	9	31	6	0	0
DERRY		35.2	20.7	28.0	- 3.0	55	6+	5	28	1142	0	10	29	0	2.75	- .92	.65	29	13.6	9	20+	8	2	0
DONEGAL		29.1	12.7	20.9		48	6	- 3	28	1361	0	24	31	1	3.47		1.29	29	17.1	6	10+	8	2	1
DONORA	AM	37.2	24.3	30.8	- 3.5	57	7	11	24+	1057	0	8	27	0	1.02	- .68	.55	30	6.3	2	10+	7	1	0
EAST BRADY		36.5	19.3	27.9		48	6	- 1	26	1144	0	7	30	1			.50	30	9.5	4	20+		1	0
EBENSBURG		29.5	16.3	22.9	- 3.3	47	30	- 2	28	1296	0	23	31	1	2.64	- .61	.50	20	14.5	7	20+	7	1	0
FARRELL SHARON		34.5	18.3	26.4	- 2.4	51	6	3	27	1189	0	10	30	0			.44	19					0	0
FORD CITY 4 S DAM	AM	33.8	17.0	25.4		52	7	- 1	26	1219	0	11	30	3	1.72		.47	30	5.5	3	20+	5	0	0
FRANKLIN		34.4	19.6	27.0	.3	47	6	3	26	1168	0	10	30	0	1.37	- 2.04	.40	20	8.0	6	23+	5	0	0
GREENVILLE		33.4	18.6	26.0	- 1.6	49	6	- 2	26	1201	0	11	29	2	1.33	- 2.00	.40	30	12.3	4	20+	6	0	0
INDIANA 3 SE		33.7	17.6	25.7	- 3.8	53	6	- 1	26+	1213	0	12	30	3	2.05	- 1.60	.54	29	11.3	4	20+	5	2	0
IRWIN		34.2	21.2	27.7	- 2.9	45	2	4	28	1147	0	11	29	0	2.30	- .58	1.01	29	10.8	4	21+	4	1	1
JAMESTOWN 2 NW	AM	31.6	15.2	23.0		47	7	- 2	23+	1266	0	16	30	3	1.12	- 1.43	.25	30	8.4	3	20+	3	0	0
JOHNSTOWN	AM	35.6	19.7	27.7	- 2.8	56	7	7	28	1151	0	11	29	0	2.00	- 2.08	.93	29	7.6	5	20	3	2	0
KANE 1 NNE	AM	30.6	12.9	21.8		42	7	-10	26	1333	0	20	31	3	1.55	- 2.10	.35	20	18.6	9	30+	5	0	0
LINESVILLE 5 WNW		31.7	16.8	24.3		45	6	- 2	26+	1251	0	17	30	3	1.65	- .99	.47	31	17.8	6	31	7	0	0
MEADVILLE 1 S	AM	31.8	16.8	24.3	- 1.3	47	7	1	23+	1257	0	17	30	0	1.23	- 1.92	.27	31	15.2	4	23+	4	0	0
MERCER 2 NNE		30.5	11.2	20.9		38	4+	- 9	28	1360	0	20	31	4									1	0
MIDLAND DAM 7		33.3	22.1	27.7	- 2.9	44	6	6	24	1151	0	10	29	0	1.58	- 1.09	.43	29	6.5	5	20	5	0	0
NEW CASTLE 1 N		35.1	19.4	27.3	- 1.1	50	6	0	26+	1165	0	9	29	2	1.66	- 1.28	.40	20	6.3			6	0	0

See Reference Notes Following Station Index

1956 - 57 CLIMATOLOGICAL DATA

TABLE 2 - CONTINUED

PENNSYLVANIA
JANUARY 1956

Station	Temperature: Average Maximum	Average Minimum	Average	Departure From Normal	Highest	Date	Lowest	Date	Degree Days	No. of Days Max. 90° or Above	Max. 32° or Below	Min. 32° or Below	Min. 0° or Below	Precipitation: Total	Departure From Normal	Greatest Day	Date	Snow, Sleet Total	Max. Depth on Ground	Date	No. of Days .10 or More	.50 or More	1.00 or More
NEWELL AM	36.1	22.9	29.5	- 3.3	57	7	9	24+	1094	0	13	30	0	3.29	.49	1.50	29		4	19	8	2	1
NEW STANTON	36.1	19.9	28.0	- 3.3	48	6+	5	27	1140	0	7	31	0	1.92	- 1.49	.46	30		4	20+	6	0	0
PITTSBURGH WB AP 2 //R	33.7	21.6	27.7	- 1.3	52	6	9	23+	1149	0	14	29	0	1.90	- .87	.38	30	7.3	4	20+	7	0	0
PITTSBURGH WB CITY R	36.6	25.2	30.9	- 2.1	55	6	15	23+	1050	0	8	27	0	1.75	- 1.08	.48	30	5.3			7	0	0
PUTNEYVILLE 2 SE DAM AM	33.3	14.8	24.1		47	7+	- 3	28+	1260	0	13	31	2	1.25		.39	30	9.5	6	23	4	0	0
RIDGWAY 3 W	32.5	14.7	23.6	- 1.0	44	30	-12	26	1278	0	17	31	3	1.36	- 1.58	.22	20	8.5	5	20+	5	0	0
SALINA 3 W	34.3	19.8	27.1		52	6	3	24+	1165	0	9	30	0	1.87		.44	20	8.5	5	20	6	0	0
SHIPPINGPORT WB	34.7	22.3	28.5		52	6	9	24	1124	0	10	29	0	1.27		.37	30	4.0	4	20+	4	0	0
SLIPPERY ROCK	33.9	18.8	26.4		40	4+	5	26+	1193	0	13	31	0	1.15		.19	30	8.0	5	20	7	0	0
SOMERSET MAIN ST	33.5	17.8	25.7	- 1.2	51	6	- 1	28	1213	0	14	31	1	2.52	- 1.70	.80	29	10.8	6	20+	9	2	0
SPRINGS 1 SW	31.0	15.3	23.2	- 3.9	51	6	- 3	28	1290	0	17	31	3	2.18	- 1.55	.53	29	15.2	11	19+	6	1	0
TIONESTA 2 SE DAM AM	32.8	16.0	24.4		46	7	- 4	26	1250	0	13	30	1	1.33	- 1.14	.33	20	6.5	4	23+	4	0	0
TITUSVILLE WATER WORKS	32.1	15.8	24.0		44	6	- 5	26	1266	0	16	31	1	1.27		.45	30	11.1	4	22+	3	0	0
UNIONTOWN	36.8	21.7	29.3	- 3.8	56	6	7	24+	1101	0	9	29	0	2.92	- .66	.67	29	7.1	5	16+	7	2	0
WARREN	31.8	18.4	25.1	- .9	46	6	2	26	1229	0	17	30	0	1.24	- 1.64	.39	31	10.2	4	31	3	0	0
WAYNESBURG 2 W	37.3	20.1	28.7	- 4.4	55	6	2	26	1117	0	8	29	0	2.63	- .69	.72	30	7.8	4	10	6	2	0
DIVISION			25.9											1.90				10.6					
LAKE DRAINAGE																							
ERIE CAA AIRPORT	30.5	20.8	25.7		44	6	6	25	1213	0	20	29	0	1.31		.66	30	11.5	6	31	4	1	0
SPRINGBORO																							
DIVISION			25.7											1.31				11.5					

See Reference Notes Following Station Index

DAILY PRECIPITATION

PENNSYLVANIA
JANUARY 1956

Table 3

Station	Total	1	2	3	4	5	6	7	8	9	10	11	12	13	14	15	16	17	18	19	20	21	22	23	24	25	26	27	28	29	30	31
ACMETONIA LOCK 3	2.21	T		.03	.05	T		T	T	.01	.35	.12	.36				T	T	T		.30	T	.01	.01	T	T	T	.02		.38	.57	.12
ALLENTOWN WB AP R	1.68	T		.01	T					.29	.01	.09	.16	.10	T	.03	T	.21		.09	.06			T						.20	.43	T
ALLENTOWN GAS CO	2.04		T	T	T					.31	.41	T	.27	.22	.02	T	T	.17			.17			T						T	.40	.27
ALTOONA HORSESHOE CURVE	2.28			.04				.03		.18	.29	.12	.20	.05				.05		.19	.18				T		T			.39	.52	.04
ARENDTSVILLE	1.51										.13	.09	.10				T	.06			.43									.19	.44	.07
ARTEMAS 1 WNW	-									.06	.03		-			.08	.04			.45	.12						.30		.25	.15	-	
AUSTINBURG 2 N	1.28	T	T	.06	T			T	.07	.32	.38	T	T	.12		T	T	T			.28	T		.07			T	T	T	T	.14	.24
BAKERSTOWN 3 WNW	-							T	T	.05	-	-	-						T	.04	T	T		.01		T	T			.48	.35	T
BARNES	1.13	T		T	.10	T		T	T	T	.06							.04			.29	T	T	.08	T			.09		T	.32	.15
BEAR GAP	.79			.02				.02		.10		.10		.03				.02		.13										.04	.20	
BEAVER FALLS	1.48	T		.01	T			T	T	.03	.34	T	.09	T	T			T	T		.35	T	T	.04	.02	T	T	T		.36	.32	.07
BEAVERTOWN	-			-	.04				-	-	.29	.03	.06	.07	.02						.10	.11								.04	.33	.15
BEECH CREEK STATION	1.56			.02	.02				T	.08	.44	.05	.06	.14				T			.25	T		T						.08	.26	.18
BELLEFONTE 4 S	1.17			T	T			T	T	.31	.38	.08		T							.22	T		T						.08	.30	
BERWICK	.87			T	.05			T		.21	.05	.06	.03	.02				.02		.09	.06			T						.02	.26	T
BETHLEHEM	2.23		T	T	T					.29	.42	T	.36	.15	.06	T		.22			.13	T			T					.01	.32	.27
BETHLEHEM LEHIGH UNIV	2.00	T		.02	T					.32	.01	.12	.22	.12	T	.05	T	.25		.14	.10									.22	.43	T
BLAIRSVILLE 6 ENE	3.21			.31				.06	T	.32	.29	.10	.05	.34			.04	.08		.32	.09	.01	.03	.02	.02	T	.04	.02		.60	.54	.19
BLOSERVILLE 1 N	1.46			T				.02		.03	.27	.09	T					T		.20	.11									.18	.55	
BOSWELL 6 WNW	3.39		T	T	.05			T	.05	.21	.35	.07	T	.35				.19	T		.55	.14			T			.06		.47	.59	.27
BRADDOCK LOCK 2	1.83	T		.02	.01			.01	.01	T	.30	.05	.10	T			T	.01	T		.31	T	.02	.01	T	T		.01	T	.36	.55	.06
BRADFORD CNTRL FIRE STA	1.31	.01		.08	.07			.01		.03	.07		.05	T				.02			.29	.02	.01	.05	T	T		T	T	.03	.27	.34
BRADFORD 4 W RES	1.40	T		.12	.03			.03	T	.12	.05	.05						.05		.05	.13		.03	.08	T			.03		.03	.55	.05
BREEZEWOOD	1.82							.02		.28	T	.12					.16	T		.46	T								.32	.46		
BROOKVILLE CAA AIRPORT	1.40		T	.16	T			.02	.02	.25	.02	.01						.04		.17	.06	.01	.09	.02	T		T	T	.08	.12	.39	.01
BRUCETON 1 S	2.10			.04	T					.04	.38	.11	.06	T			T	.04	.04		.37			.04	.05					-	1.05	.02
BUFFALO MILLS	2.21							T			.30	.05	.22	.05				.16			.46									.36	.48	.13
BURGETTSTOWN 2 W	2.01				.02				.01	.02	.32	.03	.12				.01	T	.02		.35							T		.54	.55	.02
BURNT CABINS 2 NE	1.02							.03		.30	.31	T	.03				.06			.42	.05								T	.24	.48	
BUTLER	1.84			.03	.09			.01		.01	.18	T	.13								.55			.08				.01		.35	.39	.11
CAMP HILL	2.00							.02		.14	.20	.22	.20					.02		.27	.17									.33	.43	
CANTON 1 NW	1.10	T	T	.02	T			T	T	.02	.24	.12	.10	.05				T			.25	T	.13	T				T	T	T	.12	.14
CARLISLE	1.72							.02		.05	.22	.30	.05	.01			T	T		.31	.11									.15	.50	T
CARROLLTOWN 2 SSE	1.60	T		T	.05	T		.01	T	.01	.16	.03	.05	.10				.01	T		.21	T		.05	T	T		T		.28	.47	.17
CARTER CAMP 2 W	.88	T		.17	T		T	T	T	T	T	T		T				T			.20			.07	T				T	.06	.13	.22
CEDAR RUN	1.28	T		.05	.01			.02	.03	T	.25	T	T	T				T			.15			.08						.05	.04	.80
CHADDS FORD	-										.10	.20	.25	.10	.05		T	-		T	.33	T								.10	.30	.05
CHAMBERSBURG 1 ESE	1.75							.02		.15	.09	.06	T				.13			.38	.08									.34	.30	
CHARLEROI LOCK 4	2.18	T		.02	T			T	.01	.01	.33	.07	.12	.01			.01	.09	.02		.45	T	T	T	T	T		T		.42	.57	.05
CHESTER	2.90									T	.30	.60	.36	T	D.09		.04	.11			.40									-	.94	.16
CLARENCE 1 E	1.30	T		.03	T	T		T	.02	.05	.24	.01	.04	.12				T			.35	T	T	.04					T	.06	.16	.18
CLARION 3 SW	1.36	T		.06	.15			.01	T	.03	.21	.01	.09						T		.34		T	.06	T				T	T	.27	.17
CLAUSSVILLE	-										.22	.04	.12	.28	.04			.08			.09										.35	-
CLAYSVILLE 3 W	2.12			.01	T			T	.01	.03	.34	.05	.13	.03			.02	.12	T		.35	T		T			T		T	.45	.68	.02
CLEARFIELD	1.67			.16	.05			T		.02	.25		.02	.06				T			.40			.05						.22	.22	.24
CLERMONT	1.70	.03		.15	.36			T	T	.32	.12	.06	T	T				.04	T		.30		T	.16	T	T		T	T	.10	.23	.21
COALDALE 2 NW	.88			.03	.02					.04	.05	.03	.16	.05				.01			.16									.01	.16	.18
COATESVILLE 1 SW	2.34									T	.23	.17	.45	.04	.04			.15			.40									.05	.47	.36
COBAN STATION 2 N	-			.07	.06	.05				.02	.10							.23			.11									.25	-	-
COLUMBIA	1.81			T	T			.23		T	.25	.16	.09	.07			.08	.15		.08	.12								T	.15	.45	
CONFLUENCE 1 SW DAM	2.60	T		T	T			T	T	.02	.22	.06	.04	.02			T	.25	.02	T	.36	T		T	T	T	.04	T		.76	.86	.03
CONFLUENCE 1 NW	2.61	T		T	T	T		T	.04	.01	.20	.02	.03	.04	T		T	.21	.01	T	.39	.03		T	T	T	.03	T	T	.76	.82	.02
CONNELLSVILLE	2.72				.07			T	T	.07	.06	T	.42	.06			T	.36	.06		.20	T								.56	.74	.12
CONSHOHOCKEN	3.16			T						.08	.20	.42	.45	.06	T			.40			.58									.07	.78	.12
COOKSBURG	1.51			.09	.15	.02		.02		.02	.29	T	.10	T				.03	T		.23	T	.01	.09				T		.12	.27	.13
COOKSBURG 2 NNW	1.65			.10	.12	.02		.02		.03	.25	.02	.05					.03	T		.36	T	.01	.09						.12	.29	.12
CORAOPOLIS NEVILLE IS	1.46									.01	.30						.01	T			.30	T	T	T	T		T			-	.83	T
CORRY	1.62	.05	T	.18	.06			.04	.03	.04	.03	.06	T					.04		.11	.14		.06	.03	.04		T	T		.05	.48	.16
COUDERSPORT 2 NW	1.60	.03		.02	.04			.02	.04	.16		.12	T	.06				.02	.01		.39	.03		.14						.09	.12	.31
COUDERSPORT 7 E	.89	.03	T	.08	.04				.05	T	.15	.02	T	T	T			T	T		.20	T		.07	T		T	T		T	.15	.10
COVINGTON	1.55			.02	T			T		T	.58	.11	T	.22				T	T		.26			.05				T	T	T	.13	.18
CREEKSIDE	1.96	T		.15	.09					.01	.30	.08	.04	.02				T			.40			.05						.33	.49	T
CRESSON 2 SE	2.71	T		.03	T	.06	T	T	.04	.03	.34	.08	.11	.28	.02	T		.05	.03		.50	.04	.03	.03	.03			.02		.26	.51	.22
CUSTER CITY 2 W	1.73	.07		.11	.10	.02		.03	.01	.08	.11		.06					.03	T		.25		T	.19	.02	T		.01	T	.14	.16	.34
DANVILLE	1.23			T	.03			T	.03	.04	.33	.03	.05	.26	T						.15			T						T	.21	.12
DERRY	2.79	.09		.17	.08			.06	T	.07	.16	.18	T	T				.10		.30	.28	.04		T	T		T	T		.65	.52	.05
DEVAULT 1 W	-									.30	.32	1.14	.19	.08			T	-		.03	-	.05								.07	.08	
DIXON	-	T		-	.03			T		.19	.22	.08	.29	.11	T			.06			.10	.05		.04		T		T	T	.05	.06	.12
DONEGAL	3.47		T	.03	.03			.02	.05	.20	.17	.22	.02	.03	.01		.15	.80		-.22	.02	T		T	T	T	.02	T	T	1.20	.09	.10
DONORA	1.92			T	T	T		T	T	.01	.32	.31	.05	T		T	T	.11	T	.20	.20	.01		T	T	T	T	T		.36	.55	T
DOYLESTOWN	2.34									.09	.29	.12	.30	.17	T			.18			.33									.16	.70	
DU BOIS 7 E	1.38			.15	T			.03		.09	.16	.02	T	T				.02		.08	.16		T	.14						.21	.30	.02
DUSHORE 3 NE	1.51		T	.03			T	T	T	.09	.33	.10	.12	.29	T			T	.02		.20	T		.05				T	T		.11	.12
EAGLES MERE	1.21			.13	.06			.01	.02	.04	.16	.02	T	.08	T			T			.21	T		.07				T	T	.02	.11	.26
EAST BRADY	-									.04	.31	-	-					.02		.16	.07			.04						.15	.50	.02
EBENSBURG	2.44	T	T	.09	.05	T		T	T	.05	.24	.05	.10	.20				T	.07		.50	T		T	T	T		T		.42	.47	.40
EDINBORO	1.46	.01	T	.08	.12	.02		.02	.01	.05	.06	.02	.11	.01					T		.20	.02	.03	.05	T	.01	T	.01		.02	.30	.51
ELIZABETHTOWN	1.54				.02						.10	.12	.23	.08				.09			.31									.09	.38	.12
EMPORIUM 1 E	1.13	T		.13	.02			.01	.01	.07	.05			.02	T			T			.25		T	.09				T	T	.11	.19	.18
ENGLISH CENTER	.94		T	.09	.01				T	.08	.11	T	.04	T							.28			.01					T	T	.14	.18
EPHRATA	1.84				T					.08	.18	.16	.10	.08				.10		.21	.30									.10	.53	
EQUINUNK	2.03	T		.39	.05					.06	T		.24	.11							.29	.02		.23	.12			T			-	.52
ERIE CAA AIRPORT	1.34	T	T	.12	T			.04	.03	.07	.05	.12	.01	T						.12	.03	T	.02	.02	T	T	T	T	T	.02	.66	T
EVERETT 1 SW	1.88			T				T	T	.28	.08	.17	.03	T			T	T		.52									.12	.30	.38	
FARRELL SHARON	-		.03	.03				T	T	-	.17	.04				.01		T		D.44	D.41	D.33	D.03	T						.16	.33	
FORD CITY 4 S DAM	1.72	T		.05	.03			T		.01	.32	.12	.07					T	T		.27	T	T	.03						.33	.47	.02
FRANKLIN	1.37			.05	.06			.03	.01	.03	.10		.12				T	T			.40	T	.02	.05	.01					.07	.29	.13
FREDERICKSVILLE 2 SE		RECORD MISSING																														
FREELAND	-	T	T	.10	.06					.06	.07	.04	.10	.06	.03				.04		.20	T		T			T	T	T	T	.12	-
GALETON	1.34			.12	T	T	T	.02	.01	.04	.15	.02	T	.02	T			.03			.29			.05				T		.05	.16	.22
GEIGERTOWN	2.41										.34	.13	.48	.28				.30			.29										.52	.19
GEORGE SCHOOL	2.32			.02						.16	.32	.21	.26	.12	.01			.25		.03	.32									.28	.34	
GETTYSBURG	1.42							T	.01		.26	.09	.12	.01				.10			.40									.02	.40	.01
GIFFORD	1.11	T		.01	T			T		.01	T		T	T				T			.02			T	T			T		.32	.24	.51
GLEN HAZEL 2 NE DAM	1.10	.01		.11	.06	T		T	T	.04	.06	.01	T	T				.02	T		.21	T	.01	.11	T	T		.02	T	.08	.26	.10
GLENWILLARD DASH DAM	1.40			.01	.03			T	T	T	.04	.01	.25	T			.04	.02			.35	T		.01	T			T		.35	.45	.03
GORDON		RECORD MISSING																														
GOULDSBORO	1.58	.08	T	.11	.05					.18	.20	.10	.08	.28	T			T			.10	T		.08	.02			.02	T	.02	.08	.23
GRANTVILLE 2 SW	1.09				T			.02		.03	.06	.08		T				.03		.10	.17									.10	.30	
GRATERFORD	2.83									.05	.12	.11	.48	.06	.26			.21			.33									.14	.23	.09
GRATZ 1 N	1.07			T	T				T	T	.32	T	.23	T					T		.08			T				T		T	.34	.10
GREENSBORO LOCK 7	2.76			T				T	T	.02	.20	.14	.10	.05	T		.02	.34	T	D.10	.21	T	T	T	T	T	.07			.52	.82	.17
GREENSBURG 3 SE	2.22			.10	T	T	.02	.08	T	.05	.30	.11	.09				.09	.01	T	.12	.09	.04					.01	.02		.70	.39	T
GREENVILLE	1.33		.03	.18	T			T	.01	.01	.18	.05	T							.25	.14		.03	.02	.01		T			.11	.40	.01
HANOVER	2.07								.02	T	.26	.24	.31	.03	T			.21			.44									.26	.44	.04
HARRISBURG WB AP R	1.46		T	T				T		.21	.02	.16	.08	.09			.07	T		.22	.12			T			T	T	T	.16	.38	T
HARRISBURG NORTH	1.42								.02	T	.25	.06	.15					T			.34									.09	.51	.02
HAWLEY	2.07	T		.15	.02					.12	.20	.34	.29	.46	.03	.01		.06	T		.11	T		.03	T			T	T	.03	.06	.27
HAWLEY 1 S DAM	1.63			.14						T	.29	.27	.18	.27	.02			.03			.11			.01						T	.05	.30
HOLLISTERVILLE	1.76	T	.02	.14	.01		T			.10	.22	.17	.21	.26	.06	T		.01	T		.09	T		.09	.01	T	T	T	T	T	.05	.23
HOLTWOOD	1.57				T				T	T	.18	.08	.10	.01	T			.29			.34									.06	.34	.11
HONESDALE 4 NW	1.79	T		.25	.04					.04	.02	.06	.16	.58	T			T			.09	T		.07				T		.06	.18	.23
HOOVERSVILLE	2.29	T		.01	.08	T		.01	.04	.02	.26	.06	.06	.15				.14	.02		.27	.01	T	T	T	T		.02		.50	.53	.09
HOP BOTTOM 2 SE	-			-	T	.01				.02	.03	.08	-	-	T			T			T	.10		.07				T	T	.01	T	.25
HUNTINGDON	1.46			T	T			T	.01	T	.33	.01	.02	.29							.33	T								.17	.22	.24
HUNTSDALE	1.57								.02	T	.44	.13	.10	T				.05			.27								T	.07	.42	.07
HYNDMAN	2.05							T			.17	.04	.24	.02			T	.08	D.10	T	.38						.02			.46	.03	.01
INDIANA 3 SE	2.05			.11	.06				.02	.04	.26	.65	.03	.02				T			.34			.02	T		T	T		.54	.52	.01
IRWIN	2.38			.09						.05	.38	.18	.06	T			.06	.03			.30	.03		T	T		.03	.06		1.01	.08	.02

Table 3—Continued

DAILY PRECIPITATION

PENNSYLVANIA
JANUARY 1956

Station	Total	1	2	3	4	5	6	7	8	9	10	11	12	13	14	15	16	17	18	19	20	21	22	23	24	25	26	27	28	29	30	31
JAMESTOWN 2 NW	1.12	T		.06	.08	T	T	T	T	.02	.09	T	.08								.22		.02	.03		.02		T	.01	.09	.25	.15
JIM THORPE	1.36	T		.05	.03			T		.03	.09	.13	.07	.10		T		.03	T	.06	.18			T				T	T	.04	.35	T
JOHNSTOWN	2.00	.01		T	T	T		T	.01	.04	.04	.10	T	.88	T		T	.02	.02	.01	.06	T	T	T	.01	T	T	T	T	.93	.58	.02
KANE 1 NNE	1.96	.02		.13	.08	.01		.02	.01	.05	.05		.01		T			.03	T		.35	.01	.01	.10	T	T	T	T	T	.08	.30	.29
KARTHAUS	1.54	T		.08	.02			T	T	.02	.31	.02	.02	.07	T				T		.35	T		.05						.12	.17	.28
KEATING SUMMIT	1.23			.08	.05				.02	.06	.05	T		T				T	T		.27			.12				T		.07	.30	.21
KEGG	1.81			T						.07	.09	.06	.05				.13			.50	T					T	T		.19	.23	.47	
KITTANNING LOCK 7	1.92			.01	.89	T		.01	T	.02	.38	.02	.04					T	T		.47		.02	.06				T		.38	.43	.07
KREBAR 4 SE	3.09		T	.06	.04			.13	.09	.26	.29	.16	.14	.12	.02		.20	.14	T	.48	.07	.02	T	.02	.03	T	.06	T	.04	.89	.71	.04
KRESGEVILLE 3 W	-			.07						-	.04	-	-	.22				-			.14										.17	.19
LAFAYETTE MC KEAN PARK	1.45	T		.11	.09			T	T	.08	.08		T					.03			.31		T	.09						.07	.25	.34
LAKEVILLE 1 NNE	-	T	T	.15	.03					.16	.24	.27	.18	.40	.02	T		.04	T		.13	.04		.06	T					.04	-	-
LANCASTER 2 NE PUMP STA	1.88				T					.01	.22	.22	.12	.15				.17		.08	.25									.17	.51	
LANDISVILLE	1.49									.01	.18	.01	.23	.02				.08			.30									.10	.51	.01
LATROBE	2.24			.14				.03	.01	.17	.18	.05	.07	T			.03	.05		.27	T	T		T			T	T	.22	.59	.43	T
LAWRENCEVILLE 2 S	-	T		T	.08			T	T	.07	.37	.16	T	.12				T			.15	.02		.03				T		T	.08	-
LEBANON 2 NW		RECORD MISSING																														
LEHIGHTON	.97		T	.04	T					.02	T	T	.24	.15	T			.04			.12	T		T						.03	.31	.04
LE ROY	1.47	T		T	T			T	.20	.16	.48	.25	.09	.04			.02			.01	.04				.01						.20	
LEWIS RUN 3 S	1.49	.01		.10	.08	T		T	.03	.05	.06	T	.02	T				.03	T		.26	.01	.01	.07	T	T		.02	T	.08	.26	.38
LEWISTOWN	1.38			T	.03				T	.05	.43	T	T	.09							.20	T								.13	.20	.25
LINESVILLE 5 WNW	1.66	T		.12	.10	.02		T	T	.04	.15	T	.10						T		.20	T	.04	.03	T	.03	T	T		.06	.30	.47
LOCK HAVEN	1.99			.01	.01			T	T	.09	.44	.06	.10	.14				T			.25	T		T				T	T	.08	.14	.29
LONG POND 2 W	1.16	T	.03	.09	.05					.08	.14	.03	.06	.21	.03			.02			.10			.03				T	T	.03	.11	.17
MADERA	1.78			.06	.04	T		.04		.04	.28	.05		.16				T			.25			.08						.24	.35	.13
MAHAFFEY	1.74	T		.09	.07	T		T	.01	T	.27	.05	.02	.02				.01	T		.40	T	T	.10				T		.06	.40	.24
MAPLE GLEN	2.11									.15	.20	.24	.23	.12	T			.04		T	.24									.21	.68	
MAPLETON DEPOT	1.77			.01	.01			T	.01	T	.56	T	.03	.14				T			.37	T								.15	.30	.19
MARCUS HOOK	2.14									.10	.38	.37	.12	.08	.02		T	.02		.26	.08									.36	.45	
MARION CENTER 2 SE	2.35	T		.14	.11	T			.03	.85	.34	.08	.04	.04				.07	.06	T	.26	T	.04	.09				T		.44	.45	.11
MARTINSBURG CAA AP	1.53		T	.01				.02	.02	.08	.10	.08	.13	T			.06	.01		.26	.06	T		T	T		T	T	.06	.10	.56	T
MATAMORAS	1.90			.05	.04					.06	.29	.16	.27	.24	.20			.09			.09											.41
MAYBURG	-	T		-	.20			.03	T	T	.09							.03			.28		.03	.10	T			T	T	T	.29	.43
MC CONNELLSBURG	1.73				T				.02	T	.41	.04	.03	.03				.03	T		.36									.31	.46	.04
MC KEESPORT	2.08			.02	.05			.01		.02	.32	.12	.04				T	.02	.03		.40	.02		T	T		T		T	T	T	1.03
MEADVILLE 1 S	1.23	.01		.08	.14	T		.01	T	.01	.05	T	.06	T				T	T		.24	T	.01	.06		T	T	T	T	.04	.25	.27
MEDIX RUN	1.38	T	T	.10	.06	T		.01	T	.03	.22	.02	T	.06				T	T		.29	.02	T	.08	T	T		T	T	.10	.23	.16
MERCER 2 NNE	-			.05				-		-	.05									.01	.59			-						-	-	-
MERCERSBURG	-										.30	-	-	.09				.07			.44									.78	.56	
MEYERSDALE	2.52							T	T	.05	.23	.10	.10	.10			T	.16	T	.05	.38	T	T	T			.10	T		.48	.70	.07
MIDDLETOWN OLMSTED FLD	1.99		T	T				T		.47	T	.18	.11	.22			.09	.02		.37	.13			T						.04	.33	
MIDLAND DAM 7	1.58			T	.02			T	T	.01	.19	.02	.12	.02			.01	.01			.34	T	T	.02			T	T		.43	.40	.03
MILANVILLE	2.34			.24	.08					.06	.16	.12	.17	.59	T			.06			.13			.20						.06	.06	.41
MILLHEIM	1.22	T	T	.01	.01			T	.01	.05	.20	.02	T	T	T			T	T		.24	T		T				T	T	.10	.25	.14
MILLVILLE 2 SW	.96	T	T	.03	.03	T		T	T	T	.17	.03	.03	.12				T			.16	T		T				T		.03	.10	.26
MILROY	1.16			.02	.01			T	.01	.02	.22	.01		.03	T						.25	.02							T	.09	.32	.16
MONTROSE 1 E	1.48	T	T	.10	.15		T		T	.08	.09	.12	.31	.06	T	T		T	T		.08	.01	T	.04	T	T	T	T	T	.08	.06	.32
MORGANTOWN	2.13			T						.27	.10	.16	.22	.08			T	.14		.20	.08									.19	.59	
MT GRETNA 2 SE	1.68			T				T		.13	.03	.20	.17	.12			.17	T		.26										.24	.36	
MT POCONO 2 N AP	1.29	D.10		.20						.10	.09	.07	.15	.08		T		.01		.02	.07			.01						.02	.37	
MUHLENBURG 1 SE	.92	.01	.07					.02		.08	.07	.01		.01				.02		.24	.01		.02	.01						.04	.30	.01
MYERSTOWN	1.46									T	.16	.05	.14	.18	.13			T			.31									T	.41	.08
NATRONA LOCK 4	1.74	T		.01	.03			T	T	.04	.31	.09	.09								.28	T		.03	T			T		.32	.43	.11
NESHAMINY FALLS																																
NEWBURG 3 W	2.15									.30	.08	.15					T	D.30		D.20	.47									.30	.33	
NEW CASTLE 1 N	1.66			.03	.04	T		.01	T	.05	.17	.07	.12	T	T				T	.05	.40	T		.08	.03		T	.01		.20	.18	.22
NEWELL	3.29									.01	.20	.20	.18				.16		.23	.11										1.50	.70	
NEW PARK	1.72									.08	.11	.18	.15					.11		.21	.05									.21	.66	
NEWPORT	1.42			T	T				T	T	.30	.07	.12	.02	T			T			.32									.02	.30	.27
NEW STANTON	1.92		T	.01				T	.01	.21	.18	.02	T				.09	.05		.31	.02	T			T		.02		.30	.24	.46	T
NEW TRIPOLI	1.13			T	.04					.10	.02	.11	.09	.07				.06		.04	.12			T						.08	.40	
NORRISTOWN	2.80				.01					.01	.26	.25	.62	.06	.18			.21			.38									.03	.48	.31
NORTH EAST 2 SE	1.70			.07	.12	.02		.14	.04	.04	.13	.02	.16					.02			.14	.04	.03	.03	T	T	.02	.01		.09	.25	.33
ORWELL 3 N	1.25	T	T	.04	.10				.18	T	.05	.13	.26	.09				.02			.13	.02		.04		T	T	T	T	.01	.14	.04
PALM	-									.10	-	.05	.20	.08	.28			.20			.30									.08	.32	.42
PALMERTON	.98			.05						.13	.01	.06	.20	.06			T	.04		.03	.02			T						.09	.29	T
PARKER	1.37			T	.06	T		T	T	.03	.17	.02	.04					T	T		.37	T	T	.07	T	T				.24	.28	.09
PAUPACK 2 WNW	2.10			.12						.12	.43	.10	.42	.32	.11			.02			.18			.04	.01					.02	.12	.18
PECKS POND	1.72	T		.16	T					.10	.30	.07	.19	.31	.02			.05			.07			.01								.44
PHIL DREXEL INST OF TEC	2.70			T						.22	.64	.30	.24	.07	.03		T	.20		.20	.10									.38	.41	
PHILADELPHIA WB AP R	2.30			T						.19	.35	.33	.14	.10	.03		T	.12		.19	.11									.36	.38	
PHILADELPHIA PT BREEZE	2.35			T						.17	.36	.38	.16	.04	.06			.18		*	.42									.23	.35	
PHILADELPHIA SHAWMONT	3.30									.10	.96	.60	.27	.15	.10			.20		.10	.38									.20	.65	
PHILADELPHIA CITY R	2.50			T						.18	.42	.52	.17	.07	.02		T	.13		.20	.12									.26	.41	
PHILIPSBURG CAA AP	2.25	T	.07	.01	T			.08	T	.22	.06	T	.43	T				.01		.31	.15	T	.03	.04	T	T	T	.01	.01	.31	.49	.02
PHOENIXVILLE 1 E	2.99									.02	.37	.67	.16	.24				.25		.22	.12									.29	.65	
PIKES CREEK	.95	T	T	.08	.03	T		.01	T	.02	.06	.03	.09	T	T			T	T	T	.14	T		.06			T	T	T	.02	.10	.33
PIMPLE HILL	1.79	.01	.02	.17	.03	T	T		T	.15	.15	.06	.09	.36	.01	T	T	.07	.01		.17	.01	T	.05	T	T	T	.01	T	.06	.27	.05
PINE GROVE 1 NE	1.12			T	.03				T	T	.13	.03	.08	.15				T			.21			T				T			.39	.10
PITTSBURGH WB AP 2 //R	1.90		T	T	T			.03	.01	.14	.21	.17	.02	T		T	.07	T		.33	.02	.02	.01	T	T		.02		.32	.14	.38	.01
PITTSBURGH WB CITY R	1.75		T	.01	T			T	T	.16	.15	.11	.05				.03	T		.36	.02	T	T	T	T		T		.20	.18	.48	T
PLEASANT MOUNT 1 W	1.60	.02		.15	.11		.01	T		.05	.05	.09	.22	.19	.02	T		.02	T		.13	.03		.11	.01	T	T	.02	T	.06	.10	.30
PORT CLINTON	1.42				.02					.05	.26		.15	.15				.11			.13									.05	.40	.10
PORTLAND		RECORD MISSING																														
POTTSTOWN	-			T						.02	.10	.20	-	-				.37		D.30	.31									.04	.54	.22
POTTSVILLE PALO ALTO BR	.90			.01					T	.02	.15	.07	.06	.01				.01			.15			T						.03	.36	.03
PUTNEYVILLE 2 SE DAM	1.25	T		.07	.05			T		.03	.12	.08	.02					T	T		.15	T	T	.07						.22	.39	.05
QUAKERTOWN 1 E	2.88			.10						.20	.16	.10	.25	.17	T			D.40		D.30										.20	.99	
RAYMOND	1.58	T		.10	T				.10	.20	T	.25	T	T				T			.35			.13	T		T	T	T	T	.08	.32
READING WB CITY R	1.54	T		T				T		.13	.04	.24	.11	.08	T		T	.08		.17	T			T						.22	.47	
RENOVO	1.66			.05	.04			T	T	.02	.30	.03		.04			T	T			.20	.02		.01						.03	.18	.14
REW	1.27	.01	.03	.08	.07	T		.04	.08	.09	.08	.03	.02	.01				.02	T		.20	T	T	.03	.01	T		.01	T	.03	.23	.20
RICES LANDING L 6	2.24							T	.01	.01	.26	.18	.04	.03			.03	.13			.30	.01								.55	.65	.04
RIDGWAY 3 W	1.36			.07	.09	T		.02		T	.15	.02	.01					.01			.32	T	.02	.08						.12	.20	.25
RUSH	1.78	T		.04	.11					.15	.18	.17	.42	.05				T	.03		.10			.06				T		.09	.18	.20
RUSHVILLE	1.48	T		.02	.07					.12	.20	.15	.30	.15		T		T			.12			.05				T		.05	.08	.17
SAGAMORE 1 S	1.76			.15	.18				T	T	.20	.15	T					T			.35			.08						.28	.22	.15
SALINA 3 W	1.87			.12				T		.02	.31	.09	.02							.19	.21		T	T			.01			.44	.42	.04
SAXTON	1.03	T		T		T		T	T	T	.24	.06	.05	.08				.05	T		.55	T						T		.28	.43	.09
SCHENLEY L 5	2.16	T		.02	.07			.01	.01	T	.60	.16	.06					T	T		.22	T	.01	.04				T		.37	.54	.02
SCRANTON	.98			.01	.07	T	T		T	.02	.14	.12	.16	.02				T			.02	T	T	.01	T		T				.13	.26
SCRANTON WB AIRPORT	1.01	T	T	.01	T	T		T	T	.10	.07	.08	.12	.06	T			T	T	.04	.08	.01	T	.07	T	T	T	T	T	T	.27	.01
SELINSGROVE CAA AP	1.17		T	.03	T			.01		.26	.03	.10	.02	.05				T		.15	.07			T			T	T	T	.06	.37	T
SHAMOKIN	1.26			T	.02				T	T	.38	.08	.09	.07	.07						.15			T						T	.33	.07
SHIPPENSBURG	1.77		T	T				T		.15	.38	.10	.05	T			T	.07		.23	.13									.24	.50	T
SHIPPINGPORT WB	1.27			T				T	T	.01	.13	.03	T	T			.02	.01		.28	.03	T	T	T	T		T		.34	.05	.37	T
SINNEMAHONING	1.19	T	T	.09	.05	T		T	.01	.05	.22	T	T	.06				T	T		.22	.01	T	.07		T			T	.06	.17	.16
SLIPPERY ROCK	1.15			.05	.10	.02			T	.02	.17		.10								.16		T	.08	T			T		.16	.19	.10
SOMERSET FAIRVIEW ST	2.76	T		.03				T	.03	.06	.24		.11	.12	T		D.10	.24	.07	T	.25	T		T			T	T		.06	.65	.20
SOMERSET MAIN ST	2.52			.04				.03	T	.05	.24	.16	.03	.12			.15	.11		.16	.10						.01	T		.80	.56	.02
SOUTH MOUNTAIN	2.17								.02	T	.30	.13	.12					.17			.47						T			.28	.51	.08
SPRINGBORO		RECORD MISSING																														
SPRING GROVE	1.83							.01		.04	.41	.12	.07	T				.14		.13	.24									*	.67	
SPRINGS 1 SW	2.18			T	T			.05	.03	.09	.16	.16	.08	.05			.30	.04		.39	.04				T		.03	T		.53	.23	T
STATE COLLEGE	1.39		T	T	T			.04		.33	.11	.07	.02	T				T		.25	.04	T		T				T	.04	.04	.45	T
STRAUSSTOWN	.98			T					T	T	.10	T	.07	.05				.04			.17									.05	.34	.16
STROUDSBURG	1.23			.06						.05	.27	.01	.10	.14				.03			.08									.07	.25	.17
STUMP CREEK	1.03			.03				.01		.01	.25	.03						T			.22	T		.03						.22	.25	T
SUNBURY	1.32			.02	.04			T	T	.03	.35	T	T	.14	T				T		.28	.02		T						.05	.19	.20
SUSQUEHANNA	1.62	T		.16	.06					.10	.04	.15	.20	.08		.02					.17	.02		.07	T	.02	T	.03		T	.16	.27

See Reference Notes Following Station Index

DAILY PRECIPITATION

Table 3-Continued

Station	Total	1	2	3	4	5	6	7	8	9	10	11	12	13	14	15	16	17	18	19	20	21	22	23	24	25	26	27	28	29	30	31
SUTERSVILLE	2.37			.03	.03	T		T	T	.05	.34	.08	.14	T			T	.09	.04		.39			T	.05	T		T		*	1.10	.03
TAMAQUA	1.12			.03	.03					.04	.14	.05	.18	.03				.05			.15			.02						T	.27	.13
TAMAQUA 4 N DAM	3.49			.02					.03	1.12			.02	T							1.15											1.15
TAMARACK 2 S FIRE TWR	1.12	T	T	.21	.04			T	.03	.03	.15	.01	.01	.09				.01			.29	T	T	.06				T	T	.03	.06	.14
TIONESTA 2 SE DAM	1.33			.07	.08	T		.02	T	T	.07	T	.06					.03	T		.33	T	T	.05	T	T	T	T		.11	.32	.19
TITUSVILLE WATER WORKS	1.27	T	.01	.18	T	T		T	T	.04	.05	.07	T					T		.07	.15	T	.06	.04	.02			T		.06	.45	.07
TORPEDO 4 W	1.58	.02		.20	.10			.03	.04	.05	.02	.06	T	T				.03	T		.20	T	.05	.10	T	T		T		.09	.29	.35
TOWANDA	1.50	T	T	T	.08			T	T	.09	.33	.20	.16	.16	T	T		.01	T		.16	.02		.04		T	T	T	T	.02	.05	.21
TOWER CITY 5 SW	1.18			.02	.02			T		.09	.13	.12	.02					.04		.07	.16									.05	.46	
TROY	1.96	.02		.01	.06			T	T	.10	.65	.41	.05	.09	T			.01	T		.18	T		.10				T			.12	.16
TURLEPOINT 4 NE	1.37	.02		.04	.05			.03	.03	.15	.10	T		.02				.01	T		.23			.12				.01	T	.09	.17	.34
TYRONE 4 NE BALD EAGLE	1.36			.03	T				T	T	.12	T	.01	.04				T	T		.37	T		.01						.15	.29	.34
UNION CITY	1.38	T	T	.08	.11	T		.02	T	.81	.03	T	.05	T				T	T		.31	T	.03	.03	.03	.04		T		.03	.27	.34
UNIONTOWN	2.92			T	T			.07	.02	.09	.22	.27	.09	.02			.34	T		.23	.05	T		T	T	T	.03		.20	.67	.62	T
UPPER DARBY	3.93									.17	.52	1.65	.20	.17	.04			.32		.11	.12									.09	.56	
UTICA	1.22			.01	.12			.01	.01	.01	.07		.10	.01							.24		.02	.08						.11	.28	.15
VANDERGRIFT	2.10			T	.17			T	T	T	.37	.08	.21								.38	T						T		.29	.48	.12
VIRGINVILLE	1.18				T					T	T	.09	.14	.21	.07			.07			.08									T	.38	.14
VOWINCKEL	1.81			.08	.12	.05		.02		.03	.21	T	.09					.04	T		.35	T	.01	.13						.12	.33	.23
VOWINCKEL 1 WSW	1.56			.07	.10	.02		.02	.02	.02	.18	T	.08					.02	T		.25	T	.01	.15						.12	.24	.25
WARREN	1.24	T		.03	.06			.02	.02	.04	.03	T	.09					.01			.25		T	.07			T	T		.03	.20	.39
WATSONTOWN	1.13			D.05						D.03	.20	.10									D.30										.25	.20
WAYNESBURG 2 W	2.03			.01				T	T	.07	.23	.08	.09	.03			.03	.20			.40	T	T				.10	T	T	.66	.72	.01
WELLSBORO 3 S	1.17	T	T	.08	T			T	.02	.06	.24	.12	.06	.08				T			.23	T		.05			T	T	T	T	.08	.15
WELLSVILLE	1.31							.02		.06	.27	.05	T	.10				.06		.08	.15								.16	.36	T	
WERNERSVILLE 1 W	1.78										.14	.07	.27	.10	.11		.03				.30									.04	.46	.26
WEST CHESTER	3.07			.01						.38	.46	.49	.04	.08				.26			.38									*	.56	.41
WEST GROVE 1 E	2.72									T	.21	.95	.21	.03				.22			.43									.27	.33	.47
WEST HICKORY	1.32			.04	.11			.03		.03	.04		.10					.05			.23			.08						.08	.28	.25
WHITESBURG	2.01									.10	.38	.10	.08								.34			.09				T		.45	.43	.04
WILKES BARRE	.79	T	T	T	.01				T	.05	.09	.04	.08	.07	T	T		T			.10	T		.07	T		T	T	T	T	.08	.20
WILLIAMSBURG	1.89			.05	.02			T	.02	T	.45	.05	.06	.10				T	T		.20									.29	.45	.20
WILLIAMSPORT WB AP	1.48	T	.02	.07	T			.01	T	.25	.02	.18	.06					T		.28	.10		T	.02			T	T	.01	.07	.35	.04
WOLFSBURG	1.74							T			.14	.04	.19	.05				.11			.42									.32	.46	.03
YORK 3 SSW PUMP STA	1.22							.02		.02	.08	.11	.02	.01				.10		.13	.21			T						.17	.35	
YORK HAVEN	1.24				.01				T		.13	.05	.13	.05				.09			.28									.07	.38	.05
ZION GROVE	1.01									.09	.22	.05	.14								.13									T	.25	.13
ZIONSVILLE 3 SE	1.95			T	T					.06	.30	T	.31	.12	.04		T	.24			.12									.02	.32	.42

Table 5

DAILY TEMPERATURES

PENNSYLVANIA
JANUARY 1956

Station		1	2	3	4	5	6	7	8	9	10	11	12	13	14	15	16	17	18	19	20	21	22	23	24	25	26	27	28	29	30	31	Average
ALLENTOWN WB AP	MAX	34	31	36	43	40	45	33	23	46	40	43	42	35	33	37	43	32	37	30	31	32	38	33	32	33	31	32	38	34	43	34	36.1
	MIN	12	8	20	24	29	24	17	14	17	43	39	35	29	24	25	23	24	22	19	21	18	19	18	17	17	15	18	13	26	31	22	22.3
ALLENTOWN GAS CO	MAX	34	25	31	38	43	42	45	34	27	47	48	43	42	35	34	39	43	35	38	31	32	38	40	34	34	33	30	33	35	37	43	36.8
	MIN	22	9	11	27	27	28	21	14	15	25	40	39	32	25	25	24	26	24	23	22	19	20	30	18	18	17	17	16	16	30	30	22.9
ALTOONA HORSESHOE CURVE	MAX	32	29	38	38	34	40	31	24	21	37	39	36	33	33	37	33	31	34	32	27	32	36	33	27	30	36	29	30	37	45	29	32.7
	MIN	19	12	27	29	26	23	21	13	13	18	34	29	24	17	17	23	21	19	18	22	18	27	9	12	19	9	9	5	27	28	21	19.5
ARENDTSVILLE	MAX	32	36	31	48	40	43	46	30	29	44	48	42	41	39	42	46	41	34	43	29	36	37	43	28	30	32	38	32	34	36	47	37.7
	MIN	10	11	17	27	26	20	21	17	16	24	40	38	33	28	28	25	26	24	24	25	17	19	23	11	12	10	13	12	15	31	27	21.6
ARTEMAS 1 WNW	MAX	45	43	48	45	47	47	30	27	42	44	42	41	42	40	44	38	43	38	32	34	34	44	31	30	32	36	34	30	48	39	36	38.9
	MIN	16	15	26	23	22	20	13	16	22	30	32	26	20	16	25	20	16	12	22	22	24	17	4	7	10	14	17	10	27	19	17	19.6
BAKERSTOWN 3 WNW	MAX	32	40	38	35	34	46	38	26	22	34	35	34	33	31	34	32	31	32	31	29	30	31	32	28	28	27	31	38	42	45	28	33.1
	MIN	18	24	34	28	27	28	24	14	16	16	32	30	24	19	20	27	22	21	26	24	22	26	5	10	16	9	16	11	31	28	19	21.5
BEAVERTOWN	MAX	35	31	40	37	43	40	30	27	31	45	46	40	40		45	41	35	41	31	35	32	39	38	33	36	33	33	36	34	38	35	35.4
	MIN																																
BELLEFONTE 4 S	MAX	27	33	33	40	36	40	42	28	25	36	41	39	37	35	40	44	36	30	40	26	31	39	27	28	31	31	33	31	34	37	43	34.7
	MIN	18	14	19	31	29	25	23	14	12	16	34	35	29	21	19	21	23	17	20	23	16	13	14	12	13	7	11	11	11	32	25	19.6
BERWICK	MAX	33	30	40	38	39	39	34	26	32	49	47	41	37	35	41	41	35	40	34	37	35	37	36	32	29	39	31	35	35	44	36	36.4
	MIN	21	10	29	27	27	28	25	15	12	30	39	35	31	24	27	21	23	19	18	21	13	20	21	12	10	9	19	10	25	32	28	22.0
BETHLEHEM LEHIGH UNIV	MAX	35	32	37	43	40	45	32	25	45	48	42	40	34	32	37	44	38	39	31	33	34	40	30	32	32	31	31	35	36	41	33	36.3
	MIN	19	11	30	27	30	22	14	13	20	42	39	34	29	24	28	27	25	25	22	21	19	28	21	18	19	18	20	19	25	32	26	24.0
BLAIRSVILLE 6 ENE	MAX	29	32	36	35	30	51	41	19	18	28	32	32	29	28	26	32	21	27	27	29	26	31	30	21	26	24	24	35	44	48	23	30.1
	MIN	13	20	29	26	22	24	14	9	10	18	24	26	21	15	11	24	18	17	18	19	17	23	5	8	14	14	14	10	30	21	16	17.7
BRADFORD 4 W RES	MAX	31	28	33	33	28	40	36	17	20	38	35	33	27	31	42	37	32	35	32	25	30	30	27	24	28	25	24	34	40	30	26	31.0
	MIN	15	3	23	24	23	21	14	4	6	17	28	23	17	9	3	9	15	7	6	9	6	19	5	3	8	-8	13	5	26	24	18	12.7
BROOKVILLE CAA AIRPORT	MAX	29	33	34	32	33	43	31	23	25	42	37	34	35	35	37	36	25	37	26	28	32	32	26	28	29	28	27	33	40	44	26	32.2
	MIN	15	18	32	27	16	16	15	11	13	25	34	26	23	15	13	20	20	20	18	14	16	25	4	13	14	-2	14	3	32	22	13	17.6
BURGETTSTOWN 2 W	MAX	26	38	42	40	33	39	52	27	25	33	37	36	32	36	32	35	33	28	35	33	31	34	37	24	30	28	29	30	44	44	46	34.5
	MIN	8	8	21	22	26	17	23	15	15	19	32	31	25	19	13	19	22	23	20	25	23	25	2	-5	2	-2	1	0	3	34	20	16.3
BURNT CABINS 2 NE	MAX	32	32	42	42	38	44	32	25	29	39	42	41	34	36	42	32	32	37	25	31	36	40	35	27	29	30	32	32	34	38	33	34.7
	MIN	16	14	31	27	23	19	18	15	15	28	37	32	28	23	18	25	25	21	20	22	16	23	12	3	8	5	16	8	26	27	17	19.9
BUTLER	MAX	30	35	39	37	33	48	52	27	27	39	41	37	33	36	38	38	36	37	38	31	31	33	35	25	28	30	28	44	46	37	33	35.5
	MIN	14	21	33	31	27	20	24	20	14	21	35	31	25	19	16	26	22	23	23	23	22	25	8	13	20	4	13	27	35	32	20	22.2
CANTON 1 NW	MAX	28	24	29	35	33	33	33	21	16	39	40	37	33	28	30	35	34	26	33	23	22	34	30	27	24	29	24	25	32	35	30	30.0
	MIN	17	5	10	27	26	24	20	10	7	14	35	30	25	14	14	17	19	13	14	17	11	13	8	6	8	6	8	7	9	25	21	19.5
CARLISLE	MAX	35	32	36	42	44	44	38	30	32	50	47	42	41	43	46	42	39	43	37	36	37	42	38	38	31	32	33	35	34	44	40	38.7
	MIN	23	15	24	24	32	24	24	19	16	32	32	40	35	29	32	27	29	28	24	26	20	29	24	19	10	17	22	13	28	34	30	25.3
CHAMBERSBURG 1 ESE	MAX	36	34	46	41	44	47	31	29	33	47	43	40	40	41	47	38	34	42	30	37	30	40	36	31	30	30	33	34	36	46	33	37.7
	MIN	18	14	31	26	27	19	20	18	18	33	38	35	32	26	26	25	26	24	23	25	13	25	19	10	9	7	16	19	31	30	24	22.5
CHESTER	MAX		38	48	41	45	45	47		35	48	48	45	44	40		45	48	35	40	33	41		42	37	31	34	32	34		41	54	41.1
	MIN		18	24	31	35	31	26		12	38	40	39	34	29		29	27	25	26	27	22		20	19	19	19	17	15		24	27	25.9
CLARION 3 SW	MAX	32	34	36	38	33	45	33	23	22	41	41	39	35	33	38	37	34	36	32	30	34	24	34	28	27	25	29	38	40	45	34	34.2
	MIN	11	15	32	29	23	17	18	13	15	21	33	29	22	16	9	24	22	21	19	22	13	28	3	5	17	-5	8	-1	31	29	22	18.0
CLAYSVILLE 3 W	MAX	43	43	45	38	41	55	34	30	27	37	47	36	40	40	35	33	31	37	34	35	35	38	34	31	39	29	34	42	49	51	31	37.6
	MIN	10	13	35	20	18	15	17	13	16	20	32	27	25	15	8	21	22	22	20	24	21	28	5	-3	7	-1	11	0	35	23	13	17.2
COATESVILLE 1 SW	MAX	33	38	36	46	42	44	45	34	26	47	48	43	43	37	38	42	44	34	40	31	32	35	42	33	30	31	31	32	35	37	48	38.0
	MIN	16	11	14	25	25	26	19	14	14	24	40	38	33	27	27	23	24	24	23	26	19	19	21	10	15	14	13	7	7	31	29	21.3
COLUMBIA	MAX	39	34	50	42	46	45	45	30	32	50	48	43	40	42	41	44	39	43	37	37	38	43	38	33	34	30	35	37	36	46	41	39.9
	MIN	14	12	31	24	29	26	25	17	16	31	41	38	33	27	30	25	27	25	22	26	20	26	24	10	20	18	21	13	27	34	29	24.5
CONFLUENCE 1 SW DAM	MAX	25	38	39	41	33	39	53	27	23	22	32	34	32	32	31	38	34	27	34	33	28	33	30	22	24	37	27	28	37	47	51	33.2
	MIN	16	18	32	30	26	19	27	13	15	21	25	32	26	22	6	24	22	24	14	27	20	29	17	1	7	14	19	-3	31	34	30	20.3
CORRY	MAX	30	31	35	34	30	44	36	18	20	38	35	33	31	28	37	32	23	32	30	27	32	31	26	27	27	24	27	28	30	34	25	30.6
	MIN	19	9	29	18	25	17	18	9	13	20	33	26	21	13	9	17	18	19	14	17	18	26	8	14	18	-1	15	15	32	29	21	17.9
COUDERSPORT 2 NW	MAX	27	24	31	31	31	36	30	11	24	37	34	30	25	26	35	34	26	30	24	21	28	30	25	25	27	30	32	34	37	37	27	29.0
	MIN	15	7	21	25	25	21	11	5	4	24	29	25	20	9	12	13	16	8	12	15	7	21	5	2	7	0	12	18	22	23	18	14.6
DERRY	MAX	34	38	40	37	37	55	39	22	23	27	36	35	40	36	32	37	32	34	34	34	33	37	34	30	28	27	31	40	45	55	30	35.2
	MIN	18	20	36	20	29	21	22	14	16	21	23	30	30	20	16	21	21	23	16	29	23	30	11	8	14	8	13	5	33	29	22	20.7
DEVAULT 1 W	MAX	34	36	43	43	42	44	33	39	43	48	42	40	36	36	40	43	36	41	30	31	34	41	33	29	33	31	33	33	32	40	36	37.6
	MIN																																
DIXON	MAX	29	28		38	38	34	37	28	18	39	47	40	36	30	28	35	41	28	31	26	26	30	41	27	26	28	29	31	33	40	44	32.7
	MIN	20	2		25	30	28	22	11	11	18	35	34	29	21	21	17	18	21	13	16	6	6	19	8	0	2	7	7	8	32	24	17.0
DONEGAL	MAX	30	33	34	28	30	48	31	18	16	24	30	28	25	26	31	31	23	27	28	29	29	33	28	30	23	20	24	36	42	44	22	29.1
	MIN	10	17	25	23	15	15	11	8	10	16	24	21	17	4	1	15	15	17	17	19	15	23	1	1	4	2	4	-3	31	15	2	12.7
DONORA	MAX	35	42	49	45	35	48	57	30	28	26	38	38	34	40	39	34	33	30	35	36	33	38	40	27	30	31	30	33	48	52	38	37.2
	MIN	19	21	39	29	29	26	27	18	20	23	27	34	29	23	18	23	24	26	26	28	27	32	14	11	19	15	18	11	36	37	23	24.3
DU BOIS 7 E	MAX	28	27	34	34	30	42	36	21	19	41	40	35	32	35	38	35	34	34	32	27	31	32	30	26	30	24	25	32	41	46	28	32.2
	MIN	15	10	25	28	25	22	21	10	10	18	33	29	22	14	12	14	17	19	13	22	11	24	4	3	5	-13	12	8	27	27	28	16.4
EAGLES MERE	MAX	25	24	28	32	31	30	34	22	12	36	40	33	31	25	28	32	35	25	28	23	21	29	32	22	23	29	22	26	28	34	37	28.2
	MIN	15	7	11	26	22	21	21	7	5	11	32	29	22	12	13	17	15	12	12	15	9	15	16	5	5	6	6	9	10	23	19	14.5
EAST BRADY	MAX	34	37	37	38	37	48	42	40	29	42	42	36	36	36	40	34	35	40	32	30	26	36	36	28	33	27	31	40	40	47	32	36.5
	MIN	12	15	20	31	28	19	12	14	17	22	35	32	26	18	11	25	23	23	20	24	14	28	6	6	19	-1	14	12	21	30	22	19.3
EBENSBURG	MAX	29	28	34	35	34	45	34	18	19	25	32	29	29	28	32	34	31	28	24	25	27	32	26	17	23	22	24	29	44	47	30	29.5
	MIN	16	18	26	25	18	17	18	9	11	17	30	24	21	15	14	17	6	16	15	16	18	25	7	6	12	6	14	-2	27	26	17	16.3
EMPORIUM 1 E	MAX	25	34	32	36	35	36	44	25	19	34	43	38	36	32	35	43	37	30	28	39	28	32	33	25	29	32	29	29	37	35	42	33.6
	MIN	16	8	8	31	28	26	20	12	10	13	34	34	25	14	8	8	17	11	11	19	9	15	9	8	9	-1	1	10	10	32	22	16.0
EPHRATA	MAX	39	33	45	41	45	46	37	28	34	48	43	42	41	40	40	42	39	41	34	34	38	41	37	33	34	32	34	33	35	46	38	38.5
	MIN	21	14	28	22	26	24	23	15	14	31	39	35	31	24	26	25	24	22	21	23	18	23	23	12	15	14	17	12	23	32	21	22.5
ERIE CAA AIRPORT	MAX	30	34	35	32	31	44	28	20	32	36	34	33	32	28	30	33	28	29	29	24	33	29	21	26	25	24	27	37	41	38	37	30.5
	MIN	19	23	32	29	23	24	19	16	15	34	32	27	24	20	14	22	21	20	22	22	23	20	9	14	6	16	15	14	33	29	13	20.8

See Reference Notes Following Station Index

DAILY TEMPERATURES

Table 5 - Continued

Station		Day Of Month 1	2	3	4	5	6	7	8	9	10	11	12	13	14	15	16	17	18	19	20	21	22	23	24	25	26	27	28	29	30	31	Average
EVERETT 1 SW	MAX	39	34	45	38	39	50	35	32	26	42	41	38	36	37	46	34	32	41	32	34	32	45	36	29	30	29	31	38	39	50	29	34.7
	MIN	14	16	32	30	19	19	20	17	19	28	38	31	26	26	23	27	24	25	26	27	26	24	16	11	11	10	10	-7	38	26	20	21.4
FARRELL SHARON	MAX	39	38	39	37	36	51	40	22	26	37	37	36	36	35	35	39	28	38	34	30	35	34	31	29	29	20	29	37	42	34	30	34.5
	MIN	18	22	32	28	26	16	18	16	16	11	32	26	22	18	12	24	18	13	23	20	18	26	5	9	10	8	3	4	36	19	17	18.3
FORD CITY 4 S DAM	MAX	27	34	38	37	34	34	52	27	25	29	35	36	33	37	35	35	35	27	34	33	28	33	35	24	27	29	30	30	42	42	30	33.8
	MIN	10	15	25	29	26	18	21	13	13	16	26	31	24	18	10	14	21	21	19	26	18	20	6	5	13	-1	18	9	0	33	20	17.0
FRANKLIN	MAX	35	35	36	35	35	47	38	21	22	41	40	31	35	34	42	38	35	38	38	29	34	34	31	28	31	28	30	38	42	38	30	34.4
	MIN	18	18	31	30	26	18	18	12	15	19	34	28	23	17	12	27	22	20	22	21	19	29	9	7	18	3	10	7	38	27	17	19.6
FREDERICKSVILLE 2 SE	MAX																																
	MIN																																
FREELAND	MAX	23	22	35	35	32	38	38	16	28	41	42	36	31	25	30	34	34	26	25	25	24	30	31	23	22	21	21	31	34	38	34	29.8
	MIN	12	17	20	26	25	28	15	6	8	24	32	28	22	19	20	19	20	20	20	20	13	23	20	10	8	5	10	20	18	32	22	18.8
GEORGE SCHOOL	MAX	37	35	38	45	46	45	35	27	45	47	45	43	38	36	42	43	36	39	35	31	35	48	35	31	34	34	32	34	36	50	37	38.3
	MIN	19	10	28	25	29	29	20	16	18	44	41	39	30	26	30	23	25	22	17	25	16	9	19	12	16	14	14	8	23	34	27	22.8
GETTYSBURG	MAX	33	38	34	50	42	46	48	32	31	44	46	42	42	40	42	46	42	36	44	30	37	37	42	29	31	32	31	32	34	36	42	38.4
	MIN	21	15	17	28	29	23	22	18	17	25	41	38	33	29	30	28	25	25	27	26	19	21	28	17	18	17	19	12	18	32	27	24.0
GORDON	MAX																																
	MIN																																
GRATZ 1 N	MAX	31	34	33	40	37	39	42	29	23	42	48	40	38	35	38	39	41	32	38	27	29	34	39	26	29	30	28	30	34	38	45	35.1
	MIN	20	11	14	27	30	27	25	15	13	23	39	36	29	22	22	24	24	22	22	24	17	18	26	14	13	14	14	17	17	27	27	21.7
GREENVILLE	MAX	33	36	36	34	34	48	37	22	23	36	36	35	35	35	38	36	27	37	35	30	36	31	28	29	28	27	32	37	40	35	28	33.4
	MIN	14	20	33	29	25	20	18	14	15	21	33	29	23	16	9	25	21	20	23	21	21	28	0	9	14	-2	3	3	26	26	19	18.6
HANOVER	MAX	32	37	34	51	41	44	47	26	30	41	47	41	42	39	43	46	41	36	43	31	34	37	43	35	32	32	32	34	36	38	44	38.4
	MIN	14	14	23	25	25	22	23	16	15	19	38	36	31	26	26	25	26	21	22	24	17	21	28	12	12	15	14	11	11	31	25	21.5
HARRISBURG WB AP	MAX	36	34	42	40	43	46	31	27	39	53	43	41	40	43	44	43	35	42	30	34	36	42	35	32	31	31	33	35	37	46	34	38.0
	MIN	22	14	31	24	29	28	20	18	18	39	40	37	31	28	30	29	28	27	26	27	21	31	22	19	21	19	24	16	29	39	24	26.8
HAWLEY I S DAM	MAX	25	25	26	35	38	33	34	26	21	43	43	37	36	29	29	33	38	26	28	28	28	27	35	22	23	23	22	24	33	36	42	30.5
	MIN	16	-1	-1	22	29	22	15	6	0	19	34	34	25	11	15	20	20	16	14	16	14	15	20	10	10	7	10	5	5	26	18	15.2
HOLTWOOD	MAX	35	36	43	38	43	45	34	28	37	46	43	41	38	41	39	39	35	39	30	34	35	41	32	30	30	30	32	37	35	48	35	37.1
	MIN	18	17	32	26	27	25	21	18	18	37	39	36	32	28	32	28	29	27	27	27	22	24	19	18	21	20	19	14	29	38	27	25.5
HUNTINGDON	MAX	31	35	35	41	38	41	46	33	29	34	43	40	40	40	41	46	38	33	42	29	33	36	40	29	34	32	32	33	38	36	45	36.9
	MIN	22	11	11	31	31	20	21	18	15	19	32	37	31	25	23	18	19	22	19	24	15	14	24	9	10	10	9	7	7	33	28	19.8
INDIANA 3 SE	MAX	33	35	38	36	33	53	33	25	22	27	35	35	36	34	31	36	32	34	32	33	32	35	33	27	30	26	29	40	42	50	28	33.7
	MIN	7	15	33	29	23	17	19	14	16	20	27	30	25	20	8	18	21	21	16	17	13	28	7	0	12	-1	15	-1	32	24	20	17.6
IRWIN	MAX	32	45	41	37	37	43	43	24	22	27	34	35	35	34	30	33	33	35	34	30	35	36	36	28	30	28	29	41	42	42	30	34.2
	MIN	16	23	36	28	28	22	24	15	17	22	26	30	26	20	16	22	22	24	23	22	22	30	11	9	12	10	11	4	34	30	21	21.2
JAMESTOWN 2 NW	MAX	27	33	35	34	32	35	47	24	20	35	35	35	30	32	32	34	35	24	33	30	27	34	30	24	27	29	26	29	48	39	33	31.6
	MIN	10	20	24	30	24	21	21	14	14	15	34	29	21	15	17	11	20	19	19	21	20	21	-2	-2	18	-1	2	1	6	30	38	16.2
JIM THORPE	MAX	37			43	40	50	46	27	48	47	47	42	37	31	37	45	42	40	37	32	34	41	35	35	36	34	33	40	38	41	42	39.3
	MIN	13	9	37	27	31	28	23	12	11	28	40	35	29	23	27	25	23	21	20	23	16	20	25	14	15	13	16	10	22	34	27	22.5
JOHNSTOWN	MAX	29	37	40	41	38	40	56	26	24	30	38	39	38	39	38	35	37	29	37	34	30	34	42	26	31	30	29	31	39	48	39	36.6
	MIN	11	19	28	31	27	24	26	9	11	18	28	33	25	19	11	19	21	22	20	26	22	22	12	12	16	13	15	7	9	35	20	20.7
KANE I NNE	MAX	22	28	33	33	32	31	42	23	12	32	40	35	31	30	32	42	38	24	24	26	25	30	30	22	26	31	23	25	37	40	40	30.6
	MIN	14	6	13	21	25	18	15	9	8	11	32	30	20	12	5	6	17	11	10	20	3	19	-1	1	8	-10	-3	16	12	30	21	12.9
KEGG	MAX	40	36	44	35	36	49	35	27	25	41	39	36	35	33	45	32	31	39	29	32	34	42	36	29	28	28	38	35	40	50	28	35.5
	MIN	22	11	31	27	26	20	17	9	12	19	35	30	25	21	20	25	23	21	24	25	25	28	9	7	4	12	13	5	30	23	15	19.8
LANCASTER 2 NE PUMP STA	MAX	38	35	45	43	44	44	37	33	33	48	47	43	42	40	40	41	38	42	37	34	36	42	38	30	32	38	34	36	36	48	48	38.9
	MIN	11	9	30	22	24	23	19	16	16	31	38	37	32	25	27	24	25	23	21	25	11	16	23	11	11	15	17	6	22	32	27	21.6
LANDISVILLE	MAX	32	36	35	44	41	42	45	33	27	47	49	42	41	37	39	39	40	34	39	28	34	34	41	29	28	30	28	30	35	35	46	36.7
	MIN	18	10	13	20	22	25	21	17	16	22	40	37	32	25	28	27	26	24	23	25	16	18	25	13	15	15	17	13	15	32	27	21.8
LAWRENCEVILLE 2 S	MAX	28	24	33	39	35	35	38	22	15	35	38	35	34	29	31	35	35	26	32	29	25	33	34	23	25	24	25	29	36	40	41	31.1
	MIN	18	3	7	33	29	26	21	13	10	15	33	32	27	17	17	12	14	17	15	16	8	9	11	-1	-5	-5	1	-4	-3	32	22	14.1
LEBANON 2 NW	MAX																																
	MIN																																
LEWISTOWN	MAX	31	36	33	40	39	45	44	31	30	33	47	43	40	40	44	48	40	37	44	28	34	38	41	32	35	34	34	34	38	38	48	37.8
	MIN	22	16	14	32	32	26	22	19	15	17	33	39	33	26	25	25	22	22	22	25	19	18	28	16	17	15	12	13	11	30	29	22.4
LINESVILLE 5 WNW	MAX	31	39	35	34	32	45	32	22	24	35	35	35	31	30	36	34	25	34	31	28	33	31	26	26	29	27	29	34	30	33	27	31.7
	MIN	4	16	31	28	19	16	16	13	15	24	33	27	22	11	7	25	20	20	21	21	20	24	-1	13	16	-2	-2	1	32	25	6	16.8
LOCK HAVEN	MAX	34	34	37	38	42	40	30	26	29	44	43	39	38	41	47	40	40	43	31	32	37	41	36	34	35	32	33	38	34	42	34	36.9
	MIN	23	12	30	32	30	29	20	16	14	29	38	35	30	21	18	22	22	19	20	20	11	28	17	5	8	7	22	21	30	32	30	22.2
MADERA	MAX	23	30	34	36	32	32	41	29	21	36	42	37	35	31	34	33	36	26	31	28	28	31	35	21	25	29	24	27	36	48	48	31.9
	MIN	12	11	16	28	25	14	18	9	9	11	22	30	22	11	1	2	15	18	12	20	9	14	7	4	8	-4	-4	-5	-6	12	20	14.6
MARCUS HOOK	MAX	41	38	39	47	47	44	37	28	44	50	44	45	40	39	44	42	38	42	32	32	36	43	38	33	35	35	34	36	36	51	38	39.5
	MIN	22	19	32	33	33	29	23	18	20	44	42	38	34	31	33	30	29	25	26	26	22	26	22	19	20	21	28	21	27	34	28	27.3
MARTINSBURG CAA AP	MAX	32	32	40	34	36	44	32	23	24	39	39	35	33	32	40	31	29	37	29	28	31	37	39	25	27	22	27	35	41	44	27	32.8
	MIN	21	15	30	29	22	20	15	12	13	23	35	28	24	19	22	24	21	19	21	20	19	27	10	10	12	11	16	6	30	24	17	19.8
MEADVILLE 1 S	MAX	27	31	35	35	31	33	47	24	20	34	36	36	30	32	31	38	36	24	35	30	37	33	31	29	29	27	26	30	40	30	33	31.8
	MIN	13	18	24	30	25	17	22	14	14	15	34	30	24	13	9	18	21	28	19	20	16	22	1	1	25	1	6	8	8	31	20	16.6
MERCER 2 NNE	MAX	32	35	35	38	27	35	24	19	29	36	36	31	33	32	37	38	35	34	28	27	32	38	25	27	27	22	24	26	38	52	30	30.5
	MIN	12	28	18	18	6	10	8	6	13	13	17	21	16	15	18	20	18	17	16	14	16	10	2	18	-1	-6	-8	-9	12	12	6	11.2
MIDDLETOWN OLMSTED FLD	MAX	35	34	41	39	42	41	33	26	40	51	42	42	39	42	41	41	35	41	29	35	38	42	35	31	31	38	32	33	34	42	34	37.1
	MIN	20	14	31	26	26	26	20	18	18	31	40	36	31	28	31	26	29	27	25	26	20	27	21	19	20	19	24	14	30	34	26	25.3
MIDLAND DAM 7	MAX	33	38	36	34	37	44	31	22	25	38	37	36	34	34	35	37	30	33	33	33	35	36	24	28	28	26	28	40	43	34	20	33.3
	MIN	16	24	28	30	28	26	18	17	19	26	35	28	26	22	20	24	24	26	29	23	24	24	9	6	14	15	12	10	38	25	22	22.1
MONTROSE 1 E	MAX	22	22	30	33	36	28	30	21	13	39	42	35	32	25	23	29	33	22	23	23	22	24	34	20	19	20	20	25	27	35	40	27.3
	MIN	16	2	6	30	27	21	18	4	2	13	34	30	21	15	14	18	18	15	12	13	11	13	17	8	8	8	10	10	10	25	18	15.1
MORGANTOWN	MAX	36	32	46	41	41	45	32	25	40	48	43	40	35	36	41	44	38	39	31	31	34	38	34	30	32	29	31	32	35	48	35	36.8
	MIN	13	11	29	25	29	23	18	13	14	39	38	34	29	25	28	24	24	21	22	21	15	18	16	8	12	15	11	7	24	31	22	21.3

See Reference Notes Following Station Index

Table 5 - Continued

DAILY TEMPERATURES

PENNSYLVANIA
JANUARY 1956

Station		1	2	3	4	5	6	7	8	9	10	11	12	13	14	15	16	17	18	19	20	21	22	23	24	25	26	27	28	29	30	31	Average
MT GRETNA 2 SE	MAX	35	32	45	43	49	45	36	27	40	50	43	52	50	45	47	41	38	40	29	33	35	41	42	36	44	36	38	33	35	43	35	30.6
	MIN	14	13	30	23	27	25	16	15	15	39	38	33	28	24	26	23	25	24	22	21	16	23	12	16	16	14	18	11	24	30	22	22.0
MT POCONO 2 N AP	MAX	19	23	35	35	31	42	37	15	36	40	40	36	30	23	30	39	32	28	30	25	25	34	31	21	24	21	21	33	33	40	36	30.5
	MIN	15	1	19	19	25	21	15	4	6	35	34	30	21	15	20	18	17	15	14	19	17	12	14	9	10	8	12	9	18	32	18	18.8
MUHLENBURG 1 SE	MAX	29	24	36	35	34	36	31	16	34	45	43	37	33	32	37	39	32	34	24	28	32	35	32	28	31	27	31	32	32	40	34	32.7
	MIN	16	16	22	28	24	28	11	8	7	32	34	33	19	18	21	16	19	15	10	19	8	17	16	5	6	6	10	6	28	29	23	17.5
NEWBURG 3 W	MAX	38	33	38	44	46	49	31	33	32	56	47	43	44	36	47	42	32	40	41	34	34	40	33	32	34	30	34	30	36	41	35	38.7
	MIN	26	20	24	32	26	26	20	14	21	30	39	38	30	26	29	29	20	25	25	27	26	25	23	26	20	14	16	16	24	31	20	24.8
NEW CASTLE 1 N	MAX	35	39	40	36	37	50	42	24	24	38	38	36	37	36	38	40	38	37	33	30	35	34	31	29	29	28	30	37	38	39	30	35.1
	MIN	14	21	34	31	26	22	20	15	17	22	34	28	24	17	12	25	22	21	21	22	18	29	7	7	9	0	3	0	30	29	20	19.4
NEWELL	MAX	35	46	49	43	37	46	57	28	28	29	37	36	32	38	37	31	32	29	35	34	32	37	37	28	30	29	28	31	44	48	40	36.1
	MIN	17	20	31	27	29	24	25	19	21	25	26	32	27	22	15	20	24	26	25	27	25	30	14	9	18	12	20	9	31	36	23	22.9
NEWPORT	MAX	33	37	33	40	40	45	44	31	31	39	49	43	41	42	44	47	41	35	44	28	35	38	43	43	34	35	33	35	37	36	45	38.7
	MIN	23	10	10	25	26	23	20	19	17	20	39	38	34	27	27	23	21	26	20	26	19	15	28	16	16	12	12	10	10	33	30	21.8
NEW STANTON	MAX	28	45	42	33	38	48	39	25	25	28	37	35	37	42	33	33	29	35	35	35	38	36	32	38	36	40	37	45	48	42	28	36.1
	MIN	16	20	30	28	23	21	18	15	18	22	29	30	25	22	9	23	22	18	22	22	22	26	15	11	12	11	5	12	32	24	13	20.9
NORRISTOWN	MAX																																
	MIN																																
PALMERTON	MAX	32	31	36	40	39	43	32	19	45	48	43	41	33	30	36	41	33	36	30	32	33	39	34	30	30	29	30	33	35	42	33	35.1
	MIN	15	9	18	29	32	26	14	13	15	44	38	34	29	24	28	23	25	22	22	23	17	20	19	17	16	13	17	10	25	30	24	22.3
PHIL DREXEL INST OF TEC	MAX	39	37	41	46	44	49	36	27	45	47	44	43	38	35	44	43	37	42	34	33	35	44	37	31	33	33	34	35	35	52	40	39.1
	MIN	23	19	33	37	34	32	22	18	18	44	40	37	33	28	33	30	29	27	27	28	23	28	25	21	20	21	21	20	26	33	30	27.7
PHILADELPHIA WB AP	MAX	38	36	39	44	45	45	35	26	46	48	44	43	39	34	43	41	36	40	33	32	34	41	35	30	33	32	34	35	37	51	38	38.3
	MIN	18	18	32	31	33	26	21	18	18	44	41	37	33	27	32	29	27	25	25	26	21	22	20	18	20	19	17	18	26	35	27	25.9
PHILADELPHIA PT BREEZE	MAX	38	37	40	45	45	45	36	28	42	45	43	44	39	36	43	43	35	42	35	33	35	41	36	32	34	34	35	36	38	53	40	39.0
	MIN	22	20	33	33	35	33	28	21	21	42	40	40	34	29	34	32	29	27	29	27	25	27	32	23	24	23	22	25	29	38	32	29.3
PHILADELPHIA SHAWMONT	MAX	37	37	45	44	42	47	46	33	37	48	47	44	43	35	41	43	40	40	39	32	34	41	39	30	33	32	33	35	37	52	50	39.9
	MIN	18	14	32	29	33	31	23	18	19	37	40	39	33	29	31	26	26	26	25	26	21	18	29	16	20	18	17	14	26	35	29	25.7
PHILADELPHIA CITY	MAX	39	36	42	49	46	48	38	26	46	47	44	44	39	36	44	43	37	43	34	32	34	40	36	32	35	34	34	38	38	52	38	39.4
	MIN	24	19	33	38	34	32	23	19	20	44	41	38	33	29	33	32	29	27	28	27	24	28	26	22	23	22	23	24	28	36	30	28.7
PHILIPSBURG CAA AP	MAX	28	28	35	30	32	40	30	21	23	38	37	32	32	35	39	33	24	34	22	26	28	31	30	25	28	24	26	29	43	30	24	30.5
	MIN	12	14	28	26	20	17	12	8	10	23	32	25	20	13	13	13	19	15	11	15	12	25	7	10	11	4	16	8	25	22	12	16.1
PHOENIXVILLE 1 E	MAX	38	36	43	45	45	47	35	33	37	49	48	43	41	38	44	44	41	42	37	33	35	42	40	32	35	33	38	35	36	50	47	40.0
	MIN	10	6	29	37	34	31	17	15	15	33	37	36	30	27	26	21	24	22	11	23	13	16	22	15	8	15	6	12	18	32	28	21.6
PIMPLE HILL	MAX	23	23	31	33	35	30	41	26	15	39	39	35	31	25	21	28	38	21	27	28	24	26	33	20	20	25	20	22	32	35	38	28.5
	MIN	14	3	9	28	24	20	18	2	3	14	34	30	23	14	14	17	15	14	12	17	11	14	16	7	8	6	10	9	13	24	19	14.9
PITTSBURGH WB AP 2	MAX	35	43	39	33	38	52	31	22	25	36	35	34	36	37	34	33	28	32	31	30	31	35	28	27	28	25	29	39	44	46	28	33.7
	MIN	19	24	31	29	26	25	19	15	17	25	33	28	25	20	18	24	22	24	24	23	23	28	9	9	15	11	16	12	35	23	19	21.6
PITTSBURGH WB CITY	MAX	38	45	42	36	40	55	36	25	26	40	39	37	38	37	35	37	30	36	35	35	35	38	31	29	30	28	33	42	47	51	30	36.6
	MIN	25	28	35	33	30	29	23	16	20	26	36	29	27	23	21	27	24	25	30	27	27	31	15	17	20	16	22	15	37	25	22	25.2
PLEASANT MOUNT 1 W	MAX	23	19	22	33	35	29	35	24	13	39	41	37	33	25	22	29	33	23	24	25	26	25	33	20	20	20	21	22	28	34		27.1
	MIN	15	-8	6	21	26	19	8	4	2	13	35	32	22	15	15	20	17	14	11	14	12	14	16	8	7	3	4	1	1	25		13.1
PORT CLINTON	MAX	33	35	38	34	40	42	44	48	36	48	48	51	45	42	36	40	40	46	34	41	34	32	36	41	30	30	30	32	33	38	42	38.7
	MIN	20	10	16	24	25	27	20	14	12	20	30	32	30	20	22	22	24	21	22	22	21	22	22	14	16	14	18	14	20	20	20	20.6
PUTNEYVILLE 2 SE DAM	MAX	26	34	38	35	34	33	47	32	23	31	39	35	35	35	34	35	35	27	36	30	28	32	34	24	27	28	24	30	42	43	47	33.3
	MIN	13	16	22	28	25	16	21	10	10	11	27	30	22	16	8	9	20	18	17	22	15	17	5	4	10	2	2	-3	-3	30	19	14.8
QUAKERTOWN 1 E	MAX	34	33	38	46	43	44	36	29	35	47	45	42	40	33	39	44	39	37	37	31	33	38	36	29	31	30	31	34	35	46	42	37.3
	MIN	18	4	25	20	28	25	16	12	13	32	37	35	28	23	26	23	21	21	15	20	16	10	22	11	15	13	14	17	18	31	28	20.8
READING WB CITY	MAX	37	34	42	42	45	46	35	26	43	50	45	43	38	38	42	43	36	42	32	33	36	41	36	32	33	32	34	36	37	46	36	38.4
	MIN	24	17	32	27	32	31	21	18	18	43	42	37	31	27	32	30	28	25	26	27	22	29	22	19	21	20	23	19	28	35	28	26.9
RIDGWAY 3 W	MAX	30	30	34	34	31	43	29	18	21	42	42	35	32	34	43	38	30	35	27	28	32	33	31	26	30	24	27	35	41	44	27	32.5
	MIN	17	9	26	28	21	16	16	10	12	20	21	20	23	14	3	15	20	18	13	22	4	27	3	0	0	-12	11	9	29	27	14	14.7
SALINA 3 W	MAX	33	39	40	39	35	52	36	24	23	28	36	34	36	34	31	34	34	34	33	34	33	36	34	26	29	26	30	39	43	50	29	34.3
	MIN	14	21	34	27	27	19	21	13	16	21	27	29	25	20	12	21	20	23	20	23	21	29	9	3	12	3	13	11	32	28	21	19.8
SCRANTON	MAX	28	26	40	43	45	34	33	30	18	49	53	37	35	36	32	35	38	28	31	26	28	29	37	26	25	24	25	29	32	36	43	33.2
	MIN	17	8	12	33	31	28	26	9	8	15	37	33	27	19	19	22	21	19	17	18	17	19	17	13	12	12	13	16	16	28	22	19.5
SCRANTON WB AIRPORT	MAX	26	28	36	37	33	35	28	14	37	44	40	36	30	26	32	36	27	30	26	26	28	37	32	24	24	23	27	36	35	43	31	31.0
	MIN	10	8	28	32	29	26	10	9	11	36	35	30	25	20	25	20	21	18	17	18	15	17	15	10	12	11	15	14	25	29	21	19.8
SELINSGROVE CAA AP	MAX	33	33	39	38	40	40	29	24	40	47	41	39	37	39	41	39	37	41	28	30	35	40	35	35	30	31	32	35	35	42	34	36.1
	MIN	14	8	31	25	27	20	19	15	15	39	38	35	29	23	25	21	26	20	16	10	9	24	12	12	8	10	20	17	29	32	22	21.0
SHIPPENSBURG	MAX	36	32	46	43	43	48	38	30	30	46	46	41	40	40	48	43	36	45	38	35	38	41	32	32	31	33	34	35	35	46	37	38.6
	MIN	22	12	29	30	26	22	20	17	17	28	39	38	31	26	28	26	26	24	26	25	18	28	23	15	16	10	19	11	27	33	26	23.8
SHIPPINGPORT WB	MAX	36	42	40	34	39	52	34	24	28	38	38	35	37	35	36	37	30	36	33	30	33	36	25	28	28	27	29	41	44	44	28	34.7
	MIN	15	23	30	30	25	26	20	17	20	28	35	29	23	21	27	26	24	25	27	25	24	25	11	9	12	11	14	10	36	25	17	22.3
SLIPPERY ROCK	MAX	32	36	36	40	34	40	40	24	22	38	36	34	37	37	40	38	26	37	32	40	32	32	28	28	27	29	31	37	40	40	28	33.9
	MIN	16	21	28	28	24	22	17	12	13	19	32	26	23	16	15	24	18	18	24	18	17	26	6	10	16	5	10	5	32	24	17	18.8
SOMERSET MAIN ST	MAX	36	32	38	38	37	51	44	22	20	33	34	35	29	32	36	35	32	34	29	30	31	36	33	27	28	26	27	38	44	44	27	33.5
	MIN	19	20	29	27	19	22	20	10	12	18	30	27	22	17	10	23	18	20	16	20	20	26	10	1	1	9	15	-1	28	27	17	17.8
SPRINGBORO	MAX																																
	MIN																																
SPRINGS 1 SW	MAX	30	33	37	35	36	51	41	18	18	33	34	31	26	25	36	33	26	32	27	25	28	33	30	21	28	21	25	35	46	45	21	31.0
	MIN	17	16	31	24	20	20	12	8	10	17	28	24	20	16	11	18	16	14	12	20	17	23	5	-1	-1	9	9	-3	29	19	13	15.3
STATE COLLEGE	MAX	31	33	39	38	37	41	30	25	28	42	39	36	35	40	44	36	30	39	25	31	33	34	31	30	32	29	29	30	37	42	29	34.1
	MIN	25	15	32	29	27	26	15	11	11	28	35	30	24	20	22	24	22	22	22	23	16	28	12	12	15	13	10	13	27	25	19	21.4
STROUDSBURG	MAX	31	33	31	30	40	40	45	35	29	45	48	42	41	35	33	41	45	32	39	34	32	35	41	30	32	35	32	32	37	35	42	36.5
	MIN	21	5	12	26	25	20	22	12	13	29	41	38	33	24	25	23	23	18	16	21	10	11	25	16	12	10	12	9	18	31	27	20.3
TAMARACK 2 S FIRE TWR	MAX	24	30	27	32	28	34	36	22	16	34	38	34	31	26	32	40	33	24	35	22	21	28	29	24	28	30	26	28	30	38	35	29.5
	MIN	12	9	8	27	24	21	20	8	5	8	32	29	23	12	11	15	18	10	10	17	11	14	10	5	7	5	5	14	13	26	19	14.5

See Reference Notes Following Station Index

DAILY TEMPERATURES

Table 5 - Continued

Station		1	2	3	4	5	6	7	8	9	10	11	12	13	14	15	16	17	18	19	20	21	22	23	24	25	26	27	28	29	30	31	Average
TIONESTA 2 SE DAM	MAX	25	32	35	35	33	34	46	25	20	35	41	36	32	34	33	43	37	25	37	29	28	33	32	24	27	33	25	28	40	41	40	32.8
	MIN	15	14	16	30	26	16	20	11	12	15	33	31	23	15	10	10	21	19	11	22	15	19	7	8	14	-4	2	5	6	32	21	16.0
TITUSVILLE WATER WORKS	MAX	31	33	33	35	32	44	32	20	21	42	37	37	33	33	40	36	28	32	29	29	33	32	27	23	29	24	20	33	42	36	32	32.1
	MIN	10	13	29	26	18	11	19	10	13	19	32	25	21	13	6	20	18	17	14	15	14	25	6	11	15	-5	4	5	31	24	11	15.8
TOWANDA	MAX	28	31	38	37	36	36	27	18	35	41	37	36	33	32	37	38	29	33	26	25	32	39	34	29	29	28	31	31	39	44	33	33.0
	MIN	13	4	28	32	29	24	17	11	11	34	34	31	27	20	19	17	22	19	13	20	10	14	16	10	1	8	13	4	22	31	22	18.6
UNIONTOWN	MAX	43	49	49	36	42	56	35	28	26	28	34	34	38	37	35	34	29	34	37	36	35	39	35	27	28	29	31	45	48	54	30	36.8
	MIN	23	26	34	29	23	22	19	15	18	22	28	29	26	17	11	26	24	23	24	27	25	31	13	7	15	10	15	7	39	26	20	21.7
UPPER DARBY	MAX	37	37	44	44	44	46	35	29	38	47	45	42	40	35	43	43	39	40	36	32	32	41	35	31	32	32	35	34	36	50	39	38.5
	MIN	17	15	31	29	32	31	24	16	17	37	39	38	32	27	30	27	26	24	24	25	19	18	23	16	19	18	16	15	20	34	29	24.8
WARREN	MAX	32	31	35	34	32	46	30	18	23	37	36	34	31	29	37	34	27	33	28	28	34	33	28	29	30	23	30	37	41	36	30	31.8
	MIN	14	13	28	19	25	25	17	11	12	22	33	26	22	14	9	17	19	19	16	14	12	27	6	14	18	2	18	20	30	26	21	18.4
WAYNESBURG 2 W	MAX	43	48	48	41	40	55	39	28	26	30	37	36	37	38	34	35	32	39	35	36	34	40	38	29	23	28	33	44	48	52	31	37.3
	MIN	12	14	37	23	24	18	23	15	18	22	29	29	26	22	7	26	23	24	20	26	23	28	19	3	11	2	19	3	34	28	16	20.1
WELLSBORO 3 S	MAX	28	26	29	35	33	33	37	21	13	33	37	33	33	26	29	35	34	24	33	22	21	32	31	21	24	26	25	27	30	36	39	29.2
	MIN	17	6	12	27	23	23	18	9	5	12	31	29	23	13	12	17	16	12	12	15	9	14	10	4	5	3	8	11	13	25	21	14.7
WELLSVILLE	MAX	36	33	46	42	45	47	34	30	32	51	43	42	40	43	45	42	38	42	38	35	37	40	36	32	31	31	33	35	46	39	36	38.7
	MIN	10	10	31	20	28	29	17	18	16	31	39	38	33	27	29	28	28	25	20	25	18	16	22	11	14	13	16	23	23	27	12	22.4
WEST CHESTER	MAX	40	36	44	45	46	48	36	27		47	42	42	38	39	34	34	36	31	32	32	32	34	34	34	36	35	35	37	37	40	39	37.4
	MIN	19	18	33	31	29	25	16	12		20	38	34	27	28	28	26	23	25	26	20	21	24	17	19	18	18	18	10	14	28	23	22.9
WILLIAMSPORT WB AP	MAX	33	31	36	37	40	41	30	22	35	47	42	39	35	40	42	42	34	40	28	29	35	39	34	32	32	31	34	33	34	44	34	35.6
	MIN	14	10	29	32	29	25	19	14	16	35	38	34	27	22	25	21	26	20	20	18	14	27	17	11	8	10	21	13	27	31	24	21.8
YORK 3 SSW PUMP STA	MAX	36	34	51	42	46	49	36	31	32	49	48	41	41	44	47	41	39	45	40	35	37	40	38	32	32	32	34	36	37	47	40	39.7
	MIN	12	10	32	22	27	17	19	19	18	32	40	39	34	28	29	24	28	25	20	27	18	18	26	10	12	17	16	7	27	34	29	23.1

See Reference Notes Following Station Index

Table 7

SNOWFALL AND SNOW ON GROUND

PENNSYLVANIA
JANUARY 1956

Day of month

Station		1	2	3	4	5	6	7	8	9	10	11	12	13	14	15	16	17	18	19	20	21	22	23	24	25	26	27	28	29	30	31
ALLENTOWN WB AIRPORT	SNOWFALL	T		T						.2				T	T	.1	T	3.2		.6	.9			T						.1		
	SN ON GND			T	T					T					T			3	1	T	2	2	1	T	T	T	T	T	T	T		T
	WTR EQUIV																	.2			.2	.2										
ALTOONA HORSESHOE CURVE	SNOWFALL							.5		2.5	1.0		.5					.5		4.0	1.5				T		T				T	.5
	SN ON GND							1		3	2	1	1	1	T			1		4	5	4	3	3	2	2	2	2	2	2	1	2
ARTEMAS 1 WNW	SNOWFALL									-			-			-	-			-	-						-		-	-		
	SN ON GND									T	T	T				1	T			4	1	T	T				3		T	T	T	T
BEAVERTOWN	SNOWFALL			-					-	T				-							-									T		
	SN ON GND			T					T					T							3	1	1	1	T	T	T	T	T	T	T	T
BELLEFONTE 4 S	SNOWFALL			T	T			-	-	-	-			T							-			-						T		
	SN ON GND							1	1	2	2										3	3	2	3	2	1						
BERWICK	SNOWFALL			T				T		T				T				T		1.3	3.0			T						T		
	SN ON GND	T	T	T						T				T				T		1	2	2	1	T	T	T	T	T	T	T	T	T
BRADFORD 4 W RES	SNOWFALL	T		1.7	.5			.5	T	1.5								.8		.8	2.5		.5	1.3	T			.5			.8	1.0
	SN ON GND	2	1	3	3	3	2	3	3	4	3	2	2	2	2	1	1	2	1	2	5	4	4	5	5	5	5	5	5	3	4	5
BROOKVILLE CAA AIRPORT	SNOWFALL		T	.8	T			.2	.2	2.3	.2							.4		4.0	.6	.1	.9	.2	T		T	T			.8	.1
	SN ON GND			T	T	T	T	T	T	1	1										4	4	4	5	5	4	4	4	4	3	1	T
BURGETTSTOWN 2 W	SNOWFALL									.5								T			2.5							T			-	-
	SN ON GND									1								T			3	2	2	2	2	2	2	2	2	-	1	1
BURNT CABINS 2 NE	SNOWFALL									-							-			4.5	-											
	SN ON GND									1							1			5	5	4	3	2	2	2	2	2	1	1		
BUTLER	SNOWFALL							T		T											5.0			1.0				T				1.0
	SN ON GND							T	T	T											5	5	5	6	6	6	6	6	4	1	1	2
CANTON 1 NW	SNOWFALL	T	T	.6	T			T	T	.2	1.2		T	T				T			4.0	T	1.6	T				T	T	T	.5	
	SN ON GND	T	T	1	T	T	T	T	T	T	1		T	T	T	T	T	T	T	T	4	3	4	3	3	3	2	2	2	2	3	2
CARLISLE	SNOWFALL							T		T							T	T		3.0	1.0											
	SN ON GND							T												3	3	2	2	2	2	2	2	2	2	T	T	T
CHAMBERSBURG 1 ESE	SNOWFALL							.3									1.3			4.0	.5											
	SN ON GND							T									1	1	T	4	3	3	2	1	1	1	1	1	1	T	T	T
CLARION 3 SW	SNOWFALL	T		.3					T	1.0	.5								T		4.5			1.5	T				T	T	.5	T
	SN ON GND	T	T	T	T	T	T	T		1	1	T	T	T					T		5	4	4	5	5	5	4	4	4	3	2	
COATESVILLE 1 SW	SNOWFALL																	2.6			5.5											
	SN ON GND																	3	2	1	6	5	5	3	3	3	3	2	2	2	T	T
CORRY	SNOWFALL	2.0	T	2.0	.5			1.0	1.5	1.0			T					1.0		1.5	2.0		1.5	1.0	1.0		T	T			3.0	5.0
	SN ON GND	2	2	2	3	2	2	2	3	4	2	1	1	1	1	1	1	1	1	2	4	4	5	5	6	5	5	5	3	1	4	8
COUDERSPORT 2 NW	SNOWFALL	T		.4	.5			T	.1	2.0				.5				.2	T		5.0	.5		2.0							1.7	4.8
	SN ON GND	1	1	1	2	1	1	1	2	4	2	1	1	2	2	1	1	1	1	1	6	6	6	8	7	6	6	5	4	3	4	9
DIXON	SNOWFALL	T		-	.3			T		.5	.3		T	.3	T			.6			1.0	.3		1.7		T		T	T	.2	T	T
	SN ON GND	T	T	-	T	T	T	T	T	1	T			T	T	T		1	1	T	1	1	1	2	2	2	2	2	2	T	T	T
DONEGAL	SNOWFALL		T		.1			.5	1.0	4.0	1.0	1.0					2.0	1.0		2.5	1.0	T			T	T	.5	T			2.0	.5
	SN ON GND		T		T			T	1	5	6	6	4	2	2	2	4	4	3	5	6	6	5	4	3	3	3	3	2	1	2	2
EAGLES MERE	SNOWFALL			1.6	.5			T	T	1.0				T	T			T			3.0	T		1.6				T	T	T	T	T
	SN ON GND	5	5	6	7	7	6	6	6	7	6	2	2	2	2	2	2	2	2	2	5	5	4	5	5	5	5	5	5	4	4	3
EMPORIUM 1 E	SNOWFALL	T		1.0	T			1.0	T	.5	T			T	T			T			3.0		T	1.0				T	T	.3	1.0	.3
	SN ON GND	T		1	1	T	T	1	1	2	1			T				T			3	3	2	3	3	2	2	2	1	1	2	2
EVERETT 1 SW	SNOWFALL							T	T	T				T			.5	T		4.8									T			
	SN ON GND							T	T	1				T				T		4	4	4	3	3	3	3	3	2	T	T	T	
FORD CITY 4 S DAM	SNOWFALL	T						T		.5	1.0		T					T	T		3.0	T	T	.5								.5
	SN ON GND	T	T					T	T	1	1	1	1	1	T	T	T	T	T	T	3	3	3	3	3	3	3	3	3	1	T	1
FRANKLIN	SNOWFALL									.5	T						T				4.0	T	1.0	1.0	T						1.0	.5
	SN ON GND	T	T	T	T	T		T	T	1	T						T				4	4	5	6	6	6	5	3	2	2	2	1
GEORGE SCHOOL	SNOWFALL									T					.3			3.0		.4	3.3									.3		
	SN ON GND																	3	2	2	5	5	5	5	5	4	4	4	4	3	T	
GETTYSBURG	SNOWFALL													T							4.0											
	SN ON GND																				4	3	2	1	T	T	T	T				
GRATZ 1 N	SNOWFALL			T					T	T				T					T		2.5			T				T		T		
	SN ON GND			T	T				T	T				T					T		3	3	2	2	1	1	T	T	T	T		
GREENVILLE	SNOWFALL		1.7	.8	.1			.2	.5	.4			T							3.2	1.2		.8	.5	.3		T				2.2	.4
	SN ON GND	1	1	T	T	T		T	T	1			T							3	4	3	4	4	4	4	4	3	3	1	3	3
HARRISBURG WB AIRPORT	SNOWFALL		T	T				T		T			T	.3			.5	T		3.3	1.2			T			T	T	.1	T		T
	SN ON GND									T				T				T	T		4	2	2	T	T	T	T	T	1	T		
	WTR EQUIV																				.3	.4	.3									
HAWLEY 1 S DAM	SNOWFALL			3.0						T								T			1.4			T						T		
	SN ON GND	T	T	3	2	1	T	T	T	T	T							T	T	T	1	1	1	1	1	1	1	1	1	T	T	T
HUNTINGDON	SNOWFALL			T				T	.1	T	1.0			T							3.5	T								.5		T
	SN ON GND							T	T	T	1	T	T								4	4	3	2	1	1	1	T	T	1	T	T
INDIANA 3 SE	SNOWFALL								.3	.5	3.0	2.0	1.0	.3				T			3.7			.3	T		T	T			T	.2
	SN ON GND								T	1	2	2	T	T	T	T	T	T	T	T	4	4	4	4	4	3	3	3	2	1		T
JOHNSTOWN	SNOWFALL	.1		T		T		T	.1	.5	.5	.2	T	.7	T		T	.2	.2	.3	4.5	T	T	T	.1	T	T	T				.2
	SN ON GND	T						T	T	1	1	T		1			T	T	T	T	5	T	T	T	T		T	T	T			T
KANE 1 NNE	SNOWFALL	.5		1.5	1.0	.3		1.0	.2	.6	.3		T		T			.8	T		4.4	.5	.4	2.5	.2	T	T	.4	T	T	2.2	1.8
	SN ON GND	2	2	3	4	4	4	4	4	4	3	2	2	2	2	2	2	3	3	2	5	5	6	8	8	8	8	8	8	7	9	9
LANDISVILLE	SNOWFALL									T								1.5			3.5									.2		
	SN ON GND																	2	1		4	3	3	2	2	2	2	2	1	1		
LAWRENCEVILLE 2 S	SNOWFALL	T		T				T	T	1.0			T	T				T			2.5	.3		1.0				T			1.0	
	SN ON GND	T		T				T	T	1	T			T	T	T		T	T		3	3	3	4	4	4	3	3	3	T	1	T
LEWISTOWN	SNOWFALL			T					T	.5	.5										3.0									T		T
	SN ON GND			T						T	1										3	2	1	T	T	T	T					

Station		1	2	3	4	5	6	7	8	9	10	11	12	13	14	15	16	17	18	19	20	21	22	23	24	25	26	27	28	29	30	31
LOCK HAVEN	SNOWFALL			T	T			T	T	.5	.5			T				T			2.8	T		T				T	T	T	T	T
	SN ON GND			T				T		1	1			T				T			3	3	2	1	1	1	1	1	1	1	1	T
MEADVILLE 1 S	SNOWFALL	.7		1.4	.6	.1		.3	.2	.7	.3		.2	T				T	T		3.3	T	.1	1.7		.3	.1	T	T		2.4	2.9
	SN ON GND	1	1	1	1	1	1	1	1	2	1	T	T	T	T	T	T	T	T	T	3	3	3	4	4	3	3	3	2	1	2	4
MERCER 2 NNE	SNOWFALL			-				-		-	-									-	-			-						-	-	-
	SN ON GND			1				-		-	1									1	5			-						-	-	-
MONTROSE 1 E	SNOWFALL	T	T	1.9	2.0		T		T	.5	.2		T	.7	T	T		T	T		1.6	.8	T	2.7	T	T	T	T	T	.3	T	2.3
	SN ON GND	4	4	6	7	6	6	6	6	6	5	2	1	1	1	1	1	1	1	1	3	3	3	5	5	5	5	5	5	4	3	5
MOUNT POCONO 2 N AIRPORT	SNOWFALL	1.0		2.5						-				.5				T		.3	.8			-						T		
	SN ON GND	1		2	2	1	1			1				1	T	T		T		T	1	1	T	1	1	T	T	T	T	T		
NEW CASTLE 1 N	SNOWFALL							.1		.5	T			T	T				T	.5	4.0	T		.8	.3		T	.1			T	T
	SN ON GND																		T		-	-	-	-	-	-	-	-	-	-	-	-
NEWPORT	SNOWFALL			T					T	T	T			T	T			T			3.2											T
	SN ON GND			T	T				T	T											3	2	2	T	T							
PALMERTON	SNOWFALL			T						T				T			T	.5		1.5	.5			T						T		T
	SN ON GND			T	T					T				T				1			2	T	T	T						T		
PHILADELPHIA WB AIRPORT	SNOWFALL													T	.6		T	1.8		2.8	1.6									.2		
	SN ON GND									T					1			1	1	T	4	3	3	1	1	1	T	T	T	T	T	
	WTR EQUIV																				.3	.3	.2									
PHILADELPHIA SHAWMONT	SNOWFALL									T					-			3.0		-	4.5											
	SN ON GND														-			-		-	-											
PHILIPSBURG CAA AIRPORT	SNOWFALL		1.0					1.0	T	2.0		T	.4	T				T		4.0	1.0	T	T	.5	T	T	T	T	T		T	.2
	SN ON GND			1				1	1	1	1	1	1	2	2	2	2	2	2	2	6	6	6	6	6	6	6	6	5	5	3	3
PHOENIXVILLE 1 E	SNOWFALL									T								2.5		2.5	1.0									T		
	SN ON GND																	-	1	3	4											
PITTSBURGH WB AIRPORT 2	SNOWFALL		T	T	T			T	.1	1.4	.5	T	T	T		T	.7	T		3.8	.2	.1	.1	T	T		.2				.1	.1
	SN ON GND	T		T				T	T	1	1	T	T	T			1	1	1	T	4	4	3	3	3	3	3	3	1	T	T	T
	WTR EQUIV																				.7	.7	.6	.5	.5	.5	.5	.5				
PORT CLINTON 1 S	SNOWFALL									T											2.0										T	
	SN ON GND	-	-	-	-	-	-	-	-	-	-	-	-	-	-	-	-	-	-	-	-	-	-	-	-	-	-	-	-	-	-	-
QUAKERTOWN 1 E	SNOWFALL									T				T	T			4.0			3.0									T		
	SN ON GND																	-			-											
READING WB CITY	SNOWFALL	T		T				T		T				T	T		T	.9		2.7	T			T						.2		
	SN ON GND									T								1	T	T	2	2	1	T	T	T	T	T	T	T		
RIDGWAY 3 W	SNOWFALL			T	T	T		T		T	.3							T			4.5	.2	T	.8						T	1.2	1.5
	SN ON GND			T	T	T	T	T	T	T	1							T	T		5	4	4	5	5	3	3	3	3	2	3	4
SCRANTON WB AIRPORT	SNOWFALL	.1	.1	.1		T		T	T	.4			.2	.2	T			.1	T	.5	.7	T	T	2.2	T	T	.1	T	T	T	T	T
	SN ON GND	T	T	T	T	T	T	T	T	T	T	T		-	T	T	T	T	T	T	-	1	1	-	2	1	1	1	1	1	1	T
	WTR EQUIV																							.1	.1							
SELINSGROVE CAA AIRPORT	SNOWFALL		T	T				T					T	2.0				T		2.0	1.0			T			T	T	T	T		T
	SN ON GND			T					T	T				2	T	T		T			3	3	2	1	1	1	T	T	T	T		T
SHIPPINGPORT WB	SNOWFALL							T	T	T		T	T	T			T	T		4.0	T	T	T	T	T		T				T	T
	SN ON GND							T	T	T			T	T	T	T	T	T	T	1	4	4	3	2	1	1	1	1	T			T
SOMERSET MAIN ST	SNOWFALL							.6	T	1.2	1.3	T	.2	1.0			1.6	.8		2.0	1.2						.3	.1			.1	.4
	SN ON GND									1	1	1	2	2	2	2	3	4	4	5	6	6	5	5	5	4	4	4	4	2	2	1
SPRINGS 1 SW	SNOWFALL			T	T			1.0	1.0	1.8	1.0	.5	.5	.5			3.0	.5		4.0	.4				T		.5	T			.5	T
	SN ON GND	T		T	T			1	2	4	5	5	5	5	5	5	8	8	8	11	11	10	9	8	8	8	9	9	8	3	1	1
TAMARACK 2 S FIRE TWR	SNOWFALL	T	T	2.0	.5			T	.4	.5	.3			T				.2			3.6	T	T	.8				T	T	.1	.5	.5
	SN ON GND	T	T	2	2	2	2	2	2	3	3	1	T	T	T	T	T	T	T	T	4	4	4	4	4	4	4	4	4	4	4	4
TIONESTA 2 SE DAM	SNOWFALL			T	T	T		.5	T	T	T							.5	T		3.0	T	T	.5	T	T	T	T			1.5	.5
	SN ON GND	T	T	T	T	T	T	T	T	1	1							1	T	T	3	3	3	4	4	4	3	3	3	2	2	2
TOWANDA	SNOWFALL	T	T	T	T			T	T	.4	1.3		.2	.2	T	T		.2	T		2.4	.3		1.7		T	T	T	T	.1	.3	T
	SN ON GND	T	T	T	T	T	T	T	T	T	1		T	T	T	T		T	T	T	2	2	2	3	2	2	1	1	1	T	T	T
TOWER CITY 5 SW	SNOWFALL			T				T		.5			T					.5		1.0	4.0									T		
	SN ON GND																			-	-											
UNIONTOWN	SNOWFALL				T			.8	.5	1.0	T	.5	T	.3			3.5	T		T	T	T		T	T	T	.5				T	T
	SN ON GND							1	1	2	2	2	2	2	2	2	5	5	4	3	3	3	3	2	2	2	2	2	2	T	T	T
WARREN	SNOWFALL			.4	T			.4	.4	.5		T						.4			2.2		T	1.6			.2	T			2.1	2.0
	SN ON GND	1	1	1	1	T	T	T	T	1	1	T	T	T	T	T	T	T	T		2	2	2	3	2	2	2	2	2	1	2	4
WAYNESBURG 2 W	SNOWFALL							T	T	2.0	1.5						.8	2.0			1.0	T	T				.5	T	T			
	SN ON GND							T	T	2	4	2	T	T	T	T	1	3	3	2	2	2	1	T	T	T	1	T	T	T	T	
WELLSBORO 3 S	SNOWFALL	T	T	2.0	T			T	T	1.0	.5	T	T	.5				T			4.0	T		1.0			T	T	T	T	1.0	T
	SN ON GND	T	T	2	1	1	1	T	T	1	1	T	T	1	1	T	T	T	T	T	4	4	3	4	4	4	4	4	4	4	4	2
WEST CHESTER	SNOWFALL									T				T				-			-									T		
	SN ON GND																	3			4											
WILLIAMSPORT WB AIRPORT	SNOWFALL	T	.2	.6	T			.1	T	.5			T					T		2.7	1.2		T	.2			T	T	T	.4	T	.4
	SN ON GND			1	T	T		T	T	T	T							T			4	3	3	2	2	1	1	1	1	1	T	
	WTR EQUIV																				.4	.3	.3	.2	.2							
YORK 3 SSW PUMP STA	SNOWFALL							.5		T	T		T	T				2.0		-	3.5			T						T	T	
	SN ON GND																	-		T	-											

See reference notes following Station Index.

STATION INDEX

Station	Index No.	County	Drainage	Latitude	Longitude	Elevation	Obs. time Temp.	Obs. time Precip.	Observer	Refer to tables
ACMETONIA LOCK 3	0022	ALLEGHENY	1	40 32	79 49	748		7A	CORPS OF ENGINEERS	3
ALLENS MILLS	0099	JEFFERSON	1	41 12	78 55	1600		MID	CHARLES M. ALLEN	C
ALLENTOWN WB AP	0106	LEHIGH	9	40 39	75 26	376	MID	MID	U.S. WEATHER BUREAU	2 3 5 7 C
ALLENTOWN GAS CO	0111	LEHIGH	9	40 36	75 28	254	7A	7A	LEHIGH VLY GAS DIV	2 3 5
ALTOONA HORSESHOE CURVE	0134	BLAIR	6	40 30	78 29	1500	6P	6P	ALTOONA WATER BUR.	2 3 5 7
ARDENTSVILLE	0229	ADAMS	15	39 55	77 18	710	8A	8A	PA STATE COL EXP	2 3 5
ARTEMAS 1 WNW	0259	BEDFORD	12	39 45	78 28	1250	6P	6P	GRAYSON E.NORTHCRAFT	2 3 5 7 C
AUSTINBURG 2 W	0313	TIOGA	15	42 00	77 32	1590		7A	OTTO D. BACON	3 C
AVOCA CAA AP	0319	LUZERNE	15	41 21	75 44	922	MID	MID	COMBINED WITH STA NO	7905 4/55
BAKERSTOWN 3 WNW	0355	ALLEGHENY	1	40 39	79 59	1230	7P	7P	PITT'GH CUT FLWR CO	2 3 5
BARNES	0409	WARREN	1	41 40	79 02	1310		7A	CORPS OF ENGINEERS	3
BEAR GAP	0457	NORTH'LAND	15	40 50	76 30	900		MID	ROARING CRK WTR CO	3
BEAVER FALLS	0475	BEAVER	2	40 46	80 19	760		7A	HOWARD R. KEMP	3
BEAVERTOWN	0482	SNYDER	15	40 45	77 10	640	7A	7A	MARLIN R. ETTINGER	2 3 5 7
BEECH CREEK STATION	0499	CENTRE	16	41 04	77 34	620		7A	HAROLD S. RUPERT	3
BELLEFONTE 4 S	0530	CENTRE	16	40 51	77 47	1110	8A	8A	ROCKVIEW PRISON FRM	2 3 5 7
BERWICK	0611	COLUMBIA	15	41 04	76 15	570	6P	6P	AMER CAR & FNDRY CO	2 3 5 7
BETHLEHEM	0629	NORTHAMPTON	9	40 37	75 22	400		7A	ARTHUR CROPPER	3
#BETHLEHEM LEHIGH UNI	0634	NORTHAMPTON	9	40 36	75 23	450	MID	MID	LEHIGH UNIVERSITY	2 3 5 C
BLAIN	0725	PERRY	15	40 20	77 31	750		MID	PA DEPT FRST & WTRS	C
BLAIRSVILLE 6 ENE	0736	INDIANA	4	40 27	79 09	2048	8P	8P	U.S. WEATHER BUREAU	2 3 5
BLAKESLEE CORNERS	0743	MONROE	9	41 06	75 36	1650		MID	WALTER WILDRICK	C
BLOSERVILLE 1 N	0763	CUMBERLAND	15	40 16	77 22	650		5P	MRS. B. M. WILLDERS	3
BOSWELL 6 WNW	0820	SOMERSET	1	40 11	79 08	2580		7A	MRS. MAE L. KIMMEL	3 C
BRADDOCK LOCK 2	0861	ALLEGHENY	10	40 24	79 52	725		7A	CORPS OF ENGINEERS	3
BRADFORD CNTRL FIRE STA	0867	MC KEAN	1	41 57	78 39	1500		8A	BRADFORD FIRE DEPT	3
BRADFORD 4 W RES	0868	MC KEAN	1	41 57	78 44	1680	5P	5P	BRADFORD WTR DEPT	2 3 5 7
BREEZEWOOD	0905	BEDFORD	6	40 00	78 14	1352		MID	PA TURNPIKE COMM	3
BROOKVILLE CAA AIRPORT	1002	JEFFERSON	1	41 09	79 06	1417	MID	MID	CIVIL AERO. ADM.	2 3 5 7
BRUCETON 1 S	1033	ALLEGHENY	10	40 18	79 59	1065		7A	AUSTIN R. COOPER	3
BUCKSTOWN 1 SE	1073	SOMERSET	4	40 04	78 50	2460		MID	ALVIN W. MANGES	C
BUFFALO MILLS	1087	BEDFORD	6	39 57	78 39	1318		7A	MRS. NELLE R. BROWN	3
BURGETTSTOWN 2 W	1105	WASHINGTON	11	40 23	80 26	980	7A	7A	SMITH TWP MUN AUTH	2 3 5 7
BURNT CABINS 2 NE	1115	HUNTINGDON	6	40 05	77 52	990	MID	MID	PA TURNPIKE COMM	2 3 5 7
#BUTLER	1130	BUTLER	2	40 52	79 54	1100	4P	7A	WILLIAM C. FAUST	2 3 5 7
BUTLER SUBSTATION	1135	BUTLER	2	40 51	79 53	1140		MID	WEST PENN POWER CO	C
CAMP HILL	1198	CUMBERLAND	15	40 15	76 55	461		6P	JOSEPH N. HOBART	3
CANTON 1 NW	1215	BRADFORD	15	41 40	76 52	1520	7A	7A	MRS.MILDRED SPENCER	2 3 5 7 C
CARLISLE	1234	CUMBERLAND	15	40 12	77 11	460	6P	6P	C. E. MILLER	2 3 5 7
CARROLLTOWN 2 SSE	1255	CAMBRIA	16	40 35	78 42	2040		8A	ROBERT F. MAURER	3
CARTER CAMP 2 W	1262	POTTER	16	41 37	77 45	2030		7A	RICHARD L. MENKEN	3 C
CEDAR RUN	1301	LYCOMING	16	41 31	77 27	800		7A	KATHRYN T.KREIGHBAUM	3
CHADDS FORD	1342	DELAWARE	5	39 52	75 36	160		8A	MRS. GRACE A. WICKS	3
CHAMBERSBURG 1 ESE	1354	FRANKLIN	12	39 56	77 38	640	9P	9P	CHARLES A. BENDER	2 3 5 7 C
CHARLEROI	1372	WASHINGTON	10	40 08	79 55	1040		MID	WEST PENN POWER CO	C
CHARLEROI LOCK 4	1377	WESTMORELAND	10	40 09	79 54	749		7A	CORPS OF ENGINEERS	
#CHESTER	1423	DELAWARE	5	39 50	75 21	86	8A	8A	CHESTER TIMES	2 3 5
CLARENCE 1 E	1480	CENTRE	16	41 03	77 56	1440		7A	MARGARET A. SWANCER	
CLARION 3 SW	1485	CLARION	1	41 12	79 26	1114	8P	7A	PA ELECTRIC CO	2 5 7 C
CLAUSSVILLE	1505	LEHIGH	9	40 37	75 39	670		8A	WILLIAM J. DOTTERER	
CLAYSVILLE 3 W	1512	WASHINGTON	11	40 07	80 28	1000	7P	7A	MANUFAC. L & H CO	2 3 5
CLEARFIELD	1519	CLEARFIELD	16	41 01	78 26	1100		7A	IRA TAYLOR	3
CLEARFIELD 8 NW NURSERY	1522	CLEARFIELD	16	41 07	78 32	2120	4P	4P	R. R. HOUPT	CLOSED 5/55
CLERMONT	1529	MC KEAN	1	41 41	78 30	2104		7A	MRS.TILLIE M.SIMONDS	3 C
COALDALE 2 NW	1572	SCHUYLKILL	9	40 50	75 56	1026		7A	PANTHER VLY WTR CO	3
COATESVILLE 1 SW	1589	CHESTER	5	39 58	75 50	342	8A	8A	PHILA ELECTRIC CO	2 3 5 7 C
COATESVILLE	1594	CHESTER	5	39 59	75 49	340		8A	EDWARD O. BIEDEMAN	INACTIVE 12/55
COGAN STATION 2 N	1631	LYCOMING	16	41 21	77 06	640		7A	LEON L. CARSON	3
COLUMBIA	1675	LANCASTER	15	40 02	76 30	300	5S	5S	JAMES H. RUST	2 3 5
CONFLUENCE 1 SW DAM	1705	SOMERSET	17	39 48	79 22	1490	8A	8A	CORPS OF ENGINEERS	2 3 5 6 C
CONFLUENCE 1 NW	1710	FAYETTE	17	39 50	79 22	1331		7A	JOHN L. REID	3
CONNELLSVILLE	1723	FAYETTE	17	40 01	79 36	890		7A	EMERY C. STEWART	3
CONNELLSVILLE 2 E	1729	FAYETTE	17	40 01	79 33	1300		MID	HARRY C. JOY	C
CONSHOHOCKEN	1737	MONTGOMERY	5	40 04	75 19	70		8A	PHILA ELECTRIC CO	3
CORAOPOLIS NEVILLE IS	1773	ALLEGHENY	11	40 30	80 05	720		8A	PGH. COKE & CHEM CO	3
CORRY	1790	ERIE	1	41 55	79 38	1427	6P	6P	GEORGE P. MULDERICK	2 3 5 7
COUDERSPORT 2 NW	1805	POTTER	1	41 48	78 03	2220	7P	8A	J. EDWARD TWIGGS	2 3 5 7
COUDERSPORT 7 E	1809	POTTER	1	41 46	77 53	2425		7A	CAMP POTATO	3
COVINGTON	1832	TIOGA	15	41 45	77 05	1193		7A	GROVER D. CLEVELAND	3
CREEKSIDE	1881	INDIANA	1	40 41	79 12	1035		7A	CORPS OF ENGINEERS	3
CRESSON 2 SE	1895	CAMBRIA	6	40 27	78 34	2540		7A	MILES A. VECELLIO	3 C
CUSTER CITY 2 W	1978	MC KEAN	1	41 55	78 41	2120		8A	M. D. BOOTH AND CO	3
DANVILLE	2013	MONTOUR	15	40 58	76 37	460		7A	MRS.MARIE M. LITTLE	3
DERRY	2108	WESTMORELAND	4	40 20	79 18	1150	6P	6P	MISS N. D. MINEMAN	2 3 5
DEVAULT 1 W	2116	CHESTER	14	40 05	75 33	360	MID	MID	PA TURNPIKE COMM	2 3 5
DINGMANS FERRY	2160	PIKE	5	41 13	74 52	360		MID	CLARENCE H. SMITH	C
DIXON	2171	WYOMING	15	41 34	75 54	620	7A	7A	HAROLD J. KUSCHEL	2 3 5 7 C
DONEGAL	2183	WESTMORELAND	17	40 07	79 23	1746	MID	MID	PA TURNPIKE COMM	2 3 5 7
#DONORA	2190	WASHINGTON	10	40 11	79 51	814	NOON	NOON	DONORA ZINC WORKS	2 3 5
DOYLESTOWN	2221	BUCKS	5	40 18	75 08	393		5P	GEORGE HART	3
DRIFTWOOD	2245	CAMERON	16	41 20	78 08	880		MID	SIDNEY KENNEDY	C
DU BOIS 7 E	2265	CLEARFIELD	16	41 06	78 38	1670	5P	5P	CITY OF DU BOIS	2 3 5 C
DUNLO	2298	CAMBRIA	4	40 17	78 43	2410		MID	MRS. D. L. WHITE	C
DUSHORE 3 NE	2324	SULLIVAN	16	41 33	76 21	1750		7A	PATRICK P. RYAN	3 C
EAGLES MERE	2343	SULLIVAN	16	41 24	76 35	2020	7A	7A	MRS.ELSIE P. BIGGER	2 3 5 7 C
EAST BRADY	2363	CLARION	1	40 59	79 37	820	5P	5P	A. B. KEMPEL	2 3 5
E. WATERFORD 3 E	2459	PERRY	6	40 21	77 33	2125	8A	8A	U.S. WEATHER BUREAU	INACTIVE 5/55
EBENSBURG	2466	CAMBRIA	4	40 29	78 43	2090	7P	7A	ROBERT A. WASSER	2 3 5
EDINBORO	2514	ERIE	1	41 52	80 08	1220		8A	EDINBORO ST TCHR COL	3
ELIZABETHTOWN	2560	LANCASTER	15	40 09	76 37	460		8A	MASONIC HOME	3
EMPORIUM 1 E	2633	CAMERON	16	41 31	78 13	1160	7A	7A	RUSSELL E.PALMATEER	2 5 7 C
ENGLISH CENTER	2644	LYCOMING	16	41 26	77 17	881		7A	WILLIAM SUDERS	C
EPHRATA	2662	LANCASTER	15	40 11	76 10	465	6P	6P	STANLEY L.VON NEIDA	2 3 5
EQUINUNK	2669	WAYNE	5	41 51	75 13	900		8A	MRS.ROSE M. NEILSEN	
ERIE CAA AIRPORT	2682	ERIE	8	42 05	80 12	732	MID	MID	CIVIL AERO. ADM.	2 5
EVERETT 1 SW	2721	BEDFORD	6	40 00	78 23	1020	MID	MID	PA TURNPIKE COMM	2 3 5 7 C
FARRELL-SHARON	2814	MERCER	2	41 14	80 30	865	7P	7P	SHARON STEEL CORP	2 3 5
FORD CITY 4 S DAM	2942	ARMSTRONG	1	40 43	79 30	950	8A	8A	CORPS OF ENGINEERS	2 3 5 6 7 C
FRANKLIN	3028	VENANGO	1	41 23	79 49	987	7P	7A	JAMES K. ELLIOTT	2 3 5 7 C
FREDERICKSVILLE 2 SE	3047	BERKS	14	40 26	75 40	950	8A	8A	D. P. FENSTERMACHER	2 3 5
FREELAND	3056	LUZERNE	15	41 01	75 54	1900	6P	8A	ANDREW B. EVANSHA	2 3 5
GALETON	3130	POTTER	16	41 44	77 39	1325		7A	W. GALE LUSH	3
GEIGERTOWN	3189	BERKS	14	40 13	75 50	400		8A	WALTER C. WOLF	3
GEORGE SCHOOL	3200	BUCKS	5	40 13	74 56	135	7P	7P	GEORGE M. HART	2 3 5 7
#GETTYSBURG	3218	ADAMS	12	39 50	77 14	540	9A	9A	HUGH C. MC ILHENNY	2 3 5 7
GETTYSBURG 1 S	3223	ADAMS	12	39 48	77 14	560		MID	NAT MILITARY PARK	C
GIFFORD	3237	MC KEAN	1	41 51	78 36	2220		8A	SOUTH PENN OIL CO	3
GLENCOE	3298	SOMERSET	12	39 49	78 51	1620		MID	MRS. MARY M.HARTMAN	C
GLEN HAZEL 2 NE DAM	3311	ELK	1	41 34	78 36	1725		8A	CORPS OF ENGINEERS	3 C
GLEN ROCK	3330	YORK	15	39 48	76 44	620		MID	MRS.E.C.MC WILLIAMS	C
GLENWILLARD DASH DAM	3343	ALLEGHENY	11	40 33	80 13	705		7A	CORPS OF ENGINEERS	3
GORDON	3379	SCHUYLKILL	15	40 45	76 20	900	6P	6P	MISS S. M. JOHNSON	2 3 5
GOULDSBORO	3394	WAYNE	9	41 15	75 27	1890		7A	L. H. EILENBERGER	3
GRANTVILLE 2 SW	3422	DAUPHIN	15	40 22	76 41	510		5S	EARL E. RHOADS	3
GRATERFORD	3435	MONTGOMERY	14	40 14	75 27	160		7A	CLAUDE K. KULP	3
GRATZ 1 N	3438	DAUPHIN	15	40 38	76 43	760	8A	8A	LEE M. LEITZEL	2 3 5 7 C
GREENSBORO LOCK 7	3503	GREENE	10	39 47	79 55	808		7A	CORPS OF ENGINEERS	3
GREENSBURG 2 E	3515	WESTMORELAND	10	40 18	79 31	1225		MID	PA DEPT HIGHWAYS	C
GREENSBURG 3 SE	3516	WESTMORELAND	10	40 17	79 30	1245		6P	WESTMORELAND WTR CO	3
GREENVILLE	3526	MERCER	2	41 24	80 23	1026	6P	6P	C. EARL MILLER	2 3 5 7
HANOVER	3662	YORK	15	39 48	76 59	600	8A	8A	HANOVER EVENING SUN	2 3 5
#HARRISBURG WB AP	3699	YORK	15	40 13	76 51	335	MID	MID	U.S. WEATHER BUREAU	2 3 5 7 C
HARRISBURG NORTH	3704	DAUPHIN	15	40 18	76 54	323		9A	GEORGE S. BEAL	3
HAWLEY	3758	WAYNE	5	41 29	75 10	880		7A	MRS.KATHERINE S.BATES	3
HAWLEY 1 S DAM	3761	WAYNE	5	41 28	75 11	1200	7A	7A	PA POWER & LIGHT CO	2 3 5 6 7 C
HOLLIDAYSBURG	4001	BLAIR	6	40 26	78 24	960		MID	JOHN M. RINGLER	C
HOLLISTERVILLE	4008	WAYNE	5	41 23	75 26	1360		8A	PA POWER & LIGHT CO	3
#HOLTWOOD	4019	LANCASTER	15	39 50	76 20	187	MID	8A	PA POWER & LIGHT CO	2 3 5 C
HOME	4027	INDIANA	1	40 45	79 06	1220		MID	MRS. EDNA M. BUSH	C
HONESDALE 4 NW	4043	WAYNE	5	41 37	75 19	1410		9A	GEORGE C. WILLIAMS	3

Station	Index No.	County	Drainage	Latitude	Longitude	Elevation	Obs. time Temp.	Obs. time Precip.	Observer	Refer to tables
HONESDALE 6 NNW	4044	WAYNE	5	41 39	75 17	1050		MID	FRIEND E. WALTER	C
HOOVERSVILLE	4058	SOMERSET	4	40 09	78 55	1660		7A	PA ELECTRIC CO	3
HOP BOTTOM 2 SE	4066	SUSQUEHANNA	15	41 43	75 43	900		7A	JOSEPH J. SANSUSKAS	3
HUNTINGDON	4159	HUNTINGDON	15	40 29	78 01	660	7A	7A	JOHN R. HENDERSON	2 3 5 7
HUNTSDALE	4166	CUMBERLAND	15	40 06	77 18	610		8A	METRO P. DOROSH	3 C
HYNDMAN	4190	BEDFORD	12	39 49	78 43	920		8A	MRS.GERTRUDE M.BURTON	3
INDIANA 3 SE	4214	INDIANA	4	40 36	79 07	1102	7P	7A	CLYMER WATER SVC CO	2 3 5 7 C
IRWIN	4276	WESTMORELAND	10	40 20	79 42	1100	5P	5P	WESTMORELAND WTR CO	2 3 5
JACKSON SUMMIT	4304	TIOGA	15	41 57	77 01	1690		MID	ARCHIE LAIN	C
JAMESTOWN 2 NW	4325	CRAWFORD	2	41 30	80 28	1050	8A	8A	DEPT FOREST & WTRS	2 3 5 6 C
JIM THORPE	4370	CARBON	9	40 52	75 45	830	5P	5P	HENRY S. HAAK	2 3 5
#JOHNSTOWN	4385	CAMBRIA	4	40 20	78 55	1214	9A	9A	JOHNSTOWN TRIBUNE	2 3 5 7
JOHNSTOWN 2	4390	CAMBRIA	4	40 19	78 55	1275		MID	CITY OF JOHNSTOWN	C
KANE 1 NNE	4432	MC KEAN	1	41 41	78 48	1750	8A	8A	SPRING WATER CO	2 3 5 7 C
KARTHAUS	4450	CLEARFIELD	16	41 07	78 07	950		7A	JEROME S. HOWE	3
KEATING SUMMIT	4466	POTTER	1	41 41	78 11	1840		7A	EUGENE L. KREITNER	3
KEGG	4481	BEDFORD	6	39 59	78 43	1280	MID	MID	PA TURNPIKE COMM	2 3 5
KITTANNING LOCK 7	4611	ARMSTRONG	1	40 49	79 32	790		7A	CORPS OF ENGINEERS	3
KREGAR 4 SE	4667	WESTMORELAND	17	40 06	79 14	2530		MID	PA TURNPIKE COMM	3
KRESGEVILLE 3 W	4672	CARBON	9	40 54	75 34	720		9A	CITY OF BETHLEHEM	3
LAFAYETTE MC KEAN PARK	4706	MC KEAN	1	41 48	78 40	2130		8A	CHARLES GORDON	3
LAKEVILLE 1 NNE	4733	WAYNE	5	41 27	75 16	1440		8A	MRS. GLADYS REINEKE	3
LANCASTER 2 NE PUMP STA	4758	LANCASTER	15	40 03	76 17	255	6P	6P	LANCASTER WATER BUR	2 3 5
LANCASTER 2 NE FILT PLT	4763	LANCASTER	15	40 03	76 17	270		MID	LANCASTER WATER BUR	C
LANDISVILLE	4778	LANCASTER	15	40 06	76 25	410	8A	8A	PA STATE COLLEGE	2 3 5 6 7 C
LATROBE	4832	WESTMORELAND	4	40 19	79 23	1000		MID	WEST PENN POWER CO	3
LAURELTON STATE VILLAGE	4853	UNION	15	40 54	77 13	880		MID	PA DEPT OF WELFARE	C
LAWRENCEVILLE 2 S	4873	TIOGA	15	41 59	77 07	1000	7A	7A	HARRY P. HOWLAND	2 3 5 7
LEBANON 2 NW	4891	LEBANON	15	40 22	76 28	600	6P	6P	LEBANON BDCSTG CO	2 3 5 7
LEBANON 3 SW	4896	LEBANON	15	40 19	76 28	490		MID	THOMAS DONNACHIE	C
LEHIGHTON	4934	CARBON	9	40 50	75 48	580		7A	GOODWIN S. DEFREHN	C
LE ROY	4972	BRADFORD	15	41 41	76 43	1040		6P	MRS.DIMMIS M.BAILEY	3
LEWIS RUN 3 S	4984	MC KEAN	1	41 50	78 39	1700		7A	SOUTH PENN OIL CO	C
LEWISTOWN	4992	MIFFLIN	6	40 35	77 35	480	7A	7A	AMERICAN VISCOSE CO	2 5 7 C
LINESVILLE 5 WNW	5050	CRAWFORD	2	41 41	80 31	1020	7P	8A	MISS RETTA M. CRUMB	2 5
LOCK HAVEN	5104	CLINTON	16	41 08	77 27	570	7P	7A	PETER L. STEVENSON	2 3 5 7
LOCK HAVEN 2	5109	CLINTON	16	41 08	77 27	630		MID	HUGH F. PARKER	C
LONG POND 2 W	5160	MONROE	9	41 03	75 30	1860		7A	THOMAS MECKES	3
MADERA	5336	CLEARFIELD	16	40 50	78 26	1460	7A	7A	MRS. JULIA J. SHOFF	2 3 5 C
MAHAFFEY	5342	CLEARFIELD	16	40 53	78 44	1280		7A	MISS ELLEN J. MILES	3
MAPLE GLEN	5368	MONTGOMERY	5	40 11	75 11	380		6P	FRANCES E.SCHEIBNER	3
MAPLETON DEPOT	5381	HUNTINGDON	6	40 24	77 56	580		7A	MRS. I. S. BUCHANAN	3
MARCUS HOOK	5390	DELAWARE	5	39 49	75 25	12	MID	MID	SUN OIL CO	2 3 5
MARIENVILLE	5400	FOREST	1	41 28	79 08	1690		MID	ROY A. MARKER	C
MARION CENTER 2 SE	5408	INDIANA	1	40 45	79 02	1610		7A	CORPS OF ENGINEERS	3
MARTINSBURG 1 SW	5453	BLAIR	6	40 18	78 20	1360		MID	BLUE MT CANNERIES	C
MARTINSBURG CAA AP	5454	BLAIR	6	40 18	78 19	1463	MID	MID	CIVIL AERO. ADM.	2 3 5
MATAMORAS	5470	PIKE	5	41 22	74 42	439		7A	HARRY BISLAND	3
MAYBURG	5490	FOREST	1	41 36	79 13	1150		7A	CORPS OF ENGINEERS	3
MC CONNELSBURG	5526	FULTON	12	39 56	78 00	895		8A	MRS. HELEN M.SHIVES	3
MC KEESPORT	5573	ALLEGHENY	10	40 21	79 52	720		8A	NATIONAL TUBE CO	3
MEADOW RUN PONDS	5601	LUZERNE	15	41 13	75 40	1995		MID	GEORGE PEARAGE	C
MEADVILLE 1 S	5606	CRAWFORD	1	41 38	80 10	1065	8A	8A	CITY OF MEADVILLE	2 3 5 7 C
MEDIX RUN	5627	ELK	16	41 17	78 24	1100		7A	MRS. E. M. SNYDER	3 C
MERCER 2 NNE	5651	MERCER	2	41 15	80 13	1160	7P	7A	WILLIAM K. STRUTHERS	2 3 5 7
MERCER HIWAY SHED	5654	MERCER	2	41 14	80 15	1250		MID	PA DEPT HIGHWAYS	C
MERCERSBURG	5662	FRANKLIN	12	39 50	77 54	605		8A	ROLLIN P. GILBERT	3
MERWINSBURG	5676	MONROE	9	40 58	75 28	920		MID	GERALD D. MURPHY	C
MEYERSDALE	5684	SOMERSET	17	39 49	79 02	2080		8A	JOHN M. BLOCHER	3
MIDDLETOWN OLMSTED FLD	5703	DAUPHIN	15	40 11	76 46	303	MID	MID	U. S. AIR FORCE	2 3 5
MIDLAND DAM 7	5710	BEAVER	11	40 38	80 28	689	11P	7A	CORPS OF ENGINEERS	2 3 5
MILAN	5731	BRADFORD	15	41 55	76 31	760		MID	W. S. ROBERTS	CLOSED 6/55
MILANVILLE	5738	WAYNE	5	41 40	75 04	760		8A	CHARLES W. DAVIS	3
MILLERSBURG 2 E	5775	DAUPHIN	15	40 32	76 56	560		MID	RUSSELL SHEPLEY	C
MILLHEIM	5790	CENTRE	15	40 54	77 29	1090		7A	NEVIN E. BOWERSOX	3
MILLVILLE 2 SW	5817	COLUMBIA	15	41 06	76 34	860		7A	KENNETH LEIGHOW	3 C
MILROY	5825	MIFFLIN	6	40 43	77 35	770		8A	THOMAS C. HARBESON	3
MONTROSE 1 E	5915	SUSQUEHANNA	15	41 50	75 51	1630	7A	7A	WILMER W. HOOPES,JR	2 3 5 7 C
MORGANTOWN	5956	BERKS	15	40 09	75 54	595	MID	MID	PA TURNPIKE COMM	2 3 5
MT GRETNA 2 SE	6028	LANCASTER	15	40 14	76 26	670	MID	MID	PA TURNPIKE COMM	2 3 5
MOUNT POCONO 2 N AP	6055	MONROE	5	41 09	75 22	1915	5P	5P	H. JOHN DAVIS, JR.	2 3 5 7 C
MOUNT UNION 1 N	6067	MIFFLIN	6	40 24	77 53	820		MID	MT UNION WTR WORKS	C
MUHLENBURG 1 SE	6090	LUZERNE	15	41 13	76 08	1110	6P	6P	THEODORE J. SAMPSON	2 3 5
MURRYSVILLE	6111	WESTMORELAND	10	40 26	79 42	903		MID	DAVID C. SHAW	C
MYERSTOWN	6126	LEBANON	14	40 22	76 18	480		8A	MRS.KATHLEEN WANDELL	3
NATRONA LOCK 4	6151	ALLEGHENY	1	40 37	79 43	800		7A	CORPS OF ENGINEERS	3
NEFFS MILLS 3 NE	6174	HUNTINGDON	6	40 40	77 55	900		MID	PA STATE UNIVERSITY	C
NESHAMINY FALLS	6194	BUCKS	5	40 09	74 57	60		MID	PHILA SUB WATER CO	3
NEWBURG 3 W	6225	FRANKLIN	15	40 09	77 37	745	MID	MID	PA TURNPIKE COMM	2 3 5
NEW CASTLE 1 N	6233	LAWRENCE	2	41 01	80 22	900	5P	7A	BAXTER F. JOHNSON	2 3 5 7 C
#NEWELL	6246	FAYETTE	10	40 05	79 54	805	NOON	NOON	GENERAL CHEMICAL CO	2 3 5
NEW PARK	6289	YORK	15	39 44	76 30	780		6P	CLINTON J. ALLEN	3
NEWPORT	6297	PERRY	6	40 29	77 08	400	7A	7A	MRS. FRANCES K. FRY	2 3 5 7
NEW STANTON	6310	WESTMORELAND	10	40 13	79 36	980	MID	MID	PA TURNPIKE COMM	2 3 5
NEW TRIPOLI	6326	LEHIGH	14	40 41	75 45	570		6P	FRED C. OSWALD	3
NORRISTOWN	6370	MONTGOMERY	14	40 07	75 21	75	MID	8A	GEORGE H. BOONE	2 3 5
NORTH EAST 2 SE	6396	ERIE	8	42 12	79 49	1060		9A	ELLSWORTH WEAVER	3
ORWELL 3 N	6621	BRADFORD	15	41 55	76 16	1620		8A	WILLIAM I. BROWN	3
PALM	6681	MONTGOMERY	14	40 26	75 32	390		8A	FRED C. ESCHBACH	3
#PALMERTON	6689	CARBON	9	40 48	75 37	435	MID	MID	NEW JERSEY ZINC CO	2 3 5 7 C
PARKER	6721	ARMSTRONG	1	41 05	79 41	1140		7A	LOUIS A. MALARKEY	3
PARKER 1 E	6724	CLARION	1	41 06	79 40	1100		MID	P. M. NEELY	C
PAUPACK 2 WNW	6762	PIKE	5	41 24	75 14	1360		8A	MISS L. VETTERLEIN	3
PECKS POND	6786	PIKE	5	41 17	75 06	1380		9A	MRS. CARRIE NESS	3
#PHILA DREXEL INST OF TEC	6879	PHILADELPHIA	14	39 57	75 11	30	MID	MID	FRANCIS K. DAVIS,JR	2 3 5
PHILADELPHIA WB AP	6889	PHILADELPHIA	5	39 53	75 14	13	MID	MID	U.S. WEATHER BUREAU	2 3 5 7 C
#PHILADELPHIA PT BREEZE	6899	PHILADELPHIA	5	39 55	75 12	85	MID	MID	ATLANTIC REFINING	2 3 5 C
PHILADELPHIA SHAWMONT	6904	PHILADELPHIA	5	40 02	75 15	70	7P	7P	SCHUYLKILL NAVIG CO	2 3 5 7
#PHILADELPHIA CITY	6909	PHILADELPHIA	5	39 57	75 09	26	9A	9A	USN HYDROGRAPHIC OFF	2 3 5 C
PHILIPSBURG CAA AP	6916	CENTRE	6	40 54	78 05	1918	8P	8P	CIVIL AERO. ADM.	2 3 5 7 C
PHOENIXVILLE 1 E	6927	CHESTER	14	40 07	75 30	105	6P	MID	PHILA SUB WATER CO	2 3 5 7 C
PIKES CREEK	6939	LUZERNE	15	41 18	76 08	1320		MID	HARRY SHELDON	3 C
PIMPLE HILL	6944	MONROE	9	41 02	75 30	2215	9A	9A	PA DEPT FRST & WTRS	2 3 5 6
PINE GROVE 1 NE	6954	SCHUYLKILL	15	40 34	76 22	535		8A	PA POWER & LIGHT CO	3
PITTSBURGH WB AP 2	6993	ALLEGHENY	11	40 30	80 13	1151	MID	MID	U.S. WEATHER BUREAU	2 3 5 7 C
#PITTSBURGH WB CITY	6997	ALLEGHENY	11	40 27	80 00	749	MID	MID	U.S. WEATHER BUREAU	2 3 5 C
PLEASANT MOUNT 1 W	7029	WAYNE	5	41 44	75 27	1800	8A	8A	PA FISH COMM	2 3 5 C
PORT CLINTON	7116	SCHUYLKILL	14	40 35	76 02	450	7A	7A	MRS. ADA E. RARICK	2 3 5 7 C
PORTLAND	7127	NORTHAMPTON	5	40 55	75 06	295		8A	JOINT BRIDGE COMM	3
POTTSTOWN	7149	MONTGOMERY	14	40 15	75 39	160		8A	MILES E. SMITH	3
POTTSVILLE PALO ALTO BR	7161	SCHUYLKILL	14	40 41	76 11	640		8A	JOHN H. SMITH	3
PUNXSUTAWNEY	7217	JEFFERSON	1	40 57	79 00	1298		MID	JOHN VOLANSKY	C
PUTNEYVILLE 2 SE DAM	7229	ARMSTRONG	1	40 55	79 17	1270	8A	8A	CORPS OF ENGINEERS	2 3 5 C
QUAKERTOWN 1 E	7239	BUCKS	5	40 26	75 20	490	5P	5P	DENNIS K. FLUCK	2 3 5 7
RAYMOND	7310	POTTER	13	41 52	77 52	2220		7A	ARTHUR LANGAN	3 C
#READING WB CITY	7318	BERKS	14	40 20	75 58	266	MID	MID	U.S. WEATHER BUREAU	2 3 5 7 C
RENOVO	7409	CLINTON	16	41 20	77 45	660		7A	MRS. C. W. BAIRD	3
RENOVO 5 S	7410	CLINTON	16	41 14	77 46	2035		MID	C. F. BILLETTE	C
REW	7425	MC KEAN	1	41 54	78 32	2250		8A	HAROLD C. MEALY	3
RICES LANDING LOCK 6	7443	GREENE	10	39 57	80 00	775		7A	CORPS OF ENGINEERS	3
RIDGWAY 3 W	7477	ELK	1	41 25	78 47	1420	7P	7A	BOROUGH OF RIDGWAY	2 3 5 7
ROCHESTER 1 N	7540	BEAVER	2	40 43	80 16	900		MID	DEQUESNE LIGHT CO	C
RUSH	7694	SUSQUEHANNA	15	41 47	76 03	1000		9A	MISS MAUDE MC CAIN	3
RUSHVILLE	7727	SUSQUEHANNA	15	41 47	76 07	870		7A	CARL KOPATZ	3
SAFE HARBOR	7732	LANCASTER	15	39 55	76 23	270		MID	S.H.WATER POWER CORP	C
SAGAMORE 1 S	7739	INDIANA	1	40 46	79 14	1320		7A	CORPS OF ENGINEERS	3
SALINA 3 W	7782	WESTMORELAND	7	40 31	79 33	1109	6P	6P	MUN AUTH WSTMRLD CO	2 3 5
SAXTON	7846	BEDFORD	6	40 12	78 15	780		8A	MRS.ALVERTA L.HOLMES	3 C
SCANDIA 2 E	7855	WARREN	1	41 55	79 01	2040		MID	DAVID R. ANDERSON	C
SCHENLEY LOCK 5	7863	ARMSTRONG	1	40 41	79 40	783		7A	CORPS OF ENGINEERS	3

STATION INDEX

Continued

Station	Index No.	County	Drainage‡	Latitude	Longitude	Elevation	Observation time Temp.	Observation time Precip.	Observer	Refer to tables
# SCRANTON	7902	LACKAWANNA	15	41 25	75 40	746	7A	7A	U.S. POST OFFICE	2 3 5
SELINSGROVE CAA AP	7931	SNYDER	15	40 49	76 52	437	MID	MID	CIVIL AERO. ADM.	2 3 5 7
SELLERSVILLE 2 NW	7938	BUCKS	5	40 23	75 20	550		MID	SELLERSVILLE WTR CO	C
SHADE GAP	7965	HUNTINGDON	6	40 11	77 52	1000		MID	MRS. HELEN M. PYLE	C
SHAMOKIN	7978	NORTH'LAND	15	40 46	76 33	770		8A	ROARING CRK WTR CO	3
SHEFFIELD 6 W	8026	WARREN	1	41 41	79 09	1940		MID	L. N. HANSON	C
SHIPPENSBURG	8073	FRANKLIN	15	40 03	77 32	709	4P	4P	KEITH B. ALLEN	2 3 5
SINNEMAHONING	8145	CAMERON	16	41 19	78 05	790		7A	MRS.FRANCES CALDWELL	3
SLIPPERY ROCK	8184	BUTLER	2	41 04	80 03	1345	7P	7A	WALTER D. ALBERT	2 3 5
SMETHPORT HIGHWAY SHED	8190	MC KEAN	1	41 48	78 27	1510		MID	PA DEPT HIGHWAYS	C
SOMERSET FAIRVIEW ST	8244	SOMERSET	17	40 01	79 05	2140		7A	HOWARD G. PECK	3
SOMERSET MAIN ST	8249	SOMERSET	17	40 01	79 05	2150	6P	6P	DAVID L. GROVE	2 3 5 7
SOUTH CANAAN 1 NE	8275	WAYNE	5	41 31	75 24	1400		MID	EUGENE M. COOK	C
SOUTH MOUNTAIN	8308	FRANKLIN	12	39 51	77 30	1520		7A	PA DEPT OF HEALTH	3
SPRINGBORO	8359	CRAWFORD	8	41 48	80 23	900	8A	8A	SPRINGBORO BOROUGH	2 3 5 7 C
SPRING GROVE	8379	YORK	15	39 52	76 52	470		4P	P. H. GLATFELTER CO	3 C
SPRINGS 1 SW	8395	SOMERSET	17	39 44	79 10	2500	8P	8P	ALLEN E. YODER	2 3 5 7
#STATE COLLEGE	8449	CENTRE	16	40 48	77 52	1175	MID	MID	PA STATE COLLEGE	2 3 5 C
STRAUSSTOWN	8570	BERKS	14	40 29	76 11	600		8A	JACOB KLAHR	3
STRONGSTOWN	8589	INDIANA	4	40 33	78 55	1880		MID	HARRY F. BENNETT	C
STROUDSBURG	8596	MONROE	5	40 59	75 12	440	8A	8A	PIERRE T. LAKE	2 3 5
STUMP CREEK	8610	JEFFERSON	1	41 01	78 50	1320		7A	CORPS OF ENGINEERS	3
SUNBURY	8668	NORTH'LAND	15	40 51	76 48	440		7A	CHARLES W. BAYLER	3 C
SUSQUEHANNA	8692	SUSQUEHANNA	15	41 57	75 36	1020		7A	MRS. LAURA A.BENSON	3
SUTERSVILLE	8699	ALLEGHENY	17	40 14	79 48	765		7A	MICHAEL RACKO	3
TAMAQUA	8758	SCHUYLKILL	14	40 48	75 58	830		8A	MRS. MARY L.ROBERTS	3
TAMAQUA 4 N DAM	8763	SCHUYLKILL	14	40 51	75 59	1120		7A	PANTHER VLY WTR CO	3 C
TAMARACK 2 S FIRE TWR	8770	CLINTON	16	41 24	77 51	2220	7A	7A	JAMES E. SWARTZ	2 3 5 7
TIONESTA 2 SE DAM	8873	FOREST	1	41 29	79 26	1200	8A	8A	CORPS OF ENGINEERS	2 3 5 7 C
TITUSVILLE	8885	CRAWFORD	1	41 38	79 40	1550		MID	PA ELECTRIC CO	C
TITUSVILLE WATER WORKS	8888	CRAWFORD	1	41 38	79 42	1220	7P	7P	CITY OF TITUSVILLE	2 3 5
TORPEDO 4 W	8901	WARREN	1	41 47	79 32	1735		7A	MRS. LILY B. GARBER	3
TOWANDA	8905	BRADFORD	15	41 46	76 26	755	7P	7A	MRS. M. O. PARKS	2 3 5 7 C
TOWER CITY 5 SW	8910	DAUPHIN	15	40 31	76 37	745		6P	HARRISBURG WTR DEPT	3 7
TROY	8959	BRADFORD	15	41 47	76 47	1100		7A	JENNIE L. BALLARD	3
TUNNELTON	8989	INDIANA	4	40 27	79 23	890		MID	MRS. MARY E. WEIMER	C
TURTLEPOINT 4 NE	9002	MC KEAN	1	41 54	78 16	1640		7A	ROBERT D. STRAIT	3
TYRONE 4 NE BALD EAGLE	9024	BLAIR	6	40 43	78 12	1020		7A	FREDERICK L. FRIDAY	3 C
UNION CITY	9042	ERIE	1	41 54	79 50	1325		7A	FORREST M. BRALEY	3 C
UNIONTOWN	9050	FAYETTE	10	39 54	79 44	1040	10P	10P	WM. W. MARSTELLER	2 3 5 7
UPPER DARBY	9074	DELAWARE	5	39 58	75 18	222	7P	7P	PHIL. SUB.TRANS. CO	2 3 5
VANDERGRIFT	9128	WESTMORELAND	7	40 36	79 33	800		7A	UNITED ENGGFNDRY CO	3
VANDERGRIFT 2 W	9133	WESTMORELAND	7	40 36	79 36	995		MID	EUGENE R. YOUNG	C
VIRGINVILLE	9196	BERKS	14	40 31	75 52	350		8A	MRS. MARY H. WRIGHT	3
WARREN	9298	WARREN	1	41 51	79 08	1280	7P	7A	GILBERT H. REIER	2 3 5 7
WASHINGTON	9312	WASHINGTON	11	40 11	80 14	1200		MID	PA DEPT HIGHWAYS	C
WATSONTOWN	9345	NORTH'LAND	16	41 05	76 52	470		8A	OWEN BERKENSTOCK	3
WAYNESBURG 2 W	9362	GREENE	10	39 54	80 13	980	6P	7A	RALPH L. AMOS	2 3 5 7
WAYNESBURG 1 E	9367	GREENE	10	39 54	80 10	940		MID	SEWAGE DISPOSAL PLT	C
WEBSTER MILLS 3 SW	9380	FULTON	12	39 49	78 05	920		MID	WILLIAM D. COVER	C
WELLSBORO 3 S	9408	TIOGA	16	41 43	77 16	1920	7A	7A	MARION L. SHUMWAY	2 3 5 7
WELLSBORO 2 E	9412	TIOGA	16	41 45	77 16	1550		MID	MRS. IDA S. MAYNARD	C
WELLSVILLE	9420	YORK	15	40 03	76 57	500	5P	5P	D. D. HOOVER	2 3 5
WERNERSVILLE 1 W	9430	BERKS	14	40 20	76 06	405		8A	CHARLES A. GRUBER	3
WEST CHESTER	9464	CHESTER	5	39 58	75 36	440	8A	8A	DAILY LOCAL NEWS	2 3 5 7
WEST GROVE 1 E	9503	CHESTER	5	39 49	75 49	440		8A	CONARD-PYLE CO	3
WEST HICKORY	9507	FOREST	1	41 34	79 25	1090		6A	MRS.HELEN F.KINNEAR	3
WHITESBURG	9655	ARMSTRONG	1	40 45	79 24	1530		7A	CORPS OF ENGINEERS	3
WILKES-BARRE	9702	LUZERNE	15	41 15	75 52	610		7A	MRS. MARY G. MIRMAK	3
WILLIAMSBURG	9714	BLAIR	6	40 28	78 12	860		7A	MYRON K. BIDDLE	3
WILLIAMSPORT WB AP	9728	LYCOMING	16	41 15	76 55	527	MID	MID	U.S. WEATHER BUREAU	2 3 5 7 C
WIND GAP	9781	NORTHAMPTON	5	40 51	75 18	720		MID	OWEN R. PARRY	C
WOLFESBURG	9823	BEDFORD	6	40 03	78 32	1190		7A	WALTER C. RICE	3
YORK 3 SSW PUMP STA	9933	YORK	15	39 55	76 45	390	5P	5P	YORK WATER COMPANY	2 3 5 7
YORK 2 S	9938	YORK	15	39 56	76 44	640		MID	YORK WATER COMPANY	C
YORK HAVEN	9950	YORK	15	40 07	76 43	310		6A	METROPOL EDISON CO	3
YOUNGSVILLE	9966	WARREN	1	41 51	79 20	1225		MID	HENRY CARLETT	C
ZION GROVE	9990	SCHUYLKILL	15	40 54	76 13	940		7A	JAMES D. TEETER	3
ZIONSVILLE 3 SE	9995	LEHIGH	14	40 27	75 27	660		7A	LESLIE HOWATT	3
NEW STATIONS										
SCRANTON WB AP	7905	LUZERNE	15	41 20	75 44	956	MID	MID	U.S. WEATHER BUREAU	2 3 5 7 C
COOKSBURG	1749	CLARION	1	41 20	79 13	1160		8A	PA DEPT FOR & WTRS	3
COOKSBURG 2 NNW	1752	CLARION	1	41 21	79 13	1460		8A	PA DEPT FOR & WTRS	3
SHIPPINGPORT WB	8078	BEAVER	11	40 37	80 26	740	MID	MID	U.S. WEATHER BUREAU	2 3 5 7 C
VOWINCKEL	9206	CLARION	1	41 25	79 14	1620		8A	PA DEPT FOR & WTRS	3
VOWINCKEL 1 WSW	9209	CLARION	1	41 24	79 15	1610		8A	PA DEPT FOR & WTRS	3
MILAN 4 WNW	5732	BRADFORD	15	41 56	76 35	1448		MID	CARL A. MORRIS	C
UTICA	9099	VENANGO	1	41 26	79 57	1030		7A	MRS.FLORENCE E.MILLER	3

‡ 1-ALLEGHENY; 2-BEAVER; 3- 4-CONEMAUGH; 5-DELAWARE; 6-JUNIATA; 7-KISKIMINETAS; 8-LAKE ERIE; 9-LEHIGH; 10-MONONGAHELA; 11-OHIO; 12-POTOMAC; 13-LAKE ONTARIO; 14-SCHUYLKILL; 15-SUSQUEHANNA; 16-WEST BRANCH; 17-YOUGHIOGHENY

REFERENCE NOTES

The four digit identification numbers in the index number column of the Station Index are assigned on a state basis. There will be no duplication of numbers within a state.

Figures and letters following the station name, such as 12 SSW, indicate distance in miles and direction from the post office.

Observation times given in the Station Index are in local standard time.

Delayed data and corrections will be carried only in the June and December issues of this bulletin.

Monthly and seasonal snowfall and heating degree days for the preceding 12 months will be carried in the June issue of this bulletin.

Stations appearing in the Index, but for which data are not listed in the tables, are either missing or received too late to be included in this issue.

Unless otherwise indicated, dimensional units used in this bulletin are. temperature in °F., precipitation and evaporation in inches, and wind movement in miles. Degree days are based on a daily average of 65° F.

Evaporation is measured in the standard Weather Bureau type pan of 4 foot diameter unless otherwise shown by footnote following Table 6.

Amounts in Table 3 are from non-recording gages, unless otherwise indicated.

Data in Tables 3, 5 and 6 and snowfall data in Table 7 are for the 24 hours ending at time of observation. See Station Index for observation time.

Snow on ground in Table 7 is at observation time for all except Weather Bureau and CAA stations. For these stations snow on ground values are at 7:30 A.M. E.S.T. WTR EQUIV in Table 7 means the water equivalent of snow on the ground. It is measured at selected stations when depth of snow on the ground is two inches or more. water equivalent samples are necessarily taken from different points for successive observations; consequently occasional drifting and other causes of local variability in the snowpack result in apparent inconsistencies in the record.

- \- No record in Tables 3, 6, 7 and the Station Index. No record in Tables 2 and 5 is indicated by no entry.
- \+ And also on a later date or dates.
- * Amount included in following measurement, time distribution unknown.
- @ Data in the column formerly headed No. of Days .01 or more have been changed to No. of Days .10 or more effective January 1, 1954.
- \# Thermometers are generally exposed in a shelter located a few fet above sod-covered ground; however, the reference indicates that the thermometers are exposed in a shelter located on the roof of a building.
- // Gage is equipped with a windshield.
- AM Data based on observational day ending before noon.
- B Adjusted to a full month.
- C In the "Refer to Tables" column in the Station Index the letter "C" indicates recorder stations. These stations are processed for special purposes and are published later in Hourly Precipitation Data.
- D Water equivalent of snowfall wholly or partly estimated, using a ratio of 1 inch water equivalent to every 10 inches of new snowfall.
- M One or more days of record missing; see Table 5 for detailed daily record. Degree day data, if carried for this station, have been adjusted to represent the value for a full month.
- R Amounts from recording gage (These amounts are essentially accurate but may vary slightly from the amounts to be published later in Hourly Precipitation Data).
- SS This entry in time of observation column in Station Index means sunset.
- T Trace, an amount too small to measure.
- V Includes total for previous month.

Additional information regarding the climate of Pennsylvania may be obtained by writing to any Weather Bureau Office or to the State Climatologist at Weather Bureau Airport Station, Harrisburg State Airport, New Cumberland, Pennsylvania.

Subscription Price: 20 cents per copy, monthly and annual; $2.50 per year. (Yearly subscription includes the Annual Summary.) Checks and money orders should be made payable to the Superintendent of Documents. Remittances and correspondence regarding subscriptions should be sent to the Superintendent of Documents, Government Printing office, Washington 25, D. C.

WRPC., Asheville, N. C. --- 3/14/56 --- 1225

U. S. DEPARTMENT OF COMMERCE
SINCLAIR WEEKS, Secretary
WEATHER BUREAU
F. W. REICHELDERFER, Chief

CLIMATOLOGICAL DATA

PENNSYLVANIA

FEBRUARY 1956

Volume LXI No. 2

ASHEVILLE: 1956

PENNSYLVANIA - FEBRUARY 1956

WEATHER SUMMARY

GENERAL

February's weather decisively reversed the cold, dry pattern that had characterized the three previous months of the current winter season. As might be expected with excessive precipitation, heavy cloudiness shut out much of the sunshine, holding this element considerably below average generally except at Pittsburgh WB Airport 2 where, oddly enough, more sunshine than usual was recorded. Extreme eastern areas were somewhat windier than usual throughout the month, particularly Allentown and Scranton, but the biggest wind news was on the 25th when the entire State was severely buffeted to the tune of about $10,000,000.

Precipitation fell largely as rain in most areas and resulted in the wettest February in many years at some stations. The Lake Drainage Division, comprising a small area, averaged only 2.45 inches but the Ohio Drainage averaged 5.60 inches and the Atlantic Division 4.20 inches. Of the 126 stations having long-term precipitation means, all but one registered excesses that averaged +2.16 inches, and ranged from .00 at Holtwood to +4.96 inches at Butler. Holtwood had the least monthly total, 2.41 inches, while Kregar 4 SE took honors as the wettest with 7.97 inches, closely followed by Confluence 1 NW and Vandergrift with 7.36 inches. Newell measured 2.08 inches on the 7th for the greatest daily amount, barely exceeding Pottstown's 2.03 inches on the same date. Snowfall averaged only about 70% of the usual expectancy and fell mostly in the first and fourth weeks. Some stations in the normally snowier areas measured over 20 inches during the month led by Clermont with 30.5 inches, however, amounts on the ground at any one time were generally much less than might be expected due largely to rapid thawing and rains.

Although this month's mildness was in sharp contrast to the previous three months, many Februarys have been even warmer. Of the 73 temperature stations with long-term means all except one (Bradford 4 W Res.) registered departures toward the warm side, averaging +3.6°. On an area basis, temperature averages progressed rather uniformly from 29.2° in the Lake Drainage to 32.7° in the Atlantic Division. The warmest reading, 65° at Donora on the 25th, was rather cool considering the general mildness and the much higher maxima recorded in most Februarys, while the -13° reading at Bradford 4 W Reservoir was almost typical of February minima.

WEATHER DETAILS

A moderately cold air mass lay over the State on the 1st, but its eastward passage to the Atlantic was quickly followed by warming on the 2nd. The complex low pressure system that approached from the southwest on that date spread warmth and an umbrella of clouds and moist air aloft to begin the wet mild pattern that typified this February's weather. Precipitation began in the west on the 1st and advanced eastward, occurring almost every day throughout the month due to the frequent passage of disturbances over or near the State. The prevailing warmth was interrupted by intruding Canadian air masses most noticeably on the 4th when some northern stations reached their coldest of the month, later during the 21st to 24th period when the month's lowest readings were generally experienced, and again at the close of the month. In many areas the warmest and coldest readings of the entire month came only one to three days apart, the warmest occurring practically everywhere in the State on the 25th. The 25th was also the stormiest day of the month. An intense Low moving eastward over the Great Lakes intensified still more and, changing its pace and direction, shot northeastward with widespread damage.

WEATHER EFFECTS

Above average precipitation coupled with unseasonable mildness softened the ground and prevented farmers from doing much of the field work customary at this time of year. The excessive moisture was beneficial in adding appreciably to the greatly depleted groundwater which rose sharply from the earlier record-low levels. Water standing in some fields damaged winter grains which, otherwise, were generally in good condition. Maple trees began to be tapped about mid-month and progressed so that syrup making was well under way in western counties by month's end.

DESTRUCTIVE STORMS

The State Climatologist reported that all sections suffered wind and rain damage on February 25th, resulting in injuries to 25 persons and aggregate property losses of about $10,000,000. Losses involved felled power lines, broken windows, roofs damaged or torn off, trees and utility poles snapped, automobiles smashed by felled trees, toppled billboards, several barns destroyed, and innumerable TV antennas blown down. A 4-story scaffold was partly destroyed in Philadelphia. Two light planes at Middlesex Airport were torn loose from their moorings and damaged. At Sharon, 2 large overhead cranes at the Sharon Steel Company were blown beyond the end of their tracks to crash onto parked automobiles, resulting in damage of about $100,000.

FLOODS

Moderate to heavy rains in the first week, supplemented by snow melt, produced minor flooding in the Monongahela River. A similar rainfall situation over the Allegheny basin on the 25th resulted in moderate rises but no flooding except on tributaries which overflowed into low-lying areas.

Local flooding occurred on the Perkiomen on the 6th and again about the 18th as the result of moderate to heavy precipitation that caused good rises but no flooding on the Schuylkill and Brandywine.

J. E. Stork

SUPPLEMENTAL DATA

Station	Wind direction: Prevailing	Wind direction: Percent of time from prevailing	Wind speed m. p. h.: Average	Wind speed: Fastest mile	Wind speed: Direction of fastest mile	Wind speed: Date of fastest mile	Relative humidity averages - percent: 1:30 a EST	7:30 a EST	1:30 p EST	7:30 p EST	Number of days with precipitation: Trace	.01-.09	.10-.49	.50-.99	1.00-1.99	2.00 and over	Total	Percent of possible sunshine	Average sky cover sunrise to sunset
ALLENTOWN WB AIRPORT	WNW	13	12.1	-	-	-	78	82	64	72	5	3	7	4	0	0	19	-	7.3
HARRISBURG WB AIRPORT	WNW	20	8.6	59	NW	25	68	72	54	61	6	8	2	4	0	0	20	45	7.2
PHILADELPHIA WB AIRPORT	NW	11	10.0	59	NW	25	74	78	59	64	8	1	8	2	1	0	20	46	7.3
PITTSBURGH WB AIRPORT	WSW	21	11.4	46*	SW	25	81	83	73	75	8	9	5	4	1	0	27	41	8.1
READING WB CITY	-	-	11.8	56	W	25	-	-	-	-	5	2	6	2	2	0	17	38	7.5
SCRANTON WB AIRPORT	WSW	15	8.8	60	W	25	76	79	66	71	5	8	7	3	0	0	23	33	8.0
SHIPPINGPORT WB CITY	-	-	3.9	53††	WNW	25	-	-	-	-	7	7	4	4	1	0	23	-	8.2
WILLIAMSPORT WB AIRPORT	-	-	-	-	-	-	-	80	62	69	2	9	5	4	0	0	20	-	7.6

* This datum is obtained by visual observation since recording equipment is not available. It is not necessarily the fastest mile occurring during the period.

†† Peak Gust

TABLE 2

CLIMATOLOGICAL DATA

Station		Temperature: Average Maximum	Average Minimum	Average	Departure From Long-term Mean	Highest	Date	Lowest	Date	Degree Days	No. of Days Max. 90° or Above	Max. 32° or Below	Min. 32° or Below	Min. 0° or Below	Precipitation: Total	Departure From Long-term Mean	Greatest Day	Date	Snow, Sleet: Total	Max. Depth on Ground	Date	No. of Days: .10 or More	.50 or More	1.00 or More
ATLANTIC DRAINAGE																								
ALLENTOWN WB AP	R	40.3	25.4	32.9	4.3	58	25	12	22	927	0	4	25	0	4.90	2.17	.98	18	5.7	2	2	11	4	0
ALLENTOWN GAS CO	AM	41.8	25.2	33.5	3.9	58	26	12	22	906	0	2	27	0	4.39	1.59	.94	7	4.6	3	2	10	4	0
ALTOONA HORSESHOE CURVE		38.0	24.5	31.3	3.5	54	25	8	24	973	0	7	26	0	4.75	2.40	1.22	25	11.3	3	2+	9	4	1
ARENDTSVILLE	AM	43.0	24.9	34.0	2.6	59	26	13	24	894	0	1	26	0	4.71	2.21	.93	7	5.2			10	3	0
ARTEMAS 1 WNW		42.1	32.7	37.4		57	8	10	21+	936	0	4	29	0										
BEAVERTOWN	AM	40.2		M		50	8				0	3		0	D 4.84		.85	7	7.0	5	2	12	5	0
BELLEFONTE 4 S	AM	38.8	23.3	31.1	3.8	54	26	10	24	975	0	4	27	0	4.75	2.61	.90	26		5	2	10	5	0
BERWICK		41.0	25.4	33.2		55	25	10	22	916	0	2	25	0	4.35		.74	18	6.3	2	2+	10	5	0
BETHLEHEM LEHIGH UNIV		40.8	27.8	34.3	3.2	59	25	11	22	884	0	5	20	0	4.56	1.46	1.00	18	7.4	2	2	10	4	1
BURNT CABINS 2 NE		40.0	24.9	32.5		54	25	10	24	938	0	4	29	0	3.00		.84	17	5.5	2	2+	6	2	0
CANTON 1 NW	AM	34.6	17.9	26.3		47	26	3	22	1116	0	1	28	0	D 3.18		.51	7	13.4	4	2+	13	1	0
CARLISLE		44.1	28.3	36.2	5.7	59	25	15	24	827	0	1	20	0	4.01	1.16	1.05	2	7.0	4	2+	9	3	1
CHAMBERSBURG 1 ESE		42.4	27.2	34.8	3.1	59	25	14	24	868	0	3	22	0	4.18	1.57	1.13	2	5.1	2	2	10	3	1
CHESTER	AM	47.2M	29.4M	38.3M		62	26	17	22	780	0	1		0	5.75		1.55	18	T	0		11	4	2
COATESVILLE 1 SW	AM	44.0	24.7	34.4	3.8	60	26	12	24	881	0	1	26	0	3.96	.34	.90	18		1	17	9	3	0
COLUMBIA		45.5	28.5	37.0		62	25	15	24	806	0	1	21	0	3.90		1.01	18	T	0		8	3	1
DEVAULT 1 W		43.7		M		61	25				0	0		0	4.47		1.32	18		2	24	9	3	1
DIXON	AM	38.7	18.2	28.5		54	26	0	4	1053	0	6	29	1	3.74		.68	7	7.7	4	28+	11	2	0
DU BOIS 7 E		36.6	21.2	28.9		55	25	1	1+	1041	0	8	29	0	5.86	2.96	1.73	25	10.0	3	2+	10	6	1
EAGLES MERE	AM	32.8	17.2	25.0		44	26	- 1	22	1151	0	14	28	2	4.45	.95	.75	7	17.5	12	28+	12	2	0
EMPORIUM 1 E	AM	36.9	16.2	26.6	.8	52	26	- 1	24	1107	0	7	29	2	5.77	2.98	1.26	25	16.5	7	4	10	5	1
EPHRATA		43.0	26.8	34.9	4.1	60	25	12	22	865	0	2	24	0	4.26	1.40	1.04	18	1.3	0		9	4	1
EVERETT 1 SW		40.8	24.5	32.7	4.7	59	27	10	24	934	0	4	25	0	D 5.17	3.03	1.36	2	3.5	4	2	12	4	2
FREDERICKSVILLE 2 SE	AM																							
FREELAND		34.7	21.6	28.2	3.5	44	9+	7	22+	1063	0	10	28	0						7	28+			0
GEORGE SCHOOL		44.2	27.3	35.8	4.5	61	25	12	24	840	0	1	24	0	4.45	1.65	1.12	18	1.9	1	17	9	3	1
GETTYSBURG	AM	43.6	27.6	35.6	4.0	59	26	16	22	844	0	2	24	0	4.23	1.57	.95	18	5.0	3	2	10	3	0
GRATZ 1 N	AM	40.3	22.9	31.6		58	26	10	24	960	0	2	26	0	3.01		.94	7	2.6	3	2	7	3	0
HANOVER	AM	45.1	24.8	35.0	1.9	61	26	13	22	865	0	1	28	0	4.11	1.50	.99	7	4.5	2	2	8	4	0
HARRISBURG WB AP	R	42.3	28.5	35.4	3.3	60	25	17	24	850	0	3	19	0	3.47	1.19	.97	2	4.6	3	2	6	4	0
HAWLEY 1 S DAM	AM	35.0M	16.8M	25.9M		45	10	3	4	1123	0	6	29	0			.72	28	10.4	7	28+		3	0
HOLTWOOD		42.6	29.6	36.1	3.4	59	25	19	1+	829	0	2	19	0	2.41	.00	.57	18	2.0	1	2+	6	2	0
HUNTINGDON	AM	42.0	23.3	32.7	3.2	56	9	9	24	929	0	2	29	0	4.03	1.48	.78	7	5.5	5	2	8	3	0
JIM THORPE		42.7	25.3	34.0	6.1	54	26	9	22	894	0	2	24	0	5.02	1.60	.93	18	7.1			11	4	0

See Reference Notes Following Station Index

TABLE 2 - CONTINUED

Station		Temperature: Average Maximum	Average Minimum	Average	Departure From Long-term Mean	Highest	Date	Lowest	Date	Degree Days	No. of Days Max. 90° or Above	Max. 32° or Below	Min. 32° or Below	Min. 0° or Below	Precipitation: Total	Departure From Long-term Mean	Greatest Day	Date	Snow, Sleet: Total	Max. Depth on Ground	Date	No. of Days .10 or More	.50 or More	1.00 or More
KEGG		41.1	24.5	32.8		59	25	10	24	927	0	4	29	0	5.49		1.16	2	5.5	3	2	10	3	2
LANCASTER 2 NE PUMP STA		45.5	26.6	36.1	5.0	62	25	14	24	835	0	1	25	0	D 3.81	1.20	.98	18	1.5	1	1	9	2	0
LANDISVILLE	AM	41.7	25.2	33.5		60	26	14	24	909	0	3	28	0	3.97		1.03	18	5.1			8	3	1
LAWRENCEVILLE 2 S	AM	36.6	16.6	26.6	1.6	51	9	- 1	22	1106	0	7	29	1	2.84	1.14	.56	7	8.6	4	28	10	1	0
LEBANON 2 NW																								
LEWISTOWN	AM	42.6	25.6	34.1		55	9	14	25	888	0	2	25	0	2.45		.50	2	7.0	5	2	8	1	0
LOCK HAVEN		39.5	25.6	32.6	4.2	53	8	11	24	934	0	2	22	0	4.02	1.52	.76	7	7.5	4	2+	10	3	0
MADERA	AM	36.1	17.3	26.7		52	26	3	24+	1104	0	5	29	0	4.50		.94	7	3.8	2	2+	12	2	0
MARCUS HOOK		44.9	31.5	38.2	2.6	58	10+	17	22	771	0	0	15	0	4.45	1.80	1.25	18	1.6	0		9	3	1
MARTINSBURG CAA AP		38.3	24.8	31.6		55	8	12	22+	963	0	7	26	0	4.27		.89	2	4.7	2	2	11	2	0
MIDDLETOWN OLMSTED FLD		42.3	28.7	35.5	3.9	60	25	17	24	848	0	3	21	0	3.14	.79	.92	2	3.9	3	2	7	2	0
MONTROSE 1 E	AM	32.7	17.4	25.1	2.6	47	26	1	22+	1151	0	12	28	0	3.61	1.31	.69	7	21.1	11	28	12	2	0
MORGANTOWN		41.8	24.6	33.2		59	25	11	24	916	0	4	26	0	4.04		1.10	18	3.0			8	3	1
MT GRETNA 2 SE		42.3	24.8	33.6		60	25	10	24	903	0	3	26	0	4.29		1.05	2	T	0		8	5	1
MT POCONO 2 N AP		34.3	19.9	27.1	5.3	49	25	3	22	1092	0	8	29	0	4.09	1.15	.71	28	16.3	7	28	11	4	0
MUHLENBURG 1 SE		38.1	20.9	29.5		50	25	2	22	1023	0	7	29	0	4.80		.83	18	16.5			11	4	0
NEWBURG 3 W		41.7	28.1	34.9		54	27	15	24	867	0	1	22	0	3.51		1.08	2	3.5	3	2	7	3	1
NEWPORT	AM	42.2	24.1	33.2		56	26	12	24+	916	0	2	28	0	3.33	1.14	.78	7	4.2	4	2	8	1	0
NORRISTOWN		44.4	29.5	37.0		61	25	16	22	806	0	1	20	0	3.80		1.12	18	.1	T	17	8	3	1
PALMERTON		39.0	25.0	32.0	3.0	57	25	12	22	948	0	5	23	0	3.76	1.54	.76	18	6.3	4	2	8	3	0
PHIL DREXEL INST OF TEC		46.1	32.6	39.4		63	25	16	22	738	0	0	9	0	5.10		1.35	18	.8	1	17	11	3	1
PHILADELPHIA WB AP	R	44.8	30.3	37.6	4.0	63	25	17	22	790	0	1	18	0	4.64	1.52	1.35	18	1.1	T	2+	11	3	1
PHILADELPHIA PT BREEZE		45.8	34.6	40.2		63	25	21	22	712	0	0	10	0	3.85		.93	18	.6	0		10	3	0
PHILADELPHIA SHAWMONT		46.2	29.1	37.7	4.3	62	25+	16	22+	784	0	1	21	0	4.28	1.22	1.19	18	2.0	0		11	2	1
PHILADELPHIA CITY	R AM	44.7	32.1	38.4	3.3	60	25	18	22	764	0	1	13	0	4.72	1.59	1.35	18				11	3	1
PHILIPSBURG CAA AP		34.8	18.8	26.8		49	8	- 2	24	1099	0	10	29	2	4.87		.80	25	13.8	9	2+	11	4	0
PHOENIXVILLE 1 E		46.0	24.9	35.5	3.0	62	25	10	24	850	0	1	26	0	3.98	.98	1.04	18	.1	0		9	3	1
PIMPLE HILL	AM	33.8	18.9	26.4		48	26	0	22	1113	0	13	29	1	5.20		.85	18	16.9	8	28	11	5	0
PLEASANT MOUNT 1 W	AM	33.0	13.9	23.5		48	26	- 7	4	1199	0	13	29	2	4.36	1.36	.73	7	19.0	14	28	12	2	0
PORT CLINTON	AM	43.2	23.1	33.2	3.8	54	10	10	24	918	0	1	28	0	4.29	.97	.84	18				9	3	0
QUAKERTOWN 1 E		42.2	23.8M	33.0M	4.0	56	25	10	22	927	0	1		0	D 5.26	1.94	1.43	18	4.8			10	3	2
READING WB CITY	R	43.2	30.1	36.7	3.9	61	25	17	22	815	0	2	17	0	4.88	2.11	1.13	2	3.8	3	2	10	4	2
SCRANTON	AM	35.9	21.9	28.9	.6	55	26	8	22	1039	0	8	25	0	3.52	1.50	.90	7	4.5			9	2	0
SCRANTON WB AIRPORT		37.0	23.0	30.0	2.9	53	25	8	22	1007	0	8	25	0	3.64	1.54	.62	18	8.6	4	28+	10	3	0
SELINSGROVE CAA AP		39.9	24.4	32.2	3.6	54	8	12	24	946	0	4	26	0	3.90	1.17	.64	11	8.2	5	2	10	4	0
SHIPPENSBURG		44.1	27.6	35.9	5.0	58	25	15	24	839	0	2	24	0	3.90	1.64	1.28	2	6.0	2	2+	7	3	1
STATE COLLEGE		37.6	23.6	30.6	3.4	50	8	13	22+	990	0	4	27	0	D 4.08	1.54	.89	2		6	2	11	3	0
STROUDSBURG	AM	37.8	20.5	29.2	1.4	55	25	4	24	1030	0	6	29	0	4.86	2.11	.96	18	12.4	3	28+	10	4	0
TAMARACK 2 S FIRE TWR	AM	33.1	16.8	25.0		46	26	5	22	1153	0	14	28	0	3.60		.66	7	17.3	10	12+	9	3	0
TOWANDA		38.9	21.0	30.0	4.5	54	25	1	4	1011	0	5	28	0	2.91	1.00	.50	7	11.0	4	28	11	1	0
UPPER DARBY		45.2	29.4	37.3		61	25	15	22	798	0	1	19	0	5.34		1.60	6	.5	T	24	9	3	2
WELLSBORO 3 S	AM	34.3	17.4	25.9	1.5	47	26	1	22	1127	0	10	29	0	3.64	1.51	.53	25	17.5	10	2	9	1	0
WELLSVILLE		44.5	25.3	34.9		59	25	11	24	865	0	1	27	0	3.75		1.00	2	4.0	2	2	6	4	1
WEST CHESTER	AM	45.9	29.4	37.7	6.3	60	25+	15	21	787	0	0	19	0	4.22	.59	1.24	18		1	16		3	1
WILLIAMSPORT WB AP		39.2	24.0	31.6	2.5	51	25	8	4	959	0	5	26	0	4.15	1.72	.70	18	10.4	4	2	9	4	0
YORK 3 SSW PUMP STA		45.9	27.9	36.9	5.2	62	25	15	24	811	0	1	21	0	3.09	.38	.72	2	2.8	0		7	3	0
DIVISION				32.7											4.20				6.7					
OHIO DRAINAGE																								
BAKERSTOWN 3 WNW		41.7	25.5	33.6		59	25	7	22	904	0	3	23	0	6.86		1.75	25	T	T	1+	10	7	1
BLAIRSVILLE 6 ENE		38.0	23.7	30.9		57	25	5	22	983	0	8	27	0	6.87	4.33	1.28	2	8.3			11	5	2
BRADFORD 4 W RES		34.6	15.8	25.2	- .7	52	25	-13	24	1147	0	10	29	3	4.57	1.95	.98	25	28.6	16	28	13	3	0
BROOKVILLE CAA AIRPORT		36.7	21.1	28.9	3.7	56	25	3	1	1039	0	5	29	0	5.81	3.32	1.62	25	10.6	4	2	10	4	2
BURGETTSTOWN 2 W	AM	41.7	22.1	31.9		64	25	7	1+	951	0	5	24	0	6.27		1.12	25		8	2	12	6	1
BUTLER		41.7	25.5	33.6	4.8	60	27	5	1	903	0	3	24	0	7.35	4.96	1.41	7	5.0	4	2	11	6	2
CLARION 3 SW		37.9	22.8	30.4		55	25	3	1	996	0	4	25	0	6.87	3.76	1.64	25		5	2	11	5	2
CLAYSVILLE 3 W		46.4	22.7	34.6	3.4	62	25	2	1	876	0	2	23	0	4.98	2.50	.87	7	T	T	21+	13	3	0
CONFLUENCE 1 SW DAM	AM	43.1	26.5	34.8		61	25	7	1	870	0	4	25	0			1.14	7		1	1+		4	3
CORRY		35.3	20.1	27.7	2.4	50	25	- 4	24	1076	0	8	29	1	4.65	1.62	.90	25	24.5	9	22	12	3	0
COUDERSPORT 2 NW		32.8	17.7	25.3		49	25	0	22+	1146	0	11	29	2	3.53		.59	12	27.0	13	23+	10	2	0
DERRY		44.5	26.5	35.5	5.2	63	25	9	22	0	0	2	23	0	6.11	3.14	1.33	25	1.1	1	29	10	5	2
DONEGAL		38.5	19.6	29.1		54	25	- 1	22	1036	0	5	29	1	6.30				5.1	2	1			
DONORA	AM	46.8	30.2	38.5	4.0	65	25	13	22	763	0	2	17	0	5.57	3.29	1.24	25	T	T	21	12	4	1
EAST BRADY		41.3	23.2	32.3		59	25	6	1	943	0	3	26	0	6.44		1.70	25	T	T	2+	11	5	2
EBENSBURG		37.9	22.0	30.0	2.9	53	25	5	1+	1010	0	7	29	0	5.48	2.65	.95	2		6	2	14	4	0
FARRELL SHARON		41.2	22.0	31.6	2.8	60	25	6	1	963	0	2	26	0	5.88	3.92	1.43	25	T	0		12	5	1
FORD CITY 4 S DAM	AM	40.4	22.2	31.3		58	25+	8	1	972	0	8	26	0	7.04		1.25	25	3.0	2	2	12	6	2
FRANKLIN		38.9	21.5	30.2	4.3	56	8+	3	1	1003	0	5	29	0	5.09	2.39	1.12	25		5	2	10	4	1
GREENVILLE		38.4	22.1	30.3	3.1	55	25	4	1+	1000	0	5	28	0	5.04	2.52	1.35	25	13.4	4	2+	11	4	1
INDIANA 3 SE		41.2	24.6	32.9	3.0	60	25	6	1	923	0	4	24	0	6.88	3.97	1.26	7	1.6	1	2			2
IRWIN		43.7	27.3	35.5	4.9	60	25	12	22	848	0	3	20	0	6.38	3.92	1.33	25		2	23	9	6	2
JAMESTOWN 2 NW	AM	36.6	18.3	27.5		56	26	- 1	1	1080	0	7	29	1	4.34	2.26	1.10	25	9.7	4	2	10	3	1
JOHNSTOWN	AM	44.0	24.8	34.4	4.0	63	25	10	24	882	0	5	24	0	6.00	2.44	1.23	26	7.3	2	2+	10	6	2
KANE 1 NNE	AM	34.1	15.0	24.6		51	26	-10	24	1165	0	8	29	3	5.04	2.09	.86	25	26.9	15	23	13	4	0
LINESVILLE 5 WNW		35.8	19.0	27.4		53	25	- 8	1	1084	0	9	29	1	3.79	1.47	.87	7	13.2	4	1+	9	3	0
MEADVILLE 1 S	AM	36.3	18.1	27.2	2.7	54	26	0	1	1090	0	8	29	1	4.64	1.97	1.06	25	16.9	5	2	11	3	1
MERCER 2 NNE		38.0	17.9M	28.0M		58	26	- 1	1	1070	0	6	29	1	4.24		.96	25	13.0	4	28	12	1	0
MIDLAND DAM 7		41.3	27.2	34.3	2.9	54	25	12	22	884	0	4	21	0	6.15	3.94	1.11	7	.6	T	2+	13	4	1
NEW CASTLE 1 N		41.8	23.8	32.8	3.9	60	25	6	1	929	0	3	25	0	5.53	3.17	1.20	7	.3	0		10	4	2

See Reference Notes Following Station Index

Station		Temperature: Average Maximum	Average Minimum	Average	Departure From Long-term Mean	Highest	Date	Lowest	Date	Degree Days	No. of Days Max. 90° or Above	Max. 32° or Below	Min. 32° or Below	Min. 0° or Below	Precipitation: Total	Departure From Long-term Mean	Greatest Day	Date	Snow, Sleet: Total	Max. Depth on Ground	Date	No. of Days .10 or More	.50 or More	1.00 or More
NEWELL	AM	43.7	28.1	35.9	3.4	61	25	11	22	834	0	4	19	0			2.08	7	1.0	1	23			1
NEW STANTON		44.6	23.4	34.0	2.4	55	8	7	24	894	0	0	28	0	5.32	2.48	1.08	6		1	1+	10	4	2
PITTSBURGH WB AP 2	//R	41.8	26.2	34.0	4.2	59	25	11	22+	897	0	4	24	0	5.98	3.52	1.26	25	3.2	1	2+	10	5	1
PITTSBURGH WB CITY	R	44.4	29.3	36.9	3.3	62	25	13	22	808	0	3	17	0	5.97	3.53	1.24	6	.3	0		10	6	2
PUTNEYVILLE 2 SE DAM	AM	38.9	20.1	29.5		57	26	8	24	1022	0	5	29	0	6.99		1.40	25		2	2+	12	7	2
RIDGWAY 3 W		35.7	19.3	27.5	2.6	54	25	- 7	1	1080	0	7	28	2	5.42	3.09	1.01	25	8.9	7	2	11	4	1
SALINA 3 W		41.9	25.3	33.6		58	25	8	1	905	0	4	23	0	6.45		1.43	25	4.5			10	6	2
SHIPPINGPORT WB		42.0	26.2	34.1		61	25	13	22	883	0	3	23	0	5.72		1.50	25	T	T	2+	9	5	1
SLIPPERY ROCK		38.8	22.9	30.9		57	25	6	1	984	0	5	28	0	6.02		1.16	28	4.5	3	2	9	5	2
SOMERSET MAIN ST		41.3	23.8	32.6	5.5	57	25	6	1+	933	0	4	28	0	6.02	2.48	1.50	2	7.0	2	21	11	4	1
SPRINGS 1 SW		39.6	23.0	31.3	4.0	58	25	5	22+	972	0	4	28	0	3.34	.22	.90	2	2.0	1	1+	9	2	0
TIONESTA 2 SE DAM	AM	36.4	16.9	26.7		55	26	- 1	1	1103	0	7	29	2	5.24	2.91	1.12	25	16.0	5	20	13	4	1
TITUSVILLE WATER WORKS		36.3	17.5	26.9		51	8	- 2	24	1095	0	6	29	2	5.13		1.17	25	15.2	5	17	10	4	1
UNIONTOWN		46.5	28.6	37.6	4.6	62	17+	11	22	788	0	2	18	0	5.69	2.81	1.12	2	.3	0		12	6	1
WARREN		36.2	21.5	28.9	3.7	54	25	3	24	1043	0	7	29	0	3.72	1.15	.72	7	17.0	5	2	11	2	0
WAYNESBURG 2 W		47.3	26.5	36.9	4.8	64	25	9	22	807	0	1	20	0	5.89	3.64	1.09	7	T	T	1+	12	5	1
DIVISION				31.5											5.60				7.8					
LAKE DRAINAGE																								
ERIE CAA AIRPORT		35.4	22.3	28.9		54	25	12	1	1039	0	10	28	0	2.45		.69	6	4.5	6	1	7	1	0
SPRINGBORO		37.4M	21.5M	29.5M		54	26	5	4	1024	0	6	28	0						6	1			
DIVISION				29.2											2.45				4.5					

DAILY PRECIPITATION

Table 3

Station	Total	1	2	3	4	5	6	7	8	9	10	11	12	13	14	15	16	17	18	19	20	21	22	23	24	25	26	27	28	29	30	31
ACHETONIA LOCK 3	7.21	T	.78	.30		.24		1.28	T	T	T	.03	.78	.02	T	.56	.22	.20	.74	.10		.03	.01	.02		.56	1.24		.10	T		
ALLENTOWN WB AP R	4.90		.85		.15	T	.92	.10		T		.48	.06			.16		.18	.98		T	.01		T	.16	.21	T	.05	.62			
ALLENTOWN GAS CO	4.39	T	.29	.56		.23		.94					.44			.02	.10	.16	.88	.06			T			.13	.05		.53			
ALTOONA HORSESHOE CURVE	4.75		.89	.05	.07		.59	.24				.36	.04	.01		.19		.19	.57			T	T	.03	.09	1.22			.17	.04		
ARENDTSVILLE	4.71		.78	.47		.24		.93					.45			.05	.05	.15	.86	.14		T				.41	.18		T			
ARTENAS 1 WNW	-	*	1.16			*	.87					.40		.05		.22		.62	-						.42							
AUSTINBURG 2 W	3.21	T	.23	.07		T		.64			.06	T	.53			T	.29	.13	.29	T		T	T	T		.42	.15	T	.40	T		
BAKERSTOWN 3 WNW	6.86		.90	T	.13	.01	.70	.52		.01	.03	.85	.02	.01	T	.67	T	.27	.80			T	T	.01	.17	1.75			.01	T		
BARNES	-	.16	.43	.02		.09		1.02		T	-		.20	T		.02	.06	.29	.05	T		.06	.05	.08	T	1.12	.90	T	.46	.06		
BEAR GAP	2.64		.46		.12		.23	.25				.14	.15			.09		.05	.35						T	.38			.42			
BEAVER FALLS	5.29	T	.29	.27		.09		1.05	T		.04	T	.83	T	T	.17	.19	.17	.41	.13		T	T	.02		.53	1.04		.06	T		
BEAVERTOWN	4.84		D.50	.64		.12		.85			T	.03	.53			.15	.06	D.10	.64	.02		T	T		D.10	.25	.46	.08	.33	T		
BEECH CREEK STATION	4.23	T	.41	.18		.08		.91			.06	T	.45			.08	.16	.09	.56	.08			T			.36	.45		.36	T		
BELLEFONTE 4 S	4.75	.13	.60	.07		T		.82			.03		.32	T		.28	.08	.10	.59	T		T	T	T		.50	.90	.08	.22	.03		
BERWICK	4.39		.53		.19	.05	.53	.34			.03	.20	.30			.20		.06	.74		T	T				.02			.56			
BETHLEHEM	4.23		.22	.54		.14		1.00			T		.38			.01	.07	.10	.92	.10			T			.24	.01		.50	T		
BETHLEHEM LEHIGH UNIV	4.96		.05		.15		.77	.08		T		.37	.09		T	.15		.19	1.00		T	.01			.17	.22		.05	.50			
BLAIRSVILLE 6 ENE	6.87		1.28	.06	.09	.04	.83	.44		.04	.08	.34	.09	.04	.01	.64		.28	.77		T	.04	.06	.04	.11	1.21	T	.29		.12		
BLOSERVILLE 1 N	3.80		1.24		.04	.03	.75	.10				.35	.08		T	.05		.09	.53			T			T	.50			.04			
BOSWELL 6 WNW	6.57	T	.94	.66				1.12			.03	.07	.45	T	T	.09	.27	.04	.77			.25	.05	.07	T	.50	.96		.17	.13		
BRADDOCK LOCK 2	5.72	T	.46	.24		.13		1.10	T			.02	.64	.06	.01	.12	.18	.30	.60	.15		.02	T	.02		.55	.98		.14	T		
BRADFORD CNTRL FIRE STA	-	T	.27	.07	T	.03		.79	T		-		.77	.02		.06	.09	.18	.13	.12		.05	T	.05	.10	.68	.49	T	.31	.04		
BRADFORD 4 W RES	4.57		.28		.03		.26	.76		T	.17	.52	.17	T		.22		.15	.21		T	.13	.08	.05	T	.98	.19		.36	.03		
BREEZEWOOD	3.09	.10	.39		.10		.78	T		.03		.44		.15	T		.03	.47	.20			.02		T	.18	.08		.12	T			
BROOKVILLE CAA AIRPORT	5.81	.02	.91		.12	.01	1.00	.12		.01	T	.51	.02	T	T	.28	T	.20	.49		T	.02	.01	T	.42	1.62	T	.01	.03	.01		
BRUCETON 1 S	5.43	T	.55	.24			.21	1.12	T				.70			.24		.31	*	.80		.03		T		*	1.15		.08			
BUFFALO MILLS	4.19		.88	.25		.07		.71			.03	.10	.41			.14	.02	.11	.69	.02		.02	T			.28	.23		.20	.03		
BURGETTSTOWN 2 W	6.27	.01	.47	.25			.07	.89			.01	.12	.76	T		.38	.15	.23	.60	.09		.02	T	.02		1.12	.72		.16	T		
BURNT CABINS 2 NE	3.00	.02	.78		T	T	.48	.40		T	T	.10	T		T	T	T	.84	T			T	.05		.31	T		T	.02			
BUTLER	7.35		.62	.38	.09			1.41			.04	.27	.70			.26	.13	.26	.94	.05		.03		.04		1.38	.70		.05	T		
CAMP HILL	3.52		1.00		.20		.68					.68			T	.10		.11	T			T			T	.73			.02			
CANTON 1 NW	3.18	T	.10	.12		.07		.51	D.32		.10	T	.42		D.14	T	.22	.11	.31	.03		T	T	T		.22	.20	T	.31	T		
CARLISLE	4.01		1.05		.05	.05	.80	.20				.36	.14		.02	.11		.14	.60			T			.05	.40			.04			
CARROLLTOWN 2 SSE	5.05	T	.73	.40		.15		.82				.01	.35	.02	.01	.29	.09	.13	.51			.09	T	.01		.48	.80	T	.15	.01		
CARTER CAMP 2 W	4.91	T	.35	.28		.08		.79			.15		.82	T			.24	.23	.46			T	T	T		1.10	.50		.15	T		
CEDAR RUN	4.26	.05	.10	.56		.07		.66			.06	T	.46	T		.02	.44	.10	.17	.53		.03	.02	T		.45	.45		.10	T		
CHADDS FORD	3.95		T	.80	.20	.30	.50	.20	T				T			T		.20	1.05	.10				T	T	*	*		.60			
CHAMBERSBURG 1 ESE	4.18		1.13		.15		.83	.13			T	.37	.02		.03	.12		.14	.64			T			.27	.32			.03			
CHARLEROI LOCK 4	5.39		.67	.38		.17	T	1.13		T	.02	.04	.70	.01	T	.10	.24	*	.63	.12	.01	T	T	.01		.20	.82		.14	T		
CHESTER	5.75		.24	.78	T	.50		1.38			T	T	.30			.34	.10	.05	1.55				T			.24	.12		.15			
CLARENCE 1 E	4.24	T	.44	.17		.12		.66			T	T	.55	T	T	.03	.25	.15	.40	.25		T	T	T		.48	.49		.23			
CLARION 3 SW	6.87		.68	.41		.14		1.14	T		.02	T	.98	.02		.05	.25	.18	.45	.10		.02		T		1.04	.68		.08	.03		
CLAUSSVILLE	4.33		.28	.80		.19		.85					.37			.09	.03	.16	.70							.51			.55			
CLAYSVILLE 3 W	4.98		.44	.37		.14	T	.87		T	T	.02	.35	.05		.27	.19	.22	.71	.16		T	T	T		.19	.80		.20	T		
CLEARFIELD	5.92		.86	.46		.12		1.00			.04	.03	.51	T	.02	.13	.27	.18	.68	.18						.45	1.02	.03	.08	.04		
CLERMONT	4.81	.05	.32	.12		T		.55	T		.45		.55	.03	T	.08	.23	.22	.20	.12		.06	.12	.07	T	.90	.35	T	.35	.04		
COALDALE 2 NW	4.64		.34	.40		.24	.14	.84					.51			.01	.14	.12	.61	.20			.01			.27	.19		.61	.01		
COATESVILLE 1 SW	3.96		.28	.68	T	.31		.62			T		.28			T	.09	.12	.90	.06						.17	.23		.02	T		
COGAN STATION 2 N	3.71		.50	.07		.24		.60		.14		.06	.46					.15	.44	.09						.38	.38		.20			
COLUMBIA	3.90		.96		.26	.04	.57	.23				.28	.06		T	.07		.12	1.01			T			T	.32			T			
CONFLUENCE 1 SW DAM	-	T	1.04	.59		.19	T	1.14	T		T	.08	.35	.02		-	.04	.44	1.01	.29		T	T	T	T	.43	.41		.28	T		
CONFLUENCE 1 NW	7.36	T	.98	.69		.20	T	1.36	T		.07	.09	.35	T	T	.29	.08	.39	1.06	.32		T	T	T	T	.49	.67		.32	T		
CONNELLSVILLE	5.81		.82	.54		.25		.98					.56			.32	.15	.13	.89	.12		T		T	.04	.16	.69		.06	.10		
CONSHOHOCKEN	4.77		.28	.65	T	.26		.77			T		.12			.05	T	.12	1.87	.02						.18	.20		.25			
COOKSBURG	6.04	T	.46	.38		.12	T	.95	.02		.10	T	.68	.04	T	.04	.26	.15	.40	.12	T	.02	.02	.02		1.38	.73	T	.15	.02		
COOKSBURG 2 NNW	6.86	T	.58	.14		.13	T	.95	.01	T	.10	T	.69	.04	T	.09	.26	.14	.35	.55	T	.03	.02	.01	T	1.78	.65	.10	.20	.04		
CORAOPOLIS NEVILLE IS	-		.51	*	*	*	.28	.95					*	.60	T	.70	T	.21	.92		T	T	T	T		-	-		T	T		
CORRY	4.85		.32	T	.01	.01	.34	.52		.02	.07	.65	.14	T	T	.23		.31	.33		T	.09	.13	.06	.22	.90	.01	.04	.24	.03		
COUDERSPORT 2 NW	3.53	.03	.17	.05		.08		.53			.09		.59	.03		.04	.28	.24	.13	.15		.05	.07	.07		.46	.17		.24	.06		
COUDERSPORT 7 E	3.42	T	.10	.09		.02		.50			.08		.50	T		.02	.28	.08	.10	.04		.08	.09	T	T	.04	1.08	.02	.16	.14		
COVINGTON	3.10	T	.36					.42			.08		.46			T	.26	.08	.46	T						.41	.25	T	.32	T		
CREEKSIDE	7.12		.85	.54		.22		1.26					.70	T		.53	.20	.25	.60	.10						.90	.80		.17			
CRESSON 2 SE	5.25	.03	.72	.11		.14	.03	.45			.23	.10	.50	.07	.04	.13	.11	.25	.40	.14		.05	.04	.05	.02	.65	.72	.03	.20	.04		
CUSTER CITY 2 W	4.84	.04	.17	.25		.05		.85			.11		.64	.04	.01	.11	.16	.22	.18			.03	.07	.05	T	.87	.47		.50	.02		
DANVILLE	4.46		.35	.27		.19		.83			.04		.80			.04	.16	.08	.63	.08						.16	.43		.40	T		
DERRY	6.11		1.25	T	.20	T	.55	.49			T	.51	.05	.06	T	.44		.17	.66			.03	T		.07	1.33			.23	.05		
DEVAULT 1 W	4.47		.86		.28	.10	.96	.12		T	T	.13	.06		T	.03		.05	1.32						.03	.10		T	.33			
DIXON	3.74		.25	.10		.11		.68	.02	T	.08	T	.46			.03	.42	.10	.54		T		T	T		.30	.20	T	.45	T		
DONEGAL	6.30	*	1.48		*	*	1.57	.07		T	*	.35	.03	T	.13	.24	.12	.50	.59		T	.02	.05	T	.26	.70	T	.04	.13	.02		
DONORA	5.57		.74	.31	.01	.14	.36	.78		T	T	.22	.47	T	T	.23	T	.21	.65		T	T	T	T		1.24	.02	T	.19	T		
DOYLESTOWN	4.24		.77	.01	.26	.02	.46	.38		T		.11	.04		T	.09		.21	1.01			T				.47			.41			
DU BOIS 7 E	5.86		.76		.02		.50	.52		.02	.08	.73	.15	T		.36		.12	.65			T	T		.12	1.73	.02		.06	.02		
DUSHORE 3 NE	3.93		.35	.23		.06		.58			.20		.32	T		T	.35	.08	.30	.23	T	T	T	T	T	.39	.45	T	.38	.03		
EAGLES MERE	4.45	T	.35	.30		.05		.75			.16	T	.39	T		.02	.30	.14	.47	.20		T	.02	T		.33	.50		.47	T		
EAST BRADY	6.44		1.17		.18	.12	.42	.62		.02	.01	.86	.02		.01	.28		.24	.58			.01	.01		.18	1.70				.01		
EBENSBURG	5.48	T	.95	.47		.13		.66	T			T	.40	.10		.24	.05	.20	.40	.29		T	T	T		.65	.54		.29	.11		
EDINBORO	4.57	.08	.20	.05		.01		.90	T		.09	.01	.61	.03	T	.09	.02	.28	.24	.07		.07	.10	.03	.01	1.14	.31		.20	.03		
ELIZABETHTOWN	4.37		.40	.82		.21		.81					.45					.15	.91							.26	.36					
EMPORIUM 1 E	5.77	T	.50	.24	.35	.08		.89			.07		.69	.01		.08	.27	.19	.42	.09		T	.01	T		1.20	.54		.07	.01		
ENGLISH CENTER	3.43	.02	.26	.16		.04		.58			.03	T	.59	T		T	.23	.07	.40	.12			T	T		.39	.35		.19	T		
EPHRATA	4.26		.95	.05	.15	.10	.64	.10				.25	.07		.03	.07		.10	1.04						.01	.65			.05			
EQUINUNK	4.78		.38	.42		.26		.80			.10		.40				.16	.07	.63	.27	.06			.08		.46	.27		.42	T		
ERIE CAA AIRPORT	2.45		.14	T	.01		.60	.01		.03	.04	.34	.09	T	T	T		.09	.30		T	.01	.01	T	.22	.32	T	.14	.01	T		
EVERETT 1 SW	5.17	D.20	1.36		.10		1.00	.20		.10		.40			T	.16	T	.52	.40						.63			.10				
FARRELL SHARON	5.88		.56		.03	.02	.74	.32		.05	.06	.60	.03			.23		.75	.39				.02		.17	1.43	.04	.10	.17	.11		
FORD CITY 4 S DAM	7.04	T	.83	.34		.20	T	1.13	T		.04	.03	.75	T	T	.46	.12	.21	.81	.14		T	T	.01	T	1.25	.72		T	T		
FRANKLIN	5.09		.54	.05		.03		.90			.08	.02	.70	T		.11	.25	.22	.33	.03		.01	T	.03		1.12	.36		.30	.01		
FREDERICKSVILLE 2 SE		RECORD MISSING																														
FREELAND	-		.41	.15	.15	.30		.20	.03	T	.03		.34				-	-	.05		.04	T	.01	T		.15	.23	.10	.70			
GALETON	3.83	.02	.21	.09		.10		.51			.09		.60	T		.06	.28	.14	.30	.03		.02	T	.02		.58	.38	T	.35	.05		
GEIGERTOWN	4.51			1.01		*		1.16					.30			.09		.10	1.15							.28	.25		.17			
GEORGE SCHOOL	4.45		.87		.29		.67	.30				.12	.05		.01	.06		.18	1.12				T		.03	.35			.40			
GETTYSBURG	4.23		.70	.41		.20		.88				T	.40			.11	.02	.13	.95			T	T			.31	.12					
GIFFORD	4.73	.04	.26	.09			T	.92			.13		.71	.06		.07	.19	.26	.23	.08		.03	.05	.05		.84	.44	T	.26	.02		
GLEN HAZEL 2 NE DAM	5.36	T	.39	.14		.10		.79	T	T	.16	.02	.63	.06	T	.07	.28	.16	.41	.08		.04	.03	.05	T	1.20	.49	T	.22	.04		
GLENWILLARD DASH DAM	6.04	T	.29	.25		.17		1.04			.03	.01	.97	T	T	.68	.19	.24	.50	.13		.02	T	.01		.40	1.10		.01	T		
GOULDSBORO	5.21		.25	.33		.17		.92			.02		.32				.28	.11	.60	.29	.02	.04		T		.24	.47		1.08	.07		
GRANTVILLE 2 SW	3.75		1.00		.16	.01	.65	.14		T		.38	.13			.07		.06	.70						.03	.37			.09			
GRATERFORD	4.66		.12	.19	.01	.21		1.13					.28			.03	.32	.11	1.19	.06						.31	.24			.46		
GRATZ 1 N	3.01		.26	.30		T		.94					.50			.04	.07	.04	.50	T						.16	T		.20	T		
GREENSBORO LOCK 7	5.35	T	.59	.46		.20	T	.95			.08	.06	.37			.31	.19	.14	.65	.14	.04		T			.17	.73		.27	T		
GREENSBURG 3 SE	5.91		1.13		.09	.02	.69	.45				.58	T	.01	.03	.30	.02	.30	.80	.03		.02	.01	T	.23	.99			.20	.01		
GREENVILLE	5.04		.55		.04		.50	.36		.02	.05	.82	.03	T	.02	.12		.20	.25			.10	T	T	.29	1.35		.02	.31	.01		
HANOVER	4.11		.51	.65	T	.29		.99		T		T	.37			.02	.04	.05	.78	.02						.26	.15					
HARRISBURG WB AP R	3.47		.97		.08	T	.70	.01		T	.01	.51	.01		.01	.07		.17	.59			T			.28	.05	T	T	.01	T		
HARRISBURG NORTH	3.79		.80	.16		.15		.85			T		.57			.04	.01	.09	.61			T				.44	.02		.05			
HAWLEY	3.94		.07	.16		.26		.64	.07		.04	T	.33	T			.15	.07	.64	.31	.06	T	T	T		.32	.17		.58	.07		
HAWLEY 1 S DAM	-		.10	.20		.26		.57			.05		.35				.12	.06	.55	.31	.04					.27	-		.72			
HOLLISTERVILLE	4.62	T	.22	.21	T	.28		.83			.02	T	.40	T	T	T	.18	.03	.83	.17	.03	T	T	T	T	.27	.38	.01	.72	.04		
HOLTWOOD	2.41		.17	.36	T	.27		.56		T	T		.26			T	.05	.07	.57	T		T	T			.06	.02		.02			
HONESDALE 4 NW	4.85		.30	.18		.18		.89			.10		.55				.10	.11	.81	.08	.03	T		T		.58	.42		.52	T		
HOOVERSVILLE	5.24	.01	.68	.41		.17		.82	T		.03	T	.42	.02	T	.14	.03	.22	.64	.05		.11	.02	.04	T	.57	.60		.16	.08		
HOP BOTTOM 2 SE	2.55		*	.30	T	.20	T	.20	.57			.02	.10	.25			.25	T	.06	.02		.07	T		.02	T		T	.40	.09		
HUNTINGDON	4.03	T	.55	.27		.08		.78		T	T	T	.38	T		.07	.05	.08	.45	.07		T	T			.35	.71	T	.19	T		
HUNTSDALE	3.33		.59	.49		.10		.86					.45			.02	.02	.04	.45	.02		T				.26	.03			T		
HYNDMAN	4.41		.80	.20		.08	.04	.69			.01	.18	.40			.15	.02	.15	.74	.02		.01		T		.38	.20		.30	.04		
INDIANA 3 SE	6.88	*	.67	.54		.16		1.26	.01		.02	.01	.74	.03	.03	.43	.24	.20	.55	.10		T	T	.07		.44	1.16		.22	T		
IRWIN	6.38		1.04	.06	.06	.07	.64	.76			.02	.70	.07	.01		.37		.24	.71			.04		.05	.08	1.33			.12	.01		
JAMESTOWN 2 NW	4.34		.43	.03		.02		.78		T	.11	.06	.61			.15	.07	.15	.16	.04		.02	T	.02		1.10	.28		.30	.01		

See Reference Notes Following Station Index

DAILY PRECIPITATION

Table 3—Continued

PENNSYLVANIA
FEBRUARY 1956

Day of month

Station	Total	1	2	3	4	5	6	7	8	9	10	11	12	13	14	15	16	17	18	19	20	21	22	23	24	25	26	27	28	29	30	31
JIM THORPE	5.02		.73		.17	.07	.48	.83				.29	.27			.10		.18	.93				T			.48			.53			
JOHNSTOWN	6.00	T	.65	.25		.01	T	1.03	T		.02		.53	T	T	.20	T	.25	.75			.04	.02	.03	T	.83	1.23		.13	.03		
KANE 1 NNE	5.04	.01	.44	.11		.04	T	.72	T		.11	T	.74	.04	T	.14	.21	.25	.26	.11		.01	.04	.05	T	.66	.54	T	.33	.03		
KARTHAUS	4.85	T	.43	.27		.12		1.04	T		.04	T	.44	.02	T	.07	.30	.08	.56	.08		T	T	T	T	.59	.68	T	.13	T		
KEATING SUMMIT	5.08	T	.53	.17		.10		.78			.06		.78	T	T	.17	.20	.16	.30	.16		T	.04	T	T	1.00	.44		.16	T		
KEGG	5.49	.10	1.16	1.00	.09		.69	.01		T		.48		T	T	.06	T	.44	.49			.02	T	T	.42	.30		.06	.17	T		
KITTANNING LOCK 7	8.70		.92	.34		.22		1.15	T		.02	.02	.60	.01	T	.38	.11	.19	.65	.17		T	T	T		1.17	.69		.06	T		
KREGAR 4 SE	7.97	.15	1.40	T	.33	.06	1.04	.24		.02	.07	.53	.14	T	.11	.38	.08	.61	.53		.24	.17	.07	.05	.42	.89	T	.07	.34	.03		
KRESGEVILLE 3 W	4.20		.39	.40		.21		.82					.45			.02	.05	.10	.87	.03						.27	.12		.47			
LAFAYETTE MC KEAN PARK		RECORD MISSING																														
LAKEVILLE 1 NNE	4.68		.22	.05		.29		.89					.45				.15	.15	.05	.12	.07	T	T			.35	.25		.69	.05		
LANCASTER 2 NE PUMP STA	3.81	D.10	.90		.25	.03	.48	.26				.19	.07		.02	.08		.12	.98						T	.30			.03	T		
LANDISVILLE	3.97		.37	.60		.30		.74					.33			.06	.04	.07	1.03	.02						.20	.19		.02			
LATROBE	6.03	.03	1.06		.17	T	1.03	.06		.01		.68	.01	T	.02	.32	T	.32	.63			.12	.04	.04	.33	.97		.02	.17	T		
LAWRENCEVILLE 2 S	2.84		.31	T		.08		.58			.11		.46			T	.32	.12	.32	.05			.02	T		.15	.14		.20			
LEBANON 2 NW		RECORD MISSING																														
LEHIGHTON	4.22	.02	.28	.38		.23		.77			T		.55			.05	.08	.15	1.00	T			T			.24	.10	T	.37	T		
LE ROY	2.51		.03				.18	.66					.48			.18		.06	.64						T	.24			.04			
LEWIS RUN 3 S	5.00	.02	.32	.09		.04		.80			.14	.01	.79	.04	T	.07	.22	.31	.21	.08		.04	.02	.05	T	.84	.41	T	.49	.05		
LEWISTOWN	2.45		.50	.12		.05		.17			.02		.38			T	.06	.10	.30	.06		.01				.41	.07		.20			
LINESVILLE 5 WNW	3.70	T	.29	T		.05		.87			.03	T	.53	.06		.15		.24	.31	T		.06	.03	.07	T	.72	.16		.17	.03		
LOCK HAVEN	4.02	T	.32	.20		.10		.76			.08	T	.43			.02	.23	.07	.50	.03	T	T	T			.41	.57		.32			
LONG POND 2 W	3.99	T	.24	.42				.74			.03		.46				.18	.09	.61	.13		T	.03	.05	T	.25	.21		.53	.02		
MADERA	4.50		.48	.49		.12		.94			T	T	.36	.03	T	.25	.20	.14	.59	.17				T		.49	.09	T	.15	T		
MAHAFFEY	7.35	T	.71	.56		.24		1.20	T		.06	.04	.60	.09	T	.21	.35	.25	.65	.17		T	.03	T		.95	1.08	.03	.13	T		
MAPLE GLEN	3.92		.78		.30	.03	.51	.28		T		.10	.02		T	.11		.16	1.05			T	T		T	.34			.24			
MAPLETON DEPOT	3.76	T	.51	.28		.03		.84		T	.04	.01	.42			.07	.04	.08	.42	.07		T	T	T		.36	.42		.17			
MARCUS HOOK	4.45		.90		.44	T	.73	.03		T	T	.25	.01		.01	.17		.21	1.25		T	T	T		.09	.22	T	T	.14	T		
MARION CENTER 2 SE	7.02		.74	.56		.17		1.20	T		.06	.02	.55	.15	.01	.40	.28	.15	.56	.14		T	T			.78	1.10		.15			
MARTINSBURG CAA AP	4.27	.13	.89	T	.10	T	.64	.07			T	.42	.02	T	.06	.12		.14	.46		T	.04	.04	T	.48	.42	.05	.01	.17	.01		
MATAMORAS	4.21		.04	.41		.29		.66					.64				.09		.87	.16		.04				.26	.12		.54	.09		
MAYBURG	4.80	T	.38	T		.10		.87			.10		.68	T		.11	.15	.26	.27	.06		.05	.03	.04		.95	.27		.43	.05		
MC CONNELLSBURG	3.92		.84	.15		.11		.91			T	T	.40	T		.11	.12	.09	.70	T		.05	T			.24	.09		.11			
MC KEESPORT	4.68		.51	.20		.38	T	.75	.02			.01	.53	T	T	.22	.05	.16	.35			.03	T	.06		*	1.29		.09	.03		
MEADVILLE 1 S	4.64	.01	.41	.06		.04		.87	T	T	.12	.02	.59	.01	T	.14	.09	.24	.12	.14		.04	.02	.05	T	1.06	.34	T	.25	.02		
MEDIX RUN	5.79	T	.35	.40		.08		.93			.04	T	.64	T	T	.06	.26	.16	.75	.03		T	T	T	T	1.11	.81		.16	.01		
MERCER 2 NNE	4.24		.41				.26	.43		.04		.33	.08			.30		.10	.07			.20	.12		.29	.96	.05	T	.36	.24		
MERCERSBURG	-		-	.10		.10	.20	.80		.01	.14		.15				.10	.14	.76			.01				.25	.30		.03			
MEYERSDALE	5.25		.62	.41				.81			.05		.52	T		.13	T	.15	1.20	.20	T	T	T	T	T	.42	.43	T	.31	T		
MIDDLETOWN OLMSTED FLD	3.14		.92		.25	T	.79	.04		T		.30	.01		.01	.09		.10	.37			.01			.17	.08		T	T	T		
MIDLAND DAM 7	8.15		.45	.26		.13		1.11		T	.07	.03	.85	T		.41	.13	.22	.47	.17	T	T	T	.02		.85	.82		.14	.02		
MILANVILLE	4.98		.14	.64		.24		.71			.07		.37				.12	.07	.61	.34	T		T			.45	.59	D.25	.38			
MILLHEIM	3.85	T	.56	.17		.07		.77			T		.43	T	T	.14	T	.10	.48	T	T	T	T	T	T	.30	.57	.05	.21	T		
MILLVILLE 2 SW	4.12	T	.36	.35		.12		.71			.05		.70			T	.22	.03	.54	.08	T		T			.21	.39		.36	T		
MILROY	4.23	T	.80	.18		.09		.90					.41		T	.08	.06	.08	.53	.02		.01	T	T	T	.35	.49	T	.21	.02		
MONTROSE 1 E	3.81	T	.19	.25	T	.26		.69	T	T	.13	T	.44	.02	T		.19	.05	.50	.18	T	T	T	.01	T	.35	.18	.02	.15	T		
MORGANTOWN	4.04		.90		.20		.71	.18				.25	T		T	.06		.06	1.10						.10	.48		T	T	T		
MT GRETNA 2 SE	4.29		1.05		.24		.70	T			T	.51			T	.09		.20	.72						.25	.50			.03			
MT POCONO 2 N AP	4.09		.69		.22		.28	.60			T	.31	.27			.18		.19	.10			.03	.01			.54			.71			
MUHLENBURG 1 SE	4.80		.64		.20	.04	.53	.24				.24	.37			.30		.14	.83		.01	.03	T		T	.77	.02		.44			
MYERSTOWN	3.95		.55	.45		.02		.83					.65			T	.12	.08	.72	T					.08	.35				.10		
NATRONA LOCK 4	7.32	T	.66	.35		.20		1.17	T		.01	T	.79	T		.70	.29	.20	.71	.11		T	.01	.01		.60	1.40		.12	.03		
NESHAMINY FALLS	4.86		.97		.37		.95	.12		T		.30	T		T	.09		.11	1.28			T			.10	.30		T	.27			
NEWBURG 3 W	3.51		1.08		.08		.78					.47				.10		.74	.15						.10					.01		
NEW CASTLE 1 N	5.55	T	.40	.24		.03		1.20		T	.07	.03	.73			.11	.05	.12	.32	.02		.03	T	T	T	1.15	.76		.27	T		
NEWELL	-		.63	-				2.08				.11	.15	.38		.47		.34	.44	.20	T			.01		.50			.28			
NEW PARK	3.93		1.10		.28		.89					.25	.10			.23		.55	.25			T			.04	.24						
NEWPORT	3.33		.37	.39		.06		.78					.48			.02	.04	.07	.46	.06		T				.22	.18		.20			
NEW STANTON	5.32	.10	.42		.21	T	1.08	T		1.07		.76	T	.01	.02	.27	.09	.02	.01	.05	T	.10	.02		.21	.84	.02		.01	.01		
NEW TRIPOLI	4.72		1.06		.18		.63	.08				.32	.09			.10		.18	1.06				T		.03	.48			.51			
NORRISTOWN	3.80		.08	.63		.36		.76					.11			.01	.07	.11	1.12	.03			T			.18	.08		.24	.02		
NORTH EAST 2 SE	4.56	.05	.22	.09		T		.96	T	T	.10	T	.71	.09	T		.03	.22	.44	.07	.02	.04	.11	.04		1.08	.12		.13	.04		
ORWELL 3 N	3.21		.20	.06		.11		.68			.16	T	.45			.03	.19	.08	.46							.32	.08		.39			
PALM	6.01		.30	.87	.28	1.05							.40				.12	.18	1.12	.24						.30	.40		.30	.45		
PALMERTON	3.76		.73		.16	.04	.69	.04		T		.31	.07			.12		.07	.78			T	T	T	.09	.23		T	.45			
PARKER	6.36	T	.71	.29		.14		1.19	T	T	T	T	.82	T	T	*	.24	.06	.52	T		.03	.04	.02		1.47	.78		.05	T		
PAUPACK 2 WNW	4.08		.15	.17		.55		.37	.02				.46				.08	.04	.54	.49						.20	.25		.68	.08		
PECKS POND	4.75					.81		.91			.01		.37			.12	.07	.10	1.03	T	.02	T				.33	.19		.79			
PHIL DREXEL INST OF TEC	5.10		.92		.44	T	.83	.10		T		.29	T		T	.14		.22	1.35			T			.18	.40		T	.23	T		
PHILADELPHIA WB AP R	4.04		.86		.42	.01	.69	.10		T	T	.21	T		T	.12		.20	1.35		T	T			.16	.30		T	.22	T		
PHILADELPHIA PT BREEZE	3.85		.65		.33		.55	.07		T		.16			T	.13		.15	.93						.15	.49		T	.24			
PHILADELPHIA SHAWMONT	4.28		.85		.40	.15	.33	.30				.11	.05			.09		.16	1.19						T	.20	.10	.05	.30	T		
PHILADELPHIA CITY R	4.72		.78		.30	T	.74	.12		T	T	.26	T		.01	.10		.22	1.35		T	T			.14	.47		T	.23	T		
PHILIPSBURG CAA AP	4.87	.02	.78	T	.02	.01	.59	.18		.01	T	.43	T	.02	T	.31		.08	.55	T	T	.02	T	.01	.43	.80	.13	T	.28	.20		
PHOENIXVILLE 1 E	3.98		.75		.26		.98	.07				.22	T		.01	.08		.12	1.04						.15	.11		.19				
PIKES CREEK	4.65	T	.39	.25		.20		.78			.03		.58	T		T	.20	.10	.63	.19	.01		T	T		.38	.52		.39			
PIMPLE HILL	9.20	T	.59	.33	T	.30		.82			.01	T	.53	T	T	.03	.16	.16	.85	.04	.01	T	.05	.02	T	.42	.15	T	.73	T		
PINE GROVE 1 NE	4.17		.54	.41		.17		.89					.60			.03	.06	.09	.76	.04						.31	.02		.25	T		
PITTSBURGH WB AP 2 //R	5.98	.05	.67		.16	T	.93	.01		T	T	.77	.03	.01	.10	.77	.02	.17	.46	T	T	.02	.05	.03	.39	1.26	T	T	.08	T		
PITTSBURGH WB CITY R	5.97	.10	.75		.14		1.24	.01		T	T	.68	.02	.01	.02	.50	.03	.25	.60			.01	.01	T	.35	1.18		T	.07	T		
PLEASANT MOUNT 1 W	4.36		.13	.33	T	.27		.73	T	T	.16	T	.43	T		T	.16	.06	.57	.12	T	.01	T	.02	T	.39	.47	.02	.47	.02		
PORT CLINTON	4.29		.61	.37		.17		.71					.48			.02	.08	.12	.84			.01				.36	.08		.44			
PORTLAND		RECORD MISSING																														
POTTSTOWN	6.36		.09	.87		.36		2.03					.42		T	.05	.09	.06	1.44	.05					.05	.27	.32		.26			
POTTSVILLE PALO ALTO BR	3.94		.49	.39		.19		.80					.51			.03	.05	.07	.70	.02			T			.30	.06	T	.33	T		
PUTNEYVILLE 2 SE DAM	6.99		.58	.63	T	.29		1.07		T	.05	.03	.62	.04	.01	.40	.14	.10	.75	.20		.01		T		1.40	.65		.02			
QUAKERTOWN 1 E	5.26		1.05		.16		.83	.42				.20	.06			.11		D.13	1.43							.45			.42			
RAYMOND	3.62	.05	.12	.15		.05		.45			.14		.38			.05	.28	.15	.18	.15		T	.05	.04		.90	.30	T	.38	T		
READING WB CITY R	4.88		1.13		.20		.73	.07		T	.01	.35			T	.11		.14	1.08			T			.24	.63		T	.19	T		
RENOVO	4.09	T	.28	.15		.08		.48			.23	T	.47	T		.03	.25	.07	.55	.05		T	T			.60	.62		.25			
REW	4.55	.07	.20	.20	T	.06		.85			.12	T	.50	.04	T	.12	.20	.13	.26	.02		.04	.04	.06	T	.77	.42	T	.42	.03		
RICES LANDING L 6	6.13		.75	.40		.20	.04	1.15			.02	.12	.80			.29	.14	.25	.72	.15	.05					.29	.86		.20			
RIDGWAY 3 W	5.42	T	.32	.30		.09		.94	T		.12	T	.76	.04		.03	.28	.18	.45	.07		.01	.01	T	T	1.01	.60		.19	.02		
RUSH	3.65		.13	.06		.21		.80		T	.16		.43			.02	.26	.10	.55	.08						.37	.10	.03	.35			
RUSHVILLE	2.71		.03	.13		.16		.70			.11		.37				.05	.32	.17				.02			.26	.10		.29			
SAGAMORE 1 S	-	T	.60	.36		.18		1.19	.10				.60	T	T	.24	.15	.18	.50	.12		T		T	T	.89	-		T	T		
SALINA 3 W	6.49		1.02		.10	.04	.65	.73			.02	.72	.05	T	T	.41		.29	.73			.01	T	.01	.16	1.43			.08	T		
SAXTON	3.65		.87	.19		.09		.80		T		.01	.32		T	.08	.03	.07	.56	T		T	T	.01		.31	.27	T	.08	T		
SCHENLEY L 5	7.18		.83	.33		.25	T	1.08	T		.05	.04	.76	.02	T	.58	.13	.23	.65	.14			T	T		1.15	.86		.08			
SCRANTON	3.52		.10	.25	T	T		.90	.02		.03	T	.37	.02			.31	T	.05	.20	.07	T	T	T		.21	.42		.57			
SCRANTON WB AIRPORT	3.64		.30		.10		.57	.20			.02	.22	.13			.25		.06	.62		.07	.01		.02	.04	.53	.01	.02	.47			
SELINSGROVE CAA AP	3.90		.60		.18	T	.63	.12			T	.64	.05	T		.17		.13	.59		T	T	T		.08	.40	.04	.01	.26	T		
SHAMOKIN	4.32		.37	.20		.25		.86					.49			.05	.10	.08	.64	.04						.17	*	.32	.75	T		
SHIPPENSBURG	3.90		1.28		.06	T	.76	.17	T			.37			.05	.12	T	.05	.58			T		T	T	.46		T	T			
SHIPPINGPORT WB	5.72	.08	.57		.09	.01	.99			.02		.88	.02	T	.10	.39	T	.23	.54		T	T	T	T	.18	1.90		.06	.06	T		
SINNEMAHONING	4.73	T	.48	.23		.05		.77			.02	T	.52	T	T	.05	.29	.12	.52	.04		T	T	T	T	.79	.73	T	.12	T		
SLIPPERY ROCK	6.02		.33	.39		.07		.93			.05		.60	.03		.03	.16	.08	.28	.08		.05	T	T		1.10	.74		1.16	T		
SOMERSET FAIRVIEW ST	6.33	T	1.03	.67		.19		.80				.12	.36	.03		.25	.06	.27	.88	.12		.05	.09	.07	T	.53	.52		.23	.06		
SOMERSET MAIN ST	6.02		1.50	.03	.08	.08	.60	.22			.03	.45	.04	.01	.07	.26		.37	.80			.12	.02	.04	.20	.80			.30	T		
SOUTH MOUNTAIN	4.56		.84	.49		.21		.91		T		.01	.37			.11	.05	.16	.75	.03		T		T		.39	.22		.02			
SPRINGBORO	-	-	-	-	-	-	-	-	-	-	-	-	-	-	-	-	-	-	-	-	-	-	-	-	-	-	-	-	-	-		
SPRING GROVE	3.86		1.05	T	.16	.04	.73	.26		T		.20	.06		.02	.07		.12	.90			T			T	.23			T			
SPRINGS 1 SW	3.34		.90	T	.16	.01	.77	.07				.31	T	.01	.11	.01		.12	.07			.03			.28	.38			.11	T		
STATE COLLEGE	4.08	.05	.89	D.10	.04	T	.65	.11		.01	.05	.34	T	.01	T	.24		.16	.43	T	T	T	T	T	.27	.54	.03		.15	.01		
STRAUSSTOWN	4.20		.49	.45		.22		.78					.57			.02	.06	.09	.79	.06						.32	.09		.25	.01		
STROUDSBURG	4.86		.84	T	.23	.02	.80	.14		T	.01	.35	.07	T		.08	T	.22	.96		.01	.01	T	T	.14	.37	T	.01	.60	T		
STUMP CREEK	5.89		.52	.47		.12		1.20			.05	T	.48	.07		.23	.20	.09	.62	.10		T	T			.87	.76		.09	.02		
SUNBURY	4.24	T	.43	.12		.28		.72			T		.80			.03	.16	.14	.57	.02					T	.14	.42	T	.41	T		
SUSQUEHANNA	3.96		.44	.29		.25		.80			.18		.28	T		.02	.22	.07	.53	T		.06	T	T		.35	.22	T	.25	T		
SUTERSVILLE	3.99	T	.68	.35		.35	.01	1.29					*	.54	T	.21	.18	.25	.52	.08		.01	T	T		*	1.16		.36	T		

See Reference Notes Following Station Index

DAILY PRECIPITATION

PENNSYLVANIA
FEBRUARY 1956

Table 3—Continued

Station	Total	1	2	3	4	5	6	7	8	9	10	11	12	13	14	15	16	17	18	19	20	21	22	23	24	25	26	27	28	29	30	31
TAMAQUA	4.53		.38	.37		.22		.82					.54			.08	.07	.15	.68	.15			.08			.28	.16		.49	.09		
TAMAQUA 4 N DAM		RECORD MISSING																														
TAMARACK 2 S FIRE TWR	3.60	T	.27	.15		.03		.68			.05	T	.37	T		.02	.24	.07	.44	T			T	T	T	.57	.50		.23	T		
TIONESTA 2 SE DAM	5.24	T	.50	.10		.02		.89		T	.10	T	.78		T	.11	.34	.19	.25	.10		.02	.02	T	T	1.12	.36	T	.33	.01		
TITUSVILLE WATER WORKS	5.13		.55		T		.52	.44		.05	.06	.58	.07	T		.34		.20	.29			.03	.05	T	.36	1.17	T	T	.39	.03		
TORPEDO 4 W	4.47	.08	.28	.10		.02		.89			.11		.80	T	T	.17	.08	.20	.07	.13		.05	.07	.12	T	.95	.34		.29	.05		
TOWANDA	2.91	T	.12	.16	T	.15		.50		T	.07		.36		T	T	.29	.06	.43	.12	T		T	T	T	.10	.17	.01	.36	.01		
TOWER CITY 5 SW	4.08		1.03		.06	.12	.24	.42				.54	.07		T	.18		.15	.57			T			T	.42			.23	.05		
TROY	3.92		.29	.10		.05	.38	.71			.05		.55			.01	.25	.10	.58	.09				T		.21	.13	T	.42			
TURLEPOINT 4 NE	4.49	.04	.26	.05		.06		.80			.14	.02	.77	.06		.08	.14	.19	.24	.05		.05	.06	.05	T	.63	.33		.42	.07		
TYRONE 4 NE BALD EAGLE	5.03		.63	.39		.15		.89			.02	T	.45		T	.26	.10	.18	.52	.17		T	T	T		.47	.69	T	.17	T		
UNION CITY	4.45	.03	.28	.08		T	T	.88	T		.14	T	.75	.02	T	.12	.02	.34	.11	.14		.03	.03	.05	T	.82	.28		.31	.02		
UNIONTOWN	5.69	T	1.12	.02	.20		.78	.23		.02		.33	.01		.11	.30	.01	.14	.96			.02	T	T	.16	.65		.03	.20	T		
UPPER DARBY	5.34		.85		.40	T	1.60	.18		T		.15	.05		T	.04		.20	1.22						.03	.36			.26			
UTICA	5.58		.56	.15		.03		.96			.03	.04	.65			.05	.35	.19	.24	.05		.02		.04		1.27	.50		.39	.03		
VANDERGRIFT	7.36	T	.57	.47	T			1.21	T		T	T	.72	T		.53	.22	.21	.55	T			T	.07		1.56	1.13		.12			
VIRGINVILLE	–		.12	.21		.27		.63	.09				.27			.02	.11	.03	–				T			.28			.34			
VOWINCKEL	6.90	T	.52	.15		.12	T	.93	.04		.11	T	.69	.05	T	.34	.04	.15	.41	.61	T	.03	.03	.02	T	1.70	.71	.03	.17	.05		
VOWINCKEL 1 WSW	6.88	T	.45	.13		.12	T	.97	.04		.11	T	.70	.03	T	.42	.06	.10	.42	.60	T	.03	.02	.02	T	1.68	.67	.03	.22	.04		
WARREN	3.72	.03	.29	.10		.03		.72			.08		.47	.02		.11	.09	.26	.12	.10		.04	.04	.06		.61	.21		.32	.02		
WATSONTOWN	–		D.40	.30				.80		.05			.60			.10	.05	–	–	–							.35	.35	.35			
WAYNESBURG 2 W	5.89		.73	.37		.20	T	1.09			T	.03	.45			.63	.09	.23	.76	.13	T	T	T	T		.16	.84		.18	T		
WELLSBORO 3 S	3.64	.07	.38	.12		.06		.49			.02		.48	T		.01	.30	.08	.41	.05		T	T	T		.53	.38	T	.26	T		
WELLSVILLE	3.75		1.00		.14	T	.73	.05				.37	.02		T	.07		T	.75						T	.62						
WERNERSVILLE 1 W	4.72			1.10		.24		.78					.40			.04		.15	.85	.11						.22	.64		.13			
WEST CHESTER	4.22		.19	.65	*	.34		.69		.01			.16			.05	.05	.19	1.24	.02						.21	.29		.11	.02		
WEST GROVE 1 E	4.49		.23	1.07		.43		.77		.03			.25			.05		.10	1.16							.13	.16		.08	.03		
WEST HICKORY	5.52	.06	.48	.08				.90			.10		.70			.12	.25	.20	.26	.05		.05	.05	.05		1.35	.47		.30	.05		
WHITESBURG	6.43		.66	.54		.23		1.23					.59			.26	.33	.28	.64			T		T		1.24	.43		T			
WILKES BARRE	4.27	T	.13	.55		.12		.78			.03	T	.40	T			.29	.07	.60	.19	.01	T	T	T		.15	.40		.55	T		
WILLIAMSBURG	4.32	.03	.45	.15	.03	.13		.71	T		T	.04	.44	.03		.13	T	.24	.54	.06		T	T	.02		.50	.52	.05	.23	.02		
WILLIAMSPORT WB AP	4.15	T	.45		.08	.01	.61	.18		.02	.07	.50	.08			.22		.18	.70			.01	T		.08	.44	.01	.01	.50			
WOLFSBURG	4.19		.92	.25		.08		.78			.05	.05	.46	T		.12	.06	.12	.59	.02		.02				.37	.18		.12	T		
YORK 3 SSW PUMP STA	3.09		.72		.16	T	.63	.07		T		.23	.03		T	.04		.15	.70						T	.35			.03			
YORK HAVEN	3.74		.36	.55		.22		.82		T			.39			.03	.03	.06	.77	T	T	T				.19	.32		T	T		
ZION GROVE	–		.24	.27		.27		–					.45				.15	.20	.50	.05						.22	.26		.34	.06		
ZIONSVILLE 3 SE	5.11	T	.29	.54		.31		.89					.39				.18	.12	1.08	.22						.18	.55		.42	T		

Table 5

DAILY TEMPERATURES

PENNSYLVANIA
FEBRUARY 1956

Station		1	2	3	4	5	6	7	8	9	10	11	12	13	14	15	16	17	18	19	20	21	22	23	24	25	26	27	28	29	30	31	Average
ALLENTOWN WB AP	MAX	35	34	37	29	40	35	41	49	44	49	40	45	42	49	43	40	29	43	46	44	32	28	35	37	58	45	49	36	34			40.3
	MIN	18	26	23	19	26	22	34	31	30	30	33	34	29	25	29	24	23	27	27	28	15	12	19	13	34	30	32	22	21			25.4
ALLENTOWN GAS CO	MAX	35	35	38	38	34	40	40	44	50	45	49	41	47	44	49	43	40	36	45	45	44	31	28	35	41	58	48	50	38			41.8
	MIN	20	22	27	20	21	23	27	32	30	32	33	35	30	25	27	25	23	24	30	31	24	12	14	14	18	30	29	32	21			25.2
ALTOONA HORSESHOE CURVE	MAX	32	38	42	30	40	33	35	50	47	41	36	37	36	39	42	39	35	38	43	40	31	23	28	30	54	46	48	41	28			38.0
	MIN	10	26	28	23	28	20	30	27	33	35	32	31	28	22	34	19	25	31	26	30	18	10	13	8	28	24	32	23	17			24.5
ARENDTSVILLE	MAX	33	37	38	38	35	46	39	42	51	54	53	38	47	44	45	49	43	34	52	44	46	33	30	34	42	59	50	52	39			43.0
	MIN	15	16	29	23	26	24	28	28	29	34	33	33	28	22	24	22	25	28	26	30	26	15	18	13	15	32	28	32	21			24.9
ARTEMAS 1 WNW	MAX	37	45	35	38	46	38	45	57	50	42	42	42	43	47	40	49	46	42	41	27	45	24	28	30	52	54	53	48	36			42.1
	MIN	13	29	22	20	28	25	25	22	26	30	29	30	32	19	21	29	24	31	21	20	10	12	20	10	25	17	19	25	29			32.7
BAKERSTOWN 3 WNW	MAX	35	40	38	35	41	40	39	55	48	43	40	38	35	43	45	38	49	48	46	42	31	25	32	43	59	50	53	45	33			41.7
	MIN	13	31	27	28	26	27	33	25	35	36	33	34	29	25	31	20	28	32	21	24	18	7	10	17	35	24	32	23	16			25.5
BEAVERTOWN	MAX	33	38	39	32	40	37	39	50	48	46	41	44	40	44	43	40	36	43	46	43	38	28	33	34	43	47	45	45	32			40.2
	MIN																																
BELLEFONTE 4 S	MAX	29	34	39	37	38	38	37	37	50	43	42	37	40	37	43	49	39	34	41	45	40	26	25	31	37	54	45	46	33			38.8
	MIN	14	15	31	20	25	17	25	31	31	33	33	32	30	22	25	22	24	27	23	24	21	14	16	10	15	25	26	26	18			23.3
BERWICK	MAX	35	36	38	31	40	38	39	49	47	44	42	44	40	47	44	39	33	45	44	43	38	30	35	38	55	46	49	46	33			41.0
	MIN	14	27	28	17	30	20	32	30	32	35	34	34	26	22	36	23	22	29	25	32	21	10	19	12	31	28	28	26	15			25.4
BETHLEHEM LEHIGH UNIV	MAX	37	36	38	30	42	35	41	50	45	48	39	45	42	51	43	41	30	45	48	43	29	27	38	36	59	45	50	37	32			40.8
	MIN	27	26	25	20	28	27	35	34	35	34	37	36	34	30	32	30	23	30	31	28	13	11	19	17	36	29	37	23	20			27.8
BLAIRSVILLE 6 ENE	MAX	35	41	37	32	38	36	32	52	50	41	36	33	30	44	46	38	41	41	46	32	25	18	23	36	57	45	53	41	24			38.0
	MIN	13	28	24	27	25	30	29	28	36	32	30	28	25	25	28	18	27	30	22	23	11	5	9	16	31	20	33	18	15			23.7
BRADFORD 4 W RES	MAX	27	38	35	29	32	33	34	46	46	36	34	34	31	43	39	32	33	34	41	38	30	20	24	30	52	35	38	36	24			34.6
	MIN	-2	18	21	0	20	5	27	28	28	28	21	28	22	8	26	18	17	28	5	21	11	5	10	-13	26	13	21	16	3			15.8
BROOKVILLE CAA AIRPORT	MAX	32	43	36	33	34	35	35	49	39	39	35	35	33	41	38	36	36	37	48	36	24	21	27	37	56	44	45	34	27			36.7
	MIN	3	28	19	21	18	18	32	26	30	30	31	30	19	17	21	20	25	27	18	24	12	11	9	6	29	22	30	19	16			21.1
BURGETTSTOWN 2 W	MAX	28	37	42	36	38	42	43	37	55	49	40	42	35	38	45	38	40	53	45	45	39	21	26	32	64	58	52	58	30			41.7
	MIN	7	13	27	22	23	23	32	20	21	35	33	33	30	21	33	13	13	37	20	22	20	8	7	8	28	25	28	23	16			22.1
BURNT CABINS 2 NE	MAX	36	40	34	32	44	33	38	48	48	47	36	38	39	37	38	41	38	40	42	50	45	25	30	33	54	50	51	46	28			40.0
	MIN	11	28	24	24	24	25	31	25	27	32	32	32	25	23	30	28	24	32	27	28	19	14	17	10	29	30	29	22	20			24.9
BUTLER	MAX	37	39	40	40	40	40	40	51	55	44	38	38	36	44	44	35	42	43	49	49	37	25	30	34	57	55	60	38	30			41.7
	MIN	5	29	27	27	23	30	34	27	32	33	32	30	32	24	35	20	32	35	30	21	18	12	11	12	32	25	33	22	17			25.5
CANTON 1 NW	MAX	27	28	38	29	30	35	35	38	45	39	38	35	37	37	38	38	29	33	39	41	34	22	24	26	38	47	37	39	26			34.6
	MIN	11	10	23	9	17	15	18	31	33	32	30	28	25	25	25	15	14	15	18	22	11	3	5	7	7	19	20	20	10			17.9
CARLISLE	MAX	42	35	35	35	45	40	41	51	51	48	44	47	44	48	45	48	40	53	47	47	41	32	35	38	59	52	52	49	35			44.1
	MIN	17	28	29	19	29	24	34	34	31	34	34	36	29	24	38	24	28	32	28	38	27	17	22	15	33	32	29	33	24			28.3
CHAMBERSBURG 1 ESE	MAX	36	36	39	32	46	33	42	53	54	47	38	45	43	45	47	44	35	51	44	45	32	29	34	36	59	50	57	45	34			42.4
	MIN	17	28	27	25	28	24	32	28	30	33	33	34	30	23	37	25	30	33	27	32	22	17	20	14	33	33	28	27	20			27.2
CHESTER	MAX	37	40	43	42		46	50	46	54	52	55		49	55	52	53	46	43		52	48	35	32	36	56	62		57	40			47.2
	MIN	20	28	34	30		31	36	31	35	35	37		30	25	39	28	28	30		32	26	17	22	19	30		38	30	23			29.4
CLARION 3 SW	MAX	33	38	38	33	35	35	37	49	38	40	39	36	35	42	41	37	38	38	44	38	30	25	27	34	55	46	47	43	29			37.9
	MIN	3	29	25	18	24	18	33	25	30	33	28	31	29	17	31	17	27	33	16	25	17	13	14	6	34	22	25	22	16			22.8
CLAYSVILLE 3 W	MAX	39	45	42	40	46	47	47	60	53	45	44	44	41	48	51	42	57	52	48	45	32	27	36	49	62	60	60	50	35			46.4
	MIN	2	34	23	20	20	20	32	19	27	34	33	30	25	19	29	14	33	34	21	23	19	4	8	9	35	24	29	22	15			22.7
COATESVILLE 1 SW	MAX	36	38	39	39	33	44	39	43	51	56	52	41	48	44	51	49	42	35	52	46	45	34	31	35	49	60	50	55	40			44.0
	MIN	16	17	31	25	26	23	29	26	27	29	30	36	27	21	23	26	26	27	29	29	21	14	15	12	14	32	33	36	16			24.7
COLUMBIA	MAX	40	35	39	34	48	41	44	56	53	55	48	49	45	50	46	45	37	54	45	51	42	30	37	37	62	53	56	50	38			45.5
	MIN	18	28	33	24	30	25	33	27	32	33	36	35	28	23	38	24	28	31	30	37	27	18	21	15	32	33	32	32	23			28.5
CONFLUENCE 1 SW DAM	MAX	33	39	47	35	44	45	39	35	55	54	41	40	37	40	49	50	48	43	52	53	35	26	23	30	61	60	48	58	29			43.1
	MIN	7	30	29	29	29	26	35	24	30	38	32	34	31	22	40	20	32	32	28	29	23	10	18	9	31	29	28	26	18			26.5
CORRY	MAX	28	36	33	32	33	35	36	48	42	38	35	35	33	43	39	32	38	37	41	36	23	21	25	35	50	40	40	32	27			35.3
	MIN	4	24	23	8	20	10	30	30	32	30	26	30	27	25	25	14	22	28	12	23	15	12	14	-4	30	17	26	18	13			20.1
COUDERSPORT 2 NW	MAX	25	35	34	24	35	30	34	44	38	36	33	34	35	38	37	28	28	34	40	34	21	20	27	27	49	37	31	30	34			32.8
	MIN	4	21	20	9	19	12	29	28	30	31	26	27	23	17	23	12	17	27	12	18	9	0	10	0	25	22	10	14	18			17.7
DERRY	MAX	40	45	42	39	43	43	40	57	52	46	42	41	38	48	50	42	57	50	49	42	37	25	32	40	63	50	55	52	34			44.5
	MIN	22	31	27	27	27	25	32	26	32	40	32	30	31	24	33	19	34	37	26	23	20	9	12	14	35	26	35	23	17			26.5
DEVAULT 1 W	MAX	37	33	40	40	45	43	43	52	51	53	41	49	44	49	49	40	39	48	46	45	33	33	34	40	61	49	52	43	34			43.7
	MIN																																
DIXON	MAX	31	35	37	32	34	37	35	43	50	45	40	39	44	40	44	40	34	35	42	45	38	29	26	30	42	54	42	47	31			38.7
	MIN	12	12	27	0	4	10	11	22	23	31	30	32	32	19	20	20	20	21	27	26	20	9	9	6	8	25	25	26	2			18.2
DONEGAL	MAX	34	40	30	38	38	35	35	52	50	40	36	34	33	40	44	40	50	42	44	37	22	19	29	30	54	42	51	34	24			38.5
	MIN	1	28	23	24	22	21	24	22	26	30	30	27	18	21	23	15	27	28	20	21	10	-1	3	5	28	21	28	13	9			19.6
DONORA	MAX	40	46	48	39	42	46	44	48	59	54	46	43	39	45	51	41	55	62	46	50	42	30	28	39	65	61	56	58	33			46.8
	MIN	18	33	31	31	30	32	36	29	38	38	36	35	34	30	41	23	37	42	29	30	23	13	17	19	39	30	36	26	20			30.2
DU BOIS 7 E	MAX	32	39	38	32	34	32	34	48	46	40	35	35	33	40	40	39	35	36	43	38	28	23	27	30	55	41	44	38	27			36.6
	MIN	1	26	26	20	24	13	31	26	28	32	29	30	26	12	31	18	22	32	15	24	15	8	13	1	29	19	28	20	15			21.2
EAGLES MERE	MAX	28	27	32	24	27	32	32	32	42	42	38	39	34	35	35	37	28	31	34	38	34	23	21	26	36	44	35	39	27			32.8
	MIN	11	11	21	14	17	19	21	27	27	33	29	30	23	21	23	15	14	18	17	17	11	-1	0	8	10	18	18	18	8			17.2
EAST BRADY	MAX	35	40	38	35	40	37	39	55	46	42	38	37	37	45	42	40	39	41	49	47	47	26	31	35	59	52	49	45	31			41.3
	MIN	6	32	28	19	21	20	35	26	31	34	30	22	31	22	33	22	31	22	21	27	18	12	14	11	23	13	28	24	17			23.2
EBENSBURG	MAX	36	42	34	32	38	34	32	47	45	46	36	35	34	41	45	39	35	40	46	40	32	21	26	32	53	43	48	40	26			37.9
	MIN	5	25	25	23	24	21	30	25	31	31	31	29	23	21	31	15	25	29	22	25	15	8	10	5	27	21	30	17	14			22.0
EMPORIUM 1 E	MAX	30	32	39	35	33	35	35	35	50	37	41	41	41	36	42	37	37	32	38	45	37	25	25	30	36	52	40	45	30			36.9
	MIN	3	3	28	5	7	7	10	32	28	30	29	32	26	13	16	11	16	25	14	15	16	11	13	-1	0	21	22	22	15			16.2
EPHRATA	MAX	37	34	38	31	45	34	40	52	51	54	41	48	46	47	46	45	37	48	46	48	38	31	35	35	60	50	54	41	35			43.0
	MIN	18	26	30	23	28	25	31	29	32	32	34	34	30	23	37	21	24	28	26	35	25	12	18	14	29	30	34	31	19			26.8
ERIE CAA AIRPORT	MAX	34	36	29	35	31	38	37	47	35	35	38	37	33	48	41	29	38	36	38	30	23	25	25	44	54	44	32	27	28			35.4
	MIN	12	29	14	15	20	21	31	32	31	29	29	30	25	33	24	21	25	24	17	23	16	17	13	13	27	19	24	19	15			22.3

See Reference Notes Following Station Index

DAILY TEMPERATURES

Table 5 - Continued

Station		1	2	3	4	5	6	7	8	9	10	11	12	13	14	15	16	17	18	19	20	21	22	23	24	25	26	27	28	29	30	31	Average
EVERETT 1 SW	MAX	32	44	39	34	43	34	39	53	56	44	38	43	43	45	45	45	36	40	46	40	28	27	32	34	42	50	59	38	35			40.8
	MIN	16	28	23	20	23	21	27	23	27	31	33	33	23	21	31	21	30	33	30	30	14	14	16	10	35	30	27	20	21			24.5
FARRELL SHARON	MAX	33	39	37	35	37	39	40	54	44	43	39	40	40	48	44	38	42	46	52	41	31	27	33	41	60	52	48	36	35			41.2
	MIN	6	25	24	17	22	21	32	28	33	31	33	31	30	28	24	10	13	15	24	22	16	12	12	14	33	22	26	20	13			22.0
FORD CITY 4 S DAM	MAX	29	37	41	34	38	41	39	36	54	43	39	39	39	36	45	43	43	44	42	49	32	26	25	30	58	58	49	52	32			40.4
	MIN	8	9	27	28	26	22	33	23	24	32	31	33	29	27	27	18	20	33	20	21	17	10	11	10	14	24	25	24	17			22.2
FRANKLIN	MAX	32	39	38	35	38	37	38	56	38	39	37	37	35	45	41	37	39	39	46	44	31	25	29	35	56	48	45	40	30			38.9
	MIN	3	30	25	24	14	15	32	26	30	32	28	31	28	21	29	9	27	32	16	24	15	13	13	8	25	20	23	18	13			21.5
FREDERICKSVILLE 2 SE	MAX																																
	MIN																																
FREELAND	MAX	29	34	34	27	30	31	38	43	44	42	36	36	35	39	39	32	28	35	36	37	33	27	27	29	38	35	44	43	25			34.7
	MIN	10	20	20	12	27	20	28	27	34	32	31	31	28	22	29	16	15	20	20	27	13	7	18	7	22	29	29	19	13			21.6
GEORGE SCHOOL	MAX	37	38	38	34	45	38	45	52	49	53	45	47	45	50	52	43	38	50	46	45	39	31	35	37	61	50	55	50	35			44.2
	MIN	20	28	30	26	29	26	29	25	29	30	36	33	26	24	31	24	25	33	31	32	24	14	19	12	32	30	37	35	21			27.3
GETTYSBURG	MAX	34	32	39	40	38	48	40	42	53	55	51	40	45	43	45	49	43	33	52	44	45	33	30	36	48	59	50	57	40			43.6
	MIN	18	20	32	25	28	26	25	30	32	36	36	35	32	23	30	26	28	31	29	32	27	16	20	17	25	34	32	34	22			27.6
GORDON	MAX																																
	MIN																																
GRATZ 1 N	MAX	34	35	38	35	34	40	37	38	50	46	47	40	44	40	46	42	37	34	45	44	42	30	29	33	45	58	46	48	33			40.3
	MIN	17	17	18	19	24	20	28	20	29	33	34	34	30	23	23	24	24	24	25	26	23	13	17	10	12	27	28	25	18			22.9
GREENVILLE	MAX	32	37	38	35	39	36	38	39	38	38	37	37	38	46	41	35	41	39	50	40	30	25	30	40	55	51	44	34	31			38.4
	MIN	4	29	23	14	21	19	32	27	32	32	30	32	27	27	27	4	29	32	17	24	15	12	10	14	33	22	26	17	10			22.1
HANOVER	MAX	34	39	37	39	45	49	37	42	54	56	54	40	48	45	50	52	43	35	53	45	48	34	32	36	48	61	52	59	41			45.1
	MIN	17	17	29	24	27	25	28	26	27	32	32	33	29	23	23	24	24	28	27	32	25	13	14	14	15	31	30	31	19			24.8
HARRISBURG WB AP	MAX	37	35	39	30	43	35	42	53	52	51	39	46	43	49	44	40	33	51	45	46	31	29	34	37	60	51	53	45	34			42.3
	MIN	19	28	28	25	29	26	33	33	33	34	35	35	29	25	37	27	27	30	31	31	21	18	22	17	37	33	35	26	23			28.5
HAWLEY 1 S DAM	MAX	23	31	37	36	33	35	35	37	43	45	40	35	40	35	40	40	30	38	38	40	35	24	23	24	39							35.0
	MIN	12	12	24	3	4	12	12	20	30	28	28	31	30	17	17	19	17	15	25	24	15	5	5	7	9							16.8
HOLTWOOD	MAX	40	34	39	32	43	36	43	54	46	50	40	47	43	46	45	41	35	52	45	46	35	31	34	38	59	50	52	45	35			42.6
	MIN	19	29	28	27	28	27	35	28	32	32	37	34	30	28	37	28	30	35	33	35	24	19	22	19	38	36	35	29	25			29.6
HUNTINGDON	MAX	34	37	38	41	39	45	39	41	56	51	44	38	43	41	44	42	46	35	47	50	42	32	28	35	35	54	50	55	35			42.0
	MIN	13	13	32	20	24	20	24	27	27	32	31	30	30	22	24	21	22	30	26	25	25	17	12	9	10	30	29	29	23			23.3
INDIANA 3 SE	MAX	40	43	37	34	41	38	39	53	50	42	40	39	33	45	48	43	44	43	49	42	30	24	29	36	60	48	54	44	28			41.2
	MIN	6	28	28	25	28	24	34	24	30	35	32	32	27	19	33	17	31	34	23	28	18	12	9	9	34	25	28	24	17			24.6
IRWIN	MAX	38	43	43	37	42	42	38	53	53	49	38	38	36	45	45	41	57	59	46	47	35	25	29	40	60	50	54	54	31			43.7
	MIN	14	31	29	27	29	26	34	27	31	37	33	33	30	26	33	20	34	39	27	27	20	12	17	15	36	27	35	25	18			27.3
JAMESTOWN 2 NW	MAX	26	35	37	33	34	36	38	35	48	39	35	37	35	35	46	32	33	40	36	43	32	23	24	28	54	56	47	37	27			36.6
	MIN	-1	14	21	10	20	15	29	26	26	31	29	31	28	26	30	3	8	31	15	18	13	11	4	10	20	19	21	14	10			18.3
JIM THORPE	MAX	41	34	38	32	43	39	43	53	51	51	43	46	42	44	45	43	35	41	49	45	44	30	35	37	50	54	50	46	33			42.7
	MIN	18	26	31	17	27	18	30	32	31	33	34	35	28	20	37	23	22	25	27	33	20	9	17	11	28	27	29	28	17			25.3
JOHNSTOWN	MAX	31	40	46	40	42	44	43	37	58	55	43	43	38	49	46	49	47	41	46	52	38	27	26	32	63	62	49	57	32			44.0
	MIN	11	14	29	28	28	26	33	27	29	37	33	34	31	23	29	22	24	33	29	29	20	12	15	10	15	26	27	26	18			24.8
KANE 1 NNE	MAX	26	29	36	34	33	29	34	32	44	38	34	34	33	34	38	35	35	34	35	41	33	20	23	27	40	51	38	40	28			34.1
	MIN	-5	0	24	3	19	6	26	30	28	31	31	31	25	7	24	11	13	25	4	6	13	9	12	-10	6	18	18	18	13			15.0
KEGG	MAX	37	46	36	35	45	34	38	53	57	43	37	40	40	41	43	43	37	48	48	42	28	25	30	33	59	47	58	38	32			41.1
	MIN	14	29	27	22	25	24	32	25	30	31	31	32	24	21	31	18	31	32	26	27	16	11	15	10	32	29	30	19	17			24.5
LANCASTER 2 NE PUMP STA	MAX	38	35	38	37	45	40	43	54	49	53	49	50	45	49	45	45	41	52	49	48	47	32	35	36	62	55	56	54	37			45.5
	MIN	16	26	32	23	29	23	32	26	28	29	33	34	26	22	35	23	26	30	27	34	24	16	19	14	31	32	28	30	22			26.6
LANDISVILLE	MAX	33	35	37	35	35	41	38	39	51	48	51	39	45	42	47	43	39	34	49	44	44	30	28	32	51	60	49	53	36			41.7
	MIN	18	18	27	21	26	25	27	29	30	31	31	33	29	23	28	23	25	26	27	29	24	15	19	14	19	31	31	30	21			25.2
LAWRENCEVILLE 2 S	MAX	30	40	35	32	33	36	38	39	51	39	39	39	42	38	46	37	30	34	40	40	36	28	27	28	39	39	38	40	28			36.6
	MIN	10	13	18	5	7	8	11	30	29	32	30	29	29	16	22	15	17	20	18	22	12	-1	8	3	7	21	25	21	5			16.6
LEBANON 2 NW	MAX																																
	MIN																																
LEWISTOWN	MAX	34	39	41	41	39	46	39	41	55	51	48	39	46	43	47	44	42	35	49	49	45	32	30	35	36	53	49	50	36			42.6
	MIN	17	16	28	22	25	21	25	29	29	33	33	34	33	24	27	27	26	28	30	28	26	17	17	15	14	31	31	32	25			25.6
LINESVILLE 5 WNW	MAX	28	36	32	33	34	35	37	46	37	36	35	35	35	45	39	32	39	38	42	31	27	23	28	40	53	45	39	29	30			35.8
	MIN	-8	26	18	7	18	12	32	27	31	31	29	31	27	25	20	7	27	27	13	22	13	13	4	4	31	16	24	15	10			19.0
LOCK HAVEN	MAX	34	37	38	28	40	33	39	53	49	45	39	43	41	40	39	38	34	41	44	42	35	29	34	36	49	44	48	40	33			39.5
	MIN	13	28	26	14	27	17	32	35	32	36	33	33	29	22	34	20	24	32	23	33	21	15	20	11	33	27	28	27	18			25.6
MADERA	MAX	27	35	39	34	35	35	34	34	46	45	36	35	36	35	42	40	36	34	37	42	33	23	23	27	35	52	42	45	29			36.1
	MIN	4	4	26	18	24	15	24	23	22	29	28	29	25	15	18	16	17	25	17	17	16	6	7	3	3	18	20	22	12			17.3
MARCUS HOOK	MAX	38	38	42	34	49	41	48	50	48	58	43	48	45	50	52	44	34	53	45	47	38	34	38	40	58	51	53	46	37			44.9
	MIN	24	30	31	28	32	30	36	34	34	38	37	40	36	32	38	31	27	34	33	35	24	17	21	24	40	38	38	28	24			31.5
MARTINSBURG CAA AP	MAX	34	43	36	31	42	32	36	55	49	41	35	36	35	40	44	39	32	41	49	38	26	23	28	34	51	43	53	37	27			38.3
	MIN	16	25	24	24	25	22	30	27	33	32	32	31	28	27	29	20	27	31	25	25	15	12	15	12	33	25	35	20	18			24.8
MEADVILLE 1 S	MAX	28	35	36	34	34	34	37	35	47	40	35	36	34	35	45	32	32	38	36	43	32	25	25	26	52	54	45	38	29			36.3
	MIN	0	9	23	11	20	13	29	27	28	31	29	32	28	24	32	8	8	30	16	17	13	13	11	7	11	12	14	18	12			18.1
MERCER 2 NNE	MAX	29	40	34	30	35	36	31	49	40	36	37	34	42	37	40	40	42	35	46	32	29	26	36	34	52	58	54	35	33			38.0
	MIN	-1		12	10	14	20	17	19	19	29	25	29	30	24	20	5	14	24	18	15	9	9	12	12	32	24	25	29	7			17.9
MIDDLETOWN OLMSTED FLD	MAX	37	35	38	30	42	34	42	51	50	50	40	46	44	49	45	40	33	51	45	47	32	31	34	37	60	50	53	45	35			42.3
	MIN	19	28	27	24	28	25	34	31	32	33	37	35	27	26	35	27	28	32	30	32	22	18	22	17	37	34	38	28	25			28.7
MIDLAND DAM 7	MAX	37	40	36	39	38	42	40	48	46	42	41	38	37	44	46	42	48	47	46	41	28	26	30	50	54	48	53	40	32			41.3
	MIN	18	33	28	30	27	30	33	29	36	35	35	32	29	30	25	20	35	30	27	27	18	12	15	20	34	27	33	22	19			27.2
MONTROSE 1 E	MAX	24	28	34	26	30	32	32	34	44	40	36	35	38	33	40	38	25	30	35	38	34	22	20	22	34	47	35	37	24			32.7
	MIN	13	13	22	8	12	17	18	29	28	33	30	31	28	19	20	17	14	15	22	23	12	1	1	7	9	17	16	21	10			17.4
MORGANTOWN	MAX	36	35	39	30	42	35	41	50	51	50	40	46	43	48	47	40	31	49	45	44	32	29	34	38	59	47	52	44	34			41.8
	MIN	15	26	24	22	25	21	32	26	30	29	33	33	27	22	34	22	23	28	28	30	20	13	18	11	32	16	30	24	18			24.8

See Reference Notes Following Station Index

Table 5 - Continued

DAILY TEMPERATURES

PENNSYLVANIA
FEBRUARY 1956

Station		1	2	3	4	5	6	7	8	9	10	11	12	13	14	15	16	17	18	19	20	21	22	23	24	25	26	27	28	29	30	31	Average
MT GRETNA 2 SE	MAX	40	41	40	39	43	34	40	51	50	52	39	42	43	48	50	40	42	50	46	43	36	29	32	34	60	44	51	40	29			42.3
	MIN	14	26	23	20	27	22	32	26	31	30	35	29	25	21	33	20	25	31	27	28	17	14	19	10	34	30	29	23	19			24.8
MT POCONO 2 N AP	MAX	33	33	36	23	33	30	35	44	44	38	34	37	35	38	40	33	26	34	41	36	30	21	24	29	49	38	41	35	26			34.3
	MIN	11	21	19	8	23	13	27	28	32	32	29	31	25	20	32	16	16	20	21	27	12	3	10	4	24	21	24	20	9			19.9
MUHLENBURG 1 SE	MAX	31	40	35	30	38	32	40	45	45	44	39	40	38	41	44	40	32	39	42	39	32	26	36	33	50	40	44	40	29			38.1
	MIN	10	22	22	7	26	15	29	30	31	31	31	31	24	30	31	16	18	24	20	29	10	2	10	6	21	22	28	21	8			20.9
NEWBURG 3 W	MAX	38	37	41	34	45	34	37	46	49	48	44	43	42	40	48	41	40	42	45	43	38	30	35	36	53	53	54	38	35			41.7
	MIN	17	28	27	29	28	21	32	30	31	32	36	33	32	26	30	27	25	32	31	33	22	16	18	15	33	33	34	31	26			28.1
NEW CASTLE 1 N	MAX	34	39	37	35	39	39	39	54	52	42	39	39	38	46	44	38	46	47	47	44	34	26	32	44	60	51	51	44	32			41.8
	MIN	6	32	26	18	23	22	33	27	31	33	31	31	24	25	30	14	32	34	19	24	16	12	10	15	35	25	28	19	14			23.8
NEWELL	MAX	36	42	44	36	40	44	42	45	58	53	42	43	37	42	47	42	46	58	46	45	38	26	25	32	61	56	54	57	30			43.7
	MIN	16	32	29	28	30	29	35	27	35	38	35	34	33	27	40	23	33	42	27	27	21	11	14	15	30	28	33	25	19			28.1
NEWPORT	MAX	35	37	39	40	37	44	38	41	55	52	49	40	45	42	48	43	42	33	46	47	46	30	30	35	37	56	50	50	36			42.2
	MIN	15	15	28	20	25	20	25	29	28	32	32	33	27	21	24	23	23	28	28	28	26	17	19	12	12	31	27	27	23			24.1
NEW STANTON	MAX	42	48	38	40	44	44	42	55	47	43	43	44	40	49	51	44	50	47	50	48	38	38	39	44	52	48	51	39	34			44.6
	MIN	12	24	25	28	25	26	32	26	32	31	38	32	22	21	24	17	20	30	28	28	15	8	9	7	26	26	30	18	18			23.4
NORRISTOWN	MAX	39	37	39	33	45	38	46	56	53	53	43	48	46	52	50	42	34	49	48	46	35	32	36	40	61	50	55	46	36			44.4
	MIN	21	31	29	26	32	27	36	30	34	34	38	37	30	26	36	28	28	32	31	32	23	16	21	19	38	34	38	26	23			29.5
PALMERTON	MAX	34	35	35	28	39	33	42	49	46	46	38	44	40	46	43	38	28	43	44	41	28	27	33	35	57	46	48	34	32			39.0
	MIN	15	17	22	17	25	20	33	34	32	33	33	36	27	22	30	25	23	27	30	28	15	12	20	13	35	30	30	21	20			25.0
PHIL DREXEL INST OF TEC	MAX	41	41	42	35	48	41	48	54	52	58	44	49	48	53	52	44	35	50	47	48	36	35	37	41	63	51	57	49	37			46.1
	MIN	26	33	33	31	33	34	36	35	38	38	36	39	37	33	39	28	30	33	33	37	27	16	23	23	41	37	39	33	25			32.6
PHILADELPHIA WB AP	MAX	38	38	42	35	46	41	46	53	50	54	44	48	45	52	52	42	35	50	45	46	35	30	36	42	63	51	56	47	36			44.8
	MIN	22	31	31	29	32	29	35	31	34	37	37	39	31	28	36	28	28	33	31	33	23	17	22	20	39	35	37	28	24			30.3
PHILADELPHIA PT BREEZE	MAX	40	41	44	36	47	42	47	53	51	54	46	49	46	54	54	44	36	51	46	49	37	34	38	42	63	52	57	40	36			45.8
	MIN	26	31	37	31	34	34	37	33	39	41	40	42	40	34	43	32	32	36	37	40	32	21	26	28	36	38	42	35	25			34.6
PHILADELPHIA SHAWMONT	MAX	37	40	39	38	44	43	45	54	50	52	49	48	47	51	51	51	41	49	49	45	44	31	36	38	62	62	55	54	36			46.2
	MIN	18	29	36	25	32	25	36	28	31	32	37	38	29	25	38	28	28	32	30	36	24	16	22	16	32	35	30	33	23			29.1
PHILADELPHIA CITY	MAX	39	41	44	34	47	42	45	52	48	53	43	47	45	51	51	45	34	49	46	47	36	32	35	42	60	49	55	49	36			44.7
	MIN	27	31	31	29	33	32	37	36	37	41	36	39	37	33	36	29	29	33	33	36	22	18	23	25	40	36	40	28	25			32.1
PHILIPSBURG CAA AP	MAX	30	39	35	29	34	30	33	49	47	39	33	35	31	37	42	38	30	35	42	36	21	19	25	31	46	41	41	38	23			34.8
	MIN	0	25	20	18	15	11	30	28	30	29	32	27	13	12	23	17	21	26	15	20	9	8	10	-2	29	20	29	16	13			18.8
PHOENIXVILLE 1 E	MAX	39	36	38	40	45	40	45	54	51	53	48	50	46	51	50	47	45	49	49	48	43	32	36	38	62	58	53	52	36			46.0
	MIN	13	25	24	21	26	19	33	23	26	27	32	36	23	19	32	22	24	29	31	34	19	13	19	10	30	32	31	31	19			24.9
PIMPLE HILL	MAX	26	32	34	28	31	30	32	32	43	46	37	33	37	34	41	39	29	31	34	41	33	22	21	25	38	48	37	42	24			33.8
	MIN	12	16	22	11	16	19	22	27	29	32	28	30	23	20	30	14	15	16	21	24	12	0	7	8	21	19	22	22	9			18.9
PITTSBURGH WB AP 2	MAX	36	40	35	39	40	41	39	54	49	42	40	38	36	45	45	39	52	48	46	42	29	25	30	52	59	50	52	37	32			41.8
	MIN	15	32	27	28	26	29	31	28	37	34	34	32	30	29	25	19	34	32	26	27	15	11	11	20	32	26	34	19	16			26.2
PITTSBURGH WB CITY	MAX	41	45	38	41	42	43	41	56	53	45	43	43	38	49	50	40	57	47	47	42	30	27	32	55	62	51	55	41	35			44.4
	MIN	20	33	30	31	30	32	35	33	40	36	36	35	31	34	28	22	35	34	29	28	17	13	19	22	35	26	41	24	20			29.3
PLEASANT MOUNT 1 W	MAX	23	28	34	26	31	32	32	33	42	43	37	33	38	35	39	39	28	29	35	37	32	24	21	21	36	48	34	39	27			33.0
	MIN	3	7	23	-7	5	6	8	27	27	32	29	29	27	14	14	17	14	16	20	20	2	1	5	1	2	18	19	23	0			13.9
PORT CLINTON	MAX	43	38	39	37	40	35	42	40	44	54	45	52	40	49	43	48	44	42	36	45	49	48	34	32	38	42	52	50	53			43.2
	MIN	14	20	27	16	24	17	25	24	28	30	34	32	27	20	24	24	23	24	28	30	20	12	14	10	20	30	26	30	17			23.1
PUTNEYVILLE 2 SE DAM	MAX	30	35	41	34	36	35	38	36	52	41	36	37	36	35	43	42	38	39	40	47	37	30	25	30	55	57	46	49	29			38.9
	MIN	11	11	25	22	24	19	30	25	25	24	28	30	27	21	26	17	18	30	18	18	15	9	10	8	15	20	22	20	14			20.1
QUAKERTOWN 1 E	MAX	35	35	39	34	42	38	43	50	47	49	44	47	42	49	44	44	36	44	45	45	39	28	34	36	56	47	51	47	34			42.2
	MIN	16	25	30	18	27	18	31	26	26	27	30	34	24	19	33	23	23	25	27	32	21	10	11	12	28							23.8
READING WB CITY	MAX	37	37	39	32	44	36	42	54	50	52	42	47	44	50	45	44	33	48	47	47	33	30	35	39	61	50	54	45	35			43.2
	MIN	24	28	30	26	30	27	34	34	36	36	36	37	33	29	36	27	28	32	31	33	22	17	23	20	39	33	40	28	24			30.1
RIDGWAY 3 W	MAX	31	38	36	31	34	33	34	47	37	38	35	35	35	42	37	36	35	37	42	33	25	25	27	32	54	41	44	35	27			35.7
	MIN	-7	28	22	10	24	10	30	27	28	33	28	28	23	9	28	14	23	32	9	25	14	9	13	-4	32	20	20	19	14			19.3
SALINA 3 W	MAX	38	43	40	35	39	38	40	54	50	44	41	39	36	44	48	44	47	47	45	43	31	24	29	40	58	49	52	47	30			41.9
	MIN	8	30	28	26	28	26	33	24	30	34	32	33	28	22	32	18	34	35	23	26	19	10	13	13	34	25	31	22	18			25.3
SCRANTON	MAX	30	35	36	34	32	36	37	42	42	39	42	41	38	35	40	43	32	38	34	34	22	21	17	29	39	55	42	47	29			35.9
	MIN	19	18	29	12	16	11	20	33	32	35	33	34	32	23	26	20	20	23	28	20	19	8	9	13	14	24	24	26	15			21.9
SCRANTON WB AIRPORT	MAX	32	35	36	30	36	34	40	4"	43	40	39	40	37	43	41	32	30	40	42	36	26	26	30	35	53	40	45	34	32			37.0
	MIN	17	25	14	11	24	19	32	32	32	33	32	34	28	23	24	21	21	30	28	24	9	8	14	11	34	25	33	15	15			23.0
SELINSGROVE CAA AP	MAX	36	34	38	31	40	33	39	54	45	47	40	42	41	45	42	38	32	45	47	43	29	28	36	35	52	48	46	38	33			39.9
	MIN	13	28	19	14	22	17	33	27	30	33	32	33	24	23	30	25	26	32	26	29	17	14	18	12	32	29	28	23	18			24.4
SHIPPENSBURG	MAX	37	35	40	36	48	46	44	53	53	50	43	46	43	45	47	46	41	51	46	45	37	31	35	32	58	50	55	53	33			44.1
	MIN	17	27	32	27	29	24	30	29	30	35	33	34	30	25	35	25	29	31	29	24	25	17	20	15	31	31	33	32	21			27.6
SHIPPINGPORT WB	MAX	38	38	35	38	39	42	37	53	46	43	42	42	38	46	45	38	48	45	46	39	30	27	31	54	61	53	53	36	34			42.0
	MIN	14	14	28	28	28	29	32	28	36	34	35	35	28	28	26	20	34	32	24	27	17	13	16	17	34	28	32	23	19			26.2
SLIPPERY ROCK	MAX	32	38	37	33	38	36	37	51	43	40	37	36	35	42	42	36	40	40	47	41	29	26	30	38	57	47	50	38	30			38.8
	MIN	6	29	25	21	23	23	31	27	32	30	29	29	27	26	26	16	30	28	20	22	14	9	10	15	33	21	30	19	13			22.9
SOMERSET MAIN ST	MAX	38	44	44	33	41	36	45	52	51	47	35	35	35	42	47	44	39	46	48	47	30	30	29	33	57	43	53	48	27			41.3
	MIN	6	27	26	22	27	25	30	24	29	33	30	30	27	22	32	17	29	32	27	26	19	7	14	6	32	25	31	20	15			23.8
SPRINGBORO	MAX	28	35	36	36	34	35	38	36	49	38	36	38	35	39	47	44	37	40	37	42	37	25	25	21	52	54	46	28				37.4
	MIN	12	16	16	5	18	11	31	28	30	31	27	31	28	26	29	6	20	32	17	17	17	17	17	15	45	20	26	13				21.5
SPRINGS 1 SW	MAX	35	45	42	33	43	33	36	52	51	42	34	35	34	44	44	41	40	48	49	44	25	18	26	34	58	43	52	42	25			39.6
	MIN	16	27	25	25	25	25	29	22	29	31	31	29	26	18	29	17	28	31	25	24	17	5	7	5	31	25	34	17	13			23.0
STATE COLLEGE	MAX	34	39	36	37	38	36	35	50	45	40	36	39	37	42	44	38	34	42	45	37	25	24	30	33	40	45	45	36	29			37.6
	MIN	17	26	24	21	24	20	32	31	33	34	32	31	25	25	21	22	23	26	25	22	14	13	13	13	30	24	26	20	18			23.6
STROUDSBURG	MAX	34	36	35	26	40	33	43	46	45	43	37	43	40	42	43	37	26	42	43	41	29	27	28	35	55	44	40	35	29			37.8
	MIN	9	25	20	9	24	13	30	25	25	29	28	31	23	17	27	18	18	25	25	25	10	7	11	4	30	27	30	16	14			20.5
TAMARACK 2 S FIRE TWR	MAX	23	26	35	31	30	32	31	30	45	36	35	32	34	34	38	37	34	30	32	35	37	22	21	27	33	46	38	42	31			33.1
	MIN	8	9	24	14	9	19	20	28	29	34	29	29	21	10	21	14	14	17	15	15	14	5	6	9	9	18	17	18	12			16.8

See Reference Notes Following Station Index

DAILY TEMPERATURES

Table 5 - Continued

Station		1	2	3	4	5	6	7	8	9	10	11	12	13	14	15	16	17	18	19	20	21	22	23	24	25	26	27	28	29	30	31	Average
TIONESTA 2 SE DAM	MAX	27	35	38	38	35	31	36	35	48	39	35	36	36	34	43	36	36	37	37	45	32	23	22	26	49	55	45	40	28			36.4
	MIN	- 1	0	25	11	18	12	18	26	25	30	26	32	28	17	24	14	16	27	11	12	15	10	14	1	4	19	20	20	15			16.9
TITUSVILLE WATER WORKS	MAX	30	37	34	32	34	36	37	51	40	37	35	34	34	46	42	34	37	37	45	36	29	20	19	36	50	45	45	36	25			36.3
	MIN	- 5	27	21	1	15	8	31	25	27	30	26	29	17	15	24	3	24	30	10	21	13	11	11	- 2	30	14	21	17	14			17.5
TOWANDA	MAX	34	38	38	32	39	34	43	52	42	40	38	44	41	46	41	34	31	41	43	40	30	28	32	37	54	42	43	37	33			38.9
	MIN	15	27	16	1	28	11	32	28	30	33	32	32	29	19	27	17	19	30	25	27	16	8	14	7	11	22	25	17	10			21.0
UNIONTOWN	MAX	44	49	40	45	46	43	42	58	56	46	43	42	44	49	50	46	62	55	49	44	31	29	35	50	62	50	60	44	34			46.5
	MIN	16	35	31	34	29	31	31	25	35	38	38	34	28	27	33	23	36	36	28	30	20	11	18	17	36	29	36	25	19			28.6
UPPER DARBY	MAX	38	40	41	35	45	38	46	54	53	54	45	49	46	50	52	45	38	50	47	47	40	31	36	38	61	50	55	51	35			45.2
	MIN	19	30	33	27	31	29	35	29	32	34	36	38	30	28	39	27	27	32	31	35	25	15	19	18	33	33	35	31	21			29.4
WARREN	MAX	29	37	35	31	34	35	36	50	40	37	37	36	35	45	40	32	37	37	43	36	25	25	30	35	54	40	39	33	27			36.2
	MIN	5	28	21	11	24	15	32	32	32	32	28	31	28	21	21	18	24	30	15	22	13	11	14	3	31	18	29	20	15			21.5
WAYNESBURG 2 W	MAX	40	47	46	40	46	47	45	58	56	51	45	43	42	48	50	43	61	57	49	46	36	27	36	48	64	52	59	54	35			47.3
	MIN	13	32	29	24	25	24	35	22	32	37	34	33	32	22	33	20	35	38	24	27	23	9	13	12	37	28	33	25	18			26.5
WELLSBORO 3 S	MAX	26	27	37	29	32	35	34	35	45	39	38	36	35	33	38	38	31	32	37	44	36	22	22	27	36	47	36	39	29			34.3
	MIN	9	11	23	10	18	16	18	29	30	32	31	31	26	18	25	14	14	18	18	18	12	1	4	7	9	17	17	18	11			17.4
WELLSVILLE	MAX	36	34	38	35	45	42	42	51	53	52	45	47	44	47	46	41	44	55	50	48	46	32	36	33	59	51	54	50	35			44.5
	MIN	12	27	32	23	25	21	32	24	26	27	32	32	26	20	33	21	25	25	20	35	32	19	18	11	31	31	25	31	18			25.3
WEST CHESTER	MAX	41	40	40	43	47	41	45	46	54	56	52	50	48	51	51	45	37	40	48	48	46	34	38	40	60	60	52	41	37			45.9
	MIN	27	33	26	29	29	32	31	33	36	35	37	34	28	37	26	27	29	31	35	26	15	20	20	28	32	37	35	22	23			29.4
WILLIAMSPORT WB AP	MAX	32	34	37	31	40	35	40	49	44	44	41	42	41	44	41	38	30	43	44	44	30	29	35	35	51	45	46	39	34			39.2
	MIN	13	27	14	8	21	15	32	32	32	34	33	32	27	23	29	25	23	29	26	27	16	12	21	12	34	28	29	24	19			24.0
YORK 3 SSW PUMP STA	MAX	40	37	39	35	48	41	43	55	53	54	47	47	44	50	48	45	41	54	50	49	44	31	37	37	62	52	57	54	36			45.9
	MIN	16	29	33	24	28	24	33	26	29	30	34	34	28	23	35	25	29	32	27	36	28	17	21	15	34	34	30	32	22			27.9

See Reference Notes Following Station Index

SNOWFALL AND SNOW ON GROUND

Station		Day of month 1	2	3	4	5	6	7	8	9	10	11	12	13	14	15	16	17	18	19	20	21	22	23	24	25	26	27	28	29	30	31
ALLENTOWN WB AIRPORT	SNOWFALL		1.8		.1		T											1.4				.3		T	.9				1.2			
	SN ON GND		2	1	1	1	T	T	T									1	1				T	T		T			1	T		
	WTR EQUIV		.2																													
ALTOONA HORSESHOE CURVE	SNOWFALL		4.0		.5							2.0	.5	.3				1.0				T	T	1.0	T				1.0	1.0		
	SN ON GND	1	3	2	3	2	1	1				2	1	1				1					T		T				T	1		
ARTEMAS 1 WNW	SNOWFALL	-	-			-										-																
	SN ON GND	4	3			-										-																
BEAVERTOWN	SNOWFALL		5.0								T	T						1.0				T	T		1.0				T	T		
	SN ON GND		5	3	2	2	2	1	1	1	T	T						1	1			T	T		1	T			T	T		
BELLEFONTE 4 S	SNOWFALL		-					-					T	T				-	-			T	T	T		-	-		-	-		
	SN ON GND		5	2	2	2	1	2	2	1			T					1	1							T	T		2	3		
BERWICK	SNOWFALL		2.5		.3	T												1.0				T							2.5			
	SN ON GND		2	1	1	1	T	T	T	T								1				T							2	1		
BRADFORD 4 W RES	SNOWFALL		3.1		.5							3.6	2.6	T		1.0		2.6	.5		T	3.6	1.7	1.0	T	T	3.1		4.5	.8		
	SN ON GND	5	8	7	7	5	5	5	4	4	3	7	9	9	8	9	8	11	10	9	9	12	14	15	14	11	14	12	16	15		
BROOKVILLE CAA AIRPORT	SNOWFALL	.2	4.0					.1				3.3	.2	T		.4	T	2.0			T	.2	.1	T		T	T		T	.1		
	SN ON GND	T	4	1	1	1	1	1	1				2	2	2	T		2	T			T	T	T			T		T	T		
BURGETTSTOWN 2 W	SNOWFALL		2.0											T								-								T		
	SN ON GND		1											T								1	T							T		
BURNT CABINS 2 NE	SNOWFALL	.5	5.0																			T			T							
	SN ON GND		2	2	1	1																T	T									
BUTLER	SNOWFALL		3.0										T					T				1.0		1.0					T	T		
	SN ON GND	2	4	1	1								T					T				1		1					T	T		
CANTON 1 NW	SNOWFALL	T	1.5			T		.5	3.2			T	1.0		1.4		1.0	1.0		T		T	T	T		T		T	3.8	T		
	SN ON GND	2	4	4	4	4	3	4	3	2	2	1	2	2	1	1	2	2	2	T	T	T	T	T	T	T	T	T	4	3		
CARLISLE	SNOWFALL		4.0		T		T					T						1.0	T			T			1.0	1.0			T			
	SN ON GND		4	4	4	3	2	1	T	T								1	T						1							
CHAMBERSBURG 1 ESE	SNOWFALL		3.0									.2						.9				T			1.0							
	SN ON GND	T	2	1	1	T	T											T							1							
CLARION 3 SW	SNOWFALL		3.5										.5					2.0				.3		T			T		T	-		
	SN ON GND	2	5	4	3	3	3	2	2	1	1	1	1	1	1	1	T	2	T	T		T	T	T	T		T		T	1		
COATESVILLE 1 SW	SNOWFALL		.8		T													.5											-			
	SN ON GND																	1	T										T			
CORRY	SNOWFALL		1.5	T	T			T			T	2.0	T	T		.5		4.0	T		T	3.0	5.0	2.0		.5	.5	.5	4.0	1.0		
	SN ON GND	8	5	5	5	5	4	3	2	1	1	3	3	3	1	1	1	3	2	1	1	4	9	8	5	1	T	1	4	4		
COUDERSPORT 2 NW	SNOWFALL	.5	3.2					1.3					7.3	.5			1.3	3.2		1.3		.8	1.3	1.0					4.1	1.2		
	SN ON GND	9	12	9	8	6	5	6	6	5	3	2	10	9	8	7	8	11	10	11	11	11	12	13	13	9	6	6	10	11		
DIXON	SNOWFALL		2.0	.2		.2		.8									T	1.0					T	T		T			3.5	T		
	SN ON GND		2	2	2	2	2	3	2	1	T	T					T	1	1				T	T					4	4		
DONEGAL	SNOWFALL	2.0												T							T	2.6	.2	T					.3	T		
	SN ON GND	2	T	T										T							T	1	1	T						T		
EAGLES MERE	SNOWFALL	T	4.0	2.0		T		3.0				T	T				T	2.0				T	T	T		.5			6.0	T		
	SN ON GND	3	7	9	9	9	9	11	10	8	8	8	7	7	7	7	7	9	8	8	7	7	7	7	7	7	6	6	12	12		
EMPORIUM 1 E	SNOWFALL	T	4.0	1.0	5.0	.1		.5					2.5	T				1.5	T	T		T	T	T		T	1.5		.3	.1		
	SN ON GND	1	5	5	7	4	3	4	4	3	3	3	6	5	5	4	4	5	5	4	4	2	2	2	2	2	3	2	2	2		
EVERETT 1 SW	SNOWFALL	2.0	1.5					T									T	T														
	SN ON GND	2	4	2	T			T									T															
FORD CITY 4 S DAM	SNOWFALL	T	2.5										T	T	T			T				T	T	.5	T		T			T		
	SN ON GND	T	1	T									T	T				T				T	T	1	T		T			T		
FRANKLIN	SNOWFALL		5.0										-				-	-	-					-			-		-	-		
	SN ON GND	1	5	3	3	2	2	1	1	1	T		T	T	T		1	3	T	T		T	T	1	T		T		1	1		
GEORGE SCHOOL	SNOWFALL		.1		.2													1.0					T		.2	.4			T			
	SN ON GND																	1							T							
GETTYSBURG	SNOWFALL		3.0															1.0				T	T			1.0						
	SN ON GND		3	2	T													1														
GRATZ 1 N	SNOWFALL		2.6	T		T												T											T	T		
	SN ON GND		3	2	1	1	T	T	T									T	T										T	T		
GREENVILLE	SNOWFALL		3.4									T	.2	T		2.7		.8	T			2.2	T	T		T		T	3.8	.3		
	SN ON GND	2	4	4	3	3	2	2	1	T	T	T	T	T		3	1	2	T			1	1	T				T	3	2		
HARRISBURG WB AIRPORT	SNOWFALL		2.9		T			T				T			T			.7				T			1.0				T	T		
	SN ON GND		3	1	1	1	T	T										1	T			T							T			
	WTR EQUIV		.4																													
HAWLEY 1 S DAM	SNOWFALL		1.0			1.0												1.2											7.2			
	SN ON GND	T	1	T	T	1	T	T	T	T	T	T	T	T	T	T		1	1	T	T	T	T	T	T	T			7	7		
HUNTINGDON	SNOWFALL	T	4.5			T		T					T					1.0				T	T			T	T			T		
	SN ON GND	T	5	3	2	2	1	1	T	T	T	T	T	T				1				T				T						
INDIANA 3 SE	SNOWFALL		1.2											T				.2				T		.1					.1	T		
	SN ON GND	T	1	T	T	T								T	T			T				T		T	T				T	T		
JOHNSTOWN	SNOWFALL	T	2.0						T				T	T	T		T	.5				2.3	.5	1.5	T		T			.5		
	SN ON GND	T	2										T	T	T			1				2	1	2						1		
KANE 1 NNE	SNOWFALL	.4	5.0	T		T	T	.4	T			T	3.8	.4	.2		1.5	3.2		.4		.5	1.8	2.5	.3	T	1.5	.3	3.7	1.0		
	SN ON GND	9	14	10	10	10	10	10	9	9	9	9	11	11	11	10	10	13	12	12	12	12	13	15	14	11	10	10	13	14		
LANDISVILLE	SNOWFALL		1.5			.4												.2	1.0							2.0						
	SN ON GND		2			T												T	1							-						
LAWRENCEVILLE 2 S	SNOWFALL		2.0	T				T			T		1.4				T	1.5	T	T			.2	T		T	T		3.5			
	SN ON GND		2	T	1	1	1	T	T	T	T	T	2	1	1	T	T	2	1	T	T		T	T	T				4	3		
LEWISTOWN	SNOWFALL		5.5					T										1.0				T				.5			T			
	SN ON GND		5	4	3	3	3	1	T	T	T							1	T			T				1			T			

See reference notes following Station Index.

Table 7 - Continued

SNOWFALL AND SNOW ON GROUND

Station		Day of month 1	2	3	4	5	6	7	8	9	10	11	12	13	14	15	16	17	18	19	20	21	22	23	24	25	26	27	28	29	30	31
LOCK HAVEN	SNOWFALL	T	4.0	T		T		1.5				T	T					.5	T			T	T			.5	T		1.0			
	SN ON GND	T	4	3	2	2	2	4	3	2	1	T	T	T	T			1	T			T				1	T		1	1		
MEADVILLE 1 S	SNOWFALL	.7	3.2	T				T	T			T	1.1	.2	.1	.1	1.7	2.0	T	T		1.6	.5	1.8	T		.5	T	2.8	.6		
	SN ON GND	3	5	3	3	3	3	3	3	2	2	T	T	T	T	T	1	3	1	1	1	2	2	2	2	1	1	T	3	3		
MERCER 2 NNE	SNOWFALL		3.0													2.0			T			2.0	1.0				T	T	3.0	2.0		
	SN ON GND		3													2			T			2	1				T	T	4	2		
MONTROSE 1 E	SNOWFALL	T	2.4	2.2	.2	.8		2.3	T			T	1.0	T	T		1.5	1.1	.7	.4	T	T	.5	2.0	T	.9		.6	4.5	T		
	SN ON GND	5	7	7	7	7	7	9	9	8	7	7	8	8	8	7	8	9	9	9	8	8	8	10	9	9	7	7	11	10		
MOUNT POCONO 2 N AIRPORT	SNOWFALL		4.0		.5			1.0				.8						1.5				.5							8.0			
	SN ON GND		4		2			4	3	3	2	3	-	2	-	1	1	2	2	2									7			
NEW CASTLE 1 N	SNOWFALL	T				T																.3	T	T	T				T	T		
	SN ON GND																															
NEWPORT	SNOWFALL		3.7	T		T												.5								T						
	SN ON GND		4	3	2	1	T	T										1	T													
PALMERTON	SNOWFALL		3.8		T	T												1.5				T	T	T	T				1.0			
	SN ON GND		4	2	2	2	1	1	T	T								2	T			T	T	T					1	T		
PHILADELPHIA WB AIRPORT	SNOWFALL		T		.1													.7				T			.3				T	T		
	SN ON GND		T															T														
	WTR EQUIV																															
PHILADELPHIA SHAWMONT	SNOWFALL		1.0															1.0											T	T		
	SN ON GND																															
PHILIPSBURG CAA AIRPORT	SNOWFALL	T	6.0	T	T		T	T				2.0	T	T	T	T		1.0			T	T	T	T	T	T	T	T	2.8	2.0		
	SN ON GND	3	9	9	9	9	9	6	6	4	2	2	4	3	3	2	2	3	3	3	2	2	2	2	2	2	1	1	2	4		
PHOENIXVILLE 1 E	SNOWFALL																	.1														
	SN ON GND																															
PITTSBURGH WB AIRPORT 2	SNOWFALL	.8	.3					T					T	T		T					T	.2	1.0	.5		T	T	T	.4	T		
	SN ON GND		1											T								T	T	1	T				T	T		
	WTR EQUIV																															
PORT CLINTON 1 S	SNOWFALL	-	-	-	-	-	-	-	-	-	-	-	-	-	-	-	-	-	-	-	-	-	-	-	-	-	-	-	-	-		
	SN ON GND	-	-	-	-	-	-	-	-	-	-	-	-	-	-	-	-	-	-	-	-	-	-	-	-	-	-	-	-	-		
QUAKERTOWN 1 E	SNOWFALL		2.3		T													1.3								1.2						
	SN ON GND		-																													
READING WB CITY	SNOWFALL		2.6		T													.4				T			.5				.3	T		
	SN ON GND		3	1	1	T	T											T	T										T			
RIDGWAY 3 W	SNOWFALL	T	4.0										2.0	T				2.0				.3		T	T		.5		T	.1		
	SN ON GND	4	7	2	2	2	2	2	2	1	1	1	3	3	3	3	3	5	4	3	3	3	3	3	3	2	3	2	2	2		
SCRANTON WB AIRPORT	SNOWFALL		2.3		.2			.4				T						.8				.1		.2	.4				4.2			
	SN ON GND		2	2	2	2	2	1	1	1	1							1											4	4		
	WTR EQUIV		.2	.3	.3	.4	.3																						.4	.4		
SELINSGROVE CAA AIRPORT	SNOWFALL		5.2		T		T	T				T		T				.5				T	T		.5	T			2.0	T		
	SN ON GND		5	3	2	2	2	2	2	T	T	T						1	1										2	T		
SHIPPINGPORT WB	SNOWFALL	T	T										T	T		T	T				T	T	T	T					T	T		
	SN ON GND		T																			T							T	T		
SOMERSET MAIN ST	SNOWFALL		1.7										T	.3								2.5	.5	1.2					.6	.2		
	SN ON GND	1											T									2	1	1						T		
SPRINGBORO	SNOWFALL	-	-	-	-	-	-	-	-	-	-	-	-	-	-	-	-	-	-	-	-	-	-	-	-	-	-	-	-	-		
	SN ON GND	6		4	3	2	2	2	1		1		T		T	2	1	3		1		1	1	2					3			
SPRINGS 1 SW	SNOWFALL											T	T	.5	T			T				.5				T			1.0	T		
	SN ON GND	1	T									T	T	1	T			T				1				T			1	1		
TAMARACK 2 S FIRE TWR	SNOWFALL	T	3.0	1.0		T		2.0				T	4.0	T			1.0	1.0	.3	T			T	T	T	1.0	1.0		3.0	T		
	SN ON GND	4	6	7	7	7	7	9	9	8	7	7	10	10	10	8	9	10	8	8	8	8	8	8	8	9	8	8	9	9		
TIONESTA 2 SE DAM	SNOWFALL	T	4.0	T									2.0		T		1.5	3.5		T		1.0	.5	T	T		.5	T	2.5	.5		
	SN ON GND	1	4	3	3	2	2	2	1	1	1	1	3	2	2	1	2	4	2	1	5	2	2	2	1	T	1	T	3	3		
TOWANDA	SNOWFALL	T	1.7	1.8	T	.1		1.3		T			T		T		1.0	.9	.3	T	T		T	T	T	T		T	3.7	.2		
	SN ON GND	T	2	3	2	2	2	2	1	T	T	T	T				1	1	1	T	T	T	T	T	T			T	4	3		
TOWER CITY 5 SW	SNOWFALL		4.0															1.0				T			T	T			T	1.0		
	SN ON GND	-	-	-	-	-	-	-	-	-	-	-	-	-	-	-	-	-	-	-	-	-	-	-	-	-	-	-	-	-		
UNIONTOWN	SNOWFALL	T											T									.3	T	T					T	T		
	SN ON GND																															
WARREN	SNOWFALL	1.5	3.1			T								.3			.6	2.4				1.0	1.1	1.5			1.2		3.9	.4		
	SN ON GND	4	5	3	2	2	2	2	2	1	1	T	T	T	T	T	1	3	1	1	1	1	2	4	3	1	1	T	4	4		
WAYNESBURG 2 W	SNOWFALL																					T	T							T		
	SN ON GND	T																				T	T							T		
WELLSBORO 3 S	SNOWFALL	2.0	6.0	1.0		T		1.0					2.0	T			1.0	1.0	.5	T		T	T	T		1.0	T	T	2.0	T		
	SN ON GND	4	10	8	8	7	7	8	8	7	6	5	7	7	7	6	7	8	7	6	6	6	6	6	6	6	4	4	6	6		
WEST CHESTER	SNOWFALL		T			T											-	T								T			T			
	SN ON GND																1															
WILLIAMSPORT WB AIRPORT	SNOWFALL	T	4.9		.1		.2	.9				T				T		1.6				.1	T		.3	T	.1		2.2			
	SN ON GND	T	4	3	3	3	3	3	2	T	T	T						1	1							T	T		2	1		
	WTR EQUIV		.3	.5	.5	.7	.6	.8	.7																				.3			
YORK 3 SSW PUMP STA	SNOWFALL		1.8															.5							T	.5						
	SN ON GND																															

See reference notes following Station Index.

STATION INDEX

Station	Index No.	County	Drainage†	Latitude	Longitude	Elevation	Observation time Temp.	Observation time Precip.	Observer	Refer to tables
ACMETONIA LOCK 3	0022	ALLEGHENY	1	40 32	79 49	748		7A	CORPS OF ENGINEERS	3
ALLENS MILLS	0090	JEFFERSON	1	41 12	78 55	1600		MID	CHARLES M. ALLEN	C
ALLENTOWN WB AP	0106	LEHIGH	9	40 39	75 26	376	MID	MID	U.S. WEATHER BUREAU	2 3 5 7 C
ALLENTOWN GAS CO	0111	LEHIGH	9	40 36	75 28	254	7A	7A	LEHIGH VLY GAS DIV	2 3 5
ALTOONA HORSESHOE CURVE	0134	BLAIR	6	40 30	78 29	1500	6P	6P	ALTOONA WATER BUR.	2 3 5 7
ARDENTSVILLE	0229	ADAMS	15	39 55	77 18	710	8A	8A	PA STATE COL EXP	2 3 5
ARTEMAS 1 WNW	0259	BEDFORD	12	39 45	78 28	1250	6P	6P	GRAYSON E.NORTHCRAFT	2 3 5 7 C
AUSTINBURG 2 W	0313	TIOGA	15	42 00	77 32	1590		7A	OTTO D. BACON	3 C
AVOCA CAA AP	0319	LUZERNE	15	41 21	75 44	922	MID	MID	COMBINED WITH STA NO	7905 4/55
BAKERSTOWN 3 WNW	0355	ALLEGHENY	1	40 39	79 59	1230	7P	7P	PITT'GH CUT FLWR CO	2 3 5
BARNES	0409	WARREN	1	41 40	79 02	1310		7A	CORPS OF ENGINEERS	3
BEAR GAP	0457	NORTH'LAND	15	40 50	76 30	900		MID	ROARING CRK WTR CO	3
BEAVER FALLS	0475	BEAVER	2	40 46	80 19	760		7A	HOWARD R. KEMP	3
BEAVERTOWN	0482	SNYDER	15	40 45	77 10	640	7A	7A	MARLIN R. ETTINGER	2 3 5 7
BEECH CREEK STATION	0499	CENTRE	16	41 04	77 34	620		7A	HAROLD S. RUPERT	3
BELLEFONTE 4 S	0530	CENTRE	16	40 51	77 47	1110	8A	8A	ROCKVIEW PRISON FRM	2 3 5 7
BERWICK	0611	COLUMBIA	15	41 04	76 15	570	6P	6P	AMER CAR & FNDRY CO	2 3 5 7
BETHLEHEM	0629	NORTHAMPTON	9	40 37	75 22	400		7A	ARTHUR CROPPER	3
#BETHLEHEM LEHIGH UNI	0634	NORTHAMPTON	9	40 36	75 23	450	MID	MID	LEHIGH UNIVERSITY	2 3 5 C
BLAIN	0725	PERRY	15	40 20	77 31	750		MID	PA DEPT FRST & WTRS	C
BLAIRSVILLE 6 ENE	0736	INDIANA	4	40 27	79 09	2048	8P	8P	U.S. WEATHER BUREAU	2 3 5
BLAKESLEE CORNERS	0743	MONROE	9	41 06	75 36	1650		MID	WALTER WILDRICK	C
BLOSERVILLE 1 N	0763	CUMBERLAND	15	40 16	77 22	650		5P	MRS. B. M. WILLDERS	3
BOSWELL 6 WNW	0820	SOMERSET	1	40 11	79 08	2580		7A	MRS. MAE L. KIMMEL	3 C
BRADDOCK LOCK 2	0861	ALLEGHENY	10	40 24	79 52	725		7A	CORPS OF ENGINEERS	3
BRADFORD CNTRL FIRE STA	0867	MC KEAN	1	41 57	78 39	1500		8A	BRADFORD FIRE DEPT	3
BRADFORD 4 W RES	0868	MC KEAN	1	41 57	78 44	1680	5P	5P	BRADFORD WTR DEPT	2 3 5 7
BREEZEWOOD	0905	BEDFORD	6	40 00	78 14	1352		MID	PA TURNPIKE COMM	3
BROOKVILLE CAA AIRPORT	1002	JEFFERSON	1	41 09	79 06	1417	MID	MID	CIVIL AERO. ADM.	2 3 5 7
BRUCETON 1 S	1033	ALLEGHENY	10	40 18	79 59	1065		7A	AUSTIN R. COOPER	3
BUCKSTOWN 1 SE	1073	SOMERSET	4	40 04	78 50	2460		MID	ALVIN W. MANGES	C
BUFFALO MILLS	1087	BEDFORD	6	39 57	78 39	1318		7A	MRS. NELLE R. BROWN	3
BURGETTSTOWN 2 W	1105	WASHINGTON	11	40 23	80 26	980	7A	7A	SMITH TWP MUN AUTH	2 3 5 7
BURNT CABINS 2 NE	1115	HUNTINGDON	6	40 05	77 52	990	MID	MID	PA TURNPIKE COMM	2 3 5 7
#BUTLER	1130	BUTLER	2	40 52	79 54	1100	4P	7A	WILLIAM C. FAUST	2 3 5 7
BUTLER SUBSTATION	1135	BUTLER	2	40 51	79 53	1140		MID	WEST PENN POWER CO	C
CAMP HILL	1198	CUMBERLAND	15	40 15	76 55	461		6P	JOSEPH N. HOBART	3
CANTON 1 NW	1215	BRADFORD	15	41 40	76 52	1520	7A	7A	MRS.MILDRED SPENCER	2 3 5 7 C
CARLISLE	1234	CUMBERLAND	15	40 12	77 11	460	6P	6P	C. E. MILLER	2 3 5 7
CARROLLTOWN 2 SSE	1255	CAMBRIA	16	40 35	78 42	2040		8A	ROBERT F. MAURER	3
CARTER CAMP 2 W	1262	POTTER	16	41 37	77 45	2030		7A	RICHARD L. MENKEN	3 C
CEDAR RUN	1301	LYCOMING	16	41 31	77 27	800		7A	KATHRYN T.KREIGHBAUM	3
CHADDS FORD	1342	DELAWARE	5	39 52	75 36	160		8A	MRS. GRACE A. WICKS	3
CHAMBERSBURG 1 ESE	1354	FRANKLIN	12	39 56	77 38	640	9P	9P	CHARLES A. BENDER	2 3 5 7 C
CHARLEROI	1372	WASHINGTON	10	40 08	79 55	1040		MID	WEST PENN POWER CO	C
CHARLEROI LOCK 4	1377	WESTMORELAND	10	40 09	79 54	749		7A	CORPS OF ENGINEERS	3
#CHESTER	1423	DELAWARE	5	39 50	75 21	86	8A	8A	CHESTER TIMES	2 3 5
CLARENCE 1 E	1480	CENTRE	16	41 03	77 56	1440		7A	MARGARET A. SWANCER	3
CLARION 3 SW	1485	CLARION	1	41 12	79 26	1114	8P	7A	PA ELECTRIC CO	2 3 5 7 C
CLAUSSVILLE	1505	LEHIGH	9	40 37	75 39	670		8A	WILLIAM J. DOTTERER	3
CLAYSVILLE 3 W	1512	WASHINGTON	11	40 07	80 28	1000	7P	7A	MANUFAC. L & H CO	2 3 5
CLEARFIELD	1519	CLEARFIELD	16	41 01	78 26	1100		7A	IRA TAYLOR	3
CLEARFIELD 8 NW NURSERY	1522	CLEARFIELD	16	41 07	78 32	2120	4P	4P	R. R. HOUPT	CLOSED 5/55
CLERMONT	1529	MC KEAN	1	41 41	78 30	2104		7A	MRS.TILLIE M.SIMONDS	3 C
COALDALE 2 NW	1572	SCHUYLKILL	9	40 50	75 56	1026		7A	PANTHER VLY WTR CO	3
COATESVILLE 1 SW	1589	CHESTER	5	39 58	75 50	342	8A	8A	PHILA ELECTRIC CO	2 3 5 7 C
COATESVILLE	1594	CHESTER	5	39 59	75 49	340		8A	EDWARD D. BIEDEMAN	INACTIVE 12/55
COGAN STATION 2 N	1631	LYCOMING	16	41 21	77 06	640		7A	LEON L. CARSON	3
COLUMBIA	1675	LANCASTER	15	40 02	76 30	300	5S	5S	JAMES H. RUST	2 3 5
CONFLUENCE 1 SW DAM	1705	SOMERSET	17	39 48	79 22	1490	8A	8A	CORPS OF ENGINEERS	2 3 5 6 C
CONFLUENCE 1 NW	1710	FAYETTE	17	39 50	79 22	1331		7A	JOHN L. REID	3
CONNELLSVILLE	1723	FAYETTE	17	40 01	79 36	890		7A	EMERY C. STEWART	3
CONNELLSVILLE 2 E	1729	FAYETTE	17	40 01	79 33	1300		MID	HARRY C. JOY	C
CONSHOHOCKEN	1737	MONTGOMERY	5	40 04	75 19	70		8A	PHILA ELECTRIC CO	3
CORAOPOLIS NEVILLE IS	1773	ALLEGHENY	11	40 30	80 05	720		8A	PGH. COKE & CHEM CO	3
CORRY	1790	ERIE	1	41 55	79 38	1427	6P	6P	GEORGE P. MULDERICK	2 3 5 7
COUDERSPORT 2 NW	1805	POTTER	1	41 48	78 03	2220	7P	8A	J. EDWARD TWIGGS	2 3 5 7
COUDERSPORT 7 E	1809	POTTER	1	41 46	77 53	2425		7A	CAMP POTATO	3
COVINGTON	1832	TIOGA	15	41 45	77 05	1193		7A	GROVER D. CLEVELAND	3
CREEKSIDE	1881	INDIANA	1	40 41	79 12	1035		7A	CORPS OF ENGINEERS	3
CRESSON 2 SE	1895	CAMBRIA	6	40 27	78 34	2540		7A	MILES A. VECELLIO	3 C
CUSTER CITY 2 W	1978	MC KEAN	1	41 55	78 41	2120		8A	M. D. BOOTH AND CO	3
DANVILLE	2013	MONTOUR	15	40 58	76 37	460		7A	MRS.MARIE M. LITTLE	3
DERRY	2108	WESTMORELAND	4	40 20	79 18	1150	6P	6P	MISS N. D. MINEMAN	2 3 5
DEVAULT 1 W	2116	CHESTER	14	40 05	75 33	360	MID	MID	PA TURNPIKE COMM	2 3 5
DINGMANS FERRY	2160	PIKE	5	41 13	74 52	360		MID	CLARENCE H. SMITH	C
DIXON	2171	WYOMING	15	41 34	75 54	620	7A	7A	HAROLD J. KUSCHEL	2 3 5 7 C
DONEGAL	2183	WESTMORELAND	17	40 07	79 23	1746	MID	MID	PA TURNPIKE COMM	2 3 5 7
#DONORA	2190	WASHINGTON	10	40 11	79 51	814	NOON	NOON	DONORA ZINC WORKS	2 3 5
DOYLESTOWN	2221	BUCKS	5	40 18	75 08	393		5P	GEORGE HART	3
DRIFTWOOD	2245	CAMERON	16	41 20	78 08	880		MID	SIDNEY KENNEDY	C
DU BOIS 7 E	2265	CLEARFIELD	16	41 06	78 38	1670	5P	5P	CITY OF DU BOIS	2 3 5 C
DUNLO	2298	CAMBRIA	4	40 17	78 43	2410		MID	MRS. D. L. WHITE	C
DUSHORE 3 NE	2324	SULLIVAN	16	41 33	76 21	1750		7A	PATRICK P. RYAN	3 C
EAGLES MERE	2343	SULLIVAN	16	41 24	76 35	2020	7A	7A	MRS.ELSIE P. BIGGER	2 3 5 7 C
EAST BRADY	2363	CLARION	1	40 59	79 37	820	5P	5P	A. B. KEMPEL	2 3 5
E. WATERFORD 3 E	2459	PERRY	6	40 21	77 33	2125	8A	8A	U.S. WEATHER BUREAU	INACTIVE 5/55
EBENSBURG	2466	CAMBRIA	4	40 29	78 43	2090	7P	7A	ROBERT A. WASSER	2 3 5
EDINBORO	2514	ERIE	1	41 52	80 08	1220		8A	EDINBORO ST TCHR COL	3
ELIZABETHTOWN	2560	LANCASTER	15	40 09	76 37	460		8A	MASONIC HOME	3
EMPORIUM 1 E	2633	CAMERON	16	41 31	78 13	1160	7A	7A	RUSSELL E.PALMATEER	2 3 5 7 C
ENGLISH CENTER	2644	LYCOMING	16	41 26	77 17	881		7A	WILLIAM SUDERS	3 C
EPHRATA	2662	LANCASTER	15	40 11	76 10	465	6P	6P	STANLEY L.VON NEIDA	2 3 5
EQUINUNK	2669	WAYNE	5	41 51	75 13	900		8A	MRS.ROSE M. NEILSEN	3
ERIE CAA AIRPORT	2682	ERIE	8	42 05	80 12	732	MID	MID	CIVIL AERO. ADM.	2 3 5
EVERETT 1 SW	2721	BEDFORD	6	40 00	78 23	1020	MID	MID	PA TURNPIKE COMM	2 3 5 7 C
FARRELL-SHARON	2814	MERCER	2	41 14	80 30	865	7P	7P	SHARON STEEL CORP	2 3 5
FORD CITY 4 S DAM	2942	ARMSTRONG	1	40 43	79 30	950	8A	8A	CORPS OF ENGINEERS	2 3 5 6 7 C
FRANKLIN	3028	VENANGO	1	41 23	79 49	987	7P	7A	JAMES K. ELLIOTT	2 3 5 7 C
FREDERICKSVILLE 2 SE	3047	BERKS	14	40 26	75 40	950	8A	8A	D. P. FENSTERMACHER	2 3 5
FREELAND	3056	LUZERNE	15	41 01	75 54	1900	6P	8A	ANDREW B. EVANSHA	2 3 5
GALETON	3130	POTTER	16	41 44	77 39	1325		7A	W. GALE LUSH	3
GEIGERTOWN	3189	BERKS	14	40 13	75 50	400		8A	WALTER C. WOLF	3
GEORGE SCHOOL	3200	BUCKS	5	40 13	74 56	135	7P	7P	GEORGE M. HART	2 3 5 7
#GETTYSBURG	3218	ADAMS	12	39 50	77 14	540	9A	9A	HUGH C. MC ILHENNY	2 3 5 7
GETTYSBURG 1 S	3223	ADAMS	12	39 48	77 14	560		MID	NAT MILITARY PARK	C
GIFFORD	3237	MC KEAN	1	41 51	78 36	2220		8A	SOUTH PENN OIL CO	3
GLENCOE	3298	SOMERSET	12	39 49	78 51	1620		MID	MRS. MARY M.HARTMAN	C
GLEN HAZEL 2 NE DAM	3311	ELK	1	41 34	78 56	1725		8A	CORPS OF ENGINEERS	3 C
GLEN ROCK	3330	YORK	15	39 48	76 44	620		MID	MRS.E.C.MC WILLIAMS	C
GLENWILLARD DASH DAM	3343	ALLEGHENY	11	40 33	80 13	705		7A	CORPS OF ENGINEERS	3
GORDON	3379	SCHUYLKILL	15	40 45	76 20	900	6P	6P	MISS S. M. JOHNSON	CLOSED 2/56
GOULDSBORO	3394	WAYNE	9	41 15	75 27	1890		7A	L. H. EILENBERGER	3
GRANTVILLE 2 SW	3422	DAUPHIN	15	40 22	76 41	510		5S	EARL E. RHOADS	3
GRATERFORD	3435	MONTGOMERY	14	40 14	75 27	160		7A	CLAUDE K. KULP	3
GRATZ 1 N	3438	DAUPHIN	15	40 38	76 43	760	8A	8A	LEE M. LEITZEL	2 3 5 7 C
GREENSBORO LOCK 7	3503	GREENE	10	39 47	79 55	808		7A	CORPS OF ENGINEERS	3
GREENSBURG 2 E	3515	WESTMORELAND	10	40 18	79 31	1225		MID	PA DEPT HIGHWAYS	C
GREENSBURG 3 SE	3516	WESTMORELAND	10	40 17	79 30	1245		6P	WESTMORELAND WTR CO	3
GREENVILLE	3526	MERCER	2	41 24	80 23	1026	6P	6P	C. EARL MILLER	2 3 5 7
HANOVER	3662	YORK	15	39 48	76 59	600	8A	8A	HANOVER EVENING SUN	2 3 5
#HARRISBURG WB AP	3699	YORK	15	40 13	76 51	335	MID	MID	U.S. WEATHER BUREAU	2 3 5 7 C
HARRISBURG NORTH	3704	DAUPHIN	15	40 18	76 54	323		9A	GEORGE S. BEAL	3
HAWLEY	3758	WAYNE	5	41 29	75 10	880		7A	MRS.KATHERINE S.BATES	3
HAWLEY 1 S DAM	3761	WAYNE	5	41 28	75 11	1200	7A	7A	PA POWER & LIGHT CO	2 3 5 6 7 C
HOLLIDAYSBURG	4001	BLAIR	6	40 26	78 24	960		MID	JOHN M. RINGLER	C
HOLLISTERVILLE	4008	WAYNE	5	41 23	75 26	1360		8A	PA POWER & LIGHT CO	3
† #HOLTWOOD	4019	LANCASTER	15	39 50	76 20	187	MID	8A	PA POWER & LIGHT CO	2 3 5 C
HOME	4027	INDIANA	1	40 45	79 06	1220		MID	MRS. EDNA M. BUSH	C
HONESDALE 4 NW	4043	WAYNE	5	41 37	75 19	1410		9A	GEORGE C. WILLIAMS	3
HONESDALE 6 NNW	4044	WAYNE	5	41 39	75 17	1050		MID	FRIEND E. WALTER	C
HOOVERSVILLE	4058	SOMERSET	4	40 09	78 55	1660		7A	PA ELECTRIC CO	3
HOP BOTTOM 2 SE	4066	SUSQUEHANNA	15	41 43	75 43	900		7A	JOSEPH J. SANSUSKAS	3
HUNTINGDON	4159	HUNTINGDON	15	40 29	78 01	660	7A	7A	JOHN R. HENDERSON	2 3 5 7
HUNTSDALE	4166	CUMBERLAND	15	40 06	77 18	610		8A	METRO P. DOROSH	3 C
HYNDMAN	4190	BEDFORD	12	39 49	78 43	920		8A	MRS.GERTRUDE M.BURTON	3
INDIANA 3 SE	4214	INDIANA	4	40 36	79 07	1102	7P	7A	CLYMER WATER SVC CO	2 3 5 7 C
IRWIN	4276	WESTMORELAND	10	40 20	79 42	1100	5P	5P	WESTMORELAND WTR CO	2 3 5
JACKSON SUMMIT	4304	TIOGA	15	41 57	77 01	1690		MID	ARCHIE LAIN	C
JAMESTOWN 2 NW	4325	CRAWFORD	2	41 30	80 28	1050	8A	8A	DEPT FOREST & WTRS	2 3 5 6 C
JIM THORPE	4370	CARBON	9	40 52	75 45	830	5P	5P	HENRY S. HAAK	2 3 5
#JOHNSTOWN	4385	CAMBRIA	4	40 20	78 55	1214	9A	9A	JOHNSTOWN TRIBUNE	2 3 5 7
JOHNSTOWN 2	4390	CAMBRIA	4	40 19	78 55	1275		MID	CITY OF JOHNSTOWN	C
KANE 1 NNE	4432	MC KEAN	1	41 41	78 48	1750	8A	8A	SPRING WATER CO	2 3 5 7 C
KARTHAUS	4450	CLEARFIELD	16	41 07	78 07	950		7A	JEROME S. HOWE	3
KEATING SUMMIT	4466	POTTER	1	41 41	78 11	1840		7A	EUGENE L. KREITNER	3
KEGG	4481	BEDFORD	6	39 59	78 43	1280	MID	MID	PA TURNPIKE COMM	2 3 5
KITTANNING LOCK 7	4611	ARMSTRONG	1	40 49	79 32	790		7A	CORPS OF ENGINEERS	3
KREGAR 4 SE	4667	WESTMORELAND	17	40 06	79 14	2530		MID	PA TURNPIKE COMM	3
KRESGEVILLE 3 W	4672	CARBON	9	40 54	75 34	720		9A	CITY OF BETHLEHEM	3
LAFAYETTE MC KEAN PARK	4706	MC KEAN	1	41 48	78 40	2130		8A	CHARLES GORDON	3
LAKEVILLE 1 NNE	4733	WAYNE	5	41 27	75 16	1440		8A	MRS. GLADYS REINEKE	3
LANCASTER 2 NE PUMP STA	4758	LANCASTER	15	40 03	76 17	255	6P	6P	LANCASTER WATER BUR	2 3 5
LANCASTER 2 NE FILT PLT	4763	LANCASTER	15	40 03	76 17	270		MID	LANCASTER WATER BUR	C
LANDISVILLE	4778	LANCASTER	15	40 06	76 25	410	8A	8A	PA STATE COLLEGE	2 3 5 6 7 C
LATROBE	4832	WESTMORELAND	4	40 19	79 23	1000		MID	WEST PENN POWER CO	3
LAURELTON STATE VILLAGE	4853	UNION	15	40 54	77 13	880		MID	PA DEPT OF WELFARE	C
LAWRENCEVILLE 2 S	4873	TIOGA	15	41 59	77 07	1000	7A	7A	HARRY P. HOWLAND	2 3 5 7
LEBANON 2 NW	4891	LEBANON	15	40 22	76 28	600	6P	6P	LEBANON BDCSTG CO	2 3 5 7
LEBANON 3 SW	4896	LEBANON	15	40 19	76 28	490		MID	THOMAS DONNACHIE	C
LEHIGHTON	4934	CARBON	9	40 50	75 43	580		7A	GOODVIN S. DEFREHN	3 C
LE ROY	4972	BRADFORD	15	41 41	76 43	1040		6P	MRS.DINNIS M.BAILEY	3
LEWIS RUN 3 S	4984	MC KEAN	1	41 50	78 39	1700		7A	SOUTH PENN OIL CO	3 C
LEWISTOWN	4992	MIFFLIN	6	40 35	77 35	480	7A	7A	AMERICAN VISCOSE CO	2 3 5 7 C
LINESVILLE 5 WNW	5050	CRAWFORD	2	41 41	80 31	1020	7P	8A	MISS RETTA M. CRUMB	2 3 5
LOCK HAVEN	5104	CLINTON	16	41 08	77 27	570	7P	7A	PETER L. STEVENSON	2 3 5 7
LOCK HAVEN 2	5109	CLINTON	16	41 08	77 27	630		MID	HUGH F. PARKER	C
LONG POND 2 W	5160	MONROE	9	41 03	75 30	1860		7A	THOMAS MECKES	3
MADERA	5336	CLEARFIELD	16	40 50	78 26	1460	7A	7A	MRS. JULIA J. SHOFF	2 3 5 C
MAHAFFEY	5342	CLEARFIELD	16	40 53	78 44	1280		7A	MISS ELLEN J. MILES	3
MAPLE GLEN	5368	MONTGOMERY	5	40 11	75 11	380		6P	FRANCES E.SCHEIBNER	3
MAPLETON DEPOT	5381	HUNTINGDON	6	40 24	77 56	580		7A	MRS. I. S. BUCHANAN	3
MARCUS HOOK	5390	DELAWARE	5	39 49	75 25	12	MID	MID	SUN OIL CO	2 3 5
MARIENVILLE	5400	FOREST	1	41 28	79 08	1690		MID	ROY A. MARKER	C
MARION CENTER 2 SE	5408	INDIANA	1	40 45	79 02	1610		7A	CORPS OF ENGINEERS	3
MARTINSBURG 1 SW	5453	BLAIR	6	40 18	78 20	1360		MID	BLUE MT CANNERIES	C
MARTINSBURG CAA AP	5454	BLAIR	6	40 18	78 19	1463	MID	MID	CIVIL AERO. ADM.	2 3 5
MATAMORAS	5470	PIKE	5	41 22	74 42	439		7A	HARRY BISLAND	3
MAYBURG	5490	FOREST	1	41 36	79 13	1150		7A	CORPS OF ENGINEERS	3
MC CONNELSBURG	5526	FULTON	12	39 56	78 00	895		8A	MRS. HELEN M.SHIVES	3
MC KEESPORT	5573	ALLEGHENY	10	40 21	79 52	720		8A	NATIONAL TUBE CO	3
MEADOW RUN PONDS	5601	LUZERNE	15	41 13	75 40	1995		MID	GEORGE PEARAGE	C
MEADVILLE 1 S	5606	CRAWFORD	1	41 38	80 10	1065	8A	8A	CITY OF MEADVILLE	2 3 5 7 C
MEDIX RUN	5627	ELK	16	41 17	78 24	1100		7A	MRS. E. M. SNYDER	3 C
MERCER 2 NNE	5651	MERCER	2	41 15	80 13	1160	7P	7A	WILLIAM K. STRUTHERS	2 3 5 7
MERCER HIWAY SHED	5654	MERCER	2	41 14	80 15	1250		MID	PA DEPT HIGHWAYS	C
MERCERSBURG	5662	FRANKLIN	12	39 50	77 54	605		8A	ROLLIN P. GILBERT	3
MERWINSBURG	5676	MONROE	9	40 58	75 28	920		MID	GERALD D. MURPHY	C
MEYERSDALE	5684	SOMERSET	17	39 49	79 02	2080		8A	JOHN H. BLOCHER	3
MIDDLETOWN OLMSTED FLD	5703	DAUPHIN	15	40 11	76 46	303	MID	MID	U. S. AIR FORCE	2 3 5
MIDLAND DAM 7	5710	BEAVER	11	40 38	80 28	689	11P	7A	CORPS OF ENGINEERS	2 3 5
MILAN	5731	BRADFORD	15	41 55	76 31	760		MID	W. S. ROBERTS	CLOSED 6/55
MILANVILLE	5738	WAYNE	5	41 40	75 04	760		8A	CHARLES W. DAVIS	3
MILLERSBURG 2 E	5775	DAUPHIN	15	40 32	76 56	560		MID	RUSSELL SHEPLEY	C
MILLHEIM	5790	CENTRE	15	40 54	77 29	1090		7A	NEVIN E. BOWERSOX	3
MILLVILLE 2 SW	5817	COLUMBIA	15	41 06	76 34	860		7A	KENNETH LEIGHOW	3 C
MILROY	5825	MIFFLIN	6	40 43	77 35	770		8A	THOMAS C. HARBESON	3
MONTROSE 1 E	5915	SUSQUEHANNA	15	41 50	75 51	1630	7A	7A	WILMER W. HOOPES,JR	2 3 5 7 C
MORGANTOWN	5956	BERKS	15	40 09	75 54	595	MID	MID	PA TURNPIKE COMM	2 3 5
MT GRETNA 2 SE	6028	LANCASTER	15	40 14	76 26	670	MID	MID	PA TURNPIKE COMM	2 3 5
MOUNT POCONO 2 N AP	6055	MONROE	5	41 09	75 22	1915	5P	5P	H. JOHN DAVIS, JR.	2 3 5 7 C
MOUNT UNION 1 N	6067	MIFFLIN	6	40 24	77 53	820		MID	MT UNION WTR WORKS	C
MUHLENBURG 1 SE	6090	LUZERNE	15	41 13	76 08	1110	6P	6P	THEODORE J. SAMPSON	2 3 5
MURRYSVILLE	6111	WESTMORELAND	10	40 26	79 42	903		MID	DAVID C. SHAW	C
MYERSTOWN	6126	LEBANON	14	40 22	76 18	480		8A	MRS.KATHLEEN WANDELL	3
NATRONA LOCK 4	6151	ALLEGHENY	1	40 37	79 43	800		7A	CORPS OF ENGINEERS	3
NEFFS MILLS 3 NE	6174	HUNTINGDON	6	40 40	77 55	900		MID	PA STATE UNIVERSITY	C
NESHAMINY FALLS	6194	BUCKS	5	40 09	74 57	60		MID	PHILA SUB WATER CO	3
NEWBURG 3 W	6225	FRANKLIN	15	40 09	77 37	745	MID	MID	PA TURNPIKE COMM	2 3 5
NEW CASTLE 1 N	6233	LAWRENCE	2	41 01	80 22	900	5P	7A	BAXTER F. JOHNSON	2 3 5 7 C
#NEWELL	6246	FAYETTE	10	40 05	79 54	805	NOON	NOON	GENERAL CHEMICAL CO	2 3 5
NEW PARK	6289	YORK	15	39 44	76 30	780		6P	CLINTON J. ALLEN	3
NEWPORT	6297	PERRY	6	40 29	77 08	400	7A	7A	MRS. FRANCES K. FRY	2 3 5 7
NEW STANTON	6310	WESTMORELAND	10	40 13	79 36	980	MID	MID	PA TURNPIKE COMM	2 3 5
NEW TRIPOLI	6326	LEHIGH	14	40 41	75 45	570		6P	FRED C. OSWALD	3
NORRISTOWN	6370	MONTGOMERY	14	40 07	75 21	75	MID	8A	GEORGE H. BOONE	2 3 5
NORTH EAST 2 SE	6396	ERIE	8	42 12	79 49	1060		9A	ELLSWORTH WEAVER	3
ORWELL 3 N	6621	BRADFORD	15	41 55	76 16	1620		8A	WILLIAM I. BROWN	3
PALM	6681	MONTGOMERY	14	40 26	75 32	390		8A	FRED C. ESCHBACH	3
#PALMERTON	6689	CARBON	9	40 48	75 37	435	MID	MID	NEW JERSEY ZINC CO	2 3 5 7 C
PARKER	6721	ARMSTRONG	1	41 05	79 41	1140		7A	LOUIS A. MALARKEY	3
PARKER 1 E	6724	CLARION	1	41 06	79 40	1100		MID	P. M. NEELY	C
PAUPACK 2 WNW	6762	PIKE	5	41 24	75 14	1360		8A	MISS L. VETTERLEIN	3
PECKS POND	6786	PIKE	5	41 17	75 06	1380		9A	MRS. CARRIE NESS	3
#PHILA DREXEL INST OF TEC	6879	PHILADELPHIA	14	39 57	75 11	30	MID	MID	FRANCIS K. DAVIS,JR	2 3 5
PHILADELPHIA WB AP	6889	PHILADELPHIA	5	39 53	75 14	13	MID	MID	U.S. WEATHER BUREAU	2 3 5 7 C
#PHILADELPHIA PT BREEZE	6899	PHILADELPHIA	5	39 55	75 12	85	MID	MID	ATLANTIC REFINING	2 3 5 C
PHILADELPHIA SHAWMONT	6904	PHILADELPHIA	5	40 02	75 15	70	7P	7P	SCHUYLKILL NAVIG CO	2 3 5 7
#PHILADELPHIA CITY	6909	PHILADELPHIA	5	39 57	75 09	26	9A	9A	USN HYDROGRAPHIC OFF	2 3 5 C
PHILIPSBURG CAA AP	6916	CENTRE	6	40 54	78 05	1918	8P	8P	CIVIL AERO. ADM.	2 3 5 7 C
PHOENIXVILLE 1 E	6927	CHESTER	14	40 07	75 30	105	6P	MID	PHILA SUB WATER CO	2 3 5 7 C
PIKES CREEK	6939	LUZERNE	15	41 18	76 08	1320		MID	HARRY SHELDON	3 C
PIMPLE HILL	6944	MONROE	9	41 02	75 30	2215	9A	9A	PA DEPT FRST & WTRS	2 3 5 6
PINE GROVE 1 NE	6954	SCHUYLKILL	15	40 34	76 22	535		8A	PA POWER & LIGHT CO	3
PITTSBURGH WB AP 2	6993	ALLEGHENY	11	40 30	80 13	1151	MID	MID	U.S. WEATHER BUREAU	2 3 5 7 C
#PITTSBURGH WB CITY	6997	ALLEGHENY	11	40 27	80 00	749	MID	MID	U.S. WEATHER BUREAU	2 3 5 C
PLEASANT MOUNT 1 W	7029	WAYNE	5	41 44	75 27	1800	8A	8A	PA FISH COMM	2 3 5 C
PORT CLINTON	7116	SCHUYLKILL	14	40 35	76 02	450	7A	7A	MRS. ADA E. RARICK	2 3 5 7 C
PORTLAND	7127	NORTHAMPTON	5	40 55	75 06	295		8A	JOINT BRIDGE COMM	3
POTTSTOWN	7149	MONTGOMERY	14	40 15	75 39	160		8A	MILES E. SMITH	3
POTTSVILLE PALO ALTO BR	7161	SCHUYLKILL	14	40 41	76 11	640		8A	JOHN M. SMITH	3
PUNXSUTAWNEY	7217	JEFFERSON	1	40 57	79 00	1298		MID	JOHN VOLANSKY	C
PUTNEYVILLE 2 SE DAM	7229	ARMSTRONG	1	40 55	79 17	1270	8A	8A	CORPS OF ENGINEERS	2 3 5 C
QUAKERTOWN 1 E	7239	BUCKS	5	40 26	75 20	490	5P	5P	DENNIS K. FLUCK	2 3 5 7
RAYMOND	7310	POTTER	13	41 52	77 52	2220		7A	ARTHUR LANGAN	3 C
#READING WB CITY	7318	BERKS	14	40 20	75 58	266	MID	MID	U.S. WEATHER BUREAU	2 3 5 7 C
RENOVO	7409	CLINTON	16	41 20	77 45	660		7A	MRS. C. W. BAIRD	3
RENOVO 5 S	7410	CLINTON	16	41 14	77 46	2035		MID	C. F. BILLETTE	C
REW	7425	MC KEAN	1	41 54	78 32	2250		8A	HAROLD C. MEALY	3
RICES LANDING LOCK 6	7443	GREENE	10	39 57	80 00	775		7A	CORPS OF ENGINEERS	3
RIDGWAY 3 W	7477	ELK	1	41 25	78 47	1420	7P	7A	BOROUGH OF RIDGWAY	2 3 5 7
ROCHESTER 1 N	7540	BEAVER	2	40 43	80 18	900		MID	DEQUESNE LIGHT CO	C
RUSH	7694	SUSQUEHANNA	15	41 47	76 03	1000		9A	MISS MAUDE MC CAIN	3
RUSHVILLE	7727	SUSQUEHANNA	15	41 47	76 07	870		7A	CARL KOPATZ	3
SAFE HARBOR	7732	LANCASTER	15	39 55	76 23	270		MID	S.H.WATER POWER CORP	C
SAGAMORE 1 S	7739	INDIANA	1	40 46	79 14	1320		7A	CORPS OF ENGINEERS	3
SALINA 3 W	7782	WESTMORELAND	7	40 31	79 33	1109	6P	6P	MUN AUTH WSTMRLD CO	2 3 5
SAXTON	7846	BEDFORD	6	40 12	78 15	780		6A	MRS.ALVERTA L.HOLMES	3 C
SCANDIA 2 E	7855	WARREN	1	41 55	79 01	2040		MID	DAVID R. ANDERSON	C
SCHENLEY LOCK 5	7863	ARMSTRONG	1	40 41	79 40	783		7A	CORPS OF ENGINEERS	3

STATION INDEX

Continued

Station	Index No.	County	Drainage‡	Latitude	Longitude	Elevation	Observation time Temp.	Observation time Precip.	Observer	Refer to tables
# SCRANTON	7902	LACKAWANNA	15	41 25	75 40	746	7A	7A	U.S. POST OFFICE	2 3 5
SELINSGROVE CAA AP	7931	SNYDER	15	40 49	76 52	437	MID	MID	CIVIL AERO. ADM.	2 3 5 7
SELLERSVILLE 2 NW	7935	BUCKS	5	40 23	75 20	530		MID	SELLERSVILLE WTR CO	C
SHADE GAP	7965	HUNTINGDON	6	40 11	77 52	1000		MID	MRS. HELEN H. PYLE	C
SHAMOKIN	7978	NORTH'LAND	15	40 48	76 33	770		8A	ROARING CRK WTR CO	3
SHEFFIELD 6 W	8026	WARREN	1	41 41	79 09	1940		MID	L. N. HANSON	C
SHIPPENSBURG	8073	FRANKLIN	15	40 03	77 32	709	4P	4P	KEITH B. ALLEN	2 3 5
SINNEMAHONING	8145	CAMERON	16	41 19	78 05	790		7A	MRS.FRANCES CALDWELL	3
SLIPPERY ROCK	8184	BUTLER	2	41 04	80 03	1345	7P	7A	WALTER D. ALBERT	2 3 5
SMETHPORT HIGHWAY SHED	8190	MC KEAN	1	41 48	78 27	1510		MID	PA DEPT HIGHWAYS	C
SOMERSET FAIRVIEW ST	8244	SOMERSET	17	40 01	79 05	2140		7A	HOWARD G. PECK	3
SOMERSET MAIN ST	8249	SOMERSET	17	40 01	79 05	2150	6P	6P	DAVID L. GROVE	2 3 5 7
SOUTH CANAAN 1 NE	8275	WAYNE	5	41 31	75 24	1400		MID	EUGENE M. COOK	C
SOUTH MOUNTAIN	8308	FRANKLIN	12	39 51	77 30	1520		7A	PA DEPT OF HEALTH	3
SPRINGBORO	8359	CRAWFORD	8	41 48	80 23	900	8A	8A	SPRINGBORO BOROUGH	2 3 5 7 C
SPRING GROVE	8379	YORK	15	39 52	76 52	470		4P	P. H. GLATFELTER CO	3 C
SPRINGS 1 SW	8395	SOMERSET	17	39 44	79 10	2500	8P	8P	ALLEN E. YODER	2 3 5 7
#STATE COLLEGE	8449	CENTRE	16	40 48	77 52	1175	MID	MID	PA STATE COLLEGE	2 3 5 C
STRAUSSTOWN	8570	BERKS	14	40 29	76 11	600		8A	JACOB KLAHR	3
STRONGSTOWN	8589	INDIANA	4	40 33	78 55	1880		MID	HARRY F. BENNETT	C
STROUDSBURG	8596	MONROE	5	40 59	75 12	440	8A	8A	PIERRE T. LAKE	2 3 5
STUMP CREEK	8610	JEFFERSON	1	41 01	78 50	1320		7A	CORPS OF ENGINEERS	3
SUNBURY	8668	NORTH'LAND	15	40 51	76 48	440		7A	CHARLES W. BAYLER	3 C
SUSQUEHANNA	8692	SUSQUEHANNA	15	41 57	75 36	1020		7A	MRS. LAURA A.BENSON	3
SUTERSVILLE	8695	ALLEGHENY	17	40 14	79 48	765		7A	MICHAEL RACKO	3
TAMAQUA	8758	SCHUYLKILL	14	40 48	75 58	830		8A	MRS. MARY L.ROBERTS	3
TAMAQUA 4 N DAM	8763	SCHUYLKILL	14	40 51	75 59	1120		7A	PANTHER VLY WTR CO	3 C
TAMARACK 2 S FIRE TWR	8770	CLINTON	16	41 24	77 51	2220	7A	7A	JAMES E. SWARTZ	2 3 5 7
TIONESTA 2 SE DAM	8873	FOREST	1	41 29	79 26	1200	8A	8A	CORPS OF ENGINEERS	2 3 5 7 C
TITUSVILLE	8885	CRAWFORD	1	41 38	79 40	1550		MID	PA ELECTRIC CO	C
TITUSVILLE WATER WORKS	8888	CRAWFORD	1	41 38	79 42	1220	7P	7P	CITY OF TITUSVILLE	2 3 5
TORPEDO 4 W	8901	WARREN	1	41 47	79 32	1735		7A	MRS. LILY B. GARBER	3
TOWANDA	8905	BRADFORD	15	41 46	76 26	755	7P	7A	MRS. M. O. PARKS	2 3 5 7 C
TOWER CITY 5 SW	8910	DAUPHIN	15	40 31	76 37	745		6P	HARRISBURG WTR DEPT	3 7
TROY	8959	BRADFORD	15	41 47	76 47	1100		7A	JENNIE L. BALLARD	3
TUNNELTON	8989	INDIANA	4	40 27	79 23	890		MID	MRS. MARY E. WEIMER	C
TURTLEPOINT 4 NE	9002	MC KEAN	1	41 54	78 16	1640		7A	ROBERT D. STRAIT	3
TYRONE 4 NE BALD EAGLE	9024	BLAIR	6	40 43	78 12	1020		7A	FREDERICK L. FRIDAY	3 C
UNION CITY	9042	ERIE	1	41 54	79 50	1325		7A	FORREST M. BRALEY	3 C
UNIONTOWN	9050	FAYETTE	10	39 54	79 44	1040	10P	10P	WM. W. MARSTELLER	2 3 5 7
UPPER DARBY	9074	DELAWARE	5	39 58	75 18	222	7P	7P	PHIL. SUB.TRANS. CO	2 3 5
VANDERGRIFT	9126	WESTMORELAND	7	40 36	79 33	800		7A	UNITED ENG&FNDRY CO	3
VANDERGRIFT 2 W	9133	WESTMORELAND	7	40 36	79 36	995		MID	EUGENE R. YOUNG	C
VIRGINVILLE	9196	BERKS	14	40 31	75 52	350		8A	MRS. MARY H. WRIGHT	3
WARREN	9298	WARREN	1	41 51	79 08	1280	7P	7A	GILBERT H. REIER	2 3 5 7
WASHINGTON	9312	WASHINGTON	11	40 11	80 14	1200		MID	PA DEPT HIGHWAYS	C
WATSONTOWN	9345	NORTH'LAND	16	41 05	76 52	470		8A	OWEN BERKENSTOCK	3
WAYNESBURG 2 W	9362	GREENE	10	39 54	80 13	980	6P	7A	RALPH L. AMOS	2 3 5 7
WAYNESBURG 1 E	9367	GREENE	10	39 54	80 10	940		MID	SEWAGE DISPOSAL PLT	C
WEBSTER MILLS 3 SW	9380	FULTON	12	39 49	78 05	920		MID	WILLIAM D. COVER	C
WELLSBORO 3 S	9408	TIOGA	16	41 43	77 16	1920	7A	7A	MARION L. SHUMWAY	2 3 5 7
WELLSBORO 2 E	9412	TIOGA	16	41 45	77 16	1550		MID	MRS. IDA S. MAYNARD	C
WELLSVILLE	9420	YORK	15	40 03	76 57	500	5P	5P	D. D. HOOVER	2 3 5
WERNERSVILLE 1 W	9430	BERKS	14	40 20	76 06	405		8A	CHARLES A. GRUBER	3
WEST CHESTER	9464	CHESTER	5	39 58	75 36	440	8A	8A	DAILY LOCAL NEWS	2 3 5 7
WEST GROVE 1 E	9503	CHESTER	5	39 49	75 49	440		8A	CONARD-PYLE CO	3
WEST HICKORY	9507	FOREST	1	41 34	79 25	1090		8A	MRS.HELEN F.KINNEAR	3
WHITESBURG	9655	ARMSTRONG	1	40 45	79 24	1530		7A	CORPS OF ENGINEERS	3
WILKES-BARRE	9702	LUZERNE	15	41 15	75 52	610		7A	MRS. MARY G. MIRMAK	3
WILLIAMSBURG	9714	BLAIR	6	40 28	78 12	860		7A	MYRON K. BIDDLE	3
WILLIAMSPORT WB AP	9728	LYCOMING	16	41 15	76 55	527	MID	MID	U.S. WEATHER BUREAU	2 3 5 7 C
WIND GAP	9781	NORTHAMPTON	5	40 51	75 18	720		MID	OWEN R. PARRY	C
WOLFESBURG	9823	BEDFORD	6	40 03	78 32	1190		7A	WALTER C. RICE	3
YORK 3 SSW PUMP STA	9933	YORK	15	39 55	76 45	390	5P	5P	YORK WATER COMPANY	2 3 5 7
YORK 2 S	9938	YORK	15	39 56	76 44	640		MID	YORK WATER COMPANY	C
YORK HAVEN	9950	YORK	15	40 07	76 43	310		8A	METROPOL EDISON CO	3
YOUNGSVILLE	9966	WARREN	1	41 51	79 20	1225		MID	HENRY CARLETT	C
ZION GROVE	9990	SCHUYLKILL	15	40 54	76 13	940		7A	JAMES D. TEETER	3
ZIONSVILLE 3 SE	9995	LEHIGH	14	40 27	75 27	660		7A	LESLIE HOWATT	3
NEW STATIONS										
SCRANTON WB AP	7905	LUZERNE	15	41 20	75 44	956	MID	MID	U.S. WEATHER BUREAU	2 3 5 7 C
COOKSBURG	1749	CLARION	1	41 20	79 13	1180		8A	PA DEPT FOR & WTRS	3
COOKSBURG 2 NNW	1752	CLARION	1	41 21	79 13	1460		8A	PA DEPT FOR & WTRS	3
SHIPPINGPORT WB	8078	BEAVER	11	40 37	80 26	740	MID	MID	U.S. WEATHER BUREAU	2 3 5 7 C
VOWINCKEL	9206	CLARION	1	41 25	79 14	1620		8A	PA DEPT FOR & WTRS	3
VOWINCKEL 1 WSW	9209	CLARION	1	41 24	79 15	1610		8A	PA DEPT FOR & WTRS	3
MILAN 4 WNW	5732	BRADFORD	15	41 56	76 35	1448		MID	CARL A. MORRIS	C
UTICA	9099	VENANGO	1	41 26	79 57	1090		7A	MRS.FLORENCE E.MILLER	3

‡1-ALLEGHENY; 2-BEAVER; 3- 4-CONEMAUGH; 5-DELAWARE; 6-JUNIATA; 7-KISKIMINETAS; 8-LAKE ERIE; 9-LEHIGH; 10-MONONGAHELA; 11-OHIO; 12-POTOMAC; 13-LAKE ONTARIO; 14-SCHUYLKILL; 15-SUSQUEHANNA; 16-WEST BRANCH; 17-YOUGHIOGHENY

REFERENCE NOTES

The four digit identification numbers in the index number column of the Station Index are assigned on a state basis. There will be no duplication of numbers within a state.

Figures and letters following the station name, such as 12 SSW, indicate distance in miles and direction from the post office.

Observation times given in the Station Index are in local standard time.

Delayed data and corrections will be carried only in the June and December issues of this bulletin.

Monthly and seasonal snowfall and heating degree days for the preceding 12 months will be carried in the June issue of this bulletin.

Stations appearing in the Index, but for which data are not listed in the tables, are either missing or received too late to be included in this issue.

Unless otherwise indicated, dimensional units used in this bulletin are: temperature in °F., precipitation and evaporation in inches, and wind movement in miles. Degree days are based on a daily average of 65° F.

Evaporation is measured in the standard Weather Bureau type pan of 4 foot diameter unless otherwise shown by footnote following Table 6.

Amounts in Table 3 are from non-recording gages, unless otherwise indicated.

Data in Tables 3, 5 and 8 and snowfall data in Table 7 are for the 24 hours ending at time of observation. See Station Index for observation time.

Snow on ground in Table 7 is at observation time for all except Weather Bureau and CAA stations. For these stations snow on ground values are at 7:30 A.M. E.S.T. WTR EQUIV in Table 7 means the water equivalent of snow on the ground. It is measured at selected stations when depth of snow on the ground is two inches or more. Water equivalent samples are necessarily taken from different points for successive observations; consequently occasional drifting and other causes of local variability in the snowpack result in apparent inconsistencies in the record.

Long-term means for full-time Weather Bureau stations (those shown in the Station Index as United States Weather Bureau Stations) are based on the period 1921-1950, adjusted to represent observations taken at the present location.

- \- No record in Tables 3, 6, 7 and the Station Index. No record in Tables 2 and 5 is indicated by no entry.
- \+ And also on a later date or dates.
- • Amount included in following measurement, time distribution unknown.
- Θ Data in the column formerly headed No. of Days .01 or more have been changed to No. of Days .10 or more effective January 1, 1954.
- \# Thermometers are generally exposed in a shelter located a few feet above sod-covered ground; however, the reference indicates that the thermometers are exposed in a shelter located on the roof of a building.
- // Gage is equipped with a windshield.
- AM Data based on observational day ending before noon.
- B Adjusted to a full month.
- C In the "Refer to Tables" column in the Station Index the letter "C" indicates recorder stations. These stations are processed for special purposes and are published later in Hourly Precipitation Data.
- D Water equivalent of snowfall wholly or partly estimated, using a ratio of 1 inch water equivalent to every 10 inches of new snowfall.
- M One or more days of record missing; see Table 5 for detailed daily record. Degree day data, if carried for this station, have been adjusted to represent the value for a full month.
- R Amounts from recording gage (These amounts are essentially accurate but may vary slightly from the amounts to be published later in Hourly Precipitation Data).
- SS This entry in time of observation column in Station Index means sunset.
- T Trace, an amount too small to measure.
- Y Includes total for previous month.

Additional information regarding the climate of Pennsylvania may be obtained by writing to any Weather Bureau Office or to the State Climatologist at Weather Bureau Airport Station, Harrisburg State Airport, New Cumberland, Pennsylvania.

Subscription Price: 20 cents per copy, monthly and annual; $2.50 per year. (Yearly subscription includes the Annual Summary.) Checks and money orders should be made payable to the Superintendent of Documents. Remittances and correspondence regarding subscriptions should be sent to the Superintendent of Documents, Government Printing Office, Washington 25, D. C.

NWRC., Asheville, N. C. --- 4/6/56 --- 1225

U. S. DEPARTMENT OF COMMERCE
SINCLAIR WEEKS, Secretary
WEATHER BUREAU
F. W. REICHELDERFER, Chief

CLIMATOLOGICAL DATA

PENNSYLVANIA

MARCH 1956

Volume LXI No. 3

ASHEVILLE: 1956

GENERAL

This month's weather was noteworthy for practically twice as much snow as usually falls in March, and for protracted cold that dominated the last two-thirds of the month in sharp contrast to the unseasonable mildness of the first week.

Precipitation continued the wet pattern that began in February but excesses generally were not nearly as large as last month, considering the greater expectancy in March. Areal averages were 4.23 inches in the Atlantic Drainage, 5.06 inches in the Ohio Drainage, and 3.74 inches in the Lake Drainage. All except the latter compared rather closely with February's averages. Monthly totals ranged from 7.82 inches at Kregar 4 SE to 1.98 inches at Scranton, while the greatest daily amount fell at Norristown where 1.94 inches was measured on the 19th. Most of the stations having long-term precipitation means registered excessive departures, many being +1.50 inches or more, but a few were negative and these were nearly all on the order of -0.50 inch or smaller.

Snowfall was the dominant feature of the month's precipitation, approaching long-term snowfall records in many communities, and generally this was the snowiest March since 1942. Division snowfall averages varied only 3 inches between the greatest and the least. Station totals were mostly not over 20 inches but some falls of more than 30 inches were noted, the greatest being 42 inches at Lewis Run 3 S and Rew.

This was the coldest March, generally, since 1950 with areal averages of 35° in the Atlantic and Ohio Drainage Divisions and 32° in the Lake Drainage. Extremes this month, 79° at Newburg 3 W on the 6th and -8° at Pleasant Mount 1 W on the 18th, were not unusual having been surpassed in both directions many times in the past. Departures at stations having long-term temperature means were all negative except at Somerset Main St. which had +0.2°. Minimum temperatures dropped to 32° or below every day in the month at 5 stations and generally occurred several more days than usually expected. Along the same line, maximum temperatures failed to rise as high as 32° on several more days than usual.

Skies were cloudier than usual while sunshine was moderately less than par generally except in the Pittsburgh and Harrisburg areas where approximately normal percentages were recorded.

WEATHER DETAILS

Mostly sunny skies and seasonable temperatures prevailed on March 1. However, the southerly flow in advance of a deep low pressure system moving eastward across the Great Lakes, and the influence of several other Lows, dominated the remainder of the first week. Temperatures were unseasonably warm, reaching the highs of the month generally during the 5th to 7th. Light to moderate rains were frequent, particularly during the 5th-8th and were attended by thunderstorms on several days. The combination of rains and extreme warmth early in the month caused most of the snow cover to melt, thus adding to the flood potential.

Seasonable temperatures returned on the 8th and 9th when the edge of a temperate Canadian air mass reached the State by way of the Southern Plains and Gulf of Mexico. Warming began again on the 10th and culminated in moderately above normal readings on the 11th which proved to be the last warm spell of the month. An intense storm system that moved rapidly down the St. Lawrence Valley late on the 11th trailed its cold front over Pennsylvania to pave the way for a series of cold outbreaks that kept temperatures far below normal generally on most days during the remainder of the month. Intervals between fresh cold incursions were too brief to permit more than token warming when temperatures struggled up to within a few degrees of normal on isolated dates. The lowest readings generally occurred about the 18th

SUPPLEMENTAL DATA

Station	Wind direction: Prevailing	Wind direction: Percent of time from prevailing	Wind speed m. p. h.: Average	Wind speed: Fastest mile	Wind speed: Direction of fastest mile	Wind speed: Date of fastest mile	Relative humidity averages - percent: 1:30 a EST	7:30 a EST	1:30 p EST	7:30 p EST	Number of days with precipitation: Trace	.01–.09	.10–.49	.50–.99	1.00–1.99	2.00 and over	Total	Percent of possible sunshine	Average sky cover sunrise to sunset
ALLENTOWN WB AIRPORT	WNW	11	14.1	-	-	-	74	77	59	67	6	5	6	3	1	0	21	-	6.6
HARRISBURG WB AIRPORT	W	14	9.9	34	W	8	60	67	47	53	9	1	9	3	0	0	22	55	6.9
PHILADELPHIA WB AIRPORT	N	12	11.5	47	N	16	70	73	59	60	4	6	4	3	1	0	18	51	6.8
PITTSBURGH WB AIRPORT	WSW	22	12.5	41*	W	8	74	77	58	64	11	5	6	5	0	0	27	76	7.2
READING WB CITY	-	-	13.5	42	W	8	-	-	-	-	3	3	8	2	1	0	17	50	6.8
SCRANTON WB AIRPORT	NNW	14	9.0	42	W	8	73	72	59	65	5	13	3	2	0	0	23	41	7.3
SHIPPINGPORT WB CITY	-	-	4.2	41††	WSW	1	-	-	-	-	9	3	6	3	1	0	22	-	7.9
WILLIAMSPORT WB AIRPORT	-	-	-	-	-	-	-	75	54	62	7	9	6	3	0	0	25	-	6.9

* This datum is obtained by visual observation since recording equipment is not available. It is not necessarily the fastest mile occurring during the period.
†† Peak Gust

CLIMATOLOGICAL DATA

TABLE 2

Station		Temperature: Average Maximum	Average Minimum	Average	Departure from Long-Term Mean	Highest	Date	Lowest	Date	Degree Days	No. of Days Max. 90° or Above	Max. 32° or Below	Min. 32° or Below	Min. 0° or Below	Precipitation: Total	Departure from Long-Term Mean	Greatest Day	Date	Snow, Sleet: Total	Max. Depth on Ground	Date	No. of Days: .10 or More	.50 or More	1.00 or More
ATLANTIC DRAINAGE																								
ALLENTOWN WB AP	R	43.5	26.2	34.9	- 3.0	64	5	10	21	928	0	4	26	0	4.88	1.69	1.04	14	18.1	10	19+	10	4	1
ALLENTOWN GAS CO	AM	43.5	26.5	35.0	- 3.5	65	6	13	21	924	0	5	26	0	4.30	.90	.91	19	14.1	11	19	9	3	0
ALTOONA HORSESHOE CURVE		45.9	24.9	35.4	- 2.0	66	5+	12	1	910	0	2	28	0	4.86	1.64	.83	14	24.5	7	18	12	4	0
ARENDTSVILLE	AM	46.1	27.7	36.9	- 3.0	71	6	17	1	864	0	2	25	0	4.15	.59	.76	14	9.5	6	19	13	3	0
ARTEMAS 1 WNW		53.2M	27.1M	40.2M		72	5	14	17+	792	0	0		0										
BEAVERTOWN	AM	46.4M		M		67	6				0	1		0	3.43		.70	8					2	0
BELLEFONTE 4 S	AM	44.0	24.7	34.4	- 3.5	65	8	12	21	945	0	3	27	0	3.93	.56	.90	8		7	17	11	3	0
BERWICK		45.9	26.4	36.2		62	5	10	1	885	0	1	26	0	2.18		.60	14	5.1	4	17+	6	2	0
BETHLEHEM LEHIGH UNIV		43.5	28.4	36.0	- 4.5	64	5	16	18	895	0	4	23	0	4.65	1.22	1.00	14	23.0	12	19	10	4	1
BURNT CABINS 2 NE		47.2M	25.6M	36.4M		67	7	8	21	879	0	2	25	0	4.17		.67	16		5	18	10	4	0
CANTON 1 NW	AM	36.2	19.1	27.7		49	8	5	18+	1150	0	0	28	0	4.23		.95	17	15.7	11	24+	9	3	0
CARLISLE		50.5	30.1	40.3	1.3	73	5	18	1	756	0	0	21	0	4.29	.83	.88	14	17.5	8	18	12	2	0
CHAMBERSBURG 1 ESE		47.5	28.1	37.8	- 2.3	71	5	13	20	834	0	1	23	0	4.46	1.24	.88	14	12.0	6	18	10	3	0
CHESTER	AM	47.2M	31.7M	39.5M		66	6			784	0	1		0	4.60									
COATESVILLE 1 SW	AM	45.1	26.4	35.8	- 4.1	61	6	13	20	898	0	3	26	0	4.75	.62	.81	14	14.4	11	19	11	5	0
COLUMBIA		49.3	29.5	39.4		69	5	17	21	787	0	1	20	0						7	19			
DEVAULT 1 W		45.8		M		64	5				0	0		0						15	19			
DIXON	AM	41.2	19.4	30.3		56	6	4	18	1069	0	6	28	2	3.04		.52	17	17.3	7	17+	9	1	0
DU BOIS 7 E		41.7	20.4	31.1		64	7	3	21	1045	0	4	27	2	4.32	1.14	1.22	8	23.5	13	16	9	2	1
EAGLES MERE	AM	35.9	18.5	27.2		52	6	7	25	1164	0	0	31	0	4.03	.66	.72	8	21.8	13	17	11	3	0
EMPORIUM 1 E	AM	40.7	18.7	29.7	- 5.6	62	2	4	17+	1083	0	5	29	0	5.08	1.47	1.14	8	19.6	9	17	11	4	1
EPHRATA		46.7	27.4	37.1	- 3.4	67	5	12	17	858	0	1	24	0	5.08	1.65	1.17	8	8.5			13	3	2
EVERETT 1 SW		48.2	26.5	37.4	- 1.9	70	5	18	1+	850	0	1	28	0	4.68	1.54	.96	7	8.5	4	18	15	3	0
FREDERICKSVILLE 2 SE	AM																							
FREELAND		40.3	21.4	30.9	- 2.4	55	5	8	18+	1053	0	4	29	0	2.90	1.03	.76	17	22.3	14	18+	8	1	0
GEORGE SCHOOL		46.1	28.0	37.1	- 3.5	65	5	6	21	858	0	3	23	0	6.00	2.54	1.61	14	18.9	12	19	10	4	2
GETTYSBURG	AM	46.8	29.0	37.9	- 2.7	72	6	18	1	833	0	2	23	0	4.41	1.12	.90	14	6.8	6	19	13	3	0
GRATZ 1 N	AM	43.2	25.5	34.4		69	6	14	22	943	0	5	27	0	2.69		.53	17	8.5	6	17+	9	2	0
HANOVER	AN	47.5	26.3	36.9	- 5.1	73	6	15	20	864	0	0	27	0	5.27	1.99	1.08	8	9.0	6	19	12	3	1
HARRISBURG WB AP	R	46.2	30.2	38.2	- 2.6	70	5	19	1+	824	0	2	20	0	4.41	1.54	.70	18	20.2	9	19	12	3	0
HAWLEY 1 S DAM	AM	36.7	17.4	27.1		52	6	3	18	1170	0	7	26	2	3.31		.87	17	18.5	13	20	11	1	0
HOLTWOOD		45.7	31.5	38.6	- 2.7	64	5	23	5+	810	0	2	15	0	4.11	1.13	1.04	19	23.7	15	20	12	3	1
HUNTINGDON	AM	47.5	23.9	35.7	- 3.0	69	6	13	21+	899	0	2	27	0	4.25	.78	1.61	8	12.1	5	17+	7	3	1
JIM THORPE		45.7	26.4	36.1	- 1.2	65	5	11	1	891	0	1	25	0	3.72	.49	.89	14	13.5	6	19	7	3	0
KEGG		48.6	26.2	37.4		69	5	13	20	848	0	1	27	0	4.75		1.30	7	9.0	5	16	11	3	1

See Reference Notes Following Station Index

CLIMATOLOGICAL DATA

TABLE 2 - CONTINUED

Station		Temperature: Average Maximum	Average Minimum	Average	Departure from Long-Term Mean	Highest	Date	Lowest	Date	Degree Days	No. of Days Max. 90° or Above	Max. 32° or Below	Min. 32° or Below	Min. 0° or Below	Precipitation: Total	Departure from Long-Term Mean	Greatest Day	Date	Snow, Sleet: Total	Max. Depth on Ground	Date	No. of Days .10 or More	.50 or More	1.00 or More
LANCASTER 2 NE PUMP STA		49.3	27.1	38.2	- 1.9	69	5	8	20	823	0	0	24	0	4.81	1.36	1.30	14	16.2	6	19	11	3	1
LANDISVILLE	AM	44.3	27.9	36.1		69	6	17	18+	890	0	3	25	0	4.22		.77	8	5.2	6	19	11	3	0
LAWRENCEVILLE 2 S	AM	39.9	17.2	28.6	- 6.2	56	12	- 5	21	1122	0	6	29	5	4.39	1.95	1.16	6	21.7	13	17	9	4	1
LEBANON 2 NW																								
LEWISTOWN	AM	47.0	27.1	37.1		71	6	18	18+	855	0	2	24	0	2.72		.94	8	8.0	5	17+	8	1	0
LOCK HAVEN		46.1	26.7	36.4	- 2.1	63	5+	14	21	877	0	0	26	0	3.25	- .22	.73	17	10.5	7	17	9	2	0
MADERA	AM	41.7	18.1	29.9		65	8	3	1	1079	0	6	29	0	D 4.75		.76	8	12.0	7	17	11	4	0
MARCUS HOOK		46.3	31.9	39.1	- 5.7	60	3+	21	20+	704	0	1	16	0	4.76	1.10	1.75	14	12.4	7	19	10	2	1
MARTINSBURG CAA AP		44.9	25.8	35.4		66	5+	13	21	902	0	4	26	0	4.12		1.13	7	9.7	6	18+	8	3	1
MIDDLETOWN OLMSTED FLD		46.8	29.6	38.2	- 2.0	69	5	19	21	820	0	1	19	0	4.16	.65	1.04	14	11.7	8	19	11	2	1
MONTROSE 1 E	AM	34.7	18.2	26.5	- 5.3	47	3+	3	18	1185	0	13	31	0	5.08	2.20	1.32	17	24.6	17	17+	9	4	1
MORGANTOWN		43.9	25.4	34.7		66	5	10	20+	933	0	3	26	0	5.20		1.32	14		12	19	10	4	1
MT GRETNA 2 SE		46.1M	28.3	37.2M		68	5	14	1	859	0		23	0	4.44		1.07	14	2.2			11	3	1
MT POCONO 2 N AP		37.4	20.6	29.0	- 3.0	54	5	1	1	1109	0	7	31	0	4.03	.08	1.56	14		10	19	8	3	1
MUHLENBURG 1 SE		42.3	22.7	32.5		58	5	6	18	998	0	5	28	0	3.16		.77	8	18.0	10	17+	8	2	0
NEWBURG 3 W		49.6	30.2	39.9		79	6	18	17	771	0	0	20	0	D 3.11		.76	7	12.0			10	2	0
NEWPORT	AM	46.5	25.7	36.1		72	6	12	21	887	0	2	27	0	3.24	- .23	.65	17	9.4	5	17+	11	2	0
NORRISTOWN		45.9	29.7	37.8		56	5	18	21	836	0	3	18	0	6.98		1.94	19	19.0	17	19+	9	5	2
PALMERTON		42.5	26.5	34.5	- 3.8	63	5	12	1	939	0	4	25	0	2.98	- .12	.62	8	10.7	6	19+	9	1	0
PHIL DREXEL INST OF TEC		48.2	33.4	40.8		66	5	21	25	743	0	2	13	0	4.48		1.50	14	9.2	7	19	11	3	1
PHILADELPHIA WB AP	R	46.3	31.2	38.8	- 3.5	65	5	21	25	808	0	2	14	0	4.65	1.33	1.56	14	10.9	7	19+	8	4	1
PHILADELPHIA PT BREEZE		46.4	34.2	40.3	- 3.2	65	5	24	25	760	0	2	12	0	4.41		1.47	14				11	2	1
PHILADELPHIA SHAWMONT		48.8	30.1	39.5	- 3.1	68	6	19	21	784	0	1	20	0	5.24	1.65	1.59	14				11	4	1
PHILADELPHIA CITY	R AM	45.8	32.6	39.2	- 4.3	63	5	22	25	795	0	2	13	0	4.49	1.12	1.60	14				9	4	1
PHILIPSBURG CAA AP		40.0	21.4	30.7		63	7	- 2	1+	1058	0	10	28	2	4.80		.83	8	18.6	10	19+	11	4	0
PHOENIXVILLE 1 E		48.3	25.8	37.1	- 4.4	67	5	6	22	861	0	0	24	0	5.75	2.10	1.49	14				10	4	1
PIMPLE HILL	AM	35.5	19.8	27.7		54	6	6	25	1150	0	11	31	0	4.74		.99	17	24.2	15	20	13	2	0
PLEASANT MOUNT 1 W	AM	34.6	16.1	25.4		46	6	- 8	18	1220	0	11	31	3	4.25	.28	.61	17	24.7	20	20	13	2	0
PORT CLINTON	AM	45.7	24.7	35.2	- 3.3	68	7	12	1	917	0	3	26	0	4.44	.57	.72	14				13	2	0
QUAKERTOWN 1 E		46.1	26.3	36.2	- 1.5	66	5	10	18	885	0	3	23	0	6.03	2.43	1.25	15	15.4			12	4	2
READING WB CITY	R	46.0	30.6	38.3	- 3.3	69	5	21	17+	820	1	0	17	0	4.82	1.51	1.15	14	11.2	8	20	11	3	1
SCRANTON	AM	40.9	22.5	31.7	- 5.6	56	6	7	19	1021	0	6	28	0	D 1.98	- .77	.50	14	9.8			8	1	0
SCRANTON WB AIRPORT		39.6	23.4	31.5	- 4.8	55	5	6	18	1032	0	6	27	0	2.48	- .35	.57	16	14.5	9	19+	5	2	0
SELINSGROVE CAA AP		44.8	25.9	35.4	- 3.3	66	5	11	21	911	0	3	27	0	2.70	- .99	.63	14	11.0	5	17	8	2	0
SHIPPENSBURG		50.2	28.8	39.5	- 1.5	72	5	15	20	781	0	0	22	0	3.90	.63	.92	14	12.0	5	18+	11	2	0
STATE COLLEGE		43.5	25.0	34.3	- 2.1	63	7	12	19	945	0	4	28	0	3.46	.12	.70	14	8.0	6	17+	10	3	0
STROUDSBURG	AM	39.6	20.9	30.3	- 6.9	52	3+	- 2	18	1067	0	5	28	2	3.40	- .33	.68	14	27.3	14	19	9	3	0
TAMARACK 2 S FIRE TWR	AM	37.4	18.4	27.9		58	12	5	25+	1142	0	12	28	0	3.96		.98	17	23.2	15	17+	9	2	0
TOWANDA		41.9	21.8	31.9	- 3.5	55	11	- 1	18	1018	0	4	27	2	4.62	1.96	1.03	6	23.1	13	17	9	4	1
UPPER DARBY		47.4	29.6	38.5		66	5	20	1+	814	0	2	21	0	5.06		1.68	14	11.7	6	18	10	3	1
WELLSBORO 3 S	AM	37.1	18.7	27.9	- 5.0	54	12	7	18+	1141	0	8	27	0	4.16	1.20	.89	6	26.5	14	17+	9	3	0
WELLSVILLE		48.3	26.5	37.4		68	5	14	22	847	0	1	24	0	4.34		.93	14	12.3	7	18	13	2	0
WEST CHESTER	AM	47.1	30.6	38.9	- .5	65	5	19	19+	804	0	2	18	0	5.62	1.70			19.6	15	18			
WILLIAMSPORT WB AP		43.9	26.1	35.0	- 3.3	62	5	13	1	923	0	2	26	0	3.28	- .06	.80	16	12.0	7	17	9	3	0
YORK 3 SSW PUMP STA		50.7	28.5	39.6	- 1.5	71	5	9	20	777	0	0	23	0	3.56	.28	1.11	14		8	19	9	2	1
DIVISION				35.1											4.23				15.0					
OHIO DRAINAGE																								
BAKERSTOWN 3 WNW		48.0	28.1	38.1		66	7	13	20	830	0	1	25	0	4.14		1.01	8	7.0	7	16	7	4	1
BLAIRSVILLE 6 ENE		43.8	24.6	34.2		65	6	11	20	905	0	5	27	0	6.49	2.80	1.19	8	29.4	8	16	14	5	1
BRADFORD 4 W RES		39.9	16.2	28.1	- 6.5	56	7	- 4	25	1138	0	5	31	5	6.03	2.58	1.20	6	31.6	14	24+	10	5	2
BROOKVILLE CAA AIRPORT		42.5	22.4	32.5	- 1.5	63	7	6	21	1002	0	6	29	0	4.30	1.01	.80	8	16.9	7	17+	10	2	0
BURGETTSTOWN 2 W	AM	47.4	24.6	36.0		69	6	6	20	892	0	1	28	0	5.92		.99	17				10	6	0
BUTLER		49.4	26.2	37.8	- .6	68	7	9	20	834	0	1	27	0	4.92	1.59	1.20	17	14.0	11	17	8	4	1
CLARION 3 SW		45.7	23.5	34.6		64	6+	6	20	933	0	0	27	0	4.82	1.10	1.11	8	13.1	8	17	10	3	1
CLAYSVILLE 3 W		50.7	24.2	37.5	- 3.1	70	5	6	20	848	0	1	26	0	6.11	2.57	1.00	29		5	17	11	6	1
CONFLUENCE 1 SW DAM	AM	46.0	25.2	35.6		67	6+	11	20	903	0	4	27	0	4.39		.80	29	12.0	5	17+	10	3	0
CORRY		41.4	21.0	31.2	- 2.1	58	6+	- 1	20+	1039	0	7	26	2	5.05	1.43	1.55	6	22.6	8	24	10	2	2
COUDERSPORT 2 NW		37.8	18.9	28.4		53	7	2	25	1129	0	8	28	0	5.71		1.07	8	36.2	14	17+	11	4	2
DERRY		49.1	27.6	38.4	- 1.7	70	7	9	20	816	0	1	25	0	6.21	2.15	.95	8+	16.5	11	17	14	6	0
DONEGAL		43.3	20.5	31.9		63	7	4	20	1019	0	8	29	0	7.11		1.20	7	12.6	6	17	11	6	1
DONORA	AM	52.1	31.5	41.8	- .6	71	6	16	20	711	0	0	18	0	6.36	2.81	1.21	7	6.6	3	17	10	7	2
EAST BRADY		49.7	23.9	36.8		68	6	10	20	868	0	0	25	0	4.44		1.06	8	9.0	9	16	9	3	1
EBENSBURG		44.9	21.8	33.4	- 2.0	66	7	5	21	974	0	4	29	0	5.52	2.03	1.25	7	20.5	9	17	12	4	1
FARRELL SHARON		47.4	24.1	35.8	- 2.6	68	7	12	20	899	0	1	29	0	4.01	1.27	.75	6	2.0	1	16	9	4	0
FORD CITY 4 S DAM	AM	45.6	22.8	34.2		68	7	8	20	950	0	3	29	0	4.19		.87	8	14.5	9	17	8	4	0
FRANKLIN		45.9	23.9	34.9	- .6	62	7	5	20	926	0	0	27	0	5.06	1.67	.95	17		10	17	10	4	0
GREENVILLE		44.9	24.7	34.8	- 2.1	65	6	5	20	930	0	2	26	0	4.31	.86	.94	8	19.0	8	16	9	3	0
INDIANA 3 SE		48.0	25.0	36.5	- 2.5	68	7	3	20	876	0	1	27	0	5.81	1.89	1.20	8	12.0	8	17	10	4	3
IRWIN			27.9	M		65	10+	10	20		0	0	24	0	D 5.94	2.47	1.00	8	9.6	9	17	9	6	1
JAMESTOWN 2 NW	AM	42.1	21.5	31.8		65	12	6	20+	1022	0	5	29	0	4.40	1.56	.91	8		5	17+	10	4	0
JOHNSTOWN	AM	48.2	27.0	37.6	- 1.6	71	8	16	1+	843	0	2	27	0	4.50	.34	.80	7	8.5	6	18	10	4	0
KANE 1 NNE	AM	38.7	17.0	27.9		57	12	- 5	20	1144	0	8	28	5	5.94	2.12	1.05	8	38.3	16	17+	14	5	1
LINESVILLE 5 WNW		41.5	23.0	32.3		60	7	5	1	1005	0	4	26	0	4.13	1.02	.87	8	22.2	6	17	10	3	0
MEADVILLE 1 S	AM	41.1	21.7	31.4	- 3.4	62	7	7	20	1034	0	6	29	0	4.72	1.45	.95	8	23.1	6	17	12	4	0
MERCER 2 NNE		43.4	22.8	33.1		62	6	4	1	981	0	1	28	0						8	17			
MIDLAND DAM 7		46.6	29.3	38.0	- 2.0	65	6+	15	20	831	0	0	23	0	4.83	1.23	1.05	8	10.0	9	17	9	4	1

See Reference Notes Following Station Index

CLIMATOLOGICAL DATA

TABLE 2 - CONTINUED

PENNSYLVANIA
MARCH 1956

Station	Temperature: Average Maximum	Average Minimum	Average	Departure from Long-Term Mean	Highest	Date	Lowest	Date	Degree Days	No. of Days: Max. 90° or Above	Max. 32° or Below	Min. 32° or Below	Min. 0° or Below	Precipitation: Total	Departure from Long-Term Mean	Greatest Day	Date	Snow, Sleet: Total	Max. Depth on Ground	Date	No. of Days: .10 or More	.50 or More	1.00 or More
NEW CASTLE 1 N	48.1	26.1	37.1	- .2	66	6	6	20	857	0	0	27	0	4.53	1.49	1.10	17	14.3	13	18	8	2	1
NEWELL AM	49.1	29.4	39.3	- 2.5	68	6	17	20	790	0	1	24	0	6.23	3.18	1.01	14	10.0	8	17		6	1
NEW STANTON	49.7	26.4	38.1	- 2.0	71	6	15	19+	828	0	0	26	0	5.35	1.78	1.01	7		7	16	8	5	1
PITTSBURGH WB AP 2 //R	46.5	27.8	37.2	- 1.4	67	7	15	20	857	0	2	25	0	5.31	2.11	.93	16	14.8	9	17	11	5	0
PITTSBURGH WB CITY R	49.4	31.4	40.4	- 1.2	69	7	20	17+	759	0	0	19	0	5.03	1.62	1.03	16	9.5			9	6	1
PUTNEYVILLE 2 SE DAM AM	43.9	20.4	32.2		66	7	6	20	1012	0	3	29	0	4.34		1.04	8		10	17	8	3	1
RIDGWAY 3 W	42.4	20.0M	31.2M	- 2.2	63	7	- 7	17	1040	0	3	28	4	4.61	1.50	.90	8	19.2	10	17	11	3	0
SALINA 3 W	48.2	26.6	37.4		66	7	6	20	849	0	2	26	0	6.52		1.18	17		9	16	10	7	2
SHIPPINGPORT WB	47.2	28.1	37.7		68	7	14	20	841	0	1	26	0	4.30		1.02	7	9.0	7	16	10	4	1
SLIPPERY ROCK	45.3	24.9	35.1		64	7	10	20+	919	0	2	26	0	3.82		.88	8	15.5	13	17	8	2	0
SOMERSET MAIN ST	46.8	25.5	36.2	.2	64	5+	7	20+	887	0	3	27	0	4.84	.65	.84	14	11.5	3	16+	10	4	0
SPRINGS 1 SW	43.8	21.8	32.8	- 3.0	64	7	5	21	990	0	8	28	0	2.93	- .74	.38	16	17.0	7	18	9	0	0
TIONESTA 2 SE DAM AM	42.1	19.4	30.8		63	8	3	20	1055	0	3	29	0	4.78	1.30	.97	8	23.7	13	17	11	3	0
TITUSVILLE WATER WORKS	41.6	19.1	30.4		62	7	- 4	20	1064	0	5	28	3	5.01		.96	8	17.1	12	16	12	4	0
UNIONTOWN	51.2	29.6	40.4	- 1.3	71	5	15	20	754	0	0	20	0	4.70	.77	.87	8	3.5	3	16	9	5	0
WARREN	42.2	22.0	32.1	- 2.5	61	7	0	19	1013	0	4	27	1	4.11	.83	.73	8	24.1	10	17	10	3	0
WAYNESBURG 2 W	51.9	27.6	39.8	- 1.1	70	5+	13	20+	774	0	0	24	0	5.76	1.91	1.35	29		2	17	8	5	2
DIVISION			35.0											5.06				16.1					
LAKE DRAINAGE																							
ERIE CAA AIRPORT	39.4	24.0	31.7		61	6	9	20	1027	0	7	28	0	3.74		.93	5	17.8	7	17+	7	2	0
SPRINGBORO	41.1M		M		61	7				0	5												
DIVISION			31.7											3.74				17.8					

DAILY PRECIPITATION

PENNSYLVANIA
MARCH 1956

Table 3

Station	Total	1	2	3	4	5	6	7	8	9	10	11	12	13	14	15	16	17	18	19	20	21	22	23	24	25	26	27	28	29	30	31
ACHETONIA LOCK 3	5.80	T	.01	.02	.14		.28	1.27	.85	.82				.03	.47	.07	.02	.96	.05	T				.01	.23	.02	.18		T	.93	.06	.0
ALLENTOWN WB AP R	4.88		.06	T	.06		.07	.28	.55			.22	.14	T	1.04		.84	.02	.44	.58				T	.21	T	T			.36	.01	T
ALLENTOWN GAS CO	4.30		.01	T	.02		T	.06	.33	.44		.07	.13	.11	.55	.48	.01	.89	.01	.91	.07				.05	.07					.29	
ALTOONA HORSESHOE CURVE	4.86		.12		.11		.62	.78	.78	.04			.12	.04	.83		.38	.06	.18	.03			T		.08		.07		.30	.21	.13	
ARENDTSVILLE	4.19						.05	.51	.47	.22		.12	.20	.13	.76	.30	.10	.54	.15	.22					.07	T	T			.23	.07	.0
ARTEMAS 1 WNW	-						-	.10	.08				.33	*	.72	*	.58	.06	-						.82	.46			-	-		
AUSTINBURG 2 W	4.93		.05		.40		1.30	.35	.40					T	.16	.25	T	.98	T					T	.73		T			T	T	.2
BAKERSTOWN 3 WNW	4.14		.04	.05			.58	.04	1.01				T		.37		.85	T	.01	T	T	T			T				.46	.16	.01	
BARNES	6.18		.10	.08	.02		1.20	.28	1.10	.17	T				T	.45	T	1.12	T					T	.75	T	.16			.32	.31	.1
BEAR GAP	2.30		.03		.02		.06	.04	.48			.02		.10	.50		.22	.34		.20					.15					.14		T
BEAVER FALLS	4.21	T	.01	T	.04		.20	.82	.91	T			T	T	.19	.15	T	.82	.03	T	T			T	.40	T	.06		T	.52	.03	.0
BEAVERTOWN	3.43		.02	.04	.04		.17	.20	.70	.09			.07	.08	.10	.67	*	.26	.23	.12					.31		T			.07	.22	.0
BEECH CREEK STATION	3.19		.04	T	.19			.38	.61	.03				.02	.24	.33	T	.76	T	.03					.26	T	T			.19	.09	T
BELLEFONTE 4 S	3.93	T	.02	T	.30		.37	.45	.90	T				.12	.33	.14	T	.52	.02	.10			T		.15		T			.23	.05	.0
BERWICK	2.18		.05		.03		.03	.08	.58	T		.02	T	.03	.80		.34	.12	.01	.07					.12					.13		
BETHLEHEM	4.08		T	T	.02		T	.02	.35	.44		.07	.14	.06	.40	.48		.72	T	.90	.04				T	.09					.26	
BETHLEHEM LEHIGH UNIV	4.65		.01	T	.02		.05	.30	.32			.25	.11	T	1.00		.82	T	.40	.62					.25					.29	.01	
BLAIRSVILLE 6 ENE	6.49		.02	T	T		.79	.97	1.19	.16		T	.13		.81	.01	.78	.09	.10	T	.01		.01	T	.27	.03	.26		.25	.33	.18	.1
BLOSERVILLE 1 N	3.80	T					.45	.35	.45			.12	.12	.08	.82		.55	.18	.25	.15	T				.06				.20	T	.02	
BOSWELL 6 WNW	-	T	.17	.03	.20		.50	1.20	.70	.06				.10	.58	.09	T	-	-	-				.03	.45	.08	.31		T	.40	.10	.0
BRADDOCK LOCK 2	5.14	T	.06	.04	.16		.28	1.05	.71	.01				.04	.44	.15	.02	.85	.03	T	T			.02	.26	.02	.15		.01	.76	.07	.0
BRADFORD CNTRL FIRE STA	6.17		.11	.07	.36		1.17	.93	.90	.12					.05	.40	.02	.70	T	.02				.03	.90		.09			.18	.24	.1
BRADFORD 4 W RES	6.03	T	.24	T	.32		1.20	.91	1.05	.03			T		.64		.45	.05	T				T	.03	.90	T	T			.03	.30	.1
BREEZEWOOD	3.71		.02				.34	.47	.33			.09	.32	.50	.17		.40	T	.14					T	T	.01	.85		.32	.24	.02	T
BROOKVILLE CAA AIRPORT	4.30		.07	.06		.01	.37	.40	.80	.01		T	.04	T	.35	T	.71	T	.04	T			T	.19	.13	.07	.01		.35	.47	.18	.0
BRUCETON 1 S	5.18		T	T	.09		.65	.76	*	.57				.05	.65	.10	.11	*	*	.09				T	*	*	.29		T	.87	.05	
BUFFALO MILLS	4.53			.02			.14	.90	.64				.26	.15	.60	.13	.02	.57	.09	.13					.10	T	.09			.56	.14	T
BURGETTSTOWN 2 W	3.92		.06	.05	.21		.52	.64	.94	.02				T	.61	.05	.23	.99	.08	.01					.30		.12			.98	.09	.0
BURNT CABINS 2 NE	4.17						.60	.61	.46			.12	.28	.06	.59		.67		.30	T									.33	.15	T	
BUTLER	4.92		.02		.05		.34	.61	.87	.05					.27	.09		1.20	.02					.01	.38	.02	.86	T	.05	.72	.10	.0
CAMP HILL	4.09			T			.30	.24	.10			.20	.28	.36	.95		.68		.50	.03	.14				.02				T	.32		T
CANTON 1 NW	4.23		T	T	.22		.98	.29	.28	.14				T	.20	.44	T	.95	T	.01				T	.77	T	T				T	T
CARLISLE	4.29		T		.02	T	.44	.33	.38			.15	.18	.12	.88		.60	.04	.38	.13			T		.07		T		.15	.40	.02	T
CARROLLTOWN 2 SSE	5.12	T	.08	T	.16		.52	1.08	.70	.10				.08	.54	.24	T	.44	.11	.03				.02	.27	T	.08		T	.62	.12	.0
CARTER CAMP 2 W	5.15		.10	T	.35		.91	.39	.92	.05				T	.15	.27	T	.98	T	T					.55	T	.05			.15	.23	.0
CEDAR RUN	4.55		.06	.42	.30		.30	.25	.56	.10			T	T	.05	.65	T	.85	T	.05				T	.65	T	T			T	.05	.0
CHADDS FORD	-		T	T			T	.15	.16	T			T	.70	1.70	-	.20	.70	.05	.75	.20									.08		
CHAMBERSBURG 1 ESE	4.46		.03				.33	.38	.65			.38	.28	T	.88		.72		.28	.04					.04		T		.33	.10	T	.0
CHARLEROI LOCK 4	6.85	T	.08	.01	.14		.55	1.04	.80	.02				.06	.58	.36	.07	1.07	.03	T					.22	T	.08	T	.01	1.03	.08	T
CHESTER	4.60		.04	.27		.06		.08	.32	.46			.06	.19	1.19	.24	.05	*	*	1.20	.13				.07						.26	
CLARENCE 1 E	3.57		.06	.08	.13	T	.21	.40	.74	.02			T	.07	.24	.33	.01	.60	.01	.04				T	.29	T	.01			.23	.09	.0
CLARION 3 SW	4.82		.09		.07		.41	.27	1.11	.04				.03	.18	.17	T	.66	T					T	.40		.10		.07	.92	.22	.0
CLAUSSVILLE	4.24		.02	.07	.04		.04	.09	.38	.41		.21	.25	.10	.58	.50		.65		.58	.07					.08					.19	
CLAYSVILLE 3 W	6.11		.14		.21		.65	.80	.71	.05				.04	.80	.21	.04	.90	.09	.01					.30		.10		.02	1.00	.04	T
CLEARFIELD	4.73		.10	.10	.08		.48	.60	.90	.05				.04	.28	.20	.08	.71	.03	T				T	.28		.10			.46	.13	.1
CLERMONT	5.60	T	.20	.05	.15		1.20	.60	1.10	.10				.02	.10	.20	.04	.80	T	T				T	.60	T	.06			.16	.24	.0
COALDALE 2 NW	D 3.85	D.10	.01	.01	.13			.23	.38	.43		.24	.26	.06	.38	.47		.53		.37	.04				.05						.16	
COATESVILLE 1 SW	4.75		T	T	.05			.19	.64	.30		.06	.20	.16	.81	.67	.02	.69	T	.58	.05				T	.01				.11	.21	
COLUMBIA	-		.06				.21	.41	1.01			.10	.06	.11	1.26		.62	.10	.36	.36					.09				.27	-	T	T
CONFLUENCE 1 SW DAM	4.30		T	T	.06		.07	.35	.74	.02			.19	.12	.68	.14		.39	.06	.09				T	.24	T	.36		T	.80	.06	.0
CONFLUENCE 1 NW	5.15	T	.05	T	.14		.05	.74	.80	.02			.17	.11	.68	.15	.04	.52	.03	.07	T			T	.37	T	.29	.01		.84	.06	.0
CONNELLSVILLE	4.80		.05		.08		.04	1.00	.90	.02			T		.63	.19		.55							.10	.13	.21			.74	.07	
CONSHOHOCKEN	3.89		T	.10	.06			.21	.45	.45		.02	.05	.21	.83	.73	.03	.79	.70	.85					T	T	T				.21	
COOKSBURG	5.02	T	.15	.05	.17		.55	.54	1.06	.08		T		T	.16	.17	.05	.52	.05	T				.05	.46	T	.11			.53	.24	.1
COOKSBURG 2 NNW	5.61		.12	.20	.16		.55	.44	1.10	.03		T		T	.19	.18	.20	.55	.05	T				.05	.41	T	.13			.61	.29	.1
CORAOPOLIS NEVILLE IS	4.21		T		.08		.38	.84	.77	T				T	T	.40	.29	*	.38	T				T	T	T	.23			.77	.07	
CORRY	5.05		.09	.06	.07	.05	1.95	.14	1.04	.15		.02			.40	.01	.25	.06					T	.23	.37	T	.08		T	.25	.15	.0
COUDERSPORT 2 NW	5.71		.11	.06	.44		1.04	.84	1.07	.18				.04	.08	.26	.03	.44						.03	.62	.02	.07			.14	.17	.0
COUDERSPORT 7 E	-	T	.13	T	.50		.96	.63	.82	.16				.07	.07	.30	T	.89	T	.03	-	-	-	-	.65	T	.08				.25	.1
COVINGTON	4.81		.03	T	.30		1.10	.54	.38	T				T	.05	T	T	1.49	T	.02				T	.85						.06	.0
CREEKSIDE	5.38		.07	.05	.12		.36	.84	.90	T				T	.45	.15	T	1.00	.11	T					.34	T	T			.80	.10	T
CRESSON 2 SE	6.49	.03	.03	.06	.08		.54	.80	1.20	.13			T	.20	.40	.44	.04	.91	.15	.11				.04	.22	.02	.13			.70	.12	[illegible]
CUSTER CITY 2 W	D 6.90	.06	.10	.12	D.40		1.25	.82	1.01	.12	T		T	.03	.08	.32	.06	.83		.02				.05	.67	.03	.09			.17	.23	[illegible]
DANVILLE	2.51				.17		.04	.10	.50	.23			T	T	.38	.27		.61		.16					.20						.05	
DERRY	6.21		.12		.11		.50	.80	.95				.06		.95		.85	.25	T	T					.30	T	.21	T	.22	.50	.20	.1
DEVAULT 1 W	-		.18		T		.23	.90	.56			.28	.03	.26	1.54		-	-	-	.03					.05					.29	.28	
DIXON	3.04		T	T	.21		.34	.34	.38	.30		T		.02	.27	.25		.52		T	.09				.32	T	T				T	
DONEGAL	7.11		.04	T	.15		.92	1.20	.56	T		T	.05		.80		.40	.05	.04	T			T	T	.95	.80	.15	T	.40	.42	.06	[illegible]
DONORA	6.36	T	.09	T	.10		.71	1.21	.75	T			T	.06	.89	T	.68	.54	.01	T				T	.17	T	.11	T	T	1.01	.04	[illegible]
DOYLESTOWN	5.61		.07		.04		.19	.42	.90			.13	.02	.08	1.44		.56	.38	.48	.66					.03					.20	.01	
DU BOIS 7 E	4.32		.17	.02			.47	.29	1.22	T		T	T	.03	.37		.73	.07	T				T	.07	.31		.08		.09	.33	.02	[illegible]
DUSHORE 3 NE	3.46		.06	.15	.12		.44	.25	.08	.20			T	.02	.20	.10		.84		T	T				.40		T	T				
EAGLES MERE	4.03		.06	.08	.23		.29	.13	.72	.29			T	.10	.29	.42		.65	T	.04				T	.59	T	T				.10	[illegible]
EAST BRADY	4.44		.01	.03	.08		.46	.64	1.06	.03			.01		.34		.88		.02					.07	.02	.10	.01		.20	.36	.11	[illegible]
EBENSBURG	5.52	T	T	.05	T		.43	1.25	.38	.22				.07	.59	.42	T	.85	.12	.06					.32	T	.16			.58	.22	T
EDINBORO	5.34	.01	.04	.05	.12		1.46	.24	1.07	.31		.01			T	.35	.03	.31	.01	.01				.01	.66	T	.06			.28	.11	[illegible]
ELIZABETHTOWN	4.75				.02			.34	.58	.43		.28	.14	.15	.73	.41	.07	.86	.02	.37					.08					.16	.11	
EMPORIUM 1 E	5.08		.16	.04	.29		.72	.25	1.14	.05	T			.03	.21	.26	.02	.80	.02	T				T	.58	T	.06	T		.24	.16	[illegible]
ENGLISH CENTER	4.16		.08	.05	.03		.61	.59	.53	T			T	.01	.21	.42	T	.90	T	.02					.62		.01			T	.08	T
EPHRATA	5.08						.30	.27	1.17			.30	.10	.12	1.06		.66	.10	.20	.35					.10					.48	.01	
EQUINUNK	-	T	.03				.64	.46	.29	.40			T		.42	.26		.80		.10	-				.40		.04	T		T	.11	T
ERIE CAA AIRPORT	3.74	T	.04	.01		.93	.39	.30	.46	T		T			.44		.50	.01	.02	.02			T	.45	.08	.04			T	.04	.03	T
EVERETT 1 SW	4.68						.30	.96	.40			.20	.36	.10	.67		.46	.12	.12	.12					.10	.03	.10		.50	.14		
FARRELL SHARON	4.01		.04	.07			.75	.03	.65	.62					.53	.01	.32	.02	.10				.01	.15	.03	.01			.22	.28	.06	[illegible]
FORD CITY 4 S DAM	4.19	T	.05	.02	.05		.40	.57	.87	.07				.04	.37	.04	.02	.55	.05	T					.28	T	.08		T	.63	.11	[illegible]
FRANKLIN	5.06		.05		.12		.52	.28	.94	.08		.01			.09	.38	.09	.93	.03	T				.01	.46		.09		.11	.65	.13	[illegible]
FREDERICKSVILLE 2 SE		RECORD MISSING																														
FREELAND	2.90		.15	T	.04	T	T		T	.05		.28	T	T	.28	.35	T	.76	.30	.31					.08	T	.04			.03	.18	[illegible]
GALETON	5.72			.02	.35		.02	.65	.75	.05			T	.05	.20	.32	T	1.28	T	.02					.79		.08			.08	.12	[illegible]
GEIGERTOWN	5.06			.01	.02			.49	.64	.32		.28	.06	.15	.85	.47	*	.84	.18	T	1.15			T	.01						.25	
GEORGE SCHOOL	6.00		.08				.11	.07	1.29			.07	.09	.14	1.61		.49	.38	.55	.85					.13					.16		
GETTYSBURG	4.41			T			.14	.38	.81	.07		.15	.12	.12	.90	.33	.13	.55	.15	.29					.02	.04				.15	.06	T
GIFFORD		RECORD MISSING																														
GLEN HAZEL 2 NE DAM	4.94	T	.15	.04	.29		.76	.40	1.03	.10	T			.05	.18	.17	.02	.50	T	T				.03	.50	T	.07			.39	.26	[illegible]
GLENWILLARD DASH DAM	4.96	T	.03	.04	.12		.26	.85	.85	T					.28	.12	.03	1.07	.02	T				.01	.34	T	.03			.83	.08	T
GOULDSBORO	3.66		T	.05	.05		.03	.14	.22	.48		.05	.12	.05	.28	.43		.85		.22	.36				.15	T	.05				.15	[illegible]
GRANTVILLE 2 SW	3.77		T				.18	.25	.62			.34	.18	.02	.95		.59	.02	.16	.10					.02				T	.34		
GRATERFORD	-		.03	.03	.14	.02	.17	.21	.48	.46		.12	.05	.18	.76	-	-	.87		1.49	.24				.02	.04				.11	.09	1
GRATZ 1 N	2.69	T		T	T		T	.18	.50	.18		T	T	.15	.35	.20	T	.53	T	.32					.08	T	T					
GREENSBORO LOCK 7	4.64		.06	T	.08		.01	.38	.98	T			T	.11	.60	.21	.01	.62	.03	.06					.37	T	.34	.02		.92	.04	
GREENSBURG 3 SE	5.68		.09	.01	.02		.73	.98	.95				.10		.84		.64	T	.01	T			T	.01	.20	.01	.25		.32	.47	.14	[illegible]
GREENVILLE	4.31		.08	.25	.04	.01	.84	.18	.94	T					.38		.51	.02	.02	.01			.02	.17	.01	.04	.84		.27	.42	.08	1
HANOVER	5.27			.02				.21	1.08	.42		.21	.13	.20	.86	.38	.04	.91	.21	.39					.02	.01	T			.11	.02	1
HARRISBURG WB AP R	4.41		T	.03			.31	.29	.42			.22	.27	T	.96		.60	T	.70	.14			T	T	.11	T	T		.20	.16	T	1
HARRISBURG NORTH	3.60			T			.18	.22	.45	.11		.15	.13	.11	.72	.24	.10	.40	.05	.26					.06					.29	.06	
HAWLEY	3.42		T	T	.05		.20	.44	.18	.31		.03	.04	.03	.33	.44		.73		.16	.16				.12	.01	.03	T			.15	
HAWLEY 1 S DAM	3.31				.04		.19	.34	.12	.24		.01	.04	T	.36	.40		.87		.20	.15				T	.12	T				.17	
HOLLISTERVILLE	3.40		.01	T	.02		.07	.27	.21	.44		.02	.08	.02	.38	.39		.78		.22	.27			T	.15	.03	.06				.12	
HOLTWOOD	4.11		T	T	T		T	.12	.26	.28		.14	.13	.12	.50	.31	.02	.68	.03	1.04	.19				T	T			T	.11	.09	
HONESDALE 4 NW	-			-	.05		.40	.73	.29	.32		.02	.01	T	.57	.21	T	.80		.10	.12				.17	T	D.05	T			.20	
HOOVERSVILLE	4.54	T	.02	T	.05		.45	.83	.56	.05			T	.07	.58	.16	.01	.60	.05	.03				.02	.20	.02	.20			.65	.02	
HOP BOTTOM 2 SE	-				T	.02	-	T	.07	.47	T	T		T	.04	.48	T	.05	.49	.01	.24				T	T	T	.02			.07	
HUNTINGDON	4.25		T	T	.05		.18	.50	1.61	.07			T	.08	.43	.18	T	.52	.05	.08				T	.06	T	T		T	.42	.02	
HUNTSDALE	3.92			.02	T		.08	.80	.48	.09		.04	.27	.13	.56	.20	.02	.85	.06	.28	T				.10	.01				.27	.06	
HYNDMAN	3.61						.17	.58	.20	.01			.26	.15	.56	.12	.06	.46	.10	.15					.05		.11			.61	.02	
INDIANA 3 SE	5.81	T	.05		.13		.25	1.03	1.20	.02				.08	.43	.22	T	1.03	.07					.02	.34	T	.09			.73	.12	
IRWIN	D 5.94		.03	.08			.80	.72	1.08	T			.06		.86		.91	.17		D.03					.18	.07	.08		.31	.64		
JAMESTOWN 2 NW	4.40	T	.08		.31		.61	.25	.91	.02					.02	.36	.08	.26	.03	.01				T	.58	.04	.03		.12	.51	.18	
JIM THORPE	3.72		.03				.09	.19	.68	T		.50	.04	.08	.89		.42	.37	T	.32					.05	T	T			.04	.02	
JOHNSTOWN	4.50	T	.13	T	.09		.66	.80	.38	.07	.03			.07	.75	T	T	.15	.04	.03				T	.25	T	.35		T	.60	T	

See Reference Notes Following Station Index

DAILY PRECIPITATION

PENNSYLVANIA
MARCH 1956

Total	1	2	3	4	5	6	7	8	9	10	11	12	13	14	15	16	17	18	19	20	21	22	23	24	25	26	27	28	29	30	31
													Day of month																		
3.04	T	.14	.10	.20		.02	.34	1.05	.20	T		T	.01	.12	.27	.04	.83		T				.03	.65	.02	.10			.28	.31	.07
3.79	T	.11	.04	.06		.31	.27	.66	.03			T	.03	.26	.30	T	.88	T	.02					.34	T	.04			.19	.19	T
3.02	T	.15	.09	.41		.80	.63	1.20	.15				.02	.20	.21		.71		.02				T	.35		.09			.25	.27	.07
4.79		T				.46	1.30	.20			.10	.32	T	.77		.84	.10	.10				T				.08		.38	.32	T	T
4.27	T	.04	T	.05		.32	.37	.07	T		T	T	T	.38	.04	.05	.86	.04					T	.39	T	.09		.02	.70	.14	.05
7.82		.11	.20	T		1.10	1.94	.71	.01		T	.30	T	.88	T	.99	.09	.08	T			.04		.41	.17	.22		.46	.31	.18	.11
3.22		.02		.03			.15	.29	.44		.16	.25	.02	.46	.44		.40		.26	.12				.03	.02					.15	
	RECORD MISSING																														
3.50				.05		.17	.31	.27	.37		.02	.85	.05	.93	.15	T	.69		.31	.15				.15	.06	.83				.14	.02
4.81		.03				.16	.34	.86			.14	.07	.11	1.30		.32	.31	.22	.36					.09					.29	.02	T
4.22			.06			.05	.30	.77	.38		.28	.05	.10	.76	.38	.04	.53	.01	.13					.06	T				.14	.18	
4.88		.10	.14			.66	.93	.72	T			.10		.16		.80	.02	T	T			T		.26	.08	.09		.30	.38	.09	T
4.30		T	T	.31		1.16	.74	.24	.07				T	.15	.28	T	.80	T					T	.52		T				.12	
	RECORD MISSING																														
3.41		T	.03	.05		T	.22	.30	.35		.24	.10	T	.95	.20	T	.56	T	.24	.40				.03	T	T				.14	
-				-		.98	.51	.46						.41	-	.05	.08	T				D.10	.04	-	-				.01	D.10	
6.60	.01	.14	.12	.48		1.18	.87	1.07	.11	T		T	.02	.08	.34	.02	.86	T	.01				.05	.72	.01	.06			.11	.21	.13
2.72		T	.02	.03		.02	.28	.94	.08			.10	.06	.22	.10	.01	.43	T	.09				T	.14	T	T			.09	.11	T
4.13		.02		.19		.80	.18	.87	.21					T	.24	.06	.26	.03	T					.53	.02	.08		.09	.37	.09	.12
3.25		.03	.04	.13		.18	.18	.53	.26			T	T	.25	.43	T	.73	T	.05					.36		.05			T	.03	.02
3.22		.02	.04	.12			.20	.28	.43		.18	.22	.05	.34	.30		.30		.16	.12			T	.08	T	.04	T			.12	.04
4.75		.09		.17		.27	.51	.78	.05				.13	.36	.25	T	D.66	.04	.04					.29		.08		.06	.73	.19	.05
5.46	T	.08	.05	.09		.25	.68	1.20	.05			T	.09	.31	.22	.10	.91	.07	.02	T			.02	.33	.01	.08		.04	.74	.15	.05
4.72		.07		.02		.20	.14	1.68			.06	.09	.08	1.40		.28	.13	.11	.25					.03					.21		
4.50	T	T	T	.03		.13	.57	1.50	.10			.06	.10	.41	.25	T	.57	.05	.14					.07	T	.01			.47	.07	.06
4.76		.24	T	.04		.06	.22	.46			.12	.12	.20	1.75		.69	T	.41	.09					.06				.03	.27	T	
3.56		.06		.12		.28	.70	1.08	.08	T		T	.08	.37	.15	.02	.93	.08	.02				.03	.35	T	.13		T	.74	.26	.08
4.12		T	.02			.60	1.13	.28	T		T	.08	T	.72	T	.44	.02	.23	.02			T	T	.04	.02	T		.30	.11	.02	T
3.78				.12		T	.36	.08	.46			.12		.28	.53		.74		.22	.43			T	.17	.05					.22	
3.33		.09	.09	.27		.75	.32	.90	.12				T	T	.43	T	.83						T	.56	T	.14			.38	.35	.10
3.71			T			.03	.55	.43	T			.16	.09	.57	.18	.08	.64	.08	.30					T		T		T	.54	.04	T
4.91		.02		.09		*	1.20	.82	.02		T	.02	.05	.57	.03	T	.77	.10	T				T	.16	*	.12			.72	.02	T
4.72	T	.03	.01	.32		.58	.27	.05	.15		.01		T	.01	.40	.05	.28	.01	.01				.01	.59	.01	.10		.04	.61	.13	.15
4.48	T	.18	.07	.14		.45	.19	.88	.03			T	.02	.20	.27	.01	.88	T	T				.01	.45	T	.06			.34	.29	.01
-		T	T			.62	.70	1.00	.05						.38	-	.60	T					.05	.20		.10		.10	-	.20	T
4.12						.06	.68	.40				.40	.15	*	.95	.29	.47	.14	.15					.01		.03			.38	.01	
4.17	.03	.06		.11		.10	.64	.70	.10			.29	.15	.22	.17	.04	.35	.09	.18				T	.28	T	.09	.01		.55	.01	T
4.16		T	.02			.29	.27	.61			.46	.25	.05	1.04		.38		.30	.14					.08		T		.10	T	.12	T
4.83		.02	.04	.04		.33	.90	1.05		T			T	.26	.11	.06	.76	.07	T				.01	.46	T	.10			.55	.07	T
4.11		.06	.11	.06		.40	.69	.21	.41		T	.06	T	.30	.52		.68		.07	.17				.16		.05				.10	T
3.34	T	.01	.01	.10		.18	.24	.76	.07	T		T	T	.50	.21	T	.61	T	.06					.27	T	T			.25	.07	T
2.31	T	.01	T	.11		.03	.11	.66	.27			.01	.01	.22	.29	T	.34	T	.03					.15	T	T				.07	T
3.41		.01	.02	.08		.15	.42	.05	.05			.16	.12	.33	.20	.02	.35	.01	.04				T	.17		.01			.24	.08	T
5.08	T	T	T	.16	T	.76	.66	.73	.34	T		T	T	.22	.42		1.32	T	T	T			T	.32	.01	.05	T			.07	T
5.20		.08		T		.20	.80	.72			.27	.15	T	1.32		.70	T	.40	.26					T				.05	.25		
4.44		.03	T			.34	.42	.60			.35	.18	T	1.07		.68		.35	.12					T				.15	.15		
4.03		.02				T	.15	.52			.25		.11	1.56		T	.80		.37					.08					.15	.02	
3.16		.17					.40	.77			.15			.60		.30	.30	.01	.05					.24					.08	T	.02
4.19			.05	.03		T	.20	.50			.50	.16	.15	.50	.39	T	.75	T	.56	.02				T					T	.11	
4.09		.02	T	.16		.22	1.03	.96	.02				.02	.30	.08	.08	.63	.01	T					.28	T	.16		T	.79	.10	.03
5.24		.15		.06		.24	.07	.97			.02	.11	T	1.75		.81	T	.22	.53					.04	T				.27	T	
3.11						.18	.76	.16			.20	.20	.52			.15	.08	D.40	.03									.25	.18		
4.53	T	.02		.02		.47	.34	.79	.04				T	.07	.35	.18	1.10	.05	T				T	.41	.03	.05		.03	.46	.05	.07
6.23		.11		.80		.50	.38	.80						1.01		.16	.80	.15	.07				*	.37		.30			.86	.12	
5.92						.06	.30	.74			.05	.09	.55	1.37		.76		.90	.75			.02						.08	.24		.01
3.24			.02	T		.02	.38	.62	.20		T	.18	.03	.35	.20	T	.65	T	.20					.12	T				.15	.12	T
5.39		T	.05			.97	1.01	.18			T	.07		.85		.82	.03	.02	.02			T	.01	.21	.05	.06		.34	.65	T	.01
4.29		.04		.03		.09	.15	.77			.47	.06	.08	1.08		.51	.12	.12	.56					.06					.17		
6.98		T	.07	.04			.15	1.40	.47		.03	.06	.16	.69	.77	.02	.91	T	1.94	.01				.01	.03					.22	
4.77	.02	.06	.07	.09		1.21	.64	.70	.05		.02			T	.30	.11	.38		.02			T	.04	.57		.07			.08	.07	.18
4.68				.26		.80	.76	.64	.22					.20	.21		.98							.56	.02					.03	
6.55				.08			.18	.95	.50		.18	.15	.20	.60	.80	*	.90		1.30	.30				.05	.06					.28	
2.98		.02	.02	T	T	.03	.24	.62			.38	.02	.14	.49	T	.32	.02	.28	.19					.05	T	T			.16	T	
4.10	T	T	T	T		.45	.30	.96	.03		T	T	.02	.19	.11	.06	.66						T	.26	.02	.06		T	.73	.16	
-						.12	.42	.18	.12		.19	.23		.37	.47		.81		.33	.22				-	.06	.03				.08	
3.36			.01	T		T	.31	.35	.24		.14	T	.09	.54	.22	.01	.69		.35	.08				.18	T	.01				.14	T
4.48		.17	T	.02		.10	.10	.58			.04	.10	.10	1.50		.78	T	.40	.30					.06					.23		
4.65		.20	T	.03		.06	.13	.50			.06	.09	.09	1.56		.73	T	.56	.35					.07					.22	T	T
4.41		.12		.11		.10	.15	.44			.03	.08	.12	1.47		.47		.60	.48					.06					.18		T
5.24		.25				.19	.05	.50			.05	.05	.17	1.59		.30	.65	.15	.97					.14					.16	.04	
4.40		.14	T	.03		.05	.05	.56			.03	.15	.10	1.60		.68	T	.58	.24					.04					.24	T	T
4.80		.09	.23		T	.40	.77	.83	.04			.07	.03	.62	T	.69	.01	.17	T			T	.03	.20	.02	.01		.28	.11	.11	.09
3.75		T				.28	.90	.48			.17	.19	T	1.49		.99		.82	.37					.04					.21		
3.03		.05	.06	.11		.08	.18	.40	.30			.01	.05	.33	.36	T	.63	T	.03	T			T	.36	.01	.01	T			.08	T
4.74	T	.02	.01	.16		.03	.22	.39	.28		.27	.22	.08	.82	.20	.01	.99	T	.45	.22			T	.10	T	.04	T		T	.21	.02
3.21		.01	.05	T	T	.07	.14	.49	.25		.15	.28	.09	.58	.28	.02	.56	T	.20	T				.04					T	T	T
3.31	T	.05	.19		T	.68	.87	.63	T		T	T	T	.48	T	.93	.12	.04	T			T	.07	.20	.03	.12	T	.33	.55	T	.02
5.03	T	.03	.09			.57	.67	.58	T		T	.03	.03	.51		1.03	.07	.01	.01			.02	.04	.13	.01	.10		.37	.72	.01	T
4.25	T	.03	.10	.17		.59	.44	.36	.48		T		.02	.24	.42		.61		.05	.16			T	.28	.01	.10	.07	T		.12	T
4.44		.02	.01			.10	.18	.40	.40		.46	.15	.12	.72	.32	.05	.70		.20	.40				.08					.13		
	RECORD MISSING																														
6.49		.04		.06			.25	1.03	.22		.11	.16	.22	1.07	.62	.03	.64		1.48	.16				.09	.04					.27	
3.30			.01	.09		.08	.11	.40	.35		.35	.04	.03	.82	.15	T	.55	T	.16	T				.05	T					.13	T
4.34				T	T	.26	.46	1.04	.03					.29	.03	T	.87	.05						.43		.06		.01	.55	.21	.03
6.03		.04		.06		.13	.33	.99			.21	.02	.12	1.23	1.25	.19	.22	.16	.67					.09		T			.29	.03	
5.50	T	.06	.10	.53		1.10	.75	.78	.20				.05	T	.40		.70						T	.71	T	.08				.02	.02
4.82		T	.03	T		.15	.39	.71			.44	.15	.01	1.15		.81		.27	.35					.13					.21	.02	T
4.23		.08	.05	.19		.51	.15	.65	.04			T	T	.15	.39	T	1.22	T	T				T	.62		.03			.05	.10	T
6.06	T	.15	.06	.50		1.22	.87	1.00	.08	T			.02	.05	.42	.01	.50	T	T				.05	.60	.01	.05			.13	.19	.15
5.56		.10	.02	.07		.02	.70	.84	.02				.07	.68	.29	.07	.92	.06						.28		.11	.02		1.25	.04	
4.81		.13	.06	.13		.59	.33	.90	.13				.04	.09	.16	T	.80		T				T	.44		.09			.36	.33	.03
4.56			T	.26		.85	.39	.59	.16					.36	.29		1.05							.46	T	.05				.06	.03
3.77				.24		.86	.55	.37	.21					.25	.29		.61							.35		T				.04	T
4.42		T	.29	.35		.25	.85	.95	.10	T				.20	.25	T	.62	T	T				.12	.10	T	.04			.22	.12	T
6.52		T	.02	.06		.57	.93	1.04				T		.57		.87	1.18	T				T	T	.13		.16		.35	.32	.09	.03
4.22	T	T	T	T		.32	.87	1.01	T			.08	.07	.61	.13	T	.43	.10	.10					.03	T	.02			.46	.06	.03
4.97	T	T	.07	.05		.38	.70	.88	.01				T	.52	.13	.13	.82	.01					T	.29	T	.10		T	.79	.08	.01
1.98		.10	T	.03		.07	.18	.20	.36		T	.04	D.01	.50	.10	T	.02	T	.08	.05				.12		T				.12	T
2.48		.02	.02	T	.08	.09	.08	.46	T		.03	.04		.53	T	.57	.03	.04	.22				.10	.06	.01	.01			.09	T	T
2.70		.06	T	.01	T	.16	.12	.52	T		.26	.08	T	.63		.40	.02	.14	.01				.04	.11	T	T		.05	.08	.01	T
3.13			.07	.06		.10	.08	.43	.34			.13	.05	.40	.11	T	.78		.30					.15					T	.10	.03
3.90		T				.45	.37	.60			T	.18	.08	.92		.36	.22	.21	.12			T	T	.04				.15	.12	.08	T
4.30	T	.01	T		T	.54	1.02	.57	T			T		.35		.59	.14	T				T	.25	.14	.01	.09		.23	.36	T	T
4.37	T	.16	.06	.17		.35	.24	.79	.02			.01	T	.23	.27	T	.86	T	T				T	.38		.04			.40	.17	.02
3.82	T	.03		.05		.34	.45	.88	T				T	.09	.22	.01	.48	.02					.01	.40	T	.05		.02	.62	.07	.11
5.05	T	.03		.07		.09	.89	.79	.09			.04	.10	.55	.31	T	.66	.05	.04				T	.20	.04	.24	T		.57	.25	.04
4.84		.04		.05		.20	.79	.74			T	.08	.04	.84	T	.51	.29	.07	.02			T		.21	.02	.26		.23	.43	.04	.04
5.03			.06	.01		.01	.48	.88	.10			.35	.16	.70	.26	.13	.84	.15	.36					.10	.03	.01			.34	.07	.01
-		-		.30		1.35	*	1.00	-					T	-		-					T		-		T		T	*	*	1.20
5.24		.01		T		.15	.43	.85			.19	.15	.15	1.29		.60	.34	*	.77					.09		T		.01	.21	T	T
2.93		.04		.14		.08	.06	.32	T		.27	.28	.03	.01		.38	.05	.20	T			T		.35	.01	.28		.31	.05	.04	.03
3.46		.09	.15	T	T	.32	.61	.56			.01	.15	T	.70		.36	.01	.10	T			T	.09	.04	.01	T		.12	.12	.02	T
3.98		.03		.03		.13	.11	.40	.30		.38	.14	.10	.68	.34	.02	.74		.17	.02				.08	T					.13	T
3.40		.02	T	.03	T	.03	.18	.61	T		.23	.04	.01	.68	T	.65	.01	.15	.40				.01	.14	T	T			.21	T	T
4.06	T	.10	T	.08		.38	.60	.98	.04				.03	.25	.13		.81	.01						.35		.06		.03	.52	.27	.03
3.31		T	.09	.04		.12	.12	.32	.26		T	.05	.04	.35	.25	T	1.08		.25					.25	T	T			.03	.09	T
4.93		.06	T	.23		.56	.75	.46	.54			.07	T	.26	.35		.98			.04			T	.50		.07	T			.05	.01
3.91	T	.05	.03	.04		.67	.98	.85	T			T	.05	.75	.18	.12	.75	*	.10				T	*	*	.34			.94	.04	T
4.02			.06	.16		.08	.16	.34	.45		.40	.15	.08	.48	.32	T	.79		.36	.04										.15	
2.89				.01		.15	.15	.30	.48			.09	.07	*	.40		.60		.25											.10	

DAILY PRECIPITATION

Table 3—Continued

Station	Total	1	2	3	4	5	6	7	8	9	10	11	12	13	14	15	16	17	18	19	20	21	22	23	24	25	26	27	28	29	30	31
TAMARACK 2 S FIRE TWR	3.96		.10	.08	.20		.44	.31	.46	.02				T	.16	.28	T	.98	T	.05	T			T	.60	T	.09			.06	.07	.06
TIONESTA 2 SE DAM	4.78	T	.08	.04	.20		.58	.47	.97	.05		T	T	T	.11	.35	.07	.56	T	T				T	.45	T	.08			.44	.23	.10
TITUSVILLE WATER WORKS	5.01		.05	.25	T	.09	.88	.18	.96	.11		T			.37	T	.66		T	T			T	.10	.43	.01	.07		.15	.19	.20	.02
TORPEDO 4 W	6.91	T	.08	.12	.29		1.25	1.17	.99	.30	T				.02	.53	.06	.45		.04				.02	.82	.02	.08			.37	.18	.12
TOWANDA	4.62	T	T	T	.34		1.03	.53	.18	.39				T	.17	.36	T	.93	T	T				T	.60	.03	T	T			.04	T
TOWER CITY 5 SW	3.96						.14	.32	.65				.09	.31	1.02		.70	.05	.19	.11					.04		T			.34		T
TROY	5.39		.01	.03	.29		1.16	.51	.35	.08				T	.22	.66		1.09		T				T	.90		.01				.04	.02
TURLEPOINT 4 NE	5.61	T	.16		.52		1.20	.73	.84	.17				.02	.10	.23	.02	.55	.01	T				.02	.51	T	.10			.13	.23	.13
TYRONE 4 NE BALD EAGLE	4.73	T	.03	.03	.10		.19	.51	1.04	T			T	.11	.38	.46	T	.03	.06	.14				T	.11	T	.02		T	.73	.15	.01
UNION CITY	5.32	T	.08	.02	.11		1.67	.26	.95	.15	T				T	.30		.47	T	T				T	.71	T	.07			.31	.16	.08
UNIONTOWN	4.70		.02	.05			.09	.73	.87			T	.10		.78		.52	.02	.09	.01		T			.37	T	.18		.30	.52	.04	.01
UPPER DARBY	5.08		.17		.04		.14	.07	.83			.06	.05	.17	1.68		.23	.25	.33	.75					.06					.23	T	T
UTICA	5.28		.08		.26		.57	.23	.90	.10					.03	.53	.10	.78	.04	.02					.58		.11		.15	.58	.09	.04
VANDERGRIFT	5.23		.11	.08	.06		.33	1.08	.87	T					.36	T	T	1.05	.02	T				T	.35	T	T			.77	.11	.06
VIRGINVILLE	3.72						T	.09	.62	.04			.12	.34	.94	.21	T	.70	T	.57	.09				T	T						
VOWINCKEL	5.44	T	.15	.20	.14		.53	.17	1.14	.06		T		T	.22	.12	.26	.56	.05	T				.07	.44	T	.12			.53	.42	.26
VOWINCKEL 1 WSW	5.39	T	.16	.20	.15		.51	.21	1.15	.04		T		T	.20	.15	.15	.51	.07	T				.07	.44	T	.08			.52	.32	.26
WARREN	4.11				.29		.37	.32	.73	.16			T		.02	.35		.71	T					.02	.65		.08			.25	.14	.02
WATSONTOWN	-					.10		.10	1.00	.09				.05	D.20	-		D.80	D.10						-						.05	
WAYNESBURG 2 W	5.76		.08	T	.07		.05	.60	.98	.01				.05	.75	.25	.02	1.05	.03	.02					.30	T	.11	.01		1.35	.03	T
WELLSBORO 3 S	4.16		.05	.02	.29		.89	.38	.42	.06				T	.13	.23	T	.72	T	.01				T	.75	T	.03	T			.11	.07
WELLSVILLE	4.34		.13		.03		.27	.37	.46	T		.40	.15	.10	.93		.37	.03	.28	.15									.16	.31		
WERNERSVILLE 1 W	4.44	.03		.22	.06			.22	.46	.55		.43	.04		.77	.56	.03	.60		.33	.03								.11			
WEST CHESTER	5.62		.01	.14	.03		.18	.30	.44			.21	.19	.02	.73	.04	*	.94	*	1.12	.06			.01	.01				.03	.26		
WEST GROVE 1 E	-		.12					.15	.20	.55		.13	.16	.20	1.29	.52	.56	.25	-	.37	-				.12					.37	.05	
WEST HICKORY	4.23		.10	.05	.33		.74	.20	.75	.26					.02	.45	.05	.60							.06		.03			.35	.20	.04
WHITESBURG	3.67			.02	.05		.21	.58	1.00	T				T	.22	.04	.02	.58	.01						.35		.10		T	.32	.14	.03
WILKES BARRE	2.90		.07	.05	.07		.03	.23	.15	.31		T	T	.04	.21	.28		.71		.10	T			T	.22	T		T			.12	T
WILLIAMSBURG	5.34	T	T	.04	.11		.34	.79	1.26	.06			T	.13	.58	.27	.04	.55	.15	.09					.08		.05		T	.69	.06	.05
WILLIAMSPORT WB AP	3.28		.12	.12	.02	.08	.13	.17	.09	T		.07	.02	.01	.60	T	.80	T	.05	T			T	.11	.24	.01	T			.03	.01	T
WOLFSBURG	4.58				T		.29	.84	.73	.03			.17	.13	.60	.18	T	.75	.10	.04					.03		.85			.64	T	T
YORK 3 SSW PUMP STA	3.56		.03				.05	.28	.40			.11	.10	.02	1.11		.56	.06	.23	.33					.02				.07	.19	T	
YORK HAVEN	4.28		T	T	.02		.03	.25	.58	.29		.27	.18	.13	.70	.33	.05	.72	.03	.33	T				.09	T				.17	.11	
ZION GROVE	-				.02		.06	.13	.37	.49		.08	.09		.28	-		.42		.07					.09						.14	
ZIONSVILLE 3 SE	5.01		.14				T	.12	.41	.72			.12	.16	.87	.47	T	.72	T	.78	.13				.08	.03	T				.28	

Table 5

DAILY TEMPERATURES

Station		1	2	3	4	5	6	7	8	9	10	11	12	13	14	15	16	17	18	19	20	21	22	23	24	25	26	27	28	29	30	31	Average
ALLENTOWN WB AP	MAX	47	55	56	47	64	44	48	41	47	54	53	40	36	42	42	29	30	27	27	41	43	46	49	42	35	50	47	41	34	45	45	43.5
	MIN	19	36	33	27	25	35	35	27	28	32	36	30	30	32	29	23	15	15	20	13	10	16	30	22	19	32	26	24	30	32	30	26.2
ALLENTOWN GAS CO	MAX	33	47	55	58	47	65	42	48	42	47	54	53	38	37	44	42	29	32	28	28	43	45	49	51	31	39	50	47	41	36	46	43.5
	MIN	19	23	33	37	27	30	35	35	28	30	35	30	30	30	30	26	18	17	18	18	13	18	25	31	18	19	29	27	28	32	31	26.5
ALTOONA HORSESHOE CURVE	MAX	58	52	55	50	66	53	66	56	47	55	64	43	33	43	42	37	32	28	36	41	47	48	47	40	35	49	50	44	33	37	37	45.9
	MIN	12	38	31	26	29	31	40	20	19	29	40	29	28	31	26	26	15	18	15	14	14	22	28	24	14	29	25	23	26	23	28	24.9
ARENDTSVILLE	MAX	35	53	57	57	56	71	45	52	45	50	58	59	38	37	48	44	32	35	27	35	41	46	52	55	36	43	55	54	33	38	45	46.1
	MIN	17	23	32	35	25	33	38	39	27	30	39	30	31	31	31	27	20	20	20	20	21	20	28	33	19	24	27	29	28	30	31	27.7
ARTEMAS 1 WNW	MAX	55	56	57	60	72	58	63	60	57	67	64	48	40	46	47	38	38	41	49	44	52	55	56									53.2
	MIN	19	34	38	29		37	37	26	23	35	33	27	28	25	27	22	14	14	16	20	16	31	25	27	26	25	25	32	30	41	32	27.1
BAKERSTOWN 3 WNW	MAX	58	55	52	48	65	65	66	59	46	56	63	41	41	40	42	38	36	38	32	39	45	40	46	42	35	50	49	44	60	56	40	48.0
	MIN	18	38	37	36	29	43	55	23	20	28	40	30	25	32	27	25	14	25	22	13	20	24	30	22	18	32	30	28	32	30	25	28.1
BEAVERTOWN	MAX	33	55	54	50	46	67	44	52	48	54	55	61	38	39	41	46	34	32	36	43	47	48	52	49	37	52	50	44		41	43	46.4
	MIN																																
BELLEFONTE 4 S	MAX	31	54	54	53	45	62	44	65	42	47	55	62	38	37	42	40	27	33	28	37	44	47	47	48	35	36	50	49	34	38	39	44.0
	MIN	13	19	31	28	29	37	38	41	16	25	35	31	29	30	28	24	14	17	14	18	12	19	26	24	15	18	27	23	26	29	29	24.7
BERWICK	MAX	49	54	51	47	62	54	54	54	46	53	54	52	41	39	41	38	33	32	33	42	44	51	50	46	36	51	47	41	40	45	44	45.9
	MIN	10	41	28	31	25	39	36	33	25	31	39	32	30	32	28	23	15	16	21	11	13	17	30	26	17	29	24	21	31	32	31	26.4
BETHLEHEM LEHIGH UNIV	MAX	49	54	58	46	64	45	56	39	44	52	50	39	38	42	43	29	31	28	27	41	46	47	50	39	35	50	46	41	34	44	43	43.5
	MIN	20	43	38	35	30	35	35	27	27	34	32	30	32	32	29	20	20	16	22	19	21	23	33	25	19	34	28	25	32	32	31	28.4
BLAIRSVILLE 6 ENE	MAX	54	47	50	46	64	65	60	54	43	58	58	35	37	38	39	33	26	32	30	35	41	40	43	38	31	47	45	39	54	44	32	43.8
	MIN	15	36	29	23	33	40	51	18	16	28	32	27	22	28	23	21	12	19	14	11	18	27	28	19	14	26	29	26	29	26	23	24.6
BRADFORD 4 W RES	MAX	52	53	45	37	46	44	56	47	37	47	55	35	39	37	35	33	28	28	29	37	44	42	38	34	30	44	41	35	40	38	31	39.9
	MIN	-3	32	25	21	21	31	32	18	15	22	28	23	21	27	8	14	2	2	-1	-3	-3	7	27	17	-4	21	15	15	26	24	23	16.2
BROOKVILLE CAA AIRPORT	MAX	55	48	43	43	54	57	63	57	43	56	58	33	36	36	39	28	31	31	33	41	42	41	41	36	32	47	48	32	46	35	31	42.5
	MIN	8	32	27	25	30	39	47	21	21	23	30	26	25	27	24	16	8	18	13	10	6	12	28	17	10	28	20	22	30	28	24	22.4
BURGETTSTOWN 2 W	MAX	34	61	56	55	50	69	67	64	30	49	58	63	36	42	42	45	33	37	40	33	39	47	44	51	33	38	55	52	42	64	41	47.4
	MIN	11	31	25	27	27	41	45	30	23	25	29	31	24	30	27	28	14	18	20	6	7	14	23	25	18	22	19	31	34	28	29	24.6
BURNT CABINS 2 NE	MAX	52	51	50	50	60	54	67	50	52	54	62	38	40	44	45	42	34	27	44	44	49	50	55	50	44	48	50	32	35	42		47.2
	MIN	13	37	27	27	25	34	38	25	26	34	31	29	28	33	30	22	22	18	20	9	8	16	35	20	24	27	25	28	26	30		25.6
BUTLER	MAX	57	59	53	60	60	65	68	65	38	53	59	51	41	41	40	41	32	41	41	40	44	46	45	44	40	45	51	50	60	62	39	49.4
	MIN	13	41	27	32	27	44	53	24	21	28	32	30	22	33	28	29	15	23	21	9	10	17	28	24	19	26	22	28	30	29	28	26.2
CANTON 1 NW	MAX	26	42	45	41	37	48	44	49	43	41	45	48	32	34	35	31	19	27	23	26	35	39	43	35	25	30	42	35	35	32	35	36.2
	MIN	9	13	27	20	24	33	34	34	20	21	25	26	21	23	20	15	10	5	5	10	14	17	21	20	9	12	24	12	15	27	27	19.1
CARLISLE	MAX	56	60	58	55	73	71	53	50	52	59	60	55	39	47	48	43	38	35	38	43	48	51	55	52	44	55	54	48	35	45	46	50.5
	MIN	18	43	36	36	25	39	39	33	29	31	40	32	32	33	32	27	21	20	23	20	25	22	32	31	21	36	31	30	30	32	34	30.1
CHAMBERSBURG 1 ESE	MAX	56	58	58	51	71	45	53	49	50	61	62	45	37	50	44	34	36	27	37	42	47	51	54	47	40	55	55	36	36	43	44	47.5
	MIN	18	44	31	34	24	39	38	33	28	30	39	31	31	34	32	25	21	20	20	13	16	17	31	25	20	35	24	28	29	30	31	28.1
CHESTER	MAX	37	50	55		50	66	45	53	46	50		59	41	40	50	45	42		35	32	42	47	52	53		45	58	51	42	40	48	47.2
	MIN	20	45	33		33	43	38	40	24	33		30	32	36	34	31	23		21	22	26	23	35	38		34	32	30	32	34	34	31.7
CLARION 3 SW	MAX	57	52	44	44	55	64	64	59	45	55	61	38	39	38	40	34	34	35	34	41	44	42	43	42	34	49	49	48	52	44	37	45.7
	MIN	7	37	25	25	25	40	46	22	19	23	38	29	20	32	24	25	7	22	17	6	7	14	26	23	10	28	20	24	32	27	28	23.5
CLAYSVILLE 3 W	MAX	63	56	57	51	70	65	56	60	50	61	62	40	42	46	43	40	38	40	31	42	48	45	57	54	38	57	52	46	63	57	42	50.7
	MIN	11	39	23	26	24	39	46	21	22	22	35	30	24	31	24	25	11	22	19	6	9	14	20	24	18	30	12	32	35	27	28	24.2
COATESVILLE 1 SW	MAX	36	51	55	60	49	61	43	50	45	49	59	56	36	41	46	44	34	32	28	30	42	45	51	52	40	39	54	51	38	36	46	45.1
	MIN	16	20	27	31	24	29	36	37	27	28	38	33	30	32	32	27	20	16	20	13	15	17	26	37	19	22	24	28	29	32	32	26.4
COLUMBIA	MAX	52	56	61	52	69	65	49	51	54	61	57	55	38	46	45	38	36	31	37	46	49	53	54	47	41	58	55	42	35	47	47	49.3
	MIN	18	41	28	37	27	39	38	39	28	29	40	32	31	35	33	27	22	20	23	19	17	21	31	30	21	33	27	30	30	34	33	29.5
CONFLUENCE 1 SW DAM	MAX	30	57	52	58	49	67	67	62	33	47	59	64	33	35	54	45	33	32	32	34	37	46	46	53	31	37	51	52	35	57	38	46.0
	MIN	16	18	30	29	24	38	44	33	22	18	29	29	28	33	28	31	17	18	20	11	13	19	28	26	16	31	23	25	26	29	29	25.2
CORRY	MAX	51	50	44	40	48	58	58	55	40	52	55	37	44	34	38	31	29	32	28	35	42	39	38	30	30	45	42	34	48	45	32	41.4
	MIN	5	34	29	25	34	38	44	20	19	25	34	26	22	29	7	18	8	15	12	-1	1	14	29	20	-1	25	19	18	31	25	26	21.0
COUDERSPORT 2 NW	MAX	49	47	41	37	46	40	53	46	35	46	43	32	33	33	33	28	28	25	30	34	43	40	39	32	30	43	41	30	38	36	41	37.8
	MIN	9	34	24	20	27	34	33	19	15	21	32	22	22	28	14	16	4	8	6	10	9	18	28	12	2	11	13	23	24	28	20	18.9
DERRY	MAX	60	56	53	48	68	67	70	62	45	61	63	46	33	53	42	35	32	37	36	39	47	39	49	50	38	52	49	45	58	55	35	49.1
	MIN	15	32	38	29	34	44	56	23	24	28	45	31	25	35	27	27	19	24	20	9	14	20	30	25	17	31	23	31	32	28	21	27.6
DEVAULT 1 W	MAX	48	53	59	51	64	47	49	46	47	56	54	54	38	45	42	33	34	33	35	40	46	49	49	40	35	51	49	40	35	46	52	45.8
	MIN																																
DIXON	MAX	32	46	52	47	41	56	45	55	43	47	48	52	38	40	38	35	24	28	30	29	39	43	50	41	30	35	46	40	44	38	45	41.2
	MIN	0	1	26	25	23	35	35	37	26	27	31	31	25	28	25	15	18	-4	3	2	1	5	12	26	11	17	24	13	19	32	32	19.4
DONEGAL	MAX	53	48	53	42	62	59	63	54	41	57	59	30	35	47	37	29	28	30	28	32	41	42	47	44	32	45	47	37	53	34	32	43.3
	MIN	7	28	28	22	27	43	49	16	17	23	28	23	18	24	21	16	12	17	14	4	6	14	23	14	11	23	15	26	26	21	21	20.5
DONORA	MAX	55	62	56	56	64	71	70	65	39	57	64	63	41	48	52	45	36	40	41	37	42	50	49	56	36	49	57	54	56	64	41	52.1
	MIN	22	43	34	31	37	47	55	32	25	33	44	34	30	37	31	34	20	30	19	16	20	25	31	29	21	33	27	36	36	32	32	31.5
DU BOIS 7 E	MAX	53	51	41	40	54	47	64	54	40	50	60	37	34	40	37	33	29	28	30	38	42	44	41	39	31	45	43	41	37	37	34	41.7
	MIN	0	35	25	24	28	36	40	20	19	22	36	22	27	30	23	22	2	13	7	1	-3	6	28	21	9	25	16	23	27	23	26	20.4
EAGLES MERE	MAX	27	39	45	38	36	52	40	48	41	37	44	45	32	33	33	30	22	26	27	25	34	40	44	41	25	29	42	35	35	30	37	35.9
	MIN	9	12	25	20	21	32	30	32	18	20	23	23	23	24	19	15	10	9	11	10	14	17	24	18	7	8	22	14	16	24	24	18.5
EAST BRADY	MAX	60	59	50	48	60	68	67	64	48	58	63	51	42	41	42	41	39	40	39	40	47	45	46	39	37	52	50	47	63	60	43	49.7
	MIN	13	42	16	16	26	36	45	24	24	25	33	31	24	33	28	28	12	14	20	10	11	17	29	14	18	31	22	28	34	18	19	23.9
EBENSBURG	MAX	54	52	54	52	65	58	66	57	42	56	61	35	34	42	40	30	31	30	34	39	45	44	43	42	32	45	45	40	41	42	40	44.9
	MIN	8	25	29	23	27	37	42	20	13	27	31	27	25	29	24	23	13	12	15	7	5	12	27	20	12	26	21	22	26	24	25	21.8
EMPORIUM 1 E	MAX	28	54	47	42	42	52	42	53	40	43	54	62	35	39	37	39	25	32	32	33	40	46	45	42	29	33	47	48	35	37	35	40.7
	MIN	5	5	26	26	22	26	38	38	21	22	25	27	23	27	23	21	4	5	7	4	5	11	16	21	8	12	19	14	25	26	27	18.7
EPHRATA	MAX	49	56	59	55	67	55	51	45	48	57	54	48	38	44	43	38	39	29	33	44	45	49	51	45	38	55	51	40	36	46	45	46.7
	MIN	20	38	33	34	28	36	35	33	25	32	37	30	29	32	29	24	12	17	20	15	17	19	31	31	17	32	30	25	27	30	30	27.4
ERIE CAA AIRPORT	MAX	53	45	47	44	48	61	50	36	44	46	56	33	40	35	32	25	25	28	28	31	39	37	35	29	34	42	36	38	54	35	35	39.4
	MIN	18	34	31	27	37	37	31	21	24	27	30	27	22	26	14	20	15	19	12	9	15	29	26	19	15	24	24	24	30	29	27	24.0

See Reference Notes Following Station Index

DAILY TEMPERATURES

Table 5 - Continued

Station		1	2	3	4	5	6	7	8	9	10	11	12	13	14	15	16	17	18	19	20	21	22	23	24	25	26	27	28	29	30	31	Average
EVERETT 1 SW	MAX	60	58	52	57	70	54	66	57	50	55	68	39	40	46	46	33	38	38	35	39	42	51	54	54	38	54	53	31	36	43	37	48.2
	MIN	18	40	32	25	25	40	37	25	25	32	30	30	30	32	30	25	20	19	20	18	19	19	29	22	18	27	21	27	27	31	30	26.5
FARRELL SHARON	MAX	60	58	47	49	57	65	68	58	50	54	60	39	46	40	38	32	37	38	33	41	47	44	42	43	37	53	49	38	62	41	42	47.4
	MIN	18	37	27	24	26	28	30	22	22	29	33	28	23	28	21	19	14	23	18	12	14	24	29	20	15	27	23	26	32	27	27	24.1
FORD CITY 4 S DAM	MAX	31	59	55	50	47	62	68	65	34	44	58	62	37	40	46	42	31	33	35	34	38	44	45	48	32	38	51	50	35	61	40	45.6
	MIN	13	17	25	26	24	40	42	32	21	22	29	29	21	24	27	28	11	15	19	8	10	16	19	24	18	20	20	25	27	27	27	22.8
FRANKLIN	MAX	57	55	50	44	53	60	62	56	45	54	59	38	42	40	37	37	33	35	33	38	44	43	42	41	34	49	49	43	57	56	38	45.9
	MIN	8	39	27	26	31	38	41	21	14	24	35	28	25	32	21	23	13	23	16	5	9	18	30	19	13	29	23	24	31	27	28	23.9
FREDERICKSVILLE 2 SE	MAX																																
	MIN																																
FREELAND	MAX	39	40	44	44	55	51	54	48	48	38	44	45	48	44	43	37	31	22	24	34	40	42	42	41	28	40	40	38	34	34	36	40.3
	MIN	9	33	28	29	24	24	29	28	24	19	33	24	24	24	25	19	15	8	13	12	16	23	23	19	8	23	20	14	24	26	24	21.4
GEORGE SCHOOL	MAX	48	53	60	52	65	53	48	43	47	56	58	51	39	46	46	35	31	28	29	41	46	51	52	43	36	51	50	39	40	47	46	46.1
	MIN	20	42	31	36	31	39	37	36	27	29	28	30	31	37	32	29	20	23	22	14	6	13	28	28	19	28	25	29	33	33	32	28.0
GETTYSBURG	MAX	36	55	58	60	53	72	45	51	45	51	60	61	35	37	49	44	32	35	27	35	41	46	54	55	37	46	56	57	34	38	45	46.8
	MIN	18	30	40	36	27	35	39	40	29	33	40	31	31	32	32	29	21	21	22	20	21	20	34	32	20	20	29	30	28	30	30	29.0
GRATZ 1 N	MAX	31	50	55	55	46	65	40	54	44	47	56	54	37	39	41	39	28	31	26	33	39	43	48	50	32	37	51	48	40	35	44	43.2
	MIN	15	17	30	31	28	33	35	36	25	27	36	30	30	30	30	25	19	15	20	18	18	14	22	27	17	18	30	24	28	30	32	29.5
GREENVILLE	MAX	58	52	41	48	52	65	61	53	48	57	57	41	46	38	35	30	35	35	31	39	44	40	38	37	35	51	46	39	60	39	41	44.9
	MIN	9	38	25	25	36	42	50	24	22	23	40	28	20	30	18	22	15	24	13	5	8	20	27	23	17	25	23	27	32	26	28	24.7
HANOVER	MAX	37	56	58	62	53	73	46	54	46	52	52	62	36	37	48	45	34	36	36	35	42	47	54	57	41	41	56	56	36	38	47	47.5
	MIN	19	21	32	33	29	29	36	36	25	26	33	29	29	30	30	27	19	19	19	15	20	20	23	31	18	29	26	28	28	28	29	26.3
HARRISBURG WB AP	MAX	55	57	59	50	70	48	48	44	50	56	60	43	40	47	43	32	34	27	34	41	45	50	53	46	38	53	51	37	34	43	44	46.2
	MIN	19	41	39	32	29	38	37	29	29	37	40	31	32	34	32	25	22	19	22	25	25	24	33	26	21	36	34	29	31	32	33	30.2
HAWLEY 1 S DAM	MAX						52	37	46	37	43	45	46	35	35	36	32	22	20	28	22	38	40	46	40	29	31	42	35	43	35	38	36.7
	MIN						32	30	31	21	24	27	27	25	26	22	9	12	-3	-1	6	2	4	8	22	8	14	24	10	19	27	27	17.4
HOLTWOOD	MAX	48	55	57	49	64	46	49	46	49	50	52	49	37	48	42	36	36	29	32	41	46	50	54	43	39	52	50	37	37	45	44	45.7
	MIN	41	38	32	33	23	39	38	32	30	36	42	33	33	37	35	26	23	25	23	23	23	24	33	28	25	35	32	31	33	35	35	31.5
HUNTINGDON	MAX	34	52	56	62	50	69	46	63	52	52	61	65	40	39	47	43	32	37	32	41	46	52	50	53	38	40	55	53	33	38	43	47.5
	MIN	15	14	21	26	22	22	40	41	26	28	30	34	23	30	31	28	16	16	19	15	13	13	19	29	19	19	21	21	27	31	33	23.9
INDIANA 3 SE	MAX	58	53	53	47	64	67	68	57	45	60	62	40	40	50	43	34	32	38	36	40	45	44	46	46	35	51	51	41	57	46	40	48.0
	MIN	12	39	23	29	23	43	53	24	22	27	40	31	22	32	28	24	12	20	17	3	7	15	26	24	18	29	19	28	32	24	29	25.0
IRWIN	MAX	58	54	52	58	59	57	62	62	50	65	65	45	40	40	44	44																
	MIN	18	41	30	29	32	42	44	23	23	30	45	32	26	34	29	30	12	27	20	10	15	21	28	26	19	31	23	33	33	29	30	27.9
JAMESTOWN 2 NW	MAX	29	55	52	41	45	52	63	60	29	46	55	65	38	46	35	36	30	33	34	30	36	37	37	35	29	33	50	43	35	58	38	42.1
	MIN	10	20	26	23	27	39	41	28	21	23	27	27	18	24	16	19	13	18	17	6	6	15	25	21	16	21	21	26	26	23	24	21.5
JIM THORPE	MAX	45	53	55	52	65	60	47	46	46	58	52	47	35	35	42	36	34	34	27	40	48	51	51	49	37	50	48	44	40	46	43	45.7
	MIN	11	35	31	33	23	37	34	34	25	30	36	31	29	32	27	22	18	15	21	16	19	14	32	27	16	29	25	21	31	32	31	26.4
JOHNSTOWN	MAX	33	61	56	60	56	70	69	71	31	50	61	65	39	39	50	42	35	34	35	31	42	51	51	52	34	39	54	53	37	51	41	48.2
	MIN	16	25	31	28	27	43	44	31	23	26	42	32	31	33	28	28	17	22	20	16	16	22	29	25	18	24	26	29	28	29	29	27.0
KANE 1 NNE	MAX	25	52	43	43	41	48	45	55	34	40	49	57	32	39	35	37	22	30	31	31	38	43	43	40	28	31	44	40	33	38	33	38.7
	MIN	-2	10	28	24	25	35	36	34	19	20	25	25	16	28	16	19	-3	4	7	-5	-2	7	21	20	-3	10	17	17	25	27	26	17.0
KEGG	MAX	60	53	56	54	69	57	69	59	50	60	66	37	35	52	44	34	35	28	36	41	50	50	53	55	40	51	53	39	39	41	40	48.6
	MIN	17	39	30	29	23	40	39	22	19	30	35	29	30	32	29	24	18	20	17	13	16	20	28	21	21	29	24	30	30	30	28	26.2
LANCASTER 2 NE PUMP STA	MAX	50	57	60	58	69	67	50	48	52	57	56	55	38	45	44	43	35	33	33	45	47	51	54	51	40	56	54	50	38	47	46	49.3
	MIN	17	40	26	34	24	38	36	38	26	27	38	31	30	34	31	26	18	16	21	8	10	15	32	30	20	32	24	27	29	32	30	27.1
LANDISVILLE	MAX	35	50	56	59	48	69	41	50	43	48	55	57	35	37	45	43	33	32	26	32	40	43	50	52	34	41	52	49	37	35	45	44.3
	MIN	19	27	30	35	27	37	37	37	26	32	39	31	30	31	31	26	20	17	20	17	20	20	32	30	20	22	30	29	29	31	34	27.9
LAWRENCEVILLE 2 S	MAX	28	46	50	46	37	46	47	52	46	41	47	56	42	40	35	33	24	27	31	29	36	43	49	42	26	34	46	36	41	41	40	39.9
	MIN	1	2	25	26	25	32	33	34	23	26	29	29	28	28	21	16	11	-2	-2	-4	-5	-2	12	22	12	15	26	9	14	25	24	17.2
LEBANON 2 NW	MAX																																
	MIN																																
LEWISTOWN	MAX	35	58	58	57	50	71	44	60	46	51	59	61	40	39	45	44	30	38	29	40	44	51	52	52	36	40	56	53	36	37	45	47.0
	MIN	20	19	31	29	26	26	39	39	29	31	36	36	33	33	32	28	19	18	20	21	18	18	22	33	19	19	28	28	29	32	30	27.1
LINESVILLE 5 WNW	MAX	54	50	39	42	50	59	60	45	43	52	55	37	44	34	35	27	34	32	28	36	43	36	37	31	34	47	41	33	57	35	38	41.5
	MIN	5	35	27	24	34	40	41	21	21	25	31	28	20	26	12	21	11	22	15	7	10	21	26	20	16	20	22	26	33	26	27	23.0
LOCK HAVEN	MAX	52	54	46	47	63	51	48	52	47	54	63	45	40	40	40	33	39	38	37	43	48	50	49	46	39	51	49	39	40	44	43	46.1
	MIN	15	36	29	30	26	39	38	26	26	29	42	32	31	32	30	23	16	15	18	16	14	19	33	26	16	29	25	23	31	32	32	26.7
MADERA	MAX	28	54	48	49	41	60	50	65	42	43	54	60	36	35	41	38	23	29	28	34	40	43	45	45	31	33	47	45	31	39	37	41.7
	MIN	3	5	23	24	23	24	35	40	17	19	23	27	26	27	24	22	9	9	10	7	4	6	13	20	10	11	16	18	19	23	25	18.1
MARCUS HOOK	MAX	48	47	60	51	60	46	49	44	46	56	54	50	38	49	44	36	35	28	33	42	47	54	52	44	38	54	55	39	38	50	48	46.3
	MIN	27	42	37	38	36	38	37	31	30	38	39	32	31	36	35	26	23	24	24	21	28	29	38	26	21	35	34	31	32	36	35	31.9
MARTINSBURG CAA AP	MAX	56	50	57	45	66	49	66	55	48	58	64	34	34	43	42	30	30	25	35	41	49	44	49	48	35	49	50	32	35	37	37	44.9
	MIN	16	40	30	27	34	38	40	22	23	30	34	29	29	29	27	21	16	19	17	14	13	23	30	19	15	30	26	26	25	28	29	25.8
MEADVILLE 1 S	MAX	30	54	49	41	43	51	62	59	30	44	53	56	38	44	35	34	26	32	34	29	36	42	38	37	29	33	49	42	34	55	35	41.1
	MIN	9	19	25	24	24	40	42	30	21	22	27	28	22	22	16	20	13	16	17	7	10	16	26	21	13	19	22	26	27	24	26	21.7
MERCER 2 NNE	MAX	56	52	49	46	54	62	59	48	46	57	57	37	43	38	42	32	35	33	33	37	42	39	35	34	38	40	38	35	52	35	40	43.4
	MIN	4	32	28	29	25	40	40	20	19	29	35	26	20	25	28	15	20	22	15	20	18	16	18	10	12	14	17	30	31	19	30	22.[illegible]
MIDDLETOWN OLMSTED FLD	MAX	54	57	59	49	69	50	49	47	50	58	58	43	39	45	45	33	35	27	34	41	47	53	54	45	41	53	51	37	35	45	49	46.[illegible]
	MIN	23	38	31	36	28	39	38	30	30	33	41	32	33	35	33	25	22	21	24	22	19	22	34	26	22	23	29	30	30	34	34	29.[illegible]
MIDLAND DAM 7	MAX	55	52	52	45	60	65	65	54	46	56	60	40	46	38	40	37	36	40	33	37	40	42	50	45	36	50	48	38	60	38	40	46.[illegible]
	MIN	22	36	32	30	32	46	54	26	26	32	35	31	29	31	30	20	19	27	22	15	18	26	30	20	20	34	29	35	36	33	32	29.[illegible]
MONTROSE 1 E	MAX	25	40	47	43	32	44	38	47	40	39	40	46	30	34	33	28	20	20	25	22	32	36	44	47	22	27	39	31	38	32	36	34.[illegible]
	MIN	9	9	28	23	23	31	31	32	19	21	24	24	23	24	20	10	11	3	5	10	13	13	22	20	6	7	24	13	15	27	25	18.[illegible]
MORGANTOWN	MAX	48	55	58	51	66	46	51	44	45	56	54	45	37	44	41	33	31	27	29	38	38	45	46	41	35	50	48	36	34	45	44	43.[illegible]
	MIN	16	41	28	30	29	35	35	26	25	30	36	30	28	33	29	20	18	17	19	10	10	18	14	22	18	31	24	25	29	32	29	25.[illegible]
MT GRETNA 2 SE	MAX	54	62	64	49	68	48	51	50	50	50	54	40	36	44	42	32	34	28	33	40	45	50	52	31								46.1
	MIN	14	35	30	29	27	35	37	37	33	31	38	31	30	33	30	21	19	18	21	20	26	21	32	23	20	32	30	26	32	33	32	28.[illegible]

See Reference Notes Following Station Index

Table 5 - Continued

DAILY TEMPERATURES

Station		1	2	3	4	5	6	7	8	9	10	11	12	13	14	15	16	17	18	19	20	21	22	23	24	25	26	27	28	29	30	31	Average
MT POCONO 2 N AP	MAX	38	45	45	38	54	36	50	49	37	48	45	44	31	31	34	26	20	23	20	33	39	43	40	38	27	40	38	39	37	36	34	37.4
	MIN	1	31	28	25	21	30	29	28	19	25	28	25	24	27	20	12	13	3	15	9	15	20	28	20	7	22	25	15	21	28	26	20.6
MUHLENBURG 1 SE	MAX	43	50	43	42	58	49	49	48	48	50	47	44	48	39	40	30	30	29	30	39	45	45	43	41	32	45	42	40	37	40	46	42.3
	MIN	25	31	25	24	25	34	31	30	20	34	34	28	30	30	24	15	11	6	15	9	10	14	26	22	10	24	24	13	26	29	26	22.7
NEWBURG 3 W	MAX	52	59	50	56	67	79	61	48	50	63	59	48	41	47	51	37	39	35	42	41	48	52	59	45	44	49	52	39	42	38	45	49.6
	MIN	20	36	32	32	27	35	36	35	31	31	40	31	34	33	33	24	18	21	26	25	22	29	39	29	27	33	31	30	33	31	31	30.2
NEW CASTLE 1 N	MAX	60	59	51	49	60	66	65	57	49	58	59	41	42	42	40	40	35	39	34	39	44	43	43	42	35	51	50	40	61	55	41	48.1
	MIN	14	41	26	25	30	44	53	24	22	25	38	30	24	31	25	25	15	26	21	6	10	21	27	23	18	25	21	30	32	29	29	26.1
NEWELL	MAX	50	60	53	51	63	68	64	62	37	53	60	60	37	46	50	43	34	35	35	36	40	49	43	54	32	45	54	53	54	62	39	49.1
	MIN	18	41	29	29	29	42	52	29	24	28	41	32	27	35	29	32	18	28	22	17	19	23	27	27	20	32	26	38	35	31	31	29.4
NEWPORT	MAX	35	55	57	58	50	72	43	58	44	52	60	60	37	39	43	45	31	36	30	38	43	50	52	54	36	40	55	53	37	35	45	46.5
	MIN	17	17	30	32	23	23	38	29	27	29	32	32	33	33	32	28	20	20	21	20	12	13	19	29	20	20	25	28	29	32	33	25.7
NEW STANTON	MAX	58	52	55	60	69	71	65	62	48	63	64	39	42	53	40	35	37	39	36	38	48	43	54	46	39	56	48	38	63	38	42	49.7
	MIN	22	28	27	38	40	43	48	22	25	26	33	29	24	29	28	22	18	22	15	15	16	21	24	20	16	26	24	32	32	31	23	26.4
NORRISTOWN	MAX	48	54	60	51	66	48	50	44	49	57	58	46	39	39	42	34	32	30	29	42	48	52	52	41	38	52	50	40	37	48	47	45.9
	MIN	23	41	35	35	33	38	38	30	29	34	39	32	32	37	32	24	22	22	22	19	18	19	32	24	20	33	30	29	33	35	33	29.7
PALMERTON	MAX	46	52	54	45	63	44	47	41	46	51	49	37	35	40	38	29	31	27	29	42	45	49	49	42	34	48	43	40	34	44	42	42.5
	MIN	12	38	33	29	27	36	35	27	28	30	37	32	30	33	27	22	18	15	22	15	16	17	31	21	17	30	25	23	32	32	31	26.5
PHIL DREXEL INST OF TEC	MAX	49	55	62	53	66	50	53	46	51	58	60	49	39	48	43	38	36	32	32	40	47	54	54	48	40	56	54	43	39	49	49	48.2
	MIN	28	45	40	40	37	39	39	32	31	38	41	37	33	38	36	29	25	26	25	23	26	29	40	28	21	36	37	31	34	36	35	33.4
PHILADELPHIA WB AP	MAX	49	54	61	50	65	47	51	45	49	56	59	48	38	48	42	36	33	30	30	40	45	51	52	44	37	52	51	40	39	47	46	46.3
	MIN	24	41	35	36	33	38	38	31	30	34	40	33	32	37	34	26	23	25	23	22	25	27	35	24	21	34	33	31	33	35	34	31.2
PHILADELPHIA PT BREEZE	MAX	48	52	62	50	65	49	53	44	48	57	58	39	39	49	43	36	34	31	31	41	47	52	53	47	38	53	51	41	37	45	44	46.4
	MIN	28	42	38	42	39	39	39	40	30	38	41	38	32	37	35	32	25	26	26	26	27	30	38	42	24	37	36	31	34	35	34	34.2
PHILADELPHIA SHAWMONT	MAX	48	53	60	59	66	68	50	50	47	57	57	59	38	41	47	42	36	33	31	42	51	51	51	51	39	50	52	49	40	48	47	48.8
	MIN	20	40	30	39	30	39	38	39	29	31	39	34	30	37	34	31	23	20	23	20	19	20	30	30	22	30	28	28	33	35	32	30.1
PHILADELPHIA CITY	MAX	48	52	60	50	63	47	51	44	47	55	57	47	38	48	44	35	33	29	31	42	48	50	50	46	36	51	50	40	38	46	45	45.8
	MIN	28	44	40	40	37	37	37	31	30	39	39	33	32	36	34	26	25	25	24	24	28	34	39	25	22	34	34	30	33	36	35	32.6
PHILIPSBURG CAA AP	MAX	48	45	49	40	56	40	63	48	42	53	58	33	32	39	38	24	27	24	32	38	43	42	42	41	30	43	43	30	32	32	32	40.0
	MIN	-2	33	28	24	29	36	37	18	19	27	30	27	27	27	24	17	11	15	14	13	-2	7	30	14	9	29	24	22	26	26	24	21.4
PHOENIXVILLE 1 E	MAX	49	57	60	58	67	63	50	49	48	56	55	55	40	42	47	42	35	33	33	43	46	50	50	48	36	51	50	49	39	48	47	48.3
	MIN	14	36	24	35	23	37	35	37	25	26	35	31	30	34	31	28	19	15	20	16	12	6	22	29	18	26	21	25	30	31	28	25.8
PIMPLE HILL	MAX	25	37	44	44	43	54	33	48	43	38	47	44	30	31	34	32	19	23	21	21	34	40	43	41	25	30	40	34	36	31	36	35.5
	MIN	10	19	27	23	25	30	28	29	17	22	28	24	22	25	19	15	11	8	13	9	13	24	26	21	6	13	22	14	23	24	24	19.8
PITTSBURGH WB AP 2	MAX	59	52	51	47	66	64	67	57	48	56	60	34	40	41	42	35	32	37	31	37	45	41	49	42	35	52	49	36	60	38	38	46.5
	MIN	19	36	30	28	35	43	55	23	24	30	33	30	28	29	29	20	17	25	20	15	16	24	31	19	19	34	29	32	30	29	29	27.8
PITTSBURGH WB CITY	MAX	61	55	55	49	68	68	69	59	50	60	62	38	43	48	44	38	34	38	35	40	47	46	52	49	37	53	51	40	62	41	40	49.4
	MIN	25	42	37	31	42	45	57	25	27	35	36	33	30	31	30	24	20	28	23	20	25	30	36	22	21	35	31	34	32	33	32	31.4
PLEASANT MOUNT 1 W	MAX	22	41	45	43	36	46	33	40	36	39	40	43	34	33	32	30	21	23	28	21	35	38	42	39	25	29	38	32	40	30	39	34.6
	MIN	0	1	24	24	18	31	30	30	19	22	25	24	24	25	20	3	10	-8	0	6	11	6	15	20	5	8	23	14	20	25	24	16.1
PORT CLINTON	MAX	36	44	49	58	60	49	68	48	48	42	52	58	52	40	38	42	44	30	34	31	32	42	51	54	50	40	42	54	40	38	50	45.7
	MIN	12	22	29	34	24	32	35	36	22	27	35	33	30	32	28	24	20	15	19	14	14	13	20	28	17	22	23	26	30	24	27	24.7
PUTNEYVILLE 2 SE DAM	MAX	30	57	52	47	45	61	66	64	34	44	55	62	35	38	42	39	30	33	34	34	40	43	44	44	31	37	50	47	34	52	38	43.9
	MIN	10	16	24	24	25	39	38	31	19	23	23	27	18	23	24	25	8	13	14	6	10	14	19	22	11	15	19	23	23	25	20	20.4
QUAKERTOWN 1 E	MAX	47	54	59	54	66	61	48	48	47	55	52	51	37	42	43	42	32	30	30	42	45	49	48	45	34	47	49	43	38	45	45	46.1
	MIN	26	30	33	34	33	36	36	34	21	28	34	33	28	31	28	25	27	10	19	16	12	14	28	28	17	27	21	20	28	30	29	26.3
READING WB CITY	MAX	50	55	60	50	69	48	51	43	49	56	54	45	38	44	44	34	33	28	33	44	46	52	51	44	37	52	51	38	36	46	45	46.0
	MIN	25	44	38	36	31	37	36	30	29	35	38	32	32	35	32	24	21	22	24	23	22	24	35	25	21	36	33	29	33	34	34	30.6
RIDGWAY 3 W	MAX	54	48	42	42	51	48	63	55	42	54	60	35	40	37	39	29	32	35	34	40	44	45	41	34	32	47	44	34	43	36	35	42.4
	MIN	0	32	24	23	25	37	38	20	20	21	34	28	19	30	20	20	-7	13	4	-4	-1		30	21	4	27	15	22	29	28	28	20.0
SALINA 3 W	MAX	59	55	52	49	65	64	66	59	45	58	62	41	40	48	42	37	32	38	32	37	44	43	45	49	37	50	49	44	60	55	38	48.2
	MIN	14	41	27	28	28	42	53	24	23	27	40	31	22	32	28	25	15	25	20	6	10	19	29	25	18	30	21	31	36	27	28	26.6
SCRANTON	MAX	42	52	52	42	40	56	43	51	47	43	49	50	39	40	39	34	26	22	30	25	39	40	49	46	31	32	46	39	46	37	42	40.9
	MIN	12	13	33	30	28	31	34	35	24	28	28	28	28	29	24	20	18	8	7	16	14	15	16	25	12	13	29	19	21	29	31	22.5
SCRANTON WB AIRPORT	MAX	42	49	44	40	55	42	51	42	42	47	51	37	38	37	32	24	25	28	24	35	39	46	44	40	29	44	38	44	35	42	42	39.6
	MIN	9	36	30	28	28	35	34	24	25	28	34	29	26	30	20	18	11	6	18	11	11	13	31	18	13	28	24	18	28	32	29	23.4
SELINSGROVE CAA AP	MAX	52	54	53	48	66	42	54	50	48	54	54	39	38	40	39	30	38	28	32	39	48	50	51	41	38	53	48	39	35	43	45	44.8
	MIN	13	30	29	27	26	38	38	27	26	29	39	31	31	32	28	22	17	18	21	15	11	15	34	22	18	27	24	23	32	32	29	25.9
SHIPPENSBURG	MAX	56	56	57	55	72	68	51	51	50	61	63	51	37	42	49	45	38	36	40	44	48	49	55	53	42	60	55	47	35	44	45	50.2
	MIN	18	43	38	33	26	38	38	33	27	34	38	30	30	30	30	28	19	19	21	15	18	20	32	30	19	40	28	28	29	30	30	28.8
SHIPPINGPORT WB	MAX	60	55	51	48	63	67	68	59	50	57	62	36	41	37	40	34	33	37	32	37	44	42	49	43	36	52	49	37	62	41	40	47.2
	MIN	18	31	30	30	30	45	56	24	26	30	34	30	29	30	29	22	21	27	21	14	16	23	30	22	21	31	25	33	34	31	29	28.1
SLIPPERY ROCK	MAX	57	52	45	46	48	59	64	59	45	56	59	37	40	38	40	32	32	38	35	40	40	45	42	40	34	50	47	39	59	45	40	45.3
	MIN	15	40	25	24	37	42	45	20	18	25	35	28	24	29	20	22	14	24	18	10	10	22	29	21	15	28	25	26	30	27	25	24.9
SOMERSET MAIN ST	MAX	54	52	55	51	64	60	64	58	44	58	63	42	32	49	41	39	31	30	38	38	44	44	48	48	35	48	50	44	48	44	35	46.8
	MIN	18	37	31	24	30	47	56	22	18	28	40	26	26	29	24	25	26	22	14	7	7	19	28	23	13	28	20	27	27	25	25	25.5
SPRINGBORO	MAX	35	55	49	46	43	50	61	58	42	46	55	43	38	45	40	37	27	25		35	35	40	37	28	28	35	48	31	40	57	44	41.1
	MIN																																
SPRINGS 1 SW	MAX	53	48	55	45	63	59	64	57	43	55	60	32	30	47	40	32	28	26	30	34	42	42	46	49	32	44	47	38	46	40	32	43.8
	MIN	10	34	27	25	24	36	44	17	16	26	31	25	25	27	23	20	14	15	13	6	5	15	24	17	11	26	19	26	28	23	24	21.8
STATE COLLEGE	MAX	52	50	54	44	61	42	63	48	47	55	60	37	37	42	40	27	32	27	35	41	46	46	47	42	32	48	48	33	35	38	38	43.5
	MIN	18	32	31	27	33	35	38	21	23	23	31	29	30	28	24	13	15	18	12	15	16	25	32	18	14	31	29	26	30	30	29	25.0
STROUDSBURG	MAX	42	51	52	41	42	50	47	40	42	52	48	40	36	35	36	25	29	25	28	38	45	47	44	35	29	44	42	41	33	33	37	39.6
	MIN	-1	30	29	26	22	34	34	25	24	21	34	30	29	31	25	20	9	-2	18	5	3	4	28	17	10	24	22	18	24	30	26	20.9
TAMARACK 2 S FIRE TWR	MAX	28	45	46	36	38	49	35	56	44	40	47	58	30	32	32	35	20	28	24	32	37	44	43	42	28	32	44	41	28	31	33	37.4
	MIN	11	11	27	21	21	34	33	34	16	17	23	24	23	24	19	16	8	7	10	8	12	15	25	17	5	5	23	15	17	24	24	18.4
TIONESTA 2 SE DAM	MAX	29	56	47	41	43	52	58	63	35	45	54	59	36	43	35	38	25	33	38	33	40	44	41	40	30	34	48	45	34	50	36	42.1
	MIN	4	6	25	25	16	21	39	34	21	22	27	27	21	28	19	22	7	13	15	3	6	14	18	22	8	18	20	25	21	27	27	19.4

See Reference Notes Following Station Index

DAILY TEMPERATURES

Table 5 - Continued

Station		1	2	3	4	5	6	7	8	9	10	11	12	13	14	15	16	17	18	19	20	21	22	23	24	25	26	27	28	29	30	31	Average
TITUSVILLE WATER WORKS	MAX	55	55	38	42	50	57	62	58	44	44	59	36	45	38	29	31	28	35	29	39	44	41	34	36	31	48	44	34	37	33	35	41.6
	MIN	1	37	24	23	26	36	41	20	17	19	32	25	19	27	14	17	6	18	8	- 4	0	12	23	18	- 1	26	15	23	20	24	26	19.1
TOWANDA	MAX	45	53	46	41	51	48	50	48	44	47	55	38	42	37	37	24	31	30	32	39	45	49	44	33	34	48	41	41	42	44	41	41.9
	MIN	4	37	25	27	24	35	36	25	25	26	37	29	25	31	23	15	15	- 1	14	6	0	5	28	19	12	26	26	14	28	31	30	21.8
UNIONTOWN	MAX	60	56	58	53	71	70	70	58	48	65	65	40	42	56	44	38	34	38	36	40	50	49	55	54	38	53	53	44	62	44	42	51.2
	MIN	19	40	34	30	37	50	58	26	25	30	40	33	27	34	29	25	19	27	23	15	16	21	28	23	20	33	24	34	37	31	30	29.6
UPPER DARBY	MAX	48	52	61	54	66	57	52	48	49	57	58	55	38	47	47	40	33	30	31	40	46	50	51	45	35	54	51	43	39	48	45	47.4
	MIN	20	39	30	38	31	39	37	35	27	31	39	33	31	36	33	30	22	22	21	24	24	21	31	30	20	22	25	29	32	35	31	29.6
WARREN	MAX	54	50	46	40	49	53	61	55	42	53	59	37	45	37	35	30	30	36	30	37	45	40	40	32	35	47	40	35	45	35	34	42.2
	MIN	6	37	30	25	34	38	42	20	20	26	32	27	23	28	15	20	7	16	0	3	5	17	32	20	4	27	22	22	31	26	27	22.0
WAYNESBURG 2 W	MAX	63	57	58	52	70	68	70	58	49	63	62	44	47	52	43	41	34	37	35	39	50	48	56	57	38	55	53	49	62	58	40	51.9
	MIN	16	42	27	28	25	39	50	23	22	26	42	32	29	34	28	27	19	28	23	13	13	18	23	26	18	32	21	35	37	30	31	27.6
WELLSBORO 3 S	MAX	29	44	42	39	37	46	39	49	44	39	44	54	32	34	35	33	19	30	27	27	34	39	41	42	25	32	44	38	35	41	35	37.1
	MIN	8	11	36	22	23	33	33	34	19	20	24	25	23	25	18	15	8	7	7	8	10	13	25	18	7	9	20	13	18	25	24	18.7
WELLSVILLE	MAX	55	56	58	56	68	55	51	50	49	54	59	54	39	45	48	42	34	27	35	42	45	51	54	51	39	55	53	48	35	44	46	48.3
	MIN	15	34	25	36	22	38	37	35	27	26	35	31	31	34	31	27	20	16	22	16	17	14	26	28	20	30	20	29	29	30	21	26.5
WEST CHESTER	MAX	49	55	62	52	65	43	49	44	50	60	54	56	38	45	44	35	36	29	31	42	47	53	54	41	44	55	54	39	40	48	45	47.1
	MIN	31	35	38	35	41	37	38	27	26	38	34	30	32	32	29	21	21	21	19	23	28	34	39	33	19	34	28	31	32	33	31	30.6
WILLIAMSPORT WB AP	MAX	48	55	43	47	62	44	52	50	48	51	55	38	40	39	39	27	35	29	34	42	49	49	48	42	39	52	44	38	35	43	45	43.9
	MIN	13	33	29	28	26	38	36	27	28	31	37	30	30	32	26	21	16	15	19	20	14	18	33	20	17	29	26	21	31	32	32	26.1
YORK 3 SSW PUMP STA	MAX	56	57	61	59	71	70	51	51	50	61	59	59	37	46	48	44	37	38	37	44	45	50	56	53	40	57	55	51	37	45	47	50.7
	MIN	18	44	27	35	26	40	38	37	28	29	41	32	32	35	33	29	21	21	23	9	10	17	29	30	21	32	24	30	30	32	30	28.5

See Reference Notes Following Station Index

Table 7

SNOWFALL AND SNOW ON GROUND

PENNSYLVANIA
MARCH 1956

Station		1	2	3	4	5	6	7	8	9	10	11	12	13	14	15	16	17	18	19	20	21	22	23	24	25	26	27	28	29	30	31
ALLENTOWN WB AIRPORT	SNOWFALL								T			T	.9	T	T		4.8	.2	4.3	5.7					.8	T	T			1.4		T
	SN ON GND	T											T	1				4	3	10	10	5	2	T	T	T	T	T			T	
	WTR EQUIV																	.8	.7	1.6	1.7	1.1	.7									
ALTOONA HORSESHOE CURVE	SNOWFALL								.5				.5	.5	1.0		4.5	6.0	3.5	.5					T		1.0		2.0	2.5	2.0	
	SN ON GND								1				1				5	3	7	4	2								2	2	1	
ARTEMAS 1 WNW	SNOWFALL												-			-	-	-	-						-	-			-	-		
	SN ON GND												1			2	5	T	T						-	-			-	-		
BEAVERTOWN	SNOWFALL								T					T	2.0			7.0	4.0	3.0							T			-	T	T
	SN ON GND													T	-			7	-	7	5	3	1	1	1	T	T			1	T	T
BELLEFONTE 4 S	SNOWFALL	T								T				-	-	-	-	-	-	-			T		-		T			-		
	SN ON GND	1								T				1	3	2	T	7	5	6	4	2	T		2		T			1	T	T
BERWICK	SNOWFALL									T				T	T		2.3	1.7	.1	T					1.0					T		
	SN ON GND	T													T		2	4	4	3	2	1	T		T							
BRADFORD 4 W RES	SNOWFALL				2.0				1.0	.5			T		4.0		9.5	.8	T				T	.5	6.0	T	T			.5	4.0	2.8
	SN ON GND	12	9	7	9	7	6	5	4	4	3	2	2	2	4	3	13	12	11	11	9	9	8	8	14	13	12	11	11	10	14	14
BROOKVILLE CAA AIRPORT	SNOWFALL			T					.2	.2			.4		3.0	T	7.1	T	T	T			T		.1	.7	.1		1.4	1.5	1.8	.4
	SN ON GND	T							T	T			T	T	2	1	T	7	7	7	7	7	5	T	1	T	1		1	1	2	2
BURGETTSTOWN 2 W	SNOWFALL																-								-		T					
	SN ON GND																-								1							
BURNT CABINS 2 NE	SNOWFALL												2.5	.5			3.8		-										1.5	.5		
	SN ON GND												1				4	4	5	4	3	2							2			
BUTLER	SNOWFALL														1.0			11.0	T							T	T	T	T	T	1.0	1.0
	SN ON GND														1			11	9	6	4	2	1	T		T	T	T	T	T	1	1
CANTON 1 NW	SNOWFALL		T	T	T					T				T	2.6	T	T	8.0	T	.1				T	5.0	T	T				T	T
	SN ON GND	T	T	T	T	T	T			T				T	3	2	2	10	10	10	10	8	7	6	11	11	10	8	5	4	4	4
CARLISLE	SNOWFALL												2.0	.5	T		4.0	T	4.0	2.0			T		1.0				1.0	3.0	T	T
	SN ON GND																4	4	8	5	3	1	T							2		
CHAMBERSBURG 1 ESE	SNOWFALL												1.7				3.7		4.2	.6									1.5		T	.3
	SN ON GND												1				4	2	6	3	2	1	T						1	T		
CLARION 3 SW	SNOWFALL									.3				T	.5		T	8.0	T						.5		.8		.5	1.0	.5	1.0
	SN ON GND	T								T				T	1		T	8	4	4	4	3	3	2	3	2	3	T	1	2	2	3
COATESVILLE 1 SW	SNOWFALL													.6			.3	2.5	T	10.0										1.0		
	SN ON GND													1			T	3	1	11	9	4	3	2	T	T				1		
CORRY	SNOWFALL				T				1.0	3.0					3.5	.5	4.8	1.3						1.5	3.0	T	1.0		T	T	1.5	1.5
	SN ON GND	T							1	T					4	2	7	6	5	5	4	3	3	5	8	7	5	3	3	T	2	3
COUDERSPORT 2 NW	SNOWFALL				4.7					1.6				.5	1.1	3.2	.5	10.0						.4	8.5	T	1.7			1.0	2.0	1.0
	SN ON GND	10	6	4	8	7	5	3	1	3	2	1			1	4	4	14	14	13	12	8	5	5	13	12	12	7	5	6	7	7
DIXON	SNOWFALL													.2	1.5	4.5		7.0		.1	1.0				3.0	T	T					
	SN ON GND	3	1											T	2	6	1	7	6	6	7	3	2	2	5	3	2	1	T	T	T	T
DONEGAL	SNOWFALL								T	T			.1				4.5	2.0							2.0	2.0	1.0			1.0	T	
	SN ON GND								T	T			T				4	6	4	2	T				2	2	T			T	T	
EAGLES MERE	SNOWFALL				1.0					T				1.0	2.0	2.0		10.0	T	T				T	4.0	T	T				1.0	.8
	SN ON GND	12	10	7	8	6	5	4	2	2	T	T	T	1	2	4	3	13	12	12	11	10	8	6	9	8	T	7	5	5	5	6
EMPORIUM 1 E	SNOWFALL				T				T	.5	T			.5	2.0	T	.3	9.0	.2	T				.1	3.0	T	1.0	T		1.0	1.5	.5
	SN ON GND	1	T							1				1	2	1	T	9	7	6	4	4	2	1	3	2	2	1		1	2	1
EVERETT 1 SW	SNOWFALL								T				2.5				2.0	1.0	1.5	1.5									T			
	SN ON GND												3	1	T		2	3	4	2	1	T										
FORD CITY 4 S DAM	SNOWFALL	T							T	1.0				.5	.5		.5	9.0	.5	T					1.0	T	.5		T		1.0	T
	SN ON GND	T							T	1				T	1		1	9	8	6	4	2	1	T	1	T	1	T	T		1	T
FRANKLIN	SNOWFALL									-							.5	10.0		T							1.0		T		.5	T
	SN ON GND	T								T							1	10	6	6	5	4	2	T			1		T			
GEORGE SCHOOL	SNOWFALL												T	.7			1.2	3.5	5.0	8.0					.5							
	SN ON GND												T				1	3	7	12	11	9	7	4	3	3	2	1	T			
GETTYSBURG	SNOWFALL								T				.5				1.0		2.0	3.0					T					.3		T
	SN ON GND																1	1	3	6	4	2	1	T	T					T	T	T
GRATZ 1 N	SNOWFALL	T											T	T	1.0		T	5.5	T	1.0					T	T	T			1.0	T	T
	SN ON GND	T											T	T	1		T	6	5	6	5	4	4	3	T	T	T	T	T	1	T	T
GREENVILLE	SNOWFALL			T					T	T					3.5		8.0	.8	1.0	.5			T		.4	2.0	1.0		T		1.8	T
	SN ON GND			T					T						3	T	8	4	5	4	2	T	T	T	T	T	T		T		T	
HARRISBURG WB AIRPORT	SNOWFALL								T			T	2.2	T	.2		4.4	T	9.4	2.0					.6	T	T		1.4	T	T	T
	SN ON GND												1	T			T	4	4	9	5	3	1		T					1		
	WTR EQUIV																	.7	.5	1.4	1.0	.8										
HAWLEY 1 S DAM	SNOWFALL						T			T				T	2.4	2.1		8.0		2.0	2.0				T	1.0	T				1.0	
	SN ON GND	6	4	2	1	T	T			T				T	2	5	3	11	10	11	13	11	8	6	5	4	4	4	4	3	3	2
HUNTINGDON	SNOWFALL									T				.8	T		T	5.2	.5	.8					.6	T			T	4.2		T
	SN ON GND													T	T		T	5	5	5	2	1	T	T	T					2	1	T
INDIANA 3 SE	SNOWFALL	T							T	.3				.5	T		T	8.3	.8						1.0		.7			T	.4	T
	SN ON GND	T								T				T	T		T	8	6	4	2	1	T	T	1		1				T	T
JOHNSTOWN	SNOWFALL	T							T	1.0				.5			T	5.5	1.0	.5					T	T	T		T	T	T	T
	SN ON GND	T							T	1				1			T	5	6	4	2	T	T		T		T				T	4
KANE 1 NNE	SNOWFALL	.2		T	1.5				T	7.5	T			1.0	1.2	1.0	.7	12.0		T				.3	4.2	.5	1.8			.4	4.2	1.8
	SN ON GND	14	12	10	8	8	4	3	3	7	5	4	3	3	4	4	5	16	16	15	14	13	12	11	15	14	15	14	13	13	14	15
LANDISVILLE	SNOWFALL												.3	.5			.5	1.5	.3	.4					.2					1.5	T	
	SN ON GND												T	1			1	2	2	6	5	3	2	2	T					1		
LAWRENCEVILLE 2 S	SNOWFALL				.5									T	.5	2.0	T	11.5	T					T	6.0		T				1.2	
	SN ON GND	2	T											T	1	3	2	13	12	11	10	8	7	6	10	10	8	6	4	3	2	2
LEWISTOWN	SNOWFALL													T	T		T	5.0	T	2.0							T			1.0	T	T
	SN ON GND													T	T		T	5	3	5	2	T	T							1	T	T

See reference notes following Station Index.

Table 7 - Continued

SNOWFALL AND SNOW ON GROUND

Station		1	2	3	4	5	6	7	8	9	10	11	12	13	14	15	16	17	18	19	20	21	22	23	24	25	26	27	28	29	30	31
LOCK HAVEN	SNOWFALL			T						T				T	.5	2.5	T	7.0	T	T					.5		T			T	T	T
	SN ON GND	T													1	1	T	7	5	5	4	2	T	T	1		T				T	T
MEADVILLE 1 S	SNOWFALL	T			T				T	5.3				T	T	3.2	1.0	6.5	.4	.2				T	1.5	.3	.6		T	T	2.3	1.8
	SN ON GND	3	T	T	T				T	5	T					3	2	6	4	2	2	2	2	1	2	3	2	1	1	1	2	2
MERCER 2 NNE	SNOWFALL		T	T						.5								8.0	T					T	T		1.0		.1	-	2.0	T
	SN ON GND									1	-	-	-	-	-	-	-	8	-	-	-	-	-	T	T		1	T	T		2	1
MONTROSE 1 E	SNOWFALL	T			1.1	T				T	T			T	2.6	3.5		12.0	T	T	T			T	3.0	.3	1.6	T			.5	T
	SN ON GND	10	9	7	7	6	5	5	3	3	3	2	1	1	3	7	6	17	17	16	16	15	14	13	14	14	14	12	11	10	10	9
MOUNT POCONO 2 N AIRPORT	SNOWFALL		T				T		T			T		T	7.0		T			-										.8	T	
	SN ON GND		2												7					10	-	9	7	-	-	6	-	-	5	5	-	-
NEW CASTLE 1 N	SNOWFALL	T												T	T		1.8	11.0	.5	T						.3					T	.7
	SN ON GND																-	-	13	-	-	-	-	-	-	-	-	-	-	-	-	-
NEWPORT	SNOWFALL												.2	T	T		T	4.5	T	3.0					.5	T				1.2	T	T
	SN ON GND												T					5	2	5	2	1	T		1					1		
PALMERTON	SNOWFALL								T				T	T	1.0	T	3.4	.2	2.8	1.9					.5	T	T			.9		
	SN ON GND	T											T	T	1		T	4	2	6	6	4	2	T	1					1		
PHILADELPHIA WB AIRPORT	SNOWFALL								T				T	.7			1.3	T	5.4	3.3					.2							T
	SN ON GND													T			T	1		7	7	2	T									
	WTR EQUIV																			.8	.7	.2										
PHILADELPHIA SHAWMONT	SNOWFALL												-	-	-			2.0	1.0	5.0					-							
	SN ON GND												-	-	-			-	-	-					-							
PHILIPSBURG CAA AIRPORT	SNOWFALL		T	.4					1.0	.4			.7	T	3.0	T	7.0	T	2.0	T			T		T	T	T		1.0	1.0	1.1	1.0
	SN ON GND	4	2	1						1				T	3	2	2	9	9	10	10	7	4	3	2	2	2	1	T	1	3	4
PHOENIXVILLE 1 E	SNOWFALL	-	-	-	-	-	-	-	-	-	-	-	-	-	-	-	T	-	-	-	-	-	-	-	-	-	-	-	-	-	-	-
	SN ON GND	-	-	-	-	-	-	-	-	-	-	-	-	-	-	-	-	-	-	14	-	-	-	-	-	-	-	-	-	-	-	-
PITTSBURGH WB AIRPORT 2	SNOWFALL								.3	T			T		1.5	T	9.7	1.2	.4	T			T		.5	T	T	T		1.0	T	.2
	SN ON GND	T							T	T					1		1	9	8	3	1	T	T	T	1	T	T		T		T	T
	WTR EQUIV																	.9	.7	.4												
PORT CLINTON 1 S	SNOWFALL	-	-	-	-	-	-	-	-	-	-	-	-	-	-	-	-	-	-	-	-	-	-	-	-	-	-	-	-	-	-	-
	SN ON GND	-	-	-	-	-	-	-	-	-	-	-	-	-	-	-	-	-	-	-	-	-	-	-	-	-	-	-	-	-	-	-
QUAKERTOWN 1 E	SNOWFALL													T			2.4	3.0	2.0	8.0					T							
	SN ON GND																-	-	-	-	-	-	-	-	-	-	-	-	-	-	-	-
READING WB CITY	SNOWFALL								T				.2	T			3.8		3.1	3.1					.5					.5		T
	SN ON GND												T	T			T	4	3	7	8	6	4	1	T	T	T					
RIDGWAY 3 W	SNOWFALL									1.5					2.0			10.0		T				T	1.0		1.2			T	3.0	.5
	SN ON GND	3	2	T	T	T	T	T		2	T				2	1	T	10	6	5	4	3	3	3	4	4	4	2	1	1	4	2
SCRANTON WB AIRPORT	SNOWFALL								T	T			.4		3.4	T	5.4	.4	.6	2.8				T	.7	.1	.1			.6	T	T
	SN ON GND	4	2	T	T	T							T	T	2	2	1	6	6	9	9	8	6	4	2	1	1	T	T	T	T	T
	WTR EQUIV	.4	.3												.2	.3		.6	.6	.8	.8	.7	.6	.6	.4							
SELINSGROVE CAA AIRPORT	SNOWFALL								T	T			1.0		2.0		4.2	T	2.8	T					1.0	T	T		T	T	T	T
	SN ON GND	T													2	1	T	5	2	5	3	1	1	T	1	T	T			T		
SHIPPINGPORT WB	SNOWFALL								T	T			T		T		7.5	1.5	T						T	T	T			T	T	T
	SN ON GND								T						T		7	6	4	3	T	T	T	T	T	T						
SOMERSET MAIN ST	SNOWFALL		T										.6	.4			3.0	4.0	.6	.4					T	.4	1.0				.5	.6
	SN ON GND																3	3	3	2	1											
SPRINGBORO	SNOWFALL	-	-	-	-	-	-	-	-	-	-	-	-	-	-	-	-	-	-	-	-	-	-	-	-	-	-	-	-	-	-	-
	SN ON GND	-	-	-	-	-	-	-	-	-	-	-	-	-	-	-	-	-	-	-	-	-	-	-	-	-	-	-	-	-	-	-
SPRINGS 1 SW	SNOWFALL								.5			T	3.0	.5	T		3.0	2.0	3.0	T			T		.5	.5	3.0				.5	.5
	SN ON GND								1			T	3	3	T		3	5	7	5	5	4	3	1	1	1	4	T			T	T
TAMARACK 2 S FIRE TWR	SNOWFALL			T	1.0					.4				.3	2.0	2.0	T	11.0	T	1.0	T			T	1.5	T	2.0			T	1.0	1.0
	SN ON GND	9	8	7	7	7	7	6	3	3	2	T	T	T	2	4	4	15	15	15	13	11	9	9	10	9	11	9	8	8	9	10
TIONESTA 2 SE DAM	SNOWFALL	T								2.0				T	.7	2.0	1.0	12.0	1.0	T				T	.5	T	1.0			T	2.5	1.0
	SN ON GND	3	T	T	T	T				2				T	1	2	1	13	12	6	5	3	2	2	3	2	2	T	T	T	3	3
TOWANDA	SNOWFALL	T			.4					T				T	2.0	1.7	T	13.0	T	T				T	5.1	.8	T	T			.1	T
	SN ON GND	2	T		T	T								T	2	2	1	13	12	9	8	6	5	3	7	6	4	1	T	T	T	T
TOWER CITY 5 SW	SNOWFALL												1.0		1.0		4.0		4.0	2.0							T			1.5		T
	SN ON GND	-	-	-	-	-	-	-	-	-	-	-	-	-	-	-	-	-	-	-	-	-	-	-	-	-	-	-	-	-	-	-
UNIONTOWN	SNOWFALL								T				T				2.5	.5	T	T					.5	T	T				T	T
	SN ON GND								T				T				3	2	T	T						T						
WARREN	SNOWFALL				T					2.2					T	2.5		10.1							5.6		.8			T	2.2	.7
	SN ON GND	3	T		T	T				2					T	3	T	10	6	5	4	3	2	1	6	4	4	2	1	T	2	3
WAYNESBURG 2 W	SNOWFALL	-	-	-	-	-	-	-	-	-	-	-	-	-	-	-	-	-	-	-	-	-	-	-	-	-	-	-	-	-	-	-
	SN ON GND									T				T				2	1	T					1	T						T
WELLSBORO 3 S	SNOWFALL				2.0					T				T	1.0	2.0	T	12.0	T	T				T	7.0	T	.5	T			1.0	1.0
	SN ON GND	6	5	2	4	3	T	T	T	T	T	T	T	T	1	3	2	14	14	14	14	14	12	9	14	14	14	12	10	8	9	10
WEST CHESTER	SNOWFALL												1.0			.5	3.5		14.5	.1										T		
	SN ON GND												1			1	4	2	15	14	12	7	3	1	1	1						
WILLIAMSPORT WB AIRPORT	SNOWFALL								T	T			.3	T	2.5	T	7.1	T	.5	T					1.4	.1	T			T	.1	T
	SN ON GND	T												T	1	1	T	7	4	4	4	2	T	T	1	T	T				T	
	WTR EQUIV																	.8	.6	.6	.8	.5										
YORK 3 SSW PUMP STATION	SNOWFALL												-				1.0	2.0	4.5	5.5					.5				.5	2.0		
	SN ON GND												T				1	1	5	8	6											

See Reference Notes Following Station Index

STATION INDEX

Station	Index No.	County	Drainage†	Latitude	Longitude	Elevation	Observation time: Temp.	Observation time: Precip.	Observer	Refer to tables
ACMETONIA LOCK 3	0022	ALLEGHENY	1	40 32	79 49	748		7A	CORPS OF ENGINEERS	3
ALLENS MILLS	0099	JEFFERSON	1	41 12	78 55	1600		MID	CHARLES M. ALLEN	C
ALLENTOWN WB AP	0106	LEHIGH	9	40 39	75 26	376	MID	MID	U.S. WEATHER BUREAU	2 3 5 7 C
ALLENTOWN GAS CO	0111	LEHIGH	9	40 36	75 28	254	7A	7A	LEHIGH VLY GAS DIV	2 3 5
ALTOONA HORSESHOE CURVE	0134	BLAIR	6	40 30	78 29	1500	6P	6P	ALTOONA WATER BUR.	2 3 5 7
ARDENTSVILLE	0229	ADAMS	15	39 55	77 18	710	8A	8A	PA STATE COL EXP	2 3 5
ARTEMAS 1 WNW	0259	BEDFORD	12	39 45	78 28	1250	6P	6P	GRAYSON E.NORTHCRAFT	2 3 5 7 C
AUSTINBURG 2 W	0313	TIOGA	15	42 00	77 32	1590		7A	OTTO D. BACON	3 C
AVOCA CAA AP	0319	LUZERNE	15	41 21	75 44	922	MID	MID	COMBINED WITH STA NO	7905 4/55
BAKERSTOWN 3 WNW	0355	ALLEGHENY	1	40 39	79 59	1230	7P	7P	PITT'GH CUT FLWR CO	2 3 5
BARNES	0409	WARREN	1	41 40	79 02	1310		7A	CORPS OF ENGINEERS	3
BEAR GAP	0457	NORTH'LAND	15	40 50	76 30	900		MID	ROARING CRK WTR CO	3
BEAVER FALLS	0475	BEAVER	2	40 46	80 19	760		7A	HOWARD R. KEMP	3
BEAVERTOWN	0482	SNYDER	15	40 45	77 10	640	7A	7A	MARLIN R. ETTINGER	2 3 5 7
BEECH CREEK STATION	0499	CENTRE	16	41 04	77 34	620		7A	HAROLD S. RUPERT	3
BELLEFONTE 4 S	0530	CENTRE	16	40 51	77 47	1110	8A	8A	ROCKVIEW PRISON FRM	2 3 5 7
BERWICK	0611	COLUMBIA	15	41 04	76 15	570	6P	6P	AMER CAR & FNDRY CO	2 3 5 7
BETHLEHEM	0629	NORTHAMPTON	9	40 37	75 22	400		7A	ARTHUR CROPPER	3
#BETHLEHEM LEHIGH UNI	0634	NORTHAMPTON	9	40 36	75 23	450	MID	MID	LEHIGH UNIVERSITY	2 3 5 C
BLAIN	0725	PERRY	15	40 20	77 31	750		MID	PA DEPT FRST & WTRS	C
BLAIRSVILLE 6 ENE	0736	INDIANA	4	40 27	79 09	2048	8P	8P	U.S. WEATHER BUREAU	2 3 5
BLAKESLEE CORNERS	0743	MONROE	9	41 06	75 36	1650		MID	WALTER WILDRICK	C
BLOSERVILLE 1 N	0763	CUMBERLAND	15	40 16	77 22	650		5P	MRS. B. M. WILLDERS	3
BOSWELL 6 WNW	0820	SOMERSET	1	40 11	79 08	2580		7A	MRS. MAE L. KIMMEL	3 C
BRADDOCK LOCK 2	0861	ALLEGHENY	10	40 24	79 52	725		7A	CORPS OF ENGINEERS	3
BRADFORD CNTRL FIRE STA	0867	MC KEAN	1	41 57	78 39	1500		8A	BRADFORD FIRE DEPT	3
BRADFORD 4 W RES	0868	MC KEAN	1	41 57	78 44	1680	5P	5P	BRADFORD WTR DEPT	2 3 5 7
BREEZEWOOD	0905	BEDFORD	6	40 00	78 14	1352		MID	PA TURNPIKE COMM	3
BROOKVILLE CAA AIRPORT	1002	JEFFERSON	1	41 09	79 06	1417	MID	MID	CIVIL AERO. ADM.	2 3 5 7
BRUCETON 1 S	1033	ALLEGHENY	10	40 18	79 59	1065		7A	AUSTIN R. COOPER	3
BUCKSTOWN 1 SE	1073	SOMERSET	4	40 04	78 50	2460		MID	ALVIN W. MANGES	C
BUFFALO MILLS	1087	BEDFORD	6	39 57	78 39	1318		7A	MRS. NELLE R. BROWN	3
BURGETTSTOWN 2 W	1105	WASHINGTON	11	40 23	80 26	980	7A	7A	SMITH TWP MUN AUTH	2 3 5 7
BURNT CABINS 2 NE	1115	HUNTINGDON	6	40 05	77 52	990	MID	MID	PA TURNPIKE COMM	2 3 5 7
#BUTLER	1130	BUTLER	2	40 52	79 54	1100	4P	7A	WILLIAM C. FAUST	2 3 5 7
BUTLER SUBSTATION	1135	BUTLER	2	40 51	79 53	1140		MID	WEST PENN POWER CO	C
CAMP HILL	1198	CUMBERLAND	15	40 15	76 55	461		6P	JOSEPH N. HOBART	3
CANTON 1 NW	1215	BRADFORD	15	41 40	76 52	1520	7A	7A	MRS.MILDRED SPENCER	2 3 5 7 C
CARLISLE	1234	CUMBERLAND	15	40 12	77 11	460	6P	6P	C. E. MILLER	2 3 5 7
CARROLLTOWN 2 SSE	1255	CAMBRIA	16	40 35	78 42	2040		8A	ROBERT F. MAURER	3
CARTER CAMP 2 W	1262	POTTER	16	41 37	77 45	2030		7A	RICHARD L. MENKEN	3 C
CEDAR RUN	1301	LYCOMING	16	41 31	77 27	800		7A	KATHRYN T.KREIGHBAUM	3
CHADDS FORD	1342	DELAWARE	5	39 52	75 36	160		8A	MRS. GRACE A. WICKS	3
CHAMBERSBURG 1 ESE	1354	FRANKLIN	12	39 56	77 38	640	9P	9P	CHARLES A. BENDER	2 3 5 7 C
CHARLEROI	1372	WASHINGTON	10	40 08	79 55	1040		MID	WEST PENN POWER CO	C
CHARLEROI LOCK 4	1377	WESTMORELAND	10	40 09	79 54	749		7A	CORPS OF ENGINEERS	3
#CHESTER	1423	DELAWARE	5	39 50	75 21	86	8A	8A	CHESTER TIMES	2 3 5
CLARENCE 1 E	1480	CENTRE	16	41 03	77 56	1440		7A	MARGARET A. SWANCER	3
CLARION 3 SW	1485	CLARION	1	41 12	79 26	1114	8P	7A	PA ELECTRIC CO	2 3 5 7 C
CLAUSSVILLE	1505	LEHIGH	9	40 37	75 39	670		8A	WILLIAM J. DOTTERER	3
CLAYSVILLE 3 W	1512	WASHINGTON	11	40 07	80 28	1000	7P	7A	MANUFAC. L & H CO	2 3 5
CLEARFIELD	1519	CLEARFIELD	16	41 01	78 26	1100		7A	IRA TAYLOR	3
CLEARFIELD 8 NW NURSERY	1522	CLEARFIELD	16	41 07	78 32	2120	4P	4P	R. R. HOUPT	CLOSED 5/55
CLERMONT	1529	MC KEAN	1	41 41	78 30	2104		7A	MRS.TILLIE M.SIMONDS	3 C
COALDALE 2 NW	1572	SCHUYLKILL	9	40 50	75 56	1026		7A	PANTHER VLY WTR CO	3
COATESVILLE 1 SW	1589	CHESTER	5	39 58	75 50	342	8A	8A	PHILA ELECTRIC CO	2 3 5 7 C
COATESVILLE	1594	CHESTER	5	39 59	75 49	340		8A	EDWARD D. BIEDEMAN	INACTIVE 12/55
COGAN STATION 2 N	1631	LYCOMING	16	41 21	77 06	640		7A	LEON L. CARSON	CLOSED 3/56
COLUMBIA	1675	LANCASTER	15	40 02	76 30	300	5S	5S	JAMES H. RUST	2 3 5
CONFLUENCE 1 SW DAM	1705	SOMERSET	17	39 48	79 22	1490	8A	8A	CORPS OF ENGINEERS	2 3 5 6 C
CONFLUENCE 1 NW	1710	FAYETTE	17	39 50	79 22	1331		7A	JOHN L. REID	3
CONNELLSVILLE	1723	FAYETTE	17	40 01	79 36	870		8A	MARSHALL B. MENEFEE	3
CONNELLSVILLE 2 E	1729	FAYETTE	17	40 01	79 33	1300		MID	HARRY C. JOY	C
CONSHOHOCKEN	1737	MONTGOMERY	5	40 04	75 19	70		8A	PHILA ELECTRIC CO	3
CORAOPOLIS NEVILLE IS	1773	ALLEGHENY	11	40 30	80 05	720		8A	PGH. COKE & CHEM CO	3
CORRY	1790	ERIE	1	41 55	79 38	1427	6P	6P	GEORGE P. MULDERICK	2 3 5 7
COUDERSPORT 2 NW	1805	POTTER	1	41 48	78 05	2220	7P	8A	J. EDWARD TWIGGS	2 3 5 7
COUDERSPORT 7 E	1809	POTTER	1	41 46	77 53	2425		7A	CAMP POTATO	3
COVINGTON	1832	TIOGA	15	41 45	77 05	1193		7A	GROVER D. CLEVELAND	3
CREEKSIDE	1881	INDIANA	1	40 41	79 12	1035		7A	CORPS OF ENGINEERS	3
CRESSON 2 SE	1895	CAMBRIA	6	40 27	78 34	2540		7A	MILES A. VECELLIO	3 C
CUSTER CITY 2 W	1978	MC KEAN	1	41 55	78 41	2120		8A	M. D. BOOTH AND CO	3
DANVILLE	2013	MONTOUR	15	40 58	76 37	460		7A	MRS.MARIE M. LITTLE	3
DERRY	2108	WESTMORELAND	4	40 20	79 18	1150	6P	6P	MISS N. D. WINEMAN	2 3 5
DEVAULT 1 W	2116	CHESTER	14	40 05	75 33	360	MID	MID	PA TURNPIKE COMM	2 3 5
DINGMANS FERRY	2160	PIKE	5	41 13	74 52	360		MID	CLARENCE H. SMITH	C
DIXON	2171	WYOMING	15	41 34	75 54	620	7A	7A	HAROLD J. KUSCHEL	2 3 5 7 C
DONEGAL	2183	WESTMORELAND	17	40 07	79 23	1746	MID	MID	PA TURNPIKE COMM	2 3 5 7
#DONORA	2190	WASHINGTON	10	40 11	79 51	814	NOON	NOON	DONORA ZINC WORKS	2 3 5
DOYLESTOWN	2221	BUCKS	5	40 18	75 08	393		5P	GEORGE HART	3
DRIFTWOOD	2245	CAMERON	16	41 20	78 08	880		MID	SIDNEY KENNEDY	C
DU BOIS 7 E	2265	CLEARFIELD	16	41 06	78 38	1670	5P	5P	CITY OF DU BOIS	2 3 5 C
DUNLO	2298	CAMBRIA	4	40 17	78 43	2410		MID	MRS. D. L. WHITE	C
DUSHORE 3 NE	2324	SULLIVAN	16	41 33	76 21	1750		7A	PATRICK P. RYAN	3 C
EAGLES MERE	2343	SULLIVAN	16	41 24	76 35	2020	7A	7A	MRS.ELSIE P. BIGGER	2 3 5 7 C
EAST BRADY	2363	CLARION	1	40 59	79 37	820	5P	5P	A. B. KEMPEL	2 3 5
E. WATERFORD 3 E	2459	PERRY	6	40 21	77 33	2125	8A	8A	U.S. WEATHER BUREAU	INACTIVE 5/55
EBENSBURG	2466	CAMBRIA	4	40 29	78 43	2090	7P	7A	ROBERT A. MASSER	2 3 5
EDINBORO	2514	ERIE	1	41 52	80 08	1220		8A	EDINBORO ST TCHR COL	3
ELIZABETHTOWN	2560	LANCASTER	15	40 09	76 37	460		8A	MASONIC HOME	3
EMPORIUM 1 E	2633	CAMERON	16	41 31	78 13	1160	7A	7A	RUSSELL E.PALMATEER	2 3 5 7 C
ENGLISH CENTER	2644	LYCOMING	16	41 26	77 17	881		7A	WILLIAM SUDERS	3 C
EPHRATA	2662	LANCASTER	15	40 11	76 10	465	6P	6P	STANLEY L.VON NEIDA	2 3 5
EQUINUNK	2669	WAYNE	5	41 51	75 13	900		8A	MRS.ROSE M. NEILSEN	3
ERIE CAA AIRPORT	2682	ERIE	8	42 05	80 12	732	MID	MID	CIVIL AERO. ADM.	2 3 5
EVERETT 1 SW	2721	BEDFORD	6	40 00	78 23	1020	MID	MID	PA TURNPIKE COMM	2 3 5 7 C
FARRELL-SHARON	2814	MERCER	2	41 14	80 30	865	7P	7P	SHARON STEEL CORP	2 3 5
FORD CITY 4 S DAM	2942	ARMSTRONG	1	40 43	79 30	950	8A	8A	CORPS OF ENGINEERS	2 3 5 6 7 C
FRANKLIN	3028	VENANGO	1	41 23	79 49	987	7P	7A	JAMES K. ELLIOTT	2 3 5 7 C
FREDERICKSVILLE 2 SE	3047	BERKS	14	40 26	75 40	950	8A	8A	D. P. FENSTERMACHER	2 3 5
FREELAND	3056	LUZERNE	15	41 01	75 54	1900	6P	8A	ANDREW B. EVANSHA	2 3 5
GALETON	3130	POTTER	16	41 44	77 39	1325		7A	W. GALE LUSH	3
GEIGERTOWN	3189	BERKS	14	40 13	75 50	400		8A	WALTER C. WOLF	3
GEORGE SCHOOL	3200	BUCKS	5	40 13	74 56	135	7P	7P	GEORGE M. HART	2 3 5 7
#GETTYSBURG	3218	ADAMS	12	39 50	77 14	540	9A	9A	HUGH C. MC ILHENNY	2 3 5 7
GETTYSBURG 1 S	3223	ADAMS	12	39 48	77 14	560		MID	NAT MILITARY PARK	C
GIFFORD	3237	MC KEAN	1	41 51	78 36	2220		8A	SOUTH PENN OIL CO	3
GLENCOE	3298	SOMERSET	12	39 49	78 51	1620		MID	MRS. MARY M.HARTMAN	C
GLEN HAZEL 2 NE DAM	3311	ELK	1	41 34	78 36	1725		8A	CORPS OF ENGINEERS	3 C
GLEN ROCK	3330	YORK	15	39 48	76 44	620		MID	MRS.E.C.MC WILLIAMS	C
GLENWILLARD DASH DAM	3349	ALLEGHENY	11	40 33	80 13	705		7A	CORPS OF ENGINEERS	3
GORDON	3379	SCHUYLKILL	15	40 45	76 20	900	6P	6P	MISS S. M. JOHNSON	CLOSED 2/56
GOULDSBORO	3394	WAYNE	9	41 15	75 27	1890		7A	L. H. EILENBERGER	3
GRANTVILLE 2 SW	3422	DAUPHIN	15	40 22	76 41	510		5S	EARL E. RHOADS	3
GRATERFORD	3435	MONTGOMERY	14	40 14	75 27	160		7A	CLAUDE K. KULP	3
GRATZ 1 N	3438	DAUPHIN	15	40 38	76 43	760	8A	8A	LEE M. LEITZEL	2 3 5 7 C
GREENSBORO LOCK 7	3503	GREENE	10	39 47	79 55	808		7A	CORPS OF ENGINEERS	3
GREENSBURG 2 E	3515	WESTMORELAND	10	40 18	79 31	1225		MID	PA DEPT HIGHWAYS	C
GREENSBURG 3 SE	3516	WESTMORELAND	10	40 17	79 30	1245		6P	WESTMORELAND WTR CO	3
GREENVILLE	3526	MERCER	2	41 24	80 23	1026	6P	6P	C. EARL MILLER	2 3 5 7
HANOVER	3662	YORK	15	39 48	76 59	600	8A	8A	HANOVER EVENING SUN	2 3 5
#HARRISBURG WB AP	3699	YORK	15	40 13	76 51	335	MID	MID	U.S. WEATHER BUREAU	2 3 5 7 C
HARRISBURG NORTH	3704	DAUPHIN	15	40 18	76 54	323		9A	GEORGE S. BEAL	3
HAWLEY	3758	WAYNE	5	41 29	75 10	880		7A	MRS.KATHERINE S.BATES	3
HAWLEY 1 S DAM	3761	WAYNE	5	41 28	75 11	1200	7A	7A	PA POWER & LIGHT CO	2 3 5 6 7 C
HOLLIDAYSBURG	4001	BLAIR	6	40 26	78 24	960		MID	JOHN H. RINGLER	C
HOLLISTERVILLE	4008	WAYNE	5	41 23	75 26	1360		8A	PA POWER & LIGHT CO	3
#HOLTWOOD	4019	LANCASTER	15	39 50	76 20	187	MID	8A	PA POWER & LIGHT CO	2 3 5 C
HOME	4027	INDIANA	1	40 45	79 06	1220		MID	MRS. EDNA M. BUSH	C
HONESDALE 4 NW	4043	WAYNE	5	41 37	75 19	1410		9A	GEORGE C. WILLIAMS	3
HONESDALE 6 NNW	4044	WAYNE	5	41 39	75 17	1050		MID	FRIEND E. WALTER	C
HOOVERSVILLE	4058	SOMERSET	4	40 09	78 55	1660		7A	PA ELECTRIC CO	3
HOP BOTTOM 2 SE	4066	SUSQUEHANNA	15	41 43	75 45	900		7A	JOSEPH J. SANSUSKAS	3
HUNTINGDON	4159	HUNTINGDON	15	40 29	78 01	660	7A	7A	JOHN R. HENDERSON	2 3 5 7
HUNTSDALE	4166	CUMBERLAND	15	40 06	77 18	610		8A	METRO P. DOROSH	3 C
HYNDMAN	4190	BEDFORD	12	39 49	78 43	970		8A	MRS.GERTRUDE M.BURTON	3
INDIANA 3 SE	4214	INDIANA	4	40 36	79 07	1102	7P	7A	CLYMER WATER SVC CO	2 3 5 7 C
IRWIN	4276	WESTMORELAND	10	40 20	79 42	1100	5P	5P	WESTMORELAND WTR CO	2 3 5
JACKSON SUMMIT	4304	TIOGA	15	41 57	77 01	1690		MID	ARCHIE LAIN	C
JAMESTOWN 2 NW	4325	CRAWFORD	2	41 30	80 28	1050	8A	8A	DEPT FOREST & WTRS	2 3 5 6 C
JIM THORPE	4370	CARBON	9	40 52	75 45	830	5P	5P	HENRY S. HAAK	2 3 5
#JOHNSTOWN	4385	CAMBRIA	4	40 20	78 55	1214	9A	9A	JOHNSTOWN TRIBUNE	2 3 5 7
JOHNSTOWN 2	4390	CAMBRIA	4	40 19	78 55	1275		MID	CITY OF JOHNSTOWN	C
KANE 1 NNE	4432	MC KEAN	1	41 41	78 48	1750	8A	8A	SPRING WATER CO	2 3 5 7 C
KARTHAUS	4450	CLEARFIELD	16	41 07	78 07	950		7A	JEROME S. HOWE	3
KEATING SUMMIT	4466	POTTER	1	41 41	78 11	1840		7A	EUGENE L. KREITNER	3
KEGG	4481	BEDFORD	6	39 59	78 43	1280	MID	MID	PA TURNPIKE COMM	2 3 5
KITTANNING LOCK 7	4611	ARMSTRONG	1	40 49	79 32	790		7A	CORPS OF ENGINEERS	3
KREGAR 4 SE	4667	WESTMORELAND	17	40 06	79 14	2530		MID	PA TURNPIKE COMM	3
KRESGEVILLE 3 W	4672	CARBON	9	40 54	75 34	720		9A	CITY OF BETHLEHEM	3
LAFAYETTE MC KEAN PARK	4706	MC KEAN	1	41 48	78 40	2130		8A	CHARLES GORDON	3
LAKEVILLE 1 NNE	4733	WAYNE	5	41 27	75 16	1440		8A	MRS. GLADYS REINEKE	3
LANCASTER 2 NE PUMP STA	4758	LANCASTER	15	40 03	76 17	255	6P	6P	LANCASTER WATER BUR	2 3 5
LANCASTER 2 NE FILT PLT	4763	LANCASTER	15	40 03	76 17	270		MID	LANCASTER WATER BUR	C
LANDISVILLE	4778	LANCASTER	15	40 08	76 25	410	8A	8A	PA STATE COLLEGE	2 3 5 6 7 C
LATROBE	4832	WESTMORELAND	4	40 19	79 23	1000		MID	WEST PENN POWER CO	3
LAURELTON STATE VILLAGE	4853	UNION	15	40 54	77 13	880		MID	PA DEPT OF WELFARE	C
LAWRENCEVILLE 2 S	4873	TIOGA	15	41 59	77 07	1000	7A	7A	HARRY P. HOWLAND	2 3 5 7
LEBANON 2 NW	4891	LEBANON	15	40 22	76 28	600	6P	6P	LEBANON BDCSTG CO	2 3 5 7
LEBANON 3 SW	4896	LEBANON	15	40 19	76 28	490		MID	THOMAS DONNACHIE	C
LEHIGHTON	4934	CARBON	9	40 50	75 43	580		7A	GOODWIN S. DEFREHN	3 C
LE ROY	4972	BRADFORD	15	41 41	76 43	1040		6P	MRS.DIMMIS M.BAILEY	3
LEWIS RUN 3 S	4984	MC KEAN	1	41 50	78 39	1700		7A	SOUTH PENN OIL CO	3 C
LEWISTOWN	4992	MIFFLIN	6	40 35	77 35	480	7A	7A	AMERICAN VISCOSE CO	2 3 5 7 C
LINESVILLE 5 WNW	5050	CRAWFORD	2	41 41	80 31	1020	7P	8A	MISS RETTA M. CRUMB	2 3 5
LOCK HAVEN	5104	CLINTON	16	41 08	77 27	570	7P	7A	PETER L. STEVENSON	2 3 5 7
LOCK HAVEN 2	5109	CLINTON	16	41 08	77 27	630		MID	HUGH F. PARKER	C
LONG POND 2 W	5160	MONROE	9	41 03	75 30	1860		7A	THOMAS MECKES	3
MADERA	5336	CLEARFIELD	16	40 50	78 26	1460	7A	7A	MRS. JULIA J. SHOFF	2 3 5 C
MAHAFFEY	5342	CLEARFIELD	16	40 53	78 44	1280		7A	MISS ELLEN J. MILES	3
MAPLE GLEN	5368	MONTGOMERY	5	40 11	75 11	380		6P	FRANCES E.SCHEIBNER	3
MAPLETON DEPOT	5381	HUNTINGDON	6	40 24	77 56	580		7A	MRS. I. S. BUCHANAN	3
MARCUS HOOK	5390	DELAWARE	5	39 49	75 25	12	MID	MID	SUN OIL CO	2 3 5
MARIENVILLE 1 SW	5400	FOREST	1	41 27	79 09	1700		MID	ROY A. MARKER	C
MARION CENTER 2 SE	5408	INDIANA	1	40 45	79 02	1610		7A	CORPS OF ENGINEERS	3
MARTINSBURG 1 SW	5453	BLAIR	6	40 18	78 20	1360		MID	BLUE MT CANNERIES	C
MARTINSBURG CAA AP	5454	BLAIR	6	40 18	78 19	1463	MID	MID	CIVIL AERO. ADM.	2 3 5
MATAMORAS	5470	PIKE	5	41 22	74 42	439		7A	HARRY BISLAND	3
MAYBURG	5490	FOREST	1	41 36	79 13	1150		7A	CORPS OF ENGINEERS	3
MC CONNELSBURG	5526	FULTON	12	39 56	78 00	895		8A	MRS. HELEN M.SHIVES	3
MC KEESPORT	5573	ALLEGHENY	10	40 21	79 52	720		8A	NATIONAL TUBE CO	3
MEADOW RUN PONDS	5601	LUZERNE	15	41 13	75 40	1995		MID	GEORGE PEARAGE	C
MEADVILLE 1 S	5606	CRAWFORD	1	41 38	80 10	1065	8A	8A	CITY OF MEADVILLE	2 3 5 7 C
MEDIX RUN	5627	ELK	16	41 17	78 24	1100		7A	MRS. E. M. SNYDER	3 C
MERCER 2 NNE	5651	MERCER	2	41 15	80 13	1160	7P	7A	WILLIAM K. STRUTHERS	2 3 5 7
MERCER HIWAY SHED	5654	MERCER	2	41 14	80 15	1250		MID	PA DEPT HIGHWAYS	C
MERCERSBURG	5662	FRANKLIN	12	39 50	77 54	605		8A	ROLLIN P. GILBERT	3
MERWINSBURG	5676	MONROE	9	40 58	75 28	920		MID	GERALD D. MURPHY	C
MEYERSDALE	5684	SOMERSET	17	39 49	79 02	2080		8A	JOHN H. BLOCHER	3
MIDDLETOWN OLMSTED FLD	5709	DAUPHIN	15	40 11	76 46	305	MID	MID	U. S. AIR FORCE	2 3 5
MIDLAND DAM 7	5710	BEAVER	11	40 38	80 28	689	11P	7A	CORPS OF ENGINEERS	2 3 5
MILAN	5731	BRADFORD	15	41 55	76 31	760		MID	W. S. ROBERTS	CLOSED 6/55
MILANVILLE	5738	WAYNE	5	41 40	75 04	760		8A	CHARLES W. DAVIS	3
MILLERSBURG 2 E	5775	DAUPHIN	15	40 32	76 56	560		MID	RUSSELL SHEPLEY	C
MILLHEIM	5790	CENTRE	15	40 54	77 29	1090		7A	NEVIN E. BOWERSOX	3
MILLVILLE 2 SW	5817	COLUMBIA	15	41 06	76 34	860		7A	KENNETH LEIGHOW	3 C
MILROY	5825	MIFFLIN	6	40 43	77 35	770		8A	THOMAS C. HARBESON	3
MONTROSE 1 E	5915	SUSQUEHANNA	15	41 50	75 51	1630	7A	7A	WILMER W. HOOPES,JR	2 3 5 7 C
MORGANTOWN	5956	BERKS	15	40 09	75 54	595	MID	MID	PA TURNPIKE COMM	2 3 5
MT GRETNA 2 SE	6028	LANCASTER	15	40 14	76 26	670	MID	MID	PA TURNPIKE COMM	2 3 5
MOUNT POCONO 2 N AP	6055	MONROE	5	41 09	75 22	1915	5P	5P	H. JOHN DAVIS, JR.	2 3 5 7 C
MOUNT UNION 1 N	6067	MIFFLIN	6	40 24	77 53	820		MID	MT UNION WTR WORKS	C
MUHLENBURG 1 SE	6090	LUZERNE	15	41 13	76 08	1110	6P	6P	THEODORE J. SAMPSON	2 3 5
MURRYSVILLE	6111	WESTMORELAND	10	40 26	79 42	903		MID	DAVID C. SHAW	C
MYERSTOWN	6126	LEBANON	14	40 22	76 18	480		8A	MRS.KATHLEEN WANDELL	3
NATRONA LOCK 4	6151	ALLEGHENY	1	40 37	79 43	800		7A	CORPS OF ENGINEERS	3
NEFFS MILLS 3 NE	6174	HUNTINGDON	6	40 40	77 55	900		MID	PA STATE UNIVERSITY	C
NESHAMINY FALLS	6194	BUCKS	5	40 09	74 57	60		MID	PHILA SUB WATER CO	3
NEWBURG 3 W	6225	FRANKLIN	15	40 09	77 37	745	MID	MID	PA TURNPIKE COMM	2 3 5
NEW CASTLE 1 N	6233	LAWRENCE	2	41 01	80 22	900	5P	7A	BAXTER F. JOHNSON	2 3 5 7 C
#NEWELL	6246	FAYETTE	10	40 05	79 54	805	NOON	NOON	GENERAL CHEMICAL CO	2 3 5
NEW PARK	6289	YORK	15	39 44	76 30	780		6P	CLINTON J. ALLEN	3
NEWPORT	6297	PERRY	6	40 29	77 08	400	7A	7A	MRS. FRANCES K. FRY	2 3 5 7
NEW STANTON	6310	WESTMORELAND	10	40 13	79 36	980	MID	MID	PA TURNPIKE COMM	2 3 5
NEW TRIPOLI	6326	LEHIGH	14	40 41	75 45	570		6P	FRED C. OSWALD	3
NORRISTOWN	6370	MONTGOMERY	14	40 07	75 21	75	MID	8A	GEORGE H. BOONE	2 3 5
NORTH EAST 2 SE	6396	ERIE	8	42 12	79 49	1060		9A	ELLSWORTH WEAVER	3
ORWELL 3 N	6621	BRADFORD	15	41 55	76 16	1620		8A	WILLIAM I. BROWN	3
PALM	6681	MONTGOMERY	14	40 26	75 32	390		8A	FRED C. ESCHBACH	3
#PALMERTON	6689	CARBON	9	40 48	75 37	435	MID	MID	NEW JERSEY ZINC CO	2 3 5 7 C
PARKER	6721	ARMSTRONG	1	41 05	79 41	1140		7A	LOUIS A. MALARKEY	3
PARKER 1 E	6724	CLARION	1	41 06	79 40	1100		MID	P. M. NEELY	C
PAUPACK 2 WNW	6762	PIKE	5	41 24	75 14	1360		8A	MISS L. VETTERLEIN	3
PECKS POND	6786	PIKE	5	41 17	75 06	1380		9A	MRS. CARRIE NESS	3
#PHILA DREXEL INST OF TEC	6879	PHILADELPHIA	14	39 57	75 11	30	MID	MID	FRANCIS K. DAVIS,JR	2 3 5
PHILADELPHIA WB AP	6889	PHILADELPHIA	5	39 53	75 14	13	MID	MID	U.S. WEATHER BUREAU	2 3 5 7 C
#PHILADELPHIA PT BREEZE	6899	PHILADELPHIA	5	39 55	75 12	85	MID	MID	ATLANTIC REFINING	2 3 5 C
PHILADELPHIA SHAWMONT	6904	PHILADELPHIA	5	40 02	75 15	70	7P	7P	SCHUYLKILL NAVIG CO	2 3 5 7
#PHILADELPHIA CITY	6909	PHILADELPHIA	5	39 57	75 09	26	9A	9A	USN HYDROGRAPHIC OFF	2 3 5 C
PHILIPSBURG CAA AP	6916	CENTRE	6	40 54	78 05	1918	8P	8P	CIVIL AERO. ADM.	2 3 5 7 C
PHOENIXVILLE 1 E	6927	CHESTER	14	40 07	75 30	105	6P	MID	PHILA SUB WATER CO	2 3 5 7 C
PIKES CREEK	6939	LUZERNE	15	41 18	76 08	1320		MID	HARRY SHELDON	3 C
PIMPLE HILL	6944	MONROE	9	41 02	75 30	2215	9A	9A	PA DEPT FRST & WTRS	2 3 5 6
PINE GROVE 1 NE	6954	SCHUYLKILL	15	40 34	76 22	535		8A	PA POWER & LIGHT CO	3
PITTSBURGH WB AP 2	6993	ALLEGHENY	11	40 30	80 13	1151	MID	MID	U.S. WEATHER BUREAU	2 3 5 7 C
#PITTSBURGH WB CITY	6997	ALLEGHENY	11	40 27	80 00	749	MID	MID	U.S. WEATHER BUREAU	2 3 5 C
PLEASANT MOUNT 1 W	7029	WAYNE	5	41 44	75 27	1800	8A	8A	PA FISH COMM	2 3 5 C
PORT CLINTON	7116	SCHUYLKILL	14	40 35	76 02	450	7A	7A	MRS. ADA E. RARICK	2 3 5 7 C
PORTLAND	7127	NORTHAMPTON	5	40 55	75 06	295		8A	JOINT BRIDGE COMM	3
POTTSTOWN	7149	MONTGOMERY	14	40 15	75 39	160		8A	MILES E. SMITH	3
POTTSVILLE PALO ALTO BR	7161	SCHUYLKILL	14	40 41	76 11	640		8A	JOHN M. SMITH	3
PUNXSUTAWNEY	7217	JEFFERSON	1	40 57	79 00	1298		MID	JOHN VOLANSKY	C
PUTNEYVILLE 2 SE DAM	7229	ARMSTRONG	1	40 55	79 17	1270	8A	8A	CORPS OF ENGINEERS	2 3 5 C
QUAKERTOWN 1 E	7239	BUCKS	5	40 26	75 20	490	5P	5P	DENNIS K. FLUCK	2 3 5 7
RAYMOND	7310	POTTER	13	41 52	77 52	2220		7A	ARTHUR LANGAN	3 C
#READING WB CITY	7318	BERKS	14	40 20	75 58	266	MID	MID	U.S. WEATHER BUREAU	2 3 5 7 C
RENOVO	7409	CLINTON	16	41 20	77 45	660		7A	MRS. C. W. BAIRD	3
RENOVO 5 S	7410	CLINTON	16	41 14	77 46	2035		MID	C. F. BILLETTE	C
REW	7425	MC KEAN	1	41 54	78 32	2250		8A	HAROLD C. HEALY	3
RICES LANDING LOCK 6	7443	GREENE	10	39 57	80 00	775		7A	CORPS OF ENGINEERS	3
RIDGWAY 3 W	7477	ELK	1	41 25	78 47	1420	7P	7A	BOROUGH OF RIDGWAY	2 3 5 7
ROCHESTER 1 N	7540	BEAVER	2	40 43	80 18	900		MID	DEQUESNE LIGHT CO	C
RUSH	7694	SUSQUEHANNA	15	41 47	76 03	1000		9A	MISS MAUDE MC CAIN	3
RUSHVILLE	7727	SUSQUEHANNA	15	41 47	76 07	870		7A	CARL KOPATZ	3
SAFE HARBOR	7732	LANCASTER	15	39 55	76 23	270		MID	S.H.WATER POWER CORP	C
SAGAMORE 1 S	7739	INDIANA	1	40 46	79 14	1320		7A	CORPS OF ENGINEERS	3
SALINA 3 W	7782	WESTMORELAND	7	40 31	79 33	1109	6P	6P	MUN AUTH WSTMRLD CO	2 3 5
SAXTON	7846	BEDFORD	6	40 12	78 15	780		8A	MRS.ALVERTA L.HOLMES	3 C
SCANDIA 2 E	7855	WARREN	1	41 55	79 01	2040		MID	DAVID R. ANDERSON	C
SCHENLEY LOCK 5	7863	ARMSTRONG	1	40 41	79 40	783		7A	CORPS OF ENGINEERS	3

STATION INDEX

Continued

Station	Index No.	County	Drainage‡	Latitude	Longitude	Elevation	Observation time Temp.	Observation time Precip.	Observer	Refer to tables
# SCRANTON	7902	LACKAWANNA	15	41 25	75 40	746	7A	7A	U.S. POST OFFICE	2 3 5
SELINSGROVE CAA AP	7931	SNYDER	15	40 49	76 52	437	MID	MID	CIVIL AERO. ADM.	2 3 5 7
SELLERSVILLE 2 NW	7938	BUCKS	5	40 23	75 20	530		MID	SELLERSVILLE WTR CO	C
SHADE GAP	7965	HUNTINGDON	6	40 11	77 52	1000		MID	MRS. HELEN H. PYLE	C
SHAMOKIN	7978	NORTH'LAND	15	40 48	76 33	770		8A	ROARING CRK WTR CO	3
SHEFFIELD 6 W	8026	WARREN	1	41 41	79 09	1940		MID	L. N. HANSON	C
SHIPPENSBURG	8073	FRANKLIN	15	40 03	77 32	709	4P	AP	KEITH B. ALLEN	2 3 5
SINNEMAHONING	8145	CAMERON	16	41 19	78 05	790		7A	MRS. FRANCES CALDWELL	3
SLIPPERY ROCK	8184	BUTLER	2	41 04	80 03	1345	7P	7A	WALTER D. ALBERT	2 3 5
SMETHPORT HIGHWAY SHED	8190	MC KEAN	1	41 48	78 27	1510		MID	PA DEPT HIGHWAYS	C
SOMERSET FAIRVIEW ST	8244	SOMERSET	17	40 01	79 05	2140		7A	HOWARD G. PECK	3
SOMERSET MAIN ST	8249	SOMERSET	17	40 01	79 05	2150	6P	6P	DAVID L. GROVE	2 3 5 7
SOUTH CANAAN 1 NE	8275	WAYNE	5	41 31	75 24	1400		MID	EUGENE M. COOK	C
SOUTH MOUNTAIN	8308	FRANKLIN	12	39 51	77 30	1520		7A	PA DEPT OF HEALTH	3
SPRINGBORO	8359	CRAWFORD	8	41 49	80 23	900	8A	8A	SPRINGBORO BOROUGH	2 3 5 7 C
SPRING GROVE	8379	YORK	15	39 52	76 52	470		4P	P. H. GLATFELTER CO	3 C
SPRINGS 1 SW	8395	SOMERSET	17	39 44	79 10	2500	8P	8P	ALLEN E. YODER	2 3 5 7
#STATE COLLEGE	8449	CENTRE	16	40 48	77 52	1175	MID	MID	PA STATE COLLEGE	2 3 5 C
STRAUSSTOWN	8570	BERKS	14	40 29	76 11	600		8A	JACOB KLAHR	3
STRONGSTOWN	8589	INDIANA	4	40 33	78 55	1880		MID	HARRY F. BENNETT	C
STROUDSBURG	8596	MONROE	5	40 59	75 12	440	8A	8A	PIERRE T. LAKE	2 3 5
STUMP CREEK	8610	JEFFERSON	1	41 01	78 50	1320		7A	CORPS OF ENGINEERS	3
SUNBURY	8668	NORTH'LAND	15	40 51	76 48	440		7A	CHARLES W. BAYLER	3 C
SUSQUEHANNA	8692	SUSQUEHANNA	15	41 57	75 36	1020		7A	MRS. LAURA A.BENSON	3
SUTERSVILLE	8699	ALLEGHENY	17	40 14	79 48	765		7A	MICHAEL RACKO	3
TAMAQUA	8758	SCHUYLKILL	14	40 48	75 58	830		8A	MRS. MARY L.ROBERTS	3
TAMAQUA 4 N DAM	8763	SCHUYLKILL	14	40 51	75 59	1120		7A	PANTHER VLY WTR CO	3 C
TAMARACK 2 S FIRE TWR	8770	CLINTON	16	41 24	77 51	2220	7A	7A	JAMES E. SWARTZ	2 3 5 7
TIONESTA 2 SE DAM	8873	FOREST	1	41 29	79 26	1200	8A	8A	CORPS OF ENGINEERS	2 3 5 7 C
TITUSVILLE	8885	CRAWFORD	1	41 38	79 40	1550		MID	PA ELECTRIC CO	C
TITUSVILLE WATER WORKS	8888	CRAWFORD	1	41 38	79 42	1220	7P	7P	CITY OF TITUSVILLE	2 3 5
TORPEDO 4 W	8901	WARREN	1	41 47	79 32	1735		7A	MRS. LILY B. GARBER	3
TOWANDA	8905	BRADFORD	15	41 46	76 26	755	7P	7A	MRS. M. O. PARKS	2 3 5 7 C
TOWER CITY 5 SW	8910	DAUPHIN	15	40 31	76 37	745		6P	HARRISBURG WTR DEPT	3 7
TROY	8959	BRADFORD	15	41 47	76 47	1100		7A	JENNIE L. BALLARD	3
TUNNELTON	8989	INDIANA	4	40 27	79 23	890		MID	MRS. MARY E. WEIMER	C
TURTLEPOINT 4 NE	9002	MC KEAN	1	41 54	78 16	1640		7A	ROBERT D. STRAIT	3
TYRONE 4 NE BALD EAGLE	9024	BLAIR	6	40 43	78 12	1020		7A	FREDERICK L. FRIDAY	3 C
UNION CITY	9042	ERIE	1	41 54	79 50	1325		7A	FORREST M. BRALEY	3 C
UNIONTOWN	9050	FAYETTE	10	39 54	79 44	1040	10P	10P	WM. W. MARSTELLER	2 3 5 7
UPPER DARBY	9074	DELAWARE	5	39 58	75 18	222	7P	7P	PHIL. SUB.TRANS. CO	2 3 5
VANDERGRIFT	9128	WESTMORELAND	7	40 36	79 33	800		7A	UNITED ENG&FNDRY CO	3
VANDERGRIFT 2 W	9133	WESTMORELAND	7	40 36	79 36	995		MID	EUGENE R. YOUNG	C
VIRGINVILLE	9196	BERKS	14	40 31	75 52	350		8A	MRS. MARY H. WRIGHT	3
WARREN	9298	WARREN	1	41 51	79 08	1280	7P	7A	GILBERT H. REIER	2 3 5 7
WASHINGTON	9312	WASHINGTON	11	40 11	80 14	1200		MID	PA DEPT HIGHWAYS	C
WATSONTOWN	9345	NORTH'LAND	16	41 05	76 52	470		8A	OWEN BERKENSTOCK	3
WAYNESBURG 2 W	9362	GREENE	10	39 54	80 13	980	6P	7A	RALPH L. AMOS	2 3 5 7
WAYNESBURG 1 E	9367	GREENE	10	39 54	80 10	940		MID	SEWAGE DISPOSAL PLT	C
WEBSTER MILLS 3 SW	9380	FULTON	12	39 49	78 05	920		MID	WILLIAM D. COVER	C
WELLSBORO 3 S	9408	TIOGA	16	41 43	77 16	1920	7A	7A	MARION L. SHUMWAY	2 3 5 7
WELLSBORO 2 E	9412	TIOGA	16	41 45	77 16	1550		MID	MRS. IDA S. MAYNARD	C
WELLSVILLE	9420	YORK	15	40 03	76 57	500	5P	5P	D. D. HOOVER	2 3 5
WERNERSVILLE 1 W	9430	BERKS	14	40 20	76 06	405		8A	CHARLES A. GRUBER	3
WEST CHESTER	9464	CHESTER	5	39 58	75 36	440	8A	8A	DAILY LOCAL NEWS	2 3 5 7
WEST GROVE 1 E	9503	CHESTER	5	39 49	75 49	440		8A	CONARD-PYLE CO	3
WEST HICKORY	9507	FOREST	1	41 34	79 25	1090		8A	MRS.HELEN F.KINNEAR	3
WHITESBURG	9655	ARMSTRONG	1	40 45	79 24	1530		7A	CORPS OF ENGINEERS	3
WILKES-BARRE	9702	LUZERNE	15	41 15	75 52	610		7A	MRS. MARY G. MIRMAK	3
WILLIAMSBURG	9714	BLAIR	6	40 28	78 12	860		7A	MYRON K. BIDDLE	3
WILLIAMSPORT WB AP	9728	LYCOMING	16	41 15	76 55	527	MID	MID	U.S. WEATHER BUREAU	2 3 5 7 C
WIND GAP	9781	NORTHAMPTON	5	40 51	75 18	720		MID	OWEN R. PARRY	C
WOLFESBURG	9823	BEDFORD	6	40 03	78 32	1190		7A	WALTER C. RICE	3
YORK 3 SSW PUMP STA	9933	YORK	15	39 55	76 45	390	5P	5P	YORK WATER COMPANY	2 3 5 7
YORK 2 S	9938	YORK	15	39 56	76 44	640		MID	YORK WATER COMPANY	C
YORK HAVEN	9950	YORK	15	40 07	76 43	310		8A	METROPOL EDISON CO	3
YOUNGSVILLE	9966	WARREN	1	41 51	79 20	1225		MID	HENRY CARLETT	C
ZION GROVE	9990	SCHUYLKILL	15	40 54	76 13	940		7A	JAMES D. TEETER	3
ZIONSVILLE 3 SE	9995	LEHIGH	14	40 27	75 27	660		7A	LESLIE HOWATT	3
NEW STATIONS										
SCRANTON WB AP	7905	LUZERNE	15	41 20	75 44	956	MID	MID	U.S. WEATHER BUREAU	2 3 5 7 C
COOKSBURG	1749	CLARION	1	41 20	79 13	1180		8A	PA DEPT FOR & WTRS	3
COOKSBURG 2 NNW	1752	CLARION	1	41 21	79 13	1460		8A	PA DEPT FOR & WTRS	3
SHIPPINGPORT WB	8078	BEAVER	11	40 37	80 26	740	MID	MID	U.S. WEATHER BUREAU	2 3 5 7 C
VOWINCKEL	9208	CLARION	1	41 25	79 14	1620		8A	PA DEPT FOR & WTRS	3
VOWINCKEL 1 WSW	9209	CLARION	1	41 24	79 15	1610		8A	PA DEPT FOR & WTRS	3
MILAN 4 WNW	5732	BRADFORD	15	41 56	76 35	1448		MID	CARL A. MORRIS	C
UTICA	9099	VENANGO	1	41 26	79 57	1030		7A	MRS.FLORENCE E.MILLER	3

‡1-ALLEGHENY; 2-BEAVER; 3- 4-CONEMAUGH; 5-DELAWARE; 6-JUNIATA; 7-KISKIMINETAS; 8-LAKE ERIE; 9-LEHIGH; 10-MONONGAHELA; 11-OHIO; 12-POTOMAC; 13-LAKE ONTARIO; 14-SCHUYLKILL; 15-SUSQUEHANNA; 16-WEST BRANCH; 17-YOUGHIOGHENY

REFERENCE NOTES

The four digit identification numbers in the index number column of the Station Index are assigned on a state basis. There will be no duplication of numbers within a state.

Figures and letters following the station name, such as 12 SSW, indicate distance in miles and direction from the post office.

Observation times given in the Station Index are in local standard time.

Delayed data and corrections will be carried only in the June and December issues of this bulletin.

Monthly and seasonal snowfall and heating degree days for the preceding 12 months will be carried in the June issue of this bulletin.

Stations appearing in the Index, but for which data are not listed in the tables, are either missing or received too late to be included in this issue.

Unless otherwise indicated, dimensional units used in this bulletin are: temperature in °F., precipitation and evaporation in inches, and wind movement in miles. Degree days are based on a daily average of 65° F.

Evaporation is measured in the standard Weather Bureau type pan of 4 foot diameter unless otherwise shown by footnote following Table 6.

Amounts in Table 3 are from non-recording gages, unless otherwise indicated.

Data in Tables 3, 5 and 6 and snowfall data in Table 7 are for the 24 hours ending at time of observation. See Station Index for observation time.

Snow on ground in Table 7 is at observation time for all except Weather Bureau and CAA stations. For these stations snow on ground values are at 7:30 A.M. E.S.T. WTR EQUIV in Table 7 means the water equivalent of snow on the ground. It is measured at selected stations when depth of snow on the ground is two inches or more. Water equivalent samples are necessarily taken from different points for successive observations; consequently occasional drifting and other causes of local variability in the snowpack result in apparent inconsistencies in the record.

Long-term means for full-time Weather Bureau stations (those shown in the Station Index as United States Weather Bureau Stations) are based on the period 1921-1950, adjusted to represent observations taken at the present location.

- \- No record in Tables 3, 6, 7 and the Station Index. No record in Tables 2 and 5 is indicated by no entry.
- \+ And also on a later date or dates.
- • Amount included in following measurement, time distribution unknown.
- @ Data in the column formerly headed No. of Days .01 or more have been changed to No. of Days .10 or more effective January 1, 1954.
- # Thermometers are generally exposed in a shelter located a few feet above sod-covered ground; however, the reference indicates that the thermometers are exposed in a shelter located on the roof of a building.
- // Gage is equipped with a windshield.
- AM Data based on observational day ending before noon.
- B Adjusted to a full month.
- C In the "Refer to Tables" column in the Station Index the letter "C" indicates recorder stations. These stations are processed for special purposes and are published later in Hourly Precipitation Data.
- D Water equivalent of snowfall wholly or partly estimated, using a ratio of 1 inch water equivalent to every 10 inches of new snowfall.
- M One or more days of record missing; see Table 5 for detailed daily record. Degree day data, if carried for this station, have been adjusted to represent the value for a full month.
- R Amounts from recording gage (These amounts are essentially accurate but may vary slightly from the amounts to be published later in Hourly Precipitation Data).
- SS This entry in time of observation column in Station index means sunset.
- T Trace, an amount too small to measure.
- Y Includes total for previous month.

Additional information regarding the climate of Pennsylvania may be obtained by writing to any Weather Bureau Office or to the State Climatologist at Weather Bureau Airport Station, Harrisburg State Airport, New Cumberland, Pennsylvania.

Subscription Price: 20 cents per copy, monthly and annual; $2.50 per year. (Yearly subscription includes the Annual Summary.) Checks and money orders should be made payable to the Superintendent of Documents. Remittances and correspondence regarding subscriptions should be sent to the Superintendent of Documents, Government Printing Office, Washington 25, D. C.

WRPC., Asheville, N. C. --- 5/3/56 --- 1225

U. S. DEPARTMENT OF COMMERCE
SINCLAIR WEEKS, Secretary
WEATHER BUREAU
F. W. REICHELDERFER, Chief

LIMATOLOGICAL DATA

PENNSYLVANIA

APRIL 1956
Volume LXI No. 4

ASHEVILLE: 1956

GENERAL

The month's weather was cold, windy and cloudy with frequent precipitation that included generous snowfall in northerly or mountainous sections of the State. Sunshine was slightly less than par generally but was particularly deficient in the Pittsburgh area.

Temperatures continued the cold pattern started last month, this being the coldest April since 1950 with fairly uniform temperature distribution over the State in terms of divisional averages, as may be seen in Table 2. Monthly temperature means ranged from 39.0° at Pleasant Mount 1 W to 51.7° at Donora while extreme temperatures were 5° at Kane 1 NNE on the 1st and 91° at Newport on the 29th. Not since 1925 has this month's temperature range of 86° been equaled or exceeded in April. The number of days when minimum temperature dipped to 32° or below was larger than usual at many stations; Scranton WB Airport established a new record with 16 such days. Nearly all the numerous stations having long-term temperature means registered departures toward the cold side but only five deficiencies were as large as -4.0°; Stroudsburg with -5.6° was the largest.

Precipitation was generally adequate. In terms of division averages the Ohio Drainage was more generously treated than other portions of the State even though it contained the driest station, Warren, which had only 1.48 inches for the month. The wettest station was Kregar 4 SE with a total of 7.19 inches, while Stroudsburg measured 2.38 inches on the 29th for the greatest daily amount. Considering only the stations having long-term means, precipitation was deficient at a great majority of Atlantic Division stations and predominantly excessive in the Ohio Drainage where 21 stations had departures greater than +1.00 inch. In spite of ample precipitation the latter division also had two noteworthy dry spots. Warren, mentioned above, had a deficiency of -2.06 inches and Springs 1 SW registered -2.15.

Snowfall was considerably in excess of the usual expectancy for April and was heaviest in mountainous or northern portions of the State. The greatest total was 24.9 inches at Montrose 1 E, followed by 20 inches at a few stations and 10 inches or more in a large number of localities. By contrast, many stations in the southern tier of counties recorded little or no snow.

WEATHER DETAILS

April 1 was fair and chilly, the coldest of the month at many stations. Warm southerly winds with increasing moisture content reached Western Pennsylvania on the 2nd and spread eastward on the 3rd to provide the longest warm spell of the month. Frequent light rains marked the 3rd to 6th but heavy rains attended the approach and passage of a Low to the coast just south of the State while another Low advanced eastward over the Great Lakes during the 6th-7th. The combined effects of the two disturbances drew a large mass of chilly Canadian air southeastward on the 7th to change the rain to snow and decisively end the warmth. Temperatures moderated to near normal during the 11th to 16th

SUPPLEMENTAL DATA

PENNSYLVANIA
APRIL 1956

Station	Wind direction: Prevailing	Wind direction: Percent of time from prevailing	Wind speed m. p. h.: Average	Wind speed m. p. h.: Fastest mile	Wind speed m. p. h.: Direction of fastest mile	Wind speed m. p. h.: Date of fastest mile	Relative humidity averages percent: 1:30 a EST	Relative humidity averages percent: 7:30 a EST	Relative humidity averages percent: 1:30 p EST	Relative humidity averages percent: 7:30 p EST	Number of days with precipitation: Trace	.01–.09	.10–.49	.50–.99	1.00–1.99	2.00 and over	Total	Percent of possible sunshine	Average sky cover sunrise to sunset
NTOWN WB AIRPORT	WSW	13	13.2	-	-	-	79	76	55	63	5	4	7	0	1	0	17	-	6.8
ISBURG WB AIRPORT	WNW	15	9.6	31	W	8	65	67	47	53	8	3	7	1	0	0	19	56	6.9
ADELPHIA WB AIRPORT	SW	9	10.8	42	NW	8	74	69	51	61	8	4	5	1	0	0	18	55	6.8
SBURGH WB AIRPORT	WSW	27	13.7	46*	W	28+	75	76	55	63	2	6	7	4	0	0	19	39	7.6
ING WB CITY	-	-	12.8	38	S	16	-	-	-	-	5	5	8	0	1	0	19	54	6.8
NTON WB AIRPORT	NNW	12	10.3	47	SW	29	75	73	52	61	6	5	5	3	0	0	19	45	6.8
PINGPORT WB	-	-	3.9	55††	W	28	-	-	-	-	3	3	12	1	0	0	19	-	7.9
IAMSPORT WB AIRPORT	-	-	-	-	-	-	-	77	48	56	3	7	8	0	1	0	19	-	6.8

is datum is obtained by
al observation since record-
equipment is not available.
s not necessarily the fast-
mile occurring during the
od.
eak Gust

CLIMATOLOGICAL DATA

: 2

Station		Temperature: Average Maximum	Average Minimum	Average	Departure From Long Term Means	Highest	Date	Lowest	Date	Degree Days	No. of Days Max: 90° or Above	Max: 32° or Below	Min: 32° or Below	Min: 0° or Below	Precipitation: Total	Departure From Long Term Means	Greatest Day	Date	Snow, Sleet: Total	Max. Depth on Ground	Date	No. of Days: .10 or More	.50 or More	1.00 or More
ATLANTIC DRAINAGE																								
NTOWN WB AP	R	57.9	35.5	46.7	- 1.8	84	28	26	1	548	0	0	13	0	3.42	.03	1.25	7	2.0	2	8	8	1	1
NTOWN GAS CO	AM	58.7	36.8	47.8	- 1.1	86	29	27	25	523	0	0	9	0	3.31	- .17	1.17	8	2.0	2	8	6	2	1
ONA HORSESHOE CURVE		56.9	34.7	45.8	- 2.3	85	28	23	1+	574	0	0	14	0	5.34	1.88	1.17	7	4.0	T	7+	12	4	1
DTSVILLE	AM	59.1	38.0	48.6	- 1.2	86	29	24	1+	498	0	0	10	0	2.94	- .64	1.11	7	T	T	24	7	2	1
MAS 1 WNW		62.5	34.7	48.6		89	28	18	21	490	0	0	13	0	3.25		.98	7				8	2	0
ERTOWN	AM	58.9		M		86	28+				0	0		0	2.97		1.02	7	1.0	0		6	2	1
EFONTE 4 S	AM	56.9	34.2	45.6	- 3.4	84	29	21	1	582	0	0	14	0	2.40	- 1.24	.70	7		1	23	6	1	0
ICK		61.0	36.9	49.0		88	28	24	21	489	0	0	10	0	2.88		.66	8	T	T	8	8	2	0
LEHEM LEHIGH UNIV		58.0	38.0	48.0	- 3.2	86	28	29	7+	512	0	0	6	0	3.40	.19	1.18	7	2.0	0		8	1	1
T CABINS 2 NE		60.3	34.8	47.6		88	28	19	1	520	0	0	13	0	2.87		.86	3	.0	0		6	3	0
ON 1 NW	AM	50.8	31.0	40.9		80	29	21	1+	716	0	0	20	0	2.10		.56	8	5.3	4	8+	8	1	0
ISLE		62.4	39.3	50.9	.2	90	28	25	1	434	1	0	7	0	2.85	- .68	1.03	7	T	0		7	2	1
BERSBURG 1 ESE		59.9	36.9	48.4	- 2.0	88	28	23	1	497	0	0	9	0	2.67	- .50	.98	3	.2	0		6	2	0
TER	AM	60.2M	39.9M	50.1M		84	30			448	0	0	2	0	3.73				.0	0				
ESVILLE 1 SW	AM	58.6	36.9	47.8	- 2.6	85	30	26	10	520	0	0	10	0	2.64	- 1.09	.75	7				6	2	0
MBIA		61.3	39.3	50.3		89	28	26	1	444	0	0	6	0	2.27		.79	7	T	0		6	1	0
ULT 1 W		59.2		M		84	28+				0	0		0	3.28		1.00	7	4.8			6	3	1
I	AM	55.8	32.0	43.9		85	29	21	25	635	0	0	20	0	3.01		1.21	8	6.7	5	8	8	2	1
OIS 7 E		55.6	31.7	43.7		81	28	8	1	637	0	0	20	0	4.10	.52	1.32	7	7.5	1	7+	11	1	1
ES MERE	AM	50.0	30.8	40.4		81	29	19	1	734	0	2	19	0	3.59	- .11	1.13	8	15.0	10	9	9	1	1
RIUM 1 E	AM	55.5	28.6	42.1	- 4.5	82	29	15	1	684	0	0	23	0	3.01	- .54	.60	29	1.4	1	8	8	2	0
ATA		58.9	36.6	47.8	- 2.9	85	28	23	25	515	0	0	8	0	2.94	- .41	.96	7	T	0		9	1	0
ETT 1 SW		61.5	32.7	47.1	- 1.6	88	29	20	1	530	0	0	17	0	4.70	1.61	1.25	6	T	T	16	11	4	1
ERICKSVILLE 2 SE	AM																							
LAND		52.8	32.1	42.5	- 2.1	79	28+	20	1	671	0	0	19	0	2.73	- 1.30	1.15	8	21.0	18	9	7	1	1
IE SCHOOL		59.1	37.3	48.2	- 2.1	84	28	26	21+	506	0	0	7	0	2.62	- .86	1.36	7	3.3	2	8	5	1	1
'SBURG	AM	59.9	40.3	50.1	- 1.0	86	29	25	1	458	0	0	4	0	3.44	- .15	1.05	7	T	0		10	3	1
: 1 N	AM	56.5	35.6	46.1		85	29	24	1+	570	0	0	12	0	2.67		.60	8	5.0	5	8	6	2	0
'ER	AM	60.8	36.7	48.8	- 3.5	88	29	23	1	498	0	0	10	0	3.06	- .38	.90	7	T	0		7	3	0
SBURG WB AP	R	59.0	39.1	49.1	- 1.8	87	28	29	1	484	0	0	5	0	2.66	- .31	.71	7	T	0		8	1	0
'Y 1 S DAM	AM	51.0	30.3	40.7		81	29	19	2	721	0	0	21	0	4.11		1.00	8	11.5	9	8	8	4	1
'OOD		57.8	40.7	49.3	- 2.2	82	28	30	1	469	0	0	2	0	1.86	- 1.05	.50	7	1.0	T	1+	5	1	0
NGDON	AM	59.7	33.2	46.5	- 2.9	89	29	21	1	563	0	0	15	0	3.56	.12	.85	4	T	T	23	8	3	0
HORPE		59.7M	36.1M	47.9M	- .5	84	28+	24	1+	512	0	0	13	0	5.95	2.11	1.55	30	4.0	4	8	9	5	2
		58.0	34.4	46.2		86	28	21	1	559	0	0	15	0	3.70		.96	3	T	T	18+	10	3	0
STER 2 NE PUMP STA		60.9	36.9	48.9	- .9	88	28	25	1	485	0	0	8	0	2.80	- .65	.90	7	T	0		8	1	0
SVILLE	AM	58.2	36.7	47.5		87	30	24	1	530	0	0	8	0	2.14		.79	7				6	1	0
NCEVILLE 2 S	AM	54.3	29.6	42.0	- 4.1	83	30	16	1	685	0	0	19	0	1.93	- .92	.50	8	5.0	4	8+	6	1	0
ON 2 NW																								
TOWN	AM	59.5	34.9	47.2		89	29	24	1+	539	0	0	14	0	2.54		.70	7+	T	T	8+	6	2	0
HAVEN		60.0	36.3	48.2	- 2.0	88	28+	23	1	511	0	0	11	0	1.91	- 1.46	.46	8	.2	T	24+	6	0	0
A	AM	54.5	27.6	41.1		83	29	14	1	714	0	0	24	0	3.38		.62	22	2.0	2	23	9	2	0
S HOOK		58.9	40.9	49.9	- 4.6	79	30	31	1	449	0	0	1	0	3.54	.06	1.14	7	T	0		8	2	1
NSBURG CAA AP		55.8	35.5	45.7		85	28	24	1	581	0	0	16	0	3.81		1.06	3	3.2	1	23	9	3	1
ETOWN OLMSTED FLD		58.9	39.4	49.2	- .9	87	28	27	21	480	0	0	4	0	2.41	- .97	.93	7	T	0		7	1	0

See Reference Notes Following Station Index

TABLE 2 - CONTINUED

Station		Temperature: Average Maximum	Average Minimum	Average	Departure From Long Term Means	Highest	Date	Lowest	Date	Degree Days	No. of Days Max. 90° or Above	Max. 32° or Below	Min. 32° or Below	Min. 0° or Below	Precipitation: Total	Departure From Long Term Means	Greatest Day	Date	Snow, Sleet: Total	Max. Depth on Ground	Date	No. of Days .10 or More	.50 or More	1.00 or More
MONTROSE 1 E	AM	48.9	31.4	40.2	- 3.3	79	30	21	1	739	0	1	20	0	3.32	- .12	1.07	8	24.9	12	8+	10	1	1
MORGANTOWN		57.5	35.3	46.4		84	28	23	25	557	0	0	11	0	2.37		1.10	7	1.8	2	7	6	1	1
MT GRETNA 2 SE			37.3	M		86	28	22	1		0	0	13	0	3.19		.87	6	T	0		10	2	0
MT POCONO 2 N AP		52.2	31.3	41.8	- .6	79	28	20	25	691	0	0	19	0	3.81	- .08	.92	8		9	8	7	4	0
MUHLENBURG 1 SE		56.1	31.2	43.7		84	28	20	1+	634	0	0	18	0	4.18		.83	8	7.5	3	1	7	5	0
NEWBURG 3 W		60.6	39.7	50.2		90	28	28	25	459	1	0	10	0	2.87		.85	3	1.0	0		8	2	0
NEWPORT	AM	59.0	34.6	46.8		91	29	22	1	554	1	0	13	0	2.69	- .81	.90	7	T	0		6	2	0
NORRISTOWN		60.5	39.7	50.1		86	28	30	1	453	0	0	3	0	2.72		1.01	8	T	0		5	2	1
PALMERTON		56.6	35.3	46.0	- 2.2	83	28+	26	25	569	0	0	14	0	4.11	1.04	1.11	7	2.5			9	2	1
PHIL DREXEL INST OF TEC		60.4	42.2	51.3		84	28+	34	1+	417	0	0	0	0	3.04		1.18	7	.7	T	8	7	1	1
PHILADELPHIA WB AP	R	59.6	40.2	49.9	- 1.7	84	28+	29	1	456	0	0	2	0	2.68	- .70	.90	7	T	0		6	1	0
PHILADELPHIA PT BREEZE		59.7	43.4	51.6	- 1.1	84	29	33	1	409	0	0	0	0	2.98		1.18	7	.0	0		7	1	1
PHILADELPHIA SHAWMONT		61.1	39.7	50.4	- 1.9	85	29	28	1	449	0	0	5	0	3.18	- .18	1.00	7	1.0	0		5	2	1
PHILADELPHIA CITY	RAM	57.9	41.5	49.7	- 3.0	83	28	33	7+	462	0	0	0	0	2.50	- .88	.82	7				7	1	0
PHILIPSBURG CAA AP		52.9	31.2	42.1		80	28	12	1	686	0	1	18	0	4.18		.80	7	2.9	3	23	10	3	0
PHOENIXVILLE 1 E		61.3	34.5	47.9	- 4.0	86	28	23	1+	518	0	0	14	0	3.43	.05	.90	7				6	4	0
PIMPLE HILL	AM	49.8	31.8	40.8		79	29	20	21	720	0	1	19	0	6.64		1.69	30	19.6	12	9	10	5	2
PLEASANT MOUNT 1 W	AM	48.7	29.2	39.0		78	29	15	2	775	0	0	22	0	4.21	.36	1.28	8	20.0	15	1	9	2	1
PORT CLINTON	AM	58.6	34.6	46.6	- 2.9	87	30	23	25	504	0	0	16	0	3.60	- .54	.75	30				7	4	0
QUAKERTOWN 1 E		59.8	35.5	47.7	- .9	85	28	25	25	521	0	0	13	0	3.53	.12	.96	8				8	2	0
READING WB CITY	R	59.4	39.9	49.7	- 1.6	87	28	31	1+	465	0	0	3	0	3.04	- .20	1.01	7	.5	T	8	9	1	1
SCRANTON	AM	54.8	33.8	44.3	- 3.5	84	29+	27	14	615	0	0	14	0	3.74	.71	1.00	29	5.0			8	2	1
SCRANTON WB AIRPORT		55.0	34.7	44.9	- 2.1	84	28	27	10+	602	0	0	16	0	3.16	- .09	.75	29	12.0	8	9	8	3	0
SELINSGROVE CAA AP		58.7	35.5	47.1	- 2.3	88	28	22	1	543	0	0	10	0	2.50	- 1.05	1.14	7	T	T	8+	6	1	1
SHIPPENSBURG		61.5	37.6	49.6	- 1.2	88	28	25	1	466	0	0	9	0	1.96	- 1.55	.60	3	T	0		5	2	0
STATE COLLEGE		56.3	35.8	46.1	- 1.6	86	29	24	1	569	0	0	13	0	2.67	- .74	.46	22	2.0	T	7+	8	0	0
STROUDSBURG	AM	54.8	31.1	43.0	- 5.6	83	28	20	25	656	0	0	19	0	6.43	2.75	2.38	29	7.9	3	8	13	5	2
TAMARACK 2 S FIRE TWR	AM	51.2	30.5	40.9		81	29+	18	1+	721	0	1	20	0	2.51		.52	7	9.5	9	1	8	1	0
TOWANDA		56.8	32.9	44.9	- 1.6	84	28	21	10+	604	0	0	19	0	3.13	.15	1.38	8	11.0	8	8	8	1	1
UPPER DARBY		60.0	39.5	49.8		84	28	29	1	461	0	0	3	0	2.94		.90	7	1.5	0		5	2	0
WELLSBORO 3 S	AM	51.2	31.0	41.1	- 3.3	82	29	19	1	711	0	0	19	0	2.62	- .66	.62	8	13.0	9	1+	6	1	0
WELLSVILLE		60.0	35.5	47.8		86	28	20	21	519	0	0	9	0	2.63		.68	7	T	0		9	1	0
WEST CHESTER	AM	60.7	40.7	50.7	.7	86	28	29	1	440	0	0	4	0	2.71	- .98	.76	8	1.0	1	8	6	2	0
WILLIAMSPORT WB AP		58.9	36.7	47.8	- 1.3	88	28	26	21+	520	0	0	9	0	3.08	- .46	1.00	7	2.1	T	8+	9	1	1
YORK 3 SSW PUMP STA		62.0	37.9	50.0	- 1.3	86	28	23	1	463	0	0	8	0	2.49	- .74	.68	7	T	0		10	1	0
DIVISION				46.6											3.20				3.7					
OHIO DRAINAGE																								
BAKERSTOWN 3 WNW		58.5	38.4	48.5		81	28	23	21	501	0	0	11	0	5.15		1.17	7	T	0		10	4	1
BLAIRSVILLE 6 ENE		53.8	34.6	44.2		80	28	22	1	623	0	2	16	0	6.33	2.24	1.35	3	10.1	6	23	13	4	2
BRADFORD 4 W RES		53.7	26.9	40.3	- 4.6	76	29	10	1	732	0	0	25	0	3.53	- .28	.93	16	9.1	11	1	10	2	0
BROOKVILLE CAA AIRPORT		54.7	32.3	43.5	- 1.4	79	28	17	1	639	0	0	19	0	5.29	2.11	1.20	7	7.6	2	23	13	2	1
BURGETTSTOWN 2 W	AM	58.3	33.0	45.7		86	29	17	1	577	0	0	18	0	4.93		.74	3				11	4	0
BUTLER		60.7	36.0	48.4	- .3	82	29	20	1	506	0	0	12	0	4.89	1.39	1.40	3	2.0	1	18+	11	2	1
CLARION 3 SW		58.4	33.0	45.7		81	28	17	1	575	0	0	17	0	5.38	1.63	.78	7	3.5	3	18	12	5	0
CLAYSVILLE 3 W		59.8	32.2	46.0	- 4.3	82	27+	14	1	571	0	0	18	0	3.90	.44	.70	7	1.0	1	23	10	2	0
CONFLUENCE 1 SW DAM	AM	56.8	34.7	45.8		83	29	20	1	574	0	0	16	0	3.28		.61	7	T	T	18+	10	1	0
CORRY		54.3	30.7	42.5	- 2.6	74	29	8	1	670	0	0	21	0	4.74	.95	.88	7	3.5	3	7	13	3	0
† COUDERSPORT 3 NW				M		78	28+				0	0		0										0
DERRY				M															.0	0				0
DONEGAL		53.0	28.4	40.7		80	28	13	1	723	0	0	22	0	5.32		1.17	3	7.1	1	18	14	2	1
DONORA	AM	62.5	40.8	51.7	- .5	88	29	27	1	419	0	0	8	0	4.62	1.02	1.00	3	4.8	T	18	10	3	1
EAST BRADY		61.9	33.4	47.7		84	28	19	1	513	0	0	13	0	3.94		1.28	7				9	3	1
EBENSBURG		53.2M	32.3M	42.8M	- 2.4	80	28	16	1	662	0	1	20	0	4.56	1.00	.90	22	7.0	4	23	13	3	0
FARRELL SHARON		59.6	33.7	46.7	- 2.6	83	28	20	1	550	0	0	17	0	4.49	1.35	1.40	3	T	0		10	2	2
FORD CITY 4 S DAM	AM	57.0	32.4	44.7		83	29	19	1	605	0	1	17	0	5.41		1.65	3	4.0	1	23	12	2	1
FRANKLIN		58.0	33.3	45.7	- .3	79	28	20	1	574	0	0	16	0	4.95	1.73	.85	16	2.0	1	8+	11	5	0
GREENVILLE		57.7	33.8	45.8	- .9	79	28	19	1	575	0	0	15	0	4.89	1.43	.85	7	2.6	T	7	12	4	0
INDIANA 3 SE		59.1	33.9	46.5	- 2.9	84	28	18	1	557	0	0	16	0	5.42	1.45	1.12	3	1.0	1	23	12	6	1
IRWIN			37.4	M		85	28+	25	10+		0	0	12	0			1.15	7	2.5	T	23+			1
JAMESTOWN 2 NW	AM	54.9	32.5	43.7		75	28+	19	1	631	0	0	16	0	4.48	1.18	.59	16	2.3	1	8+	16	3	0
JOHNSTOWN	AM	59.8	36.8	48.3	- 1.5	88	29	24	1	504	0	0	13	0	6.25	2.20	.94	3				14	4	0
KANE 1 NNE	AM	51.9	28.0	40.0		77	29+	5	1	745	0	0	21	0	4.22	.27	.93	16	7.9	14	1	12	2	0
LINESVILLE 5 WNW		54.7	32.5	43.6		74	27+	20	1	632	0	0	18	0	4.69	1.17	.54	16	12.9	3	8	14	2	0
MEADVILLE 1 S	AM	54.0	32.1	43.1	- 2.4	75	28	19	1	650	0	0	17	0	4.92	1.56	.90	16	7.7	3	8	14	2	0
MERCER 2 NNE		56.6	33.8	45.2		78	28	20	1+	589	0	0	13	0	6.00		1.06	3	.0	0		14	3	1
MIDLAND DAM 7		57.4	38.6	48.0	- 2.3	81	28	29	1	512	0	0	10	0	3.79	.24	.75	7	.6	T	8+	12	2	0
NEW CASTLE 1 N		60.7	35.0	47.9	- .7	83	28	20	1	516	0	0	13	0	4.63	1.54	1.10	3	.7	0		12	3	1
NEWELL	AM	62.2	40.8	51.5	.6	86	29	22	1	413	0	0	6	0	4.36	1.10	.60	7	T	T	20+	11	3	0
NEW STANTON		60.3	33.0	46.7	- 3.5	86	28	20	1	553	0	0	17	0	5.13	1.38	.90	3				11	5	0
PITTSBURGH WB AP 2	//R	56.7	37.4	47.1	- 1.7	82	28	22	1	540	0	0	12	0	4.31	1.12	.73	6	3.3	2	18	15	2	0
PITTSBURGH WB CITY	R	59.1	40.3	49.7	- 2.1	85	28	28	1	466	0	0	3	0	4.18	1.10	.66	6+	1.0			11	4	0
PUTNEYVILLE 2 SE DAM	AM	56.4	31.3	43.9		82	29	17	1	630	0	0	20	0	4.69		.72	29	1.5	1	8+	12	3	0
RIDGWAY 3 W		56.0	29.8	42.9	- 2.2	80	28	10	1	659	0	0	22	0	4.26	1.04	.91	16	5.2	2	8	10	3	0
SALINA 3 W		58.9	35.5	47.2		84	28	20	1	539	0	0	15	0	4.70		1.16	7	T	0		12	3	1
SHIPPINGPORT WB		57.8	36.6	47.2		82	28	24	1	533	0	0	12	0	3.31		.63	6	T	0		13	1	0
SLIPPERY ROCK		57.5	35.3	46.4		78	28	21	1	554	0	0	14	0	5.23		.80	3	T	T	18	12	4	0
SOMERSET MAIN ST		56.1	33.7	44.9	- 1.3	80	28	19	1	599	0	0	15	0	4.65	.26	1.06	7	6.4	T	8+	11	2	1

See Reference Notes Following Station Index

CLIMATOLOGICAL DATA

Station	Temperature: Average Maximum	Average Minimum	Average	Departure From Long Term Means	Highest	Date	Lowest	Date	Degree Days	No. of Days: Max 90° or Above	Max 32° or Below	Min 32° or Below	Min 0° or Below	Precipitation: Total	Departure From Long Term Means	Greatest Day	Date	Snow, Sleet: Total	Max Depth on Ground	Date	No. of Days: .10 or More	.50 or More	1.00 or More
NGS 1 SW	53.4	31.1	42.3	- 3.1	79	28	17	1	675	0	2	20	0	1.78	- 2.15	.35	7	7.8	1	8+	7	0	0
ESTA 2 SE DAM AM	54.6	30.2	42.4		79	30	15	1	671	0	0	19	0	4.68	1.17	.63	16	5.1	3	8	12	5	0
SVILLE WATER WORKS	56.0	29.3	42.7		77	27+	12	1	664	0	0	22	0	4.86		.91	7	3.0	1	7	14	4	0
NTOWN	60.2	38.3	49.3	- 2.3	85	28	22	1	483	0	0	9	0	3.06	- .67	.47	6	2.0	0		11	0	0
EN	55.5	32.5	44.0	- 1.0	78	29	15	1	624	0	0	16	0	1.48	- 2.06	.26	7	2.3	3	1	7	0	0
ESBURG 2 W	61.2	35.2	48.2	- 2.4	85	28	19	1	507	0	0	12	0	5.05	1.60	1.10	7		1	8	10	3	1
DIVISION			45.6											4.55				3.4					
LAKE DRAINAGE																							
CAA AIRPORT	52.2	34.2	43.2	- 1.1	74	27+	22	1	647	0	0	13	0	3.38	- .12	.80	27	4.0	3	8	10	2	0
NGBORO	54.5	35.2	44.9		72	29+	19	1	598	0	0	10	0										0
DIVISION			44.1											3.38				4.0					

TA RECEIVED TOO LATE TO BE
CLUDED IN DIVISION AVERAGES

DAILY PRECIPITA

Table 3

Station	Total	1	2	3	4	5	6	7	8	9	10	11	12	13	14	15
		Day of month														
ACMETONIA LOCK 3	5.01	.01		.51	.64			.92	.35	T						
ALLENTOWN WB AP R	3.42		T	.01	.05		.32	1.25	.25					.03		.45
ALLENTOWN GAS CO	3.31				.09	T		.60	1.17	.06					.01	
ALTOONA HORSESHOE CURVE	5.34		.06	.87	.03		.12	1.17	.05							.05
ARENDTSVILLE	2.94			.30	.57			1.11	.31							
ARTEMAS 1 WNW	3.25			.55			.48	.98								.15
AUSTINBURG 2 W	-			.05		.18		.42	.58	T				T	T	T
BAKERSTOWN 3 WNW	5.15			.90				1.17						.60		
BARNES	3.69	T	T	.44	T			.42	.25	T						
BEAR GAP	3.85		.04		.03			.40	1.58							.17
BEAVER FALLS	3.77	T	T	.66	.18			.59	.16	T						
BEAVERTOWN	2.97				.11	.01		1.02	.47	.05						
BEECH CREEK STATION	1.96	T			.01	T		.38	.36	T						
BELLEFONTE 4 S	2.40			.03	.28			.70	.30	T						T
BERWICK	2.88		T		.03			.35	.66							.01
BETHLEHEM	3.74			T	T	T		.56	1.45	.11						
BETHLEHEM LEHIGH UNIV	3.40		T	.01	.04		.30	1.18	.23							.38
BLAIRSVILLE 6 ENE	6.33		.29	1.35	.08		.28	1.30	.01							T
BLOSERVILLE 1 N	3.95			.56	.03		.09	1.32								.04
BOSWELL 6 WNW	5.61			.56	.90			.88	.05	T						
BRADDOCK LOCK 2	4.84	T		.38	.62			.90	.32	T						
BRADFORD CNTRL FIRE STA	3.43			.15	T			.42	.35	T						
BRADFORD 4 W RES	3.53		.19	.08				.53	.31							.09
BREEZEWOOD	3.55		.08	.52	.15		.58	.82	.08							.07
BROOKVILLE CAA AIRPORT	5.29		.24	.41	.14		.27	1.20	.02							.06
BRUCETON 1 S	4.41			.65	.45			*	*	.05						
BUFFALO MILLS	3.99			.63	.72			.86	.56							.07
BURGETTSTOWN 2 W	4.93			.74	.09			.71	.33							
BURNT CABINS 2 NE	2.87		T	.86			.73	.50	T							T
BUTLER	4.89			1.40	.15	.01		.86	.27	.08						
CAMP HILL	2.58			.30	T		.15	1.05	T							.08
CANTON 1 NW	2.10			.04	T	.02		.27	.56	.10						-
CARLISLE	2.85			.56	.05		.12	1.03	.10							
CARROLLTOWN 2 SSE	4.02			.52	.66	T		.44	.40	.01						
CARTER CAMP 2 W	2.63	T		.18		.03		.48	.39	T						
CEDAR RUN	2.62	T		.10		.08		.41	.45	.25						
CHADDS FORD	2.02				T	T		.85	.06							.20
CHAMBERSBURG 1 ESE	2.67		.02	.98	.05		.58	.17	T							T
CHARLEROI LOCK 4	4.98		T	.38	.82			.93	.35	T						
CHESTER	3.73				.05	.46		.86	*	.05						
CLARENCE 1 E	3.04	T		.02	.30	T		.69	.36	.01						
CLARION 3 SW	5.38			.40	.53			.78	.64							
CLAUSSVILLE	-			.02	.05			.74	-	-						
CLAYSVILLE 3 W	3.90			.46	.04			.70	.26							
CLEARFIELD	3.21	T		.22	.28	.03		.58	.35	T						
CLERMONT	3.72			.28	.03			.53	.30	.05						
COALDALE 2 NW	5.04					.05		.84	.95	.17						
COATESVILLE 1 SW	2.64		T		.13	T		.75	.71	.02						
COLUMBIA	2.27			.25			.03	.79	.47							T
CONFLUENCE 1 SW DAM	3.28			.48	.07			.61	.40	.03						.19
CONFLUENCE 1 NW	3.16	T		.61	.07			.59	.33	.05						.19
CONNELLSVILLE	4.35			.54	.43			.67	.37							.09
CONSHOHOCKEN	3.31		T		.04	.03		.77	1.17	.22						
COOKSBURG	5.23	T	.02	.39	.22	T		.59	.55							
COOKSBURG 2 NNW	5.07		.07	.40	.15	T		.56	.56							
CORAOPOLIS NEVILLE IS	4.00			*	.85			*	1.03							
CORRY	4.74		.34	.15	T			.88	.08							.46
COUDERSPORT 3 NW	-	-	-	-	-	-	-	-	-	-	-	-	-	-	-	-
COUDERSPORT 7 E	3.46	T		.22	.01	.08		.33	.50	.08						
COVINGTON	1.90	T		.05	T			.28	.73	.03						
CREEKSIDE	5.22			.97	.46			.70	.50							
CRESSON 2 SE	6.36	.02		.29	.78			.96	.47	.05						T
CUSTER CITY 2 W	3.49	T		.23				.32	.34	.02						
DANVILLE	2.93				T			.69	.60	.05						
DERRY	-		-	-	-		.30	-	-						.19	.10
DEVAULT 1 W	3.28			.06	.08		.51	1.00	.22							.27
DIXON	3.01	T		.02	T	.01		.31	1.21	.02						
DONEGAL	3.32		.37	1.17	T		.44	.28	.16							.10
DONORA	4.62		.22	1.00	.01			.94	.23	.02						T
DOYLESTOWN	3.07			T	.01			.62	1.16					T		.27
DU BOIS 7 E	4.10		.24	.30			T	1.32	.07							.11
DUSHORE 3 NE	2.51			.06	T	.02		.40	.95	T					T	
EAGLES MERE	3.59			T	T	.05		.37	1.13	.23				T	T	
EAST BRADY	3.94		.06	.55				1.28	.17							
EBENSBURG	4.56			.70	.65			.43	.33	.06						T
EDINBORO	4.84		.21	.14	.06	.07		.33	.78	.05						.15
ELIZABETHTOWN	2.17				.26			.78	.53							
EMPORIUM 1 E	3.01			.20	T	.03		.41	.28	.02						
ENGLISH CENTER	2.49			.01	.01	T		.54	.62	.04						
EPHRATA	2.94			.14	.04		.02	.96	.43							.14
EQUINUNK	4.34	T		.27	T	.12		.37	1.30	.13						
ERIE CAA AIRPORT	3.38		.25	.13	.04		.04	.77	.03							.30
EVERETT 1 SW	4.70		.10	.60			.25	.70	.20							.10
FARRELL SHARON	4.49		.41	1.40				1.01	.01							.07
FORD CITY 4 S DAM	5.41			1.65	.40			.99	.40	.08						
FRANKLIN	4.95		.02	.62	.32			.52	.67							
FREDERICKSVILLE 2 SE		RECORD MISSING														
FREELAND	2.73							.34	1.15	.33			T			
GALETON	2.72	.02		.10	T	.01		.46	.36						T	
GEIGERTOWN	-				.11	.06		.88	.87	-						
GEORGE SCHOOL	2.62			T	T		T	1.36	.43							.28
GETTYSBURG	3.44			.50	.38			1.05	.20							
GIFFORD		RECORD MISSING														
GLEN HAZEL 2 NE DAM	4.63	.01	T	.31	.09	T		.47	.34	T						
GLENWILLARD DASH DAM	4.54	T		.23	.43			.68	.27	.03						
GOULDSBORO	4.94			T	T	.03		.53	1.60	.27						
GRANTVILLE 2 SW	2.58			.21			.07	.87	.21							.04
GRATERFORD	3.49				.07	.08		.70	1.17	.08						
GRATZ 1 N	2.67			T	T			.41	.60	T						
GREENSBORO LOCK 7	3.59			.74	.08			.71	.31	.02						T
GREENSBURG 3 SE	5.07		.25	.85	.07		.27	.85	.01							.06
GREENVILLE	4.89		.34	.58				.85	T							.52
HANOVER	3.06			T	.59			.90	.38	T						
HARRISBURG WB AP R	2.66		T	.31	T		.45	.71	.02							.01
HARRISBURG NORTH	2.66			.01	.25			.84	.41	T						
HAWLEY	4.21			.09		.06		.24	.85	.06					T	
HAWLEY 1 S DAM	4.11			.11		.03		.22	1.00	.08						
HOLLISTERVILLE	4.51	T		.02	T	.03		.30	1.43	.08						
HOLTWOOD	1.86		T		.20	T		.50	.37	.07					T	
HONESDALE 4 NW	3.98			.12		.01		.37	1.60	.08					T	
HOOVERSVILLE	4.81	.01		.56	.70			.71	.47	.06					.04	.07
HOP BOTTOM 2 SE	2.29			T		T			.69	T					T	T
HUNTINGDON	3.56			T	.85			.66	.35	T						
HUNTSDALE	2.93			.14	.54			1.02	.32	T						
HYNDMAN	3.89			.64	.20			.87	.51							.02
INDIANA 3 SE	5.42			1.12	.66			.71	.58	T						.02
IRWIN	-		-	-	-		.11	1.15								.23
JAMESTOWN 2 NW	4.48		.18	.54	.15	T		.36	.35	T						.16
JIM THORPE	5.95		T		.01	.09		.77	1.23	.02						
JOHNSTOWN	6.25			.94	.24			.84	.39	.02						.03

See Reference Notes Following Station Index

PRECIPITATION

PENNSYLVANIA
APRIL 1956

Day of month

11	12	13	14	15	16	17	18	19	20	21	22	23	24	25	26	27	28	29	30	31
		T		T	.93	.20	.17	.10	T	.01	.40	.14	.03	T	.31	T		.37	.18	
					.14	.02	.07	T		T	.46	.21	.02	.03	.08	T		.16	.12	
					.69	.12	.03	.05		T	.35	.17		.04	.21	.02		.74	.22	
				.05	.15	.15	.09	T	T		.20	.09	.19		.16		.10			
				T	.30	.09	.10	.03			.27	.44	T	.05	.18			.31	.16	
				.21	.58	.39	.51	.06	.09	T	.46	.20	.36	T	.37		.02	.38		
					.85	.16					.07	.50			.40			.10	1.36	
					.11	.03	T	T	T	T	.19	.66	.14	T	.33	.04		.73	.69	
				.07	.27		T		.01		T	.11	.05		.20			.23	.18	
					.12		.06		.03			.09	.01	.02	.21	.02	T	.02	.11	
				.04	.40	.05	.20	T	.04	.02	.78	.06	.09	.01	.31			.37		
				T	.19		.03	.04			.16	.16	.09		.06				.07	
				T	.50	.05		.05	T	T	.03	.43			.05	.23	T	.03	1.09	
					.20	.03						.09			.03			.42		
				.05	1.08	.16	.20	.12	T	.01	.40	.08	.02		.20	.01	.02	.45	.32	
					.06	.04	.08	.01		T	.20	.70		.05	.02	.02		.08	.10	
				.18	.54	.18	.24	.09	T	.04	.20	.14	T		.43		.28	.43	.05	
					.11	.01	.02	T	T	T	.20	.41	T	.02	.03				.15	
					.68	.09	.02	.03			.22	.46	.02		.29			.44	1.50	
					.35	.12	.29	.06	T		.62	.42	.03	.07	.05				.34	
					.53	.06	.22	.05	.05	T	.60	.43	.03	.04	.09	T	T	.10	.16	
		T		.24	.28		.01		T	T		.05			.33		T		T	
					.03	.06	.05	.09	.03		.12	.60	T	.07	.02	.01		.16	.22	
		.03		.21	.35	T	.05		T		T	T	.07		.45				.02	
					.76	.13	.23	.10	.02	T	.41	.57	.04	.04	.05	.01		.14	.26	
				.09	.09	.03	.13	.04	.01	T	.30	.16	.05		.18		.04	.14		
					.36	.14					.18	.33	.38		.31	.07		.44	.59	
				T	.77	.32	.15	.05			.37	.08	.08		.45			.62	.22	
				.04	.20	.02	.14	.09				.40	.03	.33	.17			.07	.12	
					.28	.07	.18	.04	.11			.97	.11	.03	.34				.24	
				.26	.90	.26	.10	.04	T	.01	.25	.12	.14	T	.48	T	.07	.28	T	
					.57	.06	.55	.06		T	.30	.11	.06	.02	.20	T		.57	.22	
				.30	.89	.32	.30		T		.35	.20	.10		.35		.31	.46	T	
					.05			.10		*	.27	.23			.08			.08	.10	
				.06	.13	.09	.14	.16	.06	.01		.33	.03	.18	.26	.03			.19	
				T	.09		T		.01		.26	.14	.11	T	.21		.04	.02		
					.53	.03	.29	.05	T		.21	.35	.02	.10	.32			.31	.20	
				T	.32	.09		.01			.14	.66	.15		.27	T		.31	1.00	
					.09	T	T	T	T	T	.38	.47	T	.05	.02			.13	.06	
					.19	.11	.03	T			.18	.31	T	T	.09			.39	-	
				T	.06		.09	T		T	.31	.57	T	.05	.03				.25	
			T		.24	.13	.03	.01	T	.02	.26	.42	.06	T	.27	T		.13	.02	
				.18	.22	T	.04		T		.02	.05			.19		.07		T	
				.10	.17	.03	.03		T		.26	.13	.04	T	.19	T	.28	.15		
		T		.15	.63	.01	.01	T	T			.88			.32			.30	T	
				.05	.14	.03			T		.27	.58			.08			.74	.60	
				.10	.02							.52			.12	.01		.08	.04	
					.32	.15	.17	.16			.05	.59	T	.04	.22			.13	.18	
		T		.31	.25		.03				T	T			.40					
			.08		.40	.02					.07		.10		.15			.10		
					.68	.10	.22	.06	T	T	.25	.16	.06	.08	.25			.29	.05	
					.39	.13	.38	.14	.02			.58	.23	.03	.47				.30	
				.05	.24	.03	.15						.32		.12					
					.16	.02	.01	T	T	T	T	.65	T	.02	T	T		.01	.37	
				.01	.03	.01	.23	.04	.02	.01	.54	.22	.24	.11	.47			.56		
		T		.33	.38	T	.02				.02	.45			.27	.01		.06	.92	
					.45	.10						.04	T		.23	.03				
				.06	.80	.15	.22	.07	.02	T	.22	.02	.01		.24	.02	.87	.55	.09	
				.12	.06		.12	T		T		.83			.21			.23	.08	
					.70	.12		.15				.22	.05		.30	.05		.10	.30	
		T		.38	.44		.01	T	T		.17	.25	T		.33	T	.04	.86	T	
					.77	.12	.06	.04		T	.47	.26	.02	.11	.29			.42	.07	
					.16	.08					.37	.62	.04		.26			.32	.80	
					.63	.39	T	T	.03	T	.26	.70	T		.28			.40	.48	
		T		.40	.28	T	.03		.03		T	T	T		.30				T	
		T		.27	.30	T	.07		T		T	T	.02		.32		T		T	
		.01		.28	.29	.01	.04		.01		T		.03		.31					
				.30	.40	.07			T			.05			.30					
			T	.24	.22	.01	.04		.03		T	T	.02		.30		T		.02	
				.05	.40	.11	.05	.01	.02	.42	.36	.21	.06	T	.06		T	.25	T	
				.23	.71		.02				T	.05			.33					
					.26	.11	.08	T	T	T	.20	.52	T		.24	.01		.43	1.08	
			T		.86	.12	T	.04	T	T	.19	.51	T	T	.48	T		.41	1.69	
					.17	.02	T	T	T	T		.51	T		.12			.15	.78	
				.16	.29	.15	.23	T	.02	.22	.37	.05	.10	.19	.21		.28	.20	T	
				.03	.26	.06	.24		T	.11	.67	.10	.07	.16	.26		.08	.06		
		T		.40	.20	.03	T		.02	T	.30	.67	.08		.36	T	T	T	.08	
					.44	.08		.05				.51						.19	.75	
					.42	.28	.18	T				.35			.11				.06	
					.38	.19	.10	.05			.45	.35	.03	.03	.19			.72	.24	
				.45	.40		.11		.05		.02	.16			.24	.02	.01	.02	.36	
					.45	T	.20	.10			.40	.15			.14	T		.44	.25	
		T		.23	.34	.01	.02		T		.21	.15	T	T	.12		.03	.30		
					.22	.05	.27	T		T	.30	.23	T	T	.11			.26	.03	
				T	1.09	.08	.11	.07	T	T	.32	.08	T	T	.20	.01	T	.23	.32	
				.07	.40	.07	.21	.04	.02			.38	.04	.20	.37			.16	.19	
					.91	.08	.11	.08		T	.34	.14	.08	.02	.30	T		.52	.15	
					.23	.19	.12	.02		.03	.22	.62	.05		.29	T		.13	.01	
					.10	.09	.05			T	.18	.35	.09		.23			.15		
					.35	.10	.10				.44	.25		.12	.23			.12	.15	
					.45	.10	.25	.05	T		.42	.57	.06		.22			.10	.17	
				.03	.04	T	T	.19	T	T		.64	.02	.10	.13	T		T	.03	
					.32	.10	.18	.08		.01	.21	.43	.05	.07	.17			.35	.19	
		T	T	T	.09	.06	.04				.36	.48	.12		.18	T	T	1.00	.66	
		T		.03	.18	T	T	.01	.03	.16	.03	.53		T	.11		.43	.75		
				.02	.20	T		T		T	.35	.35	.02	.01	.04		.11	.06		
					.40	.08	.01				*	.71	.01	T	.15			*	.61	
				T	T	T	.05		T		T	.30	.21	T	.07			.11	.03	
				.19	.29	.08	.19		T	.20	.27	.05	.09	.22	.10		.19	.19		
			T		.40	.06	.29	T	T	.01	.38	.14	.02	T	.10	T		.36	.41	
					.89	.19	.20	.06			.47	.12	.03	.25	.33			.48	.07	
				.13	.10	.18	.29	.19	.04	.02		.40	.05	.20	.21			T	T	
				.11	.09	.26	.31	.07	.02		T	.40	.34		.24		T	.01		
					.07		.02	.14				-	.05	.21	.04			.07	.05	
				.15	.55	*	*	*	*	.50	.30		T		.45	.10	.20	.20	.10	
					.11		.04		T			.10		.17	.10			T	.42	
				.04	.18	.02	.16	.03	.02			.28	.19		.08		T			
				.03	.12	.09	.08	T	T	.32	.46	.20	.08		.03		.12	.04		
					.25	.17	T	.01		T		.46		T	.15	T		.01	.77	
		.01		.30	.65	.01	.10	T	T		.12	.58			.18	T	.10	2.38	.15	
					.56	.07	.09	.05			.44	.25	.01		.12			.29	.22	
					.20	.02	T				.22	.57	.01	T	.09			.05	.23	
					.17	.08	T	.05		.02	T	.91	.16		.25	.01	.06	.20		
				T	.31	T	.11	.02	T		*	.70	.04	.14	.52			T	.11	
					.42	.04						.57	.04		.30			.22	1.10	
					-	.29					.20	.43			-			.42	1.03	

See Reference Notes Following Station Index

TAMARACK 2 S FIRE TWR
TIONESTA 2 SE DAM
TITUSVILLE WATER WORKS
TORPEDO 4 W
TOWANDA

TOWER CITY 5 SW
TROY
TURLEPOINT 4 NE
TYRONE 4 NE BALD EAGLE
UNION CITY

UNIONTOWN
UPPER DARBY
UTICA
VANDERGRIFT
VIRGINVILLE

VOWINCKEL
VOWINCKEL 1 WSW
WARREN
WATSONTOWN
WAYNESBURG 2 W

WELLSBORO 3 S
WELLSVILLE
WERNERSVILLE 1 W
WEST CHESTER
WEST GROVE 1 E

WEST HICKORY
WHITESBURG
WILKES BARRE
WILLIAMSBURG
WILLIAMSPORT WB AP

WOLFSBURG
YORK 3 SSW PUMP STA
YORK HAVEN
ZION GROVE
ZIONSVILLE 3 SE

Table 5

DAILY TEMPERATURES

PENNSYLVANIA
APRIL 1956

Station		Day Of Month 1	2	3	4	5	6	7	8	9	10	11	12	13	14	15	16	17	18	19	20	21	22	23	24	25	26	27	28	29	30	31	Average
ALLENTOWN WB AP	MAX	55	54	59	64	66	64	47	41	54	58	52	61	59	60	55	65	51	52	51	50	56	61	51	48	55	52	61	84	83	67		57.9
	MIN	26	31	40	44	42	36	32	31	30	30	35	29	34	30	41	42	36	31	34	31	28	42	35	32	27	38	33	47	54	43		35.5
ALLENTOWN GAS CO	MAX	45	55	55	60	65	67	65	65	42	54	58	52	61	59	60	62	66	52	54	51	50	58	60	49	58	55	52	60	86	85		58.7
	MIN	28	33	37	44	44	37	44	32	30	30	36	30	33	31	41	46	38	33	34	32	29	34	35	37	27	38	34	45	51	61		36.8
ALTOONA HORSESHOE CURVE	MAX	53	54	67	76	65	60	48	34	52	59	54	63	58	63	61	55	43	41	47	45	60	56	41	39	52	52	68	85	83	72		56.9
	MIN	23	33	46	51	40	36	33	28	29	26	34	29	38	26	44	40	30	31	30	30	25	35	31	27	23	40	36	50	55	43		34.7
ARENDTSVILLE	MAX	45	56	56	69	79	69	64	47	42	55	59	52	63	63	62	58	59	51	49	54	50	62	64	48	45	55	61	67	86	83		59.1
	MIN	24	35	40	46	46	42	46	32	32	29	39	32	35	30	42	47	36	30	36	31	24	40	37	34	27	40	42	50	55	60		38.0
ARTEMAS 1 WNW	MAX	57	59	67	81	68	65	55	42	60	62	60	66	65	66	65	57	48	44	51	48	62	61	57	62	55	62	74	89	86	81		62.5
	MIN	21	31	43	41	45	42	39	29	30	27	38	28	39	29	36	44	35	29	28	27	18	37	34	30	26	39	41	53	44	39		34.7
BAKERSTOWN 3 WNW	MAX	55	60	72	70	62	64	52	38	52	58	57	64	60	65	64	54	46	40	52	48	60	58	44	45	57	57	79	81	74	68		58.5
	MIN	30	42	54	50	43	44	30	28	30	34	40	38	37	36	52	38	33	30	30	31	23	39	32	31	25	44	42	66	60	40		38.4
BEAVERTOWN	MAX	53	55	56	63	68	65	60	40	56	58	57	64	58	61	60	59	49	49	53	49	60	59	48	45	55	53	61	86	86	82		58.9
	MIN																																
BELLEFONTE 4 S	MAX	40	51	58	66	77	66	63	47	39	55	58	55	67	56	61	59	50	45	46	49	45	58	58	48	43	53	55	72	84	83		56.9
	MIN	21	32	40	52	40	34	43	30	28	25	33	27	40	29	36	40	34	29	33	32	27	28	27	26	24	35	36	40	57	49		34.2
BERWICK	MAX	54	55	69	76	69	69	62	40	54	58	58	64	60	62	60	61	50	54	53	51	59	59	56	49	58	53	62	88	86	82		61.0
	MIN	25	33	45	50	42	35	39	31	29	26	33	29	38	27	46	49	39	34	34	35	24	38	31	31	25	39	36	53	56	54		36.9
BETHLEHEM LEHIGH UNIV	MAX	54	55	61	65	66	63	46	38	52	59	50	64	61	58	53	65	52	52	52	49	59	62	51	49	57	51	61	86	83	67		58.0
	MIN	30	34	43	45	45	41	29	29	31	35	38	35	33	33	39	44	40	38	37	34	30	44	39	36	32	36	37	48	62	42		38.0
BLAIRSVILLE 6 ENE	MAX	51	63	64	72	63	58	45	30	48	55	52	61	48	62	66	55	38	32	44	39	56	50	34	35	55	49	77	80	75	58		53.8
	MIN	22	40	50	45	37	42	29	24	27	28	34	34	39	29	47	32	28	28	23	27	24	30	29	30	24	39	41	60	57	38		34.6
BRADFORD 4 W RES	MAX	47	51	59	66	57	61	59	39	43	51	57	61	60	60	59	57	37	36	42	42	49	45	43	42	52	50	67	71	76	72		53.7
	MIN	10	29	32	32	27	22	32	25	16	16	21	21	32	17	40	31	28	28	25	21	15	25	28	21	16	35	27	56	47	33		26.9
BROOKVILLE CAA AIRPORT	MAX	49	58	64	67	64	60	47	34	50	57	57	63	51	62	63	45	42	38	45	37	53	50	42	43	54	54	75	79	78	61		54.7
	MIN	17	38	52	44	33	29	30	28	28	22	32	25	30	24	44	34	33	30	30	24	23	32	27	27	21	36	31	53	53	38		32.3
BURGETTSTOWN 2 W	MAX	40	60	63	71	74	68	62	50	38	55	60	57	66	56	67	67	48	44	38	53	43	63	51	45	44	60	58	81	86	80		58.3
	MIN	17	29	45	52	31	31	45	29	25	20	31	23	32	22	43	37	34	32	28	28	20	37	32	30	23	34	34	51	51	45		33.0
BURNT CABINS 2 NE	MAX	57	57	70	80	71	65	48	43	55	63	53	65	64	60	61	60	49	45	45	49	64	61	52	49	54	58	68	88	80	75		60.3
	MIN	19	36	39	50	42	35	30	31	32	23	35	26	38	30	47	39	36	30	32	26	24	41	34	28	22	41	37	48	51	42		34.8
BUTLER	MAX	54	58	64	71	72	67	64	49	48	55	60	61	65	62	67	65	46	43	48	55	55	59	52	44	54	59	80	81	82	80		60.7
	MIN	20	40	53	56	34	33	40	28	28	24	39	26	39	25	49	38	34	31	30	25	25	35	33	31	25	43	35	67	54	39		36.0
CANTON 1 NW	MAX	35	43	47	62	66	61	60	43	40	44	47	49	58	49	50	57	55	43	41	45	39	51	48	42	44	50	47	56	80	72		50.8
	MIN	21	26	37	44	36	35	39	25	27	27	27	30	34	26	27	31	33	30	29	29	22	21	31	25	25	30	32	38	48	46		31.0
CARLISLE	MAX	57	58	60	72	73	69	58	45	58	63	60	65	65	65	62	61	54	50	56	54	65	62	50	48	60	57	67	90	86	82		62.4
	MIN	25	39	41	49	44	40	41	35	36	28	38	29	37	31	48	50	39	32	37	33	30	47	38	36	28	43	40	52	57	57		39.3
CHAMBERSBURG 1 ESE	MAX	56	55	70	78	70	65	49	40	56	62	53	63	59	62	61	60	49	48	54	50	62	63	48	41	54	62	68	88	83	68		59.9
	MIN	23	37	39	50	44	39	36	32	31	27	36	28	36	30	45	44	36	34	36	31	27	41	33	33	26	42	42	46	54	50		36.9
CHESTER	MAX		55	58	58	71	69	71		48	56	62	52	62	61		63	72	54	54	53	52		65	52	50	56	61	65		84		60.2
	MIN		30	43	45	42	43	46		34	34	39	36	37	36		45	37	40	37	40	32		42	37	35	41	39	48		59		39.9
CLARION 3 SW	MAX	52	57	68	72	64	63	61	36	52	60	60	64	55	64	68	50	45	40	47	50	56	50	51	46	56	56	79	81	80	68		58.4
	MIN	17	33	49	47	31	30	32	29	25	22	37	25	36	24	48	35	33	31	28	25	19	30	32	28	22	42	33	55	51	40		33.0
CLAYSVILLE 3 W	MAX	60	64	70	72	67	62	52	40	54	60	57	66	57	65	65	51	45	39	53	47	62	58	48	46	61	61	82	82	82	66		59.8
	MIN	14	34	51	47	29	28	32	28	23	19	32	20	33	22	47	35	31	30	26	24	18	35	30	26	20	45	35	60	50	42		32.2
COATESVILLE 1 SW	MAX	44	55	57	58	73	68	69	46	39	56	61	52	62	63	60	60	60	53	50	55	52	59	63	51	43	57	60	63	84	85		58.6
	MIN	27	32	39	43	36	37	45	33	32	26	36	35	37	30	40	47	38	30	35	31	29	36	38	31	28	39	38	45	55	58		36.9
COLUMBIA	MAX	57	59	57	75	73	69	54	41	60	62	55	63	64	61	58	62	53	51	57	55	60	65	53	48	58	59	66	89	85	70		61.3
	MIN	26	41	42	47	47	41	41	35	33	29	37	32	37	34	45	47	38	31	38	34	30	44	38	35	28	41	40	50	58	59		39.3
CONFLUENCE 1 SW DAM	MAX	37	60	61	71	73	66	61	52	35	50	62	56	62	53	64	63	47	45	37	47	40	59	57	44	39	57	60	80	83	82		56.8
	MIN	20	23	49	49	44	33	38	26	23	26	40	25	32	25	44	41	29	32	32	28	22	41	32	26	28	44	39	50	50	51		34.7
CORRY	MAX	48	53	68	66	59	64	58	34	45	50	60	62	55	65	64	45	40	38	45	41	49	49	41	44	54	50	73	72	74	63		54.3
	MIN	8	35	50	43	32	28	30	27	21	21	32	25	33	23	43	32	30	30	23	23	22	29	31	25	20	37	30	56	46	35		30.7
COUDERSPORT 3 NW	MAX																		39	43	38	52	46	41	52	50	48	58	78	78	41		
	MIN																		29	26	24	16	26	29	20	16	32	28	52	48	29		
DERRY	MAX																																
	MIN																																
DEVAULT 1 W	MAX	54	56	57	72	67	68	50	38	54	58	54	60	63	59	59	67	52	50	53	50	60	63	49	52	56	58	61	84	84	68		59.2
	MIN																																
DIXON	MAX	40	48	48	68	73	65	66	45	38	47	52	56	60	53	60	60	61	50	51	46	44	55	54	47	48	55	49	67	85	83		55.8
	MIN	22	25	31	43	33	28	35	31	29	23	24	24	30	22	34	48	39	30	31	29	23	32	32	27	21	29	38	39	53	56		32.0
DONEGAL	MAX	53	58	61	71	60	57	49	35	46	56	51	57	47	62	61	45	39	33	44	35	54	47	38	36	53	50	77	80	78	57		53.0
	MIN	13	33	48	41	32	30	25	21	21	19	26	19	28	20	42	29	25	26	23	19	16	29	25	25	21	34	29	48	48	37		28.4
DONORA	MAX	51	61	65	75	76	69	66	50	49	58	62	61	67	62	67	67	49	45	49	53	56	62	53	47	56	64	78	85	88	84		62.5
	MIN	27	41	57	63	42	40	49	32	31	30	43	31	42	31	54	41	35	33	34	34	28	45	34	34	29	47	42	67	59	48		40.8
DU BOIS 7 E	MAX	45	55	64	72	62	60	54	33	49	56	55	61	61	62	61	56	43	39	45	43	53	52	46	41	51	54	68	81	79	67		55.6
	MIN	8	31	45	45	37	27	32	26	26	20	35	22	31	24	48	37	31	28	28	28	21	30	30	26	18	39	30	59	51	39		31.7
EAGLES MERE	MAX	32	45	45	61	62	62	62	40	32	44	42	50	56	50	53	53	53	42	44	45	40	52	51	42	42	45	43	54	81	77		50.0
	MIN	19	22	35	43	33	36	38	26	21	24	29	31	34	26	30	41	31	30	26	28	20	24	24	24	26	24	36	37	51	56		30.8
EAST BRADY	MAX	55	63	70	74	66	65	62	51	54	60	63	65	65	67	68	65	48	43	52	49	59	59	51	45	60	58	80	84	83	74		61.9
	MIN	19	35	49	48	33	33	22	28	27	24	38	27	39	25	38	39	36	33	31	32	24	23	34	31	27	43	35	47	42	41		33.4
EBENSBURG	MAX	53	58	65	65	64	59	41	32	48	53	55	56	58	61	63	56	41	36	44	41	53	50	35	35	48	48	68	80	78			53.2
	MIN	16	37	51	42	38	35	30	25	25	24	30	24	29	32	46	32	29	29	25	27	25	32	29	25	21	39	32	57	52			32.3
EMPORIUM 1 E	MAX	36	49	54	63	72	65	64	44	36	51	58	60	66	54	64	63	47	45	42	48	42	55	52	45	47	55	54	70	82	81		55.5
	MIN	15	19	33	41	31	26	32	29	19	18	25	22	30	21	26	41	34	31	29	27	17	24	32	24	18	26	32	34	55	46		28.6
EPHRATA	MAX	54	55	54	67	67	66	51	40	56	58	55	60	62	58	55	63	51	52	55	52	60	62	55	48	54	57	62	85	83	71		58.9
	MIN	26	38	40	44	42	41	33	31	30	30	35	29	34	31	43	42	36	33	33	34	26	44	36	33	23	38	37	47	57	52		36.6
ERIE CAA AIRPORT	MAX	43	64	71	68	56	65	52	35	44	44	51	52	45	65	58	43	43	38	42	38	51	44	39	43	54	49	74	74	74	46		52.2
	MIN	22	42	54	42	38	41	31	31	26	23	35	29	34	32	40	36	33	33	33	29	30	32	29	29	27	37	37	43	43	34		34.2

See Reference Notes Following Station Index

DAILY TEMPERATURES

Table 5 - Continued

Station		Day Of Month 1	2	3	4	5	6	7	8	9	10	11	12	13	14	15	16	17	18	19	20	21	22	23	24	25	26	27	28	29	30	31	Average
EVERETT 1 SW	MAX	57	58	60	70	73	63	58	57	52	60	58	64	62	64	60	54	46	44	54	53	60	62	59	60	58	57	66	81	88	86		61.5
	MIN	20	32	49	43	34	31	34	30	25	28	23	27	34	29	45	32	34	29	27	26	29	34	28	30	27	39	36	42	38	45		32.7
FARRELL SHARON	MAX	56	63	74	70	68	67	59	37	56	60	66	68	56	68	64	48	47	42	50	44	61	52	47	47	58	57	79	83	78	63		59.6
	MIN	20	40	53	45	35	41	30	28	27	26	38	28	34	28	29	32	33	30	28	26	26	31	31	29	21	40	38	60	47	37		33.7
FORD CITY 4 S DAM	MAX	40	56	63	68	73	65	62	49	32	53	59	57	64	53	65	68	46	45	40	50	43	59	50	45	45	58	57	79	83	82		57.0
	MIN	19	26	40	52	34	31	37	28	26	23	31	26	35	25	37	39	33	30	28	29	23	36	31	27	25	28	34	42	53	44		32.4
FRANKLIN	MAX	53	55	68	70	64	64	62	38	51	59	63	64	63	64	63	47	41	41	49	48	56	56	48	44	55	55	77	79	77	67		58.0
	MIN	20	35	48	39	34	31	32	27	25	24	35	28	37	25	47	35	32	31	30	28	24	29	33	30	22	40	34	55	52	38		33.3
FREDERICKSVILLE 2 SE	MAX																																
	MIN																																
FREELAND	MAX	47	45	61	60	60	59	53	40	45	48	49	53	49	47	49	49	43	48	43	50	48	53	53	50	48	49	54	79	79	74		52.8
	MIN	20	28	35	41	35	40	28	24	25	24	30	26	29	26	38	40	29	25	29	29	28	37	29	29	23	29	36	48	56	46		32.1
GEORGE SCHOOL	MAX	55	56	55	69	66	64	52	40	55	58	51	58	61	58	56	72	52	52	52	51	55	63	56	46	55	56	65	84	83	78		59.1
	MIN	27	34	41	44	41	36	35	34	32	30	35	36	37	35	40	44	39	34	35	31	26	40	39	30	26	39	36	47	58	59		37.3
GETTYSBURG	MAX	47	56	56	70	80	70	68	49	43	57	61	53	63	64	62	60	57	49	47	55	52	62	64	49	45	55	64	68	86	84		59.9
	MIN	25	39	42	47	47	43	47	33	33	30	38	34	40	35	46	48	38	36	37	37	31	42	38	33	28	41	44	51	60	65		40.3
GRATZ 1 N	MAX	44	52	53	59	69	68	65	45	36	53	56	54	61	59	59	59	58	50	47	54	49	59	59	48	45	53	52	61	85	82		56.5
	MIN	24	31	41	46	42	35	44	31	30	28	35	27	35	28	40	45	37	30	35	36	25	34	32	32	24	33	35	42	55	56		35.6
GREENVILLE	MAX	55	61	70	68	65	64	59	37	51	55	64	65	58	67	62	45	44	39	50	46	57	50	43	46	56	55	77	79	76	67		57.7
	MIN	19	40	54	46	33	33	32	30	23	23	36	27	34	27	43	37	33	32	29	27	23	28	32	31	22	40	36	59	48	36		33.8
HANOVER	MAX	47	58	61	70	79	71	69	48	40	58	61	55	64	66	64	61	60	51	50	55	54	61	66	50	41	57	63	69	88	86		60.8
	MIN	23	40	40	43	43	42	45	30	28	29	36	29	35	32	36	49	33	31	33	34	25	33	36	32	27	33	42	45	57	60		36.7
HARRISBURG WB AP	MAX	54	56	55	70	69	65	49	40	56	61	52	64	60	63	60	62	50	49	53	51	62	60	49	42	56	55	66	87	84	69		59.0
	MIN	29	40	43	47	48	43	36	35	35	31	38	32	38	33	46	43	38	35	37	35	30	42	37	34	30	42	40	50	57	48		39.1
HAWLEY 1 S DAM	MAX	35	43	45	58	63	59	62	37	36	43	46	50	55	50	58	56	58	45	49	40	40	52	50	42	44	54	43	59	81	78		51.0
	MIN	27	19	26	35	37	27	33	28	26	21	21	24	26	23	37	45	36	27	32	27	25	30	31	29	22	32	32	34	48	50		30.3
HOLTWOOD	MAX	53	57	52	70	66	65	50	41	55	55	53	61	59	59	57	61	50	49	52	50	59	61	49	43	54	59	62	82	81	70		57.8
	MIN	30	41	43	46	43	44	37	37	37	35	39	36	39	37	46	45	41	37	39	39	32	44	41	37	34	43	45	49	55	50		40.7
HUNTINGDON	MAX	42	57	60	71	79	70	65	48	41	58	66	60	69	58	67	63	54	48	47	54	46	64	56	47	44	58	54	68	89	87		59.7
	MIN	21	22	34	45	41	34	34	32	29	24	25	25	26	27	27	49	37	37	36	32	22	24	33	28	27	37	38	40	53	56		33.2
INDIANA 3 SE	MAX	56	64	69	74	65	63	50	36	53	61	57	64	53	66	69	60	45	40	50	46	60	57	42	44	58	55	80	84	81	71		59.1
	MIN	18	34	52	46	31	32	33	30	27	21	37	24	32	24	50	36	33	30	30	29	22	38	32	28	22	43	34	53	54	43		33.9
IRWIN	MAX																		42	46	51	60	61	41	45	61	62	82	85	85	85		
	MIN	31	40	46	50	41	36	34	36	29	25	38	28	39	28	50	39	38	32	30	31	25	42	32	30	26	44	39	65	55	44		37.4
JAMESTOWN 2 NW	MAX	39	53	60	70	66	64	64	48	37	49	53	62	62	49	65	63	48	44	39	50	39	56	47	43	45	55	52	75	75	74		54.9
	MIN	19	28	39	54	36	35	44	29	22	20	37	26	33	28	40	37	32	31	28	27	23	27	32	31	22	35	34	45	46	36		32.5
JIM THORPE	MAX	54	54	63	65	67	68	63	40	51	57	57	63		63	57	62	55	53	52	53	57	61	57	57	55	50	58	84	84	72		59.7
	MIN	24	30	40	45	41	33	38	31	29	31	34	29		28	41	50	36	28	34	32	26	43	35	31	24	36	38	47	56	57		36.1
JOHNSTOWN	MAX	41	60	66	70	78	69	65	55	40	54	65	58	67	57	69	64	50	48	43	51	47	63	55	44	44	59	59	80	88	84		59.8
	MIN	24	36	43	55	43	36	45	28	30	28	37	28	38	29	48	41	33	31	31	32	28	37	32	31	28	35	39	54	56	47		36.
KANE 1 NNE	MAX	35	46	51	59	69	61	60	43	34	46	56	58	62	48	61	62	42	40	38	43	37	50	47	40	44	54	49	69	77	77		51.
	MIN	5	20	36	39	28	26	37	27	18	17	21	21	31	20	38	36	30	30	28	22	17	26	30	22	17	36	29	43	52	37		28.
KEGG	MAX	60	61	70	76	67	62	48	36	43	61	53	64	55	65	65	56	45	42	49	43	60	65	55	40	56	58	74	86	66	60		58.
	MIN	21	32	52	48	41	35	33	32	29	26	32	26	33	27	46	35	33	32	32	28	26	36	29	29	24	40	39	47	42	46		34.
LANCASTER 2 NE PUMP STA	MAX	56	57	57	72	71	69	56	43	58	61	56	63	63	59	57	65	55	51	55	54	61	64	53	48	56	59	63	88	85	73		60.
	MIN	25	35	39	45	36	37	40	33	32	26	33	29	34	31	43	46	37	31	36	34	27	44	37	35	26	40	36	48	54	59		36.
LANDISVILLE	MAX	46	54	58	55	73	68	65	46	40	56	58	53	61	62	60	62	61	51	49	52	51	59	67	50	41	56	57	64	85	87		58.
	MIN	24	35	41	45	46	39	45	33	32	32	35	31	34	32	32	47	37	33	36	33	27	39	37	35	25	34	38	35	47	63		36.
LAWRENCEVILLE 2 S	MAX	37	45	50	66	70	62	65	43	37	47	53	55	61	51	62	57	56	47	47	46	40	56	50	45	47	56	51	64	79	83		54.
	MIN	16	20	30	40	34	27	31	36	25	21	22	24	33	22	35	47	36	31	30	29	19	27	32	23	20	30	34	34	47	42		29.
LEBANON 2 NW	MAX																																
	MIN																																
LEWISTOWN	MAX	44	54	57	69	79	71	66	49	40	58	62	57	67	60	65	60	61	51	50	55	50	61	57	50	44	58	53	65	89	87		59.
	MIN	24	24	38	45	45	39	38	35	32	27	27	29	29	32	29	51	38	35	36	36	27	27	33	32	28	28	40	41	49	52		34.
LINESVILLE 5 WNW	MAX	51	59	69	66	63	64	52	35	48	51	60	60	49	64	58	44	44	38	49	39	54	46	42	45	54	50	74	71	74	67		54.
	MIN	20	38	50	43	36	33	31	29	24	22	33	27	30	30	41	35	32	31	28	24	25	26	32	31	23	39	32	52	44	35		32.
LOCK HAVEN	MAX	55	55	61	79	71	66	57	40	56	60	58	67	58	64	59	59	48	50	54	49	60	53	52	49	58	53	64	88	88	69		60.
	MIN	23	37	37	50	41	35	35	32	29	26	32	28	38	29	50	47	38	31	33	35	24	36	33	29	25	40	39	50	57	49		36.
MADERA	MAX	36	49	56	64	74	64	61	45	34	51	57	54	63	53	62	66	47	43	40	47	41	58	52	43	40	53	49	69	83	82		54.
	MIN	14	15	37	48	32	27	30	26	24	18	23	24	25	20	26	40	30	27	27	27	17	25	28	22	16	22	29	35	51	44		27.
MARCUS HOOK	MAX	56	55	54	67	67	68	50	39	58	62	50	59	57	58	57	68	54	53	54	52	54	67	53	44	54	61	62	77	78	79		58.
	MIN	31	39	43	44	49	45	35	35	34	36	39	38	37	38	46	45	41	38	39	38	33	46	42	36	36	41	43	48	62	50		40.
MARTINSBURG CAA AP	MAX	54	56	65	75	66	60	46	34	50	59	51	62	53	63	61	55	45	40	48	41	58	51	40	39	53	52	67	85	83	63		55.
	MIN	24	39	53	44	40	37	32	29	29	28	35	28	38	29	46	35	32	32	31	28	26	32	31	28	25	41	40	56	56	42		35.
MEADVILLE 1 S	MAX	37	52	59	69	67	64	66	47	36	49	52	62	63	48	64	61	45	42	37	49	37	52	47	42	45	54	52	75	74	74		54.
	MIN	19	25	39	54	32	33	44	29	24	24	27	28	34	28	39	37	33	32	28	26	20	27	32	30	23	33	33	44	49	36		32.
MERCER 2 NNE	MAX	55	56	54	65	64	65	51	39	48	54	70	67	57	64	55	48	44	38	47	40	55	56	48	47	55	56	77	78	77	67		56.
	MIN	20	42	40	36	38	28	38	34	29	26	40	30	32	34	40	40	34	30	27	29	22	30	34	30	20	37	39	57	45	34		33.
MIDDLETOWN OLMSTED FLD	MAX	55	56	55	69	69	65	49	40	56	60	54	62	60	62	57	61	51	50	54	51	61	61	51	43	56	55	64	87	85	69		58.
	MIN	28	42	43	48	48	42	37	36	35	30	38	33	37	34	47	45	40	36	38	35	27	43	38	35	30	43	40	50	58	47		39.
MIDLAND DAM 7	MAX	55	61	70	71	62	63	51	40	53	59	58	63	51	70	65	47	42	39	50	38	61	50	42	43	58	56	78	81	80	64		57.
	MIN	29	46	55	49	41	40	32	31	30	30	40	32	40	33	42	39	36	31	33	32	30	37	34	35	31	46	42	58	60	43		38.
MONTROSE 1 E	MAX	33	40	41	61	66	58	60	37	30	38	43	46	53	46	55	52	55	44	45	39	38	50	48	40	41	50	43	57	78	79		48.
	MIN	21	23	30	39	36	38	37	26	25	26	26	30	33	27	30	41	34	28	28	29	22	26	31	26	26	31	32	39	50	51		31.
MORGANTOWN	MAX	52	54	55	71	65	66	48	37	53	57	52	59	60	57	59	64	51	51	52	52	56	60	50	42	53	56	58	84	81	71		57.
	MIN	25	35	40	43	41	39	32	31	30	27	34	33	34	29	41	39	35	31	31	33	25	42	36	31	23	38	40	38	58	45		35.
MT GRETNA 2 SE	MAX																63	55	50	54	51	60	61	50	42	55	55	60	86	85	67		
	MIN	22	44	50	54	44	40	32	32	30	26	35	29	32	30	43	41	34	28	35	32	30	41	36	31	30	40	48	49	56	45		37.

See Reference Notes Following Station Index

DAILY TEMPERATURES

PENNSYLVANIA
APRIL 1956

	Day Of Month 1	2	3	4	5	6	7	8	9	10	11	12	13	14	15	16	17	18	19	20	21	22	23	24	25	26	27	28	29	30	31	Average
MAX	44	44	57	58	60	72	54	33	41	46	47	54	53	53	49	57	45	45	44	40	50	48	47	49	45	44	55	79	78	76		52.2
MIN	24	24	35	40	37	33	32	27	22	26	29	26	28	24	35	44	32	27	30	27	23	36	31	22	20	32	38	45	48	41		31.3
MAX	52	49	66	76	65	65	56	41	47	47	54	59	53	58	53	53	47	49	45	49	55	55	45	49	53	47	57	84	81	72		56.1
MIN	20	20	40	40	36	34	32	28	24	22	29	26	34	23	40	44	32	29	28	20	20	35	29	24	22	34	29	48	52	41		31.2
MAX	56	58	62	76	78	68	56	42	55	63	61	64	60	62	62	59	49	44	46	58	62	61	45	50	52	57	67	90	84	72		60.6
MIN	32	38	42	49	62	49	39	30	32	31	38	29	36	32	52	41	38	31	33	32	32	39	33	34	28	46	46	55	61	51		39.7
MAX	56	62	72	72	66	66	63	39	54	60	63	65	64	67	66	49	45	42	52	48	62	62	48	47	58	58	79	83	78	74		60.7
MIN	20	41	53	50	36	33	33	29	24	24	35	25	35	27	45	38	33	31	29	26	27	31	33	32	26	43	36	64	51	39		35.0
MAX	47	57	65	75	75	69	66	50	48	57	63	60	67	63	68	66	50	47	48	53	55	63	55	48	57	64	78	84	86	82		62.2
MIN	22	37	54	56	40	40	50	34	33	32	48	31	42	31	52	42	37	35	37	35	29	46	36	36	32	48	42	61	57	48		40.8
MAX	46	55	56	58	69	72	65	48	40	59	61	57	67	62	65	59	59	51	49	48	52	64	61	49	45	58	55	64	91	85		59.0
MIN	22	24	37	44	46	35	37	35	34	25	28	25	28	28	31	46	38	31	36	34	25	30	34	34	28	28	39	41	57	57		34.6
MAX	55	65	68	75	72	65	50	41	55	61	56	65	57	67	66	55	52	42	53	43	63	54	41	51	61	61	84	86	82	63		60.3
MIN	20	37	38	46	36	33	32	27	30	23	29	23	32	34	36	32	36	22	29	26	27	32	28	28	29	38	36	59	51	42		33.0
MAX	56	57	59	73	69	68	50	39	55	60	52	60	61	60	60	71	56	55	53	51	58	66	54	48	58	57	64	86	85	74		60.5
MIN	30	37	44	45	47	42	33	34	33	34	36	36	37	37	45	43	40	37	38	38	31	46	40	36	31	42	40	50	62	48		39.7
MAX	52	51	57	62	67	64	46	38	50	55	54	62	55	57	55	62	50	50	50	47	57	60	49	47	54	51	60	83	83	69		56.6
MIN	28	30	41	45	44	34	32	32	32	28	31	27	35	30	42	40	36	30	35	32	27	41	35	31	26	38	37	46	57	38		35.3
MAX	58	58	58	69	71	70	51	41	55	60	51	59	62	60	61	72	53	53	53	52	58	67	53	44	56	56	65	84	84	78		60.4
MIN	34	40	45	46	49	51	34	36	36	39	40	38	39	40	43	46	43	41	39	40	34	47	42	38	36	42	43	50	66	49		42.2
MAX	56	57	57	70	67	68	51	40	54	59	51	59	60	59	62	72	53	52	53	52	57	64	52	44	55	57	64	84	84	75		59.6
MIN	29	37	43	44	45	45	34	34	35	36	38	38	37	39	43	46	43	40	37	38	32	45	41	35	33	41	40	49	63	47		40.2
MAX	56	57	58	70	65	69	50	40	55	60	51	60	61	59	61	72	54	53	53	51	56	64	53	45	56	58	63	83	84	75		59.7
MIN	33	42	46	45	49	48	35	35	37	41	41	39	38	43	44	57	43	41	38	40	34	49	43	38	37	42	46	49	64	66		43.4
MAX	55	57	58	68	69	67	62	43	54	60	59	61	62	59	60	71	53	53	51	52	58	62	59	53	55	56	64	84	85	84		61.1
MIN	28	33	40	45	43	51	42	34	34	32	36	35	37	33	44	52	40	33	40	39	30	44	40	33	30	32	39	49	59	63		39.7
MAX	55	53	55	67	64	65	49	37	54	59	48	57	58	56	58	68	51	50	51	52	56	62	53	45	56	57	63	83	82	73		57.9
MIN	34	39	44	43	49	48	33	33	34	38	37	36	36	40	42	45	42	40	38	38	36	48	43	39	40	42	44	49	65	50		41.5
MAX	46	53	62	72	63	59	44	31	49	58	51	61	51	59	55	52	41	38	43	38	54	50	38	38	51	52	61	80	78	60		52.9
MIN	12	39	48	43	33	28	29	27	25	20	33	21	29	22	45	33	31	30	28	25	22	33	28	24	16	36	30	55	53	37		31.2
MAX	56	58	59	72	72	67	52	41	55	58	58	60	64	61	59	71	55	55	53	53	58	63	54	51	58	58	63	86	85	84		61.3
MIN	23	28	29	38	38	34	38	31	30	25	29	30	33	30	40	44	35	30	33	30	25	39	37	29	23	37	37	47	53	61		34.5
MAX	35	44	46	56	57	60	61	37	32	39	46	46	54	54	53	52	57	43	45	42	41	51	53	42	42	49	47	55	79	76		49.8
MIN	22	29	34	42	36	41	36	25	22	25	30	26	29	26	34	39	31	27	27	29	20	35	30	25	23	30	32	42	54	52		31.8
MAX	55	61	70	71	65	61	48	38	53	58	55	64	53	63	64	45	41	37	50	39	60	50	42	44	57	56	78	82	79	62		56.7
MIN	22	44	53	48	40	42	31	28	28	29	41	34	38	34	43	37	33	32	32	30	29	33	32	31	28	44	44	62	58	41		37.4
MAX	55	63	71	74	68	64	52	40	54	60	58	66	55	66	65	48	45	40	52	42	63	51	45	45	60	58	82	85	82	65		59.1
MIN	28	46	55	51	46	42	34	31	33	33	41	37	42	35	46	39	36	34	35	34	33	36	34	37	31	47	44	65	62	43		40.3
MAX	34	39	40	53	60	54	59	37	40	44	49	54	45	51	53	58	45	45	45	36	37	50	48	41	41	48	41	60	78	76		48.7
MIN	25	15	31	32	36	26	36	27	19	20	20	27	21	34	37	33	28	29	29	26	21	31	32	23	20	32	29	36	47	53		29.2
MAX	48	46	58	54	62	65	70	67	55	52	55	60	53	65	60	62	61	54	56	50	54	52	60	52	52	49	57	60	82	87		58.6
MIN	27	29	41	45	39	32	44	32	29	24	31	24	32	28	38	47	30	28	34	31	24	38	34	31	23	38	34	40	52	59		34.6
MAX	38	52	60	66	74	65	62	48	36	52	59	57	64	52	64	68	46	46	41	50	40	56	52	44	45	57	57	78	82	80		56.4
MIN	17	25	37	51	34	32	43	26	24	21	29	24	34	25	38	36	30	29	27	28	22	32	29	26	21	31	32	44	52	41		31.3
MAX	55	57	58	64	67	65	58	38	53	59	59	63	63	60	58	62	52	50	52	50	58	60	55	54	56	57	62	85	84	79		59.8
MIN	26	27	39	41	44	34	38	30	31	31	34	31	30	29	39	45	37	32	35	31	28	38	33	30	25	37	33	47	52	59		35.5
MAX	56	56	56	70	68	66	49	40	56	60	55	63	62	59	60	65	52	52	54	52	59	62	51	45	56	55	62	87	84	69		59.4
MIN	31	40	44	45	46	44	33	33	34	34	40	34	38	35	45	45	40	37	37	37	32	46	39	38	31	40	41	50	63	46		39.9
MAX	46	56	64	69	63	62	52	35	49	58	60	64	56	62	65	55	43	38	45	45	54	49	42	44	54	54	70	80	79	68		56.0
MIN	10	30	43	42	29	25	31	28	24	16	29	20	31	19	39	35	32	31	30	25	17	26	30	24	11	39	30	61	50	38		29.8
MAX	55	62	67	73	64	62	51	38	52	60	56	64	61	64	65	60	44	39	50	47	60	58	42	43	58	56	80	84	80	73		58.9
MIN	20	42	52	50	35	34	33	28	26	32	38	26	30	26	49	36	32	32	30	29	24	38	32	29	26	43	37	63	53	41		35.5
MAX	36	48	50	67	74	74	55	45	33	50	50	45	60	53	60	60	62	47	50	45	44	55	53	45	47	56	48	64	84	84		54.8
MIN	28	28	36	42	43	35	35	30	28	28	30	35	34	27	38	40	38	32	32	32	28	38	32	32	28	35	36	38	38	38		33.8
MAX	47	47	66	74	66	65	46	34	43	49	52	58	52	59	56	60	46	51	45	45	54	53	45	45	54	48	60	84	81	64		55.0
MIN	28	30	40	48	42	35	31	28	28	27	31	29	35	27	43	40	35	31	32	28	27	37	32	31	27	37	37	51	55	40		34.7
MAX	56	56	60	66	71	65	46	38	56	58	58	65	60	60	55	60	48	52	56	52	58	59	50	48	56	53	62	88	84	65		58.7
MIN	22	34	46	50	40	33	34	33	32	25	30	27	31	26	47	40	35	34	34	34	24	39	33	30	26	39	39	53	55	41		35.5
MAX	56	56	69	77	76	67	55	40	56	61	60	65	65	62	61	61	55	48	53	52	62	62	48	45	56	58	68	88	82	82		61.5
MIN	25	37	40	49	44	41	38	32	30	28	35	28	39	30	38	48	36	35	36	31	28	45	35	33	26	40	42	49	55	55		37.6
MAX	59	63	72	71	65	63	50	39	52	57	58	63	54	67	64	46	44	39	51	40	63	49	43	43	57	56	79	82	81	64		57.8
MIN	24	42	54	48	39	37	31	30	31	26	37	31	35	30	43	37	36	32	35	30	29	34	33	30	28	43	41	57	55	39		36.6
MAX	55	60	68	70	68	62	50	35	57	59	60	65	59	65	61	46	45	38	50	45	58	54	44	43	56	53	77	78	76	67		57.5
MIN	21	40	52	45	37	40	34	27	26	25	37	32	36	30	41	34	32	29	28	27	28	33	32	30	25	42	49	55	55	37		35.3
MAX	54	60	65	72	62	58	47	35	48	59	56	62	57	62	61	56	42	38	45	44	56	55	40	38	52	54	74	80	78	72		56.1
MIN	19	35	51	53	39	33	33	24	26	24	35	22	32	24	48	37	29	30	26	25	24	38	29	28	22	42	33	59	50	42		33.7
MAX	38	51	60	70	67	61	65	48	40	47	52	60	60	53	66	60	43	45	40	49	47	53	46	44	46	55	53	71	72	72		54.5
MIN	19	23	41	56	35	37	47	33	28	22	35	28	35	32	45	42	36	33	32	29	30	33	42	33	28	34	36	44	48	39		35.2
MAX	57	58	68	69	61	57	49	30	45	57	49	58	50	62	60	54	37	32	42	36	54	55	40	36	52	52	70	79	75	59		53.4
MIN	17	31	47	43	35	32	30	23	25	23	28	22	30	22	40	32	29	28	27	25	19	35	30	25	21	41	36	48	48	41		31.1
MAX	51	57	66	75	70	62	45	45	45	52	58	65	54	54	62	57	50	43	44	47	57	53	43	43	52	53	54	84	86	62		56.3
MIN	24	40	54	45	41	39	32	29	30	28	33	30	37	31	35	46	34	33	32	32	26	34	30	29	27	34	37	59	50	42		35.8
MAX	50	51	54	57	65	66	44	34	46	55	52	60	55	57	52	63	47	50	45	47	56	60	46	45	55	43	58	83	82	[illegible]		54.8
MIN	21	24	35	40	40	28	31	30	26	24	25	23	27	24	38	39	32	27	26	29	22	40	35	27	20	34	32	40	53	40		31.1
MAX	36	45	49	56	71	64	60	39	32	45	53	51	52	52	53	58	50	41	41	48	41	54	50	38	42	50	43	61	81	81		51.2
MIN	18	18	39	47	34	34	38	25	22	22	25	31	32	26	27	44	29	28	25	26	22	24	29	25	25	28	35	37	53	47		30.5
MAX	35	48	57	69	70	63	63	47	35	49	57	61	65	50	63	64	44	42	39	46	38	54	49	42	44	55	54	77	78	79		54.6
MIN	15	21	34	41	29	28	36	28	25	24	26	21	35	24	37	36	33	31	32	29	22	29	32	26	21	29	33	37	54	38		30.2

See Reference Notes Following Station Index

DAILY TEMPERATURES

Table 5 - Continued

Station		Day Of Month 1	2	3	4	5	6	7	8	9	10	11	12	13	14	15	16	17	18	19	20	21	22	23	24	25	26	27	28	29	30	31	Average
TITUSVILLE WATER WORKS	MAX	45	56	69	63	64	65	60	37	50	55	64	65	55	66	65	45	43	40	42	44	52	42	43	43	56	54	77	76	77	68		56.0
	MIN	12	32	48	43	31	27	29	27	19	14	25	23	33	21	42	33	31	30	22	21	21	24	31	23	18	39	29	57	50	29		29.3
TOWANDA	MAX	49	49	70	72	66	65	58	36	48	51	54	62	54	60	53	60	50	51	48	43	55	54	47	47	55	52	60	84	83	69		56.8
	MIN	23	26	40	44	41	28	33	30	25	21	25	26	31	22	46	44	36	32	32	31	24	32	32	25	21	38	30	54	49	45		32.9
UNIONTOWN	MAX	60	67	73	76	69	64	56	38	54	61	55	65	57	66	64	50	47	42	52	45	60	60	47	41	63	60	82	85	83	64		60.2
	MIN	22	44	55	50	42	38	34	27	31	28	43	28	39	28	50	39	35	34	34	31	25	38	33	34	29	48	40	65	57	47		38.3
UPPER DARBY	MAX	56	58	58	70	68	70	51	40	55	60	53	59	62	59	56	71	54	53	53	52	58	63	52	48	56	57	64	84	83	78		60.0
	MIN	29	37	42	45	42	43	39	33	33	34	37	35	36	37	42	45	39	35	36	39	32	43	43	34	31	40	39	48	61	57		39.5
WARREN	MAX	49	55	64	70	62	65	58	35	48	53	63	65	56	65	62	45	41	40	47	37	51	47	44	45	56	52	74	74	78	65		55.5
	MIN	15	35	46	45	33	30	31	29	23	23	30	27	36	26	44	35	33	32	29	25	22	29	36	24	21	39	33	59	49	37		32.5
WAYNESBURG 2 W	MAX	60	63	76	74	67	64	54	42	52	60	57	65	63	66	65	59	46	41	53	50	62	60	48	45	62	62	82	85	82	71		61.2
	MIN	19	36	51	52	33	34	36	24	29	24	35	25	37	25	47	38	34	33	32	28	21	35	32	31	26	45	38	55	54	46		35.2
WELLSBORO 3 S	MAX	34	45	49	58	65	60	59	42	35	44	48	48	57	49	57	54	52	43	43	45	39	51	48	42	45	52	48	61	82	81		51.2
	MIN	19	21	37	45	34	36	38	26	23	26	27	28	33	26	31	44	30	29	26	27	22	27	29	26	25	31	34	40	46	45		31.0
WELLSVILLE	MAX	54	57	62	76	78	67	52	41	56	58	53	61	62	61	58	61	50	48	54	52	60	62	50	46	55	58	65	86	83	74		60.0
	MIN	21	35	38	37	39	36	43	34	32	24	36	26	33	28	44	46	34	26	36	29	20	38	37	34	22	42	37	54	52	54		35.5
WEST CHESTER	MAX	57	57	56	70	69	70	46	42	58	62	52	60	64	61	61	70	56	52	53	54	61	66	52	46	59	59	61	86	85	75		60.7
	MIN	29	31	45	45	46	45	33	32	35	37	34	36	36	42	50	38	35	36	37	31	43	40	36	33	40	40	48	60	64	43		40.7
NILLIAMSPORT WB AP	MAX	55	53	66	73	71	66	48	39	55	58	57	65	58	62	56	58	50	53	55	48	60	58	51	50	55	49	60	88	84	66		58.9
	MIN	27	34	47	50	41	35	34	33	32	27	31	29	35	28	48	41	37	36	34	36	26	40	34	30	26	39	37	54	56	43		36.7
YORK 3 SSW PUMP STA	MAX	55	59	64	79	78	68	54	43	59	61	61	63	64	62	59	62	54	51	55	54	60	63	52	48	56	62	68	86	85	74		62.0
	MIN	23	37	40	49	42	38	42	35	30	27	36	28	37	31	47	46	36	29	35	33	24	37	38	34	26	43	39	57	57	61		37.9

EVAPORATION AND WIND

Table 6

Station		Day of month 1	2	3	4	5	6	7	8	9	10	11	12	13	14	15	16	17	18	19	20	21	22	23	24	25	26	27	28	29	30	31	Total or Avg.
CONFLUENCE 1 SW DAM	EVAP	.03	.10	-	.03	.24	.18	.03	.05	.29	.10	.13	.11	.14	.16	.17	.05	.04	.00	.01	.09	.10	.18	.09	.06	.00	.16	.17	.16	.22	.18		B3.38
	WIND	49	11	62	32	164	60	69	117	127	72	51	56	57	91	88	85	124	84	133	70	110	129	87	78	32	83	39	63	71	114		2408
PIMPLE HILL	EVAP	-	-	-	-	-	-	-	-	-	-	-	-	-	-	-	.09	-	.08	.06	.09	.09	.15	.19	.08	.10	.20	.01	.09	.27	-		-
	WIND	-	-	-	-	-	-	-	-	-	-	-	-	-	-	-	164	196	150	126	83	116	175	105	121	85	129	84	180	124	168		-

See Reference Notes Following Station Index

Table 7

SNOWFALL AND SNOW ON GROUND

PENNSYLVANIA
APRIL 1956

Station		1	2	3	4	5	6	7	8	9	10	11	12	13	14	15	16	17	18	19	20	21	22	23	24	25	26	27	28	29	30	31
ALLENTOWN WB AIRPORT	SNOWFALL							.9	1.1																							
	SN ON GND								2																							
	WTR EQUIV								-																							
ALTOONA HORSESHOE CURVE	SNOWFALL							T	T									T	1.5	.5	1.0			1.0	T							
	SN ON GND							T	T									T														
ARTEMAS 1 WNW	SNOWFALL																	T							-							
	SN ON GND																								-							
BEAVERTOWN	SNOWFALL								T									T				T	T	1.0	T							
	SN ON GND																															
BELLEFONTE 4 S	SNOWFALL								T									T	T					-	T							
	SN ON GND								T	T														1	T							
BERWICK	SNOWFALL								T										T					T								
	SN ON GND								T																							
BRADFORD 4 W RES	SNOWFALL								4.0								T	1.3	1.5	1.3	T			1.0								
	SN ON GND	11	9	5	5	3	2	1	4	2	1						T	1	T		T											
BROOKVILLE CAA AIRPORT	SNOWFALL							1.0	T								T	1.7	2.2	T	.1		.3	1.8	.5							
	SN ON GND	T							1	T									1	T				2	T							
BURGETTSTOWN 2 W	SNOWFALL							-											-					-								
	SN ON GND							-											1					1								
BUTLER	SNOWFALL																		1.0	T	T			1.0	T							
	SN ON GND																		1	T				1								
CANTON 1 NW	SNOWFALL								3.8	T									T	T	T			1.5	T							
	SN ON GND	3	3	T					4	4	T	T								T				2								
CARLISLE	SNOWFALL																								T							
	SN ON GND																															
CHAMBERSBURG 1 ESE	SNOWFALL								T											T					.2							
	SN ON GND																															
CLARION 3 SW	SNOWFALL								T										2.5	T				1.0								
	SN ON GND	T							T										3	T				1	T							
COATESVILLE 1 SW	SNOWFALL							-	.5																	-						
	SN ON GND							-	1																	-						
CORRY	SNOWFALL							3.0	.5									T	T	T	T			T								
	SN ON GND	T						3	2									T	T	T	T											
DIXON	SNOWFALL	T							5.0	.2										T	T			1.5	T							
	SN ON GND	T							5	2	T									T				2								
DONEGAL	SNOWFALL							T	T								T	.5	1.6	T	1.5		.5	3.0	T							
	SN ON GND							T	T								T	T	1	T	T		T	T	T							
EAGLES MERE	SNOWFALL								9.0	1.0					T				T	T	T			5.0								
	SN ON GND	5	3	T	T				9	10	4	T	T						T	T	T			5	T	T						
EMPORIUM 1 E	SNOWFALL								1.0	T								T	.2	T				T	.2	T						
	SN ON GND								1										T	T				T	T							
EVERETT 1 SW	SNOWFALL																T															
	SN ON GND																T															
FORD CITY 4 S DAM	SNOWFALL								T	T									1.0	1.0		T		2.0	T							
	SN ON GND																		T					1	T							
FRANKLIN	SNOWFALL								1.0																1.0							
	SN ON GND								1																1							
GEORGE SCHOOL	SNOWFALL							.1	3.2																							
	SN ON GND							T	2																							
GETTYSBURG	SNOWFALL							T	T																T							
	SN ON GND																															
GRATZ 1 N	SNOWFALL								5.0	T											T	T		T	T							
	SN ON GND								5	3											T			T								
GREENVILLE	SNOWFALL							T									T	T	.3	T	T			1.0	1.3							
	SN ON GND							T																								
HARRISBURG WB AIRPORT	SNOWFALL							T	T															T	T							
	SN ON GND																															
	WTR EQUIV																															
HAWLEY 1 S DAM	SNOWFALL								9.0	T											T			2.5		T						
	SN ON GND	2	2	1	T				9	7	3	1									T			3		T						
HUNTINGDON	SNOWFALL									T									T	T	T			T	T	T						
	SN ON GND																							T								
INDIANA 3 SE	SNOWFALL							T	T									T	T		T	T	T	1.0	T							
	SN ON GND																		T		T			1								
JOHNSTOWN	SNOWFALL								T	T							T	T	T	T	T	T		T	T	T	T		-			
	SN ON GND																		T	T									-			
KANE 1 NNE	SNOWFALL	T							1.5	.4				T			T	1.2	1.0	1.3	.2	.2		1.6	.5	T						
	SN ON GND	14	11	7	2	T	T	T	1	1	T	T	T	T				1	1	1	T			1	1							
LANDISVILLE	SNOWFALL	-	-	-	-	-	-	-	-	-	-	-	-	-	-	-	-	-	-	-	-	-	-	-	-	-	-	-	-	-	-	
	SN ON GND	-	-	-	-	-	-	-	-	-	-	-	-	-	-	-	-	-	-	-	-	-	-	-	-	-	-	-	-	-	-	
LAWRENCEVILLE 2 S	SNOWFALL								4.0	1.0										T				T								
	SN ON GND	2	1	T					4	4	T													T								
LEWISTOWN	SNOWFALL								T													T		T		T						
	SN ON GND								T															T								
LOCK HAVEN	SNOWFALL	T							T	T							T	T	T	T		T			T	.2						
	SN ON GND																								T	T						
MEADVILLE 1 S	SNOWFALL	.1							3.5	T							T	.6	.7	.3	T	.2		.7	1.6	T					T	
	SN ON GND	T	T						3	T								T	T	T				T	1							

See reference notes following Station Index.

Table 7- Continued

SNOWFALL AND SNOW ON GROUND

Station		1	2	3	4	5	6	7	8	9	10	11	12	13	14	15	16	17	18	19	20	21	22	23	24	25	26	27	28	29	30	31
MONTROSE 1 E	SNOWFALL	T							11.6	2.5					T			T	T	T	T	.6		8.7	.8	T	.7					
	SN ON GND	9	8	6	3	T	T	T	12	12	8	5	3	T	T	T		T		T	T	1		9	3	T	1					
MOUNT POCONO 2 N AIRPORT	SNOWFALL								-					T				T	T	T	T			2.5			1.3					
	SN ON GND								9	6	3																					
NEW CASTLE 1 N	SNOWFALL								.5	.2								T				T										
	SN ON GND																															
NEWPORT	SNOWFALL	T								T												T			T	T						
	SN ON GND																															
PALMERTON	SNOWFALL							2.0	.5										T		T											
	SN ON GND							-	T																							
PHILADELPHIA WB AIRPORT	SNOWFALL							T	T																T							
	SN ON GND																															
	WTR EQUIV																															
PHILADELPHIA SHAWMONT	SNOWFALL								1.0																							
	SN ON GND																															
PHILIPSBURG CAA AIRPORT	SNOWFALL							T	T								T	.6	.2	T	T		T	2.1	T							
	SN ON GND	2	1						1	1									1	T	T		T	3								
PHOENIXVILLE 1 E	SNOWFALL	-	-	-	-	-	-	-	-	-	-	-	-	-	-	-	-	-	-	-	-	-	-	-	-	-	-	-	-	-	-	
	SN ON GND	-	-	-	-	-	-	-	-	-	-	-	-	-	-	-	-	-	-	-	-	-	-	-	-	-	-	-	-	-	-	
PITTSBURGH WB AIRPORT 2	SNOWFALL							T	T								T	T	2.8	T	T		T	.5	T							
	SN ON GND								T										2		T			1								
	WTR EQUIV																		.1													
PORT CLINTON 1 S	SNOWFALL	-	-	-	-	-	-	-	-	-	-	-	-	-	-	-	-	-	-	-	-	-	-	-	-	-	-	-	-	-	-	
	SN ON GND	-	-	-	-	-	-	-	-	-	-	-	-	-	-	-	-	-	-	-	-	-	-	-	-	-	-	-	-	-	-	
QUAKERTOWN 1 E	SNOWFALL	-	-	-	-	-	-	-	-	-	-	-	-	-	-	-	-	-	-	-	-	-	-	-	-	-	-	-	-	-	-	
	SN ON GND	-	-	-	-	-	-	-	-	-	-	-	-	-	-	-	-	-	-	-	-	-	-	-	-	-	-	-	-	-	-	
READING WB CITY	SNOWFALL							.2	.3																T	T	T					
	SN ON GND								T																							
RIDGWAY 3 W	SNOWFALL								1.6									T	.8	1.0			T	1.0	.8							
	SN ON GND	1	T						2									T	1	1				1	1							
SCRANTON WB AIRPORT	SNOWFALL							4.7	3.7					T				T		.1	.5	T		3.0								
	SN ON GND	T	T	T					6	8	1	T									T	T		2								
	WTR EQUIV								.5	.8														.3								
SELINSGROVE CAA AIRPORT	SNOWFALL							T	T								T	T		T				T	T							
	SN ON GND								T															T	T							
SHIPPINGPORT WB	SNOWFALL							T	T									T	T		T			T	T							
	SN ON GND																															
SOMERSET MAIN ST	SNOWFALL								.7									.5	2.4	.6	.2			1.5	.5							
	SN ON GND								T										T													
SPRINGBORO	SNOWFALL	-	-	-	-	-	-	-	-	-	-	-	-	-	-	-	-	-	-	-	-	-	-	-	-	-	-	-	-	-	-	
	SN ON GND	-	-	-	-	-	-	-	-	-	-	-	-	-	-	-	-	-	-	-	-	-	-	-	-	-	-	-	-	-	-	
SPRINGS 1 SW	SNOWFALL							T	2.0	T							.5	.5	1.5	.3	1.0			1.0	1.0							
	SN ON GND								1								T	T	1	T	T			T	T							
TAMARACK 2 S FIRE TWR	SNOWFALL								4.0	1.0								T	2.0	.5		T		2.0	T	T						
	SN ON GND	9	7	4	T	T			4	4	T	T	T	T				T	2	1				2	T	T						
TIONESTA 2 SE DAM	SNOWFALL	T							3.0	T								T	.1	T				T	2.0	T						
	SN ON GND	1	T						3	T								T	T	T				T	2							
TOWANDA	SNOWFALL	T	T						8.0	1.0					T			T	T	T	T	T		1.7	.3							
	SN ON GND	T	T	T					8	6	2	T	T											2								
TOWER CITY 5 SW	SNOWFALL								6.0																T							
	SN ON GND								-																							
UNIONTOWN	SNOWFALL							T	1.0								T	T	T		.5			.5	T				T			
	SN ON GND																															
WARREN	SNOWFALL								1.4									T		.4				.3	.2							
	SN ON GND	3							1	T								T		T				T	T							
WAYNESBURG 2 W	SNOWFALL								-												T											
	SN ON GND								1												T											
WELLSBORO 3 S	SNOWFALL	T							7.0	2.0								T	T	T		T		4.0	T							
	SN ON GND	9	6	T	T				7	9	T	T	T					T	T	T				4	T							
WEST CHESTER	SNOWFALL								1.0	T																T						
	SN ON GND								1	T																						
WILLIAMSPORT WB AIRPORT	SNOWFALL							.8	.3										T	T				1.0	T							
	SN ON GND								T															T								
	WTR EQUIV																															
YORK 3 SSW PUMP STA	SNOWFALL								T										T						T							
	SN ON GND																															

See reference notes following Station Index.

STATION INDEX

Station	Index No.	County	Drainage	Latitude	Longitude	Elevation	Observation Time Temp.	Observation Time Precip.	Observer	Refer To Tables
ACMETONIA LOCK 3	0022	ALLEGHENY	1	40 32	79 49	748		7A	CORPS OF ENGINEERS	3
ALLENS MILLS	0099	JEFFERSON	1	41 12	78 55	1600		MID	CHARLES M. ALLEN	C
ALLENTOWN WB AP	0106	LEHIGH	9	40 39	75 26	376	MID	MID	U.S. WEATHER BUREAU	2 3 5 7 C
ALLENTOWN GAS CO	0111	LEHIGH	9	40 36	75 28	254	7A	7A	LEHIGH VLY GAS DIV	2 3 5
ALTOONA HORSESHOE CURVE	0134	BLAIR	6	40 30	78 29	1500	6P	6P	ALTOONA WATER BUR.	2 3 5 7
ARENDTSVILLE	0229	ADAMS	15	39 55	77 18	710	8A	8A	PA STATE COL EXP	2 3 5
ARTEMAS 1 WNW	0259	BEDFORD	12	39 45	78 28	1250	6P	6P	GRAYSON E.NORTHCRAFT	2 3 5 7 C
AUSTINBURG 2 W	0313	TIOGA	15	42 00	77 32	1640		7A	OTTO D. BACON	3 C
BAKERSTOWN 3 WNW	0355	ALLEGHENY	1	40 39	79 59	1230	7P	7P	PGH CUT FLOWER CO	2 3 5
BARNES	0409	WARREN	1	41 40	79 02	1310		7A	CORPS OF ENGINEERS	3
BEAR GAP	0457	NORTH LAND	15	40 50	76 30	900		MID	ROARING CRK WTR CO	3
BEAVER FALLS	0475	BEAVER	2	40 46	80 19	760		7A	HOWARD R. KEMP	3
BEAVERTOWN	0482	SNYDER	15	40 45	77 10	640	7A	7A	MARLIN R. ETTINGER	2 3 5 7
BEECH CREEK STATION	0499	CENTRE	16	41 04	77 34	620		7A	HAROLD S. RUPERT	3
BELLEFONTE 4 S	0530	CENTRE	16	40 51	77 47	1110	8A	8A	ROCKVIEW PRISON FARM	2 3 5 7
BERWICK	0611	COLUMBIA	15	41 04	76 15	570	6P	6P	AMER CAR + FNDRY CO	2 3 5 7
BETHLEHEM	0629	NORTHAMPTON	9	40 37	75 22	400		7A	ARTHUR CROPPER	3
# BETHLEHEM LEHIGH UNIV	0634	NORTHAMPTON	9	40 36	75 23	450	MID	MID	LEHIGH UNIVERSITY	2 3 5 C
BLAIN	0725	PERRY	15	40 20	77 31	720		MID	PA DEPT FRST + WTRS	C
BLAIRSVILLE 6 ENE	0736	INDIANA	4	40 27	79 09	2048	8P	8P	U.S. WEATHER BUREAU	2 3 5
BLAKESLEE CORNERS	0743	MONROE	9	41 06	75 36	1650		MID	WALTER WILDRICK	C
BLOSERVILLE 1 N	0763	CUMBERLAND	15	40 16	77 22	650		5P	MRS. B. M. WILLDERS	3
BOSWELL 6 WNW	0820	SOMERSET	1	40 11	79 08	2580		7A	MRS. MAE L. KIMMEL	3 C
BRADDOCK LOCK 2	0861	ALLEGHENY	10	40 24	79 52	725		7A	CORPS OF ENGINEERS	3
BRADFORD CNTRL FIRE STA	0867	MC KEAN	1	41 57	78 39	1500		8A	BRADFORD FIRE DEPT	3
BRADFORD 4 W RES	0868	MC KEAN	1	41 57	78 44	1680	5P	5P	BRADFORD WTR DEPT	2 3 5 7
BREEZEWOOD	0905	BEDFORD	6	40 00	78 14	1352		MID	PA TURNPIKE COMM	3
BROOKVILLE CAA AIRPORT	1002	JEFFERSON	1	41 09	79 06	1407	MID	MID	CIVIL AERO. ADM.	2 3 5 7
BRUCETON 1 S	1033	ALLEGHENY	10	40 18	79 59	1065		7A	AUSTIN R. COOPER	3
BUCKSTOWN 1 SE	1073	SOMERSET	4	40 04	78 50	2460		MID	ALVIN W. MANGES	C
BUFFALO MILLS	1087	BEDFORD	6	39 58	78 39	2450		7A	MRS. NELLE R. BROWN	3
BURGETTSTOWN 2 W	1105	WASHINGTON	11	40 23	80 26	980	7A	7A	SMITH TWP MUN AUTH	2 3 7
BURNT CABINS 2 NE	1115	HUNTINGDON	6	40 05	77 52	990	MID	MID	PA TURNPIKE COMM	2 3 5 7
# BUTLER	1130	BUTLER	2	40 52	79 54	1100	4P	7A	WILLIAM C. FAUST	2 3 5 7
BUTLER SUBSTATION	1135	BUTLER	2	40 51	79 53	1140		MID	WEST PENN POWER CO	C
CAMP HILL	1198	CUMBERLAND	15	40 15	76 55	461		6P	JOSEPH N. HOBART	3
CANTON 1 NW	1215	BRADFORD	15	41 40	76 52	1520	7A	7A	MRS.MILDRED SPENCER	2 3 5 7 C
CARLISLE	1234	CUMBERLAND	15	40 12	77 11	460	6P	6P	C. E. MILLER	2 3 5 7
CARROLLTOWN 2 SSE	1255	CAMBRIA	16	40 35	78 42	2040		8A	ROBERT F. MAURER	3
CARTER CAMP 2 W	1262	POTTER	16	41 37	77 45	2030		7A	RICHARD L. MENKEN	3 C
CEDAR RUN	1301	LYCOMING	16	41 31	77 27	800		7A	KATHRYN T.KREIGHBAUM	3
CHADDS FORD	1342	DELAWARE	5	39 52	75 36	180		8A	MRS.GRACE A. WICKS	3
CHAMBERSBURG 1 ESE	1354	FRANKLIN	12	39 56	77 38	640	9P	9P	CHARLES A. BENDER	2 3 5 7 C
CHARLEROI	1372	WASHINGTON	10	40 08	79 55	1040		MID	WEST PENN POWER CO	C
CHARLEROI LOCK 4	1377	WESTMORELAND	10	40 09	79 54	749		7A	CORPS OF ENGINEERS	3
# CHESTER	1423	DELAWARE	5	39 50	75 21	86	8A	8A	CHESTER TIMES	2 3 5
CLARENCE 1 E	1480	CENTRE	16	41 03	77 56	1440		7A	MARGARET A. SWANCER	3
CLARION 3 SW	1485	CLARION	1	41 12	79 26	1114	8P	7A	PA ELECTRIC CO	2 3 5 7 C
CLAUSSVILLE	1505	LEHIGH	9	40 37	75 39	670		8A	WILLIAM J. DOTTERER	3
CLAYSVILLE 3 W	1512	WASHINGTON	11	40 07	80 28	1000	7P	7A	MFGRS. L + M CO	2 3 5
CLEARFIELD	1519	CLEARFIELD	16	41 01	78 26	1100		7A	IRA TAYLOR	3
CLERMONT	1529	MC KEAN	1	41 41	78 30	2104		7A	MRS.TILLIE M.SIMONDS	3 C
COALDALE 2 NW	1572	SCHUYLKILL	9	40 50	75 56	1026		7A	PANTHER VLY WTR CO	3
COATESVILLE 1 SW	1589	CHESTER	5	39 58	75 50	342	8A	8A	PHILA ELECTRIC CO	2 3 5 7 C
COATESVILLE	1594	CHESTER	5	39 59	75 49	340		8A	EDWARD D. BIEDEMAN	INAC 12/55
COLUMBIA	1675	LANCASTER	15	40 02	76 30	300	5S	5S	JAMES H. RUST	2 3 5
CONFLUENCE 1 SW DAM	1705	SOMERSET	17	39 48	79 22	1490	8A	8A	CORPS OF ENGINEERS	2 3 5 6 C
CONFLUENCE 1 NW	1710	FAYETTE	17	39 50	79 22	1331		7A	JOHN L. REID	3
CONNELLSVILLE	1723	FAYETTE	17	40 01	79 36	870		8A	MARSHALL B. MENEFEE	3
CONNELLSVILLE 2 E	1729	FAYETTE	17	40 01	79 33	1300		MID	HARRY C. JOY	C
CONSHOHOCKEN	1737	MONTGOMERY	5	40 04	75 19	70		8A	PHILA ELECTRIC CO	3
COOKSBURG	1749	CLARION	1	41 20	79 13	1180		8A	PA DEPT FRST + WTRS	3
COOKSBURG 2 NNW	1752	CLARION	1	41 21	79 13	1460		8A	PA DEPT FRST + WTRS	3
CORAOPOLIS NEVILLE IS	1773	ALLEGHENY	11	40 30	80 05	720		8A	PGH. COKE + CHEM CO	3
CORRY	1790	ERIE	1	41 56	79 38	1427	7P	5A	LEO C. WECKERS	2 3 5 7
COUDERSPORT 7 E	1809	POTTER	1	41 46	77 53	2425		7A	CAMP POTATO	3
COVINGTON	1832	TIOGA	15	41 45	77 05	1193		7A	GROVER D. CLEVELAND	3
CREEKSIDE	1881	INDIANA	1	40 41	79 12	1035		7A	CORPS OF ENGINEERS	3
CRESSON 2 SE	1895	CAMBRIA	6	40 27	78 43	2540		7A	MILES A. VECELLIO	3 C
CUSTER CITY 2 W	1978	MC KEAN	1	41 55	78 41	2120		8A	M. D. BOOTH AND CO	3
DANVILLE	2013	MONTOUR	15	40 58	76 37	460		7A	MRS.MARIE M. LITTLE	3
DERRY	2108	WESTMORELAND	4	40 20	79 18	1150	6P	6P	MISS N. D. WINEMAN	2 3 5
DEVAULT 1 W	2116	CHESTER	14	40 05	75 33	360	MID	MID	PA TURNPIKE COMM	2 3 5
DINGMANS FERRY	2160	PIKE	5	41 13	74 52	360		MID	CLARENCE H. SMITH	C
DIXON	2171	WYOMING	15	41 34	75 54	620	7A	7A	HAROLD J. KUSCHEL	2 3 5 7 C
DONEGAL	2183	WESTMORELAND	17	40 07	79 23	1746	MID	MID	PA TURNPIKE COMM	2 3 5 7
# DONORA	2190	WASHINGTON	10	40 11	79 51	814	12M	12M	DONORA ZINC WORKS	2 3 5
DOYLESTOWN	2221	BUCKS	5	40 18	75 08	393		5P	GEORGE HART	3
DRIFTWOOD	2245	CAMERON	16	41 20	78 08	820		MID	SIDNEY KENNEDY	C
DU BOIS 7 E	2265	CLEARFIELD	16	41 06	78 38	1670	5P	5P	CITY OF DU BOIS	2 3 5 C
DUNLO	2298	CAMBRIA	4	40 17	78 43	2410		MID	MRS. D. L. WHITE	
DUSHORE 3 NE	2324	SULLIVAN	16	41 33	76 21	1750		7A	PATRICK F. RYAN	3 C
EAGLES MERE	2343	SULLIVAN	16	41 24	76 35	2020	7A	7A	MRS.ELSIE P. BIGGER	2 3 5 7 C
EAST BRADY	2363	CLARION	1	40 59	79 37	820	5P	5P	A. B. KEMPEL	2 3 5
EAST WATERFORD 3 E	2459	PERRY	6	40 21	77 33	2125	8A	8A	U.S. WEATHER BUREAU	INAC 5/55
EBENSBURG	2466	CAMBRIA	4	40 29	78 43	2090	7P	7A	ROBERT A. WASSER	2 5
EDINBORO	2514	ERIE	1	41 52	80 08	1220		8A	EDINBORO ST TCHR COL	
ELIZABETHTOWN	2560	LANCASTER	15	40 09	76 31	460		8A	MASONIC HOME	
EMPORIUM 1 E	2633	CAMERON	16	41 31	78 13	1160	7A	7A	RUSSELL E.PALMATEER	2 5 7 C
ENGLISH CENTER	2644	LYCOMING	16	41 26	77 17	881		7A	WILLIAM SUDERS	U C
EPHRATA	2662	LANCASTER	15	40 11	76 10	465	6P	6P	STANLEY L.VON NEIDA	2 3 5
EQUINUNK	2669	WAYNE	5	41 51	75 13	900		8A	MRS.ROSE M. NEILSEN	3
ERIE CAA AIRPORT	2682	ERIE	8	42 05	80 12	732	MID	MID	CIVIL AERO. ADM.	2 3 5
EVERETT 1 SW	2721	BEDFORD	6	40 00	78 23	1020	MID	MID	PA TURNPIKE COMM	2 3 5 7 C
FARRELL SHARON	2814	MERCER	2	41 14	80 30	865	7P	7P	SHARON STEEL CORP	2 3 5
FORD CITY 4 S DAM	2942	ARMSTRONG	1	40 43	79 30	950	8A	8A	CORPS OF ENGINEERS	2 3 5 6 7 C
FRANKLIN	3028	VENANGO	1	41 23	79 49	987	7P	7A	JAMES K. ELLIOTT	2 3 5 7 C
FREDERICKSVILLE 2 SE	3047	BERKS	14	40 26	75 40	950	8A	8A	D. P. FENSTERMACHER	2 3 5
FREELAND	3056	LUZERNE	15	41 01	75 54	1900	6P	8A	ANDREW B. EVANSHA	2 3 5
GALETON	3130	POTTER	16	41 44	77 39	1325		7A	W. GALE LUSH	3
GEIGERTOWN	3189	BERKS	14	40 13	75 50	400		8A	WALTER C. WOLF	3
GEORGE SCHOOL	3200	BUCKS	5	40 13	74 56	135	7P	7P	GEORGE M. HART	2 3 5 7
# GETTYSBURG	3218	ADAMS	12	39 50	77 14	540	9A	9A	HUGH C. MC ILHENNY	2 3 5 7
GETTYSBURG 1 S	3223	ADAMS	12	39 48	77 14	570		MID	NAT MILITARY PARK	C
GIFFORD	3237	MC KEAN	1	41 51	78 36	2220		8A	SOUTH PENN OIL CO	3
GLENCOE	3298	SOMERSET	12	39 49	78 51	1620		MID	MRS. MARY M.HARTMAN	C
GLEN HAZEL 2 NE DAM	3311	ELK	1	41 34	78 36	1725		8A	CORPS OF ENGINEERS	3 C
GLEN ROCK	3330	YORK	15	39 48	76 44	620		MID	MRS.E.C.MC WILLIAMS	C
GLENWILLARD DASH DAM	3343	ALLEGHENY	11	40 33	80 13	705		7A	CORPS OF ENGINEERS	3
GOULDSBORO	3394	WAYNE	9	41 15	75 27	1890		7A	L. M. EILENBERGER	3
GRANTVILLE 2 SW	3422	DAUPHIN	15	40 22	76 41	510		5S	EARL E. RHOADS	3
GRATERFORD	3435	MONTGOMERY	14	40 14	75 72	160		7A	CLAUDE K. KULP	3
GRATZ 1 N	3438	DAUPHIN	15	40 36	76 43	760	8A	8A	LEE M. LEITZEL	2 3 5 7 C
GREENSBORO LOCK 7	3503	GREENE	10	39 47	79 55	808		7A	CORPS OF ENGINEERS	3
GREENSBURG 2 E	3515	WESTMORELAND	10	40 18	79 30	1225		MID	PA DEPT HIGHWAYS	C
GREENSBURG 3 SE	3516	WESTMORELAND	10	40 17	79 30	1245		6P	WESTMORELAND WTR CO	3
GREENVILLE	3526	MERCER	2	41 24	80 23	1026	6P	6P	C. EARL MILLER	2 3 5 7
HANOVER	3662	YORK	15	39 48	76 59	600	8A	8A	HANOVER EVENING SUN	2 3 5
# HARRISBURG WB AP	3699	YORK	15	40 13	76 51	335	MID	MID	U.S. WEATHER BUREAU	2 3 5 7 C
HARRISBURG NORTH	3704	DAUPHIN	15	40 18	76 54	323		9A	GEORGE S. BEAL	3
HAWLEY	3758	WAYNE	5	41 29	75 10	880		7A	MRS.KATHERINE S.BATE	3
HAWLEY 1 S DAM	3761	WAYNE	5	41 28	75 11	1180	7A	7A	PA POWER + LIGHT CO	2 3 5 6 7 C
HOLLIDAYSBURG	4001	BLAIR	6	40 26	78 24	960		MID	JOHN M. RINGLER	C
HOLLISTERVILLE	4008	WAYNE	9	41 23	75 26	1380		8A	PA POWER + LIGHT CO	3
# HOLTWOOD	4019	LANCASTER	15	39 50	76 20	187	MID	8A	PA POWER + LIGHT CO	2 3 5 C
HOME	4027	INDIANA	1	40 45	79 06	1260		MID	MRS. EDNA M. BUSH	C
HONESDALE 4 NW	4043	WAYNE	5	41 37	75 19	1410		9A	GEORGE C. WILLIAMS	3
HONESDALE 6 N	4044	WAYNE	5	41 39	75 17	1050		MID	FRIEND E. WALTER	C
HOOVERSVILLE	4058	SOMERSET	4	40 09	78 55	1660		7A	PA ELECTRIC CO	3
HOP BOTTOM 2 SE	4066	SUSQUEHANNA	15	41 43	75 43	900		7A	JOSEPH J. SANSUSKAS	3
HUNTINGDON	4159	HUNTINGDON	15	40 29	78 01	660	7A	7A	JOHN R. HENDERSON	2 3 5 7
HUNTSDALE	4166	CUMBERLAND	15	40 06	77 18	610		8A	METRO P. DOROSH	3 C
HYNDMAN	4190	BEDFORD	12	39 49	78 43	920		8A	MRS.GERTRUDE M.BURTT	3
INDIANA 3 SE	4214	INDIANA	4	40 36	79 07	1102	7P	7A	CLYMER WATER SVC CO	2 3 5 7 C
IRWIN	4276	WESTMORELAND	10	40 20	79 42	1090	5P	5P	WESTMORELAND WTR CO	2 3 5
JACKSON SUMMIT	4304	TIOGA	15	41 57	77 01	1690		MID	ARCHIE LAIN	C
JAMESTOWN 2 NW	4325	CRAWFORD	2	41 30	80 28	1050	8A	8A	PA DEPT FRST + WTRS	2 3 5 6 C
JIM THORPE	4370	CARBON	9	40 52	75 45	830	5P	5P	HENRY S. HAAK	2 3 5
# JOHNSTOWN	4385	CAMBRIA	4	40 20	78 55	1214	9A	9A	JOHNSTOWN TRIBUNE	2 3 5 7
JOHNSTOWN 2	4390	CAMBRIA	4	40 19	78 55	1130		MID	CITY OF JOHNSTOWN	C
KANE 1 NNE	4432	MC KEAN	1	41 41	78 48	1750	8A	8A	SPRING WATER CO	2 3 5 7 C
KARTHAUS	4450	CLEARFIELD	16	41 07	78 07	950		7A	JEROME S. HOWE	3
KEATING SUMMIT	4466	POTTER	1	41 41	78 11	1840		7A	EUGENE L. KREITNER	3
KEGG	4481	BEDFORD	6	39 59	78 43	1280	MID	MID	PA TURNPIKE COMM	2 3 5
KITTANNING LOCK 7	4611	ARMSTRONG	1	40 49	79 32	790		7A	CORPS OF ENGINEERS	3
KREGAR 4 SE	4667	WESTMORELAND	17	40 06	79 14	2530		MID	PA TURNPIKE COMM	3
KRESGEVILLE 3 W	4672	CARBON	9	40 54	75 34	720		9A	CITY OF BETHLEHEM	3
LAFAYETTE MC KEAN PARK	4706	MC KEAN	1	41 48	78 40	2130		8A	CHARLES GORDON	3
LAKEVILLE 1 NNE	4733	WAYNE	5	41 27	75 16	1460		8A	MRS. GLADYS REINEKE	3
LANCASTER 2NE PUMP STA	4758	LANCASTER	15	40 03	76 17	255	6P	6P	LANCASTER WATER BUR	2 3 5
LANCASTER 2NE FILT PL	4763	LANCASTER	15	40 03	76 17	270		MID	LANCASTER WATER BUR	C
LANDISVILLE	4778	LANCASTER	15	40 06	76 25	410	8A	8A	PA STATE COLLEGE	2 3 5 6 7 C
LATROBE	4832	WESTMORELAND	4	40 19	79 23	1000		MID	WEST PENN POWER CO	3
LAURELTON STATE VILLAGE	4853	UNION	15	40 54	77 13	860		MID	PA DEPT OF WELFARE	C
LAWRENCEVILLE 2 S	4873	TIOGA	15	41 59	77 07	995	7A	7A	HARRY P. HOWLAND	2 3 5 7
LEBANON 2 NW	4891	LEBANON	15	40 22	76 28	600	6P	6P	LEBANON BOCSTG CO	2 3 5 7
LEBANON 3 SW	4896	LEBANON	15	40 19	76 28	490		MID	THOMAS DONNACHIE	C
LEHIGHTON	4934	CARBON	9	40 50	75 43	580		7A	GOODWIN S. DEFREHN	3 C
LE ROY	4972	BRADFORD	15	41 41	76 43	1040		6P	MRS.DIMMIS M.BAILEY	3
LEWIS RUN 3 SE	4984	MC KEAN	1	41 50	78 39	1740		7A	RUSSELL LINEMAN	3 C
LEWISTOWN	4992	MIFFLIN	6	40 35	77 35	480	7A	7A	AMERICAN VISCOSE CO	2 3 5 7 C
LINESVILLE 5 WNW	5050	CRAWFORD	2	41 41	80 31	1020	7P	8A	MISS RETTA M. CRUMB	2 3 5
LOCK HAVEN	5104	CLINTON	16	41 08	77 27	570	7P	7A	PETER L. STEVENSON	2 3 5 7
LOCK HAVEN 2	5109	CLINTON	16	41 08	77 27	620		MID	HUGH F. PARKER	C
LONG POND 2 W	5160	MONROE	9	41 03	75 30	1860		7A	THOMAS MECKES	3
MADERA	5336	CLEARFIELD	16	40 50	78 26	1460	7A	7A	MRS. JULIA J. SHOFF	2 3 5 C
MAHAFFEY	5342	CLEARFIELD	16	40 53	78 44	1280		7A	MISS ELLEN J. MILES	3
MAPLE GLEN	5368	MONTGOMERY	5	40 11	75 11	380		6P	FRANCES E.SCHEIBNER	3
MAPLETON DEPOT	5381	HUNTINGDON	6	40 24	77 56	580		7A	MRS. I. S. BUCHANAN	3
MARCUS HOOK	5390	DELAWARE	5	39 49	75 25	12	MID	MID	SUN OIL CO	2 3 5
MARIENVILLE 3 SW	5400	FOREST	1	41 27	79 09	1700		MID	ROY A. MARKER	C
MARION CENTER 2 SE	5408	INDIANA	1	40 45	79 02	1610		7A	CORPS OF ENGINEERS	3
MARTINSBURG 1 SW	5453	BLAIR	6	40 18	78 20	1360		MID	BLUE MT. CANNERIES	C
MARTINSBURG CAA AP	5454	BLAIR	6	40 18	78 19	1463	MID	MID	CIVIL AERO. ADM.	2 3 5
MATAMORAS	5470	PIKE	5	41 22	74 42	439		7A	HARRY BISLAND	3
MAYBURG	5490	FOREST	1	41 36	79 13	1150		7A	CORPS OF ENGINEERS	3
MC CONNELLSBURG	5526	FULTON	12	39 56	78 00	895		8A	MRS. HELEN M. SHIVES	3
MC KEESPORT	5573	ALLEGHENY	10	40 21	79 52	720		8A	NATIONAL TUBE CO	3
MEADOW RUN PONDS	5601	LUZERNE	15	41 13	75 40	2000		MID	GEORGE PEARAGE	C
MEADVILLE 1 S	5606	CRAWFORD	1	41 37	80 10	1065	8A	8A	CITY OF MEADVILLE	2 3 5 7 C
MEDIX RUN	5627	ELK	16	41 17	78 24	1100		7A	MRS.E. M. SNYDER	3 C
MERCER 2 NNE	5651	MERCER	2	41 15	80 13	1160	7P	7A	WILLIAM K. STRUTHERS	2 3 5 7
MERCER HIWAY SHED	5654	MERCER	2	41 14	80 15	1240		MID	PA DEPT HIGHWAYS	
MERCERSBURG	5662	FRANKLIN	12	39 50	77 54	605		8A	ROLLIN P. GILBERT	3
MERWINSBURG	5676	MONROE	9	40 58	75 28	920		MID	GERALD D. MURPHY	C
MIDDLETOWN OLMSTED FLD	5703	DAUPHIN	15	40 11	76 46	303	MID	MID	U. S. AIR FORCE	2 3 5
MIDLAND DAM 7	5710	BEAVER	11	40 38	80 28	689	11P	7A	CORPS OF ENGINEERS	2 3 5
MILAN 4 WNW	5732	BRADFORD	15	41 56	76 35	1448		MID	CARL A. MORRIS	C
MILANVILLE	5738	WAYNE	5	41 40	75 04	760		8A	CHARLES W. DAVIS	3
MILLERSBURG 2 E	5775	DAUPHIN	15	40 32	76 56	560		MID	RUSSELL SHEPLEY	C
MILLHEIM	5790	CENTRE	15	40 54	77 29	1090		7A	NEVIN E. BOWERSOX	3
MILLVILLE 2 SW	5817	COLUMBIA	15	41 06	76 33	860		7A	KENNETH LEIGHOW	3 C
MILROY	5825	MIFFLIN	6	40 43	77 35	770		8A	THOMAS C. HARBESON	3
MONTROSE 1 E	5915	SUSQUEHANNA	15	41 50	75 51	1630	7A	7A	WILBER W. HOOPES.JR	2 3 5 7 C
MORGANTOWN	5956	BERKS	15	40 09	75 54	595	MID	MID	PA TURNPIKE COMM	2 3 5
MT GRETNA 2 SE	6028	LANCASTER	15	40 14	76 26	670	MID	MID	PA TURNPIKE COMM	2 3 5
MT POCONO 2 N AP	6055	MONROE	5	41 09	75 22	1915	5P	5P	H. JOHN DAVIS. JR.	2 3 5 7 C
MOUNT UNION 1 N	6067	MIFFLIN	6	40 24	77 53	820		MID	MT UNION WTR WORKS	C
MUHLENBURG 1 SE	6090	LUZERNE	15	41 13	76 08	1110	6P	6P	THEODORE J. SAMPSON	2 3 5
MURRYSVILLE	6111	WESTMORELAND	10	40 26	79 42	903		MID	DAVID C. SHAW	C
MYERSTOWN	6126	LEBANON	14	40 22	76 18	480		8A	MRS.KATHLEEN MANDELL	3
NATRONA LOCK 4	6151	ALLEGHENY	1	40 37	79 43	800		7A	CORPS OF ENGINEERS	3
NEFFS MILLS 4 NE	6174	HUNTINGDON	6	40 40	77 55	900		MID	PA STATE UNIVERSITY	C
NESHAMINY FALLS	6194	BUCKS	5	40 09	74 57	60		MID	PHILA SUB WATER CO	3
NEWBURG 3 W	6225	FRANKLIN	15	40 09	77 37	745	MID	MID	PA TURNPIKE COMM	2 3 5
NEW CASTLE 1 N	6233	LAWRENCE	2	41 01	80 22	900	5P	7A	BAXTER F. JOHNSON	2 3 5 7 C
# NEWELL	6246	FAYETTE	10	40 05	79 54	805	12M	12M	GENERAL CHEMICAL CO	2 3 5
NEW PARK	6289	YORK	15	39 44	76 30	780		6P	CLINTON J. ALLEN	3
NEWPORT	6297	PERRY	6	40 29	77 08	400	7A	7A	MRS. FRANCES K. FRY	2 3 5 7
NEW STANTON	6310	WESTMORELAND	10	40 13	79 36	980	MID	MID	PA TURNPIKE COMM	2 3 5
NEW TRIPOLI	6326	LEHIGH	14	40 41	75 45	570		6P	FRED C. OSWALD	3
NORRISTOWN	6370	MONTGOMERY	14	40 07	75 20	75	MID	8A	GEORGE H. BOONE	2 3 5
NORTH EAST 2 SE	6396	ERIE	8	42 12	79 49	1060		9A	ELLSWORTH WEAVER	3
ORWELL 3 N	6621	BRADFORD	15	41 55	76 16	1620		8A	WILLIAM I. BROWN	3
PALM	6681	MONTGOMERY	14	40 26	75 32	390		8A	FRED C. ESCHBACH	3
# PALMERTON	6689	CARBON	9	40 48	75 37	435	MID	MID	NEW JERSEY ZINC CO	2 3 5 7 C
PARKER	6721	ARMSTRONG	1	41 05	79 41	1140		7A	LOUIS A. MALARKEY	3
PARKER 1 E	6724	CLARION	1	41 06	79 40	870		MID	P. M. NEELY	C
PAUPACK 2 WNW	6762	PIKE	5	41 24	75 14	1360		8A	MISS L. VETTERLEIN	3
PECKS POND	6786	PIKE	5	41 17	75 06	1380		9A	MRS. CARRIE NESS	3
# PHIL DREXEL INST OF TEC	6879	PHILADELPHIA	14	39 57	75 11	30	MID	MID	FRANCIS K. DAVIS.JR	2 3 5
PHILADELPHIA WB AP	6889	PHILADELPHIA	5	39 53	75 14	13	MID	MID	U.S. WEATHER BUREAU	2 3 5 7 C
# PHILADELPHIA PT BREEZE	6899	PHILADELPHIA	5	39 55	75 12	85	MID	MID	ATLANTIC REFINING	2 3 5 C
PHILADELPHIA SHAWMONT	6904	PHILADELPHIA	5	40 02	75 15	70	7P	7P	SCHUYLKILL NAVIG CO	2 3 5 7
# PHILADELPHIA CITY	6909	PHILADELPHIA	5	39 57	75 09	26	9A	9A	USN HYDROGRAPHIC OFF	2 3 5 C
PHILIPSBURG CAA AP	6916	CENTRE	6	40 54	78 05	1918	8P	8P	CIVIL AERO. ADM.	2 3 5 7 C
PHOENIXVILLE 1 E	6927	CHESTER	14	40 07	75 30	105	6P	MID	PHILA SUB WATER CO	2 3 5 7 C
PIKES CREEK	6939	LUZERNE	15	41 18	76 06	1320		MID	HARRY SHELDON	3 C
PIMPLE HILL	6944	MONROE	9	41 02	75 30	2215	9A	8A	PA DEPT FRST + WTRS	2 3 5 6
PINE GROVE 1 NE	6954	SCHUYLKILL	15	40 34	76 22	535		8A	PA POWER + LIGHT CO	3
PITTSBURGH WB AP 2	6993	ALLEGHENY	11	40 30	80 13	1151	MID	MID	U.S. WEATHER BUREAU	2 3 5 7 C
# PITTSBURGH WB CITY	6997	ALLEGHENY	11	40 27	80 00	914	MID	MID	U.S. WEATHER BUREAU	2 3 5 C
PLEASANT MOUNT 1 W	7029	WAYNE	5	41 44	75 27	1800	8A	8A	PA FISH COMM	2 3 5 C
PORT CLINTON	7116	SCHUYLKILL	14	40 35	76 02	450	7A	7A	MRS. ADA E. RARICK	2 3 5 7 C
PORTLAND	7127	NORTHAMPTON	5	40 55	75 06	297		8A	JOINT BRIDGE COMM	3
POTTSTOWN	7149	MONTGOMERY	14	40 15	75 39	160		8A	MILES E. SMITH	3
POTTSVILLE PALO ALTO BR	7161	SCHUYLKILL	14	40 41	76 11	640		8A	JOHN H. SMITH	INACTIVE 4/56
PUNXSUTAWNEY	7217	JEFFERSON	1	40 57	79 00	1298		MID	JOHN VOLANSKY	C
PUTNEYVILLE 2 SE DAM	7229	ARMSTRONG	1	40 55	79 17	1270	8A	8A	CORPS OF ENGINEERS	2 3 5 C
QUAKERTOWN 1 E	7239	BUCKS	5	40 26	75 20	490	5P	5P	DENNIS K. FLUCK	2 3 5 7
RAYMOND	7310	POTTER	13	41 52	77 52	2220		7A	MRS. RACHEL LANGAN	C
# READING WB CITY	7318	BERKS	14	40 20	75 56	266	MID	MID	U.S. WEATHER BUREAU	2 3 5 7 C
RENOVO	7409	CLINTON	16	41 20	77 45	660		7A	MRS. C. W. BAIRD	3
RENOVO 5 S	7410	CLINTON	16	41 14	77 46	2035		MID	C. F. BILLETTE	C
REW	7425	MC KEAN	1	41 54	78 32	2250		8A	HAROLD C. MEALY	3
RICES LANDING L 6	7443	GREENE	10	39 57	80 00	775		7A	CORPS OF ENGINEERS	3
RIDGWAY 3 W	7477	ELK	1	41 25	78 47	1420	7P	7A	BOROUGH OF RIDGWAY	2 3 5 7
ROCHESTER 1 N	7540	BEAVER	2	40 43	80 18	900		MID	DEQUESNE LIGHT CO	C
RUSH	7694	SUSQUEHANNA	15	41 47	76 03	1000		9A	MISS MAUDE MC CAIN	3
RUSHVILLE	7727	SUSQUEHANNA	15	41 46	76 07	870		7A	CARL KOPATZ	3
SAFE HARBOR	7732	LANCASTER	15	39 55	76 23	270		MID	S.W.WATER POWER CORP	C
SAGAMORE 1 S	7739	INDIANA	1	40 46	79 14	1320		7A	CORPS OF ENGINEERS	3
SALINA 3 W	7782	WESTMORELAND	7	40 31	79 33	1109	6P	6P	MUN AUTH WSTMRLD CO	2 3 5
SAXTON	7846	BEDFORD	6	40 12	78 15	780		8A	MRS.ALVERTA L.HOLMES	3 C
SCANDIA 2 E	7855	WARREN	1	41 55	79 01	2040		MID	DAVID R. ANDERSON	C
SCHENLEY LOCK 5	7863	ARMSTRONG	1	40 41	79 40	783		7A	CORPS OF ENGINEERS	3
# SCRANTON	7902	LACKAWANNA	15	41 25	75 40	746	7A	7A	U.S. POST OFFICE	2 3 5
SCRANTON WB AIRPORT	7905	LUZERNE	15	41 20	75 44	956	MID	MID	U.S. WEATHER BUREAU	2 3 5 7 C
SELINSGROVE CAA AP	7931	SNYDER	15	40 49	76 52	460	MID	MID	CIVIL AERO. ADM.	2 3 5 7
SELLERSVILLE 2 NW	7936	BUCKS	5	40 23	75 20	530		MID	SELLERSVILLE WTR CO	C

STATION INDEX

Continued

Station	Index No.	County	Drainage ‡	Latitude	Longitude	Elevation	Observation Time Temp.	Observation Time Precip.	Observer	Refer To Tables
SHADE GAP	7965	HUNTINGDON	6	40 11	77 52	1000		MID	MRS. HELEN H. PYLE	C
SHAMOKIN	7978	NORTH LAND	15	40 48	76 33	770		8A	ROARING CRK WTR CO	3
SHEFFIELD 6 W	8026	WARREN	1	41 42	79 09	1940		MID	L. N. HANSON	C
SHIPPENSBURG	8073	FRANKLIN	15	40 03	77 32	709	4P	4P	KEITH B. ALLEN	2 3 5
SHIPPINGPORT WB	8078	BEAVER	11	40 37	80 26	740	MID	MID	U.S. WEATHER BUREAU	2 3 5 7 C
SINNEMAHONING	8145	CAMERON	16	41 19	78 05	790		7A	MRS.FRANCES CALDWELL	3
SLIPPERY ROCK	8184	BUTLER	2	41 04	80 03	1345	7P	7A	WALTER D. ALBERT	2 3 5
SMETHPORT HIGHWAY SHED	8190	MC KEAN	1	41 48	78 27	1510		MID	PA DEPT HIGHWAYS	C
SOMERSET FAIRVIEW ST	8244	SOMERSET	17	40 01	79 05	2140		7A	HOWARD G. PECK	3
SOMERSET MAIN ST	8249	SOMERSET	17	40 01	79 05	2150	6P	6P	DAVID L. GROVE	2 3 5 7
SOUTH CANAAN 1 NE	8275	WAYNE	5	41 31	75 24	1400		MID	EUGENE M. COOK	C
SOUTH MOUNTAIN	8308	FRANKLIN	12	39 51	77 30	1520		7A	PA DEPT OF HEALTH	3
SPRINGBORO	8359	CRAWFORD	8	41 48	80 23	900	8A	8A	SPRINGBORO BOROUGH	2 3 5 7 C
SPRING GROVE	8379	YORK	15	39 52	76 52	470		4P	P. H. GLATFELTER CO	3 C
SPRINGS 1 SW	8395	SOMERSET	17	39 44	79 10	2500	8P	8P	ALLEN E. YODER	2 3 5 7
# STATE COLLEGE	8449	CENTRE	16	40 48	77 52	1175	MID	MID	PA STATE COLLEGE	2 3 5 C
STRAUSSTOWN	8570	BERKS	14	40 30	76 11	600		8A	JACOB KLAHR	3
STRONGSTOWN	8589	INDIANA	4	40 33	78 55	1880		MID	HARRY F. BENNETT	C
STROUDSBURG	8596	MONROE	5	40 59	75 12	480	6A	6A	WILLIAM MAGERTY	2 3 5 C
STUMP CREEK	8610	JEFFERSON	1	41 01	78 50	1320		7A	CORPS OF ENGINEERS	3
SUNBURY	8668	NORTH LAND	15	40 51	76 48	440		7A	CHARLES W. BAYLER	3 C
SUSQUEHANNA	8692	SUSQUEHANNA	15	41 57	75 36	1020		7A	MRS. LAURA A.BENSON	3
SUTERSVILLE	8699	ALLEGHENY	17	40 14	79 48	765		7A	MICHAEL RACKO	3
TAMAQUA	8758	SCHUYLKILL	14	40 48	75 58	830		6A	MRS. MARY L.ROBERTS	3
TAMAQUA 4 N DAM	8763	SCHUYLKILL	14	40 51	75 59	1120		7A	PANTHER VLY WTR CO	3 C
TAMARACK 2 S FIRE TWR	8770	CLINTON	16	41 24	77 51	2220	7A	7A	JAMES E. SWARTZ	2 3 5 7
TIONESTA 2 SE DAM	8873	FOREST	1	41 29	79 26	1200	8A	8A	CORPS OF ENGINEERS	2 3 5 7 C
TITUSVILLE	8885	CRAWFORD	1	41 38	79 40	1550		MID	PA ELECTRIC CO	C
TITUSVILLE WATER WORKS	8888	CRAWFORD	1	41 38	79 42	1220	7P	7P	CITY OF TITUSVILLE	2 3 5
TORPEDO 4 W	8901	WARREN	1	41 47	79 32	1735		7A	MRS. LILY B. GARBER	3
TOWANDA	8905	BRADFORD	15	41 46	76 26	760	7P	7A	MRS. M. O. PARKS	2 3 5 7 C
TOWER CITY 5 SW	8910	DAUPHIN	15	40 31	76 37	745		6P	HARRISBURG WTR DEPT	3 7
TROY	8959	BRADFORD	15	41 47	76 47	1100		7A	JENNIE L. BALLARD	3
TUNNELTON	8989	INDIANA	4	40 27	79 23	890		MID	MRS. MARY E. WEIMER	C
TURTLEPOINT 4 NE	9002	MC KEAN	1	41 54	78 16	1640		7A	ROBERT D. STRAIT	3
TYRONE 4 NE BALD EAGLE	9024	BLAIR	6	40 43	78 12	1080		7A	FREDERICK L. FRIDAY	3 C
UNION CITY	9042	ERIE	1	41 54	79 50	1429		7A	FORREST M. BRALEY	3 C
UNIONTOWN	9050	FAYETTE	10	39 54	79 44	1040	10P	10P	WM. W. MARSTELLER	2 3 5 7
UPPER DARBY	9074	DELAWARE	5	39 58	75 18	222	7P	7P	PHIL. SUB.TRANS. CO	2 3 5
UTICA	9099	VENANGO	1	41 26	79 57	1030		7A	MRS.FLORENCE MILLER	3
VANDERGRIFT	9128	WESTMORELAND	7	40 36	79 33	800		7A	UNITED ENG+FNDRY CO	3
VANDERGRIFT 2 W	9133	WESTMORELAND	7	40 36	79 36	995		MID	EUGENE R. YOUNG	C
VIRGINVILLE	9196	BERKS	14	40 31	75 52	350		8A	MRS. MARY H. WRIGHT	3
VOWINCKEL	9206	CLARION	1	41 25	79 14	1620		8A	PA DEPT FRST + WTRS	3
VOWINCKEL 1 SW	9209	CLARION	1	41 24	79 15	1610		8A	PA DEPT FRST + WTRS	3
WARREN	9298	WARREN	1	41 51	79 08	1280	7P	7A	GILBERT H. REIER	2 3 5 7
WASHINGTON	9312	WASHINGTON	11	40 11	80 14	1200		MID	PA DEPT HIGHWAYS	C
WATSONTOWN	9345	NORTH LAND	16	41 05	76 52	470		8A	OWEN BERKENSTOCK	3
WAYNESBURG 2 W	9362	GREENE	10	39 54	80 13	980	6P	7A	RALPH L. AMOS	2 3 5 7
WAYNESBURG 1 E	9367	GREENE	10	39 54	80 10	940		MID	SEWAGE DISPOSAL PLT	C
WEBSTER MILLS 3 SW	9380	FULTON	12	39 50	78 05	920		MID	WILLIAM D. COVER	C
WELLSBORO 3 S	9408	TIOGA	16	41 43	77 16	1920	7A	7A	MARION L. SHUMWAY	2 3 5 7
WELLSBORO 2 E	9412	TIOGA	16	41 45	77 16	1440		MID	MRS. IDA S. MAYNARD	C
WELLSVILLE	9420	YORK	15	40 03	76 57	500	5P	5P	D. D. HOOVER	2 3 5
WERNERSVILLE 1 W	9430	BERKS	14	40 20	76 06	405		8A	CHARLES A. GRUBER	3
WEST CHESTER	9464	CHESTER	5	39 58	75 36	440	8A	8A	DAILY LOCAL NEWS	2 3 5 7
WEST GROVE 1 E	9503	CHESTER	5	39 49	75 49	440		8A	CONARD-PYLE CO	3
WEST HICKORY	9507	FOREST	1	41 34	79 25	1090		8A	MRS.HELEN F.KINNEAR	3
WHITESBURG	9655	ARMSTRONG	1	40 45	79 24	1530		7A	CORPS OF ENGINEERS	3
WILKES-BARRE	9702	LAZERNE	15	41 15	75 52	610		7A	MRS. MARY G. HIRMAK	3
WILLIAMSBURG	9714	BLAIR	6	40 28	78 12	860		7A	MYRON K. BIDDLE	3
WILLIAMSPORT WB AP	9728	LYCOMING	16	41 15	76 55	527	MID	MID	U.S. WEATHER BUREAU	2 3 5 7 C
WIND GAP 2 SW	9781	NORTHAMPTON	5	40 51	75 18	720		MID	OWEN R. PARRY	C
WOLFSBURG	9823	BEDFORD	6	40 03	78 32	1190		7A	WALTER C. RICE	3
YORK 3 SSW PUMP STA	9933	YORK	15	39 55	76 45	390	5P	5P	YORK WATER COMPANY	2 3 5 7
YORK 2 S	9938	YORK	15	39 56	76 44	640		MID	YORK WATER COMPANY	C
YORK HAVEN	9950	YORK	15	40 07	76 43	310		8A	METROPOL EDISON CO	3
YOUNGSVILLE	9966	WARREN	1	41 51	79 20	1225		MID	HENRY CARLETT	C
ZION GROVE	9990	SCHUYLKILL	15	40 54	76 13	940		7A	JAMES D. TEETER	3
ZIONSVILLE 3 SE	9995	LEHIGH	14	40 27	75 27	660		7A	LESLIE HOWATT	3
NEW STATIONS										
COUDERSPORT 3 NW	1806	POTTER	1	41 49	78 03	2020	7P	8A	MISS ELIZABETH NEFF	2 3 5 7
MEYERSDALE 1 ENE	5685	SOMERSET	17	39 49	79 01	2290		8A	ARTHUR B. MC CARTER	3
CLOSED STATIONS										
COUDERSPORT 2 NW	1805	POTTER	1	41 48	78 03	2220	7P	8A	J. EDWARD TWIGGS	CLOSED 4/56
MEYERSDALE	5684	SOMERSET	17	39 49	79 02	2080		8A	JOHN H. BLOCHER	CLOSED 3/56

‡1-ALLEGHENY; 2-BEAVER; 3- 4-CONEMAUGH; 5-DELAWARE; 6-JUNIATA; 7-KISKIMINETAS; 8-LAKE ERIE; 9-LEHIGH; 10-MONONGAHELA; 11-OHIO; 12-POTOMAC; 13-LAKE ONTARIO; 14-SCHUYLKILL; 15-SUSQUEHANNA; 16-WEST BRANCH; 17-YOUGHIOGHENY

REFERENCE NOTES

The four digit identification numbers in the index number column of the Station Index are assigned on a state basis. There will be no duplication of numbers within a state.

Figures and letters following the station name, such as 12 SSW, indicate distance in miles and direction from the post office.

Observation times given in the Station Index are in local standard time.

Delayed data and corrections will be carried only in the June and December issues of this bulletin.

Monthly and seasonal snowfall and heating degree days for the preceding 12 months will be carried in the June issue of this bulletin.

Stations appearing in the Index, but for which data are not listed in the tables, are either missing or received too late to be included in this issue.

Unless otherwise indicated, dimensional units used in this bulletin are: temperature in °F., precipitation and evaporation in inches, and wind movement in miles. Degree days are based on a daily average of 65° F.

Evaporation is measured in the standard Weather Bureau type pan of 4 foot diameter unless otherwise shown by footnote following Table 6.

Amounts in Table 3 are from non-recording gages, unless otherwise indicated.

Data in Tables 3, 5 and 6 and snowfall data in Table 7 are for the 24 hours ending at time of observation. See Station Index for observation time.

Snow on ground in Table 7 is at observation time for all except Weather Bureau and CAA stations. For these stations snow on ground values are at 7:30 A.M. E.S.T. WTR EQUIV in Table 7 means the water equivalent of snow on the ground. It is measured at selected stations when depth of snow on the ground is two inches or more. Water equivalent samples are necessarily taken from different points for successive observations; consequently occasional drifting and other causes of local variability in the snowpack result in apparent inconsistencies in the record.

Long-term means for full-time Weather Bureau stations (those shown in the Station Index as United States Weather Bureau Stations) are based on the period 1921-1950, adjusted to represent observations taken at the present location.

- \- No record in Tables 3, 6, 7 and the Station Index. No record in Tables 2 and 5 is indicated by no entry.
- \+ And also on a later date or dates.
- * Amount included in following measurement, time distribution unknown.
- @ Data in the column formerly headed No. of Days .01 or more have been changed to No. of Days .10 or more effective January 1, 1954.
- \# Thermometers are generally exposed in a shelter located a few feet above sod-covered ground; however, the reference indicates that the thermometers are exposed in a shelter located on the roof of a building.
- // Gage is equipped with a windshield.
- AM Data based on observational day ending before noon.
- B Adjusted to a full month.
- C In the "Refer to Tables" column in the Station Index the letter "C" indicates recorder stations. These stations are processed for special purposes and are published later in Hourly Precipitation Data.
- D Water equivalent of snowfall wholly or partly estimated, using a ratio of 1 inch water equivalent to every 10 inches of new snowfall.
- M One or more days of record missing; see Table 5 for detailed daily record. Degree day data, if carried for this station, have been adjusted to represent the value for a full month.
- R Amounts from recording gage (These amounts are essentially accurate but may vary slightly from the amounts to be published later in Hourly Precipitation Data).
- SS This entry in time of observation column in Station Index means sunset.
- T Trace, an amount too small to measure.
- V Includes total for previous month.

Additional information regarding the climate of Pennsylvania may be obtained by writing to any Weather Bureau Office or to the State Climatologist at Weather Bureau Airport Station, Harrisburg State Airport, New Cumberland, Pennsylvania.

Subscription Price: 30 cents per copy, monthly and annual; $2.50 per year. (Yearly subscription includes the Annual Summary.) Checks and money orders should be made payable to the Superintendent of Documents. Remittances and correspondence regarding subscriptions should be sent to the Superintendent of Documents, Government Printing Office, Washington 25, D. C.

WRPC., Asheville, N. C. --- 5/25/56 --- 1225

U. S. DEPARTMENT OF COMMERCE
SINCLAIR WEEKS, Secretary
WEATHER BUREAU
F. W. REICHELDERFER, Chief

CLIMATOLOGICAL DATA

PENNSYLVANIA

MAY 1956

Volume LXI No. 5

ASHEVILLE: 1956

PENNSYLVANIA - MAY 1956

WEATHER SUMMARY

GENERAL

May weather in Pennsylvania was cooler and slightly wetter than usual expectancy.

This was the third consecutive month which has been cooler than usual. In fact, it was the tenth coolest May since 1888. Of the stations having long-term averages 95% showed negative departures. Extreme temperatures ranged from 18° on the 25th at Bradford 4 W Res to 95° on the 31st at Phoenixville 1 E. The 18° minimum along with five other years with similar readings ranked as the second lowest minimum since 1888, while the 95° maximum was not unusual. There were 14 stations at which the minimum temperature dropped to 32° or below on 10 or more days, and Emporium 1 E topped the list with 15 such days. Scranton WB Airport and Youngstown WB Airport reported that the 30° on the 25th was the latest date in the spring for such occurrences, while Pittsburgh WB Airport reported new record low temperatures for so late in the season were set with 32° readings on the 17th and 24th.

There was adequate precipitation during the month, and was the fourth consecutive month with more than the usual amount. Rainfall was more plentiful in the Ohio and Lake Drainage Divisions than it was over the Atlantic Drainage. Long-term average stations in the Ohio and Lake Drainage Divisions were all positive, while over the Atlantic Drainage Division they were predominantly on the negative side. Monthly totals ranged from 1.29 inches at Leroy to 9.10 inches at Titusville Water Works. The greatest daily amount was 2.50 inches at Stump Creek on the 13th. A number of stations reported traces of snow during the month, but Pleasant Mount 1 W with 1.0 inch on the 18th was the only station to report a measurable amount. Harrisburg WB Airport reported that the trace of snow on the 16th was the latest date ever recorded in the spring.

Based on available reports the percentage of sunshine was deficient at Pittsburgh WB Airport and Scranton WB Airport, while Harrisburg WB Airport and Reading WB City had more than usual. Except for Allentown WB Airport and Williamsport WB Airport average daytime cloudiness was greater than usual expectancy.

WEATHER DETAILS

A succession of cool air masses dominated the month's weather and were marked by unusual chill that approached or even dropped below freezing around the 1st, 8th, 17th and 25th. Noteworthy interruptions in the cool pattern occurred during the 12th to 14th and on the 22nd and 31st when pressure patterns favored the northward circulation of warm air that resulted in peak temperatures for the month on one or more of those dates.

Rain fell at frequent intervals, occurring on about half the days in connection with the numerous air mass changes and frontal passages throughout the month. Daily amounts were mostly light, however, except for an occasional heavy thundershower.

WEATHER EFFECTS

The cool weather of April continued through May, delaying plantings and hindering growth of vegetation, according to the Federal-State Crop Reporting Service at Harrisburg. The most freeze damage in years plagued the farm front, sharply reducing Pennsylvania's fruit prospects and requiring replanting of many tender crops. Pastures were in good condition but provided little grazing due to short growth, necessitating continued winter feeding of cattle in some localities. Winter grains were heading on shorter straw than usual but good yields were expected. Acreage intended for spring oats was being reduced due to weather-caused delays in planting and may be diverted to corn or buckwheat.

DESTRUCTIVE STORMS

On May 6 from 6:00 p.m. to midnight a fast moving cold front crossed the State setting off thunderstorms accompanied by high wind, hail and much lightning. Cloudbursts occurred at many places causing flash floods, highway washouts and several landslides. Many windows were broken by hailstones near Blairsville and also in southeastern counties. The 60 mph winds at Pittsburgh blew off several house roofs leaving the inside furnishings exposed to heavy rains causing additional damage. Winds of lesser intensity howled over the State, felling trees, billboards, TV antennas and miscellaneous material not tied down. Two persons were reported injured. One man was killed by lightning in Bucks County while working in a steel plant. Damage from lightning and resulting fires caused most of the destruction. The total estimated damage to property was $820,000. Damage to churches and destruction of barns accounted for some of the losses, but the most outstanding damages were sustained at Lemoyı when lightning struck a warehouse where electrical appliances valued at one-half million dollars were destroyє along with the $250,000 structure.

On May 12-13 severe thunderstorms occurred over southwestern Pennsylvania with suspected tornado and local flooding. The path of destruction was discontinuous for 80 miles, and its width varied from 30 to 300 yards. Th storms hit the Aliquippa, West Mifflin, Duquesne, and Windber areas, respectively; however, Duquesne was by fa the hardest hit. It left a swath of destruction in the city 12 blocks long and 2 blocks wide, consisting of unroofed and smashed windows in stores, homes, two churche the high school building, post office, a rectory, two funeral homes, a hotel, drugstores and bars. Approximat ly 75 buildings were heavily damaged and 200 others suffered lesser damage.

The estimated loss at Aliquippa was $500,000, of which $50,000 damage resulted at the Aliquippa-Hopewell Airpor when it was leveled; 14 planes were demolished and 3 mor badly damaged.

In West Mifflin a service station, which included certai garage and repair facilities as well as the sales, was partially demolished as the result of destruction of the roof. The stack of tires largely disappeared, however, many were recovered between West Mifflin and Duquesne. Damage was estimated at $25,000.

At Windber the hospital and nurses home suffered smashed windows and the roof was partly dislodged. A coal compa was leveled and one man injured when wind slammed him against a church.

Southwestern Pennsylvania was completely blacked out for a time due to the downed utility poles and electric and telephone wires. The torrential rains which accompanied the storm caused flash floods and several landslides, temporarily blocking some major traffic arteries. Total damage of these storms was estimated at $1,000,000 and 1 persons were reported injured.

On May 31 thunderstorms accompanying a fast moving cold front occurred from 6 p.m. to midnight. No major damage resulted from the storm in any one locality but it was widespread. Roofs, trees, utility wires and poles, and several automobiles were the major casualties. The southern sections of York and Lancaster Counties receive a shower of small hail which melted quickly and caused relatively little or no damage to crops. The Stroudsbur area was hardest hit. Other than the damage previously mentioned, flooding up to one foot occurred when an inch of rain fell in less than an hour. The toppled trees an electric wires brought traffic to a crawl for a short period of time. The damage over the State from these storms was estimated at $25,000.

FLOODS

Flood stages were exceeded by less than 1 foot on French Creek at Meadville and at Freeport on the lower Alleghen River on the 13th and 14th. Three lives were reported lost on French Creek near Meadville. Torrential rains i Southwestern Pennsylvania during this storm period cause local flash floods which are included in the descriptio of destructive storms in that area, given above.

Heavy rains ranging from 1.50 to 4.00 inches fell over t Monongahela River Basin the evening of the 27th and the 28th, bringing the river 1 foot over flood stage at Loc 5, Brownsville, and Lock 2, Braddock; and 3.3 feet abov at Charleroi. Overflows covered low areas, closing secondary roads and highways, but no serious flooding w reported.

J. E. Stork - Franklin W. Long

CLIMATOLOGICAL DATA

PENNSYLVANIA
MAY 1956

	Temperature: Average Maximum	Average Minimum	Average	Departure From Long Term Means	Highest	Date	Lowest	Date	Degree Days	No. of Days Max 90° or Above	Max 32° or Below	Min 32° or Below	Min 0° or Below	Precipitation: Total	Departure From Long Term Means	Greatest Day	Date	Snow, Sleet: Total	Max Depth on Ground	Date	No. of Days .10 or More	.50 or More	1.00 or More
R	68.9	44.6	56.0	- 3.7	87	13+	31	9	278	0	0	2	0	3.83	- .14	1.58	6	.0	0		8	2	1
AM	69.3	44.5	56.9	- 3.8	87	14	32	9	267	0	0	1	0	3.08	- .87	1.21	7	.0	0		6	2	1
	69.0	42.8	55.9	- 3.2	85	14	28	17	304	0	0	7	0	4.69	.56	1.19	2	.0	0		12	3	1
AM	70.9	45.3	58.1	- 2.9	89	15	29	17	239	0	0	2	0	2.88	- 1.44	.97	13	.0	0		4	3	0
	74.6	42.7	58.7		87	14+	26	5	211	0	0	6	0					.0	0				0
	72.2		M		87	14+				0	0		0	4.24		1.18	7	.0	0		8	4	1
AM	67.3	42.9	55.1	- 4.8	82	14	28	17	315	0	0	4	0	4.68	.79	1.76	7	.0	0		7	3	1
	71.4	45.2	58.3		87	14+	29	17	245	0	0	4	0	3.74		.89	7	.0	0		10	3	0
	68.7M	47.4M	58.1M	- 4.2	89	31	35	17	245	0	0	0	0	3.52	- .18	1.45	6	.0	0		8	2	1
	71.3	44.6	58.0		88	14	28	17	243	0	0	4	0	2.34		.71	2	.0	0		7	1	0
AM	62.0	38.2	50.1		83	15	26	8+	462	0	0	10	0	1.71		.48	7	.0	0		5	0	0
	75.4	48.5	62.0	.2	91	14	34	17+	146	2	0	0	0	3.70	- .25	.98	13	.0	0		8	3	0
	72.3	45.2	58.8	- 2.7	90	31	29	17	228	1	0	3	0	3.04	- .76	.94	2	.0	0		7	2	0
AM	70.9M	48.1M	59.5M		92	15	36	17	196	1	0	0	0	2.80		.98	13	.0	0		5	3	0
AM	70.7	44.7	57.7	- 3.7	90	15	30	17+	244	1	0	3	0	2.12	- 1.78	.81	7	.0	0		5	1	0
	75.0	48.6	61.8		92	31	32	17	155	2	0	1	0	2.06		.61	7	.0	0		6	1	0
	70.7	M	M		88	14				0	0		0	2.62		.66	31	.0	0		6	2	0
AM	66.7	38.1	52.4		85	15	25	25	401	0	0	8	0	3.04		.66	7	.0	0		7	2	0
	68.1	42.5	55.3		83	14+	24	8	320	0	0	8	0	6.36	1.80	1.10	13	.0	0		12	6	1
AM	62.2	38.4	50.3		81	14+	25	8+	455	0	0	9	0			.56	3	.0	0			1	0
AM	67.8	35.6	51.7	- 6.1	86	15	22	17+	420	0	0	15	0	5.12	.71	1.20	13	.0	0		9	3	1
	72.3	46.0	59.2	- 2.7	88	14+	31	17	210	0	0	1	0	2.72	- .89	1.07	7	.0	0		7	1	1
AM	72.8	42.1	57.5	- 2.5	88	6+	30	9+	247	0	0	3	0	4.68	.99			.0	0				
	63.4	41.4M	52.4M	- 4.5	80	13	24	8	382	0	0	6	0	4.02	- .59	.87	13	.0	0		10	4	0
	72.5	47.5	60.0	- 1.1	91	31	29	25	191	2	0	3	0	3.26	- .52	1.39	7	.0	0		9	1	1
AM	70.7	47.3	59.0	- 2.9	90	14+	32	17	216	2	0	1	0	2.51	- 1.49	.96	13	.0	0		5	2	0
AM	67.1	43.5	55.3		83	14+	28	17	309	0	0	2	0	3.87		1.14	13	.0	0		7	3	2
AM	71.7	44.8	58.3	- 4.9	89	14+	30	17	235	0	0	1	0	2.22	- 1.43	.86	13	.0	0		4	1	0
R	71.1	48.2	59.7	- 2.7	89	31	34	17	202	0	0	0	0	2.43	- 1.27	.62	2	T	0		7	1	0
AM	64.5	38.1	51.3		82	13	24	9+	425	0	0	11	0	3.19		1.17	7	.0	0		7	2	1
	69.7	50.3	60.0	- 3.1	90	31	37	17	189	1	0	0	0	1.35	- 1.79	.24	23	.0	0		4	0	0
AM	71.9	40.8	56.4	- 4.1	89	15	29	5+	286	0	0	6	0	5.24	1.08	2.41	13	.0	0		9	2	2
	71.0M	43.2M	57.1M	- 2.5	87	13+	27	9	283	0	0	5	0	3.44	- .90	.90	7	.0	0		8	2	0
	71.1	42.3	56.7		86	14	29	8+	278	0	0	6	0	4.58		1.23	27	.0	0		10	2	2
	74.4	46.7	60.6	- .7	91	31	32	9+	182	2	0	2	0	1.96	- 1.58	.60	7	.0	0		7	1	0
AM	69.6	46.5	58.1		89	15	33	17+	241	0	0	0	0	2.36		.63	7	.0	0		6	1	0
AM	65.7	36.3	51.0	- 6.6	88	15	23	25	440	0	0	13	0	2.05	- 1.88	.55	7	.0	0		6	1	0
	72.6M	48.9M	60.8M	- .4	90	15	34	17	174	1	0	0	0					.0	0				0
AM	71.5	43.5	57.5		89	15	31	17	247	0	0	2	0	4.38		1.13	24	.0	0		9	4	1
	72.8	43.7M	58.3M	- 3.4	88	12	29	17	248	0	0		0	3.90	- .21	.95	7	.0	0		8	3	0
AM	66.7	35.4	51.1		83	15+	22	17	435	0	0	14	0	5.28		1.68	13	.0	0		9	3	2
	70.3	50.3	60.3	- 5.5	92	14	38	17	186	2	0	0	0	3.10	- .66	.83	7	.0	0		7	2	0
	68.1	44.2	56.2		83	31	27	17	292	0	0	2	0	2.92		.84	2	.0	0		8	2	0
	71.5	49.1	60.3	- 1.6	91	31	34	17	190	2	0	0	0	2.43	- 1.75	.68	2	.0	0		7	2	0
AM	61.5	38.2	49.9	- 5.1	81	15	22	13	469	0	0	9	0	2.53	- 1.59	.49	7	T	T	18	7	0	0
	68.9	45.4	57.2		88	31	29	17	266	0	0	1	0	4.40		1.12	13	.0	0		9	3	1
	70.4	45.4	57.9		90	31	31	5+	250	1	0	3	0	2.46		.88	6	.0	0		5	1	0
	65.0	40.5	52.8	- 1.2	82	31	25	25	388	0	0	6	0	2.66	- 1.69	.78	7	.0	0		5	2	0
	67.1	40.6	53.9		85	13	25	17+	359	0	0	9	0	4.04		1.35	7	.0	0		10	2	1
	73.6	50.5	62.1		90	13	32	17	146	1	0	1	0	3.63		1.06	2	.0	0		7	3	1
AM	71.5	42.3	56.9		90	15	30	9+	270	1	0	7	0	2.37	- 1.94	.83	3	.0	0		8	1	0
	72.4	49.4	60.9		93	31	37	17	174	2	0	0	0	2.07		.49	7+	.0	0		6	0	0
	69.3	45.8	57.6	- 2.0	87	13+	30	9	265	0	0	3	0	3.32	- .62	.81	6	.0	0		7	2	0
	72.7	52.2	62.5		92	14+	40	17	134	3	0	0	0	3.65		1.19	31	.0	0		10	2	1
R	71.8	49.9	60.9	- 2.2	92	14	37	17	170	2	0	0	0	3.84	.26	2.00	6	.0	0		6	2	1
	71.2	52.8	62.0	- 2.4	91	14	40	17	150	2	0	0	0	3.15		.84	31	.0	0		8	2	0
	74.6	49.8	62.2	- 1.0	92	14+	35	25	143	2	0	0	0	2.37	- 1.27	.81	23	.0	0		8	1	0
RAM	70.3	51.4	60.9	- 2.8	88	14+	43	9+	163	0	0	0	0	2.97	- .61	1.01	31	.0	0		8	2	1
	65.7	40.4	53.1		84	14	22	25	381	0	0	8	0	5.17		1.04	6	.0	0		11	4	1
	75.7	45.4	60.6	- 1.8	95	31	28	25	186	2	0	3	0	2.20	- 2.03	.67	6	.0	0		7	1	0
AM	62.7	41.0	51.9		80	13+	24	8	413	0	0	5	0	3.52		.92	7	T	0		9	3	0
AM	60.9	36.7	48.8		78	13+	22	25	493	0	0	14	0	3.02	- 1.61	.57	27	1.0	1	18	10	1	0
AM	70.0	42.0	56.0	- 5.0	90	15	27	25	293	1	0	5	0	2.89	- 1.25	.60	3	.0	0		7	2	0
	72.4	45.6	59.0	- .7	87	13+	30	9+	222	0	0	3	0	2.46	- 1.65	1.18	7	.0	0		7	1	1
R	70.9	49.3	60.1	- 2.4	90	14+	37	17	197	2	0	0	0	2.95	- .74	.96	6	.0	0		6	3	0
AM	66.6	40.9	53.8	- 5.6	85	15	28	25	361	0	0	6	0	2.87	- .70	.89	7	.0	0		7	2	0
	66.6	42.8	54.7	- 4.2	85	14+	30	8+	338	0	0	4	0	2.25	- 1.86	.71	6	.0	0		6	1	0
	68.8	43.5	56.2	- 4.6	86	14+	29	17	297	0	0	3	0	3.87	- .17	.78	13	.0	0		8	4	0
	73.3	46.4	59.9	- 2.8	89	31	30	17	195	0	0	2	0	2.66	- 1.53	.90	13	.0	0		6	2	0
	68.5	46.4	57.5	- 1.5	85	14	30	17	260	0	0	1	0	4.93	.82	1.80	6	.0	0		8	4	1
	67.3	39.3	53.3	- 6.7	87	13	24	25	374	0	0	8	0	4.70	.86	1.88	31	T	0		9	4	1
AM	64.4M	36.4M	50.4M		86	15	26	8+	455	0	0	14	0					.0	0				0
	68.5	41.5	55.0	- 2.8	88	14	25	25	338	0	0	8	0	1.92	- 1.68	.41	7+	.0	0		6	0	0
	73.3	49.6	61.5		92	14	35	17	159	2	0	0	0	2.87		.72	7	.0	0		8	2	0
AM	63.2	38.3	50.8	- 5.5	83	15	25	8	447	0	0	8	0	2.53	- 1.34	.75	7	.0	0		6	2	0
	72.6	45.3	59.0		88	31	28	17	216	0	0	4	0	3.30		1.26	13	.0	0		6	2	1
AM	73.0	47.8	60.4	- .6	93	14+	33	17	180	2	0	0	0	4.35	.01	1.47	31	.0	0		8	4	2
	69.5	44.3	56.9	- 3.3	89	14	31	17+	280	0	0	2	0	3.33	- .98	.67	6+	.0	0		8	4	0

See Reference Notes Following Station Index

TABLE 2 - CONTINUED

Station	
YORK 3 SSW PUMP STA	
DIVISION	
OHIO DRAINAGE	
BAKERSTOWN 3 WNW	
BLAIRSVILLE 6 ENE	
BRADFORD 4 W RES	
BROOKVILLE CAA AIRPORT	
BURGETTSTOWN 2 W	AM
BUTLER	
CLARION 3 SW	
CLAYSVILLE 3 W	
CONFLUENCE 1 SW DAM	AM
CORRY	
COUDERSPORT 3 NW	
DERRY	
DONEGAL	
DONORA	AM
EAST BRADY	
EBENSBURG	
FARRELL SHARON	
FORD CITY 4 S DAM	AM
FRANKLIN	
GREENVILLE	
INDIANA 3 SE	
IRWIN	
JAMESTOWN 2 NW	AM
JOHNSTOWN	AM
KANE 1 NNE	AM
LINESVILLE 5 WNW	
MEADVILLE 1 S	AM
MERCER 2 NNE	
MIDLAND DAM 7	
NEW CASTLE 1 N	
NEWELL	AM
NEW STANTON	
PITTSBURGH WB AP 2	//R
PITTSBURGH WB CITY	R
PUTNEYVILLE 2 SE DAM	AM
RIDGWAY 3 W	
SALINA 3 W	
SHIPPINGPORT WB	
SLIPPERY ROCK	
SOMERSET MAIN ST	
SPRINGS 1 SW	
TIONESTA 2 SE DAM	AM
TITUSVILLE WATER WORKS	
UNIONTOWN	
WARREN	
WAYNESBURG 2 W	
DIVISION	
LAKE DRAINAGE	
ERIE CAA AIRPORT	
SPRINGBORO	
DIVISION	

Day of month

9	10	11	12	13	14	15	16	17	18	19	20	21	22	23	24	25	26	27	28	29	30	31
	.09	.26	.85	.61			.17	.10	.28			T		.50	.02			.46	.28			.10
T	.02		.01	.27	.14	.01	.04	.01	.05	.04			.12	.23				.41			.05	.20
	.03	T		.40		.05	.04		.04		.04			.04	.09			.10	.25			.12
	.18	.05	.70	.04		.06	.19	.10	.28					.25				.21	.01			.15
	.04	.08	.02	.97			.09	T	.05					.04				.40	.04			.04
	.96	.22	-			.40			.45				*	.83	.22			-			.10	-
	.16	.03	.44	.46			.12		.22		.05				.01			.05				.28
	.26		.68		.10			.37	.06					.79			.04	.48			.15	.34
	.99	.06	.89	1.02	.21		.20	.14	.25	.15				T	T				.05			.60
			.16	.70			.12		.15					.55				.21			.31	
	.16	.19	1.92	1.75	T		.32	.13	.35	.01	T			.48	.08			.17	.16			.17
	.01		.32	.70	.12		.14		.09					.04	.60			.08				.22
	.04		.36	.88			.10		.09		T			T				.31	.07			1.80
	.06	.03	.40	.60	T		.06		.08		.02			.47	.08			.05	.22			.27
	.04		.17	.49		T	.03		.18	.01				.20				.66	.18		.14	.08
	.02		.03	.31		.15	.02		T		.01			.18	.02			.06	.28			T
T	.03		.02	.32	.16		.02	.01		.03			.10	.18				.37			.06	.18
T	.49	.07	1.75	.03		.11	.25	.19	.27			T	.18			T		.82	.11		.11	.08
	T	.15		.85		T	.20						T					.40			.17	
	T	.42	.66	.45			.20	.14	.28					.92				1.42	.42			.44
	T	.24	1.11	.52			.21	.15	.20					.15				.73	.67			.10
	.89	.02	.86	.06			.19	.12	.23	.10	.01			.06	.01			.33	.11			.56
.19	.78	T	.94	.70			.43	T	.30	.11		T		T				.45	.08		.12	.60
			.49										.12				.19	.90			.60	.16
.14	.52		1.39	1.10		.15	.14	.23	.08	.05		T	.65	.06			.14	.68			.08	.72
	.04	.16	*	*	.60		T		.51							T		*	1.69			.39
	T	.02	.20	.25			.23	.03	.14					.19	T			.90	.31			.75
	.17	.24	.21	.26			.30		.37			.02		.37				1.65	.32			.51
	T		.20	.27		.09	T	T	T								T	.46			.34	.17
	.47	.16	1.40	.15			.38	.10	.18	.06				.31				.44	.66			.40
		.02	.03	.58		T	.08		.06	.09			.07					.30			.05	.50
	.02	.03	.15	.46			.02	.07	.11									.04	.04			T
	.04	T	.14	.98		T	.10	T	.05	T			T	T				.27			.38	T
	.19	.18	.76	.25			.18	.14	.46	.05				.37	.01			.43	.36			.41
	.20	.05	.40	.83			.16	T	.19		T				T			.26	.08			.08
	.03	.06	.20	.62			.12	.04	.20		.03				.04			.10	.09			.03
T	T	T		.30	T						.20			T				.20			T	
	.06		.08	.07	.02	T	.16	.04	.01	T			.01	.25				.59			.16	.33
	.02	.23	.55	.38			.21	.08	.18					.28	T			.77	.59			.45
	T			.98			T		T					.25	T				.27			T
	.11	T	.82	.67	T	T	.14	.03	.11		.07			.04	.04			.14	.19			.41
	.56	.14	.69	1.30			.17		.24	.01		T		.44	.03			.55	.19			.27
	.04		.03	.36		.01	.07		.08		.02			.02	.12			.24	.11			.13
	.19	.49	.16	.45			.23		.37				.02	.14				.77	.94			.03
	.28	.09	.80	.80	T		.22		.37		.06			.02	.02			.48	.42			.20
	.85	.11	.75	1.70			.12	.06	.16	.09	.02				T			.30	.03			.53
	.02			.62			.10		.16		.01				.31			.30	.40			.13
	.02	.01	.03	.31	T				.06		.06			.13	.09			.12	.07			T
	.03	.02		.31	.13	T	T		.04	.02			.07	T				.25			T	
	T	1.00	.25	.18	T		.43	.10	.41	.01	T			.58	.03			.95	.99			.14
		.64	T	.30			.39	.12	.45				T	.57	.04			.94	1.15			.05
	.09	.59	.66	.19			.20	.17	.12					.09				.75	.86			1.24
	.03	T	T	.30	T				.04		.12			.41	.21			.15	T			.04
	.71	.16	.66	1.37	T		.12	.14	.15	.04				T				.60	.08	T		.42
	.78	.14	.04	1.03	T		.13	.12	.17	.04		T		.04				.61	.08	T		.52
		.35	*	.87			.40	T	.21									*	1.50			T
.32	1.08		.92	.99			.40	.11	.19	.15			.03					.29				.90
	.74	.07	.71	.89			.19	.11	.15	.05					.02			.24	.24			.57
	.59	.10	.59	1.15	.02		.20	.12	.07	.03	.04				T			.18	.19			.40
	T	.03	.31	.47			.03		.04										.02			T
	.27	.11	.82				.14	.18	.40	.05				.20				.37	.50			.20
	.18	.20	.55	.13	.03		.21	.05	.24	.06				.02	.35			.16	.22			.15
	.90	.05	.75	.98			.22	.13	.26	.06	.01			.02	T			.30	.13			.46
			.29	1.10			.08		.08									.30	.10			.20
	.20	.22	.58	.10		.21	.15	.22						.42				1.21			.26	.05
		.03	T	T	T			.53		.08	T		.39	T			.15	.22			T	.66
	.15		.16	.49			.04	T	.48	.01	.05							.61	.04			
	.39		.77			.18	.08	.14	T				.03	.18			T	1.46	.25		.29	.35
	.38	.07	.61		T	T	.26	.12	.02			T	.03	T				1.35	.07		.08	.05
	.04		.03	.23			T		.06		.45			.42				.22			.04	
	.54	.10	.92	1.10	.02	.04	.35	.03	.18	.07				.27			.62	.08			T	.33
	T	.03	.16	.06			.10	.04	.34	.06					.02			.11	.04			.07
	.02	.04	.19	-			.28	.07	.14						.02			.16	.08			.02
	.54	.03	1.25	.23			.40	.05	.15	.01			.03					.83			.08	.29
	.25	.13	.73	T			.12	.11	.32	T				T	.33			.03	.20			.10
	1.24	.03	.88	1.07	.02		.38	.01	.33	.08				.01				.07	.19		.02	.11
	.02	.02	.03	.37	.05						.08							.26	.10			
	.48	.05	.49	1.20	.04		.13	.09	.23	.06	.03			.02				.31	.08			.45
	.05	.09	.26	.56	T		.10	.04	.13	T	.07				.05			.08	.03			.13
	.02	.05	.04	.33	.02				.03	T	.10			.05				.40			.12	
		.12			T	.05	T	.06	.45	.05	.33				T			.40	.24			.08
.56	.26	1.23	.46	.23		.32	.16	.36	.02	.11		T		.01			.06	.01			.07	1.14
			.40			.20	T	.10						.10			*	1.30	.10		.68	.60
.26	.31		1.16	.08		.03	.39	.30	.12	.02			.38	.02			.02	.25			.28	.90
	.45	.05	.98	.01			.18	.15	.33					.27	T			.33	.22			.20
	.83	.13	1.07	.97	T		.29	.13	.24	.08				.19				.43	.05			.13
	.03	.03	.05	.45				.25			.15		T		.18			.50	.21		.27	.87
	.27	T	-	.70	.02		.12	.02	.12	.02					T	T			.04			.51
	.03		.02	.80							.06				.24			.47				.06
			.03	.15							.16		.07	.27				.34			.10	.33
	.01	.03	T	.96			.03	T	.05	T	T			.13	.01			.38	.02			.08
	.73	.09	.69	1.01	1.37		.18	.15	.33	.09	.02			.09				.40	.18		T	.73
	.01	.31	1.00	.12			.32	.25	.43					.75				.52	.68			.09
	.10		.05	.10		T	.25		.25				.06		.16			.27	.22			
	.02	.11	.05	.46			.09	.04	.05				.01	.01				.32			.03	.13
				.33							.05			.18				.14	.08			.07
	T		.10	1.14	T		.08	T	.14	T					1.00			.14	.08			.48
		.56		.34			.12	.12	.32				T	.47	.02			.71	1.36			.46
	.32	.05	.76	.71		.15	.14	.15					.01	.01				1.73			.12	.01
.30	.70	T	1.22	.30		T	.42	.25	.03	.08		.02	.05	.11				.37			.04	.50
	T	.02	T	.86			T		.02		T			.08				.31	.03			T
	T	.01	.23	.29		.10	T	.02		.07			.01	.03			T	.31	T		.03	.46
	T		.05	.48		.06	.07	.01	.09		.01			.12				.19	.06			.11
	.10	T	.04	T		.11	.07	T	.39	.02	.03				.03			.42	.08			T
	.10		.05			.20	.07		.38	.04					.03			.33	.17			
	.19	T	.04	.34		.18	.08		.43	.02	.04				.03			.44	.14			T
	.01	.03	.01	.20	T		.01	T	.05		.02			.24	.06			.09	.09			.03
	.16		.10	.02	T	.38	.07	.02	.58	.02	.03			T	T			.66	T			
	.17	.15	.46	.10			.36	.10	.13					.74				*	.77			.18
	T	T	.21	.23			T	.09	-					T	.07				.27			.01
	.09	.06	.25	2.41	T		.12		.18	.12				.12	.13			.07	.08			.09
	.01	.02	.08	1.10	T		.12	.01	.04		T			.06	T			.29	.03			.13
	.02	.08	.28	.16			.28	.02	.30					.43				.71	.64			.35
	.25	.07	.81	.02			.15	.12	.38	T				.23				.43	.28			.07
	.14	.05	.92	.20		.15	.19	.23	.02				.02				.05	1.63	.20			.62
	1.08	.22	1.03	.61			.36	.01	.21	.03		.02		.13				.24				.20
	.05		.08	.40			.11		.18					.31				.43	.06		.07	.21
	.16	T	.55	.74			.14	.21	.30	.15			T	.51				.32	.55			.14
	.84	.07	.64	1.77	.28	T	.16	.11	.38	.12	T		T	.02				.33	.45			.70

See Reference Notes Following Station Index

DAILY PRECIPITATION

Table 3—Continued

Station	Total	1	2	3	4	5	6	7	8	9	10	11	12	13	14	15	16	17	18	19	20	21	22	23	24	25	26	27	28	29	30	31
KARTHAUS	5.00			.95		T		.73	T		.18	.02	.78	.69	.03		.23	.07	.17		.11			.03	.07			.33	.27			.3
KEATING SUMMIT	5.28	T		.56		.04		.81			.54	.09	.70	.98	T		.22	.10	.16	.07	.03		T		T			.39	.09			.5
KEGG	4.58		1.05		T		.30	.28			.04	.01	.43	.04		.25	.04	.10					.07	.28				1.23			.30	.1
KITTANNING LOCK 7	5.33			.98		.03		.75			.43	.10	1.05	.07			.17	.15	.30		T			.16	T			.43	.46			.2
KREGAR 4 SE	8.19		1.43		.17		.70	.31		T	.57		.78	.06		.26	.24	.18	.04				.09	.32			T	1.89	.28		.72	.1
KRESGEVILLE 3 W	3.23			.59				1.02			.05		.11	.22	.02		.10		.09						.28			.20	.51			.0
LAKEVILLE 1 NNE	2.33			.65		.03		.34	T		.11	T	.02	T		.03	.11		.45	.02					.05			.49	.03			
LANCASTER 2 NE PUMP STA	1.96		.26	.14				.60			.05	.02	.02	.33	T				.02		T			.11				.30			.11	
LANDISVILLE	2.36			.49	.02			.63			.02	.01	.03	.22	.01	.08	.01		.03	T	.09			.13	.03			.26	.03			.2
LATROBE	4.73		.96		.06		.66			T	.24		.70	T		.11	.12	.18					.23	.02			.11	1.15			.14	.0
LAWRENCEVILLE 2 S	2.05			.23				.55			.04	.06	.34	.44	T		.09	.04	.12													.1
LEBANON 2 NW	-		-					-			.02	T	.03	.37		.12		T	.04		.05		T		.18			.20	.10			.0
LEHIGHTON	3.09			.60		T		.77			.07	T	T	.30			.06		.07		.04				.78			T	.40			
LE ROY	1.29			.24	.05	.11	.43					.04		.30						.12												
LEWIS RUN 3 SE	5.86	.02		.42		.06		.92			.74	.10	.74	1.39			.19	.14	.30	.06	.02		.02		.02			.31	.07			.3
LEWISTOWN	4.38			.81		.02		.63			.02	.02	.24	.60			.24		.17						1.13			.02	.25			.2
LINESVILLE 5 WNW	5.43	T		.35		.01		.27			1.28	.08	1.29	1.10			.44	.03	.19	.06			T	.08				.13	.02			.1
LOCK HAVEN	3.90			.67		.01		.95			.02		.34	.67	.01		.09		.18		.02				.05			.18	.29			.4
LONG POND 2 W	2.88			.43		.05		.75	.03		.06	.02	.08	.11		.06	.05		.10	T	.05				.48			.44	.15			T
MADERA	5.28			.06		.03		1.47			.23	.08	.53	1.68	T		.14	.07	.15		.03			.20	.06			.28	.24			.0
MAHAFFEY	6.77			.87		.04		.99			.42	.08	.73	1.41			.20	.12	.20		.05	.01		.35	.10			.39	.98			.1
MAPLE GLEN	4.15		.50	.17	.23			1.13			.01	T	T	.23			T	T	.04		.07	T	T	1.17				.42			.18	
MAPLETON DEPOT	3.61			.76		T		.25	T		.04	.07	.32	1.13	T		.17		.21	.03				.16	.16			.09	.04			.1
MARCUS HOOK	3.10		.40	T	T		.40	.83			T	T	T	.93		T	T			.16	T		.07	T				.32			T	.3
MARION CENTER 2 SE	6.48	T		.89		.05		1.60	.01		.36	.21	1.10	.20	T	T	.18	.19	.42	.02	.02	T		.17	.02			.47	.43			.1
MARTINSBURG CAA AP	2.92		.84		T		.28	T			.09	.03	.35	.51		.22	.01	.23	T				.04	.05			T	.15	T		.10	.0
MATAMORAS	3.06			.59				1.31			.17					.22	.04		.23	.04					.08			.33	.07			
MAYBURG	6.21	T		.55		.03		.74			.98	.06	.93	.55	.50		.13	.16	.28	.14				T	T			.50	.11			.5
MC CONNELLSBURG	2.92			.71				.28	T		.08	.01	.18	.07			.13		.07					.17				.74	.11			.3
MC KEESPORT	5.96			.90				1.44				.12	*	1.15			.27	.03	.23										1.52			.3
MEADVILLE 1 S	7.74	T		.37		.03	.08	.61			1.52	.20	1.59	1.62			.45	.09	.17	.04			T	.05				.29	.05		.03	.5
MEDIX RUN	5.80	T		.59		.03		.44			.49	.08	.84	.85	1.07		.13	.10	.17	T	.07			.03	.04			.39	.19			.3
MERCER 2 NNE	5.87			.42		T		.75			.54	.20	1.30	.20			.05	.40	.32	.04				.35				.48	.12			.7
MERCERSBURG	3.41			.60				.27						.15			.24		.09					.07				.94	.10			.9
MEYERSDALE 1 ENE	5.77			1.39		.02		.95			.05	.28	.14	.25			.31	.10	.24	.02				.29	.12			.78	.81			.0
MIDDLETOWN OLMSTED FLD	2.43		.88	T			.57	.04			.01	.01	.28	.30		.01	T	T	T	.07			.01	.01			T	.12			.14	.1
MIDLAND DAM 7	6.67			.98		.02		1.17			.06	.30	1.33	.03			.35	.15	.20			T		.85				.31	.77			.1
MILANVILLE	2.37			.45		.04		.46			.13		.09	.21	T	T			.51	.04				T				.36	.08			
MILLHEIM	4.58			.54		T		1.91	T		.05	.02	.31	.89	.03		.10		.12		T			.05	T			.24	.06			.4
MILLVILLE 2 SW	3.25		.57			.01		.71	T		T	T	.16	.07	T		.16	.08	.07		T		T		.08			.28	.24		.10	.1
MILROY	4.89			.74		.01		1.16			.04		.38	.55	T		.19		.22					T	1.07			.25	.11			.1
MONTROSE 1 E	2.55	T		.35		.10		.49			.20	.08	.29	.06		T	.05	.05	.37	.01	.03				.03			.38	.07			
MORGANTOWN	4.40		.37		.05		.68	.85			.02	T	.03	1.12	.20		T	T		.05			.14	.18				.19			.09	.4
MT GRETNA 2 SE	2.46		.49				.88	.02			T	.04	.07	.34			.04	T		.02				.09				.32			.13	.0
MT POCONO 2 N AP	2.66			.48	.07		.03	.78			.09		.11	.03					.29	.09								.09				
MUHLENBURG 1 SE	4.04		.56	.13	.08		T	1.35			T		.12	.43		T	.15		.20	.08								.48	.20			.3
MYERSTOWN	3.17			.48		.06		.79	.03		.06			.62			.12		.04					.18	.34			.12	.08			.2
NATRONA LOCK 4	4.70			.96		.01		.99			.17	.12	.79	.05			.20	.14	.29					.27	.07			.37	.17			.1
NESHAMINY FALLS	2.52		.31		.17		.07	.40			T		T	.17	.12		.02	T		.02	.23		.17	.02				.34			.06	.4
NEWBURG 3 W	3.63		1.06				.15	.06			.07	.14		.40		.08												.63			.30	.7
NEW CASTLE 1 N	5.01			.64		.03	.02	.43			.41	.10	1.15	.16	.02		.23	.13	.31	.02			T	.45				.27	.19			.4
NEWELL	5.46		.54	.52			.20	.58			.37	.20	.58				.33	.16	.11				.09	.10				1.30	.23			.0
NEW PARK	2.23		.27	.03				.48			T			.41			.01			.06			.48	T				.31			.02	.1
NEWPORT	2.37			.83		T		.37	T		T	.01	.02	.36			.18	T	.12				T	T	T			.15	.10			.2
NEW STANTON	5.09		.88		.07		.54	T		.01	.38		.75			.02		.02				T	.03	.08			.01	1.62			.25	.4
NEW TRIPOLI	3.29		.35	.36	T		T	1.02			.04		.02	.46	.02	T	.06		.12		.03		.02	.24				.43	.02		.08	.
NORRISTOWN	2.07			.29		.04		.49	.02		.02	T	.01	.36	T		T		.04		.10			.49	.07			.11	.02			.
NORTH EAST 2 SE	4.91			.14	.04	.06	T	.28			.83	T	1.18	.82	T		.73	.03	.36	.12	T			.03				.07	.06		T	.
ORWELL 3 N	2.41	T		.28				.71			.18	.01	.32	.10			.06		.32				T					.37	.02			.
PALM	3.10			.56		.25		1.20	.08			.04	.05	.28				.05	.04					.05	.08			.20	.10		.10	
PALMERTON	3.32		.39				.81	.01		.01	.01		.05	.25	T	.05	.02	.01	.04	.18				.61				.37			.04	.
PARKER	4.31			.62		.02		.53			.36	.12	1.17	.17			.16	.04	.20	.04				.09				.56	.14			.
PAUPACK 2 WNW	3.13			.61		.08		.94			.18		.09			.18	.08		.40					.04				.55				
PECKS POND	2.70			.52		.02		.77			.15		.04	.02		.33	.06		.26	T	T				.15			.34	.04			
PHIL DREXEL INST OF TEC	3.65		.39	T	.10		.30	.56		T	T			.30		T	.01	T		.15	T		.20	.25				.20			T	1.
PHILADELPHIA WB AP R	3.84		.40	T	.07		2.00	.09		T	T	T	T	.51		T	.01	T		.09	.03		.17	T				.21			T	.
PHILADELPHIA PT BREEZE	3.15		.45	.01	.26		.02	.68						.25			.01			.07	.01		.20	.18				.16			.01	.
PHILADELPHIA SHAWMONT	2.37		.24	.16	.09		T	.39			.03		.02	.22			.02			T	.13		T	.81				.16			.10	.
PHILADELPHIA CITY R	2.07		.32	T	.18		.64	.14		T	T	T	T	.23		.01	.01	T		.04	.02		.11	.14				.08			.04	1.
PHILIPSBURG CAA AP	5.17		.72		.05		1.04	.03		T	.20	T	.99	.39		.10	.04	.11	T	.08			T	.61			T	.35			.35	.
PHOENIXVILLE 1 E	2.20		.30				.67	.18			T		T	.32					.04	.01	T		.12	.04				.16			.01	.
PIKES CREEK	2.98			.61		.08		.83	.02		T	.04	.11	.42	T		.15	T	.26	T	.01				.02			.26	.13			.
PIMPLE HILL	3.52			.53		.04		.92	.02		.07	.01	.10	.14		.03	.08	T	.10	.01	.16				.60			.42	.29			T
PINE GROVE 1 NE	2.86			.60				.55			T		T	.76			.09		.04		T				.24			.14	.10			.
PITTSBURGH WB AP 2 //R	5.90		.74		T	T	1.02			T	.24	T	.63			.23	.15	.17	T			T	.21	.16			.03	1.62	T		.20	.
PITTSBURGH WB CITY R	6.08		1.00		.02	T	1.00	T		T	.28		1.07			.20	.10	.17		T		T	.12	.08			.10	1.56			.06	.
PLEASANT MOUNT 1 W	3.02			.35		.18		.48			.17	.05	.12	.19		.02	.08	.10	.49	.04	.13			T	T			.57	.05		T	
PORT CLINTON	2.89			.60				.48			.02		.03	.43			.06		.08		.02			.11	.19			.23	.05			.
POTTSTOWN	2.57			.42		.20		1.05			.04			.59			.04				T			.04				.06	.06			.
PUTNEYVILLE 2 SE DAM	5.84			.82		.02		.72			.57	.07	1.18	.31			.19	.15	.29		.02			.07				.54	.48			.
QUAKERTOWN 1 E	2.46		.16	.26	.10			1.18			.03		.01	.21	T		.02		.02		.06			.15				.21			.05	
RAYMOND	3.87			.07				.50			.40	.24	.64	.90			.20	.10	.15		.10							.20	.12			.
READING WB CITY R	2.95		.52		.03		.96	.03		T	.05		.03	.66	T	.01	.04	.02		.03			.17	.02				.22			.10	.
RENOVO	-			.54		.02		-			.18	.05	.70	.08	T		.08		.17		.06				.05			.19	.32			.
REW	4.24	T		.37		.06		.23			.70	.05	.76	.63			.22	.10	.23	.08	.03			T	.02			.31	.13			.
RICES LANDING L 6	5.33			1.17		.05		.88			.03	.27	.51	.25			.21	.13	.18					.08				.70	.86			.
RIDGWAY 3 W	5.49			.49		.02		.46			.66	.11	.54	.65	1.08		.11	.12	.12	.05				.02				.44	.12			.
RUSH	2.80			.36		.08		.39			.18	.02	.27	.27		.02	.08	.02	.39						.07			.51				
RUSHVILLE	2.56			.36		.06		.33			.11	.02	.31	.25		.04	.04		.38		.01							.59	.03			.
SAGAMORE 1 S	6.38			1.10		.11		1.63			.30	.15	.85				.10	.35	.65	.22			.14					.25	.53			
SALINA 3 W	4.56	.02	.84	.02	.03			.53			.43	.05	.53	.28		.13	.21	.21	.17	.01			.02	.12	.01			.65	.04		.23	.
SAXTON	3.00			.68		T		.49	T		.07	.03	.25	.09		T	.24	T	.19	T	T			.13	T			.21	.09			.
SCHENLEY LOCK 5	4.91			.95		.02		1.01			.21	.05	.90	.01			.18	.15	.31	.01				.16				.45	.36			.
SCRANTON	2.87			.39		.07		.89			.03	T	.03	.30			.10	.01	.29	.01	T				.05			.20	.50			
SCRANTON WB AIRPORT	2.25		.38	T	.03		.71	T		T	.01		.05	.11		.02	.07	T	.22	.01		T		.07				.27			T	.
SELINSGROVE CAA AP	3.87		.56		T		.71	T			T	.01	.42	.78		.11	T	.03	.05					.64			T	.43			.13	
SHAMOKIN	3.60			.49				.83			T		.08	.66			.14		.12						.70			*	.38			.
SHIPPENSBURG	2.86		.50	.30				.28			T		T	.90	T	T	.12	T	T				.01	T				.48			T	.
SHIPPINGPORT WB	7.01		1.01		T		1.11			.03	.27		1.27			.35	.15	.28					.35	.15			.12	.88			.15	.
SINNEMAHONING	5.18			.67		.02		.50			.36	.08	.62	.87	.35		.14	.08	.17		.05			T	.01			.26	.08			.
SLIPPERY ROCK	4.80			.52		.01		.35			.47	.17	1.17	.10			.21	.16	.35					.36				.47	.29			.
SOMERSET FAIRVIEW ST	6.66			1.38		.02		.57				.30	.51	.27			.45	.09	.26					.52				.89	.80			.
SOMERSET MAIN ST	7.17		1.05	.20	.04			.60			.26	.04	.84			.16	.38	.18	.20				.05	.63				1.40	.34		.45	
SOUTH MOUNTAIN	3.14			.51				.25			.01	.07	.02	.14			.10		.06					.60	.10			.39	.34			
SPRINGBORO	-			-		T	T	.35			1.20	T	*	1.15	T		.40	.10	1.15	1.12		T		T				-	T		T	
SPRING GROVE	2.39		.28	.16				.47			.02		T	.90	.01		T		.03		.02			.06				.28			.05	
SPRINGS 1 SW	7.51		1.46		.06			.90			.70		.27		.03	.34	.43	.30	.15									2.45			.39	
STATE COLLEGE	4.93		.68	.01	.03		1.80	T		T	.12	T	.72	.20		.06	.01	.07	.03	.02	T		T	.76			T	.16			.04	
STRAUSSTOWN	3.76			.66		T		.58	T		.03		.03	.53		.08	.09		.03		.07			.20	.48			.26	.24			
STROUDSBURG	4.70		.56	.01	.01		.60	.57		.04	.01	T	.01	T	T	.01	.04	T	.14	.14	.02		T	.18				.35	.13		T	1
STUMP CREEK	6.89			.76		T		.70			.41	.09	.82	2.50	.02		.15	.11	.11			.04		.12				.50	.27			
SUNBURY	2.94			.30		T		.75	T		T	T	.26	.65	T		.10		.09		T			T	.19			.19	.04		.03	
SUSQUEHANNA	2.69			.23		T		.45			.13	.04	.32	.33		.02	.08	.07	.43	.02				.02	.01			.38	.12			
SUTERSVILLE	4.34			.76		.04		.44			.05	.36	*	*	.65			.08	.20		T	T		.18				*	1.43			
TAMAQUA	3.68			.66				.71	.03		.03		.14	.70			.14		.13						.43			.35	.14			
TAMAQUA 4 N DAM	4.09			.60				1.40		.03			.04	.73			.06		.16		.01				.21			.28	.43			
TAMARACK 2 S FIRE TWR	-			.98		.02		.76			.24	.06	.44	.77	T		.12	T	.09	T	.08		T	T	T			.10	.18			
TIONESTA 2 SE DAM	6.66	.01		.53				.68			.95	.10	.91	1.71	T	T	.18	.09	.20	.08				.11	T			.59	.08		T	
TITUSVILLE WATER WORKS	9.10		.34		.04		.35	.75		.44	1.01		1.16	1.87	.01	T	.50	.14	.07	.05			T	.07				.46	.01		.66	1
TORPEDO 4 W	8.26	.01		.31		.07		.65			1.18	.10	1.07	.86	.05		.27	.21	.35	.09	.03			.06	T			.38	.07			

See Reference Notes Following Station Index

DAILY PRECIPITATION

Station	Total	1	2	3	4	5	6	7	8	9	10	11	12	13	14	15	16	17	18	19	20	21	22	23	24	25	26	27	28	29	30	31
OA	1.02			.17		.09		.41			.01	.02	.27	.41			.01	.05	.17	T	.02		T		.03			.25	.01			T
CITY 3 SW	3.25		.55	.13				.02					.03	.74		T	.10		.11					.22				.28			.30	.17
	2.05			.22		.14		.47			.03	.08	.40	.38			.02	.07	.17	.02					.05			.03				T
EPOINT 4 NE	RECORD MISSING																															
E 4 NE BALD EAGLE	5.77			1.03		T		1.07			.17	.02	.33	1.08	.04		.13	T	.37	T				T	.15			.15	.34			.02
CITY	6.44	.03		.26	.02	.05		.63			1.35	.07	.92	1.20	.12		.26	.19	.34	.15				.06				.22	.14			.43
TOWN	5.65		.78		.12		.03	1.20			.57		.90			.15	.10	.24	.01				.06	.05			T	1.81			.03	T
DARBY	2.87		.27	.12	.09			.72			.01		T	.30			.02		.02		.15		.63	.23				.24			.07	
	5.72			.40				.55			1.03	.14	1.20	.76			.34	.11	.19		.10			.20				.53	.03		.02	.12
ERGRIFT	4.29			.72		.17		.84			.30	.08	.53	.02			.18	.18	.35			T		.18	T			.35	.26			.36
NVILLE	2.85			.62				.88					.03	.47		.02								.05	.08			.24	.46			
CKEL	5.61	T		.56	T	.03	.03	.42	T		.87	.10	.64	1.44	T	T	.09	.05	.16	.05				.03				.09	.14	T		.31
CKEL 1 WSW	5.58	T		.57	T	.02	.03	.43	T		.85	.09	.61	1.45	T	T	.11	.08	.15	.06				.03				.64	.15	T		.31
N	5.80			.29		.03		1.00			.92	.06	.84	.98			.21	.09	.31	.05				.03	T			.28	.19			.52
NTOWN	3.57		.60					.80					.20	.80			.20		.20					.19				.38				.20
SBURG 2 W	6.65			1.11		.04		1.10			.07	.42	.09	.45			.24	.17	.28				.02	.16				.88	1.50			.14
BORO 3 S	2.53			.18		.03		.75			.12	.06	.32	.63	.02		.07	.08	.11		.03				.02			.02	.05			.06
VILLE	3.30		.41	.20				.56			.03		.04	1.26			.16	T	.06		.06							.39	.06		.07	
RSVILLE 1 W	3.26			.45		.13		1.00	.02		.05			.80			.05		.07					.14	.10			.16	.07			.22
CHESTER	4.35		.53	T	T		.50	.01		.02	.02	.01	1.24			T		.09		.11			.10	.11				.18			T	1.47
GROVE 1 E	1.81			.45		T		.49	.04		.03	.05	.02	.20					.06		.10			.13				.24				
HICKORY	6.35			.70		.03		.90			.90	.03	1.10	.93	.04		.20	.10	.10	.20				.10				.58	.04			.40
SBURG	5.11			.83				1.26			.26	.12	.55	.05			.06	.22	.55				.06					.30	.57			.28
S BARRE	2.64			.37		.08		.95	T		T	T	.09	.31			.10		.23	T	.09			T	.13			.18	.11			T
AMSBURG	3.99			1.12		.02		.61	.02		.10	.07	.35	.52			.16		.17	.07				.42	.03			.14	.04			.15
AMSPORT WB AP	3.33		.53	T	.03		.67	T		T	.01	T	.27	.61		.07	.02	.10	.02	.01		T		.10			T	.67			.18	.04
BURG	4.20			.94				.45			.07	.04	.33	.15			.23	.07	.14					.24	.05			.61	.55			.33
3 SSW PUMP STA	2.04		.30	.16				.45			.02		.02	.70			.02		.03		.05		T	.01				.26				.02
HAVEN	2.29			.54				.79	.02		T	.02	.03	.35		T	.03	.01	.02		.06				T			.22	.03	.01		.16
GROVE	4.16			.48		.02		.85	.01				.24	.77			.09		.22					.50				.25	.47			.26
VILLE 3 SE	2.83			.56		.06		1.33	.03				.02	.21	.09		.04				T			.04	.06			.06	.22			.11

DAILY TEMPERATURES

Table 5

Station		1	2	3	4	5	6	7	8	9	10	11	12	13	14	15	16	17	18	19	20	21	22	23	24	25	26	27	28	29	30	31
ALLENTOWN WB AP	MAX	64	59	69	74	63	75	53	60	61	71	59	80	87	86	73	66	55	59	77	65	74	82	68	60	63	68	65	70	70	74	87
	MIN	39	40	43	44	33	48	42	35	31	53	44	47	63	60	51	42	32	43	38	43	47	53	44	39	33	39	52	47	41	53	65
ALLENTOWN GAS CO	MAX	67	64	60	70	75	64	77	54	59	63	74	67	82	87	86	72	67	55	60	78	65	75	83	69	59	64	70	66	70	72	75
	MIN	42	40	43	46	35	42	49	36	32	42	45	42	50	63	54	53	34	38	40	44	45	51	58	39	33	40	48	52	41	47	57
ALTOONA HORSESHOE CURVE	MAX	63	60	65	72	65	78	67	60	68	66	62	82	83	85	70	56	45	56	74	64	75	75	72	60	64	72	68	75	70	84	84
	MIN	35	41	44	39	31	44	49	30	30	52	49	53	61	60	46	40	28	40	36	32	42	50	38	31	29	38	55	53	38	51	63
ARENDTSVILLE	MAX	69	64	52	71	77	66	85	58	59	66	77	60	82	87	89	73	66	53	62	80	64	78	80	77	60	67	78	69	78	71	81
	MIN	42	40	44	44	35	41	55	38	30	44	53	52	56	61	54	55	29	42	40	43	42	48	57	36	33	36	48	57	44	50	55
ARTEMAS 1 WNW	MAX	71	66	72	75	82	85	74	62	72	70	71	86	86	87	73	69	63	66	75	76	83	79	77	56	71	79	66	79	70	87	86
	MIN	36	44	45	30	26	44	52	31	36	52	49	53	60	49	46	34	32	46	32	43	45	50	40	32	36	43	51	47	40	46	54
BAKERSTOWN 3 WNW	MAX	66	64	65	62	66	74	70	60	72	62	82	80	81	86	66	54	45	60	66	64	76	74	72	57	64	76	75	73	77	84	80
	MIN	40	51	45	40	30	52	32	42	40	59	62	64	66	48	50	30	34	45	36	50	58	60	32	36	44	44	58	52	46	54	64
BEAVERTOWN	MAX	65	64	69	73	64	71	72	62	63	70	59	84	84	87	81	60	54	59	78	73	78	80	76	76	73	79	69	75	72	82	87
	MIN																															
BELLEFONTE 4 S	MAX	56	66	55	67	71	65	78	60	62	63	71	57	78	82	76	66	56	74	57	74	67	76	76	74	55	58	65	63	63	74	80
	MIN	33	41	42	42	32	42	48	31	35	34	47	49	57	59	46	52	28	34	40	36	43	50	58	35	30	41	46	52	38	48	60
BERWICK	MAX	65	62	70	75	64	71	71	60	65	68	62	84	86	87	87	64	55	57	76	70	76	84	81	60	64	73	71	69	74	78	85
	MIN	35	42	45	42	32	50	49	33	31	52	42	51	62	62	51	53	29	43	38	41	46	53	57	35	30	41	52	48	39	56	61
BETHLEHEM LEHIGH UNIV	MAX	65	60	69	74		75	52	59	61	70	59	80	85	84	72	64	53	57	75	67	76	82	68	59	62	68	65	70	72	70	89
	MIN	50	44	44	44		46	44	36	37	52	45	47	62	63	52	44	35	46	44	44	47	55	45	41	36	47	53	52	44	54	68
BLAIRSVILLE 6 ENE	MAX	67	60	63	64	64	75	63	57	71	60	76	75	77	81	60	51	44	53	69	63	73	68	66	53	64	75	67	71	77	81	82
	MIN	35	45	50	41	32	53	42	30	40	54	54	55	64	57	46	35	28	40	40	33	48	60	45	28	32	42	57	49	42	59	64
BRADFORD 4 W RES	MAX	60	61	62	62	59	64	63	56	62	60	65	79	78	80	66	65	47	50	59	61	69	74	74	50	60	72	72	66	75	81	82
	MIN	22	31	43	33	22	42	43	24	23	49	44	49	57	54	35	34	21	35	39	26	39	43	44	23	18	26	54	38	31	55	60
BROOKVILLE CAA AIRPORT	MAX	65	56	65	60	62	76	62	57	68	60	71	81	79	83	68	52	45	52	66	64	75	69	66	54	64	75	69	76	76	83	77
	MIN	31	46	41	32	25	42	33	28	31	53	51	58	62	46	40	29	26	40	35	29	46	45	37	27	27	31	59	46	41	63	60
BURGETTSTOWN 2 W	MAX	50	69	64	70	61	69	82	60	62	74	64	84	82	85	85	62	52	54	62	72	62	80	76	65	57	69	80	67	74	80	86
	MIN	31	40	46	34	25	32	49	25	29	44	58	60	61	60	41	48	27	37	38	28	42	48	57	26	26	31	43	55	38	50	65
BURNT CABINS 2 NE	MAX	68	60	72	68	78	68	60	64	66	75	65	80	87	88	73	64	55	59	78	62	80	80	78	62	68	71	70	78	70	81	83
	MIN	42	44	46	30	40	50	40	38	39	54	54	50	66	60	48	40	28	38	35	39	44	50	48	37	30	29	55	52	41	53	62
BUTLER	MAX	68	68	65	67	70	76	80	60	68	70	76	84	82	83	85	64	45	55	68	76	76	79	74	74	72	75	79	69	79	87	76
	MIN	35	43	49	40	27	51	45	31	31	58	57	60	65	68	42	41	28	41	45	30	41	49	56	31	35	33	61	52	53	65	65
CANTON 1 NW	MAX	53	58	55	66	64	61	60	54	52	57	60	53	80	78	83	64	55	46	50	68	57	63	77	65	50	60	65	66	59	67	76
	MIN	33	32	38	40	31	38	44	26	26	38	37	39	48	61	42	43	26	29	34	32	37	48	56	29	26	30	46	45	35	40	54
CARLISLE	MAX	68	67	73	76	69	80	80	63	69	77	71	83	88	91	88	64	57	60	81	74	80	80	78	76	70	75	72	79	75	84	90
	MIN	42	46	48	45	38	46	52	39	36	55	54	55	64	63	54	57	34	45	38	46	45	51	59	43	34	44	50	58	44	55	62
CHAMBERSBURG 1 ESE	MAX	66	54	71	77	65	87	67	62	67	75	65	81	88	89	75	63	53	61	79	66	79	81	76	62	66	74	68	80	72	81	90
	MIN	40	43	49	43	32	40	52	36	33	55	53	51	61	60	52	43	29	39	36	40	41	47	58	38	30	36	55	58	39	51	62
CHESTER	MAX	75	67	63	68	77		78	53	62	64	79	64		88	92	73	70	58	65		65	75	85	77	62	63		69	74	70	78
	MIN	45	42	46	52	38		43	41	42	49	50	51		53	58	50	36	44	44		49	54	63	42	37	47		61	47	54	61
CLARION 3 SW	MAX	67	65	67	65	64	76	63	61	68	62	76	82	80	84	65	54	45	55	68	65	77	73	70	58	66	77	73	75	79	86	81
	MIN	31	42	44	38	28	41	47	28	29	53	53	59	62	57	41	38	27	42	41	30	45	46	54	26	25	31	58	45	41	56	62
CLAYSVILLE 3 W	MAX	72	65	68	67	70	83	86	61	75	69	83	81	85	85	66	50	57	62	74	68	80	75	76	59	69	78	68	77	80	85	83
	MIN	29	39	45	34	25	37	48	24	26	55	55	57	65	51	40	40	25	39	34	26	37	43	55	24	26	31	59	57	36	61	65
COATESVILLE 1 SW	MAX	71	65	60	68	75	65	79	53	61	64	78	62	84	87	90	70	68	54	64	78	78	76	83	74	61	63	72	65	74	71	78
	MIN	43	36	41	41	34	44	51	38	32	45	53	50	53	61	53	54	30	40	37	45	41	47	54	37	30	39	47	59	43	50	58
COLUMBIA	MAX	67	64	71	78	69	86	70	63	65	77	72	83	89	91	83	70	59	66	83	78	79	85	75	66	67	72	68	80	73	85	92
	MIN	42	42	48	47	35	48	52	37	37	56	52	52	64	64	52	55	32	46	40	44	45	53	59	38	33	58	56	57	44	56	64
CONFLUENCE 1 SW DAM	MAX	54	73	62	67	68	73	82	58	63	76	63	78	78	82	84	65	54	50	60	75	68	79	73	73	55	69	78	66	74	74	82
	MIN	39	47	51	41	31	41	57	29	33	54	54	55	65	59	48	50	29	44	36	31	36	44	45	32	30	36	58	58	41	42	52
CORRY	MAX	59	58	60	59	61	65	52	55	59	61	79	85	79	79	65	60	47	55	57	59	74	75	73	53	64	75	76	71	78	86	79
	MIN	26	38	45	40	25	44	39	28	28	51	48	59	62	55	43	33	25	40	47	29	44	55	47	27	24	30	59	38	41	64	63
COUDERSPORT 3 NW	MAX	63	60	64	69	61	65	56	55	62	60	54	79	76	83	65	61	46	50	63	62	71	74	69	50	61	70	67	65	72	81	76
	MIN	25	36	39	34	24	45	42	25	25	41	38	50	58	56	35	33	21	35	39	29	39	44	44	22	19	28	52	43	39	57	61
DERRY	MAX	71	65	65	67	75	75	55	61	74	69	80	79	81	84	64	56	50	58	63	66	78	75	71	62	67	78	75	75	79	83	84
	MIN	37	51	52	40	30	33	32	28	41	59	59	60	66	60	46	43	29	45	42	32	43	50	58	31	30	36	60	55	48	62	68
DEVAULT 1 W	MAX	63	59	67	74	65	78	75	60	65	73	62	82	87	88	70	68	53	63	77	75	74	81	71	59	63	69	65	72	68	76	87
	MIN																															
DIXON	MAX	61	65	61	69	67	64	66	58	56	62	65	62	84	82	85	67	64	53	55	69	63	75	84	65	55	64	70	68	58	73	78
	MIN	31	34	38	35	29	35	48	29	27	33	35	37	54	60	43	48	26	34	37	33	41	45	51	31	25	30	38	44	35	36	59
DONEGAL	MAX	67	57	61	65	63	76	55	57	73	63	77	75	80	79	60	53	44	53	69	62	74	66	64	50	62	75	68	69	75	78	80
	MIN	34	45	41	30	22	36	37	27	31	52	53	51	60	47	42	26	21	35	31	25	33	45	37	26	25	30	53	43	40	53	53
DONORA	MAX	67	72	65	69	62	81	83	65	73	79	82	87	82	88	89	65	55	56	75	77	74	82	76	74	65	77	84	72	78	82	85
	MIN	41	55	53	44	32	46	55	38	39	60	62	62	74	68	51	46	35	47	48	36	47	56	62	34	35	41	66	59	50	62	69
DU BOIS 7 E	MAX	64	64	65	65	60	75	72	58	68	66	60	78	79	83	73	57	45	50	68	64	71	73	68	60	66	75	70	74	75	82	83
	MIN	30	43	43	35	25	40	46	24	30	49	48	47	60	59	40	39	25	39	38	28	44	47	57	27	32	56	54	49	40	59	63
EAGLES MERE	MAX	57	59	55	65	66	57	69	54	51	58	58	53	78	81	81	67	56	48	49	67	59	71	79	63	51	57	65	61	59	65	69
	MIN	32	33	39	42	31	32	41	25	26	39	37	40	47	58	43	45	25	29	40	33	35	46	56	29	30	36	44	45	39	41	51
EAST BRADY	MAX	68	70	67	68	68	81	79	63	72	70	85	84	84	86	74	60	45	55	70	66	78	80	72	64	69	78	79	75	76	87	88
	MIN	34	43	46	40	30	32	50	31	31	54	55	48	51	58	44	41	30	44	42	32	48	49	57	30	29	34	50	50	48	55	63
EBENSBURG	MAX	61	55	61	65	62	74	64	55	69	64	79	75	76	80	62	54	43	51	70	61	70	70	67	55	62	70	63	70	70	78	79
	MIN	34	42	48	35	26	43	45	28	37	53	49	51	61	60	42	35	25	39	38	31	38	50	55	29	30	37	56	49	41	54	61
EMPORIUM 1 E	MAX	49	67	58	70	64	65	74	63	61	67	63	58	83	82	86	68	51	51	54	69	68	75	78	70	60	67	75	73	70	78	84
	MIN	28	31	40	37	26	29	45	25	25	29	46	46	56	56	39	41	22	27	39	27	30	40	43	25	22	26	34	43	32	37	57
EPHRATA	MAX	64	62	69	75	65	79	71	61	61	76	65	82	87	88	80	67	59	63	79	72	75	81	74	69	64	69	67	75	75	79	88
	MIN	39	40	45	43	35	47	38	34	37	52	50	50	61	62	50	54	31	44	38	42	44	53	59	38	35	42	52	54	41	54	63
ERIE CAA AIRPORT	MAX	53	57	56	53	60	58	50	45	63	64	83	81	76	79	64	50	48	56	58	52	75	77	68	49	60	75	68	63	79	83	77
	MIN	31	42	46	35	35	45	39	32	36	50	51	60	61	49	48	33	34	42	45	33	49	63	39	33	31	43	52	41	42	68	63

See Reference Notes Following Station Index

DAILY TEMPERATURES

Day Of Month

	1	2	3	4	5	6	7	8	9	10	11	12	13	14	15	16	17	18	19	20	21	22	23	24	25	26	27	28	29	30	31	Average
MAX	48	48	68	69	84	88	72	72	72	70	69	79	85	86	70	68	65	64	78	72	74	84	72	65	64	75	73	74	73	87	86	72.6
MIN	40	42	45	39	31	46	39	34	30	43	52	42	49	53	50	38	30	38	34	38	43	50	44	36	38	42	50	50	38	50	50	42.1
MAX	61	55	65	65	68	76	64	61	68	67	82	85	85	85	65	55	46	61	68	66	80	78	76	57	67	80	75	73	75	86	83	70.3
MIN	32	43	45	42	27	42	41	30	31	54	54	54	64	58	44	36	29	31	48	32	47	55	52	29	26	32	35	42	47	63	61	42.8
MAX	48	68	60	66	63	67	79	63	60	72	63	83	81	82	85	63	51	47	57	70	65	77	71	68	57	66	77	67	74	78	86	68.2
MIN	34	41	45	38	29	31	49	30	30	42	46	56	60	54	43	47	29	33	40	29	34	47	53	27	29	33	39	51	52	52	63	41.5
MAX	67	67	65	65	63	73	59	58	63	62	81	82	79	82	65	63	45	52	65	66	73	76	70	57	66	76	74	75	77	84	80	68.7
MIN	31	41	46	41	29	43	45	29	30	53	52	57	55	58	44	37	28	40	44	32	45	48	54	29	27	33	60	46	42	62	63	43.4
MAX																																
MIN																																
MAX	61	61	61	63	57	65	55	52	53	56	56	76	80	78	72	63	53	49	68	68	68	75	75	54	58	63	63	65	63	68	67	63.4
MIN	33	39	38	43	32	46	42	24	32	48	39	44	60	59	43	45	25		39	34	44	51	50	27	29	42	42	38	46	53	56	41.4
MAX	64	62	67	75	68	78	76	62	62	77	69	84	89	90	73	71	60	65	78	72	77	81	76	63	62	69	65	71	73	79	91	72.5
MIN	43	39	47	54	34	47	48	37	30	55	50	50	68	63	54	57	31	47	43	44	44	54	61	35	29	46	52	61	43	53	54	47.5
MAX	69	65	53	73	77	67	85	58	60	62	76	61	80	90	90	68	65	53	63	80	65	80	79	78	61	66	72	66	80	72	78	70.7
MIN	43	46	44	46	37	45	54	39	38	46	54	54	58	63	55	55	32	43	39	43	43	53	60	41	34	40	50	58	44	53	56	47.3
MAX	62	64	55	68	72	63	75	57	58	60	70	56	81	83	83	65	62	51	57	75	64	76	80	71	57	63	68	66	70	70	77	67.1
MIN	37	39	43	40	33	39	51	35	36	45	45	49	52	62	52	54	28	35	39	43	43	51	55	38	30	37	50	55	37	42	55	43.5
MAX	65	62	67	65	66	70	65	59	61	63	83	84	83	82	65	59	44	59	62	66	79	78	78	56	68	78	76	72	80	87	79	69.7
MIN	30	41	45	42	26	44	40	30	30	54	52	59	62	59	45	37	28	43	45	30	46	52	52	27	26	35	60	42	44	64	62	43.6
MAX	70	68	52	72	76	74	83	60	61	68	75	61	82	89	89	67	67	55	64	81	67	80	82	76	63	66	73	65	79	76	81	71.7
MIN	41	41	44	49	34	43	58	34	35	39	52	52	53	63	52	53	30	34	39	42	43	50	55	39	34	36	46	56	40	42	61	44.8
MAX	63	55	71	74	68	79	60	61	65	76	61	82	86	88	66	65	54	61	78	67	78	80	77	61	66	73	69	77	73	82	89	71.1
MIN	44	45	50	46	38	47	45	40	44	57	52	53	63	64	57	41	34	45	40	46	45	57	48	41	35	48	55	53	43	56	63	48.2
MAX	60	61	58	65	67	60	63	52	52	58	64	62	82	79	81	68	60	60	52	68	62	73	80	68	52	60	67	65	55	71	75	64.5
MIN	31	34	37	37	29	37	45	29	24	29	36	41	46	56	46	48	28	32	26	38	39	48	57	33	24	30	42	49	32	40	57	38.1
MAX	66	54	70	75	65	77	59	59	61	74	62	81	84	87	67	65	54	61	77	64	75	79	73	61	63	68	66	73	72	79	90	69.7
MIN	46	45	50	48	39	54	50	43	43	57	55	52	64	63	59	45	37	48	45	48	48	55	55	43	38	50	57	55	47	57	64	50.3
MAX	63	71	56	70	75	71	84	63	67	69	73	60	87	84	89	65	58	52	57	79	70	81	78	77	64	73	75	71	83	76	87	71.9
MIN	37	37	46	38	29	30	44	35	35	36	50	52	55	59	50	50	29	29	35	35	35	45	48	37	29	30	39	57	40	40	53	40.8
MAX	70	66	66	67	67	79	67	62	73	64	76	79	81	84	65	56	48	57	71	65	77	71	70	57	68	78	70	76	80	84	83	70.2
MIN	34	47	45	35	27	41	49	26	32	53	57	58	65	54	41	41	25	44	34	29	38	43	53	27	27	33	60	49	43	55	59	42.7
MAX	70	70	68	68	69	80	70	62	75	68	85	84	81	85	80	56	49	57	75	75	78	79	79	70	67	80	80	76	80	85	85	73.7
MIN	37	51	51	41	30	44	51	30	36	58	60	60	66	65	46	44	30	45	43	41	44	53	59	31	31	35	57	55	45	62	65	47.3
MAX	45	61	58	65	52	62	69	55	54	63	62	82	81	80	80	63	42	45	59	59	61	71	76	58	52	64	71	74	66	78	85	64.3
MIN	31	40	44	41	27	33	40	31	30	47	50	58	61	66	45	39	29	35	43	31	45	50	52	31	27	38	48	43	46	53	62	42.5
MAX	64	65	67	73		76	73	59	62	70	63	84	87	86	84	74	61	57	74	73		80	77	60	63	67	63	69	70		87	71.0
MIN	39	38	44	40	32		48	32	27	51	43	49	63	62	50	51	30	43	35	42	43		54	35	29	37	49	49	42	52		43.2
MAX	56	74	57	68	73	73	80	64	66	80	65	70	88	86	88	68	54	50	60	77	70	72	65	64	56	66	82	70	73	88	88	70.7
MIN	39	48	46	39	32	44	55	33	34	54	57	55	60	61	50	50	29	35	35	35	42	47	43	35	31	38	53	58	43	55	55	44.9
MAX	43	65	55	65	58	62	70	58	59	63	62	66	80	78	81	67	47	48	52	63	62	72	73	61	53	65	73	70	66	76	83	64.4
MIN	25	34	43	32	23	33	44	24	26	45	47	47	59	54	35	45	23	32	39	26	34	42	53	22	19	26	39	43	31	49	61	37.3
MAX	67	52	67	71	69	84	63	61	74	68	63	80	84	86	65	60	62	60	78	70	80	75	71	58	68	76	69	77	78	83	85	71.1
MIN	37	41	42	38	31	40	43	29	30	50	53	49	64	57	47	36	29	39	34	32	40	45	48	36	30	36	56	49	39	51	61	42.3
A MAX	64	62	70	78	69	79	75	63	62	81	79	85	87	90	86	68	61	65	81	75	78	81	78	71	63	68	67	78	72	80	91	74.4
MIN	42	39	48	45	34	46	52	34	32	55	51	51	64	65	52	56	33	46	37	44	42	51	58	38	32	40	53	54	41	55	59	46.7
MAX	67	65	57	70	74	66	83	55	59	62	77	60	82	87	89	69	65	52	61	80	64	75	81	72	60	61	70	68	74	71	81	69.6
MIN	45	40	44	43	35	47	52	36	35	45	51	51	58	62	53	55	33	42	38	42	43	52	58	38	33	45	53	58	42	54	59	46.5
MAX	47	62	48	67	68	62	64	57	55	65	60	60	85	80	88	68	57	56	54	68	63	76	83	60	54	65	72	74	59	76	83	65.7
MIN	28	31	38	36	26	31	45	26	25	33	34	36	55	58	38	45	24	32	39	32	36	44	51	26	23	30	37	47	32	36	50	36.3
MAX									65	77	63	80	84	88	90	71	67	54	61	79	67	78	83	74	60	66	70	66	75	72	80	72.6
MIN									41	46	49	50	53	65	56	55	34	41	43	47	47	52	60	42	38	44	52	57	43	52	58	48.9
MAX	64	67	57	72	76	70	82	62	63	67	75	60	85	87	89	67	59	55	61	79	68	80	81	78	63	69	74	69	78	76	84	71.5
MIN	41	41	44	43	35	34	45	37	36	46	51	51	55	60	50	50	31	32	40	40	44	48	47	42	34	34	43	55	42	42	55	43.5
MAX	58	56	62	58	61	66	52	63	57	61	81	81	79	78	62	56	44	56	59	61	75	75	73	52	64	74	75	64	77	87	78	66.0
MIN	30	38	42	40	28	44	39	30	30	55	49	59	62	55	55	37	29	44	49	31	46	56	43	27	26	34	60	41	42	64	65	43.5
MAX	67	67	75	71	68	77	70	64	66	72	63	88	86	83	73	62	53	57	78	73	82	83	77	68	68	74	72	76	71	85	87	72.8
MIN	35	42	45	40	31	48	50	35	32	52	46	52	62	59	47	45	29	43	39	36	46	47										43.7
MAX	49	64	54	66	69	65	78	61	59	70	61	58	79	79	83	65	54	48	53	72	74	74	75	71	55	65	72	65	74	74	83	66.7
MIN	29	29	40	32	24	25	42	25	27	37	46	46	53	55	39	41	22	24	33	29	34	42	44	27	24	26	32	45	34	36	54	35.4
MAX	62	60	65	72	61	74	58	60	62	75	65	76	90	92	76	73	53	66	75	67	71	80	78	63	63	68	65	78	69	74	88	70.3
MIN	46	44	49	49	42	50	48	42	42	54	51	50	66	67	56	50	38	48	47	50	49	53	54	45	44	48	55	54	49	54	64	50.3
MAX	65	51	65	69	69	78	60	63	68	66	62	81	80	82	62	55	46	54	73	67	77	76	70	55	63	73	68	75	73	82	83	68.1
MIN	37	43	45	38	32	46	40	34	40	56	50	54	62	54	50	34	27	40	39	35	44	54	42	34	35	43	55	50	40	54	64	44.2
MAX	44	61	55	64	53	60	68	54	55	60	62	82	81	79	81	65	41	44	55	60	62	75	73	58	50	64	75	75	65	78	86	64.0
MIN	29	36	46	44	28	33	40	29	30	43	51	57	64	64	46	40	29	35	43	32	35	50	53	28	28	34	40	42	46	50	63	41.5
MAX	62	65	64	59	65	73	54	57	64	65	81	80	81	82	68	53	51	61	64	64	75	73	65	63	63	73	72	73	77	82	78	68.0
MIN	29	34	40	34	28	40	40	29	27	40	39	59	50	45	40	34	26	41	29	27	39	52	42	24	23	34	40	40	44	55	61	38.2
MAX	65	56	72	77	67	80	59	60	65	79	61	83	86	90	69	65	53	64	78	65	78	82	75	61	66	72	67	77	72	81	91	71.5
MIN	43	46	50	46	38	49	46	39	44	58	53	53	64	65	55	43	34	47	43	46	49	57	50	40	36	49	57	53	45	57	66	49.1
MAX	67	64	65	61	66	77	58	59	72	66	82	82	84	83	64	54	52	58	66	66	76	74	64	56	66	78	70	70	79	84	83	69.2
MIN	42	49	52	42	35	48	43	40	40	60	58	59	68	57	50	38	36	46	47	36	49	56	44	36	36	42	61	58	51	66	60	48.5
MAX	55	58	58	64	64	58	57	53	48	59	57	58	80	74	81	65	58	47	49	66	55	70	80	62	48	57	66	63	50	69	76	61.5
MIN	32	34	39	39	32	35	43	25	27	36	35	39	48	61	43	45	25	29	33	34	36	46	56	30	29	35	42	46	37	42	52	38.2
MAX	62	56	66	72	62	77	58	58	59	74	60	80	86	87	71	65	53	61	75	64	73	80	73	67	62	68	64	71	68	77	88	68.9
MIN	40	39	46	43	33	45	45	36	37	54	50	51	62	69	51	42	29	45	40	43	45	54	48	38	34	43	52	51	39	53	49	45.4
MAX	62	55	70	75	64	80	57	58	61	75	60	82	88	88	68	65	52	69	79	65	75	81	73	58	64	69	78	74	69	79	90	70.4
MIN	40	39	47	44	31	44	42	36	31	59	50	51	62	62	52	39	32	40	37	41	55	58	46	35	35	44	52	54	45	54	51	45.4

See Reference Notes Following Station Index

DAILY TEMPERATURES

Table 5 - Continued

Station		Day Of Month																															Average
		1	2	3	4	5	6	7	8	9	10	11	12	13	14	15	16	17	18	19	20	21	22	23	24	25	26	27	28	29	30	31	
MT POCONO 2 N AP	MAX	61	59	65	62	60	70	60	51	56	62	54	80	79	80	79	61	54	48	69	61	71	78	76	52	59	63	62	63	66	73	82	65.0
	MIN	35	35	39	38	28	38	43	26	29	43	38	45	60	59	45	46	27	37	33	35	42	52	51	29	25	38	46	48	35	49	62	40.5
MUHLENBURG 1 SE	MAX	62	57	67	70	60	70	63	58	60	62	62	80	89	84	81	59	51	51	70	62	71	80	75	54	61	68	64	61	74	78	81	67.1
	MIN	30	40	40	39	29	47	42	27	32	48	36	43	59	60	44	29	25	34	37	32	53	51	48	29	25	38	45	44	38	56	60	40.6
NEWBURG 3 W	MAX	70	68	73	78	77	80	62	61	76	71	65	86	90	88	73	69	52	69	76	81	78	74	75	65	71	76	67	68	74	85	85	73.6
	MIN	40	41	42	41	39	55	56	34	48	56	54	52	64	68	65	53	32	45	51	56	55	46	49	38	47	55	56	59	39	64	66	50.5
NEW CASTLE 1 N	MAX	67	67	68	67	66	77	72	59	70	67	84	83	84	84	68	59	46	58	67	64	77	77	73	56	65	78	77	73	79	85	80	70.9
	MIN	31	41	46	42	29	43	45	28	30	57	55	60	66	65	47	38	30	43	46	30	46	51	53	28	27	34	60	48	45	64	62	44.8
NEWELL	MAX	64	73	64	69	65	78	84	64	70	79	78	85	81	85	87	65	55	56	74	75	72	82	76	73	64	74	82	69	78	82	85	73.8
	MIN	44	50	53	43	35	46	54	40	38	60	61	61	70	61	52	47	35	48	44	36	45	54	62	37	38	42	62	62	48	64	64	50.2
NEWPORT	MAX	64	68	56	73	75	69	80	61	65	67	71	59	86	85	90	66	62	54	62	77	68	82	83	79	65	68	75	69	78	76	83	71.5
	MIN	40	40	45	41	32	33	47	35	30	32	52	52	53	60	52	52	30	32	37	38	44	48	50	38	30	32	44	54	40	40	57	42.3
NEW STANTON	MAX	72	63	69	62	56	81	62	62	78	68	76	82	80	86	65	58	52	57	75	68	79	73	72	58	69	75	68	75	82	85	87	70.8
	MIN	37	49	47	45	32	44	37	38	40	56	50	59	60	52	45	38	36	48	35	29	41	48	39	28	29	37	51	47	43	58	54	43.6
NORRISTOWN	MAX	65	63	70	79	67	80	58	61	63	78	64	84	88	92	72	71	58	65	79	67	75	84	77	62	65	70	67	75	73	79	93	72.4
	MIN	44	44	48	47	40	50	48	39	40	55	51	52	65	65	56	47	37	48	48	47	49	55	51	41	39	48	56	53	45	56	66	49.4
PALMERTON	MAX	63	58	70	72	64	74	57	60	64	72	59	80	87	87	73	69	57	57	75	69	74	87	68	59	64	69	64	69	70	72	86	69.3
	MIN	38	39	44	42	32	51	43	36	30	55	46	50	65	63	55	43	33	43	40	44	50	57	47	40	32	41	52	47	40	56	65	45.8
PHIL DREXEL INST OF TEC	MAX	66	64	69	77	67	78	57	62	63	76	65	83	90	92	74	74	59	68	80	70	74	84	77	63	67	70	66	76	73	79	92	72.7
	MIN	47	47	48	50	45	52	48	41	44	58	56	56	69	69	59	56	40	49	49	50	51	56	54	44	45	50	54	56	51	56	68	52.2
PHILADELPHIA WB AP	MAX	65	62	68	77	65	79	57	61	62	75	66	81	89	92	73	70	58	65	80	69	74	83	76	63	65	70	66	75	71	79	91	71.8
	MIN	47	44	49	47	42	50	46	41	42	58	53	53	65	66	58	45	37	49	47	48	50	54	49	42	41	48	54	54	49	54	66	49.9
PHILADELPHIA PT BREEZE	MAX	67	63	68	75	63	79	52	62	63	74	63	80	88	91	75	70	57	64	79	68	74	83	75	61	63	69	65	76	71	78	90	71.2
	MIN	48	46	48	56	43	50	51	42	43	54	54	53	66	72	59	57	40	50	49	50	52	56	66	46	46	50	55	63	51	56	66	52.8
PHILADELPHIA SHAWMONT	MAX	67	66	69	76	75	79	79	59	62	75	75	82	87	92	92	70	64	63	79	78	75	83	83	67	65	69	68	73	74	77	89	74.6
	MIN	44	40	48	52	38	50	50	37	39	55	52	52	65	63	56	55	36	48	54	46	48	54	65	39	35	46	55	58	43	55	65	49.8
PHILADELPHIA CITY	MAX	65	60	67	74	64	77	56	62	61	74	64	79	86	88	72	69	56	64	77	67	72	82	75	62	63	68	66	75	70	76	88	70.3
	MIN	48	48	51	49	46	51	48	44	43	56	51	51	66	66	56	47	43	49	49	51	51	55	50	47	46	50	54	55	52	54	66	51.4
PHILIPSBURG CAA AP	MAX	61	50	65	68	62	74	58	59	63	60	53	80	79	84	63	52	46	51	70	64	74	75	70	54	63	69	65	72	70	83	81	65.7
	MIN	29	40	41	33	24	43	36	28	39	50	45	53	59	49	44	31	23	34	40	31	48	45	39	30	22	42	53	45	39	57	60	40.4
PHOENIXVILLE 1 E	MAX	65	65	71	79	70	80	78	62	65	79	74	85	88	92	87	72	63	65	78	78	78	85	83	70	68	71	70	77	73	80	95	75.7
	MIN	40	35	46	49	31	47	49	33	34	53	59	50	62	59	51	54	29	43	35	45	40	48	62	33	28	39	50	54	36	52	60	45.4
PIMPLE HILL	MAX	57	59	54	64	67	61	69	48	51	56	60	55	80	80	79	67	59	50	55	70	60	71	78	63	52	60	63	60	58	65	74	62.7
	MIN	33	40	37	46	30	44	42	24	36	43	37	43	54	62	43	45	25	36	39	34	40	51	55	28	30	41	42	46	37	47	61	41.0
PITTSBURGH WB AP 2	MAX	68	63	68	61	66	80	60	60	72	68	82	79	83	85	61	52	50	58	70	63	76	74	68	56	65	77	67	73	78	84	82	69.3
	MIN	38	53	52	41	36	52	41	34	43	59	59	60	70	54	49	35	32	45	43	37	47	60	38	32	35	45	58	56	48	64	59	47.6
PITTSBURGH WB CITY	MAX	70	65	69	66	69	81	61	62	75	69	85	81	86	87	63	55	53	62	72	67	80	75	70	57	68	79	69	75	80	86	85	71.7
	MIN	41	54	55	43	37	52	43	37	44	61	62	62	73	59	52	40	37	47	45	39	52	59	43	38	39	43	62	57	51	67	62	50.2
PLEASANT MOUNT 1 W	MAX	53	53	55	63	60	56	58	53	49	59	56	57	78	78	78	67	60	49	51	65	58	69	78	63	49	56	66	60	52	69	71	60.9
	MIN	29	32	36	32	29	39	43	25	23	40	30	39	50	55	42	46	25	29	32	34	37	50	51	30	22	30	44	43	30	38	54	36.7
PORT CLINTON	MAX	61	65	57	72	75	66	79	58	63	62	73	60	85	88	90	72	68	56	64	80	68	78	83	72	62	65	70	60	74	73	72	70.0
	MIN	36	36	44	37	30	39	49	29	28	42	45	50	53	59	50	52	28	38	35	40	42	49	55	34	27	39	50	48	36	46	57	42.0
PUTNEYVILLE 2 SE DAM	MAX	46	61	59	67	64	66	80	64	60	70	62	74	81	81	85	64	50	47	56	70	65	76	70	69	57	66	76	67	75	79	85	67.5
	MIN	46	39	42	38	26	28	45	27	33	44	51	51	56	63	40	40	26	31	40	27	30	47	55	26	25	31	39	45	43	49	52	39.8
QUAKERTOWN 1 E	MAX	69	64	69	74	65	77	77	60	63	75	70	81	87	87	82	67	60	61	77	70	76	83	83	65	64	70	69	70	69	72	87	72.4
	MIN	43	36	44	42	39	46	48	35	30	51	45	58	63	60	52	53	30	44	38	43	44	50	61	38	30	39	49	52	42	50	59	45.6
READING WB CITY	MAX	65	59	70	76	65	80	58	61	62	75	62	83	87	90	71	66	55	61	79	65	76	83	72	62	65	70	67	74	72	76	90	70.9
	MIN	44	45	48	47	40	52	45	38	42	56	51	52	66	66	56	42	37	48	43	46	50	58	48	43	38	48	56	52	44	58	68	49.3
RIDGWAY 3 W	MAX	61	57	67	65	63	72	64	62	66	61	66	81	80	83	67	56	49	53	66	67	74	76	68	57	66	75	72	70	77	84	75	67.7
	MIN	28	42	45	34	23	38	47	22	27	51	49	55	60	54	36	38	23	40	38	26	42	40	51	23	21	30	57	43	34	57	61	39.8
SALINA 3 W	MAX	69	67	67	66	66	78	69	60	72	67	83	81	81	84	68	56	47	57	71	65	76	75	68	58	66	76	75	74	78	84	83	70.5
	MIN	38	51	48	40	28	42	50	28	34	56	60	59	65	62	43	40	28	45	40	29	41	49	58	28	28	33	60	53	44	60	65	45.3
SCRANTON	MAX	64	65	62	63	71	63	66	58	55	63	65	65	79	83	85	70	65	55	54	71	64	76	84	67	54	64	69	55	58	75	76	66.6
	MIN	36	38	42	41	32	35	48	30	32	47	39	40	54	55	48	50	32	37	39	39	40	55	60	32	28	34	35	35	38	40	58	40.9
SCRANTON WB AIRPORT	MAX	63	59	68	71	61	68	55	53	62	63	62	81	82	85	67	62	53	52	72	61	73	83	67	53	61	70	65	58	73	76	85	66.6
	MIN	35	43	45	37	32	50	38	30	35	45	39	49	61	54	49	36	30	40	41	37	47	58	40	34	30	45	50	43	37	54	64	42.8
SELINSGROVE CAA AP	MAX	65	57	70	73	64	74	60	59	62	71	58	84	84	86	64	60	52	57	74	67	76	80	71	57	65	70	67	70	71	78	86	68.8
	MIN	35	42	45	36	33	49	40	33	31	55	43	51	63	57	46	36	29	42	40	40	44	53	44	35	30	45	52	46	37	55	61	43.5
SHIPPENSBURG	MAX	65	65	70	70	65	84	68	61	66	74	72	79	86	87	85	63	55	60	78	74	77	79	77	76	67	73	72	77	76	81	89	73.3
	MIN	40	44	45	43	33	42	50	35	35	54	54	51	62	62	51	54	30	41	38	40	44	50	59	39	32	39	55	61	40	52	64	46.4
SHIPPINGPORT WB	MAX	66	66	66	59	67	79	59	58	72	69	83	82	84	85	62	54	54	59	67	65	78	76	68	54	66	77	70	71	79	84	82	69.7
	MIN	37	45	46	34	31	47	41	32	35	60	60	60	64	50	45	32	32	45	39	33	46	53	40	31	30	37	62	48	46	64	60	44.7
SLIPPERY ROCK	MAX	61	65	67	62	74	75	65	60	66	65	80	81	81	81	64	55	44	56	55	63	76	75	70	55	78	75	72	78	75	82	84	69.0
	MIN	33	45	48	43	30	46	46	31	36	55	54	59	66	61	44	38	30	42	47	32	48	55	50	30	30	39	60	48	45	62	62	45.6
SOMERSET MAIN ST	MAX	67	67	64	68	66	79	77	60	74	69	68	75	80	82	75	56	46	56	73	67	76	75	67	64	66	75	72	73	72	79	81	70.0
	MIN	36	45	50	37	27	40	49	28	40	55	58	55	67	61	45	40	25	41	35	31	38	45	58	30	28	35	56	58	41	56	62	44.3
SPRINGBORO	MAX	57	58	57	61	48	62		53	57	58	62	82	82	79	80	65	49	48	50	55	62	77	76	72	53	66	75	75	66	78	85	65.2
	MIN	32	41	46	46	33	49		30	36	31	52	63	65	70	48	42	34	45	47	36	41	58	54	31	31	43	38	45	44	59	66	45.2
SPRINGS 1 SW	MAX	65	58	64	66	69	77	58	62	72	62	68	73	78	79	62	59	47	56	71	65	74	69	65		67	74	62	71	72	76	78	67.3
	MIN	35	45	42	35	25	39	44	30	30	51	52	49	64	55	45	37	24	40	33	27	43	44	43		27	32	50	40	38	52	66	41.2
STATE COLLEGE	MAX	66	54	67	71	63	78	60	61	64	65	57	83	81	85	65	57	50	54	74	65	76	76	73	63	68	71	66	75	71	82	83	68.5
	MIN	38	43	45	40	33	50	48	34	43	51	48	55	61	54	50	34	30	42	44	39	52	54	59	36	34	47	56	53	40	58	66	46.4
STROUDSBURG	MAX	56	60	68	72	65	68	52	50	60	70	62	82	87	83	73	66	55	60	74	64	72	77	65	58	62	67	65	66	70	72	85	67.3
	MIN	33	35	40	35	28	44	38	31	26	50	40	45	57	55	47	38	28	37	31	34	40	50	40	30	24	33	50	42	32	48	56	39.3
TAMARACK 2 S FIRE TWR	MAX	48	75	58	67	63	63	72	60	57	62	57	53	81	78	86	67	50	47	50	67	62	75	78	70	55	63	70	68				64.4
	MIN	31	31	34	43	29	30	32	26	26	39	39	39	54	60	40	42	26	27	37	31	32	46	46	27	28	36	42	45				36.4
TIONESTA 2 SE DAM	MAX	49	68	57	65	65	61	73	60	66	63	62	75	82	80	82	67	50	51	54	63	66	75	73	65	55	66	75	74	70	78	84	66.9
	MIN	36	36		37	34	38	44	28	29	36		58	58	58	43	45	27	33	43	31	34	47	52	26	25	32	37	45	38	47	62	40.0

See Reference Notes Following Station Index

Table 5 - Continued

DAILY TEMPERATURES

PENNSYLVANIA
MAY 1956

Station		1	2	3	4	5	6	7	8	9	10	11	12	13	14	15	16	17	18	19	20	21	22	23	24	25	26	27	28	29	30	31	Average
TUSVILLE WATER WORKS	MAX	67	62	60	60	64	66	67	59	55	62	81	82	80	73	69	59	46	55	58	65	77	71	71	53	65	74	74	69	81	66	79	67.4
	MIN	20	35	45	39	24	44	42	23	26	52	51	50	58	56	41	34	26	39	44	27	44	45	48	24	22	29	58	41	40	59	61	40.0
WANDA	MAX	63	62	70	68	65	63	59	55	63	63	60	80	82	88	68	61	52	55	69	62	76	85	73	55	64	73	70	70	75	62	65	68.5
	MIN	32	35	42	36	28	48	47	28	28	52	34	49	60	61	44	43	26	38	41	33	42	50	48	30	25	32	52	47	34	55	67	41.5
UNIONTOWN	MAX	73	63	69	69	70	83	64	62	77	69	84	78	83	85	66	60	57	61	77	67	77	73	70	60	71	78	67	76	80	84	83	72.[illegible]
	MIN	41	54	53	42	31	45	47	31	40	58	60	61	70	63	51	40	32	45	41	33	41	51	50	33	30	40	60	57	49	65	69	48.0
PER DARBY	MAX	65	63	69	76	64	79	78	61	63	78	73	82	89	92	81	71	58	64	79	77	75	84	75	65	65	69	64	75	71	78	90	73.3
	MIN	44	42	47	55	39	49	49	39	39	54	52	50	64	66	57	54	35	48	46	47	47	53	64	40	38	44	52	58	47	54	65	49.6
RREN	MAX	63	58	66	60	64	68	58	58	62	63	78	84	79	83	68	59	49	54	63	63	74	78	72	54	65	77	73	65	80	86	80	67.9
	MIN	28	37	45	40	27	47	44	26	31	53	48	58	63	59	44	38	28	40	48	31	40	47	49	27	25	31	58	43	40	64	64	42.9
YNESBURG 2 W	MAX	70	65	68	69	72	83	80	61	77	73	84	81	85	86	74	56	59	63	75	67	81	80	76	61	69	79	75	75	60	83	84	73.9
	MIN	35	43	49	38	28	42	51	47	31	56	57	55	66	57	48	43	30	44	37	31	39	47	59	29	32	35	60	59	42	45	69	45.3
LLSBORO 3 S	MAX	46	60	54	67	65	61	64	54	52	63	57	52	80	78	83	65	56	47	49	67	59	73	79	64	52	61	68	70	59	71	82	63.2
	MIN	31	33	39	40	30	33	43	25	27	40	36	39	52	63	41	44	26	29	33	33	35	47	57	27	29	34	44	45	36	40	57	38.3
LLSVILLE	MAX	63	56	71	73	64	82	76	59	65	78	70	81	86	87	84	61	52	63	78	78	76	81	76	76	64	71	67	73	72	79	88	72.6
	MIN	41	40	47	40	32	41	51	38	30	55	52	53	62	60	50	52	28	44	40	41	40	48	55	36	31	38	56	50	38	57	58	45.3
ST CHESTER	MAX	66	67	71	78	67	77	52	62	65	80	63	83	87	93	71	72	71	66	71	80	71	84	76	62	67	71	66	77	75	80	93	73.0
	MIN	42	47	53	40	48	49	38	39	44	52	50	56	66	55	54	35	33	45	45	46	50	52	41	38	45	46	58	46	53	51	64	47.8
LLIAMSPORT WB AP	MAX	66	60	73	69	64	75	61	61	63	66	58	87	86	89	69	62	52	56	76	66	76	84	71	59	63	69	68	69	71	76	86	69.5
	MIN	36	43	45	40	33	52	42	34	33	51	40	51	61	59	49	38	31	43	43	39	48	49	46	37	31	41	52	47	40	58	60	44.3
RK 3 SSW PUMP STA	MAX	66	68	70	75	66	84	85	61	67	78	72	83	88	89	89	66	60	63	80	78	78	83	78	75	65	73	70	79	79	81	90	75.5
	MIN	42	42	49	49	33	47	52	35	34	57	54	53	63	61	50	56	30	41	38	43	41	52	59	35	30	45	57	60	39	55	60	47.2

Table 6

EVAPORATION AND WIND

Station		1	2	3	4	5	6	7	8	9	10	11	12	13	14	15	16	17	18	19	20	21	22	23	24	25	26	27	28	29	30	31	Total or Avg.
CONFLUENCE 1 SW DAM	EVAP	.13	.17	.00	.12	.12	.15	.51	.10	.16	.22	.24	.14	.13	.16	.19	.06	*	*	.27	.20	.18	.19	.06	.15	.19	.19	*	*	.45	.15	.14	4.77
	WIND	84	45	30	53	96	32	85	101	45	94	73	57	67	72	87	60	99	53	53	92	38	39	64	112	69	45	67	61	67	34	54	2028
FORD CITY 4 S DAM	EVAP	-	-	-	-	-	-	-	-	-	-	-	-	-	-	-	-	-	-	.06	.20	.16	.16	.04	.29	.20	.17	.13	.03	.24	.17	.19	-
	WIND	-	-	-	-	-	-	-	-	-	-	-	-	-	-	-	-	79	53	47	93	18	18	29	32	88	20	52	57	50	24	76	-
HAWLEY 1 S DAM	EVAP	-	.14	.06	.12	*	.27	.07	*	*	.41	.07	.13	.07	.28	.29	.12	*	.24	.01	.12	.16	.23	.27	.09	*	.34	.19	.03	.11	.24	.11	B4.31
	WIND	-	35	40	68	115	93	38	62	73	309	107	75	111	87	121	93	153	65	69	133	51	102	147	103	73	64	112	131	96	129	149	B3104
JAMESTOWN 2 NW	EVAP	.01	*	*	.31	-	-	-	.19	.16	-	.03	.22	-	.12	.24	.07	*	*	.10	.18	.15	.17	.10	.18	.17	.17	.13	.10	.21	.14	.16	B3.82
	WIND	6	36	24	30	33	25	43	75	28	41	5	86	64	43	66	47	39	38	43	34	18	34	40	52	33	19	49	41	20	49	58	1219
PIMPLE HILL	EVAP	.24	.19	.15	.17	.18	.21	.28	.09	.17	.21	.07	.12	.25	.26	.33	.16	.23	.11	.06	.24	.21	.26	.25	.23	.21	.22	.27	.04	.20	.23	.12	5.96
	WIND	171	89	143	87	157	109	103	135	103	224	138	145	161	98	173	124	169	88	112	159	89	106	108	183	97	97	170	139	138	120	130	4065

SUPPLEMENTAL DATA

Station	Wind direction: Prevailing	Wind direction: Percent of time from prevailing	Wind speed m. p. h.: Average	Wind speed: Fastest mile	Wind speed: Direction of fastest mile	Wind speed: Date of fastest mile	Relative humidity averages - percent: 1:30 a EST	7:30 a EST	1:30 p EST	7:30 p EST	Number of days with precipitation: Trace	.01-.09	.10-.49	.50-.99	1.00-1.99	2.00 and over	Total	Percent of possible sunshine	Average sky cover sunrise to sunset
ALLENTOWN WB AIRPORT	WSW	14	11.4	-	-	-	76	75	52	62	1	11	6	1	1	0	20	-	6.0
HARRISBURG WB AIRPORT	WSW	11	8.3	44	SW	31	67	64	47	53	6	7	6	1	0	0	20	71	6.4
LADELPHIA WB AIRPORT	SW	19	11.1	47	NE	6	70	67	45	56	9	5	4	1	0	1	20	61	6.2
TSBURGH WB AIRPORT	WSW	19	12.4	40*	NW	6	73	73	55	60	7	1	7	3	2	0	20	47	7.0
DING WB CITY	-	-	11.3	45	NE	6	-	-	-	-	2	10	3	3	0	0	18	61	6.3
ANTON WB AIRPORT	WSW	20	10.4	40	NW	14	70	68	48	55	6	7	5	1	0	0	19	49	7.1
PPINGPORT WB	-	-	2.7	51††	W	30	-	-	-	-	1	1	8	2	3	0	15	-	-
LIAMSPORT WB AIRPORT	-	-	-	-	-	-	-	72	49	53	6	7	4	4	0	0	21	-	6.9

his datum is obtained by
ual observation since record-
equipment is not available.
is not necessarily the fast-
mile occurring during the
iod.
Peak Gust

See Reference Notes Following Station Index

STATION INDEX

Station	Index No.	County	Drainage 1	Latitude	Longitude	Elevation	Observation Time Temp.	Observation Time Precip.	Observer	Refer To Tables
ACMETONIA LOCK 3	0022	ALLEGHENY	1	40 32	79 49	748		7A	CORPS OF ENGINEERS	3
ALLENS MILLS	0099	JEFFERSON	1	41 12	78 55	1600		MID	CHARLES H. ALLEN	C
ALLENTOWN WB AP	0106	LEHIGH	9	40 39	75 26	376	MID	MID	U.S. WEATHER BUREAU	2 3 5 7 C
ALLENTOWN GAS CO	0111	LEHIGH	9	40 36	75 28	254	7A	7A	LEHIGH VLY GAS DIV	2 3 5
ALTOONA HORSESHOE CURVE	0134	BLAIR	6	40 30	78 29	1500	6P	6P	ALTOONA WATER BUR.	2 3 5 7
ARENDTSVILLE	0229	ADAMS	15	39 55	77 18	710	8A	8A	PA STATE COL EXP	2 3 5
ARTEMAS 1 WNW	0259	BEDFORD	12	39 45	78 28	1250	6P	6P	GRAYSON E.NORTHCRAFT	2 3 5 7 C
AUSTINBURG 2 W	0313	TIOGA	15	42 00	77 32	1590		7A	OTTO D. BACON	3 C
BAKERSTOWN 3 WNW	0355	ALLEGHENY	1	40 39	79 59	1230	7P	7P	PGH CUT FLOWER CO	2 3 5
BARNES	0409	WARREN	1	41 40	79 02	1310		7A	CORPS OF ENGINEERS	3
BEAR GAP	0457	NORTHUMBERLAND	15	40 50	76 30	900		MID	ROARING CRK WTR CO	3
BEAVER FALLS	0475	BEAVER	2	40 46	80 19	760		7A	HO ARD R. KEMP	3
BEAVERTOWN	0482	SNYDER	15	40 45	77 10	640	7A	7A	MARLIN R. ETTINGER	2 3 5 7
BEECH CREEK STATION	0499	CENTRE	16	41 04	77 34	620		7A	HAROLD S. RUPERT	3
BELLEFONTE 4 S	0530	CENTRE	16	40 51	77 47	1110	8A	8A	ROCKVIEW PRISON FARM	2 3 5 7
BERWICK	0611	COLUMBIA	15	41 04	76 15	570	6P	6P	AMER CAR + FNDRY CO	2 3 5 7
BETHLEHEM	0629	NORTHAMPTON	9	40 37	75 22	400		7A	ARTHUR CROPPER	3
#BETHLEHEM LEHIGH UNIV	0634	NORTHAMPTON	9	40 36	75 23	450	MID	MID	LEHIGH UNIVERSITY	2 3 5 C
BLAIN	0725	PERRY	15	40 20	77 31	750		MID	PA DEPT FRST + WTRS	C
BLAIRSVILLE 6 ENE	0736	INDIANA	4	40 27	79 09	2048	8P	8P	U.S. WEATHER BUREAU	2 3 5
BLAKESLEE CORNERS	0743	MONROE	9	41 06	75 36	1650		MID	WALTER WILDRICK	C
BLOSERVILLE 1 N	0763	CUMBERLAND	15	40 16	77 22	650		5P	MRS. B. M. WILLDERS	3
BOSWELL 6 WNW	0820	SOMERSET	1	40 11	79 08	2580		7A	MRS. MAE L. KIMMEL	3 C
BRADDOCK LOCK 2	0861	ALLEGHENY	10	40 24	79 52	725		7A	CORPS OF ENGINEERS	3
BRADFORD CNTRL FIRE STA	0867	MC KEAN	1	41 57	78 39	1500		8A	BRADFORD FIRE DEPT	3
BRADFORD 4 W RES	0868	MC KEAN	1	41 57	78 44	1680	5P	5P	BRADFORD WTR DEPT	2 3 5 7
BREEZEWOOD	0905	BEDFORD	6	40 00	78 14	1352		MID	PA TURNPIKE COMM	3
BROOKVILLE CAA AIRPORT	1002	JEFFERSON	1	41 09	79 06	1417	MID	MID	CIVIL AERO. ADM.	2 3 5 7
BRUCETON 1 S	1033	ALLEGHENY	10	40 18	79 59	1065		7A	AUSTIN R. COOPER	3
BUCKSTOWN 1 SE	1073	SOMERSET	4	40 04	78 50	2460		MID	ALVIN W. MANGES	C
BUFFALO MILLS	1087	BEDFORD	6	39 58	78 39	1318		7A	MRS. NELLE R. BROWN	3
BURGETTSTOWN 2 W	1105	WASHINGTON	11	40 23	80 26	980	7A	7A	SMITH TWP MUN AUTH	2 3 5 7
BURNT CABINS 2 NE	1115	HUNTINGDON	6	40 05	77 52	990	MID	MID	PA TURNPIKE COMM	2 3 5 7
#BUTLER	1130	BUTLER	2	40 52	79 54	1100	4P	7A	WILLIAM C. FAUST	2 3 5 7
BUTLER SUBSTATION	1135	BUTLER	2	40 51	79 53	1140		MID	WEST PENN PO ER CO	C
CAMP HILL	1198	CUMBERLAND	15	40 15	76 55	461		6P	JOSEPH N. HOBART	
CANTON 1 NW	1215	BRADFORD	15	41 40	76 52	1520	7A	7A	MRS.MILDRED SPENCER	2 3 5 7 C
CARLISLE	1234	CUMBERLAND	15	40 12	77 11	460	6P	6P	C. E. MILLER	2 5 7
CARROLLTOWN 2 SSE	1255	CAMBRIA	16	40 35	78 42	2040		8A	ROBERT F. MAURER	
CARTER CAMP 2 W	1262	POTTER	16	41 37	77 45	2030		7A	RICHARD L. MENKEN	3 C
CEDAR RUN	1301	LYCOMING	16	41 31	77 27	800		7A	KATHRYN T.KREIGHBAUM	3
CHADDS FORD	1342	DELAWARE	5	39 52	75 36	160		8A	MRS.GRACE A. WICKS	3
CHAMBERSBURG 1 ESE	1354	FRANKLIN	12	39 56	77 38	640	9P	9P	CHARLES A. BENDER	2 3 5 7 C
CHARLEROI	1372	WASHINGTON	10	40 08	79 55	1040		MID	WEST PENN POWER CO	C
CHARLEROI LOCK 4	1377	WESTMORELAND	10	40 09	79 54	749		7A	CORPS OF ENGINEERS	3
#CHESTER	1423	DELAWARE	5	39 50	75 21	86	8A	8A	CHESTER TIMES	2 3 5
CLARENCE 1 E	1480	CENTRE	16	41 03	77 56	1440		7A	MARGARET A. SWANCER	3
CLARION 3 SW	1485	CLARION	1	41 12	79 26	1114	8P	7A	PA ELECTRIC CO	2 3 5 7 C
CLAUSSVILLE	1505	LEHIGH	9	40 37	75 39	670		8A	WILLIAM J. DOTTERER	3
CLAYSVILLE 3 W	1512	WASHINGTON	11	40 07	80 28	1000	7P	7A	MFGRS. L + M CO	2 3 5
CLEARFIELD	1519	CLEARFIELD	16	41 01	78 26	1100		7A	IRA TAYLOR	3
CLERMONT	1529	MC KEAN	1	41 41	78 30	2104		7A	MRS.TILLIE M.SIMONDS	3 C
COALDALE 2 NW	1572	SCHUYLKILL	9	40 50	75 56	1026		7A	PANTHER VLY WTR CO	3
COATESVILLE 1 SW	1589	CHESTER	5	39 58	75 50	342	8A	8A	PHILA ELECTRIC CO	2 3 5 7 C
COATESVILLE	1594	CHESTER	5	39 59	75 49	340		8A	EDWARD D. BIEDEMAN	INAC 12/55
COLUMBIA	1675	LANCASTER	15	40 02	76 30	300	5S	5S	JAMES H. RUST	2 3 5
CONFLUENCE 1 SW DAM	1705	SOMERSET	17	39 48	79 22	1490	8A	8A	CORPS OF ENGINEERS	2 3 5 6 C
CONFLUENCE 1 NW	1710	FAYETTE	17	39 50	79 22	1331		7A	JOHN L. REID	3
CONNELLSVILLE	1723	FAYETTE	17	40 01	79 36	870		8A	MARSHALL B. MENEFEE	U
CONNELLSVILLE 2 E	1729	FAYETTE	17	40 01	79 33	1300		MID	HARRY C. JOY	C
CONSHOHOCKEN	1737	MONTGOMERY	5	40 04	75 19	70		8A	PHILA ELECTRIC CO	3
COOKSBURG	1740	CLARION	1	41 20	79 13	1180		8A	PA DEPT FRST + WTRS	3
COOKSBURG 2 NNW	1752	CLARION	1	41 21	79 13	1460		8A	PA DEPT FRST + WTRS	3
CORAOPOLIS NEVILLE IS	1773	ALLEGHENY	11	40 30	80 05	720		8A	PGH. COKE + CHEM CO	3
CORRY	1790	ERIE	1	41 56	79 38	1427	7P	5A	LEO C. NECKERS	2 3 5 7
COUDERSPORT 3 NW	1806	POTTER	1	41 49	78 03	2020	7P	8A	MISS ELIZABETH NEFF	2 3 5 7
COUDERSPORT 7 E	1809	POTTER	1	41 46	77 53	2425		7A	CAMP POTATO	3
COVINGTON	1832	TIOGA	15	41 45	77 05	1193		7A	GROVER D. CLEVELAND	3
CREEKSIDE	1881	INDIANA	1	40 41	79 12	1035		7A	CORPS OF ENGINEERS	3
CRESSON 2 SE	1895	CAMBRIA	6	40 27	78 34	2540		7A	MILES A. VECELLIO	3 C
CUSTER CITY 2 W	1978	MC KEAN	1	41 55	78 41	2120		8A	M. D. BOOTH AND CO	
DANVILLE	2013	MONTOUR	15	40 58	76 37	460		7A	MRS.MARIE M. LITTLE	3
DERRY	2108	WESTMORELAND	4	40 20	79 18	1150	6P	6P	MISS N. D. INEMAN	2 5
DEVAULT 1 W	2116	CHESTER	14	40 05	75 33	360	MID	MID	PA TURNPIKE COMM	2 5
DINGMANS FERRY	2160	PIKE	5	41 13	74 52	360		MID	CLARENCE H. SMITH	C
DIXON	2171	WYOMING	15	41 34	75 54	620	7A	7A	HAROLD J. KUSCHEL	2 3 5 7 C
DONEGAL	2183	WESTMORELAND	17	40 07	79 23	1746	MID	MID	PA TURNPIKE COMM	2 3 5 7
#DONORA	2190	WASHINGTON	10	40 11	79 51	814	12M	12M	DONORA ZINC WORKS	2 3 5
DOYLESTOWN	2221	BUCKS	5	40 18	75 08	393		5P	GEORGE HART	3
DRIFTWOOD	2245	CAMERON	16	41 20	78 08	880		MID	SIDNEY KENNEDY	C
DU BOIS 7 E	2265	CLEARFIELD	16	41 06	78 38	1670	5P	5P	CITY OF DU BOIS	2 3 5 C
DUNLO	2298	CAMBRIA	4	40 17	78 43	2410		MID	MRS. D. L. WHITE	C
DUSHORE 3 NE	2324	SULLIVAN	16	41 33	76 21	1750		7A	PATRICK P. RYAN	3 C
EAGLES MERE	2343	SULLIVAN	16	41 24	76 35	2020	7A	7A	MRS.ELSIE P. BIGGER	2 3 5 7 C
EAST BRADY	2363	CLARION	1	40 59	79 37	820	5P	5P	A. B. KEMPEL	2 3 5
EAST WATERFORD 3 E	2459	PERRY	6	40 21	77 33	2125	8A	8A	U.S. WEATHER BUREAU	INAC 5/55
EBENSBURG	2466	CAMBRIA	4	40 29	78 43	2090	7P	7A	ROBERT A. WASSER	2 3 5
EDINBORO	2514	ERIE	1	41 52	80 08	1220		8A	EDINBORO ST TCHR COL	3
ELIZABETHTOWN	2560	LANCASTER	15	40 09	76 37	460		8A	MASONIC HOME	3
EMPORIUM 1 E	2633	CAMERON	16	41 31	78 13	1160	7A	7A	RUSSELL E.PALMATEER	2 3 5 7 C
ENGLISH CENTER	2644	LYCOMING	16	41 26	77 17	881		7A	WILLIAM SUDERS	3 C
EPHRATA	2662	LANCASTER	15	40 11	76 10	465	6P	6P	STANLEY L.VON NEIDA	2 3 5
EQUINUNK	2669	WAYNE	5	41 51	75 13	900		8A	MRS.ROSE M. NEILSEN	3
ERIE CAA AIRPORT	2682	ERIE	8	42 05	80 12	732	MID	MID	CIVIL AERO. ADM.	2 3 5
EVERETT 1 SW	2721	BEDFORD	6	40 00	78 23	1020	MID	MID	PA TURNPIKE COMM	2 3 5 7 C
FARRELL SHARON	2814	MERCER	2	41 14	80 30	865	7P	7P	SHARON STEEL CORP	2 5
FORD CITY 4 S DAM	2942	ARMSTRONG	1	40 43	79 30	950	8A	8A	CORPS OF ENGINEERS	2 5 6 7 C
FRANKLIN	3028	VENANGO	1	41 23	79 49	987	7P	7A	JAMES K. ELLIOTT	2 3 5 7 C
FREDERICKSVILLE 2 SE	3047	BERKS	14	40 26	75 40	950	8A	8A	D. P. FENSTERMACHER	2 5
FREELAND	3056	LUZERNE	15	41 01	75 54	1900	6P	8A	ANDREW B. EVANSHA	2 5
GALETON	3130	POTTER	16	41 44	77 39	1325		7A	W. GALE LUSH	3
GEIGERTOWN	3189	BERKS	14	40 13	75 50	400		8A	WALTER C. WOLF	3
GEORGE SCHOOL	3200	BUCKS	5	40 13	74 56	135	7P	7P	GEORGE M. HART	2 3 5 7
#GETTYSBURG	3218	ADAMS	12	39 50	77 14	540	9A	9A	HUGH C. MC ILHENNY	2 3 5 7
GETTYSBURG 1 S	3223	ADAMS	12	39 48	77 14	560		MID	NAT MILITARY PARK	C
GIFFORD	3237	MC KEAN	1	41 51	78 36	2220		8A	SOUTH PENN OIL CO	INAC 3/56
GLENCOE	3298	SOMERSET	12	39 49	78 51	1620		MID	MRS. MARY M.HARTMAN	C
GLEN HAZEL 2 NE DAM	3311	ELK	1	41 34	78 36	1725		8A	CORPS OF ENGINEERS	3 C
GLEN ROCK	3330	YORK	15	39 48	76 44	620		MID	MRS.E.C.MC WILLIAMS	C
GLENWILLARD DASH DAM	3343	ALLEGHENY	11	40 33	80 13	705		7A	CORPS OF ENGINEERS	3
GOULDSBORO	3394	WAYNE	9	41 15	75 27	1890		7A	L. M. EILENBERGER	3
GRANTVILLE 2 SW	3422	DAUPHIN	15	40 22	76 41	510		5S	EARL E. RHOADS	3
GRATERFORD	3435	MONTGOMERY	14	40 14	75 72	160		7A	CLAUDE K. KULP	3
GRATZ 1 N	3438	DAUPHIN	15	40 38	76 43	760	8A	8A	LEE M. LEITZEL	2 3 5 7 C
GREENSBORO LOCK 7	3503	GREENE	10	39 47	79 55	808		7A	CORPS OF ENGINEERS	3
GREENSBURG 2 E	3515	WESTMORELAND	10	40 18	79 31	1225		MID	PA DEPT HIGHWAYS	C
GREENSBURG 3 SE	3516	WESTMORELAND	10	40 17	79 30	1245		6P	WESTMORELAND WTR CO	3
GREENVILLE	3526	MERCER	2	41 24	80 23	1026	6P	6P	C. EARL MILLER	2 3 5 7
HANOVER	3662	YORK	15	39 48	76 59	600	8A	8A	HANOVER EVENING SUN	2 3 5
#HARRISBURG WB AP	3699	YORK	15	40 13	76 51	335	MID	MID	U.S. WEATHER BUREAU	2 3 5 7 C
HARRISBURG NORTH	3704	DAUPHIN	15	40 18	76 54	323		9A	GEORGE S. BEAL	3
HAWLEY	3758	WAYNE	5	41 29	75 10	880		7A	MRS.KATHERINE S.BATE	3
HAWLEY 1 S DAM	3761	WAYNE	5	41 28	75 11	1200	7A	7A	PA POWER + LIGHT CO	2 3 5 6 7 C
HOLLIDAYSBURG	4001	BLAIR	6	40 26	78 24	960		MID	JOHN M. RINGLER	C
HOLLISTERVILLE	4008	WAYNE	5	41 23	75 26	1360		8A	PA POWER + LIGHT CO	3
#HOLTWOOD	4019	LANCASTER	15	39 50	76 20	187	MID	8A	PA POWER + LIGHT CO	2 3 5 C
HOME	4027	INDIANA	1	40 45	79 06	1220		MID	MRS. EDNA M. BUSH	C
HONESDALE 4 NW	4043	WAYNE	5	41 37	75 19	1410		9A	GEORGE C. WILLIAMS	3
HONESDALE 6 NNW	4044	WAYNE	5	41 39	75 17	1050		MID	FRIEND E. WALTER	C
HOOVERSVILLE	4058	SOMERSET	4	40 09	78 55	1660		7A	PA ELECTRIC CO	3
HOP BOTTOM 2 SE	4066	SUSQUEHANNA	15	41 43	75 43	900		7A	JOSEPH J. SANSUSKAS	3
HUNTINGDON	4159	HUNTINGDON	15	40 29	78 01	600	7A	7A	JOHN R. HENDERSON	2 3 5 7
HUNTSDALE	4166	CUMBERLAND	15	40 06	77 18	610		8A	METRO P. DOROSH	3
HYNDMAN	4190	BEDFORD	12	39 49	78 43	920		8A	MRS.GERTRUDE M.BURTU	3
INDIANA 3 SE	4214	INDIANA	4	40 36	79 07	1102	7P	7A	CLYMER WATER SVC CO	2 3 5 7
IRWIN	4276	WESTMORELAND	10	40 20	79 42	1100	5P	5P	WESTMORELAND WTR CO	2 3 5
JACKSON SUMMIT	4304	TIOGA	15	41 57	77 01	1690		MID	ARCHIE LAIN	
JAMESTOWN 2 NW	4325	CRAWFORD	2	41 30	80 28	1050	8A	8A	PA DEPT FRST + WTRS	2 3 5 6
JIM THORPE	4370	CARBON	9	40 52	75 45	830	5P	5P	HENRY S. MAAK	2 3 5
#JOHNSTOWN	4385	CAMBRIA	4	40 20	78 55	1214	9A	9A	JOHNSTO N TRIBUNE	2 3 5 7
JOHNSTOWN 2	4390	CAMBRIA	4	40 19	78 55	1275		MID	CITY OF JOHNSTOWN	
KANE 1 NNE	4432	MC KEAN	1	41 41	78 48	1750	8A	8A	SPRING WATER CO	2 3 5 7
KARTHAUS	4450	CLEARFIELD	16	41 07	78 07	950		7A	JEROME S. HOWE	3
KEATING SUMMIT	4468	POTTER	1	41 41	78 11	1840		7A	EUGENE L. KREITNER	3
KEGG	4481	BEDFORD	6	39 59	78 43	1280	MID	MID	PA TURNPIKE COMM	2 3 6
KITTANNING LOCK 7	4611	ARMSTRONG	1	40 40	79 32	790		7A	CORPS OF ENGINEERS	3
KREGAR 4 SE	4667	WESTMORELAND	17	40 06	79 14	2530		MID	PA TURNPIKE COMM	3
KRESGEVILLE 3 W	4672	CARBON	9	40 54	75 34	720		9A	CITY OF BETHLEHEM	3
LAFAYETTE MC KEAN PARK	4706	MC KEAN	1	41 48	78 40	2130		8A	CHARLES GORDON	INAC 2/56
LAKEVILLE 1 NNE	4733	WAYNE	5	41 27	75 16	1460		8A	MRS. GLADYS REINEKE	3
LANCASTER 2 NE PUMP STA	4758	LANCASTER	15	40 03	76 17	255	6P	6P	LANCASTER WATER BUR	2 3 5
LANCASTER 2 NE FILT PL	4763	LANCASTER	15	40 03	76 17	270		MID	LANCASTER WATER BUR	
LANDISVILLE	4778	LANCASTER	15	40 06	76 25	410	8A	8A	PA STATE COLLEGE	2 3 5 6 7
LATROBE	4832	WESTMORELAND	4	40 19	79 23	1000		MID	WEST PENN POWER CO	3
LAURELTON STATE VILLAGE	4853	UNION	15	40 54	77 13	880		MID	PA DEPT OF WELFARE	
LAWRENCEVILLE 2 S	4873	TIOGA	15	41 59	77 07	1000	7A	7A	HARRY P. HOWLAND	2 3 5 7
LEBANON 3 SW	4896	LEBANON	15	40 19	76 28	490		MID	THOMAS DONNACHIE	
LEHIGHTON	4934	CARBON	9	40 50	75 43	580		7A	GOODWIN S. DEFRENN	3
LE ROY	4972	BRADFORD	15	41 41	76 43	1040		6P	MRS.DIMMIS M.BAILEY	3
LEWIS RUN 3 S	4984	MC KEAN	1	41 50	78 39	1740		7A	RUSSELL LINEMAN	3
LEWISTOWN	4992	MIFFLIN	6	40 35	77 35	480	7A	7A	AMERICAN VISCOSE CO	2 3 5 7
LINESVILLE 5 WNW	5050	CRAWFORD	2	41 41	80 31	1020	7P	8A	MISS RETTA M. CROMS	2 3 5
LOCK HAVEN	5104	CLINTON	16	41 08	77 27	570	7P	7A	PETER L. STEVENSON	2 3 5 7
LOCK HAVEN 2	5109	CLINTON	16	41 08	77 27	630		MID	HUGH F. PARKER	
LONG POND 2 W	5160	MONROE	9	41 03	75 30	1860		7A	THOMAS MECKES	3
MADERA	5336	CLEARFIELD	16	40 50	78 26	1460	7A	7A	MRS. JULIA J. SHOFF	2 3 5
MAHAFFEY	5342	CLEARFIELD	16	40 53	78 44	1280		7A	MISS ELLEN J. MILES	3
MAPLE GLEN	5368	MONTGOMERY	5	40 11	75 11	380		6P	FRANCES E.SCHEIBNER	3
MAPLETON DEPOT	5381	HUNTINGDON	6	40 24	77 56	580		7A	MRS. I. S. BUCHANAN	3
MARCUS HOOK	5390	DELAWARE	[illegible]	39 49	75 25	12	MID	MID	SUN OIL CO	2 3 5
MARIENVILLE 1 SW	5400	FOREST	1	41 27	79 09	1700		MID	ROY A. MARKER	
MARION CENTER 2 SE	5408	INDIANA	1	40 45	79 02	1610		7A	CORPS OF ENGINEERS	3
MARTINSBURG 1 SW	5453	BLAIR	6	40 18	78 20	1360		MID	BLUE MT. CANNERIES	
MARTINSBURG CAA AP	5454	BLAIR	6	40 18	78 19	1463	MID	MID	CIVIL AERO. ADM.	2 3 5
MATAMORAS	5470	PIKE	5	41 22	74 42	439		7A	HARRY BISLAND	3
MAYBURG	5490	FOREST	1	41 36	79 13	1150		7A	CORPS OF ENGINEERS	3
MC CONNELLSBURG	5526	FULTON	12	39 56	78 00	895		8A	MRS. HELEN M. SHIVES	3
MC KEESPORT	5573	ALLEGHENY	10	40 21	79 52	720		8A	NATIONAL TUBE CO	3
MEADOW RUN PONDS	5601	LUZERNE	15	41 13	75 40	1995		MID	GEORGE PEARAGE	
MEADVILLE 1 S	5606	CRAWFORD	1	41 38	80 10	1065	8A	8A	CITY OF MEADVILLE	2 3 5 7
MEDIA RUN	5627	ELK	16	41 17	78 24	1100		7A	MRS.E. M. SNYDER	3
MERCER 2 NNE	5651	MERCER	2	41 15	80 13	1160	7P	7A	WILLIAM K. STRUTHERS	2 3 5 7
MERCER HIRAY SHED	5654	MERCER	2	41 14	80 15	1250		MID	PA DEPT HIGHWAYS	
MERCERSBURG	5662	FRANKLIN	12	39 50	77 54	605		8A	ROLLIN P. GILBERT	3
MERWINSBURG	5676	MONROE	9	40 58	75 28	970		MID	WILLIAM D. GOULD	
MEYERSDALE 1 ENE	5685	SOMERSET	17	39 49	79 01	2290		8A	ARTHUR B. MC CARTER	3
MIDDLETOWN OLMSTED FLD	5703	DAUPHIN	15	40 11	76 46	303	MID	MID	U. S. AIR FORCE	2 3 5
MIDLAND DAM 7	5710	BEAVER	11	40 38	80 28	689	11P	7A	CORPS OF ENGINEERS	2 3 5
MILAN 4 WNW	5732	BRADFORD	15	41 56	76 35	1448		MID	CARL A. MORRIS	
MILANVILLE	5738	WAYNE	5	41 40	75 04	760		8A	CHARLES W. DAVIS	3
MILLERSBURG 2 E	5775	DAUPHIN	15	40 32	76 56	560		MID	RUSSELL SHEPLEY	
MILLHEIM	5790	CENTRE	15	40 54	77 29	1090		7A	NEVIN E. BOWERSOX	3
MILLVILLE 2 SW	5817	COLUMBIA	15	41 06	76 34	860		7A	KENNETH LEIGHOW	3
MILROY	5825	MIFFLIN	6	40 43	77 35	770		8A	THOMAS C. HARBESON	3
MONTROSE 1 E	5915	SUSQUEHANNA	15	41 50	75 51	1630	7A	7A	WILBER W. HOOPES.JR	2 3 5 7
MORGANTOWN	5956	BERKS	15	40 09	75 54	595	MID	MID	PA TURNPIKE COMM	2 3 5
MT GRETNA 2 SE	6028	LANCASTER	15	40 14	76 26	670	MID	MID	PA TURNPIKE COMM	2 3 5
MT POCONO 2 N AP	6055	MONROE	5	41 09	75 22	1915	5P	5P	H. JOHN DAVIS. JR.	2 3 5 7
MOUNT UNION 1 N	6067	MIFFLIN	6	40 24	77 53	820		MID	MT UNION WTR WORKS	
MUHLENBURG 1 SE	6090	LUZERNE	15	41 13	76 08	1110	6P	6P	THEODORE J. SAMPSON	2 3 5
MURRYSVILLE	6111	WESTMORELAND	10	40 26	79 42	903		MID	DAVID C. SHAW	
MYERSTOWN	6126	LEBANON	14	40 22	76 18	480		8A	MRS.KATHLEEN WANDELL	3
NATRONA LOCK 4	6151	ALLEGHENY	1	40 37	79 43	800		7A	CORPS OF ENGINEERS	3
NEFFS MILLS 3 NE	6174	HUNTINGDON	6	40 40	77 55	900		MID	PA STATE UNIVERSITY	
NESHAMINY FALLS	6194	BUCKS	5	40 09	74 57	60		MID	PHILA SUB WATER CO	3
NEWBURG 3 W	6225	FRANKLIN	15	40 09	77 37	745	MID	MID	PA TURNPIKE COMM	2 3 5
NEW CASTLE 1 N	6233	LAWRENCE	2	41 01	80 22	900	5P	7A	BAXTER F. JOHNSON	2 3 5 7
#NEWELL	6246	FAYETTE	10	40 05	79 54	805	12M	12M	GENERAL CHEMICAL CO	2 3 5
NEW PARK	6289	YORK	15	39 44	76 30	780		6P	CLINTON J. ALLEN	3
NEWPORT	6297	PERRY	6	40 29	77 08	400	7A	7A	MRS. FRANCES K. FRY	2 3 5 7
NEW STANTON	6310	WESTMORELAND	10	40 13	79 36	980	MID	MID	PA TURNPIKE COMM	2 3 5
NEW TRIPOLI	6326	LEHIGH	14	40 41	75 45	570		6P	FRED C. OSWALD	3
NORRISTOWN	6370	MONTGOMERY	14	40 07	75 21	75	MID	8A	GEORGE H. BOONE	2 3 5
NORTH EAST 2 SE	6396	ERIE	8	42 12	79 49	1060		9A	ELLSWORTH WEAVER	3
ORWELL 3 N	6621	BRADFORD	15	41 55	76 16	1620		8A	WILLIAM I. BROWN	3
PALM	6681	MONTGOMERY	14	40 26	75 32	385		8A	FRED C. ESCHBACH	3
#PALMERTON	6689	CARBON	9	40 48	75 37	435	MID	MID	NEW JERSEY ZINC CO	2 3 5 7
PARKER	6721	ARMSTRONG	1	41 05	79 41	1140		7A	LOUIS A. MALARKEY	3
PARKER 1 E	6724	CLARION	1	41 06	79 40	1100		MID	P. M. NEELY	
PAUPACK 2 WNW	6762	PIKE	5	41 24	75 14	1360		8A	MISS L. VETTERLEIN	3
PECKS POND	6786	PIKE	5	41 17	75 06	1380		9A	MRS. CARRIE NESS	3
#PHIL DREXEL INST OF TEC	6879	PHILADELPHIA	14	39 57	75 11	30	MID	MID	FRANCIS K. DAVIS.JR	2 3 5
PHILADELPHIA WB AP	6889	PHILADELPHIA	5	39 53	75 14	13	MID	MID	U.S. WEATHER BUREAU	2 3 5 7
#PHILADELPHIA PT BREEZE	6899	PHILADELPHIA	5	39 55	75 12	32	MID	MID	ATLANTIC REFINING	2 3 5
PHILADELPHIA SHAWMONT	6904	PHILADELPHIA	5	40 02	75 15	70	7P	7P	SCHUYLKILL NAVIG CO	2 3 5 7
#PHILADELPHIA CITY	6909	PHILADELPHIA	5	39 57	75 09	26	9A	9A	USN HYDROGRAPHIC OFF	2 3 5
PHILIPSBURG CAA AP	6916	CENTRE	6	40 54	78 05	1918	8P	8P	CIVIL AERO. ADM.	2 3 5 7
PHOENIXVILLE 1 E	6927	CHESTER	14	40 07	75 30	105	6P	MID	PHILA SUB WATER CO	2 3 5 7
PIKES CREEK	6939	LUZERNE	15	41 18	76 08	1320		MID	HARRY SHELDON	3
PIMPLE HILL	6944	MONROE	9	41 02	75 30	2215	9A	9A	PA DEPT FRST + WTRS	2 3 5 6
PINE GROVE 1 NE	6954	SCHUYLKILL	15	40 34	76 22	535		8A	PA POWER + LIGHT CO	3
PITTSBURGH WB AP 2	6993	ALLEGHENY	11	40 30	80 13	1151	MID	MID	U.S. WEATHER BUREAU	2 3 5
#PITTSBURGH WB CITY	6997	ALLEGHENY	11	40 27	80 00	749	MID	MID	U.S. WEATHER BUREAU	2 3 5
PLEASANT MOUNT 1 W	7029	WAYNE	[illegible]	41 44	75 27	1800	8A	8A	PA FISH COMM	2 3 5
PORT CLINTON	7116	SCHUYLKILL	14	40 35	76 02	450	7A	7A	MRS. ADA E. RARICK	2 3 5
PORTLAND	7127	NORTHAMPTON	5	40 55	75 06	297		8A	JOINT BRIDGE COMM	INAC 1/5
POTTSTOWN	7149	MONTGOMERY	14	40 15	75 39	160		8A	MILES E. SMITH	3
POTTSVILLE PALO ALTO BR	7161	SCHUYLKILL	14	40 41	76 11	640		8A	JOHN MC SMITH	INAC 4/5
PUNXSUTAWNEY	7217	JEFFERSON	1	40 57	79 00	1298		MID	JOHN VOLANSKY	
PUTNEYVILLE 2 SE DAM	7229	ARMSTRONG	1	40 55	79 17	1270	8A	8A	CORPS OF ENGINEERS	2 3 5
QUAKERTOWN 1 E	7239	BUCKS	5	40 26	75 20	490	5P	5P	DENNIS K. FLUCK	2 3 5
RAYMOND	7310	POTTER	13	41 52	77 52	2220		7A	MRS. RACHEL LANGAN	3
#READING WB CITY	7318	BERKS	14	40 20	75 58	266	MID	MID	U.S. WEATHER BUREAU	2 3 5
RENOVO	7409	CLINTON	16	41 20	77 46	660		7A	MRS. CAROLINE BAIRD	3
RENOVO 5 S	7410	CLINTON	16	41 14	77 46	2035		MID	C. F. BILLETTE	
REW	7425	MC KEAN	1	41 54	78 32	2250		8A	HAROLD C. HEALY	3
RICES LANDING L 6	7443	GREENE	10	39 57	80 00	775		7A	CORPS OF ENGINEERS	3
RIDGWAY 3 W	7477	ELK	1	41 25	78 47	1420	7P	7A	BOROUGH OF RIDGWAY	2 3 5
ROCHESTER 1 N	7540	BEAVER	2	40 43	80 18	900		MID	DEQUESNE LIGHT CO	
RUSH	7694	SUSQUEHANNA	15	41 47	76 03	1000		9A	MISS MAUDE MC CAIN	3
RUSHVILLE	7727	SUSQUEHANNA	15	41 47	76 07	870		7A	CARL KOPATZ	3
SAFE HARBOR	7732	LANCASTER	15	39 55	76 23	270		MID	S.H.WATER POWER CORP	
SAGAMORE 1 S	7739	INDIANA	1	40 46	79 14	1320		7A	CORPS OF ENGINEERS	3
SALINA 3 W	7782	WESTMORELAND	7	40 31	79 33	1109	6P	6P	MUN AUTH WSTMRLD CO	2 3 5
SAXTON	7846	BEDFORD	6	40 12	78 15	780		8A	MRS.ALVERTA L.HOLMES	3
SCANDIA 2 E	7855	WARREN	1	41 55	79 01	2040		MID	DAVID R. ANDERSON	
SCHENLEY LOCK 5	7863	ARMSTRONG	1	40 41	79 40	783		7A	CORPS OF ENGINEERS	3
#SCRANTON	7902	LACKAWANNA	15	41 25	75 40	746	7A	7A	U.S. POST OFFICE	2 3 5
SCRANTON WB AIRPORT	7905	LUZERNE	15	41 20	75 44	956	MID	MID	U.S. WEATHER BUREAU	2 3 5
SELINSGROVE CAA AP	7931	SNYDER	15	40 49	76 52	437	MID	MID	CIVIL AERO. ADM.	2 3 5

STATION INDEX

Station	Index No.	County	Drainage ‡	Latitude	Longitude	Elevation	Observation Time Temp.	Observation Time Precip.	Observer	Refer To Tables
LERSVILLE 2 NW	7938	BUCKS	5	40 23	75 20	530		MID	SELLERSVILLE WTR CO	C
DE GAP	7965	HUNTINGDON	6	40 11	77 52	1000		MID	MRS. HELEN H. PYLE	C
MOKIN	7978	NORTHUMBLAND	15	40 48	76 33	770		8A	ROARING CRK WTR CO	3
FFIELD 6 W	8020	WARREN	1	41 41	79 09	1040		MID	L. N. HANSON	C
PPENSBURG	8073	FRANKLIN	15	40 03	77 32	709	4P	4P	KEITH B. ALLEN	2 3 5
PPINGPORT WB	8078	BEAVER	11	40 37	80 26	740	MID	MID	U.S. WEATHER BUREAU	2 3 5 7 C
NEMAHONING	8145	CAMERON	16	41 19	78 05	790		7A	MRS.FRANCES C/ OVELL	3
PPERY ROCK	8184	BUTLER	2	41 04	80 03	1345	7P	7A	WALTER D. ALBE	2 3 5
THPORT HIGHWAY SHED	8190	MC KEAN	1	41 48	78 27	1510		MID	PA DEPT HIGHWAYS	C
ERSET FAIRVIEW ST	8244	SOMERSET	17	40 01	79 05	2140		7A	HOWARD G. PECK	3
ERSET MAIN ST	8249	SOMERSET	17	40 01	79 05	2150	6P	6P	DAVID L. GROVE	2 3 5 7
TH CANAAN 1 NE	8275	WAYNE	5	41 31	75 24	1400		MID	EUGENE H. COOK	C
TH MOUNTAIN	8308	FRANKLIN	12	39 51	77 30	1520		7A	PA DEPT OF HEALTH	3
INGBORO	8359	CRAWFORD	8	41 48	80 23	900	8A	8A	SPRINGBORO BOROUGH	2 3 5 7 C
ING GROVE	8379	YORK	15	39 52	76 52	470		4P	P. H. GLATFELTER CO	3 C
INGS 1 SW	8399	SOMERSET	17	39 44	79 10	2500	8P	8P	ALLEN E. YODER	2 3 5 7
TE COLLEGE	8449	CENTRE	16	40 48	77 52	1175	MID	MID	PA STATE COLLEGE	2 3 5 C
AUSSTOWN	8570	BERKS	14	40 29	76 11	600		8A	JACOB KLAHR	3
ONGSTOWN	8589	INDIANA	4	40 33	78 55	1880		MID	HARRY F. BENNETT	C
OUDSBURG	8596	MONROE	5	40 59	75 12	480	8A	8A	WILLIAM MAGERTY	2 3 5 7 C
MP CREEK	8610	JEFFERSON	1	41 01	78 50	1320		7A	CORPS OF ENGINEERS	3
BURY	8668	NORTHUMBLAND	15	40 51	76 48	440		7A	CHARLES W. BAYLER	3 C
QUEHANNA	8692	SUSQUEHANNA	15	41 57	75 36	1020		7A	MRS. LAURA A.BENSON	3
ERSVILLE	8699	ALLEGHENY	17	40 14	79 48	765		7A	MICHAEL C. RACKO	3
AQUA	8758	SCHUYLKILL	14	40 48	75 58	830		8A	MRS. MARY L.ROBERTS	3
AQUA 4 N DAM	8763	SCHUYLKILL	14	40 51	75 59	1120		7A	PANTHER VLY WTR CO	3 C
ARACK 2 S FIRE TWR	8770	CLINTON	16	41 24	77 51	2220	7A	7A	JAMES E. SWARTZ	2 3 5 7
NESTA 2 SE DAM	8873	FOREST	1	41 29	79 26	1200	8A	8A	CORPS OF ENGINEERS	2 3 5 7 C
USVILLE	8885	CRAWFORD	1	41 38	79 40	1550		MID	PA ELECTRIC CO	C
USVILLE WATER WORKS	8888	CRAWFORD	1	41 38	79 42	1220	7P	7P	CITY OF TITUSVILLE	2 3 5
PEDO 4 W	8901	WARREN	1	41 47	79 32	1735		7A	MRS. LILY B. GARBER	3
ANDA	8905	BRADFORD	15	41 46	76 26	760	7P	7A	MRS. M. O. PARKS	2 3 5 7 C
ER CITY 5 SW	8910	DAUPHIN	15	40 31	76 37	745		6P	HARRISBURG WTR DEPT	3 7
Y	8959	BRADFORD	15	41 47	76 47	1100		7A	JENNIE L. BALLARD	3
NELTON	8989	INDIANA	4	40 27	79 23	890		MID	MRS. MARY E. WEIMER	C
TLEPOINT 4 NE	9002	MC KEAN	1	41 54	78 16	1640		7A	ROBERT D. STRAIT	3
ONE 4 NE BALD EAGLE	0024	BLAIR	6	40 43	78 12	1020		7A	FREDERICK L. FRIDAY	3 C
ON CITY	9042	ERIE	1	41 54	79 50	1325		7A	FORREST M. BRALEY	3 C
ONTOWN	9050	FAYETTE	10	39 54	79 44	1040	10P	10P	WM. W. MARSTELLER	2 3 5 7
ER DARBY	9074	DELAWARE	5	39 58	75 18	222	7P	7P	PHIL. SUB.TRANS. CO	2 3 5
CA	9099	VENANGO	1	41 26	79 57	1030		7A	MRS.FLORENCE MILLER	3
DERGRIFT	9128	WESTMORELAND	7	40 36	79 33	800		7A	UNITED ENG+FNDRY CO	3
DERGRIFT 2 W	9133	WESTMORELAND	7	40 36	79 36	995		MID	EUGENE R. YOUNG	C
SINVILLE	9196	BERKS	14	40 31	75 52	350		8A	MRS. MARY H. WRIGHT	3
INCKEL	9206	CLARION	1	41 25	79 14	1020		8A	PA DEPT FRST + WTRS	3
VOWINCKEL 1 WSW	9209	CLARION	1	41 24	79 15	1610		8A	PA DEPT FRST + WTRS	3
WARREN	9298	WARREN	1	41 51	79 08	1280	7P	7A	GILBERT H. REIER	2 3 5 7
WASHINGTON	9312	WASHINGTON	11	40 11	80 14	1200		MID	PA DEPT HIGHWAYS	C
WATSONTOWN	9345	NORTHUMBLAND	16	41 05	76 52	470		8A	OWEN BENKENSTOCK	3
WAYNESBURG 2 W	9362	GREENE	10	39 54	80 13	980	6P	7A	RALPH L. AMOS	2 3 5 7
WAYNESBURG 1 E	9367	GREENE	10	39 54	80 10	940		MID	SEWAGE DISPOSAL PLT	C
WEBSTER MILLS 3 SW	9380	FULTON	12	39 49	78 05	920		MID	WILLIAM D. COVER	C
WELLSBORO 3 S	9408	TIOGA	16	41 43	77 16	1920	7A	7A	MARION L. SHUMWAY	2 3 5 7
WELLSBORO 2 E	9412	TIOGA	16	41 45	77 16	1550		MID	MRS. IDA S. MAYNARD	C
WELLSVILLE	9420	YORK	15	40 03	76 57	500	5P	5P	D. D. HOOVER	2 3 5
WERNERSVILLE 1 W	9430	BERKS	14	40 20	76 06	405		8A	CHARLES A. GRUBER	3
WEST CHESTER	9464	CHESTER	5	39 58	75 36	440	8A	8A	DAILY LOCAL NEWS	2 3 5 7
WEST GROVE 1 E	9503	CHESTER	5	39 40	75 40	440		8A	CONARD-PYLE CO	3
WEST HICKORY	9507	FOREST	1	41 34	79 25	1090		8A	MRS.HELEN F.KINNEAR	3
WHITESBURG	9655	ARMSTRONG	1	40 45	79 24	1530		7A	CORPS OF ENGINEERS	3
WILKES-BARRE	9702	LAZERNE	15	41 15	75 52	610		7A	MRS. MARY G. MIRMAK	3
WILLIAMSBURG	9714	BLAIR	6	40 28	78 12	860		7A	MYRON K. BIDDLE	3
WILLIAMSPORT WB AP	9728	LYCOMING	16	41 15	76 55	527	MID	MID	U.S. WEATHER BUREAU	2 3 5 7 C
WIND GAP	9781	NORTHAMPTON	5	40 51	75 18	720		MID	OWEN R. PARRY	C
WOLFSBURG	9823	BEDFORD	6	40 03	78 32	1190		7A	WALTER C. RICE	3
YORK 3 SSW PUMP STA	9933	YORK	15	39 55	76 45	390	5P	5P	YORK WATER COMPANY	2 3 5 7
YORK 2 S	9938	YORK	15	39 56	76 44	640		MID	YORK WATER COMPANY	C
YORK HAVEN	9950	YORK	15	40 07	76 43	310		6A	METROPOL EDISON CO	3
YOUNGSVILLE	0060	WARREN	1	41 51	79 20	1225		MID	HENRY CARLETT	C
ZION GROVE	9990	SCHUYLKILL	15	40 54	76 13	940		7A	JAMES D. TEETER	3
ZIONSVILLE 3 SE	9995	LEHIGH	14	40 27	75 27	660		7A	LESLIE HOWATT	3
CLOSED STATIONS										
LEBANON 2 NW	4891	LEBANON	15	40 22	76 28	600	6P	6P	LEBANON BDCSTG CO	CLOSED 5/56

‡1-ALLEGHENY; 2-BEAVER; 3- 4-CONEMAUGH; 5-DELAWARE; 6-JUNIATA; 7-KISKIMINETAS; 8-LAKE ERIE; 9-LEHIGH; 10-MONONGAHELA; 11-OHIO; 12-POTOMAC; 13-LAKE ONTARIO; 14-SCHUYLKILL; 15-SUSQUEHANNA; 16-WEST BRANCH; 17-YOUGHIOGHENY

REFERENCE NOTES

The four digit identification numbers in the index number column of the Station Index are assigned on a state basis. There will be no duplication of numbers within a state.

Figures and letters following the station name, such as 12 SSW, indicate distance in miles and direction from the post office.

Observation times given in the Station Index are in local standard time.

Delayed data and corrections will be carried only in the June and December issues of this bulletin.

Monthly and seasonal snowfall and heating degree days for the preceding 12 months will be carried in the June issue of this bulletin.

Stations appearing in the Index, but for which data are not listed in the tables, are either missing or received too late to be included in this issue.

Unless otherwise indicated, dimensional units used in this bulletin are: temperature in °F., precipitation and evaporation in inches, and wind movement in miles. Degree days are based on a daily average of 65° F.

Evaporation is measured in the standard Weather Bureau type pan of 4 foot diameter unless otherwise shown by footnote following Table 6.

Amounts in Table 3 are from non-recording gages, unless otherwise indicated.

Data in Tables 3, 5 and 6 and snowfall data in Table 7 are for the 24 hours ending at time of observation. See Station Index for observation time.

Snow on ground in Table 7 is at observation time for all except Weather Bureau and CAA stations. For these stations snow on ground values are at 7:30 A.M. E.S.T. WTR EQUIV in Table 7 means the water equivalent of snow on the ground. It is measured at selected stations when depth of snow on the ground is two inches or more. Water equivalent samples are necessarily taken from different points for successive observations; consequently occasional drifting and other causes of local variability in the snowpack result in apparent inconsistencies in the record.

Long-term means for full-time Weather Bureau stations (those shown in the Station Index as United States Weather Bureau Stations) are based on the period 1921-1950, adjusted to represent observations taken at the present location.

- \- No record in Tables 3, 6, 7 and the Station Index. No record in Tables 2 and 5 is indicated by no entry.
- \+ And also on a later date or dates.
- * Amount included in following measurement, time distribution unknown.
- Φ Data in the column formerly headed No. of Days .01 or more have been changed to No. of Days .10 or more effective January 1, 1954.
- \# Thermometers are generally exposed in a shelter located a few feet above sod-covered ground; however, the reference indicates that the thermometers are exposed in a shelter located on the roof of a building.
- // Gage is equipped with a windshield.
- AM Data based on observational day ending before noon.
- B Adjusted to a full month.
- C In the "Refer to Tables" column in the Station index the letter "C" indicates recorder stations. These stations are processed for special purposes and are published later in Hourly Precipitation Data.
- D Water equivalent of snowfall wholly or partly estimated, using a ratio of 1 inch water equivalent to every 10 inches of new snowfall.
- M One or more days of record missing; see Table 5 for detailed daily record. Degree day data, if carried for this station, have been adjusted to represent the value for a full month.
- R Amounts from recording gage (These amounts are essentially accurate but may vary slightly from the amounts to be published later in Hourly Precipitation Data).
- SS This entry in time of observation column in Station index means sunset.
- T Trace, an amount too small to measure.
- V Includes total for previous month.

Additional information regarding the climate of Pennsylvania may be obtained by writing to any Weather Bureau Office or to the State Climatologist at Weather Bureau Airport Station, Harrisburg State Airport, New Cumberland, Pennsylvania.

Subscription Price: 20 cents per copy, monthly and annual: $2.50 per year. (Yearly subscription includes the Annual Summary.) Checks and money orders should be made payable to the Superintendent of Documents. Remittances and correspondence regarding subscriptions should be sent to the Superintendent of Documents, Government Printing Office, Washington 25, D. C.

WRC., Asheville, N. C. --- 7/9/56 --- 1225

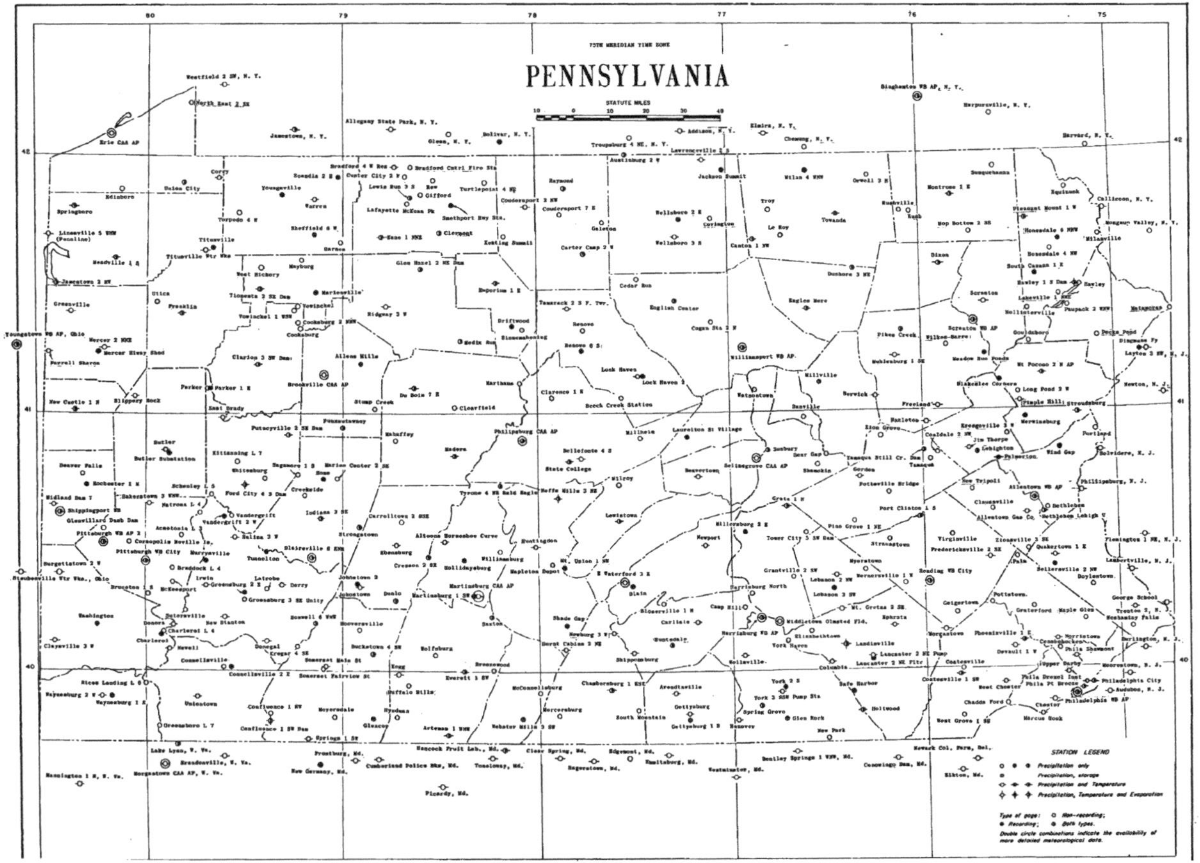
75TH MERIDIAN TIME ZONE
PENNSYLVANIA
STATUTE MILES
10 0 10 20 30 40
STATION LEGEND
Precipitation only
Precipitation, storage
Precipitation and Temperature
Precipitation, Temperature and Evaporation
Type of gage: ○ Non-recording; ● Recording; ◉ Both types.
Double circle combinations indicate the availability of more detailed meteorological data.

U. S. DEPARTMENT OF COMMERCE
SINCLAIR WEEKS, Secretary
WEATHER BUREAU
F. W. REICHELDERFER, Chief

IMATOLOGICAL DATA

PENNSYLVANIA

JUNE 1956
Volume LXI No. 6

ASHEVILLE: 1956

GENERAL

June's weather was characterized by temperature and precipitation values near the usual expectancy and was marked by severe storms on several dates. Cloudiness and sunshine were both a little above average in most localities reporting this information.

Divisional temperature averages were rather uniform and station monthly means, with few exceptions, differed little from their long-term values. The temperature extremes of 99° and 30° were not unusual but the frequency of days with 90° or above readings in the eastern part of the State exceeded the expectancy at stations having comparative figures.

While precipitation averages varied from 5-1/4 inches in the Ohio Drainage to slightly under 4 inches in the other two divisions, the comparison between smaller areas was even more marked. For instance, several eastern counties clustered around Lehigh received from 5 to 6 inches, while numerous counties in the same division, extending from Tioga to Wayne thence southward and southwestward in a crude funnel pattern, were missed by the midmonth rains and received less than 3 inches, with several counties receiving less than 2 inches. Station totals ranged from 11.07 inches at Slippery Rock to only 1.00 inch at Everett 1 SW. The greatest daily rainfall was 3.89 inches, measured at East Brady on the 24th.

WEATHER DETAILS

The leading edge of a cool Canadian air mass began moving eastward across the State on the 1st, causing generous showers along the frontal zone. Temperatures dropped well below seasonable levels on the 2nd and continued cool through the 7th in the west and through the 9th in the east under the influence of further cool air intrusions. Most stations recorded their lowest temperature of the month by the 6th, and daily maxima gradually rose to the high 70's and low 80's by the 7th.

Widespread hailstorms occurred over several eastern counties on the 10th. Hailstones ranged up to 2 inches in diameter and, at Stroudsburg, Monroe County, covered the ground for four hours with depths as much as 2 inches. A period of appreciable warmth began on the 12th and continued through the 17th while air from warm southern regions was circulated northward, resulting in the highest readings of the month during the 13th to 15th. Interaction between the warm moist air and the relatively cool air lying over the State produced numerous showers and thunderstorms with worthwhile amounts of rain generally. The southward passage of a cold front on the 18th produced some additional showers and preceded the arrival of an air mass from the Hudson Bay region of Canada that broke the warm spell and brought the lowest temperatures of the month to a goodly number of eastern stations on the 19th or 20th.

On the 21st the State came under the influence of a complex northeastward moving frontal system that lay to the west and south and sections of Allegheny County reporting widespread damage. Newspaper accounts estimated damage to White Oak's Rainbow Gardens amusement park alone at $150,000. In Westmoreland County flash floods hit Irwin, Scottdale and Delmont.

21st: A late afternoon thunderstorm caused about $5,000 property damage and unknown crop damage in the Mercer area. Lightning fired a barn with loss of $4,000 and caused lesser damages to other buildings. Hailstones up to 1-1/2 inches in diameter damaged crops and wind uprooted trees and felled utility lines.

23rd: Squall line thunderstorms affected the whole State but concentrated their fury on the western half except that flash flood damage at Willow Park, Northampton County was estimated at $20,000. Widespread, though mostly minor damage such as felled trees and power lines did occur in the eastern portion of the State. Two barns were destroyed by lightning in the Camp Run - Zelionople - Harmony areas with building losses of $37,000 plus equipment worth $12,000. High water due to heavy thunderstorm rains claimed the life of a 17-year old youth who was drowned while trying to retrieve floating debris. In Pittsburgh a man was fatally injured when he stepped on a live wire blown down by the storm. Heavy rains caused landslides in the Kittanning area and washed out a bridge. Newspaper accounts estimated heavy damages from flash flooding in western Pennsylvania - probably over a million dollars. Bridges were washed out and low-lying roads flooded. State routes 19 and 108 were closed to traffic. Hundreds of campers, including 175 small girls were stranded at the Salvation Army Camp at Wittenburg and were evacuated by State Police, volunteer firemen and Civil Defense crews. Along the Lake Erie shore 70 m.p.h. winds battered several boats and capsized a few sailboats. Lightning strikes in several localities caused various amounts of property damage, largely due to resulting fires. Six personal injuries were reported.

FLOODS

No main stream flooding was reported. Heavy thundershowers caused brief flash flooding of a damaging nature as described above.

J. E. Stork
Weather Records Processing Center
Chattanooga, Tennessee

TABLE 2

Station		Temperature: Average Maximum	Average Minimum	Average	Departure From Long Term Means	Highest	Date	Lowest	Date	Degree Days	No. of Days Max 90° or Above	Max 32° or Below	Min 32° or Below	Min 0° or Below	Precipitation: Total	Departure From Long Term Means	Greatest Day	Date	Snow, Sleet: Total	Max. Depth on Ground	Date	No. of D[ays] 10 or More	50 or More
ATLANTIC DRAINAGE																							
ALLENTOWN WB AP	R	81.0	58.3	69.7	.1	95	13	49	5+	26	6	0	0	0	4.85	.80	2.70	23	.0	0		4	3
ALLENTOWN GAS CO	AM	81.9	58.3	70.1	.4	95	14+	46	20	24	6	0	0	0	4.81	.92	2.18	24	.0	0		7	3
ALTOONA HORSESHOE CURVE		78.3	54.7	66.5	- .2	92	13	37	10	63	1	0	0	0	2.85	- 1.33	.80	18	.0	0		8	2
ARENDTSVILLE	AM	81.9	58.6	70.3	- .1	97	14	47	5	34	9	0	0	0	2.87	- 1.27	.70	24	.0	0		8	2
ARTEMAS 1 WNW		82.9	55.2	69.1		97	8	36	4	48	6	0	0	0	2.91		1.22	12	.0	0		6	2
BEAVERTOWN		83.1M	57.9M	70.5M		95	13	46	29	31	6	0	0	0	2.48		.72	3	.0	0		7	1
BELLEFONTE 4 S	AM	77.4	55.4	66.4	- 1.8	93	14	43	4	87	2	0	0	0	3.40	- .71	.77	3	.0	0		8	3
BERWICK		83.7	57.7	70.7		95	13+	49	2	18	7	0	0	0	3.38		.73	1	.0	0		8	4
BETHLEHEM LEHIGH UNIV		81.4	60.9	71.2	.6	95	14	48	19	24	6	0	0	0	4.09	.05	1.87	23	.0	0		4	2
BURNT CABINS 2 NE		79.6	54.3	67.0		95	14	45	29	60	4	0	0	0	4.83		1.34	13	.0	0		10	3
CANTON 1 NW	AM	74.9	52.6	63.8		89	14	42	4	108	0	0	0	0	1.62		.48	1	.0	0		6	0
CARLISLE		85.0	61.1	73.1	2.0	98	13	51	2	13	11	0	0	0	3.74	- .31	1.52	18	.0	0		7	2
CHAMBERSBURG 1 ESE		81.9	57.8	69.9	- .3	96	13	46	4	30	5	0	0	0	4.39	.42	2.16	24	.0	0		6	3
CHESTER	AM																						
COATESVILLE 1 SW	AM	81.5	57.9	69.7	- .6	94	14+	42	20	39	6	0	0	0	5.26	1.05	.86	3+	.0	0		9	6
COLUMBIA		85.3	60.6	73.0		99	13	50	5	10	10	0	0	0	3.14		.90	2	.0	0		7	2
DEVAULT 1 W		80.2	57.3	68.8		94	13+	44	20	37	4	0	0	0	3.01		.80	16	.0	0		9	1
DIXON	AM	80.4	51.9	66.2		94	14	39	19	58	5	0	0	0	3.45		1.06	1	.0	0		4	3
DU BOIS 7 E		77.8	53.1	65.5		90	14+	40	2	74	2	0	0	0	4.98	.62	1.20	18	.0	0		8	3
EAGLES MERE	AM	73.6	53.6	63.6		88	15	42	3	109	0	0	0	0	4.90	.39	2.31	24	.0	0		7	2
EMPORIUM 1 E	AM	79.0	50.9M	65.0M	- .9	91	14	37	19	100	3	0	0	0	6.20	1.84	2.19	17	.0	0		10	4
EPHRATA		81.7	58.3	70.0	.0	95	13	49	20	25	5	0	0	0	4.62	.26	1.68	2	.0	0		8	3
EVERETT 1 SW		80.2	53.7	67.0	- .3	94	13	44	3+	62	3	0	0	0	1.00	- 3.63	.30	2	.0	0		6	0
FREELAND		76.2	54.2	65.2	.1	89	14	43	2+	83	0	0	0	0	3.91	- .80	1.20	3	.0	0		10	3
GEORGE SCHOOL		82.6	59.1	70.9	1.4	96	14	47	19	17	5	0	0	0	3.42	- .34	1.42	24	.0	0		5	2
GETTYSBURG	AM	81.9	60.2	71.1	.7	97	14	49	5	36	9	0	0	0	3.89	.13	.91	24	.0	0		9	2
GRATZ 1 N	AM	78.8	56.4	67.6		92	14	49	5	49	3	0	0	0	5.91		2.05	24	.0	0			4
HANOVER	AM	82.3	57.9	70.1	- 1.4	97	14	49	3+	32	7	0	0	0	2.93	- 1.00	.86	24	.0	0		8	2
HARRISBURG WB AP	R	81.5	60.4	71.0	- .1	95	13+	50	5	19	4	0	0	0	2.66	- .98	.69	14	.0	0		9	2
HAWLEY 1 S DAM	AM	77.6	52.2	64.9		90	15+	36	19	89	2	0	0	0	4.03		1.65	3	.0	0		7	2
HOLTWOOD		81.1	63.7	72.4	- .1	97	13	54	5	13	7	0	0	0	4.07	.72	1.45	3	.0	0		6	3
HUNTINGDON	AM	83.4M	55.8M	69.6M	1.0	98	14	39	3	44	9	0	0	0	3.22	- .91	.53	19	.0	0		10	2
JIM THORPE		81.3M	56.5M	68.9M	1.2	95	14	43	20	35	3	0	0	0	6.07	1.68	1.71	24	.0	0		7	6
KEGG		79.0M	54.2M	66.6M		93	13	42	4	65	2	0	0	0	2.48		.78	18	.0	0		7	1
LANCASTER 2 NE PUMP STA		82.8	57.8	70.3	.1	95	13	45	20	25	8	0	0	0	3.79	- .22	1.58	2	.0	0		6	3
LANDISVILLE	AM	81.3	60.3	70.8		95	14	48	20	31	8	0	0	0	3.18		.95	3	.0	0		9	2
LAWRENCEVILLE 2 S	AM	80.8	50.0	65.4	- .9	95	15	36	19	88	7	0	0	0	1.99	- 1.82	.72	1	.0	0		6	1
LEWISTOWN	AM	82.2	57.1	69.7		98	14	48	4	39	7	0	0	0	3.87		1.01	19	.0	0		8	3
LOCK HAVEN		83.1	56.9M	70.0M	.4	98	13	44	4	37	9	0	0	0	2.70	- 1.38	.85	24	.0	0		8	1
MADERA	AM	76.5	49.0	62.8		92	14	39	2+	124	2	0	0	0	5.79		1.26	18	.0	0		12	4
MARCUS HOOK		82.0	64.1	73.1	- 2.0	98	13	54	20	9	7	0	0	0	2.54	- 1.06	.60	10	.0	0		6	1
MARTINSBURG CAA AP		78.8	56.0	67.4		94	14	45	2	60	2	0	0	0	1.67		.40	18	.0	0		6	0
MIDDLETOWN OLMSTED FLD		82.3	61.3	71.8	1.1	97	13+	53	5	15	7	0	0	0	2.93	- .96	.77	14	.0	0		8	1
MONTROSE 1 E	AM	74.8	53.6	64.2	.5	89	15	40	19	96	0	0	0	0	2.95	- 1.04	1.15	1	.0	0		7	2
MORGANTOWN		79.7	55.2	67.5		94	13+	44	1	45	4	0	0	0	5.21		1.22	2	.0	0		10	4
MT GRETNA 2 SE		77.2	56.9	67.1		90	13+	45	20	72	4	0	0	0	4.04		.93	2	.0	0		6	4
MT POCONO 2 N AP		77.4	53.6	65.5	3.7	90	14	42	19	72	1	0	0	0	5.70	.62	2.13	15	.0	0		7	4
MUHLENBURG 1 SE		80.2	53.9	67.1		93	14	44	2+	52	3	0	0	0	4.81		1.88	24	.0	0		7	4
NEWBURG 3 W		83.3	61.8	72.6		97	14	51	7+	10	8	0	0	0	2.41		.77	27	.0	0		6	2
NEWPORT	AM	83.0	57.5	70.3		98	14	49	29+	30	11	0	0	0	4.93	1.32	1.38	24	.0	0		10	2
NORRISTOWN		82.7	62.0	72.4		96	14	51	20	9	6	0	0	0	4.11		1.04	24	.0	0		7	4
PALMERTON		79.2	57.9	68.6	.1	92	14	47	20	35	2	0	0	0	5.09	.85	1.82	23	.0	0		6	4
PHIL DREXEL INST OF TEC		83.7	65.2	74.5		98	13+	55	20	4	10	0	0	0	3.05		1.02	2	.0	0		8	2
PHILADELPHIA WB AP	R	82.0	62.5	72.3	.2	95	13+	51	20	11	6	0	0	0	3.86	- .01	1.02	16	.0	0		7	3
PHILADELPHIA PT BREEZE		82.3	64.8	73.6	.7	96	13+	54	20	8	8	0	0	0	5.41		1.90	16	.0	0		9	4
PHILADELPHIA SHAWMONT		84.7	60.5	72.6	.3	96	13	49	20	7	9	0	0	0	5.09	1.55	1.35	1	.0	0		6	6
PHILADELPHIA CITY	RAM	80.8	64.7	72.8	.2	94	14+	57	9+	7	3	0	0	0	5.45	1.48	1.08	2	.0	0		9	5
PHILIPSBURG CAA AP		75.0	50.5	62.8		89	13+	40	2+	128	0	0	0	0	3.95		1.02	18	.0	0		12	1
PHOENIXVILLE 1 E		85.4	56.5	71.0	- .6	98	13	42	19	21	11	0	0	0	2.34	- 1.53	.80	24	.0	0		5	1
PIMPLE HILL	AM	75.3	55.0	65.2		90	15	43	19+	89	1	0	0	0	5.34		1.48	3	.0	0		10	6
PLEASANT MOUNT 1 W	AM	74.3	50.5	62.4		89	15	36	19	133	0	0	0	0	3.72	- .60	1.25	1	.0	0		6	2
PORT CLINTON	AM	82.0	54.6	68.3	- .9	96	14	42	20	41	7	0	0	0	4.33	- .13	1.37	3	.0	0		9	4
QUAKERTOWN 1 E		81.5	57.6	69.6	1.2	93	14+	42	20	32	5	0	0	0	3.48	- .48	.89	24	.0	0		6	4
READING WB CITY	R	81.9	61.6	71.8	.5	96	13+	52	5+	13	6	0	0	0	6.03	2.27	1.59	2	.0	0		9	5
SCRANTON	AM	78.2	55.5	66.9	- 1.2	93	14+	48	3+	47	3	0	0	0	4.09	.24	1.35	3	.0	0		6	[illegible]
SCRANTON WB AIRPORT		78.3	55.9	67.1	- .7	92	14	45	19	47	3	0	0	0	4.68	.25	1.07	23	.0	0		7	[illegible]
SELINSGROVE CAA AP		80.8	57.1	69.0	- .1	96	13	48	29	34	4	0	0	0	3.10	- .82	.69	23	.0	0		7	[illegible]
SHIPPENSBURG		82.9	58.8	70.9	- .4	96	13+	48	4	25	4	0	0	0	3.60	.04	1.32	24	.0	0		7	[illegible]
STATE COLLEGE		78.9	57.1	68.0	.9	94	13	45	2	50	3	0	0	0	5.15	1.11	1.21	23	.0	0		12	[illegible]
STROUDSBURG		79.5	52.3	65.9	- 1.7	95	14	37	19	71	7	0	0	0	3.98	- .62	1.28	27	.0	0		7	[illegible]
TAMARACK 2 S FIRE TWR	AM	81.3	53.8	67.6	1.6	95	14	39	19	46	5	0	0	0	2.28	- 1.38	.78	1	.0	0		5	[illegible]
TOWANDA		83.1	61.7	72.4		96	14	49	20	11	8	0	0	0	7.33		1.92	1	.0	0		10	[illegible]
UPPER DARBY		75.8	52.4	64.1	- .4	92	15	42	2+	111	2	0	0	0	2.12	- 1.62	.61	1	.0	0		6	[illegible]
WELLSBORO 3 S	AM	82.1	55.9	69.0		96	13	45	5	33	4	0	0	0	3.10		.86	18	.0	0		8	[illegible]
WELLSVILLE																							
WEST CHESTER	AM	83.9	61.7	72.8	3.1	97	14	49	19	9	9	0	0	0	4.81	.55	.91	22	.0	0		8	[illegible]
WILLIAMSPORT WB AP		81.9	58.0	70.0	.8	98	13	47	4	35	9	0	0	0	3.02	- .40	1.19	23	.0	0		6	[illegible]

Station		Temperature: Average Maximum	Average Minimum	Average	Departure From Long Term Means	Highest	Date	Lowest	Date	Degree Days	No. of Days Max. 90° or Above	Max. 32° or Below	Min. 32° or Below	Min. 0° or Below	Precipitation: Total	Departure From Long Term Means	Greatest Day	Date	Snow, Sleet Total	Max. Depth on Ground	Date	No. of Days .10 or More	.50 or More	1.00 or More
K 3 SSW PUMP STA		84.8	58.5	71.7	1.1	97	13+	48	5+	13	9	0	0	0	4.09	.33	.94	14	.0	0		7	5	0
DIVISION				68.9											3.90				.0					
OHIO DRAINAGE																								
ERSTOWN 3 WNW		79.6	58.2	68.9		91	13+	42	2	52	2	0	0	0	5.57		1.82	18	.0	0		6	3	3
IRSVILLE 6 ENE		75.3	55.5	65.4		88	14	39	2	77	0	0	0	0	6.20	.44	1.19	24	.0	0		10	5	2
DFORD 4 W RES		75.7	49.4	62.6	- 2.3	89	14	37	8	121	0	0	0	0	3.76	- .85	.98	17	.0	0		7	3	0
OKVILLE CAA AIRPORT		76.3	52.7	64.5	.4	90	13+	42	6	94	2	0	0	0	3.25	- 1.03	1.05	24	.0	0		8	2	1
GETTSTOWN 2 W	AM	79.1	53.4	66.3		93	15	38	6	79	2	0	0	0	5.45		1.21	25	.0	0		8	6	1
LER		82.0	57.0M	69.5M	.9	94	15	44	2	38	4	0	0	0	6.99	2.66	1.34	13	.0	0		10	2	2
RION 3 SW		78.8	53.8	66.3		92	14	42	6	65	2	0	0	0	4.20	- .50	1.00	25	.0	0		9	3	1
YSVILLE 3 W		81.4	53.8	67.6	- 1.5	98	14+	40	11	65	5	0	0	0	6.55	2.05	1.51	14	.0	0		9	5	2
FLUENCE 1 SW DAM	AM	78.0	54.0	66.0		92	15	40	4	73	2	0	0	0	4.37		.81	19	.0	0		10	4	0
RY		78.3	52.7	65.5	.0	92	14	40	6+	87	3	0	0	0	2.41	- 2.40	.80	24	.0	0		7	1	0
DERSPORT 3 NW		74.9	48.7	61.8		89	13	30	19	132	0	0	1	0	3.25		1.38	25	.0	0		6	3	1
RY				M							3	0	0	0	5.39	1.38			.0	0				
EGAL		74.0	48.5	61.3		87	14	36	4	143	0	0	0	0	3.78		.69	24	.0	0		7	4	0
ORA	AM	83.1	60.1	71.6	- .4	95	15	47	2+	33	5	0	0	0	5.13	1.10	1.03	19	.0	0		9	6	1
T BRADY		82.8	55.5	69.2		94	13+	32	2	46	4	0	1	0	9.89		3.89	24	.0	0		8	3	2
NSBURG		74.8	52.1	63.5	- 1.4	87	14	40	2	96	0	0	0	0	4.77	- .07	.98	1	.0	0		9	4	0
RELL SHARON		81.0	53.3	67.2	- 2.6	95	14	37	19	75	4	0	0	0	4.77	1.21	1.99	24	.0	0		9	1	1
D CITY 4 S DAM	AM	78.2	54.1	66.2		92	14	41	2	71	2	0	0	0	6.11		2.95	24	.0	0		9	4	1
NKLIN		79.0	55.0	67.0	.7	90	13+	40	4	59	3	0	0	0	5.17	.87	1.05	1+	.0	0		13	3	2
ENVILLE		80.2	54.2	67.2	- .1	93	14	41	6	62	3	0	0	0	6.39	2.39	1.76	22	.0	0		9	4	3
IANA 3 SE		78.9	54.1	66.5	- 1.5	91	13+	41	4	61	2	0	0	0	5.59	.68	.91	18	.0	0		12	5	0
IN		82.4	57.5	70.0	1.4	93	15	40	4	36	3	0	0	0	4.07	- .38	.76	24	.0	0		9	4	0
ESTOWN 2 NW	AM	76.5	53.9	65.2		90	15	40	6	100	1	0	0	0	6.64	2.98	1.00	23	.0	0		12	6	1
NSTOWN	AM	82.3	55.6	69.0	- .4	96	15	44	4	52	8	0	0	0	3.99	- 1.04	.80	25	.0	0		10	2	0
E 1 NNE	AM	75.6	49.2	62.4		89	14+	36	19	141	0	0	0	0	6.08	1.43	1.67	16	.0	0		9	4	2
ESVILLE 5 WNW		77.2	53.7	65.5		89	13+	39	6	84	0	0	0	0	6.40	2.62	1.20	24	.0	0		14	4	2
DVILLE 1 S	AM	76.3	54.0	65.2	- .6	90	14+	42	6	97	2	0	0	0	6.51	2.40	2.32	17	.0	0		12	3	1
CER 2 NNE		78.4	51.2	64.8		89	13	38	6	77	0	0	0	0	6.09		1.05	23	.0	0		12	4	2
LAND DAM 7		79.5	59.8	69.7	- .3	90	13+	48	1+	47	2	0	0	0	4.23	.23	1.09	25	.0	0		8	4	1
CASTLE 1 N		80.5	56.2	68.4	- .6	91	13+	43	6	43	2	0	0	0	7.15	3.00	1.08	24	.0	0		14	8	1
ELL	AM	81.6	60.2	70.9	1.3	94	14	48	2+	31	5	0	0	0	5.37	1.25	1.42	18	.0	0				
STANTON		80.9	52.9	66.9	- 1.8	94	14	43	4	61	5	0	0	0	3.79	- .68	.84	16	.0	0		9	2	0
TSBURGH WB AP 2	//R	77.7	57.7	67.7	- .9	91	13+	43	2	66	2	0	0	0	4.19	.12	.95	24	.0	0		9	4	0
TSBURGH WB CITY	R	80.2	60.6	70.4	- 1.3	94	13+	46	2+	44	3	0	0	0	4.13	.30	1.19	16	.0	0		9	3	1
NEYVILLE 2 SE DAM	AM	79.3	51.5	65.4		98	16	40	2	84	3	0	0	0	6.68		1.47	23	.0	0		11	4	3
GWAY 3 W	AM	77.6	49.5	63.6	- .9	90	13+	40	6+	96	2	0	0	0	4.95	.71	.87	1	.0	0		11	4	0
INA 3 W		79.3	56.2	67.8		91	14	42	2	47	2	0	0	0	4.22		1.33	16	.0	0		8	3	1
PINGPORT WB		77.9	56.1	67.0		91	13+	43	2	67	2	0	0	0	3.34		1.23	24	.0	0		7	2	1
PERY ROCK		78.0	56.6	67.3		93	14	42	2	64	1	0	0	0	11.07		1.90	23	.0	0		12	7	7
ERSET MAIN ST		77.6	52.9	65.3	.1	90	13	42	2+	73	1	0	0	0	3.77	- 1.26	.71	18	.0	0		8	3	0
INGS 1 SW		74.9	51.0	63.0	- .7	86	14	40	4+	105	0	0	0	0	3.99	- 1.31	.72	2	.0	0		11	4	0
IESTA 2 SE DAM	AM	77.6	53.4	65.5		95	16	43	2	84	3	0	0	0	3.13	- 1.14	.82	25	.0	0		9	2	0
JSVILLE WATER WORKS		79.2	51.7	65.5		93	14+	40	6+	78	3	0	0	0	6.49		1.44	16	.0	0		13	4	3
NTOWN		79.3	58.5	68.9	- 1.4	92	13	40	29	51	2	0	0	0	5.51	.66	.76	17	.0	0		12	4	0
REN		78.7	54.0	66.4	.9	93	14	43	6+	70	3	0	0	0	5.42	.97	1.62	18	.0	0		9	5	2
IESBURG 2 W		80.2	55.5	67.9	- 2.0	92	13	44	4	52	2	0	0	0	4.78	.45	1.01	25	.0	0		10	3	1
DIVISION				66.5											5.24				.0					
LAKE DRAINAGE																								
CAA AIRPORT		74.6	56.5	65.6	.1	88	13	44	2+	96	0	0	0	0	1.58	- 1.29	.46	24	.0	0		5	0	0
NGBORO		76.4	54.9	65.7		90	14	43	6	97	1	0	0	0	6.27		1.45	1	.0	0		9	4	4
DIVISION				65.7											3.93				.0					

See Reference Notes Following Station Index

DAILY PRECIPITATION

Table 3

Station	Total	1	2	3	4	5	6	7	8	9	10	11	12	13	14	15	16	17	18	19	20	21	22	23	24	25	26	27	28	29
ACMETONIA LOCK 3	3.96	.47		.40	.02					T								.46	.07	.60		.19			.27	1.22		.17	.01	
ALLENTOWN WB AP R	4.85	.02	1.02	.07						.06	T			T		T	T	T	T			.30		2.70	.05			.63	T	
ALLENTOWN GAS CO	4.81	.14	.06	.98							.02	.12		T			.02	T	.03	.06		T	.33		2.16	.05		.62	.22	
ALTOONA HORSESHOE CURVE	2.89	.21	.22	.05						.03					.08	.14	.04		.80			.26			.17	.24		.51		
ARENDTSVILLE	2.87	.51	.30	.44							.03		T		.23	.01	.03	.05	.14	.25		.03	.04		.70			.10	.01	
ARTEMAS 1 WNW	2.91	.34	.50							.25		.30	1.22								.30									
AUSTINBURG 2 W	1.67	.66	T	.21	.03	.09				.12				T		.10	T	.08	.03						.09	.18		.16	T	
BAKERSTOWN 3 WNW	5.57	.28	.07	.43	.01					.02							1.16	.01	1.82	.31				.05	1.41					
BARNES	6.09	.91		.06	.21	.06				.06						.18	2.60	.12	.31	.04		.34	.06	.07	.03	.79		.06	.17	
BEAR GAP	4.94	.78	.46	.35								.37										.35		.12	.90	.38		1.25		
BEAVER FALLS	6.11	1.02		.52	.13	.02				.03							T	.85	.08	1.43			.10	.07	.94	.70		.24	T	
BEAVERTOWN	2.48	.26	.06	.72											.06	.02			.17	.11		.26	.03		.46			.28	.03	
BEECH CREEK STATION	3.22	.14	.12	.42	.05											.26		T	.29	.13		.21	.29		.23	.27		.63	.22	
BELLEFONTE 4 S	3.40	.26	.10	.77						T	.02					.08	.02		.73	.10		.15			.67	.05		.47		
BERWICK	3.38	.73	.67	.09							.10							.12	.03			.33		.12	.54			.65		
BETHLEHEM	4.26	.07	.03	1.29	T						.07	T					.01	T	T	T		T	.37		1.94	.02		.43	.09	
BETHLEHEM LEHIGH UNIV	4.09	.02	1.04	.07						.09	.01			T			T	.02	T			.37		1.87	.03			.48	.09	
BLAIRSVILLE 6 ENE	6.20	.71	.41	.27	.04					.06				1.03			.42		.56			.28		.01	1.10	.44	T	.78		
BLOSERVILLE 1 N	4.21	.50	.55												.05		T		.80			.35			.60			1.36	T	
BOSWELL 6 WNW	3.08	.25	T	.32												T	T	.35	.08	.73		.03	.13	.03	.14	.32		.56	.16	T
BRADDOCK LOCK 2	8.48	.38	T	.40	.05	T				T					1.66	1.47		1.48	.99	.58		.17			.33	.74		.22	.02	
BRADFORD CNTRL FIRE STA	3.29	.42	.01	.45	.16	.02				.02								.70	.52			.02	.02		.02	.72		.15	T	.02
BRADFORD 4 W RES	3.76	.76		.50	.10	.08				.05							.45	.98	T			.06	T			.47		.18		.05
BREEZEWOOD	2.65	.42	.16							.07						.04	.06	T	.60			.06	.16	.24			.58	.22	.04	
BROOKVILLE CAA AIRPORT	3.25	.04	.10	.05	.11				T						T	T	T	.37	.40			T	.22	.37	1.05		.01	.51	.04	
BRUCETON 1 S	5.75	.32		•	.56											.84			1.80	.53						1.22		.33	.05	
BUFFALO MILLS	3.50	.33	.16	.47												.03	.57	.01		1.34					.06	.21		.29	.11	
BURGETTSTOWN 2 W	5.45	.57		.60	.08					.05						.26		.89	.64	.71			.01		.89	1.21		.34		
BURNT CABINS 2 NE	4.83	.29	.27	T										1.34			.19	1.00	.31			.05	.38	T	.12		.11	.77	T	
BUTLER	6.90	1.15		.08	.33													.38	.12	.32			.08	1.49	2.01	.84		.11	.12	
CAMP HILL	2.40	.15	.46	.63															.24			.36			.27			.30	T	
CANTON 1 NW	1.62	.48	T	.31						.04				.08		.14		.02					.03		.20	.03		.16	.13	
CARLISLE	3.74	.92	.28	.30		T	.10			T					T	T			1.92			.05		T	.38			.18	.01	
CARROLLTOWN 2 SSE	5.35	.51	.02	.34	.01					.02	T				T	.25	.56	.02	.25	.22		.48	.02	.10	1.17	.61		.71	.09	
CARTER CAMP 2 W	3.39	.83	T	.30	T											.41	.08	.18					.05		.22	.52		.73	.07	
CEDAR RUN	5.23	1.40	.05	.35	T						.05	T				.15		1.64					.02		.60	.30		.67		T
CHADDS FORD	4.11	2.50	.15	.40							T	.16					.30	T	T			T	T	.10	T	.46	T			
CHAMBERSBURG 1 ESE	4.30	.53	.27	.02										T			.39	T	.88			.03	.11		2.16			.04	T	
CHARLEROI LOCK 4	4.32	.19		.47	T					T					.16	.01		.69	.44	.36					.28	1.14		.54	.02	
CHESTER		RECORD MISSING																												
CLARENCE 1 E	5.63	.62	.10	.60	T	T					.11				.04	.19	.09	T	.38	.74		.20	.23	.53		1.14		.38	.31	
CLARION 3 SW	4.20	.56		.35	.01	.14				.04	.04							.29	.23	.03			.08	.13	.90	1.00		.39	.03	
CLAUSSVILLE	4.62	.42	.27	1.17							.01	.06					.07		.25	.02			.45		.83	.04		.73	.34	
CLAYSVILLE 3 W	6.59	.11		.45	.05					T				.05	1.51			.48	.72	.56		T			.82	1.35	T	.45	T	
CLEARFIELD	6.03	.48	T	.12	.02						1.90					.29	.23	.08	.98	.05		.18	T		.62	.46		.60	.32	
CLERMONT	4.45	.80		.96	.15	.05					.56			T	T	.20	.18	.20	.12			.05	.07		.07	.95		.36	.16	
COALDALE 2 NW	4.43	.77	.03	1.29							.08	.18						.46				.06	.34		.28			.88	.06	
COATESVILLE 1 SW	5.26	.81	.14	.86	T						.04	.70						.11	.86	.06		.12	.09	.82	.69		T	T		
COLUMBIA	3.14	.89	.90	.11								T							.17			.20			.40	.09		.38		
CONFLUENCE 1 SW DAM	4.37	.51	T	.77	T		T					.16				.03		.17	.23	.81		.07	.01	.05	.25	.80		.34	.17	
CONFLUENCE 1 NW	4.76	.51	T	.75	T		T					T				.17		.37	.24	.44		.04	.05	.22	.46	.98		.40	.13	
CONNELLSVILLE	5.15	.55		.71														.90	.20	.45		.05	.06	.07	.71	.73		.67	.05	
CONSHOHOCKEN	4.74	1.00	.20	.92								.90					.62	T		T		.09	.03	T	.90	T		T	.05	.03
COOKSBURG	4.60	.71	T	.16	.04	.11	T			.03							.95	T	.60	.12	T	.08	T		.81	.78	T	.30	T	
COOKSBURG 2 NNW	5.33	1.00	T	.13	.05	.11	T			.03							1.01	.03	1.23	.27	T	.09	T		.58	.70	T	.10	T	
CORAOPOLIS NEVILLE IS	4.35	.59		•	.54											.06		1.16				.73				1.09		.14		
CORRY	2.41	.18		.37	.10	.03			.10	.07							.10	.05	.07			.46			.80			.06		
COUDERSPORT 3 NW	3.25	.50		.61	.07					T						.15		.04					.05		.30	1.38		.15		
COUDERSPORT 7 E	5.18	.49	.01	.28	.10	.05				.02	.22					1.01	.01	.30					.06		1.73	.68		.22		T
COVINGTON	2.06	.62	.04	.43										.12		T	T	T							.38	.25		.24		
CREEKSIDE	7.03	.58		.25	.02	.03				.11						.68	.05	.20	2.05	.32		.20	.05	.22	1.37	.83		.30		
CRESSON 2 SE	5.90	.29	.08	.35	.03					.05	.03					2.79	.12	.02	.11	.27		.57		.04	.05	.40		.61	.06	
CUSTER CITY 2 W	4.19	1.10		.35	.26	.09				.01								1.23	.46						.05	.47		.13	.01	
DANVILLE	6.47	1.00	.07	.60								.34						.38					.50	1.88	.48			.86	.36	
DERRY	3.39	.45	.32	.32													1.48		•			•			•	•		•	2.04	
DEVAULT 1 W	3.01	.16	.45	.23							.46	.02					.80	.04	.33			.13	.12	.02				.23	T	
DIXON	3.45	1.06	.04	.89						T	.07	T				.06		T				T	.03		1.04			.30		T
DONEGAL	3.78	.31	.61	T					T					T			.36	.09	.48			T		.38	.69	T	.61	.06	T	
DONORA	5.13	.24	T	.52	T					T				T	T	T	.41	.14	.53	1.03		T	T		.51	.81		.91	.03	
DOYLESTOWN	3.73	.27	.70	.58						.16	T	.04					.04		.12			.45			1.06			.22	T	
DU BOIS 7 E	4.98	.88	T	.19		.02				T	.08					.41	.45	.06	1.20						.78	.47		.46		
DUSHORE 3 NE	5.91	1.00	.12	.55	T									T		2.50							T		1.66			.08		
EAGLES MERE	4.90	.93	.07	.33						T	.02	T		.04		.16	.09	.32				.04	.15		2.31	.87		.31		.06
EAST BRADY	9.89	.83		.26	.04												3.69	.06	.29				.26		3.89	.28		.01	.18	
EBENSBURG	4.77	.98		.39	T					.05	T	.06				.38	.33	T	.30	.24		.56	T	T	.07	.58		.78	.09	
EDINBORO	6.01	.98	.02	.20	.36	.03	.01			.20							2.04	.39	.19			.31	.53		.01	.67		.07	.08	
ELIZABETHTOWN	3.10	.19	.10	.76							.02									.11		.02	.14		1.01	.07		.25	.43	
EMPORIUM 1 E	6.20	.45		.71	.04	.03					.45					.70	.04	2.15	.03	.02		.11	.07	.19	.15	.41		.52	.04	T
ENGLISH CENTER	4.00	.73	.02	.41	.01										.02	.01		1.33	.24				.09		.42	.27		.41	.04	
EPHRATA	4.62	.18	1.68	.09						.04		.70						.23	.07			.44		.29	.79	.15				
EQUINUNK	4.82	.78	.02	1.43	.02						.48			.10				T					.28		1.42			.29		
ERIE CAA AIRPORT	1.98	T	T	.24	.13	T			.06						.15	T	T	T	.04			.43		T	.46		T	.07		
EVERETT 1 SW	1.00	.10	.36													.05			.10					T	.10		.25	.10		
FARRELL SHARON	4.77	.16		.45	.09	.04									.24	.08	.30	.26	.46			.44	.05		1.99	.02	.10	.07	.02	
FORD CITY 4 S DAM	6.11	.60		.33	.01													.24	.26	.30			.01	.50	2.95	.71		.20	T	
FRANKLIN	5.17	1.05	T	.47	.03	.19				.12							.02	.81	.20	.12		.15	.12	.20	.21	1.05		.36	.07	
FREELAND	3.91	.27	.10	1.20							.10						.20						.42	.20	.60		.12	.70		
GALETON	3.50	.40		.21	T	T				T	T	.02		T		.60	.32	.02					.07		.76	.51		.56	.12	
GEIGERTOWN	5.11	.34	.41	1.11								.84						.48	.46	.08			.36	.39	.30	.13		.04	.17	
GEORGE SCHOOL	3.42	.03	1.07	.37						T	.03						.04	.03	.10			.33			1.42					
GETTYSBURG	3.89	.35	.21	.72	T							.02			.07	.05	.43	.06	.49	.28		.01	.12		.91			.17		
GLEN HAZEL 2 NE DAM	5.88	1.16		.60	.04	.10				.03	.10			T		.03	1.48	.41	.17	T		.13	.01	.39	.18	.98		.42	.03	.01
GLENWILLARD DASH DAM	5.33	.59		.63	.03	T				.02							.01	.30	.11	.49			.02		1.57	1.31		.11		
GOULDSBORO	2.18	.18	.06	.35														.08	.08				.57		.36			.46	.08	
GRANTVILLE 2 SW	4.29	.20	.67	.20						T		.29		.03		.54		T	.10			1.36			.27	.26		.37		
GRATERFORD	2.68	.36	.27	.33							.02	.80										.30			.20	.01			.39	
GRATZ 1 N	5.91	•	.12	.77	T		T									.06			.05	.08		.19	.19	1.37	2.09	T		.60	.40	
GREENSBORO LOCK 7	6.32	.99	.01	.56	T										.27			.10	.84	1.45		.01			.38	1.13		.28	.29	.01
GREENSBURG 3 SE	4.45	.76	.34	.23						.02							.28		1.37			.13			.23	.58		.36	.15	
GREENVILLE	6.39		.01	.42	.17	.05			T	.02					.01	T	.40		1.22			.95	1.76		1.00	.06		.19	.13	
HANOVER	2.93	.44	.13	.67											.25		.02	T	.02	.15		.02	.16		.86			.23		
HARRISBURG WB AP R	2.66	.24	.54	.09		T				T	T			.04	.69		T	.01	.20		T	.19		.33	.10		.11	.12	T	
HARRISBURG NORTH	4.39	.41	.14	.59	T						T					.31			.22	.01		.68	.18		1.59	.07		.31		
HAWLEY	3.75	.35	T	1.77							.02	.27		.03				T					.16		.50			.33	.32	T
HAWLEY 1 S DAM	4.03	.38		1.05							.03	.30											.22		.60			.32	.33	
HOLLISTERVILLE	5.27	.47	.01	1.31			T			T	.02	.88		.04		T		.03	T				.68		1.30			.41	.03	T
HOLTWOOD	4.07	.45	.09	1.45							.03	.63			T		T		T	.21		.04	.17		1.00				T	
HONESDALE 4 NW	3.92	.87	.02	1.34	T					T	.01	.60			.02			.29					.22		.13			.38		
HOOVERSVILLE	4.47	.43	.03	.42	.02					.02					.01	T	.08	.04	.07	1.43		.05		.01	.33	.63		.71	.10	
HOP BOTTOM 2 SE	3.04	.15	.91	.92								.15				T							.15		.40			.07	.15	.05
HUNTINGDON	3.22	.15	.16	.35			.01				T				.42	.04	T	T	.55	.52	T	.23	.07		.33	.05		.21	.15	
HUNTSDALE	3.08	.66	.10	.63			T											T	.12	.43			.06	.03	.47	T		.07	.36	.06
HYNDMAN	3.60	.30	.04	.45							.48					.06	.23	.04	.02	.98			.13	T	.16	.23		.54	.03	
INDIANA 3 SE	3.59	.48	T	.29	.02					.06						.04	.26	.11	.91	.37		.07	.01	.62	.68	.67		.26	.12	
IRWIN	4.07	.22		.39						.01				.12		.02	.22	.03	.74	.02				.24	.76	.73		.52	.05	
JAMESTOWN 2 NW	6.64	.66		.34	.24	.03									.87		.10	.51	.96	.05		.40	.08	1.06	.47	.70		.21	.02	
JIM THORPE	6.07	.51	1.20	.58						.68	T	T						.55				.35			1.71			1.09		
JOHNSTOWN	3.99	.38	.01	.29						.02							.28	.04	.47	.44	T	.54	T	.12	.10	.80		.46	.04	T
KANE 1 NNE	6.08	1.47		.43	.15	.05				.02	.01					T	1.67	.51	.33	T		.34		.05	.06	.63	T	.29	.07	
KARTHAUS	5.42	.64	.03	.67	.02	T					.04					.74	.17	T	.62	.38		.03	T	.14	.76	.21		.80	.17	

See Reference Notes Following Station Index

DAILY PRECIPITATION

PENNSYLVANIA
JUNE 1956

Total	1	2	3	4	5	6	7	8	9	10	11	12	13	14	15	16	17	18	19	20	21	22	23	24	25	26	27	28	29	30	31
3.90	.80	T	.30	.14	.08					.08					.36	.30	2.10	T				.17		.06	.88		.20	.06			
2.48	.24	.37												.35	.22	T	.01	.76					.09			.23	.23				
8.09	1.14		.35	.02					T						.29	.09	.29	1.07	.01				1.81	2.90	.85		.21				
3.90	.42	.09	.15						T							.39	.18	.53			.03	T	.32	.22	.05	.84	.39	.07			
4.06	.84	.05	1.62							.05							.18	.26				.30		1.16			.68	.14			
2.95	.21	.02	1.30				.05		.02	.03	.23	.02	.02									.21		.19			.41	.24			
3.79	.90	1.58	.08						.03		.59							.06			.19			.25			.19				
3.18	.50	.11	.05							.11	.42								.02		.11	.07		.37	.06		.10	.36			
	RECORD MISSING																														
1.99	.72	.02	.27	.02					T						.15	.05	.26							.27	.23						
4.44	.82	.07	1.56						T	.05	T					T	T	T				.15		1.30	T		.49	T			
2.29	.68	.09	.30						.10							.12					.03			.36			.61				
4.66	.74		.78	.12	.05				.01							.23	1.60	.09	T		T	.04		.19	.52		.24	.05	T		
3.87	.13	.11	.69							T					T	T	T	.07	1.01		.41	.20		.90			.28	.07			
6.40	.71	T	.27	.36	.05				.07					.10	1.16	.11	.40	.25			.71	.22		1.20	.36		.14	.18			
2.70	.15	.12	.38	.01					T		T				.10		.02	T	.09		T	.19	.05	.85	.28		.41	.07			
4.17	.47	.03	1.30							.03	.25						.18					.30		.29			.39	.05			
5.70	.42	.04	.18						.04	.02					.65	.17	.16	1.26	.38		.19		.11	1.19	.36		.02				
6.88	.33	.01	.11	.13					.03					.07	.29	.02	.24	1.04	.69		.71		.40	.70	1.38		.50	.17			
4.22	.42	.74	.64								.15					.05	T				.52			1.63			.03	.04			
2.52	.09	.13	.41								T			.14	.23		.08	.34	.35		.15	.05		.38	.05		.12	T	T		
2.54	.07	.40	.01						.02	.60						.19	T	.03		.04	.25	T		.46			.47	T			
5.29	.45		.25	.04	.01				.03						.15	.01	.18	.64	.18		.13	.04	.09	2.09	.64		.36				
1.67	.27	.52	T						T						T	.01	.02	.40			.20	.01		.14		.01	.29	T			
2.75	.00		.89								.14						.51					.33		.57			.35	.07			
5.07	*		*	*	1.08		.08		.08						T	.09	1.48	.88	.07		.32	.05		.13	.73		.08	.03	T		
3.19	.32	.15	.27						T	.04	.02			.39	T			.11	.77			.10	.08	.19	T		.73	.02			
—	-	-	*	.43					T					.68	2.22		*	2.41	.49		.02			.39	.83		.21	.02			
6.51	.48	T	.33	.18	.05				.24					T		.08	2.32	.10	.01		.47	.64	T	.63	.49		.38	.11	T		
4.94	1.15		.30	.01	T					.08			T		.40	.88	.09	.84	.03	T	.01	.04	.04	.84	.43		.42	T			
6.09	.82		.48	.10	.07							.05		.25			.35	.23			.28	1.00	1.03	.44	.72		.29				
1.63	.25	.12	.34						.02									.30	.33			.01	.16			.10					
5.30	.34	.03	.66	.04		.03											.84	.06	1.15						1.60		.45	.10			
2.93	.23	.47	.17		T				T	T			.01	.77		T	.02	.16		.02	.30		.33	T		.05	.40	T			
4.23	.75		.51	.05	T				.13							.31	.10	.71	.05			.05		.40	1.09		.08				
5.45	1.78		1.86							T	.23		.15									.63		.45			.34	.01			
3.63	.13	.14	.65	.07					T	.03					.48			.37	.30		.25	.06	.01	.85	.04		.28				
3.93	.12	.06	.46						T		.14		T		.37				T		T	.77		1.28	T		.20	.27			
4.73	.10		.56						.08	.02					.20	T	T	1.05	.06		.37	.03		2.14	T		.15				
2.95	1.15	.04	.61			T			T	T	.39		T	T	.14			T				.24		.27			.19	.01	T		
5.21	.21	1.22	.16						.03	.07						.20	1.14	.13			.27	.70	.03	.89			.16				
4.04	.05	.95	.01						.07	.43				T				.05		.03	.90	.15	.53	.01			.90				
5.70	.18	.89	.99						.01	T						2.13					.38			.43			.69				
4.81	.20	.77	.14							T			T	T	T						.67		.33	1.88			.82				
4.26		.27	1.49							T	.48		T		.29			.06			.26	.02	.20	.13			.35				
5.44	.74		.37	.01	.01											1.41	.80		.32		.30			.73	.73		.02				
3.18	.39	1.10	.42							.02						.08	.04			T	.27		.20	.63				.07			
2.41	.43	.21															.03	.14			.23		.57	.03			.77				
7.15	.68	.01	.41	.10	.07				T					.17		.47	.54	.21	.78		.55	T	.59	1.08	.77		.50	.22			
5.37	.28		.17	.40										.33				1.42	.97					*	1.29		.51				
3.43	.61	1.36	.10						.05							T		.40			.26			.55							
4.93	.33	.15	.48	T						.22	.03				.08			.16	.35		.35	.12		1.36	T		1.28				
3.70	.27	.45	.04						.01							.64	.27	.38			.10		.27	.61	.01	.45	.02	.07			
4.60	.22	1.25	.19						.03		.26				.13	.29	.52	.02			.35			.56	.03		.82				
4.11	.62	.14	.90								.55					.42	.04		.01		.07	.09	T	1.04	.01		.02	.19	.01		
1.59	.63	.03	.11	.18	.02	T			.09							.03	T	T			.19			T	.31		T		T		
2.70	.46	.12	.57						.12				.04								.11			.87			.23	.06	.02		
2.57	.03	.10	.40								.38					.32					.04	.48		.20			.48	.15	.05		
5.09	.10	1.41	.05						.09	T						T	.67				.21		1.82	.01			.73				
5.82	.06		.43	.05	.07				.24								.01	.77	.13		.03	.00	.82	.59	.67		.06	.03			
4.19	.40	.03	1.31							.03	.47		.10									.87		.84			.34				
4.35	.20	.03	2.57							T	.15		.11				T					.56		.25			.45	.03			
3.05	.10	1.02	T						T	.65						.10		.05		T	.06	.32	T	.48			.15	.12			
3.86	.06	.98	T						T	.83						1.02	T	.07		.01	.18	.14	.22	.30			.05	T			
5.41	.08	.83							T	.28					.20	1.90	.66	.01			.27	.29		.90			.02	.01			
5.09	1.35	.55	.54								.77					.70	.05	.03			.07	T	T	.88				.04	.09		
5.45	.09	1.08							T	.96						1.01	.55	T		T	.04	.28	.20	.80			.16	.26			
3.95	.28	.15	.38						.01					.41		.24	.14	1.02			.24		.46	.22	T	.21	.19	T			
2.34	.09	.46	.05							.48						.01					.38	.03	.12	.80							
6.99	.82	.07	.81	.01						T	.01				.42	2.03	.01				.01	.52		1.37	.09		.85	.17			
5.34	.69	.15	1.48						T	.05	.76						.11	T			.17	.15		.63			.62	.53	T		
5.85	.51	.03	.89							.05	.88				.02				.21		.62	.15	1.40	.65	.10		.30	.04			
4.19	.02	.51	.20	T				.01						.01		.62	.84	.28			T		.43	.95	.18	.10	.04			T	
4.13	.06	.37	.09	T				.02						.16		1.19	.15	.66			.03		.41	.53	.21	.21	.04				
3.72	1.25	T	1.09	T		T			T	T	.33		.05								T	.24		.46			.26	.01	.03		
4.33	.50	.10	1.37							.07	.25				.02		.02	.05			.30	.24		.60	.20		.58	.03			
4.14	.06	.07	1.10							.02	.94					.45		.02			.02	.48		.74			.02	.22			
5.31	.56	.09	1.08							.07	.03						.17				.18	.24	1.44	.53	.06		.50	.36			
6.68	1.05		.25	.05					.04						.09	.29	1.40	.34	.10			.01	1.47	.51	.48		.46	.14			
3.48	.50	.55	.60								.05					.01	T	T			.42			.89	T		.45	.01			
4.34	.84		.38	.02	.01										.35	.08	.19					.15		1.62	.58		.08	.04			
8.03	.04	1.90	.08						T	1.02	.01			.02		.24	1.13	.06			.59	.20	.70	.02			.33				
4.16	.04	.03	.82	.03					.03	.96				.02	.17		.11		.05			.10	T	.48	.33		.39				
3.53	.77		.21	.50	.04				.01							.01	1.10	.07			.02	.01		.03	.41		.24	.02	T		
4.64	.43	.01	.53											.03			.20	.47	.53					.98	1.02		.43	.01			
4.95	.87		.01	.23	.10				.02	.14						.86	.28	.49	T			.34		.28	.68		.65				
2.37	.87	.06	.52						.03		.64											.11		.56			.12	.05	.01		
3.10	1.30	.06	.61							.01				T										.13	.83			.10	.06		
5.04	.62		.50	.12											T	T	.30	1.10	.20	.10			.30	1.78	.62						
4.22	.21	.03	.35	T					.01	T			T		.04	1.33	.52	.31			.04		.02	.45	.38	.02	.33				
2.10	.12	.10	.31	T		T			.01	.02				.31		.02		.16	.41		T	.02		.08	.12		.36	.06	T		
4.11	.52		.39	.03					.02								.53	.41	T				.03	1.18	.89		.11				
4.09	.96	.03	1.35	.02						.03	T				.17		T					.42		.42			.60	.09			
4.68	.01	1.05	.12	T	T				.06	.18		.04					.01				.86		1.07	.01			.67				
3.10	.30	.42	.31						.01	.06								.02			.45	.28	.69	T			.56				
4.74	.68	.10	.83			.05					1.14								T		.21	.14		*	.86		.73				
3.60	.79	.30	.03						T					T	.10	T		.54	T		.24	.08		1.32	T		.24	T			
3.34	.01	.36	.15	.03				.12								.37	.50	.09			.06		.33	1.23		.03	.06				
5.92	.52	.02	.72	.01	T	T			T	.28			T	.06	1.12	1.13	.11	.46	.02		T	.11	.02	.36	.32		.46	T	T		
11.07	1.03		.40	.11	.10				.06								1.08	.39	.46			1.13	1.90	1.38	1.20		1.67	.07			
3.55	.39		.55								.11				.17	T	.10	.10	.37			.02	.02	.21	.65		.62	.04			
3.77	.40	.30	.30								.09			T	T	.29	.00	.71			T	.06		.24	.64		.64	.03			
3.71	.35	.20	.48														.33	.26	.80			.35	.18	.72				.06			
6.27	1.45	T	1.25	.20	T	T		T								T	.15	1.25			.40			.10	.37		1.10	T			
2.96	.49	.62	.15											.07		.08		.80	T		.12			.53			.10				
3.99	.39	.72	.10		T											.05		.67			.13	.21	.34	.13	.50	.20	.34	.01			
5.18	.26	.20	.45	T					T					.16	.10	.53	.32	1.10			.21	T	1.21	.05		.37	.19				
4.97	.07	.05	1.14							.06	.29				.03			.03	.15		.40	.24	.97	.78	.17		.50	.14			
3.98	.02	1.20	.36	T	T				.03	.58						T	T	T			.19		.20	.12			1.28	T			
6.31	.64		.07						.03						.19	.29	.75	2.09	.57				.02	.79	.82		.20	.19			
2.77	.29	.07	.46	T						T	.05								.02		.21	.27	.03	.78	.04		.55				
3.50	1.50	.04	.76						.02		.17		.11			.01						.45		.34			.08		.02		
4.05	.22	*	*	.60										.03	.03			.88	.48						1.05		.77	.02			
5.14	.90	.55	1.00							.15	.73						.19				.05	.34		.28			.81	.14			
3.21	.37	.03	1.24							.01	.30										.01	.48		.26			.51				
	RECORD MISSING																														
3.13	.80	T	.25	.03	.10				.10						T	.22	.19	.04	.02		.30	T		.18	.82		.06	.02	T		
6.49	.11		.41	.13	.03			.06	.04					T	1.40	1.44	.10	.40			.51	.24	.24	1.10	.03		.10	.15			
2.07	.62	.03	.37	.16	.10				.09								.05	.01	.03		.17	.06		.05	.10		.10	.13			
2.28	.78	.10	.42	.03	T				.12	.01			T		.07	T	T					.06		.55	T		.08	.06	T		

See Reference Notes Following Station Index

DAILY PRECIPITATION

Table 3--Continued

Station	Total	Day of month																													
		1	2	3	4	5	6	7	8	9	10	11	12	13	14	15	16	17	18	19	20	21	22	23	24	25	26	27	28	29	30
TOWER CITY 3 SW	3.40	.49	.48	.28							T	.09							.19			.62			.19	.32		.74			
TROY	1.96	.52	.03	.38	.03					.08				.02			T	.02					.01		.61	.04		.18	.04		
TURTLEPOINT 4 NE	4.73	1.38		.44	.28	.04										.40	.01	.57					.03		.63	.53		.16	.03		
TYRONE 4 NE BALD EAGLE	3.78	.35	.13	.20											T	.47	.05	.01	1.14	.14		.22		.04	.33	.22		.43	.05		
UNION CITY	5.62	.70	.03	.24	.29	.04	.02			.15							.04	2.37	.08	.14	.02	.20	.36	.02		.84	.03	.05	.04		
UNIONTOWN	5.61	.62	.70	.13		.01								.33	.17		.29	.76	.45		T	.04	T	.42	.60	.42	.09	.45	.03		
UPPER DARBY	7.33	1.92	.46	.43							.01	.38					.66	.93	.07			.09		1.26	.85			.23	.24		
UTICA	4.75	.78	.48	.13	.17						.20							.64	.37			.21	.36	.02	.19	1.0		.15			
VANDERGRIFT	4.89	.60		.40	.20	T				.01							.12	.80	T	.32		.19	T	T	1.22	.61		.42			
VIRGINVILLE	4.19	.15	.47	1.24								.81				.02			.75			.06	.08		.14			.47			
VOWINCKEL	4.99	.79	T	.13	.04	.13	T			.10						T	.99	.04	.97	.07		.19	T		.40	.94	T	.11	.05		
VOWINCKEL 1 WSW	5.34	.84	T	.13	.04	.12	T			.10						T	1.12	.06	1.33	.07	T	.16	T		.38	.85	T	.10	.04		
WARREN	5.42	.82		.12	.60	.03				.10						1.10		.05	1.62			.15			.16	.51			.05		
WATSONTOWN	2.70	.15		.3								.20										.50	.20	.10	.80			.30	.25		
WAYNESBURG 2 W	4.78	.28	.02	.40	T					.01					.90			.20	.24	.18		T			.61	1.01		.48	.16		
WELLSBORO 3 S	2.12	.61	.03	.36	.04	.02				.07	.04					.12	.04	T	.04				.02		.26	.19		.23	.05		
WELLSVILLE	3.10	.46	.50	.06		T				T						.12	T		.86			.15			.37	.32		.26			
WERNERSVILLE 1 W	5.64	.07		1.56								.20					.05	1.12	.04	.21		.03	.57		1.10	.27	.04	.38			
WEST CHESTER	4.01	.12	.47									.82				.05	.70	.03	.07		.12	.06	.91	.77	.01		T	.65	.03		
WEST GROVE 1 E	5.48	2.50	.20	.70								.75						.03	.24			.18	.29		.54			.03			
WEST HICKORY	4.87	.75	.10	.28	.08	.06				.28							.98	.25	.40	.10		.35			.40	.75		.06	.03		
WHITESBURG	6.48	.62		.25	T					T						.29	T	.14	.05	.82		T		.74	2.75	.59		.23			
WILKES BARRE	5.12	.68	.08	1.11	.02						.02	.02					T		.06				.94		1.60			.57	.02		
WILLIAMSBURG	3.05	.38	.11	.20						.02						.03	.01	.03	.46	.61		.27	.03	T	.51	.11		.27	.01		
WILLIAMSPORT WB AP	3.02	.27	.30	.22						T	.03				T		.09		T			.18		1.19	.09			.69			
WOLFSBURG	3.49	.24	.14	.38	.04		.02								.08		.17		T	1.84			.02		.03	.19		.23	.11	T	
YORK 3 SSW PUMP STA	4.09	.60	.60	.21											.04		.03		.67			.08			.53	T		.23			
YORK HAVEN	2.48	.17	.08	.48	T										.07	.09	.01		T	.08		T	.09		.53	.12		.10	.66		
ZION GROVE	3.56	.54	.08	.72							.02							.97		.03			.44		.27	.04		.45			
ZIONSVILLE 3 SE	2.98	.47	.10	.77							.01										.01	.30			.93			.33	.06		

CORRECTIONS

ANNUAL - 1949

Table 2:
Doylestown

Precipitation annual total should be 41.94; annual departure from normal should be -3.71.

MONTH: MARCH 1956

Table 2
Pittsburgh WB AP 2

Total precipitation should be 5.28; departure from normal, +2.08; number of days with precipitation .10 or more should be 10.

Table 3
Pittsburgh WB AP 2

Precipitation on 17th should be 0.09; monthly total should be 5.28.

Table 7
Pittsburgh WB AP 2

Snowfall amount on 17th should be 0.9; total monthly snowfall should be, 14.5.

MONTH: APRIL 1956

Table 2
Pittsburgh WB AP 2

Average minimum temperature should be 37.3; average temperature should be, 47.0; temperature departure from normal should be -1.8.

Table 5
Pittsburgh WB AP 2

Minimum temperature on 28th should be ! average minimum temperature should be :

Table 7
Mt Pocono 2 N AP

Snowfall on the 30th should be 0.7.

MONTHLY AND SEASONAL SNOWFALL

Season of 1955 - 1956

October	November	December	January	February	March	April	May	June	Total
	6.0	1.9	5.9	4.3	9.8	-			-
	2.0	3.7	5.1	5.7	18.1	2.0			37.2
	.5	3.1	5.6	4.6	14.1	2.0			29.9
	7.3	3.3	11.0	11.3	24.5	4.0			61.4
	3.5	.3	4.7	5.2	9.5	T			23.2
-	-	2.0	-	-	-	-			-
1.8	4.0	9.0	9.4	13.1	21.0	5.0			63.3
	6.0	T	7.0	T	7.0	T			20.0
2.0	7.0	12.0	4.5	16.0	24.5	T			66.0
	7.0	7.5	4.0	8.0	11.0	5.5			43.0
T	5.5	.9	4.1	.7	11.7	1.0			23.9
	-	-	-	7.0	-	1.0			-
	2.0	5.2	3.8	7.0	12.0	T			30.0
	-	-	-	-	-	-			-
T	2.0	5.7	4.3	6.3	5.1	T			23.4
T	2.0	3.0	4.5	4.7	15.5	2.1			31.8
	2.0	3.3	4.5	7.4	23.0	2.0			42.2
	-	7.6	23.4	8.3	29.4	10.1			-
	4.0	2.0	-	6.0	14.0	T			-
	8.6	8.5	18.0	10.5	-	10.5			-
	-	-	-	-	-	-			-
-	-	16.5	9.0	-	-	-			-
3.0	20.6	22.8	12.4	28.6	31.6	9.1			128.1
	5.4	-	9.1	4.0	11.5	3.0			-
T	7.2	5.0	10.8	10.6	16.9	7.6	T		58.1
	T	1.0	11.0	1.7	5.5	-			-
	5.5	.5	7.1	4.0	8.3	-			-
	-	-	-	-	-	-			-
	-	-	-	5.5	-				-
T	7.0	4.5	7.0	5.0	14.0	2.0			39.5
	2.5	3.4	4.9	5.1	13.5	T			29.4
1.0	6.0	9.2	8.1	13.4	15.7	5.3			58.7
	5.0	4.0	4.0	7.0	17.5	T			37.5
T	8.0	9.0	12.7	11.1	16.7	8.5	T		66.0
.5	5.0	10.0	8.0	17.0	27.0	4.0			71.5
T	3.5	6.5	4.0	7.0	14.0	T			35.0
		-	-		-	-			-
	7.0	2.0	6.1	5.1	12.0	.2			32.4
	-	-	-	-	-	-			-
	T	T	.9	T	-				-
	3.7	4.5	3.5	5.5	15.0	T			32.2
	7.0	12.5	8.3	-	13.1	3.5			-
		-	2.8	8.4	21.5	-			-
	-	3.8	4.4	T	-	1.0			-
	4.0	3.7	7.7	8.5	11.1	T			35.0
7.0	22.0	18.7	18.0	30.5	34.5	9.5	T		140.2
	5.4	6.2	4.0	9.4	16.0	7.0			48.0
	4.0	2.0	8.1	-	14.4	-			-
	3.6	-	-	-	-	-	-	-	-
	T	—	T	-	-	-	-	-	-
	2.0	1.0	5.3	T	-	T			-
	9.0	3.5	11.5	-	12.0	T			-
	9.0	5.5	12.9	2.3	11.0	.5			41.2
	2.0	1.0	4.0	T	-	-			-
	3.3	3.1	8.0	.7	14.5	2.0			31.6
	-	8.0	-	-	19.0	3.0			-
1.0	-	7.8	-	-	-	2.5			-
		.5	5.0	T	6.5	T			12.0
1.0	28.5	50.0	24.0	24.5	22.6	3.5	T		154.1
3.0	10.5	13.2	17.7	27.0	30.2	-			-
-	-	-	-	-	-	-			-
-	11.5	11.3	10.4	17.2	-	8.7	T		-
T	9.0	9.0	9.0	16.5	29.0	8.0			80.5
-	-	3.0	7.5	-	13.5	T			-
T	-	10.0	13.0	14.4	20.0	16.5			-
5.1	-	31.5	-	21.9	34.8	7.3	T		-
	6.0	5.0	5.2	7.0	9.6	T			32.8
	7.0	3.7	13.6	1.1	16.5				41.9
	4.5	-	-	-	-	4.8			-
T	4.5	8.2	5.2	7.7	17.3	6.7			49.6
T	9.4	10.2	17.1	5.1	12.6	7.1			61.5
	.4	.9	6.3	T	6.6	4.8			19.0
	4.0	3.0	5.6	2.8	16.2	3.0			34.6
.5	12.0	10.5	10.5	10.0	23.5	7.5			74.5
.5	5.6	9.9	5.4	11.2	18.0	13.5			64.1
T	9.5	11.5	7.7	17.5	21.8	15.0			83.0
	6.5	5.0	9.5	T	9.0	-			-
T	17.5	8.5	14.5	-	20.5	7.0			-
T	16.1	43.8	20.1	18.4	24.4	7.6			130.4
	2.0	-	5.0	3.0	14.0				-
1.5	9.5	12.2	8.1	16.5	19.6	1.4			68.8
	2.6	5.6	6.3	8.2	12.5	2.0			37.2
	3.0	1.4	4.3	1.3	8.5	T			18.5
	3.6	22.1	11.0	19.5	-	13.7			-
T	6.4	18.6	11.5	4.5	17.8	4.0	T		62.8
	.8	1.0	5.3	3.5	8.5	T			19.1
T	T	-	-	T	2.0	T			-
	8.5	2.2	5.5	3.0	14.5	4.0			37.7
	-	-	8.0	-	-	2.0			-
	4.0	3.3	-	-	-	-	-	-	-
.5	12.8	11.4	-	-	22.3	21.0			-
1.2	5.4	13.3	10.1	17.6	29.5	3.9	T		81.0
	4.0	3.0	8.0	.5	8.0	-			-
	5.5	2.9	7.3	1.9	18.9	3.3			39.8
	3.0	.3	4.0	5.0	6.8	T			19.1

See Reference Notes Following Station Index

MONTHLY AND SEASONAL SNOWFALL

Season of 1955 - 1956

Continued

Station	July	August	September	October	November	December	January	February	March	April	May	June	Total
GIFFORD	-			6.0	-	23.0	-	25.0	-	-	-	-	-
GLEN HAZEL 2 NE DAM				4.0	12.5	18.0	9.8	24.5	28.0	7.0	T		103.8
GLENWILLARD DASH DAM					-	-	-	-	10.0	.4			-
GORDON					6.0	-	-	-	-	-	-	-	-
GOULDSBORO				T	10.5	17.3	12.0	22.5	31.0	20.0			112.3
GRANTVILLE 2 SW					-	-	-	-	-	-			-
GRATERFORD					3.5	3.6	8.0	1.8	20.6	1.0			38.5
GRATZ 1 N					4.6	3.0	2.5	2.6	8.5	5.0			26.2
GREENSBORO LOCK 7					1.5	1.0	20.0	T	3.5	T			26.0
GREENSBURG 3 SE					9.5	4.3	18.3	6.5	11.8	7.5			57.9
GREENVILLE				.8	14.5	16.5	12.3	13.4	19.0	2.6	T		79.1
HANOVER					3.0	1.0	6.0	4.5	9.0	T			23.5
HARRISBURG WB AP					4.6	3.4	5.4	4.6	20.2	T	T		38.2
HARRISBURG NORTH					3.0	2.2	4.2	4.3	12.2	T			25.9
HAWLEY					6.5	8.8	9.8	12.2	21.9	11.4	-		-
HAWLEY 1 S DAM					5.6	9.5	4.4	10.4	18.5	11.5			59.9
HOLLISTERVILLE				T	7.7	11.7	6.3	13.5	20.6	14.4			80.2
HOLTWOOD					3.0	1.2	9.5	2.0	23.7	1.0			40.4
HONESDALE 4 NW		T			-	12.5	6.0	12.0	17.5	-			-
HOOVERSVILLE					11.0	14.5	20.3	16.9	22.7	19.4			104.8
HOP BOTTOM 2 SE						T	-	-	-				-
HUNTINGDON					4.4	2.0	5.1	5.5	12.1	T			29.1
HUNTSDALE					7.0	2.0	5.0	4.5	15.0	T			33.5
HYNDMAN					8.0	T	7.0	-	7.0	-			-
INDIANA 3 SE					9.1	4.3	11.3	1.6	12.0	1.0			39.3
IRWIN	T				-	3.5	10.8	-	9.6	2.5			-
JAMESTOWN 2 NW					14.2	15.3	8.4	9.7	-	2.3			-
JIM THORPE	T			T	3.7	-	2.9	7.1	13.5	4.0			-
JOHNSTOWN				T	6.0	4.3	7.6	7.3	8.5	-			-
KANE 1 NNE				6.5	17.7	28.1	18.6	26.9	38.3	7.9	T		144.0
KARTHAUS				T	5.6	9.6	7.7	7.8	13.5	T			44.2
KEATING SUMMIT			T	2.0	10.2	15.8	10.5	16.7	25.2	5.7			86.1
KEGG	T				8.0	-	13.5	5.5	9.0	T			-
KITTANNING LOCK 7					5.8	3.2	6.8	1.9	9.5	T			27.2
KREGAR 4 SE				T	11.4	15.7	23.9	-	22.6	13.1	T		-
KRESGEVILLE 3 W					-	-	-	-	-	-			-
LAFAYETTE MC KEAN PARK				-	-	-	-	-	-	-	-	-	-
LAKEVILLE 1 NNE				T	8.5	12.0	12.0	18.0	25.5	19.0			96.0
LANCASTER 2NE PUMP STA					2.0	1.5	6.0	1.5	10.2	T			27.2
LANDISVILLE					T	-	5.2	5.1	5.2	-			-
LATROBE					-	-	-	2.0	-	-			-
LAWRENCEVILLE 2					4.4	11.7	5.8	8.5	21.7	5.0			57.2
LEBANON 2 NW				-	-	-	-	-	-	-		-	-
LEHIGHTON					2.5	-	3.4	-	14.0	-			-
LE ROY				.5	5.0	10.2	11.0	-	30.5	9.5			-
LEWIS RUN 3 SE				3.0	27.0	38.0	17.0	23.0	42.0	4.0	T		154.0
LEWISTOWN					3.4	2.5	4.0	7.0	8.0	T			24.9
LINESVILLE 5 WNW				T	27.2	28.0	17.8	13.2	22.2	12.9	T		121.9
LOCK HAVEN					3.4	-	3.8	7.5	10.5	.2			-
LONG POND 2 W				1.0	13.3	15.3	6.9	15.5	20.3	15.3			87.6
MADERA					6.2	4.0	4.1	3.8	12.0	2.0			32.1
MAHAFFEY					8.1	4.8	7.4	7.0	21.0	1.7			50.0
MAPLE GLEN					4.5	7.4	8.0	2.0	9.8	2.0			33.7
MAPLETON DEPOT					5.2	2.0	7.0	4.8	14.0	T			33.0
MARCUS HOOK					5.4	1.5	3.6	1.6	12.4	T			24.5
MARION CENTER 2 SE				T	15.5	7.0	13.5	12.0	-	9.7	T		-
MARTINSBURG CAA AP					5.2	1.1	8.2	4.7	9.7	3.2			32.1
MATAMORAS					3.0	8.0	4.1	9.0	21.0	8.7			51.5
MAYBURG				2.0	11.7	-	-	-	22.0	3.0			-
MC CONNELLSBURG	-	-	-	T	5.7	1.0	7.9	4.0	13.8	T			-
MC KEESPORT					-	-	-	-	-	-			-
MEADVILLE 1 S				.5	21.9	35.3	19.3	16.9	23.1	7.7	T		120.7
MEDIX RUN				T	6.0	8.5	5.8	9.3	18.7	5.0			54.3
MERCER 2 NNE					-	-	-	13.0	-				-
MERCERSBURG					5.5	1.5	5.5	-	9.5	T			-
MEYERSDALE						-	-	-	-	-	-	-	-
MEYERSDALE 1 ENE	-	-	-	-	-	-	-	-	-	-			-
MIDDLETOWN OLMSTED FLD					3.8	2.8	4.8	3.9	11.7	T			26.8
MIDLAND DAM 7		T			4.3	2.0	6.5	.6	10.0	.6			24.0
MILANVILLE					5.0	10.0	9.1	9.3	19.3	10.0			62.7
MILLHEIM				T	9.0	7.0	6.0	8.5	18.0	1.5			50.0
MILLVILLE 2 SW					4.5	4.5	3.0	7.0	11.0	4.0			34.0
MILROY			-		3.0	-	3.8	7.7	8.2	T			-
MONTROSE 1 E				T	10.2	21.3	13.0	21.1	24.0	24.9	T		115.1
MORGANTOWN					3.0	3.5	6.0	3.0	-	1.8			-
MT GRETNA 2 SE					-	-	T	T	2.2	T			-
MT POCONO 2 N AP			T	.8	8.5	6.6	-	16.3	-	-			-
MUHLENBURG 1 SE				.5	10.5	12.0	8.5	16.5	18.0	7.5			73.5
MYERSTOWN					-	-	-	-	-	-			-
NATRONA LOCK 4					5.0	T	4.5	1.0	9.1	T			19.6
NESHAMINY FALLS					-	-	-	.1	18.5	T			-
NEWBURG 3 W	T				1.6	-	5.0	3.5	12.0	1.0			-
NEW CASTLE 1 N					4.5	5.3	6.3	.3	14.3	.7			31.4
NEWELL					3.5	.5	-	1.0	10.0	T			-
NEW PARK					3.0	.5	7.0	2.5	14.5	T			27.5
NEWPORT					3.6	3.0	3.2	4.2	9.4	T			23.4
NEW STANTON					-	-	-	-	-	-			-
NEW TRIPOLI					4.0	5.5	2.6	8.6	12.8	1.0			32.5
NORRISTOWN					2.0	2.0	5.5	.1	19.0	T			28.6
NORTH EAST 2 SE				T	6.5	21.4	16.1	6.1	18.3	8.6			77.0
ORWELL 3 N					-	-	8.5	15.5	27.0	20.0			-
PALM					2.5	2.8	-	5.5	19.0	T			-
PALMERTON				T	2.5	4.6	2.5	6.3	10.7	2.5			29.1
PARKER					7.0	4.0	-	2.5	14.3	.8			-
PAUPACK 2 WNW				T			-	-	-				-

See Reference Notes Following Station Index

MONTHLY AND SEASONAL SNOWFALL

Season of 1955 - 1956

Station	July	August	September	October	November	December	January	February	March	April	May	June	Total
ECKS POND				T	5.5	9.5	7.0	15.0	24.5	19.0			80.5
HIL DREXEL INST OF TEC					5.0	.6	7.4	.8	9.2	.7			23.7
HILADELPHIA WB AP				T	2.9	1.1	7.0	1.1	10.9	T			23.0
HILADELPHIA PT BREEZE					3.0	-	5.8	.6	-				-
HILADELPHIA SHAWMONT					1.0	-	-	2.0	-	1.0			-
HILADELPHIA CITY	-	-	-	-	-	-	-	-	-	-			-
HILIPSBURG CAA AP				T	7.2	6.0	10.1	13.8	18.6	2.9			58.6
HOENIXVILLE 1 E					3.0	2.0	6.0	.1	-	-			-
IKES CREEK				T	5.7	11.2	5.3	10.8	12.5	9.3			54.8
IMPLE HILL				.8	10.9	15.0	8.5	16.9	24.2	19.6	T		95.9
INE GROVE 1 NE				T	3.0	5.3	3.0	-	7.6	2.0			-
ITTSBURGH WB AP 2				T	6.5	2.6	7.3	3.2	14.5	3.3			37.4
ITTSBURGH WB CITY					4.6	1.0	5.3	.3	9.5	1.0			21.7
LEASANT MOUNT 1 W				T	8.0	19.4	15.0	19.0	24.7	20.0	1.0		107.1
ORT CLINTON					-	2.0	2.0	-	-	-			-
ORTLAND		-	-	-	-	-	-	-	-	-	-	-	-
OTTSTOWN					2.5	.7	7.2	-	-	-			-
OTTSVILLE PALO ALTO BR	T				3.0	4.5	3.6	5.4	8.9	-	-		-
UTNEYVILLE 2 SE DAM					22.5	6.5	8.5	-	-	1.5			-
UAKERTOWN 1 E					6.2	4.6	7.0	4.8	15.4	-			-
AYMOND				3.0	-	-	12.0	-	-	-			-
EADING WB CITY					2.7	1.2	3.8	3.8	11.2	.5			23.2
ENOVO				T	3.3	5.0	5.5	8.0	13.0	T			34.8
EW				7.0	18.9	30.1	-	33.5	41.6	9.6	T		-
ICES LANDING L					-	-	-	-	-	-			-
IDGWAY 1					8.9	-	8.5	8.9	19.2	5.2			-
USH					5.5	13.7	5.5	5.5	18.0	8.5			[illegible]
USHVILLE				T	3.4	11.6	5.7	7.2	17.0	11.5			56.4
AGAMORE 1 S					-	[illegible]	7.2	2.1	12.0	.5			-
ALINA 3 W					7.0	2.0	8.5	4.5	-	T			-
AXTON					7.0	1.5	6.0	4.0	8.0	T			26.5
CHENLEY LOCK 5					3.5	2.5	4.5	1.0	8.5	T			20.0
CRANTON					T	3.0	-	4.5	9.8	5.0			-
CRANTON WB AIRPORT		T		.3	4.5	7.8	4.7	8.6	14.5	12.0			52.4
ELINSGROVE CAA AP					5.4	4.1	5.0	8.2	11.0	T			33.7
HAMOKIN					-	3.8	3.0	6.5	12.0	8.0			-
HIPPENSBURG	T				9.0	2.0	6.0	6.0	12.0	T			35.0
HIPPINGPORT WB					4.5	T	4.0	T	9.0	T			17.5
INNEMAHONING				T	5.5	6.7	6.0	8.0	15.5	T	T		41.7
LIPPERY ROCK				T	6.0	8.5	8.0	4.5	15.5	T	T		42.5
OMERSET FAIRVIEW ST				T	-	-	13.8	5.3	14.6	7.7			-
OMERSET MAIN ST				T	8.8	5.8	10.8	7.0	11.5	6.4	T		50.3
OUTH MOUNTAIN	T			T	7.4	1.5	5.7	7.5	14.4	1.8			38.3
PRINGBORO			T	T	-	-	-	-	-	-			-
PRING GROVE					2.5	1.5	6.4	3.5	10.1	-			-
PRINGS 1 SW				T	13.5	4.8	15.2	2.0	17.0	7.8	T		60.3
TATE COLLEGE					8.1	3.5	-	-	8.0	2.0			-
TRAUSSTOWN					2.2	1.2	2.0	3.2	8.0	T			16.6
TROUDSBURG					2.1	-	-	12.4	27.3	7.9	T		-
TUMP CREEK					7.5	5.0	5.3	5.5	20.5	3.0			46.8
UNBURY					4.5	4.3	3.5	7.4	12.5	T			32.2
USQUEHANNA	T				5.7	19.8	13.9	15.5	23.5	10.0			88.4
UTERSVILLE					-	1.1	11.1	-	13.0	-			-
AMAQUA				T	4.0	6.5	2.5	7.0	9.0	6.0			35.0
AMAQUA 4 N DAM			-	-	-	-	T	-	-	T			-
AMARACK 2 S FIRE TWR				3.0	7.7	7.9	9.4	17.3	23.2	9.5			78.0
IONESTA 2 SE DAM				1.5	12.0	14.0	6.5	16.0	23.7	5.1			78.8
ITUSVILLE WATER WORKS				2.0	16.8	16.8	11.1	15.2	17.1	3.0	T		82.0
ORPEDO 4 W				6.0	15.2	19.4	9.2	15.0	24.7	9.2	T		98.7
OWANDA				T	6.4	12.0	7.1	11.0	23.1	11.0			70.6
OWER CITY 5 SW					3.5	5.0	6.0	6.0	13.5	6.0			40.0
ROY	T				3.7	11.2	7.4	10.1	24.0	8.5			64.9
URTLEPOINT 4 NE				-	-	-	-	-	-	-	-		-
YRONE 4 NE BALD EAGLE				T	6.0	3.5	5.0	6.0	13.0	T			33.5
NION CITY	-			T	13.4	42.8	14.0	23.0	21.8	12.0	T		127.0
NIONTOWN					3.7	3.3	7.1	.3	3.5	2.0			19.9
PPER DARBY					2.0	1.3	9.5	.5	11.7	1.5			26.5
TICA					10.0	-	-	-	15.7	-			-
ANDERGRIFT					-	-	-	-	-	-			-
IRGINVILLE					3.0	3.0	3.0	-	-	-			-
OWINCKEL				1.5	-	8.8	-	-	-	3.0			-
OWINCKEL 1 SW				2.5	-	7.8	-	-	-	4.0			-
ARREN	T			1.7	12.9	27.2	10.2	17.0	24.1	2.3			95.4
ATSONTOWN					6.0	5.0	3.8	-	-	T			-
AYNESBURG 2 W					5.5	2.4	7.8	T	-	-			-
ELLSBORO 3 S				T	7.0	11.4	10.0	17.5	26.5	13.0			85.4
ELLSVILLE					3.5	2.3	4.3	4.0	12.3	T			26.4
ERNERSVILLE 1 W							2.0	3.0	-	2.0			-
EST CHESTER					-	1.9	-	-	19.6	1.0			-
EST GROVE 1 E					-	1.0	7.1	T	-				-
EST HICKORY				1.0	14.0	-	6.0	14.0	20.5	1.0			-
HITESBURG				T	11.0	3.5	9.8	-	13.3	-	T		-
ILKES BARRE				T	2.5	8.2	3.6	8.1	11.2	5.2			38.8
ILLIAMSBURG				T	4.8	3.0	5.5	6.0	9.5	T			28.8
ILLIAMSPORT WB AP				T	6.1	8.5	6.3	10.4	12.0	2.1			45.4
OLFSBURG	T				8.5	T	8.0	4.0	7.5	T			28.0
ORK 3 SSW PUMP STA					3.3	1.9	-	2.8	-	T			-
ORK HAVEN					1.7	2.2	3.5	4.0	11.5	T			22.9
ION GROVE	T				3.0	-	2.5	5.5	7.0	T			-
IONSVILLE 3 SE					3.2	3.5	6.6	-	18.4	4.1			-

BEGINNING WITH JANUARY 1, 1956, HAIL WAS EXCLUDED FROM THE SNOWFALL TABLES.

See Reference Notes Following Station Index

DAILY TEMPERATURES

Table 5

Station		Day Of Month																													
		1	2	3	4	5	6	7	8	9	10	11	12	13	14	15	16	17	18	19	20	21	22	23	24	25	26	27	28	29	30	31
ALLENTOWN WB AP	MAX	77	62	71	71	76	78	82	87	69	76	84	86	95	93	92	90	84	79	72	69	71	92	90	87	84	82	86	83	76	85	
	MIN	60	53	57	51	49	53	52	54	57	58	54	54	66	64	66	70	68	57	49	49	59	64	66	66	64	57	66	59	53	53	
ALLENTOWN GAS CO	MAX	89	79	65	72	71	77	80	83	89	65	77	83	89	95	95	93	91	85	78	75	70	73	90	90	88	84	84	87	83	77	
	MIN	65	54	53	51	50	53	52	55	58	57	56	54	61	65	68	72	69	63	51	46	54	61	65	66	65	58	62	61	52	53	
ALTOONA HORSESHOE CURVE	MAX	72	58	55	67	73	76	81	84	79	84	83	87	92	89	85	82	84	78	68	64	81	84	85	84	80	82	73	79	74	85	
	MIN	57	43	46	43	51	47	48	53	60	37	53	52	63	62	62	63	62	54	51	53	58	66	67	62	60	51	65	55	47	49	
ARENDTSVILLE	MAX	91	69	57	68	72	80	77	84	87	69	86	83	91	97	94	91	90	89	67	73	69	77	90	92	91	85	87	87	84	81	
	MIN	63	52	51	51	47	56	52	54	59	60	56	56	61	66	64	68	67	66	53	53	57	61	68	63	68	59	67	58	48	54	
ARTEMAS 1 WNW	MAX	73	62	62	68	71	80	87	97	93	91	86	79	78	80	87	90	87	84	86	74	84	88	89	90	86	85	87	87	87	90	
	MIN	57	50	40	36	41	49	45	52	57	60	61	53	55	57	62	60	64	70	62	50	60	66	61	60	55	54	59	44	52	64	
BAKERSTOWN 3 WNW	MAX	66	51	51	67	73	78	84	84	80	85	86	89	91	91	87	82	85	74	85	78	84	86	84	84	73	88	82	78	76	87	
	MIN	50	42	45	47	58	47	52	55	62	58	60	56	55	64	62	65	62	56	54	61	68	70	64	61	62	64	70	62	54	60	
BEAVERTOWN	MAX	87	67	61	69	76	76	86	88	87	86	85	90	95	94	92	90	86	83	72	72		90	89	88	89	84		82	78	84	
	MIN	65	49	51	59	57	74		52	58	61	51	49	69	61	61	65	67	57	47	53		64	62	64	63	52		56	46	49	
BELLEFONTE 4 S	MAX	75	58	52	49	64	64	70	84	87	78	85	85	89	93	92	89	84	85	70	66	65	80	87	86	87	81	84	80	76	76	
	MIN	60	45	47	43	52	48	47	54	52	60	52	50	69	65	58	64	65	57	45	54	56	59	64	64	62	52	57	61	58	50	
BERWICK	MAX	83	66	70	71	75	80	83	88	88	81	83	90	95	95	94	90	90	85	79	76	76	91	89	87	86	84	86	85	77	87	
	MIN	63	49	51	51	51	52	50	54	61	61	51	52	64	61	65	68	67	61	52	53	61	64	60	66	61	54	69	58	51	51	
BETHLEHEM LEHIGH UNIV	MAX	79	61	72	72	77	80	85	88	63	76	84	88	94	95	94	93	86	80	74	70	70	90	90	88	83	83	83	80	76	87	
	MIN	61	53	58	54	52	57	57	59	57	59	60	59	72	72	70	71	70	60	48	50	60	65	67	66	67	62	66	60	56	58	
BLAIRSVILLE 6 ENE	MAX	67	50	48	64	69	78	79	79	76	80	80	83	87	88	85	75	77	69	73	76	77	77	79	82	74	85	75	71	71	86	
	MIN	49	39	40	43	53	49	53	59	58	57	60	58	64	62	62	64	61	55	50	53	60	65	64	58	58	55	63	54	49	50	
BRADFORD 4 W RES	MAX	74	49	50	59	66	74	79	79	78	80	80	85	87	89	87	83	73	71	71	70	79	84	84	82	71	80	80	74	69	83	
	MIN	46	38	42	44	48	38	42	37	54	48	41	45	55	55	52	55	61	58	53	43	59	60	53	64	57	42	59	50	46	38	
BROOKVILLE CAA AIRPORT	MAX	61	52	51	63	69	78	81	82	80	83	83	87	90	90	86	80	82	69	72	70	79	80	81	81	75	82	76	69	72	89	
	MIN	43	43	45	47	49	42	46	48	59	53	47	47	58	60	57	62	63	52	47	52	63	61	62	61	56	51	64	51	44	48	
BURGETTSTOWN 2 W	MAX	84	63	51	52	70	74	79	84	84	78	86	83	88	91	93	87	83	85	74	71	77	84	84	88	86	77	86	80	75	77	
	MIN	56	43	44	44	51	38	44	48	58	44	46	48	56	61	59	63	60	65	51	59	63	64	64	59	61	49	60	56	42	46	
BURNT CABINS 2 NE	MAX	64	52	55	71	72	76	83	88	73	84	88	90	94	95	88	89	86	68	67	67	81	88	87	90	78	86	84	81	78	84	
	MIN	57	48	46	46	48	48	46	50	56	48	56	48	57	58	61	60	63	54	58	55	59	62	60	60	60	53	63	56	45	48	
BUTLER	MAX	82	60	61	70	72	80	83	86	86	82	86	87	90	93	94	90	85	83	76	78	84	86	86	85	85	86	88	80	72	89	
	MIN	57	44	46	45	57	51	49	50	63	60	51		60	64	61	68	66	63	52	60	68	68	65	63	62	50	60	50	49	50	
CANTON 1 NW	MAX	78	64	49	57	63	69	71	78	81	72	80	76	86	89	88	86	84	75	70	69	64	74	85	82	83	73	78	80	72	71	
	MIN	58	43	43	42	44	46	46	53	56	58	55	54	55	67	60	62	62	57	43	46	49	56	57	58	59	49	49	57	47	46	
CARLISLE	MAX	86	68	67	72	77	80	85	90	88	87	87	92	98	96	94	91	88	84	72	70	80	91	91	91	90	90	88	84	81	89	
	MIN	64	51	54	54	52	56	52	57	64	62	59	57	67	68	68	72	71	59	56	57	62	64	70	66	68	60	71	63	54	55	
CHAMBERSBURG 1 ESE	MAX	72	63	64	71	77	78	83	88	75	87	85	90	96	95	92	87	88	72	71	69	79	89	89	90	85	87	86	82	80	87	
	MIN	61	51	51	46	48	53	49	54	58	62	53	52	62	63	63	68	67	55	53	56	61	64	67	64	65	58	70	62	47	52	
CHESTER	MAX																															
	MIN																															
CLARION 3 SW	MAX	65	53	53	67	72	80	84	84	79	85	85	89	91	92	89	79	82	81	75	74	82	82	85	85	75	84	78	73	75	86	
	MIN	48	43	45	48	50	42	49	49	59	52	48	47	57	61	59	63	62	58	46	55	65	61	61	62	59	52	63	55	46	49	
CLAYSVILLE 3 W	MAX	72	55	54	70	76	79	84	85	90	88	85	89	96	98	98	81	94	80	70	71	85	84	88	84	80	85	80	77	78	87	
	MIN	52	43	43	42	52	42	45	45	61	58	40	46	56	57	59	61	62	63	50	51	62	69	62	62	60	52	68	65	41	45	
COATESVILLE 1 SW	MAX	90	77	64	71	72	78	80	82	88	63	71	83	88	94	94	93	88	86	69	73	68	73	90	91	88	86	87	86	85	87	
	MIN	62	56	54	50	48	54	50	51	57	58	55	50	62	66	66	70	67	66	49	42	51	62	67	66	65	66	57	58	59	52	
COLUMBIA	MAX	82	67	70	74	82	85	85	90	80	84	87	91	99	96	94	93	91	80	76	74	75	95	94	92	88	88	89	87	82	88	
	MIN	64	53	55	53	50	56	54	55	57	60	58	55	67	69	70	72	71	60	55	52	59	63	70	68	65	61	72	62	57	55	
CONFLUENCE 1 SW DAM	MAX	82	65	47	52	67	72	79	82	82	79	84	82	85	90	92	88	81	82	76	75	72	79	81	87	85	78	86	79	76	76	
	MIN	59	45	43	40	45	48	48	50	53	55	54	50	54	60	59	61	61	64	54	51	58	58	65	61	60	57	57	56	44	50	
CORRY	MAX	65	49	50	63	65	76	82	82	84	79	87	88	91	92	90	87	79	76	80	78	82	86	84	85	70	84	80	73	74	88	
	MIN	43	41	43	46	52	40	45	41	60	52	45	48	60	60	58	60	64	63	40	56	65	61	60	61	61	46	65	55	46	43	
COUDERSPORT 3 NW	MAX	63	52	49	62	68	74	81	80	79	79	78	85	89	88	85	82	72	72	68	66	77	85	82	83	71	77	77	72	70	81	
	MIN	51	39	42	44	49	39	42	41	53	51	42	44	57	53	48	54	60	57	30	42	56	64	52	59	57	43	55	49	46	41	
DERRY	MAX	75	56	52	68	72	78	82	82	79	84	83	87	90	92	88	78	75													90	
	MIN	55	45	45	46	45	47	50	53	61	56	51	51	68	63	65	64	65													45	
DEVAULT 1 W	MAX	78	62	68	70	78	78	81	89	68	74	82	88	94	94	93	87	86	80	71	67	73	80	80	90	84	84	85	80	77	84	
	MIN	59	50	51	52	53	53	53	57	56	55	52	59	69	68	66	65	58	55	47	44	54	65	64	64	62	57	65	60	52	55	
DIXON	MAX	86	69	53	72	71	73	79	84	86	69	83	79	90	94	92	92	89	83	76	75	70	79	88	88	91	78	83	86	80	78	
	MIN	60	49	49	51	52	45	46	49	52	58	49	46	50	57	58	59	65	55	39	43	54	54	53	58	59	51	52	52	47	46	
DONEGAL	MAX	60	44	50	64	69	75	77	78	75	80	78	83	86	87	84	77	79	67	65	72	77	74	80	80	74	83	75	71	71	84	
	MIN	43	37	39	36	47	38	42	43	45	45	44	42	56	56	55	58	55	55	52	50	60	62	60	57	53	46	53	45	40	42	
DONORA	MAX	87	67	53	64	75	77	84	86	88	85	89	89	90	94	95	90	84	88	80	77	79	84	84	90	88	86	89	83	81	87	
	MIN	60	47	47	49	58	49	54	55	64	56	56	56	65	64	65	68	65	68	57	63	70	71	71	64	64	57	70	66	51	54	
DU BOIS 7 E	MAX	74	60	51	63	70	78	80	82	82	82	81	85	88	90	90	85	79	78	69	67	78	82	81	82	82	82	82	75	71	85	
	MIN	56	40	43	43	52	49	44	47	57	54	45	46	57	58	55	59	64	56	46	54	60	67	59	62	59	47	67	57	43	47	
EAGLES MERE	MAX	78	61	55	59	63	69	70	78	82	66	75	74	83	87	88	85	82	75	71	68	61	72	83	80	79	73	75	77	72	67	
	MIN	61	43	42	44	45	48	50	59	59	56	54	55	62	62	62	64	63	57	46	47	49	51	51	63	57	53	52	56	46	50	
EAST BRADY	MAX	78	60	57	70	72	81	85	85	84	87	89	91	94	94	93	88	83	84	80	80	85	86	86	88	86	86	86	80	78	89	
	MIN	55	32	36	49	54	46	50	52	51	53	53	50	61	64	62	55	64	61	50	57	68	66	65	63	63	55	70	58	49	53	
EBENSBURG	MAX	71	55	50	62	69	73	78	81	82	79	77	82	86	87	83	75	79	73	66	66	75	78	78	80	75	81	77	72	70	83	
	MIN	51	40	43	42	40	46	44	50	57	54	47	46	62	57	59	62	58	52	50	52	53	51	62	59	58	48	65	54	46	46	
EMPORIUM 1 E	MAX	79	65	55	52	66	72	80	85	86	83	84	82	89	91	90	90	87	88	77	72	69	82	88	85	85	78	84	80	71	75	
	MIN	58	42	44	46	49	44	45	46	49	59	43	45	49	55	57	59	64	60	37	42	51	60	64	64		50	53	51	45	45	
EPHRATA	MAX	76	68	67	72	77	79	82	87	81	78	83	87	95	93	92	89	86	76	73	71	72	90	90	87	84	85	86	82	79	84	
	MIN	54	52	53	50	50	55	55	56	67	58	56	54	65	66	67	70	67	64	54	49	50	50	65	65	62	59	67	63	51	54	
ERIE CAA AIRPORT	MAX	64	54	52	65	58	67	73	77	74	77	82	86	88	83	83	83	74	71	73	81	83	83	82	86	68	83	75	65	67	80	
	MIN	45	44	47	49	46	44	48	53	52	55	52	62	71	70	69	67	67	52	50	58	66	66	68	64	54	50	64	54	54	55	

See Reference Notes Following Station Index

DAILY TEMPERATURES

PENNSYLVANIA
JUNE 1956

Day Of Month

		1	2	3	4	5	6	7	8	9	10	11	12	13	14	15	16	17	18	19	20	21	22	23	24	25	26	27	28	29	30	31	Average
	MAX	70	56	60	70	73	78	86	88	76	86	84	88	94	93	88	85	86	74	71	70	84	86	85	83	80	88	82	75	74	92		80.2
	MIN	48	50	44	44	46	46	48	50	64	52	50	49	54	60	63	62	62	55	52	52	60	59	66	60	52	54	56	48	46	60		53.7
	MAX	52	52	53	67	70	80	85	86	84	88	89	91	94	95	88	84	86	82	80	80	88	90	88	88	75	86	83	79	79	89		81.0
	MIN	49	43	43	45	51	41	48	49	56	48	52	54	59	65	63	65	53	47	37	44	65	67	66	58	59	49	66	58	48	52		53.3
	MAX	83	64	52	52	68	72	79	82	84	80	85	84	87	92	91	87	78	82	70	74	78	83	85	85	85	76	85	79	75	78		78.2
	MIN	57	41	45	45	47	44	47	51	54	50	50	49	56	61	60	62	61	63	49	56	61	67	64	60	60	53	55	58	46	50		54.1
	MAX	81	55	54	64	69	80	82	82	81	85	84	88	90	90	90	86	82	78	75	75	79	82	84	84	73	81	82	78	73	83		79.0
	MIN	48	43	45	40	52	44	50	49	60	51	52	51	61	64	61	63	65	59	47	58	67	62	61	61	61	51	68	57	48	50		55.0
	MAX	66	62	66	65	67	75	78	82	80	73	76	82	85	89	88	84	84	75	72	68	68	83	80	80	80	77	77	76	70	78		76.2
	MIN	46	43	46	46	46	47	52	56	54	53	53	55	65	65	64	64	63	55	43	43	55	61	62	66	52	50	62	60	49	50		54.2
	MAX	86	67	74	74	80	77	83	88	81	70	82	89	92	96	93	92	87	79	73	72	70	90	88	88	85	86	88	89	75	85		82.6
	MIN	67	53	60	50	49	54	50	60	57	60	57	53	65	67	64	67	68	64	47	49	59	66	67	63	66	57	68	60	55	51		59.1
	MAX	90	68	56	65	72	78	79	85	90	70	86	86	91	97	96	94	89	90	64	71	67	78	89	90	90	86	87	88	84	81		81.9
	MIN	65	54	50	52	49	56	52	56	61	61	59	56	64	68	66	69	69	63	54	55	58	62	70	65	69	61	69	66	51	55		60.2
	MAX	85	66	54	64	69	76	77	81	85	65	81	80	86	92	90	90	87	84	70	73	68	77	89	88	85	81	83	84	80	75		78.8
	MIN	64	52	50	50	49	50	50	53	57	59	50	51	54	61	64	67	66	62	52	54	55	61	64	64	63	55	58	58	50	50		56.4
	MAX	65	53	52	69	65	80	84	83	80	85	86	90	91	93	89	85	83	80	81	81	85	85	87	87	71	86	85	80	75	89		80.2
	MIN	46	43	45	47	51	41	47	47	58	47	48	48	62	64	60	64	63	62	49	59	66	62	63	60	58	47	65	56	51	46		54.2
	MAX	91	79	55	68	72	80	79	83	89	70	84	85	90	97	95	93	88	88	70	74	67	76	89	91	90	86	87	88	84	81		82.3
	MIN	63	51	49	50	49	54	51	54	59	60	56	56	59	62	64	66	67	66	52	54	55	62	65	64	64	60	61	61	50	52		57.9
	MAX	70	61	67	72	76	80	84	88	68	84	85	88	95	95	91	89	87	74	73	69	79	89	90	88	84	87	85	82	78	86		81.5
	MIN	59	52	53	53	50	58	54	57	61	62	60	55	68	66	67	72	70	56	57	56	61	65	69	66	66	61	69	62	53	55		60.4
	MAX	83	69	69	72	68	70	77	81	84	62	73	76	85	88	90	90	87	81	73	73	68	75	85	85	83	75	81	82	75	69		77.6
	MIN	61	47	47	47	51	45	45	43	54	54	48	47	57	62	60	62	63	56	36	43	52	60	57	57	63	46	52	57	50	43		52.2
	MAX	72	63	67	73	77	76	81	86	67	77	81	90	97	95	90	90	86	75	74	68	75	90	91	87	84	86	86	84	81	84		81.1
	MIN	63	55	57	55	54	59	55	59	64	62	63	59	67	77	71	76	75	63	60	56	63	66	70	70	68	66	73	66	58	61		63.7
	MAX	89	69	53			72	84	90	90	85	89	91	93	98	91	92	82	88	68	69	68	82	88	90	92	86	88	85	82	82		83.4
	MIN	62	48	39			48	49	49	52	69	50	50	51	60	62	63	65	65	54	54	58	62	63	63	63	56	57	58	46	47		55.8
	MAX	72	55	52	67	74	81	83	84	81	85	84	87	91	91	87	76	82	75	73	75	80	80	84	84	78	87	79	75	75	89		78.9
	MIN	55	42	46	41	50	43	45	49	61	51	47	47	56	58	60	64	60	60	48	52	63	67	62	61	60	50	70	64	44	48		54.1
	MAX	84	62	62	72	75	81	85	85	84	80	87	88	90	92	93	88	88	87	73	78	83	82	87	86	79	89	87	80	77	89		82.4
	MIN	58	49	52	40	47	45	50	54	62	61	52	53	64	62	63	66	62	63	52	60	66	68	65	62	62	54	68	60	48	58		57.5
	MAX	77	51	52	50	66	63	74	80	81	77	83	84	88	89	90	87	83	81	75	77	77	82	84	84	87	70	83	78	66	75		76.5
	MIN	49	43	44	48	49	40	46	47	54	48	48	53	60	62	60	65	64	65	51	57	61	63	65	61	59	47	54	58	45	51		53.9
	MAX	85	68	68	70	76	80	83	88	75	76	80	89	89	95	94	93	82	77	76	70	70	89	89	87	85	83	82	82	78			81.3
	MIN	63	50	51	50	46	53	49	52	58	58	50	48	66	63	60	71	64	61	47	43	57	66	61	64	63	54	66	55	50			56.5
	MAX	88	69	53	58	73	70	84	87	89	84	88	88	92	95	96	92	82	92	72	74	75	85	88	90	90	83	91	82	79	79		82.3
	MIN	58	46	46	44	52	47	48	52	62	56	52	51	59	60	63	65	60	61	51	51	59	63	65	64	61	55	62	58	47	49		55.6
	MAX	75	58	52	49	61	69	78	81	82	79	81	80	87	89	89	87	83	75	74	71	70	80	85	82	83	71	82	77	65	72		75.6
	MIN	56	40	43	44	47	37	42	38	54	49	39	43	53	55	50	56	63	60	36	45	54	63	59	64	59	42	51	48	46	40		49.2
	MAX	69	54	60	69	72	78	81	85	77	85	84	87	93	92	89	81	87	72	68	68	82	86	87		80	85	80	78	77	86		79.0
	MIN	53	45	46	42	49	46	47	54	61	54	51	49	60	59	62	65	61	56	53	51	60	66	65		59	54	59	51	47	47		54.2
A	MAX	84	66	67	72	80	79	85	87	82	77	85	89	95	93	91	90	87	80	73	69	73	92	91	90	90	84	86	84	80	83		82.8
	MIN	64	52	53	50	48	55	52	54	59	59	58	52	61	63	67	70	67	60	54	45	57	60	57	65	62	58	69	59	53	52		57.8
	MAX	89	72	60	69	72	77	78	82	82	74	82	81	90	95	94	92	90	88	68	72	68	74	91	92	90	85	86	89	84	73		81.3
	MIN	65	54	52	53	50	56	54	56	65	65	57	55	66	68	69	72	69	63	55	48	55	63	69	67	65	60	67	62	54	55		60.3
	MAX	83	63	54	62	70	75	83	87	86	84	80	85	92	94	95	93	93	72	75	72	70	82	90	89	85	72	89	92	75	83		80.8
	MIN	60	43	45	40	46	43	44	48	51	56	45	48	56	56	55	58	61	55	36	42	55	52	59	60	50	47	51	49	46	42		50.0
	MAX	88	71	54	62	72	78	80	86	89	76	89	89	92	98	96	94	87	87	69	69	68	83	91	90	90	84	87	85	82	80		82.2
	MIN	64	51	51	48	49	53	50	50	54	64	54	54	53	63	63	65	67	68	53	53	59	60	66	65	64	58	58	59	49	49		57.1
	MAX	65	54	51	65	61	73	79	82	77	81	84	87	89	89	87	83	80	77	78	76	79	85	85	84	70	83	78	74	75	84		77.2
	MIN	45	42	45	47	52	39	45	46	54	47	47	51	59	60	61	64	65	65	48	59	65	61	63	63	57	45	64	57	45	49		53.7
	MAX	72	68	61	68	75	81	89	90	88	88	88	92	98	91	92	90	84	78	74	70	81	90	88	90	83	87	85	81	81	90		83.1
	MIN		48	49	44	55	48	49	54	64	63	52	52	63	62	61	65	67	58	47	50	62	67	63	65	60	55	69	58	49	51		56.9
	MAX	81	64	49	53	66	64	77	82	85	79	84	82	87	92	90	85	80	82	65	71	68	77	83	81	82	77	82	79	75	74		76.5
	MIN	54	39	40	39	40	40	41	44	47	54	39	45	47	54	56	57	61	58	43	47	53	58	59	60	56	50	50	53	41	44		49.0
	MAX	81	64	70	72	75	82	84	89	68	70	86	86	98	95	95	85	88	76	74	73	73	92	90	90	89	83	91	80	80	82		82.0
	MIN	64	56	59	58	58	62	60	60	58	58	64	64	70	77	74	70	72	60	56	54	62	67	72	70	70	68	72	67	58	64		64.1
	MAX	66	59	54	67	73	78	83	81	78	82	85	89	91	94	86	81	83	66	70	65	81	84	87	89	89	86	78	76	75	87		78.8
	MIN	51	45	47	46	52	50	48	55	61	62	54	52	63	64	62	65	61	54	55	54	59	65	65	60	60	54	64	55	46	51		56.0
	MAX	77	50	51	51	65	66	76	81	81	78	82	83	87	90	90	88	82	79	76	78	76	79	85	84	85	70	83	78	65	73		76.3
	MIN	50	43	44	46	49	42	45	47	53	49	49	52	59	65	60	64	65	66	49	54	61	61	63	68	61	50	52	56	47	49		54.0
	MAX	70	59	54	61	75	77	81	82	81	83	84	86	89	88	86	82	82	79	76	73	85	83	84	82	72	83	80	75	75	85		78.4
	MIN	48	42	44	44	50	38	49	46	43	45	42	48	58	54	57	62	60	57	48	47	55	64	61	58	58	47	64	55	44	48		51.2
	MAX	70	60	69	72	80	80	85	88	67	84	84	91	97	97	92	90	88	73	79	69	75	91	93	89	84	88	86	84	78	86		82.3
	MIN	59	54	55	54	53	58	54	59	62	62	59	56	65	68	68	72	71	58	57	56	61	65	69	68	68	61	72	65	54	57		61.3
	MAX	60	52	54	69	71	77	82	82	80	83	83	87	90	90	89	87	87	77	75	80	84	86	89	87	77	87	78	81	76	85		79.5
	MIN	48	48	48	50	59	49	54	58	64	55	57	58	65	69	68	70	67	65	59	63	69	70	67	65	56	58	67	58	53	56		59.8
	MAX	81	63	58	69	65	69	72	77	80	66	74	72	84	87	89	86	81	75	69	70	67	74	81	83	82	72	76	81	73	68		74.8
	MIN	59	43	43	49	49	46	50	57	57	56	56	55	58	67	60	63	64	52	40	45	48	56	60	62	59	49	51	56	49	50		53.6
	MAX	76	61	67	68	76	77	82	87	68	74	81	89	94	94	92	88	84	72	68	66	72	89	90	86	83	83	86	80	76	82		79.7
	MIN	44	51	56	48	48	56	50	53	57	57	55	60	52	63	65	68	61	58	52	46	57	48	62	48	61	58	67	54	49	52		55.2
	MAX	68	58	64	68	73	75	84	87	61	67	69	74	90	90	90	88	85	70	70	65	72	87	87	93	81	83	82	79	74	82		77.2
	MIN	48	51	53	49	47	54	51	52	59	47	54	53	63	72	65	70	67	53	52	45	58	62	66	64	66	66	64	57	48	52		56.9
	MAX	76	57	67	67	70	74	80	83	80	73	71	84	87	90	89	89	79	79	69	65	70	83	82	82	80	88	79	79	71	79		77.4
	MIN	57	46	51	45	47	49	47	49	55	54	48	47	63	60	61	63	63	57	42	46	53	64	61	62	61	47	60	55	46	48		53.6
	MAX	78	64	66	68	72	76	82	85	81	78	78	86	91	93	91	88	83	79	73	69	72	88	86	84	84	82	84	80	82	83		80.2
	MIN	60	44	47	48	46	46	47	51	57	55	49	49	62	60	59	64	63	59	44	45	62	62	57	62	58	48	64	56	49	45		53.9

See Reference Notes Following Station Index

DAILY TEMPERATURES

Table 5 - Continued

Station		1	2	3	4	5	6	7	8	9	10	11	12	13	14	15	16	17	18	19	20	21	22	23	24	25	26	27	28
NEWBURG 3 W	MAX	76	66	65	79	75	82	86	88	73	82	87	92	96	97	95	96	94	79	75	76	73	89	90	87	87	90	81	80
	MIN	61	58	54	54	55	56	51	60	63	61	63	64	65	72	73	76	68	60	59	58	54	63	67	67	66	69	66	69
NEW CASTLE 1 N	MAX	79	54	54	77	70	78	83	83	81	85	85	87	91	91	86	83	84	80	76	78	84	84	87	88	75	85	85	80
	MIN	52	44	45	49	54	43	48	50	59	48	50	53	60	64	60	66	64	68	53	61	67	66	66	58	61	52	67	57
NEWELL	MAX	86	66	53	65	75	76	82	86	86	83	88	87	90	94	93	90	80	84	79	75	79	84	80	87	87	82	90	82
	MIN	61	48	48	48	58	51	53	56	64	57	56	56	64	64	65	69	65	68	60	64	69	69	68	64	65	60	71	62
NEWPORT	MAX	91	69	53	67	72	76	80	87	91	67	88	90	93	98	95	94	90	88	73	75	68	83	92	91	92	87	89	86
	MIN	64	54	51	51	51	53	50	51	56	61	55	53	53	63	65	67	69	63	53	55	57	62	65	64	65	57	58	60
NEW STANTON	MAX	66	51	55	70	76	80	85	86	80	88	86	90	93	94	90	83	87	72	77	78	82	88	89	87	81	89	76	78
	MIN	47	44	45	43	50	44	47	50	50	52	50	49	60	58	60	58	60	52	52	57	60	60	63	62	60	53	59	50
NORRISTOWN	MAX	83	65	73	73	80	80	83	88	71	76	84	88	95	96	94	90	88	75	74	72	75	90	92	89	86	87	88	83
	MIN	64	55	61	56	54	58	55	58	59	59	60	57	69	69	70	70	71	63	54	51	62	66	71	68	67	63	72	64
PALMERTON	MAX	73	61	69	69	76	77	81	85	68	74	78	88	88	92	90	89	88	75	73	67	70	89	87	84	82	82	84	80
	MIN	61	53	58	51	48	50	52	54	60	59	50	51	68	62	66	70	67	57	48	47	61	67	64	66	65	56	68	58
PHIL DREXEL INST OF TEC	MAX	85	65	73	75	79	81	84	90	69	75	85	90	98	98	97	89	91	74	75	72	74	92	93	90	86	88	93	84
	MIN	68	60	64	60	58	61	59	60	59	60	64	60	72	78	75	69	73	64	58	55	64	71	75	70	70	69	73	68
PHILADELPHIA WB AP	MAX	83	65	72	72	78	80	82	88	67	73	82	88	95	95	95	88	89	74	73	71	73	90	91	88	85	86	90	83
	MIN	64	59	62	56	54	60	55	58	58	58	60	58	68	74	70	66	71	60	55	51	62	68	71	69	67	67	71	66
PHILADELPHIA PT BREEZE	MAX	90	65	71	73	79	82	83	90	65	72	84	88	96	96	96	87	86	70	75	72	71	90	92	89	86	88	90	82
	MIN	66	59	62	60	59	63	63	63	58	59	64	66	68	78	75	66	73	67	56	54	61	67	72	68	68	68	71	67
PHILADELPHIA SHAWMONT	MAX	90	74	72	72	79	79	82	89	91	73	83	88	96	95	95	94	86	86	73	75	72	89	92	93	90	89	89	89
	MIN	65	55	59	54	52	57	53	55	59	59	61	54	65	68	66	57	69	66	52	49	61	65	69	79	64	62	72	59
PHILADELPHIA CITY	MAX	81	65	71	72	76	78	81	87	66	71	83	86	93	94	94	87	86	75	73	70	72	88	89	87	85	85	88	81
	MIN	64	58	61	59	60	62	62	65	57	58	63	67	70	77	77	65	72	59	57	57	61	68	70	69	70	68	70	68
PHILIPSBURG CAA AP	MAX	63	47	52	62	69	74	82	85	77	82	80	86	89	89	85	79	78	66	64	61	77	83	82	83	75	79	77	70
	MIN	46	40	46	45	50	40	41	48	59	52	42	43	62	60	53	61	65	45	41	52	57	64	63	59	52	44	54	48
PHOENIXVILLE 1 E	MAX	86	67	73	75	84	85	89	87	76	85	91	97	98	95	92	93	87	75	74	75	76	93	93	91	90	88	91	87
	MIN	61	52	55	50	47	47	50	61	57	56	48	62	60	63	65	66	61	48	42	49	60	60	66	65	60	56	69	60
PIMPLE HILL	MAX	82	69	60	65	67	70	75	81	83	57	71	74	84	87	90	88	82	79	74	68	63	72	83	82	82	75	77	77
	MIN	61	45	45	47	51	46	55	61	54	53	54	56	64	68	62	65	63	55	43	43	51	57	64	61	58	51	62	56
PITTSBURGH WB AP 2	MAX	60	50	51	66	73	76	81	82	79	85	83	87	91	91	86	83	85	73	69	74	82	82	84	83	77	83	79	74
	MIN	44	43	45	47	52	48	53	57	62	55	56	58	68	66	66	67	65	58	55	60	67	69	65	61	62	55	65	54
PITTSBURGH WB CITY	MAX	64	53	54	70	74	80	84	85	80	87	86	90	94	94	89	82	86	73	72	77	85	84	87	87	79	86	82	76
	MIN	49	46	46	50	56	51	57	60	65	59	70	61	71	70	70	69	65	60	56	62	68	70	68	64	65	58	69	60
PLEASANT MOUNT 1 W	MAX	80	65	59	68	65	68	73	78	80	59	74	73	83	85	89	87	85	73	69	68	66	71	81	83	82	71	75	80
	MIN	55	45	45	47	45	42	44	46	55	56	48	47	58	58	61	61	65	51	36	42	50	58	50	63	58	42	50	49
PORT CLINTON	MAX	89	74	60	71	75	78	80	85	89	66	78	84	90	96	95	95	91	85	75	75	68	74	90	90	89	85	85	86
	MIN	62	51	45	49	46	48	49	50	56	57	52	46	60	59	62	68	64	62	54	42	54	59	62	65	59	52	62	51
PUTNEYVILLE 2 SE DAM	MAX	81	63	52	50	66	73	80	83	85	81	86	85	89	92	92	98	79	83	69	74	75	83	83	84	85	78	89	80
	MIN	55	40	42	44	45	42	46	49	54	51	47	47	47	60	57	62	61	53	47	47	57	63	61	60	58	49	52	56
QUAKERTOWN 1 E	MAX	84	66	72	70	77	79	82	87	63	75	80	87	92	93	93	90	87	80	78	71	71	88	90	88	83	83	87	84
	MIN	62	52	54	48	47	56	52	60	57	57	52	59	65	61	64	67	66	60	47	42	59	65	64	66	63	60	67	58
READING WB CITY	MAX	77	64	70	73	79	79	85	91	70	77	85	89	96	96	93	89	86	71	73	68	73	90	90	89	85	85	88	83
	MIN	64	53	58	54	52	57	56	59	60	60	58	57	71	70	72	70	69	61	56	52	59	67	69	68	68	62	70	62
RIDGWAY 3 W	MAX	62	58	50	63	70	79	83	83	81	83	83	88	90	90	89	83	79	77	72	71	78	85	83	83	74	83	78	70
	MIN	58	42	45	45	47	40	40	42	44	54	41	42	43	53	54	53	61	60	40	44	55	61	61	62	57	50	50	51
SALINA 3 W	MAX	82	58	52	66	72	78	82	82	79	84	84	88	90	91	89	85	82	72	73	75	80	82	84	86	77	85	82	77
	MIN	57	42	45	46	57	44	48	51	61	52	50	51	59	60	59	64	61	62	58	57	66	69	65	62	61	51	68	59
SCRANTON	MAX	85	68	62	73	70	73	79	84	84	68	75	79	89	93	93	93	89	84	76	76	71	74	88	86	67	66	70	78
	MIN	62	49	48	52	52	48	50	55	54	57	54	54	50	63	62	63	67	61	48	52	54	62	60	61	63	52	52	59
SCRANTON WB AIRPORT	MAX	67	55	71	69	71	76	81	84	67	78	77	88	91	92	90	87	81	75	75	70	73	86	87	84	77	80	84	78
	MIN	53	49	54	52	53	47	50	53	58	58	53	51	66	63	62	67	66	52	45	49	58	66	62	65	57	51	64	54
SELINSGROVE CAA AP	MAX	68	57	64	72	76	81	86	89	67	82	83	88	96	92	92	90	84	72	74	68	78	89	86	87	85	85	86	81
	MIN	57	51	51	50	50	49	50	54	60	58	51	51	67	59	63	69	68	53	51	57	61	67	65	65	60	55	64	58
SHIPPENSBURG	MAX	87	68	65	71	77	77	82	88	81	85	85	90	96	96	92	88	88	83	71	69	77	88	89	88	88	86	85	83
	MIN	62	50	50	48	50	53	50	56	61	60	55	53	67	64	64	69	68	57	53	56	61	67	68	63	66	58	68	64
SHIPPINGPORT WB	MAX	61	51	52	67	70	77	82	82	79	85	83	86	91	91	85	83	84	75	71	76	83	84	85	86	75	84	78	72
	MIN	46	43	46	49	51	44	51	54	58	52	53	54	64	66	63	66	64	56	54	60	65	68	63	62	57	54	67	51
SLIPPERY ROCK	MAX	65	52	51	65	70	79	84	84	80	83	85	87	89	93	85	86	88	72	74	75	74	82	83	85	75	82	80	73
	MIN	47	42	44	45	54	47	52	54	60	53	55	55	65	65	65	66	62	59	50	58	65	68	65	62	59	52	65	58
SOMERSET MAIN ST	MAX	76	60	49	65	70	76	80	81	78	81	81	85	90	89	86	85	82	77	64	70	77	79	83	84	82	84	80	76
	MIN	55	42	42	42	50	42	45	48	54	50	48	48	59	59	60	59	60	56	53	52	60	65	60	59	59	50	65	56
SPRINGBORO	MAX	72	55	54	55	55	62	73	78	82	78	82	87	88	90	82	89	85	79	79	72	79	86	87	87	82	71	84	78
	MIN	50	45	50	48	45	43	45	48	57	53	50	54	62	64	61	66	65	64	49	57	59	64	60	65	59	47	66	55
SPRINGS 1 SW	MAX	69	84	59	63	68	72	78	78	76	79	78	81	84	86	80	78	80	72	61	65	74	79	82	80	78	82	74	72
	MIN	63	41	41	40	41	41	43	46	55	47	46	45	54	56	54	61	56	54	52	50	60	65	64	59	48	48	64	52
STATE COLLEGE	MAX	68	68	56	66	72	77	84	88	79	85	85	89	94	91	90	83	81	68	65	64	84	85	84	85	78	84	80	75
	MIN	60	45	47	46	54	52	51	55	62	62	57	53	70	65	60	61	61	57	50	56	59	60	65	64	62	56	64	56
STROUDSBURG	MAX	70	60	71	70	71	80	82	88	60	73	78	90	91	95	93	90	82	76	70	68	71	90	88	90	82	82	82	85
	MIN	60	50	50	45	42	47	45	50	53	54	50	45	62	56	60	61	62	52	37	40	57	56	58	62	60	50	63	53
TAMARACK 2 S FIRE TWR	MAX																												
	MIN																												
TIONESTA 2 SE DAM	MAX	80	57	54	54	64	70	80	82	82	80	82	83	88	90	91	95	83	80	76	75	75	81	84	84	84	72	82	78
	MIN	55	43	45	45	48	44	45	49	49	53	50	49	55	62	59	63	64	64	44	51	59	63	62	64	61	51	52	57
TITUSVILLE WATER WORKS	MAX	65	54	52	66	74	79	83	84	80	84	83	88	91	93	93	85	83	79	78	76	81	88	87	85	73	81	78	75
	MIN	44	41	43	41	50	40	47	42	59	48	45	45	56	58	56	61	63	60	40	53	64	59	60	60	59	48	65	54
TOWANDA	MAX	75	61	68	71	74	77	83	85	77	83	80	90	93	95	92	89	80	76	77	72	82	89	89	90	80	84	86	78
	MIN	60	47	47	44	52	45	46	51	60	58	50	47	64	58	56	62	65	55	39	47	60	62	53	65	63	50	64	52

See Reference Notes Following Station Index

able 5 - Continued

DAILY TEMPERATURES

PENNSYLVANIA
JUNE 1956

Station		Day Of Month 1	2	3	4	5	6	7	8	9	10	11	12	13	14	15	16	17	18	19	20	21	22	23	24	25	26	27	28	29	30	31	Average
IIONTOWN	MAX	71	53	53	68	74	80	83	85	82	87	83	87	92	91	87	80	84	77	66	76	80	79	86	84	80	87	81	79	76	87		79.3
	MIN	53	47	47	45	56	48	53	54	62	57	55	54	64	64	64	68	62	63	60	61	69	70	68	64	63	57	70	62	40	54		58.5
'PER DARBY	MAX	85	66	71	74	79	81	83	90	79	74	83	88	95	96	95	90	87	80	74	71	74	90	92	88	86	86	90	83	78	86		83.1
	MIN	64	55	60	55	54	60	54	58	58	59	61	57	68	73	69	66	70	64	52	49	60	66	70	68	65	66	73	63	55	58		61.7
ARREN	MAX	65	54	51	61	69	78	83	83	82	82	82	90	91	93	89	84	80	78	78	74	82	89	85	87	71	85	79	74	75	88		78.7
	MIN	46	44	45	47	53	43	49	44	60	54	47	49	59	60	58	62	66	62	43	54	62	62	62	62	61	50	67	55	48	45		54.0
AYNESBURG 2 W	MAX	80	54	53	69	75	79	83	84	81	86	84	89	92	91	88	84	87	78	68	76	82	80	86	86	80	87	81	77	77	88		80.2
	MIN	53	45	45	44	50	45	49	50	59	51	50	49	59	59	61	65	62	66	54	59	65	63	64	62	62	56	68	56	45	49		55.5
ELLSBORO 3 S	MAX	80	64	49	53	62	68	73	89	83	71	80	78	86	90	92	86	84	73	72	69	65	79	86	82	85	73	79	79	72	73		75.8
	MIN	59	42	42	43	45	44	48	50	55	57	51	53	61	63	61	61	61	55	42	44	51	58	58	60	59	47	52	55	47	48		52.4
ELLSVILLE	MAX	80	60	66	70	76	78	82	88	82	82	83	82	96	94	90	88	88	80	72	70	86	89	89	92	84	85	86	83	78	85		82.1
	MIN	59	51	53	50	45	52	48	52	56	60	51	50	58	60	63	69	66	56	52	52	51	60	65	63	60	55	69	54	46	50		55.9
EST CHESTER	MAX	80	74	71	75	81	81	86	91	90	76	85	91	96	97	95	88	87	68	75	69	73	92	91	91	88	87	89	84	80	86		83.9
	MIN	56	54	55	55	58	56	59	59	61	58	57	68	73	71	70	69	66	60	49	57	64	68	67	66	63	69	63	56	59	65		61.7
ILLIAMSPORT WB AP	MAX	69	57	64	68	75	80	87	90	73	84	86	94	98	94	93	91	86	82	74	67	76	94	90	90	84	82	86	80	79	85		81.9
	MIN	57	51	50	47	55	48	52	57	64	62	53	53	67	63	63	68	69	57	52	54	62	65	63	65	62	55	63	60	53	51		58.0
ORK 3 SSW PUMP STA	MAX	87	68	68	73	79	78	84	89	89	84	84	90	97	97	95	93	89	88	73	74	74	90	91	90	90	88	88	86	83	85		84.8
	MIN	62	53	53	51	48	54	51	54	59	60	57	53	62	62	65	68	68	59	54	55	61	61	68	65	64	58	71	57	48	54		58.5

able 6

EVAPORATION AND WIND

Station		Day of month 1	2	3	4	5	6	7	8	9	10	11	12	13	14	15	16	17	18	19	20	21	22	23	24	25	26	27	28	29	30	31	Total or Avg.
CONFLUENCE 1 SW DAM	EVAP	.21	.11	.00	.04	.11	.05	.20	.21	.19	.15	.25	.24	.21	.28	.14	.21	.07	.08	.08	.18	.12	.06	.08	.17	.28	.17	.19	.21	.23	.21		4.73
	WIND	88	73	49	35	40	31	30	33	36	39	51	41	34	25	22	29	20	27	32	80	36	47	34	45	58	56	40	72	87	41		1331
FORD CITY 4 S DAM	EVAP	.19	.13	.03	.01	.08	.17	.19	.20	.21	.16	.25	.24	.23	.22	.26	.20	.01	.16	.10	.25	.12	.09	.15	-	.25	.19	.18	.28	.25	.20		B5.17
	WIND	56	55	41	47	40	38	13	9	21	6	32	13	34	6	20	20	15	13	12	51	29	40	10	32	57	32	24	61	60	10		897
HAWLEY 1 S DAM	EVAP	.17	.09	.00	.15	.17	.12	.20	.21	.24	.02	.09	.22	.28	.25	.29	.26	.16	.20	.26	.24	.19	.02	.25	.22	.28	.20	.21	.23	.21	.17		5.60
	WIND	84	72	29	57	84	57	39	33	39	37	38	55	96	62	60	44	34	35	40	85	137	62	54	53	110	73	50	116	111	59		1905
JAMESTOWN 2 NW	EVAP	.13	.04	.05	.00	.07	.14	.17	.20	.06	.23	.21	.23	.23	.23	.18	.14	.07	.13	.13	.20	.12	.12	.16	-	.19	.13	.19	.29	.15	.20		B4.54
	WIND	35	17	26	23	22	29	4	11	12	15	15	7	18	8	8	5	4	4	15	22	20	19	11	25	23	13	30	43	18	15		517
PIMPLE HILL	EVAP	.32	.10	.05	.18	.14	.16	.24	.22	.24	*	.30	.32	.36	.30	.37	.26	.17	.21	.28	.25	.16	.05	.22	.31	.27	.23	.28	.28	.25	.26		6.78
	WIND	99	61	99	64	49	75	27	25	50	*	109	74	104	89	77	37	30	40	52	84	109	73	34	69	93	64	84	115	112	88		2086

SUPPLEMENTAL DATA

Station	Wind direction: Prevailing	Wind direction: Percent of time from prevailing	Wind speed m. p. h.: Average	Fastest mile	Direction of fastest mile	Date of fastest mile	Relative humidity averages - percent: 1:30 a EST	7:30 a EST	1:30 p EST	7:30 p EST	Number of days with precipitation: Trace	.01–.09	.10–.49	.50–.99	1.00–1.99	2.00 and over	Total	Percent of possible sunshine	Average sky cover sunrise to sunset
LLENTOWN WB AIRPORT	WSW	18	8.6	-	-	-	84	79	55	64	7	4	1	1	1	1	15	-	5.7
ARRISBURG WB AIRPORT	WSW	17	6.6	32	NW	24	79	75	51	60	6	3	7	2	0	0	18	70	5.6
HILADELPHIA WB AIRPORT	WSW	17	7.9	38	W	16	81	71	52	63	4	4	4	2	1	0	15	65	6.0
ITTSBURGH WB AIRPORT	WSW	22	8.8	31*	NW	23	82	80	57	67	3	4	5	4	0	0	16	70	6.3
EADING WB CITY	-	-	8.1	36	NW	24	-	-	-	-	1	6	3	2	3	0	15	59	6.2
RANTON WB AIRPORT	WSW	16	7.6	43	W	23	77	76	49	60	2	4	2	3	2	0	13	61	5.9
HIPPINGPORT WB	-	-	2.3	43††	W	23	-	-	-	-	0	6	5	1	1	0	13	-	6.3
ILLIAMSPORT WB AIRPORT	-	-	-	-	-	-	-	79	49	60	3	3	4	1	1	0	12	-	5.8

This datum is obtained by
isual observation since record-
ig equipment is not available.
: is not necessarily the fast-
st mile occurring during the
eriod.
† Peak Gust

MONTHLY AND SEASONAL HEATING DEGREE DAYS

Season of 1955 - 1956

Station	July	August	September	October	November	December	January	February	March	April	May	June	Total	Long-ter means July-Jun
ALLENTOWN WB AP	0	1	100	299	750	1209	1103	927	928	548	278	26	6169	5880
ALLENTOWN GAS CO	0	1	85	276	720	1169	1083	906	924	523	267	24	5978	
ALTOONA HORSESHOE CURVE	0	7	133	363	846	1203	1197	973	910	574	304	63	6573	
ARENDTSVILLE	0	0	81	307	760	1146	1088	894	864	498	239	34	5911	
ARTEMAS 1 WNW	0	0			772		1117	936	792	490	211	48		
BAKERSTOWN 3 WNW	0	2	49	325	759	1106	1160	904	830	501	234	52	5922	
BEAVERTOWN					659							31		
BELLEFONTE 4 S	0	1	131	368	829	1209	1165	975	945	582	315	87	6607	
BERWICK	0	0	84	285	752	1184	1104	916	885	489	245	18	5962	
BETHLEHEM LEHIGH UNIV	0	0	73	229	712	1156	1072	884	895	512	245	24	5802	
BLAIRSVILLE 6 ENE	0	6	90	368	854	1212	1266	983	905	623	296	77	6680	
BRADFORD 4 W RES	13	33	244	468	919	1330	1330	1147	1138	732	427	121	7902	
BROOKVILLE CAA AIRPORT	0	15	165	459	873	1210	1237	1039	1002	639	361	94	7094	
BURGETTSTOWN 2 W	0	10	119	450	865	1184	1220	981	892	577	317	79	6684	
BURNT CABINS 2 NE	0	0	89	389	804	1198	1160	938	879	520	243	60	6280	
BUTLER	0	2	84	328	750	1091	1115	903	834	506	218	38	5869	
CANTON 1 NW	2	20	259	438	899	1344	1300	1116	1150	716	462	108	7814	
CARLISLE	0	0	59	256	721	1109	1015	827	756	434	146	13	5336	
CHAMBERSBURG 1 ESE	0	0	86	314	750	1125	1072	868	834	497	228	30	5804	
CHESTER	0	0	35	172	604	1009	972	780	784	448	196			
CLARION 3 SW	1	9	152	459	863	1205	1198	996	939	575	305	65	6761	
CLAYSVILLE 3 W	0	8	78	433	796	1155	1158	876	848	571	279	[illegible]	[illegible]	
COATESVILLE 1 SW	0	0	82	295	707	1150	1088	881	898	520	244	39	5904	
COLUMBIA	0	0	58	225	668	1083	1007	806	787	444	155	10	5243	
CONFLUENCE 1 SW DAM	0	9	116	386	788	1155	1179	870	903	574	271	73	6324	
CORRY	0	4	148	392	828	1200	1251	1076	1039	670	364	87	7059	
COUDERSPORT 2 NW	1	23		448	942	1333	1332	1146	1129					
COUDERSPORT 3 NW											429	132		
DERRY	0	0	61	323	723	1103	1142		816		247			
DEVAULT 1 W	0	9	158		755	1249						37		
DIXON	0	14		366	782	1309	1237	1053	1069	635	401	58		
DONEGAL	0	25	174	532	965	1303	1361	1036	1019	723	398	143	7679	
DONORA	0	0	21	253	647	978	1057	763	711	419	157	33	5039	
DU BOIS 7 E	0	11	148	416	869	1234	1253	1041	1045	637	320	74	7046	
EAGLES MERE	0	18	223	446	924	1384	1346	1151	1164	734	455	109	7954	
EAST BRADY	0	0	53	305	728	1077	1144	943	868	513	236	46	5913	
EBENSBURG	0	14	147	431	881	1201	1296	1010	974	662	345	96	7057	
EMPORIUM 1 E	1	11	193	431	886	1289	1238	1107	1083	684	420	100	7443	
EPHRATA	0	1	95	315	721	1133	1062	865	858	515	210	25	5800	
ERIE CAA AIRPORT	0	7	112	347	765	1132	1213	1039	1027	647	365	96	6750	
EVERETT 1 SW	0	3	103	382	824	1131	1105	934	850	530	247	62	6171	
FARRELL SHARON	0	0	70	345	763	1081	1189	963	899	550	298	75	6233	
FORD CITY 4 S DAM	0	5	110	397	841	1156	1218	972	950	605	333	71	6658	
FRANKLIN	0	4	107	361	788	1121	1168	1003	926	574	302	59	6413	
FREDERICKSVILLE 2 S E	0	1	77	269	687	1144								
FREELAND	0	8	158		898	1333	1253	1063	1053	671	382	83		
GEORGE SCHOOL	0	2	83	263	695	1144	1062	840	898	506	191	17	5661	
GETTYSBURG	0	0	61	264	707	1097	1040	844	833	458	216	36	5556	
GORDON	0	2	136	385	817									
GRATZ 1 N	0	0	122	360	820	1215	1126	960	943	570	309	49	6474	
GREENVILLE	0	4	107	390	764	1135	1201	1000	930	575	294	62	6462	
HANOVER	0	0	78	293	743	1126	1075	865	864	498	235	32	5809	
HARRISBURG WB AP	0	0	67	257	718	1124	1015	850	824	484	202	19	5560	5258
HAWLEY 1 S DAM	6	55	289	413	865	1333	1300	1123	1170	721	425	89	7789	
HOLTWOOD	0	0	34	222	686	1089	1035	829	810	469	188	13	5375	
HUNTINGDON	0	0	101	347	824	1147	1127	929	899	563	286	44	6267	
INDIANA 3 SE	0	6	82	383	801	1146	1213	923	876	557	285	61	6333	
IRWIN	0	3	35	294	730	1057	1147	848			194	36		
JAMESTOWN 2 NW	0	9	150	399	860	1193	1266	1080	1022	631	383	100	7093	
JIM THORPE	0	0	86	289	733	1149	1048	894	891	512	283	35	5920	
JOHNSTOWN	0	0	77	325	785	1118	1151	882	843	504	259	52	5996	
KANE 1 NNE	14	40	267	514	907	1327	1333	1165	1144	745	445	141	8042	
KEGG	0	6	107	376	833	1149	1152	927	848	559	278	65	6300	
LANCASTER 2NE PUMP STA	0	0	84	269	700	1134	1067	835	823	485	182	25	5604	
LANDISVILLE	0	0	87	288	746	1165	1100	909	890	530	241	31	5987	
LAWRENCEVILLE 2	6	11	202	420	845	1297	1304	1106	1122	685	440	88	7526	
LEBANON 2 NW	0	0	101								174			
LEWISTOWN	0	0	83	300	768	1131	1073	888	855	539	247	39	5923	
LINESVILLE 5 WNW	0	8	150	425	795	1190	1251	1084	1005	632	344	84	6968	
LOCK HAVEN	0	0	121	331	782	1175	1092	934	877	511	248	37	6108	
MADERA	0	12	175	419	937	1304	1332	1104	1079	714	435	124	7635	
MARCUS HOOK	0	0	18	164	594	1053	972	771	704	449	186	9	4920	
MARTINSBURG CAA AP	0	4	122	356	846	1180	1191	963	902	581	292	60	6497	
MEADVILLE 1 S	0	8	164	424	864	1200	1257	1090	1034	650	398	97	7186	
MERCER 2 NNE	0	10	122	459	791	1258	1360	1070	981	589	373	77	7090	
MIDDLETOWN OLMSTED FLD	0	0	67	247	709	1125	1043	848	820	480	190	15	5544	
MIDLAND DAM 7	0	0	56	363	771	1093	1151	884	831	512	228	47	5936	
MONTROSE 1 E	0	18	224	421	903	1409	1350	1151	1185	739	469	96	7965	
MORGANTOWN	0			314	755	1205	1109	916	933	557	266	45		
MT GRETNA 2 SE	0	0	104	282	742	1133	1093	903	859		250	72		
MT POCONO 2 N AP	0	13	193	371	872	1355	1276	1092	1109	691	388	72	7432	
MUHLENBURG 1 SE	0	4	147	356	844	1306	1230	1023	998	634	359	52	6953	
NEWBURG 3 W	0	0	64	206	670	1097	1025	867	771	459	146	10	5315	
NEW CASTLE 1 N	0	3	71	350	757	1084	1165	928	857	516	266	43	6040	
NEWELL	0	0	33	295	677	1002	1094	834	790	413	167	31	5336	
NEWPORT	0	0	97	324	790	1138	1068	916	887	554	270	30	6074	
NEW STANTON	0	0	70	355	773	1152	1140	894	828	553	263	61	6089	
NORRISTOWN	0	0	38	192	628	1074		806	836	453	174	9		
PALMERTON	0	1	115	338	762	1199	1119	948	939	569	265	35	6290	
PHIL DREXEL INST OF TEC	0	0	13	143	562	1015	970	738	743	417	134	4	4739	
PHILADELPHIA WB AP	0	0	32	200	626	1061	1011	790	808	456	170	11	5165	4866
PHILADELPHIA PT BREEZE	0	0	13	155	553	1000	948	712	760	409	150	8	4708	
PHILADELPHIA SHAWMONT	0	0	34	193	607	1059	989	784	784	449	143	7	5049	
PHILADELPHIA CITY	0	0	16	156	551	1010	954	764	795	462	163	7	4878	4523
PHILIPSBURG CAA AP	5	28	213	456	937	1301	1285	1099	1098	686	381	128	7577	

See Reference Notes Following Station Index

ntinued

MONTHLY AND SEASONAL HEATING DEGREE DAYS

PENNSYLVANIA

Season of 1955 - 1956

Station	July	August	September	October	November	December	January	February	March	April	May	June	Total	Long term means July-June
HOENIXVILLE 1 E	0	0	83	263	686	1122	1055	850	861	518	186	21	5645	
IMPLE HILL	0	12	176	413	894	1373	1332	1113	1150	720	413	89	7685	
ITTSBURGH WB AP 2	0	2	59	361	775	1115	1149	897	857	540	242	66	6063	5905
ITTSBURGH WB CITY	0	0	30	275	693	1013	1050	808	759	466	184	44	5322	5048
.EASANT MOUNT 1 W	5	37	281	483	936	1435	1383	1199	1220	775	493	133	8380	
ORT CLINTON	0	11	243			1139	1090	918	917	504	293	41		
JTNEYVILLE 2 SE DAM	0	9	147	444	880	1211	1260	1022	1012	630	358	84	7057	
JAKERTOWN 1 E	0	0	86	296	731	1190	1111	927	885	521	222	32	6001	
EADING WB CITY	0	0	56	213	657	1092	995	815	820	465	197	13	5323	5060
IDGWAY 3 W	1	15	184	457	873	1275	1278	1080	1040	659	360	96	7318	
ALINA 3 W	0	5	74	345	774	1104	1165	905	849	539	260	47	6067	
CRANTON	0	0	175	332	773	1184	1192	1039	1021	615	361	47	6739	
CRANTON WB AIRPORT	0	0	133	340	815	1277	1222	1007	1032	602	338	47	6811	
ELINSGROVE CAA AP	0	0	113	362	798	1205	1124	946	911	543	297	34	6333	
HIPPENSBURG	0	0	59	261	730	1109	1038	839	781	466	195	25	5503	
HIPPINGPORT WB	0	2	73	370	766	1089	1124	888	841	533	277	67	6030	
.IPPERY ROCK	0	6	87	312	843	1140	1193	984	919	554	271	64	6373	
OMERSET MAIN ST	0	13	134	417	830	1178	1213	933	887	599	265	73	6542	
PRINGBORO	0	9	139	371	1162			1024		598	338	97		
PRINGS 1 SW	0	25	189	438	906	1251	1290	972	990	675	344	105	7185	
TATE COLLEGE	0	3	124	354	836	1188	1149	990	945	569	260	50	6468	
TROUDSBURG	0		138	331	746	1225	1129	1030	1067	656	374	71	6767	
AMARACK 2 S FIRE TWR					961	1359	1325	1153	1142	721	455			
IONESTA 2 SE DAM	9	11	158	419	871	1230	1250	1103	1055	671	363	84	7221	
ITUSVILLE WATER WORKS	1	9	165	423	895	1232	1266	1095	1064	664	356	78	7248	
OWANDA	0	4	137	337	792	1253	1207	1011	1018	604	338	46	6747	
NIONTOWN	0	2	41	330	728	1041	1101	788	754	483	200	51	5519	
PPER DARBY	0	0	40	204	633	1084	1027	798	814	461	159	11	5231	
ARREN	0	1	137	411	815	1193	1229	1043	1013	624	328	70	6864	
AYNESBURG 2	0	3	56	363	749	1095	1117	807	774	507	207	52	5730	
ELLSBORO 3 S	0	13	229	421	903	1334	1327	1127	1141	711	447	111	7764	
ELLSVILLE	0	0	87	306	755	1163	1063	865	847	519	216	33	5854	
EST CHESTER	0	0	54	220	654	1090	1037	787	804	440	180	9	5275	
ILLIAMSPORT WB AP	0	0	105	340	793	1207	1115	959	923	520	280	35	6277	5898
ORK 3 SSW PUMP STA	0	0	54	250	694	1104	1035	811	777	463	169	13	5370	

DEGREE DAY NORMALS IN THIS TABLE ARE DERIVED FROM THE PERIOD 1921-1950.

able 3

DAILY PRECIPITATION

Station	1	2	3	4	5	6	7	8	9	10	11	12	13	14	15	16	17	18	19	20	21	22	23	24	25	26	27	28	29	30	31	Total
JULY 1955																																
TICA	.31	3.32	T			.33	.75		T							.06	.05							*				*	1.97			6.79
AUGUST 1955																																
TICA		.02		.35	.43	*	.41	.13			.66	.06	.10	1.50			.24						.18					.04			.33	4.45
SEPTEMBER 1955																																
TICA											.22	.02				.04						T	.01	.91	.01			.75				1.96
OCTOBER 1955																																
TICA						1.44	.42	.50					T	.43	.74	.15	.11	.19	.01	.02					1.10					.59	.07	5.77
NOVEMBER 1955																																
TICA	.05		.31	T	.01				.02		.15	.06		.54	T	1.87	.08	.02	.25	.01		T	.05	.20		T	.11	.23	.04	.45		4.45

See Reference Notes Following Station Index

STATION INDEX

Station	Index No.	County	Drainage [1]	Latitude	Longitude	Elevation	Observation Time Temp.	Observation Time Precip.	Observer	Refer To Tables	Station
ACHETONIA LOCK 3	0022	ALLEGHENY	1	40 32	79 49	748		7A	CORPS OF ENGINEERS	3	HUNTINGDON
ALLENS MILLS	0090	JEFFERSON	1	41 12	78 55	1600		MID	CHARLES M. ALLEN	C	HUNTSDALE
ALLENTOWN WB AP	0106	LEHIGH	9	40 39	75 26	376	MID	MID	U.S. WEATHER BUREAU	2 3 5 7 C	HYNDMAN
ALLENTOWN GAS CO	0111	LEHIGH	9	40 36	75 28	254	7A	7A	LEHIGH VLY GAS DIV	2 3 5	INDIANA 3 SE
ALTOONA HORSESHOE CURVE	0134	BLAIR	6	40 30	78 29	1500	6P	6P	ALTOONA WATER BUR.	2 3 5 7	IRWIN
ARENDTSVILLE	0229	ADAMS	15	39 55	77 18	710	8A	8A	PA STATE COL EXP	2 3 5	JACKSON SUMMIT
ARTEMAS 1 WNW	0259	BEDFORD	12	39 45	78 28	1250	6P	6P	GRAYSON E.NORTHCRAFT	2 3 5 7 C	JAMESTOWN 2 NW
AUSTINBURG 2 W	0313	TIOGA	15	42 00	77 32	1590		7A	OTTO D. BACON	3 C	JIM THORPE
BAKERSTOWN 3 WNW	0355	ALLEGHENY	1	40 39	79 59	1230	7P	7P	PGH CUT FLOWER CO	2 3 5	*JOHNSTOWN
BARNES	0409	WARREN	1	41 40	79 02	1310		7A	CORPS OF ENGINEERS	3	JOHNSTOWN 2
BEAR GAP	0457	NORTHUMBLAND	15	40 50	76 30	900		MID	ROARING CRK WTR CO	3	KANE 1 NNE
BEAVER FALLS	0475	BEAVER	2	40 46	80 19	760		7A	HOWARD R. KEMP	3	KARTHAUS
BEAVERTOWN	0482	SNYDER	15	40 45	77 10	640	7A	7A	MARLIN RC ETTINGER	2 3 5 7	KEATING SUMMIT
BEECH CREEK STATION	0499	CENTRE	16	41 04	77 34	620		7A	HAROLD S. RUPERT	3	KEGG
BELLEFONTE 4 S	0530	CENTRE	16	40 51	77 47	1110	8A	8A	ROCKVIEW PRISON FARM	2 3 5 7	KITTANNING LOCK 7
BERWICK	0611	COLUMBIA	15	41 04	76 15	570	6P	6P	AMER CAR + FNDRY CO	2 3 5 7	KREGAR 4 SE
BETHLEHEM	0629	NORTHAMPTON	9	40 37	75 22	400		7A	ARTHUR CROPPER	3	KRESGEVILLE 3 W
*BETHLEHEM LEHIGH UNIV	0634	NORTHAMPTON	9	40 36	75 23	450	MID	MID	LEHIGH UNIVERSITY	2 3 5 C	LAFAYETTE MC KEAN PARK
BLAIN	0729	PERRY	15	40 20	77 31	750		MID	PA DEPT FRST + WTRS	C	LAKEVILLE 1 NNE
BLAIRSVILLE 6 ENE	0736	INDIANA	4	40 27	79 09	2048	8P	8P	U.S. WEATHER BUREAU	2 3 5	LANCASTER 2 NE PUMP ST.
BLAKESLEE CORNERS	0743	MONROE	9	41 06	75 36	1650		MID	WALTER WILDRICK	C	LANCASTER 2 NE FILT PL
BLOSERVILLE 1 N	0763	CUMBERLAND	15	40 16	77 22	650		5P	MRS. B. M. WILLDERS	3	LANDISVILLE
BOSWELL 6 WNW	0820	SOMERSET	1	40 11	79 08	2580		7A	MRS. MAE L. KIMMEL	3 C	LATROBE
BRADDOCK LOCK 2	0861	ALLEGHENY	10	40 24	79 52	725		7A	CORPS OF ENGINEERS	3	LAURELTON STATE VILLAGI
BRADFORD CNTRL FIRE STA	0867	MC KEAN	1	41 57	78 39	1500		8A	BRADFORD FIRE DEPT	3	LAWRENCEVILLE 2 S
BRADFORD 4 W RES	0868	MC KEAN	1	41 57	78 44	1680	5P	5P	BRADFORD WTR DEPT	2 3 5 7	LEBANON 3 SW
BREEZEWOOD	0905	BEDFORD	6	40 00	78 14	1352		MID	PA TURNPIKE COMM	3	LEHIGHTON
BROOKVILLE CAA AIRPORT	1002	JEFFERSON	1	41 09	79 06	1417	MID	MID	CIVIL AERO. ADM.	2 3 5 7	LE ROY
BRUCETON 1 S	1033	ALLEGHENY	10	40 18	79 59	1065		7A	AUSTIN R. COOPER	3	LEWIS RUN 3 S
BUCKSTOWN 1 SE	1073	SOMERSET	4	40 04	78 50	2460		MID	ALVIN W. MANGES	C	LEWISTOWN
BUFFALO MILLS	1087	BEDFORD	6	39 58	78 39	1318		7A	MRS. NELLE R. BROWN	3	LINESVILLE 5 WNW
BURGETTSTOWN 2 W	1105	WASHINGTON	11	40 23	80 26	980	7A	7A	SMITH TWP MUN AUTH	2 3 5 7	LOCK HAVEN
BURNT CABINS 2 NE	1115	HUNTINGDON	6	40 05	77 52	990	MID	MID	PA TURNPIKE COMM	2 3 5 7	LOCK HAVEN 2
*BUTLER	1130	BUTLER	2	40 52	79 54	1100	4P	7A	WILLIAM C. FAUST	2 3 5 7	LONG POND 2 W
BUTLER SUBSTATION	1135	BUTLER	2	40 51	79 53	1140		MID	WEST PENN POWER CO	C	MADERA
CAMP HILL	1198	CUMBERLAND	15	40 15	76 55	461		6P	JOSEPH N. HOBART	3	MAHAFFEY
CANTON 1 NW	1215	BRADFORD	15	41 40	76 52	1520	7A	7A	MRS.MILDRED SPENCER	2 3 5 7 C	MAPLE GLEN
CARLISLE	1234	CUMBERLAND	15	40 12	77 11	460	6P	6P	C. E. MILLER	2 3 5 7	MAPLETON DEPOT
CARROLLTOWN 2 SSE	1255	CAMBRIA	16	40 35	78 42	2040		8A	ROBERT F. MAURER	3	MARCUS HOOK
CARTER CAMP 2 W	1262	POTTER	16	41 37	77 45	2030		7A	RICHARD L. MENKEN	3 C	MARIENVILLE 1 SW
CEDAR RUN	1301	LYCOMING	16	41 31	77 27	800		7A	KATHRYN T.KREIGHBAUM	3	MARION CENTER 2 SE
CHADDS FORD	1342	DELAWARE	5	39 52	75 36	160		8A	MRS.GRACE A. HICKS	3	MARTINSBURG 1 SW
CHAMBERSBURG 1 ESE	1354	FRANKLIN	12	39 56	77 38	640	9P	9P	CHARLES A. BENDER	2 3 5 7 C	MARTINSBURG CAA AP
CHARLEROI	1372	WASHINGTON	10	40 08	79 55	1040		MID	WEST PENN POWER CO	C	MATAMORAS
CHARLEROI LOCK 4	1377	WESTMORELAND	10	40 09	79 54	749		7A	CORPS OF ENGINEERS	3	MAYBURG
*CHESTER	1423	DELAWARE	5	39 50	75 21	86	8A	8A	CHESTER TIMES	2 3 5	MC CONNELLSBURG
CLARENCE 1 E	1480	CENTRE	16	41 03	77 56	1440		7A	MARGARET A. SWANCER	3	MC KEESPORT
CLARION 3 SW	1485	CLARION	1	41 12	79 26	1114	8P	7A	PA ELECTRIC CO	2 3 5 7 C	MEADOW RUN PONDS
CLAUSSVILLE	1505	LEHIGH	9	40 37	75 39	670		8A	WILLIAM J. DOTTERER	3	MEADVILLE 1 S
CLAYSVILLE 3 W	1512	WASHINGTON	11	40 07	80 28	1000	7P	7A	MFGRS. L + M CO	2 3 5	MEDIX RUN
CLEARFIELD	1519	CLEARFIELD	16	41 01	78 26	1100		7A	IRA TAYLOR	3	MERCER 2 NNE
CLERMONT	1529	MC KEAN	1	41 41	78 30	2104		7A	MRS.TILLIE M.SIMONDS	3 C	MERCER HIWAY SHED
COALDALE 2 NW	1572	SCHUYLKILL	9	40 50	75 56	1026		7A	PANTHER VLY WTR CO	3	MERCERSBURG
COATESVILLE 1 SW	1589	CHESTER	5	39 58	75 50	342	8A	8A	PHILA ELECTRIC CO	2 3 5 7 C	MERWINSBURG
COATESVILLE	1594	CHESTER	5	39 59	75 49	340		8A	EDWARD D. BIEDEMAN	INAC 12/55	MEYERSDALE 1 ENE
COLUMBIA	1675	LANCASTER	15	40 02	76 30	300	SS	SS	JAMES H. RUST	2 3 5	MIDDLETOWN OLMSTED FLD
CONFLUENCE 1 SW DAM	1705	SOMERSET	17	39 48	79 22	1490	8A	8A	CORPS OF ENGINEERS	2 3 5 6 C	MIDLAND DAM 7
CONFLUENCE 1 NW	1710	FAYETTE	17	39 50	79 22	1331		7A	JOHN L. REID	3	MILAN 4 WNW
CONNELLSVILLE	1723	FAYETTE	17	40 01	79 36	870		8A	MARSHALL B. MENEFEE	3	MILANVILLE
CONNELLSVILLE 2 E	1729	FAYETTE	17	40 01	79 33	1300		MID	HARRY C. JOY	C	MILLERSBURG 2 E
CONSHOHOCKEN	1737	MONTGOMERY	5	40 04	75 19	70		8A	PHILA ELECTRIC CO	3	MILLHEIM
COOKSBURG	1749	CLARION	1	41 20	79 13	1180		8A	PA DEPT FRST + WTRS	3	MILLVILLE 2 SW
COOKSBURG 2 NNW	1752	CLARION	1	41 21	79 13	1460		8A	PA DEPT FRST + WTRS	3	MILROY
CORAOPOLIS NEVILLE IS	1773	ALLEGHENY	11	40 30	80 05	720		8A	PGH. COKE + CHEM CO	3	MONTROSE 1 E
CORRY	1790	ERIE	1	41 56	79 38	1427	7P	5A	LEO C. NECKERS	2 3 5 7	MORGANTOWN
COUDERSPORT 3 NW	1806	POTTER	1	41 49	78 03	2020	7P	8A	MISS ELIZABETH NEFF	2 5 7	MT GRETNA 2 SE
COUDERSPORT 7 E	1809	POTTER	1	41 46	77 53	2425		7A	CAMP POTATO		MT POCONO 2 N AP
COVINGTON	1832	TIOGA	15	41 45	77 05	1193		7A	GROVER D. CLEVELAND		MOUNT UNION 1 N
CREEKSIDE	1881	INDIANA	1	40 41	79 12	1035		7A	CORPS OF ENGINEERS		MUHLENBURG 1 SE
CRESSON 2 SE	1895	CAMBRIA	6	40 27	78 34	2540		7A	MILES A. VECELLIO	U C	MURRYSVILLE
CUSTER CITY 2 W	1978	MC KEAN	1	41 55	78 41	2120		8A	M. D. BOOTH AND CO	3	MYERSTOWN
DANVILLE	2013	MONTOUR	15	40 58	76 37	460		7A	MRS.MARIE M. LITTLE	3	NATRONA LOCK 4
DERRY	2108	WESTMORELAND	4	40 20	79 18	1150	6P	6P	MISS N. D. WINEMAN	2 3 5	NEFFS MILLS 3 NE
DEVAULT 1 W	2116	CHESTER	14	40 05	75 33	360	MID	MID	PA TURNPIKE COMM	2 3 5	NESHAMINY FALLS
DINGMANS FERRY	2160	PIKE	5	41 13	74 52	360		MID	CLARENCE H. SMITH	C	NEWBURG 3 W
DIXON	2171	WYOMING	15	41 34	75 54	620	7A	7A	HAROLD J. KUSCHEL	2 3 5 7 C	NEW CASTLE 1 N
DONEGAL	2183	WESTMORELAND	17	40 07	79 23	1746	MID	MID	PA TURNPIKE COMM	2 3 5 7	*NEWELL
*DONORA	2190	WASHINGTON	10	40 11	79 51	814	12M	12M	DONORA ZINC WORKS	2 3 5	NEW PARK
DOYLESTOWN	2221	BUCKS	5	40 18	75 08	393		5P	GEORGE HART	3	NEWPORT
DRIFTWOOD	2245	CAMERON	16	41 20	78 08	880		MID	SIDNEY KENNEDY	C	NEW STANTON
DU BOIS 7 E	2265	CLEARFIELD	16	41 06	78 38	1670	5P	5P	CITY OF DU BOIS	2 3 5 C	NEW TRIPOLI
DUNLO	2298	CAMBRIA	4	40 17	78 43	2410		MID	MRS. D. L. WHITE	C	NORRISTOWN
DUSHORE 3 NE	2324	SULLIVAN	16	41 33	76 21	1750		7A	PATRICK P. RYAN	3 C	NORTH EAST 2 SE
EAGLES MERE	2343	SULLIVAN	16	41 24	76 35	2020	7A	7A	MRS.ELSIE P. BIGGER	2 3 5 7 C	ORRELL 3 N
EAST BRADY	2363	CLARION	1	40 59	79 37	820	5P	5P	A. B. KEMPEL	2 3 5	PALM
EAST WATERFORD 3 E	2490	PERRY	6	40 21	77 33	2125	8A	8A	U.S. WEATHER BUREAU	INAC 5/55	*PALMERTON
EBENSBURG	2466	CAMBRIA	4	40 29	78 43	2090	7P	7A	ROBERT A. WASSER	2 3 5	PARKER
EDINBORO	2514	ERIE	1	41 52	80 08	1220		8A	EDINBORO ST TCHR COL	3	PARKER 1 E
ELIZABETHTOWN	2560	LANCASTER	15	40 09	76 37	460		8A	MASONIC HOME	3	PAUPACK 2 WNW
EMPORIUM 1 E	2633	CAMERON	16	41 31	78 13	1160	7A	7A	RUSSELL E.PALMATEER	2 3 5 7 C	PECKS POND
ENGLISH CENTER	2644	LYCOMING	16	41 26	77 17	881		7A	WILLIAM SUDERS	3 C	*PHIL DREXEL INST OF T
EPHRATA	2662	LANCASTER	15	40 11	76 10	465	6P	6P	STANLEY L.VON NEIDA	2 3 5	PHILADELPHIA WB AP
EQUINUNK	2669	WAYNE	5	41 51	75 13	900		6A	MRS.ROSE M. NEILSEN	3	*PHILADELPHIA PT BREEZ
ERIE CAA AIRPORT	2682	ERIE	8	42 05	80 12	732	MID	MID	CIVIL AERO. ADM.	2 3 5	PHILADELPHIA SHAWMONT
EVERETT 1 SW	2721	BEDFORD	6	40 00	78 23	1020	MID	MID	PA TURNPIKE COMM	2 3 5 7 C	*PHILADELPHIA CITY
FARRELL SHARON	2814	MERCER	2	41 14	80 30	865	7P	7P	SHARON STEEL CORP	2 3 5	PHILIPSBURG CAA AP
FORD CITY 4 S DAM	2942	ARMSTRONG	1	40 43	79 30	950	8A	8A	CORPS OF ENGINEERS	2 3 5 6 7 C	PHOENIXVILLE 1 E
FRANKLIN	3028	VENANGO	1	41 23	79 49	987	7P	7A	JAMES K. ELLIOTT	2 3 5 7 C	PIKES CREEK
FREDERICKSVILLE 2 SE	3047	BERKS	14	40 26	75 40	950	8A	8A	D. P. FENSTERMACHER	INAC 5/56	PIMPLE HILL
FREELAND	3056	LUZERNE	15	41 01	75 54	1900	6P	8A	ANDREW B. EVANSHA	2 3 5	PINE GROVE 1 NE
GALETON	3130	POTTER	16	41 44	77 39	1325		7A	W. GALE LUSH	3	PITTSBURGH WB AP 2
GEIGERTOWN	3189	BERKS	14	40 13	75 50	400		8A	WALTER C. WOLF	3	*PITTSBURGH WB CITY
GEORGE SCHOOL	3200	BUCKS	5	40 13	74 56	135	7P	7P	GEORGE M. HART	2 3 5 7	PLEASANT MOUNT 1 W
*GETTYSBURG	3218	ADAMS	12	39 50	77 14	540	9A	9A	HUGH C. MC ILHENNY	2 3 5 7	PORT CLINTON
GETTYSBURG 1 S	3223	ADAMS	12	39 48	77 14	560		MID	NAT MILITARY PARK	C	PORTLAND
GIFFORD	3237	MC KEAN	1	41 51	78 36	2220		8A	SOUTH PENN OIL CO	INAC 3/56	POTTSTOWN
GLENCOE	3298	SOMERSET	12	39 49	78 51	1620		MID	MRS. MARY M.HARTMAN	C	POTTSVILLE PALO ALTO
GLEN HAZEL 2 NE DAM	3311	ELK	1	41 34	78 36	1725		8A	CORPS OF ENGINEERS	3 C	PUNXSUTAWNEY
GLEN ROCK	3330	YORK	15	39 48	76 44	620		MID	MRS.E.C.MC WILLIAMS	C	PUTNEYVILLE 2 SE DAM
GLENWILLARD DASH DAM	3343	ALLEGHENY	11	40 33	80 13	705		7A	CORPS OF ENGINEERS	3	QUAKERTOWN 1 E
GOULDSBORO	3394	WAYNE	9	41 15	75 27	1890		7A	L. M. EILENBERGER	3	RAYMOND
GRATERFORD	3435	MONTGOMERY	14	40 14	75 72	160		7A	CLAUDE K. KULP	3	*READING WB CITY
GRATZ 1 N	3438	DAUPHIN	15	40 38	76 43	760	8A	8A	LEE M. LEITZEL	2 3 5 7 C	RENOVO
GREENSBORO LOCK 7	3503	GREENE	10	39 47	79 55	808		7A	CORPS OF ENGINEERS	3	RENOVO 5 S
GREENSBURG 2 E	3515	WESTMORELAND	10	40 18	79 31	1225		MID	PA DEPT HIGHWAYS	C	REW
GREENSBURG 3 SE	3516	WESTMORELAND	10	40 17	79 30	1245		8P	WESTMORELAND WTR CO	3	RICES LANDING L 6
GREENVILLE	3526	MERCER	2	41 24	80 23	1026	6P	6P	C. EARL MILLER	2 3 5 7	RIDGWAY 3 W
HANOVER	3662	YORK	15	39 48	76 59	600	8A	8A	HANOVER EVENING SUN	2 3 5	ROCHESTER 1 N
*HARRISBURG WB AP	3699	YORK	15	40 13	76 51	335	MID	MID	U.S. WEATHER BUREAU	2 3 5 7 C	RUSH
HARRISBURG NORTH	3704	DAUPHIN	15	40 18	76 54	323		9A	GEORGE S. BEAL	3	RUSHVILLE
HAWLEY	3758	WAYNE	5	41 29	75 10	880		7A	MRS.KATHERINE S.BATE	3	SAFE HARBOR
HAWLEY 1 S DAM	3761	WAYNE	5	41 28	75 11	1200	7A	7A	PA POWER + LIGHT CO	2 3 5 6 7 C	SAGAMORE 1 S
HOLLIDAYSBURG	4001	BLAIR	6	40 26	78 24	960		MID	JOHN M. RINGLER	C	SALINA 3 W
HOLLISTERVILLE	4008	WAYNE	5	41 23	75 26	1360		8A	PA POWER + LIGHT CO	3	SAXTON
*HOLTWOOD	4019	LANCASTER	15	39 50	76 20	187	MID	8A	PA POWER + LIGHT CO	2 3 5 C	SCANDIA 2 E
HOME	4027	INDIANA	1	40 45	79 06	1220		MID	MRS. EDNA M. BUSH	C	SCHENLEY LOCK 5
HONESDALE 4 NW	4043	WAYNE	5	41 37	75 19	1410		9A	GEORGE C. WILLIAMS	3	*SCRANTON
HONESDALE 6 NNW	4044	WAYNE	5	41 39	75 17	1050		MID	FRIEND E. WALTER	C	SCRANTON WB AIRPORT
HOOVERSVILLE	4058	SOMERSET	4	40 09	78 55	1660		7A	PA ELECTRIC CO	3	SELINSGROVE CAA AP
HOP BOTTOM 2 SE	4066	SUSQUEHANNA	15	41 43	75 43	900		7A	JOSEPH J. SANSUSKAS	3	SELLERSVILLE 2 NW

STATION INDEX

Station	Index No.	County	Drainage ‡	Latitude	Longitude	Elevation	Observation Time Temp.	Observation Time Precip.	Observer	Refer To Tables
ADE GAP	7965	HUNTINGDON	6	40 31	77 52	1060		MID	MRS. HELEN M. RYLC	C
AMOKIN	7978	NORTHUMBLAND	15	40 48	76 33	770		8A	ROARING CRK WTR CO	3
EFFIELD 6 W	8026	WARREN	1	41 41	79 04	1940		MID	L. N. HANSOM	C
IPPENSBURG	8073	FRANKLIN	15	40 03	77 32	709	4P	4P	KEITH B. ALLEN	2 3 3
IPPINGPORT WB	8078	BEAVER	11	40 37	80 26	740	MID	MID	U.S. WEATHER BUREAU	2 3 5 7 C
INNEMAHONING	8145	CAMERON	16	41 19	78 05	790		7A	MRS.FRANCES CALDWELL	3
IPPERY ROCK	8184	BUTLER	2	41 04	80 03	1345	7P	7A	WALTER D. ALBERT	2 3 5
ETHPORT HIGHWAY SHED	8190	MC KEAN	1	41 48	78 27	1510		MID	PA DEPT HIGHWAYS	C
MERSET FAIRVIEW ST	8244	SOMERSET	17	40 01	79 05	2140		7A	HOWARD G. PECK	3
MERSET MAIN ST	8249	SOMERSET	17	40 01	79 05	2150	6P	6P	DAVID L. GROVE	2 3 5 7
UTH CANAAN 1 NE	8275	WAYNE	5	41 31	75 24	1400		MID	EUGENE M. COOK	C
UTH MOUNTAIN	8308	FRANKLIN	12	39 51	77 30	1520		7A	PA DEPT OF HEALTH	3
RINGBORO	8359	CRAWFORD	8	41 48	80 23	900	8A	8A	SPRINGBORO BOROUGH	2 3 5 7 C
RING GROVE	8379	YORK	15	39 52	76 52	470		4P	P. H. GLATFELTER CO	3 C
RINGS 1 SW	8395	SOMERSET	17	39 44	79 10	2500	8P	8P	ALLEN E. YODER	2 3 5 7
ATE COLLEGE	8449	CENTRE	16	40 48	77 52	1175	MID	MID	PA STATE COLLEGE	2 3 5 C
RAUSSTOWN	8570	BERKS	14	40 29	76 11	600		8A	JACOB KLAHR	3
RONGSTOWN	8589	INDIANA	4	40 33	78 55	1080		MID	HARRY F. BENNETT	C
ROUDSBURG	8596	MONROE	5	40 50	75 12	480	8A	8A	WILLIAM MAGERTY	2 3 5 7 C
UMP CREEK	8610	JEFFERSON	1	41 01	78 50	1320		7A	CORPS OF ENGINEERS	3
NBURY	8668	NORTHUMBLAND	15	40 51	76 48	440		7A	CHARLES W. BAYLER	3 C
SQUEHANNA	8692	SUSQUEHANNA	15	41 57	75 36	1020		7A	MRS. LAURA A.BENSON	3
TERSVILLE	8699	ALLEGHENY	17	40 14	79 48	765		7A	FRANK E. MARSH	3
MAQUA	8758	SCHUYLKILL	14	40 48	75 58	830		8A	MRS. MARY L.ROBERTS	3
MAQUA 4 N DAM	8763	SCHUYLKILL	14	40 51	75 59	1120		7A	PANTHER VLY WTR CO	3 C
MARACK 2 S FIRE TWR	8770	CLINTON	16	41 24	77 51	2220	7A	7A	JAMES E. SWARTZ	2 3 5 7
ONESTA 2 SE DAM	8873	FOREST	1	41 29	79 26	1200	8A	8A	CORPS OF ENGINEERS	2 3 5 7 C
TUSVILLE #	8885	CRAWFORD	1	41 38	79 40	1550		MID	PA ELECTRIC CO	C
TUSVILLE WATER WORKS	8888	CRAWFORD	1	41 38	79 42	1220	7P	7P	CITY OF TITUSVILLE	2 3 5
RPEDO 4 W	8901	WARREN	1	41 47	79 32	1735		7A	MRS. LILY B. GARBER	3
WANDA	8905	BRADFORD	15	41 46	76 26	760	7P	7A	MRS. M. O. PARKS	2 3 5 7 C
WER CITY 5 SW	8910	DAUPHIN	15	40 31	76 37	745		6P	HARRISBURG WTR DEPT	3 7
OY	8959	BRADFORD	15	41 47	76 47	1100		7A	JENNIE L. BALLARD	3
NNELTON	8989	INDIANA	4	40 27	79 23	890		MID	MRS. MARY E. WEIMER	C
RTLEPOINT 4 NE	9002	MC KEAN	1	41 54	78 16	1040		7A	ROBERT D. STRAIT	3
RONE 4 NE BALD EAGLE	9024	BLAIR	8	40 43	78 12	1020		7A	FREDERICK L. FRIDAY	3 C
ION CITY	9042	ERIE	1	41 54	79 50	1325		7A	FORREST M. BRALEY	3 C
IONTOWN	9050	FAYETTE	10	39 54	79 44	1040	10P	10P	WM. W. MARSTELLER	2 3 5 7
PER DARBY	9074	DELAWARE	5	39 56	75 16	222	7P	7P	PHIL. SUB.TRANS. CO	2 3 5
ICA	9099	VENANGO	1	41 26	79 57	1030		7A	MRS.FLORENCE MILLER	3
NDERGRIFT	9128	WESTMORELAND	7	40 36	79 33	800		7A	UNITED ENG+FNDRY CO	3
NDERGRIFT 2 W	9133	WESTMORELAND	7	40 36	79 36	995		MID	EUGENE R. YOUNG	C
RGINVILLE	9196	BERKS	14	40 31	75 52	350		8A	MRS. MARY M. WRIGHT	3
WINCKEL	9206	CLARION	1	41 25	79 14	1620		8A	PA DEPT FRST + WTRS	3
WINCKEL 1 WSW	9209	CLARION	1	41 24	79 15	1610		8A	PA DEPT FRST + WTRS	3

Station	Index No.	County	Drainage ‡	Latitude	Longitude	Elevation	Observation Time Temp.	Observation Time Precip.	Observer	Refer To Tables
WARREN	9296	WARREN	1	41 51	79 08	1280	7P	7A	GILBERT H. REIER	2 3 5 7
WASHINGTON	9312	WASHINGTON	11	40 11	80 14	1200		MID	PA DEPT HIGHWAYS	C
WATSONTOWN	9345	NORTHUMBLAND	16	41 05	76 52	470		8A	OWEN BERKENSTOCK	3
WAYNESBURG 2 W	9362	GREENE	10	39 54	80 13	980	6P	7A	RALPH L. AMOS	2 3 5 7
WAYNESBURG 1 E	9367	GREENE	10	39 54	80 10	940		MID	SEWAGE DISPOSAL PLT	C
WEBSTER MILLS 3 SW	9380	FULTON	12	39 49	78 05	920		MID	WILLIAM D. COVER	C
WELLSBORO 3 S	9408	TIOGA	16	41 43	77 16	1920	7A	7A	MARION L. SHUMWAY	2 3 5 7
WELLSBORO 2 E	9412	TIOGA	16	41 45	77 16	1550		MID	MRS. IDA S. MAYNARD	C
WELLSVILLE	9420	YORK	15	40 03	76 57	500	5P	5P	D. D. HOOVER	2 3 5
WERNERSVILLE 1 W	9430	BERKS	14	40 20	76 06	405		8A	CHARLES A. GRUBER	3
WEST CHESTER	9464	CHESTER	5	39 58	75 36	440	8A	8A	DAILY LOCAL NEWS	2 3 5 7
WEST GROVE 1 E	9503	CHESTER	5	39 49	75 49	440		8A	CONARD-PYLE CO	3
WEST HICKORY	9507	FOREST	1	41 34	79 25	1090		8A	MRS.HELEN F.KINNEAR	3
WHITESBURG	9655	ARMSTRONG	1	40 45	79 24	1530		7A	CORPS OF ENGINEERS	3
WILKES-BARRE	9702	LAZERNE	15	41 15	75 52	610		7A	MRS. MARY G. MIRMAK	3
WILLIAMSBURG	9714	BLAIR	6	40 28	78 12	860		7A	MYRON K. BIDDLE	3
WILLIAMSPORT WB AP	9728	LYCOMING	16	41 15	76 55	527	MID	MID	U.S. WEATHER BUREAU	2 3 5 7 C
WIND GAP	9781	NORTHAMPTON	5	40 51	75 18	720		MID	OWEN R. PARRY	C
WOLFSBURG	9823	BEDFORD	6	40 03	78 32	1190		7A	WALTER C. RICE	3
YORK 3 SSW PUMP STA	9933	YORK	15	39 55	76 45	390	5P	5P	YORK WATER COMPANY	2 3 5 7
YORK 2 S	9938	YORK	15	39 56	76 44	640		MID	YORK WATER COMPANY	C
YORK HAVEN	9950	YORK	15	40 07	76 43	310		8A	METROPOL EDISON CO	3
YOUNGSVILLE	9966	WARREN	1	41 51	79 20	1225		MID	HENRY CARLETT	C
ZION GROVE	9990	SCHUYLKILL	15	40 54	76 13	940		7A	JAMES D. TEETER	3
ZIONSVILLE 3 SE	9995	LEHIGH	14	40 27	75 27	660		7A	LESLIE HOWATT	3
CLOSED STATIONS										
GRANTVILLE 2 SW	3422	DAUPHIN	15	40 22	76 41	510		SS	EARL E. RHOADS	3
NEW STATIONS										
LEBANON 2 NW	4891	LEBANON	15	40 22	76 28	000	8A	8A		2 3 5
PALMYRA	6694	LEBANON	15	40 18	76 35	480		7P	EARL E. RHOADS	3

‡ 1-ALLEGHENY; 2-BEAVER; 3- 4-CONEMAUGH; 5-DELAWARE; 6-JUNIATA; 7-KISKIMINETAS; 8-LAKE ERIE; 9-LEHIGH; 10-MONONGAHELA; 11-OHIO; 12-POTOMAC; 13-LAKE ONTARIO; 14-SCHUYLKILL; 15-SUSQUEHANNA; 16-WEST BRANCH; 17-YOUGHIOGHENY

REFERENCE NOTES

Additional information regarding the climate of Pennsylvania may be obtained by writing to the State Climatologist at Weather Bureau Airport Station, Harrisburg State Airport, New Cumberland, Pennsylvania, or to any Weather Bureau Office near you.

The four digit identification numbers in the index number column of the Station Index are assigned on a state basis. There will be no duplication of numbers within a state.

Figures and letters following the station name, such as 12 SSW, indicate distance in miles and direction from the post office.

Observation times given in the Station Index are in local standard time.

Delayed data and corrections will be carried only in the June and December issues of this bulletin.

Monthly and seasonal snowfall and heating degree days for the preceding 12 months will be carried in the June issue of this bulletin.

Stations appearing in the Index, but for which data are not listed in the tables, are either missing or received too late to be included in this issue.

Unless otherwise indicated, dimensional units used in this bulletin are: temperature in °F., precipitation and evaporation in inches, and wind movement in miles. Degree days are based on a daily average of 65° F.

Evaporation is measured in the standard Weather Bureau type pan of 4 foot diameter unless otherwise shown by footnote following Table 6.

Amounts in Table 3 are from non-recording gages, unless otherwise indicated.

Data in Tables 3, 5 and 6 and snowfall data in Table 7 are for the 24 hours ending at time of observation. See Station Index for observation time.

Snow on ground in Table 7 is at observation time for all except Weather Bureau and CAA stations. For these stations Snow on ground values are at 7:30 a.m. E.S.T. WTR EQUIV in Table 7 means the water equivalent of snow on the ground. It is measured at selected stations when depth of snow on the ground is two inches or more. Water equivalent samples are necessarily taken from different points for successive observations; consequently occasional drifting and other causes of local variability in the snowpack result in apparent inconsistencies in the record.

Long-term means for full-time Weather Bureau stations (those shown in the Station Index as United States Weather Bureau Stations) are based on the period 1921-1950, adjusted to represent observations taken at the present location.

- \- No record in Tables 3, 6, 7 and the Station Index. No record in Tables 2 and 5 is indicated by no entry.
- \+ And also on a later date or dates.
- * Amount included in following measurement, time distribution unknown.
- \# Thermometers are generally exposed in a shelter located a few feet above sod-covered ground; however, the reference indicates that the thermometers are exposed in a shelter located on the roof of a building.
- // Gage is equipped with a windshield.
- AM Data based on observational day ending before noon.
- B Adjusted to a full month.
- C In the "Refer to Tables" column in the Station Index the letter "C" indicates recorder stations. These stations are processed for special purposes and are published later in Hourly Precipitation Data.
- D Water equivalent of snowfall wholly or partly estimated, using a ratio of 1 inch water equivalent to every 10 inches of new snowfall.
- M One or more days of record missing; see Table 5 for detailed daily record. Degree day data, if carried for this station, have been adjusted to represent the value for a full month.
- R Amounts from recording gage (These amounts are essentially accurate but may vary slightly from the amounts to be published later in Hourly Precipitation Data).
- SS This entry in time of observation column in Station Index means sunset.
- T Trace, an amount too small to measure.
- Y Includes total for previous month.
- VAR Observations made at 2 p.m. Monday through Thursday and 7 a.m. Friday through Sunday.

Subscription Price: 20 cents per copy, monthly and annual; $2.50 per year. (Yearly subscription includes the Annual Summary.) Checks and money orders should be made payable to the Superintendent of Documents. Remittances and correspondence regarding subscriptions should be sent to the Superintendent of Documents, Government Printing Office, Washington 25, D. C.

WWRC., Asheville, N. C. --- 6/6/56 --- 1225

See Page 86 for Corrections

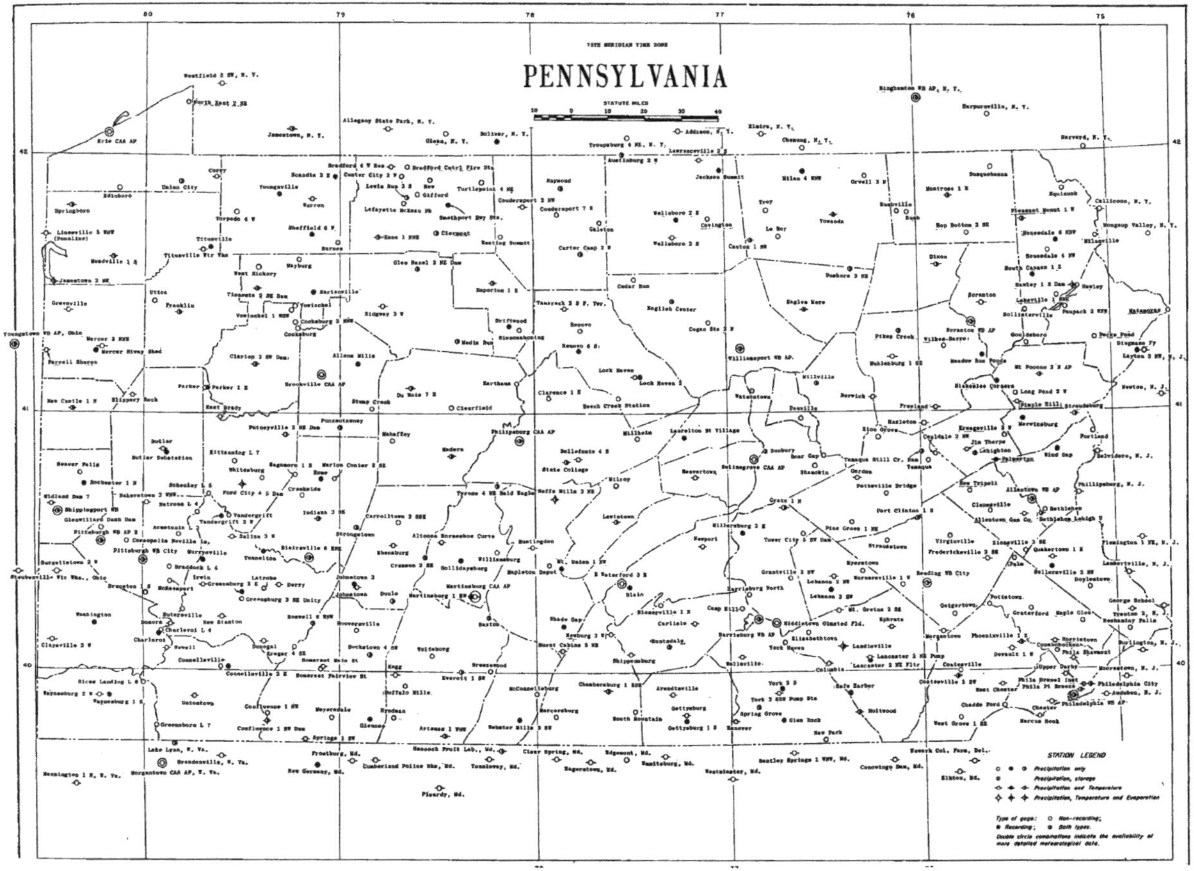

75TH MERIDIAN TIME ZONE
PENNSYLVANIA
STATUTE MILES
10 0 10 20 30 40
80
79
78
77
76
75
42
41
40
STATION LEGEND
Precipitation only
Precipitation, storage
Precipitation and Temperature
Precipitation, Temperature and Evaporation
Type of gage: Non-recording;
Recording; Both types.
Double circle combinations indicate the availability of more detailed meteorological data.

U. S. DEPARTMENT OF COMMERCE
SINCLAIR WEEKS, Secretary
WEATHER BUREAU
F. W. REICHELDERFER, Chief

IMATOLOGICAL DATA

PENNSYLVANIA

JULY 1956

Volume LXI No. 7

ASHEVILLE: 1956

WEATHER SUMMARY

GENERAL

July weather was unusually cool and wet with excessive cloudiness and greatly deficient sunshine. Thunderstorms were typically numerous and in some instances assumed violent proportions, resulting in several casualties and considerable damage over the State.

Monthly mean temperatures were coolest since well before the turn of the century at several reporting stations having records going back that far. At Harrisburg, for instance, this was the coolest July since 1891 and the second coolest of record. The number of days with readings reaching 90° or higher was well under par with a surprising number of stations recording none at all and many others only a fraction of their usual quota. Temperature extremes ranged from 99° at Phoenixville 1 E on the 2nd to 36° at Phillipsburg CAA Airport on the 18th.

Rainfall was well distributed and practically all fell as showers or thundershowers with few stations having as many as four consecutive rainless days. Precipitation was excessive at nearly all the stations having long-term figures for comparison. Departures of +1.00 inch or more were common and ranged all the way from +5.36 inches at Altoona Horseshoe Curve down to -2.15 inches at Scranton WB Airport, the driest spot in the State. Monthly totals ranged from 3.18 inches at Scranton to 12.48 inches at Bear Gap. The greatest daily amount was 5.21 inches at Waynesburg 2 W on the 27th.

WEATHER ~~DETAILS~~

Typical July temperatures with daytime readings in the 90's marked the first two days of the month. Thereafter, a procession of Canadian air masses dominated the State's temperatures on most days with readings as high as 90° extremely rare. The temperature situation was quite unusual. Maxima in the 60's generally around the 5th and 6th and prevailing daily peaks in the 70's and low 80's established an exceptionally cool pattern for July. This month's extreme readings occurred at opposite ends of the month, the warmest at the beginning and the coolest at the end.

Precipitation occurred as frequent showers, often in association with thunderstorms, due to the interaction between the prevailing cool air lying over the State and the warm moist air circulated northward by the frequently changing pressure systems. Days entirely without rain were few. Many localities experienced extremely heavy rains several times during the month.

WEATHER EFFECTS

Frequent rainfall delayed harvesting of grain and hay, causing losses in production and quality, according to the Federal-State Crop Reporting Service at Harrisburg. Sprouting of wheat in the shock was common and shelling out of overripe grain also reduced yields in some fields. Conditions were unfavorable for cultivation and spraying of crops. Blight threatened potato and tomato crops. Many row crops became weedy. Excessive moisture caused splitting of Erie County sweet cherrie and production dropped sharply. On the other hand, the abundant rainfall favored fruit sizing and rapid growth of crops. Prospects for oats, corn, potatoes, commercial vegetables, and later cuttings of hay improved materially. Picking of early peaches and apples began in southeastern counties. Tobacco varied from well above average in the Lancaster area to not so good in the Clinton County area where soil moisture was excessive and drainage poor. Lush pastures aided milk production this month, but the poor results thus far from hay crops may be keenly felt later.

DESTRUCTIVE STORMS

Noteworthy storms are listed below by dates of occurrence.

1-2nd: A squall line crossed the State in 30 hours and set off severe thunderstorms accompanied by strong winds, heavy rains and some hail. Four persons in Montoursville were burned when lightning struck a garage in which they were working. Strong winds and hail moderately damaged grapes and cheries in Erie County while in other sections crops were damaged by washing rains; total crop losses were about $10,000. Property damage was $350,000 Statewide, mostly to trees, utility lines and barns. Except for the warehouse and contents destroyed by a lightning set fire at Mt. Carmel, relatively little damage to buildings was reported.

8th: In the Mechanicsburg area, lightning killed 7 head of cattle and slightly damaged two industrial plants about 8:30 p.m. Total losses were estimated $3500.

12th: An evening thunderstorm with severe lightning and hail up to one inch in diameter caused unknown damage to crops and about $1000 damage to property in Allegheny, Westmoreland and Indiana Counties. The hailstorm was termed by some residents as the worst since the turn of the century in their locality. A boy was injured when struck on the head by a large hailstone. Lightning knocked out transformers and interrupted electric service.

14th: Lightning struck a barn in the Bloomsburg area about 10:30 a.m., burning the struc ture and its contents with total loss of $15,000.

17th: Heavy thunderstorms hit Allegheny Cou ty with extensive damage in the New Kensingt Tarentum-Natrona area. Lock 4 at Natrona reported 2.35 inches of rain in one hour. Puck Creek near New Kensington overflowed its ban and washed out the framework and forms of a bridge in the State's Route 56 By-Pass proje Landslides blocked many secondary roads and damaged several homes. Damage elsewhere in Allegheny County was limited to fallen utili wires and flooded cellars.

20th: Erie County was pounded by a straight-

windstorm and heavy rains that caused
st irreparable damage to three of its
r crops, hay, wheat and grapes.

l: Gusty thunderstorm winds caused wide-
ad damage, mostly to trees and utility
s, as the storm roared through upper
gomery and Bucks Counties from 6 to 9
Total damage was not believed to be
e.

: Severe evening thunderstorms hit ex-
e western Pennsylvania with greatly
ing amounts of rainfall that ranged up
ore than 3 inches in two hours at Waynes-
and Beaver Falls. A state of emergency
declared by the Mayor of Beaver Falls as
water and power lines were broken and
city was virtually isolated by washed
highways. Service on the Pittsburgh and
Erie Railroad was disrupted for a time.
y damage was also reported in Ambridge,
n, Midland, Aliquippa, Freedom, Monaca,
ington, Warren and Pittsburgh. Several
lies in Warren were evacuated from their
s by an army "duck" when small streams
flowed their banks. Newspaper accounts
mated $1,000,000 damage from this storm
he greater Pittsburgh area.

: A series of evening thunderstorms accompanied a cold front southeastward from the Schuylkill-Northumberland-Luzerne County area to beyond the State's border about midnight. Near Elysburg, 1 man was killed and 2 standing nearby were injured when lightning struck a shed in which they were working. Lightning killed a cow and heifer at Pottsville, and set fire to a cottage near Bloomsburg with damage of $4,000. At Phoenixville, lightning struck 6 persons in an amusement park but all recovered after treatment for shock. A lightning-set fire at Lancaster caused $3,000 damage. The thunderstorms dumped heavy rains that flooded streets and helped down wires and trees. Total reported damage amounted to $12,000.

FLOODS

Although main rivers rose as a result of the heavy rains, flood stages were not reached. The extremely heavy thunderstorm downpours caused damaging local flash floods as described above.

J. E. Stork, Climatologist
U. S. Weather Bureau
Weather Records Processing Center
Chattanooga, Tennessee

SPECIAL NOTICE

In this issue of the Climatological Data for Pennsylvania there is inaugurated a new presentation of precipitation and temperature data for the State. In January, 1956, the decision to abandon the State means of temperature and precipitation was reached after careful consideration and consultation with the Advisory Committee on Climatology. Political subdivisions generally bear no relation to natural regions of topography, vegetation or atmospheric circulation, and averages of climatic data over such areas do not form a valid time series. In addition the number and location of stations change from year to year. The charts presented herein give a general picture of the distribution of precipitation and temperature over the State.

CLIMATOLOGICAL DATA

TABLE 2

Station		Temperature: Average Maximum	Average Minimum	Average	Departure From Long Term Means	Highest	Date	Lowest	Date	Degree Days	No. of Days: Max 90° or Above	Max 32° or Below	Min 32° or Below	Min 0° or Below	Precipitation: Total	Departure From Long Term Means	Greatest Day	Date	Snow, Sleet: Total	Max Depth on Ground	Date	No. of Days: .10 or More	.50 or More
ATLANTIC DRAINAGE																							
ALLENTOWN WB AP	R	79.0	60.8	69.9	- 4.2	90	2	51	30	12	1	0	0	0	6.16	1.38	1.77	3	.0	0		10	5
ALLENTOWN GAS CO	AM	80.1	61.0	70.6	- 3.5	91	3	50	30	13	2	0	0	0	5.42	.65	1.63	21	.0	0		10	4
ALTOONA HORSESHOE CURVE		77.8	58.9	68.4	- 2.4	89	1+	45	30	17	0	0	0	0	9.36	5.36	3.26	16	.0	0		9	4
ARENDTSVILLE	AM	82.4	61.3	71.9	- 2.4	94	2+	49	30	4	4	0	0	0	4.72	.76	2.05	21	.0	0		8	2
ARTEMAS 1 WNW		81.9	57.8	69.9		92	1	46	29	7	3	0	0	0	5.82		1.70	3	.0	0		11	3
BEAVERTOWN		81.4M	59.1M	70.3M		92	1+	46	30	12	4	0	0	0	8.63				.0	0			
BELLEFONTE 4 S	AM	79.3	57.6	68.5	- 4.1	90	2	47	18+	13	1	0	0	0	4.95	1.14	1.20	20	.0	0		11	4
BERWICK		81.4	59.8	70.6		93	1	47	30	8	3	0	0	0	5.05		.82	5	.0	0		13	3
BETHLEHEM LEHIGH UNIV		78.6	62.0	70.3	- 4.7	92	1	53	31	15	2	0	0	0	3.77	- .92	.88	9	.0	0		9	3
BURNT CABINS 2 NE		80.4	57.6	69.0		92	2	45	29+	16	2	0	0	0	5.45		1.20	3	.0	0		8	4
CANTON 1 NW	AM	73.8	55.3	64.6		86	2	46	18	60	0	0	0	0	4.87		1.00	27	.0	0		10	5
CARLISLE		83.5	63.5	73.5	- 1.5	96	1	52	30	1	5	0	0	0	5.00	1.00	.98	21	.0	0		12	3
CHAMBERSBURG 1 ESE		81.9	61.2	71.6	- 3.1	94	2	48	30	3	3	0	0	0	5.94	2.18	2.20	20	.0	0		9	3
CHESTER	AM	82.4M	65.0M	73.7M		95	3	56	30	2	4	0	0	0	6.16		2.00	21	.0	0		10	4
COATESVILLE 1 SW	AM	81.7	61.3	71.5	- 3.3	95	3	47	30	10	4	0	0	0	5.71	1.05	2.18	21	.0	0		10	3
COLUMBIA		83.6	64.0	73.8		98	2	51	30	1	6	0	0	0	6.13		1.92	3	.0	0		8	4
DEVAULT 1 W		80.5	58.7	69.6		94	2	41	21	26	1	0	0	0	4.28		1.20	21	.0	0		11	2
DIXON	AM	78.7	55.6	67.2		89	2+	44	30	32	0	0	0	0	5.65		1.32	21	.0	0		12	4
DU BOIS 7 E		78.0	56.2	67.1		86	1	41	30+	31	0	0	0	0	7.25	2.71	1.80	2	.0	0		13	5
EAGLES MERE	AM	70.9	55.9	63.4		82	2	47	30	75	0	0	0	0	7.77	2.34	1.70	20	.0	0		12	6
EMPORIUM 1 E	AM	78.1M	54.5M	66.3M	- 3.4	88	2+	42	30	38	0	0	0	0	4.50	.08	1.17	9	.0	0			
EPHRATA		81.2	62.1	71.7	- 3.3	93	2	50	30	7	3	0	0	0	5.03	.36	1.80	3	.0	0		11	3
EVERETT 1 SW		80.3	58.4	69.4	- 2.1	90	1+	49	16	4	2	0	0	0	3.55	- .31	1.60	19	.0	0		11	1
FREELAND		74.0	56.1	65.1	- 4.2	82	1+	40	31	60	0	0	0	0	5.61	.08	.85	19	.0	0		15	4
GEORGE SCHOOL		80.9	61.5	71.2	- 3.0	91	2+	51	31	3	3	0	0	0	4.27	- .48	2.03	21	.0	0		7	1
GETTYSBURG	AM	83.0	63.2	73.1	- 1.5	95	3	50	30+	6	5	0	0	0	7.98	4.09	2.63	21	.0	0		8	4
GRATZ 1 N	AM	78.2M	58.5M	68.4M		89	2+	48	30+	22	0	0	0	0	4.91		1.07	21	.0	0		14	2
HANOVER	AM	82.6	61.0	71.8	- 3.9	96	3	49	30	5	3	0	0	0	6.45	2.07	2.24	21	.0	0		9	5
HARRISBURG WB AP	R	80.4	63.6	72.0	- 3.4	93	1	53	30	7	3	0	0	0	4.57	.93	1.03	8	.0	0		8	4
HAWLEY 1 S DAM	AM	75.5	54.6	65.1		86	2	41	31	63	0	0	0	0	4.11		.89	5	.0	0		11	3
HOLTWOOD		81.1	66.6	73.9	- 3.1	94	2	57	30+	0	3	0	0	0	6.23	2.34	2.05	21	.0	0		8	4
HUNTINGDON	AM	82.8	58.1	70.5	- 1.9	95	2	47	30+	6	6	0	0	0	6.95	2.94	1.92	3	.0	0		8	4
JIM THORPE		79.9M	58.9M	69.4M	- 2.5	89	1+	46	30	16	0	0	0	0	9.87	4.52	2.90	9	.0	0		11	5
KEGG		80.7	57.7	69.2		92	1+	45	30	7	2	0	0	0	3.87		1.03	17	.0	0		9	3
LANCASTER 2 NE PUMP STA		81.9	61.0	71.5	- 2.5	95	2+	51	30	4	4	0	0	0	5.04	.67	1.14	3	.0	0		11	4
LANDISVILLE 2 NW	AM	80.7	61.8	71.3		96	3	49	30	8	4	0	0	0	4.28		1.35	3	.0	0		8	2
LAWRENCEVILLE 2 S	AM	80.5	53.2	66.9	- 3.7	93	2	43	1	34	3	0	0	0	6.07	1.99	1.12	5	.0	0		12	4
LEBANON 2 NW	AM	81.7	63.5	72.6	- 1.7	94	2+	54	31	7	3	0	0	0	6.43	1.88	1.77	3	.0	0		8	5
LEWISTOWN	AM	81.8	60.0	70.9		93	2+	49	31	2	3	0	0	0	4.67		.95	27	.0	0		10	5
LOCK HAVEN		81.3	59.8	70.6	- 2.8	94	1	48	30	5	3	0	0	0	6.42	2.25	1.50	20	.0	0		11	6
MADERA	AM	77.2	52.6	64.9		88	2	40	30+	54	0	0	0	0	6.71		2.55	2	.0	0		12	2
MARCUS HOOK		82.0	66.3	74.2	- 4.8	92	2	56	6	4	2	0	0	0	5.81	1.59	2.22	21	.0	0		7	3
MARTINSBURG CAA AP		78.4	59.0	68.7		93	1	48	30	10	2	0	0	0	6.70		2.32	16	.0	0		10	5
MIDDLETOWN OLMSTED FLD		81.0	63.7	72.4	- 2.7	95	1	53	30	5	3	0	0	0	5.18	1.45	1.12	20	.0	0		12	3
MONTROSE 1 E	AM	74.0	55.4	64.7	- 3.6	86	2	48	30+	60	0	0	0	0	6.46	2.35	1.59	21	.0	0		12	4
MORGANTOWN		79.5	60.4	70.0		93	2	48	30	14	1	0	0	0	3.25		.75	2	.0	0		10	2
MT GRETNA 2 SE		79.5	60.7	70.1		90	1+	48	30	12	3	0	0	0	3.38		1.00	20	.0	0		9	2
MT POCONO 2 N AP		74.1M	55.5M	64.8M	- 1.2	84	1	43	30	60	0	0	0	0	5.98	.72	1.52	21	.0	0		11	3
MUHLENBURG 1 SE		77.9	55.2	66.6		89	1+	41	31	32	0	0	0	0	5.18		1.04	5	.0	0		14	4
NEWBURG 3 W		83.1	66.8	75.0		92	2+	56	11	0	5	0	0	0	8.13		1.90	16	.0	0		12	5
NEWPORT	AM	81.2	59.2	70.2		95	2	49	30+	9	3	0	0	0	4.67	.16	2.42	21	.0	0		8	2
NORRISTOWN		82.2	64.7	73.5		96	2	55	31	4	5	0	0	0	3.74		1.80	21	.0	0		4	3
PALMERTON		77.5	60.2	68.9	- 4.3	90	2	49	30+	21	1	0	0	0	7.47	2.74	1.98	4	.0	0		9	8
PHIL DREXEL INST OF TEC		83.6	67.6	75.6		97	2	59	6	1	5	0	0	0	5.22		2.00	21	.0	0		10	3
PHILADELPHIA WB AP	R	81.7	65.4	73.6	- 2.7	94	2	58	31	2	2	0	0	0	4.61	.41	1.92	21	.0	0		10	2
PHILADELPHIA PT BREEZE		81.6	67.5	74.6	- 2.8	95	2	58	6	4	3	0	0	0	4.80		1.92	21	.0	0		8	3
PHILADELPHIA SHAWMONT		83.6	64.1	73.9	- 2.4	96	3	53	30	2	3	0	0	0	5.85	1.26	2.40	21	.0	0		9	3
PHILADELPHIA CITY	RAM	80.5	66.6	73.6	- 3.6	93	2	59	5+	4	1	0	0	0	4.70	.49	1.46	21	.0	0		10	2
PHILIPSBURG CAA AP		74.7	53.9	64.3		87	1	36	18	73	0	0	0	0	7.44		1.67	19	.0	0		12	5
PHOENIXVILLE 1 E		84.5	60.7	72.6	- 3.1	99	2	48	30+	1	6	0	0	0	3.86	- .96	1.32	21	.0	0		10	2
PIMPLE HILL	AM	72.8	56.3	64.6		83	2	44	30	66	0	0	0	0	6.16		1.24	21	.0	0		11	5
PLEASANT MOUNT 1 W	AM	72.9	53.6	63.3		83	2	41	31	87	0	0	0	0	5.23	.16	1.59	5	.0	0		11	3
PORT CLINTON	AM	80.3	57.6	69.0	- 4.4	92	2+	45	30	20	3	0	0	0	5.18	.28	1.40	21	.0	0		8	4
QUAKERTOWN 1 E		81.0M	59.9M	70.5M	- 2.2	90	2+	49	31	11	2	0	0	0	5.73	.77	1.34	21	.0	0		11	4
READING WB CITY	R	81.2	64.4	72.8	- 2.9	94	2	55	31	6	3	0	0	0	4.01	- .42	.69	20	.0	0		12	3
SCRANTON	AM	77.3	57.0	67.2	- 5.4	90	2+	46	30+	33	2	0	0	0	6.33	1.90	1.00	14	.0	0		14	6
SCRANTON WB AIRPORT		76.7	58.3	67.5	- 4.7	89	1	47	30+	28	0	0	0	0	3.18	- 2.15	.62	5	.0	0		13	1
SELINSGROVE CAA AP		80.0	59.4	69.7	- 3.7	93	2	47	30	7	2	0	0	0	7.51	3.47	1.49	4	.0	0		12	6
SHIPPENSBURG		82.5	61.9	72.2	- 2.5	93	1+	49	30	3	4	0	0	0	4.65	.91	1.50	20	.0	0		10	2
STATE COLLEGE		78.3	59.2	68.8	- 2.2	91	1	48	18+	12	1	0	0	0	4.59	.73	.70	19	.0	0		10	5
STROUDSBURG		79.2	55.6	67.4	- 4.8	91	1	39	30	34	2	0	0	0	8.08	2.93	1.80	5	.0	0		12	6
TAMARACK 2 S FIRE TWR	AM																						
TOWANDA		79.6	56.8	68.2	- 2.5	92	1	44	30+	22	2	0	0	0	4.38	.50	1.17	5	.0	0		9	[illegible]
UPPER DARBY		82.6	65.2	73.9		95	2	56	30	2	3	0	0	0	5.81		2.35	21	.0	0		9	[illegible]
WELLSBORO 3 S	AM	75.0	55.9	65.5	- 3.3	87	2	44	30	48	0	0	0	0	3.91	.23	.89	5	.0	0		9	[illegible]
WELLSVILLE		81.7	59.7	70.7		93	2	46	30	6	4	0	0	0	5.10		1.18	21	.0	0		9	[illegible]
WEST CHESTER	AM	82.0	63.9	73.0	- 1.4	96	3	55	30	8	3	0	0	0	6.46	1.70	2.13	3	.0	0		9	[illegible]
WILLIAMSPORT WB AP		79.8	59.9	69.9	- 3.4	93	1	49	30	10	3	0	0	0	7.17	3.46	1.24	13	.0	0		10	[illegible]

See Reference Notes Following Station Index

Station	Temperature: Average Maximum	Average Minimum	Average	Departure From Long Term Means	Highest	Date	Lowest	Date	Degree Days	No. of Days: Max 90° or Above	Max 32° or Below	Min 32° or Below	Min 0° or Below	Precipitation: Total	Departure From Long Term Means	Greatest Day	Date	Snow, Sleet: Total	Max Depth on Ground	Date	No. of Days: .10 or More	.50 or More	1.00 or More
3 SSW PUMP STA	84.5	63.0	73.8	-1.0	95	2+	45	30	4	5	0	0	0	5.47	1.22	1.70	21	.0	0		10	3	2
DIVISION			70.0											5.60				.0					
OHIO DRAINAGE																							
STOWN 3 WNW	80.8	61.1	71.0		92	2	50	15	3	3	0	0	0	6.39		1.20	19	.0	0		11	5	2
SVILLE 6 ENE	76.4	59.1	67.8		85	1+	49	30	20	0	0	0	0	6.03	1.29	1.69	16	.0	0		11	4	2
ORD 4 W RES	75.8	52.2	64.0	-4.0	86	1	38	18	72	0	0	0	0	6.59	2.37	1.26	9	.0	0		9	6	1
VILLE CAA AIRPORT	76.4	56.2	66.3	-1.8	86	1+	44	30	40	0	0	0	0	7.23	2.86	1.42	4	.0	0		16	5	3
TTSTOWN 2 W AM	81.3M	57.4M	69.4M		90	3	43	30	20	1	0	0	0	5.24		1.13	27	.0	0		10	4	2
R	82.7	60.4	71.6	-.7	94	3	46	30	3	1	0	0	0	5.62	1.44	1.22	13	.0	0		11	5	2
ON 3 SW	80.6	57.8	69.2		90	1+	44	30	14	2	0	0	0	6.55	1.98	2.11	2	.0	0		11	3	3
VILLE 3 W	81.8M	57.2M	69.5M	-3.2	92	2			2	1	0	0	0					.0	0				
UENCE 1 SW DAM AM	79.8	55.4	67.6		90	3	40	31	28	1	0	0	0	6.42		1.43	27	.0	0		12	6	1
	78.1	56.6	67.4	-1.8	91	1	41	30	32	1	0	0	0	6.45	2.86	2.47	2	.0	0		10	3	2
RSPORT 3 NW	74.1	52.7	63.4		85	1	37	30	85	0	0	0	0	4.42		.89	9	.0	0		10	3	0
	80.8	62.0	71.4	-1.2	92	4	47	30	5	2	0	0	0	4.48	-.29	.95	4	.0	0		12	2	0
AL	76.0	53.4	64.7		87	2	38	30	61	0	0	0	0	3.82		.74	6	.0	0		11	2	0
A AM	84.5	64.1	74.3	-1.5	94	3	51	30	0	4	0	0	0	5.42	1.66	1.15	27	.0	0		13	3	2
BRADY	83.4	60.6	72.0		93	2	47	30	1	4	0	0	0	6.56		1.24	16	.0	0		10	4	1
BURG	74.7	56.8	65.8	-2.4	85	1	42	30	44	0	0	0	0	5.91	1.58	2.02	16	.0	0		13	3	2
LL SHARON	82.8	57.9	70.4	-3.5	93	1+	39	29	15	5	0	0	0	4.65	1.12	1.77	16	.0	0		9	3	1
CITY 4 S DAM AM	79.9	57.8	68.9		90	2+	47	30	23	2	0	0	0	6.90		2.05	16	.0	0		14	3	2
LIN	79.7	58.7	69.2	-1.4	88	1+	40	11	15	0	0	0	0	3.96	-.44	.74	9	.0	0		11	2	0
VILLE	81.2M	58.6M	69.9M	-1.4	92	1	47	14	3	3	0	0	0	4.05	-.04	1.15	15	.0	0		8	3	1
NA 3 SE	79.6	58.0	68.8	-2.9	89	2+	44	30	11	0	0	0	0	8.47	3.87	2.98	16	.0	0		16	3	1
	83.9M	62.0M	73.0M	.5	92	2			0	3	0	0	0	5.02	1.04	1.55	17	.0	0		12	3	1
TOWN 2 NW AM	78.5	58.4	68.5		89	2	44	30	25	0	0	0	0	5.98	2.09	2.31	9	.0	0		8	3	2
TOWN AM	84.7	58.8	71.8	-1.3	94	2	42	30	12	7	0	0	0	6.43	1.98	1.16	16	.0	0		11	5	3
1 NNE AM	75.5	52.2	63.9		87	2	37	18+	85	0	0	0	0	7.30	2.89	1.82	2	.0	0		10	5	2
VILLE 5 WNW	78.4	58.9	68.7		89	1	44	30	21	0	0	0	0	4.13	.38	1.04	21	.0	0		10	3	1
ILLE 1 S AM	77.9	58.1	68.0	-1.7	89	2	45	18	32	0	0	0	0	5.11	.89	1.91	9	.0	0		9	2	2
R 2 NNE	79.1	56.1	67.6		89	3+	40	30	27	0	0	0	0	6.86		1.34	16	.0	0		13	6	2
ND DAM 7	81.3	63.6	72.5	-.4	92	2	54	30	1	2	0	0	0	5.10	1.51	.98	18				12	4	0
ASTLE 1 N	81.3	60.0	70.7	-1.8	90	1+	46	30	7	4	0	0	0	8.26	4.10	1.91	27	.0	0		9	7	4
L AM	84.0	64.4	74.2	.7	95	3	53	30	0	3	0	0	0	4.12	.49	.68	27	.0	0		11	4	0
TANTON	83.2	57.3	70.3	-2.0	97	1	44	30	7	2	0	0	0	3.74	-.28	.95	8	.0	0		11	2	0
BURGH WB AP 2 //R	79.0	61.6	70.3	-2.0	88	1+	50	30	4	0	0	0	0	4.25	.34	1.32	26	.0	0		9	3	2
BURGH WB CITY R	81.6	64.5	73.1	-2.3	93	2	54	30	0	3	0	0	0	4.15	.43	.80	26	.0	0		8	3	0
YVILLE 2 SE DAM AM	79.7	55.8	67.8		90	3	43	30	25	1	0	0	0	7.70		2.17	2	.0	0		13	6	2
AY 3 W AM	77.6	52.8	65.2	-2.8	88	1+	40	31	63	0	0	0	0	6.54	2.32	1.65	27	.0	0		10	5	2
A 3 W	80.3	60.3	70.3		90	2	46	30	6	1	0	0	0	7.64		1.60	17	.0	0		14	6	1
INGPORT WB	79.1	60.8	70.0		90	2	52	15	2	1	0	0	0	5.08		1.52	17	.0	0		9	4	2
ERY ROCK	78.5	60.1	69.3		90	2+	49	30	9	2	0	0	0	9.18		2.09	5				13	6	3
SET MAIN ST	78.9	57.3	68.1	-.4	88	2	42	30	15	0	0	0	0	4.10	-.58	.95	6	.0	0		11	1	0
GS 1 SW	75.1	55.6	65.4	-1.7	86	2	41	30	49	0	0	0	0	4.72	.02	.62	26	.0	0		14	2	0
STA 2 SE DAM AM	78.1	57.1	67.6		89	2	47	30+	27	0	0	0	0	6.49	2.58	3.03	2	.0	0		7	5	1
VILLE WATER WORKS	78.8	55.4	67.1		90	1	40	30	39	1	0	0	0	6.97		1.96	9	.0	0		12	4	2
TOWN	80.7	63.0	71.9	-1.5	91	2	50	30	3	1	0	0	0	4.24	-.51	.90	28	.0	0		12	3	0
N	78.5	57.9	68.2	-1.7	90	1	46	18	20	1	0	0	0	7.31	2.84	2.75	27	.0	0		10	3	2
SBURG 2 W	81.4	59.6	70.5		92	2	48	30	3	1	0	0	0	11.13		5.21	27	.0	0		14	6	2
DIVISION			69.1											5.93				.0					
LAKE DRAINAGE																							
CAA AIRPORT	76.3	60.9	68.6	-1.8	91	1	50	18	12	1	0	0	0	7.11	3.92	1.37	20	.0	0		13	7	2
GBORO	79.3	58.3	68.8		97	3	45	18	31	2	0	0	0	5.63		1.38	9	.0	0		10	5	2
DIVISION			68.7											6.37				.0					

See Reference Notes Following Station Index

DAILY PRECIPITATION

Table 3

Station	Total	Day of month																													
		1	2	3	4	5	6	7	8	9	10	11	12	13	14	15	16	17	18	19	20	21	22	23	24	25	26	27	28	29	30
ACHETONIA LOCK 3	6.32	T		.28		T	.79			.28	.88			.38	.09		.14	.03	.89		.18	1.07	.12	.69	.03		.03	.38	.03	.03	
ALLENTOWN WB AP R	6.16	.10	.01	1.77	.50	.58	.04		.42	.57		.01	T	.26	T		.06			T	.25	1.40			.01	.01	.15	.02	T		
ALLENTOWN GAS CO	5.42		.23	.81		.62	.42	T		.53	.32			.04	.22	T		.09				1.63	.02		.04	.02	.02	.26		.15	
ALTOONA HORSESHOE CURVE	9.36		2.06	.12		.02	.17			.06			.04	.06	.03		3.26	1.43	.02	.21	1.27	.22	.02		.05	.03		.20	.09		
ARENDTSVILLE	4.72		.14	.75	.06	.44	.22	.05	.01	.08	T				.42		.11	.07	.06		.08	2.05	.03		.13	.02				T	
ARTEMAS 1 WNW	5.82			1.70	.41		.34			.08				.26				.40	.99	.24	.95	.22	.33		.34						
AUSTINBURG 2 W	5.48		.29			.60	.76			.52	.05	T	.19	.47	.31						.71	1.14	.03	.06	.12			.23			
BAKERSTOWN 3 WNW	6.39		.12		.07	.68			.04	.96	.07		.12	.08	T		.33	1.00	.02	1.20	.75	.03	.01	T	.15	.07	.15	.48	.06		
BARNES	7.03		2.70			1.11	.07			.96	.19	.06	.01	.16	.23	.06	.17	T			T	.09	.42	.08			T	.72			
BEAR GAP	12.48		.21	1.80	1.46	1.66	.18	.40		.99		.50	.60	.10	.18		.80	.40		.30	.40	.78			.50			.97	.23		
BEAVER FALLS	7.14	.04		T	T	.02	.33	.03		.57	.06	.02		.23	.01	.01	.18	.04	.93		.20	.54	.48	.15				3.23	.03	.04	
BEAVERTOWN	8.63		.48	.26	*	2.12	.05	.11		.36	.06			.01	.05		.20	.08			.87	1.56	.02	.02	.10	.02	.30	1.82		.34	
BEECH CREEK STATION	6.08		.31	.25		.81	.09	T		.14	.04		T		.24		.03	.36			1.65	.23		.53				.83		.57	
BELLEFONTE 4 S	4.95		.38	.21	T	.50			.02	.20	.02	T	.03	.14	T	.32		.80	.03		1.20	.07	T	.20	.03		.07	.07	.57	.29	
BERWICK	5.09		.22	.61	.29	.82	.08	.01		.43		T	.15	.03	.03		.05	.01		.29	.42	.49			.56	.13	.02	.24	.17		
BETHLEHEM	4.65		.09	.88		.49	.12			.08	.85			.18	.06	.06	.22	.05			.03	1.29			.02	T	T	.21	T	.04	
BETHLEHEM LEHIGH UNIV	3.77		.14	.83	.63	.46	.10		.03	.88			.02	.21	.02		.05	T		.04	T	.13			.02	T	.21		T		
BLAIRSVILLE 6 ENE	6.03		.42	.03	T	T	.09			.69	.03		.14	.05	.09		1.09	1.09		.12	.12	T	.25	.01	.02	.35	.03	.18	.03		
BLOSERVILLE 1 N	5.01		.41	T	.32	.46	T			.04	T	.04		.60	.30		.75	.07		.08	1.33	.45		.08		.08					
BOSWELL 6 WNW	4.87	T	.03	.55		.24	.90	.14		.82	.29	.04		.06	.16		.09	.07	.63		.27	.08	.36		.05		T	.16	.13	.04	
BRADDOCK LOCK 2	5.24			.17		.62	.39	.39		.23	.21	T		.02	.03		.01	.03	.21		.34	.37	.80	.35	.04		T	.92	.07	.04	
BRADFORD CNTRL FIRE STA	6.36		.68			.72	.05			.05	.16	.12	.32	.53	.12	.01	.03				.06	.07	.77	.16	.03			.48			
BRADFORD 4 W RES	6.59		.96		.02	.69	.03			.26	.46	.03	.54	.26	.08		.06				.06	.04	.91	.03	.05	.02	.29	.80			
BREEZEWOOD	5.35		.54	.12	.20	.44	.30		.04					.25			.16	1.36		.98	.39	.14	.10	.12	.11	.03	.05	.02			
BROOKVILLE CAA AIRPORT	7.23	.08	1.07	.01	.42	.32	T		.31	.17	.01		.17	.12	T		.47	.17		.53	.11	.01	.10		T	.30	.85	T	.21		
BRUCETON 1 S	7.03			.20		.84	.34			.33	.21			.04			.13	.02	*		1.10			.41	.05			.95			.41
BUFFALO MILLS	4.58		.63	.15		.50	.76	.09		.06	.01	.01		.07	.11		.13	.11	.71		.67	.13	T	.02	.18			.17		.05	.02
BURGETTSTOWN 2 W	5.24	.02		.14		.05	.21	T		.60	.49	T		.04	.03		T	.01	.12		.19	.90	.09	.10	.02			1.13	.10		
BURNT CABINS 2 NE	5.45		T	1.20	.02	.63	.16		.08	.09	.04			.22			1.10	.47		.46	.88	.04	T	T	.06		T				
BUTLER	5.62					.11				.58	.21	.03		.22	.05	T	1.09		.82		.70	.18	.12			.01	.15	.28	.07		
CAMP HILL	5.69		.23	.28	.03	.12	.21		.31	.62	T	T	.02	.63	.08		.57	T		.07	.75	.77	T		.02						
CANTON 1 NW	4.87		.32			.87	.11	T		.13	.13		.03	.27	.02	.03		.02			.78	.50	.02	.62			.02	1.00			
CARLISLE	5.00		.28	.03	.38	.22	.22		T	.20			T	.42	.26		.85	.02		T	.84	.98	T	T	.10	T	.20		T		
CARROLLTOWN 2 SSE	9.87	.10	1.70	1.15		.03	.37	.12		.39	.15	.04		.16	.08	.02	1.91	1.65	.18		.14	.02	.07	.02	.05	.01	.20	.25	.02	.04	
CARTER CAMP 2 W	6.99		.55			1.70	.21	.25		.43	.02	T	T	.26	.26		T				.62	1.17	.01	.05	T		T	1.46			
CEDAR RUN	5.69		.85	.20		.45	.15	.02		.16	.80	.03	.02	.10	.06		.10	T			.70	.45	.03	.75			.01	.75		.06	
CHADDS FORD	7.60		T	1.12	.01	.10	.80	T		1.60	.15		.10	T				.30		T		3.10				.20		.12			
CHAMBERSBURG 1 ESE	5.94		.04	1.51	.20	.47	.24			.13				.24	T		.01	.24		.50	2.20	.08	T	T	.08			T	T		
CHARLEROI LOCK 4	4.51			.24		.27	.04	.18		.96	.20	.01		.04	.10			.02	.50		.40	.15	T	.17	.06			.93	.09	.15	T
CHESTER	8.16		.07	1.20		.08	.04	.09		.86	T				.33	.16	.12		.70			2.00		.20	.12			.19			
CLARENCE 1 E	4.36		.71	.53	T	.15	.03	T		.14	T	T	T	.06	.35	T	.16	.41	T		.95	.18		.42			T	.12		.15	
CLARION 3 SW	6.55		2.11			1.08	.07	.03		.38	.08			.23	.10		.46		.04		.36	.11		.09		.10		1.17	.14		
CLAUSSVILLE	7.77		.34	.58		.69	.39	.02		1.92	.40		.01		.40			.03	.05			1.43	.01		.02		.20	.30		.02	
CLAYSVILLE 3 W	-	T		1.16	.04	.06	.57	.12		1.34	.40			.03	.21	.02		.10	.33		.63	.27	.49	.34	.04			-	-	-	-
CLEARFIELD	6.92		2.13	.98	T	.12	.18	.07		.25	.45	.03					.28		.08		1.20	.08	.35	.10		.15	.05	.13		.10	
CLERMONT	5.88		.96			.35	.28			1.60	.10	.04	.30		.22		.06	.08	T		.55	.28		.10	.05		.05	.51			
COALDALE 2 NW	9.09		.05	.66		3.44	.64	.10		.80			.03		.33			.06			.05	1.35	.05				.32	1.00		.21	
COATESVILLE 1 SW	5.71		.08	1.64	.02	.07	.11	T		.51	.10		.12		.14			.28	T			2.18	T	.02	.08	.04		.15			
COLUMBIA	6.13		.61	1.92	.20	.42				.05				.30	T		.89	T			.34	1.32	T		.03				T		
CONFLUENCE 1 SW DAM	6.42		T	.28		.62	.40	.17			.03	T	.06	.04				.67	.58		.61	.07	.26	T	.23	.10		1.43	.08	.69	T
CONFLUENCE 1 NW	6.58			.38		1.38	.41	.16		1.06	.07	T	.09	.05	.17			.18	.45		.64	.05	.10		.23	.05		.82	.11	.18	T
CONNELLSVILLE	5.61			.18		.14	.50	.90		1.29	.24			.03	.16			.02	.26		.30	.18	.01	.02	.06			1.15	.06	.15	
CONSHOHOCKEN	4.34		.28	.48		.04	.15			.57	.10							.10				1.98		.02	.04			T		.39	
COOKSBURG	7.65		2.70	T	T	.71	.04	T	T	.60	.14	.02	.12				.19	T	.22	T	.54	.20	T	.02		.83	.03	.46	.44		.19
COOKSBURG 2 NNW	5.92		1.92	T	T	.74	.02	T		.74	.10	T					.17	.07	.21	T	.25	.15	T	.02	T	.05	.03	.67	.33		.02
CORAOPOLIS NEVILLE IS	3.32			.15		.10	T			.42	.38						.18	.07	.10		T		*	.04	.06			.89		*	.09
CORRY	6.45		2.47		.10	.08	.02			1.18	.12		.37	.77	.17	.02	.05			.48	.22	.09	.05	.19	.05						
COUDERSPORT 3 NW	4.42		.71			.19	.42	T		.89	.03	.12	.08	.30	.07	.01	.07	T	T		.55	.37		.11	T		.09	.41			
COUDERSPORT 7 E	5.77		.55			.79	.28			.57	.13	.07	.08	.19	.37		.08	.02	T		.51	.62		.04	.05		.05	1.20	.15		
COVINGTON	4.72		.47	.04		.92	.16			.55	.14		.13	.06	.04			.04			.58	.30	.04	.48			.06	.65		.06	
CREEKSIDE	10.48		1.20	1.03		.40	.05	.05		.36	.38			.16	.08		2.70	.10	.30		.73	.07	.28	.62	.05	.11	.57	.20	.03	.03	
CRESSON 2 SE	8.62		.81	.68	.03	.05	.23	.51		.19	.09	.08	T	.27	.70	.03	2.49	.24	.53	.03	.76	.21	.12	.04	.06		.17	.09	.16	.09	T
CUSTER CITY 2 W	7.07		1.03			.70	.38	.01		1.06	.15	.15	.28	.40	.12	.02	.05		T		.10	.09	1.40	.05	.06		.01	.81			
DANVILLE	7.38		.86	1.00		1.60	.08			.25	.20							.09			.50	1.20	.22		.05		.34	.75		.24	
DERRY	4.48		T	.13	.95	T	.19			.47	.07		.30	.22	.03		.10	.75		.08	.20	.05	.35	.04	.05	.08		.32	.12		
DEVAULT 1 W	4.28		.13	.37	.04	.42	.10	.02	.29	.46	.10	.05	.02	.09	T	T	.11				.73	1.20	T	T	T	.02		.13			
DIXON	5.65		.15	.11		1.15	.22	.02	.04	.05	T		.06	.21	.33	.17					.86	1.32	.03	.61		.01	.14	.17			
DONEGAL	3.82		.15	.01	T	.02	.74		.31	.68	.05		.02	.27	T		.05	.32		.15	.05	.11		.03	.03	.02	.16	.15	.49	.01	
DONORA	5.42			.24	T	.20	.20	T		1.00	.18	.03	.10	.05	.06		T	.39	.72		.48	.10	.16	.05	.05			1.15	.25	.01	
DOYLESTOWN	5.40		.03	.44	.24	.34	.23			1.02	.02			.17	.18		.05			T	T	1.67			.44			.08		.49	
DU BOIS 7 E	7.25		1.80	.26	.06	.12				.23	.15		.08	.70			.37	.04		T	1.00	.06	.10	.06		.05	.40	.57	.20		
DUSHORE 3 NE	5.73		.04	.12		1.25	T	T		.02		T	.22	T	.20			T			1.05	.65	.15	.45		1.00	.10	.48			
EAGLES MERE	7.77		.15	.07		.83	.08	.03		.27	.02	T	.06	.25	.42	.20	.01	T			1.70	.93	.14	.92			.52	1.13		.04	
EAST BRADY	6.56		.90		.44				.06	.48	.05		.06	.41			1.24	.92		.54	.43		.04		.48		.02	.49			
EBENSBURG	5.91	T	1.15	.56		T	T	.13		.14	.15	T		T	.18	T	2.02	.15	.42		.41	T	.05	.09	.10	T	.23	.11	T	.06	
EDINBORO	4.20		.66			.04	.04	.01		.76	.30	.07	.11	.62	.29	.04	.05		.02		T	.91	.15	.01	.02		.01	.09			
ELIZABETHTOWN	4.81		.08	.56	.03	.50	.10	.01		.51					.43	.13	.10	.20	.04		.01	1.66	.04		.05					.36	
EMPORIUM 1 E	4.50		.62			.49	.04	.01		1.17	.08	.03		.15	.35	.01	.06	.01			*	*	.85	.28	.01			*		.34	
ENGLISH CENTER	5.59	T	.62	.16		1.31	.02	.07		.11	.28		.01	.28	.07	.12	.18	.32			.83	.56	.04	.22			.01	.32	.01	.03	
EPHRATA	5.03		.20	.80	.10	.63	.10		.05	.28				.26	.01		.14				.19	1.08			.07				.12		
EQUINUNK	4.19		.11			1.21	.52				.02			.12	.25	.11					.17	.82	.09	.15			.62				
ERIE CAA AIRPORT	7.11	.54	.35		.02	.07	.03		.53	1.07	.26	.28	.86	.52	T	T	.10	.01		T	1.37	.20	.53	.35		T	.02				
EVERETT 1 SW	3.59	.10	.25	.40	.10	.35								.05			.10	.30		1.60	.10		T		.10		.10				
FARRELL SHARON	4.65				.58	.01				.45	.01		.08	.12			1.77	.59	.02	.19	.07	.13			.43	.01	.03		.16		
FORD CITY 4 S DAM	6.90		.21	.20	T	.10	.08	T		.83	.30	T		.30	.12		2.05	T	.31		1.44	.35	.17	.07	.02		.12	.20	.03	T	
FRANKLIN	3.96		.48	T	.01	.51				.74	T	T		T	.13		.25	T	.45		.24	.38		.35		.03		.28	.11		
FREELAND	5.61		.10	.62	T	.50	.30	.04		.77	.10		.05		.05	.06	T	T	.20	.85	.13	T	.40	T	.29	.40	.29	.32			.14
GALETON	5.29		.74			1.22	.15	.02		.36	.02	T	.06	.11	.40	.04	.01	.18	T		.58	.88	.02	.08	.01	.01	.02	.32	.06		
GEIGERTOWN	3.46		.08	.41			.21		.06	.51				.19	.24			.11				1.50				.07				.08	
GEORGE SCHOOL	4.27		.01	.38	.03	.47	.17			.41				.25			.07					2.03			.03			.09	.33		
GETTYSBURG	7.98		.02	.31	.48	1.12	.51		T	.15					.41	.01	T		.06		T	2.63	.03		.14	.02		.07			.02
GLEN HAZEL 2 NE DAM	5.42		.31	.01	T	.20	.07	T		1.31	.17	.04	T	.21	.23	.01	.05	T			.28	.22	T	.38	.03		.05	.85			
GLENWILLARD DASH DAM	4.02			.13	T	.02	T			.44	.11			.12	.07		.10	.09	.27		.41	1.13	.02	.04	.02		T	.99	.05	.01	
GOULDSBORO	5.16			.40		.64	.64	.10		1.40	.07		.23	.04	.17	.37					.25	.63	.08	T	T		T	.14			
GRANTVILLE 2 SW	5.54		.04	.25	.02	.37	.04		.91	.11			.67	.40	.11		.16	.03		T	.45	.93		T	.03			.02			
GRATERFORD	4.52		.02	.57	.03	.32	.37	.03		.49	.05			.14								2.03	.05		.18				.06	.18	
GRATZ 1 N	4.91		.92	.35		.21	.18	.13		.26			.37	.11	.07	.18		.45			.11	1.07	.06					.23		.21	
GREENSBORO LOCK 7	6.25			.76		.16	.73	.19		.01	.11			.02	.10			T	.87		.03	.47	.10		.44	.01		1.40	.21	.04	T
GREENSBURG 3 SE	3.61	T		.14	.12		.26			.52	.26		.08	.18	.01		.03	.70		.15	.40		.03	.10	.05	.12	.05	.27	.15	.01	
GREENVILLE	4.05		.01	.15	.08				.40	.01	.02	.02	.22	.01		1.15	.15	.01		.10	.02	.76	.71	.05	.03	.08		.07			T
HANOVER	6.45			.71	.07	1.56	.61	.02		.21					.56		T	T	.09	T		2.24	.14	T	.10	.04		T			T
HARRISBURG WB AP R	4.57	*	.61	.03	.06	.15	.03	T	.03	T	T	.01	.18	.26	.02		.43	.01		.01	1.01	.62	T		.05	.02	T		.01		
HARRISBURG NORTH	4.86		.20	.66		.10	.09	.04		.30			.23	.40	.49	.01	.34		.05		.16	1.67		T	.04	T	.07	.01			
HAWLEY	3.89		.06	.01		.86	.60	.12	.16	.25	T		.05	.08	.18	.39	T	T			.14	.61	.12	.01			.09	.16	T		
HAWLEY 1 S DAM	4.11		.07			.89	.65	.03	.45	.34			.01	.12	.18	.25					.13	.60	.11				.05	.23			
HOLLISTERVILLE	4.40		.25	.06		.62	.56	.01	T	.13	T		.05	.28	.34	.26	T				.19	.59	.05	.06		T	.58	.37		T	
HOLTWOOD	6.23		.22	.92	.73	.07	.19	.04		.53	.03				.16		T	.02	.07		T	2.05	T	.02	.16	.02	T	T			
HONESDALE 4 NW	4.74		.14	.07		1.23	.75	.04	.02	.06			.03	.06	.37	.13					.34	.55	.14	.24	T		.53	.04			
HOOVERSVILLE	5.19		1.47	.13	.10	.05	.33	.32		.10	.13	.01		.01	.13		.20	.17	.63		.31	.01	.53	.02	.06	.01	.04	.15	.16	.05	.07
HOP BOTTOM 2 SE	3.27		.06			.36	.59	T			.10	T	.35	T	.22	.09					.02	.25	.01	.03			.59	.29	.31		
HUNTINGDON	6.95	T	1.61	.92	.06	.02	.08	.76		.08	.02			.06	.04	.08	.48	.42	.34	T	.54	.26	.03	.02	.04		T	.04		.05	
HUNTSDALE	5.80		.08	.53	.66	.32	.31	.03		.08	.01				.22		.47	.93	.10		.19	1.65	.03	.11	.08	T				T	
HYNDMAN	5.54		.54	.31		.21	.05			.05	.02			.14	.06			.25	1.62		1.45	.15	.03	.12	.22	.01		.28	.03		
INDIANA 3 SE	8.47		.92	.10		.22	.20	.03		.37	.15	.03		.26	.40		2.98		.37		.20	.06	.66	.28	.05	.03	.39	.49	T	.28	
IRWIN	5.02	T	T	.31	.19	.04	.54			.41	.32	.03	.03	.12	.03		.01	1.55	.02	.02	.56	.12	.18		.05	.07		.27	.15		
JAMESTOWN 2 NW	5.98				.02	.02		T		.31	.07	.02		.07	.12		.32	.02	.39			.62	.42	1.15			.03	.38	.02		
JIM THORPE	9.87		.06	.47		2.48	.86			.90			.16	.11	.43		.67				.32	1.07			.02			.47	.05		
JOHNSTOWN	6.43	T	1.10	.05		.15	.10	.16		.59	.09	.01		.20	.11	T	1.16	.08	.91		.10	.03	T	T	.05	T	.45	.07	.06	T	
KANE 1 NNE	7.30		1.82			.76	.20			.85	.16	.07	.06	.38	.18	T	.02	T			.58	.35	T	.04			.09	1.74		T	
KARTHAUS	5.36		.94	.60	T	.15	.07	.03		.26	.48	T	T	.03	.48	.12	.11	.39			.79	.18	.08	.26				.14		.18	

See Reference Notes Following Station Index

DAILY PRECIPITATION

Day of month

Station	Total	1	2	3	4	5	6	7	8	9	10	11	12	13	14	15	16	17	18	19	20	21	22	23	24	25	26	27	28	29	30	31
KEATING SUMMIT	4.47		.58			.29	.11			.69	.06	.03	.07	.23	.20	.04			T		.49	.57	T	.08	.60		.07	.37	.03			
KEGG	3.87		.78	.03	.03	.59	.04			.06				.15			.16	1.03		.32	.10	.04	.22	.02	.13	T	.07		.09	.01		
KITTANNING LOCK 7	6.43		.40	.01	T	.20	T			.75	.30		.07	.11	.05	T	2.17	.32	.05	T	1.50	.24	T	T		.03	.04	.15	.03	.01		
KREGAR 4 SE	5.18	T	.14	.02	.70	.12	.60		.31	1.00	.01		.03	.22	T		.18	.21		.33	.13	.14	T	.04	.03	.03	.35	.23	.34	.02		
KRESGEVILLE 3 W	9.43		.04	.58		1.63	1.23	.10		1.60	.12			.37	1.06			.04				1.20	.05		.02			1.18		.13		
LAKEVILLE 1 NNE	4.85		.05			.87	.72	.07	.31	.15				.18	.17	.57					.17	.02	.11	.22			.17	.27				
LANCASTER 2 NE PUMP STA	5.04	T	.12	1.14	.07	.50	.19	.01	.02	.19		.12		.25	.05		.57	.01			.21	1.13			.07					.43		
LANDISVILLE 2 NW	4.28		.20	1.35	.06	.16	.22			.15			T		.28	.05	.06	.27	.01			1.30	.02	.02	.07	T				.05		
LAWRENCEVILLE 2 S	6.07		.35			1.12	.87	T		.32	T	T	.08	.87	.30	.05					.02	.17	.02	.10	.25		.24	.45				
LEBANON 3 W	6.43		.04	1.77		.31	.12	T		.81			T	.90	.39	T	.08	.02	.02	T		1.21	.05	T	.65	T	T	.05		.01		
LEHIGHTON	8.59		T	.60		2.60	1.23	.10		1.52	T		.07	.50			.03	T			T	1.22	.03		.03		T	.57	T	.09		
LE ROY	4.40		.21		.11	1.04				.13	.14	.07	.31		.02						.96	.73		.30	.14		.24					
LEWIS RUN 3 SE	5.05		1.01		.02	.91	.02			.63	.09	.14	.10	.32	.10		.09				.14	.15	.11	.10	.05		.04	.85				
LEWISTOWN	4.67	T	.51	.18		.24	.02	.12		.09	.02				.01		.28	.56	.05		.50	.73	T	.01	.04			.95		.36		
LINESVILLE 5 WNW	4.13					.08	.02			.71	.41	T	T	.15	.25	T	.10	.08	.04			1.04	.93		.37		.13	.22	T			
LOCK HAVEN	6.42	.01	.39	.65		.74	.48	T		.04	.01		.01	.05	.20	T	.04	.03			1.50	.54	.01	.50			.31	.57		.25		
LONG POND 2 W	6.71		.10	.64		.66	.57	.05		.75	.15			.14	.82	.19		.02			.97	1.01	.08	.02	.05			.47		.02		
MADERA	6.71		2.95	.42		.47	.20	.07		.38	.09			.03	.41		.54	.03	.11		.41	.02	T	.42	T		.02	.43		.11		
MAHAFFEY	9.45		2.51	1.21		.11	.04	.04		.44	.20			.15	.30		.50	.02	.22		.95	.03	1.52	.26		.02	.37	.20	.25	.09		
MAPLE GLEN	3.87		.02	.49	.01	.20	T		T	.66	.02			.15	.02		.06				T	1.80			.00			.14	.01	.23		
MAPLETON DEPOT	8.47		2.12	1.20	.03	.12	.03	.69		.07	T	T		.06	.02	.22	.98	1.02	.29		.65	.32	.04	.32	.06		.04	.18		.01		
MARCUS HOOK	5.81		.02	.81	.08	.23	.01		T	1.28		.03		.09	T		.13		T		.37	2.22		.01	.04			.49	T			T
MARION CENTER 2 SE	9.20		2.38	.62		.18	.23	.03		.28	.39	.02		.09	.29	.03	1.18	.04	.23		1.57	.08	.28	.53	.03	.29	.08	.32		.03		
MARTINSBURG CAA AP	6.70	.02	.92	.01	T	.15	.77		.13	.08			T	T	T		2.32	.83		.33	.07	.06	.56	T	.07	.05	.22	.01	.10			
MATAMORAS	5.27					.68	.74			1.54	.20			.04	.65	.32					.04	.67	.04					.24	.11			
MAYBURG	6.47		2.62			1.05	.09			.91	.18	.08	T	.18	.15	.05	.14	T			T	.12		.24			T	.68				
MC CONNELLSBURG	6.81		.18	.93	.19	1.23	.09	.64		.09	.07				.27	.06	.03	.11	.42		.54	.71	.09	.87	.17		T	.08			.04	
MC KEESPORT	-	-	-	-	-	-	-	-	-	-	-	-	-	-	-	-	-	-	-	-	-	-	-	-	-	-	-	-	-	-	-	-
MEADVILLE 1 S	5.11		.33		T	.02	.01	T		1.91	.33	.04	T	.15	.03	.03	.08		.10			.25	1.24	.30	.01		.04	.24	T			
MEDIX RUN	5.65	T	1.34	.47	T	.56	T	T		.16	.19	.02	.07	.19	.25	.07	.12	.35	T		.67	.18	.03	.35				.41	T	.22		
MERCER 2 NNE	6.86			.47	.03	.72				1.00		T		.20	.12		1.34		.52		.68	.07	.10	.12		.45	.24	.80				
MERCERSBURG	4.29		.03	.04	.01	1.16	.20			.13					.15				.15		.26	1.23			.18	T		.15				
MEYERSDALE 1 ENE	-		.30	.36		.02	.12			*	.22			.08	.03			.06	.47	.34	.06	.04	.16	.06	.24	.02		.43	-	-	.10	
MIDDLETOWN OLMSTED FLD	5.18	T	.83	.11	.30	.22	.02		.81	T	T	.01	.10	.45	.12		.34	.01		T	1.12	.48	T		.04	.05	T		.17			
MIDLAND DAM 7	5.10			.57	.03	.01	.16			.66	.26	.02		.24	.10		T	.18	.98		.10	.40	.38	.07	.01			.86	.07			
MILANVILLE	3.06		.02			.09	1.11	T		.07			T	.07	.21	.05					.15	.47	.37	.25			.20					
MILLHEIM	5.91		.51	.81		.50	.09	.02			.23			.02	.11	T	.13	.04			1.05	.70		.65	.11		.07	.30		.57		
MILLVILLE 2 SW	6.05	T	.92	.40		1.14	.08			.41	.04		.19	.11	.08	.02	.01	.04			.83	1.14	.28	.10			.27	.35		.04		
MILROY	4.40		.44	.12		.09	T			.17	.05			.08	.10		.36	.40	.01		.84	.78		.08	.04		.01	.71		.14		
MONTROSE 1 E	6.46		.07			1.27	.56	T	T	T	T		.82	.20	.23	.04	T				.25	1.59	.12	.13	.27	T	.47	.44				
MORGANTOWN	9.25		.75	.22	.13	.10	.09		.11	.40		.02	T	.19	.01		.10				.45	.57			.04			.07				
MT GRETNA 2 SE	3.38	T	.15	.25	T	.31	.03		.54				.33	.40	.06		.10	T			1.00	.20		T					.01			
MT POCONO 2 N AP	5.98		.06	.29	.38	1.19	.31			1.20		.07	.03	.12	.16		T				.22	1.52	.01		.15	T	.24	.03				
MUHLENBURG 1 SE	5.18	.01	.16	.22	.14	1.04	.14	.01				.10	.11	.15	.86		.02			T	.89	.76		.18		.27	.17	.09	.06			
MYERSTOWN	7.16		.46	3.16						.87			.08	.94	.33		T	.05	T			.89			.76			.02		T		
NATRONA LOCK 4	7.54			.75	.01	T	.35	T		.14	.88			.10	.03		.72	.06	2.42		.78	.36	.45	.04	.02		.07	.31	T	.05		
NESHAMINY FALLS	4.57		.06	.36		.50	T		.05	.47	T		T	.50	T		.15				.25	1.86		.02	.02			.07	.26			
NEWBURG 3 W	8.13		1.10	.13	.14	1.13	.35			.09				.19			1.90	.12		1.38	1.10	.40			.10							
NEW CASTLE 1 N	8.26			.07	T	1.26	T			.90	.51		T	.62	.17	.01	1.46	.02	1.03		T		.02	.05		.06	.07	1.91	.10			
NEWELL	4.12			.32		.19	.67			.46	.16		.02	.08				.04	.26		.50	.50			.10			.68	.14			
NEW PARK	5.52		T	1.06	.56	.16	.15		.03	.57				.06			.11	.02		.01	.32	2.20	T	.03	.22				.02	T		
NEWPORT	4.67		.20	.78		.10	.05	.10		.07	T			T	.03	T	.25	.02	T		.40	2.42	.01	T	.06		.15	.03		T		
NEW STANTON	3.74		.17		.04	.01	.06		.95	.23	T		.13	.14	.01			.39		.15	.08		.15	.07	.03	.17	.54	.08	.34			
NEW TRIPOLI	7.94		.30	.76	.44	1.05	.48			1.41			.33	.28	.24		.19	T			.25	1.39			.04	.06	T	.54	.18			
NORRISTOWN	3.74		.02	.51	T	.21	.07			.80	.06				.08	.01		.06				1.80			.04	.01		.01		.06		
NORTH EAST 2 SE	8.16		1.87		.03	.05	.06	.02		.39	1.74	.58	.64	.84	.43	T	.04	.03				.53	.04	.50	.37		T					
ORWELL 3 N	3.80		.30			1.18	.58			.31	.12		.24	.38	.28						.71	.83	.11	.26	.06	.44						
PALM	5.77		.22	.50		.12	.44			1.20	.10				.24			.05			.38	1.48	.25		1.40	.03		.18		.18		
PALMERTON	7.47	.02	.01	.50	1.98	1.04	.65		.65	.51		T	T	.71	.04		.07				.25	.89			.01		.05	.06	.03			
PALMYRA	RECORD MISSING																															
PARKER	5.83	T	.17	.09	.03	1.41				.38	.19			.08	.07	*	.84	.05	.28		.17	.14	.02	.17		.68	.05	.19	.76	.06		
PAUPACK 2 WNW	4.03		.09			.71	.68	.01	.04	.41				.20	.32	.21					.16	.59	.09	.01			.03	.52				
PECKS POND	5.21		.06	.07		.62	.89	.09	T	1.43	.13		.01	.10	.20	.49					.07	.80	.01	.01	T		.08	.15				
PHIL DREXEL INST OF TEC	5.22		.02	.35	T	.27	.07		.14	.70	T			.45	.10		.10				.38	2.00		.01	.06			T	.57			
PHILADELPHIA WB AP R	4.61		.18	.28	.01	.28	.09	T	.13	.51	T	T		.10	.05		.23				.38	1.92		.01	.05			.04	.35			
PHILADELPHIA PT BREEZE	4.80		.05	.40	.03	.14	.02		.02	.57				.10	.04		.36				.30	1.92			.04			.02	.73			
PHILADELPHIA SHAWMONT	5.85		.12	.30	.06	.22	.02		.02	.93	.02		.02	.33	.05		.08				.02	2.40			.10			.02	.25	.80		
PHILADELPHIA CITY R	4.70		.08	.27	.01	.26	.02	T	.08	.46	T	T		.19	.12		.24				.40	1.46			.02			.16	.93			
PHILIPSBURG CAA AP	7.44	.89	.79		1.28	.11	.01		.39	.16	T		.08	.31	.02	T	.42	.03		1.67	.31	.01	.25	.02	T	.08	.07		.54			
PHOENIXVILLE 1 E	3.86		.12	.37	.09	.26	.05		.23	.25	.06		.14	.16			.12				.58	1.32			.07				.04			
PIKES CREEK	7.03		.38	.46		.77	.36	.05		.20	T		.04	.08	1.04	.15	.02	.01			1.10	1.03	.05	.20		.22	.04	.61		.02		
PIMPLE HILL	6.16		.10	.49	T	.77	.49	.03		.71	.10		.12		.89	.05	.01	.01			.76	1.24	.04	T	.03			.25		.07		
PINE GROVE 1 NE	4.91		.25	1.48		.25	.26	.05		.64			T	T	.43		.07	.07	T		.01	.67	T		.04		.05	.30		.34		
PITTSBURGH WB AP 2 //R	4.25	T	.13	T	.05	.02	T		.30	.70	T	T	T	T	T		.17	.14		.12	1.15	T	.03	.01	T		1.32	T	.11	T		T
PITTSBURGH WB CITY R	4.15	T	.14	T	.08	.04	.06		.34	.47	.01		.02	.08	.01		.07	.32		.03	.77	.22	.60	.02	.01	T	.80		.06	T		T
PLEASANT MOUNT 1 W	5.23		.15			1.59	.71	.03	.01	.02			.14	.01	.24	.16	T				.14	.98	.35	.39			.28	.03				
PORT CLINTON	5.18		.20	.88		.58	.45	.02		.48					.80		.02	.05			.01	1.40			.03			.26				
POTTSTOWN	4.87		.02	.48		.18	.08		T	.64				.34	.14			.04				2.15						.38	.28	.14		
POTTSVILLE PALO ALTO BR	6.28		.04	1.46		.64	.51	.08	.02	1.11	T		.21	.01	.24	.01	.06	.09	T		.06	1.05	.01		.04		.01	.48		.15		
PUTNEYVILLE 2 SE DAM	7.70		2.17	.02	T	.20	.04			.51	.26			.07	.12	.04	.71	.17	.46		.73	.23	.14			.05	1.10	.65	.03			
QUAKERTOWN 1 E	5.73		.23	.41	.03	.28	.03	.01	.97		.17			.23	.01		.05			.55	.02	1.34			.24			.30		.86		
RAYMOND	5.08		.45			.44	.54			.52	.07		.33	.49	.64		.06				.34	.70		.17				.33				
READING WB CITY R	4.01	.17	.20	.28	.11	.56	.04		.07	.15			.16	.24	T		.07	T		.01	.69	.60	T	.22	.04		.06		.34			
RENOVO	5.23	.08	.67	.62		1.03	.02			.18	.30			.17	.07	.31	.05	.02			.52	.23		.10			.26	.42		.18		
REW	5.01		.58			.68	.51	.01		.96	.07	.15	.25	.49	.35	T	.05				.13	.20	.10	.04	.08			.38				
RICES LANDING L 6	6.94			.33	.74	.10	.49	.75		.52	.37			.06	.09			.02	.33		.70	.20		.12	.34			.65	.47	.66		
RIDGWAY 3 W	6.54		1.38			.29	.02	T		.72	.07	.03		.20	.27	.18	.09	.18	T		.58	.06	T	.82	T		T	1.65				
RUHM	5.76		.27			1.29	.33				.03		.23	.29	.19	.17					.93	.80	.14	.11	.02		.35	.61				
RUSHVILLE	6.43		.31			1.27	.24			.02	.04		.55	.38	.05	.39					.39	1.52	.13	.10	.02		.14	.88				
SAGAMORE 1 S	11.66		1.42	1.41		.12	.32			.75	.12			.10	T		2.10	.35	*		2.80	.25	.12	.10	.25	.60	.45	.40				
SALINA 3 W	7.64			.10	T		.31			.25	.26		.92	.10	T	.03	.33	1.60	T	.03	.91	.30	.86	.58	.06	.65		.28	.07			
SAXTON	5.86		.68	.10	.11	.13	.30	.52		.12	.01	T		.01	.10		1.63	.19	.39		.92	.07	.46	T	.05		.06	.01	T	T		
SCHENLEY LOCK 5	7.14		.04	.25	T	.23	.11			.77	.32		.30	.28	.14		1.45	.88	.04		1.18	.37	.15	.07	.04	.08	.01	.38	.02	.03		
SCRANTON	6.33		.21	.22		.79	.29	.04		.21			.40	.16	1.00	.16					.25	.71	.01	.58		.04	.73	.53		T		
SCRANTON WB AIRPORT	3.18	.15	.01	T	.23	.62	.15		T	.10		.42	T	.28	.12		T			.06	.31	.19		.13	.09	T	.10	.21	.01			T
SELINSGROVE CAA AP	7.51	.13	.97	.03	1.49	.38	.02			.38				.02			.37			.12	.84	1.07			.11	T	.93	.02	.63			
SHAMOKIN	8.31		.31	.63		2.00	.20	.04		.80	.38		.19	.03	.11		.50	.08			.14	.90	.20		.02			1.67	.11			
SHIPPENSBURG	4.65		.31	.38	.27	.28	.08			T				.25			.74	T	.22	T	1.50	.43	.03		.11			.05	T	T		
SHIPPINGPORT WB	5.06	T	.28	.01	T	.18	T		.50	.16	T		.21	.05	T			1.52		.06	.44	.55	.03			T	1.07		.02			
SINNEMAHONING	4.90	.01	.83	.47	.01	.60	.03	.01		.06	.42	.04	T	.08	.18	.34	.08	.12			.64	.55	.01	.07			.05	.30		.13		
SLIPPERY ROCK	9.18	T	.04	.47	.03	2.09				.53	.47			.16	.07	T	1.92	.16	.51		.06	1.40	.04	.10		.73	.13	.20	.07			
SOMERSET FAIRVIEW ST	3.68			.18		.14	.60	.03		.41	.15			.03	.10		.16	.17	.30		.64	.03	.19	.03	.06		T	.29	.04	.13		
SOMERSET MAIN ST	4.10		.03	.20	.09	.08	.95			.37	.08			.14	T		.38	.30		.28	.39	.04	.22	T	.07			.30	.18	T		
SOUTH MOUNTAIN	4.92		.03	.15	.35	.36	.37	.09		.11					.39			.02	.13		.17	2.58		.01	.11	.03					.02	
SPRINGBORO	5.63		.40			T	.10			1.38	.35	T	T	.60	1.10	T	T		T			.75	.15				.50	.30	T			
SPRING GROVE	6.55		.26	.13	1.60	.10	.40			.37				.45	.14		.13	.20	.01		.47	2.06	.13	.01	.08			.01				
SPRINGS 1 SW	4.72		.48	.04	.04	.27	.31			.03	.20			.20	T		.05	.34		.24	.13	.20	.30	.03	.50		.62	.36	.36			
STATE COLLEGE	4.59	.61	.65		.03	.15	.04		.18	.02	T	T	.01	.09		T	.39	.02		.70	.59	.01	.03	.27	.03	.09	.56		.14			T
STRAUSSTOWN	6.22		.39	1.39		.42	.49	.01		.54	.04			.35	.64		.05	.06			.03	1.19	T		.04	T	.23	.16		.23		
STROUDSBURG	8.08		.12	.95	.22	1.80	.50		.04	1.63		.01	.21	.84	.21		.02			.01	.16	1.02	T		.02	.02	.01	.25	.04		T	
STUMP CREEK	7.76		2.09	.31		1.57	.03			.40	.33	.02		.08	.12	.02	.32		.14		.77	.10	.08	.04		.15	.30	.35	.40	.09		
SUNBURY	8.18		.45	.98		1.33	.04	T		.34	.10				T	T	.08	.38			.50	1.75	T		.08			1.70		.45		
SUSQUEHANNA	4.21		.14			1.19	.58	T	.12			.01	.09		.18	.15		.01			.16	1.03	.05	.06	T		.30	.14				
SUTERSVILLE	-			.99		.02	.03	*		.88	.20		.06	.03	*	*	.11	.03	.52		.45	-	*	.25	.02			.98	*	*	.28	
TAMAQUA	8.32		.13	.86		1.85	.89	.14			T		*	*	1.49			.14			.04	1.28	.05		.03	T	.79	.48		.15		
TAMAQUA 4 N DAM	7.88		.13	1.14		2.15	.39	.30		.85	.06		.04		.28		.02					1.11	.02		.02		.32	.90		.15		
TAMARACK 2 S FIRE TWR	RECORD MISSING																															
TIONESTA 2 SE DAM	6.49		3.03	.01	T	.71	.01			.55	.02	.04	T	.04	.08	.03	.07				.33	.68		.15	.03		.07	.64	T			
TITUSVILLE WATER WORKS	6.97	.04	1.54	.01	.01	.06				1.96	.31	.02	.24	.75	.24	.01	.10	T		.61	.03	.23	.18	.13		.01	.49					
TORPEDO 4 W	6.80		2.60			.11	.02			1.45	.22	.04	.03	.17	.15	.05	.12				T	.45	.99	.10			.20	.10				

DAILY PRECIPITATION

Table 3—Continued

Station	Total	1	2	3	4	5	6	7	8	9	10	11	12	13	14	15	16	17	18	19	20	21	22	23	24	25	26	27	28	29	30
TOWANDA	4.38	T	.16	.01		1.17	.10	.01	T	.29	.05		.08	.38	.06	.03	T				.52	.93	.18	.09		.03	.21	.06			
TOWER CITY 5 SW	6.49		.28	2.05	.37	.10	T		T	.62		.18		.15	.24		.16	.25			.42	1.43			.09			.15			
TROY	5.34		.38	.02		1.13	.60	.08		.18	.51	.02	.04	.42	.13	.05	T				.76	.62	.13	.08	T		.01	.18			
TURTLEPOINT 4 NE	7.08		.70			.42	1.25			2.40	.15	.06	.21	.46	.31	.06	.05				.21	.56		.11	.01			.10			
TYRONE 4 NE BALD EAGLE	6.76		2.28	.66		.04	.05	.02		.14	.06			.02	.09	T	.64	.04	.07		2.06	.18	.07		.05		T	.23		.06	
UNION CITY	4.95		1.44	.02	T	.09	.04			.35	.22	.09	.10	1.22	.35	.05	.05					.14	.53	.21	.02		T	.03			
UNIONTOWN	4.24		.15	.02	T	.36	.22			.63				.12				.69		.09	.27	T	.27	.12	.13		.03	.24	.90		
UPPER DARBY	5.81		.03	.55	.03	.35	.04			.84	.02			.25	.14		.14				.08	2.35		.01	.11			T	.87		
UTICA	3.67		.19			.29				.60	.05			.06	.44	.01	.26		.52		.17	.39	.04	.22				.41	.02		
VANDERGRIFT	5.49			.25	T	.16	.12	T		.32	.37			.35	T	T	1.35	T	.80		.27	.25	.08	.24	.08	T		.80	.05	T	
VIRGINVILLE	4.90		.22	.85	.06	.41	.45			.78				.14	.32		.04	.08				1.41			.08					.06	
VOWINCKEL	6.25		1.89	T	T	1.16	.02	T		.83	.09	T	T	.22	.15	T	.14	T	T		.27	.23		.46	T		T	.70	.09		T
VOWINCKEL 1 WSW	6.11		1.87	T	T	1.09	T	T		.74	.09	T	T	.28	.13	T	.12	T	T		.38	.19		.50	T		T	.65	.07		
WARREN	7.31		2.11			.16	.16			.64	.13	.06	.25	.45	.32		.08				T	.14	.05				.03	2.75			
WATSONTOWN	8.27		.30	.45		1.65	.20			.10					.25	.05	.05	.15			1.25	1.40	.07	.60			.05	1.45	.25		
WAYNESBURG 2 W	11.13	T		.65	.12	1.00	.69	.01		.42	.40			.03	.10			T	.72		.62	.07	T	.20	.41			5.21	.35	.12	.01
WELLSBORO 3 S	3.91		.39	.02		.89	.11	.03		.25	.13	.02	.06	.07	.09	.02	.04	.02	T		.03	.43	.03	.24	.02		.06	.36	T		
WELLSVILLE	5.10		.16	.54	.03	.07	.10		.15	.77				.44			.91	.05		T	.62	1.18			.08						
WERNERSVILLE 1 W	4.27	.03		.85		.58	.41			.10				.24	.28			.12				1.29	.02		.25					.10	
WEST CHESTER	6.46		.04	2.13		.25	.07	.03		.64	.09	.02	.21		.10			.38		.05		1.90	.03	.02	.21	.02		.27		T	
WEST GROVE 1 E	7.58		.18	1.74	.05	.32		.05		1.72	.05		.08		.03			.16				2.48	.02	.06	.07	.12		.26	.19		
WEST HICKORY	6.57		2.40		.01	.80	.02			.64	.35	.03		.02	.20	.05	.08				.20	.60	.10	.55			.07	.45			
WHITESBURG	7.50		.47	.34	T	T	.76			.64	.34			.10	.23		1.93		.43		1.22	.23	.14	T	T	T	.21	.46	T		
WILKES BARRE	3.39		.15	.11		.78	.29	.03		.27	T		.08	.03	.20	.46	T	T			.19	.47	T	.10		.01	T	.21		.01	
WILLIAMSBURG	7.63	.04	.71	1.23	.05	.03	.46	.42		.10	.03			.17	.51		.75	1.01	.46		1.12	.20	.06	.01	.04		.10	.13			
WILLIAMSPORT WB AP	7.17	.09	1.17	.03	.73	.33	.02		.12	.04	T	.02	.07	1.24	.29	.01	.07	T		.38	.98	1.03		.46		T	.07		.02		
WOLFSBURG	5.57		.43	.08	1.25	.23	1.14	.08		.06				.04	.10		.37	.02	.47		.46	.15	.41	.03	.12	T		.09		.04	
YORK 3 SSW PUMP STA	5.47		.05	1.06	.62	.15	.27	T	.03	.14				.47	T		.42	.03	T		.32	1.70	.09	.01	.11	T		T		T	
YORK HAVEN	4.43		.26	.30	.03	.18	.08	T		.45				.07	.39	.15	.19	.71	.01		.01	1.50	.02		.06	.02					
ZION GROVE	6.27		.24	1.10		1.18	.30	.04		.83	.07		.02		.21	.06		.05			.13	.44		.02	.03		.61	.63		.31	
ZIONSVILLE 3 SE	3.89		.17	.31		.16	.48	.02		.12				.03	.22			.04			.10	1.39	.05		.22	.02	T	.07		.48	

DAILY TEMPERATURES

Day Of Month

	1	2	3	4	5	6	7	8	9	10	11	12	13	14	15	16	17	18	19	20	21	22	23	24	25	26	27	28	29	30	31	Average
MAX	89	90	87	69	64	62	80	83	85	77	82	82	78	81	80	76	77	80	78	76	68	77	84	76	83	84	88	82	78	76	77	74.0
MIN	63	69	65	62	57	56	59	61	69	61	58	58	64	61	57	64	62	53	57	63	60	59	64	65	62	62	67	64	59	51	52	60.8
MAX	86	90	91	87	69	63	65	80	85	86	79	83	85	77	80	81	75	79	81	80	77	69	77	85	78	85	85	88	85	77	75	80.1
MIN	60	67	65	65	63	56	57	60	66	65	58	58	64	69	58	63	58	53	58	62	62	59	60	65	62	63	67	69	59	50	51	61.0
MAX	89	89	83	76	67	77	82	84	84	74	78	77	74	71	80	75	72	75	71	68	73	84	78	78	80	84	86	81	76	70	75	77.8
MIN	61	64	65	64	60	62	52	55	64	57	55	56	59	64	55	57	58	48	50	61	60	61	61	61	62	63	65	72	58	45	50	58.9
MAX	87	94	94	84	82	67	72	84	85	88	78	85	86	78	82	84	83	72	80	80	72	82	83	82	77	86	89	92	90	78	77	82.4
MIN	62	67	67	68	62	58	59	60	65	65	54	57	61	64	57	61	62	61	57	63	63	64	61	65	60	64	69	69	56	49	51	61.3
MAX	92	90	91	83	82	80	85	86	84	81	80	85	84	75	82	82	79	76	78	70	82	84	79	82	84	84	88	79	74	77	81	81.9
MIN	65	60	63	63	62	65	52	54	53	56	54	54	61	60	51	52	59	55	58	64	57	65	59	61	56	59	65	54	46	49	60	57.8
MAX	91	92	88	86	81	72	84	88	80	74	79	78	72	72	80	80	75	77	79	77	82	85	82	78	83	85	90	84	77	76	77	80.8
MIN	68	66	67	64	66	54	60	68	64	57	56	58	64	63	50	64	58	53	59	63	64	60	62	64	62	63	64	67	56	52	58	61.1
MAX	92	92	89	84	64	72	83	85	85	85	82	80	76	77	81		78	79	78	73	77	79	82	82	83	86	90	90	82	78	78	81.4
MIN	66	67	66	62	60	58	59	57	64	59	52	54	61	66	56		59	47	48	61	66	63	62	63	60	60	63	69	52	46	48	59.1
MAX	85	90	89	83	68	66	80	81	82	82	71	81	80	74	75	80	76	72	80	76	72	78	84	80	79	82	83	87	88	78	76	79.3
MIN	59	65	65	64	61	60	54	58	56	60	54	56	56	57	55	55	56	47	49	55	60	61	64	63	59	62	63	61	54	47	49	57.6
MAX	93	91	91	82	66	67	83	88	85	85	84	80	77	80	81	79	79	80	80	72	70	81	84	83	84	85	87	87	83	78	78	81.4
MIN	66	67	65	60	60	56	60	59	65	61	53	55	64	68	56	61	60	49	52	61	61	62	64	65	61	61	65	67	54	47	49	59.8
MAX	92	91	86	68	62	60	79	83	84	77	81	83	78	78	79	75	78	82	79	75	65	77	84	76	82	86	87	82	76	75	77	78.6
MIN	67	71	64	62	58	55	59	62	69	61	60	60	64	66	61	65	61	58	59	62	59	58	66	66	63	65	67	67	61	54	53	62.0
MAX	85	85	81	79	79	70	78	85	78	64	74	75	70	66	76	74	72	76	80	77	78	82	76	77	80	80	81	74	73	67	76	76.4
MIN	66	66	63	65	62	62	54	59	59	51	54	62	62	59	55	58	60	52	56	60	58	61	62	59	62	63	62	65	55	49	52	59.1
MAX	86	85	82	81	66	69	75	82	82	76	75	72	70	68	73	75	74	74	75	70	76	80	75	78	78	77	83	84	72	67	70	75.8
MIN	56	61	53	53	58	60	45	51	58	53	44	53	57	56	44	55	52	38	41	60	60	55	55	54	51	57	56	62	41	40	40	52.2
MAX	86	86	83	67	79	74	80	84	77	65	77	75	69	68	76	75	69	75	74	73	82	83	78	74	77	80	86	79	73	72	73	76.4
MIN	62	63	64	61	62	55	52	54	59	50	48	55	62	57	50	59	54	46	47	62	62	59	63	57	57	61	64	54	49	44	49	56.2
MAX	87	89	90	83	81	86	73	83	87	81	76	79	83	74	73	81	82	77	77	82	78	82	85	81	80	82	84	87	80	76		81.3
MIN	57	68	62	65	66	66	51	53	63	55	52	54	61	64	45	52	56	49	49	58	60	56	60	59	61	58	61	66	51	43		57.4
MAX	89	92	88	81	72	80	76	84	85	75	82	83	77	75	81	79	68	78	76	73	80	82	82	80	84	85	90	89	78	72	76	80.4
MIN	50	65	67	65	62	60	61	54	65	57	52	54	60	62	50	57	55	56	54	63	62	61	61	62	56	62	64	54	45	45	46	57.6
MAX	89	89	94	89	80	84	82	87	89	80	80	80	80	72	80	79	76	80	81	81	84	84	84	83	81	82	84	89	81	80	80	82.7
MIN	70	69	65	69	65	65	53	55	61	60	54	59	63	63	49	64	60	48	63	63	59	60	61	63	64	64	65	69	51	46	52	60.4
MAX	80	86	84	81	65	60	69	78	79	79	68	76	69	70	70	76	75	70	75	75	65	67	65	76	78	76	78	82	78	70	69	73.8
MIN	49	63	60	57	58	54	54	59	63	57	53	54	59	59	53	56	52	46	47	50	55	57	60	61	57	57	57	63	49	47	47	55.3
MAX	96	94	91	82	70	68	86	87	87	84	86	85	82	80	85	82	77	81	81	77	79	82	83	81	87	90	92	89	85	78	82	83.5
MIN	68	69	71	69	63	59	64	62	70	62	57	59	64	66	59	63	64	57	57	64	63	64	65	68	64	66	70	72	62	52	55	63.5
MAX	93	94	89	82	68	75	85	86	86	76	83	84	79	79	83	82	74	80	79	72	86	84	81	74	85	87	92	88	77	76	80	81.9
MIN	64	69	67	66	62	59	59	60	70	60	55	58	62	65	54	61	58	57	57	64	63	65	61	63	59	64	70	69	57	48	50	61.2
MAX		92	95	90	83	67	70	64	85	83	81	85	87	86	85		80	79	82	84	78	74	81	82	80	86	89	89	80	90	82	82.4
MIN		67	69	73	68	58	60		67	70	61	62	70	74	62		61	65	63	67	68		64	65	61	68	70	62		56	58	65.0
MAX	90	90	86	81	80	77	83	86	84	79	78	77	81	81	79	77	72	78	77	77	82	84	81	80	82	83	88	81	75	74	75	80.6
MIN	60	66	63	63	63	65	53	56	62	58	51	55	62	63	50	60	58	47	50	60	60	59	58	59	58	62	62	65	49	44	50	57.8
MAX	89	92	86	85	85	78	85	85	82	75	80	83	76	74	80	82	78	78	78	80	84	84	80	79	84	84						81.8
MIN	56	64	58	66	65	65	53	52	60	55	51	53	62	62	47	60	58	52	49	53	56	55	58	58	64	56						57.2
MAX	85	91	95	88	78	65	68	84	84	86	79	84	85	83	81	82	79	78	82	82	74	75	78	85	76	85	87	90	90	78	77	81.7
MIN	59	67	67	68	63	57	56	61	70	64	56	57	60	66	58	60	60	62	60	59	64	61	62	68	58	64	68	67	60	47	50	61.3
MAX	94	98	88	80	71	70	84	84	90	86	86	86	81	83	85	80	77	84	84	77	75	80	87	78	88	90	93	92	80	79	82	83.6
MIN	68	69	68	68	62	57	63	64	71	68	59	61	64	70	69	64	63	61	61	65	64	62	64	68	60	64	71	72	60	51	53	64.0
MAX	88	88	90	86	84	84	76	82	85	79	70	78	80	73	71	80	80	78	78	75	77	84	83	78	74	81	83	83	81	75	70	79.8
MIN	47	61	63	61	66	64	58	53	65	58	50	51	52	50	54	55	62	57	54	48	57	56	56	55	51	54	57	61	53	48	40	55.4
MAX	91	82	84	84	69	68	80	86	79	66	76	73	75	73	75	77	73	79	76	75	81	80	78	80	81	82	85	84	73	72	84	78.1
MIN	62	63	60	59	62	59	49	58	60	56	49	56	61	59	46	60	60	42	46	64	62	67	58	58	58	59	62	64	46	41	48	56.6
MAX	85	83	82	77	64	73	76	79	77	68	77	68	66	68	73	72	70	77	71	66	72	80	76	79	75	76	83	77	68	69	70	74.1
MIN	58	62	56	55	58	57	48	52	52	55	44	52	57	57	45	55	52	39	43	58	57	62	57	58	56	52	57	61	44	37	39	52.7
MAX	90	89	85	92	85	79	83	89	80	71	79	80	80	70	81	81	74	77	77	79	81	85	80	78	80	85	86	82	77	73	77	80.8
MIN	72	69	64	69	68	68	53	65	63	58	56	60	64	65	54	63	59	52	63	67	64	61	61	62	65	64	64	67	62	47	53	62.0
MAX	89	94	80	77	65	65	80	80	84	78	83	85	81	82	83	77	78	78	80	76	72	75	85	84	84	84	89	88	86	76	79	80.5
MIN	63	67	65	63	53	53	59	59	65	60	57	60	63	61	61	63	58	54	57	58	41	47	56	63	60	59	69	60	57	49	59	58.7
MAX	85	89	89	82	72	63	67	82	84	85	74	81	76	73	76	83	81	77	80	81	70	67	80	83	82	81	80	87	82	74	73	78.7
MIN	48	64	61	59	59	51	52	59	61	61	52	53	56	63	52	54	52	47	49	50	59	60	63	61	55	57	60	65	51	44	45	55.6
MAX	86	87	81	78	81	70	79	83	77	66	75	77	69	65	75	77	72	74	73	74	81	81	75	73	78	79	81	75	71	67	76	76.0
MIN	58	62	58	62	61	54	49	48	57	52	49	51	56	49	44	55	52	50	53	57	56	56	55	55	56	56	57	58	47	38	44	53.4
MAX	91	92	94	87	87	89	78	86	90	84	79	84	85	76	79	84	85	78	83	83	83	86	88	82	81	85	87	89	84	79	80	84.5
MIN	67	76	67	72	71	69	58	61	68	64	61	61	66	68	57	68	63	57	59	66	64	66	65	65	61	66	66	69	58	51	57	64.1
MAX	86	85	84	80	80	70	79	83	82	73	76	76	75	69	75	76	74	75	79	71	76	82	78	77	76	81	85	83	78	72	81	78.0
MIN	62	63	62	60	60	63	46	53	62	57	48	52	61	62	48	58	54	43	46	61	61	64	63	62	56	59	63	62	49	41	41	56.2
MAX	76	82	81	78	62	59	63	73	75	76	64	72	67	68	68	74	71	68	71	72	68	62	70	72	72	75	73	76	75	68	66	70.9
MIN	51	62	61	60	51	54	53	55	62	57	51	53	56	61	53	54	56	54	55	55	56	58	59	62	57	57	60	63	51	47	48	55.9
MAX	91	93	91	86	82	80	84	89	88	72	82	80	78	73	83	79	78	80	81	81	85	86	86	83	84	85	90	89	85	80	80	83.4
MIN	63	69	68	55	66	67	55	60	65	60	52	56	64	64	52	63	61	52	55	62	64	63	60	64	62	65	65	72	54	47	53	60.6
MAX	85	84	80	70	80	71	78	81	77	64	74	74	70	68	75	73	70	72	70	70	76	80	73	74	76	79	81	77	72	67	74	74.7
MIN	62	63	62	61	60	63	47	53	60	55	52	53	58	59	48	68	55	47	50	60	60	58	61	59	59	60	62	65	51	42	48	56.8
MAX	85	88	88	84	68	67	77	81	85	81	66	76	73	70	73	77	79					78	85	81					87	74	72	78.1
MIN	48	63	61	57	60	60	51	53	58	60	52	53	57	57	52	52	58					45	61	60					48	42	45	54.5
MAX	91	93	86	81	73	63	82	81	86	81	84	85	83	83	83	76	76	80	81	75	73	75	83	78	85	86	91	88	81	76	78	81.2
MIN	63	67	62	65	60	56	61	64	69	66	56	60	62	68	62	63	62	57	61	63	61	61	63	67	60	65	69	70	59	50	52	62.1
MAX	91	76	76	68	65	70	77	88	80	70	77	77	76	71	75	74	72	73	80	77	82	82	77	79	79	80	85	74	68	69	76	76.3
MIN	67	66	60	63	60	57	57	67	60	59	59	61	63	58	56	64	54	50	56	66	65	62	64	63	65	66	67	65	57	56	56	60.9

See Reference Notes Following Station Index

DAILY TEMPERATURES

Table 5 - Continued

Station		1	2	3	4	5	6	7	8	9	10	11	12	13	14	15	16	17	18	19	20	21	22	23	24	25	26	27	28	29	30	31
EVERETT 1 SW	MAX	90	80	89	82	70	78	88	88	82	76	77	82	82	70	82	82	76	75	76	74	82	80	82	78	84	86	90	81	82	70	76
	MIN	56	66	64	62	65	58	56	67	55	54	52	53	56	60	50	49	54	56	54	60	64	65	60	60	56	58	60	69	59	54	51
FARRELL SHARON	MAX	93	93	88	82	82	78	86	91	83	78	81	80	75	76	83	79	79	80	83	76	85	86	84	83	85	83	92	90	78	76	79
	MIN	66	72	65	64	63	60	58	55	57	52	45	61	63	61	48	62	60	48	52	60	61	68	59	62	62	67	58	52	39	41	53
FORD CITY 4 S DAM	MAX	87	90	90	84	75	83	75	82	87	82	72	79	78	73	69	80	78	70	76	79	78	82	85	80	79	81	85	88	80	75	74
	MIN	55	66	64	65	56	67	52	54	59	59	52	58	61	64	51	52	58	50	52	55	60	59	61	62	61	63	63	67	52	47	48
FRANKLIN	MAX	88	88	86	85	77	78	81	84	80	76	79	77	75	72	77	77	77	75	77	77	81	81	80	81	80	81	87	88	77	74	74
	MIN	63	59	63	63	63	64	53	58	65	58	40	59	63	58	50	61	60	48	52	62	62	60	61	62	60	64	64	68	57	46	53
FREELAND	MAX	82	82	77	77	60	60	75	77	78	78	77	77	77	73	74	74	74	73	73	68	64	72	74	77	77	75	79	77	75	68	71
	MIN	61	62	62	57	52	49	54	59	62	58	51	57	61	64	54	58	54	54	53	45	53	54	63	62	59	59	64	64	52	43	40
GEORGE SCHOOL	MAX	90	91	87	80	68	67	80	84	83	81	78	82	83	82	83	76	79	79	81	75	70	77	85	77	87	89	88	91	80	75	79
	MIN	58	68	67	66	62	58	60	63	70	57	61	60	65	67	57	65	61	52	55	58	60	59	65	63	61	62	68	70	64	52	51
GETTYSBURG	MAX	90	94	95	88	83	67	75	86	85	88	76	86	86	79	82	84	84	73	82	81	73	83	84	83	75	87	89	94	91	76	75
	MIN	65	70	68	68	62	59	60	65	70	67	60	60	63	67	57	63	63	60	58	62	64	64	65	67	60	66	72	73	60	50	50
GRATZ 1 N	MAX	85	89	89	84	69	64	67	80	84	84	75	80	80	75	77		76	75	79	77	70	68	76	82	77	83	84	87	81	75	74
	MIN	55	66	66	65	60	56	57	60	62	60	51	54	57	65	56		59	49	52	58	61	60	61	64	58	58	63	67	58	48	48
GREENVILLE	MAX	92	87	80	78	75	85	88	80	76	81	81	78	74	81	78	73	79	83	78	83	85	81	82	83	83		91	90	78	78	76
	MIN	62	64	64	63	62	51	59	62	57	53	58	63	60	47	67	59	55	52	62	61	56	57	60	59	62	63	66		50	54	51
HANOVER	MAX	86	93	96	89	82	69	72	84	86	88	78	85	86	80	83	84	82	75	82	82	72	84	78	83	76	85	88	92	89	76	77
	MIN	57	70	67	67	62	57	57	63	70	64	55	55	60	66	56	60	61	59	61	63	63	63	62	65	59	60	63	69	58	49	50
HARRISBURG WB AP	MAX	93	92	87	75	65	66	85	87	85	76	83	83	79	79	83	77	76	81	80	71	73	75	83	78	85	87	92	86	77	75	79
	MIN	68	70	69	65	58	57	62	66	70	63	58	62	64	64	62	64	65	61	60	63	63	63	66	65	62	68	70	72	63	53	55
HAWLEY 1 S DAM	MAX	82	86	85	81	68	60	61	78	80	81	72	78	75	77	73	77	76	74	74	78	70	62	80	80	76	77	80	83	78	70	70
	MIN	55	64	59	53	54	51	52	54	61	61	55	58	58	59	53	59	50	45	45	49	56	54	59	62	54	54	60	63	52	44	41
HOLTWOOD	MAX	91	94	87	84	70	70	86	85	86	77	82	86	82	81	82	77	72	79	81	73	78	77	84	75	86	81	90	87	76	75	81
	MIN	68	72	72	70	62	61	66	69	72	67	63	64	68	68	63	68	68	66	66	68	68	66	68	64	63	68	73	73	66	57	57
HUNTINGDON	MAX	90	95	93	84	71	72	84	87	87	86	75	82	82	77	73	84	80	73	84	76	70	91	84	85	81	90	89	92	88	83	78
	MIN	50	66	66	68	63	63	55	55	60	63	51	52	55	54	54	55	60	54	52	53	63	63	63	63	60	60	64	67	56	47	47
INDIANA 3 SE	MAX	88	89	85	76	83	76	82	89	81	71	79	77	74	70	80	78	73	79	78	77	85	85	79	78	78	83	87	81	76	73	78
	MIN	60	66	62	65	65	65	50	55	64	58	49	52	61	63	52	59	57	49	50	61	59	56	63	62	58	60	63	68	52	44	49
IRWIN	MAX	90	92	91	89	86	87	84	88	86	80	81	80	80	72	82	83	81	81	82	82	85	86	85	81	80	85	88	86	85	80	
	MIN	66	73	64	66	68	67	54	58	65	58	57	60	65	65	56	65	58	52	56	62	61	66	62	62	64	64	67	67	57	54	
JAMESTOWN 2 NW	MAX	84	89	85	83	70	76	70	82	87	79	74	78	79	74	72	78	77	73	77	79	75	80	83	79	82	80	81	88	78	72	71
	MIN	58	73	64	63	64	61	52	60	62	57	54	59	63	61	51	56	59	46	50	59	59	59	59	60	61	64	64	66	51	44	51
JIM THORPE	MAX	89	89	88		84	60	79	80	82	82	81	82	78	77	81	77		82	77	76	69	73	82	82		85	83	85	80	76	79
	MIN	66	67	63		57	54	58	57	64	59	52	55	63	67	56	60		53	49	62	61	58	65	64		58	65	65	57	46	48
JOHNSTOWN	MAX	93	94	93	85	89	91	81	86	92	86	73	84	85	79	68	79	84	80	83	78	82	88	91	85	84	88	89	92	85	80	80
	MIN	64	65	64	67	64	64	55	56	64	59	53	54	54	62	53	60	60	52	53	61	64	60	61	60	61	61	64	67	54	42	46
KANE 1 NNE	MAX	84	87	84	83	67	71	72	78	89	78	62	75	70	68	70	74	76	70	70	73	73	78	80	78	79	76	81	84	77	69	69
	MIN	54	57	56	54	60	60	44	52	58	56	43	52	58	59	42	54	55	37	40	50	60	55	55	58	52	58	58	61	41	37	41
KEGG	MAX	92	92	89	78	73	78	83	86	82	71	81	82	76	72	86	81	76	77	76	72	82	85	81	78	83	86	88	85	78	75	79
	MIN	62	64	64	64	62	60	52	50	62	56	54	53	59	58	51	51	59	55	53	61	62	65	59	60	58	60	64	65	52	45	48
LANCASTER 2 NE PUMP STA	MAX	90	95	95	80	70	67	81	85	87	82	85	85	82	82	81	77	76	81	79	76	76	75	84	81	85	86	90	88	82	77	79
	MIN	61	66	66	67	61	56	61	61	67	63	57	57	60	66	57	61	59	58	60	62	62	61	60	65	57	62	69	68	57	51	52
LANDISVILLE 2 NW	MAX	85	92	96	84	75	64	69	82	79	88	79	84	85	78	78	83	77	76	80	79	73	73	78	84	77	85	86	90	90	77	75
	MIN	64	69	67	70	62	57	62	61	69	65	54	56	61	73	61	57	60	59	58	64	63	62	61	68	59	61	69	68	57	49	50
LAWRENCEVILLE 2 S	MAX	90	93	85	87	73	63	75	84	87	87	79	82	78	76	79	82	72	72	82	82	69	75	84	83	80	82	90	89	83	76	75
	MIN	43	62	57	54	52	55	56	55	58	57	48	54	58	57	49	52	50	44	45	50	59	58	60	57	58	54	58	56	45	44	45
LEBANON 2 NW	MAX	87	94	94	88	73	64	67	84	85	88	80	85	84	79	82	82	77	79	84	81	74	70	78	85	80	87	89	91	89	78	76
	MIN	65	70	68	71	61	56	58	64	71	66	58	61	64	67	60	64	64	59	62	65	61	60	65	67	62	65	69	72	63	55	54
LEWISTOWN	MAX	88	93	93	87	72	68	76	84	87	87	75	85	81	75	79	84	78	77	82	78	73	79	84	84	80	86	89	90	86	80	77
	MIN	53	69	67	69	63	61	60	60	60	63	55	55	56	63	57	57	61	55	53	54	62	63	65	65	62	62	64	68	58	50	49
LINESVILLE 5 WNW	MAX	89	84	82	74	72	71	83	87	78	74	78	77	75	74	77	78	72	77	80	77	80	83	79	82	80	82	88	81	71	71	74
	MIN	65	71	63	61	64	59	51	62	64	57	52	63	63	61	47	63	60	45	48	64	62	58	61	59	63	64	67	65	50	44	51
LOCK HAVEN	MAX	94	92	86	82	65	74	85	87	86	83	82	77	74	78	82	81	76	81	79	70	75	86	83	83	83	84	90	86	82	76	79
	MIN	66	67	67	64	61	58	56	58	65	60	52	55	59	65	54	60	62	59	51	59	61	64	63	64	61	62	62	68	52	48	51
MADERA	MAX	84	88	84	82	66	74	76	80	85	81	69	79	75	71	70	77	75	74	74	73	72	78	84	77	76	80	84	83	78	73	72
	MIN	46	61	61	63	59	59	49	49	49	51	45	50	56	59	48	52	56	46	44	46	58	52	59	59	54	57	57	60	46	40	40
MARCUS HOOK	MAX	90	92	88	78	68	68	81	84	80	85	88	86	83	87	84	83	79	80	82	78	77	77	88	75	84	85	86	89	78	79	80
	MIN	66	72	71	66	60	56	64	69	65	69	63	67	68	69	64	68	68	67	66	67	64	63	70	68	66	70	70	74	67	59	60
MARTINSBURG CAA AP	MAX	93	90	84	74	70	77	85	85	81	67	77	79	74	73	82	76	72	76	75	69	78	82	79	78	81	84	86	80	74	71	77
	MIN	66	65	67	63	61	62	54	59	63	58	54	56	59	58	52	58	56	51	52	61	60	62	62	62	60	64	65	63	55	48	52
MEADVILLE 1 S	MAX	85	89	86	83	71	74	67	81	86	83	70	78	76	73	70	72	78	70	77	79	75	81	82	79	82	79	83	88	77	71	70
	MIN	58	69	64	63	64	61	52	54	63	57	56	57	62	63	53	53	59	45	49	59	63	58	58	61	59	62	65	66	50	46	51
MERCER 2 NNE	MAX	88	84	89	78	79	75	82	86	79	72	77	76	72	73	79	76	74	76	77	78	81	82	81	79	80	82	88	89	72	73	79
	MIN	70	62	66	67	62	60	49	58	60	56	50	58	62	57	44	60	57	45	50	47	60	56	51	59	62	62	62	50	48	40	50
MIDDLETOWN OLMSTED FLD	MAX	95	94	86	75	66	67	84	85	86	76	83	86	76	80	81	77	75	80	81	72	75	77	85	79	87	87	92	88	78	75	82
	MIN	67	72	69	60	59	59	64	66	72	65	56	61	64	66	65	65	65	60	60	65	65	63	65	65	62	65	71	71	60	53	55
MIDLAND DAM 7	MAX	91	92	84	80	85	85	84	88	81	74	80	80	74	73	80	78	76	78	84	79	83	84	82	81	85	86	88	79	73	73	79
	MIN	66	69	67	69	70	65	60	63	63	58	60	62	66	61	57	68	63	61	57	66	68	64	62	66	68	67	67	66	61	54	59
MONTROSE 1 E	MAX	80	86	84	82	70	58	61	76	81	82	69	76	68	71	71	78	75	71	73	76	64	62	78	79	78	77	78	80	76	68	67
	MIN	54	62	58	57	57	51	52	57	60	57	54	51	57	59	55	56	53	51	53	53	55	56	57	60	57	56	57	64	52	48	48
MORGANTOWN	MAX	88	93	85	74	66	65	81	82	84	77	82	82	79	81	80	76	77	79	77	74	70	75	83	82	83	86	88	87	77	74	78
	MIN	63	67	67	64	56	55	61	65	55	62	56	55	61	63	56	64	58	59	62	61	61	60	63	64	59	61	70	68	57	48	50
MT GRETNA 2 SE	MAX	90	90	84	75	65	66	81	85	84	75	81	83	77	80	83	75	75	80	78	72	70	75	78	75	84	85	90	88	88	75	79
	MIN	60	65	67	64	57	56	60	59	68	58	52	56	60	62	62	60	61	55	65	63	64	65	66	60	61	62	70	68	58	48	49
MT POCONO 2 N AP	MAX	84	83	83	75	60	60	77	78	76	76	75	75	74	71	77	75	72	75	73	65	64	74	77	75	78	77	77	77		67	74
	MIN	61	63	57	58	52	50	53	57	62	55	50	54	59	60	52	58	51	50	49	49	57	54	63	60	57	57	66	62		43	45

See Reference Notes Following Station Index

DAILY TEMPERATURES

Day Of Month

	1	2	3	4	5	6	7	8	9	10	11	12	13	14	15	16	17	18	19	20	21	22	23	24	25	26	27	28	29	30	31	Average
MAX	79	89		80	62	65	79	83	82	73	80	75	73	77	78	77	79	77	75	69	65	75	80	77	84	81	83	84	81	80	75	77.9
MIN	61	62	50	56	55	51	53	55	60	50	49	57	60	55	58	56	55	48	48	56	55	56	59	62	55	54	60	62	49	49	41	55.2
MAX	90	92	90	80	74	74	84	83	82	83	86	84	84	78	82	79	78	78	79	84	85	81	84	84	84	80	91	92	86	77	79	83.1
MIN	74	72	76	68	61	64	71	68	66	67	56	62	59	61	70	72	66	64	66	64	66	65	68	71	72	67	70	79	60	61	66	66.8
MAX	90	90	88	85	82	78	74	88	82	76	79	78	76	75	82	80	78	79	80	76	81	85	82	80	83	84	90	90	79	74	77	81.5
MIN	65	74	64	63	65	63	54	54	63	59	55	62	64	62	51	64	60	49	52	63	62	59	60	60	63	64	63	69	54	46	53	60.0
MAX	90	92	95	84	87	88	74	85	89	85	78	83	85	77	76	83	85	82	83	85	84	85	88	83	80	85	87	86	83	80	76	84.0
MIN	65	73	68	76	71	70	60	61	67	62	61	59	67	68	57	67	64	60	59	66	64	64	64	66	67	65	66	70	59	53	57	64.4
MAX	89	95	93	86	73	66	67	86	87	87	76	85	83	73	80	83	78	76	84	80	71	72	75	83	81	85	87	91	88	81	77	81.2
MIN	53	68	68	70	62	58	58	58	60	63	52	54	57	62	56	58	62	52	52	54	62	63	63	64	61	61	63	67	57	49	49	59.2
MAX	97	94	87	86	89	79	81	88	83	73	81	85	79	72	83	84	80	80	79	81	86	88	81	80	84	86	88	83	84	75	82	83.2
MIN	59	67	63	67	50	60	63	54	59	60	58	53	51	53	50	60	58	52	53	61	59	58	59	62	61	59	62	63	47	44	50	57.3
MAX	90	96	88	78	69	66	83	84	84	81	80	87	85	85	83	79	79	81	83	78	73	79	86	76	87	90	90	90	80	77	81	82.2
MIN	66	72	70	68	58	58	63	67	71	65	61	62	67	68	61	68	64	62	64	65	63	62	67	66	63	66	73	71	64	56	55	64.7
MAX	88	90	84	67	62	60	78	82	83	76	81	81	75	78	79	76	76	78	77	72	66	74	84	77	83	82	86	82	77	73	76	77.5
MIN	63	68	63	62	56	55	58	60	68	63	56	55	64	64	55	63	60	51	53	65	60	60	68	66	63	60	67	63	58	49	49	60.2
MAX	94	97	89	79	70	69	84	84	83	81	87	89	84	87	85	80	81	81	84	79	75	80	90	75	89	91	89	92	81	80	83	83.6
MIN	69	75	71	70	60	59	64	69	73	68	66	66	72	71	65	70	68	67	68	67	64	63	70	69	65	70	74	74	67	61	62	67.6
MAX	92	94	87	78	68	69	82	84	82	80	83	86	84	84	82	79	79	80	81	77	77	80	87	75	85	88	88	89	77	75	80	81.7
MIN	65	72	70	67	60	59	64	68	71	66	61	62	69	66	62	68	67	66	64	66	64	63	67	66	64	68	71	71	64	59	58	65.4
MAX	92	95	88	76	68	66	82	84	82	81	85	86	84	84	82	79	80	80	82	77	74	79	87	74	85	87	87	90	77	77	81	81.6
MIN	68	74	72	71	60	58	64	69	72	70	64	65	71	66	65	70	67	66	66	67	65	63	80	68	64	70	72	73	69	62	62	67.5
MAX	91	94	96	87	75	68	85	87	83	82	83	86	87	83	82	83	78	82	82	82	78	78	86	85	85	88	88	89	80	79	81	83.6
MIN	63	70	69	70	63	58	63	67	70	68	59	60	65	73	59	65	63	60	60	63	65	62	66	69	62	64	72	71	61	53	55	64.1
MAX	89	93	85	76	67	67	81	81	81	80	83	84	82	82	81	79	80	78	80	76	73	80	85	75	84	86	86	88	79	77	79	80.5
MIN	67	74	71	67	59	59	64	68	69	68	65	68	70	64	66	69	68	66	66	65	63	62	70	67	66	71	71	73	66	60	63	66.6
MAX	87	86	79	66	64	75	80	81	78	65	75	74	68	69	76	75	70	74	69	68	71	81	76	76	75	81	84	79	71	70	72	74.7
MIN	62	63	62	60	59	55	44	50	59	55	51	51	61	57	47	55	47	36	41	60	59	62	63	55	54	58	62	56	49	37	42	53.9
MAX	94	99	93	84	74	67	83	86	86	82	88	86	87	87	86	85	79	82	83	81	73	76	88	86	89	90	92	91	82	79	82	84.5
MIN	60	68	66	66	58	62	61	64	68	65	56	64	59	69	53	60	57	57	59	59	61	60	61	65	59	59	67	66	58	48	48	60.7
MAX	77	83	81	79	65	54	60	76	76	77	70	75	75	72	71	76	72	73	75	74	65	63	70	77	71	78	78	79	77	70	67	72.8
MIN	60	61	57	60	53	50	52	57	62	57	51	57	61	62	53	59	53	48	57	56	56	54	62	59	58	58	62	66	51	44	50	56.3
MAX	88	88	83	80	83	73	82	86	79	74	78	78	73	70	79	80	75	75	79	77	78	83	79	78	82	82	86	77	74	73	77	79.0
MIN	67	68	65	67	67	63	56	62	63	60	61	63	66	58	53	66	59	55	58	64	65	62	65	63	66	62	64	61	57	50	55	61.6
MAX	90	93	85	83	85	74	85	87	84	76	81	81	75	73	82	83	78	78	81	79	82	85	81	80	84	85	91	80	75	75	79	81.6
MIN	71	71	69	69	69	65	59	65	66	62	64	66	67	64	58	68	62	56	59	67	66	65	66	65	68	66	67	66	60	54	60	64.5
MAX	79	83	82	80	67	57	58	75	79	78	71	76	70	70	70	75	74	70	74	75	63	60	76	78	77	76	75	80	76	69	66	72.9
MIN	55	63	55	53	56	51	51	55	60	57	54	51	55	60	53	57	46	44	45	50	54	54	56	59	53	56	60	63	51	43	41	53.6
MAX	86	92	92	87	72	62	65	84	85	87	78	83	84	75	80	81	78	80	83	79	72	68	72	85	79	89	86	90	85	78	77	80.3
MIN	60	66	65	61	60	54	55	59	66	59	51	51	59	66	52	59	52	48	51	62	60	59	61	64	57	58	64	65	52	45	46	57.6
MAX	84	89	90	85	70	81	76	83	87	80	72	79	78	70	70	81	77	75	78	76	78	83	84	81	80	81	81	88	81	76	76	79.7
MIN	49	63	63	62	62	63	51	53	62	56	49	54	58	62	50	52	56	46	47	53	60	57	61	60	58	61	61	64	48	43	46	55.8
MAX	89	90	90	89	67	63	80	85		84	81	85	82	81	80	79	77	80	79	76	72	76	84	82	84	85	86	86	82	79	77	81.0
MIN	59	67	65	63	59	53	60	61		64	55	55	62	68	55	62	68	55	54	61	61	59	64	65	59	59	61	67	58	50	49	59.9
MAX	91	94	87	75	65	66	83	86	87	79	85	86	79	82	82	77	78	82	79	77	72	76	85	77	86	88	90	86	79	78	80	81.2
MIN	67	69	69	65	58	57	63	69	71	64	61	63	66	67	63	65	64	61	63	63	63	62	68	68	64	68	70	71	63	56	55	64.4
MAX	88	88	84	79	75	74	80	84	80	75	67	74	70	71	75	78	70	77	74	71	80	82	79	80	78	82	87	86	74	71	73	77.6
MIN	45	58	61	57	62	61	48	49	52	57	45	47	53	60	46	47	57	44	43	45	62	57	58	61	53	60	60	63	46	41	40	52.8
MAX	89	90	86	89	82	78	82	86	82	72	78	77	74	71	80	79	74	77	78	78	82	84	80	78	79	82	88	86	78	74	77	80.3
MIN	62	70	64	69	67	66	53	59	66	59	54	58	64	63	55	63	58	51	52	62	59	59	63	63	64	63	64	68	54	46	52	60.3
MAX	85	90	90	85	71	64	65	78	85	84	74	80	62	69	68	80	80	77	78	78	72	68	77	84	78	78	82	85	81	73	74	77.3
MIN	51	65	65	61	60	53	54	60	58	63	57	55	58	57	55	54	56	50	51	55	60	59	60	64	58	56	58	64	58	46	46	57.0
MAX	89	87	83	69	63	65	78	82	82	73	78	76	76	75	79	78	75	77	76	71	67	81	81	76	80	80	84	80	72	71	75	76.7
MIN	65	65	62	60	55	54	59	60	65	60	56	56	63	59	56	61	56	49	53	59	59	58	65	62	60	60	64	60	52	47	47	58.3
MAX	91	93	86	68	65	67	83	85	86	75	87	81	75	80	81	78	77	84	80	72	69	80	85	80	83	82	88	85	80	78	77	80.0
MIN	67	68	65	64	60	59	59	58	65	57	52	55	63	61	55	62	56	53	49	63	61	63	66	64	60	60	64	59	55	47	50	59.4
MAX	93	93	90	82	72	70	83	85	86	83	83	85	79	80	83	80	76	80	78	74	82	84	83	79	86	88	91	89	84	76	81	82.5
MIN	64	66	68	67	60	58	59	60	70	60	57	62	62	69	58	62	62	58	58	63	62	62	64	64	62	66	69	71	57	49	51	61.9
MAX	89	90	82	77	82	73	82	88	79	75	78	76	74	71	79	78	72	76	79	76	81	83	80	79	82	84	87	78	74	72	76	79.1
MIN	64	67	65	66	68	59	55	60	64	58	58	60	66	57	52	63	58	55	54	63	64	62	67	63	65	64	63	58	53	59	55	60.8
MAX	88	90	85	77	78	77	81	84	78	74	77	75	72	72	80	75	73	76	77	74	80	82	80	78	79	76	90	86	75	72	72	78.5
MIN	67	70	60	62	63	63	55	60	62	58	56	62	63	59	51	62	60	50	55	62	62	62	62	60	65	64	65	68	55	49	52	60.1
MAX	85	88	86	81	83	79	80	84	78	76	77	78	77	68	77	78	75	75	75	72	85	83	82	77	78	80	84	81	76	71	76	78.9
MIN	61	65	60	64	63	63	51	53	62	56	52	53	58	60	51	59	56	57	58	61	61	58	58	59	59	58	60	63	49	42	47	57.3
MAX	87	90	97	85	72	76	70	83	87	79	73	80	78	75	73	78	84	73	75	80	77	82	81	80	80	80	83	82	77	70	72	79.3
MIN	62	68	61	59	61	60	50	59	64	57	53	59	62	61	49	62	62	45	50	63	62	59	61	59	62	62	64	65	48	46	52	58.3
MAX	84	86	82	77	81	74	78	75	75	64	73	74	69	69	76	75	74	72	72	70	78	79	74	70	77	80	79	77	70	67	76	75.1
MIN	61	63	60	60	63	62	54	59	59	54	50	47	55	60	56	56	54	52	52	62	56	56	51	58	60	53	58	63	45	41	44	55.6
MAX	91	89	83	70	66	79	84	83	81	69	85	77	72	72	82	77	72	78	75	70	76	81	79	79	80	84	86	81	77	73	76	78.3
MIN	67	65	66	64	61	59	54	59	61	59	54	58	63	61	57	58	56	48	50	62	60	61	64	63	62	63	65	62	54	48	51	59.2
MAX	91	88	90	74	71	60	76	83	84	78	82	83	76	80	83	70	77	77	82	75	65	75	85	80	87	85	85	83	77	76	77	79.2
MIN	57	64	60	58	56	48	50	61	62	58	54	50	61	60	51	60	57	45	48	58	60	57	61	64	54	57	61	63	50	39	41	55.6
MAX																																
MIN																																
MAX	84	89	88	85	69	77	71	80	84	79	69	78	75	72	71	76	79	72	77	77	74	81	81	80	81	79	82	87	79	73	72	78.1
MIN	53	62	60	61	62	63	53	55	59	58	51	53	60	61	51	52	59	53	49	53	60	60	59	62	64	66	62	65	50	47	47	57.1
MAX	90	89	84	80	72	74	84	88	80	68	73	76	76	73	78	79	73	74	80	76	83	76	83	83	81	81	88	85	71	75	69	78.8
MIN	57	62	58	59	61	60	50	55	62	54	48	56	61	58	47	58	57	43	44	61	65	56	54	56	54	61	62	64	44	40	49	55.4

See Reference Notes Following Station Index

DAILY TEMPERATURES

Table 5 - Continued

Station		1	2	3	4	5	6	7	8	9	10	11	12	13	14	15	16	17	18	19	20	21	22	23	24	25	26	27	28	29	30	31	Average
TOWANDA	MAX	92	90	88	78	66	69	83	87	85	76	83	74	73	76	82	80	77	69	82	73	67	84	82	83	81	80	87	83	74	74	78	79.8
	MIN	64	65	60	57	58	56	60	59	63	58	54	53	61	62	52	60	53	45	47	58	60	65	62	50	53	57	61	66	50	44	44	56.8
UNIONTOWN	MAX	89	91	87	86	86	74	82	86	81	72	81	82	74	79	81	82	79	78	79	80	84	84	78	73	82	83	83	82	76	73	81	80.7
	MIN	64	70	66	70	71	67	60	59	65	58	61	61	65	66	54	66	61	59	65	65	64	63	65	64	64	62	65	67	59	56	55	63.0
UPPER DARBY	MAX	91	95	90	84	72	66	83	83	83	81	85	87	84	84	83	81	76	80	83	77	75	80	87	84	85	86	88	88	78	76	80	82.6
	MIN	64	70	72	70	60	57	62	67	70	68	61	62	68	70	62	65	66	64	62	69	64	63	67	69	63	68	71	72	63	56	57	65.2
WARREN	MAX	90	87	85	78	68	69	81	86	81	72	79	74	72	74	77	78	74	77	77	73	82	84	80	83	80	85	88	84	70	73	73	78.5
	MIN	62	63	58	60	62	62	52	58	69	58	49	58	62	59	50	60	59	46	50	65	63	62	61	58	58	63	62	66	49	47	48	57.9
WAYNESBURG 2 W	MAX	89	92	86	89	87	75	84	85	84	74	79	83	79	74	81	81	79	78	81	81	82	84	79	79	82	89	84	89	77	78	80	81.4
	MIN	59	69	63	68	68	66	57	56	63	58	52	53	64	66	52	63	60	57	53	61	59	58	58	62	60	58	61	65	57	48	53	59.6
WELLSBORO 3 S	MAX	80	87	84	82	66	60	71	80	79	79	70	77	70	69	70	76	74	68	75	74	67	69	77	78	79	79	77	85	80	71	72	75.0
	MIN	52	63	60	57	58	54	54	57	62	56	51	55	59	62	53	57	54	46	49	54	58	59	61	61	57	58	61	64	49	44	47	55.9
WELLSVILLE	MAX	92	93	90	81	78	75	83	84	86	80	83	84	70	76	82	78	76	80	78	72	78	80	83	75	84	86	90	89	82	75	80	81.7
	MIN	62	67	68	66	52	58	60	60	67	62	51	54	60	59	52	60	60	59	57	55	64	62	60	66	56	61	69	66	56	48	47	59.7
WEST CHESTER	MAX	86	92	96	86	79	64	67	84	89	85	82	87	88	82	81	85	78	77	80	82	74	74	76	88	73	87	89	90	86	79	79	82.9
	MIN	65	65	68	67	63	56	57	64	70	66	60	63	67	70	63	61	65	63	55	64	64	61	65	68	61	67	70	70	64	55	57	63.9
WILLIAMSPORT WB AP	MAX	93	92	85	70	63	66	84	85	87	75	85	76	72	78	83	81	77	82	79	70	69	79	83	83	85	84	90	87	79	76	77	79.8
	MIN	69	68	66	63	58	57	58	59	66	60	54	56	65	61	54	62	59	51	52	59	61	65	64	65	62	61	63	63	55	49	51	59.9
YORK 3 SSW PUMP STA	MAX	94	95	95	85	71	70	85	86	89	87	85	85	84	81	84	84	78	82	83	81	70	82	84	85	86	89	92	94	86	76	81	84.5
	MIN	65	71	78	69	64	59	64	65	71	64	56	57	62	70	55	62	60	60	60	67	65	64	62	67	58	62	76	68	56	45	50	63.0

EVAPORATION AND WIND

Table 6

Station		1	2	3	4	5	6	7	8	9	10	11	12	13	14	15	16	17	18	19	20	21	22	23	24	25	26	27	28	29	30	31	Total or Avg.
CONFLUENCE 1 SW DAM	EVAP	.19	.20	.21	.19	.09	.15	.12	.21	.22	.22	.08	.17	.13	.03	.09	.21	.16	.04	.20	.09	.04	.13	.34	.11	.08	.17	.19	.17	.19	.10	.20	4.70
	WIND	37	50	48	14	19	50	40	39	67	75	52	44	33	71	68	26	51	23	32	26	43	29	41	42	29	31	35	61	37	40	39	1292
FORD CITY 4 S DAM	EVAP	.20	.28	.16	.10	.11	.10	.11	.16	.24	.25	.10	.16	.15	.03	.19	.27	.10	-	.16	.17	-	.09	.23	.13	.08	.14	.17	.17	.11	.17	.12	B4.76
	WIND	21	33	37	5	13	27	30	3	46	83	43	30	8	42	43	20	33	7	22	10	25	8	46	33	16	20	19	35	21	34	22	835
HAWLEY 1 S DAM	EVAP	.25	.29	.17	.16	.00	.00	.02	.15	.20	.23	.23	.19	.14	.18	.19	.12	.13	.19	.18	.13	.02	.00	.11	.23	.15	.15	.14	.18	.17	.18	.15	4.63
	WIND	15	106	57	35	25	40	24	41	74	104	130	101	52	127	81	67	40	37	27	43	31	35	37	102	61	56	29	58	48	55	45	1823
JAMESTOWN 2 NW	EVAP	.19	.25	.25	.23	.03	.06	.05	.18	.19	.26	.08	.20	.11	.04	.07	.12	.15	.09	.22	.13	.01	.05	-	.11	.21	.10	.02	.22	.26	.27	.19	B4.51
	WIND	27	49	15	20	26	14	15	20	41	72	25	37	18	46	20	17	16	13	25	20	37	19	33	26	20	12	17	16	25	22	22	786
LANDISVILLE	EVAP	-	-	-	-	-	-	-	-	-	-	-	-	-	-	-	-	-	-	-	-	-	.18	.15	.05	.15	.18	.20	.23	.17	.26	.26	-
	WIND	-	-	-	-	-	-	-	-	-	-	-	-	-	-	-	-	-	-	-	-	-	5	6	17	22	25	17	13	41	47	35	-
PIMPLE HILL	EVAP	.26	.27	.24	.18	.09	.03	.02	.17	.27	.17	.20	.27	.15	.16	.23	.23	.10	.18	.25	.23	.11	.01	.09	.20	.12	.19	.16	.17	.14	.21	.17	5.27
	WIND	88	89	74	25	75	82	39	67	111	87	107	92	71	113	114	62	42	38	19	73	143	55	79	93	81	75	60	87	54	51	45	2291
STATE COLLEGE	EVAP	.30	.32	.15	.17	.03	.03	.10	.24	.22	.26	.10	.23	.08	.05	.19	.16	.07	.07	.17	.08	.01	.08	.18	.05	.11	.18	.18	.21	.19	.22	.13	4.53
	WIND	42	47	33	13	21	19	28	23	43	52	43	44	18	35	68	22	12	8	14	21	31	18	34	32	25	31	18	34	46	15	29	919

SUPPLEMENTAL DATA

Station	Wind direction		Wind speed m. p. h.				Relative humidity averages - percent				Number of days with precipitation								
	Prevailing	Percent of time from prevailing	Average	Fastest mile	Direction of fastest mile	Date of fastest mile	1:30 a EST	7:30 a EST	1:30 p EST	7:30 p EST	Trace	.01–.09	.10–.49	.50–.99	1.00–1.99	2.00 and over	Total	Percent of possible sunshine	Average sky cover sunrise to sunset
ALLENTOWN WB AIRPORT	WSW	19	8.9	-	-	-	91	84	63	75	4	7	5	3	2	0	21	-	7.1
HARRISBURG WB AIRPORT	W	14	6.6	25	NW	11	82	81	58	70	5	11	4	2	2	0	24	59	7.4
PHILADELPHIA WB AIRPORT	WSW	15	9.0	37	SW	8	84	79	60	70	3	6	8	1	1	0	19	50	7.6
PITTSBURGH WB AIRPORT	WSW	24	9.4	51*	WSW	9	86	85	63	74	13	4	6	1	2	0	26	56	7.5
READING WB CITY	-	-	8.4	43	S	1	-	-	-	-	3	6	9	3	0	0	21	42	7.3
SCRANTON WB AIRPORT	SW	20	6.1	40	N	1	83	79	62	72	6	4	11	1	0	0	22	44	7.3
SHIPPINGPORT WB	-	-	2.1	42††	W	9	-	-	-	-	6	5	5	2	2	0	20	-	-
WILLIAMSPORT WB AIRPORT	-	-	-	-	-	-	-	88	62	73	4	10	5	2	3	0	24	-	7.6

* This datum is obtained by visual observation since recording equipment is not available. It is not necessarily the fastest mile occurring during the period.
†† Peak Gust

See Reference Notes Following Station Index

STATION INDEX

Station	Index No.	County	Drainage	Latitude	Longitude	Elevation	Obs. Time Temp.	Obs. Time Precip.	Observer	Refer To Tables
ACMETONIA LOCK 3	0022	ALLEGHENY	1	40 32	79 49	748		7A	CORPS OF ENGINEERS	3
ALLENS MILLS	0099	JEFFERSON	1	41 12	78 55	1600		MID	CHARLES M. ALLEN	C
ALLENTOWN WB AP	0106	LEHIGH	9	40 39	75 26	376	MID	MID	U.S. WEATHER BUREAU	2 3 5 7 C
ALLENTOWN GAS CO	0111	LEHIGH	9	40 36	75 28	254	7A	7A	LEHIGH VLY GAS DIV	2 3 5
ALTOONA HORSESHOE CURVE	0134	BLAIR	6	40 30	78 29	1500	6P	6P	ALTOONA WATER BUR.	2 3 5 7
ARENDTSVILLE	0229	ADAMS	15	39 55	77 18	710	8A	8A	PA STATE COL EXP	2 3 5
ARTEMAS 1 WNW	0259	BEDFORD	12	39 45	78 28	1250	6P	6P	GRAYSON E.NORTHCRAFT	2 3 5 7 C
AUSTINBURG 2 W	0313	TIOGA	15	42 00	77 32	1590		7A	OTTO D. BACON	3 C
BAKERSTOWN 3 WNW	0355	ALLEGHENY	1	40 39	79 59	1230	7P	7P	PGH CUT FLOWER CO	2 3 5
BARNES	0409	WARREN	1	41 40	79 02	1310		7A	CORPS OF ENGINEERS	3
BEAR GAP	0457	NORTHUMBLAND	15	40 50	76 30	900		MID	ROARING CRK WTR CO	3
BEAVER FALLS	0475	BEAVER	2	40 46	80 19	760		7A	HOWARD R. KEMP	3
BEAVERTOWN	0482	SNYDER	15	40 45	77 10	640	7A	7A	MARLIN RC ETTINGER	2 3 5 7
BEECH CREEK STATION	0499	CENTRE	16	41 04	77 34	620		7A	HAROLD S. RUPERT	3
BELLEFONTE 4 S	0530	CENTRE	16	40 51	77 47	1110	8A	8A	ROCKVIEW PRISON FARM	2 3 5 7
BERWICK	0611	COLUMBIA	15	41 04	76 15	570	6P	6P	AMER CAR + FNDRY CO	2 3 5 7
BETHLEHEM	0629	NORTHAMPTON	9	40 37	75 22	400		7A	ARTHUR CROPPER	3
#BETHLEHEM LEHIGH UNIV	0634	NORTHAMPTON	9	40 36	75 23	450	MID	MID	LEHIGH UNIVERSITY	2 3 5 C
BLAIN	0725	PERRY	15	40 20	77 31	750		MID	PA DEPT FRST + WTRS	C
BLAIRSVILLE 6 ENE	0736	INDIANA	4	40 27	79 09	2048	6P	8P	U.S. WEATHER BUREAU	2 3 5
BLAKESLEE CORNERS	0743	MONROE	9	41 06	75 36	1650		MID	WALTER WILDRICK	C
BLOSERVILLE 1 N	0763	CUMBERLAND	15	40 16	77 22	650		5P	MRS. B. M. WILLDERS	3
BOSWELL 6 WNW	0820	SOMERSET	1	40 11	79 08	2580		7A	MRS. MAE L. KIMMEL	3 C
BRADDOCK LOCK 2	0861	ALLEGHENY	10	40 24	79 52	725		7A	CORPS OF ENGINEERS	3
BRADFORD CNTRL FIRE STA	0867	MC KEAN	1	41 57	78 39	1500		8A	BRADFORD FIRE DEPT	3
BRADFORD 4 W RES	0868	MC KEAN	1	41 57	78 44	1680	5P	5P	BRADFORD WTR DEPT	2 3 5 7
BREEZEWOOD	0905	BEDFORD	6	40 00	78 14	1352		MID	PA TURNPIKE COMM	3
BROOKVILLE CAA AIRPORT	1002	JEFFERSON	1	41 09	79 06	1417	MID	MID	CIVIL AERO. ADM.	2 3 5 7
BRUCETON 1 S	1033	ALLEGHENY	10	40 18	79 59	1065		7A	AUSTIN R. COOPER	3
BUCKSTOWN 1 SE	1073	SOMERSET	4	40 04	78 50	2460		MID	ALVIN W. MANGES	C
BUFFALO MILLS	1087	BEDFORD	6	39 58	78 39	1318		7A	MRS. NELLE R. BROWN	3
BURGETTSTOWN 2 W	1105	WASHINGTON	11	40 23	80 26	980	7A	7A	SMITH TWP MUN AUTH	2 3 5 7
BURNT CABINS 2 NE	1115	HUNTINGDON	6	40 05	77 52	990	MID	MID	PA TURNPIKE COMM	2 3 5 7
#BUTLER	1130	BUTLER	2	40 52	79 54	1100	4P	7A	WILLIAM C. FAUST	2 3 5 7
BUTLER SUBSTATION	1135	BUTLER	2	40 51	79 53	1140		MID	WEST PENN POWER CO	C
CAMP HILL	1198	CUMBERLAND	15	40 15	76 55	461		6P	JOSEPH N. HOBART	3
CANTON 1 NW	1215	BRADFORD	15	41 40	76 52	1520	7A	7A	MRS.MILDRED SPENCER	2 3 5 7 C
CARLISLE	1234	CUMBERLAND	15	40 12	77 11	460	6P	6P	C. E. MILLER	2 3 5 7
CARROLLTOWN 2 SSE	1255	CAMBRIA	16	40 35	78 42	2040		8A	ROBERT F. MAURER	3
CARTER CAMP 2 W	1262	POTTER	16	41 37	77 45	2030		7A	RICHARD L. MENKEN	3 C
CEDAR RUN	1301	LYCOMING	16	41 31	77 27	800		7A	KATHRYN T.KREIGHBAUM	3
CHADDS FORD	1342	DELAWARE	5	39 52	75 36	160		8A	MRS.GRACE A. WICKS	3
CHAMBERSBURG 1 ESE	1354	FRANKLIN	12	39 56	77 38	640	9P	9P	CHARLES A. BENDER	2 3 5 7 C
CHARLEROI	1372	WASHINGTON	10	40 08	79 55	1040		MID	WEST PENN POWER CO	C
CHARLEROI LOCK 4	1377	WESTMORELAND	10	40 09	79 54	749		7A	CORPS OF ENGINEERS	3
#CHESTER	1423	DELAWARE	5	39 51	75 21	86	8A	8A	CHESTER TIMES	2 3 5
CLARENCE 1 E	1480	CENTRE	16	41 03	77 56	1440		7A	MARGARET A. SWANCER	3
CLARION 3 SW	1485	CLARION	1	41 12	79 26	1114	8P	7A	PA ELECTRIC CO	2 3 5 7 C
CLAUSSVILLE	1505	LEHIGH	9	40 37	75 39	670		8A	WILLIAM J. DOTTERER	3
CLAYSVILLE 3 W	1512	WASHINGTON	11	40 07	80 28	1000	7P	7A	MFGRS. L + M CO	2 3 5
CLEARFIELD	1519	CLEARFIELD	16	41 01	78 26	1100		7A	IRA TAYLOR	3
CLERMONT	1529	MC KEAN	1	41 41	78 30	2104		7A	MRS.TILLIE M.SIMONDS	3 C
COALDALE 2 NW	1572	SCHUYLKILL	9	40 50	75 56	1026		7A	PANTHER VLY WTR CO	3
COATESVILLE 1 SW	1589	CHESTER	5	39 58	75 50	342	8A	8A	PHILA ELECTRIC CO	2 3 5 7 C
COATESVILLE	1594	CHESTER	5	39 59	75 49	340		8A	EDWARD D. BIEDEMAN	INAC 12/55
COLUMBIA	1675	LANCASTER	15	40 02	76 30	300	SS	SS	JAMES H. RUST	2 3 5
CONFLUENCE 1 SW DAM	1705	SOMERSET	17	39 48	79 22	1490	8A	8A	CORPS OF ENGINEERS	2 3 5 6 C
CONFLUENCE 1 NW	1710	FAYETTE	17	39 50	79 22	1331		7A	JOHN L. REID	3
CONNELLSVILLE	1723	FAYETTE	17	40 01	79 36	870		8A	MARSHALL B. MENEFEE	3
CONNELLSVILLE 2 E	1729	FAYETTE	17	40 01	79 33	1300		MID	HARRY C. JOY	C
CONSHOHOCKEN	1737	MONTGOMERY	5	40 04	75 19	70		8A	PHILA ELECTRIC CO	3
COOKSBURG	1749	CLARION	1	41 20	79 13	1180		8A	PA DEPT FRST + WTRS	3
COOKSBURG 2 NNW	1752	CLARION	1	41 21	79 13	1460		8A	PA DEPT FRST + WTRS	3
CORAOPOLIS NEVILLE IS	1773	ALLEGHENY	11	40 30	80 05	720		8A	PGH. COKE + CHEM CO	3
CORRY	1790	ERIE	1	41 56	79 38	1427	7P	5A	LEO C. NECKERS	2 3 5 7
COUDERSPORT 3 NW	1808	POTTER	1	41 49	78 03	2020	7P	8A	MISS ELIZABETH NEFF	2 3 5 7
COUDERSPORT 7 E	1809	POTTER	1	41 46	77 53	2425		7A	CAMP POTATO	3
COVINGTON	1832	TIOGA	15	41 45	77 05	1193		7A	GROVER D. CLEVELAND	3
CREEKSIDE	1881	INDIANA	1	40 41	79 12	1035		7A	CORPS OF ENGINEERS	3
CRESSON 2 SE	1895	CAMBRIA	6	40 27	78 34	2540		7A	MILES A. VECELLIO	3 C
CUSTER CITY 2 W	1978	MC KEAN	1	41 55	78 41	2120		8A	W. D. BOOTH AND CO	3
DANVILLE	2013	MONTOUR	15	40 58	76 37	460		7A	MRS.MARIE M. LITTLE	3
DERRY	2108	WESTMORELAND	4	40 20	79 18	1150	6P	6P	MISS N. D. MINEMAN	2 3 5
DEVAULT 1 W	2116	CHESTER	14	40 05	75 33	360	MID	MID	PA TURNPIKE COMM	2 3 5
DINGMANS FERRY	2160	PIKE	5	41 13	74 52	360		MID	CLARENCE H. SMITH	C
DIXON	2171	WYOMING	15	41 34	75 54	620	7A	7A	HAROLD J. KUSCHEL	2 3 5 7 C
DONEGAL	2183	WESTMORELAND	17	40 07	79 23	1746	MID	MID	PA TURNPIKE COMM	2 3 5 7
#DONORA	2190	WASHINGTON	10	40 11	79 51	814	12M	12M	DONORA ZINC WORKS	2 3 5
DOYLESTOWN	2221	BUCKS	5	40 18	75 08	393		5P	GEORGE HART	3
DRIFTWOOD	2245	CAMERON	16	41 20	78 08	880		MID	SIDNEY KENNEDY	C
DU BOIS 7 E	2265	CLEARFIELD	16	41 06	78 38	1670	5P	5P	CITY OF DU BOIS	2 3 5 C
DUNLO	2298	CAMBRIA	4	40 17	78 43	2410		MID	MRS. D. L. WHITE	C
DUSHORE 3 NE	2324	SULLIVAN	16	41 33	76 21	1750		7A	PATRICK P. RYAN	3 C
EAGLES MERE	2343	SULLIVAN	16	41 24	76 35	2020	7A	7A	MRS.ELSIE P. BIGGER	2 3 5 7 C
EAST BRADY	2363	CLARION	1	40 59	79 37	820	5P	5P	A. B. KEMPEL	2 3 5
EAST WATERFORD 3 E	2459	PERRY	6	40 21	77 33	2125	8A	8A	U.S. WEATHER BUREAU	INAC 5/55
EBENSBURG	2466	CAMBRIA	4	40 29	78 43	2090	7P	7A	ROBERT A. WASSER	2 3 5
EDINBORO	2514	ERIE	1	41 52	80 08	1220		8A	EDINBORO ST TCHR COL	3
ELIZABETHTOWN	2560	LANCASTER	15	40 09	76 37	460		8A	MASONIC HOME	3
EMPORIUM 1 E	2633	CAMERON	16	41 31	78 13	1160	7A	7A	RUSSELL E.PALMATEER	2 3 5 7 C
ENGLISH CENTER	2644	LYCOMING	16	41 26	77 17	881		7A	WILLIAM SUDERS	3 C
EPHRATA	2662	LANCASTER	15	40 11	76 10	465	6P	6P	STANLEY L.VON NEIDA	2 3 5
EQUINUNK	2669	WAYNE	5	41 51	75 13	900		8A	MRS.ROSE M. NEILSEN	3
ERIE CAA AIRPORT	2682	ERIE	8	42 05	80 12	732	MID	MID	CIVIL AERO. ADM.	2 3 5
EVERETT 1 SW	2721	BEDFORD	6	40 00	78 23	1020	MID	MID	PA TURNPIKE COMM	2 3 5 7 C
FARRELL SHARON	2814	MERCER	2	41 14	80 30	865	7P	7P	SHARON STEEL CORP	2 3 5
FORD CITY 4 S DAM	2942	ARMSTRONG	1	40 43	79 30	950	8A	8A	CORPS OF ENGINEERS	2 3 5 6 7 C
FRANKLIN	3028	VENANGO	1	41 23	79 49	987	7P	7A	JAMES K. ELLIOTT	2 3 5 7 C
FREELAND	3056	LUZERNE	15	41 01	75 54	1900	6P	8A	ANDREW B. EVANSHA	2 3 5
GALETON	3130	POTTER	16	41 44	77 39	1325		7A	W. GALE LUSH	3
GEIGERTOWN	3189	BERKS	14	40 13	75 50	400		8A	WALTER C. WOLF	3
GEORGE SCHOOL	3200	BUCKS	5	40 13	74 56	135	7P	7P	GEORGE M. HART	2 3 5 7
#GETTYSBURG	3218	ADAMS	12	39 50	77 14	540	9A	9A	HUGH C. MC ILHENNY	2 3 5 7
GETTYSBURG 1 S	3223	ADAMS	12	39 48	77 14	560		MID	NAT MILITARY PARK	C
GIFFORD	3237	MC KEAN	1	41 51	78 36	2220		8A	SOUTH PENN OIL CO	INAC 3/56
GLENCOE	3298	SOMERSET	12	39 49	78 51	1620		MID	MRS. MARY M.HARTMAN	C
GLEN HAZEL 2 NE DAM	3311	ELK	1	41 34	78 36	1725		8A	CORPS OF ENGINEERS	3 C
GLEN ROCK	3330	YORK	15	39 48	76 44	620		MID	MRS.E.C.MC WILLIAMS	C
GLENWILLARD DASH DAM	3343	ALLEGHENY	11	40 33	80 13	705		7A	CORPS OF ENGINEERS	3
GOULDSBORO	3394	WAYNE	9	41 15	75 27	1890		7A	L. M. EILENBERGER	3
GRATERFORD	3435	MONTGOMERY	14	40 14	75 27	160		7A	CLAUDE K. KULP	3
GRATZ 1 N	3438	DAUPHIN	15	40 38	76 43	760	8A	8A	LEE M. LEITZEL	2 3 5 7 C
GREENSBORO LOCK 7	3503	GREENE	10	39 47	79 55	808		7A	CORPS OF ENGINEERS	3
GREENSBURG 2 E	3515	WESTMORELAND	10	40 18	79 31	1225		MID	PA DEPT HIGHWAYS	C
GREENSBURG 3 SE	3516	WESTMORELAND	10	40 17	79 30	1245		6P	WESTMORELAND WTR CO	3
GREENVILLE	3526	MERCER	2	41 24	80 23	1026	6P	6P	C. EARL MILLER	2 3 5 7
HANOVER	3662	YORK	15	39 48	76 59	600	8A	8A	HANOVER EVENING SUN	2 3 5
#HARRISBURG WB AP	3699	YORK	15	40 13	76 51	335	MID	MID	U.S. WEATHER BUREAU	2 3 5 7 C
HARRISBURG NORTH	3704	DAUPHIN	15	40 18	76 54	323		9A	GEORGE S. BEAL	3
HAWLEY	3758	WAYNE	5	41 29	75 10	880		7A	MRS.KATHERINE B.BATE	3
HAWLEY 1 S DAM	3761	WAYNE	5	41 28	75 11	1200	7A	7A	PA POWER + LIGHT CO	2 3 5 6 7 C
HOLLIDAYSBURG	4001	BLAIR	6	40 26	78 24	960		MID	JOHN M. RINGLER	C
HOLLISTERVILLE	4008	WAYNE	5	41 23	75 26	1360		8A	PA POWER + LIGHT CO	3
#HOLTWOOD	4019	LANCASTER	15	39 50	76 20	187	MID	8A	PA POWER + LIGHT CO	2 3 5 C
HOME	4027	INDIANA	1	40 45	79 06	1220		MID	MRS. EDNA M. BUSH	C
HONESDALE 4 NW	4043	WAYNE	5	41 37	75 19	1410		9A	GEORGE C. WILLIAMS	3
HONESDALE 6 NNW	4044	WAYNE	5	41 39	75 17	1050		MID	FRIEND E. WALTER	C
HOOVERSVILLE	4058	SOMERSET	4	40 09	78 55	1660		7A	PA ELECTRIC CO	3
HOP BOTTOM 2 SE	4066	SUSQUEHANNA	15	41 43	75 43	900		7A	JOSEPH J. SANSUSKAS	3
HUNTINGDON	4159	HUNTINGDON	15	40 29	78 01	680	7A	7A	JOHN R. HENDERSON	2 3 5 7
HUNTSDALE	4168	CUMBERLAND	15	40 06	77 [illegible]	610		8A	PETRO P. [illegible]	
HYNDMAN	4190	BEDFORD	12	39 49	78 43	920		8A	MRS. GERTRUDE [illegible]	
INDIANA 3 SE	4214	INDIANA	4	40 36	79 07	1102	7P	7A	CLYMER WATER SVC CO	2 3 5 7 C
IRWIN	4276	WESTMORELAND	10	40 20	79 42	1100	5P	5P	WESTMORELAND WTR CO	2 3 5
JACKSON SUMMIT	4304	TIOGA	15	41 57	77 01	1690		MID	[illegible] LAIN	C
JAMESTOWN 2 NW	4325	CRAWFORD	2	41 30	80 28	1050	8A	8A	PA DEPT FRST + WTRS	2 3 5 6 C
JIM THORPE	4370	CARBON	9	40 52	75 45	830	5P	5P	HENRY S. HAAK	2 3 5
#JOHNSTOWN	4385	CAMBRIA	4	40 20	78 55	1214	9A	9A	JOHNSTOWN TRIBUNE	2 3 5 7
JOHNSTOWN 2	4390	CAMBRIA	4	40 19	78 55	1275		MID	CITY OF JOHNSTOWN	
KANE 1 NNE	4432	MC KEAN	1	41 41	78 48	1750	8A	8A	SPRING WATER CO	2 3 5 7 C
KARTHAUS	4450	CLEARFIELD	16	41 07	78 07	950		7A	JEROME S. HOWE	3
KEATING SUMMIT	4466	POTTER	1	41 41	78 11	1840		7A	EUGENE L. KREITNER	3
KEGG	4481	BEDFORD	6	39 59	78 43	1280	MID	MID	PA TURNPIKE COMM	2 3 5
KITTANNING LOCK 7	4611	ARMSTRONG	1	40 49	79 32	790		VAR	CORPS OF ENGINEERS	3
KREGAR 4 SE	4667	WESTMORELAND	17	40 06	79 14	2530		MID	PA TURNPIKE COMM	3
KRESGEVILLE 3 W	4672	CARBON	9	40 54	75 34	720		8A	CITY OF BETHLEHEM	3
LAFAYETTE MC KEAN PARK	4706	MC KEAN	1	41 48	78 40	2130		8A	CHARLES GORDON	INAC 2/56
LAKEVILLE 1 NNE	4733	WAYNE	5	41 27	75 16	1480		8A	MRS. GLADYS REINEKE	3
LANCASTER 2 NE PUMP STA	4758	LANCASTER	15	40 03	76 17	255	6P	6P	LANCASTER WATER BUR	2 3 5
LANCASTER 2 NE FILT PL	4763	LANCASTER	15	40 03	76 17	270		MID	LANCASTER WATER BUR	C
LANDISVILLE 2 NW	4778	LANCASTER	15	40 07	76 26	360	8A	8A	PA STATE COLLEGE	2 3 5 6 7 C
LATROBE	4832	WESTMORELAND	4	40 19	79 23	1000		MID	WEST PENN POWER CO	INAC 6/56
LAURELTON STATE VILLAGE	4853	UNION	15	40 54	77 13	880		MID	PA DEPT OF WELFARE	C
LAWRENCEVILLE 2 S	4873	TIOGA	15	41 59	77 07	1000	7A	7A	HARRY P. HOWLAND	2 3 5 7
LEBANON 3 W	4891	LEBANON	15	40 20	76 29	460	7A	7A	LEON MILLER	2 3 5 7
LEBANON 3 SW	4896	LEBANON	15	40 19	76 28	490		MID	THOMAS DONNACHIE	C
LEHIGHTON	4934	CARBON	9	40 50	75 43	580		7A	GOODWIN S. DEFREHN	3 C
LE ROY	4972	BRADFORD	15	41 41	76 43	1040		6P	MRS.DIMMIS M.BAILEY	3
LEWIS RUN 3 S	4984	MC KEAN	1	41 50	78 39	1740		7A	RUSSELL LINEMAN	3 C
LEWISTOWN	4992	MIFFLIN	6	40 35	77 35	480	7A	7A	AMERICAN VISCOSE CO	2 3 5 7 C
LINESVILLE 5 WNW	5050	CRAWFORD	2	41 41	80 31	1020	7P	8A	MISS RETTA M. CRUMB	2 3 5
LOCK HAVEN	5104	CLINTON	16	41 08	77 27	570	7P	7A	PETER L. STEVENSON	2 3 5 7
LOCK HAVEN 2	5109	CLINTON	16	41 08	77 27	630		MID	HUGH F. PARKER	C
LONG POND 2 W	5160	MONROE	9	41 03	75 30	1860		7A	THOMAS MECKES	3
MADERA	5336	CLEARFIELD	16	40 50	78 26	1460	7A	7A	MRS. JULIA J. SHOFF	2 3 5 C
MAHAFFEY	5342	CLEARFIELD	16	40 53	78 44	1280		7A	MISS ELLEN J. MILES	3
MAPLE GLEN	5368	MONTGOMERY	5	40 11	75 11	380		6P	FRANCES E.SCHEIBNER	3
MAPLETON DEPOT	5381	HUNTINGDON	6	40 24	77 56	580		7A	MRS. I. S. BUCHANAN	3
MARCUS HOOK	5390	DELAWARE	5	39 49	75 25	12	MID	MID	SUN OIL CO	2 3 5
MARIENVILLE 1 SW	5400	FOREST	1	41 27	79 09	1700		MID	ROY A. MARKER	C
MARION CENTER 2 SE	5408	INDIANA	1	40 45	79 02	1610		7A	CORPS OF ENGINEERS	3
MARTINSBURG 1 SW	5453	BLAIR	6	40 18	78 20	1360		MID	BLUE MT. CANNERIES	C
MARTINSBURG CAA AP	5454	BLAIR	6	40 18	78 19	1463	MID	MID	CIVIL AERO. ADM.	2 3 5
MATAMORAS	5470	PIKE	5	41 22	74 42	439		7A	HARRY BISLAND	3
MAYBURG	5490	FOREST	1	41 36	79 13	1150		7A	CORPS OF ENGINEERS	3
MC CONNELLSBURG	5526	FULTON	12	39 56	78 00	895		8A	MRS. HELEN M. SHIVES	3
MC KEESPORT	5573	ALLEGHENY	10	40 21	79 52	720		8A	NATIONAL TUBE CO	3
MEADOW RUN PONDS	5601	LUZERNE	15	41 13	75 40	1995		MID	GEORGE PEARAGE	C
MEADVILLE 1 S	5606	CRAWFORD	1	41 38	80 10	1065	8A	8A	CITY OF MEADVILLE	2 3 5 7 C
MEDIX RUN	5627	ELK	16	41 17	78 24	1100		7A	MRS.E. M. SNYDER	3 C
MERCER 2 NNE	5651	MERCER	2	41 15	80 13	1160	7P	7A	WILLIAM K. STRUTHERS	2 3 5 7
MERCER HIWAY SHED	5654	MERCER	2	41 14	80 15	1250		MID	PA DEPT HIGHWAYS	C
MERCERSBURG	5662	FRANKLIN	12	39 50	77 54	605		8A	ROLLIN P. GILBERT	3
MERWINSBURG	5676	MONROE	9	40 58	75 28	970		MID	WILLIAM D. GOULD	C
MEYERSDALE 1 ENE	5685	SOMERSET	17	39 49	79 01	2290		8A	ARTHUR B. MC CARTER	3
MIDDLETOWN OLMSTED FLD	5703	DAUPHIN	15	40 11	76 46	303	MID	MID	U. S. AIR FORCE	2 3 5
MIDLAND DAM 7	5710	BEAVER	11	40 38	80 28	689	11P	7A	CORPS OF ENGINEERS	2 3 5
MILAN 4 WNW	5732	BRADFORD	15	41 56	76 35	1448		MID	CARL A. MORRIS	C
MILANVILLE	5738	WAYNE	5	41 40	75 04	760		8A	CHARLES W. DAVIS	3
MILLERSBURG 2 E	5775	DAUPHIN	15	40 32	76 56	560		MID	RUSSELL SHEPLEY	C
MILLHEIM	5790	CENTRE	15	40 54	77 29	1090		7A	NEVIN E. BOWERSOX	3
MILLVILLE 2 SW	5817	COLUMBIA	15	41 06	76 34	860		7A	KENNETH LEIGHOW	3 C
MILROY	5825	MIFFLIN	6	40 43	77 35	770		8A	THOMAS C. HARBESON	3
MONTROSE 1 E	5915	SUSQUEHANNA	15	41 50	75 51	1630	7A	7A	WILBER W. HOOPES,JR	2 3 5 7 C
MORGANTOWN	5956	BERKS	15	40 09	75 54	595	MID	MID	PA TURNPIKE COMM	2 3 5
MT GRETNA 2 SE	6028	LANCASTER	15	40 14	76 26	670	MID	MID	PA TURNPIKE COMM	2 3 5
MT POCONO 2 N AP	6055	MONROE	5	41 09	75 22	1915	5P	5P	H. JOHN DAVIS, JR.	2 3 5 7 C
MOUNT UNION 1 N	6067	MIFFLIN	6	40 24	77 53	820		MID	MT UNION WTR WORKS	C
MUHLENBURG 1 SE	6090	LUZERNE	15	41 13	76 08	1110	6P	6P	THEODORE J. SAMPSON	2 3 5
MURRYSVILLE	6111	WESTMORELAND	10	40 26	79 42	903		MID	DAVID C. SHAW	C
MYERSTOWN	6126	LEBANON	14	40 22	76 18	480		8A	MRS.KATHLEEN WANDELL	3
NATRONA LOCK 4	6151	ALLEGHENY	1	40 37	79 43	800		7A	CORPS OF ENGINEERS	3
NEFFS MILLS 3 NE	6174	HUNTINGDON	6	40 40	77 55	900		MID	PA STATE UNIVERSITY	C
NEW CASTLE 1 N	6233	LAWRENCE	2	41 01	80 22	825	5P	7A	BAXTER F. JOHNSON	2 3 5 7 C
NESHAMINY FALLS	6194	BUCKS	5	40 09	74 57	60		MID	PHILA SUB WATER CO	3
NEWBURG 3 W	6225	FRANKLIN	15	40 09	77 37	745	MID	MID	PA TURNPIKE COMM	2 3 5
#NEWELL	6246	FAYETTE	10	40 05	79 54	805	12M	12M	GENERAL CHEMICAL CO	2 3 5
NEW PARK	6289	YORK	15	39 44	76 30	780		6P	CLINTON J. ALLEN	3
NEWPORT	6297	PERRY	6	40 29	77 08	400	7A	7A	MRS. FRANCES K. FRY	2 3 5 7
NEW STANTON	6310	WESTMORELAND	10	40 13	79 36	980	MID	MID	PA TURNPIKE COMM	2 3 5
NEW TRIPOLI	6326	LEHIGH	14	40 41	75 45	570		6P	FRED C. OSWALD	3
NORRISTOWN	6370	MONTGOMERY	14	40 07	75 21	75	MID	8A	GEORGE H. BOONE	2 3 5
NORTH EAST 2 SE	6396	ERIE	8	42 12	79 49	1060		9A	ELLSWORTH WEAVER	3
ORWELL 3 N	6621	BRADFORD	15	41 55	76 16	1620		8A	WILLIAM I. BROWN	3
PALM	6681	MONTGOMERY	14	40 26	75 32	385		8A	FRED C. ESCHBACH	3
#PALMERTON	6689	CARBON	9	40 48	75 37	435	MID	MID	NEW JERSEY ZINC CO	2 3 5 7 C
PALMYRA	6694	LEBANON	15	40 18	76 35	480		7P	EARL E. RHOADS	3
PARKER	6721	ARMSTRONG	1	41 05	79 41	1140		7A	LOUIS A. MALARKEY	3
PARKER 1 E	6724	CLARION	1	41 06	79 40	1100		MID	P. M. NEELY	C
PAUPACK 2 WNW	6762	PIKE	5	41 24	75 14	1360		8A	MISS L. VETTERLEIN	3
PECKS POND	6786	PIKE	5	41 17	75 06	1380		9A	MRS. CARRIE NESS	3
#PHIL DREXEL INST OF TEC	6879	PHILADELPHIA	14	39 57	75 11	30	MID	MID	FRANCIS K. DAVIS,JR	2 3 5
PHILADELPHIA WB AP	6889	PHILADELPHIA	5	39 53	75 14	13	MID	MID	U.S. WEATHER BUREAU	2 3 5 7 C
#PHILADELPHIA PT BREEZE	6899	PHILADELPHIA	5	39 55	75 12	32	MID	MID	ATLANTIC REFINING	2 3 5 C
PHILADELPHIA SHAWMONT	6904	PHILADELPHIA	5	40 02	75 15	70	7P	7P	SCHUYLKILL NAVIG CO	2 3 5 7
#PHILADELPHIA CITY	6909	PHILADELPHIA	5	39 57	75 09	26	9A	9A	USN HYDROGRAPHIC OFF	2 3 5 C
PHILIPSBURG CAA AP	6916	CENTRE	6	40 54	78 05	1918	8P	8P	CIVIL AERO. ADM.	2 3 5 7 C
PHOENIXVILLE 1 E	6927	CHESTER	14	40 07	75 30	105	6P	MID	PHILA SUB WATER CO	2 3 5 7 C
PIKES CREEK	6939	LUZERNE	15	41 18	76 08	1320		MID	HARRY SHELDON	3 C
PIMPLE HILL	6944	MONROE	9	41 02	75 30	2215	9A	9A	PA DEPT FRST + WTRS	2 3 5 6
PINE GROVE 1 NE	6954	SCHUYLKILL	15	40 34	76 22	535		8A	PA POWER + LIGHT CO	3
PITTSBURGH WB AP 2	6993	ALLEGHENY	11	40 30	80 13	1151	MID	MID	U.S. WEATHER BUREAU	2 3 5 7 C
#PITTSBURGH WB CITY	6997	ALLEGHENY	11	40 27	80 00	749	MID	MID	U.S. WEATHER BUREAU	2 3 5 C
PLEASANT MOUNT 1 W	7029	WAYNE	5	41 44	75 27	1800	8A	8A	PA FISH COMM	2 3 5 C
PORT CLINTON	7116	SCHUYLKILL	14	40 35	76 02	450	7A	7A	MRS. ADA E. RARICK	2 3 5 7 C
PORTLAND	7127	NORTHAMPTON	5	40 55	75 06	297		8A	JOINT BRIDGE COMM	INAC 1/56
POTTSTOWN	7149	MONTGOMERY	14	40 15	75 39	160		8A	MILES E. SMITH	3
POTTSVILLE PALO ALTO BR	7161	SCHUYLKILL	14	40 41	76 11	840		8A	JOHN MC SMITH	INAC 4/56
PUNXSUTAWNEY	7217	JEFFERSON	1	40 57	79 00	1298		MID	JOHN VOLANSKY	C
PUTNEYVILLE 2 SE DAM	7229	ARMSTRONG	1	40 55	79 17	1270	8A	8A	CORPS OF ENGINEERS	2 3 5 C
QUAKERTOWN 1 E	7239	BUCKS	5	40 26	75 20	490	5P	5P	DENNIS K. FLUCK	2 3 5 7
RAYMOND	7310	POTTER	13	41 52	77 52	2220		7A	MRS. RACHEL LANGAN	3 C
#READING WB CITY	7318	BERKS	14	40 20	75 56	266	MID	MID	U.S. WEATHER BUREAU	2 3 5 7 C
RENOVO	7409	CLINTON	16	41 20	77 46	660		7A	MRS. CAROLINE BAIRD	3
RENOVO 5 S	7410	CLINTON	16	41 14	77 46	2035		MID	C. F. GILLETTE	C
REW	7425	MC KEAN	1	41 54	78 32	2250		8A	HAROLD C. HEALY	3
RICES LANDING L 6	7443	GREENE	10	39 57	80 00	775		7A	CORPS OF ENGINEERS	3
RIDGWAY 3 W	7477	ELK	1	41 25	78 47	1420	7A	7A	BOROUGH OF RIDGWAY	2 3 5 7
ROCHESTER 1 N	7540	BEAVER	2	40 43	80 18	900		MID	DEQUESNE LIGHT CO	C
RUSH	7694	SUSQUEHANNA	15	41 47	76 03	1000		9A	MISS MAUDE MC CAIN	3
RUSHVILLE	7727	SUSQUEHANNA	15	41 47	76 07	870		7A	CARL KOPATZ	3
SAFE HARBOR	7732	LANCASTER	15	39 55	76 23	270		MID	S.W.WATER POWER CORP	C
SAGAMORE 1 S	7739	INDIANA	1	40 46	79 14	1320		7A	CORPS OF ENGINEERS	3
SALINA 3 W	7782	WESTMORELAND	7	40 31	79 33	1109	6P	8P	MUN AUTH WSTMRLD CO	2 3 5
SAXTON	7846	BEDFORD	6	40 12	78 15	780		8A	MRS.ALVERTA L.HOLMES	3 C
SCANDIA 2 E	7855	WARREN	1	41 55	79 01	2040		MID	DAVID R. ANDERSON	C
SCHENLEY LOCK 5	7863	ARMSTRONG	1	40 41	79 40	783		VAR	CORPS OF ENGINEERS	3
#SCRANTON	7902	LACKAWANNA	15	41 25	75 40	746	7A	7A	U.S. POST OFFICE	2 3 5
SCRANTON WB AIRPORT	7905	LUZERNE	15	41 20	75 44	956	MID	MID	U.S. WEATHER BUREAU	2 3 5 7 C
SELINSGROVE CAA AP	7931	SNYDER	15	40 49	76 52	437	MID	MID	CIVIL AERO. ADM.	2 3 5 7

STATION INDEX

Continued

Station	Index No.	County	Drainage ‡	Latitude	Longitude	Elevation	Observation Time: Temp.	Observation Time: Precip.	Observer	Refer To Tables
SELLERSVILLE 2 NW	7936	BUCKS	5	40 23	75 20	530		MID	SELLERSVILLE WTR CO	C
SHADE GAP	7965	HUNTINGDON	6	40 11	77 52	1000		MID	MRS. HELEN M. PYLE	C
SHAMOKIN	7978	NORTHUMBLAND	15	40 48	76 33	770		8A	ROARING CRK WTR CO	3
SHEFFIELD 6 W	8026	WARREN	1	41 41	79 04	1940		MID	L. N. HANSON	C
SHIPPENSBURG	8073	FRANKLIN	15	40 03	77 32	709	4P	4P	KEITH B. ALLEN	2 3 5
SHIPPINGPORT WB	8078	BEAVER	11	40 37	80 26	740	MID	MID	U.S. WEATHER BUREAU	2 3 5 7 C
SINNEMAHONING	8145	CAMERON	10	41 19	78 05	790		7A	MRS.FRANCES CALDWELL	3
SLIPPERY ROCK	8184	BUTLER	2	41 04	80 03	1345	7P	7A	WALTER D. ALBERT	2 3 5
SMETHPORT HIGHWAY SHED	8190	MC KEAN	1	41 48	78 27	1510		MID	PA DEPT HIGHWAYS	C
SOMERSET FAIRVIEW ST	8244	SOMERSET	17	40 01	79 05	2140		7A	HOWARD G. PECK	3
SOMERSET MAIN ST	8249	SOMERSET	17	40 01	79 05	2150	6P	6P	DAVID L. GROVE	2 3 5 7
SOUTH CANAAN 1 NE	8275	WAYNE	5	41 31	75 24	1400		MID	EUGENE M. COOK	C
SOUTH MOUNTAIN	8308	FRANKLIN	12	39 51	77 30	1520		7A	PA DEPT OF HEALTH	3
SPRINGBORO	8359	CRAWFORD	8	41 48	80 23	900	8A	8A	SPRINGBORO BOROUGH	2 3 5 7 C
SPRING GROVE	8379	YORK	15	39 52	76 52	470		4P	P. H. GLATFELTER CO	3 C
SPRINGS 1 SW	8395	SOMERSET	17	39 44	79 10	2500	8P	8P	ALLEN E. YODER	2 3 5 7
#STATE COLLEGE	8449	CENTRE	16	40 48	77 52	1175	MID	MID	PA STATE COLLEGE	2 3 5 6 C
STRAUSSTOWN	8570	BERKS	14	40 29	76 11	600		8A	JACOB KLAHR	3
STRONGSTOWN	8589	INDIANA	4	40 33	78 55	1880		MID	HARRY F. BENNETT	C
STROUDSBURG	8596	MONROE	5	40 59	75 12	480	8A	8A	WILLIAM HAGERTY	2 3 5 7 C
STUMP CREEK	8610	JEFFERSON	1	41 01	78 50	1320		7A	CORPS OF ENGINEERS	3
SUNBURY	8668	NORTHUMBLAND	15	40 51	76 48	440		7A	CHARLES W. BAYLER	3 C
SUSQUEHANNA	8692	SUSQUEHANNA	15	41 57	75 36	1020		7A	MRS. LAURA A.BENSON	3
SUTERSVILLE	8699	ALLEGHENY	17	40 14	79 48	765		7A	FRANK E. MARSH	3
TAMAQUA	8758	SCHUYLKILL	14	40 48	75 58	830		8A	MRS. MARY L.ROBERTS	3
TAMAQUA 4 N DAM	8763	SCHUYLKILL	14	40 51	75 59	1120		7A	PANTHER VLY WTR CO	3 C
TAMARACK 2 S FIRE TWR	8770	CLINTON	16	41 24	77 51	2220	7A	7A	JAMES E. SWARTZ	2 3 5 7
TIONESTA 2 SE DAM	8873	FOREST	1	41 29	79 26	1200	8A	8A	CORPS OF ENGINEERS	2 3 5 7 C
TITUSVILLE	8885	CRAWFORD	1	41 38	79 40	1550		MID	PA ELECTRIC CO	C
TITUSVILLE WATER WORKS	8888	CRAWFORD	1	41 38	79 42	1220	7P	7P	CITY OF TITUSVILLE	2 3 5
TORPEDO 4 W	8901	WARREN	1	41 47	79 32	1735		7A	MRS. LILY B. GARBER	3
TOWANDA	8905	BRADFORD	15	41 46	76 26	760	7P	7A	MRS. M. O. PARKS	2 3 5 7 C
TOWER CITY 5 SW	8910	DAUPHIN	15	40 31	76 37	745		6P	HARRISBURG WTR DEPT	3 7
TROY	8959	BRADFORD	15	41 47	76 47	1100		7A	JENNIE L. BALLARD	3
TUNNELTON	8989	INDIANA	4	40 27	79 23	890		MID	MRS. MARY E. WEIMER	C
TURTLEPOINT 4 NE	9002	MC KEAN	1	41 54	78 16	1640		7A	ROBERT D. STRAIT	3
TYRONE 4 NE BALD EAGLE	9024	BLAIR	8	40 43	78 12	1020		7A	FREDERICK L. FRIDAY	3 C
UNION CITY	9042	ERIE	1	41 54	79 50	1325		7A	FORREST M. BRALEY	3 C
UNIONTOWN	9050	FAYETTE	10	39 54	79 44	1040	10P	10P	WM. W. MARSTELLER	2 3 5 7
UPPER DARBY	9074	DELAWARE	5	39 58	75 18	222	7P	7P	PHIL. SUB.TRANS. CO	2 3 5
UTICA	9099	VENANGO	1	41 26	79 57	1030		7A	MRS.FLORENCE MILLER	3
VANDERGRIFT	9128	WESTMORELAND	7	40 36	79 33	800		7A	UNITED ENG+FNDRY CO	3
VANDERGRIFT 2 W	9133	WESTMORELAND	7	40 36	79 36	995		MID	EUGENE R. YOUNG	C
VIRGINVILLE	9196	BERKS	14	40 31	75 52	350		8A	MRS. MARY M. WRIGHT	3
VOWINCKEL	9206	CLARION	1	41 25	79 14	1620		8A	PA DEPT FRST + WTRS	3
VOWINCKEL 1 WSW	9209	CLARION	1	41 24	79 15	1610		8A	PA DEPT FRST + WTRS	3
WARREN	9298	WARREN	1	41 51	79 08	1280	7P	7A	GILBERT H. REIER	2 3 5 7
WASHINGTON	9312	WASHINGTON	11	40 11	80 14	1200		MID	PA DEPT HIGHWAYS	
WATSONTOWN	9345	NORTHUMBLAND	16	41 05	76 52	470		6A	OWEN BERKENSTOCK	3
WAYNESBURG 2 W	9362	GREENE	10	39 54	80 13	980	6P	7A	RALPH L. AMOS	2 3 5 7
WAYNESBURG 1 E	9367	GREENE	10	39 54	80 10	940		MID	SEWAGE DISPOSAL PLT	
WEBSTER MILLS 3 SW	9380	FULTON	12	39 49	78 05	920		MID	WILLIAM D. COVER	
WELLSBORO 3 S	9408	TIOGA	16	41 43	77 16	1920	7A	7A	MARION L. SHUMWAY	2 3 5 7
WELLSBORO 2 E	9412	TIOGA	16	41 45	77 16	1550		MID	MRS. IDA S. MAYNARD	
WELLSVILLE	9420	YORK	15	40 03	76 57	500	5P	5P	D. D. HOOVER	2 3 5
WERNERSVILLE 1 W	9430	BERKS	14	40 20	76 06	405		8A	CHARLES A. GRUBER	3
WEST CHESTER	9464	CHESTER	5	39 58	75 36	440	8A	8A	DAILY LOCAL NEWS	2 3 5 7
WEST GROVE 1 E	9503	CHESTER	5	39 49	75 49	440		8A	CONARD-PYLE CO	3
WEST HICKORY	9507	FOREST	1	41 34	79 25	1090		8A	MRS.HELEN F.KINNEAR	3
WHITESBURG	9655	ARMSTRONG	1	40 45	79 24	1530		7A	CORPS OF ENGINEERS	3
WILKES-BARRE	9702	LAZERNE	15	41 15	75 52	610		7A	MRS. MARY G. HIRMAK	3
WILLIAMSBURG	9714	BLAIR	6	40 28	78 12	860		7A	MYRON K. BIDDLE	3
WILLIAMSPORT WB AP	9728	LYCOMING	16	41 15	76 55	527	MID	MID	U.S. WEATHER BUREAU	2 3 5 7
WIND GAP	9781	NORTHAMPTON	5	40 51	75 18	720		MID	OWEN R. PARRY	
WOLFSBURG	9823	BEDFORD	6	40 03	78 32	1190		7A	WALTER C. RICE	3
YORK 3 SSW PUMP STA	9933	YORK	15	39 55	76 45	390	5P	5P	YORK WATER COMPANY	2 3 5 7
YORK 2 S	9938	YORK	15	39 56	76 44	640		MID	YORK WATER COMPANY	
YORK HAVEN	9950	YORK	15	40 07	76 43	310		8A	METROPOL EDISON CO	3
YOUNGSVILLE	9966	WARREN	1	41 51	79 20	1225		MID	HENRY GARLETT	
ZION GROVE	9990	SCHUYLKILL	15	40 54	76 13	940		7A	JAMES J. TEETER	3
ZIONSVILLE 3 SE	9995	LEHIGH	14	40 27	75 27	660		7A	LESLIE HOWATT	3
CLOSED STATIONS										
FREDERICKSVILLE 2 SE	3047	BERKS	14	40 26	75 40	950	8A	8A	D. P. FENSTERMACHER	CLOSED 7/5

‡ 1-ALLEGHENY; 2-BEAVER; 3- 4-CONEMAUGH; 5-DELAWARE; 6-JUNIATA; 7-KISKIMINETAS; 8-LAKE ERIE; 9-LEHIGH; 10-MONONGAHELA; 11-OHIO; 12-POTOMAC; 13-LAKE ONTARIO; 14-SCHUYLKILL; 15-SUSQUEHANNA; 16-WEST BRANCH; 17-YOUGHIOGHENY

REFERENCE NOTES

Additional information regarding the climate of Pennsylvania may be obtained by writing to the State Climatologist at Weather Bureau Airport Station, Harrisburg State Airport, New Cumberland, Pennsylvania, or to any Weather Bureau Office near you.

The four digit identification numbers in the index number column of the Station Index are assigned on a state basis. There will be no duplication of numbers within a state.

Figures and letters following the station name, such as 12 SSW, indicate distance in miles and direction from the post office.

Observation times given in the Station Index are in local standard time.

Delayed data and corrections will be carried only in the June and December issues of this bulletin.

Monthly and seasonal snowfall and heating degree days for the preceding 12 months will be carried in the June issue of this bulletin.

Stations appearing in the Index, but for which data are not listed in the tables, are either missing or received too late to be included in this issue.

Unless otherwise indicated, dimensional units used in this bulletin are: temperature in °F., precipitation and evaporation in inches, and wind movement in miles. Degree days are based on a daily average of 65° F.

Evaporation is measured in the standard Weather Bureau type pan of 4 foot diameter unless otherwise shown by footnote following Table 6.

Amounts in Table 3 are from non-recording gages, unless otherwise indicated.

Data in Tables 3, 5 and 6 and snowfall data in Table 7 are for the 24 hours ending at time of observation. See Station Index for observation time.

Snow on ground in Table 7 is at observation time for all except Weather Bureau and CAA stations. For these stations snow on ground values are at 7:30 a.m. E.S.T. WTR EQUIV in Table 7 means the water equivalent of snow on the ground. It is measured at selected stations when depth of snow on the ground is two inches or more. Water equivalent samples are necessarily taken from different points for successive observations; consequently occasional drifting and other causes of local variability in the snowpack result in apparent inconsistencies in the record.

Long-term means for full-time Weather Bureau stations (those shown in the Station Index as United States Weather Bureau Stations) are based on the period 1921-1950, adjusted to represent observations taken at the present location.

- \- No record in Tables 3, 6, 7 and the Station Index. No record in Tables 2 and 5 is indicated by no entry.
- \+ And also on a later date or dates.
- * Amount included in following measurement, time distribution unknown.
- \# Thermometers are generally exposed in a shelter located a few feet above sod-covered ground; however, the reference indicates that the thermometers are exposed in a shelter located on the roof of a building.
- // Gage is equipped with a windshield.
- AM Data based on observational day ending before noon.
- B Adjusted to a full month.
- C In the "Refer to Tables" column in the Station Index the letter "C" indicates recorder stations. These stations are processed for special purposes and are published later in Hourly Precipitation Data.
- D Water equivalent of snowfall wholly or partly estimated, using a ratio of 1 inch water equivalent to every 10 inches of new snowfall.
- M One or more days of record missing; see Table 5 for detailed daily record. Degree day data, if carried for this station, have been adjusted to represent the value for a full month.
- R Amounts from recording gage (These amounts are essentially accurate but may vary slightly from the amounts to be published later in Hourly Precipitation Data).
- SS This entry in time of observation column in Station Index means sunset.
- T Trace, an amount too small to measure.
- V Includes total for previous month.
- VAR Observations made at 2 p.m. Monday through Thursday and 7 a.m. Friday through Sunday.

Subscription Price: 20 cents per copy, monthly and annual; $2.50 per year. (Yearly subscription includes the Annual Summary.) Checks and money orders should be made payable to the Superintendent of Documents. Remittances and correspondence regarding subscriptions should be sent to the Superintendent of Documents, Government Printing office, Washington 25, D. C.

WWRC., Asheville, N. C. --- 9/4/56 --- 1225

Isolines are drawn through points of approximately equal values. (See Special notice following Weather Summary.)

AVERAGE MONTHLY TEMPERATURE, JULY 1956

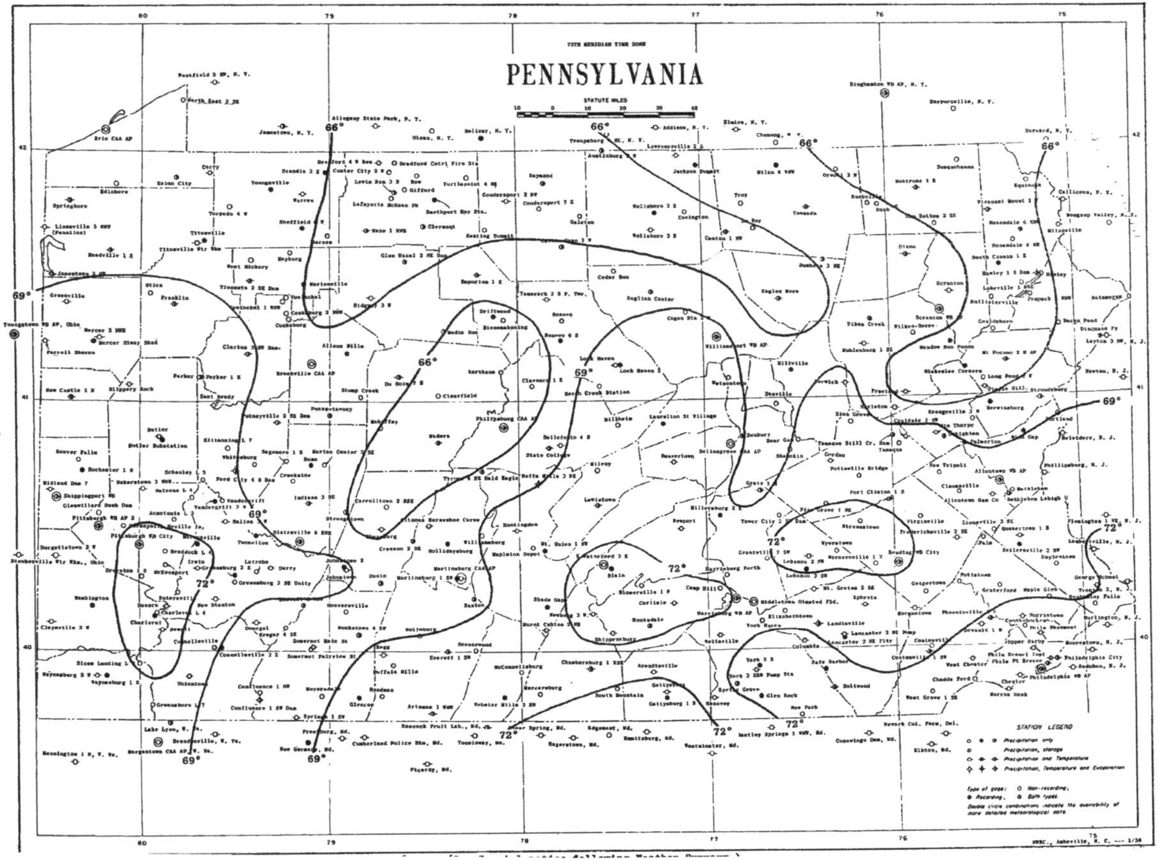

U. S. DEPARTMENT OF COMMERCE
SINCLAIR WEEKS, Secretary
WEATHER BUREAU
F. W. REICHELDERFER, Chief

CLIMATOLOGICAL DATA

PENNSYLVANIA

AUGUST 1956

Volume LXI No. 8

ASHEVILLE: 1956

PENNSYLVANIA - AUGUST 1956

WEATHER SUMMARY

GENERAL

Cool and wet were characteristics of the weather again this month - the sixth consecutive month for which these terms have been applicable. Destructive weather was associated with thunderstorms and occurred on several dates. The storms were usually of a local nature but affected considerable areas on the 5th and 18th.

Precipitation was heavy over most of the western half of the State and moderate to occasionally light over the eastern half. Totals ranged from 12.39 inches at Corry to 2.14 inches at Equinunk and at Susquehanna while the greatest amount of rain for one day was 5.70 inches at Connellsville measured on the 6th. Temperatures ranged from 100° at Wellsville to 33° at Donegal and Kane 1 NNE, both extremes being of about average value. The occurrence of maximum temperatures of 90° or higher was somewhat less frequent than is usual for August over most of the State. The percentage of sunshine was well above average at Harrisburg and Reading, and about average at other stations recording this element.

WEATHER DETAILS

Seasonal temperatures on the 1st gave way to moderately cool weather the 2nd that held through the 4th in the west and persisted through the 6th in the east. Showery weather developed in the west on the 4th, enlarged its coverage to include the entire State the 5th, and continued over most areas into the 7th. Clearing skies and rising temperatures on the 7th inaugurated a moderately warm weather regime that lasted through the 19th except for slight cooling due largely to cloudiness and showers around the 9th-10th and 13th-14th.

The leading edge of a strong polar air mass reached northwestern Pennsylvania early on the 19th and advanced southeastward into Maryland and Delaware where the frontal system became quasi-stationary and remained until the 21st. Temperatures in Pennsylvania dropped considerably by the 20th but wave disturbances moving northeastward along the frontal system to the south and east maintained cloudiness and showery weather over most of the State until the 21st. Clearing skies late on the 21st set the stage for the lowest temperature of the month at over half of the stations on the 22nd. A second polar air mass that moved into the area on the 24th caused showers in scattered localities and extended the cool weather period through the 26th.

Temperatures rose to about the usual late August levels on the 27th to introduce a warm period accompanied by frequent showers and locally severe thunderstorms that continued through the 31st.

WEATHER EFFECTS

Early fall vegetable crops, including cabbage, carrots, celery, sweet corn, spinach and tomatoes, made very good progress under generally favorable weather conditions during August. Excessive rains in many localities disrupted potato spray schedules and permitted considerable late blight, but even so, per acre yields were expected to be well above average. Some tubers were rotting in the ground in the Erie-Crawford area and much rotting was reported in the Schuylkill area.

Corn continued to show excellent promise but was maturing later than usual and much of the crop in the northern and western counties was becoming subject to probable freeze damage. Cutting for ensilage started about a week later than usual and only a few silos had been filled at the end of August. Heavy rains slowed harvests of hay and grain in the western counties. Pastures were in the best condition in several years and helped conserve supplies of hay and ensilage.

One of the best tobacco crops in years was being cut in the Lancaster area. Excessive soil moisture in the Clinton County area slowed the growth of plants but cutting got under way late in August.

Picking of apples and peaches was later than usual but adequate soil moisture enabled fruit to reach large size.

DESTRUCTIVE STORMS

5th: Western Pennsylvania was hard hit by two series of thunderstorms. The first series struck around dawn bring ing heavy rain which saturated much of the ground. The second series came around dusk bringing some hail and mor heavy rain which produced extensive flooding. Crops on high lands were badly pelted by rain and hail, and those on bottom lands were damaged due to flooding. Fields, roadways and drains were badly eroded. Lightning claimed the lives of three people and started fires that destroye or heavily damaged a number of houses, barns and other buildings. Trees, house roofs, billboards and utility lines were damaged by gusty winds on an extensive scale throughout the Western portion of the State while the Pittsburgh area appeared to have received particularly rough treatment.

12th: A 15-minute hailstorm in the Temple area near Reading broke some glass in every home in a large housing development and caused slight injury to one person. The hailstones measured 2 inches in diameter and played havoc with automobiles, greenhouses and shrubbery.

13th: A tornado cut through a section of Montgomery County east of Lansdale about 4:15 p.m. leaving a path 30 yards wide and 7 miles long. Several homes were damaged, 2 house trailers were smashed to splinters, 6 house trailers were wrecked when they were turned over and roll along the ground, electric service was disrupted, and cor was flattened in the fields. Lack of casualties and the small amount of damage was attributed to the fact that th twister was over open country most of the time.

18th: An evening thunderstorm moved from Ohio into Pennsylvania through Mercer County accompanied by 65 mph winc rain, hail and lightning. One person was killed and 12 others injured when a tree fell on a shelter house at a municipal park in Sharon. 300 trees were felled in Cook Forest in Clarion and Jefferson Counties and lightning burned a barn in Centre County. Power lines and transformers were damaged by wind and lightning through much of Western Pennsylvania.

27th-31st: Local thunderstorms developed to severe proportions during this period in several counties, including Washington, Luzerne, Schuylkill, Berks, Dauphin, Erie Bucks, Lackawanna, Montgomery, Crawford and Northumberlar Rather heavy property damage was caused primarily throug lightning strikes and resultant fires. Wind, rain and ha were added as destructive agents, singly or in combinati in several instances.

For more detailed storm information please refer to Clima tological Data, National Summary.

FLOODS

Flooding during August was confined to the Western porti of the State and was due to the heavy rains associated with thunderstorms on the 5th.

Severe flash flooding on Chartiers Creek caused the evac ation of 1200 persons at Canonsburg and several hundred more at Carnegie. Water ran 8 feet deep over key highways, bridges and residential streets in low-lying spots of these towns, claimed 6 lives through drowning, and caused extensive property damage.

The Monongahelia River was above flood stages from 24 to 40 hours and crested on the 6th from 2.0 to 7.6 feet abo flood stages.

The Youghiogheny River crested 1.3 feet above flood stag at Sutersville on the morning of the 6th and the Ohio River crested 2.7 feet above flood stage at Midland abou midnight of the 6th-7th.

J. T. B. Beard, Climatologist
U. S. Weather Bureau
Weather Records Processing Center
Chattanooga, Tennessee

Station		Temperature: Average Maximum	Average Minimum	Average	Departure From Long Term Means	Highest	Date	Lowest	Date	Degree Days	No. of Days Max 90° or Above	Max 32° or Below	Min 32° or Below	Min 0° or Below	Precipitation: Total	Departure From Long Term Means	Greatest Day	Date	Snow, Sleet Total	Max. Depth on Ground	Date	No. of Days 10 or More	50 or More	1.00 or More
ATLANTIC DRAINAGE																								
TOWN WB AP	R	81.1	60.5	70.8	- 1.0	90	17+	48	22+	12	3	0	0	0	3.56	- .93	1.00	31	.0	0		8	3	1
TOWN GAS CO	AM	81.3	60.0	70.7	- 1.3	93	19	48	26	11	3	0	0	0	3.39	- 1.14	1.07	21	.0	0		9	1	1
NA HORSESHOE CURVE		78.5	57.8	68.2	- .9	88	28	43	22	31	0	0	0	0	6.11	2.60	2.08	7	.0	0		8	3	2
TSVILLE	AM	82.5	60.3	71.4	- 1.0	94	19	49	25	9	4	0	0	0	3.90	.03	1.52	21	.0	0		4	2	2
AS 1 WNW		83.1	57.5	70.3		91	29	44	24+	16	4	0	0	0	6.29		2.00	7	.0	0				
RTOWN		81.7	57.2	69.5		90	28	42	24	21	1	0	0	0	3.81		.73	5	.0	0		10	1	0
FONTE 4 S	AM	78.7	56.4	67.6	- 2.6	89	29	44	22	36	0	0	0	0	6.96	3.07	1.40	5	.0	0		13	5	2
CK		82.2	59.0	70.6		90	31	46	26	10	1	0	0	0	3.93		.57	5	.0	0		12	2	0
EHEM LEHIGH UNIV		80.4	62.5	71.5	- 1.7	92	28	50	22	10	3	0	0	0	3.34	- .92	.83	21	.0	0		8	3	0
CABINS 2 NE		79.6	55.6	67.6		89	28+	43	22+	25	0	0	0	0	4.26		1.30	5	.0	0		8	2	2
N 1 NW	AM	74.2	54.6	64.4		84	18	44	22+	75	0	0	0	0	2.85		.80	19	.0	0		8	3	0
SLE		84.1	61.8	73.0	.2	93	28	51	22+	1	7	0	0	0	4.35	.05	2.26	5	.0	0		6	3	1
ERSBURG 1 ESE		82.4	59.5	71.0	- 1.4	92	28	46	22+	13	3	0	0	0	3.95	.02	.98	20	.0	0		6	4	0
ER	AM	83.3M	63.8M	73.6M		93	20+	54	25+	0	8	0	0	0	2.87		1.80	21	.0	0		5	2	1
SVILLE 1 SW	AM	82.2	59.2	70.7	- 2.0	92	29	49	22+	13	3	0	0	0	3.27	- 1.31	1.74	21	.0	0		6	2	1
BIA		85.2	62.5	73.9		95	12	50	25	0	9	0	0	0	4.01		1.66	21	.0	0		4	3	2
LT 1		82.0	61.8	71.9		93	12	49	26	3	3	0	0	0	3.80		1.23	21	.0	0		5	4	2
	AM	79.8	53.8	66.8				43	3+	41	1	0	0	0	3.05		.97	31	.0	0		7	1	0
IS 7 E		77.5	54.9	66.2		85	17+	38	22	43	0	0	0	0	7.51	4.23	1.90	5	.0	0		12	6	1
S MERE	AM	71.1	56.3	63.7		80	19	47	25+	78	0	0	0	0	3.62	- .70	.72	7	.0	0		10	2	0
IUM 2 SSW	AM	77.1	52.8	65.0		86	18	38	25	71	0	0	0	0	8.60		2.66	6	.0	0		13	7	2
TA		82.5	60.6	71.6	- 1.0	92	28	50	25+	9	3	0	0	0	3.90	- .61	1.70	21	.0	0		5	3	2
TT 1 SW		77.4	58.4	67.9	- 1.7	96	18	42	26	22	2	0	0	0	7.35	3.52	1.80	5	.0	0		8	5	5
AND		74.0	56.3	65.2	- 1.7	80	16	45	22	54	0	0	0	0	3.79	- .28	.90	7	.0	0		10	2	0
E SCHOOL		83.0	61.7	72.4	.2	93	28	49	25+	6	4	0	0	0	2.92	- 1.69	1.26	21	.0	0		4	3	1
SBURG	AM	82.7	62.0	72.4	.0	93	29	50	22	9	6	0	0	0	3.59	- .36	1.94	21	.0	0		3	2	2
1 N	AM	79.0	56.3	67.7		89	29	45	22+	28	0	0	0	0	5.79		1.55	29	.0	0		10	5	1
ER	AM	82.9	59.0	71.0	- 2.6	93	29	48	22+	15	4	0	0	0	3.59	- .57	2.11	21	.0	0		5	2	2
SBURG WB AP	R	82.1	62.6	72.4	- .6	91	18+	52	22+	0	3	0	0	0	3.48	.14	1.42	5	.0	0		6	2	1
Y 1 S DAM	AM	76.2	52.4	64.3		87	18	39	22	70	0	0	0	0	2.39		.59	21	.0	0		6	2	0
DOD		82.7	65.9	74.3	- .8	93	28	57	22	0	4	0	0	0	3.95	- .10	1.90	5	.0	0		4	3	2
NGDON	AM	82.1M	57.2	69.7M	- 1.0	93	29	46	25	11	2	0	0	0	5.27	1.36	1.73	5	.0	0		8	5	1
HORPE		81.7M	57.6	69.7M	.0	90	17	44	26	16	1	0	0	0	3.47	- 1.30			.0	0				
		81.5	55.9	68.7		90	18	41	22	30	1	0	0	0	4.05		1.50	5	.0	0		8	3	1
STER 2 NE PUMP STA		82.3	60.3	71.3	- .9	90	28	48	22	7	1	0	0	0	3.71	- .59	1.78	21	.0	0		4	2	2
SVILLE 2 NW	AM	81.7	59.3	70.5		91	19	47	1	14	2	0	0	0	3.17		1.80	21	.0	0		3	2	2
NCEVILLE 2 S	AM	78.0	53.7	65.9	- 2.5	89	10	42	3	53	0	0	0	0	3.79	- .02	.90	24	.0	0		9	2	0
ON 3 W	AM	83.5	60.4	72.0	- .2	98	29	51	3	0	4	0	0	0	3.80	- .46	1.00	20	.0	0		7	4	1
TOWN	AM	81.7	58.3	70.0		92	29	49	22+	10	4	0	0	0	5.21		1.32	5+	.0	0		9	4	3
HAVEN				M							0	0	0	0					.0	0				
A	AM	76.2	49.7	63.0		84	10+	38	22+	86	0	0	0	0	5.42		1.67	5	.0	0		11	4	1
S HOOK		84.1	67.2	75.7	- .9	95	28	56	22	1	8	0	0	0	2.71	- 2.74	1.10	21	.0	0		5	3	1
NSBURG CAA AP		79.2	58.1	68.7		89	28+	45	22	23	0	0	0	0	5.73		2.39	5	.0	0		11	4	2
ETOWN OLMSTED FLD		83.0	63.3	73.2	.3	94	28	52	25	0	4	0	0	0	3.20	- .84	1.40	5	.0	0		5	3	1
OSE 1 E	AM	74.4	55.1	64.8	- 2.0	84	18+	45	22	63	0	0	0	0	3.64	- .49	1.19	31	.0	0		8	3	1
NTOWN		81.2	59.4	70.3		91	28	47	25	13	1	0	0	0	2.85		1.12	21	.0	0		4	3	1
ETNA 2 SE		81.3	60.3	70.8		91	18	49	26	4	4	0	0	0	3.27		1.14	5	.0	0		5	2	2
CONO 2 N AP		75.2M	55.6M	65.4M	1.2	84	17+	42	22	54	0	0	0	0	3.06	- 1.38	.99	21	.0	0		9	3	0
BURG 1 SE		78.4	54.7	66.6		86	12+	40	22	39	0	0	0	0	4.26		1.10	31	.0	0		11	3	1
IG 3 W		84.7	65.4	75.1		94	12	52	25	0	8	0	0	0	3.60		1.40	5	.0	0		6	3	1
IT	AM	82.0	57.6	69.8		92	29	47	25	11	2	0	0	0	3.86	- .37	1.30	5	.0	0		7	2	1
STOWN		84.3	64.3	74.3		95	18	54	22+	1	9	0	0	0	3.15		1.80	21	.0	0		4	3	1
ITON		79.4	60.0	69.7	- .9	88	17+	47	26	17	0	0	0	0	4.54	.46	1.21	31	.0	0		8	4	1
DREXEL INST OF TEC		85.8	67.7	76.8		97	28	57	22	0	11	0	0	0	2.55		1.05	21	.0	0		4	3	1
DELPHIA WB AP	R	83.2	64.9	74.1	.1	93	18+	53	22	2	4	0	0	0	2.79	- 1.79	1.02	21	.0	0		5	3	1
DELPHIA PT BREEZE		83.6	67.9	75.8	.2	93	18+	58	22	1	6	0	0	0	2.17		1.11	21	.0	0		4	1	1
DELPHIA SHAWMONT		83.6M	63.2M	73.4M	- .9	93	29	53	25+	2	8	0	0	0	2.46	- 2.40	1.53	21	.0	0		4	2	1
DELPHIA CITY	RAM	83.0	68.7	75.9	.7	92	18	60	22+	0	6	0	0	0	2.63	- 1.99	1.00	21	.0	0		5	3	1
SBURG CAA AP		75.0	51.7	63.4		84	17+	35	22	93	0	0	0	0	10.28		2.41	5	.0	0		14	6	4
XVILLE 1 E		86.3	58.4	72.4	- 1.1	97	28	46	25+	2	12	0	0	0	3.27	- 1.45	1.12	21	.0	0		4	3	1
HILL	AM	73.9	57.3	65.6		83	18	46	3	48	0	0	0	0	3.11		1.26	21	.0	0		6	2	1
NT MOUNT 1 W	AM	73.6	52.2	62.9		84	18	39	22	95	0	0	0	0	2.81	- 1.30	.73	31	.0	0		7	2	0
LINTON	AM	82.1	55.2	68.7	- 2.5	93	29	43	26	24	3	0	0	0	4.65	- .52	1.20	21	.0	0		9	4	1
TOWN 1 E		81.9	59.0	70.5	.1	92	18	46	22+	13	2	0	0	0	4.09	- .40	1.77	21	.0	0		6	3	1
G WB CITY	R	82.7	64.5	73.6	.2	94	28	54	22+	0	3	0	0	0	3.30	- .58	.98	21	.0	0		6	3	0
ON	AM	78.6	55.9	67.3	- 3.0	89	18	45	22+	34	0	0	0	0	4.16	.49	1.67	31	.0	0		10	1	1
ON WB AIRPORT		78.3	57.4	67.9	- 2.1	88	18	44	22	29	0	0	0	0	3.03	- 1.05	1.22	31	.0	0		8	1	1
GROVE CAA AP		81.5	58.0	69.8	- 1.6	92	17	46	3+	16	3	0	0	0	4.50	.56	1.21	6	.0	0		11	3	1
NSBURG		84.1	61.1	72.6	- .5	94	28	47	25	2	5	0	0	0	3.77	- .24	1.36	5	.0	0		6	3	1
COLLEGE		78.6	58.8	68.7	- .3	88	17+	46	22	21	0	0	0	0	8.39	4.95	2.42	6	.0	0		13	4	3
SBURG		80.5	54.3	67.4	- 2.6	92	18	40	3+	35	1	0	0	0	3.72	- .96	1.30	21	.0	0		8	2	1
CK 2 S FIRE TWR	AM																							
A		80.6	55.4	68.0	- .6	90	17	41	26	27	1	0	0	0	4.60	1.28	1.32	29	.0	0		8	3	3
DARBY		83.7	64.3	74.0		93	28	53	22	1	7	0	0	0	2.55		1.28	21	.0	0		4	2	1
ORO 3 S	AM	75.4	54.8	65.1	- 1.3	84	29	42	3	60	0	0	0	0	4.92	1.29	1.20	7	.0	0		11	4	1
ILLE		83.1	59.3	71.2		100	28+	45	25	10	5	0	0	0	4.65		2.73	5	.0	0		4	3	1
HESTER	AM	84.6	64.5	74.6	2.4	94	18	54	21+	5	10	0	0	0	2.95	- 1.79	1.69	21	.0	0		4	2	1
MSPORT WB AP		81.4	58.6	70.0	- .9	90	17	47	3+	11	1	0	0	0	4.09	.48	.96	5	.0	0		9	3	0

See Reference Notes Following Station Index

TABLE 2 - CONTINUED

Station	Temperature: Average Maximum	Average Minimum	Average	Departure From Long Term Means	Highest	Date	Lowest	Date	Degree Days	No. of Days Max. 90° or Above	Max. 32° or Below	Min. 32° or Below	Min. 0° or Below	Precipitation: Total	Departure From Long Term Means	Greatest Day	Date	Snow, Sleet Total	Max. Depth on Ground	Date	No. of D .10 or More	.50 or More
YORK 3 SSW PUMP STA	84.7	60.6	72.7	- .1	93	18+	48	22+	4	6	0	0	0	5.16	.92	2.49	5	.0	0		5	3
DIVISION			69.9											4.11				.0				
OHIO DRAINAGE																						
BAKERSTOWN 3 WNW	80.7	58.9	69.8		88	5+	43	22	23	0	0	0	0	5.19		1.80	5	.0	0		8	4
BLAIRSVILLE 6 ENE	76.2	58.7	67.5		85	31	45	22	31	0	0	0	0	5.57	1.62	1.56	5	.0	0		9	5
BRADFORD 4 W RES	75.3M	50.9M	63.1M	- 3.2	84	31	34	3	107	0	0	0	0	8.35	5.08	1.78	7	.0	0		11	6
BROOKVILLE CAA AIRPORT	77.7	54.7	66.2	.2	88	31	39	22	47	0	0	0	0	5.31	1.58	1.96	5	.0	0		9	4
BURGETTSTOWN 2 W AM	80.3	54.8	67.6		89	6	37	22	50	0	0	0	0	7.64		2.88	6	.0	0		8	4
BUTLER	82.0	57.4	69.7	- .5	89	29	40	22	34	0	0	0	0	4.87	1.03	.99	6	.0	0		9	5
CLARION 3 SW	79.7	55.5	67.6		87	28+	42	22	40	0	0	0	0	7.29	3.40	2.51	5	.0	0		9	5
CLAYSVILLE 3 W																						
CONFLUENCE 1 SW DAM AM	78.4	56.5	67.5		88	29	42	26	35	0	0	0	0	8.69		3.18	6	.0	0		9	5
CORRY	76.9	55.5	66.2	- 1.0	86	17	38	3	49	0	0	0	0	12.39	8.99	3.12	5	.0	0		13	8
COUDERSPORT 3 NW	74.5	49.7	62.1		84	17	35	3+	121	0	0	0	0	6.46		1.00	6	.0	0		10	7
DERRY	80.1	59.9	70.0	- .8	89	31	42	22	18	0	0	0	0	7.37	3.15	3.35	5	.0	0		9	3
DONEGAL	75.3	52.0	63.7		84	17	33	22	84	0	0	0	0	6.79		3.00	5	.0	0		11	4
DONORA AM	84.1	62.5	73.3	- .6	92	18+	47	22	10	3	0	0	0	7.38	3.48	3.50	6	.0	0		9	3
EAST BRADY	83.2	58.8	71.0		91	31	44	22	9	3	0	0	0	5.78		2.25	5	.0	0		9	3
EBENSBURG	75.6	54.6	65.1	- 1.6	85	31	38	22	57	0	0	0	0	6.68	2.69	1.82	5	.0	0		9	4
FARRELL SHARON	82.7	57.5	70.1	- 1.4	91	28	42	25	22	4	0	0	0	6.99	3.16	2.17	5	.0	0		11	6
FORD CITY 4 S DAM AM	79.4	55.4	67.4		87	29	42	22	41	0	0	0	0	3.88		1.34	5	.0	0		8	2
FRANKLIN	79.4	57.1	68.3	- .2	87	17+	42	22	27	0	0	0	0	6.91	3.33	2.37	5	.0	0		10	5
GREENVILLE	80.4	57.4	68.9	- .1	89	28	42	22	29	0	0	0	0	7.70	4.19	2.30	5	.0	0		10	5
INDIANA 3 SE	80.3	56.4	68.4	- 1.6	88	31	40	22	23	0	0	0	0	5.04	1.00	2.00	5	.0	0		9	4
IRWIN	83.4	59.5	71.5	.7	90	17+	43	22	16	3	0	0	0	6.17	2.30	2.90	5	.0	0		6	3
JAMESTOWN 2 NW AM	78.5	57.2	67.9		87	29	44	25	37	0	0	0	0	6.67	2.94	1.63	5	.0	0		9	7
JOHNSTOWN AM	83.1	56.6	69.9	- 1.3	92	29	43	22	29	4	0	0	0	4.44	.07	.94	5	.0	0		12	4
KANE 1 NNE AM	74.6	49.6	62.1		83	18	33	22	114	0	0	0	0	8.45	4.82	1.63	19	.0	0		13	5
LINESVILLE 5 WNW	78.7	58.0	68.4		87	28	44	25	32	0	0	0	0	9.81	6.12	2.27	19	.0	0		12	7
MEADVILLE 1 S AM	77.5	56.5	67.0	- .7	86	29	45	22	40	0	0	0	0	8.61	4.99	3.12	19	.0	0		12	4
MERCER 2 NNE	79.5	55.5	67.5		87	28	41	25	26	0	0	0	0	7.93		3.25	5	.0	0		9	6
MIDLAND DAM 7	80.1	62.6	71.4	- .7	88	18	52	22+	8	0	0	0	0	5.57	1.91	1.96	5	.0	0		7	4
NEW CASTLE 1 N	81.6	57.8	69.7	- .8	88	17+	44	22	21	0	0	0	0	5.49	2.18	1.66	6	.0	0		9	4
NEWELL AM	82.5	63.3	72.9	.7	90	19	52	22+	5	1	0	0	0	7.67	4.10			.0	0			
NEW STANTON	82.7	56.4	69.6	- 1.0	92	31	43	25+	27	4	0	0	0	7.14	2.92	3.30	5	.0	0		5	5
PITTSBURGH WB AP 2 //R	79.9	61.7	70.8	.7	89	5	46	22	19	0	0	0	0	5.07	1.94	3.06	5	.0	0		6	3
PITTSBURGH WB CITY R	81.9	63.8	72.9	- .2	92	17	51	22	6	2	0	0	0	5.28	2.20	3.34	5	.0	0		6	2
PUTNEYVILLE 2 SE DAM AM	79.7	53.8	66.8		88	29	41	22	46	0	0	0	0	6.04		1.98	5	.0	0		9	4
RIDGWAY 3 W AM	76.7	50.3	63.5	- 3.2	87	31	38	22	91	0	0	0	0	9.73	6.48	2.90	5	.0	0		12	5
SALINA 3 W	80.3	58.8	69.6		89	17	42	22	26	0	0	0	0	5.46		2.02	6	.0	0		7	4
SHIPPINGPORT WB	79.7	59.1	69.4		88	5+	40	24	29	0	0	0	0	5.63		3.30	5	.0	0		7	4
SLIPPERY ROCK	80.1	59.0	69.6		87	28	45	22	22	0	0	0	0	5.26		1.60	5	.0	0		9	5
SOMERSET MAIN ST	77.3	55.5	66.4	- .5	85	28+	37	22	49	0	0	0	0	5.31	.82	1.40	6	.0	0		10	3
SPRINGS 1 SW	75.0	53.8	64.4	- 1.2	82	17+	37	22	66	0	0	0	0	7.68	3.18	2.63	5	.0	0		10	3
TIONESTA 2 SE DAM AM	77.5	54.7	66.1		85	6+	42	22	49	0	0	0	0	6.62	3.60	1.65	5	.0	0		10	5
TITUSVILLE WATER WORKS	78.6	54.7	66.7		87	31	39	3	45	0	0	0	0	8.71		1.92	19	.0	0		19	7
UNIONTOWN	80.1	61.2	70.7	- 1.2	87	17+	45	22	19	0	0	0	0	7.85	3.38	3.40	5	.0	0		8	3
WARREN	78.5	56.4	67.5	- .5	87	17+	40	3	40	0	0	0	0	7.68	4.03	1.73	6	.0	0		11	5
† WAYNESBURG 2 W	82.2	57.2	69.7	- 1.8	90	5	43	22	0	1	0	0	0	6.26	2.32	1.80	5	.0	0		15	4
DIVISION			68.1											6.83				.0				
LAKE DRAINAGE																						
ERIE CAA AIRPORT	76.3	61.4	68.9	- .1	86	31	49	3+	19	0	0	0	0	8.61	4.13	1.73	30	.0	0		12	1
SPRINGBORO	78.4	57.1	67.8		88	18	44	25	34	0	0	0	0	6.00		1.65	5	.0	0		13	5
DIVISION			68.4											6.31				.0				

† DATA RECEIVED TOO LATE TO BE INCLUDED IN DIVISION AVERAGES

DAILY PRECIPITATION

Day of month

2	3	4	5	6	7	8	9	10	11	12	13	14	15	16	17	18	19	20	21	22	23	24	25	26	27	28	29	30	31
		T	.60	1.74	T	T		.60		.06	T	.61						.02	T			.22				.54			.07
T			.42	.12	T		T	T		.02	.14					.10	.02	.34	.78			T			T	.60	.02	T	1.00
.05			.40	.36	.21						T	.14					.22	.09	1.07	.12		T	.01				.46		.26
			1.79	.80	2.08			.35			.17	.02						.45	.03			.12			.27			.03	.04
			1.48	.48	.21	.04						.02	.03					.08	1.52	.07									.03
			*	*	2.00		.20	.10							1.60			*	1.87						.22		.30		
			.37	.32	.02	.14		.16				.30	T				.48	T			.92		.06		.03		.72		.56
			1.80	1.17					.17		.26	.35		.01			.19					.30			.08			.04	
			.43	.38	.78	.31		.30		T	T	1.10					1.61					.65				.39	.45		.61
			1.02	.62	.12	.65		.42		.36	.92						.33	.41	.66			.04					.84		.05
			1.66	1.08	T	T		.14		.32	.04	.64						T	T			.29			T	.47			.32
			.73	.23	.48	.02		.49			.25	.32		T			.37	.03	.42			.05			T	.08	.10		.24
			.73	.98	.71	.09		.19		.16	.23	.27			1.26		.33		.12			.27				.15	.23		.47
			1.40	.55	1.10	.09		.26		.97	.09	.21			.30		.40	.02	.28	T		.15			.01	.19	.56	I	.58
			.57	.90		.03	.28	.16		.18	.30	.02	.03	.30	T	.32	.03	.12	.31			.03			T	T	.45		.30
			.32	.18	.15	T					T	.10					.09	.02	1.17	.15		T					.58		.35
T			.59	.16						T	.12					.09	.17	.40	.83							.55		T	.43
		.01	1.56	.71	.65		.04	.35	.16		.72			.02		T	.01	.41	T			.37			.55			.01	
			2.45	.71	.11						.04							.45	.70						.05		.37		
			.90	1.90	.20	.34	.10					.04	.13					.90	1.51			.34				.30			.06
			1.08	2.61		.12		.45		.17	T	.26					T	.02	.07			.14				.67			.06
			.88	2.23	2.35	.65	.01	.34		.01	.04	.45					.99	.07				.73			.01	.12	.48		.49
		.03	.94	1.60	1.78						.41	.05				.11	1.06					.82			.24	.36	.30		.65
		.03	.96	.50	1.10	.31	.04				.04	.22					.11	1.87	.14				.14			.33	.11		
		.27	1.96	.15	.08	.07	.11		.10	1.06	.26			.03				T			.60	T		T	.53	.07			
			*	4.52	.92			.32			.12	.03						.18				.20				.48			.09
			.89	1.33	.02	.18	.05					.12						.38	1.42							.15	.15		.20
			2.09	2.88	.05			.34		.11	.72	T					.04	.03	.01			.36				.03			.38
		T	1.30	.21	.42	I	T							.34			.04	1.12	.42						.13	.24	.04		
			.85	.99	T			.48		.41	.05	.50				.55						.40				.52			.12
			1.46	.30											T			.45	.80						T		.23		.13
			.50	.20	.54		.02	.01		T	.05	.17					.80					.22			T	T	.10		.24
		T	2.26	.43	.03			T			T							.84	.76			T			.04	T	.10	.09	.10
			1.04	.98	1.14	2.24	.03	.54		T	T	.34			.10		.05	.02	.34			.83			T	.32			.01
			.68	.08	.58	.10	.05	.14		T	.35	.28					.68	.02				.64				.07	.16		.25
			.60	.32	1.06	.02	.05	.06		.30	.10	.35					.04					.50			T	T	.15		.28
			.65	.70	.20	T													1.55	T	T								
			.95	.90	.12	.01	T				.04	.08					T	.98	.44						.06	.02			.75
			2.08	2.35				.18			T	.04	.15					.87	.44			.10				.54		.01	.13
					.34								.12						1.80	.50									.11
			1.00	.45	1.16	.27		.49		.21	.43	.55					.41		.09			.42				.10	.56		T
			2.51	.21	.01	.09	.02	.06		1.70		.22			.11		.78					.59				.69			.29
			.45	.22	.32	.01		.02			.15	.21					.65	.15	1.10	.03							.33		1.01
			2.05	.65	.18	1.17		1.05		.85	.10	.32					.35		.05			.30			.02	.22	.07	T	.50
			-	-	-	-		-				.48					.95	.10				1.06			T	.36	.27		.24
			.42	.16	.44	.10		.21			.14	.55					.02	.10	.80								.05		.13
			.73	.23	.29			T										T	1.74	.13							T		.15
			1.54	.16	T													.65	1.66						T				
.06	.04		.89	3.18	.05	.04		.08				.17	1.07					1.03	1.25			.03				.42		.28	.10
.07	.02		1.04	3.66	.05	.10		.09				.32	.39					.76	1.22			.07				.36	.09	.12	.10
			1.15	5.70	.02	.02		.04			.18	.02	1.35					.89	.63			.08				.45			.25
			.50	.08	.33			T											1.68	.04						T			.05
			1.78	.22	.07	.04	T	.11	T	.36	.05	.29	T		T		.74	.02				.80			T	.65	T		.27
T			1.50	.18	.06	.10	T	.09	T	.41	.05	.14	T		T		.40		T			.70			.07	.48	T	I	.47
			*	2.97	.37			1.00			.22	.08						.04	T							.60	.06		.08
		.05	3.12	.30	.03		.51			.17	.96	.16				.35	1.82					.78			.28	1.42	1.72		.70
			.65	1.00	.20	.09		.63				.76	.01				.94	.15				.85			.01	.02	.72		.43
			.65	.46	.16	.06		.31		.03	.06	.61					1.00	.20			*	*	*	*	.98	.02	.74	.01	1.21
			.46	.38	.95			.13			.21	.14					.50	.04				.67			.04	T	.22		.42
			2.50	.80		.40		.45		.13		.30							.30			.30				.30			
			2.07	.65	1.80	.65	.05	.36	.03	.03	T	.77	.02				T	.05	.45	T		.17			.02	.30			.09
			.88	1.74	1.79	.75		.40		.01	.01	.52					.75	.04				.84	.06		.02	.25	1.03		.27
			.30	.95	.56	T		.20		.10	.12	.26					.09	T	.30								.15		.17
		.03	3.35	1.23	.52			.30		.39	.08						.24	.45	.03						.46		.08	.08	.13
			.67	.66	.02													1.01	1.23							T	.02		.19
			.07	.39	.37	.02	.07				.14	.19		.01		.01	.28	.05	T			T					.45	T	.97
		.01	3.00	.60	.15		.14	.02		T	.32	.07	.13			.02	.61	.80	.01		T	.22			.49			.15	.05
			1.17	3.50	.02	T		.18		T	.06	T	.02				.29	1.28	.08			.14			.34	.18		T	.12
			.71	.10	.16						.48							.19	1.57					T			.11		.09
			1.90	.81	.77		.25	.87		.95	.21				T	.15	.34	.01				.50			.30		.02		.34
			.17	.12	.30	T					.34	.08		T			.29	T				.09			T	T	.19	1.00	.40
T			.44	.48	.72	.02		.12			.19	.20		T			.61	.03	T			.22			T	.02	.26		.31
			2.25	.45				.45		.98	.45							.20				.40			.50				.10
			1.82	1.03	.64	1.20	.08	.47		.05		.42			T			.05	.40			.15				.37			
.01			1.54	.09	.16	.03		.15		.19	.31	.47		.04	.11		.54	.06				1.03	.08		.15	.39	.21		.78
			1.32	.23	.12														1.35	.05									.05
			1.06	2.66	.38	.61	.60	.17		.20		.36			.20		.55	.05				.84				.23	.52		.08
T			.50	.63	.71	T	.01	.08		.20	.10	.17						.58				.32			.03	.08	.17		.22
			1.21	.51	.03													.35	1.70									.10	
					.10							.42					.16					.29					.50		.67
		1.52	.26	.07	.17		.28		.14	.02	.46			.03		.15	.13			T	.95			T	.29	.01		1.73	.40
		T	1.80	1.20	1.20						.05	.10						1.25	.25						.05	1.05	.35	.05	
		.15	2.17	.98	.02				.25	.40	.52			.03		.91	.12					.96			.82			.11	
			1.34	.76	T	T		.21		.23	.08	.30			.10		T	T	T			.37				.47			.02
			2.37	.19				.09		1.12	.19	.03			.05		1.07	.01				.57			.13	.39			.10
			.40	.04	.90	.18		.06	T	.05	.13	.40		.10				.02	.78	.02		.10			.03		.38		.18
			.72	.62	.50	.05		.22		T	T	.27			.01		.59	.14				.83			.02	.02	.62		.42
			.88	.28	.23													.10	1.94	.02									.21
			.72	.51	.05						.07	.01						.30	1.26										
			1.14	.36	.05	.01							.08						1.94	.01									
			1.13	1.34	1.22	.84		.30		.23	.03	.63			.05		1.11	.04				1.04				.77	.27		.03
			1.40	1.43	.07			.18		.01	.07	.46					.01	T	.02			.42				.57			.05
			T	.06	.46	.03		.02			.03	.30					.13	.04	.93			.08				T	.52		.09
			1.40	.36	T			.01			.01	.07						.45	.86			.01			T		.37	.20	.38
			.56	.09	.41							T							1.59	.08							.11		T
			.77	.60	.26	.19	.30	.50			T	.34					.38	T	.90								1.55		
.19	.09		2.90	1.94	1.00			.32				.23	.15					.65	1.08			.07				.30	T		.14
		.30	.25	2.72	.10	T		.44		.14	.07		T				.26	.47				.13			.35		.09		.02
		.09	2.30	.39	.02		.05			.88	.40			.80	T	.17	1.50					.67			.44			.05	.14
			1.01	.26	.11							T	T					T	2.11	.10									
		.07	1.42	.22	T		T				T	T		T			T	.78	.37			T		T	.02	.27		T	.33
			1.57	.18	.18							.07						.02	1.16	T		T				.02	.35		.11
				T	.10			.02	T		.02	.26					.17	T	.65	.01		.04	T		T	.09	.44	T	.63
					.25				.02			.30					.16		.59	.06		.05				.02	.36	.01	.57
			T	T	.60	.01		.03	T		T	.26		T		T	.03	.04	.50	.91		.02			T	T	.24		.53
			1.90	.55	.04			T			T	T	.01					T	1.31	.14			T						T
					.06			.04			.10	.38					.53	.02	.11	T		.09			T	.01	.87	T	.93
			1.18	1.48	.05	.17		.10			.08	.03	.11					.42	.90			.12				.32			.05
				.03	.29	T	.03		.11	.09	.01	.03	.13				T	.15	.08	.09	.01				.06		.22	T	.89
			1.73	.33	.03	.58	T	.08			.08	.10		T	T			.04	.66	T		.02		.02	.15				.55
			1.92	.40	.13	.01		T				.01						.02	1.35	.03						.05	.02		.63
			.46	1.10	.10	.13				.04		.22			.16			.60	1.03							.25	1.02		.05
			2.00	.62	.01	.18		.71		.02		.18			.53				.13			.21				.46			.01
		1.90	2.90							.03	.04						.25	.22	.03			.18			.57			.05	
		T	1.63	.33	.03			.67		.57	.52	.04			.23		1.21	T				.57			.03	.78	T		.04
T			*	1.03				.13		.03	.46			.06				*	1.03						T		.19	T	.54
			.94	.86	.10	.45		.30	T	T	T	.10					.13	.15	.57			.12	T			.42			.10
			1.20	1.31	1.37	.33	T	.21		.06	.39	.21					1.63	.19				.81			T	.25	.29		.20

See Reference Notes Following Station Index

DAILY PRECIPITATION

Table 3—Continued

Station	Total	1	2	3	4	5	6	7	8	9	10	11	12	13	14	15	16	17	18	19	20	21	22	23	24	25	26	27	28	29	30
KARTHAUS	6.19					1.10	.56	1.75	.18		.47		.30	.20	.34					.32		.05			.34				.17	.30	
KEATING SUMMIT	6.82					1.05	1.56	.35	.20		.25	T	.04		.42			T		.96	.07				.88		T		.27	.42	.0
KEGG	4.05				.09	1.50	.62	.57						.02	.13	T				.05	.40	.20						.16	.01	T	.3
KITTANNING LOCK 7	7.18					3.63	.82	.01	.07		.92		.27	.51	T			T		.11	.01				.46			.30			
KREGAR 4 SE	8.27				T	2.47	.36	.53		.02			.01	.05	.29	.23				.65	1.02	.03		.05	.08			.45			.6
KRESGEVILLE 3 W	3.48					.22	.06	.34			.12			.03	.45		.11			.02		1.16	.11							.15	
LAKEVILLE 1 NNE	3.08	T					T	.23			.06				.33					.20	.05	.59	.12		.06			T		.48	
LANCASTER 2 NE PUMP STA	3.71					1.19	.25	.02			T			T	T						.47	1.78						T			
LANDISVILLE 2 NW	3.17					1.15	.14	.05													.01	1.80	.02	T					T		
LAWRENCEVILLE 2 S	3.79					.22	.04	.15	.06		.03				.26			T	.21	.47	.05				.90					.43	.7
LEBANON 3 W	3.80					.77	.28	.32	.01	T	T				.03						1.00	.50					.02		.32		
LEHIGHTON	3.81		T			.50	.10	.45	T		.12			.12	.45					.09	.06	1.15	.04							.15	
LE ROY	3.17	.02				.39	.41	.03			.20	.06	.13							1.03					.15			.04	.19	.05	.0
LEWIS RUN 3 SE	9.68					.96	2.05	1.96	.80		.28			.04	.45					.64	.08				.85	.02		.03	.28	.88	
LEWISTOWN	3.21					1.32	.18	1.10	.01		.10			.13	1.32						.01	.54	T		.04			T	.15	.04	
LINESVILLE 5 WNW	9.81	T			T	2.25	.14	.07			.85		.67	.27	.09		.18	.20		2.27					1.03			.79	.48		
LOCK HAVEN	-		T			.61	1.00	.85	.02		.12	T	.02	.36	.74				-	-	-	-	-	-	-	-	-	-		-	-
LONG POND 2 W	2.79					.12	.08	.18	T		.24			.06	.22		.05			.18	.03	1.11	.09		.10				T	.26	
MADERA	5.42					1.67	.54	.11	.16	.02	.71		.68		.20					.47		.16			.37			.02	.25		
MAHAFFEY	7.39					1.62	.41	1.20	.23		.42		1.11	.56	.31					.57	.01	.12			.52				.31		
MAPLE GLEN	3.01					.70	.17	.29													.21	1.56							T		
MAPLETON DEPOT	4.97					1.60	.49	.20	.20		.04			.16	.13			.78			.10	.96						T	.21		
MARCUS HOOK	2.71					.67	.22	T					.04	T	.01						.52	1.10									
MARION CENTER 2 SE	5.00					1.66	.60	.30	.34	.08	.35		.06	.13	.24			.19		.03		.09			.40			.04	.30	.01	
MARTINSBURG CAA AP	5.79				.11	2.39	.58	1.06	T	.13		T	T	.06	.10				T	.10	.66	.15			T			.25			.1
MATAMORAS	2.28							.41							.26						.12	.73	.14			.04				.07	
MAYBURG	8.51	T				1.07	.40	.74	.28		.43		.14	T	1.14			T		1.50	.03				.63				.41	.30	
MC CONNELLSBURG	4.46					.97	.32	.21	.65	.03	T				.12						.13	1.39							.12	.05	.4
MC KEESPORT	5.30					*	3.60	.03	.05		.31		.30	.02	.01						.09	.02			.15				.69		
MEADVILLE 1 S	8.61	T	T		T	1.95	.14	.08	.01		.20		.50	.42	.22		T	.04		3.12					.70			.45	.35	.23	
MEDIX RUN	6.82	T				1.58	.57	1.21	.58		.48		.38	T	.35			.01		.54		T			.63			.01	.22	.25	
MERCER 2 NNE	7.93					3.25	.60				.10		1.25	.30			T			1.12					.67				.54		.1
MERCERSBURG	3.57					.80	.29	.18	.30	.07		.10						T			T	1.35							.10		
MEYERSDALE 1 ENE	6.42					.04	1.63	.12	.11		.04			.17	.23	.32					1.22	1.30			.07				.34	.17	
MIDDLETOWN OLMSTED FLD	3.20				.15	1.40	.17			T				T						T	.76	.54			.01			.05	.03		.
MIDLAND DAM 7	5.57					1.96	1.53	.08	T		.01		T	.15	.38					T	.01				.56				.63	.05	
MILANVILLE	2.65							.13						.34	.60					.38		.09	T		.08					.33	
MILLHEIM	7.73	T				.84	.40	.93	.05		.51		.35	.15	.38			.16		1.01		.20			.14			.01	.12	1.67	
MILLVILLE 2 SW	3.47	T				.39	.52	.36	T		.38			.19	.22		.01			.02	T	.14			.10				T	.34	
MILROY	5.82					1.71	.67	.47	T		.10		.10	.18	.71			T		.23		.42			.03			.17	.03		
MONTROSE 1 E	3.64	.03				T	.12	.11	.05		.03			T	.46			T		.26	.01				.18			.02		.51	.
MORGANTOWN	2.85					.51	.40														.82	1.12									
MT GRETNA 2 SE	3.27					1.14	.37	T				.01									1.00	.40							.35		
MT POCONO 2 N AP	3.06					.10	.67	.11						.20					.22	T	.14	.99			.01					.51	T
MUHLENBURG 1 SE	4.26		.02			.50	.59		.25		.27		.12	.21		.46		T	.22	.06	.02				.20					.24	
MYERSTOWN	4.28					.11	.83	.39													T	1.05	T							.35	
NATRONA LOCK 4	5.39					1.20	2.40		.07		.27		.33	T	.26		.02					T			.26				.49		.
NESHAMINY FALLS	3.22					.84	.75							T							.47	1.16							T		
NEWBURG 3 W	3.60					1.40	.45	.35							.01						.71	.59						.11			
NEW CASTLE 1 N	5.49					1.23	1.66	T	T		.10		.68	.38	.02			T		.17	.04			T	.47			.01	.61		
NEWELL	7.67					*	4.13	.46			.38			.20	.10						1.27	.24			.06				.57		
NEW PARK	4.67					2.01	.07						1.18	.05	.02						.20	1.14			T						
NEWPORT	3.86					1.30	.20	.47	T		.04			.03	.30			T			.25	.80	.04		T			T	.05	.38	
NEW STANTON	7.14				T	3.30	.01							.60						1.96	.50			T				.76			T
NEW TRIPOLI	4.19		.01			.61	.52	.05					.24	.22	.02					.22	.18	1.10			T					.27	T
NORRISTOWN	3.15					.50	.16	.51			T											1.80	.08							.03	
NORTH EAST 2 SE	4.18	T	T		T	1.14	.08	.38	.02		.28	.02	.03	.14	.23		.03		T	.12				T	.76			.05	.19	.14	T
ORWELL 3 N	2.63	.03				.10	.02		.06		.04				.35				.40	.07					.21			.02		.98	
PALM	5.04					.60	.28	.30							.15							1.80	.12							1.35	
PALMERTON	4.54	T				.44	.28			.11			T	.88		T			.04	T	.52	.80			T				.26		T
PALMYRA		RECORD MISSING																													
PARKER	7.17					3.13	.33				.14		1.55	.06	.09			.07		.73					.47			T	.31		
PAUPACK 2 WNW	2.08						.01	.20			.02				.24				.05	.02		.73	.29		.05			.01	.01	.22	
PECKS POND	2.76	T						.52			T			T	.26					.09	.02	1.00	.09		T				.05	.35	
PHIL DREXEL INST OF TEC	2.55					.56	.29						T		.01						.61	1.05									
PHILADELPHIA WB AP R	2.79					.53	.36				T		.09	T	.02						.81	1.02							T		
PHILADELPHIA PT BREEZE	2.17					.45	.13								.04						.34	1.11									
PHILADELPHIA SHAWMONT	2.46					.53	.15														.25	1.53									
PHILADELPHIA CITY R	2.69					.51	.37								.06						.58	1.00									
PHILIPSBURG CAA AP	10.26				.19	2.41	2.08	.24		.29	.04	.03	1.37	.11	T				.51	T	.19	T		.38	.01		T	.22	.91		.
PHOENIXVILLE 1 E	3.27					.73	.46														.90	1.12							T		
PIKES CREEK	5.98					.31	.30	.60			.18			.17	.20		.21			.30	T	.09			.06				T	1.22	.
PIMPLE HILL	3.11	T				.15	.05	.28	.01		.03		T	T	.75		.01			.01	.03	1.26	T		.01				T	.36	T
PINE GROVE 1 NE	4.49					.20	.96	.44	T		.10				.19					.08	.13	.96	.03		T			T		.71	
PITTSBURGH WB AP 2 //R	5.07		T		T	3.06	T	T		.60		.07		.24	.02				T	T	.02			.28	.02			.53			.
PITTSBURGH WB CITY R	5.28	T			T	3.34	.04	T		.37		.04		.46							.02			.21				.58			.
PLEASANT MOUNT 1 W	2.81	.02					T	.24			.03			T	.41					.23	.02	T			.11			.02	.01	.68	.
PORT CLINTON	4.69					.49	.53	.28			.05			.21	.24					.49	.02	1.20	.03							.52	
POTTSTOWN	3.24					.75	.20	.18			T			.08	T							1.88	.08						T		
POTTSVILLE PALO ALTO BR	3.12					.76	.24	.47	T		.13				.27					.15	.02	.81	.08		T					.07	
PUTNEYVILLE 2 SE DAM	6.04					1.98	.52	.03	.14		1.05		.68	.05	.42			.07		.09		.03			.48			.01	.36		
QUAKERTOWN 1 E	4.09					.61	.07	.16						.04	.06						.18	1.77						.02		.96	
RAYMOND	5.12					.53	.32	.21	.09		.37				.48					.73					.85					.53	
READING WB CITY R	3.30					.77	.34						.02	.02					.01		.68	.98			T			T	T		.
RENOVO	4.81		T			.82	.70	.62	.05		.64		.22	.05	.22					.53					.30			.01	.20	.35	
REW	6.48					.84	1.21	.73	.48		.30		.01	T	.35					.70	.05				.78	.01		T	.15	.52	
RICES LANDING L 6	8.83		.08	.05		2.80	2.85				.14				.06						1.06	.58			.12				.46	.07	
RIDGWAY 3 W	9.73	T				2.90	.25	1.39	.15	.05	.14		.40		.34			1.15		1.58	T				.74				.33	.30	
RUSH	3.98	.03				.31	.40	.02			.04				.35					.35	.07				.17			.04		1.05	.
RUSHVILLE	3.77	.01				.24	.33	.02	T		.08				.35					.31	.01				.15					1.15	.
SAGAMORE 1 S	4.99					2.58	.60	T	.25		.40		.15		.52			.15				T			.10				.24		
SALINA 3 W	5.46				.02	.81	2.02	.02			.71	.03	.05	.48		T	T	.48		T	.09				.20			.52	T		.
SAXTON	6.10					2.00	.45	.65	.75		.04			T	T			T			.23	.93			T				.31	.54	.
SCHENLEY LOCK 5	3.88					1.55	.72				.16		.32	.38	.01						.02				.21			.46			
SCRANTON	4.16					.10	.09	.47	.47		.14				.24		.11			.26	.03	.19	.01		.02					.36	
SCRANTON WB AIRPORT	3.03					.03	.37	.05		.11	.08		.01	.16					.10		.02	.26			.02				.28	.05	.
SELINSGROVE CAA AP	4.50				T	.98	1.21		.16	.15			.20	.37		.01	T		.57	T	.27	.16			.02		T	T	.15	.03	.
SHAMOKIN	5.27					*	1.43	.52	.14		.40			.27	.43					*	.47	.69			T					.80	
SHIPPENSBURG	3.77					1.36	.27	.27						.01	.06						.67	.74						.03		T	
SHIPPINGPORT WB	5.63				.03	3.30	.28	T		T		T		.57					T		T			.56				.60	.03		.
SINNEMAHONING	6.77	T	T			1.02	.75	.88	.36	T	.79		.30	.03	.22			.13		.96	.01	T			.42			.01	.21	.20	
SLIPPERY ROCK	5.26					1.60	.53				.25		.77	.08	.20			.01	.04	.27					.60			T	.55		
SOMERSET FAIRVIEW ST	5.45					.64	1.41	.12	.28		.03			.06	.15	.33					.41	1.31			.16				.32		
SOMERSET MAIN ST	5.31				.03	.65	1.40	.30			.03		.05	.05	.32	.28				.17	1.34	.24			.14			.31			
SOUTH MOUNTAIN	3.73					.84	.28	.38	.02		.01					.07					T	1.58	.03						.06		
SPRINGBORO	6.00	T		T		1.65	.15	T					.35	.36	.10		.51		.21	.22					.75			.79	.50		.
SPRING GROVE	4.42					1.95	.15	.01				T			.01						.82	1.69									
SPRINGS 1 SW	7.66	T	.23			2.63	1.42	.43			.07		T	.23	.09	T				.40	1.38	.28			.07			.31	.10	.04	.
STATE COLLEGE	8.39				T	1.83	2.42	.11		.11	.23	.10	1.23	.21	.02				.23	.02	.24	.01		.08	.06		T	.23	.06		.
STRAUSSTOWN	6.46					.62	.37	.42			.02				.20					.25	.03	1.17	.02					.01		2.16	
STROUDSBURG	3.72		T			.08	.36	T			.03		.18	.47	T	T			.02	T	.30	1.30			.01				.13	.29	.
STUMP CREEK	8.36					2.02	.32	.44	.64		1.42		1.57		.51					.60					.34				.35		
SUNBURY	4.33					.67	.90	.57	.13	.05	.22		.06	.30	.26		.03			.35	T	.41			T				.03	.11	
SUSQUEHANNA	2.14	T						.03						.02	.28					.13					.16			.04		.50	
SUTERSVILLE	5.90					*	3.50				.20			.06		.07					1.07	.27			.14				.59		
TAMAQUA	3.58					.48	.09	.49	.08		.20			.40	.61					.11	.09	.79	.08								
TAMAQUA 4 N DAM	3.83					.44	.06	.45	.10	.05	.18			.19	.44		.07				.28	.75								.64	
TAMARACK 2 S FIRE TWR		RECORD MISSING																													
TIONESTA 2 SE DAM	6.62	T				1.65	.14	T	.25	T	.77		.64	.11	.09			.05	T	1.57	T				.65			.04	.47	.03	
TITUSVILLE WATER WORKS	8.71	T			.03	1.53	.17	.08		1.23	.03		.66	.34	T		.07		.92	1.92	T		T		.73	T	T	.34	.04		

See Reference Notes Following Station Index

DAILY PRECIPITATION

I—Continued

PENNSYLVANIA
AUGUST 1956

Station	Total	1	2	3	4	5	6	7	8	9	10	11	12	13	14	15	16	17	18	19	20	21	22	23	24	25	26	27	28	29	30	31
4 W	8.71	.03				2.39	.31	.04	.03		1.04		.03	.21	.97			.05		1.55	.07				.60				.38	.93		.10
	4.60	T				.11	.05	.06	.10		.02		.01	.02	.25					.33	.04				.11			.01		1.32	1.08	1.09
ITY 3 SW	4.77					.80	1.30	.08	.05		.04		.04	.27	.04					.30	.15	.81						T		.78		.11
	3.92					.18	.16	.30	.08		.02			.86	.23		.18			.34	T				.25			.01		1.18	.03	.09
DINT 4 NE	5.92	.02				.98	1.21	.07	.16		.30		.03		.38					.78	.02				.97			.02	.08	.51		.39
4 NE BALD EAGLE	6.05					2.53	.63	.31	.21		.29		T	.35	.39					.04	T	.30			.14				.24			.62
ITY	8.34	T	T			2.37	.07	.08	.02		.55	.02	.15	.55	.48	.02		.30				1.32	.05		.80	.02	.02	.03	.37	.83	.02	.27
WN	7.89	.02	.06		T	3.40	1.39	T		T	.16			.01	.04				T	.44	1.48	.05			.13			.48		T	.17	
ARBY	2.59					.65	.21	.07							.04						.28	1.28										.02
	7.46	.03				1.96	.23	.04			.32		1.01	.25	.19						.15	1.28			.90				.78			.34
RIFT	7.98					1.55	1.80	T	T		1.78		.24	T	.28			.08		.12	T				.18			T	1.45			.50
ILLE	4.32					.04	.71	.24						.34	.10					.25	.09	1.24	.11							.97		.23
EL	8.60	T	T			1.80	.18	.28	.59	T	.50	T	.50	.11	.07	T		.12		.93		T	T		.97			.14	.38	T	T	.17
EL 1 WSW	6.38	T	T			1.70	.19	.09	.38	T	.48	T	.49	.09	.09	T		.12		1.12		T	T		.94			.09	.43	T	T	.17
	7.68					1.20	1.73	.20	.07	T	.43		.03	.03	.38			T		1.00	.16				.75			.02	.31	1.09		.28
DWN	5.32					.65	.80	.69			.65			.40							.10	.10						.05			1.02	
URG 2 W	6.28		.25	.06		1.80	1.16	.27	.02		.12			T	.08	.01				T	.90	.57			.13				.44	.09		.36
RO 3 S	4.92					.91	.45	1.20	.12		.22		.03	.13	.18			.08		.53	.03				.56			.04	.02	.39		.43
LLE	4.09					2.73	.21	T						T	T						.80	.91						T				
VILLE 1 W	3.15					.60	.46	.38							.02							1.53						.08				.11
ESTER	2.95					.65	.07	.21														1.69	.07									.26
OVE 1 E	2.96					.87	.12	.34			T				.03							1.41	.19									
CKORY	7.80					1.99	.11	.05	.40		.70		.34	.20	.20					1.56	.03				.60			.73	.34	.10		.45
URG	5.94			T		3.02	.72		.16		.61	.06	.12		.38			T	T						.40			T	.47	T		
BARRE	3.96	T				.15	.10	.60	.02		.18			.60	.20		.14			.08	.02	.31	T		.02	T			T	.92	T	.62
SBURG	4.75					1.66	.35	.47	.23	.16	.24			.04	.38						.03	.53			.05			.06	.19			.36
SPORT WB AP	4.09				.01	.96	.68	T		.02	T		.26	.38		T			.25	.04	.01				.23		T	.01	.16	.02	.12	.94
RG	5.00					.76	1.03	.35	.23	.07	.06			.03	.04	.04				T	.31	1.35							.18	.45	.02	.08
SSW PUMP STA	5.16					2.49	.15	.03			T		.21	T	.04						.60	1.55						T				
VEN	3.11					1.70	.16	.04					.02		T						.03	1.10	.03									.03
OVE	4.52					.43	.08	.43	.08		.15			.20	.85		.27			.05	.15	.63	.08							.60	.10	.42
LLE 3 SE	3.84					.48	.22	.24							.09							1.03	.49							.77		.52

DAILY TEMPERATURES

Table 5

Station		1	2	3	4	5	6	7	8	9	10	11	12	13	14	15	16	17	18	19	20	21	22	23	24	25	26
ALLENTOWN WB AP	MAX	84	80	80	81	68	69	84	85	87	87	86	85	78	83	86	88	90	90	86	70	70	76	75	76	75	79
	MIN	64	62	52	53	64	65	63	62	63	65	62	63	59	67	61	60	62	65	67	60	55	48	58	55	49	48
ALLENTOWN GAS CO	MAX	78	85	81	80	82	69	70	83	85	87	88	86	86	79	83	87	83	90	93	87	66	70	78	76	77	76
	MIN	56	65	51	52	58	64	62	61	62	68	62	64	60	64	61	61	63	66	68	64	58	52	52	58	50	48
ALTOONA HORSESHOE CURVE	MAX	79	77	76	76	78	70	69	82	86	81	81	82	77	81	82	84	84	86	81	72	69	72	75	69	74	76
	MIN	60	62	49	52	61	64	62	61	61	65	58	59	58	66	59	55	61	62	71	57	51	43	47	55	46	46
ARENDTSVILLE	MAX	82	86	81	80	76	71	70	76	85	90	88	89	88	83	84	86	89	90	94	87	68	72	76	78	76	78
	MIN	62	65	57	56	61	64	64	63	60	69	59	61	62	65	63	59	61	63	70	62	57	51	50	55	49	52
ARTEMAS 1 WNW	MAX	80	81	78	75	79	82	81	85	86	86	85	87	80	87	80	85	84	87	90	87	86	74	78	78	75	80
	MIN	64	65	55	66	64	67	64	59	61	64	57	60	58	59	62	57	56	58	61	53	52	52	46	44	44	48
BAKERSTOWN 3 WNW	MAX	78	80	82	81	88	86	83	81	80	82	83	81	84	79	78	86	84	82	88	69	71	74	76	73	75	78
	MIN	60	63	66	64	56	57	62	64	61	65	59	60	62	63	61	59	66	64	61	58	49	43	49	52	45	48
BEAVERTOWN	MAX	81	79	77	79	73	74	79	85	87	84	85	85	83	84	85	85	88	87	87	79	73	76	75	76	76	79
	MIN	59	57	46	46	63	64	63	58	58	65	56	63	58	64	57	55	58	61	67	60	56	46	62	42	46	47
BELLEFONTE 4 S	MAX	75	80	78	78	76	71	67	73	86	85	81	83	83	76	84	85	86	87	85	82	62	72	74	74	73	75
	MIN	54	54	46	51	49	63	63	58	61	66	58	62	58	61	59	55	58	61	66	61	53	44	48	48	47	47
BERWICK	MAX	84	83	79	82	81	70	82	84	87	87	85	84	75	84	85	86	89	88	85	79	75	75	78	77	76	78
	MIN	62	60	48	50	60	64	61	60	60	65	59	63	59	64	57	60	63	62	67	58	56	49	55	61	48	46
BETHLEHEM LEHIGH UNIV	MAX	82	81	80	79	66	68	84	85	88	86	86	84	78	82	84	89	90	90	84	65	67	76	75	74	74	78
	MIN	64	62	54	55	62	64	65	66	68	70	67	68	65	69	65	62	65	68	68	60	57	50	55	54	53	51
BLAIRSVILLE 6 ENE	MAX	76	75	77	72	80	76	72	77	83	77	80	78	75	77	79	81	83	81	74	65	65	71	76	68	70	72
	MIN	62	61	51	57	62	62	65	58	63	61	59	59	63	60	59	58	63	61	64	54	48	45	53	57	50	54
BRADFORD 4 W RES	MAX	75	75	73	75	78	79	68				80	78	76	77	76	80	82	81	72	70	65	69	73	73	68	70
	MIN	56	48	34	42	58	61	60					56	52	60	50	46	54	57	62	48	41	37	44	45	38	43
BROOKVILLE CAA AIRPORT	MAX	76	76	75	75	82	74	72	80	83	79	80	79	78	80	81	80	85	85	76	66	69	71	75	72	75	76
	MIN	60	53	47	55	62	65	61	59	56	58	51	60	58	58	54	51	56	59	53	53	46	39	44	49	43	44
BURGETTSTOWN 2 W	MAX	78	79	80	82	77	89	79	79	84	85	82	84	83	80	81	85	86	88	86	76	64	70	75	78	72	75
	MIN	58	60	51	55	63	63	64	51	56	60	55	59	57	64	57	53	58	60	67	57	46	37	42	48	38	40
BURNT CABINS 2 NE	MAX	79	88	78	77	76	71	75	84	78	76	78	78	77	81	84	85	87	88	82	75	72	73	76	74	75	78
	MIN	50	51	50	57	63	64	63	59	58	59	55	56	57	64	59	54	56	58	65	52	48	43	51	49	43	49
BUTLER	MAX	78	79	81	79	84	86	81	83	86	86	83	84	85	80	84	84	87	88	87	87	69	73	75	80	72	75
	MIN	65	58	51	57	69	66	66	56	60	66	55	62	60	66	58	57	59	61	60	57	47	40	48	53	42	44
CANTON 1 NW	MAX	71	76	70	72	75	65	66	74	80	82	79	80	76	70	78	78	80	84	80	74	63	67	70	70	68	70
	MIN	51	53	45	48	49	56	59	58	59	60	55	58	56	63	59	54	57	63	66	51	51	44	44	53	46	46
CARLISLE	MAX	85	82	81	78	76	72	79	86	90	88	87	88	85	85	88	90	91	92	88	84	73	77	80	77	79	81
	MIN	64	65	55	56	64	65	65	64	65	70	62	66	63	67	64	63	64	65	73	60	58	51	53	63	51	53
CHAMBERSBURG 1 ESE	MAX	84	82	80	79	75	71	76	86	87	86	86	88	80	82	87	89	89	90	85	72	74	76	78	77	77	80
	MIN	61	63	54	55	64	65	64	59	62	68	59	61	62	66	62	58	60	64	71	58	56	46	49	55	46	52
CHESTER	MAX	82	87	82	72		81	83	84	86	90	75	75	92	81	86	90	90	92	80	93	79	70	81	79	78	76
	MIN	58	71	61			65	64	64	63	75	65		64	70	67	64	63	67		70	60	65	56	62	54	
CLARION 3 SW	MAX	79	78	79	73	84	77	78	83	86	80	83	82	80	82	83	84	86	86	75	68	70	74	78	73	75	76
	MIN	60	53	47	45	63	65	65	56	56	63	54	60	58	61	54	53	59	60	63	53	46	42	48	51	44	46
CLAYSVILLE 3 W	MAX																										
	MIN																										
COATESVILLE 1 SW	MAX	80	85	83	80	78	70	71	83	88	89	80	87	88	85	85	87	89	90	91	88	66	70	78	76	76	77
	MIN	57	65	54	50	56	65	62	62	64	58	59	64	61	64	64	61	61	62	66	66	58	49	53	51	49	49
COLUMBIA	MAX	86	84	82	79	72	72	83	88	90	90	89	95	86	86	89	90	92	94	90	83	76	79	78	78	80	83
	MIN	65	65	55	56	64	64	65	65	64	71	62	69	64	68	62	62	63	64	74	59	58	52	59	62	50	52
CONFLUENCE 1 SW DAM	MAX	80	80	74	77	78	85	78	75	82	86	80	83	82	78	78	80	84	87	86	79	59	68	72	77	69	75
	MIN	59	63	54	53	63	63	64	58	59	56	59	55	56	65	60	60	59	56	61	57	53	47	47	57	49	42
CORRY	MAX	77	74	77	72	83	77	74	83	82	76	80	78	78	78	79	83	86	77	73	70	67	70	74	71	72	70
	MIN	60	55	38	51	60	64	63	54	55	64	54	59	57	63	53	52	61	59	64	51	49	41	56	50	41	45
COUDERSPORT 3 NW	MAX	76	72	75	72	75	70	69	78	80	76	79	76	73	77	78	82	84	83	72	65	66	67	70	68	68	70
	MIN	46	46	35	40	59	61	60	55	51	52	40	47	43	61	46	47	52	56	60	47	44	35	45	49	38	40
DERRY	MAX	78	80	78	75	81	79	76	83	85	82	82	83	80	83	84	85	85	87	80	72	69	67	74	78	79	80
	MIN	63	64	55	64	65	65	66	59	64	64	60	61	61	68	60	57	60	62	70	58	52	42	55	53	47	45
DEVAULT 1 W	MAX	84	81	79	79	68	68	82	84	89	88	86	93	84	87	86	88	89	90	88	72	67	78	76	76	71	78
	MIN	62	66	52	55	61	60	59	65	64	68	65	63	62	65	62	64	63	67	66	56						49
DIXON	MAX	79	81	75	77	82	72	70	82	84	88	84	85	83	73	84	84	85	90	88	80	68	73	70	75	73	76
	MIN	52	53	43	45	48	62	60	59	58	57	55	56	57	57	54	54	56	61	61	54	55	46	46	56	43	43
DONEGAL	MAX	76	77	77	72	79	74	71	77	82	77	80	79	74	76	78	83	84	82	72	60	64	69	73	67	71	71
	MIN	55	57	49	57	59	58	57	52	57	59	53	54	55	59	55	49	53	55	59	51	41	33	41	45	37	37
DONORA	MAX	83	82	84	84	87	90	83	83	88	88	86	83	87	82	86	87	89	92	92	89	69	74	76	80	75	78
	MIN	65	67	59	65	66	65	68	60	67	67	63	63	65	70	64	63	65	68	71	59	53	47	55	56	50	51
DU BOIS 7 E	MAX	76	75	78	74	76	78	68	80	83	81	80	79	78	79	80	82	85	84	79	72	68	70	75	75	69	73
	MIN							62	59	55	65	53	60	57	65	51	51	54	58	63	52	46	38	51	53	41	42
EAGLES MERE	MAX	68	72	69	69	73	63	65	71	77	77	76	75	74	67	75	76	75	79	80	71	61	64	65	68	66	61
	MIN	53	55	51	51	57	58	59	59	59	62	56	57	60	61	57	57	60	65	63	56	52	49	49	55	47	47
EAST BRADY	MAX	82	82	80	78	86	86	80	87	88	86	86	85	83	84	82	86	90	87	88	75	72	75	80	79	78	79
	MIN	64	58	51	58	65	67	67	57	59	64	56	61	61	64	56	57	61	64	66	58	59	44	50	52	46	48
EBENSBURG	MAX	77	74	72	71	77	74	69	78	82	76	78	77	75	75	78	80	81	80	80	76	64	69	74	69	68	73
	MIN	59	59	49	54	62	63	61	49	57	64	55	59	55	52	55	51	56	56	67	55	49	38	47	52	40	43
EMPORIUM 1 E	MAX																										
	MIN																										
EMPORIUM 2 SSW	MAX	75	80	78	78	77	70	67	74	83	85	80	83	82	76	82	83	85	86	79	77	66	68	70	83	67	70
	MIN	49	53	39	42	47	63	63	60	58	58	55	55	60	60	54	55	56	59	63	53	49	43	46	46	38	42
EPHRATA	MAX	85	82	80	80	78	71	80	83	87	86	85	86	84	84	87	86	90	91	89	80	70	75	76	76	76	78
	MIN	64	64	56	53	63	63	60	61	62	69	61	65	61	66	63	60	63	63	72	58	51	51	57	59	50	50

See Reference Notes Following Station Index

DAILY TEMPERATURES

		Day Of Month 1	2	3	4	5	6	7	8	9	10	11	12	13	14	15	16	17	18	19	20	21	22	23	24	25	26	27	28	29	30	31	Average
	MAX	74	73	78	72	79	71	74	78	83	76	80	79	80	78	77	82	82	79	71	86	68	72	79	67	72	72	77	83	82	83	86	76.3
	MIN	60	58	49	62	66	67	64	62	66	64	61	61	61	64	62	64	68	68	63	58	55	52	60	57	49	55	60	69	63	67	69	61.4
	MAX	78	82	72	79	79	78	78	76	81	80	89	90	84	78	82	80	86	96	82	80	78	72	80	73	77	80	70	84	82	88	88	77.4
	MIN	63	66	54	60	60	66	66	62	62	62	60	60	59	65	60	58	60	60	60	58	50	46	48	50	47	42	56	64	60	64	65	58.4
	MAX	80	82	81	76	88	80	81	87	89	84	87	84	82	86	86	90	90	88	75	70	73	77	81	75	77	70	81	91	87	88	90	82.7
	MIN	63	55	50	60	64	64	67	56	62	64	57	59	62	64	56	54	58	58	59	54	49	43	51	40	42	47	58	66	62	64	65	57.8
	MAX	77	78	80	78	79	83	80	77	83	85	80	83	82	80	82	83	85	86	86	76	65	71	74	77	72	74	77	73	87	89	89	79.4
	MIN	56	58	49	57	59	60	64	57	58	63	59	58	59	62	56	56	57	56	64	57	47	42	43	50	44	44	44	59	62	59	61	55.4
	MAX	76	80	77	76	84	77	77	84	84	82	83	82	78	81	82	82	87	85	74	71	70	72	76	76	74	76	78	87	84	83	85	79.4
	MIN	62	56	48	56	61	66	66	57	58	64	55	60	61	66	55	56	54	58	65	53	51	42	51	53	44	48	56	63	63	57	64	57.1
	MAX	77	76	72	73	72	67	77	78	78	76	78	74	69	76	76	80	78	78	76	74	65	68	68	68	68	68	68	78	70	79	77	74.0
	MIN	62	54	49	51	56	57	56	57	60	61	58	50	57	65	57	57	60	68	65	53	50	45	52	58	48	52	56	57	58	.52	64	56.3
	MAX	84	80	76	83	74	70	80	82	90	88	88	88	85	85	88	89	91	92	89	89	74	74	75	77	78	80	78	93	88	82	85	83.0
	MIN	64	66	52	51	65	66	66	65	65	68	64	68	67	66	62	60	61	63	72	67	63	51	53	50	49	49	59	62	63	65	71	61.7
	MAX	80	87	82	81	76	72	70	78	87	89	87	88	90	83	83	90	90	91	92	87	63	73	78	78	77	77	82	82	93	89	89	82.7
	MIN	62	66	58	57	62	65	64	63	64	72	61	64	63	68	66	62	63	64	74	62	57	50	53	59	51	54	59	63	62	65	68	62.0
	MAX	77	81	80	77	77	70	70	79	83	85	83	83	83	75	81	84	84	86	87	82	64	72	74	74	73	75	78	77	89	84	83	79.0
	MIN	53	60	47	48	56	63	60	59	56	60	57	60	58	59	57	55	58	61	63	60	56	45	48	60	45	46	51	58	61	61	63	56.3
	MAX	76	80	80	75	86	78	78	85	85	81	84	83	79	83	82	87	88	86	80	67	69	74	78	72	77	78	77	89	85	85	86	80.4
	MIN	64	55	48	58	65	65	65	55	59	63	54	58	60	62	55	57	62	63	56	53	50	42	52	50	43	47	58	66	62	65	67	57.4
	MAX	80	86	83	81	76	72	72	79	86	89	87	89	89	84	84	88	89	91	92	86	66	74	78	79	76	78	81	83	93	90	89	82.9
	MIN	52	63	55	55	62	63	63	60	60	63	60	61	64	64	62	60	61	63	67	64	55	48	48	57	48	48	58	58	62	62	64	59.0
	MAX	85	80	80	76	70	71	81	85	88	86	86	86	81	85	86	88	89	91	84	72	73	77	78	74	77	79	81	91	87	88	91	82.1
	MIN	65	66	55	55	65	65	66	64	66	67	64	66	64	68	65	61	64	65	72	59	57	52	60	59	53	52	63	63	63	66	70	62.6
	MAX	76	78	73	75	80	68	65	80	79	84	80	80	79	72	79	78	83	87	85	78	65	70	73	71	70	70	75	75	83	82	70	76.2
	MIN	46	50	42	44	52	57	56	56	57	63	60	57	51	53	54	52	55	58	56	52	53	39	40	56	40	43	50	54	58	59	60	52.4
	MAX	86	82	80	79	72	73	79	84	88	86	86	86	84	82	89	85	90	91	86	74	76	79	78	74	78	82	80	93	84	87	91	82.7
	MIN	68	67	61	61	66	67	66	68	67	72	66	68	68	71	69	66	67	68	72	61	60	57	63	63	59	59	64	66	68	70	75	65.9
	MAX	78	82	83	84	76	72	67	75	87	90		86	88	77	88	87	87	89	89	82	83	75	79	79	76	79	81	75	93	87	88	82.1
	MIN	52	62	50	50	55	65	65	60	60	60		56	61	61	60	58	59	63	65	62	56	49	49	49	46	47	52	59	60	59	65	57.2
	MAX	77	80	79	76	85	80	77	83	85	80	82	82	82	82	84	84	87	85	80	71	71	75	80	72	76	76	74	86	84	87	88	80.3
	MIN	60	60	50	55	65	65	63	58	56	66	53	58	57	62	56	53	57	58	69	58	50	40	45	52	50	44	55	57	59	57	60	56.4
	MAX	79	83	83	82	80	88	86	88	88	88	85	86	81	85	85	83	90	90	86	73	74	76	79	78	78	79	77	89	88	88	90	83.4
	MIN	64	65	60	61	57	61	55	58	64	64	65	62	64	67	65	64	59	64	69	57	50	43	45	54	45	46	60	65	64	63	65	59.5
	MAX	75	76	78	77	74	83	77	78	85	83	80	83	80	79	82	82	86	85	83	72	67	67	72	76	71	74	76	78	87	84	83	78.5
	MIN	58	52	47	58	60	65	65	57	60	64	56	59	60	63	56	59	61	65	64	55	51	45	49	48	44	50	52	60	62	64	65	57.2
	MAX	82	81	80	80		68	81		87	85	85	83	80		87	87	90	88	86			78		78	75	78	79	88		72	82	81.7
	MIN	60	61	49	48		62	61		58	65	59	60	60		56	58	61	61	66			45		56	46	44	57	58		61	70	57.6
	MAX	85	83	88	85	85	86	81	78	87	84	86	88	86	84	85	88	91	91	87	75	64	69	75	81	75	78	80	80	92	88	90	83.1
	MIN	56	64	53	57	62	64	60	57	58	65	55	59	58	61	58	55	59	59	65	57	52	43	45	55	45	45	54	59	58	59	59	56.6
	MAX	71	78	72	75	73	78	66	69	79	81	76	78	77	76	78	78	81	83	76	70	65	66	69	74	68	71	73	70	81	81	81	74.6
	MIN	48	44	34	42	50	63	62	59	50	56	48	54	52	59	47	47	53	54	58	45	44	33	43	46	37	40	45	56	56	54	59	49.6
	MAX	81	79	80	75	80	84	72	84	88	82	85	85	82	81	84	87	89	90	87	77	70	69	78	72	75	85	78	89	85	85	89	81.5
	MIN	59	62	49	55	65	65	61	58	60	61	58	57	57	63	60	54	57	58	65	55	48	41	43	52	44	43	50	63	56	56	59	55.9
TA	MAX	83	82	81	77	76	70	81	85	88	87	85	87	88	83	85	88	89	89	87	80	71	73	75	76	77	80	79	90	85	85	89	82.3
	MIN	63	64	54	55	64	64	62	61	61	70	59	63	61	65	63	59	62	63	70	58	57	48	54	59	49	50	58	61	61	63	70	60.3
	MAX	81	84	81	79	78	71	71	80	87	89	86	85	88	85	84	87	87	88	91	88	64	72	76	76	76	78	80	82	90	85	85	81.7
	MIN	47	63	53	51	64	64	64	62	61	70	57	62	60	64	62	57	60	61	69	63	58	48	54	60	48	49	58	60	61	63	66	59.3
	MAX	79	82	75	79	81	72	72	79	84	89	80	85	77	72	80	79	84	86	82	74	67	69	75	77	70	71	75	72	83	83	84	78.0
	MIN	44	51	42	47	49	61	61	59	57	62	53	56	56	59	52	55	57	60	64	50	50	43	45	51	46	45	48	56	61	62	63	53.7
	MAX	81	83	82	79	78	70	80	82	84	88	85	86	86	80	82	87	88	94	84	75	76	78	83	81	81	77	86	93	98	85	95	82.5
	MIN	63	62	51	53	62	64	60	58	61	63	58	60	61	63	59	57	58	67	69	69	58	52	59	62	53	53	53	64	63	67	69	60.4
	MAX	82	83	81	80	76	71	69	79	88	90	86	87	86	75	86	87	88	90	91	84	66	74	78	79	77	77	80	74	92	88	88	81.7
	MIN	53	62	52	51	55	65	64	62	62	62	60	60	62	61	61	57	57	61	64	64	59	49	49	52	49	49	52	61	62	64	66	58.3
	MAX	76	77	77	72	84	78	78	84	83	80	83	80	79	81	82	85	86	80	72	67	69	74	75	70	76	77	77	87	84	82	86	78.7
	MIN	63	50	46	62	64	65	65	55	60	63	63	60	59	63	55	59	64	64	58	53	48	45	58	50	44	48	58	63	62	64	66	58.0
	MAX	83	80	80	76	71	71	80	87	89	85	86	86	81	86	87	88	89															
	MIN	59	59	47	50	63	64	65	61	60	65	57	64	62	65	57	60	61															
	MAX	75	77	77	74	76	76	69	69	80	84	77	81	78	73	77	80	82	84	84	79	62	69	71	78	69	71	79	69	84	80	82	76.2
	MIN	47	56	44	44	52	60	60	56	54	53	50	50	53	54	52	48	48	54	55	54	47	38	38	45	39	39	41	53	56	55	53	49.7
	MAX	84	80	82	80	71	72	84	88	87	92	90	88	85	89	90	92	94	91	94	77	67	78	78	81	77	77	83	95	87	87	87	84.1
	MIN	69	68	62	64	64	66	65	67	70	74	70	70	71	74	71	70	71	73	77	62	60	56	60	60	60	63	65	70	69	70	71	67.2
	MAX	82	78	75	75	77	72	73	82	88	80	82	82	79	80	84	86	88	86	75	68	71	74	78	69	77	75	73	89	85	83	89	79.2
	MIN	62	60	53	55	63	64	63	63	60	62	59	61	61	64	59	55	60	61	65	56	52	45	50	52	46	48	57	63	59	60	64	58.1
	MAX	74	75	77	76	71	81	74	76	83	83	79	83	80	79	81	81	84	85	80	73	66	68	72	74	70	74	74	76	86	83	84	77.5
	MIN	56	55	46	56	59	65	65	57	58	61	54	57	60	64	56	58	62	62	65	52	50	45	49	53	46	46	50	58	60	61	64	56.5
	MAX	77	78	76	73	84	80	77	83	84	82	82	80	80	81	82	84	85	85	80	71	77	74	74	72	74	75	78	87	84	82	85	79.5
	MIN	57	50	50	57	62	66	63	55	58	53	55	50	51	64	65	52	60	57	52	53	50	58	53	47	41	43	54	64	60	60	62	55.5
	MAX	85	81	80	78	71	72	80	85	90	87	88	89	83	84	87	89	89	93	86	71	73	76	77	75	80	81	82	94	88	89	90	83.0
	MIN	67	65	59	56	66	66	65	64	60	69	63	68	64	68	67	62	66	66	73	60	57	54	60	61	52	53	63	65	64	67	71	63.3
	MAX	80	80	81	77	87	79	78	83	86	81	84	82	81	82	82	85	87	88	76	70	72	74	77	70	73	77	75	85	83	83	86	80.1
	MIN	66	65	60	64	65	67	68	58	62	68	62	66	65	69	65	64	65	68	65	62	54	52	57	56	52	53	61	64	66	66	66	62.6
	MAX	72	75	69	72	75	68	66	76	79	82	78	78	76	69	77	77	80	84	84	75	65	68	70	70	67	70	73	72	79	80	79	74.4
	MIN	51	53	47	50	57	59	59	58	58	61	57	57	58	61	57	56	58	62	63	52	52	45	46	54	47	48	49	54	58	59	63	55.1
	MAX	83	79	78	79	77	70	80	83	86	86	86	84	82	83	86	87	89	89	87	73	68	76	74	74	75	78	79	91	87	82	86	81.2
	MIN	64	64	51	53	62	63	59	59	60	64	58	57	60	66	60	59	61	63	72	59	56	48	56	54	47	48	58	64	62	63	70	59.4
	MAX	83	80	80	78	70	69	80	83	87	85	85	86	81	82	85	83	89	91	86	70	73	75	75	79	75	78	80	90	90	86	90	81.3
	MIN	61	64	54	51	63	63	62	62	61	63	58	62	60	65	62	63	66	68	71	65	54	56	55	58	50	49	57	60	60	62	63	60.3

See Reference Notes Following Station Index

DAILY TEMPERATURES

Table 5 - Continued

Station		1	2	3	4	5	6	7	8	9	10	11	12	13	14	15	16	17	18	19	20	21	22	23	24	25	26	27	28	29	30	31
MT POCONO 2 N AP	MAX	78	76	72		71	63	75	78	82	79	79	77	75	77	80	83	84	83	77	72	65	64	68	69	70	69	72	84	83	75	76
	MIN	56	55	49	47		59	58	59	54	64	58	58	55	64	52	54	59	59	63	55	53	42	52	57	43	44	55	59	60	59	66
MUHLENBURG 1 SE	MAX	79	76	75	79	70	68	79	82	85	81	81	86	71	81	81	83	84	86	82	78	79	72	72	72	72	75	73	83	83	78	83
	MIN	55	53	46	45	56	59	56	61	56	60	54	56	56	60	59	57	57	59	61	53	59	40	50	56	42	42	56	56	56	58	63
NEWBURG 3 W	MAX	84	82	78	76	81	80	78	85	87	90	90	94	84	86	88	89	91	89	92	78	85	82	82	78	80	80	78	91	90	89	90
	MIN	72	72	62	67	69	61	71	60	60	68	65	68	65	66	67	66	73	72	71	56	62	54	57	56	52	53	62	67	73	79	80
NEW CASTLE 1 N	MAX	78	80	78	78	87	83	80	84	86	82	85	83	82	83	83	87	88	88	88	70	71	73	78	78	75	79	78	87	87	84	86
	MIN	64	53	50	58	66	65	65	57	57	63	56	60	61	64	51	55	61	64	65	54	48	44	53	49	40	48	60	64	63	63	66
NEWELL	MAX	84	81	83	86	78	87	80	82	86	87	82	85	89	81	84	86	89	88	90	78	70	73	76	81	74	77	80	82	89	89	88
	MIN	67	68	61	65	67	67	68	62	66	66	62	65	66	69	66	64	65	65	71	60	57	52	54	60	52	52	61	66	67	65	66
NEWPORT	MAX	81	83	82	82	78	70	71	81	86	88	85	87	88	76	85	87	88	89	90	85	65	77	76	79	77	78	80	80	92	87	88
	MIN	51	63	50	50	53	65	65	60	60	60	58	58	62	62	59	59	59	62	65	62	58	49	49	52	47	49	50	60	60	63	67
NEW STANTON	MAX	80	84	80	79	91	87	80	86	80	83	86	86	83	85	87	90	87	90	78	71	72	75	74	79	77	80	80	89	85	89	92
	MIN	61	58	58	60	68	62	60	52	60	59	55	58	62	63	59	53	56	60	62	58	45	44	46	44	43	43	55	63	60	57	65
NORRISTOWN	MAX	87	82	82	83	72	71	83	86	91	88	88	91	85	86	90	91	93	95	90	74	69	78	78	78	79	82	85	94	91	83	88
	MIN	68	69	57	57	65	66	65	64	65	72	64	70	65	71	66	65	65	67	74	62	59	54	57	62	54	54	62	68	65	68	72
PALMERTON	MAX	82	78	77	80	68	68	81	84	87	85	85	82	75	82	84	86	88	88	85	66	72	73	74	74	75	77	78	84	86	74	82
	MIN	63	58	48	50	54	65	62	62	61	69	61	63	62	66	59	59	63	63	69	62	58	48	61	56	48	47	60	61	64	66	71
PHIL DREXEL INST OF TEC	MAX	87	83	85	84	74	71	85	89	92	93	90	91	86	87	93	92	95	94	93	77	69	80	81	80	79	82	86	97	91	86	89
	MIN	70	70	64	63	67	67	66	67	71	76	70	71	70	73	70	71	71	73	76	64	60	57	60	63	58	61	64	72	69	72	72
PHILADELPHIA WB AP	MAX	85	80	80	80	72	71	83	85	89	88	86	89	85	85	88	89	90	93	90	75	68	78	78	77	77	80	83	93	89	85	89
	MIN	68	66	60	58	66	67	66	66	67	73	66	70	67	71	67	66	68	69	75	63	58	53	57	61	54	55	62	68	66	68	72
PHILADELPHIA PT BREEZE	MAX	86	82	82	81	70	72	84	86	89	89	87	90	86	85	89	90	91	93	90	72	68	77	79	79	78	80	81	93	89	87	88
	MIN	69	72	65	65	66	68	67	69	70	74	68	70	72	71	71	69	70	71	78	70	60	58	59	63	61	61	67	70	69	71	72
PHILADELPHIA SHAWMONT	MAX	84	83	80	81	78	70	82	84	89	88	87	90	90	85	88	90	91	92	89	72	66	78	79	78	77	79	83	92	93	90	
	MIN	67	67	56	55	66	66	64	63	63	71	63	69	65	68	65	63	65	65	74	64	60	55	55	61	53	53	60	66	65	68	
PHILADELPHIA CITY	MAX	83	80	82	80	71	72	84	86	89	88	87	89	84	84	90	90	91	92	90	77	68	77	77	78	76	78	81	91	87	82	88
	MIN	69	69	64	66	66	67	67	69	73	75	71	72	74	74	71	71	73	76	77	64	61	60	60	63	61	63	69	71	70	72	72
PHILIPSBURG CAA AP	MAX	76	73	74	70	69	63	68	80	83	79	78	79	73	79	79	82	84	81	75	60	69	70	73	68	69	73	68	84	80	81	84
	MIN	56	49	42	44	60	62	58	56	51	53	59	55	52	57	48	46	52	56	58	53	43	35	47	42	36	43	55	63	58	54	60
PHOENIXVILLE 1 E	MAX	86	85	83	84	75	71	84	87	92	90	92	92	88	90	88	91	93	95	95	88	69	80	78	80	82	83	85	97	90	92	89
	MIN	63	64	49	49	63	64	60	58	58	69	58	64	64	60	58	58	59	59	59	60	58	51	51	58	46	46	55	60	60	61	68
PIMPLE HILL	MAX	72	78	74	73	75	62	68	76	78	81	78	77	78	68	75	77	80	83	82	78	60	65	71	68	68	70	72	75	82	81	68
	MIN	58	54	46	54	57	58	57	58	61	62	58	63	60	62	58	60	61	66	65	52	52	47	53	54	48	53	57	58	59	63	63
PITTSBURGH WB AP 2	MAX	79	80	79	75	89	78	78	84	84	80	83	82	79	82	82	88	88	87	76	64	69	73	77	70	75	77	78	87	83	88	85
	MIN	66	61	58	63	65	66	66	61	66	65	65	64	66	68	64	65	68	68	63	57	51	46	53	54	50	53	61	67	64	65	65
PITTSBURGH WB CITY	MAX	79	82	82	75	88	80	79	86	87	83	86	85	82	84	85	89	92	89	78	66	72	75	78	73	76	78	79	90	86	86	89
	MIN	69	65	59	65	64	67	67	63	69	68	65	65	67	71	66	65	66	69	65	59	55	51	56	57	52	52	63	71	67	70	69
PLEASANT MOUNT 1 W	MAX	74	75	71	71	75	65	65	77	76	81	79	79	76	68	76	76	80	84	83	74	66	67	69	69	66	69	72	72	76	79	73
	MIN	46	48	41	43	54	60	54	55	55	63	53	55	50	57	52	52	54	59	65	52	53	39	44	52	41	42	49	54	57	58	61
PORT CLINTON	MAX	80	84	82	81	82	69	70	85	86	89	87	88	86	74	84	87	88	92	90	81	72	75	79	76	77	77	82	80	93	89	79
	MIN	53	61	44	46	52	51	59	58	56	61	55	61	52	61	55	57	59	60	65	60	56	45	49	59	44	43	49	57	59	61	64
PUTNEYVILLE 2 SE DAM	MAX	78	80	78	78	76	83	80	75	84	86	81	84	82	79	82	83	86	87	85	78	67	71	75	77	72	74	77	74	88	85	86
	MIN	53	54	46	54	58	62	64	54	57	60	53	56	58	61	53	52	56	58	62	54	45	41	42	49	43	44	45	56	60	58	59
QUAKERTOWN 1 E	MAX	83	82	78	80	76	68	80	83	87	86	85	85	82	82	85	87	88	92	89	81	71	76	76	78	75	78	80	90	89	83	84
	MIN	62	64	49	49	63	64	63	59	60	69	58	62	58	68	58	58	59	61	68	61	58	46	52	58	46	46	58	60	62	61	70
READING WB CITY	MAX	84	82	81	79	71	71	83	84	89	88	86	87	83	84	88	88	92	92	87	72	73	77	77	77	77	80	81	94	88	80	88
	MIN	68	67	58	57	65	66	64	65	65	72	67	68	64	71	67	65	67	70	72	61	60	54	59	62	55	54	63	68	67	68	72
RIDGWAY 3 W	MAX	78	77	76	74	68	80	70	83	83	79	82	80	77	80	80	83	85	79	75	67	68	70	75	69	70	74	70	75	82	83	87
	MIN	46	51	40	41	50	63	62	61	52	53	50	50	56	56	50	50	51	55	58	49	46	38	40	43	41	41	41	55	59	56	56
SALINA 3 W	MAX	78	80	78	74	85	85	79	82	85	83	82	80	79	81	82	86	89	86	85	73	69	72	76	76	73	77	75	88	81	84	87
	MIN	62	62	55	60	65	65	65	57	61	65	58	61	61	67	59	58	60	63	71	57	49	42	47	53	45	46	59	66	63	61	61
SCRANTON	MAX	76	81	76	78	81	67	72	80	83	87	83	84	80	76	84	82	85	89	80	80	67	73	76	75	73	74	78	77	86	84	70
	MIN	48	56	48	49	49	62	61	61	58	60	61	61	58	59	56	56	58	61	63	56	57	45	45	58	45	45	46	62	62	62	64
SCRANTON WB AIRPORT	MAX	80	75	76	80	70	67	80	81	85	83	82	80	74	82	82	84	87	88	80	65	72	73	74	71	73	76	76	86	83	79	84
	MIN	60	53	47	49	62	63	61	61	60	65	61	61	58	62	56	57	61	63	59	55	51	44	56	52	46	47	59	61	61	63	66
SELINSGROVE CAA AP	MAX	80	78	81	77	69	70	82	89	89	87	87	85	74	89	87	85	92	87	84	65	74	77	77	77	76	80	76	91	86	85	90
	MIN	60	53	46	50	64	65	63	59	61	60	57	62	62	63	56	60	62	62	62	58	51	48	50	51	46	47	61	63	63	65	67
SHIPPENSBURG	MAX	85	86	81	78	75	73	75	85	88	88	89	89	85	84	89	89	92	92	88	80	75	78	79	77	80	82	78	94	90	89	93
	MIN	63	66	54	57	63	65	64	61	65	70	63	63	62	70	68	59	62	64	74	57	57	49	51	63	47	52	57	61	60	63	64
SHIPPINGPORT WB	MAX	76	79	79	75	88	79	78	83	84	80	83	82	80	82	82	86	86	86	75	65	69	76	77	70	73	76	80	86	83	84	88
	MIN	64	57	56	61	66	66	62	58	62	62	60	62	62	65	60	59	61	65	63	56	49	51	51	40	48	48	59	66	64	64	65
SLIPPERY ROCK	MAX	78	80	76	73	86	80	80	85	80	81	85	82	79	84	84	82	86	85	81	69	72	72	77	74	75	79	73	87	84	85	86
	MIN	64	56	51	60	65	65	65	57	62	64	59	60	61	66	58	60	61	65	64	51	50	45	54	51	46	50	58	67	64	65	65
SOMERSET MAIN ST	MAX	77	75	76	72	81	75	73	80	83	81	82	80	78	76	80	82	82	83	80	69	63	70	75	74	71	75	71	85	80	83	85
	MIN	57	62	49	58	62	62	62	58	60	63	57	57	57	63	59	52	55	56	66	55	50	37	44	53	40	41	53	63	58	54	59
SPRINGBORO	MAX	75	77	78	78	72	76	78	78	83	83	80	82	80	82	81	80	85	88	80	73	68	70	74	76	69	76	75	78	87	88	84
	MIN	60	49	45	58	59	65	65	56	61	63	55	60	52	64	56	58	64	64	66	50	48	45	56	52	44	48	57	60	61	64	66
SPRINGS 1 SW	MAX	76	70	72	72	78	73	72	76	81	78	78	78	75	74	76	81	82	82	73	64	64	68	75	66	69	76	75	81	76	81	82
	MIN	57	56	57	57	62	58	62	59	57	57	53	53	54	62	57	56	53	54	63	52	48	37	42	46	39	41	46	62	55	54	58
STATE COLLEGE	MAX	79	78	77	74	70	65	73	84	86	81	82	82	77	82	84	85	88	84	80	65	70	74	76	71	74	78	72	88	85	85	87
	MIN	61	60	51	55	61	62	62	58	61	62	59	63	60	65	59	56	60	66	65	58	54	46	57	53	48	50	56	66	62	62	62
STROUDSBURG	MAX	83	80	76	85	68	66	80	85	88	86	87	86	75	83	85	87	89	92	85	66	63	74	73	77	79	82	82	89	88	75	82
	MIN	56	55	40	43	60	61	56	55	54	60	56	55	56	60	54	53	58	56	62	50	53	40	55	56	49	40	50	57	60	57	61
TAMARACK 2 S FIRE TWR	MAX																															
	MIN																															
TIONESTA 2 SE DAM	MAX	73	78	77	77	73	85	73	76	83	84	78	82	80	79	79	80	83	85	82	72	67	69	72	75	70	72	75	72	85	83	82
	MIN	54	55	45	47	57	65	64	57	57	57	56	56	60	62	55	54	56	61	55	53	50	42	44	53	46	47	47	57	61	61	61

See Reference Notes Following Station Index

ıble 5 · Continued

DAILY TEMPERATURES

PENNSYLVANIA
AUGUST 1956

Station		1	2	3	4	5	6	7	8	9	10	11	12	13	14	15	16	17	18	19	20	21	22	23	24	25	26	27	28	29	30	31	Average
TUSVILLE WATER WORKS	MAX	79	75	78	73	84	73	76	84	86	79	85	77	81	84	75	86	86	84	72	70	68	73	72	71	73	75	76	85	86	83	87	78.6
	MIN	60	52	39	53	62	68	63	54	54	59	51	57	57	61	52	52	59	59	63	58	47	40	49	52	42	44	53	60	58	57	62	54.7
WANDA	MAX	81	76	78	83	69	72	79	84	88	84	86	83	76	84	84	88	90	87	79	69	73	76	78	74	76	79	76	87	86	86	89	80.6
	MIN	58	55	40	47	61	64	61	59	56	64	53	59	54	54	51	56	58	59	64	52	53	43	48	58	42	41	56	57	60	63	66	55.4
IONTOWN	MAX	80	78	81	76	86	77	80	83	86	82	84	85	78	78	83	85	87	87	75	68	70	73	78	73	75	77	76	87	82	85	87	80.1
	MIN	65	67	62	66	66	65	66	59	65	67	60	62	64	67	66	59	61	64	68	58	54	45	50	59	46	47	57	68	65	63	66	61.2
PER DARBY	MAX	86	81	81	81	75	70	83	81	90	88	88	90	85	85	88	90	91	92	90	82	68	78	78	78	78	80	83	93	89	85	89	83.7
	MIN	66	70	59	57	58	66	65	68	67	73	65	68	67	69	66	65	67	68	75	63	59	53	56	60	54	55	62	68	65	69	71	64.3
RREN	MAX	82	76	78	73	83	75	71	83	86	79	83	80	80	81	80	85	87	79	73	69	68	73	75	71	75	75	73	85	85	84	87	78.5
	MIN	62	55	40	50	61	65	63	59	56	66	55	60	58	62	54	54	60	61	65	52	49	42	53	49	44	48	57	61	61	60	65	56.4
YNESBURG 2 W	MAX	80	81	82	79	90	81	80	85	86	82	85	85	82	83	85	87	88	88	80	80	72	78	78	76	75	79	80	88	84	86	83	82.2
	MIN	61	64	54	61	65	64	62	55	60	60	56	59	60	65	61	57	59	60	65	58	48	43	45	52	44	44	54	59	59	59	59	57.2
LLSBORO 3 S	MAX	73	77	72	73	76	65	67	73	81	81	79	80	78	74	80	80	82	83	78	74	65	69	72	73	69	71	74	69	84	83	81	75.4
	MIN	53	54	42	48	54	59	59	57	59	63	55	58	58	62	55	55	59	63	64	50	48	43	47	52	46	49	54	58	59	62	64	54.8
LLSVILLE	MAX	81	80	78	75	70	71	79	84	87	86	86	87	84	84	86	87	89	90	87	74	72	75	77	76	77	80	80	100	96	100	99	83.1
	MIN	62	64	52	50	63	64	64	60	66	61	56	60	59	62	59	56	60	61	67	58	57	46	52	59	45	50	56	67	65	67	70	59.3
ST CHESTER	MAX	87	83	83	81	79	70	74	87	93	90	90	91	84	86	90	91	93	94	92	87	66	79	79	79	80	81	86	85	90	86	87	84.6
	MIN	59	68	60	64	65	63	64	67	73	66	69	67	70	66	68	67	69	71	65	59	54	57	61	56	56	54	66	66	69	70	70	64.5
LLIAMSPORT WB AP	MAX	84	85	81	80	69	73	80	85	89	87	87	86	74	86	88	87	90	84	84	68	75	75	75	75	77	79	75	86	87	85	88	81.4
	MIN	61	54	47	51	63	64	64	60	59	65	58	63	62	63	57	60	61	65	60	58	53	48	55	54	47	49	61	59	63	66	66	58.6
RK 3 SSW PUMP STA	MAX	86	84	83	81	76	73	82	85	89	87	88	89	88	85	88	89	90	93	91	83	75	77	78	78	78	81	81	93	92	89	93	84.7
	MIN	63	63	52	54	65	65	65	59	61	70	58	63	62	66	62	59	61	63	72	59	59	48	56	61	48	52	58	60	62	64	70	60.6

ıble 6

EVAPORATION AND WIND

Station		1	2	3	4	5	6	7	8	9	10	11	12	13	14	15	16	17	18	19	20	21	22	23	24	25	26	27	28	29	30	31	Total or Avg.
ONFLUENCE 1 SW DAM	EVAP	.15	.10	.06	.16	.10	-	.06	.08	.16	.18	.16	.18	.16	.06	.16	.15	.18	.18	.18	.05	.13	.15	.20	.15	.15	.16	.14	.11	.06	.12	.15	B4.16
	WIND	33	35	25	29	35	54	31	35	39	43	43	30	40	50	44	24	22	23	54	36	22	43	24	55	59	23	26	36	30	22	34	1099
ORD CITY 4 S DAM	EVAP	.09	.07	.17	.35	-	-	.02	.18	.15	.13	.19	.14	.16	.06	.16	.16	.13	.12	.13	.13	.03	.14	.12	.21	.15	.12	.13	.04	.18	.12	.11	B4.16
	WIND	13	10	28	16	15	38	30	19	30	26	29	27	37	22	26	15	9	16	52	30	16	27	16	45	31	8	32	15	33	13	27	751
AWLEY 1 S DAM	EVAP	.15	.14	.21	.21	.18	.13	.00	.16	.20	.21	.24	.21	.12	.02	.18	.16	.16	.20	.24	.12	.02	.08	.15	.14	.18	.15	.17	.13	.17	.16	.05	4.64
	WIND	32	30	36	38	45	15	33	38	50	106	79	74	16	74	53	39	27	41	139	42	17	26	58	91	70	59	66	117	79	34	21	1645
AMESTOWN 2 NW	EVAP	.10	.12	.24	.17	-	.12	.14	.21	.20	.08	.25	-	.11	.13	.17	.19	.14	.18	.00	.01	.15	.22	.15	.00	.23	.23	*	*	.24	.18	.14	B4.38
	WIND	6	13	30	15	23	18	25	23	15	32	22	21	14	43	17	17	19	16	31	23	21	24	26	50	26	18	12	40	19	22	28	709
ANDISVILLE	EVAP	.20	.20	.34	.25	.12	.01	.10	.12	.12	.30	.31	.21	.25	.07	.15	.22	.17	.32	.22	.22	-	.14	.15	.18	.26	.19	.13	.13	.24	.21	.12	B5.84
	WIND	16	29	15	56	35	11	48	21	35	14	42	26	20	18	20	18	3	31	31	52	35	21	21	52	34	18	15	13	35	10	22	817
IMPLE HILL	EVAP	.18	.19	.24	.22	.23	.03	.03	.18	.24	.26	.26	.23	.13	.15	.17	.14	*	*	*	10.3	.21	.09	.17	.04	.19	.26	.21	.10	.25	.15	.04	5.62
	WIND	49	50	46	29	67	60	63	42	25	144	121	71	35	102	73	32	*	*	*	253	32	32	75	120	61	66	57	97	74	28	93	1997
TATE COLLEGE	EVAP	.15	.11	.22	.10	.19	.01	-	.04	.18	.17	.21	.23	.19	.03	.18	.21	.18	.15	.17	.15	.01	.15	.16	.18	.20	.16	.15	.04	.19	.14	.18	B4.58
	WIND	15	17	20	15	13	10	4	8	32	29	51	35	36	30	40	33	25	12	34	53	13	14	32	64	61	28	*	53	38	24	30	869

SUPPLEMENTAL DATA

Station	Wind direction		Wind speed m. p. h.				Relative humidity averages - percent				Number of days with precipitation								
	Prevailing	Percent of time from prevailing	Average	Fastest mile	Direction of fastest mile	Date of fastest mile	1:30 a EST	7:30 a EST	1:30 p EST	7:30 p EST	Trace	.01–.09	.10–.49	.50–.99	1.00–1.99	2.00 and over	Total	Percent of possible sunshine	Average sky cover sunrise to sunset
ALLENTOWN WB AIRPORT	WSW	18	7.8	-	-	-	90	86	56	73	8	3	5	2	1	0	19	-	5.7
HARRISBURG WB AIRPORT	W	15	5.6	30	NW	28	82	80	53	68	9	2	4	1	1	0	17	73	5.5
PHILADELPHIA WB AIRPORT	SW	14	8.1	26	NW	19	83	78	51	67	3	2	2	2	1	0	10	64	5.7
PITTSBURGH WB AIRPORT	WSW	22	9.2	46*	NW	5	84	87	57	69	6	5	3	2	0	1	17	60	6.7
READING WB CITY	-	-	7.8	34	N	12	-	-	-	-	3	3	3	3	0	0	12	67	5.5
SCRANTON WB AIRPORT	SW	16	5.6	50	NE	28	86	83	56	72	3	7	7	0	1	0	18	55	6.4
SHIPPINGPORT WB	-	-	1.7	55††	NW	5	-	-	-	-	5	2	3	3	0	1	14	-	6.3
WILLIAMSPORT WB AIRPORT	-	-	-	-	-	-	-	92	56	74	4	6	6	3	0	0	19	-	6.4

* This datum is obtained by visual observation since recording equipment is not available. It is not necessarily the fastest mile occurring during the period.
†† Peak Gust

See Reference Notes Following Station Index

STATION INDEX

Station	Index No.	County	Drainage 1	Latitude	Longitude	Elevation	Observation Time Temp.	Observation Time Precip.	Observer	Refer To Tables
ACHETONIA LOCK 3	0022	ALLEGHENY	1	40 32	79 48	748		7A	CORPS OF ENGINEERS	3
ALLENS MILLS	0090	JEFFERSON	1	41 12	78 55	1600		MID	CHARLES M. ALLEN	C
ALLENTOWN WB AP	0106	LEHIGH	9	40 39	75 26	376	MID	MID	U.S. WEATHER BUREAU	2 3 5 7 C
ALLENTOWN GAS CO	0111	LEHIGH	9	40 36	75 28	294	7A	7A	LEHIGH VLY GAS DIV	2 3 5
ALTOONA HORSESHOE CURVE	0134	BLAIR	6	40 30	78 29	1500	6P	6P	ALTOONA WATER BUR.	2 3 5 7
ARENDTSVILLE	0229	ADAMS	15	39 55	77 18	710	8A	8A	PA STATE COL EXP	2 3 5
ARTEMAS 1 WNW	0259	BEDFORD	12	39 45	78 28	1250	6P	6P	GRAYSON E.NORTHCRAFT	2 3 5 7 C
AUSTINBURG 2 W	0313	TIOGA	15	42 00	77 32	1590		7A	OTTO D. BACON	3 C
BAKERSTOWN 3 WNW	0355	ALLEGHENY	1	40 39	79 59	1230	7P	7P	PGH CUT FLOWER CO	2 3 5
BARNES	0409	WARREN	1	41 40	79 02	1310		7A	CORPS OF ENGINEERS	3
BEAR GAP	0457	NORTHUMBLAND	15	40 50	76 30	900		MID	ROARING CRK WTR CO	3
BEAVER FALLS	0475	BEAVER	2	40 46	80 19	760		7A	HOWARD R. KEMP	3
BEAVERTOWN	0482	SNYDER	15	40 45	77 10	640	7A	7A	MARLIN RC ETTINGER	2 3 5 7
BEECH CREEK STATION	0499	CENTRE	16	41 04	77 34	620		7A	HAROLD S. RUPERT	3
BELLEFONTE 4 S	0530	CENTRE	16	40 51	77 47	1110	8A	8A	ROCKVIEW PRISON FARM	2 3 5 7
BERWICK	0611	COLUMBIA	15	41 04	76 15	570	6P	6P	AMER CAR + FNDRY CO	2 3 5 7
BETHLEHEM	0629	NORTHAMPTON	9	40 37	75 22	400		7A	ARTHUR CROPPER	3
#BETHLEHEM LEHIGH UNIV	0634	NORTHAMPTON	9	40 36	75 23	450	MID	MID	LEHIGH UNIVERSITY	2 3 5 C
BLAIN	0725	PERRY	15	40 20	77 31	750		MID	PA DEPT FRST + WTRS	C
BLAIRSVILLE 6 ENE	0736	INDIANA	4	40 27	79 09	2048	8P	8P	U.S. WEATHER BUREAU	2 3 5
BLAKESLEE CORNERS	0743	MONROE	9	41 05	75 36	1650		MID	WALTER WILDRICK	C
BLOSERVILLE 1 N	0763	CUMBERLAND	15	40 16	77 22	650		5P	MRS. B. M. WILLDERS	3
BOSWELL 6 WNW	0820	SOMERSET	1	40 11	79 08	2580		7A	MRS. MAE L. KIMMEL	3 C
BRADDOCK LOCK 2	0861	ALLEGHENY	10	40 24	79 52	725		7A	CORPS OF ENGINEERS	3
BRADFORD CNTRL FIRE STA	0867	MC KEAN	1	41 57	78 39	1500		8A	BRADFORD FIRE DEPT	3
BRADFORD 4 W RES	0868	MC KEAN	1	41 57	78 44	1680	5P	5P	BRADFORD WTR DEPT	2 3 5 7
BREEZEWOOD	0905	BEDFORD	6	40 00	78 14	1352		MID	PA TURNPIKE COMM	3
BROOKVILLE CAA AIRPORT	1002	JEFFERSON	1	41 09	79 06	1417	MID	MID	CIVIL AERO. ADM.	2 3 5 7
BRUCETON 1 S	1033	ALLEGHENY	10	40 18	79 59	1065		7A	AUSTIN R. COOPER	3
BUCKSTOWN 1 SE	1073	SOMERSET	4	40 04	78 50	2460		MID	ALVIN W. MANGES	C
BUFFALO MILLS	1087	BEDFORD	6	39 58	78 39	1318		7A	MRS. NELLE R. BROWN	3
BURGETTSTOWN 2 W	1105	WASHINGTON	11	40 23	80 26	980	7A	7A	SMITH TWP MUN AUTH	2 3 5 7
BURNT CABINS 2 NE	1115	HUNTINGDON	6	40 05	77 52	990	MID	MID	PA TURNPIKE COMM	2 3 5 7
#BUTLER	1130	BUTLER	2	40 52	79 54	1100	4P	7A	WILLIAM C. FAUST	2 3 5 7
BUTLER SUBSTATION	1135	BUTLER	2	40 51	79 53	1140		MID	WEST PENN POWER CO	C
CAMP HILL	1198	CUMBERLAND	15	40 15	76 55	461		6P	JOSEPH N. HOBART	3
CANTON 1 NW	1215	BRADFORD	15	41 40	76 52	1520	7A	7A	MRS.MILDRED SPENCER	2 3 5 7 C
CARLISLE	1234	CUMBERLAND	15	40 12	77 11	460	6P	6P	C. E. MILLER	2 3 5 7
CARROLLTOWN 2 SSE	1255	CAMBRIA	16	40 35	78 42	2040		8A	ROBERT F. MAURER	3
CARTER CAMP 2 W	1262	POTTER	16	41 37	77 45	2030		7A	RICHARD L. MENKEN	3 C
CEDAR RUN	1301	LYCOMING	16	41 31	77 27	800		7A	KATHRYN T.KREIGHBAUM	3
CHADDS FORD	1342	DELAWARE	5	39 52	75 36	160		8A	MRS.GRACE A. WICKS	3
CHAMBERSBURG 1 ESE	1354	FRANKLIN	12	39 56	77 38	640	9P	9P	CHARLES A. BENDER	2 3 5 7 C
CHARLEROI	1372	WASHINGTON	10	40 08	79 55	1040		MID	WEST PENN POWER CO	C
CHARLEROI LOCK 4	1377	WESTMORELAND	10	40 09	79 54	749		7A	CORPS OF ENGINEERS	3
#CHESTER	1423	DELAWARE	5	39 51	75 21	86	8A	8A	CHESTER TIMES	2 3 5
CLARENCE 1 E	1480	CENTRE	16	41 03	77 56	1440		7A	MARGARET A. SWANCER	3
CLARION 3 SW	1485	CLARION	1	41 12	79 26	1114	8P	7A	PA ELECTRIC CO	2 5 7 C
CLAUSSVILLE	1505	LEHIGH	9	40 37	75 39	670		8A	WILLIAM J. DOTTERER	3
CLAYSVILLE 3 W	1512	WASHINGTON	11	40 07	80 28	1000	7P	7A	MFGRS. L + W CO	2 3 5
CLEARFIELD	1519	CLEARFIELD	16	41 01	78 26	1100		7A	IRA TAYLOR	3
CLERMONT	1529	MC KEAN	1	41 41	78 30	2104		7A	MRS.TILLIE M.SIMONDS	3 C
COALDALE 2 NW	1572	SCHUYLKILL	9	40 50	75 56	1026		7A	PANTHER VLY WTR CO	3
COATESVILLE 1 SW	1589	CHESTER	5	39 58	75 50	342	8A	8A	PHILA ELECTRIC CO	2 3 5 7 C
COATESVILLE	1594	CHESTER	5	39 59	75 49	340		8A	EDWARD D. BIEDEMAN	INAC 12/55
COLUMBIA	1675	LANCASTER	15	40 02	76 30	300	SS	SS	JAMES H. RUST	2 3 5
CONFLUENCE 1 SW DAM	1705	SOMERSET	17	39 48	79 22	1490	8A	8A	CORPS OF ENGINEERS	2 3 5 6 C
CONFLUENCE 1 NW	1710	FAYETTE	17	39 50	79 22	1331		7A	JOHN L. REID	3
CONNELLSVILLE	1723	FAYETTE	17	40 01	79 36	870		8A	MARSHALL B. MENEFEE	3
CONNELLSVILLE 2 E	1729	FAYETTE	17	40 01	79 33	1300		MID	HARRY C. JOY	C
CONSHOHOCKEN	1737	MONTGOMERY	5	40 04	75 19	70		8A	PHILA ELECTRIC CO	3
COOKSBURG	1749	CLARION	1	41 20	79 13	1180		8A	PA DEPT FRST + WTRS	3
COOKSBURG 2 NNW	1752	CLARION	1	41 21	79 13	1460		8A	PA DEPT FRST + WTRS	3
CORAOPOLIS NEVILLE IS	1773	ALLEGHENY	11	40 30	80 05	720		8A	PGH. COKE + CHEM CO	3
CORRY	1790	ERIE	1	41 56	79 38	1427	7P	5A	LEO C. NECKERS	2 3 5 7
COUDERSPORT 3 NW	1806	POTTER	1	41 49	78 03	2020	7P	8A	MISS ELIZABETH NEFF	2 3 5 7
COUDERSPORT 7 E	1809	POTTER	1	41 46	77 53	2425		7A	CAMP POTATO	3
COVINGTON	1832	TIOGA	15	41 45	77 05	1193		7A	GROVER D. CLEVELAND	3
CREEKSIDE	1881	INDIANA	1	40 41	79 12	1035		7A	CORPS OF ENGINEERS	3
CRESSON 2 SE	1895	CAMBRIA	6	40 27	78 34	2540		7A	MILES A. VECELLIO	3 C
CUSTER CITY 2 W	1978	MC KEAN	1	41 55	78 41	2120		8A	M. D. BOOTH AND CO	3
DANVILLE	2013	MONTOUR	15	40 58	76 37	460		7A	MRS.MARIE M. LITTLE	3
DERRY	2108	WESTMORELAND	4	40 20	79 18	1150	6P	6P	MISS N. D. WINEMAN	2 3 5
DEVAULT 1 W	2116	CHESTER	14	40 05	75 33	360	MID	MID	PA TURNPIKE COMM	2 3 5
DINGMANS FERRY	2160	PIKE	5	41 13	74 52	364		MID	CLYDE T. VOORHEES	C
DIXON	2171	WYOMING	15	41 34	75 54	620	7A	7A	HAROLD J. KUSCHEL	2 3 5 7 C
DONEGAL	2183	WESTMORELAND	17	40 07	79 23	1746	MID	MID	PA TURNPIKE COMM	2 3 5 7
#DONORA	2190	WASHINGTON	10	40 11	79 51	814	12M	12M	DONORA ZINC WORKS	2 3 5
DOYLESTOWN	2221	BUCKS	5	40 18	75 08	393		5P	GEORGE HART	3
DRIFTWOOD	2245	CAMERON	16	41 20	78 08	880		MID	SIDNEY KENNEDY	C
DU BOIS 7 E	2265	CLEARFIELD	16	41 06	78 38	1670	5P	5P	CITY OF DU BOIS	2 3 5 C
DUNLO	2298	CAMBRIA	4	40 17	78 43	2410		MID	MRS. D. L. WHITE	C
DUSHORE 3 NE	2324	SULLIVAN	16	41 33	76 21	1750		7A	PATRICK F. RYAN	3 C
EAGLES MERE	2343	SULLIVAN	16	41 24	76 35	2020	7A	7A	MRS.ELSIE P. BIGGER	2 3 5 7 C
EAST BRADY	2363	CLARION	1	40 59	79 37	820	5P	5P	A. B. KEMPEL	2 3 5
EAST WATERFORD 3 E	2459	PERRY	6	40 21	77 33	2125	8A	8A	U.S. WEATHER BUREAU	INAC 5/55
EBENSBURG	2466	CAMBRIA	4	40 29	78 43	2090	7P	7A	ROBERT A. WASSER	2 3 5
EDINBORO	2514	ERIE	1	41 52	80 08	1220		8A	EDINBORO ST TCHR COL	3
ELIZABETHTOWN	2560	LANCASTER	15	40 09	76 37	460		8A	MASONIC HOME	3
ENGLISH CENTER	2644	LYCOMING	16	41 26	77 17	881		7A	WILLIAM SUDERS	3 C
EPHRATA	2662	LANCASTER	15	40 11	76 10	465	6P	6P	STANLEY L.VON NEIDA	2 3 5
EQUINUNK	2669	WAYNE	5	41 51	75 13	900		8A	MRS.ROSE M. NEILSEN	3
ERIE CAA AIRPORT	2682	ERIE	8	42 05	80 12	732	MID	MID	CIVIL AERO. ADM.	2 3 5
EVERETT 1 SW	2721	BEDFORD	6	40 00	78 23	1020	MID	MID	PA TURNPIKE COMM	2 3 5 7 C
FARRELL SHARON	2814	MERCER	2	41 14	80 30	865	7P	7P	SHARON STEEL CORP	2 3 5
FORD CITY 4 S DAM	2942	ARMSTRONG	1	40 43	79 30	950	8A	8A	CORPS OF ENGINEERS	2 3 5 6 7 C
FRANKLIN	3028	VENANGO	1	41 23	79 49	987	7P	7A	JAMES K. ELLIOTT	2 3 5 7 C
FREELAND	3056	LUZERNE	15	41 01	75 54	1900	6P	8A	ANDREW B. EVANSHA	2 3 5
GALETON	3130	POTTER	16	41 44	77 39	1325		7A	W. GALE LUSH	3
GEIGERTOWN	3189	BERKS	14	40 13	75 50	400		8A	WALTER C. WOLF	3
GEORGE SCHOOL	3200	BUCKS	5	40 13	74 56	135	7P	7P	GEORGE M. HART	2 3 5 7
#GETTYSBURG	3218	ADAMS	12	39 50	77 14	540	9A	9A	HUGH C. MC ILHENNY	2 3 5 7
GETTYSBURG 1 S	3223	ADAMS	12	39 48	77 14	560		MID	NAT MILITARY PARK	C
GIFFORD	3237	MC KEAN	1	41 51	78 36	2220		8A	SOUTH PENN OIL CO	3
GLENCOE	3298	SOMERSET	12	39 49	78 51	1620		MID	MRS. MARY M.HARTMAN	C
GLEN HAZEL 2 NE DAM	3311	ELK	1	41 34	78 36	1725		8A	CORPS OF ENGINEERS	3 C
GLEN ROCK	3330	YORK	15	39 48	76 44	620		MID	MRS.E.C.MC WILLIAMS	C
GLENWILLARD DASH DAM	3343	ALLEGHENY	11	40 33	80 13	705		7A	CORPS OF ENGINEERS	3
GOULDSBORO	3394	WAYNE	9	41 15	75 27	1890		7A	L. H. EILENBERGER	3
GRATERFORD	3435	MONTGOMERY	14	40 14	75 27	160		7A	CLAUDE K. KULP	3
GRATZ 1 N	3438	DAUPHIN	15	40 38	76 43	760	8A	8A	LEE M. LEITZEL	2 3 5 7 C
GREENSBORO LOCK 7	3503	GREENE	10	39 47	79 55	808		7A	CORPS OF ENGINEERS	3
GREENSBURG 2 E	3515	WESTMORELAND	10	40 18	79 31	1225		MID	PA DEPT HIGHWAYS	C
GREENSBURG 3 SE	3516	WESTMORELAND	10	40 17	79 30	1245		6P	WESTMORELAND WTR CO	3
GREENVILLE	3526	MERCER	2	41 24	80 23	1026	6P	6P	C. EARL MILLER	2 3 5 7
HANOVER	3662	YORK	15	39 48	76 59	600	8A	8A	HANOVER EVENING SUN	2 3 5
#HARRISBURG WB AP	3699	YORK	15	40 13	76 51	335	MID	MID	U.S. WEATHER BUREAU	2 3 5 7 C
HARRISBURG NORTH	3704	DAUPHIN	15	40 18	76 54	323		9A	GEORGE S. BEAL	3
HAWLEY	3758	WAYNE	5	41 29	75 10	880		7A	MRS.KATHERINE S.BATE	3
HAWLEY 1 S DAM	3761	WAYNE	5	41 28	75 11	1200	7A	7A	PA POWER + LIGHT CO	2 3 5 6 7 C
HOLLIDAYSBURG	4001	BLAIR	6	40 26	78 24	960		MID	JOHN M. RINGLER	C
HOLLISTERVILLE	4008	WAYNE	5	41 23	75 26	1360		8A	PA POWER + LIGHT CO	3
#HOLTWOOD	4019	LANCASTER	15	39 50	76 20	187	MID	8A	PA POWER + LIGHT CO	2 3 5 C
HOME	4027	INDIANA	1	40 45	79 06	1220		MID	MRS. EDNA M. BUSH	C
HONESDALE 4 NW	4043	WAYNE	5	41 37	75 19	1410		9A	GEORGE C. WILLIAMS	3
HONESDALE 6 NNW	4044	WAYNE	5	41 39	75 17	1050		MID	FRIEND E. WALTER	C
HOOVERSVILLE	4058	SOMERSET	4	40 09	78 55	1660		7A	PA ELECTRIC CO	3
HOP BOTTOM 2 SE	4066	SUSQUEHANNA	15	41 43	75 43	900		7A	JOSEPH J. SANSUSKAS	3
HUNTINGDON	4159	HUNTINGDON	15	40 29	78 01	660	7A	7A	JOHN R. HENDERSON	2 3 5 7
HUNTSDALE	4166	CUMBERLAND	15	40 06	77 18	610		8A	METRO P. DOROSH	3 C
HYNDMAN	4190	BEDFORD	12	39 49	78 43	920		8A	MRS.GERTRUDE M.BURTO	3
INDIANA 3 SE	4214	INDIANA	4	40 36	79 07	1102	7P	7A	CLYMER WATER SVC CO	2 3 5 7 C
IRWIN	4276	WESTMORELAND	10	40 20	79 42	1100	5P	5P	WESTMORELAND WTR CO	2 3 5
JACKSON SUMMIT	4304	TIOGA	15	41 57	77 01	1690		MID	ARCHIE LAIN	C
JAMESTOWN 2 NW	4325	CRAWFORD	2	41 30	80 28	1050	8A	8A	PA DEPT FRST + WTRS	2 3 5 6 C
JIM THORPE	4370	CARBON	9	40 52	75 45	830	5P	5P	HENRY S. HAAK	2 3 5
#JOHNSTOWN	4385	CAMBRIA	4	40 20	78 55	1214	9A	9A	JOHNSTOWN TRIBUNE	2 3 5 7
JOHNSTOWN 2	4390	CAMBRIA	4	40 19	78 55	1275		MID	CITY OF JOHNSTOWN	C
KANE 1 NNE	4432	MC KEAN	1	41 41	78 48	1750	8A	8A	SPRING WATER CO	2 3 5 7 C
KARTHAUS	4450	CLEARFIELD	16	41 07	78 07	950		7A	JEROME S. HOWE	3
KEATING SUMMIT	4466	POTTER	1	41 41	78 11	1840		7A	EUGENE L. KREITNER	3
KEGG	4481	BEDFORD	6	39 59	78 43	1280	MID	MID	PA TURNPIKE COMM	2 3 5
KITTANNING LOCK 7	4611	ARMSTRONG	1	40 49	79 32	790		VAR	CORPS OF ENGINEERS	3
KREGAR 4 SE	4667	WESTMORELAND	17	40 06	79 14	2530		MID	PA TURNPIKE COMM	3
KRESGEVILLE 3 W	4672	CARBON	9	40 54	75 34	720		9A	CITY OF BETHLEHEM	3
LAFAYETTE MC KEAN PARK	4706	MC KEAN	1	41 48	78 40	2130		8A	CHARLES GORDON	INAC 2/56
LAKEVILLE 1 NNE	4733	WAYNE	5	41 27	75 16	1480		8A	MRS. GLADYS REINEKE	3
LANCASTER 2 NE PUMP STA	4758	LANCASTER	15	40 03	76 17	255	6P	6P	LANCASTER WATER BUR	2 3 5
LANCASTER 2 NE FILT PL	4763	LANCASTER	15	40 03	76 17	270		MID	LANCASTER WATER BUR	C
LANDISVILLE 2 NW	4778	LANCASTER	15	40 07	76 26	360	8A	8A	PA STATE COLLEGE	2 3 5 6 7 C
LATROBE	4832	WESTMORELAND	4	40 19	79 23	1000		MID	WEST PENN POWER CO	INAC 6/56
LAURELTON STATE VILLAGE	4853	UNION	15	40 54	77 13	880		MID	PA DEPT OF WELFARE	C
LAWRENCEVILLE 2 S	4873	TIOGA	15	41 59	77 07	1000	7A	7A	HARRY P. HOWLAND	2 3 5 7
LEBANON 3 W	4891	LEBANON	15	40 20	76 29	460	7A	7A	LEON MILLER	2 3 5 7
LEBANON 3 SW	4896	LEBANON	15	40 19	76 28	490		MID	THOMAS DONNACHIE	C
LEHIGHTON	4934	CARBON	9	40 50	75 43	580		7A	GOODWIN S. DEFREHN	3
LE ROY	4972	BRADFORD	15	41 41	76 43	1040		6P	MRS.DIMMIS M.BAILEY	3
LEWIS RUN 3 S	4984	MC KEAN	1	41 50	78 39	1740		7A	RUSSELL LINEMAN	3 C
LEWISTOWN	4992	MIFFLIN	6	40 35	77 35	480	7A	7A	AMERICAN VISCOSE CO	2 3 5 7 C
LINESVILLE 5 WNW	5050	CRAWFORD	2	41 41	80 31	1020	7P	8A	MISS RETTA M. CRUMB	2 3 5
LOCK HAVEN	5104	CLINTON	16	41 08	77 27	570	7P	7A	PETER L. STEVENSON	2 3 5 7
LOCK HAVEN 2	5109	CLINTON	16	41 08	77 27	630		MID	HUGH F. PARKER	
LONG POND 2 W	5160	MONROE	9	41 03	75 30	1860		7A	THOMAS MECKES	3
MADERA	5336	CLEARFIELD	16	40 50	78 26	1460	7A	7A	MRS. JULIA J. SHOFF	2 3 5
MAHAFFEY	5342	CLEARFIELD	16	40 53	78 44	1280		7A	MISS ELLEN J. MILES	3
MAPLE GLEN	5368	MONTGOMERY	5	40 11	75 11	380		6P	FRANCES E.SCHEIBNER	3
MAPLETON DEPOT	5381	HUNTINGDON	6	40 24	77 56	580		7A	MRS. I. S. BUCHANAN	3
MARCUS HOOK	5390	DELAWARE	5	39 49	75 25	12	MID	MID	SUN OIL CO	2 3 5
MARIENVILLE 1 SW	5400	FOREST	1	41 27	79 09	1700		MID	RUY A. MARKER	C
MARION CENTER 2 SE	5408	INDIANA	1	40 45	79 02	1610		7A	CORPS OF ENGINEERS	3
MARTINSBURG 1 SW	5453	BLAIR	6	40 18	78 20	1360		MID	BLUE MT. CANNERIES	
MARTINSBURG CAA AP	5454	BLAIR	6	40 18	78 19	1463	MID	MID	CIVIL AERO. ADM.	2 3 5
MATAMORAS	5470	PIKE	5	41 22	74 42	439		7A	HARRY BISLAND	3
MAYBURG	5490	FOREST	1	41 36	79 13	1150		7A	CORPS OF ENGINEERS	3
MC CONNELLSBURG	5526	FULTON	12	39 56	78 00	895		8A	MRS. HELEN M. SHIVES	3
MC KEESPORT	5573	ALLEGHENY	10	40 21	79 52	720		8A	NATIONAL TUBE CO	3
MEADOW RUN PONDS	5601	LUZERNE	15	41 13	75 40	1995		MID	GEORGE PEARAGE	C
MEADVILLE 1 S	5606	CRAWFORD	1	41 38	80 10	1065	8A	8A	CITY OF MEADVILLE	2 3 5 7 C
MEDIX RUN	5627	ELK	16	41 17	78 24	1100		7A	MRS.E. M. SNYDER	3 C
MERCER 2 NNE	5651	MERCER	2	41 15	80 13	1160	7P	7A	WILLIAM K. STROTHERS	2 3 5 7
MERCER HIWAY SHED	5654	MERCER	2	41 14	80 15	1250		MID	PA DEPT HIGHWAYS	
MERCERSBURG	5662	FRANKLIN	12	39 50	77 54	605		8A	ROLLIN P. GILBERT	3
MERWINSBURG	5678	MONROE	9	40 58	75 28	970		MID	WILLIAM D. GOULD	
MEYERSDALE 1 ENE	5685	SOMERSET	17	39 49	79 01	2290		8A	ARTHUR B. MC CARTER	3
MIDDLETOWN OLMSTED FLD	5703	DAUPHIN	15	40 11	76 46	303	MID	MID	U. S. AIR FORCE	2 3 5
MIDLAND DAM 7	5710	BEAVER	11	40 38	80 28	689	11P	7A	CORPS OF ENGINEERS	2 3 5
MILAN 4 WNW	5732	BRADFORD	15	41 56	76 35	1448		MID	CARL A. MORRIS	
MILANVILLE	5738	WAYNE	5	41 40	75 04	760		8A	CHARLES W. DAVIS	3
MILLERSBURG 2 E	5775	DAUPHIN	15	40 32	76 56	560		MID	RUSSELL SHEPLEY	
MILLHEIM	5790	CENTRE	15	40 54	77 29	1090		7A	NEVIN E. BOWERSOX	3
MILLVILLE 2 SW	5817	COLUMBIA	15	41 06	76 34	860		7A	KENNETH LEIGHOW	3
MILROY	5825	MIFFLIN	6	40 43	77 35	770		8A	THOMAS C. HARBESON	3
MONTROSE 1 E	5915	SUSQUEHANNA	15	41 50	75 51	1630	7A	7A	WILBER W. HOOPES,JR	2 3 5 7
MORGANTOWN	5956	BERKS	15	40 09	75 54	595	MID	MID	PA TURNPIKE COMM	2 3 5
MT GRETNA 2 SE	6028	LANCASTER	15	40 14	76 26	670	MID	MID	PA TURNPIKE COMM	2 3 5
MT POCONO 2 N AP	6055	MONROE	5	41 09	75 22	1915	5P	5P	H. JOHN DAVIS, JR.	2 3 5 7
MOUNT UNION 1 N	6067	MIFFLIN	6	40 24	77 53	820		MID	MT UNION WTR WORKS	
MUHLENBURG 1 SE	6090	LUZERNE	15	41 13	76 08	1110	6P	6P	THEODORE J. SAMPSON	2 3 5
MURRYSVILLE	6111	WESTMORELAND	10	40 26	79 42	903		MID	DAVID C. SHAW	
MYERSTOWN	6126	LEBANON	14	40 22	76 18	480		8A	MRS.KATHLEEN WANDELL	3
NATRONA LOCK 4	6151	ALLEGHENY	1	40 37	79 43	800		7A	CORPS OF ENGINEERS	3
NEFFS MILLS 3 NE	6174	HUNTINGDON	6	40 40	77 55	900		MID	PA STATE UNIVERSITY	
NEW CASTLE 1 N	6233	LAWRENCE	2	41 01	80 22	825	5P	7A	BAXTER F. JOHNSON	2 3 5 7
NESHAMINY FALLS	6194	BUCKS	5	40 09	74 57	60		MID	PHILA SUB WATER CO	3
NEWBURG 3 W	6225	FRANKLIN	15	40 09	77 37	745	MID	MID	PA TURNPIKE COMM	2 3 5
#NEWELL	6246	FAYETTE	10	40 05	79 54	805	12M	12M	GENERAL CHEMICAL CO	2 3 5
NEW PARK	6289	YORK	15	39 44	76 30	780		6P	CLINTON J. ALLEN	3
NEWPORT	6297	PERRY	6	40 29	77 08	400	7A	7A	MRS. FRANCES K. FRY	2 3 5 7
NEW STANTON	6310	WESTMORELAND	10	40 13	79 36	980	MID	MID	PA TURNPIKE COMM	2 3 5
NEW TRIPOLI	6326	LEHIGH	14	40 41	75 45	570		6P	FRED C. OSWALD	3
NORRISTOWN	6370	MONTGOMERY	14	40 07	75 21	75	MID	8A	GEORGE H. BOONE	2 3 5
NORTH EAST 2 SE	6396	ERIE	8	42 12	79 49	1060		9A	ELLSWORTH WEAVER	3
ORWELL 3 N	6621	BRADFORD	15	41 55	76 16	1620		8A	WILLIAM I. BROWN	3
PALM	6681	MONTGOMERY	14	40 26	75 32	385		8A	FRED C. ESCHBACH	3
#PALMERTON	6689	CARBON	9	40 48	75 37	435	MID	MID	NEW JERSEY ZINC CO	2 3 5 7
PALMYRA	6694	LEBANON	15	40 18	76 35	480		7P	EARL E. RHOADS	3
PARKER	6721	ARMSTRONG	1	41 05	79 41	1140		7A	LOUIS A. MALARKEY	3
PARKER 1 E	6724	CLARION	1	41 06	79 40	1100		MID	P. M. NEELY	
PAUPACK 2 WNW	6762	PIKE	5	41 24	75 14	1360		8A	MISS L. VETTERLEIN	3
PECKS POND	6786	PIKE	5	41 17	75 06	1380		9A	MRS. CARRIE NESS	3
#PHIL DREXEL INST OF TEC	6879	PHILADELPHIA	14	39 57	75 11	30	MID	MID	FRANCIS K. DAVIS,JR	2 5
PHILADELPHIA WB AP	6889	PHILADELPHIA	5	39 53	75 14	13	MID	MID	U.S. WEATHER BUREAU	2 7
#PHILADELPHIA PT BREEZE	6899	PHILADELPHIA	5	39 55	75 12	32	MID	MID	ATLANTIC REFINING	2
PHILADELPHIA SHAWMONT	6904	PHILADELPHIA	5	40 02	75 15	70	7P	7P	SCHUYLKILL NAVIG CO	2 5 7
#PHILADELPHIA CITY	6909	PHILADELPHIA	5	39 57	75 09	26	9A	9A	USN HYDROGRAPHIC OFF	2 U 9
PHILIPSBURG CAA AP	6916	CENTRE	6	40 54	78 05	1918	8P	8P	CIVIL AERO. ADM.	2 3 5 7
PHOENIXVILLE 1 E	6927	CHESTER	14	40 07	75 30	105	6P	MID	PHILA SUB WATER CO	2 3 5 7
PIKES CREEK	6939	LUZERNE	15	41 18	76 08	1320		MID	HARRY SHELDON	3
PIMPLE HILL	6944	MONROE	9	41 02	75 30	2215	9A	9A	PA DEPT FRST + WTRS	2 3 5 6
PINE GROVE 1 NE	6954	SCHUYLKILL	15	40 34	76 22	535		8A	PA POWER + LIGHT CO	3
PITTSBURGH WB AP 2	6993	ALLEGHENY	11	40 30	80 13	1151	MID	MID	U.S. WEATHER BUREAU	2 3 5 7
#PITTSBURGH WB CITY	6997	ALLEGHENY	11	40 27	80 00	749	MID	MID	U.S. WEATHER BUREAU	2 3 5
PLEASANT MOUNT 1 W	7029	WAYNE	5	41 44	75 27	1800	8A	8A	PA FISH COMM	2 3 5
PORT CLINTON	7116	SCHUYLKILL	14	40 35	76 02	450	7A	7A	MRS. ADA E. RARICK	2 3 5 7
PORTLAND	7127	NORTHAMPTON	5	40 55	75 06	297		8A	JOINT BRIDGE COMM	INAC 1/56
POTTSTOWN	7149	MONTGOMERY	14	40 15	75 39	160		8A	MILES E. SMITH	3
POTTSVILLE PALO ALTO BR	7161	SCHUYLKILL	14	40 41	76 11	640		8A	JOHN MC SMITH	INAC 4/56
PUNXSUTAWNEY	7217	JEFFERSON	1	40 57	79 00	1298		MID	JOHN VOLANSKY	
PUTNEYVILLE 2 SE DAM	7229	ARMSTRONG	1	40 55	79 17	1270	8A	8A	CORPS OF ENGINEERS	2 3 5
QUAKERTOWN 1 E	7239	BUCKS	5	40 26	75 20	490	5P	5P	DENNIS K. FLUCK	2 3 5 7
RAYMOND	7310	POTTER	13	41 52	77 52	2220		7A	MRS. RACHEL LANGAN	3
#READING WB CITY	7318	BERKS	14	40 20	75 58	266	MID	MID	U.S. WEATHER BUREAU	2 3 5 7
RENOVO	7409	CLINTON	16	41 20	77 46	660		7A	MRS. CAROLINE BAIRD	3
RENOVO 5 S	7410	CLINTON	16	41 14	77 46	2035		MID	C. F. BILLETTE	
REW	7425	MC KEAN	1	41 54	78 32	2250		8A	HAROLD C. MEALY	3
RICES LANDING L 6	7443	GREENE	10	39 57	80 00	775		7A	CORPS OF ENGINEERS	3
RIDGWAY 3 W	7477	ELK	1	41 25	78 47	1420	7A	7A	BOROUGH OF RIDGWAY	2 3 5 7
ROCHESTER 1 N	7540	BEAVER	2	40 43	80 18	900		MID	DEQUESNE LIGHT CO	
RUSH	7694	SUSQUEHANNA	15	41 47	76 03	1000		9A	MISS MAUDE MC CAIN	3
RUSHVILLE	7727	SUSQUEHANNA	15	41 47	76 07	870		7A	CARL KOPATZ	3
SAFE HARBOR	7732	LANCASTER	15	39 55	76 23	270		MID	S.H.WATER POWER CORP	
SAGAMORE 1 S	7739	INDIANA	1	40 46	79 14	1320		7A	CORPS OF ENGINEERS	3
SALINA 3 W	7782	WESTMORELAND	7	40 31	79 33	1109	6P	6P	MUN AUTH WSTMRLD CO	2 3 5
SAXTON	7846	BEDFORD	6	40 12	78 15	780		8A	MRS.ALVERTA L.HOLMES	3
SCANDIA 2 E	7855	WARREN	1	41 55	79 01	2040		MID	DAVID R. ANDERSON	
SCHENLEY LOCK 5	7863	ARMSTRONG	1	40 41	79 40	783		VAR	CORPS OF ENGINEERS	3
#SCRANTON	7902	LACKAWANNA	15	41 25	75 40	746	7A	7A	U.S. POST OFFICE	2 3 5
SCRANTON WB AIRPORT	7905	LUZERNE	15	41 20	75 44	956	MID	MID	U.S. WEATHER BUREAU	2 3 5 7
SELINSGROVE CAA AP	7931	SNYDER	15	40 49	76 52	437	MID	MID	CIVIL AERO. ADM.	2 3 5 7
SELLERSVILLE 2 NW	7938	BUCKS	5	40 23	75 20	530		MID	SELLERSVILLE WTR CO	

STATION INDEX

Station	Index No.	County	Drainage ‡	Latitude	Longitude	Elevation	Observation Time Temp.	Observation Time Precip.	Observer	Refer To Tables
E WAP	7985	HUNTINGDON	6	40 11	77 52	1000		MID	MRS. HELEN M. PYLE	C
OKIN	7978	NORTHUMBLAND	15	40 48	76 33	770		8A	ROARING CRK WTR CO	3
FIELD 8 W	8028	WARREN	1	41 41	79 09	1040		MID	L. N. HANSON	C
PENSBURG	8073	FRANKLIN	15	40 03	77 32	709	4P	4P	KEITH B. ALLEN	2 3 5
PINGPORT WB	8078	BEAVER	11	40 37	80 20	740	MID	MID	U.S. WEATHER BUREAU	2 3 5 7 C
ENAMONING	8145	CAMERON	16	41 19	78 05	790		7A	MRS.FRANCES CALDWELL	3
PERY ROCK	8184	BUTLER	2	41 04	80 03	1345	7P	7A	WALTER D. ALBERT	2 3 5
HPORT HIGHWAY SHED	8190	MC KEAN	1	41 48	78 27	1510		MID	PA DEPT HIGHWAYS	C
RSET FAIRVIEW ST	8244	SOMERSET	17	40 01	79 05	2140		7A	HOWARD G. PECK	3
RSET MAIN ST	8249	SOMERSET	17	40 01	79 05	2150	6P	6P	DAVID L. GROVE	2 3 5 7
H CANAAN 1 NE	8275	WAYNE	5	41 31	75 24	1400		MID	EUGENE M. COOK	C
H MOUNTAIN	8308	FRANKLIN	12	39 51	77 30	1520		7A	PA DEPT OF HEALTH	3
NGBORO	8359	CRAWFORD	8	41 48	80 23	900	8A	8A	SPRINGBORO BOROUGH	2 3 5 7 C
NG GROVE	8379	YORK	15	39 52	76 52	470		4P	P. H. GLATFELTER CO	3 C
NGS 1 SW	8395	SOMERSET	17	39 44	79 10	2500	8P	8P	ALLEN E. YODER	2 3 5 7
E COLLEGE	8449	CENTRE	16	40 48	77 52	1175	MID	MID	PA STATE COLLEGE	2 3 5 6 C
USSTOWN	8570	BERKS	14	40 20	76 11	600		8A	JACOB KLAHR	3
NGSTOWN	8589	INDIANA	4	40 33	78 55	1880		MID	HARRY F. BENNETT	C
UDSBURG	8596	MONROE	5	40 59	75 12	480	11P	11P	WILLIAM MAGERTY	2 3 5 7 C
P CREEK	8610	JEFFERSON	1	41 01	78 50	1320		7A	CORPS OF ENGINEERS	3
URY	8668	NORTHUMBLAND	15	40 51	76 48	440		7A	CHARLES W. BAYLER	3 C
UEHANNA	8692	SUSQUEHANNA	15	41 57	75 36	1020		7A	MRS. LAURA A.BENSON	3
RSVILLE	8699	ALLEGHENY	17	40 14	79 48	765		7A	FRANK E. MARSH	3
QUA	8758	SCHUYLKILL	14	40 48	75 58	830		8A	MRS. MARY L.ROBERTS	3
QUA 4 N DAM	8763	SCHUYLKILL	14	40 51	75 59	1120		7A	PANTHER VLY WTR CO	3 C
RACK 2 S FIRE TWR	8770	CLINTON	16	41 24	77 51	2220	7A	7A	JAMES E. SWARTZ	2 3 5 7
ESTA 2 SE DAM	8873	FOREST	1	41 29	79 26	1200	8A	8A	CORPS OF ENGINEERS	2 3 5 7 C
SVILLE	8885	CRAWFORD	1	41 38	79 40	1550		MID	PA ELECTRIC CO •	C
SVILLE WATER WORKS	8888	CRAWFORD	1	41 38	79 42	1220	7P	7P	CITY OF TITUSVILLE	2 3 5
EDO 4 W	8901	WARREN	1	41 47	79 32	1735		7A	MRS. LILY B. GARBER	3
NDA	8905	BRADFORD	15	41 46	76 26	760	7P	7A	MRS. M. O. PARKS	2 3 5 7 C
R CITY 5 SW	8910	DAUPHIN	15	40 31	76 37	745		6P	HARRISBURG WTR DEPT	3 7
	8959	BRADFORD	15	41 47	76 47	1100		7A	JENNIE L. BALLARD	3
ELTON	8989	INDIANA	4	40 27	79 23	890		MID	MRS. MARY E. WEIMER	C
LEPOINT 4 NE	9002	MC KEAN	1	41 54	78 16	1640		7A	ROBERT D. STRAIT	3
NE 4 NE BALD EAGLE	9024	BLAIR	8	40 43	78 12	1020		7A	FREDERICK L. FRIDAY	3 C
N CITY	9042	ERIE	1	41 54	79 50	1325		7A	FORREST M. BRALEY	3 C
NTOWN	9050	FAYETTE	10	39 54	79 44	1040	10P	10P	WM. W. MARSTELLER	2 3 5 7
R DARBY	9074	DELAWARE	5	39 58	75 18	222	7P	7P	PHIL. SUB.TRANS. CO	2 3 5
A	9099	VENANGO	1	41 26	79 57	1030		7A	MRS.FLORENCE MILLER	3
ERGRIFT	9128	WESTMORELAND	7	40 36	79 33	800		7A	UNITED ENG+FNDRY CO	3
ERGRIFT 2 W	9133	WESTMORELAND	7	40 36	79 36	995		MID	EUGENE R. YOUNG	C
INVILLE	9196	BERKS	14	40 31	75 52	350		8A	MRS. MARY H. WRIGHT	3
NCKEL	9206	CLARION	1	41 25	79 14	1620		8A	PA DEPT FRST + WTRS	3
NCKEL 1 WSW	9209	CLARION	1	41 24	79 15	1610		8A	PA DEPT FRST + WTRS	3

Station	Index No.	County	Drainage ‡	Latitude	Longitude	Elevation	Observation Time Temp.	Observation Time Precip.	Observer	Refer To Tables
WARREN	9298	WARREN	1	41 51	79 08	1280	7P	7A	GILBERT H. HEIER	2 3 5 7
VASHINGTON	9312	WASHINGTON	11	40 11	80 14	1200		MID	PA DEPT HIGHWAYS	C
WATSONTOWN	9345	NORTHUMBLAND	16	41 05	76 52	470		8A	OWEN BERKENSTOCK	3
WAYNESBURG 2 W	9362	GREENE	10	39 54	80 13	980	6P	7A	RALPH L. AMOS	2 3 5 7
WAYNESBURG 1 E	9367	GREENE	10	39 54	80 10	940		MID	SEWAGE DISPOSAL PLT	C
WEBSTER MILLS 3 SW	9380	FULTON	12	39 49	78 05	920		MID	VILLIAM D. COVEN	C
WELLSBORO 3 S	9408	TIOGA	16	41 43	77 18	1920	7A	7A	MARION L. SHUMWAY	2 3 5 7
WELLSBORO 2 E	9412	TIOGA	16	41 45	77 16	1550		MID	MRS. IDA S. MAYNARD	C
WELLSVILLE	9420	YORK	15	40 03	76 57	500	5P	5P	D. D. HOOVER	2 3 5
WERNERSVILLE 1 W	9430	BERKS	14	40 20	76 06	405		8A	CHARLES A. GRUBER	3
WEST CHESTER	9464	CHESTER	5	39 58	75 36	440	8A	8A	DAILY LOCAL NEWS	2 3 5 7
WEST GROVE 1 E	9503	CHESTER	5	39 49	75 49	440		8A	CONARD-PYLE CO	3
WEST HICKORY	9507	FOREST	1	41 34	79 25	1090		8A	MRS.HELEN F.KINNEAR	3
WHITESBURG	9655	ARMSTRONG	1	40 45	79 24	1530		7A	CORPS OF ENGINEERS	3
RILKES-BARRE	9702	LAZERNE	15	41 15	75 52	610		7A	MRS. MARY G. HIRMAK	3
WILLIAMSBURG	9714	BLAIR	6	40 28	78 12	860		7A	MYRON K. BIDDLE	3
WILLIAMSPORT WB AP	9728	LYCOMING	16	41 15	76 55	527	MID	MID	U.S. WEATHER BUREAU	2 3 5 7 C
VIND GAP	9761	NORTHAMPTON	5	40 51	75 18	720		MID	OVEN R. PARRY	C
WOLFSBURG	9823	BEDFORD	6	40 03	78 32	1190		7A	WALTER C. RICE	3
YORK 3 SSW PUMP STA	9933	YORK	15	39 55	76 45	390	5P	5P	YORK WATER COMPANY	2 3 5 7
YORK 2 S	9938	YORK	15	39 56	76 44	640		MID	YORK WATER COMPANY	C
YORK HAVEN	9950	YORK	15	40 07	76 43	310		8A	METROPOL EDISON CO	3
YOUNGSVILLE	9966	WARREN	1	41 51	79 20	1225		MID	HENRY CARLETT	C
ZION GROVE	9990	SCHUYLKILL	15	40 54	76 13	940		7A	JAMES D. TEETER	3
ZIONSVILLE 3 SE	9995	LEHIGH	14	40 27	75 27	660		7A	LESLIE HOWATT	3
NEW STATIONS										
EMPORIUM 2 SSW	2634	CAMERON	16	41 28	78 15	1735	7A	7A	JACKSON THOMAS	2 3 5 7 C
CLOSED STATIONS										
EMPORIUM 1 E	2633	CAMERON	16	41 31	78 13	1160	7A	7A	RUSSELL E.PALMATEER	CLOSED 8/56

‡ 1-ALLEGHENY; 2-BEAVER; 3- 4-CONEMAUGH; 5-DELAWARE; 6-JUNIATA; 7-KISKIMINETAS; 8-LAKE ERIE; 9-LEHIGH; 10-MONONGAHELA; 11-OHIO; 12-POTOMAC; 13-LAKE ONTARIO; 14-SCHUYLKILL; 15-SUSQUEHANNA; 16-WEST BRANCH; 17-YOUGHIOGHENY

REFERENCE NOTES

Additional information regarding the climate of Pennsylvania may be obtained by writing to the State Climatologist at Weather Bureau Airport Station, Harrisburg State Airport, New Cumberland, Pennsylvania, or to any Weather Bureau Office near you.

The four digit identification numbers in the index number column of the Station Index are assigned on a state basis. There will be no duplication of numbers within a state.

Figures and letters following the station name, such as 12 SSW, indicate distance in miles and direction from the post office.

Observation times given in the Station Index are in local standard time.

Delayed data and corrections will be carried only in the June and December issues of this bulletin.

Monthly and seasonal snowfall and heating degree days for the preceding 12 months will be carried in the June issue of this bulletin.

Stations appearing in the index, but for which data are not listed in the tables, are either missing or received too late to be included in this issue.

Unless otherwise indicated, dimensional units used in this bulletin are: temperature in °F., precipitation and evaporation in inches, and wind movement in miles. Degree days are based on a daily average of 65° F.

Evaporation is measured in the standard Weather Bureau type pan of 4 foot diameter unless otherwise shown by footnote following Table 6.

Amounts in Table 3 are from non-recording gages, unless otherwise indicated.

Data in Tables 3, 5 and 6 and snowfall data in Table 7 are for the 24 hours ending at time of observation. See Station Index for observation time.

Snow on ground in Table 7 is at observation time for all except Weather Bureau and CAA stations. For these stations snow on ground values are at 7:30 a.m. E.S.T. WTR EQUIV in Table 7 means the water equivalent of snow on the ground. It is measured at selected stations when depth of snow on the ground is two inches or more. Water equivalent samples are necessarily taken from different points for successive observations; consequently occasional drifting and other causes of local variability in the snowpack result in apparent inconsistencies in the record.

Long-term means for full-time Weather Bureau stations (those shown in the Station Index as United States Weather Bureau Stations) are based on the period 1921-1950, adjusted to represent observations taken at the present location.

- \- No record in Tables 3, 6, 7 and the Station Index. No record in Tables 2 and 5 is indicated by no entry.
- \+ And also on a later date or dates.
- * Amount included in following measurement, time distribution unknown.
- \# Thermometers are generally exposed in a shelter located a few feet above sod-covered ground; however, the reference indicates that the thermometers are exposed in a shelter located on the roof of a building.
- // Gage is equipped with a windshield.
- AM Data based on observational day ending before noon.
- B Adjusted to a full month.
- C In the "Refer to Tables" column in the Station Index the letter "C" indicates recorder stations. These stations are processed for special purposes and are published later in Hourly Precipitation Data.
- D Water equivalent of snowfall wholly or partly estimated, using a ratio of 1 inch water equivalent to every 10 inches of new snowfall.
- M One or more days of record missing; see Table 5 for detailed daily record. Degree day data, if carried for this station, have been adjusted to represent the value for a full month.
- R Amounts from recording gage (These amounts are essentially accurate but may vary slightly from the amounts to be published later in Hourly Precipitation Data).
- SS This entry in time of observation column in Station Index means sunset.
- T Trace, an amount too small to measure.
- Y Includes total for previous month.
- VAR Observations made at 2 p.m. Monday through Thursday and 7 a.m. Friday through Sunday.

Subscription Price: 20 cents per copy, monthly and annual; $2.50 per year. (Yearly subscription includes the Annual Summary.) Checks and money orders should be made payable to the Superintendent of Documents. Remittances and correspondence regarding subscriptions should be sent to the Superintendent of Documents, Government Printing Office, Washington 25, D. C.

WRPC., Asheville, N. C. --- 10/10/56 --- 1100

TOTAL MONTHLY PRECIPITATION, AUGUST 1956

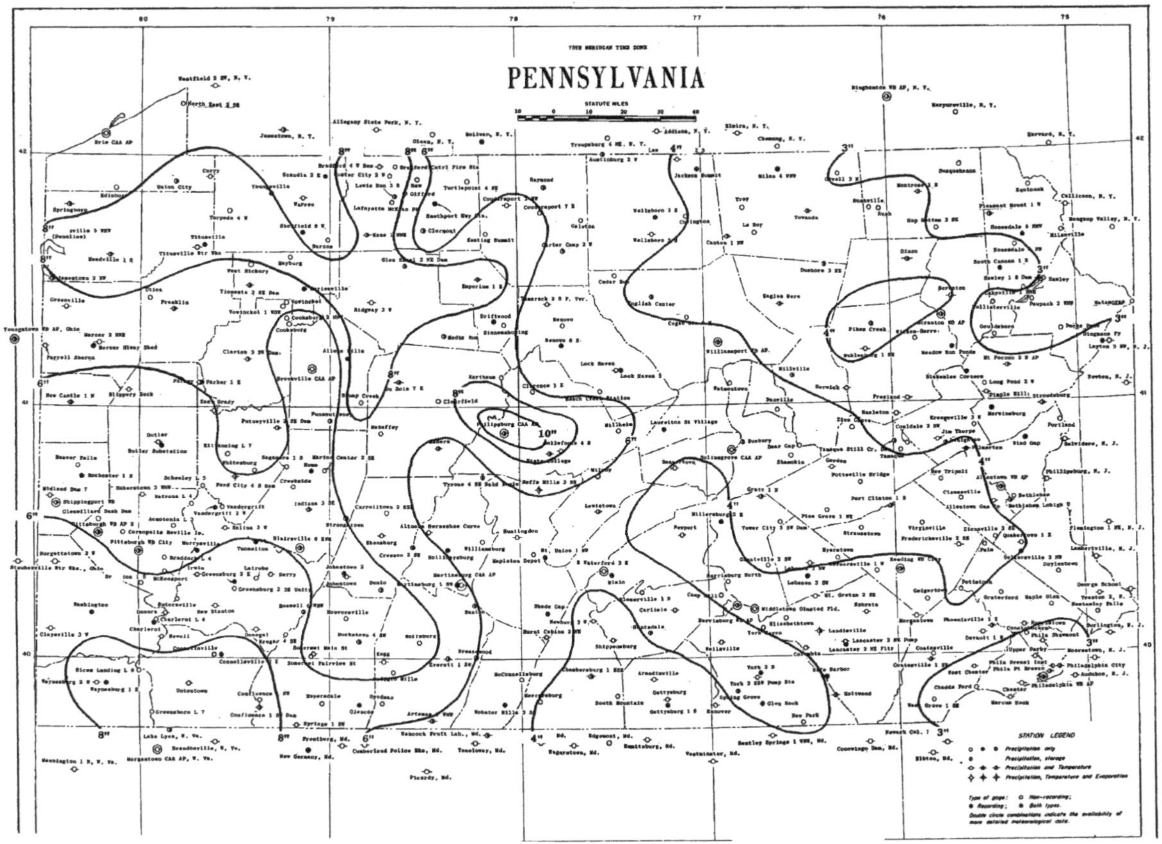

PENNSYLVANIA
STATUTE MILES
STATION LEGEND

PENNSYLVANIA
STATUTE MILES
63°
66°
69°
72°
STATION LEGEND

Isolines are drawn through points of approximately equal values.

U. S. DEPARTMENT OF COMMERCE
SINCLAIR WEEKS, Secretary
WEATHER BUREAU
F. W. REICHELDERFER, Chief

CLIMATOLOGICAL DATA

PENNSYLVANIA

SEPTEMBER 1956
Volume LXI No. 9

ASHEVILLE: 1956

PENNSYLVANIA - SEPTEMBER 1956

WEATHER SUMMARY

GENERAL

This was the coolest September in many years, featuring record-low temperatures and damaging freezes. The frequent rains along with excessive cloudiness and deficient sunshine were further adverse factors for the maturing and harvesting of crops and other outdoor activities.

Records for September coolness were broken at some stations having long records -- going back to 1900 at Scranton, for instance, while others were the coolest in 28 years or longer. Extreme temperatures ranged from 95° at Lebanon 3 W on the 1st to 22° at Madera on the 21st. Minimum temperatures of 32° or lower were recorded at least once at virtually all stations except those in the extreme east and along Lake Erie. Mercer 2 NNE led in this respect with 11 such days, followed by Kane 1 NNE and Madera with 9 each.

Precipitation varied considerably during the month at individual stations, ranging from 9.80 inches at Gifford to 1.45 inches at Newburg 3 W; however, the area averages differed much less sharply and mostly reflected ample to excessive moisture for the season. The coming of winter was foreshadowed by the traces of snowfall at numerous stations.

WEATHER DETAILS

During the first week temperatures were rather mild with nearly all stations recording their warmest readings of the month on the 1st or shortly thereafter. Beginning on the 6th, surges of chilly Canadian air flowed over the Northeast often enough to dominate the remainder of the month and set coolness records for September in Pennsylvania. Interruptions in the cool regime were few and brief, occurring on the 14th and 23rd, generally, plus the 17th in the east. Lowest readings were scattered over several dates after the first week, however, well over 100 stations experienced monthly minima on the 21st.

General rains of varying intensities occurred on the 1st-2nd and the 6th followed by dryness until about midmonth. The frequent movements of low pressure centers and their attendant frontal zones across the northeastern states brought rain virtually every day somewhere in the State after the 14th, usually over a substantial area. Hurricane Flossy, in its last stages as a weather producer, caused light rains over eastern Pennsylvania on the 27th and 28th as it moved northeastward offshore.

WEATHER EFFECTS

The unusually early advent of freezing temperatures killed much corn and other tender vegetation. For some sections the growing season was the shortest of record, according to the Federal-State Crop Reporting Service. Record breaking low temperatures for so early in the season occurred in some localities on the morning of the 10th with light damage but the general freeze on the 21st caused damage ranging from light in the southeast to severe in northern and western counties. Much corn in the milk stage was frozen and cutting for ensilage was rushed, necessitating construction of many new trench and temporary silos. The freeze reduced corn acreage for grain, lowered yield prospects and quality of ensilage. However, much corn in the southeast was reported the best in years.

Good grazing favored exceptionally high milk production with pastures better than ever before at this time of year. On the other hand the frequent rains, wet ground and low temperatures made haying difficult and reduced quality, hampered the harvesting of spring planted small grains and the seeding of fall plantings, delayed harvesting and caused rotting of late potatoes. Grape vines in the Erie Belt were well loaded with fruit that was unduly slow to ripen. Early cut tobacco cured nicely but about 10% of the crop was still in the fields and was caught by the freeze and lost or greatly reduced in value. The freeze stopped the fall nectar flow and coupled with poor spring and summer nectar conditions resulted in sharply reduced honey production and a poor outlook for bee colonies during the coming winter. Hail on several dates damaged field and fruit crops.

DESTRUCTIVE STORMS

1st: Lightning fires destroyed several buildings and contents in southeastern counties, including a meat packing plant in Reading. In western sections some local flooding resulted from thunderstorm downpours.

6th: Northwestern counties suffered heavy damage from lightning fires, particularly in Erie County where a furniture warehouse and contents and another nearby building were destroyed. Some local flooding occurred in Warren County. In the eastern half of the State, lightning struck several buildings but only minor fires resulted. Torrential rains caused much local flooding, while the combination of wet ground and wind downed many trees throughout the east.

17th: A local storm described as a twister cut a swath 3 miles long and about 50 yards wide in Lancaster County, destroying a tobacco shed and damaging several dwellings. A boy was injured when struck by flying debris. Hail up to an in in diameter fell in most southeastern counties, ruining many acres of late crops as well as breaking many windows. Also in the eastern half there were lightning fires and wind damage to trees, antennas and signs along with power disruptions in many communities. During the night severe thunderstorms, accompanied by hail in some sections, affected the whole State. Strong winds damaged roofs, felled many trees and disrupted power service.

FLOODS

No stream flooding occurred.

J. E. Stork, Climatologist
U. S. Weather Bureau
Weather Records Processing Center
Chattanooga, Tennessee

CLIMATOLOGICAL DATA

Station		Temperature: Average Maximum	Average Minimum	Average	Departure From Long Term Means	Highest	Date	Lowest	Date	Degree Days	No. of Days Max 90° or Above	Max 32° or Below	Min 32° or Below	Min 0° or Below	Precipitation: Total	Departure From Long Term Means	Greatest Day	Date	Snow, Sleet Total	Max. Depth on Ground	Date	No. of Days 10 or More	50 or More	1.00 or More
POCONO MOUNTAINS																								
AND		64.9	48.8	56.9	- 3.5	77	5+	32	21	264	0	0	1	0	6.59	2.91	3.00	7	.0	0		10	4	1
Y 1 S DAM	AM	67.8	43.1	55.5		83	2+	29	10	295	0	0	5	0	3.43		.74	7	.0	0		10	1	0
CONO 2 N AP		66.2	46.9	56.6	- 1.8	80	5	28	21	278	0	0	1	0	5.57	.78	2.88	6	.0	0		8	2	1
VBURG 1 SE		68.9	45.4	57.2		83	1+	26	21	256	0	0	2	0	4.32		1.13	6	.0	0		9	2	1
E HILL	AM	65.2	47.2	56.2		78	3+	30	21	281	0	0	1	0	5.77		1.68	7	T	0		8	4	2
ANT MOUNT 1 W	AM	64.9	43.3	54.1		81	1	29	21	338	0	0	8	0	4.53	.66	.92	16	.0	0		8	4	0
TON	AM	69.5	46.6	58.1	- 5.6	87	6	33	21	243	0	0	0	0	3.33	.40	.73	1	.0	0		7	2	0
TON WB AIRPORT		68.1	47.8	58.0	- 5.2	85	1	32	21	241	0	0	1	0	2.54	- .68	.81	6	T	0		9	1	0
DSBURG		70.2	45.0	57.6	- 5.0	85	2+	29	21	252	0	0	4	0	5.47	1.87	2.55	6	.0	0		9	4	1
DIVISION				56.7											4.62				T					
EAST CENTRAL MOUNTAINS																								
TOWN WB AP	R	71.1	50.7	60.9	- 3.8	85	2	34	21	178	0	0	0	0	3.27	- .20	1.03	6	.0	0		7	2	1
TOWN GAS CO	AM	72.4	50.4	61.4	- 3.6	86	15	35	21	172	0	0	0	0	3.15	- .32	.88	7	.0	0		7	2	0
EHEM LEHIGH UNIV		71.1	53.2	62.2	- 4.6	85	1+	39	21	157	0	0	0	0	3.08	- .29	.88	15	.0	0		6	3	0
HORPE		71.4M	49.1M	60.3M	- 3.4	85	14	31	21	180	0	0	1	0	6.95	2.93	3.64	7	.0	0		8	4	1
RTON		69.8	50.3	60.1	- 3.7	83	2+	33	21	195	0	0	0	0	3.80	.11	1.34	6	.0	0		7	3	1
CLINTON	AM	72.9	46.2	59.6	- 5.6	85	2+	28	21	203	0	0	3	0	5.76	1.71	2.70	7	.0	0		6	3	2
RTOWN 1 E		73.6	50.9	62.3	- 1.5	85	1+	31	21	156	0	0	1	0	3.23	- .39	.86	6	.0	0		8	2	0
DIVISION				61.0											4.18				.0					
SOUTHEASTERN PIEDMONT																								
ER	AM	76.3M	56.0M	66.2M		89	1			95	0	0	0	0					.0	0				
SVILLE 1 SW	AM	74.1	50.2	62.2	- 3.9	91	2	30	22	163	2	0	2	0	4.06	.35	1.00	7	.0	0		7	3	1
BIA		74.5	53.5	64.0		88	1	35	21	118	0	0	0	0	4.32		2.00	6	.0	0		7	2	1
LT 1 W		71.9	48.0	60.0		90	1	33	21	211	1	0	0	0	5.10		1.60	27	.0	0		10	4	1
TA		73.3	52.0	62.7	- 3.6	86	1	33	21	139	0	0	0	0	3.45	- .07	.80	1	.0	0		7	4	0
E SCHOOL		73.9	53.3	63.6	- 2.7	88	1	32	21	139	0	0	1	0	2.50	- 1.08	.73	24	.0	0		6	2	0
OOD		72.6	56.7	64.7	- 4.2	88	4	39	21	108	0	0	0	0	4.33	1.70	1.53	7	.0	0		9	3	1
STER 2 NE PUMP STA		72.6	51.1	61.9	- 3.5	85	1	31	21	150	0	0	1	0	4.29	.97	1.33	6	.0	0		7	3	1
SVILLE 2 NW	AM	72.3	50.9	61.6		90	1	31	21	172	1	0	1	0	3.67		.95	7	.0	0		8	3	0
ON 3 W	AM	72.1	50.2	61.2	- 4.5	95	1	32	21	184	1	0	1	0	5.22	1.83	2.46	7	.0	0		6	4	1
S HOOK		74.4	57.9	66.2	- 4.3	91	1	42	21	89	3	0	0	0	3.17	.06	1.48	6	.0	0		6	2	1
ETOWN OLMSTED FLD		71.8	53.6	62.7	- 3.2	88	1	37	21	137	0	0	0	0	2.97	- .32	.99	6	.0	0		7	2	0
NTOWN		71.4	51.1	61.3		86	1	31	21	173	0	0	1	0	4.36		1.15	6	.0	0		9	3	1
ETNA 2 SE		71.1	51.6	61.4		86	1	30	21	166	0	0	1	0	4.24		2.00	6	.0	0		7	2	1
STOWN		75.2	55.5	65.4		94	1	38	21	107	2	0	0	0	2.86		.99	28	.0	0		6	2	0
DREXEL INST OF TEC		75.8	58.6	67.2		93	1	42	21	75	2	0	0	0	3.77		1.52	6	.0	0		7	2	1
DELPHIA WB AP	R	73.9	56.4	65.2	- 2.5	91	1	38	21	107	1	0	0	0	3.75	.29	1.60	6	.0	0		7	2	1
DELPHIA PT BREEZE		74.0	59.1	66.6	- 2.9	91	1	43	21	80	1	0	0	0	3.62		1.74	6	.0	0		6	3	1
DELPHIA SHAWMONT		76.2	55.6	65.9	- 2.1	92	2+	36	21	98	2	0	0	0	2.83	- .46	.97	28	.0	0		5	3	0
DELPHIA CITY	RAM	74.1	59.7	66.9	- 2.4	90	1	46	21	73	1	0	0	0	2.75	- .68	.88	27	.0	0		7	2	0
IXVILLE 1 E		76.9	50.9	63.9	- 3.3	92	1	34	10	137	3	0	0	0	3.26	- .14	1.34	27	.0	0		7	2	1
NG WB CITY	R	72.6	54.7	63.7	- 3.4	86	4+	38	21	127	0	0	0	0	3.72	.44	1.21	6	.0	0		7	3	1
DARBY		75.8	55.9	65.9		93	1	36	21	103	1	0	0	0	4.57		1.50	6+	.0	0		6	3	2
CHESTER	AM	77.1	52.8	65.0	- .8	92	4	32	21	116	3	0	1	0	2.83	- 1.03	.83	27	.0	0		5	2	0
DIVISION				64.0											3.72				.0					
LOWER SUSQUEHANNA																								
TSVILLE	AM	73.2	51.0	62.1	- 3.6	92	1+	30	21	165	2	0	1	0	3.57	- .09	.86	7	.0	0		8	2	0
SLE		74.6	53.0	63.8	- 1.7	89	1	34	21	126	0	0	0	0	3.58	.21	1.17	6	.0	0		6	2	1
ERSBURG 1 ESE		73.1	50.4	61.8	- 4.3	91	1	30	21	159	1	0	1	0	3.06	- .05	.69	27	.0	0		8	3	0
SBURG	AM	73.9	52.7	63.3	- 2.7	93	1	32	21	146	2	0	1	0	4.00	.54	.78	24+	.0	0		9	4	0
ER	AM	74.3	50.4	62.4	- 5.0	93	1	31	21+	169	2	0	2	0	3.26	.10	1.04	28	.0	0		7	2	1
SBURG WB AP	R	71.8	53.2	62.5	- 3.6	87	1	35	21	146	0	0	0	0	3.24	.61	.99	6	.0	0		8	2	0
RG 3 W		76.3	54.1	65.2		90	1	29	21	90	1	0	1	0	1.45		.40	15+	.0	0		5	0	0
ENSBURG		75.2	51.5	63.4	- 2.8	93	1	32	21	136	1	0	1	0	2.09	- 1.19	.57	15	.0	0		6	1	0
VILLE		73.3	50.4	61.9		89	1	28	21	160	0	0	1	0	4.18		1.52	6	.0	0		7	3	1
SSW PUMP STA		76.1	52.4	64.3	- 2.2	94	1	32	21	123	1	0	1	0	3.95	.65	1.01	6	.0	0		6	4	1
DIVISION				63.1											3.24				.0					
MIDDLE SUSQUEHANNA																								
RTOWN		71.9M	48.9	60.4M		87	1	30	21	175	0	0	1	0	4.17		1.47	24	.0	0		8	2	2
CK		72.8	50.5	61.7		88	1	31	21	157	0	0	1	0	4.09		1.30	6	.0	0		8	2	1
1 N	AM	70.1	47.4	58.8		86	1	30	21+	223	0	0	2	0	2.72		.80	24	.0	0		7	2	0
TOWN	AM	73.4	49.9	61.7		90	1+	32	22	168	2	0	1	0	3.42		1.22	2	.0	0		7	2	1
RT	AM	72.6	48.9	60.8		91	1	32	21+	186	1	0	2	0	2.27	- .87	.52	24	.0	0		7	1	0
SGROVE CAA AP		71.0	49.7	60.4	- 4.4	88	1	30	21	183	0	0	1	0	3.45	.02	1.05	23	.0	0		9	3	1
AMSPORT WB AP		70.8	50.2	60.5	- 4.1	86	23	33	21	176	0	0	0	0	2.60	- .73	.36	14	.0	0		9	0	0
DIVISION				60.6											3.25				.0					
UPPER SUSQUEHANNA																								
1 NW	AM	66.1	44.8	55.5		82	1	30	21+	303	0	0	2	0	2.93		.93	16	.0	0		7	2	0
	AM	70.4M	45.6M	58.0M		88	1	30	21	263	0	0	2	0	4.60		1.52	24	.0	0		10	2	1
MERE	AM	62.3	45.4	53.9		77	1+	29	21	344	0	0	2	0	5.16	.52	1.42	7	.0	0		9	4	1
ICEVILLE 2 S	AM	68.9	43.4	56.2	- 5.6	86	1+	30	21	288	0	0	3	0	2.76	- .34	.95	16	.0	0		8	1	0
OSE 1 E	AM	65.0	45.3	55.2	- 5.1	83	1	30	21+	315	0	0	2	0	5.29	1.46	.99	7	.0	0		10	4	0

See Reference Notes Following Station Index

CLIMATOLOGICAL DATA

TABLE 2 - CONTINUED

Station		Temperature													Precipitation								
											No. of Days								Snow, Sleet			No. of I	
											Max.		Min.										
		Average Maximum	Average Minimum	Average	Departure From Long Term Means	Highest	Date	Lowest	Date	Degree Days	90° or Above	32° or Below	32° or Below	0° or Below	Total	Departure From Long Term Means	Greatest Day	Date	Total	Max. Depth on Ground	Date	.10 or More	.50 or More
TOWANDA		71.5	47.0	59.3	-3.1	89	1	29	21	207	0	0	1	0	3.71	.41	.78	18	.0	0		9	2
WELLSBORO 3 S	AM	67.7	44.8	56.3	-3.5	84	1	32	21	289	0	0	1	0	3.02	-.05	.81	16	.0	0		7	2
DIVISION				56.3											3.92				.0				
CENTRAL MOUNTAINS																							
BELLEFONTE 4 S	AM	71.2	45.8	58.5	-5.3	88	1	32	21	220	0	0	1	0	4.46	1.58	1.80	1	.0	0		7	2
DU BOIS 7 E		69.3	46.9	58.1		85	1	28	21	236	0	0	2	0	3.04	-.46	.55	17	T	0		9	1
EMPORIUM 2 SSW	AM	68.0	42.3	55.2		83	2	26	22	308	0	0	6	0	3.56		.96	24	T	0		8	3
LOCK HAVEN		71.0M	49.4M	60.2M	-4.6			31	21	171	0	0	1	0	1.97	-1.35	.68	7	.0	0		6	1
MADERA	AM	69.1	40.3	54.7		88	1	22	21	320	0	0	9	0	3.36		.70	12	.0	0		6	3
PHILIPSBURG CAA AP		65.9	43.7	54.8		84	1	25	21	315	0	0	7	0	2.50		.57	6	.0	0		9	2
RIDGWAY 3 W	AM	69.7	41.4	55.6	-4.3	85	1+	29	21+	291	0	0	6	0	3.32	.04	1.42	15	T	0		7	2
STATE COLLEGE		68.8	49.6	59.2	-3.5	86	1	32	21	209	0	0	1	0	2.73	-.23	1.10	6	.0	0		7	1
TAMARACK 2 S FIRE TWR	AM																						
DIVISION				57.0											3.12				T				
SOUTH CENTRAL MOUNTAINS																							
ALTOONA HORSESHOE CURVE		70.0	49.1	59.6	-3.4	86	1	30	21	199	0	0	1	0	4.22	1.15	1.23	6	.0	0		9	3
ARTEMAS 1 WNW		76.2	48.4	62.3		86	14	30	10+	138	0	0	3	0	3.48		2.10	14	.0	0		4	2
BURNT CABINS 2 NE		72.9	46.4	59.7		91	1	30	21	192	1	0	2	0	3.36		.70	6	.0	0		10	1
EBENSBURG		67.2	47.0	57.1	-3.9	85	1	27	21	252	0	0	4	0	4.24	1.00	1.06	7	T	0		8	3
EVERETT 1 SW		69.7	50.4	60.1	-2.5	82	5	28	21	183	0	0	1	0	3.30	.30	.80	1	.0	0		8	3
HUNTINGDON	AM																						
JOHNSTOWN	AM	72.0	47.6	59.8	-5.5	93	2	27	21	212	2	0	2	0	2.96	-.46	.98	7	.0	0		5	3
KEGG		71.4	45.7	58.6		89	1	26	21	220	0	0	4	0	2.39		.98	14	.0	0		6	2
MARTINSBURG CAA AP		69.6	48.4	59.0		87	1	30	21	212	0	0	1	0	2.44		.46	6	.0	0		9	0
DIVISION				59.5											3.30				T				
SOUTHWEST PLATEAU																							
BAKERSTOWN 3 WNW		71.4	51.9	61.7		88	1	34	21	156	0	0	0	0			.66	2	.0	0			
BLAIRSVILLE 6 ENE		67.8	49.5	58.7		86	1	31	21	220	0	0	1	0	5.13	2.07	1.79	6	.0	0		10	3
BURGETTSTOWN 2 W	AM	72.2	43.1	57.7		88	1	23	21	249	0	0	6	0	2.49		.62	2	.0	0		8	2
BUTLER		72.8	47.6	60.2	-3.9	90	1	29	21	190	1	0	1	0	3.35	.34	.74	16	T	0		9	2
CLAYSVILLE 3 W																							
CONFLUENCE 1 SW DAM	AM	71.3	48.0	59.7		89	2	32	21	189	0	0	1	0	3.25		.82	7	.0	0		6	3
DERRY		71.7	50.9	61.3	-4.1	88	1	31	21	164	0	0	1	0	5.23	2.11	1.55	6	.0	0		8	3
DONEGAL		67.2	42.7	55.0		84	1+	23	21	307	0	0	5	0	5.56		1.80	6	.0	0		9	4
DONORA	AM	76.1	54.3	65.2	-2.7	90	1+	35	21	94	2	0	0	0	4.17	1.37	1.00	7	.0	0		9	2
FORD CITY 4 S DAM	AM	72.0	45.9	59.0		89	1	29	21	220	0	0	2	0	2.43		.45	16	.0	0		7	0
INDIANA 3 SE		71.1	47.1	59.1	-5.3	88	1	27	21	207	0	0	1	0	4.57	.85	2.44	7	.0	0		8	2
IRWIN		75.8M	49.6	62.7M	-2.7	90	1	32	21	139	1	0	1	0	4.83	1.97	2.17	6	.0	0		10	2
MIDLAND DAM 7		69.6	52.7	61.2	-3.9	85	5	37	21	157	0	0	0	0	2.54	-.01	.73	16	.0	0		8	1
NEW CASTLE 1 N		73.0	47.6	60.3	-4.0	86	1	32	21	181	0	0	1	0	4.23	1.18	1.23	16	.0	0		11	2
NEWELL	AM	75.3	55.9	65.6	-1.2	90	6	38	21	82	1	0	0	0	4.46	1.46			.0	0			
NEW STANTON		73.6	47.2	60.4	-4.6	90	1+	32	21	195	2	0	1	0	5.10	1.91	1.90	6	.0	0		6	4
PITTSBURGH WB AP 2	//R	70.4	50.3	60.4	-4.5	86	1	34	21	180	0	0	0	0	1.93	-1.04	.45	1	.0	0		8	0
PITTSBURGH WB CITY	R	72.6	53.6	63.1	-4.8	89	1	39	21	127	0	0	0	0	2.91	.14	.54	1	.0	0		9	1
PUTNEYVILLE 2 SE DAM	AM	71.1	43.6	57.4		88	1	26	21	257	0	0	3	0	2.84		.63	24	.0	0		6	1
SALINA 3 W		71.9	49.0	60.5		85	5	31	21	184	0	0	1	0	4.41		1.77	6	.0	0		8	2
SHIPPINGPORT WB		70.7	49.0	59.9		86	5	32	21	189	0	0	1	0	2.59		.57	16	.0	0		10	1
SLIPPERY ROCK		70.8	49.0	59.9		86	1	34	21	191	0	0	0	0	2.85		.78	16	.0	0		8	1
SOMERSET MAIN ST		70.1	46.9	58.5	-2.1	85	1	27	21	213	0	0	2	0	4.78	1.34	2.00	15	.0	0		10	2
SPRINGS 1 SW		66.3	44.6	55.5	-4.0	83	1	23	21	291	0	0	4	0	2.67	-.82	.73	6	.0	0		9	1
UNIONTOWN		71.9	52.5	62.2	-4.2	88	1	31	21	143	0	0	1	0	4.34	1.14	1.45	6	.0	0		8	3
WAYNESBURG 2 W		73.3	48.7	61.0	-4.1	92	1	28	21	168	1	0	1	0	2.48	-1.05	.85	7	.0	0		5	2
DIVISION				60.2											3.71				T				
NORTHWEST PLATEAU																							
BRADFORD 4 W RES		67.8	41.3	54.6	-5.3	83	1+	28	19+	324	0	0	7	0	5.74	1.73	1.95	6	.0	0		12	3
BROOKVILLE CAA AIRPORT		69.1	44.4	56.8	-3.5	88	1	27	21	262	0	0	4	0	2.74	-.40	.73	6	.0	0		9	1
CLARION 3 SW		71.4	46.8	59.1		86	1	30	21	205	0	0	1	0	3.84	.26	.96	7	.0	0		8	4
CORRY		69.0	44.6	56.8	-4.3	86	1	31	27+	260	0	0	2	0	4.23	.36	.79	2	.0	0		12	2
COUDERSPORT 3 NW		66.0	40.8	53.4		81	1	28	10	347	0	0	8	0	4.82		1.26	2	T	0		9	4
EAST BRADY		75.4	49.4	62.4		91	1	31	21	144	1	0	1	0	3.54		1.30	6	.0	0		9	2
ERIE CAA AIRPORT		68.1	50.2	59.2	-4.0	84	1+	39	28	202	0	0	0	0	1.79	-1.60	.68	19	.0	0		5	1
FARRELL SHARON		73.2	45.4	59.3	-6.1	89	1+	31	22	205	0	0	1	0	2.89	.11	.63	16	.0	0		8	2
FRANKLIN		71.4	47.6	59.5	-3.1	84	1	33	21	191	0	0	0	0	4.11	.64	1.00	16	.0	0		9	5
GREENVILLE		72.6	46.9	59.8	-3.2	87	4+	32	21	191	0	0	1	0	2.66	-.71	.76	16	.0	0		7	1
JAMESTOWN 2 NW	AM	70.3	45.9	58.1		86	1	33	21	237	0	0	0	0	4.05	.63	1.24	16	.0	0		8	4
KANE 1 NNE	AM	67.1	39.7	53.4		85	1	27	27	359	0	0	9	0	7.54	3.84	3.73	6	.2	0		12	4
LINESVILLE 5 WNW		69.5	45.7	57.6		83	1+	32	28	237	0	0	1	0	1.91	-1.93	.51	20	.0	0		6	1
MEADVILLE 1 S	AM	70.1	45.2	57.7	-4.3	88	4	35	19+	246	0	0	0	0	3.73	.21	.89	1	.0	0		8	4
MERCER 2 NNE		72.1	40.8	56.5		87	1	29	8+	272	0	0	11	0					.0	0			
SPRINGBORO		70.8	44.9	57.9		86	5	30	26	249	0	0	2	0	4.11		1.60	16	.0	0		8	3
TIONESTA 2 SE DAM	AM	70.4	45.3	57.9		86	1+	32	21	237	0	0	1	0	6.67	3.48	1.42	6+	.0	0		10	5
TITUSVILLE WATER WORKS		68.9	43.0	56.0		85	1+	30	19+	283	0	0	7	0	3.61		.90	16	.0	0		10	3
WARREN		69.7	46.8	58.3	-3.9	88	1	34	21+	224	0	0	0	0	5.98	2.32	1.64	6	.0	0		10	4
DIVISION				57.6											4.11				T				

See Reference Notes Following Station Index

DAILY PRECIPITATION

Day of month

4	5	6	7	8	9	10	11	12	13	14	15	16	17	18	19	20	21	22	23	24	25	26	27	28	29	30	31
			1.08				.06	.11			.22	.53	T	.18		.35		.21	T	.11				T			
		1.03	T				T			T	.01	.02	.02		.17	.16		T	.44	.01			.36	.02	.02	T	
		.03	.88									.78	.04	.01		.29	T	.01	T	.35				.45	.04		
		1.23					.06	.19	.02	.02	.72	.22	.17	.04		.26		.04	.78	.21				.01			
		.37	.84				.02	.04			.16	.78	T			.27				.47				.48	.10		
		.10								2.10				.36						.90							
			.09		T			.10			.15	.90	.11	.15		.10	.07	.04	.10	.08							
		.06				.61						–	.18							.34							
		2.25	.26				T	.07			.42	.60	.14	.11		.39	.15	.15		.22							
		.51	.06							.09	.30	.05	.07	.36		.32				1.72				.45			
		T	.20				.08	.21		T	.16	.18	.01	.04		.29		.27	T	.51				T	T		
	.02		1.04					.04				.45		.23		.10		.18	.04	1.47				.20	.03		
			.83					.14			.35	.32	.21	.17		.27	T	.16	.05	.10				T	.07		
		.38	.91					.03		T	.08	.34	T	.08		.41	.08	.12		.04				.03	T		
		1.30								.03	.46	.11	.42			.43		.02		.59				.30			
		T	1.62					T			T	.89	.03	.05		.27	T	T	T	.36				.33	.01		
		.68						T		T	.88		.04	T		.26		T	.30								
	.05	1.79	T				.19	.02		.74	.21	.22	.27		.01	.49		.20	.76				.32	.01			
		.40						.08			.42	.11	.11			.11				.60							
		T	.90				.03	.39			.54	.96	.46	.40		.52				.55			.28	.25	T		
			1.31				.12	.04			.11	.52	T	.04		.29		.21		.72				T			
		1.48	.27	.02			.05	.02			.27	1.34		.21		.38	.13	.24	.02	.21				.02			
		1.95					.12			.36	.26	1.02	.16	.08	T	.53	.12	.27	.16	.05							
		.52					.20			.12	.76	.02			.21		.06	.02	.16							.05	
		.73				.01	.13		.03	.13	.14	.38	.01	T	.27	.06	T	.06	.40				.22	.28	.06		
		.02	.55				.20	.05					1.08	.24						.95							
			.71				.11	.12			.51	.85		.01		.10		.06		.49				.19	.02		
							.23	.12			.16	.54	.01			.35		.02		.31							
		.70					.24			.18	.45	.07	.44		.12				.45	.02			.38	.19			
			.20				.06	.06		.07	.13	.74	.11	.04		.33	.02	.23		.54					T		
		2.38							T		.53	.07	.30			.03		.02	.28	.25				.45	T		
			.24								.02	.93	.07	.39		.55	.15	.07	.03	.07							
		1.17				T	T	.08			.58	.08	.48		T	.07		.02	T	.36		T	.32	.06	.02		
		.18	.96					.09		.03	.04	.71	.04	.21		.54	.03	.03		.40				T	T		
		T	.82				T	.15			.07	.80	.07	.25			.08	.12	T	.12							
		.20	.45				T	.17			.07	1.02	.10	.08		.50	.15		.10	.08							
			.51								T	.30	T	T		.18			.10	.80	T		T	T	T	T	
	.07	.56					.11	.05		.06	.02	.14	.31		.15			.02	.06				.60	.20			
			1.29				.11	.04			.52	.60	.01	.26		.26		.01	.06	.07							
			.97				.01		.01		.07		.07		.10	.14	.10		.55		.10		.06	–	.07		
		.10	.36					.39				.35	.10			.28		.22	.03	.23			.04	T			
		.09	.96				.12	.08			.18	.53	.02	.06		.23	.02	.08		.76							
		.13	1.14									.93		.09		.28				.41				.66	.08		
		T	.82				T	.28		.06		.40	.03	.50		.12	.03	.04	T	.18				.03	T		
		.06	.35				.08	.02			.27	.85	.09		.14	.26	.06	.08	.08	.06							
			2.66								.04	.65	.26	.01		.35		.03		.62							
		.05	1.00							.02	.08	.27	.05			.13		.04	.06	.78				.60	.02		
		2.00							.03		.45	.07				.32		.02		.32				.75	.43		
		.03	.82				.02	.05			.11	.78	.08	T		.16		T	.09	.42			.10	.69			
		.02	.97				.02	.02			.13	.98	.14	T		.30			.09	.54				T			
		.20	3.35				.09	.05			1.00	1.10	.05			.35		.02	.02	.35							
			1.12	T						T	.01	.26				.39		.05	T	.73				1.10	T		
T		.09	.07	T			.06	.09	T		.36	.39	.06	.13	T	.36	.13	.05	.02	.07	T		T	T		T	
T		.21	.10			T	.05	.12	T	.06	.41	.50	.07	.09	T	.38	.12	.16	T	.06	T	T		T		T	
			.16				.15	.08			*	*	.74			.40		*	*	.33							
	.45	.11		.11			.21			.39	.36	.58		.12	.35	.47		.21	.05								
		.08	.66				.04	.33			.19	.88	T	.15		.24	.06	.14	.03	.03					.05		
		.03	.40				T	.90	.02		.10	.60	.06	.33	T	.22	.05	.24	.02	.07						T	
			.17					.08			*	.73	.07	.42			.45										
		.30	1.00					.13		.10	.10	.80		.10		.26		.10		.45							
		.21	.81					.75			.14	.93	.02	.23		.32	.06	.03		.73	.03			.05	.02		
		1.11	.81				.09	.04			.26	1.30	.04	.10		.48	.10	.22		.25							
			1.70								.16	.46		1.10		.18	.03	.05		.65				.22			
		1.55					.32		T	T	.45	.28	.32			.38			1.35								
		.76	.03						T		.45	.02	.14			.14		.50	.78	.22			1.60	.36			
			.35					.03	T		.46	.41	.25	.25		.56	.05	.01	.13	1.52				.11	.09		
		1.80					.17			1.08	.75	.30	.32		.28	.06	.03	.08	.52	.01							
		.88	1.00				.21	.04		T	.35	.44	.05	.26		.31		.03	.01	.16				T			
		.13	.17								.25	.24	.01	.12		.25		.01		.41			T	1.19	.01		
		.32					.08	.27	.04	.08	.10	.31	.55		T	.44		.06	.33	.16							
			1.98					T			.05	.57	.28	.43		.54	.08	T	T	1.13					T		
			1.42			T		.03	T		.15	.46	.32	.46		.76	T	.05		.66				.04	.02		
		1.30					.11		.27	.52	.10	.48	.21			.42			.13								
		.05	1.06					.45			.31	.69	T	.27		.38	T	.18		.75							
		.51		.02			.28				.43	1.06		.06		.75	.40	.09	.01						.01	.01	
			1.07									.57		.58		.35	.02		.17	.23				.49	.10		
			.08				T	.08			.19	.85	.05	.07		.24	.20	.11	T	.96						T	
		.09	.40					.09			.05	.48	.17	.15		.41	.05	.15	.05	.51					.02		
											.60	.07	.53			.36		.05		.35			.15	.54			
			.20								.01	1.17	.88	.20		.70			.02	.82				.05	T		
	T					.01	.07			.04	.03	.41	.02	.06	.68	.19	.10	.01	T							.02	
		.65					.20			.45	.50	.20	.05		.20				.20				T	.05			
	.37	.14					.29		.03	.17	.17	.63	.03	.01	.34	.51		.07		.02							
			.23				.02	.29		.08	.04	.45	.04	.04		.36	T	.16	T	.31					.02		
		.55	.53				.15	.02			.55	1.00	.11	.24		.50	.06	.06	T	.03							
			3.00					T				.47		.70		.90		.10		.17				.70	.17		
		.01	.20					.18			.03	.02	T	.52		.22	.02	.11	.02	.70							
			1.34							.02		.60		.32		.23				.38				.65	.06		
		.50									.07	.16	.05					.01		.73			.06	.36			
		.29	.58					.33	T		.22	.61	.01			.18				.78			.01	.78	.20	T	
	.86	1.40	3.05	1.10		.27		.01		.50					.71	.05				.82	.02		T	.30	.71		
		.12	.27		.02		.07	.12			.26	1.14	.16	.10		.28	.21	.17	.01	.11							
			.01				.08	.09			.12	.40	T	.14		.29		.09	.02	.01							
			1.55								.14	.37	.15	.09		.58	.06		T	.56				.20	.05		
			.71									.52		.19		.23		.11	.01	.08				.09	.12		
		T	.40								T	.40	T	.07		.26		.10	T	.80				.50	.10		
			.71				T	.12			.30	.83	T	.05		.32		T	.03	.76				.01			
		2.25					.16	.09			.19	.45	.13			.40		.15	T	.50							
	.49	.44					.08			.06	.04	.76	.10	.03	.19	.21		.03	T	.01						.01	
		T	.49					.13			.22	.41		.02		.51				.41			T	1.04	.03		
		.90	T					T	T	T	.56	.02	.20		.32		T	.04	.38	.01			.12	.43	.01	T	
		.84	1.34							.08	.01	.69	T	.14		.39		.02	.08	.30			T	.41	.03	T	
			.76					T	T		.01	.38	.37	.32		.44	.01		.05	.45				.24	.11	T	
			.74					.03				.48	.29	.28		.46			.07	.37				.24	.17		
			.95					.02			.27	.29	.14	.39		.63	T	T	.03	.35				.21	.07	T	
		.04	1.53								.10	.28	T	T		.11		.01	T	.61			T	.89	.23	T	
			.45					.02			.09	.88	.24	1.03		.54	.02		.04	1.24				*	.15		
	.76		.42				.08	.67			.60	1.12	.05	.23		.28		.17	.03	.30				.06	.01		
			.78					.15	T	.06	T	.12	.35	.28			.53	.04	.11	.31				T	T		
		.01	.63				T	.15			.14	.43		.37		.15		T		.23			T	.48	.08		
		.01	.50				.04	.09			.35	.78	.04	.02		.07		.07		.07				.16			
		.03	2.44					.05			.12	.51	.02	.13		.39		.10		.41							
		2.17					.10			.04	.17	.24	.37		.28		.18	.41	.62								
		.69					.19	.02		.01	.27	1.24		.06	T	.62	.10	.03		.04							
		.20	3.64							.02	.30	.42	.05			.50		.02	.01	.70			T	.70			
		T	.98				T	T			.07	.62	.05				.03	.35	.02	.62					.01		
		3.73	.62		.01		.10	.02		T	.41	.82	.03	.12		.43	.14	.18	.01	.10						T	
		.13	.64					.59			.52	.37	.06	.17		.14	T	.19	.04	.36				T	T		

See Reference Notes Following Station Index

DAILY PRECIPITATION

Table 3—Continued

Station	Total	1	2	3	4	5	6	7	8	9	10	11	12	13	14	15	16	17	18	19	20	21	22	23	24	25	26	27	28	29	30
KEATING SUMMIT	2.83	.33	.44	T				.13	T			.05	.25			.12	.67	.07	.27		.18	.05	.18	T	.09				T		
KEGG	2.39	.10	.02			T	.30					.12			.98	.54	.07	.10		.03		T	T					.04	.09		
KITTANNING LOCK 7	2.08	.03	.17				.05	.08				.10	.01	T		.03	.70	.28			.35		.09		.22						
KREGAR 4 SE	4.97	.06	.33				1.16					.12			1.10	.78	.23	.28	T	.35	T	.04	.05	.47	.02						
KRESGEVILLE 3 W	5.20	.50						2.04								.03	.71	T	.31		.41		.03		.74				.40	.03	
LAFAYETTE MC KEAN PARK	-	-	-	-	-	-	-	-	-	-	-	-	-	-		.20	.64	.04	.26	.02	.41	.07	.20	.12	.05						
LAKEVILLE 1 NNE	4.00	.12	.05					.01					.03			.05	.64	.15	.35		.50	T		.11	.68				.29	.15	
LANCASTER 2 NE PUMP STA	4.29	.83					1.33	T						T		.41	.08	T			.29		.03	.38	.41			.08	.67		
LANDISVILLE 2 NW	3.67		.18				.04	.95								.03	.54		.32		.48		.04	.29	.22				.56	.02	
LAWRENCEVILLE 2 S	2.76	.39	.42					.21		T		T	.14			.06	.95	.11			.21	.05	.03	.09	.14						
LEBANON 3 W	5.22						.01	2.46							T		.75	.03	.58		.49		.05		.23				.54	.08	
LEHIGHTON	3.78	.59	T	T				2.00								.04	.82	.06	.26		.46		.04	.04	.72				.70	.05	
LE ROY	3.06	.30	.26				.45	.04								.32	.70	.33			.33			.13							
LEWIS RUN 3 SE	4.18	.71	.31				.68	.10				.11	.07		.05	.28	1.06	.03	.10	.01	.40	.03	.18	.03	.03						
LEWISTOWN	3.42		1.22					.74					.31		.05		.37	.07	.19		.10	T	.04	.03	.09				.19	.02	
LINESVILLE 5 WNW	1.91		.31				.10					.22				.47	.23	T	.05		.51	.02	T								
LOCK HAVEN	1.97						.01	.68					.01			.13	.26		.19		.36	.05	.08	T	.12				.01	.07	
LONG POND 2 W	5.50	.50						1.54								.08	.80	.08	.54		.45		T	T	1.30				.36	.05	T
MADERA	3.36		.04				.06	.67					.70		.08	.02	.57	.01	.43		.19	.02	.08	.02	.44					.03	
MAHAFFEY	4.29		.78				T	1.71				T	.28		.09	.05	.62	T	.16		.30		.13		.16				.02	.01	
MAPLE GLEN	3.80		.17				1.27	.05								.43	.13		.06		.25		.05		.64			.03	.72		
MAPLETON DEPOT	1.95		.09					.68					.24	T			.38	T	.13		.05	T	.03		.20		T		.20	.02	
MARCUS HOOK	3.17		.02				1.48	T						T		.10	.02	.05			.15		T	.21	.19		T	.93	.02		
MARION CENTER 2 SE	4.18	.10	.12				.13	1.56				.02	.07		.04	.34	.72	.05	.23		.40	.03	.04		.33						
MARTINSBURG CAA AP	2.44	.44	.04				.46					.17		.01	.16	.27	.18	.31		.18	.02	.01	.03	.10				.03	.03		
MATAMORAS	6.19	.08	.67	.61				2.63									.51	.32	.12		.20	.03		.04	.71				.21	.06	
MAYBURG	8.19	1.90	.50				2.30	.23				.16	.05			.47	1.30		.15		.45	.13	.18		.35						
MC CONNELLSBURG	3.32		.24	T			T	.44					.54			.36	.51	.04	.12		.14		.04		.03			.03	.78	.07	
MC KEESPORT	3.35	*	.65					1.07				.15	.02			*	*	*	.72		.22		*	*	.54						
MEADVILLE 1 S	3.73	.89	.25				.68	T	T			.28	.01		T	.22	.58	.01	.03		.59	.15	.04	T	T						
MEDIX RUN	2.70	.21	.76	T		.01		.09				.02	.17	T	T	.26	.20	.06	.21		.30	.11	.12	.01	.26						
MERCER 2 NNE	-		.20				.30					.20	.16		-	.30	.52	.05	T	T	.40	.12	.07		-				-	-	
MERCERSBURG	3.45		.48					.48			T	.22				.40	.08					.10			.03			.10	.90	.06	
MEYERSDALE 1 ENE	2.70		.14				.06	.44				.05	.02			.49	.90	.06							.55				.08		
MIDDLETOWN OLMSTED FLD	2.97		.01				.99	T						.01	T	.33	T	.50		.32	T		.01	.44	T			.15	.21	T	
MIDLAND DAM 7	2.54	.08	.28					.03				.18	.18			.19	.73	.03	.04		.33		.11		.40						
MILANVILLE	5.13	.13						.55					T			T	.51	.83	.83		.45				1.49				.15	.23	
MILLHEIM	3.52	.37	.47					.86					.13			.17	.38	.04	.36		.28	T	.17	T	.20				.11	T	
MILLVILLE 2 SW	3.28	.25	.19					.98					T			.18	.31	.21	.29		.30	T	.08	T	.36				.12	.01	
MILROY	4.13	T	.89				T	1.35					.09		.08	.14	.51	.02	.07		.12	.02	.05	.01	.75				.09	T	T
MONTROSE 1 E	5.29	.42	.03	.10				.99					T		T	.38	.75	.78	.39	T	.81	.05		.06	.37					.16	
MORGANTOWN	4.36	.95					1.15							T	T	.45	.02	.25			.24		.11	.29	.16			.72	.06		
MT GRETNA 2 SE	4.24	.07					2.00									.68		.25		.40			.02	.25	.01			.42	.14		
MT POCONO 2 N AP	5.57		.38				2.88									.40	.35	.14			T		.38		.71			.02	.31		
MUHLENBURG 1 SE	4.32	.40	.04				1.13					.10		.02	.08	.24	.35	.32			.98		.02		.36				.28		
MYERSTOWN	7.85	.15						5.30									.40	.08	.39		.57		T	.06	.48				.40	.02	
NATRONA LOCK 4	2.63		.45					.61				.05	.22			.11	.44		.05		.35		.15		.20						
NESHAMINY FALLS	2.42	.29	.18				.55									.16	T	T			.12		.01	.03	.45			.57	.06		
NEWBURG 3 W	1.45						.02					.10				.40	.17	.40						.30				.04	.02		
NEW CASTLE 1 N	4.23	.10	.36				.28	.02				.20	.15		.38	.50	1.29	.22	T		.30	.05	.33	T	.05				.02	.04	
NEWELL	4.46	.46					1.14	.36				.06	.11				*	1.54			.19				.40						
NEW PARK	5.94	1.52	.07				1.01	.06								.44	.09	.02			.25				.68			1.32	.48		
NEWPORT	2.27		.25	.02			.10	.30					.03		.02	T	.41		.04		.10		.01		.52				.46	.01	
NEW STANTON	5.10	.01	.05				1.90					.14		.01	.06	.08	.90	.50	.02	.33	T	.02	.09	.99							
NEW TRIPOLI	4.50	.45					1.13									.61	.41	.04			.35		.02		.82			T	.64	.01	
NORRISTOWN	2.86			.12				.46							T		.35	T	.03		.20		.02	.02	.65			.01	.99	.01	
NORTH EAST 2 SE	4.13	1.11	.16				.73					.16					.59	T			.92	.25	.16	.05							
ORWELL 3 N	3.87	.47	.04					.68					.01			.34	.84	.09	.78		.25			.12	.21					.04	
PALM	2.98		.29					.88							.04		.60		.12		.22				.30				.52	.05	
PALMERTON	3.80	T					1.34									.61	.04	.25		.22	.12		.01	.67	.03			.45	.05	.01	
PALMYRA	4.18		.01				1.79							.01		.70	.08	.34			.40		.05	.01	.20			.03	.52	.04	
PARKER	2.35	.07	.41					.11				.06	.06		.07	.16	.49	.11	T		.17	.04	.08		.46				.02	.04	
PAUPACK 2 WNW	3.90	.20	.13					.96						.02		.07	.44	.15	.29		.46	.01		.07	.36				.27	.11	
PECKS POND	4.77	.23	.04	.07				2.34								.05	.05	.08	.08		.36	.02			.54				.24	.07	
PHIL DREXEL INST OF TEC	3.77		.38				1.52	.01								.19	.02	.02			.13		.03	.30	.20			.97	T		
PHILADELPHIA WB AP R	3.79		.48				1.60	.01						T		.13	T	.02			.15		.04	.36	.21			.79	T	T	
PHILADELPHIA PT BREEZE	3.62		.28				1.74									.17		.01			.11				.58			.03	.70		
PHILADELPHIA SHAWMONT	2.83		.07				.73	.03									.18				.20		.04	T	.57			.03	.97		
PHILADELPHIA CITY R	2.79		.15				.83									.17		.01			.10			.45	.15			.88	.01		
PHILIPSBURG CAA AP	2.50	.17	.10				.57					.11		.02	.09	.54	.24	.13		.19	.08	.01	.09	.11				.02	.03	T	
PHOENIXVILLE 1 E	3.26	.07					.55	T								.18					.14			.38	.15			1.34	.45		
PIKES CREEK	3.26	.60		T				.43					.06			.11	.21	.26	.20		.79		.01		.39				.19	.01	
PIMPLE HILL	3.77	.06	T	T			T	1.68					T	.09		.10	.83	.07	.38		.43	.01	T	T	1.32			T	.34	.05	
PINE GROVE 1 NE	4.27	.15		.01		.01	T	1.51							.02	.03	.87	.01	.21		.57		.09	.02	.49				.24	.04	
PITTSBURGH WB AP 2 //R	1.93	.45	.03								.12	.14			.01	.11	.38	T	T	.39		.15	T	.15							
PITTSBURGH WB CITY R	2.91	.54					.48				.05	.10			.19	.22	.36	.04	T	.39		.15	T	.39							
PLEASANT MOUNT 1 W	4.53	.40	.05				T	.27					T			.14	.92	.86	.16		.90	.03		.04	.65				.05	.06	
PORT CLINTON	5.76							2.70								.29	1.05		.03		.41				.95				.32	.05	
POTTSTOWN	2.84							.87									.54	.25			.14	T		.06	.24			T	.08	.06	
POTTSVILLE	6.31	1.86	.01	.15			T	1.54								.12	.80	.04	.12	T	.50				.72			T	.45	T	
PUTNEYVILLE 2 SE DAM	2.84		.24					.49				.03	.09		.06	.07	.47	.38	.01		.31	.06	.04		.63						
QUAKERTOWN 1 E	3.23	.04	.26				.86	.06								.25	.26	.01	.23		.27		.02	T	.35			.01	.60	.01	
RAYMOND	3.47	.23	.23					.68					.23			.14	1.05	.03	.25		.25	.14	.08	.06	.10						
READING WB CITY R	3.72	.05					1.21							T		.05	.03	.32		.29	.05		.07	.33	.01			.38	.10		
RENOVO	4.37	.92	1.05	T			.09	.33					.14			.31	.35		.37		.35	.05	.09		.30						
REW	4.51	.37	.15				.62	.44				.06	.09			.38	1.37		.08	T	.40	.13	.23		.19						
RICES LANDING L 6	2.47		.16					.96				T				.23	.59	T	.02		.20			.03	.28						
RIDGWAY 3 W	3.32	.11	.08	T			T	.05				.05	.05		T	1.42	.62	.03	.10	T	.24	.07	.14	T	.36						
RUSH	4.58	.60	.07	.14				.35							.04	.15	1.10	.45	.41		.55	.03		.09	.44					.14	
RUSHVILLE	4.48	.62	.12	.12				.49					.01		.01	.11	.89	.62	.39		.49	.04		.07	.39					.11	
SAGAMORE 1 S	1.99		.30				.10	.12					.15		.10	.10	.30		.12		.45		.10		.15						
SALINA 3 W	4.41	.40	.34				1.77		.03			.33	.02		.05	.70	.24	.02			.03		.20	.06	.22						
SAXTON	2.05	T	.20	T			T	.43				T	.13			.30	.59	.01	.11		.08		.03		.10				.07	T	
SCHENLEY LOCK 5	2.39		.42				.04	.08				.14	.01			.17	.52	.12			.34		.20		.35						
SCRANTON	3.33	.73						.49								.04	.04	.21	.28	T	.68	.02		.05	.45				.25	.09	
SCRANTON WB AIRPORT	2.54		.03				.81					T	T		.03	.20	.15	.28		.22	.35		T	.10	.21			.01	.15		
SELINSGROVE CAA AP	3.45	.10	.20				.55								.25	.33	.05	.34		.06	T	T	.05	1.05	.02			.12	.13		
SHAMOKIN	5.14	.92		.02			T	.78								.13	.38		.36		.28		.01		1.90				.33	.03	
SHIPPENSBURG	2.09		T				.23						.03			.57	.07	.22			.07		T		.31			.17	.41	.01	
SHIPPINGPORT WB	2.59	.29					.01				.10	.25			.11	.24	.57	.12	.05	.39		.12	T	.34							
SINNEMAHONING	3.60	.73	.37					.15				T	.05	T		.57	.37	.05	.21		.25	.12	.12	.02	.59						
SLIPPERY ROCK	2.85	.02	.12				.40					.49	.18		.03	.23	.78	.07			.34	.08	.10		.02				.01	.02	
SOMERSET FAIRVIEW ST	5.25		.62	.03		.15	.19	.49				.10				1.29	1.12	.06	.40		.34		.10		.34				.02		
SOMERSET MAIN ST	4.78					.11	.84	.06				.13	.02		.12	2.00	.22	.45			.34		.11	.05	.33						
SOUTH MOUNTAIN	5.54		.26	.02				1.45				T	.51			.38	.88		.02		.38		.01		.80				.73	.10	
SPRINGBORO	4.11	1.00	.21		T	T	T					.15			T	.10	1.60	T	.10		.85	.10	T								
SPRING GROVE	3.12						.29	T					.02			.44	.13				.40		T		.48			.11	1.27	T	
SPRINGS 1 SW	2.87		.17				.73					.22			.02	.45	.28	.10	.09	.10			.08	.25	.16			.02			
STATE COLLEGE	2.73	.15	.03				1.10					.12		.03	.14	.29	.14	.09		.49	.03	T	.07	.05				T	T		
STRAUSSTOWN	7.89	.05						4.84							.05	T	1.10	.01	.05		.51		.09	.01	.76				.41	.03	
STROUDSBURG	5.47	.71	.02				2.35	T	T			T	T		.13	.30	.07	.20		T	.28		T	.30	.08			.29	.16	.02	
STUMP CREEK	2.54		.13	.03			.03	.33				.04	.34		.10	.08	.32	.03	.44		.32		.13		.20				.02		
SUNBURY	3.95	.09	.21	T				.96								.26	.30	.03	.83		.09		.05	T	.82				.25	.08	
SUSQUEHANNA	4.61	.18	.05	.15				.33					.01		.04	.06	.71	.56	.78	.01	1.05	.02		.03	.48				T	.15	
SUTERSVILLE	3.72	*	.29					1.45				.14	.05			*	*	.67	.03		.34		*	*	.75						
TAMAQUA	6.56	1.18						2.76								T	.72		.37		.38		.03		.57				.52	.03	
TAMAQUA 4 N DAM	5.50	.54	.02					2.10								.10	.60		.34		.45				.80				.33	.02	
TAMARACK 2 S FIRE TWR		RECORD MISSING																													
TIONESTA 2 SE DAM	6.67	.39	.82				1.42	.48				.14	.02			.80	1.42	.06	.22		.50	.22	.07	.02	.09						
TITUSVILLE WATER WORKS	3.61	T	.16			.23	.03					.26		T	.90	.18	.90	.06	.13	.46	.53	T	.13	.01							

See Reference Notes Following Station Index

DAILY PRECIPITATION

3–Continued

PENNSYLVANIA
SEPTEMBER 1956

Station	Total	1	2	3	4	5	6	7	8	9	10	11	12	13	14	15	16	17	18	19	20	21	22	23	24	25	26	27	28	29	30	31
D 4 W	3.82	.03	.20				.35	T	T			.16	.04			.33	.08		.26		.03	.32	.18	.02	.04							
A	3.71	.36	.14	.05				.39					.11		.02	.07	.09	.43	.78		.15	.07	.01	.07	.31					.06		
CITY 5 SW	4.06		.22				.84									.02	.26	.07			.55		.12		.60			.24	.82	.02		
	2.70	.10	.16					.24					.10			.16	.79	.09	.29		.43	.09	.08	.08	.19							
POINT 4 NE	3.66	.16	.11	.01			.48	.24				.09	.23			.35	1.16	.06	.31	.02	.28	.09	.18	.01	.09							
4 NE BALD EAGLE	9.18	.03	.08				.62	2.26					.75		.03	T	.59	.07	.14		.43	.01	.08	T	.08				.03	T		
CITY	4.99	.82	.19	.02			.73	.03	.02			.16	.04			.58	.98	.03	.07		.62	.44	.15	.03	.03					.02	.03	
OWN	4.34	.12	.09			T	1.45					.04			.19	1.09	.18	.14		.04	.20		.04	.69	.07							
DARBY	4.57						1.50	.05						T		.30		.01	.05		.16		.03		1.50			.53	.44	T		
	4.14	.85	.26				.25	.26				.11					1.20	.03	.37		.44	.09		.08	.11							
GRIFT	4.54		.33				.42	1.65				.07	.16			.31	.45	T	.37		.40		.17		.28							
VILLE	–	.09					.21	1.80									.17	.09			–		T		.29				.78	.14		
KEL	6.12	T	.57	T		T	2.00	.50	T		T	.12	.05	T	.07	.60	.87	.22	.19	T	.37	.24	.18	.10	.04	T		T	T		T	
KEL 1 WSW	5.57	T	.47	T	T		1.64	.30	T		T	.11	.06	T	.06	.58	.81	.21	.15	T	.38	.27	.17	.12	.04	T		T	T		T	
	5.98	1.39	.37				1.64					.30	.04			.35	.80		.17		.53	.10	.21	.02	.06							
TOWN	2.35							.45								.25	.40	.10	.20		.40		.05		.45				.05			
BURG 2 W	2.48	.02	.19					.85				.03	.09			.08	.82	.02	T		.14		.03	.03	.22							
ORO 3 S	3.02	.13	.37	.01				.61		T		.03	.35			.03	.81	.04	.23		.17	.07	.06	.05	.06						T	
ILLE	4.18		.03				1.52									.54	.06	.14					.42		.88			.18	.41	.03		
SVILLE 1 W	4.66							2.26									.60	.04	.51		.41				.34				.50			
HESTER	2.83	.09					.02	.49	T					T	.09	.24		.08			.18	.02	.03	.69			.05	.83	.04	T		
ROVE 1 E	3.36							.83									.30				.22		.03	.13	.47			.67	.59	.12		
ICKORY	7.59	1.20	.88				1.68	.48				.18				.42	1.40		.20		.65	.20	.15		.18							
BURG	2.70		.68				T	.18					.09	T			.80	.15	.04		.44	T	T		.32							
BARRE	4.00	.66	T	.02				1.40					T			.11	.28	.15	.22		.50		T	T	.36				.25	.05		
MSBURG	2.62	T	.25				.16	.20					.32		.02		.31	.02	.35		.19	.18	.07		.30				.13	.12		
MSPORT WB AP	2.60		.34				.32					T			.36	.20	.32	.13		.34	.03	T	.11	.34	.03			T	.08	T	T	
URG	2.64		.06					.45				T	.49			.39	.53		.03		.09		.06		.39				.13	.02		
SSW PUMP STA	3.95	.01					1.01	T								.73	.09				.39		T		.60			.10	.99	.03	T	
AVEN	3.18						.02	.79					T		.11	.03	.44	.01	.75		.30		.01	T	.25				.37	.10	T	
ROVE	4.30	.42						1.30									.45		.26		.53		.04		.90				.35	.05		
ILLE 3 SE	3.45		.80					1.06								.60					.33				.30	.03				.31	.02	

SUPPLEMENTAL DATA

Station	Wind direction		Wind speed m. p. h.				Relative humidity averages - percent				Number of days with precipitation							Percent of possible sunshine	Average sky cover sunrise to sunset
	Prevailing	Percent of time from prevailing	Average	Fastest mile	Direction of fastest mile	Date of fastest mile	1:30 a EST	7:30 a EST	1:30 p EST	7:30 p EST	Trace	.01–.09	.10–.49	.50–.99	1.00–1.99	2.00 and over	Total		
TOWN WB AIRPORT	WSW	12	8.2	–	–	–	91	88	60	77	6	5	5	1	1	0	18	–	6.9
SBURG WB AIRPORT	W	12	6.2	27	NW	20	83	81	59	70	6	4	6	2	0	0	18	56	7.4
DELPHIA WB AIRPORT	SW	11	9.4	47	NE	27	81	81	51	70	5	3	5	1	1	0	15	54	7.2
BURGH WB AIRPORT	WSW	12	9.7	23*	SW	14	85	85	54	70	3	2	8	0	0	0	13	74	6.7
NG WB CITY	–	–	8.2	58	NW	17	–	–	–	–	1	5	4	2	1	0	13	47	7.0
TON WB AIRPORT	SW	15	7.0	31	S	19	85	84	59	77	4	3	8	1	0	0	16	43	6.9
INGPORT WB	–	–	1.8	20††	SW	14+	–	–	–	–	1	2	9	1	0	0	13	–	–
AMSPORT WB AIRPORT	–	–	–	–	–	–	–	92	62	81	5	3	9	0	0	0	17	–	7.2

st Peak
test observed one minute speed. This station is not ped with automatic record- ind instruments.

DAILY TEMPERATURES

Table 5

Station		Day Of Month 1	2	3	4	5	6	7	8	9	10	11	12	13	14	15	16	17	18	19	20	21	22	23	24	25	26	27	28	29	30	31	
ALLENTOWN WB AP	MAX	83	85	83	84	83	77	71	69	65	67	68	76	81	83	64	72	77	65	68	60	61	69	82	69	66	61	50	55	65	65		71
	MIN	66	65	57	59	62	66	53	47	44	39	48	54	53	61	54	53	57	43	38	39	34	44	52	49	44	41	45	48	52	53		5
ALLENTOWN GAS CO	MAX	85	85	85	81	85	85	78	69	69	66	68	69	77	83	86	64	73	78	65	68	61	62	70	85	70	66	62	58	59	63		7
	MIN	66	68	57	59	61	62	62	45	44	38	45	52	53	53	56	54	55	49	39	42	35	39	47	55	44	43	44	46	48	52		5
ALTOONA HORSESHOE CURVE	MAX	86	79	76	81	82	74	68	65	62	66	69	77	80	76	67	72	71	60	65	61	63	75	84	67	67	59	50	62	61	74		7
	MIN	61	65	49	54	59	66	52	41	37	35	51	52	53	64	53	51	56	44	35	36	30	45	57	51	42	43	41	45	50	54		4
ARENDTSVILLE	MAX	92	92	82	80	86	84	80	71	70	65	70	72	76	84	84	61	78	80	67	70	61	64	72	86	71	69	58	52	57	61		7
	MIN	66	68	56	58	61	65	63	48	44	40	46	52	54	57	59	54	56	43	41	44	30	36	48	57	46	45	45	46	49	54		5
ARTEMAS 1 WNW	MAX	80	83	84	85	82	83	81	81	80	80	78	85	84	86	76	76	79	67	70	67	70	74	82	70	65	55	63	76	73	70		7
	MIN	64	53	57	58	60	64	57	35	34	30	50	54	50	59	62	44	49	40	45	55	30	50	50	45	32	35	51	49	49	42		4
BAKERSTOWN 3 WNW	MAX	88	77	75	82	86	80	66	65	64	70	72	74	81	76	67	74	73	64	68	60	62	70	76	68	67	64	62	68	70	72		71
	MIN	64	62	58	60	66	62	50	46	48	41	56	58	60	66	54	58	62	48	46	38	34	46	56	52	44	45	40	46	42	48		5
BEAVERTOWN	MAX	87	85	80	84	84	76	72	68	67	67	68	76	79	79	59	76	77		66	66	62	72	85	78	67	61	57	58	60	70		7
	MIN	65	65	49	55	61	66	49	43	38	35	51	52	51	59	52	52	55	45	35	44	30	44	45	51	41	38	42	46	54	55		4
BELLEFONTE 4 S	MAX	88	87	79	79	82	82	72	70	66	68	66	70	75	76	76	76	74	82	62	64	52	61	72	82	68	66	58	54	58	69		7
	MIN	63	63	49	50	55	61	50	44	38	35	37	52	51	52	52	50	49	45	35	36	32	34	46	48	38	38	40	41	45	46		4
BERWICK	MAX	88	85	80	84	87	73	72	70	69	67	68	74	84	82	73	72	74	65	68	66	62	69	85	84	69	65	60	59	65	70		7
	MIN	64	69	55	57	60	67	59	48	42	38	48	52	51	61	50	54	55	42	38	46	31	43	51	54	43	39	44	46	52	56		5
BETHLEHEM LEHIGH UNIV	MAX	85	84	82	84	84	76	68	69	64	68	69	78	82	84	63	71	79	65	69	61	61	70	85	70	67	60	55	53	65	65		7
	MIN	70	72	63	59	61	65	49	54	46	41	50	56	55	65	52	53	60	47	41	44	39	47	58	55	48	45	44	47	52	57		5
BLAIRSVILLE 6 ENE	MAX	86	73	78	82	85	69	63	62	60	65	70	75	79	72	64	70	69	56	65	48	59	66	77	63	63	61	48	63	60	71		6
	MIN	63	61	52	59	62	60	49	41	41	39	52	55	59	61	54	57	54	43	41	36	31	43	58	50	43	41	40	43	48	49		4
BRADFORD 4 W RES	MAX	83	83	74	80	81	80	66	59	59	63	64	73	77	77	68	59	66	61	58	57	56	68	72	71	63	59	59	65	67	67		6
	MIN	58	58	41	45	45	58	38	34	31	51	48	53	45	57	34	43	48	36	28	34	30	39	48	42	31	44	28	32	38	42		4
BROOKVILLE CAA AIRPORT	MAX	88	76	76	82	85	70	64	65	60	69	70	79	80	72	55	73	71	58	63	47	62	71	79	68	64	62	58	72	65	60		6
	MIN	63	52	47	50	56	56	44	38	34	32	53	52	52	55	50	51	49	36	31	29	27	45	56	41	33	39	36	41	45	40		4
BURGETTSTOWN 2 W	MAX	88	87	76	79	83	86	77	67	65	64	69	70	80	82	77	67	75	74	63	67	50	65	70	80	70	67	63	61	71	74		7
	MIN	60	60	43	50	55	61	42	32	35	31	37	46	49	62	53	54	55	39	32	32	23	26	48	41	33	36	37	40	40	40		4
BURNT CABINS 2 NE	MAX	91	81	78	82	83	75	76	71	72	77	72	76	83	82	65	78	76	68	67	63	62	70	82	70	68	59	56	67	68	70		7
	MIN	68	54	48	54	51	66	54	34	34	32	51	50	51	52	52	52	52	33	34	52	30	42	58	41	35	39	41	43	46	44		4
BUTLER	MAX	90	85	80	80	86	79	75	67	67	67	69	75	81	83	72	77	77	66	72	55	58	65	77	70	70	69	65	65	73	68		7
	MIN	65	51	47	55	57	66	46	38	37	34	55	54	55	64	52	53	60	46	35	35	29	47	59	46	36	43	38	41	42	41		4
CANTON 1 NW	MAX	82	80	74	74	79	80	70	64	61	58	62	63	68	77	69	54	72	68	57	60	53	57	65	76	68	57	57	53	59	66		6
	MIN	61	65	50	53	52	61	50	44	38	34	34	50	52	50	42	44	52	39	36	39	30	30	44	39	40	38	38	38	41	50		4
CARLISLE	MAX	89	84	81	86	85	80	73	70	66	70	72	78	85	83	80	83	79	68	68	67	65	72	87	85	70	62	60	58	61	70		7
	MIN	69	70	56	61	64	64	63	48	44	41	53	56	57	59	55	58	58	49	41	49	34	44	52	58	47	43	44	44	53	57		5
CHAMBERSBURG 1 ESE	MAX	91	82	82	86	86	75	73	70	68	70	75	79	85	82	65	79	79	68	70	59	63	73	86	72	71	59	53	58	61	74		7
	MIN	64	60	52	56	61	67	55	43	39	36	53	59	53	63	54	54	58	44	40	45	30	41	52	50	42	43	43	47	53	55		5
CHESTER	MAX	89	81	83	83	87	88	88	74	75		74	75	80	85	87	78	80	83	67	72	68	63	69	87	68	72	62	59	58			7
	MIN	71		65	66	66	68	64	47	49		47	61	61	69	62		61	52	45	56	49		55	54	40	40	48	51	53			5
CLARION 3 SW	MAX	86	75	78	84	85	72	68	65	64	69	70	78	82	77	69	74	73	62	64	61	61	73	79	68	66	63	64	74	70	68		7
	MIN	63	62	49	51	55	62	46	40	35	37	53	55	54	61	49	52	53	41	36	37	30	45	49	48	36	39	36	38	46	45		4
CLAYSVILLE 3 W	MAX																																
	MIN																																
COATESVILLE 1 SW	MAX	90	91	86	84	86	86	74	72	71	67	69	72	79	83	85	68	79	82	68	72	62	64	70	86	71	72	59	55	55	62		7
	MIN	65	68	59	59	60	55	63	47	46	38	43	50	52	58	59	56	56	45	38	37	32	30	49	57	41	45	47	47	58	54		5
COLUMBIA	MAX	88	85	84	87	86	79	71	73	69	71	71	79	83	85	79	79	82	68	75	66	65	72	86	78	73	61	57	58	60	68		7
	MIN	69	68	58	62	65	65	63	49	44	41	51	54	56	61	56	55	58	47	49	49	35	49	52	60	44	44	45	48	52	56		5
CONFLUENCE 1 SW DAM	MAX	86	89	75	75	83	83	73	67	65	63	69	67	78	83	75	75	74	73	62	68	52	65	74	81	66	67	58	54	65	75		7
	MIN	60	56	51	54	52	58	56	45	40	38	39	50	50	60	63	57	52	43	41	41	32	40	42	49	42	44	45	43	47	50		4
CORRY	MAX	86	77	78	83	84	71	62	61	62	68	70	76	80	73	67	69	67	63	62	52	60	71	71	66	62	63	64	73	67	62		6
	MIN	62	61	48	46	50	61	44	40	36	33	53	51	53	62	39	47	51	41	35	33	34	44	54	45	35	33	31	31	40	44		4
·COUDERSPORT 3 NW	MAX	81	73	77	80	78	72	62	58	60	63	63	73	74	69	60	65	69	57	57	52	56	69	75	65	58	58	59	65	70	63		6
	MIN	58	62	40	46	48	60	39	35	31	28	47	44	49	58	37	40	48	36	31	34	29	37	37	40	30	32	29	32	39	48		4
DERRY	MAX	88	75	82	84	87	75	68	64	65	69	73	80	82	74	68	75	72	62	70	54	64	72	80	67	67	62	57	68	74	74		7
	MIN	65	65	49	59	62	62	53	43	39	36	55	59	62	64	56	60	54	50	39	39	31	47	58	51	40	46	42	47	47	46		5
DEVAULT 1 W	MAX	90	86	82	84	84	77	70	70	63	68	70	78	87	83	72	77	80	67	68	57	62	69	82	68	67	58	55	54	60	66		7
	MIN	68	60	59	60	58	63	48	45	40	39	48	53	56	63	50	52	55	43	38	37	33	35	38	47	44	38	38	37	48	48		4
DIXON	MAX	88	85		81	83	86	75	69	67	63	67	65	75	82	77	59	72	72	61	65	59	62	71	82	70	62	63	55	56	70		7
	MIN	64		85	51	55	60	47	43	37	34	35	45	49	51	43	43	54	42	38	38	30	32	43	50	42	38	38	45	43	47		4
DONEGAL	MAX	84	71	76	83	84	67	62	60	58	65	64	74	78	70	68	72	68	56	66	48	59	69	78	63	62	58	47	62	72	71		6
	MIN	59	48	40	51	55	56	47	33	28	28	46	44	50	57	53	54	41	35	31	25	23	41	51	42	33	41	38	42	46	43		4
DONORA	MAX	90	90	80	84	87	89	75	74	70	68	71	76	81	84	79	73	78	76	66	71	60	68	82	83	71	70	68	68	73	77		7
	MIN	68	66	54	62	64	68	56	46	45	44	57	55	64	69	59	62	65	49	44	40	35	52	61	50	45	49	46	50	53	51		5
DU BOIS 7 E	MAX	85	74	75	82	80	79	67	62	61	65	66	74	70	76	67	73	71	64	62	62	58	69	78	65	63	60	59	65	65	72		6
	MIN	65	64	46	54	55	64	45	37	34	35	52	56	54	62	50	50	54	40	34	32	28	44	56	46	35	35	38	43	49	50		4
EAGLES MERE	MAX	77	76	70	72	74	77	67	61	58	59	57	59	63	71	67	53	63	63	54	57	56	53	59	73	60	55	56	50	55	58		6
	MIN	62	64	54	54	58	63	50	44	40	40	40	49	53	56	42	43	51	38	38	39	29	31	41	36	43	39	38	38	41	49		4
EAST BRADY	MAX	91	88	82	85	88	87	71	66	66	71	74	80	83	83	71	78	77	70	67	65	65	73	79	73	70	68	68	75	74	73		7
	MIN	65	64	54	55	62	64	49	42	40	40	55	55	55	64	53	54	54	44	40	38	31	46	52	48	40	43	38	42	45	49		4
EBENSBURG	MAX	85	72	76	80	80	71	67	65	61	61	67	72	77	73	65	69	68	58	65	59	58	68	78	61	61	56	48	59	64	72		6
	MIN	64	62	45	53	57	61	49	44	32	31	50	51	51	63	53	52	55	42	32	36	27	43	55	48	36	40	38	42	48	50		4
EMPORIUM 2 SSW	MAX	80	83	73	74	80	80	70	66	73	60	65	65	72	78	72	72	70	68	60	62	47	56	69	75	64	60	59	56	65	67		6
	MIN	59	63	45	48	50	57	46	35	35	32	32	50	49	53	42	46	50	36	32	32	28	26	44	43	34	36	34	38	43	50		4
EPHRATA	MAX	86	85	80	83	83	81	76	72	69	67	71	76	78	85	76	75	85	71	68	67	61	70	84	74	70	64	55	56	65	65		7
	MIN	67	68	57	60	62	67	60	47	41	39	52	52	52	65	55	53	55	46	41	51	33	43	53	58	44	42	44	47	52	55		5
ERIE CAA AIRPORT	MAX	84	74	79	80	84	73	64	61	61	70	72	76	81	70	57	68	67	57	62	48	60	72	71	66	61	62	62	62	70	63		6
	MIN	66	56	52	57	61	60	55	49	42	40	56	53	64	56	47	52	52	45	46	40	42	49	56	47	43	42	42	39	49	49		5

DAILY TEMPERATURES

Day Of Month

	1	2	3	4	5	6	7	8	9	10	11	12	13	14	15	16	17	18	19	20	21	22	23	24	25	26	27	28	29	30	31	Average
MAX	80	75	72	80	82	75	68	63	65	65	64	72	80	74	68	74	73	64	60	58	62	70	78	74	74	60	56	62	62	80		69.7
MIN	66	60	52	56	66	64	54	46	38	36	52	55	55	65	62	56	52	40	39	38	28	48	52	52	38	42	46	44	54	55		50.4
MAX	89	79	80	89	89	74	63	68	67	71	72	81	85	80	68	77	73	64	67	56	64	74	78	73	70	62	67	73	73	69		73.2
MIN	64	59	46	54	49	57	45	37	37	35	52	48	56	62	45	50	58	45	38	36	33	31	38	41	35	41	38	39	43	49		45.4
MAX	89	88	76	80	84	87	70	67	65	63	68	72	78	83	78	64	77	73	61	67	52	62	73	80	68	66	64	59	75	72		72.0
MIN	63	63	50	49	56	59	46	42	37	36	36	53	54	57	54	53	59	44	36	36	29	30	47	47	38	38	38	40	43	43		45.9
MAX	84	83	77	83	82	72	65	64	65	70	69	75	80	80	73	72	73	61	63	62	60	72	75	69	68	66	65	73	74	68		71.4
MIN	65	59	50	51	56	62	47	39	38	36	54	55	55	64	48	50	55	42	36	36	33	45	53	48	38	41	36	40	48	48		47.6
MAX	76	76	74	75	77	77	63	63	57	57	61	69	73	72	69	58	60	60	59	59	55	64	70	68	66	58	53	55	61	61		64.0
MIN	64	65	51	57	62	58	50	41	38	34	47	49	58	65	45	54	56	40	39	42	32	42	58	52	44	38	39	43	47	54		48.8
MAX	88	85	83	84	83	82	72	69	66	62	72	80	85	87	80	78	83	67	72	65	65	72	87	80	68	60	58	56	63	65		73.9
MIN	68	71	61	59	71	68	60	48	45	38	48	55	52	68	58	56	62	48	38	54	32	46	52	52	43	44	46	51	51	53		53.3
MAX	93	92	83	83	87	85	80	72	70	65	70	70	80	85	84	65	78	80	69	71	61	63	74	86	72	70	60	53	56	61		73.9
MIN	68	69	59	59	65	67	64	50	45	39	50	54	55	58	61	60	63	47	42	47	32	35	49	59	45	45	45	46	49	55		52.7
MAX	86	85	80	79	82	83	73	68	68	65	67	66	74	78	81	57	72	75	64	67	57	61	67	82	70	65	61	53	56	62		70.1
MIN	65	67	51	53	59	61	60	43	43	33	35	50	52	54	53	53	55	46	35	36	30	30	46	52	39	37	39	44	47	53		47.4
MAX	86	84	81	87	87	71	68	65	67	69	70	80	82	79	69	76	70	63	65	54	64	72	75	73	71	68	70	74	73	68		72.6
MIN	66	54	47	49	55	62	47	39	38	35	54	52	58	64	48	51	56	42	38	37	32	48	55	42	37	40	36	36	45	45		46.9
MAX	93	92	84	84	87	86	80	71	70	67	70	73	79	86	84	70	79	82	68	70	60	63	74	85	72	70	63	52	55	61		74.3
MIN	69	68	58	60	60	67	63	42	44	38	39	53	56	56	60	54	59	45	41	41	31	31	49	57	43	41	44	43	47	52		50.4
MAX	87	81	82	85	83	78	71	68	65	68	71	78	81	82	67	75	79	65	69	58	63	71	85	70	67	60	55	57	61	72		71.8
MIN	70	65	58	63	65	66	55	50	48	42	53	56	58	62	58	56	57	45	41	42	35	48	54	51	47	46	48	49	54	56		53.2
MAX	82	83	78	78	80	83	74	65	62	60	63	63	73	78	78	57	65	69	67	64	53	58	69	79	64	59	57	51	55	68		67.8
MIN	59	61	49	51	52	56	55	36	34	29	30	43	46	47	44	48	50	43	34	34	32	33	44	51	36	32	32	41	44	48		43.1
MAX	86	81	81	88	87	76	70	71	65	71	73	79	81	82	70	81	81	66	70	61	66	72	87	68	66	60	55	55	62	66		72.6
MIN	74	73	64	67	69	66	57	55	50	50	56	59	62	65	57	59	62	51	48	47	39	51	57	52	50	48	50	52	55	57		56.7
MAX																																
MIN																																
MAX	88	76	81	85	87	72	67	67	63	68	72	78	81	76	66	75	72	61	69	55	51	71	80	68	67	64	57	69	73	74		71.1
MIN	63	61	48	55	58	63	50	41	34	34	52	52	53	61	55	57	54	42	35	36	27	46	50	48	36	41	35	37	47	43		47.1
MAX	90	84	82	88	89	85	70	69	67	71	72	81	82	84	78	76	78	72	73	65	72	73	75	69	67	60		76	77	74		75.8
MIN	65	67	49	58	61	64	50	41	40	38	53	53	55	59	55	59	63	40	39	33	32	47	52	41	45	42	45	44	48	49		49.6
MAX	86	84	75	77	83	84	73	65	63	63	68	69	78	81	73	59	73	70	60	64	52	61	71	74	72	66	63	63	69	70		70.3
MIN	64	60	48	50	54	60	49	42	38	37	40	52	52	66	49	50	51	42	39	37	33	35	48	41	36	40	40	34	39	50		45.9
MAX	82	82	82	83			68	69	67	70		77	80	85	76	67	70	73	65	66	63	66	81	80	69	62	60	57	65	64		71.4
MIN	63	71	55	56			57	45	43	36		47	52	62	50	52	58	44	36	49	31	39	50	54	40	38	44	47	52	55		49.1
MAX	90	93	83	82	88	87	72	69	67	62	70	73	81	81	79	79	76	74	63	54	59	65	75	85	69	50	49	52	57	77		72.0
MIN	62	62	58	48	59	62	52	42	35	34	42	50	53	57	57	57	55	45	36	41	27	31	47	48	38	43	42	44	51	51		47.6
MAX	85	83	72	75	81	82	70	61	60	58	65	66	74	77	68	56	67	69	56	60	46	58	68	75	64	61	60	61	69	67		67.1
MIN	58	62	38	43	46	51	42	34	34	29	31	52	48	53	40	42	48	34	30	32	30	33	44	40	30	30	27	29	37	43		39.7
MAX	89	78	79	83	83	75	69	67	65	69	71	80	87	77	62	72	75	64	69	56	63	77	85	68	68	58	51	61	66	74		71.4
MIN	60	40	46	52	58	62	49	40	35	31	50	49	51	58	54	52	52	40	31	32	26	45	52	43	35	41	42	45	50	50		45.7
A MAX	85	83	82	83	83	80	70	70	65	68	70	78	78	83	77	76	80	68	69	65	65	70	82	75	69	63	58	55	62	66		72.6
MIN	66	67	57	59	61	65	61	47	43	37	49	51	54	60	54	54	54	46	39	50	31	40	51	58	41	41	45	47	52	54		51.1
MAX	90	83	82	81	84	84	78	68	68	65	63	71	77	81	85	65	77	79	66	69	60	63	71	84	70	68	61	56	57	62		72.3
MIN	67	66	55	59	62	66	63	46	42	37	45	51	53	58	58	55	55	46	45	45	31	37	50	56	42	41	45	46	49	58		50.9
MAX	86	86	75	78	83	85	74	65	63	61	66	66	72	79	73	55	67	73	56	65	50	59	67	80	66	59	61	58	67	72		68.9
MIN	62	64	50	52	54	58	49	44	35	35	38	50	48	51	40	40	46	37	35	37	30	32	45	43	40	37	31	33	40	47		43.4
MAX	95	85	82	82	85	85	75	71	69	66	68	69	76	79	82	60	72	78	66	70	59	63	69	85	70	68	60	55	57	63		72.1
MIN	69	68	55	61	62	63	62	45	42	37	39	51	53	57	57	53	57	44	39	42	32	33	47	57	42	42	46	47	49	55		50.2
MAX	90	90	82	81	87	86	76	73	70	66	70	73	78	82	80	62	78	77	66	88	59	65	72	87	73	70	82	53	60	66		73.4
MIN	67	67	54	53	59	65	64	48	42	40	40	54	56	56	60	52	54	48	40	38	33	32	48	52	42	42	44	46	47	59		49.9
MAX	83	78	77	83	82	73	65	63	63	69	70	76	80	74	59	72	69	60	62	50	61	71	74	70	66	63	65	72	70	64		69.5
MIN	65	58	46	48	53	59	48	38	38	35	54	51	55	58	43	49	55	41	38	37	37	47	56	38	36	36	33	32	41	46		45.7
MAX				86	89	80	71	67	66	69	71	76	81	76	67	77	73	67	67	63	64	72	85	71	68	64	57	60	62	73		71.0
MIN				55	64	65	56	46	40	42	53	54	55	58	51	51	58	42	40	41	31	45	52	50	43	41	42	47	55	56		49.4
MAX	88	85	74	75	81	80	69	66	65	62	65	67	70	78	80	78	70	74	61	65	50	58	69	79	65	64	60	52	58	64		69.1
MIN	56	58	44	45	48	52	48	37	31	29	29	48	47	49	55	48	48	36	28	28	22	25	41	44	31	31	35	34	41	40		40.3
MAX	91	90	84	85	84	82	72	73	70	68	71	77	83	90	73	80	87	68	72	65	62	70	84	70	73	61	61	58	63	66		74.4
MIN	72	73	66	67	68	69	60	55	52	50	57	60	64	69	60	58	64	53	50	48	42	50	60	58	53	49	48	50	54	58		57.9
MAX	87	75	78	84	85	72	66	64	61	68	72	76	83	77	62	74	71	60	67	52	63	75	83	66	67	57	49	57	62	76		69.6
MIN	63	56	50	55	58	62	52	44	39	36	52	52	55	62	53	53	50	41	37	33	30	46	58	46	43	42	42	44	50	48		48.4
MAX	86	85	74	88	83	83	71	64	62	63	69	70	76	81	73	55	72	69	60	62	49	60	71	73	68	64	64	65	72	71		70.1
MIN	66	61	49	48	53	55	46	42	40	36	38	53	55	59	46	47	55	42	35	37	37	39	47	44	37	37	35	35	37	46		48.2
MAX	87	86	76	83	85	74	65	63	63	68	70	76	80	76	80	80	80	64	61	60	61	71	74	75	65	63	64	74	76	62		72.1
MIN	58	56	42	45	52	60	39	29	32	30	53	51	55	51	47	48	46	33	32	31	30	29	35	42	32	31	31	32	38	34		40.8
MAX	88	81	83	84	85	75	71	69	64	67	70	76	80	85	67	74	79	65	68	59	62	71	86	71	66	61	56	58	62	71		71.8
MIN	70	66	51	62	66	67	54	50	47	44	56	55	56	67	58	57	59	47	43	44	37	48	56	51	46	46	48	50	55	58		53.6
MAX	84	74	76	82	88	75	69	63	64	69	70	75	79	76	64	75	74	60	67	50	57	68	77	66	65	62	60	66	68	69		69.6
MIN	66	60	55	59	64	69	53	53	46	46	56	56	61	63	58	58	52	48	44	41	37	50	51	51	44	48	45	46	51	51		52.7
MAX	83	82	71	75	78	78	70	62	59	57	61	60	70	77	73	54	66	65	54	62	50	55	64	77	63	55	56	50	57	65		65.0
MIN	62	64	54	54	58	62	52	45	40	35	37	46	50	55	43	43	51	41	37	37	30	30	43	47	42	39	34	40	41	50		45.3
MAX	86	84	82	84	83	76	69	69	64	66	70	77	79	83	60	76	81	75	68	60	61	69	83	69	67	58	53	56	61	64		71.4
MIN	67	68	56	59	60	65	53	46	43	37	51	52	56	64	54	55	57	45	39	43	31	43	59	48	43	43	45	48	51	53		51.1
MAX	86	83	76	84	82	75	70	68	65	67	69	75	78	80	67	73	77	65	67	72	60	69	82	70	66	60	67	56	62	61		71.1
MIN	67	66	55	59	61	64	51	48	42	39	47	51	64	65	56	60	60	43	56	42	30	39	52	48	42	42	45	47	52	55		51.6
MAX	79	79	77	77	80	77	63	61	56	64	62	71	76	77	60	64	67	63	62	58	56	65	77	73	61	54	50	50	66	62		66.2
MIN	60	66	52	55	66	62	52	41	38	35	44	50	50	60	44	48	51	40	34	40	28	36	53	49	39	38	38	41	47	49		46.9

See Reference Notes Following Station Index

DAILY TEMPERATURES

Table 5 - Continued

Station		1	2	3	4	5	6	7	8	9	10	11	12	13	14	15	16	17	18	19	20	21	22	23	24	25	26	27	28	29	30	31	Average
MUHLENBURG 1 SE	MAX	83	80	78	81	83	76	69	65	61	65	64	72	79	72	66	68	70	60	68	65	59	66	80	78	73	60	52	57	61	55		68.9
	MIN	59	63	49	52	56	60	56	37	35	30	42	46	49	58	42	47	52	36	42	40	26	48	59	48	46	33	38	41	34	39		46.4
NEWBURG 3 W	MAX	90	84	83	84	86	83	73	71	68	70	72	78	84	83	78	76	78	69	68	67	68	75	88	86	85	66	65	65	74	71		76.3
	MIN	69	70	52	70	72	69	65	48	47	39	52	52	54	56	53	53	57	58	44	50	29	38	54	55	57	51	49	46	54	57		54.1
NEW CASTLE 1 N	MAX	86	82	78	84	84	79	67	66	66	70	70	79	82	80	65	75	79	70	67	61	62	72	78	73	70	67	68	72	72	72		73.0
	MIN	65	61	48	50	54	60	44	40	40	38	54	53	57	64	56	57	52	43	38	34	32	46	53	45	36	41	35	38	42	48		47.6
NEWELL	MAX	88	89	78	86	85	90	75	70	67	66	73	71	82	86	78	73	78	77	64	73	57	68	78	83	73	71	64	63	71	78		75.3
	MIN	68	67	58	62	65	69	57	46	46	44	59	57	62	67	62	64	65	51	46	44	38	55	57	54	48	52	49	54	58	53		56.9
NEWPORT	MAX	91	88	83	83	85	85	75	73	75	67	69	70	78	82	81	59	73	76	66	68	59	64	70	66	71	60	62	52	57	61		72.6
	MIN	66	67	53	53	59	63	63	45	40	39	39	53	54	54	57	54	56	44	38	39	32	32	47	51	42	40	40	44	48	55		48.9
NEW STANTON	MAX	90	80	83	88	90	81	71	67	67	71	72	82	87	79	69	74	70	64	70	55	64	75	85	70	69	65	55	59	77	76		73.6
	MIN	71	60	49	55	60	59	49	39	37	35	52	48	53	60	62	62	48	40	34	33	32	47	50	42	36	40	37	42	42	41		47.2
NORRISTOWN	MAX	94	90	85	86	87	81	73	72	69	71	76	81	89	88	73	80	85	68	72	63	66	73	88	72	71	63	58	58	63	67		75.2
	MIN	71	70	63	63	67	69	59	51	47	44	55	58	58	69	58	57	64	50	43	47	38	49	57	55	47	46	48	50	54	57		55.5
PALMERTON	MAX	81	83	79	83	83	74	68	66	62	67	67	78	79	83	62	73	75	62	67	59	59	66	82	76	64	59	57	55	66	63		69.8
	MIN	66	62	57	58	62	66	53	44	41	35	48	52	54	62	52	52	55	45	37	41	33	44	52	58	42	39	45	47	52	54		50.3
PHIL DREXEL INST OF TEC	MAX	93	89	82	89	89	84	74	73	69	73	76	82	86	92	74	81	86	69	74	69	65	72	86	71	70	62	61	56	65	67		75.8
	MIN	72	73	67	68	68	71	63	57	51	48	57	60	63	68	60	57	64	53	50	52	42	52	60	63	50	53	51	52	54	50		58.6
PHILADELPHIA WB AP	MAX	91	88	81	86	86	81	72	70	67	70	74	81	84	87	71	80	84	67	72	62	63	70	86	70	70	61	58	55	65	66		73.9
	MIN	73	73	65	65	67	68	60	54	49	45	55	59	61	68	59	58	62	49	45	45	38	49	58	55	50	51	49	51	54	58		56.4
PHILADELPHIA PT BREEZE	MAX	91	86	83	87	87	81	72	70	67	71	74	80	84	87	72	79	84	68	73	62	62	70	86	69	70	60	57	56	58	66		74.0
	MIN	72	74	68	69	69	66	64	55	50	50	58	61	64	70	61	59	64	55	54	55	43	51	61	62	53	51	49	51	54	50		58.1
PHILADELPHIA SHAWMONT	MAX	84	92	85	86	87	86	70	92	72	70	72	79	84	86	84	79	83	67	71	70	63	70	86	85	71	70	50	56	63	65		76.2
	MIN	71	75	62	62	66	69	68	50	45	43	52	56	58	68	60	58	49	62	43	54	36	43	58	61	47	45	40	50	53	56		55.6
PHILADELPHIA CITY	MAX	90	88	83	86	88	80	74	72	69	71	72	78	83	86	74	80	83	69	71	63	64	70	84	70	72	61	57	56	66	66		74.1
	MIN	75	73	69	69	70	71	62	56	53	51	58	61	65	70	60	60	65	57	53	49	46	52	62	60	55	52	51	55	56	60		60.7
PHILIPSBURG CAA AP	MAX	84	74	75	78	80	69	64	62	58	63	66	74	76	71	56	72	60	56	62	46	59	70	79	64	62	57	51	56	56	67		65.9
	MIN	63	49	41	55	52	59	45	33	32	28	50	50	54	57	49	50	49	32	2V	31	25	44	57	35	31	39	38	44	50	41		43.7
PHOENIXVILLE 1 E	MAX	92	90	86	88	87	84	74	74	69	72	75	82	84	90	80	82	86	80	72	70	67	72	89	84	73	68	58	55	57	68		76.9
	MIN	64	70	56	56	68	68	60	42	39	34	48	52	52	64	56	55	56	45	37	50	37	39	51	58	39	38	46	47	48	51		50.9
PIMPLE HILL	MAX	75	77	78	76	78	78	67	62	62	58	63	63	70	74	77	55	61	69	57	62	52	56	68	75	64	58	55	48	52	67		65.2
	MIN	62	67	53	59	62	63	52	42	37	37	47	52	47	53	44	48	53	39	40	40	30	41	48	46	43	37	36	40	46	49		47.2
PITTSBURGH WB AP 2	MAX	86	75	77	82	84	76	66	64	65	66	67	78	81	76	65	76	73	61	64	50	62	70	79	68	67	62	61	69	70	70		70.4
	MIN	65	62	54	59	63	59	48	43	43	40	54	53	61	60	55	58	51	44	42	35	34	49	56	46	42	47	42	48	50	45		50.3
PITTSBURGH WB CITY	MAX	89	77	79	85	87	75	69	67	65	72	70	79	84	79	60	77	74	63	68	53	63	74	82	71	69	65	60	70	73	72		72.6
	MIN	70	62	55	64	65	62	53	47	48	44	57	56	65	62	57	61	56	49	46	41	39	52	59	51	45	49	44	46	49	50		53.6
PLEASANT MOUNT 1 W	MAX	81	79	76	75	76	79	69	63	60	57	59	60	69	76	74	58	62	65	59	60	49	55	64	76	61	56	58	52	56	65		64.9
	MIN	59	66	51	51	53	57	53	39	34	30	32	46	49	50	44	47	48	40	31	31	29	30	45	48	39	32	32	41	44	46		43.3
PORT CLINTON	MAX	82	85	84	83	85	84	74	72	70	68	70	68	78	80	85	70	71	80	66	70	62	64	71	80	72	60	61	57	58	67		72.9
	MIN	63	66	52	55	57	61	59	41	37	34	36	49	50	52	53	51	54	44	35	37	28	31	41	46	38	31	40	46	47	52		46.2
PUTNEYVILLE 2 SE DAM	MAX	88	87	77	79	83	87	70	66	65	62	70	71	77	80	75	62	76	72	62	65	51	61	71	81	68	65	63	58	70	70		71.1
	MIN	61	61	47	47	54	58	44	38	32	33	37	51	53	56	48	49	54	41	35	33	26	28	44	43	35	36	37	36	44	46		43.8
QUAKERTOWN 1 E	MAX	85	85	83	84	85	82	73	69	65	68	70	77	83	82	78	74	80	78	70	67	62	70	84	80	67	66	63	55	66	64		75.6
	MIN	65	70	56	56	62	67	60	44	40	36	45	54	52	65	56	54	58	46	36	50	31	36	57	57	40	40	46	47	51	47		59.9
READING WB CITY	MAX	85	85	83	86	86	78	73	70	66	68	70	78	81	85	69	75	80	67	70	60	63	69	85	72	70	60	57	56	63	66		72.6
	MIN	69	70	61	63	65	68	57	51	47	42	56	58	56	69	56	57	59	49	43	44	38	49	58	54	48	48	47	50	54	56		54.7
RIDGWAY 3 W	MAX	85	85	77	83	82	70	64	63	61	68	68	78	79	69	67	72	72	67	60	68	59	60	67	66	63	62	60	70	66	79		69.7
	MIN	60	59	48	47	47	52	45	38	33	33	33	52	47	51	43	44	50	39	31	31	29	29	45	45	33	33	31	30	40	44		41.4
SALINA 3 W	MAX	83	75	79	83	85	82	67	65	62	68	70	77	81	79	67	76	74	64	68	61	61	72	80	68	65	63	59	76	74	72		71.
	MIN	64	64	48	56	59	64	48	39	38	38	54	53	58	66	54	58	60	41	38	35	31	47	55	47	39	45	41	42	42	47		49.
SCRANTON	MAX	84	82	80	80	33	87	75	68	65	62	65	61	77	82	79	60	66	71	60	66	55	59	67	81	68	62	61	54	58	68		69.
	MIN	63	62	54	54	58	60	57	42	41	36	36	43	44	51	49	48	53	46	36	38	33	35	45	55	40	39	42	44	49	50		46.
SCRANTON WB AIRPORT	MAX	85	79	78	81	84	73	66	64	61	64	64	74	80	79	57	69	71	59	65	56	58	66	80	66	59	61	52	57	67	67		68.
	MIN	63	61	53	59	61	62	46	42	39	34	49	53	52	56	48	52	51	41	37	35	32	44	52	47	40	37	43	44	50	50		47.
SELINSGROVE CAA AP	MAX	88	84	82	85	85	73	70	70	64	67	69	75	78	79	60	76	73	64	66	67	63	68	83	72	66	62	53	59	63	67		71.
	MIN	64	66	50	58	62	65	49	45	39	39	54	49	53	60	53	54	55	43	40	46	30	42	52	44	42	39	43	47	55	52		48.
SHIPPENSBURG	MAX	93	83	83	88	86	83	74	70	67	72	73	81	89	84	78	79	80	69	68	66	65	72	87	82	70	66	56	58	64	74		79.
	MIN	64	69	55	58	60	67	62	46	40	38	53	55	53	66	54	53	58	46	39	42	32	43	55	57	42	42	42	47	53	59		51.
SHIPPINGPORT WB	MAX	85	74	77	83	86	75	66	63	63	69	71	81	82	77	62	76	72	61	66	50	62	70	78	68	67	63	61	70	74	70		70.
	MIN	62	54	50	63	61	58	45	41	42	39	54	54	58	60	54	57	50	43	45	34	32	49	53	46	43	45	42	44	49	44		49.
SLIPPERY ROCK	MAX	86	78	78	82	80	71	66	66	65	71	69	76	85	78	68	75	70	63	70	46	62	67	76	70	68	62	63	73	71	68		70.
	MIN	65	61	50	54	60	63	47	41	41	39	53	54	59	62	50	50	58	45	40	37	34	45	60	46	40	42	39	41	47	48		49.
SOMERSET MAIN ST	MAX	85	76	75	81	80	77	68	65	64	65	67	74	80	77	70	70	71	62	67	64	58	71	79	67	66	60	57	62	71	75		70.
	MIN	60	55	49	52	59	62	50	39	33	32	49	45	52	62	57	57	57	42	33	37	27	45	53	46	36	41	40	44	50	44		46.
SPRINGBORO	MAX	85	85	74	78	86	85	72	65	63	63	70	72	77	80	73	58	74	68	61	62	52	63	72	69	69	69	66	67	77	70		70.
	MIN	66	61	47	51	53	64	57	40	36	37	36	50	56	64	59	49	50	38	35	31	33	39	44	35	34	30	33	33	40	49		44.
SPRINGS 1 SW	MAX	83	70	72	78	76	69	62	60	58	63	67	73	79	72	64	69	68	56	66	52	59	70	76	61	62	52	54	58	69	72		66.
	MIN	57	58	43	51	57	58	47	37	32	31	45	44	49	61	50	53	53	36	33	30	23	38	57	41	36	42	40	43	47	40		44.
STATE COLLEGE	MAX	86	77	79	83	83	72	67	65	62	67	69	74	79	75	62	73	72	60	60	52	61	72	83	67	66	58	53	57	58	72		66.
	MIN	62	59	51	57	61	64	53	44	41	37	55	54	54	62	50	51	54	45	37	36	32	46	61	49	44	42	42	42	53	49		48.
STROUDSBURG	MAX	83	85	85	84	84	74	66	68	63	70	65	75	80	85	58	68	73	63	65	58	64	68	83	70	66	63	52	55	70	65		70.
	MIN	61	63	50	53	56	62	50	38	34	30	42	48	50	56	46	48	50	41	32	37	29	34	47	44	36	32	42	45	46	48		45.
TAMARACK 2 S FIRE TWR	MAX																																
	MIN																																
TIONESTA 2 SE DAM	MAX	86	86	75	77	82	85	71	65	69	63	68	69	76	80	72	59	70	70	59	63	48	60	75	75	67	65	64	72	73	67		70.
	MIN	62	62	49	50	51	55	47	42	39	38	38	54	54	54	48	49	55	42	35	37	32	33	45	49	39	38	37	34	44	47		45.
TITUSVILLE WATER NORKS	MAX	85	75	79	85	85	69	65	63	63	65	65	79	76	75	62	72	73	61	64	52	52	72	71	63	66	64	65	72	68	61		68.
	MIN	62	60	44	45	47	59	43	38	34	32	51	49	50	61	42	47	49	39	30	32	32	44	47	45	33	32	30	32	40	41		43.

See Reference Notes Following Station Index

able 5 - Continued

DAILY TEMPERATURES

PENNSYLVANIA
SEPTEMBER 1956

Station		1	2	3	4	5	6	7	8	9	10	11	12	13	14	15	16	17	18	19	20	21	22	23	24	25	26	27	28	29	30	31	Average
WANDA	MAX	89	79	82	85	87	79	69	66	64	68	65	75	83	75	67	73	73	62	67	61	63	70	85	71	63	62	58	53	73	69		71.5
	MIN	61	63	50	53	59	65	53	45	38	35	47	48	50	56	42	49	52	40	36	40	29	37	51	46	41	38	39	42	52	52		47.0
IONTOWN	MAX	88	77	80	84	84	75	69	68	65	69	68	78	83	75	70	75	75	65	69	56	63	72	82	68	67	62	55	65	74	77		71.9
	MIN	66	62	51	59	66	64	56	45	41	39	54	51	60	67	60	63	58	45	40	40	31	51	63	50	42	50	48	49	57	48		52.5
PER DARBY	MAX	93	89	85	86	87	89	73	72	69	70	73	80	83	88	78	79	84	75	72	66	64	70	86	77	70	65	57	56	64	74		75.8
	MIN	71	74	65	64	67	67	63	52	47	45	45	57	59	67	59	57	62	58	43	53	36	46	58	61	46	47	48	50	53	58		55.9
RREN	MAX	88	78	79	82	85	72	68	64	61	68	68	78	80	75	62	67	71	61	61	58	60	70	76	67	62	63	63	71	67	65		69.7
	MIN	62	60	49	51	53	62	47	40	41	36	53	55	55	59	41	48	54	41	38	35	34	45	54	48	38	37	34	38	46	50		48.8
YNESBURG 2 W	MAX	92	77	82	85	88	78	71	67	66	70	69	80	83	75	73	76	75	66	71	59	65	76	82	69	69	64	56	67	75	72		73.3
	MIN	64	63	50	56	58	63	51	41	41	36	50	49	54	68	59	60	55	39	36	36	28	45	49	47	37	43	42	43	52	46		48.7
LLSBORO 3 S	MAX	84	83	76	76	82	82	70	64	62	58	64	65	70	75	70	54	70	73	59	61	61	58	68	80	67	60	56	52	61	70		67.7
	MIN	62	65	48	53	58	62	48	41	35	34	39	50	54	60	40	44	52	39	36	35	32	35	43	45	37	36	34	35	41	50		44.8
LLSVILLE	MAX	89	82	86	84	83	79	70	70	66	68	72	77	83	84	78	77	78	68	68	65	62	70	85	79	68	63	56	55	61	72		73.3
	MIN	67	60	63	65	60	69	62	43	43	35	48	53	52	56	55	54	55	41	36	40	28	39	49	56	39	43	46	48	53	55		50.4
ST CHESTER	MAX	90	91	87	92	88	87	81	82	82	73	74	80	83	89	89	80	85	79	72	63	66	70	68	86	71	69	54	54	61	67		77.1
	MIN	69	66	59	64	64	64	61	51	46	46	55	60	62	59	56	60	50	45	50	37	32	50	50	48	41	45	46	49	53	47		52.8
LLIAMSPORT WB AP	MAX	85	81	82	83	85	75	70	69	66	69	67	73	80	75	60	74	72	65	66	57	65	67	86	72	66	66	59	61	62	67		70.8
	MIN	64	60	54	56	64	67	52	47	42	41	52	53	54	60	50	52	56	44	40	37	33	46	50	49	45	41	43	48	54	52		50.2
RK 3 SSW PUMP STA	MAX	94	87	84	87	86	85	71	72	70	70	72	79	87	86	79	80	82	76	70	68	65	73	85	85	70	67	59	58	62	73		76.1
	MIN	71	68	55	59	64	66	64	45	40	38	51	53	54	62	60	56	58	44	40	49	32	43	51	59	42	42	46	49	54	56		52.4

able 6

EVAPORATION AND WIND

Station		1	2	3	4	5	6	7	8	9	10	11	12	13	14	15	16	17	18	19	20	21	22	23	24	25	26	27	28	29	30	31	Total or Avg.
ONFLUENCE 1 SW DAM	EVAP	.16	.19	.19	.10	.12	.15	.07	.20	.14	.14	.11	.03	.12	.20	.09	.03	.05	.13	.12	.14	.10	.08	.09	.14	.13	.09	.08	.03	.04	.12		3.38
	WIND	38	33	43	21	10	29	35	92	16	36	20	29	45	60	69	34	50	80	75	82	65	28	50	57	38	26	62	54	18	18		1313
ORD CITY 4 S DAM	EVAP	.18	.17	.18	.15	.11	.14	.08	.12	.14	.11	.10	.07	.08	.17	.11	.02	.09	.12	.13	.06	.07	.11	.05	.12	.12	.04	.16	.10	.08	.09		3.27
	WIND	19	25	32	22	10	12	26	44	37	22	27	13	17	35	51	21	64	50	39	23	58	18	43	48	25	23	35	34	15	18		906
AWLEY 1 S DAM	EVAP	.13	.13	.12	.15	.14	.13	.05	.12	.13	.11	.14	.06	.11	.12	.14	.02	.03	.05	.12	.11	.10	.13	.07	.06	.21	.11	.11	.01	.00	.06		2.97
	WIND	42	36	35	31	34	37	35	52	50	42	73	51	38	114	109	23	23	86	73	92	92	125	43	80	39	56	55	58	28	55		1707
AMESTOWN 2 NW	EVAP	.06	.17	.22	.18	.13	-	-	.09	.12	.13	.05	.08	.11	.21	.02	-	.07	.15	*	*	.22	.15	.08	.10	.17	.11	.08	.12	.07	.07		B3.29
	WIND	31	25	15	12	11	26	6	17	21	16	22	19	18	65	26	17	28	19	21	34	26	33	32	26	21	18	25	24	15	25		694
ANDISVILLE	EVAP	.22	.16	.12	.18	.16	.13	.12	.15	.18	.15	.12	.08	.12	.10	.17	.04	.02	.26	.13	.11	.18	.13	.10	.14	.12	.15	.14	.02	.00	.02		3.72
	WIND	17	22	15	13	11	30	16	50	45	59	3	9	22	2	41	33	5	34	51	41	62	25	18	37	29	51	125	138	44	5		1053
IMPLE HILL	EVAP	.17	.18	.19	.26	.16	.17	.27	.13	.16	.12	.15	.06	.13	.17	.20	*	*	.18	.13	.15	.14	.12	.08	.39	.11	.12	.11	.05	.01	.08		4.19
	WIND	75	84	57	45	52	79	60	43	54	36	61	61	54	115	87	67	74	118	64	128	88	80	88	100	49	65	121	130	46	68		2249
TATE COLLEGE	EVAP	.24	.16	.17	.15	.12	.16	.12	.17	.16	.11	.11	.05	.06	.14	.14	.04	.04	.10	.10	.14	.12	.09	.07	.17	.15	.10	*	*	.11	.05		3.34
	WIND	33	27	35	18	18	33	34	45	41	23	22	21	18	33	44	19	27	62	54	42	71	26	27	54	37	17	25	25	12	10		953

ble 7

SNOWFALL AND SNOW ON GROUND

Station		1	2	3	4	5	6	7	8	9	10	11	12	13	14	15	16	17	18	19	20	21	22	23	24	25	26	27	28	29	30	31
TLER	SNOWFALL																				T											
	SN ON GND																															
UDERSPORT 3 NW	SNOWFALL																				T											
	SN ON GND																															
PORIUM 2 SSW	SNOWFALL																				T											
	SN ON GND																															
NE 1 NNE	SNOWFALL																					.2										
	SN ON GND																															
DGWAY 3 W	SNOWFALL																				T											
	SN ON GND																															
RANTON WB AIRPORT	SNOWFALL																				T											
	SN ON GND																															
	WTR EQUIV																															

See Reference Notes Following Station Index

TOTAL PRECIPITATION

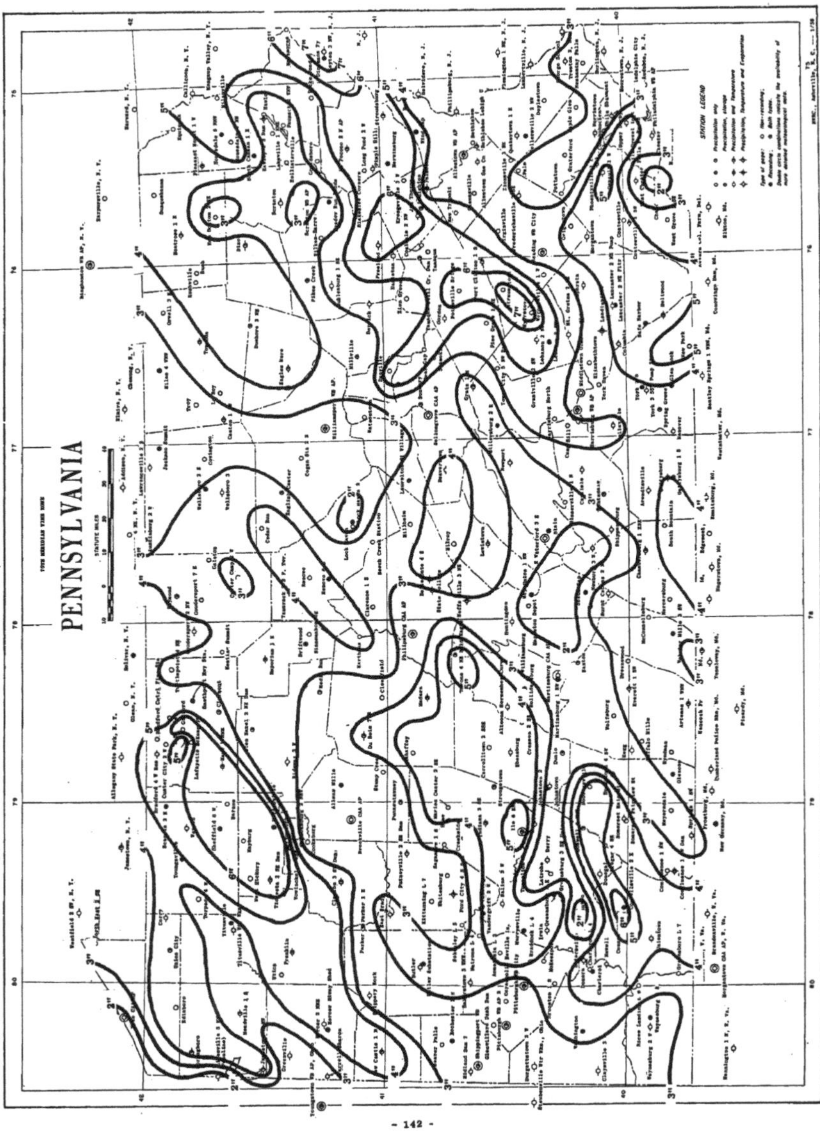

Isolines are drawn through points of approximately equal values. Hourly precipitation data from recorder substations will be available in the publication 'Hourly Precipitation

AVERAGE TEMPERATURE

PENNSYLVANIA
SEPTEMBER 1956

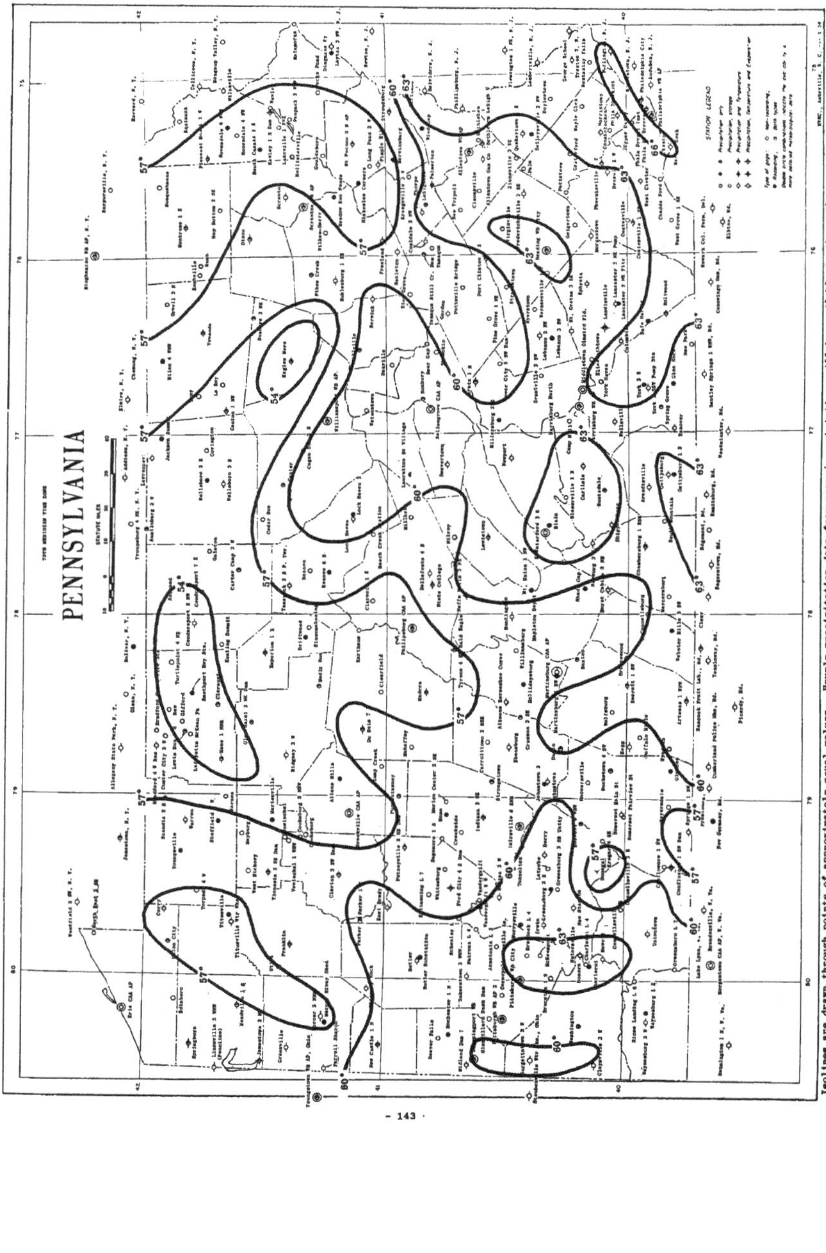

Isolines are drawn through points of approximately equal values. Hourly precipitation data from recorder substations will be available in the publication 'Hourly Precipitation Data'.

STATION INDEX

PENNSYLVANIA
SEPTEMBER 1956

Station	Index No.	County	Drainage [1]	Latitude	Longitude	Elevation	Observation Time Temp.	Observation Time Precip.	Observer	Refer To Tables
ACMETONIA LOCK 3	0022	ALLEGHENY	1	40 32	79 49	748		7A	CORPS OF ENGINEERS	3
ALLENS MILLS	0099	JEFFERSON	1	41 12	78 55	1600		MID	CHARLES M. ALLEN	C
ALLENTOWN WB AP	0106	LEHIGH	9	40 39	75 26	376	MID	MID	U.S. WEATHER BUREAU	2 3 5 7 C
ALLENTOWN GAS CO	0111	LEHIGH	9	40 36	75 28	254	7A	7A	LEHIGH VLY GAS DIV	2 3 5
ALTOONA HORSESHOE CURVE	0134	BLAIR	6	40 30	78 29	1500	6P	6P	ALTOONA WATER BUR.	2 3 5 7
ARENDTSVILLE	0229	ADAMS	15	39 55	77 18	710	8A	8A	PA STATE COL EXP	2 3 5
ARTEMAS 1 WNW	0259	BEDFORD	12	39 45	78 28	1250	6P	6P	GRAYSON E.NORTHCRAFT	2 3 5 7 C
AUSTINBURG 2 W	0313	TIOGA	15	42 00	77 32	1590		7A	OTTO D. BACON	3 C
BAKERSTOWN 3 WNW	0355	ALLEGHENY	1	40 39	79 59	1230	7P	7P	PGH CUT FLOWER CO	2 3 5
BARNES	0409	WARREN	1	41 40	79 02	1310		7A	CORPS OF ENGINEERS	3
BEAR GAP	0457	NORTHUMBLAND	15	40 50	76 30	900		MID	ROARING CRK WTR CO	3
BEAVER FALLS	0475	BEAVER	2	40 46	80 19	760		7A	HOWARD R. KEMP	3
BEAVERTOWN	0482	SNYDER	15	40 45	77 10	640	7A	7A	MARLIN RC ETTINGER	2 3 5 7
BEECH CREEK STATION	0499	CENTRE	16	41 04	77 34	620		7A	HAROLD S. RUPERT	3
BELLEFONTE 4 S	0530	CENTRE	16	40 51	77 47	1110	8A	8A	ROCKVIEW PRISON FARM	2 3 5 7
BERWICK	0611	COLUMBIA	15	41 04	76 15	570	6P	6P	AMER CAR + FNDRY CO	2 3 5 7
BETHLEHEM	0629	NORTHAMPTON	9	40 37	75 22	400		7A	ARTHUR CROPPER	3
#BETHLEHEM LEHIGH UNIV	0634	NORTHAMPTON	9	40 36	75 23	450	MID	MID	LEHIGH UNIVERSITY	2 3 5 C
BLAIN	0725	PERRY	15	40 20	77 31	750		MID	PA DEPT FRST + WTRS	C
BLAIRSVILLE 6 ENE	0736	INDIANA	4	40 27	79 09	2048	8P	8P	U.S. WEATHER BUREAU	2 3 5
BLAKESLEE CORNERS	0743	MONROE	9	41 06	75 36	1650		MID	WALTER WILDRICK	C
BLOSERVILLE 1 N	0763	CUMBERLAND	15	40 16	77 22	650		5P	MRS. B. M. WILLDERS	3
BOSWELL 6 WNW	0820	SOMERSET	1	40 11	79 08	2580		7A	MRS. MAE L. KIMMEL	3 C
BRADDOCK LOCK 2	0861	ALLEGHENY	10	40 24	79 52	725		7A	CORPS OF ENGINEERS	3
BRADFORD CNTRL FIRE STA	0867	MC KEAN	1	41 57	78 39	1500		8A	BRADFORD FIRE DEPT	3
BRADFORD 4 W RES	0868	MC KEAN	1	41 57	78 44	1680	5P	5P	BRADFORD WTR DEPT	2 3 5 7
BREEZEWOOD	0905	BEDFORD	6	40 00	78 14	1352		MID	PA TURNPIKE COMM	3
BROOKVILLE CAA AIRPORT	1002	JEFFERSON	1	41 09	79 06	1417	MID	MID	CIVIL AERO. ADM.	2 3 5 7
BRUCETON 1 S	1033	ALLEGHENY	10	40 18	79 59	1065		7A	AUSTIN R. COOPER	3
BUCKSTOWN 1 SE	1073	SOMERSET	4	40 04	78 50	2460		MID	ALVIN W. MANGES	C
BUFFALO MILLS	1087	BEDFORD	6	39 56	78 39	1318		7A	MRS. NELLE R. BROWN	3
BURGETTSTOWN 2 W	1105	WASHINGTON	11	40 23	80 26	980	7A	7A	SMITH TWP MUN AUTH	2 3 5 7
BURNT CABINS 2 NE	1115	HUNTINGDON	6	40 05	77 52	990	MID	MID	PA TURNPIKE COMM	2 3 5 7
#BUTLER	1130	BUTLER	2	40 52	79 54	1100	4P	7A	WILLIAM C. FAUST	2 3 5 7
BUTLER SUBSTATION	1135	BUTLER	2	40 51	79 53	1140		MID	WEST PENN POWER CO	C
CAMP HILL	1198	CUMBERLAND	15	40 15	76 55	461		6P	JOSEPH N. HOBART	3
CANTON 1 NW	1215	BRADFORD	15	41 40	76 52	1520	7A	7A	MRS.MILDRED SPENCER	2 3 5 7 C
CARLISLE	1234	CUMBERLAND	15	40 12	77 11	460	6P	6P	C. E. MILLER	2 3 5 7
CARROLLTOWN 2 SSE	1255	CAMBRIA	16	40 35	78 42	2040		8A	ROBERT F. MAURER	3
CARTER CAMP 2 W	1262	POTTER	16	41 37	77 45	2030		7A	RICHARD L. MENKEN	3 C
CEDAR RUN	1301	LYCOMING	16	41 31	77 27	800		7A	KATHRYN T.KREIGHBAUM	3
CHADDS FORD	1342	DELAWARE	5	39 52	75 36	160		8A	MRS.GRACE A. HICKS	3
CHAMBERSBURG 1 ESE	1354	FRANKLIN	12	39 56	77 38	640	9P	9P	CHARLES A. GENDER	2 3 5 7 C
CHARLEROI	1372	WASHINGTON	10	40 08	79 55	1040		MID	WEST PENN POWER CO	C
CHARLEROI LOCK 4	1377	WESTMORELAND	10	40 09	79 54	749		7A	CORPS OF ENGINEERS	3
#CHESTER	1423	DELAWARE	5	39 51	75 21	86	8A	8A	CHESTER TIMES	2 3 5
CLARENCE	1480	CENTRE	16	41 03	77 56	1410		7A	MISS VELDA SWANCER	3
CLARION 3 SW	1485	CLARION	1	41 12	79 26	1114	8P	7A	PA ELECTRIC CO	2 3 5 7 C
CLAUSSVILLE	1505	LEHIGH	9	40 37	75 39	670		8A	WILLIAM J. DOTTERER	3
CLAYSVILLE 3 W	1512	WASHINGTON	11	40 07	80 28	1000	7P	7A	MFGRS. L + H CO	2 3 5
CLEARFIELD	1519	CLEARFIELD	16	41 01	78 26	1100		7A	IRA TAYLOR	3
CLERMONT	1529	MC KEAN	1	41 41	78 30	2104		7A	MRS.TILLIE M.SIMONDS	3 C
COALDALE 2 NW	1572	SCHUYLKILL	9	40 50	75 56	1026		7A	PANTHER VLY WTR CO	3
COATESVILLE 1 SW	1589	CHESTER	5	39 58	75 50	342	8A	8A	PHILA ELECTRIC CO	2 3 6 7 C
COATESVILLE	1594	CHESTER	5	39 59	75 49	340		8A	EDWARD D. BIEDEMAN	INAC 12/55
COLUMBIA	1675	LANCASTER	15	40 02	76 30	300	5S	5S	JAMES H. RUST	2 3 5
CONFLUENCE 1 SW DAM	1705	SOMERSET	17	39 48	79 22	1490	8A	8A	CORPS OF ENGINEERS	2 3 5 6 C
CONFLUENCE 1 NW	1710	FAYETTE	17	39 50	79 22	1331		7A	JOHN L. REID	3
CONNELLSVILLE	1723	FAYETTE	17	40 01	79 36	870		8A	MARSHALL B. MENEFEE	3
CONNELLSVILLE 2 E	1729	FAYETTE	17	40 01	79 33	1300		MID	HARRY C. JOY	C
CONSHOHOCKEN	1737	MONTGOMERY	5	40 04	75 19	70		8A	PHILA ELECTRIC CO	3
COOKSBURG	1749	CLARION	1	41 20	79 13	1180		8A	PA DEPT FRST + WTRS	3
COOKSBURG 2 NNW	1752	CLARION	1	41 21	79 13	1460		8A	PA DEPT FRST + WTRS	3
CORAOPOLIS NEVILLE IS	1773	ALLEGHENY	11	40 30	80 05	720		8A	PGH. COKE + CHEM CO	3
CORRY	1790	ERIE	1	41 56	79 38	1427	7P	5A	LEO C. NECKERS	2 3 5 7
COUDERSPORT 3 NW	1806	POTTER	1	41 49	78 03	2020	7P	8A	MISS ELIZABETH NEFF	2 3 5 7
COUDERSPORT 7 E	1809	POTTER	1	41 46	77 53	2425		7A	CAMP POTATO	3
COVINGTON	1832	TIOGA	15	41 45	77 05	1193		7A	GROVER D. CLEVELAND	3
CREEKSIDE	1861	INDIANA	1	40 41	79 12	1035		7A	CORPS OF ENGINEERS	3
CRESSON 2 SE	1895	CAMBRIA	6	40 27	78 34	2540		7A	MILES A. VECELLIO	3 C
CUSTER CITY 2 W	1978	MC KEAN	1	41 55	78 41	2120		8A	M. D. BOOTH AND CO	3
DANVILLE	2013	MONTOUR	15	40 58	76 37	460		7A	MRS.MARIE M. LITTLE	3
DERRY	2108	WESTMORELAND	4	40 20	79 18	1150	6P	6P	MISS M. D. WINEMAN	2 3 5
DEVAULT 1 W	2116	CHESTER	14	40 05	75 33	360	MID	MID	PA TURNPIKE COMM	2 3 5
DINGMANS FERRY	2160	PIKE	5	41 13	74 52	364		MID	CLYDE T. VOORKEES	C
DIXON	2171	WYOMING	15	41 34	75 54	620	7A	7A	HAROLD J. KUSCHEL	2 3 5 7 C
DONEGAL	2183	WESTMORELAND	17	40 07	79 23	1746	MID	MID	PA TURNPIKE COMM	2 3 5 7
#DONORA	2190	WASHINGTON	10	40 11	79 51	814	12M	12M	DONORA ZINC WORKS	2 3 5
DOYLESTOWN	2221	BUCKS	5	40 18	75 08	393		5P	GEORGE HART	3
DRIFTWOOD	2245	CAMERON	16	41 20	78 08	880		MID	SIDNEY KENNEDY	C
DU BOIS 7 E	2265	CLEARFIELD	16	41 06	78 38	1670	5P	5P	CITY OF DU BOIS	2 3 5 C
DUNLO	2298	CAMBRIA	4	40 17	78 43	2410		MID	MRS. D. L. WHITE	C
DUSHORE 3 NE	2324	SULLIVAN	16	41 33	76 21	1750		7A	PATRICK F. RYAN	3 C
EAGLES MERE	2343	SULLIVAN	16	41 24	76 35	2020	7A	7A	MRS.ELSIE P. BIGGER	2 3 5 7 C
EAST BRADY	2363	CLARION	1	40 59	79 37	820	5P	5P	A. B. KEMPEL	2 3 8
EAST WATERFORD 3 E	2450	PERRY	6	40 21	77 33	2125	8A	8A	U.S. WEATHER BUREAU	INAC 5/55
EBENSBURG	2466	CAMBRIA	4	40 29	78 43	2090	7P	7A	ROBERT A. WASSER	2 3 5
EDINBORO	2514	ERIE	1	41 52	80 08	1220		8A	EDINBORO ST TCHR COL	3
ELIZABETHTOWN	2560	LANCASTER	15	40 09	76 37	460		8A	MASONIC HOME	3
EMPORIUM 2 SSW	2634	CAMERON	16	41 28	78 15	1735	7A	7A	JACKSON THOMAS	2 3 5 7 C
ENGLISH CENTER	2644	LYCOMING	16	41 26	77 17	881		7A	WILLIAM SUDERS	3 C
EPHRATA	2662	LANCASTER	15	40 11	76 10	465	6P	6P	STANLEY L.VON NEIDA	2 3 5
EQUINUNK	2669	WAYNE	5	41 51	75 13	900		8A	MRS.ROSE M. NEILSEN	3
ERIE CAA AIRPORT	2682	ERIE	8	42 05	80 12	732	MID	MID	CIVIL AERO. ADM.	2 3 5
EVERETT 1 SW	2721	BEDFORD	6	40 00	78 23	1020	MID	MID	PA TURNPIKE COMM	2 3 5 7 C
FARRELL SHARON	2814	MERCER	2	41 14	80 30	865	7P	7P	SHARON STEEL CORP	2 3 5
FORD CITY 4 S DAM	2942	ARMSTRONG	1	40 43	79 30	950	8A	8A	CORPS OF ENGINEERS	2 3 5 6 7 C
FRANKLIN	3028	VENANGO	1	41 23	79 49	987	7P	7A	JAMES K. ELLIOTT	2 3 5 7 C
FREELAND	3056	LUZERNE	15	41 01	75 54	1900	6P	8A	ANDREW B. EVANSHA	2 3 5
GALETON	3130	POTTER	16	41 44	77 39	1325		7A	W. GALE LUSH	3
GEIGERTOWN	3189	BERKS	14	40 13	75 50	400		8A	WALTER C. WOLF	3
GEORGE SCHOOL	3200	BUCKS	5	40 13	74 56	135	7P	7P	GEORGE M. HART	2 3 5 7
#GETTYSBURG	3218	ADAMS	12	39 50	77 14	540	9A	9A	HUGH C. MC ILHENNY	2 3 5 7
GETTYSBURG 1 S	3223	ADAMS	12	39 48	77 14	560		MID	NAT MILITARY PARK	C
GIFFORD	3237	MC KEAN	1	41 51	78 36	2220		8A	SOUTH PENN OIL CO	3
GLENCOE	3298	SOMERSET	12	39 49	78 51	1620		MID	MRS. MARY M.HARTMAN	C
GLEN HAZEL 2 NE DAM	3311	ELK	1	41 34	78 36	1725		8A	CORPS OF ENGINEERS	3 C
GLEN ROCK	3330	YORK	15	39 48	76 44	620		MID	MRS.E.C.MC WILLIAMS	C
GLENWILLARD DASH DAM	3343	ALLEGHENY	11	40 33	80 13	705		7A	CORPS OF ENGINEERS	3
GOULDSBORO	3394	WAYNE	9	41 15	75 27	1890		7A	L. M. EILENBERGER	3
GRATERFORD	3435	MONTGOMERY	14	40 14	75 27	160		7A	CLAUDE K. KULP	3
GRATZ 1 N	3438	DAUPHIN	15	40 38	76 43	760	8A	8A	LEE M. LEITZEL	2 3 5 7 C
GREENSBORO LOCK 7	3503	GREENE	10	39 47	79 55	808		7A	CORPS OF ENGINEERS	3
GREENSBURG 2 E	3515	WESTMORELAND	10	40 18	79 31	1225		MID	PA DEPT HIGHWAYS	C
GREENSBURG 3 SE	3516	WESTMORELAND	10	40 17	79 30	1245		6P	WESTMORELAND WTR CO	3
GREENVILLE	3526	MERCER	2	41 24	80 23	1026	6P	6P	C. EARL MILLER	2 3 5 7
HANOVER	3662	YORK	15	39 48	76 59	600	8A	8A	HANOVER EVENING SUN	2 3 5
#HARRISBURG WB AP	3699	YORK	15	40 13	76 51	335	MID	MID	U.S. WEATHER BUREAU	2 3 5 7 C
HARRISBURG NORTH	3704	DAUPHIN	15	40 18	76 54	323		9A	GEORGE S. BEAL	3
HAWLEY	3758	WAYNE	5	41 29	75 10	880		7A	MRS.KATHERINE S.BATE	3
HAWLEY 1 S DAM	3761	WAYNE	5	41 28	75 11	1200	7A	7A	PA POWER + LIGHT CO	2 3 5 6 7 C
HOLLIDAYSBURG	4001	BLAIR	6	40 26	78 24	960		MID	JOHN M. RINGLER	C
HOLLISTERVILLE	4008	WAYNE	5	41 23	75 26	1300		8A	PA POWER + LIGHT CO	3
#HOLTWOOD	4019	LANCASTER	15	39 50	76 20	187	MID	8A	PA POWER + LIGHT CO	2 3 5 C
HOME	4027	INDIANA	1	40 45	79 06	1220		MID	MRS. EDNA M. BUSH	C
HONESDALE 4 NW	4043	WAYNE	5	41 37	75 19	1410		9A	GEORGE C. WILLIAMS	3
HONESDALE 6 NNW	4044	WAYNE	5	41 39	75 17	1050		MID	FRIEND E. WALTER	C
HOOVERSVILLE	4056	SOMERSET	4	40 09	78 55	1660		7A	PA ELECTRIC CO	3
HOP BOTTOM 2 SE	4066	SUSQUEHANNA	15	41 43	75 43	900		7A	JOSEPH J. SANSUSKAS	3
HUNTINGDON	4159	HUNTINGDON	6	40 29	78 01	610	7A	7A	MRS JANET I. VAUGHN	2 3 5 7
HUNTSDALE	4166	CUMBERLAND	15	40 06	77 18	610		8A	METRO P. DOROSH	3 C
HYNDMAN	4190	BEDFORD	12	39 49	78 43	920		8A	MRS.GERTRUDE M.BURTO	3
INDIANA 3 SE	4214	INDIANA	4	40 36	79 07	1102	7P	7A	CLYMER WATER SVC CO	2 3 5 7 C
IRWIN	4276	WESTMORELAND	10	40 20	79 42	1100	5P	5P	WESTMORELAND WTR CO	2 3 5
JACKSON SUMMIT	4304	TIOGA	15	41 57	77 01	1690		MID	ARCHIE LAIN	C
JAMESTOWN 2 NW	4325	CRAWFORD	2	41 30	80 28	1050	8A	8A	PA DEPT FRST + WTRS	2 3 5 6 C
JIM THORPE	4370	CARBON	9	40 52	75 45	830	5P	5P	HENRY S. HAAK	2 3 5
#JOHNSTOWN	4385	CAMBRIA	4	40 20	78 55	1214	9A	9A	JOHNSTOWN TRIBUNE	2 3 5 7
JOHNSTOWN 2	4390	CAMBRIA	4	40 19	78 55	1275		MID	CITY OF JOHNSTOWN	C
KANE 1 NNE	4432	MC KEAN	1	41 41	78 48	1750	8A	8A	SPRING WATER CO	2 3 5 7 C
KARTHAUS	4450	CLEARFIELD	16	41 07	78 07	950		7A	JEROME S. HOWE	3
KEATING SUMMIT	4466	POTTER	1	41 41	78 11	1840		7A	EUGENE L. KREITNER	3
KEGG	4481	BEDFORD	6	39 59	78 43	1260	MID	MID	PA TURNPIKE COMM	2 3 5
KITTANNING LOCK 7	4611	ARMSTRONG	1	40 49	79 32	790		VAR	CORPS OF ENGINEERS	3
KREGAR 4 SE	4667	WESTMORELAND	17	40 06	79 14	2530		MID	PA TURNPIKE COMM	3
KRESGEVILLE 3 W	4672	CARBON	9	40 54	75 34	720		9A	CITY OF BETHLEHEM	3
LAFAYETTE MC KEAN PARK	4706	MC KEAN	1	41 48	78 40	2130		7A	ORIN A. BUTTERS	3
LAKEVILLE 1 NNE	4733	WAYNE	5	41 27	75 16	1480		8A	MRS. GLADYS REINEKE	3
LANCASTER 2 NE PUMP STA	4758	LANCASTER	15	40 03	76 17	255	6P	6P	LANCASTER WATER BUR	2 3 5
LANCASTER 2 NE FILT PL	4763	LANCASTER	15	40 03	76 17	270		MID	LANCASTER WATER BUR	C
LANDISVILLE 2 NW	4778	LANCASTER	15	40 07	76 26	360	8A	8A	PA STATE COLLEGE	2 3 5 6 7 C
LATROBE	4832	WESTMORELAND	4	40 19	79 23	1000		MID	WEST PENN POWER CO	INAC 6/56
LAURELTON STATE VILLAGE	4853	UNION	15	40 54	77 13	880		MID	PA DEPT OF WELFARE	C
LAWRENCEVILLE 2 S	4873	TIOGA	15	41 59	77 07	1000	7A	7A	HARRY P. HOWLAND	2 3 5 7
LEBANON 3 W	4891	LEBANON	15	40 20	76 29	460	7A	7A	LEON MILLER	2 3 5 7
LEBANON 3 SW	4896	LEBANON	15	40 19	76 28	490		MID	THOMAS DONNACHIE	C
LEHIGHTON	4934	CARBON	9	40 50	75 43	580		7A	GOODWIN S. DEFREHN	3 C
LE ROY	4972	BRADFORD	15	41 41	76 43	1040		6P	MRS.DIMMIS M.BAILEY	3
LEWIS RUN 3 S	4984	MC KEAN	1	41 50	78 39	1740		7A	RUSSELL LINEMAN	3 C
LEWISTOWN	4992	MIFFLIN	6	40 35	77 35	480	7A	7A	AMERICAN VISCOSE CO	2 3 5 7 C
LINESVILLE 5 WNW	5050	CRAWFORD	2	41 41	80 31	1020	7P	8A	MISS RETTA M. CRUMB	2 3 5
LOCK HAVEN	5104	CLINTON	16	41 08	77 27	570	7P	7A	PETER L. STEVENSON	2 3 5 7
LOCK HAVEN 2	5109	CLINTON	16	41 08	77 27	630		MID	HUGH F. PARKER	C
LONG POND 2 W	5160	MONROE	9	41 03	75 30	1860		7A	THOMAS MECKES	3
MADERA	5336	CLEARFIELD	16	40 50	78 26	1400	7A	7A	MRS. JULIA J. SHOFF	2 3 5 C
MAHAFFEY	5342	CLEARFIELD	16	40 53	78 44	1280		7A	MISS ELLEN J. MILES	3
MAPLE GLEN	5368	MONTGOMERY	5	40 11	75 11	380		6P	FRANCES E.SCHEIBNER	3
MAPLETON DEPOT	5381	HUNTINGDON	6	40 24	77 56	580		7A	MRS. I. S. BUCHANAN	3
MARCUS HOOK	5390	DELAWARE	5	39 49	75 25	12	MID	MID	SUN OIL CO	2 3 5
MARIENVILLE 1 SW	5400	FOREST	1	41 27	79 09	1700		MID	ROY A. MARKER	C
MARION CENTER 2 SE	5408	INDIANA	1	40 45	79 02	1610		7A	CORPS OF ENGINEERS	3
MARTINSBURG 1 SW	5453	BLAIR	6	40 18	78 20	1360		MID	BLUE MT. CANNERIES	C
MARTINSBURG CAA AP	5454	BLAIR	6	40 18	78 19	1463	MID	MID	CIVIL AERO. ADM.	2 3 5
MATAMORAS	5470	PIKE	5	41 22	74 42	439		7A	HARRY BISLAND	3
MAYBURG	5490	FOREST	1	41 36	79 13	1150		7A	CORPS OF ENGINEERS	3
MC CONNELLSBURG	5526	FULTON	12	39 56	78 00	895		8A	MRS. HELEN M. SHIVES	3
MC KEESPORT	5573	ALLEGHENY	10	40 21	79 52	720		8A	NATIONAL TUBE CO	3
MEADOW RUN PONDS	5601	LUZERNE	15	41 13	75 40	1995		MID	GEORGE PEARAGE	C
MEADVILLE 1 S	5606	CRAWFORD	1	41 38	80 10	1065	8A	8A	CITY OF MEADVILLE	2 3 5 7 C
MEDIX RUN	5627	ELK	16	41 17	78 24	1100		7A	MRS.E. M. SNYDER	3 C
MERCER 2 NNE	5651	MERCER	2	41 15	80 13	1160	7P	7A	WILLIAM K. STRUTHERS	2 3 5 7
MERCER HIWAY SHED	5654	MERCER	2	41 14	80 15	1250		MID	PA DEPT HIGHWAYS	C
MERCERSBURG	5662	FRANKLIN	12	39 50	77 54	605		8A	ROLLIN P. GILBERT	3
MERWINSBURG	5670	MONROE	9	40 58	75 28	970		MID	WILLIAM D. GOULD	C
MEYERSDALE 1 ENE	5685	SOMERSET	17	39 49	79 01	2290		8A	ARTHUR B. MC CARTER	3
MIDDLETOWN OLMSTED FLD	5703	DAUPHIN	15	40 11	76 46	303	MID	MID	U. S. AIR FORCE	2 3 5
MIDLAND DAM 7	5710	BEAVER	11	40 38	80 28	689	11P	7A	CORPS OF ENGINEERS	2 3 5
MILAN 4 WNW	5732	BRADFORD	15	41 56	76 35	1448		MID	CARL A. MORRIS	C
MILANVILLE	5738	WAYNE	5	41 40	75 04	760		8A	CHARLES W. DAVIS	3
MILLERSBURG 2 E	5775	DAUPHIN	15	40 32	76 56	560		MID	RUSSELL SHEPLEY	C
MILLHEIM	5790	CENTRE	15	40 54	77 29	1090		7A	NEVIN E. BOWERSOX	3
MILLVILLE 2 SW	5817	COLUMBIA	15	41 06	76 34	860		7A	KENNETH LEIGHOW	3 C
MILROY	5825	MIFFLIN	6	40 43	77 35	770		8A	THOMAS C. HARBESON	3
MONTROSE 1 E	5915	SUSQUEHANNA	15	41 50	75 51	1630	7A	7A	WILBER W. HOOPES.JR	2 3 5 7 C
MORGANTOWN	5956	BERKS	15	40 09	75 54	595	MID	MID	PA TURNPIKE COMM	2 3 5
MT GRETNA 2 SE	6028	LANCASTER	15	40 14	76 26	670	MID	MID	PA TURNPIKE COMM	2 3 5
MT POCONO 2 N AP	6055	MONROE	5	41 09	75 22	1915	5P	5P	M. JOHN DAVIS, JR.	2 3 5 7 C
MOUNT UNION 1 N	6067	MIFFLIN	6	40 24	77 53	820		MID	MT UNION WTR WORKS	C
MUHLENBURG 1 SE	6090	LUZERNE	15	41 13	76 08	1110	6P	6P	THEODORE J. SAMPSON	2 3 5
MURRYSVILLE	6111	WESTMORELAND	10	40 26	79 42	903		MID	DAVID C. SHAW	C
MYERSTOWN	6126	LEBANON	14	40 22	76 18	480		8A	MRS.KATHLEEN MANDELL	3
NATRONA LOCK 4	6151	ALLEGHENY	1	40 37	79 43	800		7A	CORPS OF ENGINEERS	3
NEFFS MILLS 3 NE	6174	HUNTINGDON	6	40 40	77 55	900		MID	PA STATE UNIVERSITY	C
NEW CASTLE 1 N	6233	LAWRENCE	2	41 01	80 22	825	5P	7A	BAXTER F. JOHNSON	2 3 5 7 C
NESHAMINY FALLS	6194	BUCKS	5	40 09	74 57	60		MID	PHILA SUB WATER CO	3
NEWBURG 3 W	6225	FRANKLIN	15	40 09	77 37	745	MID	MID	PA TURNPIKE COMM	2 3 5
#NEWELL	6246	FAYETTE	10	40 05	79 54	805	12M	12M	GENERAL CHEMICAL CO	2 3 5
NEW PARK	6289	YORK	15	39 44	76 30	780		6P	CLINTON J. ALLEN	3
NEWPORT	6297	PERRY	6	40 29	77 08	400	7A	7A	MRS. FRANCES K. FRY	2 3 5 7
NEW STANTON	6310	WESTMORELAND	10	40 13	79 36	980	MID	MID	PA TURNPIKE COMM	2 3 5
NEW TRIPOLI	6326	LEHIGH	14	40 41	75 45	570		6P	FRED C. OSWALD	3
NORRISTOWN	6370	MONTGOMERY	14	40 07	75 21	75	MID	8A	GEORGE M. BOONE	2 3 5
NORTH EAST 2 SE	6396	ERIE	8	42 12	79 49	1060		9A	ELLSWORTH WEAVER	3
ORWELL 3 N	6621	BRADFORD	15	41 55	76 16	1620		8A	WILLIAM I. BROWN	3
PALM	6681	MONTGOMERY	14	40 26	75 32	385		8A	FRED C. ESCHBACH	3
#PALMERTON	6689	CARBON	9	40 48	75 37	435	MID	MID	NEW JERSEY ZINC CO	2 3 5 7
PALMYRA	6694	LEBANON	15	40 18	76 35	480		7P	EARL E. RHOADS	3
PARKER	6721	ARMSTRONG	1	41 05	79 41	1140		7A	LOUIS A. MALARKEY	3
PARKER 1 E	6724	CLARION	1	41 06	79 40	1100		MID	P. M. NEELY	
PAUPACK 2 WNW	6762	PIKE	5	41 24	75 14	1360		8A	MISS L. VETTERLEIN	3
PECKS POND	6786	PIKE	5	41 17	75 06	1380		9A	MRS. CARRIE NESS	3
#PHIL DREXEL INST OF TEC	6879	PHILADELPHIA	14	39 57	75 11	30	MID	MID	FRANCIS K. DAVIS.JR	2 3 5
PHILADELPHIA WB AP	6889	PHILADELPHIA	5	39 53	75 14	13	MID	MID	U.S. WEATHER BUREAU	2 3 5 7
#PHILADELPHIA PT BREEZE	6899	PHILADELPHIA	5	39 55	75 12	32	MID	MID	ATLANTIC REFINING	2 3 5
PHILADELPHIA SHAWMONT	6904	PHILADELPHIA	5	40 02	75 15	70	7P	7P	SCHUYLKILL NAVIG CO	2 3 5 7
#PHILADELPHIA CITY	6909	PHILADELPHIA	5	39 57	75 09	26	9A	9A	USN HYDROGRAPHIC OFF	2 3 5
PHILIPSBURG CAA AP	6916	CENTRE	6	40 54	78 05	1918	8P	8P	CIVIL AERO. ADM.	2 3 5 7
PHOENIXVILLE 1 E	6927	CHESTER	14	40 07	75 30	105	6P	MID	PHILA SUB WATER CO	2 3 5 7
PIKES CREEK	6939	LUZERNE	15	41 18	76 08	1320		MID	HARRY SHELDON	3
PIMPLE HILL	6944	MONROE	9	41 02	75 30	2215	9A	9A	PA DEPT FRST + WTRS	2 3 5 6
PINE GROVE 1 NE	6954	SCHUYLKILL	15	40 34	76 22	535		8A	PA POWER + LIGHT CO	3
PITTSBURGH WB AP 2	6993	ALLEGHENY	11	40 30	80 13	1151	MID	MID	U.S. WEATHER BUREAU	2 3 5 7
#PITTSBURGH WB CITY	6997	ALLEGHENY	11	40 27	80 00	749	MID	MID	U.S. WEATHER BUREAU	2 3 5
PLEASANT MOUNT 1 W	7029	WAYNE	5	41 44	75 27	1800	8A	8A	PA FISH COMM	2 3 5
PORT CLINTON	7116	SCHUYLKILL	14	40 35	76 02	450	7A	7A	MRS. ADA E. RARICK	2 3 5 7
PORTLAND	7127	NORTHAMPTON	5	40 55	75 06	297		8A	JOINT BRIDGE COMM	INAC 1/56
POTTSTOWN	7149	MONTGOMERY	14	40 15	75 39	160		8A	MILES E. SMITH	3
POTTSVILLE	7161	SCHUYLKILL	14	40 42	76 11	690		8A	LLOYD E. WELLER	3
PUNXSUTAWNEY	7217	JEFFERSON	1	40 57	79 00	1298		MID	JOHN VOLANSKY	
PUTNEYVILLE 2 SE DAM	7229	ARMSTRONG	1	40 55	79 17	1270	8A	8A	CORPS OF ENGINEERS	2 3 5
QUAKERTOWN 1 E	7239	BUCKS	5	40 26	75 20	490	5P	5P	DENNIS K. FLUCK	2 3 5 7
RAYMOND	7310	POTTER	13	41 52	77 52	2220		7A	MRS. RACHEL LANGAN	3
#READING WB CITY	7318	BERKS	14	40 20	75 58	266	MID	MID	U.S. WEATHER BUREAU	2 3 5 7
RENOVO	7409	CLINTON	16	41 20	77 46	660		7A	MRS. CAROLINE BAIRD	3
RENOVO 5 S	7410	CLINTON	16	41 14	77 46	2035		MID	C. F. BILLETTE	
REW	7425	MC KEAN	1	41 54	78 32	2250		8A	HAROLD C. MEALY	3
RICES LANDING L 6	7443	GREENE	10	39 57	80 00	775		7A	CORPS OF ENGINEERS	3
RIDGWAY 3 W	7477	ELK	1	41 25	78 47	1420	7A	7A	BOROUGH OF RIDGWAY	2 3 5 7
ROCHESTER 1 N	7540	BEAVER	2	40 43	80 18	900		MID	DEQUESNE LIGHT CO	
RUSH	7694	SUSQUEHANNA	15	41 47	76 03	1000		9A	MISS MAUDE MC CAIN	3
RUSHVILLE	7727	SUSQUEHANNA	15	41 47	76 07	870		7A	CARL KOPATZ	3
SAFE HARBOR	7732	LANCASTER	15	39 55	76 23	270		MID	S.H.WATER POWER CORP	
SAGAMORE 1 S	7739	INDIANA	1	40 46	79 14	1320		7A	CORPS OF ENGINEERS	3
SALINA 3 W	7782	WESTMORELAND	7	40 31	79 33	1109	6P	6P	MUN AUTH WSTMRLD CO	2 3 5
SAXTON	7846	BEDFORD	6	40 12	78 15	780		8A	MRS.ALVERTA L.HOLMES	3
SCANDIA 2 E	7855	WARREN	1	41 55	79 01	2040		MID	DAVID R. ANDERSON	
SCHENLEY LOCK 5	7863	ARMSTRONG	1	40 41	79 40	783		VAR	CORPS OF ENGINEERS	3
#SCRANTON	7902	LACKAWANNA	15	41 25	75 40	746	7A	7A	U.S. POST OFFICE	2 3 5
SCRANTON WB AIRPORT	7905	LUZERNE	15	41 20	75 44	956	MID	MID	U.S. WEATHER BUREAU	2 3 5 7
SELINSGROVE CAA AP	7931	SNYDER	15	40 49	76 52	437	MID	MID	CIVIL AERO. ADM.	2 3 5 7

STATION INDEX

Station	Index No.	County	Drainage ‡	Latitude	Longitude	Elevation	Observation Time Temp.	Observation Time Precip.	Observer	Refer To Tables
ERSVILLE 2 NW	7938	BUCKS	5	40 23	75 20	530		MID	SELLERSVILLE WTR CO	C
E GAP	7965	HUNTINGDON	6	40 11	77 52	1000		MID	MRS. HELEN H. PYLE	C
OKIN	7978	NORTHUMBLAND	15	40 48	76 33	770		8A	ROARING CRK WTR CO	3
FIELD 6 W	8026	WARREN	1	41 41	79 09	1940		MID	L. N. HANSON	C
PENSBURG	8073	FRANKLIN	15	40 03	77 32	709	4P	4P	KEITH B. ALLEN	2 3 5
PINGPORT WB	8078	BEAVER	11	40 37	80 26	740	MID	MID	U.S. WEATHER BUREAU	2 3 5 7 C
EMAHONING	8145	CAMERON	16	41 19	78 05	790		7A	MRS.FRANCES CALDWELL	3
PERY ROCK	8184	BUTLER	2	41 04	80 03	1345	7P	7A	WALTER D. ALBERT	2 3 5
MPORT HIGHWAY SHED	8190	MC KEAN	1	41 49	78 27	1510		MID	PA DEPT HIGHWAYS	C
RSET FAIRVIEW ST	8244	SOMERSET	17	40 01	79 05	2140		7A	HOWARD G. PECK	3
RSET MAIN ST	8249	SOMERSET	17	40 01	79 05	2150	6P	6P	DAVID L. GROVE	2 3 5 7
H CANAAN 1 NE	8275	WAYNE	5	41 31	75 24	1400		MID	EUGENE W. COOK	C
H MOUNTAIN	8308	FRANKLIN	12	39 51	77 30	1520		7A	PA DEPT OF HEALTH	3
NGBORO	8359	CRAWFORD	8	41 48	80 23	900	8A	8A	SPRINGBORO BOROUGH	2 3 5 7 C
NG GROVE	8379	YORK	15	39 52	76 52	470		4P	P. H. GLATFELTER CO	3 C
NGS 1 SW	8395	SOMERSET	17	39 44	79 10	2500	8P	8P	ALLEN E. YODER	2 3 5 7
E COLLEGE	8449	CENTRE	16	40 48	77 52	1175	MID	MID	PA STATE COLLEGE	2 3 5 6 C
USSTOWN	8570	BERKS	14	40 29	76 11	600		8A	JACOB KLAHR	3
NGSTOWN	8589	INDIANA	4	40 33	78 55	1880		MID	HARRY F. BENNETT	C
UDSBURG	8596	MONROE	5	40 59	75 12	480	11P	11P	WILLIAM MAGERTY	2 3 5 7 C
P CREEK	8610	JEFFERSON	1	41 01	78 56	1320		7A	CORPS OF ENGINEERS	3
URY	8668	NORTHUMBLAND	15	40 51	76 48	440		7A	CHARLES W. BAYLER	3 C
UEHANNA	8692	SUSQUEHANNA	15	41 57	75 36	1020		7A	MRS. LAURA A.BENSON	3
RSVILLE	8699	ALLEGHENY	17	40 14	79 48	765		7A	FRANK E. MARSH	3
QUA	8758	SCHUYLKILL	14	40 48	75 58	830		8A	MRS. MARY L.ROBERTS	3
QUA 4 N DAM	8763	SCHUYLKILL	14	40 51	75 59	1120		7A	PANTHER VLY WTR CO	3 C
RACK 2 S FIRE TWR	8770	CLINTON	16	41 24	77 51	2220	7A	7A	JAMES E. SWARTZ	2 3 5 7
ESTA 2 SE DAM	8873	FOREST	1	41 29	79 26	1200	8A	8A	CORPS OF ENGINEERS	2 3 5 7 C
SVILLE	8885	CRAWFORD	1	41 38	79 40	1550		MID	PA ELECTRIC CO	C
SVILLE WATER WORKS	8888	CRAWFORD	1	41 38	79 42	1220	7P	7P	CITY OF TITUSVILLE	2 3 5
EDO 4 W	8901	WARREN	1	41 47	79 32	1735		7A	MRS. LILY B. GARBER	3
NDA	8905	BRADFORD	15	41 46	76 26	760	7P	7A	MRS. M. O. PARKS	2 3 5 7 C
R CITY 5 SW	8910	DAUPHIN	15	40 31	76 37	745		6P	HARRISBURG WTR DEPT	3 7
	8959	BRADFORD	15	41 47	76 47	1100		7A	JENNIE L. BALLARD	3
ELTON	8989	INDIANA	4	40 27	79 23	890		MID	MRS. MARY E. WEIMER	C
LEPOINT 4 NE	9002	MC KEAN	1	41 54	78 16	1640		7A	ROBERT D. STRAIT	3
NE 4 NE BALD EAGLE	9024	BLAIR	6	40 43	78 12	1020		7A	FREDERICK L. FRIDAY	3 C
N CITY	9042	ERIE	1	41 54	79 50	1325		7A	FORREST M. BRALEY	3 C
NTOWN	9050	FAYETTE	10	39 54	79 44	1040	10P	10P	WM. W. MARSTELLER	2 3 5 7
R DARBY	9074	DELAWARE	5	39 58	75 18	222	7P	7P	PHIL. SUB.TRANS. CO	2 3 5
A	9099	VENANGO	1	41 26	79 57	1030		7A	MRS.FLORENCE MILLER	3
ERGRIFT	9128	WESTMORELAND	7	40 36	79 33	800		7A	UNITED ENG+FNDRY CO	3
ERGRIFT 2 W	9133	WESTMORELAND	7	40 36	79 36	995		MID	EUGENE R. YOUNG	C
INVILLE	9196	BERKS	14	40 31	75 52	350		8A	MRS. MARY M. WRIGHT	3
NCKEL	9206	CLARION	1	41 25	79 14	1620		8A	PA DEPT FRST + WTRS	3
VOWINCKEL 1 WSW	9209	CLARION	1	41 24	79 15	1610		8A	PA DEPT FRST + WTRS	3
WARREN	9298	WARREN	1	41 51	79 08	1280	7P	7A	GILBERT H. REIER	2 3 5 7
WASHINGTON	9312	WASHINGTON	11	40 11	80 14	1200		MID	PA DEPT HIGHWAYS	C
WATSONTOWN	9345	NORTHUMBLAND	16	41 05	76 52	470		8A	OWEN HERKENSTOCK	3
WAYNESBURG 2 W	9362	GREENE	10	39 54	80 13	980	6P	7A	RALPH L. AMOS	2 3 5 7
WAYNESBURG 1 E	9367	GREENE	10	39 54	80 10	940		MID	SEWAGE DISPOSAL PLT	C
WEBSTER MILLS 3 SW	9380	FULTON	12	39 49	78 05	920		MID	WILLIAM D. COVER	C
WELLSBORO 3 S	9408	TIOGA	16	41 43	77 16	1920	7A	7A	MARION L. SHUMWAY	2 3 5 7
WELLSBORO 2 E	9412	TIOGA	16	41 45	77 16	1550		MID	MRS. IDA S. MAYNARD	C
WELLSVILLE	9420	YORK	15	40 03	76 57	500	5P	5P	D. D. HOOVER	2 3 5
WERNERSVILLE 1 W	9430	BERKS	14	40 20	76 06	405		8A	CHARLES A. GRUBER	3
WEST CHESTER	9464	CHESTER	5	39 58	75 36	440	8A	8A	DAILY LOCAL NEWS	2 3 5 7
WEST GROVE 1 E	9503	CHESTER	5	39 49	75 49	440		8A	CONARD-PYLE CO	3
WEST HICKORY	9507	FOREST	1	41 34	79 25	1090		8A	MRS.HELEN F.KINNEAR	3
WHITESBURG	9655	ARMSTRONG	1	40 45	79 24	1530		7A	CORPS OF ENGINEERS	3
WILKES-BARRE	9702	LAZERNE	15	41 15	75 52	610		7A	MRS. MARY G. WIRHAK	3
WILLIAMSBURG	9714	BLAIR	6	40 28	78 12	860		7A	MYRON K. BIDDLE	3
WILLIAMSPORT WB AP	9728	LYCOMING	16	41 15	76 55	527	MID	MID	U.S. WEATHER BUREAU	2 3 5 7 C
WIND GAP	9781	NORTHAMPTON	5	40 51	75 18	720		MID	OWEN R. PARRY	C
WOLFSBURG	9823	BEDFORD	6	40 03	78 32	1190		7A	WALTER C. RICE	3
YORK 3 SSW PUMP STA	9933	YORK	15	39 55	76 45	390	5P	5P	YORK WATER COMPANY	2 3 5 7
YORK 2 S FILTER PLANT	9938	YORK	15	39 56	76 44	640		MID	YORK WATER COMPANY	C
YORK HAVEN	9950	YORK	15	40 07	76 43	310		8A	METROPOL EDISON CO	3
YOUNGSVILLE	9966	WARREN	1	41 51	79 20	1225		MID	HENRY CARLETT	C
ZION GROVE	9990	SCHUYLKILL	15	40 54	76 13	940		7A	JAMES D. TEETER	3
ZIONSVILLE 3 SE	9995	LEHIGH	14	40 27	75 27	660		7A	LESLIE HOWATT	3

‡ 1-ALLEGHENY; 2-BEAVER; 3- 4-CONEMAUGH; 5-DELAWARE; 6-JUNIATA; 7-KISKIMINETAS; 8-LAKE ERIE; 9-LEHIGH; 10-MONONGAHELA; 11-OHIO; 12-POTOMAC; 13-LAKE ONTARIO; 14-SCHUYLKILL; 15-SUSQUEHANNA; 16-WEST BRANCH; 17-YOUGHIOGHENY

REFERENCE NOTES

Additional information regarding the climate of Pennsylvania may be obtained by writing to the State Climatologist at Weather Bureau Airport Station, Harrisburg State Airport, New Cumberland, Pennsylvania, or to any Weather Bureau Office near you.

The four digit identification numbers in the index number column of the Station Index are assigned on a state basis. There will be no duplication of numbers within a state.

Figures and letters following the station name, such as 12 SSW, indicate distance in miles and direction from the post office.

Observation times given in the Station Index are in local standard time.

Delayed data and corrections will be carried only in the June and December issues of this bulletin.

Monthly and seasonal snowfall and heating degree days for the preceding 12 months will be carried in the June issue of this bulletin.

Stations appearing in the Index, but for which data are not listed in the tables, are either missing or received too late to be included in this issue.

Unless otherwise indicated, dimensional units used in this bulletin are: temperature in °F., precipitation and evaporation in inches, and wind movement in miles. Degree days are based on a daily average of 65° F.

Evaporation is measured in the standard Weather Bureau type pan of 4 foot diameter unless otherwise shown by footnote following Table 6.

Amounts in Table 3 are from non-recording gages, unless otherwise indicated.

Data in Tables 3, 5 and 6 and snowfall data in Table 7 are for the 24 hours ending at time of observation. See Station Index for observation time.

Snow on ground in Table 7 is at Observation time for all except Weather Bureau and CAA stations. For these stations snow on ground values are at 7:30 a.m. E.S.T. WTR EQUIV in Table 7 means the water equivalent of snow on the ground. It is measured at selected stations when depth of snow on the ground is two inches or more. Water equivalent samples are necessarily taken from different points for successive observations; consequently occasional drifting and other causes of local variability in the snowpack result in apparent inconsistencies in the record.

Long-term means for full-time Weather Bureau stations (those shown in the Station Index as United States Weather Bureau Stations) are based on the period 1921-1950, adjusted to represent observations taken at the present location.

- \- No record in Tables 3, 6, 7 and the Station index. No record in Tables 2 and 5 is indicated by no entry.
- \+ And also on a later date or dates.
- * Amount included in following measurement, time distribution unknown.
- # Thermometers are generally exposed in a shelter located a few feet above sod-covered ground; however, the reference indicates that the thermometers are exposed in a shelter located on the roof of a building.
- // Gage is equipped with a windshield.
- AM Data based on observational day ending before noon.
- B Adjusted to a full month.
- C In the "Refer to Tables" column in the Station Index the letter "C" indicates recorder stations. These stations are processed for special purposes and are published later in Hourly Precipitation Data.
- D Water equivalent of snowfall wholly or partly estimated, using a ratio of 1 inch water equivalent to every 10 inches of new snowfall.
- M One or more days of record missing; see Table 5 for detailed daily record. Degree day data, if carried for this station, have been adjusted to represent the value for a full month.
- R Amounts from recording gage (These amounts are essentially accurate but may vary slightly from the amounts to be published later in Hourly Precipitation Data).
- SS This entry in time of observation column in Station Index means sunset.
- T Trace, an amount too small to measure.
- V Includes total for previous month.
- VAR Observations made at 2 p.m. Monday through Thursday and 7 a.m. Friday through Sunday.

Subscription Price: 20 cents per copy, monthly and annual; $2.50 per year. (Yearly subscription includes the Annual Summary.) Checks and money orders should be made payable to the Superintendent of Documents. Remittances and correspondence regarding subscriptions should be sent to the Superintendent of Documents, Government Printing Office, Washington 25, D. C.

NWRC., Asheville, N. C. --- 11/13/56 --- 1100

U. S. DEPARTMENT OF COMMERCE
SINCLAIR WEEKS, Secretary
WEATHER BUREAU
F. W. REICHELDERFER, Chief

CLIMATOLOGICAL DATA

PENNSYLVANIA

OCTOBER 1956
Volume LXI No. 10

ASHEVILLE: 1956

GENERAL

After a cool beginning carried over from the preceding month, October turned out rather mild and favorable for harvesting and other fall activities. The dry, sunny second and third weeks were particularly beneficial for outdoor work and sports events.

Average temperatures reversed the coolness that had persisted for the past several months. Extremes ranged from 17° at Philipsburg CAA Airport on the 11th to 86° at Titusville Water Works on the 15th.

Precipitation was adequate in most areas except the extreme west and along the northern tier of counties. Monthly totals varied from 0.90 inch at Slippery Rock to 5.70 inches at Mt. Pocono 2 N AP. Saxton measured the greatest daily amount, 2.80 inches on the 23rd.

WEATHER DETAILS

Cool weather marked the first twelve days of October with the month's lowest readings around the 11th or 12th at nearly all stations. Warming began on the 12th and advanced eastward over the entire State by the 14th to dominate the remainder of the month. Practically all stations recorded their highest readings during the 15th to 17th. The only noteworthy break in the warm spell was the 25th-26th when a moderately cool Canadian air mass moved across the East into the Atlantic Ocean.

Light to moderate rains fell in the latter part of the first week followed by prolonged dryness that continued until the 22nd, except in the extreme southeast where good rains fell on the 18th. Beginning on the 22nd Statewide rains occurred frequently through the end of the month, although amounts in the extreme west inclined to be scanty.

WEATHER EFFECTS

Deficient precipitation during October permitted most soils to dry out and harvesting of potatoes, apples, grapes, hay and corn progressed rapidly. Mild temperatures the latter half of the

Station		Temperature: Average Maximum	Average Minimum	Average	Departure From Long Term Means	Highest	Date	Lowest	Date	Degree Days	No. of Days Max 90° or Above	Max 32° or Below	Min 32° or Below	Min 0° or Below	Precipitation: Total	Departure From Long Term Means	Greatest Day	Date	Snow, Sleet Total	Max. Depth on Ground	Date	No. of Days 10 or More	.50 or More	1.00 or More
POCONO MOUNTAINS																								
AND		61.7M	43.4M	52.6M	3.3	79	15	30	11	368	0	0	2	0	4.42	.57	1.90	23	.0	0		8	3	1
Y 1 S DAM	AM	62.4	33.2	47.8		83	16	22	11+	527	0	0	15	0	1.39		.62	23	.0	0		3	1	0
CONO 2 N AP		60.5	40.0	50.3	1.6	78	16	22	11	454	0	0	6	0	5.70	1.19	2.45	23	.0	0		5	4	2
NBURG 1 SE		64.3	37.1	50.7		79	16+	23	11	437	0	0	10	0	4.06		2.16	23	.0	0		6	3	1
E HILL	AM	59.0	41.9	50.5		78	16	29	11	447	0	0	3	0	4.00		2.45	23	.0	0		6	2	1
ANT MOUNT 1 W	AM	58.6	34.3	46.5		78	16	22	12+	568	0	0	13	0	1.86	- 2.00	.67	23	.0	0		6	1	0
TON	AM	64.3	39.9	52.1	- .5	82	17+	27	11+	392	0	0	5	0	1.78	- 1.16	.80	23	.0	0		4	2	0
TON WB AIRPORT		63.1	41.1	52.1	- .1	80	15	26	11	394	0	0	4	0	1.35	- 2.03	.53	23	.0	0		4	2	0
DSBURG		65.1	35.8	50.5	- 1.9	82	15	18	11	446	0	0	12	0	4.21	.72	1.45	31	.0	0		6	2	2
DIVISION				50.3											3.20				.0					
EAST CENTRAL MOUNTAINS																								
TOWN WB AP	R	65.2	42.6	53.9	.7	80	15+	30	11	335	0	0	3	0	2.72	- .25	1.06	23	.0	0		5	2	1
TOWN GAS CO	AM	66.0	41.5	53.8		82	16	29	11	342	0	0	3	0	2.28	- .83	1.38	23	.0	0		6	1	1
EHEM LEHIGH UNIV		65.1	47.3	56.2	.2	83	15	35	12	268	0	0	0	0	2.57	- .50	1.21	23	.0	0		4	2	1
HORPE		67.2M	41.6M	54.4M	2.2	83	15+	26	11	313	0	0	6	0	3.71	- .08	1.55	23	.0	0		7	2	1
RTON		63.9	41.4	52.7	- .1	80	15	27	11	375	0	0	8	0	3.19	.02	1.37	23	.0	0		5	2	1
CLINTON	AM	66.1	36.9	51.5	- 1.8	80	15+	24	11	410	0	0	12	0										
RTOWN 1 E		66.9	42.2	54.6	2.2	82	15	26	11	314	0	0	5	0	3.60	.27	2.37	23	.0	0		5	1	1
DIVISION				54.3											3.01				.0					
SOUTHEASTERN PIEDMONT																								
ER	AM	67.1M	46.3M	56.7M		80	16+	34	3	242	0	0	0	0	3.14		1.25	21	.0	0		6	3	1
SVILLE 1 SW	AM	66.1	41.0	53.6	- .8	81	16	32	20	347	0	0	4	0	3.48	.05	2.12	23	.0	0		6	1	1
BIA		66.7	45.0	55.9		81	15	32	11	277	0	0	1	0	3.28		1.39	23	.0	0		6	2	1
LT 1 W		65.7	42.4	54.1		81	15	29	12	332	0	0	4	0	3.62		.94	23	.0	0		9	3	0
TA		65.6	43.8	54.7	- .2	78	15	30	11	311	0	0	1	0	3.44	.28	1.70	23	.0	0		8	1	1
E SCHOOL		66.2	45.5	55.9	.4	80	15	28	11	279	0	0	2	0	3.48	.37	1.29	23	.0	0		6	2	1
OOD		65.2	49.0	57.1	.1	83	15	38	11	238	0	0	0	0	3.24	.60	2.33	23	.0	0		5	1	1
STER 2 NE PUMP STA		65.9	41.9	53.9	.1	78	15	27	11	334	0	0	5	0	4.19	1.06	1.84	23	.0	0		8	3	1
SVILLE 2 NW	AM	64.6	41.3	53.0		80	16	27	11	365	0	0	4	0	2.94		1.87	23	.0	0		5	1	1
ON 3 W	AM	65.2	42.7	54.0		80	16	28	11	338	0	0	2	0	3.33	- .18	1.72	23	.0	0		5	2	1
S HOOK		66.4	51.0	58.7	- 1.1	79	16	41	11+	195	0	0	0	0	3.28	.75	.65	18	.0	0		8	4	0
ETOWN OLMSTED FLD		65.0	46.3	55.7	1.0	78	15+	34	11	284	0	0	0	0	3.14	- .24	.78	22	.0	0		8	2	0
NTOWN		64.5	41.5	53.0		78	15	28	11	362	0	0	3	0	2.56		.84	22	.0	0		5	2	0
ETNA 2 SE		64.8	44.4	54.6		78	15+	30	8	315	0	0	4	0	3.81		1.28	23	.0	0		5	2	2
STOWN		67.5	46.6	57.1		84	15	32	11	243	0	0	1	0	3.30		1.70	23	.0	0		7	1	1
DREXEL INST OF TEC		68.5	51.5	60.0		83	15	38	11	161	0	0	0	0	4.48		1.20	23	.0	0		6	5	1
DELPHIA WB AP	R	66.7	48.6	57.7	1.1	81	15	36	11	222	0	0	0	0	3.47	.87	.85	23	.0	0		6	3	0
DELPHIA PT BREEZE		66.9	53.0	60.0	1.5	81	15	42	11+	165	0	0	0	0	3.73		.98	23	.0	0		6	3	0
DELPHIA SHAWMONT		67.3	47.6	57.5	1.0	82	15	33	11	232	0	0	0	0	3.18	.07	1.47	23	.0	0		7	2	1
DELPHIA CITY	RAM	66.3	52.3	59.3	.8	80	15	41	11	177	0	0	0	0	4.24	1.63	1.26	23	.0	0		6	3	2
IXVILLE 1 E		68.9	42.4	55.7	.1	84	15	28	12	282	0	0	6	0	3.60	.51	1.33	23	.0	0		7	3	1
NG WB CITY	R	66.3	47.7	57.0	.9	82	15	35	11	243	0	0	0	0	3.12	.37	1.19	23	.0	0		5	2	1
DARBY		67.2	48.7	58.0		81	15	35	11	215	0	0	0	0	3.66		1.32	23	.0	0		7	2	1
CHESTER	AM	67.8	46.7	57.3	2.4	83	15	35	10+	238	0	0	0	0	2.83	- .72	1.33	23	.0	0		6	2	1
DIVISION				56.3											3.44				.0					
LOWER SUSQUEHANNA																								
TSVILLE	AM	64.8	43.5	54.2	- .3	79	16	30	12	330	0	0	3	0	4.86	1.33	1.96	23	.0	0		6	3	2
SLE		66.3	44.5	55.4	2.1	81	15	30	11	290	0	0	2	0	4.99	1.64	1.42	23	.0	0		6	4	2
ERSBURG 1 ESE		65.1	43.5	54.3	.6	79	15+	27	11	325	0	0	3	0	3.88	.60	1.06	23	.0	0		6	4	1
SBURG	AM	66.0	44.9	55.5	1.6	80	16	30	11	291	0	0	2	0	4.74	1.45	1.89	23	.0	0		6	3	2
ER	AM	66.6	41.8	54.2	- 2.1	80	16	28	11+	327	0	0	3	0	3.14	- .01	1.53	23	.0	0		6	2	1
SBURG WB AP	R	64.7	45.7	55.2		79	15	32	11	295	0	0	1	0	3.52	.45	1.08	22	.0	0		7	3	1
RG 3 W		67.4	45.0	56.2		82	16	34	11	271	0	0	0	0	3.26		1.16	23	.0	0				1
ENSBURG		67.5	43.7	55.6	.7	83	15	29	11	284	0	0	2	0	3.33	- .19	1.07	27	.0	0		5	3	1
VILLE		65.1	41.5	53.3		79	15	25	11	356	0	0	4	0	3.44		1.65	23	.0	0		7	3	1
3 SSW PUMP STA		67.9	43.3	55.6	.9	82	15	28	11	287	0	0	4	0	3.08	- .14	1.04	23	.0	0		7	2	1
DIVISION				55.0											3.82				.0					
MIDDLE SUSQUEHANNA																								
RTOWN		64.8	41.5	53.2		79	16	27	11	361	0	0	5	0	3.99		1.54	23	.0	0		6	3	1
CK		66.7	42.5	54.6		81	16+	28	11	313	0	0	2	0	3.02		1.40	23	.0	0		6	2	1
1 N	AM	63.9	40.2	52.1		79	17	26	11+	394	0	0	3	0	3.49		1.49	23	.0	0		5	2	1
TOWN	AM	67.3	41.9	54.6		81	16+	30	11+	314	0	0	2	0	3.31		1.47	23	.0	0		5	2	1
RT	AM	65.6	40.6	53.1		79	16	29	11+	360	0	0	3	0	4.62	1.18	1.96	23	.0	0		7	2	1
SGROVE CAA AP		64.5	40.7	52.6	- .3	80	15+	29	11+	377	0	0	5	0	3.96	.39	1.48	23	.0	0		7	3	1
AMSPORT WB AP		64.8	42.3	53.6	.6	80	16+	29	11	346	0	0	2	0	3.53	.16	.90	27	.0	0		7	4	0
DIVISION				53.4											3.70				.0					
UPPER SUSQUEHANNA																								
1 NW	AM	61.2	38.4	49.8		79	16	27	19	463	0	0	8	0	2.59		.54	7	.0	0		7	3	0
	AM	65.0	34.7	49.9		83	16	22	11+	464	0	0	14	0	2.43		1.32	23	.0	0		6	1	1
MERE	AM		41.0	M		75	17	31	11+		0	0	6	0	3.32	- 2.02	.99	23	.0	0		6	4	0
ICEVILLE 2 S	AM	63.7	35.7	49.7	- 1.3	80	16+	23	11	466	0	0	11	0	1.76	- 1.01	.46	23	.0	0		5	0	0
SE 1 E	AM	59.3	38.8	49.1	- .3	77	16+	28	20	488	0	0	6	0	2.22	- 1.32	.62	23	.0	0		5	2	0

See Reference Notes Following Station Index

TABLE 2 - CONTINUED

Station	Temperature: Average Maximum	Average Minimum	Average	Departure From Long Term Means	Highest	Date	Lowest	Date	Degree Days	No. of Days Max. 90° or Above	Max. 32° or Below	Min. 32° or Below	Min. 0° or Below	Precipitation: Total	Departure From Long Term Means	Greatest Day	Date	Snow, Sleet: Total	Max. Depth on Ground	Date	No. of Days .10 or More	.50 or More
TOWANDA	64.6	38.2	51.4	.2	84	16	26	12	413	0	0	6	0	2.55	-.40	.73	23	.0	0		6	1
WELLSBORO 3 S AM	60.6	39.8	50.2	1.2	79	17	27	11	448	0	0	6	0	1.90	-1.03	.82	23	.0	0		8	1
DIVISION			50.0											2.40				.0				
CENTRAL MOUNTAINS																						
BELLEFONTE 4 S AM	64.5	39.7	52.1	-.6	80	17	26	11	394	0	0	5	0	3.83	.86	1.76	23	.0	0		5	3
DU BOIS 7 E	64.8	40.6	52.7		81	16	24	11	374	0	0	5	0	2.56	-.28	.66	4	.0	0		5	4
EMPORIUM 2 SSW AM	62.6	36.1	49.4		78	16	21	11	477	0	0	9	0	2.39		1.05	23	.0	0		5	2
LOCK HAVEN	65.4	43.5	54.5	1.1	78	15+	28	11	320	0	0	3	0	2.69	-.48	.70	5	.0	0		6	2
MADERA AM	62.5	33.5	48.0		77	16+	19	11+	520	0	0	18	0	2.20		1.08	23	.0	0		4	1
PHILIPSBURG CAA AP	61.5	39.6	50.6		78	16	17	11	439	0	0	3	0	4.04		2.11	22	.0	0		6	2
RIDGWAY 3 W AM	63.8	35.1	49.5	.3	80	15	20	11+	473	0	0	13	0	1.34	-1.69	.63	7	.0	0		3	1
STATE COLLEGE	63.6	44.3	54.0	2.4	81	16	28	11	335	0	0	1	0	4.20	1.29	1.84	22	.0	0		6	2
TAMARACK 2 S FIRE TWR AM	60.4M	40.2M	50.3M		77	16	29	11	431	0	0	5	0					.0	0			
DIVISION			51.2											2.91				.0				
SOUTH CENTRAL MOUNTAINS																						
ALTOONA HORSESHOE CURVE	64.2	42.8	53.5	1.1	78	2+	27	11	349	0	0	4	0	3.40	.45	1.12	23	.0	0		6	2
ARTEMAS 1 WNW	70.2	42.3	56.3		80	2+	25	12	276	0	0	5	0	1.18		1.08	4	.0	0		2	1
BURNT CABINS 2 NE																						
EBENSBURG	60.2	40.8	50.5		74	14	25	11	442	0	0	3	0	2.18	-1.00	.59	23	.0	0		5	2
EVERETT 1 SW	63.9	42.3	53.1	1.1	78	16+	26	11	366	0	0	5	0	3.80	1.01	1.30	4+	.0	0		6	3
HUNTINGDON AM																						
JOHNSTOWN AM	67.9	40.8	54.4	.5	84	16	26	11	324	0	0	4	0	1.52	-1.48	.71	4	.0	0		4	1
KEGG	65.8M	39.5M	52.7M		80	14+	26	11	359	0	0	4	0	2.00		.95	4	.0	0		7	1
MARTINSBURG CAA AP	63.8	43.0	53.4		81	15	27	11	352	0	0	2	0	3.19		1.56	22	.0	0		6	2
DIVISION			53.4											2.47				.0				
SOUTHWEST PLATEAU																						
BAKERSTOWN 3 WNW	67.3	46.5	56.9		77	2	30	11	245	0	0	2	0	1.81		.98	4	.0	0		3	2
BLAIRSVILLE 6 ENE	63.6	45.7	54.7		79	15	31	11	318	0	0	2	0	1.68	-1.96	.81	4	.0	0		3	1
BURGETTSTOWN 2 W AM	67.5	35.6	51.6		78	15+	21	11	408	0	0	7	0	1.93		.82	4	.0	0		5	2
BUTLER	70.4	42.2	56.3	2.9	83	17	25	11	264	0	0	2	0	1.85	-1.23	.72	4	.0	0		6	1
CLAYSVILLE 3 W		42.0	M				22	11				3	0	1.61	-1.37	.49	4	.0	0		5	0
CONFLUENCE 1 SW DAM AM	66.5	42.1	54.3		81	16+	27	12	326	0	0	4	0	1.41		.48	4	.0	0		6	0
DERRY	68.9	45.2	57.1	2.7	80	15	26	11	242	0	0	2	0	1.51	-1.69	.74	4	.0	0		4	1
DONEGAL	62.8	38.6	50.7		77	15	21	10	437	0	0	7	0	1.87		.97	4	.0	0		3	2
DONORA AM	72.0	48.5	60.3	3.6	82	16+	33	11	145	0	0	0	0	1.39	-1.35	.68	4	.0	0		4	1
FORD CITY 4 S DAM AM	67.6	39.5	53.6		82	16	25	12	346	0	0	3	0	1.48		.85	4	.0	0		3	1
INDIANA 3 SE	68.0	42.0	55.0	2.2	82	15	25	11	305	0	0	2	0	1.71	-1.68	.57	4	.0	0		4	1
IRWIN	71.9	44.6	58.3	4.0	85	15	28	11	205	0	0	2	0	1.63	-1.15	.93	4	.0	0		2	1
MIDLAND DAM 7	65.8	48.1	57.0	2.8	75	2+	32	11	240	0	0	1	0	1.86	-1.25	.68	4	.0	0		4	2
NEW CASTLE 1 N	70.0	42.2	56.1	3.3	82	15+	25	11	270	0	0	2	0	1.19	-1.52	.61	7	.0	0		3	1
NEWELL AM	71.5	49.5	60.5	4.9	83	16	36	9	140	0	0	0	0	1.50	-1.08	.76	4	.0	0		4	1
NEW STANTON	70.0	42.2	56.1	2.0	84	15	31	9	268	0	0	2	0	1.47	-1.52	.79	4	.0	0		3	1
PITTSBURGH WB AP 2 //R	66.5	46.9	56.7	3.7	79	14	31	11	250	0	0	2	0	1.50	-.94	.79	4	.0	0		3	1
PITTSBURGH WB CITY R	68.5	49.3	58.9	3.0	80	15+	34	11	183	0	0	0	0	1.63	-.86	.80	4	.0	0		3	1
PUTNEYVILLE 2 SE DAM AM	65.9	38.1	52.0		80	16	22	11+	395	0	0	4	0	2.69		1.08	21	.0	0		5	3
SALINA 3 W	67.8	43.9M	55.9M		80	15	25	11	263	0	0	2	0	1.46		1.08	4	.0	0		2	1
SHIPPINGPORT WB	67.8	44.9	56.4		80	15	30	11	260	0	0	1	0	1.80		.89	4	.0	0		3	2
SLIPPERY ROCK	67.4	43.9	55.7		81	15	28	11	282	0	0	2	0	.90		.51	7	.0	0		3	1
SOMERSET MAIN ST	64.0	41.3	52.7	3.2	80	15	23	11	375	0	0	2	0	1.36	-1.69	.73	4	.0	0		4	1
SPRINGS 1 SW	60.7	40.7	50.7	1.0	74	15	23	11	437	0	0	4	0	2.11	-1.32	.95	4	.0	0		5	1
UNIONTOWN	68.3	48.2	58.3	3.1	80	15	31	10	207	0	0	2	0	1.48	-1.72	.90	4	.0	0		4	1
WAYNESBURG 2 W	70.0	41.2	55.6	1.0	82	15	24	11	286	0	0	4	0	1.65	-.99	.58	4	.0	0		5	1
DIVISION			55.7											1.63				.0				
NORTHWEST PLATEAU																						
BRADFORD 4 W RES	64.7	34.9	49.8		80	15+	22	25	463	0	0	12	0	2.19	-1.25	1.17	7	.0	0		3	2
BROOKVILLE CAA AIRPORT	65.5	38.9	52.2	2.6	82	15	22	11	389	0	0	5	0	2.10	-.89	.61	7	.0	0		4	2
CLARION 3 SW	67.2	39.9	53.6		80	15+	24	11	348	0	0	4	0	1.53	-1.88	.67	7	.0	0		5	1
CORRY	67.1	38.7	52.9	3.0	81	15+	26	11	368	0	0	7	0	2.01	-1.65	1.40	7	.0	0		3	1
COUDERSPORT 3 NW	61.9	36.1	49.0		80	17	19	11	489	0	0	10	0	1.76		.64	7	.0	0		4	2
EAST BRADY	71.5	42.9	57.2		82	17	30	10+	231	0	0	2	0	1.52		.68	4	.0	0		4	2
ERIE CAA AIRPORT	64.5	46.0	55.3	.3	78	15	32	11+	298	0	0	2	0	1.19	-1.82	.62	6	.0	0		3	1
FARRELL SHARON	70.5	40.3	55.4	1.4	84	16+	26	10+	293	0	0	3	0	.98	-1.61	.65	7	.0	0		2	1
FRANKLIN	68.4	41.4	54.9	3.5	81	18	27	11	306	0	0	2	0	1.15	-1.95	.62	7	.0	0		3	1
GREENVILLE	69.5	41.4	55.5	4.1	83	15+	25	11	289	0	0	2	0	1.02	-2.28	.70	7	.0	0		2	1
JAMESTOWN 2 NW AM	66.1	41.3	53.7		79	15+	24	11	341	0	0	2	0	1.40	-1.47	.71	7	.0	0		3	1
KANE 1 NNE AM	63.8	32.7	48.3		79	16	19	11	514	0	0	16	0	1.69	-1.89	.85	7	.0	0		4	1
LINESVILLE 5 WNW	67.4	40.4	53.9		81	16	26	11	336	0	0	6	0	1.23	-1.86	.69	7	.0	0		3	1
MEADVILLE 1 S AM	66.4	40.0	53.2	2.3	81	16+	28	10	360	0	0	3	0	1.21	-2.18	.77	7	.0	0		3	1
MERCER 2 NNE	68.8	40.2	54.5		80	15	24	10	317	0	0	5	0	1.03		.80	7	.0	0		2	1
SPRINGBORO	66.9	39.3	53.1		82	16	28	11+	360	0	0	5	0	1.43		.80	7	.0	0		4	1
TIONESTA 2 SE DAM AM	65.8	38.2	52.0		80	16+	27	26	393	0	0	7	0	.96	-2.57	.65	7	.0	0		1	1
TITUSVILLE WATER WORKS	66.3	36.2	51.3		86	15	24	19	421	0	0	11	0	1.39		1.06	7	.0	0		1	1
WARREN	66.2	40.5	53.4	2.1	80	15	27	11	355	0	0	4	0	1.36	-2.07	.82	7	.0	0		4	1
DIVISION			53.1											1.43				.0				

† DATA RECEIVED TOO LATE TO BE INCLUDED IN DIVISION AVERAGES

See Reference Notes Following Station Index

DAILY PRECIPITATION

Total	1	2	3	4	5	6	7	8	9	10	11	12	13	14	15	16	17	18	19	20	21	22	23	24	25	26	27	28	29	30	31
1.71			T	.74	.29		.34														.02		.05	.08			.19				
2.72				.17		.44	.01														T	.74	1.08			.08	.09			.01	.18
2.28				.10	.19		.33	.01															1.38	.13	T		.11	.01			.02
3.40			.04	.91		.06	.27															.39	1.12			.07	.32			.01	.21
4.88				.39	.70	T	.20																1.98			T	1.16	.08			.37
1.18				1.08		.10																									
1.73	T		.07	.05	.17		.57	.09															.85	.07		.10					T
1.81			.09	.98	.01		.53								.18																.02
.96	T		.19		T		.45	.10															.20	.02			T				
2.13							.34											T				.28	.62	.48		.23	.18				
4.10				.46			.29															.19	1.65	.76			.40	.15			.24
1.73			T	.49	.36		.52														.05		.10	.08			.13	T			T
3.99			T		.23		.43	T												T			1.54	.54			.78	.41			.06
2.60			T	.32	.62		.49								T						T		.76	.05			.34	.02			
3.83			.02	.62	.37	T	.63																1.76	.03			.33				.07
3.02				.51		.02	.23															.30	1.40	.13			.40	T			.03
2.80					.18		.37																1.84	.32			.06	T			.03
2.57				.20		.38														T		.08	1.21			.08				.05	.57
1.68		.08		.81			.44															.08	.09			.01	.11				.06
3.66				.72		.02	.28													T		.62	.78	.04		.02	.95	.05		T	.18
1.82			.07	.64	.20		.51														T	.04	.05	.19			.07				.05
1.39				.56	.31		.34														.03		.04	.04			.07				
1.69	.04		.13	.04			.75	.13															.54	.04			.02				
2.19		.17		.07		.05	1.17	.05															.60				.03				.05
3.83			.09	1.16		.13																1.00	.28			.22	.06			.18	.11
2.10		.02		.49		.35	.61													.06		.56	.01			T	T				
1.66			.01	.65	.28	*	*	.45												*	*	.10	.02	T			*	*	.14		.01
2.22				.73	.13		.41																.29				.35	.06			.25
1.93				.82	.11		.56													.13	.09	.02	.08	.01			.11				
	RECORD MISSING																														
1.89			T	.72	.19		.41	T													.18		.12	.08			.15				
3.78				.92		.10	.06															.58	1.61	.03		.03	.66			.04	.15
2.59			.08	.10	.52		.54	.02															.50	.26			.34	.23			T
4.99				.96		.04	.14															.76	1.42			.08	1.41	.04		T	.14
2.84			.05	.62	.25		.38	T													.05	.02	.84	T			.19	.20			.04
1.98			T	.09	.30		.73	.06															.60	.03			.17				
2.46	.05		.04	.15	.50		.45	.03															1.02	.08			.04	.05			.05
3.06				.22		T	.30											.50	T			T	1.72	T			.20			.02	.10
3.88			T	.81		.04	.08															.82	1.06			.10	.72			.03	.22
1.65				.48	.22		.54														.14	T	.05	.05			.15				.02
3.14			.58	.01	.25		.20											.68	.10		1.25					.07					
3.26			.05	.50	.44		.33	T													.10		1.62	T			.14			T	.08
1.53			.10	.20	.10		.67	.02													.07		.22	.08			.07				
2.80				.06	.08		.52																1.70	.18			.16				.10
1.61				.49	.31		.07												T	.16	.04	.24	.05			.25					
2.69			.18	.42	.29		.52	T													.03	T	1.15				.10	T			T
1.48	.01		.10	.08	.06		.05	.09															1.04				.05				
3.55					.23		.62	.01	.01														2.20	.18			.10				.20
3.48				.04	.32		.17											.14					2.12	.04			.16	T			.49
3.28				.36		.37	.05															.65	1.39			.07	.21			.06	.12
1.41			T	.48	.10		.30															.17	.11	.04			.20	.01			T
1.06				.52	.11		.42															.20	.13	.07			.20	.01			T
1.15				.50	.20		.35															.02	.02	.03			.03				
3.52				T	.22		.29											.54				T	2.02	.04			.16				.25
1.22			.09	.12	.04	T	.78	.07	T												T	T	.12	T			T	T	T		
1.17	T		.06	.12	.03	T	.74	.04	T												T	T	.13	T			.05	T	T		
1.55			.02	.74	.11		.36														*	.08	.07	.02			.11				.04
2.01		.36		.07		T	1.40													.02			.12				.04				
1.76			.05	.03	.07		.64	.12															.63	.17			.05				T
2.58	.02		.17	.15	.17		*	.90															.75	.25			.16				.01
1.88			.04	.17	.25		.41	.01															.49	.03			.30	.17			.01
1.89			.16	1.00	.20		.36																.09				.08				
3.43			.06	.80	.22		.36	.02														.02	1.30	.02			.30	.05	.03	.02	.23
1.78	.02		.20	.04	.01		*	.91															.52	.05			.03				
2.73				.15	.21		.35																1.20	.30			.45	.07			
1.51			.03	.74		T	.37														.10	.14	T	.04		.09					
3.62				.37		.20	.02											.28				.72	.94			.27	.11			.12	.59
2.43			.13	.03	.31		.22	T															1.32	.20			.14	.08			T
1.87		.02		.97		T	.55													T	T	.24	.03			.02	.04			T	T
1.39			T	.68	.02		.35	.01													.12	.01	.04	.01			.15	T			T
3.44		T		.32		T	.26											.16			.01	.22	2.16	.01			.03				.27
2.56			.58	.66		.07	.51	.02														T	.61			T	.11				T
2.99			.23	T	.30		.35	T															1.28	.28			.38	.17			T
3.32	T		.01	.01	.53		.58	.05															.99	.27	.01		.64	.21		T	.02
1.52				.68			.59													.10			.15								
2.18			.07	.56	.20		.45															T	.59	.03			.23				.05
1.31	.03		.10				.87	.14			.01									.04	.02		.08	.01			.01				
2.03				.13	.28		.39																1.65	.06				.02			.10
2.39			.09	.17	.20		.65	.03															1.05	.05			.15				
3.21	T		.01	.29	.73		.69	.01															1.02	.01			.31	.09			.05
3.44				.27	.03	.33	.15															.45	1.70	.05		.11	.10				.25
1.46					.47		.36																.55	.08							T
1.19		.27				.62	.08													.06		.01	.15			T					
3.80				1.30			.10															1.30				.75				.20	.15
.98				.09		.01	.65													.04		.01	.14				.04				
1.48			.02	.85	.15		.34														.03		.03	T			.06				
1.15	.03		.17	.05	.01	T	.62	.10												T	.01		.05	.05			.05		.01		
4.42				.17	.23		.30	.15															1.90	.90				.62	.03	.02	.10
2.22	.02		.10	.15	.12		.60	.18															.82	.10			.12	T			.01
2.81					.21		.42											.01					1.63	.04			.08				.42
3.48				.26		T	.42											.66			.07	.25	1.29			.03	.06				.44
4.74		.01		.31	.53	T	.19																1.89	.02		.01	1.41	.02			.39
2.27	.25		.26	.05	.02		.72	.20														.69	.02				.06				
1.86	T		.18	.13	.04		.58	.06															.63	.01			.03				T
1.66			.01	.66	.22		.43														.06		.08	.02			.18				
2.88					.17		.30	.07															1.40	.72		T	.05	.07		T	.10
3.43					.36		.31											.16	.01				1.68	.24			.14				.53
3.49			T	.06	.47		.25																1.49	.79			.28	.08			.07
1.64				.52	.23	T	.43																.27	.06			.12				.01
1.59				.82		.01	.37														.07	.18					.08				.02
1.02		.02		.05			.70													.05			.18				.02				
3.14				.12	.21		.24	T													T		1.53				.75	.03			.26
3.52				.57	.01	.20	.06														T	1.08	.90	T		.17	.38			.02	.13
3.83				.29	.47		.30																1.78	.26			.58	.04			.13
1.53			.09	T	.10		.30	T													.01		.64	.30			.02	.04			.03
1.39			.04		.08		.26																.62	.37				.02			
2.14	T		.01	T	.12		.23	.02														T	.97	.59			.05	.09			.04
3.24				.07	.16		.28	.01										.11					2.39	.02	T		.19	.02			.05
1.60	T			.03	.16		.33	.02															.80	.07			.07	.07			.05
1.57			.03	.65	.15		.37															.05	.06				.21				.05
1.53	T	T			.11		.77	T															.02	.03	.01	.57	T	.02			
	RECORD MISSING																														
4.28			T	.13	.58		.13																1.32	.05			1.49	.33			.25
1.99			.04	.80	.16		.38															.03	.09	.02		.03	.34	T			.10
1.71			.19	.57	.32		.45														.03		.08	.02			.05				

See Reference Notes Following Station Index

DAILY PRECIPITATION

Table 3–Continued

Station	Total	Day of month																											
		1	2	3	4	5	6	7	8	9	10	11	12	13	14	15	16	17	18	19	20	21	22	23	24	25	26	27	28	29	30
IRWIN	1.63			.93			.45														.05	.09	.04								
JAMESTOWN 2 NW	1.40	.02			.07			.71	.21											.01	.03		.29				.06			
JIM THORPE	3.71			.23	.02	T	.63																.41	1.55	.33			.11	T		
JOHNSTOWN	1.52		T	.71	.13	.02	.47															T	T	.01			.18			
KANE 1 NNE	1.69	.03		.18	.03	T		.85	.12														T	T	.41	.04			.03			
KARTHAUS	3.25	T		.04	.41	.33		.54	.02														.08		1.63	T			.20			
KEATING SUMMIT	2.14			.19	.17		.65	.12											T					.78	.08			.15			
KEGG	2.00	T	T	.95		.19	.22																	T	T		.27	.12			.10
KITTANNING LOCK 7	1.39		.04	.80			.43																.05		.02	T			.05			
KREGAR 4 SE	1.51			.76	T		.43																T		.08	.05	T		.02	.10	.01	T	.04
KRESGEVILLE 3 W	3.54				.31		.57																			2.34	.09			.11			
LAKEVILLE 1 NNE	1.77			T	.17		.21	T													T	T		.81	.41			.05	.04		
LANCASTER 2 NE PUMP STA	4.19			.22		.18	.23											.01				.60	1.84	.10		.05	.27			T
LANDISVILLE 2 NW	2.94			.06	.32		.38																			1.87	.09			.13	.01	.01	
LAWRENCEVILLE 2 S	1.78	T		.11	.08	.35		.41	.02																.46	.08			.20	.05		
LEBANON 3 W	3.33			.02	.50		.38																			1.72	.27			.38	.01		
LEHIGHTON	4.07			.08	.25		.65																		T	2.15	.60			.15	.04		
LE ROY	2.79		.13		.57			.36																			.84	.12			.63			.07
LEWIS RUN 3 SE	1.89	.03		.30	T	.03		.71	.18																	.58	.03			.03			
LEWISTOWN	3.31		T	.07	.60		.45																				1.47	.07			.44	.05		
LINESVILLE 5 WNW	1.23	.03		.02	.02			.69	.17			T								.02			.25	T			.03			
LOCK HAVEN	2.69		T	.43	.70		.49																.01	.01	.62				.31	.12		
LONG POND 2 W	4.21				.27		.60	.05																	2.19	.36			.51	.03		
MADERA	2.20		.02	.41	.07		.43	.02														.01		1.08				.16			
MAHAFFEY	2.48		.03	.73	.22		.48																	T	.86	T			.16			
MAPLE GLEN	3.31			.35		.01	.03											.46				.23	1.56			.14	.10			
MAPLETON DEPOT	4.24		.08	.48	.27		.26																			2.61	.05			.34	.03		
MARCUS HOOK	3.28			.32		.21	.01											T	.65			T	.58	.55			.16	.06			.15
MARION CENTER 2 SE	2.00		.08	.93	.11		.55	T														T		.28	T			.05	T		
MARTINSBURG CAA AP	3.19	.02	T	.89		.13	.19																	1.56	.02	.02		.19	.03	T		.03
MATAMORAS	1.58				.19		.64	.04																	.61	.06			.04			
MAYBURG	1.24	T		.16		.03		.79	.08																	.18	T		T	T			
MC CONNELLSBURG	5.68			.81	.34		.21																		.11	3.17				.47	.02		
MC KEESPORT	1.63		.08	.25	.65		.47																.02	T	.08	.02			.04			
MEADVILLE 1 S	1.21	.02		.03	.07			.77	.19		T	T								.01	T		.10	.02		T	T			
MEDIX RUN	2.81	T		.09	.18	.29		.57	.01														.01		1.60				.06			
MERCER 2 NNE	1.03			T		T	.80														T	.10	.05	.08	T						
MERCERSBURG	4.39			.64			.10																.01		2.65				.45	.09		
MEYERSDALE 1 ENE	1.92		.05	.64	.13		.28																	.05	.25	.05			.13	.03		.02
MIDDLETOWN OLMSTED FLD	3.14			.46		.26	.12																	.78	.77	T		.19	.32			.03
MIDLAND DAM 7	1.86		.05	.68	.22		.63																.04		.03	.10			.09			
MILANVILLE	1.11		T		.21		.23																			.47	.10			.03	.03		
MILLHEIM	2.59			.38	.36		.50	T																	.79	.03			.44	.02		T
MILLVILLE 2 SW	2.61			T	.39	.38	.02																T	T	1.05	.21			.40	.13		
MILROY	2.66			.37	.35		.35																			1.00	.02			.50	.02		
MONTROSE 1 E	2.22	T		.04	T	.52		.43	.04																	.62	.37			.06	.14		
MORGANTOWN	2.56			.21		.39	.02											T				.84	.68			.03	.02			.08
MT GRETNA 2 SE	3.81			.38		.33	.09																		1.25	1.28			.08	.06			
MT POCONO 2 N AP	5.70			.22		T	.60																		.89	2.45			.04				
MUHLENBURG 1 SE	4.06			.58		T	.25											.22			T	.17	2.16				.60			
MYERSTOWN		RECORD MISSING																												
NATRONA LOCK 4	1.64		.03	.65	.43		.34																			.01	.06			.12			
NESHAMINY FALLS	3.85			.24		.32	.03											.84			T	.69	.92	T		.05	.03			T
NEWBURG 3 W	3.26			.77	.07																				.10	1.16			*	.88	.09		
NEW CASTLE 1 N	1.19		.02	.20	.03		.61	.02														.02	.04	.16	.03			.06	T		
NEWELL	1.50			.76			.36																		.10	.08	.03			.14			
NEW PARK	4.44			.28		.19	.01												.17			1.21	1.40			.08	.74	T	T	.12
NEWPORT	4.62			.06	.45		.38																			1.96	.44			.84	.37		
NEW STANTON	1.47			.79		.01	.39														.05		.15	.01			.01	.06			
NEW TRIPOLI	3.28			.22		.12	.42																		.31	1.76	.04		T	.15			
NORRISTOWN	3.30			.02	.22		.30											.47	.01			T	1.70	.22			.14			
NORTH EAST 2 SE	1.66	.05		.30				1.02	.09												T	.07		.08	.05			T			
ORWELL 3 N	2.66		.04	.02	.48		.52																			.78	.20			.38	.24		
PALM	2.25			.05			.45																			1.25	.34			.08			
PALMERTON	3.19			.25		.42	.08																		.66	1.37	.02		.07	T			T
PALMYRA		RECORD MISSING																												
PARKER	1.38		T	.31	.09		.65	T												T	.06		.12	T			.15			
PAUPACK 2 WNW	1.73		.05		.12		.28	.05																	.81	.28			.05	.09		
PECKS POND	1.09		T	.02	.11	T	.68	.04														.05		.79	.11			.05	.01		
PHIL DREXEL INST OF TEC	4.48			.29		.59	T											.85				.80	1.20			.05	.07			.04
PHILADELPHIA WB AP R	3.47			.26		.40	T											.75			T	.65	.85			.07	.08			.02
PHILADELPHIA PT BREEZE	3.73			.29		.40	.02											.77				.70	.98			.04	.02			.02
PHILADELPHIA SHAWMONT	3.18			.19	.01		.21											.68				.20	1.47			.17				
PHILADELPHIA CITY R	4.24			.21		.45													.74				1.11	1.26			.06	.06			
PHILIPSBURG CAA AP	4.04	.04		.80		T	.31															.06		2.11	.23	.02		.11	.06			T
PHOENIXVILLE 1 E	3.60			.31		.28													.22				.62	1.33			.17	.06			.05
PIKES CREEK	3.20	T			.01	.67		.33	.02																	1.53	.22			.29	.12		
PIMPLE HILL	4.00		.01	.12	.16		.68	.03														.01	T	2.45	.08		T	.17	.01		.07
PINE GROVE 1 NE	3.36	T			.07	.21		.51												T				2.01	.16			.28	.03		
PITTSBURGH WB AP 2 //R	1.50	.02	T	.79		.48	.02														T	T	.03	.01			.11	.02			
PITTSBURGH WB CITY R	1.63	.01	T	.80		.43	.04														.06		.04	.03			.18	.02			
PLEASANT MOUNT 1 W	1.86		T	T	.38		.20	.03																	.67	.27			.14	.12		T
PORT CLINTON	-	-	-	-	-	-	-	-	-	-	-	-	-	-	-	-	-	-	-	-	-	-	-	-	-	-	-	-	-	-	-
POTTSVILLE		RECORD MISSING																												
PUTNEYVILLE 2 SE DAM	2.69		.04	.60	.17		.58	T														1.08		.19	.02			.01			
QUAKERTOWN 1 E	3.60			.24		T	.39																		.18	2.37	.03			.06			
RAYMOND	2.26	.03	.26	.10	.12		.60	.12																	.67	.20			.16			
READING WB CITY R	3.12			.16		.46	.02																		.95	1.19			.04	.04			.0
RENOVO	2.65		.16	.21	.39		.57	.02																	1.00	.03			.23			
REW	1.76	.04		.29	.03	.02		.58	.11																	.62	.02			.05			
RICES LANDING L 6	1.33			.46	.25		.32																			.07	.03			.20			
RIDGWAY 3 W	1.34	.06	.14	.08			.58	.05														.02		.33	.03			.05			
RUSH	2.77		.12	.05	.47		.56	.01																	.93	.13			.31	.17		
RUSHVILLE	2.44		.11	T	.48		.49																			.75	.27			.16	.18		
SAGAMORE 1 S	1.15		.10	.45	.25		.25							T				T					.10								
SALINA 3 W	1.46		T	1.08			.32	.01												T	T	T	T				.05			
SAXTON	4.54		T	.90	.11		.27																		T	2.80	.06			.23	.02		T
SCHENLEY LOCK 5	1.43		.01	.91			.32																.01		.03	.03			.12			
SCRANTON	1.78		.10	T	.09		.10	.06																	.80	.04			.50	.09		
SCRANTON WB AIRPORT	1.35	T		.11		.05	.08																		.50	.53	T		T	.10			
SELINSGROVE CAA AP	3.96	T		.38		.21	.19																		.72	1.48	.05		.09	.72	T		
SHAMOKIN	3.37			.06	.36		.20																			1.15	1.12			.35	.11		
SHIPPENSBURG	3.33			.76		.03																			.42	.74	.07		T	1.07	.04		.0
SHIPPINGPORT WB	1.80	.03	T	.89		.57	.01														.08		.02	.08			.12				
SINNEMAHONING	2.57	T		.01	.13	.33		.61	.02														T		1.25	T			.22			
SLIPPERY ROCK	.90			.07	.12		.51	.01																	.01	.08			.12	T		
SOMERSET FAIRVIEW ST	1.28			.59	.10		.29																		.03	.09	.06			.08			.0
SOMERSET MAIN ST	1.36		T	.73		.02	.30																		.11				.01	.10			.0
SOUTH MOUNTAIN	5.10			.58	.39		.15																			2.08	.03			.92	.13		.0
SPRINGBORO	1.43	T					.80	.30												T		.15	.18	T			T			
SPRING GROVE	3.12			.26		.02	.28																		.89	1.00			.01	.42			.0
SPRINGS 1 SW	2.11			.95	.01	.05	.48																.11	.14	.10	.03		.03	.07	.01		.0
STATE COLLEGE	4.20	T		1.05		.13	.43														T		1.84	.39			.05	.23			T
STRAUSSTOWN	4.19			.06	.26		.59																			2.18	.31			.49	T		

See Reference Notes Following Station Index

DAILY PRECIPITATION

3–Continued

PENNSYLVANIA
OCTOBER 1956

Station	Total	Day of month																														
		1	2	3	4	5	6	7	8	9	10	11	12	13	14	15	16	17	18	19	20	21	22	23	24	25	26	27	28	29	30	31
DSBURG	4.21	.01	T	T	.26	T	.37	.24	T		T											.05	.36	1.37	T		.02	.08			T	1.45
CREEK	1.99			.03	.40	.30		.44	.05															.61	T			.07				
RY	3.07				.23	.06		.37	T													T		1.74	.77			.50	.25			.05
EHANNA	2.12			.02		.45		.54	.07															.58	.20			.10	.16			
SVILLE	1.42				.69	.16		*	.32														.06	.05	.02							.12
UA		RECORD MISSING																														
JA 4 N DAM	3.10				.22			.48																2.04	.04		.04	.02				.26
ACK 2 S FIRE TWR	-			-	-	-		-	-													T	T	.71	.05			.12	T			.02
STA 2 SE DAM	.96	.02		.05	.03	.01		.65	.04												T	.03		.05	T			.08				
VILLE WATER WORKS	1.39		T		.05		.07	1.06			T										.03		T	.09				.09				T
OO 4 W	1.16	.02		.09	.05	T		.69	.12													T		.12	T			.07	T			
DA	2.59			.04	.01	.47		.39	.03															.73	.41			.23	.24			T
CITY 5 SW	5.27				.84		.10	.30															.62	2.06			.03	.57			.03	.83
	2.47			.05	.17	.44		.45	.05															.70	.12			.29	.23			.01
EPOINT 4 NE	1.84			.17	.02	.02		.72	.07															.67	.07			.10				
E 4 NE BALD EAGLE	4.21			.01	.62	.37		.19														T		2.78	T			.20				.04
CITY	1.98	.09		.18	.05	.05		1.08	.25	.03												.03		.15	.02			.03				
TOWN	1.48				.90			.32													T	T	.10	.05				.10				.01
DARBY	3.66				.22		T	.20											.78				.47	1.32	.04		T	.19		.01		.43
	1.03			.11	.07	.02		.63	.04													.04		.03	.02			.05				
RGRIFT	1.53			.09	.77	.27		.35																T	T	T		.05				
WVILLE		RECORD MISSING																														
CKEL	1.50	T	T	.34	.08	T		.85	.06	T			T									T	T	.12	T		T	.05	T	T		
CKEL 1 WSW	1.50	T		.35	.08	T		.85	.07	T			T									T	T	.11	T			.04	T	T		
W	1.38	.04		.15	.03	.03		.82	.14													T		.13				.02				
NTOWN	3.38				.20	.25		.50																1.25	.30			.50	.35			.03
SBURG 2 W	1.65			.02	.58	.20		.30														.06	.03	.19	.01			.26				T
BORO 3 S	1.90	T		.07	.16	.21		.35	.03															.62	.09			.26	.10			.01
VILLE	3.44				.66		.12	.12															.15	1.65			.05	.51			.04	.14
RSVILLE 1 W	3.65				.03	.24		.43																2.35	.35			.02				.23
CHESTER	2.83				.02		.19												.50	.01		T		1.33			.18				.46	.14
GROVE 1 E	4.27				.20			.28											.43				.34	2.36	.08			.16				.42
HICKORY	1.26			.05	.01	T		.82														.18		.10				.10				
SBURG	1.62				.95	.15		.52														T		T			T	T				
S BARRE	2.03				T	.22		.15	.03															1.26	.25			T	.12			T
AMSBURG	3.91			.07	.71	.16		.46																2.21				.22				.08
AMSPORT WB AP	3.53		.01		.55	T	.13	.25															.86	.53			.02	.90			T	.28
BURG	2.43			.03	.66	.15		.41																.61	T			.43	.02			.12
SSW PUMP STA	3.08				.30		.29	.12															.76	1.04			.02	.34	T		.03	.18
HAVEN	3.30				.08	.35		.35																1.87	.08			.45	.03			.09
GROVE	2.47					.20																		1.70	.17			.22				.18
VILLE 3 SE	3.16					.18		.45																1.46	.80			.13				.14

SUPPLEMENTAL DATA

Station	Wind direction		Wind speed m. p. h.				Relative humidity averages - — percent				Number of days with precipitation							Percent of possible sunshine	Average sky cover sunrise to sunset
	Prevailing	Percent of time from prevailing	Average	Fastest mile	Direction of fastest mile	Date of fastest mile	1:30 a EST	7:30 a EST	1:30 p EST	7:30 p EST	Trace	.01–.09	.10–.49	.50–.99	1.00–1.99	2.00 and over	Total		
TOWN WB AIRPORT	ENE	22	8.6	-	-	-	88	88	57	77	1	4	3	1	1	0	10	-	5.1
WB AIRPORT	-	-	10.6	-	-	-	-	-	-	-	1	3	2	1	0	0	7	-	4.8
SBURG WB AIRPORT	ESE	12	5.8	26	W	7	83	83	58	74	2	3	4	2	1	0	12	56	5.9
DELPHIA WB AIRPORT	ENE	20	9.9	33	NE	26	80	79	55	71	2	3	3	3	0	0	11	59	6.1
BURGH WB AIRPORT	ESE	22	9.8	27*	SW	8	79	83	53	67	3	6	2	1	0	0	12	57	5.5
NG WB CITY	-	-	9.0	35	SE	26	-	-	-	-	0	4	3	1	1	0	9	55	5.5
TON WB AIRPORT	ESE	11	8.2	36	SE	26	82	82	53	68	4	2	2	2	0	0	10	57	4.9
INGPORT WB	-	-	2.0	39††	NW	6	-	-	-	-	2	5	1	2	0	0	10	-	5.8
AMSPORT WB AIRPORT	-	-	-	-	-	-	-	90	57	78	2	2	3	4	0	0	11	-	5.6

ak Gust
test observed one minute
speed. This station is not
ped with automatic record-
ind instruments.

DAILY TEMPERATURES

Table 5

Station		1	2	3	4	5	6	7	8	9	10	11	12	13	14	15	16	17	18	19	20	21	22	23	24	25	26	27	28	29	30	31
ALLENTOWN WB AP	MAX	66	69	71	60	68	60	62	66	64	56	59	57	64	75	80	80	77	75	58	62	67	61	70	68	55	53	58	65	63	63	68
	MIN	43	39	48	49	41	35	49	40	38	33	30	31	33	38	45	44	45	48	37	32	51	53	59	42	36	41	46	46	38	52	59
ALLENTOWN GAS CO	MAX	65	62	70	72	60	68	64	64	69	64	64	58	58	66	76	82	80	78	75	59	64	68	62	69	67	55	54	58	65	65	64
	MIN	44	42	43	49	49	36	40	41	42	33	29	31	33	34	40	44	44	47	39	32	33	52	54	58	36	37	40	46	41	45	52
ALTOONA HORSESHOE CURVE	MAX	66	78	74	63	64	53	58	69	58	55	57	58	69	77	78	77	74	76	63	56	66	60	68	66	56	45	58	64	62	58	64
	MIN	40	41	48	52	47	38	44	37	43	30	27	32	35	42	46	45	45	49	38	46	41	41	53	54	30	43	43	49	43	50	54
ARENDTSVILLE	MAX	72	70	70	77	62	65	58	63	70	64	55	57	60	66	74	79	78	75	75	60	60	63	62	68	67	55	49	54	61	57	62
	MIN	41	42	44	53	49	40	47	36	38	36	31	30	32	39	45	46	47	57	43	38	41	50	56	58	37	38	42	49	43	48	52
ARTEMAS 1 WNW	MAX	76	80	72	76	71	62	64	71	63	61	60	65	71	76	80	78	78	76	72	70	70	68	72	70	66	64	68	74	64	68	70
	MIN	59	60	57	56	50	44	40	37	50	36	27	25	28	30	33	45	46	52	41	40	42	38	60	46	39	36	40	46	32	34	41
BAKERSTOWN 3 WNW	MAX	72	77	75	67	65	70	64	67	61	54	58	68	76	72	74	76	74	72	66	64	68	65	61	64	62	60	60	64	67	71	72
	MIN	37	46	49	55	44	46	43	37	42	31	30	39	40	48	52	54	53	50	42	44	51	56	54	53	42	44	46	52	52	50	58
BEAVERTOWN	MAX	68	73	73	71	83	53	60	70	65	57	56	59	66	77	78	79	76	76	64	62	66	62	64	62	57	50	52	59	62	61	67
	MIN	38	39	45	51	44	33	50	37	39	32	27	28	35	37	41	40	41	41	32	46	44	50	58	56	29	42	47	50	38	44	52
BELLEFONTE 4 S	MAX	72	70	74	72	62	62	59	56	68	60	56	54	57	68	78	78	80	76	74	58	62	66	62	71	59	56	50	55	58	60	65
	MIN	41	39	40	52	45	36	41	40	43	32	26	30	33	36	38	40	40	43	33	34	43	44	55	50	29	31	43	46	38	40	50
BERWICK	MAX	66	71	72	70	64	61	62	68	67	58	59	60	66	73	80	81	81	77	68	68	63	63	68	65	60	56	53	64	66	71	68
	MIN	41	39	45	49	45	36	52	36	39	33	28	33	34	38	42	41	43	48	34	38	45	50	59	54	31	37	48	51	38	49	62
BETHLEHEM LEHIGH UNIV	MAX	67	70	72	60	66	61	63	67	64	56	61	57	57	78	83	81	77	74	60	63	66	61	67	66	53	52	57	65	63	63	67
	MIN	48	44	55	53	45	42	51	47	48	41	36	35	40	44	51	51	52	52	43	37	53	55	60	47	39	43	46	51	45	54	59
BLAIRSVILLE 6 ENE	MAX	62	73	69	60	61	63	50	63	54	50	58	65	71	75	79	76	75	71	65	59	72	57	62	64	60	53	55	53	68	63	65
	MIN	38	49	49	54	47	47	41	39	42	32	31	38	42	50	59	53	52	54	39	44	46	51	53	51	38	39	44	46	43	49	57
BRADFORD 4 W RES	MAX	63	72	67	67	65	57	56	65	64	49	51	63	72	76	80	80	77	75	62	61	69	68	65	60	58	57	55	62	65	63	63
	MIN	33	35	38	43	35	26	42	30	30	25	24	24	31	35	36	37	36	38	24	36	38	42	54	40	22	31	45	30	30	38	55
BROOKVILLE CAA AIRPORT	MAX	65	76	71	62	66	60	56	65	56	53	56	65	75	77	82	80	78	73	63	60	72	62	65	64	58	53	58	63	66	65	66
	MIN	30	40	46	46	37	37	39	37	32	25	22	34	34	36	35	38	37	40	31	48	40	52	53	38	33	41	47	38	34	50	55
BURGETTSTOWN 2 W	MAX	73	68	76	72	65	66	71	55	67	58	52	57	69	75	78	77	78	76	76	70	62	72	62	62	65	64	63	59	63	69	73
	MIN	32	35	39	40	40	36	39	29	32	23	21	23	32	34	36	37	37	36	39	42	37	39	51	48	33	33	34	43	33	33	39
BURNT CABINS 2 NE	MAX																															
	MIN																															
BUTLER	MAX	71	75	78	75	62	65	68	65	68	68	57	65	70	78	80	82	83	81	77	70	75	70	68	64	69	64	60	67	65	71	71
	MIN	34	43	43	53	47	39	43	38	39	27	25	34	36	42	38	46	45	46	35	45	50	50	50	48	37	37	48	47	45	41	57
CANTON 1 NW	MAX	61	62	64	65	58	54	54	54	65	55	49	49	54	64	76	79	77	75	65	66	62	63	61	69	50	55	60	50	57	60	63
	MIN	39	39	46	45	43	34	42	35	35	31	30	29	35	41	45	48	46	48	27	30	34	42	43	46	29	28	29	43	39	41	48
CARLISLE	MAX	70	74	75	67	67	60	63	71	67	59	59	63	67	76	81	78	77	77	70	64	65	62	65	67	53	52	53	63	60	60	70
	MIN	45	42	49	55	50	39	52	41	42	37	30	32	38	40	43	43	47	54	38	42	44	50	58	56	34	44	49	48	38	49	52
CHAMBERSBURG 1 ESE	MAX	72	72	77	65	67	54	61	71	64	58	59	61	66	74	79	79	76	77	57	61	67	61	72	66	55	49	53	59	56	58	71
	MIN	43	43	48	54	44	39	50	37	40	32	27	30	36	38	41	41	45	53	41	44	42	51	59	48	34	43	48	47	43	51	57
CHESTER	MAX	67	68	71	76	67	71		61	70	62	62	60	68		74	80	80	75	73	60	71	67	69	69	52	55	56		65	65	66
	MIN	48	44	34	55	56	46		45	47	38	37	39	42		43	48	51	54	45	41	45	53	60	42	39	45	43		45	53	58
CLARION 3 SW	MAX	66	78	71	66	67	61	63	63	62	55	58	66	74	78	80	80	80	75	70	62	71	66	66	65	6	57	60	63	65	66	68
	MIN	34	40	43	49	38	37	43	33	35	28	24	34	34	38	39	39	39	39	31	44	41	49	54	51	29	41	47	44	38	45	58
CLAYSVILLE 3 W	MAX	74	72	84	67	76																										
	MIN	36	45	43	54	46	51	42	33	36	25	22	31	33	36	37	35	37	38	42	46	53	53	49	53	43	51	46	42	40	47	56
COATESVILLE 1 SW	MAX	66	68	70	75	64	68	64	64	70	65	57	59	62	67	76	81	79	74	75	59	64	67	65	67	67	53	52	58	65	65	64
	MIN	45	39	39	47	44	36	38	36	36	34	29	29	31	34	38	41	42	55	39	32	33	52	56	57	38	38	43	48	43	45	54
COLUMBIA	MAX	70	71	76	64	70	62	67	70	67	59	60	62	66	76	81	79	77	75	66	65	64	62	64	70	61	52	54	65	62	61	70
	MIN	46	43	47	53	51	39	54	39	44	35	32	33	36	40	43	45	47	59	43	34	45	52	59	56	34	43	51	42	40	52	58
CONFLUENCE 1 SW DAM	MAX	78	71	73	76	65	70	66	56	67	58	54	61	64	77	80	81	81	75	74	61	61	68	61	62	65	59	52	58	59	64	64
	MIN	42	44	53	55	53	43	47	36	34	31	28	27	34	30	38	43	39	39	40	46	40	54	54	45	41	44	46	44	40	46	49
CORRY	MAX	66	73	69	68	64	57	57	67	61	51	58	68	74	78	81	81	79	71	68	62	75	73	64	58	64	62	60	68	68	68	68
	MIN	31	40	36	46	36	35	44	34	31	28	26	32	37	38	39	39	38	40	28	45	40	47	56	45	33	40	47	28	42	44	54
COUDERSPORT 3 NW	MAX	63	70	66	61	58	49	54	64	57	48	52	56	71	78	78	79	80	65	60	59	67	64	62	58	55	47	54	62	60	61	61
	MIN	38	35	38	43	40	30	42	29	29	22	19	23	32	35	36	36	35	41	23	39	42	44	54	41	25	36	43	38	32	43	55
DERRY	MAX	67	76	73	65	66	69	68	69	65	54	63	66	76	79	80	79	77	76	73	62	73	63	67	68	69	58	60	60	72	68	74
	MIN	36	44	51	55	49	52	42	41	42	29	26	45	39	40	40	44	43	43	39	51	45	55	51	55	37	45	50	50	49	52	60
DEVAULT 1 W	MAX	67	68	73	64	68	64	71	68	65	58	58	59	65	74	81	77	73	73	59	63	68	64	66	66	55	57	60	59	64	61	68
	MIN	43	43	48	51	42	42	39	39	39	33	30	29	31	38	48	49	49	50	45	48	45	50	55	40	30	38	38	42	35	48	57
DIXON	MAX	69	69	68	69	60	60	61	61	68	60	51	53	59	66	78	83	82	82	70	62	62	67	63	70	60	59	54	51	65	67	66
	MIN	47	36	36	43	44	31	31	36	36	30	22	22	25	31	36	41	40	41	26	26	29	41	43	46	28	27	34	43	30	30	45
DONEGAL	MAX	63	72	68	63	63	65	59	62	53	49	57	62	70	73	77	76	72	69	61	56	69	57	59	60	57	52	53	53	65	62	69
	MIN	29	39	46	47	45	45	36	29	35	21	22	32	30	32	33	38	40	37	37	43	36	48	48	43	37	37	42	47	42	48	53
DONORA	MAX	76	77	77	75	69	72	74	65	68	63	58	68	72	78	81	82	82	81	80	74	75	77	64	64	69	68	62	65	68	74	74
	MIN	41	50	52	58	52	51	48	40	34	34	33	41	42	45	46	48	47	47	48	56	50	59	57	57	49	47	52	56	51	51	62
DU BOIS 7 E	MAX	63	75	75	68	63	60	57	63	63	52	55	59	72	75	79	81	78	75	64	57	67	63	67	63	60	53	56	60	61	61	65
	MIN	33	39	45	49	38	39	43	37	37	25	24	31	40	37	38	39	39	42	32	42	42	53	53	51	32	41	45	49	37	50	56
EAGLES MERE	MAX	57	57	60	60	55	53	54	56	60	52	47	47	52	56	71	74	75	71	61												
	MIN	39	38	45	47	44	40	40	36	37	33	31	32	36	40	47	55	55	54	32	31	38	46	50	49	32	32	39	45	41	41	47
EAST BRADY	MAX	71	80	77	71	69	67	64	70	69	57	61	71	77	80	81	81	82	80	74	70	76	75	66	69	68	65	62	65	72	73	72
	MIN	36	45	46	52	44	40	35	35	38	30	30	35	37	41	44	42	43	43	35	46	42	54	55	54	38	44	49	50	45	42	61
EBENSBURG	MAX	60	70	66	65	60	53	56	62	55	48	52	56	68	74	73	73	70	70	57	51	64	58	62	63	50	45	54	52	59	57	62
	MIN	32	39	46	56	43	43	42	37	40	26	25	37	34	34	40	42	42	45	35	44	40	50	46	43	34	39	43	45	42	48	53
EMPORIUM 2 SSW	MAX	67	65	73	67	64	67	55	50	62	56	50	54	58	72	77	78	72	72	69	60	59	62	63	68	59	56	47	55	61	60	62
	MIN	36	35	38	41	40	32	38	32	33	23	21	23	34	34	37	39	39	39	29	28	42	43	51	49	27	27	40	45	35	39	50
EPHRATA	MAX	65	69	73	63	67	63	64	67	66	58	58	60	63	71	78	77	77	74	69	63	64	63	65	71	54	55	55	66	63	63	69
	MIN	42	41	52	52	49	41	53	42	45	35	30	33	37	39	44	46	49	56	39	36	46	53	59	52	33	33	46	43	39	50	44
ERIE CAA AIRPORT	MAX	58	74	61	67	56	64	59	67	53	50	53	66	74	74	78	76	69	63	61	62	74	72	61	53	65	63	57	63	66	71	71
	MIN	36	53	47	52	42	47	45	43	42	42	32	43	50	52	54	50	48	47	34	51	52	57	53	37	32	45	39	37	48	54	61

See Reference Notes Following Station Index

DAILY TEMPERATURES

Day Of Month

Station		1	2	3	4	5	6	7	8	9	10	11	12	13	14	15	16	17	18	19	20	21	22	23	24	25	26	27	28	29	30	31	Average
	MAX	62	74	70	65	62	62	62	66	58	52	56	55	76	75	74	78	72	78	64	58	64	61	66	65	52	48	56	58	68	62	62	63.9
	MIN	40	45	48	50	40	42	38	40	38	28	26	27	32	40	40	40	45	48	40	48	40	51	57	42	30	44	48	50	42	52	59	42.3
	MAX	68	82	73	72	69	70	66	72	63	62	61	70	78	81	83	84	84	76	69	62	73	69	67	67	65	55	62	67	69	73	72	70.5
	MIN	33	40	40	46	39	40	42	36	38	26	26	29	34	39	41	42	41	41	38	47	43	51	53	44	39	39	47	43	39	44	48	40.3
	MAX	71	67	77	73	65	65	69	57	67	58	54	58	67	75	78	82	79	77	76	67	64	73	64	67	68	62	60	61	60	67	69	67.6
	MIN	37	36	42	48	41	38	45	38	37	29	27	25	33	36	39	39	39	40	37	41	42	42	52	50	40	40	42	43	45	39	43	39.5
	MAX	65	77	70	70	69	66	61	68	67	54	58	67	74	78	80	80	80	81	74	66	71	72	67	62	67	62	60	61	65	66	62	68.4
	MIN	36	42	44	50	39	37	45	35	37	30	27	34	35	40	42	43	43	43	44	44	46	42	50	56	43	43	43	48	39	40	43	41.4
	MAX		60	65	65	60	59	56	63	61	54	53	51	62	73	79	78	68	74	65	66	62	58	65	61	56	48	51	62	59	56	61	61.7
	MIN		44	47	50	46	39	50	40	45	32	30	33	37	46	46	46	51	54	44	36	44	50	56	47	33	36	41	42	37	46	55	43.4
	MAX	65	72	74	66	68	60	66	68	65	58	60	61	65	74	80	79	73	72	67	65	70	66	64	67	51	53	62	64	63	63	70	66.2
	MIN	46	39	45	52	52	36	54	40	48	33	28	29	36	42	43	47	47	60	43	33	54	53	62	57	40	43	50	50	43	52	55	45.5
	MAX	73	72	70	79	63	66	60	64	70	67	57	58	62	66	76	80	79	74	76	62	62	65	63	70	68	54	50	56	62	58	64	66.0
	MIN	45	43	47	56	50	42	47	42	44	38	30	31	35	39	43	45	49	56	44	40	45	53	56	58	38	39	44	48	44	47	53	44.9
	MAX	66	65	70	70	62	64	60	60	66	61	55	56	60	63	73	78	79	77	73	60	60	64	62	62	62	55	57	53	62	62	65	63.9
	MIN	44	39	39	45	50	37	43	38	38	33	26	26	36	37	38	42	45	45	34	34	42	47	52	57	32	34	42	48	35	36	52	40.2
	MAX	69	77	70	73	69	67	64	70	61	56	62	68	76	82	83	83	82	75	70	62	74	70	65	66	65	60	62	67	69	70	69	69.5
	MIN	35	45	40	51	37	38	44	36	34	28	25	35	38	41	41	42	42	46	33	48	44	52	55	51	36	41	48	36	38	45	57	41.4
	MAX	73	73	73	79	65	69	60	64	69	66	58	60	62	67	76	80	79	76	75	64	64	67	62	68	68	55	56	54	63	57	64	66.6
	MIN	42	41	43	52	51	40	44	37	38	35	28	28	32	37	44	44	45	52	42	37	37	52	54	55	33	33	43	43	40	44	50	41.8
	MAX	67	73	74	62	66	57	63	70	62	56	57	62	67	75	79	77	75	75	58	62	64	63	64	68	54	51	54	64	59	61	68	64.7
	MIN	46	44	51	56	45	40	50	43	44	36	32	36	38	40	44	46	49	53	43	37	48	54	60	47	40	43	48	46	44	53	60	45.7
	MAX	66	59	66	64	60	58	60	57	65	55	48	50	54	66	74	83	80	78	68	58	60	67	60	69	64	53	50	50	62	62	68	62.4
	MIN	43	31	32	40	43	27	33	37	40	30	22	22	22	28	38	38	38	40	24	23	23	41	43	54	23	23	34	40	27	28	42	33.2
	MAX	64	68	71	64	66	63	64	73	63	55	57	63	71	75	83	77	73	72	63	63	63	64	64	65	52	52	55	64	64	63	66	65.2
	MIN	49	46	52	55	48	46	55	45	47	40	38	39	43	45	49	50	55	57	45	41	51	57	61	52	43	47	52	48	46	55	63	49.0
	MAX																																
	MIN																																
	MAX	67	76	79	65	67	65	63	66	58	54	61	66	74	79	82	81	80	77	67	62	74	64	69	70	62	56	60	57	68	68	71	68.0
	MIN	34	40	47	53	43	40	46	33	36	26	25	33	38	38	40	40	40	41	38	50	44	54	51	52	42	43	48	43	39	46	58	42.0
	MAX	81	78	75	67	68	72	70	70	61	56	64	72	76	76	85	81	80	79	76	70	76	76	74	68	68	64	61	60	75	74	77	71.9
	MIN	37	46	49	55	47	46	45	39	40	30	28	38	38	37	41	45	43	43	41	50	47	56	55	53	39	44	50	52	46	46	58	44.6
	MAX	65	64	75	67	71	64	65	48	68	56	52	57	67	75	79	79	78	77	70	66	62	71	68	65	60	62	59	59	65	66	70	66.1
	MIN	33	34	40	41	38	39	42	38	34	28	24	33	41	44	45	45	41	47	37	43	45	50	55	50	40	41	45	38	44	53	53	41.3
	MAX	67	67	72	72	65	65	61	67	65	60	58	59	65	80	83	83	83	80	72	61	67	63	69	68	60	54	55	66		65	64	67.2
	MIN	44	37	43	46	51	32	52	38	40	32	26	28	33	38	43	42	43	51	32	29	51	52	59	37	34	39	45	50		40	60	41.6
	MAX	80	70	78	75	68	68	68	58	69	59	55	62	63	77	81	84	83	77	75	63	63	72	63	68	69	61	50	60	56	67	64	67.9
	MIN	36	41	49	52	48	38	38	38	45	30	26	28	33	33	39	40	39	41	36	39	38	53	51	53	32	35	44	44	42	51	54	40.8
	MAX	64	64	74	69	66	62	54	47	64	57	50	53	63	72	77	79	77	78	68	62	60	69	67	68	58	57	51	56	64	64	64	63.8
	MIN	28	30	37	40	31	30	36	29	28	23	19	20	31	33	34	35	33	34	24	25	39	41	49	48	23	23	39	32	30	37	52	32.7
	MAX	69	78	77	72	65	58	56	70	60	57	57	61	71	80	80	77	73	76	58	58	67		67	66	57	47	61		63	59	68	65.8
	MIN	35	41	46	55	40	39	45	34	35	34	26	28	31	42	35	36	38	42	33	45	36		54	41	28	42	43		37	50	55	39.5
STA	MAX	69	68	75	65	68	62	64	69	65	58	58	59	64	73	78	77	75	74	72	62	63	63	65	69	60	52	55	66	63	62	70	65.9
	MIN	41	39	45	50	49	35	52	37	39	31	27	29	33	36	39	40	44	54	35	30	42	50	58	56	32	43	48	41	37	52	56	41.9
	MAX	67	65	70	73	63	65	62	63	69	62	55	57	60	65	74	80	77	75	73	58	62	63	63	64	67	53	60	50	63	62	64	64.6
	MIN	42	40	43	51	50	36	45	36	38	32	27	31	33	36	40	40	42	56	35	31	38	49	56	58	36	38	45	42	36	43	54	41.3
	MAX	67	70	72	65	61	57	58	56	70	57	49	50	58	70	78	80	80	79	63	61	60	70	68	66	55	58	55	54	62	65	61	63.7
	MIN	42	35	38	45	40	31	32	34	34	30	23	29	30	35	39	39	40	38	24	25	35	42	47	46	28	29	38	45	31	33	49	35.7
	MAX	67	67	71	74	61	67	60	62	68	64	56	58	62	65	74	80	79	77	75	64	62	65	62	63	67	55	53	54	66	60	62	65.2
	MIN	43	41	45	53	47	38	43	37	40	32	28	34	34	37	41	42	44	53	40	34	46	50	54	55	35	37	47	47	36	52	59	42.7
	MAX	73	72	74	76	63	67	58	60	72	63	59	61	61	70	80	81	81	79	78	61	60	68	64	73	68	59	61	57	59	64	64	67.3
	MIN	42	41	43	49	50	39	39	39	37	35	30	30	33	36	42	45	45	46	39	38	44	44	57	59	35	34	45	48	43	41	52	41.9
	MAX	64	76	69	72	63	64	61	67	57	53	57	67	75	79	79	81	80	71	68	62	71	70	66	59	65	61	59	65	65	72	70	67.4
	MIN	30	46	39	49	34	37	44	38	32	30	26	34	43	40	41	43	39	43	30	48	47	48	54	42	40	42	40	31	45	43	55	40.4
	MAX	68	69	72	60	66	53	60	71	62	58	57	61	67	77	78	76	78	75	63	60	66	65	73	66	59	55	55	62	65	62	67	65.4
	MIN	39	42	49	52	47	37	49	37	43	32	28	31	36	43	46	45	44	46	35	48	45	52	53	51	33	41	47	51	39	49	59	43.5
	MAX	74	59	73	68	61	60	58	49	59	57	51	54	58	69	74	77	77	74	74	59	56	65	61	69	64	54	48	57	56	59	63	62.5
	MIN	30	29	34	43	41	31	38	27	28	22	19	19	31	30	31	31	31	32	28	28	40	40	50	50	26	28	38	42	35	39	47	33.5
	MAX	71	68	78	65	71	62	68	68	70	60	60	63	65	70	77	79	72	73	63	66	67	65	67	69	49	54	60	62	64	63	70	66.4
	MIN	52	50	58	59	52	48	53	48	51	44	41	41	46	48	50	52	58	61	45	44	54	58	62	52	41	46	52	52	48	55	59	51.0
	MAX	68	76	73	66	64	53	57	69	57	54	55	58	72	78	81	77	73	77	55	54	67	58	72	65	55	47	55	55	61	58	69	63.8
	MIN	42	43	49	53	43	42	43	40	41	32	27	35	39	39	43	40	41	47	35	47	42	54	54	43	34	43	46	45	43	50	58	43.0
	MAX	65	65	76	70	70	64	61	49	68	55	52	58	68	74	78	81	81	80	70	67	62	73	68	62	60	63	60	59	65	66	69	66.4
	MIN	35	37	40	42	36	38	44	34	34	28	29	31	41	42	42	43	41	42	34	41	45	47	55	50	37	42	45	33	37	46	49	40.0
	MAX	69	74	70	68	72	66	64	67	69	64	69	66	72	75	80	79	78	75	73	60	70	68	64	60	61	58	66	69	67	70	71	68.8
	MIN	30	38	40	42	34	41	41	30	35	24	26	34	40	50	45	48	40	45	49	52	51	48	45	42	44	43	37	40	32	34	46	40.2
LD	MAX	66	73	74	64	67	58	64	70	64	55	58	61	64	73	78	78	75	76	59	62	64	62	65	68	54	51	55	65	60	62	69	65.0
	MIN	48	45	51	57	46	41	51	42	45	38	34	35	38	43	45	47	49	56	42	38	49	54	61	46	38	44	49	48	42	53	61	46.3
	MAX	62	75	70	68	64	70	55	63	56	52	54	66	68	71	73	73	72	75	70	62	70	68	63	66	61	60	62	65	66	71	70	65.8
	MIN	42	50	49	55	48	48	45	42	45	35	32	42	44	48	50	50	49	50	46	55	48	56	58	54	46	46	53	50	45	50	59	48.1
	MAX	63	57	63	62	55	53	56	55	63	52	46	45	54	62	73	77	77	76	62	55	58	63	62	67	54	52	50	48	58	60	60	59.3
	MIN	41	39	40	46	41	35	37	34	35	33	31	32	33	35	42	51	51	48	30	28	36	47	45	50	30	29	35	42	40	40	46	38.8
	MAX	65	68	72	63	64	62	62	67	62	56	71	59	64	71	78	77	74	72	58	63	63	63	65	66	52	52	56	64	62	60	69	64.5
	MIN	45	41	45	50	40	38	35	38	40	33	28	31	34	39	39	39	49	49	39	32	48	48	47	48	37	42	48	47	43	51	44	41.5
	MAX	66	69	73	60	68	60	62	68	63	55	58	60	64	74	78	78	77	74	58	68	65	62	64	65	53	52	55	64	62	62	72	64.8
	MIN	41	40	46	51	46	31	49	30	40	32	33	41	44	50	51	53	50	54	38	35	45	55	58	49	31	42	48	46	38	51	59	44.4
	MAX	59	62	65	61	56	54	56	63	59	51	52	51	60	76	77	78	72	69	53	57	64	60	66	62	52	46	51	60	59	63	60	60.5
	MIN	41	36	43	44	42	34	48	35	45	31	22	27	38	42	40	41	42	43	33	30	47	47	56	51	32	32	39	46	37	41	55	40.0

DAILY TEMPERATURES

Table 5 - Continued

Station		1	2	3	4	5	6	7	8	9	10	11	12	13	14	15	16	17	18	19	20	21	22	23	24	25	26	27	28
MUHLENBURG 1 SE	MAX	65	67	68	66	60	56	58	64	60	54	54	66	63	68	78	79	79	70	72	72	64	59	67	66	58	55	50	62
	MIN	39	39	40	44	42	31	46	32	40	28	23	27	31	33	37	42	38	40	38	38	40	42	54	31	25	31	40	44
NEWBURG 3 W	MAX	77	68	73	66	66	66	66	69	68	66	63	65	70	70	80	82	79	79	69	61	66	64	72	70	57	52	54	60
	MIN	45	42	53	54	48	40	51	36	38	37	34	37	39	42	49	41	52	58	41	46	44	52	60	52	46	41	46	43
NEW CASTLE 1 N	MAX	66	78	73	70	68	70	69	70	72	53	59	69	76	78	82	81	82	77	70	67	72	69	64	68	65	60	63	66
	MIN	36	45	41	52	38	38	44	37	35	29	25	35	37	40	40	41	40	47	35	50	44	53	55	52	38	44	50	50
NEWELL	MAX	76	73	78	76	68	69	74	63	72	64	59	66	72	78	82	83	82	79	78	72	67	76	67	65	70	69	64	63
	MIN	46	51	54	57	53	48	48	39	36	39	37	43	43	45	47	49	49	48	51	58	51	61	60	60	50	45	45	56
NEWPORT	MAX	70	69	72	74	62	65	58	62	71	64	58	57	61	66	78	79	78	77	77	60	61	67	62	63	63	57	62	53
	MIN	41	41	41	44	49	38	39	38	38	33	29	29	31	35	40	42	43	45	37	37	43	46	51	58	33	33	45	49
NEW STANTON	MAX	80	78	77	68	73	73	62	70	59	52	62	70	78	80	84	80	76	77	69	65	75	63	63	66	64	64	62	64
	MIN	37	43	49	53	42	47	34	38	31	32	35	36	35	37	38	39	37	36	39	51	41	54	52	46	39	48	41	52
NORRISTOWN	MAX	69	72	76	65	70	65	66	71	67	59	60	61	68	78	84	79	75	75	60	68	69	66	69	69	52	54	61	65
	MIN	47	43	51	54	49	41	52	44	45	38	32	35	37	42	48	48	53	59	41	35	54	57	61	46	40	40	50	47
PALMERTON	MAX	67	67	69	59	64	59	61	66	61	54	58	55	62	75	80	78	77	73	62	60	65	61	69	64	54	52	55	63
	MIN	43	38	44	47	43	32	51	39	39	32	27	28	32	38	39	44	45	52	31	31	53	52	60	38	29	40	45	47
PHIL DREXEL INST OF TEC	MAX	70	73	80	68	72	68	69	70	69	61	61	64	67	75	83	82	75	73	61	68	71	68	70	69	54	54	62	66
	MIN	52	50	57	60	56	47	54	48	52	44	38	43	43	47	52	54	58	60	47	43	58	61	62	54	45	47	51	52
PHILADELPHIA WB AP	MAX	67	71	76	67	69	66	67	68	67	58	59	62	65	74	81	79	74	72	58	66	69	67	69	68	51	54	62	64
	MIN	49	46	55	56	47	43	51	44	47	40	36	37	40	41	49	49	57	58	45	40	56	58	61	51	43	45	52	50
PHILADELPHIA PT BREEZE	MAX	68	72	76	66	68	66	65	69	67	58	60	62	67	74	81	80	74	72	59	66	72	67	69	68	51	54	61	62
	MIN	51	52	59	60	57	51	59	48	53	47	42	44	48	50	54	55	61	61	45	46	57	59	64	63	42	46	51	53
PHILADELPHIA SHAWMONT	MAX	68	71	74	65	69	70	65	70	66	56	59	60	66	76	82	80	74	74	73	65	70	69	67	69	56	53	60	63
	MIN	46	43	50	52	54	41	57	42	47	38	33	34	39	41	47	48	52	60	43	38	54	55	63	61	38	45	51	46
PHILADELPHIA CITY	MAX	69	70	76	66	72	64	66	68	68	59	61	61	66	74	80	77	72	72	60	66	70	66	67	69	51	53	60	62
	MIN	54	53	60	59	55	51	54	51	53	47	41	44	47	51	55	58	60	56	46	47	56	57	62	51	43	46	51	52
PHILIPSBURG CAA AP	MAX	63	74	70	59	64	49	53	66	56	51	54	57	66	77	76	78	75	72	58	53	65	57	64	63	53	45	55	55
	MIN	33	35	38	52	36	41	40	39	35	25	17	38	40	33	35	37	36	40	30	44	47	52	55	40	33	40	45	42
PHOENIXVILLE 1 E	MAX	70	71	77	71	72	66	67	71	69	62	62	62	69	78	84	80	75	75	75	68	70	67	68	70	59	54	61	67
	MIN	42	37	43	47	40	37	54	38	40	31	30	28	30	35	40	39	45	52	50	42	46	51	59	55	31	42	48	40
PIMPLE HILL	MAX	56	58	59	64	54	57	55	55	63	54	47	51	51	61	75	78	76	73	67	54	56	61	58	66	57	49	45	50
	MIN	39	43	45	49	42	39	47	36	45	32	29	33	37	47	48	48	44	51	33	36	45	49	53	53	31	33	37	44
PITTSBURGH WB AP 2	MAX	66	76	70	65	65	70	54	66	57	51	56	67	74	79	78	78	76	75	68	61	71	62	61	66	63	58	59	61
	MIN	38	52	51	53	46	49	43	40	40	32	31	41	42	47	48	48	49	51	43	53	49	57	56	49	42	43	50	53
PITTSBURGH WB CITY	MAX	68	78	73	66	66	72	57	69	59	54	59	68	76	79	80	80	78	78	70	64	72	64	63	68	65	60	61	63
	MIN	44	51	54	56	49	50	47	45	43	38	34	44	44	48	49	50	50	52	45	57	51	57	58	51	45	48	52	55
PLEASANT MOUNT 1 W	MAX	59	55	63	61	55	54	57	56	60	52	45	45	51	62	72	78	76	75	65	55	57	64	58	63	58	52	46	48
	MIN	40	32	34	39	41	28	33	34	37	28	24	22	22	28	42	41	40	40	25	25	33	39	49	53	32	26	33	40
PORT CLINTON	MAX	65	67	69	75	66	68	65	64	69	65	60	61	65	71	80	80	79	74	62	64	65	63	65	63	58	60	53	55
	MIN	42	36	38	45	46	31	32	35	36	28	24	25	34	36	41	42	45	30	28	30	40	51	55	28	29	30	42	44
PUTNEYVILLE 2 SE DAM	MAX	70	65	77	72	64	65	64	55	66	58	53	57	65	74	74	80	78	78	70	63	60	71	64	68	66	60	55	59
	MIN	32	34	43	45	38	38	41	36	36	23	22	22	37	36	38	38	39	39	35	35	41	41	51	50	36	35	40	45
QUAKERTOWN 1 E	MAX	64	70	71	69	67	64	62	66	66	60	59	62	66	75	82	81	78	74	72	66	65	64	69	66	64	51	59	67
	MIN	44	36	44	46	47	34	54	41	41	31	26	27	29	36	41	41	43	56	36	29	51	50	60	56	34	36	47	46
READING WB CITY	MAX	68	70	74	63	69	62	64	70	65	59	60	60	66	76	82	80	77	77	59	63	65	65	66	68	54	54	57	66
	MIN	49	44	52	55	48	40	52	46	46	39	35	36	39	43	50	50	52	56	45	37	52	56	61	51	40	44	50	51
RIDGWAY 3 W	MAX	66	65	70	64	54	59	48	45	56	57	56	64	72	77	80	78	78	71	63	62	61	65	61	66	58	61	58	63
	MIN	32	32	37	42	35	32	39	31	33	26	20	20	32	34	37	35	36	36	27	27	39	39	49	47	28	30	45	44
SALINA 3 W	MAX	66	75	73	67	64	69	68	66	64	52	58	67	72	77	80	78	77	75	72	63	72	64	67	68	64	58	60	60
	MIN	36	45	48	52	46	46	46	39	37	28	25	37	36	40	42	42	40	42	42	50	46	56	52	52	40		49	53
SCRANTON	MAX	67	62	69	67	62	60	61	60	66	57	51	52	58	66	76	81	82	82	69	62	62	67	62	70	62	57	53	53
	MIN	45	34	38	46	42	35	40	40	42	32	27	27	33	34	40	44	45	47	32	32	38	47	50	58	34	36	37	44
SCRANTON WB AIRPORT	MAX	60	67	66	60	58	60	60	65	57	51	52	57	64	74	80	79	79	69	60	61	65	61	70	61	56	53	51	62
	MIN	41	39	46	48	38	35	44	40	40	30	26	34	36	40	46	46	47	42	32	35	47	48	58	37	32	36	44	43
SELINSGROVE CAA AP	MAX	67	70	70	61	64	62	61	69	62	55	56	60	64	75	80	80	80	73	64	61	64	61	63	60	58	52	52	60
	MIN	41	42	44	50	37	33	47	33	35	31	29	29	33	39	43	43	42	47	32	43	43	50	56	42	30	34	48	40
SHIPPENSBURG	MAX	72	71	80	70	70	65	65	66	65	66	63	65	69	77	83	81	78	79	70	63	67	65	71	65	56	50	54	63
	MIN	46	41	46	53	49	40	50	40	42	33	29	30	36	39	43	42	46	52	38	42	42	48	59	55	36	42	46	45
SHIPPINGPORT WB	MAX	66	77	70	68	64	72	56	68	57	51	57	69	75	79	80	79	77	76	70	62	72	64	63	67	64	61	60	64
	MIN	39	48	47	55	45	44	42	38	36	33	30	38	39	39	45	46	45	48	43	52	46	57	55	51	41	42	51	50
SLIPPERY ROCK	MAX	67	76	72	68	65	65	63	68	61	51	58	67	64	77	81	80	78	76	67	62	71	65	62	68	64	59	64	64
	MIN	35	48	44	52	42	44	42	37	40	29	28	37	40	45	45	48	47	52	38	48	45	54	55	51	38	40	47	44
SOMERSET MAIN ST	MAX	68	72	72	70	65	60	61	65	62	54	55	58	71	76	80	78	72	73	65	56	67	59	62	65	56	47	58	55
	MIN	33	43	47	56	48	45	43	36	43	26	23	36	33	35	38	38	39	42	38	44	38	50	44	53	36	39	42	47
SPRINGBORO	MAX	64	61	76	70	72	65	55	51	67	55	53	59	69	75	78	82	80	80	67	69	63	73	70	63	61	65	64	60
	MIN	31	42	38	43	33	40	42	35	33	30	28	34	43	42	41	44	39	41	28	39	44	46	54	49	35	36	41	28
SPRINGS 1 SW	MAX	65	68	71	64	63	57	60	63	61	49	52	56	69	73	74	73	68	60	56	54	63	56	59	60	53	53	56	51
	MIN	32	42	52	58	44	40	40	37	39	25	23	30	33	36	38	37	38	37	38	40	37	50	53	48	36	44	43	47
STATE COLLEGE	MAX	70	75	71	62	61	55	57	68	59	55	56	58	67	77	78	81	76	75	59	56	65	61	68	60	54	48	54	57
	MIN	42	41	51	53	44	39	46	41	43	35	28	35	42	42	47	45	47	45	37	47	47	54	56	43	34	43	46	47
STROUDSBURG	MAX	67	67	71	62	62	58	63	68	63	54	60	58	64	75	82	80	77	74	58	63	65	60	71	69	55	55	58	64
	MIN	40	32	41	41	38	28	48	38	35	25	18	19	28	32	38	36	39	44	26	25	47	45	50	37	25	29	42	40
TAMARACK 2 S FIRE TWR	MAX										54	48	49	55	66	76	77	76	75	71	57	55	61	60	70	55	53	44	52
	MIN										31	29	30	34	36	49	52	52	54	34	32	39	44	49	49	32	33	36	42
TIONESTA 2 SE DAM	MAX	66	64	76	69	67	67	59	50	66	55	52	58	66	74	77	80	80	80	73	66	62	71	70	63	55	61	58	61
	MIN	38	37	43	45	39	36	41	34	35	30	29	29	34	36	41	43	43	43	30	31	40	41	49	52	30	27	35	38
TITUSVILLE WATER WORKS	MAX	57	77	74	62	62	59	59	68	58	52	48	64	75	73	86	81	81	73	78	63	72	70	62	62	62	55	60	61
	MIN	31	38	37	46	31	31	38	30	30	25	25	30	32	37	35	35	35	35	24	38	35	44	52	48	36	39	46	29

See Reference Notes Following Station Index

Table 5 - Continued

DAILY TEMPERATURES

PENNSYLVANIA
OCTOBER 1956

Station		1	2	3	4	5	6	7	8	9	10	11	12	13	14	15	16	17	18	19	20	21	22	23	24	25	26	27	28	29	30	31	Average
OWANDA	MAX	65	71	69	59	60	57	60	69	62	52	54	60	71	77	78	84	78	67	59	61	69	65	71	62	57	54	52	66	66	62	65	64.6
	MIN	45	36	44	44	40	33	39	35	39	33	27	26	32	35	43	39	38	44	28	37	45	42	47	45	29	33	44	43	32	35	52	38.2
NIONTOWN	MAX	68	74	73	67	68	72	67	67	61	55	63	69	74	77	80	78	78	74	68	65	72	63	61	66	65	57	57	62	73	68	74	68.3
	MIN	39	49	55	58	53	56	47	39	41	31	32	45	40	41	43	46	46	44	50	54	47	58	57	55	47	47	51	53	52	56	62	48.2
PPER DARBY	MAX	68	71	74	65	69	65	65	69	66	58	59	62	66	76	81	79	72	72	67	66	69	66	69	68	61	57	62	65	63	63	70	67.2
	MIN	48	44	52	55	54	43	52	43	47	39	35	37	41	44	48	49	54	60	42	40	54	57	62	60	39	47	50	50	47	55	61	48.7
ARREN	MAX	63	77	67	67	63	57	56	67	60	50	55	65	73	78	80	79	78	67	69	62	73	72	63	61	62	58	59	67	68	68	67	66.2
	MIN	37	43	43	49	36	37	44	33	35	29	27	33	38	41	43	42	43	43	29	45	43	50	57	43	29	42	48	35	38	41	60	40.5
AYNESBURG 2 W	MAX	73	76	76	67	68	73	67	68	62	56	62	72	77	80	82	80	76	76	74	65	75	64	63	67	65	65	59	64	72	72	75	70.0
	MIN	38	45	45	55	48	41	43	32	38	28	24	32	33	36	37	38	38	39	40	51	42	54	52	49	34	36	50	50	39	40	49	41.2
ELLSBORO 3 S	MAX	63	63	67	67	60	55	54	51	65	56	48	49	54	67	77	77	79	77	64	57	55	63	64	65	52	54	49	53	56	59	60	60.6
	MIN	36	37	46	46	41	36	41	37	39	29	27	30	37	38	48	50	49	47	30	33	42	48	52	44	28	30	39	44	41	42	48	39.8
ELLSVILLE	MAX	69	70	75	70	66	58	63	69	64	56	58	60	65	75	79	78	75	75	67	60	63	63	64	68	57	50	52	63	58	58	70	65.1
	MIN	40	38	43	52	48	36	52	33	38	30	25	27	32	30	39	39	42	56	36	33	44	49	50	55	35	44	48	44	37	48	57	41.5
EST CHESTER	MAX	68	71	74	73	70	64	68	71	69	59	61	63	68	77	83	80	75	72	71	66	67	65	67	64	63	52	61	65	64	64	68	67.8
	MIN	48	42	44	52	44	45	43	45	40	35	37	38	45	50	51	55	56	58	41	35	45	56	59	58	39	43	47	43	47	53	53	46.7
ILLIAMSPORT WB AP	MAX	70	68	72	60	64	57	59	72	63	57	57	58	63	73	77	80	80	74	60	61	64	65	68	63	58	54	55	62	62	66	67	64.8
	MIN	43	40	46	51	41	35	48	36	40	34	29	31	37	42	46	44	43	46	34	47	47	50	59	41	33	39	47	41	38	45	59	42.3
ORK 3 SSW PUMP STA	MAX	73	72	77	76	70	59	63	71	69	63	60	62	68	78	82	81	78	77	75	62	67	65	64	69	64	52	53	65	59	59	71	67.9
	MIN	40	41	46	54	51	37	53	39	41	32	28	30	35	38	41	42	46	56	37	34	44	49	60	53	31	45	50	40	36	53	59	43.3

Table 6

EVAPORATION AND WIND

Station		1	2	3	4	5	6	7	8	9	10	11	12	13	14	15	16	17	18	19	20	21	22	23	24	25	26	27	28	29	30	31	Total or Avg.
CONFLUENCE 1 SW DAM	EVAP	.14	.10	.03	.10	.03	.11	.06	.09	.13	.11	.10	.09	.11	.07	.07	.08	.10	.14	.03	.11	.05	.07	.01	.01	.07	.14	.04	.03	.07	.07	.02	2.38
	WIND	64	14	56	19	13	48	51	88	70	70	45	44	44	17	25	26	34	35	36	64	39	45	29	66	43	99	54	44	60	69	35	1447
FORD CITY 4 S DAM	EVAP	.09	.08	.07	.11	.07	.10	.04	.07	.12	.10	.06	.07	.09	.05	.05	.07	.05	.06	.13	.09	.04	.08	.02	.05	.12	.13	.02	.06	.07	.08	.05	2.29
	WIND	46	10	36	19	3	18	60	86	48	41	19	15	10	14	15	4	9	11	21	14	75	31	13	34	68	78	54	25	35	25	58	995
HAWLEY 1 S DAM	EVAP	.07	.11	.05	.10	.00	.08	.00	.11	.17	.11	*	*	*	.26	.06	.09	.10	.10	*	*	.22	.07	.00	.03	–	–	–	–	–	–	–	B2.23
	WIND	81	60	69	45	60	58	68	113	153	78	56	32	32	43	22	25	30	20	50	35	39	22	39	24	39	–	–	–	–	–	–	B1603
JAMESTOWN 2 NW	EVAP	.08	.07	.06	.11	.07	.10	–	.03	.19	.11	.04	*	*	.25	.09	.08	.08	.09	.10	.10	.02	.04	.02	.05	.12	.13	.05	.06	.04	.07	.05	B2.38
	WIND	19	20	24	11	18	33	54	35	67	26	14	22	32	24	18	13	14	16	42	52	41	27	32	43	65	88	71	29	31	40	57	1078
LANDISVILLE	EVAP	.06	.12	.07	.11	.04	.15	*	*	.29	.16	.11	.10	.07	.06	.06	.08	.09	.08	.13	.09	.04	*	*	*	.12	.10	.08	.01	.00	.03	.02	2.27
	WIND	24	41	16	27	28	41	37	110	43	58	50	26	22	7	12	4	7	55	105	23	17	23	82	20	158	34	104	66	48	64	77	1429
PIMPLE HILL	EVAP	.07	.13	.11	.13	.01	.13	.08	.13	.16	.14	.08	.08	.07	.09	.13	.18	.15	.14	.14	.09	.07	.05	.26	.05	.18	.08	.00	.01	.10	.07	.09	3.20
	WIND	67	64	99	61	101	73	140	154	122	75	60	56	85	81	46	50	41	70	135	84	89	63	133	77	154	131	176	92	94	81	80	2834
STATE COLLEGE	EVAP	.11	.11	.07	.11	.01	.10	.04	.12	.15	.15	.10	.06	.09	.06	.07	.09	.09	.07	.09	.11	.04	.05	.17	.08	.10	.11	.00	.02	.02	.06	.04	2.49
	WIND	40	22	30	10	9	15	35	100	56	71	36	14	27	16	14	14	10	9	21	39	27	33	20	30	30	64	23	22	16	29	48	930

TOTAL PRECIPITATION

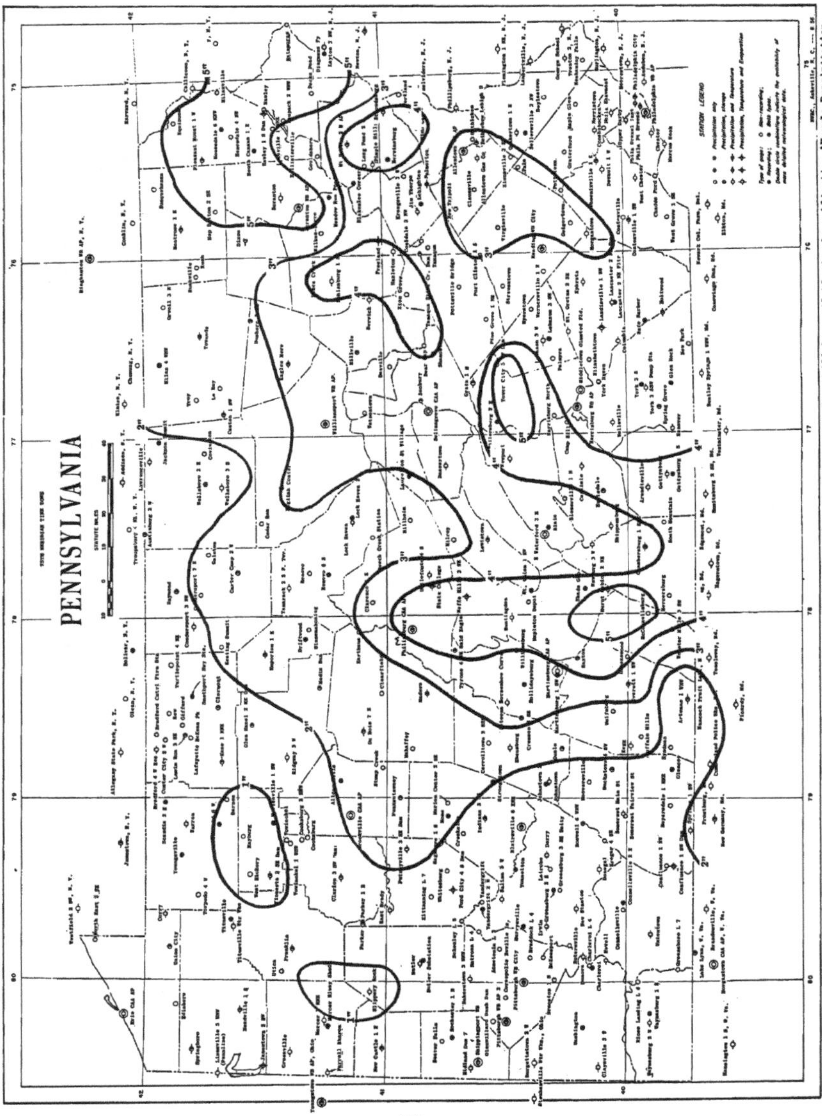

Isolines are drawn through points of approximately equal values. Hourly precipitation data from recorder substations will be available in the publication 'Hourly Precipitation

AVERAGE TEMPERATURE

PENNSYLVANIA
OCTOBER 1956

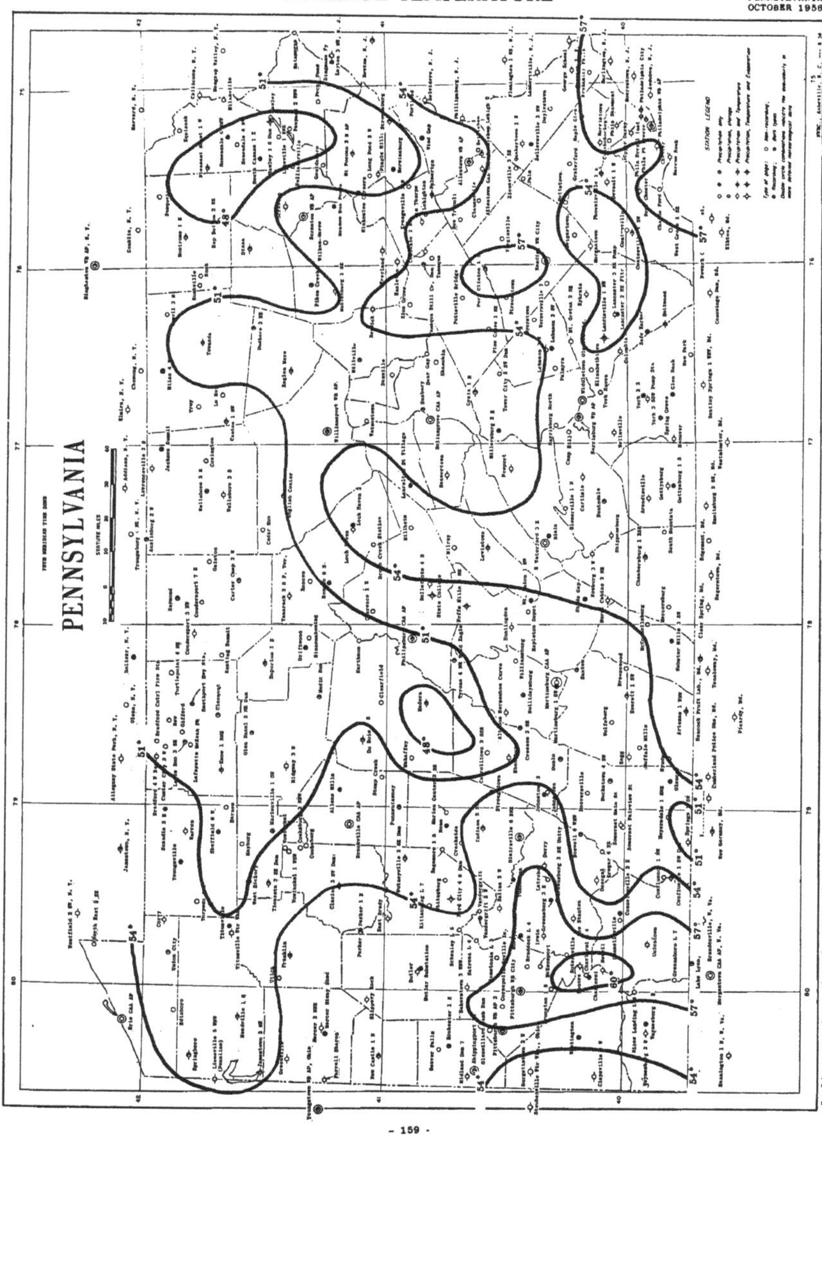

Isolines are drawn through points of approximately equal values. Hourly precipitation data from recorder substations will be available in the publication 'Hourly Precipitation Data'.

TOTAL PRECIPITATION

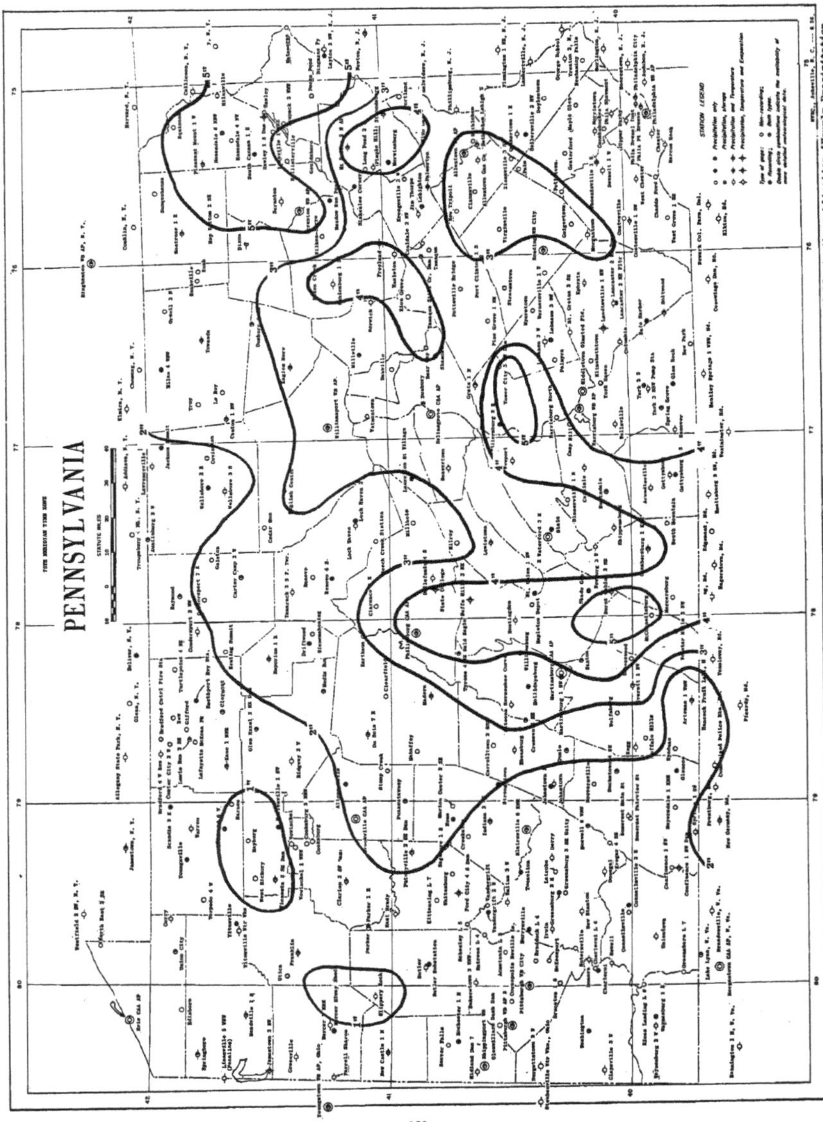

Isolines are drawn through points of approximately equal values. Hourly precipitation data from recorder substations will be available in the publication 'Hourly Precipitation Data'.

AVERAGE TEMPERATURE

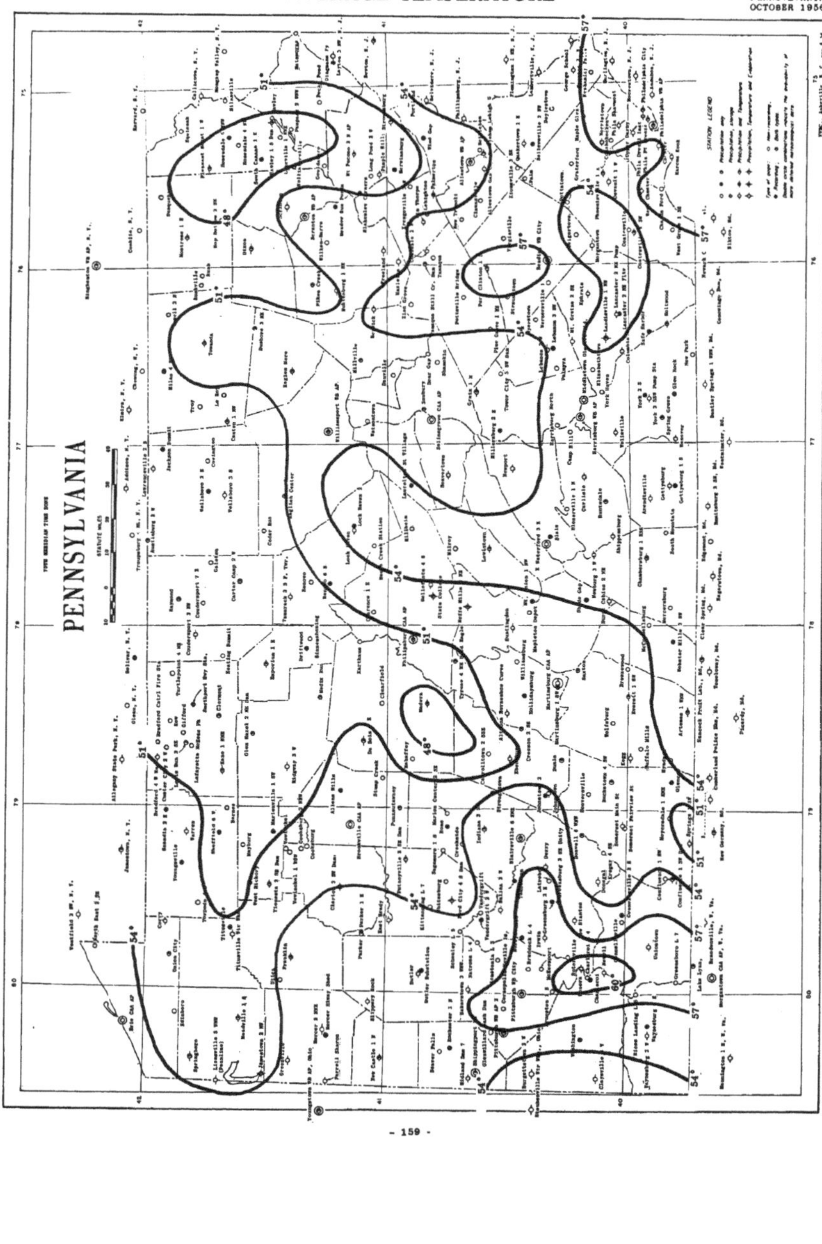

Isolines are drawn through points of approximately equal values. Hourly precipitation data from recorder substations will be available in the publication 'Hourly Precipitation Data'.

STATION INDEX

PENNSYLVANIA
OCTOBER 1956

Station	Index No.	County	Drainage 1	Latitude	Longitude	Elevation	Observation Time Temp.	Observation Time Precip.	Observer	Refer To Tables
ACHETONIA LOCK 3	0022	ALLEGHENY	1	40 32	79 40	748		7A	CORPS OF ENGINEERS	3
ALLENS MILLS	0099	JEFFERSON	1	41 12	78 55	1600		MID	CHARLES M. ALLEN	C
ALLENTOWN WB AP	0106	LEHIGH	9	40 39	75 26	376	MID	MID	U.S. WEATHER BUREAU	2 3 5 7 C
ALLENTOWN GAS CO	0111	LEHIGH	9	40 36	75 28	254	7A	7A	LEHIGH VLY GAS DIV	2 3 5
ALTOONA HORSESHOE CURVE	0134	BLAIR	6	40 30	78 29	1500	6P	6P	ALTOONA WATER BUR.	2 3 5 7
ARENDTSVILLE	0229	ADAMS	15	39 55	77 18	710	8A	8A	PA STATE COL EXP	2 3 5
ARTEMAS 1 WNW	0259	BEDFORD	12	39 45	78 28	1250	6P	6P	GRAYSON E.NORTHCRAFT	2 3 5 7 C
AUSTINBURG 2 W	0313	TIOGA	15	42 00	77 32	1590		7A	OTTO D. BACON	3 C
BAKERSTOWN 3 WNW	0355	ALLEGHENY	1	40 39	79 59	1230	7P	7P	PGH CUT FLOWER CO	2 3 5
BARNES	0409	WARREN	1	41 40	79 02	1310		7A	CORPS OF ENGINEERS	3
BEAR GAP	0457	NORTHUMBLAND	15	40 50	76 30	900		MID	ROARING CRK WTR CO	3
BEAVER FALLS	0475	BEAVER	2	40 46	80 19	760		7A	HOWARD R. KEMP	3
BEAVERTOWN	0482	SNYDER	15	40 45	77 10	640	7A	7A	MARLIN RC ETTINGER	2 3 5 7
BEECH CREEK STATION	0499	CENTRE	16	41 04	77 34	620		7A	HAROLD S. RUPERT	3
BELLEFONTE 4 S	0530	CENTRE	16	40 51	77 47	1110	8A	8A	ROCKVIEW PRISON FARM	2 3 5 7
BERWICK	0611	COLUMBIA	15	41 04	76 15	570	6P	6P	AMER CAR + FNDRY CO	2 3 5 7
BETHLEHEM	0629	NORTHAMPTON	9	40 37	75 22	400		7A	ARTHUR CROPPER	3
#BETHLEHEM LEHIGH UNIV	0634	NORTHAMPTON	9	40 36	75 23	450	MID	MID	LEHIGH UNIVERSITY	2 3 5 C
BLAIN	0725	PERRY	15	40 20	77 31	750		MID	PA DEPT FRST + WTRS	C
BLAIRSVILLE 6 ENE	0736	INDIANA	4	40 27	79 09	2048	8P	8P	U.S. WEATHER BUREAU	2 3 5
BLAKESLEE CORNERS	0743	MONROE	9	41 06	75 36	1650		MID	WALTER WILDRICK	C
BLOSERVILLE 1 N	0763	CUMBERLAND	15	40 16	77 22	650		5P	MRS. B. M. WILLDERS	3
BOSWELL 6 WNW	0820	SOMERSET	1	40 11	79 08	2580		7A	MRS. MAE L. KIMMEL	3 C
BRADDOCK LOCK 2	0861	ALLEGHENY	10	40 24	79 52	725		7A	CORPS OF ENGINEERS	3
BRADFORD CNTRL FIRE STA	0867	MC KEAN	1	41 57	78 39	1500		8A	BRADFORD FIRE DEPT	3
BRADFORD 4 W RES	0868	MC KEAN	1	41 57	78 44	1680	5P	5P	BRADFORD WTR DEPT	2 3 5 7
BREEZEWOOD	0905	BEDFORD	6	40 00	78 14	1352		MID	PA TURNPIKE COMM	3
BROOKVILLE CAA AIRPORT	1002	JEFFERSON	1	41 09	79 06	1417	MID	MID	CIVIL AERO. ADM.	2 3 5 7
BRUCETON 1 S	1033	ALLEGHENY	10	40 18	79 59	1065		7A	AUSTIN R. COOPER	3
BUCKSTOWN 1 SE	1073	SOMERSET	4	40 04	78 50	2460		MID	ALVIN W. MANGES	C
BUFFALO MILLS	1087	BEDFORD	6	39 58	78 39	1318		7A	MRS. NELLE R. BROWN	3
BURGETTSTOWN 2 W	1105	WASHINGTON	11	40 23	80 26	980	7A	7A	SMITH TWP MUN AUTH	2 3 5 7
BURNT CABINS 2 NE	1115	HUNTINGDON	6	40 05	77 52	990	MID	MID	PA TURNPIKE COMM	2 3 5 7
#BUTLER	1130	BUTLER	2	40 52	79 54	1100	4P	7A	WILLIAM C. FAUST	2 3 5 7
BUTLER SUBSTATION	1135	BUTLER	2	40 51	79 53	1140		MID	WEST PENN POWER CO	C
CAMP HILL	1198	CUMBERLAND	15	40 15	76 55	461		6P	JOSEPH N. HOBART	3
CANTON 1 NW	1215	BRADFORD	15	41 40	76 52	1520	7A	7A	MRS.MILDRED SPENCER	2 3 5 7 C
CARLISLE	1234	CUMBERLAND	15	40 12	77 11	460	6P	6P	C. E. MILLER	2 3 5 7
CARROLLTOWN 2 SSE	1255	CAMBRIA	16	40 35	78 42	2040		8A	ROBERT F. MAURER	3
CARTER CAMP 2 W	1262	POTTER	16	41 37	77 45	2030		7A	RICHARD L. MENKEN	3 C
CEDAR RUN	1301	LYCOMING	16	41 31	77 27	800		7A	KATHRYN T.KREIGHBAUM	3
CHADDS FORD	1342	DELAWARE	5	39 52	75 36	160		8A	MRS.GRACE A. WICKS	3
CHAMBERSBURG 1 ESE	1354	FRANKLIN	12	39 56	77 38	640	9P	9P	CHARLES A. BENDER	2 3 5 7 C
CHARLEROI	1372	WASHINGTON	10	40 08	79 55	1040		MID	WEST PENN POWER CO	C
CHARLEROI LOCK 4	1377	WESTMORELAND	10	40 09	79 54	749		7A	CORPS OF ENGINEERS	3
#CHESTER	1423	DELAWARE	5	39 51	75 22	86	8A	8A	CHESTER TIMES	2 3 5
CLARENCE	1480	CENTRE	16	41 03	77 56	1410		7A	MISS VELDA SWANCER	3
CLARION 3 SW	1485	CLARION	1	41 12	79 26	1114	8P	7A	PA ELECTRIC CO	2 3 5 7 C
CLAUSSVILLE	1505	LEHIGH	9	40 37	75 39	670		8A	WILLIAM J. DOTTERER	3
CLAYSVILLE 3 W	1512	WASHINGTON	11	40 07	80 28	1000	7P	7A	MFGRS. L + M CO	2 3 5
CLEARFIELD	1519	CLEARFIELD	16	41 01	78 26	1100		7A	IRA TAYLOR	3
CLERMONT	1529	MC KEAN	1	41 41	78 30	2104		7A	MRS.TILLIE M.SIMONDS	3 C
COALDALE 2 NW	1572	SCHUYLKILL	9	40 50	75 56	1026		7A	PANTHER VLY WTR CO	3
COATESVILLE 1 SW	1589	CHESTER	5	39 58	75 50	342	8A	8A	PHILA ELECTRIC CO	2 3 5 7 C
COATESVILLE	1594	CHESTER	5	39 59	75 49	340		8A	EDWARD D. BIEDEMAN	INAC 12/55
COLUMBIA	1675	LANCASTER	15	40 02	76 30	300	SS	SS	JAMES H. RUST	2 3 5
CONFLUENCE 1 SW DAM	1705	SOMERSET	17	39 48	79 22	1490	8A	8A	CORPS OF ENGINEERS	2 3 5 6 C
CONFLUENCE 1 NW	1710	FAYETTE	17	39 50	79 22	1331		7A	JOHN L. REID	3
CONNELLSVILLE	1723	FAYETTE	17	40 01	79 36	870		8A	MARSHALL B. MENEFEE	3
CONNELLSVILLE 2 E	1729	FAYETTE	17	40 01	79 33	1300		MID	HARRY C. JOY	C
CONSHOHOCKEN	1737	MONTGOMERY	5	40 04	75 19	70		8A	PHILA ELECTRIC CO	
COOKSBURG	1740	CLARION	1	41 20	79 13	1180		8A	PA DEPT FRST + WTRS	
COOKSBURG 2 NNW	1752	CLARION	1	41 21	79 13	1460		8A	PA DEPT FRST + WTRS	
CORAOPOLIS NEVILLE IS	1773	ALLEGHENY	11	40 30	80 05	720		8A	PGH. COKE + CHEM CO	3
CORRY	1790	ERIE	1	41 56	79 36	1427	7P	5A	LEO C. NECKERS	2 3 5 7
COUDERSPORT 3 NW	1806	POTTER	1	41 49	78 03	2020	7P	8A	MISS ELIZABETH NEFF	2 3 5 7
COUDERSPORT 7 E	1809	POTTER	1	41 46	77 53	2425		7A	CAMP POTATO	3
CREEKSIDE	1881	INDIANA	1	40 41	79 12	1035		7A	CORPS OF ENGINEERS	3
CRESSON 2 SE	1895	CAMBRIA	6	40 27	78 34	2540		7A	MILES A. VECELLIO	3 C
CUSTER CITY 2 W	1978	MC KEAN	1	41 55	78 41	2120		8A	M. D. BOOTH AND CO	3
DANVILLE	2013	MONTOUR	15	40 58	76 37	460		7A	MRS.MARIE M. LITTLE	
DERRY	2108	WESTMORELAND	4	40 20	79 18	1150	6P	6P	MISS N. D. WINEMAN	2 3 5
DEVAULT 1 W	2116	CHESTER	14	40 05	75 33	360	MID	MID	PA TURNPIKE COMM	2 3 5
DINGMANS FERRY	2160	PIKE	5	41 13	74 52	364		MID	CLYDE T. VOORHEES	C
DIXON	2171	WYOMING	15	41 34	75 54	620	7A	7A	HAROLD J. KUSCHEL	2 3 5 7 C
DONEGAL	2183	WESTMORELAND	17	40 07	79 23	1746	MID	MID	PA TURNPIKE COMM	2 3 5 7
#DONORA	2190	WASHINGTON	10	40 11	79 51	814	12M	12M	DONORA ZINC WORKS	2 3 5
DOYLESTOWN	2221	BUCKS	5	40 18	75 08	393		5P	GEORGE HART	3
DRIFTWOOD	2245	CAMERON	16	41 20	78 08	880		MID	SIDNEY KENNEDY	C
DU BOIS 7 E	2265	CLEARFIELD	16	41 06	78 38	1670	5P	5P	CITY OF DU BOIS	2 3 5 C
DUNLO	2298	CAMBRIA	4	40 17	78 43	2410		MID	MRS. D. L. WHITE	C
DUSHORE 3 NE	2324	SULLIVAN	16	41 33	76 21	1750		7A	PATRICK F. RYAN	3 C
EAGLES MERE	2343	SULLIVAN	16	41 24	76 35	2020	7A	7A	MRS.ELSIE P. BIGGER	2 3 5 7 C
EAST BRADY	2363	CLARION	1	40 59	79 37	820	5P	5P	A. B. KEMPEL	2 3 5
EAST WATERFORD 3 E	2450	PERRY	6	40 21	77 33	2125	8A	8A	U.S. WEATHER BUREAU	INAC 5/55
EBENSBURG	2466	CAMBRIA	4	40 29	78 43	2090	7P	7A	ROBERT A. WASSER	2 5
EDINBORO	2514	ERIE	1	41 52	80 08	1220		8A	EDINBORO ST TCHR COL	
ELIZABETHTOWN	2560	LANCASTER	15	40 09	76 37	460		8A	MASONIC HOME	3
EMPORIUM 2 SSW	2634	CAMERON	16	41 28	78 15	1735	7A	7A	JACKSON THOMAS	2 3 5 7 C
ENGLISH CENTER	2644	LYCOMING	16	41 26	77 17	881		7A	WILLIAM SUDERS	U C
EPHRATA	2662	LANCASTER	15	40 11	76 10	465	6P	6P	STANLEY L.VON NEIDA	2 3 5
EQUINUNK	2669	WAYNE	5	41 51	75 13	900		8A	MRS.ROSE M. NEILSEN	3
ERIE CAA AIRPORT	2682	ERIE	8	42 05	80 12	732	MID	MID	CIVIL AERO. ADM.	2 3 5
EVERETT 1 SW	2721	BEDFORD	6	40 00	78 23	1020	MID	MID	PA TURNPIKE COMM	2 3 5 7 C
FARRELL SHARON	2814	MERCER	2	41 14	80 30	865	7P	7P	SHARON STEEL CORP	2 3 5
FORD CITY 4 S DAM	2942	ARMSTRONG	1	40 43	79 30	950	8A	8A	CORPS OF ENGINEERS	2 3 5 6 7 C
FRANKLIN	3028	VENANGO	1	41 23	79 49	987	7P	7A	GEORGE S. SMITH JR.	2 3 5 7 C
FREELAND	3056	LUZERNE	15	41 01	75 54	1900	6P	8A	ANDREW B. EVANSHA	2 3 5
GALETON	3130	POTTER	16	41 44	77 39	1325		7A	W. GALE LUSH	3
GEIGERTOWN	3189	BERKS	14	40 13	75 50	400		8A	WALTER C. WOLF	3
GEORGE SCHOOL	3200	BUCKS	5	40 13	74 56	135	7P	7P	GEORGE M. HART	2 3 5 7
#GETTYSBURG	3218	ADAMS	12	39 50	77 14	540	9A	9A	HUGH C. MC ILHENNY	2 3 5 7
GETTYSBURG 1 S	3223	ADAMS	12	39 48	77 14	560		MID	NAT MILITARY PARK	C
GIFFORD	3237	MC KEAN	1	41 51	78 36	2220		8A	SOUTH PENN OIL CO	3
GLENCOE	3298	SOMERSET	12	39 49	78 51	1620		MID	MRS. MARY M.HARTMAN	C
GLEN HAZEL 2 NE DAM	3311	ELK	1	41 34	78 36	1725		8A	CORPS OF ENGINEERS	3 C
GLEN ROCK	3330	YORK	15	39 48	76 44	620		MID	MRS.E.C.MC WILLIAMS	C
GLENWILLARD DASH DAM	3343	ALLEGHENY	11	40 33	80 13	705		7A	CORPS OF ENGINEERS	3
GOULDSBORO	3394	WAYNE	9	41 15	75 27	1890		7A	L. H. EILENBERGER	3
GRATERFORD	3435	MONTGOMERY	14	40 14	75 27	160		7A	CLAUDE K. KULP	3
GRATZ 1 N	3438	DAUPHIN	15	40 38	76 43	760	8A	8A	LEE M. LEITZEL	2 3 5 7 C
GREENSBORO LOCK 7	3503	GREENE	10	39 47	79 55	808		7A	CORPS OF ENGINEERS	3
GREENSBURG 2 E	3515	WESTMORELAND	10	40 18	79 31	1225		MID	PA DEPT HIGHWAYS	C
GREENSBURG 3 SE UNITY	3516	WESTMORELAND	10	40 17	79 30	1245		6P	WESTMORELAND WTR CO	3
GREENVILLE	3526	MERCER	2	41 24	80 23	1026	6P	6P	C. EARL MILLER	2 3 5 7
HANOVER	3662	YORK	15	39 48	76 59	600	8A	8A	HANOVER EVENING SUN	2 5
#HARRISBURG WB AP	3699	YORK	15	40 13	76 51	335	MID	MID	U.S. WEATHER BUREAU	2 3 5 7 C
HARRISBURG NORTH	3704	DAUPHIN	15	40 18	76 54	323		9A	GEORGE S. BEAL	
HAWLEY	3758	WAYNE	5	41 29	75 10	880		7A	MRS.KATHERINE S.BATE	3 5
HAWLEY 1 S DAM	3761	WAYNE	5	41 28	75 11	1200	7A	7A	PA POWER + LIGHT CO	2 U 5 6 7 C
HOLLIDAYSBURG	4001	BLAIR	6	40 26	78 24	960		MID	JOHN M. RINGLER	C
HOLLISTERVILLE	4008	WAYNE	5	41 23	75 26	1360		8A	PA POWER + LIGHT CO	3
#HOLTWOOD	4019	LANCASTER	15	39 50	76 20	187	MID	8A	PA POWER + LIGHT CO	2 3 5 C
HOME	4027	INDIANA	1	40 45	79 06	1220		MID	MRS. EDNA M. BUSH	C
HONESDALE 4 NW	4043	WAYNE	5	41 37	75 19	1410		8A	GEORGE C. WILLIAMS	3
HONESDALE 6 NNW	4044	WAYNE	5	41 39	75 17	1050		MID	FRIEND E. WALTER	C
HOOVERSVILLE	4058	SOMERSET	4	40 09	78 55	1660		7A	PA ELECTRIC CO	3
HOP BOTTOM 2 SE	4066	SUSQUEHANNA	15	41 43	75 43	900		7A	JOSEPH J. SANSUSKAS	3
HUNTINGDON	4159	HUNTINGDON	6	40 29	78 01	610	7A	7A	MRS JANET I. VAUGHN	2 3 5 7
HUNTSDALE	4166	CUMBERLAND	15	40 06	77 18	610		8A	METRO P. DOROSH	3 C
HYNDMAN	4190	BEDFORD	12	39 49	78 43	920		8A	MRS.GERTRUDE M.BURTO	3
INDIANA 3 SE	4214	INDIANA	4	40 36	79 07	1102	7P	7A	CLYMER WATER SVC CO	2 3 5 7 C
IRWIN	4276	WESTMORELAND	10	40 20	79 42	1100	5P	5P	WESTMORELAND WTR CO	2 3 5
JACKSON SUMMIT	4304	TIOGA	15	41 57	77 01	1690		MID	ARCHIE LAIN	C
JAMESTOWN 2 NW	4325	CRAWFORD	2	41 30	80 28	1050	8A	8A	PA DEPT FRST + WTRS	2 3 5 6 C
JIM THORPE	4370	CARBON	9	40 52	75 45	830	5P	5P	HENRY S. HAAK	2 3 5
#JOHNSTOWN	4385	CAMBRIA	4	40 20	78 55	1214	9A	9A	JOHNSTOWN TRIBUNE	2 3 5 7
JOHNSTOWN 2	4390	CAMBRIA	4	40 19	78 55	1275		MID	CITY OF JOHNSTOWN	C
KANE 1 NNE	4432	MC KEAN	1	41 41	78 48	1750	8A	8A	SPRING WATER CO	2 3 5 7 C
KARTHAUS	4450	CLEARFIELD	16	41 07	78 07	850		7A	JEROME S. HOWE	3
KEATING SUMMIT	4466	POTTER	1	41 41	78 11	1840		7A	EUGENE L. KREITNER	3
KEGG	4481	BEDFORD	6	39 59	78 43	1280	MID	MID	PA TURNPIKE COMM	2 3 5
KITTANNING LOCK 7	4611	ARMSTRONG	1	40 49	79 32	790		VAR	CORPS OF ENGINEERS	3
KREGAR 4 SE	4667	WESTMORELAND	17	40 06	79 14	2530		MID	PA TURNPIKE COMM	3
KRESGEVILLE 3 W	4672	CARBON	9	40 54	75 34	720		8A	CITY OF BETHLEHEM	3
LAFAYETTE MC KEAN PARK	4706	MC KEAN	1	41 48	78 40	2130		7A	ORIN A. BUTTERS	3
LAKEVILLE 1 NNE	4733	WAYNE	5	41 27	75 16	1480		8A	MRS. GLADYS REINEKE	3
LANCASTER 2 NE PUMP STA	4758	LANCASTER	15	40 03	76 17	255	6P	6P	LANCASTER WATER BUR	2 3 5
LANCASTER 2 NE FILT PL	4763	LANCASTER	15	40 03	76 17	270		MID	LANCASTER WATER BUR	C
LANDISVILLE 2 NW	4778	LANCASTER	15	40 07	76 26	360	8A	8A	PA STATE COLLEGE	2 3 5 6 7 C
LATROBE	4832	WESTMORELAND	4	40 19	79 23	1000		MID	WEST PENN POWER CO	INAC 6/56
LAURELTON STATE VILLAGE	4853	UNION	15	40 54	77 13	880		MID	PA DEPT OF WELFARE	C
LAWRENCEVILLE 2 S	4873	TIOGA	15	41 59	77 07	1000	7A	7A	HARRY P. HOWLAND	2 3 5 7
LEBANON 3 W	4891	LEBANON	15	40 20	76 29	460	7A	7A	LEON MILLER	2 3 5 7
LEBANON 3 SW	4896	LEBANON	15	40 19	76 28	490		MID	THOMAS DONNACHIE	C
LEHIGHTON	4934	CARBON	9	40 50	75 43	580		7A	GOODWIN S. DEFREHN	3 C
LE ROY	4972	BRADFORD	15	41 41	76 43	1040		6P	MRS.DIMMIS M.BAILEY	3
LEWIS RUN 3 S	4984	MC KEAN	1	41 50	78 39	1740		7A	RUSSELL LINEMAN	3 C
LEWISTOWN	4992	MIFFLIN	6	40 35	77 35	480	7A	7A	AMERICAN VISCOSE CO	2 3 5 7 C
LINESVILLE 5 WNW	5050	CRAWFORD	2	41 41	80 31	1020	7P	8A	MISS RETTA M. CRUMB	2 3 5
LOCK HAVEN	5104	CLINTON	16	41 08	77 27	570	7P	7A	PETER L. STEVENSON	2 3 5 7
LOCK HAVEN 2	5109	CLINTON	16	41 08	77 27	630		MID	HUGH F. PARKER	C
LONG POND 2 W	5160	MONROE	9	41 03	75 30	1860		7A	THOMAS MECKES	3
MADERA	5336	CLEARFIELD	16	40 50	78 26	1460	7A	7A	MRS. JULIA J. SHOFF	2 3 5 C
MAHAFFEY	5342	CLEARFIELD	16	40 53	78 44	1280		7A	MISS ELLEN J. MILES	3
MAPLE GLEN	5368	MONTGOMERY	5	40 11	75 11	380		6P	FRANCES E.SCHEIBNER	3
MAPLETON DEPOT	5381	HUNTINGDON	6	40 24	77 56	580		7A	MRS. I. S. BUCHANAN	3
MARCUS HOOK	5390	DELAWARE	5	39 49	75 25	12	MID	MID	SUN OIL CO	2 3 5
MARIENVILLE 1 SW	5400	FOREST	1	41 27	79 09	1700		MID	ROY A. MARKER	C
MARION CENTER 2 SE	5408	INDIANA	1	40 45	79 02	1610		7A	CORPS OF ENGINEERS	3
MARTINSBURG 1 SW	5453	BLAIR	6	40 18	78 20	1360		MID	BLUE MT. CANNERIES	C
MARTINSBURG CAA AP	5454	BLAIR	6	40 18	78 19	1463	MID	MID	CIVIL AERO. ADM.	2 3 5
MATAMORAS	5470	PIKE	5	41 22	74 42	439		7A	HARRY BISLAND	3
MAYBURG	5490	FOREST	1	41 36	79 13	1150		7A	CORPS OF ENGINEERS	3
MC CONNELLSBURG	5526	FULTON	12	39 56	78 00	895		8A	MRS. HELEN M. SHIVES	3
MC KEESPORT	5573	ALLEGHENY	10	40 21	79 52	720		8A	NATIONAL TUBE CO	3
MEADOW RUN PONDS	5601	LUZERNE	15	41 13	75 40	1995		MID	GEORGE PEARAGE	C
MEADVILLE 1 S	5606	CRAWFORD	1	41 38	80 10	1065	8A	8A	CITY OF MEADVILLE	2 3 5 7 C
MEDIX RUN	5627	ELK	16	41 17	78 24	1100		7A	MRS.E. M. SNYDER	3 C
MERCER 2 NNE	5651	MERCER	2	41 15	80 13	1160	7P	7A	WILLIAM K. STRUTHERS	2 3 5 7
MERCER HIWAY SHED	5654	MERCER	2	41 14	80 15	1250		MID	PA DEPT HIGHWAYS	C
MERCERSBURG	5662	FRANKLIN	12	39 50	77 54	605		8A	ROLLIN P. GILBERT	3
MERWINSBURG	5676	MONROE	9	40 58	75 28	970		MID	WILLIAM D. GOULD	C
MEYERSDALE 1 ENE	5685	SOMERSET	17	39 49	79 01	2290		8A	ARTHUR B. MC CARTER	3
MIDDLETOWN OLMSTED FLD	5703	DAUPHIN	15	40 11	76 46	303	MID	MID	U. S. AIR FORCE	2 3 5
MIDLAND DAM 7	5710	BEAVER	11	40 38	80 28	689	11P	7A	CORPS OF ENGINEERS	2 3 5
MILAN 4 WNW	5732	BRADFORD	15	41 56	76 35	1448		MID	CARL A. MORRIS	C
MILANVILLE	5738	WAYNE	5	41 40	75 04	760		8A	CHARLES W. DAVIS	3
MILLERSBURG 2 E	5775	DAUPHIN	15	40 32	76 56	560		MID	RUSSELL SHEPLEY	C
MILLHEIM	5790	CENTRE	15	40 54	77 29	1090		7A	NEVIN E. BOWERSOX	3
MILLVILLE 2 SW	5817	COLUMBIA	15	41 06	76 34	860		7A	KENNETH LEIGHOW	3 C
MILROY	5825	MIFFLIN	6	40 43	77 35	770		8A	THOMAS C. HARBESON	3
MONTROSE 1 E	5915	SUSQUEHANNA	15	41 50	75 51	1630	7A	7A	WILBER W. HOOPES,JR	2 3 5 7 C
MORGANTOWN	5936	BERKS	15	40 09	75 54	595	MID	MID	PA TURNPIKE COMM	2 3 5
MT GRETNA 2 SE	6028	LANCASTER	15	40 14	76 26	670	MID	MID	PA TURNPIKE COMM	2 3 5
MT POCONO 2 N AP	6055	MONROE	5	41 09	75 22	1915	5P	5P	H. JOHN DAVIS, JR.	2 3 5 7 C
MOUNT UNION 1 N	6067	MIFFLIN	6	40 24	77 53	820		MID	MT UNION WTR WORKS	C
MUHLENBURG 1 SE	6090	LUZERNE	15	41 13	76 08	1110	6P	6P	THEODORE J. SAMPSON	2 3 5
MURRYSVILLE	6111	WESTMORELAND	10	40 26	79 42	903		MID	DAVID C. SHAW	C
MYERSTOWN	6126	LEBANON	14	40 22	76 18	480		8A	MRS.KATHLEEN WANDELL	3
NATRONA LOCK 4	6151	ALLEGHENY	1	40 37	79 43	800		7A	CORPS OF ENGINEERS	3
NEFFS MILLS 3 NE	6174	HUNTINGDON	6	40 40	77 55	900		MID	PA STATE UNIVERSITY	C
NESHAMINY FALLS	6194	BUCKS	5	40 09	74 57	60		MID	PHILA SUB WATER CO	3
NEWBURG 3 W	6225	FRANKLIN	15	40 09	77 37	745	MID	MID	PA TURNPIKE COMM	2 3 5
NEW CASTLE 1 N	6233	LAWRENCE	2	41 01	80 22	825	5P	7A	BAXTER F. JOHNSON	2 3 5 7 C
#NEWELL	6246	FAYETTE	10	40 05	79 54	805	12M	12M	GENERAL CHEMICAL CO	2 3 5
NEW PARK	6289	YORK	15	39 44	76 30	780		6P	CLINTON J. ALLEN	3
NEWPORT	6297	PERRY	6	40 29	77 08	400	7A	7A	MRS. FRANCES K. FRY	2 3 5 7
NEW STANTON	6310	WESTMORELAND	10	40 13	79 36	980	MID	MID	PA TURNPIKE COMM	2 3 5
NEW TRIPOLI	6326	LEHIGH	14	40 41	75 45	570		6P	FRED C. OSWALD	3
NORRISTOWN	6370	MONTGOMERY	14	40 07	75 21	75	MID	8A	GEORGE H. BOONE	2 3 5
NORTH EAST 2 SE	6396	ERIE	8	42 12	79 49	1060		8A	ELLSWORTH WEAVER	3
ORWELL 3 N	6621	BRADFORD	15	41 55	76 16	1620		8A	WILLIAM I. BROWN	3
PALM	6661	MONTGOMERY	14	40 26	75 32	385		8A	FRED C. ESCHBACH	3
#PALMERTON	6689	CARBON	9	40 48	75 37	435	MID	MID	NEW JERSEY ZINC CO	2 3 5 7 C
PALMYRA	6694	LEBANON	15	40 18	76 35	480		7P	EARL E. RHOADS	3
PARKER	6721	ARMSTRONG	1	41 05	79 41	1140		7A	LOUIS A. MALARKEY	3
PARKER 1 E	6724	CLARION	1	41 06	79 40	1100		MID	P. M. NEELY	C
PAUPACK 2 WNW	6762	PIKE	5	41 24	75 14	1360		8A	MISS L. VETTERLEIN	3
PECKS POND	6786	PIKE	5	41 17	75 06	1380		8A	MRS. CARRIE NESS	3
#PHIL DREXEL INST OF TEC	6879	PHILADELPHIA	14	39 57	75 11	30	MID	MID	FRANCIS K. DAVIS,JR	2 3 5
PHILADELPHIA WB AP	6889	PHILADELPHIA	5	39 53	75 14	13	MID	MID	U.S. WEATHER BUREAU	2 3 5 7 C
#PHILADELPHIA PT BREEZE	6899	PHILADELPHIA	5	39 55	75 12	32	MID	MID	ATLANTIC REFINING	2 3 5 C
PHILADELPHIA SHAWMONT	6904	PHILADELPHIA	5	40 02	75 15	70	7P	7P	SCHUYLKILL NAVIG CO	2 3 5 7
#PHILADELPHIA CITY	6909	PHILADELPHIA	5	39 57	75 09	26	9A	9A	USN HYDROGRAPHIC OFF	2 3 5 C
PHILIPSBURG CAA AP	6916	CENTRE	6	40 54	78 05	1918	8P	8P	CIVIL AERO. ADM.	2 3 5 7 C
PHOENIXVILLE 1 E	6927	CHESTER	14	40 07	75 30	105	6P	MID	PHILA SUB WATER CO	2 3 5 7 C
PIKES CREEK	6939	LUZERNE	15	41 18	76 08	1320		MID	HARRY SHELDON	3 C
PIMPLE HILL	6944	MONROE	9	41 02	75 30	2215	9A	9A	PA DEPT FRST + WTRS	2 3 5 6
PINE GROVE 1 NE	6954	SCHUYLKILL	15	40 34	76 22	535		8A	PA POWER + LIGHT CO	3
PITTSBURGH WB AP 2	6993	ALLEGHENY	11	40 30	80 13	1151	MID	MID	U.S. WEATHER BUREAU	2 3 5 7 C
#PITTSBURGH WB CITY	6997	ALLEGHENY	11	40 27	80 00	749	MID	MID	U.S. WEATHER BUREAU	2 3 5 C
PLEASANT MOUNT 1 W	7029	WAYNE	5	41 44	75 27	1800	8A	8A	PA FISH COMM	2 3 5 C
PORT CLINTON	7116	SCHUYLKILL	14	40 35	76 02	450	7A	7A	MRS. ADA E. RARICK	2 3 5 7 C
PORTLAND	7127	NORTHAMPTON	5	40 55	75 06	297		8A	JOINT BRIDGE COMM	INAC 1/56
POTTSVILLE	7161	SCHUYLKILL	14	40 42	76 11	690		8A	LLOYD E. WELLER	3
PUNXSUTAWNEY	7217	JEFFERSON	1	40 57	79 00	1298		MID	JOHN VOLANSKY	C
PUTNEYVILLE 2 SE DAM	7229	ARMSTRONG	1	40 55	79 17	1270	8A	8A	CORPS OF ENGINEERS	2 3 5 C
QUAKERTOWN 1 E	7239	BUCKS	5	40 26	75 20	490	5P	5P	DENNIS K. FLUCK	2 3 5 7
RAYMOND	7310	POTTER	13	41 52	77 52	2220		7A	MRS. RACHEL LANGAN	3 C
#READING WB CITY	7318	BERKS	14	40 20	75 58	266	MID	MID	U.S. WEATHER BUREAU	2 3 5 7 C
RENOVO	7409	CLINTON	16	41 20	77 46	660		7A	MRS. CAROLINE BAIRD	3
RENOVO 5 S	7410	CLINTON	16	41 14	77 46	2035		MID	C. F. GILLETTE	C
REW	7425	MC KEAN	1	41 54	78 32	2250		8A	HAROLD C. MEALY	3
RICES LANDING L 6	7443	GREENE	10	39 57	80 00	775		7A	CORPS OF ENGINEERS	3
RIDGWAY 3 W	7477	ELK	1	41 25	78 47	1420	7A	7A	BOROUGH OF RIDGWAY	2 3 5 7
ROCHESTER 1 N	7540	BEAVER	2	40 43	80 18	900		MID	DEQUESNE LIGHT CO	C
RUSH	7694	SUSQUEHANNA	15	41 47	76 03	1000		8A	MISS MAUDE MC CAIN	3
RUSHVILLE	7727	SUSQUEHANNA	15	41 47	76 07	870		7A	CARL KOPATZ	3
SAFE HARBOR	7732	LANCASTER	15	39 55	76 23	270		MID	S.H.WATER POWER CORP	C
SAGAMORE 1 S	7739	INDIANA	1	40 46	79 14	1320		7A	CORPS OF ENGINEERS	3
SALINA 3 W	7782	WESTMORELAND	7	40 31	79 33	1109	6P	6P	MUN AUTH WSTMRLD CO	2 3 5
SAXTON	7846	BEDFORD	6	40 12	78 15	780		8A	MRS.ALVERTA L.HOLMES	3 C
SCANDIA 2 E	7855	WARREN	1	41 55	79 01	2040		MID	DAVID R. ANDERSON	C
SCHENLEY LOCK 5	7863	ARMSTRONG	1	40 41	79 40	783		VAR	CORPS OF ENGINEERS	3
#SCRANTON	7902	LACKAWANNA	15	41 25	75 40	746	7A	7A	U.S. POST OFFICE	2 3 5
SCRANTON WB AIRPORT	7905	LUZERNE	15	41 20	75 44	956	MID	MID	U.S. WEATHER BUREAU	2 3 5 7 C
SELINSGROVE CAA AP	7931	SNYDER	15	40 49	76 52	437	MID	MID	CIVIL AERO. ADM.	2 3 5 7
SELLERSVILLE 2 NW	7938	BUCKS	5	40 23	75 20	530		MID	SELLERSVILLE WTR CO	C

STATION INDEX

Station	Index No.	County	Drainage ‡	Latitude	Longitude	Elevation	Observation Time Temp.	Observation Time Precip.	Observer	Refer To Tables
SHADE GAP	7965	HUNTINGDON	6	40 11	77 52	1000		MID	MRS. HELEN M. PYLE	C
SHAMOKIN	7978	NORTHUMBLAND	15	40 48	76 33	770		8A	ROARING CRK WTR CO	3
SHEFFIELD 6 W	8026	WARREN	1	41 41	79 09	1940		MID	L. N. HANSON	C
SHIPPENSBURG	8073	FRANKLIN	15	40 03	77 32	709	4P	4P	KEITH B. ALLEN	2 3 5
SHIPPINGPORT WB	8078	BEAVER	11	40 37	80 26	740	MID	MID	U.S. WEATHER BUREAU	2 3 5 7 C
SINNEMAHONING	8145	CAMERON	16	41 19	78 05	790		7A	MRS.FRANCES CALDWELL	3
SLIPPERY ROCK	8184	BUTLER	2	41 04	80 03	1345	7P	7A	WALTER D. ALBERT	2 3 5
SMETHPORT HIGHWAY SHED	8190	MC KEAN	1	41 48	78 27	1510		MID	PA DEPT HIGHWAYS	C
SOMERSET FAIRVIEW ST	8244	SOMERSET	17	40 01	79 05	2140		7A	HOWARD G. PECK	3
SOMERSET MAIN ST	8249	SOMERSET	17	40 01	79 05	2150	6P	6P	DAVID L. GROVE	2 3 5 7
SOUTH CANAAN 1 NE	8275	WAYNE	5	41 31	75 24	1400		MID	EUGENE M. COOK	C
SOUTH MOUNTAIN	8308	FRANKLIN	12	39 51	77 30	1520		7A	PA DEPT OF HEALTH	3
SPRINGBORO	8359	CRAWFORD	8	41 48	80 23	900	8A	8A	SPRINGBORO BOROUGH	2 3 5 7 C
SPRING GROVE	8379	YORK	15	39 52	76 52	470		4P	P. H. GLATFELTER CO	3 C
SPRINGS 1 SW	8395	SOMERSET	17	39 44	79 10	2500	8P	8P	ALLEN E. YODER	2 3 5 7
STATE COLLEGE	8449	CENTRE	16	40 48	77 52	1175	MID	MID	PA STATE COLLEGE	2 3 5 6 C
STRAUSSTOWN	8570	BERKS	14	40 29	76 11	600		8A	JACOB KLAHR	3
STRONGSTOWN	8589	INDIANA	4	40 33	78 55	1860		MID	HARRY F. BENNETT	C
STROUDSBURG	8596	MONROE	5	40 59	75 12	460	11P	11P	WILLIAM MAGERTY	2 3 5 7 C
STUMP CREEK	8610	JEFFERSON	1	41 01	78 50	1320		7A	CORPS OF ENGINEERS	3
SUNBURY	8668	NORTHUMBLAND	15	40 51	76 48	440		7A	CHARLES W. BAYLER	3 C
SUSQUEHANNA	8692	SUSQUEHANNA	15	41 57	75 36	1020		7A	MRS. LAURA A.BENSON	3
SUTERSVILLE	8699	ALLEGHENY	17	40 14	79 48	765		7A	FRANK E. MARSH	3
TAMAQUA	8758	SCHUYLKILL	14	40 48	75 58	830		8A	MRS. MARY L.ROBERTS	3
TAMAQUA 4 N DAM	8763	SCHUYLKILL	14	40 51	75 59	1120		7A	PANTHER VLY WTR CO	3 C
TAMARACK 2 S FIRE TWR	8770	CLINTON	16	41 24	77 51	2220	7A	7A	JAMES E. SWARTZ	2 3 5 7
TIONESTA 2 SE DAM	8873	FOREST	1	41 29	79 26	1200	8A	8A	CORPS OF ENGINEERS	2 3 5 7 C
TITUSVILLE	8885	CRAWFORD	1	41 38	79 40	1550		MID	PA ELECTRIC CO	C
TITUSVILLE WATER WORKS	8888	CRAWFORD	1	41 38	79 42	1220	7P	7P	CITY OF TITUSVILLE	2 3 5
TORPEDO 4 W	8901	WARREN	1	41 47	79 32	1735		7A	MRS. LILY B. GARBER	3-
TOWANDA	8905	BRADFORD	15	41 46	76 26	760	7P	7A	MRS. M. O. PARKS	2 3 5 7 C
TOWER CITY 5 SW	8910	DAUPHIN	15	40 31	76 37	745		6P	HARRISBURG WTR DEPT	3 7
TROY	8959	BRADFORD	15	41 47	76 47	1100		7A	JENNIE L. BALLARD	3
TUNNELTON	8989	INDIANA	4	40 27	79 23	890		MID	MRS. MARY E. WEIMER	C
TURTLEPOINT 4 NE	9002	MC KEAN	1	41 54	78 16	1640		7A	ROBERT D. STRAIT	3
TYRONE 4 NE BALD EAGLE	9024	BLAIR	6	40 43	78 12	1020		7A	FREDERICK L. FRIDAY	3 C
UNION CITY	9042	ERIE	1	41 54	79 50	1325		7A	FORREST M. BRALEY	3 C
UNIONTOWN	9050	FAYETTE	10	39 54	79 44	1040	10P	10P	WM. W. MARSTELLER	2 3 5 7
UPPER DARBY	9074	DELAWARE	5	39 58	75 18	222	7P	7P	PHIL. SUB.TRANS. CO	2 3 5
UTICA	9099	VENANGO	1	41 26	79 57	1030		7A	MRS.FLORENCE MILLER	3
VANDERGRIFT	9128	WESTMORELAND	7	40 36	79 33	800		7A	UNITED ENG+FNDRY CO	3
VANDERGRIFT 2 W	9133	WESTMORELAND	7	40 36	79 36	995		MID	EUGENE R. YOUNG	C
VIRGINVILLE	9196	BERKS	14	40 31	75 52	350		8A	MRS. MARY M. WRIGHT	3
VOWINCKEL	9206	CLARION	1	41 25	79 14	1620		8A	PA DEPT FRST + WTRS	3
VOWINCKEL 1 WSW	9209	CLARION	1	41 24	79 15	1610		8A	PA DEPT FRST + WTRS	3
WARREN	9298	WARREN	1	41 51	79 08	1280	7P	7A	GILBERT H. KLIER	2 3 5 7
WASHINGTON	9312	WASHINGTON	11	40 11	80 14	1200		MID	PA DEPT HIGHWAYS	C
WATSONTOWN	9345	NORTHUMBLAND	16	41 05	76 52	470		8A	OWEN BERKENSTOCK	3
WAYNESBURG 2 W	9362	GREENE	10	39 54	80 13	980	6P	7A	RALPH L. AMOS	2 3 5 7
WAYNESBURG 1 E	9367	GREENE	10	39 54	80 10	940		MID	SEWAGE DISPOSAL PLT	C
WEBSTER MILLS 3 SW	9380	FULTON	12	39 40	78 05	920		MID	WILLIAM D. COVER	C
WELLSBORO 3 S	9408	TIOGA	16	41 43	77 16	1920	7A	7A	MARION L. SHUMWAY	2 3 5 7
WELLSBORO 2 E	9412	TIOGA	16	41 45	77 16	1550		MID	MRS. IDA S. MAYNARD	C
WELLSVILLE	9420	YORK	15	40 03	76 57	500	5P	5P	D. D. HOOVER	2 3 5
WERNERSVILLE 1 W	9430	BERKS	14	40 20	76 06	405		8A	CHARLES A. GRUBER	3
WEST CHESTER	9464	CHESTER	5	39 58	75 36	440	8A	8A	DAILY LOCAL NEWS	2 3 5 7
WEST GROVE 1 E	9503	CHESTER	5	39 49	75 49	440		8A	CONARD-PYLE CO	3
WEST HICKORY	9507	FOREST	1	41 34	79 25	1090		8A	MRS.HELEN F.KINNEAR	3
WHITESBURG	9655	ARMSTRONG	1	40 [illegible]	79 24	1530		7A	CORPS OF ENGINEERS	3
WILKES-BARRE	9702	LUZERNE	15	41 15	75 52	610		7A	MRS. MARY G. MIGMAK	3
WILLIAMSBURG	9714	BLAIR	6	40 28	78 12	860		7A	MYRON K. BIDDLE	3
WILLIAMSPORT WB AP	9728	LYCOMING	16	41 15	76 55	527	MID	MID	U.S. WEATHER BUREAU	2 3 5 7 C
WIND GAP	9781	NORTHAMPTON	5	40 51	75 18	720		MID	OWEN R. PARRY	C
WOLFSBURG	9823	BEDFORD	6	40 03	78 32	1190		7A	WALTER C. RICE	3
YORK 3 SSW PUMP STA	9933	YORK	15	39 55	76 45	390	5P	5P	YORK WATER COMPANY	2 3 5 7
YORK 2 S FILTER PLANT	9938	YORK	15	39 56	76 44	640		MID	YORK WATER COMPANY	C
YORK HAVEN	9950	YORK	15	40 07	76 43	310		8A	METROPOL EDISON CO	3
YOUNGSVILLE	9966	WARREN	1	41 51	79 20	1225		MID	HENRY CARLETT	C
ZION GROVE	9990	SCHUYLKILL	15	40 54	76 13	940		7A	JAMES D. TEETER	3
ZIONSVILLE 3 SE	9995	LEHIGH	14	40 27	75 27	660		7A	LESLIE HOWATT	3
NEW STATIONS										
BARTO 4 NW	0428	BERKS	14	40 26	75 39	312		7A	MARIE B. NICHLAS	3
COVINGTON 2 WSW	1833	TIOGA	15	41 44	77 07	1745		7A	CALVIN R. PACKARD	3
CLOSED STATIONS										
COVINGTON 3 W	1832	TIOGA	15	41 45	77 07	1575		7A	GROVER D. CLEVELAND	CLOSED 9/56
POTTSTOWN	7149	MONTGOMERY	14	40 15	75 39	160		8A	MILES E. SMITH	CLOSED 10/56

‡ 1-ALLEGHENY; 2-BEAVER; 3- 4-CONEMAUGH; 5-DELAWARE; 6-JUNIATA; 7-KISKIMINETAS; 8-LAKE ERIE; 9-LEHIGH; 10-MONONGAHELA; 11-OHIO; 12-POTOMAC; 13-LAKE ONTARIO; 14-SCHUYLKILL; 15-SUSQUEHANNA; 16-WEST BRANCH; 17-YOUGHIOGHENY

REFERENCE NOTES

Additional information regarding the climate of Pennsylvania may be obtained by writing to the State Climatologist at Weather Bureau Airport Station, Harrisburg State Airport, New Cumberland, Pennsylvania, or to any Weather Bureau Office near you.

Figures and letters following the station name, such as 12 SSW, indicate distance in miles and direction from the post office.

Delayed data and corrections will be carried only in the June and December issues of this bulletin.

Monthly and seasonal snowfall and heating degree days for the preceding 12 months will be carried in the June issue of this bulletin.

Stations appearing in the Index, but for which data are not listed in the tables, either are missing or were received too late to be included in this issue.

Divisions, as used in Table 2, became effective with data for September 1956.

Unless otherwise indicated, dimensional units used in this bulletin are: Temperature in °F, precipitation and evaporation in inches, and wind movement in miles. Degree days are negative departures of average daily temperature from 65° F.

Evaporation is measured in the standard Weather Bureau type pan of 4 foot diameter unless otherwise shown by footnote following Table 6.

Long-term means for full-time stations (those shown in the Station Index as "U. S. Weather Bureau") are based on the period 1921-1950, adjusted to represent observations taken at the present location. Long-term means for all stations except full-time Weather Bureau stations are based on the period 1931-155.

Water equivalent samples published in Table 7 are necessarily taken from different points for successive observations; consequently occasional drifting and other causes of local variability in the snowpack result in apparent inconsistencies in the record. Water equivalent of snow on the ground is measured at selected stations when two or more inches of snow are on the ground.

Data in Tables 3, 5, and 6 and snowfall in Table 7, when published, are for the 24 hours ending at time of observation. The Station Index lists observation times in the standard of time in local use..

Snow on ground in Table 7 is at observation time for all except Weather Bureau and CAA stations. For these stations snow on ground values are at 7:30 a.m., E.S.T.

- \- No record in Tables 3, 6, 7 and the Station Index. No record in Tables 2 and 5, is indicated by no entry. Consult the annual issue of this publication for interpolated monthly precipitation totals.
- + And also on a later date or dates.
- • Amount included in following measurement, time distribution unknown.
- // Gage is equipped with a windshield.
- # Thermometers are generally exposed in a shelter located a few feet above sod-covered ground; however, the reference indicates that the thermometers are exposed in a shelter located on the roof of a building.
- AM Data based on observational day ending before noon.
- B Adjusted to a full month.
- C In the "Refer to Tables" column in the Station Index the letter "C" indicates recorder stations. These stations are processed for special purposes and are published later in "Hourly Precipitation Data".
- D Water equivalent of snowfall wholly or partly estimated, using a ratio of 1 inch water equivalent to every 10 inches of new snowfall.
- G In the "Refer to Tables" column in the Station Index the letter "G" indicates that soil temperatures are published.
- M One to nine days of record missing; see Table 5 for detailed daily record. Degree day data, if carried for this station, have been adjusted to represent the valur for a full month.
- R Amounts from recording gage (These amounts are essentially accurate but may vary slightly from the amounts to be published later in Hourly Precipitation Data.
- SS This entry in time of observation column in Station Index means observation made near sunset.
- T Trace, an amount too small to measure.
- Y Includes total for previous month.
- VAR This entry in time of observation column in Station index means variable.

Information concerning the history of changes in locations, elevations, exposure etc. of substations through 1955 may be found in the publication 'Substation History' for this state, soon to be issued. That publication, when available, may be obtained from the Superintendent of Documents, Government Printing Office, Washington 25, D. C. at a price to be announced. Similar information for regular Weather Bureau stations may be found in the latest issues of Local Climatological Data, Annual for the respective stations, obtained as indicated above, price 15 cents.

Subscription Price: 20 cents per copy, monthly and annual; $2.50 per year. (Yearly subscription includes the Annual Summary). Checks, and money orders should be made payable to the Superintendent of Documents. Remittance and correspondence regarding subscriptions should be sent to the Superintendent of Documents, Government Printing Office, Washington 25, D. C.

WRPC., Asheville, N. C. --- 12/7/56 --- 1100

U. S. DEPARTMENT OF COMMERCE
SINCLAIR WEEKS, Secretary
WEATHER BUREAU
F. W. REICHELDERFER, Chief

CLIMATOLOGICAL DATA

PENNSYLVANIA

NOVEMBER 1956
Volume LXI No. 11

ASHEVILLE: 1957

PENNSYLVANIA - NOVEMBER 1956

WEATHER SUMMARY

GENERAL

Extremely heavy snow with deep drifts in Erie County the 22nd-23rd, heavy thunderstorm rains in central and southeastern Pennsylvania the 1st-2nd, unseasonably warm weather at the beginning of the month, and a hard cold snap the 23rd-25th were the major weather features of November.

Temperature extremes ranged from 80° at Berwick on the 1st to -4° at Springs 1 SW on the 24th. Average temperatures were generally less than 3° above or below the long term mean with positive and negative departures presenting a random distribution except for a preponderance of pluses across the northern portion of the State and in the Southeastern Piedmont Division.

Precipitation was considerably above average in the Southeastern Piedmont Division, near average in the Susquehanna Valley-Central Mountains region, and appreciably less than average elsewhere. Station totals ranged from 6.82 inches at Watsontown to 0.32 inch at Coraopolis Neville Island and the greatest amount for one day was 3.36 inches measured at Beavertown on the 2nd. Snowfall was relatively light in the southeastern section, very heavy in the extreme northwest, and light to locally heavy in a spotty distribution over the intervening area.

WEATHER DETAILS

Very high temperatures at the beginning of November declined gradually to slightly below the seasonal average by the 9th, and a cold snap the 10th-11th dropped minima into the twenties and upper teens. Temperatures were moderate the 12th-14th and the combined effects of southerly winds and bright sunshine on the 15th sent maxima above the 70° mark, approximately duplicating the high readings at the beginning of the month. Changes were of a moderate nature with temperatures averaging near the seasonal value the 16th-20th and appreciably warmer weather the 21st was the last occurrence of higher than average temperatures this month. The change on the 22nd established very cold weather over Pennsylvania that held through the 25th and moderately cold weather prevailed the remainder of November.

Precipitation occurrences were even more frequent than temperature changes. Amount of precipitation were generally light except that rains were heavy over the eastern half of Pennsylvania the 1st-2nd, and snow was extremely heavy near the shore of Lake Erie the 22nd.

WEATHER EFFECTS

Rainy weather hampered field work generall the first week and corn harvesting progressed slowly. Milk production dropped considerably this month and much of the drop was attributed to the poor quality of hay and ensilage harvested under adverse weather conditions earlier in the fall season. Ground-water levels in observation wells were a little lower than average at the end of the month. Stream flow averaged near median.

DESTRUCTIVE STORMS

Heavy rains accompanying local thunderstorms in central and southeastern Pennsylvania the 1st-2nd caused flash flooding on several creeks, mostly in the vicinity of Williamsport, and local flooding of streets in the Philadelphia area. Property damages were substantial in the relatively small areas affected. Streets, highways, bridges, buildings, homes, driveways, lawns, winter wheat fields, stored grain, and a few motor vehicles were reported as damaged.

A snowstorm the 22nd-23rd deposited up to 27 inches of snow in Erie County while accompanying strong winds piled the snow into drifts up to 12 feet high. The city of Erie was hardest hit and virtually stranded by the mounds of snow which closed all roads. Most businesses and factories were closed for several days while roads were being reopened.

FLOODS

None on main streams.

J. T. B. Beard, Climatologist
Weather Records Processing Center
Chattanooga, Tennessee

Temperature: Average Maximum	Average Minimum	Average	Departure From Long Term Means	Highest	Date	Lowest	Date	Degree Days	No. of Days Max 90° or Above	Max 32° or Below	Min 32° or Below	Min 0° or Below	Precipitation: Total	Departure From Long Term Means	Greatest Day	Date	Snow, Sleet: Total	Max Depth on Ground	Date	No. of Days .10 or More	.50 or More	1.00 or More
48.3	32.8	40.6	2.9	68	1+	11	24	728	0	4	17	0										
48.8	26.4	37.6		72	2+	5	25	816	0	3	25	0	1.81		.54	1	3.7	2	18+	5	1	0
47.2	30.1	38.7	2.2	69	15	8	24+	784	0	6	18	0	3.03	-.32	.89	2	4.9	2	25+	7	2	0
50.2	29.7	40.0		76	1	6	24	758	0	3	16	0	1.66		.46	2	4.0	2	18+	5	0	0
46.4	28.2	37.3		66	16	9	24	824	0	5	21	0	3.78		.85	2	4.6	1	18+	6	4	0
46.1	26.7	36.4		69	16	5	24+	852	0	4	22	0	2.14	-1.78	.86	22	4.8	3	18	5	1	0
50.7	30.1	40.4	-1.5	74	16	12	24+	731	0	2	18	0	1.47	-1.43	.56	22	.8	0		4	1	0
49.0	31.7	40.4	-.3	76	1	13	25	736	0	2	17	0	1.31	-1.90	.48	21	2.7	2	18	4	0	0
49.0	29.0	39.0	-2.0	70	1	7	24	775	0	3	20	0	2.13	-1.68	.60	21	2.2	1	25	5	1	0
		38.9											2.17				3.5					
51.0	32.3	41.7	-.3	74	4	16	25	694	0	1	16	0	2.41	-.66	.68	1	T	T	25	6	2	0
52.7	33.0	42.9	.9	70	2	17	25	658	0	1	15	0	3.19	.12	1.20	2	.3	3	26	5	3	1
51.7	35.6	43.7	-.8	74	4	15	30	633	0	1	12	0	2.87	-.29	1.00	1	.1	0		5	4	1
53.6M	31.8M	42.7M	1.5	72	4+	12	25	664	0	1	17	0	2.20	-1.51	1.13	2	1.2	T	23+	4	1	1
49.8	32.2	41.0	-.8	72	4	12	25	714	0	3	17	0	2.52	-.61	.97	1	T	T	25+	5	2	0
54.2	29.6	41.9	.1	75	2	10	25	687	0	0	21	0										
51.9	33.7	42.8	1.2	72	4	13	25	661	0	0	15	0	4.25	.97	1.67	2	T	0		6	3	2
		42.4											2.91				.3					
57.9M	39.3M	48.6M		74	3			487	0	0	11	0	3.74		2.10	2				5	2	1
53.8	32.5	43.2	.1	72	5	13	25	652	0	2	17	0	5.22	1.98	2.78	2	.0	0		5	3	1
54.4	35.4	44.9		74	1	14	25+	597	0	0	12	0	3.00		1.15	2	.0	0		6	1	1
54.5	30.7	42.6		72	1+	12	25	665	0	1	15	0	5.14		2.27	1	T	0		7	3	1
52.7	35.4	44.1	.3	69	1+	15	24+	619	0	0	11	0	3.18	.44	1.25	2	.0	0		6	3	1
54.8	35.2	45.0	.9	72	2	15	25	596	0	0	13	0	4.20	1.08	1.73	2	.0	0		6	3	1
52.3	37.2	44.8	-.7	70	1	19	25	604	0	1	14	0	4.86	2.38	1.81	2	T	T	26	6	4	2
53.3	33.7	43.5	.2	72	1	15	25	639	0	1	13	0	3.13	.42	1.42	2	T	0		5	2	1
51.6	31.4	41.5		73	2	13	24	701	0	2	17	0	3.00		.76	3	.0	0		6	4	0
52.6	33.6	43.1	.3	74	2	15	24+	653	0	2	14	0	2.36	-.65	.54	18	T	0		6	1	0
53.8	39.0	46.4	-2.0	73	2	20	24	551	0	1	8	0	5.69	2.46	1.63	2	T			7	5	2
51.8	35.7	43.8	.2	72	1	17	25	632	0	1	14	0	2.52	-.42	.77	1	.9	1	25	5	2	0
51.5	32.1	41.8		69	15	13	24+	690	0	0	15	0	3.59		1.22	1	T	0		6	4	1
51.7	32.5	42.1		70	1	11	24	681	0	2	16	0	2.94		.68	2	T	0		7	2	0
55.1	36.9	46.0		74	4	19	25	565	0	0	13	0	4.32		1.97	2	T	0		5	2	2
56.3	41.5	48.9		75	2	22	24	480	0	0	6	0	6.77		2.70	2	T	0		7	4	2
54.6	37.9	46.3	.4	74	2	20	24	556	0	0	11	0	5.71	2.63	1.81	1	T	0		7	4	2
55.2	43.8	49.5	1.8	74	2	25	24	461	0	0	4	0	6.08		2.02	1	.0	0		6	4	3
57.0	38.5	47.8	2.4	73	2	18	25	520	0	0	10	0	5.89	2.81	2.77	2	.0	0		6	5	1
54.9	41.9	48.4	.6	73	4	25	24	491	0	0	5	0	5.15	2.07	1.65	1				7	4	2
57.2	33.5	45.4	1.2	74	4	11	25	587	0	0	11	0	3.84	.51	1.20	1	.0	0		8	3	1
52.9	36.6	44.8	-.6	74	1	17	25	604	0	0	14	0	3.86	.81	1.28	2	T	0		5	4	2
55.2	37.8	46.5		73	2	19	24	552	0	0	10	0	5.18		2.40	2	.0	0		7	4	1
53.7	32.9M	43.3M	-.1	69	1+	18	23	649	0	1	14	0	4.02	.42	2.24	1	T	0		4	3	1
		45.1											4.31				T					
52.7	33.0	42.9	.0	71	3	13	25	657	0	1	15	0	2.67	-.48	1.52	2	.0	0		5	1	1
53.8	34.4	44.1	2.4	72	2	14	25	621	0	1	16	0	2.54	-.61	1.20	2	2.0	1	26	6	1	1
52.9	31.9	42.4	-.1	74	2	14	25	670	0	1	16	0	3.54	.71	2.73	1	T	T	25	3	1	1
53.7	34.5	44.1	1.3	71	1	14	25	619	0	1	12	0	2.33	-.54	1.39	2	T	0		4	1	1
54.2	32.2	43.2	-1.8	74	16	15	24+	646	0	1	15	0	2.64	.10	.94	3	.5	T	26	5	3	0
52.2	35.2	43.7	-.3	73	15	18	25	631	0	1	15	0	1.97	-.76	.59	1	1.0	1	26	5	1	0
54.1	33.7	43.9	.5	74	1	12	25	631	0	1	15	0	2.76	-.43	1.21	2	1.0	0		5	2	1
53.3	31.5	42.4		72	2	11	25	674	0	3	18	0	2.55		1.00	2	T	T	22+	6	2	1
55.6	34.1	44.9	1.2	74	15	14	25	596	0	0	14	0	2.64	-.06	.71	3	T	0		6	2	0
		43.5											2.63				.5					
51.7	33.0	42.4		74	1	12	25	672	0	2	18	0	5.66		3.36	2	3.0	3	26	7	2	2
52.6	33.9	43.3		80	1	15	24+	654	0	0	15	0	1.27		.49	22	T	T	23+	4	0	0
51.8	32.1	42.0		75	2	13	25	686	0	2	17	0	2.35		.59	2				5	3	0
53.9	32.6	43.3		73	2+	16	26	645	0	1	17	0	2.37		1.10	2	.9	1	26	5	1	1
52.8	31.1	42.0		74	2	12	25	683	0	1	18	0	2.87	-.47	1.45	2	2.5			7	1	1
50.7	30.9	40.8	-1.0	76	1	11	25	719	0	1	18	0	2.90	.06	1.32	2	3.0	3	26	6	2	1
50.3	33.4	41.9	.2	76	1	14	25	688	0	2	16	0	4.75	1.49	3.00	2	5.0	5	26	6	2	1
		42.2											3.17				2.4					
47.2	30.3	38.8		72	2	9	24	779	0	5	18	0	3.24		1.05	3	4.7	4	26	6	3	1
52.2	29.3	40.8		79	2	10	24+	720	0	1	19	0	1.19		.39	2+	1.0	1	18	4	0	0
42.2M	29.7	36.0M				8	24	951	0	7	20	0	5.63	1.17	2.81	3	7.2	4	26	8	4	1
50.7	29.3	40.0	.7	75	2	8	24	743	0	3	20	0	1.35	-.93	.34	22	3.0	3	26+	5	0	0
46.9	29.5	38.2	.8	73	2	8	24+	795	0	4	21	0	.97	-1.90	.32	22	4.9	2	18+	4	0	0

See Reference Notes Following Station Index

TABLE 2 - CONTINUED

Station		Temperature: Average Maximum	Average Minimum	Average	Departure From Long Term Means	Highest	Date	Lowest	Date	Degree Days	No. of Days Max. 90° or Above	Max. 32° or Below	Min. 32° or Below	Min. 0° or Below	Precipitation: Total	Departure From Long Term Means	Greatest Day	Date	Snow, Sleet: Total	Max. Depth on Ground	Date	No. of Days: .10 or More	.50 or More	1.00 or More
TOWANDA		51.5	31.2	41.4	1.4	79	1	12	25	704	0	1	18	0	3.83	1.53	2.74	3	3.4	2	26	6	1	1
WELLSBORO 3 S	AM	47.3	30.2	38.8	1.2	70	2+	9	24+	782	0	4	18	0	3.45	.83	1.70	2	5.0	5	26	6	1	1
DIVISION				39.1											2.81				4.2					
CENTRAL MOUNTAINS																								
BELLEFONTE 4 S	AM	51.1	32.2	41.7	.7	73	16	16	24+	694	0	4	18	0	2.55	.24	.85	2	1.5	2	26	7	1	0
DU BOIS 7 E		49.3	30.6	40.0		77	15	11	24+	743	0	5	17	0	2.82	- .42	1.24	2	3.5	1	22+	6	2	1
EMPORIUM 2 SSW	AM	47.9	28.2	38.1		72	2	7	25	802	0	5	21	0	2.01		.74	2	4.5	4	26	6	2	0
LOCK HAVEN		50.9	33.5	42.2	.5	78	1	13	25	674	0	2	15	0	3.95	1.35	1.68	2	3.0	3	26	8	2	1
MADERA	AM	48.0	25.1	36.6		72	2	6	24	847	0	4	25	0	1.60		.78	2				2	1	0
PHILIPSBURG CAA AP		46.3	27.7	37.0		71	15	9	30	832	0	6	21	0	2.39		.56	1	3.9	2	26+	5	1	0
RIDGWAY 3 W	AM	47.6	28.4	38.0	- .1	68	2+	5	25	803	0	4	18	0	2.22	- .81	.97	2	1.5	2	26	6	1	0
STATE COLLEGE		49.1	33.6	41.4	1.2	74	15	15	24	703	0	4	14	0	2.26	- .30	.66	2	3.1	T	18+	5	1	0
TAMARACK 2 S FIRE TWR	AM	47.1	29.6	38.4		70	16	10	24	794	0	5	19	0	2.31		1.15	2	5.1	3	26+	6	1	1
DIVISION				39.3											2.46				3.3					
SOUTH CENTRAL MOUNTAINS																								
ALTOONA HORSESHOE CURVE		49.9	31.3	40.6	.1	78	15	12	25	726	0	4	18	0	2.53	.00	1.03	2	3.7	1	22+	6	1	1
ARTEMAS 1 WNW			28.9	M				11	23				23	0	1.79		1.05	2	.0	0		4	1	1
BURNT CABINS 2 NE																								
EBENSBURG		47.2	28.7	38.0	- .6	69	15	8	24	802	0	5	19	0	1.78	- 1.42	.92	2	4.0	3	29	3	2	0
EVERETT 1 SW		50.8	30.1	40.5	- .1	78	15	14	23+	734	0	3	19	0	.64	- 1.58	.25	21	.0	0		3	0	0
HUNTINGDON	AM																							
JOHNSTOWN	AM	51.9	30.5	41.2	- .9	77	16	8	25	707	0	2	18	0	1.20	- 1.77	.48	2	2.5	2	23+	4	0	0
KEGG		50.8	27.0	38.9		77	15	8	25	777	0	3	20	0	1.26		.75	1	T	0		3	1	0
MARTINSBURG CAA AP		49.3	31.1	40.2		75	15	13	23+	739	0	4	15	0	1.04		.40	1	.1	T	10+	4	0	0
DIVISION				39.9											1.46				1.5					
SOUTHWEST PLATEAU																								
BAKERSTOWN 3 WNW		51.5	33.4	42.5		73	15	9	24	670	0	3	13	0	.88		.40	21	T	T	22+	3	0	0
BLAIRSVILLE 6 ENE		48.2	31.0	39.6		71	15	9	23+	757	0	7	19	0	5.41	2.32	2.50	22	8.2	3	22+	11	3	1
BURGETTSTOWN 2 W	AM	52.2	27.1	39.7		75	4	4	24	753	0	4	20	0	1.04		.47	22		1	23+	1	0	0
BUTLER		53.1	32.3	42.7	1.3	72	4+	7	24	661	0	3	15	0	1.28	- 1.64	.40	21				3	0	0
CLAYSVILLE 3 W		52.6	28.6	40.6	- 1.4	79	15	5	24	726	0	3	19	0	1.10	- 1.46	.60	22	3.0			2	1	0
CONFLUENCE 1 SW DAM	AM	52.0	31.8	41.9		74	16	4	24	685	0	4	15	0	1.52		.69	2	2.5	1	22+	3	1	0
DERRY		53.2	33.9	43.6	1.2	75	15	11	25	635	0	3	14	0	1.55	- 1.40	.60	21	.5	T	11+	3	2	0
DONEGAL		47.0	24.6	35.8		70	1	- 2	24	868	0	7	23	2	2.16		.73	21	5.5	3	29+	7	2	
DONORA	AM	56.7	36.8	46.8	1.6	76	16	15	24	542	0	2	12	0	1.00	- 1.60	.44	22	1.1	T	22+	3	0	
FORD CITY 4 S DAM	AM	53.5	30.0	41.8		74	16	12	24+	690	0	4	17	0	.97		.34	22	.5	1	11	3	0	
INDIANA 3 SE		52.2	30.1	41.2	- .3	74	1+	6	24	708	0	3	18	0	1.66	- 1.27	.72	2	1.9	1	23+	3	1	
† IRWIN		54.1	33.2	43.7	1.4	75	3	11	24	632	0	1	14	0	.98	- 1.59	.46	21	1.7	1	26	2	0	
MIDLAND DAM 7		50.6	35.6	43.1	.6	72	3	16	24	649	0	3	13	0	.83	- 1.71	.35	22	.5	1	26	2	0	
NEW CASTLE 1 N		53.6	33.8	43.7	3.1	73	15	16	23	633	0	3	14	0	1.30	- 1.20	.39	21	3.1	1	27	4	0	
NEWELL	AM	57.8	39.5	48.7	4.8	78	16	19	24	486	0	1	8	0					1.5	T	26			
NEW STANTON		53.4	29.2	41.3	- 1.4	74	6	8	24	704	0	3	17	0	.81	- 1.88	.53	21	T	T	26+	1	1	
PITTSBURGH WB AP 2	//R	50.8	33.1	42.0	1.0	72	3+	13	24	683	0	3	14	0	1.03	- 1.56	.33	21	3.4	1	23+	4	0	
PITTSBURGH WB CITY	R	53.2	36.6	44.9	.3	74	15	18	24	595	0	2	11	0	.76	- 1.85	.30	21	1.2			2	0	
PUTNEYVILLE 2 SE DAM	AM	51.6	28.2	39.9		73	16	9	25	747	0	5	20	0	1.92		.52	22	1.8	1	22+	5	1	
SALINA 3 W		52.0	30.6	41.3		73	15	5	24+	701	0	3	18	0	1.12		.45	21	2.8	1	22+	3	0	
SHIPPINGPORT WB		51.9	33.2	42.6		73	3+	12	24	667	0	3	14	0	.83		.39	21	T	T	22+	2	0	
SLIPPERY ROCK		51.0	31.7	41.4		72	15	8	24	704	0	4	15	0	.99		.36	21	3.5	1	11+	3	0	
SOMERSET MAIN ST		49.7	29.5	39.6	.9	72	15	3	24	752	0	5	19	0	1.51	- 1.74	.40	1	6.7	2	23+	4	0	
SPRINGS 1 SW		47.9	26.2	37.1	- 1.3	71	15	- 4	24	830	0	5	23	2	1.22	- 1.90	.33	1	5.3	2	26+	2	0	
UNIONTOWN		54.3	32.9	43.6	- .4	77	15	9	24	638	0	2	17	0	1.34	- 1.76	.53	21	1.3	T	22+	3	1	
WAYNESBURG 2 W		53.7	30.1	41.9	- 1.2	75	3+	6	24	682	0	3	19	0	.92	- 1.68	.35	22		1	26+	3	0	
DIVISION				41.9											1.38				2.5					
NORTHWEST PLATEAU																								
BRADFORD 4 W RES		48.4	27.9	38.2	- .5	72	1	2	25	795	0	5	19	0	2.97	- .64	1.65	21	10.7	6	27+	7	1	
BROOKVILLE CAA AIRPORT		49.1	28.7	38.9	1.0	75	1	11	23	774	0	7	20	0	1.87	- 1.25	.52	21	3.7	2	28+	5	1	
CLARION 3 SW		51.8	29.9	40.9		75	1	11	24	715	0	4	18	0	1.54	- 1.47	.44	2	1.8	1	26+	5	0	
CORRY		49.9	29.8	39.9	1.1	73	5	6	25	748	0	5	18	0	2.84	- 1.21	1.27	21	11.0	8	24	7	1	
COUDERSPORT 3 NW		46.5	26.2	36.4		70	1	0	30	851	0	7	20	1	1.89		.58	2	4.2	4	26+	5	1	
EAST BRADY		54.6	32.8	43.7		75	5+	14	24+	630	0	2	15	0	.60		.27	1	T	T	11+	2	0	
ERIE CAA AIRPORT		49.7	34.8	42.3	1.3	73	3	18	23+	675	0	4	14	0	5.60	2.34	2.62	22	34.8	24	24	8	2	
FARRELL SHARON		53.7	30.8	42.3	.6	75	5	14	30	677	0	3	16	0	1.03	- 1.34	.62	21	T	0		3	1	
FRANKLIN		52.3	32.6	42.5	2.8	72	5+	13	30	670	0	5	15	0	1.33	- 1.79	.41	21		1	23+	5	0	
GREENVILLE		52.3	31.4	41.9	1.8	75	5	15	24	686	0	4	15	0	1.38	- 1.65	.86	21	4.5	1	29+	1	1	
JAMESTOWN 2 NW	AM	50.3	30.6	40.5		71	4	12	23	726	0	6	16	0	1.70	- .92	.94	21	4.1	1	29+	3	1	
KANE 1 NNE	AM	48.5	27.0	37.8		71	2	5	25	809	0	5	21	0	2.16	- 1.38	.67	2	10.7			6	2	
LINESVILLE 5 WNW		51.0	30.6	40.8		71	3	14	25	722	0	4	16	0	2.37	- .83	1.00	21	14.5	5	23+	7	1	
MEADVILLE 1 S	AM	50.5	31.2	40.9	1.8	72	5	14	25	716	0	5	17	0	2.20	- 1.22	1.03	21	9.9	3	24+	6	1	
MERCER 2 NNE		50.3	28.8	39.6		74	2+	11	30	756	0	4	22	0	1.19		.52	21	.0	0		6	1	
SPRINGBORO		51.5	30.6	41.1		74	4	17	23+	713	0	3	19	0	D 3.35		1.20	23	20.0			8	2	
TIONESTA 2 SE DAM	AM	50.9	29.1	40.0		74	2	10	25+	743	0	6	19	0	1.17	- 1.90	.46	21	1.3	1	24+	3	0	
TITUSVILLE WATER WORKS		50.0	27.2	38.6		72	4	6	25	785	0	5	21	0	3.06		1.23	21	3.9	2	29+	10	2	
WARREN		50.4	31.9	41.2	1.8	75	1	13	24	710	0	4	15	0	2.29	- 1.24	.75	21	4.4	2	24+	5	2	
DIVISION				40.4											2.13				7.8					

† DATA RECEIVED TOO LATE TO BE INCLUDED IN DIVISION AVERAGES

See Reference Notes Following Station Index

DAILY PRECIPITATION

Total	1	2	3	4	5	6	7	8	9	10	11	12	13	14	15	16	17	18	19	20	21	22	23	24	25	26	27	28	29	30	31
R .90	.01	.17					.03		T		.05		T			.04	.02				.10	.42	.03	T	T	T	.02	T	T	.01	
2.41	.08	.32	T					T	T		T	T	T			T	.60	.18		T	.49	T	T		.14	T	T		T		
3.18	.12	1.20	.36						T				T				.01	.79				.63	T	T		.08					
2.53	.20	1.03	.22							.02	.04	.02	.13			.22		.04		.01	.47	.03	.01			.02			.06	.01	
2.67	.11	1.52	.30	.04				.04	.05									.37				.19				.05					
1.79	.29	1.05														.35									.10						
2.83	.10	1.80	.05				T			T			.10			.05	T				.10	.28	T	T	T	.37	T				
.88					.09						.08					.10				.21	.40	T	T	T	T					T	
2.38	T	.51					.10		T	T	T		.41			.05					1.01	.06	.06	.06	T	.06	T		.06	T	
-	.68	.42																.43				-									
2.89	.43	.96	.13					.06				.04				.07		.22				.59		.04		.35					
1.09	.01	.12					.04		T	.01	.02		T			T	T				.30	.28	T	.02		.20	.03	T	T	T	
5.66	.16	3.30	1.05					T				T				.14	.15	.08				.33	T		T	.39					
2.90	.19	1.54	.16				T	.01			T					.07	.22				.08	.37	T	T		.26					
2.55	.12	.85	.33				.01			T			.03			.24	.17	.06			T	.44	T	T		.30	T			T	
4.44	.06	.78	2.35						T								T	.55				.52				.18					
1.27	.05	.27	.04				.02	.02				T				.03		.20		.01	T	.49	T		T	.14	T				
3.60	.62	1.38	.09						T		T	T	T			T	T	.83				.58	T	T		.10					
2.87	1.00	.52						T	T			T				T	.70	.15			.50	T			T						
5.41	.42	.01					.10		T	.01	.10	T	.01			.42		.04		.01	.51	2.50	.80		T	.12	.19	.02	.10	.05	
3.19	.25	1.55	.72				T	.03				T				.11	T	.15		T	.26	T	T			.12			T		
1.50		.31							T	.02	.04		T			.11	.05	.04				.65	.10	.03	T	.02	T	.06	.02	.05	
.86	.01	.22					.07				.07		.04			.03	.02				.05	.28	.02	T		.01	.04				
-	.04	.22	T				.08		T	.06			.22			-	-			T	.75	.57	.09	.12		.10	.04			.12	
2.97		.32					.10	T	T	T		.08	.14			.10				T	1.65		.08	.17		.12	.08	T	.08	.05	
.37	.09	.12	.14							T		.02									T	T	T				T	T	T		
1.87	.43						.09	T	.03	.01	T	.11	T			.24				.19	.52	.05	.01	T	.02	.06	.07	T	.04	T	
.69	T	.24					.02						.01			.04					.04	*	.34			.05	T	T	T	T	
1.77	.02	1.21	.13				.08				T		.03			.03	.09	.05				.11	.02			T					
1.04	.01	.08					.03			T	.08		.02			.07	.01				.06	.47	.04			.09	.05		.01		
	RECORD MISSING																														
1.28	.11	.06					.05				.06		.08			.04					.40	.36	.02	.02		.05	.02		.01		
2.26	.03	.80	.45					.06								.03	.03	.27			.07	.02			.02	.48					
3.24	.13	.90	1.05	T						.02	T		.02			.02	.20	.02			T	.53		.03		.32	T	T	T	T	
2.54	.15	1.20	.35				T	.05								.04	.03	.15			.08	.17			T	.32	T	T	T		
2.13	.03	1.03	.03	T			.03			T	.05		T			.14	.03	.04			.01	.50	.08	T		.04	.04	.03	.03	.02	
2.25	.21	.71	.15	.01			T	T	T	T						.20	.12	T			.18	.43	T			.24		T			
5.04	.33	2.30	.40				T	.04		.07			.01			.12	.25	.01			.30	.71	T	.05		.41	T	.02	T	.02	
4.97	.10	2.80	.72	T					T				T				T	.85	T			.50			T						
3.54	2.73	.08	.06				T	.03		T						.07	.12	.06			.36	T			.03				T		
.92		.22					T			T	.09		T			.01	.03				.03	.44	.02	T		.03	.03		T		
3.74	.21	2.10	.45						.17													.77				.04					
2.80	.11	1.46	.12	T	T		.01	T	T				.02			.11	.03	.05			.15	.55	.04	T		.11	T	.03	.01		
1.54		.44					.13		.01	.04	.03	T	.16			.02	.05				.27	.25	T	T		.03	.02	.07		.02	
2.89	.14	1.18	.36						.02									.67				.45				.07					
1.10	.03	.12								T	T		.04			.07	.03				.05	.60	.02			.09	.05		T	T	
1.53	.02	.35	T				.08	T	T	.06			.08			.08	.15	.03			.23	.38	.02			.03	T	.02	T		
2.56	.02	.72	.01				.15		.06	.08			.10			.14	T				.35	.46	.10	.08		.11	.06	.04	T	.08	
2.65	.15	.88	.48						.05	.02						.01	.06	.41				.41		.01		.17					
5.22	.07	2.78	.69	.08					.01	T								.85			.04	.41				.29					
3.00	.08	1.15	.29					T				T				.04	.18	.45		T	T	.47			.02	.32					
1.52	T	.69	T				.07	T	T	.02	.03		.01			.12	T					.49	T	T		.03	.04		.02	T	
1.83	T	.67	T				.09	.05		.01	.03		T			.14	.01	.02				.68	.03	T		.02	.04		.02	.02	
.97		.25					.02			.02	.02					.03	.03	.01				.43	.05	.03		.03	.03	T	.02		
4.56	.28	2.36	.43						.06								T	.89				.46				.08					
1.74		.37	T		T		.11	T	.03	.02		T	.08			.13	.07	T	T	T	.31	.41	T	.02		.05	.02	.06	T	.06	
1.89	T	.36	T		T		.12	.15	.03	.03			.08	T		.16	.03	T		T	.32	.34	T	.03		.17	.02	.02		.03	
.32		.10					.03						T								.05	*	.14			T	T		T		
2.84	.05	.03					.15	.02	.20	.02		.23	.08			.07				.03	1.27	.22	.22	T		.03	.11		.08	.03	
1.89	.02	.58	T				.03		.02	.04			.06			.11	.06				.32	.43	.03	.03	T	.15	.01	T		T	
2.21	.11	.84		.13			.02		T	.08			.03			.31	.11					.39	T	.02	T	.17	T	T	T	T	
4.20	.13	1.96	.67	.02						T			.12			.03	.25	T			.05	.61		.01		.35			T		
1.30		.40					.10			.05	.06		.04			.06		.10			.07	.30	.11	T		.01	T		T	T	
2.15	.23	.68	.16	.04	.02		.02		T	.01	.02		.02			.07	.17	.03	.04		.02	.33	.04	.03		.07	.04	.03	.05	.03	
3.48	.02	.31	.02				.08		.04	.08			1.03	T		.07	.09				.68	.57	.05	.14		.13	.05	.03	T	.09	
5.03	.99	.97	1.97															.30			.03	.45				.32					
1.55	.51	.03							T	T	T	.07	.08			.13	.02			.05	.60	T		T	T	.06		T	T	T	
5.14	2.27	.72	.17					.06									.94	.38			.42			.16	.02						
1.19	.10	.39	.03	T				T		T	T	T	T					.21			.03	.39		T		.04					
2.16	.50						.07		T	.10	.03	.05				.17	.05			.05	.73	.10	.01		T	.10	T	T	.15	.05	
1.00	.14	.16					T			.04	.06		.01			.06				T	T	.44	.01	T		.06	.02	T	T	T	
4.35	.53	2.12	.04					.08					T			T	.17	.84				.46			.01	.10					
2.82	.38	1.24					.10		.04	T						.17		T	T	.16	.51	.09	.02			.06	.03	T	.02	T	
1.79	.32	.16						T		.03			T				.32	.20			.04	.52			T	.20					
5.63	.54	.49	2.81	.02	.01			T		T	T		.11			T	.51	.11			.06	.52		.02		.43	T	T	T	T	
.60	.27						.05				.01	.01				.01				.18			.01			.03	.02		.01		
1.78	.05	.92	.06	T					T	T	T		T			.10	T	T			T	.54	T	T	T	.06	T	T	T	.05	
3.73	.02	.02	.02				.15		.34		.01		.41			.11					.94	.52	.45	.20	T	.04	.15	.11	.08	.16	
3.62	.23	.75	.53	.12														.58				.61				.80					
2.01	.02	.74	.10	.02			.03	T	T				T			.12	.02				.14	.59	T	.02		.19	.02	T	T		
4.84	.42	2.52	.44	T			T	.02		.05			T			.15	.31	.05			.04	.49		T		.35		T	T	T	
3.18	.04	1.25	.30					T								.02	.15					.51			.08	.24					
2.64	.35	.88	.13					.02		T							.03	.40			.07	.67				.09				T	
5.60	.03	T		T		.02	.08	.25	T	T	T	T			T	.15				.04	1.08	2.62	.39	.09	.11	.05	.03	.02	.26	.38	
.64	.20															.10					.25								.09		
1.03							.01			.01	.03					.07				.16	.62	T	T	T	T	.10	T	.01	.02		
.97		.25					.06				.02		.07			.05	.06				.10	.34	.01	T		.01			T	T	
1.33		.14					.12		T		.01		.13			.03					.41	.31	.01	.01		.04	.02	.07		.03	
-	.13	.75	.25						.05	-		-	-	-		.08	T	.65			-	1.03		-	-	.11	T		-		
2.50	.06	.68	.05	.01			T		.02	T						.48	.03	T			.02	.82	T	.01		.31			T	.01	
4.17	.05	1.52	.95	.10					.02	.03							T	.80				.46	.02			.22					
4.20	.26	1.73						.08				.01				.02	.22	.88			.07	.74			.06	.13					
2.33	.06	1.39	.21	.04				T	.02								.02	.42				.11				.06					
2.63	.04	.44					.09		T	.15			.17			.17	.05				.75	.52	.01	.04		.05	.09	.02		.04	
1.94	.02	.61	.01	T			.05		.05	T			.08			.11	.06				.25	.45	.02	.03	T	.12	.03	.03	T	.02	
.90	.07	.06					.02			T	.02		.05			.02					.14	.43	.01			.04	.04		T	T	
2.65	.32	.55	.14					.02	.06	T			.09					.46			.04	.75		T		.23				.03	
3.53		1.56	.37						.09									.97				.46				.08					
2.35	.29	.59	.51	T				T	.06	T			T				T	.05			T	.50	T	T		.35				T	
1.10	.12	.37					T			T	.02					.07	.04				.05	.39	.01	T		.01	T	T	.01	.01	
.69	.35								.02	.05						.19					.01	.02		.01	T	.04	T	T		T	
1.38	.02						.07		T		.03	.07				.05				.08	.86	.01	.02	T	T	.07	.01		.09		
2.64	.02	.67	.94	.02														.56				.32				.11					
1.97	.50	.45	.02	T			T	.04		T		T	T			T	.39	.02			.20	T	T		.26	T			T		
2.00	.03	.74	.19	.04				.04	T				T				.02	.27				.32	.05			.30				T	
1.99	.54	.19	.04	T				.06	.07	.03	T		.01			T	T	.30			.02	.57	T	T		.16	T	T		T	
1.81	.84	.12	.04						.07				.07					.40				.39				.18					
2.15	.13	.33	.05					.01	.03	.01	.01	T	.18				.01	.43			.04	.67	T	.02		.22	T	T		.01	
4.86	.23	1.81	1.28	.05					T								T	.68				.28	T			.53					
1.84	.14	.30	.04					.03	.06	.02								.45			.02	.64		T	T	.14	T				
1.24	.03	.50	.04	.02						T	.04		.05			.08	.03	.04				.30	.01	.01		.01	T	T	.03	.05	
1.21	T	*	.42	.01					T			T	.59	T			.04				T	.10	T			.05	T			T	
	RECORD MISSING																														
1.92	.14	.97	.14	T				.02	T				T				T	.24				.32	.01			.08				T	
1.66		1.03	.21	T	.01		.03		.02	.04	T		.04			.07		.05				.10	.01			.01	T	T	.01	.03	

See Reference Notes Following Station Index

DAILY PRECIPITATION

Table 3—Continued

Station	Total	Day of month																													
		1	2	3	4	5	6	7	8	9	10	11	12	13	14	15	16	17	18	19	20	21	22	23	24	25	26	27	28	29	30	31
INDIANA 3 SE	1.86	.02	.72					.10			.01	.04					.06	.08	.02			.07	.43	.04				.06	.01		T	
IRWIN	.98	.28							.04					.02							.07	.46					.08	.03				
JAMESTOWN 2 NW	1.70		.02	T				.15		T		T		.09			.03					.94	.31	.02	.03		.02	.03	.01	.04	.01	
JIM THORPE	2.20	.07	1.13						.03								T	T	.42				.40	T	T	.02	.13	T	T	T		
JOHNSTOWN	1.20	T	.48	.03				.03		T	T	.03		T			.13	T	T			T	.26	.20	T		.04	T	T	T	T	
KANE 1 NNE	2.18	.03	.67					.13		.06	.01			.13			.16	.05			T	.53	.08	.06		.10	.05	.03	T	.05	.02	
KARTHAUS	2.23	.11	1.05	.03				.05	.04	T		T	T	T			.08	.16	T			.19	.41	T	T		.11	T	T	T	T	
KEATING SUMMIT	2.10	.12	.38	.04				.03			.05			.02			.24	.08				.18	.52	.16	.02		.16	.06	.02		.02	
KEGG	1.26	.75		.16				.06		T	T		.01				.07	.13				.08	T	T		T	T			T		
KITTANNING LOCK 7	1.08		.16					.07			T	.04		.03			.02	.05				.29	.35	.03	T		T	.02	T	T		
KREGAR 4 SE	2.48	.43		T				.03		T	.11	.03	.01				.20	.07	T		.01	.73	.19	.22		.04	.08	.05	T	.25	.05	
KRESGEVILLE 3 W	2.50	.45	.80	.10														T	.54				.49				.12					
LAKEVILLE 1 NNE	2.07	.36	.35	T					.06	T	.04			.02					.43			.02	.59		.02		.18	T	T			
LANCASTER 2 NE PUMP STA	3.13	.04	1.42	.21					.01				T				.02	.09	.62				.41			.01	.30					
LANDISVILLE 2 NW	3.00	.22	.37	.76	.05					.04								.03	.53				.50				.50					
LAWRENCEVILLE 2 S	1.35	.20	.06	.09				.03			T						.12	.07	T			.18	.34		.02		.24		T			
LEBANON 3 W	2.36	.14	.46	.37	.01				T	.03				.01				.03	.54				.36	.01			.40					
LEHIGHTON *	2.86	.25	.80	.60					T								T	T	.53				.50	T	.03		.15					
LE ROY	3.07		2.85	.13							T			T				.01				.06				T	.04	T	T	T		
LEWIS RUN 3 SE	2.93	.05	.65	T				.10	.01	.13	.11	T		.10			.07	.08			T	.61	.63	.03	.11	T	.16	.02	.02		.05	
LEWISTOWN	2.37	.42	1.10	.16							T			.02				.38	.06				.23	T			T	T				
LINESVILLE 5 WNW	2.37		.02					.12	T	.04	.03			.12			.07					.00	.26	.25	.17		.04	.15	.02	.05	.03	
LOCK HAVEN	3.95	.12	1.68	.74				.01	.01		T			T			.05	.35	.14			.12	.39	T	T		.34		T		T	
LONG POND 2 W	3.01	.75	.72	.36					T	.02	T			.02				T	.44				.53		.05		.12					
MADERA	1.60	.02	.78					.05		T		T		.06			.09	.05	.04			.06	.34	.07			.01			.03		
MAHAFFEY	2.84	.02	1.10					.12		.03	.02	T		.11			.08	.18	.02			.14	.49	.05	.03		.06	.02	.08	T	T	
MAPLE GLEN	4.24	.68	2.35	.01					.13				T				T	.20	.80				T			T	.07					
MAPLETON DEPOT	1.38	.13	.78	T	T						T			.01			.04	.17	.03				.16	T	T		.04				T	
MARCUS HOOK	5.69	1.49	1.63	.52					.24				.01				.01	.79	.25			.72	T	T		•	.01					
MARION CENTER 2 SE	1.82	.02	.36					.09			T	.04		.02			.09	.07	.05			.09	.56	.06	.01		.03	.05	.05		.03	
MARTINSBURG CAA AP	1.04	.40	T	.10						T	T	T	T				.20	.04	.01			.27	.04	T		•	T	T	T	T		
MATAMORAS	2.74	.21	.86	.04						.04			.03	.05					.76				.69				.08					
MAYBURG	2.53	T	.47					.09		T	T	T		.39			.05					.93	.42		.13		.05	T	T	T	T	
MC CONNELLSBURG	2.61	.15	1.59	.18	.02			.01	.04				T	.02			.05	.11	.04				.40	T	T			T			T	
MC KEESPORT	.97	T	.23					.04				.05		.08			.07	.02				.09	.36	T			.03	T			T	
MEADVILLE 1 S	2.20	T	.01					.15		.11	T	.04		.13	T		.04					1.03	.31	.02	.09	T	.03	.11	.07	.05	.01	
MEDIX RUN	1.78	T	.56	T				.03		T	.01	T		.11			.06	.07	T			.25	.50	T	T	T	.12	.01	.01	.05	T	
MERCER 2 NNE	1.19	.10						.10	T			T		.12			T					.52	.20	T			.10	.05		T		
MERCERSBURG	1.73	.10	1.14	.07													.05		.15				.22									
MEYERSDALE 1 ENE	1.34	.02	.54	.04	.06			.03			T	T		T			•	.23					.11	.18				T		.06	.07	
MIDDLETOWN OLMSTED FLD	2.52	.77	.59	.04	T				.02				T				.02	.33	.02			.37	.03	T		•	.04			T		
MIDLAND DAM 7	.83	.02	.03					.04				.01		.02			.03	.01				.25	.35	T			.04	.03				
MILANVILLE	2.32	.37	.62	.03					.03	.04	T			.05			T		.45			.01	.04				.08	T				
MILLHEIM	4.51	.26	2.85	.39	T			T	T		.03			.07			.07	.20	.05			.01	.35	T	T		.23	T	T		T	
MILLVILLE 2 SW	4.10	.50	1.04	1.29	.03				.01	T	.01		T	T				.27	.28			.03	.34	T	T		.30		T			
MILROY	3.32	.32	1.62	.31	.01						.01			T			.20	.25	.05			.01	.39	T	T		.15		T	T	T	
MONTROSE 1 E	.97	.02	.22	T	T				T	T	.03	T	T	.04				.10	.08			.03	.32	T	.01		.12	T	T		T	
MORGANTOWN	3.59	1.22	.69	.09					T		T						T	.61	.15			.63				.20	T					
MT GRETNA 2 SE	2.94	.39	.68	.27					.02								.03	.45	.11			.62	.02			.35						
MT POCONO 2 N AP	3.03	.31	.89	.11					.09		T		T	T					.47		T	.70	T	.05		.10	.31			T		
MUHLENBURG 1 SE	1.66		.46	.08									.01	.02			.02		.22		.02	.40	.22	.01		T	.20					
MYERSTOWN	2.45	.54	.40	.18															.57				.39			.37	T					
NATRONA LOCK 4	.77		.17					.04				.02		.03			.03	.02				.04	.39	.02	T			.01	T		T	
NESHAMINY FALLS	4.83	1.42	1.17	.14					.20				.04				T	.45	.68			.59	.03			.11						
NEWBURG 3 W		RECORD MISSING																														
NEW CASTLE 1 N	1.30	T	.08					.05	T	T	T	.04		.09			.05					.39	.29	.05	.10		.06	.10	T	T	T	
NEWELL	-	.15	.17									.08					.08						-				.34			•		
NEW PARK	3.64	.08	2.40	.06													T	.35	.24				.21	T		.05	.25					
NEWPORT	2.87	.12	1.45	.34	.01					.02				T			T	.10	.12			.03	.43				.25				T	
NEW STANTON	.81	.02						.02		T	.01	.02	.01				.08	T			.06	.53	.01	T		.01	.03			T	.01	
NEW TRIPOLI	2.63	.03	1.36	.02					.02		T		T				.01	.08	.53				.49	T		.05	.04					
NORRISTOWN	4.32	.43	1.97	.35	T					.07				.01					1.03				.44				.02					
NORTH EAST 2 SE	4.09		.06					.17		.34				.21			.13				T	.78	.49	1.10	.13	T	.03	.15	•	•	.14	
ORWELL 3 N	1.94	.06	.14	.86							T			.11				.13	.12			.14	.21		T		.17		T	T		
PALM	3.70	.38	.40	1.38	.32													.72					.40				.10					
PALMERTON	2.52	.97	.35						.01	T			T	T			T	.58	.11			.44	T	T		.03	.03			T		
PALMYRA		RECORD MISSING																														
PARKER	1.15	.02	.17					.11		T	T	.04		.02			.06					.27	.34	.05	T		.02	.03	T	T	.02	
PAUPACK 2 WNW	1.80	.36	.32	.04					.02	.06	.01			.02				.03	.04			.04	.67				.19					
PECKS POND	2.31	.65	.31	.11					.09	T	T			T					.51				.51		T		.13					
PHIL DREXEL INST OF TEC	6.77	1.70	2.70	.15					.18				.01				T	.71	.37			.87	T			.08						
PHILADELPHIA WB AP R	5.71	1.81	1.65	.21					.17		T		.01				T	.69	.43			.72	T			.02						
PHILADELPHIA PT BREEZE	6.08	2.02	1.73	.24					.18								T	.03	1.08			.73	.02			.05						
PHILADELPHIA SHAWMONT	5.89	.58	2.77	.93					.05				.04					.10	.78			T	.57			.05	.02					
PHILADELPHIA CITY R	5.15	1.65	1.33	.23					.23				.01					.59	.33			.73				.05						
PHILIPSBURG CAA AP	2.39	.56	.49	.04	.01			.03	T	T	.03	T	.07	.02			.20	.04	.03		.05	.43	.08	.03	T	.20	.01	.03	.01	.03	T	
PHOENIXVILLE 1 E	3.84	1.20	.70	.14					.14									.81	.36			.36				.13						
PIKES CREEK	1.43	.10	.19	.10					T		T	T		.02				.07	.15			.03	.52		.02		.22				.01	
PIMPLE HILL	3.78	.83	.85	.41					.02	.02	.02	T	T	.04	T			.01	.56			T	.73	T	.01	T	.26	T	T		.02	
PINE GROVE 1 NE	3.23	.87	.92	.28				T		.01	.02			T				.30	.20				.30	.01			.32				T	
PITTSBURGH WB AP 2 //R	1.03	.10						.02	T	T	T	.02	.04				.04				.11	.33	.08	.06		.03	.15	T	T	T	.05	
PITTSBURGH WB CITY R	.76	.16						.03			T	.04	.02				.04				.07	.30	.04	.02		.01	.03			T	T	
PLEASANT MOUNT 1 W	2.14	.26	.29	.14					T	.03	.02	T		.02				.03	.30			.05	.86	T	.04		.08		.01		.01	
PORT CLINTON	-	-	-	-	-	-	-	-	-	-	-	-	-	-	-	-	-	-	-	-	-	-	-	-	-	-	-	-	-	-	-	
POTTSVILLE	1.89	.19	.48	.57					T	.08	.02								.05				-	T			.30					
PUTNEYVILLE 2 SE DAM	1.92		.37					.08			.01	T		.02			.10	.06	T			.41	.52	.03	.25		.02	.02	.02	.01		
QUAKERTOWN 1 E	4.25	1.06	1.67	.14					.01								.03	.10	.73			T	.39			.03	.09					
RAYMOND	2.51	.10	.65	.12	.06						.15			.10			.13	.07				.18	.50	.04	.04	.04	.25	.03	.02		.03	
READING WB CITY R	3.86	1.12	1.28	.05					T		.01		T				.01	.57	.08			.54	T	T		.20						
RENOVO	2.15	.22	.69	.05				T	T	T	.02			T			.15	.12	.04			.11	.50	T	.01		.24		T	T	T	
REW	2.19	.06	.21	T	.02			.07			.08			.16	T		.09	.06				.69	.48	.03	.06	T	.10	.02	.03	.02	.01	
RICES LANDING L 6	1.05		.36									.03		.02			.05	.03					.40	.02	.02		.04	.02			.06	
RIDGWAY 3 W	2.22	T	.97					.05		.01	T			.10			.11	.13				.22	.48	.01	.02		.02	T	.08		.02	
RUSH	1.37	.04	.29	.04	.01				.02					.12				.11	.15			.07	.29		.01		.22					
RUSHVILLE	1.08	.02	.22	.04					.02					.09				.02	.27			.04	.21		T		.15				T	
SAGAMORE 1 S	1.36		.50					.10			T	T		.15								.15	.25	.15			.06					
SALINA 3 W	1.12	.28	.04					.02		T		.05	T	.02			.10				.05	.45	.04	.05			.02	T		T	.02	
SAXTON	1.34	.01	.58	.04	T						T	T		T			.10	.07	T				.50	.04	T		T	T		T	T	
SCHENLEY LOCK 5	.89		.17					.06				.06					.04	.01				.10	.34	.02	.01		.01	.01	T	T	T	
SCRANTON	1.47	.40		.01	T					.04			.01	.08				.01	.21			.04	.56				.11					
SCRANTON WB AIRPORT	1.31	.09	.35		T			T	.03	T	T		T	T			.04	.10	.15		.01	.48		T		T	.05	T	T	.01		
SELINSGROVE CAA AP	2.90	.55	1.32	.03	T			T	T	.01	T		.01				.15	.09	.04		T	.23		T		.33	.14			T		
SHAMOKIN	3.21	.81	1.08	.13					T	.02				.01				.06	.19				.57	T			.34			T		
SHIPPENSBURG	2.76	.62	1.21	.31	T			T	T								.05	.03	.15			T	.39				T			T		
SHIPPINGPORT WB	.83	.03					T	.02			T	T	.05				.05				.20	.39	T			.02	.07			T	T	
SINNEHAMONING	2.36	.13	1.15	.16	T			.07	T	T	T	T	T	.03	T		.06	.09	T			.12	.41	T	T		.09	T	•	.01	.03	
SLIPPERY ROCK	.99	.10	.02					.06				.05		.05		T	.02					.36	.26	T	.01		.03	.03			T	
SOMERSET FAIRVIEW ST	1.34	T	.51						.02	T	.03	.04		.02			.04	.02	T				.39	.05	.04	T	.03	.04		.02	.09	
SOMERSET MAIN ST	1.51	.40	.17					T	T	.03	.07	.03	T	.04			.16		.03			.33	.06	.05			.06	T		.08		
SOUTH MOUNTAIN	2.80	.17	1.49	.15	T				.06	.01								.02	.39				.50				.01					
SPRINGBORO	D 3.35							.15		.25		D.05	T	T			T					.95	D.20	D1.20	D.05	D.20		T		.10	.20	
SPRING GROVE	2.38	.07	.70	.57					T				.02				.01	.23	.35				.32	T		T	.11					
SPRINGS 1 SW	1.22	.33		.01				.07	.02	.04	.05	.02	.01				.05	.07	.02			.27	.05	.05		T	.02	.07		.06	.01	
STATE COLLEGE	2.26	.32	.66	.23	T			.01	T				.03				.39	.04	.01		.01	.49	.01	T		.06	T	T		T	T	
STRAUSSTOWN	2.82	.24	.51	.56						.08	.03							.02	.57				.59	T			.22					

See Reference Notes Following Station Index

DAILY PRECIPITATION

3—Continued

Station	Total	1	2	3	4	5	6	7	8	9	10	11	12	13	14	15	16	17	18	19	20	21	22	23	24	25	26	27	28	29	30	31
)SBURG	2.13	.08	.45	T				T	.01	T	T	T	T	T			T	.34	.43		T	.60	T	.02	T	.06	.14	T	T	T		.
CHEEK	2.06		.95					.08		.05		T		.06			.09	.08	T			.30	.38	T			.01	T	.04	.02		.
RY	2.41	.10	.75	.37	.07				.05	.02	T			T			T	.12	.17			T	.38	T	.03		.35					.
HANNA	1.25	.03	.27	T	.01	T			.04		.03		T	.05				.08	.17			.04	.45		.01		.05	T	.02		T	.
VILLE	1.05		.27					.02				.05		T			.18	.02					.39	.03			.06	.03				.
IA	2.04	.13	.07	.55						.07	T							.05	.47				.30				.20				T	.
IA 4 N DAM	2.18	.08	.72							.02			.04				.02	T	.36				.76	T			.18					.
ICK 2 S FIRE TWR	2.31	.12	1.15	.06	.01			.02		T	T			T			.06	.10	T			.10	.38	T	.02		.23	T	.02	.01	.03	.
STA 2 SE DAM	1.17	.02	.22	T				.08		.02	T	T		.18			.08	T				.46	T	.01	.01		.03	.01	.03	T	.02	.
ILLE WATER WORKS	3.06	.10			T		T	.19	T	.10	.02	T	.21	.04	T		.16				.12	1.23	.57	.05	T		.10	.10		.05	.02	.
IO 4 W	2.71	.02	.19					.13		.19	T	T		.23			.07	.03				.85	.54	.10	.16		.02	.05	.04		.09	.
IA	3.83	.16	.17	2.74	.03	T			.01		.03	T		.01	T			.09	.13			.03	.21		T		.22		T	T	T	.
CITY 5 SW	3.51	.13	1.56	.11					.09								.08	.03	.30			.04	.69			T	.52					.
	3.41	.12	.75	1.16	T	T			T		.03			.04			T	.17	.04			.03	.54		.02	T	.48			.01		.
POINT 4 NE	1.74	.02	.26	.04				.03		.02	.06			.06			.05					.48	.44	.05	.03		.15	.02			.01	.
4 NE BALD EAGLE	.95	.09	.25	.01				.01	T			T		.04			.07	.08	.02			T	.33	T	T		.05	T		T		.
CITY	3.25	.03	.03	.02				.21		.34	T	T		.20			.05	T				.93	.60	.42	.18		.05	.04	.05	T	.10	.
TOWN	1.34	.35						.02			.05	.02	T				.19		.01		T	.53	T	.02			.06	.02		.07	T	.
DARBY	5.18	.60	2.40	.40					.14				.02				T	.18	.75			T	.65			.04						.
	1.99	.03	.05					.13		.02		.04		.16			.11					.65	.48	.02	.03		.10	.07	.03	.04	.03	.
IGRIFT	.82		.33					T			T	T		T			T					.05	.41	.03			T	T			T	.
IVILLE	2.52	.21	.58	.07															.21				1.20	.04			.21					.
KEL	2.12	T	.33	T		T		.14	.11	.02	.04			.12	T		.19	T		T		.35	.36	T	.03		.20	.06	.08	.04	.05	.
KEL 1 WSW	1.79	T	.36	T		T		.16	.11	.03	.03			.10	.03		.17	T	T				.35	T	.04		.21	.03	.07	.05	.05	.
(	2.29	.03	.20	.05				.10		.03	.05			.10			.05	.05				.75	.64	.04	.08		.03	.02	.02		.05	.
ITOWN	6.82	1.10	*	4.62				T		T	T	T	.05				.19	.07	T		.04	.19	T	T	T	.30	.26	T		T	T	.
BURG 2 W	.92	T	.26								.02	.04		T			.06	.02					.35	T	T		.10	.05			.02	.
IORO 3 S	3.45	.42	1.70	.19	.03	.02		T	.02		.02			.04	T		.09	.15	T			.06	.36		.02		.31	T	.02	T	T	.
ILLE	2.55	.15	1.00	.52													.06	.08	.36				.26			T	.12					.
ISVILLE 1 W	3.26	.07	.65	.83							.50								.77				.46									.
CHESTER	4.02	2.24	.51	.02					.05										.88				T			.32						.
GROVE 1 E	4.84	.12	2.44	.47	.05				.04					.03					.90				.47				.32					.
HICKORY	2.14		.28					.10		.05				.20			.10					.85	.35	.05	.03		.04	.01	.05	.02	.01	.
BURG	1.34		.73					T		T	T	.06					T					.15	.27	.13	T	T	T	T		T	T	.
BARRE	1.92	T	.59	.24					T	T	.03	T		T				.12	.34			.03	.53	T	T		.04	T	T		T	.
IMSBURG	1.32	.03	.30	T				.05				.06		T			.10	.14	.15			.02	.38	.02	.02		.03	T	T	.02	T	.
IMSPORT WB AP	4.75	.50	3.00	T				.01		.02	.01	T	.03	T			.25	.04	T		.09	.27	T	.01		.36	.15	.01		T		.
BURG	.88	.02	.33	.08	T			.04				T		.02			.06	T	.06				.09	T	T		T				.01	.
SSW PUMP STA	2.64	.06	.59	.71	T				.01				.02				.01	.12	.46				.47			.03	.16					.
HAVEN	2.78	.17	.63	.64	.06					.07								.01	.43				.38	T		T	.39	T				.
GROVE	2.10	.11	-.29	.22					.05									.20	.28				.80				.15					.
ILLE 3 SE	3.36	.25	1.34	.26														.01	.81				.40				.29					.

SUPPLEMENTAL DATA

Station	Wind direction		Wind speed m. p. h.				Relative humidity averages - percent				Number of days with precipitation							Percent of possible sunshine	Average sky cover sunrise to sunset
	Prevailing	Percent of time from prevailing	Average	Fastest mile	Direction of fastest mile	Date of fastest mile	1:30 a EST	7:30 a EST	1:30 p EST	7:30 p EST	Trace	.01-.09	.10-.49	.50-.99	1.00-1.99	2.00 and over	Total		
TOWN WB AIRPORT	W	14	9.8	-	-	-	81	84	59	71	13	0	4	2	0	0	19	-	6.8
WB AIRPORT	-	-	11.3	-	-	-	-	-	-	-	7	8	6	0	1	1	23	-	7.9
SBURG WB AIRPORT	WNW	17	7.6	39	SW	21	72	75	53	64	10	3	4	1	0	0	18	52	6.9
DELPHIA WB AIRPORT	SSW	13	10.3	49	SW	21	75	76	53	64	3	2	3	2	2	0	12	57	6.6
SBURGH WB AIRPORT	WSW	25	11.7	40*	W	12	71	77	56	62	6	8	4	0	0	0	18	54	6.5
IG WB CITY	-	-	10.6	42	S	21	-	-	-	-	4	4	1	2	2	0	13	40	6.9
ON WB AIRPORT	WSW	22	8.6	34	SW	16	71	76	54	66	10	6	4	0	0	0	20	42	7.0
NGPORT WB	-	-	3.3	39††	NW	12	-	-	-	-	6	6	2	0	0	0	14	-	7.2
MSPORT WB AIRPORT	-	-	-	-	-	-	-	79	56	67	6	8	4	1	0	1	20	-	6.7

k Gust
test observed one minute
peed. This station is not
ed with automatic record-
nd instruments.

DAILY TEMPERATURES

Table 5

Station		Day Of Month																													
		1	2	3	4	5	6	7	8	9	10	11	12	13	14	15	16	17	18	19	20	21	22	23	24	25	26	27	28	29	30	31
ALLENTOWN WB AP	MAX	70	68	58	74	67	65	57	56	47	39	48	54	47	60	69	66	43	45	47	49	64	43	30	33	35	37	39	41	43	36	
	MIN	63	53	48	48	42	37	42	43	35	21	19	39	33	27	32	41	33	28	22	25	42	29	18	17	16	25	22	30	25	17	
ALLENTOWN GAS CO	MAX	69	70	68	58	72	67	65	59	52	48	39	48	55	47	63	71	67	42	44	47	51	65	43	32	35	37	38	40	41	47	
	MIN	61	62	47	47	43	36	41	44	36	34	21	25	38	28	32	36	37	35	24	25	27	34	22	18	17	21	25	29	27	18	
ALTOONA HORSESHOE CURVE	MAX	69	70	62	64	66	65	65	53	44	40	52	61	43	69	78	64	40	43	47	43	58	38	25	28	29	37	34	43	39	27	
	MIN	55	54	50	48	45	36	42	39	34	28	24	35	32	29	43	39	24	29	22	28	30	23	15	13	12	24	27	23	23	13	
ARENDTSVILLE	MAX	69	68	71	57	64	65	66	60	61	45	44	52	66	48	65	67	58	41	47	48	46	61	40	31	33	33	44	41	43	47	
	MIN	59	61	50	49	49	40	37	43	37	38	22	32	37	27	32	37	39	33	25	25	28	33	20	16	13	21	26	20	24	17	
ARTEMAS 1 WNW	MAX																															
	MIN	44	56	38	39	51	52	38	24	26	30	22	26	22	29	29	30	22	20	16	12	19	21	11	23	26	30	28	31	28	24	
BAKERSTOWN 3 WNW	MAX	64	65	68	64	66	67	63	52	48	44	64	60	47	68	73	65	45	50	55	49	65	38	27	30	33	34	33	40	38	30	
	MIN	48	44	46	50	48	42	51	40	34	33	30	37	34	36	47	39	21	24	27	36	38	24	15	9	16	29	28	27	26	24	
BEAVERTOWN	MAX	74	66	62	69	66	66	65	57	48	44	47	60	48	64	70	57	46	46	48	42	58	54	32	34	32	40	39	41	43	33	
	MIN	57	60	50	51	42	34	45	44	38	29	20	31	37	26	31	44	24	32	21	25	39	31	21	17	12	30	32	24	28	15	
BELLEFONTE 4 S	MAX	68	72	67	54	65	65	66	63	53	43	42	50	62	44	65	73	62	40	47	47	50	58	32	26	31	31	39	38	41	40	
	MIN	60	55	53	50	42	34	39	43	36	31	22	28	35	30	35	38	26	29	22	23	32	31	18	16	16	20	27	26	29	19	
BERWICK	MAX	80	71	67	71	68	69	62	60	51	45	46	55	45	64	72	55	48	46	44	45	63	52	34	34	36	37	39	42	43	35	
	MIN	62	63	51	50	43	37	37	44	38	31	20	35	35	27	33	46	26	32	22	25	40	33	21	15	15	31	29	28	31	17	
BETHLEHEM LEHIGH UNIV	MAX	69	70	56	74	66	68	58	55	47	41	49	57	47	62	70	66	45	45	49	50	64	42	30	35	38	38	39	41	44	36	
	MIN	63	52	48	51	47	35	45	44	40	29	17	43	40	36	39	45	37	36	30	31	42	32	23	21	21	23	22	33	28	15	
BLAIRSVILLE 6 ENE	MAX	69	67	62	67	67	68	62	52	41	38	60	54	40	65	71	55	40	39	54	51	65	33	19	27	27	31	29	42	28	24	
	MIN	53	49	50	47	45	42	49	32	30	26	23	36	30	35	53	32	23	27	28	36	31	19	9	9	10	25	22	21	20	18	
BRADFORD 4 W RES	MAX	72	69	62	66	65	66	63	57	40	37	52	52	37	60	69	67	43	40	49	49	53	39	27	26	29	33	32	38	35	25	
	MIN	51	52	46	45	44	27	40	34	31	20	14	34	28	31	36	38	22	17	17	23	36	24	13	9	2	25	24	21	20	13	
BROOKVILLE CAA AIRPORT	MAX	75	65	58	69	68	67	61	48	43	38	58	54	41	64	72	61	44	44	51	52	64	32	23	28	32	32	31	38	35	26	
	MIN	51	52	52	45	37	30	38	34	32	19	20	34	32	38	41	30	18	21	18	31	31	15	11	12	17	26	25	25	13	14	
BURGETTSTOWN 2 W	MAX	73	62	65	75	65	68	70	62	49	46	40	64	57	49	68	73	46	45	45	56	64	65	29	26	28	31	34	34	43	33	
	MIN	47	41	40	42	36	30	31	34	31	32	21	35	27	27	41	42	14	12	15	17	35	25	16	4	5	22	28	23	23	17	
BURNT CABINS 2 NE	MAX																															
	MIN																															
BUTLER	MAX	71	70	70	72	63	71	72	62	47	47	62	64	54	60	71	64	47	49	49	57	66	38	24	28	30	34	35	40	44	33	
	MIN	58	46	47	49	45	32	49	38	36	33	22	40	34	35	43	44	18	19	24	30	35	21	17	7	13	28	27	26	30	22	
CANTON 1 NW	MAX	63	72	60	54	60	61	61	56	56	43	30	46	57	42	59	68	57	40	40	43	43	50	37	24	27	30	34	32	35	36	
	MIN	56	58	50	41	45	40	40	44	34	24	18	25	31	30	36	50	25	25	21	20	34	30	15	9	10	17	27	22	21	11	
CARLISLE	MAX	68	72	68	68	67	68	60	62	56	44	52	60	53	62	69	65	52	48	49	45	62	59	30	35	33	41	40	43	44	38	
	MIN	60	62	47	52	47	37	39	47	39	38	22	34	40	27	32	47	27	32	24	26	41	28	22	19	14	31	27	24	28	19	
CHAMBERSBURG 1 ESE	MAX	72	74	61	66	65	65	65	60	47	46	53	63	48	68	72	57	43	48	49	47	61	53	30	33	33	44	41	43	44	36	
	MIN	48	60	50	47	42	34	38	41	39	26	23	34	33	27	33	39	28	28	24	24	39	28	19	15	14	27	30	23	27	17	
CHESTER	MAX	71	70	74		72	69	69	68	60	49		55	68	49	64	72	70		48	50	57	65	47	33		45	45	43	44	48	
	MIN	62	62	49		54	42	41	49	41	33		49	39	35	39	54	41		30	28	38	37	26	20		36	32	30	30	26	
CLARION 3 SW	MAX	75	69	62	70	69	68	63	58	45	47	60	60	43	60	73	67	46	44	52	53	64	39	26	30	31	35	36	40	41	28	
	MIN	50	51	45	49	40	31	42	35	33	22	21	33	32	30	39	40	20	18	20	30	36	26	16	11	13	26	27	25	22	14	
CLAYSVILLE 3 W	MAX	68	70	70	71	70	69	64	50	50	51	63	57	42	70	79	50	44	51	49	54	67	38	28	31	33	33	36	46	42	31	
	MIN	47	43	43	41	37	29	45	35	32	25	23	36	26	35	35	31	15	25	15	24	36	23	12	5	9	28	28	26	26	22	
COATESVILLE 1 SW	MAX	69	71	67	55	72	65	67	65	58	48	42	50	63	48	64	71	65	42	47	52	52	64	44	32	32	40	39	42	43	45	
	MIN	63	62	49	46	47	35	36	40	37	32	18	28	37	27	32	33	42	35	29	24	26	32	23	15	13	18	25	23	24	23	
COLUMBIA	MAX	74	68	63	67	68	67	58	60	50	46	51	61	52	67	71	67	56	49	50	52	63	52	35	36	36	41	43	45	46	38	
	MIN	62	61	48	48	47	37	43	48	39	33	22	40	38	30	34	54	35	34	24	26	45	34	23	17	14	32	26	25	30	14	
CONFLUENCE 1 SW DAM	MAX	68	68	71	63	71	71	67	64	49	44	38	64	60	51	66	74	57	41	42	56	46	71	29	23	29	33	35	31	44	33	
	MIN	50	49	53	53	42	34	34	44	33	31	25	39	34	27	38	46	23	24	21	22	41	28	18	4	9	26	27	26	33	20	
CORRY	MAX	71	70	68	71	73	69	64	53	44	40	56	55	40	63	70	62	45	42	54	48	54	37	25	28	30	35	32	38	35	25	
	MIN	54	52	44	49	37	30	39	36	32	25	19	34	32	36	51	34	27	18	18	25	36	24	15	8	6	26	27	22	20	17	
COUDERSPORT 3 NW	MAX	70	68	58	65	65	62	58	48	38	32	54	55	40	59	69	65	43	38	44	44	52	36	24	26	28	31	30	35	36	23	
	MIN	57	53	52	45	39	29	36	34	31	13	13	28	29	29	42	34	17	19	16	16	35	22	13	6	4	15	25	21	14	0	
DERRY	MAX	73	70	68	70	71	71	66	59	46	42	66	62	40	69	75	67	46	42	59	55	71	40	25	29	33	34	34	46	38	30	
	MIN	56	47	53	43	40	45	53	40	35	33	24	40	33	40	54	43	20	28	23	31	39	23	18	13	11	29	30	28	25	21	
DEVAULT 1 W	MAX	72	68	55	70	72	69	70	64	40	45	52	64	48	62	70	67	49	48	49	50	62	42	31	47	46	44	43	45	45	45	
	MIN	59	47	42	42	42	51	51	38	33	34	18	35	33	30	39	44	32	25	25	22	33	31	22	13	12	14	13	14	13	14	
DIXON	MAX	66	79	70	65	69	67	66	61	61	47	34	51	60	45	62	75	60	43	41	47	50	62	34	29	33	37	34	35	40	44	
	MIN	55	54	50	50	40	32	34	38	31	29	14	28	33	27	31	41	21	23	16	18	33	34	20	10	10	13	26	26	30	13	
DONEGAL	MAX	70	68	65	66	65	65	59	45	38	35	57	54	39	63	69	56	38	37	51	49	66	27	18	24	28	30	30	39	33	25	
	MIN	45	38	44	37	37	32	39	30	27	26	16	29	25	32	42	25	14	17	16	24	27	13	0	-2	6	22	21	20	25	10	
DONORA	MAX	74	66	73	74	69	71	73	68	48	48	59	66	62	65	74	76	51	46	54	58	70	61	30	27	37	37	39	40	47	37	
	MIN	57	48	51	45	43	39	55	43	37	34	32	50	35	41	55	45	24	26	24	34	47	29	20	15	22	32	31	30	34	26	
DU BOIS 7 E	MAX	71	67	66	66	65	64	60	55	41	40	50	55	40	63	77	65	42	42	47	48	63	38	24	28	30	34	32	40	39	26	
	MIN	52	49	53	47	40	30	45	38	31	28	18	39	31	34	41	40	19	22	18	35	38	23	14	11	11	26	27	22	24	12	
EAGLES MERE	MAX							68	61	61	53	32	48	54	39	54		54	40	37	39	42	50	34	23	25	31	30	30	30	35	
	MIN	57	57	50	47	46	41	42	44	32	23	21	21	28	28	33	47	25	25	23	20	32	27	13	8	9	16	24	21	20	12	
EAST BRADY	MAX	71	74	68	73	75	74	65	60	48	45	65	63	46	70	75	71	51	48	58	51	67	36	28	35	35	35	35	45	42	30	
	MIN	54	49	47	52	43	34	47	39	37	34	23	39	36	34	40	43	21	21	23	32	32	28	18	14	14	28	30	27	28	18	
EBENSBURG	MAX	67	65	58	64	60	60	60	55	40	36	51	55	40	62	69	59	38	38	45	50	62	36	20	25	29	31	30	40	38	34	
	MIN	52	52	38	49	41	34	45	32	30	24	22	33	30	31	43	34	21	25	20	33	32	14	11	8	14	21	22	20	19	12	
EMPORIUM 2 SSW	MAX	62	72	68	56	67	66	64	59	48	40	36	48	56	42	61	70	58	42	41	45	44	48	30	19	28	29	34	33	38	32	
	MIN	57	54	55	47	39	30	30	34	32	26	15	27	30	26	38	40	18	19	17	20	35	28	13	8	7	17	26	22	24	12	
EPHRATA	MAX	69	68	64	69	66	65	58	58	50	43	48	55	47	62	69	62	52	48	46	49	61	62	37	34	35	40	40	42	45	38	
	MIN	61	62	46	46	46	38	41	47	36	35	21	43	36	35	38	51	35	33	25	27	45	33	21	15	15	31	27	26	30	18	
ERIE CAA AIRPORT	MAX	71	64	73	61	62	69	59	51	45	38	59	56	45	65	70	67	42	40	54	52	56	35	28	28	31	36	34	38	34	28	
	MIN	57	50	52	50	43	46	42	36	37	23	31	39	37	44	58	35	30	28	31	40	34	19	18	18	20	30	27	25	23	22	

See Reference Notes Following Station Index

DAILY TEMPERATURES

PENNSYLVANIA
NOVEMBER 1956

		Day Of Month																														
		1	2	3	4	5	6	7	8	9	10	11	12	13	14	15	16	17	18	19	20	21	22	23	24	25	26	27	28	29	30	31	Average
	MAX	70	68	58	60	66	62	60	54	45	44	54	61	44	66	78	62	40	50	44	48	58	34	28	32	32	38	39	48	42	38		50.8
	MIN	56	52	45	44	38	28	36	36	36	30	27	31	28	26	35	38	28	27	22	25	28	24	14	16	14	24	25	28	20	15		30.1
	MAX	70	71	74	69	75	73	65	54	53	44	65	57	47	69	73	67	48	49	57	50	61	38	27	33	32	37	37	44	40	31		53.7
	MIN	52	44	47	47	45	34	43	42	34	29	23	39	33	35	50	37	20	20	20	24	29	24	16	15	18	26	19	24	22	14		30.8
	MAX	71	72	69	66	70	69	70	64	62	47	41	63	57	49	68	74	49	45	45	56	65	69	30	24	30	33	35	32	44	36		53.5
	MIN	51	49	46	42	39	30	32	37	34	32	21	34	34	34	40	45	18	19	19	19	36	29	16	12	12	23	28	25	26	18		30.0
	MAX	70	68	71	65	72	71	68	62	50	46	49	62	47	64	65	72	45	48	57	53	61	42	30	27	32	32	35	34	41	30		52.3
	MIN	60	54	51	47	50	43	33	46	37	34	29	33	36	34	38	43	28	21	20	20	31	27	16	15	15	24	27	27	25	13		32.6
	MAX	68	67	60	65	65	60	56	56	48	39	40	54	49	61	68	60	44	38	44	45	55	55	28	24	29	32	35	35	35	33		48.3
	MIN	60	59	42	46	46	42	40	46	38	20	19	38	32	30	46	43	28	30	22	30	41	24	16	11	14	27	23	23	29	19		32.8
	MAX	70	72	61	71	63	69	67	57	51	45	52	67	50	63	71	70	54	48	51	53	62	62	33	34	40	44	42	40	46	37		54.8
	MIN	65	61	48	47	52	46	39	42	40	28	18	47	35	31	37	50	38	34	23	23	35	33	22	16	15	29	27	28	25	22		35.2
	MAX	71	68	69	57	65	69	67	62	62	48	46	53	63	49	68	70	60	42	49	48	48	62	40	30	33	34	46	41	44	46		53.7
	MIN	59	61	50	50	49	38	38	45	38	39	24	37	38	33	35	40	37	34	26	26	30	35	23	18	14	25	29	23	22	20		34.5
	MAX	67	75	68	53	67	65	65	58	58	46	39	49	58	47	65	70	65	42	44	46	49	66	38	29	32	35	37	38	41	42		51.8
	MIN	60	62	49	48	47	35	38	45	36	33	20	28	37	32	35	40	31	31	21	20	28	30	19	14	13	19	28	23	25	15		32.1
	MAX	70	74	72	73	75	70	62	51	48	44	62	55	45	66	71	66	48	48	55	50	57	36	26	32	32	36	34	41	38	32		52.3
	MIN	56	43	46	45	39	37	39	38	34	28	22	37	34	35	54	36	18	18	20	32	36	25	17	15	19	27	28	24	23	18		31.4
	MAX	72	70	71	54	65	68	68	63	60	48	45	54	61	50	68	74	61	41	49	51	52	63	40	32	35	35	44	39	45	47		54.2
	MIN	58	58	49	48	45	36	37	42	35	33	22	35	35	31	34	38	36	30	24	24	28	30	19	15	15	23	24	22	23	18		32.2
	MAX	72	70	59	67	69	64	58	60	46	45	52	62	47	64	73	63	44	47	48	49	64	42	30	33	35	40	41	44	44	35		52.2
	MIN	61	59	50	52	45	39	43	43	39	26	24	39	37	31	36	44	34	30	26	30	42	29	20	19	18	31	32	27	28	21		35.2
	MAX	62	72	65	56	67	65	62	58	55	38	30	48	56	42	52	72	60	41	37	45	45	59	37	24	28	35	43	33	38	38		48.8
	MIN	53	53	43	43	39	32	29	30	31	25	11	22	31	28	31	32	27	25	14	14	23	31	17	6	5	7	21	27	27	14		26.4
	MAX	70	64	62	64	66	66	63	57	47	45	52	63	47	63	66	63	47	47	51	50	60	44	32	35	37	43	40	42	46	36		52.3
	MIN	63	59	50	53	46	44	45	46	43	29	28	44	36	36	37	47	37	32	30	31	44	32	22	21	19	29	28	27	31	26		37.2
	MAX																																
	MIN																																
	MAX	74	71	64	72	72	71	64	48	45	41	63	58	44	67	74	64	46	44	54	53	69	39	26	30	33	34	34	44	40	28		52.2
	MIN	49	53	51	43	38	31	47	36	31	26	20	36	29	36	35	34	17	27	20	29	38	25	14	6	10	28	27	26	25	15		30.1
	MAX	68	65	75	70	71	75	71	52	48	39	69	55	42	69	76	68	50	49	60	52	69	41	30	34	35	35	35	46	45	29		54.1
	MIN	54	50	47	43	45	35	52	39	36	34	26	37	34	37	47	33	21	21	23	32	40	25	20	11	17	30	30	27	30	20		33.2
	MAX	70	70	70	71	68	70	68	60	44	46	37	61	51	44	65	70	44	45	45	53	53	56	29	23	30	31	35	32	39	29		50.3
	MIN	55	43	45	46	37	39	38	36	34	32	22	34	32	33	41	37	19	19	24	26	40	27	12	16	13	23	28	23	25	18		30.6
	MAX	70	71		72	72	67	61	58	56	46			47	65	70	69	54	45	50	49			35	37	32	42	40	41	47	45		53.6
	MIN	63	61		47	49	37	34	42	38	17			32	26	32	47	28	24	21	22		33	20	16	12	30	25	29	27	16		31.8
	MAX	69	75	72	57	60	62	69	57	47	44	44	59	58	51	67	77	49	49	41	60	50	66	32	25	34	33	37	35	42	35		51.9
	MIN	52	52	50	51	41	30	35	43	32	31	23	33	33	28	37	45	23	23	21	27	33	24	15	11	8	20	26	28	26	14		30.5
	MAX	64	71	68	60	67	67	66	59	47	40	33	53	53	42	61	70	47	43	40	48	49	58	29	21	27	39	34	32	38	30		48.5
	MIN	49	50	46	46	36	27	29	33	31	25	15	30	30	27	36	40	17	15	15	17	34	28	14	13	5	16	27	23	24	12		27.0
	MAX	71	70	61	63	66	65	65	53	45	42	56	63	46	69	77	57	39	45	50	44	60	35	25	32	34	37	37	45	41	32		50.8
	MIN	48	46	50	44	39	30	40	35	33	22	23	29	26	24	33	27	21	25	18	21	33	21	12	10	8	19	19	25	15	13		27.0
STA	MAX	72	68	64	68	68	65	59	58	55	45	50	60	57	62	70	64	55	47	43	50	63	43	36	32	35	40	41	43	46	41		53.3
	MIN	59	61	48	47	42	34	34	42	37	33	20	37	36	28	31	42	37	35	24	25	42	34	24	17	15	32	24	25	26	19		33.7
	MAX	69	73	69	54	67	65	63	56	57	46	40	49	60	46	62	70	61	39	45	46	49	63	41	32	30	35	38	39	42	43		51.6
	MIN	61	63	48	47	43	34	36	43	35	31	20	23	36	27	30	33	35	33	22	24	28	31	22	13	14	25	25	22	22	15		31.4
	MAX	64	75	63	60	64	65	67	63	56	44	32	50	60	43	65	73	56	45	43	49	47	55	38	25	31	34	39	35	40	39		50.7
	MIN	52	55	52	50	42	30	31	36	35	23	16	30	32	33	35	42	22	23	16	19	29	30	15	8	10	21	26	25	27	15		29.3
	MAX	69	74	69	58	70	69	66	56	59	47	43	49	55	48	64	69	62	41	47	48	48	62	41	31	30	35	38	41	44	45		52.6
	MIN	61	62	49	50	45	35	36	43	35	34	21	35	38	28	32	44	39	32	23	25	33	33	21	15	15	31	26	25	27	16		33.6
	MAX	68	73	68	56	70	68	69	68	58	49	44	52	64	51	73	73	54	42	51	51	44	60	38	30	36	33	43	41	46	43		53.9
	MIN	57	57	56	53	43	36	35	41	40	36	25	28	33	28	29	33	30	28	26	24	26	35	22	19	17	16	29	28	29	19		32.6
	MAX	70	69	71	69	69	69	64	50	46	42	60	54	46	65	70	64	45	45	53	48	55	35	29	30	31	39	37	39	36	29		51.0
	MIN	52	48	45	49	39	38	34	34	36	22	21	34	30	37	48	33	25	21	23	25	34	23	16	18	14	27	26	23	23	19		30.6
	MAX	78	64	60	69	70	65	64	55	47	43	48	61	49	66	68	60	43	49	48	45	58	35	21	33	34	40	40	43	40	32		50.9
	MIN	56	59	53	52	43	34	39	43	37	29	22	30	38	38	35	41	26	30	23	28	38	28	18	16	13	31	33	28	27	18		33.5
	MAX	66	72	65	55	63	64	63	60	41	41	38	50	51	41	62	70	54	40	40	44	48	57	31	22	28	30	36	33	41	34		48.0
	MIN	53	49	49	45	35	25	25	31	29	25	15	27	29	25	31	31	17	16	15	15	29	26	9	6	8	15	22	19	23	8		25.1
	MAX	68	73	56	71	66	58	66	58	51	44	51	66	51	61	70	67	52	50	47	50	64	46	31	33	42	44	46	44	49	39		53.8
	MIN	63	55	50	50	53	46	47	46	39	30	29	44	39	38	45	52	37	37	33	35	44	30	24	20	25	35	33	30	34	27		39.0
	MAX	69	69	60	64	65	66	66	51	42	39	53	60	42	68	75	57	38	41	51	45	58	34	23	30	30	35	34	44	40	29		49.3
	MIN	54	51	50	48	42	35	48	35	34	23	23	36	34	36	49	33	26	28	23	27	33	20	13	13	17	21	25	25	18	14		31.1
	MAX	71	70	71	70	72	70	69	60	44	45	38	60	52	45	64	70	44	45	45	54	51	56	28	24	29	31	35	34	39	30		50.5
	MIN	57	49	46	48	40	35	39	38	32	30	23	34	32	33	45	41	21	22	21	25	34	28	17	17	14	22	28	24	25	16		31.2
	MAX	70	74	71	68	74	68	63	41	44	46	48	44	45	64	60	65	50	48	55	56	57	39	25	34	30	35	34	40	30	31		50.3
	MIN	45	47	49	42	38	39	28	30	29	28	26	27	26	30	32	34	23	21	25	30	39	20	16	18	20	25	26	19	21	11		28.8
LD	MAX	72	70	59	66	66	64	58	60	47	46	52	60	48	65	69	63	41	48	46	48	65	42	31	34	34	38	41	42	44	35		51.8
	MIN	62	61	51	53	45	40	40	45	40	25	24	40	38	32	36	43	34	30	26	27	44	30	23	21	17	32	33	29	29	22		35.7
	MAX	66	65	72	62	65	65	60	50	47	40	62	56	47	66	69	63	44	44	50	49	63	39	29	29	34	37	33	43	37	32		50.6
	MIN	61	49	50	52	48	43	50	38	38	30	35	38	36	38	48	36	25	28	31	39	36	23	18	16	22	32	29	27	26	27		35.6
	MAX	61	73	65	60	63	60	60	56	56	41	26	42	55	37	59	70	54	37	33	40	42	56	35	31	28	33	35	30	34	35		46.9
	MIN	56	57	46	46	46	40	40	41	31	23	16	20	28	28	32	48	26	26	20	21	29	29	15	8	8	16	27	24	25	14		29.5
	MAX	71	69	55	68	64	65	61	58	46	41	48	58	47	63	69	64	48	45	47	48	62	46	34	33	38	38	38	41	45	35		51.5
	MIN	62	54	46	48	40	37	41	42	35	23	21	36	34	33	32	45	34	27	22	27	42	27	16	13	13	26	23	24	24	16		32.1
	MAX	73	68	58	69	66	64	58	59	52	43	48	58	48	61	68	62	48	45	45	48	60	48	30	32	37	40	40	42	45	36		51.7
	MIN	62	56	47	50	41	38	38	41	42	22	24	40	30	32	35	43	34	25	22	25	40	27	17	11	13	29	29	23	26	14		32.5
	MAX	65	62	59	65	62	60	57	55	47	32	38	54	47	60	69	57	43	36	44	46	56	56	26	27	25	39	30	33	36	29		47.2
	MIN	59	56	42	47	42	37	38	44	31	23	11	36	28	30	40	41	27	29	16	26	37	26	14	8	8	24	26	23	26	8		30.1

See Reference Notes Following Station Index

DAILY TEMPERATURES

Table 5 - Continued

Station		1	2	3	4	5	6	7	8	9	10	11	12	13	14	15	16	17	18	19	20	21	22	23	24	25	26	27
		Day Of Month																										
MUHLENBURG 1 SE	MAX	76	70	62	66	5	64	59	59	47	41	41	54	54	60	71	61	44	41	44	45	58	52	33	28	32	34	34
	MIN	56	56	45	42	61	34	44	44	33	17	13	35	28	35	48	40	27	25	16	25	33	22	10	6	8	24	23
NEWBURG 3 W	MAX																											
	MIN																											
NEW CASTLE 1 N	MAX	70	70	72	69	71	70	64	59	48	45	64	62	47	69	73	68	48	48	56	51	63	40	29	30	34	36	36
	MIN	54	46	45	46	48	42	48	37	36	31	36	38	35	38	48	40	19	20	20	32	39	27	16	18	28	29	23
NEWELL	MAX	74	63	72	77	70	74	76	69	50	50	58	67	62	67	73	78	54	48	49	62	71	70	34	29	37	38	39
	MIN	56	52	54	49	49	42	55	47	41	39	34	47	40	42	47	50	29	31	29	35	50	33	28	19	23	34	34
NEWPORT	MAX	67	74	70	54	69	61	61	61	60	48	44	50	63	49	68	69	56	42	49	49	47	61	39	31	35	34	42
	MIN	55	55	52	51	43	34	36	41	39	37	20	29	34	26	31	32	26	26	21	22	24	35	21	16	12	15	31
NEW STANTON	MAX	68	71	73	69	70	74	68	49	45	47	65	60	66	68	72	66	46	40	59	54	47	36	27	32	36	36	38
	MIN	46	45	46	39	35	30	39	35	35	34	32	33	38	33	35	24	18	20	30	30	25	20	10	8	11	29	28
NORRISTOWN	MAX	70	73	57	74	67	67	68	59	51	43	52	69	50	67	72	71	52	48	50	53	66	47	33	35	42	45	43
	MIN	64	55	48	50	44	42	42	47	40	28	25	44	40	37	39	51	38	32	29	28	44	31	22	20	19	31	29
PALMERTON	MAX	70	67	55	72	67	64	55	57	45	38	47	55	46	60	67	63	45	41	45	47	63	42	29	30	32	38	38
	MIN	63	53	48	50	40	35	37	43	37	20	19	44	33	27	31	42	29	28	21	23	42	29	18	15	12	32	21
PHIL DREXEL INST OF TEC	MAX	71	75	58	74	67	70	68	58	52	45	53	68	53	65	73	71	54	49	52	53	66	48	36	38	44	46	45
	MIN	65	58	52	49	56	51	47	49	45	34	31	50	42	41	45	54	42	36	31	33	46	35	26	22	28	38	36
PHILADELPHIA WB AP	MAX	70	74	57	72	65	70	67	57	49	42	52	68	48	64	71	70	52	48	52	53	67	46	33	34	43	45	43
	MIN	65	55	50	49	48	46	44	46	40	30	27	44	38	35	41	52	39	34	30	30	44	31	22	20	22	35	32
PHILADELPHIA PT BREEZE	MAX	70	74	57	73	66	70	66	58	49	53	53	67	48	64	71	71	52	49	49	53	67	46	33	36	44	45	44
	MIN	63	64	51	52	57	53	50	54	43	51	34	52	41	42	48	57	41	40	34	39	50	39	30	25	31	39	35
PHILADELPHIA SHAWMONT	MAX	72	73	72	72	69	66	67	58	55	46	50	66	64	63	71	69	65	47	47	52	66	65	39	38	39	45	42
	MIN	65	63	48	52	55	49	41	47	41	38	23	47	40	33	37	50	39	38	27	28	44	37	25	20	18	36	28
PHILADELPHIA CITY	MAX	68	72	56	73	68	69	66	58	51	45	53	66	50	63	72	69	53	50	50	54	66	45	33	36	43	45	44
	MIN	64	55	51	53	54	52	50	49	42	34	32	47	42	42	48	53	41	39	36	41	46	33	28	25	29	39	36
PHILIPSBURG CAA AP	MAX	70	66	57	64	64	63	61	48	39	35	47	55	39	64	71	54	39	42	44	46	51	31	21	27	27	33	31
	MIN	54	54	49	43	34	28	42	32	32	15	15	32	31	34	38	31	21	20	15	34	31	18	12	10	14	26	22
PHOENIXVILLE 1 E	MAX	71	71	70	74	73	72	71	60	56	47	52	67	62	66	73	69	60	50	51	53	66	45	37	35	36	44	44
	MIN	63	60	46	41	39	40	43	44	37	34	18	42	35	38	39	44	36	34	21	21	39	31	21	15	11	33	22
PIMPLE HILL	MAX	61	65	61	54	63	61	61	56	51	41	28	46	52	42	58	66	55	37	32	43	44	55	35	22	28	34	38
	MIN	57	55	41	42	43	34	32	35	30	23	17	21	28	28	32	36	26	28	20	18	34	27	12	9	14	21	25
PITTSBURGH WB AP 2	MAX	64	65	72	64	67	68	62	50	47	39	63	57	44	67	72	63	45	46	55	50	66	35	23	28	33	35	34
	MIN	52	48	52	49	49	43	49	36	36	29	30	36	33	35	50	33	22	22	26	39	35	19	14	13	19	29	27
PITTSBURGH WB CITY	MAX	67	68	72	65	69	70	66	54	49	41	65	59	47	69	74	64	47	48	57	54	69	37	26	31	36	37	36
	MIN	56	51	54	50	48	42	52	39	38	35	34	37	36	41	58	38	30	29	29	39	37	21	19	18	23	33	30
PLEASANT MOUNT 1 W	MAX	59	68	61	52	63	61	58	55	56	38	26	46	52	38	55	69	57	38	35	42	43	56	37	22	26	33	35
	MIN	55	58	43	43	43	32	31	33	30	24	11	18	28	25	34	35	23	26	12	13	23	30	16	5	5	15	24
PORT CLINTON	MAX	68	75	68	57	71	69	66	60	58	47	43	48	55	50	62	68	61	57	46	49	55	52	48	40	35	48	40
	MIN	60	60	47	48	41	33	31	37	31	30	15	30	36	27	30	40	27	30	19	20	26	31	18	12	10	15	19
PUTNEYVILLE 2 SE DAM	MAX	68	72	68	61	70	69	68	62	48	45	39	61	58	48	65	73	48	45	45	53	60	66	30	25	29	32	34
	MIN	51	49	49	47	37	32	35	38	31	28	19	31	17	30	41	44	17	19	19	21	36	25	12	10	9	18	24
QUAKERTOWN 1 E	MAX	70	69	55	72	65	66	59	56	55	44	48	61	47	62	69	66	45	40	47	49	64	43	34	33	35	40	39
	MIN	63	60	46	48	41	35	38	43	36	30	18	45	37	26	28	45	37	35	29	31	42	31	21	16	13	24	20
READING WB CITY	MAX	74	69	56	73	68	66	59	59	48	43	51	57	48	65	73	64	47	47	49	51	64	44	31	34	39	39	41
	MIN	65	56	40	53	45	41	42	44	40	28	25	42	40	36	38	47	36	32	28	30	43	30	23	20	17	32	31
RIDGWAY 3 W	MAX	62	68	68	57	68	65	60	57	41	34	35	55	53	41	60	64	53	42	49	51	48	51	33	18	30	34	33
	MIN	59	51	48	48	40	29	30	33	34	30	16	38	33	28	36	42	16	16	15	17	33	30	16	10	5	14	26
SALINA 3 W	MAX	71	69	63	68	69	69	64	53	45	42	62	60	45	66	73	65	48	44	57	52	66	37	27	31	33	34	34
	MIN	53	48	50	41	32	30	40	38	34	29	22	40	34	39	44	42	20	23	23	31	31	24	14	5	5	29	28
SCRANTON	MAX	68	67	60	53	69	63	66	59	60	46	34	48	56	44	54	74	64	43	39	45	48	63	43	28	30	40	39
	MIN	58	60	47	47	48	38	38	39	35	20	18	14	36	31	35	43	28	27	18	18	28	30	17	12	12	16	26
SCRANTON WB AIRPORT	MAX	76	68	60	66	65	62	58	58	45	34	47	55	43	61	71	62	41	37	42	46	60	40	27	28	35	37	34
	MIN	61	54	47	50	43	38	43	38	33	19	18	38	31	31	39	37	27	24	19	29	38	26	16	14	13	31	29
SELINSGROVE CAA AP	MAX	76	66	60	68	67	67	60	60	45	40	48	60	48	64	69	55	40	46	47	44	61	40	29	34	33	37	39
	MIN	55	61	51	50	38	35	37	40	35	20	18	38	31	29	31	34	25	24	21	24	40	27	20	14	11	32	30
SHIPPENSBURG	MAX	74	72	66	68	70	66	65	60	48	46	52	62	57	69	70	62	48	50	51	46	60	58	33	34	32	43	40
	MIN	50	60	50	48	44	37	37	44	38	36	22	37	37	29	37	44	30	32	22	24	38	32	22	16	12	29	30
SHIPPINGPORT WB	MAX	65	66	73	63	68	70	63	52	49	41	64	59	46	68	73	66	45	46	58	50	66	36	25	30	33	37	34
	MIN	50	47	51	48	45	38	46	38	37	28	31	37	35	34	49	34	22	24	26	36	36	21	16	12	19	30	29
SLIPPERY ROCK	MAX	66	70	69	70	70	69	60	51	47	40	62	53	51	66	72	66	40	47	55	50	62	36	25	28	31	33	34
	MIN	54	44	51	50	44	39	47	35	34	29	24	33	30	37	49	36	22	22	25	38	34	22	14	8	15	27	25
SOMERSET MAIN ST	MAX	70	69	60	68	66	63	61	56	40	38	58	58	42	65	72	61	47	44	54	55	54	36	21	32	30	33	32
	MIN	52	47	52	50	37	32	46	35	30	28	21	35	29	31	39	41	19	27	19	24	36	21	13	3	15	24	25
SPRINGBORO	MAX	72	70	69	74	70	71	70	61	42	45	40	59	52	47	62	70	51	49	41	55	54	55	38	24	31	37	37
	MIN	59	45	46	44	39	33	36	37	32	30	18	29	30	25	43	37	29	23	20	25	34	25	17	17	23	26	28
SPRINGS 1 SW	MAX	65	65	58	65	61	60	59	51	39	35	59	58	40	63	71	56	36	38	49	55	69	34	20	34	28	32	28
	MIN	47	48	48	44	38	31	38	30	28	21	18	32	26	25	39	30	16	22	19	24	31	19	- 1	- 4	3	21	23
STATE COLLEGE	MAX	70	66	62	64	64	64	63	53	43	39	49	60	43	65	74	59	39	45	45	46	57	35	25	29	32	37	35
	MIN	58	57	52	51	47	38	49	38	36	27	25	36	35	36	42	35	28	29	25	34	35	23	18	15	18	26	28
STROUDSBURG	MAX	70	68	58	66	66	63	63	58	44	35	43	53	44	60	65	64	41	40	41	47	63	41	27	30	32	38	37
	MIN	62	53	46	47	40	30	32	40	30	17	10	38	32	22	38	41	24	22	17	27	40	22	11	7	8	24	27
TAMARACK 2 S FIRE TWR	MAX	60	69	62	52	62	67	63	57	47	39	33	46	58	42	62	70	50	40	42	43	43	52	39	29	27	30	29
	MIN	56	54	52	45	44	44	42	41	31	24	19	22	29	29	38	39	24	22	23	25	33	26	13	10	11	13	25
TIONESTA 2 SE DAM	MAX	67	74	69	61	71	70	68	61	48	43	38	60	52	44	64	71	50	47	45	52	52	61	31	28	30	32	34
	MIN	52	52	45	47	42	33	33	39	34	29	21	32	32	29	32	40	20	19	19	20	35	28	17	15	10	10	27
TITUSVILLE WATER WORKS	MAX	70	71	66	72	71	67	62	46	43	41	60	53	41	65	71	65	46	48	52	45	59	39	23	25	30	38	31
	MIN	50	48	38	48	37	26	38	33	30	23	18	31	29	32	39	33	17	14	15	25	32	22	14	13	6	28	24

able 5 - Continued

DAILY TEMPERATURES

PENNSYLVANIA
NOVEMBER 1956

Station		1	2	3	4	5	6	7	8	9	10	11	12	13	14	15	16	17	18	19	20	21	22	23	24	25	26	27	28	29	30	31	Average
WANDA	MAX	79	66	60	67	65	64	64	59	47	37	47	62	40	64	75	59	45	43	48	45	59	47	32	37	33	43	38	39	42	34		51.5
	MIN	54	54	49	51	43	34	38	39	35	20	16	30	31	32	33	41	24	27	18	30	38	30	18	14	12	29	27	27	27	15		31.2
IONTOWN	MAX	66	72	74	73	71	75	68	51	48	41	65	63	48	70	77	65	49	47	61	53	71	36	26	33	34	36	36	46	41	32		54.3
	MIN	52	40	46	45	45	49	50	39	36	31	29	39	32	35	39	32	22	25	24	28	36	24	12	9	17	32	30	29	28	25		32.9
'PER DARBY	MAX	68	73	65	72	66	66	66	57	53	43	51	66	54	63	71	69	56	48	48	48	65	63	37	33	40	45	42	44	47	37		55.2
	MIN	65	60	48	49	50	42	41	50	40	33	25	47	39	34	34	52	38	36	29	29	45	35	23	19	20	35	30	29	31	25		37.8
RREN	MAX	75	68	65	71	72	69	61	54	44	35	57	54	41	64	72	64	45	44	53	48	57	36	26	30	32	36	33	39	38	28		50.4
	MIN	52	54	48	50	43	39	45	37	33	25	21	35	33	36	50	37	24	20	19	29	36	26	16	13	14	28	27	25	22	19		31.9
YNESBURG 2 W	MAX	68	71	75	73	70	73	66	52	47	44	66	61	41	70	75	64	46	49	57	52	69	42	26	32	35	35	34	46	41	32		53.7
	MIN	47	44	43	44	40	30	47	37	32	32	24	40	26	27	33	38	16	26	26	23	40	25	16	6	10	28	28	27	28	21		30.1
LLSBORO 3 S	MAX	62	70	61	63	61	62	63	58	51	41	30	48	57	42	60	70	53	41	39	45	43	50	33	23	27	30	33	33	35	34		47.3
	MIN	57	55	53	47	47	38	42	43	33	22	18	25	29	29	37	48	25	25	21	22	34	28	13	9	9	16	26	21	22	12		30.2
LLSVILLE	MAX	70	72	63	66	67	66	61	61	49	45	51	61	53	67	70	61	51	48	48	48	63	61	31	32	31	42	40	43	43	35		53.3
	MIN	56	61	49	49	43	34	34	45	37	21	18	31	37	24	29	45	30	32	20	21	39	29	20	13	11	30	20	20	25	23		31.5
ST CHESTER	MAX	69	69	61	61	67	67	67	59	55	43	41	56	60	54	62	67	62	40	51	53	59	62	43	36	31	42	44	42	42	47		53.7
	MIN	60		49	49	45	38	40	38	36	35	25	27	35	30	38	40	34	29	30	36	32	33	18	20	22	19	27	25	20	24		32.9
LLIAMSPORT WB AP	MAX	76	65	61	69	68	64	59	58	48	40	47	61	48	61	68	57	42	46	45	44	59	41	29	33	34	38	39	38	40	32		50.3
	MIN	62	55	52	52	46	38	43	43	37	21	21	36	37	32	35	39	27	27	23	28	40	28	20	18	14	31	28	30	23	17		33.4
RK 3 SSW PUMP STA	MAX	71	72	63	68	69	70	60	62	53	47	52	64	58	69	74	63	54	50	52	51	64	62	35	33	37	44	41	45	46	40		55.6
	MIN	61	61	50	51	40	34	37	45	38	32	21	32	32	30	33	51	32	33	23	26	45	33	22	16	14	33	24	23	33	17		34.1

See Reference Notes Following Station Index

Table 7

SNOWFALL AND SNOW ON GROUND

Station		1	2	3	4	5	6	7	8	9	10	11	12	13	14	15	16	17	18	19	20	21	22	23	24	25	26	27	28	29	30	31
ALLENTOWN WB AIRPORT	SNOWFALL									T		T		T					T			T	T	T		T		T				
	SN ON GND																									T						
	WTR EQUIV																															
AUSTINBURG 2 W	SNOWFALL										T			T										T	T	T	7.0	T				
	SN ON GND										T			T										T	T	T	7	4	3	2	2	
BEACH CREEK STATION	SNOWFALL											T												T	T		3.0					
	SN ON GND											T												T	T		3	1	T	T	T	
BRADFORD 4 W RESVR	SNOWFALL										T			1.7										1.3	2.6		1.7	1.3	T	1.3	.8	
	SN ON GND																							1	4	3	5	6	5	6	5	
BROOKVILLE CAA AIRPORT	SNOWFALL								T	.3	.1	T	T	T								T	1.0	.1	T	.2	.6	1.0	T	.4	T	
	SN ON GND										T	T												1	1		1	1	2	2	1	
CANTON 1 NW	SNOWFALL										T			T					T						.6		4.1	T	T	T		
	SN ON GND										T			T					T						T	T	4	3	3	2	2	
CARROLLTOWN 2 SSE	SNOWFALL										T	.5		.5					.5				1.0	1.0	T		2.0	.5	.5	1.0	.5	
	SN ON GND										T	T		T					T				1	2	2	2	3	3	3	2	2	
COALDALE 2 NW	SNOWFALL										T								.3						T		2.0					
	SN ON GND																		T						T		2					
CORRY	SNOWFALL									T				T									3.0	3.0	2.0			1.0		1.5	.5	
	SN ON GND																						3	6	8	5	4	3	2	4	4	
DONEGAL	SNOWFALL									T	T	T	T										T	1.0		T	1.0	T	T	3.5	T	
	SN ON GND									T	T	T	T										T	1	T	T	1	T	T	3	3	
DU BOIS 7 E	SNOWFALL									T	T								T	T			1.0	.5			1.0	.5	T	.5	T	
	SN ON GND																						1	1	1	1	1	1	1	1	1	
ERIE CAA AIRPORT	SNOWFALL								T	T	T	T										T	20.0	3.0	.9	1.1	.3	.5	T	3.0	6.0	
	SN ON GND																						6	23	24	17	16	12	12	12	14	
FORD CITY 4 S DAM	SNOWFALL											.5											T	T	T		T			T	T	
	SN ON GND											1											T	T	T		T			T	T	
GALETON	SNOWFALL										T							T					T	T	.3		3.8			T	.3	
	SN ON GND																															
GRATERFORD	SNOWFALL	-	-	-	-	-	-	-	-	-	-	-	-	-	-	-	-	-	-	-	-	-	-	-	-	-	-	-	-	-	-	
	SN ON GND	-	-	-	-	-	-	-	-	-	-	-	-	-	-	-	-	-	-	-	-	-	-	-	-	-	-	-			-	
GREENSBORO LOCK 7	SNOWFALL																								-	-	-	-			T	
	SN ON GND																								T	T	T	T				
HANOVER	SNOWFALL																										.5					
	SN ON GND																										T					
HARRISBURG WB AIRPORT	SNOWFALL																	.2	T				T	T		.8	T			T		
	SN ON GND																							T			1	T				
	WTR EQUIV																															
HAWLEY 1 S DAM	SNOWFALL																		2.2								1.5					
	SN ON GND																		2	1	T						2	T				
HOLTWOOD	SNOWFALL																							T			T					
	SN ON GND																										T					
HOOVERSVILLE	SNOWFALL										T	.5		T					T				1.5	.5	1.4		1.0	T	T	1.7	2.4	
	SN ON GND																		T				1	1	1		1	1	1	2	2	
INDIANA 3 SE	SNOWFALL										T	T							T				.4	1.3				.2			T	
	SN ON GND											T											T	1	1	1	1	1	T	T	T	
KANE 1 NNE	SNOWFALL									.4	.3			.6								.2	1.5	2.0		2.5	.7	.5	.2	1.5	.3	
	SN ON GND										T			T									-	-	-	-	-	-	-	-	-	
KEATING SUMMIT	SNOWFALL										1.0													.7			4.0	.4	.4		.3	
	SN ON GND										1													1	1	1	4	4	3	2	2	
LANCASTER 2 NE PUMP STA	SNOWFALL																	T					T				T					
	SN ON GND																															
LAWRENCEVILLE 2 S	SNOWFALL										T								T						T		3.0		T			
	SN ON GND										T								T						T	T	3	3	2	2	1	
LEWISTOWN	SNOWFALL																							T			.9					
	SN ON GND																										1	T				
MARTINSBURG CAA AIRPORT	SNOWFALL									T	T	T	T					T	.1			T	T	T		T	T	T	T	T		
	SN ON GND										T	T							T								T			T		
MATAMORAS	SNOWFALL																		1.0								.5					
	SN ON GND																		1								1					
MEADVILLE 1 S	SNOWFALL									.7	T	.5		T	T								.3	.7	2.5	.1	.6	1.3	1.6	1.0	.6	
	SN ON GND									T		T											T	1	3	2	2	2	2	3	3	
MEDIX RUN	SNOWFALL											T		T					T				T	T	T	T	3.0	T	T	.5	T	
	SN ON GND											T		T					T					T	T	T	3	1	1	T	T	
MONTROSE 1 E	SNOWFALL										.7	T	T	T					1.7					T	1.1		1.3	T	.1		T	
	SN ON GND										1	T		T					2	T	T			T	1	T	2	T	T	T	T	
MUHLENBURG 1 SE	SNOWFALL													T					2.0					.5		.5	1.0					
	SN ON GND																		2					1	1	1	2	1				
NEWPORT	SNOWFALL																										2.5					
	SN ON GND																															
PHILADELPHIA WB AIRPORT	SNOWFALL																									T						
	SN ON GND																															
	WTR EQUIV																															
PHILADELPHIA CITY	SNOWFALL	-	-	-	-	-	-	-	-	-	-	-	-	-	-	-	-	-	-	-	-	-	-	-	-	-	-	-	-	-	-	
	SN ON GND	-	-	-	-	-	-	-	-	-	-	-	-	-	-	-	-	-	-	-	-	-	-	-	-	-	-	-	-	-	-	
PHILIPSBURG CAA AIRPORT	SNOWFALL								T	T	T	T	T	T				T	T				.8	.3	T	2.0	.1	.3	.1	.3	T	
	SN ON GND																		T					1	1	1	2	2	2	2	2	
PIMPLE HILL	SNOWFALL									T	.4	.1	T	T	T				1.1				T	.1	.4	T	1.6	T	.2		.7	
	SN ON GND									T	T	T		T					1	1	T	T	T	T	T	T	1	1	1	1	1	

See reference notes following Station Index.

SNOWFALL AND SNOW ON GROUND

Station		1	2	3	4	5	6	7	8	9	10	11	12	13	14	15	16	17	18	19	20	21	22	23	24	25	26	27	28	29	30	31
PITTSBURGH WB AIRPORT 2	SNOWFALL								T	T	T	T										T	.8	.6		T	1.5	T		T	.5	
	SN ON GND											T											T	1	T	T	1	T	T	T	T	
	WTR EQUIV																															
PLEASANT MOUNT 1 W	SNOWFALL										T	T		T					3.0					T	1.0		.8		T		T	
	SN ON GND										T	T		T					3	1	1			T	1	1	1	T	T	T	T	
READING WB CITY	SNOWFALL																						T			T						
	SN ON GND																															
SCRANTON WB AIRPORT	SNOWFALL									T	T		T					1.0	1.5					T		.1	T	T	T	.1		
	SN ON GND										T								2	T	T				T	T	T					
	WTR EQUIV																		.2													
SELINSGROVE CAA AIRPORT	SNOWFALL										T							T	T					T		3.0	T					
	SN ON GND																										3	2	1	T		
SHIPPENSBURG	SNOWFALL																	T	.5				.5									
	SN ON GND																										T			T		
SHIPPENSBURG WB	SNOWFALL										T	T										T	T			T	T			T	T	
	SN ON GND																						T	T	T	T	T	T	T			
SLIPPERY ROCK	SNOWFALL											1.0												.5	.5		1.0	.5				
	SN ON GND											1												T	1	1	1	1	1			
SPRING 1 SW	SNOWFALL									T	.5	.5	T					T	T			T	.5	1.0		T	.5	1.0		1.0	.3	
	SN ON GND									T	1	1	T					T	T			T	1	1	1	1	2	2	1	2	2	
TAMARACK 2 S FIRE TWR	SNOWFALL									T	T			T					T						.4		3.4	T	.4	.3	.6	
	SN ON GND									T	T			T					T						T		3	3	3	3	2	
TIONESTA 2 SE DAM	SNOWFALL									T	T	T											T	T	.5		.6	.2		T	T	
	SN ON GND																							T	1	T	1	T	T	T	T	
TOWANDA	SNOWFALL										T	T		T	T				1.4						T		2.0		T	T	T	
	SN ON GND										T			T					1	T	T						2	1	T	T	T	
TOWER CITY 5 SW	SNOWFALL																						T			T	3.0					
	SN ON GND																															
WILLIAMSPORT WB AIRPORT	SNOWFALL									T	T	T		T				.1	T				T	.1		3.6	1.2	T		T		
	SN ON GND																								T		5	3	2	1	T	
	WTR EQUIV																										.5	.4				

See reference notes following Station Index.

TOTAL PRECIPITATION

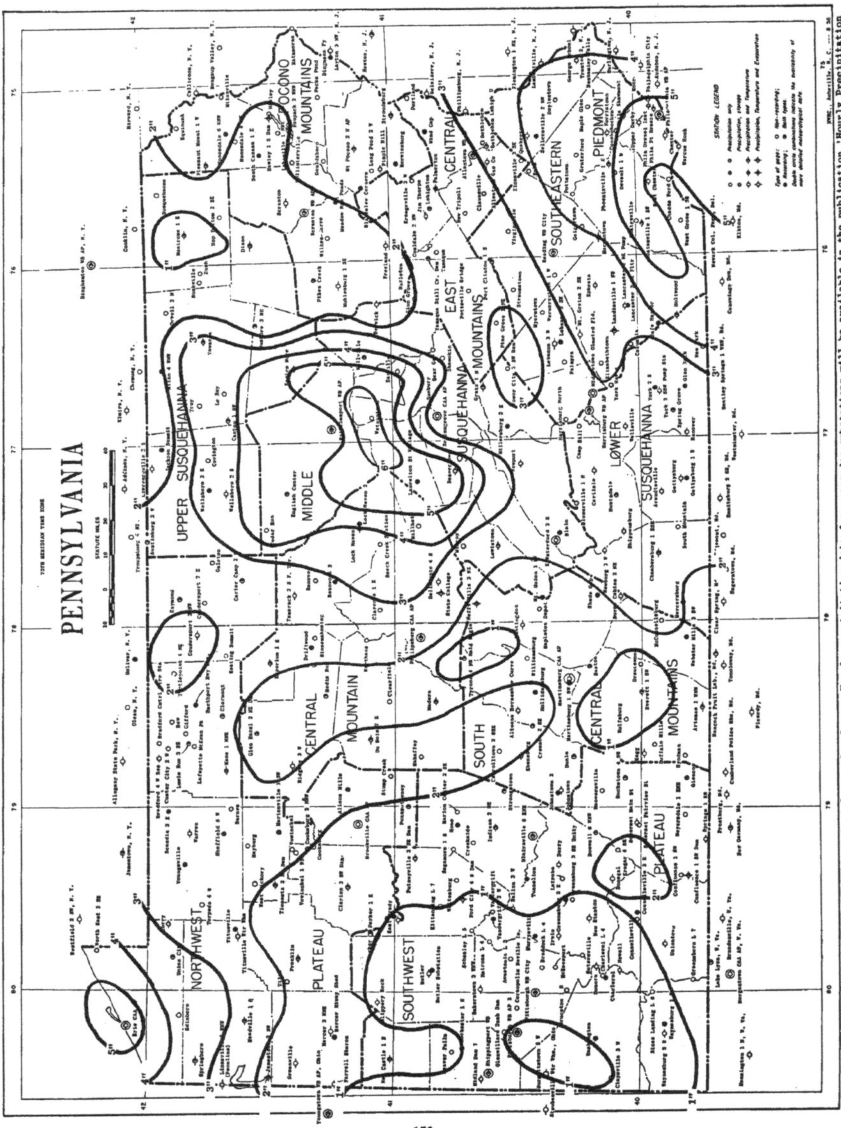

Isolines are drawn through points of approximately equal values. Hourly precipitation data from recorder substations will be available in the publication 'Hourly Precipitation Data'.

AVERAGE TEMPERATURE

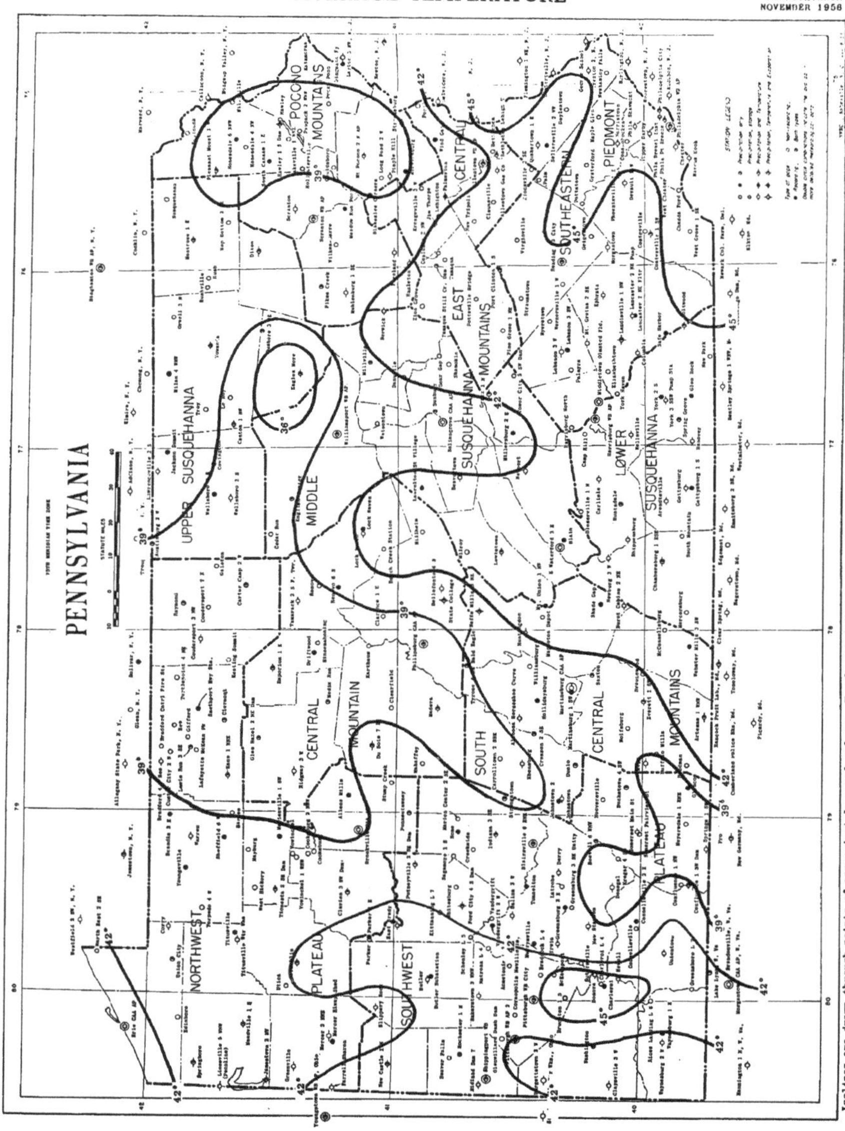

Isolines are drawn through points of approximately equal values. Hourly precipitation data from recorder substations will be available in the publication 'Hourly Precipitation Data'.

STATION INDEX

Station	Index No.	County	Drainage 1	Latitude	Longitude	Elevation	Observation Time Temp.	Observation Time Precip.	Observer	Refer To Tables
ACHETONIA LOCK 3	0022	ALLEGHENY	1	40 32	79 49	748		7A	CORPS OF ENGINEERS	3
ALLENS MILLS	0099	JEFFERSON	1	41 12	78 55	1600		MID	CHARLES M. ALLEN	C
ALLENTOWN WB AP	0106	LEHIGH	9	40 39	75 26	376	MID	MID	U.S. WEATHER BUREAU	2 3 5 7 C
ALLENTOWN GAS CO	0111	LEHIGH	9	40 36	75 28	254	7A	7A	LEHIGH VLY GAS DIV	2 3 5
ALTOONA HORSESHOE CURVE	0134	BLAIR	6	40 30	78 29	1500	6P	6P	ALTOONA WATER BUR.	2 3 5
ARENDTSVILLE	0229	ADAMS	15	39 55	77 16	710	8A	8A	PA STATE COL EXP	2 3 5
ARTEMAS 1 WNW	0259	BEDFORD	12	39 45	78 28	1250	6P	6P	GRAYSON E.NORTHCRAFT	2 3 5 C
AUSTINBURG 2 W	0313	TIOGA	15	42 00	77 32	1590		7A	OTTO D. BACON	3 7 C
BAKERSTOWN 3 WNW	0355	ALLEGHENY	1	40 39	79 59	1230	7P	7P	PGH CUT FLOWER CO	2 3 5
BARNES	0409	WARREN	1	41 40	79 02	1310		7A	CORPS OF ENGINEERS	3
BARTO 4 NW	0428	BERKS	14	40 26	75 39	312		7A	MARIE B. NICHLAS	3
BEAR GAP	0457	NORTHUMBLAND	15	40 50	76 30	900		MID	ROARING CRK WTR CO	3
BEAVER FALLS	0475	BEAVER	2	40 46	80 19	760		7A	HOWARD R. KEMP	3
BEAVERTOWN	0482	SNYDER	15	40 45	77 10	640	7A	7A	MARLIN RC ETTINGER	2 3 5
BEECH CREEK STATION	0499	CENTRE	16	41 04	77 34	620		7A	HAROLD S. RUPERT	3 7
BELLEFONTE 4 S	0530	CENTRE	16	40 51	77 47	1110	8A	8A	ROCKVIEW PRISON FARM	2 3 5
BERWICK	0611	COLUMBIA	15	41 04	76 15	570	6P	6P	AMER CAR + FNDRY CO	2 3 5
BETHLEHEM	0629	NORTHAMPTON	9	40 37	75 22	400		7A	ARTHUR CROPPER	3
#BETHLEHEM LEHIGH UNIV	0634	NORTHAMPTON	9	40 36	75 23	450	MID	MID	LEHIGH UNIVERSITY	2 3 5 C
BLAIN	0725	PERRY	15	40 20	77 31	750		MID	PA DEPT FRST + WTRS	C
BLAIRSVILLE 6 ENE	0736	INDIANA	4	40 27	79 09	2048	8P	8P	U.S. WEATHER BUREAU	2 3 5
BLAKESLEE CORNERS	0743	MONROE	9	41 06	75 36	1650		MID	WALTER WILDRICK	C
BLOSERVILLE 1 N	0763	CUMBERLAND	15	40 16	77 22	650		5P	MRS. B. M. WILLDERS	3
BOSWELL 6 WNW	0820	SOMERSET	1	40 11	79 08	2580		7A	MRS. MAE L. KIMMEL	3 C
BRADDOCK LOCK 2	0861	ALLEGHENY	10	40 24	79 52	725		7A	CORPS OF ENGINEERS	3
BRADFORD CNTRL FIRE STA	0867	MC KEAN	1	41 57	78 39	1500		8A	BRADFORD FIRE DEPT	3
BRADFORD 4 W RES	0868	MC KEAN	1	41 57	78 44	1680	5P	5P	BRADFORD WTR DEPT	2 3 5 7
BREEZEWOOD	0905	BEDFORD	6	40 00	78 14	1352		MID	PA TURNPIKE COMM	3
BROOKVILLE CAA AIRPORT	1002	JEFFERSON	1	41 09	79 06	1417	MID	MID	CIVIL AERO. ADM.	2 3 5 7
BRUCETON 1 S	1033	ALLEGHENY	10	40 18	79 59	1065		7A	AUSTIN R. COOPER	3
BUCKSTOWN 1 SE	1073	SOMERSET	4	40 04	78 50	2460		MID	ALVIN W. MANGES	C
BUFFALO MILLS	1087	BEDFORD	6	39 58	78 39	1318		7A	MRS. NELLE R. BROWN	3
BURGETTSTOWN 2 W	1105	WASHINGTON	11	40 23	80 26	980	7A	7A	SMITH TWP MUN AUTH	2 3 5
BURNT CABINS 2 NE	1115	HUNTINGDON	6	40 05	77 52	990	MID	MID	PA TURNPIKE COMM	2 3 5
#BUTLER	1130	BUTLER	2	40 52	79 54	1100	4P	7A	WILLIAM C. FAUST	2 3 5
BUTLER SUBSTATION	1135	BUTLER	2	40 51	79 53	1140		MID	WEST PENN POWER CO	C
CAMP HILL	1198	CUMBERLAND	15	40 15	76 55	461		6P	JOSEPH N. HOBART	3
CANTON 1 NW	1215	BRADFORD	15	41 40	76 52	1520	7A	7A	MRS.MILDRED SPENCER	2 3 5 7 C
CARLISLE	1234	CUMBERLAND	15	40 12	77 11	460	6P	6P	C. E. MILLER	2 3 5
CARROLLTOWN 2 SSE	1255	CAMBRIA	16	40 35	78 42	2040		8A	ROBERT F. MAURER	3 7
CARTER CAMP 2 W	1262	POTTER	16	41 37	77 45	2030		7A	RICHARD L. MENKEN	3 C
CEDAR RUN	1301	LYCOMING	16	41 31	77 27	800		7A	KATHRYN T.KREIGHBAUM	3
CHADDS FORD	1342	DELAWARE	5	39 52	75 36	160		8A	MRS.GRACE A. HICKS	3
CHAMBERSBURG 1 ESE	1354	FRANKLIN	12	39 56	77 38	640	9P	9P	CHARLES A. BENDER	2 3 5 C
CHARLEROI	1372	WASHINGTON	10	40 08	79 55	1040		MID	WEST PENN POWER CO	C
CHARLEROI LOCK 4	1377	WESTMORELAND	10	40 09	79 54	749		7A	CORPS OF ENGINEERS	3
#CHESTER	1423	DELAWARE	5	39 51	75 22	86	8A	8A	CHESTER TIMES	2 3 5
CLARENCE	1480	CENTRE	16	41 03	77 56	1410		7A	MISS VELDA SWANCER	3
CLARION 3 SW	1485	CLARION	1	41 12	79 26	1114	8P	7A	PA ELECTRIC CO	2 3 5 C
CLAUSSVILLE	1505	LEHIGH	9	40 37	75 39	670		8A	WILLIAM J. DOTTERER	3
CLAYSVILLE 3 W	1512	WASHINGTON	11	40 07	80 28	1000	7P	7A	MFGRS. L + H CO	2 3 5
CLEARFIELD	1519	CLEARFIELD	16	41 01	78 26	1100		7A	IRA TAYLOR	3
CLERMONT	1529	MC KEAN	1	41 41	78 30	2104		7A	MRS.TILLIE M.SIMONDS	3 C
COALDALE 2 NW	1572	SCHUYLKILL	9	40 50	75 56	1026		7A	PANTHER VLY WTR CO	3 7
COATESVILLE 1 SW	1589	CHESTER	5	39 58	75 50	342	8A	8A	PHILA ELECTRIC CO	2 3 5 C
COATESVILLE	1594	CHESTER	5	39 59	75 49	340		8A	EDWARD D. BIEDEMAN	INAC 12/55
COLUMBIA	1675	LANCASTER	15	40 02	76 30	300	SS	SS	JAMES H. RUST	2 3 5
CONFLUENCE 1 SW DAM	1705	SOMERSET	17	39 48	79 22	1490	8A	8A	CORPS OF ENGINEERS	2 3 5 6 C
CONFLUENCE 1 NW	1710	FAYETTE	17	39 50	79 22	1331		7A	JOHN L. REID	3
CONNELLSVILLE	1723	FAYETTE	17	40 01	79 36	870		8A	MARSHALL B. MENEFEE	3
CONNELLSVILLE 2 E	1729	FAYETTE	17	40 01	79 33	1300		MID	HARRY C. JOY	C
CONSHOHOCKEN	1737	MONTGOMERY	5	40 04	75 19	70		8A	PHILA ELECTRIC CO	3
COOKSBURG	1749	CLARION	1	41 20	79 13	1180		8A	PA DEPT FRST + WTRS	3
COOKSBURG 2 NNW	1752	CLARION	1	41 21	79 13	1460		8A	PA DEPT FRST + WTRS	3
CORAOPOLIS NEVILLE IS	1773	ALLEGHENY	11	40 30	80 05	720		8A	PGH. COKE + CHEM CO	3
CORRY	1790	ERIE	1	41 56	79 38	1427	7P	8A	LEO C. MECKERS	2 3 5 7
COUDERSPORT 3 NW	1806	POTTER	1	41 49	78 03	2020	7P	8A	MISS ELIZABETH NEFF	2 3 5
COUDERSPORT 7 E	1809	POTTER	1	41 46	77 53	2425		7A	CAMP POTATO	3
COVINGTON 2 WSW	1833	TIOGA	15	41 44	77 07	1745		7A	CALVIN R. PACKARD	3
CREEKSIDE	1881	INDIANA	1	40 41	79 12	1035		7A	CORPS OF ENGINEERS	3
CRESSON 2 SE	1895	CAMBRIA	6	40 27	78 34	2540		7A	MILES A. VECELLIO	3 C
CUSTER CITY 2 W	1978	MC KEAN	1	41 55	78 41	2120		8A	W. D. BOOTH AND CO	3
DANVILLE	2013	MONTOUR	15	40 58	76 37	460		7A	MRS.MARIE M. LITTLE	3
DERRY	2108	WESTMORELAND	4	40 20	79 18	1150	6P	6P	MISS N. D. WINEMAN	2 3 5
DEVAULT 1 W	2116	CHESTER	14	40 05	75 33	360	MID	MID	PA TURNPIKE COMM	2 3 5
DINGMANS FERRY	2160	PIKE	5	41 13	74 52	364		MID	CLYDE T. VOORHEES	C
DIXON	2171	WYOMING	15	41 34	75 54	620	7A	7A	HAROLD J. KUSCHEL	2 3 5 C
DONEGAL	2183	WESTMORELAND	17	40 07	79 23	1746	MID	MID	PA TURNPIKE COMM	2 3 5 7
#DONORA	2190	WASHINGTON	10	40 11	79 51	814	12M	12M	DONORA ZINC WORKS	2 3 5
DOYLESTOWN	2221	BUCKS	5	40 18	75 08	393		5P	GEORGE HART	3
DRIFTWOOD	2245	CAMERON	16	41 20	78 08	880		MID	SIDNEY KENNEDY	
DU BOIS 7 E	2265	CLEARFIELD	16	41 06	78 38	1670	5P	5P	CITY OF DU BOIS	2 3 5 7
DUNLO	2298	CAMBRIA	4	40 17	78 43	2410		MID	MRS. D. L. WHITE	
DUSHORE 3 NE	2324	SULLIVAN	16	41 33	76 21	1750		7A	PATRICK P. RYAN	3 C
EAGLES MERE	2343	SULLIVAN	16	41 24	76 35	2020	7A	7A	MRS.ELSIE P. BIGGER	2 3 5
EAST BRADY	2363	CLARION	1	40 59	79 37	820	5P	5P	A. B. KEMPEL	2 3 5
EAST WATERFORD 3 E	2459	PERRY	6	40 21	77 33	2125	8A	8A	U.S. WEATHER BUREAU	INAC 5/55
EBENSBURG	2466	CAMBRIA	4	40 29	78 43	2090	7P	7A	ROBERT A. WASSER	2 3 5
EDINBORO	2514	ERIE	1	41 52	80 08	1220		8A	EDINBORO ST TCHR COL	3
ELIZABETHTOWN	2560	LANCASTER	15	40 09	76 37	460		8A	MASONIC HOME	3
EMPORIUM 2 SSW	2634	CAMERON	16	41 28	78 15	1735	7A	7A	JACKSON THOMAS	2 3 5 C
ENGLISH CENTER	2644	LYCOMING	16	41 26	77 17	881		7A	WILLIAM SUDERS	3 7 C
EPHRATA	2662	LANCASTER	15	40 11	76 10	465	6P	6P	STANLEY L.VON NEIDA	2 3 5
EQUINUNK	2669	WAYNE	5	41 51	75 13	900		8A	MRS.ROSE M. NEILSEN	3
ERIE CAA AIRPORT	2682	ERIE	8	42 05	80 12	732	MID	MID	CIVIL AERO. ADM.	2 3 5 7
EVERETT 1 SW	2721	BEDFORD	6	40 00	78 23	1020	MID	MID	PA TURNPIKE COMM	2 3 5 7 C
FARRELL SHARON	2814	MERCER	2	41 14	80 30	865	7P	7P	SHARON STEEL CORP	2 3 5
FORD CITY 4 S DAM	2942	ARMSTRONG	1	40 43	79 30	950	8A	8A	CORPS OF ENGINEERS	2 3 5 6 7 C
FRANKLIN	3028	VENANGO	1	41 23	79 49	987	7P	7A	GEORGE S. SMITH JR.	2 3 5 C
FREELAND	3056	LUZERNE	15	41 01	75 54	1900	6P	8A	ANDREW B. EVANSHA	2 3 5
GALETON	3130	POTTER	16	41 44	77 39	1325		7A	W. GALE LUSH	3 7
GEIGERTOWN	3189	BERKS	14	40 13	75 50	400		8A	WALTER C. WOLF	3
GEORGE SCHOOL	3200	BUCKS	5	40 13	74 56	135	7P	7P	GEORGE M. HART	2 3 5 7
#GETTYSBURG	3218	ADAMS	12	39 50	77 14	540	9A	9A	HUGH C. MC ILHENNY	2 3 5
GETTYSBURG 1 S	3223	ADAMS	12	39 48	77 14	560		MID	NAT MILITARY PARK	C
GIFFORD	3237	MC KEAN	1	41 51	78 36	2220		8A	SOUTH PENN OIL CO	3
GLENCOE	3298	SOMERSET	12	39 49	78 51	1620		MID	MRS. MARY M.HARTMAN	C
GLEN HAZEL 2 NE DAM	3311	ELK	1	41 34	78 36	1725		8A	CORPS OF ENGINEERS	3 C
GLEN ROCK	3330	YORK	15	39 48	76 44	620		MID	MRS.E.C.MC WILLIAMS	C
GLENWILLARD DASH DAM	3343	ALLEGHENY	11	40 33	80 13	705		7A	CORPS OF ENGINEERS	3
GOULDSBORO	3394	WAYNE	9	41 15	75 27	1890		7A	L. M. EILENBERGER	3
GRATERFORD	3435	MONTGOMERY	14	40 14	75 27	160		7A	CLAUDE K. KULP	3 7
GRATZ 1 N	3438	DAUPHIN	15	40 38	76 43	760	8A	8A	LEE M. LEITZEL	2 3 5 C
GREENSBORO LOCK 7	3503	GREENE	10	39 47	79 55	808		7A	CORPS OF ENGINEERS	3 7
GREENSBURG 2 E	3515	WESTMORELAND	10	40 18	79 31	1225		MID	PA DEPT HIGHWAYS	C
GREENSBURG 3 SE UNITY	3516	WESTMORELAND	10	40 17	79 30	1245		6P	WESTMORELAND WTR CO	3
GREENVILLE	3526	MERCER	2	41 24	80 23	1026	6P	6P	C. EARL MILLER	2 3 5
HANOVER	3662	YORK	15	39 48	76 59	600	8A	8A	HANOVER EVENING SUN	2 3 5 7
#HARRISBURG WB AP	3699	YORK	15	40 13	76 51	335	MID	MID	U.S. WEATHER BUREAU	2 3 5 7 C
HARRISBURG NORTH	3704	DAUPHIN	15	40 18	76 54	323		9A	GEORGE S. BEAL	3
HAWLEY	3758	WAYNE	5	41 29	75 10	880		7A	MRS.KATHERINE S.BATE	3 5
HAWLEY 1 S DAM	3761	WAYNE	5	41 28	75 11	1200	7A	7A	PA POWER + LIGHT CO	2 3 5 6 7 C
HOLLIDAYSBURG	4001	BLAIR	6	40 26	78 24	960		MID	JOHN M. RINGLER	C
HOLLISTERVILLE	4008	WAYNE	5	41 23	75 26	1360		8A	PA POWER + LIGHT CO	3
#HOLTWOOD	4019	LANCASTER	15	39 50	76 20	187	MID	8A	PA POWER + LIGHT CO	2 3 5 7 C
HOME	4027	INDIANA	1	40 45	79 06	1220		MID	MRS. EDNA M. BUSH	C
HONESDALE 4 NW	4043	WAYNE	5	41 37	75 19	1410		9A	GEORGE C. WILLIAMS	3
HONESDALE 6 NNW	4044	WAYNE	5	41 39	75 17	1050		MID	FRIEND E. WALTER	C
HOOVERSVILLE	4058	SOMERSET	4	40 09	78 55	1660		7A	PA ELECTRIC CO	3 7
HOP BOTTOM 2 SE	4066	SUSQUEHANNA	15	41 43	75 43	900		7A	JOSEPH J. SANSUSKAS	3
HUNTINGDON	4159	HUNTINGDON	6	40 29	78 01	610	7A	7A	MRS JANET I. VAUGHN	2 3 5
HUNTSDALE	4166	CUMBERLAND	15	40 06	77 18	610		8A	METRO P. DOROSH	3 C
HYNDMAN	4190	BEDFORD	12	39 49	78 43	920		8A	MRS.GERTRUDE M.BURTON	3
INDIANA 3 SE	4214	INDIANA	4	40 36	79 07	1102	7P	7A	CLYMER WATER SVC CO	2 3 5 7 C
IRWIN	4276	WESTMORELAND	10	40 20	79 42	1100	5P	5P	WESTMORELAND WTR CO	2 3 5
JACKSON SUMMIT	4304	TIOGA	15	41 57	77 01	1690		MID	ARCHIE LAIN	C
JAMESTOWN 2 NW	4325	CRAWFORD	2	41 30	80 28	1050	8A	8A	PA DEPT FRST + WTRS	2 3 5 6 C
JIM THORPE	4370	CARBON	9	40 52	75 45	830	5P	5P	HENRY S. HAAK	2 3 5
#JOHNSTOWN	4385	CAMBRIA	4	40 20	78 55	1214	9A	9A	JOHNSTOWN TRIBUNE	2 3 5
JOHNSTOWN 2	4390	CAMBRIA	4	40 19	78 55	1275		MID	CITY OF JOHNSTOWN	C
KANE 1 NNE	4432	MC KEAN	1	41 41	78 48	1750	8A	8A	SPRING WATER CO	2 3 5 7 C
KARTHAUS	4450	CLEARFIELD	16	41 07	78 07	950		7A	JEROME S. HOWE	3
KEATING SUMMIT	4466	POTTER	1	41 41	78 11	1840		7A	EUGENE L. KREITNER	3 7
KEGG	4481	BEDFORD	6	39 59	78 43	1280	MID	MID	PA TURNPIKE COMM	2 3 5
KITTANNING LOCK 7	4611	ARMSTRONG	1	40 49	79 32	790		VAR	CORPS OF ENGINEERS	3
KREGAR 4 SE	4667	WESTMORELAND	17	40 06	79 14	2530		MID	PA TURNPIKE COMM	3
KRESGEVILLE 3 W	4672	CARBON	9	40 54	75 34	720		9A	CITY OF BETHLEHEM	3
LAFAYETTE MC KEAN PARK	4706	MC KEAN	1	41 48	78 40	2130		7A	ORIN A. BUTTERS	3
LAKEVILLE 1 NNE	4733	WAYNE	5	41 27	75 16	1460		8A	MRS. GLADYS REINEKE	3
LANCASTER 2 NE PUMP STA	4758	LANCASTER	15	40 03	76 17	255	6P	6P	LANCASTER WATER BUR	2 3 5 7
LANCASTER 2 NE FILT PL	4763	LANCASTER	15	40 03	76 17	270		MID	LANCASTER WATER BUR	C
LANDISVILLE 2 NW	4778	LANCASTER	15	40 07	76 26	360	8A	8A	PA STATE COLLEGE	2 3 5 6 C
LATROBE	4832	WESTMORELAND	4	40 19	79 23	1000		MID	WEST PENN POWER CO	INAC 6/56
LAURELTON STATE VILLAGE	4853	UNION	15	40 54	77 13	880		MID	PA DEPT OF WELFARE	C
LAWRENCEVILLE 2 S	4873	TIOGA	15	41 59	77 07	1000	7A	7A	HARRY P. HOWLAND	2 3 5 7
LEBANON 3 W	4891	LEBANON	15	40 20	76 29	460	7A	7A	LEON MILLER	2 3 5 7
LEBANON 3 SW	4896	LEBANON	15	40 19	76 28	490		MID	THOMAS DONNACHIE	C
LEHIGHTON	4934	CARBON	9	40 50	75 43	580		7A	GOODWIN S. DEFREHN	3 C
LE ROY	4972	BRADFORD	15	41 41	76 43	1040		6P	MRS.DIMMIS M.BAILEY	3
LEWIS RUN 3 S	4984	MC KEAN	1	41 50	78 39	1740		7A	RUSSELL LINEMAN	3 C
LEWISTOWN	4992	MIFFLIN	6	40 35	77 35	480	7A	7A	AMERICAN VISCOSE CO	2 3 5 7 C
LINESVILLE 5 WNW	5050	CRAWFORD	2	41 41	80 31	1020	7P	8A	MISS RETTA M. CRUMB	2 3 5
LOCK HAVEN	5104	CLINTON	16	41 08	77 27	570	7P	7A	PETER L. STEVENSON	2 3 5
LOCK HAVEN 2	5109	CLINTON	16	41 08	77 27	630		MID	HUGH F. PARKER	C
LONG POND 2 W	5160	MONROE	9	41 03	75 30	1860		7A	THOMAS MECKES	
MADERA	5336	CLEARFIELD	16	40 50	78 26	1460	7A	7A	MRS. JULIA J. SHOFF	2 3 5 C
MAHAFFEY	5342	CLEARFIELD	16	40 53	78 44	1280		7A	MISS ELLEN J. MILES	3
MAPLE GLEN	5368	MONTGOMERY	5	40 11	75 11	380		6P	FRANCES E.SCHEIBNER	3
MAPLETON DEPOT	5381	HUNTINGDON	6	40 24	77 56	580		7A	MRS. I. S. BUCHANAN	3
MARCUS HOOK	5390	DELAWARE	5	39 49	75 25	12	MID	MID	SUN OIL CO	2 3 5
MARIENVILLE 1 SW	5400	FOREST	1	41 27	79 09	1700		MID	ROY A. MARKER	C
MARION CENTER 2 SE	5408	INDIANA	1	40 45	79 02	1610		7A	CORPS OF ENGINEERS	3
MARTINSBURG 1 SW	5453	BLAIR	6	40 18	78 20	1360		MID	BLUE MT. CANNERIES	C
MARTINSBURG CAA AP	5454	BLAIR	6	40 18	78 19	1463	MID	MID	CIVIL AERO. ADM.	2 3 5 7
MATAMORAS	5470	PIKE	5	41 22	74 42	439		7A	HARRY GISLAND	3 7
MAYBURG	5490	FOREST	1	41 36	79 13	1150		7A	CORPS OF ENGINEERS	3
MC CONNELLSBURG	5526	FULTON	12	39 56	78 00	895		8A	MRS. HELEN M. SHIVES	3
MC KEESPORT	5573	ALLEGHENY	10	40 21	79 52	720		8A	NATIONAL TUBE CO	3
MEADOW RUN PONDS	5601	LUZERNE	15	41 13	75 40	1995		MID	GEORGE PEARAGE	C
MEADVILLE 1 S	5606	CRAWFORD	1	41 38	80 10	1065	8A	8A	CITY OF MEADVILLE	2 3 5 7 C
MEDIX RUN	5627	ELK	16	41 17	78 24	1100		7A	MRS.E. M. SNYDER	3 7 C
MERCER 2 NNE	5651	MERCER	2	41 15	80 13	1100	7P	7A	WILLIAM K. STRUTHERS	2 3 5
MERCER HIWAY SHED	5654	MERCER	2	41 14	80 15	1250		MID	PA DEPT HIGHWAYS	C
MERCERSBURG	5662	FRANKLIN	12	39 50	77 54	605		8A	ROLLIN P. GILBERT	3
MERWINSBURG	5676	MONROE	9	40 58	75 28	970		MID	WILLIAM D. GOULD	C
MEYERSDALE 1 ENE	5685	SOMERSET	17	39 49	79 01	2290		8A	ARTHUR B. MC CARTER	3
MIDDLETOWN OLMSTED FLD	5703	DAUPHIN	15	40 11	76 46	303	MID	MID	U. S. AIR FORCE	2 3 5
MIDLAND DAM 7	5710	BEAVER	11	40 38	80 28	689	11P	7A	CORPS OF ENGINEERS	2 3 5
MILAN 4 WNW	5732	BRADFORD	15	41 56	76 35	1448		MID	CARL A. MORRIS	C
MILANVILLE	5738	WAYNE	5	41 40	75 04	760		8A	CHARLES W. DAVIS	3
MILLERSBURG 2 E	5775	DAUPHIN	15	40 32	76 56	560		MID	RUSSELL SHEPLEY	C
MILLHEIM	5790	CENTRE	15	40 54	77 29	1090		7A	NEVIN E. BOWERSOX	3
MILLVILLE 2 SW	5817	COLUMBIA	15	41 06	76 34	860		7A	KENNETH LEIGHOW	3 C
MILROY	5825	MIFFLIN	6	40 43	77 35	770		8A	THOMAS C. HARBESON	3
MONTROSE 1 E	5915	SUSQUEHANNA	15	41 50	75 51	1630	7A	7A	WILBER W. HOOPES,JR	2 3 5 7 C
MORGANTOWN	5956	BERKS	15	40 09	75 54	595	MID	MID	PA TURNPIKE COMM	2 3 5
MT GRETNA 2 SE	6028	LANCASTER	15	40 14	76 26	670	MID	MID	PA TURNPIKE COMM	2 3 5
MT POCONO 2 N AP	6055	MONROE	5	41 09	75 22	1915	5P	5P	H. JOHN DAVIS, JR.	2 3 5 C
MOUNT UNION 1 N	6067	MIFFLIN	6	40 24	77 53	820		MID	MT UNION WTR WORKS	C
MUHLENBURG 1 SE	6090	LUZERNE	15	41 13	76 08	1110	6P	6P	THEODORE J. SAMPSON	2 3 5 7
MURRYSVILLE	6111	WESTMORELAND	10	40 26	79 42	903		MID	DAVID C. SHAW	C
MYERSTOWN	6126	LEBANON	14	40 22	76 18	480		8A	MRS.KATHLEEN MANDELL	3
NATRONA LOCK 4	6151	ALLEGHENY	1	40 37	79 43	800		7A	CORPS OF ENGINEERS	3
NEFFS MILLS 3 NE	6174	HUNTINGDON	6	40 40	77 55	900		MID	PA STATE UNIVERSITY	C
NESHAMINY FALLS	6194	BUCKS	5	40 09	74 57	60		MID	PHILA SUB WATER CO	3
NEWBURG 3 W	6225	FRANKLIN	15	40 09	77 37	745	MID	MID	PA TURNPIKE COMM	2 3 5
NEW CASTLE 1 N	6233	LAWRENCE	2	41 01	80 22	825	5P	7A	BAXTER F. JOHNSON	2 3 5 C
#NEWELL	6246	FAYETTE	10	40 05	79 54	805	12M	12M	GENERAL CHEMICAL CO	2 3 5
NEW PARK	6289	YORK	15	39 44	76 30	780		6P	CLINTON J. ALLEN	3
NEWPORT	6297	PERRY	6	40 29	77 08	400	7A	7A	MRS. FRANCES A. FRY	2 3 5 7
NEW STANTON	6310	WESTMORELAND	10	40 13	79 36	980	MID	MID	PA TURNPIKE COMM	2 3 5
NEW TRIPOLI	6326	LEHIGH	14	40 41	75 45	570		6P	FRED C. OSWALD	3
NORRISTOWN	6370	MONTGOMERY	14	40 07	75 21	75	MID	8A	GEORGE M. BOONE	2 3 5
NORTH EAST 2 SE	6396	ERIE	8	42 12	79 49	1060		9A	ELLSWORTH WEAVER	3
ORWELL 3 N	6621	BRADFORD	15	41 55	76 16	1620		8A	WILLIAM I. BROWN	3
PALM	6681	MONTGOMERY	14	40 26	75 32	385		8A	FRED C. ESCHBACH	3
#PALMERTON	6689	CARBON	9	40 48	75 37	435	MID	MID	NEW JERSEY ZINC CO	2 3 5 C
PALMYRA	6694	LEBANON	15	40 18	76 35	480		7P	CARL E. RHOADS	3
PARKER	6721	ARMSTRONG	1	41 05	79 41	1140		7A	LOUIS A. MALARKEY	3
PARKER 1 E	6724	CLARION	1	41 06	79 40	1100		MID	P. M. NEELY	C
PAUPACK 2 WNW	6762	PIKE	5	41 24	75 14	1360		8A	MISS L. VETTERLEIN	
PECKS POND	6786	PIKE	5	41 17	75 06	1380		9A	MRS. CARRIE NESS	
#PHIL DREXEL INST OF TEC	6879	PHILADELPHIA	14	39 57	75 11	30	MID	MID	FRANCIS K. DAVIS,JR	2 3 5
PHILADELPHIA WB AP	6889	PHILADELPHIA	5	39 53	75 14	13	MID	MID	U.S. WEATHER BUREAU	2 3 5 7 C
#PHILADELPHIA PT BREEZE	6899	PHILADELPHIA	5	39 55	75 12	32	MID	MID	ATLANTIC REFINING	2 3 5 C
PHILADELPHIA SHAWMONT	6904	PHILADELPHIA	5	40 02	75 15	70	7P	7P	SCHUYLKILL NAVIG CO	2 3 5
#PHILADELPHIA CITY	6909	PHILADELPHIA	5	39 57	75 09	26	9A	9A	USN HYDROGRAPHIC OFF	2 3 5 C
PHILIPSBURG CAA AP	6916	CENTRE	6	40 54	78 05	1918	8P	8P	CIVIL AERO. ADM.	2 3 5 7 C
PHOENIXVILLE 1 E	6927	CHESTER	14	40 07	75 30	105	6P	MID	PHILA SUB WATER CO	2 3 5 C
PIKES CREEK	6939	LUZERNE	15	41 18	76 08	1320		MID	HARRY SHELDON	3 C
PIMPLE HILL	6944	MONROE	9	41 02	75 30	2215	9A	9A	PA DEPT FRST + WTRS	2 3 5 6 7
PINE GROVE 1 NE	6954	SCHUYLKILL	15	40 34	76 22	535		8A	PA POWER + LIGHT CO	3
PITTSBURGH WB AP 2	6993	ALLEGHENY	11	40 30	80 13	1151	MID	MID	U.S. WEATHER BUREAU	2 3 5 7 C
#PITTSBURGH WB CITY	6997	ALLEGHENY	11	40 27	80 00	749	MID	MID	U.S. WEATHER BUREAU	2 3 5 C
PLEASANT MOUNT 1 W	7029	WAYNE	5	41 44	75 27	1800	8A	8A	PA FISH COMM	2 3 5 7 C
PORT CLINTON	7116	SCHUYLKILL	14	40 35	76 02	450	7A	7A	MRS. ADA E. RARICK	2 3 5 C
PORTLAND	7127	NORTHAMPTON	5	40 55	75 06	297		8A	JOINT BRIDGE COMM	INAC 1/56
POTTSTOWN	7149	MONTGOMERY	14	40 15	75 39	160		8A	MILES E. SMITH	3
POTTSVILLE	7161	SCHUYLKILL	14	40 42	76 11	690		8A	LLOYD E. HELLER	3
PUNXSUTAWNEY	7217	JEFFERSON	1	40 57	79 00	1298		MID	JOHN VOLANSKY	C
PUTNEYVILLE 2 SE DAM	7229	ARMSTRONG	1	40 55	79 17	1270	8A	8A	CORPS OF ENGINEERS	2 3 5 C
QUAKERTOWN 1 E	7239	BUCKS	5	40 26	75 20	490	5P	5P	DENNIS K. FLUCK	2 3 5
RAYMOND	7310	POTTER	13	41 52	77 52	2220		7A	MRS. RACHEL LANGAN	C
#READING WB CITY	7318	BERKS	14	40 20	75 58	266	MID	MID	U.S. WEATHER BUREAU	2 3 5 7 C
RENOVO	7409	CLINTON	16	41 20	77 46	660		7A	MRS. CAROLINE BAIRD	3
RENOVO 5 S	7410	CLINTON	16	41 14	77 46	2035		MID	C. F. GILLETTE	C
REW	7425	MC KEAN	1	41 54	78 32	2250		8A	HAROLD C. MEALY	3
RICES LANDING L 6	7443	GREENE	10	39 57	80 00	775		7A	CORPS OF ENGINEERS	3
RIDGWAY 3 W	7477	ELK	1	41 25	78 47	1420	7A	7A	BOROUGH OF RIDGWAY	2 5
ROCHESTER 1 N	7540	BEAVER	2	40 43	80 18	900		MID	DUQUESNE LIGHT CO	C
RUSH	7694	SUSQUEHANNA	15	41 47	76 03	1000		9A	MISS MAUDE MC CAIN	3
RUSHVILLE	7727	SUSQUEHANNA	15	41 47	76 07	870		7A	CARL KOPATZ	3
SAFE HARBOR	7732	LANCASTER	15	39 55	76 23	270		MID	S.H.WATER POWER CORP	C
SAGAMORE 1 S	7739	INDIANA	1	40 46	79 14	1320		7A	CORPS OF ENGINEERS	3
SALINA 3 W	7782	WESTMORELAND	7	40 31	79 33	1109	6P	6P	MUN AUTH WSTMRLD CO	2 3 5
SAXTON	7846	BEDFORD	6	40 12	78 15	780		8A	MRS.ALVERTA L.HOLMES	3 C
SCANDIA 2 E	7855	WARREN	1	41 55	79 01	2040		MID	DAVID R. ANDERSON	C
SCHENLEY LOCK 5	7863	ARMSTRONG	1	40 41	79 40	783		VAR	CORPS OF ENGINEERS	3
#SCRANTON	7902	LACKAWANNA	15	41 25	75 40	746	7A	7A	U.S. POST OFFICE	2 3 5
SCRANTON WB AIRPORT	7905	LUZERNE	15	41 20	75 44	956	MID	MID	U.S. WEATHER BUREAU	2 3 5 7 C

STATION INDEX

Station	Index No.	County	Drainage ‡	Latitude	Longitude	Elevation	Observation Time Temp.	Observation Time Precip.	Observer	Refer To Tables
.INSGROVE CAA AP	7931	SNYDER	15	40 49	76 52	437	MID	MID	CIVIL AERO. ADM.	2 3 5 7
.LLERSVILLE 2 NW	7938	BUCKS	5	40 23	75 20	530		MID	SELLERSVILLE WTR CO	C
ADE GAP	7965	HUNTINGDON	6	40 11	77 52	1000		MID	MRS. HELEN M. PYLE	C
AMOKIN	7978	NORTHUMBLAND	15	40 48	76 33	770		8A	ROARING CRK WTR CO	3
EFFIELD 6 W	8026	WARREN	1	41 41	79 09	1940		MID	L. N. HANSON	C
IPPENSBURG	8073	FRANKLIN	15	40 03	77 32	709	4P	4P	KEITH D. ALLEN	2 3 5 7
IPPINGPORT WB	8078	BEAVER	11	40 37	80 26	740	MID	MID	U.S. WEATHER BUREAU	2 3 5 7 C
NNEMAHONING	8145	CAMERON	16	41 19	78 05	790		7A	MRS.FRANCES CALDWELL	3
IPPERY ROCK	8184	BUTLER	2	41 04	80 03	1345	7P	7A	WALTER D. ALBERT	2 3 5 7
ETHPORT HIGHWAY SHED	8190	MC KEAN	1	41 48	78 27	1510		MID	PA DEPT HIGHWAYS	C
MERSET FAIRVIEW ST	8244	SOMERSET	17	40 01	79 05	2140		7A	HOWARD G. PECK	3
MERSET MAIN ST	8249	SOMERSET	17	40 01	79 05	2150	6P	6P	DAVID L. GROVE	2 3 5
UTH CANAAN 1 NE	8275	WAYNE	5	41 31	75 24	1400		MID	EUGENE M. COOK	C
UTH MOUNTAIN	8308	FRANKLIN	12	39 51	77 30	1520		7A	PA DEPT OF HEALTH	3
RINGBORO	8359	CRAWFORD	8	41 48	80 23	900	8A	8A	SPRINGBORO BOROUGH	2 3 5 C
RING GROVE	8379	YORK	15	39 52	76 52	470		4P	P. H. GLATFELTER CO	3 C
RINGS 1 SW	8395	SOMERSET	17	39 44	79 10	2500	8P	8P	ALLEN E. YODER	2 3 5 7
ATE COLLEGE	8449	CENTRE	16	40 48	77 52	1175	MID	MID	PA STATE COLLEGE	2 3 5 6 C
RAUSSTOWN	8570	BERKS	14	40 29	76 11	600		8A	JACOB KLAHR	3
RONGSTOWN	8589	INDIANA	4	40 33	78 55	1880		MID	HARRY F. BENNETT	C
ROUDSBURG	8596	MONROE	5	40 59	75 12	480	11P	11P	WILLIAM MAGERTY	2 3 5 C
UMP CREEK	8610	JEFFERSON	1	41 01	78 50	1320		7A	CORPS OF ENGINEERS	3
NBURY	8668	NORTHUMBLAND	15	40 51	76 48	440		7A	CHARLES W. BAYLER	3 C
SQUEHANNA	8692	SUSQUEHANNA	15	41 57	75 36	1020		7A	MRS. LAURA A.BENSON	3
TERSVILLE	8699	ALLEGHENY	17	40 14	79 48	765		7A	FRANK E. MARSH	3
MAQUA	8758	SCHUYLKILL	14	40 48	75 58	830		8A	MRS. MARY L.ROBERTS	3
MAQUA 4 N DAM	8763	SCHUYLKILL	14	40 51	75 59	1120		7A	PANTHER VLY WTR CO	3 C
MARACK 2 S FIRE TWR	8770	CLINTON	16	41 24	77 51	2220	7A	7A	JAMES E. SWARTZ	2 3 5 T
ONESTA 2 SE DAM	8873	FOREST	1	41 29	79 26	1200	8A	8A	CORPS OF ENGINEERS	2 3 5 7 C
TUSVILLE	8885	CRAWFORD	1	41 38	79 40	1550		MID	PA ELECTRIC CO	C
TUSVILLE WATER WORKS	8888	CRAWFORD	1	41 38	79 42	1220	7P	7P	CITY OF TITUSVILLE	2 3 5
RPEDO 4 W	8901	WARREN	1	41 47	79 32	1735		7A	MRS. LILY B. GARBER	3
WANDA	8905	BRADFORD	15	41 46	76 26	760	7P	7A	MRS. M. O. PARKS	2 3 5 7 C
WER CITY 5 SW	8910	DAUPHIN	15	40 31	76 37	745		6P	HARRISBURG WTR DEPT	3 7
OY	8959	BRADFORD	15	41 47	76 47	1100		7A	JENNIE L. BALLARD	3
WNELTON	8989	INDIANA	4	40 27	79 23	890		MID	MRS. MARY E. WEIMER	C
RTLEPOINT 4 NE	9002	MC KEAN	1	41 54	78 16	1640		7A	ROBERT D. STRAIT	3
RONE 4 NE BALD EAGLE	9024	BLAIR	6	40 43	78 12	1020		7A	FREDERICK L. FRIDAY	3 C
ION CITY	9042	ERIE	1	41 54	79 50	1325		7A	FORREST M. BRALEY	3 C
IONTOWN	9050	FAYETTE	10	39 54	79 44	1040	10P	10P	WM. W. MARSTELLER	2 3 5
PER DARBY	9074	DELAWARE	5	39 58	75 18	222	7P	7P	PHIL. SUB.TRANS. CO	2 3 5
ICA	9099	VENANGO	1	41 26	79 57	1030		7A	MRS.FLORENCE MILLER	3
NDERGRIFT	9128	WESTMORELAND	7	40 36	79 33	800		7A	UNITED ENG+FNDRY CO	3
NDERGRIFT 2 W	9133	WESTMORELAND	7	40 36	79 36	995		MID	EUGENE R. YOUNG	C
RGINVILLE	9196	BERKS	14	40 31	75 52	350		8A	MRS. MARY M. WRIGHT	3

Station	Index No.	County	Drainage ‡	Latitude	Longitude	Elevation	Observation Time Temp.	Observation Time Precip.	Observer	Refer To Tables
VOWINCKEL	9206	CLARION	1	41 25	79 14	1620		8A	PA DEPT FRST + WTRS	3
VOWINCKEL 1 WSW	9209	CLARION	1	41 24	79 15	1610		8A	PA DEPT FRST + WTRS	3
WARREN	9298	WARREN	1	41 51	79 08	1280	7P	7A	GILBERT H. NEILER	2 3 5
WASHINGTON	9312	WASHINGTON	11	40 11	80 14	1200		MID	PA DEPT HIGHWAYS	C
WATSONTOWN	9345	NORTHUMBLAND	16	41 05	76 52	490		7A	WILLIAM BIRD	3
WAYNESBURG 2 W	9362	GREENE	10	39 54	80 13	980	6P	7A	RALPH L. AMOS	2 3 5
WAYNESBURG 1 E	9367	GREENE	10	39 54	80 10	940		MID	SEWAGE DISPOSAL PLT	C
WEBSTER MILLS 3 SW	9380	FULTON	12	39 49	78 05	920		MID	WILLIAM D. COVER	C
WELLSBORO 3 S	9408	TIOGA	16	41 43	77 16	1920	7A	7A	MARION L. SHUMWAY	2 3 5
WELLSBORO 2 E	9412	TIOGA	16	41 45	77 16	1550		MID	MRS. IDA S. MAYNARD	C
WELLSVILLE	9420	YORK	15	40 03	76 57	500	5P	5P	D. D. HOOVER	2 3 5
WERNERSVILLE 1 W	9430	BERKS	14	40 20	76 06	405		8A	CHARLES A. GRUBER	3
WEST CHESTER	9464	CHESTER	5	39 58	75 36	440	8A	8A	DAILY LOCAL NEWS	2 3 5
WEST GROVE 1 E	9503	CHESTER	5	39 49	75 49	440		8A	CONARD-PYLE CO	3
WEST HICKORY	9507	FOREST	1	41 34	79 25	1090		8A	MRS.HELEN F.KINNEAR	3
WHITESBURG	9655	ARMSTRONG	1	40 45	79 24	1530		7A	CORPS OF ENGINEERS	3
WILKES-BARRE	9702	LAZERNE	15	41 15	75 52	610		7A	MRS. MARY G. MIRHAK	3
WILLIAMSBURG	9714	BLAIR	6	40 28	78 12	860		7A	MYRON K. BIDDLE	3
WILLIAMSPORT WB AP	9728	LYCOMING	16	41 15	76 55	527	MID	MID	U.S. WEATHER BUREAU	2 3 5 7 C
WIND GAP	9781	NORTHAMPTON	5	40 51	75 18	720		MID	OWEN R. PARRY	C
WOLFSBURG	9823	BEDFORD	6	40 03	78 32	1190		7A	WALTER C. RICE	3
YORK 3 SSW PUMP STA	9933	YORK	15	39 55	76 45	390	5P	5P	YORK WATER COMPANY	2 3 5
YORK 2 S FILTER PLANT	9938	YORK	15	39 56	76 44	640		MID	YORK WATER COMPANY	C
YORK HAVEN	9950	YORK	15	40 07	76 43	310		8A	METROPOL EDISON CO	3
YOUNGSVILLE	9966	WARREN	1	41 51	79 20	1225		MID	HENRY GARLETT	C
ZION GROVE	9990	SCHUYLKILL	15	40 54	76 13	940		7A	JAMES D. TEETER	3
ZIONSVILLE 3 SE	9995	LEHIGH	14	40 27	75 27	660		7A	LESLIE HOWATT	3
NEW STATIONS										
BERNE	0599	BERKS	14	40 31	76 00	325		7A	FLOYD W. TRUMP	3

‡ 1-ALLEGHENY; 2-BEAVER; 3- 4-CONEMAUGH; 5-DELAWARE; 6-JUNIATA; 7-KISKIMINETAS; 8-LAKE ERIE; 9-LEHIGH; 10-MONANGAHELA; 11-OHIO; 12-POTOMAC; 13-LAKE ONTARIO; 14-SCHUYLKILL; 15-SUSQUEHANNA; 16-WEST BRANCH; 17-YOUGHIOGHENY

REFERENCE NOTES

Additional information regarding the climate of Pennsylvania may be obtained by writing to the State Climatologist at Weather Bureau Airport Station, Harrisburg State Airport, New Cumberland, Pennsylvania, or to any Weather Bureau Office near you.

Figures and letters following the station name, such as 12 SSW, indicate distance in miles and direction from the post office.

Delayed data and corrections will be carried only in the June and December issues of this bulletin.

Monthly and seasonal snowfall and heating degree days for the preceding 12 months will be carried in the June issue of this bulletin.

Stations appearing in the Index, but for which data are not listed in the tables, either are missing or were received too late to be included in this issue.

Divisions, as used in Table 2, became effective with data for September 1956.

Unless otherwise indicated, dimensional units used in this bulletin are: Temperature in °F, precipitation and evaporation in inches, and wind movement in miles. Monthly degree day totals are the sums of the negative departures of average daily temperatures from 65° F

Evaporation is measured in the standard Weather Bureau type pan of 4 foot diameter unless otherwise shown by footnote following Table 6.

Long-term means for full-time stations (those shown in the Station Index as "U. S. Weather Bureau") are based on the period 1921-1950, adjusted to represent observations taken at the present location. Long-term means for all stations except full-time Weather Bureau stations are based on the period 1931-155.

Water equivalent samples published in Table 7 are necessarily taken from different points for successive observations; consequently occasional drifting and other causes of local variability in the snowpack result in apparent inconsistencies in the record. Water equivalent of snow on the ground is measured at selected stations when two or more inches of snow are on the ground.

Data in Tables 3, 5, and 6 and snowfall in Table 7, when published, are for the 24 hours ending at time of observation. The Station Index lists observation times in the standard of time in local use.

Snow on ground in Table 7 is at observation time for all except Weather Bureau and CAA stations. For these stations snow on ground values are at 7:30 a.m., E.S.T.

- \- No record in Tables 3, 6, 7 and the Station Index. No record in Tables 2 and 5, is indicated by no entry. Consult the annual issue of this publication for interpolated monthly precipitation totals.
- \+ And also on a later date or dates.
- * Amount included in following measurement, time distribution unknown.
- // Gage is equipped with a windshield.
- \# Thermometers are generally exposed in a shelter located a few feet above sod-covered ground; however, the reference indicates that the thermometers are exposed in a shelter located on the roof of a building.
- AM Data based on observational day ending before noon.
- B Adjusted to a full month.
- C In the "Refer to Tables" column in the Station Index the letter "C" indicates recorder stations. These stations are processed for special purposes and are published later in "Hourly Precipitation Data".
- D Water equivalent of snowfall wholly or partly estimated, using a ratio of 1 inch water equivalent to every 10 inches of new snowfall.
- G In the "Refer to Tables" column in the Station Index the letter "G" indicates that soil temperatures are published.
- M One to nine days of record missing; see Table 5 for detailed daily record. Degree day data, if carried for this station, have been adjusted to represent the valur for a full month.
- R Amounts from recording gage (These amounts are essentially accurate but may vary slightly from the amounts to be published later in Hourly Precipitation Data.
- SS This entry in time of observation column in Station Index means observation made near sunset.
- T Trace, an amount too small to measure.
- Y Includes total for previous month.
- VAR This entry in time of observation column in Station Index means variable.

Information concerning the history of changes in locations, elevations, exposure etc. of substations through 1955 may be found in the publication 'Substation History' for this state, soon to be issued. That publication, when available, may be obtained from the Superintendent of Documents, Government Printing Office, Washington 25, D. C. at a price to be announced. Similar information for regular Weather Bureau stations may be found in the latest issues of Local Climatological Data, Annual for the respective stations, obtained as indicated above, price 15 cents.

Subscription Price: 20 cents per copy, monthly and annual; $2.50 per year. (Yearly subscription includes the Annual Summary). Checks, and money orders should be made payable to the Superintendent of Documents. Remittance and correspondence regarding subscriptions should be sent to the Superintendent of Documents, Government Printing Office, Washington 25, D. C.

WRC., Asheville, N. C. --- 1/10/57 --- 1100

U. S. DEPARTMENT OF COMMERCE
SINCLAIR WEEKS, Secretary
WEATHER BUREAU
F. W. REICHELDERFER, Chief

CLIMATOLOGICAL DATA

PENNSYLVANIA

DECEMBER 1956
Volume LXI No. 12

ASHEVILLE: 1957

PENNSYLVANIA - DECEMBER 1956

WEATHER SUMMARY

GENERAL

Very warm weather, interrupted by short periods with temperatures that were down to only about seasonal values, far outweighed cold weather at the beginning and end of the month to produce average temperatures that were generally four to eight degrees higher than the long-term means. Comparative data in records of full time Weather Bureau stations indicated this as the warmest December since 1923 at Reading, since 1931 at Allentown, Philadelphia and Harrisburg, and since 1941 at Pittsburgh and Erie. Temperature extremes ranged from 74° on the 7th at Norristown to -6° on the 31st at Pleasant Mount 1 W.

Precipitation totals in the Northwest Plateau Division were fairly close to the long-term mean values in most instances, but elsewhere an appreciable excess of precipitation was generally indicated. The greatest amount for one day was 2.08 inches measured at Springs on the 14th. Totals for the month ranged from 1.94 inches at Farrell-Sharon to 6.23 inches at Kregar 4 SE. The total snowfall was generally very light in southeastern Pennsylvania and varied from light to fairly heavy in other areas of the State. Deficient sunshine and heavy daytime cloudiness were indicated at all stations recording data pertinent to these phenomena.

WEATHER DETAILS

Moderately cold weather on the 1st became mild by the 3rd and very warm the 6th to the 8th. Light precipitation, mostly in the form of snow, occurred the 1st and 2nd except in the southeastern section. Moderate amounts of precipitation fell as rain the 7th-8th and mostly as snow the 9th. Colder air moved into the State late on the 8th and seasonal temperatures prevailed the 9th and 10th. Mild weather reappeared the 11th and continued on the scene, with the exception of minor interruptions the 14th and 19th, through the 24th. Precipitation occurred very frequently, almost daily in some areas, during the 2-week period ending the 24th. Daily amounts were generally light to moderate with the exception of heavy falls over much of the State on the 14th. Most of the precipitation occurred as rain; however, a combination of sleet and freezing rain reached serious proportions as an ice storm in the Pocono Mountain area the 14th-15th.

Temperatures were down to seasonal levels the 25th through the 29th. An Arctic air mass that was centered just south of Hudson Bay early on the 29th drifted southeastward and spread over Pennsylvania to produce the coldest weather of the month in most areas on the 30th. Considerable warming on the 31st raised temperatures to about the seasonal average as the month ended. Precipitation occurrences continued on an almost daily basis the final week of December, generally as light to moderate amounts of snow.

WEATHER EFFECTS

Very warm weather and above average rainfall kept farm lands too soft for use of equipment most of the month and caused delays in hauling of manure and picking of corn. Rainfall on the unfrozen ground added much moisture to ground supplies and caused runoff to be excessive in most streams. Low quality roughage continued to affect milk production and the output was below the levels of a year ago for the third consecutive month. Wet weather made it difficult for poultrymen to keep litter dry and reports of disease in flocks were common. Conditions were favorable for late plantings of winter grains to attain good root systems but some early stands showed excessive fall growth.

DESTRUCTIVE STORMS

Tree limbs and wires were coated with up to 6 inches of ice in the Pocono Mountain area the 14th-15th. Many trees and wire lines were felled during the two day ice storm. Property damages were rather light but inconveniences due to failures of electric power were great. Many residences were without electricity for many hours, and for several days in some instances.

FLOODS

Flood stages were exceeded on the Monongahela and Youghiogheny Rivers as a result of moderate to heavy rains the 13th-14th. Low-lying areas and highways in the Meyersdale-Confluence section of the Youghiogheny River Basin were under water. Flood stages on the Monongahela River were exceeded by 3 feet at Lock 4, Charleroi; 1 foot at Lock 5, Brownsville, and Lock 2, Braddock; while flood stage was just reached at Lock 3, Elizabeth.

Small streams in Green and Washington Counties overflowed as a result of heavy rains the 14th causing minor property damage, and one man was killed when he slipped from a bridge where he had been clearing debris.

J. T. B. Beard, Climatologist
Weather Records Processing Center
Chattanooga, Tennessee

CLIMATOLOGICAL DATA

TABLE 2

PENNSYLVANIA
DECEMBER 1956

Station	Temperature: Average Maximum	Average Minimum	Average	Departure From Long Term Means	Highest	Date	Lowest	Date	Degree Days	No. of Days Max 90° or Above	Max 32° or Below	Min 32° or Below	Min 0° or Below	Precipitation: Total	Departure From Long Term Means	Greatest Day	Date	Snow, Sleet: Total	Max Depth on Ground	Date	No. of Days: 10 or More	50 or More	1.00 or More
POCONO MOUNTAINS																							
FREELAND	41.0	26.8	33.9	6.6	61	7+	5	30	957	0	6	23	0	6.07	2.49	.95	15	5.3	3	29	14	6	0
HAWLEY 1 S DAM AM	40.5	23.6	32.1		64	8	2	31	1012	0	5	28	0	4.20		1.21	15	2.6	2	10	9	2	1
MT POCONO 2 N AP	39.5	23.6	31.6	5.9	62	7	-3	31	1031	0	9	26	1	3.93	.37			5.9					
MUHLENBURG 1 SE	41.7	23.9	32.8		58	7	3	30+	989	0	4	27	0	4.45		1.32	14	10.0	4	29+	10	3	1
PIMPLE HILL AM	38.6	24.9	31.8		60	8	0	30	1026	0	11	25	1	5.18		1.11	15	7.2	3	31	12	4	1
PLEASANT MOUNT 1 W AM	37.2	21.9	29.6		58	7	-6	31	1093	0	8	28	1	4.19	.92	.70	15	15.0	6	31	14	2	0
SCRANTON AM	42.7	26.5	34.6	3.7	60	8	6	30	937	0	3	25	0	3.80	1.54	.95	15	3.2			11	1	0
SCRANTON WB AIRPORT	41.9	26.5	34.2	4.6	60	7	5	30	943	0	4	22	0	3.24	.87	1.26	14	5.6	2	10+	7	1	1
STROUDSBURG	42.8	24.1	33.5	3.2	64	7	4	30+	969	0	2	24	0	4.71	1.28	1.90	14	3.5	1	9+	9	3	1
DIVISION			32.7											4.42				6.5					
EAST CENTRAL MOUNTAINS																							
ALLENTOWN WB AP R	45.1	28.5	36.8	5.7	63	7	14	30	864	0	1	21	0	4.74	1.72	1.72	14	1.1	T	10+	9	3	1
ALLENTOWN GAS CO AM	45.5	29.2	37.4	5.3	64	8	14	30+	849	0	1	19	0	4.66	1.43	1.13	15	T	T	10	9	3	1
BETHLEHEM LEHIGH UNIV	45.4	32.2	38.8	5.5	64	7	16	30	805	0	1	13	0	4.57	1.30			.3	0				
JIM THORPE	46.2M	28.0M	37.1M	6.7	65	7	11	30+	869	0	1	15	0	3.89	.09	1.42	14	1.0	1	27+	9	2	1
PALMERTON	44.4	27.9	36.2	4.9	63	7	12	30	889	0	1	22	0	4.39	1.66	1.46	14	T	T	3+	9	3	1
PORT CLINTON AM																							
QUAKERTOWN 1 E	47.2	29.7	38.5	7.1	62	7+	14	19+	814	0	1	18	0	4.32	.93	1.43	14				10	2	1
DIVISION			37.5											4.43				.5					
SOUTHEASTERN PIEDMONT																							
CHESTER AM	50.0M	32.6M	41.3M		69	8	16	20	730	0	0	11	0	3.45		.85	14						0
COATESVILLE 1 SW AM	47.2	30.1	38.7	5.9	69	8	14	31	811	0	1	16	0	3.09	-.67	.67	14	.0	0		9	2	0
COLUMBIA	49.0	32.0	40.5		66	7	12	31	752	0	1	16	0	3.49		1.38	14	T	0		10	2	1
DEVAULT 1 W	48.8	27.1	38.0		70	7	11	30	831	0	0	23	0	3.49		.70	9	T	0		11	2	0
EPHRATA	47.7	32.2	40.0	7.1	64	7	16	31	769	0	1	16	0	4.83	1.72	1.53	14	T	0		11	2	1
GEORGE SCHOOL	49.3	31.7	40.5	7.1	69	7	14	31	751	0	1	16	0	3.57	.29	1.17	14	.0	0		8	2	1
HOLTWOOD	47.3	34.1	40.7	6.1	64	7	21	30	744	0	1	13	0	3.27	.73	.83	14	T	T	28	9	2	0
LANCASTER 2 NE PUMP STA	48.6	31.7	40.2	7.1	65	7	17	31	763	0	1	16	0	3.45	.33	1.34	14	T	0		12	2	1
LANDISVILLE 2 NW AM	45.3	28.9	37.1		62	8	13	31	859	0	1	18	0	3.87		.75	15	.2	0		9	3	0
LEBANON 3 W AM	45.4	31.1	38.3	6.3	62	8	16	31	822	0	1	15	0	4.89	1.55	.94	15	.4	T	10+	11	5	0
MARCUS HOOK	48.8	35.0	41.9	3.4	65	8	21	30+	706	0	1	10	0	3.80	.84	1.21	14	T	T	26	11	2	1
MIDDLETOWN OLMSTED FLD	47.0	33.2	40.1	7.1	61	8	20	19+	763	0	1	13	0	4.39	1.68	1.26	14	.7	T	9	10	3	1
MORGANTOWN	46.6	29.9	38.3		68	7	14	30	821	0	1	20	0	2.97		1.00	14				10	2	1
MT GRETNA 2 SE	47.0	31.6	39.3		68	8	12	30	789	0	1	18	0	4.64		1.40	14	.0	0		10	3	1
NORRISTOWN	50.0	34.0	42.0		74	7	19	30	703	0	1	13	0	3.62		.79	15	T	0			4	0
PHIL DREXEL INST OF TEC	50.6	37.7	44.2		70	7	24	30	635	0	1	5	0	3.13		1.00	14	T	0		9	2	1
PHILADELPHIA WB AP R	49.3	34.0	41.7	5.8	69	7	20	30	718	0	1	11	0	3.70	1.03	1.25	14	.2	T	27	10	2	1
PHILADELPHIA PT BREEZE	50.5	38.2	44.4	7.8	69	7	25	30	632	0	0	8	0	3.60		1.37	14	T	0				1
PHILADELPHIA SHAWMONT	50.5	34.3	42.4	7.5	72	7	18	19	693	0	0	11	0										
PHILADELPHIA CITY RAM	49.6	37.2	43.4	6.0	68	7	23	30	659	0	1	8	0	2.69	-.08	1.10	14	.0	0		7	1	1
PHOENIXVILLE 1 E	51.2	32.4M	41.8M	8.0	65	7	16	31	729	0	0	12	0	3.76	.55	1.57	14	.0	0		10	2	1
READING WB CITY R	47.7	34.0	40.9	6.1	66	7	20	30	741	0	1	12	0	4.27	1.47	1.26	14	.1	T	27	10	3	1
UPPER DARBY	49.8	34.2	42.0		72	7	19	31	707	0	1	13	0	3.44		1.43	14	T	0		8	1	1
WEST CHESTER AM	46.8	32.1	39.5	6.1	60	7+	17	30	784	0	0	11	0	3.73	-.03	.84	13	T	0		8	3	0
DIVISION			40.7											3.70				.1					
LOWER SUSQUEHANNA																							
ARENDTSVILLE AM	47.7	30.6	39.2	6.5	70	8	12	31	796	0	1	18	0	4.12	1.02	.90	14	.2	T	1	9	4	0
CARLISLE	48.0	32.3	40.2	8.3	68	7	15	31	762	0	1	17	0	5.47	2.55	1.85	14	1.0	T	27	8	5	1
CHAMBERSBURG 1 ESE	48.1	31.5	39.8	6.7	69	7	17	30	773	0	1	17	0	5.05	2.30	1.55	14	1.5	0				1
GETTYSBURG AM	49.2	32.7	41.0	8.2	70	8	18	30	739	0	1	15	0	3.64	.50	.91	14	.4			7	T	0
HANOVER AM	49.5	31.3	40.4	5.9	70	8	17	30+	754	0	1	18	0	3.86	.82	.91	24	T	T	27	9	3	0
HARRISBURG WB AP R	47.4	32.9	40.2	6.3	66	7	19	30	762	0	1	13	0	4.26	1.70	1.24	14	.7	T	10+	12	4	1
NEWBURG 3 W																							
SHIPPENSBURG	49.2	32.5	40.9	8.0	70	7	15	31	743	0	1	15	0	5.39	2.27	1.81	14	1.0	T	30	9	4	2
WELLSVILLE	49.0	30.4	39.7		65	3+	13	31	779	0	1	19	0	4.52		1.45	14	.5	0		7	3	1
YORK 3 SSW PUMP STA	51.0	32.5	41.8	8.4	70	7	16	31	713	0	1	17	0	3.38	.46	1.46	14	T	0		9	1	1
DIVISION			40.4											4.41				.6					
MIDDLE SUSQUEHANNA																							
BEAVERTOWN	44.8M	29.2M	37.0M		66	7	14	19	860	0	1	19	0										
BERWICK	45.1	29.3	37.2		60	7	11	30	854	0	1	19	0	4.16		1.50	14	2.0	2	9	10	2	1
GRATZ 1 N AM	44.0	28.8	36.4		64	8	13	31	879	0	2	19	0	2.31		.41	9	T	T	1+	8	0	0
LEWISTOWN AM	46.4	31.2	38.8		69	8	17	31	804	0	1	16	0	3.68		.89	15	.8	1	10	8	1	0
NEWPORT AM	45.7	30.2	38.0		69	8	16	19+	830	0	1	17	0	4.05	1.02	.97	15	.5	0		10	3	0
SELINSGROVE CAA AP	44.4	28.1	36.3	4.7	65	7	14	19	884	0	1	22	0	4.06	1.02	1.38	14	1.0	1	10	8	4	1
WILLIAMSPORT WB AP	43.1	28.4	35.8	4.9	57	8	12	30	899	0	1	21	0	4.28	1.61	1.17	14	6.5	2	10	10	2	1
DIVISION			37.1											3.76				1.8					
UPPER SUSQUEHANNA																							
CANTON 1 NW AM	39.1	25.1	32.1		58	8	0	30	1013	0	9	23	1	D 3.79		.65	15	11.6	4	29+	14	2	0
DIXON AM	43.0	24.4	33.7		65	7+	1	31	962	0	3	23	0	3.75		.85	15	4.5	4	10	11	3	0
EAGLES MERE AM	37.2	24.1	30.7		56	8	-1	31	1058	0	12	25	2	4.75	.91	.97	23	14.8	8	31	13	3	0
LAWRENCEVILLE 2 S AM	41.2	24.7	33.0	4.8	62	7	2	31	985	0	4	23	0	3.25	1.32	.68	15	4.6	4	10	8	2	0
MONTROSE 1 E AM	37.1	23.3	30.2	4.1	59	7+	0	31	1073	0	13	25	1	4.15	1.51	.98	15	14.9	8	31	10	3	0

See Reference Notes Following Station Index

CLIMATOLOGICAL DATA

TABLE 2 - CONTINUED

Station		Temperature: Average Maximum	Average Minimum	Average	Departure From Long Term Means	Highest	Date	Lowest	Date	Degree Days	No. of Days Max. 90° or Above	Max. 32° or Below	Min. 32° or Below	Min. 0° or Below	Precipitation: Total	Departure From Long Term Means	Greatest Day	Date	Snow, Sleet: Total	Max. Depth on Ground	Date	No. of Days .10 or More	.50 or More	1.00 or More
TOWANDA		44.5	25.7	35.1	6.1	64	6+	1	31	920	0	1	23	0	3.65	1.45	.79	15	8.9	4	10	9	2	0
WELLSBORO 3 S	AM	38.8	24.5	31.7	4.1	59	7+	-3	31	1025	0	10	24	2	3.30	.92	.58	15	11.5	5	3+	8	2	0
DIVISION				32.4											3.81				10.1					
CENTRAL MOUNTAINS																								
BELLEFONTE 4 S	AM	44.9	28.4	36.7	6.4	62	8	12	30	873	0	1	21	0	3.94	1.39	.55	22	T			9	3	0
DU BOIS 7 E		42.4	28.1	35.3		62	8	5	30	915	0	6	20	0	4.44	1.54	1.15	9	15.0	4	9+	11	3	1
EMPORIUM 2 SSW	AM	39.8	24.1	32.0		59	7	4	30	1018	0	8	25	0	4.96		.76	9	14.4	6	10+	15	3	0
LOCK HAVEN		44.7	30.0	37.4	6.5	61	7	13	30	850	0	1	18	0	3.27	.37	.61	15	2.0	2	9+	10	1	0
MADERA	AM	42.1	23.8	33.0		59	7	4	31	986	0	5	26	0	3.99		.68	9	5.0	3	10	15	1	0
PHILIPSBURG CAA AP		39.9	27.6	33.8		60	7	7	30	959	0	7	25	0	3.30		.51	14	8.8	4	29+	11	1	0
RIDGWAY 3 W	AM	42.6	26.1	34.4	6.6	59	7+	7	19	942	0	4	22	0	4.37	1.66			11.5	6	10			0
STATE COLLEGE		43.5	31.7	37.6	7.7	62	7	12	30	842	0	3	16	0	3.45	.81	.85	14	8.0	1	26+	8	2	0
TAMARACK 2 S FIRE TWR	AM	37.7	25.2	31.5		56	8	2	31	1033	0	12	24	0	3.86		.60	9	16.5	6	3	13	1	0
DIVISION				34.6											3.95				9.0					
SOUTH CENTRAL MOUNTAINS																								
ALTOONA HORSESHOE CURVE		44.1	29.9	37.0	7.1	63	6	11	30	859	0	2	19	0	3.98	1.16	.83	14	11.5	3	29+	13	3	0
ARTEMAS 1 WNW			29.0	M				11	31				24	0					T	0				
BURNT CABINS 2 NE																								
EBENSBURG		43.3	28.8	36.1	7.7	59	6+	8	30	892	0	4	20	0	4.32	1.18	.60	21				17	2	0
EVERETT 1 SW		48.1	31.0	39.6	9.7	68	7	10	31	783	0	1	20	0	D4.12	1.38	1.30	15	2.1			11	4	1
HUNTINGDON	AM	47.8	29.1	38.5	6.9	73	8	14	31	816	0	0	20	0	3.80	.90	.78	15				13	2	0
JOHNSTOWN	AM	48.6	28.8	38.7	6.3	65	8+	10	30	811	0	1	20	0	3.23	-.35	.55	14	3.4	2	27	11	2	0
KEGG		47.6M	28.9M	38.3M		66	6	7	30	822	0	1	18	0	5.09		1.88	14	3.5	2	29	9	3	2
MARTINSBURG CAA AP		44.9	31.1	38.0		64	7	12	30	828	0	2	19	0	4.83		1.31	24	1.0	1	27	7	3	2
DIVISION				38.0											4.20				3.6					
SOUTHWEST PLATEAU																								
BAKERSTOWN 3 WNW		46.5	33.9	40.2		67	5	10	30	764	0	3	15	0	3.77		.65	9	4.5	3	30+	11	3	0
BLAIRSVILLE 6 ENE		42.7	29.3	36.0		60	6	6	30	893	0	5	18	0	4.89	1.82	.80	9	16.0	5	2+	14	2	0
BURGETTSTOWN 2 W	AM	45.7	28.2	37.0		67	6	9	30+	861	0	3	21	0	4.17		.48	9				14	0	0
BUTLER		46.1	32.7	39.4	7.9	66	6	12	30	784	0	3	18	0	3.53	.83	.47	9	15.0	5	27+	14	0	0
CLAYSVILLE 3 W		48.7	31.7	40.2	7.8	69	5	13	19	762	0	2	18	0	3.46	.60	.67	9				10	1	0
CONFLUENCE 1 SW DAM	AM	48.0	30.6	39.3		64	7	10	31	790	0	4	18	0	4.83		1.55	14	8.5	4	30+	10	2	1
DERRY		48.3	32.7	40.5	8.1	67	7	11	30	751	0	1	14	0	3.67	.48	.80	9	9.4	4	30	10	2	0
DONEGAL		43.2	26.3	34.8		58	5	4	30	931	0	6	24	0	5.29		.71	14	16.5	8	30	17	3	0
DONORA	AM	50.8	36.1	43.5	7.7	70	6	13	30	657	0	1	13	0	3.33	.85	.76	9	4.7	1	29+	10	2	0
FORD CITY 4 S DAM	AM	46.1	29.9	38.0		68	6	11	30	830	0	3	16	0	3.89		.53	9	13.5	3	27	13	1	0
INDIANA 3 SE		46.6	30.4	38.5	7.5	63	6	10	31	813	0	1	19	0	4.30	1.00	.83	9	6.8	3	27	15	1	0
IRWIN				M							0	1	11	0					2.0					
MIDLAND DAM 7		45.2	33.8	39.5	6.3	64	6	14	30	782	0	2	13	0	3.57	1.19	.53	9	8.5	4	30	13	1	0
NEW CASTLE 1 N		46.8	30.8	38.8	7.8	68	5+	14	19+	804	0	1	19	0	2.67	.09	.50	10	14.5			10	1	0
NEWELL	AM	50.7	38.7	44.7	9.7	70	6	21	30	621	0	1	6	0	3.95	1.52	.92	9				8	3	0
NEW STANTON		50.3	29.8	40.1	7.3	70	5	10	30	767	0	1	18	0	3.41	.29	.61	9	3.5			10	2	0
PITTSBURGH WB AP 2	//R	46.1	32.7	39.4	8.5	66	5+	10	30	785	0	5	15	0	3.35	.84	.57	9	11.2	4	30	11	1	0
PITTSBURGH WB CITY	R	49.5	36.0	42.8	7.6	68	5+	14	30	682	0	2	13	0	3.43	.86	.72	9	7.5			11	2	0
PUTNEYVILLE 2 SE DAM	AM	43.8	26.9	35.4		62	7+	8	30+	912	0	3	23	0	4.47		.77	9	18.5	4	10+	15	2	0
SALINA 3 W		46.9	31.9	39.4		65	5	12	30	786	0	3	15	0	3.47		.61	9	5.3	2	29+	8	3	0
SHIPPINGPORT WB		47.2	32.0	39.6		67	5+	13	30	781	0	2	16	0	3.31		.58	9	10.8	6	9	13	2	0
SLIPPERY ROCK		44.4	29.8	37.1		67	5	10	30	860	0	5	18	0	2.95		.58	9	14.0	5	10	11	1	0
SOMERSET MAIN ST		45.9	30.4	38.2	9.3	60	6+	7	30	826	0	3	17	0	4.82	1.17	1.26	14	11.2	4	30	14	2	1
SPRINGS 1 SW		44.8M	28.3M	36.6M	7.4	60	6+	6	30	872	0	4	20	0	5.05	1.80	2.08	14	8.1	4	30+	11	2	1
UNIONTOWN		50.5	34.5	42.5	7.6	72	5	12	30	690	0	2	14	0	4.76	1.51	.94	9	5.5	3	29+	12	2	0
WAYNESBURG 2 W		50.6	31.7	41.2	7.2	68	6+	13	19+	731	0	2	18	0	4.01	1.22	.80	14	5.0	3	30	9	2	0
DIVISION				39.3											3.93				9.6					
NORTHWEST PLATEAU																								
BRADFORD 4 W RES		39.7	24.7	32.2	4.6	57	7	2	30	1006	0	8	24	0										
BROOKVILLE CAA AIRPORT		41.7	28.3	35.0	7.0	60	6	6	30	920	0	6	20	0	4.51	1.44	.71	9	15.6	6	30	15	2	0
CLARION 3 SW		44.0	28.3	36.2		61	5+	7	30	887	0	2	21	0	3.73	.43	.74	9	11.7	5	30	14	1	0
CORRY		40.5	26.7	33.6	5.0	59	6+	7	30	966	0	7	21	0	4.04	.61	.62	7	11.0	6	2	12	2	0
COUDERSPORT 3 NW		38.8	22.7	30.8		58	7	-1	30	1055	0	10	27	1	3.54		.59	9	12.1	5	10+	11	1	0
EAST BRADY		46.9	30.6	38.8		67	5	16	19+	809	0	2	19	0	3.49		1.05	28	16.4	5	30	11	2	1
ERIE CAA AIRPORT		41.7	30.3	36.0	5.3	61	6	12	30	891	0	3	19	0	2.81	.42	.87	7	10.2			10	1	0
FARRELL SHARON		46.7	29.0	37.9	6.7	67	5	13	30	835	0	2	19	0	1.94	-.40	.59	7	T	0		7	1	0
FRANKLIN		45.3	30.0	37.7	8.2	64	6	10	31	840	0	4	18	0	3.01	-.12	.82	9		8	9+	8	1	0
GREENVILLE		44.4	30.2	37.3	6.5	66	6	12	30	848	0	2	19	0	2.68	-.05	.54	9	14.3	4	9	8	1	0
JAMESTOWN 2 NW	AM	42.6	28.4	35.5		66	7	12	30	906	0	7	21	0	2.30	.05	.49	9	9.8	4	9	7	0	0
KANE 1 NNE	AM	38.9	23.9	31.4		60	6	6	30	1034	0	10	24	0	4.57	1.28	.53	8	22.4	7	31	16	2	0
LINESVILLE 5 WNW		42.6	29.0	35.8		65	6	12	30	898	0	5	21	0	2.75	.10	.40	30	22.9	10	30	9	0	0
MEADVILLE 1 S	AM	41.6	28.3	35.0	6.0	64	7	9	30+	924	0	7	20	0	2.64	-.37	.46	21	19.2	5	30	10	0	0
MERCER 2 NNE		44.8	28.4	36.6		66	5	9	19+	870	0	2	19	0	3.75		.87	9						0
SPRINGBORO		42.2	28.4	35.3		65	7	11	30	912	0	2	21	0										
TIONESTA 2 SE DAM	AM	41.7	25.9	33.8		60	7+	4	30	961	0	7	22	0	3.85	.86	.63	9	18.6	7	10	14	2	0
TITUSVILLE WATER WORKS		41.9	26.6	34.3		61	6	1	30	943	0	6	22	0	3.57		.64	7	19.1	7	30	11	2	0
WARREN		41.9	28.7	35.3	6.7	60	6	14	1	915	0	3	20	0	2.99	-.08	.46	9	14.4	6	31	14	0	0
DIVISION				35.2											3.30				14.5					

See Reference Notes Following Station Index

DAILY PRECIPITATION

Day of month

Total	1	2	3	4	5	6	7	8	9	10	11	12	13	14	15	16	17	18	19	20	21	22	23	24	25	26	27	28	29	30	31
3.75	.05	.02	.14			.01	.42	.19	.48	.45		.02	.08	.19	.28	.20				T	.28	.19	T	.27	.05	.02	.20	T	.15	.06	
4.74		T	T		T	T		.24	.82		.01	.22	.06	1.72	.42	.02		T		.10	.11	.62	.03	.32			.05	T	T		T
4.66			T			T		T	.31	.78		.07	.22	.47	1.13	.38					.28	T	.50	.42	.06		T	.04	T		T
3.98	.02	.12				.02	.10	.28	.73				.17	.83	.01	.19					.50	.26		.32	.10	.02	.10	.05	.11	.04	.01
4.12	T								.70	.50		.13	.11	.90	.05	.31					.39	.07	.08	.18	.03		.04			.03	
-								*	1.45					-								*		*	*	*	.84				T
3.45			.12			.06	.08	.11	.55	.17	T		.18		.50	.11		T			.44	.08	.33	.20	T		T	T	.27	T	.05
3.77	.08	.04		.04	.52			.40	.05			T		.48	.10					.06	T	.05	.62	.33	.02	.08	.10	.12	.10	.10	T
4.13	.15	.35			.03	.00	.30	.62	.18			T	.03	.02	.12	T		T	T		.31	.55	.21	.23	.08	.05	.12	.01	.11	.05	.04
-									-	-			-	-	-	-				.04	-		-	-	-		.24	.41			
4.49			.09						1.22				.18	1.32	.20	.15					.30	.44		.28			.15	.12	.04		
3.04	.01	T	.10			.02	.22	.27	.43	.36		T	.22	T	.26	.11	T	T	T	.01	.16	.10	.01	T	T	.02	.35	T	.28	.11	T
-			-			.07		-	.68	.39			.07	.39	.97	.05					.36	.31	.27	.14	.14		.06		.10		
3.01	T	T	.04			T	T	.06	.49	.32		T	.08	.29	.54						.36	.32	.19	.18	.03		T	T	.11		T
3.94	T	T	.09		T		.20	.05	.50	.32			.08	.47	.46	T	T				.41	.55	.50	.19			.03	T	.09		
4.48			T			T			.42	.64		.09	.19	.44	1.25	.44					.29	T	.39	.22	.06			.05			
4.16		T	.05			T	.02	.14	.88			T	.10	1.50	.14	.04		T			.27	.42	.15	.18	.10		.02	.06	.09		T
4.61			T	T				T	.24	.81		.05	.16	.43	1.31	.54		T			.26		.44	.33	.03			.01	T		
4.57	T	T					T	.30	.61			.29	*	1.67	.54					.08	*	.58	.03	.47			T			T	
4.89	.27	.05					.39	.30	.80		.01	.02	.24	.06	T	.16	T			.05	.46	.29	.06	.73	.15	.19	.14	.05	.32	.05	.10
5.02	T	.05				T		.30	.91		T	.02	.17	1.75	.09	.15					.60	.60	.05	.22			.11	T	T		
-	.10	.04	.15			.02	.01	.20	.80	.42		.02	.28	.55	.16	.14		-	-	-	-	-	-	-	-	-	-	-	-	-	-
3.70	.03	.01	.15			.02	.32	.18	.43	.36		.04	.10	.40	.28	.11				.02	.32	.21	.01		.04	.04	.12	.26	.16	.09	
-	.01	.10	.19			.04	.33	.09	.47	-		.05	.19	T	.21	.20		.04			.44	.13	.34	.29	.08	.01	.08	.03	.10	.12	.12
-	.10	.18	.13				.45	.08	.69		.11		.23	.20	.10	.23		.08			.47	.51	-	-	-	-	-	-	-	-	.26
5.14		T	.21		.16	.28		.78	.49			.09	.57	1.18	.24					.38	.05	.14	.31	.22		.04			T	T	T
4.51	.06	.13			.02		.49	.38	.71		.13	.06	.21	.23	.06			T		.12	.21	.42	T	.51	.08	.11	.13	.25	.02	.08	.10
3.60			.16			T	.01			1.13	T	.02	.10	.64			.14			.01	T	*	*	*	*	1.01	.16				.22
4.51	T		.08			T	.07	.02	.87	.36			.06	1.48	.53	.01					.33	.10	.08	.32	.07		.06			.07	
4.17	.03	.01	.06				.44	.37	.48	.32		.03	.11	.13	.43	.19				.03	.34	.22	.21	.11	.03	.05	.19		.32	.07	
	RECORD MISSING																														
3.53	.03	T	.11				.25	.18	.47	.37	T	.04	.28	.16	.10	.30		T			.27	.24	.07	.09	.09	.10	.15		.21	.02	T
4.07	T	T				T		.48	.74		T	.08	.15	1.52	.05	.70					.46	.23	.10	.11	.03		.02	T			
D 3.79	D.18	D.16	.10	T			T	.50	.40	.17			.10	.03	.65			T			.30	.15	.37	.18	.03		T	.12	.35	T	T
5.47	T	.03	.02			.03	T	.50	.82		T	.08	.18	1.85	.08	.82				T	.50	.24	.10	.08	.04	T	.08	.02	T		
4.53	.06	.04	.13			T	.24	.14	.71	.37		.02	.26	.67	.17	.10		T			.43	.26	.08	.14	.26	.05	.10		.15	.12	.03
-	T	T	.24			T	.12	.26	.53	.14			.23	.03	-						.38	.14	.45	.34	.03		.07	.07	.34	T	.14
4.32	T	T	.04			.03	.07	.20	.80	.33		.02	.06	.08	.55	.10		.06	T		.30	.20	.55	.35	.04		.03	.01	.40	T	.10
-	-	-	-	-	-	-	-	-	-	-	-	-	-	-	-	-	-	-	-	-	-	-	-	-	-	-	-	-	-	-	-
5.05	T	.01			.02	.04	T	.57	.81		.09	.14	.21	1.55	*	.56				.26	.19	.20	.13	.18		.02	.06	T	.01		
3.58	.03	T	.05			.08	T	.12	.40	.46		T	.17	.58	.19	.23				.04	.40	.12	.05	.31	.04	T	.06	T	.18	.03	
3.45									*	.35		.14	.06	.85	.61	*	.70				.16	.02	*	.51			.02	.03	T		
3.79	.05	.07	.11			T	.22	.12	.43	*	.43		.05	.16	.40	.04					.43	.34	.27	.25	.05	T	.09	T	.19	.07	.02
3.73	.02	.03	.16			.03	.25	.28	.74	.41		.03	.32	.01	.11	.18		T	T		.25	.12	.14	.05	.10	.04	.18	.02	.18	.03	.05
4.35									.41	.61		.06	.19	.30	1.41	.28					.27		.45	.25	.06			.06			
3.46	.04	.02	T			T	.05	.04	.67	.40	T	T	.13	.43	.29	.15				.04	.43	.09	.03	.15	.04	.03	.10		.28	.05	
4.70	T	.02	.18				.22	.09	.69	.87		T	.08	.09	.25	.08		T			.44	.40	.18	.62	.05	.05	.08	.03	.22	.02	.04
4.66	T	.14	.15			T	.40	.15	.65	.28		.07	.42		.11	.20		T	T		.56	.25	.42	.31	T	T	.18	.05	.22	.03	.07
4.54			.05			.01			.36	.50		.04	.20	.38	1.10	.42					.25		.76	.17	.13		.01	.12	.04		
3.09			T			T			.03	.32		.25	.07	.67	.66	.35					.25	T	.17	.18	.12		T	.02			
3.49		T				T		.21	.55			.13	.12	1.38	.06	.18					.27	.14	.08	.26	.11		T	T			
4.83	.06	.01	.01			.03	.06	.10	.84	.36		.03	.16	1.55	.38	.05				.02	.33	.14	.08	.22	.19	.02	.08	T	.08	.03	
5.36	.03	T	.05			.02	.10	.15	.83	.48		.03	.25	1.42	.40	.04				.02	.38	.16	.07	.28	.32	.02	.11	T	.14	.06	T
3.82	.04	.02	.03			.02	.01	.08	.83	.40		.02	.04	.61	.13	.13				.08	.45	.13	.02	.05	.18	.02	.05	.03	.32	.13	
3.96						T		.02	.05	.56		.20	.11	.79	.73	.55					.31	T	.26	.23	.13			T		T	
4.59	.03	.11	.13		T	.03	.38	.26	.73	.28	T	.08	.40	.02	.10	.23	T	T	T		.26	.22	.26	.08	.13	.06	.16	.08	.26	.20	.10
4.32	.04	.13	.14		T	.02	.31	.28	.73	.12	T	.04	.38	.02	.05	.21	T	T			.34	.27	.21	.07	.14	.05	.22	.07	.26	.15	.07
-	*	*	.08				.46	*	*	.44	T	T	.05	.26	*	*	.18	-	-	-	-	-	-	-	-	-	-	-	-	-	-
4.04	.06	.17	.12				.02	.23	.35		T			.09	.09	.06		.44			.61	.19			.17	.04	.19	.36	.02	.04	.19
3.54	.06	.02	.12				.09	.26	.59	.20	T				.24	.13		.02			.45	.23	.44	.28	.05	T	.07	.05	.20	.02	.02
4.12	.01	T	.14				.10	.55	.33	.21			.23		.37	.12	T	T			.56	.12	*	*	*	.90	.07	.05	.20	.07	.09
3.21			.08			T	.07	.14	.47	.16			.07	.02	.59	T					.42	.06	.49	.22	.04		T	.04	.25	.04	.05
4.46	.13	T	.15				.30	.15	.65	.42			.15	.35	.16	.10					.33	.40		.53	.10	.07	.15		.20	.07	.07
4.49	.03	.06	.12			.03	.07	.20	.55	.52		.03	.16	.50	.27	.15		.02			.64	.18	.10	.20	.16	.06	.17	T	.15	.12	
-	.04	.12	.25			.02	.35	.27	.55	.21		.04	.22		.21	.11	T	.05	T		.41	.08	.61		.13	.01	.12	.15	.21	-	.14
3.61			T						.35	.47			.04	.50	.94	T					.32	.19	.44	.16	.15		T	T	.05		
3.67	.05	.10			T		.10	.28	.80	T	T	T	.19	.04	T	.00				T	.35	.15	.09	.37	.06	.04	.07	T	.24	.05	T
3.49		T			T	.02		.03	.70		.23	.25	.28	.52	.41	.02				.13	.21	.24	.16	.27	T		.02				
3.75		T	.03			T	T	.13	.36	.51			.02	.13	.85	.04		.07			.34	.02	.54	.12	.18		T	T	.29		.12
5.29	.14	.17			.03	T	.13	.43	.66		.02	.14	.45	.71	.09	T		T	T	.40	T	.18		.56	.25	.08	.10	.20	.15	.20	.20
3.33	.03	.03	.04			T	.04	.15	.76	.05	T	T	.15	.71	.02	.22		T		.02	.37	T	.12	.24	.01	.02	.12	.01	.18	.04	
3.45								.04	.74			.21	.11	.93	.28	.32					.36	.23	.07	.06	.06		.04		T	T	
4.44	.03	.12					.41	.21	1.15		T			.53	T	.12		T			.33	.52	.01	.40	.16	.05	.09	.07	.17		.07
2.85			.04			T		.08	.07	.70			.10	.15	.20	.08		T	T		.30	.08	.45	.08	.05		.02	.05	.35	.05	
4.75	T	T	.18					.24	.52	.37			.19	.08	.91			T			.37	.05	.97	.10	.10		.11	.10	.38	T	.08
3.49		.04				.02	.60	.18	.16		.02	.10	.30	.22	.02	.13				.01	.25				.03	.04	.14	1.05	.04	.12	.02
4.32	.05	.05	.15		T	T	.15	.14	.57	.44			.18	.47	.10	.12		T	T	T	.60	.22		.30	.13	.20	.10	T	.10	.16	.09
3.36	.01	.08	.10			.04	.52	.16	.30	.15	T		.04			.10		.02	T	T	.30	.30	T	T	.30	.16	.05	.16	.05	.34	.16
4.90			.14						.47	.79		.11	.10	.74	.90	.36					.49		.19	.41	.20						
4.96	T	.06	.25			T	.21	.14	.76	.32		.07	.32	.01	.25	.12		T			.40	.65	.50	.34	.11		.11	.04	.21	T	.09
2.72	T	T	.13			T	.06	.10	.30	.18		T	.05	.06	.33	.04		T			.34	.14	.42	.21	.05		T	.04	.21		.06
4.83			.03			.03		.28	.90			.16	.23	1.53	.05	.20					.46	.23	.33	.15	.07		.18				
4.47		T	.18				T	.10	.65	.35		.04	T	T	1.10	.10					.26	.06	.68	.22	.12	T	.03	T	.43	T	.15
2.81	.04	.08			.07	T	.87	.15	.24	T	T	T	T		.01	T	T	T	T	.11	.13	.20		.08	.13	.02	.38	.12	.04	.03	.11
D4.12		.11				.10		.20	D.19			.05	.55	.15	1.30					.55		.10	.15	.65			D.02				
1.94	.03	.13			.02		.59	.34	.04					.10	.11			T	T	.05	.08	.16		.01	.02	.02	.13	.07	.04	T	
3.89	.03	.01	.08			T	.43	.21	.53	.20		T	.06	.19	.17	.45				.01	.38	.29	.02	.32	.08	.12	.15	T	.14	.02	T
3.01	.02	.06	.07			.01	.40	.21	.82	.09			.07	T	.20	T		.01			.30	.30	.02	T	.10	.02	.10	.02	.09	.08	.02
6.07		.11				.22		.20	.85	.55	.05	.03	.50	.77	.95	.30		T	T	T	.22	T	.51	.18	.03	T	T	.18	.38		.04
4.00	.01		.16			.09	.15	.03	.49	.18	T	.02	.28	T	.52			T			.48	.20	.68	.12	.01	.01	.06	.05	.20		.26
3.54									.28	.50		.13	.24	.57	.79	.17					.32		.24	.20	.10		T	T			
3.57		.01						.02	.60			.16	.08	1.17	.12	.44					.19	.23	.33	.07	.09		.06				
3.64	.01					T			.51	.40		.03	.09	.91	.73	.25					.31	.05	.09	.21	.02		.03			T	
4.54	.01	.07	.15			.07	.50	.25	.64	.22			.20	T	.40	.20		.08			.37	.15	.41	.22	.05	T	.10	.06	.22	.05	.12
4.30	.01	.09	.24			T	.23	.28	.53	.20		.04	.47	T	.12	.20		.03		T	.36	.20	.38	.36	.08	T	.07	.06	.23	.04	.10
4.04	.05	.01	.14			.01	.47	.28	.52	.37		.03	.10	.08	.22	.08		T		.03	.30	.22	.23	.13	.03	.03	.35	T	.22	.14	
4.54			.10			.02		.02	.41	.73		.05	.15	.47	1.11	.35		.03			.24	T	.32	.12	.18			.12	.10		.02
3.26									.21	.48		.32	.11	.48	.12	.78					.22	.33	.12	.09				T			
2.31	T	T	.05	T					.41	.16	T	.21	.09	.23	T	.28		T			.30	.05	.29	.24	T		T	T	T	T	T
4.62	.01	.01	.01			.03	.10	.17	.56	.50		.02	.18	1.11	.26	.09				.03	.45	.20	.03	.23	.25	T	.05	T	.30	.03	T
3.48	.01	.04	.01		.05	T	.10	.28	.77			.14	.15	.31		.20						.15	.05	.59	T		.27	.18	.07	.01	.10
2.68	.08	.15			T		.47	.35	.54		T		T	.03	.05	T					.34	.11	T	.01	.22	.06	.17	.01	.04	.05	T
3.86									.34	.26		.14	.07	.80	.86	.16					T	.02	.11	.91	.19		T	T			
4.26	.01	.02			.01	T		.54	.62		.10	.11	.17	1.24	.62	T		T		.28	.11	.20	.10	.12		T	T	.01	T	T	T
5.07	T		.04			T			.80	.37		.08	.20	1.04	.71	.87					.49	.20	.05	.17	.01		.04		T		
4.58		T	.09					.01	.32	.52		.02	.09	.31	1.22	.40		.02	T		.44	T	.67	.17	.19	T	T	.03	.08		T
4.20			.06						.35	.39			.08	.35	1.21	.39					.42		.64	.19	.12			T			T
4.79		T	.12			T	T	.01	.45	.54		.02	.15	.49	1.15	.22		.03	.01		.36	.03	.49	.23	.24	T	T	.03	.18	T	T
3.27			T			.02		T	.02	.18		.25	.05	.83	.82	.32	.03			T	.21	.03	.12	.23	.15		T	.01		T	
4.50		T	.14					.08	.43	.36		.02	.17	.21	.92	.12	T	.02			.40	.06	.73	.35	.10		.04	.01	.31		.03
4.08	.02	.01	.13			.03		.05	.72	.30		T	.19	.85	.21	.15					.42	.20	.03	.22	.22	.05	.09		.10	.09	T
2.45		.15	T	.04			T	T	.78	.69		.05	.15	.13	.05			T	.03		*	.30	T		.02			.02	.03	T	.01
3.80	T	.13	.11			.02	.07	.10	.32	.15			.09		.78	.21				T	.60	.30	.12	.30	.40			T	.10	T	T
4.60	T	T	.02			.01	T		.89	.55		.04	.08	.87	.72	.75					.35	T	.14	.14	.01		.03	T	T		
4.24	.01		.05			.05	.05	.02	1.01	.14			.06	1.34	.47	.06					.31	.11	.06	.29	.05	.01	.10		.01	.04	

See Reference Notes Following Station Index

DAILY PRECIPITATION

Table 3—Continued

Station	Total	1	2	3	4	5	6	7	8	9	10	11	12	13	14	15	16	17	18	19	20	21	22	23	24	25	26	27	28	29	30	31
INDIANA 3 SE	4.30	.07	.02	.10	T		T	.30	.13	.83	.17		.03	.07	.43	.14	.16				T	.34	.32	.12	.38	.18	.04	.16		.14	.08	
IRWIN	-			.25					-	-	T	.02	.03	.24	.70			.30			.04	.50	-	.30	-	.11	.19	.03		-		
JAMESTOWN 2 NW	2.30	.04	.08	.08			T	.35	.19	.49	.03			.06			.12	T				.41	.14			.04	.04	.14	T	.06	.03	T
JIM THORPE	3.89		T	.03			.12			.03				.27	1.42	.18	.40					.25	.65	.14	.23	.03		.03	.09			.02
JOHNSTOWN	3.23	.03	.01	.27			.05	T	.07	.05	T		.17	.14	.55	.03	.27				T	.51	.22	.07	.12	.10	.04	.20	T	.25	.08	
KANE 1 NNE	4.57	.12	.23			.03	.48	.30	.53	.27	.01	.03	.30	.03	.10	.05	T	.04	T	T	.52	.22	.43	.10	.08	.01	.14	.04	.20	.05	.10	.16
KARTHAUS	3.93	.02	.03	.18			T	.15	.16		.89		.03	.09	.07	.33	.17			T		.40	.33	.28	.39	.05	T	.09	T	.23	T	.04
KEATING SUMMIT	4.62	.03	.03	.24				.16	.27	.50	.18		.03	.43	T	.26	.25	.02	.04			.38	.32	.48	.41	.04		.13	.06	.22	T	.14
KEGG	5.09					.10	T	.52	1.04		T		.04	.32	1.88						.35	.15	.21	.04	.35	T	T	.04	.02	.03		T
KITTANNING LOCK 7	3.93	.03	.01	.09			T	.47	.23	.60	.29		.02	.09	.17	.20	.22		T		T	.29	.26	.08	.44	.07	.04	.23	T	.10	T	T
KREGAR 4 SE	6.23	.12	.19			.02	.01	.21	.58	.88		.03	.18	.52	.84	.22	T	T	T	T	.37	.13	.17	.05	.45	.26	.08	.16	.20	.32	.15	.09
KRESGEVILLE 3 W	4.58			.06						.24	.53		.03	.18	.30	1.26	.48					.24		.90	.18	.08			.10			T
LAKEVILLE 1 NNE	4.84			.13					.13	.41	.38	T		.16	.69	1.01	.27		.01			.44	.05	.59	.28	.13		.02	.03	.11		
LANCASTER 2 NE PUMP STA	3.45						T		.11	.62			.16	.14	1.34	.11	.20					.29	.14	.10	.10	.13		.01				
LANDISVILLE 2 NW	3.87									.43	.56		.12	.09	.60	.75	.27					.42	.02	.15	.35	.09		.02				
LAWRENCEVILLE 2 S	3.25		T	.04			T	.03	.19	.28	.40			.06	T	.68	.04		T			.47	.03	.50	.21	.07		T	T	.23	.02	T
LEBANON 3 W	4.89	T		.03			.03			.64	.60		.11	.17	.68	.94	.50		T			.41	.02	.26	.30	.15		.02	.03			
LEHIGHTON	4.68			.07			T	T	T	.60	.28		.05	.21	.30	1.15	.47		T	T		.23	.43	.35	.25	.06		.05	.10	.09		.03
LE ROY	2.68							.25	.30	.07		.15			.55	.18						.31		.33	.16	.02		T	.01	.34		.01
LEWIS RUN 3 SE	4.11	T	.11	.15			.08	.36	.31	.62	.05	T	.03	.31	T	.16	.05	T	.05	T	T	.39	.09	.40	.20	.07	T	.11	.06	.20	.23	.08
LEWISTOWN	3.68	T		.08			.02		T	.43	.46			.04	.46	.89	.03		T			.45	.03	.27	.11	.33		T	T	.08	T	T
LINESVILLE 5 WNW	2.75	.03	.10	.06			T	.30	.17	.29	T			.03		T	.08		T	.02		.35	.36		T	.21	.08	.15	.03	.09	.40	T
LOCK HAVEN	3.27	.02		.16			.05	.02	.18	.42			T	.07	.16	.61	.07		T			.40	.12	.49	.16	.03		.02	.05	.21	T	.03
@LONG POND 2 W	4.21			.05			T		T	.30	.48		.05	.15	.47	1.09	.42		.02	.02		.22	.02	.49	.13	.11	T	.03	.13	.05		.02
MADERA	3.99	.05	.03	.19			T	.25	.14	.68	.33		.02	.07	.31	.26	.10		.03			.44	.30	.25	.16	.13	T	.11	.02	.12	T	T
@LYNDELL 2 NW	5.95						.18			.20	.48		.20	.10	.56	.96	.38					.35	.08	.08	.24	.14						
MAHAFFEY	4.60	.02	.05	.11				.35	.25	.78	.36		.09	.12	.25	.25	.07	T	.02		T	.44	.39	.15	.47	.13	.08	.04	.05	.04	.07	.02
MAPLE GLEN	3.64								.02	.64			.30	.09	1.18	.17	.49					.29	.19	.05	.13	.06		.02		.01		
MAPLETON DEPOT	3.73	T		.07			T	T	T	.58	.37			.01	.64	.73	T					.49	.10	.15	.21	.29		.02	T	.07	T	T
MARCUS HOOK	3.80		T			T	T	T	T	.27		.01	.30	.25	1.21	.69	.15	T			.12	.10	.32	.15	.16		T	.03		.04		T
MARION CENTER 2 SE	5.36	.05	.05	.14			.01	.39	.24	.81	.35		.04	.14	.35	.14	.07	.01	T	T	.01	.41	.48	.08	.64	.18	.11	.18	.04	.24	.15	.05
MARTINSBURG CAA AP	4.83	.01	.07			T	T	T	.48	.57	T	T	.04	.23	1.16	.05	T				.37	.03	.30	.04	1.31	T	.01	.08	.03	.03	T	.02
MATAMORAS	4.31			.17						.44	.54			.08	.37	1.10	.24					.34		.61	.10	.24				.08		
MAYBURG	3.81	T	.26	.22			.05	.51	.25	.57	.19		T	.15	T	.05	.03		T			.29	.18	.18	.45	.08	.06	.12	T	.09	.03	.05
MC CONNELLSBURG	4.89		T	T			.08	.01	.02	1.06	.31		T	.12	.76	.82	.33					.74	.16	.07	.24	.09	.01	T	T	T	.07	
MC KEESPORT	4.44	.17		.60			T	.27			.72		.02	.20		.70	.03			T	.03	.50			.45	.05		.25			.45	
MEADVILLE 1 S	2.64	.04	.16	.09			T	.29	.15	.37	.05	T	T	.03	T	T	.17		T	T		.46	.18	T	T	.19	.05	.16	.03	.03	.14	.05
MEDIX RUN	4.23	.01	.03	.18			T	.25	.16	.69	.35	T	.04	.25	.08	.24	.20		T	T		.35	.26	.30	.35	.09	T	.08	.03	.21	.03	.05
MERCER 2 NNE	3.75	T	.10					*	.70	.87			T	.10	.12	.40						.54	.05		.12	.05	.10	.35		.20	.05	
MERCERSBURG	4.05							.02		1.07	.15			.20	1.48	.07	.40					.35		.16				.15				
MEYERSDALE 1 ENE	5.72	.08						.05	.09	.99	.19			.11	1.97	.47	.06					.27	.12	.10	.39	.20	.20	.18		T	.25	
MIDDLETOWN OLMSTED FLD	4.39	T	.02			.01	T		.57	.75		.15	.06	.16	1.26	.42					.20	.30	.19	.04	.23		T	.03	T	T	T	T
MIDLAND DAM 7	3.57	.01	.01	.12			.08	.40	.31	.53	.30		.01	.29	.03	.26	.23		T			.26	.14		.05	.02	.03	.11		.23	.15	
MILANVILLE	4.08			.10					.09	.38	.38		.06	.10	.14	.93	.13		T			.33		.66	.23	.19		T	.08	.23		.05
MILLHEIM	3.85	T	T	.10			T	.02	.07	.68	.14		T	.20	.39	.64	.12					.38	.35	.35	.11	.18	T	T	.04	.08	T	T
MILLVILLE 2 SW	3.86		T	.10			T		.12	.54	.39			.06	.27	.96			T			.32	T	.61	.07	.23		T	.02	.16	T	.01
MILROY	3.65	T	T	.08			.03	.03	.02	.62	.18			.08	.53	.03	.16					.43	.37	.07	.12	.11		.07	.02	.10		T
MONTROSE 1 E	4.15	T	.01	.11	T			T	.23	.57	.17	T	T	.06	.06	.98	.07	T	T	.02		.35	.04	.63	.13	.20	T	.01	.09	.37	T	.05
MORGANTOWN	2.97		T						.15	.55		.03	.18	.12	1.00	.13	T				.12	.20	.19	.08	.22			T				
MT GRETNA 2 SE	4.64								.51	.81		.09	.13	.15	1.40	.34	.05				.17	.26	.21	.09	.40			.03				
MT POCONO 2 N AP	3.93		T	.06				T	.08	.83			.17	*	1.56	.16	T		T			.25	.41	.04	.17	.07		.03	.07	.05		T
MUHLENBURG 1 SE	4.45		.01	.12				.04		.89		.01	.04	.13	1.32	.11			.07			.33	.60	.04	.33	.03		.06	.16	.10	.03	.03
MYERSTOWN	4.06			.04			.03			.45	.75		.16	.17	.58	.60	.36					.35	.08	.30	.19							
NATRONA LOCK 4	3.84	.05	.01	.12			T	.41	.16	.45	.47		T	.04	.19	.27	.30				T	.34	.22	.02	.42	.02	.03	.14	T	.14	.04	
NESHAMINY FALLS	3.61					T			.07	.41		.15	.20	.17	1.31	.27	.10				.13	.15	.35	.06	.15	T		.09		T		
NEWBURG 3 W		RECORD MISSING																														
NEW CASTLE 1 N	2.67	.10	.02	.01				.03	.20	.39	.50			.15	T	.23	.02		T	T	T	.20	.20	.03		.05	.04	.25	.05	.18	.04	T
NEWELL	3.95			.09			.06	.05	T	.92			.04	.13	.88		.18				.09	.44	T	T		.68		.13				.26
NEW PARK	3.70	.01	.04						.05	.25			.10	.12	1.46	.56	.18					.15	.12	.08	.11	.44		.03				
NEWPORT	4.05	T		.02			T			.50	.36		T	.14	.65	.97	.24					.43	.06	.25	.23	.11		.03	.01	.04	T	
NEW STANTON	3.41	.03	.15			.04	T	.10	.21	.61		.05	.03	.20	.59	.06				T	.24	.08	.31	T	.37	.03	.02	.06	.04	.17	T	T
NEW TRIPOLI	5.27		T	.01					.14	.88			.05	.17	1.81	.13	.60		T			.35	.67	.11	.18	.09		.08	T			T
NORRISTOWN	3.62						T			.62			.19	.05	.66	.79	.55					.24	*	.20	.15	.16			.01	T	T	
NORTH EAST 2 SE	3.67	.31	T	.22			.12	.76	.22	.37	T			T			.08	.02	.03		.01	.10	.11	.06		.78	.02	.04	.23	.10	.04	.05
ORWELL 3 N	3.82			.12				.03	.24	.46	.20			T	.03	1.02			.03			.39	.05	.56	.24			.04	.04	.37	T	T
PALM	4.78									.57	.72		.10	.30	.53	1.18	.38					.30		.40	.15	.08			.07			
PALMERTON	4.39		.01	.02			.02	T	.18	.65		.05	.10	.10	1.46	.42	.02		T		.09	.14	.79	.02	.24		T	.08		T		T
PALMYRA		RECORD MISSING																														
PARKER	3.14	.04	.04	.09			T	.33	.18	.52	.22		.05	.28	.02	.12	.18		T		.03	.24	.16	.06	.03	.10	.08	.15	T	.17	.05	T
PAUPACK 2 WNW	4.20			.08					.03	.43	.13		.35	.08	.42	1.02	.35		.05			.33	.60		.25			.02	.03	.03		
PECKS POND	4.31			.10			T		T	.66	.19		.02	.15	.87	.81	.34		.01			.22	.03	.50	.20	.09			.07	.03	T	
PHIL DREXEL INST OF TEC	3.13					T	T		T	.35		.02	.10	.28	1.00	.60	.18	T			.07	.05	.20	.12	.15		T	T		.01		
PHILADELPHIA WB AP R	3.70					T	T		T	.31		.02	.14	.23	1.25	.72	.21	T	T		.11	.06	.35	.11	.15		T	.02		.02		T
PHILADELPHIA PT BREEZE	3.60		T			.01			.02	.30		.05	.12	.22	1.37	.03	*	.72			.16	.06	.29	.12	.10	.02		T		.01		T
PHILADELPHIA SHAWMONT	-		T				.02		.08	.35		T	.20	.10	-	*	.39					.25	.23	.17	.18	.10		T		.12		
PHILADELPHIA CITY R	2.69					.01	.01			.22		.02	.03	.12	1.10	.45	.20				.11	.07	.25	.06	.04							
PHILIPSBURG CAA AP	3.30	.03	.07			T	T	.23	.33	.34	T	T	T	.15	.51	.08	T		T		.24	.15	.44	T	.23	.03	.02	.09	.14	.15	.03	.06
PHOENIXVILLE 1 E	3.76								.16	.56		.02	.23	.23	1.57	.32	.03				.13	.14	.23	.10	.04							
PIKES CREEK	3.77		T	.10					.02	.50	.34		.05	.19	.35	.85	.19	T	.01	T		.34	.02	T	.20	.10	T	.14	.10	.23	T	.04
PIMPLE HILL	5.18		.01	.11			.01	T	.01	.43	.52	T	.05	.18	.72	1.11	.49		.03	T	T	.22	.04	.59	.23	.11	T	.04	.14	.08	.03	.03
PINE GROVE 1 NE	4.69	T	T	.04			T			.55	.38		.06	.20	.53	1.10	.55					.27	.05	.51	.32	.06	T	.03	.04	T	T	T
PITTSBURGH WB AP 2 //R	3.35	.04	.10			.01	T	.62	.12	.57	T	.03	.01	.02	.37	.13			T	T	.21	.03	.38	T	.18	.03	.06	.11	.13	.17	T	.03
PITTSBURGH WB CITY R	3.43	.02	.12			T		.58	.15	.72		.02		.05	.42	.25				.02	.26	.03	.16		.16	.01	.03	.16	.07	.18	T	T
PLEASANT MOUNT 1 W	4.19		.01	.17					.21	.49	.24	T	.18	.11	.12	.70	.10		.03	T		.31	.05	.57	.21	.18	.03	T	.09	.33	.01	.05
PORT CLINTON		RECORD MISSING																														
POTTSTOWN		RECORD MISSING																														
POTTSVILLE	5.35			.04					T	.60	.64		.32	.18	.57	1.04	.43					.28	.05	.64	.35	.11		.02	.08	T		
PUTNEYVILLE 2 SE DAM	4.47	.02	.01	.10		.20	.01	.47	.23	.77	.32		.03	.14	.13	.16	.12					.31	.27	.10	.64	.08	.06	.11	.07	.02	.04	.06
QUAKERTOWN 1 E	4.32			T					.25	.76	.03		.10	.20	1.43	.33	.18					.30	.40	.05	.13	.09		.03	.01		.03	
RAYMOND	4.13	.03	.05	.18			.03	.25	.15	.50	.30			.30	.07	.28	.23		.04			.22	.27	.32	.30		.03	.09	.11	.23	.05	.10
READING WB CITY R	4.27	T	.01						.47	.90		.05	.14	.18	1.26	.54	T		T		.10	.13	.24	.05	.18			.02	T	T		
RENOVO	3.69	T	.01	.20			T	.02	.35	.48	.31		.02	.06	.08	.43	.13		T			.42	.26	.24	.39	.06		T	.02	.15	T	.06
REW	4.23	.01	.08	.11			.07	.54	.22	.70	.07	T	.01	.32		.18	.06	T	.06	T		.42	.13	.47	.17	.07	T	.10	.06	.09	.20	.09
RICES LANDING L 6	4.23	.01		.04			.04	.01	.03	.61	.38		.03	.12	.78	.20	.20				.11	.43	.12	.04	.68	.05		.07		.25	.03	
RIDGWAY 3 W	4.37	.02	.10	.25			.10	.30	*	.60	.30		.08	.35	T	.14	.25		T		T	.32	.16	.54	.26	.11		.09	.05	.24	.03	.08
RUSH	4.20		.02	.13			T	T	.18	.62	.32			.05	.07	.73	.10		.04			.35	.15	.59	.19	.14		.07	.04	.37		.04
RUSHVILLE	3.94		T	.11					.13	.53	.32			.03	.03	.86	.16		.03			.35	.10	.58	.14	.20		.02	.04	.29	T	.02
SAGAMORE 1 S	4.22	.08	T					1.05	.98	.35	.10						T	.15	.10			.25	.35	.15	.15	.20		.13		.10	.08	
SALINA 3 W	3.47	.02	.09			T		.57	.13	.61			.02	.11	.60		.05				T	.30	.25	T	.42	.06	.06	.04	.06	.05		.03
SAXTON	4.25	T	T	.07			T		.02	.68	.30		T	.04	1.14	.72	.02		T			.50	.18	.03	.29	.10	T	.04	T	.07	.05	T
SCHENLEY LOCK 5	4.30	.03	.02	.14			T	.37	.28	.55	.35		.02	.07	.18	.22	.13		T	.02	.04	.40	.25	.05	.70	.07	.04	.15		.20	.02	T
SCRANTON	3.80			.11					.04	.04	.40		.30	.04	.23	.95	.05		.01			.40	.04	.38	.11	.28	.19		.03	.19		.01
SCRANTON WB AIRPORT	3.24		.02	.02		T		T	.35	.38		.03	.08	.05	1.26	.01	.03		.03		.03	.27	.20	T	.22	T	T	.08	.15	.01	T	.02
SELINSGROVE CAA AP	4.06	T	.04			T	.01	.04	.50	.57		T	.04	.11	1.38	.05	.04		.01		.23	.12	.58	.03	.16		T	.02	.08	.05		T
SHAMOKIN	4.16			.03			.01			*	1.00		T	.14	.55	1.07	.13		T			.27	.10	*	.60	.08		.06	.03	.09		T
SHIPPENSBURG	3.39	T	T	.02			T		.55	1.08		T		.22	1.81	.08	.57					.47	.16	.10	.20	T	T	.05	T	T	.08	
SHIPPINGPORT WB	3.31	T	.14			.15		.55	.25	.58		T	.13	.08	.33	.20					.22	.01	.14	.02	.03	T	.06	.15	.15	.12		T
SINNEMAHONING	3.64	.01	.01	.19	T		T	.30	.12	.58	.29	T	.02	.14	.15	.31	.15		T	T		.37	.21	.28	.32	.07	T	.04	.03	T	T	.03
SLIPPERY ROCK	2.95	.04	.01	.11			T	.32	.31	.58	.36			.12		.15	.02		T			.21	.20	.02		.08	.06	.18	.01	.15	.02	
SOMERSET FAIRVIEW ST	4.86	.05	.02	.15			.04	.03	.09	.78	.39		.03	.17	1.04	.36					.03	.50	.20		.23	.12	.11	.16		.13	.23	
SOMERSET MAIN ST	4.82	.05	.14				.10	.04	.48	.69		T	.02	.24	1.26		.11				.01	.48	.20	.02	.23	.12	.02	.17	.04	.16	.24	T
SOUTH MOUNTAIN	3.97		T				T	T		.49	.68		.08	.12	.82	.72	.23					.33	.09	.09	.19			.10		.02	.01	
SPRINGBORO	-							.60	.10	T				T		T	.17					.36	.35			T	-	-	-	-	-	-
SPRING GROVE	3.87	T							T	.66	T		.13	.07	1.60	.05	.17					.25	.16	.21	.51			.06				
SPRINGS 1 SW	5.05	.04	T				.07	.08	.20	.16	T	T	.04	.41	2.08	.12		.05			.19	.23	.26	.15	.54	.08	.04	.05	.03	.15	.08	T
STATE COLLEGE	3.45	T	.08			T	T	.19	.44	.31		T	.09	.08	.85	.13			T	T	.42	T	.55	T	.25	T	.01	.02	.08	T	.01	T

See Reference Notes Following Station Index

DAILY PRECIPITATION

ble 3—Continued

PENNSYLVANIA
DECEMBER 1956

Station	Total	1	2	3	4	5	6	7	8	9	10	11	12	13	14	15	16	17	18	19	20	21	22	23	24	25	26	27	28	29	30	31
AUSSTOWN	4.74			.04			T			.59	.34		.09	.20	.63	1.05	.42					.33	.03	.35	.24	.13		.03	.07		T	T
OUDSBURG	4.71	T	.01	.03		T	.01	T	.16	.64	T	.02	.02	.18	1.90	.28	.14	T	.01			.22	.81	.02	.18	T	T	.04	.02	.01	T	.01
NP CREEK	4.63	.01	.02	.08				.36	.27	.89	.32		.05	.16	.12	.21	.19					.35	.38	.02	.08	.11	T	.10	T	.29	.02	
BURY	4.37	T		.03			T		T	.68	.55		T	.05	.41	1.17	.05					.33	.25	.41	.15	.10		.08	.03	.09	.02	T
QUEHANNA	4.47		.04	.12			T		.21	.47	.31		.04	.03	.13	1.16	.06		.04			.21	.05	.54	.16	.28	T	.03	.04	.46	.02	.07
ERSVILLE	3.80			.13			.02				1.15		T	.14	.56		.18				.04	.28			.92			.11	T		.27	
AQUA	4.96			.05						.53	.43		.06	.22	.46	1.22	.49					.25	.72		.23	.15		T	.10	.05		
AQUA 4 N DAM	4.52		.05							.02	.80		.03	.22	.46	1.03	.40					.22		.79	.22	.20	.02	.05				.01
ARACK 2 S FIRE TWR	3.86	T	.04	.30			T	.14	.17	.60	.39		.01	.12	.05	.27	.18		T			.30	.13	.38	.28	.06	T	.05	.05	.31	.03	.02
NESTA 2 SE DAM	3.85	.01	.10	.13	T		.03	.52	.22	.63	.23		.03	.12	.02	.16	.05		T			.40	.16	.09	.33	.06	.02	.14	.09	.15	.10	.06
USVILLE WATER WORKS	3.57	.08	.17		T	T	T	.64	.27	.46	T	T			.23	.08			T			.55	.23		.06	.12	.04	.24	.04	.07	.17	.12
PEDO 4 W	3.13	.03	.14	.29	T		T	.38	.20	.40	.10			T		.27	.05		.04	T		.37	.14	.14	.05	.18	.01	.15	.08	.04	.06	
ANDA	3.65	T	T	.05					.16	.72	.28			.01	.01	.79	.04		.01	T		.41	.01	.45	.14	.20	T	T	T	.33	.04	T
ER CITY 5 SW	4.24		T	.11			.03		.08	.88			.09	.16	1.47	.08	.32					.33	.28	.04	.08	.20		.04	.05	T		
Y	3.78			.08				.07	.19	.57	.27			.02	.06	.83	.06		.03			.42	.05	.44	.19	.11		.02	T	.32		.05
TLEPOINT 4 NE	3.59	.02	.03	.13			.04	.19	.25	.35	.15	.11		.25		.21	.08		.04			.45	.12	.41	.17	.05		.05	.07	.16	.05	.21
ONE 4 NE BALD EAGLE	4.11	T	T	.21			.01	.07	.14	.58	.36		T	.10	.48	.59	.13		T			.46	.29	.14	.23	.04		.13	T	.14	.01	
ON CITY	3.01	T	.15	.17			.03	.40	.21	.48	.06			.05			.06	T	.04	T	T	.46	.08	.13		.13	T	.10	.17	.04	.15	.10
ONTOWN	4.76	.03	.03			.06	.08	.10	.37	.94		.03	.10	.35	.84	.02	.05				.40	.16	.17	.02	.47	.04	.01	.06	.17	.24	.02	T
ER DARBY	3.44						T		.02	.30			.17	.08	1.43	.27	.35					.22	.30	.09	.17	.01		.03		T	T	
CA	3.85	.10	.12	.04			.04	.16	.73	.90	.02		.02			.21	.15					.28	.18	.04	.07	.16	.01	.21		.10	.10	.01
DERGRIFT	3.08	.04	T	.12			T	.38	.14	.37	.42			.08	.21	.21	.10		T	T	T	T	.24		.28	.07	T	.12	.06	.19	.05	T
GINVILLE	4.27									1.00	.05			.21	.62	1.16	.09					.08	.12	.45	.39	.08		T	.02			
INCKEL	4.45	.04	.13	.21		T	.02	.47	.23	.75	.13	T	.03	.38	.03	.02	.22	T	T			.30	.22	.17	.07	.17	.09	.19	.08	.26	.17	.07
INCKEL 1 WSW	4.32	.04	.15	.18		T	.03	.40	.24	.75	.12	T	.03	.35	.03	.02	.22	T	T			.30	.23	.17	.09	.16	.07	.16	.07	.28	.17	.06
REN	2.99	T	.09	.17				.22	.21	.46	.18		.05	.11		.27	.05		T			.38	.12	.15	T	.11		.11	.02	.10	.02	.17
SONTOWN	4.17	T	.04	T		T	.02	.08	.36	.62		T		.09	1.25	.12	T		T			.28	.78	T	.18		T	.08	.18	.06		.03
NESBURG 2 W	4.01	.09	T	.03			.04	.01	.05	.47	.38		.02	.11	.80	.25	.10				.06	.46	.09	.03	.59	.04	.01	.07		.29	.02	T
LSBORO 3 S	3.30	T	T	.05			.02	.07	.08	.55	.28		T	.09	.04	.58	.04		T			.41	.14	.25	.26	.03	T	T	.04	.29	.02	.06
LSVILLE	4.52		T				T		.34	.90		T	.09	.08	1.45	.05	.27					.37	T	.72	.15	.07	T	.03				
NERSVILLE 1 W	5.17									.97	.65		.35	.19	.60	1.14	*	.33				.33		.28	.33							
T CHESTER	3.73	T	T			.02			T	.44	.24		.07	.84	.62	.59		.04		.01	.24	.05	.01	.38	.18		T					
T GROVE 1 E	4.28						T			.37			.29	.30	1.05	.80	.50		T			.29	.03	.24	.26	.10		.05				
T HICKORY	3.77	.04	.10	.06			T	.55	.15	.55	.15			.10	.05	.15	.15					.50	.30	.05	.35	.05	.02	.15	.05	.15	.05	.05
TESBURG	4.43	.06	.04	.08				.45	.28	.53	.20	T		.06	.29	.13	.33			T		.37	.30	T	.55	.13	.12	.30		.17	.04	
KES BARRE	3.86			.03			T		T	.48	.46		.06	.10	.37	1.19	.04		.02	T		.30	.01	.37	.10	.11	T	T	.07	.14	T	.01
LIAMSBURG	4.24	.03	.02	.12			.14	.03	.05	.59	.38		T	.24	.56	.47	.15		T			.60	.29	.04	.25	.09	T	.10	T	.04	.05	T
LIAMSPORT WB AP	4.28	T	.04	.01		.03		.16	.47	.40	T	T	.10	.02	1.17	.06	.02		.01		.14	.26	.74	.01	.23			.04	.28	.05	T	.04
FSBURG	4.49	T		.09			T	.01	T	.79	.33			.04	1.47	.57	.01					.44	.14	.11	.32	.07	T	.06		.03	.01	
K 3 SSW PUMP STA	3.38	T	T				T		.13	.43			.10	.08	1.46	.04	.14					.27	.15	.08	.38	.10	T	.02	T			
K HAVEN	4.17	T	T	T			.03			.51	.75		.10	.06	.63	.83	.30					T	.37	.16	.27	.15	T	.01	T	T		
N GROVE	3.37							.02		.38	.48			.14	*	1.03	.25					.24	.06	.46	.25	.06						
NSVILLE 3 SE	4.54									.61	.73		.07	.22	.66	1.08	.37					.26		.35	.18				.03			

SUPPLEMENTAL DATA

Station	Wind direction: Prevailing	Wind direction: Percent of time from prevailing	Wind speed m. p. h.: Average	Wind speed m. p. h.: Fastest mile	Wind speed m. p. h.: Direction of fastest mile	Wind speed m. p. h.: Date of fastest mile	Relative humidity averages - percent: 1:30 a EST	Relative humidity averages - percent: 7:30 a EST	Relative humidity averages - percent: 1:30 p EST	Relative humidity averages - percent: 7:30 p EST	Number of days with precipitation: Trace	Number of days with precipitation: .01–.09	Number of days with precipitation: .10–.49	Number of days with precipitation: .50–.99	Number of days with precipitation: 1.00–1.99	Number of days with precipitation: 2.00 and over	Number of days with precipitation: Total	Percent of possible sunshine	Average sky cover sunrise to sunset
ENTOWN WB AIRPORT	ENE	19	10.5	-	-	-	87	87	70	82	8	4	5	2	1	0	20	-	7.6
E WB AIRPORT	-	-	9.7	-	-	-	-	-	-	-	9	8	9	1	0	0	27	-	9.3
RISBURG WB AIRPORT	WNW	13	6.8	34	NW	30	78	80	65	73	8	4	8	3	1	0	24	35	8.2
LADELPHIA WB AIRPORT	WSW	16	10.0	40	NW	29	86	87	69	79	7	4	8	1	1	0	21	37	7.8
TSBURGH WB AIRPORT	WSW	31	12.3	35++	WSW	11	83	83	73	80	3	8	9	2	0	0	22	19	8.7
DING WB CITY	-	-	9.1	38	NW	30	-	-	-	-	5	4	7	2	1	0	19	33	7.7
ANTON WB AIRPORT	WSW	20	8.5	38	NW	18	85	83	72	80	6	12	6	0	1	0	25	25	8.0
PPINGPORT WB	-	-	3.1	27††	W	31	-	-	-	-	4	5	11	2	0	0	22	-	-
LIAMSPORT WB AIRPORT	-	-	-	-	-	-	-	85	70	79	4	11	8	1	1	0	25	-	8.0

Peak Gust
Fastest observed one minute
d speed. This station is not
ipped with automatic record-
wind instruments.

DAILY TEMPERATURES

Table 5

Station		1	2	3	4	5	6	7	8	9	10	11	12	13	14	15	16	17	18	19	20	21	22	23	24	25	26	27	28	29	30	31
ALLENTOWN WB AP	MAX	35	38	56	34	45	58	63	59	38	39	47	54	56	35	37	55	52	45	36	32	54	46	42	43	42	37	36	40	36		45
	MIN	23	31	30	26	26	37	38	37	23	21	26	41	34	32	33	32	32	19	15	30	37	37	34	36	28	20	25	27	23		18
ALLENTOWN GAS CO	MAX	36	36	36	57	55	47	58	64	55	38	41	47	54	57	37	39	55	53	46	39	53	55	48	38	45	41	38	38	42	37	25
	MIN	21	26	30	27	27	27	39	40	34	22	26	34	41	31	32	33	33	32	17	19	36	38	36	35	36	23	24	29	29	14	14
ALTOONA HORSESHOE CURVE	MAX	34	33	53	56	51	63	62	60	40	38	42	48	48	38	38	47	49	39	39	46	57	52	45	48	40	32	38	37	33	23	38
	MIN	16	27	30	33	28	40	45	39	25	24	23	39	38	30	32	35	33	26	15	30	42	44	36	39	29	23	26	30	22	11	18
ARENDTSVILLE	MAX	36	37	41	61	62	43	59	70	62	38	44	49	56	54	36	40	57	56	43	51	57	60	52	43	46	41	39	43	42	34	26
	MIN	20	25	27	29	27	31	39	45	37	24	25	30	44	33	33	34	35	32	17	19	44	44	43	38	34	27	25	29	30	17	12
ARTEMAS 1 WNW	MAX																															
	MIN	26	28	31	28	30	42	43	35	31	30	18	40	32	31	34	26	32	30	19	32	45	37	30	30	21	15	22				
BAKERSTOWN 3 WNW	MAX	34	35	52	54	67	64	62	59	42	35	44	48	52	46	56	52	50	48	42	47	54	54	57	52	39	31	36	36	32	23	37
	MIN	26	30	32	30	40	56	58	40	28	27	40	42	34	35	37	40	42	27	16	41	44	46	41	39	30	26	28	30	22	10	14
BEAVERTOWN	MAX	35	37	57	55	40	58	66		38	38	43	52	52	39	38	53	51	47	38	52	46	50	44	48	44	37	38	38	35	29	43
	MIN	18	31	26	30	25	35	37		28	24	26	39	38	31	33	36	29	28	14	25	36	41	37	37	35	23	28	27	27	15	16
BELLEFONTE 4 S	MAX	30	34	45	52	53	48	58	62	48	37	37	45	52	52	40	41	49	49	39	45	49	52	52	48	52	44	33	39	37	33	38
	MIN	18	25	29	31	26	32	43	46	31	22	18	19	41	30	32	34	33	33	15	15	39	40	35	38	26	24	21	31	27	12	14
BERWICK	MAX	35	38	55	50	45	58	60	56	39	36	46	52	53	39	41	53	50	43	37	48	50	51	49	44	45	37	38	39	36	28	
	MIN	19	30	28	24	27	42	41	37	28	18	25	39	38	31	35	38	31	28	14	27	33	43	40	37	35	21	24	25	28	11	
BETHLEHEM LEHIGH UNIV	MAX	35	38	56	55	46	59	64	61	37	40	48	53	55	36	38	53	53	46	39	52	53	46	38	44	40	37	37	42	37	23	
	MIN	28	34	35	25	30	44	44	36	28	25	35	43	33	33	34	37	39	25	20	36	40	39	37	38	31	29	31	34	19	16	
BLAIRSVILLE 6 ENE	MAX	28	35	49	52	59	60	58	57	46	31	44	43	46	38	51	46	45	42	43	44	53	52	46	46	34	27	33	34	31		38
	MIN	18	25	34	24	29	45	53	42	22	21	26	37	32	32	33	38	37	21	19	37	40	41	37	34	25	21	22	28	17		11
BRADFORD 4 W RES	MAX	29	31	40	43	49	56	57	54	30	28	43	42	47	36	39	45	42	41	38	38	45	50	46	46	41	29	33	33	30		
	MIN	6	24	27	25	30	33	41	27	19	9	20	35	25	22	32	34	28	18	7	26	28	37	44	39	25	24	26	29	18		
BROOKVILLE CAA AIRPORT	MAX	31	36	47	43	56	60	59	48	34	32	44	45	53	38	42	48	45	43	37	42	48	52	47	49	32	30	34	34	28		35
	MIN	19	29	26	22	28	51	48	33	20	24	19	38	31	31	35	36	36	15	10	37	42	38	34	32	25	23	28	27	15		20
BURGETTSTOWN 2 W	MAX	31	34	48	53	56	67	66	59	43	34	40	44	53	39	44	55	45	51	34	47	54	58	55	54	50	32	33	40	34		
	MIN	23	27	30	19	20	31	45	38	31	23	22	36	34	32	31	38	36	31	12	12	40	42	34	39	28	27	26	27	23		
BURNT CABINS 2 NE	MAX																															
	MIN																															
BUTLER	MAX	32	35	48	52	64	66	65	51	43	34	45	45	50	44	45	48	50	52	50	50	51	52	53	55	46	32	36	36	35	30	35
	MIN	24	30	34	23	27	52	57	37	30	25	26	38	32	32	37	43	45	27	13	43	43	47	34	41	28	24	28	31	24	12	28
CANTON 1 NW	MAX	28	30	33	47	44	43	55	58	50	25	31	41	49	50	33	37	49	45	35	36	45	45	48	40	41	36	30	32	32		
	MIN	12	15	26	29	22	30	41	39	23	13	24	30	35	24	25	31	29	34	15	19	33	35	38	35	32	18	20	25	25		
CARLISLE	MAX	37	38	60	60	52	55	68	65	45	44	42	55	55	44	38	55	53	51	38	54	53	52	47	45	45	40	39	41	39	30	47
	MIN	26	32	29	32	28	38	39	45	30	25	29	37	44	33	34	37	36	32	18	29	42	44	39	37	36	26	28	32	30	18	15
CHAMBERSBURG 1 ESE	MAX	38	40	61	64	42	59	69	63	44	43	39	55	54	36	38	56	55	50	41	57	61	52	45	47	43	38	45	43	38	26	
	MIN	27	31	27	30	29	34	42	43	29	27	25	38	34	33	35	35	35	24	18	30	44	43	41	38	34	29	29	31	26	17	
CHESTER	MAX	37		44	63	61	53	60	69		35	45	53	55	60	43		59	50	49	44	57	53		42		47	38		50	40	
	MIN	25		27	31	35	39	44	53		17	26	26	46	35	35		39	40	21	16	42	43		38		26	20		37	20	
CLARION 3 SW	MAX	32	34	48	43	61	60	61	51	42	36	44	44	50	40	45	47	47	43	38	44	48	54	50	50	43	34	35	38	38		37
	MIN	18	29	30	21	25	42	42	36	20	18	24	32	32	31	36	39	36	25	11	29	38	43	34	39	30	24	27	26	22		12
CLAYSVILLE 3 W	MAX	36	42	50	51	69	68	65	60	43	36	49	48	56	45	66	59	52	43	50	48	56	55	57	57	38	32	41		35	28	38
	MIN	25	30	38	21	24	51	58	40	29	28	26	31	34	34	41	41	32	22	13	36	48	37	36	37	29	29	29		23	14	18
COATESVILLE 1 SW	MAX	37	37	42	58	59	50	60	69	61	39	44	49	55	55	40	40	57	54	46	42	55	57	50	40	40	40	35	40	45	37	29
	MIN	21	22	30	26	28	34	40	47	37	19	26	28	44	34	34	36	35	36	16	15	38	40	40	36	37	21	21	29	30	19	14
COLUMBIA	MAX	39	41	63	60	53	53	66	65	47	43	49	56	57	43	39	56	57	47	45	54	53	52	48	47	45	36	43		41	28	50
	MIN	23	31	29	28	27	43	39	45	30	23	30	42	43	33	34	37	34	34	19	32	44	42	38	37	36	25	26		28	19	12
CONFLUENCE 1 SW DAM	MAX	29	32	51	55	60	61	64	63	60	60	35	48	57	47	39	53	51	50	38	53	59	59	56	47	50	28	33	41			
	MIN	19	27	31	25	25	29	48	48	39	27	23	25	43	35	36	42	34	33	19	18	43	43	37	40	28	28	27	31			
CORRY	MAX	30	32	40	41	56	59	59	49	29	32	42	43	39	40	46	44	44	39	38	39	46	51	55	46	38	30	33	33	29		33
	MIN	9	28	30	22	30	50	47	28	21	19	27	33	26	23	35	34	33	22	13	33	34	33	26	34	27	24	26	23	18		13
COUDERSPORT 3 NW	MAX	28	30	42	43	50	55	58	53	30	27	38	43	48	34	35	42	42	40	37	40	45	48	42	48	35	28	32	32	32	15	
	MIN	2	25	25	24	25	37	44	28	13	11	21	29	25	24	31	30	27	13	9	18	28	40	32	34	23	22	24	22	15	- 1	
DERRY	MAX	33	35	48	54	61	66	67	60	46	38	54	47	58	44	59	55	51	45	49	47	58	56	57	56	40	34	40		36	24	39
	MIN	24	30	33	28	38	39	57	44	27	27	33	42	37	35	35	43	34	25	16	37	44	48	37	38	28	26	28		23	11	16
DEVAULT 1 W	MAX	47	45	60	60	50	62	70	62	48	43	49	53	56	41	39	56	54	46	41	56	54	50	46	44	41	36	38		38	37	
	MIN	25	22	30	30	30	38	38	42	21	13	29	41	29	28	30	30	34	18	14	20	30	37	35	33	26	21	23		21	11	
DIXON	MAX	35	36	39	52	44	50	65	65	42	31	37	41	55	55	35	41	53	48	38	38	48	48	49	42	45	39	34	38	37	31	
	MIN	13	13	29	31	19	20	40	42	31	10	18	26	35	28	31	34	30	26	10	10	26	35	37	38	37	16	20	22	23	6	
DONEGAL	MAX	30	40	49	54	58	57	57	50	42	30	44	50	52	37	52	47	44	42	46	50	51	48	45	47	29	30	34		28	26	35
	MIN	17	23	26	23	28	44	50	40	21	20	18	36	30	31	29	30	26	12	10	36	42	40	32	27	21	21	24		12	4	18
DONORA	MAX	33	38	54	58	64	70	68	64	46	35	52	51	58	48	56	67	48	54	42	52	60	59	58	58	58	34	38		40	30	
	MIN	26	33	33	30	32	53	61	44	32	29	34	42	41	37	43	48	38	34	21	31	49	50	43	50	32	31	31		26	13	
DU BOIS 7 E	MAX	30	32	48	43	50	58	61	62	40	32	44	46	54	35	39	47	44	42	38	42	48	52	48	49	41	30	34		32	23	
	MIN	13	27	31	19	25	43	43	38	23	21	26	38	33	30	33	37	33	26	15	30	38	43	32	41	28	19	26		21	5	
EAGLES MERE	MAX	28	27	29	46	44	42	53	56	50	28	29	37	47	48	34	35	44	41	31	33	40	45	46	41	38	32	29	30	31	25	
	MIN	13	11	24	27	25	28	40	37	20	12	21	29	36	23	29	31	30	31	14	15	32	39	37	33	30	18	20	20	23	0	- 1
EAST BRADY	MAX	36	35	53	53	67	64	62	58	43	38	45	50	53	44	50	50	53	47	47	45	50	57	54	49	41	32	36		34	29	38
	MIN	25	31	32	25	27	45	44	38	17	24	24	36	35	33	38	30	39	29	16	25	40	43	36	36	31	26	30		25	23	16
EBENSBURG	MAX	29	33	48	51	49	59	59	57	47	32	45	44	54	35	47	48	45	45	45	44	53	52	45	48	36	29	35	35	34	23	35
	MIN	20	25	33	31	31	40	48	47	21	22	19	37	32	30	31	36	32	21	13	36	42	42	35	34	25	21	23	30	19	8	9
EMPORIUM 2 SSW	MAX	25	31	42	45	43	46	59	58	38	26	30	40	50	40	35	44	45	44	34	40	44	47	52	42	49	32	30	33	31	25	33
	MIN	8	18	26	24	26	26	43	38	24	13	16	21	32	27	30	33	28	28	9	10	32	41	34	34	29	22	22	20	20	4	8
EPHRATA	MAX	37	40	60	59	48	54	64	61	45	44	47	56	54	44	38	55	55	47	41	51	54	51	49	44	40	37	40		42	29	50
	MIN	23	31	31	31	28	45	41	43	30	24	33	40	40	32	33	36	38	35	18	32	42	40	36	35	35	24	28		28	17	16
ERIE CAA AIRPORT	MAX	35	38	42	40	53	61	57	40	31	38	44	44	33	38	55	46	47	40	43	41	45	49	53	53	34	33	35		30	24	37
	MIN	24	31	34	28	32	51	40	30	25	27	37	31	25	25	38	34	34	21	20	37	39	40	37	33	28	27	30		17	12	22

See reference notes following Station Index.

DAILY TEMPERATURES

PENNSYLVANIA
DECEMBER 1956

		1	2	3	4	5	6	7	8	9	10	11	12	13	14	15	16	17	18	19	20	21	22	23	24	25	26	27	28	29	30	31	Average
	MAX	37	36	54	62	62	62	68	54	38	44	54	56	53	44	40	50	48	50	42	58	58	58	48	50	34	38	45	40	35	26	48	48.1
	MIN	28	30	34	27	24	37	48	32	29	25	22	41	35	32	34	28	30	22	17	48	48	44	40	36	29	29	29	32	26	15	10	31.0
	MAX	35	35	52	54	67	64	64	52	37	38	45	47	43	44	54	55	53	48	43	47	51	56	55	53	41	43	38	36	32	26	40	46.7
	MIN	22	25	28	23	32	49	47	33	24	24	21	25	33	26	35	37	37	22	15	34	36	42	35	35	25	24	28	26	19	13	24	29.0
	MAX	30	36	49	52	54	68	65	61	45	35	40	48	55	38	44	57	46	50	35	*43	54	58	56	52	52	32	33	38	37	28	37	46.1
	MIN	23	26	29	21	21	38	51	39	34	25	39	36	35	33	36	37	39	30	13	13	38	44	33	35	29	25	27	31	24	11	12	29.9
	MAX	29	33	35	47	56	64	62	60	50	37	44	44	45	48	51	47	49	48	45	49	43	58	55	53	49	39	31	35	36	30	32	45.3
	MIN	17	20	29	22	23	37	47	43	35	25	25	24	36	30	38	35	38	36	21	23	32	38	41	37	38	27	26	28	28	21	10	30.0
	MAX	28	31	49	46	42	60	61	61	37	28	38	48	51	34	33	45	45	41	38	41	45	47	45	43	41	31	31	36	33	23	38	41.0
	MIN	15	25	28	27	25	34	50	34	25	15	25	38	29	29	29	31	33	22	13	28	33	40	40	31	30	18	21	26	19	5	12	26.8
	MAX	36	42	62	60	51	58	69	62	51	47	53	54	58	47	40	57	50	50	43	'56	51	50	48	45	45	38	40	47	41	30	48	49.3
	MIN	20	28	31	30	27	45	38	41	32	23	26	45	43	34	36	37	37	32	16	28	39	42	37	36	35	21	25	36	30	18	14	31.7
	MAX	37	38	40	63	65	45	60	70	63	40	44	52	56	56	38	51	56	57	45	53	59	60	53	45	47	39	37	44	45	35	31	49.2
	MIN	21	27	28	32	30	32	41	46	38	28	31	34	44	33	33	35	36	38	19	23	45	45	43	38	35	31	29	30	33	18	19	32.7
	MAX	33	36	36	55	53	48	57	64	53	35	39	46	54	52	37	39	51	50	43	38	51	51	50	40	44	37	34	39	40	32	26	44.0
	MIN	15	23	27	26	28	30	42	44	34	18	25	36	40	31	32	34	35	31	15	16	36	40	40	36	35	20	20	21	30	19	13	28.8
	MAX	33	34	48	53	65	66	60	50	36	37	42	44	36	43	51	52	51	45	41	42	47	54	56	50	37	42	35	35	30	23	37	44.4
	MIN	24	30	33	23	32	52	50	35	25	23	29	24	29	26	37	38	36	24	14	37	40	44	39	37	28	25	28	26	21	12	16	30.2
	MAX	38	38	42	63	64	49	63	70	62	39	44	48	56	56	37	47	57	59	48	55	57	62	56	44	47	40	38	44	45	37	30	49.5
	MIN	20	25	29	32	28	30	41	45	37	23	28	34	43	32	32	34	36	36	20	21	41	45	41	37	33	28	26	29	30	17	17	31.3
	MAX	37	41	61	59	46	54	66	63	42	43	49	55	55	37	39	54	55	48	41	55	54	49	45	44	44	36	42	42	38	27	48	47.4
	MIN	27	33	28	33	31	40	41	41	28	28	31	40	35	34	35	38	38	25	22	34	43	44	37	37	35	29	30	35	27	19	22	32.9
	MAX	30	31	36	48	48	48	61	64	42	34	37	44	53	52	33	34	45	44	40	40	42	44	43	35	43	35	30	35	36	30	19	40.5
	MIN	14	21	28	29	19	19	32	39	29	12	20	33	36	25	27	29	27	29	6	16	27	30	30	30	31	19	17	25	28	4	2	23.6
	MAX	37	41	61	58	48	52	64	59	45	45	48	48	54	40	40	55	57	47	45	54	48	48	46	46	44	37	41	43	38	29	49	47.3
	MIN	26	33	33	31	31	40	41	45	30	26	32	43	36	36	37	39	38	28	25	36	43	43	39	39	36	28	32	34	29	21	26	34.1
	MAX	33	39	39	60	61	47	55	73	52	38	42	50	69	63	42	41	57	54	39	47	53	55	55	45	42	38	42	44	39	33	34	47.8
	MIN	17	25	30	25	24	25	38	43	35	28	20	25	42	30	34	36	32	31	15	15	41	41	36	38	34	25	26	30	30	16	14	29.1
	MAX	34	34	52	53	61	63	62	60	47	35	48	48	57	47	53	51	48	45	44	47	56	56	49	51	39	34	37	39	34	24	38	46.6
	MIN	19	30	30	21	28	44	52	44	24	26	24	36	36	35	37	40	32	24	14	30	43	39	36	38	30	26	29	30	23	11	10	30.4
	MAX			56	65	62	65	57			44	48	48	53	45	65		53	50	51	48	57		54	47		40	41			28		
	MIN			30	30	34	33	42			27	28	39	35	34	25		37	31	16	40	45		40		27	30	27			16		
	MAX	29	32	42	47	49	65	66	58	42	31	39	43	43	35	42	53	42	50	30	41	43	49	53	54	45	32	32	35	34	27	38	42.6
	MIN	18	25	30	21	22	40	53	36	25	23	23	34	30	25	35	37	36	26	15	26	37	40	31	37	29	26	27	25	23	12	13	28.4
	MAX	38	36	57	55	50	63	65			38	40	55	54		39	55	52		37	52	54	53	45	42	43	38	37	37	38	30	45	46.2
	MIN	20	28	29	27	27	39	40			20	24		39		33	34			12	28	35	41	35	34	34	20	25	25	28	11	11	28.0
	MAX	32	36	52	55	56	55	61	65	65	34	40	51	59	43	42	52	50	53	37	54	58	58	58	50	52	42	35	41	40	40	40	48.6
	MIN	18	18	30	27	27	28	45	43	35	24	23	29	38	32	34	34	34	29	15	18	42	44	37	42	26	23	25	30	22	10	12	28.8
	MAX	25	29	37	42	43	60	58	58	34	25	30	41	49	32	36	46	43	43	25	36	40	47	51	44	48	30	30	33	35	23	32	38.9
	MIN	7	20	27	18	24	32	40	34	23	14	18	25	30	27	31	34	33	24	8	9	30	37	33	35	28	22	23	22	20	6	7	23.9
	MAX	37	37	60	55	62	66	61	45	40	50	50	54	58	37		48	53	49	44	54	59	57	46	54	36	36	43	38	36	21	42	47.6
	MIN	30	23	25	25	34	44	43	35	23	19	24	42	34	34		32	30	19	13	41	44	37	37	34	30	25	24	30	17	7	11	28.9
STA	MAX	38	41	62	58	48	52	65	61	48	43	49	55	55	47	39	56	55	46	44	54	52	49	49	46	47	40	41	45	44	32	45	48.6
	MIN	22	29	28	25	25	41	36	38	32	25	27	41	45	34	35	38	34	35	18	31	40	42	39	37	36	24	28	30	31	19	17	31.7
	MAX	33	35	39	60	58	46	53	62	59	37	41	46	55	56	37	39	53	54	45	39	54	54	48	42	44	37	35	41	41	35	27	45.3
	MIN	17	25	26	24	24	28	35	37	37	22	24	31	38	33	33	33	34	30	16	21	39	42	40	36	39	21	23	29	28	17	13	28.9
	MAX	30	39	39	48	43	46	62	60	37	28	36	43	46	44	38	42	40	46	34	38	47	47	50	45	49	36	35	38	36	27	27	41.2
	MIN	13	15	28	24	20	23	42	35	23	15	22	34	32	26	28	35	31	30	11	14	28	35	33	36	34	17	23	28	27	3	2	24.7
	MAX	36	36	38	58	58	45	53	62	60	38	42	47	55	54	36	38	55	55	44	40	55	54	47	39	44	39	35	39	43	36	25	45.4
	MIN	22	31	28	26	29	42	37	38	37	22	28	38	35	33	34	36	33	32	17	27	42	42	38	36	36	21	27	30	34	17	16	31.1
	MAX	34	37	38	58	66	44	57	69	55	36	43	49	55	54	37	39	54	55	45	45	56	53	50	45	47	40	36	42	39	35	24	46.4
	MIN	20	26	31	28	28	32	38	42	35	28	24	34	45	33	33	37	33	32	18	18	42	42	40	39	36	27	27	29	34	18	17	31.2
	MAX	34	34	44	47	60	65	60	45	32	32	42	44	33	42	52	52	49	43	39	42	46	51	55	49	40	32	34	35	29	22	38	42.6
	MIN	23	30	29	20	32	51	44	31	25	24	28	30	26	24	36	35	35	15	14	37	39	41	34	39	27	26	29	24	19	12	19	29.0
	MAX	36	36	55	52	49	49	61	59	37	37	45	53	50	37	40	51	50	45	34	51	60	51	52	45	39	36	39	37	34	24	41	44.7
	MIN	20	31	32	27	28	40	48	36	25	19	21	34	36	30	35	35	33	27	16	25	39	42	37	39	35	28	29	30	24	13	15	30.0
	MAX	27	31	44	48	47	48	59	58	46	33	31	45	53	47	35	45	47	45	35	39	50	50	52	44	50	33	31	35	36	27	35	42.1
	MIN	12	16	24	19	19	32	39	40	29	19	16	20	34	26	29	31	29	26	9	19	34	40	29	30	25	17	21	25	21	5	4	23.8
	MAX	38	42	64	63	51	56	64	68	49	46	51	51	59	42	40	58	47	51	42	54	51	50	46	46	46	36	40	47	41	28	50	48.8
	MIN	28	33	39	38	36	45	45	46	27	27	34	44	38	35	38	40	42	28	24	38	43	42	37	39	34	30	30	35	28	21	21	35.0
	MAX	34	35	55	55	51	60	64	57	38	39	45	50	50	36	37	49	51	47	46	48	58	56	43	51	34	32	40	37	33	21	39	44.9
	MIN	23	29	32	32	30	39	54	38	25	27	31	41	32	31	34	36	33	21	19	42	43	41	38	34	28	23	27	31	16	12	21	31.1
	MAX	30	31	41	45	49	62	64	56	38	30	38	42	43	35	41	50	41	48	28	42	41	47	52	56	46	32	32	34	34	27	35	41.6
	MIN	20	26	30	23	24	38	52	36	25	24	24	36	30	26	34	37	36	26	15	17	37	41	36	37	30	26	26	25	23	9	9	28.3
	MAX	31	33	50	54	66	64	65	50	38	39	45	49	45	45	50	45	47	42	35	49	45	54	49	47	40	38	40	35	33	30	37	44.8
	MIN	19	22	31	19	29	37	46	34	33	19	18	23	26	25	37	35	32	24	9	34	38	39	40	34	32	30	34	30	22	9	20	28.4
LD	MAX	38	41	59	57	47	51	60	61	42	42	50	55	56	37	39	53	55	48	43	54	52	51	45	45	43	36	42	43	38	27	48	47.0
	MIN	27	34	30	31	28	40	40	42	28	28	34	40	35	34	36	37	41	25	20	34	44	45	38	38	36	28	32	34	28	20	22	33.2
	MAX	34	39	51	48	61	64	61	50	38	34	44	47	45	45	50	51	50	45	43	48	56	55	55	51	35	34	38	38	30	24	38	45.2
	MIN	29	34	34	30	35	48	51	40	29	28	28	39	33	35	37	42	41	24	22	43	49	42	40	35	32	31	33	30	20	14	19	33.8
	MAX	28	30	31	44	38	44	59	59	37	26	30	38	48	50	32	37	44	41	32	34	39	41	44	36	41	32	28	32	32	26	16	37.1
	MIN	13	15	25	30	21	24	40	35	21	13	20	29	34	24	27	31	28	22	10	12	31	36	33	33	32	18	20	22	21	1	0	23.3
	MAX	35	39	58	57	48	57	68	62	40	41	47	52	55	37	38	54	54	45	39	54	51	51	44	45	42	36	40	43	38	27	47	46.6
	MIN	21	20	31	29	28	46	44	40	24	21	30	41	32	32	33	35	35	21	15	32	40	41	36	36	31	22	26	30	25	14	16	29.9
	MAX	36	38	50	58	48	55	65	68	45	42	47	48	59	38	40	56	55	45	48	55	57	50	44	44	42	35	39	42	38	28	49	47.0
	MIN	23	29	28	31	28	45	46	38	26	31	43	42	32	31	34	36	36	21	30	33	43	43	36	36	31	21	24	30	25	12	16	31.6
	MAX	28	30	47	44	40	60	62	57	35	27	36	47	51	33	31	43	44	40	32	43	49	42	37	43	41	28	29	35	32	21	36	39.5
	MIN	12	22	28	31	21	33	46	33	19	13	18	36	30	25	24	30	28	18	8	27	29	37	30	30	28	17	19	21	20	1	-3	23.6

See reference notes following Station Index.

DAILY TEMPERATURES

Table 5-Continued

Station		1	2	3	4	5	6	7	8	9	10	11	12	13	14	15	16	17	18	19	20	21	22	23	24	25	26	27	28	29	30	31
MUHLENBURG 1 SE	MAX	31	34	54	43	42	55	58	55	34	31	47	49	51	38	36	50	48	40	34	44	50	47	44	41	41	33	34	35	32	22	40
	MIN	10	24	23	29	29	39	43	28	25	10	18	29	27	27	29	37	31	18	6	25	30	38	32	31	28	13	18	20	18	3	3
NEWBURG 3 W	MAX																															
	MIN																															
NEW CASTLE 1 N	MAX	35	35	55	54	68	68	65	54	42	38	45	49	42	44	53	53	52	52	43	47	50	55	55	51	40	33	37	36	34	27	39
	MIN	18	30	30	21	27	46	52	37	28	22	30	36	31	28	33	40	39	26	14	35	42	46	36	40	30	23	29	28	24	14	19
NEWELL	MAX	34	36	55	59	62	70	69	64	47	38	51	52	58	46	52	67	53	56	41	54	57	58	57	56	52	36	38	44	40	30	41
	MIN	28	34	36	34	34	50	57	47	38	35	32	44	46	42	44	50	41	40	27	36	48	51	47	51	34	33	34	35	30	21	22
NEWPORT	MAX	35	38	38	58	58	43	56	69	55	36	43	46	56	55	37	39	54	55	44	40	55	51	50	44	46	39	35	40	41	34	27
	MIN	18	26	27	26	25	26	39	43	35	25	27	30	45	33	33	36	33	30	16	16	35	44	43	38	37	26	27	30	34	18	16
NEW STANTON	MAX	37	52	56	60	70	68	65	60	42	40	54	53	58	47	62	55	50	46	51	48	59	57	55	57	35	35	42	40	34	30	42
	MIN	24	29	26	20	25	36	52	40	27	24	22	37	34	35	44	38	31	18	14	38	44	37	36	33	29	27	30	28	17	10	19
NORRISTOWN	MAX	38	43	62	60	52	65	74	61	43	44	52	55	59	46	41	58	56	49	43	57	54	51	47	46	46	40	43	47	41	28	48
	MIN	25	32	37	30	31	46	46	43	28	26	37	44	46	35	36	38	39	26	20	36	44	42	37	38	33	27	30	36	27	19	20
PALMERTON	MAX	34	36	56	51	45	57	63	58	37	38	46	54	55	35	37	54	51	44	35	48	53	47	42	47	43	36	36	38	34	22	43
	MIN	20	30	31	25	27	40	40	35	22	20	25	40	33	30	31	32	32	16	14	29	35	39	35	35	29	19	26	25	22	12	15
PHIL DREXEL INST OF TEC	MAX	41	43	63	61	54	60	70	64	47	45	55	55	60	43	43	60	52	51	43	58	52	51	47	47	47	41	43	49	44	30	51
	MIN	32	36	40	42	39	48	49	47	33	30	35	48	40	36	38	41	45	33	25	39	44	44	40	39	36	34	35	38	34	24	26
PHILADELPHIA WB AP	MAX	38	43	63	60	52	58	69	63	46	45	54	54	59	42	41	58	50	50	43	58	51	51	46	46	45	37	41	48	41	27	50
	MIN	25	33	36	33	34	45	43	46	28	26	31	44	37	34	37	40	41	27	21	36	43	44	38	38	33	27	30	34	27	20	22
PHILADELPHIA PT BREEZE	MAX	38	43	62	59	52	56	69	62	46	46	55	53	57	43	43	58	50	50	47	58	52	52	55	49	43	39	43	50	46	38	52
	MIN	27	35	42	38	36	49	49	47	30	28	38	46	50	36	37	42	45	35	27	43	46	45	41	44	41	34	32	38	30	25	28
PHILADELPHIA SHAWMONT	MAX	37	42	62	58	56	62	72	69	55	44	50	55	58	49	42	56	52	46	43	55	52	50	50	46	45	41	40	47	47	35	49
	MIN	22	29	37	39	31	48	43	51	37	26	32	44	45	33	36	38	36	34	18	33	39	42	34	37	39	24	28	31	34	22	22
PHILADELPHIA CITY	MAX	38	42	61	59	52	58	68	64	48	45	53	53	58	43	42	58	51	50	42	57	53	50	49	47	47	38	42	49	44	28	50
	MIN	31	34	40	42	36	49	50	47	30	30	37	46	38	36	38	41	44	30	27	40	43	44	46	39	36	33	34	37	29	23	25
PHILIPSBURG CAA AP	MAX	29	36	46	48	44	54	60	50	32	31	40	45	50	33	35	45	45	42	39	44	49	49	40	47	30	29	33	33	29	15	36
	MIN	19	27	29	26	35	42	53	31	21	24	29	37	29	28	32	30	30	14	11	38	42	31	31	32	27	19	25	26	14	7	16
PHOENIXVILLE 1 E	MAX	46	42	58	60	58	61	65	59	58	53	51	55	58	47	41	60	55	50	42	59	56	50	50	46	47	42	42	46	47	35	49
	MIN	30	34	38	29	30	41	42	48	32	33	48								24	18	36	39	37	37	38	21	26	31	31	19	16
PIMPLE HILL	MAX	28	28	34	46	45	48	59	60	40	31	29	40	50	50	32	39	45	45	30	40	40	47	44	37	41	31	28	30	34	26	19
	MIN	16	19	26	30	22	26	47	38	29	13	22	28	38	26	27	29	33	30	11	26	33	39	30	29	36	17	20	22	25	0	1
PITTSBURGH WB AP 2	MAX	35	42	52	56	66	66	63	50	38	32	45	46	54	43	56	51	50	45	46	48	58	54	54	53	32	31	38	38	28	24	37
	MIN	25	31	35	34	36	51	49	38	27	27	29	39	33	35	35	42	40	22	18	41	48	41	40	32	30	28	30	28	17	10	24
PITTSBURGH WB CITY	MAX	38	46	55	58	68	68	63	52	41	38	49	52	57	46	64	55	53	48	51	54	60	58	57	57	35	34	42	38	31	27	40
	MIN	26	32	38	34	36	55	52	41	29	30	37	43	35	37	40	46	43	29	23	45	54	46	44	35	32	30	32	31	21	14	27
PLEASANT MOUNT 1 W	MAX	28	29	31	43	38	44	58	57	38	29	33	38	50	51	33	34	39	41	32	35	37	40	39	33	41	34	36	32	33	27	20
	MIN	12	19	26	27	18	21	38	33	28	9	18	33	31	25	26	30	25	27	8	16	26	32	31	31	32	15	16	16	16	1	-6
PORT CLINTON	MAX																															
	MIN																															
PUTNEYVILLE 2 SE DAM	MAX	29	34	45	51	49	61	62	62	43	33	37	45	55	37	40	55	46	47	33	41	51	51	55	49	30	33	32	35	35	27	35
	MIN	18	22	26	20	21	38	48	37	29	21	21	31	32	30	32	34	36	27	12	13	37	43	31	36	27	21	23	29	22	8	8
QUAKERTOWN 1 E	MAX	35	38	56	54	48	61	62	62	44	38	47	54	56	43	48	55	53	47	37	52	55	50	45	42	44	40	38	43	40	30	45
	MIN	20	27	29	24	25	42	36	43	29	20	25	42	42	33	33	35	32	30	14	28	32	36	35	35	35	19	26	38	29	14	14
READING WB CITY	MAX	37	40	60	59	49	55	66	62	40	44	49	55	57	39	40	56	55	47	41	56	56	48	45	45	43	37	40	44	38	28	49
	MIN	27	34	32	33	32	41	41	40	28	27	37	44	36	35	36	39	42	28	21	38	43	44	38	38	35	28	31	36	28	20	22
RIDGWAY 3 W	MAX	30	40	45	49	43	50	59	59	38	33	44	51	51	38	38	46	44	43	38	44	48	51	51	49	53	31	34	34	30	24	34
	MIN	8	21	29	19	23	30	41	39	26	18	16	21	32	30	35	35	33	29	7	19	36	42	34	37	30	24	26	25	25	9	11
SALINA 3 W	MAX	35	34	53	54	65	64	63	60	44	35	49	46	54	45	58	54	49	44	45	47	57	55	51	52	40	32	38	37	32	24	38
	MIN	24	30	33	24	33	48	50	41	26	25	25	39	34	34	39	43	38	26	15	35	44	44	36	39	29	26	28	31	22	12	17
SCRANTON	MAX	34	34	37	52	45	49	59	60	46	39	36	49	53	55	38	42	48	47	42	38	46	48	48	42	41	40	32	32	40	36	20
	MIN	19	18	27	28	24	26	42	40	28	18	18	32	39	29	28	35	30	29	12	12	35	40	32	32	32	32	22	28	22	6	8
SCRANTON WB AIRPORT	MAX	31	36	50	46	47	59	60	58	34	32	42	49	53	36	40	46	46	40	35	46	45	40	40	44	41	32	35	36	33	18	40
	MIN	19	29	29	27	25	44	43	31	16	15	25	37	29	29	33	33	32	15	12	31	35	38	35	35	24	19	22	27	16	5	12
SELINSGROVE CAA AP	MAX	35	37	57	53	44	57	65	58	35	39	42	54	52	37	38	55	52	45	35	51	47	48	42	43	41	35	37	38	34	24	46
	MIN	19	31	25	23	24	38	38	34	18	18	24	40	32	32	35	30	28	19	14	30	39	40	38	38	28	20	29	28	24	13	21
SHIPPENSBURG	MAX	37	41	62	65	55	62	70	65	47	36	37	55	52	45	37	56	57	49	45	56	62	58	48	46	43	38	42	43	39	29	47
	MIN	27	30	28	38	29	35	41	47	31	29	27	36	41	31	33	36	35	35	18	29	44	42	40	38	36	27	29	34	28	17	15
SHIPPINGPORT WB	MAX	35	45	53	53	67	67	63	51	38	34	47	48	50	45	54	52	52	47	47	50	57	56	56	57	34	33	38	37	30	28	40
	MIN	27	31	30	28	33	33	50	37	28	28	27	38	33	35	35	41	42	21	17	41	47	39	38	34	30	29	32	29	20	13	27
SLIPPERY ROCK	MAX	30	32	48	52	67	64	61	50	37	36	45	50	47	42	49	53	49	45	42	44	50	54	52	51	38	30	34	34	32	22	36
	MIN	19	28	31	28	34	50	50	36	24	22	30	36	29	29	33	39	37	23	16	34	41	40	36	36	28	22	24	26	20	10	13
SOMERSET MAIN ST	MAX	30	37	53	58	57	60	60	58	57	37	47	48	54	37	42	48	47	46	50	49	56	55	46	49	38	30	38	40	38	21	38
	MIN	19	26	34	32	30	39	49	45	27	24	27	38	34	33	34	38	31	26	14	39	47	43	36	36	25	24	23	29	20	7	13
SPRINGBORO	MAX	29	33	41	42	45	60	65	53	45	38	39	43	41	33	42	50	41	49	40	42	43	49	52	46	43	36	33	35	35	29	37
	MIN	18	27	30	21	28	41	51	37	24	24	28	34	29	23	32	33	35	26	15	18	36	42	34	39	29	26	28	26	23	11	13
SPRINGS 1 SW	MAX	30			56	56	60	60	57	58	32	48	49	54	34	39	52	47	45	48	48	55	56	43	50	34	27	36	39	34	16	36
	MIN	18	25		25	29	39	49	45	24	23	22	39	33	30	32	29	29	18	15	42	46	36	37	33	23	21	23	29	15	6	13
STATE COLLEGE	MAX	34	35	51	52	46	56	62	57	33	37	45	51	50	36	38	49	48	48	39	49	52	51	44	49	37	32	38	37	32	22	40
	MIN	24	31	35	35	31	43	51	33	23	27	31	42	33	30	34	36	36	25	18	37	40	42	37	37	32	24	30	32	20	12	22
STROUDSBURG	MAX	36	36	51	52	41	61	64	58	35	33	46	54	55	32	33	53	50	43	35	45	50	44	38	42	37	38	34	37	33	15	46
	MIN	14	24	28	25	22	37	35	34	20	13	18	40	31	30	32	32	28	18	10	23	29	34	33	33	28	15	17	22	15	4	4
TAMARACK 2 S FIRE TWR	MAX	24	27	36	45	44	46	55	56	41	23	28	37	48	45	32	40	41	43	31	36	43	45	47	38	46	30	27	31	30	25	28
	MIN	13	17	24	31	27	28	45	40	22	16	20	26	35	24	26	30	31	31	15	18	34	40	34	35	26	20	20	24	21	4	2
TIONESTA 2 SE DAM	MAX	29	31	42	45	42	59	60	60	39	29	34	44	50	34	39	50	45	47	30	40	44	48	55	51	49	32	32	35	35	27	35
	MIN	15	24	30	21	25	28	40	37	21	20	18	31	32	26	33	35	35	27	12	12	35	40	35	35	30	25	24	26	22	4	5
TITUSVILLE WATER WORKS	MAX	32	33	42	42	59	61	60	48	30	32	45	44	41	40	45	49	45	42	38	41	47	52	53	51	39	32	35	35	30	21	35
	MIN	14	27	28	19	24	46	46	31	23	17	25	30	28	23	34	35	30	16	10	34	37	41	35	36	29	27	26	24	19	1	14

See reference notes following Station Index.

Table 5 - Continued

DAILY TEMPERATURES

PENNSYLVANIA
DECEMBER 1956

Station		Day Of Month 1	2	3	4	5	6	7	8	9	10	11	12	13	14	15	16	17	18	19	20	21	22	23	24	25	26	27	28	29	30	31	Average
TOWANDA	MAX	36	36	53	49	45	64	64	61	33	35	43	52	53	36	40	49	47	45	41	49	47	48	47	51	45	38	39	37	34	21	41	44.5
	MIN	13	29	31	25	21	40	42	31	22	14	22	36	29	27	33	33	25	18	14	29	29	38	37	37	28	19	28	25	19	2	1	25.7
UNIONTOWN	MAX	38	46	60	62	72	67	65	59	47	40	50	50	58	44	67	56	53	46	50	51	58	58	57	57	36	32	43	42	35	27	40	50.5
	MIN	26	32	34	29	37	54	59	46	30	29	28	42	36	38	40	42	35	24	18	46	50	43	41	36	30	30	31	33	22	12	17	34.5
UPPER DARBY	MAX	37	42	63	59	52	60	72	62	48	44	52	54	59	44	42	57	52	49	42	56	54	53	46	46	46	40	40	48	45	30	49	49.8
	MIN	24	30	37	31	33	46	44	47	32	25	33	45	42	34	36	39	39	30	27	35	45	43	34	38	38	25	27	30	31	20	19	34.2
WARREN	MAX	33	33	42	45	55	60	59	51	34	33	42	46	48	39	42	49	45	43	39	41	45	53	53	45	35	32	34	35	30	22	35	41.9
	MIN	14	28	31	24	29	46	51	34	18	17	29	32	26	25	35	36	35	18	15	35	35	43	37	35	28	25	28	29	20	15	17	28.7
WAYNESBURG 2 W	MAX	36	45	57	63	60	68	68	61	46	36	52	49	59	47	67	59	54	47	52	50	60	56	58	59	41	32	44	42	36	25	41	50.6
	MIN	25	32	33	24	27	42	60	39	28	29	23	40	35	34	41	43	29	28	13	32	47	40	37	40	29	28	29	27	22	13	13	31.7
WELLSBORO 3 S	MAX	26	29	37	45	45	44	59	59	37	25	30	40	49	47	32	40	45	44	32	37	45	45	49	41	45	34	30	33	30	26	24	38.8
	MIN	14	15	25	30	22	30	40	34	21	14	22	29	34	23	26	31	30	31	15	17	34	37	34	34	30	19	22	25	23	0	- 3	24.5
WELLSVILLE	MAX	40	40	65	61	49	56	65	64	48	44	48	55	55	45	38	56	56	48	43	55	51	52	52	45	45	38	42	44	39	30	50	49.0
	MIN	20	27	25	23	23	42	35	47	30	20	23	40	45	32	34	37	32	31	15	28	45	40	39	37	35	22	25	28	30	18	13	30.4
WEST CHESTER	MAX	36	44	49	58	51	50	60	60	60	36	48	56	53	53	40	47	54	53	42	48	57	44	42	41	39	35	35	45	37	34	45	46.8
	MIN	26	24	36	31	36	34	40	36	34	26	35	34	43	34	35	39	41	20	22	36	43	38	36	36	36	23	26	34	18	17	26	32.1
WILLIAMSPORT WB AP	MAX	35	37	54	51	42	48	52	57	35	39	42	52	51	37	40	51	49	42	34	50	49	51	43	43	41	36	38	38	34	23	42	43.1
	MIN	18	32	29	27	28	37	38	34	19	20	27	38	33	29	35	30	30	20	16	25	35	40	39	38	29	21	29	28	23	12	20	28.4
YORK 3 SSW PUMP STA	MAX	38	42	63	63	54	60	70	65	50	44	49	56	57	47	39	58	57	49	46	57	57	55	52	48	48	40	45	45	44	32	51	51.0
	MIN	22	29	28	27	25	38	38	50	31	23	29	43	47	34	36	39	34	32	18	31	45	42	40	38	37	26	27	30	31	20	16	32.5

See reference notes following Station Index.

Day of month

Station		1	2	3	4	5	6	7	8	9	10	11	12	13	14	15	16	17	18	19	20	21	22	23	24	25	26	27	28	29	30	31
ALLENTOWN WB AIRPORT	SNOWFALL		T	T						.6				T	T													.5	T	T		T
	SN ON GND										T				T																	
	WTR EQUIV																															
AUSTINBURG 2 W	SNOWFALL			1.0						1.0	2.0	T																T	T	2.0	T	1.
	SN ON GND	2	1	2	T					1	3	2	T															T	T	2	2	3
BEACH CREEK STATION	SNOWFALL	T	T	1.0							1.5																	T	T	.5		T
	SN ON GND	T	T	1	T	T					2	1	T															T	T	1	1	1
BRADFORD 4 W RESVR	SNOWFALL	1.3	2.6	1.7						5.0									1.3					-	-	-	-	-	-	-	-	3.
	SN ON GND	5	7	5	3	2	1			5	4	3	1	1					1	T				-	-	-	-	-	-	-	-	8
BROOKVILLE CAA AIRPORT	SNOWFALL	.6	1.3							6.0									T						T	.8	1.1	1.3	2.5	.2	.8	1.
	SN ON GND	1	2	1						1	5	5													T	1	1	3	2	5	6	4
CANTON 1 NW	SNOWFALL	1.8	1.6	1.3	T					2.1	.9					T												T	.9	3.0	T	
	SN ON GND	2	2	3	T	T				2	3	3	T		T	T												T	1	4	4	4
CARROLLTOWN 2 SSE	SNOWFALL	2.0	1.0								1.0				.5				T							.5	.5	1.0		1.0	1.0	T
	SN ON GND	4	4	2	T	T					1	1			T	T			T							T	1	2	2	3	4	4
COALDALE 2 NW	SNOWFALL			.5							.8																	.2	1.5	1.0		
	SN ON GND			1							1																	T	2	1	1	
CORRY	SNOWFALL	.5	1.0							4.0																2.0	.5	.5	1.5	T	T	1.
	SN ON GND	5	6	2	2	T				4	3	T														2	2	3	4	4	4	5
DONEGAL	SNOWFALL	T	2.5							1.0									T							1.0	1.0	2.0	2.0	2.0	4.0	1.
	SN ON GND	3	5	4	T					1	T															1	2	2	4	6	8	3
DU BOIS 7 E	SNOWFALL	.5	2.0							5.0									T							.5	1.0	1.5	1.0	2.5		1.
	SN ON GND	1	3	T	T					4	3															T	1	2	3	4	4	4
ENGLISH CENTER	SNOWFALL	-	-	-	-	-	-	-	-	-	-	-	-	-	-	-	-	-	-	-	-	-	-	-	-	-	-	-	-	-	-	-
	SN ON GND	-	-	-	-	-	-	-	-	-	-	-	-	-	-	-	-	-	-	-	-	-	-	-	-	-	-	-	-	-	-	-
ERIE CAA AIRPORT	SNOWFALL	.7	1.6						T	3.0	T								T						T	1.3	T	1.0	1.0	.6	T	1.
	SN ON GND	19	20	12	9	6				2	2	T	T													1	1	1	1	2	3	3
EVERETT 1 SW	SNOWFALL									1.9			T	T														.2				
	SN ON GND	-	-	-	-	-	-	-	-	-	-	-	-	-	-	-	-	-	-	-	-	-	-	-	-	-	-	-	-	-	-	-
FORD CITY 4 S DAM	SNOWFALL	1.0	.5	.5							3.0															.5	1.0	4.5	T	2.0	.5	T
	SN ON GND	1	1								2	1														1	1	3	T	1	2	T
GALETON	SNOWFALL	.3		1.9					T	3.5	2.3	T			T												T	.6	.5	2.5		2.
	SN ON GND	3		2	1					3	4	3	T														T	1	1	3	1	[illegible]
GRATERFORD	SNOWFALL										T																		T			
	SN ON GND																															
GREENSBORO LOCK 7	SNOWFALL	.5	.5	T																									T	3.0	1.0	1
	SN ON GND	T																										T		2	2	
HANOVER	SNOWFALL																											T	T			
	SN ON GND																											T				
HARRISBURG WB AIRPORT	SNOWFALL	.2	T							.4																	T	.1		T	T	[illegible]
	SN ON GND										T																	T				
	WTR EQUIV																															
HAWLEY 1 S DAM	SNOWFALL			1.0							1.6																		T			[illegible]
	SN ON GND			1							2	T			T														T			[illegible]
HOLTWOOD	SNOWFALL			T					T																			T	T		T	
	SN ON GND																												T			
HOOVERSVILLE	SNOWFALL	1.5	1.0	.7							.4															1.8	1.6	3.0		1.0	3.5	
	SN ON GND	2	2	1							T															1	1	3	1	1	3	
INDIANA 3 SE	SNOWFALL	1.1	.4							1.0	T															.6	.5	1.7		.3	1.2	
	SN ON GND	1	1							1	T															1	1	3	1	1	2	
KANE 1 NNE	SNOWFALL	2.0	1.5						3.8	2.7	.2							T	T						1.0	.3	2.1	.5	3.7	1.5	.6	2
	SN ON GND	3	4	4	3	2	1		4	6	5	4	1						T	T						1	1	2	5	6	6	
KEATING SUMMIT	SNOWFALL	.5		3.0						4.0	1.0															.5		1.3	1.0	2.1		1
	SN ON GND	2	2	5	2	1				4	5	4	1													1		1	2	4	4	
LANCASTER 2 NE PUMP STA	SNOWFALL									T																		T				
	SN ON GND																															
LAWRENCEVILLE 2 S	SNOWFALL		T	T						1.8	1.2																	T	T	1.2	.4	
	SN ON GND	1	T	T	T					2	3	3	T															T	T	1	1	
LEWISTOWN	SNOWFALL	T									.5																	T	.3		T	
	SN ON GND	T									1																	T			T	
MARTINSBURG CAA AIRPORT	SNOWFALL	T	T							T	T														T	T	T	1.0	T	T	T	
	SN ON GND		T								T															T	T	1		T	T	
MATAMORAS	SNOWFALL			1.0							1.5				1.0																	
	SN ON GND			1							1	1			1	1																
MEADVILLE 1 S	SNOWFALL	.7	3.0	.6						2.8	.7				T				T	T						2.0	.7	2.0	.2	.5	5.1	
	SN ON GND	3	4	2	1	T				3	3	2							T							2	2	3	2	2	5	
MEDIX RUN	SNOWFALL	.2	.5	.5						1.5	3.0	T			T				T	T						T	T	.7	T	1.5	.5	
	SN ON GND	T	1	2	T					2	4	3	T						T							T		1	T	2	2	
MONTROSE 1 E	SNOWFALL	T	.3	1.7						T	3.2	T			T				T	T						T	T	.4	2.6	4.7	T	2
	SN ON GND	T	T	2	T	T				T	3	3	2		T	T			T	T	T					T	T	T	3	7	7	
MUHLENBURG 1 SE	SNOWFALL		T	2.0						4.0																		1.0	2.0	.5		
	SN ON GND			2	1																							1	3	4	4	
NEWPORT	SNOWFALL	T		T																								.5			T	
	SN ON GND																															
PHILADELPHIA WB AIRPORT	SNOWFALL									T																	T	.2		T		
	SN ON GND																											T				
	WTR EQUIV																															
PHILIPSBURG CAA AIRPORT	SNOWFALL	.3	.7							3.4	T			T					T						T	T	T	.9	2.0	1.5	T	
	SN ON GND	2	2	2							3	2														T	T	1	1	4	4	

See reference notes following Station Index.

Table 7 - Continued

SNOWFALL AND SNOW ON GROUND

PENNSYLVANIA
DECEMBER 1956

Station		1	2	3	4	5	6	7	8	9	10	11	12	13	14	15	16	17	18	19	20	21	22	23	24	25	26	27	28	29	30	31
PIMPLE HILL	SNOWFALL		.2	1.1							1.4	T			.5				.1	.1						T	.1	.5	1.5	.8	.4	.5
	SN ON GND	1	1	2	T	T	T				1	1	T		T	T	T	T	T	T	T	T	T	T	T	T	T	T	2	2	2	3
PITTSBURGH WB AIRPORT	SNOWFALL	.4	.8							3.2	T								T						T	.3	.6	1.6	1.3	2.7	T	.3
	SN ON GND	1	T								2	1														T	T	2	1	2	4	2
	WTR EQUIV										.2																	.2		.2	.4	.3
PLEASANT MOUNT 1 W	SNOWFALL		T	5.0						T	3.0	T			T	T	T		T	T							T	T	2.0	4.0	T	1.0
	SN ON GND	T	T	5	T	T	T			T	3	3	T		T	T	T	T	T	T							T	T	2	5	5	6
READING WB CITY	SNOWFALL	T	T							T				T	T													.1		T		
	SN ON GND										T																					
SCRANTON WB AIRPORT	SNOWFALL		.4	.4						1.9					.4				T							T	T	.7	1.2	.1	T	.5
	SN ON GND			1							2	2			T													T		1	1	1
	WTR EQUIV										.2	.1																				
SELINSGROVE CAA AIRPORT	SNOWFALL	T	T							1.0				T	T												T	T	T	T		T
	SN ON GND			T							1	T			T													T		T		T
SHIPPENSBURG	SNOWFALL	T	T	T						T																	T	T			1.0	
	SN ON GND																														T	
SHIPPENSBURG WB	SNOWFALL	T	1.3							6.0																T	T	1.5	1.0	1.0		T
	SN ON GND		1							6	T	T														T	T	T	T	2	1	T
SLIPPERY ROCK	SNOWFALL	.5	.5	T						T	5.0															1.0	1.0	3.0		3.0	T	
	SN ON GND	1	1	T						T	5	3	2													1	1	4	1	3	3	3
SPRING 1 SW	SNOWFALL	.6								.5	T														T	1.0	.5	1.0	T	3.0	1.5	T
	SN ON GND	2	2							1															T	1	1	1	T	3	4	4
TAMARACK 2 S FIRE TWR	SNOWFALL	T	.7	4.0						1.0	4.0				T	.2			T							.3	.2	.8	.8	3.5	.5	.5
	SN ON GND	2	3	6	3	2	T			1	4	4	2	T	T	T			T							T	T	1	2	5	5	5
TIONESTA 2 SE DAM	SNOWFALL	.2	1.8	2.0	T					5.0	2.0								T							1.0	.3	1.3	.5	2.0	2.0	.5
	SN ON GND	T	2	3	T					5	7	4	T						T							1	1	2	2	3	5	4
TOWANDA	SNOWFALL	T	T	.7						.5	3.8			T	T	.5			T	T							T	T	T	3.0	.4	T
	SN ON GND	T	T	1	T					T	4	3	T		T														T	3	3	3
TOWER CITY 5 SW	SNOWFALL		T							2.0																		.5		T		
	SN ON GND	-	-	-	-	-	-	-	-	-	-	-	-	-	-	-	-	-	-	-	-	-	-	-	-	-	-	-	-	-	-	-
WILLIAMSPORT WB AIRPORT	SNOWFALL	T	.2	.1						2.4	T				.4													.3	2.2	.5	T	.4
	SN ON GND	T	T	T							2	T			T													T		1	1	1
	WTR EQUIV										.2																					

CLIMATOLOGICAL DATA

TABLE 2

PENNSYLVANIA
DELAYED DATA

Station	Temperature													Precipitation									
										No. of Days								Snow, Sleet			No. of Days		
										Max.		Min.											
	Average Maximum	Average Minimum	Average	Departure From Long Term Means	Highest	Date	Lowest	Date	Degree Days	90° or Above	32° or Below	32° or Below	0° or Below	Total	Departure From Long Term Means	Greatest Day	Date	Total	Max. Depth on Ground	Date	10 or More	50 or More	1.00 or More
JUNE 1956																							
CHESTER	83.8M	61.6M	72.7M		96	14+	50	20	8	10	0	0	0	3.05		.70	3+	.0	0		7	2	0
LEBANON	82.5	61.0	71.8	+1.9	96	14+	52	3+	20	8	0	0	0	4.11	-.02	1.15	11	.0	0		9	3	1
NOVEMBER 1956																							
HUNTINGDON	55.5	29.6	42.6	+0.8	78	16	10	25	667	0	1	19	0	1.99	-.69	1.13	2	.7			5	1	1

See reference notes following Station Index.

DAILY PRECIPITATION

Table 3

Station	1	2	3	4	5	6	7	8	9	10	11	12	13	14	15	16	17	18	19	20	21	22	23	24	25	26	27	28	29	30	31	Total
FEBRUARY 1955																																
WATSONTOWN	.03	.16				.91	.20				.60			.05	T	.33	T				T	T	.52			T	.03	T				2.83
MARCH 1955																																
WATSONTOWN	.40			.55	T	.10	.01		.02	T	.15	T			.13	.40		.20			.45	1.00	T	T		.28	T		T			3.69
FEBRUARY 1956																																
LAFAYETTE MCKEAN PARK	T	.37			.15		.83	T				.82	T		.15	.14	.26	.25	.10		.02	.03	.04	T	.99	.38		.36	T			4.89
MARCH 1956																																
LAFAYETTE MCKEAN PARK	T	.15	.09	.40		1.09	.78	1.10	.13	T			T	.12	.23	.02	.87						-	-	-	-	-	-	-	-	-	-
MAY 1956																																
GIFFORD	.01		.46				.76			.78	.07	.74	1.09			.30	.11	.33	.08				.02				.34	.08			.35	5.5[illegible]
JUNE 1956																																
CHESTER	.43	.11	.70								.70					.38		.02		.02		.07	.03		.48			.11				3.0[illegible]
GIFFORD	.70		.53	.23	.07												.61	.26			.07			.08	.56		.26	.03				3.4[illegible]
LEBANON	.14	.07	.93							.02	1.15				.51			.12	T		.34	.34		.13	.02		.34					4.1[illegible]
JULY 1956																																
BARTO	-	-	-	-	-	-	-	-	-	-	-	-	-	-	-	-	-	-	-	-	-	-	-	-	-	-	.08	.06	.09			-
AUGUST 1956																																
BARTO						.30						.06	.20							1.30	.42								1.80			4.0[illegible]
PAUPACK 2 NNW						.01	.20		.02					.24				.05	.02		.73	.29		.05			.01	.01	.22		.23	2.0[illegible]
SEPTEMBER 1956																																
GIFFORD	.45	.23				.58	.07				.09	.02			.25	1.11	.01	.14		.44	.10	.21	.02	.03								3.7[illegible]
HUNTINGDON	T	.78	.04									.12		.09	T	.28	.02	.29		.09	.02	.04		.36				.03				2.1[illegible]
NOVEMBER 1956																																
HUNTINGDON	.10	1.13	T													.13		.15			.03	.42	T	T		.03				T		1.9[illegible]

DAILY TEMPERATURES

Table 5

Station		1	2	3	4	5	6	7	8	9	10	11	12	13	14	15	16	17	18	19	20	21	22	23	24	25	26	27	28	29	30	31	Average
JUNE 1956																																	
CHESTER	MAX	91	82		73	73	79	82	85	89		75	83	89	96	96	96		90	71	75	70	74	90		92	86	87	90	85	80		83.8
	MIN	65	58		55	52	59	55	57	58		58	58	69	74	69	67		67	55	50	60	67	70		66	64	71	63	56	59		61.6
LEBANON	MAX	90	71	62	68	73	78	80	87	89	69	82	84	91	96	96	95	93	89	72	75	68	75	92	92	89	85	86	87	84	78		82.5
	MIN	66	54	52	54	52	58	56	59	61	59	58	58	69	69	69	72	71	62	57	53	57	63	69	67	66	61	66	63	54	56		61.0
NOVEMBER 1956																																	
HUNTINGDON	MAX	72	76	74	57	67	71	69	67	58	47	56	67	65	59	70	78	55	54	48	48	45	59	37	29	34	34	41	41	47	41		55.5
	MIN	51	52	55	51	40	33	34	43	38	35	18	25	28	24	22	31	25	24	20	19	29	34	18	14	10	15	27	28	29	15		29.6

EVAPORATION AND WIND

Table 6

Station		1	2	3	4	5	6	7	8	9	10	11	12	13	14	15	16	17	18	19	20	21	22	23	24	25	26	27	28	29	30	31	Total or Avg.
JUNE 1956																																	
STATE COLLEGE	EVAP	-	-	-	-	-	-	-	-	-	-	-	-	-	-	-	-	-	-	.10	*	*	.29	.10	.32	.25	.19	.20	.29	.26	.12		-
	WIND	-	-	-	-	-	-	-	-	-	-	-	-	-	-	-	-	-	-	-	-	-	-	40	31	61	58	24	70	83	41		-

CORRECTIONS

ANNUAL 1955

Table 2:	Watsontown	Precipitation total for February should be 2.83; total for March, 3.69; Annual total, E37.69.

TOTAL PRECIPITATION

PENNSYLVANIA
DECEMBER 1956

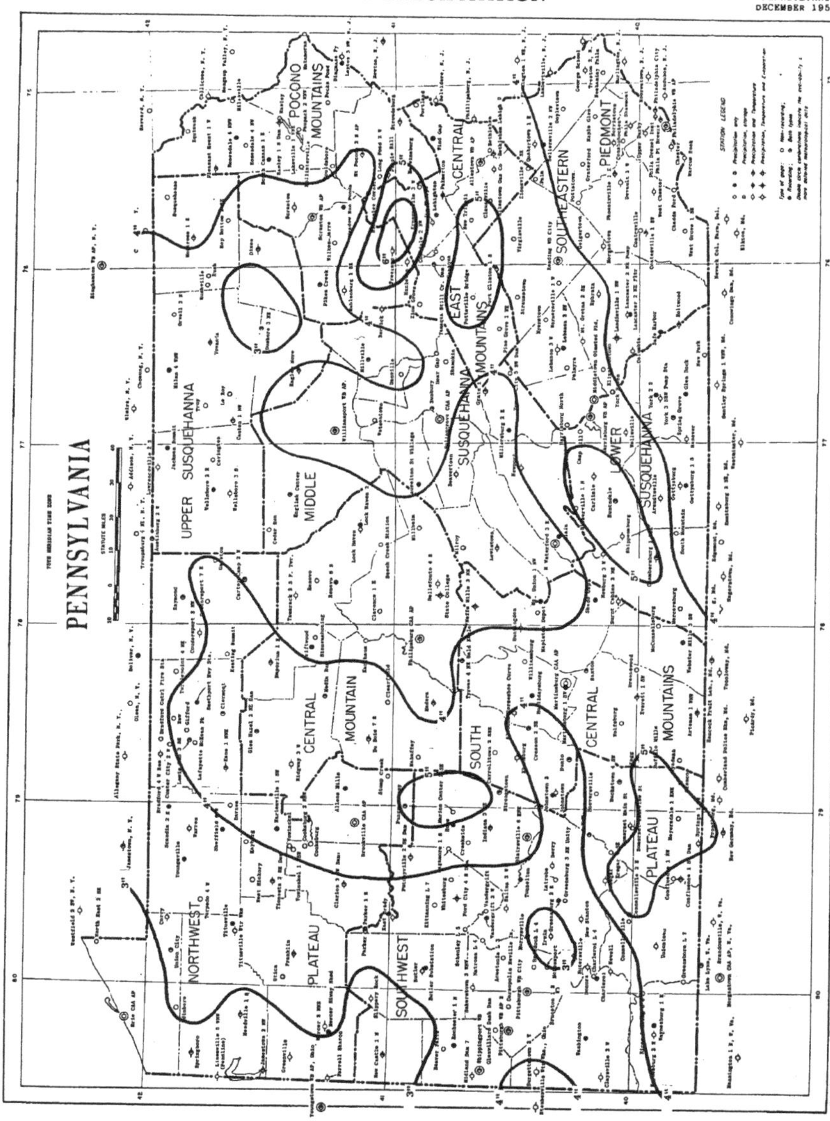

Isolines are drawn through points of approximately equal values. Hourly precipitation data from recorder substations will be available in the publication 'Hourly Precipitation Data'.

AVERAGE TEMPERATURE

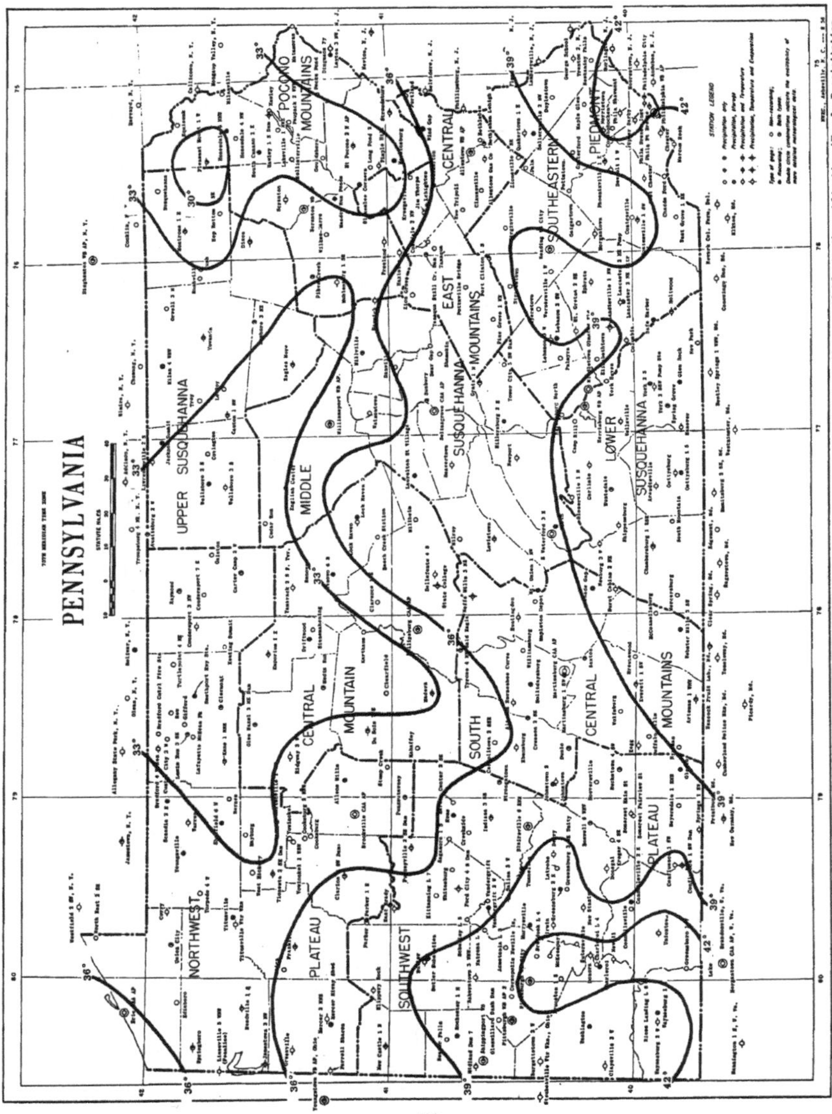

Isolines are drawn through points of approximately equal values. Hourly precipitation data from recorder substations will be available in the publication 'Hourly Precipitation Data'.

STATION INDEX

Station	Index No.	County	Drainage	Latitude	Longitude	Elevation	Observation Time: Temp.	Observation Time: Precip.	Observer	Refer To Tables
ACMETONIA LOCK 3	0022	ALLEGHENY	1	40 32	79 49	748		7A	CORPS OF ENGINEERS	3
ALLENS MILLS	0099	JEFFERSON	1	41 12	78 55	1000		MID	CHARLES H. ALLEN	C
ALLENTOWN WB AP	0106	LEHIGH	9	40 39	75 26	376	MID	MID	U.S. WEATHER BUREAU	2 3 5 7 C
ALLENTOWN GAS CO	0111	LEHIGH	9	40 36	75 28	254	7A	7A	LEHIGH VLY GAS DIV	2 3 5
ALTOONA HORSESHOE CURVE	0134	BLAIR	6	40 30	78 29	1500	6P	6P	ALTOONA WATER BUR.	2 3 5
ARENDTSVILLE	0229	ADAMS	15	39 55	77 18	710	8A	8A	PA STATE COL EXP	2 3 5
ARTEMAS 1 WNW	0259	BEDFORD	12	39 45	78 28	1250	6P	6P	GRAYSON E.NORTHCRAFT	2 3 5 C
AUSTINBURG 2 W	0313	TIOGA	15	42 00	77 32	1590		7A	OTTO D. BACON	3 7 C
BAKERSTOWN 3 WNW	0355	ALLEGHENY	1	40 39	79 59	1230	7P	7P	PGH CUT FLOWER CO	2 3 5
BARNES	0409	WARREN	1	41 40	79 02	1310		7A	CORPS OF ENGINEERS	3
BARTO 4 NW	0428	BERKS	14	40 26	75 39	312		7A	MARIE B. NICHLAS	3
BEAR GAP	0457	NORTHUMBERLAND	15	40 50	76 30	900		MID	ROARING CRK WTR CO	3
BEAVER FALLS	0475	BEAVER	2	40 46	80 19	760		7A	HOWARD R. KEMP	3
BEAVERTOWN	0482	SNYDER	15	40 45	77 10	640	7A	7A	MARLIN RC ETTINGER	2 3 5
BEECH CREEK STATION	0499	CENTRE	16	41 04	77 34	620		7A	HAROLD S. RUPERT	3 7
BELLEFONTE 4 S	0530	CENTRE	16	40 51	77 47	1110	8A	8A	ROCKVIEW PRISON FARM	2 3 5
BERNE	0599	BERKS	14	40 31	76 00	325		7A	FLOYD W. TRUMP	3
BERWICK	0611	COLUMBIA	15	41 04	76 15	570	6P	6P	AMER CAR + FNDRY CO	2 3 5
BETHLEHEM	0629	NORTHAMPTON	9	40 37	75 22	400		7A	ARTHUR CROPPER	3
#BETHLEHEM LEHIGH UNIV	0634	NORTHAMPTON	9	40 36	75 23	450	MID	MID	LEHIGH UNIVERSITY	2 3 5 C
BLAIN	0725	PERRY	15	40 20	77 31	750		MID	PA DEPT FRST + WTRS	C
BLAIRSVILLE 6 ENE	0736	INDIANA	4	40 27	79 09	2048	8P	8P	U.S. WEATHER BUREAU	2 3 5
BLAKESLEE CORNERS	0743	MONROE	9	41 06	75 36	1650		MID	WALTER WILDRICK	C
BLOSERVILLE 1 N	0763	CUMBERLAND	15	40 16	77 22	650		5P	MRS. B. M. WILLDERS	3
BOSWELL 6 WNW	0820	SOMERSET	1	40 11	79 08	2580		7A	MRS. MAE L. KIMMEL	3 C
BRADDOCK LOCK 2	0861	ALLEGHENY	10	40 24	79 52	725		7A	CORPS OF ENGINEERS	3
BRADFORD CNTRL FIRE STA	0867	MC KEAN	1	41 57	78 39	1500		8A	BRADFORD FIRE DEPT	3
BRADFORD 4 W RES	0868	MC KEAN	1	41 57	78 44	1680	5P	5P	BRADFORD WTR DEPT	2 3 5 7
BREEZEWOOD	0905	BEDFORD	6	40 00	78 14	1352		MID	PA TURNPIKE COMM	3
BROOKVILLE CAA AIRPORT	1002	JEFFERSON	1	41 09	79 06	1417	MID	MID	CIVIL AERO. ADM.	2 3 5 7
BRUCETON 1 S	1033	ALLEGHENY	10	40 18	79 59	1065		7A	AUSTIN R. COOPER	3
BUCKSTOWN 1 SE	1073	SOMERSET	4	40 04	78 50	2460		MID	ALVIN N. MANGES	C
BUFFALO MILLS	1087	BEDFORD	6	39 57	78 39	1318		7A	MRS. NELLE R. BROWN	3
BURGETTSTOWN 2 W	1105	WASHINGTON	11	40 23	80 26	980	7A	7A	SMITH TWP MUN AUTH	2 3 5
BURNT CABINS 2 NE	1115	HUNTINGDON	6	40 05	77 52	990	MID	MID	PA TURNPIKE COMM	INAC 10/56
#BUTLER	1130	BUTLER	2	40 52	79 54	1100	4P	7A	WILLIAM C. FAUST	2 3 5
BUTLER SUBSTATION	1135	BUTLER	2	40 51	79 53	1140		MID	WEST PENN POWER CO	C
CAMP HILL	1198	CUMBERLAND	15	40 15	76 55	461		6P	JOSEPH N. HOBART	3
CANTON 1 NW	1215	BRADFORD	15	41 40	76 52	1520	7A	7A	MRS.MILDRED SPENCER	2 3 5 7 C
CARLISLE	1234	CUMBERLAND	15	40 12	77 11	460	6P	6P	C. E. MILLER	2 3 5
CARROLLTOWN 2 SSE	1255	CAMBRIA	16	40 35	78 42	2040		8A	ROBERT F. MAURER	3 7
CARTER CAMP 2 W	1262	POTTER	16	41 37	77 45	2030		7A	RICHARD L. MENKEN	3 C
CEDAR RUN	1301	LYCOMING	16	41 31	77 27	800		7A	KATHRYN T.KREIGHBAUM	3
CHADDS FORD	1342	DELAWARE	5	39 52	75 36	160		8A	MRS.GRACE A. WICKS	3
CHAMBERSBURG 1 ESE	1354	FRANKLIN	12	39 56	77 38	640	9P	9P	CHARLES A. BENDER	2 3 5 C
CHARLEROI	1372	WASHINGTON	10	40 08	79 55	1040		MID	WEST PENN POWER CO	C
CHARLEROI LOCK 4	1377	WESTMORELAND	10	40 09	79 54	749		7A	CORPS OF ENGINEERS	3
#CHESTER	1423	DELAWARE	5	39 51	75 22	86	8A	8A	CHESTER TIMES	2 3 5
CLARENCE	1480	CENTRE	16	41 03	77 56	1410		7A	MISS VELDA SWANCER	3
CLARION 3 SW	1485	CLARION	1	41 12	79 26	1114	8P	7A	PA ELECTRIC CO	2 3 5 C
CLAUSSVILLE	1505	LEHIGH	9	40 37	75 39	670		8A	WILLIAM J. DOTTERER	3
CLAYSVILLE 3 W	1512	WASHINGTON	11	40 07	80 28	1000	7P	7A	MFGRS. L + H CO	2 3 5
CLEARFIELD	1519	CLEARFIELD	16	41 01	78 26	1100		7A	IRA TAYLOR	3
CLERMONT	1529	MC KEAN	1	41 41	78 30	2104		7A	MRS.TILLIE M.SIMONDS	3 C
COALDALE 2 NW	1572	SCHUYLKILL	9	40 50	75 56	1026		7A	PANTHER VLY WTR CO	3 7
COATESVILLE 1 SW	1589	CHESTER	5	39 58	75 50	342	8A	8A	PHILA ELECTRIC CO	2 3 5 C
COATESVILLE	1594	CHESTER	5	39 59	75 49	340		8A	EDWARD D. BIEDEMAN	INAC 12/55
COLUMBIA	1675	LANCASTER	15	40 02	76 30	300	SS	SS	JAMES H. RUST	2 3 5
CONFLUENCE 1 SW DAM	1705	SOMERSET	17	39 48	79 22	1490	8A	8A	CORPS OF ENGINEERS	2 3 5 6 C
CONFLUENCE 1 NW	1710	FAYETTE	17	39 50	79 22	1331		7A	JOHN L. REID	3
CONNELLSVILLE	1723	FAYETTE	17	40 01	79 36	870		8A	MARSHALL B. MENEFEE	3
CONNELLSVILLE 2 E	1729	FAYETTE	17	40 01	79 33	1300		MID	HARRY C. JOY	C
CONSHOHOCKEN	1737	MONTGOMERY	5	40 04	75 19	70		8A	PHILA ELECTRIC CO	3
COOKSBURG	1749	CLARION	1	41 20	79 13	1180		8A	PA DEPT FRST + WTRS	3
COOKSBURG 2 NNW	1752	CLARION	1	41 21	79 13	1460		8A	PA DEPT FRST + WTRS	3
CORAOPOLIS NEVILLE IS	1773	ALLEGHENY	11	40 30	80 05	720		8A	PGH. COKE + CHEM CO	3
CORRY	1790	ERIE	1	41 56	79 38	1427	7P	8A	LEO C. HECKERS	2 3 5 7
COUDERSPORT 3 NW	1806	POTTER	1	41 49	78 03	2020	7P	8A	MISS ELIZABETH NEFF	2 3 5
COUDERSPORT 7 E	1809	POTTER	1	41 46	77 53	2425		7A	CAMP POTATO	3
COVINGTON 2 WSW	1833	TIOGA	15	41 44	77 07	1745		7A	CALVIN R. PACKARD	3
CREEKSIDE	1881	INDIANA	1	40 41	79 12	1035		7A	CORPS OF ENGINEERS	3
CRESSON 2 SE	1895	CAMBRIA	6	40 27	78 34	2540		7A	TALMAGE R. FRAZER	3 C
CUSTER CITY 2 W	1978	MC KEAN	1	41 55	78 41	2120		8A	M. D. BOOTH AND CO	3
DANVILLE	2013	MONTOUR	15	40 58	76 37	460		7A	MRS.MARIE M. LITTLE	3
DERRY	2108	WESTMORELAND	4	40 20	79 18	1150	6P	6P	MISS N. D. WINEMAN	2 3 5
DEVAULT 1 W	2116	CHESTER	14	40 05	75 33	360	MID	MID	PA TURNPIKE COMM	2 3 5
DINGMANS FERRY	2160	PIKE	5	41 13	74 52	364		MID	CLYDE T. VOORHEES	C
DIXON	2171	WYOMING	15	41 34	75 54	620	7A	7A	HAROLD J. KUSCHEL	2 3 5 C
DONEGAL	2183	WESTMORELAND	17	40 07	79 23	1746	MID	MID	PA TURNPIKE COMM	2 3 5 7
#DONORA	2190	WASHINGTON	10	40 11	79 51	814	12M	12M	DONORA ZINC WORKS	2 3 5
DOYLESTOWN	2221	BUCKS	5	40 18	75 08	393		5P	GEORGE HART	3
DRIFTWOOD	2245	CAMERON	16	41 20	78 08	880		MID	SIDNEY KENNEDY	C
DU BOIS 7 E	2265	CLEARFIELD	16	41 06	78 38	1670	5P	5P	CITY OF DU BOIS	2 3 5 7 C
DUNLO	2298	CAMBRIA	4	40 17	78 43	2410		MID	MRS. D. L. WHITE	C
DUSHORE 3 NE	2324	SULLIVAN	16	41 33	76 21	1750		7A	PATRICK F. RYAN	3 C
EAGLES MERE	2343	SULLIVAN	16	41 24	76 35	2020	7A	7A	MRS.ELSIE P. BIGGER	2 3 5 C
EAST BRADY	2363	CLARION	1	40 59	79 37	820	5P	5P	A. B. KEMPEL	2 3 5
EAST WATERFORD 3 E	2459	PERRY	6	40 21	77 33	2125	8A	8A	U.S. WEATHER BUREAU	INAC 5/55
EBENSBURG	2466	CAMBRIA	4	40 29	78 43	2090	7P	7A	ROBERT A. WASSER	2 3 5
EDINBORO	2514	ERIE	1	41 52	80 08	1220		8A	EDINBORO ST TCHR COL	3
ELIZABETHTOWN	2560	LANCASTER	15	40 09	76 37	460		8A	MASONIC HOME	3
EMPORIUM 2 SSW	2634	CAMERON	16	41 28	78 15	1735	7A	7A	JACKSON THOMAS	2 3 5 C
ENGLISH CENTER	2644	LYCOMING	16	41 26	77 17	881		7A	WILLIAM SUDERS	3 7 C
EPHRATA	2662	LANCASTER	15	40 11	76 10	465	6P	6P	STANLEY L.VON NEIDA	2 3 5
EQUINUNK	2669	WAYNE	5	41 51	75 13	900		8A	MRS.ROSE M. NEILSEN	3
ERIE CAA AIRPORT	2682	ERIE	8	42 05	80 12	732	MID	MID	CIVIL AERO. ADM.	2 3 5 7
EVERETT 1 SW	2721	BEDFORD	6	40 00	78 23	1020	MID	MID	PA TURNPIKE COMM	2 3 5 7 C
FARRELL SHARON	2814	MERCER	2	41 14	80 30	865	7P	7P	SHARON STEEL CORP	2 3 5
FORD CITY 4 S DAM	2942	ARMSTRONG	1	40 43	79 30	950	8A	8A	CORPS OF ENGINEERS	2 3 5 6 7 C
FRANKLIN	3028	VENANGO	1	41 23	79 49	987	7P	7A	GEORGE S. SMITH, JR	2 3 5 C
FREELAND	3056	LUZERNE	15	41 01	75 54	1900	6P	8A	ANDREW B. EVANSHA	2 3 5
GALETON	3130	POTTER	16	41 44	77 39	1325		7A	W. GALE LUSH	3 7
GEIGERTOWN	3189	BERKS	14	40 13	75 50	400		8A	WALTER C. WOLF	3
GEORGE SCHOOL	3200	BUCKS	5	40 13	74 56	135	7P	7P	GEORGE M. HART	2 3 5 7
#GETTYSBURG	3218	ADAMS	12	39 50	77 14	540	9A	9A	HUGH C. MC ILHENNY	2 3 5
GETTYSBURG 1 S	3223	ADAMS	12	39 48	77 14	560		MID	NAT MILITARY PARK	C
GIFFORD	3237	MC KEAN	1	41 51	78 36	2220		8A	SOUTH PENN OIL CO	3
GLENCOE	3298	SOMERSET	12	39 49	78 51	1620		MID	MRS. MARY M.HARTMAN	C
GLEN HAZEL 2 NE DAM	3311	ELK	1	41 34	78 36	1725		8A	CORPS OF ENGINEERS	3 C
GLEN ROCK	3330	YORK	15	39 48	76 44	620		MID	MRS.E.C.MC WILLIAMS	C
GLENWILLARD DASH DAM	3343	ALLEGHENY	11	40 33	80 13	705		7A	CORPS OF ENGINEERS	3
GOULDSBORO	3394	WAYNE	9	41 15	75 27	1890		7A	L. H. EILENBERGER	3
GRATERFORD	3435	MONTGOMERY	14	40 14	75 27	160		7A	CLAUDE K. KULP	3 7
GRATZ 1 N	3438	DAUPHIN	15	40 38	76 43	760	8A	8A	LEE M. LEITZEL	2 3 5 C
GREENSBORO LOCK 7	3503	GREENE	10	39 47	79 55	808		7A	CORPS OF ENGINEERS	3 7
GREENSBURG 2 E	3515	WESTMORELAND	10	40 18	79 31	1225		MID	PA DEPT HIGHWAYS	C
GREENSBURG 3 SE UNITY	3516	WESTMORELAND	10	40 17	79 30	1245		6P	WESTMORELAND WTR CO	3
GREENVILLE	3526	MERCER	2	41 24	80 23	1026	6P	6P	C. EARL MILLER	2 3 5
HANOVER	3662	YORK	15	39 48	76 59	600	8A	8A	HANOVER EVENING SUN	2 3 5 7
#HARRISBURG WB AP	3699	YORK	15	40 13	76 51	335	MID	MID	U.S. WEATHER BUREAU	2 3 5 7 C
HARRISBURG NORTH	3704	DAUPHIN	15	40 18	76 54	323		8A	GEORGE S. BEAL	3
HAWLEY	3758	WAYNE	5	41 29	75 10	880		7A	MRS.KATHERINE S.BATES	3 5
HAWLEY 1 S DAM	3761	WAYNE	5	41 28	75 11	1200	7A	7A	PA POWER + LIGHT CO	2 3 5 6 7 C
HOLLIDAYSBURG	4001	BLAIR	6	40 26	78 24	960		MID	JOHN M. RINGLER	C
HOLLISTERVILLE	4008	WAYNE	5	41 23	75 26	1300		8A	PA POWER + LIGHT CO	3
HOLTWOOD	4019	LANCASTER	15	39 50	76 20	187	MID	8A	PA POWER + LIGHT CO	2 3 5 7 C
HOME	4027	INDIANA	1	40 45	79 06	1220		MID	MRS. EDNA M. BUSH	C
HONESDALE 4 NW	4043	WAYNE	5	41 37	75 10	1410		9A	GEORGE C. WILLIAMS	3
HONESDALE 6 NNW	4044	WAYNE	5	41 39	75 17	1050		MID	FRIEND E. WALTER	C
HOOVERSVILLE	4058	SOMERSET	4	40 09	78 55	1660		7A	PA ELECTRIC CO	3 7
HOP BOTTOM 2 SE	4066	SUSQUEHANNA	15	41 43	75 43	900		7A	JOSEPH J. SANSUSKAS	3
HUNTINGDON	4159	HUNTINGDON	6	40 29	78 01	610	7A	7A	MRS JANET I. VAUGHN	2 3 5
HUNTSDALE	4166	CUMBERLAND	15	40 06	77 18	610		8A	METRO P. DOROSH	3 C
HYNDMAN	4190	BEDFORD	12	39 49	78 43	920		8A	MRS.GERTRUDE M.BURTON	3
INDIANA 3 SE	4214	INDIANA	4	40 36	79 07	1102	7P	7A	CLYMER WATER SVC CO	2 3 5 7 C
IRWIN	4276	WESTMORELAND	10	40 20	79 42	1100	5P	5P	WESTMORELAND WTR CO	2 3 5
JACKSON SUMMIT	4304	TIOGA	15	41 57	77 01	1690		MID	ARCHIE LAIN	C
JAMESTOWN 2 NW	4325	CRAWFORD	2	41 30	80 28	1050	8A	8A	PA DEPT FRST + WTRS	2 3 5 6 C
JIM THORPE	4370	CARBON	9	40 52	75 45	830	5P	5P	HENRY S. HAAK	2 3 5
#JOHNSTOWN	4385	CAMBRIA	4	40 20	78 55	1214	9A	9A	JOHNSTOWN TRIBUNE	2 3 5
JOHNSTOWN 2	4390	CAMBRIA	4	40 19	78 55	1275		MID	CITY OF JOHNSTOWN	C
KANE 1 NNE	4432	MC KEAN	1	41 41	78 48	1750	8A	8A	SPRING WATER CO	2 3 5 7 C
KARTHAUS	4450	CLEARFIELD	16	41 07	78 07	950		7A	JEROME S. HOWE	3
KEATING SUMMIT	4466	POTTER	16	41 41	78 11	1840		7A	EUGENE L. KREITNER	3 7
KEGG	4481	BEDFORD	6	39 59	78 43	1280	MID	MID	PA TURNPIKE COMM	2 3 5
KITTANNING LOCK 7	4611	ARMSTRONG	1	40 49	79 32	790		VAR	CORPS OF ENGINEERS	3
KREGAR 4 SE	4667	WESTMORELAND	17	40 06	79 14	2530		MID	PA TURNPIKE COMM	3
KRESGEVILLE 3 W	4672	CARBON	9	40 54	75 34	720		9A	CITY OF BETHLEHEM	3
LAFAYETTE MC KEAN PARK	4706	MC KEAN	1	41 48	78 40	2130		7A	ORIN A. BUTTERS	3
LAKEVILLE 1 NNE	4733	WAYNE	5	41 27	75 16	1440		8A	MRS. GLADYS REINEKE	3
LANCASTER 2 NE PUMP STA	4758	LANCASTER	15	40 03	76 17	255	6P	6P	LANCASTER WATER BUR	2 3 5 7
LANCASTER 2 NE FILT PL	4763	LANCASTER	15	40 03	76 17	270		MID	LANCASTER WATER BUR	C
LANDISVILLE 2 NW	4778	LANCASTER	15	40 07	76 26	360	8A	8A	PA STATE COLLEGE	2 3 5 6 C
LATROBE	4832	WESTMORELAND	4	40 19	79 23	1000		MID	WEST PENN POWER CO	INAC 6/56
LAURELTON STATE VILLAGE	4853	UNION	15	40 54	77 13	880		MID	PA DEPT OF WELFARE	C
LAWRENCEVILLE 2 S	4873	TIOGA	15	41 59	77 07	1000	7A	7A	HARRY P. HOWLAND	2 3 5 7
LEBANON 3 W	4891	LEBANON	15	40 20	76 29	460	7A	7A	LEON MILLER	2 3 5 7
LEBANON 3 SW	4896	LEBANON	15	40 19	76 28	490		MID	THOMAS DONNACHIE	C
LEHIGHTON	4934	CARBON	9	40 50	75 43	580		7A	GOODWIN S. DEFREHN	3 C
LE ROY	4972	BRADFORD	15	41 41	76 43	1040		6P	MRS.DIMMIS M.BAILEY	3
LEWIS RUN 3 SE	4984	MC KEAN	1	41 50	78 39	1740		7A	RUSSELL LINEMAN	3 C
LEWISTOWN	4992	MIFFLIN	6	40 35	77 35	480	7A	7A	AMERICAN VISCOSE CO	2 3 5 7 C
LINESVILLE 5 WNW	5050	CRAWFORD	2	41 41	80 31	1020	7P	8A	MISS RETTA M. CRUMB	2 3 5
LOCK HAVEN	5104	CLINTON	16	41 08	77 27	570	7P	7A	PETER L. STEVENSON	2 3 5
LOCK HAVEN 2	5109	CLINTON	16	41 08	77 27	630		MID	HUGH F. PARKER	C
LONG POND 2 W	5160	MONROE	9	41 03	75 30	1860		7A	THOMAS MECKES	3
MADERA	5336	CLEARFIELD	16	40 50	78 26	1460	7A	7A	MRS. JULIA J. SHOFF	2 3 5 C
MAHAFFEY	5342	CLEARFIELD	16	40 53	78 44	1280		7A	MISS ELLEN J. MILES	3
MAPLE GLEN	5368	MONTGOMERY	5	40 11	75 11	380		6P	FRANCES E.SCHEIBNER	3
MAPLETON DEPOT	5381	HUNTINGDON	6	40 24	77 56	580		7A	MRS. I. S. BUCHANAN	3
MARCUS HOOK	5390	DELAWARE	5	39 49	75 25	12	MID	MID	SUN OIL CO	2 3 5
MARIENVILLE 1 SW	5400	FOREST	1	41 27	79 09	1700		MID	ROY A. MARKER	C
MARION CENTER 2 SE	5408	INDIANA	1	40 45	79 02	1610		7A	CORPS OF ENGINEERS	3
MARTINSBURG 1 SW	5453	BLAIR	6	40 18	78 20	1360		MID	BLUE MT. CANNERIES	C
MARTINSBURG CAA AP	5454	BLAIR	6	40 18	78 19	1463	MID	MID	CIVIL AERO. ADM.	2 3 5 7
MATAMORAS	5470	PIKE	5	41 22	74 42	439		7A	HARRY BISLAND	3 7
MAYBURG	5490	FOREST	1	41 36	79 13	1150		7A	CORPS OF ENGINEERS	3
MC CONNELLSBURG	5526	FULTON	12	39 56	78 00	895		7A	MRS. HELEN M. SHIVES	3
MC KEESPORT	5573	ALLEGHENY	10	40 21	79 52	720		8A	NATIONAL TUBE CO	3
MEADOW RUN PONDS	5601	LUZERNE	15	41 13	75 40	1995		MID	GEORGE PEARAGE	C
MEADVILLE 1 S	5606	CRAWFORD	1	41 38	80 10	1065	8A	8A	CITY OF MEADVILLE	2 3 5 7 C
MEDIX RUN	5627	ELK	16	41 17	78 24	1100		7A	MRS.E. M. SNYDER	3 7 C
MERCER 2 NNE	5651	MERCER	2	41 15	80 13	1160	7P	7A	WILLIAM K. STRUTHERS	2 3 5
MERCER HIWAY SHED	5654	MERCER	2	41 14	80 15	1250		MID	PA DEPT HIGHWAYS	C
MERCERSBURG	5662	FRANKLIN	12	39 50	77 54	605		8A	ROLLIN P. GILBERT	3
MERWINSBURG	5676	MONROE	9	40 58	75 28	970		MID	WILLIAM D. GOULD	C
MEYERSDALE 1 ENE	5685	SOMERSET	17	39 49	79 01	2290		8A	ARTHUR B. MC CARTER	3
MIDDLETOWN OLMSTED FLD	5703	DAUPHIN	15	40 11	76 46	303	MID	MID	U. S. AIR FORCE	2 3 5
MIDLAND DAM 7	5710	BEAVER	11	40 38	80 28	689	11P	7A	CORPS OF ENGINEERS	2 3 5
MILAN 4 WNW	5732	BRADFORD	15	41 56	76 35	1448		MID	CARL A. MORRIS	C
MILANVILLE	5738	WAYNE	5	41 40	75 04	760		8A	CHARLES W. DAVIS	3
MILLERSBURG 2 E	5775	DAUPHIN	15	40 32	76 56	560		MID	RUSSELL SHEPLEY	C
MILLHEIM	5790	CENTRE	15	40 54	77 29	1090		7A	NEVIN E. BOWERSOX	3
MILLVILLE 2 SW	5817	COLUMBIA	15	41 06	76 34	860		7A	KENNETH LEIGHOW	3 C
MILROY	5825	MIFFLIN	6	40 43	77 35	770		8A	THOMAS C. HARBESON	3
MONTROSE 1 E	5915	SUSQUEHANNA	15	41 50	75 51	1630	7A	7A	WILBER W. HOOPES,JR	2 3 5 7 C
MORGANTOWN	5956	BERKS	15	40 09	75 54	595	MID	MID	PA TURNPIKE COMM	2 3 5
MT GRETNA 2 SE	6028	LANCASTER	15	40 14	76 26	670	MID	MID	PA TURNPIKE COMM	2 3 5
MT POCONO 2 N AP	6055	MONROE	5	41 09	75 22	1915	5P	5P	H. JOHN DAVIS, JR.	2 3 5 C
MOUNT UNION 1 N	6067	MIFFLIN	6	40 24	77 53	820		MID	MT UNION WTR WORKS	C
MUHLENBURG 1 SE	6090	LUZERNE	15	41 13	76 08	1110	6P	6P	THEODORE J. SAMPSON	2 3 5 7
MURRYSVILLE	6111	WESTMORELAND	10	40 26	79 42	903		MID	DAVID C. SHAW	C
MYERSTOWN	6126	LEBANON	14	40 22	76 18	480		8A	MRS.KATHLEEN WANDELL	3
NATRONA LOCK 4	6151	ALLEGHENY	1	40 37	79 43	800		7A	CORPS OF ENGINEERS	3
NEFFS MILLS 3 NE	6174	HUNTINGDON	6	40 40	77 55	900		MID	PA STATE UNIVERSITY	C
NESHAMINY FALLS	6194	BUCKS	5	40 09	74 57	60		MID	PHILA SUB WATER CO	3
NEWBURG 3 W	6225	FRANKLIN	15	40 09	77 37	745	MID	MID	PA TURNPIKE COMM	2 3 5
NEW CASTLE 1 N	6233	LAWRENCE	2	41 01	80 22	825	5P	7A	BAXTER F. JOHNSON	2 3 5 C
NEWELL	6246	FAYETTE	10	40 05	79 54	805	12M	12M	GENERAL CHEMICAL CO	2 3 5
NEW PARK	6289	YORK	15	39 44	76 30	780		8P	CLINTON J. ALLEN	3
NEWPORT	6297	PERRY	6	40 29	77 08	400	7A	7A	MRS. FRANCES K. FRY	2 3 5 7
NEW STANTON	6310	WESTMORELAND	10	40 13	79 36	980	MID	MID	PA TURNPIKE COMM	2 3 5
NEW TRIPOLI	6326	LEHIGH	14	40 41	75 45	570		6P	FRED C. OSWALD	3
NORRISTOWN	6370	MONTGOMERY	14	40 07	75 21	75	MID	8A	GEORGE H. BOONE	2 3 5
NORTH EAST 2 SE	6396	ERIE	8	42 12	79 49	1060		9A	ELLSWORTH WEAVER	3
ORWELL 3 N	6621	BRADFORD	15	41 55	76 16	1620		8A	WILLIAM I. BROWN	3
PALM	6681	MONTGOMERY	14	40 26	75 32	385		8A	FRED C. ESCHBACH	3
#PALMERTON	6689	CARBON	9	40 48	75 37	435	MID	MID	NEW JERSEY ZINC CO	2 3 5 C
PALMYRA	6694	LEBANON	15	40 18	76 35	480		7P	EARL E. RHOADS	3
PARKER	6721	ARMSTRONG	1	41 05	79 41	1140		7A	LOUIS A. MALARKEY	3
PARKER 1 E	6724	CLARION	1	41 06	79 40	1100		MID	P. M. NEELY	C
PAUPACK 2 WNW	6762	PIKE	5	41 24	75 14	1360		8A	MISS L. VETTERLEIN	3
PECKS POND	6786	PIKE	5	41 17	75 06	1380		9A	MRS. CARRIE NESS	3
#PHIL DREXEL INST OF TEC	6879	PHILADELPHIA	14	39 57	75 11	30	MID	MID	FRANCIS K. DAVIS,JR	2 3 5
PHILADELPHIA WB AP	6889	PHILADELPHIA	5	39 53	75 14	13	MID	MID	U.S. WEATHER BUREAU	2 3 5 7 C
#PHILADELPHIA PT BREEZE	6899	PHILADELPHIA	5	39 55	75 12	32	MID	MID	ATLANTIC REFINING	2 3 5 C
PHILADELPHIA SHAWMONT	6904	PHILADELPHIA	5	40 02	75 15	70	7P	7P	SCHUYLKILL NAVIG CO	2 3 5
#PHILADELPHIA CITY	6909	PHILADELPHIA	5	39 57	75 09	26	9A	9A	USN HYDROGRAPHIC OFF	2 3 5 C
PHILIPSBURG CAA AP	6916	CENTRE	6	40 54	78 05	1918	8P	8P	CIVIL AERO. ADM.	2 3 5 7 C
PHOENIXVILLE 1 E	6927	CHESTER	14	40 07	75 30	105	6P	MID	PHILA SUB WATER CO	2 3 5 C
PIKES CREEK	6939	LUZERNE	15	41 18	76 08	1320		MID	HARRY SHELDON	3 C
PIMPLE HILL	6944	MONROE	9	41 02	75 30	2215	9A	9A	PA DEPT FRST + WTRS	2 3 5 6 7
PINE GROVE 1 NE	6954	SCHUYLKILL	15	40 34	76 22	535		8A	PA POWER + LIGHT CO	3
PITTSBURGH WB AP 2	6993	ALLEGHENY	11	40 30	80 13	1151	MID	MID	U.S. WEATHER BUREAU	2 3 5 7 C
#PITTSBURGH WB CITY	6997	ALLEGHENY	11	40 27	80 00	749	MID	MID	U.S. WEATHER BUREAU	2 3 5 C
PLEASANT MOUNT 1 W	7029	WAYNE	5	41 44	75 27	1800	8A	8A	PA FISH COMM	2 3 5 7 C
PORT CLINTON	7116	SCHUYLKILL	14	40 35	76 02	450	7A	7A	MRS. ADA E. RARICK	2 3 5 C
PORTLAND	7127	NORTHAMPTON	5	40 55	75 06	297		8A	JOINT BRIDGE COMM	INAC 1/56
POTTSTOWN	7149	MONTGOMERY	14	40 15	75 39	160		8A	MILES E. SMITH	3
POTTSVILLE	7161	SCHUYLKILL	14	40 42	76 11	690		8A	LLOYD E. WELLER	3
PUNXSUTAWNEY	7217	JEFFERSON	1	40 57	79 00	1298		MID	JOHN VOLANSKY	C
PUTNEYVILLE 2 SE DAM	7229	ARMSTRONG	1	40 55	79 17	1270	8A	8A	CORPS OF ENGINEERS	2 3 5 C
QUAKERTOWN 1 E	7239	BUCKS	5	40 26	75 20	490	5P	5P	DENNIS K. FLUCK	2 3 5
RAYMOND	7310	POTTER	13	41 52	77 52	2220		7A	MRS. RACHEL LANGAN	3 C
#READING WB CITY	7318	BERKS	14	40 20	75 58	266	MID	MID	U.S. WEATHER BUREAU	2 3 5 7 C
RENOVO	7409	CLINTON	16	41 20	77 46	660		7A	MRS. CAROLINE BAIRD	3
RENOVO 5 S	7410	CLINTON	16	41 14	77 46	2035		MID	C. F. BILLETTE	C
REW	7425	MC KEAN	1	41 54	78 32	2250		8A	HAROLD C. HEALY	3
RICES LANDING L 6	7443	GREENE	10	39 57	80 00	775		7A	CORPS OF ENGINEERS	3
RIDGWAY 3 W	7477	ELK	1	41 25	78 47	1420	7A	7A	BOROUGH OF RIDGWAY	2 3 5
ROCHESTER 1 N	7540	BEAVER	2	40 43	80 18	900		MID	DEQUESNE LIGHT CO	C
RUSH	7694	SUSQUEHANNA	15	41 47	76 03	1000		9A	MISS MAUDE MC CAIN	3
RUSHVILLE	7727	SUSQUEHANNA	15	41 47	76 07	870		7A	CARL KOPATZ	3
SAFE HARBOR	7732	LANCASTER	15	39 55	76 23	270		MID	S.H.WATER POWER CORP	C
SAGAMORE 1 S	7739	INDIANA	1	40 46	79 14	1320		7A	CORPS OF ENGINEERS	3
SALINA 3 W	7782	WESTMORELAND	7	40 31	79 33	1109	6P	6P	MUN AUTH WSTMRLD CO	2 3 5
SAXTON	7846	BEDFORD	6	40 12	78 15	780		8A	MRS.ALVERTA L.HOLMES	3 C
SCANDIA 2 E	7855	WARREN	1	41 55	79 01	2040		MID	DAVID R. ANDERSON	C
SCHENLEY LOCK 5	7863	ARMSTRONG	1	40 41	79 40	783		VAR	CORPS OF ENGINEERS	3
#SCRANTON	7902	LACKAWANNA	15	41 25	75 40	746	7A	7A	U.S. POST OFFICE	2 3 5

Isolines are drawn through points of approximately equal values. Hourly precipitation data from recorder substations will be available in the publication 'Hourly Precipitation

STATION INDEX

CONTINUED

Station	Index No.	County	Drainage ‡	Latitude	Longitude	Elevation	Observation Time Temp.	Observation Time Precip.	Observer	Refer To Tables
SCRANTON WB AIRPORT	7905	LUZERNE	15	41 20	75 44	956	MID	MID	U.S. WEATHER BUREAU	2 3 5 7 C
SELINSGROVE CAA AP	7931	SNYDER	15	40 49	76 52	437	MID	MID	CIVIL AERO. ADM.	2 3 5 7
SELLERSVILLE 2 NW	7938	BUCKS	5	40 23	75 20	330		MID	SELLERSVILLE WTR CO	C
SHADE GAP	7965	HUNTINGDON	6	40 11	77 52	1000		MID	MRS. HELEN M. PYLE	C
SHAMOKIN	7978	NORTHUMBLAND	15	40 48	76 33	770		8A	ROARING CRK WTR CO	3
SHEFFIELD 6 W	8026	WARREN	1	41 41	79 09	1940		MID	L. N. HANSON	C
SHIPPENSBURG	8073	FRANKLIN	15	40 03	77 32	709	4P	4P	KEITH B. ALLEN	2 3 5 7
SHIPPINGPORT WB	8078	BEAVER	11	40 37	80 26	740	MID	MID	U.S. WEATHER BUREAU	2 3 5 7 C
SINNEMAHONING	8145	CAMERON	16	41 19	78 05	790		7A	MRS.FRANCES CALDWELL	3
SLIPPERY ROCK	8184	BUTLER	2	41 04	80 03	1345	7P	7A	WALTER D. ALBERT	2 3 5 7
SMETHPORT HIGHWAY SHED	8190	MC KEAN	1	41 48	78 27	1510		MID	PA DEPT HIGHWAYS	C
SOMERSET FAIRVIEW ST	8244	SOMERSET	17	40 01	79 05	2140		7A	HOWARD G. PECK	3
SOMERSET MAIN ST	8249	SOMERSET	17	40 01	79 05	2150	6P	6P	DAVID L. GROVE	2 3 5
SOUTH CANAAN 1 NE	8275	WAYNE	5	41 31	75 24	1400		MID	EUGENE M. COOK	C
SOUTH MOUNTAIN	8308	FRANKLIN	12	39 51	77 30	1920		7A	PA DEPT OF HEALTH	3
SPRINGBORO	8359	CRAWFORD	8	41 48	80 23	900	8A	8A	SPRINGBORO BOROUGH	2 3 5 C
SPRING GROVE	8379	YORK	15	39 52	76 52	470		4P	P. H. GLATFELTER CO	3 C
SPRINGS 1 SW	8395	SOMERSET	17	39 44	79 10	2500	8P	8P	ALLEN E. YODER	2 3 5 7
#STATE COLLEGE	8449	CENTRE	16	40 48	77 52	1175	MID	MID	PA STATE COLLEGE	2 3 5 6 C
STRAUSSTOWN	8570	BERKS	14	40 29	76 11	600		8A	JACOB KLAHR	3
STRONGSTOWN	8589	INDIANA	4	40 33	78 55	1880		MID	HARRY F. BENNETT	C
STROUDSBURG	8596	MONROE	5	40 59	75 12	480	11P	11P	WILLIAM HAGERTY	2 3 5 C
STUMP CREEK	8610	JEFFERSON	1	41 01	78 50	1320		7A	CORPS OF ENGINEERS	3
SUNBURY	8668	NORTHUMBLAND	15	40 51	76 48	440		7A	CHARLES W. BAYLER	3 C
SUSQUEHANNA	8692	SUSQUEHANNA	15	41 57	75 36	1020		7A	MRS. LAURA A.BENSON	3
SUTERSVILLE	8699	ALLEGHENY	17	40 14	79 48	765		7A	FRANK E. MARSH	3
TAMAQUA	8758	SCHUYLKILL	14	40 48	75 58	830		8A	MRS. MARY L.ROBERTS	3
TAMAQUA 4 N DAM	8763	SCHUYLKILL	14	40 51	75 59	1120		7A	PANTHER VLY WTR CO	3 C
TAMARACK 2 S FIRE TWR	8770	CLINTON	16	41 24	77 51	2220	7A	7A	JAMES E. SWARTZ	2 3 5 7
TIONESTA 2 SE DAM	8873	FOREST	1	41 29	79 26	1200	8A	8A	CORPS OF ENGINEERS	2 3 5 7 C
TITUSVILLE	8885	CRAWFORD	1	41 38	79 40	1550		MID	PA ELECTRIC CO	C
TITUSVILLE WATER WORKS	8888	CRAWFORD	1	41 38	79 42	1220	7P	7P	CITY OF TITUSVILLE	2 3 5
TORPEDO 4 W	8901	WARREN	1	41 47	79 32	1735		7A	MRS. LILY B. GARBER	3
TOWANDA	8905	BRADFORD	15	41 46	76 26	760	7P	7A	MRS. M. O. PARKS	2 3 5 7 C
TOWER CITY 5 SW	8910	DAUPHIN	15	40 31	76 37	745		6P	HARRISBURG WTR DEPT	3 7
TROY	8959	BRADFORD	15	41 47	76 47	1100		7A	JENNIE L. BALLARD	3
TUNNELTON	8989	INDIANA	4	40 27	79 23	890		MID	MRS. MARY E. WEIMER	C
TURTLEPOINT 4 NE	9002	MC KEAN	1	41 54	78 16	1640		7A	ROBERT D. STRAIT	3
TYRONE 4 NE BALD EAGLE	9024	BLAIR	6	40 43	78 12	1020		7A	FREDERICK L. FRIDAY	3 C
UNION CITY	9042	ERIE	1	41 54	79 50	1325		7A	FORREST M. BRALEY	3 C
UNIONTOWN	9050	FAYETTE	10	39 54	79 44	1040	10P	10P	WM. W. MARSTELLER	2 3 5
UPPER DARBY	9074	DELAWARE	5	39 58	75 16	222	7P	7P	PHIL. SUB.TRANS. CO	2 3 5
UTICA	9099	VENANGO	1	41 26	79 57	1030		7A	MRS.FLORENCE HILLER	3
VANDERGRIFT	9128	WESTMORELAND	7	40 36	79 33	800		7A	UNITED ENG+FNDRY CO	3
VANDERGRIFT 2 W	9133	WESTMORELAND	7	40 36	79 36	995		MID	EUGENE R. YOUNG	C
VIRGINVILLE	9196	BERKS	14	40 31	75 52	350		8A	MRS. MARY M. WRIGHT	3
VOWINCKEL	9206	CLARION	1	41 25	79 14	1620		8A	PA DEPT FRST + WTRS	3
VOWINCKEL 1 WSW	9209	CLARION	1	41 24	79 15	1610		8A	PA DEPT FRST + WTRS	3
WARREN	9298	WARREN	1	41 51	79 08	1280	7P	7A	GILBERT H. REIER	2 3 5
WASHINGTON	9312	WASHINGTON	11	40 11	80 14	1200		MID	PA DEPT HIGHWAYS	C
WATSONTOWN	9345	NORTHUMBLAND	16	41 05	76 52	490		9P	WILLIAM BIRD	3
WAYNESBURG 2 W	9362	GREENE	10	39 54	80 13	980	6P	7A	RALPH L. AMOS	2 3 5
WAYNESBURG 1 E	9367	GREENE	10	39 54	80 10	940		MID	SEWAGE DISPOSAL PLT	C
WEBSTER MILLS 3 SW	9380	FULTON	12	39 49	78 05	920		MID	WILLIAM D. COVER	C
WELLSBORO 3 S	9408	TIOGA	16	41 43	77 16	1920	7A	7A	MARION L. SHUMWAY	2 3 5
WELLSBORO 2 E	9412	TIOGA	16	41 45	77 16	1550		MID	MRS. IDA S. MAYNARD	C
WELLSVILLE	9420	YORK	15	40 03	76 57	500	5P	5P	D. D. HOOVER	2 3 5
WERNERSVILLE 1 W	9430	BERKS	14	40 20	76 06	405		8A	CHARLES A. GRUBER	3
WEST CHESTER	9464	CHESTER	5	39 58	75 36	440	8A	8A	DAILY LOCAL NEWS	2 3 5
WEST GROVE 1 E	9503	CHESTER	5	39 49	75 49	440		8A	CONARD-PYLE CO	3
WEST HICKORY	9507	FOREST	1	41 34	79 25	1090		8A	MRS.HELEN F.KINNEAR	3
WHITESBURG	9655	ARMSTRONG	1	40 45	79 24	1530		7A	CORPS OF ENGINEERS	3
WILKES-BARRE	9702	LUZERNE	15	41 15	75 52	610		7A	MRS. MARY G. MIRMAK	3
WILLIAMSBURG	9714	BLAIR	6	40 28	78 12	860		7A	MYRON K. BIDDLE	3
WILLIAMSPORT WB AP	9728	LYCOMING	16	41 15	76 55	527	MID	MID	U.S. WEATHER BUREAU	2 3 5 7 C
WIND GAP	9781	NORTHAMPTON	5	40 51	75 18	720		MID	OWEN R. PARRY	C
ROLFSBURG	9823	BEDFORD	6	40 03	78 32	1190		7A	WALTER C. RICE	3
YORK 3 SSW PUMP STA	9933	YORK	15	39 55	76 45	390	5P	5P	YORK WATER COMPANY	2 3 5
YORK 2 S FILTER PLANT	9938	YORK	15	39 50	76 44	640		MID	YORK WATER COMPANY	C
YORK HAVEN	9950	YORK	15	40 07	76 43	310		8A	METROPOL EDISON CO	3
YOUNGSVILLE	9966	WARREN	1	41 51	79 20	1225		MID	HENRY CARLETT	C
ZION GROVE	9990	SCHUYLKILL	15	40 54	76 13	940		7A	JAMES D. TEETER	3
ZIONSVILLE 3 SE	9995	LEHIGH	14	40 27	75 27	660		7A	LESLIE HOWATT	3
NEW STATIONS										
LYNDELL 2 NW	5279	CHESTER	5	40 05	75 46	-		8A	MRS. DOROTHY HARPLE	3

‡ 1-ALLEGHENY; 2-BEAVER; 3- 4-CONEMAUGH; 5-DELAWARE; 6-JUNIATA; 7-KISKIMINETAS; 8-LAKE ERIE; 9-LEHIGH; 10-MONONGAHELA; 11-OHIO; 12-POTOMAC; 13-LAKE ONTARIO; 14-SCHUYLKILL; 15-SUSQUEHANNA; 16-WEST BRANCH; 17-YOUGHIOGHENY

REFERENCE NOTES

Additional information regarding the climate of Pennsylvania may be obtained by writing to the State Climatologist at Weather Bureau Airport Station, Harrisburg State Airport, New Cumberland, Pennsylvania, or to any Weather Bureau Office near you.

Figures and letters following the station name, such as 12 SSW, indicate distance in miles and direction from the post office.

Delayed data and corrections will be carried only in the June and December issues of this bulletin.

Monthly and seasonal snowfall and heating degree days for the preceding 12 months will be carried in the June issue of this bulletin.

Stations appearing in the Index, but for which data are not listed in the tables, either are missing or were received too late to be included in this issue.

Divisions, as used in Table 2, became effective with data for September 1956.

Unless otherwise indicated, dimensional units used in this bulletin are: Temperature in °F, precipitation and evaporation in inches, and wind movement in miles. Monthly degree day totals are the sums of the negative departures of average daily temperatures from 65° F.

Evaporation is measured in the standard Weather Bureau type pan of 4 foot diameter unless otherwise shown by footnote following Table 6.

Long-term means for full-time stations (those shown in the Station Index as "U. S. Weather Bureau") are based on the period 1921-1950, adjusted to represent observations taken at the present location. Long-term means for all stations except full-time weather Bureau stations are based on the period 1931-155.

Water equivalent samples published in Table 7 are necessarily taken from different points for successive observations; consequently occasional drifting and other causes of local variability in the snowpack result in apparent inconsistencies in the record. Water equivalent of snow on the ground is measured at selected stations when two or more inches of snow are on the ground.

Data in Tables 3, 5, and 6 and snowfall in Table 7, when published, are for the 24 hours ending at time of observation. The Station Index lists observation times in the standard of time in local use.

Snow on ground in Table 7 is at observation time for all except Weather Bureau and CAA stations. For these stations snow on ground values are at 7:30 a.m., E.S.T.

- \- No record in Tables 3, 6, 7 and the Station Index. No record in Tables 2 and 5, is indicated by no entry. Consult the annual issue of this publication for interpolated monthly precipitation totals.
- \+ And also on a later date or dates.
- ♦ Amount included in following measurement, time distribution unknown.
- // Gage is equipped with a windshield.
- \# Thermometers are generally exposed in a shelter located a few feet above sod-covered ground; however, the reference indicates that the thermometers are exposed in a shelter located on the roof of a building.
- AM Data based on observational day ending before noon.
- B Adjusted to a full month.
- C In the "Refer to Tables" column in the Station Index the letter "C" indicates recorder stations. These stations are processed for special purposes and are published later in "Hourly Precipitation Data".
- D Water equivalent of snowfall wholly or partly estimated, using a ratio of 1 inch water equivalent to every 10 inches of new snowfall.
- G In the "Refer to Tables" column in the Station Index the letter "G" indicates that soil temperatures are published.
- M One to nine days of record missing; see Table 5 for detailed daily record. Degree day data, if carried for this station, have been adjusted to represent the valur for a full month.
- R Amounts from recording gage (These amounts are essentially accurate but may vary slightly from the amounts to be published later in Hourly Precipitation Data.
- SS This entry in time of observation column in Station Index means observation made near sunset.
- T Trace, an amount too small to measure.
- Y Includes total for previous month.
- VAR This entry in time of observation column in Station Index means variable.

Information concerning the history of changes in locations, elevations, exposure etc. of substations through 1955 may be found in the publication 'Substation History' for this state, soon to be issued. That publication, when available, may be obtained from the Superintendent of Documents, Government Printing Office, Washington 25, D. C. at a price to be announced. Similar information for regular Weather Bureau stations may be found in the latest issues of Local Climatological Data, Annual for the respective stations, obtained as indicated above, price 15 cents.

Subscription Price: 30 cents per copy, monthly and annual; $2.50 per year. (Yearly subscription includes the Annual Summary). Checks, and money orders should be made payable to the Superintendent of Documents. Remittance and correspondence regarding subscriptions should be sent to the Superintendent of Documents, Government Printing Office, Washington 25, D. C.

WWRC., Asheville, N. C. --- 2/11/57 --- 1100

U. S. DEPARTMENT OF COMMERCE
SINCLAIR WEEKS, Secretary
WEATHER BUREAU
F. W. REICHELDERFER, Chief

CLIMATOLOGICAL DATA

PENNSYLVANIA

ANNUAL SUMMARY 1956
Volume LXI No. 13

ASHEVILLE: 1957

GENERAL

Most of Pennsylvania received abundant precipitation during 1956. In spite of predominantly cool weather during the growing season, crops recorded a good year, and the average corn yield for the State was record high. Destructive storms were numerous and costly; the casualty toll was high, although not as great as in the hurricane-plagued previous year. A major flood on the upper Allegheny and several flash floods caused extremely great damages and took many lives.

WEATHER EFFECTS

Winter grains were injured in January by cold, dry weather and the absence of snow cover much of the time. Field preparation work that usually begins in February was postponed due to softened, wet ground. An excellent maple sirup season began in the middle of February, and continued unusually late, into early April. Heavy snowfall in March further postponed field work, but the improved soil moisture supplies and snow cover aided winter grains. Planting of spring crops was hindered in April by cool weather and frequent rainfall, with the result that field activities lagged about two weeks behind schedule. Poor pasture conditions forced farmers to buy hay. Freezes marked continued cool weather in May; apple and cherry crops were sharply reduced, peaches and grapes were damaged to a lesser extent, and replanting of many tender crops was required. The growth of tobacco in seed beds was retarded, and transplanting was delayed in May and June. The condition of pastures improved in May, but it was not until June that they provided sufficient grazing for cattle. Wet weather in June hindered hay making and cultivation of row crops, and some fields were eroded by particularly heavy rains, but commercial vegetables generally made good progress under the stimulus of seasonal warmth. More frequent rainfall in July caused losses in production and quality of grains and hay. Cultivation and spraying of crops was hindered. On the other hand, fruit sized nicely and other crops put on rapid growth as a result of the abundant rainfall. Lush pastures aided milk production. Cool, wet weather in August was favorable for growth and harvesting of fruit, truck, and corn crops, but the harvests of hay and small grains were slowed. The unusually early advent of freezing temperatures in September killed much corn and other tender vegetation. About 10% of the tobacco crop was caught still in the field, and was either lost completely or greatly reduced in value. Pastures continued to afford good grazing in September, but chilly, wet weather made haying difficult, caused rotting of late potatoes, and hampered the harvesting of spring planted small grains and the seeding of fall plantings. Soils dried out in October, and harvesting operations progressed rapidly. Much of the corn intended for grain was converted to ensilage because of freeze damage in September. Corn harvesting was hampered by rainy weather in November and December. Low quality of hay and ensilage adversely affected milk production at the end of the year. Wet weather in December made it difficult to keep poultry litter dry, and disease spread through flocks. The same wet conditions, however, were favorable for late plantings of winter grains, which developed good root systems.

The growing season was favorable for most commercial vegetable crops, and for quality in the apple crop. The average corn yield for the State was record high due to especially good conditions in central and southeastern counties. The tobacco crop was particularly good, the best in years. Grape production was higher than in the previous year, but with lowered quality.

TEMPERATURE

Predominantly cool weather from early in March

eceding months, but
e usual seasonal ex-
distributed in July,
many as 4 consecutive
was excessive at
itation in August was
rn portion, and moder-
er the east portion.
of the precipitation
iderable variation in
wever, received more
od from the 8th to the
her, but goodly amounts
inning and ending of
ly the west and ex-
led to accumulate the
tation in November was
portion, but occur-
out the State, in light
frequency and amount
in December; the
found in the north-
r proportion of the

amounts (0.10 inch
ently at Kregar 4 SE,
ation reported the
inches. Daily amounts
corded 16 times during
Dam, to take the top
e greatest daily pre-
nches measured at

r in 1956 than in the
y heavy snowstorms
in March and the Lake
r.

t in January, giving
usual. In February,
and less frequent,
ith a vengeance in
he middle of the month.
ice the customary
nd long-term snowfall
ached or exceeded at
in April was heaviest
rn portion of the
n the south had little
tions reported Traces
cord for latest occur-
at Harrisburg WB Air-
nowfall were reported
r, but the first snow-
in the second week of
emely heavy November
Lake Erie, and heavy
on until the end of
n the southeast. In
y heavy in the west
the southeast.

total was 125.0
e greatest depth on

the ground was 24 inches, reported at Gouldsboro on March 20 and 21, and at Erie CAA AP on November 24.

DESTRUCTIVE STORMS

Violent weather features took 33 lives and injured at least 107 persons during the year. Property losses were very great, far exceeding the damages wrought by storms other than hurricanes during the previous year.

Heavy rains and flash floods caused extremely great damages in June and July, and took the lives of 11 persons. Ice and snow storms in January, March, November, and December each caused extremely great property damages; these storms cost 12 persons their lives, and injuries in automobile accidents on slick roads and highways were innumerable. The most spectacular of these storms was the snowstorm that struck Erie County on November 22-23, depositing up to 27 inches of snow. Strong winds piled the snow into drifts up to 12 feet high, and the City of Erie was virtually stranded.

Lightning strikes took 7 lives and injured at least 36 others. Electrical storms caused major property damages in May, June, and September, and some damage in each month, March through October. Tornadoes were neither frequent nor particularly destructive: Only one was reported during the year, on August 13, and three other storms were suspected to be tornadoes; 3 persons were injured by these storms. Other windstorms caused 3 deaths and 66 reported injuries; extremely great damage was done by the windstorms of February 25, and damage of major proportions occurred in each month, April through August. Hailstorms were reported in each month, May through September; damage of major amounts was done by hailstorms on June 10. Two persons were injured by hail during the year.

FLOODS

During the middle of March, major flooding occurred on the upper Allegheny, and lesser flooding was reported on the lower Allegheny and on the Ohio River below Pittsburgh. At Warren, the second highest crest of historic record caused mass evacuation of 500 families and 70 hospital patients without loss of life; damages in this area were severe. Minor damages resulted downstream and along the Ohio. Flash floods resulting from extremely heavy thunderstorm rainfall caused locally severe damage in May, June, July, and August. Minor flooding was reported along the Monongahela in January, February, May, August, and December, but damages were light. Minor floods were reported on other Pennsylvania streams in February, March, April, August, and December, with only minor damages.

Details of each month's weather may be found in the monthly issues of this publication.

Harold S. Lippmann, Climatologist
Weather Records Processing Center
Chattanooga, Tennessee

AVERAGE TEMPERATURES AND DEPARTURES FROM LONG-TERM MEANS

Table 1

Station	January Temperature	January Departure	February Temperature	February Departure	March Temperature	March Departure	April Temperature	April Departure	May Temperature	May Departure	June Temperature	June Departure	July Temperature	July Departure	August Temperature	August Departure	September Temperature	September Departure	October Temperature	October Departure	November Temperature	November Departure	December Temperature	December Departure	Annual Temperature	Annual Departure
ALLENTOWN WB AP	29.2	.7	32.9	4.3	34.9	-3.0	46.7	-1.8	56.0	-3.7	69.7	.1	69.9	-4.2	70.8	-1.0	60.9	-3.8	53.9	.7	41.7	-.3	36.8	5.7	50.3	-
ALLENTOWN GAS CO	29.9	.4	33.5	3.9	35.0	-3.5	47.8	-1.1	56.9	-3.8	70.1	.4	70.6	-3.5	70.7	-1.3	61.4	-3.6	53.8	.0	42.9	.9	37.4	5.3	50.8	-
ALTOONA HORSESHOE CURV	26.1	-1.8	31.3	3.5	35.4	-2.0	45.8	-2.3	55.9	-3.2	66.5	-.2	68.4	-2.4	68.2	-.9	59.6	-3.4	53.5	1.1	40.6	.1	37.0	7.1	49.0	-
ARENDTSVILLE	29.7	-.8	34.0	2.6	36.9	-3.0	48.6	-1.2	58.1	-2.9	70.3	-.1	71.9	-2.4	71.4	-1.0	62.1	-3.6	54.2	-.3	42.9	.0	39.2	6.5	51.6	-
ARTEMAS 1 WNW	28.8		37.4		40.2M		48.6		58.7		69.1		69.9		70.3		62.3		56.3							
BAKERSTOWN 3 WNW	27.3		33.6		38.1		48.5		58.4		68.9		71.0		69.8		61.7		56.9		42.5		40.2		51.4	
BEAVERTOWN	M		M		M		M		M		70.5M		70.3M		69.5		60.4M		53.2		42.4		37.0M			
BELLEFONTE 4 S	27.2	-1.8	31.1	3.8	34.4	-3.5	45.6	-3.4	55.1	-4.8	66.4	-1.8	68.5	-4.1	67.6	-2.6	58.9	-5.3	52.1	-.6	41.7	.7	36.7	6.4	48.8	-1
BERWICK	29.2		33.2		36.2		49.0		58.3		70.7		70.6		70.6		61.7		54.6		43.3		37.2		51.2	
BETHLEHEM LEHIGH UNIV	30.2	-.5	34.3	3.2	36.0	-4.5	48.0	-3.2	58.1M	-4.2	71.2	.6	70.3	-4.7	71.5	-1.7	62.2	-4.6	56.2	.2	43.7	-.8	38.8	5.5	51.7	-1
BLAIRSVILLE 6 ENE	23.9		30.9		34.2		44.2		56.0		65.4		67.8		67.5		58.7		54.7		39.6		36.0		48.3	
BRADFORD 4 W RES	21.9	-2.6	25.2	-.7	28.1	-6.5	40.3	-4.6	51.5	-3.8	62.6	-2.3	64.0	-4.0	63.1M	-3.2	54.6	-5.3	49.8	.0	38.2	-.5	32.2	4.6	44.3	-2
BROOKVILLE CAA AIRPORT	24.9	-.1	26.9	3.7	32.5	-1.5	43.5	-1.4	53.8	-2.1	64.5	.4	66.3	-1.8	66.2	.2	56.8	-3.5	52.2	2.6	38.9	1.0	35.0	7.0	47.0	
BURGETTSTOWN 2 W	25.4		31.9		36.0		45.7		55.7		66.3		69.4M		67.6		57.7		51.6		39.7		37.0		48.6	
BURNT CABINS 2 NE	27.3		32.5		36.4M		47.6		58.0		67.0		69.0		67.6		59.7									
BUTLER	28.9	-1.0	33.6	4.8	37.8	-.6	48.4	-.3	59.4	-.4	69.5M	.9	71.6	-.7	69.7	-.5	60.2	-3.9	56.3	2.9	42.7	1.3	39.4	7.9	51.5	
CANTON 1 NW	22.8		26.3		27.7		40.9		50.1		63.8		64.6		64.4		55.5		49.8		38.8		32.1		44.7	
CARLISLE	32.1	3.2	36.2	5.7	40.3	1.3	50.9	.2	62.0	.2	73.1	2.0	73.5	-1.5	73.0	.2	63.8	-1.7	55.4	2.1	44.1	2.4	40.2	8.3	53.7	1
CHAMBERSBURG 1 ESE	30.1	.0	34.8	3.1	37.8	-2.3	48.4	-2.0	58.8	-2.7	69.9	-.3	71.6	-3.1	71.0	-1.4	61.8	-4.3	54.3	.6	42.4	-.1	39.8	6.7	51.7	-
CHESTER	33.5M		38.3M		39.5M		50.1M		59.5M		72.7M		73.7M		73.6M		66.2M		56.7M		48.6M		41.3M		54.5	
CLARION 3 SW	26.1		30.4		34.6		45.7		56.0		66.3		69.2		67.6		59.1		53.6		40.9		36.2		48.8	
CLAYSVILLE 3 W	27.4	-3.6	34.6	3.4	37.5	-3.1	46.0	-4.3	57.2	-3.3	67.6	-1.5	69.5M	-3.2					M		40.6	-1.4	40.2	7.8		
COATESVILLE 1 SW	29.7	-.8	34.4	3.8	35.8	-4.1	47.8	-2.6	57.7	-3.7	69.7	-.6	71.5	-3.3	70.7	-2.0	62.2	-3.9	53.6	-.8	43.2	.1	38.7	5.9	51.2	-1
COLUMBIA	32.2		37.0		39.4		50.3		61.8		73.0		73.8		73.9		64.0		55.9		44.9		40.5		53.9	
CONFLUENCE 1 SW DAM	26.8		34.8		35.6		45.8		56.8		66.0		67.6		67.5		59.7		54.3		41.9		39.3		49.7	
CORRY	24.4	-.7	27.7	2.4	31.2	-2.1	42.5	-2.6	54.1	-1.3	65.5	.0	67.4	-1.8	66.2	-1.0	56.8	-4.3	52.9	3.0	39.9	1.1	33.6	5.0	48.8	-
COUDERSPORT 2 NW	21.8		25.3		28.4																					
COUDERSPORT 3 NW							M		51.4		61.8		63.4		62.1		53.4		49.0		36.4		30.8			
DERRY	28.0	-3.0	35.5	5.2	38.4	-1.7	M		58.3	-2.5	M		71.4	-1.2	70.0	-.8	61.3	-4.1	57.1	2.7	43.6	1.2	40.5	8.1		
DEVAULT 1 W	M		M		M		M		M		68.8		69.6		71.9		60.0		54.1		42.6		38.0			
DIXON	24.9M		28.5		30.3		43.9		52.4		66.2		67.2		66.8		58.0M		49.9		40.8		33.7		46.9	
DONEGAL	20.9		29.1		31.9		40.7		52.2		61.3		64.7		63.7		55.0		50.7		35.8		34.8		45.1	
DONORA	30.8	-3.5	38.5	4.0	41.8	-.6	51.7	-.5	62.8	-.2	71.6	-.4	74.3	-1.5	73.3	-.6	65.2	-2.7	60.3	3.6	46.8	1.6	43.5	7.7	55.1	
DU BOIS 7 E	24.3		28.9		31.1		43.7		55.3		65.5		67.1		66.2		58.1		52.7		40.0		35.3		47.4	
EAGLES MERE	21.4		25.0		27.2		40.4		50.3		63.6		63.4		63.7		53.9		M		36.0M		30.7			
EAST BRADY	27.9		32.3		36.8		47.7		58.2		69.2		72.0		71.0		62.4		57.2		43.7		38.8		51.4	
EBENSBURG	22.9	-3.3	30.0	2.9	33.4	-2.0	42.8M	-2.4	54.1	-2.3	63.5	-1.4	65.8	-2.4	65.1	-1.6	57.1	-3.9	50.5	.0	38.0	-.6	36.1	7.7	46.6	-
EMPORIUM 1 E	24.8	-1.4	26.6	.8	29.7	-5.6	42.1	-4.5	51.7	-6.1	65.0M	-.9	66.3M	-3.4												
EMPORIUM 2 SSW															65.0		55.2		49.4		38.1		32.0			
EPHRATA	30.5	-.3	34.9	4.1	37.1	-3.4	47.8	-2.9	59.2	-2.7	70.0	.0	71.7	-3.3	71.6	-1.0	62.7	-3.6	54.7	-.2	44.1	.3	40.0	7.1	52.0	-
ERIE CAA AIRPORT	25.7	-1.5	28.9	2.4	31.7	-2.4	43.2	-1.1	54.1	-1.0	69.6	.1	68.6	-1.8	68.9	-.1	59.2	-4.0	55.3	3.0	42.3	1.3	36.0	5.2	48.3	
EVERETT 1 SW	29.1	.3	32.7	4.7	37.4	-1.9	47.1	-1.0	57.5	-2.5	67.0	-.3	69.4	-2.1	67.9	-1.7	60.1	-2.5	53.1	1.1	40.5	-.1	39.6	9.7	50.1	
FARRELL SHARON	26.4	-2.4	31.6	2.8	35.8	-2.6	46.7	-2.6	56.6	-3.6	67.2	-2.6	70.4	-3.5	70.1	-1.4	59.3	-6.1	55.4	1.4	42.3	.8	37.9	6.7	50.0	-1
FORD CITY 4 S DAM	25.4		31.3		34.2		44.7		54.9		66.2		68.9		67.4		59.0		53.6		41.8		36.0		48.8	
FRANKLIN	27.0	.3	30.2	4.3	34.9	-.6	45.7	-.3	56.1	-1.4	67.0	.7	69.2	-1.4	68.3	-.2	59.5	-3.1	54.9	3.5	42.5	2.8	37.7	8.2	49.4	
FREELAND	24.3	-.3	28.2	3.5	30.9	-2.4	42.5	-2.1	52.4M	-4.5	65.2	.1	65.1	-4.2	65.2	-1.7	56.9	-3.5	52.6M	3.3	40.6	2.9	33.9	8.6	46.5	-
GEORGE SCHOOL	30.6	-.8	35.8	4.5	37.1	-3.5	48.2	-2.1	60.0	-1.1	70.9	1.4	71.2	-3.0	72.4	.2	63.6	-2.7	55.9	.4	45.0	.9	40.5	7.1	52.6	
GETTYSBURG	31.2	.8	35.6	4.0	37.9	-2.7	50.1	-1.0	59.0	-2.9	71.1	.7	73.1	-1.5	72.4	.0	63.3	-2.7	55.5	1.6	44.1	1.3	41.0	8.2	52.9	
GRATZ 1 N	28.4		31.6		34.4		46.1		55.3		67.6		68.4M		67.7		58.8		52.1		42.0		36.4		49.1	
GREENVILLE	26.0	-1.6	30.3	3.1	34.8	-2.1	45.8	-.9	56.7	-1.4	67.2	-.1	69.9M	-1.4	68.9	-.1	59.8	-3.2	55.5	4.1	41.9	1.8	37.3	6.3	49.5	
HANOVER	30.0	-2.7	35.0	1.9	36.9	-5.1	48.8	-3.5	58.3	-4.9	70.1	-1.4	71.8	-3.9	71.0	-2.6	62.4	-5.0	54.2	-2.1	43.2	-1.8	40.4	5.9	51.8	-1
HARRISBURG WB AP	32.0	.9	35.4	3.3	38.2	-2.6	49.1	-1.8	59.7	-2.7	71.0	-.1	72.0	-3.4	72.4	-.6	62.8	-3.6	55.2	.0	43.7	-.3	40.2	6.3	52.6	-
HAWLEY 1 S DAM	22.9		25.9M		27.1M		40.7		51.3		64.9		65.1		64.3		55.5		47.8		37.6		32.1		44.6	
HOLTWOOD	31.3	-.7	36.1	3.4	38.6	-2.7	49.3	-2.2	60.0	-3.1	72.4	-.1	73.9	-3.1	74.3	-.8	64.7	-4.2	57.1	.1	44.8	-.7	40.7	6.1	53.6	-
HUNTINGDON	28.4	-.8	32.7	3.2	35.7	-3.0	46.5	-2.9	56.4	-4.1	69.6M	1.0	70.5	-1.9	69.7M	-1.0	60.6	-3.9			42.6	.8	38.5	6.9		
INDIANA 3 SE	25.7	-3.8	32.9	3.0	36.5	-2.5	46.5	-2.9	56.5	-3.3	66.5	-1.5	68.8	-2.9	68.4	-1.6	59.1	-5.3	55.0	2.2	41.2	-.3	38.5	7.5	49.6	-1
IRWIN	27.7	-2.9	35.5	4.9	M		M		60.5	.1	70.0	1.4	72.0M	.5	71.5	.7	62.7M	-2.7	58.3	4.0	43.7	1.4	M			
JAMESTOWN 2 NW	23.9		27.5		31.8		43.7		53.4		65.2		68.5		67.9		58.1		53.7		40.5		39.5		47.5	
JIM THORPE	30.9M	3.1	34.0	6.1	38.1	-1.2	47.9M	-.5	57.1M	-2.5	68.9M	1.2	69.4M	-2.5	69.7M	.0	60.3M	-3.4	54.4M	2.2	42.7M	1.5	37.1M	6.7	50.7	1
JOHNSTOWN	27.7	-2.8	34.4	4.0	37.6	-1.6	48.3	-1.5	57.8	-3.2	69.0	-.4	71.8	-1.3	69.9	-1.3	59.8	-5.5	54.4	.5	41.2	-.9	38.7	6.3	50.8	-
KANE 1 NNE	21.8		24.6		27.9		40.0		50.9		62.4		63.9		62.1		53.4		48.3		37.8		31.4		43.7	
KEGG	27.7		32.8		37.4		46.2		56.7		66.6M		69.2		68.7		58.6		52.7M		38.9		36.3M		49.5	
LANCASTER 2NE PUMP STA	30.3	-.1	36.1	5.0	38.2	-1.9	48.9	-.9	60.6	-.7	70.3	.1	71.5	-2.5	71.3	-.9	61.9	-3.5	53.9	.1	43.5	.2	40.2	7.1	52.2	
LANDISVILLE 2 NW	29.3		33.5		36.1		47.5		58.1		70.8		71.3		70.5		61.6		53.0		41.5		37.1		50.9	
LAWRENCEVILLE 2 S	22.6	-2.9	26.6	1.6	28.6	-6.2	42.0	-4.1	51.0	-6.6	65.4	-.9	66.9	-3.7	65.9	-2.5	56.2	-5.6	49.7	-1.3	40.0	.7	33.0	4.8	45.7	-1
LEBANON 3 W									60.8M	-.4	71.8	1.9	72.6	-1.7	72.0	-.2	61.2	-4.5	54.0	.0	43.1	.3	38.3	6.3		
LEWISTOWN	30.1		34.1		37.1		47.2		57.5		69.7		70.9		70.0		61.7		54.6		43.3		38.8		51.3	
LINESVILLE 5 WNW	24.3		27.4		32.3		43.6		54.8		65.5		68.7		68.4		57.6		53.9		40.8		35.8		47.8	
LOCK HAVEN	29.6	1.2	32.6	4.2	36.4	-2.1	48.2	-2.0	58.3M	-3.4	70.0M	.4	70.6	-2.8	M		60.2M	-4.6	54.5	1.1	42.2	.5	37.4	6.5		
MADERA	21.8		26.7		29.9		41.1		51.1		62.8		64.9		63.0		54.7		48.0		36.6		33.0		44.5	
MARCUS HOOK	33.4	-2.3	38.2	2.6	39.1	-5.7	49.9	-4.6	60.3	-5.5	73.1	-2.0	74.2	-4.8	75.7	-.9	66.2	-4.3	58.7	-1.1	46.4	-2.0	41.9	3.4	54.8	-1
MARTINSBURG CAA AP	26.3		31.6		35.4		45.7		56.2		67.4		68.7		68.7		59.0		53.4		40.2		38.0		49.2	
MEADVILLE 1 S	24.3	-1.3	27.2	2.7	31.4	-3.4	43.1	-2.4	52.8	-4.1	65.2	-.6	68.0	-1.7	67.0	-.7	57.7	-4.3	53.2	2.3	40.9	1.8	35.0	6.8	47.2	-
MERCER 2 NNE	20.9		28.0M		33.1		45.2		53.1		64.8		67.6		67.5		56.5		54.5		39.6		36.6		47.5	
MIDDLETOWN OLMSTED FLD	31.2	.1	35.5	3.9	38.2	-2.0	49.2	-.9	60.3	-1.6	71.8	1.1	72.4	-2.7	73.2	.3	62.7	-3.2	55.7	1.0	43.8	.2	40.1	7.1	52.8	
MIDLAND DAM 7	27.7	-2.9	34.3	2.9	38.0	-2.0	48.0	-2.3	58.9	-1.9	69.7	-.3	72.5	-.4	71.4	-.7	61.2	-3.9	57.0	2.8	43.1	.6	39.5	6.3	51.8	-
MONTROSE 1 E	21.2	-1.9	25.1	2.6	26.5	-5.3	40.2	-3.3	49.9	-5.1	64.2	.5	64.7	-3.6	64.8	-2.0	55.2	-5.1	49.1	-.3	38.2	.8	30.2	4.1	44.1	-1
MORGANTOWN	29.1		33.2		34.7		46.4		57.2		67.5		70.0		70.3		61.3		53.0		41.8		38.3		50.2	
MT GRETNA 2 SE	30.8		33.6		37.2M		M		57.9		67.1		70.1		70.8		61.4		54.6		42.1		39.3			
MT POCONO 2 N AP	23.7	.4	27.1	5.3	29.0	-3.0	41.8	-.6	52.8	-1.2	65.5	3.7	64.8M	-1.2	65.4M	1.2	56.6	-1.8	50.3	1.6	38.7	2.2	31.6	5.9	45.6	1
MUHLENBURG 1 SE	25.1		29.5		32.5		43.7		53.9		67.1		66.6		66.6		57.2		50.7		40.0		32.8		47.2	
NEWBURG 3 W	31.8		34.9		39.9		50.2		62.1		72.6		76.0		75.1		65.2		56.2							
NEW CASTLE 1 N	27.3	-1.1	32.8	3.9	37.1	-.2	47.9	-.7	57.9	-1.7	68.4	-.6	70.7	-1.8	69.7	-.8	60.3	-4.0	56.1	3.3	43.7	3.1	38.8	7.8	50.8	
NEWELL	29.5	-3.3	35.9	3.4	39.3	-2.5	51.5	.6	62.0	.7	70.9	1.3	74.2	.7	72.9	.7	65.6	-1.2	60.5	4.9	48.7	4.8	44.7	9.7	54.6	1
NEWPORT	30.3		33.2		36.1		46.8		56.9		70.3		70.2		69.8		60.8		53.1		42.0		38.0		50.6	
NEW STANTON	28.0	-3.3	34.0	2.4	38.1	-2.0	46.7	-3.5	57.2	-3.3	66.9	-1.8	70.3	-2.0	69.6	-1.0	60.4	-4.6	56.1	2.0	41.3	-1.4	40.1	7.3	50.7	-1
NORRISTOWN	M		37.0		37.8		50.1		60.9		72.4		73.5		74.3		65.4		57.1		46.0		42.6			
PALMERTON	28.7	.1	32.0	3.0	34.5	-3.8	46.0	-2.2	57.6	-2.0	68.6	.1	68.9	-4.3	69.7	-.9	60.1	-3.7	52.7	-.1	41.0	-.8	38.2	4.9	49.7	-
PHIL DREXEL INST OF TE	33.4		39.4		40.8		51.3		62.5		74.5		75.6		76.8		67.2		60.0		48.9		44.2		54.2	
PHILADELPHIA WB AP	32.1	-1.1	37.6	4.0	38.8	-3.5	49.9	-1.7	60.9	-2.2	72.3	.2	73.6	-2.7	74.1	.1	65.2	-2.9	57.7	1.1	46.3	.4	41.7	3.8	54.2	-
PHILADELPHIA PT BREEZE	34.2	.0	40.2	5.0	40.3	-3.2	51.6	-1.1	62.0	-2.4	73.6	.7	74.6	-2.8	75.8	.2	66.6	-2.9	60.0	1.5	49.5	1.8	44.4	7.8	56.1	
PHILADELPHIA SHAWMONT	32.8	.3	37.7	4.3	39.5	-3.1	50.4	-1.9	62.2	-1.0	72.6	.3	72.9	-2.4	72.4M	-.9	65.9	-2.1	57.5	1.0	47.8	2.4	42.4	7.5	54.7	
PHILADELPHIA CITY	34.1	-.8	38.4	3.3	39.2	-4.3	49.7	-3.0	60.9	-2.8	72.8	.2	73.6	-3.6	75.9	.7	66.9	-2.4	59.5	.8	48.4	.6	43.4	6.0	55.2	-
PHILIPSBURG CAA AP	23.3		26.8		30.7		42.1		53.1		62.8		64.3		65.4		54.8		50.6		37.0		33.8		49.2	
PHOENIXVILLE 1 E	30.8	-.6	35.5	3.0	37.1	-4.4	47.9	-4.0	60.6	-1.8	71.0	-.6	72.6	-3.1	72.4	-1.1	68.9	-3.3	55.7	.1	45.4	1.2	41.6M	8.0	52.9	-
PIMPLE HILL	21.7		26.4		27.7		40.8		51.9		65.2		64.6		65.6		56.2		50.5		37.5		31.6		48.8	
PITTSBURGH WB AP 2	27.7	-1.3	34.0	4.2	37.2	-1.4	47.0	-1.8	58.5	-1.3	67.7	-.9	70.3	-2.0	70.8	.7	60.4	-4.5	56.7	3.7	42.0	1.8	39.4	8.5	51.0	
PITTSBURGH WB CITY	30.9	-2.1	36.9	3.3	40.4	-1.2	49.7	-2.1	61.0	-1.6	70.4	-1.3	73.1	-2.3	72.9	-.2	63.1	-4.8	58.9	3.0	44.9	.3	42.8	7.6	53.8	-
PLEASANT MOUNT 1 W	20.1M		23.5		25.4		39.0		48.8		62.4		63.3		62.9		54.1		46.5		36.4		29.8		42.7	
PORT CLINTON	29.7	.9	33.2	3.8	35.2	-3.3	46.6	-2.9	56.0	-5.0	68.3	-.9	69.0	-4.4	68.7	-2.5	59.6	-5.6	51.5	-1.8	41.9	.1				
PUTNEYVILLE 2 SE DAM	24.1		29.5		32.2		43.9		53.7		65.4		67.8		66.8		57.4		52.8		39.9		30.4		47.4	
QUAKERTOWN 1 E	28.9	.9	33.0M	4.0	36.2	-1.5	47.7	-.9	59.0	-.7	69.6	1.2	70.5M	-2.2	70.5	.1	62.3	-1.5	54.6	2.2	42.8	1.2	38.5	7.1	51.1	
READING WB CITY	32.7	.5	36.7	3.9	38.3	-3.3	49.7	-1.6	60.1	-2.4	71.8	.5	72.8	-2.9	73.6	.2	63.7	-3.4	57.0	.9	44.8	-.6	40.9	8.1	53.5	-
RIDGWAY 3 W	23.6	-1.9	27.5	2.6	31.2M	-2.2	42.9	-2.2	53.8	-2.1	63.6	-.9	65.2	-2.8	63.5	-3.2	55.6	-4.3	49.5	.3	38.0	-.1	34.4	6.6	48.7	-
SALINA 3 W	27.1		33.6		37.4		47.2		57.9		67.8		70.3		69.6		60.5		55.9M		41.3		30.4		50.7	
SCRANTON	26.4	-1.8	28.9	.6	31.7	-5.6	44.3	-3.5	53.8	-5.6	66.9	-1.2	67.2	-5.4	67.3	-3.0	58.1	-5.6	52.1	-.3	40.4	-1.5	34.6	3.7	47.6	-1
SCRANTON WB AIRPORT	25.4	-1.5	30.0	2.9	31.5	-4.8	44.9	-2.1	54.7	-4.2	67.1	-.7	67.5	-4.7	67.9	-2.1	58.0	-5.2	52.1	-.1	40.4	-.3	34.2	4.6	47.8	-1
SELINSGROVE CAA AP	28.6	-.1	32.2	3.6	35.4	-3.3	47.1	-2.3	56.2	-4.6	69.0	-.1	69.7	-3.7	69.8	-1.6	60.4	-4.4	52.6	-.3	40.8	-1.0	36.3	4.7	49.8	-1
SHIPPENSBURG	31.2	.5	35.9	3.0	39.5	-1.5	49.6	-1.2	59.9	-2.8	70.9	-.4	72.2	-2.5	72.6	-.5	63.4	-2.8	55.6	.7	43.9	.5	40.9	8.0	53.0	
SHIPPINGPORT WB	28.5		34.1		37.7		47.2		57.2		67.0		70.0		69.4		59.9		56.4		42.6		39.6		50.8	

See Reference Notes Following Station Index

AVERAGE TEMPERATURES AND DEPARTURES FROM LONG-TERM MEANS

Station	January		February		March		April		May		June		July		August		September		October		November		December		Annual	
	Temperature	Departure	Temperature	Departure	Temperature	Departure	Temperature	Departure	Temperature	Departure	Temperature	Departure	Temperature	Departure	Temperature	Departure	Temperature	Departure	Temperature	Departure	Temperature	Departure	Temperature	Departure	Temperature	Departure
ERY ROCK	26.4		30.9		35.1		40.4		57.3		67.3		69.2		69.6		59.9		55.7		41.4		37.1		49.7	
ISET MAIN ST	25.7	- 1.2	32.6	5.5	36.2	.2	44.9	- 1.3	57.2	.5	65.3	.1	68.1	- .4	66.4	- .5	58.5	- 2.1	52.7	3.2	39.6	.9	38.2	9.3	48.8	1.2
BBORO			29.5M		M		44.9		55.2M		65.7		68.8		67.8		57.9		53.1		41.1		39.3			
IGS 1 SW	23.2	- 3.9	31.3	4.0	32.8	- 3.0	42.3	- 3.1	54.3M	- 1.1	63.0	- .7	65.4	- 1.7	64.4	- 1.2	55.5	- 4.0	50.7	1.0	37.1	- 1.3	34.0M	7.4	46.4	- .6
COLLEGE	27.8	.7	30.6	3.4	34.3	- 2.1	46.1	- 1.6	57.5	- 1.5	68.0	.9	68.8	- 2.2	68.7	- .3	59.2	- 3.5	54.0	2.4	41.4	1.2	37.6	7.7	49.5	.4
IDSBURG	28.4	1.0	29.2	1.4	30.3	- 6.9	43.0	- 5.6	53.3	- 6.7	65.9	- 1.7	67.4	- 4.8	67.4	- 2.6	57.6	- 5.0	50.5	- 1.9	39.0	- 2.0	33.5	3.2	47.1	- 2.7
IACK 2 S FIRE TWR	22.0		25.0		27.9		40.9		50.4M										50.3M		38.4		31.5			
ISTA 2 SE DAM	24.4		26.7		30.8		42.4		53.5M		65.5		67.6		66.1		57.9		52.0		40.0		33.8		46.7	
IVILLE WATER WORKS	24.0		26.9		30.4		42.7		54.0		65.5		67.1		66.7		56.0		51.3		38.6		34.3		46.8	
IDA	25.8	- .2	30.0	4.5	31.9	- 3.5	44.9	- 1.6	55.0	- 2.8	67.6	1.6	68.2	- 2.5	68.0	- .8	59.3	- 3.1	51.4	.2	41.4	1.4	35.1	6.1	48.2	- .1
ITOWN	29.3	- 3.8	37.6	4.6	40.4	- 1.3	49.3	- 2.3	60.1	- 2.0	68.9	- 1.4	71.9	- 1.5	70.7	- 1.2	62.2	- 4.2	58.3	3.1	43.6	- .4	42.5	7.6	52.9	- .2
DARBY	31.7		37.3		38.5		49.8		61.5		72.4		73.9		74.0		65.9		58.0		46.5		42.0		54.2	
IN	28.1	- .9	28.9	3.7	32.1	- 2.5	44.0	- 1.0	55.4	- 1.3	66.4	.9	68.2	- 1.7	67.5	- .5	58.3	- 3.9	53.4	2.1	41.2	1.8	35.3	6.7	48.0	.3
ESBURG 2 W	28.7	- 4.4	36.9	4.8	39.8	- 1.1	48.2	- 2.4	59.6	- 1.2	67.9	- 2.0	70.5	- 2.4	69.7	- 1.8	61.0	- 4.1	55.6	1.0	41.9	- 1.2	41.2	7.2	51.8	- .6
BORO 3 S	22.0	- 2.3	25.9	1.5	27.9	- 5.0	41.1	- 3.3	50.8	- 5.5	64.1	- .4	65.5	- 3.3	65.1	- 1.3	56.3	- 3.5	50.2	1.2	38.8	1.2	31.7	4.1	44.9	- 1.4
IVILLE	30.6		34.9		37.4		47.8		59.0		69.0		70.7		71.2		61.9		53.3		42.4		30.7		51.5	
CHESTER	30.2M	- .6	37.7	6.3	38.9	- .5	50.7	.7	60.4	- .6	72.8	3.1	73.0	- 1.4	74.6	2.4	65.0	- .8	57.3	2.4	43.3M	- .1	39.5	6.1	53.6	1.4
AMSPORT WB AP	28.7	.2	31.6	2.5	35.0	- 3.3	47.8	- 1.3	56.9	- 3.3	70.0	.8	69.9	- 3.4	70.0	- .9	60.5	- 4.1	53.6	.6	41.9	.2	35.8	4.9	50.1	- .6
3 SSW PUMP STA	31.4	.6	36.9	5.2	39.6	- 1.5	50.0	- 1.3	61.4	- .6	71.7	1.1	73.8	- 1.0	72.7	- .1	64.3	- 2.2	55.6	.9	44.9	1.2	41.8	8.4	53.7	.9

See Reference Notes Following Station Index

TOTAL PRECIPITATION AND DEPARTURES FROM LONG-TERM MEANS

ACMETONIA LOCK 3							
ALLENTOWN WB AP							
ALLENTOWN GAS CO							
ALTOONA HORSESHOE CURV							
ARENDTSVILLE							
ARTEMAS 1 WNW							
AUSTINBURG 2 W							
BAKERSTOWN 3 WNW							
BARNES							
BARTO 4 NW							
BEAR GAP							
BEAVER FALLS							
BEAVERTOWN							
BEECH CREEK STATION							
BELLEFONTE 4 S							
BERNE							
BERWICK							
BETHLEHEM							
BETHLEHEM LEHIGH UNIV							
BLAIRSVILLE 6 ENE							
BLOSERVILLE 1 N							
BOSWELL 6 WNW							
BRADDOCK LOCK 2							
BRADFORD CNTRL FIRE ST							
BRADFORD 4 W RES							
BREEZEWOOD							14
BROOKVILLE CAA AIRPORT			1				13
BRUCETON 1 S			1				
BUFFALO MILLS							
BURGETTSTOWN 2 W							
BURNT CABINS 2 NE							
BUTLER			2				
CAMP HILL							
CANTON 1 NW							
CARLISLE							
CARROLLTOWN 2 SSE							
CARTER CAMP 2 W							
CEDAR RUN			1				
CHADDS FORD							
CHAMBERSBURG 1 ESE							
CHARLEROI LOCK 4							
CHESTER							
CLARENCE							
CLARION 3 SW							
CLAUSSVILLE							11
CLAYSVILLE 3 W			2				14
CLEARFIELD			1				
CLERMONT							
COALDALE 2 NW							
COATESVILLE 1 SW			1				
COGAN STATION 2 N							
COLUMBIA							
CONFLUENCE 1 SW DAM							
CONFLUENCE 1 NW							
CONNELLSVILLE							
CONSHOHOCKEN			1				
COOKSBURG							
COOKSBURG 2 NNW							
CORAOPOLIS NEVILLE IS							
CORRY			2				
COUDERSPORT 2 NW							
COUDERSPORT 3 NW							
COUDERSPORT 7 E							
COVINGTON 3 W							
COVINGTON 2 WSW							
CREEKSIDE							
CRESSON 2 SE							
CUSTER CITY 2 W							
DANVILLE							
DERRY		2			2		
DEVAULT 1 W							
DIXON							
DONEGAL							
DONORA		1	1	1	1		
DOYLESTOWN	1						
DU BOIS 7 E	1			2		1	
DUSHORE 3 NE							
EAGLES MERE	2			2			
EAST BRADY				1	1	1	
EBENSBURG		1					
EDINBORO			1		1		
ELIZABETHTOWN							
EMPORIUM 1 E	2		1				
EMPORIUM 2 SSW							
ENGLISH CENTER						1	
EPHRATA	1						
EQUINUNK				3	1		
ERIE CAA AIRPORT	1						
EVERETT 1 SW		1	3				
FARRELL SHARON		1	1	1			
FORD CITY 4 S DAM							
FRANKLIN	2	1			2	2	
FREELAND	2	1				1	
GALETON	1			1			
GEIGERTOWN							
GEORGE SCHOOL	1				1		
GETTYSBURG	1			4			
GIFFORD							
GLEN HAZEL 2 NE DAM							
GLENWILLARD DASH DAM							
GOULDSBORO	1	1	2			1	
GRANTVILLE 2 SW					1		
GRATERFORD	1		1				
GRATZ 1 N						1	
GREENSBORO LOCK 7			1	1			
GREENSBURG 3 SE UNITY	1	1			1		
GREENVILLE	2	1	2	2			
HANOVER	1		1			1	
HARRISBURG WB AP	1				1	2	
HARRISBURG NORTH	1						

See Reference Notes Following Station Index

Station	January Precipitation	January Departure	February Precipitation	February Departure	March Precipitation	March Departure	April Precipitation	April Departure	May Precipitation	May Departure	June Precipitation	June Departure	July Precipitation	July Departure	August Precipitation	August Departure	September Precipitation	September Departure	October Precipitation	October Departure	November Precipitation	November Departure	December Precipitation	December Departure	Annual Precipitation	Annual Departure
HAWLEY	2.07	- .69	3.94	1.34	3.42	.20	4.21	.88	2.94	-1.04	3.75	- .11	3.89	- .54	2.43	-1.67	3.31	- .22	1.53	-1.70	1.99	-1.08	4.58	1.63	38.06	- 2.04
HAWLEY 1 S DAM	1.63		E 3.90		3.31		4.11		3.19		4.03		4.11		2.39		3.43		1.30		1.81		4.20		E37.50	
HOLLISTERVILLE	1.76	-1.07	4.62	1.94	3.49	- .07	4.51	.76	3.50	- .69	5.27	.90	4.40	- .78	2.27	-1.47	3.88	.11	2.14	-1.02	2.19	-1.17	4.79	1.76	42.94	- .80
HOLTWOOD	1.57	-1.43	2.41	.00	4.11	1.13	1.86	-1.05	1.35	-1.79	4.07	.72	6.23	2.34	3.95	- .10	4.33	1.70	3.24	.60	4.86	2.38	3.27	.73	41.25	5.23
HONESDALE 4 NW	1.73		4.85		E 4.11		3.98		4.83		3.92		4.74		3.16		5.28		1.60		1.84		4.50		E44.54	
HOOVERSVILLE	2.25		5.24		4.54		4.81		4.91		4.47		5.19		5.01		5.13		1.57		1.24		4.08		48.44	
HOP BOTTOM 2 SE	E 1.05		2.55		E 3.65		2.29		1.07		3.04		3.27		2.22		2.76		1.53		1.21		2.45		E27.99	
HUNTINGDON	1.48	-1.60	4.03	1.48	4.25	.78	3.56	.12	5.24	1.08	3.22	- .91	6.95	2.94	5.27	1.36	2.16	-1.11	E 3.30	.37	1.09	- .59	3.80	.90	E45.25	4.02
HUNTSDALE	1.57		3.33		3.92		2.93		3.39		3.08		5.80		4.57		3.38		4.28		1.92		4.60		42.73	
HYNDMAN	E 2.05	- .77	4.41	2.25	3.61	.48	3.80	.45	4.69	1.49	3.69	- .38	5.54	2.29	6.06	2.17	3.39	.60	1.99	- .09	1.68	- .50	4.24	1.72	E45.13	8.81
INDIANA 3 SE	2.05	-1.60	6.88	3.97	5.81	1.89	5.42	1.45	4.47	.28	5.59	.68	8.47	3.87	5.04	1.00	4.57	.85	1.71	-1.68	1.66	-1.27	4.30	1.00	55.97	10.44
IRWIN	2.38	- .58	6.38	3.92	E 5.94	2.47	E 4.58	1.26	6.47	2.95	4.07	- .38	5.02	1.04	6.17	2.30	4.83	1.97	1.63	-1.15	.98	-1.59	E 3.37	.45	E51.82	12.68
JAMESTOWN 2 NW	1.12	-1.43	4.34	2.26	4.40	1.50	4.48	1.18	5.04	1.07	5.64	2.98	5.98	2.09	6.67	2.94	4.05	.63	1.40	-1.47	1.70	- .92	2.30	.05	48.12	10.94
JIM THORPE	1.16	-2.45	5.02	1.60	3.72	- .49	5.95	2.11	3.44	- .90	6.07	1.68	9.87	4.52	3.47	-1.30	6.95	2.93	3.71	- .08	2.20	-1.51	3.89	.09	55.45	6.20
JOHNSTOWN	2.00	-2.08	6.00	2.44	4.50	.34	6.25	2.20	6.15	1.68	3.99	-1.04	6.43	1.98	4.44	.07	2.96	- .46	1.52	-1.48	1.20	-1.77	3.23	- .35	48.67	1.53
KANE 1 NNE	1.55	-2.10	5.04	2.09	5.94	2.12	4.22	.27	7.33	2.61	6.08	1.43	7.30	2.89	8.45	4.82	7.54	3.84	1.69	-1.89	2.16	-1.38	4.57	1.28	61.87	15.98
KARTHAUS	1.51		4.85		3.79		2.08		5.00		5.42		5.36		6.19		4.06		3.25		2.23		3.93		47.67	
KEATING SUMMIT	1.23		5.06		5.92		4.29		5.28		5.90		4.47		6.82		2.83		2.14		2.10		4.62		50.66	
KEGG	1.81		5.49		4.75		3.70		4.58		2.48		3.87		4.05		2.39		2.00		1.26		5.09		41.47	
KITTANNING LOCK 7	1.92	-1.43	6.70	4.11	4.27	.65	4.65	1.30	5.33	1.14	8.09	3.91	6.43	2.54	7.18	3.49	2.08	- .55	1.39	-1.95	1.06	-1.72	3.93	.85	53.03	12.34
KREGAR 4 SE	3.95		7.97		7.82		7.19		8.19		3.90		5.18		6.27		4.97		1.51		2.48		6.23		65.66	
KRESGEVILLE 3 W	E 1.41		4.20		3.22		5.17		3.23		4.96		9.43		3.48		5.20		3.54		2.50		4.58		E50.92	
LAFAYETTE MC KEAN PARK	1.43		4.89		-		-		-		-		-		-		-		-		-		-		-	
LAKEVILLE 1 NNE	E 2.15	- .55	4.68	2.09	3.50	- .04	3.96	.18	2.33	-1.96	2.95	-1.50	4.85	- .21	3.08	-1.09	4.00	.39	1.77	-1.61	2.07	-1.21	4.84	1.98	E40.18	- 3.53
LANCASTER 2NE PUMP STA	1.88	-1.28	E 3.81	1.20	4.81	1.36	2.80	- .65	1.96	-1.58	3.79	- .22	5.04	.67	3.71	- .59	4.29	.97	4.19	1.06	3.13	.42	3.45	.33	E42.86	1.69
LANDISVILLE 2 NW	1.45		3.97		4.22		2.14		2.56		3.18		4.28		3.17		3.67		2.04		3.00		3.87		38.25	
LATROBE	2.24		6.03		4.85		4.77		4.73		-		-		-		-		-		-		-		-	
LAWRENCEVILLE 2 S	E 1.26	- .61	2.84	1.14	4.39	1.95	1.93	- .92	2.05	-1.88	1.99	-1.82	6.07	1.99	3.79	- .02	2.76	- .34	1.76	-1.01	1.35	- .93	3.25	1.32	E33.44	- 1.13
LEBANON 3 W	-		-		-		-		-		4.11	- .02	6.43	1.88	3.80	- .46	5.22	1.83	3.33	- .18	2.36	- .65	4.89	1.55	-	
LEHIGHTON	.97	-2.97	4.22	1.71	3.41	- .64	4.27	1.06	3.09	-1.68	4.44	- .47	8.59	2.66	3.81	- .79	5.78	2.14	4.07	.41	2.86	-1.08	4.68	1.12	50.19	1.47
LE ROY	1.47		2.51		E 3.08		1.87		1.29		2.29		4.40		3.17		3.06		2.75		3.07		2.68		E31.64	
LEWIS RUN 3 SE	1.45		5.00		6.60		4.47		5.86		4.66		5.65		9.68		4.18		1.89		2.93		4.11		56.48	
LEWISTOWN	1.38		2.45		2.72		2.54		4.38		3.87		4.67		5.21		3.42		3.31		2.37		3.68		40.00	
LINESVILLE 5 WNW	1.66	- .99	3.79	1.47	4.13	1.02	4.69	1.17	5.43	1.58	6.40	2.62	4.13	.38	9.81	6.12	1.91	-1.93	1.23	-1.86	2.37	- .83	2.75	.10	48.30	8.85
LOCK HAVEN	1.55	-1.38	4.02	1.52	3.25	- .22	1.91	-1.46	3.90	- .21	2.70	-1.38	6.42	2.25	E 7.70	3.66	1.97	-1.35	2.69	- .48	3.95	1.35	3.27	.27	E43.33	2.67
LONG POND 2 W	1.16		3.09		3.22		5.38		2.88		4.17		6.71		2.75		5.50		4.21		3.01		4.21		47.19	
MADERA	1.70		4.50		4.75		3.38		5.28		5.79		6.71		5.42		3.36		2.20		1.60		3.99		48.68	
MAHAFFEY	1.74		7.35		5.48		4.37		6.77		6.88		9.45		7.39		4.29		2.48		2.64		4.60		63.44	
MAPLE GLEN	2.11		3.92		4.72		2.58		4.15		4.22		3.87		3.01		3.80		3.31		4.24		3.64		43.57	
MAPLETON DEPOT	1.77		3.76		4.59		3.28		3.61		2.52		8.47		4.97		1.95		4.24		1.38		3.73		44.27	
MARCUS HOOK	2.14	-1.31	4.45	1.80	4.76	1.10	3.54	.06	3.10	- .66	2.54	-1.06	5.81	1.59	2.71	-2.74	3.17	.06	3.28	.75	5.69	2.46	3.80	.84	44.99	2.89
MARION CENTER 2 SE	2.35		7.02		5.56		5.25		6.48		5.29		9.20		5.00		4.18		2.00		1.62		5.36		59.31	
MARTINSBURG CAA AP	1.53		4.27		4.12		3.81		2.92		1.67		6.70		5.73		2.44		3.19		1.04		4.83		42.25	
MATAMORAS	1.90	- .91	4.21	1.68	3.78	.63	4.94	1.46	3.08	- .65	2.75	-1.29	5.27	1.28	2.28	-1.52	6.19	2.70	1.58	-1.57	2.74	- .33	4.31	1.26	43.03	2.74
MAYBURG	E 1.51		4.80		5.33		4.32		6.21		5.07		6.47		8.51		8.19		1.24		2.53		3.81		E57.99	
MC CONNELLSBURG	1.73	- .99	3.92	1.71	3.71	.16	4.39	1.30	2.92	-2.34	3.19	-1.38	6.81	3.00	4.46	.22	3.32	.75	5.66	2.02	2.61	- .58	4.89	2.04	47.61	5.91
MC KEESPORT	2.08	- .41	4.68	2.48	4.51	1.08	4.68	1.52	5.96	2.49	E 8.00	4.28	E 5.76	2.27	5.30	1.65	3.35	.42	1.63	- .67	.97	-1.60	4.44	1.97	E51.36	15.48
MEADVILLE 1 S	1.23	-1.92	4.64	1.97	4.72	1.45	4.92	1.56	7.74	3.62	6.51	2.40	5.11	.89	8.61	4.99	3.73	.21	1.21	-2.18	2.20	-1.22	2.64	- .37	53.28	11.40
MEDIX RUN	1.38		5.79		4.48		4.10		5.89		4.94		5.65		6.82		2.79		2.81		1.78		4.23		50.66	
MERCER 2 NNE	E 1.19		4.24		E 4.72		6.00		5.87		6.09		6.86		7.93		E 2.44		1.03		1.19		3.75		E51.31	
MERCERSBURG	E 2.46		E 4.03		4.12		3.19		3.41		1.63		4.29		3.57		3.45		4.39		1.75		4.05		E40.32	
MEYERSDALE 1 ENE	2.52		5.25		4.17		3.58		5.77		5.30		E 5.56		6.42		2.79		1.92		1.34		5.72		E50.34	
MIDDLETOWN OLMSTED FLD	1.93	-1.12	3.14	.79	4.16	.65	2.41	- .97	2.43	-1.75	2.93	- .96	5.18	1.45	3.20	- .84	2.97	- .32	3.14	- .24	2.52	- .42	4.39	1.68	38.40	- 2.05
MIDLAND DAM 7	1.58	-1.09	6.15	3.94	4.83	1.23	3.79	.24	6.67	2.28	4.23	.23	5.10	1.51	5.57	1.91	2.54	- .01	1.86	-1.25	.83	-1.71	3.57	1.19	46.72	8.47
MILANVILLE	2.34		E 4.98		4.11		4.57		2.37		5.45		3.66		2.65		5.13		1.11		2.32		4.08		E42.77	
MILLHEIM	1.22		3.85		3.34		2.49		4.58		3.63		5.91		7.73		3.52		2.59		4.51		3.85		47.22	
MILLVILLE 2 SW	.96		4.12		2.31		E 2.61		3.25		3.93		6.05		3.47		3.28		2.61		4.10		3.86		E40.55	
MILROY	1.16		4.23		3.41		2.74		4.89		4.73		4.40		5.82		4.13		2.66		3.32		3.65		45.14	
MONTROSE 1 E	1.48	-1.15	3.61	1.31	5.08	2.20	3.32	- .12	2.53	-1.59	2.95	-1.04	6.46	2.35	3.64	- .49	5.29	1.46	2.22	-1.32	.97	-1.90	4.15	1.51	41.70	1.22
MORGANTOWN	2.13		4.04		5.20		2.37		4.40		5.21		3.25		2.85		4.36		2.56		3.59		2.97		42.93	
MT GRETNA 2 SE	1.68		4.29		4.44		3.19		2.46		4.04		3.38		3.27		4.24		3.81		2.94		4.64		42.38	
MT POCONO 2 N AP	E 1.29	-2.08	4.09	1.15	4.03	.08	3.81	- .08	2.66	-1.69	5.70	.62	5.98	.72	3.06	-1.38	5.57	.78	5.70	1.19	3.03	- .32	3.93	.37	E48.85	- .64
MUHLENBURG 1 SE	.92		4.80		3.16		4.18		4.04		4.81		5.18		4.26		4.32		4.06		1.66		4.45		45.84	
MYERSTOWN	1.46		3.95		4.19		E 2.05		3.17		4.20		7.16		4.28		7.85		E 3.72		2.45		4.06		E48.60	
NATRONA LOCK 4	1.74	-1.38	7.32	4.71	4.89	1.15	4.76	1.16	4.70	.73	5.44	.90	7.54	3.40	5.39	1.82	2.63	- .04	1.64	-1.26	.77	-2.10	3.84	1.08	50.66	10.17
NESHAMINY FALLS	E 2.22	-1.04	4.86	2.06	5.24	1.79	2.86	- .59	2.52	-1.27	3.18	- .97	4.57	- .27	3.22	-1.47	2.42	-1.22	3.85	.67	4.83	1.86	3.61	.58	E43.38	.13
NEWBURG 3 W	E 2.13		3.51		E 3.11		2.87		3.63		2.41		8.13		3.60		1.45		3.26		E 2.82		E 4.06		E41.58	
NEW CASTLE 1 N	1.66	-1.28	5.53	3.17	4.53	1.49	4.63	1.54	5.01	1.46	7.15	3.00	8.26	4.10	5.49	2.18	4.23	1.18	1.19	-1.52	1.30	-1.20	2.67	.09	51.65	14.21
NEWELL	3.29	.49	E 5.70	3.50	6.23	3.18	4.36	1.10	5.46	2.17	5.37	1.25	4.12	.49	7.67	4.10	4.46	1.46	1.50	-1.08	E 1.05	-1.54	3.95	1.52	E53.16	16.64
NEW PARK	1.72	-1.53	3.93	1.31	5.92	2.53	2.77	-1.00	2.23	-1.74	3.43	- .64	5.92	1.33	4.67	- .17	5.94	2.37	4.44	1.00	3.64	.39	3.70	.76	47.91	4.61
NEWPORT	1.42	-1.55	3.33	1.14	3.24	- .23	2.69	- .81	2.37	-1.94	4.93	1.32	4.67	.16	3.86	- .37	2.27	- .87	4.62	1.18	2.87	- .47	4.05	1.02	40.32	- 1.42
NEW STANTON	1.92	-1.49	5.32	2.48	5.35	1.78	5.13	1.38	5.09	1.05	3.79	- .68	3.74	- .28	7.14	2.92	5.10	1.91	1.47	-1.52	.81	-1.88	3.41	.29	48.27	5.96
NEW TRIPOLI	1.13		4.72		4.29		4.37		3.29		4.69		7.94		4.19		4.50		3.28		2.63		3.27		50.30	
NORRISTOWN	2.80		3.80		6.98		2.72		2.07		4.11		3.74		3.15		2.86		3.30		4.32		3.62		43.47	
NORTH EAST 2 SE	1.70		4.56		4.77		4.45		4.91		1.59		8.16		4.18		4.13		1.66		4.09		3.67		47.87	
ORWELL 3 N	1.25		3.21		4.68		3.57		2.41		2.70		5.80		2.63		3.87		2.66		1.94		3.82		38.54	
PALM	E 2.26		6.01		6.55		3.86		3.10		2.57		5.77		5.04		2.98		2.25		3.70		4.78		E48.87	
PALMERTON	.98	-1.86	3.76	1.54	2.98	- .12	4.11	1.04	3.32	- .62	5.09	.85	7.47	2.74	4.54	.46	3.80	.11	3.19	.02	2.52	- .61	4.39	1.66	46.15	5.21
PALMYRA	-		-		-		-		-		-		-		-		4.18		-		-		-		-	
PARKER	1.37	-2.12	6.36	3.46	4.10	.44	4.89	1.39	4.31	.37	5.82	1.60	5.83	1.70	7.17	3.36	2.35	- .90	1.38	-1.49	1.15	-1.86	3.14	- .06	47.87	5.89
PAUPACK 2 WNW	2.19	- .54	4.08	1.50	E 3.67	.31	4.78	1.22	3.13	- .91	4.19	.12	4.03	- .52	2.08	-2.30	3.50	- .18	1.73	-1.85	1.80	-1.49	4.20	1.18	E39.38	- 3.46
PECKS POND	1.72		4.75		3.36		4.97		2.70		4.35		5.21		2.76		4.77		1.89		2.31		4.31		43.10	
PHIL DREXEL INST OF TE	2.79		5.10		4.48		3.04		3.65		3.05		5.22		2.59		3.77		4.48		6.77		3.13		48.03	
PHILADELPHIA WB AP	2.30	-1.07	4.64	1.52	4.65	1.33	2.68	- .70	3.84	.26	3.86	- .01	4.61	.41	2.79	-1.79	3.75	.29	3.47	.87	5.71	2.63	3.70	1.03	46.00	4.77
PHILADELPHIA PT BREEZE	2.35		3.85		4.41		2.98		3.15		5.41		4.80		2.17		3.62		3.73		6.08		3.60		46.15	
PHILADELPHIA SHAWMONT	3.30	- .03	4.28	1.22	5.24	1.65	3.18	- .18	2.37	-1.27	5.09	1.55	5.85	1.26	2.46	-2.40	2.83	- .46	3.18	.07	5.89	2.81	E 3.28	- .18	E46.95	4.04
PHILADELPHIA CITY	2.50	- .89	4.72	1.59	4.49	1.12	2.50	- .88	2.97	- .61	5.45	1.48	4.70	.49	2.63	-1.99	2.75	- .68	4.24	1.63	5.15	2.07	2.69	- .08	44.79	3.29
PHILIPSBURG CAA AP	2.25		4.87		4.80		4.18		3.17		3.95		7.44		10.28		2.50		4.04		2.39		3.30		55.17	
PHOENIXVILLE 1 E	2.99	- .60	3.98	.98	5.75	2.10	3.43	.05	2.20	-2.03	2.34	-1.53	3.86	- .96	3.27	-1.45	3.26	- .14	3.60	.51	3.84	.51	3.76	.55	42.28	- 2.01
PIKES CREEK	.95		4.65		3.03		4.35		2.98		6.99		7.03		5.58		3.26		3.20		1.43		3.77		47.22	
PIMPLE HILL	1.75		5.20		4.74		6.64		3.52		5.34		6.16		3.11		5.77		4.00		3.78		5.18		55.19	
PINE GROVE 1 NE	1.12	-2.07	4.17	1.56	3.21	- .44	2.76	- .90	2.86	-1.59	5.85	1.22	4.91	- .08	4.49	.58	4.27	.57	3.36	- .48	3.23	- .60	4.69	1.47	44.92	- .76
PITTSBURGH WB AP 2	1.90	- .87	5.98	3.52	5.28	2.08	4.31	1.12	5.90	2.13	4.19	.12	4.25	.34	5.07	1.94	1.93	-1.04	1.50	- .94	1.03	-1.56	3.35	.84	44.69	7.68
PITTSBURGH WB CITY	1.75	-1.08	5.97	3.53	5.03	1.62	4.18	1.10	6.08	2.59	4.13	.30	4.15	.43	5.28	2.20	2.91	.14	1.63	- .86	.76	-1.85	3.43	.86	45.30	8.98
PLEASANT MOUNT 1 W	1.69	-1.93	4.36	1.36	4.25	.28	4.21	.36	3.02	-1.61	3.72	- .60	5.23	.16	2.81	-1.30	4.53	.68	1.86	-2.00	2.14	-1.78	4.19	.92	42.01	- 5.48
PORT CLINTON	1.42	-2.10	4.29	.97	4.44	.57	3.60	- .54	2.69	-1.25	4.33	- .13	5.18	.28	4.65	- .52	5.76	1.71	E 3.10	- .87	E 3.18	.37	E 3.83	.22	E46.67	- 1.29
POTTSTOWN	E 2.54	- .79	6.36	3.18	6.49	2.87	3.74	.55	2.57	-1.56	4.14	.35	4.87	- .04	5.24	1.45	2.84	- .41	-		-		-		-	
POTTSVILLE	.90		3.94		3.30		E 3.18		E 2.88		5.31		6.28		3.12		6.31		E 3.23		E 2.09		5.35		E45.89	
PUTNEYVILLE 2 SE DAM	1.25		6.99		4.34		4.69		5.84		6.68		7.70		6.04		2.84		2.69		1.92		4.47		55.45	
QUAKERTOWN 1 E	E 2.85	- .61	E 5.26	1.94	6.03	2.43	3.53	.12	2.46	-1.65	3.46	- .48	5.73	.77	4.09	- .40	3.23	- .39	3.60	.27	4.25	.97	4.32	.93	E48.83	3.90
RAYMOND	1.53		3.62		5.50		3.37		3.87		4.34		5.08		5.12		3.47		2.26		2.51		4.13		44.80	
READING WB CITY	1.54	-1.61	4.88	2.11	4.82	1.51	3.04	- .20	2.95	- .74	6.03	2.27	4.01	- .42	3.30	- .58	3.72	.44	3.12	.37	3.86	.81	4.27	1.47	45.54	5.43
RENOVO	1.06	-1.58	4.09	1.82	4.23	1.14	2.61	- .71	E 4.17	.21	4.16	.07	5.23	1.11	4.81	1.30	4.37	1.44	2.65	- .39	2.15	- .60	3.69	1.10	E43.22	4.91
REW	1.27		4.55		6.06		3.58		4.24		3.53		5.01		6.48		4.51		1.76		2.19		4.23		47.41	
RICES LANDING L 6	2.24		6.13		5.56		3.96		5.33		4.64		6.94		8.83		2.47		1.33		1.05		4.23		52.71	
RIDGWAY 3 W	1.36	-1.58	5.42	3.09	4.61	1.50	4.26	1.04	5.49	1.47	4.95	.71	6.54	2.32	9.73	6.48	3.32	.04	1.34	-1.69	2.22	- .81	4.37	1.66	53.61	14.23
RUSH	1.78		3.65		4.55		4.12		2.60		2.37		5.76		3.95		4.58		2.77		1.37		4.20		41.70	
RUSHVILLE	1.48		2.71		3.77		3.34		2.56		3.10		6.43		3.77		4.48		2.44		1.08		3.94		39.10	
SAGAMORE 1 S	1.76		E 5.89		4.42		3.99		6.38		5.64		11.66		4.99		1.99		1.15		1.36		4.22		E53.45	
SALINA 3 W	1.87		6.45		6.52		4.70		4.56		4.22		7.64		5.46		4.41		1.46		1.12		3.47		51.88	

See Reference Notes Following Station Index

Table 2—Continued

TOTAL PRECIPITATION AND DEPARTURES FROM LONG–TERM MEANS

Station	January		February		March		April		May		June		July		August		September		October		November		December		Annual	
	Precipitation	Departure	Precipitation	Departure	Precipitation	Departure	Precipitation	Departure	Precipitation	Departure	Precipitation	Departure	Precipitation	Departure	Precipitation	Departure	Precipitation	Departure	Precipitation	Departure	Precipitation	Departure	Precipitation	Departure	Precipitation	Departure
SAXTON	1.83		3.65		4.22		3.63		3.00		2.10		5.86		6.10		2.05		4.54		1.34		4.29		42.57	
SCHENLEY LOCK 5	2.16	-1.47	7.18	4.17	4.97	1.27	4.85	1.38	4.91	1.01	4.11	- .19	7.14	3.09	3.88	.24	2.39	- .02	1.43	-1.41	.89	-2.04	4.30	1.06	48.21	6.
SCRANTON	.98	-1.28	3.52	1.50	E 1.98	- .77	3.74	.71	2.87	- .70	4.09	.24	6.33	1.90	4.16	.49	3.33	.40	1.78	-1.16	1.47	-1.43	3.80	1.54	E38.05	1.
SCRANTON WB AIRPORT	1.01	-1.25	3.64	1.54	2.48	- .35	3.16	- .09	2.25	-1.86	4.68	.25	3.18	-2.15	3.03	-1.05	2.54	- .68	1.35	-2.03	1.31	-1.80	3.24	.87	31.87	- 8.
SELINSGROVE CAA AP	1.17	-1.84	3.90	1.17	2.70	- .99	2.50	-1.05	3.87	- .17	3.10	- .82	7.51	3.47	4.50	.56	3.45	.02	3.96	.39	2.90	.08	4.08	1.02	43.62	1.
SHAMOKIN	1.26	-1.63	4.32	1.70	3.13	- .24	3.61	- .13	3.60	- .72	4.74	.31	8.31	3.71	5.27	1.32	5.14	1.70	3.37	- .10	3.21	.16	4.16	1.17	50.12	7.
SHIPPENSBURG	1.77	-1.32	3.90	1.64	3.90	.63	1.96	-1.55	2.66	-1.53	3.60	.04	4.65	.91	3.77	- .24	2.09	-1.19	3.33	- .19	2.76	- .43	3.39	2.27	39.78	-
SHIPPINGPORT WB	1.27		5.72		4.30		3.31		7.01		3.34		5.08		5.63		2.59		1.80		.83		3.21		44.19	
SINNEMAHONING	1.19		4.73		4.37		3.24		5.18		5.92		4.99		8.77		3.60		2.57		2.36		3.84		48.56	
SLIPPERY ROCK	1.15		6.02		3.82		5.23		4.80		11.07		9.18		5.26		2.85		.90		.99		2.95		54.22	
SOMERSET FAIRVIEW ST	E 2.76		6.33		5.05		4.62		6.66		3.55		3.68		5.45		5.25		1.28		1.34		4.86		E50.83	
SOMERSET MAIN ST	2.52	-1.70	6.02	2.48	4.84	.65	4.65	.26	7.17	2.35	3.77	-1.26	4.10	- .58	5.31	.82	4.78	1.34	1.36	-1.69	1.51	-1.74	4.82	1.17	50.89	2
SOUTH MOUNTAIN	2.17		4.56		5.03		E 3.25		3.14		3.71		4.92		3.73		5.54		5.10		2.80		3.97		E47.92	
SPRINGBORO	-		-		-		-		-		6.27		5.63		6.00		4.11		1.43		E 3.35		-		-	
SPRING GROVE	1.83		3.86		5.24		2.65		2.33		2.96		6.55		4.43		3.12		3.12		2.38		3.87		42.34	
SPRINGS 1 SW	2.18	-1.55	3.34	.22	2.93	- .74	1.78	-2.15	7.51	3.21	3.99	-1.31	4.72	.02	7.68	3.18	2.67	- .82	2.11	-1.32	1.22	-1.90	5.05	1.80	45.16	- 1
STATE COLLEGE	1.39	-1.52	E 4.08	1.54	3.46	.12	2.67	- .74	4.93	.82	5.15	1.11	4.59	.73	8.39	4.95	2.73	- .23	4.20	1.29	2.26	- .30	3.45	.81	E47.30	8
STRAUSSTOWN	.98		4.20		3.99		2.98		3.76		4.97		6.22		6.66		7.89		4.19		2.82		4.74		53.48	
STROUDSBURG	1.23	-2.06	4.86	2.11	3.40	- .33	6.43	2.75	4.70	.86	3.98	- .62	8.08	2.93	3.72	- .96	5.47	1.87	4.21	.72	2.13	-1.68	4.71	1.28	52.92	6
STUMP CREEK	1.03		5.89		4.65		3.88		6.89		6.31		7.76		8.36		2.54		1.99		2.06		4.63		55.99	
SUNBURY	1.32	-1.70	4.24	1.85	3.31	.00	2.97	- .65	2.94	-1.67	2.77	-1.12	8.18	4.09	4.33	.56	3.95	.74	3.87	.68	2.41	- .85	4.57	1.31	44.76	3
SUSQUEHANNA	1.62	- .45	3.96	1.89	4.93	1.73	3.82	1.09	2.65	-1.05	3.50	- .57	4.21	.33	2.14	-1.38	4.81	1.62	2.12	-1.07	1.25	-1.90	4.47	1.88	39.28	2
SUTERSVILLE	2.37		5.99		5.91		4.21		4.34		4.05		E 4.93		5.90		3.72		1.42		1.05		3.80		E47.69	
TAMAQUA	1.12		4.53		4.02		4.53		3.68		5.14		8.32		3.58		6.56		E 3.29		2.64		4.96		E52.37	
TAMAQUA 4 N DAM	3.49		E 4.08		2.69		E 4.66		4.09		3.21		7.88		3.83		5.50		3.10		2.18		4.82		E40.21	
TAMARACK 2 S FIRE TWR	1.12		3.60		3.96		2.51		-		-		-		-		-		-		2.31		3.84		-	
TIONESTA 2 SE DAM	1.33	-1.14	5.24	2.91	4.78	1.30	4.66	1.17	6.66	1.89	3.13	-1.14	6.49	2.58	6.62	3.60	6.67	3.48	.96	-2.57	1.17	-1.90	3.85	.86	51.58	11
TITUSVILLE WATER WORKS	1.27		5.13		5.01		4.86		9.10		6.49		6.97		8.71		3.61		1.39		3.08		3.57		50.17	
TORPEDO 4 W	1.58		4.47		6.91		5.13		6.26		2.07		6.80		8.71		3.82		1.16		2.71		3.13		52.75	
TOWANDA	1.50	- .48	2.91	1.00	4.62	1.96	3.13	.15	1.92	-1.68	2.28	-1.38	4.38	.50	4.60	1.28	3.71	.41	2.55	- .40	3.83	1.53	3.65	1.45	39.08	4
TOWER CITY 5 SW	1.18		4.08		3.96		3.96		3.25		3.40		6.49		4.77		4.06		3.27		3.51		4.24		48.17	
TROY	1.96		3.92		5.39		2.66		2.05		1.96		5.34		3.92		2.79		2.47		3.41		3.78		39.65	
TURTLEPOINT 4 NE	1.27		4.49		5.61		3.64		E 4.06		4.73		7.08		5.52		3.86		1.84		1.74		3.59		E47.51	
TYRONE 4 NE BALD EAGLE	1.36		5.03		4.73		3.69		5.77		3.76		6.76		6.05		5.18		4.21		.95		4.11		51.62	
UNION CITY	1.38		4.45		5.32		4.81		6.44		5.62		4.95		8.34		4.99		1.96		3.25		3.01		54.52	
UNIONTOWN	2.92	- .66	5.69	2.81	4.70	.77	3.06	- .67	5.65	1.51	5.51	.66	4.24	- .51	7.85	3.38	4.34	1.14	1.48	-1.72	1.34	-1.76	4.76	1.91	51.54	8
UPPER DARBY	3.93		5.34		5.06		2.94		2.87		7.33		5.81		2.55		4.57		3.66		5.18		3.44		52.08	
UTICA	1.22		5.55		5.28		5.45		5.72		4.75		3.67		7.46		4.14		1.03		1.99		3.65		49.91	
VANDERGRIFT	2.10	- .59	7.36	4.89	5.23	2.00	4.23	1.13	4.29	.71	4.89	.42	5.49	1.40	7.98	3.97	4.59	1.43	1.53	-1.59	.82	-1.72	3.08	.30	51.59	12
VIRGINVILLE	1.18		2.37		3.72		2.33		2.85		4.19		4.90		4.32		E 3.89		E 3.47		2.52		4.27		E40.01	
VOWINCKEL	1.81		6.90		5.44		5.60		5.61		4.99		6.25		6.60		6.12		1.50		2.12		4.45		57.39	
VOWINCKEL 1 SW	1.55		6.88		5.39		5.43		5.58		5.34		6.11		6.38		5.57		1.50		1.79		4.32		55.84	
WARREN	1.24	-1.64	3.72	1.15	4.11	.83	1.48	-2.06	5.80	1.60	5.42	.97	7.31	2.84	7.68	4.03	5.98	2.32	1.36	-2.07	2.29	-1.24	2.99	- .08	49.38	6
WATSONTOWN	E 1.13		E 4.12		E 2.83		2.75		3.57		2.70		8.27		5.32		2.35		3.38		6.82		4.17		E47.41	
WAYNESBURG 2 W	2.63	- .69	5.89	3.64	5.76	1.91	5.05	1.80	6.65	2.56	4.78	.45	11.13	6.77	6.26	2.32	2.48	-1.05	1.65	- .99	.92	-1.68	4.01	1.22	57.21	16
WELLSBORO 3 S	1.17	-1.18	3.64	1.51	4.16	1.20	2.62	- .66	2.53	-1.34	2.12	-1.62	3.91	.23	4.92	1.29	3.02	- .05	1.90	-1.03	3.45	.83	3.30	.92	36.74	
WELLSVILLE	1.31		3.75		4.34		2.63		3.30		3.10		5.10		4.65		4.18		3.44		2.55		4.52		42.87	
WERNERSVILLE 1 W	1.78		4.72		4.44		2.76		3.26		5.64		4.27		3.15		4.66		3.65		3.28		5.17		46.78	
WEST CHESTER	3.07	- .69	4.22	.59	5.62	1.70	2.71	- .98	4.35	.01	4.81	.59	6.46	1.70	2.95	-1.79	2.83	-1.03	2.83	- .72	4.02	.42	3.73	- .03	47.60	-
WEST GROVE 1 E	2.72	- .67	4.49	1.99	E 5.19	1.42	3.18	- .11	1.81	-2.38	5.45	1.53	7.58	2.61	2.96	-2.23	3.36	- .02	4.27	1.12	4.84	1.65	4.28	1.21	E50.13	6
WEST HICKORY	1.32		5.52		4.23		5.08		6.35		4.87		6.57		7.60		7.59		1.26		2.14		3.77		56.50	
WHITESBURG	2.01		6.43		3.67		5.19		5.11		6.48		7.50		5.94		2.70		1.62		1.34		4.43		52.42	
WILKES BARRE	.79	-1.76	4.27	1.64	2.59	- .51	3.65	.75	2.64	-1.10	5.12	1.09	3.39	-1.04	3.96	.05	4.00	.72	2.03	-1.05	1.92	- .75	3.86	1.07	38.22	-
WILLIAMSBURG	1.89		4.32		5.34		4.50		3.99		3.05		7.63		4.75		2.62		3.91		1.32		4.24		47.56	
WILLIAMSPORT WB AP	1.48	-1.11	4.15	1.72	3.28	- .06	3.08	- .46	3.33	- .98	3.02	- .40	7.17	3.46	4.09	.48	2.60	- .73	3.53	.16	4.75	1.49	4.28	1.61	44.76	5
WOLFSBURG	1.74		4.19		4.58		3.85		4.20		3.49		5.57		5.00		2.64		2.43		.68		4.49		42.86	
YORK 3 SSW PUMP STA	1.22	-1.86	3.09	.38	3.56	.28	2.49	- .74	2.04	-1.68	4.09	.33	5.47	1.22	5.16	.92	3.95	.65	3.08	- .14	2.64	- .06	3.38	.44	40.17	-
YORK HAVEN	1.24	-1.51	3.74	1.40	4.28	1.19	2.22	-1.17	2.29	-1.66	2.48	-1.63	4.43	.22	3.11	- .72	3.18	.00	3.30	- .08	2.78	.01	4.17	1.44	37.22	- 2
ZION GROVE	1.01	-2.82	3.01	- .53	E 2.46	-1.78	4.02	.06	4.16	- .26	3.56	- .93	6.27	1.18	4.52	- .21	4.30	.42	2.47	-1.66	2.10	-1.35	3.37	- .55	E41.25	- 5
ZIONSVILLE 3 SE	1.95	-2.11	5.11	1.44	5.01	.47	4.01	.20	2.83	-1.77	2.98	-1.69	3.89	-1.12	3.84	- .78	3.45	- .37	3.16	- .17	3.36	- .82	4.84	1.07	44.13	- 5

See Reference Notes Following Station Index

TEMPERATURE EXTREMES AND FREEZE DATA

Station	Highest	Date	Lowest	Date	Last spring minimum of 16° or below Date	Temp.	20° or below Date	Temp.	24° or below Date	Temp.	28° or below Date	Temp.	32° or below Date	Temp.	First fall minimum of 32° or below Date	Temp.	28° or below Date	Temp.	24° or below Date	Temp.	20° or below Date	Temp.	16° or below Date	Temp.	Number of days between dates 16° or below	20° or below	24° or below	28° or below	32° or below
ALLENTOWN WB AIRPORT	95	6-13	8	1- 2	3-22	16	3-25	19	3-28	24	4-25	27	5-17	32	10-11	30	11-10	21	11-10	21	11-11	19	11-25	16	248	231	227	199	147
ALLENTOWN GAS CO	95	6-14+	9	1- 2	3-21	13	3-26	19	3-26	19	4-25	27	5- 9	32	10-11	29	11-11	21	11-11	21	11-24	18	12-30	14	284	243	230	200	155
ALTOONA HORSESHOE CURVE	92	6-13	5	1-28	3-25	14	3-25	14	4-25	23	5-17	28	5-25	29	9-21	30	10-11	27	11-11	24	11-23	15	11-23	15	243	243	200	147	119
ARENDTSVILLE	97	6-14	10	1- 1+	2-25	15	3-25	19	4-21	24	4-25	27	5-17	29	9-21	30	11-11	22	11-11	22	11-23	20	11-24	16	273	243	204	200	127
ARTEMAS 1 WNW	97	6- 8	4	1-23	3-21	16	4-21	18	4-21	18	5- 5	26	5-24	32	9-10	30	10-11	27	11- 8	24	11-18	20	11-19	16	243	211	201	159	109
BAKERSTOWN 3 WNW	92	7- 2	5	1-23	3-20	13	3-25	18	4-21	23	4-25	25	5-23	32	10-10	31	11-17	21	11-17	21	11-23	15	11-23	15	248	243	210	206	140
BEAVERTOWN	95	6-13	-	-	-		-		-		-		-		9-21	30	10-11	27	11-11	20	11-11	20	11-25	12	-	-	-	-	-
BELLEFONTE 4 S	93	6-14	7	1-26	3-25	15	3-26	18	4-25	24	5-17	28	5-25	30	9-21	32	10-11	26	11-11	22	11-23	18	11-24	16	244	242	200	147	119
BERWICK	95	6-13+	9	1-26	3-21	13	3-25	17	4-21	24	4-25	25	5-25	30	9-21	31	10-11	28	11-11	20	11-11	20	11-24	15	248	231	204	169	119
BETHLEHEM LEHIGH UNIV	95	6-14	11	1- 2+	3-18	16	3-25	19	3-25	19	3-28	25	4-25	32	11-10	29	11-11	17	11-11	17	11-11	17	11-30	15	257	231	231	228	199
BLAIRSVILLE 6 ENE	88	6-14	5	1-23+	3-25	14	3-25	14	4-25	24	5-24	28	5-25	32	9-21	31	11-10	26	11-11	23	11-22	19	11-23	9	243	242	200	170	119
BRADFORD 4 W RES	89	6-14	-13	2-24	4-25	16	5-25	18	5-25	18	5-26	26	5-29	31	9- 9	31	9-19	28	10-10	23	11-10	20	11-11	14	200	169	138	116	103
BROOKVILLE CAA AIRPORT	90	6-13+	- 2	1-26	3-25	10	4- 1	17	4-25	21	5-25	27	5-26	31	9-10	32	9-21	27	10-11	22	11-10	19	11-22	15	242	223	169	119	107
BURGETTSTOWN 2 W	93	6-15	- 5	1-24	3-22	14	4-21	20	4-25	23	5-25	26	5-26	31	9- 8	32	9-21	23	9-21	23	11-17	14	11-17	14	240	210	149	119	105
BURNT CABINS 2 NE	95	6-14	3	1-24	3-22	16	4- 1	19	4-25	22	5-17	28	5-26	29	9-10	32	-		-		-		-		-	-	-	-	107
BUTLER	94	6-15+	4	1-26	3-21	10	4- 1	20	4-10	24	5-17	28	5-24	31	9-21	29	10-10	27	11-11	22	11-17	18	11-24	7	248	230	215	146	120
CANTON 1 NW	89	6-14	0	12-30	3-29	15	3-29	15	4-22	21	5-25	26	5-26	30	9-21	30	10-19	27	11-10	24	11-11	18	11-23	15	239	227	202	147	118
CARLISLE	98	6-13	13	1-28	2-24	15	3-20	20	3-25	21	4-25	28	4-25	28	10-11	30	11-11	22	11-11	22	11-24	19	11-25	14	275	249	231	200	169
CHAMBERSBURG 1 ESE	96	6-13	7	1-26	3-21	16	3-25	20	4- 1	23	4-25	26	5-25	30	9-21	30	10-11	27	11-11	23	11-23	19	11-24	15	248	243	224	169	119
CHESTER	96	6-14+	-	-	1-28	15	3- 1	20	-		-		4-21	32	-		-		-		-		-		-	-	-	-	-
CLARION 3 SW	92	6-14	- 5	1-26	3-25	10	4-21	19	4-25	22	5-25	25	5-26	31	9-21	30	10-10	28	10-11	24	11-17	20	11-23	16	243	210	169	138	118
CLAYSVILLE 3 W	98	6-14+	- 3	1-24	4- 1	14	4-25	20	5-24	24	5-25	26	5-26	31	-		-		10-11	22	11-17	15	11-17	15	230	206	140	-	-
COATESVILLE 1 SW	95	7- 3	7	1-28+	3-21	15	3-25	19	3-27	24	4-25	28	5-25	30	9-21	32	11-11	18	11-11	18	11-11	18	11-24	15	248	231	229	200	119
COLUMBIA	99	6-13	10	1-24	2-24	15	3-21	17	3-25	21	4-25	28	5-17	32	10-11	32	11-11	22	11-11	22	11-24	17	11-25	14	275	248	231	200	147
CONFLUENCE 1 SW DAM	92	6-15	- 3	1-28	3-25	16	4- 1	20	4-21	22	4-25	28	5-25	30	9-21	32	10-11	28	11-17	23	11-23	18	11-24	4	244	236	210	169	119
CORRY	92	6-14	- 4	2-24	4- 1	8	4-25	20	5-25	24	5-25	24	5-26	30	9-27	31	10-10	28	11-11	19	11-11	19	11-23	15	236	200	170	138	124
COUDERSPORT 2 NW	-	-	-	-	-		-		-		-		-		-		-		-		-		-		-	-	-	-	-
COUDERSPORT 3 NW	89	6-13	-	-	4-25	16	5-25	19	5-25	19	5-26	28	6-19	30	9- 9	31	9-10	28	10-10	22	10-11	19	11-10	13	199	139	138	107	82
DERRY	-	-	5	1-28	-		-		-		5- 8	28	5-25	30	9-21	31	10-11	26	11-11	24	11-17	20	11-24	13	-	-	-	156	119
DEVAULT 1 W	94	6-13+	-	-	-		-		-		-		-		10-11	30	11-11	18	11-11	18	11-11	18	11-24	13	-	-	-	-	-
DIXON	94	6-14	- 4	3-18	3-28	13	3-29	19	4-25	21	5-25	25	5-26	30	9-21	30	10-11	22	10-11	22	11-11	14	11-11	14	228	227	169	139	118
DONEGAL	87	6-14+	- 3	1-28	4-21	16	4-21	16	5-17	21	5-25	25	5-26	30	9- 9	28	9- 9	28	9-21	23	11-11	16	11-11	16	204	204	127	107	106
DONORA	95	6-15	11	1-24+	3-20	16	3-21	20	3-25	21	4-21	28	5- 5	32	11-11	32	11-17	24	11-17	24	11-23	20	11-24	15	249	247	237	210	190
DU BOIS 7 E	90	6-14+	-13	1-26	4- 1	8	4-25	18	5- 8	24	5-24	27	5-25	32	9-20	32	9-21	28	10-11	24	11-11	18	11-23	14	236	200	156	120	118
EAGLES MERE	88	6-15	- 1	2-22+	3-29	16	4-21	20	4-26	24	5-17	25	5-25	30	9-21	29	11-10	23	11-10	23	11-20	20	11-23	13	239	213	198	177	119
EAST BRADY	94	6-13+	- 1	1-26	3-24	14	4- 1	19	4-22	23	4-25	27	6- 2	32	9-21	31	11-11	23	11-11	23	11-23	18	11-24	14	245	236	203	200	111
EBENSBURG	87	6-14	- 2	1-28	4- 1	16	4- 1	16	4-25	21	5-17	25	5-25	30	9- 9	32	9-21	27	11-10	24	11-19	20	11-22	14	235	232	199	127	107
EMPORIUM 1 E	91	6-14	-	-	4- 1	15	4-25	18	5-25	22	5-26	26	5-29	32	-		-		-		-		-		-	-	-	-	-
EMPORIUM 2 SSW	-	-	-	-	-		-		-		-		-		9-10	32	9-21	28	10-10	23	11-11	15	11-11	15	-	-	-	-	-
EPHRATA	95	6-13	12	1-24+	3-20	15	3-25	17	4-25	23	4-25	23	5-17	31	10-11	30	11-11	21	11-11	21	11-24	15	11-24	15	249	244	200	200	147
ERIE CAA AIRPORT	91	7- 1	6	1-25	3-25	15	3-25	15	4-10	23	4-25	27	5-25	31	10-11	32	11-10	23	11-10	23	11-22	19	12-30	12	280	242	214	199	139
EVERETT 1 SW	96	8-18	- 7	1-28	2-24	10	4- 1	20	4-11	23	4-25	27	5-17	30	9-21	28	9-21	28	11-19	22	11-23	14	11-23	14	273	236	222	149	127
FARRELL SHARON	95	6-14	3	1-27	3-25	15	4- 1	20	4-25	21	5-25	26	5-26	32	9-22	31	10-10	26	11-11	23	11-17	20	11-23	16	243	230	200	138	119
FORD CITY 4 S DAM	92	6-14	- 1	1-26	3-22	16	4- 1	19	4-21	23	5-24	27	5-25	29	9-21	29	10-11	27	11-11	21	11-17	18	11-23	16	246	230	204	140	119
FRANKLIN	90	6-13+	3	1-26+	3-25	13	4- 1	20	4-25	22	5-25	27	5-25	27	10-10	30	10-11	27	11-18	21	11-19	20	11-23	16	243	232	207	139	138
FREELAND	89	6-14	5	1-26+	3-28	14	4- 1	20	5- 8	24	5-24	27	5-25	29	9-21	32	11-10	20	11-10	20	11-10	20	11-23	16	240	223	186	170	119
GEORGE SCHOOL	96	6-14	6	3-21	3-22	13	3-25	19	3-25	19	4-25	26	5-25	29	9-21	32	10-11	28	11-11	18	11-11	18	11-24	16	247	231	231	169	119
GETTYSBURG	97	6-14	12	1-28	2-22	16	3-26	20	3-26	20	4-25	28	5-17	32	9-21	32	11-11	24	11-11	24	11-24	18	11-25	14	277	243	230	200	127
GRATZ 1 N	92	6-14	10	2-24	3-22	14	3-26	18	4-25	24	5-17	28	5-25	30	9-21	30	10-11	26	11-11	20	11-11	20	11-24	14	247	230	200	147	119
GREENVILLE	93	6-14	- 2	1-26	3-21	8	4- 1	19	4-25	22	5-25	26	5-25	26	9-21	32	10-10	28	11-11	22	11-17	18	11-24	15	248	230	200	138	119
HANOVER	97	6-14	11	1-28+	3-20	15	3-25	18	4- 1	23	4-25	27	5-17	30	9-21	31	10-11	28	11-11	22	11-23	19	11-24	15	249	243	224	169	127
HARRISBURG WB AIRPORT	95	6-13+	14	1- 2	1-28	16	3-18	19	3-25	21	3-25	21	4-25	30	10-11	32	11-10	26	11-11	24	11-23	20	None		-	250	231	230	169
HAWLEY 1 S DAM	90	6-15+	- 3	3-18	3-28	10	4- 2	19	5-25	24	5-25	24	5-29	32	9-10	29	10- 6	27	10-11	22	11-11	11	11-11	11	228	223	139	134	104
HOLTWOOD	97	6-13	14	1-28	1-28	14	2-24	19	3-22	24	3-25	25	4-21	32	11-10	29	11-11	28	11-23	22	11-25	19	None		-	275	246	231	203
HUNTINGDON	98	6-14	7	1-28+	3-22	13	3-26	19	4-22	24	4-25	27	5-26	30	9-21	31	-		11-11	18	11-11	18	11-24	14	247	230	203	-	118
INDIANA 3 SE	91	6-13+	- 1	1-26+	3-22	15	4- 1	18	4-25	22	5-25	27	5-25	27	9-21	27	9-21	27	11-11	20	11-11	20	11-23	14	246	224	200	119	119
IRWIN	93	6-15	4	1-28	3-21	15	3-25	19	3-27	23	4-25	26	5-25	31	9-21	32	10-11	28	11-17	21	11-23	20	11-24	11	248	243	235	169	119
JAMESTOWN 2 NW	90	6-15	- 2	1-23+	3-25	16	4-10	20	4-25	22	5-25	27	5-25	27	10-10	28	10-10	28	10-11	24	11-17	19	11-23	12	243	221	169	138	138
JIM THORPE	95	6-14	9	1- 2+	3-25	16	3-25	16	4-25	24	5- 9	27	5-25	29	9-21	31	10-11	26	11-10	17	11-10	17	11-24	16	244	230	199	155	119
JOHNSTOWN	96	6-15	7	1-28	3-21	16	3-25	18	4- 1	24	4-25	28	5-25	31	9-21	27	9-21	27	11-11	23	11-23	15	11-23	15	247	243	224	149	119
KANE 1 NNE	89	6-14+	-10	1-26+	4- 1	5	5-25	19	5-25	19	5-26	26	5-29	31	9-10	29	9-27	27	10-10	23	10-11	19	11-11	15	224	139	138	124	104
KEOG	93	6-13	4	1-25	3-21	16	3-22	20	4-25	24	4-25	24	5-25	30	9-10	31	9-21	26	11-10	22	11-19	18	11-23	12	247	242	199	149	108
LANCASTER 2 NE PUMP STA	95	6-13+	6	1-28	3-22	15	3-25	20	3-27	24	4-25	26	5-25	32	9-21	31	10-11	27	11-11	20	11-11	20	11-25	15	248	231	229	169	119
LANDISVILLE 2 NW	96	7- 3	10	1- 2	2-24	14	3-25	20	4- 1	24	4-25	25	4-25	25	9-21	31	10-11	27	11-11	20	11-11	20	11-24	13	274	231	224	169	149
LAWRENCEVILLE 2 S	95	6-15	- 5	1-25+	4- 1	16	4-25	20	5-25	23	5-25	23	5-29	32	9-21	30	10-11	23	10-11	23	11-11	16	11-11	16	224	200	139	139	115
LEBANON 3 W	96	6-14+	-	-	-		-		-		-		-		9-21	32	10-11	28	11-11	21	11-24	15	11-24	15	-	-	-	-	-
LEWISTOWN	98	6-14	11	1-29	2-25	14	3-26	19	4- 2	24	4-26	28	5-18	32	9-22	32	11-11	25	11-20	24	11-24	19	11-26	16	275	243	232	199	127
LINESVILLE 5 WNW	89	6-13+	- 8	2- 1	3-25	16	4- 1	20	4-25	23	5-25	26	5-25	26	9-28	32	10-11	26	11-10	22	11-23	16	11-23	16	243	236	199	139	126
LOCK HAVEN	98	6-13	5	1-24	3-25	16	3-25	16	4-21	24	4-25	25	-		9-21	31	10-11	28	11-11	22	11-23	18	11-24	16	244	243	204	169	-
MADERA	92	6-14	- 6	1-29	4-25	16	4-25	16	5-25	24	5-26	26	5-27	32	9- 9	31	9-19	28	9-21	22	10-11	19	11-11	15	200	169	119	116	105
MARCUS HOOK	98	6-13	17	2-22	None		2-22	17	3-25	21	3-25	21	4- 1	31	11-10	30	11-23	24	11-23	24	11-24	20	None		-	276	243	243	223
MARTINSBURG CAA AIRPORT	94	6-14	6	1-28	3-25	15	3-25	15	4- 1	24	5-17	27	5-17	27	9-21	30	10-11	27	11-10	23	11-22	20	11-23	13	243	242	223	147	127
MEADVILLE 1 S	90	6-14+	0	2- 1	3-25	13	4-21	20	4-25	23	5-25	28	5-25	28	10-10	28	10-10	28	11-11	23	11-23	17	11-25	14	245	216	200	138	138
MERCER 2 NNE	89	6-13+	- 9	1-28	3-26	14	4-25	20	5-25	23	5-25	23	5-25	23	9- 8	29	10-10	24	10-10	24	11-22	20	11-23	16	242	211	138	138	106
MIDDLETOWN OLMSTED FLD	97	6-13+	14	1- 2+	1-28	14	3-21	19	3-26	23	4-21	27	4-25	30	11-10	25	11-10	25	11-11	24	11-25	17	None		-	249	230	203	199
MIDLAND DAM 7	92	7- 2	6	1-24	3-20	15	3-25	20	3-25	20	3-25	20	4-25	31	10-11	32	11-17	25	11-22	23	11-23	18	11-24	16	249	243	242	237	169
MONTROSE 1 E	89	6-15	0	12-31	3-29	15	3-29	15	4-21	22	5-17	25	5-25	29	9-21	30	10-20	28	11-10	23	11-11	16	11-11	16	227	227	203	156	119
MORGANTOWN	94	6-13+	7	1-28	3-23	14	3-25	18	4-25	23	4-25	23	5-17	29	9-21	31	10-11	28	11-10	23	11-23	16	11-23	16	245	243	199	169	127
MT GRETNA 2 SE	91	8-18	10	2-24	3- 1	14	3-25	20	4- 1	22	4-18	28	5-17	32	9-21	30	11-10	22	11-10	22	11-23	17	11-24	11	268	243	223	206	127
MT POCONO 2 N AP	90	6-14	- 3	12-31	3-28	15	4-25	20	4-25	20	5-25	25	5-25	25	9-21	28	9-21	28	10-11	22	11-11	11	11-11	11	228	200	169	119	119
MUHLENBURG 1 SE	93	6-14	2	2-22	3-28	13	4-21	20	4-25	22	5-25	25	5-25	25	9-10	30	9-21	26	10-11	23	11-10	17	11-11	13	228	203	169	119	108
NEWBURG 3 W	97	6-14	-	-	2-24	15	3-17	18	3-21	22	4-25	28	5-17	32	9-21	29	-		-		-		-		-	-	-	-	127
NEW CASTLE 1 N	91	6-13+	0	1-26+	3-21	10	4- 1	20	4-10	24	5-25	27	5-25	27	9-21	32	10-11	25	11-17	19	11-17	19	11-23	16	247	230	221	139	119
NEWELL	95	7- 3	9	1-24+	2-24	15	3-25	20	4- 1	22	4- 1	22	4-25	32	11-17	29	11-23	28	11-24	19	11-24	19	None		-	244	237	236	206
NEWPORT	98	6-14	10	1- 2+	3-22	13	3-26	20	4- 2	24	4-26	28	5-26	32	9-21	32	11-11	20	11-11	20	11-11	20	11-24	16	247	230	223	199	118
NEW STANTON	97	7- 1	5	1-27	3-25	16	4- 1	20	4-18	22	5-24	28	5-25	29	9-21	32	11-16	24	11-16	24	11-17	18	11-23	10	243	230	212	176	119
NORRISTOWN	96	6-14+	-	-	2-22	16	3-25	20	3-25	20	3-25	20	4-25	31	10-11	32	11-10	28	11-23	22	11-24	20	None		-	244	243	230	169
PALMERTON	92	6-14	9	1- 2	3-21	16	3-25	17	3-28	23	4-25	26	5-25	32	10- 6	32	10-11	27	11-10	20	11-10	20	11-24	15	248	230	227	169	134
PHIL DREXEL INST OF TECH	98	6-13+	16	2-22	2-22	16	2-22	16	3-25	21	3-25	21	3-28	31	11-11	31	11-23	26	11-24	22	None		None		-	-	244	243	228
PHILADELPHIA WB AIRPORT	95	6-13+	17	1-27+	None		2-24	20	3-25	21	3-25	21	4-21	32	11-10	30	11-11	27	11-23	22	11-24	20	None		-	274	243	231	203
PHILADELPHIA PT BREEZE	96	6-13+	20	1- 2	None		1- 2	20	3-25	24	3-25	24	3-28	31	11-23	30	11-24	25	None		None		None		-	-	-	244	240
PHILADELPHIA SHAWMONT	96	6-13+	14	1- 2+	2-24	16	3-22	20	3-25	22	4- 1	28	4-26	32	11-11	23	11-11	23	11-11	23	11-24	20	None		-	247	231	224	199
PHILADELPHIA CITY	94	6-14+	18	2-22	None		2-22	18	3-25	22	3-25	22	3-28	30	11-11	32	11-23	28	12-30	23	None		None		-	-	280	243	228
PHILIPSBURG CAA AIRPORT	89	6-13+	- 2	2-24+	4-25	16	4-25	16	5-25	22	5-25	22	5-25	22	9- 9	32	9-10	28	10-11	17	10-11	17	11-10	15	199	169	139	108	107
PHOENIXVILLE 1 E	99	7- 2	6	1- 2+	3-22	6	3-25	18	4-25	23	5-25	28	5-25	28	10-10	31	10-12	28	11-11	18	11-11	18	11-24	15	247	231	200	140	138

See reference notes following Station Index.

FREEZE DATA

First fall minimum of

PIMPLE HILL
PITTSBURGH WB AP 2
PITTSBURGH WB CITY
PLEASANT MOUNT 1 W
PORT CLINTON

PUTNEYVILLE 2 SE DAM
QUAKERTOWN 1 E
READING WB CITY
RIDGWAY 3 W
SALINA 3 W

SCRANTON
SCRANTON WB AIRPORT
SELINSGROVE CAA AIRPORT
SHIPPENSBURG
SHIPPINGPORT WB

SLIPPERY ROCK
SOMERSET MAIN ST
SPRINGBORO
SPRINGS 1 SW
STATE COLLEGE

STROUDSBURG
TAMARACK 2 S FIRE TWR
TIONESTA 2 SE DAM
TITUSVILLE WATER WORKS
TOWANDA

UNIONTOWN
UPPER DARBY
WARREN
WAYNESBURG 2 W
WELLSBORO 3 S

WELLSVILLE
WEST CHESTER
WILLIAMSPORT WB AIRPORT
YORK 3 SSW PUMP STA

See reference notes following Station Index.

TOTAL EVAPORATION AND WIND MOVEMENT

Station		Jan.	Feb.	Mar.	Apr.	May	June	July	Aug.	Sept.	Oct.	Nov.	Dec.	Annual
ONFLUENCE 1 SW DAM	EVAP	-	-	-	B3.38	4.77	4.73	4.70	B4.16	3.38	2.38	-	-	-
	DEP	-	-	-	-	-	-	-	-	-	-	-	-	-
	WIND	-	-	-	2408	2028	1331	1292	1099	1313	1447	-	-	-
ORD CITY 4 S DAM	EVAP	-	-	-	-	-	B5.17	B4.76	B4.16	3.27	2.29	-	-	-
	DEP	-	-	-	-	-	-	-	-	-	-	-	-	-
	WIND	-	-	-	-	-	897	835	751	906	995	-	-	-
AWLEY 1 S DAM	EVAP	-	-	-	-	B4.31	5.60	4.63	4.64	2.97	B2.23	-	-	-
	DEP	-	-	-	-	-1.19	- .26	-1.90	-1.01	-1.08	- .26	-	-	-
	WIND	-	-	-	-	B3104	1905	1823	1645	1707	B1603	-	-	-
AMESTOWN 2 NW	EVAP	-	-	-	-	B3.82	B4.54	B4.51	B4.38	B3.29	B2.38	-	-	-
	DEP	-	-	-	-	- .31	- .50	-1.31	- .31	- .07	-	-	-	-
	WIND	-	-	-	-	1219	517	786	709	694	1078	-	-	-
ANDISVILLE 2 NW	EVAP	-	-	-	-	-	-	-	B5.84	3.72	2.27	-	-	-
	DEP	-	-	-	-	-	-	-	-	-	-	-	-	-
	WIND	-	-	-	-	-	-	-	817	1053	1429	-	-	-
IMPLE HILL	EVAP	-	-	-	-	5.96	6.78	5.27	5.62	4.19	3.20	-	-	-
	DEP	-	-	-	-	-	-	-	-	-	-	-	-	-
	WIND	-	-	-	-	4065	2086	2291	1997	2249	2834	-	-	-
TATE COLLEGE	EVAP	-	-	-	-	-	-	4.53	B4.58	3.34	2.49	-	-	-
	DEP	-	-	-	-	-	-	-	-	-	-	-	-	-
	WIND	-	-	-	-	-	-	919	869	953	930	-	-	-

† CHANGES IN STATION NAMES

NEW NAME	OLD NAME	DATE
CLARENCE	CLARENCE 1 E	September 1956
GREENSBURG 3 SE UNITY	GREENSBURG 3 SE	October 1956
LANDISVILLE 2 NW	LANDISVILLE	June 1956
LEBANON	LEBANON 2 NW	May 1956
LEBANON 3 W	LEBANON	July 1956
LEWIS RUN 3 SE	LEWIS RUN 3 S	April 1956
MARIENVILLE 1 SW	MARIENVILLE	March 1956
NEFFS MILLS 3 NE	NEFFS MILLS 4 NE	May 1956
POTTSVILLE	POTTSVILLE PALO ALTO	September 1956
YORK 2 S FILTER PLANT	YORK 2 S	September 1956

RELOCATION AND CHANGES OF EQUIPMENT

CLARENCE	All equipment moved 0.7 mile WNW	September 7, 1956
CONNELSVILLE	All equipment moved 0.4 mile SSW	March 22, 1956
CORRY	All equipment moved 1.0 mile N	April 1, 1956
DINGMANS FERRY	All equipment moved 300 feet SSW	August 8, 1956
HUNTINGDON	All equipment moved 0.7 mile WSW	September 6, 1956
LAFAYETTE MC KEAN PARK	All equipment moved 50 feet W	September 14, 1956
LANDISVILLE 2 NW	All equipment moved 1.9 miles NW	July 9, 1956
LEBANON	All equipment moved 2 miles SE	May 8, 1956
LEBANON 3 W	All equipment moved 3 miles W	July 27, 1956
LEWIS RUN 3 SE	All equipment moved 150 feet W	April 18, 1956
MERWINSBURG	All equipment moved 300 feet	May 10, 1956
POTTSVILLE	All equipment moved 1.0 mile	September 1, 1956
STROUDSBURG	All equipment moved 750 feet	February 10, 1956
WATSONTOWN	All equipment moved 0.6 mile NW	November 15, 1956
YOUNGSVILLE	All equipment moved 250 feet NNW	January 26, 1956

TOTAL PRECIPITATION

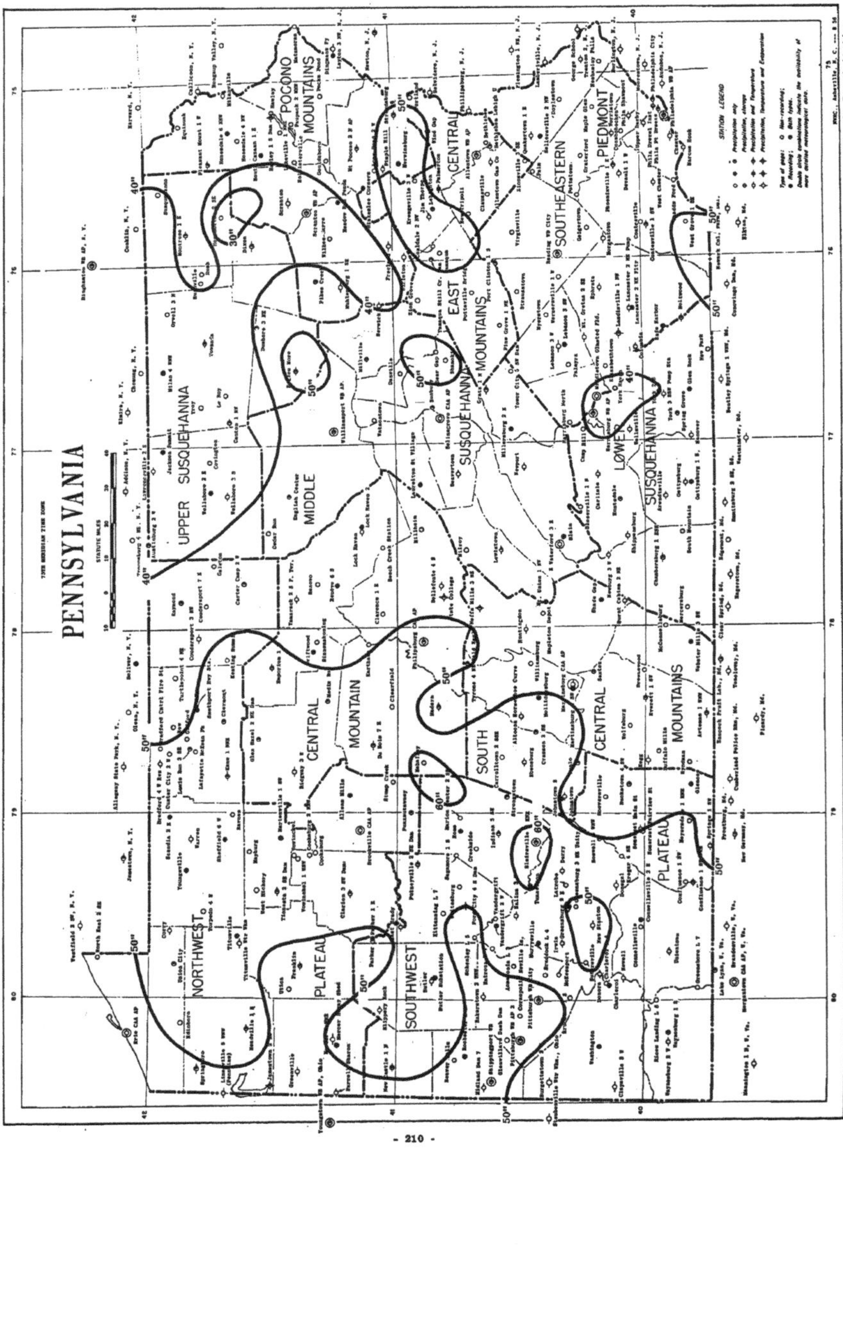

Isolines are drawn through points of approximately equal values. Hourly precipitation data from recorder substations will be available in the publication 'Hourly Precipitation Data'.

AVERAGE TEMPERATURE

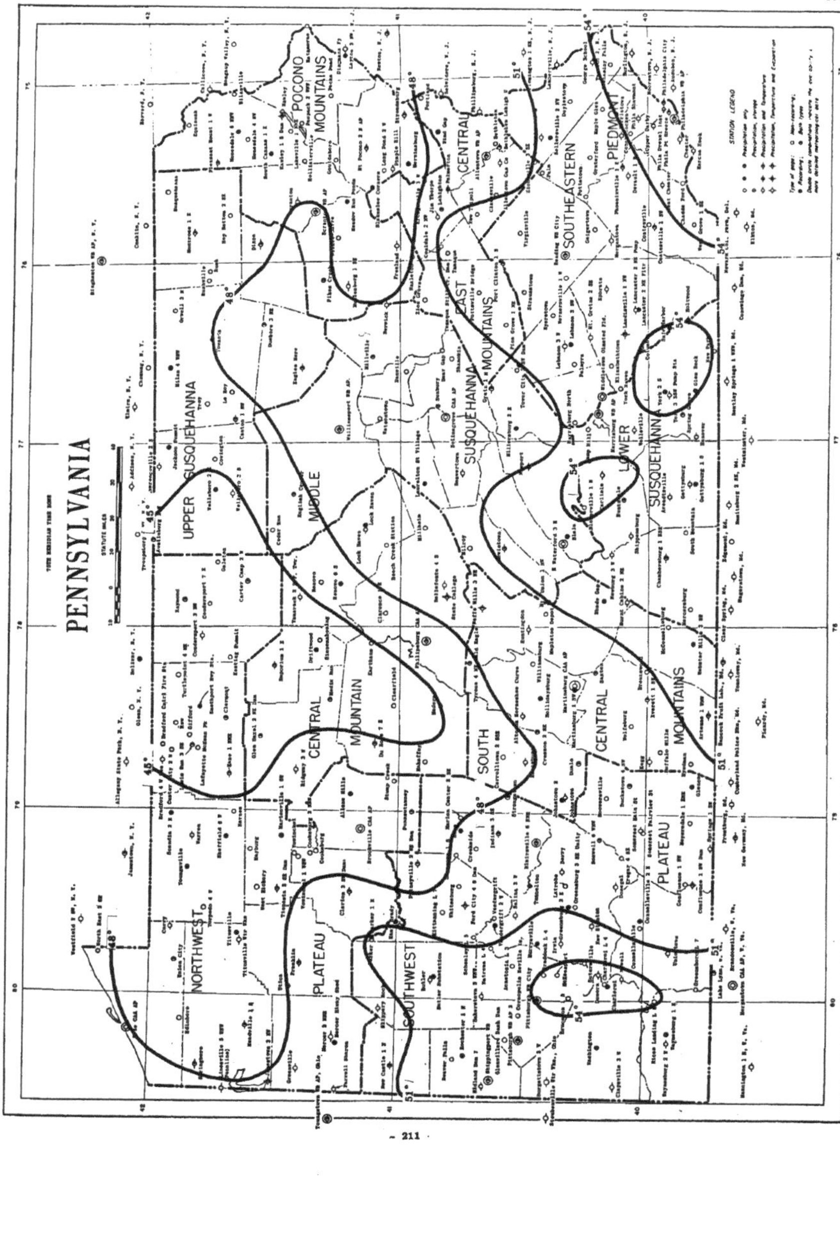

Isolines are drawn through points of approximately equal values. Hourly precipitation data from recorder substations will be available in the publication 'Hourly Precipitation Data'.

STATION INDEX

Station	Index No.	County	Drainage†	Latitude	Longitude	Elevation	Years of record: Temp.	Years of record: Precip.	Years of record: Evap.	Opened or closed during yr.: Month opened	Opened or closed during yr.: Month closed	Refer to tables
ACHETONIA LOCK 3	0022	ALLEGHENY	1	40 32	79 49	748		52				2
ALLENS MILLS	0099	JEFFERSON	1	41 12	78 55	1600						C
ALLENTOWN WB AIRPORT	0106	LEHIGH	9	40 39	75 26	376	18	16				1 2 3 C
ALLENTOWN GAS CO	0111	LEHIGH	9	40 36	75 28	254	35	45				1 2 3
ALTOONA HORSESHOE CURVE	0134	BLAIR.	6	40 30	78 29	1500	61	72				1 2 3
ARENDTSVILLE	0229	ADAMS	15	39 55	77 18	710	34	34				1 2 3
ARTEMAS 1 WNW	0256	BEDFORD	12	39 45	78 28	1250	4	4				1 2 3 C
AUSTINBURG 2 W	0313	TIOGA	15	42 00	77 32	1590		20				2 C
BAKERSTOWN 3 WNW	0355	ALLEGHENY	1	40 39	79 59	1230	9	9				1 2 3
BARNES	0409	WARREN	1	41 40	79 02	1310		16				2
BARTO 4 NW	0428	BERKS	14	40 26	75 39	310		0		JULY		2
BEAR GAP	0457	NORTH'LAND	15	40 50	76 30	900		11				2
BEAVER FALLS	0475	BEAVER	2	40 46	80 19	760		48				2
BEAVERTOWN	0482	SNYDER	15	40 45	77 10	640	10	10				1 2 3
BEECH CREEK STATION	0499	CENTRE	16	41 04	77 34	620		4				2
BELLEFONTE 4 S	0530	CENTRE	16	40 51	77 47	1110	28	40				1 2 3
BERNE	0599	BERKS	14	40 31	76 00	325		0		OCT		2
BERWICK	0611	COLUMBIA	15	41 04	76 15	570	11	11				1 2 3
BETHLEHEM	0629	NORTHAMPTON	9	40 37	75 22	400		–				2
#BETHLEHEM LEHIGH UNIVERSITY	0634	NORTHAMPTON	9	40 36	75 23	450	55	72				1 2 3 C
BLAIN	0725	PERRY	15	40 20	77 31	750						C
BLAIRSVILLE 6 ENE	0736	INDIANA	4	40 27	79 09	2048	11	20				1 2 3
BLAKESLEE CORNERS	0743	MONROE	9	41 06	75 36	1650						C
BLOSERVILLE 1 N	0763	CUMBERLAND	15	40 16	77 22	650		44				2
BOSWELL 6 WNW	0820	SOMERSET	1	40 11	79 08	2580		19				2 C
BRADDOCK LOCK 2	0861	ALLEGHENY	10	40 24	79 52	725		22				2
BRADFORD CENTRAL FIRE STA	0867	MC KEAN	1	41 57	78 39	1500		9				2
BRADFORD 4 W RESERVOIR	0868	MC KEAN	1	41 57	78 44	1680	30	30				1 2 3
BREEZEWOOD	0905	BEDFORD	6	40 00	78 14	1352	10	15				2
BROOKVILLE CAA AIRPORT	1002	JEFFERSON	1	41 09	79 06	1417	44	65				1 2 3
BRUCETON 1 S	1033	ALLEGHENY	10	40 18	79 59	1065		21				2
BUCKSTOWN 1 SE	1073	SOMERSET	4	40 04	78 50	2460						C
BUFFALO MILLS	1087	BEDFORD	6	39 57	78 39	1318		32				2
BURGETTSTOWN 2 W	1105	WASHINGTON	11	40 23	80 26	980	9	9				1 2 3
BURNT CABINS 2 NE	1115	HUNTINGDON	6	40 05	77 52	990	15	15				1 2 3
#BUTLER	1130	BUTLER	2	40 52	79 54	1100	33	43				1 2 3
BUTLER SUBSTATION	1135	BUTLER	2	40 51	79 53	1140						C
CAMP HILL	1198	CUMBERLAND	15	40 15	76 55	461		11				2
CANTON 1 NW	1215	BRADFORD	15	41 40	76 52	1520	13	17				1 2 3 C
CARLISLE	1234	CUMBERLAND	15	40 12	77 11	460	88	68				1 2 3
CARROLLTOWN 2 SSE	1255	CAMBRIA	16	40 35	78 42	2040		13				2
CARTER CAMP 2 W	1262	POTTER	16	41 37	77 45	2030		18				2 C
CEDAR RUN	1301	LYCOMING	16	41 31	77 27	800		38				2
CHADDS FORD	1342	DELAWARE	5	39 52	75 36	160		11				2
CHAMBERSBURG 1 ESE	1354	FRANKLIN	12	39 56	77 38	640	56	61				1 2 3 C
CHARLEROI	1372	WASHINGTON	10	40 08	79 55	1040						C
CHARLEROI LOCK 4	1377	WESTMORELAND	10	40 09	79 54	749		71				2
#CHESTER	1423	DELAWARE	5	39 51	75 22	86	6	6				1 2 3
†CLARENCE	1480	CENTRE	16	41 03	77 56	1410		7				2
CLARION 3 SW	1485	CLARION	1	41 12	79 26	1114	14	49				1 2 3 C
CLAUSSVILLE	1505	LEHIGH	9	40 37	75 39	670		11				2
CLAYSVILLE 3 W	1512	WASHINGTON	11	40 07	80 28	1000	54	54				1 2 3
CLEARFIELD	1519	CLEARFIELD	16	41 01	78 26	1100		48				2
CLERMONT	1529	MC KEAN	1	41 41	78 30	2104		6				2 C
COALDALE 2 NW	1572	SCHUYLKILL	9	40 50	75 56	1026		34				2
COATESVILLE 1 SW	1589	CHESTER	5	39 58	75 50	342	69	69				1 2 3 C
COATESVILLE	1594	CHESTER	5	39 59	75 49	340		9			INAC	2
COGAN STATION 2 N	1631	LYCOMING	16	41 21	77 06	640		8			MAR	2
COLUMBIA	1675	LANCASTER	15	40 02	76 30	300	14	14				1 2 3
CONFLUENCE 1 SW DAM	1705	SOMERSET	17	39 48	79 22	1490	11	11	–			1 2 3 4 C
CONFLUENCE 1 NW	1710	FAYETTE	17	39 50	79 22	1331		82				2
CONNELLSVILLE	1723	FAYETTE	17	40 01	79 36	870		18				2
CONNELLSVILLE 2 E	1729	FAYETTE	17	40 01	79 33	1300						C
CONSHOHOCKEN	1737	MONTGOMERY	5	40 04	75 19	70		33				2
COOKSBURG	1749	CLARION	1	41 20	79 13	1180		2				2
COOKSBURG 2 NNW	1752	CLARION	1	41 21	79 13	1460		2				2
CORAOPOLIS NEVILLE ISLAND	1773	ALLEGHENY	11	40 30	80 05	720		48				2
CORRY	1790	ERIE	1	41 56	79 38	1427	41	41				1 2 3
COUDERSPORT 2 NW	1805	POTTER	1	41 48	78 03	2220	1	1			APR	1 2 3
COUDERSPORT 3 NW	1806	POTTER	1	41 49	78 03	2020	1	1		APR		1 2 3
COUDERSPORT 7 E	1809	POTTER	1	41 46	77 53	2425		10				2
COVINGTON	1832	TIOGA	15	41 45	77 07	1575		18			SEPT	2
COVINGTON 2 WSW	1833	TIOGA	15	41 44	77 07	1745		0		SEPT		2
CREEKSIDE	1881	INDIANA	1	40 41	79 12	1035		16				2
CRESSON 2 SE	1895	CAMBRIA	6	40 27	78 34	2540		19				2 C
CUSTER CITY 2 W	1978	MC KEAN	1	41 55	78 41	2120		9				2
DANVILLE	2013	MONTOUR	15	40 58	76 37	460		16				2
DERRY	2108	WESTMORELAND	4	40 20	79 18	1150	59	59				1 2 3
DEVAULT 1 W	2116	CHESTER	14	40 05	75 33	360	6	6				1 2 3
DINGMANS FERRY	2160	PIKE	5	41 13	74 52	364						C
DIXON	2171	WYOMING	15	41 34	75 54	620	8	8				1 2 3 C
DONEGAL	2183	WESTMORELAND	17	40 07	79 23	1746	13	13				1 2 3
#DONORA	2190	WASHINGTON	10	40 11	79 51	814	30	30				1 2 3
DOYLESTOWN	2221	BUCKS	5	40 18	75 08	393		66				2
DRIFTWOOD	2245	CAMERON	16	41 20	78 08	880						C
DU BOIS 7 E	2265	CLEARFIELD	16	41 06	78 38	1670	1	19				1 2 3 C
DUNLO	2298	CAMBRIA	4	40 17	78 43	2410		17				C
DUSHORE 3 NE	2324	SULLIVAN	16	41 33	76 21	1750		7				2 C
EAGLES MERE	2343	SULLIVAN	16	41 24	76 35	2020	14	20				1 2 3 C
EAST BRADY	2363	CLARION	1	40 59	79 37	820	8	8				1 2 3
EAST WATERFORD 3 E	2459	PERRY	6	40 21	77 33	2125	11	18			INAC	1 2 3
EBENSBURG	2466	CAMBRIA	4	40 29	78 43	2090	39	39				1 2 3
EDINBORO	2514	ERIE	1	41 52	80 08	1220	10	15				2
ELIZABETHTOWN	2560	LANCASTER	15	40 09	76 37	460		11				2
EMPORIUM 1 E	2633	CAMERON	16	41 31	78 13	1160	68	66			AUG	1 2 3 C
EMPORIUM 2 SSW	2634	CAMERON	16	41 28	78 15	1735	0	0		AUG		1 2 3 C
ENGLISH CENTER	2644	LYCOMING	16	41 26	77 17	881		17				2 C
EPHRATA	2662	LANCASTER	15	40 11	76 10	465	54	63				1 2 3
EQUINUNK	2669	WAYNE	5	41 51	75 13	900		11				2
ERIE CAA AIRPORT	2682	ERIE	8	42 05	80 12	732	12	12				1 2 3
EVERETT 1 SW	2721	BEDFORD	6	40 00	78 23	1020	36	36				1 2 3 C
FARRELL-SHARON	2814	MERCER	2	41 14	80 30	865	44	45				1 2 3
FORD CITY 4 S DAM	2942	ARMSTRONG	1	40 43	79 30	950	13	13	11			1 2 3 4 C
FRANKLIN	3028	VENANGO	1	41 23	79 49	987	62	83				1 2 3 C
FREDERICKSVILLE 2 SE	3047	BERKS	14	40 26	75 40	950	14	19			JULY	1 2 3
FREELAND	3056	LUZERNE	15	41 01	75 54	1900	62	42				1 2 3
GALETON	3130	POTTER	16	41 44	77 39	1325		26				2
GEIGERTOWN	3189	BERKS	14	40 13	75 50	400		11				2
GEORGE SCHOOL	3200	BUCKS	5	40 13	74 56	135	50	50				1 2 3
#GETTYSBURG	3218	ADAMS	12	39 50	77 14	540	80	82				1 2 3
GETTYSBURG 1 S	3223	ADAMS	12	39 48	77 14	560						C
GIFFORD	3237	MC KEAN	1	41 51	78 36	2220		9				2
GLENCOE	3298	SOMERSET	12	39 49	78 51	1620						C
GLEN HAZEL 2 NE DAM	3311	ELK	1	41 34	78 36	1725		5				2 C
GLEN ROCK	3330	YORK	15	39 48	76 44	620						C
GLENWILLARD DASH DAM	3343	ALLEGHENY	11	40 33	80 13	705		12				2
GORDON	3379	SCHUYLKILL	15	40 45	76 20	900	52	52			FEB	1 2 3
GOULDSBORO	3394	WAYNE	9	41 15	75 27	1890	20	41				2
GRANTVILLE 2 SW	3422	DAUPHIN	15	40 22	76 41	510		19			JUNE	2
GRATERFORD	3435	MONTGOMERY	14	40 14	75 27	160		41				2

Station	Index No.	County	Drainage†	Latitude	Longitude	Elevation	Years of record: Temp.	Years of record: Precip.	Years of record: Evap.	Opened or closed during yr.: Month opened	Opened or closed during yr.: Month closed	Refer to tables
GRATZ 1 N	3438	DAUPHIN	15	40 38	76 43	760	6	8				1 2 3 C
GREENSBORO LOCK 7	3503	GREENE	10	39 47	79 55	808		75				2
GREENSBURG 2 E	3515	WESTMORELAND	10	40 18	79 31	1225						C
†GREENSBURG 3 SE UNITY	3516	WESTMORELAND	10	40 17	79 30	1245	37	48				2
GREENVILLE	3526	MERCER	2	41 24	80 23	1026	58	58				1 2 3
HANOVER	3662	YORK	15	39 48	76 59	600	53	53				1 2 3
#HARRISBURG WB AIRPORT	3699	YORK	15	40 13	76 51	335	68	68				1 2 3 C
HARRISBURG NORTH	3704	DAUPHIN	15	40 18	76 54	323		39				2
HAWLEY	3758	WAYNE	5	41 29	75 10	880	34	47				2
HAWLEY 1 S DAM	3761	WAYNE	5	41 28	75 11	1200	21	25	2			1 2 3 4 C
HOLLIDAYSBURG	4001	BLAIR	6	40 26	78 24	960						C
HOLLISTERVILLE	4008	WAYNE	5	41 23	75 26	1360		29				2
#HOLTWOOD	4019	LANCASTER	15	39 50	76 20	187	37	42				1 2 3 C
HOME	4027	INDIANA	1	40 45	79 06	1220						C
†HONESDALE 4 NW	4043	WAYNE	5	41 37	75 19	1410		11				2
HONESDALE 6 NNW	4044	WAYNE	5	41 39	75 17	1050						C
HOOVERSVILLE	4058	SOMERSET	4	40 09	78 55	1660		18				2
HOP BOTTOM 2 SE	4066	SUSQUEHANNA	15	41 43	75 43	900		12				2
HUNTINGDON	4159	HUNTINGDON	6	40 29	78 01	610	69	69				1 2 3
HUNTSDALE	4166	CUMBERLAND	15	40 06	77 18	610		16				2 C
HYNDMAN	4190	BEDFORD	12	39 49	78 43	920		44				2
INDIANA 3 SE	4214	INDIANA	4	40 36	79 07	1102	54	57				1 2 3 C
IRWIN	4276	WESTMORELAND	10	40 20	79 42	1100	54	60				1 2 3
JACKSON SUMMIT	4304	TIOGA	15	41 57	77 01	1690						C
JAMESTOWN 2 NW	4325	CRAWFORD	2	41 30	80 28	1050	15	17	15			1 2 3 4 C
JIM THORPE	4370	CARBON	9	40 52	75 45	830	64	64				1 2 3
#JOHNSTOWN	4385	CAMBRIA	4	40 20	78 55	1214	63	75				1 2 3
JOHNSTOWN 2	4390	CAMBRIA	4	40 19	78 55	1275						C
KANE 1 NNE	4432	MC KEAN	1	41 41	78 48	1750	13	41				1 2 3 C
KARTHAUS	4450	CLEARFIELD	16	41 07	78 07	950		16				2
KEATING SUMMIT	4466	POTTER	16	41 41	78 11	1840		7				2
KEGG	4481	BEDFORD	6	39 59	78 43	1280	6	6				1 2 3
KITTANNING LOCK 7	4611	ARMSTRONG	1	40 49	79 32	790		6				2
KREGAR 4 SE	4667	WESTMORELAND	17	40 06	79 14	2530		15				2
KRESGEVILLE 3 W	4672	CARBON	9	40 54	75 34	720		14				2
LAFAYETTE MC KEAN PARK	4706	MC KEAN	1	41 48	78 40	2130		9				2
LAKEVILLE 1 NNE	4733	WAYNE	5	41 27	75 16	1440		29				2
LANCASTER 2 NE PUMP STA	4758	LANCASTER	15	40 03	76 17	255	55	69				1 2 3
LANCASTER 2 NE FILTER PLT	4763	LANCASTER	15	40 03	76 17	270						C
†LANDISVILLE 2 NW	4778	LANCASTER	15	40 07	76 26	360	11	11	6			1 2 3 4 C
LATROBE	4832	WESTMORELAND	4	40 19	79 23	1000		14			INAC	2
LAURELTON STATE VILLAGE	4853	UNION	15	40 54	77 13	880						C
LAWRENCEVILLE 2 S	4873	TIOGA	15	41 59	77 07	1000	59	59				1 2 3
†LEBANON 3 W	4891	LEBANON	15	40 20	76 29	460	66	73				1 2 3
LEBANON 3 SW	4896	LEBANON	15	40 19	76 28	490						C
LEHIGHTON	4934	CARBON	9	40 50	75 43	580		22				2 C
LE ROY	4972	BRADFORD	15	41 41	76 43	1040		19				2
†LEWIS RUN 3 SE	4984	MC KEAN	1	41 50	78 39	1740		9				2 C
LEWISTOWN	4992	MIFFLIN	6	40 35	77 35	480	18	18				1 2 3 C
LINESVILLE 5 WNW	5050	CRAWFORD	2	41 41	80 31	1020	5	39				1 2 3
LOCK HAVEN	5104	CLINTON	16	41 08	77 27	570	65	65				1 2 3
LOCK HAVEN 2	5109	CLINTON	16	41 08	77 27	630						C
LONG POND 2 W	5160	MONROE	9	41 03	75 30	1860		10				2
LYNDELL 2 NW	5279	CHESTER	5	40 05	75 46	–		0		DEC		2
MADERA	5336	CLEARFIELD	16	40 50	78 26	1460	–	–				1 2 3 C
MAHAFFEY	5342	CLEARFIELD	16	40 53	78 44	1280		7				2
MAPLE GLEN	5368	MONTGOMERY	5	40 11	75 11	380		11				2
MAPLETON DEPOT	5381	HUNTINGDON	6	40 24	77 56	580		18				2
MARCUS HOOK	5390	DELAWARE	5	39 48	75 25	12	30	30				1 2 3
†MARIENVILLE 1 SW	5400	FOREST	1	41 27	79 09	1700						C
MARION CENTER 2 SE	5408	INDIANA	1	40 45	79 02	1610		14				2
MARTINSBURG 1 SW	5453	BLAIR	6	40 18	78 20	1360						C
MARTINSBURG CAA AIRPORT	5454	BLAIR	6	40 18	78 19	1463	14	14				1 2 3
MATAMORAS	5470	PIKE	5	41 22	74 42	439		52				2
MAYBURG	5490	FOREST	1	41 36	79 13	1150		11				2
MC CONNELLSBURG	5526	FULTON	12	39 56	78 00	895		24				2
MC KEESPORT	5573	ALLEGHENY	10	40 21	79 52	720		28				2
MEADOW RUN PONDS	5601	LUZERNE	15	41 13	75 40	1995						C
MEADVILLE 1 S	5606	CRAWFORD	1	41 38	80 10	1065	62	63				1 2 3 C
MEDIX RUN	5627	ELK	16	41 17	78 24	1100		15				2 C
MERCER 2 NNE	5651	MERCER	2	41 15	80 13	1160	5	5				1 2 3
MERCER HIGHWAY SHED	5654	MERCER	2	41 14	80 15	1250						C
MERCERSBURG	5662	FRANKLIN	12	39 50	77 54	605		14				2
MERWINSBURG	5676	MONROE	9	40 58	75 28	970						C
MEYERSDALE	5684	SOMERSET	17	39 49	79 02	2080		17			MAR	2
MEYERSDALE 1 ENE	5685	SOMERSET	17	39 49	79 01	2290		1		MAR		2
MIDDLETOWN OLMSTED FIELD	5703	DAUPHIN	15	40 11	76 46	303	26	26				1 2 3
MIDLAND DAM 7	5710	BEAVER	11	40 38	80 28	689	19	20				1 2 3
MILAN 4 WNW	5732	BRADFORD	15	41 56	76 35	1448						C
MILANVILLE	5738	WAYNE	5	41 40	75 04	760		11				2
MILLERSBURG 2 E	5775	DAUPHIN	15	40 32	76 56	560						C
MILLHEIM	5790	CENTRE	15	40 54	77 29	1090		–				2
MILLVILLE 2 SW	5817	COLUMBIA	15	41 06	76 34	860		7				2 C
MILROY	5825	MIFFLIN	6	40 43	77 35	770		14				2
MONTROSE 1 E	5915	SUSQUEHANNA	15	41 50	75 51	1630	51	51				1 2 3 C
MORGANTOWN	5956	BERKS	15	40 09	75 54	595	6	6				1 2 3
MOUNT GRETNA 2 SE	6028	LANCASTER	15	40 14	76 26	670	6	6				1 2 3
MOUNT POCONO 2 N AIRPORT	6055	MONROE	5	41 09	75 22	1915	–	–				1 2 3 C
MOUNT UNION 1 N	6067	MIFFLIN	6	40 24	77 53	820						C
MUHLENBURG 1 SE	6090	LUZERNE	15	41 13	76 08	1110	4	4				1 2 3
MURRYSVILLE	6111	WESTMORELAND	10	40 26	79 42	905						C
MYERSTOWN	6126	LEBANON	14	40 22	76 18	480		16				2
NATRONA LOCK 4	6151	ALLEGHENY	1	40 37	79 43	800		29				2
†NEFFS MILLS 3 NE	6174	HUNTINGDON	6	40 40	77 55	900	15	15	–			C
NESHAMINY FALLS	6194	BUCKS	5	40 09	74 57	60	29	41				2
NEWBURG 3 W	6225	FRANKLIN	15	40 09	77 37	745	15	15				1 2 3
NEW CASTLE 1 N	6233	LAWRENCE	2	41 01	80 22	825	73	70				1 2 3 C
NEWELL	6246	FAYETTE	10	40 05	79 54	805	43	35				1 2 3
NEW PARK	6289	YORK	15	39 44	76 30	780		32				2
NEWPORT	6397	PERRY	6	40 29	77 08	400	9	26				1 2 3
NEW STANTON	6310	WESTMORELAND	10	40 13	79 36	980	5	18				1 2 3
NEW TRIPOLI	6326	LEHIGH	14	40 41	75 45	570		18				2
NORRISTOWN	6370	MONTGOMERY	14	40 07	75 21	75	6	9				1 2 3
NORTH EAST 2 SE	6396	ERIE	8	42 12	79 49	1060		7				2
ORWELL 3 N	6621	BRADFORD	15	41 55	76 16	1620		13				2
PALM	6681	MONTGOMERY	14	40 26	75 32	385		15				2
#PALMERTON	6689	CARBON	9	40 48	75 37	435	39	40				1 2 3 C
PALMYRA	6694	LEBANON	15	40 18	76 35	480		1		JUNE		2
PARKER	6721	ARMSTRONG	1	41 05	79 41	1140		6				2
PARKER 1 E	6724	CLARION	1	41 06	79 40	1100						C
PAUPACK 2 WNW	6762	PIKE	5	41 24	75 14	1360		40				2
PECKS POND	6786	PIKE	5	41 17	75 06	1380		11				2
#PHIL DREXEL INST OF TEC	6879	PHILADELPHIA	14	39 57	75 11	30	–	–				1 2 3
PHILADELPHIA WB AIRPORT	6889	PHILADELPHIA	5	39 53	75 14	13	15	15				1 2 3 C
#PHILADELPHIA POINT BREEZE	6899	PHILADELPHIA	5	39 55	75 12	32	32	32				1 2 3 C
PHILADELPHIA SHAWMONT	6904	PHILADELPHIA	5	40 02	75 15	70	40	61				1 2 3
#PHILADELPHIA CITY	6909	PHILADELPHIA	5	39 57	75 09	26	85	85				1 2 3 C
PHILIPSBURG CAA AIRPORT	6916	CENTRE	6	40 54	78 05	1918	14	14				1 2 3 C
PHOENIXVILLE 1 E	6927	CHESTER	14	40 07	75 30	105	45	47				1 2 3 C
PIKES CREEK	6939	LUZERNE	15	41 18	76 08	1320		19				2 C

STATION INDEX

Station	Index No.	County	Drainage†	Latitude	Longitude	Elevation	Years of record: Temp.	Years of record: Precip.	Years of record: Evap.	Opened or closed during yr.: Month opened	Opened or closed during yr.: Month closed	Refer to tables
.E HILL	6944	MONROE	9	41 02	75 30	2215	-	-	6			1 2 3 4
GROVE 1 NE	6954	SCHUYLKILL	15	40 34	76 22	535		32				2
IBURGH WB AIRPORT 2	6993	ALLEGHENY	11	40 30	80 13	1151	5	5				1 2 3 C
IBURGH WB CITY	6997	ALLEGHENY	11	40 27	80 00	749	86	86				1 2 3 C
ANT MOUNT 1 W	7029	WAYNE	5	41 44	75 27	1800	6	35				1 2 3 C
CLINTON	7116	SCHUYLKILL	14	40 35	76 02	450	18	18				1 2 3 C
.AND	7127	NORTHAMPTON	5	40 55	75 06	297		12			INAC	2
TOWN	7149	MONTGOMERY	14	40 15	75 39	160		65			OCT	2
VILLE	7161	SCHUYLKILL	14	40 42	76 11	690		13				2
UTAWNEY	7217	JEFFERSON	1	40 57	79 00	1298		35				C
YVILLE 2 SE DAM	7229	ARMSTRONG	1	40 55	79 17	1270	13	13				1 2 3 C
RTOWN 1 E	7239	BUCKS	5	40 26	75 20	490	70	72				1 2 3
ND	7310	POTTER	13	41 52	77 52	2220		3				2 C
ING WB CITY	7318	BERKS	14	40 20	75 58	266	59	87				1 2 3 C
O	7409	CLINTON	16	41 20	77 46	660		59				2
O 5 S	7410	CLINTON	16	41 14	77 46	2035						C
	7425	MC KEAN	1	41 54	78 32	2250		9				2
LANDING LOCK 6	7443	GREENE	10	39 57	80 00	775		22				2
AY 3 W	7477	ELK	1	41 25	78 47	1420	41	50				1 2 3
STER 1 N	7540	BEAVER	2	40 43	80 18	900						C
	7694	SUSQUEHANNA	15	41 47	76 03	1000		12				2
VILLE	7727	SUSQUEHANNA	15	41 47	76 07	870		-				2
HARBOR	7732	LANCASTER	15	39 55	76 23	270						C
ORE 1 S	7739	INDIANA	1	40 46	79 14	1320		16				2
A 3 W	7782	WESTMORELAND	7	40 31	79 33	1109	4	4				1 2 3
N	7846	BEDFORD	6	40 12	78 15	780		16				2 C
IA 2 E	7855	WARREN	1	41 55	79 01	2040						C
LEY LOCK 5	7863	ARMSTRONG	1	40 41	79 40	783		78				2
TON	7902	LACKAWANNA	15	41 25	75 40	746	56	56				1 2 3
TON WB AIRPORT	7905	LUZERNE	15	41 20	75 44	956	9	9				1 2 3 C
SGROVE CAA AIRPORT	7931	SNYDER	15	40 49	76 52	437	66	66				1 2 3
RSVILLE 2 NW	7938	BUCKS	5	40 23	75 20	530						C
GAP	7965	HUNTINGDON	6	40 11	77 52	1000						C
KIN	7978	NORTH'LAND	15	40 48	76 33	770		52				2
IELD 6 W	8026	WARREN	1	41 41	79 09	1940						C
ENSBURG	8073	FRANKLIN	15	40 03	77 32	709	24	28				1 2 3
ENPORT WB	8078	BEAVER	11	40 37	80 26	740	2	2				1 2 3 C
MAHONING	8145	CAMERON	16	41 19	78 03	790		6				2
ERY ROCK	8184	BUTLER	2	41 04	80 03	1345	-	-				1 2 3
PORT HIGHWAY SHED	8190	MC KEAN	1	41 48	78 27	1310						C
SET FAIRVIEW STREET	8244	SOMERSET	17	40 01	79 05	2140		-				2
SET MAIN STREET	8249	SOMERSET	17	40 01	79 05	2150	86	73				1 2 3
CANAAN 1 NE	8275	WAYNE	5	41 31	75 24	1400						C
MOUNTAIN	8308	FRANKLIN	12	39 51	77 30	1520		17				2
GBORO	8359	CRAWFORD	8	41 48	80 23	900	2	2				1 2 3 C
G GROVE	8379	YORK	15	39 52	76 52	470		16				2 C
GS 1 SW	8395	SOMERSET	17	39 44	79 10	2500	37	37				1 2 3
E COLLEGE	8449	CENTRE	16	40 48	77 52	1175	69	72	0			1 2 3 4 C
USSTOWN	8570	BERKS	14	40 29	76 11	600		11				2
GSTOWN	8589	INDIANA	4	40 33	78 55	1880						C
OSBURG	8596	MONROE	5	40 59	75 12	480	39	39				1 2 3 C

Station	Index No.	County	Drainage†	Latitude	Longitude	Elevation	Years of record: Temp.	Years of record: Precip.	Years of record: Evap.	Opened or closed during yr.: Month opened	Opened or closed during yr.: Month closed	Refer to tables
STUMP CREEK	8610	JEFFERSON	1	41 01	78 50	1320		16				2
SUNBURY	8668	NORTH'LAND	15	40 51	76 48	440		34				2 C
SUSQUEHANNA	8692	SUSQUEHANNA	15	41 57	75 36	1020		22				2
SUTERSVILLE	8699	ALLEGHENY	17	40 14	79 48	765		16				2
TAMAQUA	8758	SCHUYLKILL	14	40 48	75 58	830		15				2
TAMAQUA 4 N DAM	8763	SCHUYLKILL	14	40 51	75 59	1120		24				2 C
TAMARACK 2 S FIRE TOWER	8770	CLINTON	16	41 24	77 51	2270	14	15				1 2 3
TIONESTA 2 SE DAM	8873	FOREST	1	41 29	79 26	1200	13	20				1 2 3 C
TITUSVILLE	8885	CRAWFORD	1	41 38	79 40	1550						C
TITUSVILLE WATER WORKS	8888	CRAWFORD	1	41 38	79 42	1220	3	3				1 2 3
TORPEDO 4 W	8901	WARREN	1	41 47	79 32	1735		6				2
TOWANDA	8905	BRADFORD	15	41 46	76 26	760	62	62				1 2 3 C
TOWER CITY 5 SW	8910	DAUPHIN	15	40 31	76 37	745		11				2
TROY	8959	BRADFORD	15	41 47	76 47	1100		6				2
TUNNELTON	8989	INDIANA	4	40 27	79 23	890						C
TURTLEPOINT 4 NE	9002	MC KEAN	1	41 54	78 16	1640		6				2
TYRONE 4 NE BALD EAGLE	9024	BLAIR	6	40 43	78 12	1020		19				2 C
UNION CITY	9042	ERIE	1	41 54	79 50	1325		7				2 C
UNIONTOWN	9050	FAYETTE	10	39 54	79 44	1040	67	68				1 2 3
UPPER DARBY	9074	DELAWARE	5	39 58	75 18	222	7	7				1 2 3
UTICA	9099	VENANGO	1	41 26	79 57	1030		1				2
VANDERGRIFT	9128	WESTMORELAND	7	40 36	79 33	800		17				2
VANDERGRIFT 2 W	9133	WESTMORELAND	7	40 36	79 36	995						C
VIRGINVILLE	9196	BERKS	14	40 31	75 52	350		11				2
VOWINCKEL	9206	CLARION	1	41 25	79 14	1620		2				2
VOWINCKEL 1 WSW	9209	CLARION	1	41 24	79 15	1610		2				2
WARREN	9298	WARREN	1	41 51	79 08	1280	60	68				1 2 3
WASHINGTON	9312	WASHINGTON	11	40 11	80 14	1200		·				C
WATSONTOWN	9345	NORTH'LAND	16	41 05	76 52	490		9				2
WAYNESBURG 2 W	9362	GREENE	10	39 54	80 13	980	27	29				1 2 3
WAYNESBURG 1 E	9367	GREENE	10	39 54	80 10	940	·					C
WEBSTER MILLS 3 SW	9380	FULTON	12	39 49	78 05	920						C
WELLSBORO 3 S	9408	TIOGA	16	41 43	77 16	1920	7	7				1 2 3
WELLSBORO 2 E	9412	TIOGA	16	41 45	77 16	1550						C
WELLSVILLE	9420	YORK	15	40 03	76 57	500	10	10				1 2 3
WERNERSVILLE 1 W	9430	BERKS	14	40 20	76 06	405		19				2
WEST CHESTER	9464	CHESTER	5	39 58	75 36	440	101	106				1 2 3
WEST GROVE 1 E	9503	CHESTER	5	39 49	75 49	440		27				2
WEST HICKORY	9507	FOREST	1	41 34	79 25	1090		5				2
WHITESBURG	9655	ARMSTRONG	1	40 45	79 24	1530		16				2
WILKES-BARRE	9702	LUZERNE	15	41 15	75 52	610		71				2
WILLIAMSBURG	9714	BLAIR	6	40 28	78 12	860		-				2
WILLIAMSPORT WB AIRPORT	9728	LYCOMING	16	41 15	76 55	527	16	16				1 2 3 C
WIND GAP	9781	NORTHAMPTON	5	40 51	75 18	720						C
WOLFSBURG	9823	BEDFORD	6	40 03	78 32	1190		7				2
YORK 3 SSW PUMP STATION	9933	YORK	15	39 55	76 45	390	58	69				1 2 3
†YORK 2 S FILTER PLANT	9938	YORK	15	39 56	76 44	640						C
YORK HAVEN	9950	YORK	15	40 07	76 43	310		36				2
YOUNGSVILLE	9966	WARREN	1	41 51	79 20	1225						C
ZION GROVE	9990	SCHUYLKILL	15	40 54	76 13	940		6				2
ZIONSVILLE 3 SE	9995	LEHIGH	14	40 27	75 27	660		7				2

† 1-ALLEGHENY; 2-BEAVER; 3- 4-CONEMAUGH; 5-DELAWARE; 6-JUNIATA; 7-KISKIMINETAS; 8-LAKE ERIE; 9-LEIGH; 10-MONONGAHELA; 11-OHIO; 12-POTOMAC; 13-ST. LAWRENCE; 14-SCHUYLKILL; 15-SUSQUEHANNA; 16-WEST BRANCH; 17-YOUGHIOGHENY

REFERENCE NOTES

Additional information regarding the climate of Pennsylvania may be obtained by writing to the State Climatologist at Weather Bureau Airport Station, Harrisburg State Airport, New Cumberland, Pennsylvania or to any Weather Bureau Office near you.

Unless otherwise indicated, dimensional units used in this bulletin are: Temperature in °F; precipitation and evaporation in inches, and wind movement in miles.

Evaporation is measured in the standard Weather Bureau type pan of 4 foot diameter unless otherwise shown by footnote following Table 4.

Figures and letters following the station name, such as 12 SSW, indicate distance in miles and direction from the post office.

Delayed data and corrections will be carried in the June and December issues of Climatological Data.

- \- No record.
- \+ Also later date (dates) or months.
- * Amount included in following measurement.
- \# Thermometers are generally exposed in a shelter located a few feet above sod covered ground; however the reference indicates that the thermometers are exposed in a shelter located on the roof of a building.
- B Adjusted to full month.
- C Data for recorder stations denoted by 'C' in the Refer to Tables column of the Station Index are processed for special purposes and published in "Hourly Precipitation Data". Length of record for recorder - only stations may be found in the annual issue of "Hourly Precipitation Data".
- E Amount is wholly or partially estimated.
- M One or more days' record missing; if average value is entered, less than 10 days record is missing. See monthly Climatological Data for detailed daily record.
- T Trace, an amount too small to measure.
- V Includes total for previous month. V in annual column means total is for a two-year period.

Information concerning the history of changes in locations, elevations, exposures, etc., of substations through 1955 may be found in the publication 'Substation History' for this state, soon to be issued. That publication, when available, may be obtained from the Superintendent of Documents, Government Printing Office, Washington, D. C. at a price to be announced. Similar information for regular Weather Bureau stations may be found in the latest issue of Local Climatological Data annuals, obtained as indicated above, price 15 cents.

Subscription Price: 20 cents per copy, monthly and annual; $2.50 per year. (Yearly subscription includes the Annual Summary.) Checks, and money orders should be made payable to the Superintendent of Documents. Remittances and correspondence regarding subscriptions should be sent to the Superintendent of Documents, Government Printing Office, Washington 25, D. C.

WRC., Asheville, N. C. --- 3/5/57 --- 1250

U. S. DEPARTMENT OF COMMERCE
SINCLAIR WEEKS, Secretary
WEATHER BUREAU
F. W. REICHELDERFER, Chief

CLIMATOLOGICAL DATA

PENNSYLVANIA

JANUARY 1957
Volume LXII No. 1

ASHEVILLE: 1957

GENERAL

The number one weather story for January was the bitter cold of the 14th-20th, which brought sub-zero temperatures to all but the southeastern portion of the State. Precipitation was deficient over most areas, but the frequent occurrence of small amounts gave the impression that it was a wet month.

Average monthly temperatures were below the long-term means for all stations for which departures are shown, ranging from -0.3° at Carlisle to -6.9° at Waynesburg 2 W. Individual monthly station averages were topped by 31.6° at Philadelphia City, while Pleasant Mount 1 W trailed the pack with a goose-pimply 15.4°. The highest temperature for the month, a balmy 63°, was reported by Uniontown on the 22nd. The lowest for the month, -25°, was the lowest January reading since 1948, and was recorded at both Bradford 4 W Res. and Coudersport 3 NW on the 15th. Kane 1 NNE and Coudersport 3 NW had the somewhat dubious distinction of having 11 days with the temperature 0° or below, to lead the field in that category. Tamarack 2 S Fire Twr took honors for the most days when the temperature failed to crawl up to the freezing mark, with 27.

Precipitation occurred somewhere in the State every day in the month and, outside of the rains which accompanied the warm wave of the 22nd-23rd, was mostly in the form of snow. Only seven stations, all in the western third of the State, reported positive departures from long-term means, with the greatest being +0.74 inch at Blairsville 6 ENE. The greatest negative departure was -2.56 inches at Coatesville 1 SW. Monthly totals ranged between 5.25 inches at Kregar 4 SE and 0.67 inch at Le Roy. The most days with 0.10 inch or more, 15, occurred at Kregar 4 SE. Only about 15% of the stations reported as much as 1.00 inch in any 24-hour period, and there were none with more than one such day. Further, 30% of the stations failed to record a single day with as much as 0.50 inch in any one day. The greatest reported snowfall total was 33.1 inches at Hooversville, while the least was 0.5 inch at Chadds Ford. The greatest accumulation on the ground was 22 inches at Bradford 4 W Res on the 18th, but by the 24th the snow cover at this station had dwindled to a mere 4 inches.

In sharp contrast with December, most sections reported more sunshine in January than is usual for the time of year, with the percentage of possible sunshine ranging from 46 to near 60 at stations equipped with recording devices.

WEATHER DETAILS

The year bowed in on a cold and windy note as a High moved in from the west. Temperatures were 8° to 15° below seasonal values, and light snow was noted over most of the State until the 3rd when temperatures returned to near normal

CLIMATOLOGICAL DATA

Station		Temperature: Average Maximum	Average Minimum	Average	Departure From Long Term Means	Highest	Date	Lowest	Date	Degree Days	No. of Days Max. 90° or Above	Max. 32° or Below	Min. 32° or Below	Min. 0° or Below	Precipitation: Total	Departure From Long Term Means	Greatest Day	Date	Snow, Sleet Total	Max. Depth on Ground	Date	No. of Days .10 or More	.50 or More	1.00 or More
POCONO MOUNTAINS																								
ELAND		29.0	13.5	21.3	- 3.3	56	23	-10	15	1349	0	22	30	4	1.98	- 1.31	.70	23	16.0	6	9+	7	1	0
LEY 1 S DAM	AM	29.0	6.5	17.8		56	23	-20	19	1461	0	20	30	7	1.44		.30	10				5	0	0
POCONO 2 N AP		28.0M	10.2M	19.1M	- 4.2	55	23	-14	15	1415	0	22	30	5	2.36									
LENBURG 1 SE		30.7	11.5	21.1		51	22+	-14	15	1353	0	19	30	5	2.11		.83	23	13.5	8	18	6	1	0
PLE HILL	AM	26.6	10.8	18.7		53	23	-12	15	1428	0	25	30	6	3.13		1.71	23	15.5	9	16+	7	1	1
ASANT MOUNT 1 W	AM	25.8	4.9	15.4		54	23	-21	15	1534	0	26	30	10	1.84	- 1.78	.37	29	19.5	10	13+	5	0	0
ANTON	AM	31.5	14.1	22.8	- 5.4	59	23	- 6	15	1300	0	17	29	6	1.26	- 1.00	.65	23	8.5			2	1	0
ANTON WB AIRPORT		30.3	12.9	21.6	- 5.3	58	23	-10	15	1337	0	19	30	4	1.49	- .77	.25	22	11.1	4	11+	7	0	0
DUDSBURG		31.0	10.2	20.6	- 6.8	57	23	-22	18	1369	0	16	30	8	1.98	- 1.31	.77	23	12.4	5	16+	8	1	0
DIVISION				19.8											1.95				13.8					
EAST CENTRAL MOUNTAINS																								
ENTOWN WB AP	R	33.4	16.7	25.1	- 3.4	59	23	- 6	18	1230	0	11	30	3	1.87	- 1.34	.49	23	7.3	1	6+	7	0	0
ENTOWN GAS CO	AM	34.7	17.1	25.9	- 3.6	60	23	- 1	15+	1203	0	12	30	4	1.54	- 1.85	.52	23	6.3	2	16+	5	1	0
HLEHEM LEHIGH UNIV				M											1.70	- 1.71	.46	23				8	0	0
THORPE		36.3	16.3	26.3	- 1.5	59	22	-10	18	1192	0	10	30	3	2.25	- 1.36	1.25	23	10.9	3	16+	6	1	1
MERTON		32.8	16.0	24.4	- 4.2	59	22	-10	18	1251	0	13	30	3	2.18	- .66	.71	23	7.0	2	16+	5	1	0
T CLINTON	AM	36.7	15.6	26.2	- 2.6	60	23	- 6	19	1195	0	11	30	3					7.5	2	9+			
DIVISION				25.6											1.91				7.8					
SOUTHEASTERN PIEDMONT																								
STER	AM	38.7	22.8	30.8		61	23+	5	14+	1055	0	8	25	0	1.80		.83	23				7	1	0
TESVILLE 1 SW	AM	36.0	18.5	27.3	- 3.2	59	23+	- 4	18	1162	0	9	29	2	1.31	- 2.56	.46	23	3.5	2	16	4	0	0
UMBIA		37.0	21.1	29.1		61	23	- 4	18	1106	0	11	29	2	2.09		.80	23	2.0	1	14+	6	1	0
AULT 1 W		36.8	14.9	25.9		60	23	- 5	15	1205	0	8	30	2	2.02		.43	29		3	7+	7	0	0
RATA		35.3	19.8	27.6	- 3.2	57	23	- 1	15+	1152	0	11	30	2	2.33	- .71	.96	23				6	2	0
RGE SCHOOL		35.7	18.7	27.2	- 4.2	60	23	- 8	18	1161	0	10	29	3	1.67	- 1.70	.76	23	6.7	1	9+	3	1	0
TWOOD		35.1	22.2	28.7	- 3.3	57	23	3	17+	1118	0	11	30	0	1.48	- 1.52	.43	10	5.5	3	16+	4	0	0
CASTER 2 NE PUMP STA		36.8	20.8	28.8	- 1.6	59	23	- 6	18	1114	0	7	29	2	D 1.71	- 1.45	.58	23	4.3	1	7+	5	1	0
DISVILLE 2 NW	AM	33.3	15.9	24.6		58	23	- 9	18	1244	0	13	30	4	1.73		.73	23	5.9	2	16	3	1	0
ANON 3 W	AM	35.0	18.3	26.7	- 2.6	57	23	- 3	18	1180	0	11	29	2	1.83	- 1.52	.63	23	5.9	2	7+	5	1	0
CUS HOOK		36.3	22.7	29.5	- 6.2	59	23	4	15	1093	0	10	28	0	1.82	- 1.63	.48	23	4.6	2	14+	6	0	0
DLETOWN OLMSTED FLD		35.0	21.5	28.3	- 2.8	61	23	1	18	1130	0	11	28	0	1.99	- 1.06	.30	9	7.2	2	15+	8	0	0
GANTOWN		34.1	17.7	25.9		58	22+	- 4	17+	1205	0	12	29	3	1.42		.46	23	2.8	1	6+	5	0	0
GRETNA 2 SE		36.0	18.0	27.0		58	23	0	16+	1170	0	9	30	2	1.32		.39	23				6	0	0
RISTOWN		36.8	21.6	29.2		61	23	2	15	1104	0	9	28	0	1.19		.45	23	2.8	1	7+	3	0	0
L DREXEL INST OF TEC		38.5	23.4	31.0		61	23	4	15	1046	0	7	26	0	1.63		.41	23	4.2	1	7+	8	0	0
LADELPHIA WB AP	R	36.4	21.9	29.2	- 4.0	61	23	5	15+	1103	0	9	29	0	1.67	- 1.70	.46	23	4.7	2	9+	6	0	0
LADELPHIA PT BREEZE		37.0	25.0	31.0	- 3.2	62	23	5	15	1047	0	7	26	0	1.62		.47	23	3.3	1	14	6	0	0
LADELPHIA SHAWMONT		37.6	21.6	29.6	- 2.9	60	23	2	18	1088	0	6	28	0	2.09	- 1.24	.55	23				12	1	0
LADELPHIA CITY	RAM	37.6	25.6	31.6	- 3.3	60	23	8	15	1025	0	8	24	0	1.31	- 2.08	.27	23				5	0	0
ENIXVILLE 1 E		39.1	18.9	29.0	- 2.4	62	23	- 6	18	1108	0	7	29	2	1.45	- 2.14	.44	23	1.2			6	0	0
KERTOWN 1 E		34.1	18.0	26.1	- 1.9	59	23	- 3	15	1200	0	11	30	1	1.92	- 1.54	.73	23	6.7			6	1	0
DING WB CITY	R	35.7	22.0	28.9	- 3.3	60	22+	2	15	1113	0	10	28	0	1.49	- 1.66	.40	23	6.4	2	7	7	0	0
ER DARBY		36.4	21.5	29.0		60	23	- 2	15	1110	0	10	29	1	1.61		.54	23	5.5			5	1	0
T CHESTER	AM	36.1	20.2	28.2	- 2.6	59	22	1	14	1135	0	7	29	0	1.59	- 2.17	.45	23	4.0	2	16+		0	0
DIVISION				28.4											1.68				4.6					
LOWER SUSQUEHANNA																								
NDTSVILLE	AM	35.6	17.0	26.3	- 4.2	59	23	-10	18	1192	0	10	30	4	2.56	- .31	.84	23	7.6	4	16+	7	2	0
LISLE		36.5	20.5	28.5	- .4	58	23	- 7	18	1123	0	7	30	2	2.01	- 1.14	.70	10	7.5	2	7+	7	1	0
MBERSBURG 1 ESE		35.6	19.5	27.6	- 2.5	58	23	- 6	17	1153	0	8	31	3	2.64	- .21	.56	10	8.0	3	15+	8	2	0
TYSBURG	AM	36.3	19.7	28.0	- 2.4	59	23	- 7	18	1139	0	10	29	3	2.42	- .67	.93	10	6.6	4	16+	7	2	0
OVER	AM	36.8	18.7	27.8	- 4.9	60	23	- 1	17+	1146	0	11	29	2	2.52	- .64	.71	23	9.0	4	14+	7	2	0
RISBURG WB AP	R	34.9	21.0	28.0	- 3.1	62	23	- 2	18	1139	0	11	29	2	1.64	- .98	.30	10	10.8	3	7+	7	0	0
BURG 3 W																								
PENSBURG		37.6	20.0	28.8	- 1.9	57	23	- 2	17	1114	0	7	30	3	2.12	- .97	.82	10	9.0	3	16+	7	2	0
.SVILLE		37.4	16.9	27.2		62	22	-14	18	1163	0	10	30	6	1.46		.48	23	7.5	3	14+	5	0	0
K 3 SSW PUMP STA		38.2	20.1	29.2	- 1.6	60	23	-10	18	1103	0	7	28	4	2.16	- .92	.75	23	7.7	5	16	9	1	0
DIVISION				27.9											2.17				8.2					
MIDDLE SUSQUEHANNA																								
VERTOWN		34.2	17.8	26.0		56	23	- 9	18	1201	0	12	30	3	D 1.91		.86	23	4.5	4	16	6	1	0
VICK		34.0	17.0	25.5		60	23	- 7	18	1217	0	12	30	4	1.35		.33	10	5.9	2	13+	5	0	0
TZ 1 N	AM	32.6M	15.2M	23.9M		58	23	- 7	18	1267	0	16	29	5	1.43		.84	23		2	7+	2	1	0
ISTOWN	AM	35.2	17.6	26.4		60	23	- 2	18+	1192	0	11	31	2	D 1.40		.41	10	3.7	3	16+	3	0	0
PORT	AM	35.7	17.5	26.6		58	23	- 7	18	1183	0	10	29	3	1.63	- 1.34	.61	23	5.3	2	9+	4	1	0
INSGROVE CAA AP		33.3	16.7	25.0	- 3.7	55	22+	- 7	18	1233	0	12	30	3	1.59	- 1.42	.63	22	9.7	4	16+	4	1	0
.IAMSPORT WB AP		32.4	15.7	24.1	- 4.4	57	23	-10	18	1263	0	14	29	4	1.59	- 1.00	.37	10	9.3	5	16+	6	0	0
DIVISION				25.4											1.56				6.4					
UPPER SUSQUEHANNA																								
TON 1 NW	AM	26.9	10.5	18.7		52	23	-14	15	1429	0	22	30	7	1.98		1.05	23	9.1	9	11+	4	1	1
ON	AM	31.9	7.4	19.7		58	23	-19	18	1399	0	15	30	9	1.79		.58	23	12.0	7	16	6	1	0
.ES MERE	AM	25.7	9.5	17.6		50	23	-12	15	1464	0	26	30	8	D 3.38	- .39	2.03	23	12.0	12	11+	6	1	1
RENCEVILLE 2 S	AM	30.0	8.4	19.2	- 6.3	55	23	-23	15	1414	0	17	30	8	1.03	- .84	.36	10	9.2	7	11+	3	0	0
ROSE 1 E	AM	25.4	8.3	16.9	- 6.2	54	23	-18	15	1485	0	24	30	9	1.42	- 1.21	.39	23	18.7	12	13+	4	0	0

See Reference Notes Following Station Index

TABLE 2 - CONTINUED

Station	Temperature: Average Maximum	Average Minimum	Average	Departure From Long Term Means	Highest	Date	Lowest	Date	Degree Days	No. of Days Max 90° or Above	Max 32° or Below	Min 32° or Below	Min 0° or Below	Precipitation: Total	Departure From Long Term Means	Greatest Day	Date	Snow, Sleet: Total	Max Depth on Ground	Date	No. of Days: 10 or More	50 or More	1.00
TOWANDA	32.8	10.8	21.8	- 4.2	57	23	-19	14	1332	0	13	30	7	1.22	- .76	.37	29	11.4	6	11+	4	0	0
WELLSBORO 3 S AM	27.2	10.1	18.7	- 5.6	55	23	-16	15	1430	0	25	30	7	1.59	- .76	.46	23+	15.5	15	11+	4	0	0
DIVISION			18.9											1.77				12.6					
CENTRAL MOUNTAINS																							
BELLEFONTE 4 S AM	31.7	15.1	23.4	- 5.6	59	23	-13	15	1281	0	14	31	4	D 1.56	- 1.05	.55	23	5.4	2	14+	4	1	0
DU BOIS 7 E	29.5	11.8	20.7		55	23	-17	17+	1369	0	23	29	6	1.96	- .96	.72	29	13.5	11	16+	6	1	0
EMPORIUM 2 SSW AM	26.9	8.3	17.6		53	23	-16	17	1463	0	24	31	7	2.76		.94	23	13.2	10	10	6	3	0
LOCK HAVEN	33.2	16.6	24.9	- 3.5	53	22+	- 9	17+	1233	0	11	31	3	1.52	- 1.41	.39	23	7.0	5	16+		0	0
MADERA AM	29.7	8.5	19.1		52	23	-16	18	1415	0	19	30	9	2.31		.47	23	9.9	6	14+	8	0	0
PHILIPSBURG CAA AP	27.4	11.3	19.4		53	23	-16	15+	1408	0	25	30	7	1.95		.48	22	11.0	10	11+	5	0	0
RIDGWAY 3 W AM	28.5	10.3	19.4	- 6.1	54	23	-18	17	1406	0	21	30	8	2.61	- .33	.81	23	17.6	12	19	6	1	0
STATE COLLEGE	31.7	18.0	24.9	- 2.2	57	23	- 4	15+	1236	0	18	29	2	D 1.53	- 1.38	.47	22	8.8	2	9+	4	0	0
TAMARACK 2 S FIRE TWR AM	25.5	9.5	17.5		50	23	-12	15	1467	0	27	30	8	2.02		.54	10	13.3	12	11+	4	2	0
DIVISION			20.8											2.02				11.1					
SOUTH CENTRAL MOUNTAINS																							
ALTOONA HORSESHOE CURVE	31.6	15.0	23.3	- 4.6	56	23	- 7	17	1287	0	16	31	5	2.24	- .73	.61	10	20.7	5	16+	7	1	0
ARTEMAS 1 WNW	41.1M	18.5M	29.8M		60	22	1	17	1084	0	5	31	0	1.71		1.20	10	2.8	2	14	4	1	1
BURNT CABINS 2 NE	35.7M	16.3M	26.0M		60	22	- 7	17	1200	0	8	31	2										
EBENSBURG	29.4	13.1	21.3	- 4.9	53	23	- 9	15+	1348	0	18	30	3	2.96	- .29	.66	23	13.3	9	9+	10	2	0
EVERETT 1 SW	35.4	17.5	26.5	- 2.3	59	22	- 4	17	1191	0	12	31	2	2.70	- .14	1.15	9		2	7+		2	1
HUNTINGDON AM																							
JOHNSTOWN AM	33.4	14.4	23.9	- 6.6	56	22	- 7	17	1270	0	13	31	3	3.28	- .80	.70	10	13.2	3	9+	9	2	0
KEGG	34.4	16.9	25.7		59	23	- 1	15	1213	0	11	31	1	1.79		.54	9	5.0	1	1+	5	2	0
MARTINSBURG CAA AP	32.3	17.0	24.7		56	23	- 5	17	1242	0	18	29	1	1.49		.44	22	4.3	2	9	4	0	0
DIVISION			25.2											2.31				9.9					
SOUTHWEST PLATEAU																							
BAKERSTOWN 3 WNW	32.1	18.9	25.5		54	22	- 6	17	1219	0	16	29	1	1.46		.52	22	5.0	2	1+		1	0
BLAIRSVILLE 6 ENE	28.5	14.1	21.3		52	21+	-12	17	1349	0	22	29	2	3.68	.74	.99	29	21.3	7	14+	11	1	0
BURGETTSTOWN 2 W AM	31.8	13.6	22.7		56	23	-19	17	1304	0	16	30	4	1.99		.64	23	5.0	3	7+	7	1	0
BUTLER	31.9	17.6	24.8	- 5.1	54	23	-10	15	1239	0	16	29	2	2.04	- .83	.65	23	17.0	12	9	6	1	0
CLAYSVILLE 3 W	34.6	15.6	25.1	- 5.9	59	22	-20	17	1229	0	10	29	5	2.03	- 1.14	.57	23		4	7	7	1	0
CONFLUENCE 1 SW DAM AM	33.4	17.2	25.3		58	23	- 8	18	1222	0	15	31	3	3.79		1.63	10	13.0	5	9	6	2	1
DERRY	34.2	18.8	26.5	- 4.5	60	23	- 6	17	1187	0	14	29	2	2.31	- 1.36	.60	29	9.4	6	8		1	0
DONEGAL	29.4	10.4	19.9		52	22	-16	17	1390	0	20	31	7	4.17		.57	29	29.2	10	16	13	1	0
DONORA AM	36.4	22.6	29.5	- 4.8	60	23	- 3	17	1092	0	10	28	1	1.75	- .85	.30	29	3.7	2	7	6	0	0
FORD CITY 4 S DAM AM	31.5	14.8	23.2		58	23	-15	17	1293	0	18	30	2	1.88		.48	23	15.6	5	9	7	0	0
INDIANA 3 SE	32.9	15.0	24.0	- 5.5	58	22	-15	17	1263	0	16	30	5	2.69	- .96	.57	29	12.0	4	9	9	2	0
IRWIN			M		59	22	- 7	17		0	15	31	2	2.10	- .86	.47	29	16.1	5	7	7	0	0
MIDLAND DAM 7	32.4	20.8	26.6	- 4.0	54	22+	- 2	17	1181	0	16	29	1	1.84	- .83	.79	23	4.5	3	9	5	1	0
NEW CASTLE 1 N	32.1	16.4	24.3	- 4.1	56	23	-10	17	1254	0	17	29	4	2.47	- .47	.45	23	15.3			9	0	0
NEWELL AM	36.9	21.8	29.4	- 3.4	60	22+	- 5	17	1097	0	10	29	1					10.0	4	7		0	0
NEW STANTON	35.7	15.8	25.8	- 5.5	60	22	- 7	15+	1209	0	9	30	4	2.10	- 1.31	.50	29		3	7+	7	1	0
PITTSBURGH WB AP 2 //R	31.8	18.2	25.0	- 4.0	57	22+	- 6	17	1234	0	17	29	2	1.65	- 1.12	.48	22	9.3	3	8+	5	0	0
PITTSBURGH WB CITY R	35.0	21.9	28.5	- 4.5	59	22+	- 1	17	1124	0	12	29	1	1.50	- 1.33	.33	22	5.5			5	0	0
PUTNEYVILLE 2 SE DAM AM	30.6	12.0	21.3		50	22+	-15	17	1346	0	19	30	5	2.31		.65	23	20.5	6	9+	8	2	0
SALINA 3 W	32.5	17.7	25.1		56	22	- 9	17	1228	0	16	29	2	2.10		.55	29	9.2	3	7	9	1	0
SHIPPINGPORT WB	32.9	19.0	26.0		57	22+	- 3	17	1202	0	15	29	1	1.52		.52	22	3.1	2	7	5	1	0
SLIPPERY ROCK	30.3	14.8	22.6		55	22	- 9	17	1309	0	21	29	3	2.07		.64	23	16.1	6	13+	5	2	0
SOMERSET MAIN ST	32.5	14.9	23.7	- 3.2	54	22	-10	17+	1272	0	16	30	3	3.09	- 1.13	1.15	10	13.7	4	15+	9	1	1
SPRINGS 1 SW	31.8	14.1	23.0	- 4.1	54	23	-12	17	1297	0	18	30	1	3.74	.01	1.86	10	9.4	8	9+	7	1	1
UNIONTOWN	36.7	20.4	28.6	- 4.5	63	22	- 6	17	1126	0	9	29	2	2.61	- .97	.39	31	10.3	5	15+	10	0	0
WAYNESBURG 2 W	35.5	16.8	26.2	- 6.9	60	22+	-17	17	1197	0	10	29	5	1.97	- 1.35	.60	10	10.7	3	7+	6	1	0
DIVISION			25.0											2.35				11.9					
NORTHWEST PLATEAU																							
BRADFORD 4 W RES	28.1	7.2	17.7	- 6.8	54	22	-25	15	1462	0	25	31	7	3.40	.21	.72	23	29.6	22	18	6	2	0
BROOKVILLE CAA AIRPORT	29.3	12.9	21.1	- 3.9	55	23	-12	17	1351	0	20	29	5	2.73	- .47	.77	22	14.4	9	10+	8	1	0
CLARION 3 SW	32.0	12.8	22.4		53	23	-14	17	1313	0	14	29	4	2.31	- 1.19	.60	23	13.0	8	13+	8	1	0
CORRY	27.7	11.7	19.7	- 5.4	51	22	-17	15	1400	0	24	29	5	2.65	- .73	.75	22	16.0	11	11+	7	1	0
COUDERSPORT 3 NW	26.2	5.9	16.1		50	22	-25	15	1512	0	24	30	11	1.97		.68	23	15.4	11	11+	4	1	0
EAST BRADY	33.7	16.2	25.0		55	23	-17	17	1235	0	12	29	4	1.58		.78	29	10.3	4	13+		1	0
ERIE CAA AIRPORT	28.6	17.2	22.9	- 4.3	56	22	- 5	17	1298	0	22	29	2	2.93	.59	.83	22	25.6	15	20	10	1	0
FARRELL SHARON	32.6	15.0	23.8	- 5.0	56	22	- 9	15	1269	0	15	30	4	2.62	.04	.48	13				8	0	0
FRANKLIN	30.9	14.5	22.7	- 4.0	53	23	-11	14	1306	0	18	30	5	2.26	- 1.15	.81	23		8	13+	5	1	0
GREENVILLE	30.9	14.8	22.9	- 4.7	53	22+	-12	15	1298	0	18	29	4	2.22	- 1.11	.51	22	19.5	8	13+	7	1	0
JAMESTOWN 2 NW AM	28.1	12.7	20.4		54	23	-14	15	1374	0	23	30	5	D 1.81	- .74	.80	23	16.1	7	13+	4	1	0
KANE 1 NNE AM	27.6	6.7	17.2		52	23	-22	17	1477	0	21	30	11	2.64	- 1.01			20.9	9	10+			
LINESVILLE 5 WNW	29.3	13.7	21.5		53	22+	-14	15	1339	0	22	29	6	2.43	- .22	1.04	23	20.9	8	13+	4	1	1
MEADVILLE 1 S AM	28.3	13.3	20.8	- 4.8	53	23	-10	15	1364	0	21	30	5	2.25	- .90	.97	23	26.9	7	10+	6	1	0
MERCER 2 NNE	32.4	13.8	23.1		62	22	-19	15	1291	0	14	29	7	2.47		.70	23	7.0	6	9		2	0
SPRINGBORO AM	31.7M	14.4M	23.1M		53	22	-13	17	1278	0	18	30	3	D 2.00		.30	13	20.0	11	14+	10	0	0
TIONESTA 2 SE DAM AM	29.1	11.0	20.1		50	22	-17	17	1388	0	19	30	6	2.57	.10	.93	23	15.0	10	19+	5	2	0
TITUSVILLE WATER WORKS	29.3	10.0	19.7		53	23	-17	17	1400	0	23	29	7	2.87		.98	22	17.8	12	18	7	1	0
WARREN	30.6	13.9	22.3	- 3.7	55	22	-11	14+	1315	0	20	29	4	2.66	- .22	1.25	23	24.4	8	13	6	1	1
DIVISION			21.2											2.44				18.4					

See Reference Notes Following Station Index

DAILY PRECIPITATION

Day of month

	Total	1	2	3	4	5	6	7	8	9	10	11	12	13	14	15	16	17	18	19	20	21	22	23	24	25	26	27	28	29	30	31
R	1.81	.05	.03	T			T	.17	.13	.06	.19	T	T	.02	.02	T	.06	T	.03	.04		.04		.30	T		.12	T		.31	.15	T
	1.87	T					.07	T	T	.10	.29			T	.01	.08	.03		T			T	.15	.49		.06		.15	.03	.15		.17
	1.94		T					.08	T	.09	.31	T	.03	T	.01		.10	T		T		T		.52			.08	.19		.14	.05	T
VE	2.24	.12	.02				T	.13	.03	.16	.81			.02	.09	.03	.02		.06				.17	.29		.08	T	.01	.07	.34		.02
	2.98							.11		.11	.78				.22		.12						.01	.84						.37	T	T
	1.71						T	.04		.15	1.20				.10													.22		T		
	1.46	.08	T						.05	T	.55	.06		T			T	T						.45			T	T		.27	T	
	1.40	T		T	.01			T		*	.10	T								T		.11	.92	.12	T	.28	T	T		*	*	.32
	2.70	.15	.06	.07		T	T	.06	.06	.10	.40	T		.04	T		.02	.03		T		T	T	1.15	T					.43	.04	
	1.06						.10			.06	*	.28											*	.42				*		.20		
	1.89							.14		.06	.38						.06							.94		.04		.06		.10		.11
	1.83	.07	.02	T	T		T	.20	.13	.09	.17	T	.01	.08	.02	T	.03	T	.02	.01		.03	T	.48	.06		.04	T	T	.28	.09	T
D	1.91	.05						D.10	.08		.42	D.10			.13		.03							.86		T		.06	T	.10		T
	1.22	T						.03	.02	.14	.39	.12		T	T		.02							.47			T	T		.02	.01	
D	1.56		T					.03		.10	.40	.02		D.03	D.07		.03		D.01	D.02				.55			T			.30	T	T
	2.03							.11	T	.09	.37	T			.04		.08			T		T	T	1.02			T	.10		.08	.14	T
	1.35	T						.10		.06	.33			.05			.04		T				T	.30		.06	T	.09		.21		.11
	1.25	T						.05	T	.05	.28	T		T	.03		.11	T		T		T	T	.39			.03	.17		.11	.01	T
	1.70	T					.06			.13	.30				.01	.11	.02		T				.13	.46		.04		.17	.03	.14		.10
	3.88	.07	.07	.01		T	.12	.22		.17	.34	.02		.22	.08	.05	.25		.15	.01			.22	.31		.18	.08	.04	.03	.09	.01	.04
	-	T RECORD MISSING						.10	T	.11	.71				.03	T	.06					T		-	.10			.02	.05	-		.25
	1.05		T	T				.09	.07	.09	.25	T			.08		.06	.01	T	.01		.05		.62	.02		.12	.04	T	.27	.16	.01
TA	2.81	.27	.04	.03		.04		.04	.08	.05	.40	.04	T	.14	.04	.04	.02	.02		.01		T	.05	1.00	T		.04	.06		.31	.03	
	3.40	.23	.08	.05	.08		T	.08	.05	.05	.58		T	.24	.05		.08	T	.08	T		.03	.48	.72		T	.08	.03		.38		.03
	1.90	T				T		.05		.76	.17			.04	.02								.37	.04		.02			.27		.01	.24
T	2.73	.15	.03	.01	T	.01	.07	.17	.07	.26	.16	.02	.02	.15	T	.01	.01		.03	T	T	.01	.77	.06		.04	.01	.02	.33	.23	.04	.05
	1.47		.01					.16	.02	.08	.25	T			.04	T	.04	T	T			.02		.38					T	.35	T	.12
	1.84		.01					.04	.01	.18	.95				.08		.06		T					.29			T	.02	T	.20		T
	1.99	.01	T	T				.15	.10	.08	.28	.01			.05		.04	.02	.02	.02		.05		.64	.01		.10			.26	.15	T
	-	D.05						*		D.20	.76				*		D.30	D.05	T					.27				.01	-	-		.01
	2.04	.08	.03					.15	.05	.18	.20	T		.11	T	T	.01	.01	.04					.65		.03	.04		T	.39	.07	T
	2.18							.18		.10	.58				.08		.20		T			T	.02	.61			.02		.10	.12		.17
	1.98	.02	T	T		T		.12	.02	T	.35	.07		T	T		.02	T		T				1.05	T	T	T	T		.33	T	
	2.01					T	T	.12		.08	.70			T	.12	T	.10		T	T			T	.42		T		.07	.06	.22		.12
	3.25	.17	.05	.10	.01		T	.09	.14	.16	.54	.08	T	.03	.11		.06	.03	.04	.17			.01	.73	T		.15	.01		.49	.08	T
	2.19	.14	T					T	.05	.07	.45	T		T			T			T				.90	T		T	T		.52	.06	
	2.20	.03	T	T				T	.08	.03	.65	.20		T	T		T	T		.03				.72	T		T	T		.40	.08	T
	-							.20		.10	-				-		-				T	T	T	1.20	T			-		-		
	2.64	T					.02	.08		.55	.56				.12	.10	T		T			.03	.20	.47		T		T	.24	.09		.18
	1.76	.01	T	T				.16	.08	.14	.30	.01		T	.05		.04	.01	T			.03	T	.32	T		.11	.01	T	.28	.20	.01
	1.80							.11		.12	.32					.10				T		T	.03	.83			.03			.12	.10	.04
	2.25	.05	.01	.06			T	.07	.07	.12	.41	.10	T	.04	.04		.03	T		.09	T			.45	T		.03	.05	T	.35	.24	.02
	2.31	.05	.02	.01			.01	.20	.11	.19	.29	.03		.14	T	T	T	T	T	T				.60	T		.03	.01		.38	.22	.02
	1.97							.10		.08	.32						.08							1.05		.08		.10		.15	.01	
	2.03							.12	.07	.12	.40	.02		T	.07		.05	T	T	T		.05		.57	T	T	.17	T	T	.25	.14	T
	2.61		.06		T			.09	T	.25	.42	.03		.06	.01		T		.02	.02		T		.84			.05	T		.68	.08	
	2.65	.12	.07	.04	T	T	T	.05	.07	.11	.25	.12	T	.06	T	T	.03	.06	T	.03		T	.04	.98	.03		.06	T		.43	.05	
	1.92							.10	.01	.01	.27	.05		.01			.06							1.13			.07	.08		.12	.01	.03
	1.31							.03	T	.04	.30				.04		.10					.07	T	.46			T	.03		.23	T	.01
	2.09							.09		.07	.35				.09	T	.12					.04	.07	.80				T	.12	.22	T	.12
	3.79	T	T	T				.14	.06	.27	1.63	.01			.08		.08	T	T	T		.08		.54	T		.06	.07	T	.42	.30	.05
	3.26	T	T	.02			T	.12	.05	.23	1.20	.03			.15	T	.06	T	T	T		.10	T	.55	T		.04	.06	T	.40	.23	.02
	2.20	.02		.02				.16	.11	.12	.50	.02			.14		.05	.03				.13	.02	.27	.01	T	.12	.03	.02	.30	.11	.02
	1.41							.08		.08	.30				T	T	.12						T	.61		T	T	T		.14	.06	.02
	2.40	.06	.04	.03	T		T	.09	.03	.15	.41	.04		.18	T	T	.02	.02	.02	.02		T	T	.70	T		T	.08		.45	.08	T
	2.69	.04	.02	.03	T			.11	.05	.18	.46	.02		.16	T	T	.02	.04	.02	.02	T		T	.82	.02			.06		.50	.12	
	1.13	T	T					.12		.06	.12				T		.02					.02		.38				.08		.22	.11	
	2.05	.16	.06	.03	.09	T	.03	.12		.09	.32	.03		.10	.04		.03		.05			T	.75	.39		T	.05	.04		.27	T	
	1.97	.20	.01	T		T	T	T	.04	.03	.36	.09		.09		T	.01	.01		.02				.08	T		T	.05		.34	.04	
	1.72	.11	T	T					.08	.07	.17	.21		.05	T		T	T	T	T			.02	.50	.03		.07	T		.31	.10	T
	1.58	.13	T	T				.02	.04	.02	.32	.11		.02				T						.58	T		T	T		.32	.02	
	2.41	.05		.02				.15	.15	.15	.28			.10	.06		.05		.03					.70			.15	.02		.50		
D	2.87	.19	D.05	.05			D.05	.07	.17	.19	.80	.10		.02	.15		.05	.02	.02	.18				.42	.01	D.05	.09	.02		.32	.06	
	2.94	.24	.08	.02		.05		.02	.04	.09	.48	.04	T	.14	.01	T		.02	.01	.02				1.15	.02		.05	.02		.36	.08	T
	1.02							.09	T	.10	.32						.11							.35			T	T		.05		
	2.31		.04				.15	.20	T	*	.40			.15	.10	T	.05	.03	.05				.05	.30		.05		.10	T	.60	T	.04
	2.02							.04		.14	.05			T								.37	.16	.29		T		.01	.24	.43		.29
	1.79		T	T				.14		T	.27	.18		.06			.17	T						.58			.09	.04		.26		
	4.17	.20	.30	T		T	.08	.25	.30	.38	.35	.20		.15	.08	.05	.06		.06			.08	.40	.18		.18	T	.07	.22	.57	T	.03
	1.75	.02	.01	T				.19	.02	.17	.29	.01	T	T	.09	T	.03	.01	T	T		.02	T	.25	T	.03	.08	T	.02	.30	.17	.04
	2.13	T						.04		.11	.35				.02		.12		T			.10	.02	.97		.01		.13	T	.14		.12
	1.96	.02	.02	T			T	.18		.09	.25			.12	T	T	.02		.02				.13	.38		.02				.72		.02
	2.03		T			T	T	.05	.04	T	.34	.08	T				T	T	T	T				1.12			.02	T		.38	T	
D	3.38	.03	T	T		T	T	.10	.08	D.10	.41	.18	T	.06	T		.02	.02		T				2.03	T		.04	.03		.26	.02	T
	1.58		.02				.01	.18		.18	.03			.08		.01	.03						*	.22		.01	.02			.78		.01
	2.96	.17	T	.06				.10	.17	.20	.59	.10		T	.20	T	.08	T	T	T			T	.66	T		.10	.07		.43	.05	T
	2.97	.10	.29	.05	T	.08	.01	.01	.06	.04	.35	.06	T	.19	.04	.03	.01	.15	.01	.01		.01		1.04	.02		.04	.06		.26	.05	T
	1.87							.09		.06	.53				.10		.11							.64			.03	.04		.27		
	2.76	.12	T					.08	.05	.14	.58	.06		.07			.02	T	T	.04		T		.94			.04	.02		.50	.10	
	1.79	T	.03					.05	.02	.03	.42	.16		T			T	T						.71			T	T		.33	.04	
	2.33							.08		.10	.50					.03	.08					.10	.02	.96		.03		.05	.12	.06		.22
		RECORD MISSING																														
	2.93	T	T	T	T	.07	T	.04	T	.36	.15	.02	.21	.18	.07	T	.23	T	.04	.06	T	.01	.83	.25		.05	T	.10	.12	.14	T	T
	2.70							.10		1.15	.20				*	.05							.55	.15					*	.25		.25
	2.62		.25				.05	.05		.22	.29	.04	.18	.48	.01	.01	.01						.44	.10					.02	.38	.07	.02
	1.88	.02	T	T	T		T	.15	.05	.12	.17	T	T	.07	T	T	.02	T	.05	T		.01		.48		T	.18	T	T	.40	.16	T
	2.26	.08	.01	.02			T	.06	.09	.10	.32	T		.28	T		.01	.01	.03	.01		.03	T	.81			.02	T		.35	.03	
	1.98	.03		T		.05	T	.05	.03	.10	.22	.10	.03	.05	T		.05	.02					T	.70	T		.10	.10		T		.35
	2.46	.15		T	T	T	T	.03	.01	.05	.40	.10		.03	T		T	.01						1.05			.01	T		.40	.22	
	1.32							.03	T	.10	.28				.03		.06						.01	.63			.02	.09		.07		T
	1.67						.05	.09		.05	.37				.04	T	.11							.76		.01		.09	.01	.05		.04
	2.42							.10	T	.10	.93				.14		.13	T				.04	T	.98				T	T	.34	T	.06
	2.81	.17	T	T	T	T		T	.10	.08	.59			.15			T	T		.07		T	T	1.10						.50	.05	
	2.57	.09	.04	.04	T	T	T	.06	.07	.12	.36	.05	T	.12	.03	T	.04	.02	T	.04		.02	T	.68	T		.08	.02		.59	.08	.02
	1.62	T	T	T	T		.01	.11	.07	.05	.22	T		T	.01		.03	.01	.02	.01		.05	T	.59	T		.08	T		.21	.15	T
	1.87	.06	T	.02				.02	.02	.02	.11	.03		.09			.08							.85	.03		.13	.16		.22	.03	
	1.87		T					.07	.12	.04	.07				.01			.16				.14		.78	.02		.08	.10		.21	.09	
	1.43							.09	T	.05	.30	T		T	T		.07	T						.84			T	.08		T	T	T
	2.42			T				.20	.08	.18	.65	.03			.15		.08	T	T	T		.05		.42	T	T	.07	.08	.01	.27	.13	.02
	1.92	.03	.01				.10	.01	.20	.19	.02	T	.05	.04	.04	.02	.05	T	.04			.04	.15	.22	T	.09	.01	.02	.06	.43	.01	.09
	2.22	.01	.08		T	T	.05	.29		.11	.14	T		.32	T		.03		.05			.01	.51	.29		.01	T	.01	T	.31	T	T
	2.52							.17	T	.16	.68				.23		.18						T	.71				T	T	.34		.05
R	1.84	T					.05	.06		.29	.30			.03	.11	.10	T		T			.01	.18	.20		T		.05	.07	.05		.14
	2.05							.15	.03	.13	.56	.01			.07		.08			T		T		.68				.05		.23	.01	.05
	1.57	.01		T		T		.08	T	.02	.30	.08		.03			.09	.02		T		T		.32	T		.16	.10		.30	.05	
	1.44							.08		.02	.30	.14		T			.08	T						.26	.02		.17	.08		.29		
	1.93	T	T	T		T		.10	.03	.02	.35	.15		.08			.07					T		.48	T		.07	.17	T	.34	.07	
	1.48		T					.06	T	.03	.43				.08	T	.12	T				.07	.04	.41			T	.02	.01	.18	.02	.01
	1.96	.04						.08		.03	.34	.14		.07			.08							.54			.11	.05		.41	.07	
	2.44	.07	.03	.01			T	.10	.14	.19	.77	.10	T		.11	.02	.06	.01	.01	T		.04	T	.28	.01		.06	.02	T	.31	.04	.04
	1.37	.09	T	.01	.03	.02	T		T	T	.29	.01	T	.01	.05			.05	T	T	.01	T	.15	.38	T	T	.03	.10		.18	T	
		RECORD MISSING																														
	1.61							.03	T	.04	.72	T			.12		.07			T		.02		.43				.02	T	.16	T	T
	2.41							.04		.22	1.30	.01			.03		.07		.01			.04		.29			.01	.03		.28	.06	.02

See Reference Notes Following Station Index

DAILY PRECIPITATION

Table 3—Continued

Day of month

Station	Total	1	2	3	4	5	6	7	8	9	10	11	12	13	14	15	16	17	18	19	20	21	22	23	24	25	26	27	28	29	30	31
INDIANA 3 SE	2.69	.09	.01	.01				.15	.12	.14	.39	.01			.11	.01	.04	.01	.04	.01				.50	T		.18	.03		.57	.28	
IRWIN	2.10		T	.04				.30		.13	.34	.01			.17		.04		.02			.03	.14	.22		.07			.05	.47	.02	.04
JAMESTOWN 2 NW	D 1.81	.05	.02	.01		T	.01	.06	.07	.10	.25	.02		.22	.03		.01	.01	.02	.01		.02		.80		T	.02	D.05		D.03	.02	
JIM THORPE	2.29							.10	T	.06	.33			T			.05	T	T				.01	1.25		.02	.04	.15	T	.14		.10
JOHNSTOWN	3.28	.15	.07	.05				.14	.04	.20	.70	.08	T	.02	.26	T	.09	.08	.04	.07		.25	T	.95	T	T	.15	.02	T	.28	.03	.01
KANE 1 NNE	2.64	.07	.01		T	T	.06	.07	.12	.43	.05	T	.15	.01	T	.01	.02	.01	.01		T	.02	•	1.01	T	.03	.01	T	.46	.07	T	T
KARTHAUS	1.92	T	T	T	T		T	.06	.05	.17	.44	.07	T	.03	T	T	T	T	T	T	T			.64	T		.02	T		.44	T	
KEATING SUMMIT	2.78	.17	.01	T				T	T	.14	.43	T		.08			.02	T		.03			T	1.17	T					.61	.06	.06
KEGG	1.79	.01	T					T	.06	.94	.53				T	.02			T				.20	.10		.03			.20	.04	T	.06
KITTANNING LOCK 7	2.12	.02	.03	T			T	.18	.10	.19	.13	T		.19	T		.02	T	.02	.01		.01		.65	T		.14	T	T	.35	.12	T
KREGAR 4 SE	5.25	.08	.09	T		T	.11	.37	.11	.42	.79	.50		.24	.21	.08	.09	.01	.01	.01	.02	.19	.44	.23		.21	.04	.07	.21	.64	.02	.10
KRESGEVILLE 3 W	1.99							.06		.04	.26	.06					.02							1.18			.06	.14		.10	.03	
LAFAYETTE MC KEAN PARK	-	-	-	-	-	-	-	-	-	-	-	-	-	-	-	-	-	-	-	-	-	-	.06	1.05	.01		.04	.01	T	.36	.07	
LAKEVILLE 1 NNE	1.54	T	.01					.10		.03	.32	.15		.05			.09	T						.30	T		.18	.11		.11		
LANCASTER 2 NE PUMP STA	D 1.71							.06		.04	.33				.07	.01	.10					.07		.58		T		.01	.09	.24		.11
LANDISVILLE 2 NW	1.73							.07		.05	.38				.06		.06					.04	.01	.73				.04	.03	.06	.19	.01
LAWRENCEVILLE 2 S	1.03	T	T	T				T	T	T	.36	.07			T	T	T			T				.30	T			T		.26	.04	
LEBANON 3 W	1.83							.14	T	.08	.47				.08		.07					.01	T	.63				.08		.14	.13	T
LEHIGHTON	1.01	T	T					.09		.05	.26	T					.15	T		T		T	T	1.05			.05	.14		.09		.03
LE ROY	D .67	T	.10								.05									.05			.06	.20						.15	.02	.04
LEWIS RUN 3 SE	2.91	.28	.03	.05		.03	T	.05	.04	.08	.30	.13		.13	T	.02	T	.02	T	.02	T	.01	.06	1.05	.04		.05	.04		.43	.05	T
LEWISTOWN	D 1.40							D .05	.02	.09	.41	.05			.09		.04			T		T		.39			T	.01		.25		
LINESVILLE 5 WNW	2.43	.03	.08	.04		T	.03	.05	.04	.06	.24	.03		.25	.04	.01	.01	T	.02	.01			.02	1.04	T		.02	.06	T	.33	.02	
LOCK HAVEN	1.52	T	T	T				.05	.09	.12	.33	.03		.08	T		.04	T		.02			•	.39	T		.02	.02		.31	.02	T
LONG POND 2 W	2.31							.05	.03	.03	.16	.09		.03			.11	.05		T				1.34	T		.11	.12		.17	.02	
LYNDELL 2 NW	1.46							.09		.10	.31				.09		.10					.10	.04	.27				.10		.11	.15	T
MADERA	2.31	T						.08	.11	.20	.42	.05		.10	.08		.02	T	.02	T	•			.47			.12	.03		.42	.15	
MAHAFFEY	2.86	.01	T	.02	T		.01	.12	.13	.21	.42	T	T	.08	.05		.03	T		.08				.87	T		.11	.03		.45	.17	.07
MAPLE GLEN	1.62							.05		.08	.26				.13	T	.07					T		.61		.03		.03	.11	.13		.10
MAPLETON DEPOT	1.35	T						.03	.03	.09	.45	.01			.11		.07		T	.02		.01		.28			.01	T		.24		T
MARCUS HOOK	1.82	T					.01	.05		.26	.17	T		.06	.08	.08	.01		T			.01	.09	.48		.03		.04	.11	.15		.27
MARION CENTER 2 SE	3.12	.07	.04	.04	.01		T	.18	.16	.15	.25	.02	T	.18	.09	T	.04	.01	.04	.03	T	.02	T	.77	T		.18	.04		.49	.30	.03
MARTINSBURG CAA AP	1.49	.01	T	T		T	.01	.11	.03	.30	.21	T		.03	.01	.02	T		.01	T		T	.44	.02		T	T	.01	.03	.09	T	.07
MATAMORAS	2.17							.06			.27	.14					.26	.16						.92			.09	.12		.07	.08	
MAYBURG	2.61	.10	.05	.04			T	.05	.08	.18	.33	T		.18	T		T			.05		T	T	1.02			T	T		.48	.05	T
MC CONNELLSBURG	2.11	T	T				T	.06	.02	.21	.95				.04	.13	T	T	T	T		.02		.38			T	T	T	.25	.03	.02
MC KEESPORT	2.32	.10	T	T				.40	.02	.14	.20	T			.12		.11	.04	T			.02	T	.70	T		.17			.26	.02	.02
MEADVILLE 1 S	2.25	.04	.10	.02		.03	T	.03	.08	.13	.19	.01	T	.21	.01	.01	T	.01	.01	.01	T	.01	T	.97	T		.01	.02	T	.32	.03	T
MEDIX RUN	2.00	.04	T	.02	T	T	T	.08	.04	.17	.43	.08	T	.08	T		.01	.01	T	.01		T	.01	.50	T		.03	T		.39	.10	T
MERCER 2 NNE	2.47	.10						.10	.20	•	.30			.62					.10			.10		.70				.10		.15		
MERCERSBURG	2.72							.13		.19	.97				.04		.10					T		.79					T	.38	.02	.10
MEYERSDALE 1 ENE	3.14							.02	.13	.21	1.46	.04			.03		.09	.03	T			.04		.34			.06	.10		.39	.20	T
MIDDLETOWN OLMSTED FLD	1.99	T					.06	.13		.30	.28			.04	.12	.06	T					.01	.25	.15		T		.04	.18	.09		.25
MIDLAND DAM 7	1.84	T	T					.12	.08	.05	.15	T		.02	T		T		.04	T		.03	.04	.79	T		.05			.35	.12	T
MILANVILLE	1.62	.07	T					.06	T	T	.23	.23		.05			.09	.03						.36			.07	.07		.36	T	
MILLHEIM	1.20	T	T	T			T	.05	.02	.10	.34	.06	T	T	.07	T	.04	T	T	T				.30			.01	.03		.18	T	T
MILLVILLE 2 SW	1.43	T	T					.06	.02	.07	.30	.07		T			.03	T		T				.58	T		.04	.03		.23	T	T
MILROY	1.70	T	T	T				.08	.01	.17	.36	.04			.04		.04		T	.05				.09			.02	.01		.19	T	T
MONTROSE 1 E	1.42	.03	T	T		T	T	.03	.02	.02	.23	.10		.08	T	T	.05	T		T				.39	•		.05	.02	T	.33	.05	T
MORGANTOWN	1.42						.02	.02		.19	.12				T	.04	T					.08	.12	.46		T		.05	.07	.16		.08
MT GRETNA 2 SE	1.32						.06			.03	.10			.01	.10	.08						.01	.14	.39				.05	.12	.06		.17
MT POCONO 2 N AP	2.36							.08			.42						.13		T								•	•		.61		.12
MUHLENBURG 1 SE	2.11	.02						.13			.43			.12			.02		.01				.07	.83		.02	.01	.07		.25		.11
MYERSTOWN	1.54							.14	T	•	.18				.07		.08						T	.78			T	T		.29		
NATRONA LOCK 4	1.79	.06	.01	T				.11	.12	.09	.17	T		.04	.02		.04	T	.03	T		.01		.40	T		.11	T		.33	.16	
NESHAMINY FALLS	1.87						T	.09		.12	.30			T	.05	.07	.02					T	.17	.68		T		.06	.01	.19		.11
NEWBURG 3 W		RECORD MISSING																														
NEW CASTLE 1 N	2.47	.05	.30	T		T	T	.15	.20	.20	.30	.03		.21	T		.05	T	.01	T		T	T	.45	T		.03	T		.38	.11	T
NEWELL	-							.20			-		.14		.04		.09						.05	.24		.04			.08	.14	.12	.02
NEW PARK	2.21							.10		.08	.65				.15	.15	.07						T	.46		.02			.05	•		
NEWPORT	1.63							.15	.01	.03	.42	T	T		.06		.08			•				.61			T	T		.26		T
NEW STANTON	2.10	.01	T				.20	.20	.05	.38	.01			.06	.01	.05	.06	T	.01		.01	.03	.24	.03		.12	T	T	.11	.50	T	.02
NEW TRIPOLI	2.19							.10		.07	.37			T	T	T	.11						.06	1.04		.05		.13	T	.15		
NORRISTOWN	1.19	T						.05	T	.05	.29				.04		.09					.02	.01	.45	T		T	.05		.11	.03	
NORTH EAST 2 SE	4.35	.38	.05		.02	.06	.09	.02	.01	.01	.32	.11		.54	.24	.02	.02	.16	T	•	T	.02	.02	1.57			.12	.09	.02	.36	.04	
ORWELL 3 N	1.32	T	.02	.03					.02	.04	.32	.04	T	.06										.38	T	T				.37	.04	
PALM	2.41							.08		.12	.08	.38					.12						.05	.85	.04		.12	.15		.20	.22	
PALMERTON	2.18	T					.04	.02		.07	.26			T		.06	.09		T			T	.47	.71		.09		.17	.01	.12		
PALMYRA		RECORD MISSING																														
PARKER	1.98	T	T	T	T	T	T	.13	.09	.16	.24	.02		.14	.01		.02	T	.02	T				.53	T		.01	.03		.46	.12	
PAUPACK 2 WNW	2.20	.01						.27		.05	.27	.12		.03			.10							.79			.18	.06		.32	.04	
PECKS POND	-	T						-		-	-	-		-			-	-						1.08	T		.11	.12		.22		
PHIL DREXEL INST OF TEC	1.63						.01	.05		.20	.10			.02	.10	.10	.02		T			.01	.18	.41		.08		.02	.05	.15		.15
PHILADELPHIA WB AP R	1.67	T					.03	.05		.27	.15	T		.01	.08	.07	.01		T			T	.12	.46		.04		.04	.07	.14		.13
PHILADELPHIA PT BREEZE	1.62	T					.02	.05	.01	.21					.29	.05	.01	T	.01				.11	.47		.02		.04	.08	.14		
PHILADELPHIA SHAWMONT	2.09								.10	.30					.06		.13					.10	.10	.55	.10		.05	.15	.10	.15	.10	.10
PHILADELPHIA CITY R	1.31						.03	.02		.22	.17			.01	.09	.08	.02						.07	.27		.01		.04	.06	.12		.10
PHILIPSBURG CAA AP	1.95	.01	.02	.01		T	.02	.08	.09	.23	.26	T	T	.15	T	.02	.02	T	.03	T		T	.48	T		.05	T	.06	.04	.36	T	
PHOENIXVILLE 1 E	1.45						.03	.04		.23	.15				.03	.02							.18	.44				.04	.05	.14		
PIKES CREEK	1.94	T		T	T			.05	T	.09	.33	.07		.05	T		.04	.02		T		T	T	.95	T		.05	.07		.23	.03	
PIMPLE HILL	3.13	.02	T	T	T	T	T	.09	.05	.09	.31	.14		.05	T	T	.12	.02		.02		T	.01	1.71	T	T	.12	.15	T	.20	.02	
PINE GROVE 1 NE	1.85							.11	T	.07	.33	.01			.02		.06						T	1.02			.02	.02		.18	.01	
PITTSBURGH WB AP 2 //R	1.65	T	T	T	T	T	.09	.18	T	.15	.06	T		.02	.01	.05	.03	T	.08			.02	.48	.05	T	.12	T	T	.01	.26	T	
PITTSBURGH WB CITY R	1.50	T	T				.06	.14	.02	.18	.10	T		T	.04	.04	T		.03		.01	.01	.33	.06		.09	T	T	.07	.32	T	
PLEASANT MOUNT 1 W	1.84	.09	T	.01		T		.08	.04	.02	.25	.20		.11	T	T	.06	T		T			T	.35	.03		.09	.09		.37	.07	
PORT CLINTON	-							.13		D.20	.44					D.10	.22							1.19				-		-	.05	
POTTSTOWN		RECORD MISSING																														
POTTSVILLE	1.82							.10	T	.07	.30						.10			T				.97		T	.08	.07		.13		
PUTNEYVILLE 2 SE DAM	2.31	.11	T	T		T	T	.08	.08	.14	.23	T		.13	.11	T	.01	.02	.01	T	—	.01	.01	.85			.02	.01		.50	.17	
QUAKERTOWN 1 E	1.92	T						.04		.07	.16				T		.15					.05	.04	.73		.03		.13		.40		
RAYMOND	2.46	.25	.03	.03		.02		.02	.04	.07	.42	.17		.08				.03		.02				.72	.05	T	.05	.02	T	.36	.08	
READING WB CITY R	1.49	T					.06	.03		.25	.12	T		T	.02	.06	T		T			T	.13	.40		.01		.11	.07	.12		
RENOVO	1.66	T	T	T				.04	.02	.09	.48	.08	T			T	.02		T	T				.48			T	T		.39	.06	
REW	2.79	.25	.04	.03	T	.01	.01	.06	.02	.07	.38	.09	T	.13	.01	T	T	.02	T	.02		T	.10	1.10	.02	T	.04	.03	.01	.30	.07	
RICES LANDING L 6	1.67							.14	.06	.08	.48	.02			.08		.10					.05		.27			.10	.03	.01	.14	.10	
RIDGWAY 3 W	2.61	.05	T	.02			T	.06	.07	.14	.45	.08		.13			.01	.02		.03			T	.81	T		.07	.02		.48	.17	
RUSH	1.53	.05	T	.03				.04	.02	.10	.35	.11		.05			.04							.32	T		.06	.02		.34	T	
RUSHVILLE	1.08	.02		T				.02	T	.07	.27	.12		.01			.02							.19			.01	T		.35		
SAGAMORE 1 S	-	T					T	.08	.10	T	-		T	.10	.08		.08		.02	T				.55		T	.08	T		.15		
SALINA 3 W	2.10	.04	.03				.04	.16		.10	.25	T		T	T	T	.10		.10				.16	.39		.15		.01	.02	.55		
SAXTON	1.78	T	T	T			T	.04	.02	.20	.74	T		T	.06		.09	T	T	T		T		.40		T	T	T	T	.23	T	
SCHENLEY LOCK 5	1.91	.05	.01	T				.15	.08	.11	.14	T		.05	.02	T	.01	T	.03	.01		.02		.54	T		.12	.02		.40	.15	
SCRANTON	1.26							.08	T	T	.01	.03		.02			.03							.65	.09			.02		.33		
SCRANTON WB AIRPORT	1.49	.02	.02	T	T	T	.06	.10	T	.10	.24	T		.05		.03	.02		T			T	.25	.12	T	.07	.02	.10	.06	.18		
SELINSGROVE CAA AP	1.59	T					.07	.05		.18	.26			T	T	.05	.01		.01				.63	.04		.02	T	.05	.06	.10	T	
SHAMOKIN	1.76							.09		.07	.26	.11		T	.03		.04			.01				.88	.01		.01	.12		.12	.01	
SHIPPENSBURG	2.12							.09		.11	.82			T	.15	T	.06	T	T			T	T	.51		T		.02	.12	.12		
SHIPPINGPORT WB	1.52	T	T				.07	.10	.03	.15	.07	T	T	.03	T	.01	T	T	.06			T	.52	.06		.04		T	.13	.25	T	
SINNEMAHONING	2.07	.04	T	T		T	T	.09	.02	.12	.49	.09	T	.05	T		.01	T		.01			T	.68	T		.02	T		.39	.10	
SLIPPERY ROCK	2.07	.03	.02					.09	.09	.09	.21	.01		.10	.01		.01	T	.01	T				.64			.04	T		.52	.11	
SOMERSET FAIRVIEW ST	3.26	.04	.08	.04				.11	.13	.20	1.01	.13			.12		.12	.03	.02	.02		.10		.39	.02	T	.03	.02	T	.30	.08	[illegible]
SOMERSET MAIN ST	3.09	.05	.02	.04			T	.20	.01	.20	1.15	.01		.03	.08	.03	.02	T	.03			.11	.10	.32		.06	.02	.01	.18	.31	.02	.11
SOUTH MOUNTAIN	2.84							.08	.01	.16	.96				.16	T	.13					.08		.92				T	.01	.35	T	
SPRINGBORO	D 2.00		D.10		T			D.05		D.20	D.20	D.05	T	D.30	D.20			T						.20	T		.10	.20	.20	.20		
SPRING GROVE	2.35							.12	T	.05	.65				.24	T	.15					.03		.66				T	.15	.19	T	

DAILY PRECIPITATION

le 3–Continued

PENNSYLVANIA
JANUARY 1957

Station	Total	1	2	3	4	5	6	7	8	9	10	11	12	13	14	15	16	17	18	19	20	21	22	23	24	25	26	27	28	29	30	31
NGS 1 SW	3.74	T	T	T			T	.18	T	.30	1.88	T		.02	.08	.10	T	T	.02				.10	.38	T	.03	T	.05	.02	.45		.06
E COLLEGE	D 1.53	T	T	T			.02	.01	.02	.24	.31	T		T	.09	.03	D.08		T			T	.47	.02		.02	T	.02	.12	.09	T	.03
USSTOWN	2.21							.12	.01	.10	.35	.02			.07		.08			T		T	T	1.00			.03	.11		.30	T	.02
UOSBURG	1.98	T	T	T		T	.02	.04	T	.10	.30			T	T	.05	.10		.01				.19	.77		.03	T	.13	T	.15		.13
P CREEK	2.23	.07	T					.06	.06	.17	.24	.04		.12	.02		T			.01				.63			.07			.66	.08	
URY	1.60							.12	T	.07	.30	.08		T	T		.11	T		T				.70			.05	.08		.09		T
UEHANNA	1.95	.12	.01	.01		T		.04	.05	.02	.24	.20		.10		T	.04	T						.47	.02		.04	.07		.43	.09	
RSVILLE	1.58	T	T	T				.18	.08	.19	.30				.03		.07		.01	T		•	•	.26	T		T	•	.11	.17	.11	.08
QUA	1.80							.10		.08	.27	.05					.07							.93		.05		.19	.15	T		T
QUA 4 N DAM	D 1.93							.05	D.08	.05	.29						.05							1.37			.02	.05				
RACK 2 S FIRE TWR	2.02	.06	T	.02	T		T	.03	.08	.07	.54	.18		.03	T		.08	T		.03	T			.52	T		.01	T		.38	.05	T
ESTA 2 SE DAM	2.57	.06	.06	.01		T	T	.07	.08	.16	.39	.04		.16	.01	T	.02	T	.02	.03	T	T	T	.93			T	T		.52	.03	
SVILLE WATER WORKS	2.87	.09	.04	T	T	T	T	.18		.16	.25	T		.19	T		.03		.06	T		.04	.96	.42		.03	T	.02	.04	.33	T	.01
EDO 4 W	3.42	.25	.10	.02		.08	T	.05	.11	.15	.20	.02	T	.21	.02	T	T	.10	.02	.02		.02		1.50	.02		.05	.05		.38	.05	
NDA	1.22	T	T	T	T	T	T	.02	.01	T	.31	.18		.02	T	T	.01	T						.26	.03	T	.02	T	T	.37	.02	
R CITY 3 SW	2.17	T						.21	T	.09	.39				.03	.04	.05		T				.23	.69		T		.08	.03	.21		.12
	1.68	.08					.04		.04	.40	.25			.03			.01							.46			T			.39		
LEPOINT A NE	2.24	.20	.03	.02		.02		.03	.08	.06	.30	.08		.11	.02		.02			.03	.02		.08	.72	.01		.04	.03		.36	.03	
NE 4 NE BALD EAGLE	2.07	.02	T				T	.06	.09	.08	.47	.10		T	.08		.04	T	T	.05				.66	T		.07	T		.34	.03	
N CITY	2.91	.13	.15	.09		T	T		.06	.07	.58	.18	T	.08	.03	.03	.06	T	T	T		.02	.03	1.02	T		.02	.05		.30	.03	
NTOWN	2.61		T			T	.10	.20	T	.27	.37			.10	.08	.10	T		T			.07	.25	.06		.08	T	.05	.20	.30	.01	.39
R DARBY	1.61							.04		.06	.33				.09	.02	.08					.02	.01	.54		T			.14	.18		.14
A	3.36	.08	.02	.04		.02	.03	.08	.12	.15	.35	.02		.38	.03		.02	.01	.06	.02		.06	.02	1.15			.02	.05		.43	.20	
ERGRIFT	1.55	.06	T	T	T		T	.08	.10	.05	.20	T	T	T	.06		.05		.05	T	T			.35			.13			.28	.14	
INVILLE	1.78							.12		.08	.35	.08			.03		.04		T	T			•	.87	T		.03	.06		.12		T
NCKEL	2.99	.08	.02	.03	T		T	.13	.07	.17	.41	.04		.17	T	T	.03	.03	.03	.02			T	1.03	T			.09		.55	.12	
NCKEL 1 WSW	2.93	.04	.03	.03	T		T	.11	.07	.17	.41	.03		.17	T	T	.04	.04	.03	.02			T	.99	.02			.07		.55	.11	
EN	2.66	.17	.06	.02		.04		.03	.03	.10	.21	.06	.01	.14		.02	.01	.02	T	T			.05	1.25	.01		.03	.02		.33	.05	
ONTOWN	2.19	T	T				.09	.02		.23	.29			.02	T	.05	T		T	T		T	.30	.77		.04	T	T	.03	.29	T	.06
ESBURG 2 W	1.97							.17	.07	.15	.60	T			.09	T	.10	T	T	T		.04		.38	T	T	.09	.02	.01	.16	.09	T
SBORO 3 S	1.59	.09	T	T			T	.05	.03	.04	.26	.16		.02	T		T		T				T	.44		T	T			.46	.02	T
SVILLE	1.46							.11		.03	.09				.24	T	.09		T				.02	.48		T		T	.08	.20		.14
ERSVILLE 1 W	D 1.89							.10		.05	.25						D.20					.15		.85						.25		
CHESTER	1.59							.06	T	.07	.28				.08	•	.11				.03	.01	•	.45		.01	.04			.19	.01	.25
GROVE 1 E	1.92							.07		.07	.37				.26		.28					.03		.36				.04	.17	.13		.16
HICKORY	2.59	.03	.06	.02				.08	.03	.20	.22	.02	.01	.15	.02		.03		.02	.04		.01	.06	1.10			.03	.02		.40	.04	
ESBURG	–	.11		T	T	T		.10	.19	.14	.17			.12	–	T	.10		.10					.64			.15			.47	.11	T
ES BARRE	1.42	T	T	T				.05	T	.01	.27	.14		.06	T		.03	T		T				.45	.01		.06	.12		.17	.05	
IAMSBURG	1.64	.09	T	T			T	.15	T	.16	.57	.03	T	T	.10	T	.06	T	.01	T		T		.36			T	.02	T	.09	T	T
IAMSPORT WB AP	1.50	T					.11	.07	T	.20	.37			.06		.04	.01		T				.24	.02		.02	T	.03	.19	.22	T	.01
SBURG	1.62	T	.01					.02		.12	.92				.04		.05							.30			T	T		.16		T
3 SSW PUMP STA	2.16							.11	T	.10	.40			T	.15	.01	.10					.03	.01	.75		T		.02	.15	.22		.11
HAVEN	1.78							.11	.01	.06	.50				.09		.10					.02		.61			T	.04	T	.24	T	T
GROVE	1.69							.16		.05	.21	.04		.03			.02							.90			.05	.12		.11		
SVILLE 3 SE	2.26							.13		.11	.35	.06			.04		.11					T	.09	.76	T		T	.09		.45	.03	.04

SUPPLEMENTAL DATA

Station	Wind direction		Wind speed m. p. h.				Relative humidity averages - percent				Number of days with precipitation							Percent of possible sunshine	Average sky cover sunrise to sunset
	Prevailing	Percent of time from prevailing	Average	Fastest mile	Direction of fastest mile	Date of fastest mile	1:30 a EST	7:30 a EST	1:30 p EST	7:30 p EST	Trace	.01–.09	.10–.49	.50–.99	1.00–1.99	2.00 and over	Total		
NTOWN WB AIRPORT	WNW	13	10.7	–	–	–	72	78	60	69	6	6	7	0	0	0	19	–	7.0
WB AIRPORT	–	–	10.6	24	S	22	–	–	–	–	12	8	9	1	0	0	30	–	9.4
ISBURG WB AIRPORT	WNW	21	7.7	34	NW	23	66	69	55	61	4	7	7	0	0	0	18	58	7.4
ADELPHIA WB AIRPORT	N	12	9.0	42	NW	23	72	75	62	67	4	9	6	0	0	0	19	57	7.3
SBURGH WB AIRPORT	WSW	23	10.8	32++	WNW	23	76	75	67	72	13	11	5	0	0	0	29	46	8.9
ING WB CITY	–	–	10.7	47	W	23	–	–	–	–	6	6	7	0	0	0	19	52	6.9
NTON WB AIRPORT	WSW	24	8.9	35	NW	23	70	73	59	67	8	10	7	0	0	0	25	44	7.5
PINGPORT WB	–	–	3.2	33††	NNW	23	–	–	–	–	12	8	4	1	0	0	25	–	9.6
IAMSPORT WB AIRPORT	–	–	–	–	–	–	–	73	58	65	5	8	6	0	0	0	19	–	7.8

eak Gust
astest observed one minute speed. This station is not pped with automatic record- wind instruments.

DAILY TEMPERATURES

Table 5

Station		1	2	3	4	5	6	7	8	9	10	11	12	13	14	15	16	17	18	19	20	21	22	23	24	25	26	27	28	29	30	31
ALLENTOWN WB AP	MAX	34	28	33	47	35	30	33	39	38	36	27	35	33	21	12	26	15	23	28	38	42	57	59	26	26	34	36	35	38	30	34
	MIN	12	11	18	27	18	11	21	27	27	18	13	11	15	4	-2	5	0	-6	6	5	30	36	16	13	20	25	28	28	29	27	28
ALLENTOWN GAS CO	MAX	45	29	29	35	47	35	31	35	39	38	37	28	36	35	22	13	28	17	24	30	40	43	60	59	26	30	35	39	35	39	37
	MIN	21	9	16	23	28	13	13	22	27	30	16	13	18	10	-1	0	1	-1	0	7	10	32	37	14	14	21	28	26	28	27	27
ALTOONA HORSESHOE CURVE	MAX	33	21	29	40	31	28	32	33	34	36	22	40	36	24	14	19	12	19	32	36	48	52	56	24	27	33	29	29	44	35	33
	MIN	11	7	15	18	26	17	23	24	25	20	10	8	22	-6	-6	-5	-7	-4	9	10	29	32	18	7	10	23	24	26	28	25	24
ARENDTSVILLE	MAX	48	28	29	35	52	35	31	38	36	40	40	28	43	36	22	13	27	15	25	34	35	44	59	56	27	35	41	46	35	42	37
	MIN	25	12	16	21	23	20	21	24	27	28	13	11	19	5	0	1	-6	-10	-2	2	13	32	35	14	14	23	29	29	30	29	29
ARTEMAS 1 WNW	MAX	41	30	40	47	41	32	30	42	38	40	37	45	46	21	22	20	23	38	50	56	59	60		39	38	40	37	49	50	46	56
	MIN	10	9	17	22	21	24	20	26	27	28	11	12	8	10	6	4	1	13	17	22	21	30	20	10		28	25	28	27	28	30
BAKERSTOWN 3 WNW	MAX	31	24	29	36	31	34	35	34	39	34	24	38	34	24	18	17	10	18	30	44	52	54	51	26	34	32	30	30	34	31	38
	MIN	12	8	10	26	28	24	27	26	28	22	10	12	22	6	2	8	-6	4	10	18	37	48	18	10	24	26	22	25	26	26	26
BEAVERTOWN	MAX	38	29	32	48	37	31	34	36	37	35	28	30	34	22	18	25	19	23	32	35	48	49	56	28	28	36	36	33	41	40	34
	MIN	19	13	20	20	29	10	23	30	27	27	17	6	21	1	-3	3	-4	-9	16	5	32	34	27	10	18	26	27	26	29	27	26
BELLEFONTE 4 S	MAX	41	22	26	39	40	33	29	34	33	36	36	23	38	29	17	12	21	11	21	31	37	49	59	39	25	33	32	34	33	39	32
	MIN	19	10	15	18	27	16	17	23	27	23	13	8	22	6	-13	-2	-3	-2	2	9	9	30	29	8	9	22	24	25	27	29	25
BERWICK	MAX	38	27	33	49	38	31	32	36	37	35	26	36	33	21	18	23	20	22	30	40	49	57	60	29	27	34	36	34	35	37	34
	MIN	17	10	15	22	25	11	24	25	25	26	13	8	21	-1	-3	9	-3	-7	6	7	30	36	29	12	10	21	26	26	29	25	25
BETHLEHEM LEHIGH UNIV	MAX	36	29	33																												
	MIN	16	16	24																												
BLAIRSVILLE 6 ENE	MAX	26	15	26	34	27	30	27	28	36	41	19	36	32	18	18	13	6	11	27	40	32	52	30	29	32	25	26	31	38	28	38
	MIN	5	5	10	22	20	16	23	21	22	14	5	12	12	2	-2	5	-12	1	4	15	38	42	10	4	21	20	20	20	25	17	20
BRADFORD 4 W RES	MAX	26	19	27	32	30	35	30	30	32	31	23	28	28	11	10	16	10	15	26	40	43	54	50	25	29	28	25	26	32	28	35
	MIN	8	2	8	19	8	-5	21	20	23	11	8	2	7	-22	-25	-6	-18	-19	2	15	32	32	12	-8	12	16	13	12	21	15	8
BROOKVILLE CAA AIRPORT	MAX	22	23	26	35	30	30	30	29	35	33	18	33	29	13	15	15	8	16	30	41	47	54	55	28	31	27	27	33	34	27	35
	MIN	5	5	14	26	11	11	24	24	26	14	6	5	6	-6	-9	-2	-12	-6	4	4	36	46	8	5	21	22	21	22	24	22	24
BURGETTSTOWN 2 W	MAX	38	21	22	37	38	31	33	35	34	37	31	28	38	25	19	23	20	14	18	33	43	54	56	27	30	35	31	29	37	37	31
	MIN	16	6	3	4	23	23	23	20	17	29	2	2	23	-2	-8	5	-19	-4	7	6	29	36	27	7	8	25	23	20	25	23	23
BURNT CABINS 2 NE	MAX	45	26		40	40	34		36	38	40	34		34			27	18	24	38	38		60		30	32	39	38		44		35
	MIN	12	10		24	27	18		21	27	28	13		8			2	-7	-3	7	8		27		8	20	29	27		26		26
BUTLER	MAX	38	23	25	37	37	30	31	33	36	37	25	32	35	30	15	18	16	17	35	45	47	53	54	24	29	30	28	28	34	34	34
	MIN	15	6	12	23	26	21	25	23	27	23	9	7	24	2	-10	9	-6	3	9	20	34	47	24	7	20	23	20	22	27	27	26
CANTON 1 NW	MAX	36	14	18	28	36	25	21	30	34	33	30	22	31	19	13	7	21	5	18	25	32	41	52	36	23	25	30	33	30	37	29
	MIN	9	0	9	15	21	4	7	19	23	25	5	9	14	-10	-14	-12	-9	-5	-3	3	21	31	36	5	5	17	18	21	22	20	18
CARLISLE	MAX	43	29	35	51	44	33	35	37	39	39	31	36	37	30	19	26	18	24	33	36	47	51	58	36	33	40	39	36	40	42	38
	MIN	24	14	22	23	29	18	24	31	28	31	17	13	29	6	3	9	0	-7	3	8	31	34	32	14	22	29	29	29	32	29	29
CHAMBERSBURG 1 ESE	MAX	36	28	34	52	36	33	37	36	39	39	27	41	37	23	14	27	17	24	33	35	49	56	58	30	33	40	39	34	45	38	34
	MIN	16	14	21	27	25	22	24	29	29	23	17	14	23	5	0	6	-6	0	10	8	32	28	22	14	23	30	29	29	32	30	30
CHESTER	MAX	52	51	30	37	48	39	39	36	42	39	42	31	41	25	25	30	21	28	41	39	41	43	61	61	29	37	36	40	37	40	38
	MIN	20	13	19	23	33	20	18	27	30	34	20	22	15	5	8	8	5	13	21	23	33	36	41	18	23	27	25	33	31	31	31
CLARION 3 SW	MAX	36	25	26	32	35	33	32	34	37	38	28	34	35	20	18	20	12	19	30	42	46	48	53	26	31	34	33	32	34	34	35
	MIN	14	5	8	20	18	10	21	21	25	19	10	4	16	-10	-10	5	-14	-8	2	3	34	33	15	4	18	22	20	21	28	21	22
CLAYSVILLE 3 W	MAX	36	24	31	41	34	36	35	33	39	36	27	39	33	20	24	21	14	20	35	45	57	59	58	29	35	34	31	33	39	33	41
	MIN	12	7	8	26	25	24	25	20	30	18	6	9	12	-3	-5	0	-20	-2	5	6	37	36	18	8	25	25	25	21	31	28	27
COATESVILLE 1 SW	MAX	49	30	30	36	51	36	34	34	40	36	38	30	43	38	24	16	27	16	25	33	39	43	59	59	29	33	37	38	35	40	38
	MIN	27	14	15	23	28	16	16	26	25	31	19	13	16	11	2	2	4	-4	0	7	13	33	42	14	14	24	27	27	30	30	28
COLUMBIA	MAX	30	30	36	51	40	32	34	38	37	37	32	43	38	28	20	28	24	26	27	39	49	54	61	53	32	39	40	36	37	39	36
	MIN	23	15	22	27	29	14	25	28	28	32	19	14	28	11	3	11	0	-4	6	10	32	34	33	14	23	27	30	30	30	30	30
CONFLUENCE 1 SW DAM	MAX	40	22	20	40	44	30	35	33	30	47	37	25	39	31	15	22	18	14	19	33	47	50	58	32	32	33	32	31	46	47	33
	MIN	20	10	11	12	28	27	26	26	26	30	12	8	29	8	-1	5	-7	-8	10	8	12	27	27	8	23	24	27	26	28	25	25
CORRY	MAX	26	21	26	33	30	27	30	31	33	32	21	29	28	13	15	14	8	14	21	38	46	51	50	26	29	25	23	28	32	27	33
	MIN	10	10	13	21	20	5	23	24	25	14	11	8	4	-16	-17	4	-10	-2	5	3	34	45	10	-2	18	19	13	14	22	18	19
COUDERSPORT 3 NW	MAX	23	16	25	32	28	22	28	29	33	30	22	28	29	11	6	17	4	14	24	35	42	50	48	21	25	25	26	26	33	26	33
	MIN	-2	-6	1	8	7	-5	20	19	22	8	9	1	-6	-23	-25	-5	-18	-9	1	-3	30	38	8	-2	15	17	18	15	21	15	14
DERRY	MAX	31	22	30	40	32	36	32	32	38	42	27	39	35	19	21	20	13	20	33	45	58	59	60	33	35	34	30	34	42	32	36
	MIN	9	8	13	24	26	22	27	26	28	23	10	13	19	5	-4	10	-6	6	8	17	37	52	17	9	26	26	25	25	32	22	27
DEVAULT 1	MAX	35	28	33	48	37	38	32	38	37	37	38	41	38	33	15	28	28	25	31	42	43	59	60	44	31	37	38	35	30	38	35
	MIN	9	8	13	23	16	10	20	23	24	18	12	11	12	2	-5	4	5	0	4	5	30	36	14	9	13	23	24	24	26	23	26
DIXON	MAX	42	19	20	32	41	29	29	34	40	41	32	29	36	22	17	12	28	15	23	34	38	48	58	45	25	28	33	37	33	36	34
	MIN	18	2	13	18	19	3	3	18	20	20	-8	-8	12	-17	-18	-15	-14	-19	-10	-10	3	28	45	6	6	15	16	22	24	19	17
DONEGAL	MAX	24	16	29	36	25	31	26	28	37	42	21	45	31	12	16	14	8	16	27	40	49	52	51	25	30	26	25	35	37	24	34
	MIN	1	-3	3	24	20	19	21	16	23	9	-2	6	9	-9	-11	-3	-16	-1	5	7	31	32	8	1	20	21	16	17	21	18	22
DONORA	MAX	39	24	26	43	44	35	36	35	40	40	30	38	42	29	22	26	20	20	32	45	53	58	60	29	38	38	34	33	42	40	39
	MIN	21	13	14	26	29	30	29	26	30	29	12	18	25	7	7	15	-3	10	13	22	40	50	28	13	24	28	28	27	33	26	32
DU BOIS 7 E	MAX	29	21	25	35	30	29	30	31	34	32	20	32	32	19	12	15	11	17	28	39	48	52	55	23	28	29	26	28	37	31	35
	MIN	10	4	12	20	22	6	22	22	24	18	8	0	18	-13	-16	6	-17	-17	5	-4	34	37	18	3	16	20	20	19	27	21	20
EAGLES MERE	MAX	35	15	20	29	34	23	19	27	32	28	29	20	28	24	13	7	20	4	14	20	30	39	50	49	19	26	28	29	27	32	27
	MIN	12	-1	2	13	18	7	7	18	20	23	4	8	12	-5	-12	-11	-8	-10	-4	0	20	28	39	3	3	16	18	20	21	17	17
EAST BRADY	MAX	36	28	29	38	34	34	33	35	38	35	24	38	38	30	20	19	14	20	35	44	50	48	55	41	34	32	30	32	34	32	35
	MIN	16	8	15	25	27	13	24	24	28	23	10	6	20	-7	-5	7	-17	-5	8	9	34	34	20	8	23	25	22	25	30	24	27
EBENSBURG	MAX	28	17	35	35	28	30	29	30	35	36	19	35	33	16	14	14	7	14	26	37	48	49	53	23	33	30	27	30	40	26	34
	MIN	6	3	12	19	21	13	20	20	24	12	7	10	15	3	-9	5	-9	-5	6	10	31	38	10	10	10	20	21	20	24	18	22
EMPORIUM 2 SSW	MAX	30	17	19	34	35	27	25	29	28	32	30	20	30	20	15	14	16	5	15	27	36	45	53	30	24	27	29	27	34	35	27
	MIN	12	1	7	6	14	2	10	20	22	25	8	-1	13	-14	-15	-9	-16	-12	-7	3	15	32	30	1	2	17	19	15	20	20	17
EPHRATA	MAX	32	30	36	51	39	34	32	40	36	36	32	40	34	26	17	29	23	26	32	36	44	51	57	34	30	37	38	33	36	38	34
	MIN	23	12	20	25	28	13	22	23	27	30	17	14	25	9	-1	8	2	-1	8	14	32	36	32	12	19	25	29	28	29	26	29
ERIE CAA AIRPORT	MAX	22	25	33	35	29	29	33	31	35	29	21	31	29	14	17	16	10	17	25	40	53	56	37	24	30	24	21	28	32	28	33
	MIN	14	18	21	29	22	22	29	27	30	18	15	21	5	3	0	4	-5	5	9	25	37	36	11	3	18	21	16	20	21	16	23

See reference notes following Station Index.

Table 5 - Continued

DAILY TEMPERATURES

PENNSYLVANIA
JANUARY 1957

Station		1	2	3	4	5	6	7	8	9	10	11	12	13	14	15	16	17	18	19	20	21	22	23	24	25	26	27	28	29	30	31	Average
EVERETT 1 SW	MAX	24	28	32	46	30	34	34	37	45	44	28	40	40	22	21	26	16	26	38	40	50	59	54	31	36	36	30	35	40	34	36	35.4
	MIN	10	9	8	25	25	20	28	26	27	20	9	12	20	6	8	6	-4	0	10	10	30	28	15	10	22	20	26	30	30	26	30	17.5
FARRELL SHARON	MAX	32	26	29	38	32	31	38	34	37	35	24	35	34	19	18	20	14	21	33	43	49	56	55	30	33	32	32	33	35	31	35	32.6
	MIN	11	12	10	25	24	20	24	24	23	16	2	11	10	-8	-9	4	-8	0	5	11	31	42	16	13	26	21	18	22	24	19	24	15.0
FORD CITY 4 S DAM	MAX	30	20	23	39	39	30	33	32	32	38	32	24	36	25	16	21	17	13	22	34	44	55	58	30	28	33	30	30	38	37	31	31.5
	MIN	16	6	13	13	26	21	23	21	22	29	10	7	22	1	3	3	-15	-8	9	6	14	39	28	6	8	23	22	22	24	23	23	14.8
FRANKLIN	MAX	37	31	28	36	37	31	30	30	33	35	33	33	34	32	16	17	16	10	19	32	42	47	53	32	25	31	29	27	31	34	39	30.9
	MIN	17	10	9	12	25	15	14	24	26	27	18	17	10	-11	-2	-4	-5	-8	1	7	28	34	27	14	13	20	22	19	22	26	22	14.5
FREELAND	MAX	35	20	27	38	33	25	27	33	32	32	21	33	32	14	14	20	17	15	23	30	47	46	56	23	23	29	30	30	33	32	30	29.0
	MIN	12	10	12	27	21	8	18	21	21	20	7	12	10	-2	-10	2	-5	-2	4	11	27	36	20	4	13	19	23	21	23	17	18	13.5
GEORGE SCHOOL	MAX	40	30	38	49	37	30	36	40	35	38	30	40	34	23	16	29	22	25	31	39	42	54	60	34	30	39	38	37	37	38	36	35.7
	MIN	22	13	17	24	30	15	27	23	28	27	13	11	23	9	1	11	-2	-8	-1	3	33	34	18	16	19	24	29	32	28	30	31	16.7
GETTYSBURG	MAX	51	29	30	36	54	36	31	39	37	41	37	30	44	37	23	14	29	12	26	33	37	45	59	51	28	37	40	40	35	45	39	36.3
	MIN	25	14	18	23	29	21	24	25	28	32	17	14	23	10	3	4	0	-7	-1	7	14	33	42	15	17	25	32	32	31	30	31	19.7
GRATZ 1	MAX	44	26	28	32	46	32	29	34	35	34	34	24	39	32	19	12	24	11	22	30	37	48	58	55	25	31	36		32	38	35	32.6
	MIN	22	11	17	19	24	9	9	23	24	28	17	7	15	6	-2	0	-2	-7	-3	8	6	33	43	11	11	21	27		28	26	25	15.2
GREENVILLE	MAX	29	28	28	35	32	30	33	32	36	35	21	33	33	18	18	17	12	18	37	40	46	53	53	26	32	28	27	31	33	29	35	30.9
	MIN	13	8	11	24	23	17	25	25	26	18	8	9	12	-8	-12	2	-10	0	4	15	35	44	16	5	15	22	18	21	27	21	24	14.8
HANOVER	MAX	51	30	31	36	54	37	32	35	37	40	32	30	46	37	25	15	28	17	27	33	39	50	60	58	29	37	42	40	34	42	38	36.8
	MIN	24	11	13	17	27	17	24	24	21	27	18	18	20	10	3	3	-1	-1	5	9	24	33	43	13	14	23	30	29	31	28	28	18.7
HARRISBURG WB AP	MAX	35	29	35	51	35	30	37	35	39	37	27	37	36	21	14	25	13	24	32	38	49	59	62	26	31	39	38	34	43	37	35	34.9
	MIN	17	15	23	29	25	17	25	30	29	23	19	16	19	10	5	12		-2	11	12	34	38	21	15	23	30	31	30	32	30	32	21.0
HAWLEY 1 S DAM	MAX	39	16	18	31	37	27	28	30	33	37	31	23	34	26	14	10	21	12	18	24	35	50	56	42	26	25	27	33	32	35	30	29.0
	MIN	12	3	10	14	21	1	1	12	18	25	3	1	10	-15	-13	-15	-19	-19	-20	-9	7	38	41	4	4	15	10	18	20	19	13	6.5
HOLTWOOD	MAX	37	30	36	49	36	31	36	36	37	41	29	42	36	23	16	27	16	26	34	37	44	54	57	28	32	37	39	32	38	37	35	35.1
	MIN	19	17	23	31	23	18	28	29	32	25	20	19	20	14	7	13	3	3	6	13	32	35	21	25	25	31	31	31	32	30	32	22.2
HUNTINGDON	MAX																																
	MIN																																
INDIANA 3 SE	MAX	31	22	28	39	31	33	32	31	38	39	22	38	35	18	23	18	10	18	31	46	54	58	57	30	34	33	30	33	40	31	38	32.9
	MIN	9	0	15	22	24	18	27	20	27	20	9	4	18	-2	-8	9	-15	-3	9	2	34	30	18	8	25	24	23	21	30	23	25	15.0
IRWIN	MAX			30	41		*	34	34	39	36	29	40			28	22	15	20			57	59	58	29	35			35	39	33	39	
	MIN			11	25			26	26	28	23	9			5	-1	13	-7	5			12	42	20	9	25			25	31	24	28	
JAMESTOWN 2 NW	MAX	38	18	23	35	34	30	29	32	31	36	24	25	18	20	14	17	15	11	17	32	40	51	54	23	26	31	27	25	32	34	29	28.1
	MIN	14	10	9	10	21	19	20	25	25	22	9	6	16	-6	-14	-1	-10	-5	2	14	30	36	22	4	6	18	18	18	23	18	18	12.7
JIM THORPE	MAX	40	30	36	46	40	32	37	41	42	39	32	38	36	22	21	30	24	25	32	36	48	59	57	36	30	36	38	37	34	38	33	36.3
	MIN	19	10	18	24	25	9	19	25	26	30	12	7	17	5	-4	5	0	-10	1	3	30	37	15	11	18	24	27	27	27	24	24	16.3
JOHNSTOWN	MAX	35	19	23	40	44	44	44	35	34	40	35	21	44	30	17	20	20	11	22	34	42	56	48	31	32	34	29	29	44	43	34	33.4
	MIN	8	7	9	15	20	21	22	23	24	29	9	7	16	5	-2	6	-7	-5	7	8	14	28	28	7	11	24	23	23	25	20	20	14.4
KANE 1 NNE	MAX	33	16	20	32	33	27	27	30	29	33	28	33	31	23	13	11	15	8	15	29	40	45	52	35	25	29	27	25	34	33	26	27.6
	MIN	11	5	1	9	21	-1	8	22	22	22	8	-3	15	-20	-21	-13	-22	-19	-9	-1	18	33	24	-6	-2	18	17	16	21	19	16	6.7
KEGG	MAX	31	22	34	45	33	32	35	34	36	41	26	43	38	18	19	22	14	21	34	36	57	54	59	30	32	35	34	33	49	34	35	34.4
	MIN	10	9	16	23	27	29	22	29	25	17	9	7	15	3	-1	4	5	1	10	10	27	29	13	8	24	26	24	24	29	24	27	16.9
LANCASTER 2 NE PUMP STA	MAX	42	31	36	51	41	33	33	37	37	38	33	41	41	31	20	27	25	23	34	39	46	51	59	36	31	38	38	37	37	37	37	36.8
	MIN	24	15	23	25	29	13	25	30	27	32	21	14	28	12	3	12	3	-6	-5	8	31	35	35	15	22	28	29	29	31	30	28	20.8
LANDISVILLE 2 NW	MAX	47	27	27	33	49	34	31	33	34	34	35	27	37	35	20	13	23	12	21	31	36	47	58	56	26	32	34	36	31	36	36	33.3
	MIN	23	12	15	20	26	8	13	22	23	29	17	10	16	9	1	1	-2	-9	-6	-3	6	32	38	14	12	23	26	27	29	28	27	15.9
LAWRENCEVILLE 2 S	MAX	42	18	21	33	40	29	26	33	37	37	25	26	35	18	15	10	23	12	22	27	38	45	55	45	25	29	30	34	34	38	29	30.0
	MIN	13	-3	12	16	21	5	6	23	23	24	2	9	15	-20	-23	-19	-17	-14	-10	-7	6	37	32	5	7	20	19	19	23	22	13	8.4
LEBANON 3 W	MAX	47	28	30	33	49	37	29	35	38	38	36	28	37	35	22	14	25	17	24	32	40	49	57	55	28	34	38	38	34	39	37	35.0
	MIN	24	13	18	22	26	12	15	28	28	32	18	11	19	9	2	3	-2	-3	1	3	17	34	42	13	13	26	29	28	30	28	28	18.3
LEWISTOWN	MAX	45	27	30	35	47	35	30	37	37	36	36	26	45	35	22	13	26	17	24	34	36	51	60	58	28	31	38	37	37	41	37	35.2
	MIN	25	15	17	23	23	19	18	24	29	29	19	11	14	9	2	2	2	-2	-2	8	7	31	30	14	13	21	28	29	29	29	29	17.6
LINESVILLE 5 WNW	MAX	27	23	25	34	31	28	33	33	36	32	20	31	28	13	16	15	9	19	31	40	45	53	53	25	32	27	25	30	32	29	33	29.3
	MIN	13	12	5	24	23	21	25	25	27	15	10	7	5	0	-14	0	-8	-4	4	10	34	43	14	0	18	20	16	19	24	16	22	13.7
LOCK HAVEN	MAX	34	30	33	43	36	27	34	38	35	34	28	38	34	23	13	25	13	24	35	36	42	53	53	27	28	36	37	32	38	38	33	33.2
	MIN	13	11	18	22	25	12	23	29	28	25	16	6	20	1	-5	5	-9	-9	10	6	31	30	21	9	19	24	26	26	29	27	27	16.6
MADERA	MAX	37	20	22	36	36	30	30	32	30	36	34	20	37	27	14	15	18	8	19	26	38	50	52	40	23	30	30	30	34	38	29	29.7
	MIN	12	0	7	9	22	15	16	20	20	24	2	-3	7	-8	-14	-5	-15	-16	-4	-4	1	31	33	2	2	17	17	17	20	19	18	8.5
MARCUS HOOK	MAX	38	31	38	45	40	31	35	42	37	40	30	39	42	25	17	31	19	2	34	38	40	54	59	26	30	42	41	35	40	40	38	36.3
	MIN	17	16	23	29	27	20	28	30	29	25	20	23	19	13	4	14	8	8	14	20	34	34	24	16	24	30	33	30	30	32	30	22.7
MARTINSBURG CAA AP	MAX	28	22	30	44	32	32	33	31	36	36	23	40	35	16	14	18	12	18	32	37	55	55	56	27	33	32	31	32	46	31	34	32.3
	MIN	9	9	18	26	24	21	23	24	26	17	11	13	15	3	1	3	-5	7	10	11	33	38	13	9	19	24	24	25	27	23	27	17.0
MEADVILLE 1 S	MAX	37	20	25	34	34	29	29	33	32	35	24	25	31	21	8	17	15	9	18	30	40	50	53	22	27	31	28	25	33	33	30	28.3
	MIN	14	11	7	12	24	17	18	25	25	22	11	5	17	-2	-10	3	-9	-7	-2	12	28	37	22	6	7	21	18	18	23	20	19	13.3
MERCER 2 NNE	MAX	20	21	25	34	37	33	34	36	40	32	28	34	30	27	24	30	10	20	33	36	45	62	30	30	32	34	40	34	36	37	40	32.4
	MIN	10	9	12	19	27	23	27	29	29	10	3	8	20	-16	-19	-12	-16	-10	0	0	34	37	25	10	12	24	29	26	29	26	24	13.8
MIDDLETOWN OLMSTED FLD	MAX	36	29	35	49	38	30	36	37	38	36	28	40	36	22	13	25	14	25	32	39	45	57	61	26	31	39	40	35	43	38	35	35.0
	MIN	18	16	24	29	25	15	25	30	30	24	19	17	21	10	6	12	5	1	7	11	34	37	23	15	25	29	31	31	32	31	33	21.5
MIDLAND DAM 7	MAX	27	23	32	38	32	31	33	35	38	39	27	37	33	16	23	17	14	18	29	45	51	54	54	28	33	32	30	33	36	31	36	32.4
	MIN	14	13	15	32	29	27	30	30	31	14	14	18	14	8	8	4	-2	10	15	21	38	47	17	13	26	26	24	27	28	24	30	20.8
MONTROSE 1 E	MAX	35	12	16	25	35	20	22	28	32	34	28	20	28	19	10	8	16	6	16	22	32	42	54	43	19	23	26	29	29	33	26	25.4
	MIN	10	-1	7	12	20	4	4	18	20	23	4	4	15	-10	-18	-16	-8	-9	-3	-1	15	25	39	1	0	16	16	16	21	17	15	8.3
MORGANTOWN	MAX	39	28	34	49	35	32	32	37	35	36	31	40	33	22	13	26	14	24	29	36	44	58	58	28	29	35	37	34	39	35	34	34.1
	MIN	15	11	21	22	20	11	22	25	28	14	15	17	16	8	-2	8	-4	-4	5	11	33	41	17	12	21	25	28	27	29	26	30	17.7
MT GRETNA 2 SE	MAX	35	29	35	50	44	36	36	36	36	35	28	35	43	38	18	27	30	25	33	36	41	54	58	26	29	36	38	32	39	37	42	36.0
	MIN	14	11	21	25	20	11	22	28	29	20	12	11	17	8	1	0	0	5	2	12	31	39	18	11	21	27	28	27	30	26	32	18.0
MT POCONO 2 N AP	MAX		14	23	37	31	24	28	32	36	31	21	33	28	12	5	22	16	14	23	31	46	45	55	25	23	27	31	31	33	33	30	28.0
	MIN		1	9	16	18	1	16	22	19	18	3	9	9	-7	-14	-1	-11	-9	1	5	25	33	15	3	11	18	19	20	23	18	16	10.2

See reference notes following Station Index.

DAILY TEMPERATURES

Table 5 - Continued

Station		1	2	3	4	5	6	7	8	9	10	11	12	13	14	15	16	17	18	19	20	21	22	23	24	25	26	27	28	29	30	31	Average
MUHLENBURG 1 SE	MAX	35	23	30	40	35	28	31	35	33	32	30	31	29	18	10	21	19	18	26	37	49	51	51	24	24	31	33	31	33	33	32	30
	MIN	7	1	10	18	16	2	16	18	20	11	7	15	10	-11	-14	1	-10	-10	-2	10	29	39	20	6	15	19	23	22	26	19	25	11
NEWBURG 3 W	MAX																																
	MIN																																
NEW CASTLE 1 N	MAX	32	26	26	38	33	32	35	32	37	35	23	36	36	21	17	15	12	20	33	43	52	55	56	28	31	31	30	32	34	31	34	32
	MIN	14	5	9	26	24	24	26	21	27	21	6	10	17	0	-7	3	-10	-2	4	8	37	48	18	15	23	24	19	23	29	21	26	14
NEWELL	MAX	40	25	27	44	44	36	36	35	39	41	31	38	43	31	25	24	23	22	32	41	56	60	60	29	36	37	38	33	41	40	38	34
	MIN	22	14	14	26	31	29	29	29	31	30	15	12	25	11	9	19	-5	11	8	11	35	37	27	13	22	28	31	26	30	27	28	21
NEWPORT	MAX	47	28	30	35	49	35	29	36	38	38	34	29	42	35	23	15	27	17	26	35	36	57	58	57	27	35	38	37	34	41	39	35
	MIN	25	15	19	22	29	13	13	25	28	30	18	9	15	7	2	3	0	-7	-3	5	7	35	37	14	14	25	30	28	30	30	27	17
NEW STANTON	MAX	24	32	39	41	33	35	34	35	40	45	30	36	37	18	28	20	15	19	34	46	58	60	59	31	38	36	34	35	41	34	40	35
	MIN	7	9	10	26	26	25	25	21	29	15	13	8	15	-6	-7	0	-7	11	9	14	37	32	12	4	18	25	14	22	31	22	29	15
NORRISTOWN	MAX	39	30	38	51	38	35	35	41	38	40	31	43	39	26	16	30	22	22	33	42	43	58	61	29	31	38	39	37	40	40	36	34
	MIN	15	16	21	30	24	17	26	28	30	26	19	19	19	10	2	11	6	4	11	16	35	40	20	17	25	28	32	30	31	30	33	23
PALMERTON	MAX	31	25	32	46	34	29	33	38	38	35	26	33	33	19	11	25	14	21	27	37	44	59	58	26	27	35	38	34	39	35	34	32
	MIN	11	11	18	24	16	8	20	26	26	18	15	10	13	3	-2	4	-3	-10	3	5	30	38	15	12	20	26	30	28	30	26	26	14
PHIL DREXEL INST OF TEC	MAX	41	32	39	49	41	36	37	43	38	42	35	41	41	27	21	31	24	29	35	43	43	59	61	30	33	42	41	40	42	41	38	36
	MIN	18	16	22	26	30	20	22	31	32	30	22	24	21	15	4	8	13	10	15	17	38	40	25	17	19	30	33	33	33	30	32	21
PHILADELPHIA WB AP	MAX	38	30	36	47	38	33	35	41	38	40	31	40	40	24	17	31	19	27	33	40	42	58	61	28	31	40	39	37	41	38	36	34
	MIN	17	15	20	30	26	20	27	29	30	25	19	21	19	12	5	13	7	5	12	13	35	36	21	17	23	27	32	30	30	31	32	21
PHILADELPHIA PT BREEZE	MAX	51	34	36	47	38	33	37	40	37	39	33	39	40	26	19	30	20	24	30	38	42	53	62	30	33	39	40	36	42	39	40	3
	MIN	32	20	26	32	22	27	32	30	30	33	20	23	24	16	5	14	10	10	13	22	35	36	28	19	25	30	33	33	31	32	32	2
PHILADELPHIA SHAWMONT	MAX	47	30	35	49	45	34	35	40	36	39	34	40	37	32	24	29	28	27	33	40	43	52	60	40	33	37	39	35	36	40	36	3
	MIN	24	11	19	26	30	16	26	26	28	25	18	28	29	13	3	10	5	2	10	14	33	34	39	6	22	25	30	30	30	29	30	2
PHILADELPHIA CITY	MAX	39	31	37	48	40	35	36	42	38	40	32	41	41	26	20	31	22	29	33	42	45	57	60	30	33	40	40	37	42	41	39	3
	MIN	20	19	26	32	29	22	30	33	31	27	23	26	22	15	8	16	13	13	18	24	38	41	23	21	25	33	35	32	32	33	33	2
PHILIPSBURG CAA AP	MAX	20	20	25	35	28	23	29	29	33	32	18	32	28	12	10	15	7	16	27	31	44	52	53	20	28	28	27	28	38	28	32	2
	MIN	5	4	13	24	15	14	21	23	25	12	9	0	10	-7	-16	-1	-16	-10	-2	2	31	41	8	1	16	19	20	21	23	20	25	1
PHOENIXVILLE 1 E	MAX	45	32	39	51	42	39	42	42	43	39	33	43	38	31	22	31	28	29	33	41	43	56	62	42	31	39	39	38	35	40	42	3
	MIN	22	14	14	24	14	20	24	26	26	31	16	13	26	10	1	2	-2	-6	2	4	29	34	37	16	21	23	29	28	30	28	31	1
PIMPLE HILL	MAX	36	17	15	25	36	25	23	28	32	32	29	19	33	20	13	15	20	11	14	22	31	42	53	49	23	22	26	30	29	30	25	2
	MIN	12	0	8	14	18	5	10	19	20	24	3	8	17	-3	-12	-8	-6	-5	1	6	17	31	40	2	5	14	19	20	21	16	18	1
PITTSBURGH WB AP 2	MAX	27	21	33	37	30	31	33	30	36	34	25	39	33	17	22	16	12	17	31	43	53	57	57	26	33	29	28	32	37	29	37	3
	MIN	9	9	10	29	26	25	26	27	28	12	10	18	12	6	6	0	-6	7	10	22	35	47	14	10	25	25	23	23	26	23	27	1
PITTSBURGH WB CITY	MAX	30	25	36	40	34	35	37	34	39	37	27	41	37	20	26	21	15	20	32	45	56	59	59	31	36	32	32	35	41	33	41	3
	MIN	15	13	15	32	30	28	30	30	31	18	14	22	16	10	9	6	-1	11	13	23	39	51	16	13	28	28	26	28	29	26	31	2
PLEASANT MOUNT 1 W	MAX	32	14	15	26	35	26	22	27	32	34	29	20	29	20	11	5	20	10	15	20	31	42	54	45	18	24	25	31	29	32	28	2
	MIN	8	-2	8	11	20	-6	6	19	12	25	-2	2	18	-20	-21	-20	-18	-18	-17	-8	14	26	42	1	1	16	8	11	21	12	4	[illegible]
PORT CLINTON	MAX	49	30	32	35	50	40	35	36	40	38	35	30	35	35	30	22	28	24	22	32	37	46	60	58	32	32	40	40	35	40	39	34
	MIN	21	9	16	21	25	7	12	24	23	24	14	8	14	6	6	9	7	-1	-6	-1	6	31	39	11	12	19	28	24	27	25	24	
PUTNEYVILLE 2 SE DAM	MAX	37	26	24	36	36	30	32	32	32	37	33	20	35	24	20	20	18	10	18	31	43	50	50	30	26	33	30	30	37	37	31	
	MIN	13	4	9	10	23	25	19	21	21	28	9	4	16	-5	-11	0	-15	-12	1	11	15	35	26	3	3	20	19	19	21	20	19	
QUAKERTOWN 1 E	MAX	41	25	33	45	40	31	33	38	36	36	27	36	37	24	17	26	22	23	29	39	39	52	59	29	29	35	37	35	35	33	35	
	MIN	17	11	18	24	25	11	20	27	27	27	9	8	24	6	-3	5	1	9	4	2	27	36	29	14	18	24	27	29	29	26	26	
READING WB CITY	MAX	37	30	36	49	37	32	37	39	38	38	29	41	36	24	15	28	16	25	33	40	45	60	60	29	30	37	38	36	40	37	35	
	MIN	15	14	24	30	24	17	26	32	30	23	21	18	19	12	2	11	7	5	12	12	36	43	21	16	24	29	32	32	32	29	33	
RIDGWAY 3 W	MAX	34	19	22	35	35	28	30	31	30	34	33	21	31	23	14	14	17	8	17	27	41	49	54	31	25	30	28	28	34	34	27	
	MIN	15	4	11	15	23	1	8	24	25	29	10	-7	18	-11	-12	-2	-18	-12	-6	-3	15	36	32	1	1	21	21	19	21	22	18	
SALINA 3 W	MAX	31	22	28	39	32	33	33	31	38	37	24	38	35	19	22	19	12	18	25	43	54	56	55	28	34	33	30	31	39	31	38	
	MIN	13	9	11	24	27	21	26	26	27	21	9	21	18	5	-4	11	-9	1	7	7	36	45	18	7	23	24	24	22	30	23	25	
SCRANTON	MAX	43	22	20	32	41	30	30	33	35	38	30	25	34	28	12	13	25	13	20	28	37	49	59	58	25	24	32	36	35	37	33	
	MIN	16	6	8	16	25	9	22	26	24	28	4	6	19	-4	-6	-4	0	0	-2	8	10	34	43	9	8	20	22	21	22	25	22	
SCRANTON WB AIRPORT	MAX	29	18	28	39	32	28	30	35	35	32	24	33	32	16	11	23	10	18	25	35	45	57	58	22	26	30	35	33	35	32	34	
	MIN	6	7	16	26	12	6	20	25	26	9	2	8	3	-8	-10	6	-3	-4	3	6	31	40	11	7	18	18	25	24	27	21	22	
SELINSGROVE CAA AP	MAX	32	31	35	46	35	28	35	36	38	34	25	38	33	22	13	25	14	22	31	35	48	55	55	25	28	36	37	33	38	37	33	
	MIN	10	10	22	28	19	9	23	25	28	19	15	7	14	3	-1	8	-5	-7	6	5	32	39	15	11	20	26	25	27	30	27	28	
SHIPPENSBURG	MAX	40	28	36	52	43	33	36	37	37	39	30	43	38	30	18	31	22	30	34	35	51	54	57	36	35	41	41	36	43	43	36	3
	MIN	17	14	20	24	29	20	23	29	28	30	16	14	22	9	0	8	-2	0	9	8	29	28	36	13	21	30	29	29	30	28	30	2
SHIPPINGPORT WB	MAX	28	24	36	39	32	32	34	33	37	36	27	37	34	17	21	17	13	17	32	45	55	57	57	27	33	31	30	33	38	31	36	
	MIN	13	16	9	31	28	25	27	28	29	14	9	16	13	3	3	2	-3	6	13	18	37	50	14	10	25	26	23	25	27	24	27	
SLIPPERY ROCK	MAX	30	24	26	35	31	30	31	30	35	33	20	33	32	18	17	15	10	16	31	42	49	55	54	26	30	30	28	30	33	30	33	
	MIN	10	6	10	24	22	20	24	22	25	16	5	9	10	0	-6	5	-9	4	6	7	35	44	13	6	22	21	19	22	25	19	23	
SOMERSET MAIN ST	MAX	32	18	27	42	32	32	30	30	40	42	23	37	36	22	17	16	13	17	30	43	52	54	52	26	35	34	29	34	44	33	36	
	MIN	10	6	11	23	25	23	24	20	25	20	6	9	19	4	-6	3	-10	-10	6	8	29	34	17	5	15	24	23	22	31	20	25	
SPRINGBORO	MAX	37	33	26	35	33	30	29	33	32	35	27	26	30	26		26	18	16	18	33	46	53	51	40	38	31	28	25	33	32	31	
	MIN	15	13	6	15	24	19	21	25	25	20	12	8	17		5	6	-13	0	5	9	32	38	19	0	2	20	17	15	24	15	17	
SPRINGS 1 SW	MAX	29	15	28	39	31	32	27	27	39	45	28	36	35	17	15	15	7	15	29	45	50	53	54	25	35	31	28	44	45	30	36	3
	MIN	6	4	9	18	23	22	23	21	24	16	7	6	3	2	1	7	-12	2	6	9	33	30	11	3	18	24	22	24	29	20	25	1
STATE COLLEGE	MAX	30	25	30	40	32	28	33	32	36	33	22	38	35	17	12	20	11	20	31	38	49	55	57	25	31	31	33	32	40	32	34	3
	MIN	14	10	18	28	23	16	24	27	27	19	13	13	15	4	-4	6	-4	6	14	12	37	38	14	9	22	24	25	27	28	25	29	1
STROUDSBURG	MAX	27	19	29	43	32	30	33	37	38	34	25	36	28	16	5	25	14	20	28	35	47	47	57	25	25	34	37	31	34	36	33	3
	MIN	8	7	7	24	12	5	17	20	22	10	0	2	11	-4	-11	0	-13	-22	-13	-6	29	35	16	8	15	21	20	23	27	23	22	1
TAMARACK 2 S FIRE TWR	MAX	31	15	21	31	31	28	20	27	28	30	28	21	28	22	9	4	18	5	15	27	31	42	50	38	20	23	28	28	31	33	28	
	MIN	10	1	8	11	16	8	9	18	20	23	8	8	14	-6	-12	-10	-11	-11	-3	5	16	31	38	0	0	14	17	18	19	17	18	
TIONESTA 2 SE DAM	MAX	36	20	23	36	35	30	30	32	33	35	25	23	33	22	15	16	16	10	18	30	42	50	45	35	26	31	28	27	35	34	30	
	MIN	15	7	13	14	25	7	14	23	25	24	10	1	18	-13	-12	-4	-17	-11	-5	4	9	36	25	3	4	21	19	20	23	22	21	
TITUSVILLE WATER WORKS	MAX	30	23	26	35	30	30	31	33	29	23	22	32	32	15	16	17	9	17	28	40	47	50	53	25	32	27	27	31	33	29	36	2
	MIN	9	5	8	21	13	9	20	22	25	12	6	-2	4	-13	-12	-1	-17	-12	4	0	33	40	9	1	17	18	17	17	22	16	19	1

See reference notes following Station Index.

Table 5 - Continued

DAILY TEMPERATURES

PENNSYLVANIA
JANUARY 1957

Station		1	2	3	4	5	6	7	8	9	10	11	12	13	14	15	16	17	18	19	20	21	22	23	24	25	26	27	28	29	30	31	Average
TOWANDA	MAX	31	22	32	42	35	27	33	38	40	34	29	36	34	19	10	28	17	23	30	37	48	53	57	24	29	33	37	33	38	34	34	32.8
	MIN	7	4	12	22	17	12	21	23	25	14	-2	13	5	-19	-17	4	-10	-15	-6	-4	30	40	14	9	17	18	22	24	25	16	13	10.8
UNIONTOWN	MAX	34	23	37	48	35	35	33	34	41	51	27	42	36	23	26	21	15	23	36	47	59	63	58	32	38	35	32	37	44	33	41	36.7
	MIN	15	11	13	32	30	28	29	20	31	21	13	15	19	3	-3	7	-6	9	11	15	39	49	18	12	30	29	26	26	32	21	31	20.4
UPPER DARBY	MAX	42	29	36	49	41	34	34	40	38	39	30	39	39	27	18	29	22	27	32	40	42	52	60	31	32	38	39	36	37	40	37	36.4
	MIN	20	14	18	29	30	17	25	30	29	28	18	20	25	13	-2	11	6	4	9	14	34	36	30	16	23	25	26	30	30	28	31	21.5
WARREN	MAX	26	24	30	35	35	29	32	34	35	33	27	31	30	16	15	15	10	19	31	41	51	55	52	28	31	29	28	30	34	30	36	30.6
	MIN	10	10	11	23	15	9	25	25	27	15	11	10	8	-11	-11	8	-8	-8	8	14	36	48	13	1	20	20	19	20	23	20	21	13.9
WAYNESBURG 2 W	MAX	37	23	31	44	33	34	34	34	41	41	22	42	34	24	23	22	14	20	36	46	57	60	60	31	37	35	32	34	44	33	44	35.5
	MIN	16	8	7	27	27	24	27	15	28	24	10	11	20	-3	-6	6	-17	-2	-1	9	33	36	22	10	26	27	27	24	32	25	28	16.8
WELLSBORO 3 S	MAX	33	15	20	32	33	32	23	31	32	32	28	24	32	22	14	6	18	6	17	25	31	42	55	35	23	27	29	32	31	36	28	27.2
	MIN	10	-1	10	15	17	5	6	19	22	24	7	10	15	-8	-16	-13	-7	-7	-5	5	19	31	35	4	4	16	19	19	21	19	19	10.1
WELLSVILLE	MAX	39	30	35	53	42	31	35	42	43	45	38	44	35	30	18	27	23	25	32	38	46	62	58	32	32	39	39	33	37	40	35	37.4
	MIN	21	13	18	20	25	12	24	30	24	32	13	11	10	0	-1	10	-11	-14	-7	-1	28	36	31	14	19	29	26	25	32	29	26	16.9
WEST CHESTER	MAX	49	33	35	37	47	33	36	39	36	37	30	33	27	25	18	26	19	24	35	40	54	59	56	30	36	38	36	35	33	38	35	36.1
	MIN	14	17	22	22	16	25	26	28	31	28	19	21	11	1	2	5	3	4	13	21	34	40	14	15	17	32	30	29	28	28	30	20.2
WILLIAMSPORT WB AP	MAX	30	28	34	43	35	26	34	37	34	33	27	32	32	22	11	25	13	21	30	36	44	54	57	24	26	36	37	33	37	38	34	32.4
	MIN	12	12	22	27	17	11	22	27	28	19	8	4	10	-5	-6	6	-6	-10	3	2	34	40	15	11	22	25	26	28	29	27	27	15.7
YORK 3 SSW PUMP STA	MAX	45	31	35	53	46	33	35	37	37	41	33	47	41	32	20	29	25	26	32	39	52	55	60	34	36	39	40	38	38	39	36	38.2
	MIN	25	15	22	26	27	13	26	31	28	32	16	13	27	5	-1	12	-9	-10	0	4	33	35	34	15	25	30	31	28	32	29	29	20.1

See reference notes following Station Index.

Table 7

SNOWFALL AND SNOW ON GROUND

Station		Day of month 1	2	3	4	5	6	7	8	9	10	11	12	13	14	15	16	17	18	19	20	21	22	23	24	25	26	27	28	29	30	31
ALLENTOWN WB AIRPORT	SNOWFALL	T					.9	T	T	1.7	.4			T	.1	.9	.5		T			T				1.0		1.2	T			.6
	SN ON GND	T					1	1	T	1	1	1	1	T	T	T	1	1	1	1	1	T	T				1	1	T	T	T	T
	WTR EQUIV																															
BEACH CREEK STATION	SNOWFALL	T						1.0	T	2.0	2.5	1.0		T	T		1.0										T	T				
	SN ON GND	T	T					1	1	2	4	4	4	4	2	2	3	3	3	3	3	3	2	T	T		T	T	T	T		
BRADFORD 4 W RESVR	SNOWFALL	3.6	1.3	.8	1.3		T	1.3	.8	.8	7.0		T	3.0	1.0		1.3	T	1.3	T				1.0		T	1.3	.8		2.5		.5
	SN ON GND	12	14	14	15	14	14	15	15	15	21	19	17	20	20	20	21	21	22	20	18	15	10	5	4	4	5	4	4	7	6	6
BROOKVILLE CAA AIRPORT	SNOWFALL	1.5	.3	.1	T	.1	.7	1.6	.7	2.6	.5	.2	.2	1.5	T	.1	.1		.3	T				T		.4	.1	.2	.3	1.5	.4	1.0
	SN ON GND	4	5	5	5	5	3	4	6	7	9	9	8	9	9	9	9	9	9	9	9	6	2	T	T		1	1	1	1	1	1
CANTON 1 NW	SNOWFALL	T	T	T		T		1.0	.3	T	4.0	1.0		T	T		T	T		T					T	T	T			1.8	1.0	
	SN ON GND	4	4	4	4	4	3	4	4	4	8	9	9	9	9	9	9	9	9	9	9	8	3		T	T	T	T	T	2	1	1
CARROLLTOWN 2 SSE	SNOWFALL	2.0	.5	1.0	T		T	1.0	2.0	2.0	1.0	1.0	T	.5	2.0		1.0	.5	.5	1.0					T		2.0	.5		T	1.0	T
	SN ON GND	6	6	6	5	4	4	5	7	8	7	7	7	7	9	9	10	10	11	12	11	9	6	T	T	T	2	2	2	1	1	1
COALDALE 2 NW	SNOWFALL							2.0	.1	.8	1.0			.1			1.5										1.0	1.5				
	SN ON GND							2	2	3	3	3	3	3	3	3	4	3	3	3	3	3	2				1	2	2	1	1	1
CORRY	SNOWFALL	2.0	1.0	.5	.5		.5	.5		.5	4.0	.5		1.5	.5		.5		.5					T		T	1.0	1.0		1.0	T	
	SN ON GND	7	8	9	6	5	6	6	6	6	10	11	11	10	11	10	11	11	11	11	10	7	T	T	T	T	1	2	2	3	3	3
DONEGAL	SNOWFALL	1.0	3.0				3.0	2.0	2.0	2.0	1.0	T		4.2	4.0	2.0	3.0		T					T		1.0		T		1.0		
	SN ON GND	4	7	5	3	2	5	7	5	2	3	1	T	4	8	9	10	8	7	6	2	T		T	T	1	1	1	T	1	1	T
DU BOIS 7 E	SNOWFALL	.5	.5	T			T	2.0		3.0	1.0			3.0	T	T	1.0		.5							.5				1.0		.5
	SN ON GND	4	5	4	3	3	3	5	4	7	7	7	7	10	10	10	11	11	11	11	10	5	T	T	T	1	1	1	1	1	1	1
ENGLISH CENTER	SNOWFALL	-	-	-	-	-	-	-	-	-	-	-	-	-	-	-	-	-	-	-	-	-	-	-	-	-	-	-	-	-	-	-
	SN ON GND	2	2	2	2	1	1	2	3	2	6	7	6	6	6	6	6	6	6	4	4	4					T	T		1	T	1
ERIE CAA AIRPORT	SNOWFALL	T	T	T	T	1.4	T	.8	T	3.5	1.5	1.2	2.6	3.0	1.3	T	2.3	T	.5	1.0				2.5		.5	.5	1.0	1.0	1.0	T	T
	SN ON GND	2	2	2	1	1	2	2	3	3	8	8	7	9	12	12	12	14	13	14	15	4		2	2	2	2	3	2	3	3	3
EVERETT 1 SW	SNOWFALL	-	-	-	-	-	-	-	-	-	-	-	-	-	-	-	-	-	-	-	-	-	-	-	-	-	-	-	-	-	-	-
	SN ON GND							2		2	1				1	1												1				1
FORD CITY 4 S DAM	SNOWFALL	1.5	T	T	T		T	2.5	1.5	1.0		T	T	1.5	T	T	.5	T	1.0	T				T		T	3.0	2.0	.1	T	1.0	T
	SN ON GND	1	1	1	1	T	T	3	4	5	2	2	2	3	3	3	3	3	4	4	4	1	T	T		T	3	2	2	1	1	1
GALETON	SNOWFALL	2.2		T	T	T	T	.5	.2	.7	4.6	1.5		.4	T		T	.2									.2	T		3.9	.3	
	SN ON GND	4	4	3	3	3	3	3	3	3	6	8	7	6	6	6	6	6	6	6	6	6	5				T			4	2	2
GEORGE SCHOOL	SNOWFALL							.5		1.3	1.5				.5	T	1.6									.1		1.0		.2		T
	SN ON GND							T		1	T	T			T	T	1	1	1	1	T					T		T		T	T	T
GRATERFORD	SNOWFALL							2.0		.5					.3			2.0									.5	1.0				
	SN ON GND							1		T					T			1									T	T				
GREENSBORO LOCK 7	SNOWFALL			T				5.0			T				3.0		3.0									T	T	1.0	T	T		T
	SN ON GND							5	4	4	T				3	1	4	3	3	3	1					T		1	T			
HANOVER	SNOWFALL							2.0	T	1.5	T				3.5		2.0											T	T			T
	SN ON GND							2	1	1	T				4	2	4	2	2	2	1	1										T
HARRISBURG WB AIRPORT	SNOWFALL	T					1.5	1.5		2.9	.2			.3	1.1	2.3	T		T							.1		.5	T			.4
	SN ON GND							3	2	2	2	T	T	T	1	1	3	2	1	1	1	T						1		T		T
	WTR EQUIV							.1	.2	.2	.4						.2	.2														
HAWLEY 1 S DAM	SNOWFALL	-	-	-	-	-	-	-	-	-	-	-	-	-	-	-	-	-	-	-	-	-	-	-	-	-	-	-	-	-	-	-
	SN ON GND	-	-	-	-	-	-	-	-	-	-	-	-	-	-	-	-	-	-	-	-	-	-	-	-	-	-	-	-	-	-	-
HOLTWOOD	SNOWFALL							1.0	T	1.0	T				2.0	T	1.5	T									T	T	T			T
	SN ON GND							1	T	1	T				2	2	3	3	2	1	1	T	T					T				T
HOOVERSVILLE	SNOWFALL	2.6	2.8	1.4			T	2.0	4.0	3.2		2.8	T		3.0	.9	2.5	.9	1.2	.4		T	T	T	1.0		.7	1.2	T		1.2	1.3
	SN ON GND	3	4	3	2	1	1	2	5	5	2	4	2	2	3	3	4	3	3	2	2	1	T	T	T			1	1		T	1
INDIANA 3 SE	SNOWFALL	1.6	.1	T				1.8	1.5	1.5	T	T			1.4		.6	T	.6	T				T			2.0	.4			.5	
	SN ON GND	2	2	2	2	T	T	2	3	4	1	1	1	T	1	1	2	2	2	2	2	T	T				2	2			T	T
KANE 1 NNE	SNOWFALL	2.9	1.1		T	T	.5	1.0	1.1	4.1	1.0	T	2.0	.3	T	.5	.3	.2	1.0		T		.5	.2	T	.7	.5	T	2.5	.5	T	T
	SN ON GND	7	7	7	6	6	6	7	7	5	9	9	9	9	9	9	9	9	9	9	9	7	6	2	1	1	2	2	2	4	4	4
KEATING SUMMIT	SNOWFALL	2.0	.6					.4	.4	1.5	3.3			.9			.5			.4					T					3.0	.9	
	SN ON GND	6	6	6	4	4	4	4	4	5	8	8	8	8	8	8	8	8	8	9	9	8	5	1	1	1	1	1	1	3	3	3
LANCASTER 2 NE PUMP STA	SNOWFALL							1.0		.5	1.0				.8	T	1.0									T						
	SN ON GND							1	T	T	T				1		1	1	1	1	T											
LAWRENCEVILLE 2 S	SNOWFALL	T	T	T				T	T	T	3.8	2.5			T	T	T			T					T			T		2.9		
	SN ON GND	2	2	2	2	1	1	1	1	1	5	7	7	7	7	7	7	7	7	7	7	6	T		T			T		3	1	1
LEWISTOWN	SNOWFALL							.5							2.0		1.0			.2								T		T		
	SN ON GND							1	1	1	1	1			2	2	3	3	3	1	1	1	T					T				
MARTINSBURG CAA AIRPORT	SNOWFALL	T	T	T		T	.1	1.1	.4	2.0	T	T		.3	.1	.2	T		.1	T		T				T	T	T	T	T	T	T
	SN ON GND	T	T	T	T			1	T	2	1	1	1	1	1	1	1	1	1	1	1	1	T				T	T	T		T	T
MATAMORAS	SNOWFALL							.5			2.5	1.0					3.0	2.0									1.0	1.5				
	SN ON GND							1	1		3	3	2	2	2	2	4	6	5	5	4	4	1				1	2	1	1	1	1
MEADVILLE 1 S	SNOWFALL	.7	3.5	1.3		.6	.2	.6	1.4	2.0	3.7	1.4	.6	2.5	.7	.8	.6	.6	.5	.7	T	T		T	T		.3	1.7	.1	1.4	1.0	T
	SN ON GND	3	6	5	4	4	4	4	5	5	7	7	6	7	7	7	7	7	7	7	7	5	1	T	T	T	T	1	1	2	2	2
MEDIX RUN	SNOWFALL	.1	.1	1.0	T	T	.2	1.0	.5	2.2	1.5	.5	T	1.0	.1		.5	.5	.1	.3		T			T		.1	T		.5	T	T
	SN ON GND	1	1	2	2	1	1	2	2	4	5	5	5	6	6	6	6	6	6	6	6	5	3	T	T	T	T	T	T	T	T	T
MONTROSE 1 E	SNOWFALL	1.5	T	.2		T	T	1.0	.8	.4	3.4	1.5		1.5	T	T	1.9	T		T					.4		.9	1.0	T	3.9	.3	T
	SN ON GND	8	8	7	6	5	5	6	7	7	10	11	11	12	12	12	12	12	11	11	10	10	8	2	2	2	2	3	2	6	5	5
MUHLENBURG 1 SE	SNOWFALL							2.0			5.0			1.0			.5		.5							2.0	.5	1.0		1.0		
	SN ON GND	3	3	3	1	1	1	3	3	1	6	6	6	7	7	7	7	7	8	7	5	4	2			2	3	4	3	4	4	4
NEWPORT	SNOWFALL							2.0		.8		T	T		.5		1.5			.5							T	T				T
	SN ON GND							-	-	2	2	T		T	-	1	2	1	1	2	1	1	T				T	T				T
PHILADELPHIA WB AIRPORT	SNOWFALL	T					.3	.6		1.5		T		.1	1.7	.3	.1		T							.1		T	T			T
	SN ON GND						T	1	T	2					2	1	1	1	1	1	T						T					T
	WTR EQUIV									.1					.1																	
PHILADELPHIA CITY	SNOWFALL	-	-	-	-	-	-	-	-	-	-	-	-	-	-	-	-	-	-	-	-	-	-	-	-	-	-	-	-	-	-	-
	SN ON GND	-	-	-	-	-	-	-	-	-	-	-	-	-	-	-	-	-	-	-	-	-	-	-	-	-	-	-	-	-	-	-

See reference notes following Station Index.

SNOWFALL AND SNOW ON GROUND

Station		1	2	3	4	5	6	7	8	9	10	11	12	13	14	15	16	17	18	19	20	21	22	23	24	25	26	27	28	29	30	31
PHILIPSBURG CAA AIRPORT	SNOWFALL	T	T	T		T	T	.8	.9	3.0	3.0	T	T	2.0	T	T	T	T	.3	T		T		T		T	T	.6	.4	T	T	T
	SN ON GND	4	4	4	4	4	4	5	5	7	8	10	8	9	10	10	10	10	10	10	9	8	4					1	1	1	1	1
PIMPLE HILL	SNOWFALL	.7	.1	.2	T	T	T	1.0	.8	.7	2.4	1.4		.8	.1	T	2.5	.7		.5		T			.1	T	1.8	1.4	T	.2	T	.1
	SN ON GND	3	3	3	3	2	2	3	4	4	6	7	7	7	7	7	9	9	9	9	9	9	4	T	T	T	2	3	2	2	2	2
PITTSBURGH WB AIRPORT 2	SNOWFALL	T	T	T	T	T	1.0	1.3	T	.4	.1	T		T	T	.8	1.1	T	2.3					T	T	1.4	T	T		.5	T	.4
	SN ON GND	1	T	T	T	T	T	2	3	2	T	T	T	T	T	T	2	2	2	3	1	T		T	T	T	1	1	T	T	T	T
	WTR EQUIV							.2	.3	.3								.2	T	T												
PLEASANT MOUNT 1 W	SNOWFALL	1.0	T	T		T		.5	.5	T	4.0	2.0		1.0	T	T	3.0	T		T					T		1.0	2.0		4.0	.5	T
	SN ON GND	7	6	6	6	5	5	5	5	5	8	9	9	10	8	8	10	9	9	9	9	8	5	T	T	T	1	3	2	6	6	6
READING WB CITY	SNOWFALL	T					1.4	.7		1.5	T	T		T	.3	1.6	T		T							.2		.7				T
	SN ON GND							2	1	1	1	T	T	T	T	T	1	1	1	1	T	T					T	1	T	T	T	T
SCRANTON WB AIRPORT	SNOWFALL	.4	.2	T	T	T	.9	.8	T	1.6	2.4	T		.5		.5	.3		T			T		T	T	1.3	.3	1.2	T	.2		.5
	SN ON GND	T	1	T	T	T	T	1	1	T	2	4	3	4	4	3	3	3	3	3	3	2	T		T	T	2	2	2	2	1	1
	WTR EQUIV										.2	.3	.3	.4	.3	.3	.3	.3	.3	.3	.2	.2					.1	.2	.2	.3		
SELINSGROVE CAA AIRPORT	SNOWFALL	T					1.3	1.8		1.8	2.5			T	T	.6	.2		.1							.4	T	1.0	T		T	T
	SN ON GND							2	1	2	3	3	3	3	3	3	4	4	4	4	4	2	T					1	T	T		T
SHIPPENSBURG	SNOWFALL							1.5		1.0	2.0			T	2.5	T	1.0	T	T							T		.5	T			.5
	SN ON GND							1	T	T	T	T	T	T	2	2	3	3	3	2	2	T										
SHIPPENSBURG WB	SNOWFALL	T	T				.5	1.3	T	T	T	T	T	T	T	T	T	T	.7					T		.6		T	T	T	T	T
	SN ON GND	T	T	T	T	T	T	2	1	T	T	T	T	T	T	T	T	T	1	T	T	T		T	T	1	T	T	T	T	T	T
SLIPPERY ROCK	SNOWFALL	1.0	.1					1.0	1.0	1.0	1.0	1.0		3.0	T		T	T	T	T							5.0	T		T	2.0	
	SN ON GND	3	3	3	2	2	2	3	4	5	5	5	4	6	6	6	6	6	6	6	5	3					T	T	T	T	2	1
SPRING 1 SW	SNOWFALL	T	.1	T			T	2.5	T	2.0		T		.2	1.0	1.8	.1	T	.4					T	T	T	T	1.0		T		.3
	SN ON GND	4	4	4	3	3	3	6	6	8	5	5	5	5	8	8	8	8	8	8	7	5	2	T	T	T	T	1	T	T	T	T
TAMARACK 2 S FIRE TWR	SNOWFALL	1.0	T	.3	T		T	.5	.8	1.0	5.0	2.0		.4	T		.8	T		.5	T				T		.3	T		.5	.2	T
	SN ON GND	6	6	6	6	6	6	6	7	8	10	12	12	12	12	12	12	12	12	12	12	11	9	T	T	T	T	T	T	1	1	1
TIONESTA 2 SE DAM	SNOWFALL	1.0	1.5	T			T	1.0	1.5	3.0	2.5	.5		2.0	T	T	.3	T	.1	.5	T						T			.8	.3	
	SN ON GND	3	5	5	4	4	3	4	5	6	8	8	7	9	9	9	9	9	9	10	10	7	2	T	T	T	T		T		1	
TOWANDA	SNOWFALL	.1	.1	T	T	T	T	.6	.1	T	4.3	1.6		.3	T	T	.3	T							.3	T	.2	T	T	3.5		
	SN ON GND	1	1	1	1	1	1	1	1	1	5	6	6	5	5	5	5	5	5	4	4	4	1		T	T	T	T	T	4	3	2
TOWER CITY 5 SW	SNOWFALL	T						3.0	T	2.0	3.0				.5	.5	2.0		T							.5		1.0				1.0
	SN ON GND	-	-	-	-	-	-	-	-	-	-	-	-	-	-	-	-	-	-	-	-	-	-	-	-	-	-	-	-	-	-	-
WILLIAMSPORT WB AIRPORT	SNOWFALL	T					.9	.6	T	2.0	3.2			.5		.9	.1		T							.2	T	.4	.3	.2	T	T
	SN ON GND	T						1	2	1	4	4	4	4	4	4	5	5	5	5	4	3	T			T	T	T		T	T	T
	WTR EQUIV										.5	.3	.3	.3	.3	.3	.3	.3	.3	.3	.3	.4										

See reference notes following Station Index.

TOTAL PRECIPITATION

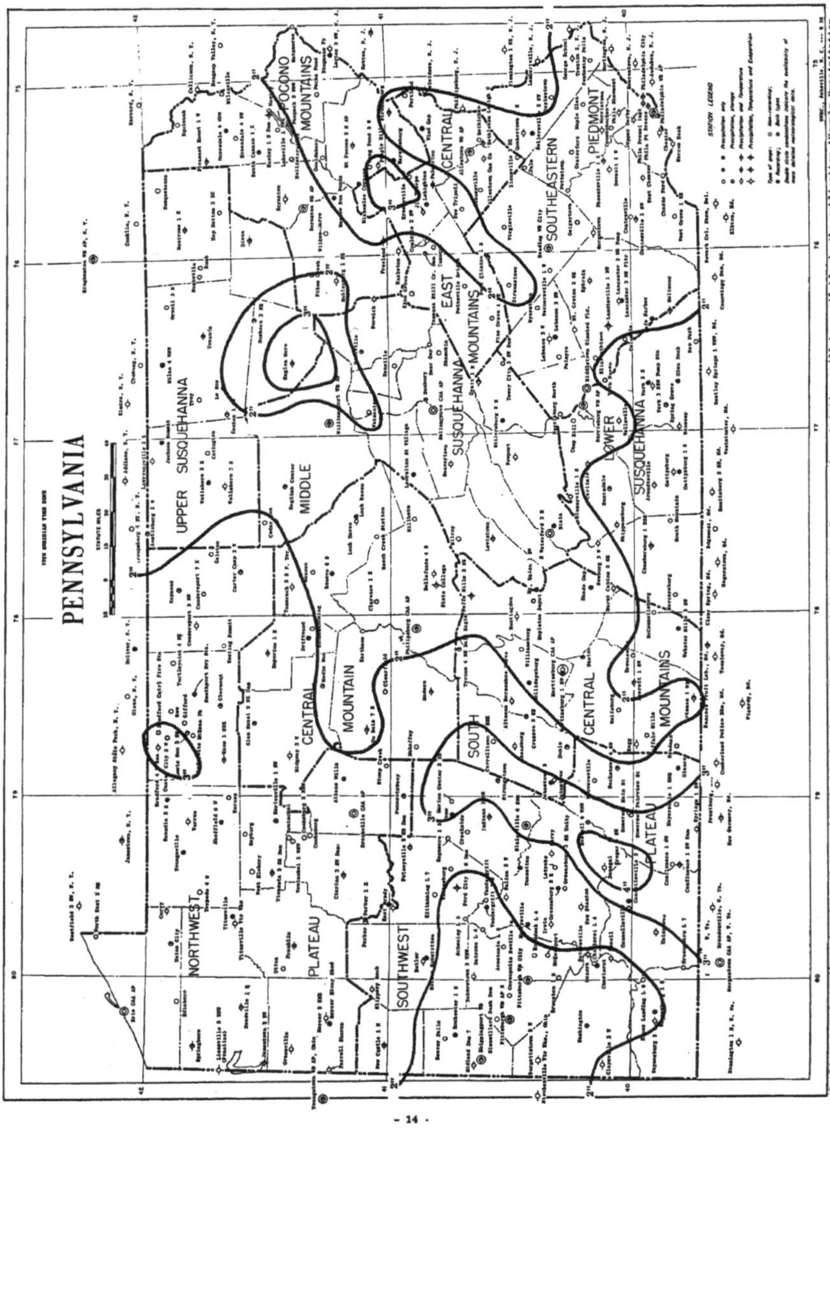

Isolines are drawn through points of approximately equal values. Hourly precipitation data from recorder substations will be available in the publication 'Hourly Precipitation Data'.

AVERAGE TEMPERATURE

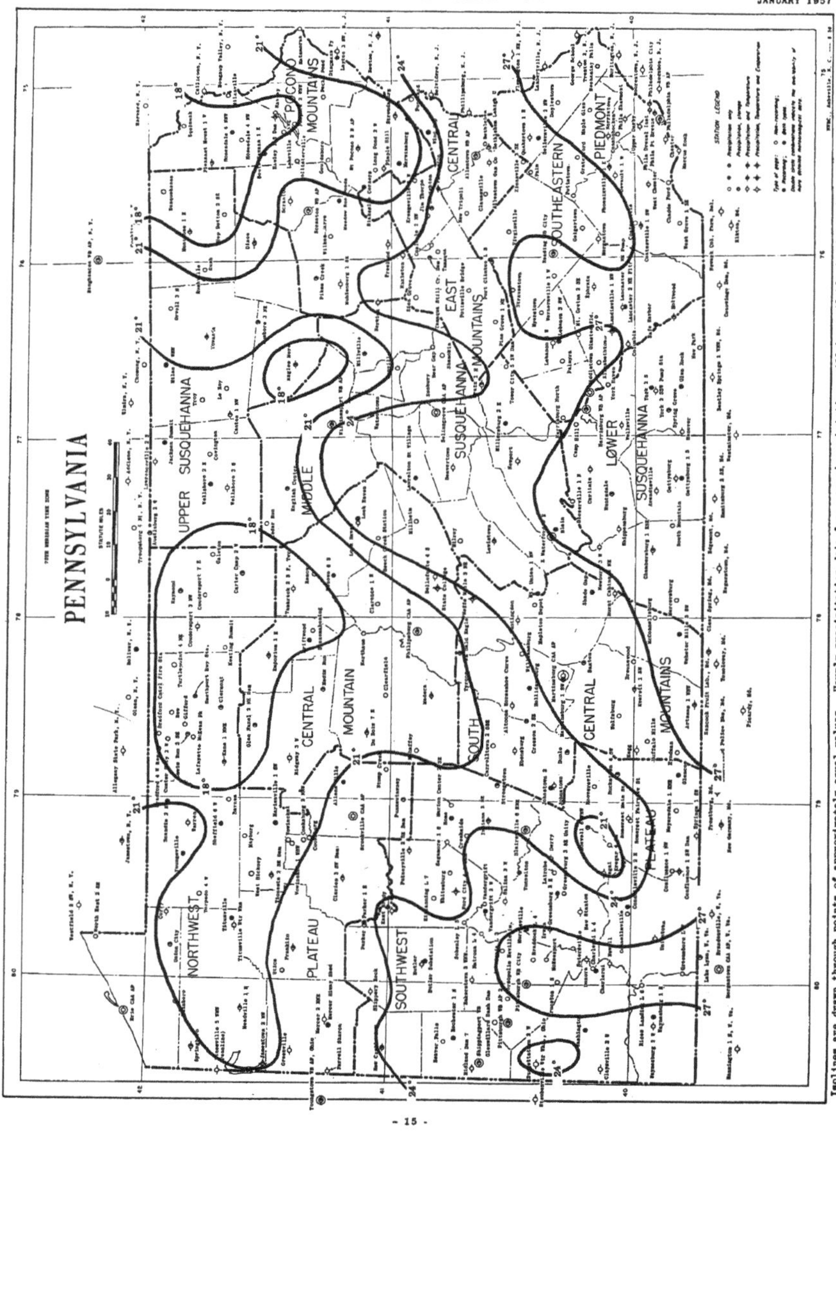

Isolines are drawn through points of approximately equal values. Hourly precipitation data from recorder substations will be available in the publication 'Hourly Precipitation Data'.

STATION INDEX

Station	Index No.	County	Drainage 1	Latitude	Longitude	Elevation	Observation Time: Temp.	Observation Time: Precip.	Observer	Refer To Tables
ACHETONIA LOCK 3	0022	ALLEGHENY	1	40 32	79 49	748		7A	CORPS OF ENGINEERS	3
ALLENS MILLS	0099	JEFFERSON	1	41 12	78 55	1600		MID	CHARLES H. ALLEN	C
ALLENTOWN WB AP	0106	LEHIGH	9	40 39	75 26	376	MID	MID	U.S. WEATHER BUREAU	2 3 5 7 C
ALLENTOWN GAS CO	0111	LEHIGH	9	40 36	75 28	294	7A	7A	LEHIGH VLY GAS DIV	2 3 5
ALTOONA HORSESHOE CURVE	0134	BLAIR	6	40 30	78 29	1500	6P	6P	ALTOONA WATER BUR.	2 3 5
ARENDTSVILLE	0229	ADAMS	15	39 55	77 18	710	8A	8A	PA STATE COL EXP	2 3 5
ARTEMAS 1 WNW	0259	BEDFORD	12	39 45	78 28	1250	6P	6P	GRAYSON E.NORTHCRAFT	2 3 5 C
AUSTINBURG 2 W	0313	TIOGA	15	42 00	77 32	1590		7A	OTTO D. BACON	3 7 C
BAKERSTOWN 3 WNW	0355	ALLEGHENY	1	40 39	79 59	1230	7P	7P	PGH CUT FLOWER CO	2 3 5
BARNES	0409	WARREN	1	41 40	79 02	1310		7A	CORPS OF ENGINEERS	3
BARTO 4 NW	0428	BERKS	14	40 26	75 39	312		7A	MARIE B. NICHLAS	3
BEAR GAP	0457	NORTHUMBLAND	15	40 50	76 30	900		MID	ROARING CRK WTR CO	3
BEAVER FALLS	0475	BEAVER	2	40 46	80 19	760		7A	HOWARD R. KEMP	3
BEAVERTOWN	0482	SNYDER	15	40 45	77 10	640	7A	7A	MARLIN RC ETTINGER	2 3 5
BEECH CREEK STATION	0499	CENTRE	16	41 04	77 34	620		7A	HAROLD S. RUPERT	3 7
BELLEFONTE 4 S	0590	CENTRE	16	40 51	77 47	1110	8A	8A	ROCKVIEW PRISON FARM	2 3 5
BERNE	0599	BERKS	14	40 31	76 00	325		7A	FLOYD W. TRUMP	3
BERWICK	0611	COLUMBIA	15	41 04	76 15	570	6P	6P	AMER CAR + FNDRY CO	2 3 5
BETHLEHEM	0629	NORTHAMPTON	9	40 37	75 22	400		7A	ARTHUR CROPPER	3
#BETHLEHEM LEHIGH UNIV	0634	NORTHAMPTON	9	40 36	75 23	450	MID	MID	LEHIGH UNIVERSITY	2 3 5 C
BLAIN	0725	PERRY	15	40 20	77 31	750		MID	PA DEPT FRST + WTRS	C
BLAIRSVILLE 6 ENE	0736	INDIANA	4	40 27	79 09	2048	8P	8P	U.S. WEATHER BUREAU	2 3 5
BLAKESLEE CORNERS	0743	MONROE	9	41 06	75 36	1650		MID	WALTER WILDRICK	C
BLOSERVILLE 1 N	0763	CUMBERLAND	15	40 16	77 22	650		5P	MRS. B. M. WILLDERS	3
BOSWELL 6 WNW	0820	SOMERSET	1	40 11	79 08	2580		7A	MRS. MAE L. KIMMEL	3 C
BRADDOCK LOCK 2	0861	ALLEGHENY	10	40 24	79 52	725		7A	CORPS OF ENGINEERS	3
BRADFORD CNTRL FIRE STA	0867	MC KEAN	1	41 57	78 39	1500		8A	BRADFORD FIRE DEPT	3
BRADFORD 4 W RES	0868	MC KEAN	1	41 57	78 44	1680	5P	5P	BRADFORD WTR DEPT	2 3 5 7
BREEZEWOOD	0905	BEDFORD	6	40 00	78 14	1352		MID	PA TURNPIKE COMM	3
BROOKVILLE CAA AIRPORT	1002	JEFFERSON	1	41 09	79 06	1417	MID	MID	CIVIL AERO. ADM.	2 3 5 7
BRUCETON 1 S	1033	ALLEGHENY	10	40 18	79 59	1065		7A	AUSTIN R. COOPER	3
BUCKSTOWN 1 SE	1073	SOMERSET	4	40 04	78 50	2460		MID	ALVIN W. HANGES	C
BUFFALO MILLS	1087	BEDFORD	6	39 57	78 39	1318		7A	MRS. NELLE R. BROWN	3
BURGETTSTOWN 2 W	1105	WASHINGTON	11	40 23	80 26	980	7A	7A	SMITH TWP MUN AUTH	2 3 5
BURNT CABINS 2 NE	1115	HUNTINGDON	6	40 05	77 52	990	MID	MID	PA TURNPIKE COMM	2 3 5
#BUTLER	1130	BUTLER	2	40 52	79 54	1100	4P	7A	WILLIAM C. FAUST	2 3 5
BUTLER SUBSTATION	1135	BUTLER	2	40 51	79 53	1140		MID	WEST PENN POWER CO	C
CAMP HILL	1198	CUMBERLAND	15	40 15	76 55	461		6P	JOSEPH N. HOBART	3
CANTON 1 NW	1215	BRADFORD	15	41 40	76 52	1520	7A	7A	MRS.MILDRED SPENCER	2 3 5 7 C
CARLISLE	1234	CUMBERLAND	15	40 12	77 11	460	6P	6P	C. E. MILLER	2 3 5
CARROLLTOWN 2 SSE	1255	CAMBRIA	16	40 35	78 42	2040		8A	ROBERT F. MAURER	3 7
CARTER CAMP 2 W	1262	POTTER	16	41 37	77 45	2030		7A	RICHARD L. MENKEN	3 C
CEDAR RUN	1301	LYCOMING	16	41 31	77 27	800		7A	KATHRYN T.KREIGHBAUM	3
CHADDS FORD	1342	DELAWARE	5	39 52	75 36	160		8A	MRS.GRACE A. WICKS	3
CHAMBERSBURG 1 ESE	1354	FRANKLIN	12	39 56	77 38	640	9P	9P	CHARLES A. BENDER	2 3 5 C
CHARLEROI	1372	WASHINGTON	10	40 08	79 55	1040		MID	WEST PENN POWER CO	C
CHARLEROI LOCK 4	1377	WESTMORELAND	10	40 09	79 54	749		7A	CORPS OF ENGINEERS	3
#CHESTER	1423	DELAWARE	5	39 51	75 22	86	8A	8A	CHESTER TIMES	2 3 5
CLARENCE	1480	CENTRE	16	41 03	77 56	1410		7A	MISS VELDA SWANCER	3
CLARION 3 SW	1485	CLARION	1	41 12	79 26	1114	6P	7A	PA ELECTRIC CO	2 3 5 C
CLAUSSVILLE	1505	LEHIGH	9	40 37	75 39	670		8A	WILLIAM J. DOTTERER	3
CLAYSVILLE 3 W	1512	WASHINGTON	11	40 07	80 28	1000	7P	7A	MFGRS. L + H CO	2 3 5
CLEARFIELD	1519	CLEARFIELD	16	41 01	78 26	1100		7A	IRA TAYLOR	3
CLERMONT	1529	MC KEAN	1	41 41	78 30	2104		7A	MRS.TILLIE M.SIMONDS	3 C
COALDALE 2 NW	1572	SCHUYLKILL	9	40 50	75 56	1026		7A	PANTHER VLY WTR CO	3 7
COATESVILLE 1 SW	1589	CHESTER	5	39 58	75 50	342	8A	8A	PHILA ELECTRIC CO	2 3 5 C
COATESVILLE	1594	CHESTER	5	39 59	75 49	340		8A	EDWARD D. BIEDEMAN	INAC 12/55
COLUMBIA	1675	LANCASTER	15	40 02	76 30	300	SS	SS	JAMES H. RUST	2 3 5
CONFLUENCE 1 SW DAM	1705	SOMERSET	17	39 48	79 22	1490	8A	8A	CORPS OF ENGINEERS	2 3 5 6 C
CONFLUENCE 1 NW	1710	FAYETTE	17	39 50	79 22	1331		7A	JOHN L. REID	3
CONNELLSVILLE	1723	FAYETTE	17	40 01	79 36	870		8A	MARSHALL B. MENEFEE	3
CONNELLSVILLE 2 E	1729	FAYETTE	17	40 01	79 33	1300		MID	HARRY C. JOY	C
CONSHOHOCKEN	1737	MONTGOMERY	5	40 04	75 19	70		8A	PHILA ELECTRIC CO	3
COOKSBURG	1749	CLARION	1	41 20	79 13	1180		8A	PA DEPT FRST + WTRS	3
COOKSBURG 2 NNW	1752	CLARION	1	41 21	79 13	1460		8A	PA DEPT FRST + WTRS	3
CORAOPOLIS NEVILLE IS	1773	ALLEGHENY	11	40 30	80 05	720		8A	PGH. COKE + CHEM CO	3
CORRY	1790	ERIE	1	41 56	79 38	1427	7P	5A	LEO C. HECKERS	2 3 5 7
COUDERSPORT 3 NW	1806	POTTER	1	41 49	78 03	2020	7P	8A	MISS ELIZABETH NEFF	2 3 5
COUDERSPORT 7 E	1809	POTTER	1	41 46	77 53	2425		7A	CAMP POTATO	3
COVINGTON 2 WSW	1833	TIOGA	15	41 44	77 07	1745		7A	CALVIN R. PACKARD	3
CREEKSIDE	1881	INDIANA	1	40 41	79 12	1035		7A	CORPS OF ENGINEERS	3
CRESSON 2 SE	1895	CAMBRIA	6	40 27	78 34	2540		7A	TALMAGE R. FRAZER	3 C
CUSTER CITY 2 W	1978	MC KEAN	1	41 55	78 41	2120		8A	M. D. BOOTH AND CO	3
DANVILLE	2013	MONTOUR	15	40 58	76 37	460		7A	MRS.MARIE M. LITTLE	3
DERRY	2108	WESTMORELAND	4	40 20	79 18	1160	6P	6P	MISS M. D. WINEMAN	2 3 5
DEVAULT 1 W	2116	CHESTER	14	40 05	75 33	360	MID	MID	PA TURNPIKE COMM	2 3 5
DINGMANS FERRY	2160	PIKE	5	41 13	74 52	364		MID	CLYDE T. VOORHEES	C
DIXON	2171	WYOMING	15	41 34	75 54	620	7A	7A	HAROLD J. KUSCHEL	2 3 5 C
DONEGAL	2183	WESTMORELAND	17	40 07	79 23	1746	MID	MID	PA TURNPIKE COMM	2 3 5 7
#DONORA	2190	WASHINGTON	10	40 11	79 51	814	12M	12M	DONORA ZINC WORKS	2 3 5
DOYLESTOWN	2221	BUCKS	5	40 18	75 08	393		5P	GEORGE HART	3
DRIFTWOOD	2245	CAMERON	16	41 20	78 08	880		MID	SIDNEY KENNEDY	C
DU BOIS 7 E	2265	CLEARFIELD	16	41 06	78 38	1670	5P	5P	CITY OF DU BOIS	2 3 5 7 C
DUNLO	2290	CAMBRIA	4	40 17	78 43	2410		MID	MRS. D. L. WHITE	C
DUSHORE 3 NE	2324	SULLIVAN	16	41 33	76 21	1750		7A	PATRICK F. RYAN	3 C
EAGLES MERE	2343	SULLIVAN	16	41 24	76 35	2020	7A	7A	MRS.ELSIE P. BIGGER	2 3 5 C
EAST BRADY	2363	CLARION	1	40 59	79 37	820	5P	5P	A. B. KEMPEL	2 3 5
EAST WATERFORD 3 E	2459	PERRY	6	40 21	77 33	2125	8A	8A	U.S. WEATHER BUREAU	INAC 5/55
EBENSBURG	2466	CAMBRIA	4	40 29	78 43	2090	7P	7A	ROBERT A. WASSER	2 3 5
EDINBORO	2514	ERIE	1	41 52	80 08	1220		8A	EDINBORO ST TCHR COL	3
ELIZABETHTOWN	2560	LANCASTER	15	40 09	76 37	460		8A	MASONIC HOME	3
EMPORIUM 2 SSW	2634	CAMERON	16	41 28	78 15	1735	7A	7A	JACKSON THOMAS	2 3 5 C
ENGLISH CENTER	2644	LYCOMING	16	41 26	77 17	881		7A	WILLIAM SUDERS	3 7 C
EPHRATA	2662	LANCASTER	15	40 11	76 10	465	6P	6P	STANLEY L.VON NEIDA	2 3 5
EQUINUNK	2669	WAYNE	5	41 51	75 13	900		8A	MRS.ROSE M. NEILSEN	3
ERIE CAA AIRPORT	2682	ERIE	8	42 05	80 12	732	MID	MID	CIVIL AERO. ADM.	2 3 5 7
EVERETT 1 SW	2721	BEDFORD	6	40 00	78 23	1020	MID	MID	PA TURNPIKE COMM	2 3 5 7 C
FARRELL SHARON	2814	MERCER	2	41 14	80 30	865	7P	7P	SHARON STEEL CORP	2 3 5
FORD CITY 4 S DAM	2942	ARMSTRONG	1	40 43	79 30	950	8A	8A	CORPS OF ENGINEERS	2 3 5 6 7 C
FRANKLIN	3028	VENANGO	1	41 23	79 49	987	7P	7A	GEORGE S. SMITH, JR	2 3 5 C
FREELAND	3056	LUZERNE	15	41 01	75 54	1900	6P	8A	ANDREW B. EVANSHA	2 3 5
GALETON	3130	POTTER	16	41 44	77 39	1325		7A	W. GALE LUSH	3 7
GEIGERTOWN	3189	BERKS	14	40 13	75 50	400		8A	WALTER C. WOLF	3
GEORGE SCHOOL	3200	BUCKS	5	40 13	74 56	135	7P	7P	GEORGE M. HART	2 3 5 7
#GETTYSBURG	3218	ADAMS	12	39 50	77 14	540	9A	9A	HUGH C. MC ILHENNY	2 3 5
GETTYSBURG 1 S	3223	ADAMS	12	39 48	77 14	560		MID	NAT MILITARY PARK	C
GIFFORD	3237	MC KEAN	1	41 51	78 36	2220		8A	SOUTH PENN OIL CO	3
GLENCOE	3298	SOMERSET	12	39 49	78 51	1620		MID	MRS. MARY M.HARTMAN	C
GLEN HAZEL 2 NE DAM	3311	ELK	1	41 34	78 36	1725		8A	CORPS OF ENGINEERS	3 C
GLEN ROCK	3330	YORK	15	39 48	76 44	620		MID	MRS.E.C.MC WILLIAMS	C
GLENWILLARD DASH DAM	3343	ALLEGHENY	11	40 33	80 13	705		7A	CORPS OF ENGINEERS	3
GOULDSBORO	3394	WAYNE	9	41 15	75 27	1890		7A	L. H. EILENBERGER	3
GRATERFORD	3435	MONTGOMERY	14	40 14	75 27	160	7A	7A	CLAUDE K. KULP	2 3 5 7 C
GRATZ 1 N	3438	DAUPHIN	15	40 38	76 43	760	8A	8A	LEE M. LEITZEL	2 3 5 C
GREENSBORO LOCK 7	3503	GREENE	10	39 47	79 55	808		7A	CORPS OF ENGINEERS	3 7
GREENSBURG 2 E	3515	WESTMORELAND	10	40 18	79 31	1225		MID	PA DEPT HIGHWAYS	C
GREENSBURG 3 SE UNITY	3516	WESTMORELAND	10	40 17	79 30	1245		6P	WESTMORELAND WTR CO	3
GREENVILLE	3526	MERCER	2	41 24	80 23	1026	6P	6P	C. EARL MILLER	2 3 5
HANOVER	3662	YORK	15	39 48	76 59	600	8A	8A	HANOVER EVENING SUN	2 3 5 7
#HARRISBURG WB AP	3699	YORK	15	40 13	76 51	335	MID	MID	U.S. WEATHER BUREAU	2 3 5 7 C
HARRISBURG NORTH	3704	DAUPHIN	15	40 18	76 54	323		9A	GEORGE S. BEAL	3
HAWLEY	3758	WAYNE	5	41 29	75 10	880		7A	MRS.KATHERINE S.BATE	3 5
HAWLEY 1 S DAM	3761	WAYNE	5	41 28	75 11	1200	7A	7A	PA POWER + LIGHT CO	2 3 5 6 7 C
HOLLIDAYSBURG	4001	BLAIR	6	40 26	78 24	960		MID	JOHN M. RINGLER	C
HOLLISTERVILLE	4008	WAYNE	5	41 23	75 26	1360		8A	PA POWER + LIGHT CO	3
#HOLTWOOD	4019	LANCASTER	15	39 50	76 20	187	MID	8A	PA POWER + LIGHT CO	2 3 5 7 C
HOME	4027	INDIANA	1	40 45	79 06	1220		MID	MRS. EDNA M. BUSH	C
HONESDALE 4 NW	4043	WAYNE	5	41 37	75 19	1410		9A	GEORGE C. WILLIAMS	3
HONESDALE 6 NNW	4044	WAYNE	5	41 39	75 17	1050		MID	FRIEND E. WALTER	C
HOOVERSVILLE	4058	SOMERSET	4	40 09	78 55	1660		7A	PA ELECTRIC CO	3 7
HOP BOTTOM 2 SE	4066	SUSQUEHANNA	15	41 43	75 43	900		7A	JOSEPH J. SANSUSKAS	3
HUNTINGDON	4159	HUNTINGDON	6	40 29	78 01	610	7A	7A	MRS JANET I. VAUGHN	2 3 5
HUNTSDALE	4166	CUMBERLAND	15	40 06	77 18	610		8A	METRO P. DOROSH	3 C
HYNDMAN	4190	BEDFORD	12	39 49	78 43	920		8A	MRS.GERTRUDE M.BURTO	3
INDIANA 3 SE	4214	INDIANA	4	40 36	79 07	1102	7P	7A	CLYMER WATER SVC CO	2 3 5 7 C
IRWIN	4276	WESTMORELAND	10	40 20	79 42	1100	5P	5P	WESTMORELAND WTR CO	2 3 5
JACKSON SUMMIT	4304	TIOGA	15	41 57	77 01	1690		MID	ARCHIE LAIN	C
JAMESTOWN 2 NW	4325	CRAWFORD	2	41 30	80 28	1050	8A	8A	PA DEPT FRST + WTRS	2 3 5 6 C
JIM THORPE	4370	CARBON	9	40 52	75 45	830	5P	5P	HENRY S. HAAK	2 3 5
#JOHNSTOWN	4385	CAMBRIA	4	40 20	78 55	1214	9A	9A	JOHNSTOWN TRIBUNE	2 3 5
JOHNSTOWN 2	4390	CAMBRIA	4	40 19	78 55	1275		MID	CITY OF JOHNSTOWN	C
KANE 1 NNE	4432	MC KEAN	1	41 41	78 48	1750	8A	8A	SPRING WATER CO	2 3 5 7 C
KARTHAUS	4450	CLEARFIELD	16	41 07	78 07	950		7A	JEROME S. HOWE	3
KEATING SUMMIT	4466	POTTER	16	41 41	78 11	1840		7A	EUGENE L. KREITNER	3 7
KEGG	4481	BEDFORD	6	39 59	78 43	1280	MID	MID	PA TURNPIKE COMM	2 3 5
KITTANNING LOCK 7	4611	ARMSTRONG	1	40 49	79 32	790		VAR	CORPS OF ENGINEERS	3
KREGAR 4 SE	4667	WESTMORELAND	17	40 06	79 14	2530		MID	PA TURNPIKE COMM	3
KRESGEVILLE 3 W	4672	CARBON	9	40 54	75 34	720		9A	CITY OF BETHLEHEM	3
LAFAYETTE MC KEAN PARK	4706	MC KEAN	1	41 48	78 40	2130		7A	ORIN A. BUTTERS	3
LAKEVILLE 1 NNE	4733	WAYNE	5	41 27	75 16	1440		8A	MRS. GLADYS REINEKE	3
LANCASTER 2 NE PUMP STA	4758	LANCASTER	15	40 03	76 17	255	6P	6P	LANCASTER WATER BUR	2 3 5 7
LANCASTER 2 NE FILT PL	4763	LANCASTER	15	40 03	76 17	270		MID	LANCASTER WATER BUR	C
LANDISVILLE 2 NW	4778	LANCASTER	15	40 07	76 26	380	8A	8A	PA STATE COLLEGE	2 3 5 6 C
LATROBE	4832	WESTMORELAND	4	40 19	79 23	1000		MID	WEST PENN POWER CO	INAC 6/56
LAURELTON STATE VILLAGE	4853	UNION	15	40 54	77 13	880		MID	PA DEPT OF WELFARE	C
LAWRENCEVILLE 2 S	4873	TIOGA	15	41 59	77 07	1000	7A	7A	HARRY P. HOWLAND	2 3 5 7
LEBANON 3 W	4891	LEBANON	15	40 20	76 29	460	7A	7A	LEON MILLER	2 3 5 7
LEBANON 3 SW	4896	LEBANON	15	40 19	76 28	490		MID	THOMAS DONNACHIE	C
LEHIGHTON	4934	CARBON	9	40 50	75 43	580		7A	GOODWIN S. DEFREHN	3 C
LE ROY	4972	BRADFORD	15	41 41	76 43	1040		6P	MRS.DIMMIS M.BAILEY	3
LEWIS RUN 3 SE	4984	MC KEAN	1	41 50	78 39	1740		7A	RUSSELL LINEMAN	3 C
LEWISTOWN	4992	MIFFLIN	6	40 35	77 35	460	7A	7A	AMERICAN VISCOSE CO	2 3 5 7 C
LINESVILLE 5 WNW	5050	CRAWFORD	2	41 41	80 31	1020	7P	8A	MISS RETTA M. CRUMB	2 3 5
LOCK HAVEN	5104	CLINTON	16	41 08	77 27	570	7P	7A	PETER L. STEVENSON	2 3 5
LOCK HAVEN 2	5109	CLINTON	16	41 08	77 27	630		MID	HUGH F. PARKER	C
LONG POND 2 W	5160	MONROE	9	41 03	75 30	1860		7A	THOMAS MECKES	3
LYNDELL 2 NW	5279	CHESTER	5	40 05	75 46	-		8A	MRS. DOROTHY MARPLE	3
MADERA	5336	CLEARFIELD	16	40 50	78 26	1460	7A	7A	MRS. JULIA J. SHOFF	2 3 5 C
MAHAFFEY	5342	CLEARFIELD	16	40 53	78 44	1280		7A	MISS ELLEN J. MILES	3
MAPLE GLEN	5368	MONTGOMERY	5	40 11	75 11	380		6P	FRANCES E.SCHEIBNER	3
MAPLETON DEPOT	5381	HUNTINGDON	6	40 24	77 56	580		7A	MRS. I. S. BUCHANAN	3
MARCUS HOOK	5390	DELAWARE	5	39 49	75 25	12	MID	MID	SUN OIL CO	2 3 5
MARIENVILLE 1 SW	5400	FOREST	1	41 27	79 09	1700		MID	ROY A. MARKER	C
MARION CENTER 2 SE	5408	INDIANA	1	40 45	79 02	1610		7A	CORPS OF ENGINEERS	3
MARTINSBURG 1 SW	5453	BLAIR	6	40 18	78 20	1360		MID	BLUE MT. CANNERIES	C
MARTINSBURG CAA AP	5454	BLAIR	6	40 18	78 19	1463	MID	MID	CIVIL AERO. ADM.	2 3 5 7
MATAMORAS	5470	PIKE	5	41 22	74 42	430		7A	HARRY BISLAND	3 7
MAYBURG	5490	FOREST	1	41 36	79 13	1150		7A	CORPS OF ENGINEERS	3
MC CONNELLSBURG	5526	FULTON	12	39 56	78 00	895		7A	MRS. HELEN M. SHIVES	3
MC KEESPORT	5573	ALLEGHENY	10	40 21	79 52	720		8A	NATIONAL TUBE CO	3
MEADOW RUN PONDS	5601	LUZERNE	15	41 13	75 40	1995		MID	GEORGE PEARAGE	C
MEADVILLE 1 S	5606	CRAWFORD	1	41 38	80 10	1065	8A	8A	CITY OF MEADVILLE	2 3 5 7 C
MEDIX RUN	5627	ELK	16	41 17	78 24	1100		7A	MRS.E. M. SNYDER	3 7 C
MERCER 2 NNE	5651	MERCER	2	41 15	80 13	1160	7P	7A	WILLIAM K. STRUTHERS	2 3 5
MERCER HIWAY SHED	5654	MERCER	2	41 14	80 15	1250		MID	PA DEPT HIGHWAYS	C
MERCERSBURG	5662	FRANKLIN	12	39 50	77 54	605		8A	ROLLIN P. GILBERT	3
MERWINSBURG	5676	MONROE	9	40 58	75 28	970		MID	WILLIAM D. GOULD	C
MEYERSDALE 1 ENE	5685	SOMERSET	17	39 49	79 01	2290		8A	ARTHUR B. MC CARTER	3
MIDDLETOWN OLMSTED FLD	5703	DAUPHIN	15	40 11	76 46	303	MID	MID	U. S. AIR FORCE	2 3 5
MIDLAND DAM 7	5710	BEAVER	11	40 38	80 28	689	11P	7A	CORPS OF ENGINEERS	2 3 5
MILAN 4 WNW	5732	BRADFORD	15	41 56	76 35	1448		MID	CARL A. MORRIS	C
MILANVILLE	5738	WAYNE	5	41 40	75 04	760		8A	CHARLES W. DAVIS	3
MILLERSBURG 2 E	5775	DAUPHIN	15	40 32	76 56	560		MID	RUSSELL SHEPLEY	C
MILLHEIM	5790	CENTRE	15	40 54	77 29	1090		7A	NEVIN E. BOWERSOX	3
MILLVILLE 2 SW	5817	COLUMBIA	15	41 06	76 34	860		7A	KENNETH LEIGHOW	3 C
MILROY	5825	MIFFLIN	6	40 43	77 35	770		8A	THOMAS C. HARBESON	3
MONTROSE 1 E	5915	SUSQUEHANNA	15	41 50	75 51	1630	7A	7A	WILBER W. HOOPES,JR	2 3 5 7 C
MORGANTOWN	5956	BERKS	15	40 09	75 54	595	MID	MID	PA TURNPIKE COMM	2 3 5
MT GRETNA 2 SE	6028	LANCASTER	15	40 14	76 26	670	MID	MID	PA TURNPIKE COMM	2 3 5
MT POCONO 2 N AP	6055	MONROE	5	41 09	75 22	1915	5P	5P	H. JOHN DAVIS, JR.	2 3 5 C
MOUNT UNION 1 N	6067	MIFFLIN	6	40 24	77 53	820		MID	MT UNION WTR WORKS	C
MUHLENBURG 1 SE	6090	LUZERNE	15	41 13	76 08	1110	6P	6P	THEODORE J. SAMPSON	2 3 5 7 C
MURRYSVILLE	6111	WESTMORELAND	10	40 26	79 42	903		MID	DAVID C. SHAW	C
MYERSTOWN	6126	LEBANON	14	40 22	76 18	480		8A	MRS.KATHLEEN MANDELL	3
NATRONA LOCK 4	6151	ALLEGHENY	1	40 37	79 43	800		7A	CORPS OF ENGINEERS	3
NEFFS MILLS 3 NE	6174	HUNTINGDON	6	40 40	77 55	900		MID	PA STATE UNIVERSITY	C
NESHAMINY FALLS	6194	BUCKS	5	40 09	74 57	60		MID	PHILA SUB WATER CO	3
NEWBURG 3 W	6225	FRANKLIN	15	40 09	77 37	745	MID	MID	PA TURNPIKE COMM	2 3 5
NEW CASTLE 1 N	6233	LAWRENCE	2	41 01	80 22	825	5P	7A	BAXTER F. JOHNSON	2 3 5 C
NEWELL	6240	FAYETTE	10	40 05	79 54	805	12M	12M	GENERAL CHEMICAL CO	2 3 5
NEW PARK	6289	YORK	15	39 44	76 30	780		8P	CLINTON J. ALLEN	3
NEWPORT	6297	PERRY	6	40 29	77 08	400	7A	7A	MRS. FRANCES K. FRY	2 3 5 7
NEW STANTON	6310	WESTMORELAND	10	40 13	79 36	980	MID	MID	PA TURNPIKE COMM	2 3 5
NEW TRIPOLI	6326	LEHIGH	14	40 41	75 45	570		6P	FRED C. OSWALD	3
NORRISTOWN	6370	MONTGOMERY	14	40 07	75 21	75	MID	8A	GEORGE H. BOONE	2 3 5
NORTH EAST 2 SE	6396	ERIE	8	42 12	79 48	1060		8A	ELLSWORTH WEAVER	3
ORWELL 3 N	6621	BRADFORD	15	41 55	76 16	1620		8A	WILLIAM I. BROWN	3
PALM	6681	MONTGOMERY	14	40 26	75 32	385		8A	FRED C. ESCHBACH	3
#PALMERTON	6689	CARBON	9	40 48	75 37	435	MID	MID	NEW JERSEY ZINC CO	2 3 5 C
PALMYRA	6694	LEBANON	15	40 18	76 35	480		7P	EARL E. RHOADS	3
PARKER	6721	ARMSTRONG	1	41 05	79 41	1140		7A	LOUIS A. MALARKEY	3
PARKER 1 E	6724	CLARION	1	41 06	79 40	1100		MID	P. M. NEELY	C
PAUPACK 2 WNW	6762	PIKE	5	41 24	75 14	1360		8A	MISS L. VETTERLEIN	3
PECKS POND	6786	PIKE	5	41 17	75 06	1380		9A	MRS. CARRIE NESS	3
#PHIL DREXEL INST OF TEC	6879	PHILADELPHIA	14	39 57	75 11	30	MID	MID	FRANCIS K. DAVIS,JR	2 3 5
PHILADELPHIA WB AP	6889	PHILADELPHIA	5	39 53	75 14	13	MID	MID	U.S. WEATHER BUREAU	2 3 5 7 C
#PHILADELPHIA PT BREEZE	6899	PHILADELPHIA	5	39 55	75 12	32	MID	MID	ATLANTIC REFINING	2 3 5 C
PHILADELPHIA SHAWMONT	6904	PHILADELPHIA	5	40 02	75 15	70	7P	7P	SCHUYLKILL NAVIG CO	2 3 5
#PHILADELPHIA CITY	6909	PHILADELPHIA	5	39 57	75 09	26	9A	9A	USN HYDROGRAPHIC OFF	2 3 5 C
PHILIPSBURG CAA AP	6916	CENTRE	6	40 54	78 05	1918	8P	8P	CIVIL AERO. ADM.	2 3 5 7 C
PHOENIXVILLE 1 E	6927	CHESTER	14	40 07	75 30	105	6P	MID	PHILA SUB WATER CO	2 3 5 C
PIKES CREEK	6939	LUZERNE	15	41 18	76 08	1320		MID	HARRY SHELDON	3 C
PIMPLE HILL	6944	MONROE	9	41 02	75 30	2215	9A	9A	PA DEPT FRST + WTRS	2 3 5 6 7
PINE GROVE 1 NE	6954	SCHUYLKILL	15	40 34	76 22	535		8A	PA POWER + LIGHT CO	3
PITTSBURGH WB AP 2	6993	ALLEGHENY	11	40 30	80 13	1151	MID	MID	U.S. WEATHER BUREAU	2 3 5 7 C
#PITTSBURGH WB CITY	6997	ALLEGHENY	11	40 27	80 00	749	MID	MID	U.S. WEATHER BUREAU	2 3 5 C
PLEASANT MOUNT 1 W	7029	WAYNE	5	41 44	75 27	1800	8A	8A	PA FISH COMM	2 3 5 7 C
PORT CLINTON	7116	SCHUYLKILL	14	40 35	76 02	450	7A	7A	MRS. ADA E. RARICK	2 3 5 C
PORTLAND	7127	NORTHAMPTON	5	40 55	75 06	297		8A	JOINT BRIDGE COMM	INAC 1/56
POTTSTOWN	7149	MONTGOMERY	14	40 15	75 39	160		8A	MILES E. SMITH	3
POTTSVILLE	7161	SCHUYLKILL	14	40 42	76 11	690		8A	LLOYD E. HELLER	3
PUNXSUTAWNEY	7217	JEFFERSON	1	40 57	79 00	1298		MID	JOHN VOLANSKY	C
PUTNEYVILLE 2 SE DAM	7229	ARMSTRONG	1	40 55	79 17	1270	8A	8A	CORPS OF ENGINEERS	2 3 5 C
QUAKERTOWN 1 E	7239	BUCKS	5	40 26	75 20	490	5P	5P	DENNIS K. FLUCK	2 3 5
RAYMOND	7310	POTTER	15	41 52	77 52	2220		7A	MRS. RACHEL LANGAN	3 C
#READING WB CITY	7318	BERKS	14	40 20	75 58	266	MID	MID	U.S. WEATHER BUREAU	2 3 5 7 C
RENOVO	7409	CLINTON	16	41 20	77 46	660		7A	MRS. CAROLINE BAIRD	3
RENOVO 5 S	7410	CLINTON	16	41 14	77 46	2035		MID	C. F. BILLETTE	C
REW	7425	MC KEAN	1	41 54	78 32	2250		8A	HAROLD C. MEALY	3
RICES LANDING L 6	7443	GREENE	10	39 57	80 00	775		7A	CORPS OF ENGINEERS	3
RIDGWAY 3 W	7477	ELK	1	41 25	78 47	1420	7A	7A	BOROUGH OF RIDGWAY	2 3 5
ROCHESTER 1 N	7540	BEAVER	2	40 43	80 18	900		MID	DEQUESNE LIGHT CO	C
RUSH	7694	SUSQUEHANNA	15	41 47	76 03	1000		9A	MISS MAUDE MC CAIN	3
RUSHVILLE	7727	SUSQUEHANNA	15	41 47	76 07	870		7A	CARL KOPATZ	3
SAFE HARBOR	7732	LANCASTER	15	39 55	76 23	270		MID	S.W.WATER POWER CORP	C
SAGAMORE 1 S	7739	INDIANA	1	40 46	79 14	1320		7A	CORPS OF ENGINEERS	3
SALINA 3 W	7782	WESTMORELAND	7	40 31	79 33	1109	6P	6P	MUN AUTH WSTMRLD CO	2 3 5
SAXTON	7846	BEDFORD	6	40 12	78 15	780		8A	MRS.ALVERTA L.HOLMES	3 C
SCANDIA 2 E	7855	WARREN	1	41 55	79 01	2040		MID	DAVID R. ANDERSON	C
SCHENLEY LOCK 5	7863	ARMSTRONG	1	40 41	79 40	783		VAR	CORPS OF ENGINEERS	3

STATION INDEX

Station	Index No.	County	Drainage I	Latitude	Longitude	Elevation	Observation Time Temp.	Observation Time Precip.	Observer	Refer To Tables
ANTON	7902	LACKAWANNA	15	41 25	75 40	746	7A	7A	U.S. POST OFFICE	2 3 5
ANTON WB AIRPORT	7905	LUZERNE	15	41 20	75 44	956	MID	MID	U.S. WEATHER BUREAU	2 3 5 7 C
INSGROVE CAA AP	7931	SNYDER	15	40 49	76 52	437	MID	MID	CIVIL AERO. ADM.	2 3 5 7
LERSVILLE 2 NW	7938	BUCKS	5	40 25	75 20	530		MID	SELLERSVILLE WTR CO	C
DE GAP	7963	HUNTINGDON	6	40 11	77 52	1000		MID	MRS. HELEN M. PYLE	C
MOLIN	7978	NORTHUMBLAND	15	40 48	76 33	770		8A	ROARING CRK WTR CO	3
FFIELD 6 W	8026	WARREN	1	41 41	79 09	1940		MID	L. N. HANSON	C
PPENSBURG	8073	FRANKLIN	15	40 03	77 32	709	4P	4P	KEITH B. ALLEN	2 3 5 7
PPINGPORT WB	8078	BEAVER	11	40 37	80 26	740	MID	MID	U.S. WEATHER BUREAU	2 3 5 7 C
NEMAHONING	8145	CAMERON	16	41 19	78 05	790		7A	MRS.FRANCES CALDWELL	3
PPERY ROCK	8184	BUTLER	2	41 04	80 03	1345	7P	7A	WALTER D. ALBERT	2 3 5 7
THPORT HIGHWAY SHED	8190	MC KEAN	1	41 48	78 27	1510		MID	PA DEPT HIGHWAYS	C
ERSET FAIRVIEW ST	8244	SOMERSET	17	40 01	79 05	2140		7A	HOWARD G. PECK	3
ERSET MAIN ST	8249	SOMERSET	17	40 01	79 05	2150	6P	6P	DAVID L. GROVE	2 3 5
TH CANAAN 1 NE	8275	WAYNE	5	41 31	75 24	1400		MID	EUGENE M. COOK	C
TH MOUNTAIN	8308	FRANKLIN	12	39 51	77 30	1920		7A	PA DEPT OF HEALTH	3
INGBORO	8359	CRAWFORD	8	41 48	80 23	900	8A	8A	SPRINGBORO BOROUGH	2 3 5 C
ING GROVE	8379	YORK	15	39 52	76 52	470		4P	P. H. GLATFELTER CO	3 C
INGS 1 SW	8395	SOMERSET	17	39 44	79 10	2500	6P	6P	ALLEN E. YODER	2 3 5 7
TE COLLEGE	8449	CENTRE	16	40 48	77 52	1175	MID	MID	PA STATE COLLEGE	2 3 5 6 C
AUSSTOWN	8570	BERKS	14	40 29	76 11	600		8A	JACOB KLAHR	3
ONGSTOWN	8589	INDIANA	4	40 33	78 55	1080		MID	HARRY F. BENNETT	C
OUDSBURG	8596	MONROE	5	40 59	75 12	480	11P	11P	WILLIAM MAGERTY	2 3 5 C
MP CREEK	8610	JEFFERSON	1	41 01	78 50	1320		7A	CORPS OF ENGINEERS	3
BURY	8668	NORTHUMBLAND	15	40 51	76 48	440		7A	CHARLES W. BAYLER	3 C
QUEHANNA	8692	SUSQUEHANNA	15	41 57	75 36	1020		7A	MRS. LAURA A.BENSON	3
ERSVILLE	8699	ALLEGHENY	17	40 14	79 48	765		7A	FRANK E. MARSH	3
AQUA	8758	SCHUYLKILL	14	40 48	75 58	830		8A	MRS. MARY L.ROBERTS	3
AQUA 4 N DAM	8763	SCHUYLKILL	14	40 51	75 59	1120		7A	PANTHER VLY WTR CO	3 C
ARACK 2 S FIRE TWR	8770	CLINTON	16	41 24	77 51	2220	7A	7A	JAMES E. SWARTZ	2 3 5 7
NESTA 2 SE DAM	8873	FOREST	1	41 29	79 26	1200	8A	8A	CORPS OF ENGINEERS	2 3 5 7 C
USVILLE	8885	CRAWFORD	1	41 38	79 40	1550		MID	PA ELECTRIC CO	C
USVILLE WATER WORKS	8888	CRAWFORD	1	41 38	79 42	1220	7P	7P	CITY OF TITUSVILLE	2 3 5
PEDO 4 W	8901	WARREN	1	41 47	79 32	1735		7A	MRS. LILY B. GARBER	3
ANDA	8905	BRADFORD	15	41 46	76 26	760	7P	7A	MRS. M. O. PARKS	2 3 5 7 C
ER CITY 5 SW	8910	DAUPHIN	15	40 31	76 37	745		6P	HARRISBURG WTR DEPT	3 7
Y	8959	BRADFORD	15	41 47	76 47	1100		7A	JENNIE L. BALLARD	3
NELTON	8989	INDIANA	4	40 27	79 23	890		MID	MRS. MARY E. WEIMER	C
TLEPOINT 4 NE	9002	MC KEAN	1	41 54	78 16	1640		7A	ROBERT D. STRAIT	3
ONE 4 NE BALD EAGLE	9024	BLAIR	6	40 43	78 12	1020		7A	FREDERICK L. FRIDAY	3 C
ON CITY	9042	ERIE	1	41 54	79 50	1325		7A	FORREST M. BRALEY	3 C
ONTOWN	9050	FAYETTE	10	39 54	79 44	1040	10P	10P	WM. W. MARSTELLER	2 3 5
ER DARBY	9074	DELAWARE	5	39 58	75 18	222	7P	7P	PHIL. SUB.TRANS. CO	2 3 5
CA	9099	VENANGO	1	41 26	79 57	1030		7A	MRS.FLORENCE MILLER	3
DERGRIFT	9128	WESTMORELAND	7	40 36	79 33	800		7A	UNITED ENG+FNDRY CO	3
VANDERGRIFT 2 W	9133	WESTMORELAND	7	40 36	79 36	995		MID	EUGENE R. YOUNG	C
VIRGINVILLE	9196	BERKS	14	40 31	75 52	350		8A	MRS. MARY H. WRIGHT	3
VOWINCKEL	9206	CLARION	1	41 25	79 14	1620		8A	PA DEPT FRST + WTRS	3
VOWINCKEL 1 WSW	9209	CLARION	1	41 24	79 15	1610		8A	PA DEPT FRST + WTRS	3
WARREN	9298	WARREN	1	41 51	79 08	1280	7P	7A	GILBERT H. WEIDE	2 3 5
WASHINGTON	9312	WASHINGTON	11	40 11	80 14	1200		MID	PA DEPT HIGHWAYS	C
WATSONTOWN	9345	NORTHUMBLAND	16	41 05	76 52	490		9P	WILLIAM BIRD	3
WAYNESBURG 2 W	9362	GREENE	10	39 54	80 13	980	6P	7A	RALPH L. AMOS	2 3 5
WAYNESBURG 1 E	9367	GREENE	10	39 54	80 10	940		MID	SEWAGE DISPOSAL PLT	C
WEBSTER MILLS 3 SW	9380	FULTON	12	39 49	78 05	920		MID	WILLIAM D. COVER	C
WELLSBORO 3 S	9408	TIOGA	16	41 43	77 16	1920	7A	7A	MARION L. SHUMWAY	2 3 5
WELLSBORO 2 E	9412	TIOGA	16	41 45	77 16	1550		MID	MRS. IDA S. MAYNARD	C
WELLSVILLE	9420	YORK	15	40 03	76 57	500	5P	5P	D. D. HOOVER	2 3 5
WERNERSVILLE 1 W	9430	BERKS	14	40 20	76 06	405		8A	CHARLES A. GRUGER	3
WEST CHESTER	9464	CHESTER	5	39 58	75 36	440	8A	8A	DAILY LOCAL NEWS	2 3 5
WEST GROVE 1 E	9503	CHESTER	5	39 49	75 49	440		8A	CONARD-PYLE CO	3
WEST HICKORY	9507	FOREST	1	41 34	79 25	1090		8A	MRS.HELEN F.KINNEAR	3
WHITESBURG	9655	ARMSTRONG	1	40 45	79 24	1530		7A	CORPS OF ENGINEERS	3
WILKES-BARRE	9702	LAZERNE	15	41 15	75 52	610		7A	MRS. MARY G. MIRMAK	3
WILLIAMSBURG	9714	BLAIR	6	40 28	78 12	860		7A	MYRON K. BIDDLE	3
WILLIAMSPORT WB AP	9728	LYCOMING	16	41 15	76 55	527	MID	MID	U.S. WEATHER BUREAU	2 3 5 7 C
WIND GAP	9781	NORTHAMPTON	5	40 51	75 18	720		MID	OWEN R. PARRY	C
WOLFSBURG	9823	BEDFORD	6	40 03	78 32	1190		7A	WALTER C. RICE	3
YORK 3 SSW PUMP STA	9933	YORK	15	39 55	76 45	390	5P	5P	YORK WATER COMPANY	2 3 5
YORK 2 S FILTER PLANT	9938	YORK	15	39 56	76 44	640		MID	YORK WATER COMPANY	C
YORK HAVEN	9950	YORK	15	40 07	76 43	310		8A	METROPOL EDISON CO	3
YOUNGSVILLE	9966	WARREN	1	41 51	79 20	1225		MID	HENRY CARLETT	C
ZION GROVE	9990	SCHUYLKILL	15	40 54	76 13	940		7A	JAMES D. TEETER	3
ZIONSVILLE 3 SE	9995	LEHIGH	14	40 27	75 27	660		7A	LESLIE HOWATT	3
NEW STATIONS										
EQUINUNK 2	2671	WAYNE	5	41 51	75 13	910		7A	MRS.HENRIETTA MURRAY	
COMBINED STATIONS										
EQUINUNK	2669	WAYNE	5	41 51	75 13	900		8A	COMBINED W/STA 2671 1/57	

I 1-ALLEGHENY; 2-BEAVER; 3- 4-CONEMAUGH; 5-DELAWARE; 6-JUNIATA; 7-KISKIMINETAS; 8-LAKE ERIE; 9-LEHIGH; 10-MONONGAHELA; 11-OHIO; 12-POTOMAC; 13-LAKE ONTARIO; 14-SCHUYLKILL; 15-SUSQUEHANNA; 16-WEST BRANCH; 17-YOUGHIOGHENY

REFERENCE NOTES

Additional information regarding the climate of Pennsylvania may be obtained by writing to the State Climatologist at Weather Bureau Airport Station, Harrisburg State Airport, New Cumberland, Pennsylvania, or to any Weather Bureau Office near you.

Figures and letters following the station name, such as 12 SSW, indicate distance in miles and direction from the post office.

Delayed data and corrections will be carried only in the June and December issues of this bulletin.

Monthly and seasonal snowfall and heating degree days for the preceding 12 months will be carried in the June issue of this bulletin..

Stations appearing in the Index, but for which data are not listed in the tables, either are missing or were received too late to be included in this issue.

Divisions, as used in Table 2, became effective with data for September 1956.

Unless otherwise indicated, dimensional units used in this bulletin are: Temperature in °F, precipitation and evaporation in inches, and wind movement in miles. Monthly degree day totals are the sums of the negative departures of average daily temperatures from 65° F.

Evaporation is measured in the standard Weather Bureau type pan of 4 foot diameter unless otherwise shown by footnote following Table 6.

Long-term means for full-time stations (those shown in the Station Index as "U. S. Weather Bureau") are based on the period 1921-1950, adjusted to represent observations taken at the present location. Long-term means for all stations except full-time Weather Bureau stations are based on the period 1931-155.

Water equivalent samples published in Table 7 are necessarily taken from different points for successive observations; consequently occasional drifting and other causes of local variability in the snowpack result in apparent inconsistencies in the record. Water equivalent of snow on the ground is measured at selected stations when two or more inches of snow are on the ground.

Data in Tables 3, 5, and 6 and snowfall in Table 7, when published, are for the 24 hours ending at time of observation. The Station Index lists observation times in the standard of time in local use.

Snow on ground in Table 7 is at observation time for all except Weather Bureau and CAA stations. For these stations snow on ground values are at 7:30 a.m., E.S.T.

- – No record in Tables 3, 6, 7 and the Station Index. No record in Tables 2 and 5, is indicated by no entry. Consult the annual issue of this publication for interpolated monthly precipitation totals.
- + And also on a later date or dates.
- * Amount included in following measurement, time distribution unknown.
- // Gage is equipped with a windshield.
- # Thermometers are generally exposed in a shelter located a few feet above sod-covered ground; however, the reference indicates that the thermometers are exposed in a shelter located on the roof of a building.
- AM Data based on observational day ending before noon.
- B Adjusted to a full month.
- C In the "Refer to Tables" column in the Station Index the letter "C" indicates recorder stations. These stations are processed for special purposes and are published later in "Hourly Precipitation Data".
- D Water equivalent of snowfall wholly or partly estimated, using a ratio of 1 inch water equivalent to every 10 inches of new snowfall.
- G In the "Refer to Tables" column in the Station Index the letter "G" indicates that soil temperatures are published.
- M One to nine days of record missing; see Table 5 for detailed daily record. Degree day data, if carried for this station, have been adjusted to represent the valur for a full month.
- R Amounts from recording gage (These amounts are essentially accurate but may vary slightly fram the amounts to be published later in Hourly Precipitation Data.
- SS This entry in time of observation column in Station Index means observation made near sunset.
- T Trace, an amount too small to measure.
- Y Includes total for previous month.
- VAR This entry in time of observation column in Station Index means variable.

Information concerning the history of changes in locations, elevations, exposure etc. of substations through 1955 may be found in the publication 'Substation History' for this state, soon to be issued. That publication, when available, may be obtained from the Superintendent of Documents, Government Printing Office, Washington 25, D. C. at a price to be announced. Similar information for regular weather Bureau stations may be found in the latest issues of Local Climatological Data, Annual for the respective stations, obtained as indicated above, price 15 cents.

Subscription Price: 20 cents per copy, monthly and annual; $2.50 per year. (Yearly subscription includes the Annual Summary). Checks, and money orders should be made payable to the Superintendent of Documents. Remittance and correspondence regarding subscriptions should be sent to the Superintendent of Documents, Government Printing Office, Washington 25, D. C.

WWRC., Asheville, N. C. --- 3/21/57 --- 1100

U. S. DEPARTMENT OF COMMERCE
SINCLAIR WEEKS, Secretary
WEATHER BUREAU
F. W. REICHELDERFER, Chief

CLIMATOLOGICAL DATA

PENNSYLVANIA

FEBRUARY 1957
Volume LXII No. 2

ASHEVILLE: 1957

GENERAL

Very frequent occurrences of light precipitation gave this month's weather a wet characteristic even though totals were below average at about 75 percent of the stations. Totals ranged from 0.53 inch at Hop Botton 2 SE to 5.14 inches at Kregar 4 SE. Only 14 of 254 stations recorded precipitation measurements of as much as one inch for one day, and Confluence 1 NW topped the list with a measurement of 1.71 inches on the 10th. Snowfall totals ranged from 0.3 inch at Donora to 20.0 inches at Kregar 4 SE but totals were generally from 5 to 12 inches.

Warm periods far outweighed the rather puny cold periods and the average temperature was above the long-term mean at every station for which the comparative figure is available. Temperature extremes ranged from -4° at Hawley 1 S Dam on the 3rd to 72° at Newell on the 26th.

Deficiencies in sunshine and excesses of cloudiness were great in eastern Pennsylvania but values relative to these elements were near average in the western part of the State.

WEATHER DETAILS

The weather was quite warm on the 4th, the 8th through the 10th, and from the 23rd through the 27th, while moderately cold weather the 11th-12th and 28th and some relatively low minimum temperatures from about the 18th to the 22nd represented the colder portions of the temperature cycles. Additional wintry features appeared in the form of a snowstorm over the eastern half of the State on the 1st and an icestorm on the 28th that reached practically all areas.

Precipitation occurrences were very

CLIMATOLOGICAL DATA

Temperature													Precipitation									
									No. of Days								Snow, Sleet			No. of Days		
									Max		Min											
Average Maximum	Average Minimum	Average	Departure From Long Term Means	Highest	Date	Lowest	Date	Degree Days	90° or Above	32° or Below	32° or Below	0° or Below	Total	Departure From Long Term Means	Greatest Day	Date	Total	Max Depth on Ground	Date	.10 or More	.50 or More	1.00 or More
37.3	23.0	30.2	5.5	54	25	7	12	970	0	9	25	0					7.5	5	2+			
37.2	17.4	27.3		56	26	- 4	3	1048	0	9	27	1	1.17		.52	27	4.7	6	2+	4	1	0
37.6	21.8	29.7	7.9	56	25	5	12	982	0	7	26	0	D 2.50	- .44	.85	26		6	1+	9	1	0
38.8	23.2	31.0		55	25	5	12	945	0	6	26	0	2.09		.66	26	10.0	5	1+	5	2	0
35.0	20.1	27.6		55	26	5	12	1043	0	12	26	0	3.13		1.16	27	10.9	8	2	6	2	1
33.8	16.9	25.4		53	26	1	3	1105	0	13	26	0	2.04	- .96	.77	27	13.0	10	2	5	2	0
39.9	24.9	32.4	4.1	59	27	11	12+	908	0	3	24	0	D 1.35	- .67	.46	27	4.1				0	0
39.0	23.1	31.1	4.0	58	25	7	12	946	0	8	26	0	.89	- 1.13	.34	26	3.3	4	2	5	0	0
40.1	21.6	30.9	3.1	54	25	7	3	947	0	3	27	0	2.51	- .24	.92	26	8.6	6	1+	5	1	0
		29.5											1.96				7.8					
41.2	24.7	33.0	4.4	55	27	8	3	892	0	2	27	0	2.16	- .48	.75	26	7.8	7	2	5	2	0
42.8	25.9	34.4	4.8	57	27	15	12+	851	0	0	26	0	2.11	- .69	.73	27	7.1	7	2	5	3	0
													2.27	- .83	.74	26				5	2	0
43.3M	26.2M	34.8M	6.9	56	27	9	12	843	0	0	20	0	2.25	- 1.17	.55	26	10.4	5	2+	8	1	0
40.8	25.1	33.0	4.0	57	26	10	12	891	0	1	25	0	2.39	.17	.87	26	8.3	6	1+	5	2	0
42.8M	23.2M	33.0M	3.6	58	26	10	12	890	0	0	26	0	2.86	- .46			7.5					
		33.6											2.34				8.2					
45.4	29.9	37.7		64	28	20	13	759	0	0	21	0	D 2.56		1.10	27				5	2	1
44.1	26.7	35.4	4.8	60	28	18	12+	822	0	0	24	0	2.72	- .90	1.16	10	3.8	1	3+	5	3	1
44.6	29.3	37.0		59	26	15	12	779	0	0	20	0	2.50		.66	15	9.0	4	1	6	1	0
43.5	23.1	33.3		60	26	10	12	878	0	0	27	0	2.59		.87	26		7	1	8	1	0
43.5	27.4	35.5	4.7	58	26	14	12	819	0	0	23	0	2.09	- .77	.68	26				5	1	0
44.6	28.9	36.8	5.5	63	27	16	12	786	0	0	21	0	2.95	.15	.77	1	8.1	7	1	5	3	0
45.2	27.3	36.3		58	26	16	3+	801	0	0	25	0	2.53	- .20	.81	27	5.0	3	2+			0
42.8	30.6	36.7	4.0	55	26	21	12	786	0	0	20	0	3.06	.65	.97	10	13.0	3	15+	6	3	0
44.7	28.6	36.7	5.6	60	27	17	12	787	0	0	20	0	2.21	- .40	.43	10	3.6	2	2	7	0	0
42.0	26.9	34.5		58	27	13	3	848	0	1	23	0	2.51		.62	10	9.7	4	2+	8	1	0
42.4	27.0	34.7	5.0	58	27	15	12	843	0	0	24	0	2.82	- .23	.68	27	10.9	6	2	6	3	0
46.2	33.1	39.7	4.1	66	27	22	12	703	0	0	15	0	3.85	1.20	1.18	26	.7	T	5	6	3	1
42.7	29.8	36.3	4.7	59	27	18	12	797	0	1	21	0	3.02	.67	.80	14	13.8	5	1+	6	3	0
42.0	26.3	34.2		58	26+	14	12	859	0	2	24	0	1.93		.55	26	5.5	5	1	4	1	0
42.2	27.3	34.8		55	27	16	12	840	0	0	23	0	2.70		.68	26				7	2	0
44.8	29.8	37.3		63	27	18	12	769	0	0	18	0	2.45		.86	27	4.3	4	2			0
46.1	32.2	39.2		67	27	20	12	719	0	0	16	0	2.97		.85	9	3.0	2	1	6	3	0
44.4	30.4	37.4	3.8	64	27	20	12	765	0	0	20	0	2.81	- .21	.80	9	1.8	1	6	6	3	0
45.6M	33.0M	39.3M	4.1	65	26+	24	12	711	0	0	16	0	2.92		.87	9				5	2	0
45.6	30.1	37.9	4.5	60	26+	17	12	752	0	0	21	0	3.00	- .06	.60	2	2.5			9	3	0
45.6	33.1	39.4	4.3	64	27	22	12	710	0	0	17	0	2.86	- .17	.78	9				5	3	0
46.7	27.4	37.1	4.6	60	27	16	12	777	0	0	23	0	2.78	- .22	.93	26				5	3	0
42.3	25.9	34.1	5.1	55	26	6	3	860	0	0	24	0	2.23	- 1.09	.68	26	7.5			6	1	0
43.4	30.0	36.7	3.9	59	26+	18	12	785	0	1	19	0	2.19	- .49	.58	26	7.6	5	2	7	2	0
44.9	30.4	37.7		63	27	18	12	757	0	0	20	0	2.97		.93	26	2.1	2	1	5	3	0
44.4	28.1M	36.3M	4.9	59	26	16	11	804	0	0	21	0	3.35	- .28	1.13	10	2.8	1	1+			1
		36.6											2.71				6.0					
43.2	26.8	35.0	3.6	58	28	15	12	833	0	0	24	0	3.04	.54	.97	27	8.7	3	2+	8	2	0
44.4	29.6	37.0	6.5	57	25	15	12	777	0	0	20	0	2.46	- .39	.60	26	10.5	5	1	6	1	0
44.2	27.6	35.9	4.2	58	25	15	12	808	0	0	23	0	2.79	.18	.81	26	7.7	2	1+	8	1	0
44.8	29.5	37.2	5.6	59	27+	17	12	771	0	0	20	0	2.89	.23	.72	10	7.7	3	6	7	2	0
45.2	27.0	36.1	3.0	62	26	15	12+	802	0	0	23	0	2.71	.10	1.04	10	7.0	4	15	6	1	1
42.5	29.2	35.9	3.8	58	26	17	12	809	0	1	21	0	2.64	.40	.60	26	16.4	7	15	7	2	0
45.1	28.0	36.6	5.7	57	25+	14	12	790	0	0	22	0	2.58	.32	.86	26	11.5	3	14	6	2	0
44.5	26.8	35.7		59	26	13	12	812	0	0	22	0	2.53		.70	1	11.0	4	1	6	2	0
46.9	29.6	38.3	6.6	62	25+	12	12	742	0	0	19	0	2.44	- .27	.58	10	6.8			6	1	0
		36.4											2.68				9.7					
42.1	25.9	34.0		59	25	10	12	860	0	0	23	0	D 2.47					5	15			0
42.8	26.0	34.4		60	25	12	12	851	0	0	22	0	1.68		.50	9	5.3	4	2	5	1	0
40.9	25.0	33.0		58	27	11	12	890	0	2	24	0	1.84		.62	2		7	15	4	2	0
43.3	26.3	34.8		61	26	15	12+	838	0	0	25	0	1.92		.56	27	5.1	2	2+	5	2	0
43.2	26.3	34.8		57	26+	13	12+	842	0	1	24	0	2.25	.06	.70	27	10.0			4	1	0
41.3	23.4	32.4	3.8	57	26	11	2+	906	0	2	26	0	1.80	- .93	.43	26	8.8	4	2	4	0	0
40.8	25.3	33.1	4.0	56	26	12	12	889	0	1	25	0	2.20	- .14	.76	26	9.5	4	2	5	1	0
		33.8											2.02				7.7					
35.4	20.5	28.0		55	26	6	12+	1030	0	10	27	0	1.41		.67	27	5.1	4	2+	4	1	0
40.0	20.8	30.4		63	26	6	12+	962	0	4	25	0	1.36		.55	27	4.5	5	2	4	1	0
33.5	19.1	26.3		53	27	5	12	1076	0	15	26	0	1.95	- 1.55	.65	27	13.0	7	17	7	1	0
39.0	19.7	29.4	4.4	64	26	4	12	991	0	6	28	0	1.21	- .49	.77	27	6.5	4	17	3	1	0

See Reference Notes Following Station Index

TABLE 2 - CONTINUED

Station	Temperature: Average Maximum	Average Minimum	Average	Departure From Long Term Means	Highest	Date	Lowest	Date	Degree Days	No. of Days Max. 90° or Above	Max. 32° or Below	Min. 32° or Below	Min. 0° or Below	Precipitation: Total	Departure From Long Term Means	Greatest Day	Date	Snow, Sleet: Total	Max. Depth on Ground	Date	No. of Days: 10 or More	50 or More
MONTROSE 1 E AM	34.1	18.8	26.5	4.0	56	26	2	12	1077	0	13	27	0	1.68	-.62	.55	10	9.7	9	2	4	1
TOWANDA	41.9	22.2	32.1	6.6	65	25	7	12	916	0	3	25	0	.90	-1.01	.41	27	4.7	6	2	3	0
WELLSBORO 3 S AM	35.7	19.6	27.7	3.3	56	26	4	12	1039	0	8	27	0	1.13	-1.00	.41	27	5.5	5	2+	4	0
DIVISION			28.6											1.38				7.0				
CENTRAL MOUNTAINS																						
BELLEFONTE 4 S AM	40.3	24.8	32.6	5.3	63	26	10	12	901	0	3	24	0	1.46	-.68	.59	27	4.6	3	2	3	1
DU BOIS 7 E	40.5	22.2	31.4		66	25	3	3+	934	0	5	24	0	1.81	-1.09	.39	26	11.5	4	15+	5	0
EMPORIUM 2 SSW AM	37.5	19.6	28.6		62	26	4	12	1012	0	8	26	0	1.99		.65	27	9.0	6	17	6	1
LOCK HAVEN	42.4	26.2	34.3	5.9	57	25	11	12	854	0	1	23	0	2.00	-.50	.72	2	6.1	3	2	5	1
MADERA AM	39.0	18.4	28.7		64	26	4	13+	1012	0	6	26	0	2.40		.62	4	9.5	6	2	6	1
PHILIPSBURG CAA AP	37.5	21.1	29.3		60	25	2	12	995	0	11	26	0	2.40		.77	26	10.0	6	15+	7	1
RIDGWAY 3 W AM	38.4	19.1	28.8	3.9	64	26	2	3	1007	0	7	26	0	1.73	-.60	.44	27	7.2	6	17	6	0
STATE COLLEGE	40.5	26.5	33.5	6.3	63	25	12	12	874	0	3	23	0	D 2.62	.08	.60	26	10.3	4	2	8	1
TAMARACK 2 S FIRE TWR AM	35.1	19.5	27.3		57	26	5	12+	1051	0	11	26	0	1.50		.44	27	9.7	6	17+	6	0
DIVISION			30.5											1.99				8.7				
SOUTH CENTRAL MOUNTAINS																						
ALTOONA HORSESHOE CURVE	41.4	25.5	33.5	5.7	64	25	9	12	874	0	3	22	0	2.79	.44	.70	26	12.3	4	14	8	1
† ARTEMAS 1 WNW	47.3	26.2	36.8		62	24+	13	20	786	0	0	24	0	2.98		1.00	1					3
BURNT CABINS 2 NE	44.5	26.4	35.5		62	25	8	12	819	0	0	23	0									
EBENSBURG	39.6	24.4	32.0	4.9	64	25	9	12	918	0	6	25	0	2.99	.16	.60	2	16.0	5	1+	8	3
EVERETT 1 SW	43.8	27.0	35.4	7.4	64	25	14	12	827	0	3	23	0	3.39	1.25	.75	9		4	5	9	3
HUNTINGDON AM			M																			
JOHNSTOWN AM	40.3	24.8	32.6	2.2	67	26	12	18	902	0	5	24	0	2.93	-.63	.50	2	6.6	3	15	9	1
KEGG	44.2	23.7	34.0		67	25	11	12	864	0	2	24	0	1.98		.58	1	8.8	3	6	5	2
MARTINSBURG CAA AP	40.8	24.6	32.7		67	25	10	12	897	0	4	24	0	2.14		.60	26	10.9	4	2	8	1
DIVISION			33.7											2.70				10.9				
SOUTHWEST PLATEAU																						
BAKERSTOWN 3 WNW	44.5	28.0	36.3		71	25	16	12	801	0	3	21	0	1.33		.42	26	3.0	3	14	6	0
BLAIRSVILLE 6 ENE	40.6	25.3	33.0		70	25	13	20	888	0	7	24	0	3.38	.84	.55	4	12.2	6	15+	9	2
BURGETTSTOWN 2 W AM	42.9	22.8	32.9		71	26	9	12+	894	0	3	24	0	1.79		.29	4				6	0
BUTLER	43.0	26.1	34.6	5.8	70	26	8	18	845	0	3	23	0	1.86	-.53	.44	27	14.5	6	15	7	0
CLAYSVILLE 3 W	46.5	25.7	36.1	4.9	68	25+	10	20+	803	0	1	23	0	1.30	-1.18	.48	10		1	14+	6	0
CONFLUENCE 1 SW DAM AM	44.0	26.6	35.3		67	26	12	18	825	0	3	22	0	3.53		1.38	10	9.0	3	15	9	2
DERRY	45.2	28.6	36.9	6.6	69	25	13	18	781	0	1	21	0	2.49	-.48	.44	4	6.8	6	16+	8	0
DONEGAL	39.6	21.4	30.5		64	25	8	12+	960	0	8	25	0	3.97		.85	9	11.5	8	14	10	3
DONORA AM	47.4	31.7	39.6	5.1	71	26	19	20	707	0	0	16	0	1.77	-.51	.34	26	.3	T	14+	6	0
FORD CITY 4 S DAM AM	42.5	23.3	32.9		70	26	10	18	893	0	3	25	0	1.92		.42	27	8.5	4	15	6	0
INDIANA 3 SE	43.8	26.4	35.1	5.2	70	25	9	18	831	0	2	20	0	2.59	-.32	.67	4	5.6	3	15	6	1
IRWIN			M		71	25	16	12		0	0	15	0					4.9	3	14		
MIDLAND DAM 7	42.8	28.4	35.6	4.2	68	26	17	21	816	0	2	20	0	1.32	-.89	.43	27	3.0	2	2	5	0
NEW CASTLE 1 N	44.0	24.8	34.4	5.5	70	25	12	12+	851	0	2	23	0	1.82	-.54	.48	27	4.8			8	0
NEWELL AM	47.7	30.1	38.9	6.4	72	26	17	20+	725	0	1	17	0	2.57	.37	.66	10					
NEW STANTON	47.4	24.2	35.8	4.2	70	25	13	12	811	0	1	24	0	2.86	.02	.80	26	4.0			9	1
PITTSBURGH WB AP 2 //R	42.4	26.8	34.6	4.8	68	25	15	12	843	0	4	22	0	1.35	-1.02	.25	26	4.3	2	2	6	0
PITTSBURGH WB CITY R	45.0	30.6	37.8	4.2	70	25	20	19	757	0	1	19	0	1.74	-.61	.47	26	2.8			6	0
PUTNEYVILLE 2 SE DAM AM	40.6	20.6	30.6		68	26	6	18	957	0	3	26	0	2.10		.41	4	15.5	5	15+	7	0
SALINA 3 W	44.4	26.3	35.4		69	25	11	18	821	0	2	20	0	1.95		.38	4	3.0	3	14	7	0
SHIPPINGPORT WB	43.1	26.3	34.7		70	25	14	21	843	0	2	22	0	1.40		.35	28	4.3	2	1+	5	0
SLIPPERY ROCK	42.0	24.8	33.4		67	25	11	18	881	0	6	25	0	1.72				12.0	5	15+		0
SOMERSET MAIN ST	43.8	25.8	34.8	7.7	66	25	13	12	839	0	2	21	0	2.98	-.56	.56	9	10.7	4	14	8	3
SPRINGS 1 SW	42.0M	24.7M	33.4M	6.1	63	25	11	12+	883	0	4	23	0	3.87	.75	.83	9	13.2	7	14	10	2
UNIONTOWN	47.5	30.6	39.1	6.1	70	25	16	20+	719	0	0	16	0	2.76	-.12	.73	9	1.0	1	14	8	2
WAYNESBURG 2 W	48.0	27.1	37.6	5.5	70	25	11	21	760	0	0	20	0	2.32	.07	.85	10	3.0	1	6+	5	2
DIVISION			35.2											2.27				6.9				
NORTHWEST PLATEAU																						
BRADFORD 4 W RES	38.8	17.6	28.2	2.3	63	25	-2	12	1022	0	9	28	1	1.74	-.88	.45	26	9.0	7	1+	4	0
BROOKVILLE CAA AIRPORT	39.4	22.3	30.9	5.7	67	25	6	18	950	0	7	25	0	1.98	-.51	.60	9	5.4	4	2	5	1
CLARION 3 SW	42.0	21.9	32.0		67	25	4	18	917	0	2	26	0	2.13	-.98	.56	27	7.5	4	2+	7	1
CORRY	38.6	20.6	29.6	4.3	64	25	7	12	984	0	6	25	0	1.93	-1.10	.36	9	7.5	6	20	6	0
COUDERSPORT 3 NW	37.2	18.6	27.9		61	25	1	12	1034	0	12	26	0	1.53		.87	27	3.4	4	2+	5	1
EAST BRADY	45.1	26.7	35.9		70	25	9	17	808	0	1	21	0	1.71		.43	9	9.5	4	14	6	0
ERIE CAA AIRPORT	37.6	24.0	30.8	4.3	67	25	11	12	951	0	7	25	0	1.73	-.34	.78	26	6.7	3	1+	3	1
FARRELL SHARON	44.4	24.5	34.5	5.7	69	25	11	12+	849	0	2	25	0	.80	-1.16	.28	14				3	0
FRANKLIN	41.9	24.3	33.1	7.2	66	26	15	21+	887	0	4	26	0	1.64	-1.06	.41	27				6	0
GREENVILLE	42.5	24.1	33.3	6.1	66	25	9	18	884	0	3	25	0	1.54	-.98	.30	27	7.7	5	14	7	0
JAMESTOWN 2 NW AM	39.1	21.7	30.4		67	26	9	12	960	0	7	26	0	1.77	-.31	.44	27	9.7	7	15	8	0
KANE 1 NNE AM	36.9	17.9	27.4		63	26	2	12	1048	0	10	28	0	2.24	-.71	.63	26	17.9	9	17+	7	1
LINESVILLE 5 WNW	39.8	20.8	30.3		64	25	1	21	965	0	6	25	0	1.71	-.61	.44	27		6	15	7	0
MEADVILLE 1 S AM	38.4	21.4	29.9	5.4	67	26	7	18	974	0	5	26	0	1.97	-.70	.39	27	16.4	7	17	8	0
MERCER 2 NNE	39.5	25.5	32.5		64	25	9	17	902	0	7	25	0	2.23		.59	4				10	1
SPRINGBORO AM	39.0M	21.8M	30.4M		69	26	7	18	945	0	6	23	0	D 2.75		.85	27				8	2
TIONESTA 2 SE DAM AM	38.9	19.4	29.2		67	26	5	18	997	0	6	27	0	1.71	-.62	.45	27	9.5	4	17+	7	0
TITUSVILLE WATER WORKS	40.5	19.3	29.9		68	25	6	12+	976	0	3	27	0	1.96		.45	9	10.7	7	17	7	0
WARREN	40.5	23.2	31.9	6.7	68	25	8	12	920	0	4	25	0	1.01	-1.56	.28	10	5.6	3	2+	4	0
DIVISION			31.0											1.79				9.0				

† DATA RECEIVED TOO LATE TO BE INCLUDED IN DIVISION AVERAGES

See Reference Notes Following Station Index

DAILY PRECIPITATION

	Total	1	2	3	4	5	6	7	8	9	10	11	12	13	14	15	16	17	18	19	20	21	22	23	24	25	26	27	28	29	30	31
	1.94	.03	.32		.45		.03			T	.32			.07		.12	T	T	T	.06	T	T			.04		.01	.41	.08			
R	2.18	.34	T	.04	.19	T	.02			.36	.18	T		.04	.01	T	T	T						T			.75	T	.03			
	2.11	.13	.30		.15		.03	T		T	.52			.02	.02		T	.01							T		T	.73				
VE	2.79	.37	.06	.05	.33	T	.17			.42	.23			.10	.13		.04	.02		.08							.70	.09	T			
	3.04	.19	.41		T		.32			.13	.53			.03		.33	T	T									.13	.97				
	2.98	1.00		.06		*	.42			.80				*	.15													.55				
	1.37	T	.20	T	T						.17				T	.11	T	.07		T								.82	T			
	1.33	T	.21		.20		T			.14	.13	T		.03	.16	T	T	T	T	.02	T			.01			.42	.01	T			
	2.00	T	.10		.24	.08				.03	.39	T		.09		.20	.10	.25	T	.02	.03	.05					T	.40				
	-	*	.72			-				.38										-								.38				
	2.15	.20	.16		.15		.05			.45	.23			.06		.15	.05										.46	.15				
	1.25	T	.18		.15	T				.01	.28	T	T	.04	T	.15	T	T	T	T	T	T			.05		T	.30	T			
D	2.47	.14	.29		.15		D.10			.30		T		.10		.46		.03	T								*	.90				
	1.62	.01	.31		.27	T	T			T	.27			.02	.03	.10		.08										.53				
	1.46		.35		.29		.05	T		.04	.06	T		.05		.03											T	.59				
	2.26	.16	.52		.14		.03			.04	.56			.03	.03	.03		T							T			.70				
	1.48	.24	.08	T	.16		T	T		.80	.29			.03		T	.03							T		T	.30	.05				
	2.10	.11	.45		.31		.03			T	.50			T	T	T		T							T			.70				
	2.27	.62		.32		.02	T			.34	.17			.04	T		T							T			.74		.02			
	3.38	.46	.02	.02	.55	.06	.06			.21	.30	T		.39	.24	.10	.07	.07	T	T	T	T		.01			.52	.28	.02			
	-	.35	T		.08		.23	T		.42	.02			.18	.18	-	T										.60	.08	.02			
	RECORD MISSING																															
	1.98	T	.37		.30		.10			.05	.35	.01		.06		.06	.03	.02	.01	.05	T	T			.04	T	.02	.39	.03			
TA	1.50		.04		.06	T					.36			.04		.10	.01	.11	T	.06	T	T			T			.72				
	1.74	.05			.08					.35	T	T		.08	.08	T	.18	.08	.03	T	.08						.45	.28				
	2.51	.32		.02		.28				.68		.08		.12	.22	T											.74	.01	.04			
T	1.98	.25	T	.20	.11			T		.60	.01		.03	.08	.07	.01	.06	.03	.04	T	.02	T		.01		.01	.36	T	.09			
	1.40	T	*	*	.49	T	T	.07		*	*	.36		.04	.04	.02			T	.01	.01	.02				T	.03	.39	.01			
	2.52	.08	.50		.04		.31			.05	.71			.04		.12		T									.07	.54	.06			
	1.70	.02	.27		.29		.03			.13	.18			.07	.05	.05				.05					.05		.06	.27	.27			
	-	-	.24	.01		.01	-			.36	.37			-	.50		.01	.01	.01								.88	T	-			
	1.66		.24	.25						.11	.31			.11		.31		T	T	.02					.07			.44				
	2.72	.33	.03				.17			.50	.04			.07	.23	.30	.42							T			.58	.05				
	1.41	.09	.30		T					T	.12			.02	T	.14		.07			T							.67	T			
	2.46	.42	.06	T	.08	T	.20	T		.44	.26		T	.06	.08	.18	.02							T			.60	.06	T			
	2.72	.02	.42		.45		.10			.08	.46	T		.12	T	.14	.02	.19	.05	.05	T	T			T		.03	.58	.01			
	1.72	.03	.24		.14					T	.33			.05	T	.13		.05	T	T	T	T						.65	.10			
	1.79	.05	.35		.03					.02	.25		T	.04	.05	.30		.10	T	T							T	.60	T			
	-	.20	.10	.10	.20		-	D.15	T	T	.70			T		T		.10									T	.95				
	2.79	.35		T	.02	.20	.10	T		.49	.27			.04	.25		.01							T			.81		.25			
	2.04	.01	.37		.24		.15			.01	.50	.02		.02		.05	T	.01	T	.04	T				.02		.01	.56	.03			
D	2.56	.15	.72		.08	T	.33	T		.08	D.10		T	T	T	T	T										T	1.10				
	2.00	.03	.38		.28		.03	T		.01	.32			.04	.02	.20	T	T		.05	T	T				T		.63	.01			
	2.13	.02	.18		.25					.15	.47			.19	.03	.19		.04		.03	T				T			.56	.02			
	2.21	.10	.51		.21		.03			.01	.60			.02														.73				
	1.30	T	.32		.18		.14	T		.10	.48			.05	.01	.07	T	T		.02	T				.02	T	.05	.12	.04			
	2.45	T	.30		.40		T			.08	.40			.13	.03	.40		T		.10					.02	.02	.02	.55	T			
	1.99		.20		.20			T	T	.02	.35	T		.06	.02	.10	T	.05	.06	.02	.04	.02		T	T		T	.82	.03			
	2.20	.12	.58		.15		.02			.01	.54			.05	.05			.04										.72				
	2.72	.10	.52		.09		.09	T		T	1.16			.02		.15		T							.02		T	.57				
	2.50	.41	.06		.02	T	.17	T	T	.32	.30				.06	.66								.03			.38		T			
	3.53	.05	.58		.15	T	.36	T		.24	1.38		T	.13	T	.14	T	.03	T	T	T	T					.15	.30	.02			
	3.81	.03	.63		.17		.32			.15	1.71	T	T	.11	T	.18	T	.03	T		T	T	T				.18	.29	.01			
	2.17	.03	.42		.32		.04			.01	.90			.07		.04		.01			.02						.02	.27	.02			
	2.66	.07	.55		.27		.10	T		T	.78			T	T		T	T							T			.89				
	2.09	.02	.22		.25	T	T			.23	.29	T		.10	.02	.17	T	.07	T	.05	T	T			.03	.03	T	.55	.06			
	2.32	.03	.26		.25					.25	.32	T		.13	.02	.20	.03	.05	T	.05	.02	T			.04	T	T	.57	.10			
	1.13		*		.43		T			*	*	.12		.02	.07					.05							.05	.31	.08			
	1.93	.03		T	.07					.36	.07			.23	.24	T	.10	.06	.07	T	.06						.30	.34				
	1.53		.20		.14					T	.16	T		.02		.01	T	.11		.02	T							.87	T			
	2.04	.18	.25		.09	.07					.25	T	T	.08	.04	.14	T	.21	T	T	T							.63	.10			
	.82		.24								.06			T		.05		.08										.34	.05			
	2.81	.25	.40		.64		T	.02		.14	.35			.20	T	.20	T			.10	T				.06			.45				
	2.55	.04	.47		.36		.19			.06	.42			.06		.19		.15							T			.61				
	1.75		.05		.08					.01	.40	.01		.05	T	.12	.03	.11		.09	.02	.03			T			.73	.02			
	2.11	.05	.30		.43		T			.16	.47			T		.38												.32				
	2.49	.38	T	.06	.44	.05	.07			.40	.20			.11	.20		.05	.03		.04	T	T		T			.31	.15				
	2.59	.21	.22	.23	.16		.05	.02	T	.28	.25			T	.02	.02								.15			.87	.09	.02			
	1.36	.11	.31	T	.07						.27	T		T				.05							T		T	.55				
	3.97	.62	T	.03	.43	.18	T	T		.85	.14		.14	T	.44	T	T	.06	T	T	T	T		T			.44	.12	.52			
	1.77	.04	.29	.02	.20		.16	T		.22	.26	T	T	.02	.04	T	.02	.01	T	.04	.01	T		.02	T		.34	.08	T			
	2.13	.33	.28	.03			.13	.01		.35				.22	T	T	T							T			.43	.33				
	1.81	.16	.07	.01	.34					.37	.06			.07	.09	.03	.04	T			T			.02			.39	.10	.06			
	1.21	T	.35		T					T	.20	T		T	T	.06		.15			T							.45	T			
	1.95	.16	.27		.13		T			T	.39	T		T	.07	.13	T	.15			T	T			T		T	.05	T			
	1.71	.16		.29	.02			.01		.43				.16	.16	.02	.02	.03									.41					
	2.99	T	.60		.45	T	.15			.09	.55		T	.15	T	.14	T	.15	T	.07	T				T		.09	.55	T			
	2.17	T	.01		.01	.01				.25	.24	T		.18	.02	.44	T	.19	.03	.04	.01	.01						.72	.01			
	2.70	.15	.47		.05		.14			.19	.50			.01		.67									.01			.51				
	1.90	.06	.21		.24					.09	.39	T		.08		.11		.16	T	T	T							.65	T			
	1.93	.05	.24		.15					T	.22			.05	.04	.21		.05		T								.92	T			
	2.09	.45			.04		.12			.45	.05			.04	.01	.21	.02							T			.68	.02				
	RECORD MISSING																															
	1.73	T	T	T	T			T		.36	T	T	.04	.07	.30	.01	.03	.05	.07	T	T			T			.78	.02	T			
	3.39	.35			.10	.30				.75	.11			.11	.39												.65	.05	.58			
	.80	.01			.21					.15					.28			.05	.03	.01				.03			.03	T				
	1.92	.03	.39		.33		T	T		.15	.26			.14	T	.08	T	T		.04	T				.01		T	.42	.07			
	1.84		.08		.23					.16	.17			.12	.01	.23	.01	.06		.04		.01			.03	.01		.41	.07			
	-	.10	.28		.35	-								.04	.04		.03	.04			T				-		-	.60				
	1.52	.02	.30		.12					T	.14	T	T	.05	.02	.12		.10	T		T	T						.65	T			
	2.26	.29	.53		.10		.08			.02	.50			T		.18									.01			.55				
	2.95	.77	.02	.04	.04	.06	.07	T		.26	.71			.06			T							.02			.60	.21	.09			
	2.89	.12	.39		.04		.31	T		.13	.72			.02		.36									T		.09	.71				
	RECORD MISSING																															
	2.15	.03	.24		.17	.02		T	T	.13	.35	T		.06	.02	.12	T	.16	T	.03	.02	T			.02			.73	.05			
	1.29	.01	.20		.15		T			.02	.23			.05	T	.08		T	T	.03					.04	T	.02	.37	.09			
	2.24	.20	.28		.18						.70			.03	.03	T		.21			T							.61				
	2.53	*	.58		.14	.02	.09	T		.14	.59			.07	.09		T											.81				
	1.84	T	.62		T		.06	T		T	.52			T	T	.30		T									T	.34				
	2.75	.02	.52		.06	T	.21			.03	1.01			.02		.05		.05	T	T							.04	.67	.07			
	2.61	.39	.02	.09	.33	.01	.09			.39	.41			.10	.15	.02	.01							.15			.39	.04	.02			
	1.54	T			.15			T		.28	.15	T	T	.14	.26		.01	.02	.03					.02			.18	.30				
	2.71	.11	.46			T	.29	T		T	1.04			T	T	.35											.02	.44	T			
R	2.64	.47		T	.06	.06	.04	T		.45	.11	T	T	.07	.54	.13	T	T						T			.60	T	.11			
	2.62	.18	.43		.10		.17	T		.20	.45			.05	T	.39		.01							T		.09	.55				
	1.42	.11	.25		.07	T					.26	T		.04	.05	.02	T	.04			T	T						.58				
	1.17	.14	.26		.05						.16			T	.04			T										.52				
	1.60	.09	.27	T	.20						.42	T		T	.07	.03	T	.03	T	T	T	T			T	T	T	.49				
	3.06	.02	.52		.10		.12	T		.04	.97			T	.01	.77	T	T						T	T	T	.04	.47	T			
	1.69	.21	.20		.04	T					.37			.04	.04	T	T	.09			T	T						.70				
D	2.43	D.03	.48		.30		.21			.10	.60	T	T	.09	.02	.18	T	.02	T	.03	T	T			.02		.05	.26	.04			
	.53	.02	.04	T	T	.11			T	T	.02	.03				T	T	.08	.01	T		T			T			.05	.15			
	-	-	-	-	-	-	-	-	-	-	-	-	-	-	-	-	-	-	-	-	-	-	-	-	-	-	.03	.39	.05			
	2.00	.04	.26		.03		.18	T		.09	.45		T	.01	T	.26		.01									.04	.63				
	2.90	.03	.47		.04		.36			.16	.68		.03	.10	T	.22	.02	.02									.04	.73				

See Reference Notes Following Station Index

DAILY PRECIPITATION

Table 3—Continued

Station	Total	1	2	3	4	5	6	7	8	9	10	11	12	13	14	15	16	17	18	19	20	21	22	23	24	25	26	27	28	29	30	31
INDIANA 3 SE	2.59	T	.40		.67		.03			.06	.49			.17		.29		.01	.02	.04	T				.04		T	.37	.01			
IRWIN	-	.34		-	-	.01	.04	T		-				.04	.16	.01			.02	.05	.01					-	.39	.11				
JAMESTOWN 2 NW	1.77	.01			.11					.28	.27	T		.13	.13	.14	T	.05	T	T	.02	T		T	.03	.03	.01	.44	.12			
JIM THORPE	2.25	.30	.20	.02	.17		.02			.38	.25	T		.12	T	T	.06					T		T			.55	.18				
JOHNSTOWN	2.93	T	.50		.34	T	.17			.33	.33	T		.16	T	.25	T	.06	.03	.25	.05				T		.07	.41	T			
KANE 1 NNE	2.24	.14		.16	.01				.09	.27	.01	T	.04	.03	.31	T	.17	.02	.06	.01	.01			T	T		.63	.09	.23			
KARTHAUS	1.95	T	.30		.32					.06	.42	T		.04	T	.12		.04		T	T	T			T	T		.65				
KEATING SUMMIT	2.03	.03	.22		.18					.12	.28			.12	.03	.04		.14	T	T	T							.82	.05			
KEGG	1.98	.58			T	.37	T			.57		T	.03	.03	.11		T			T	T							.04	.25			
KITTANNING LOCK 7	1.95	.02	.25		.32					.20	.25			.22	T	.10	T	.02	T	T	T	T			.04		.01	.40				
KREGAR 4 SE	5.14	.63	.30	.02	.36	.38	.04	T		.83	.44	T	.22	.06	.72	.03	.07	.04	T	T	.04	T		.02		T	.71	.06	.17			
KRESGEVILLE 3 W	2.48	*	.39		.56		.02				.06			.02	.03			.03										.77				
LAFAYETTE MC KEAN PARK	2.12		.12		.16						.42	T		.06	.02	.18		.21	.12	.05	T	T						.78				
LAKEVILLE 1 NNE	1.69	.18	.29		.11						.22			.03	.08	.01	T	.13									T	.64				
LANCASTER 2 NE PUMP STA	2.21	.29	.17	T	.04		.11			.29	.43			.01	.03	.39								.03			.42		T			
LANDISVILLE 2 NW	2.51	.11	.42		.06		.14			.12	.62					.45	.11								.03		.05	.40				
LAWRENCEVILLE 2 S	1.21	.02	.20		T					T	.19			T		T		.03									T	.77	T			
LEBANON 3 W	2.82	.20	.57		.11		.09	T		.07	.62			.02	.01	.45		T							T			.88	T			
LEHIGHTON	2.26	.14	.46		T		.08			T	.65			.05	T	T	T	.03							T		T	.85				
LE ROY	.92	.02		T						.10				T	.03		.01										.56	.20				
LEWIS RUN 3 SE	1.95	T	.10		.12	T					.44	.01		.05	.03	.08	.02	.16	.03	.05	.03	.02			.02			.73	.05			
LEWISTOWN	1.92	.02	.23		.14		.08			.02	.59			.06	.03	.21		.02							T		T	.56				
LINESVILLE 5 WNW	1.71	T			.04					.34	.10	T		.14	.10	.36	T	.12	.02	.03	.02	T			T		T	.44				
LOCK HAVEN	2.00	T	.72		.23		T		T	.02	.35	T		.01	.03	.18		.06							T	T	T	.40	T			
LONG POND 2 W	2.41	.11	.25		.18		T				.63	T		.03	.08	T		.08			T							1.07	T			
LYNDELL 2 NW	2.29	.15	.43		T		.22			.25	.57			T		T										*	*	*	.67			
MADERA	2.40	.04	.30		.62	T	.03			.05	.41			.17		.20		.08		T					T			.41				
MAHAFFEY	2.52	.02	.38	T	.52	T	T		T	.10	.51	T		.14	T	.15	T	.09	T	.02	T	T			.02	T	T	.53	.04			
MAPLE GLEN	2.34	.44	.07	.06	.11		.08	T		.29	.30			.02		.01	.01							T			.70	.15	.01			
MAPLETON DEPOT	1.87	.04	.19		.12		.03			.05	.47			.02	.01	.36		.02	T								.01	.53	.02			
MARCUS HOOK	3.85	.76		.04	.11	.06	.07	.01		.90	.31		T	.02	.08	T	.01	T						T			1.18	.05	.25			
MARION CENTER 2 SE	2.50	.04	.34	.01	.03		.01			.19	.33	.02		.13	T	.17	.03	.05	T	.09	.01	T	T		.04		.04	.34	.03			
MARTINSBURG CAA AP	2.14	.38	T	T	.15	.18	.03	T		.19	.16	T	.02	.07	.13	T	.06	.02	T	T	T	T				T	.60	.02	.13			
MATAMORAS	1.65		.41								.52					.08		.03										.59				
MAYBURG	1.65	T	.09		.20					.03	.40			.10		.22	T	.10	T	T	T	.05						.44				
MC CONNELLSBURG	2.69	.16	.22		.07		.25	T	T	.12	.55			.09		.29		.13									.28	.41	.12			
MC KEESPORT	2.07		*		.70		.05				.75			.02		.05			.05	.03				T		T		.40	.02			
MEADVILLE 1 S	1.97	.01	T		.12	T				.24	.28	T		.15	.06	.36	T	.18	.01	.02	T	T			.02	T	T	.39	.13			
MEDIX RUN	1.88	.05	.25		.24					.08	.41	T		.05	.04	.13	T	.14	T	.01	T	T			T	T	T	.46	.04			
MERCER 2 NNE	2.23		.10		.59					.30	.10				.10	.24		.10	.20	T					.10			.40				
MERCERSBURG	3.26	.07	.35		.02		.34			.56	.24			T		.24									.01		.63	.80				
MEYERSDALE 1 ENE	3.22	.06	.64		.07		.26			.23	1.11		.04	.06	T	.13	T	.10	.02		T						.08	.35	.07			
MIDDLETOWN OLMSTED FLD	3.02	.55		T	.06	.08	.08	.01		.30	.07	T		.04	.80	.21	T							.06			.59	T	.12			
MIDLAND DAM 7	1.32	T	.20		.10					.08	.25			.06	.02	.11	T	.01		.03	T				.04	T	.01	.43				
MILANVILLE	1.71	.23	.21		.04						.44			T	.04			.07										.68				
MILLHEIM	1.91	T	.37		.24		T			.16	.30	T	T	T	.08	.16	T	T							T		T	.60	T			
MILLVILLE 2 SW	1.76	.11	.28		.11		T	T		T	.60			.03	.02	.09	T	.03							T	T		.47				
MILROY	2.13	.06	.27		.16		.09			.16	.37			.05	.04	.19		.06			T							.66	.02			
MONTROSE 1 E	1.68	.17	.15	.07	.07	T					.55	.01		.04	.04	.03	T	.08	T		.01	T			T			.48	T			
MORGANTOWN	1.95	.48		.01	.09	T	.05			.47	.08			T	.15	T	T							.02			.55		.03			
MT GRETNA 2 SE	2.70		.47		.15	.05	.05			.55	.12			.08	.40												.68		.15			
MT POCONO 2 N AP	2.50	.20		.10	.15					D.20	.30			.09	.11	.05	.10			T				T		T	.85	.35				
MUHLENBURG 1 SE	2.09	.27	T	T	.01		.04	.08		.55				.25			.07										.66	.16				
MYERSTOWN	2.74	*	.60		.12		.09				.75			.08	T	.35	T											.75				
NATRONA LOCK 4	1.77	.02	.30		.29		.01			.01	.28			.08		.14	T	T		.05		T			.02		.01	.41	.15			
NESHAMINY FALLS	2.51	.56		.03	.04	.03	.05			.45	.40			.02	T	T	T										.84	.04	.05			
NEWBURG 3 W	-	-	-	-	-	-	-	-	-	-	-	-	-	-	-	-	-	-	-	-	-	-	-	-	-	-	-	-	-			
NEW CASTLE 1 N	1.82	T	.20		.24			T	T	.18	.12	T		.08	.10	.02	T	.10	T	T	T	T		.04	.22	T	.04	.48	T			
NEWELL	2.57	.02	*		.54	.19					.66			.03	.04	.02				.02		.15		.18			.37	.34	.09			
NEW PARK	3.37	.18	.02		.05	.03	.15	T		1.10		T		.03	.15	.40											.78		.48			
NEWPORT	2.25	.05	.37		.08	T	.04	.01		.06	.42			.08	T	.42		T	T						T		.02	.70				
NEW STANTON	2.86	.40	T	.05	.27	.08	.06			.39	.21		.11	.01	.11	.02	.10	.01	.05	T	.02			.02		T	.80	.02	.15			
NEW TRIPOLI	2.17	.48	.04		.12		.03			.46	.15			.08		T	.06							T			.69	.06				
NORRISTOWN	2.46	.09	.55		.13		.08	.01		*	.73			T	T			T							T		*	.86				
NORTH EAST 2 SE	2.27	.02	.03		T	.01				.28	.10	.01	T	.22	.11	.37	.02	.02	.03	T	T	.02						1.03				
ORWELL 3 N	.77	.05	.14		.02					.03	.12		T	T	T	T												.41				
PALM	2.20	.18	.44			.27				.49					.08													.74				
PALMERTON	2.39	.60		T	.13	T	.04	T		.35	.25	T		.06	T	T	.07							T			.87		.02			
PALMYRA	2.36	.22	.10		.05		.12			.48	.17			.04	.05	.49	.01							.03			.61	.02	T			
PARKER	1.57	T	.16		.22	T		T		.21	.11	.02		.15	T	.24	T	.06			T	T	T		T		T	.34	.06			
PAUPACK 2 WNW	1.61	.12	.25		.11	.11					.42			.01	.04			.05										.50				
PECKS POND	2.08	.10	.24		.09					T	.68			T	.11	.02		.06										.78				
PHIL DREXEL INST OF TEC	2.97	.64		.02	T	.10	.05			.85	.30			T	.01	T	T							T			.79	T	.21			
PHILADELPHIA WB AP R	2.81	.60	T	.03	.03	.03	.10	T		.80	.32	T		.01	T	T	T							T			.74	T	.15			
PHILADELPHIA PT BREEZE	2.92	.47	.04	.03	.07	.07	.06			.87	.36			.02	T									T		T	.77	.01	.15			
PHILADELPHIA SHAWMONT	3.00	.15	.60	.10	.14		.15			.25	.56					T	.05										.55	.45				
PHILADELPHIA CITY R	2.88	.65		.02	.02	.02	.08			.78	.37			.01													.73		.18			
PHILIPSBURG CAA AP	2.40	.33	T	.09	.33	T	T	T		.19	T	T	.02	.12	.31	T	.06	T	T	T	T	T		T			.77	.04	.14			
PHOENIXVILLE 1 E	2.78	.69			.10	.06	.07			.57	.17			.05		.02								.03			.93		.09			
PIKES CREEK	1.89	.11	.25		.15						.49	T		.03	.04	T		.16			T				T			.72				
PIMPLE HILL	3.13	.14	.45	T	.22		.01	T	T	.13	.72	T		.08	.07	.04	T	.09	T	T	.01	.01			T		T	1.16				
PINE GROVE 1 NE	2.25	.11	.51		.14	T	.04	T		.20	.37			.03	.02	.23		T							T			.60				
PITTSBURGH WB AP 2 //R	1.35	.23	T	.02	.15	T	T	T		.19	.03	T	.05	.02	.05	.01	.01	T	.03	T	T	T		.01	T	T	.25	.14	.16			
PITTSBURGH WB CITY R	1.74	.27	T	.28	T		.04	T		.23	.03		.04		.13		T	T	.03	T	T	T		.01		T	.47	.05	.16			
PLEASANT MOUNT 1 W	2.04	.15	.21		.13					T	.55	T		.06	.03	T		.08	T		.03	.03				T	T	.77				
PORT CLINTON	2.86	*	1.05		.23		.04			.09	.50			.10		.02		.03										.80				
POTTSTOWN	RECORD MISSING																															
POTTSVILLE	2.21	.12	.49		.09		.04	T		.13	.51			.06	.04	.06		.06							T			.61				
PUTNEYVILLE 2 SE DAM	2.10	T	.27		.41					.22	.31	.01		.15	.01	.17	.01	.04		.02	.01	.07			T	.02	.01	.35	.02			
QUAKERTOWN 1 E	2.23	.39	.28	T	.04		.08			.38	.15	T		.04		.02	.02							.02			.68	.13				
RAYMOND	1.88		.21		.15					.02	.25	.02		.05		.11		.16		.02		.02		T	T	T	T	.80	.07			
READING WB CITY R	2.19	.51		T	.12	.03	.03	T		.48	.11			.04	.13		.01				T			.03			.38		.14			
RENOVO	1.55	.03	.25		.16					T	.26	T		.02	.09	.08		.06		T					.01	T		.58	.02			
REW	1.77	.05	.04	.02	.05	.01				T	.42	T	T	.04	.01	.06	T	.14	.01	.02	.01	T			T			.87	.02			
RICES LANDING L 6	2.41		.38		.26		.20			.02	.70			.01		.02		.02									.03	.70	.07			
RIDGWAY 3 W	1.73	T	.25		.20	T				.07	.30			.03	.02	.18	T	.15	.01	.03	T	T			T		T	.44	.05			
RUSH	1.47	.22	.21		.06					T	.35	T		.04		.02		.06										.51				
RUSHVILLE	1.31	.18	.17		.04						.31			T	.03			.02				T						.56				
SAGAMORE 1 S	3.60		.20		1.21	T				.15	.45			.25	T	.10	.15	.26	.15	.05		T					T	.72				
SALINA 3 W	1.95	.35	.02	.15	.38		.06			.22	.13			.08	.17		.01			.01				.02			.33	.02	T			
SAXTON	2.19	.05	.38		.11	T	.27	T		.05	.43		T	.03	T	.21	T	.04			T	T					.03	.55	.02			
SCHENLEY LOCK 5	1.96	.03	.30		.25		.01			.14	.25	T		.15	T	.21		T		.06					.05		.02	.41	.10			
SCRANTON	1.35	*	.35		.18						.27							D.08							.01			.46				
SCRANTON WB AIRPORT	.80	.14	T	T	.11			T	T	.15	.10			T	T		.03	T	T		T			T			.34	.02	T			
SELINSGROVE CAA AP	1.80	.38	T	T.	.09	.03	.03	T		.39	.08			.04	.21	.04	.02							T			.43	.01	.05			
SHAMOKIN	1.99	.13	.45		.13		.03			.12	.36			.03	.01	.07		T							.01			.45				
SHIPPENSBURG	2.58	.22	.08		.02	T	.24	.02		.56	.24			.09	.21	.04	T										.86	T	T			
SHIPPINGPORT WB	1.40	.21		.04	.07			T		.15	T		.06		.14		T	T	T		.01			.04		T	.31	T	.35			
SINNEMAHONING	1.99	.04	.25	T	.20					.09	.30	T		.04	.06	.07	T	.08	T	T		T			T	T	T	.73	.04			
SLIPPERY ROCK	1.72	.01	.12		.22					.24	.29			.11		.20		.07		.02					.08	.01	*	.37				
SOMERSET FAIRVIEW ST	3.28	.05	.50	T	.45	.02	.25			.05	.98			.34	.03	.27	T	.05	.04	T	.03	.02			T		.08	.21	.06			
SOMERSET MAIN ST	2.98	.54	.05	.02	.30	.08	.08			.56	.32			.18	.20	.08	.06	.03			T			T			.21	.10	.01			
SOUTH MOUNTAIN	3.02	.17	.36		.04		.30			.38	.71			.03		.48											.12	.63				
SPRINGBORO	2.75	D.20								.70	.10	T		.30	D.30	D.20	T	D.10									T	.85	T			
SPRING GROVE	2.71	.31	.16		.08		.32			.26	.69	T		T	.10	.28	T							T			.39	T	.12			

See Reference Notes Following Station Index

DAILY PRECIPITATION

le 3—Continued

PENNSYLVANIA
FEBRUARY 1957

Station	Total	1	2	3	4	5	6	7	8	9	10	11	12	13	14	15	16	17	18	19	20	21	22	23	24	25	26	27	28	29	30	31
IGS 1 SW	3.87	.79		.07	.14	.37	.05			.85	.41	.01		.18	.29		.04	.03			.01						.38	.20	.17			
I COLLEGE	2.82	.30	D.35	.08	.19	.04	.01	T		.31	.04	T	.01	.04	.13	D.30	.03	T	.01		T				T	T	.60	.04	.17			
ISSTOWN	2.63	.16	.46		.16		.07			.12	.50			.07	.04	.23		.04							.02		T	.76				
IOSBURG	2.51	.40	T	.01	.21		T	T		.42	.30	T		.06	.04		.09	T		T	T			T			.92	.06	T			
I CREEK	1.72		.25		.44					.16	.42			.09		.06		.02			T							.32				
	2.00	.07	.48		.08		.06			.11	.45			.04	.02	.34		T							T		T	.47				
	1.81	.16	.17		.11	T					.52	T		.04	.01			.09	T		.01	.03						.47	T			
	1.49		.16		.40		.02			.01	.39	.02		.03	T	.06	T	T	.01	.02	.01	T	T		.02	T	.02	.32	T			
	2.29	.09	.48		.12		.05			T	.67			.08	.06	T		.06										.68				
	2.69	*	.80		.19		.01				.74			.02	.01					.10								.78				
ACK 2 S FIRE TWR	1.90	.09	.29		.12	T				T	.17	T		.09	.02	.16	T	.16	T	T	T	T					T	.44	.02			
STA 2 SE DAM	1.71	T	.11		.21					.12	.30	T		.15	T	.19	T	.08	T	.05	T	T			.02	.01		.45	.02			
VILLE WATER WORKS	1.96	.02	T	T	.11					.48	.09		T	.15	.28	T	.12	.06	T	T	.03			T			.24	.41				
DO 4 W	1.94	.03	.01		.07	T		T		.21	.37	.02		.20		.17	T	.20	.03	.03	.02	.02			T			.53	.03			
DA	.90	.07	.24		.01						.11	T		T	T	T	T	.03				T			T			.41	.03			
I CITY 5 SW	3.05	.44	T				.18			.50				.19	.08	.64	.03										.82	.17				
	1.54		.30		.02					.02	.14			T		.10		.05										.85				
EPOINT 4 NE	1.44	T	.13		.11						.32	.01		.03		.01	.03	.11	.01	.02	.02							.00	.04			
E 4 NE BALD EAGLE	2.82	.03	.41		.38		.09	T		.07	.50			.10	.03	.49		T		T								.72	T			
I CITY	1.56	T	T		.04					.20	.24	T		.18		.15	T	T	T	T	.07	.03			T			.65	T			
ITOWN	2.76	.50		.02	.28	.21	T			.73	.30	T	T	T	.07	T	.02	T			T			T			.24	.20	.19			
I DARBY	2.97	.59	.03	.04	.05		.16			.25	.85			.01		T	T							T			.93	.06	T			
	2.13		.08		.20						.47	.02		.19		.52	.02	.08	.02		.03	.01			.02			.45	.02			
	1.72	T	.27	T	.45					T	.30	T		.09		.23	T								T		T	.38	T			
INVILLE	1.24	.15	.30		.19		T			.08	.47			T	T										T			.11				
ICKEL	2.58	.04	.18		.22	T				.18	.34			.16	T	.22	.03	.10	T	.08	.05	T			.04	T	T	.84	.10			
ICKEL 1 WSW	2.46	.04	.17		.23	T				.18	.35	T		.15	.02	.21	.03	.08	T	.07	.04	T			.08	T	T	.75	.09			
	1.01		.04		.04	.03				T	.28	T		.07	.01	.11		.10	T	.03	T	.03						.29	.02			
	2.05	.38	T	.02	.10		T			.52	T			.10	.10	.05	.05	.03						T		T	.70	T	T			
ISBURG 2 W	2.32	.01	.38		.21		.23	T		.03	.85	T		T		.06	.01	.02			T						.02	.53	T			
IBORO 3 S	1.13	.03	.26		.05					T	.11		T	.02	T	.07		.06			T				T			.41	.12			
IVILLE	2.53	.70	.05		.06	T	.20			.38	.23			T	T	.30	T							T			.55	.06	T			
IRSVILLE 1 W	3.40	.34	.48		.12						.75			.10		.45								.10			.85	.21				
CHESTER	3.35	*	.57	.10		.13	.02				1.13		T		.11												.77	.52				
GROVE 1 E	2.79	*	.62		.08		.12			.29	.79			.03		.22											.56	.08				
HICKORY	1.87		.03		.30					.25	.20			.15		.20	.03	.10	.01		.05							.50	.05			
	2.16	T	.38		.38					.18	.26			.22		.35				T								.39				
IS BARRE	1.52	.10	.33	T	.07	T					.59	T		T	T			.07										.36				
IAMSBURG	2.96	T	.71		.22		.19	T		.12	.39			.06	T	.23	.03	.32		T						.03	.10	.53	.03			
IANSPORT WB AP	2.20	.34	.02	.03	.09	T	T			.41	.08		T	.13	.18	.04	.06	T	T					.01		T	.76	.01	.03			
IBURG	2.45	.05	.51		.08		.29			.04	.64			.06		.06		.03									.09	.53	.07			
3 SSW PUMP STA	2.44	.32	.09	T	.05	T	.18			.20	.58	T		T	.09	.39								.03			.43	.03	.05			
HAVEN	2.49	.13	.41		.04		.13			.11	.64			T		.60		T							T		.03	.40	T			
	1.62	.13	.44		.15		.02			.15	.46																	.27				
VILLE 3 SE	2.48	.22	.46		.19		.01		T	.09	.63			T	.04	T		.01										.83				

SUPPLEMENTAL DATA

Station	Wind direction		Wind speed m. p. h.				Relative humidity averages - percent				Number of days with precipitation							Percent of possible sunshine	Average sky cover sunrise to sunset
	Prevailing	Percent of time from prevailing	Average	Fastest mile	Direction of fastest mile	Date of fastest mile	1:30 a EST	7:30 a EST	1:30 p EST	7:30 p EST	Trace	.01–.09	.10–.49	.50–.99	1.00–1.99	2.00 and over	Total		
NTOWN WB AIRPORT	WSW	68	9.9	-	-	-	81	82	66	74	8	5	3	2	0	0	18	-	7.4
WB AIRPORT	-	-	9.4	25++	NNE	27	-	-	-	-	11	7	2	1	0	0	21	-	8.1
ISBURG WB AIRPORT	ESE	14	7.0	41	NW	10	76	77	62	68	8	4	5	2	0	0	19	42	7.5
ADELPHIA WB AIRPORT	NNE	76	9.1	35	NW	10	79	80	65	72	8	4	3	3	0	0	18	34	7.5
SBURGH WB AIRPORT	WSW	12	10.0	25++	W	9+	80	81	68	74	11	9	6	0	0	0	26	44	8.4
ING WB CITY	-	-	9.7	35	NW	10	-	-	-	-	3	5	5	2	0	0	15	39	7.8
NTON WB AIRPORT	WSW	17	8.9	30	SW	3	77	78	64	72	11	2	5	0	0	0	18	37	7.8
PINGPORT WB	-	-	3.0	31††	WNW	16	-	-	-	-	7	5	5	0	0	0	17	-	-
IAMSPORT WB AIRPORT	-	-	-	-	-	-	-	79	62	69	6	9	4	1	0	0	20	-	7.8

eak Gust

See Reference Notes Following Station Index

Table 5

DAILY TEMPERATURES

Station		1	2	3	4	5	6	7	8	9	10	11	12	13	14	15	16	17	18	19	20	21	22	23	24	25	26	27	28	29	30	31
ALLENTOWN WB AP	MAX	33	38	36	46	35	37	38	45	38	47	39	35	32	40	43	36	35	42	47	37	43	47	46	49	51	54	55	30			
	MIN	25	9	8	30	25	28	32	29	28	28	21	15	25	29	26	26	25	23	26	21	21	20	26	29	32	37	27	20			
ALLENTOWN GAS CO	MAX	35	34	38	43	48	35	37	40	44	42	46	38	35	33	42	43	40	35	44	46	38	48	50	48	52	53	57	55			
	MIN	30	27	16	18	27	28	29	31	28	32	25	15	15	24	29	29	26	24	26	22	23	24	27	31	33	39	25	21			
ALTOONA HORSESHOE CURVE	MAX	34	34	36	41	35	32	45	42	45	51	37	34	39	33	38	37	29	47	45	28	41	49	44	52	64	57	53	36			
	MIN	30	23	17	34	21	27	30	29	34	34	27	9	24	26	23	21	18	15	26	17	20	21	32	29	37	39	35	17			
ARENDTSVILLE	MAX	34	34	39	39	53	36	35	37	41	47	49	37	35	42	36	39	45	35	49	43	38	43	48	53	54	53	57	58			
	MIN	31	27	22	33	26	28	28	32	29	34	31	15	17	26	27	23	23	20	22	20	21	23	26	28	32	35	47	25			
ARTEMAS 1 WNW	MAX	40	40	38	52	50	36	41	43	52	50	46	40	44	39	40	41	40	53	54	40	48	54	55	62	60	54	62	50			
	MIN	29	22	27	40	21	28	30	29	30	31	28	14	25	26	16	28	20	21	22	13	14	21	29	34	40	31	44	20			
BAKERSTOWN 3 WNW	MAX	32	33	42	43	36	48	40	50	61	56	36	39	45	38	38	36	31	44	42	28	38	56	48	58	71	64	58	34			
	MIN	24	26	22	35	22	26	34	31	38	34	27	16	31	26	23	28	21	18	24	18	22	26	36	27	46	48	32	24			
BEAVERTOWN	MAX	34	37	37	44	39	34	39	42	39	46	43	36	38	37	39	38	35	44	43	38	42	47	48	52	59	56	55	37			
	MIN	27	26	14	33	23	28	31	27	29	36	27	10	25	22	24	18	22	19	32	20	27	20	27	27	36	40	36	18			
BELLEFONTE 4 S	MAX	34	32	36	39	42	34	34	45	45	47	42	35	33	40	33	34	33	29	46	32	35	43	48	44	53	63	55	43			
	MIN	29	26	15	34	22	24	29	29	31	36	27	10	15	24	21	21	20	19	21	19	22	22	23	29	31	39	40	15			
BERWICK	MAX	34	36	39	43	41	37	38	43	42	46	42	37	34	39	39	39	37	43	42	38	43	50	50	53	60	58	58	36			
	MIN	25	26	14	33	22	29	32	28	28	36	25	12	26	19	29	25	22	20	33	19	21	21	27	30	34	36	36	19			
BETHLEHEM LEHIGH UNIV	MAX																															
	MIN																															
BLAIRSVILLE 6 ENE	MAX	33	31	46	42	35	38	47	50	54	35	33	42	35	31	30	32	24	41	37	24	36	56	38	57	70	55	52	32			
	MIN	28	20	23	30	24	25	32	28	33	27	24	15	26	20	19	23	15	18	18	13	16	27	33	29	44	48	29	20			
BRADFORD 4 W RES	MAX	31	34	40	40	32	34	46	44	45	45	28	34	37	37	31	31	26	34	32	25	40	47	47	45	63	60	49	30			
	MIN	18	16	6	29	10	11	19	24	26	23	18	-2	23	23	16	16	13	15	17	12	16	11	24	23	30	27	22	7			
BROOKVILLE CAA AIRPORT	MAX	32	30	40	38	33	35	40	47	54	42	36	38	38	34	29	32	26	39	34	27	39	49	37	54	67	53	51	30			
	MIN	27	10	10	24	19	29	31	29	37	30	18	9	26	24	19	21	17	6	16	16	20	19	31	28	39	36	18	15			
BURGETTSTOWN 2 W	MAX	38	33	38	45	39	35	45	42	50	61	38	35	40	43	33	37	36	31	48	27	32	41	55	43	62	71	66	36			
	MIN	31	25	18	36	19	19	19	30	30	36	29	9	11	31	24	23	21	10	11	9	17	16	20	23	27	35	35	23			
BURNT CABINS 2 NE	MAX	35	37	40	43	39	35	42	45	47	48	42	37	44	41	38	42	37	46	55	34	44	49	51	56	62	57	57	42			
	MIN	31	28	21	32	24	28	30	27	34	38	29	8	25	22	23	25	21	12	31	18	23	18	28	24	37	44	39	20			
BUTLER	MAX	34	31	40	36	38	45	47	40	51	51	40	38	40	41	34	37	37	37	42	27	31	47	55	55	68	70	59	34			
	MIN	31	22	17	32	20	24	31	30	37	24	26	12	31	30	24	28	21	8	23	17	20	20	31	36	46	37	33	19			
CANTON 1 NW	MAX	31	24	32	35	40	32	34	38	37	42	35	20	31	31	34	35	34	28	36	28	28	35	42	42	46	55	53	33			
	MIN	21	20	19	29	17	16	26	25	24	32	20	6	6	22	26	23	16	15	18	15	15	15	19	25	26	37	32	10			
CARLISLE	MAX	34	38	39	50	45	35	38	45	43	50	46	38	39	38	40	43	38	46	45	39	47	51	51	54	57	55	56	42			
	MIN	30	28	20	34	31	30	33	33	30	40	31	15	28	28	30	26	26	23	35	23	28	24	30	28	38	41	42	25			
CHAMBERSBURG 1 ESE	MAX	35	40	42	53	37	36	38	46	48	49	40	38	46	37	40	43	35	49	44	37	44	49	53	57	58	54	56	33			
	MIN	29	25	23	33	27	29	32	31	36	39	25	15	26	23	26	28	25	22	27	21	23	22	29	27	32	41	33	24			
CHESTER	MAX	38	39	42	44	53	39	39	42	44	46	50	37	36	39	45	45	39	36	48	49	40	45	49	51	54	57	60	64			
	MIN	31	29	30	30	32	30	32	36	33	30	21	21	20	29	23	30	28	23	30	23	24	26	34	35	34	42	53	29			
CLARION 3 SW	MAX	36	36	39	39	34	38	39	47	54	53	35	38	40	38	33	34	30	41	38	28	38	49	43	53	67	62	59	36			
	MIN	26	17	9	28	16	19	27	29	31	33	24	9	27	27	24	18	18	4	17	16	20	13	26	26	34	31	29	15			
CLAYSVILLE 3 W	MAX	36	37	50	45	37	40	44	49	63	55	39	42	42	37	37	38	34	50	44	36	41	56	43	66	68	68	57	48			
	MIN	31	26	21	29	21	25	36	31	33	36	27	13	31	25	22	30	21	13	22	10	10	15	29	25	42	38	31	26			
COATESVILLE 1 SW	MAX	35	35	40	38	51	36	39	40	45	45	49	38	37	39	42	41	43	35	48	46	40	45	48	48	56	56	59	60			
	MIN	31	28	20	24	26	29	29	33	26	33	27	18	18	24	28	24	25	22	23	21	20	20	24	29	31	38	48	28			
COLUMBIA	MAX	35	42	37	52	42	36	40	43	45	50	43	36	40	41	40	45	42	49	45	40	44	47	49	54	56	59	57	39			
	MIN	30	28	23	34	25	29	33	34	29	40	28	15	27	27	28	26	25	22	36	27	24	23	29	30	38	44	39	26			
CONFLUENCE 1 SW DAM	MAX	37	41	38	53	45	35	39	56	56	60	38	33	40	39	34	36	36	29	49	32	30	43	55	47	63	67	58	42			
	MIN	33	28	26	37	28	28	30	31	32	37	31	17	13	26	21	22	20	12	13	16	16	18	32	31	36	37	42	31			
CORRY	MAX	30	33	43	40	35	36	35	48	42	41	26	35	38	36	31	30	25	34	34	24	39	48	42	45	64	59	53	36			
	MIN	20	9	19	29	15	14	27	25	34	25	18	7	27	27	22	16	16	13	18	11	18	11	25	25	39	33	22	11			
COUDERSPORT 3 NW	MAX	29	32	37	38	30	32	45	45	45	42	43	30	38	30	30	32	24	34	32	25	35	44	38	44	61	50	49	27			
	MIN	19	15	9	26	10	22	27	22	31	25	14	1	20	22	22	16	13	5	14	13	16	14	28	24	34	34	16	8			
DERRY	MAX	38	36	52	48	37	42	45	53	50	40	38	44	41	39	35	35	30	47	44	33	39	57	47	63	69	65	60	39			
	MIN	31	27	24	35	25	29	29	31	40	34	30	15	29	24	22	28	21	13	27	18	17	23	37	25	51	53	34	29			
DEVAULT 1 W	MAX	33	42	40	49	37	37	40	43	36	46	37	36	38	47	43	40	35	48	47	41	44	49	48	54	57	60	59	33			
	MIN	24	16	20	29	24	24	29	25	26	25	18	10	23	25	23	25	20	17	23	18	15	20	22	27	31	41	26	22			
DIXON	MAX	35	28	38	38	44	32	40	41	43	42	39	31	37	37	36	44	40	33	42	35	30	35	47	45	52	63	57	37			
	MIN	18	20	8	32	15	16	23	23	23	34	19	6	6	26	22	22	21	21	25	18	12	14	15	22	30	40	37	15			
DONEGAL	MAX	33	29	46	40	32	36	47	55	53	48	28	38	34	28	32	34	22	40	33	24	34	50	36	57	64	56	47	32			
	MIN	26	20	26	25	19	23	32	27	34	28	15	8	21	17	15	20	10	8	12	12	11	18	23	19	38	40	27	24			
DONORA	MAX	41	38	49	52	44	40	45	49	57	64	41	38	43	44	33	38	39	43	52	33	35	50	60	52	69	71	68	40			
	MIN	34	28	29	43	30	31	39	34	42	39	32	20	35	34	25	32	23	20	30	19	20	26	38	28	48	41	40	27			
DU BOIS 7 E	MAX	33	30	38	40	35	34	45	44	52	51	33	33	40	35	29	35	29	40	39	28	40	49	44	50	66	58	53	32			
	MIN	26	20	3	33	11	28	30	28	34	29	24	4	24	24	22	11	15	3	20	15	20	14	31	26	42	39	32	14			
EAGLES MERE	MAX	29	24	31	35	39	28	30	34	37	38	38	21	30	27	31	30	30	28	34	31	27	31	38	37	43	52	53	33			
	MIN	20	19	18	27	16	17	24	23	23	30	18	5	6	21	22	20	14	11	16	12	12	13	20	26	26	35	33	9			
EAST BRADY	MAX	34	34	35	40	39	44	42	53	58	56	44	40	43	43	40	37	37	45	43	29	40	52	45	56	70	64	57	42			
	MIN	30	23	16	33	20	25	32	32	35	35	28	14	32	30	26	27	9	20	24	19	22	20	36	31	38	34	34	20			
EBENSBURG	MAX	33	33	43	42	35	35	47	44	54	50	32	33	35	30	30	32	25	42	35	24	35	47	40	50	64	54	52	33			
	MIN	28	21	19	32	20	26	30	28	32	30	29	9	22	25	20	21	15	12	20	13	17	21	33	29	40	45	30	15			
EMPORIUM 2 SSW	MAX	33	27	33	40	39	30	34	45	44	49	37	30	32	33	32	35	34	27	33	29	29	38	49	40	49	62	51	35			
	MIN	23	20	10	30	14	17	22	22	23	32	20	4	5	20	21	13	15	15	19	15	18	17	22	25	29	33	34	11			
EPHRATA	MAX	36	41	37	50	41	37	39	43	42	49	41	36	37	40	39	41	36	46	46	40	44	46	48	54	54	58	56	42			
	MIN	30	26	19	33	21	27	32	31	31	36	27	14	24	25	26	28	23	20	36	19	23	23	30	30	35	43	32	25			
ERIE CAA AIRPORT	MAX	28	32	44	36	34	42	35	42	49	37	26	35	40	37	32	33	26	36	28	25	33	43	39	49	67	54	35	36			
	MIN	23	15	27	22	20	20	32	26	37	26	16	11	32	25	25	21	21	19	17	21	20	21	30	27	49	35	18	15			

See reference notes following Station Index.

DAILY TEMPERATURES

n		1	2	3	4	5	6	7	8	9	10	11	12	13	14	15	16	17	18	19	20	21	22	23	24	25	26	27	28	29	30	31	Average
	MAX	35	45	42	50	38	40	49	40	48	54	40	36	44	34	38	40	32	50	38	30	46	46	48	62	64	54	50	30				43.8
	MIN	32	32	28	28	28	28	30	28	36	38	24	14	26	26	20	28	18	16	20	20	20	20	28	25	38	48	33	26				27.0
	MAX	34	34	46	42	34	50	40	51	58	50	49	36	44	41	37	38	33	42	29	24	48	52	44	55	69	61	60	41				44.4
	MIN	24	26	20	29	26	26	30	33	30	30	19	11	28	25	22	27	18	11	16	15	13	21	31	27	45	48	21	15				24.5
	MAX	39	34	33	38	40	35	43	44	52	61	47	38	41	41	38	35	36	29	45	29	29	39	55	40	59	70	60	40				42.5
	MIN	27	22	17	31	19	22	23	30	31	35	27	12	15	31	23	24	20	10	12	17	20	19	20	25	25	37	38	20				23.3
	MAX	35	32	32	43	40	34	43	40	49	54	46	34	36	41	36	34	35	30	39	26	36	41	49	49	62	66	58	52				41.9
	MIN	22	25	18	25	32	20	22	29	29	33	32	22	21	31	27	23	22	18	20	18	15	19	19	32	30	36	26	15				24.3
	MAX	28	32	32	40	37	32	34	43	40	44	38	31	27	30	35	33	33	35	37	28	36	42	42	50	54	53	53	26				37.3
	MIN	21	22	19	32	18	21	28	26	26	34	18	7	19	25	20	23	23	17	27	14	15	21	32	26	33	42	21	14				23.0
	MAX	38	39	38	54	45	38	39	40	45	50	40	35	37	44	43	42	35	46	48	39	44	48	50	52	54	59	63	45				44.6
	MIN	30	28	22	37	26	30	34	30	29	40	26	16	26	26	29	28	24	21	34	21	24	20	30	30	34	46	45	23				28.9
	MAX	35	36	41	42	54	38	35	40	44	48	50	38	36	43	37	39	45	38	50	46	39	45	49	56	56	57	59	59				44.8
	MIN	33	28	27	35	30	29	31	33	35	35	31	17	23	26	28	29	25	25	25	20	23	24	30	30	39	42	47	27				29.5
	MAX	35	38	35	39	38	40	42	47	50	52	52	38	42	44	42	38	38	44	42	44	51	54	48	55	54	58	56	50				45.2
	MIN	30	27	16	30	26	30	34	31	28	30	26	16	21	26	24	22	21	26	28	21	23	22	26	28	32	44	48	28				27.3
	MAX	34	32	33	37	44	34	35	38	43	45	45	35	35	35	37	37	37	31	42	38	37	49	47	48	51	57	58	50				40.9
	MIN	31	27	15	33	25	25	28	31	31	33	28	11	12	25	27	22	21	18	19	19	20	20	21	29	28	40	40	20				25.0
	MAX	33	35	45	43	36	51	37	51	53	49	32	34	42	40	34	36	30	37	36	25	41	50	42	56	66	60	57	39				42.5
	MIN	24	14	20	27	19	25	31	29	33	30	22	10	30	27	24	26	21	9	18	15	17	21	30	30	44	40	23	15				24.1
	MAX	35	36	41	42	56	37	35	40	45	46	50	39	38	44	37	41	46	36	49	45	40	45	51	54	57	62	59	60				45.2
	MIN	31	26	27	34	28	27	28	32	32	33	28	15	15	23	26	26	22	21	22	17	18	22	24	28	39	39	49	25				27.0
	MAX	34	37	39	49	36	35	39	44	41	49	40	34	40	40	38	41	35	48	44	38	43	49	49	51	53	58	57	30				42.5
	MIN	29	25	26	35	31	30	33	34	33	38	24	17	28	29	29	29	25	25	28	22	27	24	32	30	39	42	28	26				29.2
	MAX	32	28	28	39	41	32	37	38	40	43	35	34	33	30	32	40	34	28	39	35	25	31	45	46	48	56	52	41				37.2
	MIN	17	18	-4	20	17	17	20	26	17	30	20	1	2	18	14	14	17	17	22	15	14	11	13	23	28	31	35	13				17.4
	MAX	36	38	36	52	37	37	38	46	42	48	38	37	39	41	39	43	36	49	44	39	41	48	45	54	52	55	53	34				42.8
	MIN	30	27	28	36	30	30	34	31	31	37	27	21	29	28	35	29	28	25	31	24	28	27	32	33	38	43	34	30				30.6
	MAX																										67	54	50				
	MIN																										35	42	20				
	MAX	35	33	41	42	37	39	48	53	59	54	39	42	40	35	36	35	29	45	39	29	40	55	40	60	70	61	55	35				43.8
	MIN	31	23	21	29	21	23	35	33	38	34	25	12	28	25	23	24	21	9	22	12	21	20	31	36	42	44	34	23				26.4
	MAX	37			47	39	41	45	54		60			44	42	38			49	47	33	41				71	67	64	42				
	MIN	32			24	25	22	37	31		29		16		26	19			16	26	18	18	23				46	35	24				
	MAX	34	32	37	45	39	34	47	35	50	52	36	30	34	41	32	33	34	27	36	24	24	37	57	39	54	67	57	29				39.1
	MIN	23	12	12	34	17	16	28	28	27	32	21	9	15	30	23	22	18	10	16	15	18	16	24	29	32	42	23	13				21.7
	MAX	34	40	39	47	46	36	38	47	47	47	40	37	33	35	45	43	40	44	45	39	43	46		55	54	55	56	37				43.3
	MIN	28	25	13	33	25	28	32	33	28	35	24	9	24	29	27	23	22	21	37	19	20	20		27	34	36	36	20				26.2
	MAX	37	35	37	44	43	35	36	48	44	54	41	33	35	36	31	32	32	24	45	42	26	37	51	35	54	67	53	40				40.3
	MIN	30	22	22	22	26	27	31	32	33	33	29	14	19	28	16	24	18	12	20	16	19	21	25	28	26	40	40	22				24.8
	MAX	35	30	32	38	37	35	36	42	45	48	34	29	35	38	32	30	32	25	35	27	26	39	48	34	45	63	51	31				36.9
	MIN	21	14	8	28	12	15	20	26	28	31	20	2	5	24	15	15	15	16	16	14	18	11	21	24	28	29	11	13				17.9
	MAX	35	40	44	47	35	35	50	44	51	56	42	37	42	35	38	40	31	51	42	32	44	52	48	59	67	55	52	33				44.2
	MIN	31	20	20	20	25	27	28	26	34	35	19	11	22	23	14	26	20	16	19	16	19	20	27	23	33	37	31	22				23.7
STA	MAX	36	39	37	51	46	36	41	42	44	49	47	36	38	41	39	45	41	50	45	40	45	47	46	53	54	59	60	45				44.7
	MIN	32	27	19	34	27	29	33	34	27	39	27	17	26	24	28	26	25	22	35	22	25	22	27	28	34	41	45	27				28.6
	MAX	32	33	36	37	48	40	37	40	43	46	48	37	34	35	40	35	41	34	46	42	38	42	48	46	52	53	58	56				42.0
	MIN	30	25	13	33	27	28	29	31	27	32	26	15	21	25	27	22	33	20	25	21	24	21	24	27	33	40	49	26				26.9
	MAX	32	28	35	39	42	34	38	48	42	43	38	22	36	39	38	39	37	31	41	31	28	37	48	44	52	64	53	33				39.0
	MIN	21	19	8	32	14	15	19	22	24	31	20	4	8	22	28	22	16	17	21	16	13	15	21	26	28	29	30	10				19.7
	MAX	34	34	38	37	47	35	36	37	44	48	48	39	36	36	39	39	41	34	46	44	40	44	48	47	53	51	58	55				42.4
	MIN	31	25	26	33	26	29	32	30	28	36	28	15	16	27	27	23	24	18	22	21	22	22	27	28	29	39	48	25				27.0
	MAX	34	34	38	38	45	37	36	43	47	48	48	38	37	40	36	39	41	34	49	41	39	47	52	47	55	61	56	52				43.3
	MIN	29	29	19	30	25	25	31	30	29	35	32	15	15	26	25	22	25	23	22	22	22	24	24	29	29	37	41	21				26.3
	MAX	31	31	45	41	34	45	34	49	50	42	29	33	41	36	32	37	29	35	34	23	41	48	40	47	64	54	49	40				39.8
	MIN	23	11	21	28	17	16	27	25	33	28	18	10	28	26	24	25	19	6	9	9	1	14	29	28	38	36	20	13				20.8
	MAX	33	40	38	45	39	37	42	45	49	47	36	36	36	36	40	41	35	46	45	37	41	51	46	54	57	53	52	29				42.4
	MIN	27	27	17	34	21	30	33	27	30	35	26	11	26	22	27	25	21	20	28	20	27	22	31	30	37	35	27	17				26.2
	MAX	37	32	32	39	38	33	35	47	44	51	39	34	34	38	33	31	36	21	43	29	30	36	47	39	51	64	54	46				39.0
	MIN	23	20	8	21	14	15	25	26	26	30	25	5	4	22	19	15	14	5	4	12	15	15	15	23	23	37	42	12				18.4
	MAX	38	45	40	58	40	39	44	44	46	53	36	35	40	44	47	44	39	47	50	45	47	48	51	54	57	59	66	37				46.2
	MIN	32	32	31	39	32	31	38	35	34	36	30	22	30	31	33	33	31	28	34	26	27	31	35	39	39	50	37	30				33.1
	MAX	33	39	38	41	32	34	45	44	52	45	37	36	39	34	35	35	27	45	36	28	42	50	42	55	67	53	51	26				40.8
	MIN	29	18	18	29	24	27	30	27	35	33	20	10	25	23	18	24	19	16	19	17	21	22	31	26	39	45	25	20				24.6
	MAX	33	33	34	42	38	34	45	37	50	50	36	29	34	40	33	34	33	28	35	25	26	38	48	39	49	67	56	30				38.4
	MIN	23	17	17	34	19	17	18	26	26	32	21	11	16	31	24	24	18	7	9	10	19	17	23	29	32	36	29	14				21.4
	MAX	32	32	38	44	35	45	38	48	46	42	40	34	36	34	39	37	30	31	30	28	40	38	37	46	64	62	49	32				39.5
	MIN	23	20	22	30	28	30	30	32	34	32	27	25	29	28	30	28	9	12	16	10	20	30	30	30	35	35	30	10				25.5
FLD	MAX	34	39	39	50	36	36	39	43	44	48	39	35	38	41	39	43	35	47	44	38	43	46	49	51	53	58	59	30				42.7
	MIN	29	25	23	35	31	30	33	36	33	38	28	18	28	30	29	29	27	27	29	23	28	25	32	29	38	43	30	27				29.8
	MAX	35	34	41	42	37	46	41	48	60	54	36	35	41	35	36	36	28	46	39	30	36	50	42	56	66	68	41	40				42.8
	MIN	31	26	27	31	28	32	36	33	38	36	24	19	34	26	26	28	22	20	19	19	17	27	27	33	44	43	26	24				28.4
	MAX	31	24	35	35	38	29	35	38	36	39	34	23	29	30	31	38	32	24	35	28	22	28	40	40	42	56	50	32				34.1
	MIN	17	18	19	23	16	17	21	25	27	29	18	2	3	20	21	20	15	16	20	14	12	14	17	22	22	36	32	10				18.8
	MAX	34	38	32	48	36	38	38	42	42	47	37	33	37	40	46	39	33	45	46	37	42	47	45	52	56	58	58	29				42.0
	MIN	27	18	21	33	26	28	32	28	31	33	22	14	25	26	25	24	23	16	26	20	24	21	31	28	36	46	27	24				26.3
	MAX	33	38	36	50	36	35	38	43	43	46	38	34	35	40	39	41	34	45	43	40	42	46	48	52	52	54	55	45				42.2
	MIN	28	20	25	35	28	32	32	29	34	36	22	16	26	20	24	24	23	18	27	20	25	22	20	30	45	50	28	26				27.3

See reference notes following Station Index.

DAILY TEMPERATURES

Table 5 - Continued

Station		1	2	3	4	5	6	7	8	9	10	11	12	13	14	15	16	17	18	19	20	21	22	23	24	25	26	27	28	29	30	31
MT POCONO 2 N AP	MAX	30	31	33	39	36	34	35	42	37	41	30	30	27	29	40	35	30	36	37	33	37	43	43	48	56	54	53	35			
	MIN	21	21	18	32	18	24	29	26	25	29	19	5	17	25	21	20	16	16	13	13	13	15	28	25	33	43	30	15			
MUHLENBURG 1 SE	MAX	32	34	35	42	32	38	35	42	48	41	31	35	31	35	38	35	30	38	42	38	38	36	36	50	55	54	54	32			
	MIN	24	24	18	30	19	26	30	26	29	30	19	5	22	22	24	26	18	15	28	11	15	15	28	31	39	40	25	14			
NEWBURG 3 W	MAX																															
	MIN																															
NEW CASTLE 1 N	MAX	33	34	44	43	39	48	38	49	57	55	35	37	42	44	37	37	30	43	42	29	39	51	50	56	70	63	48	38			
	MIN	27	19	18	25	19	24	32	30	33	34	24	12	31	27	18	29	19	12	20	14	15	21	33	30	40	42	28	18			
NEWELL	MAX	41	38	48	54	45	40	46	50	56	62	42	40	45	45	34	38	40	44	51	32	37	49	58	53	68	72	67	41			
	MIN	34	28	21	42	25	32	38	34	38	38	31	21	33	32	22	28	28	19	29	17	17	23	38	26	42	41	38	28			
NEWPORT	MAX	35	32	40	38	49	36	35	39	46	48	48	39	37	39	37	42	44	35	46	42	40	46	50	49	53	57	57	51			
	MIN	30	28	17	34	27	29	31	31	30	35	31	13	13	23	29	23	25	22	24	22	22	21	22	27	28	37	41	21			
NEW STANTON	MAX	38	37	52	46	38	51	49	56	55	56	48	46	43	38	37	39	31	50	38	33	41	58	40	64	70	67	60	47			
	MIN	31	23	22	30	23	26	25	28	40	36	20	13	22	19	14	25	15	19	18	15	14	19	21	25	38	41	30	25			
NORRISTOWN	MAX	36	42	39	51	38	39	40	45	44	49	37	36	37	44	45	41	37	50	50	40	45	50	48	54	58	60	63	35			
	MIN	29	24	24	35	30	30	35	33	35	33	26	18	28	29	29	31	27	25	30	23	24	25	33	34	35	50	33	26			
PALMERTON	MAX	34	38	36	46	34	36	39	43	39	45	36	33	33	37	42	39	34	43	44	35	41	46	47	48	51	57	55	30			
	MIN	25	11	12	32	25	29	33	30	30	29	21	10	25	30	30	25	23	23	24	21	22	19	27	30	35	36	24	21			
PHIL DREXEL INST OF TEC	MAX	40	41	41	56	40	39	41	43	48	52	37	38	40	46	45	43	38	50	49	43	47	49	50	54	57	61	67	36			
	MIN	32	29	31	40	31	32	36	35	33	36	30	20	30	30	31	33	30	26	34	24	25	29	35	36	38	50	35	30			
PHILADELPHIA WB AP	MAX	38	40	40	54	37	39	40	43	46	50	34	35	38	44	44	41	36	47	48	40	45	48	50	53	55	59	64	36			
	MIN	30	29	29	37	29	31	36	31	31	34	28	20	28	29	31	30	27	23	31	23	25	26	33	33	37	48	36	27			
PHILADELPHIA PT BREEZE	MAX	38		39	53	40	40	43	46	47	51	38	38	39	44	43	40	37	48	49	40	46	48	49	54	57	65	65	33			
	MIN	30	29	29	39	33	31		37	37	42	32	24	31	30	30	30	30	28	40	26	29	33	36	38	31	44	45	27			
PHILADELPHIA SHAWMONT	MAX	35	39	39	50	47	40	42	44	45	48	46	36	37	44	43	44	39	49	46	43	44	50	49	53	57	60	60	49			
	MIN	32	28	23	35	29	30	35	32	28	40	28	17	29	30	28	22	27	24	37	24	24	23	30	32	35	45	49	27			
PHILADELPHIA CITY	MAX	39	42	41	54	41	40	42	45	48	51	37	38	37	44	48	42	38	47	48	41	47	50	50	54	55	59	64	36			
	MIN	31	31	32	41	32	32	38	36	35	36	28	22	31	31	32	34	29	28	32	25	27	32	37	39	38	53	34	29			
PHILIPSBURG CAA AP	MAX	30	32	40	40	29	30	43	43	50	40	33	30	36	30	28	32	24	40	34	28	37	44	39	49	60	52	52	24			
	MIN	25	10	24	25	13	26	29	27	32	30	15	2	22	22	12	21	16	8	15	15	18	14	29	25	41	45	19	12			
PHOENIXVILLE 1 E	MAX	35	44	42	54	48	39	41	45	44	51	50	38	37	44	46	43	40	50	50	43	47	50	49	54	57	59	60	48			
	MIN	32	28	20	26	25	30	33	29	24	37	27	16	24	26	27	23	26	20	34	22	20	19	26	28	32	41	44	27			
PIMPLE HILL	MAX	29	25	29	39	40	30	33	34	40	42	35	28	29	25	29	39	29	26	37	34	26	32	41	41	46	55	51	35			
	MIN	20	19	19	24	16	19	25	24	24	28	15	5	15	18	19	22	15	15	19	12	12	18	26	24	28	36	34	13			
PITTSBURGH WB AP 2	MAX	32	31	44	42	34	43	41	47	62	46	35	37	43	35	35	36	28	46	36	31	38	53	41	60	68	63	45	36			
	MIN	30	24	27	29	25	26	33	31	40	33	21	15	33	25	24	23	18	17	17	16	17	26	32	26	49	45	26	22			
PITTSBURGH WB CITY	MAX	36	34	47	46	37	42	45	51	63	47	38	40	44	38	36	38	30	50	40	33	40	55	46	60	70	64	49	40			
	MIN	32	26	30	33	30	31	36	33	44	36	26	22	35	28	26	28	23	24	20	21	23	28	36	30	54	48	29	24			
PLEASANT MOUNT 1 W	MAX	31	26	29	34	37	30	34	34	35	39	34	26	29	27	29	38	30	26	35	30	23	28	41	43	41	53	50	34			
	MIN	17	18	1	25	11	14	14	22	14	27	18	6	7	17	14	17	15	17	18	15	13	7	13	25	25	36	34	13			
PORT CLINTON	MAX	36	34	40	37	48	40	38	39	46	45	49	39	35	36	40	44	41	35	46	45	39	45	48	50	49	58	53				
	MIN	28	24	12	18	21	26	29	27	21	32	25	10	15	25	27	22	23	20	25	19	22	18	24	26	27	40	21				
PUTNEYVILLE 2 SE DAM	MAX	37	34	33	42	37	33	37	43	50	57	40	36	40	40	35	33	36	30	42	30	28	36	52	38	55	68	55	40			
	MIN	25	19	15	30	17	20	22	28	27	32	24	10	12	28	21	20	15	6	7	8	17	16	20	24	25	38	36	15			
QUAKERTOWN 1 E	MAX	35	36	35	48	43	39	38	43	40	41	40	40	36	41	41	39	36	44	41	37	42	45	46	50	54	55	53	45			
	MIN	28	24	6	32	25	28	32	29	26	36	24	14	23	28	24	23	24	22	34	21	22	19	28	29	29	37	36	23			
READING WB CITY	MAX	36	40	37	51	37	38	41	45	41	48	41	35	35	41	42	41	35	47	47	39	46	49	48	51	54	59	59	32			
	MIN	29	22	24	36	31	31	35	36	34	34	26	18	27	31	32	21	26	25	30	23	28	27	33	36	36	44	31	25			
RIDGWAY 3 W	MAX	36	31	30	39	37	34	36	41	46	50	38	32	36	38	33	30	35	27	38	29	29	40	49	37	50	64	52	37			
	MIN	25	22	2	21	13	16	29	28	26	33	23	3	3	21	18	13	16	14	12	15	20	13	18	27	30	30	33	11			
SALINA 3 W	MAX	35	33	45	45	35	38	44	50	60	58	36	39	42	38	33	35	31	47	44	29	37	53	48	58	69	62	60	39			
	MIN	30	22	22	35	21	21	35	30	37	35	23	14	29	26	23	26	20	11	23	18	16	20	34	26	42	42	33	22			
SCRANTON	MAX	34	30	34	39	43	33	40	38	42	42	42	32	37	34	37	43	37	33	40	37	30	35	48	45	52	58	59	42			
	MIN	24	24	16	30	23	22	29	32	34	36	25	11	11	25	29	28	21	20	24	19	19	19	21	28	28	40	41	18			
SCRANTON WB AIRPORT	MAX	32	32	36	41	32	37	37	40	41	40	30	35	32	35	42	35	30	40	39	29	34	47	44	51	58	57	54	31			
	MIN	23	14	16	27	20	27	31	28	30	24	13	7	24	27	25	24	20	22	20	17	16	17	29	28	38	44	19	16			
SELINSGROVE CAA AP	MAX	32	40	37	43	34	34	38	46	39	48	35	36	36	39	39	37	33	43	43	39	40	48	48	51	56	57	54	30			
	MIN	27	11	11	26	23	29	32	27	27	32	18	12	25	24	20	20	23	17	24	20	22	21	28	27	37	34	21	18			
SHIPPENSBURG	MAX	35	36	41	53	41	38	39	44	45	51	41	38	45	38	48	46	38	49	48	38	44	50	52	54	57	54	57	43			
	MIN	30	26	20	34	28	28	31	29	32	40	30	14	25	24	27	24	24	23	36	20	22	22	29	27	34	40	42	23			
SHIPPINGPORT WB	MAX	33	33	44	41	35	49	41	47	61	45	35	39	43	37	37	36	29	46	39	32	40	53	41	59	70	64	41	38			
	MIN	31	23	24	27	24	28	32	31	37	34	20	15	33	26	25	26	17	15	19	18	14	24	33	30	44	40	25	22			
SLIPPERY ROCK	MAX	32	32	41	38	32	49	39	52	55	50	36	36	40	34	30	35	28	40	36	27	38	51	53	53	67	62	55	35			
	MIN	25	16	19	30	22	25	31	28	36	32	22	15	30	24	22	23	22	11	18	15	19	23	29	29	43	43	26	16			
SOMERSET MAIN ST	MAX	38	38	48	48	37	39	55	46	56	56	34	36	40	33	34	37	30	46	42	28	37	51	44	58	66	58	54	36			
	MIN	31	24	25	34	23	27	33	30	33	32	28	13	23	21	17	25	17	17	22	14	15	20	33	24	39	45	35	23			
SPRINGBORO	MAX	34	31	39	44	36	35	35	36	50	50	38	35	35	40	33	34	29	25	30	25	30	38	49	40	55	69	57				
	MIN	25	11	18	33	18	17	17	24	31	30	21	10	21	30	26	26	9	7	9	13	16	17	29	35	40	36	20				
SPRINGS 1 SW	MAX	41	37	50	50	33	37	53	45	55	47	34	33	33	30	34	32	26	44	41	26		49	44	58	63	53	52	35			
	MIN	31	23	25	32	26	26	32	29	32	32	24	11	23	19	16	21	15	14	18	11			26	28	33	37	34	24			
STATE COLLEGE	MAX	34	35	37	42	33	34	45	44	50	41	34	32	39	34	34	34	28	45	39	34	43	47	44	53	63	56	54	27			
	MIN	27	23	25	32	24	29	32	31	35	35	20	12	26	26	22	25	20	18	23	19	25	25	34	31	42	43	23	16			
STROUDSBURG	MAX	31	37	36	48	35	37	38	44	38	44	35	34	34	34	44	36	34	45	41	32	40	46	45	48	54	53	53	28			
	MIN	24	13	7	33	20	27	32	25	23	26	16	9	17	28	20	21	22	20	25	17	14	15	23	28	27	32	26	16			
TAMARACK 2 S FIRE TWR	MAX	31	24	33	37	35	29	31	40	40	44	38	28	28	35	28	27	33	27	36	29	28	37	42	38	45	57	50	34			
	MIN	23	20	19	25	17	18	24	24	24	30	20	5	5	19	20	19	12	11	14	10	14	17	22	26	27	40	33	7			
TIONESTA 2 SE DAM	MAX	37	33	34	41	36	34	40	38	50	53	38	33	32	40	35	30	30	26	38	27	27	40	50	38	51	67	55	35			
	MIN	24	15	12	20	19	20	20	27	27	27	21	7	10	29	24	15	18	5	7	15	20	11	19	22	30	32	33	13			

See reference notes following Station Index.

'able 5-Continued

DAILY TEMPERATURES

PENNSYLVANIA
FEBRUARY 1957

Station		1	2	3	4	5	6	7	8	9	10	11	12	13	14	15	16	17	18	19	20	21	22	23	24	25	26	27	28	29	30	31	Average
ITUSVILLE WATER WORKS	MAX	33	34	44	37	34	37	48	48	52	45	31	33	40	35	34	33	28	38	35	27	40	51	36	49	68	55	53	37				40.5
	MIN	21	9	11	28	15	14	21	27	30	29	19	6	26	25	17	13	16	6	10	11	19	12	28	25	35	31	23	13				19.3
OWANDA	MAX	33	37	39	46	37	38	45	42	44	46	31	35	38	38	42	41	32	40	40	32	38	49	46	50	65	60	54	34				41.9
	MIN	19	18	9	33	15	23	32	25	28	29	18	7	26	24	26	23	19	22	23	17	14	14	27	27	37	35	19	12				22.2
NIONTOWN	MAX	38	39	55	48	38	43	53	54	60	50	38	45	43	39	39	39	34	51	43	37	40	58	46	67	70	65	56	42				47.5
	MIN	34	29	34	31	27	34	40	34	42	37	32	18	34	27	22	30	23	19	23	16	16	25	40	29	46	51	35	30				30.6
PPER DARBY	MAX	36	40	38	53	43	38	40	44	45	50	41	36	37	44	42	40	39	49	48	40	42	48	49	54	56	59	63	44				44.9
	MIN	31	28	25	36	30	30	35	34	30	39	28	18	27	29	29	29	26	23	30	23	24	25	30	34	42	47	44	25				30.4
ARREN	MAX	33	35	42	41	34	38	46	49	48	45	30	37	41	35	32	36	30	36	34	27	37	51	41	48	68	55	50	35				40.5
	MIN	23	16	20	32	20	18	30	28	35	29	19	8	28	29	23	22	16	19	18	18	22	20	28	26	40	34	19	10				23.2
AYNESBURG 2 W	MAX	40	38	54	50	38	41	46	51	62	60	41	40	43	38	37	38	33	51	48	35	42	57	51	67	70	69	60	44				48.0
	MIN	33	27	22	40	23	32	37	32	35	38	30	14	31	27	15	30	20	14	25	12	11	18	29	27	40	36	34	27				27.1
ELLSBORO 3 S	MAX	36	26	36	38	39	30	34	41	37	44	35	23	30	33	33	32	33	26	37	27	26	35	43	40	45	56	51	34				35.7
	MIN	20	17	18	26	17	17	22	25	25	32	19	4	5	22	23	22	14	14	16	13	15	15	22	26	26	37	31	7				19.6
ELLSVILLE	MAX	35	38	39	54	42	35	38	44	43	50	42	35	41	39	39	45	36	47	45	39	44	52	53	58	57	59	58	40				44.5
	MIN	29	29	16	35	26	29	32	35	26	40	29	13	26	24	24	21	23	20	34	18	18	20	24	25	32	38	39	26				28.8
EST CHESTER	MAX	37	34	42	37	46	39	44	44	46	48	45	35	36	42	41	37	38	40	46	41	46	48	49	56	56	59	55	55				44.4
	MIN	27	27	29	29	28	30	33	30	35	26	16	20	26	27	29	24	22	28	21	19	26	31	34	36	39	41		26				28.1
ILLIAMSPORT WB AP	MAX	33	39	37	45	33	36	39	45	39	46	34	33	35	38	39	39	35	42	41	36	42	45	45	50	54	56	54	31				40.8
	MIN	27	17	15	30	22	29	31	28	33	32	18	12	26	26	23	26	23	23	24	20	24	22	30	28	40	41	19	18				25.3
ORK 3 SSW PUMP STA	MAX	36	41	40	55	49	37	41	46	46	52	48	38	43	41	41	46	41	47	47	41	47	52	53	57	62	62	60	43				46.9
	MIN	33	28	25	38	27	30	33	35	29	42	30	12	27	27	30	24	26	21	36	20	25	21	30	27	37	45	43	27				29.6

See reference notes following Station Index.

Table 7

SNOWFALL AND SNOW ON GROUND

Station		1	2	3	4	5	6	7	8	9	10	11	12	13	14	15	16	17	18	19	20	21	22	23	24	25	26	27	28	29	30	31
ALLENTOWN WB AIRPORT	SNOWFALL	7.2	T			T	.3			T		T		.3	T	T	T	T											T			
	SN ON GND	1	7	5	3	T	T	T	T	T				T	T		T	T														
	WTR EQUIV		.5	.5	.3																											
AUSTINBURG 2 W	SNOWFALL	T	1.0	T	T										T	.8	T	.5		T									T			
	SN ON GND	1	2	1	T	T	T								T	1	1	1	1	1												
BEACH CREEK STATION	SNOWFALL		3.0				T							1.0	.5	1.0		.5														
	SN ON GND		3	2	1	T	T	T						1	1	1	1	1	1	T												
BRADFORD 4 W RESVR	SNOWFALL	.8									T	T		1.3	1.3	T	2.5	1.3	.5	T	1.3							T				
	SN ON GND	7	6	4	3	3	2	2	1	1	1	1	1	2	3	3	5	6	6	6	7	6	5	4	4	3	3	3	3			
BROOKVILLE CAA AIRPORT	SNOWFALL	2.5	T								T		.3	.8	.7	.1	.6	.3	T	T	.1	T										
	SN ON GND	2	4	3	1	T								1	T	1	1	2	2	1	1	1	T									
CANTON 1 NW	SNOWFALL	1.0	2.2											T		1.9					T											
	SN ON GND	2	4	4	3	2	2	2	1	T				T	T	2	T	1	T	T	T	T	T									
CARROLLTOWN 2 SSE	SNOWFALL	T	4.0				1.0					T		2.0	T	2.0	T	2.0	.5		T	T										
	SN ON GND	1	5	5	1	1	2	1	T	T				2	1	3	3	4	4	2	2	2	1	T								
COALDALE 2 NW	SNOWFALL	1.0	5.5				.5			T				1.0	.5			.7														
	SN ON GND	2	8	6	4	3	3	2	2	1				1	2	1		1														
CORRY	SNOWFALL	T												3.0	1.5	T	1.0	1.0		T	1.0											
	SN ON GND	3	3	1	T									2	3	3	4	5	5	5	6	5	4	3	1							
DONEGAL	SNOWFALL	T				1.5					T		2.0		8.0	T	T	T		T	T	T							T			
	SN ON GND	T				1							2	T	8	6	4	2	T	T	T	T							T			
DU BOIS 7 E	SNOWFALL	2.0	1.0											3.0	3.0	1.0	1.0	T			T								.5			
	SN ON GND	3	3	2	1	1	1	T	T	T	T			T	3	4	4	4	2	2	2	2	1	1	T				1			
ENGLISH CENTER	SNOWFALL	-	-	-	-	-	-	-	-	-	-	-	-	-	-	-	-	-	-	-	-	-	-	-	-	-	-	-	-			
	SN ON GND	1	5	4	1	T	T	T	T					2	2	5	3	3	3	1	1	T	T	T								
ERIE CAA AIRPORT	SNOWFALL	T	T								T	T	.5	1.0	3.0	.1	.3	.5	1.0	.3	T							T				
	SN ON GND	3	3	2	T	T	T	T	T		T	T		2	1	3	3	3	3	3	3	3	1	T	T							
EVERETT 1 SW	SNOWFALL					4.0								-	-														-			
	SN ON GND	2				4								2	3																	
FORD CITY 4 S DAM	SNOWFALL	T	2.0				T							3.0	T	3.5	T	T			T											
	SN ON GND	T	1	1	T	T	T	T						3	T	4	1	1	1	T	T	T	T	T	T				T			
GALETON	SNOWFALL	T	2.9											.7	.4	1.3		1.4	T		T								T			
	SN ON GND	3	5	4	3	2	1	1	1					1	T	1		1	1	T	T											
GEORGE SCHOOL	SNOWFALL	6.5	.3				.6							.4			T												.3			
	SN ON GND	7	6	5	4	2	2	1	T					T	T														T			
GRATERFORD	SNOWFALL		4.0				.5							.5			T															
	SN ON GND		3	3	2	T	T	T						T	T																	
GREENSBORO LOCK 7	SNOWFALL																	1.0														
	SN ON GND																	1														
HANOVER	SNOWFALL		1.0				2.5							T		3.5																
	SN ON GND		1				2	T						T		4																
HARRISBURG WB AIRPORT	SNOWFALL	6.2				1.1	.9					T	T	.9	4.1	3.2	T	T											T			
	SN ON GND	T	5	3	1		2	T						1		7	2	T	T													
	WTR EQUIV		.5	.5			.1									.5	.3															
HAWLEY 1 S DAM	SNOWFALL	1.4	2.5											T	.8			T														
	SN ON GND	3	6	6	5	3	3	2	2	2	T	T	T	T	1	1	T	T	T	T	T	T	T	T	T							
HOLTWOOD	SNOWFALL		1.0				3.0							T	T	9.0		T														
	SN ON GND		1	T	T	T	T	T						T		3	3	3	2	T	T	T	T	T	T	T						
HOOVERSVILLE	SNOWFALL	.3	T				3.0					T	T	3.0	1.0	5.0	T	2.0	.5		.2	T										
	SN ON GND	T	T				3	T				T		3	1	5	3	4	3	1	1	T	T									
INDIANA 3 SE	SNOWFALL	T					.4							2.0		3.2		T			T											
	SN ON GND	T	T				T							2	T	3	1	1	1	T	T											
KANE 1 NNE	SNOWFALL	1.8			T						.2	T	.1	1.3	5.5	.5	3.4	1.0	.6	1.0	.5			T					2.0			
	SN ON GND	4	4	4	4	3	3	3	2	2	1	1	1	2	7	7	9	9	9	8	8	8	6	4	2	1						
KEATING SUMMIT	SNOWFALL		2.5											1.1		.5		3.0		.3												
	SN ON GND	3	5	5	3	2	2	1	1	1	1	1		1	1	1	1	4	4	4	4	4	2	1	1							
LANCASTER 2 NE PUMP STA	SNOWFALL	.2	2.0				.2							.5	.5	.2																
	SN ON GND		2	1											1	T																
LAWRENCEVILLE 2 S	SNOWFALL	.3	2.2											T		T		4.0									T		T			
	SN ON GND	1	3	3	1	1	T	T	T					T		T		4											T			
LEWISTOWN	SNOWFALL	T	2.3				.8							2.0		T																
	SN ON GND	T	2	2	1		1							2		T																
MARTINSBURG CAA AIRPORT	SNOWFALL	3.8	T			1.8	.3				T	T	.2	.9	2.5	T	1.0	T		T	T	T							.4			
	SN ON GND		4	3	T		2	1	T					1		2	T	T	T		T	T										
MATAMORAS	SNOWFALL		4.0															.6														
	SN ON GND	1	5	5	3	2	2	1	1									1														
MEADVILLE 1 S	SNOWFALL	.3	.1			T					T	T		2.4	1.8	3.7	.1	5.8	.8	.4	.1	.1			T			T	.8			
	SN ON GND	2	2	2	1	1	1	1	T	T	T	T		2	2	5	4	7	6	6	5	5	4	2	2	T		T	1			
MEDIX RUN	SNOWFALL	T	3.2									T		1.0	T	2.5	T	4.5	T	T	T	T										
	SN ON GND	T	3	2	T	T	T	T	T			T		1	T	2	1	5	2	1	T	T	T									
MONTROSE 1 E	SNOWFALL	2.1	2.4	T	T						1.7	.2		.9	.5	.5	T	1.0	T		.4	T			T				T			
	SN ON GND	7	9	6	6	4	4	4	3	3	4	4	4	5	5	5	5	6	6	5	5	5	5	5	3	3	1	T	T			
MUHLENBURG 1 SE	SNOWFALL	4.0					1.0							3.0			2.0															
	SN ON GND	5	5	3	2	1	2							3	2	1	3	2	1													
NEWPORT	SNOWFALL	T	4.5		.5	T	1.0							1.5	T	2.5		T	T													
	SN ON GND	-	-	-	-	-	-	-	-	-	-	-	-	-	-	-	-	-	-	-	-	-	-	-	-	-	-	-	-			
PHILADELPHIA WB AIRPORT	SNOWFALL	.8				.3	.7					T		T			T												T			
	SN ON GND		T	T			1							T																		
	WTR EQUIV																															

See reference notes following Station Index.

Station		Day of month 1	2	3	4	5	6	7	8	9	10	11	12	13	14	15	16	17	18	19	20	21	22	23	24	25	26	27	28	29	30	31
ILADELPHIA CITY	SNOWFALL	-	-	-	-	-	-	-	-	-	-	-	-	-	-	-	-	-	-	-	-	-	-	-	-	-	-	-	-			
	SN ON GND	-	-	-	-	-	-	-	-	-	-	-	-	-	-	-	-	-	-	-	-	-	-	-	-	-	-	-	-			
ILIPSBURG CAA AIRPORT	SNOWFALL	3.0	T			T	T				T	T	.2	1.2	5.0	T	.6	T	T	T	T	T		T				T	T			
	SN ON GND	1	4	4	1									1	1	6	6	6	6	4	4	4	2	T								
PLE HILL	SNOWFALL	1.0	4.6	T			.1	T		1.0	.9	T		.9	.6	.4	T	.8	T	T	.4	.2			T							
	SN ON GND	3	8	7	5	3	3	3	2	3	1	1	1	2	2	3	2	3	2	2	2	2	1	1	T	T	T	T	T			
TTSBURGH WB AIRPORT 2	SNOWFALL	2.0	T			T	T					T	.5	.2	.5	.1	.1	T		T	T	T						.9				
	SN ON GND	T	2	1	1		T							1	T	1	T	T	T		T	T							T			
	WTR EQUIV		.2																													
EASANT MOUNT 1 W	SNOWFALL	2.0	3.0							T	2.0	T		1.5	.5	T		2.0	T		1.0	1.0										
	SN ON GND	7	10	9	7	5	5	5	5	4	5	5	5	7	7	7	7	9	8	7	7	8	7	6	5	4	2	T	T			
ADING WB CITY	SNOWFALL	5.6				.5	.4			T				.7	.4		T				T								T			
	SN ON GND	T	5	3	2	T	1	T	T	T				1	T	T																
RANTON WB AIRPORT	SNOWFALL	2.6	T							T	T			T	T		.7	T	T		T											
	SN ON GND	1	4	3	1	T	T	T	T	T	T	T	T	T	T	T	T	1	T	T	T	T										
	WTR EQUIV		.4	.3																												
LINSGROVE CAA AIRPORT	SNOWFALL	4.3	T			.3	1.0			T				.8	2.4	T	T												T			
	SN ON GND	T	4	3	1	T	1	T						1	1	3	1	T	T	T												
IPPENSBURG	SNOWFALL	2.5	1.0			T	3.0							1.0	3.0	1.0	T												T			
	SN ON GND	2	2	1			2	T							3	2	T	T											T			
IPPENSBURG WB	SNOWFALL	1.8											.4		2.1		T	T										T				
	SN ON GND	2	T	T										T	2	T	T	T	T	T												
IPPERY ROCK	SNOWFALL	1.0	1.0											2.0		5.0		2.0		1.0												
	SN ON GND	1	2	2										2		5	3	5	2	1	1	1										
RING 1 SW	SNOWFALL	T				4.5								2.5	5.0		.5	.5			.2		-									
	SN ON GND	T				5	2							2	7	6	6	6	5	5	5		2	1	T							
MARACK 2 S FIRE TWR	SNOWFALL	1.3	3.0							T		T		1.0	.4	2.0	T	2.0	T	T	T	T										
	SN ON GND	2	4	4	3	3	2	2	2	2	2	2	2	1	2	4	4	6	6	5	5	5	4	3	2	T	T					
ONESTA 2 SE DAM	SNOWFALL	T	1.0								T	T		3.0	T	2.5	.3	1.5	T	.4	.8	T										
	SN ON GND		1	1	T	T	T	T	T	T	T	T	T	3	1	3	3	4	4	4	4	4	3	1	T	T						
WANDA	SNOWFALL	1.0	2.7								T	T		T	T	T	T	.8				T							.2			
	SN ON GND	3	6	5	3	2	2	1	T	T				T		T		1	T			T							T			
TER CITY 5 SW	SNOWFALL	6.5	T				1.8			T				1.0	1.0	6.0	.5															
	SN ON GND	-	-	-	-	-	-	-	-	-	-	-	-	-	-	-	-	-	-	-	-	-	-	-	-	-	-	-	-			
LLIAMSPORT WB AIRPORT	SNOWFALL	3.7	.2			T	T			T			T	1.8	2.6	.4	.8	T						T				T				
	SN ON GND	T	4	2	1	T	T							1		2	1	1	T													
	WTR EQUIV		.4	.3												.3																

See reference notes following Station Index.

TOTAL PRECIPITATION

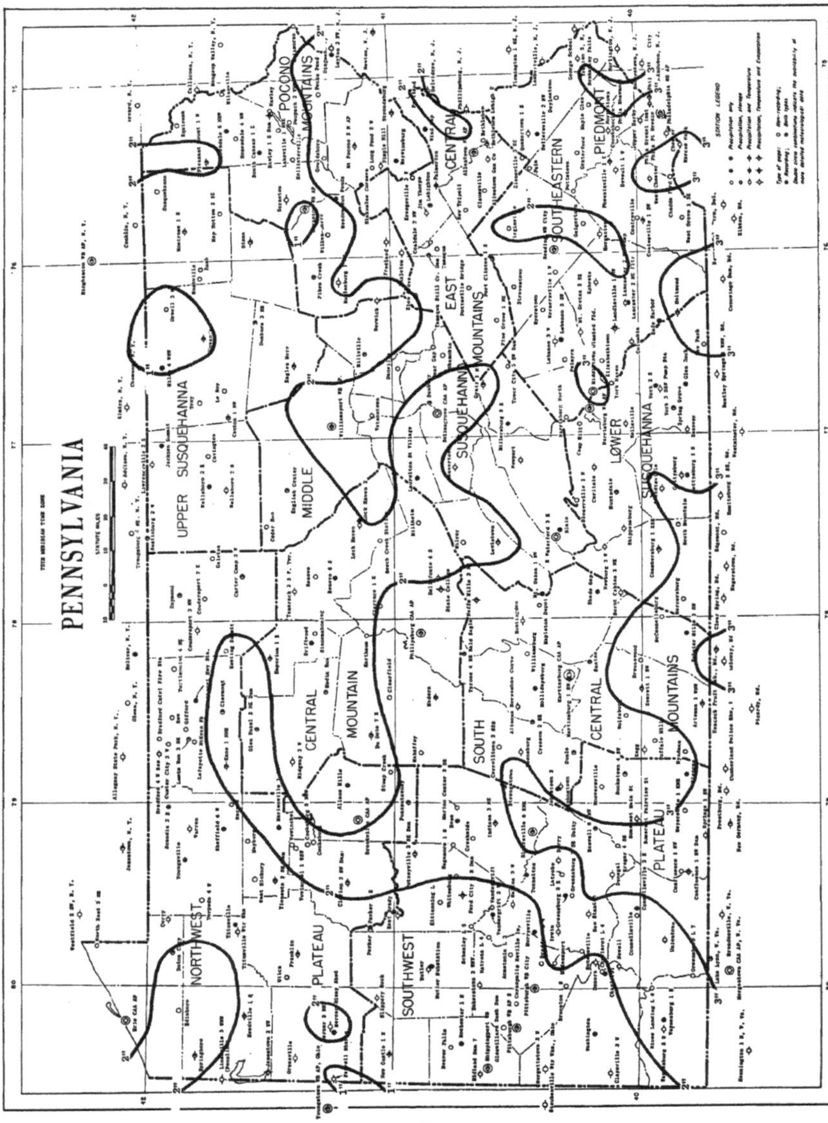

Isolines are drawn through points of approximately equal values. Hourly precipitation data from recorder substations will be available in the publication 'Hourly Precipitation

AVERAGE TEMPERATURE

PENNSYLVANIA
FEBRUARY 1957

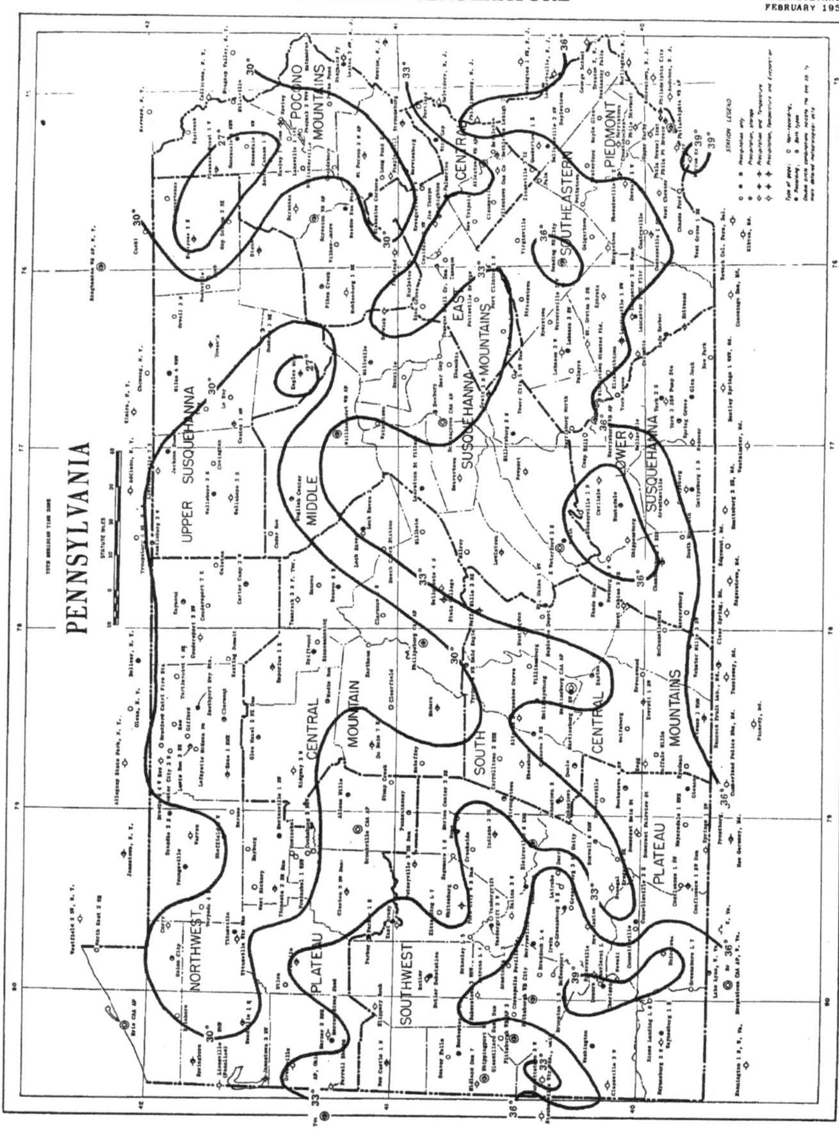

Isolines are drawn through points of approximately equal values. Hourly precipitation data from recorder substations will be available in the publication 'Hourly Precipitation Data'.

STATION INDEX

Station	Index No.	County	Drainage	Latitude	Longitude	Elevation	Obs. Time Temp.	Obs. Time Precip.	Observer	Refer To Tables
ACMETONIA LOCK 3	0022	ALLEGHENY	1	40 32	79 49	748		7A	CORPS OF ENGINEERS	3
ALLENS MILLS	0099	JEFFERSON	1	41 12	78 55	1600		MID	CHARLES M. ALLEN	C
ALLENTOWN WB AP	0106	LEHIGH	9	40 39	75 26	376	MID	MID	U.S. WEATHER BUREAU	2 3 5 7 C
ALLENTOWN GAS CO	0111	LEHIGH	9	40 36	75 28	254	7A	7A	LEHIGH VLY GAS DIV	2 3 5
ALTOONA HORSESHOE CURVE	0134	BLAIR	6	40 30	78 29	1500	6P	6P	ALTOONA WATER BUR.	2 3 5
ARENDTSVILLE	0229	ADAMS	15	39 55	77 18	710	8A	8A	PA STATE COL EXP	2 3 5
ARTEMAS 1 WNW	0259	BEDFORD	12	39 45	78 28	1250	6P	6P	GRAYSON E.NORTHCRAFT	2 3 5 C
AUSTINBURG 2 W	0313	TIOGA	15	42 00	77 32	1590		7A	OTTO D. BACOM	3 7 C
BAKERSTOWN 3 WNW	0355	ALLEGHENY	1	40 39	79 59	1230	7P	7P	PGH CUT FLOWER CO	2 3 5
BARNES	0409	WARREN	1	41 40	79 02	1310		7A	CORPS OF ENGINEERS	3
BARTO 4 NW	0428	BERKS	14	40 26	75 39	312		7A	MARIE B. NICHLAS	3
BEAR GAP	0457	NORTHUMBLAND	15	40 50	76 30	900		MID	ROARING CRK WTR CO	3
BEAVER FALLS	0475	BEAVER	2	40 46	80 19	760		7A	HOWARD R. KEMP	3
BEAVERTOWN	0482	SNYDER	15	40 45	77 10	640	7A	7A	MARLIN RC ETTINGER	2 3 5
BEECH CREEK STATION	0499	CENTRE	16	41 04	77 34	620		7A	HAROLD S. RUPERT	3 7
BELLEFONTE 4 S	0530	CENTRE	16	40 51	77 47	1110	8A	8A	ROCKVIEW PRISON FARM	2 3 5
BERNE	0599	BERKS	14	40 31	76 00	325		7A	FLOYD W. TRUMP	3
BERWICK	0611	COLUMBIA	15	41 04	76 15	570	6P	6P	AMER CAR + FNDRY CO	2 3 5
BETHLEHEM	0629	NORTHAMPTON	9	40 37	75 22	400		7A	ARTHUR CROPPER	3
#BETHLEHEM LEHIGH UNIV	0634	NORTHAMPTON	9	40 36	75 23	450	MID	MID	LEHIGH UNIVERSITY	2 3 5 C
BLAIN	0725	PERRY	15	40 20	77 31	750		MID	PA DEPT FRST + WTRS	C
BLAIRSVILLE 6 ENE	0736	INDIANA	4	40 27	79 09	2048	8P	8P	U.S. WEATHER BUREAU	2 3 5
BLAKESLEE CORNERS	0743	MONROE	9	41 06	75 36	1650		MID	WALTER WILDRICK	C
BLOSERVILLE 1 N	0763	CUMBERLAND	15	40 16	77 22	650		5P	MRS. B. M. WILLDERS	3
BOSWELL 6 WNW	0820	SOMERSET	1	40 11	79 08	2580		7A	MRS. MAE L. KIMMEL	3 C
BRADDOCK LOCK 2	0861	ALLEGHENY	10	40 24	79 52	725		7A	CORPS OF ENGINEERS	3
BRADFORD CNTRL FIRE STA	0867	MC KEAN	1	41 57	78 39	1500		8A	BRADFORD FIRE DEPT	3
BRADFORD 4 W RES	0868	MC KEAN	1	41 57	78 44	1680	5P	5P	BRADFORD WTR DEPT	2 3 5 7
BREEZEWOOD	0905	BEDFORD	6	40 00	78 14	1352		MID	PA TURNPIKE COMM	3
BROOKVILLE CAA AIRPORT	1002	JEFFERSON	1	41 09	79 06	1417	MID	MID	CIVIL AERO. ADM.	2 3 5 7
BRUCETON 1 S	1033	ALLEGHENY	10	40 18	79 59	1065		7A	AUSTIN R. COOPER	3
BUCKSTOWN 1 SE	1073	SOMERSET	4	40 04	78 50	2460		MID	ALVIN W. MANGES	C
BUFFALO MILLS	1087	BEDFORD	6	39 57	78 39	1318		7A	MRS. NELLE R. BROWN	3
BURGETTSTOWN 2 W	1103	WASHINGTON	11	40 23	80 26	980	7A	7A	SMITH TWP MUN AUTH	2 3 5
BURNT CABINS 2 NE	1115	HUNTINGDON	6	40 05	77 52	990	MID	MID	PA TURNPIKE COMM	2 3 5
#BUTLER	1130	BUTLER	2	40 52	79 54	1100	4P	7A	WILLIAM C. FAUST	2 3 5
BUTLER SUBSTATION	1135	BUTLER	2	40 51	79 53	1140		MID	WEST PENN POWER CO	C
CAMP HILL	1198	CUMBERLAND	15	40 15	76 55	461		6P	JOSEPH N. HOBART	3
CANTON 1 NW	1215	BRADFORD	15	41 40	76 52	1520	7A	7A	MRS.MILDRED SPENCER	2 3 5 7 C
CARLISLE	1234	CUMBERLAND	15	40 12	77 11	460	6P	6P	C. E. MILLER	2 3 5
CARROLLTOWN 2 SSE	1255	CAMBRIA	16	40 35	78 42	2040		8A	ROBERT F. MAURER	3 7
CARTER CAMP 2 W	1262	POTTER	16	41 37	77 45	2030		7A	RICHARD L. MENKEN	3 C
CEDAR RUN	1301	LYCOMING	16	41 31	77 27	800		7A	KATHRYN T.KREIGHBAUM	3
CHADDS FORD	1342	DELAWARE	5	39 52	75 36	160		8A	MRS.GRACE A. WICKS	3
CHAMBERSBURG 1 ESE	1354	FRANKLIN	12	39 56	77 38	640	9P	9P	CHARLES A. BENDER	2 3 5 C
CHARLEROI	1372	WASHINGTON	10	40 08	79 55	1040		MID	WEST PENN POWER CO	C
CHARLEROI LOCK 4	1377	WESTMORELAND	10	40 09	79 54	749		7A	CORPS OF ENGINEERS	3
#CHESTER	1423	DELAWARE	5	39 51	75 22	86	8A	8A	CHESTER TIMES	2 3 5
CLARENCE	1480	CENTRE	16	41 03	77 56	1410		7A	MISS VELDA SWANCER	3
CLARION 3 SW	1485	CLARION	1	41 12	79 26	1114	8P	7A	PA ELECTRIC CO	2 3 5 C
CLAUSSVILLE	1505	LEHIGH	9	40 37	75 39	670		8A	WILLIAM J. DOTTERER	3
CLAYSVILLE 3 W	1512	WASHINGTON	11	40 07	80 28	1000	7P	7A	MFGRS. L + H CO	2 3 5
CLEARFIELD	1519	CLEARFIELD	16	41 01	78 26	1100		7A	IRA TAYLOR	3
CLERMONT	1529	MC KEAN	1	41 41	78 30	2104		7A	MRS.TILLIE M.SIMONDS	3 C
COALDALE 2 NW	1572	SCHUYLKILL	9	40 50	75 56	1026		7A	PANTHER VLY WTR CO	3 7
COATESVILLE 1 SW	1589	CHESTER	5	39 58	75 50	342	8A	8A	PHILA ELECTRIC CO	2 3 5 C
COATESVILLE	1594	CHESTER	5	39 59	75 49	340		8A	EDWARD D. BIEDEMAN	INAC 12/55
COLUMBIA	1675	LANCASTER	15	40 02	76 30	300	SS	SS	JAMES H. RUST	2 3 5
CONFLUENCE 1 SW DAM	1705	SOMERSET	17	39 48	79 22	1490	8A	8A	CORPS OF ENGINEERS	2 3 5 6 C
CONFLUENCE 1 NW	1710	FAYETTE	17	39 50	79 22	1331		7A	JOHN L. REID	3
CONNELLSVILLE	1723	FAYETTE	17	40 01	79 36	870		8A	MARSHALL B. MENEFEE	3
CONNELLSVILLE 2 E	1729	FAYETTE	17	40 01	79 33	1300		MID	HARRY C. JOY	C
CONSHOHOCKEN	1737	MONTGOMERY	5	40 04	75 19	70		8A	PHILA ELECTRIC CO	3
COOKSBURG	1749	CLARION	1	41 20	79 13	1180		8A	PA DEPT FRST + WTRS	3
COOKSBURG 2 NNW	1752	CLARION	1	41 21	79 13	1460		8A	PA DEPT FRST + WTRS	3
CORAOPOLIS NEVILLE IS	1773	ALLEGHENY	11	40 30	80 05	720		8A	PGH. COKE + CHEM CO	3
CORRY	1790	ERIE	1	41 56	79 38	1427	7P	5A	LEO C. NECKERS	2 3 5 7
COUDERSPORT 3 NW	1806	POTTER	1	41 49	78 03	2020	7P	8A	MISS ELIZABETH NEFF	2 3 5
COUDERSPORT 7 E	1809	POTTER	1	41 46	77 53	2425		7A	CAMP POTATO	3
COVINGTON 2 WSW	1833	TIOGA	15	41 44	77 07	1745		7A	CALVIN R. PACKARD	3
CREEKSIDE	1881	INDIANA	1	40 41	79 12	1035		7A	CORPS OF ENGINEERS	3
CRESSON 2 SE	1895	CAMBRIA	6	40 27	78 34	2540		7A	TALMAGE R. FRAZER	3 C
CUSTER CITY 2 W	1978	MC KEAN	1	41 55	78 41	2120		8A	M. D. BOOTH AND CO	3
DANVILLE	2013	MONTOUR	15	40 58	76 37	460		7A	MRS.MARIE M. LITTLE	3
DERRY	2108	WESTMORELAND	4	40 20	79 18	1150	6P	6P	MISS M. D. WINEMAN	2 3 5
DEVAULT 1 W	2116	CHESTER	14	40 05	75 33	360	MID	MID	PA TURNPIKE COMM	2 3 5
DINGMANS FERRY	2160	PIKE	5	41 13	74 52	364		MID	CLYDE T. VOORHEES	C
DIXON	2171	WYOMING	15	41 34	75 54	620	7A	7A	HAROLD J. KUSCHEL	2 3 5 C
DONEGAL	2183	WESTMORELAND	17	40 07	79 23	1746	MID	MID	PA TURNPIKE COMM	2 3 5 7
#DONORA	2190	WASHINGTON	10	40 11	79 51	814	12M	12M	DONORA ZINC WORKS	2 3 5
DOYLESTOWN	2221	BUCKS	5	40 18	75 08	393		5P	GEORGE HART	3
DRIFTWOOD	2245	CAMERON	16	41 20	78 08	880		MID	SIDNEY KENNEDY	C
DU BOIS 7 E	2265	CLEARFIELD	16	41 06	78 38	1670	5P	5P	CITY OF DU BOIS	2 3 5 7 C
DUNLO	2298	CAMBRIA	4	40 17	78 43	2410		MID	MRS. D. L. WHITE	C
DUSHORE 3 NE	2324	SULLIVAN	16	41 33	76 21	1750		7A	PATRICK F. RYAN	3 C
EAGLES MERE	2343	SULLIVAN	16	41 24	76 35	2020	7A	7A	MRS.ELSIE P. BIGGER	2 3 5 C
EAST BRADY	2363	CLARION	1	40 59	79 37	820	5P	5P	A. B. KEMPEL	2 3 5
EAST WATERFORD 3 E	2450	PERRY	6	40 21	77 33	2125	8A	8A	U.S. WEATHER BUREAU	INAC 5/55
EBENSBURG	2466	CAMBRIA	4	40 29	78 43	2090	7P	7A	ROBERT A. WASSER	2 3 5
EDINBORO	2514	ERIE	1	41 52	80 08	1220		8A	EDINBORO ST TCHR COL	3
ELIZABETHTOWN	2560	LANCASTER	15	40 09	76 37	460		8A	MASONIC HOME	3
EMPORIUM 2 SSW	2634	CAMERON	16	41 28	78 15	1735	7A	7A	JACKSON THOMAS	2 3 5 C
ENGLISH CENTER	2644	LYCOMING	16	41 26	77 17	881		7A	WILLIAM SUDERS	3 7 C
EPHRATA	2662	LANCASTER	15	40 11	76 10	465	6P	6P	STANLEY L.VON NEIDA	2 3 5
ERIE CAA AIRPORT	2682	ERIE	8	42 05	80 12	732	MID	MID	CIVIL AERO. ADM.	2 3 5 7
EVERETT 1 SW	2721	BEDFORD	6	40 00	78 23	1020	MID	MID	PA TURNPIKE COMM	2 3 5 7 C
FARRELL SHARON	2814	MERCER	2	41 14	80 30	865	7P	7P	SHARON STEEL CORP	2 3 5
FORD CITY 4 S DAM	2942	ARMSTRONG	1	40 43	79 30	950	8A	8A	CORPS OF ENGINEERS	2 3 5 6 7 C
FRANKLIN	3028	VENANGO	1	41 23	79 49	987	7P	7A	GEORGE S. SMITH, JR	2 3 5 C
FREELAND	3056	LUZERNE	15	41 01	75 54	1900	6P	8A	ANDREW B. EVANSHA	2 3 5
GALETON	3130	POTTER	16	41 44	77 39	1325		7A	W. GALE LUSH	3 7
GEIGERTOWN	3189	BERKS	14	40 13	75 50	400		8A	WALTER C. WOLF	3
GEORGE SCHOOL	3200	BUCKS	5	40 13	74 56	135	7P	7P	GEORGE M. HART	2 3 5 7
#GETTYSBURG	3218	ADAMS	12	39 50	77 14	540	9A	9A	HUGH C. MC ILHENNY	2 3 5
GETTYSBURG 1 S	3223	ADAMS	12	39 48	77 14	560		MID	NAT MILITARY PARK	C
GIFFORD	3237	MC KEAN	1	41 51	78 36	2220		8A	SOUTH PENN OIL CO	3
GLENCOE	3298	SOMERSET	12	39 49	78 51	1620		MID	MRS. MARY M.HARTMAN	C
GLEN HAZEL 2 NE DAM	3311	ELK	1	41 34	78 36	1725		8A	CORPS OF ENGINEERS	3 C
GLEN ROCK	3330	YORK	15	39 48	76 44	620		MID	MRS.E.C.MC WILLIAMS	C
GLENWILLARD DASH DAM	3343	ALLEGHENY	11	40 33	80 13	705		7A	CORPS OF ENGINEERS	3
GOULDSBORO	3394	WAYNE	9	41 15	75 27	1890		7A	L. M. EILENBERGER	3
GRATERFORD	3435	MONTGOMERY	14	40 14	75 27	160	7A	7A	CLAUDE K. KULP	2 3 5 7 C
GRATZ 1 N	3438	DAUPHIN	15	40 38	76 43	760	8A	8A	LEE M. LEITZEL	2 3 5 C
GREENSBORO LOCK 7	3503	GREENE	10	39 47	79 55	808		7A	CORPS OF ENGINEERS	3 7
GREENSBURG 2 E	3515	WESTMORELAND	10	40 18	79 31	1225		MID	PA DEPT HIGHWAYS	C
GREENSBURG 3 SE UNITY	3516	WESTMORELAND	10	40 17	79 30	1245		6P	WESTMORELAND WTR CO	3
GREENVILLE	3526	MERCER	2	41 24	80 23	1026	6P	6P	C. EARL MILLER	2 3 5
HANOVER	3662	YORK	15	39 48	76 59	600	8A	8A	HANOVER EVENING SUN	2 3 5 7
#HARRISBURG WB AP	3699	YORK	15	40 13	76 51	335	MID	MID	U.S. WEATHER BUREAU	2 3 5 7 C
HARRISBURG NORTH	3704	DAUPHIN	15	40 18	76 54	323		9A	GEORGE S. BEAL	3
HAWLEY	3758	WAYNE	5	41 29	75 10	880		7A	MRS.KATHERINE S.BATE	3 5
HAWLEY 1 S DAM	3761	WAYNE	5	41 28	75 11	1200	7A	7A	PA POWER + LIGHT CO	2 3 5 6 7 C
HOLLIDAYSBURG	4001	BLAIR	6	40 26	78 24	960		MID	JOHN H. RINGLER	C
HOLLISTERVILLE	4008	WAYNE	5	41 23	75 26	1360		8A	PA POWER + LIGHT CO	3
#HOLTWOOD	4019	LANCASTER	15	39 50	76 20	187	MID	8A	PA POWER + LIGHT CO	2 3 5 7 C
HOME	4027	INDIANA	1	40 45	79 06	1220		MID	MRS. EDNA M. BUSH	C
HONESDALE 4 NW	4043	WAYNE	5	41 37	75 19	1410		9A	GEORGE C. WILLIAMS	3
HONESDALE 6 NNW	4044	WAYNE	5	41 39	75 17	1050		MID	FRIEND E. WALTER	C
HOOVERSVILLE	4058	SOMERSET	4	40 09	78 55	1660		7A	PA ELECTRIC CO	3 7
HOP BOTTOM 2 SE	4066	SUSQUEHANNA	15	41 43	75 43	900		7A	JOSEPH J. SANSUSKAS	3
HUNTINGDON	4159	HUNTINGDON	6	40 30	78 01	678	7A	7A	DANIEL I. GROVE	2 3 5
HUNTSDALE	4166	CUMBERLAND	15	40 06	77 18	610		8A	METRO P. GOROSH	3 C
HYNDMAN	4190	BEDFORD	12	39 49	78 43	920		8A	MRS.GERTRUDE M.BURTO	3
INDIANA 3 SE	4214	INDIANA	4	40 36	79 07	1102	7P	7A	CLYMER WATER SVC CO	2 3 5 7 C
IRWIN	4276	WESTMORELAND	10	40 20	79 42	1100	5P	5P	WESTMORELAND WTR CO	2 3 5
JACKSON SUMMIT	4304	TIOGA	15	41 57	77 01	1690		MID	ARCHIE LAIN	C
JAMESTOWN 2 NW	4325	CRAWFORD	2	41 30	80 28	1050	8A	8A	PA DEPT FRST + WTRS	2 3 5 6 C
JIM THORPE	4370	CARBON	9	40 52	75 45	830	5P	5P	HENRY S. HAAK	2 3 5
#JOHNSTOWN	4385	CAMBRIA	4	40 20	78 55	1214	9A	9A	JOHNSTOWN TRIBUNE	2 3 5
JOHNSTOWN 2	4390	CAMBRIA	4	40 19	78 55	1275		MID	CITY OF JOHNSTOWN	C
KANE 1 NNE	4432	MC KEAN	1	41 41	78 48	1750	8A	8A	SPRING WATER CO	2 3 5 7 C
KARTHAUS	4450	CLEARFIELD	16	41 07	78 07	950		7A	JEROME S. HOWE	3
KEATING SUMMIT	4466	POTTER	16	41 41	78 11	1840		7A	EUGENE L. KREITNER	3 7
KEGG	4481	BEDFORD	6	39 59	78 43	1280	MID	MID	PA TURNPIKE COMM	2 3 5
KITTANNING LOCK 7	4611	ARMSTRONG	1	40 49	79 32	790		VAR	CORPS OF ENGINEERS	3
KREGAR 4 SE	4667	WESTMORELAND	17	40 06	79 14	2530		MID	PA TURNPIKE COMM	3
KRESGEVILLE 3 W	4672	CARBON	9	40 54	75 34	720		9A	CITY OF BETHLEHEM	3
LAFAYETTE MC KEAN PARK	4706	MC KEAN	1	41 48	78 40	2130		7A	ORIN A. BUTTERS	3
LAKEVILLE 1 NNE	4733	WAYNE	5	41 27	75 16	1440		8A	MRS. GLADYS REINEKE	3
LANCASTER 2 NE PUMP STA	4758	LANCASTER	15	40 03	76 17	255	6P	6P	LANCASTER WATER BUR	2 3 5 7
LANCASTER 2 NE FILT PL	4763	LANCASTER	15	40 03	76 17	270		MID	LANCASTER WATER BUR	C
LANDISVILLE 2 NW	4778	LANCASTER	15	40 07	76 26	300	8A	8A	PA STATE COLLEGE	2 3 5 6 C
LATROBE	4832	WESTMORELAND	4	40 19	79 23	1000		MID	WEST PENN POWER CO	INAC 6/56
LAURELTON STATE VILLAGE	4853	UNION	15	40 54	77 13	880		MID	PA DEPT OF WELFARE	C
LAWRENCEVILLE 2 S	4873	TIOGA	15	41 59	77 07	1000	7A	7A	HARRY P. HOWLAND	2 3 5 7
LEBANON 3 W	4891	LEBANON	15	40 20	76 29	460	7A	7A	LEON MILLER	2 3 5 7
LEBANON 3 SW	4896	LEBANON	15	40 19	76 28	490		MID	THOMAS DONNACHIE	C
LEHIGHTON	4934	CARBON	9	40 50	75 43	580		7A	GOODWIN S. DEFRENN	3 C
LE ROY	4972	BRADFORD	15	41 41	76 43	1040		6P	MRS.DINNIS M.BAILEY	3
LEWIS RUN 3 SE	4984	MC KEAN	1	41 50	78 39	1740		7A	RUSSELL LINEMAN	3 C
LEWISTOWN	4992	MIFFLIN	6	40 35	77 35	480	7A	7A	AMERICAN VISCOSE CO	2 3 5 7 C
LINESVILLE 5 WNW	5050	CRAWFORD	2	41 41	80 31	1020	7P	8A	MISS RETTA M. CRUMB	2 3 5
LOCK HAVEN	5104	CLINTON	16	41 08	77 27	570	7P	7A	PETER L. STEVENSON	2 3 5
LOCK HAVEN 2	5109	CLINTON	16	41 08	77 27	630		MID	HUGH F. PARKER	C
LONG POND 2 W	5160	MONROE	9	41 03	75 30	1860		7A	THOMAS MECKES	3
LYNDELL 2 NW	5279	CHESTER	5	40 05	75 46	-		8A	MRS. DOROTHY MARPLE	3
MADERA	5336	CLEARFIELD	16	40 50	78 26	1460	7A	7A	MRS. JULIA J. SHOFF	2 3 5 C
MAHAFFEY	5342	CLEARFIELD	16	40 53	78 44	1280		7A	MISS ELLEN J. MILES	3
MAPLE GLEN	5368	MONTGOMERY	5	40 11	75 11	380		6P	FRANCES E.SCHEIBNER	3
MAPLETON DEPOT	5381	HUNTINGDON	6	40 24	77 56	580		7A	MRS. I. S. BUCHANAN	3
MARCUS HOOK	5390	DELAWARE	5	39 49	75 25	12	MID	MID	SUN OIL CO	2 3 5
MARIENVILLE 1 SW	5400	FOREST	1	41 27	79 09	1700		MID	ROY A. MARKER	C
MARION CENTER 2 SE	5408	INDIANA	1	40 45	79 02	1610		7A	CORPS OF ENGINEERS	3
MARTINSBURG 1 SW	5453	BLAIR	6	40 18	78 20	1360		MID	BLUE MT. CANNERIES	C
MARTINSBURG CAA AP	5454	BLAIR	6	40 18	78 19	1463	MID	MID	CIVIL AERO. ADM.	2 3 5 7
MATAMORAS	5470	PIKE	5	41 22	74 42	439		7A	HARRY BISLAND	3 7
MAYBURG	5490	FOREST	1	41 36	79 13	1150		7A	CORPS OF ENGINEERS	3
MC CONNELLSBURG	5526	FULTON	12	39 56	78 00	895		7A	MRS. HELEN M. SHIVES	3
MC KEESPORT	5573	ALLEGHENY	10	40 21	79 52	720		8A	NATIONAL TUBE CO	3
MEADOW RUN PONDS	5601	LUZERNE	15	41 13	75 40	1995		MID	GEORGE PEARAGE	C
MEADVILLE 1 S	5606	CRAWFORD	1	41 38	80 10	1065	8A	8A	CITY OF MEADVILLE	2 3 5 7 C
MEDIX RUN	5627	ELK	16	41 17	78 24	1100		7A	MRS.E. M. SNYDER	3 7 C
MERCER 2 NNE	5651	MERCER	2	41 15	80 13	1160	7P	7A	WILLIAM K. STRUTHERS	2 3 5
MERCER HIWAY SHED	5654	MERCER	2	41 14	80 15	1250		MID	PA DEPT HIGHWAYS	C
MERCERSBURG	5662	FRANKLIN	12	39 50	77 54	605		8A	ROLLIN P. GILBERT	3
MERWINSBURG	5676	MONROE	9	40 58	75 28	970		MID	WILLIAM D. GOULD	C
MEYERSDALE 1 ENE	5685	SOMERSET	17	39 49	79 01	2290		8A	ARTHUR B. MC CARTER	3
MIDDLETOWN OLMSTED FLD	5703	DAUPHIN	15	40 11	76 46	303	MID	MID	U. S. AIR FORCE	2 3 5
MIDLAND DAM 7	5710	BEAVER	11	40 38	80 28	689	11P	7A	CORPS OF ENGINEERS	2 3 5
MILAN 4 WNW	5732	BRADFORD	15	41 56	76 35	1448		MID	CARL A. MORRIS	C
MILANVILLE	5738	WAYNE	5	41 40	75 04	760		8A	CHARLES W. DAVIS	3
MILLERSBURG 2 E	5775	DAUPHIN	15	40 32	76 56	560		MID	RUSSELL SHEPLEY	C
MILLHEIM	5790	CENTRE	15	40 54	77 29	1090		7A	NEVIN E. BOWERSOX	3
MILLVILLE 2 SW	5817	COLUMBIA	15	41 06	76 34	860		7A	KENNETH LEIGHOW	3 C
MILROY	5825	MIFFLIN	6	40 43	77 35	,770		8A	THOMAS C. HARBESON	3
MONTROSE 1 E	5915	SUSQUEHANNA	15	41 50	75 51	1630	7A	7A	WILBER W. HOOPES,JR	2 3 5 7 C
MORGANTOWN	5956	BERKS	15	40 09	75 54	595	MID	MID	PA TURNPIKE COMM	2 3 5
MT GRETNA 2 SE	6028	LANCASTER	15	40 14	76 26	670	MID	MID	PA TURNPIKE COMM	2 3 5
MT POCONO 2 N AP	6055	MONROE	5	41 09	75 22	1915	5P	5P	H. JOHN DAVIS, JR.	2 3 5 C
MOUNT UNION 1 N	6067	MIFFLIN	6	40 24	77 53	820		MID	MT UNION WTR WORKS	C
MUHLENBURG 1 SE	6090	LUZERNE	15	41 13	76 08	1110	6P	6P	THEODORE J. SAMPSON	2 3 5 7
MURRYSVILLE	6111	WESTMORELAND	10	40 26	79 42	903		MID	DAVID C. SHAW	C
MYERSTOWN	6126	LEBANON	14	40 22	76 18	480		8A	MRS.KATHLEEN MANDELL	3
NATRONA LOCK 4	6151	ALLEGHENY	1	40 37	79 43	800		7A	CORPS OF ENGINEERS	3
NEFFS MILLS 3 NE	6174	HUNTINGDON	6	40 40	77 55	900		MID	PA STATE UNIVERSITY	C
NESHAMINY FALLS	6194	BUCKS	5	40 09	74 57	60		MID	PHILA SUB WATER CO	3
NEWBURG 3 W	6225	FRANKLIN	15	40 09	77 37	745	MID	MID	PA TURNPIKE COMM	2 3 5
NEW CASTLE 1 N	6233	LAWRENCE	2	41 01	80 22	825	5P	7A	BAXTER F. JOHNSON	2 3 5 C
NEWELL	6246	FAYETTE	10	40 05	79 54	805	12M	12M	GENERAL CHEMICAL CO	2 3 5
NEW PARK	6289	YORK	15	39 44	76 30	780		6P	CLINTON J. ALLEN	3
NEWPORT	6297	PERRY	6	40 29	77 08	400	7A	7A	MRS. FRANCES K. FRY	2 3 5 7
NEW STANTON	6310	WESTMORELAND	10	40 13	79 36	980	MID	MID	PA TURNPIKE COMM	2 3 5
NEW TRIPOLI	6326	LEHIGH	14	40 41	75 45	570		6P	FRED C. OSWALD	3
NORRISTOWN	6370	MONTGOMERY	14	40 07	75 21	75	MID	8A	GEORGE H. BOONE	2 3 5
NORTH EASY 2 SE	6396	ERIE	8	42 12	79 49	1060		9A	ELLSWORTH WEAVER	3
ORWELL 3 N	6621	BRADFORD	15	41 55	76 16	1620		8A	WILLIAM I. BROWN	3
PALM	6681	MONTGOMERY	14	40 26	75 32	385		8A	FRED C. ESCHBACH	3
#PALMERTON	6689	CARBON	9	40 48	75 37	435	MID	MID	NEW JERSEY ZINC CO	2 3 5 C
PALMYRA	6694	LEBANON	15	40 18	76 35	480		7P	EARL E. RHOADS	3
PARKER	6721	ARMSTRONG	1	41 05	79 41	1140		7A	LOUIS A. MALARKEY	3
PARKER 1 E	6724	CLARION	1	41 06	79 40	1100		MID	P. M. NEELY	C
PAUPACK 2 WNW	6762	PIKE	5	41 24	75 14	1360		8A	MISS L. VETTERLEIN	3
PECKS POND	6786	PIKE	5	41 17	75 06	1380		6A	MRS. CARRIE NESS	3
#PHIL DREXEL INST OF TEC	6879	PHILADELPHIA	14	39 57	75 11	30	MID	MID	FRANCIS K. DAVIS,JR	2 3 5
PHILADELPHIA WB AP	6889	PHILADELPHIA	5	39 53	75 14	13	MID	MID	U.S. WEATHER BUREAU	2 3 5 7 C
#PHILADELPHIA PT BREEZE	6899	PHILADELPHIA	5	39 55	75 12	32	MID	MID	ATLANTIC REFINING	2 3 5 C
PHILADELPHIA SHAWMONT	6904	PHILADELPHIA	5	40 02	75 15	70	7P	7P	SCHUYLKILL NAVIG CO	2 3 5
#PHILADELPHIA CITY	6909	PHILADELPHIA	5	39 57	75 09	26	9A	9A	USN HYDROGRAPHIC OFF	2 3 5 C
PHILIPSBURG CAA AP	6916	CENTRE	6	40 54	78 05	1918	8P	8P	CIVIL AERO. ADM.	2 3 5 7 C
PHOENIXVILLE 1 E	6927	CHESTER	14	40 07	75 30	105	6P	MID	PHILA SUB WATER CO	2 3 5 C
PIKES CREEK	6939	LUZERNE	15	41 18	76 08	1320		MID	HARRY SHELDON	3 C
PIMPLE HILL	6944	MONROE	9	41 02	75 30	2215	9A	9A	PA DEPT FRST + WTRS	2 3 5 6 7
PINE GROVE 1 NE	6954	SCHUYLKILL	15	40 34	76 22	535		8A	PA POWER + LIGHT CO	3
PITTSBURGH WB AP 2	6993	ALLEGHENY	11	40 30	80 13	1151	MID	MID	U.S. WEATHER BUREAU	2 3 5 7 C
#PITTSBURGH WB CITY	6997	ALLEGHENY	11	40 27	80 00	749	MID	MID	U.S. WEATHER BUREAU	2 3 5 C
PLEASANT MOUNT 1 W	7029	WAYNE	5	41 44	75 27	1800	8A	8A	PA FISH COMM	2 3 5 7 C
PORT CLINTON	7116	SCHUYLKILL	14	40 35	76 02	450	7A	7A	MRS. ADA E. RARICK	2 3 5 C
PORTLAND	7127	NORTHAMPTON	5	40 55	75 06	297		8A	JOINT BRIDGE COMM	INAC 1/56
POTTSTOWN	7149	MONTGOMERY	14	40 15	75 39	160		8A	MILES E. SMITH	3
POTTSVILLE	7161	SCHUYLKILL	14	40 42	76 11	600		8A	LLOYD E. HELLER	3
PUNXSUTAWNEY	7217	JEFFERSON	1	40 57	79 00	1298		MID	JOHN VOLANSKY	C
PUTNEYVILLE 2 SE DAM	7229	ARMSTRONG	1	40 55	79 17	1270	8A	8A	CORPS OF ENGINEERS	2 3 5 C
QUAKERTOWN 1 E	7239	BUCKS	5	40 26	75 20	490	5P	5P	DENNIS K. FLUCK	2 3 5
RAYMOND	7310	POTTER	13	41 52	77 52	2220		7A	MRS. RACHEL LANGAN	3 C
#READING WB CITY	7318	BERKS	14	40 20	75 58	266	MID	MID	U.S. WEATHER BUREAU	2 3 5 7 C
RENOVO	7409	CLINTON	16	41 20	77 46	660		7A	MRS. CAROLINE BAIRD	3
RENOVO 5 S	7410	CLINTON	16	41 14	77 46	2035		MID	C. F. BILLETTE	C
REW	7425	MC KEAN	1	41 54	78 32	2250		8A	HAROLD C. MEALY	3
RICES LANDING L 6	7443	GREENE	10	39 57	80 00	775		7A	CORPS OF ENGINEERS	3
RIDGWAY 3 W	7477	ELK	1	41 25	78 47	1420	7A	7A	BOROUGH OF RIDGWAY	2 3 5
ROCHESTER 1 N	7540	BEAVER	2	40 43	80 18	900		MID	DEQUESNE LIGHT CO	C
RUSH	7694	SUSQUEHANNA	15	41 47	76 03	1000		9A	MISS MAUDE MC CAIN	3
RUSHVILLE	7727	SUSQUEHANNA	15	41 47	76 07	870		7A	CARL KOPATZ	3
SAFE HARBOR	7732	LANCASTER	15	39 55	76 23	270		MID	S.H.WATER POWER CORP	C
SAGAMORE 1 S	7739	INDIANA	1	40 46	79 14	1320		7A	CORPS OF ENGINEERS	3
SALINA 3 W	7782	WESTMORELAND	7	40 31	79 33	1109	6P	6P	MUN AUTH WSTMRLD CO	2 3 5
SAXTON	7846	BEDFORD	6	40 12	78 15	780		8A	MRS.ALVERTA L.HOLMES	3 C
SCANDIA 2 E	7855	WARREN	1	41 55	79 01	2040		MID	DAVID R. ANDERSON	C
SCHENLEY LOCK 5	7863	ARMSTRONG	1	40 41	79 40	783		VAR	CORPS OF ENGINEERS	3
#SCRANTON	7902	LACKAWANNA	15	41 25	75 40	746	7A	7A	U.S. POST OFFICE	2 3 5

STATION INDEX

IMMED

PENNSYLVANIA
FEBRUARY 1957

Station	Index No.	County	Drainage ‡	Latitude	Longitude	Elevation	Observation Time Temp.	Observation Time Precip.	Observer	Refer To Tables
INTON WB AIRPORT	7005	LUZERNE	15	41 20	75 44	950	MID	MID	U.S. WEATHER BUREAU	2 3 5 7 C
INSGROVE CAA AP	7031	SNYDER	15	40 49	76 52	437	MID	MID	CIVIL AERO. ADM.	2 3 5 7
ERSVILLE 2 NW	7038	BUCKS	5	40 23	75 20	530		MID	SELLERSVILLE WTR CO	C
E GAP	7065	HUNTINGDON	6	40 11	77 52	1000		MID	MRS. HELEN M. PYLE	C
OKIN	7078	NORTHUMBLAND	15	40 48	76 33	770		8A	ROARING CRK WTR CO	3
FIELD 6 W	8026	WARREN	1	41 41	79 09	1940		MID	L. N. HANSON	C
PENSBURG	8073	FRANKLIN	15	40 03	77 32	709	4P	4P	KEITH B. ALLEN	2 3 5 7
PINGPORT WB	8078	BEAVER	11	40 37	80 26	740	MID	MID	U.S. WEATHER BUREAU	2 3 5 7 C
EMAHONING	8145	CAMERON	16	41 19	78 05	790		7A	MRS.FRANCES CALDWELL	3
PERY ROCK	8184	BUTLER	2	41 04	80 03	1345	7P	7A	WALTER D. ALBERT	2 3 5 7
NPORT HIGHWAY SHED	8190	MC KEAN	1	41 48	78 27	1510		MID	PA DEPT HIGHWAYS	C
RSET FAIRVIEW ST	8244	SOMERSET	17	40 01	79 05	2140		7A	HOWARD G. PECK	3
RSET MAIN ST	8249	SOMERSET	17	40 01	79 05	2150	6P	6P	DAVID L. GROVE	2 3 5
H CANAAN 1 NE	8275	WAYNE	5	41 31	75 24	1400		MID	EUGENE M. COOK	C
H MOUNTAIN	8308	FRANKLIN	12	39 51	77 30	1520		7A	PA DEPT OF HEALTH	3
NGBORO	8359	CRAWFORD	8	41 48	80 23	900	8A	8A	SPRINGBORO BOROUGH	2 3 5 C
NG GROVE	8379	YORK	15	39 52	76 52	470		4P	P. H. GLATFELTER CO	3 C
NGS 1 SW	8395	SOMERSET	17	39 44	79 10	2500	8P	8P	ALLEN E. YODER	2 3 5 7
E COLLEGE	8449	CENTRE	16	40 48	77 52	1175	MID	MID	PA STATE COLLEGE	2 3 5 6 C
USSTOWN	8570	BERKS	14	40 29	76 11	600		8A	JACOB KLAHR	3
NGSTOWN	8589	INDIANA	4	40 33	78 55	1880		MID	HARRY F. BENNETT	C
UDSBURG	8596	MONROE	5	40 59	75 12	480	11P	11P	WILLIAM HAGERTY	2 3 5 C
P CREEK	8610	JEFFERSON	1	41 01	78 50	1320		7A	CORPS OF ENGINEERS	3
URY	8668	NORTHUMBLAND	15	40 51	76 48	440		7A	CHARLES W. BAYLER	3 C
UEHANNA	8692	SUSQUEHANNA	15	41 57	75 36	1020		7A	MRS. LAURA A.BENSON	3
RSVILLE	8699	ALLEGHENY	17	40 14	79 48	765		7A	FRANK E. MARSH	3
QUA	8758	SCHUYLKILL	14	40 48	75 58	830		8A	MRS. MARY L.ROBERTS	3
OUT 4 N DAM	8763	SCHUYLKILL	14	40 51	75 59	1120		7A	PANTHER VLY WTR CO	3 C
RACK 2 S FIRE TWR	8?70	CLINTON	16	41 24	77 51	2220	7A	7A	JAMES E. SWARTZ	2 3 5 7
ESTA 2 SE DAM	8873	FOREST	1	41 29	79 26	1200	8A	8A	CORPS OF ENGINEERS	2 3 5 7 C
SVILLE	8885	CRAWFORD	1	41 38	79 40	1550		MID	PA ELECTRIC CO	C
SVILLE WATER WORKS	8888	CRAWFORD	1	41 38	79 42	1220	7P	7P	CITY OF TITUSVILLE	2 3 5
EDO 4 W	8901	WARREN	1	41 47	79 32	1735		7A	MRS. LILY B. GARBER	3
NDA	8905	BRADFORD	15	41 46	76 26	760	7P	7A	MRS. M. O. PARKS	2 3 5 7 C
R CITY 5 SW	8910	DAUPHIN	15	40 31	76 37	745		6P	HARRISBURG WTR DEPT	3 7
[illegible]	8959	BRADFORD	15	41 47	76 47	1100		7A	JENNIE L. BALLARD	3
ELTON	8989	INDIANA	4	40 27	79 23	890		MID	MRS. MARY E. WEIMER	C
LEPOINT 4 NE	9002	MC KEAN	1	41 54	78 16	1640		7A	ROBERT D. STRAIT	3
NE 4 NE BALD EAGLE	9024	BLAIR	6	40 43	78 12	1020		7A	FREDERICK L. FRIDAY	3 C
N CITY	9042	ERIE	1	41 54	79 50	1325		7A	FORREST M. BRALEY	3 C
NTOWN	9050	FAYETTE	10	39 54	79 44	1040	10P	10P	WM. W. MARSTELLER	2 3 5
R DARBY	9074	DELAWARE	5	39 58	75 18	222	7P	7P	PHIL. SUB.TRANS. CO	2 3 5
A	9099	VENANGO	1	41 26	79 57	1030		7A	MRS.FLORENCE MILLER	3
ERGRIFT	9128	WESTMORELAND	7	40 36	79 33	800		7A	UNITED ENG+FNDRY CO	3
ERGRIFT 2 W	9133	WESTMORELAND	7	40 36	79 36	995		MID	EUGENE R. YOUNG	C

Station	Index No.	County	Drainage ‡	Latitude	Longitude	Elevation	Observation Time Temp.	Observation Time Precip.	Observer	Refer To Tables
VIRGINVILLE	9196	BERKS	14	40 31	75 52	350		8A	MRS. MARY M. WRIGHT	3
VOWINCKEL	9206	CLARION	1	41 25	79 14	1620		8A	PA DEPT FRST + WTRS	3
VOWINCKEL 1 WSW	9209	CLARION	1	41 24	79 15	1610		8A	PA DEPT FRST + WTRS	3
WARREN	9298	WARREN	1	41 51	79 08	1280	7P	7A	GILBERT H. REILR	2 3 5
WASHINGTON	9312	WASHINGTON	11	40 11	80 14	1200		MID	PA DEPT HIGHWAYS	C
WATSONTOWN	9345	NORTHUMBLAND	16	41 05	76 52	490		9P	WILLIAM BIRD	3
WAYNESBURG 2 W	9362	GREENE	10	39 54	80 13	980	6P	7A	RALPH L. AMOS	2 3 5
WAYNESBURG 1 E	9367	GREENE	10	39 54	80 10	940		MID	SEWAGE DISPOSAL PLT	C
WEBSTER MILLS 3 SW	9380	FULTON	12	39 49	78 05	920		MID	WILLIAM D. COVER	C
WELLSBORO 3 S	9408	TIOGA	16	41 43	77 16	1920	7A	7A	MARION L. SHUMWAY	2 3 5
WELLSBORO 2 E	9412	TIOGA	16	41 45	77 16	1550		MID	MRS. IDA S. MAYNARD	C
WELLSVILLE	9420	YORK	15	40 03	76 57	500	5P	5P	D. D. HOOVER	2 3 5
WERNERSVILLE 1 W	9430	BERKS	14	40 20	76 06	405		8A	CHARLES A. GRUBER	3
WEST CHESTER	9464	CHESTER	5	39 58	75 36	440	8A	8A	DAILY LOCAL NEWS	2 3 5
WEST GROVE 1 E	9503	CHESTER	5	39 49	75 49	440		8A	CONARD-PYLE CO	3
WEST HICKORY	9507	FOREST	1	41 34	79 25	1090		8A	MRS.HELEN F.KINNEAR	3
WHITESBURG	9655	ARMSTRONG	1	40 45	79 24	1530		7A	CORPS OF ENGINEERS	3
WILKES-BARRE	9702	LAZERNE	15	41 15	75 52	610		7A	MRS. MARY G. MIRMAK	3
WILLIAMSBURG	9714	BLAIR	6	40 28	78 12	860		7A	MYRON K. BIDDLE	3
WILLIAMSPORT WB AP	9728	LYCOMING	16	41 15	76 55	527	MID	MID	U.S. WEATHER BUREAU	2 3 5 7 C
WIND GAP	9781	NORTHAMPTON	5	40 51	75 18	720		MID	OWEN R. PARRY	C
WOLFSBURG	9823	BEDFORD	6	40 03	78 32	1190		7A	WALTER C. RICE	3
YORK 3 SSW PUMP STA	9933	YORK	15	39 55	76 45	390	5P	5P	YORK WATER COMPANY	2 3 5
YORK 2 S FILTER PLANT	9938	YORK	15	39 56	76 44	640		MID	YORK WATER COMPANY	C
YORK HAVEN	9950	YORK	15	40 07	76 43	310		8A	METROPOL EDISON CO	3
YOUNGSVILLE	9966	WARREN	1	41 51	79 20	1225		MID	HENRY CARLETT	C
ZION GROVE	9990	SCHUYLKILL	15	40 54	76 13	940		7A	JAMES D. TEETER	3
ZIONSVILLE 3 SE	9995	LEHIGH	14	40 27	75 27	660		7A	LESLIE HOWATT	3
NEW STATIONS										
EQUINUNK 2	2671	WAYNE	5	41 51	75 13	910		7A	MRS. HENRIETTA MURRY	3
COMBINED STATIONS										
EQUINUNK	2669	WAYNE	5	41 51	75 13	900		8A	COMBINED W/STA 2671	1/57

‡ 1-ALLEGHENY; 2-BEAVER; 3- 4-CONEMAUGH; 5-DELAWARE; 6-JUNIATA; 7-KISKIMINETAS; 8-LAKE ERIE; 9-LEHIGH; 10-MONONGAHELA; 11-OHIO; 12-POTOMAC; 13-LAKE ONTARIO; 14-SCHUYLKILL; 15-SUSQUEHANNA; 16-WEST BRANCH; 17-YOUGHIOGHENY

REFERENCE NOTES

Additional information regarding the climate of Pennsylvania may be obtained by writing to the State Climatologist at Weather Bureau Airport Station, Harrisburg State Airport, New Cumberland, Pennsylvania, or to any Weather Bureau Office near you.

Figures and letters following the station name, such as 12 SSW, indicate distance in miles and direction from the post office.

Delayed data and corrections will be carried only in the June and December issues of this bulletin.

Monthly and seasonal snowfall and heating degree days for the preceding 12 months will be carried in the June issue of this bulletin.

Stations appearing in the Index, but for which data are not listed in the tables, either are missing or were received too late to be included in this issue.

Divisions, as used in Table 2, become effective with data for September 1956.

Unless otherwise indicated, dimensional units used in this bulletin are: Temperature in °F, precipitation and evaporation in inches, and wind movement in miles. Monthly degree day totals are the sums of the negative departures of average daily temperatures from 65° F.

Evaporation is measured in the standard Weather Bureau type pan of 4 foot diameter unless otherwise shown by footnote following Table 6.

Long-term means for full-time stations (those shown in the Station Index as "U. S. Weather Bureau") are based on the period 1921-1950, adjusted to represent observations taken at the present location. Long-term means for all stations except full-time Weather Bureau stations are based on the period 1931-1955.

Water equivalent values published in Table 7 are the water equivalent of snow, sleet or ice on the ground. Samples for obtaining measurements are taken from different points for successive observations; consequently occasional drifting and other causes of local variability in the snowpack result in apparent inconsistencies in the record. Water equivalent of snow on the ground is measured at selected stations when two or more inches of snow are on the ground.

Entries of Snowfall in Tables 2 and 7, and in the seasonal snowfall table, include snow and sleet. Entries of snow on ground include snow, sleet and ice.

Data in Tables 3, 5, and 6 and snowfall in Table 7, when published, are for the 24 hours ending at time of observation. The Station Index lists observation times in the standard of time in local use.

Snow on ground in Table 7 is at observation time for all except Weather Bureau and CAA stations. For these stations snow on ground values are at 7:30 a.m., E.S.T.

- – No record in Tables 3, 6, 7 and the Station Index. No record in Tables 2 and 5, is indicated by no entry. Consult the annual issue of this publication for interpolated monthly precipitation totals.
- \+ And also on a later date or dates.
- ++ Fastest observed one minute wind speed. This station is not equipped with automatic wind instruments.
- * Amount included in following measurement, time distribution unknown.
- // Gage is equipped with a windshield.
- \# Thermometers are generally exposed in a shelter located a few feet above sod-covered ground; however, the reference indicates that the thermometers are exposed in a shelter located on the roof of a building.
- AM Data based on observational day ending before noon.
- B Adjusted to a full month.
- C In the "Refer to Tables" column in the Station Index the letter "C" indicates recorder stations. These stations are processed for special purposes and are published later in "Hourly Precipitation Data".
- D Water equivalent of snowfall wholly or partly estimated, using a ratio of 1 inch water equivalent to every 10 inches of new snowfall.
- G In the "Refer to Tables" column in the Station Index the letter "G" indicates that soil temperatures are published.
- M One or more days of record missing; if average value is entered, less than 10 days record is missing. See Table 5 for detailed daily record. Degree day data, if carried for this station, have been adjusted to represent the value for a full month.
- R Amounts from recording gage (These amounts are essentially accurate but may vary slightly from the amounts to be published later in "Hourly Precipitation Data".)
- SS This entry in time of observation column in Station Index means observation made near sunset.
- T Trace, an amount too small to measure.
- Y Includes total for previous month.
- VAR This entry in time of observation column in Station Index means variable.

Information concerning the history of changes in locations, elevations, exposure etc. of substations through 1955 may be found in the publication "Substation History" for this state, soon to be issued. That publication, when available, may be obtained from the Superintendent of Documents, Government Printing Office, Washington 25, D. C. at a price to be announced. Similar information for regular Weather Bureau stations may be found in the latest issues of Local Climatological Data, Annual for the respective stations, obtained as indicated above, price 15 cents.

Subscription Price: 20 cents per copy, monthly and annual; $2.50 per year. (Yearly subscription includes the Annual Summary). Checks, and money orders should be made payable to the Superintendent of Documents. Remittance and correspondence regarding subscriptions should be sent to the Superintendent of Documents, Government Printing Office, Washington 25, D. C.

WRC., Asheville, N. C. --- 4/5/57 --- 1100

U. S. DEPARTMENT OF COMMERCE
SINCLAIR WEEKS, Secretary
WEATHER BUREAU
F. W. REICHELDERFER, Chief

CLIMATOLOGICAL DATA

PENNSYLVANIA

MARCH 1957
Volume LXII No. 3

ASHEVILLE: 1957

PENNSYLVANIA - MARCH 1957

WEATHER SUMMARY

GENERAL

Blustery conditions traditionally attributed to March were mostly missing with the exception of excessive snowfall in the Central Mountain, Northwest Plateau, and Upper Susquehanna areas.

A brief cold snap early in the month was more than offset by a mid-month warm spell and the average temperature at the majority of the stations was higher than the 25-year (1931-1955) average. Temperature extremes ranged from -3° on the 4th at Bradford 4 W and Ridgway 3 W to 79° on the 15th at West Chester. The amount of precipitation was below average at nearly all stations with totals occurring in a relatively narrow bracket ranging from 1.03 inches at Hop Bottom 2 SE to 3.81 inches at Kregar 4 SE. The greatest amount for one day was 1.45 inches measured at Chester on the 16th.

WEATHER DETAILS

Temperatures were moderate at the beginning of the month but dropped quite low during a cold snap the 3rd through the 5th. Moderate temperatures prevailed from the 6th through the 11th and a period of very warm weather from the 12th through the 15th sent maximum thermometers above the 70° mark over most of the State on the 14th. Changes in temperatures after mid-month were of a minor to moderate character and values were never very far from the seasonal ave age.

Precipitation occurred very frequent and the only statewide dry period of significance was from the 21st throu the 24th. Daily measurements were generally quite small but reached mo erate proportions on a wide scale th 8th-9th and the 27th.

WEATHER EFFECTS

Light precipitation in March allowed much ground to dry sufficiently to permit plowing and some planting. Good progress was made in hauling an spreading manure, lime, and fertiliz Snow cover was generally light but there was less than usual damage fro alternate freezing and thawing. The mid-month warm spell caused much win grain and grasses to green up and sh some growth. Sugar camps operated during the month but operators repor below average production due to the flow of sap being hindered by the mi month warm spell and the lack of sha fluctuating temperatures.

DESTRUCTIVE STORMS AND FLOODS

None reported.

J. T. B. Beard, Climatologist
Weather Records Processing Cente
Chattanooga, Tennessee

Temperature: Average Maximum	Average Minimum	Average	Departure From Long Term Means	Highest	Date	Lowest	Date	Degree Days	No. of Days Max 90° or Above	Max 32° or Below	Min 32° or Below	Min 0° or Below	Precipitation: Total	Departure From Long Term Means	Greatest Day	Date	Snow, Sleet: Total	Max Depth on Ground	Date	No. of Days: .10 or More	.50 or More	1.00 or More
44.2	27.3	35.8	2.5	71	14	13	4+	902	0	3	25	0	D 2.94	- .99	.50	15	13.6	3	9+	10	1	0
41.9	21.8	31.9		73	15	7	5	1022	0	5	31	0	2.04		.64	9	7.2	3	9+	5	1	0
42.5M	24.6M	33.6M	1.6	70	14	5	4	968	0	5	28	0	3.13	- .82	.56	9				10	2	0
46.2	27.2	36.7		72	14	10	4	869	0	0	27	0	2.56		.57	15	5.0	2	1+	7	1	0
40.4	24.5	32.5		70	15	8	4+	1001	0	10	27	0	3.06		.64	16	17.2	5	27	9	2	0
39.0M	20.7M	29.9M		68	15	3	4	1082	0	7	30	0	2.15	- 1.82	.57	9	9.2	6	10	6	1	0
46.2	27.5	36.9	- .4	77	15	8	5	863	0	0	23	0	2.25	- .50	.70	9	.4	0		9	1	0
45.0	27.3	36.2	- .1	73	14	13	5	886	0	2	25	0	1.66	- 1.17	.34	8	6.7	2	9+	7	0	0
47.3	26.1	36.7	- .5	75	14	8	5	870	0	0	27	0	2.63	- 1.10	.60	8	3.7	1	1	9	2	0
		34.5											2.80				7.9					
48.9	29.5	39.2	1.3	75	14	19	4+	792	0	0	22	0	2.31	- .88	.41	8	1.9	T	1+	7	0	0
47.8	30.9	39.4	.9	75	15	20	4	786	0	0	17	0	2.52	- .88	.70	9	.9	T	1+	7	1	0
51.7M	29.0M	40.4M	3.1	78	14	16	5	762	0	0	19	0	2.37	- 1.84	.37	27	1.2	1	1	8	0	0
48.2	29.0	38.6	.3	72	14	15	5	811	0	0	19	0	2.11	- .99	.55	15	1.3	1	1	8	1	0
49.6	26.8	38.2	- .3	75	15	12	4	823	0	0	28	0	2.86	- 1.01	.90	16	1.5				1	0
		39.2											2.43				1.4					
50.5	32.7	41.6		73	15	23	1	720	0	0	11	0	3.54		1.45	16				9	2	1
49.6	29.7	39.7	- .2	74	15	17	4	777	0	1	19	0	1.77	- 2.36	.47	1				6	0	0
51.4	31.9	41.7		76	14	17	4	717	0	0	15	0	1.87		.56	1				6	1	0
49.7	28.2	39.0		76	14	16	4+	797	0	0	24	0	3.20		.70	8				9	3	0
50.3	30.7	40.5	.0	73	14	17	4	750	0	0	18	0	3.62	.19	.90	15				7	3	0
50.2	32.0	41.1	.5	71	14	18	4	734	0	0	16	0	2.41	- 1.05	.74	9	2.2	1	1	6	2	0
51.9	30.0	41.0		78	15	18	4	745	0	0	22	0	2.65	- .81	.79	9				7	2	0
48.9	34.7	41.8	.5	71	14	23	4	711	0	0	9	0	2.79	- .19	1.29	9	.3	T	1+	8	2	1
52.1	30.5	41.3	1.2	75	14	18	4+	726	0	0	19	0	2.56	- .89	.62	8				7	2	0
48.2	29.1	38.7		74	15	17	4	808	0	1	21	0	2.24		.84	9	1.3	1	2+	8	1	0
48.5	29.2	38.9	- .4	74	15	16	4	804	0	1	21	0	3.30	- .29	.95	16	.2	T	1+	6	2	0
51.5	37.3	44.4	- .4	69	14	26	4	633	0	0	6	0	2.89	- .77	1.01	15	T	0		6	2	1
49.8	33.2	41.5	1.3	74	14	20	4	721	0	0	14	0	2.81	- .70	.74	8	6.5	T	1+	7	2	0
48.5	30.2	39.4		72	14	19	4	789	0	1	23	0	1.44		.35	1				5	0	0
49.0	30.6	39.8		73	14	21	4	775	0	0	21	0	3.06		1.04	8				6	2	1
50.5	33.4	42.0		77	14	22	4	706	0	0	12	0	2.44		.88	9				9	2	0
51.3	35.8	43.6		75	14	24	4	658	0	0	8	0	2.99		.90	15	T	T	1+	7	2	0
50.1	34.5	42.3	.0	73	14	23	4	695	0	0	9	0	3.24	- .08	1.32	15	1.2	T	1+	6	2	1
50.8	37.3	44.1	.6	72	14	27	4	641	0	0	6	0	3.19		1.19	15	T	0		6	2	1
51.1	32.6	41.9	- .7	74	14	20	4	715	0	1	13	0					1.0	0				
50.5	37.5	44.0	.5	73	14	26	4	644	0	0	5	0	3.39	.02	1.31	15				7	2	1
53.5	31.4	42.5	1.0	78	14	18	4+	692	0	0	15	0	2.52	- 1.13	.72	8				7	2	0
50.5	29.9	40.2	2.5	74	14	18	5	763	0	0	21	0	3.00	- .60	.79	9				9	1	0
50.5	34.4	42.5	.9	75	14	23	4	690	0	0	10	0	2.31	- 1.00	.66	15	1.1	T	1+	7	1	0
50.4	33.7	42.1		73	14	22	4	705	0	0	10	0	2.99		.79	1	1.5	T	1	8	1	0
52.3	32.0	42.2	2.8	79	15	16	4	699	0	0	12	0	1.66	- 2.26			.7	0				0
		41.5											2.72				1.2					
48.5	30.4	39.5	- .4	72	15	15	4	786	0	1	19	0	1.87	- 1.69	.52	9	1.0	0		8	2	0
52.5	32.3	42.4	3.4	75	14	19	4+	692	0	0	15	0	2.40	- 1.06	.80	8	3.0	T	1+	8	1	0
49.9	30.5	40.2	.1	72	14	17	4	762	0	0	21	0	1.70	- 1.52	.38	1	4.2	T	1+	7	0	0
49.9	32.3	41.1	.5	72	15	19	4	735	0	1	14	0	1.84	- 1.45	.56	1	2.5	2	7	6	1	0
50.2	29.6	39.9	- 2.1	75	15	18	4+	769	0	1	22	0	2.45	- .83	.68	1	1.0	1	7	7	2	0
49.5	33.0	41.3	.5	74	14	21	4	730	0	0	12	0	1.97	- .90	.64	8	2.4	1	7	5	1	0
52.3	30.9	41.6		75	14	14	4	718	0	0	18	0	2.55									0
50.8	30.9	40.9	- .1	72	14	17	4	741	0	0	17	0	1.81	- 1.46	.68	1	6.0	2	8	7	1	0
50.7	28.4	39.6		72	14	14	4	782	0	0	21	0	2.20		.57	8	2.5	T	1+	7	2	0
52.7	31.0	41.9	.8	75	14	17	4+	710	0	0	18	0	1.84	- 1.44	.47	1	2.5	0		7	0	0
		40.8											2.06				2.8					
48.6	28.3	38.5		73	14	12	4	815	0	0	24	0	3.02		.97	9	8.0	4	9		1	0
50.5	28.9	39.7		76	14	15	4+	779	0	0	21	0	2.49		.71	15	1.8	1	1	8	1	0
46.7	28.2	37.5		72	15	14	5	848	0	1	22	0	2.18		.47	9		2	27	6	0	0
49.0	30.0	39.5		75	15	16	5	781	0	1	21	0	2.49		.62	9	3.2	2	2		1	0
49.4	28.1	38.8		75	15	14	4	806	0	1	25	0	2.63	- .84	.68	9	2.5			8	1	0
48.4	27.4	37.9	- .8	74	14	13	4	832	0	0	25	0	2.62	- 1.07	.91	8	4.9	2	9	7	1	0
48.7	29.2	39.0	.7	71	14	17	5	799	0	0	23	0	2.87	- .47	1.12	8	14.5	3	9	8	1	1
		38.7											2.61				5.8					
41.9	24.5	33.2		69	15	9	4	980	0	3	28	0	D 2.82		1.10	9	21.1	10	9+	7	2	1
46.0	23.3	34.7		76	15	9	5	934	0	1	29	0	2.69		1.01	9	4.5	2	9	8	1	1
40.6	24.3	32.5		66	15	8	4	1003	0	7	29	0	2.23	- 2.46	.42	9	18.0	7	9+	8	0	0
44.2	20.9	32.6	- 2.2	71	15	5	5	997	0	2	30	0	2.14	- .30	.63	9	7.4	4	9+	7	1	0

See Reference Notes Following Station Index

TABLE 2 - CONTINUED

Station	
MONTROSE 1 E	AM
TOWANDA	
WELLSBORO 3 S	AM
DIVISION	
CENTRAL MOUNTAINS	
BELLEFONTE 4 S	AM
DU BOIS 7 E	
EMPORIUM 2 SSW	AM
LOCK HAVEN	
MADERA	AM
PHILIPSBURG CAA AP	
RIDGWAY 3 W	AM
STATE COLLEGE	
TAMARACK 2 S FIRE TWR	AM
DIVISION	
SOUTH CENTRAL MOUNTAINS	
ALTOONA HORSESHOE CURVE	
ARTEMAS 1 WNW	
BURNT CABINS 2 NE	
EBENSBURG	
EVERETT 1 SW	
HUNTINGDON	AM
JOHNSTOWN	AM
KEGG	
MARTINSBURG CAA AP	
DIVISION	
SOUTHWEST PLATEAU	
BAKERSTOWN 3 WNW	
BLAIRSVILLE 6 ENE	
BURGETTSTOWN 2 W	AM
BUTLER	
CLAYSVILLE 3 W	
CONFLUENCE 1 SW DAM	AM
DERRY	
DONEGAL	
DONORA	AM
FORD CITY 4 S DAM	AM
INDIANA 3 SE	
IRWIN	
MIDLAND DAM 7	
NEW CASTLE 1 N	
NEWELL	AM
NEW STANTON	
PITTSBURGH WB AP 2	//R
PITTSBURGH WB CITY	R
PUTNEYVILLE 2 SE DAM	AM
SALINA 3 W	
SHIPPINGPORT WB	
SLIPPERY ROCK	
SOMERSET MAIN ST	
SPRINGS 1 SW	
UNIONTOWN	
WAYNESBURG 2 W	
DIVISION	
NORTHWEST PLATEAU	
BRADFORD 4 W RES	
BROOKVILLE CAA AIRPORT	
CLARION 3 SW	
CORRY	
COUDERSPORT 3 NW	
EAST BRADY	
ERIE WB AIRPORT	
FARRELL SHARON	
FRANKLIN	
GREENVILLE	
JAMESTOWN 2 NW	AM
KANE 1 NNE	AM
LINESVILLE 5 WNW	
MEADVILLE 1 S	AM
MERCER 2 NNE	
SPRINGBORO	AM
TIONESTA 2 SE DAM	AM
TITUSVILLE WATER WORKS	
WARREN	
DIVISION	

See Reference Notes Following Station Index

DAILY PRECIPITATION

Day of month

	Total	1	2	3	4	5	6	7	8	9	10	11	12	13	14	15	16	17	18	19	20	21	22	23	24	25	26	27	28	29	30	31
R	3.32	.27	.03	.01				.21	.52	.34	T		.07			.07	.11			.16	.12	.02					.16	.05		.05	.33	
	2.31	.38	.02					.01	.41	.33		T	T			.27			T	.18	.09					.22	.02	.31	T	.06	.01	
	2.52	.22	.18	.04					.04	.70	T						.27			.05	.20	.06					.33	.27	.07		.09	
VE	2.48	.33	.07	.02				.10	.46	.04			.04			.13				.11	.12					.12	.15	.51	.02	.19	.07	
	1.87	.51						.17	.18	.52						T	.12			.13	.10							.14				
		RECORD MISSING																														
	2.90	.34	.15	.04				.13	.13	.82	T		.06				.19			T	.31						.21	.14	T	.20	.18	
	1.84	T	.15	T		T	.20	T	T	.21			.13				T		T	.15	.05					.01	.26	.46		.20	.02	
	1.30	.19	T	.06	.04			.19	.10	.29	.02	T				T	.09				.06	T					.07	.10		.05	.04	
	-	-	.08						-	.31							-			.23	T							-				
	3.04	.37							.28	.45		.05				.55	.30				.18						.21	.48	.03		.14	
	2.26	.33	.03	.04	T			.06	.19	.45	T	T	.02			.02	T			.16	.15	.02					.19	.42	T	T	.18	
	3.02	*	.18	T					.12	.97			.03			.03	.35			.07	.22	T					.25	.38	.31		.11	
	2.94	.44	.10					.20	.15	.73			T				.28			T							.22	.49	.19		.16	
	3.00	.41						.20	.14	.90						T	.28			.18	.09						.06	.53	T	T	.21	
	2.54	.31	.05	.11					.08	.47			.05			T	.70			T	.20	T					.18	.27	.08		.06	
	2.40	.34		T				T	.27	.25		.02				.71				.03	.10						.19	.40	.04	T	.14	
	2.24	.29	.08	.03					.02	.74	T						.25			.03	.16	.04					.20	.26	.07		.07	T
		RECORD MISSING																														
	2.52	.48	.11	.02			T	.21	.37	.09		T	.02			.05			.01	.10	.27	.01				.15	.20	.52	.22	.22	.02	
	2.23	.46	.02					.36	.50	.04						.50				.06						T	.05	.24				
		RECORD MISSING																														
	3.77	.38	.09	.03				.14	.64	.46	T	.01	.03			.02	.10			.10	.12	.01					.14	1.29		.09	.10	
TA	1.90	.25	.04	.05				.17	.06	.42	.10	*	.09				.11			T	.18						.20	.03	.05	.04	.11	
	2.08	.26	.08	.13				.22	.41	.13	.05					.08				.05	.18						.21	.05	.08	.10	.05	
	1.62	.36	D.10					.18	.44							.14											.22	.18				
T	2.84	.22	.02	T			T	.10	.65	.09	T	T	.01			.16			.01	.18	.07	.01				.04	.42	.66	.04	.20		
	2.60	.40			.04				.78			.03				T					.19	T					.14	.99		.03		
	1.86	.45	.03					.12	.37	.13							.08			.10	.11	T					.07	.35			.05	T
	2.78	.47						.19	.61	.25		.02	.01				T			.15	.18	.02					.18	.50		.11	.11	
	1.75	D.10		.05				.15	.53	.10						.29				.08	.11					.02	*	.25		.04	.03	
	2.99	.31		.02				.05	.65	.34		.01	.02				.09			.17	.31	.01					.17	.47	.05	.09	.23	
	3.22	.48	.03					1.03	.65	.04		T				.37			T	.08	.02					T		.50		.02		
	2.82	.23	T	T				T	T	1.10			D.16				.19			T	.07						.15	.26	.05	.07	.50	.02
	2.40	.28	.10					.18	.80	.08						.28				.15	.12					.04	.02	.29	.02	.04	T	
	2.27	.43	.04	.09	T			.05	.16	.10	.05	T	.05				.04			.04	.17	.06					.39	.40	.01	.08	.13	
	2.90	.35	.17	T				.15	.12	.58	T						.37			.07	.20						.20	.21	.13	T	.35	
	3.37	.55	.15	.01				.10	.04	.80	T		T				.42			T	.10						.06	.50	.10	.04	.50	
	-	-	-	-	-	-	-	-	-	-	-	-	-	-	-	-	.80			.10	.35						T	.20			T	T
	1.70	.38	T					.24	.22	.03						.20			.02	.24	.05					.10		.17		.05		
	2.77	.40	.09	.01				.06	.71	.30	.02		T			.04	.09			.10	.08	.04					.09	.62	.01	.08	.05	
	3.94	.39	.30					.04	.19	.50							1.45			.14	.11	.05					T	.17	T	T	.20	
	3.31	.51	.05	.13				.25	.19	.65	T	T	.01			T	.20			.04	.13	T					.30	.65	.12	.03	.05	
	2.71	.15	.11	.05				.08	.21	.59	T		.02			.05	.09			.12	.09	.01					.27	.49		.05	.33	
	2.42	.33	.06	.07					.05	.56							.54			.06	.12						.19	.33	.03		.08	
	2.38	.55	.01	T				.14	.60	.11		T	.02		T					.16	.10	T					.12	.48	.02	T	.07	
	2.60	.35	.05	.02				.11	.17	.29	T	T	.02			T	.15			.07	.15	T					.20	.66	.04	.12	.20	
	1.81	.18	.05	.12	T			.14	.15	.55	.03	T	.05			.04				.04	.05	T					.08	.16	.04	.06	.07	
	2.38	.24	.06						.03	.38							.74				.11	.02					.24	.38	.10		.08	
	1.77	.47	T					T	.12	.33							.35			.09	.10	T					.04	.20	T		.07	
	1.87	.56						.04	.48	.18						.09			T	.18	.11					T	.03	.20	T	T		
	1.87	.44	.04	.04				.05	.17	.10	T		.01				T			.05	.20	.04		T			.06	.55	.04	.06	.02	
	2.00	.35	.10	.06	T		T	.04	.19	.16	.03	T	.03				T			.05	.24	.04					.03	.50	.05	.05	.08	
	1.48	.27	.04	.03				.02	.21	.03	.02									.02	.09	.02						.59		.07	.04	
	2.60	.75		.12					.16	.68			T				.29			.18	.09	T				T	T	T	.24	.09	T	T
	2.88	.28	.07	.14	T			.08	.24	.51		T	.02	T	T	.14	.10			.14	.08	.04	.02				.25	.45	.02	.05	.25	
	2.76	.32	.02	.05	.02			.09	.40	.40		.02	.05	T		.10	.10			.13	.11	.03					.30	.43	T	.03	.18	
	2.32	.31		T				.10	.76			T	T				T			.13							.10	.72		.19	T	
	1.91	.12		.10				.12	.26	.09	T	T	.13			.20				.14	.20						.24	.04	.02	.19	.06	
	2.68	.26	.24	.03	T			.14	.14	1.00	.01		.04			T	.16			T	.15						.08	.12	.11	T	.20	
	-	.20	.19	T				.16	.13	.50	-		.08				.26			.09	.15	T					.27	.14	.07	.08		
	2.46	.39		.05				.03	.05	.66	T						.14			.02	.06	T					.10	.35	.22	T	.39	T
	2.90	.27		.02				.08	.45	.14			.03			.10				.10	.30						.15	.85		.13	.28	
	3.03	.31	.14	.17	T			.11	.34	.44	.05		.06				.08			.08	.09	.05				T	.17	.49		.15	.30	
	1.98	.24	.08	.10	T			.09	.06	.50	.02	.01	.09			.01	.12			.01	.20	.04					.20			.03	.17	
	2.96	.29	.09						.10	.82						.06	.46				.24						.34	.30	.12		.14	
	1.72	.30		.04				.04	.21	.06		.06				.05			T		.05	T				.12	T	.67	.08		.06	
	3.20	.20	.60					.06	.70	.03						.56	.04			.35	.11					.09	.11	.26		.13		
	2.69	.15	T	.01				T	.02	1.01			.03				.34			.02	.03	.16					.15	.19	.10	.04	.41	.03
	2.39	.30	.18	T			.03	.10	.17	.27	T		T			.06			.02	.25	T	.02				.02	.63	.19	.15	T	T	
	2.61	.44	.01	T				.08	1.11	.03	T	T	T			.08				.06	.04	.02					.07	.58	T	.09	T	
	2.79	.57	.11						.19	1.04		T				T	.15			.25	.10	T					.07	.22			.09	
	2.50	.35		.02				.06	.48			.02				.09				T	.20					T	.14	.77	.04	.33		
	3.17	.30	.25	T				T	T	.82	T					T	.38			T	.06	.10					.06	.31	.08	.06	.70	.05
	2.23	.32	.04	.03	T			T	T	.42	T	T	.19			.02	.24			T	.12	.02					.17	.28	.09	T	.27	.02
	2.44	.18						.10	.79	.04						.03				.20	.22					.01	.15	.52		.20		
	1.95	.30	.11	.08				T	.14	.14	T						T			T	.16	T					.18	.55		T	.29	
	2.01	.12	T	.16	.01			.11	.04	.21		T	.22			.01	.06			.23	.18	.05					.21		.02	.01	.27	
	2.25	.35	.18	.02				.02	.13	.43						.07	.46			.07	.24						.04	.23			.01	
	3.21	.53	.14	.05				.23	.17	.58	.01		.02			.05	.10			.04	.18						.25	.29	.12	.10	.37	
	2.65	.34	.09	T				.10	.09	.80			.02				.18			T	.10						.26	.32	.10	T	.25	T
	3.62	.48	.55					.03	.65	.20						.90	.04			.25	.08						.06	.35		.03		
	-	.10	.01						.69	.06		T					.50			T	.13	.02					.10	T	.07		-	
	1.97	.10	.08	.01				.19	.42	.02		.17	.02			.12			.01	.29	.01					T	.25	.02	T	.26		
	1.97	D.40	.05					.25	.65							.01				.19	.02					.11	.17	.12				
	-	.25	T	.01				.18	-	.04		.02	.08			.08			.04	.02	.25					.02	.24		.02	.39		
	3.01	.30	.02	.02				.14	.48	.23	T	T	.06			.02	.10			.17	.10	T					.11	.89		.06	.30	
	2.32	.23	.01	.05				.17	.21	.57			.06				.03			.17	.16	.02					.32	.10		T	.20	
	2 94	.18	D.05					.04	.04	.23	.05					.50					.02	.03			.10	.24	.40	.20	.20	.46	.20	T
	2.97	.40	.15	.08				.12	.15	.70	.03	.02	T			T	.27			.05	.18						.22	.22	.20	.18	T	
	1.80	.40	.02						.12	.41							.28			.09	.08						.10	.19	.04		.07	
	2.41	.56	.15						.23	.74						.03	.29			.24	.07					.06	.01	.01		.02		
	1.84	.56	.03					.19	.30	.43						.04	.03			.10	.16						T				T	
		RECORD MISSING																														
	2.18	.31	.08	.08	T			.16	.20	.40	.02	T	.06			.02	.10			.02	.09	.02					.09	.21	.07	.09	.16	
	2.66	.39	T	T				.12	.52	.18	T	T	.04				.04			.20	.10	.01					.14	.67		.07	.18	
	2.29	.11	.10	.05				.04	.60	.07							.42			.07	.05	.11					.12	.20	.05	.03	.22	.05
	2.65	.16	T						.27	.79							.21			.07	.66	.08					.06	.23	.12			
	2.18	.30	T	T				T	.07	.47			.05			.04	.45			T	.17	T					.15	.40	T	T	.08	
	2.37	.37	.12	.04				.01	.37	.15	.01		.05				.07			.07	.12	.03		T			.02	.86	.04	.02	.02	
	2.40	.39	T					.13	.39	.01		.01	.06			.09				.04	.09					.09	.23	.59	.15	.10	.03	
	1.87	.16	.02	.02				.17	.38	.14		.01	.15			.11			.02	.19	.10	T				.02	.21	T		.16	.01	
	2.45	.68	.02					.16	.18	.57							.24			.08	.21						T	.28			.03	
R	1.97	.36	.05	T				.11	.64	.01		T			T	.30	T		T	.09	.06					.09	.02	.25	T	.03	T	
	2.27	.42	.09					.09	.20	.54			T			.22	.19			.04	.14						.05	.27			.02	
	2.19	.08	.09	.05					.03	.65	.05		.09				.40			.01	.10	.08					.03	.04	.03	.03	.43	T
	2.04	T	.16	.02					T	.64			.09				.34			T	.14	.08					.04	.03	.04	.01	.45	
	2.66	.12	.07	.03					.05	.72	.06	T					.53			.03	.19	.12					.10	.17	.04	T	.33	.10
	2.79	.52	.05	.05				.01	.10	1.29			T		T	.21	-			.10	.21	T					.03	.13	.04	T	.05	
	1.98	.07	.03	T					.06	.58	.05		.10				.47			.03	.20	.11					.09	.05	.02	.04	.08	T
	2.38	.44	.07	.12	T			.09	.10	.09	.05	T	.02				.02			.08	.13	.06					.13	.72	.02	.05	.10	T
	1.03	.17	T	T	T				.25	.15	T		.05			T	.01				.02	.09			T			.07	.22	T		
	2.51	.47	.08	T				.15	.13	.37	T		T			T	.21			.06	.07	.01					.44	.40	.03	.02	.07	
	1.98	.37	.09	T				.12	.13	.68	T					T	.12			.09	.15						.02	.19	T		.02	
	2.17	.45	.05					.13	.55	.04			T				.08			.10	.12	.01		.02			.08	.43		.05	.06	

See Reference Notes Following Station Index

DAILY PRECIPITATION

Table 3—Continued

INDIANA 3 SE																		
IRWIN																		
JAMESTOWN 2 NW																		
JIM THORPE																		
JOHNSTOWN																		
KANE 1 NNE																		
KARTHAUS																		
KEATING SUMMIT																		
KEGG																		
KITTANNING LOCK 7																		
KREGAR 4 SE																		
KRESGEVILLE 3 W																		
LAFAYETTE MC KEAN PARK																		
LAKEVILLE 1 NNE																		
LANCASTER 2 NE PUMP STA																		
LANDISVILLE 2 NW																		
LAWRENCEVILLE 2 S																		
LEBANON 3 W																		
LEHIGHTON																		
LE ROY																		
LEWIS RUN 3 SE																		
LEWISTOWN																		
LINESVILLE 5 WNW																		
LOCK HAVEN																		
LONG POND 2 W																		
LYNDELL 2 NW																		
MADERA																		
MAHAFFEY																		
MAPLE GLEN																		
MAPLETON DEPOT																		
MARCUS HOOK																		
MARION CENTER 2 SE																		
MARTINSBURG CAA AP																		
MATAMORAS																		
MAYBURG																		
MC CONNELLSBURG																		
MC KEESPORT																		
MEADVILLE 1 S																		
MEDIX RUN																		
MERCER 2 NNE																		
MERCERSBURG																		
MEYERSDALE 1 ENE																		
MIDDLETOWN OLMSTED FLD																		
MIDLAND DAM 7																		
MILANVILLE																		
MILLHEIM																		
MILLVILLE 2 SW																		
MILROY																		
MONTROSE 1 E																		
MORGANTOWN								.30										
MT GRETNA 2 SE								.80										
MT POCONO 2 N AP								.30	.14		[illegible]	[illegible]						
MUHLENBURG 1 SE							.04	.57			.07	.19	.0					
MYERSTOWN								.03	.85		.08	.27	.0					
NATRONA LOCK 4								.10	.13		.19	.20	.0					
NESHAMINY FALLS								.40	T		.37	.11	.0			.03	.03	.32
NEWBURG 3 W								•			•	•				.79	.25	.32
NEW CASTLE 1 N								.02	.03		.18	.20	.0				.32	.12
NEWELL								.09			.05	.04						.50
NEW PARK											.20	.09				.01		.10
NEWPORT								T			.08	.11					.08	
NEW STANTON								.11		.01	.06	.02			T	.02	.42	.01
NEW TRIPOLI		.40	.26		.01			.70	.02		.15	.07	T			T	.29	.35
NORRISTOWN		.12	.88			T			.15		.11	.16	.0				.03	.13
NORTH EAST 2 SE	.09	.10	.43	T		.88		.09	.04		.15	.15	.0				.20	
ORWELL 3 N		.13	.72					.01			.02	.24	T				.09	.02
PALM		.05	.80						.40		.05	.22	.0				.18	.20
PALMERTON	T	.37	.15		T			.33		T	.11	.08				.31		
PALMYRA	.05	.47	-		-	-		-	-		-	-	-	-	-			-
PARKER	.14	.46	.41		T	T			.03		.18	.04	T				.22	.39
PAUPACK 2 WNW		.28	.40	.06					.43			.13	.0					.12
PECKS POND		.03	.50	T					.52		T	.17	.0				.14	.15
PHIL DREXEL INST OF TEC	.05	.46	.16		T			.90	T		.33	.10				.02	.05	.25
PHILADELPHIA WB AP R	.02	.42	.04		T			1.32	T	T	.28	.08				.02	.02	.2
PHILADELPHIA PT BREEZE		.44	.08		T			1.19			.32	.06				.03	.02	.25
PHILADELPHIA SHAWMONT	.05	.20	.60		.03			-			.25	.10	.05			.05	.05	.20
PHILADELPHIA CITY	.02	.47	.20					1.31	.01		.31	.05				.03		.22
PHILIPSBURG CAA AP	.12	.60	.02	.02	T	.01		.21		T	.08	.09	T				.60	.35
PHOENIXVILLE 1 E	.01	.72	.29					.12			.28	.07				.03	.01	.24
PIKES CREEK		.06	.50	T	T	.02			.63		.02	.17	.03	T				.32
PIMPLE HILL	T	.11	.63	.07		T		T	.64		.09	.17		T				.35
PINE GROVE 1 NE		.04	.70			.06		.04	.90		.02	.22					.14	.39
PITTSBURGH WB AP 2 //R	.05	.40	.02	T	.02	T		T		.05	.10	.05				.03	.63	.09
PITTSBURGH WB CITY R	.22	.77	.01	T	.01	T		.07		.06	.11	.02				.06	.65	.16
PLEASANT MOUNT 1 W		.03	.57	.08	T	.07			.46		.03	.14	.13	T			.14	.03
PORT CLINTON		.10	.40			.05		.05	.90		.03	.15					.16	
POTTSTOWN																		
POTTSVILLE		T	.69			.07		.10	.85		.05	.18	.01					.48
PUTNEYVILLE 2 SE DAM	.07	.38	.36	T	T	.03		.10	.06		.09	.19	.02				.02	1.10
QUAKERTOWN 1 E	T	.36	.79		T			.02	.24		.18	.16	.06				.21	.22
RAYMOND	.17	.20	.64	.06		.06			.22		.04	.17	.0				.02	.09
READING WB CITY	.02	.37	.12		.02			.66			.15	.07				.17	.03	.38
RENOVO	.03	.19	.89	T	T	.02			.23		.03	.11					.18	.51
REW	.14	.08	.37	.03	.02	.05		.04	.05		.01	.18	.0				.10	.07
RICES LANDING L	.04	.78	.25					.01	.05		.09	.06	.0				.01	.38
RIDGWAY 3 W	.13	.12	.40	T	T	.02		.07	.14		.08	.08	.0				.27	.37
RUSH		T	.85	.05		.08			.17		.03	.23	.0				.08	.10
RUSHVILLE		.02	.84			.06			.08		T	.15	.0				.04	.07
SAGAMORE 1 S		.45	•	•	•	.99		.15	.05		.30	.13					.12	.90
SALINA 3 W	.18	.74	T			T		.05		.01	.11	.10	T			.08	.00	.49
SAXTON	.19	.19	.23	T	T	T		T	.15		.07	.07	T				.19	.38
SCHENLEY LOCK 5	.15	.57	.25			.07		.08	.09		.19	.21	T				.15	1.10
SCRANTON			.70			.10			.43		.03	.05	.1				.10	.10
SCRANTON WB AIRPORT	T	.34	.10	T	.02	.02		.32		T	.02	.15				.06	.01	.22
SELINSGROVE CAA AP	.04	.01	T		.04	T		.24		T	.17	.13				.20	.09	.42
SHAMOKIN		.02	.40			.03		.10	.50		.02	.28					.21	.40
SHIPPENSBURG	.20	.26	T		T			.26			.12	.12				T	T	.17
SHIPPINGPORT WB	.10	.63	.02		T	.04		.03		.10	.22	.02				.09	.50	.03
SINNEMAHONING	.12	.12	.60	T	T	.04		T	.12		.03	.14	T				.18	•
SLIPPERY ROCK	.07	.15	.20			.04		.05	.01		.13	.14	.0				.16	.15
SOMERSET FAIRVIEW ST	.10	.15	.08	.18					.04		.06	.18	.1				.05	.61
SOMERSET MAIN ST	.14	.20	.22	T				.02			.16	.15	.0			.11	.11	.16
SOUTH MOUNTAIN	.26	.15	.32					.04	.08		.11	.09					.02	.18
SPRINGBORO	-	.20	.20	.19	.10	.09		T			.25	.35					.20	.28
SPRING GROVE	.22	.30	.04		T			.04	T		.17	.10					T	.22

See Reference Notes Following Station Index

DAILY PRECIPITATION

• 3—Continued

PENNSYLVANIA
MARCH 1957

Station	Total	1	2	3	4	5	6	7	8	9	10	11	12	13	14	15	16	17	18	19	20	21	22	23	24	25	26	27	28	29	30	31
GS 1 SW	2.24	.47	.12	T				.15	.15	.04						.03			.11	.08	.11		.03			.03	.30	.20	.18	.04	T	
COLLEGE	2.53	.30	.01	T				.13	.68	T	T	T	T		T	.21			T	.12	.02	T				.20	.26	.41	.02	.17	T	
SSTOWN	3.27	.34	.09	.09					.08	.67			.06			.10	1.04			.03	.15	T					.12	.39	.03		.08	
DSBURG	2.63	.32	T	T				T	.60	.23	T	T	T			.34				.20	.12	.01				.10	.12	.28	T	.09	.02	
CREEK	2.52	.42	.04	T				.09	.13	.19			T			.10	.05			.04	.14						.09	.73	.16	.16	.24	
RY	2.39	.20	.09	T				T	.10	.63			.03			T	.27			T	.21	.02					.29	.41	.05	T	.09	T
EMANNA	1.50	.10	.06	.01	T				T	.57	.12		.14				.28			T	.09	.09					.04	.01	.02	.05	.01	
SVILLE	-	.27	-	-				.08	.32	*	*	.15				-	-			.10	.05	.03					.09	.50		.07	-	
UA	2.89	.30	.03						.05	.49						.09	.85			.05	.20	T					.25	.46	.08		.11	
UA 4 N DAM	1.70								.01	.90	.09						.06				.13						.23	.03				
ACK 2 S FIRE TWR	2.85	.35	.14	.02				.14	.03	.68	T	T	T				.20			T	.05	.04					.16	.45	.12	.07	.40	
STA 2 SE DAM	2.37	.24	.03	.03	T			.10	.28	.44	T	.02	.06			.02	.09			.13	.16	T					.24	.08	.01	T	.45	
VILLE WATER WORKS	2.12	.19	.05	.02				.21	.48	.04			.09			.19	T			.21	.16	T				T	.28	.01	T	.20	.03	
DO 4 W	1.53	.15	.03	.10	.02			.15	.08	.15	T	T	.13			.05	.09			.10	.13	.04					.18			.05	.08	
DA	2.37	.20	.13	.02	T	T		T	.02	.90	T	T	.07			T	.07			.02	.15	.06					.05	.13	.07	.04	.44	T
CITY 5 SW	3.17	.50	.10	T				T	1.05							.66				.11	.12					T	.11	.40		.06	.06	
	2.93	.39	.11	.05				.01	.08	1.01		.01					.12			.04	.11	T					.16	.26	.08	.08	.44	
EPOINT 4 NE	2.02	.28	.15	.09	.02			.14	.09	.41	.06	.01				.01	.06			.04	.14						.08	.04	.09	.11	.20	
E 4 NE BALD EAGLE	3.01	.33	.05	T				.13	.25	.52			T			T	.17			.05	.18	T					.39	.79	T	T	.18	
CITY	1.58	.15	T	.06	.03			.18	.06	.30	T		.12			.08	.11			.11	.12	T					.17			.02	.07	
TOWN	1.83	.34	.05	T			T	.06	.31	.15			.01			.07			.02	.16	.02		T			T	.41	.22	.01	T		
DARBY	2.99	.79	.08					T	.45	.30		T				.49	.14			.23	.09	T				.02	.02	.24		.10	.04	
	2.08	.25	.10	.05	.01			.28	.36	.40	.04		.09			.03				.21	.22	.03					.40	.04		.01	.19	
RGRIFT	2.84	.26	T	T				.10	.53	.34			.03			.06				.13	.07	.06	T				.07	1.11	T	T	.06	T
NVILLE	1.60	.03	.12	.09					.07	.41						.04	.85										T	.06	.02			
CKEL	2.69	.30	.03	.07	T			.13	.38	.35		.03	.08	T		.08	.11			.12	.10	.04					.32	.33	T	.02	.20	
CKEL 1 WSW	2.59	.26	.03	.07	T			.11	.36	.33		.02	.09	T		.08	.12			.12	.09	.04					.32	.32	T	.02	.19	
N	1.41	.17	.03	.05				.13	.07	.32	.03	T	.05			.01				.01	.11	.03					.23	.04	.02	.03	.08	
NTOWN	3.00	.38	T					.09	.82	T	T	.04	T			.30				.02	.20					.45	.17	.40	.08	.04	T	
SBURG 2 W	2.14	.46	.05	T				.03	.60	.20			T				.01			.10	.05	T					.07	.84	.02	T	.01	
BORO 3 S	2.50	.44	.05	.02				.04	.08	.36	.03		.04	T			.23			.02	.09	T					.12	.46	.18	.04	.30	T
VILLE	2.20	.52	.08					.16	.57							.34			T	.16	.10					T		.27		T		
RSVILLE 1 W	D 1.84	D.05	D.08						.12	.13						*	.65			*	.33						.18	.30				
CHESTER	1.66	.09						.11	*	.29						*	.51		.12	.17	.02					.02	.21	.02	.05	.05	T	
GROVE 1 E	2.78		.76	.12					.33	.23							.66			.26	.12						.04	.22			.04	
HICKORY	1.92	.28	.02	.05				.12	.20	.30		.01	.05			.02	.09			.05	.12						.15	.15	.01	.10	.20	
SBURG	2.71	.17						.18	.45	.20						T				.12	T	.17					.10	.94		*	.38	
5 BARRE	1.89	.13	.10	T				T	T	.39	T	T	T				.43			.01	.06	.13					.13	.27	.15	T	.09	T
AMSBURG	2.61	.41	.04	.08				.16	.15	.37	T	T	.03			.05	.03			.14	.11	.04					.41	.47			.12	
AMSPORT WB AP	2.87	.36	.03	.01				.06	1.12		T	.05	T			.36			T	.10	.13					.06	.10	.29	T	.16	.02	
BURG	2.04	.40	.07					.12	.31	.10	T									.09	.10	T					.09	.38			.13	.07
3 SSW PUMP STA	1.84	.47	T	T				.16	.39	.08						.12	.02			.21	.10					T	.02	.25		.02		
HAVEN	2.29	.38	.08	.06				.04	.12	.35						.08	.40			.07	.17						.02	.27	.27		T	
GROVE	1.73	.03	.30							.03							.44										.21	.47			.29	
VILLE 3 SE	2.50	.37	.12	.11					.08	.62	.07						.33			.09	.23	.06					.22	.23	.04		.02	

SUPPLEMENTAL DATA

Station	Wind direction		Wind speed m. p. h.				Relative humidity averages - percent				Number of days with precipitation							Percent of possible sunshine	Average sky cover sunrise to sunset
	Prevailing	Percent of time from prevailing	Average	Fastest mile	Direction of fastest mile	Date of fastest mile	1:30 a EST	7:30 a EST	1:30 p EST	7:30 p EST	Trace	.01–.09	.10–.49	.50–.99	1.00–1.99	2.00 and over	Total		
NTOWN WB AIRPORT	ENE	15	11.4	-	-	-	78	80	55	68	4	6	7	0	0	0	17	-	6.0
WB AIRPORT	-	-	12.0	26++	WSW	12	-	-	-	-	2	7	8	0	0	0	17	-	6.5
ISBURG WB AIRPORT	WNW	19	8.8	38	W	9	65	69	48	51	7	7	4	1	0	0	19	57	6.3
ADELPHIA WB AIRPORT	N	11	9.7	42	NW	10	71	72	51	63	5	6	4	1	1	0	17	53	6.7
SBURGH WB AIRPORT	WSW	22	11.6	39++	W	2	71	75	52	63	5	10	4	1	0	0	20	61	6.7
ING WB CITY	-	-	10.1	42	NW	10	-	-	-	-	2	6	6	1	0	0	15	54	6.4
NTON WB AIRPORT	NW	15	8.4	34	NW	10	74	76	56	61	5	7	7	0	0	0	19	53	6.3
PINGPORT WB	-	-	3.7	37††	NW	12	-	-	-	-	1	9	5	2	0	0	17	-	-
IAMSPORT WB AIRPORT	-	-	-	-	-	-	-	81	50	59	4	6	7	0	1	0	18	-	6.4

eak Gust

DAILY TEMPERATURES

Station		1	2	3	4	5	6	7	8	9	10	11	12	13	14	15	16	17	18	19	20	21	22	23	24	25	26	27	28	29	30	31	Average
ALLENTOWN WB AP	MAX	34	42	38	38	44	44	44	38	40	41	49	62	67	79	54	56	60	54	45	39	48	52	62	57	50	40	43	53			53	46.
	MIN	28	24	24	19	19	24	31	34	32	26	23	33	29	32	39	33	26	27	34	32	32	30	28	30	28	34	32	38			24	29.
ALLENTOWN GAS CO	MAX	33	34	43	38	38	43	44	44	39	41	41	43	62	68	79	45	52	60	53	37	42	48	52	59	58	49	40		53	52	54	47.
	MIN	22	27	25	20	22	24	31	35	34	30	26	30	30	35	41	35	32	31	35	33	34	31	31	33	30	33	34		36	37	28	30.
ALTOONA HORSESHOE CURVE	MAX	36	37	31	37	42	44	39	34	35	36	39	58	69	70	62	55	56	50	48	38	45	46	60	57	49	48	42	41	40	45		46.
	MIN	22	30	16	8	13	27	29	30	30	22	20	34	33	34	46	33	36	27	35	31	30	30	28	30	26	30	32	31	33	30		28.
ARENDTSVILLE	MAX	30	38	46	37	38	42	43	37	38	41	41	49	63	68	72	57	60	65	50	39	44	51	48	59	62	42	44	49	48			48.
	MIN	25	28	21	15	20	22	29	31	32	30	24	32	31	31	45	33	30	33	37	36	33	34	33	35	30	34	36	31	32			30.
ARTEMAS 1 WNW	MAX																																
	MIN																																
BAKERSTOWN 3 WNW	MAX	40	39	34	33	46	55	50	40	35	34	58	57	71	68	66	58	54	50	49	50	45	51	60	56	47	60	45		43		58	49.
	MIN	32	34	16	15	22	30	34	32	28	25	28	52	34	42	44	34	30	33	40	32	30	32	30	29	28	32	35		31		24	31.
BEAVERTOWN	MAX	38	41	38	37	41	46	43	36	39	39	38	57	69	79	70	56	59	54	50	41	51	49	61	58	45	40	45			50	51	48.
	MIN	26	24	22	12	14	23	31	32	32	28	19	29	26	29	48	32	29	25	37	36	35	27	24	26	24	32	32			34	20	28.
BELLEFONTE 4 S	MAX	28	39	40	38	37	43	43	36	35	38	37	41	55	68	71	58	54	55	52	40	40	50	50	61	56	46	41	41	45	45		46.
	MIN	17	28	22	12	15	22	30	31	32	20	19	25	38	32	42	35	34	26	34	36	33	28	25	27	25	31	32	34	33	31		28.
BERWICK	MAX	35	41	39	39	43	47	46	45	39	41	41	60	68	76	74	57	58	57	49	40	50	53	65	61	52	44	44	52	51	49	53	50.
	MIN	27	21	22	15	15	23	32	36	32	27	22	33	26	31	42	35	26	24	37	34	36	29	26	27	28	33	32	37	31	35	21	28.
BETHLEHEM LEHIGH UNIV	MAX																																
	MIN																																
BLAIRSVILLE 6 ENE	MAX	31	31	28	36	46	52	36	36	31	33	49	55	67	75	57	51	54	53	42	42	42	46	55	52	40	59	37		35		53	46.
	MIN	26	26	11	12	19	28	28	29	25	19	24	41	32	32	40	27	29	29	36	27	25	29	28	28	24	26	30		29		25	27.
BRADFORD 4 W RES	MAX	35	35	25	32	37	48	47	34	33	30	42	50	62	69	67	54	44	48	47	38	43	50	56	54	41	42	36		37	41	49	44.
	MIN	25	20	12	3	0	9	28	28	25	20	6	31	27	24	41	28	22	14	32	28	27	20	23	21	13	28	31		23	21	13	21.
BROOKVILLE CAA AIRPORT	MAX	35	35	27	36	43	49	34	37	36	34	47	53	67	70	56	49	50	50	42	40	48	49	59	51	44	51	37	40	35			46.
	MIN	28	19	10	5	13	23	31	32	23	18	18	33	28	27	38	32	27	20	37	30	30	28	26	23	22	31	32	32	32			25.
BURGETTSTOWN 2 W	MAX	37	43	40	34	30	48	56	38	37	38	49	64	58	71	72	61	54	57	50	53	36	44	51	58	52	43	56		43		49	48.
	MIN	23	30	11	6	9	15	24	32	29	25	24	34	25	28	30	33	25	24	32	33	24	28	25	21	25	30	32		31		13	25.
BURNT CABINS 2 NE	MAX	40	42	40	38	44	45	42	36	39	40		63	70	73	74	71	68			41	49	49	60	63	45		48	47	48	50		50.
	MIN	25	29	19	9	14	28	29	31	31	26	21		26	27	53	32		32		35	32	28	21	30	29		33	27	30	31		27.
BUTLER	MAX	34	38	28	38	42	50	50	36	37	33	51	59	70	69	70	58	52	50	50	50	45	45	58	58	58	52	54	41	45	50		49.
	MIN	29	31	17	10	12	21	32	32	30	25	23	42	40	40	48	33	28	22	39	31	29	30	24	22	29	31	35	35	33	31		29.
CANTON 1 NW	MAX	28	35	34	36	31	34	40	34	34	34	31	39	53	60	69	51	50	48	45	35	37	43	45	55	45	40	36		46		41	41.
	MIN	10	23	15	9	10	12	16	29	29	22	15	19	35	39	43	30	27	22	24	31	31	27	27	31	22	23	29		27		21	24.
CARLISLE	MAX	39	44	47	40	45	46	45	40	43	42	49	64	71	75	72	61	68	62	50	44	53	52	63	62	53	47	47			50		52.
	MIN	28	32	24	19	19	29	32	32	34	32	26	35	30	31	45	39	33	35	39	37	36	35	29	33	30	36	36			38		32.
CHAMBERSBURG 1 ESE	MAX	39	45	37	38	44	44	38	35	42	42	50	63	68	72	68	60	64	52	45	45	51	48	59	62	42	51	48			51	53	48.
	MIN	26	32	23	17	18	30	31	32	34	30	24	32	29	29	42	37	36	35	36	36	35	32	25	30	30	35	36			31	21	30.
CHESTER	MAX	35	40	42	46	40	47	47	45	42	40	45	50	65	67	73	60	60	64	55	43	43	52	55	58	62	47	44		52			50.
	MIN	23	29	26	24	24	28	33	34	26	27	26	38	34	39	36	30	32	36	39	33	35	35	41	36	34	35	36		36			32.
CLARION 3 SW	MAX	38	37	33	37	50		52	39	38	35	47	53	70	71	64	55	50	50	44	43	49	52	61	59	53	52	50	45	45		55	46.
	MIN	27	27	11	6	20		30	32	29	22	19	34	25	26	41	30	22	20	37	31	30	27	25	22	24	30	32	32	32		18	26.
CLAYSVILLE 3 W	MAX	31	41	36	39	51	55	45	40	38	42	67	61	71	69	61	55	60	40	52	51	45	51	60	55	45	57	44			47		50.
	MIN	36	31	12	9	12	20	34	32	29	25	23	49	24	25	42	34	23	24	42	32	23	30	26	22	31	30	36			28		27.
COATESVILLE 1 SW	MAX	31	33	46	39	30	46	46	43	40	43	43	51	62	64	74	54	56	64	63	40	43	51	52	62	61	47	41		52			49.
	MIN	26	20	21	17	19	23	29	33	36	30	24	31	28	31	34	36	28	32	35	35	34	29	31	28	31	35	35		33			29.
COLUMBIA	MAX	35	46	40	40	44	45	44	42	43	42	49	64	68	76	65	60	66	57	49	44	52	52	62	63	50	41	47			51		51.
	MIN	28	27	25	17	20	29	31	34	35	30	26	35	30	31	48	36	32	34	37	35	36	33	35	31	31	36	35			37		31.
CONFLUENCE 1 SW DAM	MAX	35	38	37	32	41	48	48	40	41	34	38	60	58	69	65	60	54	60	54	47	35	42	44	57	57	39	57					47.
	MIN	30	32	16	12	13	18	27	32	28	26	23	30	26	27	28	35	35	27	29	33	30	30	29	27	29	32	34					27.
CORRY	MAX	37	35	29	31	42	52	43	34	34	32	46	52	65	72	62	49	42	47	45	43	45	53	56	48	44	48	46	42	42			46.
	MIN	28	25	8	2	9	16	30	29	28	21	15	40	38	27	40	30	23	16	37	29	28	23	23	22	20	31	33	31	28			24.
COUDERSPORT 3 NW	MAX	35	32	30	28	30	44	35	33	32	29	38	50	61	65	58	46	45	48	42	35	43	49	54	44	42	36	38		35	42		41.
	MIN	19	19	13	0	4	15	28	29	25	11	3	29	30	27	40	28	23	15	32	29	27	21	20	22	15	29	32		21	20		21.
DERRY	MAX	40	40	30	39	51	54	46	46	40	40	51	57	72	72	66	54	57	58	55	50	44	48	64	57	46	58	46				57	50.
	MIN	31	30	18	11	21	34	34	32	30	25	24	36	31	30	41	33	34	34	36	32	31	30	29	24	31	34	36				20	30.
DEVAULT 1 W	MAX	34	42	42	37	43	45	43	41	41	44	49	62	67	76	54	60	66	55	43	42	49	51	61	59	47	40	43	50		50		46.
	MIN	25	22	21	16	16	24	28	28	28	20	23	30	35	43	39	38	33	36	30	29	30	28	29	32	25	31	29	35		20		28.
DIXON	MAX	32	35	40	33	34	40	49	47	38	36	35	45	59	65	76	53	56	51	48	38	37	46	50	58	48	49	40		53	50		46.
	MIN	14	17	19	11	9	13	19	33	32	27	15	16	24	26	29	32	20	19	26	32	32	22	22	22	19	28	32		31	32		23.
DONEGAL	MAX	32	30	26	33	42	47	36	36	31	31	55	54	65	66	57	56	52	50	42	40	35	42	50	50	38	54	33		38		50	48
	MIN	27	16	10	4	15	23	29	27	22	18	17	30	25	27	31	28	29	26	36	25	25	26	18	21	27	26	29		28		16	23.
DONORA	MAX	45	37	41	37	48	55	50	41	48	40	49	67	66	73	73	63	56	60	54	54	40	49	58	62	50	60	62		43	47	52	52.
	MIN	33	33	17	16	25	28	38	35	31	28	29	45	26	35	45	37	33	33	45	35	33	35	30	31	34	37	39		36	34	24	32.
DU BOIS 7 E	MAX	33	38	30	32	40	45	40	37	36	32	42	53	66	68	65	53	50	50	47	40	45	46	57	51	44	42	41	43				44.
	MIN	23	28	12	1	9	19	28	31	28	20	13	40	35	26	43	31	27	19	36	29	29	26	23	21	23	31	32	31				25.
EAGLES MERE	MAX	28	31	34	29	28	34	40	35	32	30	32	37	52	59	66	47	49	50	47	34	33	43	46	54	44	44	34		45	42	39	40.
	MIN	10	23	13	8	9	14	24	28	27	19	15	20	32	38	46	31	28	24	25	30	29	27	29	30	20	20	30		26	28	20	24.
EAST BRADY	MAX	40	40	37	42	46	58	52	48	38	38	48	58	72	73	69	61	54	53	50	47	48	54	63	60	52	54	51		42			51.
	MIN	31	33	15	12	16	21	33	33	32	25	25	38	30	29	44	35	26	24	40	33	33	31	27	25	27	32	37		35			29.
EBENSBURG	MAX	30	34	28	30	48	53	35	34	35	31	52	53	64	65	59	49	52	51	44	41	40	45	64	51	49	58	40	38	39	40	57	46.
	MIN	22	23	12	2	14	27	28	28	25	29	16	39	32	30	42	31	33	34	35	28	26	27	24	25	23	28	31	32	30	27	19	28.
EMPORIUM 2 SSW	MAX	26	36	34	27	33	40	46	32	35	33	32	45	52	63	63	51	50	49	50	38	36	44	47	52	42	42	37	37	42	37		41.
	MIN	13	23	12	4	8	14	26	29	28	22	12	22	27	27	34	30	22	17	26	33	29	25	23	22	20	25	31	31	21	28		22.
EPHRATA	MAX	37	44	40	37	43	48	45	38	42	44	48	63	67	73	58	50	63	55	49	44	52	52	61	61	47	41	46		52			50.
	MIN	27	25	22	17	19	27	30	33	34	28	25	34	32	38	46	34	33	30	36	33	34	31	32	32	27	34	32		32			30.
ERIE WB AIRPORT	MAX	38	34	24	26	33	41	33	32	34	30	50	53	64	73	58	39	36	37	51	37	40	45	51	40	36	45	36			41	52	41.
	MIN	30	21	17	10	15	20	30	31	27	21	25	44	45	47	39	31	26	21	34	32	28	27	28	29	23	32	30					28.

See reference notes following Station Index.

DAILY TEMPERATURES

Day Of Month

		1	2	3	4	5	6	7	8	9	10	11	12	13	14	15	16	17	18	19	20	21	22	23	24	25	26	27	28	29	30	31	Average
	MAX	42	44	36	38	40	46	40	44	36	40	42	60	64	72	66	62	60	54	40	44	46	52	64	58	40	58	44	45	46	45	50	49.0
	MIN	28	28	20	14	20	34	34	32	30	28	28	34	28	30	38	38	38	32	40	32	32	30	30	30	32	36	36	38	34	32	24	31.0
	MAX	46	41	32	40	52	54	44	37	37	38	57	55	72	72	63	54	53	48	51	50	47	55	61	49	43	34	47	47	42	49	50	49.7
	MIN	18	25	20	16	22	22	29	28	27	22	26	44	42	32	43	33	27	25	38	32	31	33	30	29	25	31	38	34	32	31	21	29.2
	MAX	36	40	40	32	38	48	55	37	39	37	37	60	58	70	72	60	54	55	51	47	38	46	50	60	53	44	56	42	41	44	47	48.0
	MIN	22	29	14	10	13	21	25	31	29	22	22	30	27	27	31	33	26	22	25	33	30	28	24	23	27	29	34	34	33	31	19	25.9
	MAX	37	39	37	28	37	48	56	45	37	36	35	48	65	69	70	61	50	50	49	45	43	47	54	61	49	43	53	44	42	40	47	47.3
	MIN	15	28	26	15	13	15	31	32	31	28	20	43	37	36	41	29	31	24	32	39	32	31	28	28	25	24	32	36	34	33	28	28.9
	MAX	30	37	32	33	38	38	40	40	34	32	39	52	62	71	64	50	51	50	47	45	42	51	50	49	38	39	44	45	41	38	48	44.2
	MIN	22	27	22	13	13	18	26	30	30	20	19	38	30	37	39	31	25	24	30	32	30	30	36	21	28	30	27	30	35	20	24	27.3
	MAX	34	47	44	38	44	46	41	41	44	43	45	61	66	71	60	57	61	54	47	39	49	50	59	60	55	49	51	50	51	49	49	50.2
	MIN	31	31	26	18	23	26	32	36	33	30	26	31	34	35	41	36	36	40	37	34	35	28	34	30	31	32	33	37	32	34	29	32.0
	MAX	31	41	47	39	41	44	45	39	39	43	45	52	66	67	72	58	60	65	52	41	44	54	49	60	64	43	45	50	48	52	53	49.9
	MIN	26	31	23	19	21	27	30	32	33	31	27	34	32	33	49	38	32	36	38	37	34	34	32	33	35	36	37	36	35	35	25	32.3
	MAX	36	42	53	38	42	52	46	38	40	42	52	56	62	74	78	68	66	66	48	38	52	58	62	64	56	38	40	54	52	46	49	51.9
	MIN	28	32	22	18	21	26	30	32	26	26	28	32	32	34	38	30	26	34	36	34	34	32	34	30	32	32	34	34	32	26	24	30.0
	MAX	30	34	40	35	35	43	45	38	37	40	40	42	60	66	72	51	57	59	51	37	42	49	50	59	54	49	40	45	49	50	48	46.7
	MIN	28	24	20	16	14	19	30	30	33	27	23	28	28	33	38	34	35	26	31	34	34	29	24	27	26	32	32	33	30	33	23	28.2
	MAX	44	38	28	37	49	54	43	36	37	38	53	57	69	70	64	54	51	48	49	46	48	56	60	48	42	52	43	46	42	48	56	48.6
	MIN	28	26	16	16	16	22	31	30	29	22	24	45	36	32	41	31	23	22	38	31	26	28	26	24	24	30	33	33	32	28	18	27.8
	MAX	31	37	47	39	41	45	45	41	40	42	43	54	66	68	75	58	61	65	53	42	44	54	48	63	64	44	44	49	49	53	51	50.2
	MIN	25	26	21	18	18	21	29	30	32	29	24	30	31	33	46	36	33	34	34	35	32	32	28	29	30	31	35	32	27	34	24	29.6
	MAX	37	43	37	39	44	45	40	38	43	41	46	63	68	74	59	59	64	51	46	43	51	50	60	58	44	41	47	49	51	50	52	49.5
	MIN	29	28	25	21	24	32	31	34	34	31	29	36	34	35	45	37	38	35	36	36	37	33	32	33	32	36	35	38	35	37	27	33.0
	MAX	25	33	39	28	28	37	45	43	35	33	31	41	53	61	73	45	50	47	45	32	34	39	47	54	46	46	36	40	48	45	40	41.9
	MIN	14	13	15	10	7	9	11	28	29	21	13	20	25	27	30	28	24	20	27	28	28	22	24	24	20	24	29	30	31	29	16	21.8
	MAX	36	46	39	37	41	45	43	39	43	41	46	62	64	71	54	59	64	52	44	43	50	48	59	61	45	43	45	48	50	48	50	48.9
	MIN	30	29	28	23	25	32	32	37	36	34	30	37	34	36	46	40	37	37	38	37	37	36	38	37	35	38	38	37	36	36	29	34.7
	MAX	29	42	43	36	39	44	42	37	38	41	40	46	62	72	75	66	58	61	54	42	44	50	53	62	61	46	47	48	48	48	51	49.1
	MIN	22	28	23	9	11	13	30	32	33	29	21	28	23	25	30	34	40	24	27	37	35	27	21	23	25	32	34	30	31	35	17	26.7
	MAX	36	38	33	39	48	53	41	40	39	38	53	60	69	73	63	53	56	55	46	47	46	50	60	56	46	57	42	42	42	47	36	49.2
	MIN	30	31	14	8	15	26	33	33	31	24	20	43	25	27	44	34	24	23	41	31	32	29	23	22	27	33	33	34	33	32	18	28.2
	MAX	40			41	53	57	47	42			65	63	73	71	69			61	52	52	45	49	59			60	44	42	45			
	MIN	31			12	19	25	35	32			26	51	35	34	43			28	42	33	32	31			27	34	37	35	38			
	MAX	38	43	36	26	32	43	52	33	35	34	34	56	55	68	70	56	49	48	46	52	33	45	53	57	45	41	49	40	45	42	47	45.3
	MIN	16	26	16	10	16	17	27	29	28	21	22	31	35	36	42	30	20	20	25	31	25	28	25	26	23	27	33	32	33	26	17	25.6
	MAX	37	45	39	40	48	48	50	46	38	43	43	61	67	78	73	57	58	58	57	37	49	57	63	61		47	43	54	52	47	56	51.7
	MIN	27	23	21	17	16	19	32	34	34	24	24	34	27	32	41	33	25	25	34	32	35	31	32		27	33	33	36	32	34	22	29.0
	MAX	30	34	34	34	34	42	43	33	35	31	33	51	51	68	67	61	48	51	51	45	41	39	41	53	50	38	51	37	37	37	40	43.2
	MIN	24	28	15	9	15	13	29	31	27	21	23	29	30	29	38	33	37	27	35	30	28	29	20	26	29	29	31	33	32	29	20	26.7
	MAX	39	35	33	27	32	40	48	33	35	35	33	45	51	64	70	55	46	45	50	40	34	45	51	57	41	43	41	36	37	36	42	42.5
	MIN	16	19	13	0	5	8	24	31	28	22	21	26	27	25	29	30	19	15	23	31	28	23	21	19	16	25	31	32	26	20	13	21.5
	MAX	38	39	35	40	45	46	36	36	37	38	37	59	70	70	65	56	60	61	45	44	44	46	59	60	42	55	44	43	44	46	55	48.2
	MIN	25	24	17	9	14	25	29	31	28	23	23	33	27	26	37	35	32	27	37	32	31	29	21	27	28	31	34	30	33	27	25	27.4
STA	MAX	35	45	43	40	49	46	45	43	43	43	48	65	70	79	60	62	67	63	52	44	57	52	64	63	48	43	45	51	54	51	54	52.1
	MIN	28	23	23	18	18	27	31	35	35	30	24	32	27	29	45	37	29	30	38	35	36	30	29	29	30	36	35	37	33	35	23	30.5
	MAX	31	34	41	36	38	43	45	44	39	42	40	48	62	68	74	50	59	63	51	39	44	50	50	59	59	45	41	46	51	53	50	48.2
	MIN	25	19	24	17	19	25	31	32	36	30	23	31	26	28	37	33	26	29	37	34	35	29	29	27	28	35	34	36	31	34	21	29.1
	MAX	32	39	40	37	30	39	47	36	35	36	34	42	54	65	71	54	52	46	46	38	39	46	51	56	45	44	39	43	45	44	45	44.2
	MIN	13	16	12	6	5	11	12	30	30	24	9	15	25	24	29	28	20	18	21	34	32	21	21	22	20	25	31	28	24	28	13	20.9
	MAX	31	35	42	38	39	45	46	44	38	43	42	45	62	67	74	46	58	62	53	38	44	52	51	61	60	47	40	48	51	51	51	48.5
	MIN	28	22	23	16	20	21	32	34	35	25	30	34	27	29	32	31	28	32	33	35	35	30	26	29	28	33	34	36	30	35	23	29.2
	MAX	28	41	42	37	39	44	48	37	39	43	41	42	62	71	79	57	59	61	55	43	43	54	52	63	60	46	45	45	46	49	51	49.0
	MIN	21	28	24	17	16	23	32	32	33	31	26	29	29	29	31	40	40	32	32	38	36	33	27	27	29	30	33	33	37	36	25	30.0
	MAX	42	38	26	34	40	54	37	34	33	33	47	55	69	71	57	48	45	46	50	43	46	50	58	43	42	47	40	43	42	47	53	45.6
	MIN	28	23	17	8	12	19	30	29	29	19	21	40	38	30	41	30	21	19	37	31	23	27	25	25	24	32	31	32	33	27	18	26.4
	MAX	40	43	37	38	43	47	42	35	40	41	39	61	71	76	61	57	59	53	51	42	51	51	64	56	49	41	44	50				49.4
	MIN	27	28	21	13	11	25	32	32	32	28	22	33	27	30	50	32	29	25	38	37	36	29	26	28	28	33	32	36				29.3
	MAX	29	35	38	29	34	39	45	35	36	30	33	49	59	69	70	62	51	52	52	41	38	46	42	57	53	42	45	39	44	38	45	44.1
	MIN	13	24	10	2	1	8	21	23	27	20	14	21	21	21	22	24	25	17	17	31	26	24	17	18	20	21	29	28	28	24	13	19.7
	MAX	36	50	42	42	46	47	44	42	45	45	48	65	62	69	59	62	64	54	45	42	54	51	65	66	48	42	46	52	57	53	53	51.5
	MIN	33	33	30	26	27	32	36	38	36	32	30	38	40	41	47	43	42	40	39	37	40	40	44	43	36	39	38	42	39	39	35	37.3
	MAX	35	37	30	39	47	45	36	37	34	35	43	56	69	71	61	52	56	51	41	41	43	46	58	56	43	50	40	40	42	42	54	46.1
	MIN	26	24	17	11	16	30	30	31	27	23	22	35	34	35	41	34	37	30	36	31	31	30	26	31	27	31	32	33	32	30	23	28.9
	MAX	39	43	34	27	35	46	54	35	36	36	35	53	55	68	70	56	48	47	48	48	33	47	52	59	44	42	52	39	44	38	40	45.5
	MIN	16	25	13	15	14	17	28	30	29	21	21	31	31	30	34	31	23	21	24	32	27	27	27	24	24	27	34	33	34	28	19	25.5
	MAX	33	35	32	34	39	44	42	32	38	42	40	47	64	69	60	50	50	48	47	42	39	51	58	54	38	50	50	38	36	48	54	45.3
	MIN	10	24	26	16	22	24	29	27	26	22	24	42	30	32	34	30	25	24	29	30	30	26	28	30	27	28	30	28	26	30	32	27.1
FLD	MAX	38	44	37	36	42	46	41	39	43	40	46	63	67	74	58	59	63	53	48	44	51	51	61	60	46	42	47	50	54	50	53	49.8
	MIN	28	28	26	20	23	32	32	36	35	32	29	36	32	34	46	39	36	34	37	37	38	33	32	32	32	37	36	40	34	38	25	33.2
	MAX	42	38	29	34	44	54	41	39	35	35	59	58	47	69	58	50	53	51	52	48	42	53	56	48	46	52	42	42	42	48	54	47.7
	MIN	32	22	18	18	23	28	35	32	31	26	33	40	34	36	44	35	33	32	42	34	31	36	33	31	31	36	36	36	35	32	26	32.0
	MAX	29	32	34	26	26	32	43	40	34	31	28	36	51	56	69	48	50	43	40	32	34	39	45	52	40	41	35	46	46	44	40	39.9
	MIN	11	21	13	10	8	10	17	29	30	20	15	16	34	37	43	31	26	22	24	29	29	26	28	30	18	20	28	30	30	29	22	23.7
	MAX	32	42	37	36	43	44	42	38	41	42	48	61	66	72	56	57	61	54	48	42	49	49	62	59	45	39	43	50	50	49	50	48.5
	MIN	26	22	23	19	21	26	31	32	32	29	24	32	32	42	42	34	31	32	35	33	30	29	28	30	29	34	32	38	30	34	23	30.2
	MAX	35	42	40	37	43	44	42	38	41	42	40	62	68	73	55	60	63	52	46	43	48	50	60	59	45	40	46	51	52	50	51	49.0
	MIN	27	31	26	21	22	30	30	32	32	29	24	23	22	32	43	32	31	32	34	34	33	30	34	32	27	34	33	38	36	35	31	30.6

See reference notes following Station Index.

MT POCONO 2 N AP						
MUHLENBURG 1 SE						
NEWBURG 3 W						
NEW CASTLE 1 N						
NEWELL						
NEWPORT						
NEW STANTON						
NORRISTOWN						
PALMERTON	51 28	60 25	54 27	49 29	41 34	41 33
PHIL DREXEL INST OF TEC	51 38	62 39	66 36	48 34	42 39	44 36
PHILADELPHIA WB AP	50 35	61 39	63 35	47 34	42 37	44 36
PHILADELPHIA PT BREEZE	52 40	61 43	62 44	49 36	42 38	44 37
PHILADELPHIA SHAWMONT	52 32	62 34	60 32	58 31	47 37	44 34
PHILADELPHIA CITY	51 41	62 42	63 41	49 35	42 38	45 37
PHILIPSBURG CAA AP	45 24	56 17	51 20	40 17	36 [illegible]	35 32
PHOENIXVILLE 1 E	50 28	65 37	65 26	60 28	46 36	46 34
PIMPLE HILL	34 25	44 30	52 33	48 18	46 28	32 29
PITTSBURGH WB AP 2	52 34	58 30	51 33	44 30	35 32	43 36
PITTSBURGH WB CITY	51 36	60 35	55 35	45 31	37 36	44 38
PLEASANT MOUNT 1 W	35 19		51 23	40 18	44 21	34 30
PORT CLINTON	50 25	54 33	60 34	62 24	30 30	40 30
PUTNEYVILLE 2 SE DAM	48 27	50 23	59 22	50 22	43 26	52 30
QUAKERTOWN 1 E	51 28	63 27	63 27	52 28	46 34	47 33
READING WB CITY	52 34	63 34	60 35	49 32	41 37	45 34
RIDGWAY 3 W	47 23	49 21	59 18	49 17	44 18	44 32
SALINA 3 W	48 29	58 24	54 24	48 29	57 33	42 36
SCRANTON	45 30	50 31	58 30	55 25	50 27	40 33
SCRANTON WB AIRPORT	48 27	57 27	48 27	47 23	40 31	42 32
SELINSGROVE CAA AP	51 28	64 23	53 26	45 24	41 33	46 32
SHIPPENSBURG	48 32	62 24	62 29	53 29	50 35	48 36
SHIPPINGPORT WB	52 33	58 31	50 39	45 30	53 32	42 36
SLIPPERY ROCK	52 30	59 28	50 29	40 24	52 29	40 34
SOMERSET MAIN ST	44 28	56 25	57 25	50 26	53 29	45 32
SPRINGBORO	45 25	55 27	57 20	43 23	43 29	49 31
SPRINGS 1 SW	39 28	52 23	54 26	38 27	50 29	36 32
STATE COLLEGE	49 31	60 28	55 33	44 26	40 33	40 32
STROUDSBURG	51 22	55 22	55 24	51 25	36 32	42 33
TAMARACK 2 S FIRE TWR	44 27	46 27	58 28	47 19	41 18	32 28
TIONESTA 2 SE DAM	46 26	52 29	60 23	49 23	44 25	48 34

See reference notes following Station Index.

Table 5 - Continued

DAILY TEMPERATURES

PENNSYLVANIA
MARCH 1957

Station		1	2	3	4	5	6	7	8	9	10	11	12	13	14	15	16	17	18	19	20	21	22	23	24	25	26	27	28	29	30	31	Average
ITUSVILLE WATER NORKS	MAX	39	36	27	35	47	54	38	38	34	34	46	54	68	72	58	48	47	50	45	43	46	53	60	47	44	52	38	42	38	46	54	46.2
	MIN	23	25	12	8	10	16	30	30	29	20	18	37	39	25	41	29	20	16	25	31	29	23	23	20	22	32	34	31	29	20	15	24.6
OWANDA	MAX	37	40	34	33	39	47	41	39	37	37	38	58	67	79	58	56	51	48	41	38	47	50	60	48	47	42	45	52	48	46	51	46.8
	MIN	25	18	18	12	10	15	30	32	32	24	14	23	24	26	41	26	20	19	32	32	34	23	25	23	20	31	32	30	29	30	18	24.8
NIONTOWN	MAX	40	39	37	41	54	58	44	45	38	44	66	64	72	72	64	58	64	53	52	49	43	49	59	57	44	62	42	42	44	50	60	51.8
	MIN	34	31	17	15	26	36	37	34	30	29	27	40	31	33	45	35	37	33	45	34	33	35	29	29	36	38	38	36	36	32	21	32.6
PPER DARBY	MAX	34	44	39	40	45	45	43	40	43	44	48	63	67	73	63	59	63	54	50	39	51	51	61	62	48	41	45	52	53	50	53	50.4
	MIN	30	26	26	22	24	29	34	36	34	30	29	36	35	37	45	41	35	34	37	34	37	35	39	35	32	36	35	40	36	36	30	33.7
ARREN	MAX	40	36	29	32	43	58	40	36	36	34	46	54	66	73	65	47	46	49	45	40	48	54	57	50	46	47	41	40	39	45	54	46.3
	MIN	28	27	18	9	11	18	30	31	29	24	19	42	34	30	43	31	22	19	39	32	29	24	24	22	19	32	34	34	30	26	18	26.7
AYNESBURG 2 W	MAX	41	41	37	40	54	55	48	40	38	42	69	68	72	70	67	59	61	57	53	53	45	51	59	57	52	60	39	45	47	48	59	52.5
	MIN	32	31	14	11	15	23	38	31	29	26	23	51	25	26	43	33	25	27	40	33	24	31	28	26	34	31	36	35	33	28	17	29.0
ELLSBORO 3 S	MAX	28	35	33	31	30	34	42	33	33	32	31	39	51	59	65	51	48	48	46	36	35	44	46	54	44	40	34	45	43	41	42	41.1
	MIN	9	23	13	9	10	10	18	28	28	22	18	22	37	39	45	30	27	21	25	32	29	25	26	29	20	23	30	29	26	28	20	24.2
ELLSVILLE	MAX	36	44	41	38	44	45	42	38	43	42	50	63	66	72	68	60	65	59	48	42	51	49	59	61	53	41	48	51	51	51	52	50.7
	MIN	26	21	22	14	16	25	30	34	32	30	21	30	24	25	46	33	26	30	37	36	35	29	25	25	29	35	35	33	25	34	18	28.4
EST CHESTER	MAX	37	46	49	45	47	46	43	42	44	43	51	62	65	74	79	60	64	61	50	44	55	49	62	60	57	41	43	54	52	46	51	52.3
	MIN	26	24	20	16	20	29	34	33	28	26	31	39	41	44	36	29	33	34	33	34	36	35	40	31	35	34	34	35	36	30	37	32.0
ILLIAMSPORT WB AP	MAX	39	41	39	39	45	45	38	36	40	41	36	60	69	71	60	57	59	53	44	42	52	52	62	53	49	42	46	50	49	50	51	48.7
	MIN	28	22	23	18	17	22	32	33	31	27	25	32	27	32	44	32	26	26	37	35	32	29	29	29	27	33	33	38	33	29	23	29.2
ORK 3 SSW PUMP STA	MAX	37	48	42	39	45	46	44	42	43	43	53	64	68	75	72	60	65	62	52	43	54	54	62	63	60	43	49	49	52	51	54	52.7
	MIN	28	25	25	17	17	29	32	35	36	31	25	34	28	30	52	34	34	29	39	37	37	30	26	27	32	37	37	34	29	35	21	31.0

See reference notes following Station Index.

Table 7

SNOWFALL AND SNOW ON GROUND

Station		Day of month																														
		1	2	3	4	5	6	7	8	9	10	11	12	13	14	15	16	17	18	19	20	21	22	23	24	25	26	27	28	29	30	31
ALLENTOWN WB AIRPORT	SNOWFALL	1.0	T						T	T		T								T	T					T	T	.9			.T	
	SN ON GND	T	T																									T				
	WTR EQUIV																															
AUSTINBURG 2 W	SNOWFALL	1.5	1.8	.5				2.0	1.5	7.8	T									T							3.0		T	T	1.0	
	SN ON GND	2	3	3	2	1	T	2	3	11	11	10	5	T						T							3	1	T	T	1	
BEACH CREEK STATION	SNOWFALL	1.0	.5					2.0	1.0	2.5			T														T	1.0				
	SN ON GND	1	1	1	1	T	T	2	2	5	4	3	3	T													T	1				
BRADFORD 4 W RESVR	SNOWFALL	2.5	1.3	2.0				2.6	4.5	1.7	.8										T						3.0	T	T	T		
	SN ON GND	5	6	7	6	6	5	8	11	13	12	11	9	7	5	3	2	1	1	T	T						2	1	1	T		
BROOKVILLE CAA AIRPORT	SNOWFALL	2.2	.2	T			T	1.0	6.5	.4	T										.2	T				.4	T	3.8	T	2.0		
	SN ON GND	1	1	1	1			1	4	5	5	2	T														1	3		T	T	
CANTON 1 NW	SNOWFALL	1.4	1.4					T	T	10.2			1.8							T							1.2	2.3			2.8	
	SN ON GND	1	1	1	1	1	T	T	T	10	10	7	6	2						T							1	2			3	
CARROLLTOWN 2 SSE	SNOWFALL	1.0	1.0	1.0	T			1.0	3.0	1.0	.5	T	T								T	T					.5	3.0	T	.5	2.0	
	SN ON GND	1	2	2	2	1	T	1	4	4	4	3	T								T	T					1	3	1	T	2	
COALDALE 2 NW	SNOWFALL	.3	1.0							.3												.5					.5	2.5			T	
	SN ON GND	T	1							T												1					1	3				
CORRY	SNOWFALL			2.0				1.0	2.5	1.0	T										T						2.5			T		
	SN ON GND	T		2	T				3	4	3	2									T									T		
DONEGAL	SNOWFALL	T	3.0	T				T	2.0	2.0	T										T					T		T	1.0	T	T	
	SN ON GND	T	3	T	T			T	T	T	T										T					T		T	1	T	T	
DU BOIS 7 E	SNOWFALL	1.5		.5				1.0	9.0												T					T	.5	3.0	.5	2.0		
	SN ON GND	1	1	1	1	T	T	1	6	4	4	3	T													T		1	T	1		
ENGLISH CENTER	SNOWFALL	-	-	-	-	-	-	-	-	-	-	-	-	-	-	-	-	-	-	-	-	-	-	-	-	-	-	-	-	-	-	-
	SN ON GND	1	2	1	1	T	T	1	2	4	3	2	1														1	1				
ERIE WB AIRPORT	SNOWFALL	.8	2.0	1.0				2.0	3.2	.2											T					T	3.0	T		1.3		
	SN ON GND	1	T	2	1	T		2	2	4	2	2															3				1	
EVERETT 1 SW	SNOWFALL	4.0						3.0	2.0																							
	SN ON GND	4						3	5																							
FORD CITY 4 S DAM	SNOWFALL	2.0	T	.5				2.0	3.0	3.0	T	T									T	T					.5			T	1.0	
	SN ON GND	1		1				1	2	1	T	T															T				T	
GALETON	SNOWFALL	1.5	1.3	1.0				1.3	1.2	6.5	.5	.3	T							.2							2.0	.8	T	1.0	T	
	SN ON GND	1	2	2	2	2	1	2	2	7	7	7	3							T							2	1	T	1		
GEORGE SCHOOL	SNOWFALL	1.0	.2							1.0																T		T				
	SN ON GND	1	T							T																						
GRATERFORD	SNOWFALL	-	-	-	-	-	-	-	-	-	-	-	-	-	-	-	-	-	-	-	-	-	-	-	-	-	-	-	-	-	-	-
	SN ON GND	-	-	-	-	-	-	-	-	-	-	-	-	-	-	-	-	-	-	-	-	-	-	-	-	-	-	-	-	-	-	-
GREENSBORO LOCK 7	SNOWFALL									T																						
	SN ON GND									T																						
HANOVER	SNOWFALL		T					1.0																								
	SN ON GND							1																								
HARRISBURG WB AIRPORT	SNOWFALL	1.1	T	T				1.2	.1	T		T														T		T				
	SN ON GND	T	T					1																								
	WTR EQUIV																															
HAWLEY 1 S DAM	SNOWFALL	T	1.2	T					T	3.0										T	T	T					T				3.0	
	SN ON GND	T	1	1	T	T			T	3	3	2	T							T	T	T					T				3	
HOLTWOOD	SNOWFALL	T	T					.3																			T					
	SN ON GND	T	T					T																								
HOOVERSVILLE	SNOWFALL	2.0	2.4	2.6	T			1.8	1.6	2.0	1.6	T	T									1.6					.8	T	T	1.2	2.4	T
	SN ON GND	2	3	4	3	2	1	2	2	2	2	T										1					T	T		1	2	
INDIANA 3 SE	SNOWFALL	T	.4					.2	1.5	.3											T					T	T	T			.5	
	SN ON GND	T	T	T				T		T																T	T	T			T	
KANE 1 NNE	SNOWFALL	2.0	1.2	.2				1.7	1.2	4.4	.5	.2	T									.1	T			1.8	.5	T	.7		1.0	
	SN ON GND		2	3	3	2	1	3	3	7	8	7	3									T					2		T		1	
KEATING SUMMIT	SNOWFALL	1.5	.3	1.2				2.4	1.5	4.0	T																1.0			.4	.5	
	SN ON GND	2	2	3	2	1	1	2	4	8	8	7	3	1													1	1		1	1	
LANCASTER 2 NE PUMP STA	SNOWFALL	-	-	-	-	-	-	-	-	-	-	-	-	-	-	-	-	-	-	-	-	-	-	-	-	-	-	-	-	-	-	-
	SN ON GND	-	-	-	-	-	-	-	-	-	-	-	-	-	-	-	-	-	-	-	-	-	-	-	-	-	-	-	-	-	-	-
LAWRENCEVILLE 2 S	SNOWFALL	.3	.8	T				T	.5	3.3	T																2.5	T				
	SN ON GND		1	1	1	1	1	T	1	4	4	3	2	T													3	T				
LEWISTOWN	SNOWFALL	1.0	.9	.1					1.2				T															T				
	SN ON GND	1	2	T					1																			T				
MARTINSBURG CAA AIRPORT	SNOWFALL	3.0	.2	T				1.2	3.5	T	T	T									T					T	T	T	T	T	T	
	SN ON GND	3	2	1	T	T		1	2	2	1	1															T	T			T	
MATAMORAS	SNOWFALL		1.0							1.0																						
	SN ON GND		1							1																						
MEADVILLE 1 S	SNOWFALL	.4	.2	3.8	.1			.8	1.0	1.9	T	T	T									T					3.3		T	T	.3	
	SN ON GND	T	T	4	2	T	T	1	1	3	1	T	T									T					3					
MEDIX RUN	SNOWFALL	1.0	.3	.5				1.5	.8	1.5	.5	T	T									T					.7	1.7	T		T	
	SN ON GND	1	2	2	1	T	T	2	2	3	3	2	T														1	2	T		T	
MONTROSE 1 E	SNOWFALL	.7	1.0	.2	T	T			T	7.8	.5	T								.2	T	1.3					1.2	.1	T	.8	1.9	T
	SN ON GND	1	1	1	1	1	T	T	T	T	8	7	6	4	T	T	T			T	T	1	T				1	T		1	2	
MUHLENBURG 1 SE	SNOWFALL	2.0										T															2.0	1.0			T	
	SN ON GND	2																									2					
NEWPORT	SNOWFALL	1.0		T				.5		1.0																		T				
	SN ON GND	-	-	-	-	-	-	-	-	-	-	-	-	-	-	-	-	-	-	-	-	-	-	-	-	-	-	-	-	-	-	-
PHILADELPHIA WB AIRPORT	SNOWFALL	1.1						.1		T		T																				
	SN ON GND	T	T																													
	WTR EQUIV																															

See reference notes following Station Index.

SNOWFALL AND SNOW ON GROUND

Station		1	2	3	4	5	6	7	8	9	10	11	12	13	14	15	16	17	18	19	20	21	22	23	24	25	26	27	28	29	30	31
PHILADELPHIA CITY	SNOWFALL	-	-	-	-	-	-	-	-	-	-	-	-	-	-	-	-	-	-	-	-	-	-	-	-	-	-	-	-	-	-	-
	SN ON GND	-	-	-	-	-	-	-	-	-	-	-	-	-	-	-	-	-	-	-	-	-	-	-	-	-	-	-	-	-	-	-
PHILIPSBURG CAA AIRPORT	SNOWFALL	2.8	.2	T			T	1.0	6.2	.6	.2									T	T	T				2.6	5.0	.6	T	.4	T	
	SN ON GND	1	1	1	1	1		1	8	9	9	9	6														3	8	4	3	3	
PIMPLE HILL	SNOWFALL	1.2	1.3	.2	T			T	.6	3.7	.9		T							.2	.2	.7	T				1.4	3.7	.2	.1	2.3	.5
	SN ON GND	1	2	1	1	1	T	T	1	4	4	3	2	T	T	T	T			T	T	1	1	T	T	T	1	5	2	T	2	T
PITTSBURGH WB AIRPORT 2	SNOWFALL	.2	.3	T				.1	5.4	.2	T										.5					T			.1	.5	T	
	SN ON GND	T		T					4	2	1	T										T										
	WTR EQUIV								.8																							
PLEASANT MOUNT 1 W	SNOWFALL	.5	1.0	1.0	T				T	4.7	1.5	T								T	T	.5	T				T	T	T	T	T	
	SN ON GND	1	1	2	2	2	T	T	T	5	6	5	3	1	T	T	T	T	T	T	T	1	1				T	T	T	T	T	
READING WB CITY	SNOWFALL	.1	1.0					T				T									T					T		T				
	SN ON GND	T	T	T																												
SCRANTON WB AIRPORT	SNOWFALL	.9	.1	.5				T	1.1	1.2	T								T	T	1.6					.3	.1	.6		T	.3	
	SN ON GND	1	1	1	T	T	T	T	T	2	2	2	1	T							T	T					T	T				
	WTR EQUIV									.3	.3	.2																				
SELINSGROVE CAA AIRPORT	SNOWFALL	.9	T					T	3.0			T														T		1.0				
	SN ON GND	1	1					T	T	2	T																T	1				
SHIPPENSBURG	SNOWFALL	1.0	T	T				2.0	3.0	T		T														T						
	SN ON GND	1	T					T	2																							
SHIPPENSBURG WB	SNOWFALL	T	T					T	T	T		T									T					T			T	T		
	SN ON GND								T	T																						
SLIPPERY ROCK	SNOWFALL	1.0		1.0				.5	2.0	5.0																	1.0				1.0	
	SN ON GND	1		1				T	2	5	2																1				1	
SPRING 1 SW	SNOWFALL	2.5	1.5	T				1.5	2.5	.5											1.0		T			T		1.0	2.0	T	T	
	SN ON GND	3	4	4	4	2		2	4	4	3										1					T		1	2	T		
TAMARACK 2 S FIRE TWR	SNOWFALL	1.5	1.5	.4				2.0	.5	8.0	T	T								T		T					1.7	5.0	2.0	1.	4.0	
	SN ON GND	2	3	3	3	3	2	3	4	11	11	10	7	3	T					T	T						2	6	5	4	7	4
TIONESTA 2 SE DAM	SNOWFALL	2.0	T	.5	T			2.0	2.5	2.0	.3	T										T					2.5			T	.4	
	SN ON GND	2	1	1	T	T	T	2	4	3	2	2	T														3				T	
TOWANDA	SNOWFALL	.5	.5	.2	T	T		T	.2	4.0	T	T	T							T	T	T					T	T	T		1.2	T
	SN ON GND	1	1	T	T	T	T	T	T	3	2	2	1	T						T	T						T	T			1	
TOWER CITY 5 SW	SNOWFALL	1.0	1.0	T				T																		T						
	SN ON GND	-	-	-	-	-	-	-	-	-	-	-	-	-	-	-	-	-	-	-	-	-	-	-	-	-	-	-	-	-	-	-
WILLIAMSPORT WB AIRPORT	SNOWFALL	1.8	.1	.1				.5	10.5		T	T														T	T	1.5		T	T	
	SN ON GND	1	1	1	T			T	T	3	2	T	T															1		T		
	WTR EQUIV									.4	.2																					

See reference notes following Station Index.

TOTAL PRECIPITATION

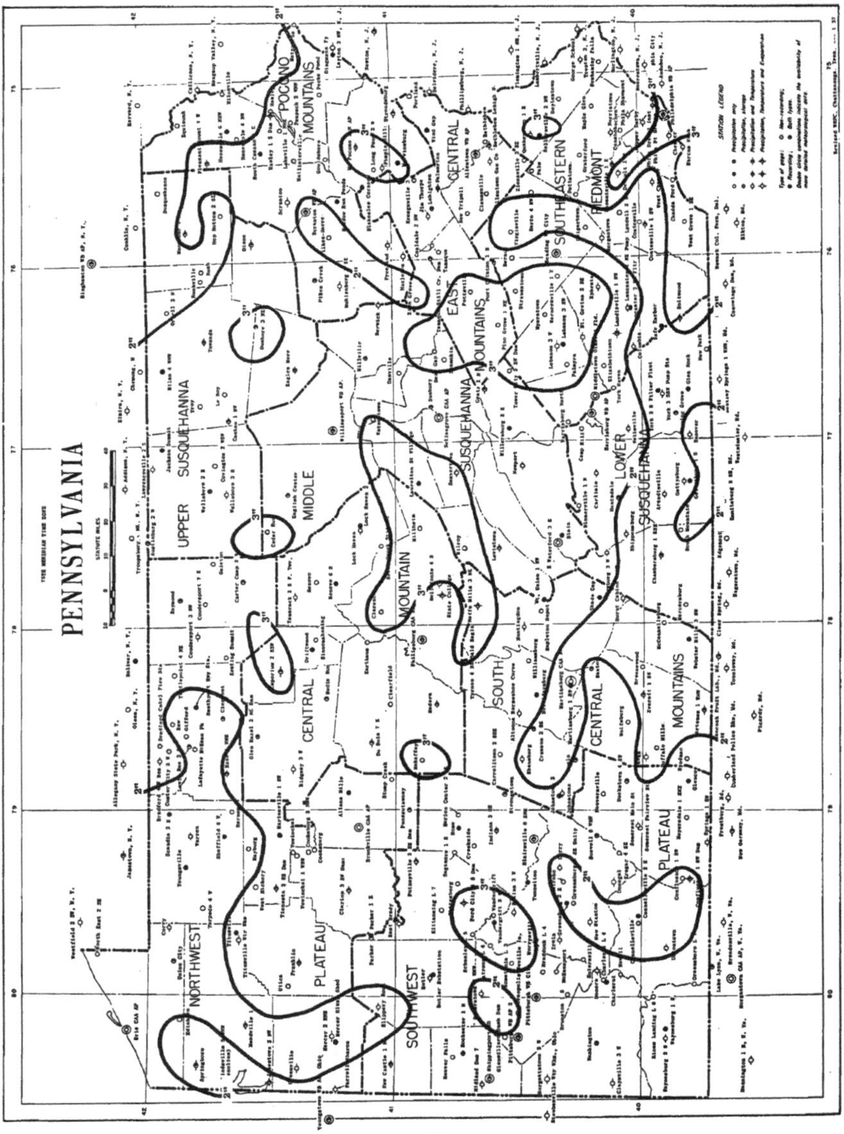

AVERAGE TEMPERATURE

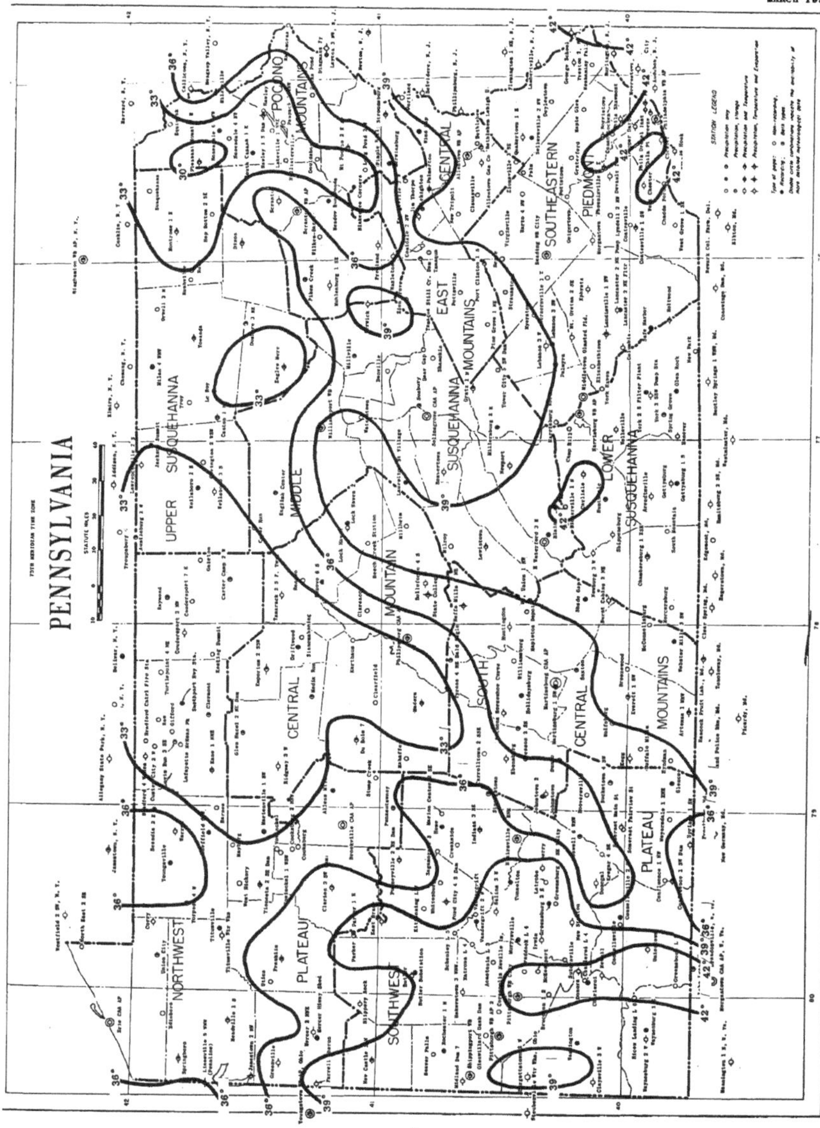

Isolines are drawn through points of approximately equal values. Hourly precipitation data from recorder substations will be available in the publication "Hourly Precipitation Data".

STATION INDEX

Station	Index No.	County	Drainage 1	Latitude	Longitude	Elevation	Observation Time Temp.	Observation Time Precip.	Observer	Refer To Tables
ACMETONIA LOCK 3	0022	ALLEGHENY	1	40 32	79 49	748		7A	CORPS OF ENGINEERS	3
ALLENS MILLS	0099	JEFFERSON	1	41 12	78 55	1600		MID	CHARLES M. ALLEN	C
ALLENTOWN WB AP	0106	LEHIGH	9	40 39	75 26	376	MID	MID	U.S. WEATHER BUREAU	2 3 5 7 C
ALLENTOWN GAS CO	0111	LEHIGH	9	40 36	75 28	254	7A	7A	LEHIGH VLY GAS DIV	2 3 5
ALTOONA HORSESHOE CURVE	0134	BLAIR	6	40 30	78 29	1500	6P	6P	ALTOONA WATER BUR.	2 3 5
ARENDTSVILLE	0229	ADAMS	15	39 55	77 18	710	8A	8A	PA STATE COL EXP	2 3 5
ARTEMAS 1 WNW	0259	BEDFORD	12	39 45	78 28	1250	6P	6P	GRAYSON E.NORTHCRAFT	2 3 5 C
AUSTINBURG 2 W	0313	TIOGA	15	42 00	77 32	1590		7A	OTTO D. BACON	3 7 C
BAKERSTOWN 3 WNW	0355	ALLEGHENY	1	40 39	79 59	1230	7P	7P	PGH CUT FLOWER CO	2 3 5
BARNES	0409	WARREN	1	41 40	79 02	1310		7A	CORPS OF ENGINEERS	3
BARTO 4 NW	0428	BERKS	14	40 26	75 39	312		7A	MARIE B. NICHLAS	3
BEAR GAP	0457	NORTHUMBERLAND	15	40 50	76 30	900		MID	ROARING CRK WTR CO	3
BEAVER FALLS	0475	BEAVER	2	40 46	80 19	760		7A	HOWARD R. KEMP	3
BEAVERTOWN	0482	SNYDER	15	40 45	77 10	640	7A	7A	MARLIN RC ETTINGER	2 3 5
BEECH CREEK STATION	0499	CENTRE	16	41 04	77 34	620		7A	HAROLD S. RUPERT	3 7
BELLEFONTE 4 S	0530	CENTRE	16	40 51	77 47	1110	8A	8A	ROCKVIEW PRISON FARM	2 3 5
BERNE	0599	BERKS	14	40 31	76 00	325		7A	FLOYD W. TRUMP	3
BERWICK	0611	COLUMBIA	15	41 04	76 15	570	6P	6P	AMER CAR + FNDRY CO	2 3 5
BETHLEHEM	0629	NORTHAMPTON	9	40 37	75 22	400		7A	ARTHUR CROPPER	3
#BETHLEHEM LEHIGH UNIV	0634	NORTHAMPTON	9	40 36	75 23	450	MID	MID	LEHIGH UNIVERSITY	2 3 5 C
BLAIN	0725	PERRY	15	40 20	77 31	750		MID	PA DEPT FRST + WTRS	C
BLAIRSVILLE 6 ENE	0736	INDIANA	4	40 27	79 09	2048	6P	6P	U.S. WEATHER BUREAU	2 3 5
BLAKESLEE CORNERS	0743	MONROE	9	41 06	75 36	1650		MID	WALTER WILDRICK	C
BLOSERVILLE 1 N	0763	CUMBERLAND	15	40 16	77 22	650		5P	MRS. B. M. WILLDERS	3
BOSWELL 6 WNW	0820	SOMERSET	1	40 10	79 08	2570		8A	CLARK N. ST. CLAIR	3 C
BRADDOCK LOCK 2	0861	ALLEGHENY	10	40 24	79 52	725		7A	CORPS OF ENGINEERS	3
BRADFORD CNTRL FIRE STA	0867	MC KEAN	1	41 57	78 39	1500		8A	BRADFORD FIRE DEPT	3
BRADFORD 4 W RES	0868	MC KEAN	1	41 57	78 44	1680	5P	5P	BRADFORD WTR DEPT	2 3 5 7
BREEZEWOOD	0905	BEDFORD	6	40 00	78 14	1352		MID	PA TURNPIKE COMM	3
BROOKVILLE CAA AIRPORT	1002	JEFFERSON	1	41 09	79 06	1417	MID	MID	CIVIL AERO. ADM.	2 3 5 7
BRUCETON 1 S	1033	ALLEGHENY	10	40 18	79 59	1065		7A	AUSTIN R. COOPER	3
BUCKSTOWN 1 SE	1073	SOMERSET	4	40 04	78 50	2460		MID	ALVIN W. MANGES	C
BUFFALO MILLS	1087	BEDFORD	6	39 57	78 39	1318		7A	MRS. NELLE R. BROWN	3
BURGETTSTOWN 2 W	1105	WASHINGTON	11	40 23	80 26	980	7A	7A	SMITH TWP MUN AUTH	2 3 5
BURNT CABINS 2 NE	1115	HUNTINGDON	6	40 05	77 52	990	MID	MID	PA TURNPIKE COMM	2 3 5
#BUTLER	1130	BUTLER	2	40 52	79 54	1100	4P	7A	WILLIAM C. FAUST	2 3 5
BUTLER SUBSTATION	1135	BUTLER	2	40 51	79 53	1140		MID	WEST PENN POWER CO	C
CAMP HILL	1198	CUMBERLAND	15	40 15	76 55	461		6P	JOSEPH N. HOBART	3
CANTON 1 NW	1215	BRADFORD	15	41 40	76 52	1520	7A	7A	MRS.MILDRED SPENCER	2 3 5 7 C
CARLISLE	1234	CUMBERLAND	15	40 12	77 11	460	6P	6P	C. E. MILLER	2 3 5
CARROLLTOWN 2 SSE	1255	CAMBRIA	16	40 35	78 42	2040		8A	ROBERT F. MAURER	3 7
CARTER CAMP 2 W	1262	POTTER	16	41 37	77 45	2030		7A	RICHARD L. MENKEN	3 C
CEDAR RUN	1301	LYCOMING	16	41 31	77 27	800		7A	KATHRYN T.KREIGHBAUM	3
CHADDS FORD	1342	DELAWARE	5	39 52	75 36	160		8A	MRS.GRACE A. WICKS	3
CHAMBERSBURG 1 ESE	1354	FRANKLIN	12	39 56	77 38	640	9P	9P	CHARLES A. BENDER	2 3 5 C
CHARLEROI	1372	WASHINGTON	10	40 08	79 55	1040		MID	WEST PENN POWER CO	C
CHARLEROI LOCK 4	1377	WESTMORELAND	10	40 09	79 54	749		7A	CORPS OF ENGINEERS	3
#CHESTER	1423	DELAWARE	5	39 51	75 22	86	8A	8A	CHESTER TIMES	2 3 5
CLARENCE	1480	CENTRE	16	41 03	77 56	1410		7A	MISS VELDA SWANCER	3
CLARION 3 SW	1485	CLARION	1	41 12	79 26	1114	8P	7A	PA ELECTRIC CO	2 3 5 C
CLAUSSVILLE	1505	LEHIGH	9	40 37	75 39	670		8A	WILLIAM J. DOTTERER	3
CLAYSVILLE 3 W	1512	WASHINGTON	11	40 07	80 28	1000	7P	7A	MFGRS. L + H CO	2 3 5
CLEARFIELD	1519	CLEARFIELD	16	41 01	78 26	1100		7A	IRA TAYLOR	3
CLERMONT	1529	MC KEAN	1	41 41	78 30	2104		7A	MRS.TILLIE M.SIMONDS	3 C
COALDALE 2 NW	1572	SCHUYLKILL	9	40 50	75 56	1026		7A	PANTHER VLY WTR CO	3 7
COATESVILLE 1 SW	1589	CHESTER	5	39 58	75 50	342	8A	8A	PHILA ELECTRIC CO	2 3 5 C
COATESVILLE	1594	CHESTER	5	39 59	75 49	340		8A	EDWARD O. BIEDEMAN	INAC 12/55
COLUMBIA	1675	LANCASTER	15	40 02	76 30	300	SS	SS	JAMES H. RUST	2 3 5
CONFLUENCE 1 SW DAM	1705	SOMERSET	17	39 48	79 22	1490	8A	8A	CORPS OF ENGINEERS	2 3 5 6 C
CONFLUENCE 1 NW	1710	FAYETTE	17	39 50	79 22	1331		7A	JOHN L. REID	3
CONNELLSVILLE	1723	FAYETTE	17	40 01	79 36	870		8A	MARSHALL B. MENEFEE	3
CONNELLSVILLE 2 E	1729	FAYETTE	17	40 01	79 33	1300		MID	HARRY C. JOY	C
CONSHOHOCKEN	1737	MONTGOMERY	5	40 04	75 19	70		8A	PHILA ELECTRIC CO	3
COOKSBURG	1740	CLARION	1	41 20	79 13	1180		8A	PA DEPT FRST + WTRS	3
COOKSBURG 2 NNW	1752	CLARION	1	41 21	79 13	1400		8A	PA DEPT FRST + WTRS	3
CORAOPOLIS NEVILLE IS	1773	ALLEGHENY	11	40 30	80 05	720		8A	PGH. COKE + CHEM CO	3
CORRY	1790	ERIE	1	41 56	79 38	1427	7P	5A	LEO C. MECKERS	2 3 5 7
COUDERSPORT 3 NW	1806	POTTER	1	41 49	78 03	2020	7P	8A	MISS ELIZABETH NEFF	2 3 5
COUDERSPORT 7 E	1809	POTTER	1	41 48	77 53	2425		7A	CAMP POTATO	3
COVINGTON 2 WSW	1833	TIOGA	15	41 44	77 07	1745		7A	CALVIN R. PACKARD	3
CREEKSIDE	1881	INDIANA	1	40 41	79 12	1035		7A	CORPS OF ENGINEERS	3
CRESSON 2 SE	1895	CAMBRIA	6	40 27	78 34	2540		7A	TALMAGE R. FRAZER	3 C
CUSTER CITY 2 W	1978	MC KEAN	1	41 55	78 41	2120		8A	M. D. BOOTH AND CO	3
DANVILLE	2013	MONTOUR	15	40 58	76 37	460		7A	MRS.MARIE M. LITTLE	3
DERRY	2108	WESTMORELAND	4	40 20	79 18	1150	6P	6P	MISS N. D. WINEMAN	2 3 5
DEVAULT 1 W	2116	CHESTER	14	40 05	75 33	360	MID	MID	PA TURNPIKE COMM	2 3 5
DINGMANS FERRY	2160	PIKE	5	41 13	74 52	364		MID	CLYDE T. VOORHEES	C
DIXON	2171	WYOMING	15	41 34	75 54	620	7A	7A	HAROLD J. KUSCHEL	2 3 C
DONEGAL	2183	WESTMORELAND	17	40 07	79 23	1746	MID	MID	PA TURNPIKE COMM	2 3 5 7
#DONORA	2190	WASHINGTON	10	40 11	79 51	814	12M	12M	DONORA ZINC WORKS	2 3 5
DOYLESTOWN	2221	BUCKS	5	40 18	75 08	393		5P	GEORGE HART	3
DRIFTWOOD	2245	CAMERON	16	41 20	78 08	880		MID	SIDNEY KENNEDY	
DU BOIS 7 E	2265	CLEARFIELD	16	41 06	78 38	1670	5P	5P	CITY OF DU BOIS	2 3 5 7
DUNLO	2298	CAMBRIA	4	40 17	78 43	2410		MID	MRS. D. L. WHITE	C
DUSHORE 3 NE	2324	SULLIVAN	16	41 33	76 21	1750		7A	PATRICK F. RYAN	3 C
EAGLES MERE	2343	SULLIVAN	16	41 24	76 35	2020	7A	7A	MRS.ELSIE P. BIGGER	2 3 5 C
EAST BRADY	2363	CLARION	1	40 59	79 37	820	5P	5P	A. B. KEMPEL	2 3 5
EAST WATERFORD 3 E	2459	PERRY	6	40 21	77 33	2125	8A	8A	U.S. WEATHER BUREAU	INAC 3/55
EBENSBURG	2466	CAMBRIA	4	40 29	78 43	2090	7P	7A	ROBERT A. WASSER	2 3 5
EDINBORO	2514	ERIE	1	41 52	80 08	1220		8A	EDINBORO ST TCHR COL	3
ELIZABETHTOWN	2560	LANCASTER	15	40 09	76 37	460		8A	MASONIC HOME	3
EMPORIUM 2 SSW	2634	CAMERON	16	41 28	78 15	1735	7A	7A	JACKSON THOMAS	2 3 5 C
ENGLISH CENTER	2644	LYCOMING	16	41 26	77 17	881		7A	WILLIAM SUDERS	3 7 C
EPHRATA	2662	LANCASTER	15	40 11	76 10	465	6P	6P	STANLEY L.VON NEIDA	2 3 5
EQUINUNK 2	2671	WAYNE	5	41 51	75 13	910		7A	MRS. HENRIETTA MURRY	3
ERIE WB AIRPORT	2682	ERIE	8	42 05	80 12	732	MID	MID	U. S. WEATHER BUREAU	2 3 5 7
EVERETT 1 SW	2721	BEDFORD	6	40 00	78 23	1020	MID	MID	PA TURNPIKE COMM	2 3 5 7 C
FARRELL SHARON	2814	MERCER	2	41 14	80 30	865	7P	7P	SHARON STEEL CORP	2 3 5
FORD CITY 4 S DAM	2942	ARMSTRONG	1	40 43	79 30	950	8A	8A	CORPS OF ENGINEERS	2 3 5 6 7 C
FRANKLIN	3028	VENANGO	1	41 23	79 49	987	7P	7A	GEORGE S. SMITH, JR	2 3 5 C
FREELAND	3056	LUZERNE	15	41 01	75 54	1900	6P	8A	ANDREW B. EVANSHA	2 5
GALETON	3130	POTTER	16	41 44	77 39	1325		7A	W. GALE LUSH	7
GEIGERTOWN	3189	BERKS	14	40 13	75 50	400		8A	WALTER C. WOLF	
GEORGE SCHOOL	3200	BUCKS	5	40 13	74 56	135	7P	7P	GEORGE M. HART	2 3 5 7
#GETTYSBURG	3218	ADAMS	12	39 50	77 14	540	9A	9A	HUGH C. MC ILHENNY	2 U 5
GETTYSBURG 1 S	3223	ADAMS	12	39 48	77 14	560		MID	NAT MILITARY PARK	C
GIFFORD	3237	MC KEAN	1	41 51	78 36	2220		8A	SOUTH PENN OIL CO	3
GLENCOE	3298	SOMERSET	12	39 49	78 51	1620		MID	MRS. MARY M.HARTMAN	C
GLEN HAZEL 2 NE DAM	3311	ELK	1	41 34	78 36	1725		8A	CORPS OF ENGINEERS	3 C
GLEN ROCK	3330	YORK	15	39 48	76 44	620		MID	MRS.E.C.MC WILLIAMS	C
GLENWILLARD DASH DAM	3343	ALLEGHENY	11	40 33	80 13	705		7A	CORPS OF ENGINEERS	
GOULDSBORO	3394	WAYNE	9	41 15	75 27	1890		7A	L. M. EILENBERGER	
GRATERFORD	3435	MONTGOMERY	14	40 14	75 27	160	7A	7A	CLAUDE K. KULP	2 5 7 C
GRATZ 1 N	3438	DAUPHIN	15	40 38	76 43	760	8A	8A	LEE M. LEITZEL	2 5 C
GREENSBORO LOCK 7	3503	GREENE	10	39 47	79 55	808		7A	CORPS OF ENGINEERS	U 7
GREENSBURG 2 E	3515	WESTMORELAND	10	40 18	79 31	1225		MID	PA DEPT HIGHWAYS	C
GREENSBURG 3 SE UNITY	3516	WESTMORELAND	10	40 17	79 30	1245		6P	WESTMORELAND WTR CO	3
GREENVILLE	3526	MERCER	2	41 24	80 23	1026	6P	6P	C. EARL MILLER	2 3 5
HANOVER	3662	YORK	15	39 48	76 59	600	8A	8A	HANOVER EVENING SUN	2 3 5 7
#HARRISBURG WB AP	3699	YORK	15	40 13	76 51	335	MID	MID	U.S. WEATHER BUREAU	2 3 5 7 C
HARRISBURG NORTH	3704	DAUPHIN	15	40 18	76 54	323		9A	GEORGE S. BEAL	3
HAWLEY	3758	WAYNE	5	41 29	75 10	880		7A	MRS. KATHERINE BATES	3
HAWLEY 1 S DAM	3761	WAYNE	5	41 28	75 11	1200	7A	7A	PA POWER + LIGHT CO	2 3 5 6 7 C
HOLLIDAYSBURG	4001	BLAIR	6	40 26	78 24	960		MID	JOHN M. RINGLER	C
HOLLISTERVILLE	4008	WAYNE	5	41 23	75 26	1360		8A	PA POWER + LIGHT CO	3
#HOLTWOOD	4019	LANCASTER	15	39 50	76 20	187	MID	8A	PA POWER + LIGHT CO	2 3 5 7 C
HOME	4027	INDIANA	1	40 45	79 08	1220		MID	MRS. EDNA M. BUSH	C
HONESDALE 4 NW	4043	WAYNE	5	41 37	75 19	1410		9A	GEORGE C. WILLIAMS	3
HONESDALE 6 NNW	4044	WAYNE	5	41 39	75 17	1050		MID	FRIEND E. WALTER	C
HOOVERSVILLE	4058	SOMERSET	4	40 09	78 55	1660		7A	PA ELECTRIC CO	3 7
HOP BOTTOM 2 SE	4066	SUSQUEHANNA	15	41 43	75 43	900		7A	JOSEPH J. SANSUSKAS	3
HUNTINGDON	4159	HUNTINGDON	6	40 30	78 01	678	7A	7A	DANIEL I. GROVE	2 3 5
HUNTSDALE	4166	CUMBERLAND	15	40 06	77 18	610		8A	METRO P. DOROSH	3 C
HYNDMAN	4190	BEDFORD	12	39 49	78 43	920		8A	MRS.GERTRUDE M.BURTON	3
INDIANA 3 SE	4214	INDIANA	4	40 36	79 07	1102	7P	7A	CLYMER WATER SVC CO	2 3 5 7 C
IRWIN	4276	WESTMORELAND	10	40 20	79 42	1100	5P	5P	WESTMORELAND WTR CO	2 3 5
JACKSON SUMMIT	4304	TIOGA	15	41 57	77 01	1690		MID	ARCHIE LAIN	C
JAMESTOWN 2 NW	4325	CRAWFORD	2	41 30	80 28	1050	8A	8A	PA DEPT FRST + WTRS	2 3 5 6 C
JIM THORPE	4370	CARBON	9	40 52	75 45	830	5P	5P	HENRY S. HAAK	2 3 5
#JOHNSTOWN	4385	CAMBRIA	4	40 20	78 55	1214	9A	9A	JOHNSTOWN TRIBUNE	2 3 5
JOHNSTOWN 2	4390	CAMBRIA	4	40 19	78 55	1275		MID	CITY OF JOHNSTOWN	C
KANE 1 NNE	4432	MC KEAN	1	41 41	78 48	1750	8A	8A	SPRING WATER CO	2 3 5 7 C
KARTHAUS	4450	CLEARFIELD	16	41 07	78 07	950		7A	JEROME S. HOWE	3
KEATING SUMMIT	4466	POTTER	16	41 41	78 11	1840		7A	EUGENE L. KREITNER	3 7
KEGG	4481	BEDFORD	6	39 59	78 43	1280	MID	MID	PA TURNPIKE COMM	2 3 5
KITTANNING LOCK 7	4611	ARMSTRONG	1	40 49	79 32	790		VAR	CORPS OF ENGINEERS	3
KREGAR 4 SE	4667	WESTMORELAND	17	40 06	79 14	2530		MID	PA TURNPIKE COMM	3
KRESGEVILLE 3 W	4672	CARBON	9	40 54	75 34	720		9A	CITY OF BETHLEHEM	3
LAFAYETTE MC KEAN PARK	4706	MC KEAN	1	41 48	78 40	2130		7A	ORIN A. BUTTERS	3
LAKEVILLE 1 NNE	4733	WAYNE	5	41 27	75 16	1440		8A	MRS. GLADYS REINEKE	3
LANCASTER 2 NE PUMP STA	4758	LANCASTER	15	40 03	76 17	255	6P	6P	LANCASTER WATER BUR	2 3 5 7
LANCASTER 2 NE FILT PL	4763	LANCASTER	15	40 03	76 17	270		MID	LANCASTER WATER BUR	C
LANDISVILLE 2 NW	4778	LANCASTER	15	40 07	76 26	380	8A	8A	PA STATE COLLEGE	2 3 5 6 C
LATROBE	4832	WESTMORELAND	4	40 19	79 23	1000		MID	WEST PENN POWER CO	INAC 6/56
LAURELTON STATE VILLAGE	4853	UNION	15	40 54	77 13	880		MID	PA DEPT OF WELFARE	C
LAWRENCEVILLE 2 S	4873	TIOGA	15	41 59	77 07	1000	7A	7A	HARRY P. HOWLAND	2 3 5 7
LEBANON 3 W	4891	LEBANON	15	40 20	76 29	460	7A	7A	LEON MILLER	2 3 5 7
LEBANON 3 SW	4896	LEBANON	15	40 19	76 28	490		MID	THOMAS DONNACHIE	C
LEHIGHTON	4934	CARBON	9	40 50	75 43	580		7A	GOODWIN S. DEFREHN	3 C
LE ROY	4972	BRADFORD	15	41 41	76 43	1040		6P	MRS.DIMMIS M.BAILEY	3
LEWIS RUN 3 SE	4984	MC KEAN	1	41 50	78 39	1740		7A	RUSSELL LINEMAN	3 C
LEWISTOWN	4992	MIFFLIN	6	40 35	77 35	480	7A	7A	AMERICAN VISCOSE CO	2 3 5 7 C
LINESVILLE 5 WNW	5050	CRAWFORD	2	41 41	80 31	1020	7P	8A	MISS RETTA M. CRUMB	2 3 5
LOCK HAVEN	5104	CLINTON	16	41 08	77 27	570	7P	7A	PETER L. STEVENSON	2 3 5
LOCK HAVEN 2	5109	CLINTON	16	41 08	77 27	630		MID	HUGH F. PARKER	C
LONG POND 2 W	5160	MONROE	9	41 03	75 30	1860		7A	THOMAS MECKES	3
LYNDELL 2 NW	5279	CHESTER	5	40 05	75 48	-		8A	MRS. DOROTHY MARPLE	3
MADERA	5336	CLEARFIELD	16	40 50	78 26	1460	7A	7A	MRS. JULIA J. SHOFF	2 3 5 C
MAHAFFEY	5342	CLEARFIELD	16	40 53	78 44	1280		7A	MISS ELLEN J. MILES	3
MAPLE GLEN	5368	MONTGOMERY	5	40 11	75 11	380		6P	FRANCES E.SCHEIBNER	3
MAPLETON DEPOT	5381	HUNTINGDON	6	40 24	77 56	580		7A	MRS. I. S. BUCHANAN	3
MARCUS HOOK	5390	DELAWARE	5	39 49	75 25	12	MID	MID	SUN OIL CO	2 3 5
MARIENVILLE 1 SW	5400	FOREST	1	41 27	79 09	1700		MID	ROY A. MARKER	C
MARION CENTER 2 SE	5408	INDIANA	1	40 45	79 02	1610		7A	CORPS OF ENGINEERS	3
MARTINSBURG 1 SW	5453	BLAIR	6	40 18	78 20	1360		MID	BLUE MT. CANNERIES	C
MARTINSBURG CAA AP	5454	BLAIR	6	40 18	78 19	1463	MID	MID	CIVIL AERO. ADM.	2 3 5 7
MATAMORAS	5470	PIKE	5	41 22	74 42	439		7A	HARRY BISLAND	3 7
MAYBURG	5490	FOREST	1	41 36	79 13	1150		7A	CORPS OF ENGINEERS	3
MC CONNELLSBURG	5526	FULTON	12	39 56	78 00	895		7A	MRS. HELEN M. SHIVES	3
MC KEESPORT	5573	ALLEGHENY	10	40 21	79 52	720		8A	NATIONAL TUBE CO	3
MEADOW RUN PONDS	5601	LUZERNE	15	41 13	75 40	1995		MID	GEORGE PEARAGE	C
MEADVILLE 1 S	5606	CRAWFORD	1	41 38	80 10	1065	8A	8A	CITY OF MEADVILLE	2 3 5 7 C
MEDIX RUN	5627	ELK	16	41 17	78 24	1100		7A	MRS.E. M. SNYDER	3 7 C
MERCER 2 NNE	5651	MERCER	2	41 15	80 13	1160	7P	7A	WILLIAM K. STRUTHERS	2 3 5
MERCER HIWAY SHED	5654	MERCER	2	41 14	80 15	1250		MID	PA DEPT HIGHWAYS	C
MERCERSBURG	5662	FRANKLIN	12	39 50	77 54	605		8A	ROLLIN P. GILBERT	3
MERWINSBURG	5676	MONROE	9	40 58	75 28	970		MID	WILLIAM D. GOULD	C
MEYERSDALE 1 ENE	5685	SOMERSET	17	39 49	79 01	2290		8A	ARTHUR B. MC CARTER	3
MIDDLETOWN OLMSTED FLD	5703	DAUPHIN	15	40 11	76 46	303	MID	MID	U. S. AIR FORCE	2 3 5
MIDLAND DAM 7	5710	BEAVER	11	40 38	80 28	689	11P	7A	CORPS OF ENGINEERS	2 3 5
MILAN 4 WNW	5732	BRADFORD	15	41 56	76 35	1448		MID	CARL A. MORRIS	C
MILANVILLE	5738	WAYNE	5	41 40	75 04	760		8A	CHARLES W. DAVIS	3
MILLERSBURG 2 E	5775	DAUPHIN	15	40 32	76 56	560		MID	RUSSELL SHEPLEY	C
MILLHEIM	5790	CENTRE	15	40 54	77 29	1090		7A	NEVIN E. BOWERSOX	3
MILLVILLE 2 SW	5817	COLUMBIA	15	41 06	76 34	860		7A	KENNETH LEIGHOW	3 C
MILROY	5825	MIFFLIN	6	40 43	77 35	770		8A	THOMAS C. HARBESON	3
MONTROSE 1 E	5915	SUSQUEHANNA	15	41 50	75 51	1630	7A	7A	WILBER W. HOOPES,JR	2 3 5 7 C
MORGANTOWN	5956	BERKS	15	40 09	75 54	595	MID	MID	PA TURNPIKE COMM	2 3 5
MT GRETNA 2 SE	6028	LANCASTER	15	40 14	76 26	670	MID	MID	PA TURNPIKE COMM	2 3 5
MT POCONO 2 N AP	6055	MONROE	5	41 09	75 22	1915	5P	5P	H. JOHN DAVIS, JR.	2 3 5 C
MOUNT UNION 1 N	6067	MIFFLIN	6	40 24	77 53	820		MID	MT UNION WTR WORKS	C
MUHLENBURG 1 SE	6090	LUZERNE	15	41 13	76 08	1110	6P	6P	THEODORE J. SAMPSON	2 3 5 7
MURRYSVILLE	6111	WESTMORELAND	10	40 26	79 42	903		MID	DAVID C. SHAW	C
MYERSTOWN	6126	LEBANON	14	40 22	76 18	480		8A	MRS.KATHLEEN WANDEL	3
NATRONA LOCK 4	6151	ALLEGHENY	1	40 37	79 43	800		7A	CORPS OF ENGINEERS	3
NEFFS MILLS 3 NE	6174	HUNTINGDON	6	40 40	77 55	900		MID	PA STATE UNIVERSITY	C
NESHAMINY FALLS	6194	BUCKS	5	40 09	74 57	60		MID	PHILA SUB WATER CO	3
NEWBURG 3 W	6225	FRANKLIN	15	40 09	77 37	745	MID	MID	PA TURNPIKE COMM	2 3 5
NEW CASTLE 1 N	6233	LAWRENCE	2	41 01	80 22	825	5P	7A	BAXTER F. JOHNSON	2 3 5 C
NEWELL	6246	FAYETTE	10	40 05	79 54	805	12M	12M	GENERAL CHEMICAL CO	2 3 5
NEW PARK	6289	YORK	15	39 44	76 30	780		6P	CLINTON J. ALLEN	3
NEWPORT	6297	PERRY	6	40 29	77 08	400	7A	7A	MRS. FRANCES K. FRY	2 3 5 7
NEW STANTON	6310	WESTMORELAND	10	40 13	79 36	980	MID	MID	PA TURNPIKE COMM	2 3 5
NEW TRIPOLI	6326	LEHIGH	14	40 41	75 45	570		6P	FRED C. OSWALD	3
NORRISTOWN	6370	MONTGOMERY	14	40 07	75 21	75	MID	8A	GEORGE H. BOONE	2 3 5
NORTH EAST 2 SE	6396	ERIE	8	42 12	79 49	1060		8A	ELLSWORTH WEAVER	3
ORWELL 3 N	6621	BRADFORD	15	41 55	76 16	1620		8A	WILLIAM I. BROWN	3
PALM	6681	MONTGOMERY	14	40 26	75 32	385		8A	FRED C. ESCHBACH	3
#PALMERTON	6689	CARBON	9	40 48	75 37	435	MID	MID	NEW JERSEY ZINC CO	2 3 5 C
PARKER	6721	ARMSTRONG	1	41 05	79 41	1140		7A	LOUIS A. MALARKEY	3
PARKER 1 E	6724	CLARION	1	41 06	79 40	1100		MID	P. M. NEELY	C
PAUPACK 2 WNW	6762	PIKE	5	41 24	75 14	1360		8A	MISS L. VETTERLEIN	3
PECKS POND	6786	PIKE	5	41 17	75 06	1380		8A	MRS. CARRIE NESS	3
#PHIL DREXEL INST OF TEC	6879	PHILADELPHIA	14	39 57	75 11	30	MID	MID	FRANCIS K. DAVIS,JR	2 3 5
PHILADELPHIA WB AP	6889	PHILADELPHIA	5	39 53	75 14	13	MID	MID	U.S. WEATHER BUREAU	2 3 5 7 C
#PHILADELPHIA PT BREEZE	6899	PHILADELPHIA	5	39 55	75 12	32	MID	MID	ATLANTIC REFINING	2 3 5 C
PHILADELPHIA SHAWMONT	6904	PHILADELPHIA	5	40 02	75 15	70	7P	7P	SCHUYLKILL NAVIG CO	2 3 5
#PHILADELPHIA CITY	6909	PHILADELPHIA	5	39 57	75 09	26	9A	9A	USN HYDROGRAPHIC OFF	2 3 5 C
PHILIPSBURG CAA AP	6916	CENTRE	6	40 54	78 05	1918	8P	8P	CIVIL AERO. ADM.	2 3 5 7 C
PHOENIXVILLE 1 E	6927	CHESTER	14	40 07	75 30	105	6P	MID	PHILA SUB WATER CO	2 3 5 C
PIKES CREEK	6939	LUZERNE	15	41 18	76 08	1320		MID	HARRY SHELDON	C
PIMPLE HILL	6944	MONROE	9	41 02	75 30	2215	9A	9A	PA DEPT FRST + WTRS	2 5 6 7
PINE GROVE 1 NE	6954	SCHUYLKILL	15	40 34	76 22	535		8A	PA POWER + LIGHT CO	
PITTSBURGH WB AP 2	6993	ALLEGHENY	11	40 30	80 13	1151	MID	MID	U.S. WEATHER BUREAU	2 5 7 C
#PITTSBURGH WB CITY	6997	ALLEGHENY	11	40 27	80 00	749	MID	MID	U.S. WEATHER BUREAU	2 U 5 C
PLEASANT MOUNT 1 W	7029	WAYNE	5	41 44	75 27	1800	8A	8A	PA FISH COMM	2 3 5 7 C
PORT CLINTON	7116	SCHUYLKILL	14	40 35	76 02	450	7A	7A	MRS. ADA E. RARICK	2 5 C
PORTLAND	7127	NORTHAMPTON	5	40 55	75 06	297		8A	JOINT BRIDGE COMM	INAC 1/56
POTTSTOWN	7149	MONTGOMERY	14	40 15	75 39	160		8A	MILES E. SMITH	3
POTTSVILLE	7161	SCHUYLKILL	14	40 42	76 11	690		8A	LLOYD E. WELLER	U
PUNXSUTAWNEY	7217	JEFFERSON	1	40 57	79 00	1298		MID	JOHN VOLANSKY	C
PUTNEYVILLE 2 SE DAM	7229	ARMSTRONG	1	40 55	79 17	1270	8A	8A	CORPS OF ENGINEERS	2 3 5 C
QUAKERTOWN 1 E	7239	BUCKS	5	40 26	75 20	490	5P	5P	DENNIS K. FLUCK	2 3 5
RAYMOND	7310	POTTER	13	41 52	77 52	2220		7A	MRS. RACHEL LANGAN	3 C
#READING WB CITY	7318	BERKS	14	40 20	75 56	266	MID	MID	U.S. WEATHER BUREAU	2 3 5 7 C
RENOVO	7409	CLINTON	16	41 20	77 46	660		7A	MRS. CAROLINE BAIRD	3
RENOVO 5 S	7410	CLINTON	16	41 14	77 46	2035		MID	C. F. BILLETTE	C
REW	7425	MC KEAN	1	41 54	78 32	2250		8A	HAROLD C. MEALY	3
RICES LANDING L 6	7443	GREENE	10	39 57	80 00	775		7A	CORPS OF ENGINEERS	3
RIDGWAY 3 W	7477	ELK	1	41 25	78 47	1420	7A	7A	BOROUGH OF RIDGWAY	2 3 5
ROCHESTER 1 N	7540	BEAVER	2	40 43	80 18	900		MID	DEQUESNE LIGHT CO	C
RUSH	7694	SUSQUEHANNA	15	41 47	76 03	1000		9A	MISS MAUDE MC CAIN	3
RUSHVILLE	7727	SUSQUEHANNA	15	41 47	76 07	870		7A	CARL KOPATZ	3
SAFE HARBOR	7732	LANCASTER	15	39 55	76 23	270		MID	S.H.WATER POWER CORP	C
SAGAMORE 1 S	7739	INDIANA	1	40 46	79 14	1320		7A	CORPS OF ENGINEERS	3
SALINA 3 W	7782	WESTMORELAND	7	40 31	79 33	1109	6P	6P	MUN AUTH WSTMRLD CO	2 3 5
SAXTON	7846	BEDFORD	6	40 12	78 15	780		8A	MRS.ALVERTA L.HOLMES	3 C
SCANDIA 2 E	7855	WARREN	1	41 55	79 01	2040		MID	DAVID R. ANDERSON	C
SCHENLEY LOCK 5	7863	ARMSTRONG	1	40 41	79 40	783		VAR	CORPS OF ENGINEERS	3
#SCRANTON	7902	LACKAWANNA	15	41 25	75 40	746	7A	7A	U.S. POST OFFICE	2 3 5

INUED

STATION INDEX

PENNSYLVANIA
MARCH 1957

Station	Index No.	County	Drainage 1	Latitude	Longitude	Elevation	Observation Time Temp.	Observation Time Precip.	Observer	Refer To Tables
INTON WB AIRPORT	7905	LUZERNE	15	41 20	75 44	956	MID	MID	U.S. WEATHER BUREAU	2 3 5 7 C
INSGROVE CAA AP	7931	SNYDER	15	40 49	76 52	437	MID	MID	CIVIL AERO. ADM.	2 3 5 7
ERSVILLE 2 NW	7936	BUCKS	5	40 23	75 20	530		MID	SELLERSVILLE WTR CO	C
IE GAP	7965	HUNTINGDON	6	40 11	77 52	1000		MID	MRS. HELEN M. PYLE	C
IOKIN	7978	NORTHUMBLAND	15	40 48	76 33	770		6A	ROARING CRK WTR CO	3
FIELD 6 W	8026	WARREN	1	41 41	79 09	1040		MID	L. N. HANSON	C
PENSBURG	8073	FRANKLIN	15	40 03	77 32	700	4P	4P	KEITH B. ALLEN	2 3 5 7
PINGPORT WB	8078	BEAVER	11	40 37	80 26	740	MID	MID	U.S. WEATHER BUREAU	2 3 5 7 C
IEMAHONING	8145	CAMERON	16	41 10	78 05	790		7A	MRS.FRANCES CALDWELL	3
PERY ROCK	8184	BUTLER	2	41 04	80 03	1345	7P	7A	WALTER D. ALBERT	2 3 5 7
HPORT HIGHWAY SHED	8190	MC KEAN	1	41 48	78 27	1910		MID	PA DEPT HIGHWAYS	C
RSET FAIRVIEW ST	8244	SOMERSET	17	40 01	79 05	2140		7A	HOWARD G. PECK	3
RSET MAIN ST	8249	SOMERSET	17	40 01	79 05	2150	6P	6P	DAVID L. GROVE	2 3 5
H CANAAN 1 NE	8275	WAYNE	5	41 31	75 24	1400		MID	EUGENE M. COOK	C
H MOUNTAIN	8308	FRANKLIN	12	39 51	77 30	1520		7A	PA DEPT OF HEALTH	3
NGBORO	8359	CRAWFORD	8	41 48	80 23	900	8A	8A	SPRINGBORO BOROUGH	2 3 5 C
NG GROVE	8379	YORK	15	39 52	76 52	470		4P	P. H. GLATFELTER CO	3 C
NGS 1 SW	8395	SOMERSET	17	39 44	79 10	2500	8P	8P	ALLEN E. YODER	2 3 5 7
E COLLEGE	8449	CENTRE	16	40 48	77 52	1175	MID	MID	PA STATE COLLEGE	2 3 5 6 C
USSTOWN	8570	BERKS	14	40 29	76 11	600		8A	JACOB KLAHR	3
INGSTOWN	8589	INDIANA	4	40 33	78 55	1880		MID	HARRY F. BENNETT	C
UDSBURG	8596	MONROE	5	40 59	75 12	480	11P	11P	WILLIAM HAGERTY	2 3 5 C
P CREEK	8610	JEFFERSON	1	41 01	78 50	1320		7A	CORPS OF ENGINEERS	3
URY	8668	NORTHUMBLAND	15	40 51	76 48	440		7A	CHARLES W. BAYLER	3 C
UEHANNA	8692	SUSQUEHANNA	15	41 57	75 36	1020		7A	MRS. LAURA A.BENSON	3
RSVILLE	8699	ALLEGHENY	17	40 14	79 48	765		7A	FRANK E. MARSH	3
QUA	8758	SCHUYLKILL	14	40 48	75 58	830		8A	MRS. MARY L.ROBERTS	3
QUA 4 N DAM	8763	SCHUYLKILL	14	40 51	75 59	1120		7A	PANTHER VLY WTR CO	3 C
RACK 2 S FIRE TWR	8770	CLINTON	16	41 24	77 51	2220	7A	7A	JAMES E. SWARTZ	2 3 5 7
ESTA 2 SE DAM	8873	FOREST	1	41 29	79 20	1200	8A	8A	CORPS OF ENGINEERS	2 3 5 7 C
SVILLE	8885	CRAWFORD	1	41 38	79 40	1550		MID	PA ELECTRIC CO	C
SVILLE WATER WORKS	8888	CRAWFORD	1	41 38	79 42	1220	7P	7P	CITY OF TITUSVILLE	2 3 5
EDO 4 W	8901	WARREN	1	41 47	79 32	1735		7A	MRS. LILY B. GARBER	3
NDA	8905	BRADFORD	15	41 46	76 26	760	7P	7A	MRS. M. O. PARKS	2 3 5 7 C
R CITY 5 SW	8910	DAUPHIN	15	40 31	76 37	745		8P	HARRISBURG WTR DEPT	3 7
	8959	BRADFORD	15	41 47	76 47	1100		7A	JENNIE L. BALLARD	3
ELTON	8989	INDIANA	4	40 27	79 23	890		MID	MRS. MARY E. WEIMER	C
LEPOINT 4 NE	9002	MC KEAN	1	41 54	78 16	1640		7A	ROBERT D. STRAIT	3
NE 4 NE BALD EAGLE	9024	BLAIR	6	40 43	78 12	1020		7A	FREDERICK L. FRIDAY	3 C
N CITY	9042	ERIE	1	41 54	79 50	1325		7A	FORREST M. BRALEY	3 C
NTOWN	9050	FAYETTE	10	39 54	79 44	1040	10P	10P	WM. W. MARSTELLER	2 3 5
R DARBY	9074	DELAWARE	5	39 58	75 18	222	7P	7P	PHIL. SUB.TRANS. CO	2 3 5
A	9099	VENANGO	1	41 26	79 57	1030		7A	MRS.FLORENCE MILLER	3
ERGRIFT	9128	WESTMORELAND	7	40 36	79 33	800		7A	UNITED ENG+FNDRY CO	3
ERGRIFT 2 W	9133	WESTMORELAND	7	40 36	79 36	995		MID	EUGENE R. YOUNG	C
VIRGINVILLE	9196	BERKS	14	40 31	75 52	350		8A	MRS. MARY M. WRIGHT	3
VOWINCKEL	9208	CLARION	1	41 25	79 14	1620		8A	PA DEPT FRST + WTRS	3
VOWINCKEL 1 WSW	9209	CLARION	1	41 24	79 15	1610		8A	PA DEPT FRST + WTRS	3
WARREN	9298	WARREN	1	41 51	79 08	1780	7P	7A	GILBERT H. REIER	2 3 5
WASHINGTON	9312	WASHINGTON	11	40 11	80 14	1200		MID	PA DEPT HIGHWAYS	C
WATSONTOWN	9345	NORTHUMBLAND	16	41 05	76 52	490		9P	WILLIAM BIRD	3
WAYNESBURG 2 W	9362	GREENE	10	39 54	80 13	980	6P	7A	RALPH L. AMOS	2 3 5
WAYNESBURG 1 E	9367	GREENE	10	39 54	80 10	940		MID	SEWAGE DISPOSAL PLT	C
WEBSTER MILLS 3 SW	9380	FULTON	12	39 49	78 05	920		MID	WILLIAM D. COVER	C
WELLSBORO 3 S	9408	TIOGA	16	41 43	77 16	1920	7A	7A	MARION L. SHUMWAY	2 3 5
WELLSBORO 2 E	9412	TIOGA	16	41 45	77 16	1550		MID	MRS. IDA S. MAYNARD	C
WELLSVILLE	9420	YORK	15	40 03	76 57	500	5P	5P	D. D. HOOVER	2 3 5
WERNERSVILLE 1 W	9430	BERKS	14	40 20	76 06	405		8A	CHARLES A. GRUBER	3
WEST CHESTER	9464	CHESTER	5	39 58	75 36	440	8A	8A	DAILY LOCAL NEWS	2 3 5
WEST GROVE 1 E	9503	CHESTER	5	39 49	75 49	440		8A	CONARD-PYLE CO	3
WEST HICKORY	9507	FOREST	1	41 34	79 25	1090		8A	MRS.HELEN F.KINNEAR	3
WHITESBURG	9655	ARMSTRONG	1	40 45	79 24	1530		7A	CORPS OF ENGINEERS	3
WILKES-BARRE	9702	LAZERNE	15	41 15	75 52	610		7A	MRS. MARY G. MIRMAK	3
WILLIAMSBURG	9714	BLAIR	6	40 28	78 12	860		7A	MYRON K. BIDDLE	3
WILLIAMSPORT WB AP	9728	LYCOMING	16	41 15	76 55	527	MID	MID	U.S. WEATHER BUREAU	2 3 5 7 C
WIND GAP	9781	NORTHAMPTON	5	40 51	75 18	720		MID	OWEN R. PARRY	C
WOLFSBURG	9823	BEDFORD	6	40 03	78 32	1190		7A	WALTER C. RICE	3
YORK 3 SSW PUMP STA	9933	YORK	15	39 55	76 45	390	5P	5P	YORK WATER COMPANY	2 3 5
YORK 2 S FILTER PLANT	9938	YORK	15	39 56	76 44	640		MID	YORK WATER COMPANY	C
YORK HAVEN	9950	YORK	15	40 07	76 43	310		6A	METROPOL EDISON CO	3
YOUNGSVILLE	9966	WARREN	1	41 51	79 20	1225		MID	HENRY CARLETT	C
ZION GROVE	9990	SCHUYLKILL	15	40 54	76 13	940		7A	JAMES D. TEETER	3
ZIONSVILLE 3 SE	9995	LEHIGH	14	40 27	75 27	660		7A	LESLIE HOWATT	3
CLOSED STATIONS										
PALMYRA	6694	LEBANON	15	40 18	76 35	480		7P	EARL E. RHOADS	CLOSED 3/57

1 1-ALLEGHENY; 2-BEAVER; 3- 4-CONEMAUGH; 5-DELAWARE; 6-JUNIATA; 7-KISKIMINETAS; 8-LAKE ERIE; 9-LEHIGH; 10-MONONGAHELA; 11-OHIO; 12-POTOMAC; 13-LAKE ONTARIO; 14-SCHUYLKILL; 15-SUSQUEHANNA; 16-WEST BRANCH; 17-YOUGHIOGHENY

REFERENCE NOTES

Additional information regarding the climate of Pennsylvania may be obtained by writing to the State Climatologist at Weather Bureau Airport Station, Harrisburg State Airport, New Cumberland, Pennsylvania, or to any Weather Bureau Office near you.

Figures and letters following the station name, such as 12 SSW, indicate distance in miles and direction from the post office.

Delayed data and corrections will be carried only in the June and December issues of this bulletin.

Monthly and seasonal snowfall and heating degree days for the preceding 12 months will be carried in the June issue of this bulletin.

Stations appearing in the Index, but for which data are not listed in the tables, either are missing or were received too late to be included in this issue.

Divisions, as used in Table 2, become effective with data for September 1956.

Unless otherwise indicated, dimensional units used in this bulletin are: Temperature in °F, precipitation and evaporation in inches, and wind movement in miles. Monthly degree day totals are the sums of the negative departures of average daily temperatures from 65° F.

Evaporation is measured in the standard Weather Bureau type pan of 4 foot diameter unless otherwise shown by footnote following Table 6.

Long-term means for full-time stations (those shown in the Station Index as "U. S. Weather Bureau") are based on the period 1921-1950, adjusted to represent observations taken at the present location. Long-term means for all stations except full-time Weather Bureau stations are based on the period 1931-1955.

Water equivalent values published in Table 7 are the water equivalent of snow, sleet or ice on the ground. Samples for obtaining measurements are taken from different points for successive observations; consequently occasional drifting and other causes of local variability in the snowpack result in apparent inconsistencies in the record. Water equivalent of snow on the ground is measured at selected stations when two or more inches of snow are on the ground.

Entries of Snowfall in Tables 2 and 7, and in the seasonal snowfall table, include snow and sleet. Entries of snow on ground include snow, sleet and ice.

Data in Tables 3, 5, and 6 and snowfall in Table 7, when published, are for the 24 hours ending at time of observation. The Station Index lists observation times in the standard of time in local use.

Snow on ground in Table 7 is at observation time for all except Weather Bureau and CAA stations. For these stations snow on ground values are at 7:30 a.m., E.S.T.

- − No record in Tables 3, 6, 7 and the Station Index. No record in Tables 2 and 5, is indicated by no entry. Consult the annual issue of this publication for interpolated monthly precipitation totals.
- + And also on a later date or dates.
- ++ Fastest observed one minute wind speed. This station is not equipped with automatic wind instruments.
- * Amount included in following measurement, time distribution unknown.
- // Gage is equipped with a windshield.
- # Thermometers are generally exposed in a shelter located a few feet above sod-covered ground; however, the reference indicates that the thermometers are exposed in a shelter located on the roof of a building.
- AM Data based on observational day ending before noon.
- B Adjusted to a full month.
- C In the "Refer to Tables" column in the Station Index the letter "C" indicates recorder stations. These stations are processed for special purposes and are published later in "Hourly Precipitation Data".
- D Water equivalent of snowfall wholly or partly estimated, using a ratio of 1 inch water equivalent to every 10 inches of new snowfall.
- G In the "Refer to Tables" column in the Station Index the letter "G" indicates that soil temperatures are published.
- M One or more days of record missing; if average value is entered, less than 10 days record is missing. See Table 5 for detailed daily record. Degree day data, if carried for this station, have been adjusted to represent the value for a full month.
- R Amounts from recording gage (These amounts are essentially accurate but may vary slightly from the amounts to be published later in "Hourly Precipitation Data".)
- SS This entry in time of observation column in Station Index means observation made near sunset.
- T Trace, an amount too small to measure.
- Y Includes total for previous month.
- VAR This entry in time of observation column in Station Index means variable.

Information concerning the history of changes in locations, elevations, exposure etc. of substations through 1955 may be found in the publication "Substation History" for this state, soon to be issued. That publication, when available, may be obtained from the Superintendent of Documents, Government Printing Office, Washington 25, D. C. at a price to be announced. Similar information for regular Weather Bureau stations may be found in the latest issues of Local Climatological Data, Annual for the respective stations, obtained as indicated above, price 15 cents.

Subscription Price: 20 cents per copy, monthly and annual; $2.50 per year. (Yearly subscription includes the Annual Summary). Checks, and money orders should be made payable to the Superintendent of Documents. Remittance and correspondence regarding subscriptions should be sent to the Superintendent of Documents, Government Printing Office, Washington 25, D. C.

WWRC., Asheville, N. C. --- 5/3/57 --- 1100

U. S. DEPARTMENT OF COMMERCE
SINCLAIR WEEKS, Secretary
WEATHER BUREAU
F. W. REICHELDERFER, Chief

CLIMATOLOGICAL DATA

PENNSYLVANIA

APRIL 1957
Volume LXII No. 4

ASHEVILLE: 1957

GENERAL

Large scale features of the weather included a stormy period early in the month with strong winds, heavy precipitation, snow, and ice cast in discomforting roles; predominantly cold weather the first half of April; and a long period with unseasonably high temperatures the latter part of the month.

The average temperature at the majority of the stations was between two and four degrees higher than the seasonal value. Extreme temperatures ranged from 13° at Bradford 4 W Res and Coudersport on the 13th to 93° at Port Clinton on the 28th.

Precipitation totals were from one to three inches larger than average and ranged from 3.19 inches at Connellsville to 9.47 at Boswell 6 WNW. The greatest amount for one day was 2.28 inches measured at East Brady on the 4th.

WEATHER DETAILS

Precipitation was an almost daily feature through the 9th with many stations recording amounts that indicated heavy falls on more than one day of this period. Rain was the usual form of the precipitation but frozen forms such as snow, sleet, and frozen rain were rather heavy and widespread in the northern and mountainous portions of the State on the 4th and the 7th-8th. Precipitation was somewhat less frequent and lighter the middle and latter periods of April.

Temperature changes of appreciable magnitude were relatively frequent up to mid-month even though the weather was predominantly cold. A major warm-up from the 15th to the 20th boosted temperatures from late winter values to those applicable to early summer and warm weather persisted through the remainder of the month.

WEATHER EFFECTS

The persistent rainy weather of early April hindered field work in all areas and delayed planting of oats, peas, and gardens. Delays were most pronounced in the northwest. Lighter precipitation the latter half of April permitted planting of oats, potatoes, and peas at a rapid pace. Warm weather the latter part of the month brought a sudden surge of growth to winter grains, grasses, and fruit trees. Peach, cherry, pear, and early apple trees burst into bloom in the southern and some central areas. Pasture conditions at the end of April were the best for the time of year since 1945 and milk production had increased sharply in some herds

CLIMATOLOGICAL DATA

Temperature: Average Maximum	Average Minimum	Average	Departure From Long Term Means	Highest	Date	Lowest	Date	Degree Days	No. of Days Max 90° or Above	Max 32° or Below	Min 32° or Below	Min 0° or Below	Precipitation: Total	Departure From Long Term Means	Greatest Day	Date	Snow, Sleet Total	Max Depth on Ground	Date	No. of Days .10 or More	.50 or More	1.00 or More
58.0	41.0	49.5	4.9	83	28	24	13	469	0	0	8	0					8.5	6	5			
56.2	34.8	45.5		85	28	20	16	584	0	0	15	0			1.57	5	8.0	7	5		3	1
56.6M	36.3M	46.5M	4.1	84	27	21	13	557	0	0	12	0	6.58	2.69	1.44	4	10.6	10	4	9	5	3
60.3	40.3	50.3		85	27	23	11	450	0	0	11	0	6.93		1.47	2	7.5	4	4	11	6	2
55.3	35.8	45.6		84	28	19	13	587	0	0	15	0	7.49		2.07	5	12.1	8	5	9	6	2
53.6	34.5	44.1		81	28	19	10	624	0	2	14	0	5.82	1.97	1.43	5	11.0	8	5	11	5	2
60.6	39.8	50.2	2.4	88	28	26	1	460	0	0	11	0	6.24	3.21	1.60	5				13	4	1
59.3	38.9	49.1	2.1	84	27	25	3+	485	0	0	12	0	5.81	2.56	1.27	4	8.0	4	5	12	4	1
61.0	38.2	49.6	1.0	86	27	21	16	467	0	0	12	0	6.89	3.21	1.52	4	9.5	6	4	8	6	2
		47.8											6.54				9.4					
62.2	40.7	51.5	3.0	87	27+	26	11	420	0	0	10	0	6.49	3.10	1.71	5	3.1	2	4	9	5	3
61.4	42.0	51.7	2.8	88	28+	29	11+	420	0	0	7	0	6.66	3.18	1.55	5	2.1	1	4	10	5	3
65.5	40.2	52.9	1.7	90	28	27	1+	392	1	0	12	0	6.54	3.33	1.74	5		0		10	5	3
64.2	40.5	52.4	4.0	91	27	24	16	403	1	0	11	0	6.77	2.93	1.54	5	3.0	3	4	9	5	2
61.3	41.4	51.4	3.2	88	27	25	11+	427	0	0	9	0	6.65	3.58	1.86	5	4.0	3	4	10	6	1
62.6	37.7	50.2	.7	93	28	22	11+	460	1	0	12	0	6.41	2.27	1.72	2	2.5	0		8	4	2
		51.7											6.59				2.9					
64.5	42.5	53.5		89	29	24	15	368	0	0	3	0	5.00		1.31	2	.0	0		9	4	1
64.0	41.2	52.6	2.2	89	28+	24	11+	394	0	0	7	0	4.69	.96	1.13	2	T	T	14	10	4	1
66.4	43.6	55.0		91	28	27	11	332	2	0	7	0	4.78		1.56	5	.0	0		7	5	1
64.0	38.3	51.2		88	27	25	14	427	0	0	12	0	6.07		1.70	5	T	0		11	4	1
63.1	42.3	52.7	2.0	88	27	27	11+	394	0	0	10	0	5.72	2.37	1.45	5				10	5	1
64.4	42.1	53.3	3.0	89	27	24	11+	371	0	0	7	0	5.36	1.88	1.18	2	.8	0		11	5	2
65.6	43.0	54.3		90	28	26	10	363	1	0	7	0	5.86	2.67	1.57	5				10	5	1
62.8	45.2	54.0	2.5	86	27	32	11+	352	0	0	2	0	4.46	1.55	.99	5	T	0		6	5	0
66.2	42.3	54.3	4.5	90	28	26	11	349	1	0	8	0	4.52	1.07	1.33	5	T	0		10	2	1
61.8	40.6	51.2		87	28+	23	11	426	0	0	8	0	4.07		1.07	6	T	0		7	3	2
62.0	40.7	51.4	1.2	91	28	24	11	425	1	0	10	0	5.47	2.01	1.29	6	.5	1	4	8	4	3
65.5	46.3	55.9	1.4	92	21	34	15	306	1	0	0	0	4.72	1.24	1.29	2	T	0		10	4	1
63.8	45.0	54.4	4.3	91	27	27	11	348	1	0	3	0	4.37	.99	1.28	5	.4	0		10	3	1
62.3	40.9	51.6		87	27+	25	11+	418	0	0	9	0	4.28		1.30	5				11	2	1
63.5	42.2	52.9		88	27+	24	11	384	0	0	7	0	5.04		1.75	5				9	3	1
64.5	43.8	54.2		89	27	30	11	349	0	0	5	0	4.43		1.01	2	.0	0		9	3	1
65.6	46.1	55.9		91	27+	34	15	307	3	0	0	0	5.26		1.23	2	T	0		11	4	1
64.3	44.1	54.2	2.6	89	27	31	11+	346	0	0	2	0	4.22	.84	1.09	2	T	0		9	3	1
64.3	46.6	55.5	2.8	88	27+	34	13+	322	0	0	0	0	4.23		1.04	2	T	T	4	11	3	1
66.8	43.6	55.2	2.9	89	27	29	11+	328	0	0	7	0	4.39	1.03	1.00	2	.0	0				1
63.8	46.1	55.0	2.3	88	27	35	13+	326	0	0	0	0	4.40	1.02	.75	2				10	3	0
68.8	41.6	55.2	3.3	90	27+	24	16	328	3	0	8	0	5.17	1.79	1.28	5	.0	0		12	3	1
65.2	41.0	53.1	4.5	88	27	23	11	380	0	0	10	0	6.67	3.26	1.32	5				11	6	2
64.0	45.0	54.5	3.2	91	27	31	11	353	2	0	4	0	5.63	2.39	1.83	5	1.0	1	4	9	4	1
66.6	44.5	55.6		89	27	30	14	318	0	0	4	0	4.23		1.11	2	.0	0		8	3	1
																	.0	0				
		53.9											4.89				.1					
62.8	42.1	52.5	2.7	90	28	24	15	403	1	0	8	0	4.57	.99	.92	5	.0	0		8	4	0
66.9	44.9	55.9	5.2	92	27+	27	11	335	2	0	6	0	4.62	1.09	1.05	5				10	4	1
64.0	43.1	53.6	3.2	91	27	23	15	371	1	0	6	0	4.08	.91	1.21	5	T	0		10	3	1
64.5	44.3	54.4	3.3	91	28+	28	11	354	2	0	5	0	4.00	.41	1.13	5	T	0		6	4	1
64.9	42.0	53.5	1.2	92	28	26	15	374	1	0	7	0	4.18	.74	1.02	6				7	4	1
63.8	44.8	54.3	3.4	92	27	27	11	358	2	0	4	0	3.89	.92	1.43	5	.7	T	4+	8	2	1
66.5	43.3	54.9		90	27+	25	11	359	3	0	8	0										
65.8	42.9	54.4	3.6	92	27	26	11	353	1	0	7	0	3.62	.11	.99	5	.7	0		8	3	0
65.2	40.7	53.0		88	27	20	15	379	0	0	8	0	4.22		1.35	5	T	0		9	3	1
67.6	42.8	55.2	3.9	92	27	24	15	324	1	0	8	0	4.55	1.32	1.40	5				9	5	1
		54.2											4.19				.2					
63.7	41.7	52.7		89	27	23	11	399	0	0	10	0	6.10		1.59	5	4.0	4	4			
64.3	41.8	53.1		89	27	25	11	387	0	0	10	0	6.25		1.14	4	4.6	4	4	10	6	1
60.3	40.5	50.4		87	28	24	11	450	0	0	11	0	3.57		.62	6		4	4	10	2	0
62.9	41.6	52.3		90	28	24	1	418	1	0	10	0	5.00		1.10	2		1	4	9	4	2
63.8	41.4	52.6		90	28+	24	11	410	2	0	11	0	5.15	1.65	1.02	5	.5	0		8	5	1
61.9	41.1	51.5	2.1	88	27	22	11	425	0	0	10	0	5.48	1.93	1.18	4	5.2	5	4	9	5	1
61.6	41.9	51.8	2.7	88	27	24	11	418	0	0	10	0	6.30	2.76	1.74	4	5.9	3	4+	11	5	1
		52.1											5.41				4.0					
54.9	36.5	45.7		83	28	20	3	582	0	1	13	0	5.71		1.33	5				11	4	1
60.1	37.2	48.7		85	25+	20	1+	497	0	0	12	0	5.95		1.74	5	13.8	6	5	12	4	2
54.8	35.0	44.9		82	28	19	9+	601	0	1	14	0	6.67	2.97	1.61	5	10.0	5	5	10	5	2
57.7	35.3	46.5	.4	86	28	20	10+	568	0	0	14	0	5.04	2.19	1.38	5	15.3	8	9	9	5	1

See Reference Notes Following Station Index

TABLE 2 - CONTINUED

Station		
MONTROSE 1 E	AM	
TOWANDA		
WELLSBORO 3 S	AM	
DIVISION		
CENTRAL MOUNTAINS		
BELLEFONTE 4 S	AM	
DU BOIS 7 E		
EMPORIUM 2 SSW	AM	
LOCK HAVEN		
MADERA	AM	
PHILIPSBURG CAA AP		
RIDGWAY 3 W	AM	
STATE COLLEGE		
TAMARACK 2 S FIRE TWR	AM	
DIVISION		
SOUTH CENTRAL MOUNTAINS		
ALTOONA HORSESHOE CURVE		
ARTEMAS 1 WNW		
BURNT CABINS 2 NE		
EBENSBURG		
EVERETT 1 SW		
HUNTINGDON	AM	
JOHNSTOWN	AM	
KEGG		
MARTINSBURG CAA AP		
DIVISION		
SOUTHWEST PLATEAU		
BAKERSTOWN 3 WNW		63.9
BLAIRSVILLE 6 ENE		60.4
BURGETTSTOWN 2 W	AM	62.6
BUTLER		63.4
CLAYSVILLE 3 W		65.3
CONFLUENCE 1 SW DAM	AM	62.6
DERRY		64.4
DONEGAL		57.6
DONORA	AM	68.3
FORD CITY 4 S DAM	AM	61.2
INDIANA 3 SE		63.9
IRWIN		66.9M
MIDLAND DAM 7		61.8
NEW CASTLE 1 N		63.5
NEWELL	AM	68.7
NEW STANTON		65.9
PITTSBURGH WB AP 2	//R	62.2
PITTSBURGH WB CITY	R	64.3
PUTNEYVILLE 2 SE DAM	AM	60.5
SALINA 3 W		63.5
SHIPPINGPORT WB		62.8
SLIPPERY ROCK		60.9
SOMERSET MAIN ST		63.0
SPRINGS 1 SW		59.8
UNIONTOWN		66.7
WAYNESBURG 2 W		66.7
DIVISION		
NORTHWEST PLATEAU		
BRADFORD 4 W RES		57.0
BROOKVILLE CAA AIRPORT		59.0
CLARION 3 SW		61.8
CORRY		57.5
COUDERSPORT 3 NW		55.3
EAST BRADY		65.3
ERIE WB AIRPORT		55.7
FARRELL SHARON		60.4
FRANKLIN		60.6
GREENVILLE		62.1
JAMESTOWN 2 NW	AM	57.9
KANE 1 NNE	AM	56.4
LINESVILLE 5 WNW		58.8
MEADVILLE 1 S	AM	58.1
MERCER 2 NNE		59.3
SPRINGBORO	AM	
TIONESTA 2 SE DAM	AM	
TITUSVILLE WATER WORKS		
WARREN		
DIVISION		

† DATA RECEIVED TOO LATE TO BE INCLUDED IN DIVISION AVERAGES

DAILY PRECIPITATION

Day of month

	Total	1	2	3	4	5	6	7	8	9	10	11	12	13	14	15	16	17	18	19	20	21	22	23	24	25	26	27	28	29	30	31
	8.01		.87	.10	.88	1.06	.62	.03	.05	.72	.08			T	.01			.16	.54	.17				.01	.71	T	.02	T				
R	8.40	.20	1.12		1.23	1.71	.19	T	.61	.05			.06					.13	.73	.01	T	T	T	.31	.08	T	.06			T		
	8.66		1.53	.12	.24	1.59	1.27	.01		.65				.07					.56	.25			T	.14	.05	.03	.19		T	T		
E	5.07	.05	.85		1.05	.26	.27		.54	.35					.04			.10	.67		.02			.03	.37	.39	.08			.02		
	4.57		.80		T	.02	.75			.77								T	.14	.19					.44		.48		.08			
	5.00		*		*	1.50			.82																							
	5.71		.21	T	.31	1.35	.26		.40	.85	T	T		T	T			.18	.05	.50	.55				1.44	.50		.05				
	8.85	.26	1.78	.11	1.13				.75	.06					.04			.15	T	.04		.12		T	.16	1.03	.11	.32				
	5.06		.40	.07	.70	.65	.40	T	.50	.77			.01	T	.08	T	T	.10	.19	.12		.02		1.44	.28	.54	.18		.09			
	-	-	-			.32	.44								-				.29	.17		T		T	.04	T	1.00	.68				
	5.71		.04		1.02	.84	.34		.83	.44								.07	.54	.10				.48								
	5.98	T	.57	.04	.01	.70	.30	T	.12	.06	T		T	T	.05	T		.06	.38	.09		.13		T	1.05	.23	.03			.05		
	8.10		1.15		*	1.59	.71	T	.05	1.02					T			.02	.47	.16				.20	.05	.13	.24	.13		.03		
	-		.74	.02	.89	1.31	.49		.18	.87								T	.62	-		-	-	-	-	-	.03	.67	-	-	-	
	5.03		.85	T	.53	.94	.30	.07	.09	.73					T			.02	.60	.06	T	T		.18	.16	.03	T	.49				
	5.90		1.30	T	.40	1.33	1.08			.77				T																		
	6.25	T	.88		1.14	.01	.32	T	.75	.19			T						.30	.50				T	T	T	.17			.09		
	8.23		1.11	.14	.12	1.49	1.50			.59				.07				.03	.40	.15		T		.75		.66	T	T				
	6.54	.21	1.15	T	1.26	1.74	.19		.66				.00	T					.55	.26				.27	T	T	.13			T		
	5.36	.23	.07	.02	.73	.29	.04	.01	.46	.13			.01	.02	.02			.15	.68	T				.27			.14					
																	.02	.42		.01	.01		.05	.43	.46	.24	.11		T			
	4.20	T	.72		.46	.08	.32		.52	.20			T					.08	.14	.10				T	.68	T	.06	.04				
	9.47		*	1.13	.23	.12	.85	.53	.02	.84	.08	.01		.05	.19			.17	1.02	.08		.08	.05	.05	.55	1.89	1.53					
	5.09		1.09	.10	.59	.90	.26	T	.02	.51	.04			T	.04			.16	.97	.12					.07	.18	.08					
A	6.15		.48	.46	*	.76	.54	.09	.50	.78	.02		.06		.02			.08	.18	.22		.17		.07	.01	.40	1.21	.10		T		
	8.09		.48		.71	.14	.68	.08	.94	.41		.05	.03	.02	.02			.13	.21	.06	.12	.05		.12		.42	1.30	.12		T		
	3.53	.38	.14	.03	.52	.47	.16		.37				.04				.03	.36	.07	.03	.20	.04	.01	.03	.31	.22	.12					
	5.02	.23	.12	.03	1.54	.35	.05	.21	1.01	.06	T		T	.06	.01		.03	.22	.19			T		.20	.58	.09	.02					
	4.43	.01	1.15	.05	.59	.69	*	*	.16	.45	T					T		.19	.68	.09					T	.08	.08		.02			
	5.31		.75	.01	.03	.57	.18			.69					T			T	.21	.01		.42		.03	.06	2.07	.28			.01		
	5.84		.87	.11	.77	1.14	.75		.21	.64				.02	.01			.19	.47	.21		.03			.01		.38	.02		.01		
	-		.62		.24	.80	.33		.75						.01			.45		-	-	-		.35		.12	.17					
	7.18		.83		1.55	.99	.79		.30	.83				.02	.01			.27	.28	.08		.06			.93	.01	.17	.06				
	4.04	.10	.65		.35	1.43	.35		.63				T	.03				.04	.17					.12	.10		.07	T				
	5.71		.28	.03	.24	1.33	.45		.41	.87			T		T			T	.18	.37		.02		.52	.02	.67	.32					
	4.62	.04	.70		.40	1.05	.38		.68	.20			T					.08	.15	.10	.02			.02	.50	T	.30					
	5.52		.09	.12	.83	.93	.36	T		.60				.01	.05	T		.07	.46	.27			T	T	.60	.16	.06			.01		
	5.98		.74	.05	.45	1.23	.47	T	.48	.50	T	T			T			T	.35	.20				.20		*	1.22	T				
	7.00		.60		.40	1.33	.42	T	.50	.85	.01	.02			T			.01	.40	.15		.05	T	.06	.25	1.20	.58	.15	.05			
	3.79		.45			.75	.80	.20										T	T	.20	T			.05		T	.65			.69		
	4.08	.55	.26		.24	1.21	.08		.81				T	T				.11	.21		.05			.18	.03	.11	.24		T			
	5.11		1.01	.00	.39	.58	.48	.04	.04	.70	.02				.02			.19	1.12	.11		.05	.01	T	T	.08	.10	.08		.03		
	5.00	.17	1.31	T	T	.81	.78			.36								T	.05	.18	T			.12		T	.82			.40		
	5.22		.60	.03	.78	1.39	.20		.16	.78	T				.03			T	.60	.09		.03		.43	.06	.01	.04	.04				
	6.64		.47	.03	.84	1.49	.84	.06	.47	1.02	.03			.05	.05	.03		.08	.24	.12				.03	.60	.02	.14	.03		.02		
	6.12		1.24	.05	.52	1.36	.91	.02		.76				.03					.58	.23	.02			.15	.02	.06	.10		.09			
	4.77	T	.85	.12	.45	.78	.47		.06	.42	.05		T		T			.15	1.12	.04		.01	.14	.02	.01			.04		.01		
	6.10		.96		.72	1.27	.28	.03	.12	.95					.04			.08	.62	.11		.03	.08	.32	.25	.08	T	.16				
	-		.65	T	.40	.60	.36	.05	.50	.68	.05		.08	T	.06			.14	.23	.11		.10	.02	.05		.62	-	.56	.02			
	6.85		1.44		.20	1.50	.98			.83				.10					.60	.33		.04		.39		.29	.14					
	4.69		1.13	.02	T	.90	.88			.45				T	T			T	.11	.27				.11	.06	.10	.56			.13	T	
	4.78	T	.98		.19	1.56	.70		.46	.09			T	T				T	T	.52				.02	T		.64			.08		
	3.41		.85	.04	.02	.25	.39	.02	T	.77	T			.01	.02			.04	.41	T		.10		T	T	.48	.01					
	4.24		.99	.06	.03	.28	.57	T	T	.79	T			T	.03			.08	.45			.17	.08	T		.68	.05					
	3.10		.65	.05	.12	.14	.19		.01	.66	.02				.02			.11	.85	.05			.06			.08	.21			.01		
	4.58		1.14	T	.10	.09	.85	T		.40				.02					.18	.18				.30	T		.29	.02		.18		
	6.46	T	.45	.04	.55	.94	.62	.09	.70	1.12	T		T	.04	.08	T		.10	.29	.14	T	.15	T	.03	.70	.04	.38	T		T		
	5.74	T	.43	.03	.63	.87	.52	.03	.79	.93	.15	T	T	.02	.15	T		.11	.22	.18	T	.01		.06	.56	.83	.02	T		T		
	5.09		.75	.04	1.10	.82	*	*	.48	.84	.03							.22	.36	.15					.52		.08					
	5.89		.34		1.01		.29	.31	.60	.34	T	.08	T	.11	.20			.13	.21	.27	T	.03		.10	.05	.73	.89	.15	.05			
	5.68		.40		.36	.80	.25	.02	.40	.60	.02	T	.02	T	T			.02	.22	.28		.14	T	.07	T	1.31	.59	.09		T		
	6.02		.96	.02	.23	1.10	.27	.01	.58	.79	.01	T	.01					.03	.23	.27		.11	.01	.12		.88	.27	.31	.21			
	4.62		.18	.12	.17	.65	.22		.39	.56					T				.15	.35		.40		.16	.27	.60	.17		.14			
	6.96		1.29	*	1.00	.95	.33		.02	.77					.06			.10	.62	.25					.30	1.00	.07					
	4.53		.73		.49	.47	.32	.02		.78					.05			.02	.40	.29		.08		.02	.48	.24	.14					
	6.09		.56	.05	.36	1.02	.45	.13	.56	.99	.05		.02	.02				.13	.18	.16		.05	T	.04	.01	.30	.88	.13				
	5.94		.94	.05	.20	1.32	.51		.08	.92									.67	.13				.38	.10	.05	.12	.42		.05		
	5.36	T	1.09		.62	.19	.05		.41	.20			.02	T	T	.06	T	.45	.55	.02	.05	.03		T	.99	.67						
	6.07	.17	.90		.47	1.70	.46		.63	.11			.02					.08	.52	.21				.46		.05	.27		.02	T		
	5.95		.49	.10	.15	1.74	.88	.09	.18	1.02				.03		T		T	.12	.55		.06		.23		.15	.14		.02			
	6.15	.64	.62	T	.50	.49	.15		.98	.10	T		.07	.07	.10		.07	1.15	.32		.01	.17	T	T	.39	.32			T			
	4.67	T	1.07	T	.74	.23	.45	T	.26	.41	.04		T	T	.01		T	.21	1.00	.04		.01		T	.02	.11	.05	.02		T		
	5.23	T	.01		.55	.01	.71		.39	.12				.06				.03	.29	.71				.12	T		.07	.01		.35		
	5.20	T	.73		1.44	.09	.33	T	.71	.35				T	.04		T	.14	.42		T	.02		.20	.55	.02	T	.16				
	5.50		.42	.20	.35	1.15	.75		.27	1.07				T	T				.22	.36		.15				.15	.30	.11				
	6.67		.85	.05	.29	1.61	.91	T	.13	1.14					T	T		.02	.32	.34				.57	.07	.30			T	T		
	5.65		.58		2.28				1.45	.39			.01		.02	.01	.01	.25	.22					.03	.30	.03	.10					
	5.97		.01	T	.70	.86	.37	T	T	.70				T	.11			T	.45	.25				T	.53	.77	.23			T		
	5.77		.29		.71	.60	.21	.22	.80	.53	T		.13	.03	.05			.06	.12	.04		.03		.02	.26	.25	1.01	.07	.34			
	-	.02	.23	.19	.34	.54	.23	.19	-	.42			.02		.04			-	.20	-				.31	.20	.46	1.30		.28			
	4.85		.89		.05	.93	1.14			.64								T	.16	.16				.02		.07	.73		.08			
	5.43		.65	.02	.55	1.10	.22	T	.60	.86	T		T		T			.06	.29	.19		.05		.27		.27	.84	.26	.02			
	6.64		.63	.03	.32	1.25	.40		.33	.96	T								.29	.29	T	.02		.32	.16	1.32	.14	.18				
	5.72		.98		.31	1.45	.50		.95	.12				.03				.03	.20	.12				.05			.20			.78		
	4.35		.46	.12	*	1.45	.71		.07	.89	.02			.02	T				.06	.21							.18		.20			
	6.33	.05	.20		1.43	.28	.38	.54	.52	.05	T	.03	.18	T			T	.19	.09			T		.13	.65	1.05	.27	.27	.02			
	4.88	.56	.31		.24	.71			.75									.31	.01		.19				1.35	.35						
	6.47	.08	.44		1.46	.11	.04	.41	.80	.20				.30	.03			.26	.21			T		.24	1.60	.08	.01		T			
	5.95		.77	.03	.06	1.12	.60	.02	.16	.60				T	.07	T		.17	.40	.18					.60	.11	.03	.04				
	6.16		.37	.06	1.13	.65	.29	.06	.82	.90			T	.01	.06			.05	.16	.07		.07			.40	.11	.74	.24		.01		
	-		.40	.03	.03	1.20	.13		-	-	T		T	.05	T	T			.45	.35				-			.10	.38	.10	.14		
	6.37		.62	.02	.38	1.09	.64	.02	.38	.80			T	T	T	T		T	.37			.22	.18			1.28	.10	.25	.02	T		
	4.79		.89		.21	1.00	.77			.59				.02					.19	.25				.05			.42			.44		
	5.36		1.18		.82	1.07	.67		.30	.11			T	.03				.09	.18	.62				.29		T	.11			.23		
	4.00		.72		T	1.13	.94			.71					T				.08	.02	T	T			.11		.29					
	6.86		.57	.03	1.28	.25	.40	.05	.55	1.10	T		T	T	.05			.10	.22	.16		.11		.08	T	.29	1.09	.53				
	5.13		.35	.03	.81	.66	.37	.06	.69	.61	T		.02	.04	.05	T		.12	.25	.17		.01		.10	.01	.70	.20	.18		T		
	5.74		.78	.00	.06	1.13	.31	.01	.05	.90	.08			.02	.02	T		.12	.42	.25		.13		T	.25	.16	.04	.01		.01		
	6.16		.60	.10	.16	1.64	.59		.04	.93				.20					.23	.45		.23		.40	.45		T					
	5.86		.69	.71	.12	1.57	.96			.57									.19	.38				.08				.11		.48		
	3.57		.60	T	.43	.48	.62		T	.17				T				T	.37	.15				T	.15	.06	.33	.21		T		
	3.62		.76	.03	.12	.27	.18	.02	.01	.77	T			.01	.02			.07	.58	.02		.18		.11	.18	.04	.20	.04		.01		
	4.62	.20	.83	T	.78	.37	.03		.46	.28	T				.02		.06	.42	.72	.03	T				.01	.30	.03					
	6.10		.69		1.33	.16	.08	.20	1.28	.28	T	T	.07	T	.02		.01	.21	.15		.02	.02		.21	.63	.27	.32		.15			
	4.18		.79	T	T	.01	1.02			.58				T					.12	.07		T			.37					.32		
R	3.89	.47	.27		.27	1.43	.39		.62	.04	T		.02		T			.06	.14	T	T			.03	.08	.13	T	T	T	T		
	4.34		.70		.10	.84	1.08			.87				.06				T	.18	.20	T			.03	.11		.03	.05				
	4.94		.40	.05	.12	1.57	.59	.02	.05	1.05	T			.12	T	T			.07	.22		.03		.17	.01	.23	.10	T	.05			
	-		.37	.05	.10	1.57	.68		.04	.93				.05					.07	-		.02		.18		.44	.30					
	6.11		.69	.01	.22	1.77	.76	.02	.11	1.05	T			.18	T	T		T	.14	.33		.08		.36	.27	T	.16		T			
	4.46		.74	T	T	.09	.86			.59	.01			.02	T			.01	.18	.08		T		.02	.03	T	.92		T	.01		
	5.42		.73	.02	.11	1.69	.86	T	.11	1.03	T			.14					.05	.28		.06		.01	.27		.06					
	4.88		.80	.06	.24	.41	.33	T		.90	.03			T	.07	T		.06	.78	.09		.03	.05	.04	.11	.58	.30			T		
	5.13			.95	.05	.67	.41		.95	.70	.05			.01	.02	T			T	.15		.03	.17	.21	.03	.15	.28	T	.30	T		
	5.51		1.11	.01	.68	.81	.25	.02	.01	1.05	.01				T			.01	.45	.32		.02			.58	.10	.07	.01				
	4.33		.71		.08	.81	.71			.79				T				.01	.27	.13					.80		.09		.13			

DAILY PRECIPITATION

Table 3—Continued

Station	Total	1	2	3	4	5	6	7	8	9	10	11	12	13	14	15	16	17	18	19	20	21	22	23	24	25	26	27	28	29	30
HYNDMAN	4.57		.76	.01	.03	.52	.19	.01	T	.55	T				T			.03	.21	.01		.36	.03	.02		1.64	.20				
INDIANA 3 SE	5.62	T	1.05	.10	.87	.86	.30	.02		.65				T	.06	T		.11	.56	.23				.01	.56	.16	.05			.01	
IRWIN	4.85	.14	1.24		1.21	.09			.48	.09			.02				.02	.48	.67					.05	.04	.23	.09				
JAMESTOWN 2 NW	3.46		.61		.02	.50	.14	.04	.86	.45	T		.09	.04	.02			.04	.20	.10	.02			.01	.90	.22	.30				
JIM THORPE	6.77		1.39		.48	1.54	.49		.57	.30			T	.09				.02	.63	.31				.80		.08	.06				
JOHNSTOWN	7.03		.97	.15	.89	.68	.21		.26	.76				T	.05			.16	.56	.26		T		T	.55	1.21	.32				
KANE 1 NNE	6.38		.35	.20	.98	.98	.16	.18	.65	.81	T		.02	.02	.07	T		.12	.20	.06		.21	T	.14	.05	.10	.75	.33	T		
KARTHAUS	5.11		.71	.03	.84	1.23	.28	T	.17	.80					T			.02	.44	.07		.10		.37	.06	.06	.03	.10		T	
KEATING SUMMIT	6.69		.75	.09	.44	1.03	.33	.06	.39	.88	T		.04	T				.08	.25	.18		.15	.02	.21		1.13	.37	.08	.21		
KEGG	3.83	.64	.22	T	.28	.47	.01		.74	.04			T	T				.23	.09		.25	.08	.01	.03	T	.74	T				
KITTANNING LOCK 7	6.62		.81	.02	1.15	1.20	.85	.02	.24	.73				T	.02	T		.24	.35	.14		.10		T	.72	.05	.06	.12			
KREGAR 4 SE	6.77	.74	.48	.06	.38	.60	.09		.94	.17	T		.05	.10	.02		.04	1.09	.35		.12	.10	.03	.09	.80	.60			.02		
KRESGEVILLE 3 W	6.62		1.11	.13	.09	1.60	1.14			.83				.13					.46	.25		.08		.46	.23	.03	.08				
LAFAYETTE MC KEAN PARK	7.45		.45		.36	.96	.41	*	.65	1.68	.04		T	.60				.13	.20	.14		.14	T	.28		.10	.81	.41			
LAKEVILLE 1 NNE	5.31		.59	T	.24	1.89	.66	T	.06	1.12		T			T	T	T	T	.08	.24		.06		.18	T	T	.19	T			
LANCASTER 2 NE PUMP STA	4.52	.01	.72		.14	1.33	.42		.40	.09				.02	.01			.05	.12	.31				.04	.18		.21			.47	
LANDISVILLE 2 NW	4.07		.75	T	.05	1.01	1.07	T		.45					T				.18	.14				.02		.06	.26			.08	
LAWRENCEVILLE 2 S	5.04		.09		.19	1.38	.21		.33	.63			.03						.06	.60		.52		T	.08	.70	.04	.19	.05		
LEBANON 3 W	5.47		1.00	.01	.24	1.06	1.29			.80				.08	T				.23	.28				.09		.01	.36	.02			
LEHIGHTON	6.42		1.33	T	.16	1.80	.67	T	T	.80	T			.08					.52	.28		T		.60	.03	.10	.02	.03			
LE ROY	4.91				.60	.55	.09		.89	.64										.69				.60		.58	.26	.01			
LEWIS RUN 3 SE	6.91		.54	T	.27	1.12	.43	.09	.57	.93	.03		T	.01	.07	T		.08	.18	.08		.08	T	.07	.02	.26	1.05	1.03		T	
LEWISTOWN	5.00		1.10	.02	.40	1.03	.34		T	.45					.01			.01	.34	.25				.03	.08	.16	.05	.53		T	
LINESVILLE 5 WNW	5.83	T	.31		.98	.38	.37	.15	.84	.51	T		.08	.04	.04			.07	.19	.04				.02	.30	.18	.98	.18	.17		
LOCK HAVEN	6.30		.79	T	.32	1.52	.42	T	.16	.83						T	.02		.47	.08		.20		.15	.30		.10	1.03	T	T	
LONG POND 2 W	5.89		1.07	.09	.15	1.47	.81		.02	.75				.11	.03			T	.34	.60		.03		.40	T	T	.02			T	
LYNDELL 2 NW	5.27		.40	.20	.47	1.53	.86			.53									.20	.40				.19			.49				
MADERA	6.31		.80	.06	.45	1.12	.41	.02	.15	.70	.10			T	.02	.02		.08	.50	.13		.03		.12	1.25	.11	T	.06			
MAHAFFEY	8.09		1.05	.07	.74	1.96	.36	.07	.11	.95	.03			T	.05	T		.12	.62	.12		.01		.12	1.35	.15	.08	.13			
MAPLE GLEN	4.55		.90		.35	.81	.65		.25	.03			T	T				.02	.20	.37		.01		.29		T	.15	.01		.51	
MAPLETON DEPOT	4.15		1.05	T	.47	.72	.16			.76					.02			T	.32	.10				.02	.19	.14	.13	.01		.02	
MARCUS HOOK	4.72	.12	1.29		.27	.53	.62		.33	.02			.02	T				.03	.11	T				.12	T	.02	.40		.82	.02	
MARION CENTER 2 SE	6.69		1.13	.02	.94	.72	.38	.08	.13	.78	T			.03	.09	T		.22	.64	.19					.73	.60	.01				
MARTINSBURG CAA AP	5.01	.62	.28	T	.61	.57	T		.80	.03	T		T	.03	T		T	.29	.27		.10			.19	.81	.15	.26				
MATAMORAS	5.10		.58	.14	*	1.38	.95	.06		.74									.08	.42				.21	.04		.31		.21		
MAYBURG	6.05		.28		.75	.45	.80	T	.55	.75			T		.08	T		.12	.05	.03		T	T	T	.05	T	1.52	.62			
MC CONNELLSBURG	3.38		.69	.02	.05	.77	.47			.54								.07	.23	.02	.11	.03	.01		.09	.17	.11				
MC KEESPORT	4.59		1.20	.05	1.04	.10	T		.38	.46	.03			.02	T			.20	.77	.12		.03		T	.04	.14	T				
MEADVILLE 1 S	6.60	T	.49	T	.99	.53	.25	.10	.82	.37	T		.06	.02	.04	T		.06	.25	.07		.01	T	.03	.38	.82	1.06	.14	.03	T	
MEDIX RUN	5.03		.47	.03	.69	1.07	.21	.02	.32	.84	T			T	.01	T		.03	.31	.05		.07	T	.56	.02	.12	.03	.18		T	
MERCER 2 NNE	-		-		1.35	.40	1.80	.20	.20	.45				T					.02	.10					.46	1.65	.20			T	
MERCERSBURG	4.32		.64		.30	1.00	.58			.75								.10	.10	.05		.25			.30		.06		.10		
MEYERSDALE 1 ENE	3.49		.73	.86		.57	.29		.05	.85	.04				.09			.05	.18							.35	.27				
MIDDLETOWN OLMSTED FLD	4.37	.50	.40		.39	1.28	.24		.74	.10			.07		T			.14	.19	T				T	.05	.19	.03	.04	.01	T	
MIDLAND DAM 7	5.61		.66	.06	1.16	1.01	.26		.16	.78	T			T	.03			.12	.44	.16		T			.08	.09	.56	T		T	
MILANVILLE	5.50		.74	.15		1.53	.77	.06	.06	1.03				.08					.07	.20		T		T	.24	T	.42		.15		
MILLHEIM	5.57		1.00	T	.72	1.11	.49	T	.06	.66					T	T		.01	.64	.07		.01		.35	.04		.07	.38			
MILLVILLE 2 SW	6.02		.95	.14	.18	1.57	.84	T	.13	.95		T						.01	.55	.18		T		.13	.34	.24	.03	.08			
MILROY	5.62		1.31		.56	1.04	.41		.03	.87					T	.02		.05	.56	.14				.11	.12	.03	T	.37			
MONTROSE 1 E	5.70		.47	.21	.03	1.68	.67	T	.24	.74	.01	T	T	.07	T	T		.03	.07	.37		.12		.01	.01	.08	.33		.56		
MORGANTOWN	4.28	.14	.56		.32	1.30	.26		.43	.05			.04		T			.11	.32	.05				.10		.02	.21		.37		
MT GRETNA 2 SE	5.04	.34	.60		.38	1.75	.10		.64	.04			.08		.03			.13	.23	.07				.05	.01		.47	.05			
MT POCONO 2 N AP	6.58	T	1.03		1.44	1.42	.35		.70	.18			.07	.05	T				.36	.25		.09		.54		.06	.04	T			
MUHLENBURG 1 SE	6.93		1.47		1.41	.87	.50	.01	.81	.24			.01					.02	.40	.34				.55	.10	.16	.04				
MYERSTOWN	6.11		.85	.10	.25	1.80	1.20			.72				.08					.25	.29				.09	.01		.47				
NATRONA LOCK 4	6.46		.80	.07	.94	1.07	.61	.08	.02	.73				T	.07			.14	.52	.21					.79	.46					
NESHAMINY FALLS	4.50	.08	.94		.52	.84	.57		.30	.05			T					.05	.35				T	.46	T	.02			.11	.12	
NEWBURG 3 W	-	-	-	-	-	-	-	-	-	-	-	-	-	-	-	-	-	-	-	-	-	-	-	-	-	-	-	-	-	-	-
NEW CASTLE 1 N	5.53		.38	T	1.15	.78	.45	.03	.75	.82	T		T	T	.05	T		.13	.26	.16					.47	.04	.04			T	
NEWELL	4.62		1.06		.74	.22	.30		.21	.35								.26	.99	.04				.10		.07	.25			.03	
NEW PARK	4.76	.02	.88		.06	1.90	.49		.43	.20								.30	.25	.05					.18						
NEWPORT	5.15		.74	.01	.47	1.02	.77		T	.97					T			T	.35	.18	T			.03	.03	T	.01	.57		T	
NEW STANTON	4.10	.62	.31	.04	.68	.29	T		.62	.02	T			.02	T		.03	.80	.41	.01	T	.22	T		.04	.08					
NEW TRIPOLI	8.97	T	1.40		1.08	1.45	.60		.76	.16			.02	.02				.03	.64	.26		T		.30	T	.09	.08				
NORRISTOWN	4.43		1.01	T	.08	.93	.83			.34				.03					.13	.23				.37	.01		.18			.29	
NORTH EAST 2 SE	5.51		.24	.10	.65	.47	.22	.26	.60	.39			.30	.04	.07			.04	.04	.09						.19	1.16	.08	.47	.01	
ORWELL 3 N	4.85		.47	.02	.06	.77	.37		.44	1.00								T	.04	.39		.06		T	.17	.14	.13		.79		
PALM	7.08		1.30	.17	.32	1.54	1.35			.90									.38	.70				.15		.05	.22				
PALMERTON	8.65	.28	.99		.80	1.86	.12	T	.63	.09			.04	T	T			.11	.64	.02	.02	.01		.65	.33	.02	.06				
PARKER	5.95		.49		.98	.96	.62	.02	.42	.87	T		T	T	.09			.04	.15	.05				T	.85	.08	.16	.17		T	
PAUPACK 2 WNW	5.12		.54		.14	2.00	.60			1.02									.11	.26		.07		.28				.08			
PECKS POND	5.17		.85		.22	1.60	.77		.03	.80				.09					.11	.31	T	.04		.29	.06		T		T		
PHIL DREXEL INST OF TEC	5.26	.10	1.25		.30	.48	.85		.21				.02					.06	.20	T				.15			.76		.80	.10	
PHILADELPHIA WB AP R	4.22	.06	1.09		.32	.42	.70		.32	T			.0'					.01	.18	.04	T	T		.17	T	T	.63		.22	.05	
PHILADELPHIA PT BREEZE	4.23	.05	1.04		.34	.43	.66		.33				.02					.01	.18	.14				.18		T	.62		.10	.13	
PHILADELPHIA SHAWMONT	4.39		1.00		.86	*	.95		.15	.20								.05	.11	.18				.28			.28		.30	.05	
PHILADELPHIA CITY R	4.40	.05	.75		.35	.45	.73		.31									.01	.23	.12				.20			.49		.65	.06	
PHILIPSBURG CAA AP	5.14	.63	.31	.06	1.56	.34	.02	.09	.70	.08	T		T	.03	T		T	.26	.23	T	T			.12	.22	.09	.20				
PHOENIXVILLE 1 E	5.17	.15	.86		.55	1.28	.42		.48	.04			.06					.16	.24	.01				.29	T	T	.18	.11	.33	.01	
PIKES CREEK	7.57		1.23	.07	.39	2.03	.87	T	.16	1.07				T	T	T		T	.25	.37				.43	T	.29	.08	T	.35		
PIMPLE HILL	7.49		1.40	T	.52	2.07	.78	T	T	.95	T	T		.15	T	T		T	.41	.68	T	.01		.48	T	.02	.04			T	T
PINE GROVE 1 NE	6.42		1.23	T	.50	1.26	1.09			.89				.09		T		T	.35	.88				.03	.02	T	.06	T		.02	
PITTSBURGH WB AP 2 //R	4.58	.45	.24	.30	1.57	.26	.03	T	.73	.08			.02	.02	T		.03	.40	.32		.05			.06	T	.01	T		T	.01	
PITTSBURGH WB CITY R	4.94	.55	.43	.15	1.54	.33	.03		.67	.02			T	.03			.02	.31	.46		T			.07	T	.09	.01		.01		
PLEASANT MOUNT 1 W	5.82		.54	.13	.02	1.43	1.08	.04	.13	.75	.04	T		.12		T		T	.05	.34		.07		T	.13	T	.67		.28		
PORT CLINTON	6.41		1.72		.45	1.43	.95			.89				.02					.49	.30				.03		.05	.10				
POTTSVILLE	6.62		1.11	.01	.41	1.37	1.51	T		.98				.08				T	.57	.22	T			.08	.04	.14	.10	.02			
PUTNEYVILLE 2 SE DAM	5.95		.66		.94	.97	.34	.01	.26	.88	.04			T	.03				.39	.12			.04	.04	.58	.01	.20	.44			
QUAKERTOWN 1 E	8.67	T	1.12		.89	1.32	.38		.59	.12				.08				.08	.44	.87				.16	.70		.16	T			
RAYMOND	6.58		.40	.07	.20	1.15	.40	.04	.36	.94		.03			.01			.03	.20	.35		.16		.08		1.33	.35	.48			
READING WB CITY R	5.63	.24	.93		.74	1.83	.16		.53	.03			.03		T			.09	.46	.04		T		.14	.01	T	.34	T	.08	.01	
RENOVO	5.19		.63	.05	.48	1.37	.39	T	.30	.94								T	.29	.14		.05		.27	.05	.17	.05	.05			
REW	5.60		.58	.07	.30	.97	.35	.05	.50	.76	T	T	.02	.02	.01	.01		.05	.17	.17		.13		.05		.26	.97	.14			
RICES LANDING L 6	4.03		.69	.07	.21	.30	.33		.05	.57					.02			.15	.99	.03		.10				.09	.40			.03	
RIDGWAY 3 W	6.24		.46	.04	.66	.86	.37	.07	.55	.88				.01	.06			.08	.21	.33		.05		.33	.02	1.02	.26				
RUSH	5.19		.43	.08	.19	1.45	.32		.40	.94				.11				T	.05	.38		.18		.05	.12	.20	.17		.12		
RUSHVILLE	4.76		.33	.15	T	1.17	.36		.32	.87				.02					.03	.44		.09		.07	.35	.18	.22		.16		
SAGAMORE 1 S	8.51		1.15	.35	.20	1.29	.15	.20	.94	T					.08			.20	.40	.10					1.20	.69					
SALINA 3 W	6.20	.10	1.25	.02	1.80	.83	.05		.40	.12	T				.01		.02	.36	.60						.65	.02	.03				
SAXTON	4.05		.93	T	.18	.70	.17	T		.73	T			T	T	T		T	.44	.09		T		.01	.14	.62	.04	T		T	
SCHENLEY LOCK 5	8.20		.80	.04	1.22	1.10	.34	.01	.18	.70				T	.07	T		.23	.35	.15			T	T	.91	.10	T				
SCRANTON	6.24		.90	.10	.25	1.60	.80	.03	.15	.85				.15					.12	.40		.17		.41	.20	.06	.02		.03		
SCRANTON WB AIRPORT	5.81	.14	.81		1.27	.72	.25	.15	.83	.05	T		.14	T	T			.01	.47		.26			.38		.03	T	.30	T		
SELINSGROVE CAA AP	5.48	.62	.38		1.18	.87	.06	.03	.95	.07								.19	.51	T				.39	T	T	.18	.05	T		
SHAMOKIN	5.36		.87	.01	.50	1.13	.48		.02	1.03								T	.53	.12				.25	.05	.27		.10			
SHIPPENSBURG	3.62	T	.70		.22	.99	.33		.58	.05			T	T	T			.06	.21	.13	T	T		T	.26	T		T		T	
SHIPPINGPORT WB	5.46	.45	.22	.72	1.57	.38	T	T	.66	.02			T	.02	T		.06	.37	.21					.07	.11	.50			.01		
SINNEMAHONING	5.15		.75	.05	.57	1.02	.29	.02	.30	.80	T	T	T	T	.02	T		.02	.32	.07		.09	T	.36	.06	.11	.15	.15			
SLIPPERY ROCK	4.63		.34		.58	.68	.39		.40	.78				.02	.10			.08	.33	.18	.01				.32	.04	.62			.02	
SOMERSET FAIRVIEW ST	5.19		.77	.11	.11	.33	.41	.03		.99	T			T	.11			.10	.50	.07		.04	.64	T		.66	.27				
SOMERSET MAIN ST	-	.10	-		.25	.17	.57		.65	.31	T		T	T	.08		T	.16	.53		.03	.53		T	T	.98	.04				
SOUTH MOUNTAIN	4.19		.72		T	.92	.73			.74				T	.01				.17	.03		.10			.16	.09	.15		.25	.12	
SPRINGBORO	D 5.81	.27	T	T	.48	.45	T	.27	*	*	1.13		.10	D.10	D.20			.28	.25	T				.16	T	.10	1.23	.10	.60		
SPRING GROVE	4.18	.02	.50		.07	1.53	.65		.57	.05				.02				.10	.15	.15					.14	T	.14			T	
SPRINGS 1 SW	4.91	.35	.45		.26	.71	.20	.03	.77	.08			T	T	.06		T	.20	.21		.28	.05	.09			1.17					

See Reference Notes Following Station Index

DAILY PRECIPITATION

Station	Total	1	2	3	4	5	6	7	8	9	10	11	12	13	14	15	16	17	18	19	20	21	22	23	24	25	26	27	28	29	30	31
E COLLEGE	9.31	.88	.48	.27	1.11	.30	.02	.07	.65	.05				T	T		T	.36	.34	T	.05		T	.17	.11	.05	.60					
USSTOWN	6.17		1.31	T	.44	1.30	1.07			.82				.06					.27	.53				.02	T	.07	.22		T			
UOSBURG	6.89	.02	.98		1.52	1.40	.59	T	.72	.14	T		.05	T	T			T	.88	.02	.08			.46	.02	.02	T	.01		.02		
P CREEK	5.82		.75	.03	.37	1.07	.32	.03	.11	.95					.02			.08	.44	.09		.04		.33	.62	.31	.10	.22				
URY	6.20		1.05	T	.61	1.33	.60	T	.05	1.00								T	.59	.08		T		.29	.07		.03	.50				
UEHANNA	4.40		.42	.15		1.25	.60	.07	.19	.79	T	.01		.10		T		.03	.03	.24		.04				.03	.36		.07			
RSVILLE	5.59		1.08	.14	.51	.82	*	*	.42	.61	T				.02			.25	1.06	.14						.36	.18					
QUA	7.37		1.38	T	.40	1.35	1.26			.63				.20					.61	.27				.43	.15	.25	.14					
QUA 4 N DAM	6.87		1.18		.05	1.63	1.22			.80				.40					.63	.32		.03		.43	.16		.02					
RACK 2 S FIRE TWR	5.40		.58	.06	.45	1.20	.70	.08	.34	.65	T	T		T	T	T		.01	.28	.12		.11		.46	.07	.16	.07	.08	T			
ESTA 2 SE DAM	7.39		.25	.04	.86	.90	.75	.09	.76	.87	T		.01	T	.10	T		.10	.25	.10		T	T	.02	.45	.06	1.32	.46				
SVILLE WATER WORKS	6.72	T	.76	T	1.34	.36	.23	.29	1.04	.21		T		T	.05		.01	.19	.20	T	T	T		.16	1.02	.51	.35			T		
EDO 4 W	8.79		.54	.03	.50	.78	.38	.19	.74	.63	T		.04	.02	.15	.03		.08	.16	.15		.02	T	.29	.36	1.48	2.10	.18				
NOA	5.44		.15	.13	.10	1.21	.57	T	.47	.92	T			T	T	T		T	.05	.47		.08		.12	T	.45	.25	T	.47			
R CITY 3 SW	5.70	.04	1.03		.90	1.21	.42		.72	.15			T	.04				.09	.19	.30				.05	.18	.06	.05	.27				
	6.41		.25	.12	.18	1.64	.40		.43	.97									.08	.50		.04		.22	.04	.69	.23	.02	.60			
LEPOINT 4 NE	5.64		.36	.08	.28	1.03	.34	.08	.36	.90	.01				.01			.02	.22	.34		.11		.14		.42	.70	.21	.03			
NE 4 NE BALD EAGLE	6.34		1.25	.03	.88	1.29	.18	T	T	.95					T			T	.75	.20				.09	.71	.03	T					
N CITY	6.24		.33	.02	.68	.95	.27	.10	.75	.28			.11	.03	.05			.07	.14	.07		.03		.04	.33	.22	1.52	.11	.14			
NTOWN	3.31	.52	.18		.20	.10	.05		.87	.04	T		.01	T	.02		.01	.31	.28		.03	.03	.02	T	.10	.30	T		.04			
R DARBY	4.23		1.11		.25	.74	.83		.33	.06			T					.02	.05	.14				.30			.32	T		.08		
A	5.20		.68		.30	.72	.38	.08	.86	.87				.06	.05			.08	.21	.10					.45	.10	.29	.05		.01		
ERGRIFT	8.07		.78	.17	.98	.90	.09	.04	T	.64	T				T	.07	T	.09	.45	.26				T	.39	.55	T					
INVILLE	6.40		1.87	.12	.44	1.38	.78	.02		.71								.03	.21	.68				.01	.01		.14			T		
NCKEL	8.45	T	.40	.03	.64	.88	.64	.11	.66	.68	.15	T	T	.03	.11		T	.15	.27	.18		.06		.07	.35	.03	.90	.03		.02		
NCKEL 1 WSW	8.06	T	.46	.03	.58	.83	.55	.06	.73	.62	.14	T	T	.02	.11			.13	.29	.18		.06		.04	.35	.02	.87	.03		T		
EN	7.27		.37	.03	.40	.79	.86	.15	.68	.70	.02		.04	.03	.06			.05	.13	.08		T	T	.08	.05	.58	1.63	.54				
ONTOWN	6.57	.16	.70		1.74	.74	.58	.02	1.00	.10	T					T	T	T	.50	.12	T			.40		T	.21	.30				
ESBURG 2 W	4.19		.90	.06	.17	.34	.25	T	.05	.51				T	T			.09	1.02	.03		.07	.25	.02	.03		.28			.12		
SBORO 3 S	5.47		.42	.08	.19	1.25	.17	T	.47	.57	T	T	T		T			T	.19	.34	.02	.39	T	.17	.02	.93	.18	.06	.02			
SVILLE	4.22	T	.70		.13	1.35	.45		.67	.12			T	.08				.06	.22	.14					.14		.04		.03			
ERSVILLE 1 W	6.05		1.31	.12		1.70	1.10			.60									.25	.42					.10	.45						
CHESTER	–	–	–	–	–	–	–	–	–	–	–	–	–	–	–	–	–	–	–	–	–	–	–	–	–	–	–	–	–	–	–	
GROVE 1 E	4.54		1.36			.70	.90	.37		.07					T				.08	.13				.12	.03	.16	.54			.08		
HICKORY	6.00		.42	.04	.50	.65	.78	.04	.96	.73			.05		.04			.10	.20	.10				.04	.25	.10	.50	.50				
ESBURG	5.34		.78		.88	.89	.41		.18	.64					.05			.21	.45	.16					.56	.15	T					
ES BARRE	6.77		1.04	.09	.20	1.76	.91	.02	.10	.89				.12					.21	.38		T		.47	T	.25	.01		.32			
IANSBURG	4.95		.90	T	.45	.82	.27		.05	.92				T				.03	.48	.31		.03		T	.26	.17	.08	.07		T		
IANSPORT WB AP	6.30	.48	.21		1.74	.84	.01	.21	.89	T	.01			T	T		T	.11	.78	.02	.02		T	.53	T	.35	.16	.02	T			
SBURG	4.40		.84	.05	.10	.63	.22	.05		.64					.04			.02	.38	.06		.05	T		.19	1.03	.10	T				
3 SSW PUMP STA	4.58	.02	.64		.06	1.40	.57		.50	.06			T	.02	T			.12	.20	.11				T	.03		.70		T	.12		
HAVEN	4.82		.78		.05	.93	1.09			.70				T					.14	.15				.01	.01	.12	.67		.02	.15		
GROVE	–		.65		.27	1.25	1.10		.07	–				.06					.70	.25		.02		.26	.25	.14						
SVILLE 3 SE	6.18		1.46	.08	.39	1.24	.50			.76				.12					.24	.96				.22	.02		.19					

SUPPLEMENTAL DATA

Station	Wind direction: Prevailing	Wind direction: Percent of time from prevailing	Wind speed m. p. h.: Average	Wind speed m. p. h.: Fastest mile	Wind speed m. p. h.: Direction of fastest mile	Wind speed m. p. h.: Date of fastest mile	Relative humidity averages - percent: 1:30 a EST	Relative humidity averages - percent: 7:30 a EST	Relative humidity averages - percent: 1:30 p EST	Relative humidity averages - percent: 7:30 p EST	Number of days with precipitation: Trace	Number of days with precipitation: .01–.09	Number of days with precipitation: .10–.49	Number of days with precipitation: .50–.99	Number of days with precipitation: 1.00–1.99	Number of days with precipitation: 2.00 and over	Number of days with precipitation: Total	Percent of possible sunshine	Average sky cover sunrise to sunset
ENTOWN WB AIRPORT	E	11	12.5	-	-	-	80	79	56	68	7	5	4	2	3	0	21	-	6.6
E WB AIRPORT	-	-	12.3	35++	SSE	4	-	-	-	-	4	5	8	3	2	0	22	-	7.4
RISBURG WB AIRPORT	WNW	13	9.3	34	NW	9	69	69	52	57	8	5	6	1	1	0	21	54	6.9
LADELPHIA WB AIRPORT	SW	12	11.1	42	N	9	75	74	53	62	5	5	6	2	1	0	19	58	6.4
TSBURG WB AIRPORT	WSW	14	11.2	40++	WSW	5	79	79	56	67	5	9	6	1	1	0	22	50	7.5
DING WB CITY	-	-	11.7	42	NW	9	-	-	-	-	4	7	5	3	1	0	20	54	6.5
ANTON WB AIRPORT	WSW	14	10.2	47	NW	5	73	75	56	65	5	3	8	2	1	0	19	55	7.0
PPINGPORT WB	-	-	3.0	37%	WSW	25	-	-	-	-	4	5	6	3	1	0	19	-	-
LIAMSPORT WB AIRPORT	-	-	-	-	-	-	-	77	53	62	7	5	6	4	1	0	23	-	7.1
eak Gust																			

Table 5

DAILY TEMPERATURES

Station		1	2	3	4	5	6	7	8	9	10	11	12	13	14	15	16	17	18	19	20	21	22	23	24	25	26	27	28	29	30	31	Average
ALLENTOWN WB AP	MAX	60	59	48	39	62	51	60	45	47	53	62	69	47	47	55	61	54	56	62	68	83	67	73	80	57	78	87	87	77	71		62
	MIN	27	35	31	31	33	42	42	35	32	32	26	35	30	29	27	28	46	49	46	43	51	50	46	57	51	52	60	55	53	48		40
ALLENTOWN GAS CO	MAX	53	60	60	47	38	62	51	61	43	47	52	62	70	46	47	50	62	54	56	61	69	83	67	76	81	57	80	88	88	72		61
	MIN	33	39	33	32	32	38	43	41	33	34	29	37	32	32	29	29	40	50	50	44	49	59	47	50	53	52	54	57	59	50		42
ALTOONA HORSESHOE CURVE	MAX	55	54	48	46	38	43	61	50	40	47	68	63	40	37	51	56	56	53	58	82	79	72	82	83	77	81	88	83	75	77		61
	MIN	35	43	28	30	30	31	35	33	29	32	29	34	22	27	25	29	45	48	47	53	60	55	52	59	58	57	55	58	53	51		41
ARENDTSVILLE	MAX	52	53	62	50	38	58	51	65	45	48	52	67	70	47	46	54	65	58	59	60	76	87	71	77	81	60	79	90	88	77		62
	MIN	32	39	29	33	33	37	41	40	33	30	25	37	30	28	24	29	40	48	50	52	54	54	51	54	55	54	55	64	58	55		42
ARTEMAS 1 WNW	MAX	52	50	62	49	47	49	50	50	43	51	71	70	44	45	55	58	59	70	66	83	83	82	84	84	81	82	89	87	85	82		65
	MIN	35	32	32	33	34	35	32	31	30	28	27	39	27	22	25	32	45	46	47	50	49	50	52	55	60	57	59	47	48	46		40
BAKERSTOWN 3 WNW	MAX	56	54	40	44	66	56	58	40	42	44	68	68	42	37	52	54	58	61	80	85	79	80	82	84	83	86	87	84	72	77		63
	MIN	42	38	24	32	40	38	36	34	30	32	29	32	26	28	24	36	46	52	47	58	60	48	60	62	62	60	62	58	53	49		43
BEAVERTOWN	MAX	56	58	48	43	43	55	57	52	46	49	67	63	45	43	56	59	57	56	58	78	81	79	85	83	80	83	89	87	80	77		63
	MIN	38	40	28	30	32	38	40	36	32	28	23	34	29	30	27	26	46	49	50	54	54	43	46	61	57	54	57	56	57	53		41
BELLEFONTE 4 S	MAX	52	57												42	40	46	58	59	57	62	80	77	68	80	82	65	85	89	88	78		
	MIN	34	43	29	29	32	37	35	35	30	32	23	33	25	28	28	28	37	46	50	53	58	45	51	53	60	60	50	60	55	54		43
BERWICK	MAX	60	56	47	43	54	61	54	48	47	52	67	65	47	46	55	62	59	58	63	75	82	79	75	82	81	80	89	85	80	76		64
	MIN	30	44	29	30	33	44	40	36	31	30	25	36	28	28	26	27	42	49	51	48	52	48	47	59	54	55	59	60	57	57		41
BETHLEHEM LEHIGH UNIV	MAX	60	62	58	49	43	61	61	56	61	48	59	70	70	46	52	59	62	54	59	62	84	80	69	81	80	73	88	90	89	78		65
	MIN	27	31	29	28	29	39	39	35	29	32	27	39	28	29	28	28	45	48	48	41	53	51	44	59	48	49	63	54	55	52		40
BLAIRSVILLE 6 ENE	MAX	59	49	42	38	60	55	58	39	39	43	65	54	38	32	51	54	50	56	74	80	75	76	80	82	78	83	85	75	71	74		60
	MIN	39	35	24	32	33	30	28	35	35	29	30	27	21	21	20	36	43	45	50	67	65	49	55	59	59	60	63	61	49	46		41
BRADFORD 4 W RES	MAX	57	55	37	36	47	49	38	33	36	38	55	47	36	34	47	49	47	52	70	79	76	76	77	82	82	78	82	80	67	68		57
	MIN	24	31	16	21	28	29	30	27	23	25	28	26	13	21	15	21	35	35	35	47	58	38	51	51	55	55	47	53	34	35		33
BROOKVILLE CAA AIRPORT	MAX	58	54	40	35	52	45	48	35	37	44	63	36	37	34	52	52	58	57	77	80	75	75	80	83	78	82	85	77	72	75		59
	MIN	35	31	22	38	34	33	34	31	28	23	22	23	19	25	21	25	44	49	40	54	48	46	54	59	59	57	51	53	48	44		38
BURGETTSTOWN 2 W	MAX	57	59	51	41	50	71	41	61	39	46	47	69	37	43	40	55	52	56	63	82	81	77	78	85	87	87	87	87	75	73		62
	MIN	24	44	23	29	37	34	35	34	31	26	23	33	25	25	15	25	32	47	43	47	50	41	53	54	54	54	51	50	51	36		37
BURNT CABINS 2 NE	MAX	69	68	57	48	44	60	67	58	40	51	73	72	51	44	38	63	60							83	81	84	89	88	87	80		64
	MIN	34	36	25	31	33	37	36	32	31	29	21	39	27	26	19	27	47							55	58	54	54	55	57	45		37
BUTLER	MAX	55	57	45	44	61	63	55	37	37	47	65	66	40	40	52	52	56	57	78	76	80	81	84	86	83	84	85	86	75	75		63
	MIN	41	45	24	32	36	33	35	33	28	30	24	31	23	26	20	26	45	50	47	51	55	40	59	60	59	55	53	55	50	42		40
CANTON 1 NW	MAX	47	51	50	37	48	54	42	46	32	36	40	50	46	39	38	47	55	52	57	59	71	75	67	72	78	61	74	83	71	68		54
	MIN	29	31	20	23	25	36	34	35	25	24	24	29	22	21	24	28	37	43	45	49	49	43	44	46	55	52	54	57	47	43		38
CARLISLE	MAX	57	61	51	47	47	59	64	62	49	54	71	68	48	47	56	60	59	58	62	74	85	78	82	85	84	84	92	92	87	83		66
	MIN	39	41	37	33	39	43	44	40	35	32	27	37	32	32	30	30	48	51	53	53	53	50	54	64	58	55	59	61	60	60		44
CHAMBERSBURG 1 ESE	MAX	53	63	50	40	52	49	67	49	46	52	68	68	47	46	55	62	59	58	60	75	84	71	79	82	71	79	91	88	79	77		64
	MIN	35	40	33	33	33	42	43	39	34	31	25	36	30	27	23	29	49	49	52	54	57	51	51	59	57	53	54	59	57	55		43
CHESTER	MAX	55	59	60	55	42	63	60	66	50	51	55	65	73	50	48	56	62	62	60	64	87	84	68	70	85	61	79	80	89	79		64
	MIN	34	34	35	35	36	40	42	44	33	34	33	36	34	26	24	32	48	47	51	46	53	52	45	51	53	51	58	60	60	48		42
CLARION 3 SW	MAX	50	53	41	42	56	46	49	39	39	42	66	51	41	35	58	63	54	58	78	84	79	78	84	89	82	83	87	77	74	77		61
	MIN	30	35	21	30	35	33	32	31	27	28	22	30	20	24	19	25	43	45	45	46	51	40	54	57	58	54	60	61	42	39		37
CLAYSVILLE 3 W	MAX	60	55	42	55	70	53	66	44	47	50	69	50	49	48	53	52	52	68	82	82	80	76	84	86	85	86	87	79	79	78		65
	MIN	31	40	26	36	46	36	36	35	31	29	25	32	25	25	16	24	43	54	41	52	50	48	54	53	57	54	51	50	52	37		39
COATESVILLE 1 SW	MAX	53	57	65	51	40	64	65	66	48	51	54	66	73	47	46	55	61	60	58	62	71	87	71	75	83	59	80	89	89	77		64
	MIN	28	38	33	33	34	40	42	42	34	28	24	38	31	25	29	24	42	49	51	43	47	56	49	50	52	52	54	58	59	50		41
COLUMBIA	MAX	58	65	52	44	50	63	65	59	50	55	67	71	51	48	56	63	58	58	61	74	88	78	79	83	70	80	90	91	80	75		66
	MIN	37	43	32	33	34	45	42	39	33	31	27	44	31	32	29	30	48	48	52	48	52	52	51	61	53	53	57	62	57	52		43
CONFLUENCE 1 SW DAM	MAX	54	59	54	50	45	63	43	68	46	43	47	66	43	40	39	52	54	57	70	80	81	79	73	83	86	76	84	86	82	73		62
	MIN	24	39	31	27	36	35	36	42	29	27	24	27	25	24	20	27	34	47	46	49	49	47	49	54	59	56	53	53	51	38		38
CORRY	MAX	58	55	40	37	58	50	36	33	35	37	52	41	35	34	46	50	50	54	77	79	75	76	78	84	83	81	82	80	67	68		57
	MIN	29	33	20	30	35	31	31	29	24	29	21	26	18	22	20	25	43	45	47	54	61	39	54	57	58	59	54	55	35	40		37
COUDERSPORT 3 NW	MAX	52	52	36	32	47	48	39	33	36	38	56	46	38	33	47	51	48	50	67	79	74	69	75	80	72	75	83	69	69	67		59
	MIN	30	29	15	25	30	31	30	28	23	27	15	23	13	23	16	23	40	42	44	51	51	34	48	52	57	53	48	49	36	40		34
DERRY	MAX	60	54	45	44	65	59	62	45	47	48	69	63	44	40	45	47	56	63	81	82	81	77	84	85	83	86	86	88	75	77		64
	MIN	45	42	29	35	40	34	34	38	30	33	25	33	23	27	25	27	47	51	46	52	58	44	59	60	64	66	55	57	54	47		42
DEVAULT 1 W	MAX	58	60	50	42	60	55	64	40	49	50	65	67	46	47	55	61	61	56	64	71	85	76	76	80	59	79	88	86	84	71		64
	MIN	29	31	29	29	30	38	39	31	28	27	27	34	29	25	26	33	44	46	45	39	41	48	42	61	47	44	56	51	51	50		38
DIXON	MAX	53	58	55	42	39	57	50	51	36	42	46	63	58	45	43	51	56	55	60	67	79	81	71	77	85	61	83	85	78	72		60
	MIN	20	41	26	28	28	38	38	35	29	22	20	28	26	26	21	21	33	44	46	50	51	39	44	50	53	55	58	54	50	46		37
DONEGAL	MAX	53	47	40	36	65	40	59	40	37	40	64	40	36	33	46	51	50	58	74	76	72	70	77	82	73	80	88	75	66	70		57
	MIN	32	29	24	29	37	28	32	26	24	28	19	22	19	21	14	25	41	47	43	50	50	41	53	53	57	50	50	50	47	36		35
DONORA	MAX	61	62	55	46	62	75	60	69	48	47	67	72	41	45	51	56	54	61	76	86	84	82	84	88	89	88	90	91	83	77		68
	MIN	43	52	31	38	45	38	40	40	33	34	31	37	29	29	24	29	48	53	50	56	59	50	60	59	67	58	57	59	56	46		45
DU BOIS 7 E	MAX	53	51	43	39	48	49	49	37	37	41	65	61	38	33	50	55	52	54	71	81	76	71	78	80	77	82	84	80	75	73		59
	MIN	34	43	20	28	32	33	32	32	26	30	21	38	18	21	20	25	43	46	46	54	60	45	52	55	60	57	50	50	50	41		38
EAGLES MERE	MAX	46	50	48	36	37	54	42	47	32	35	44	57	51	30	30	46	53	50	57	54	71	78	66	72	78	58	77	82	75	69		54
	MIN	22	33	20	23	26	35	32	29	19	19	24	27	22	22	22	27	38	41	46	46	47	44	42	44	50	51	50	59	46	42		35
EAST BRADY	MAX	59	58	43	43	64	52	55	45	42	45	70	64	42	41	55	54	59	59	80	84	85	83	85	84	87	86	89	87	80	79		65
	MIN	33	42	25	33	39	36	37	34	31	31	25	34	22	28	22	28	43	46	47	47	52	42	56	60	60	57	55	58	52	43		40
EBENSBURG	MAX	55	50	44	33	60	59	56	40	37	42	63	54	37	34	54	53	53	56	78	78	76	79	78	77	71	80	83	78	71	70		60
	MIN	35	37	25	29	30	32	32	32	25	29	22	29	19	23	21	27	42	47	42	52	56	45	50	51	58	57	55	54	48	38		38
EMPORIUM 2 SSW	MAX	49	55	49	38	36	49	40	43	33	36	40	62	38	38	37	49	54	50	51	70	80	78	72	79	81	73	80	84	73	70		56
	MIN	28	38	18	25	28	31	32	30	25	27	18	27	17	23	24	25	35	44	48	50	55	39	49	50	59	54	50	51	46	42		36
EPHRATA	MAX	55	61	51	41	53	51	62	47	49	52	62	70	48	46	55	59	56	56	62	68	86	72	74	80	71	80	88	87	78	73		63.
	MIN	33	42	29	31	32	46	40	40	31	32	27	41	30	28	27	29	45	48	49	46	53	50	48	59	51	51	59	60	56	55		42.
ERIE WB AIRPORT	MAX	50	51	35	41	60	44	38	34	36	38	54	38	38	36	43	55	54	58	71	80	70	63	72	76	85	78	79	59	65	60		55
	MIN	41	31	27	33	41	34	32	31	29	30	32	27	27	30	24	36	46	48	45	59	46	43	59	60	59	59	58	46	40	40		40

See reference notes following Station Index.

DAILY TEMPERATURES

PENNSYLVANIA
APRIL 1957

1

		Day Of Month																														Average
		1	2	3	4	5	6	7	8	9	10	11	12	13	14	15	16	17	18	19	20	21	22	23	24	25	26	27	28	29	30	31	
	MAX	55	54	48	40	48	48	66	44	48	56	74	52	45	44	58	60	60	68	68	85	82	78	86	86	75	78	87	84	87	88		65.1
	MIN	36	34	30	32	32	40	42	38	32	30	24	30	28	28	28	30	48	50	45	44	48	54	54	60	54	48	56	48	52	52		40.9
	MAX	55	51	46	38	58	48	42	38	37	40	59	42	37	32	49	48	51	63	79	85	78	81	82	82	84	87	90	80	79	76		60.4
	MIN	36	34	24	30	40	34	33	28	29	30	29	29	25	27	32	31	46	50	47	56	61	44	60	60	58	57	59	57	48	48		41.3
	MAX	55	59	53	44	43	65	42	56	40	42	46	68	38	42	38	53	52	55	60	78	83	76	79	84	82	82	85	86	77	74		61.2
	MIN	28	40	24	30	34	31	31	35	28	30	24	33	23	24	21	26	34	47	46	48	53	42	50	58	58	55	54	54	52	40		38.4
	MAX	53	58	51	42	60	57	48	36	35	39	52	62	46	41	45	52	53	52	67	76	77	78	78	81	82	82	84	85	75	71		60.6
	MIN	19	32	27	25	31	35	37	33	31	28	30	24	28	21	28	24	38	44	48	44	56	42	42	58	59	59	56	54	47	46		38.2
	MAX	53	50	40	36	45	52	49	45	38	43	58	56	39	39	49	54	51	50	57	74	76	73	71	76	77	75	77	83	80	73		58.0
	MIN	43	39	26	25	28	35	37	30	31	35	28	35	24	36	26	43	42	45	46	42	60	56	42	54	58	50	51	57	53	53		41.0
	MAX	58	63	52	45	61	81	64	57	50	53	62	72	46	46	54	61	56	54	62	65	88	77	74	80	67	81	89	87	76	72		64.4
	MIN	30	45	31	33	37	46	40	39	34	30	24	46	34	28	24	25	47	50	50	51	49	49	47	60	51	51	54	52	57	49		42.1
	MAX	53	57	64	51	39	59	61	67	44	49	54	68	72	49	48	57	62	59	61	62	76	87	72	78	83	82	79	91	91	80		64.5
	MIN	37	40	33	34	35	37	42	40	34	36	28	47	31	30	29	31	45	50	52	52	52	54	52	56	56	55	58	64	60	60		44.3
	MAX	56	58	62	56	44	61	62	58	46	54	60	68	64	52	46	56	62	60	64	66	88	88	72	74	82	66	88	90	86	79		65.6
	MIN	32	34	32	32	36	34	38	32	34	26	32	35	38	34	32	34	46	50	48	50	56	54	54	56	54	58	60	64	56	48		43.0
	MAX	51	57	56	45	36	63	50	60	40	46	49	65	62	45	45	52	60	54	54	59	70	79	68	77	82	58	79	87	85	74		60.3
	MIN	35	40	29	29	31	35	37	38	30	29	24	31	29	28	26	29	44	45	49	51	50	48	48	48	54	53	55	59	56	54		40.5
	MAX	59	58	40	40	61	59	45	36	40	44	60	46	40	39	55	53	52	62	79	82	76	80	83	84	84	86	86	84	74	75		62.1
	MIN	34	37	22	30	39	33	31	30	25	30	26	28	23	26	22	30	44	49	46	55	59	40	57	60	56	55	54	55	41	44		39.4
	MAX	54	56	65	51	40	64	56	67	45	50	55	69	71	49	48	56	62	57	61	63	79	87	73	80	64	63	81	92	89	79		64.9
	MIN	36	39	31	34	33	39	39	40	33	33	29	31	31	29	26	30	39	48	48	50	50	52	52	50	57	54	55	61	59	51		42.0
	MAX	56	61	48	39	65	53	64	47	47	51	68	67	46	45	56	62	58	56	61	71	84	68	78	81	68	80	92	90	77	75		63.8
	MIN	38	41	35	33	35	43	44	39	34	37	27	37	32	31	30	33	50	50	52	50	56	55	52	64	54	54	59	63	60	56		44.8
	MAX	50	57	52	40	33	45	45	48	35	35	42	55	58	39	38	46	54	51	60	63	78	75	67	74	80	57	79	85	75	69		56.2
	MIN	22	38	25	25	25	31	34	32	25	26	25	30	24	25	22	20	29	41	42	38	45	38	41	43	50	47	50	55	51	44		34.8
	MAX	54	63	49	43	63	63	63	48	47	51	63	69	46	46	52	57	59	55	57	68	82	70	73	81	64	77	86	83	77	74		62.8
	MIN	37	41	36	37	40	45	45	39	36	36	32	40	34	34	33	32	46	49	49	48	52	54	53	60	55	55	61	64	58	55		45.2
	MAX	56	60	58	50	37	48	48	64	40	46	53	72	56	47	44	57	63	59	54	62	83	84	75	87	84	71	86	91	88	79		63.4
	MIN	28	40	25	32	33	36	40	39	33	31	21	29	28	30	21	24	32	48	51	52	50	43	55	57	61	57	57	54	57	44		40.3
	MAX	61	53	47	40	61	59	59	46	42	46	68	55	42	39	54	57	56	60	80	83	77	79	84	85	81	85	86	80	74	77		63.9
	MIN	41	41	24	34	37	36	35	37	29	32	23	32	20	26	19	26	44	49	46	55	51	43	55	59	59	54	53	52	52	39		40.1
	MAX	60	54	44	47	72		68		46	50	70	68			56	55	54	61				83	85	89	86	88	88			80		66.9
	MIN	41	43	27	37	41			36	30	34	27	34			24	31	46	51				45	58	60	63	56			53	49		42.0
	MAX	54	58	43	39	42	60	39	42	34	38	40	56	34	40	37	49	52	52	61	77	82	74	78	83	84	82	84	84	67	71		57.9
	MIN	31	42	23	29	34	34	29	30	25	29	26	29	21	25	19	31	38	46	45	53	60	38	55	58	59	58	53	54	39	43		38.5
	MAX	58	60	54	47	43	52	57	54	47	50	60	69	49	46	54	59	59	54	59	72	82	80	76	80	80	85	91	89	81	78		64.2
	MIN	27	43	29	30	32	41	39	36	30	31	25	34	28	27	27	24	45	48	50	44	50	50	40	58	51	52	60	57	56	51		40.5
	MAX	49	54	47	43	30	49	52	58	39	35	40	64	38	35	35	50	53	52	55	73	79	75	70	79	81	71	82	83	78	70		57.6
	MIN	33	41	29	30	31	33	37	37	27	27	24	33	24	24	27	27	41	47	47	52	52	44	51	56	59	60	53	55	53	53		40.2
	MAX	50	57	56	38	36	48	37	40	33	38	40	57	35	37	35	48	50	48	51	73	80	76	74	79	83	80	78	83	73	78		56.4
	MIN	22	40	17	25	32	31	31	30	25	26	18	29	15	24	18	24	36	38	41	47	51	34	51	53	56	56	46	46	35	35		34.3
	MAX	58	54	48	30	47	48	70	44	43	48	70	50	42	44	62	56	61	64	63	83	82	73	85	84	71	84	88	87	86	86		64.0
	MIN	31	34	30	32	33	35	38	34	30	28	23	30	25	32	25	27	47	48	46	49	50	46	51	52	*59	58	55	50	51	48		39.9
STA	MAX	57	64	56	49	56	65	66	64	50	54	64	72	50	48	55	59	58	57	61	70	86	79	78	80	78	77	87	90	84	73		66.2
	MIN	32	43	30	33	35	47	40	38	34	29	26	38	32	30	29	27	47	49	51	46	48	47	51	59	53	53	56	59	57	49		42.3
	MAX	51	57	62	50	40	63	50	63	45	47	51	65	71	47	46	53	62	57	56	62	68	84	66	76	80	59	77	87	87	70		61.8
	MIN	31	43	30	33	33	39	42	39	33	27	23	35	31	24	25	25	41	49	49	48	46	45	50	51	54	52	55	58	57	51		40.6
	MAX	50	60	50	41	40	54	45	46	36	38	43	60	46	42	39	42	47	58	60	65	82	77	72	78	84	68	82	86	70	71		57.7
	MIN	22	33	22	27	29	35	36	30	25	20	21	26	20	22	21	24	30	34	46	50	54	37	40	50	56	52	56	56	43	43		35.3
	MAX	53	57	60	51	36	61	49	62	44	46	52	67	69	47	46	55	61	56	59	61	68	82	70	76	82	58	79	91	88	76		62.0
	MIN	32	39	31	32	33	36	41	41	33	29	24	32	30	25	25	27	39	50	50	49	48	48	49	50	54	53	56	61	56	49		40.7
	MAX	55	60	59	49	38	47	49	61	41	47	52	72	57	47	44	58	63	57	57	60	80	84	71	85	83	65	87	90	89	80		62.9
	MIN	24	41	32	33	33	37	40	40	34	32	26	26	29	30	30	30	31	47	50	52	52	50	50	52	61	56	56	59	60	56		41.6
	MAX	57	49	39	39	58	49	41	34	39	40	54	42	40	38	50	53	52	61	76	82	74	74	81	83	83	86	86	67	70	68		58.8
	MIN	31	33	19	32	38	33	29	30	22	28	24	27	21	26	23	29	44	48	44	53	53	38	55	56	55	54	55	54	36	41		37.7
	MAX		58	46	42	44	47	56	40	47	50	71	54	46	45	56	61	57	57	63	80	79	74	84	87	89	87	92	86	80	80		63.4
	MIN		42	27	30	34	38	39	35	31	31	25	38	26	29	26	28	46	50	51	55	55	45	49	60	55	55	58	57	56	47		42.0
	MAX	50	58	54	44	35	46	41	47	42	43	44	67	47	40	36	51	57	54	55	70	82	79	71	80	80	72	82	88	81	72		58.8
	MIN	16	33	19	23	28	29	28	32	24	25	16	27	15	19	16	21	25	41	43	45	50	41	43	49	55	53	47	49	49	40		35.4
	MAX	58	69	54	46	63	61	66	53	54	60	62	70	51	50	58	61	64	59	61	69	92	70	67	80	61	76	88	86	80	77		65.5
	MIN	38	42	37	37	41	46	46	40	38	38	37	42	36	35	34	39	50	53	48	47	54	52	50	58	54	54	62	56	63	62		46.3
	MAX	55	54	47	34	51	45	60	39	40	46	68	47	41	36	51	56	55	55	58	80	77	70	82	82	72	85	88	81	72	74		60.0
	MIN	37	35	29	31	33	36	37	35	29	28	25	27	25	25	23	34	46	49	50	53	57	49	51	58	57	57	55	60	55	51		41.2
	MAX	55	58	46	39	40	57	39	42	34	39	42	57	36	40	36	51	52	52	60	78	82	75	78	83	85	83	84	85	65	70		58.1
	MIN	28	41	21	28	34	34	31	30	25	28	26	29	23	27	23	29	37	46	48	50	60	40	53	58	58	58	55	56	38	41		38.5
	MAX	55	46	42	48	52	50	46	39	40	49	54	46	38	36	50	56	59	55	68	70	79	70	74	78	80	82	84	78	80	78		59.3
	MIN	40	30	26	30	34	30	30	31	30	34	36	25	26	30	26	31	38	41	42	55	58	40	42	55	50	52	47	45	37	35		37.5
FLD	MAX	57	63	49	40	64	53	64	45	48	53	68	68	47	46	54	61	58	56	61	73	85	69	77	82	68	77	91	88	74	73		63.8
	MIN	39	40	34	34	35	44	45	39	34	33	27	38	32	33	33	32	50	51	53	52	52	53	53	64	55	55	58	64	60	58		45.0
	MAX	60	52	44	49	60	47	53	40	42	43	69	43	40	37	51	50	57	62	78	82	74	78	84	84	85	85	86	74	71	73		61.8
	MIN	42	36	30	35	46	38	40	32	31	32	30	29	28	29	26	34	48	50	50	55	59	48	60	62	62	62	60	58	56	46		43.8
	MAX	46	53	48	36	33	50	43	46	32	33	39	55	48	38	36	45	57	51	57	65	77	75	68	74	78	58	78	82	70	66		54.3
	MIN	29	32	22	23	25	33	33	29	23	23	24	27	22	24	25	26	35	44	45	46	48	42	42	44	48	51	53	57	47	39		35.4
	MAX	55	61	49	40	64	54	62	46	48	51	61	69	52	45	52	58	56	54	62	69	83	67	73	80	60	75	87	87	75	74		62.3
	MIN	35	36	32	31	34	41	39	36	32	29	25	37	28	28	25	27	47	49	48	44	55	47	47	59	50	51	58	57	52	49		40.9
	MAX	56	62	56	40	62	56	64	46	54	52	67	70	47	45	53	61	56	57	61	68	85	68	74	81	68	76	88	88	72	73		63.5
	MIN	36	34	39	32	33	41	41	37	31	28	24	35	34	29	27	28	45	49	51	48	53	52	50	61	52	54	58	59	55	50		42.2

See reference notes following Station Index.

Table 5-Continued

DAILY TEMPERATURES

Station		1	2	3	4	5	6	7	8	9	10	11	12	13	14	15	16	17	18	19	20	21	22	23	24	25	26	27	28	29	30	31	Average
MT POCONO 2 N AP	MAX	52	50	37	34	35	52	49	39	33	42	54	62	38	37	46	54	50	53	60	75	77	74	75	75	74	80	84	77	73			54
	MIN	28	35	22	25	27	35	33	30	23	24	23	35	21	23	24	26	41	45	45	38	56	44	40	54	47	48	54	56	51			34
MUHLENBURG 1 SE	MAX	58	54	42	39	52	55	52	44	41	49	63	61	45	45	51	58	54	57	61	72	67	69	74	79	77	79	85	80	75	72		60
	MIN	49	40	24	28	31	40	37	32	27	26	23	37	25	24	24	28	44	47	49	49	53	45	47	58	51	54	57	57	57	47		40
NEWBURG 3 W	MAX	54	61	60	50	51	62	65	65	46	52	68	68	50	46	49	54	58	59	54	71	86	80	85	87	82	86	90	90	90	79		64
	MIN	38	45	39	32	36	41	39	31	32	35	25	37	29	30	32	29	44	40	49	46	51	51	59	63	56	55	61	57	58	60		43
NEW CASTLE 1 N	MAX	60	50	42	46	65	64	48	38	43	45	63	54	42	40	54	54	54	61	80	84	82	80	84	84	84	85	87	85	74	74		63
	MIN	35	39	20	32	41	35	35	32	29	30	26	30	22	25	21	29	45	50	46	53	54	49	58	57	55	56	55	57	44	41		40
NEWELL	MAX	65	60	56	45	59	75	62	70	50	47	67	71	42	47	50	59	55	64	77	84	86	83	83	89	91	86	84	92	84	79		68
	MIN	38	48	30	40	43	38	36	39	32	33	28	37	33	27	23	30	47	51	49	50	58	50	57	55	61	58	58	58	56	44		43
NEWPORT	MAX	57	57	63	51	35	58	50	63	42	48	52	72	63	48	46	59	64	59	56	61	73	86	72	84	86	82	85	90	90	82		63
	MIN	25	40	29	32	33	35	42	40	33	29	24	28	31	28	30	28	32	50	50	52	51	48	52	54	61	55	56	59	57	58		41
NEW STANTON	MAX	65	55	46	50	71	52	63	45	46	49	60	58	58	41	54	55	56	65	82	84	80	79	85	87	80	88	88	80	80	78		65
	MIN	40	30	19	38	40	34	33	32	34	25	28	29	23	23	18	25	46	49	48	50	42	44	50	56	51	55	62	55	56	38		36
NORRISTOWN	MAX	57	63	52	44	63	62	65	49	51	54	65	74	48	48	55	63	59	56	62	70	86	67	76	82	59	80	89	88	78	73		64
	MIN	35	39	35	34	38	45	44	38	35	32	30	40	33	32	31	32	49	53	48	47	53	52	48	58	53	52	62	55	58	54		43
PALMERTON	MAX	58	57	46	39	56	52	59	42	46	50	61	68	46	47	53	39	53	56	60	68	82	67	74	78	80	81	88	86	76	70		61
	MIN	30	37	31	31	34	43	43	35	31	33	25	35	30	31	25	25	48	50	51	45	51	49	46	57	52	52	62	58	53	50		41
PHIL DREXEL INST OF TEC	MAX	59	64	54	46	64	61	66	52	51	56	62	75	50	50	57	61	62	59	63	69	90	68	72	83	63	78	91	91	79	72		65
	MIN	37	40	35	37	40	47	46	42	40	39	36	42	35	35	34	38	48	52	51	48	55	54	51	60	53	54	61	55	60	58		46
PHILADELPHIA WB AP	MAX	59	65	51	44	63	61	65	51	50	55	62	74	47	47	54	60	61	59	63	70	88	67	70	82	60	77	89	87	77	72		64
	MIN	36	40	36	35	40	45	44	39	36	33	31	41	33	33	31	34	48	52	46	46	53	51	49	57	52	53	61	55	60	54		44
PHILADELPHIA PT BREEZE	MAX	54	65	52	45	65	62	66	54	50	54	62	74	48	47	54	60	60	58	62	68	85	66	69	83	60	78	88	88	78	73		64
	MIN	38	42	38	35	39	46	46	39	36	37	36	53	34	35	34	39	49	53	48	46	55	54	50	60	54	54	64	58	64	61		46
PHILADELPHIA SHAWMONT	MAX	59	62	57	49	62	62	69	62	50	53	63	73	48	48	54	60	58	59	62	70	86	84	74	83	82	80	89	88	87	72		66
	MIN	35	45	34	34	35	47	44	39	30	30	29	49	32	30	29	29	48	51	51	46	56	51	48	67	52	52	51	55	57	51		43
PHILADELPHIA CITY	MAX	59	63	52	45	63	60	64	50	51	54	62	73	49	47	55	59	60	57	61	70	85	64	70	80	59	77	88	86	78	73		63
	MIN	38	41	38	36	40	45	45	39	37	39	37	42	39	36	35	44	48	52	51	46	57	51	50	57	52	53	60	56	61	61		46
PHILIPSBURG CAA AP	MAX	53	50	40	30	47	44	49	35	36	42	63	40	38	34	51	53	51	51	61	80	74	68	79	79	66	81	85	79	73	73		56
	MIN	36	30	22	27	30	32	35	31	26	25	17	23	19	24	25	24	44	48	47	52	55	46	49	57	54	53	54	51	51	41		37
PHOENIXVILLE 1 E	MAX	61	65	50	51	60	62	66	64	53	57	67	75	50	54	58	65	60	59	64	73	87	82	78	85	84	83	90	90	90	80		68
	MIN	29	47	29	32	34	46	42	39	34	26	26	43	33	28	29	24	46	49	51	40	48	45	48	57	53	52	58	55	57	46		41
PIMPLE HILL	MAX	48	51	48	37	33	53	41	48	34	34	42	57	63	38	39	47	53	49	51	55	71	76	62	72	74	57	82	84	80	80		55
	MIN	28	37	20	23	24	32	32	30	22	22	24	32	19	21	22	32	40	42	45	40	53	44	39	46	46	46	57	59	49	49		35
PITTSBURGH WB AP 2	MAX	57	52	41	49	68	46	57	39	44	45	68	43	41	37	53	51	54	64	80	80	78	77	83	83	83	84	87	76	72	75		62
	MIN	43	34	27	34	45	34	38	31	30	30	32	28	27	25	24	36	46	52	50	57	54	48	60	61	63	61	60	58	54	52		43
PITTSBURGH WB CITY	MAX	60	54	45	49	72	49	60	43	45	47	70	48	43	38	55	53	55	65	81	83	77	78	85	85	83	87	89	78	75	78		64
	MIN	48	36	30	36	47	38	42	32	31	34	34	31	30	29	30	37	48	55	50	59	58	51	62	65	67	62	61	63	57	53		45
PLEASANT MOUNT 1 W	MAX	45	54	49	37	31	40	40	45	34	32	41	54	54	37	35	43	54	55	51	63	74	74	65	72	78	56	76	81	71	66		53
	MIN	23	35	22	24	25	31	33	31	24	19	21	30	21	23	20	21	33	42	45	37	54	40	42	47	49	49	50	54	48	41		
PORT CLINTON	MAX	55	59	60	50	42	55	52	64	45	50	53	62	70	55	42	56	60	55	56	60	69	83	69	75	82	58	80	93	89	78		
	MIN	24	31	29	30	30	35	40	39	30	26	22	33	28	26	26	22	38	47	48	41	42	45	44	47	51	50	54	55	54	44		
PUTNEYVILLE 2 SE DAM	MAX	54	59	52	42	42	60	41	55	38	40	44	68	38	42	38	54	53	55	59	77	83	76	78	83	82	81	85	86	77	72		
	MIN	26	39	22	27	27	32	30	31	26	26	23	31	20	23	19	24	38	44	46	49	55	45	53	57	57	53	51	52	48	42		
QUAKERTOWN 1 E	MAX	59	59	50	46	60	56	62	60	49	51	64	70	48	45	56	61	57	55	60	68	82	78	77	82	82	83	88	87	84	76		
	MIN	29	35	31	31	33	44	42	37	32	30	23	44	30	31	28	24	46	48	50	40	48	50	46	56	51	51	59	54	58	48		
READING WB CITY	MAX	57	61	52	42	64	54	63	48	50	53	65	71	48	47	56	60	57	56	61	69	85	68	77	82	61	80	91	90	79	74		
	MIN	38	40	35	33	37	44	44	38	34	35	31	39	32	33	32	32	50	51	51	48	58	53	49	61	54	54	65	61	61	58		
RIDGWAY 3 W	MAX	51	58	49	40	36	51	39	44	35	38	41	62	36	38	35	51	53	50	55	75	81	75	74	80	83	80	80	85	75	71		
	MIN	14	32	16	17	32	33	33	31	28	30	18	26	17	21	20	23	27	45	46	50	52	37	52	53	56	56	49	49	38	33		
SALINA 3 W	MAX	58	53	44	43	66	57	58	42	43	46	69	66	41	38	52	51	53	60	79	82	77	76	82	82	81	85	87	82	77	76		
	MIN	40	40	25	32	40	35	36	36	29	32	26	32	23	27	20	29	45	50	47	50	53	44	45	58	60	55	53	55	53	42		
SCRANTON	MAX	57	60	55	43	37	56	49	54	39	40	47	65	62	41	43	51	60	59	61	66	77	80	70	72	84	62	83	88	80	74		
	MIN	26	39	28	29	28	37	40	36	29	28	30	33	27	27	30	29	34	42	49	48	52	52	45	48	55	54	56	61	55	48		
SCRANTON WB AIRPORT	MAX	57	52	40	36	58	49	54	38	40	46	63	59	43	42	49	60	53	59	66	76	79	70	75	80	63	80	84	77	70	63		5
	MIN	33	32	25	27	34	37	35	31	27	27	25	27	25	27	27	28	46	45	48	46	52	45	43	57	53	52	59	56	53	45		38
SELINSGROVE CAA AP	MAX	56	59	45	38	58	48	56	41	47	50	67	58	46	45	57	61	54	57	61	71	81	71	80	84	67	81	88	84	78	70		61
	MIN	38	33	28	31	33	40	40	35	32	28	22	30	29	30	25	25	47	49	50	52	52	47	48	59	56	55	59	58	53	50		41
SHIPPENSBURG	MAX	55	62	56	48	45	55	65	64	47	53	68	67	47	50	55	62	60	59	61	75	84	78	79	82	79	80	92	89	80	78		65
	MIN	35	38	32	32	33	38	40	37	33	33	26	42	30	28	27	30	48	48	52	52	56	50	50	59	56	54	55	61	57	56		42
SHIPPINGPORT WB	MAX	68	52	41	50	68	47	56	39	44	46	69	43	41	37	54	51	56	65	81	83	76	80	84	86	84	84	85	76	73	74		62
	MIN	40	34	28	35	45	35	38	33	32	30	28	29	27	26	25	33	48	50	48	53	53	44	58	60	58	59	56	56	50	46		41
SLIPPERY ROCK	MAX	57	50	40	40	62	48	50	35	39	45	59	48	41	38	53	51	55	59	77	82	76	79	83	82	82	84	84	82	72	74		68
	MIN	40	36	22	30	37	32	31	30	27	30	27	29	24	26	28	22	44	49	47	54	61	44	58	60	60	57	66	57	48	48		40
SOMERSET MAIN ST	MAX	56	54	46	42	54	54	64	57	41	45	65	64	39	37	50	54	56	64	77	79	79	70	80	82	78	83	84	83	78	75		63
	MIN	36	40	29	30	34	30	32	36	26	31	23	30	22	24	22	28	43	49	45	53	54	45	53	53	59	54	53	52	51	47		39
SPRINGBORO	MAX	56	59	53	39	43	60	39	39	37	40	45	49	38	39	39	49	54	55	64	79	78	70	76	80	82	84	83	84	74	70		58
	MIN	29	40	20	30	34	34	31	30	23	30	29	29	23	25	22	28	40	44	43	56	58	37	56	58	58	54	55	54	37	38		38
SPRINGS 1 SW	MAX	55	51	45	39	52	48	64	54	39	43	63	45	36	35	41	52	54	66	72	77	75	68	78	82	75	81	82	80	69	73		59
	MIN	32	35	29	31	33	28	32	37	23	30	22	28	20	23	21	25	42	47	45	53	50	42	50	50	55	50	50	51	50	38		37
STATE COLLEGE	MAX	57	55	43	34	49	43	56	37	42	47	66	49	41	39	55	56	55	55	61	79	77	68	83	81	68	84	88	84	76	77		60
	MIN	40	36	29	29	33	30	39	34	30	32	27	28	26	26	27	35	47	50	50	55	56	49	51	60	57	54	56	61	56	55		41
STROUDSBURG	MAX	53	62	47	33	40	47	57	41	43	54	62	71	45	45	55	63	53	60	65	70	80	69	77	78	63	83	86	88	75	70		61
	MIN	24	33	26	28	31	39	38	34	30	29	23	31	28	28	22	21	44	46	45	38	50	47	44	53	53	50	59	52	52	47		38
TAMARACK 2 S FIRE TWR	MAX	44	51	50	38	32	49	38	35	31	35	40	58	38	38	35	49	53	50	50	59	76	75	68	77	79	67	80	86	79	73		54
	MIN	24	33	19	19	25	31	31	29	22	22	23	26	18	21	21	23	35	42	45	49	50	43	45	45	53	51	52	59	45	44		34
TIONESTA 2 SE DAM	MAX	53	59	49	41	39	52	39	45	35	39	40	60	40	40	35	51	52	51	57	76	81	75	78	83	82	82	81	84	74	70		58
	MIN	27	34	21	24	32	34	33	31	27	28	22	30	19	25	21	25	31	44	47	46	53	40	46	56	57	58	53	54	41	42		36

See reference notes following Station Index.

ıble 5 - Continued

DAILY TEMPERATURES

PENNSYLVANIA
APRIL 1957

Station		1	2	3	4	5	6	7	8	9	10	11	12	13	14	15	16	17	18	19	20	21	22	23	24	25	26	27	28	29	30	31	Average
TUSVILLE WATER WORKS	MAX	58	53	40	48	55	48	42	34	39	39	57	44	38	35	50	52	53	59	79	82	75	79	80	86	83	83	85	76	71	73		59.9
	MIN	24	36	19	30	35	32	32	30	25	29	22	28	17	23	18	25	43	45	50	49	58	34	54	57	52	58	52	55	36	38		36.9
WANDA	MAX	59	52	42	37	48	56	30	43	41	48	63	54	44	43	52	60	56	60	69	81	81	74	79	84	74	84	88	75	73	66		61.1
	MIN	27	35	24	27	31	37	38	31	27	22	22	34	25	26	25	23	47	45	49	51	58	39	47	55	53	53	56	58	47	44		38.5
IONTOWN	MAX	61	57	47	49	75	53	70	50	46	51	71	51	43	44	54	55	59	68	83	86	83	79	85	87	83	87	87	84	76	77		66.7
	MIN	42	40	33	39	48	35	39	35	33	34	28	34	28	29	21	34	45	54	54	57	60	51	63	59	64	57	63	58	56	43		44.5
PER DARBY	MAX	59	64	52	48	62	63	65	59	50	55	64	70	47	55	60	62	60	58	59	69	87	80	76	83	73	80	89	88	84	76		66.6
	MIN	35	49	35	34	37	46	43	38	35	33	39	33	32	30	32	31	47	53	50	46	53	56	48	60	53	52	63	56	58	57		44.5
RREN	MAX	61	54	40	38	53	49	39	39	40	41	57	45	39	37	50	52	50	56	78	81	75	79	80	89	85	83	86	74	71	70		59.6
	MIN	35	33	21	30	35	34	34	31	27	31	24	29	21	24	24	29	44	44	48	55	59	42	54	58	63	60	53	57	39	41		39.3
YNESBURG 2 W	MAX	61	55	45	56	74	56	70	58	47	50	70	44	44	44	58	54	56	70	86	82	82	77	83	87	84	87	88	84	74	76		66.7
	MIN	31	43	29	39	45	34	35	38	32	29	24	35	25	25	17	25	45	52	48	47	49	47	54	54	60	56	53	53	54	39		40.6
LLSBORO 3 S	MAX	46	51	47	37	36	52	40	44	32	38	43	58	42	40	37	46	54	50	51	57	75	76	67	76	79	62	77	84	72	69		54.6
	MIN	25	35	20	23	25	35	29	29	23	23	24	29	20	23	19	27	37	43	46	49	50	43	44	46	53	52	54	57	44	42		35.6
LLSVILLE	MAX	56	64	53	46	63	63	64	62	49	52	67	71	48	47	54	61	58	58	60	72	85	70	75	80	69	78	88	87	82	73		65.2
	MIN	29	40	32	33	34	43	40	37	33	26	21	35	30	24	20	25	46	46	52	51	49	48	50	52	55	54	54	59	55	49		40.7
ST CHESTER	MAX																																
	MIN																																
LLIAMSPORT WB AP	MAX	56	55	45	38	57	48	54	40	47	51	69	55	47	48	55	60	55	57	60	72	82	70	73	84	69	80	88	82	78	73		61.6
	MIN	37	38	29	29	33	41	40	35	32	32	24	32	29	30	28	28	48	50	51	54	53	45	48	59	54	56	59	59	57	49		41.9
RK 3 SSW PUMP STA	MAX	56	61	57	48	65	65	67	66	49	54	68	70	48	47	55	62	70	59	63	77	85	80	81	84	71	81	92	89	81	78		67.6
	MIN	35	44	29	35	31	43	41	39	34	29	25	43	32	28	24	28	49	50	53	51	53	48	52	60	56	54	56	60	58	45		42.6

ble 6

EVAPORATION AND WIND

Station		1	2	3	4	5	6	7	8	9	10	11	12	13	14	15	16	17	18	19	20	21	22	23	24	25	26	27	28	29	30	31	Total or Avg.
TATE COLLEGE	EVAP	-	-	.12	-	-	-	.12	.05	-	.11	.13	.12	.11	.06	.09	.10	*	*	.04	.04	.07	.21	.16	.11	.11	.11	.19	.10	.38	.32		B3.42
	WIND	34	48	89	50	45	47	233	65	103	113	84	56	95	109	101	29	31	8	13	32	47	73	50	33	29	48	15	27	56	76		1839

See reference notes following Station Index.

ALLENTOWN WB AIRPORT

AUSTINBURG 2 W

BEACH CREEK STATION

BRADFORD 4 W RESVR

BROOKVILLE CAA AIRPORT

CANTON 1 NW

CARROLLTOWN 2 SSE

COALDALE 2 NW

CORRY

DONEGAL

DU BOIS 7 E

ENGLISH CENTER

ERIE WB AIRPORT

EVERETT 1 SW

FORD CITY 4 S DAM

GALETON

GEORGE SCHOOL

GRATERFORD

GREENSBORO LOCK 7

HANOVER

HARRISBURG WB AIRPORT

HAWLEY 1 S DAM

HOLTWOOD

HOOVERSVILLE

INDIANA 3 SE

KANE 1 NNE

KEATING SUMMIT

LANCASTER 2 NE PUMP STA

LAWRENCEVILLE 2 S

LEWISTOWN

MARTINSBURG CAA AIRPORT

MATAMORAS

MEADVILLE 1 S

MEDIX RUN

MONTROSE 1 E

MUHLENBURG 1 SE

NEWPORT

PHILADELPHIA WB AIRPORT

See reference notes following Station Index.

SNOWFALL AND SNOW ON GROUND

Station		1	2	3	4	5	6	7	8	9	10	11	12	13	14	15	16	17	18	19	20	21	22	23	24	25	26	27	28	29	30	31
ILADELPHIA CITY	SNOWFALL	-	-	-	-	-	-	-	-	-	-	-	-	-	-	-	-	-	-	-	-	-	-	-	-	-	-	-	-	-	-	
	SN ON GND	-	-	-	-	-	-	-	-	-	-	-	-	-	-	-	-	-	-	-	-	-	-	-	-	-	-	-	-	-	-	
ILIPSBURG CAA AIRPORT	SNOWFALL			.6	11.0	2.0	T		.5	.8	T		T	.3	T																	
	SN ON GND				6	10	3	3	T	1					T																	
APLE HILL	SNOWFALL				4.6	4.3	T	T	T	1.8	.1	T		1.1	.2	T																
	SN ON GND	T	T		5	8	3	1	T	2	1	T	T	1	T	T	T															
TTSBURGH WB AIRPORT 2	SNOWFALL			.5			T		.5	.8			.2	.2	T																	
	SN ON GND						T			T					T																	
	WTR EQUIV																															
EASANT MOUNT 1 W	SNOWFALL				T	8.0		T	T	3.0	T	T		T		T																
	SN ON GND				T	8	5	4	2	5	5	2	T	T	T	T	T	T														
ADING WB CITY	SNOWFALL				1.0					T			T		T																	
	SN ON GND																															
ANTON WB AIRPORT	SNOWFALL				6.9				.6	.5	T			T	T																	
	SN ON GND				2	4				T					T																	
	WTR EQUIV				.1	1.0																										
INSGROVE CAA AIRPORT	SNOWFALL				5.2					T																						
	SN ON GND				5	3				T																						
IPPENSBURG	SNOWFALL				.7									T	T																	
	SN ON GND																															
IPPINGPORT WB	SNOWFALL			1.4	T		T		T	T			T	T	T																	
	SN ON GND				T																											
IPPERY ROCK	SNOWFALL				3.0					3.0					1.0																	
	SN ON GND				3					3					1																	
IINGS 1 SW	SNOWFALL						T			2.0			T	T	1.0																	
	SN ON GND						T			2			T		1																	
IARACK 2 S FIRE TWR	SNOWFALL				5.0	2.5		T	T	2.0	T	T		T	T	T																
	SN ON GND	3	T		5	7	4	4	3	5	4	3	T	T	T	T	T	T														
ONESTA 2 SE DAM	SNOWFALL				4.0	T		T	3.0	4.0	T		T	T	1.0	T																
	SN ON GND				4	2			3	6	3	1	T	T	1	T	T															
'ANDA	SNOWFALL				1.5	7.7			1.0	3.0	T				T	T																
	SN ON GND				2	6	T		1	4	1																					
ER CITY 5 SW	SNOWFALL				3.0					1.0																						
	SN ON GND				-					-																						
LIAMSPORT WB AIRPORT	SNOWFALL				5.7				.2	T	T			T	T																	
	SN ON GND				3	3				T	T																					
	WTR EQUIV				.3	.4																										

See reference notes following Station Index.

TOTAL PRECIPITATION

PENNSYLVANIA
APRIL 1957

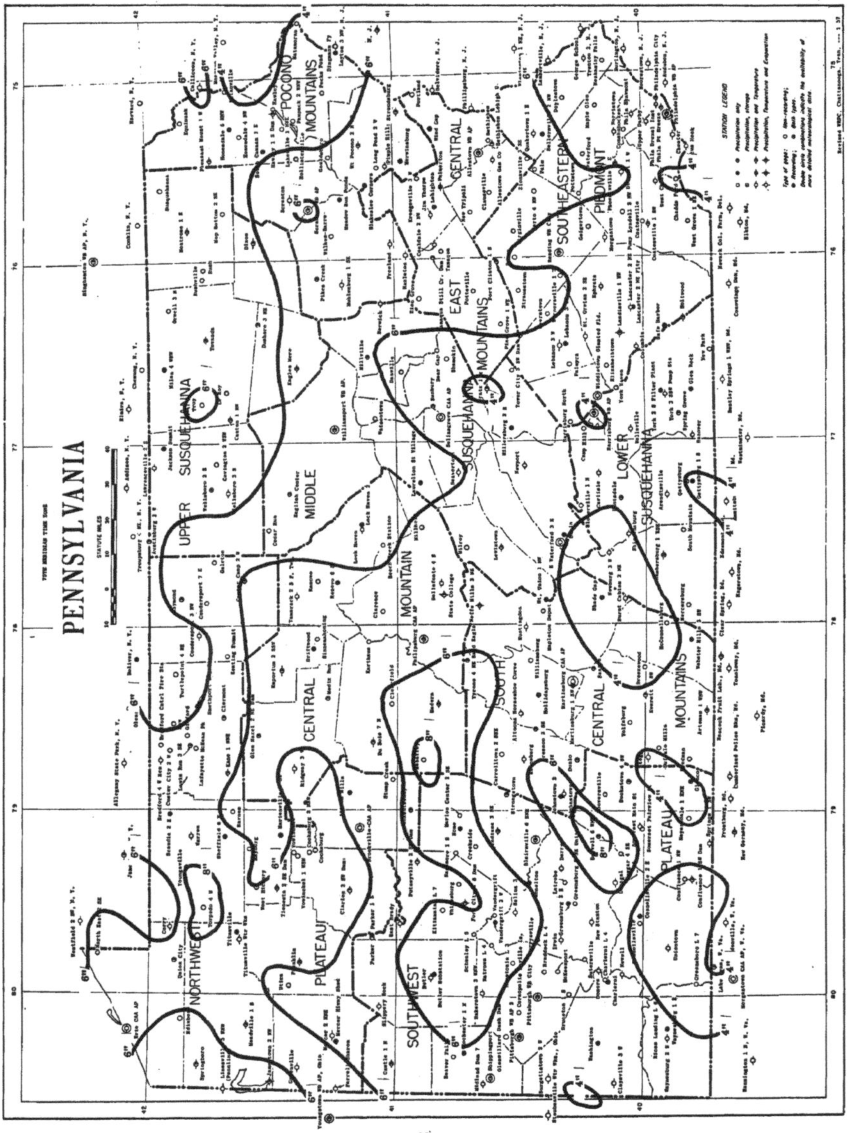

AVERAGE TEMPERATURE

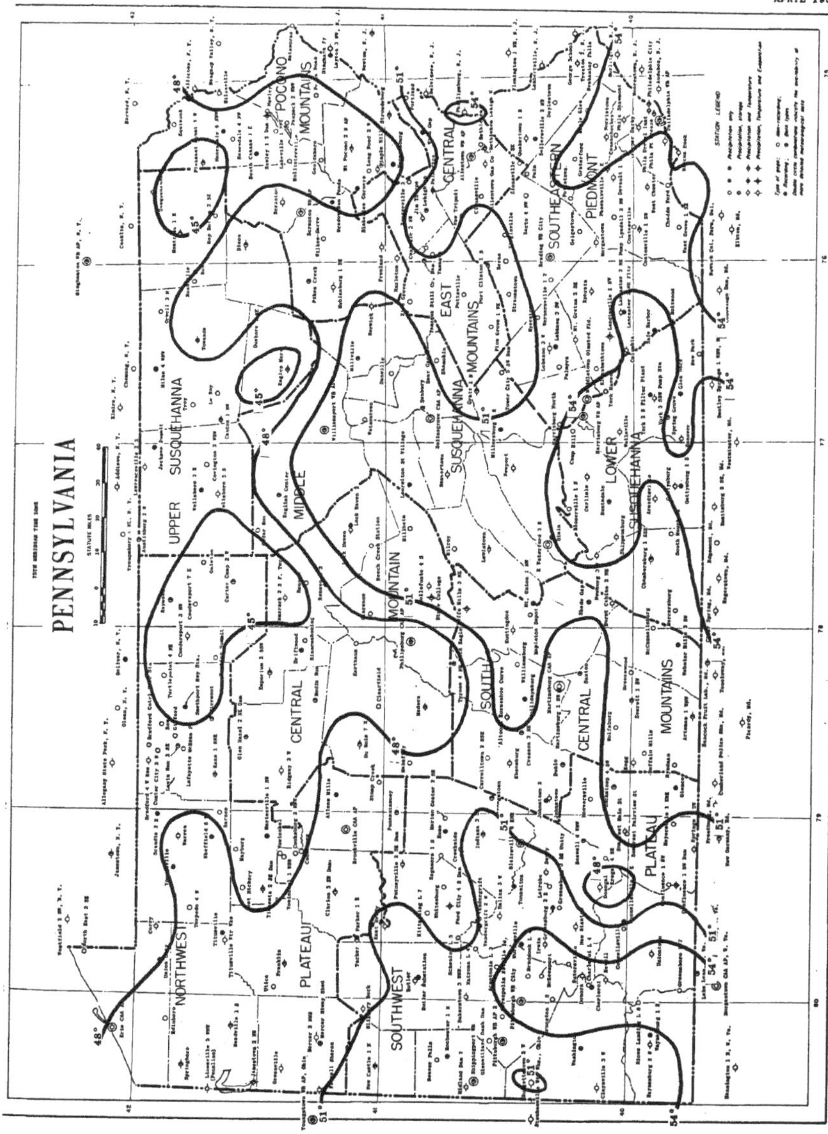

Isolines are drawn through points of approximately equal values. Hourly precipitation data from recorder substations will be available in the publication "Hourly Precipitation Data".

STATI

Station	Index No.	County	Drainage	Latitude	Longitude	Elevation	Observation Time Temp.	Observation Time Precip.	Observer	Refer To Tables
ACMETONIA LOCK 3	0022	ALLEGHENY	1	40 32	79 49	748		7A	CORPS OF ENGINEERS	3
ALLENS MILLS	0099	JEFFERSON	1	41 12	78 55	1600		MID	CHARLES M. ALLEN	C
ALLENTOWN WB AP	0106	LEHIGH	9	40 39	75 26	376	MID	MID	U.S. WEATHER BUREAU	2 3 5 7 C
ALLENTOWN GAS CO	0111	LEHIGH	9	40 36	75 28	254	7A	7A	LEHIGH VLY GAS DIV	2 3 5
ALTOONA HORSESHOE CURVE	0134	BLAIR	6	40 30	78 29	1500	6P	6P	ALTOONA WATER BUR.	2 3 5
ARENDTSVILLE	0229	ADAMS	15	39 55	77 18	710	8A	8A	PA STATE COL EXP	2 3 5
ARTEMAS 1 WNW	0259	BEDFORD	12	39 45	78 28	1250	6P	6P	GRAYSON E.NORTHCRAFT	2 3 5 C
AUSTINBURG 2 W	0313	TIOGA	15	42 00	77 32	1590		7A	OTTO D. BACON	3 7 C
BAKERSTOWN 3 WNW	0355	ALLEGHENY	1	40 39	79 59	1230	7P	7P	PGH CUT FLOWER CO	2 3 5
BARNES	0409	WARREN	1	41 40	79 02	1310		7A	CORPS OF ENGINEERS	3
BARTO 4 NW	0428	BERKS	14	40 26	75 39	312		7A	MARIE B. NICHLAS	3
BEAR GAP	0457	NORTHUMBLAND	15	40 50	76 30	900		MID	ROARING CRK WTR CO	3
BEAVER FALLS	0475	BEAVER	2	40 46	80 19	760		7A	HOWARD R. KEMP	3
BEAVERTOWN	0482	SNYDER	15	40 45	77 10	640	7A	7A	MARLIN RC ETTINGER	2 3 5
BEECH CREEK STATION	0499	CENTRE	16	41 04	77 34	620		7A	HAROLD S. RUPERT	3 7
BELLEFONTE 4 S	0530	CENTRE	16	40 51	77 47	1110	8A	8A	ROCKVIEW PRISON FARM	2 3 5
BERNE	0599	BERKS	14	40 31	76 00	325		7A	FLOYD W. TRUMP	3
BERWICK	0611	COLUMBIA	15	41 04	76 15	570	6P	6P	AMER CAR + FNDRY CO	2 3 5
BETHLEHEM	0629	NORTHAMPTON	9	40 37	75 22	400		7A	ARTHUR CROPPER	3
#BETHLEHEM LEHIGH UNIV	0634	NORTHAMPTON	9	40 36	75 23	490	MID	MID	LEHIGH UNIVERSITY	2 3 5 C
BLAIN	0725	PERRY	15	40 20	77 31	750		MID	PA DEPT FRST + WTRS	C
BLAIRSVILLE 6 ENE	0736	INDIANA	4	40 27	79 09	2048	8P	8P	U.S. WEATHER BUREAU	2 3 5
BLAKESLEE CORNERS	0743	MONROE	9	41 06	75 36	1650		MID	WALTER WILDRICK	C
BLOSERVILLE 1 N	0763	CUMBERLAND	15	40 16	77 22	650		5P	MRS. B. M. WILLDERS	3
BOSWELL 6 WNW	0820	SOMERSET	1	40 10	79 08	2570		8A	CLARK N. ST. CLAIR	3 C
BRADDOCK LOCK 2	0861	ALLEGHENY	10	40 24	79 52	725		7A	CORPS OF ENGINEERS	3
BRADFORD CNTRL FIRE STA	0867	MC KEAN	1	41 57	78 39	1500		8A	BRADFORD FIRE DEPT	3
BRADFORD 4 W RES	0868	MC KEAN	1	41 57	78 44	1680	5P	5P	BRADFORD WTR DEPT	2 3 5 7
BREEZEWOOD	0905	BEDFORD	6	40 00	78 14	1352		MID	PA TURNPIKE COMM	3
BROOKVILLE CAA AIRPORT	1002	JEFFERSON	1	41 09	79 06	1417	MID	MID	CIVIL AERO. ADM.	2 3 5 7
BRUCETON 1 S	1033	ALLEGHENY	10	40 18	79 59	1065		7A	AUSTIN R. COOPER	3
BUCKSTOWN 1 SE	1073	SOMERSET	4	40 04	78 50	2460		MID	ALVIN W. MANGES	C
BUFFALO MILLS	1087	BEDFORD	6	39 57	78 39	1318		7A	MRS. NELLE R. BROWN	3
BURGETTSTOWN 2 W	1105	WASHINGTON	11	40 23	80 26	980	7A	7A	SMITH TWP MUN AUTH	2 3 5
BURNT CABINS 2 NE	1115	HUNTINGDON	6	40 05	77 52	990	MID	MID	PA TURNPIKE COMM	2 3 5
#BUTLER	1130	BUTLER	2	40 52	79 54	1100	4P	7A	WILLIAM C. FAUST	2 3 5
BUTLER SUBSTATION	1135	BUTLER	2	40 51	79 53	1140		MID	WEST PENN POWER CO	C
CAMP HILL	1198	CUMBERLAND	15	40 15	76 55	461		6P	JOSEPH N. HOBART	3
CANTON 1 NW	1215	BRADFORD	15	41 40	76 52	1520	7A	7A	MRS.MILDRED SPENCER	2 3 5 7 C
CARLISLE	1234	CUMBERLAND	15	40 12	77 11	460	6P	6P	C. E. MILLER	2 3 5
CARROLLTOWN 2 SSE	1259	CAMBRIA	16	40 35	78 42	2040		8A	ROBERT F. MAURER	3 7
CARTER CAMP 2 W	1262	POTTER	16	41 37	77 45	2030		7A	RICHARD L. MENKEN	3 C
CEDAR RUN	1301	LYCOMING	16	41 31	77 27	800		7A	KATHRYN T.KREIGHBAUM	3
CHADDS FORD	1342	DELAWARE	5	39 52	75 36	160		8A	MRS.GRACE A. HICKS	3
CHAMBERSBURG 1 ESE	1354	FRANKLIN	12	39 56	77 38	640	9P	9P	CHARLES A. BENDER	2 3 5 C
CHARLEROI	1372	WASHINGTON	10	40 08	79 55	1040		MID	WEST PENN POWER CO	C
CHARLEROI LOCK 4	1377	WESTMORELAND	10	40 09	79 54	749		7A	CORPS OF ENGINEERS	3
#CHESTER	1423	DELAWARE	5	39 51	75 22	86	8A	8A	CHESTER TIMES	2 3 5
CLARENCE	1480	CENTRE	16	41 03	77 56	1410		7A	MISS VELDA SWANCER	3
CLARION 3 SW	1485	CLARION	1	41 12	79 26	1114	8P	7A	PA ELECTRIC CO	2 3 5 C
CLAUSSVILLE	1505	LEHIGH	9	40 37	75 39	670		8A	WILLIAM J. DOTTERER	3
CLAYSVILLE 3 W	1512	WASHINGTON	11	40 07	80 28	1000	7P	7A	MFGRS. L + H CO	2 3 5
CLEARFIELD	1519	CLEARFIELD	16	41 01	78 26	1100		7A	IRA TAYLOR	3
CLERMONT	1529	MC KEAN	1	41 41	78 30	2104		7A	MRS.TILLIE M.SIMONDS	3 C
COALDALE 2 NW	1572	SCHUYLKILL	9	40 50	75 56	1026		7A	PANTHER VLY WTR CO	3 7
COATESVILLE 1 SW	1589	CHESTER	5	39 58	75 50	342	8A	8A	PHILA ELECTRIC CO	2 3 5 C
COATESVILLE	1594	CHESTER	5	39 59	75 49	340		8A	EDWARD D. BIEDEMAN	INAC 12/55
COLUMBIA	1675	LANCASTER	15	40 02	76 30	300	SS	SS	JAMES M. RUST	2 3 5
CONFLUENCE 1 SW DAM	1705	SOMERSET	17	39 48	79 22	1490	8A	8A	CORPS OF ENGINEERS	2 3 5 6 C
CONFLUENCE 1 NW	1710	FAYETTE	17	39 50	79 22	1331		7A	JOHN L. REID	3
CONNELLSVILLE	1723	FAYETTE	17	40 01	79 36	870		8A	MARSHALL B. MENEFEE	3
CONNELLSVILLE 2 E	1729	FAYETTE	17	40 01	79 33	1300		MID	HARRY C. JOY	C
CONSHOHOCKEN	1737	MONTGOMERY	5	40 04	75 19	70		8A	PHILA ELECTRIC CO	3
COOKSBURG	1749	CLARION	1	41 20	79 13	1180		8A	PA DEPT FRST + WTRS	3
COOKSBURG 2 NNW	1752	CLARION	1	41 21	79 13	1460		8A	PA DEPT FRST + WTRS	3
CORAOPOLIS NEVILLE IS	1773	ALLEGHENY	11	40 30	80 05	720		8A	PGH. COKE + CHEM CO	3
CORRY	1790	ERIE	1	41 56	79 38	1427	7P	8A	LEO C. NECKERS	2 3 5 7
COUDERSPORT 3 NW	1806	POTTER	1	41 49	78 03	2020	7P	8A	MISS ELIZABETH NEFF	2 3 5
COUDERSPORT 7 E	1809	POTTER	1	41 46	77 53	2425		7A	CAMP POTATO	3
COVINGTON 2 WSW	1833	TIOGA	15	41 44	77 07	1745		7A	CALVIN R. PACKARD	3
CREEKSIDE	1881	INDIANA	1	40 41	79 12	1035		7A	CORPS OF ENGINEERS	3
CRESSON 2 SE	1895	CAMBRIA	6	40 27	78 34	2540		7A	MILES M. LINGLE	3 C
CUSTER CITY 2 W	1978	MC KEAN	1	41 55	78 41	2120		8A	M. D. BOOTH AND CO	3
DANVILLE	2013	MONTOUR	15	40 58	76 37	460		7A	MRS.MARIE H. LITTLE	3
DERRY	2108	WESTMORELAND	4	40 20	79 18	1150	6P	6P	MISS N. D. WINEMAN	2 3 5
DEVAULT 1 W	2116	CHESTER	14	40 05	75 33	360	MID	MID	PA TURNPIKE COMM	2 3 5
DINGMANS FERRY	2160	PIKE	5	41 13	74 52	364		MID	CLYDE T. VOORHEES	C
DIXON	2171	WYOMING	15	41 34	75 54	620	7A	7A	HAROLD J. KUSCHEL	2 3 5 C
DONEGAL	2183	WESTMORELAND	17	40 07	79 23	1746	MID	MID	PA TURNPIKE COMM	2 3 5 7
#DONORA	2190	WASHINGTON	10	40 11	79 51	814	12M	12M	DONORA ZINC WORKS	2 3 5
DOYLESTOWN	2221	BUCKS	5	40 18	75 08	393		5P	GEORGE HART	3
DRIFTWOOD	2245	CAMERON	16	41 20	78 08	880		MID	SIDNEY KENNEDY	C
DU BOIS 7 E	2265	CLEARFIELD	16	41 06	78 38	1670	5P	5P	CITY OF DU BOIS	2 3 5 7 C
DUNLO	2298	CAMBRIA	4	40 17	78 43	2410		MID	MRS. D. L. WHITE	C
DUSHORE 3 NE	2324	SULLIVAN	16	41 33	76 21	1750		7A	PATRICK F. RYAN	3 C
EAGLES MERE	2343	SULLIVAN	16	41 24	76 35	2020	7A	7A	MRS.ELSIE P. BIGGER	2 3 5 C
EAST BRADY	2363	CLARION	1	40 59	79 37	820	5P	5P	A. B. KEMPEL	2 3 5
EAST WATERFORD 3 E	2459	PERRY	6	40 21	77 33	2125	8A	8A	U.S. WEATHER BUREAU	INAC 5/55
EBENSBURG	2466	CAMBRIA	4	40 29	78 43	2090	7P	7A	ROBERT A. WASSER	2 3 5
EDINBORO	2514	ERIE	1	41 52	80 08	1220		8A	EDINBORO ST TCHR COL	3
ELIZABETHTOWN	2560	LANCASTER	15	40 09	76 37	460		8A	MASONIC HOME	3
EMPORIUM 2 SSW	2634	CAMERON	16	41 28	78 15	1735	7A	7A	JACKSON THOMAS	2 3 5 C
ENGLISH CENTER	2644	LYCOMING	16	41 26	77 17	881		7A	WILLIAM SUDERS	3 7 C
EPHRATA	2662	LANCASTER	15	40 11	76 10	465	6P	6P	STANLEY L.VON NEIDA	2 3 5
EQUINUNK 2	2671	WAYNE	5	41 51	75 13	910		7A	MRS. HENRIETTA MURRY	3
ERIE WB AIRPORT	2682	ERIE	8	42 05	80 12	732	MID	MID	U. S. WEATHER BUREAU	2 3 5 7
EVERETT 1 SW	2721	BEDFORD	6	40 00	78 23	1020	MID	MID	PA TURNPIKE COMM	2 3 5 7 C
FARRELL SHARON	2814	MERCER	2	41 14	80 30	865	7P	7P	SHARON STEEL CORP	2 3 5
FORD CITY 4 S DAM	2942	ARMSTRONG	1	40 43	79 30	950	8A	8A	CORPS OF ENGINEERS	2 3 5 6 7 C
FRANKLIN	3028	VENANGO	1	41 23	79 49	987	7P	7A	GEORGE S. SMITH. JR	2 3 5 C
FREELAND	3056	LUZERNE	15	41 01	75 54	1900	6P	8A	ANDREW B. EVANSHA	2 3 5
GALETON	3130	POTTER	16	41 44	77 39	1325		7A	W. GALE LUSH	3 7
GEIGERTOWN	3189	BERKS	14	40 13	75 50	400		8A	WALTER C. WOLF	3
GEORGE SCHOOL	3200	BUCKS	5	40 13	74 56	135	7P	7P	GEORGE M. HART	2 3 5 7
#GETTYSBURG	3218	ADAMS	12	39 50	77 14	540	9A	9A	HUGH C. MC ILHENNY	2 3 5
GETTYSBURG 1 S	3223	ADAMS	12	39 48	77 14	560		MID	NAT MILITARY PARK	C
GIFFORD	3237	MC KEAN	1	41 51	78 36	2220		8A	SOUTH PENN OIL CO	3
GLENCOE	3298	SOMERSET	12	39 49	78 51	1620		MID	MRS. MARY M.HARTMAN	C
GLEN HAZEL 2 NE DAM	3311	ELK	1	41 34	78 36	1725		8A	CORPS OF ENGINEERS	3 C
GLEN ROCK	3330	YORK	15	39 48	76 44	620		MID	MRS.E.C.MC WILLIAMS	C
GLENWILLARD DASH DAM	3343	ALLEGHENY	11	40 33	80 13	705		7A	CORPS OF ENGINEERS	3
GOULDSBORO	3394	WAYNE	9	41 15	75 27	1890		7A	L. H. EILENBERGER	3
GRATERFORD	3435	MONTGOMERY	14	40 14	75 27	160	7A	7A	CLAUDE K. KULP	2 3 5 7 C
GRATZ 1 N	3438	DAUPHIN	15	40 38	76 43	760	8A	8A	LEE M. LEITZEL	2 3 5 C
GREENSBORO LOCK 7	3503	GREENE	10	39 47	79 55	808		7A	CORPS OF ENGINEERS	3 7
GREENSBURG 2 E	3515	WESTMORELAND	10	40 18	79 31	1225		MID	PA DEPT HIGHWAYS	C
GREENSBURG 3 SE UNITY	3516	WESTMORELAND	10	40 17	79 30	1245		6P	WESTMORELAND WTR CO	3
GREENVILLE	3526	MERCER	2	41 24	80 23	1026	6P	6P	C. EARL MILLER	2 3 5
HANOVER	3662	YORK	15	39 48	76 50	600	8A	8A	HANOVER EVENING SUN	2 3 5 7
#HARRISBURG WB AP	3699	YORK	15	40 13	76 51	335	MID	MID	U.S. WEATHER BUREAU	2 3 5 7 C
HARRISBURG NORTH	3704	DAUPHIN	15	40 18	76 54	323		9A	GEORGE S. BEAL	3
HAWLEY	3758	WAYNE	5	41 29	75 10	880		7A	MRS. KATHERINE BATES	3
HAWLEY 1 S DAM	3761	WAYNE	5	41 28	75 11	1200	7A	7A	PA POWER + LIGHT CO	2 3 5 6 7 C
HOLLIDAYSBURG	4001	BLAIR	6	40 26	78 24	960		MID	JOHN M. RINGLER	C
HOLLISTERVILLE	4008	WAYNE	5	41 23	75 26	1360		8A	PA POWER + LIGHT CO	3
#HOLTWOOD	4019	LANCASTER	15	39 50	76 20	187	MID	8A	PA POWER + LIGHT CO	2 3 5 7 C
HOME	4027	INDIANA	1	40 45	79 06	1220		MID	MRS. EDNA M. BUSH	C
HONESDALE 4 NW	4043	WAYNE	5	41 37	75 19	1410		8A	GEORGE C. WILLIAMS	3
HONESDALE 6 NNW	4044	WAYNE	5	41 39	75 17	1050		MID	FRIEND E. WALTER	C
HOOVERSVILLE	4058	SOMERSET	4	40 09	78 55	1660		7A	PA ELECTRIC CO	3 7

STATION INDEX

Station	Index No.	County	Drainage I	Latitude	Longitude	Elevation	Observation Time Temp.	Observation Time Precip.	Observer	Refer To Tables
ANTON WB AIRPORT	7905	LUZERNE	15	41 20	75 44	956	MID	MID	U.S. WEATHER BUREAU	2 3 5 7 C
INSGROVE CAA AP	7931	SNYDER	15	40 49	76 52	437	MID	MID	CIVIL AERO. ADM.	2 3 5 7
LERSVILLE 2 NW	7938	BUCKS	5	40 25	75 20	530		MID	SELLERSVILLE WTR CO	C
DE GAP	7965	HUNTINGDON	6	40 11	77 52	1000		MID	MRS. HELEN M. PYLE	C
MOKIN	7978	NORTHUMBLAND	15	40 48	76 33	770		8A	ROARING CRK WTR CO	3
FFIELD 6 W	8026	WARREN	1	41 41	79 09	1940		MID	L. N. HANSON	C
PPENSBURG	8073	FRANKLIN	15	40 03	77 32	709	4P	4P	KEITH B. ALLEN	2 3 5 7
PPINGPORT WB	8078	BEAVER	11	40 37	80 26	740	MID	MID	U.S. WEATHER BUREAU	2 3 5 7 C
NEMAHONING	8145	CAMERON	16	41 19	78 05	790		7A	MRS.FRANCES CALDWELL	3
PPERY ROCK	8184	BUTLER	2	41 04	80 03	1345	7P	7A	WALTER D. ALBERT	2 3 5 7
THPORT HIGHWAY SHED	8190	MC KEAN	1	41 48	78 27	1510		MID	PA DEPT HIGHWAYS	C
ERSET FAIRVIEW ST	8244	SOMERSET	17	40 01	79 05	2140		7A	HOWARD G. PECK	3
ERSET MAIN ST	8249	SOMERSET	17	40 01	79 05	2150	6P	6P	DAVID L. GROVE	2 3 5
TH CANAAN 1 NE	8275	WAYNE	5	41 31	75 24	1400		MID	EUGENE M. COOK	C
TH MOUNTAIN	8308	FRANKLIN	12	39 51	77 30	1520		7A	PA DEPT OF HEALTH	3
INGBORO	8359	CRAWFORD	8	41 48	80 23	900	8A	8A	SPRINGBORO BOROUGH	2 3 5 C
ING GROVE	8379	YORK	15	39 52	76 52	470		4P	P. H. GLATFELTER CO	3 C
INGS 1 SW	8395	SOMERSET	17	39 44	79 10	2500	8P	8P	ALLEN E. YODER	2 3 5 7
TE COLLEGE	8449	CENTRE	16	40 48	77 52	1175	MID	MID	PA STATE COLLEGE	2 3 5 6 C
AUSSTOWN	8570	BERKS	14	40 29	76 11	600		8A	JACOB KLAHR	3
ONGSTOWN	8589	INDIANA	4	40 33	78 55	1880		MID	HARRY F. BENNETT	C
OUDSBURG	8596	MONROE	5	40 59	75 12	480	11P	11P	WILLIAM MAGERTY	2 3 5 C
MP CREEK	8610	JEFFERSON	1	41 01	78 50	1320		7A	CORPS OF ENGINEERS	3
BURY	8668	NORTHUMBLAND	15	40 51	76 48	440		7A	CHARLES W. BAYLER	3 C
QUEHANNA	8692	SUSQUEHANNA	15	41 57	75 36	1020		7A	MRS. LAURA A.BENSON	3
ERSVILLE	8699	ALLEGHENY	17	40 14	79 48	765		7A	FRANK E. MARSH	3
AQUA	8758	SCHUYLKILL	14	40 48	75 58	830		8A	MRS. MARY L.ROBERTS	3
AQUA 4 N DAM	8763	SCHUYLKILL	14	40 51	75 59	1120		7A	PANTHER VLY WTR CO	3 C
ARACK 2 S FIRE TWR	8770	CLINTON	16	41 24	77 51	2220	7A	7A	JAMES E. SWARTZ	2 3 5 7
NESTA 2 SE DAM	8873	FOREST	1	41 29	79 26	1200	8A	8A	CORPS OF ENGINEERS	2 3 5 7 C
USVILLE	8885	CRAWFORD	1	41 38	79 40	1550		MID	PA ELECTRIC CO	C
USVILLE WATER WORKS	8888	CRAWFORD	1	41 38	79 42	1220	7P	7P	CITY OF TITUSVILLE	2 3 5
PEDO 4 W	8901	WARREN	1	41 47	79 32	1735		7A	MRS. LILY B. GARBER	3
ANDA	8905	BRADFORD	15	41 46	76 26	760	7P	7A	MRS. M. O. PARKS	2 3 5 7 C
ER CITY 5 SW	8910	DAUPHIN	15	40 31	76 57	745		6P	HARRISBURG WTR DEPT	3 7
Y	8959	BRADFORD	15	41 47	76 47	1100		7A	JENNIE L. BALLARD	3
NELTON	8989	INDIANA	4	40 27	79 23	890		MID	MRS. MARY E. WEIMER	C
TLEPOINT 4 NE	9002	MC KEAN	1	41 54	78 16	1640		7A	ROBERT D. STRAIT	3
ONE 4 NE BALD EAGLE	9024	BLAIR	6	40 43	78 12	1020		7A	FREDERICK L. FRIDAY	3 C
ON CITY	9042	ERIE	1	41 54	79 50	1325		7A	FORREST M. BRALEY	3 C
ONTOWN	9050	FAYETTE	10	39 54	79 44	1040	10P	10P	WM. W. MARSTELLER	2 3 5
ER DARBY	9074	DELAWARE	5	39 58	75 18	222	7P	7P	PHIL. SUB.TRANS. CO	2 3 5
CA	9099	VENANGO	1	41 26	79 57	1030		7A	MRS.FLORENCE MILLER	3
DERGRIFT	9128	WESTMORELAND	7	40 36	79 33	800		7A	UNITED ENG+FNDRY CO	3
DERGRIFT 2 W	9133	WESTMORELAND	7	40 36	79 36	995		MID	EUGENE R. YOUNG	C
VIRGINVILLE	9196	BERKS	14	40 31	75 52	350		8A	MRS. MARY H. WRIGHT	3
VOWINCKEL	9206	CLARION	1	41 25	79 14	1620		8A	PA DEPT FRST + WTRS	3
VOWINCKEL 1 WSW	9209	CLARION	1	41 24	79 15	1610		8A	PA DEPT FRST + WTRS	3
WARREN	9298	WARREN	1	41 51	79 08	1280	7P	7A	GILBERT M. REIER	2 3 5
WASHINGTON	9312	WASHINGTON	11	40 11	80 14	1200		MID	PA DEPT HIGHWAYS	C
WATSONTOWN	9345	NORTHUMBLAND	16	41 05	76 52	490		9P	WILLIAM BIRD	3
WAYNESBURG 2 W	9362	GREENE	10	39 54	80 13	980	6P	7A	RALPH L. AMOS	2 3 5
WAYNESBURG 1 E	9367	GREENE	10	39 54	80 10	940		MID	SEWAGE DISPOSAL PLT	C
WEBSTER MILLS 3 SW	9380	FULTON	12	39 49	78 05	920		MID	WILLIAM D. COVER	C
WELLSBORO 3 S	9408	TIOGA	16	41 43	77 16	1920	7A	7A	MARION L. SHUMWAY	2 3 5
WELLSBORO 2 E	9412	TIOGA	16	41 45	77 16	1550		MID	MRS. IDA S. MAYNARD	C
WELLSVILLE	9420	YORK	15	40 03	76 57	500	5P	5P	D. D. HOOVER	2 3 5
WERNERSVILLE 1 W	9430	BERKS	14	40 20	76 08	405		8A	CHARLES A. GRUBER	3
WEST CHESTER	9464	CHESTER	5	39 58	75 36	440	8A	8A	DAILY LOCAL NEWS	2 3 5
WEST GROVE 1 E	9503	CHESTER	5	39 49	75 49	440		8A	CONARD-PYLE CO	3
WEST HICKORY	9507	FOREST	1	41 34	79 25	1090		8A	MRS.HELEN F.KINNEAR	3
WHITESBURG	9655	ARMSTRONG	1	40 45	79 24	1530		7A	CORPS OF ENGINEERS	3
WILKES-BARRE	9702	LAZERNE	15	41 15	75 52	610		7A	MRS. MARY G. MIRMAK	3
WILLIAMSBURG	9714	BLAIR	6	40 28	78 12	860		7A	MYRON K. BIDDLE	3
WILLIAMSPORT WB AP	9728	LYCOMING	16	41 15	76 55	527	MID	MID	U.S. WEATHER BUREAU	2 3 5 7 C
WIND GAP	9781	NORTHAMPTON	5	40 51	75 18	720		MID	OWEN R. PARRY	C
WOLFSBURG	9823	BEDFORD	6	40 03	78 32	1190		7A	WALTER C. RICE	3
YORK 3 SSW PUMP STA	9933	YORK	15	39 55	76 45	390	5P	5P	YORK WATER COMPANY	2 3 5
YORK 2 S FILTER PLANT	9938	YORK	15	39 56	76 44	640		MID	YORK WATER COMPANY	C
YORK HAVEN	9950	YORK	15	40 07	76 43	310		6A	METROPOL EDISON CO	3
YOUNGSVILLE	9966	WARREN	1	41 51	79 20	1225		MID	HENRY CARLETT	C
ZION GROVE	9990	SCHUYLKILL	15	40 54	76 13	940		7A	JAMES D. TEETER	3
ZIONSVILLE 3 SE	9995	LEHIGH	14	40 27	75 27	660		7A	LESLIE HOWATT	3
NEW STATIONS										
EDINBORO 3 SW	2519	CRAWFORD	1	41 50	80 13	1325		8A	WILLIAM HAGER	3

I 1-ALLEGHENY; 2-BEAVER; 3- 4-CONEMAUGH; 5-DELAWARE; 6-JUNIATA; 7-KISKIMINETAS; 8-LAKE ERIE; 9-LEHIGH; 10-MONONGAHELA; 11-OHIO; 12-POTOMAC; 13-LAKE ONTARIO; 14-SCHUYLKILL; 15-SUSQUEHANNA; 16-WEST BRANCH; 17-YOUGHIOGHENY

REFERENCE NOTES

Additional information regarding the climate of Pennsylvania may be obtained by writing to the State Climatologist at Weather Bureau Airport Station, Harrisburg State Airport, New Cumberland, Pennsylvania, or to any Weather Bureau Office near you.

Figures and letters following the station name, such as 12 SSW, indicate distance in miles and direction from the post office.

Delayed data and corrections will be carried only in the June and December issues of this bulletin.

Monthly and seasonal snowfall and heating degree days for the preceding 12 months will be carried in the June issue of this bulletin.

Stations appearing in the Index, but for which data are not listed in the tables, either are missing or were received too late to be included in this issue.

Divisions, as used in Table 2, become effective with data for September 1956.

Unless otherwise indicated, dimensional units used in this bulletin are: Temperature in °F, precipitation and evaporation in inches, and wind movement in miles. Monthly degree day totals are the sums of the negative departures of average daily temperatures from 65° F.

Evaporation is measured in the standard Weather Bureau type pan of 4 foot diameter unless otherwise shown by footnote following Table 6.

Long-term means for full-time stations (those shown in the Station Index as "U. S. Weather Bureau") are based on the period 1921-1950, adjusted to represent observations taken at the present location. Long-term means for all stations except full-time Weather Bureau stations are based on the period 1931-1955.

Water equivalent values published in Table 7 are the water equivalent of snow, sleet or ice on the ground. Samples for obtaining measurements are taken from different points for successive observations; consequently occasional drifting and other causes of local variability in the snowpack result in apparent inconsistencies in the record. Water equivalent of snow on the ground is measured at selected stations when two or more inches of snow are on the ground.

Entries of Snowfall in Tables 2 and 7, and in the seasonal snowfall table, include snow and sleet. Entries of snow on ground include snow, sleet and ice.

Data in Tables 3, 5, and 6 and snowfall in Table 7, when published, are for the 24 hours ending at time of observation. The Station Index lists observation times in the standard of time in local use.

Snow on ground in Table 7 is at observation time for all except Weather Bureau and CAA stations. For these stations snow on ground values are at 7:30 a.m., E.S.T.

- \- No record in Tables 3, 6, 7 and the Station Index. No record in Tables 2 and 5, is indicated by no entry. Consult the annual issue of this publication for interpolated monthly precipitation totals.
- \+ And also on a later date or dates.
- ++ Fastest observed one minute wind speed. This station is not equipped with automatic wind instruments.
- * Amount included in following measurement, time distribution unknown.
- // Gage is equipped with a windshield.
- \# Thermometers are generally exposed in a shelter located a few feet above sod-covered ground; however, the reference indicates that the thermometers are exposed in a shelter located on the roof of a building.
- AM Data based on observational day ending before noon.
- B Adjusted to a full month.
- C In the "Refer to Tables" column in the Station Index the letter "C" indicates recorder stations. These stations are processed for special purposes and are published later in "Hourly Precipitation Data".
- D Water equivalent of snowfall wholly or partly estimated, using a ratio of 1 inch water equivalent to every 10 inches of new snowfall.
- G In the "Refer to Tables" column in the Station Index the letter "G" indicates that soil temperatures are published.
- M One or more days of record missing; if average value is entered, less than 10 days record is missing. See Table 5 for detailed daily record. Degree day data, if carried for this station, have been adjusted to represent the value for a full month.
- R Amounts from recording gage (These amounts are essentially accurate but may vary slightly from the amounts to be published later in "Hourly Precipitation Data".)
- SS This entry in time of observation column in Station Index means observation made near sunset.
- T Trace, an amount too small to measure.
- Y Includes total for previous month.
- VAR This entry in time of observation column in Station Index means variable.

Information concerning the history of changes in locations, elevations, exposure etc. of substations through 1955 may be found in the publication "Substation History" for this state, soon to be issued. That publication, when available, may be obtained from the Superintendent of Documents, Government Printing Office, Washington 25, D. C. at a price to be announced. Similar information for regular Weather Bureau stations may be found in the latest issues of Local Climatological Data, Annual for the respective stations, obtained as indicated above, price 15 cents.

Subscription Price: 30 cents per copy, monthly and annual; $2.50 per year. (Yearly subscription includes the Annual Summary). Checks, and money orders should be made payable to the Superintendent of Documents. Remittance and correspondence regarding subscriptions should be sent to the Superintendent of Documents, Government Printing Office, Washington 25, D. C.

WRPC, Asheville, N. C. --- 6/11/57 --- 1100

U. S. DEPARTMENT OF COMMERCE
SINCLAIR WEEKS, Secretary
WEATHER BUREAU
F. W. REICHELDERFER, Chief

CLIMATOLOGICAL DATA

PENNSYLVANIA

MAY 1957

Volume LXII No. 5

ASHEVILLE: 1957

PENNSYLVANIA - MAY 1957

WEATHER SUMMARY

GENERAL

May was a very dry month in the southeast portion of the State. Other areas were rather dry and only five stations indicated precipitation totals of as much as four inches. The greatest total was 4.92 inches at New Park which was less than an inch above average while deficiencies in excess of two inches occurred at one or more stations in each division except the Northwest Plateau. The driest station was York Haven with only 0.51 inch for the month. The greatest amount for one day was 2.52 inches measured at New Park the 27th. Measurable snowfall was limited to a few stations in the northern portion of the State.

Average temperatures were generally a little higher than seasonal in the southern and western areas and near seasonal elsewhere. Extreme temperatures ranged from 19° at Madera to 92° at Carlisle, Jim Thorpe and Newburg 3 W.

WEATHER DETAILS

The first ten days of May were almost rainless; the next ten days brought frequent but usually light rains; and the last ten days furnished little rain other than showers associated with considerable thunderstorm activity around the 23rd and 26th.

The temperature factor appeared as well defined warm and cool periods of relatively short to moderate duration with the exception of a warm period extending from the 7th through the 15th. The major cold snap was around the 3rd-4th and secondary cool periods occurred around the 16th-17th, the 19th-21st, and the 28th-29th. Cool periods around the 3rd-4th and 19th-21st dropped temperatures to 10 to 15 degrees below the seasonal level over most of the State and the warm periods, in most instances, caused thermometers to climb to 10 to 15 degrees above average.

WEATHER EFFECTS

Fruits, alfalfa, clover and tobacco suffered some freeze damage but losse were not great. Precipitation, or th lack of it, played the major role. Moisture was generally adequate for good crop growth in the northern and in most central counties. In the driest area, the southeastern portion of the State, hay growth was slow, corn planting was delayed, and newly set tobacco and tomato plants made little growth.

DESTRUCTIVE STORMS

Thunderstorms were statewide during the afternoon and evening of the 14th and enacted destructive roles in scattered localities. Trees and several structures were blown down and a number of homes were damaged. Lightning knocked out many power tran formers and fired several buildings.

Thunderstorms in the central and east central portions of the State on the 23rd developed damaging winds that partially unroofed a school, downed trees, and broke utility lines. Ligh ning strikes injured three persons.

Severe thunderstorms in southeastern Pennsylvania on the 26th caused heavy damages to crops and property in scat tered areas and widespread minor dama Winds unroofed a manufacturing plant and several houses, blew down a barn and a restaurant, moved 3 house trail ers and a home off their foundations, broke trees and utility lines, and badly damaged a small airplane. Ligh ning interrupted electric service for several hours in some communities. Hail occurred in widely separated areas and caused damage to fruit. Heavy rain caused serious erosion in York County and smashed grain crops to the ground.

FLOODS

None reported.

J. T. B. Beard, Climatologist
Weather Records Processing Center
Chattanooga, Tennessee

CLIMATOLOGICAL DATA

Temperature: Average Maximum	Average Minimum	Average	Departure From Long Term Means	Highest	Date	Lowest	Date	Degree Days	No. of Days Max 90° or Above	Max 32° or Below	Min 32° or Below	Min 0° or Below	Precipitation: Total	Departure From Long Term Means	Greatest Day	Date	Snow, Sleet: Total	Max Depth on Ground	Date	No. of Days .10 or More	.50 or More	1.00 or More
69.5	46.0	57.8	.9	82	26	26	3	239	0	0	2	0	3.32	- 1.29	1.28	24	.0	0		5	3	1
66.7	41.5	54.1		80	10+	26	17	337	0	0	5	0	2.60		.70	20	.0	0		7	3	0
68.7	43.9	56.3	2.3	81	9	26	3	281	0	0	4	0	2.21	- 2.14	.99	20	.0	0		5	2	0
71.7	45.9	58.8		85	13	28	3	216	0	0	3	0	2.48		1.12	20	.0	0		4	2	1
66.1	44.1	55.1		81	10+	24	3	317	0	0	3	0	2.47		.83	24	T	0		5	2	0
63.4	40.6	52.0		79	10	26	3+	398	0	0	5	0	2.93	- 1.70	.80	20	.0	0		7	2	0
70.0	46.2	58.1	- 1.3	85	10+	32	3	242	0	0	1	0	2.30	- 1.27	.73	20	.0	0		7	2	0
69.4	45.2	57.3	- 1.6	84	10	28	3	264	0	0	2	0	1.44	- 2.87	.98	20	.0	0		2	1	0
72.1	41.6	56.9	- 3.1	86	10+	29	3	264	0	0	6	0	2.51	- 1.33	1.03	20	.0	0		5	2	1
		56.3											2.47				T					
72.2	47.5	59.9	- .6	88	13	31	4	184	0	0	1	0	2.35	- 1.62	1.30	14	.0	0		5	1	1
72.2	49.4	60.8	.1	88	14	34	4	175	0	0	0	0	2.40	- 1.55	1.50	15	.0	0		5	1	1
73.2	47.6	60.4	- 1.9	87	11	32	4	169	0	0	1	0	2.08	- 1.62	1.42	14	.0	0		2	1	1
75.1M	47.1M	61.1M	1.5	92	26	33	3	165	1	0	0	0	1.79	- 2.55	.70	20	T	T	4	5	1	0
71.6	46.7	59.2	- .4	87	13	34	3	208	0	0	0	0	1.90	- 2.04	.69	20	.0	0		5	2	0
73.0	43.8	58.4	- 2.6	90	27	28	3	230	1	0	5	0	2.57	- 1.57	.98	15	.0	0		7	2	0
		60.0											2.18				T					
74.9	51.8	63.4		90	27	35	4	126	1	0	0	0	1.54		.67	20	.0	0		3	2	0
73.5	48.2	60.9	- .5	89	14	32	3+	174	0	0	2	0	1.83	- 2.07	.57	20	.0	0		5	1	0
77.2	50.4	63.8		90	13+	31	4	109	2	0	1	0	.88		.41	20	.0	0		3	0	0
73.8	44.5	59.2		88	13	26	4	221	0	0	4	0	1.50		.37	14	.0	0		5	0	0
74.3	49.0	61.7	- .2	87	13+	30	3+	153	0	0	2	0	1.04	- 2.57	.40	27	.0	0		4	0	0
74.8	48.1	61.5	.4	89	26	30	3+	157	0	0	2	0	1.26	- 2.52	.52	20	.0	0		4	1	0
75.3	48.5	61.9		88	10+	34	3	153	0	0	0	0	1.34	- 2.72	.47	21	.0	0		4	0	0
73.4	53.6	63.5	.4	86	10+	37	4	111	0	0	0	0	1.58	- 1.56	.49	20	.0	0		4	0	0
76.4	49.0	62.7	1.4	89	24	32	4	137	0	0	1	0	1.06	- 2.48	.45	27	.0	0		4	0	0
72.8	47.2	60.0		89	27	28	4	195	0	0	2	0	.93		.37	20	.0	0		2	0	0
72.9	47.0	60.0	- 1.2	88	24+	31	4	192	0	0	3	0	2.10	- 1.91	.79	27	.0	0		5	2	0
75.4	55.4	65.4	- .4	91	13	38	4	92	1	0	0	0	1.68	- 2.08	.72	20+	.0	0		2	2	0
74.3	51.8	63.1	1.2	91	13	32	4	131	1	0	1	0	.82	- 3.36	.42	20	.0	0		2	0	0
72.0	46.9	59.5		86	13+	30	4	205	0	0	2	0	1.20		.48	26	.0	0		4	0	0
72.9	50.3	61.6		88	26	32	3	162	0	0	1	0	.89		.51	20	.0	0		2	1	0
74.6	51.9	63.3		89	10	35	4	123	0	0	0	0	.87		.44	20	.0	0		3	0	0
75.9	54.7	65.3		91	13	38	4	96	1	0	0	0	2.03		.84	14	.0	0		4	2	0
74.5	52.4	63.5	.4	90	26	35	4	126	1	0	0	0	1.21	- 2.37	.66	26	.0	0		3	1	0
74.4	55.7	65.1	.7	88	13+	40	4	97	0	0	0	0	1.35		.50	20	.0	0		3	1	0
76.1	51.9	64.0	.8	87	10	36	3+	109	0	0	0	0	1.62	- 2.02	.78	20	.0	0		4	1	0
73.2	54.3	63.8	.1	89	26	39	4	113	0	0	0	0	1.27	- 2.31	.45	14	.0	0		3	0	0
80.0	48.7	64.4	2.0	91	13	30	4	102	3	0	1	0	1.13	- 3.10	.41	20	.0	0		4	0	0
75.7	47.5	61.6	1.9	87	10	31	4	154	0	0	1	0	2.05	- 2.06	.74	20	.0	0		4	2	0
74.0	52.3	63.2	.7	89	26	36	4	133	0	0	0	0	1.71	- 1.98	.89	26	.0	0		4	1	0
76.4M	52.4M	64.4M		89	26	35	4	105	0	0	0	0	2.12		.89	20	.0	0		4	2	0
75.3	48.6	62.0	1.0	90	26	31	4	161	1	0	1	0	1.18	- 3.16	.34	20	.0	0		5	0	0
		62.7											1.40				.0					
73.8	48.5	61.2	.2	90	14	29	4	163	1	0	2	0	1.87	- 2.45	.75	27	.0	0		4	2	0
79.6	52.4	66.0	4.2	92	23	33	4	88	4	0	0	0	1.67	- 2.28	.74	15	.0	0		4	1	0
74.8	48.4	61.6	.1	89	13	27	4	152	0	0	3	0	1.34	- 2.46	.55	14	.0	0		4	1	0
74.4	50.6	62.5	.6	91	14	32	4	140	1	0	1	0	1.36	- 2.64	.72	20	.0	0		4	1	0
74.5	50.2	62.4	- .8	89	14+	33	4	142	0	0	0	0	2.43	- 1.22	.91	27	.0	0		6	2	0
73.6	51.7	62.7	.3	89	23	36	4	137	0	0	0	0	.84	- 2.86	.39	20	.0	0		2	0	0
78.7	49.7	64.2		92	13+	28	4	108	3	0	2	0	3.93		1.10	27	.0	0		4	4	1
77.4	50.0	63.7	1.0	89	13+	29	4	117	0	0	2	0	1.08	- 3.11	.44	20	.0	0		3	0	0
75.9	47.2	61.6		88	13	26	4	152	0	0	3	0	.94		.45	20	.0	0		2	0	0
78.0	49.2	63.6	1.6	89	13+	28	4	125	0	0	3	0	1.02	- 2.70	.46	20	.0	0		4	0	0
		63.0											1.65				.0					
75.7M	46.3M	61.0M		89	13	26	4	178	0	0	3	0	1.78		.50	15	T	0		5	1	0
76.8	47.8	62.3		88	13	32	3	152	0	0	1	0	3.23		1.20	20	.0	0		3	3	1
70.6	45.7	58.2		85	14	33	4+	230	0	0	0	0	1.41		.52	20	.0	0		5	1	0
74.5	47.1	60.8		90	27	32	4+	168	1	0	2	0	1.47		.62	20	.0	0		5	1	0
75.2	46.1	60.7		90	24+	30	4	175	2	0	3	0	1.21	- 3.10	.52	15	.0	0		4	1	0
72.4	45.8	59.1	- 1.7	88	13	30	4	207	0	0	3	0	1.48	- 2.56	.71	14	T	0		3	1	0
72.6	48.0	60.3	.1	88	13	34	3	185	0	0	0	0	1.93	- 2.38	.75	14	T	0		5	1	0
		60.3											1.79				T					
65.0	42.9	54.0		80	10	27	3	343	0	0	4	0	2.18		.59	20	.0	0		5	2	0
68.7	41.7	55.2		83	16+	28	3	305	0	0	8	0	2.77		.98	15	T	T	5	8	2	0
64.5	43.3	53.9		80	10+	22	4	344	0	0	4	0	1.70	- 4.24	.52	15	.2	0		5	1	0
67.7	40.4	54.1	- 3.5	85	10	27	5+	336	0	0	7	0	2.84	- 1.09	.64	21	.0	0		7	3	0

See Reference Notes Following Station Index

TABLE 2 - CONTINUED

Station		Temperature													Precipitation								
											No. of Days								Snow, Sleet			No. of Days	
											Max.		Min.										
		Average Maximum	Average Minimum	Average	Departure From Long Term Means	Highest	Date	Lowest	Date	Degree Days	90° or Above	32° or Below	32° or Below	0° or Below	Total	Departure From Long Term Means	Greatest Day	Date	Total	Max. Depth on Ground	Date	.10 or More	.50 or More
MONTROSE 1 E	AM	63.5	42.2	52.9	-2.1	80	10+	26	3	376	0	0	5	0	3.40	-.72	.88	20	T	0		7	3
TOWANDA		71.2	43.5	57.4	-.4	86	26	28	3	255	0	0	4	0	3.39	-.21	.79	20	T	0		9	3
WELLSBORO 3 S	AM	65.8	42.4	54.1	-2.2	79	11+	25	3	337	0	0	5	0	2.89	-.98	.72	21	2.0	T	4	8	2
DIVISION				54.5											2.74				.3				
CENTRAL MOUNTAINS																							
BELLEFONTE 4 S	AM	72.8	47.5	60.2	.3	88	2+	28	4+	190	0	0	3	0	2.10	-1.79	.85	15	T	0		4	2
DU BOIS 7 E		71.7	44.3	58.0		80	10+	23	4	231	0	0	6	0	2.04	-2.52	.57	15	T	0		5	1
EMPORIUM 2 SSW	AM	67.6	39.7	53.7		80	27	24	3+	348	0	0	9	0	2.49		.60	15	2.5	1	4	8	1
LOCK HAVEN		76.3	47.7	62.0	.3	90	23+	29	4	150	2	0	2	0	1.17	-2.94	.58	15	T	0		3	1
MADERA	AM	70.2	36.9	53.6		84	14	19	4+	352	0	0	12	0	3.18		1.16	15	.0	0		6	2
PHILIPSBURG CAA AP		68.1	42.8	55.5		84	13	22	4	304	0	0	5	0	1.91		.67	14	T	0		5	2
RIDGWAY 3 W	AM	70.4	39.1	54.8	-1.1	81	13	22	3	314	0	0	9	0	2.14	-1.88	.70	15	T	T	4	8	1
STATE COLLEGE		71.4	49.9	60.7	1.7	85	13+	30	4	178	0	0	1	0	1.64	-2.47	.69	14	T	0		5	1
TAMARACK 2 S FIRE TWR	AM	66.9M	42.3M	54.6M		84	14	25	3	329	0	0	4	0	1.99		.77	15	1.5	T	4+	5	1
DIVISION				57.0											2.07				.4				
SOUTH CENTRAL MOUNTAINS																							
ALTOONA HORSESHOE CURVE		72.6	46.9	59.8	.7	86	23	25	4	194	0	0	2	0	4.04	-.09	1.85	15	.0	0		6	2
ARTEMAS 1 WNW																							
BURNT CABINS 2 NE		77.7M	45.3M	61.5M		88	13+	24	4	135	0	0	3	0	1.24		.56	20	.0	0		3	1
EBENSBURG		70.0	44.4	57.2	.8	80	23	24	4	247	0	0	5	0	2.82	-1.55	1.13	15	.0	0		7	1
EVERETT 1 SW		74.4	48.0	61.2	1.2	88	9+	30	5	164	0	0	2	0	1.68	-2.02	1.12	19	.0	0		4	1
HUNTINGDON	AM	74.8	44.6	59.7	-.8	90	24	25	4	198	1	0	4	0	1.50	-2.66	.60	15	.0	0		4	1
JOHNSTOWN	AM	73.4	45.2	59.3	-1.7	89	14+	27	4+	213	0	0	4	0	2.18	-2.29	1.20	15	.0	0		4	1
KEGG		73.9	45.6	59.8		88	26	25	4	198	0	0	3	0	1.92		.90	19	.0	0		5	1
MARTINSBURG CAA AP		70.8	48.1	59.5		87	23	28	4	205	0	0	3	0	1.88		1.01	14	.0	0		4	1
DIVISION				59.8											2.16				.0				
SOUTHWEST PLATEAU																							
BAKERSTOWN 3 WNW		75.9	50.6	63.3		86	13+	30	4	130	0	0	3	0	2.20		1.13	14	.0	0		5	1
BLAIRSVILLE 6 ENE		70.1	48.0	59.1		82	30	26	4	208	0	0	3	0	2.74	-2.51	.94	14	.0	0		9	1
BURGETTSTOWN 2 W	AM	73.6	43.8	58.7		86	14	23	6	217	0	0	5	0	3.68		1.55	12	.0	0		8	1
BUTLER		74.6	46.5	60.6	.8	84	14+	30	3+	169	0	0	3	0	1.70	-1.99	.46	14	.0	0		7	0
CLAYSVILLE 3 W		76.3	44.7	60.5	.0	87	13	25	5	174	0	0	5	0	1.67	-2.14	.40	20	.0	0		6	0
CONFLUENCE 1 SW DAM	AM	73.0	44.4	58.7		85	15	26	4	212	0	0	5	0	3.50		.97	27	.0	0		8	3
DERRY		75.5	48.9	62.2	1.4	86	23	25	3	149	0	0	3	0	2.17	-1.89	.49	16	.0	0		9	0
DONEGAL		68.8	42.4	55.6		88	23	21	4	298	0	0	7	0	2.39		.82	14	.0	0		4	2
DONORA	AM	78.4	52.5	65.5	2.5	89	14	32	5	100	0	0	1	0	2.60	-1.13	.80	12	.0	0		5	3
FORD CITY 4 S DAM	AM	73.3	44.8	59.1		85	24	28	4+	208	0	0	5	0	2.35		.65	14	.0	0		6	2
INDIANA 3 SE		74.0	44.8	59.4	-.4	84	23	20	3	191	0	0	5	0	2.14	-2.05	.77	15	.0	0		6	1
IRWIN		79.8M	46.4M	63.1M	2.7	87	13+	28	6	113	0	0	2	0	1.18	-2.34	.68	20	.0	0		3	1
MIDLAND DAM 7		72.8	51.4	62.1	1.3	85	13	35	6	150	0	0	0	0	2.86	-1.53	.69	12	.0	0		7	2
NEW CASTLE 1 N		75.1	46.9	61.0	1.4	83	10+	28	3+	168	0	0	4	0	3.97	.42	.94	15	.0	0		8	4
NEWELL	AM	78.8	50.7	64.8	3.5	91	14	30	4	111	1	0	2	0	4.02	.73	1.82	12	.0	0		7	2
NEW STANTON		75.9	44.3	60.1	-.4	88	23	24	4	186	0	0	5	0	3.75	-.29	1.92	14	.0	0		6	1
PITTSBURGH WB AP 2	//R	71.9	49.9	60.9	1.1	84	13	32	4	173	0	0	1	0	2.73	-1.04	1.34	11	.0	0		5	2
PITTSBURGH WB CITY	R	74.8	52.9	63.9	1.3	86	13+	38	3+	118	0	0	0	0	2.72	-.77	.86	11	.0			6	2
PUTNEYVILLE 2 SE DAM	AM	72.7	42.6	57.7		83	24+	26	3+	238	0	0	8	0	2.40		.65	15	.0	0		6	1
SALINA 3 W		74.8	47.2	61.0		85	13	26	4	162	0	0	4	0	2.16		.80	15	.0	0		5	1
SHIPPINGPORT WB		72.6	48.0	60.3		85	13	31	6	183	0	0	1	0	3.33		1.29	11	.0	0		5	2
SLIPPERY ROCK		72.6	47.6	60.1		82	1	29	3	178	0	0	1	0	3.60		.87	20	.0	0		9	2
SOMERSET MAIN ST		72.6	45.0	58.8	2.1	82	13+	24	4	212	0	0	4	0	3.15	-1.67	1.27	15	.0	0		8	2
SPRINGS 1 SW		69.2	43.2	56.2	.8	82	14	24	5	271	0	0	4	0	4.00	-.30	1.02	27	.0	0		9	2
UNIONTOWN		75.4	50.2	62.8	.7	88	13	29	4	130	0	0	2	0	2.45	-1.69	1.03	14	.0	0		4	1
WAYNESBURG 2 W		76.9	46.0	61.5	.7	87	13	25	4	151	0	0	5	0	1.90	-2.19	.76	20	.0	0		4	1
DIVISION				60.7											2.74				.0				
NORTHWEST PLATEAU																							
BRADFORD 4 W RES		69.4	39.5	54.5	-.8	79	30	24	3+	321	0	0	10	0	3.16	-.86	.60	15	.5	0		6	2
BROOKVILLE CAA AIRPORT		70.2	43.6	56.9	1.0	80	13+	26	5	262	0	0	6	0	2.31	-1.45	.94	14	T	0		7	1
CLARION 3 SW		74.0	44.2	59.1		84	10+	26	3	204	0	0	7	0	2.98	-1.25	1.06	15	.0	0		9	1
CORRY		69.4	43.2	56.3	.9	81	30+	25	6	276	0	0	8	0	2.11	-1.85	.43	20	T	0		6	0
COUDERSPORT 3 NW		66.5	39.8	53.2		78	9+	24	3	362	0	0	10	0	2.47		.68	21	T	T	4	8	2
EAST BRADY		77.1	47.7	62.4		85	26+	32	3+	131	0	0	4	0	2.33		.93	15	.0	0		5	1
ERIE WB AIRPORT		64.8	45.7	55.3	.2	82	26	31	6+	314	0	0	2	0	3.29	.10	1.44	14	T	0		6	2
FARRELL SHARON		71.9M	48.2M	60.1M	-.1	87	23	29	6	184	0	0	1	0	3.03	-.56	1.10	11	.0	0		7	3
FRANKLIN		73.0	45.3	59.2	1.7	81	14+	30	3+	192	0	0	4	0	4.11	.35	1.00	11	.0	0		7	3
GREENVILLE		73.9M	45.8M	59.9M	1.8	88	27	26	6	194	0	0	3	0	2.66	-1.10	.75	11	T	0		7	3
JAMESTOWN 2 NW	AM	68.7	45.2	57.0		80	11+	25	6	259	0	0	5	0	2.64	-1.33	.65	11	.0	0		8	3
KANE 1 NNE	AM	68.8	40.0	54.4		80	13	24	4	321	0	0	10	0	3.31	-1.41	.92	19	1.5	1	4+	8	2
LINESVILLE 5 WNW		69.3	44.5	56.9		80	26	25	6	266	0	0	4	0	2.18	-1.67	.49	15	T	T	4	8	0
MEADVILLE 1 S	AM	69.0	44.0	56.5	-.4	81	31	28	6	271	0	0	5	0	3.01	-1.11	.66	21	.5	T	4	8	2
MERCER 2 NNE		73.6M	45.6M	59.6M		83	26	29	1	186	0	0	5	0	2.88		1.00	11	.0	0		9	2
SPRINGBORO	AM	68.3	45.1	56.7		82	27+	27	6	269	0	0	3	0	2.44		.50	11+	T	0		9	2
TIONESTA 2 SE DAM	AM	70.3	43.3	56.8		81	11+	29	3+	260	0	0	5	0	3.24	-1.53	.70	11	T	T	4	8	3
TITUSVILLE WATER WORKS		71.9	42.5	57.2		83	30	24	3+	256	0	0	8	0	3.21		.82	10	T	0		7	3
WARREN		71.2	44.2	57.7	1.0	83	26	29	3+	239	0	0	6	0	4.03	-.17	1.54	15	.4	T	4	9	2
DIVISION				57.4											2.91				.2				

† DATA RECEIVED TOO LATE TO BE INCLUDED IN DIVISION AVERAGES

See Reference Notes Following Station Index

DAILY PRECIPITATION

Day of month

	Total	1	2	3	4	5	6	7	8	9	10	11	12	13	14	15	16	17	18	19	20	21	22	23	24	25	26	27	28	29	30	31
	1.99												.23		.25	.98			.03	.06	.39	.09		.03			T	.31				
R	2.35				.03	T					T	.10	.05		1.30	.01		T		.15	.49		T	.17			.05	T				
	2.40					.02	T						.16			1.50				.11	.30	.22		T	.04			.05				
VL	4.04											.06	.07	.01	.12	1.85			.02	.05	1.23	.18	.04		.17		.02	.22				
	1.87												T		T	.21			.06	T	.70	.13	.02	T				.79				
		RECORD MISSING																														
	2.76				T							.20	.06			.54	.06		.14	.20	.38	.55		.03								
	2.20											.29		.12	1.13			.06	.11	.36					.02	.05					.06	
	2.27				.07	T					.02	.07	.03		.23	.60	.30			.07	.36	.42	T	T	T		.10		T			
	-												.21							.19	-	-										
	2.08				.14								.15			.49	.14			.08	.78	.11			.05			.14				
	2.65										.09	.28	.41		.38	.33	T		.03	.06	.55	.26	.02	.10	.02		.09	.03				
	1.78					.07						T	.10			.50	.43				.31	.28			.08			.01				
	-					-						-	T			.83			.03	T	.19	.24	T		.05			T				
	2.10				T								.04			.85	.76		.02	T	.19	.15	.01		.08							
	2.72												.20			1.23	.02			.10	.49	.12		T	.05			.51				
	3.23				.01							.02	.05		.07	.80	T			.02	1.20	.08	T		.98				T			
	2.08					T							.12			1.51			T	.03	.22	.13		T	.06			.01	T			
	2.08											.09	.06		1.42	.02				.06	.40			.01			.02					
	2.74											.11	.04		.94	.27	.02	T	.02	.22	.41	.10	T	.28	.10		.07	.12	.04			
	2.00											T	.12			.82				.06	.35	.08	.02				.50	.05				
	2.53											T	.55		.02	.86	.01	T		.05	.34	.24	.04	.03	.10		.11	.15	.03			
	2.51												.73		.22	.19	.09		T	.03	.66	.18		.10	.07		.05	.19				
TA	2.97				.01						.05	.30	.23		.16		.84			.33	.42	.52		.05	.01		.01		.01			.03
	3.16				.03						.08	.35	.44		.34	.60				.48	.55		.07		.05		.06	T	.08			.03
	1.11											.12			.52				.07	.09	.29			.02								
T	2.31				.02					T	.32	.23			.94	T	T	.08		.16	.16	T	.13	.22			.05	T				
	2.06												.27		.03	.10	.26				.78	.12	.03		.12			.35				
	2.00												.20			.31	.17		.29		.75	.18			.09			.05				
	3.68												1.55		.45	.31	.13		.02	.21	.20	.37	.04	.03			.31	.06				
	1.24												.06			.34					.56	.08					.20					
	1.70										.01	.22	.21	.02	.46	.15	.04		.05	.13	.19	.12	.09									
	2.77											.02	T			1.47				T	1.07	.03			.02		.16		.01			
	2.18					T						.11	.09	.06		.49	.17		.04	.08	.59	.51							.04			
	1.67					T						T	.05		T	.74				.07	.46	.10	T	T	.03		.20	.02				
	2.48												.16	.03	.08	1.06			.12	.01	.25	.39		.02	.31			.05	T			
	3.12				T	.23						.18	.16			.72	.22		T	.05	.70	.81					.05	T				
	2.17				T	.20						.07	.03			.68	.15		.02	T	.48	.53	T	T	T				.01			
	2.62												.30			1.05			.10	.42	.15	.20	.05	.10				.25				
	1.34					T	T					.01	.02		.55	.09			.10	.08	.34						.15					
	2.66												.78			.83	.09			.02	.44	.11		.02			.12	.25				
	1.54						T					T	T	.05		.13			T		.67	.09	T					.64	T			
	1.71					T							.04		.08	.93	.01		.04		.28	.18	.01	.04	.10							
	2.96				T	T					.02	.36	.16	.01	.25	1.06	.24		.09	.01	.11	.21		.14	.01		.25		.04			
	2.53					.08							.16			1.25				.14	.28	.25		.03	.21			.13				
	1.67											.01	.20		.04	.10	.25		.01	.05	.40	.31	.02	.05	T		.16	.07				
	1.86											.02	.04			1.12	T		.12		.18	.30	T	.02	.06		T					
	3.02				.04	.11						.38	.08	T		.78	.10		.03	.15	.18	.98		.06	.07		.03		.03			
	2.04					.10							.17			.29				.02	1.04	.21		.04	.09			.12				
	1.83						T						.06		.45	.47			.04	.02	.57	.12		T				.10	T			
	.88											T								.19	.41	.05			T			.23				
	3.50												.07			.35	.47		.50	.01	.84	.11		.02	.23		.14	.87				
	2.93												.08			.58	.27		.24	.02	.54	.06	T	.04	.36		.18	.56				
	2.42												.60			.85	.17		.03	.03	.21	.16			.10		.06	.21				
	1.14												.04		.02	.23			T	.01	.66	.02						.18				
	2.11				.02	T	T	T			.01	.48	.13	.02	.30	.55	T		.11	T	.09	.12	T	.12	T		.10	.03	.05			
	2.53				.04	T		T			.01	.45	.09	.02	.55	.42	.21	T	.12	.01	.12	.16	.11	.04	T		.08	.08	.02	T		
	2.47												1.30			.29	T			*	.29	.25	.05	.03	T			.26				
	2.11				T						.40	.10	.02		.35	.24	T	.05		.30	.43		.08		.04		.07	.03				
	2.47				T	.12					.04	.26	.13			.65	.11	T	T	.10	.22	.68		.06	.05		.05		T			
	2.86				T	.15					T	.17	.15			.57	.26		.03	.05	.40	.87		.03	.01		T	.15	.02			
	2.46				T	.15						.27	.06			.57	.23		.03	.27	.28	.60					T	T	T			
	2.38												.22		.21	1.05					.18	.25		.12	.17		T	.18				
	2.73											.03	.08		.09	1.10	.03		.02	.06	.30	.64	.03	.03	.27			.05				
	2.86				.06	.02					.05	.29	.12		.16	.73	.18		.05	.26	.31	.49		.02	.04				.08			
	2.05					.26							.09			.70					.33	.38			.24			.03				
	2.17											.32	T		.12		.49		.04	.37	.30	.10	.04		.17		.12	.10				
	1.50				T							.05		T	.37	.02			.06	.25	.36	.20					.19	T				
	2.77					T						.08	.22	.02		.98	.12		.03	.26	.52	.30		.10	T		.02	.12				
	2.39											.53			.82	.04	T	T	T	.04	.48	T	T	.03		.01	.44	T				
	2.60												.80		.11	.60	.07		.02	.08	.52	.05	.04				.29	.02				
	1.07											T				.19				T	.62	.02						.24				
	2.04				.03						.06	.28	.08	.05	.31	.57		T	.19	.04	.36	.04	.06		.04							
	2.13					.04						.02	.07			.35	.48		.08	.04	.45	.40		T	.06			.14				
	1.70					.02							.10	.01		.52	.06		.03	.09	.37	.37		.01	.02			.10	T			
	2.33										.02	.42	.09	.03	.43	.93		.02	.02		.18		.09		.16							
	2.82												.20	T	.32	1.13			.05	T	.28	.37	T	T	.23			.24				
	2.56				T						.36	.91	.03		.18	.86			.05	.13	.33	.22	.01	.03	.04		.06	.02	.03			
		RECORD MISSING																														
	.56												.01			.17			.03	.02	.35	.08										
	2.49				.03	.20						.25	.17			.60	.14		.07	.06	.24	.41	T	.05	T		.17	.07	.03			
	1.49					.13						.05	.01			.57			T		.41	.29			.03							
	1.04											.02				.10			T	.14	.35	.03						.40				
	3.05											.17	.28			.66	.22		.27	.12	.99	.27		.07	T			T	T			
	3.29			T	T						.05	.14	T		1.44	.03	T	T	.10	1.10	.32		T	T	T	T	.11	T				
	1.56											.29						.01		1.12	.21	.11										
	3.03									.12	.57	1.10			.72	.21	.01	.14		.02	.02		.10				T	.02				
	2.35												.32		.65	.30	.03		.04	T	.45	.08	T	.15	.10		T	.01	T			
	4.11				T						.01	1.00	.08	.05	.48	.87	.05		.15	.12	.45	.69	.02	.08			.04		.02			
	3.32					.03							.08			.80	T			.15	.80	.15	T		1.28			.03				
	3.52				T	.15						T	.44	T		.64	.30		.02	.10	.60	.84					.45	T	T			
	1.05												.03		.17	.06				.06	.48	.12						.13				
	1.26											.03			.06	.18					.32						.12	.35				
	1.36														.11	.12			.07	.18	.72	.08						.08				
	3.26				.10	T					.08	.35	.28			.82				.49	.20	.62		.05	.22		.06	T	.05			
	2.79				.10	.10					T	.31	.13	.10	T	.92	.18		.13	.02	.09	.53		.06	T		.10	.01	.01			
	2.60											.01	.77		.38	.34	T		.08	.12	.14	.25		.07	.32		.07	.05				
	3.14											T	.10			.45	.08		T	.10	.88	.38		.03	1.04			.08				
	1.34															.14					.44	.47						.29				
	1.41					.06							.08		T	.25	.14			T	.52	.19		T	T			.17				
	3.41												.07			.66	.15		.27	.03	.64	.09	T	.03	.07		.14	1.24				
	2.82											.02	.40		.07	.99			.07	.10	.65	.09			.10		.18	.13				
	2.66				T					T	.90	.75	.03	.03	.56	.04		.12		.15	.29		.12				.03	.04				
	2.43												.02		.29	.21			.04	.34	.28	.14						.91				
R	.84				T	T	T					.05	T		.27	.07			T	.06	.39	T		T			T					
	3.40												.09			1.34				.01	.90	.07		T	.15			.84				
	2.59					T						T	.20	.02		.64	.09		T	.03	.74	.48		T	.17			.22				
	2.60												.21			.63	.10			.11	.70	.30			.27			.08				
	2.73											T	.25			.57	.12		.02	.01	.87	.52	.03	.02	.29			.03				
	1.58					T	T						.01		.26	.33			.04	.02	.49	.07		.01				.31	.04			
	2.77											.28	.19	.04		.59	.11		.04	.07	1.01	.37		.04	.03			T				
	2.63											.20				1.51	.02			T	.37	.20	.02	.03	.11		.03	.12	.02			
	1.89			T	T							.10	.20	.10		.33	.15		T	T	.35	.39		.05	.02							
	1.50												.04		.02	.60				.02	.35	.20	.01		.23			.02	.01			
	.81						.02						.06			.26			.03	.01	.30	.11						.02				

See Reference Notes Following Station Index

DAILY PRECIPITATION

Table 3—Continued

Station	Total	1	2	3	4	5	6	7	8	9	10	11	12	13	14	15	16	17	18	19	20	21	22	23	24	25	26	27	28	29	30
HYNDMAN	2.39												.03		.20	.37	.24		.33		.69	.05			.37			.11			
INDIANA 3 SE	2.14												.30		.20	.77			.05		.23	.33		.04	.06			.16			
IRWIN	1.18														.06	.24					.68	.20									
JAMESTOWN 2 NW	2.64										.04	.85	.02	.01	.13	.55	.07		.14	.22	.10	.30	.10	.02	.04		.01		.04		
JIM THORPE	1.79				.05	T						.03	.11		.02	.30	.01			.06	.70	T	T	.13	.36			.02	T		
JOHNSTOWN	2.18												.09		T	1.20	T		.01	T	.26	.30	T	.16	.09		.03	.04	T		
KANE 1 NNE	3.31				.07	.03			.04	.50	.18	T	.32	.49	.18	.01	.10	.12	.09	.92	T	.06	.09		.07		T	.04			
KARTHAUS	1.58					.02						.03	.04		T	1.03			.05		.13	.20	T	.04	.04			T	T		
KEATING SUMMIT	3.37				T	.20					.07	.29	.10			1.05	.31		.03	.11	.16	.78		.04			.15		.08		
KEGG	1.92											.19			.39	.19				.90	.15	.04	.01	.05	T			T			
KITTANNING LOCK 7	2.33											.07	.66	T	.41	.32	.02		.08	.14	.29	.19	T	.12	.03		T	T	T		
KREGAR 4 SE	3.16											.50			1.08	.02	T	T	.03	.34	.44	.20	T	.10			.45	T			
KRESGEVILLE 3 W	2.34												.11			.18				.17	.67	.21			.90			.10			
LAFAYETTE MC KEAN PARK		RECORD MISSING																													
LAKEVILLE 1 NNE	3.16												.21			.76	.15			.15	.87	.55			.18			.29			
LANCASTER 2 NE PUMP STA	1.06											.01			T	.16			T	.10	.32	.02		T				.45			
LANDISVILLE 2 NW	.93												.01			.09			.02	.05	.37	.04		T				.35			
LAWRENCEVILLE 2 S	2.84											.21	.40			.52	.04		.21	.16	.60	.64		.06					T		
LEBANON 3 W	2.10						.02						.14		.06	.34				.04	.57	.10		T		.04		.79			
LEHIGHTON	2.43					.08							.12			.17			T	.17	.73	.18	.03		.65			.30			
LE ROY	2.33											.25		.20		.51				.44	.80	.13									
LEWIS RUN 3 SE	3.52				.03	.05					.06	.33	.40			.85	.07		.05	.40	.18	.70		.05	.27		T	.07	.03		
LEWISTOWN	1.47												.11			.30	.17		T	T	.62	.18			.07			.02			
LINESVILLE 5 WNW	2.18				T						.40	.26	.11	.01	.10	.49	T		.07	.11	.15	.38	.04		.02		.02	T	.02		
LOCK HAVEN	1.17					.08						T	.01			.58			.01	.02	.18	.25	T	.01	.03		T	T	T		
LONG POND 2 W	2.32					T						T	.11	T		.45				.07	.70	.31		.03	.65			T			
LYNDELL 2 NW	1.13													.20	.09				.02	.51								.31			
MADERA	3.18												.05			1.16	1.01		.11		.17	.46	.02	.06	.10			.04			
MAHAFFEY	3.32					T						.03	.09		.01	1.07	.80		.10	.02	.16	.79	.02	.06	.17			T			
MAPLE GLEN	.86											.01			.08	.11					.40	.08	T					.18			
MAPLETON DEPOT	1.23											T	.05			.63					.37	.13	T		.01			.04			
MARCUS HOOK	1.68					T	T					.02	T	.01	.06				.05	.09	.72	.01					.72	T			
MARION CENTER 2 SE	3.32					T						T	.27	T	.49	.94	.05		.08	.02	.34	.88		.10	.05			.08	.02		
MARTINSBURG CAA AP	1.88											.11			1.01	.03	T	T	T	.37	.31	.04	T	.01			T				
MATAMORAS	1.95												.15			.29					.41	.87			.23						
MAYBURG	3.76					T					T	.83	.85		.25	.70	T		.12	.10	.32	.40		.05	T		.14		T		
MC CONNELLSBURG	1.03												.06			.24			.07		.54	.05					.01	.06			
MC KEESPORT	2.43												.37		.15	.72	.10				.47	.17	T	.02	.08			.35	T		
MEADVILLE 1 S	3.01				.02	T					.08	.30	.18	.01	.17	.58	.07		.11	.26	.25	.66	.08	.04	.04		.03	T	.04		
MEDIX RUN	2.01				T	.19					.04	.23	.12	T	T	.82	.05		.06	.09	.09	.23		.01	.07		T	T	.01		
MERCER 2 NNE	2.88									.12	.15	1.00	.20		.51	.15			.15	.24	.24		.09					.03			
MERCERSBURG	1.21															.24			.27	.15	.43	.07	.05								
MEYERSDALE 1 ENE	2.12															.19	.14		.56		.67	.06			.18			.32			
MIDDLETOWN OLMSTED FLD	.82											.01			.07	.09			T	.06	.42	T		T			.17				
MIDLAND DAM 7	2.86										T	.18	.69		.50	.31	.02		.05	.18	.44	.22	.02	.09	.05		.08	.03			
MILANVILLE	2.93											.20	.15			.57	.54		.02		1.02	.39		T	.04			T			
MILLHEIM	2.14					T							.06		.05	.50	.42		T		.30	.21	T		.37			.23			
MILLVILLE 2 SW	2.38					.10						T	.07			1.19	.01		.01	T	.24	.33		T	.40			.03			
MILROY	2.00												.10		.02	.58	.19		.05		.48	.24			.27			.07			
MONTROSE 1 E	3.40					.01					T	.09	.47	.02		.81	.16		.16	.13	.88	.53	T	.09	T		.01	T	.04		
MORGANTOWN	1.20				T		T					T	T	.02	.10	.03				.22	.33	T	T	T			.48	.02			
MT GRETNA 2 SE	.89					.02							.08		.09	.09				.15	.51						.01				
MT POCONO 2 N AP	2.21				T							.10	.04		.09	.18	.03			.08	.99	.10			.60						
MUHLENBURG 1 SE	2.48				.03							T	.10		.01	.33	.04		T	.04	1.12	.04		.01	.76						
MYERSTOWN	3.46												.14		.09	.26					.55	.05	.02					2.35			
NATRONA LOCK 4	2.27												.18		T	.99			.03	.06	.47	.13		.14	.18		T	.09			
NESHAMINY FALLS	1.17					T						.05	T		.15	.05			T	T	.74						.18				
NEWBURG 3 W	3.93											.90				.90					.98	.05						1.10			
NEW CASTLE 1 N	3.97										.07	.70	.16	.04	.54	.94			.12	.05	.66	.36	.02	.13	.09		.09		T		
NEWELL	4.02												1.82		.08	.63	.22			.05	.30	.07	.07		.29		.39	.10			
NEW PARK	4.92													.27	.49	.34			.13	.10	.50	.08					.49	2.52			
NEWPORT	1.21						T						.27	T		.52	.02				.29	.11	T	T							
NEW STANTON	3.75											.46			1.92	.01		T	.10	.35	.42	.02	.03	.07		T	.39				
NEW TRIPOLI	2.36				.03							.05	.09		.02	.62				.29	.78	.05		.02	.26		.06	.09			
NORRISTOWN	.87												T			.16			.01	T	.44	.08					.18				
NORTH EAST 2 SE	3.62										.04	.12	.04		1.04	.42	.07	T	.05	.46	1.14	.11	.02	T	.02		.04	.03	.02		
ORWELL 3 N	3.39											.34	.29	.06		.50	.08		.32	.21	.85	.76									
PALM	2.11												.24			.32				.12	.30	.17		.04				.92			
PALMERTON	1.90				.10	T						.06	.02		.18	T				.08	.69		T	.63			.14	T			
PARKER	3.40					T					.03	.20	.17	T	1.08	.59			.08	.03	.19	.37	T	.17	.38		.11		T		
PAUPACK 2 WNW	2.62												.22			.62	.07		.02	.12	.65	.66			.26						
PECKS POND	2.24											T	.11			.38	T		T	.12	.58	.44		T	.61			T			
PHIL DREXEL INST OF TEC	2.03					T	T					.08		T	.84	T				.10	.63	T					.38	T			
PHILADELPHIA WB AP R	1.21					T	T					.05	T	T	.12				T	.07	.31	T					.66	T			
PHILADELPHIA PT BREEZE	1.35											.03	.03		.31					.01	.50						.47				
PHILADELPHIA SHAWMONT	1.62											.05	.03	.03	.07	.33				.05	.78	.14						.14			
PHILADELPHIA CITY R	1.27											.07	.02		.45					.02	.44	.01					.26				
PHILIPSBURG CAA AP	1.91				T	T						.02			.67	.61	T	.07	.01	.25	.10	.01	.04	.12	T		.01	T			
PHOENIXVILLE 1 E	1.13											.02			.33					.19	.41	.03					.15				
PIKES CREEK	2.60					T						.02	.12			.80	.05		.01	.09	.75	.37		.03	.36						
PIMPLE HILL	2.47					.01	T					T	.10			.28	.01		T	.08	.75	.37		.04	.85			T			
PINE GROVE 1 NE	2.49					T	T						.06		.01	.99	.02			.01	.85	.17	T	T	.15			.23			
PITTSBURGH WB AP 2 //R	2.73									T	T	1.34			.67	.04	T	T	.06	.14	.12	.02	.08	.01			.25	T			
PITTSBURGH WB CITY R	2.72											.86			.52	.31		T	.05	.49	.19	T	.08	.03			.19				
PLEASANT MOUNT 1 W	2.93											.15	.29			.79	.30		.08	.11	.80	.28	T	.06	T			T	.07		
PORT CLINTON	2.57					.02							.19			.98				.11	.66	.14		.03	.30			.14			
POTTSVILLE	2.07					.02							.06			.50		T			1.10	.23	T	.03	.02			.11			
PUTNEYVILLE 2 SE DAM	2.40										T	.06	.25		.38	.65	.02		.08	.07	.26	.42		.15	.06		T				
QUAKERTOWN 1 E	2.05											.05	.03		T	.35				.14	.74	.07	T	T	.01			.66			
RAYMOND	2.72				.04	.04						.33	.26			.53	.34		.10		.34	.56		.06	.03			.04	.03		
READING WB CITY R	1.71											.04	.11	.02	.07	.01				.19	.38		T	T			.89	T			
RENOVO	1.81				T	.17						.05	.03			.92	.03		.05	T	.12	.29		.02	.10			.03			
REW	3.13				.04	.02					.02	.41	.23			.82	.27		.04	.40	.20	.44		.04	.09		T	.01	.10		
RICES LANDING L 6	2.41												.45			.90	.03		.03	.01	.58	.10		.01	.05		.18	.07			
RIDGWAY 3 W	2.14				T	.12					T	.35	.15			.70	.11	.10		T	.06	.33		.04	T		.16		.02		
RUSH	3.28					T						.22	.35	.11		.52	.26		.11	.38	.60	.52		.10				.07	.04		
RUSHVILLE	3.05											.15	.29	.09		.71	.18		.09	.33	.56	.56		.08				.01			
SAGAMORE 1 S	2.29												.19		T	.80	T		.15		.33	.60		.12	.10						
SALINA 3 W	2.16											.03	.24		.23	.80		.03	.08	.03	.48	.02	.05				.14	.03			
SAXTON	1.57											T	.23			.64	T	T		T	.48	.20	T	T	.02		T	T	T		
SCHENLEY LOCK 5	2.22												.58		.45	.25			.02	.02	.37	.09	T	.17	.23		T	.04			
SCRANTON	2.30												.13			.46	.12		.01	.01	.73	.50			.14			.20			
SCRANTON WB AIRPORT	1.44				T						T	.03	.02		.29	.05		T	T	T	.98		T	.05			T				
SELINSGROVE CAA AP	1.48				.12							.09			.71	.04			T	.05	.47	T		T			T				
SHAMOKIN	2.17					.12							.11			.72	.06				.58	.33			.03			.22			
SHIPPENSBURG	1.08											T	.04			.41			.11	T	.44				.05		.01	.02			
SHIPPINGPORT WB	3.33										.16	1.29			.81	.03		.03	.09	.48	.26	T	.04	.05		.06	.03				
SINNEMAHONING	2.08				T	.17					T	.14	.06			.80	.03		.06	.04	.14	.49		.01	.12		T	.01	.01		
SLIPPERY ROCK	3.60										.03	.40	.25	.01	.24	.77			.14	.02	.87	.43		.18	.20		.05		.01		
SOMERSET FAIRVIEW ST	2.90												.56			1.02	.16		.06		.43	.21	.04	.03	.18			.21			
SOMERSET MAIN ST	3.15											.24	.34			1.27	.10		.05	T	.56	.07	.02		.22		.14	.14			
SOUTH MOUNTAIN	1.17						.01						.01			.14			.15	.05	.56	.10	T					.15			
SPRINGBORO	2.44				T			.34				.50	T		.20	.50	T		.10		.20	.40	.10		.10		T	T			
SPRING GROVE	1.35											.02	T		.20	.18			.03	.29	.54	.05						.04			
SPRINGS 1 SW	4.00											.30			.28	.30	.24	.44	.50	.49	.29	.05	.03				.06	1.02			

See Reference Notes Following Station Index

DAILY PRECIPITATION

3--Continued

PENNSYLVANIA
MAY 1957

Station	Total	1	2	3	4	5	6	7	8	9	10	11	12	13	14	15	16	17	18	19	20	21	22	23	24	25	26	27	28	29	30	31
COLLEGE	1.84				T							.06		T	.69	.40		.02	.01								.02					
SSTOWN	2.30					.01							.17		.02	1.03	.05															
DSBURG	2.51				T	T						.05	.08		.12	.11			T													
CREEK	2.14											.09	.12	T		1.17	.12		.13													
RY	1.30					.20							.12		T	.48	T		T													
EHANNA	3.79												[illegible]	.01		.62	.16		.24										.03			
SVILLE	2.32														.09	.52	.04															
UA	2.07															.20																
A 4 N	2.24				.05											.57																
ACK 2 S FIRE TWR	1.90				T	.17										.77	.10		.05													
STA 2 SE DAM	3.24				.05	T									.40	.61	.20		.14										.03			
VILLE WATER WORKS	3.21				.06										.67	.21		.13														
DO 4 W	3.30				.05	T									.30	.41	.32		.10										.05			
DA	3.30				T	T								.26		.66	.14		.13										T			
CITY	2.97				.02										[illegible]	.40	[illegible]															
	2.68					.07																										
EPOINT 4 NE	3.42																															
E 4 NE BALD EAGLE	1.84																															
CITY	2.70																															
TOWN	2.45																															
DARBY																																
	3.99																															
RGRIFT	2.04																															
NVILLE	1.72																															
KEL	2.99																															
KEL 1	2.93																															
	4.03																															
TOWN	1.47																															
BURG	1.90																															
ORO 3	2.89																															
ILLE	.94																															
RSVILLE 1 W	1.83																															
CHESTER	1.18																															
GROVE 1 E	1.87																															
HIC	3.91																															
SBURG	2.03																															
S BARRE	1.86																															
AMS	1.72																															
AMSPORT WB AP	1.93																															
BUR	1.70																															
3 SSW PUMP STA	1.02																															
HAVEN	.51																															
GROVE	1.44																															

SUPPLEMENTAL DATA

Station	Wind direction		Wind speed m. p. h.				Relative humidity averages - percent				Number of days with precipitation							Percent of possible sunshine	Average sky cover sunrise to sunset
	Prevailing	Percent of time from prevailing	Average	Fastest mile	Direction of fastest mile	Date of fastest mile	1:30 a EST	7:30 a EST	1:30 p EST	7:30 p EST	Trace	.01-.09	.10-.49	.50-.99	1.00-1.99	2.00 and over	Total		
NTOWN WB AIRPORT	WSW	12	10.6	-	-	-	76	73	50	60	5	4	4	0	1	0	14	-	5.6
WB AIRPORT	-	-	11.6	33++	SSE	21+	-	-	-	-	10	2	4	0	2	0	18	-	6.5
ISBURG WB AIRPORT	WSW	11	8.2	31	NW	27	68	67	47	53	8	3	2	0	0	0	13	63	5.8
ADELPHIA WB AIRPORT	WSW	16	10.3	56	SW	26	72	69	48	57	7	2	2	1	0	0	12	63	6.2
SBURGH WB AIRPORT	WSW	17	9.9	42++	WSW	14	75	73	50	59	5	5	3	1	1	0	15	60	6.4
ING WB CITY	-	-	9.9	53	NW	26	-	-	-	-	3	4	3	1	0	0	11	57	5.6
NTON WB AIRPORT	WSW	18	9.7	35	NW	15	72	68	48	57	7	4	1	1	0	0	13	67	5.8
PINGPORT WB	-	-	2.5	45%	W	14	-	-	-	-	1	7	3	1	1	0	13	-	-
IAMSPORT WB AIRPORT	-	-	-	-	-	-	-	74	49	57	6	3	4	1	0	0	14	-	5.7
ak Gust																			

See Reference Notes Following Station Index

Table 5

Station																					
ALLENTOWN WB AP																					
ALLENTOWN GAS CO																					
ALTOONA HORSESHOE CURVE																					
ARENDTSVILLE																					
ARTEMAS 1 WNW																					
BAKERSTOWN 3 WNW																					
BEAVERTOWN																					
BELLEFONTE 4 S																					
BERWICK																					
BETHLEHEM LEHIGH UNIV																					
BLAIRSVILLE 6 ENE																					
BRADFORD 4 W RES																					
BROOKVILLE CAA AIRPORT																					
BURGETTSTOWN 2 W																					
BURNT CABINS 2 NE																					
BUTLER																					
CANTON 1 NW																					
CARLISLE																					
CHAMBERSBURG 1 ESE																					
CHESTER																					
CLARION 3 SW																					
CLAYSVILLE 3 W		87	86	81	72	80	75														
		53	57	61	45	34	52														
COATESVILLE 1 SW		76	89	74	86	69	71														
		52	62	64	59	40	48														
COLUMBIA		90	80	88	84	69	78														
		55	64	65	54	43	57														
CONFLUENCE 1 SW DAM		83	82	89	81	58	83														
		53	52	55	48	39	38														
CORRY		75	76	78	64	63	65														
		49	54	58	37	28	45														
COUDERSPORT 3 NW		75	68	74	65	63	66														
		49	52	57	35	26	41														
DERRY		81	85	80	73	79	71				78	86	83		85	74					
		56	65	59	47	37	59				52	59	56	40	65	54					
DEVAULT 1		88	87	85	71	74	76				64	86	78	76	86	79					
		54	58	55	45	32	36				39	55	54	53		53					
DIXON		79	79	70	83	59	68				63	63	72	72	75						
		55	50	53	44	30	35				45	51	56	39	41	61					
DONEGAL	MAX	79	79	78	57	76	70				74	88	64	76	77	65					
	MIN	53	54	54	36	30	55	55	44	45	46	52	45	34	58	52					
DONORA		86	89	88	84	74	83	77	77	69	73	82	88	78	86	86					
		61	63	62	49	43	60	62	60	50	56	62	60	46	66	65					
DU BOIS 7 E	MAX	79	77	79	72	67	68	70	62	54	69	80	80	75	80	80		72	77	77	71
	MIN	49	59	57	41	34	51	52	47	44	50	55	54	34	63	54		34	52		44
EAGLES MERE	MAX	70	77	63	76	54	62	63	49	47	50	56	75	69	67	75	70	62		70	64
	MIN	50	53	55	37	34	41	42	41	39	40	44	52	43	49	58	42	39		53	43
EAST BRADY	MAX	84	81	83	81	75	74	75	65	60	79	83	83	82		83	67	78		85	77
	MIN	55	61	58	45	45	54	59	55	49	51	56	56	42	61	55	50	39		51	47
EBENSBURG	MAX	78	75	77	69	69	70	65	66	55	74	80	77	73	79	76	62	70		75	70
	MIN	56	55	55	42	35	54	49	47	43	46	54	53	37	59	53	44	35	50	47	44
EMPORIUM 2 SSW	MAX	78	78	73	72	60	66	70	53	49	55	62	79		75	80	67	65	72		67
	MIN	51	51	55	39	29	30	48	45	42	42	49	49	33	34	55	43	33			39
EPHRATA	MAX	87	80	85	73	69	76	70	56	57	61	86	78	77	87	79		73	76	78	74
	MIN	56	61	61	55	42	55	52	44	43	48	57	64	48	54	61	51		50	46	49
ERIE WB AIRPORT	MAX	72	78	74	51	54	57	55	51	63	77	77	63	73		83			77	78	
	MIN	52	55	43	33	31	45	46	45	45	55	54	46	46	60		42	40		61	45

See reference notes following Station Index.

DAILY TEMPERATURES

	Day Of Month 1	2	3	4	5	6	7	8	9	10	11	12	13	14	15	16	17	18	19	20	21	22	23	24	25	26	27	28	29	30	31	Average
MAX	87	72	60	52	66	70	72	76	88	86	78	78	88	74	82	70	78	74	62	60	60	68	80	78	87	84	80	68	78	76	74	74.4
MIN	42	46	36	32	30	46	38	38	58	58	58	52	58	48	54	47	34	42	56	52	50	52	60	60	46	60	52	50	42	46	46	48.0
MAX	83	76	55	51	66	72	70	81	83	80	74	78	78	73	74	63	58	62	61	64	51	69	87	81	80	81	78	68	75	84		71.9
MIN	38	43	36	35	40	29	37	43	53	61	55	59	57	54	58	44	37	51	58	49	48	48	63	52	44	66	51	50	39	49		48.2
MAX	76	79	65	54	47	61	64	76	79	80	82	75	80	84	82	80	65	75	73	72	71	62	77	85	70	80	84	69	67	77	80	73.3
MIN	37	39	29	28	29	28	30	38	42	51	56	53	54	56	58	47	37	42	56	54	48	49	54	55	41	44	60	48	37	41	49	44.8
MAX	74	79	62	50	60	62	74	75	78	79	71	71	77	81	77	80	72	73	72	69	68	69	76	81	75	76	81	68	79	75	79	73.0
MIN	34	35	30	31	33	33	30	32	40	48	56	58	60	55	61	38	42	44	51	46	53	53	53	56	43	60	50	51	38	46	43	45.3
MAX	76	68	56	48	58	63	76	80	79	79	75	75	80	74	75	73	64	68	64	45	53	55	77	76	73	82	76	72	72	70	74	69.5
MIN	48	40	26	28	37	45	44	53	55	57	56	46	58	53	55	39	35	46	42	39	39	43	50	54	44	56	62	41	39	48	47	46.0
MAX	83	74	60	53	67	69	75	82	84	87	77	78	88	80	86	76	69	76	65	54	58	65	85	81	77	89	77	75	74	76	79	74.8
MIN	41	39	30	30	40	46	37	43	48	51	52	50	56	60	58	57	37	52	52	49	45	38	55	69	50	57	63	53	42	45	47	48.1
MAX	76	85	66	58	64	66	71	80	83	85	87	70	77	91	72	88	87	66	79	57	56	59	64	89	80	78	87	81	74	73	77	74.4
MIN	42	46	36	32	40	50	44	48	50	56	59	53	57	62	61	52	41	52	54	46	45	46	54	64	49	61	67	51	48	53	50	50.6
MAX	76	82	68	56	62	72	78	80	84	88	82	80	78	84	79	88	66	66	72	60	56	56	70	82	84	88	86	80	78	78	76	75.3
MIN	46	36	34	38	38	43	48	52	54	56	54	58	56	60	62	40	38	44	42	44	45	46	50	62	50	56	60	48	42	48	52	48.5
MAX	70	83	61	54	49	66	68	77	80	83	83	72	73	85	71	82	63	65	70	54	56	56	60	84	75	75	84	76	69	72	74	70.6
MIN	39	40	35	33	33	37	35	42	45	51	57	52	52	55	57	47	33	38	53	45	43	45	50	59	45	52	63	49	39	45	47	45.7
MAX	82	77	54	51	69	66	78	80	80	79	72	79	83	80	80	69	87	68	70	58	61	77	81	79	77	82	88	67	79	83		73.9
MIN	33	39	28	33	34	26	33	40	54	59	53	56	54	60	58	41	31	48	57	50	46	50	60	50	40	61	48	46	35	52		45.8
MAX	77	84	67	60	56	65	70	79	82	85	87	70	79	89	73	87	69	67	79	61	58	60	63	88	81	80	89	79	74	75	78	74.5
MIN	49	46	36	33	35	50	42	44	51	56	59	53	58	60	61	61	42	45	55	47	45	45	50	60	52	53	66	52	49	50	50	50.2
MAX	83	64	57	50	65	69	79	83	85	86	71	75	88	74	86	69	67	75	65	53	60	64	89	77	79	87	80	70	73	78	80	73.6
MIN	50	45	40	36	40	48	49	50	51	56	54	53	57	64	64	49	42	60	46	46	46	52	61	61	52	62	58	54	47	57	52	51.7
MAX	61	73	52	44	54	61	62	74	75	80	80	58	75	76	68	79	58	68	61	56	45	63	60	80	67	74	79	79	60	70	75	66.7
MIN	35	32	28	29	35	38	39	42	51	53	53	47	51	47	50	44	26	35	44	37	38	35	46	52	38	45	60	46	32	37	42	41.5
MAX	83	64	56	50	64	68	82	77	84	86	72	79	84	77	85	75	72	77	64	57	60	63	84	75	74	86	77	70	75	77	77	73.4
MIN	53	48	41	37	45	51	52	48	55	57	55	52	61	65	65	51	49	58	52	51	47	54	62	61	54	61	63	55	49	56	54	53.6
MAX	80	84	69	60	50	64	70	80	85	86	88	72	84	88	76	86	70	73	72	59	59	59	65	90	76	80	89	79	73	74	80	74.8
MIN	35	41	28	25	29	33	30	37	41	48	56	57	52	55	57	50	33	43	57	48	48	48	53	60	40	45	59	51	37	43	43	44.6
MAX	80	70	55	49	60	64	75	78	80	81	73	80	83	83	81	71	72	75	70	71	63	76	84	72	81	83	75	67	78	82	81	74.0
MIN	34	40	20	25	27	30	29	36	39	48	54	51	50	57	55	47	36	57	57	54	48	51	55	55	38	61	53	48	35	50	49	44.8
MAX	82	82	68			67	77	81	82	82			87	87	82	75	80			79	72	79	87	84		85		72	81		85	79.8
MIN	40	46	31			28	35	43	48	55			55	62	59	47	39			49	49	52	59	58	43			41	39		42	46.4
MAX	69	79	56	45	51	58	62	76	77	77	80	71	72	80	78	79	55	64	65	68	57	61	76	78	67	74	80	61	63	72	80	68.7
MIN	32	40	31	32	34	25	34	41	52	50	52	58	52	57	58	40	29	42	51	54	45	47	56	48	41	55	54	46	35	46	54	45.2
MAX	82	82	65	54	64	71	79	82	85	85	82	72	87	87	83	82	70	75	72	50	58	57	78	79	75	92	81	77	71	77		75.1
MIN	37	39	33	34	39	40	38	48	46	52	55	50	55	58	57	47	36	55	48	43	43	48	56	62	44	54	64	50	39	42		47.1
MAX	72	75	60	49	46	54	57	74	73	85	79	65	85	89	85	86	66	80	77	65	72	58	72	88	89	82	87	74	70	78	82	73.4
MIN	38	43	29	27	27	34	32	38	42	49	56	53	53	55	54	46	38	47	58	50	47	48	52	56	41	47	62	47	38	48	45	45.2
MAX	70	77	47	46	62	63	75	77	78	79	71	77	80	74	72	61	67	70	55	50	56	72	77	66	76	78	63	64	74	78	79	68.8
MIN	28	28	30	24	25	26	32	38	46	51	55	47	52	57	38	27	38	49	46	41	43	52	50	30	43	45	42	28	39	44	46	40.0
MAX	80	69	57	53	60	65	76	80	83	84	71	84	84	80	84	68	81	75	70	65	55	74	87	72	77	88	72	69	75	77	77	73.9
MIN	41	43	28	25	30	36	40	38	41	50	58	58	54	62	66	44	35	43	49	50	48	45	53	50	41	58	52	46	39	46	44	45.6
A MAX	83	80	62	55	67	70	80	84	86	88	79	74	87	83	86	84	69	78	74	58	60	62	88	89	77	88	82	74	72	74	76	76.4
MIN	42	43	33	32	37	46	37	43	45	50	56	51	55	62	62	57	42	54	54	46	44	50	59	64	47	58	62	52	44	48	45	49.0
MAX	72	82	63	55	52	67	68	78	82	84	87	69	74	87	75	87	66	69	75	59	54	61	65	87	76	78	89	79	69	72	76	72.8
MIN	40	43	29	28	33	44	42	41	43	48	54	51	52	57	61	55	36	49	54	45	45	48	52	64	45	57	62	52	42	48	44	47.2
MAX	61	72	54	45	51	64	65	78	82	85	84	69	74	77	69	79	57	62	60	52	48	57	61	80	69	72	83	74	63	72	80	67.7
MIN	33	29	28	32	27	27	30	36	42	48	46	46	50	51	55	38	29	33	45	43	42	44	52	50	37	41	52	46	34	39	47	40.4
MAX	73	83	64	57	54	67	70	79	83	85	87	70	72	87	74	85	67	68	76	57	52	61	62	88	77	78	88	78	69	72	78	72.9
MIN	41	42	32	31	32	40	36	42	45	50	52	52	52	56	60	50	40	46	54	45	44	46	51	61	46	57	63	52	43	51	46	47.0
MAX	79	86	69	60	53	64	71	81	84	85	87	71	79	88	76	86	69	68	73	61	56	59	63	88	76	80	90	78	73	75	81	74.5
MIN	42	42	37	32	32	34	40	38	44	45	51	57	56	58	61	60	39	39	57	48	47	47	54	58	47	45	58	52	46	45	48	47.1
MAX	77	63	47	52	58	61	76	78	78	79	70	76	79	75	78	56	61	65	65	58	60	76	77	69	74	80	71	60	72	79	78	69.3
MIN	34	37	29	33	37	25	32	39	54	55	48	55	51	58	56	39	28	45	49	45	43	52	58	46	39	61	49	44	34	43	61	44.5
MAX	87	71	64	54	66	73	83	84	86	86	79	80	88	75	86	72	74	74	68	53	58	63	90	86	80	90	79	73	76	83	85	76.3
MIN	39	39	32	29	34	42	37	44	47	54	58	56	55	58	58	46	35	53	51	47	46	54	58	61	51	57	60	49	41	46	51	47.7
MAX	73	78	59	55	45	59	64	75	79	80	82	73	79	84	75	79	64	70	69	57	55	56	70	82	70	78	82	72	66	72	77	70.2
MIN	29	29	22	19	19	24	25	26	33	38	44	48	46	48	52	43	29	30	51	42	41	41	45	47	34	35	55	42	31	32	43	36.9
MAX	86	69	60	55	70	75	81	82	88	85	71	74	91	77	88	76	72	78	61	56	60	64	85	85	78	87	80	73	74	77	80	75.4
MIN	56	49	41	38	46	53	51	61	60	62	54	53	60	66	64	56	52	57	52	49	47	49	62	68	60	64	64	57	54	55	56	55.4
MAX	76	65	54	46	60	62	75	78	79	81	70	82	84	74	80	67	70	71	60	58	54	67	87	68	77	83	70	66	75	77	80	70.8
MIN	44	41	32	28	32	41	40	49	59	56	58	59	57	60	57	46	38	56	50	46	46	49	52	50	44	61	48	46	41	53	52	48.1
MAX	70	79	55	44	50	58	63	76	78	78	79	71	77	79	78	79	55	65	68	68	55	61	74	78	67	76	80	62	63	73	81	69.0
MIN	34	39	30	32	33	28	30	38	45	56	53	56	53	56	59	40	30	37	49	54	46	46	57	50	40	41	55	46	37	40	53	44.0
MAX	80	70	58			72	74	82	78	79	71	76	80	78	78	73	65	70	72	64	59	72	79	78	72	83	75	64	73	80	79	73.6
MIN	29	34	30			32	32	36	48	56	54	56	52	52	51	41	31	49	58	42	42	56	59	50	38	66	48	48	33	46	54	45.6
MAX	86	65	57	51	68	70	79	85	87	87	71	73	91	74	85	69	67	76	64	54	60	64	86	78	83	88	81	71	74	78	81	74.3
MIN	50	48	38	32	41	50	44	44	52	56	56	53	58	65	65	50	43	60	48	47	46	53	61	64	53	60	62	54	48	55	51	51.8
MAX	78	66	48	48	59	65	73	78	79	82	76	79	85	83	79	62	70	72	73	71	65	80	81	69	78	83	69	66	74	83	83	72.8
MIN	43	46	36	38	38	35	40	46	50	59	62	59	61	62	59	46	43	57	63	48	49	56	64	56	48	66	53	53	46	54	57	51.4
MAX	58	71	48	39	47	59	60	74	77	80	78	56	73	73	65	77	52	63	54	47	45	57	58	74	66	70	80	71	58	65	74	63.5
MIN	39	31	26	27	31	37	43	44	53	55	47	48	50	49	53	38	28	33	41	39	39	40	45	50	43	47	58	43	39	44	49	42.2
MAX	81	68	56	50	67	69	77	80	82	85	70	74	86	72	84	73	68	74	61	51	55	61	83	78	75	86	76	68	72	74	75	72.0
MIN	45	42	32	30	35	44	38	46	48	55	50	49	58	56	61	46	36	40	45	45	43	42	59	56	46	59	58	50	43	51	46	46.9
MAX	84	64	55	52	64	69	78	78	85	87	69	73	87	74	85	67	67	75	64	52	58	62	86	78	80	88	79	74	72	75	78	72.9
MIN	44	42	32	35	35	50	48	48	42	53	52	51	54	62	61	43	40	56	45	45	43	49	62	62	59	68	60	51	51	58	57	50.3

See reference notes following Station Index.

DAILY TEMPERATURES

Table 5 - Continued

Station		1	2	3	4	5	6	7	8	9	10	11	12	13	14	15	16	17	18	19	20	21	22	23	24	25	26	27	28	29	30	31	Average
MT POCONO 2 N AP	MAX	76	75	50	45	58	62	72	76	81	80	77	73	78	74	79	77	66	67	58	41	56	51	76	75	73	77	77	69	69	70	73	68
	MIN	44	31	26	30	38	43	38	38	58	59	49	46	58	53	54	41	30	50	41	38	37	38	51	52	48	54	62	44	33	42	44	43
MUHLENBURG 1 SE	MAX	81	73	54	51	64	67	78	79	83	83	79	77	85	80	80	64	68	68	60	50	57	57	81	81	73	81	71	70	78	75	77	71
	MIN	38	33	28	32	35	37	40	48	53	54	53	50	57	52	56	42	31	48	48	42	40	46	55	56	43	56	61	47	46	46	49	45
NEWBURG 3 W	MAX	84	83	69	60	68	70	84	83	86	86	81	84	92	90	92	88	70	80	78	61	59	62	88	88	79	83	78	78	78	78	80	78
	MIN	45	40	32	28	39	45	44	45	51	54	49	52	54	65	68	53	42	55	56	47	44	50	58	62	58	58	56	54	42	47	48	49
NEW CASTLE 1 N	MAX	81	79	59	48	60	66	76	79	80	83	82	79	83	81	82	81	68	73	75	65	65	77	83	78	78	82	80	67	75	80	82	75
	MIN	32	37	28	36	32	28	34	41	56	56	56	56	54	60	59	43	34	50	60	56	47	52	59	51	40	64	46	49	38	47	52	46
NEWELL	MAX	82	83	71	58	60	60	72	80	84	85	85	82	85	91	88	83	68	84	80	76	71	74	82	89	86	86	84	71	72	84	87	78
	MIN	42	50	36	30	31	35	35	40	45	51	62	61	61	61	60	48	44	60	65	59	51	53	59	60	46	67	62	52	43	52	52	50
NEWPORT	MAX	78	83	68	63	54	69	72	83	87	88	88	69	77	88	75	87	68	67	74	59	54	61	62	90	80	81	90	80	74	78	81	75
	MIN	40	41	32	30	32	34	37	38	44	47	52	54	53	57	59	52	37	39	56	46	46	46	52	61	45	47	63	52	43	46	48	46
NEW STANTON	MAX	80	68	55	48	60	67	78	80	83	84	75	84	87	86	85	65	82	75	72	70	68	80	88	73	85	85	77	69	82	82	81	75
	MIN	46	38	28	24	26	30	29	34	40	48	56	52	52	60	56	43	38	56	52	46	49	42	55	44	40	64	52	42	40	43	47	44
NORRISTOWN	MAX	83	66	58	52	68	71	78	84	87	89	73	77	88	76	87	74	73	77	61	53	58	64	86	79	79	88	80	71	74	78	81	74
	MIN	48	47	38	35	43	50	44	51	56	58	52	51	62	60	61	57	44	56	50	46	45	48	61	64	53	61	61	56	48	53	51	51
PALMERTON	MAX	83	70	51	53	63	69	84	82	85	85	70	71	87	71	83	66	68	71	59	47	57	58	82	77	75	84	78	70	70	75	77	71
	MIN	38	39	34	35	39	38	37	44	48	53	50	50	55	57	60	38	35	57	47	43	43	47	58	56	46	58	58	51	41	46	47	46
PHIL DREXEL INST OF TEC	MAX	85	68	59	55	70	71	79	86	89	89	74	78	91	76	89	76	74	78	62	54	58	66	86	83	82	89	79	73	76	80	80	75
	MIN	55	49	40	38	45	54	49	55	60	62	53	53	61	63	63	58	51	57	52	48	46	47	63	68	59	62	66	56	54	54	55	54
PHILADELPHIA WB AP	MAX	83	65	57	54	68	70	78	83	87	88	72	78	89	76	87	73	71	77	61	54	58	65	86	79	78	90	79	70	74	78	80	74
	MIN	52	45	38	35	44	50	46	54	57	61	52	51	60	63	61	53	45	56	50	47	45	45	60	63	64	62	61	56	52	52	53	52
PHILADELPHIA PT BREEZE	MAX	82	68	57	54	68	71	78	81	85	86	72	76	88	77	86	77	71	76	62	54	58	65	85	79	77	88	79	70	75	78	84	74
	MIN	55	49	43	40	50	54	52	56	59	63	52	52	62	63	63	56	50	58	53	48	47	48	62	68	65	64	64	58	56	58	58	55
PHILADELPHIA SHAWMONT	MAX	82	81	65	55	65	70	71	82	86	87	86	76	82	76	86	85	72	74	73	59	58	65	85	84	77	85	84	78	75	78	78	76
	MIN	47	44	36	36	42	47	42	52	53	56	54	52	60	64	60	57	43	56	55	49	46	46	60	67	59	60	66	55	45	50	49	51
PHILADELPHIA CITY	MAX	81	66	58	53	67	70	76	80	83	85	71	76	87	73	84	71	69	75	60	53	58	64	84	78	77	89	78	71	74	78	81	73
	MIN	56	46	41	39	48	53	54	58	60	63	51	51	60	62	60	55	51	57	51	47	47	47	60	67	68	63	61	55	53	54	55	54
PHILIPSBURG CAA AP	MAX	79	61	51	44	57	62	74	77	78	80	68	76	84	71	79	63	65	68	54	54	52	59	81	69	73	80	68	65	70	74	75	68
	MIN	31	35	26	22	28	38	36	36	45	48	53	54	48	56	57	39	33	53	44	44	43	47	55	47	33	61	46	43	30	51	44	42
PHOENIXVILLE 1 E	MAX	86	85	68	60	70	74	80	86	89	89	82	79	91	81	90	88	74	79	77	64	62	65	88	86	83	90	85	82	84	79	83	80
	MIN	41	43	33	30	36	46	45	44	48	52	53	51	56	63	60	56	36	55	55	55	40	42	58	63	45	56	63	54	42	46	43	48
PIMPLE HILL	MAX	69	77	54	45	50	57	65	73	77	81	80	57	71	81	69	79	59	65	69	46	43	54	61	74	70	72	78	73	63	69	69	66
	MIN	38	29	24	27	34	39	43	53	58	59	54	45	54	52	53	39	34	47	45	37	36	39	45	50	42	55	61	42	37	48	49	44
PITTSBURGH WB AP 2	MAX	81	63	50	46	57	64	74	79	79	80	75	80	84	82	79	61	74	69	72	66	63	75	82	69	79	82	66	66	74	70	78	71
	MIN	44	42	33	32	35	35	40	48	54	59	59	59	61	61	54	43	41	56	60	48	47	53	61	55	47	64	50	49	42	56	58	49
PITTSBURGH WB CITY	MAX	81	67	53	50	59	66	77	81	81	83	77	82	86	85	82	64	78	73	75	69	65	79	86	72	81	84	71	68	80	82	81	74
	MIN	50	45	36	36	38	41	43	50	58	63	63	60	62	63	57	47	45	59	62	51	50	55	64	58	50	67	51	52	46	56	62	52
PLEASANT MOUNT 1 W	MAX	58	70	49	40	47	57	59	72	74	79	77	55	73	73	65	77	55	64	59	45	42	56	59	77	66	70	77	71	57	67	74	63
	MIN	35	30	26	27	33	34	32	38	42	49	50	47	51	46	52	40	26	33	43	38	38	38	45	51	37	53	60	44	34	44	43	40
PORT CLINTON	MAX	73	85	66	57	52	65	70	81	82	85	88	72	70	87	76	84	68	70	75	58	50	58	60	85	78	78	90	80	70	72	78	73
	MIN	34	39	28	30	32	41	31	39	43	47	57	49	51	55	52	48	31	41	51	43	42	43	50	58	40	50	60	49	36	45	43	43
PUTNEYVILLE 2 SE DAM	MAX	76	79	64	53	46	65	64	75	78	80	81	77	80	82	80	81	60	73	73	67	72	59	76	83	70	80	83	70	67	78	81	72
	MIN	32	38	26	26	27	31	30	39	43	50	54	53	51	52	56	42	31	40	53	50	45	45	52	54	36	43	58	45	32	39	49	42
QUAKERTOWN 1 E	MAX	82	82	62	56	67	69	79	82	85	87	81	75	86	86	84	83	70	74	71	55	57	62	82	80	76	84	85	78	70	77	79	75
	MIN	39	41	34	31	39	46	35	44	45	50	53	50	58	54	57	53	36	55	52	45	44	41	57	66	45	55	64	52	40	45	45	47
READING WB CITY	MAX	84	66	58	55	68	70	80	83	85	88	73	74	88	77	87	70	70	76	60	52	58	62	87	78	78	89	80	71	72	76	79	74
	MIN	52	44	38	36	41	52	49	54	57	60	53	52	62	64	64	50	44	57	47	46	46	49	60	63	53	63	60	54	48	53	51	52
RIDGWAY 3 W	MAX	78	80	50	47	63	64	76	78	78	80	71	78	81	76	78	64	69	70	57	52	56	70	80	68	78	80	66	65	75	75	80	70
	MIN	29	30	22	23	27	27	26	27	34	40	50	53	50	51	56	41	30	33	49	48	43	44	51	53	34	36	49	44	33	36	44	39
SALINA 3 W	MAX	78	77	63	53	56	63	75	78	80	80	78	80	85	83	80	72	77	70	71	69	63	77	84	80	80	83	80	65	78	80	81	74
	MIN	38	45	30	26	29	33	32	40	46	51	56	54	53	60	60	45	35	57	57	55	49	50	56	57	41	65	55	49	36	51	51	47
SCRANTON	MAX	66	78	56	46	52	61	61	79	81	85	84	66	80	82	75	84	62	71	65	55	50	62	62	85	72	76	85	72	66	72	79	70
	MIN	40	37	32	33	37	43	40	43	49	57	56	52	53	58	60	45	35	39	49	43	44	45	50	56	45	48	61	50	41	44	48	44
SCRANTON WB AIRPORT	MAX	78	55	47	49	64	64	78	79	83	84	65	79	80	69	81	61	69	66	55	48	60	58	83	70	74	83	75	65	72	77	79	69
	MIN	38	35	28	33	37	38	40	49	55	58	50	50	58	55	57	37	32	47	43	41	38	47	56	53	44	60	49	45	38	40	49	45
SELINSGROVE CAA AP	MAX	85	62	54	51	65	71	81	82	85	86	67	72	88	72	86	63	67	72	58	53	59	61	84	78	75	85	77	72	75	78	79	72
	MIN	36	35	31	30	32	37	34	40	43	49	55	55	54	56	58	41	35	56	47	46	45	52	59	51	44	60	54	50	41	45	48	45
SHIPPENSBURG	MAX	83	81	64	60	67	69	81	84	87	88	82	77	89	83	86	79	68	78	72	57	61	64	88	85	79	89	80	79	76	80	82	77
	MIN	47	42	32	29	34	47	40	45	56	54	61	52	58	60	62	52	38	59	54	45	44	52	58	65	48	58	65	51	45	49	48	50
SHIPPINGPORT WB	MAX	80	63	49	47	58	65	75	79	80	81	73	79	83	83	80	60	72	72	72	69	63	78	83	69	80	82	67	66	75	82	82	72
	MIN	40	41	33	38	39	31	35	43	47	57	58	56	57	61	54	42	37	54	60	48	48	53	60	48	43	65	52	45	40	50	54	48
SLIPPERY ROCK	MAX	82	75	52	49	61	65	77	78	79	80	71	78	79	78	79	71	66	70	68	63	65	75	81	74	80	80	75	67	74	80	80	72
	MIN	40	42	29	34	34	35	39	41	55	59	57	56	55	60	55	37	36	50	55	50	45	50	61	57	44	63	48	47	38	51	54	47
SOMERSET MAIN ST	MAX	77	75	64	52	56	61	65	76	77	78	78	79	82	82	80	66	72	75	71	70	60	78	82	79	75	80	78	64	72	75	74	72
	MIN	37	43	28	24	26	36	37	33	32	49	56	55	56	56	55	45	35	48	59	50	48	47	56	55	39	60	55	45	36	50	45	45
SPRINGBORO	MAX	70	78	55	45	53	58	61	78	79	78	78	66	74	78	78	75	55	60	65	65	55	62	78	78	66	75	82	60	59	72	82	68
	MIN	35	43	29	33	40	27	34	40	53	59	48	53	51	57	59	39	28	42	46	49	44	49	58	48	40	51	54	46	48	43	51	45
SPRINGS 1 SW	MAX	74	67	52	49	52	59	70	74	76	77	71	78	80	82	77	60	72	74	62	66	53	76	81	68	74	79	66	62	70	73	72	69
	MIN	47	39	29	26	24	30	34	35	45	46	53	52	56	56	53	39	33	50	53	50	46	49	49	47	35	53	51	43	33	43	41	43
STATE COLLEGE	MAX	82	85	56	48	63	66	77	80	81	84	69	79	85	73	82	64	68	68	57	57	56	62	85	72	77	85	74	68	74	78	78	71
	MIN	51	39	33	30	37	43	44	53	60	57	58	56	57	59	58	45	38	53	48	46	45	51	58	57	46	64	62	47	43	54	56	49
STROUDSBURG	MAX	83	61	56	55	65	70	80	83	85	86	68	75	85	70	86	66	68	72	55	47	64	60	81	73	76	82	82	70	74	76	80	72
	MIN	32	40	29	31	40	36	31	35	40	50	50	48	52	53	52	41	30	44	46	40	40	35	53	44	36	52	56	47	31	35	40	41
TAMARACK 2 S FIRE TWR	MAX	70	81	58	50	45	60	65	77	79	81	71	68	77	84	67	78	59	65	66	49	45	50	56	78	70	74	81	69				66
	MIN	43	30	25	26	28	34	39	42	49	56	49	50	54	53	54	37	33	36	43	42	40	39	46	51	42	44	58	40				42
TIONESTA 2 SE DAM	MAX	73	77	60	49	47	63	63	76	78	78	81	71	77	81	77	79	63	67	73	65	55	60	76	80	68	77	81	65	64	73	80	70
	MIN	34	35	29	31	30	29	31	37	43	49	55	58	54	57	59	41	33	40	51	50	45	45	51	52	39	40	53	46	37	39	50	43

See reference notes following Station Index.

Table 5 - Continued

DAILY TEMPERATURES

PENNSYLVANIA
MAY 1957

Station	1	2	3	4	5	6	10	11	12	13	14	15	16	17	18	19	20	21	22	23	24	25	26	27	28	29	30	31	Average
TUSVILLE WATER WORKS	[illegible]	[illegible]	[illegible]	[illegible]	[illegible]	[illegible]	81	72	78	80	80	80	65	67	72	66	55	61	77	80	75	78	82	74	63	76	83	82	71.9
							51	57	58	51	55	57	38	28	48	52	49	42	49	54	50	42	61	50	44	31	40	42	42.5
WANDA							84	72	82	79	69	81	66	66	62	57	50	58	63	82	76	77	86	79	66	70	81	82	71.2
							51	49	52	58	50	54	41	30	45	45	43	42	47	54	53	38	59	58	47	37	41	47	43.5
IONTOWN							82	74	84	88	84	84	67	82	76	75	69	68	79	85	72	84	84	71	69	78	81	81	75.4
							54	62	57	58	64	61	49	40	60	61	55	51	55	60	59	45	64	57	51	42	54	54	50.2
PER DARBY							88	81	77	88	85	86	82	71	76	72	54	58	64	85	84	78	89	84	74	74		80	76.4
							58	52	52	60	62	60	59	45	55	53	49	45	43	60	68	53	61	66	55	49		50	52.4
RREN							80	73	80	79	78	79	61	66	68	59	54	58	77	80	72	78	83	77	64	75	82	82	71.2
							55	54	60	52	56	52	39	31	48	51	48	45	51	56	52	37	58	50	44	35	40	50	44.2
YNESBURG ;							81	76	83	87	86	82	75	83	79	77	67	70	78	86	83	84	84	75	68	78	84	85	76.9
							49	60	54	53	56	54	46	38	55	60	53	50	49	53	58	41	60	58	49	38	47	47	46.0
LLSBORO 3							78	79	66	74	79	65	76	55	65	60	50	47	53	57	78	69	71	79	70	64	68	74	65.8
							57	46	48	53	52	55	36	30	33	41	42	40	40	48	51	40	43	58	42	36	40	53	42.4
LLSVILLE							86	81	75	88	73	86	76	66	76	72	57	59	63	87	81	86	86	84	78	72	78	79	75.9
										52	60	61	51	35	55	55	45	44	50	61	62	54	55	54	52	41	46	49	47.2
ST CHESTER										88	84	88	72	72	80	59	50	57	64	89	80	82	90	82	71	79	80	83	75.3
										58	62	61	53	38	41	38	46	42	44	58	54	53	56	60	51	47	49	49	48.6
LLIAMSPORT WB AP										88	68	85	64	68	72	57	52	57	60	85	79	74	86	80	72	71	78	80	72.6
										59	57	59	44	35	52	47	46	45	52	58	56	45	63	56	51	41	47	53	48.0
RK 3 SSW PUMP STA										89	85	87	86	69	78	78	59	60	64	88	87	79	89	85	79	74	77	79	78.0
										54	61	63	54	39	54	55	47	46	51	61	64	45	59	67	54	44	52	47	49.2

WIND

NFLUENCE 1 SW DAM	5.22 1742
RD CITY 4 S DAM	B5.08 B1598
WLEY 1 S DAM	5.40 2586
AMESTOWN 2 NW	
ANDISVILLE	B6.31 1875
IMPLE HILL	7.12 3192
TATE COLLEGE	5.54 1337

See reference notes following Station Index.

Table 7

SNOWFALL AND SNOW ON GROUND

AUSTINBURG 2 W

BRADFORD 4 W RESVR

BROOKVILLE CAA AIRPORT

COALDALE 2 NW

CORRY

DU BOIS 7 E

ERIE WB AIRPORT

GALETON

KANE 1 NNE

MEADVILLE 1 S

MEDIX RUN

MONTROSE 1 E

PHILIPSBURG CAA AIRPORT

PIMPLE HILL

SELINSGROVE CAA AIRPORT

TAMARACK 2 S FIRE TWR

TIONESTA 2 SE DAM

TOWANDA

WILLIAMSPORT WB AIRPORT

See reference notes following Station Index.

TOTAL PRECIPITATION

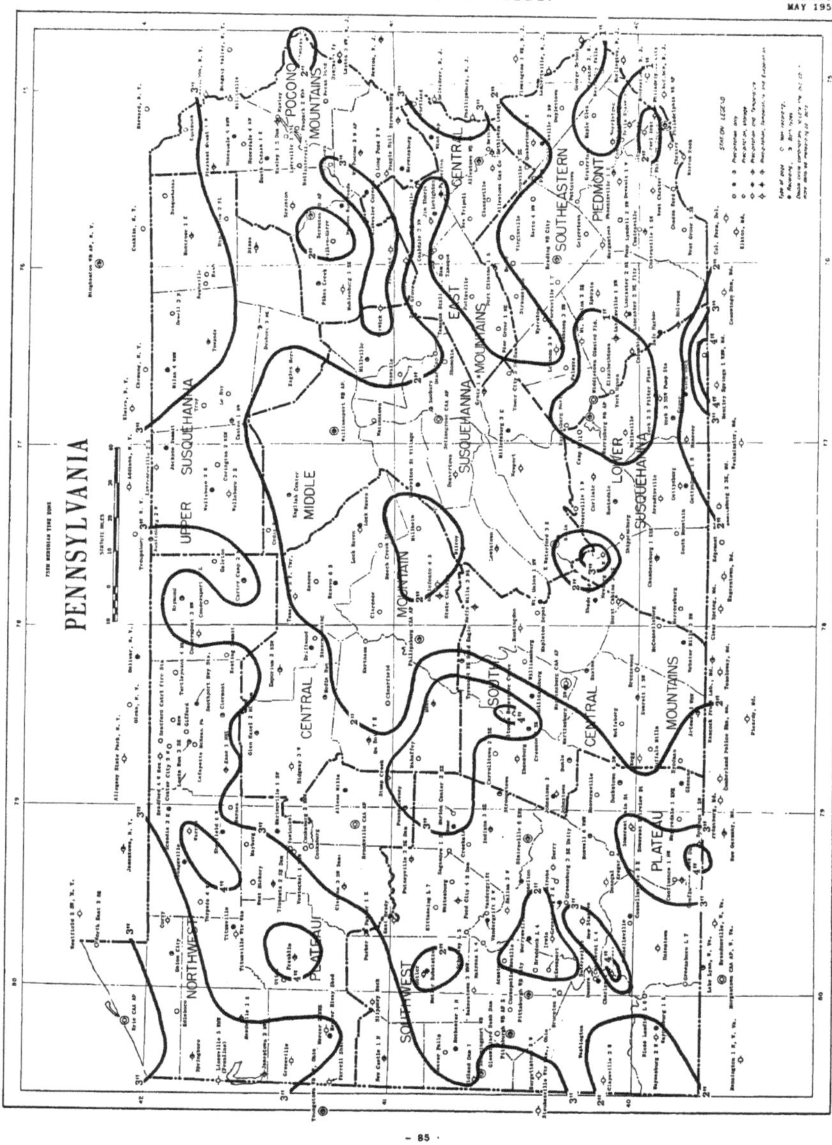

Isolines are drawn through points of approximately equal values. Hourly precipitation data from recorder substations will be available in the publication "Hourly Precipitation Data".

AVERAGE TEMPERATURE

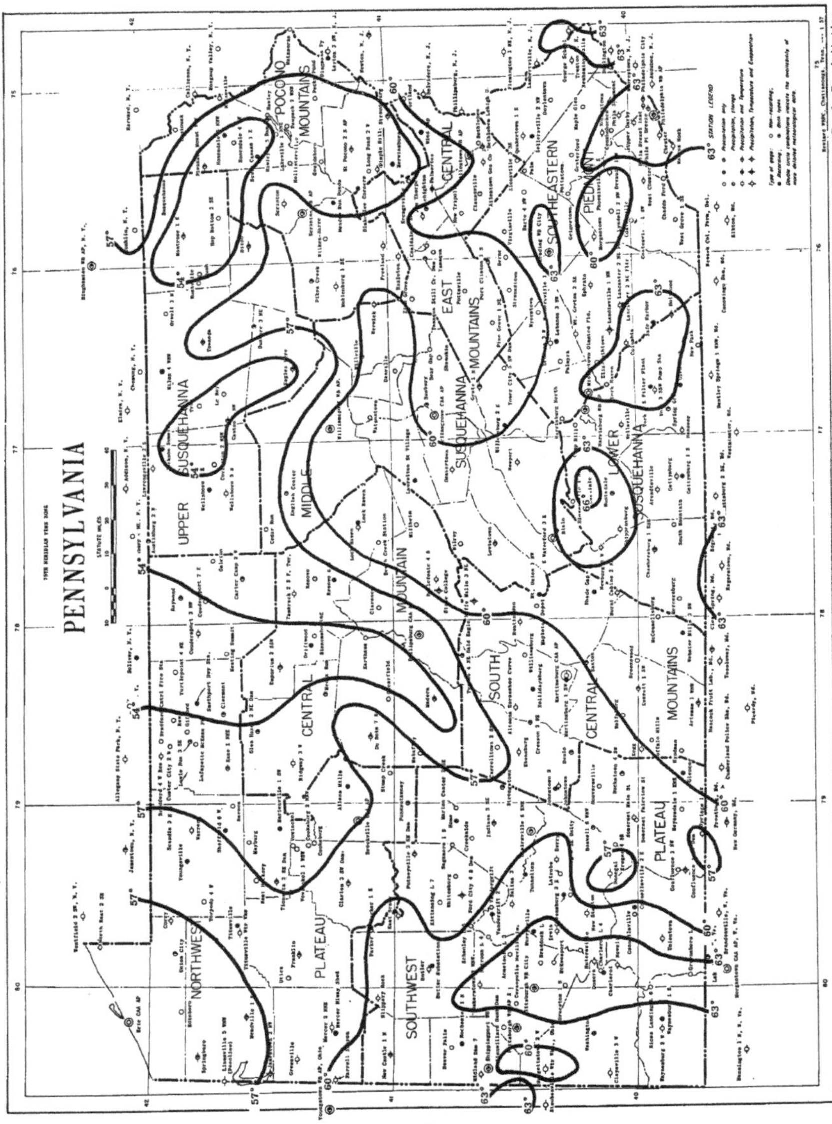

Isolines are drawn through points of approximately equal values. Hourly precipitation data from recorder substations will be available in the publication "Hourly Precipitation Data".

STATION INDEX

Index No.	County	Drainage 1	Latitude	Longitude	Elevation	Obs. Time Temp.	Obs. Time Precip.	Observer	Refer To Tables
0022	ALLEGHENY	1	40 32	79 49	748		7A	CORPS OF ENGINEERS	3
0099	JEFFERSON	1	41 12	78 55	1600		MID	CHARLES H. ALLEN	C
0106	LEHIGH	9	40 39	75 26	376	MID	MID	U.S. WEATHER BUREAU	2 3 5 7 C
0111	LEHIGH	9	40 36	75 28	254	7A	7A	LEHIGH VLY GAS DIV	2 3 5
E 0134	BLAIR	6	40 30	78 29	1500	6P	6P	ALTOONA WATER BUR.	2 3 5
0229	ADAMS	15	39 55	77 18	710	8A	8A	PA STATE COL EXP	2 3 5
0259	BEDFORD	12	39 45	78 28	1250	6P	6P	GRAYSON E.NORTHCRAFT	2 3 5
0313	TIOGA	15	42 00	77 32	1590		7A	OTTO D. BACON	3 7 C
0355	ALLEGHENY	1	40 39	79 59	1230	7P	7P	PGH CUT FLOWER CO	2 3 5
0409	WARREN	1	41 40	79 02	1310		7A	CORPS OF ENGINEERS	3
0428	BERKS	14	40 28	75 39	312		7A	MARIE B. NICHLAS	3
0457	NORTHUMBERLAND	15	40 50	76 30	900		MID	ROARING CRK WTR CO	3
0475	BEAVER	2	40 46	80 19	760		7A	HOWARD R. KEMP	3
0482	SNYDER	15	40 45	77 10	640	5P	7A	MARLIN R. ETTINGER	2 3 5
0499	CENTRE	16	41 04	77 34	620		7A	HAROLD S. RUPERT	3 7
0530	CENTRE	16	40 51	77 47	1110	8A	8A	ROCKVIEW PRISON FARM	2 3 5
0599	BERKS	14	40 31	76 00	325		7A	FLOYD W. TRUMP	3
0611	COLUMBIA	15	41 04	76 15	570	6P	8P	AMER CAR + FNDRY CO	2 3 5
0629	NORTHAMPTON	9	40 37	75 22	400		7A	ARTHUR CROPPER	3
0634	NORTHAMPTON	9	40 36	75 23	450	MID	MID	LEHIGH UNIVERSITY	2 3 5 C
0729	PERRY	15	40 20	77 31	750		MID	PA DEPT FRST + WTRS	C
0736	INDIANA	4	40 27	79 09	2048	6P	6P	U.S. WEATHER BUREAU	2 3 5
0743	MONROE	9	41 08	75 36	1650		MID	WALTER WILDRICK	C
0763	CUMBERLAND	15	40 16	77 22	650		5P	MRS. B. M. WILLDERS	3
0820	SOMERSET	1	40 10	79 08	2570		8A	CLARK N. ST. CLAIR	3 C
0861	ALLEGHENY	10	40 24	79 52	725		7A	CORPS OF ENGINEERS	3
0867	MC KEAN	1	41 57	78 39	1500		8A	BRADFORD FIRE DEPT	3
0868	MC KEAN	1	41 57	78 44	1680	5P	5P	BRADFORD WTR DEPT	2 3 5 7
0905	BEDFORD	6	40 00	78 14	1352		MID	PA TURNPIKE COMM	3
1002	JEFFERSON	1	41 09	79 06	1417	MID	MID	CIVIL AERO. ADM.	2 3 5 7
1033	ALLEGHENY	10	40 18	79 59	1065		7A	AUSTIN R. COOPER	3
1073	SOMERSET	4	40 04	78 50	2400		MID	ALVIN W. MANGES	C
1087	BEDFORD	6	39 57	78 39	1318		7A	MRS. NELLE R. BROWN	3
1105	WASHINGTON	11	40 25	80 26	980	7A	7A	SMITH TWP MUN AUTH	2 3 5
1115	HUNTINGDON	6	40 05	77 52	990	MID	MID	PA TURNPIKE COMM	2 3 5
1130	BUTLER	2	40 52	79 54	1100	4P	7A	WILLIAM C. FAUST	2 3 5
1135	BUTLER	2	40 51	79 53	1140		MID	WEST PENN POWER CO	C
1198	CUMBERLAND	15	40 15	76 55	461		6P	JOSEPH N. HOBART	3
1215	BRADFORD	15	41 40	76 52	1520	7A	7A	MRS.MILDRED SPENCER	2 3 5 7 C
1234	CUMBERLAND	15	40 12	77 11	460	6P	6P	C. E. MILLER	2 3 5
1255	CAMBRIA	16	40 35	78 42	2040		8A	ROBERT F. MAURER	3 7
1262	POTTER	16	41 37	77 45	2030		7A	RICHARD L. MENKEN	3 C
1301	LYCOMING	16	41 31	77 27	800		7A	KATHRYN T.KREIGHBAUM	3
1342	DELAWARE	5	39 52	75 36	160		8A	MRS.GRACE A. WICKS	3
1354	FRANKLIN	12	39 56	77 38	640	9P	9P	CHARLES A. BENDER	2 3 5 C
1372	WASHINGTON	10	40 08	79 55	1040		MID	WEST PENN POWER CO	C
1377	WESTMORELAND	10	40 09	79 54	749		7A	CORPS OF ENGINEERS	3
1423	DELAWARE	5	39 51	75 22	86	8A	8A	CHESTER TIMES	2 3 5
1480	CENTRE	16	41 03	77 56	1410		7A	MISS VELDA SWANCER	3
1485	CLARION	1	41 12	79 26	1114	8P	7A	PA ELECTRIC CO	2 3 5 C
1505	LEHIGH	9	40 37	75 39	670		8A	WILLIAM J. DOTTERER	3
1512	WASHINGTON	11	40 07	80 28	1000	7P	7A	MFGRS. L + H CO	2 3 5
1519	CLEARFIELD	16	41 01	78 26	1100		7A	IRA TAYLOR	3
1529	MC KEAN	1	41 41	78 30	2104		7A	MRS.TILLIE M.SIMONDS	3 C
1572	SCHUYLKILL	9	40 50	75 56	1026		7A	PANTHER VLY WTR CO	3 7
1589	CHESTER	5	39 58	75 50	342	8A	8A	PHILA ELECTRIC CO	2 3 5 C
1594	CHESTER	5	39 59	75 49	340		8A	EDWARD O. BIEDEMAN	INAC 12/55
1675	LANCASTER	15	40 02	76 30	300	SS	SS	JAMES H. RUST	2 3 5
1705	SOMERSET	17	39 48	79 22	1490	8A	8A	CORPS OF ENGINEERS	2 3 5 6 C
1710	FAYETTE	17	39 50	79 22	1331		7A	JOHN L. REID	3
1723	FAYETTE	17	40 01	79 36	870		8A	MARSHALL B. MENEFEE	3
1729	FAYETTE	17	40 01	79 33	1300		MID	HARRY C. JOY	C
1737	MONTGOMERY	5	40 04	75 19	70		8A	PHILA ELECTRIC CO	3
1749	CLARION	1	41 20	79 13	1180		8A	PA DEPT FRST + WTRS	3
1752	CLARION	1	41 21	79 13	1460		8A	PA DEPT FRST + WTRS	3
1773	ALLEGHENY	11	40 30	80 05	720		8A	PGH. COKE + CHEM CO	3
1790	ERIE	1	41 58	79 38	1427	7P	5A	LEO C. MECKERS	2 3 5 7
1806	POTTER	1	41 49	78 03	2020	7P	8A	MISS ELIZABETH NEFF	2 3 5
1809	POTTER	1	41 40	77 53	2425		7A	CAMP POTATO	3
1833	TIOGA	15	41 44	77 07	1745		7A	CALVIN R. PACKARD	3
1881	INDIANA	1	40 41	79 12	1035		7A	CORPS OF ENGINEERS	3
1895	CAMBRIA	8	40 27	78 34	2540		7A	MILES M. LINGLE	3 C
1978	MC KEAN	1	41 55	78 41	2120		8A	M. D. BOOTH AND CO	3
2013	MONTOUR	15	40 58	76 37	460		7A	MRS.MARIE M. LITTLE	3
2108	WESTMORELAND	4	40 20	79 18	1150	6P	6P	MISS N. D. WINEMAN	2 3 5
2116	CHESTER	14	40 05	75 33	340	MID	MID	PA TURNPIKE COMM	2 3 5
2160	PIKE	5	41 13	74 52	364		MID	CLYDE T. VOORHEES	C
2171	WYOMING	15	41 34	75 54	620	7A	7A	HAROLD J. KUSCHEL	2 3 5 C
2183	WESTMORELAND	17	40 07	79 23	1746	MID	MID	PA TURNPIKE COMM	2 3 5 7
2190	WASHINGTON	10	40 11	79 51	814	12M	12M	DONORA ZINC WORKS	2 3 5
2221	BUCKS	5	40 18	75 08	393		5P	GEORGE HART	3
2245	CAMERON	16	41 20	78 08	880		MID	SIDNEY KENNEDY	C
2265	CLEARFIELD	16	41 06	78 38	1670	5P	5P	CITY OF DU BOIS	2 3 5 7 C
2298	CAMBRIA	4	40 17	78 43	2410		MID	MRS. O. L. WHITE	C
2324	SULLIVAN	16	41 33	76 21	1750		7A	PATRICK P. RYAN	3 C
2343	SULLIVAN	16	41 24	76 35	2020	7A	7A	MRS.ELSIE P. BIGGER	2 3 5 C
2363	CLARION	1	40 59	79 37	820	5P	5P	A. B. KEMPEL	2 3 5
2459	PERRY	6	40 21	77 33	2125	8A	8A	U.S. WEATHER BUREAU	INAC 5/55
2466	CAMBRIA	4	40 29	78 43	2090	7P	7A	ROBERT A. WASSER	2 3 5
2514	ERIE	1	41 52	80 08	1220		8A	EDINBORO ST TCHR COL	3
2519	CRAWFORD	1	41 30	80 13	1325		8A	WILLIAM HAGER	3
2560	LANCASTER	15	40 09	76 37	440		8A	MASONIC HOME	3
2634	CAMERON	16	41 28	78 15	1735	7A	7A	JACKSON THOMAS	2 3 5 C
2644	LYCOMING	16	41 26	77 17	881		7A	WILLIAM SUDERS	3 7 C
2662	LANCASTER	15	40 11	76 10	465	6P	6P	STANLEY L.VON NEIDA	2 3 5
2671	WAYNE	5	41 51	75 13	910		7A	MRS. HENRIETTA MURRY	3
2682	ERIE	8	42 05	80 12	732	MID	MID	U. S. WEATHER BUREAU	2 3 5 7
2721	BEDFORD	6	40 00	78 23	1020	MID	MID	PA TURNPIKE COMM	2 3 5 7 C
2814	MERCER	2	41 14	80 30	865	7P	7P	SHARON STEEL CORP	2 3 5
2942	ARMSTRONG	1	40 45	79 30	950	8A	8A	CORPS OF ENGINEERS	2 3 5 6 7 C
3028	VENANGO	1	41 23	79 49	987	7P	7A	GEORGE S. SMITH, JR	2 3 5 C
3058	LUZERNE	15	41 01	75 54	1900	6P	8A	ANDREW B. EVANSHA	2 3 5
3130	POTTER	16	41 44	77 39	1325		7A	W. GALE LUSH	3 7
3189	BERKS	14	40 13	75 50	400		8A	WALTER C. WOLF	3
3200	BUCKS	5	40 15	74 56	135	7P	7P	GEORGE M. HART	2 3 5 7
3218	ADAMS	12	39 50	77 14	540	9A	9A	HUGH C. MC ILHENNY	2 3 5
3223	ADAMS	12	39 48	77 14	560		MID	NAT MILITARY PARK	C
3237	MC KEAN	1	41 51	78 36	2220		8A	SOUTH PENN OIL CO	3
3289	SOMERSET	12	39 40	78 51	1620		MID	MRS. MARY M.MARTMAN	C
3311	ELK	1	41 34	78 36	1725		8A	CORPS OF ENGINEERS	3 C
3330	YORK	15	39 48	76 44	620		MID	MRS.E.C.MC WILLIAMS	C
3343	ALLEGHENY	11	40 33	80 13	705		7A	CORPS OF ENGINEERS	3
3394	WAYNE	9	41 15	75 27	1890		7A	L. M. EILENBERGER	3
3435	MONTGOMERY	14	40 14	75 27	160	7A	7A	CLAUDE K. KULP	2 3 5 7 C
3438	DAUPHIN	15	40 38	76 43	760	8A	8A	LEE M. LEITZEL	2 3 5 C
3503	GREENE	10	39 47	79 55	808		7A	CORPS OF ENGINEERS	3 7
3515	WESTMORELAND	10	40 18	79 31	1225		MID	PA DEPT HIGHWAYS	C
3516	WESTMORELAND	10	40 17	79 30	1245		6P	WESTMORELAND WTR CO	3
3526	MERCER	2	41 24	80 23	1026	6P	6P	C. EARL MILLER	2 3 5
3662	YORK	15	39 48	76 59	600	8A	8A	HANOVER EVENING SUN	2 3 5 7
3699	YORK	15	40 13	76 51	335	MID	MID	U.S. WEATHER BUREAU	2 3 5 7 C
3704	DAUPHIN	15	40 18	76 54	323		9A	GEORGE S. BEAL	3
3758	WAYNE	5	41 29	75 10	880		7A	MRS. KATHERINE BATES	3
3761	WAYNE	5	41 28	75 11	1200	7A	7A	PA POWER + LIGHT CO	2 3 5 6 7 C
4001	BLAIR	6	40 28	78 24	960		MID	JOHN M. RINGLER	C
4008	WAYNE	5	41 23	75 26	1360		8A	PA POWER + LIGHT CO	3
4019	LANCASTER	15	39 50	76 20	187	MID	8A	PA POWER + LIGHT CO	2 3 5 7 C
4027	INDIANA	1	40 45	79 06	1220		MID	MRS. EDNA M. BUSH	C
4043	WAYNE	5	41 37	75 19	1410		9A	GEORGE C. WILLIAMS	3
4044	WAYNE	5	41 30	75 17	1050		MID	FRIEND E. WALTER	C

Station	Index No.	County	Drainage 1	Latitude	Longitude	Elevation	Obs. Time Temp.	Obs. Time Precip.	Observer	Refer To Tables
HOOVERSVILLE	4058	SOMERSET	4	40 09	78 55	1060		7A	PA ELECTRIC CO	3 7
HOP BOTTOM 2 SE	4086	SUSQUEHANNA	15	41 43	75 43	900		7A	JOSEPH J. SANSUSKAS	3
HUNTINGDON	4159	HUNTINGDON	6	40 30	78 01	678	7A	7A	DANIEL I. GROVE	2 3 5
HUNTSDALE	4166	CUMBERLAND	15	40 06	77 18	610		8A	METRO P. DOROSH	3 C
HYNDMAN	4190	BEDFORD	12	39 49	78 43	920		8A	MRS.GERTRUDE M.BURTO	3
INDIANA 3 SE	4214	INDIANA	4	40 36	79 07	1102	7P	7A	CLYMER WATER SVC CO	2 3 5 7 C
IRWIN	4276	WESTMORELAND	10	40 20	79 42	1100	5P	5P	WESTMORELAND WTR CO	2 3 5
JACKSON SUMMIT	4304	TIOGA	15	41 57	77 01	1690		MID	ARCHIE LAIN	C
JAMESTOWN 2 NW	4325	CRAWFORD	2	41 30	80 28	1050	8A	8A	PA DEPT FRST + WTRS	2 3 5 6 C
JIM THORPE	4370	CARBON	9	40 52	75 45	830	5P	5P	HENRY S. HAAK	2 3 5
#JOHNSTOWN	4385	CAMBRIA	4	40 20	78 55	1214	9A	9A	JOHNSTOWN TRIBUNE	2 3 5
JOHNSTOWN 2	4390	CAMBRIA	4	40 19	78 55	1275		MID	CITY OF JOHNSTOWN	C
KANE 1 NNE	4432	MC KEAN	1	41 41	78 48	1750	8A	8A	RUDOLPH A. ANDERSON	2 3 5 7 C
KARTHAUS	4450	CLEARFIELD	16	41 07	78 07	950		7A	JEROME S. HOWE	3
KEATING SUMMIT	4466	POTTER	16	41 41	78 11	1840		7A	EUGENE L. KREITNER	3 7
KEGG	4481	BEDFORD	6	39 59	78 43	1280	MID	MID	PA TURNPIKE COMM	2 3 5
KITTANNING LOCK 7	4611	ARMSTRONG	1	40 49	79 32	790		VAR	CORPS OF ENGINEERS	3
KREGAR 4 SE	4667	WESTMORELAND	17	40 06	79 14	2530		MID	PA TURNPIKE COMM	3
KRESGEVILLE 3 W	4672	CARBON	9	40 54	75 34	720		7A	CITY OF BETHLEHEM	3
LAFAYETTE MC KEAN PARK	4706	MC KEAN	1	41 48	78 40	2130		7A	ORIN A. BUTTERS	3
LAKEVILLE 1 NNE	4733	WAYNE	5	41 27	75 16	1440		8A	MRS. GLADYS REINEKE	3
LANCASTER 2 NE PUMP STA	4758	LANCASTER	15	40 03	76 17	255	6P	6P	LANCASTER WATER BUR	2 3 5 7
LANCASTER 2 NE FILT PL	4763	LANCASTER	15	40 03	76 17	270		MID	LANCASTER WATER BUR	C
LANDISVILLE 2 NW	4778	LANCASTER	15	40 07	76 26	360	8A	8A	PA STATE COLLEGE	2 3 5 6 C
LATROBE	4832	WESTMORELAND	4	40 19	79 23	1000		MID	WEST PENN POWER CO	INAC 6/56
LAURELTON STATE VILLAGE	4853	UNION	15	40 54	77 13	880		MID	PA DEPT OF WELFARE	C
LAWRENCEVILLE 2 S	4873	TIOGA	15	41 59	77 07	1000	7A	7A	HARRY P. HOWLAND	2 3 5 7
LEBANON 3 W	4891	LEBANON	15	40 20	76 29	460	7A	7A	LEON MILLER	2 3 5 7
LEBANON 3 SW	4896	LEBANON	15	40 19	76 28	490		MID	THOMAS DONNACHIE	C
LEHIGHTON	4934	CARBON	9	40 50	75 43	580		7A	GOODWIN S. DEFREHN	3 C
LE ROY	4972	BRADFORD	15	41 41	76 43	1040		6P	MRS.DIMMIS M.BAILEY	3
LEWIS RUN 3 SE	4984	MC KEAN	1	41 50	78 39	1740		7A	RUSSELL LINEMAN	3 C
LEWISTOWN	4992	MIFFLIN	6	40 35	77 35	480	7A	7A	AMERICAN VISCOSE CO	2 3 5 7 C
LINESVILLE 5 WNW	5050	CRAWFORD	2	41 41	80 31	1020	7P	8A	MISS RETTA M. CRUMB	2 3 5
LOCK HAVEN	5104	CLINTON	16	41 08	77 27	570	7P	7A	PETER L. STEVENSON	2 3 5
LOCK HAVEN 2	5109	CLINTON	16	41 08	77 27	630		MID	HUGH F. PARKER	C
LONG POND 2 W	5160	MONROE	9	41 03	75 30	1860		7A	THOMAS HECKES	3
LYNDELL 2 NW	5279	CHESTER	5	40 05	75 46	-		8A	MRS. DOROTHY MARPLE	3
MADERA	5336	CLEARFIELD	16	40 50	78 26	1460	7A	7A	MRS. JULIA J. SHOFF	2 3 5 C
MAHAFFEY	5342	CLEARFIELD	16	40 53	78 44	1280		7A	MISS ELLEN J. MILES	3
MAPLE GLEN	5368	MONTGOMERY	5	40 11	75 11	380		6P	FRANCES E.SCHEIBNER	3
MAPLETON DEPOT	5381	HUNTINGDON	6	40 24	77 56	580		7A	MRS. I. S. BUCHANAN	3
MARCUS HOOK	5390	DELAWARE	5	39 49	75 25	12	MID	MID	SUN OIL CO	2 3 5
MARIENVILLE 1 SW	5400	FOREST	1	41 27	79 09	1700		MID	ROY A. MARKER	C
MARION CENTER 2 SE	5408	INDIANA	1	40 45	79 02	1610		7A	CORPS OF ENGINEERS	3
MARTINSBURG 1 SW	5453	BLAIR	6	40 18	78 20	1360		MID	BLUE MT. CANNERIES	C
MARTINSBURG CAA AP	5454	BLAIR	6	40 18	78 19	1463	MID	MID	CIVIL AERO. ADM.	2 3 5 7
MATAMORAS	5470	PIKE	5	41 22	74 42	439		7A	HARRY BISLAND	3 7
MAYBURG	5490	FOREST	1	41 36	79 13	1150		7A	CORPS OF ENGINEERS	3
MC CONNELLSBURG	5526	FULTON	12	39 56	78 00	895		7A	MRS. HELEN M. SHIVES	3
MC KEESPORT	5573	ALLEGHENY	10	40 21	79 52	720		8A	NATIONAL TUBE CO	3
MEADOW RUN PONDS	5601	LUZERNE	15	41 13	75 40	1995		MID	GEORGE PEARAGE	C
MEADVILLE 1 S	5606	CRAWFORD	1	41 38	80 10	1065	8A	8A	CITY OF MEADVILLE	2 3 5 7 C
MEDIX RUN	5627	ELK	16	41 17	78 24	1100		7A	MRS.E. M. SNYDER	3 7 C
MERCER 2 NNE	5651	MERCER	2	41 15	80 13	1160	7P	7A	WILLIAM K. STRUTHERS	2 3 5
MERCER HIWAY SHED	5654	MERCER	2	41 14	80 15	1250		MID	PA DEPT HIGHWAYS	C
MERCERSBURG	5662	FRANKLIN	12	39 50	77 54	605		8A	ROLLIN P. GILBERT	3
MERWINSBURG	5676	MONROE	9	40 58	75 20	970		MID	WILLIAM D. GOULD	C
MEYERSDALE 1 ENE	5685	SOMERSET	17	39 49	79 01	2290		8A	ARTHUR B. MC CARTER	3
MIDDLETOWN OLMSTED FLD	5703	DAUPHIN	15	40 11	76 46	303	MID	MID	U. S. AIR FORCE	2 3 5
MIDLAND DAM 7	5710	BEAVER	11	40 38	80 28	689	11P	7A	CORPS OF ENGINEERS	2 3 5
MILAN 4 WNW	5732	BRADFORD	15	41 56	76 35	1448		MID	CARL A. MORRIS	C
MILANVILLE	5738	WAYNE	5	41 40	75 04	760		8A	CHARLES W. DAVIS	3
MILLERSBURG 2 E	5775	DAUPHIN	15	40 32	76 56	560		MID	RUSSELL SHEPLEY	C
MILLHEIM	5790	CENTRE	15	40 54	77 29	1090		7A	NEVIN E. BOWERSOX	3
MILLVILLE 2 SW	5817	COLUMBIA	15	41 06	76 34	860		7A	KENNETH LEIGHOW	3 C
MILROY	5825	MIFFLIN	6	40 43	77 35	770		8A	THOMAS C. HARBESON	3
MONTROSE 1 E	5915	SUSQUEHANNA	15	41 50	75 51	1630	7A	7A	WILBER W. HOOPES,JR	2 3 5 7 C
MORGANTOWN	5956	BERKS	15	40 09	75 54	595	MID	MID	PA TURNPIKE COMM	2 3 5
MT GRETNA 2 SE	6028	LANCASTER	15	40 14	76 26	670	MID	MID	PA TURNPIKE COMM	2 3 5
MT POCONO 2 N AP	6055	MONROE	5	41 09	75 22	1915	5P	5P	M. JOHN DAVIS, JR.	2 3 5 C
MOUNT UNION 1 N	6067	MIFFLIN	6	40 24	77 53	820		MID	MT UNION WTR WORKS	C
MUHLENBURG 1 SE	6090	LUZERNE	15	41 13	76 08	1110	6P	6P	THEODORE J. SAMPSON	2 3 5 7
MURRYSVILLE	6111	WESTMORELAND	10	40 26	79 42	903		MID	DAVID C. SHAW	C
MYERSTOWN	6126	LEBANON	14	40 22	76 18	480		8A	MRS.KATHLEEN WANDELL	3
NATRONA LOCK 4	6151	ALLEGHENY	1	40 37	79 43	800		7A	CORPS OF ENGINEERS	3
NEFFS MILLS 3 NE	6174	HUNTINGDON	6	40 40	77 55	900		MID	PA STATE UNIVERSITY	C
NESHAMINY FALLS	6194	BUCKS	5	40 09	74 57	60		MID	PHILA SUB WATER CO	3
NEWBURG 3 W	6225	FRANKLIN	15	40 09	77 37	745	5P	5P	PA TURNPIKE COMM	2 3 5
NEW CASTLE 1 N	6233	LAWRENCE	2	41 01	80 22	825	5P	7A	BAXTER F. JOHNSON	2 3 5 C
NEWELL	6246	FAYETTE	10	40 05	79 54	805	12M	12M	GENERAL CHEMICAL CO	2 3 5
NEW PARK	6289	YORK	15	39 44	76 30	780		6P	CLINTON J. ALLEN	3
NEWPORT	6297	PERRY	6	40 29	77 08	400	7A	7A	MRS. FRANCES K. FRY	2 3 5 7
NEW STANTON	6310	WESTMORELAND	10	40 13	79 36	980	MID	MID	PA TURNPIKE COMM	2 3 5
NEW TRIPOLI	6326	LEHIGH	14	40 41	75 45	570		6P	FRED C. OSWALD	3
NORRISTOWN	6370	MONTGOMERY	14	40 07	75 21	75	MID	8A	GEORGE H. BOONE	2 3 5
NORTH EAST 2 SE	6396	ERIE	8	42 12	79 49	1060		9A	ELLSWORTH WEAVER	3
ORWELL 3 N	6621	BRADFORD	15	41 55	76 16	1620		8A	WILLIAM I. BROWN	3
PALM	6681	MONTGOMERY	14	40 26	75 32	385		6A	FRED C. ESCHBACH	3
#PALMERTON	6689	CARBON	9	40 48	75 37	435	MID	MID	NEW JERSEY ZINC CO	2 3 5 C
PARKER	6721	ARMSTRONG	1	41 05	79 41	1140		7A	LOUIS A. MALARKEY	3
PARKER 1 E	6724	CLARION	1	41 06	79 40	1100		MID	P. M. NEELY	C
PAUPACK 2 WNW	6762	PIKE	5	41 24	75 14	1360		8A	MISS L. VETTERLEIN	3
PECKS POND	6786	PIKE	5	41 17	75 06	1380		9A	MRS. CARRIE NESS	3
#PHIL DREXEL INST OF TEC	6879	PHILADELPHIA	14	39 57	75 11	30	MID	MID	FRANCIS K. DAVIS,JR	2 3 5
PHILADELPHIA WB AP	6889	PHILADELPHIA	5	39 53	75 14	13	MID	MID	U.S. WEATHER BUREAU	2 3 5 7 C
#PHILADELPHIA PT BREEZE	6890	PHILADELPHIA	5	39 55	75 12	32	MID	MID	ATLANTIC REFINING	2 3 5 C
PHILADELPHIA SHAWMONT	6904	PHILADELPHIA	5	40 02	75 15	70	7P	7P	SCHUYLKILL NAVIG CO	2 3 5
#PHILADELPHIA CITY	6909	PHILADELPHIA	5	39 57	75 09	26	9A	9A	USN HYDROGRAPHIC OFF	2 3 5 C
PHILIPSBURG CAA AP	6916	CENTRE	6	40 54	78 05	1918	MID	MID	CIVIL AERO. ADM.	2 3 5 7 C
PHOENIXVILLE 1 E	6927	CHESTER	14	40 07	75 30	105	6P	MID	PHILA SUB WATER CO	2 3 5 C
PIKES CREEK	6939	LUZERNE	15	41 18	76 08	1320		MID	HARRY SHELDON	3 C
PIMPLE HILL	6944	MONROE	9	41 02	75 30	2215	9A	9A	PA DEPT FRST + WTRS	2 3 5 6 7
PINE GROVE 1 NE	6954	SCHUYLKILL	15	40 34	76 22	535		8A	PA POWER + LIGHT CO	3
PITTSBURGH WB AP 2	6993	ALLEGHENY	11	40 30	80 13	1151	MID	MID	U.S. WEATHER BUREAU	2 3 5 7 C
#PITTSBURGH WB CITY	6997	ALLEGHENY	11	40 27	80 00	749	MID	MID	U.S. WEATHER BUREAU	2 3 5 C
PLEASANT MOUNT 1 W	7029	WAYNE	5	41 44	75 27	1800	8A	8A	PA FISH COMM	2 3 5 7 C
PORT CLINTON	7116	SCHUYLKILL	14	40 35	76 02	450	7A	7A	MRS. ADA E. RARICK	2 3 5 C
PORTLAND	7127	NORTHAMPTON	5	40 55	75 06	297		8A	JOINT BRIDGE COMM	INAC 1/56
POTTSVILLE	7161	SCHUYLKILL	14	40 42	76 11	690		8A	LLOYD E. WELLER	3
PUNXSUTAWNEY	7217	JEFFERSON	1	40 57	79 00	1298		MID	JOHN VOLANSKY	C
PUTNEYVILLE 2 SE DAM	7229	ARMSTRONG	1	40 55	79 17	1270	8A	8A	CORPS OF ENGINEERS	2 3 5 C
QUAKERTOWN 1 E	7239	BUCKS	5	40 26	75 20	400	5P	5P	DENNIS K. FLUCK	2 3 5
RAYMOND	7310	POTTER	13	41 52	77 52	2220		7A	MRS. RACHEL LANGAN	3 C
#READING WB CITY	7318	BERKS	14	40 20	75 58	266	MID	MID	U.S. WEATHER BUREAU	2 3 5 7 C
RENOVO	7409	CLINTON	16	41 20	77 46	660		7A	MRS. CAROLINE BAIRD	3
RENOVO 5 S	7410	CLINTON	16	41 14	77 46	2035		MID	C. F. BILLETTE	C
REW	7425	MC KEAN	1	41 54	78 32	2250		8A	HAROLD C. MEALY	3
RICES LANDING L 6	7443	GREENE	10	39 57	80 00	775		7A	CORPS OF ENGINEERS	3
RIDGWAY 3 W	7477	ELK	1	41 25	78 47	1420	7A	7A	BOROUGH OF RIDGWAY	2 3 5
ROCHESTER 1 N	7540	BEAVER	2	40 43	80 18	900		MID	DEQUESNE LIGHT CO	C
RUSH	7694	SUSQUEHANNA	15	41 47	76 03	1000		9A	MISS MAUDE MC CAIN	3
RUSHVILLE	7727	SUSQUEHANNA	15	41 47	76 07	870		7A	CARL KOPATZ	3
SAFE HARBOR	7732	LANCASTER	15	39 55	76 23	270		MID	S.M.WATER POWER CORP	C
SAGAMORE 1 S	7739	INDIANA	1	40 46	79 14	1320		7A	CORPS OF ENGINEERS	3
SALINA 3 W	7782	WESTMORELAND	7	40 31	79 33	1109	6P	6P	MUN AUTH WSTMRLD CO	2 3 5
SAXTON	7846	BEDFORD	6	40 12	78 15	780		8A	MRS.ALVERTA L.HOLMES	3 C
SCANDIA 2 E	7855	WARREN	1	41 55	79 01	2040		MID	DAVID R. ANDERSON	C
SCHENLEY LOCK 5	7863	ARMSTRONG	1	40 41	79 40	783		VAR	CORPS OF ENGINEERS	3

STATION INDEX

CONTINUED

Station	Index No.	County	Drainage ‡	Latitude	Longitude	Elevation	Observation Time: Temp.	Observation Time: Precip.	Observer	Refer To Tables
#SCRANTON	7902	LACKAWANNA	15	41 25	75 40	746	7A	7A	U.S. POST OFFICE	2 3 5
SCRANTON WB AIRPORT	7905	LUZERNE	15	41 20	75 44	956	MID	MID	U.S. WEATHER BUREAU	2 3 5 7 C
SELINSGROVE CAA AP	7931	SNYDER	15	40 49	76 52	437	MID	MID	CIVIL AERO. ADM.	2 3 5 7
SELLERSVILLE 2 NW	7938	BUCKS	5	40 23	75 20	530		MID	SELLERSVILLE WTR CO	C
SHADE GAP	7965	HUNTINGDON	6	40 11	77 52	1000		MID	MRS. HELEN M. PYLE	C
SHAMOKIN	7978	NORTHUMBLAND	15	40 48	76 33	770		8A	ROARING CRK WTR CO	3
SHEFFIELD 6 W	8026	WARREN	1	41 41	79 09	1940		MID	L. N. HANSON	C
SHIPPENSBURG	8073	FRANKLIN	15	40 03	77 32	709	4P	4P	KEITH B. ALLEN	2 3 5 7
SHIPPINGPORT WB	8078	BEAVER	11	40 37	80 26	740	MID	MID	U.S. WEATHER BUREAU	2 3 5 7 C
SINNEMAHONING	8145	CAMERON	16	41 19	78 05	790		7A	MRS.FRANCES CALDWELL	3
SLIPPERY ROCK	8184	BUTLER	2	41 04	80 03	1345	7P	7A	WALTER D. ALBERT	2 3 5 7
SMETHPORT HIGHWAY SHED	8190	MC KEAN	1	41 48	78 27	1510		MID	PA DEPT HIGHWAYS	C
SOMERSET FAIRVIEW ST	8244	SOMERSET	17	40 01	79 05	2140		7A	HOWARD G. PECK	3
SOMERSET MAIN ST	8249	SOMERSET	17	40 01	79 05	2150	6P	6P	DAVID L. GROVE	2 3 5
SOUTH CANAAN 1 NE	8275	WAYNE	5	41 31	75 24	1400		MID	EUGENE M. COOK	C
SOUTH MOUNTAIN	8308	FRANKLIN	12	39 51	77 30	1520		7A	PA DEPT OF HEALTH	3
SPRINGBORO	8359	CRAWFORD	8	41 48	80 23	900	8A	8A	SPRINGBORO BOROUGH	2 3 5 C
SPRING GROVE	8379	YORK	15	39 52	76 52	470		4P	P. H. GLATFELTER CO	3 C
SPRINGS 1 SW	8395	SOMERSET	17	39 44	79 10	2500	8P	8P	ALLEN E. YODER	2 3 5 7
#STATE COLLEGE	8449	CENTRE	16	40 48	77 52	1175	MID	MID	PA STATE COLLEGE	2 3 5 6 C
STRAUSSTOWN	8570	BERKS	14	40 29	76 11	600		8A	JACOB KLAHR	3
STRONGSTOWN	8589	INDIANA	4	40 33	78 55	1880		MID	HARRY F. BENNETT	C
STROUDSBURG	8596	MONROE	5	40 59	75 12	480	11P	11P	WILLIAM MAGERTY	2 3 5 C
STUMP CREEK	8610	JEFFERSON	1	41 01	78 50	1320		7A	CORPS OF ENGINEERS	3
SUNBURY	8668	NORTHUMBLAND	15	40 51	76 48	440		7A	CHARLES W. BAYLER	3 C
SUSQUEHANNA	8692	SUSQUEHANNA	15	41 57	75 36	1020		7A	MRS. LAURA A.BENSON	3
SUTERSVILLE	8699	ALLEGHENY	17	40 14	79 48	765		7A	FRANK E. MARSH	3
TAMAQUA	8758	SCHUYLKILL	14	40 48	75 58	830		8A	MRS. MARY L.ROBERTS	3
TAMAQUA 4 N DAM	8763	SCHUYLKILL	14	40 51	75 59	1120		7A	PANTHER VLY WTR CO	3 C
TAMARACK 2 S FIRE TWR	8770	CLINTON	16	41 24	77 51	2220	7A	7A	JAMES E. SWARTZ	2 3 5 7
TIONESTA 2 SE DAM	8873	FOREST	1	41 29	79 26	1200	8A	8A	CORPS OF ENGINEERS	2 3 5 7 C
TITUSVILLE	8885	CRAWFORD	1	41 38	79 40	1550		MID	PA ELECTRIC CO	C
TITUSVILLE WATER WORKS	8888	CRAWFORD	1	41 38	79 42	1220	7P	7P	CITY OF TITUSVILLE	2 3 5
TORPEDO 4 W	8901	WARREN	1	41 47	79 32	1735		7A	MRS. LILY B. GARBER	3
TOWANDA	8905	BRADFORD	15	41 46	76 26	760	7P	7A	MRS. M. O. PARKS	2 3 5 7 C
TOWER CITY 5 SW	8910	DAUPHIN	15	40 31	76 37	745		6P	HARRISBURG WTR DEPT	3 7
TROY	8959	BRADFORD	15	41 47	76 47	1100		7A	JENNIE L. BALLARD	3
TUNNELTON	8989	INDIANA	4	40 27	79 23	890		MID	MRS. MARY E. WEIMER	C
TURTLEPOINT 4 NE	9002	MC KEAN	1	41 54	78 16	1640		7A	ROBERT D. STRAIT	3
TYRONE 4 NE BALD EAGLE	9024	BLAIR	6	40 43	78 12	1020		7A	FREDERICK L. FRIDAY	3 C
UNION CITY	9042	ERIE	1	41 54	79 50	1325		7A	FORREST M. BRALEY	3 C
UNIONTOWN	9050	FAYETTE	10	39 54	79 44	1040	10P	10P	WM. W. MARSTELLER	2 3 5
UPPER DARBY	9074	DELAWARE	5	39 58	75 18	222	7P	7P	PHIL. SUB.TRANS. CO	2 3 5
UTICA	9099	VENANGO	1	41 26	79 57	1030		7A	MRS.FLORENCE MILLER	3
VANDERGRIFT	9128	WESTMORELAND	7	40 36	79 33	800		7A	UNITED ENG+FNDRY CO	3
VANDERGRIFT 2 W	9133	WESTMORELAND	7	40 36	79 36	995		MID	EUGENE R. YOUNG	C
VIRGINVILLE	9196	BERKS	14	40 31	75 52	350		8A	MRS. MARY M. WRIGHT	3
VOWINCKEL	9206	CLARION	1	41 25	79 14	1620		8A	PA DEPT FRST + WTRS	3
VOWINCKEL 1 WSW	9209	CLARION	1	41 24	79 15	1610		8A	PA DEPT FRST + WTRS	3
WARREN	9298	WARREN	1	41 51	79 08	1280	7P	7A	GILBERT H. REIER	2 3 5
WASHINGTON	9312	WASHINGTON	11	40 11	80 14	1200		MID	PA DEPT HIGHWAYS	C
WATSONTOWN	9345	NORTHUMBLAND	16	41 05	76 52	490		9P	WILLIAM BIRD	3
WAYNESBURG 2 W	9362	GREENE	10	39 54	80 13	980	6P	7A	RALPH L. ANOS	2 3 5
WAYNESBURG 1 E	9367	GREENE	10	39 54	80 10	940		MID	SEWAGE DISPOSAL PLT	C
WEBSTER MILLS 3 SW	9380	FULTON	12	39 49	78 05	920		MID	WILLIAM D. COVER	C
WELLSBORO 3 S	9408	TIOGA	16	41 43	77 16	1920	7A	7A	MARION L. SHUMWAY	2 3 5
WELLSBORO 2 E	9412	TIOGA	16	41 45	77 16	1550		MID	MRS. IDA S. MAYNARD	C
WELLSVILLE	9420	YORK	15	40 03	76 57	500	5P	5P	D. D. HOOVER	2 3 5
WERNERSVILLE 1 W	9430	BERKS	14	40 20	76 06	405		8A	CHARLES A. GRUBER	3
WEST CHESTER	9464	CHESTER	5	39 58	75 36	440	8A	8A	DAILY LOCAL NEWS	2 3 5
WEST GROVE 1 E	9503	CHESTER	5	39 49	75 49	440		8A	CONARD-PYLE CO	3
WEST HICKORY	9507	FOREST	1	41 34	79 25	1090		8A	MRS.HELEN F.KINNEAR	3
WHITESBURG	9655	ARMSTRONG	1	40 45	79 24	1530		7A	CORPS OF ENGINEERS	3
WILKES-BARRE	9702	LAZERNE	15	41 15	75 52	610		7A	MRS. MARY G. HIRMAK	3
WILLIAMSBURG	9714	BLAIR	6	40 28	78 12	860		7A	MYRON K. BIDDLE	3
WILLIAMSPORT WB AP	9728	LYCOMING	16	41 15	76 55	527	MID	MID	U.S. WEATHER BUREAU	2 3 5 7 C
WIND GAP	9781	NORTHAMPTON	5	40 51	75 18	720		MID	OWEN R. PARRY	C
WOLFSBURG	9823	BEDFORD	6	40 03	78 32	1190		7A	WALTER C. RICE	3
YORK 3 SSW PUMP STA	9933	YORK	15	39 55	76 45	390	5P	5P	YORK WATER COMPANY	2 3 5
YORK 2 S FILTER PLANT	9938	YORK	15	39 56	76 44	640		MID	YORK WATER COMPANY	C
YORK HAVEN	9950	YORK	15	40 07	76 43	310		8A	METROPOL EDISON CO	3
YOUNGSVILLE	9966	WARREN	1	41 51	79 20	1225		MID	HENRY CARLETT	C
ZION GROVE	9990	SCHUYLKILL	15	40 54	76 13	940		7A	JAMES D. TEETER	3
ZIONSVILLE 3 SE	9995	LEHIGH	14	40 27	75 27	660		7A	LESLIE HOWATT	3

‡ 1-ALLEGHENY; 2-BEAVER; 3- 4-CONEMAUGH; 5-DELAWARE; 6-JUNIATA; 7-KISKIMINETAS; 8-LAKE ERIE; 9-LEHIGH; 10-MONONGAHELA; 11-OHIO; 12-POTOMAC; 13-LAKE ONTARIO; 14-SCHUYLKILL; 15-SUSQUEHANNA; 16-WEST BRANCH; 17-YOUGHIOGHENY

REFERENCE NOTES

Additional information regarding the climate of Pennsylvania may be obtained by writing to the State Climatologist at Weather Bureau Airport Station, Harrisburg State Airport, New Cumberland, Pennsylvania, or to any Weather Bureau Office near you.

Figures and letters following the station name, such as 12 SSW, indicate distance in miles and direction from the post office.

Delayed data and corrections will be carried only in the June and December issues of this bulletin.

Monthly and seasonal snowfall and heating degree days for the preceding 12 months will be carried in the June issue of this bulletin.

Stations appearing in the Index, but for which data are not listed in the tables, either are missing or were received too late to be included in this issue.

Divisions, as used in Table 2, became effective with data for September 1956.

Unless otherwise indicated, dimensional units used in this bulletin are: Temperature in °F, precipitation and evaporation in inches, and wind movement in miles. Monthly degree day totals are the sums of the negative departures of average daily temperatures from 65° F.

Evaporation is measured in the standard Weather Bureau type pan of 4 foot diameter unless otherwise shown by footnote following Table 6. Max and Min in Table 6 refer to extremes of temperature of water in pan as recorded during 24 hours ending at time of observation.

Long-term means for full-time stations (those shown in the Station Index as "U. S. Weather Bureau") are based on the period 1921-1950, adjusted to represent observations taken at the present location. Long-term means for all stations except full-time Weather Bureau stations are based on the period 1931-1955.

Water equivalent values published in Table 7 are the water equivalent of snow, sleet or ice on the ground. Samples for obtaining measurements are taken from different points for successive observations; consequently occasional drifting and other causes of local variability in the snowpack result in apparent inconsistencies in the record. Water equivalent of snow on the ground is measured at selected stations when two or more inches of snow are on the ground.

Entries of Snowfall in Tables 2 and 7, and in the seasonal snowfall table, include snow and sleet. Entries of snow on ground include snow, sleet and ice.

Data in Tables 3, 5, and 6 and snowfall in Table 7, when published, are for the 24 hours ending at time of observation. The Station Index lists observation times in the standard of time in local use. During the summer months some observers take the observations on daylight saving time.

Snow on ground in Table 7 is at observation time for all except Weather Bureau and CAA stations. For these stations snow on ground values are at 7:30 a.m., E.S.T.

- \- No record in Tables 3, 6, 7 and the Station Index. No record in Tables 2 and 5, is indicated by no entry. Consult the annual issue of this publication for interpolated monthly precipitation totals.
- \+ And also on a later date or dates.
- ++ Fastest observed one minute wind speed. This station is not equipped with automatic wind instruments.
- * Amount included in following measurement, time distribution unknown.
- // Gage is equipped with a windshield.
- \# Thermometers are generally exposed in a shelter located a few feet above sod-covered ground; however, the reference indicates that the thermometers are exposed in a shelter located on the roof of a building.
- AM Data based on observational day ending before noon.
- B Adjusted to a full month.
- C In the "Refer to Tables" column in the Station Index the letter "C" indicates recorder stations. These stations are processed for special purposes and are published later in "Hourly Precipitation Data".
- D Water equivalent of snowfall wholly or partly estimated, using a ratio of 1 inch water equivalent to every 10 inches of new snowfall.
- G In the "Refer to Tables" column in the Station Index the letter "G" indicates that soil temperatures are published.
- M One or more days of record missing; if average value is entered, less than 10 days record is missing. See Table 5 for detailed daily record. Degree day data, if carried for this station, have been adjusted to represent the value for a full month.
- R Amounts from recording gage (These amounts are essentially accurate but may vary slightly from the amounts to be published later in "Hourly Precipitation Data".)
- SS This entry in time of observation column in Station Index means observation made near sunset.
- T Trace, an amount too small to measure.
- Y Includes total for previous month.
- VAR This entry in time of observation column in Station Index means variable.

Information concerning the history of changes in locations, elevations, exposure etc. of substations through 1955 may be found in the publication "Substation History" for this state, soon to be issued. That publication, when available, may be obtained from the Superintendent of Documents, Government Printing Office, Washington 25, D. C. at a price to be announced. Similar information for regular Weather Bureau stations may be found in the latest issues of Local Climatological Data, Annual for the respective stations, obtained as indicated above, price 15 cents.

Subscription Price: 20 cents per copy, monthly and annual; $2.50 per year. (Yearly subscription includes the Annual Summary). Checks, and money orders should be made payable to the Superintendent of Documents. Remittance and correspondence regarding subscriptions should be sent to the Superintendent of Documents, Government Printing Office, Washington 25, D. C.

WRC., Asheville, N. C. --- 7/10/57 --- 1100

U. S. DEPARTMENT OF COMMERCE
SINCLAIR WEEKS, Secretary
WEATHER BUREAU
F. W. REICHELDERFER, Chief

CLIMATOLOGICAL DATA

PENNSYLVANIA

JUNE 1957
Volume LXII No. 6

ASHEVILLE: 1957

PENNSYLVANIA - JUNE 1957

WEATHER SUMMARY

GENERAL

A mid-month heat wave and numerous destructive thunderstorms were the highlight features of June's weather in Pennsylvania.

Average temperatures were 2 to 4 degrees higher than the 25-year (1931 - 1955) mean at over half of the stations for which comparative data are available. Extreme temperatures ranged from 28° at Bradford 4 W Res on the 9th to 100° which was recorded at nine stations on the 16th, 17th, or 18th.

Precipitation totals varied greatly over relatively short distances in a number of instances as is usually the case when thunderstorm activity contributes a large part of the total. Division averages indicated an important deficiency in the Southeastern Piedmont and a considerable excess on the Northwest Plateau. The greatest rainfall for one day was 3.92 inches measured at South Mountain on the 7th. Station totals ranged from 8.74 inches at Edinboro to 1.23 inches at Hawley.

WEATHER DETAILS

Cool periods the 3rd-4th and 8th-10th were far outweighed by excess heat from the 12th to the 19th and the 22nd-24th. Temperatures were of heat wave proportions the 15th through the 18th with maximum temperatures in the nineties at most stations and a top reading of 100° made at 9 locations.

A slow rain over the southern portion of the State lasted most of the day the 8th to relieve a drought threat that was becoming serious. Most of the precipitation from the 11th to the end of the month was associated with widespread and frequent thunderstorm activity with numerous instances of thunderstorm elements enacting destructive roles. Hurricane Audrey raced through western Pennsylvania as an extratropical storm during the night of the 28th-29th spawning destructive thunderstorms on a statewide basis.

WEATHER EFFECTS

Conditions favored field work in southeastern and central areas during June and harvesting of hay and barley progressed rapidly. Combining of wheat began earlier than usual and was underway at the end of June. In some southeast localities pastures dried up as near drought conditions prevailed. Late June rainfall provided much needed moisture in many sections but the heavy showers missed some localities. Above normal rainfall in western counties hindered hay making and barley harvest at times but the situation there was vastly improved over last year's wet season. In nearly all sections spray schedules were maintained and control of insects, disease and weeds was satisfactory to good. Pastures were exceptionally good in most western counties but declined elsewhere due to summer heat and lack of moisture.

Most of the corn acreage was planted on time and a few early stands were shoulder high by the end of June. There were some irregular stands in central and southeastern counties due to lack of moisture at planting, but development of corn in most areas was satisfactory to excellent. Above normal temperatures during the spring season caused winter wheat to develop rapidly and combining began earlier than usual. Winds from hurricane Audrey caused some shelling of wheat prior to harvest. Weather conditions did not favor spread of rust and only light damage was indicated. Harvesting of winter oats was underway in the southeast by June 30 and most spring oats were in head. In the southeast some oats were short due to lack of moisture. Prospects for potatoes were good in most areas and best in the northwest where rainfall was plentiful. The southeast lacked moisture for best development and early digging of Cobblers showed small size. A plentiful supply of tobacco plants favored timely setting of plant and only a few fields remained to be planted at the end of June. The Lancaster area was dry but most stands were making good growth. Rains of June 23-24 were very beneficial to the tobacco crop in the Clinton County area. Legumes and grasses in northern and western counties made heavy growth and good yields were common as hay making advanced. Considerable grass silage was made in June. Condition were favorable for drying hay until late June and the quality of hay was above average in nearly all sections.

DESTRUCTIVE STORMS

Thunderstorms monopolized the stormy weather scene with destructive performances reported only in small areas the 6th, 12th, 14th, 19th and 27th, but extending to sizable portions of the State the 13th, 16th, 18th and 23rd, and becoming statewide the 24th and 28th-29th. Reports indicated 6 deaths and 25 injuries due to lightning and 6 additional injuries for which the storm element was not specified. Property losses were quite large due to the destruction of costly installations by fires started by lightning.

For more detailed storm information and a report on hurricane Audrey see Climatological Data National Summary for June 1957.

FLOODS

None reported on larger streams. Local flooding occurred in a number of instances as a result of heavy thunderstorm rains.

J. T. B. Beard, Climatologist
Weather Records Processing Center
Chattanooga, Tennessee

CLIMATOLOGICAL DATA

Temperature: Average Maximum	Average Minimum	Average	Departure From Long Term Means	Highest	Date	Lowest	Date	Degree Days	No. of Days Max 90° or Above	Max 32° or Below	Min 32° or Below	Min 0° or Below	Precipitation: Total	Departure From Long Term Means	Greatest Day	Date	Snow, Sleet: Total	Max. Depth on Ground	Date	No. of Days .10 or More	.50 or More	1.00 or More
77.7M	57.6	67.7M	2.6	89	17	40	10	90	0	0	0	0	8.17	3.46	2.87	28	.0	0		10	5	3
79.9	52.3	66.1		91	19	33	10	85	1	0	0	0	1.36		.32	14	.0	0		6	0	0
78.2M	55.5M	66.9M	5.1	90	16	40	4	64	1	0	0	0	4.02	- 1.06	2.08	28	.0	0		6	2	1
81.9	58.1	70.0		96	18	37	9	27	4	0	0	0	4.04		.84	23	.0	0		6	5	0
77.0	56.7	66.9		91	17	40	9	67	1	0	0	0	3.13		.69	28	.0	0		6	3	0
76.8M	51.9M	64.4M		90	19	35	9+	107	1	0	0	0					.0	0				
83.4	59.1	71.3	3.2	97	19	41	9	23	7	0	0	0	4.87	1.02	1.30	17	.0	0		10	3	1
81.1	57.4	69.3	1.5	93	18	39	9	41	4	0	0	0	4.01	- .42	1.18	15	.0	0		10	3	1
83.2	54.7	69.0	1.4	97	16	36	9	50	6	0	0	0	2.81	- 1.79	.95	14	.0	0		7	1	0
		68.0											4.05				.0					
83.5	60.2	71.9	2.3	98	17	40	9	30	5	0	0	0	3.88	- .17	2.25	24	.0	0		5	2	1
84.5	61.6	73.1	3.4	98	18	42	9	24	9	0	0	0	3.60	- .29	1.75	25	.0	0		6	2	1
85.9	59.1	72.5	1.9	99	17+	40	9	17	10	0	0	0	4.48	.44	1.76	18	.0	0		7	2	2
83.0M	57.5M	70.3M	2.6	95	16+	38	9	34	5	0	0	0	4.37	- .02	2.18	25	.0	0		6	2	1
82.1	59.8	71.0	2.5	94	17+	40	9	34	5	0	0	0	4.56	.32	2.38	24	.0	0		6	1	1
84.1	57.0	70.6	1.4	97	18+	41	9+	39	9	0	0	0	3.15	- 1.31	1.04	15	.0	0		8	1	1
		71.6											4.01				.0					
85.5	64.2	74.9		100	16	50	4	7	13	0	0	0	3.25		1.71	17	.0	0		5	2	1
84.3	60.2	72.3	2.0	97	17+	42	9	31	11	0	0	0	4.91	.70	2.80	24	.0	0		8	3	1
85.7	62.8	74.3		99	16	46	9	7	10	0	0	0	2.72		.86	8	.0	0		8	1	0
	57.6	M				38	9			0	0	0	1.37		.45	8	.0	0		4	0	0
84.1	60.8	72.5	2.5	96	16+	42	9	19	8	0	0	0	2.34	- 2.02	.55	8	.0	0		6	2	0
84.5	60.7	72.6	3.1	98	16	40	9	21	8	0	0	0	1.90	- 1.86	.55	14	.0	0		8	1	0
87.3	63.0	75.2		100	17	54	4+	0	14	0	0	0	1.57	- 2.25	.38	9	.0	0		5	0	0
84.0	66.7	75.4	2.9	98	18	50	9	7	9	0	0	0	4.64	1.29	1.75	17	.0	0		8	3	1
84.3	60.7	72.5	2.3	96	15	45	9	13	7	0	0	0	2.90	- 1.11	1.02	24	.0	0		7	3	1
83.4	60.6	72.0		99	19	45	9	30	8	0	0	0	3.56		1.83	24	.0	0		6	2	1
83.3	60.2	71.8	1.9	97	19	41	9	27	8	0	0	0	4.97	.84	2.45	24	.0	0		8	2	1
86.0	67.0	76.5	1.4	99	16	50	9	7	12	0	0	0	2.55	- 1.05	.84	8	.0	0		6	2	0
84.5	64.8	74.7	4.0	100	18	50	9	11	9	0	0	0	3.08	- .81	.73	23	.0	0		6	3	0
81.1M	60.3	70.7M		96	16	40	9	43		0	0	0	2.00		.77	24	.0	0		4	2	0
82.4	62.0	72.2		95	17+	42	9	19	5	0	0	0	6.18		3.66	23	.0	0		7	3	1
85.6	64.3	75.0		100	16	45	9	17	12	0	0	0	3.43		.94	15	.0	0			3	0
86.5	66.4	76.5		100	16	49	9	8	15	0	0	0	2.68		1.12	16	.0	0		8	1	1
85.6	64.2	74.9	2.8	100	16	44	9	15	13	0	0	0	2.41	- 1.46	1.31	16	.0	0		4	1	1
84.8	67.7	76.3		99	16	49	9	17	12	0	0	0	1.43		.55	8	.0	0		4	1	0
85.6	63.9	74.8	2.5	100	16	44	9	12	10	0	0	0			.54	24	.0	0			1	0
84.4	66.0	75.2	2.6	98	17	50	9	16	10	0	0	0	1.83	- 2.14	.55	24				5	1	0
87.0	60.1	73.6	2.0	100	16+	40	9+	23	13	0	0	0	1.85	- 2.02	.49	8	.0	0		7	0	0
85.1	59.3	72.2	3.8	99	16	37	9	23	9	0	0	0	1.90	- 2.06	.45	19	.0	0		7	0	0
84.4	63.6	74.0	2.7	98	16	43	9	21	9	0	0	0	3.05	- .71	1.33	25	.0	0		7	2	1
87.2M	64.9M	76.1M						3		0	0	0	1.92		.39	8	.0	0		7	0	0
		74.0											2.85				.0					
83.2	60.8	72.0	1.6	96	19	49	9+	22	9	0	0	0	4.52	.38	1.08	6	.0	0		10	3	1
86.8	64.1	75.5	4.4	98	18	48	9	3	13	0	0	0	4.39	.34	1.39	24	.0	0		6	4	1
83.7	60.9	72.3	2.1	95	16	49	8+	13	8	0	0	0	7.03	3.06	2.05	6	.0	0		12	5	1
84.1	63.3	73.7	3.3	98	16+	50	9	12	10	0	0	0	4.16	.40	.76	29	.0	0		9	4	0
83.9	62.1	73.0	1.5	97	16	50	9	12	9	0	0	0	3.43	- .50	.92	6	.0	0		9	2	0
83.5	63.7	73.6	2.5	97	18	49	9	13	9	0	0	0	3.38	- .26	1.27	23	.0	0		6	3	1
86.2	63.9	75.1		98	14	48	8	1	10	0	0	0			.91	24	.0	0			3	0
84.8	61.8	73.3	2.0	96	17	49	8+	5	9	0	0	0	5.11	1.55	1.91	24	.0	0		9	4	1
83.2	59.2	71.2		96	18	46	11	16	7	0	0	0	3.33		.86	8	.0	0		8	3	0
85.9	62.0	74.0	3.4	97	16+	49	9	7	11	0	0	0	2.42	- 1.34	1.10	8	.0	0		7	1	1
		73.4											4.20				.0					
83.9	59.2	71.6		96	17	40	9	15	7	0	0	0	3.08		.67	29	.0	0		9	2	0
86.2	60.3	73.3		98	18	40	9	9	11	0	0	0	4.08		1.58	25	.0	0		6	2	1
81.6	58.5	70.1		95	19	37	9	37	5	0	0	0	3.57		.77	29	.0	0		9	3	0
83.7	59.0	71.4		97	19	45	9+	21	7	0	0	0	6.34		2.92	25	.0	0		9	3	2
84.6	59.9	72.3		97	16+	45	9	17	9	0	0	0	5.81	2.20	1.75	24	.0	0		8	4	1
82.9	58.4	70.7	1.6	97	17	43	8	29	6	0	0	0	3.71	- .21	1.18	13	.0	0		7	2	1
83.1	60.0	71.6	2.4	97	18	43	9	20	6	0	0	0	5.74	2.32	1.61	24	.0	0		10	3	1
		71.3											4.71				.0					
77.5	55.1	66.3		90	19	37	9	57	1	0	0	0	3.51		1.05	29	.0	0		5	4	1
82.4	54.7	68.6		95	19	40	10	43	5	0	0	0	3.37		.89	25	.0	0		9	2	0
74.5	57.1	65.8		87	19	42	9	65	0	0	0	0	7.34	2.83	2.12	28	.0	0		10	5	3
81.0	53.8	67.4	1.1	94	19	40	8+	46	4	0	0	0	2.92	- .89	1.03	29	.0	0		8	2	1

See Reference Notes Following Station Index

TABLE 2 - CONTINUED

Station	
MONTROSE 1 E	AM
TOWANDA	
WELLSBORO 3 S	AM
DIVISION	
CENTRAL MOUNTAINS	
BELLEFONTE 4 S	AM
DU BOIS 7 E	
EMPORIUM 2 SSW	AM
LOCK HAVEN	
MADERA	AM
PHILIPSBURG CAA AP	
RIDGWAY 3 W	AM
STATE COLLEGE	
TAMARACK 2 S FIRE TWR	AM
DIVISION	
SOUTH CENTRAL MOUNTAINS	
ALTOONA HORSESHOE CURVE	
BURNT CABINS 2 NE	
EBENSBURG	
EVERETT 1 SW	
HUNTINGDON	AM
JOHNSTOWN	AM
KEGG	
MARTINSBURG CAA AP	
DIVISION	
SOUTHWEST PLATEAU	
BAKERSTOWN 3 WNW	
BLAIRSVILLE 6 ENE	
BURGETTSTOWN 2 W	AM
BUTLER	
CLAYSVILLE 3 W	
CONFLUENCE 1 SW DAM	AM
DERRY	
DONEGAL	
DONORA	AM
FORD CITY 4 S DAM	AM
INDIANA 3 SE	
IRWIN	
MIDLAND DAM 7	
NEW CASTLE 1 N	
NEWELL	AM
NEW STANTON	
PITTSBURGH WB AP 2	//R
PITTSBURGH WB CITY	R
PUTNEYVILLE 2 SE DAM	AM
SALINA 3 W	
SHIPPINGPORT WB	
SLIPPERY ROCK	
SOMERSET MAIN ST	
SPRINGS 1 SW	
UNIONTOWN	
WAYNESBURG 2 W	
DIVISION	
NORTHWEST PLATEAU	
BRADFORD 4 W RES	
BROOKVILLE CAA AIRPORT	
CLARION 3 SW	
CORRY	
COUDERSPORT 3 NW	
EAST BRADY	
ERIE WB AIRPORT	
FARRELL SHARON	
FRANKLIN	
GREENVILLE	
JAMESTOWN 2 NW	AM
KANE 1 NNE	AM
LINESVILLE 5 WNW	
MEADVILLE 1 S	AM
MERCER 2 NNE	
SPRINGBORO	AM
TIONESTA 2 SE DAM	AM
TITUSVILLE WATER WORKS	
WARREN	
DIVISION	

† DATA RECEIVED TOO LATE TO BE INCLUDED IN DIVISION AVERAGES

See Reference Notes Following Station Index

DAILY PRECIPITATION

	Total	Day of month																														
		1	2	3	4	5	6	7	8	9	10	11	12	13	14	15	16	17	18	19	20	21	22	23	24	25	26	27	28	29	30	31
	4.63		.02					T	.06	.69			.20	T	.46			1.87		.22				.14	.08	.25	T			.62	.09	.
R	3.88		.01						.02			.05	.15	.20	T		T		.78					T	2.25	.08	T	T	T	.27	T	.
	3.60								T	.06			.20		.25	.02				.57				T		1.78	.09		.38	.16	.08	.
E	7.21						.32	.63	.74	.02		.10	.20	1.09	.35					.38				.02	1.93	.05			.03	1.08	.19	.
	4.52						1.08	.25	.11	.81			.24	T	.28	.01		.08							.39	.38	.32			.56	T	.
	1.95						T						.31		.21	T				.05	T					.17	T		T	.88	.03	.
	5.10						.25		1.55			.12	.07	.87	.01		.60			.27			T	T		.50			.28	.95	.02	.
	6.36		.90										.20		.60			.26		T	T					.91				3.20		.
	-		T							-			-		-						.17				-		-			-		.
	4.16								.06						.39	.03									.19	1.32	.10		1.25	.27	T	.
	3.75							.15	.04	.34			.08	T	.42	.02		T		.35	T			.03		1.03	T		T	1.21	.06	.
	3.08							.02	.06	.30			.63		.29										.16	.25	.41		.19	.67	.10	.
	5.44							.56	.03	.15			.60		.94	T				.04						1.96	.04		.38	.62	.07	.
	4.11							.22	.07	.38			.50		.61	T							T			1.20			.09	1.04		.
	3.40								T	.26					.46	.98									.21	.08	.57			.25	T	.
	4.08							.02	.02				.38		.38	.06								.09	.18	1.58	.08		.99	.26	.02	.
	3.08								T	.04			.14	.07	.20	.01				2.31					.01	1.43	.14		.48	.13	.11	.
	4.48		.01						.04				.15	.28	.04	T			1.76						1.33	.15			.45	.27		.
	6.20		.35					.03	1.18			.32		.35	.02	.10	.08			.52					1.71	.48			T	.76	.31	.
	4.76							T	.76	.06			.36		.85		.70			.03					.82	.20			.22	.70	.06	.
	6.69		.05	T				.00	.40	1.29	T		.70	1.06	.30	T		T						.04		1.17	.11		T	1.07	.32	.
	4.81		.02	.03			.01	.01	.23	1.04			.28	.22	.35	T		1.03		.02	.36			.22	.01	.18				.60	.22	.
	4.45							.09					.13		.52			.02		.02	.08					.31				2.81	.03	.
	5.75						.06	.04					.30		.46		.30			.25				.06	.06	.38			.35	2.98		.
	6.60								1.03			.56	.10	.34	.43	.52	.96			.24				.68	.31	.08			1.14	.28	.02	.
	4.74						.56		.07			.30		.37			.02		.01	.51			T	.03	1.51	.15			.86	.08	.02	.
	5.05							.46		1.40			.24	.83	.61			.50		.04					.41	.28						.
	4.46						.01	.26	.08	1.67			.42	.16	.34	.09		.17								.35	.08			.74	.09	.
	5.10							.10	.70	.59		.09	.09	1.10	.56	.08		.07		.04	.12			.11	.02	.27				.95		.
	6.09						1.52		.85	.28			.82		.64									.34		.39			.01	1.04	.20	.
	4.67								.16	.32			.35	.34	.47			.31		.04				.24	.11	.22				1.94	.17	.
	4.00						.08		.68	.03			.36		.78	T				T				.02	.95	.53	.03		.33	.25	.02	.
	3.51		.08					.03					.17		.54	T		T							.62	.86	.06		.05	1.05		.
	4.30		T				.04	.01	.72	.08		T	.20	T	.76	.04	.02			.02				T	1.39	.73			.05	.29	.04	.
	5.85							1.11	.08	.53			.31		.44	T		.06		.20	.16			.09	T	1.86	.06			.52	.08	.
	4.38		.30										.84		.35			.22		.05	.18				.12	.01	T			1.51		.
	3.20		.05					T	T				.45	T	.33	.23		T		.41	T				.30	.37	.01		T	1.05		.
	1.97					T	.20		T	.82	T		T					T									T			.70	.25	.
	7.03					.31	2.05		.92			.12	.08	.72	.92		.50							.16	.42	.19		T	.34	.30	T	.
	3.18							.46	.48	.69			.09	.04	.36			.05		.12	.02			.03		.22				.57	.03	.
	3.25						.12	T	T	.62				.02	T	.32		1.71									.08			.30		.
	4.62		.10					.47	.04	.17			.47		.37	.09		.01		.21	.03				.04	.80	.01			1.73	.08	.
	4.79		.22	.06									.20	.01	.75			.13		.09	.12			.03		1.27				1.51	.04	.
	4.75			.06						.08			.20		.30	.15				.01					.02	3.28	.40			.25		.
	2.57							.26	.30	.18			.08	.06	.46	.03			T	.04	.01				T	.20				.96		.
	4.57		.18					.72		.36			.58		.03			.15						T	.03	1.78	.02			.60	.12	.
	3.77		.88										1.05		1.25			.15		.03				.01	T	.71	T		.25	1.42	.02	.
	3.70									.01			.34		.63	.04									.12	1.52	.30		.10	.94	.10	.
	4.91					T	14	T	T	.72			.10					.02		.03					2.60		.94			.21	.19	.
	2.72					.43			.86	T			.03		.15					T					.48		.26		.18	.21		.
	2.26		T						.15	.67			.28	T	.22		T							.06		.37	.01		T	.37	.13	.
	3.17		.05					.08	.11	.69			.28	.12	.18		T			.02				.22		.33	.01			.42	.66	.
	2.80						4	.25	.21	.92			.15		.03		.17	.02		.03				.03	.02	.45				.43	.05	.
	4.08			.26						.45			.15	.05		1.27		1.40							T	.03	T	T	T	.45	T	.
	3.56			T				.28	T				.23	T	.45	T		.02		.12	.07	T		.04	T	.84	T			1.18	.04	.
	3.77							.18	T				.21	T	.38	T	T	.10	T	.12	T			.05	T	.85	T			1.40	.03	.
	3.25									1.02		.07		.03	.73		.04	.04							*	.79					.53	.
	7.11											.08	.23	.68	.02		.51		.27	.30				.49	.33	.08		T	1.32	2.11		.
	4.21						.75	.02					.40		.29	.22		.13		.08	.02	.02			.05	.34	.04		.16	1.24		.
	4.05						.21	.02					.71	.01	.45	.25		.08			T				.22	.50	.02			1.25	.03	.
	3.37		.10	.09				.05					.25	T	.25	.04		T		.30	.03				.23	.31	.24		.06	1.42		.
	3.69		.28					.10	.13	.66			.11		.14			.03		.04				.04		1.30				.65	.15	.
	8.18		.01					1.83	.04	.85			.34		.64	.03		.13		.12	.21				.52	2.61	.04			.64	.17	.
	5.20		.42				24	.24					.28		.67					.04	.07					.38	.01			2.80	.05	.
	3.54							.13	T				.40		.57										.08	1.52	.36		T	.45	.05	.
	5.98							.35	1.32	*		*	*	*	*					*			1.46	.10	1.09	.29			.48	.35	.03	.
	1.37		.39						.45			T	.14			.02	.02						T	.09	.02	.09				.19		.
	3.37		.21					.02					.23		.28			.16			T				.45	.89	.63		.06	.31		.
	4.87							.32	1.57			.27	.01	.25	T	T			.20					T	.65	.15			.40	.15	T	.
	3.88							.46	.74	.88			.18	.26	.40	T	T	.17		.11				.10	T	.36		T	T	.51	.01	.
	1.67		.01						.27	.06			.11		.01					.20					.35	.33	.16		T	.31	.06	.
	4.75		.42				38	.08	.25				.49		.28		T	.03		.14				.15	.75	.90				.88	T	.
	2.96		T	18			5	T					.30	T	.40					T					.54	.38	.28		T	.45		.
	7.34		.30	15				.25					.68		.40	.01		.02			T				1.42	1.08	.53		2.12	.40		.
	2.96							.04	.16				.25		.15			.20		.11				.26	.08	.41				1.30		.
	5.23		.07					.67	.10	.73			.33		.45	T		.08		.17	.50			.23		1.47	.06			.39	T	.
	8.74	.05	1.65										.18		.41		.06	.15		1.18				.01		1.70			.38	2.95	.02	.
		RECORD MISSING																														.
	2.59			.02			4			.68			.04		.28										.87	.26	.23			.17		.
	3.55		.25	.06				.34					.70	T	.20			.06		.05	.07	.02			.03	.86	.02		.01	.88		.
	5.00							.33					.45		.21			.41								1.41	.02		.31	1.51		.
	2.34								.55	.16			.54				.09	.10							.37	.48	.05					.
	3.26		T	.21				.16					.10		.48	T	.04	.23							.95	.34	.46		.06	.25	.01	.
	7.74	1.09						.02				.24		.99	T		.21		.77	.10				.28	1.23	.01			2.72	.08		.
	4.62								1.15			.51	.69	.62			.10								.22				1.33			.
	5.40	.11	.15					.06				.03		.04	.15		.36		.06	.47				.08	1.04	.75			.54	1.56		.
	3.83		.17					.20	.16	.63			.18		.58			.68		.05				.09		.27	T			1.32	.10	.
	6.16		.31					.02	T				.07		.67	.04	.04	.24	T	.71	.04	.01		.09	.02	1.69	T		T	2.20	.01	.
	8.17			.01						T	.10		.20		.53	.40				1.28					.10	1.70	.45		2.87	.53	T	.
	3.52		.35					T					.65	T	.12			.10		.02	.06				.02	.70	.02			1.46	.01	.
	1.25									.40			.26		.02			.01							.28		.07			.10		.
	1.90		.14						.27	.02			.11		.55		.25								.16	.10	.02			.28		.
	4.18			T				.66	.14	.40			.16		.57			.65							.07	.43	.30			.76		.
	4.44							.15					.22		.80	.05		T		T	T					.90				1.88	.05	.
	-						10	.35	.01				-		.41	.01		.02		.09	.01			.04	.07	.97	.03			1.28		.
	5.03		.19						.10	.67			.24		.62			.53		.36	.03			.34		.66				1.29		.
	3.00			.21					.05				.22		.28	.20	T								.06	.46	.54		.36	.62		.
	1.57			4					.06	.38			.25							.03					.09	.28				.24		.
	3.57							T	T	.31			.60		.35	.20					T				.22	.51	.43			.77	.10	.
	2.67			2					.16	.27			.38		.12			.34			.06			.26		.22	T	T		.54	.30	.
	5.47	.01	.10					.31	1.29	.03		.02	.73	1.20	.02		T			.47			T	.02	.02	.39			.02	.73	.11	.
	7.08						01	.10	T			T	.12	.42	.06		1.01		.28	.38				.07	1.16	.30			.78	1.70		.
	3.42						92	.16	.12	.31			.14	T	.39										.49	.08	.34			.28		.
	3.38							T	.50			.06	.04	.51	.08					T				1.27	.11	.42		T	.23	.07	T	.
	4.50								.02	.59			.44		.55	.31									1.22	.40	.38		.01	.58		.
	1.23			.07				.01					.14	T	.21	T	.18	T			T				.09	.13	.28		.02	.10		.
	1.36			.08									.11		.32	.05	.04								.11	.16	.30			.19		.
	2.68			0				.01					.12		.34	T	T	.29			T				.14	.30	1.08		.02	.28		.
	4.64						32		.13	.66			T	T	.09			1.75			.09				.37	.10	.92			.15	.06	.
	2.70		.05	.19				.20					.09		.42			.30							.11	.65	.47		.09	.22		.
	5.00		T	.04				.08	.44	.82			1.42	.62	.37		.04	.06		.08	T			.04		.36	.07			.44	.14	.
	2.87			.20			02								.13								.01		.67	.06	.61	.35		.45	.35	.
	4.93			1				.22	.04	.50			*		*	*		.54			.21			.01	.14	2.24	.04		.04	.78	.16	.
	4.09						26	.01	.14	.80			.08		.80	T		.08							.09	.46	.14		.03	.43	.07	.
	5.32		.07	.08				.10	.18	.71			.22		1.00		1.67				.01					.40	.02			.86	.04	.

See Reference Notes Following Station Index

DAILY PRECIPITA

Table 3—Continued

Day of month

Station																		
INDIANA 3 SE																		
IRWIN																		
JAMESTOWN 2 NW																		
JIM THORPE																		
JOHNSTOWN																		
KANE 1 NNE																		
KARTHAUS																		
KEATING SUMMIT																		
KEGG																		
KITTANNING LOCK 7																		
KREGAR 4 SE																		
KRESGEVILLE 3 W																		
LAFAYETTE MC KEAN PARK																		
LAKEVILLE 1 NNE																		
LANCASTER 2 NE PUMP STA																		
LANDISVILLE 2 NW																		
LAWRENCEVILLE 2 S																		
LEBANON 3 W																		
LEHIGHTON																		
LE ROY																		
LEWIS RUN 3 SE																		
LEWISTOWN																		
LINESVILLE 5 WNW																		
LOCK HAVEN																		
LONG POND 2 W																		
LYNDELL 2 NW																		
MADERA																		
MAHAFFEY																		
MAPLE GLEN																		
MAPLETON DEPOT																		
MARCUS HOOK		*																
MARION CENTER 2 SE																		
MARTINSBURG CAA AP		T	26	42														
MATAMORAS																		
MAYBURG			55															
MC CONNELLSBURG			01															
MC KEESPORT																		
MEADVILLE 1 S																		
MEDIX RUN																		
MERCER 2 NNE																		
MERCERSBURG			60															
MEYERSDALE 1 ENE																		
MIDDLETOWN OLMSTED FLD		T		06														
MIDLAND DAM 7																		
MILANVILLE																		
MILLHEIM		*				.33												
MILLVILLE 2 SW						.59												
MILROY						.36												
MONTROSE 1 E						.80			.12									
MORGANTOWN		T																
MT GRETNA 2 SE				02		02				.43								
MT POCONO 2 N AP						27	11			.01								
MUHLENBURG 1 SE						79												
MYERSTOWN							62											
NATRONA LOCK 4						39					.17	.03		.13				
NESHAMINY FALLS		T				.24									.49			
NEWBURG 3 W						.82								.50	.91			
NEW CASTLE 1 N						.41			.05		.85	.02			T			
NEWELL						.27			.12		.14			.33				
NEW PARK		.34							.15						.65			
NEWPORT					T				.04			.25			1.75			
NEW STANTON				15	.35			.02			.13		.18	T	.08			
NEW TRIPOLI							.56	.14							.30			
NORRISTOWN							.94		.37			T			T			
NORTH EAST 2 SE	T					41			.17		.54				.01			
ORWELL 3 N									.95						.24			
PALM						05									.15			
PALMERTON				02	39	48								.03	2.38			
PARKER						37			.20		.11	.12				1.07	T	
PAUPACK 2 WNW						30									13	.32	.35	
PECKS POND						30									12	.18	.21	
PHIL DREXEL INST OF TEC		.10				10		1.12		.20					12	.04	.03	
PHILADELPHIA WB AP R		.07			02	04		1.31		.12				T	03	T	.01	
PHILADELPHIA PT BREEZE		.03				02				T					18	.01	.01	
PHILADELPHIA SHAWMONT					12		45								54	.05	.29	
PHILADELPHIA CITY R		.03				01		.10		.33					55		.01	
PHILIPSBURG CAA AP	*	T		19		05		.22			.05				84	.03		
PHOENIXVILLE 1 E						12								.01	02		.06	
PIKES CREEK						53									1 25	.66	.61	
PIMPLE HILL						41	14				.04				02	.63	.38	
PINE GROVE 1 NE						48	49								60	.24	.31	
PITTSBURGH WB AP 2 //R	T			16	69			.03		.05	.04		.12	T	53	.04		
PITTSBURGH WB CITY R	*	.13		18	48			.12			.15				67	.11		
PLEASANT MOUNT 1 W						45									19	.27	.90	
PORT CLINTON						35	04							.30	42			.26
POTTSVILLE						.33	.04								63	.80		T
PUTNEYVILLE 2 SE DAM						.48			.15		.48	.06		.10		1.26		
QUAKERTOWN 1 E					T	.03	.02				.45				07	.35	.11	
RAYMOND				10				.16	.10		.04	.03			03	.33	.03	
READING WB CITY R					.18			.02						.17		1.33		
RENOVO						.38					.37	.02			32		.02	
REW						.80			.04		.01	.05				.85	.01	
RICES LANDING L 6						.21			.18					.15	09	.15		
RIDGWAY 3 W						.39			.43		.10	.04		.03	04	1.38	.03	
RUSH						.62			.13						65	.63	.27	
RUSHVILLE						.89									35	.77	.30	
SAGAMORE 1 S												.16				2.01		
SALINA 3 W				10		.33	T	.98	.01		.08				19	.14	.01	
SAXTON					.29	.77		.34	.02		T	T				.45	.01	
SCHENLEY LOCK 5						.37			.35		.19			.04	16	1.05		
SCRANTON						.90		.21	1.30						36	.45	.78	
SCRANTON WB AIRPORT		T		11	.50	T	.18				T			.29	21	.75		.38
SELINSGROVE CAA AP				79	.19	.04					T			.34	38	.30		T
SHAMOKIN						.30	.02								13	.55	.49	
SHIPPENSBURG		*			T	.64									1 91	.20		
SHIPPINGPORT WB				22	.61			.07		.27	.11		.12		1 83	.04		
SINNEMAHONING					T	.04	T		T			.07				.55	.03	
SLIPPERY ROCK						.48	.01		.26		.25	.23				.78		
SOMERSET FAIRVIEW ST					.45	.20		.31	.42		.04	T				.22	.07	
SOMERSET MAIN ST					.36	.18	.26				T				11	.21		
SOUTH MOUNTAIN						.90		.05							34	.55	.15	
SPRINGBORO					.07	–		T	.13		.41					.60		
SPRING GROVE		*			T	.17					.20				25	.16	.15	
SPRINGS 1 SW		T		38	.05	.14	.76	.03		.06	.02				07	.22		
STATE COLLEGE				08	.98	.20		.01				.01		.02	2 28	.01	.03	

See Reference Notes Following Station Index

DAILY PRECIPITATION

Station	Total	1	2	3	4	5	6	7	8	9	10	11	12	13	14	15	16	17	18	19	20	21	22	23	24	25	26	27	28	29	30	31
AUSSTOWN	4.58			.10				T	.07	.28			.73		.68	.70									.89	.42	.18		.17	.27	.09	
DUDSBURG	2.81		.46				T	.06	T				.02		.95	.07	T		.07		T			T	.40	.13	T	.21	.15	.29	T	
P CREEK	5.34		.26					.40	T	.37			.48		.30			.90						.15		1.54	.04			.79	.11	
BURY	3.04			.16				.02	.03	.10			.61		.60	T									.10	.39	.32		T	.89	.02	
DUEHANNA	4.56		.01	.27				.04					.09		.62			1.48			.03				.62	.26	.61			.37	.16	
ERSVILLE	4.98			.11				.26		1.46			.21	.97	.14			.84		.09	.07				.13	.72						
AQUA	4.54			T						.05			.40		.82	.10									.45	1.64	.14		.21	.45	.19	
AQUA 4 N DAM	5.89								.02				.39		.45	.02									.28	2.80	.41	.62	.50		.40	
ARACK 2 S FIRE TWR		RECORD MISSING																														
NESTA 2 SE DAM	7.34		1.07					.20	T				.23		.71	.02	.02	.61		.15	.05				.02	1.95			T	2.31		
USVILLE WATER WORKS	8.55	T	1.05									T	.26	.40	.30		1.45		.15	.40				.06	1.05	.24	T	T	1.15	1.07		
PEDO 4 W	8.73		.96					.05					.25		.79	.32	.02	.45		.84	.08			.09	.02	1.40			.02	3.44		
ANDA	2.90		.07	.12				.02					.20	T	.82	T		.11			T				.02	.86	.21		T	.47		
ER CITY 5 SW	5.11		T					.06	.36				.90		.67	.88				T				.09	.60	.83	.03		.06	.61	.02	
r	2.60		.05	.03				.03					.10		.20	.02									.73	.52	.06		.01	.85		
TLEPOINT 4 NE	4.55		.40				.44	.16					.28		.64	.09		.08			.03				.02	.45	.02		.18	1.59	.06	
ONE 4 NE BALD EAGLE	5.02			.09				.43	.16	.47			.75		.07	.01		.06		.04	.02					.88	.01		.28	1.73	.06	
ON CITY	6.96		.97	.02				.03					.22		.74		.03	.26		1.19	.10			.23	.02	.45	.02		.06	2.52	.10	
ONTOWN	2.60	.01	T				.01	.03	1.02			.36	.02	.07		.19	.09			.10			.05		.06	.21			.15	.23	T	
ER DARBY	1.92		.12			.03	.01		.39				.19	T	.36		.17		.08						T		.27			.30		
CA	-		.29					.06					.11		.43		.02	.14		.88	-				-	-	-		-	-	-	
DERGRIFT	4.90		.13	.08				.88	.09	1.01			.16		.42			.61		.07	.07			.03	.02	.16	.02			.83	.32	
GINVILLE		RECORD MISSING																														
INCKEL	6.12		.77	T	T			.18	T				.34	T	.40		T	.18	T	.05	T		T			.85	T			3.32	.03	
INCKEL 1 WSW	6.23		.75	T	T			.24	T	T			.35	T	.41		T	.25	T	.08	T		T		T	.80	T			3.35	T	
REN	5.73		.80					.03					.12		.78	.22		.43		.51	.06					1.31				1.47		
SONTOWN	5.73		.05				.35	.12	.07			.07	.31	.42	.18	T				.02				.55	.45	.62		.32	.20	T	T	
NESBURG 2 W	2.79		.02	.04				T	.33	.30			.17		.39					.07				.01		.37	.01			.59	.47	
LSBORO 3 S	2.91		.21	.14				.06					.32	.01	.41	.06		.04		.44	.10				.21	.28	.04			.59		
LSVILLE	3.35					.59	.02		.86	.09			.08		.52					T				.27	.20	.24			.10	.40	T	
NERSVILLE 1 W	2.72									.39			.56			.50									.25		.50		.30	.22		
T CHESTER		RECORD MISSING																														
T GROVE 1 E	3.28		.12			.53	.12	.03	.86	.10							.52										.26			.60	.14	
T HICKORY	7.35		.63				.10	.17					.12		.75		.08	.65		.45	.05					2.65				1.70		
TESBURG	4.45		.12					T	.21	.53			.26		1.05			.27		T						.66				1.35		
KES BARRE	4.00			.19				T	.21				.43		.58		T				T				.49	.30	.50		.88	.42		
LIAMSBURG	6.13		T					.43	.07	.58	T		.34		.60	T		.09							.22	2.53	T		.05	1.20	.02	
LIAMSPORT WB AP	5.74		.05				.46	.03	T			.30	.22	.96	.01		T			T				.50	1.61	.37		.47	.33	.43	T	
FSBURG	4.04			T				.10	.18	1.14			.41	.95	.27			.04								.26	.07			.55	.07	
K 3 SSW PUMP STA	2.42		.16	T		.28	.03	.01	1.10	.10			.02		.19			T		T					.09	.13	.09		T	.22		
K HAVEN	4.08			.13			.12		.02	.78			.04		.41					T	T				1.11	1.08	.21			.17	.01	
N GROVE	3.29			.02					.01	.02			.28		.43	.28									.18	.43	.44		.30	.80	.10	
NSVILLE 3 SE	4.72			.46						.25			.25		.21					2.65					.04	.40	.19	.06		.20	.01	

SUPPLEMENTAL DATA

Station	Wind direction		Wind speed m. p. h.				Relative humidity averages - percent				Number of days with precipitation							Percent of possible sunshine	Average sky cover sunrise to sunset
	Prevailing	Percent of time from prevailing	Average	Fastest mile	Direction of fastest mile	Date of fastest mile	1:00 a EST	7:00 a EST	1:00 p EST	7:00 p EST	Trace	.01-.09	.10-.49	.50-.99	1.00-1.99	2.00 and over	Total		
LENTOWN WB AIRPORT	13	WSW	8.7	-	-	-	85	85	54	62	7	4	3	1	0	1	16	-	6.0
IE WB AIRPORT	-	-	11.1	28	SW	13	-	-	-	-	1	3	4	2	2	1	13	-	6.6
RRISBURG WB AIRPORT	10	WSW	6.7	34	SW	29	80	79	53	58	7	4	2	2	1	0	16	54	6.3
ILADELPHIA WB AIRPORT	15	WSW	9.2	36	S	28	79	81	51	62	4	9	3	0	1	0	17	62	6.6
TTSBURGH WB AIRPORT	18	WSW	9.6	40++	W	18	80	83	55	62	4	6	4	3	1	0	18	70	7.0
ADING WB CITY	-	-	9.4	46	S	29	-	-	-	-	4	2	5	1	1	0	13	48	6.5
RANTON WB AIRPORT	17	SW	9.1	40	SW	29	81	78	53	60	8	0	7	2	1	0	18	72	6.3
IPPINGPORT WB	-	-	2.4	63%	NW	28	-	-	-	-	2	4	4	2	2	0	14	-	-
LLIAMSPORT WB AIRPORT	-	-	-	-	-	-	-	85	53	62	4	3	7	2	1	0	17	-	6.6
Peak Gust																			

See Reference Notes Following Station Index

MONTHLY AND SEASONAL SNOWFALL

Season of 1956 - 1957

Station	July	August	September	October	November	December	January	February	March	April	May	June	Total
ACMETONIA LOCK 3					1.0	7.3	9.9	-	-	.3			-
ALLENTOWN WB AP					T	1.1	7.3	7.8	1.9	3.1			21.2
ALLENTOWN GAS CO					.3	T	6.3	7.1	.9	2.1			16.7
ALTOONA HORSESHOE CURVE					3.7	11.5	20.7	12.3	10.5	3.5			62.2
ARENDTSVILLE						.2	7.6	8.7	1.0				17.5
ARTEMAS 1 WNW						T	2.8	-	-				-
AUSTINBURG 2 W					7.0	7.0	9.0	2.3	19.1	17.0	T		61.4
BAKERSTOWN 3 WNW					T	4.5	5.0	3.0	7.0	-			-
BARNES					1.5	16.0	11.6	9.0	9.0	13.5	T		60.6
BARTO 4 NW	-		-		-	-	-	-	-	-			-
BEAR GAP					T	4.0	9.0	11.0	7.0	4.0			35.0
BEAVER FALLS					.9	12.3	6.1	3.7	T	1.3			24.3
BEAVERTOWN					3.0	-	4.5	-	8.0	4.0	T		-
BEECH CREEK STATION					3.0	3.0	7.5	6.0	8.0	6.0			33.5
BELLEFONTE 4 S					1.5	T	5.4	4.6	12.9	5.5	T		29.9
BERNE	-	-	-	-		-	-	-	-	-			-
BERWICK					T	2.0	5.9	5.3	1.8	4.6			19.6
BETHLEHEM					T	T	7.0	6.0	T	1.5			14.5
BETHLEHEM LEHIGH UNIV					.1	.3	-	-		-			-
BLAIRSVILLE 6 ENE					6.2	16.0	21.3	12.2	-	7.6			-
BLOSERVILLE 1 N					.8	1.0	9.4	-	4.0	-			-
BOSWELL 6 WNW					6.5	-				-			-
BRADDOCK LOCK 2					T	-	-	-	-	-			-
BRADFORD CNTRL FIRE STA					-	13.0	20.0	-	-	-			-
BRADFORD 4 W RES					10.7	-	29.6	9.0	18.4	16.3	.5		-
BREEZEWOOD					T	2.0	5.0	10.0	9.5	-			-
BROOKVILLE CAA AIRPORT					3.7	15.6	14.4	5.4	16.7	5.5	T		61.3
BRUCETON 1 S					T	3.2	5.5	-	4.0	-			-
BUFFALO MILLS					T	2.3	4.0	6.9	5.1	T			18.3
BURGETTSTOWN 2 W					-	-	5.0	-	-	-			-
BURNT CABINS 2 NE				-	-	-	-	-	-	-			-
BUTLER			T		-	15.0	17.0	14.5	7.5	4.0			-
CAMP HILL					1.7	1.0	9.8	15.0	3.8	T			31.3
CANTON 1 NW					4.7	11.6	9.1	5.1	21.1	-			-
CARLISLE					2.0	1.0	7.5	10.5	3.0	-			-
CARROLLTOWN 2 SSE					8.0	8.5	19.5	11.5	14.5	4.0			66.0
CARTER CAMP 2 W					4.0	10.0	14.0	6.0	16.0	10.0			60.0
CEDAR RUN					5.0	6.0	6.0	8.0	9.0	9.0			43.0
CHADDS FORD						-	.5	-	-	-			-
CHAMBERSBURG 1 ESE					T	1.5	8.0	7.7	4.2	T			21.4
CHARLEROI LOCK 4					1.0	2.7	-	-	-	.9			-
CHESTER					-	-	-	-	-				-
CLARENCE					5.5	15.0	13.0	7.0	20.5	7.0			68.0
CLARION 3 SW					1.8	11.7	13.0	7.5	4.6	4.5			43.1
CLAUSSVILLE						-	-	-	-	-			-
CLAYSVILLE 3 W		-	-		3.0	-	-	-	-	T			-
CLEARFIELD					T	-	-	-	-	-			-
CLERMONT					11.0	20.0	20.0	8.5	21.0	22.5	4.0		107.0
COALDALE 2 NW					2.3	4.0	8.0	9.2	5.1	5.5	T		34.1
COATESVILLE 1 SW							3.5	3.8	-	T			-
COLUMBIA						T	2.0	9.0	-				-
CONFLUENCE 1 SW DAM					2.5	8.5	13.0	9.0	2.0	1.0			36.0
CONFLUENCE 1 NW					4.0	7.0	10.9	8.2	.8	2.5			33.4
CONNELLSVILLE					-	-	-	-	-	-			-
CONSHOHOCKEN							3.2	3.5		-			-
COOKSBURG					1.5	18.0	10.0	-	11.0	6.5	T		-
COOKSBURG 2 NNW					3.0	21.5	11.5	11.0	15.5	10.5	T		73.0
CORAOPOLIS NEVILLE IS					1.0	-	2.0	-	-	-			-
CORRY					11.0	11.0	16.0	7.5	9.0	19.5	T		74.0
COUDERSPORT 3 NW			T		4.2	12.1	15.4	3.4	16.8	-	T		-
COUDERSPORT 7 E			T		5.5	12.0	12.8	10.5	-	17.0	1.0		-
COVINGTON 3 W				-	-	-							-
COVINGTON 2 WSW	-	-	-		5.8	9.3	10.4	3.7	18.9	13.2	T		-
CREEKSIDE					T	-		7.0	-	-			-
CRESSON 2 SE					-	-	6.5	7.5	8.5	-			-
CUSTER CITY 2 W					8.3	-	20.2	-	17.3	17.0	1.0		-
DANVILLE					1.0	4.0	5.1	7.0	2.0	2.0			21.1
DERRY					.5	9.4	9.4	6.8	-	1.5			-
DEVAULT 1					T	T	-	-	-	T			-
DIXON					1.0	4.5	12.0	4.5	4.5	13.8	T		40.3
DONEGAL					5.5	16.5	29.2	11.5	8.0	T			70.7
DONORA					1.1	4.7	3.7	.3	.4	.1			10.3
DOYLESTOWN						.3	5.0	6.8	1.8	1.2			15.1
DU BOIS 7 E			T		3.5	15.0	13.5	11.5	18.0	7.5	T		69.0
DUSHORE 3 NE					3.8	9.0	5.4	4.8	-	10.6	T		-
EAGLES MERE					7.2	14.8	12.0	13.0	18.0	10.0	.2		75.2
EAST BRADY					T	16.4	10.5	9.5	7.0	3.0			46.4
EBENSBURG			T		4.0	-	13.3	16.0	-	1.0			-
EDINBORO					26.3	17.4	30.0	16.3	13.4	20.7	T		124.1
ELIZABETHTOWN					-		6.2	-	-	T			-
EMPORIUM 1 E		-	-	-	-	-							-
EMPORIUM 2 SSW	-		T		4.5	14.4	13.2	9.0	19.5	9.0	2.5		-
ENGLISH CENTER						-	-	-	-	-			-
EPHRATA						T	-	-	-	-			-
EQUINUNK					4.9	7.6							-
EQUINUNK 2									-	-			-
ERIE WB AIRPORT					34.8	10.2	25.6	6.7	13.5	17.2	T		108.0
EVERETT 1 SW						2.1	-	-	9.0	-			-
FARRELL SHARON					T	T	-	-	-	-			-
FORD CITY 4 S DAM					.5	13.5	15.6	8.5	12.0	4.5			54.6
FRANKLIN					-	-	-	-	-	-			-
FREELAND					-	5.3	16.0	7.5	13.6	8.5			-
GALETON			T		4.4	14.4	14.7	6.7	17.6	16.6	1.0		75.4
GEIGERTOWN					T	T	6.8	7.5	-	.5			-
GEORGE SCHOOL							6.7	8.1	2.2	.8			17.8

See Reference Notes Following Station Index

MONTHLY AND SEASONAL SNOWFALL

Season of 1956 - 1957

PENNSYLVANIA

July	August	September	October	November	December	January	February	March	April	May	June	Total
				T	.4	8.6	7.7	2.5	T			17.2
-	-			-	16.0	18.5		16.8	-	1.5		-
		T		7.1	22.5	27.5	12.5	17.0	20.5	2.5		109.6
				.7	10.0	4.6	3.1	7.9	-			-
				6.0	9.0	14.0	11.5	12.0	14.0			66.5
												-
				-	T	6.3	5.0	-	-			-
				-	T	-	-	-	-			-
				-	5.0	12.0	1.0	T	T			-
				3.0	9.7	26.2	10.5	4.5	T			53.9
				4.5	14.3	19.5	7.7	8.4	13.2	T		67.6
				.5	T	9.0	7.0	1.0	-			-
				1.0	.7	10.8	16.4	2.4	.7			32.0
				1.0	.2	6.7	11.2	.9	T			20.0
				5.0	-	-	-	-	-			T
				3.7	2.6	-	4.7	7.2	8.0			-
				5.9	5.7	12.9	5.5	8.6	13.5			52.1
				T	T	5.5	13.0	.3	T			18.8
				T	8.0	16.1	7.0	-	-			-
				9.0	14.5	33.1	15.0	20.0	5.1			96.7
				-		-	-	-	-			-
				.7	-		-	8.0	1.0			-
				.4	.3	6.9	8.1	5.2	T			20.9
				T	3.0	5.0	-	-	T			-
				1.9	6.8	12.0	5.6	2.9	1.6			30.6
				1.7	2.0	16.1	4.9	3.3	T			28.0
				4.1	9.8	16.1	9.7	9.8	9.9			59.4
				1.2	1.0	10.9	10.4	1.2	3.0	T		27.7
				2.5	3.4	13.2	6.6	3.4	.5			29.6
				10.7	22.4	20.9	17.9	15.5	20.7	1.5		109.8
				-	-	-	-	-	-			-
				6.8	14.4	13.9	7.4	12.8	13.2			68.5
				T	3.5	5.0	8.8	4.5	T			21.8
				.6	5.3	14.7	8.3	1.2	1.2			31.3
				10.6	16.4	29.0	20.0	18.7	4.2			98.9
				-	-	-	-	-	-			-
				-	-	-	10.0	-	-			-
				6.0	4.0	13.8	7.5	12.0	8.5			51.8
				T	T	4.3	3.6	-	T			-
					.2	5.9	9.7	1.3	T			17.1
				3.0	4.6	9.2	6.5	7.4	15.3			46.0
				T	.4	5.9	10.9	.2	.5			17.9
				-	1.2	-	-	-	-			-
				8.5	7.0	13.5	6.5	12.6	14.0			62.1
				12.0	23.0	31.0	13.0	17.0	20.0	1.0		117.0
				.9	.8	3.7	5.1	3.2	-			-
				14.5	22.9	20.9	-	14.0	23.0	T		-
				3.0	2.0	7.0	6.1	4.3	3.0	T		25.4
				4.0	7.8	16.0	10.0	12.5	14.5	T		64.8
					-	-	6.3	-	-			-
				-	5.0	9.9	9.5	-	6.0			-
				2.7	7.9	18.2	8.4	12.9	4.8	T		52.9
				T	.3	8.0	9.5	3.3	.5			21.6
				T	T	5.8	-	2.0	T			-
				T	T	4.6	.7	T	T			5.3
				3.9	16.3	22.7	10.2	17.6	7.0			77.7
				.1	1.0	4.3	10.9	7.9	.3			24.5
				1.5	3.5	11.5	4.6	2.0	6.0			29.1
				3.0	23.5	14.0	-	-	14.0			-
				T	T	4.4	11.1	5.1	-			-
				-	-	-	-	-	-			-
				9.9	19.2	26.9	16.4	11.8	17.5	.5		102.2
				3.5	8.6	10.2	11.2	8.5	11.8	T		53.8
					-	7.0	-	-	-			-
					2.0	12.5	11.0	7.5				39.0
				4.0	7.8	14.0	15.7	14.1	4.0			-
				.9	.7	7.2	13.8	6.5	.4			29.5
				.5	8.5	4.5	3.0	.8	T			-
				3.5	9.2	19.0	7.6	3.0	9.1			51.4
				3.0	2.5	9.5	10.0	16.0	7.5	T		48.5
				3.0	2.0	5.0	8.0	9.0	4.0	T		31.0
				2.5	3.9	6.4	12.8	7.0	-			-
				4.9	14.9	18.7	9.7	15.7	17.1	T		81.0
				T	-	2.8	5.5	-	-			-
				T		-	-	-	-			-
				4.9	5.9	-	-	-	10.6			-
				4.0	10.0	13.5	10.0	5.0	7.5			50.0
					-	-	-	-	-			-
				T	8.0	12.2	-	4.5	1.0			-
					T	-	-		-			-
				-	-		-	-	-			-
				3.1	14.5	15.3	4.8	6.4	T			44.1
				1.5	-	10.0	-	-	T			-
				T	.5	8.0	9.5	T				18.0
				2.5	.5	5.3	10.0	2.5	.5			21.3
				T	3.5	-	4.0	-	-			-
				.5	1.0	6.7	10.0	1.0	3.0			22.2
				T	T	2.8	4.3	-				-
				0.6	15.0	22.9	12.6	11.7	16.1			88.9
				3.0	13.5	10.7	4.0	-	-			-
				-	-	-	7.5	-	-			-
				T	T	7.0	8.3	1.3	4.0			20.6
				-	-	-	-	-				-
				1.0	11.6	8.0	8.0	9.0	-	T		-
					T	-	-	-	-			-

See Reference Notes Following Station Index

PECKS POND
PHIL DREXEL INST OF TEC
PHILADELPHIA WB AP
PHILADELPHIA PT BREEZE
PHILADELPHIA SHAWMONT

PHILADELPHIA CITY
PHILIPSBURG CAA AP
PHOENIXVILLE 1 E
PIKES CREEK
PIMPLE HILL

PINE GROVE 1 NE
PITTSBURGH WB AP 2
PITTSBURGH WB CITY
PLEASANT MOUNT 1 W
PORT CLINTON

POTTSVILLE
PUTNEYVILLE 2 SE DAM
QUAKERTOWN 1 E
RAYMOND

READING WB CITY
RENOVO
REW
RICES LANDING L 6
RIDGWAY 3 W

RUSH
RUSHVILLE
SAGAMORE 1 S
SALINA 3 W
SAXTON

SCHENLEY LOCK 5
SCRANTON
SCRANTON WB AIRPORT
SELINSGROVE CAA AP
SHAMOKIN

SHIPPENSBURG
SHIPPINGPORT WB
SINNEMAHONING
SLIPPERY ROCK
SOMERSET FAIRVIEW ST

SOMERSET MAIN ST
SOUTH MOUNTAIN
SPRINGBORO
SPRING GROVE
SPRINGS 1 SW

STATE COLLEGE
STRAUSSTOWN
STROUDSBURG
STUMP CREEK
SUNBURY

SUSQUEHANNA
SUTERSVILLE
TAMAQUA
TAMAQUA 4 N DAM
TAMARACK 2 S FIRE TWR

TIONESTA 2 SE DAM
TITUSVILLE WATER WORKS
TORPEDO 4 W
TOWANDA
TOWER CITY 5 SW

TROY
TURTLEPOINT 4 NE
TYRONE 4 NE BALD EAGLE
UNION CITY
UNIONTOWN

UPPER DARBY
UTICA
VANDERGRIFT
VIRGINVILLE
VOWINCKEL

VOWINCKEL 1 SW
WARREN
WATSONTOWN
WAYNESBURG 2 W
WELLSBORO 3 S

WELLSVILLE
WERNERSVILLE 1
WEST CHESTER
WEST GROVE 1 E
WEST HICKORY

WHITESBURG
WILKES BARRE
WILLIAMSBURG
WILLIAMSPORT WB AP
WOLFSBURG

YORK 3 SSW PUMP STA
YORK HAVEN
ZION GROVE
ZIONSVILLE 3 SE

See Reference Notes Following Station Index

DAILY TEMPERATURES

		Day Of Month																														Average
		1	2	3	4	5	6	7	8	9	10	11	12	13	14	15	16	17	18	19	20	21	22	23	24	25	26	27	28	29	30	31	
	MAX	78	77	71	73	74	79	87	58	74	79	83	88	86	89	95	96	98	95	85	78	85	89	88	90	86	84	86	87	82	82		83.5
	MIN	53	60	54	48	55	57	57	46	40	44	49	65	64	65	67	70	70	71	66	57	55	59	67	68	69	67	69	70	64	61		60.2
	MAX	78	80	79	73	74	75	81	85	58	75	81	84	88	88	90	95	97	98	97	89	79	86	90	91	93	93	86	87	83	82		84.5
	MIN	55	61	57	47	54	59	62	54	42	48	52	59	65	68	68	70	72	72	71	59	55	60	64	69	70	68	69	70	67	62		61.6
RVE	MAX	75	72	70	80	74	75	77	69	70	75	81	82	87	80	90	88	90	90	82	76	82	88	86	79	74	79	85	81	76	77		79.7
	MIN	53	58	50	57	56	58	60	48	46	48	50	67	63	60	65	67	63	66	68	51	50	55	66	66	63	54	58	61	60	59		58.2
	MAX	80	82	81	69	71	66	80	86	53	72	79	82	88	92	91	95	94	93	96	86	81	87	92	94	89	72	86	88	90	82		83.2
	MIN	58	56	57	57	57	61	63	51	49	52	49	61	67	66	67	68	67	69	67	54	55	58	67	66	66	63	63	68	64	59		60.8
	MAX	82	78	82	80	84	84	79	80	74	80	77	88	86	81	92	91	91	90	79	79	83	90	84	86	86	83	87	88	79	80		82.7
	MIN	64	48	47	56	58	62	60	54	56	53	57	68	63	64	66	68	63	67	64	53	52	62	70	68	62	53	57	67	60	57		60.0
	MAX	78	77	75	76	76	80	82	78	72	78	83	85	88	89	94	93	96	95	94	83	85	90	91	87	78	83	86	85	80	81		83.9
	MIN	57	61	47	60	56	58	64	50	40	49	50	67	62	62	63	66	64	67	61	51	50	55	72	65	68	60	62	67	64	59		59.2
	MAX	79	78	77	73	80	71	78	80	52	70	78	82	82	88	89	94	92	95	92	81	80	84	89	89	82	74	82	86	83	78		81.3
	MIN	49	55	47	55	54	54	59	48	39	39	52	63	62	62	62	63	63	62	71	51	49	50	50	65	69	56	59	62	63	59		56.5
	MAX	81	79	77	77	77	82	81	76	77	83	86	89	91	91	94	95	96	98	95	86	88	93	93	90	79	85	90	89	84	83		86.2
	MIN	55	62	50	50	54	53	63	51	40	51	52	67	63	64	66	65	68	70	71	55	52	56	73	68	69	65	64	68	65	59		60.3
V	MAX	80	79	77	76	75	78	83	85	74	80	80	85	89	90	92	97	99	99	99	86	81	88	91	91	92	91	86	89	81	84		85.9
	MIN	51	51	51	45	55	55	62	50	40	42	49	63	62	63	71	71	70	65	66	57	53	57	63	71	67	64	65	65	66	63		59.1
	MAX	76	68	81	79	79	77	75	62	66	80	78	76	87	81	87	86	89	90	82	72	84	89	80	82	72	80	84	87	70	73		79.1
	MIN	56	49	49	55	54	54	60	45	45	49	58	65	62	62	68	67	67	67	63	53	58	63	67	66	60	55	62	66	56	58		58.6
	MAX	78	74	75	75	74	75	69	63	70	76	78	78	84	83	85	84	90	90	89	71	82	86	85	80	75	78	78	83	70	72		78.3
	MIN	45	47	37	44	39	47	53	34	28	45	50	64	50	56	61	58	58	53	61	51	40	45	62	58	60	51	50	57	56	53		50.8
R	MAX	78	72	77	78	77	79	70	54	70	78	77	78	85	82	88	90	94	91	75	74	85	90	82	78	75	81	85	87	73	75		79.3
	MIN	53	50	44	50	49	54	54	45	42	50	53	64	61	61	67	62	62	63	53	47	44	52	68	63	57	52	54	61	60	58		55.1
	MAX	81	81	71	80	79	82	82	76	56	76	83	77	85	88	85	89	91	91	92	78	78	85	91	85	85	77	84	81	87	79		81.8
	MIN	55	48	44	45	45	53	59	54	47	52	57	65	58	63	63	64	59	63	67	47	48	52	65	65	61	47	51	60	59	53		55.6
	MAX	79	79	76	71	70	77	82	81	71	80	80	86	88	88	92	93	94	92	92	80	79	89	90	90	82	81	86	88	80	82		83.2
	MIN	57	58	51	56	62	59	60	43	46	50	50	65	62	63	64	64	62	63	68	48	48	54	66	64	60	58	63	66	64	52		58.2
	MAX	82	80	80	81	78	81	80	75	75	80	82	80	85	87	90	92	91	91	93	80	84	89	91	90	84	80	83	85	88	78		83.8
	MIN	55	48	46	46	47	55	64	49	48	56	56	68	64	63	68	69	59	63	64	48	46	53	63	65	61	49	55	62	59	54		56.8
	MAX	75	72	68	71	73	73	75	70	62	70	75	78	80	83	80	88	87	88	90	80	72	81	84	85	83	71	78	80	80	74		77.5
	MIN	54	58	45	51	49	51	54	44	37	43	52	58	56	52	62	64	64	65	66	49	48	52	58	63	65	56	54	66	59	57		55.1
	MAX	84	81	75	73	70	83	86	81	76	85	85	88	94	93	97	95	97	98	96	85	91	95	96	92	75	87	90	91	82	84		86.8
	MIN	61	62	56	60	63	63	64	52	48	57	53	67	71	67	70	73	69	72	72	59	57	60	71	70	69	66	69	71	68	61		64.1
	MAX	81	81	74	74	67	80	85	67	71	79	82	88	91	91	94	95	94	94	85	81	86	92	92	88	73	88	87	89	82	83		83.7
	MIN	56	57	54	58	62	60	62	49	49	55	51	66	66	65	66	67	67	67	69	52	52	57	67	68	68	65	63	64	65	59		60.9
	MAX	81	80	74	70	75	72	77	86	70	73	80	80	91	91	93	100	97	99	97	92	82	88	87	93	92	90	87	90	89	90		85.5
	MIN	56	53	60	50	60	63	63	56	60	53	53	67	69	70	70	72	74	75	75	61	60	64	70	68	71	71	70	69	61	62		64.2
	MAX	79	72	80	79	81	78	73	62	72	80	79	79	88	84	90	91	94	92	79	77	85	90	84	83	78	81	85	87	76	78		81.2
	MIN	53	48	43	48	47	54	57	50	45	48	53	62	59	59	63	62	61	63	64	49	48	51	64	63	61	51	55	60	59	52		55.1
	MAX	80	76	82	82	82	83	82	69	72	83	82	86	89	86	91	93	96	92	86	80	85	92	87	85	78	84	88	87	81	83		84.1
	MIN	51	49	45	52	46	53	62	53	58	51	55	70	59	65	66	68	60	63	67	46	45	51	51	65	55	46	52	61	60	54		56.0
	MAX	79	81	79	70	71	72	78	86	55	74	78	80	90	90	91	96	97	97	97	88	81	87	91	94	91	90	87	89	87	82		84.3
	MIN	52	58	60	49	57	57	62	53	42	43	46	58	70	66	63	69	68	68	69	60	53	55	63	69	70	67	66	67	66	60		60.2
	MAX	81	81	72	71	70	79	88	75	75	79	82	90	92	92	98	99	98	98	92	85	87	90	92	87	86	86	88	89	85	85		85.7
	MIN	56	61	58	53	61	61	66	56	46	51	53	62	69	67	67	72	69	72	71	57	56	60	68	69	70	67	68	71	65	62		62.8
	MAX	78	80	72	77	82	76	80	80	57	63	77	78	82	88	85	87	90	92	93	80	78	84	93	87	84	79	85	88	85	78		81.1
	MIN	45	53	50	54	53	57	56	57	49	47	51	54	64	61	63	64	64	64	65	54	48	51	59	66	65	56	56	54	59	58		56.6
	MAX	77	64	75	76	80	80	76	66	74	82	79	74	87	83	86	84	92	93	75	76	84	88	83	79	75	80	78	77	74	73		79.1
	MIN	53	45	36	43	42	49	51	37	38	54	56	64	51	61	68	62	59	63												60		
	MAX	70	67	70	74	71	71	65	61	68	73	76	78	81	78	87	85	90	87	75	72	80	82	79	80	70	75	80	80	84	73		76.1
	MIN	45	48	34	44	41	48	44	35	32	44	49	63	52	59	61	57	57	61	63	47	40	46	61	60	59	48	53	59	56	57		50.8
	MAX	80	74	79	79	80	81	77	69														92	85	83	75	85	87	87	79	78		
	MIN	65	52	50	57	50	57	65	52														69	70	72	63	54	62	71	61	61		
	MAX	80	82	72	72	71	78	86	63	73	77	79	89	89	90	90	98	98	96	87													
	MIN	48	49	49	44	56	55	57	44	38	39	51	60	62	62	69	64	65	69	65	53	55	56	64	60	61	70	66	69	65	63		57.6
	MAX	79	80	69	75	78	75	79	78	68	75	79	83	83	87	86	91	91	93	95	84	76	85	89	89	91	77	84	87	87	79		82.4
	MIN	46	50	46	47	49	48	51	43	41	40	45	51	56	58	62	65	66	67	68	48	50	49	54	66	66	63	59	61	65	61		54.7
	MAX	75	62	74	75	75	76	72	65	62	74	74	78	82	80	84	84	87	86	73	72	72	87	82	82	71	79	82	82	72	73		76.4
	MIN	50	46	44	50	46	51	54	43	45	48	50	63	58	59	62	58	57	59	48	43	44	50	64	61	54	47	55	54	58	52		52.3
	MAX	86	84	81	84	83	84	85	82	74	81	86	81	87	90	90	96	94	96	95	82	84	91	95	88	89	83	89	92	92	82		86.9
	MIN	62	51	54	58	54	63	67	55	52	59	64	72	68	67	72	67	65	72	70	56	56	67	72	71	65	58	63	71	64	62		63.2
	MAX	76	74	72	76	74	77	72	67	67	75	78	76	86	84	88	88	90	91	89	74	81	88	88	81	73	78	83	83	78	75		79.4
	MIN	56	53	46	57	50	52	61	48	44	56	58	62	59	62	65	61	57	61	66	46	45	57	65	64	62	50	62	65	60	57		56.9
	MAX	72	70	65	68	68	72	72	70	57	68	71	75	78	78	76	84	84	86	87	75	71	76	81	82	79	68	73	76	77	75		74.5
	MIN	54	56	47	49	52	54	54	45	42	49	52	58	60	60	61	69	67	69	67	49	55	57	63	65	65	60	58	61	58	56		57.1
	MAX	84	81	83	83	84	84	82	69	75	84	84	83	90	89	93	94	95	95	91	78	88	93	93	85	84	84	89	90	78	80		85.5
	MIN	55	50	47	49	50	56	63	51	49	50	56	61	64	63	67	66	64	67	67	52	52	55	69	66	63	54	58	62	63	57		58.2
	MAX	72	70	70	77	69	75	75	69	64	72	78	79	85	78	83	86	88	91	82	73	78	87	82	76	71	78	78	82	77	75		77.4
	MIN	55	54	46	56	60	55	61	44	44	49	52	65	60	60	64	60	59	60	64	47	43	54	65	64	60	49	52	56	57	56		55.7
	MAX	78	74	69	74	75	73	75	70	57	68	75	79	78	85	80	88	86	90	90	75	73	81	86	83	76	75	77	82	82	73		77.6
	MIN	47	53	41	44	45	47	51	44	32	39	45	51	58	58	60	61	58	59	65	46	44	44	51	61	64	51	54	56	59	52		51.3
	MAX	79	79	72	70	70	79	87	72	73	78	81	87	90	90	94	96	95	96	86	81	87	91	91	89	83	86	86	89	83	84		84.1
	MIN	53	58	54	50	57	57	64	51	42	49	51	65	66	65	67	69	67	67	71	56	54	60	68	66	69	65	68	69	64	61		60.8
	MAX	78	59	70	75	74	78	65	67	76	84	83	71	88	84	82	82	89	92	70	71	83	90	84	73	71	82	80	82	76	73		77.7
	MIN	51	45	42	47	51	53	50	43	45	60	65	56	55	67	72	69	67	70	59	56	55	64	71	63	60	57	62	62	63	61		58.0
	MAX	80	74	72	78	72	85	84	70	78	74	79	86	90	92	94	89	92	94	84	80	84	80	82	82	78	84	83	88	74	80		82.1
	MIN	54	52	56	60	64	56	58	46	52	56	54	70	68	68	72	67	70	70	66	56	58	60	64	70	62	60	68	66	58	52		61.1

See reference notes following Station Index.

FARRELL SHARON										
FORD CITY 4 S DAM										
FRANKLIN										
FREELAND										
GEORGE SCHOOL										
GETTYSBURG										
GRATERFORD										
GRATZ 1 N										
GREENVILLE										
HANOVER										
HARRISBURG WB AP										
HAWLEY 1 S DAM										
HOLTWOOD										
HUNTINGDON										
INDIANA 3 SE										
IRWIN										
JAMESTOWN 2 NW										
JIM THORPE										
JOHNSTOWN										
KANE 1 NNE										
KEGG										
LANCASTER 2 NE PUMP STA										
LANDISVILLE 2 NW										
LAWRENCEVILLE 2 S										
LEBANON 3 W										
LEWISTOWN										
LINESVILLE 3 WNW	88 54	69	79 63	76 60	80 51	78 55				
LOCK HAVEN	94		68	77 70	87 61	89 59				
MADERA	81 42	89 48	85 58	75 60	71 50	80 50				
MARCUS HOOK	91 66	92 70	92 77	91 72	86 73	89 74				
MARTINSBURG CAA AP	89 58	86 69	82 68	74 61	82 54	86 60	82 62	74 61	75 58	
MEADVILLE 1 S	54	62	83 65	74 61	78 52	81 57	79 62	77 60	55	78 56
MERCER 2 NNE	87 54	83 66	81 65	75 61	80 49	84 63	83 64	76 60	77 57	79 55
MIDDLETOWN OLMSTED FLD	93 62	93 71	85 70	76 70		90 72	89 73	81 68	82 65	84
MIDLAND DAM 7	92 64	63	86 71	79 65	83 60	87 62		78 64	78 62	82 62
MONTROSE 1 E	80 55	62	63	85 65	71 59	60	81 63	82 60	73 55	77 55
MORGANTOWN	59	59		67	66	85 68	85 70	83 64	83 61	81 60
MT GRETNA 2 SE	89 63	90 70	86 71	79 67	84 68	86 71	87 71	80 65	82 62	82 62
MT POCONO 2 N AP		81 61		77 64		81 61	79 65	77 59	74 56	78 55

See reference notes following Station Index.

DAILY TEMPERATURES

tion		1	2	3	4	5	6	7	8	9	10	11	12	13	14	15	16	17	18	19	20	21	22	23	24	25	26	27	28	29	30	31	Average
	MAX	77	74	74	74	71	78	77	74	74	79	82	85	86	86	91	91	91	96	86	85	84	88	89	85	75	81	84	83	78	79		81.9
	MIN	56	59	48	48	55	47	60	48	37	47	59	64	55	60	65	66	66	68	69	58	51	54	66	65	66	62	61	66	62	55		58.1
	MAX	80	81	78	75	74	84	92	82	78	78	82	88	92	98	96	93	96	92	81	85	92	93	88	88	82	92	89	88	84	85		86.2
	MIN	58	66	64	69	61	65	69	48	50	56	52	66	69	65	66	66	68	75	72	52	57	66	72	68	68	63	71	67	68	61		63.9
	MAX	80	78	79	79	82	82	81	68	73	83	80	80	88	82	90	88	93	92	79	79	84	91	89	83	82	82	85	85	78	78		82.4
	MIN	61	48	43	46	48	55	62	51	49	58	59	66	60	64	70	68	62	66	66	52	50	55	70	66	62	52	55	66	61	57		58.3
	MAX	88	88	78	84	85	87	86	87	73	79	89	81	87	93	85	92	98	98	97	83	82	92	98	90	90	81	90	92	93	83		87.6
	MIN	55	58	55	57	54	61	67	57	55	55	59	70	67	65	69	68	66	68	69	54	54	59	70	70	64	56	61	66	59	60		61.6
	MAX	84	83	78	76	75	75	82	85	55	77	83	85	87	93	91	97	93	97	97	85	83	90	92	92	83	74	87	88	88	82		84.6
	MIN	60	59	52	55	58	60	63	54	45	48	50	54	67	65	66	68	66	68	69	54	52	55	58	67	67	64	64	66	64	59		59.9
	MAX	82	73	79	82	83	85	80	64	71	83	80	85	91	88	91	92	100	95	93	80	84	93	88	89	79	88	92	89	80	82		84.6
	MIN	53	51	48	53	49	55	61	52	48	51	55	68	61	66	65	66	59	62	54	50	48	59	63	64	59	50	57	61	60	55		56.8
	MAX	80	84	70	76	73	79	88	64	73	79	82	90	92	91	96	100	97	97	91	82	86	90	91	93	89	87	89	90	84	85		85.6
	MIN	56	63	58	51	63	64	63	52	45	48	56	67	68	71	70	68	72	73	73	63	62	64	70	72	71	69	72	71	68	65		64.3
	MAX	79	72	71	71	73	79	81	57	73	78	82	85	88	88	92	93	94	94	94	77	84	88	87	87	82	84	85	84	80	81		82.1
	MIN	55	58	52	46	56	55	57	46	40	43	49	68	62	67	67	69	69	70	68	55	52	55	68	69	68	67	67	72	64	60		59.8
OF TEC	MAX	80	84	72	75	72	80	87	64	75	80	81	92	92	93	98	100	99	97	92	84	90	92	91	92	91	87	93	90	85	86		86.5
	MIN	59	62	63	57	65	65	66	55	49	56	57	66	73	71	70	70	75	76	77	63	64	67	69	74	71	70	73	74	68	67		66.4
P	MAX	80	82	70	74	71	79	86	65	74	78	81	90	92	93	97	100	98	96	91	82	88	91	92	92	90	87	91	89	84	84		85.6
	MIN	59	62	58	54	63	63	64	50	44	53	53	66	69	68	69	68	70	74	72	61	60	65	68	74	71	70	72	72	65	68		64.2
REEZE	MAX	81	82	70	70	67	73	82	62	70	78	79	89	92	93	98	99	97	95	92	83	87	92	92	93	90	88	90	89	86	86		84.8
	MIN	61	64	57	56	63	61	62	50	49	54	57	68	77	74	73	78	76	79	77	69	70	69	72	78	75	75	76	76	66	70		67.7
MONT	MAX	77	82	72	72	72	77	85	76	73	80	80	89	90	92	95	100	96	98	90	87	87	92	92	92	89	87	89	89	85	84		85.6
	MIN	56	64	62	50	63	63	65	54	44	45	55	65	66	69	67	71	67	72	74	62	58	68	69	72	71	70	71	72	67	66		63.9
	MAX	77	81	66	73	70	76	87	62	71	80	80	91	91	92	97	97	98	97	89	82	86	90	92	90	88	85	88	87	84	84		84.4
	MIN	58	61	57	55	63	63	63	51	50	53	59	66	75	72	71	74	74	77	74	65	69	66	69	73	71	73	74	73	62	69		66.0
P	MAX	72	71	69	78	67	75	74	55	67	72	78	78	84	78	88	86	89	88	75	74	80	85	84	74	72	78	82	78	72	74		76.6
	MIN	58	50	45	52	51	48	54	43	41	51	51	59	57	62	62	59	55	59	52	47	39	51	63	61	56	47	60	61	59	57		53.7
	MAX	74	80	78	80	78	76	83	68	76	83	84	84	93	94	98	100	100	98	94	85	86	88	94	94	92	90	93	91	88	88		87.0
	MIN	50	51	55	50	58	59	58	42	40	40	51	60	66	70	68	70	66	67	72	56	64	58	66	68	68	68	66	70	65	61		60.1
	MAX	72	72	64	66	71	69	73	74	62	69	74	77	80	85	81	88	91	88	89	78	71	79	82	82	86	77	80	80	77	72		77.0
	MIN	52	55	46	45	53	51	59	43	40	45	52	60	60	60	65	66	67	69	67	48	52	59	60	64	64	60	63	65	56	56		56.7
2	MAX	77	70	79	78	81	81	77	57	71	79	75	82	87	82	88	90	90	90	75	78	83	89	84	81	78	81	84	84	77	77		80.1
	MIN	62	49	49	54	55	62	57	50	49	57	62	69	62	67	70	70	66	71	61	56	55	64	71	69	61	57	61	62	61	60		60.6
Y	MAX	79	73	82	81	84	83	77	62	72	81	78	84	88	85	92	93	93	93	81	79	85	91	85	85	79	85	89	87	80	80		82.9
	MIN	65	52	54	58	57	63	62	52	51	59	65	71	65	69	72	72	67	75	64	61	59	66	73	70	64	61	65	64	64	63		63.4
W	MAX	75	71	66	67	72	71	73		69	69	73	78	76	81			88	86	90	78	68	79	84	82	86	78	77	82				76.8
	MIN	44	52	46	40	42	46	52		35	35	45	59	49	55			59	62	68	50	46	47	57	64	65	61	56	62				51.9
	MAX	80	80	75	74	70	75	80	85	62	75	80	84	87	90	91	95	96	97	97	85	80	87	90	91	90	85	86	87	86	82		84.1
	MIN	49	53	45	44	52	53	58	49	41	41	45	56	58	62	71	64	66	65	65	59	48	60	63	68	66	63	63	67	62	53		57.0
DAM	MAX	80	80	74	80	80	78	82	76	53	70	80	80	82	86	83	92	90	94	91	78	78	85	90	85	81	76	83	86	88	87		81.6
	MIN	53	49	45	50	47	51	57	48	44	49	55	63	61	59	64	63	59	61	65	46	47	50	64	64	60	52	56	61	58	55		55.2
	MAX	80	80	72	74	73	80	84	79	72	79	82	87	89	90	92	99	96	97	88	80	85	89	91	92	89	85	92	93	82	83		85.1
	MIN	49	60	56	44	55	59	64	51	37	40	48	65	62	64	64	67	67	67	69	59	52	56	63	68	67	67	65	69	65	60		59.3
	MAX	80	78	72	71	72	80	86	61	74	79	81	88	90	91	95	98	97	97	87	81	87	90	91	90	86	86	89	89	83	84		84.4
	MIN	58	62	58	53	60	60	61	49	43	47	55	68	67	68	71	74	74	75	69	61	59	62	71	70	69	69	71	73	67	65		63.6
	MAX	80	76	71	77	75	77	77	70	58	71	78	80	80	86	82	89	88	92	91	76	76	83	89	82	78	75	80	83	85	75		79.3
	MIN	47	50	40	43	43	45	53	49	36	40	45	50	57	58	61	61	60	61	64	45	45	46	50	60	61	50	50	54	59	55		51.3
	MAX	78	75	79	77	80	80	79	70	68	81	79	82	87	84	90	90	92	91	89	76	84	90	89	87	78	83	87	88	79	77		82.3
	MIN	57	49	48	52	47	55	66	50	49	54	56	69	64	64	70	67	60	66	64	52	50	58	71	69	63	54	58	63	61	59		58.8
	MAX	81	80	71	76	76	74	80	76	68	76	81	85	83	88	88	91	92	93	97	89	75	87	90	90	91	85	83	88	88	81		83.4
	MIN	53	55	52	50	53	53	55	50	41	45	50	56	61	62	66	69	69	70	72	59	53	56	61	70	70	65	64	67	65	62		59.1
RT	MAX	79	69	73	75	72	78	75	65	75	79	83	83	87	86	90	90	90	93	82	73	84	87	88	88	81	82	85	85	78	79		81.1
	MIN	54	50	48	47	53	50	50	45	39	45	53	65	58	63	65	66	67	69	59	53	51	59	67	67	64	63	64	66	63	59		57.4
P	MAX	81	72	75	74	75	80	83	57	75	79	82	85	89	88	94	95	97	96	85	80	88	90	90	87	73	85	85	85	80	82		82.9
	MIN	54	52	47	54	56	58	57	43	44	48	49	67	62	64	67	67	65	68	62	50	49	53	71	66	65	64	61	68	62	60		58.4
	MAX	82	79	77	72	70	82	85	79	73	80	82	88	91	91	96	94	96	94	92	85	88	92	93	86	76	84	87	88	84	80		84.8
	MIN	58	58	53	58	62	60	62	49	49	56	50	68	66	65	68	68	68	68	72	55	54	59	68	68	68	64	65	66	66	62		61.8
	MAX	80	70	80	77	81	80	72	57	74	82	77	82	88	84	90	90	91	92	75	78	86	92	85	83	76	82	85	85	79	79		81.1
	MIN	58	51	46	50	50	60	56	49	49	55	60	68	64	65	69	67	65	68	57	54	53	58	69	69	57	53	58	64	61	59		58.7
	MAX	78	74	79	78	80	81	82	62	72	84	76	80	88	83	90	90	92	91	78	77	84	89	84	82	75	80	84	82	76	77		80.9
	MIN	60	48	46	48	52	57	54	50	48	53	60	66	60	63	68	67	62	69	62	52	54	58	70	68	61	52	58	65	60	58		58.3
	MAX	77	74	72	78	75	78	78	72	58	72	78	80	86	85	86	88	89	89	86	75	81	86	83	82	73	80	84	85	79	74		79.5
	MIN	54	55	48	56	55	57	60	46	45	48	52	67	67	62	63	61	61	61	65	47	46	56	67	65	61	50	56	60	58	56		56.8
	MAX	82	78	65	72	78	80	81	73	74	75	81	80	76	84	85	87	88	94	92	84	73	84	88	85		80	80	80	80	77		80.6
	MIN	58	45	30	42	45	47	52	42	41	56	59	62	54	64	69	66	61	65	63	53	52	53	68		61	52	57	65	60	45		54.7
	MAX	75	69	71	77	68	76	76	61	56	72	77	76	85	81	84	85	86	89	76	74	79	88	84	83	72	81	84	84	73	75		77.3
	MIN	44	52	46	56	55	56	59	45	45	42	48	67	58	59	62	58	58	58	61	45	44	53	64	64	61	47	54	56	56	57		54.3
	MAX	77	76	74	78	70	79	77	57	69	76	82	82	88	84	92	89	95	94	80	77	84	89	88	81	73	81	87	83	77	77		80.5
	MIN	62	56	50	59	57	57	57	46	42	59	57	68	64	62	68	68	64	70	60	54	54	58	73	68	65	59	61	68	61	57		60.1
	MAX	81	72	73	76	75	80	81	61	72	81	84	88	89	86	96	97	93	93	86	74	85	90	84	93	85	85	86	88	80	81		83.2
	MIN	47	54	45	37	47	47	54	48	36	41	52	62	56	62	64	61	63	65	64	50	46	45	60	62	64	64	61	66	61	57		54.7
TWR	MAX																																
	MIN																																
	MAX	80	77	69	77	77	79	76	68	60	71	79	78	78	86	83	88	85	91	90	80	73	80	88	81	79	75	80	83	85	75		79.0
	MIN	52	49	43	47	47	49	55	49	42	45	53	60	60	60	65	65	62	63	67	52	49	52	60	64	62	53	56	57	62	58		55.3
WORKS	MAX	80	74	78	78	82	81	76	64	73	81	80	78	88	86	89	85	93	91	75	73	82	88	83	82	76	79	81	83	76	75		80.3
	MIN	50	47	40	46	42	49	57	44	40	47	55	62	55	60	65	64	59	65	59	52	46	51	60	62	60	49	53	62	54	53		53.6

See reference notes following Station Index.

TEMPERATURES

Day Of Month

TOWANDA

UNIONTOWN

UPPER DARBY

WARREN

WAYNESBURG 1

WELLSBORO 3

WELLSVILLE

WEST CHESTER

WILLIAMSPORT WB AP

YORK 3 SSW PUMP STA

EVAPORATION AND WIND

Table 6

Station		Day of month 1	2	3	4	5	6	7	8	9	10	11	12	13	14	15	16	17	18	19	20	21	22	23	24	25	26	27	28	29	30	31	Total or Avg.
CONFLUENCE 1 SW DAM	EVAP	.25	.09	.13	.19	.15	.09	.20	.22	.05	.37	.22	.09	.18	.22	.15	.18	.19	.25	.27	.23	.19	.23	.25	.14	.09	.12	.17	.24	.21	.17		5.53
	WIND	8	33	35	43	26	23	45	58	50	74	68	78	37	53	22	30	40	13	61	77	107	5	35	42	62	30	42	46	137	102		1482
FORD CITY 4 S DAM	EVAP	.24	-	.22	.16	.20	.17	.16	.19	.04	.19	.17	.11	.10	.33	.16	.23	.16	-	.30	.21	.16	.22	.25	.16	.20	.04	.20	.19	.30	.22		B5.68
	WIND	17	38	54	10	34	24	27	68	47	64	29	56	26	26	31	26	17	16	40	60	23	28	25	46	18	25	20	63	107	102		1167
HAWLEY 1 S DAM	EVAP	.13	.14	.07	.21	.14	.10	.14	.19	.14	.21	.25	.25	.17	.23	.17	.15	.19	.22	.27	.22	.12	.21	.25	.16	.17	.16	.17	.16	.28	.33		5.60
	WIND	52	46	20	63	47	14	98	72	44	34	78	124	48	40	56	36	13	32	66	89	41	21	52	39	35	46	28	73	122	164		1693
JAMESTOWN 2 NW	EVAP	.14	.16	.16	.19	.17	.21	.14	.12	.10	.16	.16	.06	.12	.18	.19	.27	.50	.18	.25	.20	.19	.23	.22	.13	-	.16	.23	.10	-	.26		B5.55
	WIND	13	29	20	14	8	11	24	17	28	42	24	34	7	34	31	18	9	3	17	19	10	15	21	25	9	22	19	9	97	16		645
LANDISVILLE	EVAP	.25	.40	.07	.09	.08	.01	.19	.32	.01	.26	.26	.24	.28	.30	.26	.30	.27	.27	.33	.32	.19	.30	.30	.18	.61	.18	.25	.24	.29	.39		7.44
	WIND	36	33	64	34	18	13	40	107	21	55	34	63	51	35	37	34	44	18	29	82	66	22	58	41	24	26	-	-	-	-		B1252
PIMPLE HILL	EVAP	.31	*	.32	.21	.17	.14	.22	.20	.10	.28	.27	.32	.21	.31	.27	.27	.28	.28	.22	.24	.18	.30	.30	.17	.24	.12	.24	.26	.27	.45		7.15
	WIND	82	*	144	91	50	30	88	72	38	97	73	97	34	67	63	31	30	12	57	90	38	43	89	51	72	47	48	78	175	97		1984
STATE COLLEGE	EVAP	-	.19	.19	.19	.15	.08	.14	.27	*	.14	.30	.19	.22	.38	.12	.29	.19	.23	.31	.24	.21	.25	.25	.22	-	.09	.24	.20	.33	-		B6.23
	WIND	35	37	29	38	23	18	26	67	*	58	28	46	51	41	12	38	11	11	30	67	45	18	29	22	8	17	19	29	107	-		B 993

DAILY SOIL TEMPERATURES

STATION AND DEPTH	TIME	Day of month 1	2	3	4	5	6	7	8	9	10	11	12	13	14	15	16	17	18	19	20	21	22	23	24	25	26	27	28	29	30	31	Average
STATE COLLEGE																																	
MEASURED UNDER SOD																																	
2 INCHES	8 AM	62	64	64	62	64	63	66	57	58	61	64	69	68	69	72	74	73	74	73	67	66	68	73	72	69	67	69	71	66	66		67.0
4 INCHES	8 AM	62	64	63	62	63	62	65	58	57	61	63	68	68	68	71	72	71	74	73	66	65	67	72	71	69	67	69	71	67	66		66.5
8 INCHES	8 AM	62	63	62	62	63	62	64	61	57	60	61	66	66	67	69	70	70	72	73	67	65	67	70	70	69	67	69	70	68	66		65.9
16 INCHES	8 AM	61	62	62	62	62	62	63	62	60	61	61	64	65	66	67	69	69	70	71	69	67	67	68	69	69	68	69	69	70	68		65.7

Ground Cover: Bluegrass Sod.

See reference notes following Station Index.

MONTHLY AND SEASONAL HEATING DEGREE DAYS

Season of 1956 - 1957

PENNSYLVANIA

July	August	September	October	November	December	January	February	March	April	May	June	Total	Normal July-June
12	9	178	335	694	864	1230	892	792	420	184	30	5640	5880
13	11	172	342	658	849	1203	891	786	420	175	24	5504	
37	31	199	349	726	859	1287	874	848	435	194	23	5842	
4	9	165	330	657	796	1192	833	786	403	163	22	5300	
7	16	138	276			1084	786	720	395				
3	23	156	245	670	764	1219	801	748	396	130	10	5165	
12	21	175	361	672	860	1201	860	815	399	178	15	5569	
13	36	220	394	694	873	1281	901	856		190	37		
8	10	157	313	654	894	1217	851	779	387	152			
15	19	157	268	633	805				392	169	17		
20	31	220	318	757	893	1349	888	887	459	208	30	6060	
72	07	324	463	795	1008	1462	1022	993	594	321	87	7246	
40	47	262	389	774	920	1351	950	910	503	262	44	6452	
20	50	249	408	753	861	1304	894	858	468	217	34	6116	
16	25	192				1200	819	804	446	135	13		
3	34	190	264	661	784	1239	845	795	425	169	13	5422	
60	75	303	463	779	1013	1429	1030	980	582	343	57	7114	
1	1	126	290	621	762	1123	777	692	335	88	3	4819	
3	13	159	325	670	773	1153	808	762	371	152	13	5202	
2	0	95	242	487	730	1055	759	720	368	126	7	4591	
14	40	205	348	715	887	1313	917	839	480	204	28	5990	
2				726	762	1229	803	790	397	174	10		
10	13	163	347	652	811	1162	822	777	394	174	31	5356	
1	0	118	277	597	752	1106	779	717	332	109	7	4795	
28	35	189	326	685	790	1222	825	846	448	212	32	5638	
32	49	260	368	748	966	1400	984	915	546	276			
85	21	347	489	851	1055	1512	1034	1030	600	362	111	7597	
5	18	164	242	635	751	1187	781	757	387	149			
26	3	211	332	665	831	1205	878	797	427	221			
32	41	263	464	720	962	1399	962	934	497	305	43	6622	
61	84	307	437	868	931	1390	960	968	544	298	82	6930	
0	10	94	145	542	697	1092	707	684	318	100	2	4351	
31	43	236	374	743	915	1369	934	920	493	231	34	6323	
75	78	344		951	1058	1464	1076	1003	601	344	65		
1	9	144	231	630	809	1235	808	758	404	131	8	5168	
44	57	252	442	802	892	1348	918	896	483	247	44	6425	
38													
	71	308	477	802	1018	1463	1012	1010	563	348	91		
7	9	139	311	619	769	1152	819	750	394	153	19	5141	
12	19	202	298	675	891	1298	951	920	526	314	51	6157	6558
4	22	183	366	734	783	1191	827	774	389	164	10	5447	
15	22	205	293	677	835	1269	849	786	467	184	17	5619	
23	41	220	346	690	830	1293	893	863	476	208	27	5910	
15	27	191	306	670	840	1306	887	825	490	192	36	5785	
60	54	264	368	728	957	1349	970	902	469	239	90	6450	
3	6	139	279	596	751	1161	786	734	371	157	21	5004	
6	9	146	291	619	739	1139	771	735	354	140	12	4961	
						1134	801	745	363	153	0		
22	28	223	394	686	879	1267	890	848	450	230	37	5954	
3	29	191	289	686	848	1298	884	827	461	194	23	5733	
5	15	160	327	646	754	1146	802	769	374	142	12	5161	
7	0	146	295	631	762	1139	809	730	358	137	13	5027	5258
63	70	295	527	816	1012	1461	1048	1022	584	337	85	7320	
0	0	108	238	604	744	1118	786	711	352	111	7	4779	
6	11	184		667	816			831	426	198	18		
11	23	207	305	708	813	1263	831	808	416	191	17	5593	
0	16	139	205	632					385	113			
25	37	237	341	726	906	1374	960	912	533	259	49	6359	
16	16	180	313	664	869	1192	843	762	403	165	34	5457	
12	29	212	324	707	811	1270	902	923	492	213	19	5914	
85	14	359	514	809	1034	1477	1048	1015	595	321	66	7437	
7	30	220	359	777	822	1213	864	835	416	198	28	5769	
4	7	150	334	639	763	1114	787	726	349	137	13	5023	
8	14	172	365	701	859	1244	848	808	426	195	30	5670	
34	53	288	466	743	985	1414	991	997	568	336	46	6921	
7	0	184	338	653	822	1180	843	804	425	192	27	5475	
2	10	168	314	649	804	1192	838	781	418	168	21	5361	
21	32	237	336	722	898	1339	965	890	522	266	55	6283	
5		171	320	674	850	1233	854	789	404	150	15		
54	86	320	520	847	988	1415	1012	1020	566	352	81	7259	
4	1	89	195	551	706	1093	703	633	306	92	7	4380	
10	23	212	352	739	828	1242	897	844	453	205	25	5830	
32	40	246	360	716	924	1364	974	908	528	271	49	6412	
27	26	272	317	756	870	1291	902	887	500	186	35	6069	
5	0	137	284	632	763	1130	797	721	348	131	11	4959	
1	8	157	240	649	782	1161	816	773	408	150	6	5171	
60	63	315	488	795	1073	1485	1077	1020	599	376	61	7412	
14	13	173	362	690	821	1205	859	789	418	205	43	5592	
12	4	166	315	681	789	1170	840	775	384	162	19	5317	
60	54	278	454	784	1031	1415	982	968	557	281	64	6928	
32	39	256	437	758	989	1353	945	869	450	216	27	6371	
0	0	90	271				903		359	108	1		
7	21	181	270	653	804	1254	851	773	430	168	17	5409	
0	5	82	140	488	621	1097	725	693	322	111	1	4283	
9	11	186	360	683	830	1183	842	806	410	175	17	5512	
7	27	195	268	704	767	1209	811	788	405	186	16	5383	
4	1	107	243	565	703	1104	769	706	349	123	17	4691	
21	17	195	375	714	889	1251	891	811	427	208	34	5833	
1	0	75	161	480	635	1046	719	658	307	96	8	4186	
2	2	107	222	556	718	1103	765	695	346	126	15	4657	4866
4	1	80	165	461	632	1047	711	641	322	97	17	4178	
2	2	98	232	520	693	1088	752	715	328	109	12	4551	
4	0	73	177	491	659	1025	710	644	326	113	16	4238	4523
73	93	315	439	832	959	1408	995	985	540	304	65	7008	
1	2	137	282	587	729	1108	777	692	328	102	23	4768	

See Reference Notes Following Station Index

MONTHLY AND SEASONAL HEATING DEGREE DAYS

CONTINUED

Season of 1956 - 1957

PENNSYLVANIA

Station	July	August	September	October	November	December	January	February	March	April	May	June	Total	Normal July-June
PIMPLE HILL	66	48	281	447	824	1026	1428	1043	1001	587	317	67	7135	
PITTSBURGH WB AP 2	4	19	180	290	683	785	1234	843	778	409	173	22	5380	5905
PITTSBURGH WB CITY	0	6	127	183	595	682	1124	757	694	355	118	13	4654	5048
PLEASANT MOUNT 1 W	87	95	338	568	852	1093	1534	1105	1082	624	398	107	7883	
PORT CLINTON	20	24	203	410	687		1195	890	823	460	230	39		
PUTNEYVILLE 2 SE DAM	25	46	257	395	747	912	1346	957	914	502	238	36	6375	
QUAKERTOWN 1 E	11	13	156	314	661	814	1200	860	763	380	154	23	5349	
READING WB CITY	6	0	127	243	604	741	1113	785	690	353	133	21	4816	5060
RIDGWAY 3 W	63	91	291	473	803	942	1406	1007	1022	578	314	72	7062	
SALINA 3 W	6	26	184	263	701	786	1228	821	789	413	162	17	5396	
SCRANTON	33	34	243	392	731	937	1300	908	863	460	242	23	6166	
SCRANTON WB AIRPORT	28	29	241	394	736	943	1337	946	886	485	264	41	6330	
SELINSGROVE CAA AP	7	16	183	377	719	884	1233	906	832	425	207	29	5818	
SHIPPENSBURG	3	2	136	284	631	743	1114	790	741	353	117	5	4919	
SHIPPINGPORT WB	2	29	189	260	667	781	1202	843	779	410	183	23	5368	
SLIPPERY ROCK	9	22	191	282	704	860	1309	881	829	463	178	22	5750	
SOMERSET MAIN ST	15	49	213	375	752	826	1272	839	874	428	212	34	5889	
SPRINGBORO	31	34	249	360	713	912	1278	945	910	519	269	56	6276	
SPRINGS 1 SW	49	66	291	437	830	872	1297	883	942	489	271	62	6489	
STATE COLLEGE	12	21	209	335	703	842	1236	874	827	441	178	26	5704	
STROUDSBURG	34	35	252	446	775	969	1369	947	870	487	284	50	6478	
TAMARACK 2 S FIRE TWR				431	794	1033	1467	1051	1011	615	329			
TIONESTA 2 SE DAM	27	49	237	393	743	961	1388	997	933	545	260	50	6583	
TITUSVILLE WATER WORKS	39	45	283	421	785	943	1400	976	909	517	256	41	6615	
TOWANDA	22	27	207	413	704	920	1332	916	895	471	255	29	6191	
UNIONTOWN	3	19	143	207	638	690	1126	719	700	341	130	11	4727	
UPPER DARBY	2	1	103	215	552	707	1110	757	705	318	105	3	4578	
WARREN	20	40	224	355	710	915	1315	920	876	498	239	30	6142	
WAYNESBURG 2 W	3	0	168	286	682	731	1197	760	745	368	151	5	5098	
WELLSBORO 3 S	48	60	289	448	782	1025	1430	1039	996	594	337	65	7113	
WELLSVILLE	6	10	160	356	674	779	1163	812	782	379	152	16	5289	
WEST CHESTER	8	5	116	238	649	784	1135	804	699					
WILLIAMSPORT WB AP	10	11	176	346	688	899	1263	889	799	418	185	20	5704	5898
YORK 3 SSW PUMP STA	4	4	123	287	596	713	1103	742	710	324	125	7	4738	

See Reference Notes Following Station Index

CLIMATOLOGICAL DATA

ABLE 2

PENNSYLVANIA
DELAYED DATA

Station	Temperature													Precipitation									
	Average Maximum	Average Minimum	Average	Departure From Long Term Means	Highest	Date	Lowest	Date	Degree Days	No. of Days Max. 90° or Above	No. of Days Max. 32° or Below	No. of Days Min. 32° or Below	No. of Days Min. 0° or Below	Total	Departure From Long Term Means	Greatest Day	Date	Snow, Sleet Total	Snow, Sleet Max. Depth on Ground	Snow, Sleet Date	No. of Days .10 or More	No. of Days .50 or More	No. of Days 1.00 or More
OCTOBER 1956																							
)ORT CLINTON	66.1	38.5	52.3	- 1.8	80	15+	24	11	385	0	0	9	0										
JANUARY 1957																							
;RATERFORD	37.8	18.9	28.4		60	23	- 8	17	1134	0	6	29	4	1.84	- .46	.78	23	6.3	1	7+	6	1	0
MARCH 1957																							
ARTEMAS 1 WNW	52.2	31.0	41.6		70	13+	14	4	720	0	0	20	0										

DAILY PRECIPITATION

'able 3

Station	Day of month 1	2	3	4	5	6	7	8	9	10	11	12	13	14	15	16	17	18	19	20	21	22	23	24	25	26	27	28	29	30	31	Total
OCTOBER 1956																																
'ALMYRA				.57		.30												.08				.35	1.76			.03	.26			.02	.37	3.74
'ORT CLINTON	-	-	-	-	-	-	-	-	-	-	-	-	-	-	-	-	-	-	-	-	-	-	-	-	-	-	-	-	-	-	-	-
NOVEMBER 1956																																
.YNDELL 2 NW	-	-	-	-	-	-	-	-	-	-	-	-	-	-				.88				.44				.26				-		-
'ALMYRA	.05	.71	.43					.04				T				T	.10	.43				.43			T	.34						2.53
DECEMBER 1956																																
'ALMYRA		T				T		.20	.89			.10	.14	1.38	.04	.50					T	.59	.08	.21	.08		.05	T				4.26
JANUARY 1957																																
;IFFORD	.17	T	T	T	T		T	.10	.08	.59			.15			T	T		.07		T	T	1.10						.50	.05		2.81
'ALMYRA						T	.12		.10	.50				.05	T	.05		T				T	.50		T		.07	T	T		.39	1.78
MARCH 1957																																
.RTEMAS 1 WNW		.40					-	-				-			-				-	-		-	-			-	-		-			-
;IFFORD	.22	.07	.12				.17	.18	.76	T	T	.10			.05	.08				.04	.02					.20	.12		.10	.14		2.37

OCTOBER 1956

PORT CLINTON

JANUARY 1957

GRATERFORD

MARCH 1957

ARTEMAS 1 WNW

NEWBURG 3 W

CORRECTIONS

MONTH: NOVEMBER 1956 THRU MARCH 1957

Table 7: Shippingport WB	Name published as Shippensburg WB should be Shippingport WB.

MONTH: MAY 1957

Table 2, 3, 5: West Chester	Delete all data for these tables.

See reference notes following Station Index.

TOTAL PRECIPITATION

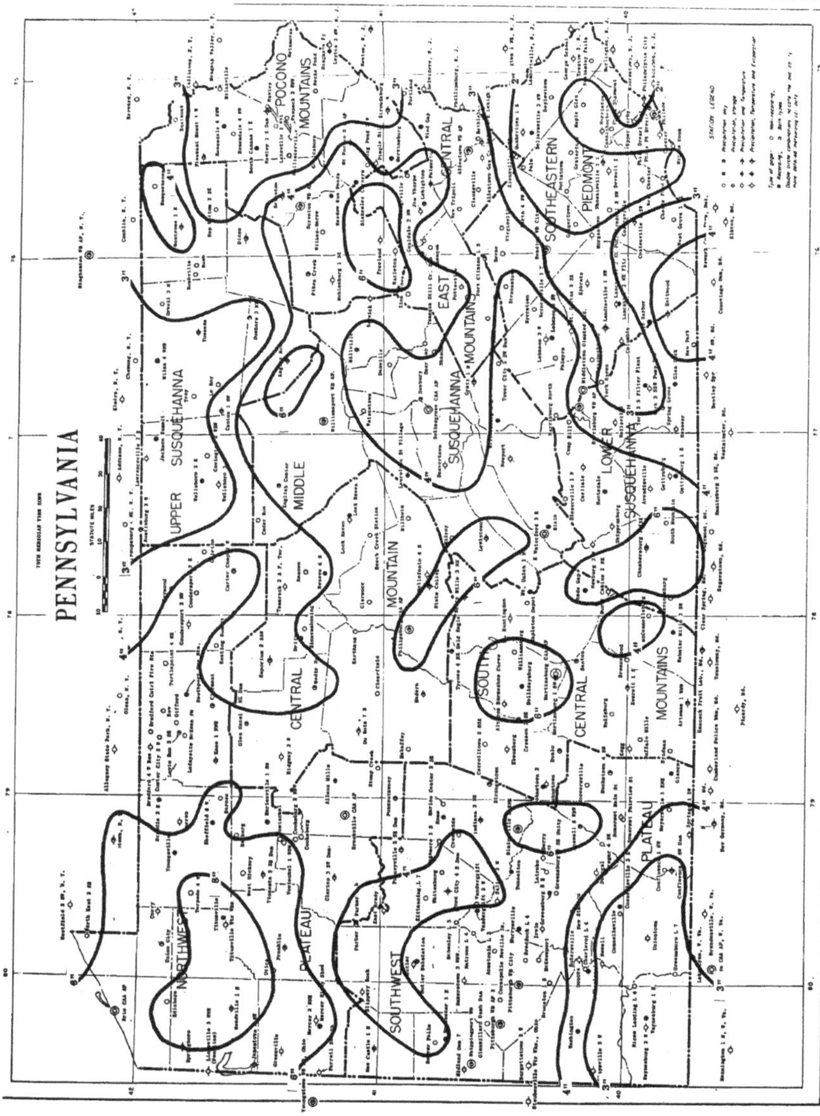

Isolines are drawn through points of approximately equal values. Hourly precipitation data from recorder substations will be available in the publication "Hourly Precipitation Data".

AVERAGE TEMPERATURE

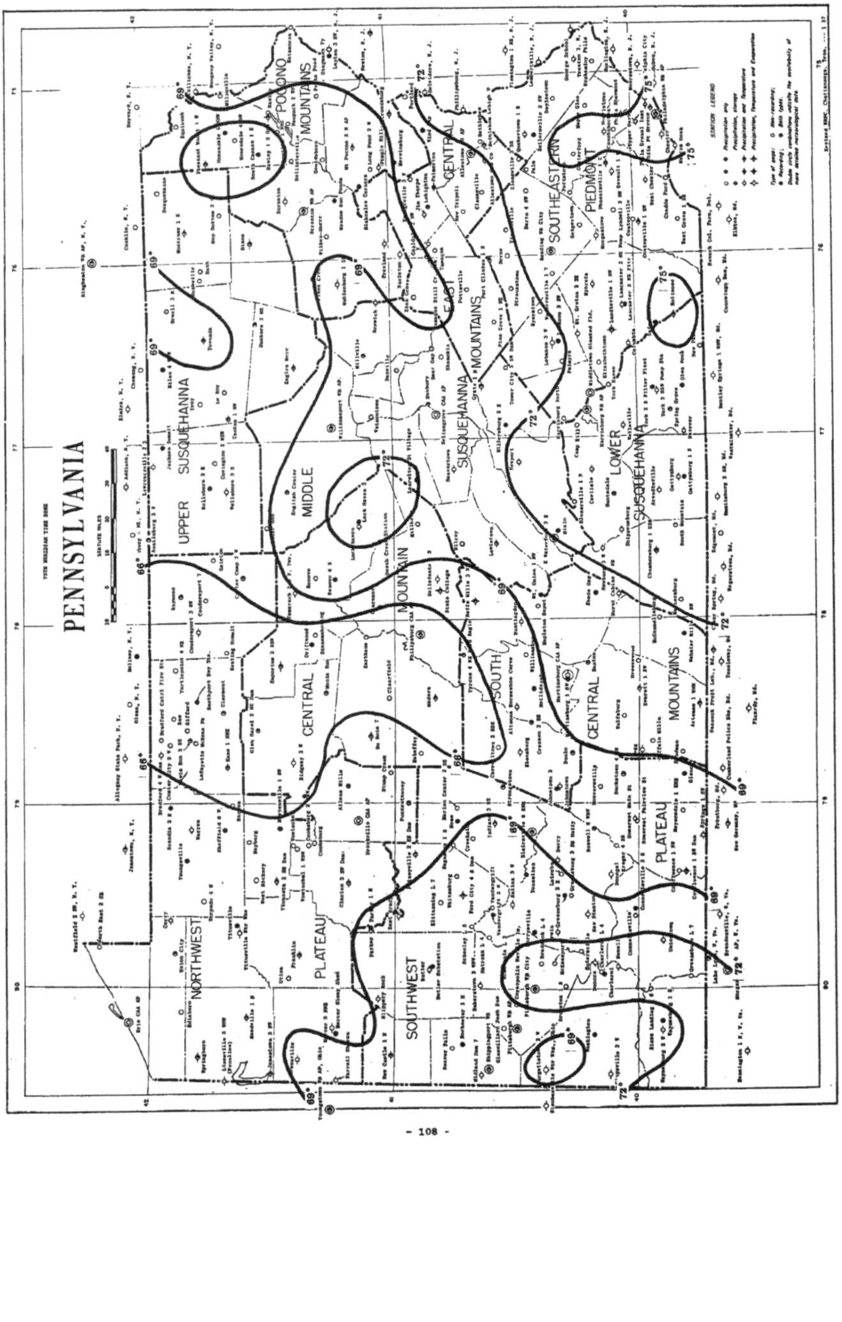

STATION INDEX

Index No.	County	Drainage [1]	Latitude	Longitude	Elevation	Observation Time Temp.	Observation Time Precip.	Observer	Refer To Tables
0022	ALLEGHENY	1	40 32	79 40	748		7A	CORPS OF ENGINEERS	3
0099	JEFFERSON	1	41 12	78 55	1660		MID	CHARLES M. ALLEN	C
0106	LEHIGH	9	40 36	75 26	376	MID	MID	U.S. WEATHER BUREAU	2 3 5 7 C
0111	LEHIGH	9	40 36	75 28	254	7A	7A	LEHIGH VLY GAS DIV	2 3 5
B 0134	BLAIR	6	40 30	78 29	1600	6P	6P	ALTOONA WATER BUR.	2 3 5
0229	ADAMS	15	39 55	77 10	710	8A	8A	PA STATE COL EXP	2 3 5
0259	BEDFORD	12	39 49	78 28	1290	6P	6P	GRAYSON E.NORTHCRAFT	2 3 5
0313	TIOGA	15	42 00	77 32	1500		7A	OTTO D. BACON	3 7 C
0355	ALLEGHENY	1	40 30	79 50	1250	7P	7P	PGH CUT FLOWER CO	2 3 5
0409	WARREN	1	41 40	79 02	1310		7A	CORPS OF ENGINEERS	3
0428	BERKS	14	40 26	75 30	312		7A	MARIE B. NICHLAS	3
0457	NORTHUMBLAND	15	40 50	76 50	900		3P	ROARING CRK WTR CO	3
0475	BEAVER	2	40 46	80 19	760		7A	HOWARD R. KEMP	3
0482	SNYDER	15	40 45	77 10	640	5P	7A	MARLIN R. ETTINGER	2 3 5
0499	CENTRE	16	41 04	77 34	620		7A	HAROLD S. RUPERT	3 7
0530	CENTRE	16	40 51	77 47	1110	6A	6A	ROCKVIEW PRISON FARM	2 3 5
0599	BERKS	14	40 31	76 00	325		7A	FLOYD W. TRUMP	3
0611	COLUMBIA	15	41 04	76 15	570	6P	6P	AMER CAR + FNDRY CO	2 3 5
0629	NORTHAMPTON	9	40 37	75 22	400		7A	ARTHUR CROPPER	3
0634	NORTHAMPTON	9	40 36	75 23	490	MID	MID	LEHIGH UNIVERSITY	2 3 5 C
0728	PERRY	15	40 28	77 31	750		MID	PA DEPT FRST + WTRS	C
0736	INDIANA	4	40 27	79 09	2048	8P	8P	U.S. WEATHER BUREAU	2 3 5
0763	MONROE	9	41 08	75 36	1480		MID	WALTER WILDRICK	C
0765	CUMBERLAND	15	40 14	77 22	650		5P	MRS. G. M. WILLDERS	3
0820	SOMERSET	1	40 10	79 08	2570		8A	CLARK M. ST. CLAIR	3 C
0861	ALLEGHENY	10	40 24	79 52	725		7A	CORPS OF ENGINEERS	3
A 0867	MC KEAN	1	41 57	78 38	1500		8A	BRADFORD FIRE DEPT	3
0868	MC KEAN	1	41 57	78 44	1680	5P	5P	BRADFORD WTR DEPT	2 3 5 7
0905	BEDFORD	6	40 00	78 14	1352		MID	PA TURNPIKE COMM	3
1002	JEFFERSON	1	41 00	79 06	1417	MID	MID	CIVIL AERO. ADM.	2 3 5 7
1033	ALLEGHENY	10	40 18	79 59	1065		7A	AUSTIN R. COOPER	3
1073	SOMERSET	4	40 04	78 50	2460		MID	ALVIN W. MANGES	C
1087	BEDFORD	6	39 57	78 30	2318		7A	MRS. NELLE R. BROWN	3
1105	WASHINGTON	11	40 23	80 26	980	7A	7A	SMITH TWP MUN AUTH	2 3 5
1115	HUNTINGDON	6	40 05	77 52	990	MID	MID	PA TURNPIKE COMM	2 3 5
1130	BUTLER	2	40 52	79 54	1100	6P	7A	WILLIAM C. FAUST	2 3 5
1135	BUTLER	2	40 51	79 53	1140		MID	WEST PENN POWER CO	C
1198	CUMBERLAND	15	40 15	76 55	461		6P	JOSEPH N. HOBART	3
1215	BRADFORD	15	41 40	76 52	1520	7A	7A	MRS.MILDRED SPENCER	2 3 5 7 C
1234	CUMBERLAND	15	40 12	77 11	460	6P	6P	C. E. MILLER	2 3 5
1255	CAMBRIA	16	40 35	78 42	2040		8A	ROBERT F. MAURER	3 7
1262	POTTER	16	41 37	77 45	2030		7A	RICHARD L. MENKEN	3 C
1301	LYCOMING	16	41 31	77 27	800		7A	KATHRYN T.KREIGHBAUM	3
1342	DELAWARE	5	39 52	75 38	180		8A	ALFRED C. WEEKS	3
1354	FRANKLIN	12	39 56	77 38	640	9P	9P	CHARLES A. BENDER	2 3 5 C
1372	WASHINGTON	10	40 08	79 55	1040		MID	WEST PENN POWER CO	C
1377	WESTMORELAND	10	40 00	79 54	740		7A	CORPS OF ENGINEERS	3
1423	DELAWARE	5	39 51	75 22	86	8A	8A	CHESTER TIMES	2 3 5
1480	CENTRE	16	41 05	77 56	1410		7A	MISS VELDA SWANCER	3
1485	CLARION	1	41 12	79 26	1134	8P	7A	PA ELECTRIC CO	2 3 5 C
1505	LEHIGH	9	40 37	75 30	670		8A	WILLIAM J. DOTTERER	3
1512	WASHINGTON	11	40 07	80 28	1000	7P	7A	MFGRS. L + H CO	2 3 5
1519	CLEARFIELD	16	41 01	78 26	1100		7A	IRA TAYLOR	3
1529	MC KEAN	1	41 41	78 30	2104		7A	MRS.TILLIE M.SIMONDS	3 C
1572	SCHUYLKILL	9	40 50	75 58	1026		7A	PANTHER VLY WTR CO	3 7
1589	CHESTER	5	39 58	75 50	342	8A	8A	PHILA ELECTRIC CO	2 3 5 C
1594	CHESTER	5	39 59	75 40	340		8A	EDWARD O. DIEDEMAN	INAC 12/55
1675	LANCASTER	15	40 02	76 30	300	SS	SS	JAMES H. RUST	2 3 5
1705	SOMERSET	17	39 48	79 22	1490	8A	8A	CORPS OF ENGINEERS	2 3 5 6 C
1710	FAYETTE	17	39 50	79 22	1381		7A	JOHN L. REID	3
1723	FAYETTE	17	40 01	79 36	870		8A	MARSHALL B. MENEFEE	3
1729	FAYETTE	17	40 01	79 33	1300		MID	HARRY C. JOY	C
1737	MONTGOMERY	5	40 04	75 19	70		8A	PHILA ELECTRIC CO	3
1749	CLARION	1	41 20	79 13	1180		8A	PA DEPT FRST + WTRS	3
1752	CLARION	1	41 21	79 13	1480		8A	PA DEPT FRST + WTRS	3
1773	ALLEGHENY	11	40 30	80 05	720		8A	PGH. COKE + CHEM CO	3
1790	ERIE	1	41 56	79 38	1427	7P	5A	LEO C. NECKERS	2 3 5 7
1806	POTTER	1	41 49	78 03	2020	7P	8A	MISS ELIZABETH NEFF	2 3 5
1809	POTTER	1	41 48	77 55	2425		7A	CAMP POTATO	3
1833	TIOGA	15	41 44	77 07	1745		7A	CALVIN R. PACKARD	3
1881	INDIANA	1	40 41	79 12	1035		7A	CORPS OF ENGINEERS	3
1895	CAMBRIA	8	40 27	78 34	2540		7A	MILES M. LINGLE	3 C
1978	MC KEAN	1	41 59	78 41	2120		8A	M. G. BOOTH AND CO	3
2013	MONTOUR	15	40 58	76 37	460		7A	MRS.MARIE M. LITTLE	3
2108	WESTMORELAND	4	40 20	79 18	1150	6P	6P	MISS N. G. WINEMAN	2 3 5
2116	CHESTER	14	40 05	75 33	360	MID	MID	PA TURNPIKE COMM	2 3 5
2160	PIKE	5	41 15	74 52	384		MID	CLYDE T. VOORHEES	C
2171	WYOMING	15	41 34	75 54	620	7A	7A	HAROLD J. KUSCHEL	2 3 5 C
2183	WESTMORELAND	17	40 07	79 23	1746	MID	MID	PA TURNPIKE COMM	2 3 5 7
2190	WASHINGTON	10	40 11	79 51	814	12M	12M	DONORA ZINC WORKS	2 3 5
2221	BUCKS	5	40 18	75 08	393		5P	GEORGE HART	3
2245	CAMERON	16	41 20	78 08	880		MID	SIDNEY KENNEDY	C
2265	CLEARFIELD	16	41 06	78 38	1670	5P	5P	CITY OF DU BOIS	2 3 5 7 C
2298	CAMBRIA	4	40 17	78 43	2410		MID	MRS. D. L. WHITE	C
2324	SULLIVAN	16	41 35	76 21	1750		7A	PATRICK P. RYAN	3 C
2343	SULLIVAN	16	41 24	76 35	2020	7A	7A	MRS.ELSIE P. BIGGER	2 3 5 C
2363	CLARION	1	40 58	79 37	820	5P	5P	A. G. KEMPEL	2 3 5
2450	PERRY	6	40 21	77 33	2125	8A	8A	U.S. WEATHER BUREAU	INAC 5/55
2466	CAMBRIA	4	40 29	78 43	2000	7P	7A	ROBERT A. VASSER	2 3 5
2514	ERIE	1	41 52	80 08	1220		8A	EDINBORO ST TCHR COL	3
2519	CRAWFORD	1	41 50	80 13	1325		8A	WILLIAM HAGER	3
2560	LANCASTER	15	40 09	76 37	466		6A	MASONIC HOME	3
2634	CAMERON	16	41 28	78 15	1735	7A	7A	JACKSON THOMAS	2 3 5 C
2644	LYCOMING	16	41 26	77 17	881		7A	WILLIAM SNDERS	3 7 C
2662	LANCASTER	15	40 11	76 10	465	6P	6P	STANLEY L.VON NEIDA	2 3 5
2671	WAYNE	5	41 51	75 13	910		7A	MRS. HENRIETTA MURRY	3
2682	ERIE	8	42 05	80 12	732	MID	MID	U. S. WEATHER BUREAU	2 3 5 7
2721	BEDFORD	6	40 00	78 23	1020	MID	MID	PA TURNPIKE COMM	2 3 5 7 C
2814	MERCER	2	41 14	80 30	865	7P	7P	SHARON STEEL CORP	2 3 5
2942	ARMSTRONG	1	40 48	79 30	950	8A	8A	CORPS OF ENGINEERS	2 3 5 6 7 C
3028	VENANGO	1	41 23	79 40	987	7P	7A	ROBERT D. RHOADS	2 3 5 C
3056	LUZERNE	15	41 01	75 54	1900	6P	8A	ANDREW B. EVANSHA	2 3 5
3130	POTTER	16	41 44	77 30	1325		7A	M. GALE LUSH	3 7
3189	BERKS	14	40 13	75 50	400		8A	WALTER C. WOLF	3
3200	BUCKS	5	40 13	74 56	135	7P	7P	GEORGE M. HART	2 3 5 7
3218	ADAMS	12	39 50	77 14	540	9A	9A	HUGH C. MC ILHENNY	2 3 5
3223	ADAMS	12	39 48	77 14	560		MID	NAT MILITARY PARK	C
3237	MC KEAN	1	41 51	78 36	2220		8A	SOUTH PENN OIL CO	3
3298	SOMERSET	12	39 49	78 51	1620		MID	MRS. MARY M.HARTMAN	C
3311	ELK	1	41 34	78 36	1725		8A	CORPS OF ENGINEERS	3 C
3330	YORK	15	39 48	76 44	420		MID	MRS.E.C.MC WILLIAMS	C
3343	ALLEGHENY	11	40 33	80 13	705		7A	CORPS OF ENGINEERS	3
3394	WAYNE	9	41 15	75 27	1400		7A	L. H. EILENBERGER	3
3435	MONTGOMERY	14	40 14	75 27	100	7A	7A	CLAUDE K. KULP	2 3 5 7 C
3438	DAUPHIN	15	40 38	76 43	760	8A	8A	LEE M. LEITZEL	2 3 5 C
3503	GREENE	10	39 47	79 55	880		7A	CORPS OF ENGINEERS	3 7
3515	WESTMORELAND	10	40 18	79 31	1225		MID	PA DEPT HIGHWAYS	C
3516	WESTMORELAND	10	40 17	79 30	1245		6P	WESTMORELAND WTR CO	3
3526	MERCER	2	41 24	80 23	1026	6P	6P	C. EARL MILLER	2 3 5
3662	YORK	15	39 46	76 59	600	8A	8A	HANOVER EVENING SUN	2 3 5 7
3699	YORK	15	40 13	76 51	355	MID	MID	U.S. WEATHER BUREAU	2 3 5 7 C
3704	DAUPHIN	15	40 18	76 54	323		9A	GEORGE S. BEAL	3
3758	WAYNE	5	41 29	75 10	880		7A	MRS. KATHERINE BATES	3
3761	WAYNE	5	41 28	75 11	1200	7A	7A	PA POWER + LIGHT CO	2 3 5 6 7 C
4001	BLAIR	6	40 26	78 24	980		MID	JOHN M. RINGLER	C
4008	WAYNE	5	41 25	75 26	1360		8A	PA POWER + LIGHT CO	3
4019	LANCASTER	15	39 58	76 20	187	MID	8A	PA POWER + LIGHT CO	2 3 5 7 C
4027	INDIANA	1	40 45	79 06	1220		MID	MRS. EDNA M. BUSH	C
4043	WAYNE	5	41 37	75 19	1410		9A	GEORGE C. WILLIAMS	3
4044	WAYNE	5	41 39	75 17	1050		MID	FRIEND E. WALTER	C

Station [1]	Index No.	County	Drainage [1]	Latitude	Longitude	Elevation	Observation Time Temp.	Observation Time Precip.	Observer	Refer To Tables
HOOVERSVILLE	4058	SOMERSET	4	40 09	78 55	1660		7A	PA ELECTRIC CO	3 7
HOP BOTTOM 2 SE	4066	SUSQUEHANNA	15	41 43	75 43	900		7A	JOSEPH J. SANSUSKAS	3
HUNTINGDON	4159	HUNTINGDON	6	40 30	78 01	678	7A	7A	DANIEL I. GROVE	2 3 5
HUNTSDALE	4166	CUMBERLAND	15	40 06	77 18	610		8A	METRO P. DOROSH	3 C
HYNDMAN	4190	BEDFORD	12	39 49	78 43	920		8A	MRS.GERTRUDE M.BURTO	3
INDIANA 3 SE	4214	INDIANA	4	40 36	79 07	1102	7P	7A	CLYMER WATER SVC CO	2 3 5 7 C
IRWIN	4276	WESTMORELAND	10	40 20	79 42	1100	5P	5P	WESTMORELAND WTR CO	2 3 5
JACKSON SUMMIT	4304	TIOGA	15	41 57	77 01	1690		MID	ARCHIE LAIN	C
JAMESTOWN 2 NW	4325	CRAWFORD	2	41 30	80 28	1050	8A	8A	PA DEPT FRST + WTRS	2 3 5 6 C
JIM THORPE	4370	CARBON	9	40 52	75 45	830	5P	5P	HENRY S. HAAK	2 3 5
#JOHNSTOWN	4385	CAMBRIA	4	40 20	78 55	1214	9A	9A	JOHNSTOWN TRIBUNE	2 3 5
JOHNSTOWN 2	4390	CAMBRIA	4	40 19	78 55	1275		MID	CITY OF JOHNSTOWN	C
KANE 1 NNE	4432	MC KEAN	1	41 41	78 48	1750	8A	8A	RUDOLPH A. ANDERSON	2 3 5 7 C
KARTHAUS	4450	CLEARFIELD	16	41 07	78 07	950		7A	JEROME S. HOWE	3
KEATING SUMMIT	4466	POTTER	16	41 41	78 11	1840		7A	EUGENE L. KREITNER	3 7
KEGG	4481	BEDFORD	6	39 59	78 43	1280	MID	MID	PA TURNPIKE COMM	2 3 5
KITTANNING LOCK 7	4611	ARMSTRONG	1	40 49	79 32	790		VAR	CORPS OF ENGINEERS	3
KREGAR 4 SE	4667	WESTMORELAND	17	40 06	79 14	2530		MID	PA TURNPIKE COMM	3
KRESGEVILLE 3 W	4672	CARBON	9	40 54	75 34	720		7A	CITY OF BETHLEHEM	3
LAFAYETTE MC KEAN PARK	4706	MC KEAN	1	41 46	78 40	2130		7A	ORIN A. BUTTERS	3
LAKEVILLE 1 NNE	4733	WAYNE	5	41 27	75 16	1440		8A	MRS. GLADYS REINEKE	3
LANCASTER 2 NE PUMP STA	4758	LANCASTER	15	40 03	76 17	255	6P	6P	LANCASTER WATER BUR	2 3 5 7
LANCASTER 2 NE FILT PL	4763	LANCASTER	15	40 03	76 17	270		MID	LANCASTER WATER BUR	C
LANDISVILLE 2 NW	4778	LANCASTER	15	40 07	76 26	360	8A	8A	PA STATE COLLEGE	2 3 5 6 C
LATROBE	4832	WESTMORELAND	4	40 19	79 23	1000		MID	WEST PENN POWER CO	INAC 6/56
LAURELTON STATE VILLAGE	4853	UNION	15	40 54	77 13	880		MID	PA DEPT OF WELFARE	C
LAWRENCEVILLE 2 S	4873	TIOGA	15	41 59	77 07	1000	7A	7A	HARRY P. HOWLAND	2 3 5 7
LEBANON 3 W	4891	LEBANON	15	40 20	76 29	460	7A	7A	LEON MILLER	2 3 5 7
LEBANON 3 SW	4896	LEBANON	15	40 19	76 28	490		MID	THOMAS DONNACHIE	C
LEHIGHTON	4934	CARBON	9	40 50	75 43	580		7A	GOODWIN S. DEFREHN	3 C
LE ROY	4972	BRADFORD	15	41 41	76 43	1040		6P	MRS.DIMMIS M.BAILEY	3
LEWIS RUN 3 SE	4984	MC KEAN	1	41 50	78 39	1740		7A	RUSSELL LINEMAN	3 C
LEWISTOWN	4992	MIFFLIN	6	40 35	77 35	480	7A	7A	AMERICAN VISCOSE CO	2 3 5 7 C
LINESVILLE 5 WNW	5050	CRAWFORD	2	41 41	80 31	1020	7P	8A	MISS RETTA M. CRUMB	2 3 5
LOCK HAVEN	5104	CLINTON	16	41 08	77 27	570	7P	7A	PETER L. STEVENSON	2 3 5
LOCK HAVEN 2	5109	CLINTON	16	41 08	77 27	630		MID	HUGH F. PARKER	C
LONG POND 2 W	5160	MONROE	9	41 03	75 30	1860		7A	THOMAS MECKES	3
LYNDELL 2 NW	5279	CHESTER	5	40 05	75 46	-		8A	MRS. DOROTHY MARPLE	3
MADERA	5336	CLEARFIELD	16	40 50	78 26	1460	7A	7A	MRS. JULIA J. SHOFF	2 3 5 C
MAHAFFEY	5342	CLEARFIELD	16	40 53	78 44	1280		7A	MISS ELLEN J. MILES	3
MAPLE GLEN	5368	MONTGOMERY	5	40 11	75 11	380		6P	FRANCES E.SCHEIBNER	3
MAPLETON DEPOT	5381	HUNTINGDON	6	40 24	77 56	580		7A	MRS. I. S. BUCHANAN	3
MARCUS HOOK	5390	DELAWARE	5	39 49	75 25	12	MID	MID	SUN OIL CO	2 3 5
MARIENVILLE 1 SW	5400	FOREST	1	41 27	79 09	1700		MID	ROY A. MARKER	C
MARION CENTER 2 SE	5408	INDIANA	1	40 45	79 02	1610		7A	CORPS OF ENGINEERS	3
MARTINSBURG 1 SW	5453	BLAIR	6	40 18	78 20	1360		MID	BLUE MT. CANNERIES	C
MARTINSBURG CAA AP	5454	BLAIR	6	40 18	78 19	1463	MID	MID	CIVIL AERO. ADM.	2 3 5 7
MATAMORAS	5470	PIKE	5	41 22	74 42	439		7A	HARRY BISLAND	3 7
MAYBURG	5490	FOREST	1	41 36	79 13	1150		7A	CORPS OF ENGINEERS	3
MC CONNELLSBURG	5526	FULTON	12	39 56	78 00	895		7A	MRS. HELEN M. SHIVES	3
MC KEESPORT	5573	ALLEGHENY	10	40 21	79 52	720		8A	NATIONAL TUBE CO	3
MEADOW RUN PONDS	5601	LUZERNE	15	41 13	75 40	1995		MID	GEORGE PEARAGE	C
MEADVILLE 1 S	5606	CRAWFORD	1	41 38	80 10	1065	8A	8A	CITY OF MEADVILLE	2 3 5 7 C
MEDIX RUN	5627	ELK	16	41 17	78 24	1100		7A	MRS.E. M. SNYDER	3 7 C
MERCER 2 NNE	5651	MERCER	2	41 15	80 13	1160	7P	7A	MRS. FRAN. STRUTHERS	2 3 5
MERCER HIWAY SHED	5654	MERCER	2	41 14	80 15	1250		MID	PA DEPT HIGHWAYS	C
MERCERSBURG	5662	FRANKLIN	12	39 50	77 54	605		8A	ROLLIN P. GILBERT	3
MERWINSBURG	5676	MONROE	9	40 58	75 28	970		MID	WILLIAM D. GOULD	C
MEYERSDALE 1 ENE	5685	SOMERSET	17	39 49	79 01	2290		8A	ARTHUR B. MC CARTER	3
MIDDLETOWN OLMSTED FLD	5703	DAUPHIN	15	40 11	76 46	303	MID	MID	U. S. AIR FORCE	2 3 5
MIDLAND DAM 7	5710	BEAVER	11	40 38	80 28	689	11P	7A	CORPS OF ENGINEERS	2 3 5
MILAN 4 WNW	5732	BRADFORD	15	41 56	76 35	1448		MID	CARL A. MORRIS	C
MILANVILLE	5738	WAYNE	5	41 40	75 04	760		8A	CHARLES W. DAVIS	3
MILLERSBURG 2 E	5775	DAUPHIN	15	40 32	76 56	560		MID	RUSSELL SHEPLEY	C
MILLHEIM	5790	CENTRE	15	40 54	77 29	1090		7A	NEVIN E. BOWERSOX	3
MILLVILLE 2 SW	5817	COLUMBIA	15	41 06	76 34	860		7A	KENNETH LEIGHOW	3 C
MILROY	5825	MIFFLIN	6	40 43	77 35	770		8A	THOMAS C. HARBESON	3
MONTROSE 1 E	5915	SUSQUEHANNA	15	41 50	75 51	1630	7A	7A	WILBER W. HOOPES,JR	2 3 5 7 C
MORGANTOWN	5956	BERKS	15	40 09	75 54	595	MID	MID	PA TURNPIKE COMM	2 3 5
MT GRETNA 2 SE	6028	LANCASTER	15	40 14	76 26	670	MID	MID	PA TURNPIKE COMM	2 3 5
MT POCONO 2 N AP	6055	MONROE	9	41 09	75 22	1915	5P	5P	H. JOHN DAVIS, JR.	2 3 5 C
MOUNT UNION 1 N	6067	MIFFLIN	6	40 24	77 53	820		MID	MT UNION WTR WORKS	C
MUHLENBURG 1 SE	6090	LUZERNE	15	41 13	76 08	1110	6P	6P	THEODORE J. SAMPSON	2 3 5 7
MURRYSVILLE	6111	WESTMORELAND	10	40 26	79 42	903		MID	DAVID C. SHAW	C
MYERSTOWN	6126	LEBANON	14	40 22	76 18	480		8A	MRS.KATHLEEN WANDELL	3
NATRONA LOCK 4	6151	ALLEGHENY	1	40 37	79 43	800		7A	CORPS OF ENGINEERS	3
NEFFS MILLS 3 NE	6174	HUNTINGDON	6	40 40	77 55	900		MID	PA STATE UNIVERSITY	C
NESHAMINY FALLS	6194	BUCKS	5	40 09	74 57	60		MID	PHILA SUB WATER CO	3
NEWBURG 3 W	6225	FRANKLIN	15	40 09	77 37	745	5P	5P	PA TURNPIKE COMM	2 3 5
NEW CASTLE 1 N	6233	LAWRENCE	2	41 01	80 22	825	5P	7A	BAXTER F. JOHNSON	2 3 5 C
NEWELL	6246	FAYETTE	10	40 05	79 54	805	12M	12M	GENERAL CHEMICAL CO	2 3 5
NEW PARK	6289	YORK	15	39 44	76 30	780		6P	CLINTON J. ALLEN	3
NEWPORT	6297	PERRY	6	40 29	77 08	400	7A	7A	MRS. FRANCES K. FRY	2 3 5 7
NEW STANTON	6310	WESTMORELAND	10	40 13	79 36	980	MID	MID	PA TURNPIKE COMM	2 3 5
NEW TRIPOLI	6326	LEHIGH	14	40 41	75 45	570		6P	FRED C. OSWALD	3
NORRISTOWN	6370	MONTGOMERY	14	40 07	75 21	75	MID	8A	GEORGE H. BOONE	2 3 5
NORTH EAST 2 SE	6396	ERIE	8	42 12	79 49	1060		9A	ELLSWORTH WEAVER	3
ORWELL 3 N	6621	BRADFORD	15	41 55	76 16	1620		8A	WILLIAM I. BROWN	3
PALM	6681	MONTGOMERY	14	40 26	75 32	385		6A	FRED C. ESCHBACH	3
#PALMERTON	6689	CARBON	9	40 48	75 37	435	MID	MID	NEW JERSEY ZINC CO	2 3 5 C
PARKER	6721	ARMSTRONG	1	41 05	79 41	1140		7A	LOUIS A. MALARKEY	3
PARKER 1 E	6724	CLARION	1	41 06	79 40	1100		MID	P. M. NEELY	C
PAUPACK 2 WNW	6762	PIKE	5	41 24	75 14	1360		8A	MISS L. VETTERLEIN	3
PECKS POND	6786	PIKE	5	41 17	75 06	1380		9A	MRS. CARRIE NESS	3
#PHIL DREXEL INST OF TEC	6879	PHILADELPHIA	14	39 57	75 11	30	MID	MID	FRANCIS K. DAVIS,JR	2 3 5
PHILADELPHIA WB AP	6889	PHILADELPHIA	5	39 53	75 14	13	MID	MID	U.S. WEATHER BUREAU	2 3 5 7 C
#PHILADELPHIA PT BREEZE	6899	PHILADELPHIA	5	39 55	75 12	32	MID	MID	ATLANTIC REFINING	2 3 5 C
PHILADELPHIA SHAWMONT	6904	PHILADELPHIA	5	40 02	75 15	70	7P	7P	SCHUYLKILL NAVIG CO	2 3 5
#PHILADELPHIA CITY	6909	PHILADELPHIA	5	39 57	75 09	26	9A	9A	USN HYDROGRAPHIC OFF	2 3 5 C
PHILIPSBURG CAA AP	6916	CENTRE	6	40 54	78 05	1918	MID	MID	CIVIL AERO. ADM.	2 3 5 7 C
PHOENIXVILLE 1 E	6927	CHESTER	14	40 07	75 30	105	6P	MID	PHILA SUB WATER CO	2 3 5 C
PIKES CREEK	6939	LUZERNE	15	41 18	76 08	1320		7A	HARRY SHELDON	3 C
PIMPLE HILL	6944	MONROE	9	41 02	75 30	2215	9A	9A	PA DEPT FRST + WTRS	2 3 5 6 7
PINE GROVE 1 NE	6954	SCHUYLKILL	15	40 34	76 22	535		8A	PA POWER + LIGHT CO	3
PITTSBURGH WB AP 2	6993	ALLEGHENY	11	40 30	80 13	1151	MID	MID	U.S. WEATHER BUREAU	2 3 5 7 C
#PITTSBURGH WB CITY	6997	ALLEGHENY	11	40 27	80 00	749	MID	MID	U.S. WEATHER BUREAU	2 3 5 C
PLEASANT MOUNT 1 W	7029	WAYNE	5	41 44	75 27	1800	8A	8A	PA FISH COMM	2 3 5 7 C
PORT CLINTON	7116	SCHUYLKILL	14	40 35	76 02	450	7A	7A	MRS. ADA E. RARICK	2 3 5 C
PORTLAND	7127	NORTHAMPTON	5	40 55	75 06	297		8A	JOINT BRIDGE COMM	INAC 1/56
POTTSVILLE	7161	SCHUYLKILL	14	40 42	76 11	690		8A	LLOYD E. HELLER	3
PUNXSUTAWNEY	7217	JEFFERSON	1	40 57	79 00	1298		MID	JOHN VOLANSKY	C
PUTNEYVILLE 2 SE DAM	7229	ARMSTRONG	1	40 55	79 17	1270	8A	8A	CORPS OF ENGINEERS	2 3 5 C
QUAKERTOWN 1 E	7239	BUCKS	5	40 26	75 20	490	5P	7A	DENNIS K. FLUCK	2 3 5
RAYMOND	7310	POTTER	15	41 52	77 52	2220		7A	MRS. RACHEL LANGAN	3 C
#READING WB CITY	7318	BERKS	14	40 20	75 58	266	MID	MID	U.S. WEATHER BUREAU	2 3 5 7 C
RENOVO	7409	CLINTON	16	41 20	77 46	660		7A	MRS. CAROLINE BAIRD	3
RENOVO 5 S	7410	CLINTON	16	41 14	77 46	2035		MID	C. F. BILLETTE	C
REW	7425	MC KEAN	1	41 54	78 32	2250		8A	HAROLD C. MEALY	3
RICES LANDING L 6	7443	GREENE	10	39 57	80 00	775		7A	CORPS OF ENGINEERS	3
RIDGWAY 3 W	7477	ELK	1	41 25	78 47	1420	7A	7A	BOROUGH OF RIDGWAY	2 3 5
ROCHESTER 1 N	7540	BEAVER	2	40 43	80 18	900		MID	DUQUESNE LIGHT CO	C
RUSH	7694	SUSQUEHANNA	15	41 47	76 03	1000		8A	MISS MAUDE MC CAIN	3
RUSHVILLE	7727	SUSQUEHANNA	15	41 47	76 07	870		7A	CARL KOPATZ	3
SAFE HARBOR	7732	LANCASTER	15	39 55	76 23	270		MID	S.H.WATER POWER CORP	C
SAGAMORE 1 S	7739	INDIANA	1	40 46	79 14	1320		7A	CORPS OF ENGINEERS	3
SALINA 3 W	7782	WESTMORELAND	7	40 31	79 33	1109	6P	6P	MUN AUTH WSTMRLD CO	2 3 5
SAXTON	7846	BEDFORD	6	40 12	78 15	780		8A	MRS.ALVERTA L.HOLMES	3 C
SCANDIA 2 E	7855	WARREN	1	41 55	79 01	2040		MID	DAVID R. ANDERSON	C
SCHENLEY LOCK 5	7863	ARMSTRONG	1	40 41	79 40	783		VAR	CORPS OF ENGINEERS	3
#SCRANTON	7902	LACKAWANNA	15	41 25	75 40	746	7A	7A	U.S. POST OFFICE	2 3 5

STATION INDEX

CONTINUED

Station	Index No.	County	Drainage ‡	Latitude	Longitude	Elevation	Observation Time Temp.	Observation Time Precip.	Observer	Refer To Tables
SCRANTON WB AIRPORT	7905	LUZERNE	15	41 20	75 44	956	MID	MID	U.S. WEATHER BUREAU	2 3 5 7 C
SELINSGROVE CAA AP	7931	SNYDER	15	40 49	76 52	437	MID	MID	CIVIL AERO. ADM.	2 3 5 7
SELLERSVILLE 2 NW	7938	BUCKS	5	40 23	75 20	530		MID	SELLERSVILLE WTR CO	C
SHADE GAP	7965	HUNTINGDON	6	40 11	77 52	1000		MID	MRS. HELEN H. PYLE	C
SHAMOKIN	7978	NORTHUMBLAND	15	40 48	76 33	770		8A	ROARING CRK WTR CO	3
SHEFFIELD 6 W	8026	WARREN	1	41 41	79 09	1940		MID	L. N. HANSON	C
SHIPPENSBURG	8073	FRANKLIN	15	40 03	77 32	709	4P	4P	KEITH B. ALLEN	2 3 5 7
SHIPPINGPORT WB	8078	BEAVER	11	40 37	80 26	740	MID	MID	U.S. WEATHER BUREAU	2 3 5 7 C
SINNEMAHONING	8145	CAMERON	16	41 19	78 05	790		7A	MRS.FRANCES CALDWELL	3
SLIPPERY ROCK	8184	BUTLER	2	41 04	80 03	1345	7P	7A	WALTER O. ALBERT	2 3 5 7
SMETHPORT HIGHWAY SHED	8190	MC KEAN	1	41 48	78 27	1510		MID	PA DEPT HIGHWAYS	C
SOMERSET FAIRVIEW ST	8244	SOMERSET	17	40 01	79 05	2140		7A	HOWARD G. PECK	3
SOMERSET MAIN ST	8249	SOMERSET	17	40 01	79 05	2150	6P	6P	DAVID L. GROVE	2 3 5
SOUTH CANAAN 1 NE	8275	WAYNE	5	41 31	75 24	1400		MID	EUGENE M. COOK	C
SOUTH MOUNTAIN	8308	FRANKLIN	12	39 51	77 30	1520		7A	PA DEPT OF HEALTH	3
SPRINGBORO	8359	CRAWFORD	6	41 48	80 23	900	8A	8A	SPRINGBORO BOROUGH	2 3 5 C
SPRING GROVE	8379	YORK	15	39 52	76 52	470		4P	P. H. GLATFELTER CO	3 C
SPRINGS 1 SW	8395	SOMERSET	17	39 44	79 10	2500	8P	8P	ALLEN E. YODER	2 3 5 7
#STATE COLLEGE	8449	CENTRE	16	40 48	77 52	1175	MID	MID	PA STATE COLLEGE	2 3 5 6 C G
STRAUSSTOWN	8570	BERKS	14	40 29	76 11	600		8A	JACOB KLAHR	3
STRONGSTOWN	8589	INDIANA	4	40 33	78 55	1880		MID	HARRY F. BENNETT	C
STROUDSBURG	8596	MONROE	5	40 59	75 12	480	11P	11P	WILLIAM HAGERTY	2 3 5 C
STUMP CREEK	8610	JEFFERSON	1	41 01	78 50	1320		7A	CORPS OF ENGINEERS	3
SUNBURY	8668	NORTHUMBLAND	15	40 51	76 48	440		7A	CHARLES W. BAYLER	3 C
SUSQUEHANNA	8692	SUSQUEHANNA	15	41 57	75 36	1020		7A	MRS. LAURA A.BENSON	3
SUTERSVILLE	8699	ALLEGHENY	17	40 14	79 48	765		7A	FRANK E. MARSH	3
TAMAQUA	8758	SCHUYLKILL	14	40 48	75 58	830		8A	MRS. MARY L.ROBERTS	3
TAMAQUA 4 N DAM	8763	SCHUYLKILL	14	40 51	75 59	1120		7A	PANTHER VLY WTR CO	3 C
TAMARACK 2 S FIRE TWR	8770	CLINTON	16	41 24	77 51	2220	7A	7A	JAMES E. SWARTZ	2 3 5 7
TIONESTA 2 SE DAM	8873	FOREST	1	41 29	79 26	1200	8A	8A	CORPS OF ENGINEERS	2 3 5 7 C
TITUSVILLE	8885	CRAWFORD	1	41 38	79 40	1550		MID	PA ELECTRIC CO	C
TITUSVILLE WATER WORKS	8888	CRAWFORD	1	41 38	79 42	1220	7P	7P	CITY OF TITUSVILLE	2 3 5
TORPEDO 4 W	8901	WARREN	1	41 47	79 32	1735		7A	MRS. LILY B. GARBER	3
TOWANDA	8905	BRADFORD	15	41 46	76 26	760	7P	7A	MRS. M. O. PARYS	2 3 5 7 C
TOWER CITY 5 SW	8910	DAUPHIN	15	40 31	76 37	745		6P	HARRISBURG WTR DEPT	3 7
TROY	8990	BRADFORD	15	41 47	76 47	1100		7A	JENNIE L. BALLARD	3
TUNNELTON	8989	INDIANA	4	40 27	79 23	890		MID	MRS. MARY E. WEIMER	C
TURTLEPOINT 4 NE	9002	MC KEAN	1	41 54	78 16	1040		7A	ROBERT D. STRAIT	3
TYRONE 4 NE BALD EAGLE	9024	BLAIR	6	40 43	78 12	1020		7A	FREDERICK L. FRIDAY	3 C
UNION CITY	9042	ERIE	1	41 54	79 50	1325		7A	FORREST M. BRALEY	3 C
UNIONTOWN	9050	FAYETTE	10	39 54	79 44	1040	10P	10P	WM. W. MARSTELLER	2 3 5
UPPER DARBY	9074	DELAWARE	5	39 58	75 18	222	7P	7P	PHIL. SUB.TRANS. CO	2 3 5
UTICA	9099	VENANGO	1	41 26	79 57	1030		7A	MRS.FLORENCE MILLER	3
VANDERGRIFT	9128	WESTMORELAND	7	40 36	79 33	800		7A	UNITED ENG+FNDRY CO	3
VANDERGRIFT 2 W	9133	WESTMORELAND	7	40 36	79 36	995		MID	EUGENE R. YOUNG	C
VIRGINVILLE	9196	BERKS	14	40 31	75 52	350		8A	MRS. MARY M. WRIGHT	3
VOWINCKEL	9206	CLARION	1	41 25	79 14	1620		8A	PA DEPT FRST + WTRS	3
VOWINCKEL 1 WSW	9209	CLARION	1	41 24	79 15	1610		8A	PA DEPT FRST + WTRS	3
WARREN	9298	WARREN	1	41 51	79 08	1280	7P	7A	GILBERT H. REIER	2 3 5
WASHINGTON	9312	WASHINGTON	11	40 11	80 14	1200		MID	PA DEPT HIGHWAYS	C
WATSONTOWN	9345	NORTHUMBLAND	16	41 05	76 52	490		9P	WILLIAM BIRD	3
WAYNESBURG 2 W	9362	GREENE	10	39 54	80 13	980	6P	7A	RALPH L. AMOS	2 3 5
WAYNESBURG 1 E	9367	GREENE	10	39 54	80 10	940		MID	SEWAGE DISPOSAL PLT	C
WEBSTER MILLS 3 SW	9380	FULTON	12	39 49	78 05	920		MID	WILLIAM D. COVER	C
WELLSBORO 3 S	9408	TIOGA	16	41 43	77 16	1920	7A	7A	MARION L. SHUMWAY	2 3 5
WELLSBORO 2 E	9412	TIOGA	16	41 45	77 16	1550		MID	MRS. IDA S. MAYNARD	C
WELLSVILLE	9420	YORK	15	40 03	76 57	500	5P	5P	D. D. HOOVER	2 3 5
WERNERSVILLE 1 W	9430	BERKS	14	40 20	76 06	405		8A	CHARLES A. GRUBER	3
WEST CHESTER	9464	CHESTER	5	39 58	75 36	440	8A	8A	DAILY LOCAL NEWS	2 3 5
WEST GROVE 1 E	9503	CHESTER	5	39 49	75 49	440		8A	CONARD-PYLE CO	3
WEST HICKORY	9507	FOREST	1	41 34	79 25	1090		8A	MRS.HELEN F.KINNEAR	3
WHITESBURG	9655	ARMSTRONG	1	40 45	79 24	1530		7A	CORPS OF ENGINEERS	3
WILKES-BARRE	9702	LAZERNE	15	41 15	75 52	610		7A	MRS. MARY G. MIRMAK	3
WILLIAMSBURG	9714	BLAIR	6	40 28	78 12	860		7A	MYRON K. BIDDLE	3
WILLIAMSPORT WB AP	9728	LYCOMING	16	41 15	76 55	527	MID	MID	U.S. WEATHER BUREAU	2 3 5 7 C
WIND GAP	9781	NORTHAMPTON	5	40 51	75 18	720		MID	OWEN R. PARRY	C
WOLFSBURG	9823	BEDFORD	6	40 03	78 32	1190		7A	WALTER C. RICE	3
YORK 3 SSW PUMP STA	9933	YORK	15	39 55	76 45	390	5P	5P	YORK WATER COMPANY	2 3 5
YORK 2 S FILTER PLANT	9938	YORK	15	39 56	76 44	640		MID	YORK WATER COMPANY	C
YORK HAVEN	9950	YORK	15	40 07	76 43	310		8A	METROPOL EDISON CO	3
YOUNGSVILLE	9966	WARREN	1	41 51	79 20	1225		MID	HENRY CARLETT	C
ZION GROVE	9990	SCHUYLKILL	15	40 54	76 13	940		7A	JAMES D. TEETER	3
ZIONSVILLE 3 SE	9995	LEHIGH	14	40 27	75 27	660		7A	LESLIE HOWATT	3

‡ 1-ALLEGHENY; 2-BEAVER; 3- 4-CONEMAUGH; 5-DELAWARE; 6-JUNIATA; 7-KISKIMINETAS; 8-LAKE ERIE; 9-LEHIGH; 10-MONONGAHELA; 11-OHIO; 12-POTOMAC; 13-LAKE ONTARIO; 14-SCHUYLKILL; 15-SUSQUEHANNA; 16-WEST BRANCH; 17-YOUGHIOGHENY

REFERENCE NOTES

Additional information regarding the climate of Pennsylvania may be obtained by writing to the State Climatologist at Weather Bureau Airport Station, Harrisburg State Airport, New Cumberland, Pennsylvania, or to any Weather Bureau Office near you.

Figures and letters following the station name, such as 12 SSW, indicate distance in miles and direction from the post office.

Delayed data and corrections will be carried only in the June and December issues of this bulletin.

Monthly and seasonal snowfall and heating degree days for the preceding 12 months will be carried in the June issue of this bulletin.

Stations appearing in the Index, but for which data are not listed in the tables, either are missing or were received too late to be included in this issue.

Divisions, as used in Table 2, became effective with data for September 1956.

Unless otherwise indicated, dimensional units used in this bulletin are: Temperature in °F, precipitation and evaporation in inches, and wind movement in miles. Monthly degree day totals are the sums of the negative departures of average daily temperatures from 65° F.

Evaporation is measured in the standard Weather Bureau type pan of 4 foot diameter unless otherwise shown by footnote following Table 6. Max and Min in Table 6 refer to extremes of temperature of water in pan as recorded during 24 hours ending at time of observation.

Long-term means for full-time stations (those shown in the Station Index as "U. S. Weather Bureau") are based on the period 1921-1950, adjusted to represent observations taken at the present location. Long-term means for all stations except full-time Weather Bureau stations are based on the period 1931-1955.

Water equivalent values published in Table 7 are the water equivalent of snow, sleet or ice on the ground. Samples for obtaining measurements are taken from different points for successive observations; consequently occasional drifting and other causes of local variability in the snowpack result in apparent inconsistencies in the record. Water equivalent of snow on the ground is measured at selected stations when two or more inches of snow are on the ground.

Entries of Snowfall in Tables 2 and 7, and in the seasonal snowfall table, include snow and sleet. Entries of snow on ground include snow, sleet and ice.

Data in Tables 3, 5, and 6 and snowfall in Table 7, when published, are for the 24 hours ending at time of observation. The Station Index lists observation times in the standard of time in local use. During the summer months some observers take the observations on daylight saving time.

Snow on ground in Table 7 is at observation time for all except Weather Bureau and CAA stations. For these stations snow on ground values are at 7:30 a.m., E.S.T.

- – No record in Tables 3, 6, 7 and the Station Index. No record in Tables 2 and 5, is indicated by no entry. Consult the annual issue of this publication for interpolated monthly precipitation totals.
- + And also on a later date or dates.
- ++ Fastest observed one minute wind speed. This station is not equipped with automatic wind instruments.
- * Amount included in following measurement, time distribution unknown.
- // Gage is equipped with a windshield.
- # Thermometers are generally exposed in a shelter located a few feet above sod-covered ground; however, the reference indicates that the thermometers are exposed in a shelter located on the roof of a building.
- AM Data based on observational day ending before noon.
- B Adjusted to a full month.
- C In the "Refer to Tables" column in the Station Index the letter "C" indicates recorder stations. These stations are processed for special purposes and are published later in "Hourly Precipitation Data".
- D Water equivalent of snowfall wholly or partly estimated, using a ratio of 1 inch water equivalent to every 10 inches of new snowfall.
- G In the "Refer to Tables" column in the Station Index the letter "G" indicates that soil temperatures are published.
- M One or more days of record missing; if average value is entered, less than 10 days record is missing. See Table 5 for detailed daily record. Degree day data, if carried for this station, have been adjusted to represent the value for a full month.
- R Amounts from recording gage (These amounts are essentially accurate but may vary slightly from the amounts to be published later in "Hourly Precipitation Data".)
- SS This entry in time of observation column in Station Index means observation made near sunset.
- T Trace, an amount too small to measure.
- V Includes total for previous month.
- VAR This entry in time of observation column in Station Index means variable.

Information concerning the history of changes in locations, elevations, exposure etc. of substations through 1955 may be found in the publication "Substation History" for this state, soon to be issued. That publication, when available, may be obtained from the Superintendent of Documents, Government Printing Office, Washington 25, D. C. at a price to be announced. Similar information for regular Weather Bureau stations may be found in the latest issues of Local Climatological Data, Annual for the respective stations, obtained as indicated above, price 15 cents.

Subscription Price: 20 cents per copy, monthly and annual; $2.50 per year. (Yearly subscription includes the Annual Summary). Checks, and money orders should be made payable to the Superintendent of Documents. Remittance and correspondence regarding subscriptions should be sent to the Superintendent of Documents, Government Printing Office, Washington 25, D. C.

WRPC., Asheville, N. C. — 8/14/57 — 1100

U. S. DEPARTMENT OF COMMERCE
SINCLAIR WEEKS, Secretary
WEATHER BUREAU
F. W. REICHELDERFER, Chief

CLIMATOLOGICAL DATA

PENNSYLVANIA

JULY 1957
Volume LXII No. 7

ASHEVILLE: 1957

GENERAL

Deficient precipitation was the major feature of this month's weather. Rainfall totals exceeded the long-term means at very few stations and deficiencies of more than three inches were common in the southeastern portion of the State. Pleasant Mount 1 W was far ahead as the wet spot with a total of 6.27 inches since the closest contender, Lawrenceville 2 S, accumulated only 4.62 inches. The greatest amount for one day was 2.71 inches at Pittsburgh WB AP 2 on the 8th. Philadelphia WB AP qualified as the driest spot with a total of only 0.64 inch while nine other stations reported totals of less than one inch.

Average temperatures were higher than the long-term mean in the extreme southeastern section and frequently a little lower than the long-term mean in other areas. Extreme temperatures ranged from 32° on the 2nd at Kane 1 NNE to 105° on the 21st at Phoenixville 1 E.

WEATHER DETAILS

Significantly cool weather around the 2nd-3rd, 10th-11th, 16th-17th, and 24th-25th was only partially offset by hot weather the 20th-22nd and 29th-31st. The frequency of thunderstorms was well below average and rains were mostly very light with the exception of a few locally heavy thundershowers. Scattered light showers provided some moisture the 3rd-4th; statewide rains the 8th-9th, 13th, and 23rd were mostly in the light to moderate category; and showers reached most areas during the three-day period ending the 29th. Philadelphia received some rain during each of the above periods but accumulated a total of only 0.64 inch which takes first place for

CLIMATOLOGICAL DATA

PENNSYLVANIA
JULY 1957

Temperature: Average Maximum	Average Minimum	Average	Departure From Long Term Means	Highest	Date	Lowest	Date	Degree Days	No. of Days Max 90° or Above	No. of Days Max 32° or Below	No. of Days Min 32° or Below	No. of Days Min 0° or Below	Precipitation: Total	Departure From Long Term Means	Greatest Day	Date	Snow, Sleet Total	Max Depth on Ground	Date	No. of Days .10 or More	.50 or More	1.00 or More
80.5	58.8M	69.7M	.4	91	21	46	2	16	1	0	0	0	1.17	- 4.36	.51	14	.0	0		4	1	0
79.2	53.2	66.2		90	21+	36	3	51	2	0	0	0	3.44		1.08	14	.0	0		6	4	1
78.9M	55.7M	67.3M	1.3	91	21	41	3	33	1	0	0	0	2.41	- 2.85	1.14	28	.0	0		5	2	1
84.0	57.1	70.6		95	21	45	3	11	5	0	0	0	1.76		.45	9	.0	0		5	0	0
77.9	56.8	67.4		91	22	44	2	44	1	0	0	0	1.55		.46	14	.0	0		6	0	0
		M								0	0	0	6.27	1.20			.0	0				
81.5	57.6	69.6	- 2.6	94	21	45	3	11	3	0	0	0	2.05	- 3.28	.84	28	.0	0		5	1	0
85.3	52.1	68.7	- 3.5	100	21	36	3	22	7	0	0	0	1.95	- 3.20	.65	28	.0	0		4	2	0
		68.5											2.58				.0					
86.2	61.0	73.6	- .5	100	21+	49	3	0	7	0	0	0	1.05	- 3.73	.33	28	.0	0		5	0	0
86.3	61.5	73.9	- .2	99	22+	50	3	0	10	0	0	0	1.29	- 3.48	.52	29	.0	0		3	1	0
87.4	61.6	74.5	- .5	101	21	48	3	0	12	0	0	0	1.12	- 3.57	.39	27	.0	0		4	0	0
85.6M	58.4M	72.0M	.1	96	21+	44	3	3	7	0	0	0	1.48	- 3.87	.71	13	.0	0		5	1	0
83.9	59.6	71.8	- 1.4	97	21	46	3	3	5	0	0	0	1.70	- 3.03	.53	28	.0	0		6	1	0
87.0	55.6	71.3	- 2.1	100	22	42	3	10	10	0	0	0	1.34	- 3.56	1.10	9	.0	0		2	1	1
		72.6											1.34				.0					
87.7	64.8	76.3		101	22	53	3	0	12	0	0	0	1.21		.64	29	.0	0		3	1	0
86.9	60.2	73.6	- 1.2	99	22+	46	3	1	9	0	0	0	1.31	- 3.35	.67	9	.0	0		3	1	0
88.9	62.4	75.7		101	21	51	3	0	15	0	0	0	1.73		.98	9	.0	0		2	2	0
	62.8M	M				53	16				0	0	1.09		.39	23	.0	0		4	0	0
87.7	61.4	74.6	- .4	99	21+	49	3	0	10	0	0	0	.92	- 3.75	.50	9	.0	0		2	1	0
87.7	60.4	74.1	- .1	103	21	46	3	4	9	0	0	0	1.11	- 3.64	.77	9	.0	0		3	1	0
91.5	63.3	77.4		102	21+	52	3	0	23	0	0	0	3.62	- 1.37	2.57	29	.0	0		4	2	1
85.7	66.8	76.3	- .7	96	21+	57	3	0	7	0	0	0	1.25	- 2.64	.59	9	.0	0		3	1	0
87.4	59.7	73.6	- .4	98	21	49	3	0	8	0	0	0	2.13	- 2.24	1.24	23	.0	0		2	2	1
85.9	60.4	73.2		99	22	47	3	3	7	0	0	0	1.53		.83	24	.0	0		2	2	0
85.8	59.4	72.6	- 1.7	99	22+	49	3	2	6	0	0	0	1.30	- 3.25	.65	24	.0	0		3	2	0
89.3	69.1	79.2	.2	103	21+	60	2	0	14	0	0	0	1.13	- 3.09	.45	28	.0	0		4	0	0
87.4	65.7	76.6	1.5	99	21	54	3	0	10	0	0	0	1.29	- 2.44	.86	23	.0	0		2	1	0
85.6	60.7	73.2		98	21	48	3	0	6	0	0	0	1.03		.36	23	.0	0		4	0	0
85.5	63.5	74.5		98	21	48	16	0	6	0	0	0	1.14		.60	23	.0	0		3	1	0
88.5	65.3	76.9		103	21	53	3	0	13	0	0	0	1.48		.48	9	.0	0		4	0	0
89.6	68.4	79.0		102	22	57	2	0	14	0	0	0	.93		.45	28	.0	0		2	0	0
87.9	65.2	76.6	.3	101	21	54	3	0	11	0	0	0	.64	- 3.56	.17	9+	.0	0		3	0	0
88.8	69.9	79.4	2.0	102	21	62	3	0	16	0	0	0	.77		.19	28	.0	0		4	0	0
87.1	69.9	78.5	1.3	98	21+	62	2+	0	8	0	0	0	.95	- 3.26	.27	28				5	0	0
91.1	60.6	75.9	.2	105	21	45	3	0	20	0	0	0	1.26	- 3.56	.44	23	.0	0		5	0	0
87.8	59.6	73.7	1.0	98	21+	44	3	0	9	0	0	0	2.17	- 2.79	.75	14	.0	0		4	3	0
87.4	66.0	76.7	1.0	99	21	54	3	0	10	0	0	0	1.36	- 3.07	.48	9	.0	0		4	0	0
88.3M	65.7M	77.0M		102	21	53	3	0	12	0	0	0	1.30		.47	8	.0	0		5	0	0
91.1M	65.7M	78.4M	4.0	104	21			0	16	0	0	0					.0	0				
		76.1											1.36				.0					
85.9	60.2	73.1	- 1.2	98	22	50	2	1	7	0	0	0	2.42	- 1.54	.95	24	.0	0		4	2	0
89.0	63.6	76.3	1.3	100	21	54	2	0	13	0	0	0	2.05	- 1.95	.98	9	.0	0		2	2	0
86.5	59.4	73.0	- 1.7	98	22	48	2	1	9	0	0	0	2.24	- 1.52	.91	9	.0	0		4	2	0
86.8	62.6	74.7	.1	100	22	52	24	3	9	0	0	0	2.18	- 1.71	.99	24	.0	0		3	2	0
86.5	62.1	74.3	- 1.4	99	22	53	2	0	9	0	0	0	1.99	- 2.39	.81	9	.0	0		4	2	0
85.6	64.3	75.0	- .4	97	21+	53	3	0	5	0	0	0	1.68	- 1.96	1.23	23	.0	0		3	1	1
87.3M	59.5	73.4M		99	21	48	2	0	6	0	0	0	2.00		1.09	23	.0	0		3	2	1
86.6	60.9	73.8	- .9	97	21	51	3+	0	8	0	0	0	2.18	- 1.56	1.22	23	.0	0		2	2	1
87.5	58.4	73.0		99	21	46	3	1	9	0	0	0	2.19		1.22	23	.0	0		2	2	1
89.0	59.9	74.5	- .3	100	21+	47	2	1	15	0	0	0	1.59	- 2.66	.81	23	.0	0		3	2	0
		74.1											2.05				.0					
86.6	57.4	72.0		97	21+	47	3	2	7	0	0	0	1.61		.72	23	.0	0		4	1	0
87.8	59.6	73.7		99	21	48	3	0	10	0	0	0	1.38		.54	9	.0	0		3	1	0
85.0	58.5	71.8		99	22	46	3	2	5	0	0	0	1.10		.58	23	.0	0		3	1	0
85.9	58.2	72.1		98	22	51	2+	0	8	0	0	0	.90		.28	9	.0	0		4	0	0
87.1	58.3	72.7		100	21	49	2+	1	11	0	0	0	1.09	- 3.42	.41	9	.0	0		4	0	0
85.7	59.7	72.7	- .6	97	21+	49	3	0	10	0	0	0	1.65	- 2.06	.55	13	.0	0		3	1	0
		72.5											1.29				.0					
77.5	55.3	66.4		91	22	46	16	45	1	0	0	0	3.46		1.32	28	.0	0		6	3	1
82.6	53.9	68.3		94	22	40	2+	34	5	0	0	0	2.72		.45	14	.0	0		9	0	0
76.9	56.3	66.6		89	22	43	2	44	0	0	0	0	2.15	- 3.28	.55	14	.0	0		7	1	0
80.4	53.8	67.1	- 3.5	92	21+	39	2	46	2	0	0	0	4.62	.54	1.50	28	.0	0		7	4	1

See Reference Notes Following Station Index

TABLE 2 - CONTINUED

Station		
MONTROSE 1 E	AM	
TOWANDA		
WELLSBORO 3 S	AM	
DIVISION		
CENTRAL MOUNTAINS		
BELLEFONTE 4 S	AM	
DU BOIS 7 E		
EMPORIUM 2 SSW	AM	
LOCK HAVEN		
MADERA	AM	
PHILIPSBURG CAA AP		78.9
RIDGWAY 3 W	AM	79.9
STATE COLLEGE	AM	82.3
TAMARACK 2 S FIRE TWR	AM	
DIVISION		
SOUTH CENTRAL MOUNTAINS		
ALTOONA HORSESHOE CURVE		81.7
BURNT CABINS 2 NE		
EBENSBURG		79.2
EVERETT 1 SW		85.5
HUNTINGDON	AM	85.4M
JOHNSTOWN	AM	86.5
KEGG		84.4
MARTINSBURG CAA AP		90.5
DIVISION		
SOUTHWEST PLATEAU		
BAKERSTOWN 3 WNW		85.2
BLAIRSVILLE 6 ENE		79.1
BURGETTSTOWN 2 W	AM	82.7
BUTLER		83.7
CLAYSVILLE 3 W		85.7
CONFLUENCE 1 SW DAM	AM	82.5
DERRY		83.4
DONEGAL		79.8
DONORA	AM	87.8
FORD CITY 4 S DAM	AM	83.0
INDIANA 3 SE		83.1
IRWIN		
MIDLAND DAM 7		82.5
NEW CASTLE 1 N		84.3
NEWELL	AM	86.3
NEW STANTON		85.8
PITTSBURGH WB AP 2	//R	81.6
PITTSBURGH WB CITY	R	84.7
PUTNEYVILLE 2 SE DAM	AM	82.7
SALINA 3 W		83.7
SHIPPINGPORT WB		81.9
SLIPPERY ROCK		83.2
SOMERSET MAIN ST		81.2
SPRINGS 1 SW		79.1
UNIONTOWN		85.1
WAYNESBURG 2 W		86.0
DIVISION		
NORTHWEST PLATEAU		
BRADFORD CAA AIRPORT		75.7
BRADFORD 4 W RES		78.2
BROOKVILLE CAA AIRPORT		80.5
CLARION 3 SW		82.2
CORRY		80.4
COUDERSPORT 3 NW		76.8
EAST BRADY		86.1
ERIE WB AIRPORT		77.8
FARRELL SHARON		85.6
FRANKLIN		82.4
GREENVILLE		85.2
JAMESTOWN 2 NW	AM	80.6
KANE 1 NNE	AM	79.8
LINESVILLE 5 WNW		81.2
MEADVILLE 1 S	AM	79.8
MERCER 2 NNE		82.0
SPRINGBORO	AM	80.6
TIONESTA 2 SE DAM	AM	79.9
TITUSVILLE WATER WORKS		80.9
WARREN		81.2
DIVISION		

† DATA RECEIVED TOO LATE TO BE INCLUDED IN DIVISION AVERAGES

See Reference Notes Following Station Index

DAILY PRECIPITATION

PENNSYLVANIA
JULY 1957

Day of month

	Total	1	2	3	4	5	6	7	8	9	10	11	12	13	14	15	16	17	18	19	20	21	22	23	24	25	26	27	28	29	30	31
	2.44	.10				.11		1.02		.86					.01									.12	.11							.01
R	1.05					.02			.18	.09				.14	T								T	.16					.33	.11	T	
	1.29	.07				.02				.23				.07	.06									.09	.05					.52	.18	T
&	1.80								.01	1.33			.13											.33								
	2.42							.09		.86														.06	.93				.35		.15	
	2.60				1.10	.43		T		.20					.31								.14	.27					.15			
	3.42					1.85	.82															.10		.44				.03			T	.18
	3.00				.06	2.00		T		.37			T	T	T									.41								1.05
	–									.23				.13									.07		–				1.63	T		
	1.49	.05							.12	.40				.19										.64								
	2.50				T	.15		.49		1.37	T		T	T	.09	T							.03	.42	.12				T			
	1.61	.40			.04					.22					.07									.72	.11				T		.05	
	2.19				.02	.08				.92				.03	.46									.65	T				.03			
	2.84				.04	.06				.07					.74									1.60						.33		
	1.12					T				.79														.22	.11							
	1.38				.03	.02		T	.08	.84				.34	.04									.35					T		T	
	1.08	T				T				.21	T			.02	.03									.10	.04					.37	.31	
	1.12								.09	.21				.02										.16				.39	.25			
	1.54					.04	T	.59	.03	.65				T										.21								T
	1.08								T	.85					.07														.04	T		T
	3.17	.27				.01	.02	.41		.57	.02		.12										.10	.22	.48			.87	.03			.05
	2.98	.13			T	.12		.53		1.76					T									.06	.19			.19				T
	–	–	–	–	–	–	–	–	–	–	–	–	–	–	–	–	–	–	–	–	–	–	–	–	–	–	–	–	–	–	–	–
A	3.12	.02			1.15	.87		.04		.36			.03	.05	.43	.02							.06	.05								.04
	3.40			.04	.85	.80	.08	.19	.13	.38		.01	.09	.58								.04	.03	.05								.18
	2.59							.22	.18	.50														.86				.11		.68		
	1.97				.03	.19	.02		.08				T	.49								.27	.39	.39				.11			T	T
	4.20	.70				.05	*	*	.13	2.10	.42					.02								.28	.17							.33
	1.50	.02						.22		.45														.23	.27				.23		.08	
	2.39	.02				.09		.33		1.21	.27		.04	.02	.04									.27	.06							
		RECORD MISSING																														
	2.02					.27		T		1.20				.01	T									.30				.02				.22
	1.92								.12	.43					.06									.91					T			
	3.46				.25	.58				.25					.67								.08	.31					1.32			
	2.05								.03	.98				.01	.05									.95					.03			
	3.11	.02			.01	.08		T		2.55	.04		.01		.01									.34	.03				.01			.01
	3.30				.14	.34		T		.50					.82								.16	.17					.85	.32		T
	2.81				.15	.50	T	T		.55					.70	T								.21					.70			
	1.88		T						T		T			.70										.58	.60				T			
	2.24					T		.19	.05	.91			.05	T								T		.74				.28				.02
	2.98	.01			T	T		.09		1.82	.14												.23	.18	.21							.30
	1.21									.38			T												.19					.64		
	2.23	.02			.33	.13	.29			.20					.80									.50								
	2.84					.80	.03	.02		.24			T		.21								1.04	.66								.04
	1.92	.08								.41				.06	.06									.14						1.12	.05	
	1.97					.02		.45		.30			.06		.02									.35	.28				.05			.44
	1.68	.06			T	.25	T	T		.08			T		.37								.02	.88	.02				T			T
	2.18				.36	.25		T		.43			T		.52								.36	.26					T			
	1.34					.05				.29					.34									.54	.09					.03		
	1.31					.03				.07					.20										.32					.09		
	1.73				T				.08	.98														.63	.04				T			
	4.46	T				T				1.92	.57					T							.34	.28	.95				.32			.08
	4.01	.09				.01	.01	.09		1.77	.55		.02										.03	.40	.90				.05			.13
	2.80	.02			T	T		.04		1.30													.35	.05	1.00							.04
	1.31	T								.41	.18		.02		T										.05					.58	T	.07
	2.87	T			.02	1.03	T	.08	T	.19	T		T	.03	.12	T							.47	.92	T							.01
	2.20	T			.02	1.10	T	.08	T	.27	T			.11	.05		T			T	T		.25	.30	T	T	T					.02
	2.82	T						.44		1.98			T		T									.17	.23							
	2.99				1.46	.34			.46	.05		T		.30									.38								T	
	3.75				.35	.65	.32	.25		.81			.01		.69	.04								.25				.36	.02			
	3.13				.38	.29	.02			.77			.02		1.18									.32				.07	.08			
	3.04				.37	.53	T			.10					1.00								.09	.94					.61			
	3.70	.10				.62		.03		2.35					.10									.50								
	2.05	.06						.09		1.00	.51				.02									.08	.22				.07			
	2.46				.46	.45		.01		.60			.06	.02	.51								.02	.23								.04
	1.24									.38					.35									.46	.05							
	2.10						.12	.73	.03	.91				T										.21					.10			
	1.09							T	.20	.31				T										.39					.19			
	2.72	.02			.23	T	.15		.08	.25				T	.45	.27							.43	.31					.11		.03	.39
	1.45				T	T	.11		.52	.14		T		T	T									.54				.09		.05		
	2.79	T			T		T	.08	.01	1.22	T	T	T	T	.01								T	.32	.18			T	T			.93
	.84									.62				T	T									.19					.03			T
	1.54				.04	.27	.02		.06	.03				.21	.09							.01		.85								
	1.89	T			.38	.02		T		.16					.56							.09		.38					.32			
	2.15	.01			.28	.10	.15	.02		.39					.55									.16					.49			
	1.14					.08		.02	.08	.49			.01	.04										.24							.18	
	2.40	.12				.09	T	T		1.20	.26				T								.14	.16	T				.34			
	2.16				.42	.35		.02	.01	.75			T	.13	.02									.46								
	1.69									.65															.98							
	3.73				.54	1.12		.17		.70			.03	.01	.29								.32	.39					.13			.03
	3.47				.12	.79		.30		.27					1.01									.26					.72			
	.92									.60														.40					.02			
	4.30	.33		.25	.12	.29	T			.44			.95	.87	.04									.35	.14			.09			.37	.06
	1.75			.15	.41	.42			.39			T		.10									.28	T							T	
	2.02									1.10	.12													.58				.22				
	1.88				.27	.12			.80	.16			.01	.05								.02		.45							.02	
	2.90					.46				1.83	T				.08									.48	.05							
	1.90					.52		.17		.83			T	.16	.08						.01			.37				T				.08
	1.17	T								.36				.10	.51									.18	.02							T
	4.61	.02			.29	.26	T	.07		.60					1.18	.14								.10				T	1.92			.01
	.86									.26															.33						.27	
	1.11									.77	.01			.11										.21					.01			
	2.18	.01						.02		.87														.08	.99				.06		.15	
	2.83				.64	T				1.40			T		.62									.17								
		RECORD MISSING																														
	2.83					.11		.34		1.54				.11	.02									.18	.39			.12				.02
	2.70	.04			.30	.04				.65				.03	.33									.18					.05	.95	.02	
	3.62									.57					.04									.23	.21					2.57		
	1.10	T			T	.07				.30														.58	.15							
	3.88	.02				.01		.51		.82	.50		.29											.25	1.27				.21			
	1.95					.03	.08	.42	.06	.89				.01	.04							T		.41				.04			T	
	1.51				T	.16	.01		.89	.03		.01	T	.17								.05	.03	.07							.09	
	1.99							.13		.81															.79						.26	
R	1.60					T			.28	.07				.10										1.23								
	1.59	.02								.59					.03									.46	.49							
	3.90	.18			.35	T	.01	T		.24				.41	1.20	T							T	.08					T	.27	1.24	.01
	3.44	.07			.58					.24				.40	1.08									.04						.52	.34	
	4.16				.27	T	T	T		.43	T			.29	.99								T	.12					.78		1.28	T
	1.25	T						T		.50			T												.47					.17		.02
	3.90	.06			.23	.03	.09			.36				1.28	.58									.22					.36		.87	.11
	2.17	.11					T	.34		.68	.05		.05		T								.01	.30	.19			.37	.07			.02
	3.04	.09						.35		.40	.36	.05	.02										.56	.77					.35		.05	.04
	1.31	.01								.37					.02								.34	.34	.19			.02		.02		
	2.14							.04		.84					.03										1.20				T			.03
	1.33	.08						.04		.17														.42	.44			.08	.05	.05		T

See Reference Notes Following Station Index

DAILY PRECIPITATION

Table 3—Continued

Station	Total	Day of month,																														
		1	2	3	4	5	6	7	8	9	10	11	12	13	14	15	16	17	18	19	20	21	22	23	24	25	26	27	28	29	30	31
INDIANA 3 SE	2.61	.17				.10		.04		1.86					.05									.26	.03				.10			
IRWIN	2.84								.50	1.61														.44								
JAMESTOWN 2 NW	2.60					.12		.07		1.16			T	.24										.30					.13	.26		[illegible]
JIM THORPE	1.48				.02					.22				.71										.12								T
JOHNSTOWN	1.98	.52				T		.30		.38	T			.02	T	.01							T	.08	.27							
KANE 1 NNE	1.46				.45	.08			.28			.03	.06	.28								T	.21								.07	
KARTHAUS	2.76				.11	.38	.07	T		.38					.30								T	.54	.09				.64			
KEATING SUMMIT	2.78	.04			.23	.30		.08		.50				.03	.61						T		.79	.20				.04	.61			
KEGG	1.59							.25	.20	.25			.02									T		.38				.48				
KITTANNING LOCK 7	2.19					.18		.03	.08	1.33				T	.12									.44								[illegible]
KREGAR 4 SE	1.64				T	.03	.30	.09	.13	.22				T	.82									.68				.17				
KRESGEVILLE 3 W	1.88	.03			.05	.07				.27				.04	.31								.07	.14					.03	.87		
LAFAYETTE MC KEAN PARK		RECORD MISSING																														
LAKEVILLE 1 NNE	3.54				.59		.09			.31			.22		.01									.12				.54		.32	.46	[illegible]
LANCASTER 2 NE PUMP STA	2.13								.06	.85														1.24								
LANDISVILLE 2 NW	1.53									.60														.01	.83							
LAWRENCEVILLE 2 S	4.62				.02	.68	.02			.34					.33								.16	.67					1.50			
LEBANON 3 W	1.30	.10					T			.52														.05	.65							
LEHIGHTON	1.43					.07				.17				.40										.50					.07	.20	.02	
LE ROY	2.95			.30		.51				.10				.41								.48		.34					.81			
LEWIS RUN 3 SE	2.34				.66	.35	.01	.06		.48			.83		.60									.23								
LEWISTOWN	.90	.12			T	.01				.28					.08									.17	.23			T	.01			T
LINESVILLE 5 WNW	1.82				.03	.04		T	T	1.31			.03	.20	T									.21								
LOCK HAVEN	3.09				.06	.19	.04	T		.51					1.37									.67	.02				.03			
LONG POND 2 W	2.01	T			.15	.05		T		.17	.01			.12	.46									.18	T				T	.87		
LYNDELL 2 NW	2.02									.66															1.34							
MADERA	1.63	.21				.30				.11			.02		.35									.58	.06							
MAHAFFEY	1.40	.16				.29				.18			T	T	.09								T	.06	.03							
MAPLE GLEN	1.62									.37				.01										.26					.90	T	.08	[illegible]
NAPLETON DEPOT	2.13	.03								1.08					.02								.28	.02	.38				T		.01	[illegible]
MARCUS HOOK	1.13				T	T		T	.10	.28				T										.30					.46			T
MARION CENTER 2 SE	3.59	.02				.61		.01		.66			.05		.20								1.47	.38	.02			.11	.06			T
MARTINSBURG CAA AP	2.77				T			.11	.48	1.37		.01		T										.56				.10		.01		[illegible]
MATAMORAS	4.18	.15			.39					.43				1.29	.77									.18						.64	.33	
MAYBURG	2.07				.10	.50		T		.05			T	T	.19								T	.38								[illegible]
MC CONNELLSBURG	2.28	.27				.05		.16		.86													.26		.56				.10		T	
MC KEESPORT	3.07	.21				.04		.74		1.70					T									.11	.24			.03	T			T
MEADVILLE 1 S	1.90				.51	.09		.06		.96	.01	T	T	.18	.03									.19								
MEDIX RUN	3.04	T			.04	.21	T	T		1.21			T		.30	T							T	1.00					T			[illegible]
MERCER 2 NNE	-				.18	.34		-		1.02				.04	.15									.15								[illegible]
MERCERSBURG	1.49	.01								.66													.09		.73							
MEYERSDALE	-	-	-	-	-	-	-	-	-	-	-	-	-	-	-	-	-	-	-	-	-	-	.02	.05	.63	-	-	-	2.16	.08	-	-
MEYERSDALE 1 ENE	-	.05						.08	.41				-	-	-	-							-	-	-				-	-		
MIDDLETOWN OLMSTED FLD	1.29				T				.36	.07				T										.86								T
MIDLAND DAM 7	3.20					.49		.20		1.83			.06	.07	T									.21	.34							
MILANVILLE	2.97	T			.47	.03	.03			.27				.86	.93									.05		T				.08	.29	
MILLHEIM	2.15				.12	.05		T		.33					.55									1.06	.04				T			
MILLVILLE 2 SW	1.44	T			.02	.04	T	.03		.92					.18									.22	.02				.01			
MILROY	1.08									.14					.04								.75	.08					.05		T	
MONTROSE 1 E	2.99	.02			.41	.27	.37	.18		.22				.46	.55								.19	.24					.09		.01	[illegible]
MORGANTOWN	1.03					T			.21	.28				.06										.36						.12		
MT GRETNA 2 SE	1.14								.13	.35				.06										.60								
MT POCONO 2 N AP	2.41				.08	.03		.01		.22				.30	.28								T	.15					1.14			
MUHLENBURG 1 SE	1.76				.13			.06	.01	.45				.36	.03									.27				.09	.36			
MYERSTOWN	.68									.27				.08										.16	.17							
NATRONA LOCK 4	1.79	.02				.36		.57		.66				T	.01									.03	.10			.04				T
NESHAMINY FALLS	.91					T		.12	.06	.30		T		.03										.37					.03			T
NEWBURG 3 W	2.00							.03	.03	.70														1.09				.03				[illegible]
NEW CASTLE 1 N	2.93				T	.53		.27		.86	T		.03	T	.11								T	.16	.06							[illegible]
NEWELL	1.33									.33													.02	.60	.15				.81			[illegible]
NEW PARK	2.11					T		T		.62														.39	.05				.71			[illegible]
NEWPORT	1.09	.03				.02				.41					T									.12	.35				T		.16	
NEW STANTON	2.17				T	.01	.19	.35	.45	.40				.09	.01									.40				.06	.01	.26	.29	
NEW TRIPOLI	1.18					.01			.02	.33				.12	.11									.30						.08	.02	[illegible]
NORRISTOWN	1.48									.48	.21				.03										.34						.06	
NORTH EAST 2 SE	2.27			T	.63	.91			T	.16			.01	.11	.04									.41					.03			T
ORWELL 3 N	2.76				.42	.46		.07	.22	.14				.18	.60								.24	.40	.02							
PALM	3.90									1.04					.82									.12	.15					1.80	.27	
PALMERTON	1.70				T	.11			.25	.05				.45	.03								T	.15					.53	.13		
PARKER	3.52					.45	T	.02	.04	.40			.09	T	.06									.39								2.
PAUPACK 2 WNW	4.47				.60					.36				.60	1.56	.01							T	.12					.73	.49		
PECKS POND	2.90	.60			.24	T				.41				.36	.55								T	.08					.45	.02	.19	
PHIL DREXEL INST OF TEC	.93					T		T	T	.33				.01										.05					.45			[illegible]
PHILADELPHIA WB AP R	.64				T	T		T	.12	.17				.01	T									.17	T				.09	T		[illegible]
PHILADELPHIA PT BREEZE	.77								.10	.17				.15										.09					.19			[illegible]
PHILADELPHIA CITY R	.95								.15	.15				.13										.07					.27			[illegible]
PHILIPSBURG CAA AP	2.98				T	.19	.01		.14	.02		T		.15								T	.20	.82				1.36	.19	T	.03	T
PHOENIXVILLE 1 E	1.26								.15	.25				.20										.44					.85			
PIKES CREEK	2.69				.20	.05			.31	.47					.34									.45					.40	.01	T	
PIMPLE HILL	1.59	.02			.11	.04		T		.20	T		.01	.13	.46									.17	T							
PINE GROVE 1 NE	1.11	T								.33					.03									.58	.17				T			
PITTSBURGH WB AP 2 //R	3.97				.04	.14	.41		2.71	.02		.09	.02	.07										.38			.13	T			T	
PITTSBURGH WB CITY R	2.83				.08	T	.30		1.85	.10		T		.03										.27							T	
PLEASANT MOUNT 1 W	6.27	.63			.33				.20	.28				[illegible]	2.06								T	.17					[illegible]	.32	1.78	[illegible]
PORT CLINTON	1.34									1.10				.03										.16	.05							
POTTSVILLE	1.47	.31			T	.04				.95			T	.06	.14	T								.32	.04						.01	[illegible]
PUTNEYVILLE 2 SE DAM	1.70					.25			.03	.72			.10	.02	.14								.15	.25	T					.60	T	
QUAKERTOWN 1 E	2.17										.86	T			.75									.06	.10				.15			
RAYMOND	2.96				.48	.50	.10			.24			.05		.78	.21								.47					T	.33	T	
READING WB CITY R	1.36					T			.06	.48		T		.27										.22								
RENOVO	2.10				.23	.21		T		.30	T		.04		.90									.31					.02			
REW	2.28				.62	.40		T		.35			.01	T	.48								.04	.16								
RICES LANDING L 6	2.38					T		.63		.48	.02													.57	.68							
RIDGWAY 3 W	2.79				.05	.93		.08		1.06			.02	.01	.16									.40					.01			[illegible]
RUSH	2.80	.14			.35	.51	.04	.88		.25				.15	.80	.09							.13	.34					.10			[illegible]
RUSHVILLE	2.80	.11			.28	.25	.30	.06		.25				.12	.85								.20	.34					.13			[illegible]
SAGAMORE 1 S	3.40					T				1.50					.10									1.80								T
SALINA 3 W	2.22				T	.08		.93	.11	.67					.01							T		.18				.20				[illegible]
SAXTON	1.76	.05						.18		.88	T													.14	.26			.20	.05		T	
SCHENLEY LOCK 5	2.59					.57		.04	.08	1.33				T	.15								.03	.37								
SCRANTON		RECORD MISSING																														
SCRANTON WB AIRPORT	2.05				.25	T	T	.13	.07	.09				.46	T							T	T	.16				T	.84	.02	.03	
SHAMOKIN	2.57	.42				.05				1.32					.05									.08	.04							T
SHIPPENSBURG	2.18							T	T	.91				T	T									1.22					.05			
SHIPPINGPORT WB	2.86				.30		.10		1.81	.83	.84	T		.02										.59							.17	
SINNEMAHONING	2.63	.02			.18	.25	.05	.03	.01	.35	T		T	T	.68								.25	.42					.36		T	[illegible]
SLIPPERY ROCK	2.25					.56		T		.99			.04		.06								.06	.14								[illegible]
SOMERSET FAIRVIEW ST	3.23	.43					T	.40		.40			.04			T							.02	.41	.35			.22	.96	T		
SOMERSET MAIN ST	2.49							.40		.38			.06											.74				.91				
SOUTH MOUNTAIN	2.97	.03						.16		1.13	.38		.05		.03									.09	1.13				.06			[illegible]
SPRINGBORO	1.20				.20	.10	T		.80	T			T	.10										T								
SPRING GROVE	1.36				T			.03		.68														.58	.09							
SPRINGS 1 SW	3.47							.03	.30	1.07			.03		.07									1.95	.02			T	T			
STATE COLLEGE	1.43				.01	.06	T	T		.09			T	T	.12									.99	.06			T	.18		T	
STRAUSSTOWN	.93									.38														.46	.09							

See Reference Notes Following Station Index

DAILY PRECIPITATION

Station	Total	1	2	3	4	5	6	7	8	9	10	11	12	13	14	15	16	17	18	19	20	21	22	23	24	25	26	27	28	29	30	31
														.40	.04							T		.11	T				.65	.52	T	
															.57								.02	.55								
															.16									.67	.06						T	
														1.34	.23	.01							.02	.49					.04		.63	
															.02									.21	.21							
																																.37
															.26									.40	.05				.03		.16	
														.08	.40									.41	.04							
														.07	.12								.04	.32								T
														.77			T		T			.04	T	.30			T				.13	
														.05	.15									.22								.32
														T	.47	.01							.27	.76					.13			.17
														T										.69								
														T	.47								.57	.60					1.07			.06
															.55								.03	.25				.	.09			
																							.13	.33	.12				.			
														.04	.13									.31	.02							.24
														T	.01									.88				.			T	.82
														.22										.13					.35			.13
														.26	.03									.18								.25
ERGRIFT															.12								T	.15	.07							
INVILLE														.06										T	.28							
NCKEL														.15	.03	T	T						.03	.38	T			T				
NCKEL 1 WSW														.15	.04		T			T	T		.03	.42	T			T				T
EN															.60									.45								.32
ONTOWN														.22	.26									.42					T			
ESBURG 2 W																	.							.48	1.20				.02			
SBORO 3 S															.89								.10	.18					.04			
SVILLE																								1.22								
ERSVILLE 1														.03										.14	.32							
CHESTER															.05										.22					.02		
GROVE 1 E														.02											.31				.11	.23		
HICKORY														.10										.20								.02
ESBURG														T										.44								T
ES BARRE														.05	.36									.44	T				.38	.02		
IAMSBURG															.05								.14	.21	.11							.03
IAMSPORT WB AP														.55									T	.41				.01	.08			
SBURG																							T	.49	.43				.17		.09	
3 SSW PUMP STA																								.81	.16				T			
HAVEN														.01	.01									.02	1.51							
GROVE																								.33	.05							
SVILLE 3 SE																									.11					.39		

SUPPLEMENTAL DATA

Station	Wind direction		Wind speed m. p. h.				Relative humidity averages - percent				Number of days with precipitation								
	Prevailing	Percent of time from prevailing	Average	Fastest mile	Direction of fastest mile	Date of fastest mile	1:00 a EST	7:00 a EST	1:00 p EST	7:00 p EST	Trace	.01-.09	.10-.49	.50-.99	1.00-1.99	2.00 and over	Total	Percent of possible sunshine	Average sky cover sunrise to sunset
NTOWN WB AIRPORT	WSW	15	8.7	-	-	-	76	78	45	51	3	2	5	0	0	0	10	-	5.1
WB AIRPORT	-	-	9.7	25++	S	8	-	-	-	-	3	0	6	0	0	0	9	-	5.3
ISBURG WB AIRPORT	WNW	16	6.1	24	W	5	67	72	45	48	1	1	2	0	1	0	5	75	5.8
ADELPHIA WB AIRPORT	WSW	17	8.9	28	NW	1	72	73	43	50	6	3	3	0	0	0	12	69	5.8
TSBURGH WB AIRPORT	WSW	21	8.2	27++	WSW	5	79	83	51	56	2	5	4	0	0	1	12	73	6.2
DING WB CITY	-	-	9.3	45	SE	29	-	-	-	-	4	1	4	0	0	0	9	70	5.5
NTON WB AIRPORT	WSW	13	8.6	30	W	5	75	77	47	55	6	4	4	1	0	0	15	62	5.8
PINGPORT WB	-	-	1.9	29%	SSW	30	-	-	-	-	1	3	3	1	1	0	9	-	-
IAMSPORT WB AIRPORT	-	-	-	-	-	-	-	85	46	55	2	6	2	1	0	0	11	-	5.8
ak Gust .																			

See Reference Notes Following Station Index

DAILY TEMPERATURES

Table 5

Station		1	2	3	4	5	6	7	8	9	10	11	12	13	14	15	16	17	18	19	20	21	22	23	24	25	26	27	28	29	30	31
ALLENTOWN WB AP	MAX	80	79	85	88	89	84	86	88	90	77	81	87	80	89	83	82	85	88	90	95	100	100	78	82	85	84	85	82	87	90	92
	MIN	58	52	49	67	65	57	60	60	68	60	55	62	63	68	59	55	54	57	59	62	66	73	64	56	55	59	62	67	66	64	69
ALLENTOWN GAS CO	MAX	82	79	79	88	91	89	85	87	90	90	76	80	87	82	88	83	81	85	90	90	95	99	99	78	82	82	85	88	85	90	90
	MIN	59	52	50	57	71	64	60	61	67	63	56	62	65	67	65	53	53	57	60	61	63	73	71	54	55	59	63	66	67	65	69
ALTOONA HORSESHOE CURVE	MAX	73	75	85	83	79	80	81	73	83	76	75	83	86	83	81	78	79	80	85	91	93	91	84	76	76	77	79	83	89	89	87
	MIN	54	43	49	66	67	50	58	59	66	50	53	61	65	65	61	49	51	54	56	60	62	70	65	50	48	54	58	57	61	62	66
ARENDTSVILLE	MAX	84	79	79	88	91	89	86	86	84	91	76	81	88	86	89	88	83	84	87	89	95	98	97	72	78	80	83	84	86	90	92
	MIN	55	50	51	62	69	54	61	60	65	60	52	64	67	68	64	52	55	60	58	57	63	74	68	58	56	57	57	60	62	62	65
BAKERSTOWN 3 WNW	MAX	76	78	88	87	84	85	84	84	82	78	76	88	86	84	83	80	89	92	92	91	94	92	84	77	80	80	88	90	91	90	88
	MIN	60	48	58	68	70	58	62	64	70	54	58	62	72	71	66	54	60	64	66	67	68	69	67	51	50	60	66	64	63	62	64
BEAVERTOWN	MAX	79	79	87	90	88	83	85	84	89	86	78	86	86	88	88	83	85	88	89	95	97	97	95	79	81	83	82	86	89	90	91
	MIN	57	48	47	63	71	49	55	56	62	59	50	60	64	64	61	48	50	51	56	56	62	69	66	50	48	51	61	61	63	60	62
BELLEFONTE 4 S	MAX	79	77	80	88	87	80	82	85	76	88	76	75	86	84	89	83	82	84	86	88	95	95	92	76	79	79	82	80	86	89	83
	MIN	57	48	50	56	70	57	55	56	61	54	54	62	60	65	62	49	57	52	56	56	60	58	60	49	48	56	57	59	61	60	65
BERWICK	MAX	82	79	87	91	90	85	86	85	89	89	79	85	85	88	88	81	83	88	90	96	99	98	93	80	83	86	88	88	93	94	93
	MIN	59	50	48	66	71	51	55	58	68	58	53	58	64	67	64	49	51	55	58	60	65	69	68	53	50	56	62	68	65	66	64
BETHLEHEM LEHIGH UNIV	MAX	79	80	89	91	88	84	88	91	91	75	80	86	80	90	83	83	86	91	92	96	101	100	77	81	89	90	89	87	86	92	93
	MIN	60	55	48	68	69	61	60	60	66	62	58	60	64	68	62	54	53	56	60	63	68	78	65	58	55	58	61	65	64	62	68
BLAIRSVILLE 6 ENE	MAX	69	73	81	80	73	76	75	70	78	68	70	81	82	81	78	78	82	85	87	89	89	89	70	73	75	79	83	84	87	86	82
	MIN	51	46	55	67	64	53	65	65	66	47	53	61	68	64	64	53	55	59	60	65	67	70	64	54	52	56	62	60	64	65	64
BRADFORD CAA AIRPORT	MAX	67	71	79	77	70	70	77	68	76	67	63	77	69	79	72	74	78	80	82	85	85	81	71	70	73	76	80	82	85	83	80
	MIN	44	35	44	62	52	50	53	53	53	49	49	49	63	64	48	41	48	48	52	56	45	63	51	45	43	54	59	55	58	57	59
BRADFORD 4 W RES	MAX	70	70	80	80	77	73	76	77	78	76	67	77	78	80	80	74	77	78	83	86	87	85	81	71	72	77	80	83	84	85	83
	MIN	52	35	41	62	60	44	49	49	62	48	43	56	61	59	59	38	45	42	50	52	50	60	59	40	40	49	56	51	53	52	55
BROOKVILLE CAA AIRPORT	MAX	72	75	84	81	77	75	80	73	80	70	70	81	79	84	78	79	82	85	88	91	93	87	74	75	77	80	84	87	88	83	85
	MIN	50	38	47	66	57	47	56	58	60	47	48	63	65	62	54	46	51	52	55	59	56	65	53	46	45	57	58	62	58	57	57
BURGETTSTOWN 2 W	MAX	80	75	78	86	84	80	82	83	75	84	74	75	86	81	84	80	81	84	88	89	91	94	92	75	76	77	79	85	88	89	89
	MIN	48	39	48	59	68	44	54	54	65	47	46	55	63	66	56	42	48	56	57	58	60	64	66	47	45	52	57	57	58	58	59
BURNT CABINS 2 NE	MAX																															
	MIN																															
BUTLER	MAX	78	76	79	84	84	80	84	82	78	82	73	86	88	88	84	79	84	87	88	90	91	93	90	77	77	79	81	88	88	90	87
	MIN	47	41	51	68	66	49	59	63	67	50	51	59	68	65	60	49	50	54	57	58	60	63	66	47	45	56	58	58	60	58	60
CANTON 1 NW	MAX	75	70	70	82	81	77	75	78	75	81	69	72	79	71	82	70	72	76	81	82	89	91	88	70	71	76	77	77	78	83	84
	MIN	53	47	48	53	63	51	53	55	57	49	50	51	55	62	60	46	47	51	56	60	63	66	64	49	50	54	55	59	62	62	62
CARLISLE	MAX	83	82	90	92	89	87	90	83	90	89	82	89	89	89	89	87	87	90	92	99	100	98	96	81	84	83	85	88	91	93	93
	MIN	66	54	55	71	73	61	66	63	67	63	56	67	69	69	67	57	57	62	60	61	67	75	71	57	55	60	63	62	64	65	68
CHAMBERSBURG 1 ESE	MAX	78	80	88	90	87	85	86	81	89	77	80	89	87	90	88	83	84	85	89	95	97	98	94	79	81	82	83	85	91	92	90
	MIN	60	48	49	65	72	53	62	58	65	62	51	65	66	66	61	50	54	60	55	59	62	70	67	54	49	56	57	58	62	62	64
CHESTER	MAX	85	80	81	81	93	92	88	86	90	91	80	84	89	86	90	88	85	90	90	91	96	101	100	80	83	85	85	82	86	89	92
	MIN	63	56	53	62	73	62	62	60	68	64	58	66	71	68	69	58	60	62	64	69	72	72	74	63	62	63	64	66	67	69	68
CLARION 3 SW	MAX	73	76	85	83	79	78	80	77	81	73	72	85	81	85	84	81	85	85	90	91	92	88	77	76	79	80	85	86	89	86	86
	MIN	47	40	49	62	66	45	56	58	67	47	48	60	64	63	58	46	51	53	54	59	54	64	64	47	45	55	56	59	58	59	60
CLAYSVILLE 3 W	MAX	78	80	86	85	80	83	85	83	87	81	77	89	85	88	85	85	89	91	93	95	95	94	86	79	80	81	88	81	89	88	90
	MIN	49	40	45	66	67	44	56	55	67	47	46	57	62	65	55	42	44	53	57	58	59	63	64	45	45	50	57	57	58	57	62
COATESVILLE 1 SW	MAX	83	79	82	87	92	90	85	87	88	90	78	81	88	87	89	87	85	88	90	90	94	99	99	76	81	84	83	87	85	89	92
	MIN	57	50	46	58	68	57	62	58	67	64	53	61	68	63	67	58	52	57	56	58	63	71	71	59	54	55	56	63	62	66	65
COLUMBIA	MAX	81	82	89	94	92	92	89	84	92	84	82	90	90	90	89	85	87	89	92	98	101	100	93	80	83	83	83	85	91	94	93
	MIN	61	56	51	65	63	62	66	62	67	63	57	66	66	68	66	53	56	60	59	61	66	73	67	57	58	59	63	64	65	65	68
CONFLUENCE 1 SW DAM	MAX	79	73	75	86	83	80	80	83	82	84	72	77	85	84	83	82	83	88	84	91	91	94	91	73	76	79	79	84	85	86	87
	MIN	58	45	47	57	62	47	57	53	58	53	48	51	61	65	60	49	50	57	58	59	55	58	63	50	49	50	57	56	61	60	59
CORRY	MAX	81	83	81	81	73	82	81	73	76	76	67	81	80	80	72	76	80	85	88	87	88	84	79	72	77	80	85	87	87	86	83
	MIN	57	48	59	58	60	53	48	57	66	48	50	58	64	59	58	41	46	47	54	55	54	66	61	43	43	55	57	52	55	55	58
COUDERSPORT 3 NW	MAX	69	72	82	78	74	74	72	68	78	69	70	78	70	80	72	74	78	80	83	88	87	83	75	70	74	76	75	82	84	83	83
	MIN	52	35	39	62	59	45	47	47	64	48	43	57	61	62	57	39	41	45	49	54	52	62	58	43	39	50	57	55	54	52	57
DERRY	MAX	74	77	87	87	83	80	81	77	82	75	75	85	85	85	82	79	86	85	89	91	93	94	79	77	79	82	85	88	88	87	89
	MIN	54	42	51	68	64	55	61	59	69	45	52	62	71	65	61	49	54	61	64	62	62	70	67	60	46	58	60	68	64	65	62
DEVAULT 1 W	MAX																															
	MIN	61	54	55	68	69	54	60	65	73	60	57	63	68	70	66	53	57	59	62	69		74		63	55	63	61	64	66	64	68
DIXON	MAX	81	74	75	86	87	84	83	83	84	87	71	78	70	79	87	75	76	82	87	87	93	94	92	76	76	81	83	84	85	90	90
	MIN	56	40	40	46	68	47	52	51	57	52	49	52	53	58	61	47	47	48	50	55	58	65	67	51	48	49	54	63	64	61	62
DONEGAL	MAX	68	70	80	88	74	75	88	70	77	86	70	81	80	89	76	78	81	82	86	86	92	86	72	70	78	86	80	90	90	85	80
	MIN	48	35	45	58	53	47	54	54	64	47	45	60	62	59	48	42	50	58	58	56	57	64	58	48	43	51	60	60	57	56	58
DONORA	MAX	84	79	85	89	87	83	85	89	83	88	78	88	92	87	89	86	87	90	93	96	97	98	98	78	81	84	85	89	91	90	94
	MIN	57	47	57	70	71	55	62	65	70	56	54	60	71	71	63	54	56	64	72	67	70	72	70	57	54	60	68	66	66	67	64
DU BOIS 7 E	MAX	72	74	83	83	77	77	79	78	80	78	72	80	80	83	82	77	80	80	84	91	90	89	88	74	75	75	79	82	88	87	84
	MIN	52	37	45	62	59	47	54	54	67	49	47	58	66	64	57	44	53	53	56	56	55	65	64	46	43	54	63	62	58	55	60
EAGLES MERE	MAX	74	72	71	79	79	76	76	78	75	82	68	72	78	74	81	71	71	78	82	82	87	89	87	70	70	74	76	70	76	81	84
	MIN	50	43	48	55	61	50	54	58	62	48	48	52	56	62	59	48	52	57	60	62	65	68	64	51	52	54	60	59	60	63	63
EAST BRADY	MAX	80	79	88	86	84	82	80	81	84	83	77	86	86	86	86	83	88	89	91	95	96	93	92	79	82	83	88	90	92	92	88
	MIN	53	44	52	66	69	50	60	61	69	53	51	61	67	67	62	51	54	55	61	63	62	68	68	52	50	57	61	63	62	60	64
EBENSBURG	MAX	72	70	81	80	77	77	78	72	79	79	71	79	83	86	78	75	77	78	83	88	88	87	87	71	73	78	80	80	84	83	82
	MIN	50	41	46	62	65	50	58	55	65	48	49	60	63	64	58	41	51	56	58	56	56	61	63	47	43	51	57	54	57	57	60
EMPORIUM 2 SSW	MAX	75	70	74	83	82	74	75	73	70	79	70	70	80	78	82	74	75	78	80	84	88	89	85	72	73	74	72	80	80	86	84
	MIN	52	35	41	53	64	45	49	51	56	50	45	55	60	62	60	42	47	49	52	58	56	59	63	46	41	48	55	58	57	57	58
EPHRATA	MAX	80	81	87	91	90	86	86	85	90	85	82	87	90	90	86	84	87	89	89	95	99	99	89	81	84	83	85	85	89	92	92
	MIN	60	52	49	65	74	58	63	60	65	60	54	63	66	67	65	51	56	58	60	61	66	72	68	56	55	56	60	64	65	67	67
ERIE WB AIRPORT	MAX	70	73	83	81	73	76	80	75	76	68	70	80	76	81	70	73	76	80	83	87	88	82	70	74	75	81	80	80	86	85	80
	MIN	58	45	60	67	62	60	60	67	60	58	58	61	65	63	52	49	52	58	65	62	67	68	61	53	52	62	61	59	62	64	63

See reference notes following Station Index.

DAILY TEMPERATURES

PENNSYLVANIA
JULY 1957

		Day Of Month																															
		1	2	3	4	5	6	7	8	9	10	11	12	13	14	15	16	17	18	19	20	21	22	23	24	25	26	27	28	29	30	31	Average
	MAX	82	78	88	86	85	86	84	78	76	82	76	84	78	89	88	84	86	84	94	94	104	98	76	82	84	84	88	87	90	90	88	85.5
	MIN	60	50	52	66	66	56	64	58	58	52	48	62	62	61	56	48	62	56	64	62	70	72	65	52	55	60	65	65	66	61	60	59.8
	MAX	81	81	92	84	80	82	85	83	84	80	80	90	85	89	84	82	87	90	91	92	92	93	85	78	79	80	83	88	93	92	88	85.6
	MIN	56	45	62	72	59	58	60	63	69	51	56	65	67	65	65	50	57	58	63	61	68	69	65	52	50	60	57	58	61	63	59	60.1
	MAX	80	75	77	87	84	79	81	82	75	83	74	76	85	84	84	80	81	84	86	89	92	93	92	77	76	80	82	86	86	90	90	83.0
	MIN	57	42	45	57	68	50	61	59	63	49	48	59	61	66	61	49	50	56	57	60	60	65	67	50	48	55	59	58	58	59	61	56.7
	MAX	78	73	77	84	82	78	80	81	76	80	77	82	85	78	85	80	81	85	86	90	91	92	89	79	78	80	79	84	86	91	87	82.4
	MIN	51	41	44	52	66	57	50	58	61	59	51	52	63	67	64	51	47	55	53	53	62	62	67	56	49	48	58	58	61	59	61	56.0
	MAX	74	71	80	82	79	78	89	80	80	80	75	78	73	80	79	74	78	83	82	88	91	89	86	78	77	77	79	78	82	87	87	80.5
	MIN	53	46	48	68	63	58	59	60	63	52	50	55	63	63	66	48	52	50	61	63	67	73	67	50		57	59	62	62	66	60	58.8
	MAX	78	76	80	84	92	88	85	86	89	85	82	86	87	88	89	84	88	91	90	92	103	102	95	82	85	85	86	85	88	93	95	87.7
	MIN	56	49	46	60	71	53	61	59	63	58	52	61	65	64	61	54	58	59	59	66	69	73	57	60	55	56	62	69	66	65	66	60.4
	MAX	83	79	81	88	90	89	86	89	84	92	78	81	90	88	91	89	85	87	87	89	97	100	99	72	79	81	82	84	86	90	95	86.8
	MIN	61	55	53	53	75	58	65	61	66	64	57	67	69	71	66	58	58	62	59	65	65	77	71	52	56	58	59	61	65	66	68	62.6
	MAX	91	88	92	90	91	94	93	93	91	88	92	92	90	90	88	88	90	92	94	94	102	102	96	88	92	93	89	88	86	90	90	91.5
	MIN	54	58	52	64	66	68	72	58	64	60	66	66	64	62	62	58	60	62	64	66	70	67	72	56	64	66	64	62	66	64	66	63.3
	MAX	80	78	79	84	89	86	84	84	81	88	78	79	87	86	87	82	82	85	88	89	96	99	98	75	79	81	82	82	85	90	93	85.0
	MIN	61	52	46	52	66	55	57	57	63	60	52	57	62	65	64	49	49	55	58	58	62	70	68	54	50	55	58	64	65	65	63	58.5
	MAX	76	81	85	83	80	81	85	79	84	82	76	88	85	88	88	83	89	90	92	94	93	91	79	78	81	83	86	90	92	91	88	85.2
	MIN	51	42	52	67	64	49	56	59	67	49	53	61	65	61	59	42	52	55	58	57	61	65	62	46	45	55	54	55	58	59	60	56.1
	MAX	81	79	81	88	89	89	85	87	84	90	79	80	87	90	90	87	85	85	88	90	95	99	98	76	81	82	84	85	86	90	93	86.5
	MIN	60	53	54	55	76	56	61	61	65	62	55	58	67	69	66	57	59	63	62	66	67	72	72	56	54	59	60	62	65	66	67	62.1
	MAX	78	79	86	89	86	84	86	83	88	77	79	87	86	87	84	83	87	89	89	95	97	97	79	78	82	82	83	85	89	91	90	85.6
	MIN	65	56	53	69	71	62	65	63	67	63	58	67	69	69	68	56	57	63	62	67	68	76	65	58	58	61	66	66	67	70	69	64.3
	MAX	76	70	70	83	83	80	78	81	84	82	67	74	79	70	82	71	72	80	85	84	90	90	89	76	75	78	80	83	76	82	86	79.2
	MIN	55	45	36	45	65	54	52	49	57	52	48	50	52	62	61	46	44	47	49	53	60	64	64	50	48	48	51	60	63	60	59	53.2
	MAX	77	79	89	88	87	84	86	86	90	75	77	86	90	87	85	82	85	87	91	95	96	96	77	81	82	82	87	82	89	91	89	85.7
	MIN	64	59	57	66	72	66	69	66	71	67	61	67	69	72	68	60	63	64	64	67	70	77	69	63	64	64	66	72	70	72	72	66.8
	MAX	83	78	80	90	90	85	84	87	76	88	78	78	88	86	88	87	83	86	86	90	95	96	95	76	79	80	82		86	89	92	85.4
	MIN	58	43	45	53	68	49	55	55	58	56	47	56	63	65	59	46	49	55	55	54	55	62	67	47	45	50	56		58	60	62	55.0
	MAX	75	77	85	83	78	80	81	75	83	75	75	85	85	86	81	81	84	85	90	92	94	91	80	78	80	81	83	87	90	90	87	83.1
	MIN	49	39	47	60	67	46	59	57	67	42	46	60	64	66	58	47	52	56	56	58	58	63	66	45	45	54	59	58	59	58	59	55.5
	MAX			80		79			73	82	84	79	88			88	83	86	91	91			94	94	78	81	83			90	91	92	
	MIN			44		66			54	69	53	52	62			61	51	54	61	64			62	67	51	49	57			57	66	61	
	MAX	77	72	77	84	82	76	79	82	76	80	71	73	84	75	83	73	79	82	85	87	91	92	88	75	73	78	81	84	86	87	86	80.6
	MIN	51	42	53	64	64	51	56	61	64	55	53	60	65	64	61	43	55	56	60	55	60	65	65	49	46	56	54	55	56	60	59	56.7
	MAX	79	78	82	90	88	83	84	86	87	87	77	85	84	86	85	79	84		87	93	96	96	96	78	82	82	85	83	86	90	90	85.6
	MIN	56	50	44		62	53	54	56	67	57	55	59	60	66	65	51	50		52	56	68	69	67	56	53	54	60	67	65	62		58.4
	MAX	80	76	80	90	88	84	85	83	79	87	75	79	89	90	89	89	88	90	90	84	98	98	96	75	80	85	84	89	90	95	96	86.5
	MIN	56	42	46	63	66	50	58	57	62	52	47	60	64	64	58	48	48	49	58	58	58	65	65	48	45	52	56	56	59	59	60	55.8
	MAX	74	70	83	81	74	75	78	80	78	80	69	71	84	81	84	74	80	81	86	89	89	85	85	73	73	75	79	82	88	86	86	79.8
	MIN	48	32	41	55	64	40	48	48	58	49	43	52	60	59	54	40	45	42	49	50	49	51	62	39	38	49	55	52	52	51	56	49.4
	MAX	80	78	87	86	82	82	85	81	87	75	79	87	88	87	85	86	83	82	90	95	96	94	71	80	79	80	81	84	88	90	88	84.4
	MIN	53	42	46	59	60	50	56	57	65	57	49	62	64	64	59	53	62	58	58	56	58	69	63	48	48	53	59	56	60	60	62	57.0
STA	MAX	80	82	89	91	92	87	86	84	90	86	80	87	87	89	86	85	87	88	86	95	98	97	93	80	83	81	84	90	87	89	89	87.4
	MIN	59	54	49	61	69	57	63	58	65	60	54	62	65	66	63	50	54	56	56	56	63	69	65	55	53	56	58	63	62	64	65	59.7
	MAX	80	78	79	87	92	89	85	85	84	89	78	81	86	89	89	84	82	86	89	91	95	99	98	73	78	80	83	85	85	90	93	85.9
	MIN	60	52	47	60	70	56	63	58	67	60	53	64	67	68	64	62	54	57	56	57	59	71	70	55	53	56	59	63	63	64	65	60.4
	MAX	77	72	74	82	84	80	78	82	79	83	69	73	81	84	85	74	73	79	85	87	92	92	88	71	73	76	81	81	81	87	86	80.4
	MIN	52	39	43	51	63	50	51	55	59	52	51	54	57	64	62	46	45	47	52	54	59	62	63	50	45	48	56	56	59	60	62	53.8
	MAX	82	77	80	86	89	87	84	85	83	89	77	81	86	88	88	85	84	86	88	91	95	99	99	72	80	82	83	85	86	92	92	85.8
	MIN	59	50	49	53	68	53	57	59	62	62	52	61	65	66	62	51	54	56	58	58	64	70	70	56	52	57	59	64	65	65	65	59.4
	MAX	82	78	81	88	90	84	85	86	78	89	79	80	87	82	90	85	84	87	88	90	96	98	97	77	80	81	84	83	88	92	93	85.9
	MIN	56	51	51	51	68	56	56	59	60	60	53	52	64	67	64	53	53	57	59	60	60	62	68	53	51	51	58	62	62	64	62	58.2
	MAX	72	78	85	82	76	79	82	76	80	72	70	84	77	84	78	77	82	89	88	90	90	88	72	73	78	81	85	86	89	88	85	81.2
	MIN	50	41	52	65	64	52	57	61	67	52	53	61	65	63	60	42	48	52	57	53	58	66	62	46	44	57	54	54	55	58	58	55.7
	MAX	79	82	91	86	85	85	76	73	89	84	76	86	81	91	83	84	85	88	90	96	96	95	78	79	81	85	84	88	93	90	93	85.5
	MIN	57	46	49	66	70	50	56	59	68	55	51	61	65	68	64	51	54	54	58	63	63	69	68	52	49	58	60	63	64	63	65	59.3
	MAX	76	78	75	84	83	78	79	81	72	83	73	71	81	85	82	80	80	81	81	86	90	92	91	75	79	77	76	80	83	87	86	80.8
	MIN	47	35	36	42	61	42	44	50	50	45	41	48	57	59	53	40	42	46	48	50	50	50	60	40	38	39	50	55	52	53	54	47.6
	MAX	85	85	86	91	94	91	86	88	94	82	86	92	88	95	91	88	90	92	90	92	103	103	85	85	84	84	86	85	87	89	90	89.3
	MIN	68	60	61	70	74	66	71	70	70	69	61	71	73	76	71	62	66	67	70	72	73	79	71	66	66	67	68	69	70	72	73	69.1
	MAX	73	72	86	84	77	78	79	75	81	70	72	82	82	85	80	78	80	82	86	90	91	89	71	76	78	78	79	85	86	87	85	80.5
	MIN	55	47	50	67	61	55	59	60	64	53	51	62	65	64	59	52	54	58	60	62	62	68	58	50	48	55	61	57	62	63	64	58.3
	MAX	76	71	76	84	81	75	78	80	75	79	70	70	83	75	82	72	77	84	86	88	89	90	87	73	72	77	80	84	86	88	87	79.8
	MIN	49	42	49	57	66	50	55	60	65	51	53	57	65	64	61	43	47	54	57	58	58	63	64	48	45	52	55	56	58	60	61	55.6
	MAX	72	76	84	84	77	80	81	78	79	75	76	85	82	83	79	78	82	85	88	89	90	88	88	75	78	80	85	85	88	87	84	82.0
	MIN	53	40	50	65	67	60	56	59	68	50	50	61	66	64	60	43	56	59	60	58	60	69	65	46	43	43	52	54	58	59	61	56.6
FLD	MAX	78	80	89	92	89	85	88	85	91	78	80	89	89	88	86	85	89	91	91	97	99	98	80	80	82	83	85	86	91	94	92	87.4
	MIN	66	57	54	70	70	60	67	66	69	65	60	68	72	70	65	57	59	62	65	69	70	78	66	61	59	63	66	69	69	74	72	65.7
	MAX	73	77	84	84	78	81	83	78	81	75	72	86	79	84	79	79	83	87	90	91	92	92	78	76	80	80	85	86	89	91	86	82.5
	MIN	58	53	58	73	72	57	64	64	68	56	56	66	70	69	63	54	58	66	66	68	71	72	64	58	55	62	65	65	67	66	67	63.6
	MAX	74	68	68	81	80	76	75	77	79	80	64	72	75	67	80	68	69	75	82	82	87	89	85	69	70	74	77	76	80	83	86	76.4
	MIN	54	46	47	49	62	52	53	56	60	51	49	51	52	60	59	50	48	53	57	60	65	67	64	50	53	56	56	60	61	62	61	55.8
	MAX	77	79	84	91	88	83	87	85	88	76	80	86	85	88	86	82	86	87	89	94	98	97	78	78	83	82	83	85	88	91	90	85.6
	MIN	57	52	48	64	70	58	61	59	66	62	53	61	66	67	63	51	54	57	59	64	67	70	66	57	54	56	56	66	68	62	67	50.7
	MAX	75	78	85	89	86	84	84	86	96	83	79	85	87	86	83	82	85	87	89	94	98	94	79	78	81	80	83	84	89	90	90	85.5
	MIN	65	52	52	69	68	62	65	68	73	62	56	62	64	65	63	48	54	64	64	60	69	74	63	62	59	62	63	67	70	70	73	63.5

See reference notes following Station Index.

Table 5 - Continued

DAILY TEMPERATURES

Station		1	2	3	4	5	6	7	8	9	10	11	12	13	14	15	16	17	18	19	20	21	22	23	24	25	26	27	28	29	30	31	Average
MT POCONO 2 N AP	MAX	71	69	80	82	79	75	79	81	82	80	73	77	76	81	71	72	77	81	81	88	91	89	75	71		79	80	78	79	85	84	78.9
	MIN	55	45	41	61	66	50	53	52	63	52	46	52	57	64	61	48	48	51	55	59	64	67	61	51		50	58	59	59	61	63	55.7
MUHLENBURG 1 SE	MAX	78	74	83	85	82	85	83	81	84	84	78	82	79	85	86	84	80	85	87	93	95	94	86	76	80	81	80	83	88	92	90	84.0
	MIN	51	47	45	62	61	50	53	55	65	55	50	55	61	64	64	48	48	53	57	60	64	69	65	46	50	55	65	63	63	64	63	57.1
NEWBURG 3 W	MAX	88	84	85	94	86	84	86	83	88	84	78	87	84	86	89	86	88	88	89	98	99	98	96	78	80	81		84	89	90	89	87.3
	MIN	62	48	49	64	64	53	60	59	64	59	56	63	63	59	71	57	56	61	57	59	64	70	65	52	53	54	59	58	61	62	64	59.5
NEW CASTLE 1 N	MAX	78	78	85	84	81	81	84	83	81	81	78	87	87	85	85	80	85	88	90	91	91	92	86	78	78	80	85	87	90	89	86	84.3
	MIN	52	44	54	66	68	52	59	61	66	49	53	60	68	65	60	45	52	55	59	61	61	67	66	48	46	57	57	59	61	61	62	57.9
NEWELL	MAX	81	77	81	88	87	82	82	86	81	87	77	83	90	87	89	86	87	92	92	94	94	95	97	74	80	84	83	87	90	91	90	86.3
	MIN	62	50	56	66	72	54	61	61	71	59	54	66	68	71	63	55	58	65	68	68	68	71	71	59	56	59	64	65	66	66	66	63.2
NEWPORT	MAX	85	81	83	90	91	86	85	87	80	91	79	81	91	84	91	88	86	89	90	91	100	99	98	73	81	83	83	84	89	89	93	87.1
	MIN	64	49	49	52	67	54	57	59	61	61	51	54	65	66	63	51	53	55	57	59	60	64	71	54	49	•51	59	61	63	64	64	58.3
NEW STANTON	MAX	70	79	89	88	82	84	86	78	86	75	80	89	88	87	85	85	89	90	93	95	96	99	76	80	82	84	86	88	89	94	89	85.8
	MIN	50	40	49	60	57	46	58	58	69	50	47	60	65	64	51	46	51	58	60	61	61	65	63	49	46	54	59	58	58	60	59	55.9
NORRISTOWN	MAX	81	81	89	95	91	88	89	91	91	79	82	89	83	91	87	85	88	90	92	97	103	100	80	83	86	87	87	85	90	93	92	88.5
	MIN	63	55	53	69	72	61	65	63	68	64	58	68	70	71	67	58	60	62	64	67	71	76	70	62	61	62	66	69	68	69	71	65.3
PALMERTON	MAX	76	76	85	88	87	83	84	85	88	73	77	83	73	85	78	78	84	87	88	95	97	96	78	79	82	84	85	81	86	90	90	83.9
	MIN	56	47	46	65	64	53	57	58	69	59	52	59	63	69	58	54	51	56	57	59	65	71	64	55	54	57	63	68	68	64	67	59.6
PHIL DREXEL INST OF TEC	MAX	81	84	88	96	93	87	90	92	93	80	85	89	89	93	89	86	91	92	93	93	101	102	88	85	89	88	87	82	87	92	94	89.6
	MIN	65	57	60	68	78	60	70	66	70	66	60	70	74	74	74	63	65	67	70	70	73	79	70	67	65	68	70	69	69	71	73	68.4
PHILADELPHIA WB AP	MAX	79	81	86	93	91	86	88	89	91	78	83	88	88	91	87	85	89	90	90	94	101	100	82	82	85	85	86	84	89	93	91	87.9
	MIN	63	56	54	68	71	59	67	63	68	62	58	66	71	71	67	59	62	63	64	65	70	76	69	65	62	63	64	67	67	70	71	65.2
PHILADELPHIA PT BREEZE	MAX	80	82	86	91	92	91	88	91	91	90	83	88	85	91	88	86	90	91	92	92	102	100	99	80	84	84	86	83	86	90	90	88.8
	MIN	70	63	62	69	80	68	71	73	71	70	63	70	75	75	75	64	68	69	70	70	73	80	71	66	65	66	69	69	70	72	71	69.9
PHILADELPHIA CITY	MAX	81	83	85	91	91	86	87	88	90	78	82	86	83	90	88	85	89	89	89	92	98	98	85	84	86	84	85	81	86	90	89	87.1
	MIN	67	62	65	71	75	71	73	72	69	69	64	73	74	75	70	62	67	70	73	71	74	82	71	66	66	67	69	67	69	71	73	69.9
PHILIPSBURG CAA AP	MAX	71	73	83	83	75	76	77	71	82	71	70	81	79	82	79	78	79	80	83	91	92	89	71	72	73	75	77	80	86	84	83	78.9
	MIN	50	36	40	64	49	41	48	49	59	49	52	56	63	65	50	39	50	50	54	53	53	64	52	42	38	51	60	56	57	53	53	51.5
PHOENIXVILLE 1 E	MAX	85	86	91	97	94	90	91	92	92	79	85	91	85	92	89	87	91	94	94	99	105	104	95	84	87	89	90	87	92	93	93	91.1
	MIN	56	50	45	65	72	54	61	56	67	59	53	61	64	70	63	50	52	55	65	66	67	70	69	56	54	57	60	66	66	65	66	60.6
PIMPLE HILL	MAX	73	70	70	81	82	79	77	80	82	81	66	73	78	71	80	71	72	79	82	83	88	91	88	73	73	76	79	79	73	79	86	77.9
	MIN	50	44	47	60	65	52	57	59	61	50	48	55	61	62	59	47	50	59	61	61	68	67	59	48	48	57	58	61	60	63	64	56.8
PITTSBURGH WB AP 2	MAX	73	77	85	82	77	79	82	74	81	72	74	85	80	82	78	79	84	86	88	90	92	91	75	76	78	78	83	86	88	88	87	81.6
	MIN	55	50	58	70	62	56	61	65	64	54	56	63	70	68	58	53	59	63	67	67	70	73	60	54	55	61	63	64	68	68	66	62.0
PITTSBURGH WB CITY	MAX	75	79	89	86	81	82	85	77	84	74	77	89	85	85	82	83	88	88	92	93	95	94	77	78	81	79	87	90	92	92	88	84.7
	MIN	59	53	61	73	67	61	63	67	67	57	59	66	72	70	64	57	60	65	69	70	70	77	63	57	57	63	69	68	70	71	71	65.0
PLEASANT MOUNT 1 W	MAX	82	68	68		80			79	80	80	63	71			79	69	71	76	80			88	86		73	75			77	82	84	
	MIN	53	45	37	49				48	62	52	45	48	54			46	45	48	50	51				53	46	50	55			59	58	
PORT CLINTON	MAX	84	79	80	86	90	88	85	87	86	90	79	80	87	82	89	84	84	89	90	90	96	100	99	79	80	85	84	87	90	92	95	87.0
	MIN	52	45	42	54	68	48	54	55	65	53	48	55	60	64	58	47	48	50	53	54	57	66	67	49	48	51	52	66	67	63	64	55.6
PUTNEYVILLE 2 SE DAM	MAX	78	74	78	85	85	79	81	82	73	85	74	74	85	82	86	80	80	84	84	90	92	95	91	77	77	79	83	85	87	90	89	82.7
	MIN	51	39	43	54	65	48	57	58	61	47	47	56	62	62	51	45	48	53	56	57	56	61	63	45	42	51	58	59	58	55	58	53.7
QUAKERTOWN 1 E	MAX	80	82	88	92	90	87	86	91	88	87	83	86	85	88	85	80	83	89	89	94	98	98	96	80	84	87	89	87	88	91	90	87.8
	MIN	58	49	44	67	73	55	57	57	60	62	54	60	61	67	64	53	51	53	57	59	63	68	68	57	54	57	60	66	63	64	67	59.6
READING WB CITY	MAX	80	81	89	92	90	85	87	87	90	78	81	87	86	89	86	84	87	89	90	96	99	98	81	82	85	84	86	86	90	91	92	87.4
	MIN	65	59	54	72	71	64	67	65	69	65	60	66	69	71	66	58	60	61	66	71	73	78	66	60	61	62	65	69	70	72	72	66.0
RIDGWAY 3 W	MAX	75	71	75	84	83	76	77	79	72	79	70	71	81	79	84	77	79	82	83	87	91	89	87	76	75	77	78	82	85	88	86	79.9
	MIN	48	37	37	46	63	43	44	51	53	44	46	50	60	64	55	45	46	48	49	53	57	57	62	45	43	43	55	58	57	56	56	50.7
SALINA 3 W	MAX	76	76	86	85	81	80	81	79	82	80	76	86	84	84	82	82	86	86	88	91	93	91	89	77	79	80	84	87	89	88	87	83.7
	MIN	53	43	51	65	69	51	60	60	69	51	51	60	68	65	59	49	52	58	60	62	62	67	67	50	47	58	62	61	62	62	61	58.5
SCRANTON	MAX																																
	MIN																																
SCRANTON WB AIRPORT	MAX	73	72	83	85	83	81	80	84	85	70	76	81	70	86	73	74	81	84	86	92	94	93	76	76	80	82	84	81	87	88	88	81.5
	MIN	54	49	45	64	61	55	56	54	65	55	54	54	62	65	56	49	48	54	58	61	66	69	57	53	50	55	64	62	64	65	63	57.6
SHIPPENSBURG	MAX	79	80	86	88	86	85	87	83	90	83	80	88	87	89	88	83	85	86	89	96	97	96	93	78	82	81	84	85	91	90	91	86.6
	MIN	59	52	51	68	71	59	63	59	65	59	54	66	68	67	64	52	56	62	58	59	62	74	68	53	51	58	60	58	62	65	66	60.9
SHIPPINGPORT WB	MAX	71	79	84	82	77	79	83	77	81	73	74	86	80	82	78	78	85	86	90	91	92	90	76	76	77	79	84	85	90	88	86	81.9
	MIN	53	47	55	69	58	53	60	60	64	54	54	62	67	65	53	48	53	63	63	65	66	70	59	52	50	58	61	62	65	64	61	59.2
SLIPPERY ROCK	MAX	75	78	85	81	78	79	83	77	82	78	74	85	83	85	79	86	86	85	91	91	92	92	82	77	78	80	84	88	90	86	88	83.2
	MIN	53	45	56	67	65	54	60	61	68	50	55	62	67	65	61	50	55	59	61	60	65	69	65	52	49	59	60	61	63	63	64	59.5
SOMERSET MAIN ST	MAX	73	73	83	82	78	77	79	78	82	79	78	83	83	82	81	80	85	80	86	88	90	89	88	75	76	76	78	82	85	86	83	81.2
	MIN	54	40	47	60	65	50	58	57	66	51	49	59	64	64	55	45	50	58	58	57	59	66	64	46	44	52	53	55	59	56	60	55.5
SPRINGBORO	MAX	75	71	77	86	83	75	80	80	77	79	69	70	84	74	83	70	76	84	88	90	90	90	87	74	74	78	82	87	87	90	89	80.6
	MIN	49	42	53	55	64	48	54	62	64	50	53	60	65	64	60	44	49	53	56	55	60	67	63	47	46	57	55	54	57	59	59	55.6
SPRINGS 1 SW	MAX	69	73	82	79	76	78	79	80	81	68	74	82	81	81	79	81	82	75	82	89	90	88	73	71	74	77	79	82	84	84	80	79.1
	MIN	52	39	44	56	52	50	51	52	65	52	56	60	62	59	53	44	49	57	54	55	52	65	59	45	43	48	54	52	55	53	53	52.9
STATE-COLLEGE	MAX	77	74	78	86	86	80	79	83	75	85	74	74	85	82	87	81	82	84	84	87	94	94	92	75	74	78	79	80	85	89	87	82.3
	MIN	56	49	51	54	67	54	57	60	62	55	54	59	65	66	64	51	54	57	58	62	62	62	66	52	50	55	60	61	62	64	65	58.5
STROUDSBURG	MAX	78	79	88	91	88	87	87	88	86	72	80	86	75	86	81	80	85	86	90	95	100	99	77	78	85	83	88	81	85	90	91	85.3
	MIN	55	43	36	55	62	47	50	50	61	51	40	51	54	60	54	44	40	47	47	52	59	62	60	47	44	47	53	61	63	59	62	52.1
TAMARACK 2 S FIRE TWR	MAX																																
	MIN																																
TIONESTA 2 SE DAM	MAX	75	70	75	84	82	75	78	80	75	79	70	70	82	79	82	76	77	82	84	87	89	89	87	75	75	78	78	84	85	88	87	79.9
	MIN	51	41	43	53	67	48	52	58	61	49	50	55	65	64	59	48	48	53	54	60	61	61	65	49	48	49	58	59	60	60	62	55.2
TITUSVILLE WATER WORKS	MAX	71	75	85	82	75	79	81	75	78	75	72	82	80	83	76	78	82	84	90	90	90	88	75	74	77	79	85	85	89	90	84	80.9
	MIN	40	38	48	65	65	48	55	58	56	45	49	62	65	63	60	45	48	44	55	60	57	66	65	46	44	55	55	56	57	57	61	54.5
TOWANDA	MAX	75	74	88	87	82	81	85	83	86	79	78	82	73	87	77	78	82	86	88	95	95	91	86	76	81	84	84	88	89	91	89	83.8
	MIN	55	42	41	64	67	52	53	54	64	51	52	53	60	65	60	47	48	51	51	57	63	65	65	50	47	52	59	62	60	60	61	55.8

See reference notes following Station Index.

ble 5-Continued

DAILY TEMPERATURES

PENNSYLVANIA
JULY 1957

Station		1	2	3	4	5	6	7	8	9	10	11	12	13	14	15	16	17	18	19	20	21	22	23	24	25	26	27	28	29	30	31	Average
IONTOWN	MAX	76	79	87	85	83	82	86	80	87	77	78	80											80	77	79	81	86	88	89	88	85	85.1
	MIN	58	46	53	65	69	54	62	59	70	57	51	67													54	67	65	62	65	64	66	62.1
ER DARBY								91	90	89	82	87	86													85	85	87	85	87	92	91	88.3
								66	68	64	67	65	70													61	62	65	67	68	70	71	65.7
RREN								82	76	81	71	70	83													78	82	86	86	89	88	85	81.2
								55	57	64	49	50	60													47	56	59	58	59	58	64	56.2
YNESBURG 1								85	83	86	76	78	88													80	80	87	87	89	89		86.0
								54	56	69	51	47	60													49	53	60	61	62	60		57.1
LLSBORO 3								76	78	73	81	68	72													72	75	77	79	80		86	78.3
								53	57	61	49	49	50													49	52	56	59	60		63	55.2
LLSVILLE								90	85	89	85	81	86													91	83	82	86	90	91	89	87.5
								62	55	66	58	52	69													51	56	56	58	61	62	63	58.4
ST CHESTER										90	89	85	90													85	87	88	88	90	94	92	91.1
																										61	63	66	65	67	69	67	65.7
LLIAMSPORT WB AP																										82	84	83		93	93	93	85.7
																										53	58	64		66	65	65	59.7
RK 3 SSW PUMP STA																																	89.0
																																	59.9

N AND WIND

Day of month

NFLUENCE 1 SW DAM	5.75 1458
RD CITY 4 S DAM	6.04 1156
WLEY 1 S DAM	6.37 1875
AMESTOWN 2 NW	5.37 516
ANDISVILLE	8.29 1449
IMPLE HILL	B8.16 1779
TATE COLLEGE	- 940

DAILY SOIL TEMPERATURES

Station And Depth	Time	Day of month																															Average
		1	2	3	4	5	6	7	8	9	10	11	12	13	14	15	16	17	18	19	20	21	22	23	24	25	26	27	28	29	30	31	
STATE COLLEGE																																	
EASURED UNDER SOD																																	
2 INCHES	8 AM	64	61	64	69	70	65	67	67	69	64	62	67	69	69	70	66	67	67	69	70	72	75	71	65	65	66	67	69	71	71	72	67.7
4 INCHES	8 AM	64	62	64	69	70	64	66	67	69	64	62	66	69	68	69	66	67	67	69	70	71	73	72	66	65	67	67	69	71	71	72	67.6
8 INCHES	8 AM	65	63	64	68	69	65	65	67	67	66	63	65	68	67	68	67	67	68	68	69	70	72	72	67	66	68	68	69	70	71	71	67.5
16 INCHES	8 AM	67	66	66	67	68	67	66	67	67	67	66	66	67	67	68	68	68	69	69	69	70	71	72	70	69	69	69	69	70	71	71	68.3

Ground Cover: Bluegrass Sod.

See reference notes following Station Index.

TOTAL PRECIPITATION

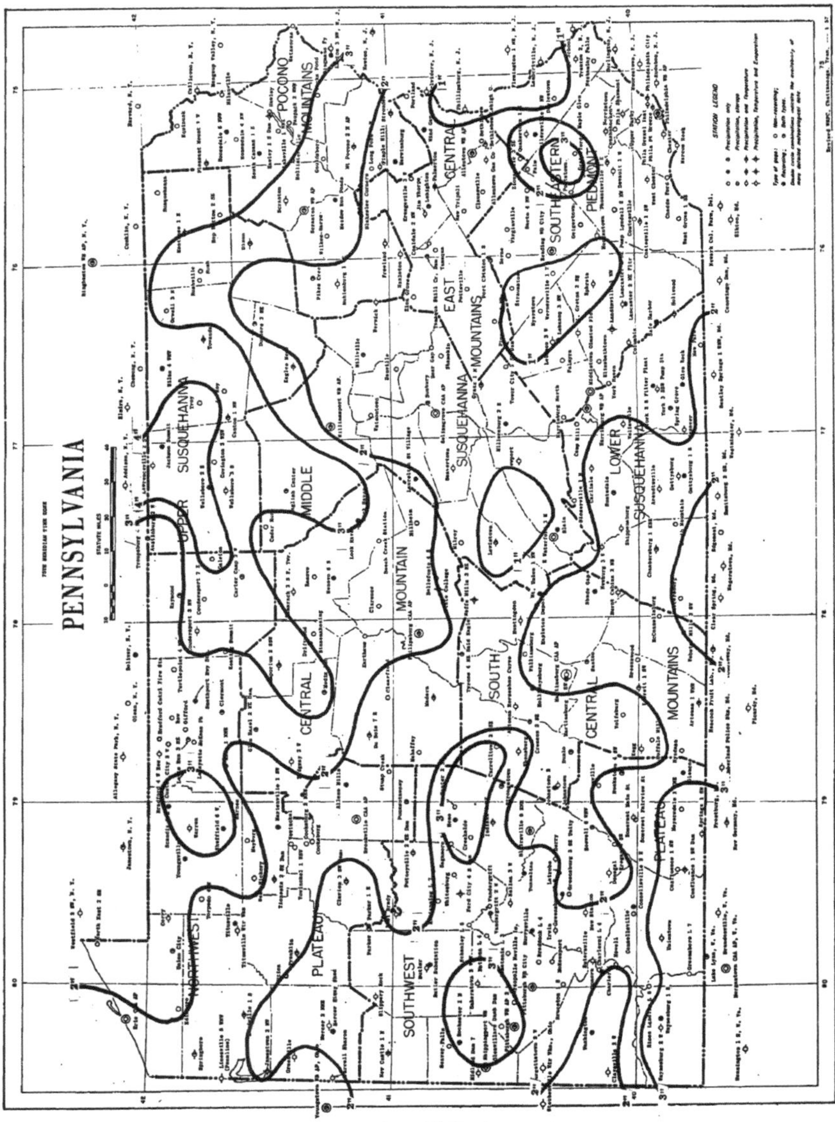

Isolines are drawn through points of approximately equal values. Hourly precipitation data from recorder substations will be available in the publication "Hourly Precipitation Data".

AVERAGE TEMPERATURE

PENNSYLVANIA
JULY 1957

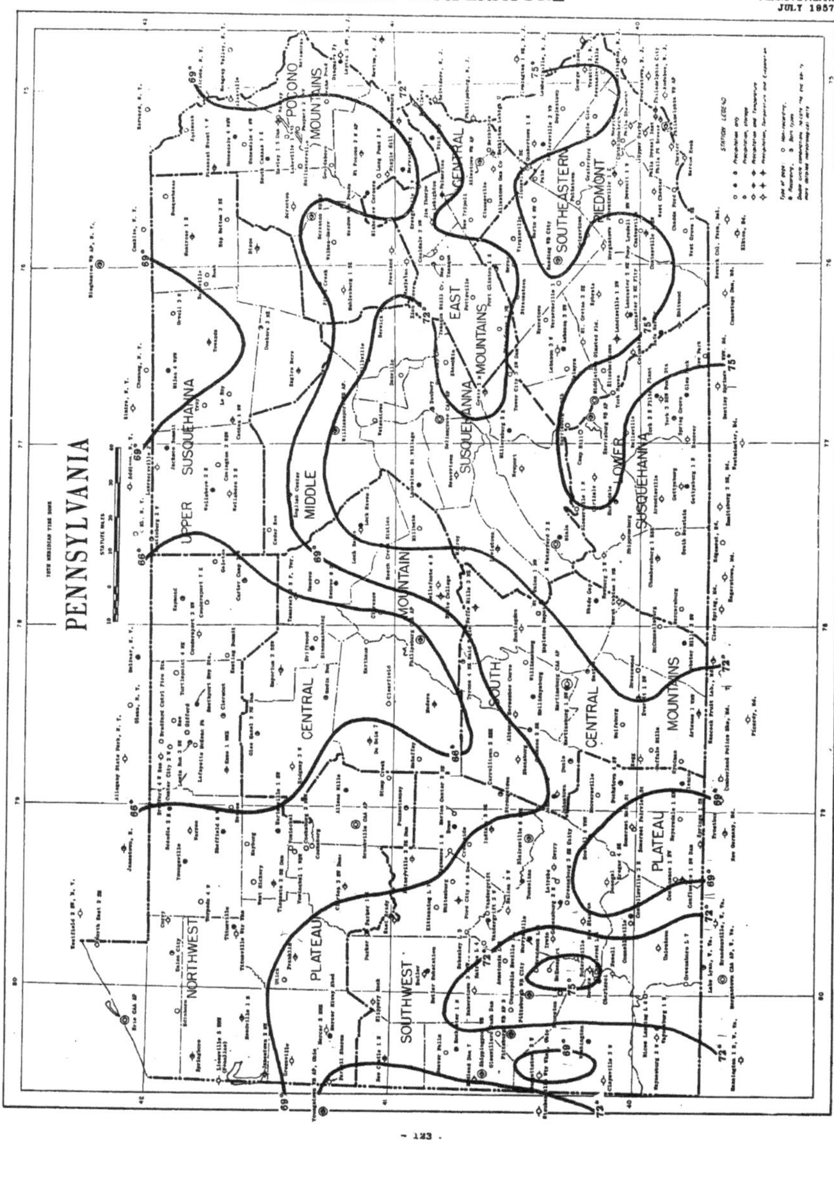

Isolines are drawn through points of approximately equal values. Hourly precipitation data from recorder substations will be available in the publication "Hourly Precipitation Data".

STATION INDEX

Station	Index No.	County	Drainage 1	Latitude	Longitude	Elevation	Observation Time Temp.	Observation Time Precip.	Observer	Refer To Tables
ACHETONIA LOCK 3	0022	ALLEGHENY	1	40 32	79 49	748		7A	CORPS OF ENGINEERS	3
ALLENS MILLS	0099	JEFFERSON	1	41 12	78 55	1600		MID	CHARLES M. ALLEN	C
ALLENTOWN WB AP	0106	LEHIGH	9	40 39	75 26	376	MID	MID	U.S. WEATHER BUREAU	2 3 5 7 C
ALLENTOWN GAS CO	0111	LEHIGH	9	40 36	75 28	254	7A	7A	LEHIGH VLY GAS DIV	2 3 5
ALTOONA HORSESHOE CURVE	0134	BLAIR	6	40 30	78 29	1500	6P	6P	ALTOONA WATER BUR.	2 3 5
ARENDTSVILLE	0229	ADAMS	15	39 55	77 18	710	8A	8A	PA STATE COL EXP	2 3 5
AUSTINBURG 2 W	0313	TIOGA	15	42 00	77 32	1590		7A	OTTO D. BACON	3 7 C
BAKERSTOWN 3 WNW	0355	ALLEGHENY	1	40 39	79 59	1230	7P	7P	PGH CUT FLOWER CO	2 3 5
BARNES	0409	WARREN	1	41 40	79 02	1310		7A	CORPS OF ENGINEERS	3
BARTO 4 NW	0428	BERKS	14	40 26	75 39	312		7A	MARIE B. NICHLAS	3
BEAR GAP	0457	NORTHUMBLAND	15	40 50	76 30	900		5P	ROARING CRK WTR CO	3
BEAVER FALLS	0475	BEAVER	2	40 46	80 19	760		7A	HOWARD R. KEMP	3
BEAVERTOWN	0482	SNYDER	15	40 45	77 10	640	5P	7A	MARLIN R. ETTINGER	2 3 5
BEECH CREEK STATION	0490	CENTRE	16	41 04	77 34	620		7A	HAROLD S. RUPERT	3 7
BELLEFONTE 4 S	0530	CENTRE	16	40 51	77 47	1110	8A	8A	ROCKVIEW PRISON FARM	2 3 5
BERNE	0599	BERKS	14	40 31	76 00	325		7A	FLOYD W. TRUMP	3
BERWICK	0611	COLUMBIA	15	41 04	76 15	570	6P	6P	AMER CAR + FNDRY CO	2 3 5
BETHLEHEM	0629	NORTHAMPTON	9	40 37	75 22	400		7A	ARTHUR CROPPER	3
#BETHLEHEM LEHIGH UNIV	0634	NORTHAMPTON	9	40 36	75 23	450	MID	MID	LEHIGH UNIVERSITY	2 3 5 C
BLAIN	0725	PERRY	15	40 20	77 31	750		MID	PA DEPT FRST + WTRS	C
BLAIRSVILLE 6 ENE	0736	INDIANA	4	40 27	79 09	2048	8P	8P	U.S. WEATHER BUREAU	2 3 5
BLAKESLEE CORNERS	0743	MONROE	9	41 06	75 36	1650		MID	WALTER WILDRICK	C
BLOSERVILLE 1 N	0763	CUMBERLAND	15	40 16	77 22	650		5P	MRS. B. M. WILLDERS	3
BOSWELL 6 WNW	0820	SOMERSET	1	40 10	79 08	2570		8A	CLARK N. ST. CLAIR	3 C
BRADDOCK LOCK 2	0861	ALLEGHENY	10	40 24	79 52	725		7A	CORPS OF ENGINEERS	3
BRADFORD CNTRL FIRE STA	0867	MC KEAN	1	41 57	78 39	1500		8A	BRADFORD FIRE DEPT	3
BRADFORD 4 W RES	0868	MC KEAN	1	41 57	78 44	1680	5P	5P	BRADFORD WTR DEPT	2 3 5 7
BREEZEWOOD	0905	BEDFORD	6	40 00	78 14	1352		MID	PA TURNPIKE COMM	3
BROOKVILLE CAA AIRPORT	1002	JEFFERSON	1	41 09	79 06	1417	MID	MID	CIVIL AERO. ADM.	2 3 5 7
BRUCETON 1 S	1033	ALLEGHENY	10	40 18	79 59	1065		7A	AUSTIN R. COOPER	3
BUCKSTOWN 1 SE	1073	SOMERSET	4	40 04	78 50	2460		MID	ALVIN W. MANGES	C
BUFFALO MILLS	1087	BEDFORD	6	39 57	78 39	1318		7A	MRS. NELLE R. BROWN	3
BURGETTSTOWN 2 W	1105	WASHINGTON	11	40 23	80 26	980	7A	7A	SMITH TWP MUN AUTH	2 3 5
BURNT CABINS 2 NE	1115	HUNTINGDON	6	40 05	77 52	990	MID	MID	PA TURNPIKE COMM	2 3 5
#BUTLER	1130	BUTLER	2	40 52	79 54	1100	4P	7A	WILLIAM C. FAUST	2 3 5
BUTLER SUBSTATION	1135	BUTLER	2	40 51	79 53	1140		MID	WEST PENN POWER CO	C
CAMP HILL	1198	CUMBERLAND	15	40 15	76 55	461		6P	JOSEPH N. HOBART	3
CANTON 1 NW	1215	BRADFORD	15	41 40	76 52	1520	7A	7A	MRS.MILDRED SPENCER	2 3 5 7 C
CARLISLE	1234	CUMBERLAND	15	40 12	77 11	460	6P	6P	C. E. MILLER	2 3 5
CARROLLTOWN 2 SSE	1255	CAMBRIA	16	40 35	78 42	2040		8A	ROBERT F. MAURER	3 7
CARTER CAMP 2 W	1262	POTTER	16	41 37	77 45	2030		7A	RICHARD L. MENKEN	3 C
CEDAR RUN	1301	LYCOMING	16	41 31	77 27	800		7A	KATHRYN T.KREIGHBAUM	3
CHADDS FORD	1342	DELAWARE	5	39 52	75 36	160		8A	ALFRED C. WEEKS	3
CHAMBERSBURG 1 ESE	1354	FRANKLIN	12	39 56	77 38	640	9P	9P	CHARLES A. BENDER	2 3 5 C
CHARLEROI	1372	WASHINGTON	10	40 08	79 55	1040		MID	WEST PENN POWER CO	C
CHARLEROI LOCK 4	1377	WESTMORELAND	10	40 09	79 54	749		7A	CORPS OF ENGINEERS	3
#CHESTER	1423	DELAWARE	5	39 51	75 22	80	8A	8A	CHESTER TIMES	2 3 5
CLARENCE	1480	CENTRE	16	41 03	77 56	1410		7A	MISS VELDA SWANCER	3
CLARION 3 SW	1485	CLARION	1	41 12	79 26	1114	8P	7A	PA ELECTRIC CO	2 3 5 C
CLAUSSVILLE	1505	LEHIGH	9	40 37	75 39	670		8A	WILLIAM J. DOTTERER	3
CLAYSVILLE 3 W	1512	WASHINGTON	11	40 07	80 28	1000	7P	7A	MFGRS. L + H CO	2 3 5
CLEARFIELD	1519	CLEARFIELD	16	41 01	78 26	1100		7A	IRA TAYLOR	3
CLERMONT	1529	MC KEAN	1	41 41	78 30	2104		7A	MRS.TILLIE M.SIMONDS	3 C
COALDALE 2 NW	1572	SCHUYLKILL	9	40 50	75 56	1026		7A	PANTHER VLY WTR CO	3 7
COATESVILLE 1 SW	1589	CHESTER	5	39 58	75 50	342	8A	8A	PHILA ELECTRIC CO	2 3 5 C
COATESVILLE	1594	CHESTER	5	39 59	75 49	340		8A	EDWARD D. BIEDEMAN	INAC 12/55
COLUMBIA	1675	LANCASTER	15	40 02	76 30	300	SS	SS	JAMES H. RUST	2 3 5
CONFLUENCE 1 SW DAM	1705	SOMERSET	17	39 48	79 22	1490	8A	8A	CORPS OF ENGINEERS	2 3 5 6 C
CONFLUENCE 1 NW	1710	FAYETTE	17	39 50	79 22	1331		7A	JOHN L. REID	3
CONNELLSVILLE	1723	FAYETTE	17	40 01	79 36	870		8A	MARSHALL B. MENEFEE	3
CONNELLSVILLE 2 E	1729	FAYETTE	17	40 01	79 33	1300		MID	HARRY C. JOY	C
CONSHOHOCKEN	1737	MONTGOMERY	5	40 04	75 19	70		8A	PHILA ELECTRIC CO	3
COOKSBURG	1749	CLARION	1	41 20	79 13	1180		8A	PA DEPT FRST + WTRS	3
COOKSBURG 2 NNW	1752	CLARION	1	41 21	79 13	1460		8A	PA DEPT FRST + WTRS	3
CORAOPOLIS NEVILLE IS	1773	ALLEGHENY	11	40 30	80 05	720		8A	PGH. COKE + CHEM CO	3
CORRY	1790	ERIE	1	41 56	79 38	1427	7P	8A	LEO C. HECKERS	2 3 5 7
COUDERSPORT 3 NW	1806	POTTER	1	41 49	78 03	2020	7P	8A	MISS ELIZABETH NEFF	2 3 5
COUDERSPORT 7 E	1809	POTTER	1	41 46	77 53	2425		7A	CAMP POTATO	3
COVINGTON 2 WSW	1833	TIOGA	15	41 44	77 07	1745		7A	CALVIN R. PACKARD	3
CREEKSIDE	1881	INDIANA	1	40 41	79 12	1035		7A	CORPS OF ENGINEERS	3
CRESSON 2 SE	1895	CAMBRIA	6	40 27	78 34	2540		7A	MILES M. LINGLE	3 C
CUSTER CITY 2 W	1978	MC KEAN	1	41 55	78 41	2120		8A	M. D. BOOTH AND CO	3
DANVILLE	2013	MONTOUR	15	40 58	76 37	460		7A	MRS.MARIE M. LITTLE	3
DERRY	2108	WESTMORELAND	4	40 20	79 18	1150	6P	6P	MISS N. D. WINEMAN	2 3 5
DEVAULT 1 W	2116	CHESTER	14	40 05	75 33	360	MID	MID	PA TURNPIKE COMM	2 3 5
DINGMANS FERRY	2160	PIKE	5	41 13	74 52	364		MID	CLYDE T. VOORHEES	C
DIXON	2171	WYOMING	15	41 34	75 54	620	7A	7A	HAROLD J. KUSCHEL	2 3 5 C
DONEGAL	2183	WESTMORELAND	17	40 07	79 23	1746	MID	MID	PA TURNPIKE COMM	2 3 5 7
#DONORA	2190	WASHINGTON	10	40 11	79 51	814	12M	12M	DONORA ZINC WORKS	2 3 5
DOYLESTOWN	2221	BUCKS	5	40 18	75 08	393		5P	GEORGE HART	3
DRIFTWOOD	2245	CAMERON	16	41 20	78 08	880		MID	SIDNEY KENNEDY	C
DU BOIS 7 E	2265	CLEARFIELD	16	41 06	78 38	1670	5P	5P	CITY OF DU BOIS	2 3 5 7 C
DUNLO	2298	CAMBRIA	4	40 17	78 43	2410		MID	MRS. D. L. WHITE	C
DUSHORE 3 NE	2324	SULLIVAN	16	41 33	76 21	1750		7A	PATRICK F. RYAN	3 C
EAGLES MERE	2343	SULLIVAN	16	41 24	76 35	2020	7A	7A	MRS.ELSIE P. BIGGER	2 3 5 C
EAST BRADY	2363	CLARION	1	40 59	79 37	820	5P	5P	A. B. KEMPEL	2 3 5
EAST WATERFORD 3 E	2459	PERRY	6	40 21	77 33	2125	8A	8A	U.S. WEATHER BUREAU	INAC 5/55
EBENSBURG	2466	CAMBRIA	4	40 29	78 43	2090	7P	7A	ROBERT A. WASSER	2 3 5
EDINBORO	2514	ERIE	1	41 52	80 08	1220		8A	EDINBORO ST TCHR COL	3
ELIZABETHTOWN	2560	LANCASTER	15	40 09	76 37	460		8A	MASONIC HOME	3
EMPORIUM 2 SSW	2634	CAMERON	16	41 28	78 15	1735	7A	7A	JACKSON THOMAS	2 3 5 C
ENGLISH CENTER	2644	LYCOMING	16	41 26	77 17	881		7A	WILLIAM SUDERS	3 7 C
EPHRATA	2662	LANCASTER	15	40 11	76 10	465	6P	6P	STANLEY L.VON NEIDA	2 3 5
EQUINUNK 2	2671	WAYNE	5	41 51	75 13	910		7A	MRS. HENRIETTA HURRY	3
ERIE WB AIRPORT	2682	ERIE	8	42 05	80 12	732	MID	MID	U. S. WEATHER BUREAU	2 3 5 7
EVERETT 1 SW	2721	BEDFORD	6	40 00	78 23	1020	MID	MID	PA TURNPIKE COMM	2 3 5 7 C
FARRELL SHARON	2814	MERCER	2	41 14	80 30	865	7P	7P	SHARON STEEL CORP	2 3 5
FORD CITY 4 S DAM	2942	ARMSTRONG	1	40 43	79 30	950	8A	8A	CORPS OF ENGINEERS	2 3 5 6 7 C
FRANKLIN	3028	VENANGO	1	41 23	79 49	987	7P	7A	ROBERT D. RHOADS	2 3 5 C
FREELAND	3056	LUZERNE	15	41 01	75 54	1900	6P	8A	ANDREW B. EVANSHA	2 3 5
GALETON	3130	POTTER	16	41 44	77 39	1325		7A	W. GALE LUSH	3 7
GEIGERTOWN	3189	BERKS	14	40 13	75 50	400		8A	WALTER C. WOLF	3
GEORGE SCHOOL	3200	BUCKS	5	40 13	74 56	135	7P	7P	GEORGE M. HART	2 3 5 7
#GETTYSBURG	3218	ADAMS	12	39 50	77 14	540	9A	9A	HUGH C. MC ILHENNY	2 3 5
GETTYSBURG 1 S	3223	ADAMS	12	39 48	77 14	560		MID	NAT MILITARY PARK	C
GIFFORD	3237	MC KEAN	1	41 51	78 36	2220		8A	SOUTH PENN OIL CO	3
GLENCOE	3298	SOMERSET	12	39 49	78 51	1620		MID	MRS. MARY M.HARTMAN	C
GLEN HAZEL 2 NE DAM	3311	ELK	1	41 34	78 36	1725		8A	CORPS OF ENGINEERS	3 C
GLEN ROCK	3330	YORK	15	39 48	76 44	620		MID	MRS.E.C.MC WILLIAMS	C
GLENWILLARD DASH DAM	3343	ALLEGHENY	11	40 33	80 13	705		7A	CORPS OF ENGINEERS	3
GOULDSBORO	3394	WAYNE	9	41 15	75 27	1890		7A	L. H. EILENBERGER	3
GRATERFORD	3435	MONTGOMERY	14	40 14	75 27	160	7A	7A	CLAUDE K. KULP	2 3 5 7 C
GRATZ 1 N	3438	DAUPHIN	15	40 38	76 43	760	8A	8A	LEE M. LEITZEL	2 3 5 C
GREENSBORO LOCK 7	3503	GREENE	10	39 47	79 55	808		7A	CORPS OF ENGINEERS	3 7
GREENSBURG 2 E	3515	WESTMORELAND	10	40 18	79 31	1225		MID	PA DEPT HIGHWAYS	C
GREENSBURG 3 SE UNITY	3516	WESTMORELAND	10	40 17	79 30	1245		6P	WESTMORELAND WTR CO	3
GREENVILLE	3526	MERCER	2	41 24	80 23	1026	6P	6P	C. EARL MILLER	2 3 5
HANOVER	3662	YORK	15	39 48	76 59	600	8A	8A	HANOVER EVENING SUN	2 3 5 7
#HARRISBURG WB AP	3699	YORK	15	40 13	76 51	335	MID	MID	U.S. WEATHER BUREAU	2 3 5 7 C
HARRISBURG NORTH	3704	DAUPHIN	15	40 18	76 54	323		9A	GEORGE S. BEAL	3
HAWLEY	3758	WAYNE	5	41 29	75 10	880		7A	MRS. KATHERINE BATES	3
HAWLEY 1 S DAM	3761	WAYNE	5	41 28	75 11	1200	7A	7A	PA POWER + LIGHT CO	2 3 5 6 7 C
HOLLIDAYSBURG	4001	BLAIR	6	40 26	78 24	960		MID	JOHN M. RINGLER	C
HOLLISTERVILLE	4008	WAYNE	5	41 23	75 26	1360		8A	PA POWER + LIGHT CO	3
#HOLTWOOD	4019	LANCASTER	15	39 50	76 20	187	MID	8A	PA POWER + LIGHT CO	2 3 5 7 C
HOME	4027	INDIANA	1	40 45	79 06	1220		MID	MRS. EDNA M. BUSH	C
HONESDALE 4 NW	4043	WAYNE	5	41 37	75 19	1410		8A	GEORGE C. WILLIAMS	3
HONESDALE 6 NNW	4044	WAYNE	5	41 39	75 17	1050		MID	FRIEND E. WALTER	C
HOOVERSVILLE	4058	SOMERSET	4	40 09	78 55	1660		7A	PA ELECTRIC CO	3 7
HOP BOTTOM 2 SE	4066	SUSQUEHANNA	15	41 43	75 43	900		7A	JOSEPH J. SANSUSKAS	3

Station	Index No.	County	Drainage 1	Latitude	Longitude	Elevation	Temp.	Precip.	Observer	Refer To Tables
HUNTINGDON										
HUNTSDALE										
HYNDMAN										
INDIANA 3 SE										
IRWIN										
JACKSON SUMMIT										
JAMESTOWN 2 NW										
JIM THORPE										
#JOHNSTOWN										
JOHNSTOWN 2										
KANE 1 NNE										
KARTHAUS										
KEATING SUMMIT										
KEGG										
KITTANNING LOCK 7										
KREGAR 4 SE										
KRESGEVILLE 3 W										
LAFAYETTE MC KEAN PARK										
LAKEVILLE 1 NNE										
LANCASTER 2 NE PUMP STA										
LANCASTER 2 NE FILT PL										
LANDISVILLE 2 NW										
LATROBE										
LAURELTON STATE VILLAGE										
LAWRENCEVILLE 2 S										
LEBANON 3 W										
LEBANON 3 SW										
LEHIGHTON										
LE ROY										
LEWIS RUN 3 SE										
LEWISTOWN										
LINESVILLE 5 WNW										
LOCK HAVEN										
LOCK HAVEN 2										
LONG POND 2 W										
LYNDELL 2 NW										
MADERA										
MAHAFFEY										
MAPLE GLEN										
MAPLETON DEPOT	5381									
MARCUS HOOK	5390		5	39 49	75 25	12	MID	MID	SUN OIL CO	2 3 5
MARIENVILLE 1 SW	5400	FOREST	1	41 27	79 09	1700		MID	ROY A. MARKER	C
MARION CENTER 2 SE	5408	INDIANA	1	40 45	79 02	1610		7A	CORPS OF ENGINEERS	3
MARTINSBURG 1 SW	5453	BLAIR	6	40 18	78 20	1360		MID	BLUE MT. CANNERIES	C
MARTINSBURG CAA AP	5454	BLAIR	6	40 18	78 19	1463	MID	MID	CIVIL AERO. ADM.	2 3 5 7
MATAMORAS	5470	PIKE	5	41 22	74 42	439		7A	HARRY BISLAND	3 7
MAYBURG	5490	FOREST	1	41 36	79 13	1150		7A	CORPS OF ENGINEERS	3
MC CONNELLSBURG	5526	FULTON	12	39 56	78 00	895		7A	MRS. HELEN M. SHIVES	3
MC KEESPORT	5573	ALLEGHEN	10	40 21	79 52	720		8A	NATIONAL TUBE CO	3
MEADOW RUN PONDS	5601	LUZERNE	15	41 13	75 40	1995		MID	GEORGE PEARAGE	C
MEADVILLE 1 S	5606	CRAWFORD	1	41 38	80 10	1065	8A	8A	CITY OF MEADVILLE	2 3 5 7 C
MEDIX RUN	5627	ELK	16	41 17	78 24	1100		7A	MRS.E. M. SNYDER	3 7 C
MERCER 2 NNE	5651	MERCER	2	41 15	80 13	1160	7P	7A	MRS. FRAN. STRUTHERS	2 3 5
MERCER HIWAY SHED	5654	MERCER	2	41 14	80 15	1250		MID	PA DEPT HIGHWAYS	C
MERCERSBURG	5662	FRANKLIN	12	39 50	77 54	605		8A	ROLLIN P. GILBERT	3
MERWINSBURG	5676	MONROE	9	40 58	75 28	970		MID	WILLIAM D. GOULD	C
MIDDLETOWN OLMSTED FLD	5703	DAUPHIN	15	40 11	76 46	303	MID	MID	U. S. AIR FORCE	2 3 5
MIDLAND DAM 7	5710	BEAVER	11	40 38	80 28	689	11P	7A	CORPS OF ENGINEERS	2 3 5
MILAN 4 WNW	5732	BRADFORD	15	41 56	76 35	1448		MID	CARL A. MORRIS	C
MILANVILLE	5738	WAYNE	5	41 40	75 04	760		8A	CHARLES W. DAVIS	3
MILLERSBURG 2 E	5775	DAUPHIN	15	40 32	76 56	560		MID	RUSSELL SHEPLEY	
MILLHEIM	5790	CENTRE	15	40 54	77 29	1090		7A	NEVIN E. BOWERSOX	3
MILLVILLE 2 SW	5817	COLUMBIA	15	41 06	76 34	860		7A	KENNETH LEIGHOW	3
MILROY	5825	MIFFLIN	6	40 43	77 35	770		8A	THOMAS C. HARBESON	3
MONTROSE 1 E	5915	SUSQUEHANNA	15	41 50	75 51	1630	7A	7A	WILBER W. HOOPES,JR	2 3 5
MORGANTOWN	5956	BERKS	15	40 09	75 54	595	MID	MID	PA TURNPIKE COMM	2 3 5
MT GRETNA 2 SE	6028	LANCASTER	15	40 14	76 26	670	MID	MID	PA TURNPIKE COMM	2 3 5
MT POCONO 2 N AP	6055	MONROE	5	41 09	75 22	1915	5P	5P	H. JOHN DAVIS, JR.	2 3 5 C
MOUNT UNION 1 N	6067	MIFFLIN	6	40 24	77 53	820		MID	MT UNION WTR WORKS	C
MUHLENBURG 1 SE	6090	LUZERNE	15	41 13	76 08	1110	6P	6P	THEODORE J. SAMPSON	2 3 5 7
MURRYSVILLE	6111	WESTMORELAND	10	40 26	79 42	903		MID	DAVID C. SHAW	C
MYERSTOWN	6126	LEBANON	14	40 22	76 18	480		8A	MRS.KATHLEEN MANDELL	3
NATRONA LOCK 4	6151	ALLEGHENY	1	40 37	79 43	800		7A	CORPS OF ENGINEERS	3
NEFFS MILLS 3 NE	6174	HUNTINGDON	6	40 40	77 55	900		MID	PA STATE UNIVERSITY	C
NESHAMINY FALLS	6194	BUCKS	5	40 09	74 57	60		MID	PHILA SUB WATER CO	3
NEWBURG 3 W	6225	FRANKLIN	15	40 09	77 37	745	5P	5P	PA TURNPIKE COMM	2 3 5
NEW CASTLE 1 N	6233	LAWRENCE	2	41 01	80 22	825	5P	7A	BAXTER F. JOHNSON	2 3 5 C
NEWELL	6246	FAYETTE	10	40 05	79 54	805	12M	12M	GENERAL CHEMICAL CO	2 3 5
NEW PARK	6289	YORK	15	39 44	76 30	780		6P	CLINTON J. ALLEN	3
NEWPORT	6297	PERRY	6	40 29	77 08	400	7A	7A	MRS. FRANCES K. FRY	2 3 5 7
NEW STANTON	6310	WESTMORELAND	10	40 13	79 36	980	MID	MID	PA TURNPIKE COMM	2 3 5
NEW TRIPOLI	6326	LEHIGH	14	40 41	75 45	570		6P	FRED C. OSWALD	3
NORRISTOWN	6370	MONTGOMERY	14	40 07	75 21	75	MID	8A	GEORGE H. BOONE	2 3 5
NORTH EAST 2 SE	6396	ERIE	8	42 12	79 49	1060		9A	ELLSWORTH WEAVER	3
ORWELL 3 N	6621	BRADFORD	15	41 55	76 16	1620		8A	WILLIAM I. BROWN	3
PALM	6681	MONTGOMERY	14	40 26	75 32	385		8A	FRED C. ESCHBACH	3
#PALMERTON	6689	CARBON	9	40 48	75 37	435	MID	MID	NEW JERSEY ZINC CO	2 3 5 C
PARKER	6721	ARMSTRONG	1	41 05	79 41	1140		7A	LOUIS A. MALARKEY	3
PARKER 1 E	6724	CLARION	1	41 06	79 40	1100		MID	P. M. NEELY	C
PAUPACK 2 WNW	6762	PIKE	5	41 24	75 14	1360		8A	MISS L. VETTERLEIN	3
PECKS POND	6786	PIKE	5	41 17	75 06	1380		9A	MRS. CARRIE NESS	3
#PHIL DREXEL INST OF TEC	6879	PHILADELPHIA	14	39 57	75 11	30	MID	MID	FRANCIS K. DAVIS,JR	2 3 5
PHILADELPHIA WB AP	6889	PHILADELPHIA	5	39 53	75 14	13	MID	MID	U.S. WEATHER BUREAU	2 3 5 7 C
#PHILADELPHIA PT BREEZE	6899	PHILADELPHIA	5	39 55	75 12	32	MID	MID	ATLANTIC REFINING	2 3 5 C
PHILADELPHIA SHAWMONT	6904	PHILADELPHIA	5	40 02	75 15	70	7P	7P	SCHUYLKILL NAVIG CO	2 3 5
#PHILADELPHIA CITY	6909	PHILADELPHIA	5	39 57	75 09	26	9A	9A	USN HYDROGRAPHIC OFF	2 5 C
PHILIPSBURG CAA AP	6916	CENTRE	6	40 54	78 05	1918	MID	MID	CIVIL AERO. ADM.	2 5 7 C
PHOENIXVILLE 1 E	6927	CHESTER	14	40 07	75 30	105	6P	MID	PHILA SUB WATER CO	2 3 5 C
PIKES CREEK	6939	LUZERNE	15	41 18	76 08	1320		7A	HARRY SHELDON	C
PIMPLE HILL	6944	MONROE	9	41 02	75 30	2215	9A	9A	PA DEPT FRST + WTRS	2 5 6 7
PINE GROVE 1 NE	6954	SCHUYLKILL	15	4[illegible] 34	76 22	535		8A	PA POWER + LIGHT CO	3
PITTSBURGH WB AP 2	6993	ALLEGHENY	11	4[illegible] 30	80 13	1151	MID	MID	U.S. WEATHER BUREAU	2 3 5 7 C
#PITTSBURGH WB CITY	6997	ALLEGHENY	11	40 27	80 00	749	MID	MID	U.S. WEATHER BUREAU	2 3 5 C
PLEASANT MOUNT 1 W	7029	WAYNE	5	41 44	75 27	1800	8A	8A	PA FISH COMM	2 3 5 7 C
PORT CLINTON	7116	SCHUYLKILL	14	40 35	76 02	450	7A	7A	MRS. ADA E. RARICK	2 3 5 C
PORTLAND	7127	NORTHAMPTON	5	40 55	75 06	297		8A	JOINT BRIDGE COMM	INAC 1/56
POTTSVILLE	7161	SCHUYLKILL	14	40 42	76 11	690		8A	LLOYD E. MELLER	3
PUNXSUTAWNEY	7217	JEFFERSON	1	40 57	79 00	1298		MID	JOHN VOLANSKY	C
PUTNEYVILLE 2 SE DAM	7229	ARMSTRONG	1	40 55	79 17	1270	8A	8A	CORPS OF ENGINEERS	2 3 5 C
QUAKERTOWN 1 E	7239	BUCKS	5	40 26	75 20	490	5P	7A	DENNIS K. FLUCK	2 3 5
RAYMOND	7310	POTTER	13	41 52	77 52	2220		7A	MRS. RACHEL LANGAN	3 C
#READING WB CITY	7318	BERKS	14	40 20	75 58	266	MID	MID	U.S. WEATHER BUREAU	2 3 5 7 C
RENOVO	7409	CLINTON	16	41 20	77 46	660		7A	MRS. CAROLINE BAIRD	3
RENOVO 5 S	7410	CLINTON	16	41 14	77 46	2035		MID	C. F. BILLETTE	C
REW	7425	MC KEAN	1	41 54	78 32	2250		8A	HAROLD C. HEALY	3
RICES LANDING L 6	7443	GREENE	10	39 57	80 00	775		7A	CORPS OF ENGINEERS	3
RIDGWAY 3 W	7477	ELK	1	41 25	78 47	1420	7A	7A	BOROUGH OF RIDGWAY	2 3 5
ROCHESTER 1 N	7540	BEAVER	2	40 43	80 18	900		MID	DEQUESNE LIGHT CO	C
RUSH	7694	SUSQUEHANNA	15	41 47	76 03	1000		9A	MISS MAUDE MC CAIN	3
RUSHVILLE	7727	SUSQUEHANNA	15	41 47	76 07	870		7A	CARL KOPATZ	3
SAFE HARBOR	7732	LANCASTER	15	39 55	76 23	270		MID	S.M.WATER POWER CORP	C
SAGAMORE 1 S	7739	INDIANA	1	40 46	79 14	1320		7A	CORPS OF ENGINEERS	3
SALINA 3 W	7782	WESTMORELAN	7	40 31	79 33	1109	6P	6P	MUN AUTH WSTMRLD CO	2 3 5
SAXTON	7846	BEDFORD	6	40 12	78 15	780		8A	MRS.ALVERTA L.HOLMES	3 C
SCANDIA 2 E	7855	WARREN	1	41 55	79 01	2040		MID	DAVID R. ANDERSON	C
SCHENLEY LOCK 5	7863	ARMSTRONG	1	40 41	79 40	783		VAR	CORPS OF ENGINEERS	3
#SCRANTON	7902	LACKAWANNA	15	41 25	75 40	746	7A	7A	U.S. POST OFFICE	2 3 5
SCRANTON WB AIRPORT	7905	LUZERNE	15	41 20	75 44	956	MID	MID	U.S. WEATHER BUREAU	2 3 5 7 C
SELINSGROVE CAA AP	7931	SNYDER	15	40 40	76 52	437	MID	MID	CIVIL AERO. ADM.	2 3 5 7
SELLERSVILLE 2 NW	7938	BUCKS	5	40 23	75 20	530		MID	SELLERSVILLE WTR CO	C

Observer	Refer To Tables
[illegible]	2 3 5 6
HENRY S. HAAK	2 3 5
JOHNSTOWN TRIBUNE	2 3 5
CITY OF JOHNSTOWN	
RUDOLPH A. ANDERSON	2 3 5
JEROME S. HOWE	3
EUGENE L. KREITNER	3
PA TURNPIKE COMM	2 3 5
CORPS OF ENGINEERS	3
PA TURNPIKE COMM	3
CITY OF BETHLEHEM	3
ORIN A. BUTTERS	3
MRS. GLADYS REINEKE	3
LANCASTER WATER BUR	2 3 5
LANCASTER WATER BUR	C
PA STATE COLLEGE	2 3 5 6 C
WEST PENN POWER CO	INAC /
PA DEPT OF WELFARE	C
HARRY P. HOWLAND	2 3 4
LEON MILLER	2 3
THOMAS DONNACHIE	C
GOODWIN S. DEFREHN	3 C
RS.DIMMIS M.BAILEY	3
USSELL LINEMAN	3
MERICAN VISCOSE CO	2 3 5
ISS RETTA M. CRUMB	2 3 5
PETER L. STEVENSON	2 3 5
HUGH F. PARKER	
THOMAS MECKES	3
MRS. DOROTHY HARPLE	3
MRS. JULIA J. SHOFF	2 3 5
MISS ELLEN J. MILES	3
FRANCES E.SCHEIBNER	3
MRS. I. S. BUCHANAN	3

STATION INDEX

Station	Index No.	County			rver	Refer To Tables
E GAP 2 NE	7965	HUNTINGDON	7	0	S. HELEN M. PYLE	C
AIN	7978	NORTHUMBLAN	7	0	ARING CRK WTR CO	3
FIELD 6 W	8026	WARREN	7	0	N. HANSON	C
PENSBURG	8073	FRANKLIN	7	0	ITH B. ALLEN	2 3 5 7
PINGPORT W	8078	BEAVER	8	0	S. WEATHER BUREAU	2 3 5 7 C
LMAHONING	8145	CAMERON	7	0	S.FRANCES CALDWELL	3
PERY ROCK	8184	BUTLER	8	5	LTER D. ALBERT	2 3 5 7
HPORT HIGHWAY SHED	8190	MC KEAN	7	0	DEPT HIGHWAYS	C
RSET FAIRVIEW ST	8244	SOMERSET	7	0	WARD G. PECK	3
RSET MAIN	8249	SOMERSET	7	0	VID L. GROVE	2 3 5
H CANAAN 1 NE	8275	WAYNE	7	0	EUGENE M. COOK	C
H MOUNTAIN	8308	FRANKLIN	7	0	PA DEpt OF HEALTH	3
NGBORO	8359	CRAWFORD	8	0	SPRINGBORO BOROUGH	2 3 5 C
NG GROVE	8379	YORK	7	0	P. H. GLATFELTER CO	3 C
NGS 1 SW	8395	SOMERSET	7	0	ALLEN E. YOCOM	2 3 5 7
E COLL	8449	CENTRE	-			2 3 5 6 CG
USSTOW	8570	BERKS				3
NGSTON	8589	INDIANA				C
UDSBUR	8596	MONROE				2 3 5 C
CREE	8610	JEFFERSON				3
URY	8668	NORTHUMBLA				3 C
UEHANNA	8692	SUSQUEHANN				3
RSVILLE	8699	ALLEGHENY				3
QUA	8758	SCHUYLKILL				3
QUA 4 N DAM	8763	SCHUYLKILL				3 -
RACK 2 S FIRE TWR	8770	CLINTON				2 3 5 7
ESTA 2 SE DAM	8873	FOREST				2 3 5 7 C
SVILLE	8885	CRAWFORD				C
SVILLE WATER WORKS	8888	CRAWFORD				2 3 5
E	8901	WARREN				3
N	8905	BRADFORD				2 3 5 7 C
R CITY 5 SW	8910	DAUPHIN				3 7
						3 -
						-
						3 C
						3 C
						2 3 5
						2 3 5
						3
						3
						3
						3
						3

Station	Index No.	County	Drainage 1	Latitude	Longitude	Elevation	Observation Time Temp.	Observation Time Precip.	Observer	Refer To Tables
WARREN	9708	WARREN	1	41 51	79 08	1280	7P	7A	GILBERT H. MEIER	2 3 5
WASHINGTON	9312	WASHINGTON	11	40 11	80 14	1200		MID	PA DEPT HIGHWAYS	C
WATSONTOWN	9345	NORTHUMBLAND	16	41 05	76 52	490		VP	WILLIAM BIRD	3
WAYNESBURG 2 W	9362	GREENE	10	39 54	80 13	980	6P	7A	RALPH L. AMOS	2 3 5
WAYNESBURG 1 E	9367	GREENE	10	39 54	80 10	940		MID	SEWAGE DISPOSAL PLT	C
WEBSTER MILLS 3 SW	9380	FULTON	12	39 49	76 05	920		MID	WILLIAM D. COVER	C
WELLSBORO 3 S	9408	TIOGA	16	41 43	77 16	1920	7A	7A	MARION L. SHUMWAY	2 3 5
WELLSBORO 2 E	9412	TIOGA	16	41 45	77 16	1550		MID	MRS. IDA S. MAYNARD	C
WELLSVILLE	9420	YORK	15	40 03	76 57	500	5P	5P	D. D. HOOVER	2 3 5
WERNERSVILLE 1 W	9430	BERKS	14	40 20	76 06	405		8A	CHARLES A. GRUBER	3
WEST CHESTER	9464	CHESTER	5	39 58	75 36	440	8A	8A	DAILY LOCAL NEWS	2 3 5
WEST GROVE 1 E	9503	CHESTER	5	39 49	75 49	440		8A	CONARD-PYLE CO	3
WEST HICKORY	9507	FOREST	1	41 34	79 25	1090		8A	MRS.HELEN F.KINNEAR	3
WHITESBURG	9655	ARMSTRONG	1	40 45	79 24	1530		7A	CORPS OF ENGINEERS	3
WILKES-BARRE	9702	LAZERNE	15	41 15	75 52	610		7A	MRS. MARY G. MIRMAK	3
WILLIAMSBURG	9714	BLAIR	6	40 28	78 12	860		7A	MYRON K. BIDDLE	3
WILLIAMSPORT WB AP	9728	LYCOMING	16	41 15	76 55	527	MID	MID	U.S. WEATHER BUREAU	2 3 5 7 C
WIND GAP	9781	NORTHAMPTON	5	40 51	75 18	720		MID	OWEN R. PARRY	C
WOLFSBURG	9823	BEDFORD	6	40 03	78 32	1190		7A	WALTER C. RICE	3
YORK 3 SSW PUMP STA	9933	YORK	15	39 55	76 45	390	5P	5P	YORK WATER COMPANY	2 3 5
YORK 2 S FILTER PLANT	38	YORK	15	39 56	76 44	640		MID	YORK WATER COMPANY	C
YORK HAVEN			15	40 07	76 43	310		8A	METROPOL EDISON CO	3
YOUNGSVILLE			1	41 51	79 20	1225		MID	HENRY CARLETT	C
ZION GROVE			15	40 54	76 13	940		7A	JAMES D. TEETER	3
ZIONSVILLE 3 SE			[illegible]	[illegible] 32	75 27	660		7A	LESLIE HOWATT	3
NEW STATIONS										
BRADFORD CAA AIRPORT					8	2150	MID	MID	CIVIL AERO. ADM.	2 3 5 7
MEYERSDALE					2	2040		8A	ARTHUR J. POTTER	3
CLOSED STATIONS										
ARTEMAS 1 WNW						0	6P	6P	GRAYSON E.NORTHCRAFT	CLOSED 7/57
EDINBORO 5 SW						5		8A	WILLIAM HAGER	CLOSED 6/57
MEYERSDALE 1 ENE						n		8A	ARTHUR B. MC CARTER	CLOSED 7/57

1 1-ALLEGHENY; 2-BEAVER; 3- 4-CONEMAUGH; 5-DELAWARE; 6-JUNIATA; 7-KISKIMINETAS; 8-LAKE ERIE; 9-LEHIGH; 10-MONONGAHELA; 11-OHIO; 12-POTOMAC; 13-LAKE ONTARIO; 14-SCHUYLKILL; 15-SUSQUEHANNA; 16-WEST BRANCH; 17-YOUGHIOGHENY

REFERENCE NOTES

Additional information regarding the climate of Pennsylvania may be obtained by writing to the State Climatologist at Weather Bureau Airport Station, Harrisburg State Airport, New Cumberland, Pennsylvania, or to any Weather Bureau Office near you.

Figures and letters following the station name, such as 12 SSW, indicate distance in miles and direction from the post office.

Delayed data and corrections will be carried only in the June and December issues of this bulletin.

Monthly and seasonal snowfall and heating degree days for the preceding 12 months will be carried in the June issue of this bulletin.

Stations appearing in the Index, but for which data are not listed in the tables, either are missing or were received too late to be included in this issue.

Divisions, as used in Table 2, became effective with data for September 1956.

Unless otherwise indicated, dimensional units used in this bulletin are: Temperature in °F, precipitation and evaporation in inches, and wind movement in miles. Monthly degree day totals are the sums of the negative departures of average daily temperatures from 65° F.

Evaporation is measured in the standard Weather Bureau type pan of 4 foot diameter unless otherwise shown by footnote following Table 6. Max and Min in Table 6 refer to extremes of temperature of water in pan as recorded during 24 hours ending at time of observation.

Long-term means for full-time stations (those shown in the Station Index as "U. S. Weather Bureau") are based on the period 1921-1950, adjusted to represent observations taken at the present location. Long-term means for all stations except full-time Weather Bureau stations are based on the period 1931-1955.

Water equivalent values published in Table 7 are the water equivalent of snow, sleet or ice on the ground. Samples for obtaining measurements are taken from different points for successive observations; consequently occasional drifting and other causes of local variability in the snowpack result in apparent inconsistencies in the record. Water equivalent of snow on the ground is measured at selected stations when two or more inches of snow are on the ground.

Entries of Snowfall in Tables 2 and 7, and in the seasonal snowfall table, include snow and sleet. Entries of snow on ground include snow, sleet and ice.

Data in Tables 3, 5, and 6 and snowfall in Table 7, when published, are for the 24 hours ending at time of Observation. The Station Index lists observation times in the standard of time in local use. During the summer months some observers take the observations on daylight saving time.

Snow on ground in Table 7 is at observation time for all except Weather Bureau and CAA stations. For these stations snow on ground values are at 7:30 a.m., E.S.T.

- \- No record in Tables 3, 6, 7 and the Station Index. No record in Tables 2 and 5, is indicated by no entry. Consult the annual issue Of this publication for interpolated monthly precipitation totals.
- + And also on a later date or dates.
- ++ Fastest observed one minute wind speed. This station is not equipped with automatic wind instruments.
- * Amount included in following measurement, time distribution unknown.
- // Gage is equipped with a windshield.
- # Thermometers are generally exposed in a shelter located a few feet above sod-covered ground; however, the reference indicates that the thermometers are exposed in a shelter located on the roof of a building.
- AM Data based on observational day ending before noon.
- B Adjusted to a full month.
- C In the "Refer to Tables" column in the Station Index the letter "C" indicates recorder stations. These stations are processed for special purposes and are published later in "Hourly Precipitation Data".
- D Water equivalent of snowfall wholly or partly estimated, using a ratio of 1 inch water equivalent to every 10 inches of new snowfall.
- G In the "Refer to Tables" column in the Station index the letter "G" indicates that soil temperatures are published.
- M One or more days of record missing; if average value is entered, less than 10 days record is missing. See Table 5 for detailed daily record. Degree day data, if carried for this station, have been adjusted to represent the value for a full month.
- R Amounts from recording gage (These amounts are essentially accurate but may vary slightly from the amounts to be published later in "Hourly Precipitation Data".)
- This entry in time of observation column in Station Index means observation made near sunset.
- SS Trace, an amount too small to measure.
- T Includes total for previous month.
- VAR This entry in time of observation column in Station Index means variable.

Information concerning the history Of changes in locations, elevations, exposure etc. of substations through 1955 may be found in the publication "Substation History" for this state, soon to be issued. That publication, when available, may be obtained from the Superintendent of Documents, Government Printing Office, Washington 25, D. C. at a price to be announced. Similar information for regular Weather Bureau stations may be found in the latest issues of Local Climatological Data, Annual for the respective stations, obtained as indicated above, price 15 cents.

Subscription Price: 20 cents per copy, monthly and annual; $2.50 per year. (Yearly subscription includes the Annual Summary). Checks, and money orders should be made payable to the Superintendent Of Documents. Remittance and correspondence regarding subscriptions should be sent to the Superintendent of Documents, Government Printing Office, Washington 25, D. C.

WPRC, Asheville, N. C. --- 9/4/57 --- 1100

U. S. DEPARTMENT OF COMMERCE
SINCLAIR WEEKS, Secretary
WEATHER BUREAU
F. W. REICHELDERFER, Chief

CLIMATOLOGICAL DATA

PENNSYLVANIA

AUGUST 1957
Volume LXII No. 8

ASHEVILLE: 1957

PENNSYLVANIA - AUGUST 1957

WEATHER SUMMARY

GENERAL

August 1957 was characterized by a continuation of the summer dry spell in the east portion, and the spread of the dryness westward throughout the State. At Philadelphia WB AP only 0.02 inch was recorded between August 1 and 24; Allentown WB AP noted this as the driest August since 1916; Reading WB City reported this August to be the driest since 1951, and the 5th driest of record; Scranton WB AP also found this to be the 5th driest August of record. At Harrisburg WB AP, this was the driest August since 1923, and third driest of record; the summer at that station was the driest since 1909, and the 4th driest of record. At Pittsburgh WB AP 2, this was the 3rd driest August since 1871. Thirty-three percent of the stations for which long-term precipitation means are available registered deficiencies of 3 inches or more for the month, and all but 4 of these stations had deficiencies greater than 0.50 inch. Monthly totals ranged from 0.03 inch at Bakerstown 3 WNW to 3.52 inches at Wellsville. The greatest daily amount was 2.55 inches at Tionesta 2 SE Dam on the 4th.

The month was also significantly cooler than usual. Minimum temperatures reached 32° at Madera on the 18th and at Kane 1 NNE on the 22nd, making this the first August since 1954 that temperatures of 32° or below were recorded so early in the fall. Temperature averages in the northeast portion reflected the prevailing coolness more strongly than did other regions of the State, and the greatest negative departure was noted at Stroudsburg where the monthly average temperature, 64.6°, was 5.4° below the long-term mean. At the other extreme, the highest temperature for the month was 99°, noted at Phoenixville 1 E and Wellsville on the 3rd.

WEATHER DETAILS

Seasonable mildness at the start of the month gave way to excessive heat on August 3 in advance of an active cold front that was accompanied by scattered showers. Temperatures in the warm air reached their highest levels of the month, but the cooler air that overspread the State on the 4th inaugurated a 3-day cool snap that plunged thermometers to their lowest values for the month at many locations. The return circulation brought warmer air on the 9th, but there was an immediate return to seasonable mildness with a few scattered thundershowers in the extreme west portion on the 10th. Another frontal passage on the 12th was accompanied by scattered light showers in all except the southeast portion, and after a 2-day cool snap an extended period of seasonable mildness ensued. Scattered light showers on August 19-21 resulted from an offshore Low moving northeastward along the coast. A fresh mass of cool air resulted in another cool snap in the east portion during the period August 22-24. On the 25th, another offshore Low moved northeastward from a point near Cape Hatteras, reaching the southern New Jersey coast by the 26th, and then moving more rapidly northeastward during the day. Rains were general over the southeast portion of the State on the 25th and during the early hours of the next day, with moderate or heavy amounts. Following another 2-day cool period, the month closed with cloudy, mild weather.

WEATHER EFFECTS

Although the rainfall in the southeast on August 25 and 26 brought some relief to that parched area, the damaging depletion of soil moisture spread westward so that all areas were dry by the end of the month. The rains came too late to help most of the corn crop, and much of the crop intended for grain was diverted to silage. Hay and pastures suffered from the dryness: the yields of the first cutting of hay were below par in the southeast, although good elsewhere in the State, but later cuttings were poor. New seedings for the 1958 hay crop were hard hit by the dryness, as the dry ground hindered re-seeding, and in the southeast delayed fall planting of alfalfa. Erie County peaches attained good size, but dry weather in most other areas limited development of peaches and apples. Grapes in the Erie Belt ripened early due to dry weather. Potatoes were hard hit by the prolonged dryness in all sections except the northwest and in Potter County. Some late tobacco was helped by the rains of the 25th and 26th, but for many fields it came too late.

DESTRUCTIVE STORMS

Thunderstorms and associated phenomena accounted for all of the violent features of the month's weather. Scattered thunderstorms in northwestern counties on the night of August 3 injured 1 person and blew down trees, while lightning-set fires caused moderate damage to homes and barns. In the Meshoppen area on the night of the 6th, another lightning-set fire destroyed a barn and several dairy cattle, with moderate losses. A "baby twister" ripped a large carnival tent near Allentown on the afternoon of August 7, but nobody was injured. Two barns and a house were destroyed by lightning-set fires at Washington on the evening of August 11, with moderate losses. Another "baby twister" caused minor damage near Harrisburg on the afternoon of the 21st, while a strong windstorm near Pine Grove damaged trees. Another lightning-set fire destroyed a barn and its contents near York on the evening of August 25, with moderate loss.

FLOODS

None reported.

Harold S. Lippmann, Climatologist
Weather Records Processing Center
Chattanooga, Tennessee

Temperature: Average Maximum	Average Minimum	Average	Departure From Long Term Means	Highest	Date	Lowest	Date	Degree Days	No. of Days Max 90° or Above	Max 32° or Below	Min 32° or Below	Min 0° or Below	Precipitation: Total	Departure From Long Term Means	Greatest Day	Date	Snow, Sleet Total	Max Depth on Ground	Date	No. of Days .10 or More	.50 or More	1.00 or More
79.2	55.0	67.1	.2	91	3	43	27+	25	1	0	0	0	2.48	- 1.59	1.15	26	.0	0		7	1	1
76.6	47.5	62.1		90	4	37	24	118	1	0	0	0	1.23		.36	26	.0	0		4	0	0
76.3	52.3	64.3	.1	88	3	41	6+	69	0	0	0	0	1.26	- 3.18	.64	26	.0	0		3	1	0
81.0	54.2	67.6		94	3	42	6	30	2	0	0	0	1.89		.67	26	.0	0		6	1	0
75.3	54.0	64.7		91	4	40	28	60	1	0	0	0	1.42		.66	26	.0	0		3	1	0
72.5M	47.0M	59.8M		86	4	39	28	175	0	0	0	0	2.16	- 1.95	.69	20	.0	0			1	0
80.2	54.2	67.2	- 3.1	95	4	46	6+	19	1	0	0	0	1.14	- 2.53	.40	5	.0	0		3	0	0
78.3	54.0	66.2	- 3.8	93	3	43	6	37	1	0	0	0	1.38	- 2.70	.52	4	.0	0		4	1	0
80.7	48.5	64.6	- 5.4	96	3	35	6	79	5	0	0	0	.72	- 3.96	.23	12	.0	0		3	0	0
		64.8											1.52				.0					
82.6	57.2	69.9	- 1.9	96	3	47	6+	8	3	0	0	0	1.39	- 3.10	.64	26	.0	0		4	1	0
83.2	57.8	70.5	- 1.5	95	4	48	13	3	3	0	0	0	1.22	- 3.31	.74	26	.0	0		3	1	0
83.3	57.8	70.6	- 2.6	95	3	48	24	2	3	0	0	0	.69	- 3.57	.37	25	.0	0		2	0	0
82.4M	55.1M	68.8M	- .9	94	3	43	6	14	3	0	0	0	1.47	- 3.30	1.00	26	.0	0		3	1	1
80.8	55.4	68.1	- 2.5	95	3	45	6	21	2	0	0	0	1.09	- 2.99	.66	25	.0	0		3	1	0
85.4	51.6	68.5	- 2.7	98	4	39	6	16	8	0	0	0					.0	0				
		69.4											1.17				.0					
84.8	62.5	73.7		93	4	50	24	0	7	0	0	0	1.63		1.35	26	.0	0		2	1	1
84.6	56.1	70.4	- 2.3	96	4	45	24	6	7	0	0	0	2.68	- 1.90	2.45	26	.0	0		2	1	1
85.4	59.7	72.6		97	3	48	28	1	7	0	0	0	1.10		.75	10	.0	0		3	1	0
	58.5	M				48	28			0	0	0	2.08		1.58	25	.0	0		2	1	1
84.8	57.3	71.1	- 1.5	95	3	45	28	1	5	0	0	0	.79	- 3.72	.39	26	.0	0		3	0	0
83.8	56.0	69.9	- 2.3	97	3	44	24	9	6	0	0	0	2.00	- 2.61	1.44	26	.0	0		3	1	1
85.8	58.0	71.9		96	3	46	6	1	12	0	0	0	1.72	- 2.41	1.27	26	.0	0		3	1	1
82.7	64.4	73.6	- 1.5	97	3	53	21	0	3	0	0	0	1.35	- 2.70	.44	11	.0	0		4	0	0
84.2	57.8	71.0	- 1.2	96	3	46	6	5	4	0	0	0	.56	- 3.74	.21	26	.0	0		3	0	0
84.0	56.1	70.1		97	4	45	6	5	7	0	0	0	.43		.18	11	.0	0		2	0	0
85.1	55.9	70.5	- 1.7	98	4	44	6	4	6	0	0	0	.55	- 3.71	.46	26	.0	0		1	0	0
85.7	66.1	75.9	- .7	95	3	56	6	0	10	0	0	0	2.05	- 3.40	1.80	25	.0	0		2	1	1
85.1	61.5	73.3	.4	97	3	53	6+	0	5	0	0	0	.69	- 3.35	.49	25	.0	0		2	0	0
82.3	57.7	70.0		94	3	45	6+	10	1	0	0	0	2.12		1.79	25	.0	0		3	1	1
82.5	58.5	70.5		95	3	46	13+	5	2	0	0	0	.67		.39	10	.0	0		2	0	0
84.4	61.6	73.0		97	3	51	23+	0	3	0	0	0	1.43		1.23	26	.0	0		1	1	1
85.3	65.2	75.3		96	3	57	6+	0	8	0	0	0	1.19		.62	25	.0	0		2	2	0
83.8	62.6	73.2	- .8	96	3	50	24	0	4	0	0	0	3.38	- 1.20	1.78	25	.0	0		2	2	2
82.9	66.2	74.6	- 1.0	93	3	58	23+	0	2	0	0	0	1.94		1.30	26	.0	0		3	1	1
83.6	66.0	74.8	- .4	93	3	57	28	0	3	0	0	0	1.32	- 3.30	1.05	25				2	1	1
86.4	57.0	71.7	- 1.8	99	3	44	6+	7	9	0	0	0	1.67	- 3.05	1.26	25	.0	0		3	1	1
84.5	56.4	70.5	.1	95	3+	43	24	5	5	0	0	0	1.26	- 3.23	.98	26	.0	0		2	1	0
83.8	61.9	72.9	- .5	97	3	53	6+	0	5	0	0	0	.88	- 3.00	.73	25	.0	0		2	1	0
84.8M	62.5M	73.7M		96	3	51	24	0	5	0	0	0	1.62		1.24	26	.0	0		2	1	1
85.8M	61.1M	73.5M	1.3	97	3	48	6	0	5	0	0	0	1.42	- 3.32	.98	26	.0	0		3	1	0
		72.4											1.46				.0					
84.8	57.4	71.1	- 1.3	96	4	47	24	2	7	0	0	0	1.88	- 1.99	1.56	26	.0	0		2	1	1
87.7	59.5	73.6	.8	98	3	50	24	0	11	0	0	0	1.86	- 2.44	1.36	26	.0	0		3	1	1
84.6	56.6	70.6	- 1.8	95	3	46	24	5	6	0	0	0	1.33	- 2.60	.97	25	.0	0		3	1	0
85.0	59.0	72.0	- .4	96	4	49	24	0	7	0	0	0	1.39	- 2.56	.82	26	.0	0		2	1	0
85.4	58.6	72.0	- 1.6	97	4	50	6	1	10	0	0	0	1.90	- 2.26	1.16	26	.0	0		3	1	1
83.4	61.1	72.3	- .7	95	3	52	6	0	3	0	0	0	.93	- 2.41	.69	25	.0	0		2	1	0
86.5	58.6	72.6		96	3	46	13	2	7	0	0	0	.14		.09	25	.0	0		0	0	0
85.5	58.2	71.9	- 1.2	97	3	48	6+	1	5	0	0	0	1.70	- 2.31	.56	26	.0	0		4	1	0
85.1	55.2	70.2		99	3	44	6+	12	6	0	0	0	3.52		1.15	25	.0	0		4	4	2
87.0	57.5	72.3	- .5	97	3	46	6	2	8	0	0	0	2.32	- 1.92	1.67	26	.0	0		3	1	1
		71.9											1.70				.0					
85.5	54.4	70.0		95	3	42	6	13	9	0	0	0	1.04		.72	26	.0	0		2	1	0
84.3	56.1	70.2		97	3	41	28	11	6	0	0	0	1.88		.58	26	.0	0		6	1	0
84.0	54.3	69.2		97	4	43	6	9	5	0	0	0	.47		.33	26	.0	0		2	0	0
85.4	54.5	70.0		95	4	47	6+	4	5	0	0	0	.53		.28	26	.0	0		1	0	0
86.7	53.6	70.2		97	4	45	24	4	7	0	0	0	1.51	- 2.72	1.42	26	.0	0		1	1	1
84.5M	51.5M	68.0M		98	4	44	6+	14	5	0	0	0	1.32	- 2.45	.85	26	.0	0		2	1	0
82.3	55.7	69.0	- 1.9	96	3	45	6	11	3	0	0	0	1.25	- 2.36	.40	25	.0	0		4	0	0
		69.5											1.14				.0					
75.4	52.0	63.7		87	4	43	28	79	0	0	0	0	2.46		.88	20	.0	0		7	2	0
79.3	48.8	64.1		94	4	41	6+	71	2	0	0	0	1.96		.63	26	.0	0		4	1	0
73.8	53.9	63.9		88	4	45	6+	80	0	0	0	0	2.12	- 2.20	.96	26	.0	0		3	2	0
77.4	49.5	63.5	- 4.9	91	4	41	6+	95	1	0	0	0	2.11	- 1.70	.63	22	.0	0		8	1	0

See Reference Notes Following Station Index

TABLE 2 - CONTINUED

Station	
MONTROSE 1 E	AM
TOWANDA	
WELLSBORO 3 S	AM
DIVISION	
CENTRAL MOUNTAINS	
BELLEFONTE 4 S	AM
DU BOIS 7 E	
EMPORIUM 2 SSW	AM
LOCK HAVEN	
MADERA	AM
PHILIPSBURG CAA AP	
RIDGWAY 3 W	AM
STATE COLLEGE	AM
TAMARACK 2 S FIRE TWR	AM
DIVISION	
SOUTH CENTRAL MOUNTAINS	
ALTOONA HORSESHOE CURVE	
BURNT CABINS 2 NE	
EBENSBURG	
EVERETT 1 SW	
HUNTINGDON	AM
JOHNSTOWN	AM
KEGG	
MARTINSBURG CAA AP	
DIVISION	
SOUTHWEST PLATEAU	
BAKERSTOWN 3 WNW	
BLAIRSVILLE 6 ENE	
BURGETTSTOWN 2 W	AM
BUTLER	
CLAYSVILLE 3 W	
CONFLUENCE 1 SW DAM	AM
DERRY	
DONEGAL	
DONORA	AM
FORD CITY 4 S DAM	AM
INDIANA 3 SE	
IRWIN	
MIDLAND DAM 7	
NEW CASTLE 1 N	
NEWELL	AM
NEW STANTON	
PITTSBURGH WB AP 2	//R
PITTSBURGH WB CITY	R
PUTNEYVILLE 2 SE DAM	AM
SALINA 3 W	
SHIPPINGPORT WB	
SLIPPERY ROCK	
SOMERSET MAIN ST	
SPRINGS 1 SW	
UNIONTOWN	
WAYNESBURG 2 W	
DIVISION	
NORTHWEST PLATEAU	
BRADFORD CAA AP	
BRADFORD 4 W RES	
BROOKVILLE CAA AIRPORT	
CLARION 3 SW	
CORRY	
COUDERSPORT 3 NW	
EAST BRADY	
ERIE WB AIRPORT	
FARRELL SHARON	
FRANKLIN	
GREENVILLE	
JAMESTOWN 2 NW	AM
KANE 1 NNE	AM
LINESVILLE 5 WNW	
MEADVILLE 1 S	AM
MERCER 2 NNE	
SPRINGBORO	AM
TIONESTA 2 SE DAM	AM
TITUSVILLE WATER WORKS	
WARREN	
DIVISION	

See Reference Notes Following Station Index

DAILY PRECIPITATION

Day of month

	Total	1	2	3	4	5	6	7	8	9	10	11	12	13	14	15	16	17	18	19	20	21	22	23	24	25	26	27	28	29	30	31
	.65										.15	.01									.38										.01	.10
R	1.39				.07	T				T	.03		.17							T	.12	T				.36	.64			T	T	
	1.22					.08				.01	.02	.04		.05						T		.12	.04				.74	.11			.01	
	1.47				1.08						.21					.02						.06								.02	.06	
	1.88				.03	.18					.09	.02															1.56					
	1.95				.21	T					.30	.30	.21	T		.16					.63		.09								.05	
	.03															.03				T			T									
	2.99				1.87						.03	.02				.48					.48		.11									
	3.12				1.46							T										.09					1.57			T		T
	2.44				.59	.64					.07		.18			.02	.25										.66				.03	
	.31				T	T					.02	T				.11					T						.18	T			T	T
	1.04				.05	.11								.05			.09						.02				.72				T	
	.98				.12	.06					.03	.01		.16		.26	.11				.19	T	.02				T				T	T
	1.43			.32	.08											.07					.04		.22				.10					
	.89					T					T	T											T				.69					
	1.88				.47			T			.20		.27			.11						.07				.15	.58				.03	
	.90					.12				T	.03	.02		.07						T		T				T	.61	.05			T	
	.69				.03						.05		.07								.04					.37	.12	.01				
	1.87			T	.86						.60									.07	.11										.23	
	1.44				.23					T	.09												T			.70	.42					
	1.63				.65	.73					.02	.23																				T
	.33				.01						.08	T				.02					.05											.17
	2.06			.74	T				T		T		.22		.29					.41	.31	T							T	.09	T	
A	1.66				.48								.64	.05		.10	.06				.07		.15							.06	.05	
	2.08				.74						T		.77		.08	.12	.06				.09	.04								.15	.03	
	.44				.10						.13																.13				.08	
	2.30			.58	.02						.01				.55	.12				.79	.06	.02								.13	.02	
	.09					T							.08								.01											
	.46				.28	.13					.03																	T				.02
	1.45				.06	.04					.05		.39			.03					.12						.67					.09
		RECORD MISSING																														
	.76										T					.57					.13										.06	
	1.37				.17						.03												.04			.15	.98					
	2.46				.08					T	.02	.12	.15	.13		.34					.88	.11	.07				.50			T	.06	
	1.86				.23						.09											T	.03			.15	1.36					
	2.86				2.07	.16					.21	T				.06	T				.16									T	.08	.12
	2.07				.34								T	.53			.30				.85	T								.05	T	
	1.47				.08	.01	T	.01			.05	T	T	.30		.15	.05				.60	.02	.20				T			T	T	
	2.45					T											.10										2.35	T				
	1.33				.05	.04					.17					T										.97				T	.10	
	.88				.28	.16					.07		.22			.01	T				.14						T					
	1.63					.08																	.20				1.35	T			T	T
	2.00				.10						.10					1.20	.10				.10		.30				.10					
	2.70				.57	.01										1.14					.55		.18								.22	.03
	2.65					.16					.10	.03		.05						.06			.02				2.19				.04	
	1.54				.12	.17					.08		.45			.05											.67					
	2.52				.50	T						T				.35					1.50		.09								.08	
	2.06				.42									.12		.27	.11				.80		.14							.04	T	.10
	2.09				.05	.13					.06	.09															1.76					
	2.68					.12					.02												.05				2.45		.04			
	1.10				.10						.75															.19	.06					
	.91				.36	.49						T				.06																T
	1.31				.60	.49					.03					.11																.08
	2.07				.84	.80					.03					.02					.36											.02
	1.62					.32					T	.03					.03						T				1.24					
	2.94				1.95	T					T	T				.19	T				.71	T	.06	T							.03	T
	3.12			T	2.20	T	T				.02	T	T	T		.17	T				.65	T	.08	T								
	.05			T							T					.02					.03										T	
	2.56			.16	1.20						.04		.13		.91						.08					T				.04		
	1.99				.31						.07	.02	.41	.20		.09	.07				.64		T							.11	.07	
	–				.36	.02		.05			.11		.32	.22		.04	.37				.37		.05							–	–	
	2.41				.21						.02	.17	.21	.12		.10	.02				.61	.06	.22				.59				.08	T
	.70										.20					.05					.45											
	1.89				.90	.65					.24	T				.07	T						.02									.01
	1.49				.52						T		.42	.07		.17					.10		.04							.08	.04	.01
	1.64				.10	.25					T			.54		T	T										.75				T	
	2.17				1.44											.10				.60											.03	
	2.08				.09		T	T							.32											1.58	.09					
	1.96				.03	.48				T	.04	T	.03	.23		.08	T				.29		.06				.63	.09				
	1.02			T	.68	T					T		.20			.07				T							T			T	T	.07
	.72				.29	.06				.04					.01						.26						T					.06
	1.11				.02					.02	.07					.02	.06				T					.01	.91					
	2.91				1.17						.12					.35				.21	.74	.07									.23	.02
	2.33					.48				T	.03	T	.04	.34		.08					.25		.11				.92	.04			.04	
	2.12										.01	.07	.02	.33		.04					.59		.04				.96			T	.06	
	.55				.03											.22			.30													
	2.50				1.50	.62					.23					.05	.10															
	1.34				.09	.02					T				.20	.79				T	.09					.03	.04			.05	.03	T
	.54															.54																T
	.81					.14						.55															.12					
	2.73				.34	.04						T		.23		1.00					.74		.24							.02	.10	.02
	2.17				.24	.19		T			.01	.02		.30		.28					.87	T	.19				.02			T	.05	
	.79				.19						.02					.10										.09	.39					
	1.84				.15	.37		.07			.07	.02	.06	.09							.92	.01	.03				.04	T			.01	
	1.43			.36	T					T	T		.06		.72										.05	.10			.03	.11	T	T
	.48				.18																										.30	
	1.38				.14										.15	.42				.23		.01				.03	T				.40	
	1.72										.32					.23					1.05											.12
	.80				.09											.06					T		.22			T	.01				.01	.41
	2.48				.22	.05					.10			.37			.30						.10			.10	1.15	.04			.05	
	2.47				.35			.14			.03	.11	.40	.05		.10					.85		.20				T			.06	.18	
	2.48					.07																.11					2.30					
	2.00				.10						.06										.03					.37	1.44					T
	1.39	.02				.36					.09	.05											.03			T	.82					
	1.53				.48								.40	.18		.16	T				.18		T							.08	.05	.02
	2.05				.70						.02	.01	.03	.08		.28					.88		.02							.01	.01	.01
	.45				.03						.20	T				.08					.10						.02					.02
	.73				.13	.10		T			.02	.02		.23		.05				T							.15				.03	
	1.72					.23											.08										1.27	.14				
	.47				.14	T					T	T															.33					
	2.19				.64	.25					.08	.04	.06	.29		.18					.58						.07					
	.96			.43	T					T	.15									.31	.01											.06
	1.07				.04						.01				.25					.16	.02	.27				.11	T			.19	.02	T
	1.90				.21	.46					T	.07														T	1.16					
	.93				.17	.01				T	.03											.02				.69	.01			T		
	1.96				.02	.20					T	.07											.08				1.59					
	.82				.10	.11					.03	.02	.02	.16		T	T			T			.07				.21	.02		T	.08	
	1.23				.09	.11					.04	.02		.25			.05						.22				.36	.03			.06	
	.79				.04	.08		T		T	T	T	.02	.24		.05	T						.01				.22	.03			.10	
	1.35				T	.36				T	T	.44					.13					T				T	.42					
	1.82				.37	.33					.03		.11			.01	.09					.12					.70	.04			.02	
	–	–	–	–	–	–	–	–	–			T					T						.11				1.64					
	1.38				.88	.36					.05	.03					.06															
	2.41					.01	.02								.10	.20		.08	.21		.01	.10	.67	.01	.02	.01	.51	.41			.05	
	.82				.17	.19					.11	.02											.25				.08					

See Reference Notes Following Station Index

DAILY PRECIPITATION

Table 3—Continued

Day of month

Station	Total	1	2	3	4	5	6	7	8	9	10	11	12	13	14	15	16	17	18	19	20	21	22	23	24	25	26	27	28	29	30	3
HUNTSDALE	3.25				.01	1.40				.02	.10	T															1.72	T				.
HYNDMAN	.43				.13	.14	T				.05			.03		.04											.02					.
INDIANA 3 SE	.83				.06	.03					.53										.19											
IRWIN	.39																			.17	.22											
JAMESTOWN 2 NW	2.69				.35															T	.09		1.97			T	.14				.02	.
JIM THORPE	1.47				.10	.07				T	.05		.20			T	T			T						T	1.00				.05	
JOHNSTOWN	1.44				.75	.26					.10	.06				.06	.03				T										T	.
KANE 1 NNE	1.75				.80					T		.05		.17		.27					.42		.02							.02	T	T
KARTHAUS	2.08				.27	.04					.05	T		T		.45	.48				.43		.21								.13	
KEATING SUMMIT	1.80				.28						.03	.02	.36	.14		.13	.05				.60									.10	.11	
KEGG	.27				.25	T					T															T					.02	.
KITTANNING LOCK 7	2.11				T	.01										.30					1.68		.05									.
KREGAR 4 SE	1.29			.30	.83	T					.14		T			T				T							T					.
KRESGEVILLE 3 W	1.37				.04	.09					.05			.23			.07						.05				.69	.09			.06	
LAFAYETTE MC KEAN PARK		RECORD MISSING																														
LAKEVILLE 1 NNE	1.44				.11	.12		.04			.03	T	T	.27			.29						.17				.27				.14	
LANCASTER 2 NE PUMP STA	.56				.03	.05					.13										.01					.13	.21					
LANDISVILLE 2 NW	.43					.08					.01	.18										.02				T	.14					
LAWRENCEVILLE 2 S	2.11				.30	T				.04		.16	.20	.09		.11					.35		.63			.10					.13	
LEBANON 3 W	.55				.02	.05					.01	.01															.46					
LEHIGHTON	1.84				.06					.06	.06			.19									.02				1.45	T		T	T	
LE ROY	1.73				.08						.17		.25				.12					.64				.44					.03	
LEWIS RUN 3 SE	1.57				.52								.51	T		.21					.19		.03							.05	.06	
LEWISTOWN	.53				.04	.03				T		.02				.02	.06						.08				.28			T		
LINESVILLE 5 WNW	.91				T										.50	.12				.06	.07					.04	.07			.02	.03	
LOCK HAVEN	1.68				.26	.12				T	.10			.08		.08	.04				.89	T	.01				.06				.04	.
LONG POND 2 W	1.09				.03	.27				.05	.01	.04		.18		T	.01						.04				.28	.12		T	.03	
LYNCH	-	-	-	-	-	-	-	-	-	-	-	-	-	-	-	-	-	-	-	-	-	-										
LYNDELL 2 NW	2.15				.35						T																1.80				.05	
MADERA	1.48				1.01						T	.04				.14					.26											
MAHAFFEY	1.20				.14	.03						.02				.15					.83	T	T								.03	T
MAPLE GLEN	1.57				.13					.02	.01					.05							.01			.03	1.32					
MAPLETON DEPOT	.86				.22	.25					.11	.01											.10				.14				T	.
MARCUS HOOK	2.05				.06					T	.01					T				.04	.01	.12	T			1.80	.01				T	
MARION CENTER 2 SE	.60				.02	.08					.02	.01				.08	.02				.19										.05	.
MARTINSBURG CAA AP	.90				.47						.35					T										T	.01			T	.07	
MATAMORAS	.97				.18	.10						.07					.06										.34	.05			.17	
MAYBURG	-				2.85						.05			T		.75					.50		.14	-	-	-	-	-	-	-	-	-
MC CONNELLSBURG	.50				.08	.07					.11	T					.02										.12					.
MC KEESPORT	.16				T	T					.10										T						T					.
MEADVILLE 1 S	1.28				.29	T					T				.01	.73					.13		.09			T	T	T		.01	T	T
MEDIX RUN	1.99				.36	.01				T	.01	.02		.02		.08	.13				.91		.37								.07	.
MERCER 2 NNE	.62				.07											.17					.08		.05				.05				.17	.
MERCERSBURG	.80				.19	.26																	.02				.23					.
MEYERSDALE	.67				.22	.30					.11	.01				.02																.
MIDDLETOWN OLMSTED FLD	.69				.09	T				T	.11											T				.49	T				.01	.
MIDLAND DAM 7	.87				.01						.16					.10					T						.33				.20	
MILANVILLE	2.27				.64	.81					.12	.05		.13		.04	.02						.16				.10					
MILLHEIM	.97				.30	T					.03	T		.01		.35	.20						T				.08					
MILLVILLE 2 SW	1.10				T	.07					.02	.02		.11		.15					T	.04	T				.65			T	.04	
MILROY	.44	T			.05	.15						.04		T		.01					T		.07				.12				T	T
MONTROSE 1 E	1.34				T	T				T	.06	.16	T	.16		.02	.13				T	T	.27				.52	T		T	.02	
MORGANTOWN	2.12				.22																	.11				1.79	T					
MT GRETNA 2 SE	.67				.07						.39								.03							.18						
MT POCONO 2 N AP	1.26				.21						.07		.27			T							.05			T	.64				.02	
MUHLENBURG 1 SE	1.89				.18					T	.05		.25			.26						.25				.22	.67	.01				
MYERSTOWN	.45					.08																					.37					
NATRONA LOCK 4	.33										.03										.30											
NESHAMINY FALLS	1.59				.07					T	.05										T		T			1.10	.37				T	
NEWBURG 3 W	.14				.05																					.09						
NEW CASTLE 1 N	2.35				T						.04	T		T		1.22					.08	T	.10	T		T	.16	T		T	.72	.(
NEWELL	1.54				.27	.20					.22		.30		.05						.30						.20					
NEW PARK	2.25				.32	.41					.75		.03			.23										.17	.34					
NEWPORT	1.51				T	.07				T	T	.02											T				1.42					
NEW STANTON	1.29				.15						.08									.99	.03						.01					.(
NEW TRIPOLI	1.95				.24	.07					.10		.06									T	.04			T	1.43				.01	
NORRISTOWN	1.43					.08					T	.03									T		.09				1.23					T
NORTH EAST 2 SE	2.71				1.29	.02					.05		.53		.13	.24	.20					T				.06	.01			.09	.13	T
ORWELL 3 N	1.72					.01				.01		.14	.24			.12	.02				.14		.10				.86	.02			.06	
PALM	1.97					.05								.05			.08						.15				1.60	.04				
PALMERTON	1.09				.04						.06		.17			T				T		T				.66	.13				.03	
PARKER	.64										.02					.14					.19		.13							T	.16	
PAUPACK 2 WNW	1.43				.06	.08		.04			.04	.08				.24	.04		.08				.06				.31	.30			.10	
PECKS POND	1.18				.08	.03		.45			.01	.04	.17	.03		T				T			.14				.16	.04			.03	
PHIL DREXEL INST OF TEC	1.19				.01					T	T											.02				.62	.54					
PHILADELPHIA WB AP R	3.38				.02					T	T					T				T		T	T			1.78	1.58					T
PHILADELPHIA PT BREEZE	1.94				.03					T	T					T						.20				.41	1.30					
PHILADELPHIA CITY R	1.32				.01						.03															1.05	.23					
PHILIPSBURG CAA AP	1.29			.37	.07						.01		.01		.35	.37				.01	T	T				T				.10	T	
PHOENIXVILLE 1 E	1.67				.09						.02					.02						.14				1.26	.14					
PIKES CREEK	1.51				.06	.10					.01	T		.22		.02							.62				.45			.01	.02	
PIMPLE HILL	1.42				.02	.08		T		.02	.03	.01	.32	.01						T	T		.21			T	.66	.01		T	.05	
PINE GROVE 1 NE	.42				.01	.01					.04			T													.36				T	
PITTSBURGH WB AP 2 //R	.78				.03					.06	.45				.10	T				.03						.03	T			T	T	.(
PITTSBURGH WB CITY R	.29				T						.09				.05					.08							T					.(
PLEASANT MOUNT 1 W	2.16				•	.40						•	.23	.10		T	.03				.69	.01	.28				.31	.01		T	.10	
PORT CLINTON	-											-															.80					
POTTSVILLE	.95				.07	.01					.03	.01		.08			T										.74	.01				
PUTNEYVILLE 2 SE DAM	1.97										.02					.43					1.35									.01	.14	.(
QUAKERTOWN 1 E	1.26				T	.02					.04	.06	T										.16				.98					
RAYMOND	1.84				.22			.26			.06	.07	.18	.13							.45		.27							.06	.14	
READING WB CITY R	.88				.12					T	.01								T		T	T				.73						.(
RENOVO	2.19				.22						.03	.02		.30		.11					1.20	.05	T								.24	.(
REW	1.20				.21								.54	.14		.02	.09				.11									.06	.03	T
RICES LANDING L 6	.89				.32	.11					.04		.09			.10					.10						.13					
RIDGWAY 3 W	2.76				1.38	.02						T		T		.45					.77		.11							T	.03	
RUSH	1.67					.05				.02	.04	.10	.17			.12	.05				.03	.03	.22				.73			.03	.08	
RUSHVILLE	2.60					.03				.02	.02		.08	.09		.06	.02				.60		.87				.93	T			.08	
SAGAMORE 1 S		RECORD MISSING																														
SALINA 3 W	.59				.08		T				.08					.01				.08	.34											
SAXTON	1.69				.80	.39					.30															.05	T		T	T	.15	
SCHENLEY LOCK 5	1.27				T						.36					.14					.75										.02	
SCRANTON	1.14				.04	.40		.01		.02	.04	.01		.30		.06							.05				.14	.05			.02	
SCRANTON WB AIRPORT	1.38			T	.52		T	T		T	T		.46			T	T				T	.19				.15	.06			T	T	
SHAMOKIN	-				.60						.04		.16				.22										.52				-	
SHIPPENSBURG	1.70				.41	.09					.13															.48	.56					.(
SHIPPINGPORT WB	.71										.18	T			.09												.26				.18	
SINNEMAHONING	1.47				.29	.15					.04	T		.12		.06					.68	T	.04								.07	.(
SLIPPERY ROCK	1.20				T						.02					.80					.01		.10				.05				.18	.(
SOMERSET FAIRVIEW ST	.97				.36	.19					.12	T		.15		.08																.(
SOMERSET MAIN ST	.83				.51	.04					.12		.14			.02											1.25					T
SOUTH MOUNTAIN	1.79				.01	.30					.13																T		T	.30		.1
SPRINGBORO	1.04										T				.74	T	T															
SPRING GROVE	1.98				T	.33					.15		.01				.12						.09			.06	1.20					
SPRINGS 1 SW	1.18				.85						.26	.02																				.(

See Reference Notes Following Station Index

DAILY PRECIPITATION

3--Continued

[illegible]
AUGUST 1957

Stati	Total	1	2	3	4	5	6	7	8
LLEVUE	.81				.40	.03			
STOWN	.71					.02			
SBURG	.72				.05		T		
CREEK	2.15			.01	.24	.11			
V	1.32				T	.09		T	
HA	1.30					.08		T	
VI	.39					.24			
A	2.49				.05	.33			
A 4 N DAM	2.14				.41	.10			
CK 2 S FIRE TWR		RECORD MISSING							
TA 2 SE DAM	3.14				2.55				
ILLE WATER WORKS	2.35			1.18	.62				
O	3.46				2.22				
A	3.17				.04	T			
CITY 3 SW	.00				.30				
	2.45				.10				
POINT 4 NE	1.31				.26				
4 NE BALD EAGLE	.62				.41	.06			
CITY	2.62				.99	.04			
	.80				.37	.08			
DARBY	1.62				.02				
	.91				.25				
GRIFT	1.42				.02				
VILLE	.94								
	2.94				1.73	T			
CKEL 1 WSW	2.49			T	1.25	T			
N	2.98				1.90				
	1.34				.14				
	2.10				.41	.54			
	2.55				.22	.01			
	3.52				.53				
	1.20					.03			
	1.42	.11			.08				
	2.30				.05	.30			
	2.11				1.62				
	-								
	1.95				.63	.33			
	.72				.24	.08			
	1.29			T	.19		T		
	.65				.11	.19			
	2.32				.07	.33			
	.76					.13			

Day of month

10	11	12	13	14	15	16	17	18	19	20	21	22	23	24	25	26	27	28	29	30	31
T	.01		T		.26					.03		.01				.05			T	.04	
.02	T		.01								T					.66				T	
.06		.23				T		T	.03		.17				.06	.12			T		
	.09				.55					1.06											
.03	.04		.22		T	.05				T	.02	T								.05	.04
																.85				.02	
.05	.08	.16	.08		T	.08				.56	.01	.06				.16	.04			.03	
		.09								.06											
[illegible]	[illegible]																				
			.08			.05						.05				1.76	.02			.02	
			.19													1.34					
					.11					.20		.24									
			T	.47	T				.05	T	T								.02	.02	T
			T	T	1.03					.09		T							.03	T	
																.03			.02	T	
			.20		.12	.08				1.00	.14	.31				1.13			T	.03	
															.10	.23					
			.03		.16	.10				.62	.27	.41				.32			.02	.06	T
			.09		.05					.30		.01							.09	.09	
												T				.02				.13	
			.04		1.36					.10					.02				.03	.04	
									.10							T					.04
												.05			.30	1.24					.01
										.06		.12									.10
										1.10											.10
									.02			T				.92	-				
						T				.76	T	.30									.02
						T				.77	T	.27									.03
										.17									.03	.01	
									T	T	T				.20	.25				.07	
																.18					
										1.23	.04	.15				.11			.01	.07	T
															.15	1.04					
									.05		.12	.05				.95					
																.98			T		
																1.75	T				
										.20											
										1.10										-	
												.20				.23	.05			T	
												.11				.03				T	.03
									.05	.01	.15								.07		T
																					.27
												.04									
												.02									
												.02									
											[illegible]	[illegible]									

SUPPLEMENTAL DATA

Station	Wind direction		Wind speed m. p. h.				Relative humidity averages - percent				Number of days with precipitation							Percent of possible sunshine	Average sky cover sunrise to sunset
	Prevailing	Percent of time from prevailing	Average	Fastest mile	Direction of fastest mile	Date of fastest mile	1:00 a EST	7:00 a EST	1:00 p EST	7:00 p EST	Trace	.01-.09	.10-.49	.50-.99	1.00-1.99	2.00 and over	Total		
ENTOWN WB AIRPORT	ENE	9	7.1	-	-	-	81	84	46	54	6	2	3	1	0	0	12	-	5.7
E WB AIRPORT	-	-	9.2	21++	NNE	21	-	-	-	-	5	3	3	1	0	0	12	-	5.9
RISBURG WB AIRPORT	NW	13	5.5	21	N	21	68	75	44	46	2	4	1	1	0	0	8	72	6.2
LADELPHIA WB AIRPORT	NNE	16	8.0	37	NE	21	74	78	45	52	7	1	0	0	2	0	10	61	6.1
TSBURGH WB AIRPORT	WSW	13	7.0	20++	WSW	3+	78	81	50	56	4	5	2	0	0	0	11	70	6.1
DING WB CITY	-	-	8.0	47	N	21	-	-	-	-	4	2	1	1	0	0	8	55	6.5
ANTON WB AIRPORT	ESE	13	7.5	26	N	21	79	81	50	57	10	1	3	1	0	0	15	50	6.2
PPINGPORT WB	-	-	-	-	-	-	-	-	-	-	0	1	3	0	0	0	4	-	-
LIAMSPORT WB AIRPORT	-	-	-	-	-	-	-	87	47	54	6	4	4	0	0	0	14	-	6.0

See Reference Notes Following Station Index

ALLENTOWN WB AP																			
ALLENTOWN GAS CO														83	78	85	89	86	82
														48	55	59	70	52	55
ALTOONA HORSESHOE CURVE														76	90	84	80	79	78
														44	48	66	65	51	45
ARENDTSVILLE														90	80	92	90	89	84
														51	49	56	66	54	51
BAKERSTOWN 3 WNW														84	92	90	86	76	78
														54	56	70	68	56	52
BEAVERTOWN														81	90	90	88	82	82
														43	52	67	63	48	44
BELLEFONTE 4														84	80	90	87	82	80
														45	47	55	65	50	44
BERWICK														79	87	87	85	83	82
	MIN	59	55	59										46	54	69	65	51	50
BETHLEHEM LEHIGH UNIV	MAX	86	89	95										80	85	91	86	84	85
	MIN	65	57	60										50	54	66	65	55	53
BLAIRSVILLE 6 ENE	MAX	83	86	91										78	88	85	77	76	77
	MIN	56	57	64										48	57	65	64	52	50
BRADFORD CAA AP	MAX	78	81	84										80	75	81	73	69	74
	MIN	50	49	55										37	46	59	51	41	39
BRADFORD 4 W RES	MAX	80	81	85										73	74	81	81	71	71
	MIN	49	46	51										38	44	56	50	40	36
BROOKVILLE CAA AIRPORT	MAX	82	87	91										77	87	85	78	75	75
	MIN	51	50	54										39	46	65	53	46	39
BURGETTSTOWN 2 W	MAX	86	83	87										82	81	90	85	81	77
	MIN	46	49	56										41	44	53	59	45	41
BURNT CABINS 2 NE	MAX																		
	MIN																		
BUTLER	MAX	85	87	88										80	88	90	88	78	78
	MIN	50	51	55										40	44	63	54	50	41
CANTON 1 NW	MAX	83	78	83										71	72	78	83	75	73
	MIN	59	55	55										45	46	57	57	48	45
CARLISLE	MAX	92	94	98										84	93	93	91	88	87
	MIN	63	60	62										51	52	68	70	58	51
CHAMBERSBURG 1 ESE	MAX	88	90	95										80	90	91	88	85	
	MIN	56	54	58										48	50	68	67	53	47
CHESTER	MAX	91	91	91										88	81	85	90	90	87
	MIN	69	64	66										57	57	61	72	61	60
CLARION 3 SW	MAX	84	88	92										81	90	86	76	74	76
	MIN	51	53	55										41	45	63	59	47	42
CLAYSVILLE 3 W	MAX	60	86	94										82	93	88	84	81	80
	MIN	47	48	54										42	47	66	62	49	41
COATESVILLE 1 SW	MAX	92	89	92										89	80	86	90	90	
	MIN	62	57	60										53	49	56	69	54	50
COLUMBIA	MAX	89	92	97										80	85	92	89	84	
	MIN	66	59	64										51	54	68	69	55	54
CONFLUENCE 1 SW DAM	MAX	84	83	86				73	78	85	85	82	87	83	83	90	87	81	77
	MIN	56	55	51				47	46	50	57	57	56	48	48	53	63	53	45
CORRY	MAX	80	86	89				81	79	78	82	85	80	76	77	85	75	75	74
	MIN	52	49	54				45	48	58	64	50	51	38	48	55	56	45	40
COUDERSPORT 3 NW	MAX	80	84	87				76	73	80	78	85	75	73	76		75	74	75
	MIN	45	45	49				38	41	56	53	44	51	35	46	56	52	38	34
DERRY	MAX	85	88	93				82	85	87	85	87	84	82	91	86	81	80	80
	MIN	56	53	58				49	52	60	63	55	64	47	54	68	69	59	43
DEVAULT 1 W	MAX																	83	83
	MIN	65	61	71				54	58	68	67	58	57	58	55	58		53	53
DIXON	MAX	87	83	87	94	79	71	77	78	81	86	73	70	76	77	85	88	80	78
	MIN	57	50	53	55	55	41	42	45	48	59	55	55	42	42	50	57	43	41
DONEGAL	MAX	78	82	88	78		68	74	79	82	76	82	77	80	84	82	87	84	83
	MIN	54	46	52	58	50	35	40	46	52	60	54	52	44	44	60	55	48	41
DONORA	MAX	92	88	93	96	86	75	79	86	90	93	90	93	89	90	95	91	87	81
	MIN	58	59	65	72	60	47	51	57	61	70	62	72	53	57	72	68	56	49
DU BOIS 7 E	MAX	82	85	91	84	77	72	77	81	80	78	84	81	75	87	85	82	74	72
	MIN	56	50	58	53	52	40	42	47	59	64	50	55	40	53	63	61	46	40
EAGLES MERE	MAX	85	78	82	88	75	65	71	73	74	78	71	84	70	70	72	82	75	72
	MIN	60	60	61	63	54	45	47	54	60	62	60	61	45	47	57	58	50	50
EAST BRADY	MAX	87	89	95	95	84	78	83	85	84	87	91	91	85	92	[illegible]	87	79	78
	MIN	56	58	57	68	55	43	48	53	57	67	55	59	47	48	68	65	57	45
EBENSBURG	MAX	80	83	89	82	69	70	75	79	80	77	83	78	71	84	83	77	74	72
	MIN	53	50	54	61	53	42	45	48	58	63	50	61	44	48	65	64	47	40
EMPORIUM 2 SSW	MAX	83	80	84	88	78	67	73	78	75	80	79	84	75	73	80	81	75	73
	MIN	50	47	51	56	51	37	39	39	50	60	54	54	38	50	50	50	44	40
EPHRATA	MAX	89	91	95	86	81	80	83	84	91	88	90	89	81	85	89	90	84	
	MIN	62	59	61	68	60	48	51	51	64	68	58	64	48	54	66	66	53	54
ERIE WB AIRPORT	MAX	79	83	87	76	68	73	77	78	81	76	83	71	73	80	81	72	71	73
	MIN	57	58	67	63	60	49	57	59	66	62	59	53	49	57	65	63	49	49

COUDERSPORT 3 NW	MAX	74	75	77	80	80	72					
	MIN	36	40	43	47	52	50					
DERRY	MAX	80	84	86	80	80	77					
	MIN	50	61	60	55	54	56					
DEVAULT 1 W	MAX	78	81	80	72	75	84					
	MIN	55	49	53	61	64	55					
DIXON	MAX	82	77	81	84	74	76					
	MIN	45	45	42	43	60	56					
DONEGAL	MAX	77	80	82	80	78	72					
	MIN	46	52	48	46	58	50					
DONORA	MAX	84	85	85	87	84	76					
	MIN	55	53	56	58	64	57					
DU BOIS 7 E	MAX	72	77	79	78	78	76					
	MIN	44	48	57	55	57	55					
EAGLES MERE	MAX	74	71	72	75	67	71					
	MIN	47	49	50	52	55	56					
EAST BRADY	MAX	84	85	88	87	82	82					
	MIN	50	54	53	55	62	54					
EBENSBURG	MAX	73	76	79	72	76						
	MIN	46	50	46	51	57	55					
EMPORIUM 2 SSW	MAX	74	72	75	77	75	80	71	[illegible]	71	75	7
	MIN	38	40	40	44	53	50	37	50	52	56	4
EPHRATA	MAX	80	82	81	79	78	86	84	80	85	87	6
	MIN	54	49	49	59	57	57	45	58	64	61	5
ERIE WB AIRPORT	MAX	75	80		76	73	68	68	78	73	70	7
	MIN	42	54	62	64	61	54	52	59	63	58	5

See reference notes following Station Index.

DAILY TEMPERATURES

Day Of Month

		1	2	3	4	5	6	7	8	9	10	11	12	13	14	15	16	17	18	19	20	21	22	23	24	25	26	27	28	29	30	31	Average
	MAX	87	96	98	85	78	78	84	86	84	82	90	87	82	96	92	88	84	75	78	79	80	82	78	88	82	78	81	80	90	81	84	84.3
	MIN	58	53	55	70	58	42	50	58	62	68	56	58	46	46	62	65	46	46	50	58	45	48	50	48	58	62	58	46	56	61	61	54.8
	MAX	88	90	96	89	73	75	80	83	88	88	90	88	83	90	89	85	80	78	74	82	83	83	88	88	80	81	76	77	92	82	78	83.8
	MIN	54	60	61	68	53	46	46	52	57	58	54	61	42	49	63	64	53	47	58	49	48	50	51	59	67	63	54	51	58	59	65	55.5
	MAX	88	84	90	95	84	74	78	85	86	85	85	90	84	82	93	88	82	78	78	80	79	83	79	83	85	82	78	77	75	92	85	83.5
	MIN	51	53	55	61	53	41	46	50	55	60	54	55	43	46	52	66	50	42	42	53	49	46	46	48	51	55	53	43	45	55	63	51.0
	MAX	86	86	88	90	85	80	77	85	81	83	85	89	79	79	85	86	85	71	73	72	80	80	79	81	84	75	80	79	89	80	81	81.7
	MIN	55	56	55	58	57	45	44	51	52	59	57	55	49	46	59	65	61	50	43	47	45	48	48	45	53	62	50	45	56	59	61	52.8
	MAX	86	87	91	89	77	78	83	85	83	78	86	79	76	79	80	80	78	76	73	75	80	74	78	78	71	76	85	71	75	75	76	79.2
	MIN	60	61	65	64	55	45	50	56	64	67	60	57	45	52	60	58	50	53	56	56	52	49	49	55	57	57	43	43	50	56	59	55.0
	MAX	90	91	97	87	82	83	84	88	84	80	92	92	80	80	84	90	84	85	78	87	85	77	76	80	74	79	87	80	75	80	86	83.8
	MIN	63	56	59	63	59	47	49	50	65	58	57	62	47	49	61	67	50	52	54	59	55	60	47	44	59	62	60	50	50	60	63	56.0
	MAX	92	89	91	96	88	79	79	82	87	89	85	93	93	80	89	92	88	84	87	75	81	87	80	81	81	70	80	87	77	83	90	85.0
	MIN	64	61	62	72	59	52	52	54	58	69	60	70	53	51	58	70	57	54	60	61	54	56	56	49	51	59	62	52	59	66	68	59.0
	MAX	90	92	96	93	84	83	86	88	92	93	92	90	92	90	92	90	88	84	82	72	80	82	84	80	76	76	82	84	74	86	88	85.8
	MIN	62	64	68	62	58	46	52	54	58	62	60	64	54	62	66	57	54	54	56	58	56	56	58	56	54	62	60	52	54	58	62	58.0
	MAX	91	88	92	97	85	76	78	82	85	90	81	92	85	79	87	89	85	83	85	81	80	87	83	82	82	70	80	84	78	81	85	84.0
	MIN	59	53	58	67	61	43	47	48	52	63	55	57	46	50	60	65	53	48	57	52	48	49	47	48	53	61	59	46	50	62	67	54.3
	MAX	87	90	91	87	80	80	85	84	85	88	92	85	82	87	89	84	80	79	79	83	83	83	85	85	79	81	78	74	87	81	79	83.6
	MIN	50	50	57	65	50	41	45	50	55	65	49	56	40	47	60	59	46	42	54	46	45	45	44	54	61	66	52	45	55	56	61	52.0
	MAX	91	90	92	97	89	79	79	83	84	90	84	92	87	82	89	90	90	85	86	75	83	90	83	84	85	68	80	87	79	83	90	85.4
	MIN	62	60	62	67	63	50	51	54	56	67	59	67	54	57	63	69	58	55	59	60	55	55	53	52	53	60	61	52	53	63	67	58.6
	MAX	86	91	95	85	76	79	81	85	89	80	91	85	80	89	89	84	84	83	78	80	85	81	83	83	68	82	84	77	82	85	85	83.4
	MIN	67	61	65	68	62	52	57	54	65	67	62	65	53	57	69	71	58	56	62	59	56	59	54	53	61	62	63	56	62	68	71	61.1
	MAX	83	79	82	90	74	68	71	74	81	82	74	85	74	72	79	82	82	74	76	78	74	80	74	79	80	68	72	74	71	70	74	76.6
	MIN	55	49	52	60	54	38	44	44	46	61	53	55	39	41	45	57	43	41	48	46	44	45	40	37	44	57	54	40	41	47	52	47.5
	MAX	86	91	97	88	77	79	81	84	88	81	90	84	78	84	88	84	81	84	73	80	83	81	83	80	70	78	84	79	79	84	84	82.7
	MIN	72	68	68	74	64	55	58	60	68	68	68	69	59	61	73	70	63	64	64	63	53	63	57	57	64	64	68	56	63	70	73	64.4
	MAX	90	85	90	95	84	75	79	83	82	86	83	91	86	81	94	89	84	83	80	82	81	85	80	84	85	74	85	82	79	88	86	84.2
	MIN	52	51	54	60	56	42	43	48	53	61	54	56	42	44	51	61	49	40	45	45	44	48	48	41	44	52	53	43	45	49	61	49.5
	MAX	84	90	93	82	74	72	83	87	82	84	88	83	80	92	88	82	80	80	82	79	85	82	84	87	82	79	79	78	91	85	80	83.1
	MIN	50	51	54	65	53	39	43	48	58	65	51	60	43	48	66	61	46	40	48	54	45	46	46	51	50	59	58	43	58	62	62	52.4
	MAX	90	90	94			83	85	88	91			91	87	92	92	89			85	80	85	85	86	89			79	82	94	93		
	MIN	55	55			56	44	47	52	59			57	47	52	69	69			45	57	50	52	49			53	57	45	60	65		54.3
	MAX	84	81	87	90	79	68	75	80	82	83	81	86	75	78	88	85	76	75	75	66	79	79	78	84	83	74	79	71	72	84	80	79.3
	MIN	52	51	58	66	55	43	48	52	58	61	50	57	42	49	58	62	46	43	51	44	47	47	49	53	59	63	54	47	51	58	60	52.7
	MAX			94	93	81	78	80	85	85	82	90	88	79	82	83	84	80	80	78	80	86	83	83	82	80	75	82	81	74	80	83	82.4
	MIN		52	56	68	60	43	49	48	63	67	59	57	44	48	67	61	50	49	58	49	48	53	54	44	64	64	57	48	48	62	63	55.1
	MAX	90	88	94	97	86	74	79	85	90	90	87	90	88	86	95	92	85	82	82	83	82	88	85	86	83	78	81	80	85	96	89	86.3
	MIN	52	51	55	64	56	41	45	48	56	57	51	60	45	45	51	64	50	41	45	54	45	45	46	44	50	59	52	43	54	55	61	51.1
	MAX	80	84	89	86	75	72	77	77	79	79	84	82	75	80	82	83	71	72	71	74	76	75	77	80	79	78	79	72	70	73	74	77.6
	MIN	48	45	49	54	45	33	36	39	47	58	48	51	36	43	52	51	44	33	39	47	41	32	37	43	45	51	48	35	44	53	58	44.7
	MAX	86	90	94	86	75	72	86	86	87	85	89	85	82	94	89	86	84	81	76	80	79	83	83	84	75	78	79	85	93	81	87	83.9
	MIN	57	55	56	64	52	42	49	49	62	60	53	56	46	47	68	59	52	44	48	53	52	46	50	46	52	59	58	43	58	62	64	53.6
	MAX	86	91	96	86	83	80	84	81	91	85	92	87	83	84	89	88	83	82	79	80	88	83	80	78	75	77	86	81	80	86	86	84.2
	MIN	60	56	58	69	60	46	49	48	62	66	68	63	51	53	67	65	54	53	58	60	50	56	48	48	63	62	61	49	56	65	67	57.8
	MAX	92	87	90	97	87	79	78	81	83	91	82	91	86	80	90	90	87	82	84	76	81	85	81	86	82	70	79	87	78	82	81	84.0
	MIN	62	56	59	71	63	45	49	49	56	66	60	61	47	51	59	64	51	50	56	60	48	54	46	46	53	64	62	46	56	61	68	56.1
	MAX	84	79	83	91	81	68	74	78	80	83	78	85	71	72	83	85	76	73	75	78	76	75	75	78	79	78	80	72	67	70	72	77.4
	MIN	55	52	53	58	56	41	44	49	58	60	55	55	43	45	53	58	44	42	45	50	50	42	43	44	45	54	54	41	43	48	55	49.5
	MAX	92	90	93	98	87	81	80	83	84	93	82	91	87	80	88	89	88	84	83	80	83	88	81	83	83	70	81	85	77	87	87	85.1
	MIN	58	60	67	65	61	44	48	50	53	65	55	61	47	51	56	65	51	53	57	59	49	53	47	47	53	62	60	46	58	65	67	55.9
	MAX	92	87	91	95	84	76	80	84	86	88	83	93	87	82	93	89	87	85	83	81	83	86	82	84	86	75	85	85	78	88	89	85.4
	MIN	59	57	59	60	62	47	47	51	53	64	58	58	49	49	49	66	55	49	49	51	52	51	51	50	50	58	58	51	51	61	66	54.5
	MAX	82	87	92	82	69	77	83	84	83	82	90	79	80	84	87	80	77	76	69	80	78	78	84	84	74	77	72	73	83	79	78	80.1
	MIN	50	49	59	67	51	40	47	49	56	66	49	56	40	47	61	58	43	41	50	43	45	41	43	54	62	63	52	42	57	58	59	51.5
	MAX	87	92	95	90	74	79	83	84	86	83	92	82	80	86	89	83	82	78	83	82	84	81	84	85	77	86	82	76	80	82	82	83.5
	MIN	57	56	59	67	56	45	49	52	62	67	56	60	47	54	68	62	51	47	50	60	51	47	50	47	55	59	59	47	58	63	65	55.7
	MAX	85	80	86	92	78	71	73	73	78	83	78	86	81	75	87	81	78	70	76	77	76	80	76	78	80	75	81	76	74	86	80	79.0
	MIN	45	45	45	48	48	34	34	37	43	55	47	47	35	35	40	56	40	32	33	39	38	38	37	39	41	45	51	37	37	53	54	42.2
	MAX	94	93	95	86	87	82	89	90	86	86	90	93	82	85	89	92	83	84	72	84	91	78	82	82	72	77	92	79	82	88	91	85.7
	MIN	71	70	70	76	64	56	62	64	74	74	68	70	60	61	70	74	65	63	63	64	68	63	60	58	68	68	69	57	60	66	73	66.1
	MAX	83	89	92	80	70	72	80	80	81	80	85	80	78	92	88	80	79	78	76	78	82	79	80	83	74	78	78	76	89	85	80	80.8
	MIN	60	56	60	63	54	45	49	52	61	65	57	58	47	51	67	60	53	46	48	56	49	50	54	53	54	58	56	46	61	65	62	55.4
	MAX	84	82	86	90	78	67	74	80	80	83	81	87	73	78	84	85	75	72	72	70	77	76	78	81	83	76	78	70	73	82	79	78.5
	MIN	53	52	58	62	53	44	48	51	53	57	52	54	42	45	56	59	48	43	48	50	48	40	45	48	55	62	54	48	50	58	61	51.5
	MAX	82	86	91	83	72	75	82	83	83	83	88	85	79	87	85	82	75	75	74	79	78	78	82	85	80	79	74	76	89	83	78	81.0
	MIN	49	49	56	70	53	49	43	49	55	67	48	54	37	46	63	61	44	39	51	48	41	47	46	53	62	63	51	45	56	57	62	52.1
FLD	MAX	89	91	97	87	78	80	83	86	92	88	93	87	80	89	90	87	83	85	78	82	88	82	81	82	79	82	85	78	82	86	88	85.1
	MIN	66	62	68	69	61	53	57	55	67	66	64	63	53	57	70	70	58	57	64	62	58	58	55	53	62	65	63	53	57	69	72	61.5
	MAX	82	87	92	82	70	75	81	86	87	84	87	81	82	84	86	79	77	78	78	78	82	80	83	84	80	75	72	73	90	83	79	81.2
	MIN	60	61	65	68	58	51	53	58	62	70	64	64	53	56	68	66	58	55	51	55	54	57	56	58	62	60	56	54	62	66	68	59.6
	MAX	82	76	81	88	77	65	72	73	78	80	72	84	69	70	81	83	73	72	75	75	74	75	72	76	79	69	70	70	64	68	68	74.5
	MIN	60	57	60	62	56	45	47	51	57	63	57	58	44	46	54	57	48	50	50	52	52	45	46	48	49	56	57	42	42	53	57	52.3
	MAX	86	89	94	86	78	78	81	82	87	80	88	80	83	83	87	87	86	82	80	83	85	76	80	79	73	75	84	75	77	83	83	82.3
	MIN	60	57	62	69	59	45	50	51	65	69	57	64	51	58	67	68	53	58	52	56	51	56	45	47	63	63	62	49	56	63	64	57.7
	MAX	85	89	95	86	80	77	81	82	90	80	89	84	78	84	88	85	82	83	76	80	82	80	80	80	69	78	85	76	81	85	86	82.5
	MIN	65	65	61	66	55	50	56	51	60	63	60	60	46	56	64	65	46	51	56	55	53	62	57	52	62	62	62	55	61	70	65	58.5

See reference notes following Station Index.

Table 5 - Continued

DAILY TEMPERATURES

Station		1	2	3	4	5	6	7	8	9	10	11	12	13	14	15	16	17	18	19	20	21	22	23	24	25	26	27	28	29	30	31	Average
MT POCONO 2 N AP	MAX	82	79	88	81	70	70	72	80	80	81	84	82	72	77	80	79	73	73	73	73	78	76	76	76	75	70	74	72	69	73	76	76.3
	MIN	56	54	61	57	56	41	45	48	60	62	57	56	41	48	65	56	47	49	54	48	51	50	43	44	57	60	56	42	46	57	53	52.3
MUHLENBURG 1 SE	MAX	86	88	94	88	73	76	78	80	87	80	90	87	77	85	84	80	79	78	80	78	83	81	79	78	80	75	81	73	75	77	81	81.0
	MIN	60	53	56	65	55	42	48	50	60	69	55	60	44	52	62	62	49	47	56	54	58	54	45	47	58	57	48	43	50	61	60	54.2
NEWBURG 3 W	MAX	88	90	96	91	88	78	81	87	88	83	94	92	86	91	92	88	84	84	83	82	85	81	83	85	83	84	85	84	87	89	88	86.5
	MIN	61	58	64	70	61	47	54	54	68	67	57	63	46	52	71	68	54	49	58	63	54	50	54	47	52	57	66	56	66	64	66	58.6
NEW CASTLE 1 N	MAX	86	89	93	91	84	78	83	83	88	86	89	86	81	89	89	88	77	77	77	77	82	80	84	86	85	78	77	76	90	90	90	84.2
	MIN	52	52	61	68	51	43	46	52	57	60	52	59	42	47	64	64	51	47	53	49	48	46	47	54	62	62	52	48	57	60	63	53.8
NEWELL	MAX	90	88	94	95	85	77	82	90	91	91	88	89	86	87	94	89	85	82	83	83	82	85	87	86	89	86	74	78	85	95	90	86.6
	MIN	58	59	63	71	60	46	49	57	60	69	60	68	55	54	70	67	58	50	55	59	54	57	53	53	57	65	57	56	62	65	68	59.2
NEWPORT	MAX	94	90	94	97	87	78	82	86	88	89	85	95	88	85	93	91	89	88	88	82	85	88	85	86	85	73	83	85	78	84	88	86.7
	MIN	60	55	57	60	59	46	47	49	51	63	55	56	48	48	50	66	53	48	48	51	49	50	51	45	46	59	62	50	50	62	68	53.6
NEW STANTON	MAX	90	90	97	90	75	78	85	90	92	89	93	88	87	95	91	86	83	82	85	80	85	84	86	89	85	76	79	82	96	90	82	86.5
	MIN	50	51	56	67	49	39	45	53	53	60	53	57	44	57	66	56	49	40	48	52	48	50	48	48	49	58	48	44	58	62	64	52.3
NORRISTOWN	MAX	88	91	97	85	82	80	85	89	86	80	93	87	81	86	89	89	84	86	75	86	89	79	83	81	74	75	86	78	79	85	87	84.4
	MIN	67	61	66	74	62	52	56	56	68	70	62	67	55	57	68	71	59	60	62	61	58	60	51	51	65	66	61	54	56	66	69	61.6
PALMERTON	MAX	85	88	95	81	74	76	80	85	88	76	90	80	78	85	86	82	80	81	77	80	84	76	81	80	73	74	82	73	74	80	82	80.8
	MIN	61	54	58	66	50	45	51	49	64	63	57	56	47	53	64	60	51	50	58	52	50	52	46	46	64	62	57	46	49	64	73	55.4
PHIL DREXEL INST OF TEC	MAX	92	93	96	85	86	84	88	90	87	81	92	90	81	85	90	89	86	85	75	85	89	77	83	82	73	77	91	79	82	86	85	85.3
	MIN	70	69	72	71	69	57	59	62	71	71	65	71	58	59	71	71	65	64	68	63	63	64	57	58	67	66	65	60	58	66	70	65.2
PHILADELPHIA WB AP	MAX	90	91	96	86	82	80	84	88	84	82	91	88	80	85	89	88	85	84	73	85	86	77	81	81	73	76	87	76	80	85	86	83.8
	MIN	67	65	66	74	64	53	55	59	68	69	63	67	56	58	69	71	62	59	62	61	60	62	55	50	67	67	65	50	56	66	69	62.6
PHILADELPHIA PT BREEZE	MAX	88	91	93	86	82	80	84	87	84	80	89	87	80	82	87	86	82	82	73	82	88	76	80	79	72	75	86	78	80	86	86	82.9
	MIN	74	71	71	77	71	60	64	66	70	72	68	68	59	60	69	72	64	62	65	63	66	63	58	59	66	67	67	58	62	66	73	66.2
PHILADELPHIA CITY	MAX	88	92	93	87	83	80	84	87	84	81	90	87	81	83	86	89	85	84	73	85	87	77	82	80	73	75	87	76	80	85	87	83.6
	MIN	73	70	73	76	64	59	63	66	73	71	67	66	60	61	70	72	66	62	66	64	66	63	61	60	67	66	64	57	62	66	72	66.0
PHILIPSBURG CAA AP	MAX	79	85	91	77	65	70	76	76	80	76	85	79	75	84	83	77	74	71	76	73	78	71	77	79	75	80	75	72	84	78	75	77.3
	MIN	47	45	50	55	47	37	40	44	58	51	45	49	34	50	61	55	42	35	42	46	39	39	46	55	55	55	47	37	60	60	58	47.9
PHOENIXVILLE 1 E	MAX	90	92	99	90	83	82	84	90	88	83	94	88	87	89	90	90	88	90	79	89	89	81	83	82	78	74	87	84	80	86	88	86.4
	MIN	60	53	58	72	63	44	48	48	63	69	56	64	48	54	66	60	64	60	57	56	50	45	44	44	65	65	60	48	51	65	66	57.0
PIMPLE HILL	MAX	83	79	82	91	77	69	70	75	82	81	73	85	73	71	77	80	76	73	75	72	75	79	71	75	75	66	67	75	69	67	71	75.3
	MIN	60	55	65	63	54	44	51	55	60	61	56	57	43	51	57	57	47	54	56	51	53	48	51	51	56	58	56	40	52	55	57	54.0
PITTSBURGH WB AP 2	MAX	83	87	93	83	71	75	81	85	88	85	88	82	81	90	86	79	76	77	71	80	81	81	83	85	75	74	73	73	90	84	81	81.3
	MIN	58	61	66	63	54	50	54	58	64	68	62	60	51	55	68	63	56	52	55	55	53	55	57	60	62	59	55	51	63	65	67	58.7
PITTSBURGH WB CITY	MAX	86	90	95	84	72	77	82	89	89	86	89	84	84	93	88	83	79	80	76	80	84	82	83	86	81	75	76	76	93	86	81	83.5
	MIN	62	63	67	67	58	53	56	61	67	71	64	63	54	59	71	66	61	54	59	59	57	56	57	64	63	65	59	54	65	68	70	61.7
PLEASANT MOUNT 1 W	MAX	80	76		86		65	69	71	78			82	70	69	75	80			73	70	71	75	70			65	66	72	67	64		72.5
	MIN	56	52			53	41	43	46	57			55	41	44	43	55		41		53	45	44	42	41			53	39	40	51		47.0
PORT CLINTON	MAX	95	90	93	98	88	80	80	85	86	90	80	94	88	84	89	90	86	85	85	80	84	90	81	84	84	75	81	85	77	80	80	85.4
	MIN	55	49	54	60	59	39	44	45	54	65	53	55	40	50	57	60	46	45	59	50	45	42	43	44	54	60	59	40	51	59	63	51.6
PUTNEYVILLE 2 SE DAM	MAX	88	85	89	95	82	74	77	83	85	85	84	80	82	80	92	87	80	77	76	78	80	79	77	82	85	80	80	77	75	89	83	82.1
	MIN	49	49	54	59	49	39	43	48	48	61	50	52	39	45	48	62	47	37	42	48	46	42	47	48	50	53	53	42	48	56	61	48.9
QUAKERTOWN 1 E	MAX	90	89	95	95	81	78	82	86	85	85	90	90	81	86	88	86	83	85	84	82	88	83	85	85	78	75	83	81	78	80	84	84.5
	MIN	60	53	61	71	64	49	51	49	63	67	55	60	50	48	64	64	50	53	59	53	49	56	49	43	64	64	60	46	47	63	64	56.4
READING WB CITY	MAX	89	91	97	85	80	79	84	85	91	80	92	87	80	85	90	88	83	83	79	83	87	79	82	81	73	76	85	76	80	84	85	83.8
	MIN	68	63	68	72	61	53	57	57	69	69	63	64	56	59	70	68	58	57	63	61	57	60	53	53	65	65	61	54	59	67	69	61.9
RIDGWAY 3 W	MAX	84	83	86	90	78	67	73	79	80	77	80	84	76	76	83	84	75	73	73	78	76	76	76	79	81	78	77	72	72	80	78	78.2
	MIN	49	50	51	53	46	39	39	41	45	57	53	53	40	40	45	56	48	39	39	47	45	42	42	42	46	47	52	40	41	56	58	46.5
SALINA 3 W	MAX	85	88	93	90	80	78	82	84	88	85	87	87	82	91	90	85	78	79	80	78	82	80	83	84	82	76	77	76	93	91	82	83.7
	MIN	52	55	59	69	60	42	46	51	57	67	55	62	46	50	66	66	50	42	50	56	48	54	47	50	54	60	59	48	57	62	64	55.0
SCRANTON	MAX	88	83	88	95	79	76	76	78	83	85	77	89	80	76	83	83	81	78	80	79	78	83	78	79	84	72	72	78	72	75	77	80.2
	MIN	63	57	58	61	62	46	49	52	55	60	59	63	50	49	51	60	51	50	51	49	52	52	49	50	50	63	58	46	48	56	60	54.2
SCRANTON WB AIRPORT	MAX	81	85	93	78	70	74	76	80	85	74	87	76	74	81	83	78	76	77	78	78	83	76	80	82	71	73	77	70	74	75	81	78.3
	MIN	60	54	60	62	49	43	49	52	63	62	56	52	45	55	66	57	47	49	58	53	49	51	48	49	60	60	51	44	51	61	59	54.0
SHIPPENSBURG	MAX	85	92	97	89	86	79	83	87	87	83	92	88	84	90	90	87	86	85	80	80	87	85	84	85	77	80	83	80	85	88	87	85.5
	MIN	58	57	61	69	59	48	50	53	63	68	58	68	51	52	70	70	57	50	57	57	53	53	53	48	58	60	61	50	58	67	66	58.2
SHIPPINGPORT WB	MAX	83	88	91	82	71	77	82	86	87	84	87	81	82	91	86	80	76	77	69	79	86	80	84	86	70	76	73	74	89	83	79	81.8
	MIN	56	58	61	65	53	47	50	55	59	62	60	53	46	50	65	58	51	49	53	51	53	57	52	54	59	54	53	50	58	67	66	55.6
SLIPPERY ROCK	MAX	85	89	92	85	77	79	86	83	85	87	89	85	82	89	86	81	79	78	75	81	79	79	82	90	80	80	81	77	89	80	77	82.8
	MIN	54	54	62	67	53	47	49	55	60	67	55	63	45	54	64	62	53	53	55	54	49	49	52	58	60	62	55	48	59	60	62	56.1
SOMERSET MAIN ST	MAX	83	84	88	85	73	72	77	81	82	81	83	81	80	87	86	82	79	76	75	77	82	79	79	82	77	71	77	81	87	86	81	80.5
	MIN	50	50	53	63	55	40	42	47	56	63	50	65	44	48	65	65	52	41	46	54	43	45	53	46	51	58	49	43	57	59	61	52.1
SPRINGBORO	MAX	84	82	89	94	79	70	75	80	83	83	80	87	75	80	85	87	75	73	78	73	78	80	80	84	86	76	75	70	73	83	80	79.9
	MIN	55	52	59	66	42	41	50	51	58	66	51	56	41	48	57	56	45	43	50	44	47	46	45	53	62	63	54	45	56	60	62	52.4
SPRINGS 1 SW	MAX	80	83	89	76	67	70	74	82	82	80	83	80	77	87	84	79	74	75	70	74	78	78	77	79	73	67	77	81	87	84	80	78.5
	MIN	53	48	51	60	53	39	39	48	51	56	50	60	43	47	64	61	50	42	44	49	43	44	44	42	47	54	54	41	52	57	52	49.6
STATE COLLEGE	MAX	87	84	88	92	80	70	76	80	80	83	80	88	82	77	90	85	80	77	76	77	78	82	78	80	82	74	82	78	74	86	81	80.9
	MIN	59	58	61	61	59	47	50	54	57	65	56	61	48	49	56	68	52	48	50	54	52	50	52	56	57	58	59	48	48	60	64	55.4
STROUDSBURG	MAX	91	89	96	80	75	77	80	90	90	76	93	80	80	84	87	85	82	73	78	74	82	72	78	83	69	76	80	70	71	77	83	80.7
	MIN	55	48	52	63	47	35	42	41	60	61	49	54	37	44	63	58	42	43	52	47	42	48	42	37	58	57	51	38	42	47	50	48.5
SUNBURY	MAX		89	90	98	87	78	77	83	84	87	80	92	85	80	92	89	85	83	84	84	82	87	84	84	86	75	82	84	76	80	87	84.5
	MIN		55	55	62	55	44	46	44	44	55	55	58	46	46	53	65	51	46	47	48	49	49	48	47	52	60	59	45	47	55	58	51.5
TAMARACK 2 S FIRE TWR	MAX																																
	MIN																																
TIONESTA 2 SE DAM	MAX	85	82	85	90	79	68	75		80	78	80	85	75	75	83	83	76	75	74	74	77	78	75	74	83	79	79	72	73	80	79	78.4
	MIN	55	55	55	51	51	45	45		55	60	56	57	45	45	52	60	49	44	45	51	50	45	45	47	51	58	54	44	47	59	62	51.3
TITUSVILLE WATER WORKS	MAX	83	87	93	79	72	75	80	80	80	82	86	82	76	80	85	81	74	74	72	78	78	78	82	84	75	80	72	75	80	80	79	79.4
	MIN	55	50	56	64	51	44	46	49	56	65	54	55	41	46	63	56	45	41	48	52	46	42	40	48	60	60	51	42	58	59	60	51.7

See reference notes following Station Index.

able 3 - Continued

DAILY TEMPERATURES

Station		2	3	4	5	6	7	8	9	10	11	12	13	14	15	17	18	19	20	27	28	29	30	31	Average
WANDA	MAX	88	94	86	72	78	81	84	87	80	89	75				70	80	81	80	76	68	71	73	81	80.5
	MIN	57	55	65	52	40	40	45	58	63	57	57								59	43	47	61	60	51.9
IONTOWN	MAX	87	92	84	73	75	80	84	89	85	87	85									84	93	89	87	83.6
	MIN	57	60	70	60	46	48	54	58	69	59	68									51	59	64	69	58.4
PER DARBY	MAX	90	90	90	82	80	84	88	86	82	92	90										79	84	86	84.8
	MIN	65	65	74	67	53	57	59	68	72	64	69										55	65	68	62.5
RREN	MAX	88	92	79	71	74	80	80	79	80	85	78									72	72	73	75	76.0
	MIN					45	46	49	59	55	55	65									41	56	59	60	53.0
YNESBURG 2							83	87	89	87	87	85									82	93	92	90	84.6
							43	48	51	63	57	67									50	56	58	63	52.9
ELLSBORO 3							74	77	78	83	75	86													76.2
							46	49	59	62	55	57													51.6
ELLSVILLE																									85.1
																									55.2
EST CHESTER																									85.8
																									61.1
ILLIAMSPORT WB AP																									82.3
																									55.7
ORK 3 SSW PUMP STA																									87.0
																									57.5

NFLUENCE 1 SW DAM	5.41 1265
RD CITY 4 S DAM	6.07 1051
WLEY 1 S DAM	4.76 1265
JAMESTOWN 2 NW	B4.56 359
LANDISVILLE	7.69 1622
PIMPLE HILL	5.82 1397
STATE COLLEGE	5.71 887

DAILY SOIL TEMPERATURES

Station And Depth	Time	Day of month																															Average
		1	2	3	4	5	6	7	8	9	10	11	12	13	14	15	16	17	18	19	20	21	22	23	24	25	26	27	28	29	30	31	
STATE COLLEGE																																	
MEASURED UNDER SOD																																	
2 INCHES	8 AM	69	68	71	71	65	61	62	64	67	68	65	66	61	64	69	68	62	61	62	64	61	61	64	63	65	65	65	61	65	69	70	65.1
4 INCHES	8 AM	69	69	70	71	66	61	62	65	67	68	65	66	63	64	69	68	64	62	63	64	63	60	65	64	65	65	66	61	65	68	69	65.4
8 INCHES	8 AM	70	69	70	72	68	64	64	66	67	67	67	66	65	65	69	69	66	65	65	66	65	61	66	66	67	66	66	64	66	68	69	66.6
16 INCHES	8 AM	71	71	71	72	70	68	67	68	67	67	67	66	68	67	68	69	68	68	67	67	67	64	67	68	68	67	68	67	67	68	68	67.9

Ground Cover: Bluegrass Sod.

See reference notes following Station Index.

TOTAL PRECIPITATION

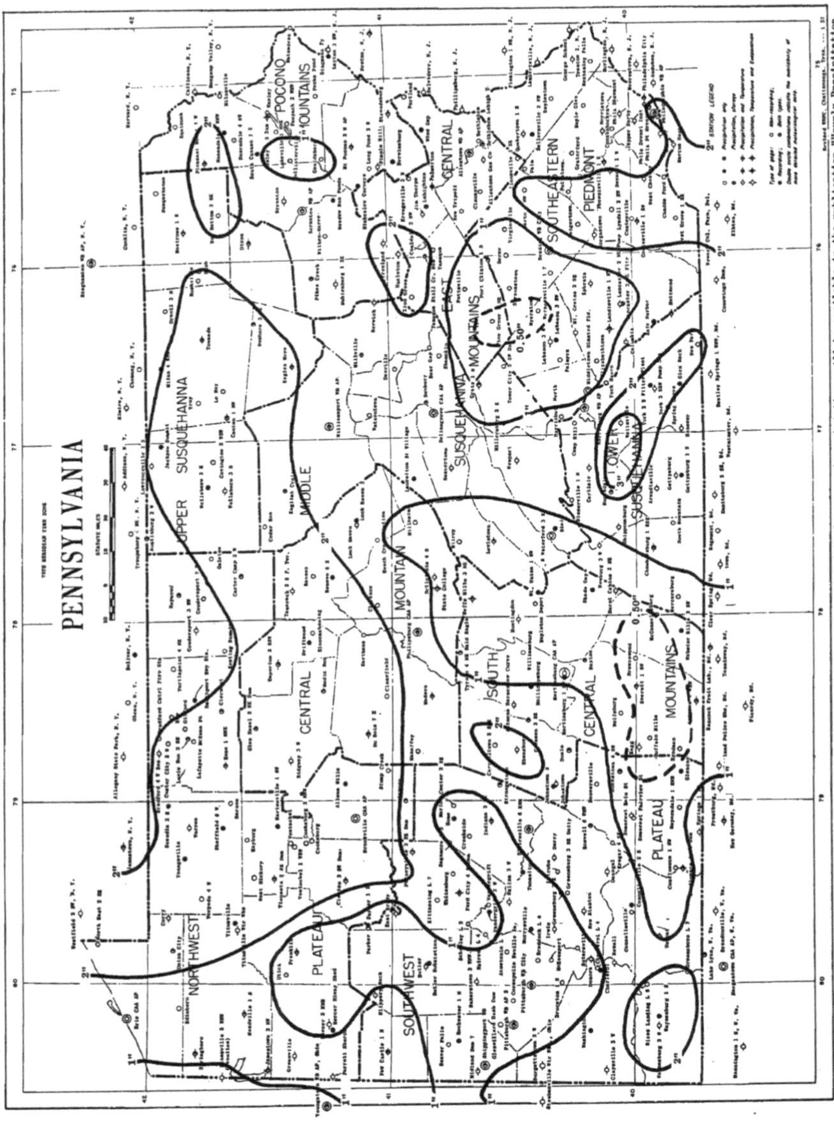

Isolines are drawn through points of approximately equal values. Hourly precipitation data from recorder substations will be available in the publication "Hourly Precipitation Data".

AVERAGE TEMPERATURE

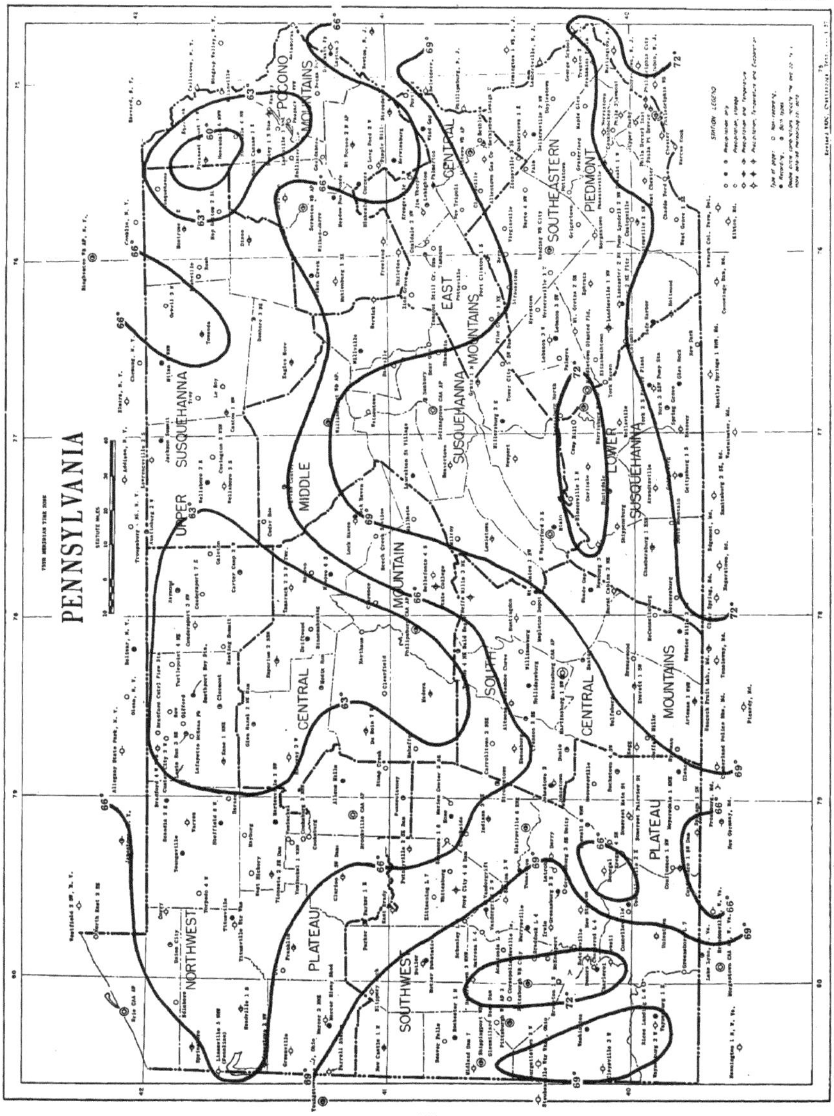

Isolines are drawn through points of approximately equal values. Hourly precipitation data from recorder substations will be available in the publication "Hourly Precipitation Data".

STATION INDEX

Station	Index No.	County	Drainage	Latitude	Longitude	Elevation	Observation Time Temp.	Observation Time Precip.	Observer	Refer To Tables
ACMETONIA LOCK 3	0022	ALLEGHENY	1	40 32	79 49	748		7A	CORPS OF ENGINEERS	3
ALLENS MILLS	0069	JEFFERSON	1	41 12	78 55	1600		MID	CHARLES M. ALLEN	C
ALLENTOWN WB AP	0106	LEHIGH	9	40 39	75 26	376	MID	MID	U.S. WEATHER BUREAU	2 3 5 7 C
ALLENTOWN GAS CO	0111	LEHIGH	9	40 36	75 28	254	7A	7A	LEHIGH VLY GAS DIV	2 3 5
ALTOONA HORSESHOE CURVE	0134	BLAIR	6	40 30	78 29	1500	6P	6P	ALTOONA WATER BUR.	2 3 5
ARENDTSVILLE	0229	ADAMS	15	39 55	77 18	710	8A	8A	PA STATE COL EXP	2 3 5
AUSTINBURG 2 W	0313	TIOGA	15	42 00	77 32	1590		7A	OTTO D. BACON	3 7 C
BAKERSTOWN 3 WNW	0355	ALLEGHENY	1	40 39	79 59	1230	7P	7P	PGH CUT FLOWER CO	2 3 5
BARNES	0409	WARREN	1	41 40	79 02	1310		7A	CORPS OF ENGINEERS	3
BARTO 4 NW	0428	BERKS	14	40 26	75 39	312		7A	MARIE B. NICHLAS	3
BEAR GAP	0457	NORTHUMBLAND	15	40 50	76 30	900		3P	ROARING CRK WTR CO	3
BEAVER FALLS	0475	BEAVER	2	40 46	80 19	760		7A	HOWARD R. KEMP	3
BEAVERTOWN	0482	SNYDER	15	40 45	77 10	640	5P	7A	MARLIN R. ETTINGER	2 3 5
BEECH CREEK STATION	0499	CENTRE	16	41 04	77 34	620		7A	HAROLD S. RUPERT	3 7
BELLEFONTE 4 S	0530	CENTRE	16	40 51	77 47	1110	8A	8A	ROCKVIEW PRISON FARM	2 3 5
BERNE	0599	BERKS	14	40 31	76 00	325		7A	FLOYD W. TRUMP	3
BERWICK	0611	COLUMBIA	15	41 04	76 13	570	6P	6P	AMER CAR + FNDRY CO	2 3 5
BETHLEHEM	0629	NORTHAMPTON	9	40 37	75 22	400		7A	ARTHUR CROPPER	3
#BETHLEHEM LEHIGH UNIV	0634	NORTHAMPTON	9	40 36	75 23	450	MID	MID	LEHIGH UNIVERSITY	2 3 5 C
BLAIN	0725	PERRY	15	40 20	77 31	750		MID	PA DEPT FRST + WTRS	C
BLAIRSVILLE 6 ENE	0736	INDIANA	4	40 27	79 09	2048	8P	8P	U.S. WEATHER BUREAU	2 3 5
BLAKESLEE CORNERS	0743	MONROE	9	41 06	75 36	1650		MID	WALTER WILDRICK	C
BLOSERVILLE 1 N	0763	CUMBERLAND	15	40 16	77 22	650		5P	MRS. B. M. WILLDERS	3
BOSWELL 6 WNW	0820	SOMERSET	1	40 10	79 08	2570		8A	CLARK N. ST. CLAIR	3 C
BRADDOCK LOCK 2	0861	ALLEGHENY	10	40 24	79 52	725		7A	CORPS OF ENGINEERS	3
BRADFORD CAA AIRPORT	0865	MC KEAN	1	41 48	78 38	2150	MID	MID	CIVIL AERO. ADM.	2 3 5 7
BRADFORD CNTRL FIRE STA	0867	MC KEAN	1	41 57	78 39	1500		8A	BRADFORD FIRE DEPT	3
BRADFORD 4 W RES	0868	MC KEAN	1	41 57	78 44	1680	5P	5P	BRADFORD WTR DEPT	2 3 5 7
BREEZEWOOD	0905	BEDFORD	6	40 00	78 14	1352		MID	PA TURNPIKE COMM	3
BROOKVILLE CAA AIRPORT	1002	JEFFERSON	1	41 09	79 06	1417	MID	MID	CIVIL AERO. ADM.	2 3 5 7
BRUCETON 1 S	1033	ALLEGHENY	10	40 18	79 59	1065		7A	AUSTIN R. COOPER	3
BUCKSTOWN 1 SE	1073	SOMERSET	4	40 04	78 50	2460		MID	ALVIN W. MANGES	C
BUFFALO MILLS	1087	BEDFORD	6	39 57	78 39	1318		7A	MRS. NELLE R. BROWN	3
BURGETTSTOWN 2 W	1105	WASHINGTON	11	40 23	80 26	980	7A	7A	SMITH TWP MUN AUTH	2 3 5
BURNT CABINS 2 NE	1115	HUNTINGDON	6	40 05	77 52	990	MID	MID	PA TURNPIKE COMM	2 3 5
#BUTLER	1130	BUTLER	2	40 52	79 54	1100	4P	7A	WILLIAM C. FAUST	2 3 5
BUTLER SUBSTATION	1135	BUTLER	2	40 51	79 53	1140		MID	WEST PENN POWER CO	C
CAMP HILL	1198	CUMBERLAND	15	40 15	76 55	461		6P	JOSEPH N. HOBART	3
CANTON 1 NW	1215	BRADFORD	15	41 40	76 52	1920	7A	7A	MRS.MILDRED SPENCER	2 3 5 7 C
CARLISLE	1234	CUMBERLAND	15	40 12	77 11	460	6P	6P	C. E. MILLER	2 3 5
CARROLLTOWN 2 SSE	1255	CAMBRIA	16	40 35	78 42	2040		8A	ROBERT F. MAURER	3 7
CARTER CAMP 2 W	1262	POTTER	16	41 37	77 45	2030		7A	RICHARD L. MENKEN	3 C
CEDAR RUN	1301	LYCOMING	16	41 31	77 27	800		7A	KATHRYN T.KREIGHBAUM	3
CHADDS FORD	1342	DELAWARE	5	39 52	75 36	160		8A	ALFRED C. WEEKS	3
CHAMBERSBURG 1 ESE	1354	FRANKLIN	12	39 56	77 38	640	9P	9P	CHARLES A. BENDER	2 3 5 C
CHARLEROI	1372	WASHINGTON	10	40 08	79 55	1040		MID	WEST PENN POWER CO	C
CHARLEROI LOCK 4	1377	WESTMORELAND	10	40 09	79 54	749		7A	CORPS OF ENGINEERS	3
#CHESTER	1423	DELAWARE	5	39 51	75 22	86	8A	8A	CHESTER TIMES	2 3 5
CLARENCE	1480	CENTRE	16	41 03	77 56	1410		7A	MISS VELDA SWANCER	3
CLARION 3 SW	1485	CLARION	1	41 12	79 26	1114	8P	7A	PA ELECTRIC CO	2 3 5 C
CLAUSSVILLE	1505	LEHIGH	9	40 37	75 39	670		8A	WILLIAM J. DOTTERER	3
CLAYSVILLE 3 W	1512	WASHINGTON	11	40 07	80 28	1000	7P	7A	MFGRS. L + H CO	2 3 5
CLEARFIELD	1519	CLEARFIELD	16	41 01	78 26	1100		7A	IRA TAYLOR	3
CLERMONT	1529	MC KEAN	1	41 41	78 30	2104		7A	MRS.TILLIE M.SIMONDS	3 C
COALDALE 2 NW	1572	SCHUYLKILL	9	40 50	75 56	1026		7A	PANTHER VLY WTR CO	3 7
COATESVILLE 1 SW	1589	CHESTER	5	39 58	75 50	342	8A	8A	PHILA ELECTRIC CO	2 3 5 C
COLUMBIA	1675	LANCASTER	15	40 02	76 30	300	5S	5S	JAMES H. RUST	2 3 5
CONFLUENCE 1 SW DAM	1705	SOMERSET	17	39 48	79 22	1490	8A	8A	CORPS OF ENGINEERS	2 3 5 6 C
CONFLUENCE 1 NW	1710	FAYETTE	17	39 50	79 22	1331		7A	JOHN L. REID	3
CONNELLSVILLE	1723	FAYETTE	17	40 01	79 36	870		8A	MARSHALL B. MENEFEE	3
CONNELLSVILLE 2 E	1729	FAYETTE	17	40 01	79 33	1300		MID	HARRY C. JOY	C
CONSHOHOCKEN	1737	MONTGOMERY	5	40 04	75 19	70		8A	PHILA ELECTRIC CO	3
COOKSBURG	1749	CLARION	1	41 20	79 13	1180		8A	PA DEPT FRST + WTRS	3
COOKSBURG 2 NNW	1752	CLARION	1	41 21	79 13	1460		8A	PA DEPT FRST + WTRS	3
CORAOPOLIS NEVILLE IS	1773	ALLEGHENY	11	40 30	80 05	720		8A	PGH. COKE + CHEM CO	3
CORRY	1790	ERIE	1	41 56	79 38	1427	7P	8A	LEO C. MECKERS	2 3 5 7
COUDERSPORT 3 NW	1804	POTTER	1	41 49	78 03	2020	7P	8A	MISS ELIZABETH NEFF	2 3 5
COUDERSPORT 7 E	1809	POTTER	1	41 46	77 53	2425		7A	CAMP POTATO	3
COVINGTON 2 WSW	1833	TIOGA	15	41 44	77 07	1745		7A	CALVIN R. PACKARD	3
CREEKSIDE	1861	INDIANA	1	40 41	79 12	1035		7A	CORPS OF ENGINEERS	3
CRESSON 2 SE	1895	CAMBRIA	8	40 27	78 34	2540		7A	MILES M. LINGLE	3 C
CUSTER CITY 2 W	1978	MC KEAN	1	41 55	78 41	2120		8A	M. D. BOOTH AND CO	3
DANVILLE	2013	MONTOUR	15	40 58	76 37	460		7A	MRS.MARIE M. LITTLE	3
DERRY	2108	WESTMORELAND	4	40 20	79 18	1150	6P	6P	MISS M. D. WINEMAN	2 3 5
DEVAULT 1 W	2116	CHESTER	14	40 05	75 33	360	MID	MID	PA TURNPIKE COMM	2 3 5
DINGMANS FERRY	2160	PIKE	5	41 13	74 52	364		MID	CLYDE T. VOORHEES	C
DIXON	2171	WYOMING	15	41 34	75 54	620	7A	7A	HAROLD J. KUSCHEL	2 3 5 C
DONEGAL	2183	WESTMORELAND	17	40 07	79 23	1746	MID	MID	PA TURNPIKE COMM	2 3 5 7
#DONORA	2190	WASHINGTON	10	40 11	79 51	814	12M	12M	DONORA ZINC WORKS	2 3 5
DOYLESTOWN	2221	BUCKS	5	40 18	75 08	393		5P	GEORGE HART	3
DRIFTWOOD	2245	CAMERON	16	41 20	78 08	880		MID	SIDNEY KENNEDY	C
DU BOIS 7 E	2265	CLEARFIELD	16	41 06	78 38	1670	5P	5P	CITY OF DU BOIS	2 3 5 7 C
DUNLO	2298	CAMBRIA	4	40 17	78 43	2410		MID	MRS. D. L. WHITE	C
DUSHORE 3 NE	2324	SULLIVAN	16	41 33	76 21	1750		7A	PATRICK F. RYAN	3 C
EAGLES MERE	2343	SULLIVAN	16	41 24	76 35	2020	7A	7A	MRS.ELSIE P. BIGGER	2 3 5 C
EAST BRADY	2363	CLARION	1	40 59	79 37	820	5P	5P	A. B. KEMPEL	2 3 5
EAST WATERFORD 3 E	2459	PERRY	6	40 21	77 33	2125	8A	8A	U.S. WEATHER BUREAU	INAC 5/55
EBENSBURG	2466	CAMBRIA	4	40 29	78 43	2090	7P	7A	ROBERT A. WASSER	2 3 5
EDINBORO	2514	ERIE	1	41 52	80 08	1220		8A	EDINBORO ST TCHR COL	3
ELIZABETHTOWN	2560	LANCASTER	15	40 09	76 37	460		8A	MASONIC HOME	3
EMPORIUM 2 SSW	2634	CAMERON	16	41 28	78 15	1735	7A	7A	JACKSON THOMAS	2 3 5 C
ENGLISH CENTER	2644	LYCOMING	16	41 26	77 17	881		7A	WILLIAM SUDERS	3 7 C
EPHRATA	2662	LANCASTER	15	40 11	76 10	465	6P	6P	STANLEY L.VON NEIDA	2 3 5
EQUINUNK 2	2671	WAYNE	5	41 51	75 13	910		7A	MRS. HENRIETTA MURRY	3
ERIE WB AIRPORT	2682	ERIE	8	42 05	80 12	732	MID	MID	U. S. WEATHER BUREAU	2 3 5 7
EVERETT 1 SW	2721	BEDFORD	6	40 00	78 23	1020	MID	MID	PA TURNPIKE COMM	2 3 5 7 C
FARRELL SHARON	2814	MERCER	2	41 14	80 30	865	7P	7P	SHARON STEEL CORP	2 3 5
FORD CITY 4 S DAM	2942	ARMSTRONG	1	40 43	79 30	950	8A	8A	CORPS OF ENGINEERS	2 3 5 6 7 C
FRANKLIN	3028	VENANGO	1	41 23	79 49	987	7P	7A	ROBERT D. RHOADS	2 3 5 C
FREELAND	3056	LUZERNE	15	41 01	75 54	1900	6P	8A	ANDREW B. EVANSHA	2 3 5
GALETON	3130	POTTER	16	41 44	77 39	1325		7A	W. GALE LUSH	3 7
GEIGERTOWN	3189	BERKS	14	40 13	75 50	400		8A	WALTER C. WOLF	3
GEORGE SCHOOL	3200	BUCKS	5	40 13	74 56	135	7P	7P	GEORGE M. HART	2 3 5 7
#GETTYSBURG	3218	ADAMS	12	39 50	77 14	540	9A	9A	HUGH C. MC ILHENNY	2 3 5
GETTYSBURG 1 S	3223	ADAMS	12	39 48	77 14	560		MID	NAT MILITARY PARK	C
GIFFORD	3237	MC KEAN	1	41 51	78 36	2220		8A	SOUTH PENN OIL CO	3
GLENCOE	3298	SOMERSET	12	39 49	78 51	1620		MID	MRS. MARY M.MARTMAN	C
GLEN HAZEL 2 NE DAM	3311	ELK	1	41 34	78 36	1725		8A	CORPS OF ENGINEERS	3 C
GLEN ROCK	3330	YORK	15	39 48	76 44	620		MID	MRS.E.C.MC WILLIAMS	C
GLENWILLARD DASH DAM	3343	ALLEGHENY	11	40 33	80 13	705		7A	CORPS OF ENGINEERS	3
GOULDSBORO	3394	WAYNE	9	41 15	75 27	1890		7A	L. M. EILENBERGER	3
GRATERFORD	3435	MONTGOMERY	14	40 14	75 27	160	7A	7A	CLAUDE K. KULP	2 3 5 7 C
GRATZ 1 N	3438	DAUPHIN	15	40 38	76 43	760	8A	8A	LEE M. LEITZEL	2 3 5 C
GREENSBORO LOCK 7	3503	GREENE	10	39 47	79 55	808		7A	CORPS OF ENGINEERS	3 7
GREENSBURG 2 E	3515	WESTMORELAND	10	40 18	79 31	1225		MID	PA DEPT HIGHWAYS	C
GREENSBURG 3 SE UNITY	3516	WESTMORELAND	10	40 17	79 30	1245		6P	WESTMORELAND WTR CO	3
GREENVILLE	3526	MERCER	2	41 24	80 23	1026	6P	6P	C. EARL MILLER	2 3 5
HANOVER	3662	YORK	15	39 48	76 59	600	8A	8A	HANOVER EVENING SUN	2 3 5 7
#HARRISBURG WB AP	3699	YORK	15	40 13	76 51	335	MID	MID	U.S. WEATHER BUREAU	2 3 5 7 C
HARRISBURG NORTH	3704	DAUPHIN	15	40 18	76 54	323		9A	GEORGE S. BEAL	3
HAWLEY	3758	WAYNE	5	41 29	75 10	880		7A	MRS. KATHERINE BATES	3
HAWLEY 1 S DAM	3761	WAYNE	5	41 28	75 11	1200	7A	7A	PA POWER + LIGHT CO	2 3 5 6 7 C
HOLLIDAYSBURG	4001	BLAIR	6	40 26	78 24	960		MID	JOHN M. RINGLER	C
HOLLISTERVILLE	4008	WAYNE	5	41 23	75 26	1360		8A	PA POWER + LIGHT CO	3
#HOLTWOOD	4019	LANCASTER	15	39 50	76 20	187	MID	8A	PA POWER + LIGHT CO	2 3 5 7 C
HOME	4027	INDIANA	1	40 45	79 06	1220		MID	MRS. EDNA M. BUSH	C
HONESDALE 4 NW	4043	WAYNE	5	41 37	75 19	1410		8A	GEORGE C. WILLIAMS	3
HONESDALE 6 NNW	4044	WAYNE	5	41 39	75 17	1050		MID	FRIEND E. WALTER	C
HOOVERSVILLE	4056	SOMERSET	4	40 09	78 55	1660		7A	PA ELECTRIC CO	3 7
HOP BOTTOM 2 SE	4066	SUSQUEHANNA	15	41 43	75 43	900		7A	JOSEPH J. SANSUSKAS	3
HUNTINGDON										
HUNTSDALE										
HYNDMAN										
INDIANA 3 SE										
IRWIN										
JACKSON SUMMIT	4304	TIOGA	15	41 57						
JAMESTOWN 2 NW	4325	CRAWFORD	2	41 30						
JIM THORPE	4370	CARBON	9	40 52						
#JOHNSTOWN	4385	CAMBRIA	4	40 20						
JOHNSTOWN 2	4390	CAMBRIA	4	40 19						
KANE 1 NNE	4432	MC KEAN	1	41 41						
KARTHAUS	4450	CLEARFIELD	16	41 07						
KEATING SUMMIT	4466	POTTER	16	41 41						
KEGG	4481	BEDFORD	6	39 59						
KITTANNING LOCK 7	4611	ARMSTRONG	1	40 49	79 32					
KREGAR 4 SE	4667	WESTMORELA	17	40 06	79 14					
KRESGEVILLE 3 W	4672	CARBON	9	40 54	75 34					
LAFAYETTE MC KEAN PARK	4706	MC KEAN	1	41 48	78 40	2130		7A	ORIN A. BUTTERS	3
LAKEVILLE 1 NNE	4733	WAYNE	5	41 27	75 16	1440		8A	MRS. GLADYS REINEKE	3
LANCASTER 2 NE PUMP STA	4758	LANCASTER	15	40 03	76 17	255	6P	6P	LANCASTER WATER BUR	2 3 5 7
LANCASTER 2 NE FILT PL	4763	LANCASTER	15	40 03	76 17	270		MID	LANCASTER WATER BUR	C
LANDISVILLE 2 NW	4778	LANCASTER	15	40 07	76 26	360	8A	8A	PA STATE COLLEGE	2 3 5 6 C
LATROBE	4832	WESTMORELA	4	40 19	79 23	1000		MID	WEST PENN POWER CO	INAC 6/56
LAURELTON STATE VILLAGE	4853	UNION	15	40 54	77 13	880		MID	PA DEPT OF WELFARE	C
LAWRENCEVILLE 2 S	4873	TIOGA	15	41 59	77 07	1000	7A	7A	HARRY P. HOWLAND	2 3 5 7
LEBANON 3 W	4891	LEBANON	15	40 20	76 29	460	7A	7A	LEON MILLER	2 3 5 7
LEBANON 3 SW	4896	LEBANON	15	40 19	76 28	490		MID	THOMAS DONNACHIE	C
LEHIGHTON	4934	CARBON	9	40 50	75 43	580		7A	GOODWIN S. DEFREHN	3 C
LE ROY	4972	BRADFORD	15	41 41	76 43	1040		6P	MRS.DIMMIS M.BAILEY	3
LEWIS RUN 3 SE	4984	MC KEAN	1	41 50	78 39	1740		7A	RUSSELL LINEMAN	3 C
LEWISTOWN	4992	MIFFLIN	6	40 35	77 35	480	7A	7A	AMERICAN VISCOSE CO	2 3 5 7
LINESVILLE 5 WNW	5050	CRAWFORD	2	41 41	80 31	1020	7P	8A	MISS RETTA M. CRUMB	2 3 5
LOCK HAVEN	5104	CLINTON	16	41 08	77 27	570	7P	7A	PETER L. STEVENSON	2 3 5
LOCK HAVEN 2	5109	CLINTON	16	41 08	77 27	630		MID	HUGH F. PARKER	
LONG POND 2 W	5160	MONROE	9	41 03	75 30	1860		7A	THOMAS MECKES	3
LYNDELL 2 NW	5279	CHESTER	5	40 05	75 46	-		8A	MRS. DOROTHY MARPLE	
MADERA	5336	CLEARFIELD	16	40 50	78 26	1460	7A	7A	MRS. JULIA J. SNOFF	2 5
MAHAFFEY	5342	CLEARFIELD	16	40 53	78 44	1280		7A	MISS ELLEN J. MILES	3
MAPLE GLEN	5368	MONTGOMERY	5	40 11	75 11	380		6P	FRANCES E.SCHEIBNER	
MAPLETON DEPOT	5381	HUNTINGDON	6	40 24	77 56	580		7A	MRS. I. S. BUCHANAN	
MARCUS HOOK	5390	DELAWARE	5	39 49	75 25	12	MID	MID	SUN OIL CO	2 3 5
MARIENVILLE 1 SW	5400	FOREST	1	41 27	79 09	1700		MID	ROY A. MARKER	
MARION CENTER 2 SE	5408	INDIANA	1	40 45	79 02	1610		7A	CORPS OF ENGINEERS	3
MARTINSBURG 1 SW	5453	BLAIR	6	40 18	78 20	1360		MID	BLUE MT. CANNERIES	
MARTINSBURG CAA AP	5454	BLAIR	6	40 18	78 19	1463	MID	MID	CIVIL AERO. ADM.	2 3 5
MATAMORAS	5470	PIKE	5	41 22	74 42	439		7A	HARRY BISLAND	3
MC CONNELLSBURG	5526	FULTON	12	39 56	78 00	895		7A	MRS. HELEN M. SHIVES	3
MC KEESPORT	5573	ALLEGHENY	10	40 21	79 52	720		8A	NATIONAL TUBE CO	3
MEADOW RUN PONDS	5601	LUZERNE	15	41 13	75 40	1995		MID	GEORGE PEARAGE	
MEADVILLE 1 S	5606	CRAWFORD	1	41 38	80 10	1065	8A	8A	CITY OF MEADVILLE	2 3 5
MEDIX RUN	5627	ELK	16	41 17	78 24	1100		7A	MRS.E. M. SNYDER	3
MERCER 2 NNE	5651	MERCER	2	41 15	80 13	1160	7P	7A	MRS. FRAN. STRUTHERS	2 3 5
MERCER HIWAY SHED	5654	MERCER	2	41 14	80 15	1250		MID	PA DEPT HIGHWAYS	
MERCERSBURG	5662	FRANKLIN	12	39 50	77 54	605		8A	ROLLIN P. GILBERT	3
MERWINSBURG	5676	MONROE	9	40 58	75 28	970		MID	WILLIAM D. GOULD	
MEYERSDALE	5684	SOMERSET	17	39 49	79 02	2040		8A	ARTHUR J. POTTER	3
MIDDLETOWN OLMSTED FLD	5703	DAUPHIN	15	40 11	76 46	303	MID	MID	U. S. AIR FORCE	2 3 5
MIDLAND DAM 7	5710	BEAVER	11	40 38	80 28	689	11P	7A	CORPS OF ENGINEERS	2 3 5
MILAN 4 WNW	5732	BRADFORD	15	41 56	76 35	1448		MID	CARL A. MORRIS	
MILANVILLE	5738	WAYNE	5	41 40	75 04	760		8A	CHARLES W. DAVIS	3
MILLERSBURG 2 E	5775	DAUPHIN	15	40 32	76 56	560		MID	RUSSELL SHEPLEY	
MILLHEIM	5790	CENTRE	15	40 54	77 29	1090		7A	NEVIN E. BOWERSOX	3
MILLVILLE 2 SW	5817	COLUMBIA	15	41 06	76 34	860		7A	KENNETH LEIGHOW	3
MILROY	5825	MIFFLIN	6	40 43	77 35	770		8A	THOMAS C. HARBESON	3
MONTROSE 1 E	5915	SUSQUEHANNA	15	41 50	75 51	1630	7A	7A	WILBER W. HOOPES.JR	2 3 5
MORGANTOWN	5956	BERKS	15	40 09	75 54	595	MID	MID	PA TURNPIKE COMM	2 3 5
MT GRETNA 2 SE	6028	LANCASTER	15	40 14	76 26	670	MID	MID	PA TURNPIKE COMM	2 3 5
MT POCONO 2 N AP	6055	MONROE	5	41 09	75 22	1915	5P	5P	H. JOHN DAVIS. JR.	2 3 5
MOUNT UNION 1 N	6067	MIFFLIN	6	40 24	77 53	820		MID	MT UNION WTR WORKS	
MUHLENBURG 1 SE	6090	LUZERNE	15	41 13	76 08	1110	6P	6P	THEODORE J. SAMPSON	2 3 5
MURRYSVILLE	6111	WESTMORELAND	10	40 26	79 42	903		MID	DAVID C. SHAW	
MYERSTOWN	6126	LEBANON	14	40 22	76 18	480		8A	MRS.KATHLEEN MANDELL	3
NATRONA LOCK 4	6151	ALLEGHENY	1	40 37	79 43	800		7A	CORPS OF ENGINEERS	3
NEFFS MILLS 3 NE	6174	HUNTINGDON	6	40 40	77 55	900		MID	PA STATE UNIVERSITY	
NESHAMINY FALLS	6194	BUCKS	5	40 09	74 57	60		MID	PHILA SUB WATER CO	3
NEWBURG 3 W	6225	FRANKLIN	15	40 09	77 37	745	5P	5P	PA TURNPIKE COMM	2 3 5
NEW CASTLE 1 N	6233	LAWRENCE	2	41 01	80 22	825	5P	7A	BAXTER F. JOHNSON	2 3 5
NEWELL	6240	FAYETTE	10	40 05	79 54	805	12M	12M	GENERAL CHEMICAL CO	2 3 5
NEW PARK	6289	YORK	15	39 44	76 30	780		6P	CLINTON J. ALLEN	3
NEWPORT	6297	PERRY	6	40 29	77 08	400	7A	7A	MRS. FRANCES K. FRY	2 3 5
NEW STANTON	6310	WESTMORELAND	10	40 13	79 36	980	MID	MID	PA TURNPIKE COMM	2 3 5
NEW TRIPOLI	6326	LEHIGH	14	40 41	75 45	570		6P	FRED C. OSWALD	3
NORRISTOWN	6370	MONTGOMERY	14	40 07	75 21	75	MID	8A	GEORGE M. BOONE	2 3 5
NORTH EAST 2 SE	6396	ERIE	8	42 12	79 49	1060		9A	ELLSWORTH WEAVER	3
ORRELL 3 N	6621	BRADFORD	15	41 55	76 16	1620		8A	WILLIAM I. BROWN	3
PALM	6681	MONTGOMERY	14	40 26	75 32	385		8A	FRED C. ESCHBACH	3
#PALMERTON	6689	CARBON	9	40 48	75 37	435	MID	MID	NEW JERSEY ZINC CO	2 3 5
PARKER	6721	ARMSTRONG	1	41 05	79 41	1140		7A	LOUIS A. MALARKEY	3
PARKER 1 E	6724	CLARION	1	41 06	79 40	1100		MID	P. M. NEELY	
PAUPACK 2 WNW	6762	PIKE	5	41 24	75 14	1360		8A	MISS L. VETTERLEIN	3
PECKS POND	6786	PIKE	5	41 17	75 06	1380		8A	MRS. CARRIE NESS	3
#PHIL DREXEL INST OF TEC	6879	PHILADELPHIA	14	39 57	75 11	30	MID	MID	FRANCIS K. DAVIS.JR	2 5
PHILADELPHIA WB AP	6889	PHILADELPHIA	5	39 53	75 14	13	MID	MID	U.S. WEATHER BUREAU	2 3 5
#PHILADELPHIA PT BREEZE	6899	PHILADELPHIA	5	39 55	75 12	32	MID	MID	ATLANTIC REFINING	2 3 5
#PHILADELPHIA CITY	6909	PHILADELPHIA	5	39 57	75 09	26	9A	9A	USN HYDROGRAPHIC OFF	
PHILIPSBURG CAA AP	6916	CENTRE	6	40 54	78 05	1918	MID	MID	CIVIL AERO. ADM.	2 5
PHOENIXVILLE 1 E	6927	CHESTER	14	40 07	75 30	105	6P	MID	PHILA SUB WATER CO	2 5
PIKES CREEK	6939	LUZERNE	15	41 18	76 08	1320		7A	HARRY SHELDON	C
PIMPLE HILL	6944	MONROE	9	41 02	75 30	2215	9A	9A	PA DEPT FRST + WTRS	2 3 5 6 7
PINE GROVE 1 NE	6954	SCHUYLKILL	15	40 34	76 22	535		8A	PA POWER + LIGHT CO	
PITTSBURGH WB AP 2	6993	ALLEGHENY	11	40 30	80 13	1151	MID	MID	U.S. WEATHER BUREAU	2 3 5 7 C
#PITTSBURGH WB CITY	6997	ALLEGHENY	11	40 27	80 00	749	MID	MID	U.S. WEATHER BUREAU	2 3 5 C
PLEASANT MOUNT 1 W	7029	WAYNE	5	41 44	75 27	1800	8A	8A	PA FISH COMM	2 3 5 7 C
PORT CLINTON	7116	SCHUYLKILL	14	40 35	76 02	450	7A	7A	MRS. ADA E. RARICK	2 3 5 C
PORTLAND	7127	NORTHAMPTON	5	40 55	75 06	297		8A	JOINT BRIDGE COMM	INAC 1/56
POTTSVILLE	7161	SCHUYLKILL	14	40 42	76 11	690		8A	LLOYD E. WELLER	3
PUNXSUTAWNEY	7217	JEFFERSON	1	40 57	79 00	1298		MID	JOHN VOLANSKY	C
PUTNEYVILLE 2 SE DAM	7229	ARMSTRONG	1	40 55	79 17	1270	8A	8A	CORPS OF ENGINEERS	2 3 5 C
QUAKERTOWN 1 E	7239	BUCKS	5	40 26	75 20	490	5P	7A	DENNIS K. FLUCK	2 3 5
RAYMOND	7310	POTTER	13	41 52	77 52	2220		7A	MRS. RACHEL LANGAN	3 C
#READING WB CITY	7318	BERKS	14	40 20	75 58	266	MID	MID	U.S. WEATHER BUREAU	2 3 5 7 C
RENOVO	7409	CLINTON	16	41 20	77 46	660		7A	MRS. CAROLINE BAIRD	3
RENOVO 5 S	7410	CLINTON	16	41 14	77 46	2035		MID	C. F. BILLETTE	C
REW	7425	MC KEAN	1	41 54	78 32	2250		8A	HAROLD C. MEALY	3
RICES LANDING L 6	7443	GREENE	10	39 57	80 00	775		7A	CORPS OF ENGINEERS	3
RIDGWAY 3 W	7477	ELK	1	41 25	78 47	1420	7A	7A	BOROUGH OF RIDGWAY	2 3 5
ROCHESTER 1 N	7540	BEAVER	2	40 43	80 18	900		MID	DEQUESNE LIGHT CO	C
RUSH	7694	SUSQUEHANNA	15	41 47	76 03	1000		9A	MISS MAUDE MC CAIN	3
RUSHVILLE	7727	SUSQUEHANNA	15	41 47	76 07	870		7A	CARL KOPATZ	3
SAFE HARBOR	7732	LANCASTER	15	39 55	76 23	270		MID	S.W.WATER POWER CORP	C
SAGAMORE 1 S	7739	INDIANA	1	40 46	79 14	1320		7A	CORPS OF ENGINEERS	3
SALINA 3 W	7782	WESTMORELAND	7	40 31	79 33	1109	6P	6P	MUN AUTH WSTMRLD CO	2 3 5
SAXTON	7846	BEDFORD	6	40 12	78 15	780		8A	MRS.ALVERTA L.HOLMES	3 C
SCANDIA 2 E	7855	WARREN	1	41 55	79 01	2040		MID	DAVID R. ANDERSON	C
SCHENLEY LOCK 5	7863	ARMSTRONG	1	40 41	79 40	783		VAR	CORPS OF ENGINEERS	3
#SCRANTON	7902	LACKAWANNA	15	41 25	75 40	746	7A	7A	U.S. POST OFFICE	2 3 5
SCRANTON WB AIRPORT	7905	LUZERNE	15	41 20	75 44	956	MID	MID	U.S. WEATHER BUREAU	2 3 5 7 C
SELLERSVILLE 2 NW	7938	BUCKS	5	40 25	75 20	530		MID	SELLERSVILLE WTR CO	C
SHADE GAP 2 NE	7965	HUNTINGDON	6	40 12	77 52	920		MID	MRS. HELEN M. PYLE	C
SHAMOKIN	7978	NORTHUMBLAND	15	40 48	76 33	770		8A	ROARING CRK WTR CO	3

STATION INDEX

INUED

Station	Index No.	County	Drainage †	Latitude	Longitude	Elevation	Observation Time Temp.	Observation Time Precip.	Observer	Refer To Tables
FFIELD 6 W	8020	WARREN	1	41 41	79 08	1940		MID	L. N. HANSON	C
PPENSBURG	8073	FRANKLIN	15	40 03	77 32	700	4P	4P	KEITH B. ALLEN	2 3 5 7
PPINGPORT WB	8078	BEAVER	11	40 37	80 26	740	MID	MID	U.S. WEATHER BUREAU	2 3 5 7 C
EMAHONING	8145	CAMERON	16	41 19	78 05	780		7A	MRS.FRANCES CALDWELL	3
PPERY ROCK	8184	BUTLER	2	41 04	80 03	1345	7P	7A	WALTER D. ALBERT	2 3 5 7
THPORT HIGHWAY SHED	8190	MC KEAN	1	41 48	78 27	1510		MID	PA DEPT HIGHWAYS	C
ERSET FAIRVIEW ST	8244	SOMERSET	17	40 01	79 05	2140		7A	HOWARD G. PECK	3
ERSET MAIN ST	8249	SOMERSET	17	40 01	79 05	2150	8P	8P	DAVID L. GROVE	2 3 5
TH CANAAN 1 NE	8275	WAYNE	5	41 31	75 24	1400		MID	EUGENE W. COOK	C
TH MOUNTAIN	8308	FRANKLIN	12	39 51	77 30	1520		7A	PA DEPT OF HEALTH	3
INGBORO	8350	CRAWFORD	8	41 48	80 23	900	8A	8A	SPRINGBORO BOROUGH	2 3 5 C
ING GROVE	8379	YORK	15	39 52	76 52	470		4P	P. H. GLATFELTER CO	3 C
INGS 1 SW	8395	SOMERSET	17	39 44	79 10	2500	8P	8P	ALLEN E. YODER	2 3 5 7
TE COLLEGE	8449	CENTRE	16	40 48	77 52	1175	7A	7A	PA STATE COLLEGE	2 3 5 6 CG
AUSSTOWN	8570	BERKS	14	40 29	76 11	400		8A	JACOB KLAHR	3
GSTOWN	8589	INDIANA	4	40 33	78 55	1880		MID	HARRY F. BENNETT	C
UDSBURG	8596	MONROE	5	40 59	75 12	480	11P	11P	WILLIAM MAGERTY	2 3 5 C
P CREEK	8610	JEFFERSON	1	41 01	78 50	1320		7A	CORPS OF ENGINEERS	3
URY	8668	NORTHUMBERLAND	15	40 51	76 48	440	7A	7A	CHARLES W. BAYLER	2 3 5 C
UEHANNA	8692	SUSQUEHANNA	15	41 57	75 36	1020		7A	MRS. LAURA A.BENSON	3
RSVILLE	8699	ALLEGHENY	17	40 14	79 48	765		7A		3
QUA	8758	SCHUYLKILL	14	40 48	75 58					3
QUA 4 N DAM	8763	SCHUYLKILL	14	40 51	75 59					3 C
RACK 2 S FIRE TWR	8770	CLINTON	16	41 24	77 51					2 3 5 7
ESTA 2 SE DAM	8873	FOREST	1	41 28	79 26					2 3 5 7 C
SVILLE	8885	CRAWFORD	1	4						C
USVILLE WATER WORKS	8888	CRAWFORD	1	4						2 3 5
PEDO 4 W	8901	WARREN	1	41						3
ANDA	8905	BRADFORD	15	41						2 3 5 7 C
ER CITY 5 SW	8910	DAUPHIN	15	40						3 7
Y	8950	BRADFORD	15	41						3
WNELTON	8969	INDIANA	4	40						C
RTLEPOINT 4 NE	9002	MC KEAN	1	41						3
RONE 4 NE BALD EAGLE	9024	BLAIR	6	40						3 C
ION CITY	9042	ERIE	1	41						3 C
IONTOWN	9050	FAYETTE	10							2 3 5
PER DARBY	9074	DE								2 3 5
ICA	9099	VE								3
NOERGRIET	9124	W								3
		W								
										3
										3
										3
										2 3 5

Station	Index No.	County	Drainage †	Latitude	Longitude	Elevation	Observation Time Temp.	Observation Time Precip.	Observer	Refer To Tables
WATSONTOWN	9345	NORTHUMBERLAND	16	41 05	76 52	490		9P	WILLIAM BIRD	3
WAYNESBURG 2 W	9367	GREENE	10	39 54	80 13	980	8P	7A	RALPH L. AMOS	2 3 5
WAYNESBURG 1 E	9387	GREENE	10	39 54	80 10	940		MID	SEWAGE DISPOSAL PLT	C
WEBSTER MILLS 3 SW	9380	FULTON	12	39 49	78 05	920		MID	WILLIAM D. COVER	C
WELLSBORO 3 S	9408	TIOGA	16	41 43	77 16	1920	7A	7A	MARION L. SHUMWAY	2 3 5
WELLSBORO 2 E	9412	TIOGA	16	41 45	77 16	1550		MID	MRS. IDA S. MAYNARD	C
WELLSVILLE	9420	YORK	15	40 03	76 57	500	5P	5P	U. D. HOOVER	2 3 5
WERNERSVILLE 1 W	9430	BERKS	14	40 20	76 06	405		8A	CHARLES A. GRUBER	3
WEST CHESTER	9464	CHESTER	5	39 58	75 36	440	8A	8A	DAILY LOCAL NEWS	2 3 5
WEST GROVE 1 E	9503	CHESTER	5	39 49	75 49	440		8A	CONARD-PYLE CO	3
REST HICKORY	9507	FOREST	1	41 34	79 25	1090		8A	MRS.HELEN F.KINNEAR	3
WHITESBURG	9655	ARMSTRONG	1	40 45	79 24	1530		7A	CORPS OF ENGINEERS	3
WILKES-BARRE	9702	LAZERNE	15	41 15	75 52	610		7A	MRS. MARY G. HIRMAK	3
WILLIAMSBURG	9714	BLAIR	6	40 28	78 12	860		7A	MYRON K. BIDDLE	3
WILLIAMSPORT WB AP	9728	LYCOMING	16	41 15	76 55	527	MID	MID	U.S. WEATHER BUREAU	2 3 5 7 C
WIND GAP	9781	NORTHAMPTON	5	40 51	75 18	740		MID	W. L. TEMPLETON	C
WOLFSBURG	9823	BEDFORD	6	40 03	78 32	1190		7A	WALTER C. RICE	3
YORK 3 SSW PUMP STA	9933	YORK	15	39 55	76 45	390	5P	5P	YORK WATER COMPANY	2 3 5
YORK 2 S FILTER PLANT	9938	YORK	15	39 56	76 44	640		MID	YORK WATER COMPANY	C
YORK HAVEN	9950	YORK	15	40 07	76 43	310		8A	METROPOL EDISON CO	3
YOUNGSVILLE	9966	WARREN						MID	HENRY CARLETT	C
ZION GROVE	9990	SCHUYLKILL						7A	JAMES D. TEETER	3
ZIONSVILLE 3 SE	9995	LEHIGH						7A	LESLIE HOWATT	3
NEW STATIONS										
EDINBORO 7 SW	2520	CRAWFORD						8A	THOMAS H. YOUNG	3
HONEY BROOK 1 W	4047	CHESTER						7A	S. H. KURTZ	3
LYNCH	5275	FOREST						7A	CORPS OF ENGINEERS	3
CLOSED STATIONS										
COATESVILLE	1594	CHESTER				0		8A	EDWARD D. BIEDEMAN	CLOSED 8/57
MAYBURG	5490	FOREST				0		7A	CORPS OF ENGINEERS	CLOSED 8/57
PHILADELPHIA SHAWMONT	6904	PHILADELPHIA				0	7P	7P	SCHUYLKILL NAVIG CO	CLOSED 6/57
COMBINED STATIONS										
SELINSGROVE CAA AP	7931	SNYDER					D	MID	COMBINED W/STA 8668	8/57

† 1-ALLEGHENY; 2-BEAVER; 3- 4-CONEMAUGH; 5-DELAWARE; 6-JUNIATA; 7-KISKIMINETAS; 8-LAKE ERIE; 9-LEHIGH; 10-MONONGAHELA; 11-OHIO; 12-POTOMAC; 13-LAKE ONTARIO; 14-SCHUYLKILL; 15-SUSQUEHANNA; 16-WEST BRANCH; 17-YOUGHIOGHENY

REFERENCE NOTES

Additional information regarding the climate of Pennsylvania may be obtained by writing to the State Climatologist at Weather Bureau Airport Station, Harrisburg State Airport, New Cumberland, Pennsylvania, or to any Weather Bureau Office near you.

Figures and letters following the station name, such as 12 SSW, indicate distance in miles and direction from the post office.

Delayed data and corrections will be carried only in the June and December issues of this bulletin.

Monthly and seasonal snowfall and heating degree days for the preceding 12 months will be carried in the June issue of this bulletin.

Stations appearing in the Index, but for which data are not listed in the tables, either are missing or were received too late to be included in this issue.

Divisions, as used in Table 2, became effective with data for September 1956.

Unless otherwise indicated, dimensional units used in this bulletin are: Temperature in °F, precipitation and evaporation in inches, and wind movement in miles. Monthly degree day totals are the sums of the negative departures of average daily temperatures from 65° F.

Evaporation is measured in the standard Weather Bureau type pan of 4 foot diameter unless otherwise shown by footnote following Table 6. Max and Min in Table 6 refer to extremes of temperature of water in pan as recorded during 24 hours ending at time of observation.

Long-term means for full-time stations (those shown in the Station Index as "U. S. Weather Bureau") are based on the period 1921-1950, adjusted to represent observations taken at the present location. Long-term means for all stations except full-time Weather Bureau stations are based on the period 1931-1955.

Water equivalent values published in Table 7 are the water equivalent of snow, sleet or ice on the ground. Samples for obtaining measurements are taken from different points for successive observations; consequently occasional drifting and other causes of local variability in the snowpack result in apparent inconsistencies in the record. Water equivalent of snow on the ground is measured at selected stations when two or more inches of snow are on the ground.

Entries of Snowfall in Tables 2 and 7, and in the seasonal snowfall table, include snow and sleet. Entries of snow on ground include snow, sleet and ice.

Data in Tables 3, 5, and 6 and snowfall in Table 7, when published, are for the 24 hours ending at time of observation. The Station Index lists observation times in the standard of time in local use. During the summer months some observers take the observations on daylight saving time.

Snow on ground in Table 7 is at observation time for all except Weather Bureau and CAA stations. For these stations snow on ground values are at 7:30 a.m., E.S.T.

- \- No record in Tables 3, 6, 7 and the Station Index. No record in Tables 2 and 5, is indicated by no entry. Consult the annual issue of this publication for interpolated monthly precipitation totals.
- \+ And also on a later date or dates.
- ++ Fastest observed one minute wind speed. This station is not equipped with automatic wind instruments.
- ‡ Amount included in following measurement, time distribution unknown.
- // Gage is equipped with a windshield.
- \# Thermometers are generally exposed in a shelter located a few feet above sod-covered ground; however, the reference indicates that the thermometers are exposed in a shelter located on the roof of a building.
- AM Data based on observational day ending before noon.
- B Adjusted to a full month.
- C In the "Refer to Tables" column in the Station Index the letter "C" indicates recorder stations. These stations are processed for special purposes and are published later in "Hourly Precipitation Data".
- D Water equivalent of snowfall wholly or partly estimated, using a ratio of 1 inch water equivalent to every 10 inches of new snowfall.
- G In the "Refer to Tables" column in the Station Index the letter "G" indicates that soil temperatures are published.
- M One or more days of record missing; if average value is entered, less than 10 days record is missing. See Table 5 for detailed daily record. Degree day data, if carried for this station, have been adjusted to represent the value for a full month.
- R Amounts from recording gage (These amounts are essentially accurate but may vary slightly from the amounts to be published later in "Hourly Precipitation Data".)
- SS This entry in time of observation column in Station Index means observation made near sunset.
- T Trace, an amount too small to measure.
- Y Includes total for previous month.
- VAR This entry in time of observation column in Station Index means variable.

Information concerning the history of changes in locations, elevations, exposure etc. of substations through 1955 may be found in the publication "Substation History" for this state, soon to be issued. That publication, when available, may be obtained from the Superintendent of Documents, Government Printing Office, Washington 25, D. C. at a price to be announced. Similar information for regular Weather Bureau stations may be found in the latest issues of Local Climatological Data, Annual for the respective stations, obtained as indicated above, price 15 cents.

Subscription Price: 20 cents per copy, monthly and annual; $2.50 per year. (Yearly subscription includes the Annual Summary). Checks, and money orders should be made payable to the Superintendent of Documents. Remittance and correspondence regarding subscriptions should be sent to the Superintendent of Documents, Government Printing Office, Washington 25, D. C.

WRPC., Asheville, N. C. --- 10/7/57 --- 1100

U. S. DEPARTMENT OF COMMERCE
SINCLAIR WEEKS, Secretary
WEATHER BUREAU
F. W. REICHELDERFER, Chief

CLIMATOLOGICAL DATA

PENNSYLVANIA

SEPTEMBER 1957
Volume LXII No. 9

ASHEVILLE: 1957

PENNSYLVANIA - SEPTEMBER 1957

WEATHER SUMMARY

GENERAL

Highlights of September's weather in Pennsylvania were rainy weather the second week and frosts near the end of the month.

Moderate amounts of precipitation were indicated in most areas since totals at nearly ninety percent of the stations were between two and five inches. Large differences over relatively short distances appeared in a few instances; one of the extreme cases was West Grove 1 E with 7.15 inches and Lebanon 3 W with 1.58 inches, the largest and smallest totals for the State, both of these stations being in the Southeastern Piedmont Division. The greatest amount for one day was 3.25 inches measured at Troy on the 23rd.

Temperature averages generally qualified as moderate with a preponderance of negative departures from the long-term mean in the northern counties and mostly positive departures in the southern half of the State. Extreme temperatures ranged from 97° on the 3rd at Marcus Hook to 17° on the 27th at Kane 1 NNE.

WEATHER DETAILS

Summer heat at the beginning of September was followed by a moderately cool period extending from the 5th through the 9th. Rather warm weather prevailed from the 12th through the 16th in most areas and made a brief appearance again the 21st-22nd. A cooling trend beginning on the 23rd, closely coinciding with the astronomical change of season, dropped minimum temperatures to frosty levels in all areas the 27th and 28th. Light rains occurred at nearly all stations during the three day period ending the 4th and light to moderate rains were widespread and frequent from the 10th through the 16th. Widespread showers and thunderstorms the 20th-22nd practically completed September's precipitation.

WEATHER EFFECTS

Precipitation in late August and during September was sufficient to green up pas tures and alfalfa. The moderate rainfal improved conditions for planting of fall grains and insured germination of winter oats, barley and early seedings of wheat Late tobacco in the Lancaster area made considerable growth and some late plante corn filled out better than expected. Despite some improvement, subsoil moistu in most areas was deficient and water su plies continued short. Hauling of water for livestock was common in scattered localities. Pastures supplied some graz and briefly relieved the strain on winte feed supplies. A few late cuttings of alfalfa bolstered hay supplies. Freezin temperatures came early to southeastern Pennsylvania again this year. The cool nights of September 27-29 brought killin frosts to all areas of the State. Damag was most severe in the Lancaster area wh about 10 percent of tobacco remained in fields.

DESTRUCTIVE STORMS

Damaging thunderstorms were reported the 1st through the 4th, on the 10th, 12th, 22nd. Lightning was the primary damagin element with wind in a secondary role. Tornadoes were reported at Germania (Pot County) and in the Selinsgrove-Sunbury a on the 15th, and at Erie on the 21st. F more detailed storm information see Clim tological Data National Summary for Sept ber 1957.

FLOODS

None reported.

J. T. B. Beard, Climatologist
Weather Records Processing Center
Chattanooga, Tennessee

SPECIAL NOTICE

A survey has indicated that the comprehensive narrative weather story carried in each issue of Climatological Data is of value to only a small number of recipients. This story will be discontinued, therefore, with the January 1958 issue. A table of extremes will be carried each month and a text will be carried whenever unusual and outstanding weather events have occurred. General weather conditions in the U. S. for each month are described in the publications MONTHLY WEATHER REVIEW and the MONTHLY CLIMATOLOGICAL DATA, NATIONAL SUMMARY, either of which may be obtained from the Superintendent of Documents, Government Printing Office, Washington, D. C.

Temperature: Average Maximum	Average Minimum	Average	Departure From Long Term Means	Highest	Date	Lowest	Date	Degree Days	No. of Days Max 90° or Above	Max 32° or Below	Min 32° or Below	Min 0° or Below	Precipitation: Total	Departure From Long Term Means	Greatest Day	Date	Snow, Sleet Total	Max Depth on Ground	Date	No. of Days .10 or More	.50 or More	1.00 or More
72.8M	52.6M	62.7M	2.3	84	2	29	27	129	0	0	1	0	4.64	.96	.99	13	.0	0		9	5	0
72.0	46.1	59.1		84	23	26	27	205	0	0	4	0	2.47		.88	3	.0	0		5	2	0
71.5	49.4	60.5	2.1	81	2	25	27	175	0	0	2	0	2.65	- 2.14	1.30	3	.0	0		4	1	1
													3.19				.0	0				
69.9	51.2	60.6M		81	3+	27	27	161	0	0	2	0	4.80		2.38	3	.0	0		6	2	2
										0	3	0	3.49	- .38			.0	0				
75.6	51.0	63.3M	- .4	89	23	32	27+	122	0	0	2	0	3.64	.71	2.04	23	.0	0		4	2	1
74.1	51.0	62.6	- .6	87	2+	30	28	139	0	0	2	0	2.18	- 1.04	.79	22	.0	0		4	2	0
75.4	47.5	61.5	- 1.1	90	1+	20	29	170	2	0	3	0	4.38	.78	2.27	23	.0	0		7	3	1
		61.5											3.49				.0					
76.8	54.9	65.9	1.2	90	3	33	27	93	1	0	0	0	2.06	- 1.41	.79	16	.0	0		5	2	0
77.9	55.0	66.5	1.5	91	14	33	27	86	2	0	0	0	1.90	- 1.57	.96	17	.0	0		3	1	0
78.2	57.0	67.6	.8	93	13	34	27	80	5	0	0	0	2.54	- .83	.89	16	.0	0		5	3	0
77.4M	52.1M	64.8M	1.1	87	2+	30	27+	114	0	0	3	0	2.54	- 1.48	.64	23	.0	0		9	1	0
75.0	53.0	64.0	.2	88	2+	31	27+	118	0	0	3	0	4.39	.70	2.80	22	.0	0		5	2	1
78.6	48.8	63.7	- 1.5	92	4	25	27	131	2	0	4	0	2.81	- 1.24	1.02	23	.0	0		4	2	1
		65.4											2.71				.0					
79.9	58.8	69.4		94	4	38	27	55	2	0	0	0	3.96		1.30	11	.0	0		5	3	3
78.1	54.9	66.5	.4	92	4	31	28	92	2	0	2	0	5.65	1.94	1.59	14	.0	0		7	5	2
78.8	56.9	67.9		92	2	32	28	76	3	0	1	0	2.35		.82	14	.0	0		7	1	0
78.1	56.3	67.2		90	3+	32	27	87	2	0	1	0	3.39		.89	16	.0	0		8	3	0
78.1	55.4	66.8	.5	90	3	31	27	84	1	0	2	0	2.17	- 1.35	.55	10	.0	0		6	1	0
78.7	56.9	67.8	1.5	94	3	31	27+	80	1	0	2	0	2.72	- .86	1.04	11	.0	0		5	3	1
81.6	55.8	68.7		92	13	27	27	66	3	0	2	0	3.16	.02	.96	17	.0	0		6	3	0
77.6	61.4	69.5	.6	91	3	41	28	51	1	0	0	0	5.35	2.72	1.52	17	.0	0		7	5	1
78.3	56.1	67.2	1.8	90	3+	31	27+	83	3	0	2	0	3.42	.10	1.02	14	.0	0		6	4	1
78.5	53.7	66.1		92	4+	27	28	108	4	0	3	0	1.61		.43	13	.0	0		5	0	0
78.9	53.0	66.0	.3	93	3	28	27	101	5	0	3	0	1.58	- 1.81	.62	11	.0	0		4	1	0
79.1	63.2	71.2	.7	97	3	43	27	41	2	0	0	0	3.56	.45	1.14	10	.0	0		6	3	1
78.4	58.5	68.5	2.6	92	2+	34	27	74	5	0	0	0	1.62	- 1.67	.51	10+	.0	0		5	2	0
77.0	54.7	65.9		89	3+	29	27	100	0	0	2	0	2.21		.80	10	.0	0		4	2	0
77.3	56.7	67.0		93	2	38	28	87	2	0	0	0	1.92		.80	10	.0	0		5	1	0
78.7	59.9	69.3		94	3	37	28	64	4	0	0	0	5.21		1.38	11	.0	0		6	4	3
79.7	63.3	71.5		96	3	41	28+	42	3	0	0	0	3.96		1.33	23	.0	0		5	3	2
78.2	60.2	69.2	1.5	94	3	37	28	64	2	0	0	0	3.10	- .36	.86	10	.0	0		5	4	0
78.8	64.3	71.6	2.1	94	3	49	29	30	1	0	0	0	3.55		1.03	23	.0	0		5	4	1
78.6	63.2	70.9	1.6	92	3	44	27+	40	2	0	0	0	2.71	- .72	.78	23				5	4	0
79.9	54.7	67.3	.1	95	3	29	28	83	5	0	2	0	3.68	.28	1.00	10	.0	0		7	3	1
79.1	54.0	66.6	2.8	90	3+	27	27	98	3	0	3	0	1.64	- 1.98	.75	11	.0	0		3	2	0
78.1	59.4	68.8	1.7	91	3	38	27+	64	3	0	0	0	2.56	- .72	1.44	16	.0	0		6	2	1
78.4	60.2	69.3		93	3	38	27+	68	1	0	0	0	5.56		1.92	23	.0	0		6	4	2
79.3	56.8	68.1	2.3	94	3	36	27	64	2	0	0	0	6.52	2.66	2.17	23	.0	0		7	4	3
		68.3											3.33				.0					
78.5	54.4	66.5	.8	93	3	32	27	95	4	0	1	0	2.85	- .81	1.00	11	.0	0		6	2	1
81.1	56.9	69.0	3.5	93	2+	33	27	66	5	0	0	0	2.12	- 1.25	.98	10	.0	0		7	1	0
78.7	54.8	66.8	.7	92	3	30	27	87	4	0	2	0	3.77	.66	1.03	10	.0	0		9	3	1
78.8	57.3	68.1	2.1	92	3+	34	27	72	2	0	0	0	3.32	- .14	.96	10	.0	0		7	2	0
79.5	56.8	68.2	.8	91	3+	34	27+	70	3	0	0	0	3.14	- .02	.92	23	.0	0		6	4	0
77.9	57.6	67.8	1.7	91	2+	34	28	76	2	0	0	0	2.19	- .44	.99	10	.0	0		3	1	0
80.1	57.6	68.9		94	2	29	27	57	2	0	1	0	3.44		.92	23	.0	0		5	4	0
79.4	55.7	67.6	1.4	91	2	32	27	76	2	0	1	0	3.19	- .09	1.01	23	.0	0		8	2	1
79.0	52.2	65.6		91	2	26	27	103	2	0	3	0	4.18		2.06	14	.0	0		5	3	1
80.5	55.7	68.1	1.6	91	2	30	27+	80	4	0	2	0	2.77	- .53	.53	12	.0	0		6	1	0
		67.7											3.10				.0					
77.3	51.5	64.4		92	2	27	27	119	1	0	3	0	4.20		1.07	11	.0	0		11	2	1
78.3	54.0	66.2		92	2	30	27+	92	3	0	2	0	3.48		1.11	3	.0	0		9	1	1
77.1	52.1	64.6		91	4	28	28	125	2	0	4	0	2.21		.71	23	.0	0		6	2	0
78.5	54.2	66.4		94	3	31	28	95	2	0	3	0	3.48		.87	11	.0	0		8	2	0
78.8	52.2	65.5		93	3	30	27+	105	2	0	3	0	3.44	.30	1.13	11	.0	0		7	2	1
78.8	53.2	66.0		92	3	28	28	95	2	0	3	0	4.65	1.44	1.30	16	.0	0		10	4	1
75.9	53.0	64.5	- .1	90	2	34	27+	109	1	0	0	0	3.80	.47	2.34	22	.0	0		6	2	1
		65.4											3.61				.0					
71.4	47.4	59.4		83	3	31	27+	186	0	0	3	0	2.97		.97	23	.0	0		5	2	0
75.6	46.8	61.2		88	23	25	27+	159	0	0	4	0	4.24		2.22	23	.0	0		6	2	1
67.7	50.2	59.0		81	3	31	27+	195	0	0	3	0	5.15	.51	1.59	23	.0	0		7	3	2
73.1	45.5	59.3	- 2.5	84	4+	23	27	195	0	0	4	0	3.75	.65	1.75	23	.0	0		6	2	2

See Reference Notes Following Station Index

TABLE 2 - CONTINUED

Station	
MONTROSE 1 E	AM
TOWANDA	
WELLSBORO 3 S	AM
DIVISION	
CENTRAL MOUNTAINS	
BELLEFONTE 4 S	AM
DU BOIS 7 E	
EMPORIUM 2 SSW	AM
LOCK HAVEN	
MADERA	AM
PHILIPSBURG CAA AP	
RIDGWAY 3 W	AM
STATE COLLEGE	AM
TAMARACK 2 S FIRE TWR	AM
DIVISION	
SOUTH CENTRAL MOUNTAINS	
ALTOONA HORSESHOE CURVE	
BURNT CABINS 2 NE	
EBENSBURG	
EVERETT 1 SW	
HUNTINGDON	AM
JOHNSTOWN	AM
KEGG	
MARTINSBURG CAA AP	
DIVISION	
SOUTHWEST PLATEAU	
BAKERSTOWN 3 WNW	
BLAIRSVILLE 6 ENE	
BURGETTSTOWN 2 W	AM
BUTLER	
CLAYSVILLE 3 W	
CONFLUENCE 1 SW DAM	AM
DERRY	
DONEGAL	
DONORA	AM
FORD CITY 4 S DAM	AM
INDIANA 3 SE	
IRWIN	
MIDLAND DAM 7	
NEW CASTLE 1 N	
† NEWELL	AM
NEW STANTON	
PITTSBURGH WB AP 2	//R
PITTSBURGH WB CITY	R
PUTNEYVILLE 2 SE DAM	AM
SALINA 3 W	
SHIPPINGPORT WB	
SLIPPERY ROCK	
SOMERSET MAIN ST	
SPRINGS 1 SW	
UNIONTOWN	
WAYNESBURG 2 W	
DIVISION	
NORTHWEST PLATEAU	
BRADFORD CAA AP	
BRADFORD 4 W RES	
BROOKVILLE CAA AIRPORT	
CLARION 3 SW	
CORRY	
COUDERSPORT 3 NW	
EAST BRADY	
ERIE WB AIRPORT	
FARRELL SHARON	
FRANKLIN	
GREENVILLE	
JAMESTOWN 2 NW	AM
KANE 1 NNE	AM
LINESVILLE 5 WNW	
MEADVILLE 1 S	AM
MERCER 2 NNE	
SPRINGBORO	AM
TIONESTA 2 SE DAM	AM
TITUSVILLE WATER WORKS	
WARREN	
DIVISION	

† DATA RECEIVED TOO LATE TO BE INCLUDED IN DIVISION AVERAGES

See Reference Notes Following Station Index

DAILY PRECIPITATION

Day of month

Total	1	2	3	4	5	6	7	8	9	10	11	12	13	14	15	16	17	18	19	20	21	22	23	24	25	26	27	28	29	30	31
3.52			.03							T	.14		.03	.16	.05	.46	.07			T	1.54		1.04								
2.06		.13								.55	T		T	.08	.04	.79	.11			T	.31	T	.05								
1.90			.03							.01	.44		.03	.08	.02	.02	.96				.21		.07								
2.54			.16							.56			.30	.06	.15	.30	.02			.71	.09		.14			.05					
2.89									T	.94	1.00		.17	.31	.26		.45				.08		.03								
2.89			1.22											.06	.08	.34	.07				.26		.69	.05							
5.41			.16							.20			.18		.40	T			.30	2.50		1.50	T								
3.02			.15							T	.04		.01	.71	.33	.06	.05	.01		.31	.41	.30	.29	.04							
	RECORD MISSING																														
3.02			.43							.08	.63		.09	.24		.39	.29			.05	.05	.05	.70								
3.96			.01		.08						.11		.08	.15	.04	.01	.08			.09	1.70	.09	1.50			.02					
4.20			.47		.09					.19	1.07	.22	.12	.15	.07	.75	.32				.31	.30	.14								
3.50			T							T	.11	T	.37	.12		1.37	.01				.40	T	1.12								
2.36			.35								.17		.04	.20	.05	.81	.10				.30	.06	.28								
1.61										.05	.39		T	.09	T		.46				.14		.05								
3.48			1.11							.07	.48		.01	.13	T	.32	.20			.02	.12	.05	.39								
2.30										T	.59		T	.19	T	.06	.95				.22		.26								
2.54										.63	T		.21		.02	.89					.22	T	.54								
2.48										.12			.17	.04	T	.65	.13			.95	.04	.01	.33								
2.84									T	1.44	.16			.17	.03	.05	.17			.13	.19		.50							T	
2.61			.20							T	.23		.15	.12	.03	.31	.37				.75	T	.45								
3.89			.14								.28		T	.09	.08	.15	.40			T	1.80		.95								
2.88			T										.32		.33	.10			T	.49	.02	.95	.29								
2.23			.39										T	.06	.06	.14	.28			.22	.12	.05	.66	.08							
3.21										.01	.04		.20	.04	.16	.67				.33	.12	.36	.48								
1.76		.09	.04						.03	.40			.04	.38	.02	.41	.04			.21		.08									
4.49		.01	.14						T	.01			.21		.28	.29				.89	.03	2.60	.01								
-			.08										T			.62	.43			.04	-		1.27								
1.69			T							.06	.19		.30	.26	.32	.06	.30				.17	.02	.01								
3.24													.14	.17	.21	.28	.03			.29	1.12	.03	.61								
3.12										.35	.24		.05	.23	.05	.04	.20			.15	.07		1.05								
5.48										T	.47	.02	.19	.07	.21	.42	.30			.49	1.76	.57	.87								
2.02										.88		T		.12		.22	.20			.08			.27								
2.97			.81								.40		.05	.06		.38	.07				.23		.97								
2.12			T						T	.98	.12			.24	.12	.05	.22			.16	.08	T	.15								
2.45			.19							.01	.33		.04	.23	.02	.62	.17				.51	.16	.17								
3.16			.60		.07					T	.05		T	.22	T	.42	.26				.58	T	.93	.03							
3.53					T					T	.30			.20		.45	.05				.55	.06	1.47	.15							
-								.50	T	*	*		.62	2.30			1.25	T					-								
3.77								.28	T	1.03				.81	.21	.16	.17			.12		.78	.19								
2.85			.16								.11		T	.23		.15	.64				1.09		.40								
3.96			T							.12	1.30		.06	.02			1.00	T		T			1.03								
2.44										T	.20		.30	.20		.52	.12				.60		.30	T							
3.62											.24		.02	.75	.15	.07	.03			.01	.82	.05	1.37	.03							
2.25										.03	.40		.15	.21	.07	.05	.78				.12		.09								
3.00			.19								.18		T	.21	.06	.03	.48				.82	.03	.83								
2.91			.32							T	.32		T	.06	T	.44	.49				.84	T	.44								
2.87			.29							.04	.14		T	.28	.35	.04	.05			.38	.25	.15	.94	T							
2.34			.30					.28		.01	.51	.32	.16			.05	.24				.20	.05	.17								
5.65								.25		.18	.87	.03	.71	1.59	.02		1.11						.85	T							
2.35										.33	.19		.02	.82	.04	T	.40				T		.11							T	
2.75	.10		.08							.01	.23		.31	.29	.28	.37	.36			T	.38	.05	.29	T						T	
2.94	.11		.21							T	.16		.33	.36	.18	.36	.38			.16	.34	.05	.30								
2.05											.10		.10	.29	.01	.15	.21				.74		.35								
4.51										.40	1.12		.09	.55			1.07						1.13								
3.83			.13		.03					.03	.12		T	.46	.21	.05	.02	T		.08	.54	.90	1.26	T	T						
2.54			.03		.06					.02	.11		.02	.31	.17	.03	T	T		.33	.27	.03	1.16	T	T				T		
4.00			T								.04		T		*	.93	T			T	*	*	3.03								
2.59			.19							.08	.22		.17		.18	.05				.28	.29	.30	.15	.03							
2.43										T	.03			.08	.23	.16	.22				.51	.06	.85	.06							
3.31			*		*					.01	.07			.20	.15	.58	.12				.51	.01	1.05	.11							
3.07			.57		.05						.04		.02	.03		.46	.05				.11	T	1.74	T							
3.02			.40								.10				.20	.05	.20				1.37		.70								
3.01			.09							.05	.19		.14	.14	.01	.27	.26				1.55	.04	.27	T							
2.52														.14	.05	.06	.13			.21	.20	.13	.66	.19							
4.61			1.15										.74	.15	.06	.58	.36				.14	T	.22								
2.63									.12				.07	T	.80	.17				.95	.52										
3.39									T	.81			.17	.24	.30	.89	.34						.51								
4.24			.71								.33		T	.44		.07	.14				.06		2.22								
2.58			.35										.35		.10	.48				.70	T	.29	.01							T	
2.65			.03							.10	.03		.05	.24	.03	.22	.40			.62	.44	.03	.46							T	
2.21			T							.28	.67		.06	.15			.67				.01		.27							T	
4.05			.32							.33	.02		.07	.09	.21	.71	.02			.80	.12	.53	.74								
2.49			.52							.20				.14		.43	.09				.06		1.05								
5.15			1.49	.05	.02						.62		T	.24	.01	.42	.37				.30	.04	1.59								
5.14										.14			.15		.40	.39				.94	.38	.87	1.87								
2.41			.07							T	.18		.09	.13		.86	.24				.68		.16								
3.84			.36		.50					.13	.72		.14	.12	.52	.24				.34	.05	.05	.58	.07							
	RECORD MISSING																														
2.07			.42							.18	.50		.11	.22	.07		.52				.03	.01									
4.63			.45		.07					.05	.30			.70	.03	.40	.11				.62	.03	1.87								
3.07			.45		.08						.26			.15		.50	.08				.29	.08	1.18	T							
2.17										.55	.18		.03	.24	.05	.48	.40						.20								
2.51			.44	.02	.31						.04			.04		.06	.16				.02		1.40	.02							
4.63		.16	T	.81						.72			.62		.10	.13			T	.45	.80	.47	.35								
2.13		.22								.28			.21	.50		.31				.28											
2.25				.06						.33			.93							.48		.40	.04	.01							
4.46			T		.10						.11		.20	.17	.32	.07	.06			T	1.87	T	1.56								
4.03	T		.02		.17	.01				.04	.13		.06	.54	.26	.04	.04			.64	.02	.02	1.12	.02		T					
4.64						.02							.99	.16	.03	.90	.55				.15	.23	.70								
2.89			.10		.18								.10			.77	.12				.58	.05	.93	.06							
2.29										.09	.68		.02	.30	.02		1.10				T		.08								
2.72										.25	1.04		.03	.22		.01	.55						.57								
3.32			T							.98	.43		.09	.49	.28		.65				.06		.13							T	
2.86			.45		.17								.02	.36	.14	.09	.08			.24	.25	.08	.65	.25							
2.65			.06		.09					.02	.05		T	.32	.36	.04	.12			.17	.39	T	.95	.08							
3.86	.02		.03		.01								.73	.24	.06	.14	.04			.03	1.37	.01	.74			T					
2.69			.91	.05	.03			.10			.25		.09	.04	.03	T	.51				.27	T	.41								
3.16										.06	.87		.16	.34			.96	.03					.53								
2.21			.25		T					T	.70		T	.10	T	T	.35				.10	T	.71								
3.19	.32		.15								.18		.28	.48	T	.38	.38				.30		.74								
3.35			.05							.08			.07	.33	.02	1.01	.23			1.10	T	.06	.40						T	T	
3.02			T	.16						.47	.02	T	1.04		.04	.11				.77	.05	.26	.10								
3.14									T	.52	.71	.11	.02	T	.23		.63				T		.92								
2.19		T	T						.06	.99	T	T	.07	.06	.04	.45	.06			.06	T	.40	T							T	
2.27			T					.20		.38	.67	T	T	.05	.06		.53				.06		.32								
2.49			.78	.01	.02			.04			.15		T	.29	.03	.08	.54				.05		.50								
2.47			.88	.03							.16		T	.25		.07	.53				.07		.48								
2.05			.64	T	T						.12		T	.17	.02	.09	.43				.03	T	.55	T							
5.35								.42		.41	.80		.74	.77	T		1.52				T		.69								
3.39			.45		.12					T	.09		T	.40		.09	.23				.22	.02	1.77								
3.27								T		.07	.64		.16	1.28	.02		.93						.17								
3.32			.04		.05						.19		.21	.33	.19	.82	.33			.02	1.01		.33								
1.78			.07	.70	T			.02	T		.03	.07	.02	T		T	.16	.17			T		.54								
2.59			.18		.06					.06	.39		.07	.14	.02	.27	.18	.03			1.10	.01	.08								

See Reference Notes Following Station Index

DAILY PRECIPITATION

Table 3—Continued

HUNTSDALE									
HYNDMAN									
INDIANA 3 SE									
IRWIN									
JAMESTOWN 2 NW									
JIM THORPE									
JOHNSTOWN									
KANE 1 NNE									
KARTHAUS									
KEATING SUMMIT									
KEGG									
KITTANNING LOCK 7									
KREGAR 4 SE									
KRESGEVILLE 3 W									
LAFAYETTE MC KEAN PARK									
LAKEVILLE 1 NNE									
LANCASTER 2 NE PUMP STA									
LANDISVILLE 2 NW									
LAWRENCEVILLE 2 S									
LEBANON 3 W									
LEHIGHTON									
LE ROY									
LEWIS RUN 3 SE									
LEWISTOWN									
LINESVILLE 5 WNW									
LOCK HAVEN									
LONG POND 2 W									
LYNCH									
LYNDELL 2 NW									
MADERA									
MAHAFFEY									T
MAPLE GLEN									
MAPLETON DEPOT									.06
MARCUS HOOK									
MARION CENTER 2 SE									
MARTINSBURG CAA AP									
MATAMORAS									
MC CONNELLSBURG									
MC KEESPORT	T			.45	.87				
MEADVILLE 1 S	.13	.37	.13	.02			.41	[illegible]	
MEDIX RUN	T	.08	.03	.20	.09			6	
MERCER 2 NNE	.08	.57	.02	.08	.04		.40	23	
MERCERSBURG	.10	.14	.30	.38				13	
MEYERSDALE	.28	.15	.39	.49	.49			22	
MIDDLETOWN OLMSTED FLD	.10	.03		.51	.25		.04		
MIDLAND DAM 7	.04	.16	.11	.05	.04		.05	72	
MILANVILLE		.51	T	.06	.73			16	
MILLHEIM	.14	.20	.02	1.24	.09			39	
MILLVILLE 2 SW	.09	.08		.18	.24			13	
MILROY	T	.14	.01	1.07	.22			48	
MONTROSE 1 E	T	.02		.23	.53			02	
MORGANTOWN		.39	T	.67	.23				
MT GRETNA 2 SE		.23	.05	.23	.13		.02	02	
MT POCONO 2 N AP	.02		.09	.01	.17		T	09	
MUHLENBURG 1 SE	•	•	•	•	•		•		
MYERSTOWN	.02	.07	.03		.28		T		
NATRONA LOCK 4	.27	.18	.01	.58	.06			63	
NESHAMINY FALLS	.33	.05		.13	.50				
NEWBURG 3 W		.07	.47				.58		
NEW CASTLE 1 N	.14	1.56	.17	.02			.53	91	
NEWELL	.14	.10	•	.54	.36		•	63	
NEW PARK	.21	.10		1.65	.60		T		
NEWPORT	T	.09	.01	.95	.21			22	
NEW STANTON	.28	.14	.35	.73			.26	03	
NEW TRIPOLI	.74	.03	.03	.14	.26		T	07	
NORRISTOWN	.05	.90	.02		1.10				
NORTH EAST 2 SE	.19	.58	.06	.16			.41	06	
ORWELL 3 N		.07		.18	.32			13	
PALM	.10	.10	.15		.65			12	
PALMERTON		.03	.02	.53	.04		.02	06	
PARKER	.06	.65	.22	.19	.03			98	
PAUPACK 2 WNW	.05	.18		.16	.46			17	
PECKS POND	.02	.05	T	.01	.21			22	
PHIL DREXEL INST OF TEC	.04	T		.12	.80				
PHILADELPHIA WB AP R	.02		T	.15	.77				.03
PHILADELPHIA PT BREEZE	.02	.02		.16	.81				.02
PHILADELPHIA CITY R	.03			.15	.62			02	.04
PHILIPSBURG CAA AP	.20	.04	.95	.13			.53	05	
PHOENIXVILLE 1 E	.60	.26		.83	.34				
PIKES CREEK	.01	.19	.03	.20	.28			15	
PIMPLE HILL	1.02	.08	.02	T	.25		T	15	
PINE GROVE 1 NE	.01	.08	.03	.01	.16			17	
PITTSBURGH WB AP 2 //R	.27	T	.42	.09			.64	01	
PITTSBURGH WB CITY R	.09		.45	.04			.50		
PLEASANT MOUNT 1 W		•	•	.13	.35				
PORT CLINTON	.48	.05	.08		.26			09	
POTTSVILLE	.93	.15	.04	.27				20	
PUTNEYVILLE 2 SE DAM	.02	.05	.10	.13	.25		.15	35	
QUAKERTOWN 1 E		.13	T		.63		T	03	
RAYMOND		.03	.12	.68	.20			47	
READING WB CITY	.02	.20	T	1.44	.11		T	16	
RENOVO	.03	.39		.69	.15			47	
REW	T	.16	.18	.07	.09		.17	30	
RICES LANDING L	.07	.12		.20	.18			72	
RIDGWAY 3 W	T	.49	.24	.02	.12		T	81	
RUSH	.01	.05		.40	.21			05	
RUSHVILLE		.01		.39	.02			0	
SAGAMORE 1 S		.30	.15	.15	.80			8	
SALINA 3 W	.09	.01	.15	.47	.01		.33	0	
SAXTON	.20	.11	.03	.01	.27			5	
SCHENLEY LOCK 5	.79	.16	.25	.37				0	
SCRANTON		.22		.08	.46			0	
SCRANTON WB AIRPORT	.06	.05	.02	.33			T	0	
SHAMOKIN	.59	.21		.33	.25				
SHIPPENSBURG	T	.26	.05	.10	.21		.16	0	
SHIPPINGPORT WB	.19		.19	.07			.39	0	
SINNEMAHONING		.05	T	.19	.35			5	
SLIPPERY ROCK	.09	.90	.04	.08	.02		.02	93	
SOMERSET FAIRVIEW ST	.44	.22		.45	.38			41	
SOMERSET MAIN ST	.28	.27	.10	.68	.07		.42		
SOUTH MOUNTAIN	1.34	.17	.23		.43			10	
SPRINGBORO	.15		.10	T			.36		
SPRING GROVE	.09	T	.21	.21	.40		T	01	
SPRINGS 1 SW	.31	.57	.06	.47	.04		.27	02	
STATE COLLEGE	.01	.05	T	1.50	.08	T		36	

See Reference Notes Following Station Index

le 3—Continued

DAILY PRECIPITATION

PENNSYLVANIA
SEPTEMBER 1957

Station	tal				7	8	9	10	11	12	13	14	15	16	17	18	19	20	21	22	23	24	25	26	27	28	29	30	31
USSTOWN											.04	.09	.06		.26				.13		.48								
UDSBURG											.03	.06	.07	.52	.10			T	.14	.01	2.27								
P CREEK											T	.04	.04	.14	.34				.87		1.28								
URY											.80	.11	T	1.30	.39				.24	.12	.20								
UEHANNA												.02		.15	.28				.01		1.96	T							
RSVILLE											.05	*	*	.82	.48			.03	.48		.79								
OUA											.45	.17			.25				.37	.07	.32								
OUA 4 N DAM																			.04	.26	.44								
RACK 2 S FIRE TWR											-	-	-	-	-				-	-	1.20	.02							
ESTA 2 SE DAM											.03	.43	.20	.04	.05					.11	.41	.02							
SVILLE WATER WORKS											.28		.18	.06						.23	.11								
EDO 4 W											.13	.25	.12	.05	.05					.05	.35	.12							
NDA											T	.02		.39	.02					T	1.25	.01							
R CITY 5 SW	3.00		.03	.10							T	.11	.02	T	.22					T	.98								
	4.73			.64							.01	.01		.20	.02						3.25								
LEPOINT 4 NE	2.74			.73							.02	.12	.22	.02	.08					.03	.81	.15							
NE 4 NE BALD EAGLE	2.28			.22							.04	.13		.72	.13					.02	.15								
	2.99	T		.25								.20	.24	.09						.30	.49	.06							
R DARBY											.49	.11	.18	.46						.38	.11								
											.03	.17			.86					.03	1.92								
A											.04	1.80	.10	.05						.02	.60	.02							
ERGRIFT											.12	.07		.27	.10					.01	1.40	.02							
INVILLE											.24	T	.04		.83														
NCKEL											.20	.34	.35	.10	.04	T				.01	.98	T							
NCKEL 1 WSW											.14	.39	.36	.08	.05	T				.01	.97	T							
EN											.04	.09	.20	.11	.08					.04	1.07	.06							
ONTOWN											.11	.11	.45	.54						.35	T								
ESBURG 2 W											.08	.17		.19	.21						.41								
SBORO 3 S											.09	.06		.20	.12					.01	1.25	.04							
SVILLE												2.06	.08	.26	.28														
ERSVILLE 1													.14	.03	1.05						.06								
CHESTER											.18	.90	T		1.16	T					2.17								
GROVE 1 E											.07		.27		1.18	.05					1.80								
HICKORY											.03	.50	.40	.15	.02					.05	.70	.01							
ESBURG											.17	.26	.66	.07															
ES BARRE											.03	.05	.04	.03	.44														
IAMSBURG											.05	.16	.08	.45	.16														
IAMSPORT WB AP											.02	.10	.20	.05															
SBURG											.39	.14	.12	.15	.33														
3 SSW PUMP STA											.07	.04	.07	.08	.42														
HAVEN												[illegible]	.09	[illegible]	[illegible]														
GROVE																													
SVILLE 3 SE																													

SUPPLEMENTAL DATA

Station	Wind direction		Wind speed m. p. h.				Relative humidity averages - percent				Number of days with precipitation							Percent of possible sunshine	Average sky cover sunrise to sunset
	Prevailing	Percent of time from prevailing	Average	Fastest mile	Direction of fastest mile	Date of fastest mile	1:00 a EST	7:00 a EST	1:00 p EST	7:00 p EST	Trace	.01–.09	.10–.49	.50–.99	1.00–1.99	2.00 and over	Total		
LENTOWN WB AIRPORT	SSW	10	7.7	-	-	-	85	89	55	69	7	3	3	2	0	0	15	-	6.3
IE WB AIRPORT	-	-	10.9	28++	SSE	10	-	-	-	-	3	1	6	4	0	0	14	-	5.6
RRISBURG WB AIRPORT	WSW	11	5.2	25	W	2+	79	83	51	62	8	6	2	1	0	0	17	52	6.8
ILADELPHIA WB AIRPORT	SW	18	8.4	33	NW	23	86	88	58	71	4	4	1	4	0	0	13	60	6.7
TTSBURGH WB AIRPORT	WSW	13	7.8	25++	W	4	79	84	58	64	4	4	4	0	1	0	13	71	7.0
ADING WB CITY	-	-	8.8	38	SW	4	-	-	-	-	7	3	4	1	1	0	16	42	6.8
RANTON WB AIRPORT	WSW	17	8.0	38	SW	4	81	84	52	65	1	8	2	2	0	0	13	56	6.2
IPPINGPORT WB	-	-	1.9	24%	W	3	-	-	-	-	1	2	4	0	1	0	8	-	-
LLIAMSPORT WB AIRPORT	-	-	6.3	-	-	-	-	90	53	69	2	5	4	1	0	1	13	-	6.3
Peak Gust																			

DAILY TEM

Station		1	2	3	4	5	6	7	8	9	10	11	
ALLENTOWN WB AP	MAX	86	86	90	87	75	80	75	77	73	68	82	80
	MIN	57	57	70	61	51	47	59	57	50	62	61	60
ALLENTOWN GAS CO	MAX	84	86	87	90	88	76	81	75	76	73	68	82
	MIN	57	58	61	67	54	48	55	59	55	57	60	60
ALTOONA HORSESHOE CURVE	MAX	88	94	87	78	74	80	79	78	69	66	84	89
	MIN	61	59	64	56	45	42	50	49	49	57	55	58
ARENDTSVILLE	MAX	87	85	93	92	89	78	82	79	76	65	71	86
	MIN	67	60	64	64	47	47	54	57	52	56	55	60
BAKERSTOWN 3 WNW	MAX	90	95	89	81	75	81	72	76	81	79	86	85
	MIN	62	64	68	58	47	43	45	45	52	65	55	59
BEAVERTOWN	MAX	86	92	89	88	75	81	79	79	78	67	82	85
	MIN	54	56	69	56	45	42	53	52	44	57	57	58
BELLEFONTE 4 S	MAX	81	85	87	86	84	73	80	79	77	68	69	83
	MIN	55	57	62	59	48	45	46	52	45	49	52	54
BERWICK	MAX	86	92	90	88	76	78	78	79	78	72	80	80
	MIN	54	57	67	63	48	47	52	57	49	61	62	58
BETHLEHEM LEHIGH UNIV	MAX	90	88	91	90	76	83	74	77	70	65	84	81
	MIN	57	59	70	68	53	49	61	60	56	61	59	61
BLAIRSVILLE 6 ENE	MAX	84	87	83	75	71	79	72	73	74	70	81	88
	MIN	61	64	65	56	45	46	52	49	52	60	57	65
BRADFORD CAA AP	MAX	80	80	79	70	66	72	63	67	77	68	75	79
	MIN	45	53	62	44	40	32	39	38	36	58	53	53
BRADFORD 4 W RES	MAX	80	82	79	79	66	71	70	68	74	74	75	79
	MIN	50	49	56	45	34	37	34	35	27	57	56	47
BROOKVILLE CAA AIRPORT	MAX	84	88	85	75	69	79	71	72	74	72	79	83
	MIN	53	56	57	49	38	35	39	39	41	60	50	52
BURGETTSTOWN 2 W	MAX	79	85	89	84	78	71	72	71	74	83	81	84
	MIN	60	58	63	51	43	35	36	38	43	54	47	50
BURNT CABINS 2 NE	MAX	86	93	90	89	85	80	81	80	76	71	83	88
	MIN	61	58	64	59	46	41	52	46	49	60	54	61
BUTLER	MAX	90	89	87	85	73	74	76	74	75	81	76	82
	MIN	57	64	68	58	39	34	38	39	45	61	54	56
CANTON 1 NW	MAX	75	79	83	81	80	70	72	73	72	73	63	76
	MIN	47	50	59	59	42	43	45	45	42	44	50	54
CARLISLE	MAX	89	93	93	93	87	83	82	82	77	70	86	90
	MIN	67	61	71	69	54	48	57	57	52	60	61	65
CHAMBERSBURG 1 ESE	MAX	85	91	92	90	78	80	81	81	68	75	86	90
	MIN	67	61	71	66	51	44	53	52	52	61	55	63
CHESTER	MAX	85	89	86	94	87	79	81	80	78	77	70	87
	MIN	66	64	68	74	58	52	62	62	60	62	64	60
CLARION 3 SW	MAX	89	90	84	75	71	77	72	74	78	75	81	86
	MIN	58	57	68	52	41	38	38	41	41	61	53	55
CLAYSVILLE 3 W	MAX	88	93	87	79	76	80	77	78	84	83	85	85
	MIN	64	60	61	53	44	37	39	39	45	66	50	56
COATESVILLE 1 SW	MAX	86	87	87	92	89	78	79	72	75	68	69	86
	MIN	58	58	68	67	49	45	48	61	54	59	63	62
COLUMBIA	MAX	89	92	90	90	80	83	75	76	70	69	86	87
	MIN	63	63	71	69	55	48	58	60	53	60	62	65
CONFLUENCE 1 SW DAM	MAX	83	85	89	85	81	74	81	79	81	77	75	84
	MIN	56	56	53	62	48	41	39	44	47	53	55	53
CORRY	MAX	85	88	84	79	68	76	71	70	79	76	78	82
	MIN	50	54	67	56	40	34	38	39	32	60	56	52
COUDERSPORT 3 NW	MAX	81	82	82	75	69	74	67	72	74	64	77	78
	MIN	47	48	62	50	38	32	35	34	34	55	58	46
DERRY	MAX	88	92	88	85	74	82	75	76	79	80	78	
	MIN	62	65	69	62	48	40	40	45	54	65	64	
DEVAULT 1 W	MAX	85	86	90	90	80	88	87	80	74	74		
	MIN	59	66	69	68	51	56	61	61	57	59		
DIXON	MAX	80	83	84	87	84	75	76	71	75	79	67	81
	MIN	50	49	52	58	44	43	43	48	39	40	56	52
DONEGAL	MAX	79	87	85	76	68	76	72	72	69	78	78	82
	MIN	60	57	63	50	40	36	40	42	47	58	48	58
DONORA	MAX	87	89	94	88	82	76	81	77	81	82		
	MIN	66	66	69	66	48	46	46	51	56	58		
DU BOIS 7 E	MAX	82	88	87	82	68	75	75	70	68			83
	MIN	52	54	67	56	39	39	40	41	44			52
EAGLES MERE	MAX	73	75	81	78	77	66	66	73	68	70	62	
	MIN	56	57	60	62	42	42	48	50	47	47	57	
EAST BRADY	MAX	88	92	92	88	74	79	79	76	83		84	
	MIN	60	61	68	55	42	43	42	45	43		57	
EBENSBURG	MAX	82	88	83	79	68	77	72	71	69	68	80	
	MIN	59	55	65	56	43	37	44	44	46	53	53	
EMPORIUM 2 SSW	MAX	76	80	85	80	77	68	73	70	70	74	67	76
	MIN	46	48	58	48	38	34	38	36	36	43	50	50
EPHRATA	MAX	86	89	90	89	81	80	76	76	76	68	83	85
	MIN	58	58	70	67	51	47	59	59	54	57	60	64
ERIE WB AIRPORT	MAX	75	85	80	72	65	66	65	65	78	78	73	81
	MIN	54	61	69	58	46	43	48	45	44	62	60	65

See reference notes following Station Index.

Table 5 - Continued

DAILY TEMPERATURES

PENNSYLVANIA
SEPTEMBER 1957

Station		1	2	3	4	5	6	7	8	9	10	11	12	13	14	15	16	17	18	19	20	21	22	23	24	25	26	27	28	29	30	31	Average
EVERETT 1 SW	MAX	90	92	92	84	76	80	82	78	70	69	86	86	82	74	87	80	74	78	72	74	82	85	74	68	72	78	58	70	60	68		77.4
	MIN	72	56	72	62	46	42	54	50	58	57	58	64	66	68	70	68	60	52	54	62	70	69	60	46	35	42	28	32	40	48		55.4
FARRELL SHARON	MAX	88	92	88	81	74	77	70	76	79	82	83	84	80	80	84	79	72	75	81	75	75	71	68	61	73	71	61	66	76	80		76.7
	MIN	58	62	71	61	42	37	46	41	45	62	55	58	65	57	59	65	50	58	53	66	68	53	52	40	44	49	30	28	33	42		51.7
FORD CITY 4 S DAM	MAX	80	88	92	87	82	73	78	72	76	81	80	85	85	75	79	83	71	75	77	86	71	82	80	69	64	75	61	59	65	70		76.7
	MIN	59	57	61	58	46	41	41	43	43	49	51	51	58	61	58	63	53	42	44	56	64	66	51	41	38	40	27	27	28	30		48.2
FRANKLIN	MAX	78	86	89	80	73	71	71	71	74	79	75	80	82	79	78	80	75	70	70	82	77	77	74	69	69	74	61	60	67	70		74.7
	MIN	54	55	59	50	42	44	38	42	44	41	53	55	57	56	61	57	46	53	47	54	67	56	57	42	40	39	27	29	29	32		47.5
FREELAND	MAX	80	84	82	80	73	75	72	71	71	69	75	74	79	77	77	77	67	69	73	71	71	81	77	60	68	67	64	63	63			72.8
	MIN	58	60	62	65	44	46	54	50	47	55	56	58	63	61	59	65	55	48	50	54	63	66	55	41	41	39	29	38	42			52.6
GEORGE SCHOOL	MAX	85	88	94	87	80	77	82	75	77	73	85	81	87	83	88	85	77	74	78	77	83	87	81	75	75	75	62	63	64	64		78.7
	MIN	62	65	69	68	45	50	65	60	57	63	63	62	64	68	70	72	65	60	55	54	67	68	59	47	40	48	31	31	34	44		56.9
GETTYSBURG	MAX	88	88	92	92	88	79	80	79	77	66	73	85	89	89	79	87	81	73	74	79	76	86	88	70	69	75	74	63	63	61		78.8
	MIN	68	64	71	70	53	48	55	58	54	55	58	61	66	68	68	69	65	57	56	61	65	70	60	48	43	53	34	35	38	49		57.3
GRATERFORD	MAX	86	88	90	88	86	89	88	87	82	72	78	76	92	88	88	90	74	78	78	76	84	88	80	76	74	76	76	74	73	74		81.6
	MIN	62	58	64	62	54	58	64	60	62	62	62	62	62	60	62	70	64	66	62	58	62	64	62	47	37	37	27	28	33	42		55.8
GRATZ 1	MAX	86	87	90	91	86	76	79	79	79	67	70	83	85	86	75	84	80	74	77	77	74	83	88	68	66	72	67	60	62	63		77.1
	MIN	55	63	68	63	48	42	43	56	47	53	62	61	63	64	63	68	63	49	50	52	65	67	57	49	37	37	29	28	30	30		52.1
GREENVILLE	MAX	89	92	89	85	75	77	72	75	83	81	82	82	79	80	82	76	78	80	84	80	80	79	71	67	75	73	61	68	74	75		78.1
	MIN	52	58	65	56	38	32	40	38	39	60	50	55	62	55	65	57	45	43	54	63	64	54	47	35	37	37	25	25	21	36		46.9
HANOVER	MAX	87	88	91	91	89	80	80	77	77	74	75	86	89	91	79	88	83	73	76	81	75	88	89	74	70	75	73	64	62	59		79.5
	MIN	68	66	69	69	53	49	49	58	58	55	61	61	66	67	67	69	66	57	57	57	63	69	60	48	44	44	34	34	35	50		56.8
HARRISBURG WB AP	MAX	86	91	91	88	76	80	79	79	68	71	85	89	88	77	88	82	75	74	80	76	86	89	71	67	76	69	61	63	62	69		77.9
	MIN	66	64	73	63	56	49	61	57	56	61	61	67	67	68	68	68	62	55	55	62	70	70	58	49	43	48	36	34	37	45		57.6
HAWLEY 1 S DAM	MAX	76	79	80	83	80	69	75	71	71	75	63	77	73	82	74	76	78	70	68	75	72	78	84	64	59	70	58	53	60	68		72.0
	MIN	45	47	53	59	49	45	44	51	39	42	53	49	49	62	53	63	58	42	42	45	54	64	53	43	34	35	26	27	27	30		46.1
HOLTWOOD	MAX	88	88	91	88	77	79	75	75	69	71	84	86	88	79	88	84	73	76	81	74	86	88	72	68	76	72	62	61	63	67		77.6
	MIN	68	66	70	69	59	55	62	61	60	65	67	68	68	72	70	67	66	63	61	64	73	72	61	52	49	50	44	41	46	54		61.4
HUNTINGDON	MAX	86	88	94	90	87	76	82	83	80	77	80	85	90	83	76	85	77	72	73	75	72	84	86	70	67	77	69	60	62	63		78.3
	MIN	60	54	52	55	41	38	41	50	43	48	50	57	61	65	60	64	62	48	48	52	60	54	57	41	34	36	24	24	25	35		48.0
INDIANA 3 SE	MAX	88	93	87	83	73	81	75	76	79	75	83	87	77	80	83	71	75	76	82	72	80	83	69	63	74	63	60	66	69	74		76.6
	MIN	61	58	67	53	45	38	40	44	47	64	51	57	61	63	58	65	55	45	56	63	62	57	54	37	34	46	25	27	30	46		50.3
IRWIN	MAX											87	87	85		85		77	79	87	85	83			70	78					77		
	MIN											53	62	66			64	57	48	58	65			55	40	43		32		31			
JAMESTOWN 2 NW	MAX	77	83	89	84	71	69	71	67	69	81	79	80	81	70	77	81	74	74	76	83	74	78	78	70	64	74	56	51	61	69		73.7
	MIN	53	58	63	61	39	34	39	40	44	53	52	55	61	56	58	62	46	44	54	62	66	66	49	37	39	42	27	28	30	39		48.6
JIM THORPE	MAX	86	87	87	85		80			75	72	82	79	85	83	80	83	81	76	77	77	75	84	82	69	74	72	63	67	66	64		77.4
	MIN	56	55		64	49	46		51	47	62	58	56	63	66	62	71	61	48	48	53	67	68	57	43	37	45	30	30	31	38		52.1
JOHNSTOWN	MAX	83	89	94	89	85	85	85	81	82	78	82	86	90	82	82	86	73	75	78	79	71	77	88	71	66	78	67	64	68	68		79.4
	MIN	55	56	65	57	45	39	46	47	44	52	44	59	61	60	58	60	55	45	47	56	59	51	53	39	33	42	26	25	27	36		47.9
KANE 1 NNE	MAX	74	82	86	81	72	66	73	64	69	77	70	77	80	71	75	78	66	71	72	78	73	68	71	69	59	71	55	54	56	67		70.8
	MIN	47	48	55	49	33	31	34	33	29	35	52	52	55	57	46	59	44	35	38	53	61	59	52	31	31	34	17	18	20	24		41.1
KEGG	MAX	88	93	91	86	79	80	81	82	67	72	86	90	81	73	86	73	72	74	71	72	86	88	69	67	68	69	67	62	62	67		76.6
	MIN	66	57	67	59	45	43	53	50	50	57	53	57	64	62	62	62	52	50	55	60	62	60	51	42	42	41	28	29	33	48		51.9
LANCASTER 2 NE PUMP STA	MAX	87	88	90	90	85	81	75	77	71	68	83	83	90	83	87	85	74	75	78	75	85	86	82	70	75	71	64	63	61	66		78.3
	MIN	59	59	70	66	50	44	57	61	61	60	63	64	63	67	66	69	66	55	53	58	67	70	58	48	40	48	31	31	34	44		56.1
LANDISVILLE 2 NW	MAX	87	86	91	92	92	78	84	74	77	87	69	86	86	90	77	87	85	77	75	78	74	88	87	68	68	75	72	61	63	62		78.5
	MIN	58	58	71	65	48	42	47	59	49	59	63	63	63	63	66	71	65	55	51	49	63	76	60	44	36	42	28	27	30	40		53.7
LAWRENCEVILLE 2 S	MAX	73	80	83	84	83	70	74	72	71	76	64	80	83	77	75	78	73	70	75	79	71	82	84	69	61	72	52	54	60	69		73.1
	MIN	50	50	52	51	43	40	42	42	39	41	54	51	53	61	53	57	53	46	44	45	65	60	53	39	37	40	23	25	27	29		45.5
LEBANON 3 W	MAX	89	89	93	92	90	78	82	79	79	67	68	80	86	90	79	87	80	77	76	79	74	86	90	69	69	75	71	62	65	65		78.9
	MIN	58	61	65	61	50	43	44	57	52	60	62	65	63	65	65	69	64	52	50	50	63	68	59	46	37	38	28	29	32	34		53.0
LEWISTOWN	MAX	87	88	94	92	88	77	82	82	81	66	68	85	88	84	77	86	80	73	74	79	73	83	89	71	69	79	69	62	64	64		78.5
	MIN	63	61	61	65	54	48	46	56	56	55	62	62	65	66	65	67	64	52	51	53	65	68	61	48	41	41	32	31	32	36		54.2
LINESVILLE 5 WNW	MAX	87	90	84	75	71	71	65	70	82	81	78	80	73	78	82	74	74	79	82	74	78	72	68	63	75	58	55	61	70	73		74.1
	MIN	51	57	67	58	38	36	40	39	35	61	53	55	64	54	54	62	45	42	55	67	67	54	42	33	40	39	26	26	30	37		47.6
LOCK HAVEN	MAX	86	92	90	88	77	82	88		77	69	82	86	81	80	83	79	73	74	79	71	84	86	78	66	77	65	62	63	68	62		77.2
	MIN	57	61	68	57	45	44	50		45	61	58	57	64	65	60	66	60	51	50	60	66	67	57	46	40	50	30	31	32	41		53.1
MADERA	MAX	76	85	90	83	84	70	77	75	74	73	68	80	65	76	73	77	71	69	70	75	69	79	82	66	61	71	63	56	59	62		73.3
	MIN	49	49	49	53	39	35	35	40	39	39	51	51	55	61	55	62	54	41	41	48	61	57	52	37	32	32	23	21	22	27		43.7
MARCUS HOOK	MAX	90	86	97	87	82	81	75	80	70	71	85	84	88	88	88	85	77	76	80	77	85	86	74	70	73	81	65	63	66	63		79.1
	MIN	68	68	74	71	61	58	67	66	64	66	67	70	70	73	72	70	68	64	62	64	70	72	64	56	51	50	43	44	48	54		63.2
MARTINSBURG CAA AP	MAX	87	87	86	82	72	80	79	79	67	78	84	90	79	72	85	73	70	72	70	70	84	85	66	64	75	65	61	61	60	66		74.7
	MIN	64	60	69	54	47	44	51	53	52	58	53	57	64	61	63	62	53	48	56	62	63	59	53	43	39	40	29	30	35	47		52.3
MEADVILLE 1 S	MAX	77	84	89	84	73	70	71	66	70	80	78	79	81	70	79	81	72	76	78	82	74	77	75	68	63	74	56	55	63	72		73.8
	MIN	51	55	61	57	41	38	38	41	38	46	53	54	59	58	56	62	48	43	44	60	66	66	50	36	36	46	27	27	27	38		47.4
MERCER 2 NNE	MAX	85	90	86	80	71	74	68	72	80	78	80	82	79	78	80	78	74	75	83	78	76	75	69	63	75	63	56	63	70	73		75.1
	MIN	54	58	68	58	36	31	40	36	42	62	51	56	65	57	57	62	46	42	57	65	67	55	50	34	39	45	23	23	29	39		48.2
MIDDLETOWN OLMSTED FLD	MAX	87	92	92	90	77	82	79	79	68	70	84	87	91	78	87	85	76	76	80	76	86	90	72	68	76	71	61	63	63	67		78.4
	MIN	65	64	76	64	56	50	60	59	57	63	63	69	68	69	69	69	62	57	57	64	71	71	59	49	44	46	34	35	37	48		58.5
MIDLAND DAM 7	MAX	84	90	84	76	69	73	70	74	82	80	81	83	78	78	82	72	75	77	84	73	81	75	69	62	73	59	57	60	66	70		74.5
	MIN	67	66	68	57	54	47	49	49	55	64	59	62	67	65	64	65	58	53	62	68	68	57	56	46	46	47	38	38	40	50		56.2
MONTROSE 1 E	MAX	74	78	81	81	80	68	71	71	70	73	64	76	79	76	73	74	74	67	71	75	69	77	83	63	57	69	53	50	56	65		70.6
	MIN	53	53	59	61	44	44	47	52	43	44	55	55	58	61	57	61	54	48	45	48	57	65	50	41	39	39	28	28	31	36		48.4
MORGANTOWN	MAX	82	85	89	87	75	80	72	74	86	69	83	82	89	87	86	86	74	75	75	79	82	84	76	72	72	71	70	62	61	65		77.0
	MIN	59	55	67	66	51	46	49	57	53	60	63	64	64	67	68	66	61	55	51	61	68	68	57	46	40	45	29	30	35	41		54.7
MT GRETNA 2 SE	MAX	83	93	90	87	77	80	75	77	67	67	83	85	86	85	85	82	75	74	84	73	84	88	75	67	74	70	61	62	62	68		77.3
	MIN	64	63	69	63	50	46	54	54	52	59	61	67	62	66	71	68	59	60	57	68	71	74	55	44	39	45	40	38	40	41		56.7

See reference notes following Station Index.

Station		1	2	3	4	5	6	7	8	9	10	11	12	13	14	15	16	17	18	19	20	21	22	23	24	25	26	27	28	29	30	31	Average
MT POCONO 2 N AP	MAX	80	81	80	80	74	74	73	71	69	64	76	73	80	76	71	77	69	67	73	72	72	80	79	59	69	66	54	60	63	62		71.5
	MIN	50	52	62	60	45	40	51	52	43	56	55	53	64	62	56	67	55	46	45	53	64	67	50	40	35	37	25	26	33	38		49.4
MUHLENBURG 1 SE	MAX	81	88	87	81	73	75	77	79	76	68																						
	MIN	48	51	63	64	43	49	62	52	46	58																						
NEWBURG 3 W	MAX	89	94	90	89	77	80	82	79	79	70	84	88	86	82	85	79	77	77	78	84	86	88	82	78	74	74	71	65	65	72		80.1
	MIN	64	62	68	62	50	46	54	51	56	59	60	64	70	63	72	70	70	56	61	62	68	75	62	55	53	44	29	36	38	47		57.6
NEW CASTLE 1 N	MAX	85	91	88	83	72	75	72	75	82	80	83	84	83	80	82	82	77	77	85	82	82	75	72	68	75	72	60	66	70	74		77.7
	MIN	57	61	68	60	45	37	43	40	42	62	54	57	66	60	58	64	51	42	55	65	66	59	50	38	40	47	26	28	30	40		50.4
NEWELL	MAX	88	87	93	89	81	76	82	78	79	84	84	88	87	78	80	84	73	78	81	90	78	85	83	72								82.4
	MIN	67	66	68	60	50	48	47	51	55	70	57	63	68	66	65	69	62	57	58	68	66	65	58	45								60.4
NEWPORT	MAX	88	89	93	92	87	80	82	80	83	67	68	84	87	86	76	88	80	73	75	80	73	87	89	70	70	76	70	64	65	63		78.8
	MIN	61	59	60	65	46	44	44	51	50	50	61	61	65	66	67	59	61	51	51	53	65	65	60	45	40	41	30	30	30	34		52.2
NEW STANTON	MAX	88	95	91	84	77	84	79	80	80	85	88	89	82	79	85	75	80	78	89	79	86	83	72	67	78	66	62	68	71	70		79.7
	MIN	62	60	63	51	45	38	39	44	50	56	52	58	62	61	62	64	54	48	50	64	62	55	48	34	34	37	28	29	33	47		49.7
NORRISTOWN	MAX	88	87	94	91	79	82	75	77	69	69	85	82	92	84	90	87	76	75	80	78	85	87	76	69	75	74	63	64	64	65		78.7
	MIN	62	69	73	70	57	52	67	62	60	63	65	66	67	70	71	70	66	60	58	62	69	72	61	52	45	46	38	37	40	47		59.9
PALMERTON	MAX	86	88	88	87	74	79	73	76	73	66	81	71	87	75	83	83	73	74	76	72	79	84	67	66	72	66	59	65	65	63		75.0
	MIN	53	55	69	60	51	45	54	53	46	62	61	58	63	65	64	69	56	50	49	58	68	70	55	45	40	37	31	31	32	41		53.0
PHIL DREXEL INST OF TEC	MAX	90	87	96	88	80	83	77	78	70	73	86	86	89	86	91	87	76	78	81	81	86	88	76	71	74	79	62	64	63	66		79.7
	MIN	67	68	73	73	61	59	67	67	63	66	66	67	71	73	72	74	69	65	62	62	70	72	62	57	54	56	42	41	41	59		63.3
PHILADELPHIA WB AP	MAX	38	86	94	87	78	81	75	77	69	70	84	84	89	84	90	87	75	76	80	79	85	88	75	67	73	75	61	62	64	64		78.2
	MIN	66	68	74	68	57	51	65	62	61	64	64	66	69	70	70	69	66	64	60	60	70	71	59	51	46	47	38	37	41	51		60.2
PHILADELPHIA PT BREEZE	MAX	89	85	94	85	85	79	78	76	75	70	85	84	89	87	89	89	86	74	75	80	78	84	73	69	73	74	62	64	65	68		78.8
	MIN	69	68	74	72	59	60	66	65	62	66	66	70	71	74	74	70	68	64	63	64	70	73	66	59	54	59	50	50	49	55		64.3
PHILADELPHIA CITY	MAX	87	86	92	86	80	81	75	78	69	70	85	84	90	86	89	86	77	76	81	77	86	88	74	70	73	75	63	65	65	64		78.6
	MIN	69	67	74	69	61	62	66	65	62	66	66	70	70	73	72	71	67	64	62	63	70	73	63	57	53	49	44	44	49	55		63.2
PHILIPSBURG CAA AP	MAX	83	86	82	79	68	77	74	72	67	64	77	83	74	73	76	71	67	66	71	67	74	79	65	60	72	60	56	60	61	60		70.8
	MIN	48	52	56	46	39	32	43	42	40	55	46	51	62	52	62	60	45	37	54	62	61	55	47	34	30	30	19	19	24	42		44.8
PHOENIXVILLE 1 E	MAX	89	88	95	90	81	82	75	76	69	70	79	84	93	88	90	87	85	76	86	77	85	90	85	70	72	76	64	65	64	67		79.9
	MIN	57	53	61	68	50	44	61	60	63	62	63	60	61	63	64	67	61	51	51	56	67	71	58	47	40	48	30	29	33	43		54.7
PIMPLE HILL	MAX	76	79	81	79	80	67	73	68	70	70	64	75	71	81	69	75	77	68	67	71	68	71	80	60	59	69	58	52	60	60		69.9
	MIN	52	60	61	64	43	45	55	50	47	54	54	59	62	61	60	61	53	48	50	53	58	64	50	40	42	49	27	28	41	45		51.2
PITTSBURGH WB AP 2	MAX	86	90	86	76	71	77	70	74	79	78	84	82	73	77	80	71	76	76	84	72	81	77	69	63	75	63	59	62	68	72		75.0
	MIN	65	68	66	54	48	47	47	48	54	61	56	64	67	63	66	61	58	52	61	66	67	57	52	43	44	42	34	35	40	49		54.5
PITTSBURGH WB CITY	MAX	87	92	87	80	73	79	74	76	79	80	85	85	76	78	82	72	76	77	87	74	83	80	71	67	78	65	61	65	70	75		77.1
	MIN	68	69	70	59	54	50	52	54	56	66	61	67	70	67	70	65	61	53	64	67	70	59	55	48	49	44	37	37	40	53		57.8
PLEASANT MOUNT 1 W	MAX			79	79	77	66			69	71	61	75	75			78	76	65	68	73			81	61	58	67	53			66		
	MIN	42			55	43	43			32	38	54	48	50			59	53	39	39	39			52	40	33	35	26			28		
PORT CLINTON	MAX	86	88	91	92	89	79	82	77	80	70	65	85	80	88	78	86	85	75	74	79	74	83	88	68	69	75	70	69	67	65		78.6
	MIN	51	52	57	63	48	40	44	50	45	50	57	56	60	63	61	66	60	47	46	46*	60	66	56	40	35	37	25	26	28	30		48.8
PUTNEYVILLE 2 SE DAM	MAX	78	86	90	90	80	72	78	71	75	77	77	82	87	74	79	82	70	76	75	85	71	79	79	67	64	75	60	58	64	70		75.7
	MIN	55	56	58	56	36	35	37	39	41	50	52	52	58	58	55	62	50	40	40	56	62	62	48	34	35	37	22	22	24	29		45.4
QUAKERTOWN 1 E	MAX	85	88	90	90	85	81	78	75	74	69	82	85	90	86	88	87	80	77	80	77	83	88	83	67	74	72	61	64	64	70		79.1
	MIN	60	55	64	64	47	43	59	58	59	62	60	58	62	67	66	71	64	56	48	54	66	71	58	44	36	46	27	28	30	37		54.0
READING WB CITY	MAX	87	88	91	90	78	82	76	77	69	68	84	84	90	79	87	86	78	75	79	75	84	88	73	68	75	73	63	64	64	68		78.1
	MIN	62	64	75	65	57	53	66	61	58	63	64	68	69	70	69	69	65	60	55	61	70	73	61	52	46	46	38	38	39	46		59.4
RIDGWAY 3 W	MAX	75	82	87	83	75	69	75	69	72	74	71	78	83	73	77	80	79	74	74	78	71	76	75	65	62	71	57	56	62	60		73.1
	MIN	54	51	52	50	38	37	37	37	36	37	52	49	55	59	50	58	50	41	40	49	62	60	53	37	33	33	22	23	25	26		43.5
SALINA 3 W	MAX	88	92	90	84	76	78	76	75	77	79	83	84	79	79	81	79	75	76	85	83	81	80	76	67	75	73	58	65	69	73		77.9
	MIN	63	61	69	59	45	39	42	44	53	65	53	58	67	64	60	68	55	43	59	65	64	65	54	48	40	51	29	29	32	48		53.1
SCRANTON	MAX	80	86	88	86	85	72	78	74	75	79	67	80	82	83	77	81	80	72	72	78	74	79	89	67	63	72	61	56	62	70		75.6
	MIN	50	52	59	62	50	48	49	54	46	48	60	56	56	66	60	65	61	48	48	49	62	66	55	49	40	40	32	32	33	34		51.0
SCRANTON WB AIRPORT	MAX	81	87	85	83	74	76	73	75	77	66	80	80	83	75	81	80	71	72	78	74	77	87	66	62	70	61	56	61	66	65		74.1
	MIN	50	56	66	55	49	46	51	50	45	59	59	57	65	59	59	66	53	46	48	59	66	59	53	42	39	38	31	30	33	40		51.0
SHIPPENSBURG	MAX	86	91	89	88	82	81	81	80	76	75	85	90	89	83	87	82	74	74	80	78	87	88	85	70	76	73	65	63	61	66		79.4
	MIN	66	61	71	69	51	47	54	53	53	59	57	63	64	65	67	64	65	53	53	62	66	65	59	46	40	52	32	33	34	46		55.7
SHIPPINGPORT WB	MAX	85	91	85	74	71	76	69	74	81	81	84	82	73	79	81	73	76	79	84	75	81	76	70	64	76	59	58	62	69	74		75.4
	MIN	63	64	63	51	48	42	45	46	51	60	55	59	66	60	62	61	52	49	60	67	66	57	52	41	42	41	31	32	35	46		52.2
SLIPPERY ROCK	MAX	86	89	86	80	74	77	72	77	82	72	82	82	77	78	82	74	76	75	84	78	76	72	74	64	76	70	61	65	66	75		76.1
	MIN	58	69	68	57	45	38	44	43	49	62	58	60	65	52	58	66	52	48	57	65	65	55	51	40	44	48	30	30	34	45		51.9
SOMERSET MAIN ST	MAX	84	88	85	82	72	79	76	80	74	70	81	84	76	75	80	76	71	72	72	73	74	80	75	63	71	69	60	61	61	67		74.4
	MIN	62	57	64	58	45	38	45	46	49	57	48	57	60	62	61	62	57	50	56	57	56	58	53	37	38	50	25	26	33	45		50.4
SPRINGBORO	MAX	78	84	90	85	69	68	69	65	69	81	80	79	80	72	78	82	73	74	80	83	75	80	74	69	61	74	63	57	63	73		74.3
	MIN	60	57	67	65	41	34	36	44	34	44	52	54	61	56	54	61	48	45	54	63	67	66	55	45	44	50	25		34	36		50.1
SPRINGS 1 SW	MAX	80	81	81	75	71	78	77	77	68	68	80	83	77	67	81	71	68	70	73	70	78	81	65	59	69	63	57	57	63	68		71.9
	MIN	57	56	60	54	43	37	45	42	44	52	49	55	64	60	61	60	57	52	52	58	55	55	53	35	32	40	23	23	32	38		48.1
STATE COLLEGE	MAX	80	83	88	85	83	72	79	77	75	66	68	81	85	79	77	81	75	67	70	73	69	80	84	68	64	74	63	59	62	63		74.3
	MIN	59	59	61	64	47	45	46	54	49	49	55	55	60	64	62	64	59	49	50	54	65	64	56	46	41	42	30	30	31	35		51.5
STROUDSBURG	MAX	90	85	90	87	68	80	77	80	76	65	84	75	80	72	82	84	69	75	80	74	80	88	72	65	70	66	58	60	66	64		75.4
	MIN	47	50	61	57	43	40	53	53	41	57	55	51	64	58	57	65	53	45	44	50	62	60	50	39	33	34	23	20	26	34		47.5
SUNBURY	MAX	84	87	92	91	87	78	82	80	81	75	71	83	87	85	79	86	79	75	75	79	74	87	89	71	69	75	67	64	69	66		78.8
	MIN	57	56	65	65	50	45	54	57	48	54	62	60	63	66	64	67	61	52	50	54	67	67	59	45	41	42	29	28	31	38		53.2
TAMARACK 2 S FIRE TWR	MAX																							74	63	59	69	56	54	74	62		
	MIN																							51	41	39	42	30	30	31	30		
TIONESTA 2 SE DAM	MAX	77	84	89	83	73	69	75	68	71	78	75	79	82	71	78	80	69	73	74	82	75	76	74	68	62	73	58	58	63	70		73.6
	MIN	55	55	59	54	42	41	40	42	40	40	55	56	58	60	55	60	52	47	46	56	64	54	51	40	38	39	28	27	30	33		47.2
TITUSVILLE WATER WORKS	MAX	85	90	86	75	70	74	68	70	79	74	79	82	75	78	81	76	74	75	83	76	76	75	70	62	75	63	57	64	71			74.6
	MIN	53	56	69	52	39	36	38	41	31	61	51	54	64	60	52	67	49	43	50	66	64	53	49	36	35	42	21	21	27			47.6

See reference notes following Station Index.

Table 5 - Continued

DAILY TEMPERATURES

PENNSYLVANIA
SEPTEMBER 1957

Station		1	2	3	4	5	6	7	8	9	10	11	12	13	14	15	16	17	18	19	20	21	22	23	24	25	26	27	28	29	30	31	Average
TOWANDA	MAX	84	84	86	85	74	77	78	77	77	69	83	84																63	68	66		75.5
	MIN	50	52	61	53	46	43	46	48	41	61	54	51																28	29	34		49.0
UNIONTOWN		[illegible]	[illegible]	[illegible]	84	76	82	78	78	73	79	86	87																65	66	75		77.3
					63	49	43	46	50	58	64	55	67																35	42	53		56.2
UPPER DARBY					87	83	81	76	76	73	69	85	82																62	62	64		78.4
					72	56	54	65	64	65	65	65	65																38	39	43		60.2
WARREN					78	68	73	67	70	80	75	77	81																62	70	72		74.1
					57	42	40	39	43	37	62	60	53																27	30	34		48.8
WAYNESBURG 2					86	76	81	77	78	83	86	86	86																				79.3
					54	46	39	40	46	48	63	53	57																				51.6
WELLSBORO 3					82	78	70	74	74	71	73	63	76																				71.5
					61	43	44	45	43	40	41	56	56																				47.6
WELLSVILLE					90	85	81	78	76	76																							79.0
					65	44	41	53	56	50																							52.2
WEST CHESTER					88	81	86	82	75	78																							79.3
																																	56.8
WILLIAMSPORT WB AP																																	75.9
																																	53.0
YORK 3 SSW PUMP STA																																	80.5
																																	55.7

Table 6

EVAPORATION AND WIND

Station		1	2	3	4	5	6	7	8	9	10	11	12	13	14	15	16	17	18	19	20	21	22	23	24	25	26	27	28	29	30	31	Total or Avg.
CONFLUENCE 1 SW DAM	EVAP	.22	.13	.10	.22	.23	.16	.15	.15	.15	.04	.05	.13	.15	.08	.00	.09	.01	.09	.11	*	*	.18	.15	.08	.10	.11	.17	.13	.08	.06		3.32
	WIND	47	45	36	65	98	57	43	59	30	61	50	35	73	41	8	31	25	29	49	38	31	34	57	51	54	44	69	50	42	37		1389
FORD CITY 4 S DAM	EVAP	.11	.22	.28	.31	.19	.17	.17	.16	.15	.14	.06	.05	.21	.00	.04	.18	.01	.13	.12	.15	-	.05	.17	.12	.12	.11	.08	.20	.10	.08		B4.01
	WIND	26	24	58	92	84	24	24	48	30	75	50	10	47	23	20	50	10	18	26	30	18	28	40	43	32	45	60	39	19	20		1113
HAWLEY 1 S DAM	EVAP	.14	.17	.14	.18	.19	.16	.16	.02	.15	.15	.03	.13	.00	.18	.07	.03	.09	.10	.00	.19	.06	.09	.22	.07	.13	.15	*	.21	.10	.10		3.41
	WIND	24	22	110	95	106	54	32	26	32	17	35	19	30	58	11	116	77	26	26	36	71	48	97	38	42	88	68	78	20	20		1522
JAMESTOWN 2 NW	EVAP	.12	.17	.15	.26	.09	.14	.05	.15	.14	.13	.06	.11	.05	.05	.08	.15	.06	.12	.15	.07	.04	.06	.06	.11	.11	.11	.12	.10	.10	.08		3.19
	WIND	6	10	38	58	29	14	13	5	18	45	34	11	36	9	7	60	10	11	22	18	51	16	2	31	15	25	32	24	17	14		681
LANDISVILLE 2 NW	EVAP	.21	.30	.23	.27	.37	.29	.22	.11	.18	.03	.00	.16	.17	.20	.08	.17	.15	.14	.14	.11	.10	.16	.20	.08	.20	.18	.24	.17	.13	.06		5.05
	WIND	39	46	66	56	97	52	48	44	35	44	55	23	32	40	20	86	51	48	22	58	29	43	94	31	48	34	55	101	36	1		1434
PIMPLE HILL	EVAP	.18	.23	*	.23	.22	.18	.17	.10	.14	.16	.05	.16	.12	.16	.05	.04	.12	.11	.11	.15	.01	.00	.20	.07	.11	*	*	*	*	.63		3.70
	WIND	29	37	97	69	112	49	46	38	31	88	87	45	58	44	37	114	50	31	54	85	78	70	89	52	27	*	*	*	*	220		1737

DAILY SOIL TEMPERATURES

Station And Depth	Time	1	2	3	4	5	6	7	8	9	10	11	12	13	14	15	16	17	18	19	20	21	22	23	24	25	26	27	28	29	30	31	Average
STATE COLLEGE																																	
MEASURED UNDER SOD																																	
2 INCHES	8 AM	65	68	70	66	58	57	63	61	58	63	60	64	67	66	66	68	66	61	60	65	57	66	64	58	55	58	49	47	49	52		61.2
4 INCHES	8 AM	66	68	70	67	60	59	64	63	60	63	61	64	67	66	66	68	66	62	61	65	66	66	65	60	57	59	51	49	50	53		62.1
8 INCHES	8 AM	67	69	70	68	64	62	65	65	63	64	63	65	67	67	66	66	67	64	63	65	66	67	67	62	60	61	55	53	54	55		63.7
16 INCHES	8 AM	69	69	69	69	68	67	67	67	67	66	65	66	67	67	66	67	67	67	66	65	66	67	68	66	64	63	61	59	59	59		65.8

Ground Cover: Bluegrass Sod.

See reference notes following Station Index.

TOTAL PRECIPITATION

PENNSYLVANIA
SEPTEMBER 1957

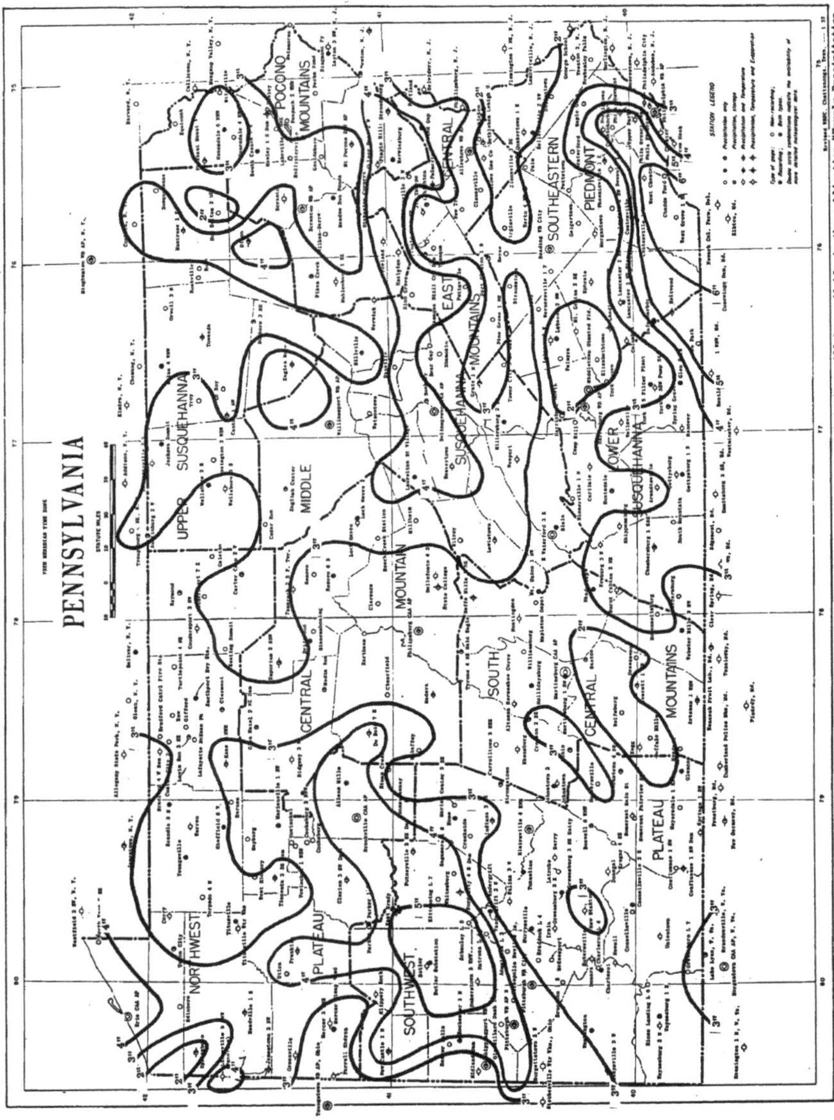

Isolines are drawn through points of approximately equal values. Hourly precipitation data from recorder substations will be available in the publication "Hourly Precipitation Data".

AVERAGE TEMPERATURE

PENNSYLVANIA
SEPTEMBER 1957

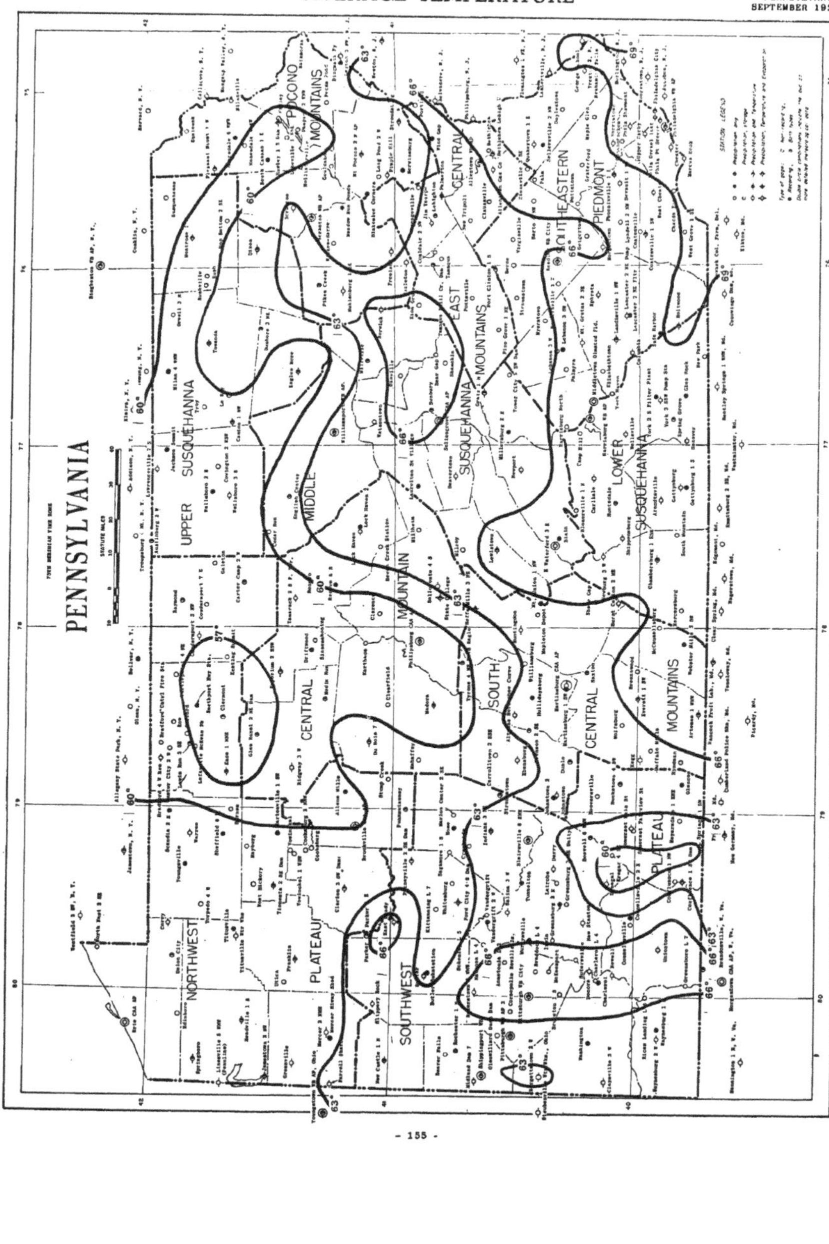

Isolines are drawn through points of approximately equal values. Hourly precipitation data from recorder substations will be available in the publication "Hourly Precipitation Data".

STATION INDEX

Station	Index No.	County	Drainage [1]	Latitude	Longitude	Elevation	Observation Time Temp.	Observation Time Precip.	Observer	Refer To Tables
ACMETONIA LOCK 3	0022	ALLEGHENY	1	40 32	79 49	748		7A	CORPS OF ENGINEERS	3
ALLENS MILLS	0099	JEFFERSON	1	41 12	78 55	1600		MID	CHARLES M. ALLEN	C
ALLENTOWN WB AP	0106	LEHIGH	9	40 39	75 26	376	MID	MID	U.S. WEATHER BUREAU	2 3 5 7 C
ALLENTOWN GAS CO	0111	LEHIGH	9	40 36	75 28	254	7A	7A	LEHIGH VLY GAS DIV	2 3 5
ALTOONA HORSESHOE CURVE	0134	BLAIR	6	40 30	78 29	1500	6P	6P	ALTOONA WATER BUR.	2 3 5
ARENDTSVILLE	0229	ADAMS	15	39 55	77 18	710	8A	8A	PA STATE COL EXP	2 3 5
AUSTINBURG 2 W	0313	TIOGA	15	42 00	77 32	1590		7A	OTTO D. BACON	3 7 C
BAKERSTOWN 3 WNW	0355	ALLEGHENY	1	40 39	79 59	1230	7P	7P	PGH CUT FLOWER CO	2 3 5
BARNES	0409	WARREN	1	41 40	79 02	1310		7A	CORPS OF ENGINEERS	3
BARTO 4 NW	0428	BERKS	14	40 26	75 39	312		7A	MARIE B. NICHLAS	3
BEAR GAP	0457	NORTHUMBLAND	15	40 50	76 30	900		3P	ROARING CRK WTR CO	3
BEAVER FALLS	0475	BEAVER	2	40 46	80 19	760		7A	HOWARD R. KEMP	3
BEAVERTOWN	0482	SNYDER	15	40 45	77 10	640	5P	7A	MARLIN R. ETTINGER	2 3 5
BEECH CREEK STATION	0499	CENTRE	16	41 04	77 34	620		7A	HAROLD S. RUPERT	3 7
BELLEFONTE 4 S	0530	CENTRE	16	40 51	77 47	1110	8A	8A	ROCKVIEW PRISON FARM	2 3 5
BERNE	0599	BERKS	14	40 31	76 00	325		7A	FLOYD W. TRUMP	3
BERWICK	0611	COLUMBIA	15	41 04	76 15	570	6P	6P	AMER CAR + FNDRY CO	2 3 5
BETHLEHEM	0629	NORTHAMPTON	9	40 37	75 22	400		7A	ARTHUR CROPPER	3
#BETHLEHEM LEHIGH UNIV	0634	NORTHAMPTON	9	40 36	75 23	450	MID	MID	LEHIGH UNIVERSITY	2 3 5 C
BLAIN	0725	PERRY	15	40 20	77 31	750		MID	PA DEPT FRST + WTRS	C
BLAIRSVILLE 6 ENE	0736	INDIANA	4	40 27	79 09	2048	8P	8P	U.S. WEATHER BUREAU	2 3 5
BLAKESLEE CORNERS	0743	MONROE	9	41 06	75 36	1650		MID	WALTER WILDRICK	C
BLOSERVILLE 1 N	0763	CUMBERLAND	15	40 16	77 22	650		5P	MRS. B. M. WILLDERS	3
BOSWELL 6 WNW	0820	SOMERSET	1	40 10	79 08	2570		8A	CLARK N. ST. CLAIR	3 C
BRADDOCK LOCK 2	0861	ALLEGHENY	10	40 24	79 52	725		7A	CORPS OF ENGINEERS	3
BRADFORD CAA AIRPORT	0865	MC KEAN	1	41 48	78 38	2150	MID	MID	CIVIL AERO. ADM.	2 3 5 7
BRADFORD CNTRL FIRE STA	0867	MC KEAN	1	41 57	78 39	1500		8A	BRADFORD FIRE DEPT	3
BRADFORD 4 W RES	0868	MC KEAN	1	41 57	78 44	1680	5P	5P	BRADFORD WTR DEPT	2 3 5 7
BREEZEWOOD	0905	BEDFORD	6	40 00	78 14	1352		MID	PA TURNPIKE COMM	3
BROOKVILLE CAA AIRPORT	1002	JEFFERSON	1	41 09	79 06	1417	MID	MID	CIVIL AERO. ADM.	2 3 5 7
BRUCETON 1 S	1033	ALLEGHENY	10	40 18	79 59	1065		7A	AUSTIN R. COOPER	3
BUCKSTOWN 1 SE	1073	SOMERSET	4	40 04	78 50	2460		MID	ALVIN W. MANGES	C
BUFFALO MILLS	1087	BEDFORD	6	39 57	78 39	1318		7A	MRS. NELLE R. BROWN	3
BURGETTSTOWN 2 W	1105	WASHINGTON	11	40 23	80 26	980	7A	7A	SMITH TWP MUN AUTH	2 3 5
BURNT CABINS 2 NE	1115	HUNTINGDON	6	40 05	77 52	990	MID	MID	PA TURNPIKE COMM	2 3 5
#BUTLER	1130	BUTLER	2	40 52	79 54	1100	4P	7A	WILLIAM C. FAUST	2 3 5
BUTLER SUBSTATION	1135	BUTLER	2	40 51	79 53	1140		MID	WEST PENN POWER CO	C
CAMP HILL	1198	CUMBERLAND	15	40 15	76 55	461		6P	JOSEPH M. HOBART	3
CANTON 1 NW	1215	BRADFORD	15	41 40	76 52	1520	7A	7A	MRS.MILDRED SPENCER	2 3 5 7 C
CARLISLE	1234	CUMBERLAND	15	40 12	77 11	460	6P	6P	C. E. MILLER	2 3 5
CARROLLTOWN 2 SSE	1255	CAMBRIA	16	40 35	78 42	2040		8A	ROBERT F. MAURER	3 7
CARTER CAMP 2 W	1262	POTTER	16	41 37	77 45	2030		7A	RICHARD L. MENKEN	3 C
CEDAR RUN	1301	LYCOMING	16	41 31	77 27	800		7A	KATHRYN T.KREIGHBAUM	3
CHADDS FORD	1342	DELAWARE	5	39 52	75 36	160		8A	ALFRED C. WEEKS	3
CHAMBERSBURG 1 ESE	1354	FRANKLIN	12	39 56	77 38	640	9P	9P	CHARLES A. BENDER	2 3 5 C
CHARLEROI	1372	WASHINGTON	10	40 08	79 55	1040		MID	WEST PENN POWER CO	C
CHARLEROI LOCK 4	1377	WESTMORELAND	10	40 09	79 54	749		7A	CORPS OF ENGINEERS	3
#CHESTER	1423	DELAWARE	5	39 51	75 22	86	8A	8A	CHESTER TIMES	2 3 5
CLARENCE	1480	CENTRE	16	41 03	77 56	1410		7A	MISS VELDA SWANCER	3
CLARION 3 SW	1485	CLARION	1	41 12	79 26	1114	8P	7A	PA ELECTRIC CO	2 3 5 C
CLAUSSVILLE	1505	LEHIGH	9	40 37	75 39	670		8A	WILLIAM J. DOTTERER	3
CLAYSVILLE 3 W	1512	WASHINGTON	11	40 07	80 28	1000	7P	7A	MFGRS. L + H CO	2 3 5
CLEARFIELD	1519	CLEARFIELD	16	41 01	78 26	1100		7A	IRA TAYLOR	3
CLERMONT	1529	MC KEAN	1	41 41	78 30	2104		7A	MRS.TILLIE M.SIMONDS	3 C
COALDALE 2 NW	1572	SCHUYLKILL	9	40 50	75 56	1026		7A	PANTHER VLY WTR CO	3 7
COATESVILLE 1 SW	1589	CHESTER	5	39 58	75 50	342	8A	8A	PHILA ELECTRIC CO	2 5 C
COLUMBIA	1675	LANCASTER	15	40 02	76 30	300	SS	SS	JAMES H. RUST	2 5
CONFLUENCE 1 SW DAM	1705	SOMERSET	17	39 48	79 22	1490	8A	8A	CORPS OF ENGINEERS	2 5 6 C
CONFLUENCE 1 NW	1710	FAYETTE	17	39 50	79 22	1331		7A	JOHN L. REID	
CONNELLSVILLE	1723	FAYETTE	17	40 01	79 36	870		8A	MARSHALL B. MENEFEE	U
CONNELLSVILLE 2 E	1729	FAYETTE	17	40 01	79 33	1300		MID	HARRY C. JOY	C
CONSHOHOCKEN	1737	MONTGOMERY	5	40 04	75 19	70		8A	PHILA ELECTRIC CO	3
COOKSBURG	1749	CLARION	1	41 20	79 13	1180		8A	PA DEPT FRST + WTRS	3
COOKSBURG 2 NNW	1752	CLARION	1	41 21	79 13	1460		8A	PA DEPT FRST + WTRS	3
CORAOPOLIS NEVILLE IS	1773	ALLEGHENY	11	40 30	80 05	720		8A	PGH. COKE + CHEM CO	3
CORRY	1790	ERIE	1	41 55	79 39	1440	6P	6P	RICHARD T. MOUNTAIN	2 5 7
COUDERSPORT 3 NW	1806	POTTER	1	41 49	78 03	2020	7P	8A	MISS ELIZABETH NEFF	2 5
COUDERSPORT 7 E	1809	POTTER	1	41 46	77 53	2425		7A	CAMP POTATO	
COVINGTON 2 WSW	1833	TIOGA	15	41 44	77 07	1745		7A	CALVIN R. PACKARD	
CREEKSIDE	1881	INDIANA	1	40 41	79 12	1035		7A	CORPS OF ENGINEERS	U
CRESSON 2 SE	1895	CAMBRIA	6	40 27	78 34	2540		7A	MILES M. LINGLE	3 C
CUSTER CITY 2 W	1978	MC KEAN	1	41 55	78 41	2120		8A	M. D. BOOTH AND CO	3
DANVILLE	2013	MONTOUR	15	40 58	76 37	460		7A	MRS.MARIE M. LITTLE	3
DERRY	2108	WESTMORELAND	4	40 20	79 18	1150	6P	6P	MISS M. D. WINEMAN	2 3 5
DEVAULT 1 W	2116	CHESTER	14	40 05	75 33	360	MID	MID	PA TURNPIKE COMM	2 3 5
DINGMANS FERRY	2160	PIKE	5	41 13	74 52	364		MID	CLYDE T. VOORHEES	C
DIXON	2171	WYOMING	15	41 34	75 54	620	7A	7A	HAROLD J. KUSCHEL	2 3 5 C
DONEGAL	2183	WESTMORELAND	17	40 07	79 23	1746	MID	MID	PA TURNPIKE COMM	2 3 5 7
#DONORA	2190	WASHINGTON	10	40 11	79 51	814	12M	12M	DONORA ZINC WORKS	2 3 5
DOYLESTOWN	2221	BUCKS	5	40 18	75 08	393		5P	GEORGE HART	3
DRIFTWOOD	2245	CAMERON	16	41 20	78 08	880		MID	SIDNEY KENNEDY	C
DU BOIS 7 E	2265	CLEARFIELD	16	41 06	78 38	1670	5P	5P	CITY OF DU BOIS	2 3 5 7 C
DUNLO	2298	CAMBRIA	4	40 17	78 43	2410		MID	MRS. D. L. WHITE	C
DUSHORE 3 NE	2324	SULLIVAN	16	41 33	76 21	1750		7A	PATRICK F. RYAN	3 C
EAGLES MERE	2343	SULLIVAN	16	41 24	76 35	2020	7A	7A	MRS.ELSIE P. BIGGER	2 3 5 C
EAST BRADY	2363	CLARION	1	40 59	79 37	820	5P	5P	A. B. KEMPEL	2 3 5
EAST WATERFORD 3 E	2459	PERRY	6	40 21	77 33	2125	8A	8A	U.S. WEATHER BUREAU	INAC 5/55
EBENSBURG	2466	CAMBRIA	4	40 29	78 43	2090	7P	7A	ROBERT A. WASSER	2 3 5
EDINBORO	2514	ERIE	1	41 52	80 08	1220		8A	EDINBORO ST TCHR COL	3
EDINBORO 7 SW	2519	CRAWFORD	1	41 47	80 13	1200		8A	THOMAS H. YOUNG	3
ELIZABETHTOWN	2560	LANCASTER	15	40 09	76 37	460		8A	MASONIC HOME	
EMPORIUM 2 SSW	2634	CAMERON	16	41 29	78 13	1735	7A	7A	JACKSON THOMAS	2 5 C
ENGLISH CENTER	2644	LYCOMING	16	41 26	77 17	881		7A	WILLIAM SUDERS	7 C
EPHRATA	2662	LANCASTER	15	40 11	76 10	465	6P	6P	STANLEY L.VON NEIDA	2 5
EQUINUNK 2	2671	WAYNE	5	41 51	75 13	910		7A	MRS. HENRIETTA MURRY	[illegible]
ERIE WB AIRPORT	2682	ERIE	8	42 05	80 12	732	MID	MID	U. S. WEATHER BUREAU	2 3 7
EVERETT 1 SW	2721	BEDFORD	6	40 00	78 23	1020	MID	MID	PA TURNPIKE COMM	2 3 7 C
FARRELL SHARON	2814	MERCER	2	41 14	80 30	865	7P	7P	SHARON STEEL CORP	2 3
FORD CITY 4 S DAM	2942	ARMSTRONG	1	40 43	79 30	950	8A	8A	CORPS OF ENGINEERS	2 3 5 6 7 C
FRANKLIN	3028	VENANGO	1	41 23	79 49	987	7P	7A	ROBERT D. RHOADS	2 3 5 C
FREELAND	3056	LUZERNE	15	41 01	75 54	1900	6P	8A	ANDREW B. EVANSHA	2 3 5
GALETON	3130	POTTER	16	41 44	77 39	1325		7A	W. GALE LUSH	3 7
GEIGERTOWN	3189	BERKS	14	40 13	75 50	400		8A	WALTER C. WOLF	3
GEORGE SCHOOL	3200	BUCKS	5	40 13	74 56	135	7P	7P	GEORGE M. HART	2 3 5 7
#GETTYSBURG	3218	ADAMS	12	39 50	77 14	540	9A	9A	HUGH C. MC ILHENNY	2 3 5
GETTYSBURG 1 S	3223	ADAMS	12	39 48	77 14	560		MID	NAT MILITARY PARK	C
GIFFORD	3237	MC KEAN	1	41 51	78 36	2220		8A	SOUTH PENN OIL CO	3
GLENCOE	3296	SOMERSET	12	39 49	78 51	1620		MID	MRS. MARY M.HARTMAN	C
GLEN HAZEL 2 NE DAM	3311	ELK	1	41 34	78 36	1725		8A	CORPS OF ENGINEERS	3 C
GLEN ROCK	3330	YORK	15	39 48	76 44	620		MID	MRS.E.C.MC WILLIAMS	C
GLENWILLARD DASH DAM	3343	ALLEGHENY	11	40 33	80 13	705		7A	CORPS OF ENGINEERS	3
GOULDSBORO	3394	WAYNE	9	41 15	75 27	1890		7A	L. H. EILENBERGER	3
GRATERFORD	3435	MONTGOMERY	14	40 14	75 27	160	7A	7A	CLAUDE K. KULP	2 3 5 7 C
GRATZ 1 N	3438	DAUPHIN	15	40 38	76 43	760	8A	8A	LEE M. LEITZEL	2 3 5 C
GREENSBORO LOCK 7	3503	GREENE	10	39 47	79 55	808		7A	CORPS OF ENGINEERS	3 7
GREENSBURG 2 E	3515	WESTMORELAND	10	40 18	79 31	1225		MID	PA DEPT HIGHWAYS	C
GREENSBURG 3 SE UNITY	3516	WESTMORELAND	10	40 17	79 30	1245		6P	WESTMORELAND WTR CO	3
GREENVILLE	3526	MERCER	2	41 24	80 23	1026	6P	6P	C. EARL MILLER	2 3
HANOVER	3662	YORK	15	39 48	76 59	600	8A	8A	HANOVER EVENING SUN	2 3 5 7
#HARRISBURG WB AP	3699	YORK	15	40 13	76 51	335	MID	MID	U.S. WEATHER BUREAU	2 3 5 7 C
HARRISBURG NORTH	3704	DAUPHIN	15	40 18	76 54	323		8A	GEORGE S. BEAL	3
HAWLEY	3758	WAYNE	5	41 29	75 10	880		7A	MRS. KATHERINE BATES	3
HAWLEY 1 S DAM	3761	WAYNE	5	41 28	75 11	1200	7A	7A	PA POWER + LIGHT CO	2 3 5 6 7 C
HOLLIDAYSBURG	4001	BLAIR	6	40 26	78 24	960		MID	JOHN M. RINGLER	C
HOLLISTERVILLE	4008	WAYNE	5	41 23	75 26	1360		8A	PA POWER + LIGHT CO	3
#HOLTWOOD	4019	LANCASTER	15	39 50	76 20	187	MID	8A	PA POWER + LIGHT CO	2 3 5 7 C
HOME	4027	INDIANA	1	40 45	79 06	1220		MID	MRS. EDNA M. BUSH	C
HONESDALE 4 NW	4043	WAYNE	5	41 37	75 19	1410		9A	GEORGE C. WILLIAMS	3
HONESDALE 6 NNW	4044	WAYNE	5	41 39	75 17	1050		MID	FRIEND E. WALTER	C
HONEY BROOK 1 W	4047	CHESTER	5	40 06	75 50	700		7A	S. H. KURTZ	3
HOOVERSVILLE	4058	SOMERSET	4	40 09	78 55	1670		8A	JAMES A. MAHN	3 7
HOP BOTTOM 2 SE	4066	SUSQUEHANNA	15	41 43	75 43	900		7A	JOSEPH J. SANSUSKAS	3
HUNTINGDON	4159	HUNTINGDON	6	40 30	78 01	678	7A	7A	DANIEL I. GROVE	2 3 5
HUNTSDALE	4166	CUMBERLAND	15	40 06	77 18	610		8A	METRO P. DOROSH	3 C
HYNDMAN	4190	BEDFORD	12	39 49	78 43	920		8A	MRS.GERTRUDE M.BURTO	3
INDIANA 3 SE	4214	INDIANA	4	40 36	79 07	1102	7P	7A	CLYMER WATER SVC CO	2 3 5 7 C
IRWIN	4276	WESTMORELAND	10	40 20	79 42	1100	5P	5P	WESTMORELAND WTR CO	2 3 5
JACKSON SUMMIT	4304	TIOGA	15	41 57	77 01	1690		MID	ARCHIE LAIN	C
JAMESTOWN 2 NW	4325	CRAWFORD	2	41 30	80 28	1050	8A	8A	PA DEPT FRST + WTRS	2 3 5 6 C
JIM THORPE	4370	CARBON	9	40 52	75 45	830	5P	5P	HENRY S. HAAK	2 3 5
#JOHNSTOWN	4385	CAMBRIA	4	40 20	78 55	1214	9A	9A	JOHNSTOWN TRIBUNE	2 3 5
JOHNSTOWN 2	4390	CAMBRIA	4	40 19	78 55	1275		MID	CITY OF JOHNSTOWN	C
KANE 1 NNE	4432	MC KEAN	1	41 41	78 48	1750	8A	8A	RUDOLPH A. ANDERSON	2 3 5 7 C
KARTHAUS	4450	CLEARFIELD	16	41 07	78 07	950		7A	JEROME S. HOWE	3
KEATING SUMMIT	4466	POTTER	16	41 41	78 11	1840		7A	EUGENE L. KREITNER	3 7
KEGG	4481	BEDFORD	6	39 59	78 43	1280	MID	MID	PA TURNPIKE COMM	2 3 5
KITTANNING LOCK 7	4611	ARMSTRONG	1	40 49	79 32	790		VAR	CORPS OF ENGINEERS	3
KREGAR 4 SE	4667	WESTMORELAND	17	40 06	79 14	2530		MID	PA TURNPIKE COMM	3
KRESGEVILLE 3 W	4672	CARBON	9	40 54	75 34	720		7A	CITY OF BETHLEHEM	3
LAFAYETTE MC KEAN PARK	4706	MC KEAN	1	41 48	78 40	2130		7A	ORIN A. BUTTERS	3
LAKEVILLE 1 NNE	4733	WAYNE	5	41 27	75 16	1440		8A	MRS. GLADYS REINEKE	3
LANCASTER 2 NE PUMP STA	4758	LANCASTER	15	40 03	76 17	255	6P	6P	LANCASTER WATER BUR	2 3 5 7
LANCASTER 2 NE FILT PL	4763	LANCASTER	15	40 03	76 17	270		MID	LANCASTER WATER BUR	C
LANDISVILLE 2 NW	4778	LANCASTER	15	40 07	76 26	360	8A	8A	PA STATE COLLEGE	2 3 5 6 C
LATROBE	4832	WESTMORELAND	4	40 19	79 23	1000		MID	WEST PENN POWER CO	INAC 6/56
LAURELTON STATE VILLAGE	4853	UNION	15	40 54	77 13	880		MID	PA DEPT OF WELFARE	C
LAWRENCEVILLE 2 S	4873	TIOGA	15	41 59	77 07	1000	7A	7A	HARRY P. HOWLAND	2 3 5 7
LEBANON 3 W	4891	LEBANON	15	40 20	76 29	460	7A	7A	LEON MILLER	2 3 5 7
LEBANON 3 SW	4896	LEBANON	15	40 19	76 28	490		MID	THOMAS DONNACHIE	C
LEHIGHTON	4934	CARBON	9	40 50	75 43	580		7A	GOODWIN S. DEFREHN	3 C
LE ROY	4972	BRADFORD	15	41 41	76 43	1040		6P	MRS.DIMMIS M.BAILEY	3
LEWIS RUN 3 SE	4984	MC KEAN	1	41 50	78 39	1740		7A	RUSSELL LINEMAN	3 C
LEWISTOWN	4992	MIFFLIN	6	40 35	77 35	480	7A	7A	AMERICAN VISCOSE CO	2 3 5 7 C
LINESVILLE 5 WNW	5050	CRAWFORD	2	41 41	80 31	1020	7P	8A	MISS RETTA M. CRUMB	2 3 5
LOCK HAVEN	5104	CLINTON	16	41 08	77 27	570	7P	7A	PETER L. STEVENSON	2 3 5
LOCK HAVEN 2	5109	CLINTON	16	41 08	77 27	630		MID	HUGH F. PARKER	C
LONG POND 2 W	5160	MONROE	9	41 03	75 30	1860		7A	THOMAS MECKES	3
LYNCH	5275	FOREST	1	41 36	79 03	1205		7A	CORPS OF ENGINEERS	3
LYNDELL 2 NW	5279	CHESTER	5	40 05	75 46	-		8A	MRS. DOROTHY HARPLE	3
MADERA	5336	CLEARFIELD	16	40 50	78 26	1460	7A	7A	MRS. JULIA J. SHOFF	2 3 5 C
MAHAFFEY	5342	CLEARFIELD	16	40 53	78 44	1280		7A	MISS ELLEN J. MILES	3
MAPLE GLEN	5368	MONTGOMERY	5	40 11	75 11	380		6P	FRANCES E.SCHEIBNER	3
MAPLETON DEPOT	5381	HUNTINGDON	6	40 24	77 56	580		7A	MRS. I. S. BUCHANAN	3
MARCUS HOOK	5390	DELAWARE	5	39 49	75 25	12	MID	MID	SUN OIL CO	2 3 5
MARIENVILLE 1 SW	5400	FOREST	1	41 27	79 09	1700		MID	ROY A. MARKER	C
MARION CENTER 2 SE	5408	INDIANA	1	40 45	79 02	1610		7A	CORPS OF ENGINEERS	3
MARTINSBURG 1 SW	5453	BLAIR	6	40 18	78 20	1360		MID	BLUE MT. CANNERIES	C
MARTINSBURG CAA AP	5454	BLAIR	6	40 18	78 19	1463	MID	MID	CIVIL AERO. ADM.	2 3 5 7
MATAMORAS	5470	PIKE	5	41 22	74 42	439		7A	HARRY BISLAND	3 7
MC CONNELLSBURG	5526	FULTON	12	39 56	78 00	895		7A	MRS. HELEN M. SHIVES	3
MC KEESPORT	5573	ALLEGHENY	10	40 21	79 52	720		8A	NATIONAL TUBE CO	3
MEADOW RUN PONDS	5601	LUZERNE	15	41 13	75 40	1995		MID	GEORGE PEARAGE	C
MEADVILLE 1 S	5606	CRAWFORD	1	41 38	80 10	1065	8A	8A	CITY OF MEADVILLE	2 3 5 7 C
MEDIX RUN	5627	ELK	16	41 17	78 24	1100		7A	MRS.E. M. SNYDER	3 7 C
MERCER 2 NNE	5651	MERCER	2	41 15	80 13	1160	7P	7A	MRS. FRAN. STRUTHERS	2 3 5
MERCER HIWAY SHED	5654	MERCER	2	41 14	80 15	1250		MID	PA DEPT HIGHWAYS	C
MERCERSBURG	5662	FRANKLIN	12	39 50	77 54	605		8A	ROLLIN P. GILBERT	3
MERWINSBURG	5676	MONROE	9	40 58	75 28	970		MID	WILLIAM D. GOULD	C
MEYERSDALE	5684	SOMERSET	17	39 49	79 02	2040		8A	ARTHUR J. POTTER	3
MIDDLETOWN OLMSTED FLD	5703	DAUPHIN	15	40 11	76 46	303	MID	MID	U. S. AIR FORCE	2 3 5
MIDLAND DAM 7	5710	BEAVER	11	40 38	80 28	689	11P	7A	CORPS OF ENGINEERS	2 3 5
MILAN 4 WNW	5732	BRADFORD	15	41 56	76 33	1448		MID	CARL A. MORRIS	
MILANVILLE	5738	WAYNE	5	41 40	75 04	760		8A	CHARLES W. DAVIS	3
MILLERSBURG 2 E	5775	DAUPHIN	15	40 32	76 56	560		MID	RUSSELL SHEPLEY	
MILLHEIM	5790	CENTRE	15	40 54	77 29	1090		7A	NEVIN E. BOWERSOX	3
MILLVILLE 2 SW	5817	COLUMBIA	15	41 06	76 34	860		7A	KENNETH LEIGHOW	3
MILROY	5825	MIFFLIN	6	40 43	77 35	770		8A	THOMAS C. HARBESON	3
MONTROSE 1 E	5915	SUSQUEHANNA	15	41 50	75 51	1630	7A	7A	WILBER W. HOOPES,JR	2 3 5 7
MORGANTOWN	5956	BERKS	15	40 09	75 54	595	MID	MID	PA TURNPIKE COMM	2 3 5
MT GRETNA 2 SE	6028	LANCASTER	15	40 14	76 26	670	MID	MID	PA TURNPIKE COMM	2 3 5
MT POCONO 2 N AP	6055	MONROE	5	41 09	75 22	1915	5P	5P	H. JOHN DAVIS, JR.	2 3 5
MOUNT UNION 1 N	6067	MIFFLIN	6	40 24	77 53	820		MID	MT UNION WTR WORKS	
MUHLENBURG 1 SE	6090	LUZERNE	15	41 13	76 08	1110	6P	6P	THEODORE J. SAMPSON	2 3 5 7
MURRYSVILLE	6111	WESTMORELAND	10	40 26	79 42	903		MID	DAVID C. SHAW	
MYERSTOWN	6126	LEBANON	14	40 22	76 18	480		8A	MRS.KATHLEEN MANDELL	3
NATRONA LOCK 4	6151	ALLEGHENY	1	40 37	79 43	800		7A	CORPS OF ENGINEERS	3
NEFFS MILLS 3 NE	6174	HUNTINGDON	6	40 40	77 55	900		MID	PA STATE UNIVERSITY	
NESHAMINY FALLS	6194	BUCKS	5	40 09	74 57	60		MID	PHILA SUB WATER CO	3
NEWBURG 3 W	6225	FRANKLIN	15	40 09	77 37	745	5P	5P	PA TURNPIKE COMM	2 3 5
NEW CASTLE 1 N	6233	LAWRENCE	2	41 01	80 22	825	5P	7A	BAXTER F. JOHNSON	2 3 5
NEWELL	6246	FAYETTE	10	40 05	79 54	805	12M	12M	GENERAL CHEMICAL CO	2 3 5
NEW PARK	6289	YORK	15	39 44	76 30	780		6P	CLINTON J. ALLEN	3
NEWPORT	6297	PERRY	6	40 29	77 08	400	7A	7A	MRS. FRANCES K. FRY	2 3 5 7
NEW STANTON	6310	WESTMORELAND	10	40 13	79 36	980	MID	MID	PA TURNPIKE COMM	2 3 5
NEW TRIPOLI	6326	LEHIGH	14	40 41	75 45	570		6P	FRED C. OSWALD	3
NORRISTOWN	6370	MONTGOMERY	14	40 07	75 21	75	MID	8A	GEORGE H. BOONE	2 3 5
NORTH EAST 2 SE	6396	ERIE	8	42 12	79 49	1060		9A	ELLSWORTH WEAVER	3
ORWELL 3 N	6621	BRADFORD	15	41 55	76 16	1620		8A	WILLIAM I. BROWN	3
PALM	6681	MONTGOMERY	14	40 26	75 32	385		6A	FRED C. ESCHBACH	3
#PALMERTON	6689	CARBON	9	40 48	75 37	435	MID	MID	NEW JERSEY ZINC CO	2 3 5
PARKER	6721	ARMSTRONG	1	41 05	79 41	1140		7A	LOUIS A. MALARKEY	3
PARKER 1 E	6724	CLARION	1	41 06	79 40	1100		MID	P. M. NEELY	
PAUPACK 2 WNW	6762	PIKE	5	41 24	75 14	1360		8A	MISS L. VETTERLEIN	3
PECKS POND	6786	PIKE	5	41 17	75 06	1380		9A	MRS. CARRIE NESS	3
#PHIL DREXEL INST OF TEC	6879	PHILADELPHIA	14	39 57	75 11	30	MID	MID	FRANCIS K. DAVIS,JR	2 3 5
PHILADELPHIA WB AP	6889	PHILADELPHIA	5	39 53	75 14	13	MID	MID	U.S. WEATHER BUREAU	2 3 5 7
#PHILADELPHIA PT BREEZE	6899	PHILADELPHIA	5	39 55	75 12	32	MID	MID	ATLANTIC REFINING	2 3 5
#PHILADELPHIA CITY	6909	PHILADELPHIA	5	39 57	75 09	26	9A	9A	USN HYDROGRAPHIC OFF	2 3 5
PHILIPSBURG CAA AP	6916	CENTRE	6	40 54	78 05	1918	MID	MID	CIVIL AERO. ADM.	2 3 5 7
PHOENIXVILLE 1 E	6927	CHESTER	14	40 07	75 30	105	6P	MID	PHILA SUB WATER CO	2 3 5
PIKES CREEK	6939	LUZERNE	15	41 18	76 08	1320		7A	HARRY SHELDON	
PIMPLE HILL	6944	MONROE	9	41 02	75 30	2215	9A	9A	PA DEPT FRST + WTRS	2 5 6 7
PINE GROVE 1 NE	6954	SCHUYLKILL	15	40 34	76 22	535		8A	PA POWER + LIGHT CO	
PITTSBURGH WB AP 2	6993	ALLEGHENY	11	40 30	80 13	1151	MID	MID	U.S. WEATHER BUREAU	2 5 7
#PITTSBURGH WB CITY	6997	ALLEGHENY	11	40 27	80 00	749	MID	MID	U.S. WEATHER BUREAU	2 U 5
PLEASANT MOUNT 1 W	7029	WAYNE	5	41 44	75 27	1800	8A	8A	PA FISH COMM	2 3 5 7
PORT CLINTON	7116	SCHUYLKILL	14	40 35	76 02	450	7A	7A	MRS. ADA E. RARICK	2 3 5
PORTLAND	7127	NORTHAMPTON	5	40 55	75 06	297		6A	JOINT BRIDGE COMM	INAC 1/56
POTTSVILLE	7161	SCHUYLKILL	14	40 42	76 11	690		8A	LLOYD E. HELLER	3
PUNXSUTAWNEY	7217	JEFFERSON	1	40 57	79 00	1298		MID	JOHN VOLANSKY	
PUTNEYVILLE 2 SE DAM	7229	ARMSTRONG	1	40 55	79 17	1270	8A	8A	CORPS OF ENGINEERS	2 3 5
QUAKERTOWN 1 E	7239	BUCKS	5	40 26	75 20	490	5P	7A	DENNIS K. FLUCK	2 3 5
RAYMOND	7310	POTTER	13	41 52	77 52	2220		7A	MRS. RACHEL LANGAN	3
#READING WB CITY	7318	BERKS	14	40 20	75 58	266	MID	MID	U.S. WEATHER BUREAU	2 3 5 7
RENOVO	7409	CLINTON	16	41 20	77 44	660		7A	MRS. CAROLINE BAIRD	3
RENOVO 5 S	7410	CLINTON	16	41 14	77 46	2035		MID	C. F. BILLETTE	
REW	7425	MC KEAN	1	41 54	78 32	2250		8A	HAROLD C. MEALY	3
RICES LANDING L 6	7443	GREENE	10	39 57	80 00	775		7A	CORPS OF ENGINEERS	3
RIDGWAY 3 W	7477	ELK	1	41 25	78 47	1420	7A	7A	BOROUGH OF RIDGWAY	2 3 5
ROCHESTER 1 N	7540	BEAVER	2	40 43	80 18	900		MID	DEQUESNE LIGHT CO	
RUSH	7694	SUSQUEHANNA	15	41 47	76 03	1000		9A	MISS MAUDE MC CAIN	3
RUSHVILLE	7727	SUSQUEHANNA	15	41 47	76 07	870		7A	CARL KOPATZ	3
SAFE HARBOR	7732	LANCASTER	15	39 55	76 23	270		MID	S.H.WATER POWER CORP	
SAGAMORE 1 S	7739	INDIANA	1	40 46	79 14	1320		7A	CORPS OF ENGINEERS	3
SALINA 3 W	7782	WESTMORELAND	7	40 31	79 33	1109	6P	6P	MUN AUTH WSTMRLD CO	2 3 5
SAXTON	7846	BEDFORD	6	40 12	78 15	780		8A	MRS.ALVERTA L.HOLMES	3
SCANDIA 2 E	7855	WARREN	1	41 55	79 01	2040		MID	DAVID R. ANDERSON	
SCHENLEY LOCK 5	7863	ARMSTRONG	1	40 41	79 40	783		VAR	CORPS OF ENGINEERS	3
#SCRANTON	7902	LACKAWANNA	15	41 25	75 40	746	7A	7A	U.S. POST OFFICE	2 3 5
SCRANTON WB AIRPORT	7905	LUZERNE	15	41 20	75 44	956	MID	MID	U.S. WEATHER BUREAU	2 3 5 7

STATION INDEX

Station	Index No.	County	Drainage ‡	Latitude	Longitude	Elevation	Observation Time Temp.	Observation Time Precip.	Observer	Refer To Tables
ELLERSVILLE 2		KS	5	40 23	75 20	530		MID	SELLERSVILLE WTR CO	C
HADE GAP 2 NE		TINGDON	6	40 12	77 52	920		MID	MRS. HELEN H. PYLE	C
HAMOKIN		THUMBLAN	15	40 48	76 33	770		8A	ROARING CRK WTR CO	3
HEFFIELD 6 W		REN	1	41 41	79 09	1940		MID	L. N. HANSON	C
HIPPENSBURG		NKLIN	15	40 03	77 32	709	4P	4P	KEITH B. ALLEN	2 3 5 7
HIPPINGPORT WB		VER	11	40 37	80 26	740	MID	MID	U.S. WEATHER BUREAU	2 3 5 7 C
		CRON	10	41 10	78 05	790		7A	MRS.FRANCES CALDWELL	3
LIPPERY ROCK		LER	2	41 04	80 03	1345	7P	7A	WALTER D. ALBERT	2 3 5 7
METHPORT HIGHWAY SHED		KEAN	1	41 48	78 27	1510		MID	PA DEPT HIGHWAYS	C
OMERSET FAIRVIEW ST		ERSET	17	40 01	79 05	2140		7A	HOWARD G. PECK	3
OMERSET MAIN ST		ERSET	17	40 01	79 05	2150	6P	6P	DAVID L. GROVE	2 3 5
OUTH CANAAN 1 NE		NE	5	41 31	75 24	1400		MID	EUGENE M. COOK	C
OUTH MOUNTAIN		NKLIN	12	39 51	77 30	1520		7A	PA DEPT OF HEALTH	3
		WFORD	8	41 48	80 23	900	8A	8A	SPRINGBORO BOROUGH	2 3 5 C
PRING GROVE		K	15	39 52	76 52	470		4P	P. H. GLATFELTER CO	3 C
PRINGS 1 SW		ERSET	17	39 44	79 10	2900	8P	8P	ALLEN E. YODER	2 3 5 7
TATE COLLEGE	8449	TRE	16	40 48	77 52	1175	7A	7A	PA STATE COLLEGE	2 3 5 6 CG
TRAUSSTOWN	8570	KS	14	40 29	76 11	800		8A	JACOB KLAHR	3
TRONGSTOWN	8589	IANA	4	40 33	78 55	1080		MID	HARRY F. BENNETT	C
TROUDSBURG	8596	ROE	5	40 59	75 12	480	11P	11P	WILLIAM HAGERTY	2 3 5 C
STUMP CREEK	8610	JEFFERSON	1	41 01	78 50	1320		7A	CORPS OF ENGINEERS	3
UNBURY	8668	NORTHUMBLA	15	40 51	76 48	440	7A	7A	CHARLES W. BAYLER	2 3 5 C
USQUEHANNA	8692	SUSQUEHANN	15	41 57	75 36	1020		7A	MRS. LAURA A.BENSON	3
UTERSVILLE	8699	ALLEGHENY	17	40 14	79 48	765		7A	FRANK E. MARSH	3
AMAQUA	8758	SCHUYLKILL	14	40 48	75 58	830		8A	MRS. MARY L.ROBERTS	3
AMAQUA 4 N DAM	8763	SCHUYLKILL	14	40 51	75 59	1120		7A	PANTHER VLY WTR CO	3 C
AMARACK 2 S FIRE TWR	8770	CLINTON	16	41 24	77 51	2220	7A	7A	JAMES E. SWARTZ	2 3 5 7
TIONESTA 2 SE DAM	8873	FOREST	1	41 29	79 26	1200	8A	8A	CORPS OF ENGINEERS	2 3 5 7 C
TITUSVILLE	8885	CRAWFORD	1	41 38	79 40	1550		MID	PA ELECTRIC CO	C
TITUSVILLE WATER WORKS	8888	CRAWFORD	1	41 38	79 42	1220	7P	7P	CITY OF TITUSVILLE	2 3 5
TORPEDO 4 W	8901	WARREN	1	41 47	79 32					3
TOWANDA	8905	BRADFORD	15	41 46	76 26					2 3 5 7 C
TOWER CITY 5 SW	8910	DAUPHIN	15	40 31	76 37					3 7
TROY	8959	BRADFORD	15	41 47	76 47					3
TUNNELTON	8989	INDIANA	4	40 27	79 23					
TURTLEPOINT 4 NE	9002	MC KEAN	1	41 54	78 16					3
TYRONE 4 NE BALD EAGLE	9024	BLAIR	6	40 43	78 12					3 C
UNION CITY	9042	ERIE	1	41 54	79 50					3 C
UNIONTOWN	9050	FAYETTE	10	39 54	79 44					2 3 5
UPPER DARBY	9074	DELAWARE	5	39 58	[illegible]					2 3 5
UTICA	9099	VENANGO	1	41 26						3
	9128	WESTMORELAND	7	40 36						3
	9133	WESTMORELAND	7	40 36						
	9196	BERKS	14	40 31						3
	9206	CLARION	1	41 25						3

Station	Index No.	County	Drainage ‡	Latitude	Longitude	Elevation	Observation Time Temp.	Observation Time Precip.	Observer	Refer To Tables
VOWINCKEL 1 WSW	9204	CLARION	1	41 24	79 15	1610		8A	PA DEPT FRST + WTRS	3
WARREN	9208	WARREN	1	41 51	79 08	1280	7P	7A	GILBERT H. REIER	2 3 5
WASHINGTON	9312	WASHINGTON	11	40 11	80 14	1200		MID	PA DEPT HIGHWAYS	
WATSONTOWN	9345	NORTHUMBLAND	16	41 05	76 52	490		[illegible]	WILLIAM BIRD	3
WAYNESBURG 2 W	9367	GREENE	10	39 54	80 13	980	[illegible]	7A	RALPH L. AMOS	2 3 5
WAYNESBURG 1 E	9367	GREENE	10	39 54	80 10	940		MID	SEWAGE DISPOSAL PLT	C
WEBSTER MILLS 3 SW	9380	FULTON	12	39 49	78 05	920		MID	WILLIAM D. COVER	C
WELLSBORO 3 S	9408	TIOGA	16	41 43	77 16	1920	7A	7A	MARION L. SHUMWAY	2 3 5
WELLSBORO 2 E	9412	TIOGA	16	41 45	77 16	1550		MID	MRS. IDA S. MAYNARD	C
WELLSVILLE	9420	YORK	15	40 03	76 57	500	5P	5P	D. D. HOOVER	2 3 5
WERNERSVILLE 1 W	9430	BERKS	14	40 20	76 06	405		8A	CHARLES A. GRUBER	3
WEST CHESTER	9464	CHESTER	5	39 58	75 36	440	8A	8A	DAILY LOCAL NEWS	2 3 5
WEST GROVE 1 E	9503	CHESTER	5	39 44	75 49	440		8A	CONARD-PYLE CO	3
WEST HICKORY	9507	FOREST	1	41 34	79 25	1090		8A	MRS.HELEN F.KINNEAR	3
WHITESBURG	9655	ARMSTRONG	1	40 45	79 24	1530		7A	CORPS OF ENGINEERS	3
WILKES-BARRE	9702	LUZERNE	15	41 15	75 52	610		7A	MRS. MARY G. MIRMAX	3
WILLIAMSBURG	9714	BLAIR	6	40 28	78 12	860		7A	MYRON K. BIDDLE	3
WILLIAMSPORT WB AP	9728	LYCOMING	16	41 15	76 55	527	MID	MID	U.S. WEATHER BUREAU	2 3 5 7 C
WIND GAP	9781	NORTHAMPTON	5	40 51	75 18	740		MID	W. L. TEMPLETON	C
WOLFSBURG	9823	BEDFORD	6	40 03	78 32	1190		7A	WALTER C. RICE	3
YORK 3 SSW PUMP STA	9933	YORK	15	39 55	76 45	390	5P	5P	YORK WATER COMPANY	2 3 5
YORK 2 S FILTER PLANT	9938	YORK	15	39 56	76 44	640		MID	YORK WATER COMPANY	C
YORK HAVEN	9950	YORK	15	40 07	[illegible]	[illegible]		8A	METROPOL EDISON CO	3
YOUNGSVILLE	9966	WARREN	[illegible]	[illegible]				MID	HENRY CARLETT	C
ZION GROVE	9990	SCHUYLKILL						7A	JAMES D. TEETER	
ZIONSVILLE 3 SE	9995	LEHIGH						7A	LESLIE HOWATT	

‡ 1-ALLEGHENY; 2-BEAVER; 3- 4-CONEMAUGH; 5-DELAWARE; 6-JUNIATA; 7-KISKIMINETAS; 8-LAKE ERIE; 9-LEHIGH; 10-MONONGAHELA; 11-OHIO; 12-POTOMAC; 13-LAKE ONTARIO; 14-SCHUYLKILL; 15-SUSQUEHANNA; 16-WEST BRANCH; 17-YOUGHIOGHENY

REFERENCE NOTES

Additional information regarding the climate of Pennsylvania may be obtained by writing to the State Climatologist at Weather Bureau Airport Station, Harrisburg State Airport, New Cumberland, Pennsylvania, or to any Weather Bureau Office near you.

Figures and letters following the station name, such as 12 SSW, indicate distance in miles and direction from the post office.

Delayed data and corrections will be carried only in the June and December issues of this bulletin.

Monthly and seasonal snowfall and heating degree days for the preceding 12 months will be carried in the June issue of this bulletin.

Stations appearing in the Index, but for which data are not listed in the tables, either are missing or were received too late to be included in this issue.

Divisions, as used in Table 2, became effective with data for September 1956.

Unless otherwise indicated, dimensional units used in this bulletin are: Temperature in °F, precipitation and evaporation in inches, and wind movement in miles. Monthly degree day totals are the sums of the negative departures of average daily temperatures from 65° F.

Evaporation is measured in the standard Weather Bureau type pan of 4 foot diameter unless otherwise shown by footnote following Table 6. Max and Min in Table 6 refer to extremes of temperature of water in pan as recorded during 24 hours ending at time of observation.

Long-term means for full-time stations (those shown in the Station Index as "U. S. Weather Bureau") are based on the period 1921-1950, adjusted to represent observations taken at the present location. Long-term means for all stations except full-time Weather Bureau stations are based on the period 1931-1955.

Water equivalent values published in Table 7 are the water equivalent of snow, sleet or ice on the ground. Samples for obtaining measurements are taken from different points for successive observations; consequently occasional drifting and other causes of local variability in the snowpack result in apparent inconsistencies in the record. Water equivalent of snow on the ground is measured at selected stations when two or more inches of snow are on the ground.

Entries of Snowfall in Tables 2 and 7, and in the seasonal snowfall table, include snow and sleet. Entries of snow on ground include snow, sleet and ice.

Data in Tables 3, 5, and 6 and snowfall in Table 7, when published, are for the 24 hours ending at time of observation. The Station Index lists observation times in the standard of time in local use. During the summer months some observers take the observations on daylight saving time.

Snow on ground in Table 7 is at observation time for all except Weather Bureau and CAA stations. For these stations snow on ground values are at 7:30 a.m., E.S.T.

- \- No record in Tables 3, 6, 7 and the Station Index. No record in Tables 2 and 5, is indicated by no entry. Consult the annual issue of this publication for interpolated monthly precipitation totals.
- \+ And also on a later date or dates.
- ++ Fastest observed one minute wind speed. This station is not equipped with automatic wind instruments.
- * Amount included in following measurement, time distribution unknown.
- // Gage is equipped with a windshield.
- \# Thermometers are generally exposed in a shelter located a few feet above sod-covered ground; however, the reference indicates that the thermometers are exposed in a shelter located on the roof of a building.
- AM Data based on observational day ending before noon.
- B Adjusted to a full month.
- C In the "Refer to Tables" column in the Station Index the letter "C" indicates recorder stations. These stations are processed for special purposes and are published later in "Hourly Precipitation Data".
- D Water equivalent of snowfall wholly or partly estimated, using a ratio of 1 inch water equivalent to every 10 inches of new snowfall.
- G In the "Refer to Tables" column in the Station Index the letter "G" indicates that soil temperatures are published.
- M One or more days of record missing; if average value is entered, less than 10 days record is missing. See Table 5 for detailed daily record. Degree day data, if carried for this station, have been adjusted to represent the value for a full month.
- R Amounts from recording gage (These amounts are essentially accurate but may vary slightly from the amounts to be published later in "Hourly Precipitation Data".)
- SS This entry in time of observation column in Station Index means observation made near sunset.
- T Trace, an amount too small to measure.
- Y Includes total for previous month.
- VAR This entry in time of observation column in Station Index means variable.

Information concerning the history of changes in locations, elevations, exposure etc. of substations through 1955 may be found in the publication "Substation History" for this state, soon to be issued. That publication, when available, may be obtained free the Superintendent of Documents, Government Printing Office, Washington 25, D. C. at a price to be announced. Similar information for regular Weather Bureau stations may be found in the latest issues of Local Climatological Data, Annual for the respective stations, obtained as indicated above, price 15 cents.

Subscription Price: 20 cents per copy, monthly and annual; $2.50 per year. (Yearly subscription includes the Annual Summary). Checks, and money orders should be made payable to the Superintendent of Documents. Remittance and correspondence regarding subscriptions should be sent to the Superintendent of Documents, Government Printing Office, Washington 25, D. C.

WRPC., Asheville, N. C. --- 11/8/57 --- 1100

U. S. DEPARTMENT OF COMMERCE
SINCLAIR WEEKS, Secretary
WEATHER BUREAU
F. W. REICHELDERFER, Chief

IMATOLOGICAL DATA

PENNSYLVANIA

OCTOBER 1957
Volume LXII No. 10

ASHEVILLE: 1957

PENNSYLVANIA - OCTOBER 1957

WEATHER SUMMARY

GENERAL

Predominantly cool weather plus two periods with unseasonably low temperatures gave October a cold label. Average temperatures were generally two to five degrees lower than long-term mean values and extremes ranged from 81° on the 9th at Marcus Hook to 17° on the 14th at Kane 1 NNE. Precipitation was generally near average in the East Central Mountains, Lower Susquehanna, and South Central Mountains Divisions. Significant deficiencies of moisture were apparent in other areas of the State. The greatest amount of precipitation for one day was 2.35 inches at Meyerdale measured on the 7th and station totals ranged from 1.00 inch at Turtlepoint 4 NE to 6.04 inches at Springs 1 SW.

WEATHER DETAILS

The major portion of October's precipitation fell in three well defined periods which were the 6th-8th, 17th-18th, and the 23rd-24th, but light precipitation was rather frequent from the 26th through the 30th. Precipitation was in the form of rain except the 26th through the 28th when snowfall ranged from a trace to about 2 inches. Temperatures were predominantly below seasonal levels but warm weather appeared briefly around the 9th in the eastern half of the State and on a statewide scale around the 17th and the 23rd. Heavy frosts occurred in most areas the 11th to 13th and sub-freezing temperatures were widespread the 26th to the 28th.

WEATHER EFFECTS

Rainfall was generally adequate for the growth of grasses and winter grain but insufficient to relieve dry subsoils or raise the levels of wells and streams. Many farmers continued to haul water for livestock. Weather conditions were favorable for field work and harvesting was more advanced than usual at the end of October. Pastures were good in most areas and showed lush growth in southeastern Pennsylvania.

DESTRUCTIVE STORMS

An extratropical storm brought winds of 50 mph to eastern Pennsylvania the 6th-7th causing light but widespread damage to trees and wire lines. Many boats tied up on the Susquehanna River were damaged when high winds slammed them into piers. Large quantities of apples were blown from the trees in the York-Adams County area.

FLOODS

None reported.

J. T. B. Beard, Climatologist
Weather Records Processing Center
Chattanooga, Tennessee

SPECIAL NOTICE

A survey has indicated that the comprehensive narrative weather story carried in each issue of Climatological Data is of value to only a small number of recipients. This story will be discontinued, therefore, with the January 1958 issue. A table of extremes will be carried each month and a text will be carried whenever unusual and outstanding weather events have occurred. General weather conditions in the U. S. for each month are described in the publications MONTHLY WEATHER REVIEW and the MONTHLY CLIMATOLOGICAL DATA; NATIONAL SUMMARY, either of which may be obtained from the Superintendent of Documents, Government Printing Office, Washington, D. C.

CLIMATOLOGICAL DATA

PENNSYLVANIA
OCTOBER 1957

Temperature: Average Maximum	Average Minimum	Average	Departure From Long Term Means	Highest	Date	Lowest	Date	Degree Days	No. of Days: Max. 90° or Above	Max. 32° or Below	Min. 32° or Below	Min. 0° or Below	Precipitation: Total	Departure From Long Term Means	Greatest Day	Date	Snow, Sleet: Total	Max Depth on Ground	Date	No. of Days: 10 or More	50 or More	1.00 or More
57.9	37.4M	47.7M	- 1.6	72	9	23	26+	530	0	0	9	0	3.05	- .80	1.00	8	T	0		7	2	1
57.1	34.1	45.6		71	10	23	12	596	0	0	17	0	3.11		1.37	19	.0	0		7	2	1
57.2	37.0	47.1	- 1.6	70	9	22	12	544	0	0	8	0	4.65	.14	1.35	18	T	0		5	4	2
61.0	37.2	49.1		75	9	25	12+	489	0	0	13	0	3.32		1.41	8	T	0		3	3	2
54.6	38.3	46.5		68	10	23	26	568	0	0	9	0	4.84		1.12	19	.3	T	27+	7	5	2
55.4M	32.9M	44.2M		68	2	23	12	636	0	1	17	0	2.88	- .98	.81	19	T	T	27+	7	3	0
60.5	39.5	50.0	- 2.6	74	10	30	12+	461	0	0	7	0	3.15	.21	1.40	8	.0	0		6	3	1
59.2	39.2	49.2	- 3.0	72	9+	28	12	479	0	0	6	0	2.54	- .84	1.26	8	T	T	27+	4	2	1
60.8	34.7	47.8	- 4.6	75	9	21	12	528	0	0	16	0	3.60	.11	1.40	18	T	0		6	2	2
		47.5											3.46				T					
62.2	40.7	51.5	- 1.7	77	9	29	12	410	0	0	4	0	2.85	- .12	1.26	18	T	0		4	3	1
62.3	40.8	51.6	- 2.2	77	10	31	12	411	0	0	4	0	2.85	- .26	1.25	19	.0	0		6	3	1
62.7	43.0	52.9	- 3.1	79	9	31	27	371	0	0	2	0	2.92	- .15	1.16	18	.0	0		4	3	1
64.2	38.9	51.6	- .6	76	9	27	12+	409	0	0	10	0	3.71	- .08	1.36	24	.0	0		5	3	2
60.8	39.6	50.2	- 2.6	75	9	28	12	453	0	0	7	0	3.62	.45	1.22	18	.0	0		5	3	2
63.0	34.5	48.8	- 4.5	77	10	23	12	495	0	0	17	0	3.50	- .47	.94	19	.0	0		7	3	0
		51.1											3.24				T					
64.2	43.6	53.9		77	10	32	21	335	0	0	1	0	3.13		1.27	7	T	0		3	3	1
62.7	39.5	51.1	- 3.3	76	10	29	12+	425	0	0	9	0	2.12	- 1.31	.86	19	.0	0		6	1	0
64.0	41.0	52.5		76	9	27	28	382	0	0	6	0	2.47		1.22	18	.0	0		5	2	1
59.5	40.7	50.1		76	9	28	26	456	0	0	7	0	2.02		.84	18	.0	0		3	2	0
61.8	39.9	50.9	- 4.0	75	9	28	26+	434	0	0	7	0	1.65	- 1.51	.75	24	.0	0		5	2	0
63.3	41.6	52.5	- 3.0	76	9	29	12	381	0	0	6	0	2.02	- 1.09	.68	24	.0	0		5	2	0
66.2	39.5	52.9		76	1+	25	12+	375	0	0	6	0	1.79	- 1.14	.62	19	.0	0		4	2	0
62.5	45.8	54.2	- 2.8	73	1+	34	29	329	0	0	0	0	2.08	- .56	.81	19	.0	0		5	1	0
63.1	38.8	51.0	- 2.8	75	9	28	12+	429	0	0	10	0	2.67	- .46	1.09	18	.0	0		4	3	1
61.4	37.1	49.3		73	2+	24	13	483	0	0	12	0	2.45		.64	19	.0	0		7	2	0
62.6	37.9	50.3	- 3.7	76	10	26	12	449	0	0	10	0	2.86	- .65	.69	19	T	0		7	2	0
64.9	48.0	56.5	- 3.3	81	9	33	28	265	0	0	0	0	2.63	.10	.91	6	.0	0		3	3	0
62.2	43.3	52.8	- 1.9	74	1+	31	26+	370	0	0	3	0	2.09	- 1.29	.64	18	.0	0		5	2	0
61.3	40.2	50.8		74	9	28	12	435	0	0	6	0	1.85		.65	18	T	0		4	2	0
61.5	41.8	51.7		74	9	28	26+	404	0	0	6	0	2.04		.65	8	.0	0		4	2	0
64.5	44.5	54.5		78	9	33	26	320	0	0	0	0	2.17		1.00	19	.0	0		3	2	1
65.2	48.1	56.7		80	9	35	26+	255	0	0	0	0	2.67		1.29	6	.0	0		3	3	1
63.5	44.6	54.1	- 2.5	77	9	32	28	335	0	0	1	0	2.05	- .55	.73	6	T	0		3	3	0
64.2	49.2	56.7	- 1.8	72	3	32	26	256	0	0	1	0	2.23		.88	6	.0	0		3	3	0
64.4	49.0	56.7	- 1.8	80	9	36	26+	256	0	0	0	0										
64.9	39.0	52.0	- 3.6	74	2+	28	13	399	0	0	10	0	1.85	- 1.24	.77	18	.0	0		3	2	0
64.4	38.7	51.6	- .8	76	9	25	12+	408	0	0	9	0	1.98	- 1.35	.83	19	T	0		4	1	0
63.2	44.8	54.0	- 2.1	77	9	34	12+	338	0	0	0	0	2.09	- .66	.67	18	.0	0		4	2	0
64.0	44.5	54.3		78	9	33	26+	326	0	0	0	0	2.83		1.05	18	.0	0		3	3	1
64.0	43.0	53.5	- 1.4	78	9	30	26	352	0	0	2	0	1.54	- 2.01	.59	7	.0	0		3	2	0
		53.0											2.22				T					
62.0	39.0	50.5	- 4.0	74	10	28	28	442	0	0	5	0	4.14	.61	1.34	8	.0	0		6	3	1
65.4	41.8	53.6	.3	76	1+	30	28	348	0	0	4	0	3.05	- .30	.82	8	.0	0		5	3	0
62.8	39.9	51.4	- 2.3	75	9	28	12	415	0	0	6	0	2.72	- .56	.81	24	.0	0		6	3	0
62.5	41.4	52.0	- 1.9	76	10	31	12+	395	0	0	3	0	4.53	1.24	2.04	8	T	0		5	4	2
63.1	40.5	51.8	- 4.5	76	10	28	28	402	0	0	4	0	3.62	.47	1.61	8	.0	0		7	2	1
62.4	42.9	52.7	- 2.5	74	1+	30	27+	376	0	0	2	0	1.78	- 1.29	.61	18	T	0		5	1	0
64.5	45.1	54.8		78	9+	27	26	317	0	0	4	0	2.72		1.54	18	.0	0		3	2	2
64.0	40.3	52.2	- 2.7	75	9	30	12+	391	0	0	6	0	3.77	.25	.99	8	.0	0		6	3	0
62.9	36.5	49.7		75	9	21	28	468	0	0	13	0	2.12		.60	24	.0	0		6	1	0
65.5	39.1	52.3	- 2.4	76	9	24	28	388	0	0	9	0	2.73	- .49	.93	18	T	0		5	3	0
		52.1											3.12				T					
61.8	37.0	49.4		75	1	23	28	477	0	0	13	0	2.41		.81	18	T	0		7	1	0
63.1	39.6	51.4		76	9	28	12+	416	0	0	8	0	2.95		1.43	8	T	0		4	2	1
60.9	38.3	49.6		76	10	26	12+	472	0	0	10	0	2.70		.67	9	T	T	27	6	1	0
63.2	38.8	51.0		78	2	29	13+	425	0	0	8	0	4.16		1.55	8	T	0		6	3	1
63.1	37.6	50.4		76	10	28	12+	446	0	0	9	0	2.25	- .19	.53	18	T	0		7	1	0
63.0	38.3	50.7		78	10	27	12+	436	0	0	9	0	2.30	- .99	.80	8	T	0		6	1	0
61.8	40.4	51.1		77	9	30	12+	424	0	0	5	0	1.50	- .87	.44	24	T	T	27	4	0	0
		50.5											2.61				T					
56.6	35.6	46.1		71	2	25	26+	579	0	0	12	0	1.65		.42	9	T	T	27	6	0	0
60.7	32.9	46.8		75	2	24	12+	559	0	0	18	0	1.61		.64	8	T	T	27	6	1	0
52.9	36.7	44.8		66	2	23	28	620	0	0	9	0	5.16	- .18	1.66	18	•	1	28	6	5	1
60.5	33.1	46.8		77	2	24	12+	555	0	0	19	0	1.38	- .39	.34	19	•	1	27	6	0	0

See Reference Notes Following Station Index

ABLE 2 - CONTINUED

Station	
MONTROSE 1 E	AM
TOWANDA	
WELLSBORO 3 S	AM
DIVISION	
CENTRAL MOUNTAINS	
BELLEFONTE 4 S	AM
DU BOIS 7 E	
EMPORIUM 2 SSW	AM
LOCK HAVEN	
MADERA	AM
PHILIPSBURG CAA AP	
RIDGWAY 3 W	AM
STATE COLLEGE	AM
TAMARACK 2 S FIRE TWR	AM
DIVISION	
SOUTH CENTRAL MOUNTAINS	
ALTOONA HORSESHOE CURVE	
BURNT CABINS 2 NE	
EBENSBURG	
EVERETT 1 SW	
HUNTINGDON	AM
JOHNSTOWN	AM
KEGG	
MARTINSBURG CAA AP	
DIVISION	
SOUTHWEST PLATEAU	
BAKERSTOWN 3 WNW	
BLAIRSVILLE 6 ENE	
BURGETTSTOWN 2 W	AM
BUTLER	
CLAYSVILLE 3 W	
CONFLUENCE 1 SW DAM	AM
DERRY	
DONEGAL	
DONORA	AM
FORD CITY 4 S DAM	AM
INDIANA 3 SE	
IRWIN	
MIDLAND DAM 7	
NEW CASTLE 1 N	
NEWELL	AM
NEW STANTON	
PITTSBURGH WB AP 2	//R
PITTSBURGH WB CITY	R
PUTNEYVILLE 2 SE DAM	AM
SALINA 3 W	
SHIPPINGPORT WB	
SLIPPERY ROCK	
SOMERSET MAIN ST	
SPRINGS 1 SW	
UNIONTOWN	
† WAYNESBURG 2 W	
DIVISION	
NORTHWEST PLATEAU	
BRADFORD CAA AP	
BRADFORD 4 W RES	
BROOKVILLE CAA AIRPORT	
CLARION 3 SW	
CORRY	
COUDERSPORT 3 NW	
EAST BRADY	
ERIE WB AIRPORT	
FARRELL SHARON	
FRANKLIN	
GREENVILLE	
JAMESTOWN 2 NW	AM
KANE 1 NNE	AM
LINESVILLE 5 WNW	
MEADVILLE 1 S	AM
MERCER 2 NNE	
SPRINGBORO	AM
TIONESTA 2 SE DAM	AM
TITUSVILLE WATER WORKS	
WARREN	
DIVISION	

† DATA RECEIVED TOO LATE TO BE INCLUDED IN DIVISION AVERAGES

See Reference Notes Following Station Index

DAILY PRECIPITATION

Total	1	2	3	4	5	6	7	8	9	10	11	12	13	14	15	16	17	18	19	20	21	22	23	24	25	26	27	28	29	30	31
1.95							.29	.01									.03	.48	.03	.08				.77			.02				.07
2.85						.22	.05	.72									.02	1.26		T			T	.58			T				T
2.85							.28	.50										.15	1.25					.02							
2.70						.42	.48	.27									.22	.27	.02					.96							
4.14							.95	1.34									.03	.82	.15												
1.01							T	.10										.30	.19	.02				.25	.02		T				
2.02																	.25	.19	.20	.10			.31	.82	.05		.01				
1.49							.04										T	.40	.10												
-							.17	-																							
3.50						.05	.05	1.60									.03	.97	.10												
1.55							.15										.02	.32	.13				T	.67	.07			.05			.08
2.41							.23	.40	.18								.03	.81	.12					.31	.21			T			.03
2.40							.29	.46	.27									.62	.04					.39	.33		T				
2.36							.32	.38	.17								.02	.64	.02					.61	.18		.01				.01
2.81							.20	.38	.24									.26	.86												T
2.95						.13	.03	1.43									.07	.92	.04					.32							T
2.87							.28	.59										.08	1.17					T							T
2.92						.34	.04	.53									.03	1.16						.82							
2.57							.20	.05									.52	.61					.10	.74			.12				.02
4.89						.24	1.12	1.15									.20	1.02						1.12			T				.04
4.23							1.37	.02									.01	.85	.35	.19				.89	.39		.07	.04			.03
2.20							.29	.01									.02	.41	.60	.06				.63	.07		.03	.05			.03
1.98																	.41	.20	.06				.39	.96	T						
1.99																	T	.42	.05						.23						
2.17																	.08	.49					T	1.47							
2.93						1.22	.05										.68	.09					.02	.76			.06	.05			
2.03						.05	.02										.43	.18					.33	.94			.03	T			
1.68							.34	.01									.07	.49						.81	T						
-						-	-	-										.56						1.08	.14						.02
1.73																	.06	.20													.05
2.46						1.35											.11							.70							
1.79							.18										.06	.36						1.00							.05
2.57						.15	.02	.37									.20	.90						.91							.02
1.65							.03	.40										.23						.20	.20						T
3.05						.20	.40										.09	.82					T	.72	T						
2.49							.76	.16									T	.45	.03	.03					.03		T				
2.01							.07	.06										.72	T	T				.80	.26		.10				
2.36							.27	.35	.12										.11					.50	.30						
-						-	-	-	-								-	-	-					.10	.90						
2.72						.68	.17										.33	.55					T	.81							
2.37							.69	.09									.02	.53	.13						.09		.01				.02
3.13							1.27	.04	.04									T	.98					T	.80		T				
1.32						.15	.20	.20	.10									.22	.05					.35	T						
2.04							.17	T									.02	.42	.06					.96	.23	.03					T
3.16							.15	.83																.24							
2.48							.50	.01									.08	.46	.08	.06					.05	.02	.06				.86
1.95							.32	.05									T	.72	.04	T			T	.58	.22	T	.02				
1.88							.02										.01	.45	.05					1.05	.20						.06
3.66							.37	.85											.81					.35	.70						.02
2.12						.08	.46	.10																T							
2.47						.11	.14	.39									.08	1.22	.02					.51							
4.41							1.99	.14									.05	.60	.03	.06				1.33	.07		.01				.03
4.54							1.99	.11									.02	.64	.09	.12					.12		T				.01
3.53								.10									.02	.62	.08	.05				.95			.04				.04
1.70						.06	.58													.01				.07			T				
1.97							.13	.02									.01	.57	.03	.02			T	1.08	.08		.05				T
1.99							.10	T									.01	.55	.02	.03			T	1.16	.09		.03				
1.30							.27																								.07
1.70																	.14	.39	.10	T			.39	.60	T		.03				.02
1.20																			.14	.01					.17		.01				
1.82							.10	.02	.11									.62	.10					.62	.10		.10	.02			
1.18							.05	.19	.04									.28	.23					.19	.07		.07	.06			
1.94							.32											.05	.05					.79	.07						.10
3.96							1.43											1.41	.04					.69	.25		.08				
2.32																	.05	.46						1.18			.09				
2.74							.05	1.02										.43	.30												
2.67						.50	.28										.30	.57	.12				T	.82							
2.02						.64		.06															T	.48							
1.61							.07	.64										.11	.41					.11	.10		T				
4.57						1.40	.39										.60	.62	.11				.20	1.10	T		.15				
2.65						T	.58	.06									.29	.24	.63					.67	.02						T
1.58						.11	.44	.18									T	.50	.02					.34	.01						T
1.98							.23	.02									.13	.65	.04				.03	.81	.02		.05				
2.98							.10	.98										.39	.40					.06	.20		.02	.03			
5.16							.07	.62										1.66					T	.79				.05			
1.73						.03											.18	.32	.06					1.09	.02		.03				
2.34							.85	.07									.04	.43	T	.05				.55	.35		T	T			T
2.14							.08	.02									.05	.45		.02			.02	.99				.11			.07
	RECORD MISSING																														
2.51							.29	.20																							
1.75							.08	T	.04									.54	.02					.82	.24		.01				
1.70							.28	.32	.07								T	.43	.13					.36	.11		T				
1.65						.10	.10	.53									.02	.15						.75							
2.68																		T	2.50					.07		.01					
1.98																	.50	.24	T				.62	.22	T	.06					T
3.90						1.14											.56	.14						1.05						1.01	
1.72							.10										.14	.13	.09				.58	.50	.05		.05				.08
1.99							.26	.02									.01	.72	.03	.02				.89	T		.02	.02			
1.53							.11										.04	.28	.08	.02			T	.82	.11	.01		T			.05
3.05							.30	1.00										.15	.70												
1.73							.10	.04										.68	.13					.49	.17						
2.28						.13	.58	.03										.15	.65					.03	.60						
2.02						.24	.53	.13									.01	.43													
4.53						T	1.03	2.04									.04	.55	.07					.60	.13						T
1.83																	T	.52	.11					.90	.22						T
1.52							.02										.01	.44	.01	T				.80	.21		.03	T			T
1.67							.23										.02	.19	.04	.01				.92	.10	T	.05	.09			.06
4.10							.43	1.22										.23	1.01	.04				.23	.66						T
1.79						.01	.57	.11										.09	.62					.05	.34						
2.70							.09	.33										.45	.44												
3.20							1.13	.07									.01	.59	.02					1.04			.06	.15			.07
2.59						.39	.43	T									.41	.30	.06				.10	.80			.08	.01			.01
2.41							.10		T								.18	.15	.11				.83	.67	.06						.14
3.62						T	.76	1.61	.11								T	.42	.26					.13	.33						T
1.78						.26	T	.32									.13	.61					T	.46							
3.18							.22	.37	.12								.02	1.25	.21					.70	.28			T			.01
3.11							.15	.91	.14									.26	1.33					.16	.15			.01			T
3.11							.14	.94	.19									.25	1.37					.12	.10						
2.52							.12	1.05	.07									.09	.86					.06	.22						T
2.08							.34	.04										.20	.81												T
2.52							.08	.96	.03									.34	.88					.06	.17						T
2.03							.47	.02	.24									.20	.62					.03	.45						
-							1.20										-	-	-												-
2.49								.35	.07									.45	.71												T
3.01							.75	.47	.10								.03	.73	T												T

See Reference Notes Following Station Index

DAILY PRECIPITATION

Table 3—Continued

HUNTSDALE							
HYNDMAN							
INDIANA 3 SE							
IRWIN							
JAMESTOWN 2 NW	.05	1.24	.12	.01			
JIM THORPE -	T	1.36					
JOHNSTOWN		.91	.07		T		
KANE 1 NNE		1.08	.18	.02	T		
KARTHAUS		.50	.13		.03		
KEGG		1.10			T		
KITTANNING LOCK 7		.99	.02		.02		
KREGAR 4 SE	.10	1.22	.18		.26		
KRESGEVILLE 3 W		.28	.75				
LAFAYETTE MC KEAN PARK							
LAKEVILLE 1 NNE		.17	.18		.02		
LANCASTER 2 NE PUMP STA		.52					
LANDISVILLE 2 NW		.20	.40				
LAWRENCEVILLE 2 S		.19	.07		.12		
LEBANON 3 W		.34	.34		.02		
LEHIGHTON		.47	.40				
LE ROY		.25			.25		
LEWIS RUN 3 SE		1.06	.26		.03		
LEWISTOWN		.42	.34		T		
LINESVILLE 5 WNW		.95	.38		.01		
LOCK HAVEN		.30	.28		.01		
LONG POND 2 W		.37	.85		-		
LYNCH		1.20	.08	.05			
LYNDELL 2 NW							
MADERA		.41	.22		.03		
MAHAFFEY		.84	.18		.06		
MAPLE GLEN		.52					
MAPLETON DEPOT		.55	.14				
MARCUS HOOK	.01	.79					
MARION CENTER 2 SE		.85	.11		.05		
MARTINSBURG CAA AP	.02	.84			.03		
MATAMORAS		.08	.40				
MC CONNELLSBURG		.51	.34		T		
MC KEESPORT		.70	.01		T		
MEADVILLE 1 S	.01	1.45	.12		T		
MEDIX RUN		.55	.21		.03		
MERCER 2 NNE		.90	.22		.06		
MERCERSBURG		.90					
MEYERSDALE		1.30	.07	.03	.01		
MIDDLETOWN OLMSTED FLD		.50					
MIDLAND DAM 7		.76	.09	-	.05		
MILANVILLE		.10	.25				
MILLHEIM		.51	.23				
MILLVILLE 2 SW		.42	.50				
MILROY		.87	.47				
MONTROSE 1 E		.18	.22		.01		
MORGANTOWN		.53			*		
MT GRETNA 2 SE		.56					
MT POCONO 2 N AP		.75			T		
MUHLENBURG 1 SE		.79			T		
MYERSTOWN		.17	.38				
NATRONA LOCK 4		.76	.20		.02		
NESHAMINY FALLS		.72			T		
NEWBURG 3 W		1.05					
NEW CASTLE 1 N	.02	.63	.09	.01	T		
NEWELL		.94	.03		T		
NEW PARK		.56					
NEWPORT		.49	.35				
NEW STANTON	.10	.74	.19		.06		
NEW TRIPOLI		.98			T		
NORRISTOWN		.02	.40				
NORTH EAST 2 SE		.83	.19	.03	.14	.02	
ORWELL 3 N		.43	.25		.06	T	
PALM		.05	.97				
PALMERTON		1.13					
PARKER		1.00	.06		.01		
PAUPACK 2 WNW			.20			.04	
PECKS POND		.31	.52		T	T	
PHIL DREXEL INST OF TEC	T	.82					
PHILADELPHIA WB AP R	T	.70			T		
PHILADELPHIA PT BREEZE		.74					
PHILADELPHIA CITY *	-	-	-	-	-	-	
PHILIPSBURG CAA AP	.07	.86	T	T	.07	.01	
PHOENIXVILLE 1 E		.37					
PIKES CREEK		.49	.61			T	
PIMPLE HILL		.70	.96		T	.01	
PINE GROVE 1 NE		.54	.48			T	
PITTSBURGH WB AP 2 //R	.34	.45	.02	T	.15	T	03
PITTSBURGH WB CITY R	.42	.32		.01	.03		05
PLEASANT MOUNT 1 W		.24	.16		T	T	
PORT CLINTON		.47	.76				
POTTSVILLE		.55	.43				
PUTNEYVILLE 2 SE DAM		1.02	.07		.04	.07	
QUAKERTOWN 1 E		.02	.47		T		
RAYMOND		.55	.15		.06		
READING WB CITY	T	.62					
RENOVO		.35	.09		.03	T	
REW		1.00	.26		.01		
RICES LANDING L 6		.85	.05		.05	.16	
RIDGWAY 3 W		.62	.35		T		
RUSH		.27	.17		T	.07	
RUSHVILLE		.15	.20			T	
SAGAMORE 1 S		1.10	.20				
SALINA 3 W	.16	.80	T		.02	T	
SAXTON		.87	.08		T	.01	
SCHENLEY LOCK 5		1.05	.04		.01		
SCRANTON		.12	.52				
SCRANTON WB AIRPORT	T	.30			T	T	
SHAMOKIN		.44	.48			T	
SHIPPENSBURG		.77					
SHIPPINGPORT WB	.37	.40	T	T	.08	.01	04
SINNEMAHONING		.41	.17		.04	T	
SLIPPERY ROCK		.64	.16	.01	T	.07	
SOMERSET FAIRVIEW ST		1.24	.15		T	.07	
SOMERSET MAIN ST	.05	1.26	.07		.08		
SOUTH MOUNTAIN		.39	.67		T		
SPRINGBORO		.15	T	.20		.10	11
SPRING GROVE		.43				T	
SPRINGS 1 SW	.05	1.70	T		.17	T	
STATE COLLEGE		.61	.38		.03	T	
STRAUSSTOWN		.42	.56				

See Reference Notes Following Station Index

3—Continued

DAILY PRECIPITATION

PENNSYLVANIA
OCTOBER 1957

Total	1	2	13	14	15	16	17	18	19	20	21	22	23	24	25	26	27	28	29	30	31
							.10	1.40					T	.46	T		T	T		T	T
							T	.93					T	.68	.26		.04				.02
								.41						.75	.20		T	.07			T
								.18						.16	.24		.06	.07			.01
							.07	.42							.02			.12			.06
								.28							.68					.04	
								.31							.68						
								.68							.20		.08	T			
							.02	.35							.09		.01	T			T
							.19	.23									T				.06
							.04	.34							.08		.04				.03
								.16							.05	T	.03	.01			T
							.11	.94													T
								.22							.09		.07	.07			
							-	.22													
							T	.70													
							.05	.31													
							.38	.27													.06
								1.05													.03
							.03	.24													.06
							.01	.87													
								.14													T
			T				.02	.57													T
			T				.03	.55													
							T	.41													
							.22	.94													T
							.07	.33													.03
							T	.29													.01
							.20	.42													.03
																					.02
																					.03
																					-
																					T
																					T

LENTOWN WB AIRPORT
IE WB AIRPORT
RRISBURG WB AIRPORT
ILADELPHIA WB AIRPORT
ITTSBURGH WB AIRPORT
ADING WB CITY
RANTON WB AIRPORT
IPPINGPORT WB
LLIAMSPORT WB AIRPORT
Peak Gust

5.6
6.6
6.3
6.1
6.8
5.7
6.0
6.3

DAILY SOIL TEMPERATURES

Station And Depth	Time	1	2	3	4	5	6	7	8	9	10	11	12	13	14	15	16	17	18	19	20	21	22	23	24	25	26	27	28	29	30	31	Average
STATE COLLEGE																																	
ASURED UNDER SOD																																	
2 INCHES	8 AM	55	52	50	48	48	51	52	54	55	55	48	44	43	44	45	47	52	55	48	45	45	47	50	54	48	43	42	40	41	44	43	48.0
4 INCHES	8 AM	55	53	51	49	49	52	53	55	56	56	50	45	45	45	46	48	53	55	50	46	46	48	51	55	49	45	44	41	42	44	44	49.1
8 INCHES	8 AM	56	56	54	53	52	53	54	55	56	57	53	49	49	48	49	50	53	55	52	48	48	50	52	54	52	48	46	44	44	46	46	51.0
16 INCHES	8 AM	58	59	58	57	57	56	56	57	58	59	58	55	54	53	53	53	54	55	55	53	52	53	53	55	55	53	51	49	49	49	49	54.4

Ground Cover: Bluegrass Sod.

See Reference Notes Following Station Index

ALLENTOWN WB AP																							
ALLENTOWN GAS CO																							
ALTOONA HORSESHOE CURVE																							
ARENDTSVILLE																							
BAKERSTOWN 3 WNW																							
BEAVERTOWN																							
BELLEFONTE 4																							
BERWICK																							
BETHLEHEM LEHIGH UNIV																							
BLAIRSVILLE 6 ENE																							
BRADFORD CAA AP																							
BRADFORD 4 W RES																							
BROOKVILLE CAA AIRPORT																							
BURGETTSTOWN 2 W																							
BURNT CABINS 2 NE																							
BUTLER																							
CANTON 1 NW																							
CARLISLE																							
CHAMBERSBURG 1 ESE																							
CHESTER																							
CLARION 3 SW																							
CLAYSVILLE 3 W																							
COATESVILLE 1 SW																							
COLUMBIA				51	39	31	30	34	35														
CONFLUENCE 1 SW DAM	50 41	50 37	64 40	67 44	54 32	53 25	59 22	66 26	71 29														
CORRY	50	66 38	70 41	59 45	49 35	56 29	62 23	69 24	73 29														
COUDERSPORT 3 NW	60 51	60 45	72 39	58 41	46 34	56 18	59 18	65 22	66 22														
DERRY	56 49	47	67 48	60 47	57 36	57 26	66 29	70 26	72 35				47	6 53	48	40	25	30					
DEVAULT 1	69 51	65 53	76 54	75 45	54 28	50 32	50 31	41	57 42				42	64 47	60 54	54 34	40 28	44 30					
DIXON	63 45	68 53	61 45	74 41	59 33	52 24	58 25	62 28	66 31	60 40	51 39	57 25	62 25	70 32	67 45	63 40	43 28	40 28					
DONEGAL	47 40	56 40	61 36	50 28	44 23	52 19	59 19	66 20	68 28	42 34	50 27	62 20	65 35	62 42	61 36	38 28	34 20	32 23					
DONORA	57 51	60 46	69 44	73 51	61 40	59 31	61 30	66 32	69 36	61 45	57 36	62 34	68 43	71 51	68 59	68 43	46 31	41 32					
DU BOIS 7 E	61 50	65 47	69 42	68 46	54 30	55 23	62 25	65 27	68 29	52 38	58 33	63 29	68 40	66 49	63 52	52 33	40 20	38 27	46 27	55 33	50 33	58 35	59 36
EAGLES MERE	56 44	57 50	55 46	66 47	54 33	47 29	50 30	35	58 42	55 39	45 33	52 32	53 32	53 41	59 47	57 33	38 24	34 24	35 23	42 25	49 31	51 37	52 36
EAST BRADY	62 53	70 44	74 45	72 53	60 38	62 29	31	70 31	73 33	54 44	62 32	33	72 37	68 47	65 52	53 39	44 28	42 32	51 30	57 29	53 36	63 40	64 39
EBENSBURG	56 44	63 46	63 47	53 43	48 32	50 22	58 23	60 25	64 32	47 35	53 34	59 26	65 40	65 45	62 41	44 23	38 23	35 25	40 27	51 32	49 34	55 34	54 35
EMPORIUM 2 SSW	64 44	60 47	64 44	71 40	60 33	50 20	57 20	60 20	66 23	57 37	50 32	23	60 25	62 37	65 44	63 34	47 22	37 23	38 21	45 25	53 29	49 32	58 31
EPHRATA	70 50	66 50	75 53	70 48	60 35	56 30	62 29	32	68 32	54 44	62 38	61 34	64 38	65 44	62 50	53 45	45 28	44 28	49 28	60 34	56 40	63 36	61 39
ERIE WB AIRPORT	65 48	43	67 49	57 46	52 33	51 32	56 33		68 42	50 45	54 42	39	67 48	63 56	65 42	42 38	39 33	39 31	51 30	55 40	55 43	56 38	58 41

See reference notes following Station Index.

Table 5 - Continued

DAILY TEMPERATURES

Station		1	2	3	4	5	6	7	8	9	10	11	12	13	14	15	16	17	18	19	20	21	22	23	24	25	26	27	28	29	30	31	Average
EVERETT 1 SW	MAX	78	72	68	68	64	58	60	69	67	64	52	54	60	64	64	66	62	62	52	58	58	68	70	70	56	46	46	55	57	52	62	61.4
	MIN	45	40	38	28	46	50	52	49	50	47	34	24	24	28	29	40	48	48	50	42	38	38	40	50	40	34	36	38	35	38	46	40.2
FARRELL SHARON	MAX	68	65	65	62	58	57	60	67	66	61	56	60	65	72	75	76	66	61	50	61	67	70	63	64	46	42	39	55	58	55	58	61.0
	MIN	55	40	30	32	39	40	42	44	41	46	40	37	29	26	38	44	50	47	43	34	31	46	54	45	37	35	33	30	36	46	44	39.8
FORD CITY 4 S DAM	MAX	74	74	70	62	65	64	57	60	60	70	61	55	59	64	70	73	72	62	58	60	60	65	70	66	65	44	40	40	45	55	50	61.3
	MIN	47	38	34	29	32	38	44	44	44	49	35	27	28	27	28	32	40	52	41	33	28	29	39	46	38	24	25	29	31	36	36	35.6
FRANKLIN	MAX	71	70	64	64	66	63	63	70	72	64	55	59	65	70	73	73	67	55	49	60	64	69	64	64	45	40	41	52	55	54	60	61.3
	MIN	43	36	35	29	45	40	45	42	44	48	33	29	27	28	29	39	52	48	41	31	29	38	48	44	33	25	31	29	33	38	40	37.2
FREELAND	MAX	66	66	63	63	65	57	61	60	72	68	54	53	58	63	68	66	52	57	57	54	58	62	60	59	50	38	38	44	48	53	62	57.9
	MIN	48	42	33	35	38	43	47	49	48	46	33	27	31	37	43	43	44	50	43	35	31	39		40	33	23	25	23	30	32	32	37.4
GEORGE SCHOOL	MAX	70	72	64	63	66	62	65	71	76	70	59	58	65	66	70	69	64	62	60	61	62	66	71	65	59	48	44	49	62	61	65	63.3
	MIN	46	42	39	39	45	53	51	58	51	52	36	29	31	37	36	36	54	55	48	36	30	32	41	50	42	32	33	31	36	39	42	41.6
GETTYSBURG	MAX	68	73	73	63	67	65	57	64	65	76	65	58	61	65	68	67	67	59	62	58	63	63	68	70	65	50	44	45	51	61	56	62.5
	MIN	48	49	46	38	42	49	49	51	55	49	37	31	31	34	35	40	44	53	48	41	34	40	43	45	40	33	33	32	39	39	36	41.4
GRATERFORD	MAX	76	74	76	72	75	64	68	72	76	72	70	67	65	70	72	70	68	62	64	58	62	62	60	68	66	56	58	62	50	60	56	66.2
	MIN	42	44	42	40	44	49	54	54	54	46	44	25	25	30	32	36	38	43	40	28	36	38	42	40	42	40	38	34	32	34	40	39.5
GRATZ 1	MAX	65	72	73	62	66	67	58	68	63	76	64	55	56	61	65	69	67	60	59	54	62	61	66	65	64	45	43	40	48	59	55	60.9
	MIN	43	45	43	32	30	36	50	57	50	48	40	26	26	27	27	33	36	54	47	40	34	34	43	45	44	30	30	30	32	39	37	38.3
GREENVILLE	MAX	74	71	64	70	68	64	69	73	70	58	53	59	67	71	75	76	68	59	50	60	64	68	63	61	44	41	39	53	57	53	60	62.0
	MIN	52	33	30	25	34	38	41	38	43	40	27	25	21	24	28	41	51	43	38	27	24	38	48	44	33	30	28	24	29	39	40	34.7
HANOVER	MAX	67	70	72	65	67	67	57	70	63	76	66	59	59	64	68	69	68	61	61	56	60	64	69	73	66	53	48	45	51	62	59	63.1
	MIN	49	45	45	37	39	41	48	50	50	49	39	31	31	35	35	39	42	54	45	38	36	36	44	46	45	33	32	28	34	41	38	40.5
HARRISBURG WB AP	MAX	74	74	62	67	65	60	70	65	74	65	56	57	63	68	72	68	61	62	55	64	63	68	69	67	53	45	41	49	62	55	61	62.4
	MIN	47	51	44	37	42	52	54	53	57	50	38	33	33	34	36	41	52	54	46	43	35	42	47	53	38	36	30	30	43	40	38	42.9
HAWLEY 1 S DAM	MAX	56	70	63	57	63	64	54	61	62	71	58	50	54	58	63	69	70	57	58	50	53	59	56	65	58	42	40	35	44	55	55	57.1
	MIN	36	40	36	28	28	42	45	51	48	44	36	23	25	31	30	29	32	35	42	38	27	27	28	47	36	28	28	28	30	29	31	34.1
HOLTWOOD	MAX	73	72	64	68	64	61	71	64	72	64	55	57	64	64	73	66	61	61	57	63	64	66	68	63	57	45	44	50	63	59	63	62.5
	MIN	52	52	48	45	46	43	55	55	57	51	42	38	38	43	44	45	48	57	48	48	41	44	49	57	40	37	36	36	34	41	49	45.8
HUNTINGDON	MAX	64	75	72	62	63	60	57	66	68	72	65	56	56	63	66	67	67	60	60	55	62	64	71	67	70	50	43	43	48	60	54	61.5
	MIN	40	33	33	26	32	38	45	52	53	43	31	26	23	26	26	31	34	50	45	41	29	33	37	42	39	25	26	28	35	31	34	35.1
INDIANA 3 SE	MAX	73	70	65	66	65	55	60	68	70	61	54	59	64	70	73	72	61	61	52	60	66	69	69	64	47	40	40	44	55	51	61	60.8
	MIN	48	33	30	28	35	39	49	47	44	43	33	23	24	25	32	38	54	50	40	32	26	39	44	46	39	23	30	30	28	32	37	36.2
IRWIN	MAX	76	75	66	71	67			65	72	71	57			74	75	77	70	62			69	74	72	66	52			45	52	56	55	66.0
	MIN	55	40	41	40			35	34	38	49	35			25	33	40	55	50			30	42	48	50	39			28	29	37	39	39.7
JAMESTOWN 2 NW	MAX	73	69	68	61	64	69	65	61	67	70	55	53	55	62	69	72	73	59	52	48	59	63	68	61	61	40	41	40	50	55	53	59.9
	MIN	47	34	33	29	39	43	52	45	41	46	32	30	25	26	35	40	49	50	42	30	29	34	45	54	36	32	30	31	29	29	29	37.0
JIM THORPE	MAX	71	72	72	67	69	65	66	63	76	73	60	56	65	69	75	74	71	59	59	60	64	65	65	64	62	45	44	52	60	59	67	64.2
	MIN	41	43	40	33	39	48	52	54	52	49	32	27	27	30	31	33	40	54	46	40	31	32	44	56	39	30	32	29	33	34	35	38.9
JOHNSTOWN	MAX	74	75	73	68	69	65	64	62	69	72	61	57	57	66	74	73	72	63	61	55	60	69	76	73	69	47	44	36	45	60	55	63.4
	MIN	45	35	35	27	33	39	36	44	42	40	30	23	23	22	27	32	40	48	38	36	25	29	39	44	36	25	27	27	30	33	36	33.7
KANE 1 NNE	MAX	71	68	65	58	62	62	61	62	63	70	54	48	57	61	67	69	70	58	53	45	55	62	61	66	60	40	35	37	47	53	50	57.7
	MIN	33	28	25	20	21	27	38	41	35	38	31	24	18	17	20	24	31	50	38	28	28	36	38	46	34	18	22	24	22	28	39	29.7
KEGG	MAX	76	74	77	71	60	55	59	68	71	61	54	57	66	67	67	68	60	61	50	59	64	73	72	69	47	41	40	46	60	52	61	61.5
	MIN	46	46	28	30	39	42	46	47	46	41	32	25	24	24	30	34	48	49	43	38	29	37	34	42	37	26	32	33	35	36	39	36.7
LANCASTER 2 NE PUMP STA	MAX	70	72	67	67	66	60	69	65	75	71	63	58	64	66	69	67	63	60	59	62	63	61	67	66	63	45	44	50	62	57	65	63.1
	MIN	45	43	40	33	38	49	51	51	53	45	37	28	28	30	32	32	41	54	45	40	30	34	39	57	44	30	30	28	31	33	33	38.8
LANDISVILLE 2 NW	MAX	67	73	73	62	67	67	59	68	65	73	65	56	58	62	66	70	67	59	59	52	61	62	66	68	64	48	41	40	48	61	55	61.4
	MIN	43	42	40	29	33	41	50	54	52	47	35	26	24	25	30	32	35	49	45	39	31	32	41	43	47	29	31	27	32	33	33	37.1
LAWRENCEVILLE 2 S	MAX	69	77	65	70	62	61	67	67	66	71	67	49	56	61	67	73	69	58	57	48	56	64	69	68	66	39	37	38	48	57	55	60.5
	MIN	30	33	30	27	30	35	37	52	43	43	41	24	24	26	27	29	30	49	40	30	25	29	37	48	37	30	29	26	28	28	30	33.1
LEBANON 3 W	MAX	67	72	74	64	68	68	60	70	65	76	68	57	60	65	68	71	69	59	60	55	63	63	67	66	65	50	45	42	50	61	56	62.6
	MIN	43	44	38	32	35	40	51	50	53	45	35	26	27	29	31	34	36	51	45	40	31	36	43	44	46	31	30	29	30	35	34	37.9
LEWISTOWN	MAX	66	78	76	65	66	63	58	66	67	77	66	58	60	65	69	70	68	59	69	54	64	67	71	67	66	50	44	43	49	62	55	63.2
	MIN	45	42	41	34	33	40	52	53	50	47	36	30	29	30	31	36	40	52	47	42	34	32	38	46	45	29	29	33	32	38	38	38.8
LINESVILLE 5 WNW	MAX	69	68	58	62	65	65	59	68	73	58	52	55	63	68	71	72	63	56	48	58	62	67	60	61	46	38	41	50	55	52	55	59.3
	MIN	45	32	30	26	33	35	51	44	39	45	30	33	24	24	31	42	54	44	41	30	29	43	44	43	36	33	28	27	34	41	39	36.5
LOCK HAVEN	MAX	74	73	64	66	65	61	65	66	77	66	57	60	64	68	69	70	59	60	54	62	65	70	67	70	46	43	43	48	59	53	63	62.2
	MIN	44	38	38	33	37	45	53	53	48	46	40	29	29	30	33	36	47	55	45	36	31	38	47	46	37	33	31	27	35	36	36	39.1
MADERA	MAX	65	70	62	58	60	58	55	62	65	68	59	52	53	58	64	65	64	57	58	50	56	60	68	65	65	43	39	38	43	52	52	57.5
	MIN	42	31	29	25	25	29	43	48	48	42	31	20	20	20	21	25	32	50	39	32	25	27	35	42	33	25	23	27	29	30	37	31.8
MARCUS HOOK	MAX	68	76	67	66	67	64	69	67	81	74	60	61	67	70	72	69	70	64	59	64	64	66	69	63	60	48	45	53	63	60	65	64.9
	MIN	56	54	50	47	52	53	57	58	59	54	44	41	42	48	48	49	49	58	44	44	44	48	49	60	41	36	35	33	38	46	50	48.0
MARTINSBURG CAA AP	MAX	72	68	63	61	57	54	63	67	68	58	52	59	66	66	69	64	57	57	49	58	63	72	65	67	45	41	37	43	59	50	60	59.0
	MIN	49	40	40	33	40	44	48	50	52	40	33	27	28	31	35	38	52	45	41	37	33	39	46	43	32	26	29	30	37	40	39	38.6
MEADVILLE 1 S	MAX	73	69	69	59	65	65	63	62	69	72	56	51	54	64	70	73	74	59	52	49	59	65	68	63	61	41	40	40	51	55	52	60.1
	MIN	43	35	33	27	35	43	47	42	43	49	28	28	24	26	28	40	46	50	41	29	28	32	41	55	35	30	31	29	31	36	41	36.3
MERCER 2 NNE	MAX	71	69	61	65	64	63	60	67	71	62	51	56	62	69	71	74	71	71	48	59	64	69	62	62	45	39	40	50	55	53	56	60.6
	MIN	55	32	32	27	39	37	50	40	39	44	26	30	20	22	31	44	52	41	40	30	25	41	52	40	33	27	29	26	29	40	42	36.0
MIDDLETOWN OLMSTED FLD	MAX	74	74	62	67	65	60	70	65	73	66	55	57	62	67	70	68	61	62	55	63	63	67	69	65	56	43	42	50	60	56	62	62.2
	MIN	49	51	45	39	46	53	54	55	55	49	40	33	33	36	37	40	51	55	48	44	37	41	48	56	38	31	32	31	37	40	39	43.3
MIDLAND DAM 7	MAX	70	67	62	62	64	61	59	67	68	57	53	55	58	63	66	72	64	57	48	56	62	68	63	65	45	40	37	48	53	53	56	58.7
	MIN	56	47	48	43	47	47	50	49	47	44	44	40	35	37	40	49	57	48	41	37	36	45	55	45	38	34	34	31	35	46	42	43.5
MONTROSE 1 E	MAX	66	70	60	53	55	59	61	64	57	68	54	47	52	56	59	66	67	57	56	43	50	56	64	64	59	37	34	32	42	52	51	55.2
	MIN	42	41	33	31	31	36	40	51	51	48	38	31	32	33	40	41	43	46	39	35	32	29	38	48	33	24	23	25	27	33	39	36.5
MORGANTOWN	MAX	69	72	62	64	66	61	67	66	74	66	55	56	63	65	67	66	61	60	59	61	60	63	65	62	59	45	42	48	58	56	63	61.3
	MIN	45	45	41	38	41	47	53	52	52	46	35	28	30	33	37	37	49	54	38	38	31	41	45	52	35	33	31	29	31	43	36	40.2
MT GRETNA 2 SE	MAX	71	73	66	65	65	59	68	63	74	65	55	58	62	66	69	67	58	59	54	63	62	65	66	65	56	45	41	49	61	55	62	61.5
	MIN	48	45	44	48	52	44	50	51	52	46	30	29	29	34	41	45	47	54	43	47	42	42	47	49	38	28	29	28	38	42	35	41.8

See reference notes following Station Index.

DAILY TEMPERATURES

Table 5 - Continued

Station		1	2	3	4	5	6	7	8	9	10	11	12	13	14	15	16	17	18	19	20	21	22	23	24	25	26	27	28	29	30	31	Average
MT POCONO 2 N AP	MAX	67	66	61	60	60	56	57	60	70	65	51	54	57	61	68	66	59	56	54	51	59	60	65	60	50	37	33	43	54	57	57	57.2
	MIN	45	41	34	35	42	47	49	51	49	46	27	22	30	35	37	38	42	50	39	36	28	35	44	37	35	24	27	26	32	33	36	37.0
MUHLENBURG 1 SE	MAX	71	70	64	65	65	60	66	62	75	67	57	56	62	65	68	68	64	58	58	60	58	60	66	64	61	39	38	49	55	59	62	61.0
	MIN	41	40	36	32	38	47	46	52	48	47	31	25	28	31	32	36	48	52	42	38	32	31	38	46	37	27	26	25	31	38	31	37.2
NEWBURG 3 W	MAX	65	74	70	65	65	70	68	73	78	78	66	65	63	72	68	72	69	65	58	62	61	68	68	65	54	48	46	51	62	55	56	64.5
	MIN	39	42	57	52	50	45	60	60	62	57	45	46	32	34	41	54	57	55	42	40	35	39	41	51	41	27	29	28	46	49	43	45.1
NEW CASTLE 1 N	MAX	74	71	69	67	67	65	61	69	73	72	55	60	65	70	71	74	69	61	51	61	64	68	65	62	49	41	42	53	58	53	58	62.5
	MIN	54	37	34	28	35	39	52	40	42	50	33	32	24	26	30	39	54	49	41	30	28	38	49	46	37	29	29	28	27	39	41	37.4
NEWELL	MAX													62	68	75	74	76	64	59	55	61	60	73	68	67	56	42	41	51	60	57	
	MIN													34	35	36	42	55	54	44	36	35	41	47	59	43	33	34	32	33	44	42	
NEWPORT	MAX	67	75	75	64	67	66	58	69	65	76	66	59	60	66	69	70	67	59	61	59	65	65	68	65	67	49	45	43	51	64	55	63.1
	MIN	44	42	40	33	33	35	50	52	49	45	33	28	28	29	30	32	35	52	45	41	32	33	37	43	43	32	31	29	35	37	38	37.6
NEW STANTON	MAX	78	71	67	68	68	55	59	67	72	59	60	59	66	73	74	76	64	62	59	64	69	72	69	59	50	40	38	41	59	55	59	62.2
	MIN	48	34	34	35	33	36	46	43	39	33	29	22	22	24	34	43	54	46	36	31	26	30	43	35	37	24	29	29	28	39	34	34.7
NORRISTOWN	MAX	70	73	65	66	67	60	70	68	78	72	59	60	65	70	72	72	65	65	58	64	63	69	71	64	61	47	44	52	63	61	67	64.5
	MIN	51	49	46	42	49	53	55	50	56	51	41	35	35	38	41	42	47	57	42	41	37	42	49	60	39	33	36	34	38	48	44	44.5
PALMERTON	MAX	70	71	61	64	65	61	65	63	75	63	54	58	63	66	69	69	59	60	52	59	60	65	64	62	56	48	39	48	59	54	63	60.8
	MIN	44	41	38	33	43	47	53	56	53	47	35	28	29	31	33	35	43	52	44	42	31	33	46	56	35	30	31	31	35	36	38	39.6
PHIL DREXEL INST OF TEC	MAX	70	76	67	66	67	63	71	69	80	70	60	61	66	70	74	72	67	65	59	65	63	66	71	63	61	47	46	53	65	61	67	65.2
	MIN	56	52	47	47	54	52	57	58	59	52	45	40	38	49	49	49	53	60	48	44	43	46	50	60	40	35	37	35	38	47	50	48.1
PHILADELPHIA WB AP	MAX	68	73	64	65	65	63	70	66	77	69	57	59	64	67	70	71	67	66	57	63	61	66	71	64	59	46	44	50	60	60	66	63.5
	MIN	51	49	46	47	53	52	56	56	58	52	42	38	35	41	40	41	47	57	42	39	37	40	47	59	39	34	33	32	35	43	43	44.6
PHILADELPHIA PT BREEZE	MAX	68	68	72	66	65	67	71	66	78	71	58	60	64	69	72	70	67	64	58	62	61	65	70	63	60	46	48	52	61	61	67	64.2
	MIN	54	56	50	48	55	53	57	58	61	59	47	43	44	51	47	49	52	58	46	45	47	51	51	60	46	32	34	35	38	48	51	49.2
PHILADELPHIA CITY	MAX	66	73	67	66	67	63	71	67	80	72	59	61	66	71	73	72	66	64	57	63	62	66	71	64	60	48	44	50	60	60	66	64.4
	MIN	57	55	50	48	53	51	57	58	60	52	46	42	45	49	51	51	51	57	46	46	47	48	51	60	40	36	38	36	39	47	51	49.0
PHILIPSBURG CAA AP	MAX	70	69	59	59	57	53	60	61	71	58	51	55	60	64	65	63	55	56	48	56	60	65	61	62	46	36	35	41	54	47	37	56.6
	MIN	44	42	30	25	30	38	49	49	47	35	26	18	19	21	27	41	50	44	38	31	30	39	49	41	28	24	26	28	29	33	31	34.3
PHOENIXVILLE 1 E	MAX	71	74	74	68	69	62	72	66	74	73	67	60	64	69	71	72	64	65	60	62	62	66	70	68	62	47	45	50	60	59	66	64.9
	MIN	47	42	41	32	39	49	49	54	50	45	36	30	28	31	30	34	38	53	48	36	29	35	41	58	42	29	29	32	31	36	35	39.0
PIMPLE HILL	MAX	60	66	63	55	60	60	53	59	58	68	55	48	53	56	61	67	64	53	54	45	51	58	60	60	55	38	37	33	42	51	50	54.6
	MIN	48	40	31	33	39	44	45	49	48	44	31	27	32	39	44	47	45	48	38	34	32	40	48	51	33	23	24	24	28	38	40	38.3
PITTSBURGH WB AP 2	MAX	72	70	63	64	62	58	56	66	70	58	54	57	62	67	69	72	62	56	48	59	62	69	63	62	42	38	35	46	54	50	56	58.8
	MIN	50	43	43	39	44	47	50	47	44	41	37	31	31	32	39	47	55	45	38	35	32	44	54	42	33	29	31	28	35	45	40	40.4
PITTSBURGH WB CITY	MAX	75	71	65	67	63	57	57	67	71	59	57	58	63	71	71	73	63	58	50	59	66	71	66	66	45	40	39	46	58	51	59	60.7
	MIN	55	46	46	41	48	49	53	50	49	45	42	34	37	35	41	47	57	47	42	39	36	47	58	44	35	32	34	31	38	47	46	43.6
PLEASANT MOUNT 1 W	MAX	63	68	60	53		63		59	61	67	55			55	59	65	67	55			55	52	61	64	53	38	37	32	40	52	50	55.4
	MIN	40	32	30	28	28			50	49	43	30	23			31	34	35	41			25	25	35	44	33	26	26	26	27	29	32	32.9
PORT CLINTON	MAX	65	73	74	65	69	67	62	68	60	77	67	60	62	66	70	73	70	60	61	57	62	65	67	66	62	50	45	43	50	63	55	63.0
	MIN	39	42	33	29	30	41	46	51	54	43	30	23	24	25	29	30	32	41	40	39	28	30	35	40	42	28	29	26	27	31	32	34.5
PUTNEYVILLE 2 SE DAM	MAX	74	73	75	62	64	63	58	59	69	71	60	54	57	62	68	72	70	61	59	50	60	64	70	65	64	44	37	40	48	55	50	60.6
	MIN	47	35	29	30	31	35	44	43	43	48	34	23	22	23	25	32	39	51	38	30	26	26	38	46	34	20	20	25	27	32	35	33.3
QUAKERTOWN 1 E	MAX	71	71	69	70	70	64	69	67	76	73	63	58	62	67	74	73	66	65	61	60	62	66	68	66	61	46	45	48	59	59	67	64.4
	MIN	40	43	39	36	41	46	47	55	53	46	36	25	25	30	30	32	37	53	47	41	29	33	43	57	42	29	30	30	37	33	34	38.7
READING WB CITY	MAX	72	73	66	67	67	61	69	67	77	68	59	59	64	68	71	70	62	61	56	63	64	66	68	63	55	45	43	50	62	58	65	63.2
	MIN	50	51	47	43	48	54	57	56	58	48	40	34	34	40	41	42	48	56	45	44	39	42	48	55	39	35	35	34	40	43	42	44.8
RIDGWAY 3 W	MAX	70	70	68	71	64	62	62	64	64	71	56	51	58	63	68	70	70	59	56	47	56	62	67	65	64	43	37	39	48	53	50	59.8
	MIN	36	33	30	25	24	32	38	45	42	41	34	24	22	22	22	24	31	51	40	28	29	31	37	42	36	20	28	27	28	30	37	31.9
SALINA 3 W	MAX	73	70	66	65	64	57	56	66	68	67	55	57	63	71	71	72	70	62	52	57	64	69	68	65	48	42	38	45	54	50	61	60.8
	MIN	51	38	37	36	41	39	48	44	43	43	32	24	25	25	31	39	54	50	42	31	28	41	38	47	37	24	29	30	34	38	35	37.2
SCRANTON	MAX	67	72	66	60	65	68	64	68	65	74	60	52	56	61	65	72	73	60	58	49	56	62	68	68	63	44	40	38	47	56	58	60.5
	MIN	43	46	40	35	36	40	53	54	52	52	42	30	30	31	36	36	38	48	46	40	34	34	37	52	41	30	30	30	32	38	38	39.5
SCRANTON WB AIRPORT	MAX	71	66	59	64	65	61	66	62	72	58	51	57	60	63	70	72	59	58	49	55	60	67	65	62	50	38	36	46	55	57	62	59.2
	MIN	44	43	37	33	38	47	52	54	49	43	33	28	29	34	36	36	48	48	42	38	30	40	50	49	33	29	30	29	36	38	39	39.2
SHIPPENSBURG	MAX	74	74	71	66	65	60	65	65	75	74	64	60	65	67	70	67	64	64	58	64	64	70	68	67	64	49	42	48	62	56	62	64.0
	MIN	47	47	43	34	38	47	47	50	47	47	33	30	30	31	37	37	47	55	45	38	33	40	42	55	42	30	32	30	40	38	38	40.3
SHIPPINGPORT WB	MAX	72	70	62	64	63	61	59	68	71	58	54	58	62	68	71	73	62	58	49	60	64	69	66	63	43	39	38	50	55	53	56	60.0
	MIN	48	40	43	36	43	42	47	45	41	39	35	32	32	32	35	43	54	45	40	35	32	42	53	43	35	31	32	29	35	44	39	39.4
SLIPPERY ROCK	MAX	74	74	63	64	64	64	69	67	72	66	56	60	65	71	72	73	65	60	50	62	65	70	63	60	45	40	40	47	55	50	58	61.4
	MIN	57	38	39	32	40	44	51	44	48	46	34	32	27	31	37	45	52	45	38	32	31	34	53	42	35	26	30	26	33	40	40	38.8
SOMERSET MAIN ST	MAX	71	69	65	61	56	50	51	65	65	59	52	56	63	65	67	66	59	58	48	55	62	67	67	65	49	40	35	39	54	49	57	57.6
	MIN	48	35	35	29	41	40	45	41	41	38	25	22	22	24	30	36	49	45	38	35	26	36	38	43	35	23	27	27	30	38	38	34.8
SPRINGBORO	MAX	74	63	67	60	63	66	66	62	68	72	59	53	55	62	70	74	74	63	55	58	65	70		63	54	46	40	52	56	53	52	61.2
	MIN	52	33	30	24	39	41	47	40	41	49	46	28	22	24	30	41	51	49	43	31	29	41	37		33	31	27	30	32	34	31	36.2
SPRINGS 1 SW	MAX	69	65	64	59	54	47	49	60	64	52	50	53	61	62	64	64	59	56	45	52	61	66	66	63	42	36	36	37	53	46	54	55.1
	MIN	44	32	34	27	37	37	40	39	38	38	24	20	22	24	27	36	46	42	37	32	24	33	42	41	35	24	27	26	31	33	38	33.2
STATE COLLEGE	MAX	64	73	71	62	62	58	55	63	64	73	61	54	57	62	66	67	64	58	58	51	60	61	69	64	65	46	40	39	45	57	51	59.4
	MIN	45	44	40	35	35	40	47	52	53	49	38	29	29	30	33	35	40	53	43	37	38	38	44	49	40	30	29	29	32	36	38	39.0
STROUDSBURG	MAX	70	70	61	65	66	59	64	60	75	65	54	60	64	70	73	70	53	60	53	58	62	65	66	61	55	44	39	45	60	56	62	60.8
	MIN	38	36	30	28	36	41	50	53	45	41	30	21	23	28	27	30	41	51	38	34	25	27	45	55	32	26	26	26	30	30	34	34.7
SUNBURY	MAX	65	76	75	65	68	69	68	70	64	78	67	59	60	65	68	70	66	62	61	55	65	60	68	67	64	45	45	42	50	60	56	63.0
	MIN	44	39	41	30	38	46	52	56	47	45	34	27	27	32	32	34	39	44	47	42	31	33	39	45	44	32	32	28	34	37	37	38.3
TAMARACK 2 S FIRE TWR	MAX	59	69	65	55	59	57	60	58	59	70	57	50	54	58	64	67	62	55	53	45	55	59	65	61	61	43	34	36	39	53	49	55.8
	MIN	45	41	35	35	34	39	45	49	47	46	36	30	30	33	42	42	44	46	37	33	33	34	44	50	33	24	24	23	25	32	37	37.0
TIONESTA 2 SE DAM	MAX	73	70	68	61	66	65	63	62	69	73	58	54	59	65	70	72	71	60	54	47	59	64	69	64	63	47	38	43	50	55	53	60.8
	MIN	37	38	35	30	30	36	41	43	43	47	39	28	30	23	28	30	32	51	40	30	30	30	38	47	32	23	25	28	31	35	42	34.6
TITUSVILLE WATER WORKS	MAX	70	69	60	66	66	62	65	69	73	57	55	58	64	71	74	74	63	58	46	59	65	69	63	65	43	39	40	50	55	56	59	60.7
	MIN	48	34	30	22	28	36	53	41	43	50	29	24	19	26	26	33	53	48	40	26	25	33	47	43	32	23	30	25	28	34	38	34.4

See reference notes following Station Index.

Table 5 - Continued

DAILY TEMPERATURES

PENNSYLVANIA
OCTOBER 1957

Station		1	2	3	4	5	6	7	8	9	10	11	12	13	14	15	16	17	18	19	20	21	22	23	24	25	26	27	28	29	30	31	Average
TOWANDA	MAX	75	68	61	62	63	66	69	61	75	60	52	59	62	67	69	71	58	60	54	57	61	70	69	66	61	41	41	48	58	59	63	61.5
	MIN	37	34	33	29	32	38	53	53	46	47	35	25	25	29	30	29	43	52	41	37	27	32	48	54	36	27	29	27	31	31	32	36.2
UNIONTOWN	MAX	76	70	67	66	61	55	53	64	69	57	54	58	64	70	71	73	64	60	50	60	67	70	70	67	47	43	37	43	59	53	63	60.7
	MIN	56	39	40	39	47	47	47	46	42	43	31	29	27	29	35	40	56	45	43	36	30	39	48	46	40	28	32	31	37	41	39	39.6
UPPER DARBY	MAX	69	73	65	66	67	66	70	66	78	71	62	59	64	68	70	70	65	64	59	63	61	66	69	66	61	46	43	50	60	60	67	64.0
	MIN	57	46	45	44	50	50	50	55	56	56	41	37	37	42	40	42	46	57	48	42	36	39	46	58	44	33	34	33	34	40	42	44.5
WARREN	MAX	71	66	58	64	64	67	65	64	73	61	50	56	60	69	71	72	64	59	49	57	63	69	66	65	45	39	42	50	55	56	60	60.3
	MIN	48	35	34	28	32	39	54	42	43	47	39	30	25	26	28	36	53	49	40	32	35	41	54	44	34	23	30	28	29	39	42	37.4
WAYNESBURG 2 W	MAX	77	71	69	68	65	59	55	68	71	66	57	58	64	72	73	74	63	61	51	60	67	71	67	66	47	41	39	45	58	50	59	61.7
	MIN	50	38	35	29	32	41	47	40	36	44	27	22	21	23	27	30	52	49	42	27	24	31	42	46	39	27	31	27	26	38	40	34.9
WELLSBORO 3 S	MAX	64	72	55	68	59	56	61	64	60	72	57	49	55	59	64	66	64	55	54	46	55	59	66	62	62	38	34	37	43	53	50	56.7
	MIN	41	41	31	35	33	35	44	50	47	46	36	27	29	32	38	41	47	49	36	35	30	33	45	51	34	26	25	24	25	34	36	36.6
WELLSVILLE	MAX	72	73	70	65	65	57	68	64	75	66	58	56	63	62	68	66	61	61	58	62	62	66	69	66	64	59	45	49	62	56	62	62.9
	MIN	42	40	40	28	39	50	52	49	49	44	30	24	24	26	29	34	40	41	40	39	28	34	38	58	45	31	27	21	27	32	31	36.5
WEST CHESTER	MAX	69	75	65	68	64	61	69	65	78	72	60	63	66	70	73	72	63	62	57	63	64	66	67	61	54	42	48	52	64	64	67	64.0
	MIN	48	45	42	45	49	54	55	54	55	41	35	37	42	44	45	43	51	47	41	36	34	38	43	45	33	30	32	35	44	44	44	43.0
WILLIAMSPORT WB AP	MAX	75	74	63	67	66	62	68	65	77	63	56	60	65	67	69	66	60	61	53	63	61	65	64	65	51	43	40	50	59	54	64	61.8
	MIN	43	41	38	35	40	47	56	55	53	46	36	30	32	34	35	36	46	52	46	38	32	38	48	51	38	33	31	30	37	37	37	40.4
YORK 3 SSW PUMP STA	MAX	72	74	73	69	68	64	69	68	76	74	66	60	65	69	71	71	67	62	60	64	65	69	72	69	66	49	43	50	62	59	64	65.5
	MIN	46	40	39	31	35	49	51	49	49	44	33	28	28	31	33	36	45	58	43	39	32	38	42	59	47	31	29	24	30	39	34	39.1

Table 6

EVAPORATION AND WIND

Station		1	2	3	4	5	6	7	8	9	10	11	12	13	14	15	16	17	18	19	20	21	22	23	24	25	26	27	28	29	30	31	Total or Avg.
CONFLUENCE 1 SW DAM	EVAP	.12	.06	.12	.13	.11	*	*	.08	.07	.09	.03	.12	.06	.07	.08	.07	.15	-	.07	.05	.07	.07	*	*	.14	.06	*	*	.04	.05	.04	B2.02
	WIND	40	31	44	52	55	46	43	21	51	55	41	51	34	41	32	30	32	20	107	116	70	26	30	21	100	74	74	38	109	44	68	1596
FORD CITY 4 S DAM	EVAP	.09	.11	.10	.12	.11	.23	-	-	.09	.08	.11	.07	.06	.07	.05	.08	*	*	.15	.04	.06	.06	-	-	.09	-	.13	.04	.02	.06	.02	B2.43
	WIND	17	32	27	46	50	30	60	0	35	21	54	32	16	2	20	10	20	40	66	55	44	10	28	42	108	47	30	25	46	51	44	1108
BAYLEY 1 S DAM	EVAP	.06	.08	.14	.11	.09	.11	.00	.04	.06	.10	.09	-	-	-	-	-	-	-	-	-	-	-	-	-	-	-	-	-	-	-	-	-
	WIND	22	72	77	52	31	42	98	4	30	35	14	117	36	-	-	-	-	-	-	-	-	-	-	-	-	-	-	-	-	-	-	-
LANDISVILLE 2 NW	EVAP	.06	.09	.19	.10	.14	.17	.03	.09	.04	.16	.16	.12	.10	.11	.09	.09	.04	.04	.02	.11	.17	.09	.08	.06	.12	.10	.07	.02	.08	.08	.03	2.85
	WIND	14	46	48	74	37	101	209	64	63	51	82	91	17	36	4	13	39	15	42	147	166	19	37	106	111	67	14	71	105	77	57	2023
PIMPLE HILL	EVAP	.11	.09	.13	.12	.11	.12	.01	.07	.01	.12	.10	*	*	.26	.09	.13	.14	.02	.07	.07	.11	.10	.09	.09	.01	*	*	*	.17	.07	.04	2.45
	WIND	45	68	66	59	59	88	131	39	54	48	73	*	*	118	38	23	100	127	102	191	114	73	78	135	159	150	50	97	150	100	71	2606
STATE COLLEGE	EVAP	-	.11	.17	.10	.11	*	*	.06	.07	.11	.14	.09	.06	.07	.08	.08	.08	.00	.08	.08	.11	.08	.07	.06	.08	.07	.03	.03	.04	.06	.03	B2.22
	WIND	-	34	57	16	16	15	55	15	46	15	52	36	9	7	9	12	36	25	57	89	52	14	12	35	78	50	30	36	80	29	21	B1073

Table 7

SNOWFALL AND SNOW ON GROUND

Station		1	2	3	4	5	6	7	8	9	10	11	12	13	14	15	16	17	18	19	20	21	22	23	24	25	26	27	28	29	30	31
ALLENTOWN WB AIRPORT	SNOWFALL																											T				
	SN ON GND																															
	WTR EQUIV																															
AUSTINBURG 2 W	SNOWFALL																											T	T			
	SN ON GND																															
BEECH CREEK STATION	SNOWFALL																											T	T			
	SN ON GND																											T				
BRADFORD CAA AIRPORT	SNOWFALL																									T	T	T	T			
	SN ON GND																									T	T	T	T			
BRADFORD 4 W RES	SNOWFALL																											.5				
	SN ON GND																															
BROOKVILLE CAA AIRPORT	SNOWFALL																										T	T	T			
	SN ON GND																															
CANTON 1 NW	SNOWFALL																											T	T			
	SN ON GND																											T	T			
CARROLLTOWN 2 SSE	SNOWFALL																											T	1.0			
	SN ON GND																											T	1			
CORRY	SNOWFALL																										T	T				
	SN ON GND																															
DONEGAL	SNOWFALL																											T	T			
	SN ON GND																											T	T			
DU BOIS 7 E	SNOWFALL																											.5				
	SN ON GND																															

See reference notes following Station Index.

Station		Day of month																													
		1	2	3	4	5	6	7	8	9	10	11	12	13	14	15	16	17	18	19	20	21	22	23	24	25	26	27	28	29	30	31
ENGLISH CENTER	SNOWFALL																											T	T			
	SN ON GND																											T	T			
ERIE WB AIRPORT	SNOWFALL																									T	T	1.2				
	SN ON GND																											T	T			
FORD CITY 4 S DAM	SNOWFALL																											.1				
	SN ON GND																											T				
GALETON	SNOWFALL																											1.3	T			
	SN ON GND																											1	T			
HARRISBURG WB AIRPORT	SNOWFALL																											T	T			
	SN ON GND																															
	WTR EQUIV																															
HOOVERSVILLE	SNOWFALL															-	-	-	-	-	-	-	-	-	-	-	-	-	-	-	-	-
	SN ON GND																															
INDIANA 3 SE	SNOWFALL																												.3			
	SN ON GND																												T			
KANE 1 NNE	SNOWFALL																										.5	T				
	SN ON GND																										1	T				
LAWRENCEVILLE 2 S	SNOWFALL																										T	1.2	T			
	SN ON GND																											1				
LEWISTOWN	SNOWFALL																											T				
	SN ON GND																															
MARTINSBURG CAA AIRPORT	SNOWFALL																											.3	T			
	SN ON GND																											T				
MEADVILLE 1 S	SNOWFALL																										T	.1	.3			
	SN ON GND																										T	T	T			
MEDIX RUN	SNOWFALL																											.5	T	T		
	SN ON GND																											T	T			
MONTROSE 1 E	SNOWFALL																										T	.3	.2			
	SN ON GND																											T	T			
MUHLENBURG 1 SE	SNOWFALL																											T				
	SN ON GND																															
NEWPORT	SNOWFALL																												T			
	SN ON GND																															
PHILADELPHIA WB AIRPORT	SNOWFALL																											T				
	SN ON GND																															
	WTR EQUIV																															
PHILADELPHIA CITY	SNOWFALL	-	-	-	-	-	-	-	-	-	-	-	-	-	-	-	-	-	-	-	-	-	-	-	-	-	-	-	-	-	-	-
	SN ON GND	-	-	-	-	-	-	-	-	-	-	-	-	-	-	-	-	-	-	-	-	-	-	-	-	-	-	-	-	-	-	-
PHILIPSBURG CAA AIRPORT	SNOWFALL																										T	T	T			
	SN ON GND																															
PIMPLE HILL	SNOWFALL																				T							T	.3	T		
	SN ON GND																											T	T	T		
PITTSBURGH WB AIRPORT 2	SNOWFALL																										T	1.5	T			
	SN ON GND																															
	WTR EQUIV																															
PLEASANT MOUNT 1 W	SNOWFALL																											T	T	T		
	SN ON GND																											T	T			
SCRANTON WB AIRPORT	SNOWFALL																											T	T			
	SN ON GND																											T	T			
	WTR EQUIV																															
SHIPPINGPORT WB	SNOWFALL																										T	T	T			
	SN ON GND																															
SLIPPERY ROCK	SNOWFALL																												T			
	SN ON GND																												T			
SPRINGS 1 SW	SNOWFALL																											1.0	T			
	SN ON GND																											1	T			
TAMARACK 2 S FIRE TWR	SNOWFALL																											1.0	T			
	SN ON GND																											1				
TIONESTA 2 SE DAM	SNOWFALL																											T				
	SN ON GND																											T				
TOWANDA	SNOWFALL																											.2	.1			
	SN ON GND																											T	T			
WILLIAMSPORT WB AIRPORT	SNOWFALL																											T				
	SN ON GND																											T				
	WTR EQUIV																															

See reference notes following Station Index.

TOTAL PRECIPITATION

PENNSYLVANIA
OCTOBER 1957

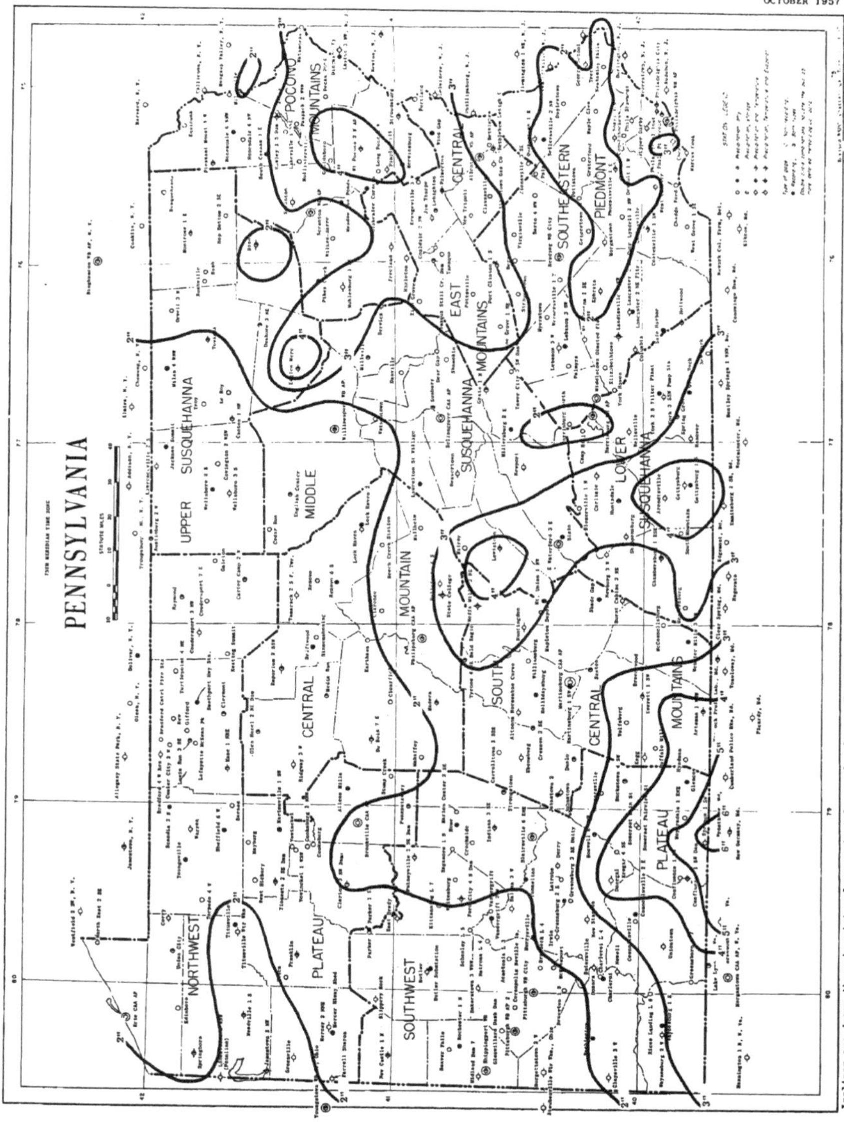

Isolines are drawn through points of approximately equal values. Hourly precipitation data from recorder substations will be available in the publication "Hourly Precipitation Data".

AVERAGE TEMPERATURE

PENNSYLVANIA
OCTOBER 1957

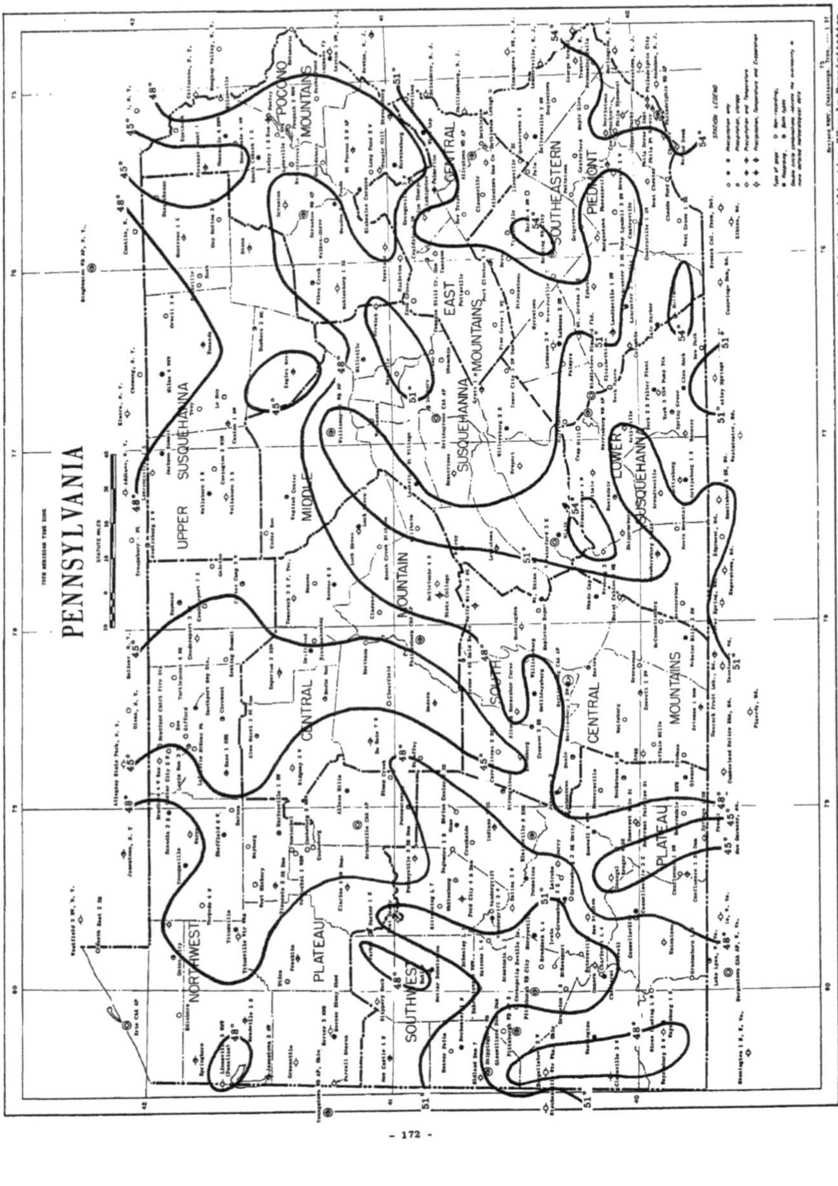

Isolines are drawn through points of approximately equal values. Hourly precipitation data from recorder substations will be available in the publication "Hourly Precipitation Data".

STATION INDEX

Station	Index No.	County	Drainage	Latitude	Longitude	Elevation	Observation Time Temp.	Observation Time Precip.	Observer	Refer To Tables
CMETONIA LOCK 3	0022	ALLEGHENY	1	40 32	79 49	748		7A	CORPS OF ENGINEERS	3
LLENS MILLS	0099	JEFFERSON	1	41 12	78 55	1600		MID	CHARLES H. ALLEN	C
LLENTOWN WB AP	0106	LEHIGH	9	40 39	75 26	376	MID	MID	U.S. WEATHER BUREAU	2 3 5 7 C
LLENTOWN GAS CO	0111	LEHIGH	9	40 36	75 28	254	7A	7A	LEHIGH VLY GAS DIV	2 3 5
LTOONA HORSESHOE CURVE	0134	BLAIR	8	40 30	78 29	1500	6P	6P	ALTOONA WATER BUR.	2 3 5
RENDTSVILLE	0229	ADAMS	15	39 55	77 18	710	8A	8A	PA STATE COL EXP	2 3 5
USTINBURG 2 W	0313	TIOGA	15	42 00	77 32	1590		7A	OTTO D. BACON	3 7 C
AKERSTOWN 3 WNW	0355	ALLEGHENY	1	40 39	79 59	1230	7P	7P	PGH CUT FLOWER CO	2 3 5
ARNES	0409	WARREN	1	41 40	79 02	1310		7A	CORPS OF ENGINEERS	3
ARTO 4 NW	0428	BERKS	14	40 26	75 39	312		7A	MARIE B. NICHLAS	3
EAR GAP	0457	NORTHUMBLAND	15	40 50	76 30	900		3P	ROARING CRK WTR CO	3
EAVER FALLS	0475	BEAVER	2	40 46	80 19	760		7A	HOWARD R. KEMP	3
EAVERTOWN	0482	SNYDER	15	40 45	77 10	640	5P	7A	MARLIN R. ETTINGER	2 3 5
EECH CREEK STATION	0499	CENTRE	16	41 04	77 34	620		7A	HAROLD S. RUPERT	3 7
ELLEFONTE 4 S	0530	CENTRE	16	40 51	77 47	1110	8A	8A	ROCKVIEW PRISON FARM	2 3 5
ERNE	0599	BERKS	14	40 31	76 00	325		7A	FLOYD W. TRUMP	3
ERWICK	0611	COLUMBIA	15	41 04	76 15	570	6P	6P	AMER CAR + FNDRY CO	2 3 5
ETHLEHEM	0629	NORTHAMPTON	9	40 37	75 22	400		7A	ARTHUR CROPPER	3
ETHLEHEM LEHIGH UNIV	0634	NORTHAMPTON	9	40 36	75 23	450	MID	MID	LEHIGH UNIVERSITY	2 3 5 C
LAIN	0725	PERRY	15	40 20	77 31	750		MID	PA DEPT FRST + WTRS	C
LAIRSVILLE 6 ENE	0736	INDIANA	4	40 27	79 09	2048	8P	8P	U.S. WEATHER BUREAU	2 3 5
LAKESLEE CORNERS	0743	MONROE	9	41 06	75 36	1650		MID	WALTER WILDRICK	C
LOSERVILLE 1 N	0763	CUMBERLAND	15	40 16	77 22	650		5P	MRS. B. M. WILLDERS	3
OSWELL 6 WNW	0820	SOMERSET	1	40 10	79 08	2570		8A	CLARK N. ST. CLAIR	3 C
RADDOCK LOCK 2	0861	ALLEGHENY	10	40 24	79 52	725		7A	CORPS OF ENGINEERS	3
RADFORD CAA AIRPORT	0865	MC KEAN	1	41 48	78 38	2150	MID	MID	CIVIL AERO. ADM.	2 3 5 7
BRADFORD CNTRL FIRE STA	0867	MC KEAN	1	41 57	78 39	1500		8A	BRADFORD FIRE DEPT	3
BRADFORD 4 W RES	0868	MC KEAN	1	41 57	78 44	1680	5P	5P	BRADFORD WTR DEPT	2 3 5 7
BREEZEWOOD	0905	BEDFORD	6	40 00	78 14	1352		MID	PA TURNPIKE COMM	3
BROOKVILLE CAA AIRPORT	1002	JEFFERSON	1	41 09	79 06	1417	MID	MID	CIVIL AERO. ADM.	2 3 5 7
BRUCETON 1 S	1033	ALLEGHENY	10	40 18	79 59	1065		7A	AUSTIN R. COOPER	3
BUCKSTOWN 1 SE	1073	SOMERSET	4	40 04	78 50	2460		MID	ALVIN W. MANGES	C
BUFFALO MILLS	1087	BEDFORD	12	39 57	78 39	1318		8A	CLIFFORD C. ADAMS	3
BURGETTSTOWN 2 W	1109	WASHINGTON	11	40 23	80 26	980	7A	7A	SMITH TWP MUN AUTH	2 3 5
BURNT CABINS 2 NE	1115	HUNTINGDON	6	40 05	77 52	990	5P	5P	PA TURNPIKE COMM	2 3 5
BUTLER	1130	BUTLER	2	40 52	79 54	1100	4P	7A	WILLIAM C. FAUST	2 3 5
BUTLER SUBSTATION	1135	BUTLER	2	40 51	79 53	1149		MID	WEST PENN POWER CO	C
CAMP HILL	1198	CUMBERLAND	15	40 15	76 55	461		6P	JOSEPH N. HOBART	3
CANTON 1 NW	1215	BRADFORD	15	41 40	76 52	1520	7A	7A	MRS.MILDRED SPENCER	2 3 5 7 C
CARLISLE	1234	CUMBERLAND	15	40 12	77 11	460	6P	6P	C. E. MILLER	2 3 5
CARROLLTOWN 2 SSE	1255	CAMBRIA	16	40 35	78 42	2040		8A	ROBERT F. MAURER	3 7
CARTER CAMP 2 W	1262	POTTER	16	41 37	77 45	2030		7A	RICHARD L. MENKEN	3 C
CEDAR RUN	1301	LYCOMING	16	41 31	77 27	800		7A	KATHRYN T.KREIGHBAUM	3
CHADDS FORD	1342	DELAWARE	5	39 52	75 37	170		7A	E. EARL TOUCHTON	3
CHAMBERSBURG 1 ESE	1354	FRANKLIN	12	39 56	77 38	640	9P	9P	CHARLES A. BENDER	2 3 5 C
CHARLEROI	1372	WASHINGTON	10	40 08	79 55	1040		MID	WEST PENN POWER CO	C
CHARLEROI LOCK 4	1377	WESTMORELAND	10	40 09	79 54	749		7A	CORPS OF ENGINEERS	3
CHESTER	1423	DELAWARE	5	39 51	75 22	86	8A	8A	CHESTER TIMES	2 3 5
CLARENCE	1480	CENTRE	16	41 03	77 56	1410		7A	MISS VELDA SWANCER	3
CLARION 3 SW	1485	CLARION	1	41 12	79 26	1114	8P	7A	PA ELECTRIC CO	2 3 5 C
CLAUSSVILLE	1505	LEHIGH	9	40 37	75 39	670		8A	WILLIAM J. DOTTERER	3
CLAYSVILLE 3 W	1512	WASHINGTON	11	40 07	80 28	1000	7P	7A	MFGRS. L + H CO	2 3 5
CLEARFIELD	1519	CLEARFIELD	16	41 01	78 26	1100		7A	IRA TAYLOR	3
CLERMONT	1529	MC KEAN	1	41 41	78 30	2104		7A	MRS.TILLIE M.SIMONDS	3 C
COALDALE 2 NW	1572	SCHUYLKILL	9	40 50	75 56	1026		7A	PANTHER VLY WTR CO	3 7
COATESVILLE 1 SW	1589	CHESTER	5	39 58	75 50	342	8A	8A	PHILA ELECTRIC CO	2 3 5 C
COLUMBIA	1675	LANCASTER	15	40 02	76 30	300	5S	5S	JAMES H. RUST	2 3 5
CONFLUENCE 1 SW DAM	1705	SOMERSET	17	39 48	79 22	1490	8A	8A	CORPS OF ENGINEERS	2 3 5 6 C
CONFLUENCE 1 NW	1710	FAYETTE	17	39 50	79 22	1331		7A	JOHN L. REID	3
CONNELLSVILLE	1723	FAYETTE	17	40 01	79 36	870		8A	MARSHALL B. MENEFEE	3
CONNELLSVILLE 2 E	1729	FAYETTE	17	40 01	79 33	1300		MID	HARRY C. JOY	C
CONSHOHOCKEN	1737	MONTGOMERY	5	40 04	75 19	70		8A	PHILA ELECTRIC CO	3
COOKSBURG	1749	CLARION	1	41 20	79 13	1180		8A	PA DEPT FRST + WTRS	3
COOKSBURG 2 NNW	1752	CLARION	1	41 21	79 13	1460		8A	PA DEPT FRST + WTRS	3
CORAOPOLIS NEVILLE IS	1773	ALLEGHENY	11	40 30	80 05	720		8A	PGH. COKE + CHEM CO	3
CORRY	1790	ERIE	1	41 55	79 39	1440	6P	6P	RICHARD T. MOUNTAIN	2 3 5 7
COUDERSPORT 3 NW	1806	POTTER	1	41 49	78 03	2020	7P	8A	MISS ELIZABETH NEFF	2 3 5
COUDERSPORT 7 E	1809	POTTER	1	41 46	77 53	2425		7A	CAMP POTATO	3
COVINGTON 2 WSW	1833	TIOGA	15	41 44	77 07	1745		7A	CALVIN R. PACKARD	3
CREEKSIDE	1881	INDIANA	1	40 41	79 12	1035		7A	CORPS OF ENGINEERS	3
CRESSON 2 SE	1895	CAMBRIA	6	40 27	78 34	2540		7A	MILES M. LINGLE	3 C
CUSTER CITY 2 W	1978	MC KEAN	1	41 55	78 41	2120		8A	W. D. BOOTH AND CO	3
DANVILLE	2013	MONTOUR	15	40 58	76 37	460		7A	MRS.MARIE M. LITTLE	3
DERRY	2108	WESTMORELAND	4	40 20	79 18	1150	6P	6P	MISS M. D. WINEMAN	2 3 5
DEVAULT 1 W	2116	CHESTER	14	40 05	75 33	360	MID	MID	PA TURNPIKE COMM	2 3 5
DINGMANS FERRY	2160	PIKE	5	41 13	74 52	364		MID	CLYDE T. VOORHEES	C
DIXON	2171	WYOMING	15	41 34	75 54	620	7A	7A	HAROLD J. KUSCHEL	2 3 5 C
DONEGAL	2183	WESTMORELAND	17	40 07	79 23	1746	MID	MID	PA TURNPIKE COMM	2 3 5 7
#DONORA	2190	WASHINGTON	10	40 11	79 51	814	12M	12M	DONORA ZINC WORKS	2 3 5
DOYLESTOWN	2221	BUCKS	5	40 18	75 08	393		5P	GEORGE HART	3
DRIFTWOOD	2245	CAMERON	16	41 20	78 08	880		MID	SIDNEY KENNEDY	C
DU BOIS 7 E	2265	CLEARFIELD	16	41 06	78 38	1670	5P	5P	CITY OF DU BOIS	2 3 5 7 C
DUNLO	2298	CAMBRIA	4	40 17	78 43	2410		MID	MRS. D. L. WHITE	C
DUSHORE 3 NE	2324	SULLIVAN	16	41 33	76 21	1750		7A	PATRICK F. RYAN	3 C
EAGLES MERE	2343	SULLIVAN	16	41 24	76 35	2020	7A	7A	MRS.ELSIE P. BIGGER	2 3 5 C
EAST BRADY	2363	CLARION	1	40 59	79 37	820	5P	5P	A. B. KEMPEL	2 3 5
EAST WATERFORD 3 E	2459	PERRY	6	40 21	77 33	2125	8A	8A	U.S. WEATHER BUREAU	INAC 5/55
EBENSBURG	2466	CAMBRIA	4	40 29	78 43	2090	7P	7A	ROBERT A. WASSER	2 3 5
EDINBORO	2514	ERIE	1	41 52	80 08	1220		8A	EDINBORO ST TCHR COL	3
EDINBORO 7 SW	2519	CRAWFORD	1	41 47	80 13	1200		8A	THOMAS H. YOUNG	3
ELIZABETHTOWN	2560	LANCASTER	15	40 09	76 37	460		8A	MASONIC HOME	3
EMPORIUM 2 SSW	2634	CAMERON	16	41 28	78 15	1735	7A	7A	JACKSON THOMAS	2 3 5 C
ENGLISH CENTER	2644	LYCOMING	16	41 26	77 17	881		7A	WILLIAM SUDERS	3 7 C
EPHRATA	2662	LANCASTER	15	40 11	76 10	465	6P	6P	STANLEY L.VON NEIDA	2 3 5
EQUINUNK 2	2671	WAYNE	5	41 51	75 13	910		7A	MRS. HENRIETTA MURRY	3
ERIE WB.AIRPORT	2682	ERIE	8	42 05	80 12	732	MID	MID	U. S. WEATHER BUREAU	2 3 5 7
EVERETT 1 SW	2721	BEDFORD	6	40 00	78 23	1020	MID	MID	PA TURNPIKE COMM	2 3 5 7 C
FARRELL SHARON	2814	MERCER	2	41 14	80 30	865	7P	7P	SHARON STEEL CORP	2 3 5
FORD CITY 4 S DAM	2942	ARMSTRONG	1	40 43	79 30	950	8A	8A	CORPS OF ENGINEERS	2 3 5 6 7 C
FRANKLIN	3028	VENANGO	1	41 23	79 49	987	7P	7A	ROBERT D. RHOADS	2 3 5 C
FREELAND	3056	LUZERNE	15	41 01	75 54	1900	6P	8A	ANDREW B. EVANSHA	2 3 5
GALETON	3130	POTTER	16	41 44	77 39	1325		7A	W. GALE LUSH	3 7
GEIGERTOWN	3189	BERKS	14	40 13	75 50	400		8A	WALTER C. WOLF	3
GEORGE SCHOOL	3200	BUCKS	5	40 13	74 56	135	7P	7P	GEORGE M. HART	2 3 5 7
#GETTYSBURG	3218	ADAMS	12	39 50	77 14	540	9A	9A	HUGH C. MC ILHENNY	2 3 5
GETTYSBURG 1 S	3223	ADAMS	12	39 48	77 14	560		MID	NAT MILITARY PARK	C
GIFFORD	3237	MC KEAN	1	41 51	78 36	2220		8A	SOUTH PENN OIL CO	3
GLENCOE	3298	SOMERSET	12	39 49	78 51	1620		MID	MRS. MARY M.HARTMAN	C
GLEN HAZEL 2 NE DAM	3311	ELK	1	41 34	78 36	1725		8A	CORPS OF ENGINEERS	3 C
GLEN ROCK	3330	YORK	15	39 48	76 44	620		MID	MRS.E.C.MC WILLIAMS	C
GLENWILLARD DASH DAM	3343	ALLEGHENY	11	40 33	80 13	705		7A	CORPS OF ENGINEERS	3
GOULDSBORO	3394	WAYNE	9	41 15	75 27	1890		7A	L. H. EILENBERGER	3
GRATERFORD	3435	MONTGOMERY	14	40 14	75 27	160	7A	7A	CLAUDE K. KULP	2 3 5 7 C
GRATZ 1 N	3438	DAUPHIN	15	40 38	76 43	760	8A	8A	LEE M. LEITZEL	2 3 5 C
GREENSBORO LOCK 7	3503	GREENE	10	39 47	79 55	808		7A	CORPS OF ENGINEERS	3 7
GREENSBURG 2 E	3515	WESTMORELAND	10	40 18	79 31	1225		MID	PA DEPT HIGHWAYS	C
GREENSBURG 3 SE UNITY	3516	WESTMORELAND	10	40 17	79 30	1245		6P	WESTMORELAND WTR CO	3
GREENVILLE	3526	MERCER	2	41 24	80 23	1026	6P	6P	C. EARL MILLER	2 3 5
HANOVER	3662	YORK	15	39 48	76 59	600	8A	8A	HANOVER EVENING SUN	2 3 5 7
#HARRISBURG WB AP	3699	YORK	15	40 13	76 51	335	MID	MID	U.S. WEATHER BUREAU	2 3 5 7 C
HARRISBURG NORTH	3704	DAUPHIN	15	40 18	76 54	323		9A	GEORGE S. BEAL	3
HAWLEY	3758	WAYNE	5	41 29	75 10	880		7A	MRS. KATHERINE BATES	3
HAWLEY 1 S DAM	3761	WAYNE	5	41 28	75 11	1200	7A	7A	PA POWER + LIGHT CO	2 3 5 6 7 C
HOLLIDAYSBURG	4001	BLAIR	6	40 26	78 24	960		MID	JOHN M. RINGLER	C
HOLLISTERVILLE	4008	WAYNE	5	41 23	75 26	1360		8A	PA POWER + LIGHT CO	3
#HOLTWOOD	4019	LANCASTER	15	39 50	76 20	187	MID	8A	PA POWER + LIGHT CO	2 3 5 7 C
HOME	4027	INDIANA	1	40 45	79 06	1220		MID	MRS. EDNA M. BUSH	C
HONESDALE 4 NW	4043	WAYNE	5	41 37	75 19	1410		9A	GEORGE C. WILLIAMS	3
HONESDALE 6 NNW	4044	WAYNE	5	41 39	75 17	1050		MID	FRIEND E. WALTER	C
HONEY BROOK 1 W	4047	CHESTER	5	40 06	75 56	700		7A	S. M. KURTZ	3
HOOVERSVILLE	4058	SOMERSET	4	40 09	78 55	1670		8A	JAMES A. MAHN	3 7
HOP BOTTOM 2 SE	4066	SUSQUEHANNA	15	41 43	75 43	900		7A	JOSEPH J. SANSUSKAS	3
HUNTINGDON	4159	HUNTINGDON	6	40 30	78 01	678	7A	7A	DANIEL I. GROVE	2 3 5
HUNTSDALE	4166	CUMBERLAND	15	40 06	77 18	610		8A	METRO P. DOROSH	3 C
HYNDMAN	4190	BEDFORD	12	39 49	78 43	920		8A	MRS.GERTRUDE M.BURTO	3
INDIANA 3 SE	4214	INDIANA	4	40 36	79 07	1102	7P	7A	CLYMER WATER SVC CO	2 3 5 7 C
IRWIN	4276	WESTMORELAND	10	40 20	79 42	1100	5P	5P	WESTMORELAND WTR CO	2 3 5
JACKSON SUMMIT	4304	TIOGA	15	41 57	77 01	1690		MID	ARCHIE LAIN	C
JAMESTOWN 2 NW	4325	CRAWFORD	2	41 30	80 28	1050	8A	8A	PA DEPT FRST + WTRS	2 3 5 6 C
JIM THORPE	4370	CARBON	9	40 52	75 45	830	5P	5P	HENRY S. HAAK	2 3 5
#JOHNSTOWN	4385	CAMBRIA	4	40 20	78 55	1214	9A	9A	JOHNSTOWN TRIBUNE	2 3 5
JOHNSTOWN 2	4390	CAMBRIA	4	40 19	78 55	1275		MID	CITY OF JOHNSTOWN	C
KANE 1 NNE	4432	MC KEAN	1	41 41	78 48	1750	8A	8A	RUDOLPH A. ANDERSON	2 3 5 7 C
KARTHAUS	4450	CLEARFIELD	16	41 07	78 07	950		7A	JEROME S. HOWE	3
KEATING SUMMIT	4466	POTTER	16	41 41	78 11	1840		7A	EUGENE L. KREITNER	INAC 10/57
KEGG	4481	BEDFORD	6	39 59	78 43	1280	MID	MID	PA TURNPIKE COMM	2 3 5
KITTANNING LOCK 7	4611	ARMSTRONG	1	40 49	79 32	790		VAR	CORPS OF ENGINEERS	3
KREGAR 4 SE	4667	WESTMORELAND	17	40 06	79 14	2530		MID	PA TURNPIKE COMM	3
KRESGEVILLE 3 W	4672	CARBON	9	40 54	75 34	720		7A	CITY OF BETHLEHEM	3
LAFAYETTE MC KEAN PARK	4706	MC KEAN	1	41 48	78 40	2130		7A	ORIN A. BUTTERS	3
LAKEVILLE 1 NNE	4733	WAYNE	5	41 27	75 16	1440		8A	MRS. GLADYS REINEKE	3
LANCASTER 2 NE PUMP STA	4758	LANCASTER	15	40 03	76 17	255	6P	6P	LANCASTER WATER BUR	2 3 5 7
LANCASTER 2 NE FILT PL	4763	LANCASTER	15	40 03	76 17	270		MID	LANCASTER WATER BUR	C
LANDISVILLE 2 NW	4778	LANCASTER	15	40 07	76 26	360	8A	8A	PA STATE COLLEGE	2 3 5 6 C
LATROBE	4832	WESTMORELAND	4	40 19	79 23	1000		MID	WEST PENN POWER CO	INAC 6/56
LAURELTON STATE VILLAGE	4853	UNION	15	40 54	77 13	880		MID	PA DEPT OF WELFARE	C
LAWRENCEVILLE 2 S	4873	TIOGA	15	41 59	77 07	1000	7A	7A	HARRY P. HOWLAND	2 3 5 7
LEBANON 3 W	4891	LEBANON	15	40 20	76 29	460	7A	7A	LEON MILLER	2 3 5
LEBANON 3 SW	4896	LEBANON	15	40 19	76 28	490		MID	THOMAS DONNACHIE	C
LEHIGHTON	4934	CARBON	9	40 50	75 43	580		7A	GOODWIN S. DEFREHN	3 C
LE ROY	4972	BRADFORD	15	41 41	76 43	1040		6P	MRS.DIMMIS M.BAILEY	3
LEWIS RUN 3 SE	4984	MC KEAN	1	41 50	78 39	1740		7A	RUSSELL LINEMAN	3 C
LEWISTOWN	4992	MIFFLIN	6	40 35	77 35	480	7A	7A	AMERICAN VISCOSE CO	2 3 5 7 C
LINESVILLE 5 WNW	5050	CRAWFORD	2	41 41	80 31	1020	7P	8A	MISS RETTA M. CRUMB	2 3 5
LOCK HAVEN	5104	CLINTON	16	41 08	77 27	570	7P	7A	PETER L. STEVENSON	2 3 5
LOCK HAVEN 2	5109	CLINTON	16	41 08	77 27	630		MID	HUGH F. PARKER	C
LONG POND 2 W	5160	MONROE	9	41 03	75 30	1860		7A	THOMAS MECKES	3
LYNCH	5275	FOREST	1	41 36	79 03	1295		7A	CORPS OF ENGINEERS	3
LYNDELL 2 NW	5279	CHESTER	5	40 05	75 46	-		8A	MRS. DOROTHY HARPLE	3
MADERA	5336	CLEARFIELD	16	40 50	78 26	1460	7A	7A	MRS. JULIA J. SNOFF	2 3 5 C
MAHAFFEY	5342	CLEARFIELD	16	40 53	78 44	1280		7A	MISS ELLEN J. MILES	3
MAPLE GLEN	5368	MONTGOMERY	5	40 11	75 11	380		6P	FRANCES E.SCHEIBNER	3
MAPLETON DEPOT	5381	HUNTINGDON	6	40 24	77 56	580		7A	MRS. I. S. BUCHANAN	3
MARCUS HOOK	5390	DELAWARE	5	39 49	75 25	12	MID	MID	SUN OIL CO	2 3 5
MARIENVILLE 1 SW	5400	FOREST	1	41 27	79 09	1700		MID	ROY A. MARKER	C
MARION CENTER 2 SE	5408	INDIANA	1	40 45	79 02	1610		7A	CORPS OF ENGINEERS	3
MARTINSBURG 1 SW	5453	BLAIR	6	40 18	78 20	1360		MID	BLUE MT. CANNERIES	C
MARTINSBURG CAA AP	5454	BLAIR	6	40 18	78 19	1463	MID	MID	CIVIL AERO. ADM.	2 3 5 7
MATAMORAS	5470	PIKE	5	41 22	74 42	439		7A	HARRY BISLAND	3 7
MC CONNELLSBURG	5526	FULTON	12	39 56	78 00	895		7A	MRS. HELEN M. SHIVES	3
MC KEESPORT	5573	ALLEGHENY	10	40 21	79 52	720		8A	NATIONAL TUBE CO	3
MEADOW RUN PONDS	5601	LUZERNE	15	41 13	75 40	1995		MID	GEORGE PEARAGE	C
MEADVILLE 1 S	5606	CRAWFORD	1	41 38	80 10	1065	8A	8A	CITY OF MEADVILLE	2 3 5 7 C
MEDIX RUN	5627	ELK	16	41 17	78 24	1100		7A	MRS.E. M. SNYDER	3 7 C
MERCER 2 NNE	5651	MERCER	2	41 15	80 13	1160	7P	7A	MRS. FRAN. STRUTHERS	2 3 5
MERCER HIWAY SHED	5654	MERCER	2	41 14	80 15	1250		MID	PA DEPT HIGHWAYS	C
MERCERSBURG	5662	FRANKLIN	12	39 50	77 54	605		8A	ROLLIN P. GILBERT	3
MERWINSBURG	5676	MONROE	9	40 58	75 28	970		MID	WILLIAM D. GOULD	C
MEYERSDALE	5684	SOMERSET	17	39 49	79 02	2040		8A	ARTHUR J. POTTER	3
MIDDLETOWN OLMSTED FLD	5703	DAUPHIN	15	40 11	76 46	303	MID	MID	U. S. AIR FORCE	2 3 5
MIDLAND DAM 7	5710	BEAVER	11	40 38	80 28	689	11P	7A	CORPS OF ENGINEERS	2 3 5
MILAN 4 WNW	5732	BRADFORD	15	41 56	76 35	1448		MID	CARL A. MORRIS	C
MILANVILLE	5738	WAYNE	5	41 40	75 04	760		8A	CHARLES W. DAVIS	3
MILLERSBURG 2 E	5775	DAUPHIN	15	40 32	76 56	560		MID	RUSSELL SHEPLEY	C
MILLHEIM	5790	CENTRE	15	40 54	77 29	1090		7A	NEVIN E. BOWERSOX	3
MILLVILLE 2 SW	5817	COLUMBIA	15	41 06	76 34	860		7A	KENNETH LEIGHOW	3 C
MILROY	5825	MIFFLIN	6	40 43	77 35	770		8A	THOMAS C. HARBESON	3
MONTROSE 1 E	5915	SUSQUEHANNA	15	41 50	75 51	1630	7A	7A	WILBER W. HOOPES.JR	2 3 5 7 C
MORGANTOWN	5956	BERKS	15	40 09	75 54	595	MID	MID	PA TURNPIKE COMM	2 3 5
MT GRETNA 2 SE	6028	LANCASTER	15	40 14	76 26	670	MID	MID	PA TURNPIKE COMM	2 3 5
MT POCONO 2 N AP	6055	MONROE	5	41 09	75 22	1915	5P	5P	H. JOHN DAVIS. JR.	2 3 5 C
MOUNT UNION 1 N	6067	MIFFLIN	6	40 24	77 53	820		MID	MT UNION WTR WORKS	C
MUHLENBURG 1 SE	6090	LUZERNE	15	41 13	76 08	1110	6P	6P	THEODORE J. SAMPSON	2 3 5 7
MURRYSVILLE	6111	WESTMORELAND	10	40 26	79 42	903		MID	DAVID C. SHAW	C
MYERSTOWN	6126	LEBANON	14	40 22	76 18	480		8A	MRS.KATHLEEN MANDELL	3
NATRONA LOCK 4	6151	ALLEGHENY	1	40 37	79 43	800		7A	CORPS OF ENGINEERS	3
NEFFS MILLS 3 NE	6174	HUNTINGDON	6	40 40	77 55	900		MID	PA STATE UNIVERSITY	C
NESHAMINY FALLS	6194	BUCKS	5	40 09	74 57	60		MID	PHILA SUB WATER CO	3
NEWBURG 3 W	6225	FRANKLIN	15	40 09	77 37	745	5P	5P	PA TURNPIKE COMM	2 3 5
NEW CASTLE 1 N	6233	LAWRENCE	2	41 01	80 22	825	5P	7A	BAXTER F. JOHNSON	2 3 5 C
NEWELL	6246	FAYETTE	10	40 05	79 54	805	12M	12M	GENERAL CHEMICAL CO	2 3 5
NEW PARK	6289	YORK	15	39 44	76 30	780		6P	CLINTON J. ALLEN	3
NEWPORT	6297	PERRY	6	40 29	77 08	400	7A	7A	MRS. FRANCES K. FRY	2 3 5 7
NEW STANTON	6310	WESTMORELAND	10	40 13	79 36	980	MID	MID	PA TURNPIKE COMM	2 3 5
NEW TRIPOLI	6326	LEHIGH	14	40 41	75 45	570		6P	FRED C. OSWALD	3
NORRISTOWN	6370	MONTGOMERY	14	40 07	75 21	75	MID	8A	GEORGE H. BOONE	2 3 5
NORTH EAST 2 SE	6396	ERIE	8	42 12	79 49	1060		9A	ELLSWORTH WEAVER	3
ORWELL 3 N	6621	BRADFORD	15	41 55	76 16	1620		8A	WILLIAM I. BROWN	3
PALM	6681	MONTGOMERY	14	40 26	75 32	385		8A	FRED C. ESCHBACH	3
#PALMERTON	6689	CARBON	9	40 48	75 37	435	MID	MID	NEW JERSEY ZINC CO	2 3 5 C
PARKER	6721	ARMSTRONG	1	41 05	79 41	1140		7A	LOUIS A. MALARKEY	3
PARKER 1 E	6724	CLARION	1	41 06	79 40	1100		MID	P. M. NEELY	C
PAUPACK 2 WNW	6762	PIKE	5	41 24	75 14	1360		8A	MISS L. VETTERLEIN	3
PECKS POND	6786	PIKE	5	41 17	75 06	1380		9A	MRS. CARRIE NESS	3
#PHIL DREXEL INST OF TEC	6879	PHILADELPHIA	14	39 57	75 11	30	MID	MID	FRANCIS K. DAVIS.JR	2 3 5
PHILADELPHIA WB AP	6889	PHILADELPHIA	5	39 53	75 14	13	MID	MID	U.S. WEATHER BUREAU	2 3 5 7 C
#PHILADELPHIA PT BREEZE	6899	PHILADELPHIA	5	39 55	75 12	32	MID	MID	ATLANTIC REFINING	2 3 5 C
#PHILADELPHIA CITY	6909	PHILADELPHIA	5	39 57	75 09	26	9A	9A	USN HYDROGRAPHIC OFF	2 3 5 7 C
PHILIPSBURG CAA AP	6916	CENTRE	6	40 54	78 05	1918	MID	MID	CIVIL AERO. ADM.	2 3 5 7 C
PHOENIXVILLE 1 E	6927	CHESTER	14	40 07	75 30	105	6P	MID	PHILA SUB WATER CO	2 3 5 C
PIKES CREEK	6939	LUZERNE	15	41 18	76 08	1320		7A	HARRY SHELDON	3 C
PIMPLE HILL	6944	MONROE	9	41 02	75 30	2215	9A	9A	PA DEPT FRST + WTRS	2 3 5 6 7
PINE GROVE 1 NE	6954	SCHUYLKILL	15	40 34	76 22	535		8A	PA POWER + LIGHT CO	3
PITTSBURGH WB AP 2	6993	ALLEGHENY	11	40 30	80 13	1151	MID	MID	U.S. WEATHER BUREAU	2 3 5 7 C
#PITTSBURGH WB CITY	6997	ALLEGHENY	11	40 27	80 00	749	MID	MID	U.S. WEATHER BUREAU	2 3 5 C
PLEASANT MOUNT 1 W	7029	WAYNE	5	41 44	75 27	1800	8A	8A	PA FISH COMM	2 3 5 7 C
PORT CLINTON	7116	SCHUYLKILL	14	40 35	76 02	450	7A	7A	MRS. ADA E. RARICK	2 3 5 C
PORTLAND	7127	NORTHAMPTON	5	40 55	75 06	297		8A	JOINT BRIDGE COMM	INAC 1/56
POTTSVILLE	7161	SCHUYLKILL	14	40 42	76 11	690		8A	LLOYD E. WELLER	3
PUNXSUTAWNEY	7217	JEFFERSON	1	40 57	79 00	1298		MID	JOHN VOLANSKY	C
PUTNEYVILLE 2 SE DAM	7229	ARMSTRONG	1	40 55	79 17	1270	8A	8A	CORPS OF ENGINEERS	2 3 5 C
QUAKERTOWN 1 E	7239	BUCKS	5	40 26	75 20	490	5P	7A	DENNIS K. FLUCK	2 3 5
RAYMOND	7310	POTTER	13	41 52	77 52	2220		7A	MRS. RACHEL LANGAN	3 C
#READING WB CITY	7318	BERKS	14	40 20	75 58	266	MID	MID	U.S. WEATHER BUREAU	2 3 5 7 C
RENOVO	7409	CLINTON	16	41 20	77 46	660		7A	MRS. CAROLINE BAIRD	3
RENOVO 5 S	7410	CLINTON	16	41 14	77 46	2035		MID	C. F. BILLETTE	C
REW	7425	MC KEAN	1	41 54	78 32	2250		8A	HAROLD C. MEALY	3
RICES LANDING L 6	7443	GREENE	10	39 57	80 00	775		7A	CORPS OF ENGINEERS	3
RIDGWAY 3 W	7477	ELK	1	41 25	78 47	1420	7A	7A	BOROUGH OF RIDGWAY	2 3 5
ROCHESTER 1 N	7540	BEAVER	2	40 43	80 18	900		MID	DEQUESNE LIGHT CO	C
RUSH	7694	SUSQUEHANNA	15	41 47	76 03	1000		9A	MISS MAUDE MC CAIN	3
RUSHVILLE	7727	SUSQUEHANNA	15	41 47	76 07	870		7A	CARL KOPATZ	3
SAFE HARBOR	7732	LANCASTER	15	39 55	76 23	270		MID	S.H.WATER POWER CORP	C
SAGAMORE 1 S	7739	INDIANA	1	40 46	79 14	1320		7A	CORPS OF ENGINEERS	3
SALINA 3 W	7782	WESTMORELAND	7	40 31	79 33	1109	6P	6P	MUN AUTH WSTMRLD CO	2 3 5
SAXTON	7846	BEDFORD	6	40 12	78 15	780		8A	MRS.ALVERTA L.HOLMES	3 C
SCANDIA 2 E	7855	WARREN	1	41 55	79 01	2040		MID	DAVID R. ANDERSON	C
SCHENLEY LOCK 5	7863	ARMSTRONG	1	40 41	79 40	783		VAR	CORPS OF ENGINEERS	3
#SCRANTON	7902	LACKAWANNA	15	41 25	75 40	746	7A	7A	U.S. POST OFFICE	2 3 5
SCRANTON WB AIRPORT	7905	LUZERNE	15	41 20	75 44	956	MID	MID	U.S. WEATHER BUREAU	2 3 5 7 C

STATION INDEX

CONTINUED

Station	Index No.	County	Drainage †	Latitude	Longitude	Elevation	Observation Time Temp.	Observation Time Precip.	Observer	Refer To Tables
SELLERSVILLE 2 NW	7938	BUCKS	5	40 23	75 20	530		MID	SELLERSVILLE WTR CO	C
SHADE GAP 2 NE	7965	HUNTINGDON	6	40 12	77 52	920		MID	MRS. HELEN M. PYLE	C
SHAMOKIN	7978	NORTHUMBLAND	15	40 48	76 33	770		8A	ROARING CRK WTR CO	3
SHEFFIELD 6 W	8026	WARREN	1	41 41	79 09	1940		MID	L. N. HANSON	C
SHIPPENSBURG	8073	FRANKLIN	15	40 03	77 32	709	4P	4P	KEITH B. ALLEN	2 3 5 7
SHIPPINGPORT WB	8078	BEAVER	11	40 37	80 26	740	MID	MID	U.S. WEATHER BUREAU	2 3 5 7 C
SINNEMAHONING	8145	CAMERON	16	41 19	78 05	790		7A	MRS.FRANCES CALDWELL	3
SLIPPERY ROCK	8184	BUTLER	2	41 04	80 03	1345	7P	7A	WALTER D. ALBERT	2 3 5 7
SMETHPORT HIGHWAY SHED	8190	MC KEAN	1	41 48	78 27	1510		MID	PA DEPT HIGHWAYS	C
SOMERSET FAIRVIEW ST	8244	SOMERSET	17	40 01	79 03	2140		7A	HOWARD G. PECK	3
SOMERSET MAIN ST	8249	SOMERSET	17	40 01	79 05	2150	6P	6P	DAVID L. GROVE	2 3 5
SOUTH CANAAN 1 NE	8275	WAYNE	5	41 31	75 24	1400		MID	EUGENE M. COOK	C
SOUTH MOUNTAIN	8308	FRANKLIN	12	39 51	77 30	1520		7A	PA DEPT OF HEALTH	3
SPRINGBORO	8359	CRAWFORD	8	41 48	80 23	900	8A	8A	SPRINGBORO BOROUGH	2 3 5 C
SPRING GROVE	8379	YORK	15	39 52	76 52	470		4P	P. H. GLATFELTER CO	3 C
SPRINGS 1 SW	8395	SOMERSET	17	39 44	79 10	2500	8P	8P	ALLEN E. YODER	2 3 5 7
#STATE COLLEGE	8449	CENTRE	16	40 48	77 52	1175	7A	7A	PA STATE COLLEGE	2 3 5 6 CG
STRAUSSTOWN	8570	BERKS	14	40 29	76 11	600		8A	JACOB KLAHR	3
STRONGSTOWN	8589	INDIANA	4	40 33	78 55	1880		MID	HARRY F. BENNETT	C
STROUDSBURG	8596	MONROE	5	40 59	75 12	480	11P	11P	WILLIAM MAGERTY	2 3 5 C
STUMP CREEK	8610	JEFFERSON	1	41 01	78 50	1320		7A	CORPS OF ENGINEERS	3
SUNBURY	8668	NORTHUMBLAND	15	40 51	76 48	440	7A	7A	CHARLES W. BAYLER	2 3 5 C
SUSQUEHANNA	8692	SUSQUEHANNA	15	41 57	75 36	1020		7A	MRS. LAURA A.BENSON	3
SUTERSVILLE	8699	ALLEGHENY	17	40 14	79 48	785		7A	FRANK E. MARSH	3
TAMAQUA	8758	SCHUYLKILL	14	40 48	75 58	830		8A	MRS. MARY L.ROBERTS	3
TAMAQUA 4 N DAM	8763	SCHUYLKILL	14	40 51	75 59	1120		7A	PANTHER VLY WTR CO	3 C
TAMARACK 2 S FIRE TWR	8770	CLINTON	16	41 24	77 51	2220	7A	7A	JAMES E. SWARTZ	2 3 5 7
TIONESTA 2 SE DAM	8873	FOREST	1	41 29	79 26	1200	8A	8A	CORPS OF ENGINEERS	2 3 5 7 C
TITUSVILLE	8885	CRAWFORD	1	41 38	79 40	1550		MID	PA ELECTRIC CO	C
TITUSVILLE WATER WORKS	8888	CRAWFORD	1	41 38	79 42	1220	7P	7P	CITY OF TITUSVILLE	2 3 5
TORPEDO 4 W	8901	WARREN	1	41 47	79 32	1735		7A	MRS. LILY B. GARBER	3
TOWANDA	8905	BRADFORD	15	41 46	76 26	760	7P	7A	MRS. M. O. PARKS	2 3 5 7 C
TOWER CITY 5 SW	8910	DAUPHIN	15	40 31	76 37	745		6P	HARRISBURG WTR DEPT	3 7
TROY	8959	BRADFORD	15	41 47	76 47	1100		7A	JENNIE L. BALLARD	3
TUNNELTON	8989	INDIANA	4	40 27	79 23	890		MID	MRS. MARY E. WEIMER	C
TURTLEPOINT 4 NE	9002	MC KEAN	1	41 54	78 16	1640		7A	ROBERT D. STRAIT	3
TYRONE 4 NE BALD EAGLE	9024	BLAIR	6	40 43	78 12	1020		7A	FREDERICK L. FRIDAY	3 C
UNION CITY	9042	ERIE	1	41 54	79 50	1325		7A	FORREST M. BRALEY	3 C
UNIONTOWN	9050	FAYETTE	10	39 54	79 44	1040	10P	10P	WM. W. MARSTELLER	2 3 5
UPPER DARBY	9074	DELAWARE	5	39 58	75 18	222	7P	7P	PHIL. SUB.TRANS. CO	2 3 5
UTICA	9099	VENANGO	1	41 26	79 57	1030		7A	MRS.FLORENCE MILLER	3
VANDERGRIFT	9128	WESTMORELAND	7	40 36	79 33	800		7A	UNITED ENG+FNDRY CO	3
VANDERGRIFT 2 W	9133	WESTMORELAND	7	40 36	79 34	995		MID	EUGENE R. YOUNG	C
VIRGINVILLE	9196	BERKS	14	40 31	75 52	350		8A	MRS. MARY M. WRIGHT	3
VOWINCKEL	9206	CLARION	1	41 25	79 14	1620		8A	PA DEPT FRST + WTRS	3
VOWINCKEL 1 WSW	9209	CLARION	1	41 24	79 15	1610		8A	PA DEPT FRST + WTRS	3
WARREN	9298	WARREN	1	41 51	79 08	1280	7P	7A	GILBERT H. REIER	2 3 5
WASHINGTON	9312	WASHINGTON	11	40 11	80 14	1200		MID	PA DEPT HIGHWAYS	C
WATSONTOWN	9345	NORTHUMBLAND	16	41 05	76 52	490		9P	WILLIAM BIRD	3
WAYNESBURG 2 W	9362	GREENE	10	39 54	80 13	980	6P	7A	RALPH L. AMOS	2 3 5
WAYNESBURG 1 E	9367	GREENE	10	39 54	80 10	940		MID	SEWAGE DISPOSAL PLT	C
WEBSTER MILLS 3 SW	9380	FULTON	12	39 49	78 05	920		MID	WILLIAM D. COVER	C
WELLSBORO 3 S	9408	TIOGA	16	41 43	77 16	1920	7A	7A	MARION L. SHUMWAY	2 3 5
WELLSBORO 2 E	9412	TIOGA	16	41 45	77 16	1550		MID	MRS. IDA S. MAYNARD	C
WELLSVILLE	9420	YORK	15	40 03	76 57	500	5P	5P	D. D. HOOVER	2 3 5
WERNERSVILLE 1 W	9430	BERKS	14	40 20	76 06	405		8A	CHARLES A. GRUBER	3
WEST CHESTER	9464	CHESTER	5	39 58	75 36	440	8A	8A	DAILY LOCAL NEWS	2 3 5
WEST GROVE 1 E	9503	CHESTER	5	39 49	75 49	440		8A	CONARD-PYLE CO	3
WEST HICKORY	9507	FOREST	1	41 34	79 25	1090		8A	MRS.HELEN F.KINNEAR	3
WHITESBURG	9655	ARMSTRONG	1	40 45	79 24	1530		7A	CORPS OF ENGINEERS	3
WILKES-BARRE	9702	LAZERNE	15	41 15	75 52	610		7A	MRS. MARY G. HIRMAK	3
WILLIAMSBURG	9714	BLAIR	6	40 28	78 12	860		7A	MYRON K. BIDDLE	3
WILLIAMSPORT WB AP	9728	LYCOMING	16	41 15	76 55	527	MID	MID	U.S. WEATHER BUREAU	2 3 5 7 C
WIND GAP	9781	NORTHAMPTON	5	40 51	75 18	740		MID	W. L. TEMPLETON	C
WOLFSBURG	9823	BEDFORD	6	40 03	78 32	1190		7A	WALTER C. RICE	3
YORK 3 SSW PUMP STA	9933	YORK	15	39 55	76 45	390	5P	5P	YORK WATER COMPANY	2 3 5
YORK 2 S FILTER PLANT	9938	YORK	15	39 56	76 44	640		MID	YORK WATER COMPANY	C
YORK HAVEN	9950	YORK	15	40 07	76 43	310		8A	METROPOL EDISON CO	3
YOUNGSVILLE	9966	WARREN	1	41 51	79 20	1225		MID	HENRY CARLETT	C
ZION GROVE	9990	SCHUYLKILL	15	40 54	76 13	940		7A	JAMES D. TEETER	3
ZIONSVILLE 3 SE	9995	LEHIGH	14	40 27	75 27	660		7A	LESLIE HOWATT	3

† 1-ALLEGHENY; 2-BEAVER; 3- 4-CONEMAUGH; 5-DELAWARE; 6-JUNIATA; 7-KISKIMINETAS; 8-LAKE ERIE; 9-LEHIGH; 10-MONONGAHELA; 11-OHIO; 12-POTOMAC; 13-LAKE ONTARIO; 14-SCHUYLKILL; 15-SUSQUEHANNA; 16-WEST BRANCH; 17-YOUGHIOGHENY

REFERENCE NOTES

Additional information regarding the climate of Pennsylvania may be obtained by writing to the State Climatologist at Weather Bureau Airport Station, Harrisburg State Airport, New Cumberland, Pennsylvania, or to any Weather Bureau Office near you.

Figures and letters following the station name, such as 12 SSW, indicate distance in miles and direction from the post office.

Delayed data and corrections will be carried only in the June and December issues of this bulletin.

Monthly and seasonal snowfall and heating degree days for the preceding 12 months will be carried in the June issue of this bulletin.

Stations appearing in the Index, but for which data are not listed in the tables, either are missing or were received too late to be included in this issue.

Divisions, as used in Table 2, became effective with data for September 1956.

Unless otherwise indicated, dimensional units used in this bulletin are: Temperature in °F, precipitation and evaporation in inches, and wind movement in miles. Monthly degree day totals are the sums of the negative departures of average daily temperatures from 65° F.

Evaporation is measured in the standard Weather Bureau type pan of 4 foot diameter unless otherwise shown by footnote following Table 6. Max and Min in Table 6 refer to extremes of temperature of water in pan as recorded during 24 hours ending at time of observation.

Long-term means for full-time stations (those shown in the Station Index as "U. S. Weather Bureau") are based on the period 1921-1950, adjusted to represent observations taken at the present location. Long-term means for all stations except full-time Weather Bureau stations are based on the period 1931-1955.

Water equivalent values published in Table 7 are the water equivalent of snow, sleet or ice on the ground. Samples for obtaining measurements are taken from different points for successive observations; consequently occasional drifting and other causes of local variability in the snowpack result in apparent inconsistencies in the record. Water equivalent of snow on the ground is measured at selected stations when two or more inches of snow are on the ground.

Entries of Snowfall in Tables 2 and 7, and in the seasonal snowfall table, include snow and sleet. Entries of snow on ground include snow, sleet and ice.

Data in Tables 3, 5, and 6 and snowfall in Table 7, when published, are for the 24 hours ending at time of observation. The Station Index lists observation times in the standard of time in local use. During the summer months some observers take the observations on daylight saving time.

Snow on ground in Table 7 is at observation time for all except Weather Bureau and CAA stations. For these stations snow on ground values are at 7:30 a.m., E.S.T.

- \- No record in Tables 3, 6, 7 and the Station Index. No record in Tables 2 and 5, is indicated by no entry. Consult the annual issue of this publication for interpolated monthly precipitation totals.
- And also on a later date or dates.
- Fastest observed one minute wind speed. This station is not equipped with automatic wind instruments.
- +‡ Amount included in following measurement, time distribution unknown.
- // Gage is equipped with a windshield.
- \# Thermometers are generally exposed in a shelter located a few feet above sod-covered ground; however, the reference indicates that the thermometers are exposed in a shelter located on the roof of a building.
- AM Data based on observational day ending before noon.
- B Adjusted to a full month.
- C In the "Refer to Tables" column in the Station Index the letter "C" indicates recorder stations. These stations are processed for special purposes and are published later in "Hourly Precipitation Data".
- D Water equivalent of snowfall wholly or partly estimated, using a ratio of 1 inch water equivalent to every 10 inches of new snowfall.
- G In the "Refer to Tables" column in the Station Index the letter "G" indicates that soil temperatures are published.
- M One or more days of record missing: if average value is entered, less than 10 days record is missing. See Table 3 for detailed daily record. Degree day data, if carried for this station, have been adjusted to represent the value for a full month.
- R Amounts from recording gage (These amounts are essentially accurate but may vary slightly from the amounts to be published later in "Hourly Precipitation Data".)
- SS This entry in time of observation column in Station Index means observation made near sunset.
- T Trace, an amount too small to measure.
- Y Includes total for previous month.
- VAR This entry in time of observation column in Station Index means variable.

Information concerning the history of changes in locations, elevations, exposure etc. of substations through 1955 may be found in the publication "Substation History" for this state, soon to be issued. That publication, when available, may be obtained from the Superintendent of Documents, Government Printing Office, Washington 25, D. C. at a price to be announced. Similar information for regular Weather Bureau stations may be found in the latest issues of Local Climatological Data, Annual for the respective stations, obtained as indicated above, price 15 cents.

Subscription Price: 20 cents per copy, monthly and annual; $2.50 per year. (Yearly subscription includes the Annual Summary). Checks, and money orders should be made payable to the Superintendent of Documents. Remittance and correspondence regarding subscriptions should be sent to the Superintendent of Documents, Government Printing Office, Washington 25, D. C.

WRC., Asheville, N. C. --- 12/9/57 --- 1100

See Page 165 for Soil Temperatures

S

U. S. DEPARTMENT OF COMMERCE
SINCLAIR WEEKS, Secretary
WEATHER BUREAU
F. W. REICHELDERFER, Chief

CLIMATOLOGICAL DATA

PENNSYLVANIA

NOVEMBER 1957
Volume LXII No. 11

ASHEVILLE: 1958

PENNSYLVANIA - NOVEMBER 1957

WEATHER SUMMARY

GENERAL

Damaging winds associated with major storm systems in the Great Lakes area highlighted November weather in Pennsylvania. Precipitation was generally moderate over the eastern half of the State but significant deficiencies continued over much of the western half. Station totals ranged from 1.18 inches at Tamarack 2 S Fire Twr to 5.49 inches at Devault 1 W and the greatest amount for one day was 2.29 inches measured at Pimple Hill on the 15th. Average temperatures were generally slightly above the seasonal level. Temperature extremes ranged from 72° which was recorded at four stations in the Southeastern Piedmont Division to 3° recorded at Coudersport 3 NW.

WEATHER DETAILS

Precipitation occurred rather frequently throughout the month but amounts were generally light except on the 8th-9th and 14th. A major storm system moving through the Great Lakes region the 8th-9th brought near half an inch of precipitation to most of the State, and deposited about 5 inches of snow in the Erie area. Rainy weather on the 14th produced about a quarter of an inch of moisture on the Northwest Plateau and generally better than half an inch elsewhere with totals approaching an inch at many stations east of the Central Mountains. Unseasonably cold weather around the 10th-12th and moderately low temperatures the 22nd-23rd and 26th-27th only partially offset warm periods of the 1st-3rd, 14th-19th, and 28th-29th.

WEATHER EFFECTS

Winter grains showed good growth except during the cold weather of the second week. Corn picking was practically completed by mid-month and many farmers turned their attention to well drilling the latter part of the month in an effort to alleviate water shortages. Ground water levels continued quite low in most areas and stream flow was again deficient.

DESTRUCTIVE STORMS

Winds of 40 to 70 mph lashed the major portion of the State during the afternoon and evening of the 8th as a major storm system moved through the Great Lakes area. Flying glass from broken plate glass windows injured 9 persons. Several buildings were unroofed and many utility lines were snapped.

A second major storm system in the Grea Lakes area on the 19th caused damaging winds over the eastern half of Pennsylvania. Numerous utility lines and poles, trees, and TV antennas were downed, and many house roofs were damaged. Tornadoes associated with this storm system struck in the Palmyra area of Lebanon County and in the Potts- ville area of Schylkill County just after noon causing considerable propert damage but no casualties.

FLOODS

None reported.

J. T. B. Beard, Climatologist
Weather Records Processing Cente
Chattanooga, Tennessee

SPECIAL NOTICE

A survey has indicated that the comprehensive narrative weather story carried in each issue of Climatological Data is of value to only a small number of recipients. This story will be discontinued, therefore, with the January 1958 issue. A table of extremes will be carried each month and a text will be carried whenever unusual and outstanding weather events have occurred. General weather conditions in the U. S. for each month are described in the publications MONTHLY WEATHER REVIEW and the MONTHLY CLIMATOLOGICAL DATA, NATIONAL SUMMARY, either of which may be obtained from the Superintendent of Documents, Government Printing Office, Washington, D. C.

CLIMATOLOGICAL DATA

Temperature													Precipitation									
									No. of Days								Snow, Sleet			No. of Days		
									Max		Min.											
Average Maximum	Average Minimum	Average	Departure From Long Term Means	Highest	Date	Lowest	Date	Degree Days	90° or Above	32° or Below	32° or Below	0° or Below	Total	Departure From Long Term Means	Greatest Day	Date	Total	Max Depth on Ground	Date	.10 or More	.50 or More	1.00 or More
47.4M	32.4M	39.9M	2.2	62	19	17	11+	747	0	0	17	0	3.35	- .44	1.60	15	.8	1	11	5	2	1
49.5	30.3	39.9		65	20	12	27	745	0	1	19	0	1.85		.66	15	T	0		5	1	0
47.8	32.0	39.9	3.4	62	19	11	27	743	0	0	16	0	D 4.66	1.31	1.80	15	.8	1	10	7	3	1
				64	19				0	0		0					.0	0				
46.5	31.5	39.0M		60	19+	16	11	772	0	2	18	0	5.31		2.29	15	.8	T	10+	7	2	2
46.9	28.0	37.5		63	20	10	27	819	0	2	21	0	3.21	- .71	1.29	15	.5	1	26	7	1	1
52.2	35.1	43.7	1.8	70	20	19	27	633	0	0	13	0	D 2.55	- .35	.95	15	.3	0		5	1	0
50.1	33.7	41.9	1.2	68	19	18	27	685	0	0	14	0	2.42	- .79	.83	14	.3	T	11+	6	1	0
51.6	29.8	40.7	- .3	68	19	15	11+	723	0	0	20	0	3.92	.11	1.42	14	.8	1	10	9	2	1
		40.3											3.41				.5					
52.9	34.9	43.9	1.9	70	19	22	13+	626	0	0	14	0	3.28	.21	.91	14	T	0		9	1	0
54.5	35.7	45.1	2.2	71	20	23	13+	589	0	0	13	0	3.64	.64	1.31	15	T	0		8	2	1
54.2	37.9	46.1	1.6	69	19	25	26+	560	0	0	10	0	3.31	.15	1.01	14	T	0		8	3	1
				67	19				0	0		0					T	0				
51.4	34.4	42.9M	1.1	70	19	20	27	656	0	0	14	0	4.56	1.43	1.89	14	T	T	10+	8	2	1
55.2	31.1	43.2	1.4	69	20	17	13	645	0	0	18	0	3.79	.98	1.09	15	.0	0		7	4	1
		44.2											3.72				T					
57.3M	39.8M	48.6M		71	20	25	12+	487	0	0	7	0	3.71		.75	2	.0	0		11	2	0
54.7	34.0	44.4	1.3	71	20	19	12	611	0	0	15	0	2.50	- .74	.82	15	.0	0		7	2	0
54.3	35.8	45.1		68	19	21	11+	592	0	0	13	0	3.31		.50	15	T	0		11	1	0
50.5	35.2	42.9		67	19	21	11	658	0	0	15	0	5.49		1.26	2	1.0	0		9	5	1
53.1	34.8	44.0	.2	69	19	22	11+	623	0	0	15	0	3.17	.43	.72	15	T	0		9	2	0
55.5	35.1	45.3	1.2	69	20	19	13+	583	0	0	13	0	4.23	1.11	.98	2	.0	0		8	3	0
53.2M	33.1M	43.2M		72	19+	24	10+	653	0	0	20	0	3.04	.00	.74	2+	.5	0		8	2	0
53.7	38.2	46.0	.5	68	19	27	27	564	0	0	9	0	2.91	.43	1.20	15				8	2	1
54.9	33.9	44.4	1.1	70	19	19	12+	609	0	0	16	0	2.76	.05	.70	15	T	T	23	10	1	0
53.4	32.8	43.1		70	20	20	12	652	0	0	16	0	2.53		.70	9	2.0	0		7	2	0
53.3	32.0	42.7	- .1	68	20	19	12	662	0	0	17	0	3.72	.71	.93	9	T	0		7	2	0
56.6	42.3	49.5	1.1	70	19	30	11	459	0	0	3	0	3.66	.43	.77	1	T	0		10	4	0
52.8	37.4	45.1	1.5	69	19	23	12	589	0	0	9	0	3.65	.71	1.03	14	.1	0		7	3	1
53.8	34.4	44.1		69	19	22	11+	621	0	0	15	0	2.56		.58	14	T	0		8	2	0
53.0	35.3	44.2		68	19	20	27	617	0	0	14	0	3.32		.83	14	.0	0		7	2	0
55.9	39.4	47.7		72	19	26	13	513	0	0	8	0	3.35		.82	15	T	0		7	4	0
57.3	42.6	50.0		72	19	28	11	446	0	0	2	0	3.56		.67	30	.2	0		10	3	0
55.9	39.6	47.8	1.9	70	19	26	11+	510	0	0	6	0	2.98	- .10	.54	1	T	0		9	2	0
55.7	43.1	49.4	1.7	70	19	30	10+	461	0	0	3	0	3.01		.56	14	T	0		9	2	0
56.1	34.4	45.3	1.1	72	19	18	12+	584	0	0	15	0	3.95	.62	1.03	14	.0	0		8	4	1
53.7	35.4	44.6	3.0	70	19	14	12	604	0	0	13	0	3.23	- .05	1.14	15	.0	0		8	3	1
54.2	39.7	47.0	1.6	71	19	27	13+	534	0	0	7	0	3.07	.02	.92	14	T	0		8	2	0
55.0	38.7	46.9		69	19	25	12+	536	0	0	8	0	3.91		.60	30	T	0		12	3	0
56.3M	37.5	46.9M	3.5	70	20	27	10+	542	0	0	9	0	4.80	1.20	1.76	3				9	4	1
		45.8											3.43				.2					
53.4	33.0	43.2	.3	65	4+	18	12	649	0	0	17	0	3.77	.62	1.78	15	.3	0		8	2	1
54.0	35.7	44.9	3.2	67	19	20	13	598	0	0	13	0	3.17	.02	1.02	15	T	0		11	2	1
52.9	34.4	43.7	1.2	66	19	19	11+	632	0	0	13	0	1.95	- .88	.87	14	.2	0		6	1	0
54.3	36.4	45.4	2.6	68	20	20	12	581	0	0	12	0	3.31	.44	1.15	15	T	0		8	2	1
55.0	35.0	45.0	.0	69	20	22	11	590	0	0	11	0	2.97	.43	.92	9	T	0		8	2	0
52.6	37.2	44.9	.9	70	19	22	12	594	0	0	8	0	2.81	.08	.94	14	T	0		7	1	0
55.9M	35.7M	45.8M		70	3	19	11	569	0	0	10	0	1.37				.0	0				
53.1	35.2	44.2	.8	68	19	20	13	617	0	0	14	0	2.22	- .97	.50	14	T	0		8	1	0
53.2	30.3	41.8		70	19	15	11	688	0	0	18	0	3.31		.67	15	T	0		10	3	0
55.1	35.1	45.1	1.4	70	19	19	12	590	0	0	14	0	3.02	.32	.46	19	T	T	23	10	0	0
		44.4											2.79				.1					
52.2	32.1	42.2		67	19	16	11+	680	0	0	16	0	3.18		.86	20	T	0		6	3	0
53.1	34.6	43.9		70	19	20	12	626	0	0	14	0	2.92		.82	19	T	0		8	2	0
51.9	32.7	42.3		67	19+	20	12	672	0	0	16	0	3.42		1.36	15	T	T	26	8	2	1
53.5	32.5	43.0		68	2+	18	14	653	0	0	17	0	1.64		.68	15	T	0		4	1	0
53.4	31.7	42.6		67	20	18	13+	665	0	0	18	0	3.46	.12	1.22	15	.0	0		6	2	1
53.8	32.4	43.1		68	2+	20	13	650	0	0	16	0	2.91	- .35	.98	15	T	T	26	7	2	0
51.3	33.9	42.6	.9	68	1	21	11+	664	0	0	14	0	3.12	- .14	1.07	14	.2	T	11+	6	3	1
		42.8											2.95				T					
48.4	30.6	39.5		64	20	15	27	759	0	0	18	0	2.01		.75	15	T	T	26	6	1	0
52.9	27.5	40.2		68	20	13	27+	738	0	0	22	0	2.83		1.13	15	T	T	11+	7	2	1
45.8	29.8	37.8		61	20	16	11+	808	0	1	19	0	2.73	- 1.73	.72	9	1.5	1	26	7	1	0
50.6	27.6	39.1	- .2	67	20	12	27	770	0	0	22	0	1.49	- .79	.42	9	T	T	10+	4	0	0

See Reference Notes Following Station Index

TABLE 2 - CONTINUED

Station	
MONTROSE 1 E	AM
TOWANDA	
WELLSBORO 3 S	AM
DIVISION	
CENTRAL MOUNTAINS	
BELLEFONTE 4 S	AM
DU BOIS 7 E	
EMPORIUM 2 SSW	AM
LOCK HAVEN	
MADERA	AM
PHILIPSBURG CAA AP	
RIDGWAY 3 W	AM
STATE COLLEGE	AM
TAMARACK 2 S FIRE TWR	AM
DIVISION	
SOUTH CENTRAL MOUNTAINS	
ALTOONA HORSESHOE CURVE	
BURNT CABINS 2 NE	
EBENSBURG	
EVERETT 1 SW	
HUNTINGDON	AM
JOHNSTOWN	AM
KEGG	
MARTINSBURG CAA AP	
DIVISION	
SOUTHWEST PLATEAU	
BAKERSTOWN 3 WNW	
BLAIRSVILLE 6 ENE	
BURGETTSTOWN 2 W	AM
BUTLER	
CLAYSVILLE 3 W	
CONFLUENCE 1 SW DAM	AM
DERRY	
DONEGAL	
DONORA	
FORD CITY 4 S DAM	AM
INDIANA 3 SE	
IRWIN	
MIDLAND DAM 7	
NEW CASTLE 1 N	
NEWELL	AM
NEW STANTON	
PITTSBURGH WB AP 2	//R
PITTSBURGH WB CITY	R
PUTNEYVILLE 2 SE DAM	AM
SALINA 3 W	
SHIPPINGPORT WB	
SLIPPERY ROCK	
SOMERSET MAIN ST	
SPRINGS 1 SW	
UNIONTOWN	
WAYNESBURG 2 W	
DIVISION	
NORTHWEST PLATEAU	
BRADFORD CAA AP	
BRADFORD 4 W RES	
BROOKVILLE CAA AIRPORT	
CLARION 3 SW	
CORRY	
COUDERSPORT 3 NW	
EAST BRADY	
ERIE WB AIRPORT	
FARRELL SHARON	
FRANKLIN	
GREENVILLE	
JAMESTOWN 2 NW	AM
KANE 1 NNE	AM
LINESVILLE 5 WNW	
MEADVILLE 1 S	AM
MERCER 2 NNE	
SPRINGBORO	AM
TIONESTA 2 SE DAM	AM
TITUSVILLE WATER WORKS	
WARREN	
DIVISION	

See Reference Notes Following Station Index

DAILY PRECIPITATION

PENNSYLVANIA
NOVEMBER 1957

Total	1	2	3	4	5	6	7	8	9	10	11	12	13	14	15	16	17	18	19	20	21	22	23	24	25	26	27	28	29	30	31
2.20					T	.19		.10	.28	.01				.04	.40				.88	.01	T				T	.09			.20		
3.26					.10			.40		T				.91	.01	T		.13	.23				T	T		T		.35	.01	.38	
3.64		.49	.32			.09			.54		T				1.31				.12	.38				T			T		.31	.10	
2.27		.06	.01		.22	.09		.51	.03	.01				.46	.03			.38	.16							.02			.25	.04	
3.77								.03	.32						1.78			.03	.39	.53				.13		T			.30		
1.29							.07		.31	T	.02				.29				.22	.11	.02			T		.06	T		T	.09	
1.20					.05	.27		.18										.06	.02							.01	.01	T		T	
3.21			.09		.06	.16	.02	.18	.30	.10	.08			.08	.68				.61	.19	.02			T		.09	T		.41	.05	
-		.88	.08			-	-	-	-	-	-	-	-	-	-	-	-	-	-	-	-	-	-	-	-	.17			.24	T	
4.04		.23				.37			.47		.02			.54	.76			•	.93										.52	.20	
2.74						.21		.27	.53	.02	T			.11	.41				.91	T	T			T	T	.07		.06	.15	T	
3.18			.06			.05		.01	.67					.01	.78				.45	.86			T	T		T	T		.19		
2.03			T			.01		T	.52	T	T				.49				.51	.42									.03	T	
1.66		.05	.04			.04		.03	.25						.63				.30	.21				.02		.01			.04	.04	
2.77		.21	.03						.55						.79				.30	.18									.49	.07	
2.92		.12				.09		.18	.30	T				.04	.64			.10	.82									.04	.32	.26	
3.01		.58				.11			.43		T				.94				.09	.09				T			T		.26	T	
3.31					.11					T				1.01				.13	.17				T			T		.20	.03	.48	
2.23					.31	.02		.30	T	.01				.21	.08			.36	.21	T				T		.11			.23	.10	
2.24						.13		.83						.50	.35			.13	T				T			T		.10	.10		
2.43						.55		.03	.49	T				.01	.43				.46	.03				T	.01	.08		T	.17	.03	
1.73						.24		.08	.23	T				.02	.28				.70	.05						.04			.09		
2.85		.25	T		.15	.06		.36	.01	.24			.01	.29		T	T	.10	.27	.01	T	T	T	.05	.03	.01		.03	.64	.07	
2.84		T	.20		.09	.18	T	.06	.37	.17	.10			.03	.53		.01	.01	.44	.09				.09	T	.07	T		.40	T	
4.14								.48	.05	.82				.21	.45			.07	.57	T				.09		.08		T	.51		
1.85		.03			.14			.52		.03				.66				.38	.07											.02	
2.08		.09			.21	T		.31	T	.02			.05	.45				.34	.36	T	T	T		.05	.04	.03		.02	.08	.03	
1.97						.42		.07					.01	T	.26				1.05							T			.16		
1.35						.09		.01	.26						.50				.22	.15									.10		
2.91						.23		.36	.03					.10	.42				1.45							.02			.30		
1.81					T	.13		.40						.41	.50			.10					T					.10	.07		
2.05					.05	.12		.43	.15		T				.06				1.03	T				T		.02			.19		
2.78		.50						.30	.12					.35	.53			.10	.43				T					.15	.05	.03	
2.01		.01				.12		T	.44		T				.75				.26	.31				T		T			T	.11	
3.17						.13		.43	.13					.30	1.02			.11	.34				T					.06	.10	.10	
2.08		.04				.29		.04	.41	.01	T			.01	.27		T	.01	.41	.01	T			T	T	.05		T	.30	.10	
1.85		T				.05		T	.30	.10	.06			T	.44				.40	.13				T	T	T	T		T	.17	
2.02		.01	.05			.03		T	.35	T	T				.40				.50	.20	T	T			.05	.01	T		.02	.20	
3.96		.83	.41			.20		.01	.47						1.00			.01	.23	.49									.21	.10	
1.95								.43						.87	T			.11	.17				.04	.20				.10	.06		
2.28						.40		.05	.36					T	.36				.90	.05						.01			.15	T	
3.71		.79	.25			.16		.17	.37					T	.64				.49	.31		T		.24		T		T	.16	.17	
2.20		.20	T			.15		.05	.45	.05					.50				.50	.05	T			.05		.05			.10	.09	
2.43			.01			.19		.17	.42		.01			.02	.63				.09	.05				.04	T	.07	T	T	.17	T	
3.00			.12						.66						.70				.45	.12									.43	.05	
2.18						.23		.18	.02					.03	.41				1.12							T			.19		
1.51		.02	.08			.06		.08	.32	T	.03			T	.26				.43	.06				T	.01	.04		T	.07	.03	
2.67		.03	.22						.53	.12	.05			.02	.53		T		.32	.05	.04	T		.05	.02	.06	.03		.56	.04	
4.87		.24	.05			.20			1.05					.03	1.61				.43	.62									.55	.09	
2.50		.56	.03			.19		T	.22						.82			T	.30	.19									.17	.02	
3.31		.28				.23		.28	.19					.38	.50			.28	.34				.11					.06	.12	.06	
1.60		T	.04			.32		.03	.20	T				T	.31				.40	.04						T		T	.22	.04	
1.80			.01			.40		T	.30	T				T	.37				.37	.04					T	T			.30	.01	
1.53						.36		.02	.33					T	.15				.34	.05						.01			.25	.02	
4.84		1.33							.49						1.10			.05	.22	.74								.10	.12		
2.65			.09			.15	T	.14	.47	.04	.04	T		.03	.66	T			.52	.06	T			T	.01	.08	T	T	.36	T	
2.46			.07			.14	T	.25	.34	.02	.02	T		.04	.69	T	T		.62	T	T			T		.01	T	T	.26	T	
1.49						.17								.06	.23				.97										.06		
4.12					.07	.07		.67	.04	1.14	.04			.14	.12			.09	.32					.16	T	.16		.32	.66	.09	
1.70					.02			.01	.37	.08	.10			T	.33				.15	.17	T			.04		T	.05		.09	.12	
-		.04		.01				T	T	.08	.08	T			-				.33	.13	T			.04	.04	.03	-	-	-	-	
1.38		.07		T		.12			.37	T	T				.35				.20	.13						.01			T	.10	
2.16						.20		.10	.45					.02	.48				.63										.28		
1.98		.04	.08			.24		.04	.45	.02	.03			T	.36				.33	.19	T					.04		T	.12	.04	
3.47		T	.39			.24		.02	.33	.41	.06			.02	.65				.38	.12				.11		.10			.50	.04	
2.66		.05				.20			.37						.80				.33	.52									.21	.18	
1.99		.10			.31	.07		.37						.17				.31	.23										.33	T	
5.49	.87	1.26			.22	.02		.26	.05					.82	.02			.29	.57				.02					.22		.87	
2.83		.13	.04			.05			.56	T	T				1.13				.29	.37						T			.15	.11	
1.60		T	T					.30	T				T	.20				.35	T					T						.31	
1.82		T				.31		.27	T	T				•	.24			.37	.51						T	T		T	.12	T	
3.90	.25	.57	.55			.13		.01		T				.31	.59			.04	.73				.03					.02	.08	.61	
1.68		.02	.01		.05	.05		.25	T	.02				.53	.21	T		.14	.11		T			.05		.05			.19	T	
2.94	.14	.05	.02		.03	.12		T	.59	T	T				.72				.24	.60				T	T				.38	.05	
2.73			.03					.05	.72	T	.02				.39		.02		.44	.43		T			T	.01			.32	.11	
1.85								.43		.03	.01			.30	.29			.23	.45							.01					
1.78			.20			.27		T	.25	T	T			T	.24				.35							.07		T	.30	.10	
3.45			.01			.37		.28	.13	.75	.01			.04	.38	.01			.37		T	T	T	.09		.10	.01		.90		
	RECORD MISSING																														
2.87		.34	.01						.65						.57			.01	.34	.31			T	.05		T			.29	.03	
1.66		T	T			.09		.02	.25	.07	.04			.01	.39				.44	.12	T			.04	T	.07	T		.05	.06	
2.62		.22	.01			.04		T	.70	T	T				1.07				.36	.17						T			.04	.01	
3.17	.03	.32				.22		.04	.60					.20	.72			.25	.30				T					.09	.20	.20	
2.82		.06	.01			.01			.36	.02					1.05				.53	.46						.06			.23	.03	
2.26								.26	.37	.04			.01	.26		T		.03	.25	T	.08	.02	T	.09	.18	.01		.18	.35	.02	
2.14					.12			1.01						.73				.23										.05			
2.08					.03	.02		.41		T			.03	•	.44			.15	.28		T					.06		.22	.42	.02	
1.86			.03			.13		.10	.32	T	T			.03	.30				.66	T						.07			.22	T	
3.20	.02							.28	.85	.03	T			.05	.43				.70	.03				.01		.09			.52		
3.35								T	T		.07				1.60				.30	.85						.03			.32	.14	
1.50		.05	T			.05	T	T	.43	.08	.03			T	.35				.35	.07	T	T	T	T	T	.04	T		T	.05	
3.16		1.35				.25			.26						.75			T	.22	.11				.08					.14		
4.23		.98	.22			.20			.30						.91				.24	.28				.07					.09	.94	
3.31		.12				.11		.02	.72						1.15			.01	.38	.49				.10		T			.21	T	
3.46			.21					T	.62	.26					.70				.30	.10	T			.05	T	.05	.03		.85	.06	
1.92		.03	.22		.08	.05		.02	.18	.10	.05			.01	.50		.02	.35	.08	T	.02	T		.02		.07	.02		.09	.01	
2.56					.01	.19		.28	.11	T				.11	.48				1.14	.01						.04			.19		
3.52		.27	.04			.07			.67		T				1.33				.18	.51						.05			.33	.07	
3.04		.74	.23			.22			.24						.74			.01	.23	.37				.09					.17		
3.42		.16	.09					T	.40	T					1.36				.12	.50						T			.22	.17	
1.79						.31		.03	.34					T	.21				.49	.04						T		T	.37	T	
1.77		T	.02		.29	T		.26	T					.21				.41	.39							.02		.01	.16	T	
2.47					.14	.12		.51	T	.10			.05	.29	.13	.02		.10	.26							.04		.31	.40	T	
2.97		.24	.02			.23		T	.92						.65			T	.30	.17				.12					.32	T	
2.81	.44	.02	T					.48		T				.94	T			.14	.33				T	T		T		.17	.02	.07	
2.85		.35	T			.28		T	.44						.85			T	.28	.33				T		T			.25	.07	
2.18		.25	.01			.02			.43	T	.01				.05				.36	.24						.09	T		.11	.05	
1.85		.29							.39						.66				.31	.12						T			.08		
2.09		.12	.02			.09		T	.44	T	T				.48				.19	.45					T	T	T		.16	.13	
2.91		.52	T			.18		.02	.22						1.20			T	.30	.10				.07		T			.19	.11	
2.26		.06	T			.02			.43	T					.84			T	.49	.40					T	.02				T	
2.25		.56	.03			.24			.10						.64		T	.01	.23	.08				.11					.12	.04	
D 1.39						.46		.04	.14	.02				.22	T		T		.49			T							D.02		
2.22		.31	T			.07					T				.54				.01	.43	.55	T	.17	.14		T					
1.82		.03				0		.08	.14						.64				.48	.24									.06	.05	

See Reference Notes Following Station Index

DAILY PRECIPITATION

Table 3—Continued

Station	Total	1	2	3	4	5	6	7	8	9	10	11	12	13	14	15	16	17	18	19	20	21	22	23	24	25	26	27	28	29	30	31
HUNTSDALE	2.57		.30	.01			.19		T	.30		T				1.18			T	.13	.32				T					.14		
HYNDMAN	1.58	.02	.02				.10		.03	.35					.04	.55			.01	.25	.09		T	T	.01					.11	T	
INDIANA 3 SE	1.78		T	.10			.18		.04	.21	T	T			T	.26				.54	.18						.04			.23		
IRWIN	2.37					.23	.04		.41						.21				.65	.68							.01			.14		
JAMESTOWN 2 NW	2.44						.26		.30	.08	.06				.15	.25				.35		T					.09			.90		
JIM THORPE	-		.42			T	.09		.04	.89	T				.07	1.98			.03	.80			-	-	-	-	-	-	-	-	-	
JOHNSTOWN	1.98		.05	.06		.08	.34		.08	.29					T	.32				.41	T						.09		T	.21	.05	
KANE 1 NNE	3.57		T	.41	T	.05	.10		.07	.51	.26	.11			.04	.83				.46	.05	.03	T	T	.04	T	.10	.02		.42	.07	
KARTHAUS	1.46		.08	T			.08	T	.02	.32	T	T			T	.28		T		.38	.13	T	T		.03	T	.02	T		.09	.05	
KEGG	1.19	T	.05			.08	T		.19					T	.39				.28	.10							T				.10	
KITTANNING LOCK 7	1.89			.02		T	.14		.18	.25	T	T			.03	.47				.57	T				.02	T	.02		T	.10		
KREGAR 4 SE	2.32		.15		T	.50	T		.40	.02	T			T	.50				.30	.12	T	T			T	T	T		.06	.14	.13	
KRESGEVILLE 3 W	4.68		.30	.03			.11			1.20		.07				1.90				.44	.26									.39		
LAFAYETTE MC KEAN PARK		RECORD MISSING																														
LAKEVILLE 1 NNE	2.36		.26				.01		T	.38					T	.58				.49	.28						T			.14	.22	
LANCASTER 2 NE PUMP STA	2.76	.04	.30				.20		.01	.37					.13	.70			.12	.48				.10			T		.04	.15	.12	
LANDISVILLE 2 NW	2.53		.18				.24		.02	.70						.67			.05	.28	.12				.06					.21		
LAWRENCEVILLE 2 S	1.49		.09	.08		T	.03			.42	T	T				.30				.28	.20						T				.09	
LEBANON 3 W	3.72		.38	.01			.30		.01	.93						.87				.38	.46				.05					.31		
LEHIGHTON	4.50		.37	.04			.11		T	1.24		T				1.58				.48	.21				T		T	T		.32	.15	
LE ROY	2.67		.16		.17					.80	T					.74	.08			.63									T	.01	.08	
LEWIS RUN 3 SE	3.48			.24		.09	.17	T	.04	.39	.23	.05			.13	.54		.01		.33	.13	.10	T	.10	.08	T	.08	T		.71	.06	
LEWISTOWN	1.84		.02				.02		T	.39						.68				.32	.14						T			.03	.04	
LINESVILLE 5 WNW	2.95						.33		.30	.07	.51	.06			.10	.56				.22		.04	T	T	T		.08			.68		
LOCK HAVEN	1.80		.01	.01			.02		.01	.39	T	T				.53				.43	.35	T			T	T	T			.03	.02	
LONG POND 2 W	4.74		.32				.11			.98	T	.03				2.16				.34	.43						.02	T		.22	.13	
LYNCH	3.51			.07		.03	.20	.03	.14	.44	.30				.10	.70				.65	.24	.01			T		.11			.45	.04	
LYNDELL 2 NW		RECORD MISSING																														
MADERA	1.76		.10	.12			.17		.08	.28		T			T	.26				.36	.22						.08			.09	.02	
MAHAFFEY	1.59			.02			.12		.08	.27	T	T			.04	.41		T		.45	.07	T	T	T	.02	T	.09			.04		
MAPLE GLEN	3.86	.27	.46	.38			.20		.01	.32						1.06				.20	.79				.08			T		.08	.01	
MAPLETON DEPOT	1.75		.04	.02			.14		.02	.28	T	T				.60				.30	.31									.02	.02	
MARCUS HOOK	3.66	.77	.13	T		.16	.02		.25						.61				.54	.35		T		.16	T		T		.15		.52	
MARION CENTER 2 SE	2.00		.01	.11	T	.01	.19		.04	.31	.01	T			.02	.35				.55	.10	T			.05	.03	.08	.01		.13	T	
MARTINSBURG CAA AP	1.38	T	.06	T	T	.09			.21	T	T				.42			T	.42	.06					T	T	T		T	.02	.10	
MATAMORAS	2.33		.26	.12						.50						.74				.14	.17						T			.32	.08	
MC CONNELLSBURG	2.22		.07				.13		.03	.54	T					.60		.02	.13	.43				T	T					.18	T	
MC KEESPORT	1.53			T			.21	.02	.07	.18					T	.25				.71	T						.02			.07		
MEADVILLE 1 S	2.70				T	T	.22		.32	.17	.14	.08			.07	.24	T	T		.29	T	T	T	T	.01	T	.10		T	1.06		
MEDIX RUN	1.80		.01	T		T	.10		.03	.23	.02	T			T	.74				.20	.04	T	T	T	.01	T	.04	T	T	T	.09	
MERCER 2 NNE	2.98						.32		.36	.55	T				.13	.45				.54							T			.63		
MERCERSBURG	2.70		.15				.18		.05	.63						.90			.07	.55	.05				.02					.10		
MEYERSDALE	1.45		.08	.01			.27		.03	.19	.03					.40				.21	.01		.01							.18	.02	
MIDDLETOWN OLMSTED FLD	3.85	.80	.01			.26			.60						1.03	T			.21		.46			.02			T		.16	.06	.04	
MIDLAND DAM 7	2.93						.23		.35	.27					.11	.40				1.09	T	T					.04			.35		
MILANVILLE	2.53	.02	.13	.05	T		.04			.41		T				.74				.54	.32						T			.25	.03	
MILLHEIM	2.46		.02				.15		.01	.53	T	T				.81			T	.32	.38	T			T	T	T	T	T	.18	.06	
MILLVILLE 2 SW	2.77		.10	T			.15		T	.41	T	.01				.78				.34	.70		T				T			.19	.09	
MILROY	2.36		.02	T			.14		.02	.45	.04	.01				.92				.43	.15				T		T	T		.17	.01	
MONTROSE 1 E	2.56		.09	.04	.01	T	.09			.33	T	T				1.01				.45	.35					T	.02	T		.12	.05	
MORGANTOWN	2.56	.86	.03			.19			.26						.58				.14	.11				.10			T		.06	T	.23	
MT GRETNA 2 SE	3.32	.31	.02			.30			.65						.83				.28	.35				.02			.04		.38	.05	.09	
MT POCONO 2 N AP	D 4.66		.33		T	.02				.54	D.08				.42	1.80			.08	.62								T	.06	.36	.35	
MUHLENBURG 1 SE	-		.05			.03				.53					.08	1.01		T	.24	.53							-	-	-	-	-	
MYERSTOWN	-		.23				.28			.79						-			T	.29	.23				.05					.37		
NATRONA LOCK 4	1.80			.01		T	.19		.08	.27	T	T			T	.47				.67	.03						.03					
NESHAMINY FALLS	3.64	.73	.41			.11	T		.26						.50	.15			.41	.23				.11			T		.12		.61	
NEWBURG 3 W	1.37		.01				.14		.61						-	-			-	.41									.20			
NEW CASTLE 1 N	2.58					T	.24		.50	.66						.19				.54	T	T	T				.10		T	.35		
NEWELL	2.23					.03	.28		.09			.45			.12	.10				1.02	.03						.02			.09		
NEW PARK	4.12	.10	.59			T	.16		.25	.60					.35	.87			.13	.38				.11			T		.19	.08	.35	
NEWPORT	3.46		.08				.28		T	.95						1.22				.28	.44									.16	.03	
NEW STANTON	1.64		.02			.36			.31	.01	T			.01	.23				.33	.26	T					T	.01		T	.08	.02	
NEW TRIPOLI	4.82	.21	.22			T	.16		.24	.97					.59	.92		T	.09	.58					T				.38	.17	.29	
NORRISTOWN	3.35		.68	.51			.20		T	.22						.82			.05	.17	.55				.07					.09	.01	
NORTH EAST 2 SE	2.88					.04	.13		.11	.11	.43	.02			T	.27	.01			.34	.09	.11	.02	.12			.26			.82		
ORWELL 3 N	1.71		.12	.16	.02	.03	.14			.26	T					.17				.44	.14	T	T							.02	.21	
PALM	3.56		.88	.40			.15			.40						.09				.24	.12									.34	.08	
PALMERTON	4.56	.20	.05			.11			.91		T				1.89	.02			.25	.47							T		.38	.02	.26	
PARKER	2.65					T	.04		.47	.23	.02	.01			.04	.62				.89	.03	T			T		.03			.27	T	
PAUPACK 2 WNW	2.18		.32	.03			.05			.56						.85				.02	.17						.02			.08	.08	
PECKS POND	4.03		.31	.01			.01			1.02	T	T				1.54				.39	.19						.01			.30	.25	
PHIL DREXEL INST OF TEC	3.56	.57	.41			.15			.30						.58				.30	.20		T	T	.20			T		.18		.67	
PHILADELPHIA WB AP R	2.98	.54	.37			.21	.01		.25		T				.50	T			.26	.08		T	T	.20	T		T		.14	T	.42	
PHILADELPHIA PT BREEZE	3.01	.48	.39			.18	.01		.21						.56				.26	.09				.18					.13		.52	
PHILIPSBURG CAA AP	2.72	T	.05	.03	T	.24	T		.61	T	T	.01		T	1.01		T		.34	.21	.01	T			T	.01	.03		T	.15	.02	
PHOENIXVILLE 1 E	3.95	.65	.77			.25			.17						1.03				.28					.07					.14		.39	
PIKES CREEK	3.32		.15			T	.07		T	.43	T	T				1.27				.56	.39					T	T	T	T	.35	.10	
PIMPLE HILL	5.31		.26	T	T	T	.09		T	1.20	T	.02			T	2.29				.46	.29		T	T	T	T	.02	T		.43	.25	
PINE GROVE 1 NE	4.09		.18				.13			.84		T				1.37			T	.56	.45									.48	.08	
PITTSBURGH WB AP 2 //R	2.50			T	T	.24			.33	T	T			.05	.52				.98	.13	T		T		T	.06	.03		.04	.10	.02	
PITTSBURGH WB CITY R	1.80		T			.17			.33	T					.39				.50	.19	T				T	.06	T		.08	.08		
PLEASANT MOUNT 1 W	3.21		T	T	.01	T	.10			.40	.02	T				1.29				.44	.43		T			T	.03	T		.21	.28	
PORT CLINTON	3.79		.30	.07			.21			.80						1.09				.51	.05									.60	.16	
POTTSVILLE	4.60		.13	.03			.17			.89		T				1.76				.55	.50	.02						T		.49	.06	
PUTNEYVILLE 2 SE DAM	1.92			.03			.20		.08	.31	T	T			.03	.56				.56					.01		.05			.09	T	
QUAKERTOWN 1 E	3.23		.70	.64			.11			.24		T				1.14				.13	.11			.05					T	.01	.10	
RAYMOND	1.78			.08		.02	.06			.10	.30	.12				.40				.25	.12				.03		.06	.03			.21	
READING WB CITY R	3.07	.47	.03			.19			.53		T				.92				.20	.16				.03					.31	.01	.22	
RENOVO	1.80		.10			T	.13			.35	T	.02				.58				.35	.09				T	.02	T			.04	.12	
REW	2.60		T	.13	T	.06	.16		T	.45	.20	.17			.02	.51				.29	.09	T	T		.04	T	.05	.02		.39	.02	
RICES LANDING L 6	2.18						.30		.04	.34					T	.19				1.15	.02						T			.14		
RIDGWAY 3 W	2.22			.12		.04	.12	T	.03	.33	.06	.05			.03	.59	T			.31	.11				.02	T	.08	T		.13	.20	
RUSH	2.48		.45			T	.17			.32	T	T				.49				.42	.44						.01			.10	.08	
RUSHVILLE	2.30		.26	.12		.02	.10			.33		.02				.28				.31	.85						T			.06	.04	
SAGAMORE 1 S	2.25					T			T	.20					.10	1.25				.60	T				T	T					.10	
SALINA 3 W	2.30		.03	T	.01	.20	.01	T	.35	.04					.30	.24			.40	.49							.05			.16	.02	
SAXTON	1.70		.05	T	T			.08	.03	.41	T	T			T	.65			T	.29	.11	T					T		T	.09	.01	
SCHENLEY LOCK 5	2.02			.03			.20		.18	.20					.03	.49				.67	.01				T		.03			.18		
SCRANTON	D 2.55		.04	.01			.05			.46						.95				.31	.34						D.03			.36		
SCRANTON WB AIRPORT	2.42	.03	.05	T	T	.04	T		.46	T	T				.83				.18	.43			T			T	T		.16	.08	.18	
SHAMOKIN	3.14		.14		.05		.31			.36						.95				.22	.60									.42		
SHIPPENSBURG	2.22		.19			.03			.30	.45					.50	.18			.11	.26		T		T					.12	.08	T	
SHIPPINGPORT WB	2.80					.17			.34					.03	.72				1.03	.11						.05			.14	.21	T	
SINNEMAHONING	1.79		.01	T		T	.15	T	T	.44	.01	.01				.58		T		.27	.09	T	T		T	T	.02	T		T	.21	
SLIPPERY ROCK	2.22						.16		.22	.42	T	.01			.07	.31				.72							.05			.26		
SOMERSET FAIRVIEW ST	1.64		T	.05			.14		.01	.35	T					.23				.31	.04					T	.03		T	.28	T	
SOMERSET MAIN ST	1.64		.05			.10	.05		.38		T				.41	.01			.20	.12							.01		T	.27	.04	
SOUTH MOUNTAIN	3.37		.16				.25		.04	.38					T	1.25	.03		.04	.16	.66				.10		T			.30		
SPRINGBORO	D 3.28					T	T		.47	T	D.55	D.20			.18	.65	T	T		.20		T		T	T		T		.15	.78	D.10	
SPRING GROVE	2.88	.01	.32				.28		.05	.72					.21	.43			.10	.41				.12			T		.06	.15	.02	
SPRINGS 1 SW	1.81		.03			.30	T		.25						.45	.05			.18	.09	T	T				T				.38	.08	
STATE COLLEGE	1.65		.03	.02		T	.05		.02	.14	T	T				.62			T	.35	.16	T			T	T	T			.17	.09	
STRAUSSTOWN	3.69		.34	.02			.28		.02	.66						1.12				.41	.29						T			.48	.07	
STROUDSBURG	3.92	.26	.27	T		.05	T		.58	T	.03				1.42	.10		T	.20	.35	T	T	T	T	T		T		.25	.03	.38	

See Reference Notes Following Station Index

le 3—Continued

DAILY PRECIPITATION

PENNSYLVANIA
NOVEMBER 1957

Station	Total	1	2	3	4	5	6	7	8	9	10	11	12	13	14	15	16	17	18	19	20	21	22	23	24	25	26	27	28	29	30	31
MP CREEK	1.87		.02	.07			.13		.03	.27	T				.05	.60		T		.37	.15					T	.02			.13	.03	.
BURY	2.01		.04				.15		T	.58		T				.98				.41	.46		T			T	T			.19	.10	.
QUEMANNA	2.02		.08	T	.03	.02	.04			.52	.03	T				.92				.28	.32					T	.07	T		.20	.16	.
ERSVILLE	-						.12		.10	.26					T	-				.90							T			.23		.
AQUA	4.48		.24	.06			.25			.88						1.45				.40	--									.48	.15	.
AQUA 4 N	3.25					.09	.25									2.23														.06		.
ARACK 2 S FIRE TWR	1.18		.04	.01		T	.10			.38	.02	.05				.20							T	T			.07	T		.05	.07	.
NESTA 2 SE DAM	3.79			T	T	.01	.09		.29	.07	.04	T			.05	.76				1...	...		T	T	.01		.06		T	.70	T	.
USVILLE WATER WORKS	3.41			T	T	.22	.03	.01	1.01	.03	.08			T	.26	.22	T		.20	.47	T	T	.01		T		.09		.1	.60	.02	.
PEDO 4 W	3.86					.11	.17		.21	.54	.20	.19			.03	.32							T	T	.08	T	.12	T		1.01	.04	.
ANDA	1.40		.13	.00	T	T	.11			.30	T	.01				.29		T								T	.02	T		T	.03	.
ER CITY	3.44		.26			.10	.30		.11	.54					.88	1.40			.20										.3	.24	.20	.
Y	2.08		.10	.03		T	.17			.63	T	.03				.50											.02			.02	.10	.
TLEPOINT 4 NE	2.15		.03	.12		.02	.20		.03	.42	.18	.17			.01	.42									.04		.04	.		.02	.17	.
ONE 4 NE BALD EAGLE	2.10		.06	.05			.04		.03	.50	T	T				.59										T	T			.10	.10	.
ON CI		ECOR MISSING																														.
ONTOWN	1.45		T			.35			.30	T				T	.07				.16						T		T		T	.28	.06	.
ER DARBY	3.91	.35	.55	.10			.20		.09	.25					.90	.49			.17					.			T		.1	.02	.60	.
CA	-	.06							.41	.58	.05	.02				-									.03		.09					.
DERGR	2.25					T	.23		.06	.50	T				.02	.45											.06			.10	T	.
GINVI	2.57			.03		.07	.11		T	.78		T				1.00															.27	.
INCKEL	2.68	T	T	.04	T	.02	.15	T	.25	.28	.04	.02	T		.06	.59	T	T					T		T	.05	.10	T	T	.31	T	.
INCKEL 1 WSW	2.53	T	T	.04	T	.02	.14	T	.23	.28	.04	.02	T		.05	.59	T	T							T	.02	.11	T	T	.27	T	.
REN	3.54					.10	.22		.06	.85	.39	.05			.02	.03											.11	.		.58	.06	.
SONTO	2.30	.02	.04			.03	T		.43	.10	T				.40	.03			.52								T		T	.20	.05	.
NESBU	2.05						.33		.09	.11					.01	.21											T			.09		.
LSBORO	1.28		.10	.04	T		.07		T	.39	T	.01				.19											.01			T		
LSVILLE	3.31	.05	.33			.09	.17		.43	.13					.23	.87			.13											.10		
NERSVILLE 1 W	3.32		.53													.86														.45		
T CHESTER	4.80		.51	1.76												.94	T		--							T				.14		.
T GROVE 1 E	4.55		.71	[illegible]																												
T HICKORY	2.91																															
TESBURG																																
KES BARRE																																
LIAMSBURG																																
LIANSPORT WB AP																																
FSBURG																																
K 3 SSW PUMP STA																																
K HAVEN																																
N GROVE																																
NSVILLE 3 SE																																

Station	
LENTOWN WB AIRPORT	
IE WB AIRPORT	6.6
RRISBURG WB AIRPORT	8.4
ILADELPHIA WB AIRPORT	7.2
TTSBURGH WB AIRPORT	6.6
ADING WB CITY	7.5
RANTON WB AIRPORT	6.8
IPPINGPORT WB	7.3
LLIAMSPORT WB AIRPORT	
Peak Gust	7.4

DAILY SOIL TEMPERATURES

Station And Depth	Time	1	2	3	4	5	6	7	8	9	10	11	12	13	14	15	16	17	18	19	20	21	22	23	24	25	26	27	28	29	30	31	Average
STATE COLLEGE																																	
ASURED UNDER SOD																																	
2 INCHES	8 AM	47	49	50	46	45	41	39	44	39	35	33	34	34	42	46	42	45	44	51	40	37	35	34	37	34	35	33	36	44	37		40.3
4 INCHES	8 AM	46	49	50	47	46	42	40	44	41	36	35	35	35	42	46	43	45	44	49	41	39	37	35	37	35	35	34	37	44	38		40.9
8 INCHES	8 AM	46	49	50	48	47	45	43	45	44	40	38	38	38	42	46	45	46	46	48	44	41	40	38	39	38	38	36	38	43	40		41.4
16 INCHES	8 AM	49	50	51	50	50	49	48	48	48	45	44	43	43	43	46	47	47	47	47	47	45	44	43	42	42	41	41	41	42	43		45.5

Ground Cover: Bluegrass Sod.

See Reference Notes Following Station Index

DAILY TEMPERATURES

Table 5

Station		1	2	3	4	5	6	7	8	9	10	11	12	13	14	15	16	17	18	19	20	21	22	23	24	25	26	27	28	29	30	31	Average
ALLENTOWN WB AP	MAX	64	63	61	55	54	52	56	63	52	42	44	54	52	62	63	60	58	56	70	46	53	41	36	50	40	42	44	57	60	44		52.9
	MIN	45	54	53	49	40	37	33	34	32	28	24	24	22	47	41	37	41	40	42	30	26	31	30	34	29	28	22	32	33	30		34.9
ALLENTOWN GAS CO	MAX	66	64	63	62	54	55	52	57	64	47	42	45	54	53	63	64	60	58	66	71	47	53	42	39	50	40	43	44	57	59		54.8
	MIN	43	54	54	51	45	40	33	34	36	28	26	27	29	27	48	39	40	41	44	35	28	32	32	32	34	29	23	25	35	32		35.7
ALTOONA HORSESHOE CURVE	MAX	68	57	57	51	45	50	58	56	54	33	43	52	50	56	60	60	61	47	58	42	49	39	41	43	40	37	47	58	52	38		50.1
	MIN	37	49	47	44	36	34	30	35	28	24	16	22	23	42	46	36	42	41	41	31	26	26	23	28	25	29	19	32	33	27		32.4
ARENDTSVILLE	MAX	60	62	62	68	65	52	52	59	57	45	41	45	50	51	59	64	56	57	62	64	46	52	43	40	51	41	42	46	53	59		53.4
	MIN	40	52	52	41	36	35	26	33	31	28	20	18	21	25	47	40	42	44	44	31	26	27	29	31	31	27	22	23	36	31		33.8
BAKERSTOWN 3 WNW	MAX	64	63	58	54	48	46	52	60	38	41	45	48	50	55	56	52	47	50	58	45	44	41	48	40	38	36	60	62	60	39		49.6
	MIN	44	45	48	45	36	34	31	32	28	30	36	34	33	48	36	24	30	45	40	34	36	32	24	32	27	28	26	53	38	18		34.9
BEAVERTOWN	MAX	65	62	57	60	50	52	55	57	58	38	44	53	50	57	62	59	56	49	67	49	49	45	41	46	44	41	46	57	55	43		52.2
	MIN	33	51	50	47	42	34	24	34	28	28	16	17	16	44	46	31	36	39	43	35	22	26	25	29	27	27	18	29	40	25		32.1
BELLEFONTE 4 S	MAX	61	65	55	56	48	47	50	54	50	35	35	43	50	50	60	60	61	52	66	66	42	46	40	42	43	40	37	47	55	53		50.3
	MIN	31	31	48	44	42	33	29	31	32	27	13	20	20	22	49	33	35	40	44	36	33	30	24	25	27	28	19	21	34	28		31.0
BERWICK	MAX	65	62	59	55	52	52	53	62	60	40	43	52	53	60	63	62	59	50	70	51	50	41	42	46	44	40	48	59	56	43		53.1
	MIN	36	53	52	47	41	34	29	34	34	30	22	20	21	46	48	37	39	41	45	32	27	25	27	35	31	27	22	31	43	30		34.4
BETHLEHEM LEHIGH UNIV	MAX	62	60	60	53	51	56	55	63	46	42	50	55	59	62	62	60	56	67	69	50	50	49	49	47	40	43	55	56	57	41		54.2
	MIN	53	53	51	44	40	36	37	37	29	27	31	26	47	53	41	49	43	44	38	29	34	31	31	33	29	25	36	52	33	25		37.[illegible]
BLAIRSVILLE 6 ENE	MAX	61	52	51	47	41	45	53	53	30	30	41	57	57	52	55	66	49	49	58	37	43	33	45	40	40	32	55	61	54	35		47.4
	MIN	41	42	44	38	32	31	28	41	25	20	19	29	33	44	44	42	38	41	34	29	31	25	21	32	23	26	27	43	32	26		32.1
BRADFORD CAA AP	MAX	61	53	51	43	40	46	50	53	31	27	37	52	47	54	52	59	47	48	57	33	37	31	40	38	29	33	47	55	51	34		44.[illegible]
	MIN	29	43	43	38	33	28	30	31	23	19	10	18	28	40	30	39	35	35	32	30	29	20	15	27	24	14	14	40	26	19		28.4
BRADFORD 4 W RES	MAX	62	58	53	50	42	47	51	53	53	30	40	52	48	55	56	60	60	50	59	39	38	36	43	40	35	32	48	54	54	39		47.[illegible]
	MIN	24	34	40	38	35	26	24	28	25	22	6	13	16	33	43	26	38	33	37	29	27	26	10	28	22	23	10	27	35	26		20.[illegible]
BROOKVILLE CAA AIRPORT	MAX	65	56	58	46	42	47	52	56	34	32	40	54	55	56	55	62	49	54	60	39	42	34	44	41	38	36	54	60	53	34		48.[illegible]
	MIN	30	46	43	40	36	29	30	35	26	25	12	17	21	47	34	31	37	39	35	33	30	19	16	33	26	22	19	39	27	23		30.[illegible]
BURGETTSTOWN 2 W	MAX	58	64	66	52	49	43	40	54	63	34	37	44	53	62	58	58	66	52	61	46	43	45	38	46	47	37	43	62	66	45		51.[illegible]
	MIN	26	27	32	39	39	21	19	19	29	21	8	9	11	24	46	33	37	39	44	32	30	24	16	22	17	18	19	20	40	22		26.[illegible]
BURNT CABINS 2 NE	MAX	65	65	60	58	48	53	59	65	59	38	45	52	51	57	64	64	61	53					42	47	42	41		59	57	48		54.[illegible]
	MIN	33	51	51	46	41	32	23	36	31	26	15	15	18	42	46	35	42	42					27	29	26	25		30	48	27		33.[illegible]
BUTLER	MAX	65	65	65	62	45	46	48	60	60	40	40	49	55	58	57	58	60	64	60	43	40	42	43	45	45	37	49	60	60	58		52.[illegible]
	MIN	28	40	45	42	38	30	22	34	30	20	12	15	18	46	46	32	36	37	40	32	33	28	17	22	20	27	18	42	37	23		30.[illegible]
CANTON 1 NW	MAX	58	61	54	49	49	44	48	45	54	50	37	40	47	48	57	56	56	50	61	64	40	44	38	37	43	35	36	43	53	54		48.[illegible]
	MIN	37	35	45	43	39	29	28	30	30	29	17	23	25	39	47	35	40	35	36	30	30	27	20	23	21	25	15	17	41	29		30.[illegible]
CARLISLE	MAX	64	63	62	58	53	54	59	60	58	45	45	50	52	59	64	60	57	53	67	53	51	46	41	50	45	42	48	54	61	47		54.[illegible]
	MIN	42	54	44	45	43	38	30	35	35	29	22	21	20	43	46	38	40	44	45	47	25	31	31	31	33	28	22	31	47	31		39.[illegible]
CHAMBERSBURG 1 ESE	MAX	62	61	65	55	50	54	58	59	56	40	45	51	53	60	63	57	57	50	66	46	51	43	42	51	41	43	49	56	58	46		52.[illegible]
	MIN	42	52	51	47	41	34	25	33	33	28	19	19	20	42	45	38	43	44	44	35	27	30	31	32	28	30	22	34	39	31		34.[illegible]
CHESTER	MAX	63	62		64	58	58	54	60	65		44	45	55	62	65	67		63	66	71	50	55	45		54	43	44	52	60	65		57.[illegible]
	MIN	55	55		45	46	40	34	39	42		26	25	25	39	55	41		44	46	41	35	40	38		38	31	27	37	54	37		39.[illegible]
CLARION 3 SW	MAX	67	61	59	56	46	48	53	59	54	33	42	56	58	55	57	63	60	53	62	42	42	39	45	44	40	38	56	61	58	40		51.[illegible]
	MIN	30	36	45	40	36	28	25	34	27	23	13	17	20	40	49	31	40	35	39	31	29	28	15	30	25	26	18	31	36	25		29.[illegible]
CLAYSVILLE 3 W	MAX	66	68	56	53	48	48	57	64	42	40	46	56	64	62	62	68	60	62	60	43	44	36	46	48	42	47	63	66	55	36		53.[illegible]
	MIN	27	32	47	44	38	23	19	36	31	21	11	10	18	46	40	35	40	43	40	30	27	20	20	27	18	27	19	39	29	25		29.[illegible]
COATESVILLE 1 SW	MAX	65	60	62	59	56	55	52	58	65	47	42	44	53	53	61	65	60	58	67	71	48	55	42	38	52	40	43	49	59	62		54.[illegible]
	MIN	37	55	52	44	42	37	31	32	31	29	25	19	20	23	47	37	39	39	39	38	26	30	33	32	31	25	21	22	46	39		34.[illegible]
COLUMBIA	MAX	63	59	61	56	53	53	61	63	59	42	46	53	50	58	64	59	59	49	68	54	54	47	39	52	40	44	47	61	63	52		54.[illegible]
	MIN	48	53	51	45	43	36	26	39	34	28	21	21	21	45	46	40	39	41	46	34	28	30	31	32	29	26	22	39	49	31		35.[illegible]
CONFLUENCE 1 SW DAM	MAX	60	65	55	57	50	47	47	60	64	36	35	45	58	60	60	59	67	56	69	57	40	45	38	45	45	43	44	63	63	50		52.[illegible]
	MIN	33	32	48	45	42	33	24	26	32	23	16	15	17	21	35	34	36	44	44	34	28	30	27	28	28	27	21	22	47	37		31.[illegible]
CORRY	MAX	64	56	53	49	43	48	52	55	47	32	38	51	49	56	57	63	53	53	59	38	41	35	42	40	36	34	53	55	52	40		48.[illegible]
	MIN	28	36	45	40	35	28	28	38	25	24	12	16	24	40	42	37	39	37	36	32	32	26	18	31	27	27	20	46	36	26		31.[illegible]
COUDERSPORT 3 NW	MAX	60	52	53	45	40	46	50	52	35	30	37	49	45	54	55	57	57	47	59	38	38	33	38	38	32	32	41	55	51	38		45.[illegible]
	MIN	26	43	40	38	33	29	25	32	25	19	3	14	23	38	39	30	30	30	36	28	25	24	10	30	22	21	9	31	38	23		27.[illegible]
DERRY	MAX	63	58	54	54	45	50	57	62	54	37	45	59	65	59	60	69	62	56	67	44	49	43	49	47	42	48	65	66	57	40		54.[illegible]
	MIN	33	44	48	43	37	33	24	40	32	25	17	17	25	50	42	40	43	44	43	35	35	30	25	35	25	26	22	50	39	30		34.[illegible]
DEVAULT 1 W	MAX	53	54	58	56	51	50	53	61	50	45	40	49	48	58	62	58	54	51	67	44	51	40	35	48	37	39	43	57	59	43		50.[illegible]
	MIN	48	47	48	43	39	35	32	42	28	26	21	27	29	47	48	44	43	40	42	32	31	32	29	28	25	25	24	37	33	30		35.[illegible]
DIXON	MAX	65	63	57	57	50	49	52	56	59	46	40	44	58	56	58	64	62	54	62	68	44	49	44	42	47	36	39	47	59	60		52.[illegible]
	MIN	31	30	50	46	35	33	19	20	29	28	14	14	16	16	42	30	31	34	39	29	28	21	24	24	29	23	13	13	40	25		27.[illegible]
DONEGAL	MAX	59	48	48	44	40	42	52	56	30	30	40	52	59	52	54	62	48	54	59	39	43	34	40	40	40	40	57	58	48	33		46.[illegible]
	MIN	30	44	41	36	28	24	18	40	20	14	7	8	18	46	35	32	36	40	28	28	24	20	19	30	19	18	15	42	24	16		26.[illegible]
DONORA	MAX	70	64	58	55	50	55	58	62	58	41	46	51	65	63	62	69	66	60	69	49	51	45	47	51	46	43	64	66	63	47		56.[illegible]
	MIN	41	47	47	46	38	32	28	45	36	24	20	20	27	52	49	42	42	47	44	35	35	29	28	37	27	39	27	50	44	32		37.[illegible]
DU BOIS 7 E	MAX	61	60	55	51	44	47	51	55	54	31	38	52	50	52	59	61	60	45	59	42	43	37	45	40	38	34	46	58	53	37		48.[illegible]
	MIN	29	45	45	38	37	31	30	32	28	24	13	12	25	42	45	32	37	34	41	31	30	27	16	32	24	22	11	34	36	24		30.[illegible]
EAGLES MERE	MAX	57	60	52	56	45	43	45	46	51	35	33	36	47	46	56	55	54	52	58	61	37	41	35	34	37	30	34	39	50	49		45.[illegible]
	MIN	39	40	45	41	35	28	27	27	28	24	16	16	27	28	45	40	41	35	35	28	28	26	21	22	23	22	19	19	38	30		29.[illegible]
EAST BRADY	MAX	68	64	60	59	47	52	56	62	58	37	45	56	59	57	59	65	63	57	63	44	45	42	48	47	46	38	61	67	61	44		54.[illegible]
	MIN	33	40	46	44	40	31	29	36	20	15	16	19	21	41	48	34	44	39	43	35	33	29	19	26	29	31	20	35	30	25		31.[illegible]
EBENSBURG	MAX	62	53	53	48	41	44	52	55	49	30	39	48	50	53	55	63	58	47	57	39	43	35	44	40	36	35	45	58	52	37		47.[illegible]
	MIN	34	45	44	39	32	31	26	37	16	20	14	12	23	42	42	35	38	39	37	30	29	25	21	32	23	25	19	37	31	25		30.[illegible]
EMPORIUM 2 SSW	MAX	60	62	56	53	45	43	50	52	54	36	36	39	52	50	51	55	60	50	60	60	40	40	33	42	40	35	34	47	60	50		48.[illegible]
	MIN	30	34	44	38	37	25	22	30	28	22	10	11	17	24	44	28	33	33	38	31	22	21	12	14	25	25	15	18	31	21		26.[illegible]
EPHRATA	MAX	62	62	60	59	56	53	55	62	48	42	45	51	50	59	65	60	59	49	69	48	54	42	37	51	41	43	46	59	62	43		53.[illegible]
	MIN	45	51	48	42	39	34	29	30	30	25	22	23	23	44	49	39	43	40	45	33	29	32	30	30	30	26	22	39	41	31		34.[illegible]
ERIE WB AIRPORT	MAX	57	52	56	48	49	47	52	60	35	35	40	50	54	60	55	67	47	57	64	42	42	34	43	44	35	35	58	58	54	37		48.[illegible]
	MIN	33	42	47	45	40	37	36	34	27	30	27	29	36	50	41	47	41	41	38	34	31	29	23	33	30	28	28	51	36	26		35.[illegible]

See reference notes following Station Index.

Table 5 - Continued

DAILY TEMPERATURES

PENNSYLVANIA
NOVEMBER 1957

Station		1	2	3	4	5	6	7	8	9	10	11	12	13	14	15	16	17	18	19	20	21	22	23	24	25	26	27	28	29	30	31	Average
EVERETT 1 SW	MAX	62	66	62	54	50	50	50	60	42	34	44	52	50	52	60	66	58	62	62	45	50	42	40	46	40	42	44	64	52	42		51.4
	MIN	40	54	55	48	40	34	24	38	28	28	20	15	18	42	40	36	50	46	45	32	25	25	32	24	28	26	18	32	32	28		33.4
FARRELL SHARON	MAX	68	69	58	53	46	51	56	61	45	37	46	56	57	60	57	68	57	56	65	45	44	41	47	48	41	40	61	59	55	40		52.8
	MIN	32	38	48	45	39	35	30	42	28	27	19	22	26	49	46	44	43	43	39	35	37	29	22	37	30	30	26	47	38	28		35.1
FORD CITY 4 S DAM	MAX	63	66	62	58	48	45	48	56	50	35	36	44	51	62	58	58	67	51	64	48	43	46	37	47	46	39	37	61	64	42		51.1
	MIN	31	31	46	44	41	30	24	25	31	25	15	16	17	21	47	30	34	38	43	33	34	26	21	21	21	21	18	19	45	25		29.1
FRANKLIN	MAX	67	63	60	50	45	50	54	58	43	35	42	55	55	57	58	64	55	55	61	41	43	39	45	45	39	37	57	58	54	39		50.8
	MIN	31	30	47	43	37	30	27	35	27	25	17	20	23	45	42	33	39	40	37	34	34	24	17	34	30	28	22	35	37	25		31.6
FREELAND	MAX	59	57	54	46	45	46	50	53	53	33	38	52	47	51	58	56	52	46	62	46	45	41	35	39	38	33	35	53	52			47.4
	MIN	42	48	44	40	35	30	29	37	27	22	17	26	30	39	46	46	40	35	39	28	28	25	21	27	23	21	17	32	46			32.4
GEORGE SCHOOL	MAX	58	60	61	65	56	56	53	57	66	44	43	47	53	55	63	65	59	60	65	69	49	65	43	40	52	44	42	48	62	64		55.5
	MIN	50	55	53	51	43	37	30	30	37	30	22	20	19	24	50	35	39	39	44	35	26	28	33	33	30	26	19	26	48	42		35.1
GETTYSBURG	MAX	60	63	60	65	56	52	54	59	61	45	41	45	51	53	60	64	61	58	65	68	47	53	43	45	50	41	45	50	55	60		54.3
	MIN	46	53	54	48	42	37	28	32	37	29	24	20	22	30	49	42	45	46	45	37	32	36	34	27	34	29	24	29	49	33		36.4
GRATERFORD	MAX	54	56	66	54	52	50	48	47	50	46	48	50	54	52	62	58	54	56	72	72	54	48	42	44	46	52	48	54	53			53.2
	MIN	38	50	44	32	28	28	28	30	27	24	26	28	24	25	32	36	43	45	56	38	34	32	32	30	28	30	26	32	34			33.1
GRATZ 1	MAX	63	63	56	57	51	50	50	54	59	43	39	42	51	53	61	62	60	54	67	67	44	50	41	37	46	36	41	46	58	56		51.9
	MIN	37	46	51	44	42	36	28	33	29	28	21	20	22	26	46	37	39	41	44	33	27	28	26	27	32	26	22	22	40	29		32.7
GREENVILLE	MAX	66	66	61	49	44	49	55	60	42	35	44	54	56	58	57	67	55	55	63	42	38	45	44	44	39	36	59	57	53	39		51.1
	MIN	27	30	42	40	33	29	23	37	24	20	17	22	26	47	48	38	42	42	38	38	28	29	26	38	28	30	28	49	39	31		33.0
HANOVER	MAX	64	62	57	66	56	54	54	60	63	46	41	46	52	55	60	65	60	57	66	69	48	54	44	43	53	43	40	50	60	61		55.0
	MIN	38	47	52	43	39	33	29	30	34	27	22	23	24	24	47	43	43	45	45	34	33	33	34	32	34	28	25	26	48	35		35.0
HARRISBURG WB AP	MAX	64	58	59	53	51	52	56	63	49	40	44	52	52	62	64	57	56	49	70	46	52	43	38	50	43	42	48	58	61	45		52.6
	MIN	46	53	53	48	42	39	33	39	34	29	26	22	25	45	45	41	44	44	46	37	31	35	33	33	31	31	25	39	34	33		37.2
HAWLEY 1 S DAM	MAX	61	60	60	53	46	48	46	54	57	40	36	38	53	51	59	58	61	50	55	65	42	46	40	40	43	32	35	45	55	55		49.5
	MIN	36	39	49	43	39	33	30	27	31	27	20	18	19	19	47	32	32	37	38	31	33	27	27	29	28	24	12	14	41	27		30.3
HOLTWOOD	MAX	59	60	59	56	53	52	64	61	57	42	45	53	50	60	64	57	57	54	68	48	56	47	38	62	42	42	42	58	61	45		53.7
	MIN	54	55	55	50	45	38	34	42	33	32	30	28	28	39	39	42	42	43	47	35	32	35	35	37	30	30	27	40	37	31		38.2
HUNTINGDON	MAX	62	66	60	59	58	50	53	58	58	42	40	45	54	53	59	64	62	58	64	65	45	50	43							55		55.1
	MIN	29	32	52	45	42	29	20	22	34	30	15	14	14	17	47	30	30	43	44	39	22	23	25							24		30.1
INDIANA 3 SE	MAX	67	56	56	53	45	49	54	59	50	35	43	58	60	58	60	68	61	55	65	43	47	37	47	44	41	37	58	64	56	37		52.1
	MIN	30	41	48	44	38	32	21	35	29	26	11	16	21	45	41	32	40	39	42	30	27	27	21	35	22	27	20	32	34	28		31.1
IRWIN	MAX	67	68			48	51	58	65				59	66	61	61			68	68	55	50	45			49	42	64		67			
	MIN	27				38	31	25	42				19	24	51	49			40	43	40	34	29			25	30	25		42			
JAMESTOWN 2 NW	MAX	56	63	62	58	47	43	49	53	59	34	34	43	53	56	57	54	66	48	62	52	40	41	37	45	45	35	34	57	56	46		49.5
	MIN	28	29	40	45	42	28	27	28	29	23	16	20	25	32	46	39	40	38	41	31	31	28	16	21	27	28	23	28	38	31		30.6
JIM THORPE	MAX	66	65	60	55	54	53	62	58	58	44	47	61	60	55	64	64	60	53	67		53											
	MIN	48	53	52	47	41	37	33	30	30	28	23	19	19	45	47	36	44	42	42		25											
JOHNSTOWN	MAX	65	70	58	51	48	49	51	61	60	40	31	47	59	59	58	63	67	67	61	53	45	49	40	53	51	43	42	56	65	52		53.8
	MIN	28	34	34	34	38	32	22	30	29	21	13	15	18	25	51	31	40	40	47	37	36	32	28	29	29	32	23	26	40	33		30.9
KANE 1 NNE	MAX	57	63	55	53	45	44	47	51	54	32	31	39	51	48	55	53	61	47	59	50	35	39	32	42	37	33	46	55	54	35		46.8
	MIN	25	27	43	40	38	24	23	30	29	24	4	11	13	24	45	28	35	30	43	32	28	27	11	14	26	11	16	39	25	16		26.0
KEGG	MAX	65	58	61	52	47	48	61	58	40	37	48	53	55	58	62	70	57	48	62	44	44	42	43	47	41	40	50	60	49	42		51.4
	MIN	34	50	51	43	37	33	24	40	29	25	17	15	18	40	39	34	44	43	39	25	25	28	26	29	28	24	19	28	34	25		31.5
LANCASTER 2 NE pump STA	MAX	62	62	60	59	55	52	56	64	62	50	42	51	50	60	65	60	57	55	70	54	54	48	41	51	46	42	47	60	61	52		54.9
	MIN	45	53	50	42	41	35	25	31	32	26	24	19	19	43	43	36	35	38	46	34	28	28	32	30	30	25	20	31	48	29		33.9
LANDISVILLE 2 NW	MAX	61	63	60	60	54	52	51	57	62	45	41	42	50	49	62	63	60	55	65	70	46	54	41	47	49	38	41	44	59	60		53.4
	MIN	38	53	49	43	41	35	27	33	31	27	22	20	21	27	44	38	37	39	43	34	24	26	31	31	29	26	22	24	39	30		32.8
LAWRENCEVILLE 2 S	MAX	63	63	53	52	48	46	50	56	56	40	38	41	59	52	58	60	61	51	63	67	42	46	41	44	44	37	33	45	54	54		50.6
	MIN	26	27	46	44	40	27	22	25	30	27	13	13	18	20	44	30	31	34	40	33	28	27	18	19	25	24	12	13	45	26		27.6
LEBANON 3 W	MAX	63	63	62	61	55	53	51	56	61	45	41	45	51	51	61	64	59	56	64	68	46	52	42	37	50	41	41	46	56	59		53.3
	MIN	45	53	49	42	40	33	26	27	30	26	22	19	20	21	46	37	37	40	45	30	24	26	29	31	31	25	21	22	34	30		32.0
LEWISTOWN	MAX	63	68	60	62	52	51	55	59	60	41	41	46	57	52	60	64	58	57	55	68	46	50	44	42	46	41	43	51	57	56		53.5
	MIN	36	33	53	48	45	36	29	27	37	30	23	20	20	18	47	36	34	45	43	40	25	25	29	30	27	32	24	23	29	30		32.5
LINESVILLE 5 WNW	MAX	62	61	58	49	44	49	54	60	36	34	40	49	51	57	54	65	52	58	62	43	40	38	43	45	36	35	54	55	52	38		49.1
	MIN	27	35	48	43	37	31	31	36	26	24	14	20	24	43	41	37	40	40	36	32	33	26	21	33	28	28	23	47	37	27		32.3
LOCK HAVEN	MAX	67	58	58	51	50	54	57	57	54	40	46	51	52	60	64	52	58	48	68	46	50	43	46	47	40	42	49	49	52	43		51.7
	MIN	33	51	47	41	42	31	31	31	34	29	21	21	21	37	48	34	41	42	45	37	28	29	26	39	32	30	22	30	42	29		34.1
MADERA	MAX	57	62	55	56	47	44	47	50	54	35	32	36	50	49	55	56	65	49	57	60	40	42	37	44	41	36	35	45	59	50		48.2
	MIN	26	26	41	40	39	31	20	20	30	24	12	11	14	16	46	28	28	35	41	33	27	25	20	20	22	21	15	16	37	24		26.3
MARCUS HOOK	MAX	62	63	67	61	61	57	59	65	57	46	45	54	54	61	68	60	63	56	70	52	58	50	42	55	44	45	47	58	66	51		56.6
	MIN	55	57	54	51	46	41	40	44	36	32	30	35	31	50	51	46	49	47	49	41	40	42	34	40	36	33	33	45	43	37		42.3
MARTINSBURG CAA AP	MAX	65	56	58	48	46	47	58	56	36	33	46	54	51	56	59	63	54	48	61	42	46	40	40	42	37	38	47	60	52	38		49.2
	MIN	37	49	48	42	37	33	27	37	27	23	19	21	23	46	45	38	42	43	37	32	32	28	26	33	27	25	22	38	28	23		32.9
MEADVILLE 1 S	MAX	58	64	65	60	46	43	50	54	61	35	34	41	54	53	58	54	65	47	61	48	42	41	37	43	44	36	25	55	56	41		49.4
	MIN	31	33	35	45	42	29	26	29	30	24	14	16	23	29	47	34	41	38	46	32	32	30	16	19	28	28	23	26	31	32		30.3
MERCER 2 NNE	MAX	65	66	58	53	45	48	52	62	50	33	42	53	55	57	57	63	64	51	63	44	42	38	44	44	38	36	58	58	54	39		51.1
	MIN	29	33	46	38	30	31	23	41	27	23	21	19	23	45	45	36	40	35	36	31	32	25	14	34	24	27	23	46	35	28		31.3
MIDDLETOWN OLMSTED FLD	MAX	64	60	60	55	53	51	55	62	50	41	42	51	51	62	65	58	56	52	69	47	58	44	37	50	44	42	47	55	60	44		52.8
	MIN	48	55	51	49	42	38	34	38	35	31	27	23	24	45	46	42	42	44	50	37	31	33	33	35	30	30	25	40	30	34		37.4
MIDLAND DAM 7	MAX	64	66	55	49	48	48	52	63	40	36	40	47	58	57	55	70	51	57	63	44	44	37	43	46	38	41	56	62	54	37		50.7
	MIN	38	42	49	46	38	34	31	39	30	26	22	24	31	49	44	42	45	46	40	37	36	29	26	35	28	31	30	44	33	25		35.7
MONTROSE 1 E	MAX	58	57	55	49	43	44	45	50	54	36	33	37	50	48	55	57	58	48	54	64	40	42	39	36	40	30	31	40	52	53		46.6
	MIN	36	37	45	39	36	31	28	29	28	26	17	17	24	28	44	40	41	35	35	30	27	26	21	21	24	21	13	14	36	29		29.3
MORGANTOWN	MAX	59	63	60	55	54	51	53	64	55	41	43	49	50	62	62	60	56	54	69	67	52	46	39	51	41	42	45	59	64	47		53.8
	MIN	51	51	48	41	38	33	30	38	30	26	22	22	23	42	44	39	39	40	43	29	31	30	30	33	25	26	24	43	31	31		34.4
MT GRETNA 2 SE	MAX	64	61	61	55	52	52	55	61	51	42	45	48	49	60	64	59	56	54	68	55	54	44	40	51	42	43	44	57	61	43		53.0
	MIN	49	53	49	46	39	32	36	38	31	30	25	25	28	49	42	39	39	38	42	28	30	36	34	34	30	24	20	30	32	32		35.3

See reference notes following Station Index.

MT POCONO 2 N AP																													
MUHLENBURG 1 SE																													
NEWBURG 3																													
NEW CASTLE 1 N																													
NEWELL																													
NEWPORT																													
NEW STANTON																													
NORRISTOWN																													
PALMERTON																													
PHIL DREXEL INST OF TEC																													
PHILADELPHIA WB AP																													
PHILADELPHIA PT BREEZE																													
PHILIPSBURG CAA AP																													
PHOENIXVILLE 1 E																													
PIMPLE HILL																													
PITTSBURGH WB AP 2																													
PITTSBURGH WB CITY																													
PLEASANT MOUNT 1																													
PORT CLINTON																													
PUTNEYVILLE 2 SE DAM																													
QUAKERTOWN 1 E																													
READING WB CITY																													
RIDGWAY 3 W																													
SALINA 3																													
SCRANTON																													
SCRANTON WB AIRPORT																													
SHIPPENSBURG																													
SHIPPINGPORT WB																													
SLIPPERY ROCK								54	62	62	35	42	56				60	40	42	39	45	46							
								27	40	27	23	16	23				34	31	32	27	18	35							
SOMERSET MAIN ST								54	57	52	33	42	53				63	43	43	40	43	42				60	54	40	50
	MIN							24	35	27	20	13	13				40	31	30	24	24	33				36	37	28	31
SPRINGBORO	MAX	58	64	58	58	49	44	49	54	61	49	37	40				58	57	43	40	32	43				56	58	45	50
	MIN	27	30	48	45	42	31	28	36	30	25	20	17				43	33	33	30	23	23				43	39	39	32
SPRINGS 1 SW	MAX	61	55	52	48	42	45	54	56	45	30	42	50				62	37	43		43	41					60	40	49
	MIN	29	47	46	39	32	30	22	32	24	19	16	14				33	25	24		24	33	21	21	20		27	24	28
STATE COLLEGE	MAX	59	63	55	55	48	46	51	55	56	36	35	43				62	63	40		38	41	42	37	37	47	57	51	49
	MIN	36	36	49	45	43	34	31	32	32	27	22	23	24	26	49	42	36	34	30	27	27	30	29	23	23	42	31	33
STROUDSBURG	MAX	64	60	63	54	55	48	57	62	53	36	41	58	51	62	65	68	44	46	40	35	45	37	40	43	55	60	41	51
	MIN	38	49	50	46	36	30	26	27	29	24	15	16	15	44	35	41	25	19	21	27	30	26	21	15	29	30	25	29
SUNBURY	MAX	66	68	60	58	54	52	54	58	59	45	41	46	55	53	61	68	68	47	50	43	41	45	38	43	47	58	56	53
	MIN	36	42	53	45	42	35	26	29	35	31	22	22	20	24	44	44	36	27	27	28	29	32	29	22	21	34	28	32
TAMARACK 2 S FIRE TWR	MAX	56	60	52	50	43	41	47	47	50	32	30	38	50		54	55	58	36	40	33	39	37	33	33	42	54	48	45
	MIN	37	40	43	39	36	28	29	30	27	22	16	16	28	28	43	37	30	28	25	17	18	24	24	22	22	41	28	29
TIONESTA 2 SE DAM	MAX	60	67	62	60	47	44	49	53	57	34	32	42	55	55	56	60	50	39	42	36	40	43	39	36	55	58	44	49
	MIN	31	32	39	43	40	28	27	30	31	25	17	20	19	24	47	39	34	31	29	15	15	29	28	22	25	32	27	29
TITUSVILLE WATER WORKS	MAX	65	61	60	52	43	49	53	57	41	43	41	54	53	56	53	59	38	41	35	43	40	36	36	55	59	54	40	49
	MIN	29	30	47	43	35	25	22	31	26	24	13	19	20	43	38	38	32	33	26	13	33	28	27	19	29	38	30	29
TOWANDA	MAX	67	57	54	51	47	52	57	57	57	39	45	55	53	59	64	69	45	48	44	45	45	40	39	48	57	59	43	52
	MIN	31	48	48	44	39	31	26	31	31	27	18	20	18	40	38	40	31	30	24	21	34	26	23	13	39	38	25	31

See reference notes following Station Index.

Table 5 - Continued

DAILY TEMPERATURES

PENNSYLVANIA
NOVEMBER 1957

Station		Day Of Month																															Average
		1	2	3	4	5	6	7	8	9	10	11	12	13	14	15	16	17	18	19	20	21	22	23	24	25	26	27	28	29	30	31	
UNIONTOWN	MAX	67	58	52	51	48	49	60	67	41	41	48	58	67	64	63	69	58	66	71	44	49	42	47	50	44	48	65	67	56	41		55.0
	MIN	33	44	48	45	37	33	24	40	30	24	18	16	26	54	43	40	40	48	37	35	36	29	28	33	27	28	23	51	33	28		34.3
UPPER DARBY	MAX	61	60	63	54	56	56	58	65	61	43	44	55	54	60	65	61	60	51	69	54	55	43	40	52	42	44	48	60	63	52		55.0
	MIN	46	59	53	47	45	45	35	36	39	30	27	25	25	48	50	41	43	44	50	38	31	36	32	33	35	30	26	40	40	36		38.7
WARREN	MAX	64	54	56	50	44	50	55	55	47	40	42	54	52	56	57	63	58	53	59	40	40	37	45	42	34	37	52	56	52	39		49.4
	MIN	33	57	46	42	38	30	27	37	28	25	15	10	24	42	42	34	38	38	37	33	33	27	18	32	28	27	21	39	39	26		31.8
WAYNESBURG 2 W	MAX	60	64	61	52	50	46	58	65	49	38	46	55	64	63	63	68	65	64	68	42	49	41	48	47	41	48	64	67	59	37		54.9
	MIN	28	36	42	45	36	25	19	35	30	22	11	10	19	46	46	34	35	43	39	34	31	21	24	38	22	32	19	36	33	27		30.6
WELLSBORO 3 S	MAX	59	60	50	40	45	43	47	51	53	33	35	30	52	46	55	56	53	50	57	60	38	41	34	38	38	34	34	42	52	52		46.5
	MIN	32	35	44	41	37	27	29	30	28	24	17	19	29	29	44	39	41	36	36	32	29	27	19	20	20	20	18	23	39	28		29.7
WELLSVILLE	MAX	62	59	61	56	53	52	56	61	60	42	44	51	51	58	63	58	51	49	70	53	53	43	39	52	41	42	47	58	62	48		53.2
	MIN	41	53	48	36	34	35	21	30	26	27	15	16	16	41	40	35	38	39	46	28	22	27	30	30	30	24	20	20	20	20		30.3
WEST CHESTER	MAX		56	57	62	59	59	55	64	64	51	45	48	56	57	61	68	60	62	65	70	51	58	45	43	54	41	44	53	60	64		56.3
	MIN	50	51	46	44	39	36	40	39	30	27	29	29	41	33	44	46	44	44	40	35	37	33	32	37	30	27	31	47	38	27		37.5
WILLIAMSPORT WB AP	MAX	68	59	58	53	51	53	54	59	43	40	45	51	49	60	62	56	58	49	66	45	50	42	40	47	41	43	44	55	56	42		51.3
	MIN	37	51	50	45	41	36	29	36	34	29	21	22	21	47	39	34	40	42	41	30	28	25	27	33	32	29	22	35	31	29		33.9
YORK 3 SSW PUMP STA	MAX	64	58	65	58	52	53	60	64	62	41	46	52	52	59	64	59	58	52	70	53	55	47	40	53	46	45	50	60	62	53		55.1
	MIN	42	54	54	37	37	34	25	34	31	29	20	19	21	45	48	40	40	40	48	30	29	27	33	32	30	26	22	44	51	31		35.1

Table 6

EVAPORATION AND WIND

Station		Day of month																															Total or Avg.
		1	2	3	4	5	6	7	8	9	10	11	12	13	14	15	16	17	18	19	20	21	22	23	24	25	26	27	28	29	30	31	
LANDISVILLE 2 NW	EVAP	.09	.03	.04	.07	.11	.01	.06	.04	.21	-	-	-	-	-	-	-	-	-	-	-	-	-	-	-	-	-	-	-	-	-		-
	WIND	61	62	82	85	104	60	47	44	101	-	-	-	-	-	-	-	-	-	-	-	-	-	-	-	-	-	-	-	-	-		-

Table 7

SNOWFALL AND SNOW ON GROUND

Station		Day of month																														
		1	2	3	4	5	6	7	8	9	10	11	12	13	14	15	16	17	18	19	20	21	22	23	24	25	26	27	28	29	30	31
ALLENTOWN WB AIRPORT	SNOWFALL										T													T	T		T					
	SN ON GND																															
	WTR EQUIV																															
AUSTINBURG 2 W	SNOWFALL										T														T		T	T			T	
	SN ON GND										T	T													T		T	T			T	
BEECH CREEK STATION	SNOWFALL										T	T																			T	
	SN ON GND										T																				T	
BRADFORD CAA AIRPORT	SNOWFALL					T	T		T	T	6.3										T	T	T	T	1.0	.5	.2				1.7	
	SN ON GND									T	3	4	3	T								T	T		T	1	1	1			2	
BRADFORD 4 W RES	SNOWFALL									T	11.5										T				1.3		1.3					
	SN ON GND									T	12	8	6	3							T				1	T	1	1				
BROOKVILLE CAA AIRPORT	SNOWFALL									T	T										T	T	T		T	T	T				.3	
	SN ON GND										T	T													T		T					
CANTON 1 NW	SNOWFALL																										T					
	SN ON GND																										T					
CARROLLTOWN 2 SSE	SNOWFALL						T				T	T										T			T	T	1.0				T	
	SN ON GND						T				T	T													T		1	T				
CORRY	SNOWFALL									2.0	9.0														1.0	T	1.5				2.0	
	SN ON GND									2	11	8	5	3											T	T	2				2	
DONEGAL	SNOWFALL					T			T	T																					-	
	SN ON GND					T			T	T																					1	
DU BOIS 7 E	SNOWFALL						T			T	.5											T			.5		1.0				T	
	SN ON GND										1	T													T	T	1	T			T	
ERIE WB AIRPORT	SNOWFALL								T	4.8	.8										T	T	T	T	T	2.0	T				.3	
	SN ON GND										5	2	1										T	T	T		2	1				
FORD CITY 4 S DAM	SNOWFALL										T	T															.5					
	SN ON GND										T																1					
GALETON	SNOWFALL						T			T		.6										T	T	T	T	T	.4	T		T		
	SN ON GND						T					T											T				T					
GRATERFORD	SNOWFALL																								.5							
	SN ON GND																															
GREENSBORO LOCK 7	SNOWFALL																										T					
	SN ON GND																															
HANOVER	SNOWFALL																								T							
	SN ON GND																															

See reference notes following Station Index.

Table 7 - Continued

SNOWFALL AND SNOW ON GROUND

Day of month

Station		1	2	3	4	5	6	7	8	9	10	11	12	13	14	15	16	17	18	19	20	21	22	23	24	25	26	27	28	29	30	31
HARRISBURG WB AIRPORT	SNOWFALL										T													T			T				T	
	SN ON GND																															
	WTR EQUIV																															
HAWLEY 1 S DAM	SNOWFALL																										T					
	SN ON GND																															
BOLTWOOD	SNOWFALL	-	-	-	-	-	-	-	-	-	-	-	-	-	-	-	-	-	-	-	-	-	-	-	-	-	-	-	-	-	-	
	SN ON GND	-	-	-	-	-	-	-	-	-	-	-	-	-	-	-	-	-	-	-	-	-	-	-	-	-	-	-	-	-	-	
HOOVERSVILLE	SNOWFALL																													.2		
	SN ON GND																													-		
INDIANA 3 SE	SNOWFALL									T	T																.5					
	SN ON GND																										T					
KANE 1 NNE	SNOWFALL						T			T	4.5	1.5										.3	T	T	.5	T	1.5	.3			1.0	
	SN ON GND										5	5	3	2	T							T	T	T	T	T	2	2	1	T	T	
LANCASTER 2 NE PUMP STA	SNOWFALL																							T			T					
	SN ON GND																							T								
LAWRENCEVILLE 2 S	SNOWFALL										T	T															T					
	SN ON GND										T	T															T	T				
LEWISTOWN	SNOWFALL																										T					
	SN ON GND																															
MARTINSBURG CAA AIRPORT	SNOWFALL									T	T														T	T	T				.1	
	SN ON GND										T																T					
MATAMORAS	SNOWFALL																										T					
	SN ON GND																															
MEADVILLE 1 S	SNOWFALL									T	3.5	2.1										T	.1	T	.1		1.9					
	SN ON GND									T	3	2	1	T								T			T		2	T				
MEDIX RUN	SNOWFALL										.8	T										T	T	T		T	.6	T				
	SN ON GND										1	T										T					1	T				
MONTROSE 1 E	SNOWFALL										.1	.1														T	.3	T				
	SN ON GND										T	T															T	T				
PHILADELPHIA WB AIRPORT	SNOWFALL										T													T			T					
	SN ON GND																															
	WTR EQUIV																															
PHILIPSBURG CAA AIRPORT	SNOWFALL					T				T	T	T									T	T			T	T	T				T	
	SN ON GND																															
PIMPLE HILL	SNOWFALL						T				.1	.4											T	T	T	T	.3	T				
	SN ON GND										T	T	T	T									T		T		T	T				
PITTSBURGH WB AIRPORT 2	SNOWFALL									T	T										T		T		T	.5	.3			T	.2	
	SN ON GND										T																1					
	WTR EQUIV																															
PLEASANT MOUNT 1 W	SNOWFALL										T	T														T	.5	T				
	SN ON GND										T	T															1	T	T			
READING WB CITY	SNOWFALL										T													T								
	SN ON GND																															
SCRANTON WB AIRPORT	SNOWFALL									T	.3												T			T	T				T	
	SN ON GND											T															T					
	WTR EQUIV																															
SHIPPENSBURG	SNOWFALL									T												T		T								
	SN ON GND																															
SHIPPINGPORT WB	SNOWFALL																									T					T	
	SN ON GND																															
SLIPPERY ROCK	SNOWFALL										T																T					
	SN ON GND										T																T					
SPRINGS 1 SW	SNOWFALL																				T	T				T					2.0	
	SN ON GND																					T				T					2	
TAMARACK 2 S FIRE TWR	SNOWFALL						T				.5	1.5										T	T	T			.3	T				
	SN ON GND										T	2	1	T	T									T	T	T	T	T				
TIONESTA 2 SE DAM	SNOWFALL										1.0												T	T	T		1.0					
	SN ON GND										1	T	T										T		T		1	T				
TOWANDA	SNOWFALL										T	.3															.2	T				
	SN ON GND											T															T					
WILLIAMSPORT WB AIRPORT	SNOWFALL									T	T																.2				T	
	SN ON GND											T															T					
	WTR EQUIV																															

TOTAL PRECIPITATION

PENNSYLVANIA
NOVEMBER 1957

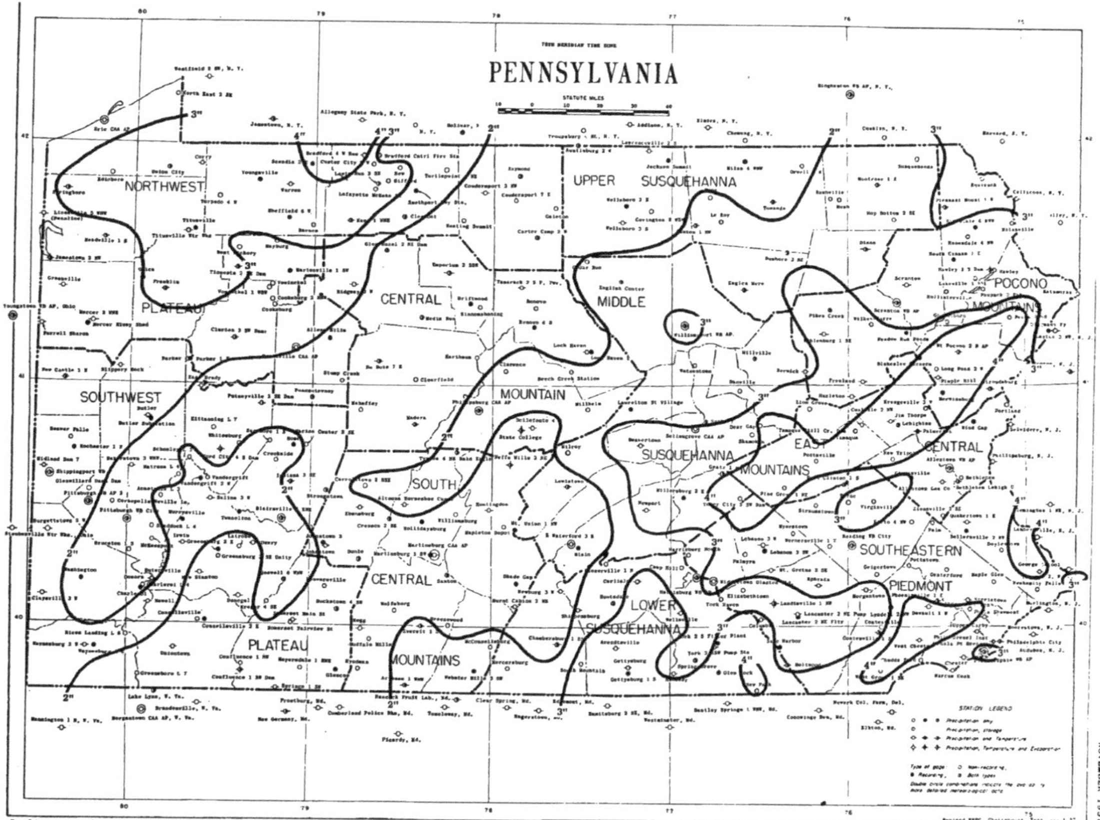

Isolines are drawn through points of approximately equal values. Hourly precipitation data from recorder substations will be available in the publication "Hourly Precipitation Data".

AVERAGE TEMPERATURE

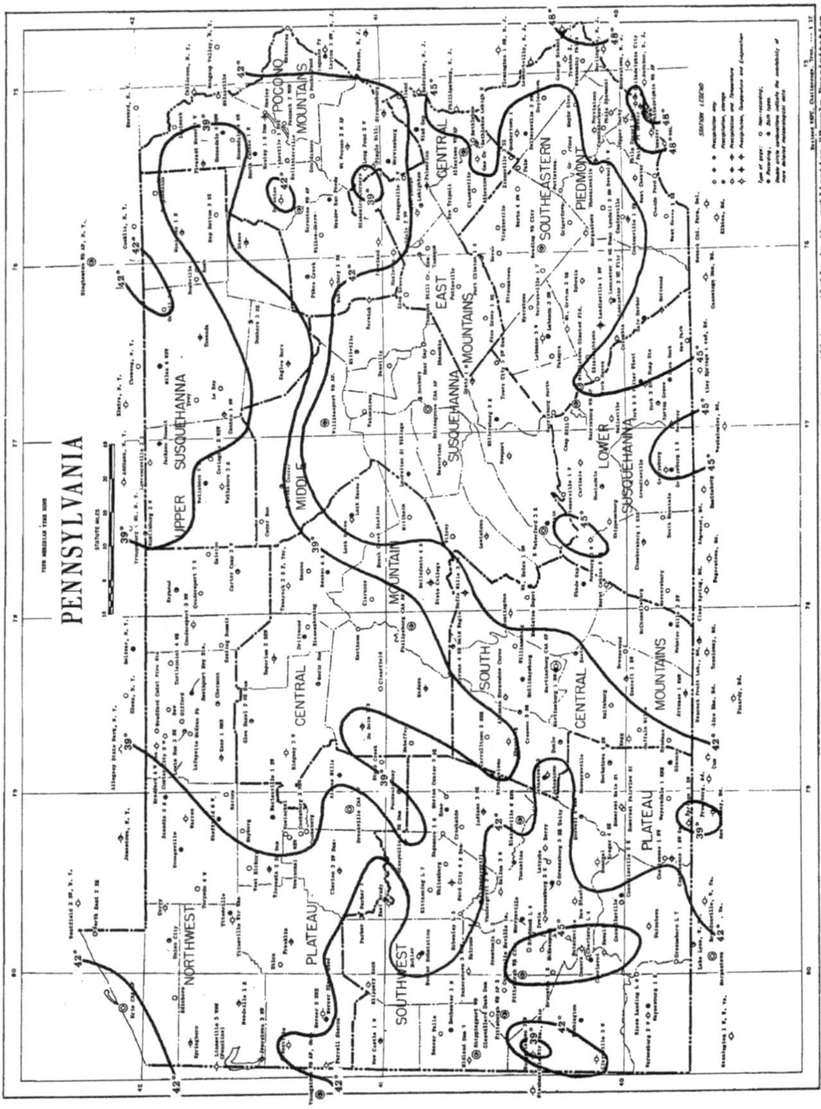

Isolines are drawn through points of approximately equal values. Hourly precipitation data from recorder substations will be available in the publication "Hourly Precipitation Data".

STATION INDEX

Station	Index No.	County	Drainage ‡	Latitude	Longitude	Elevation	Observation Time Temp.	Observation Time Precip.	Observer	Refer To Tables
ACMETONIA LOCK 3	0022	ALLEGHENY	1	40 32	79 49	748		7A	CORPS OF ENGINEERS	3
ALLENS MILLS	0090	JEFFERSON	1	41 12	78 55	1600		MID	CHARLES H. ALLEN	C
ALLENTOWN WB AP	0106	LEHIGH	9	40 39	75 26	376	MID	MID	U.S. WEATHER BUREAU	2 3 5 7 C
ALLENTOWN GAS CO	0111	LEHIGH	9	40 36	75 28	254	7A	7A	LEHIGH VLY GAS DIV	2 3 5
ALTOONA HORSESHOE CURVE	0134	BLAIR	8	40 30	78 29	1500	6P	6P	ALTOONA WATER BUR.	2 3 5
ARENDTSVILLE	0229	ADAMS	15	39 55	77 18	710	8A	8A	PA STATE COL EXP	2 3 5
AUSTINBURG 2 W	0313	TIOGA	15	42 00	77 32	1590		7A	OTTO D. BACON	3 7 C
BAKERSTOWN 3 WNW	0355	ALLEGHENY	1	40 39	79 59	1230	7P	7P	PGH CUT FLOWER CO	2 3 5
BARNES	0409	WARREN	1	41 40	79 02	1310		7A	CORPS OF ENGINEERS	3
BARTO 4 NW	0428	BERKS	14	40 28	75 39	312		7A	MARIE B. NICHLAS	3
BEAR GAP	0457	NORTHUMBERLAND	15	40 50	76 30	900		3P	ROARING CRK WTR CO	3
BEAVER FALLS	0475	BEAVER	2	40 46	80 19	760		7A	HOWARD R. KEMP	3
BEAVERTOWN	0482	SNYDER	15	40 45	77 10	640	5P	7A	MARLIN R. ETTINGER	2 3 5
BEECH CREEK STATION	0499	CENTRE	16	41 04	77 34	620		7A	HAROLD S. RUPERT	3 7
BELLEFONTE 4 S	0530	CENTRE	16	40 51	77 47	1110	8A	8A	ROCKVIEW PRISON FARM	2 3 5
BERNE	0599	BERKS	14	40 31	76 00	325		7A	FLOYD W. TRUMP	3
BERWICK	0611	COLUMBIA	15	41 04	76 15	570	6P	6P	AMER CAR + FNDRY CO	2 3 5
BETHLEHEM	0629	NORTHAMPTON	9	40 37	75 22	400		7A	ARTHUR CROPPER	3
#BETHLEHEM LEHIGH UNIV	0634	NORTHAMPTON	9	40 36	75 23	450	MID	MID	LEHIGH UNIVERSITY	2 3 5 C
BLAIN	0725	PERRY	15	40 20	77 31	750		MID	PA DEPT FRST + WTRS	C
BLAIRSVILLE 6 ENE	0736	INDIANA	4	40 27	79 09	2048	8P	8P	U.S. WEATHER BUREAU	2 3 5
BLAKESLEE CORNERS	0743	MONROE	9	41 06	75 36	1650		MID	WALTER WILDRICK	C
BLOSERVILLE 1 N	0763	CUMBERLAND	15	40 16	77 22	650		5P	MRS. B. M. WILLDERS	3
BOSWELL 6 WNW	0820	SOMERSET	1	40 10	79 08	2570		8A	CLARK N. ST. CLAIR	3 C
BRADDOCK LOCK 2	0861	ALLEGHENY	10	40 24	79 52	725		7A	CORPS OF ENGINEERS	3
BRADFORD CAA AIRPORT	0865	MC KEAN	1	41 48	78 38	2150	MID	MID	CIVIL AERO. ADM.	2 3 5 7
BRADFORD CNTRL FIRE STA	0867	MC KEAN	1	41 57	78 39	1500		8A	BRADFORD FIRE DEPT	3
BRADFORD 4 W RES	0868	MC KEAN	1	41 57	78 44	1680	5P	5P	BRADFORD WTR DEPT	2 3 5 7
BREEZEWOOD	0905	BEDFORD	6	40 00	78 14	1352		MID	PA TURNPIKE COMM	3
BROOKVILLE CAA AIRPORT	1002	JEFFERSON	1	41 09	79 06	1417	MID	MID	CIVIL AERO. ADM.	2 3 5 7
BRUCETON 1 S	1033	ALLEGHENY	10	40 18	79 59	1065		7A	AUSTIN R. COOPER	3
BUCKSTOWN 1 SE	1073	SOMERSET	4	40 04	78 50	2460		MID	ALVIN W. MANGES	C
BUFFALO MILLS	1087	BEDFORD	12	39 57	78 39	1318		8A	CLIFFORD C. ADAMS	3
BURGETTSTOWN 2 W	1105	WASHINGTON	11	40 23	80 26	980	7A	7A	SMITH TWP MUN AUTH	2 3 5
BURNT CABINS 2 NE	1115	HUNTINGDON	6	40 05	77 52	990	5P	5P	PA TURNPIKE COMM	2 3 5
#BUTLER	1130	BUTLER	2	40 52	79 54	1100	4P	7A	WILLIAM C. FAUST	2 3 5
BUTLER SUBSTATION	1135	BUTLER	2	40 51	79 53	1140		MID	WEST PENN POWER CO	C
CAMP HILL	1190	CUMBERLAND	15	40 15	76 55	461		6P	JOSEPH N. HOBART	3
CANTON 1 NW	1215	BRADFORD	15	41 40	76 52	1520	7A	7A	MRS.MILDRED SPENCER	2 3 5 7 C
CARLISLE	1234	CUMBERLAND	15	40 12	77 11	460	6P	6P	C. E. MILLER	2 3 5
CARROLLTOWN 2 SSE	1255	CAMBRIA	16	40 35	78 42	2040		8A	ROBERT F. MAURER	3 7
CARTER CAMP 2 W	1262	POTTER	16	41 37	77 45	2030		7A	RICHARD L. MENKEN	3 C
CEDAR RUN	1301	LYCOMING	16	41 31	77 27	800		7A	KATHRYN T.KREIGHBAUM	3
CHADDS FORD	1342	DELAWARE	5	39 52	75 37	170		7A	E. EARL TOUCHTON	3
CHAMBERSBURG 1 ESE	1354	FRANKLIN	12	39 56	77 38	640	9P	9P	CHARLES A. BENDER	2 3 5 C
CHARLEROI	1372	WASHINGTON	10	40 08	79 55	1040		MID	WEST PENN POWER CO	C
CHARLEROI LOCK 4	1377	WESTMORELAND	10	40 09	79 54	749		7A	CORPS OF ENGINEERS	3
#CHESTER	1423	DELAWARE	5	39 51	75 22	86	8A	8A	CHESTER TIMES	2 3 5
CLARENCE	1480	CENTRE	16	41 03	77 56	1410		7A	MISS VELDA SWANCER	3
CLARION 3 SW	1485	CLARION	1	41 12	79 26	1114	8P	7A	PA ELECTRIC CO	2 3 5 C
CLAUSSVILLE	1505	LEHIGH	9	40 37	75 39	670		8A	WILLIAM J. DOTTERER	3
CLAYSVILLE 3 W	1512	WASHINGTON	11	40 07	80 28	1000	7P	7A	MFGRS. L + H CO	2 3 5
CLEARFIELD	1519	CLEARFIELD	16	41 01	78 26	1100		7A	IRA TAYLOR	3
CLERMONT	1529	MC KEAN	1	41 41	78 39	2104		7A	MRS.TILLIE M.SIMONDS	3 C
COALDALE 2 NW	1572	SCHUYLKILL	9	40 50	75 56	1026		7A	PANTHER VLY WTR CO	3 7
COATESVILLE 1 SW	1589	CHESTER	5	39 58	75 50	342	8A	8A	PHILA ELECTRIC CO	2 3 5 C
COLUMBIA	1675	LANCASTER	15	40 02	76 30	300	5S	5S	JAMES H. RUST	2 3 5
CONFLUENCE 1 SW DAM	1705	SOMERSET	17	39 48	79 22	1490	8A	8A	CORPS OF ENGINEERS	2 3 5 6 C
CONFLUENCE 1 NW	1710	FAYETTE	17	39 50	79 22	1331		7A	JOHN L. REID	3
CONNELLSVILLE	1723	FAYETTE	17	40 01	79 36	870		8A	MARSHALL B. MENEFEE	3
CONNELLSVILLE 2 E	1729	FAYETTE	17	40 01	79 33	1300		MID	HARRY C. JOY	C
CONSHOHOCKEN	1737	MONTGOMERY	5	40 04	75 19	70		8A	PHILA ELECTRIC CO	3
COOKSBURG	1749	CLARION	1	41 20	79 13	1180		8A	PA DEPT FRST + WTRS	3
COOKSBURG 2 NNW	1752	CLARION	1	41 21	79 13	1460		8A	PA DEPT FRST + WTRS	3
CORAOPOLIS NEVILLE IS	1773	ALLEGHENY	11	40 30	80 05	720		8A	PGH. COKE + CHEM CO	3
CORRY	1790	ERIE	1	41 55	79 39	1440	6P	6P	RICHARD T. MOUNTAIN	2 3 5 7
COUDERSPORT 3 NW	1806	POTTER	1	41 48	78 03	2020	7P	8A	MISS ELIZABETH NEFF	2 3 5
COUDERSPORT 7 E	1809	POTTER	1	41 46	77 53	2425		7A	CAMP POTATO	3
COVINGTON 2 WSW	1833	TIOGA	15	41 44	77 07	1745		7A	CALVIN R. PACKARD	3
CREEKSIDE	1881	INDIANA	1	40 41	79 12	1035		7A	CORPS OF ENGINEERS	3
CRESSON 2 SE	1895	CAMBRIA	6	40 27	78 34	2540		7A	MILES M. LINGLE	3 C
CUSTER CITY 2 W	1978	MC KEAN	1	41 55	78 41	2120		8A	M. D. BOOTH AND CO	3
DANVILLE	2013	MONTOUR	15	40 58	76 37	460		7A	MRS.MARIE M. LITTLE	3
DERRY	2108	WESTMORELAND	4	40 20	79 18	1150	6P	6P	MISS M. D. WINEMAN	2 3 5
DEVAULT 1 W	2116	CHESTER	14	40 05	75 33	360	MID	MID	PA TURNPIKE COMM	2 3 5
DINGMANS FERRY	2160	PIKE	5	41 13	74 52	364		MID	CLYDE T. VOORHEES	C
DIXON	2171	WYOMING	15	41 34	75 54	620	7A	7A	HAROLD J. KUSCHEL	2 3 5 C
DONEGAL	2183	WESTMORELAND	17	40 07	79 23	1746	MID	MID	PA TURNPIKE COMM	2 3 5 7
DONORA	2190	WASHINGTON	10	40 10	79 52	900	5P	5P	THEODORE F. MATHUES	2 3 5
DOYLESTOWN	2221	BUCKS	5	40 18	75 08	393		5P	GEORGE HART	3
DRIFTWOOD	2245	CAMERON	16	41 20	78 08	880		MID	SIDNEY KENNEDY	C
DU BOIS 7 E	2265	CLEARFIELD	16	41 06	78 38	1670	5P	5P	CITY OF DU BOIS	2 3 5 7 C
DUNLO	2298	CAMBRIA	4	40 17	78 43	2410		MID	MRS. D. L. WHITE	C
DUSHORE 3 NE	2324	SULLIVAN	16	41 33	76 21	1750		7A	PATRICK p. RYAN	3 C
EAGLES MERE	2343	SULLIVAN	16	41 24	76 35	2020	7A	7A	MRS.ELSIE p. BIGGER	2 3 5 C
EAST BRADY	2363	CLARION	1	40 59	79 37	820	5P	5P	A. B. KEMPEL	2 3 5
EAST WATERFORD 3 E	2459	PERRY	6	40 21	77 33	2125	8A	8A	U.S. WEATHER BUREAU	INAC 5/55
EBENSBURG	2466	CAMBRIA	4	40 29	78 43	2090	7P	7A	ROBERT A. MASSER	2 3 5
EDINBORO	2514	ERIE	1	41 52	80 08	1220		8A	EDINBORO ST TCHR COL	3
EDINBORO 7 SW	2518	CRAWFORD	1	41 47	80 13	1200		8A	THOMAS H. YOUNG	3
ELIZABETHTOWN	2560	LANCASTER	15	40 09	76 37	460		8A	MASONIC HOME	3
EMPORIUM 2 SSW	2634	CAMERON	16	41 28	78 15	1735	7A	7A	JACKSON THOMAS	2 3 5 C
ENGLISH CENTER	2644	LYCOMING	16	41 26	77 17	881		7A	WILLIAM SUDERS	3 7 C
EPHRATA	2662	LANCASTER	15	40 11	76 10	465	6P	6P	STANLEY L.VON NEIDA	2 3 5
EQUINUNK 2	2671	WAYNE	5	41 51	75 13	910		7A	MRS. HENRIETTA MURRY	3
ERIE WB AIRPORT	2682	ERIE	8	42 05	80 12	732	MID	MID	U. S. WEATHER BUREAU	2 3 5 7
EVERETT 1 SW	2721	BEDFORD	6	40 00	78 23	1020	MID	MID	PA TURNPIKE COMM	2 3 5 7 C
FARRELL SHARON	2814	MERCER	2	41 14	80 30	865	7P	7P	SHARON STEEL CORP	2 3 5
FORD CITY 4 S DAM	2942	ARMSTRONG	1	40 43	79 30	950	8A	8A	CORPS OF ENGINEERS	2 3 5 6 7 C
FRANKLIN	3028	VENANGO	1	41 23	79 49	987	7P	7A	ROBERT D. RHOADS	2 3 5 C
FREELAND	3056	LUZERNE	15	41 01	75 54	1900	6P	8A	ANDREW B. EVANSHA	2 3 5
GALETON	3130	POTTER	16	41 44	77 39	1325		7A	W. GALE LUSH	3 7
GEIGERTOWN	3189	BERKS	14	40 13	75 50	400		8A	WALTER C. WOLF	3
GEORGE SCHOOL	3200	BUCKS	5	40 13	74 56	135	8A	8A	GEORGE M. HART	2 3 5 7
#GETTYSBURG	3218	ADAMS	12	39 50	77 14	540	9A	9A	HUGH C. MC ILHENNY	2 3 5
GETTYSBURG 1 S	3223	ADAMS	12	39 48	77 14	560		MID	NAT MILITARY PARK	C
GIFFORD	3237	MC KEAN	1	41 51	78 36	2220		8A	SOUTH PENN OIL CO	3
GLENCOE	3298	SOMERSET	12	39 49	78 51	1620		MID	MRS. MARY M.HARTMAN	C
GLEN HAZEL 2 NE DAM	3311	ELK	1	41 34	78 36	1725		8A	CORPS OF ENGINEERS	3 C
GLEN ROCK	3330	YORK	15	39 48	76 44	620		MID	MRS.E.C.MC WILLIAMS	C
GLENWILLARD DASH DAM	3343	ALLEGHENY	11	40 33	80 13	705		7A	CORPS OF ENGINEERS	3
GOULDSBORO	3394	WAYNE	9	41 15	75 27	1890		7A	L. H. EILENBERGER	3
GRATERFORD	3435	MONTGOMERY	14	40 14	75 27	160	7A	7A	CLAUDE K. KULP	2 3 5 7 C
GRATZ 1 N	3438	DAUPHIN	15	40 38	76 43	760	8A	8A	LEE M. LEITZEL	2 3 5 C
GREENSBORO LOCK 7	3503	GREENE	10	39 47	79 55	808		7A	CORPS OF ENGINEERS	3 7
GREENSBURG 2 E	3515	WESTMORELAND	10	40 18	79 31	1225		MID	PA DEPT HIGHWAYS	C
GREENSBURG 3 SE UNITY	3516	WESTMORELAND	10	40 17	79 30	1245		6P	WESTMORELAND WTR CO	3
GREENVILLE	3526	MERCER	2	41 24	80 23	1026	6P	6P	C. EARL MILLER	2 3 5
HANOVER	3662	YORK	15	39 48	76 59	600	8A	8A	HANOVER EVENING SUN	2 3 5 7
#HARRISBURG WB AP	3699	YORK	15	40 13	76 51	335	MID	MID	U.S. WEATHER BUREAU	2 3 5 7 C
HARRISBURG NORTH	3704	DAUPHIN	15	40 18	76 54	323		9A	GEORGE S. BEAL	3
HAWLEY	3758	WAYNE	5	41 29	75 10	880		7A	MRS. KATHERINE BATES	3
HAWLEY 1 S DAM	3761	WAYNE	5	41 28	75 11	1200	7A	7A	PA POWER + LIGHT CO	2 3 5 6 7 C
HOLLIDAYSBURG	4001	BLAIR	6	40 26	78 24	960		MID	JOHN H. RINGLER	C
HOLLISTERVILLE	4008	WAYNE	5	41 23	75 26	1360		8A	PA POWER + LIGHT CO	3
#HOLTWOOD	4019	LANCASTER	15	39 50	76 20	187	MID	8A	PA POWER + LIGHT CO	2 3 5 7 C
HOME	4027	INDIANA	1	40 45	79 06	1220		MID	MRS. EDNA M. BUSH	C
HONESDALE 4 NW	4043	WAYNE	5	41 37	75 19	1410		9A	GEORGE C. WILLIAMS	3
HONESDALE 6 NNW	4044	WAYNE	5	41 39	75 17	1050		MID	FRIEND E. WALTER	C
HONEY BROOK 1 W	4047	CHESTER	5	40 06	75 56	700		7A	S. H. KURTZ	3
HOOVERSVILLE	4058	SOMERSET	4	40 09	78 55	1670		8A	JAMES A. HAHN	3 7
HOP BOTTOM 2 SE	4086	SUSQUEHANNA	15	41 43	75 43	900		7A	JOSEPH J. SANAUSKAS	3
HUNTINGDON	4159	HUNTINGDON	6	40 30	78 01	678	7A	7A	DANIEL I. GROVE	2 3 5
HUNTSDALE	4166	CUMBERLAND	15	40 06	77 16	610		8A	METRO P. DOROSH	3
HYNDMAN	4190	BEDFORD	12	39 49	78 43	920		8A	MRS.GERTRUDE M.BURTU	3 C
INDIANA 3 SE	4214	INDIANA	4	40 36	79 07	1102	7P	7A	CLYMER WATER SVC CO	2 3 5 7 C
IRWIN	4276	WESTMORELAND	10	40 20	79 42	1100	5P	5P	WESTMORELAND WTR CO	2 3 5
JACKSON SUMMIT	4304	TIOGA	15	41 57	77 01	1690		MID	ARCHIE LAIN	C
JAMESTOWN 2 NW	4325	CRAWFORD	2	41 30	80 28	1050	8A	8A	PA DEPT FRST + WTRS	2 3 5 6 C
JIM THORPE	4370	CARBON	9	40 52	75 45	830	5P	5P	HENRY S. HAAK	2 3 5
#JOHNSTOWN	4385	CAMBRIA	4	40 20	78 55	1214	9A	9A	JOHNSTOWN TRIBUNE	2 3 5
JOHNSTOWN 2	4390	CAMBRIA	4	40 19	78 55	1275		MID	CITY OF JOHNSTOWN	C
KANE 1 NNE	4432	MC KEAN	1	41 41	78 48	1750	8A	8A	RUDOLPH A. ANDERSON	2 3 5 7 C
KARTHAUS	4450	CLEARFIELD	16	41 07	78 07	950		7A	JEROME S. HOWE	3
KEATING SUMMIT	4466	POTTER	16	41 41	78 11	1840		7A	EUGENE L. KREITNER	INAC 10/57
KEGG	4481	BEDFORD	6	39 59	78 43	1280	MID	MID	PA TURNPIKE COMM	2 3 5
KITTANNING LOCK 7	4611	ARMSTRONG	1	40 49	79 32	790		VAR	CORPS OF ENGINEERS	3
KREGAR 4 SE	4667	WESTMORELAND	17	40 06	79 14	2530		MID	PA TURNPIKE COMM	3
KRESGEVILLE 3 W	4672	CARBON	9	40 54	75 34	720		7A	CITY OF BETHLEHEM	3
LAFAYETTE MC KEAN PARK	4706	MC KEAN	1	41 48	78 40	2130		7A	ORIN A. BUTTERS	3
LAKEVILLE 1 NNE	4733	WAYNE	5	41 27	75 16	1440		8A	MRS. GLADYS REINEKE	3
LANCASTER 2 NE PUMP STA	4758	LANCASTER	15	40 03	76 17	255	6P	6P	LANCASTER WATER BUR	2 3 5 7
LANCASTER 2 NE FILT PL	4763	LANCASTER	15	40 03	76 17	270		MID	LANCASTER WATER BUR	C
LANDISVILLE 2 NW	4778	LANCASTER	15	40 07	76 26	360	8A	8A	PA STATE COLLEGE	2 3 5 6 C
LATROBE	4832	WESTMORELAND	4	40 19	79 23	1000		MID	WEST PENN POWER CO	INAC 6/56
LAURELTON STATE VILLAGE	4853	UNION	15	40 54	77 13	880		MID	PA DEPT OF WELFARE	C
LAWRENCEVILLE 2 S	4873	TIOGA	15	41 59	77 07	1000	7A	7A	HARRY P. HOWLAND	2 3 5 7
LEBANON 3 W	4891	LEBANON	15	40 20	76 29	460	7A	7A	LEON MILLER	2 3 5
LEBANON 3 SW	4896	LEBANON	15	40 19	76 28	490		MID	THOMAS DONNACHIE	C
LEHIGHTON	4934	CARBON	9	40 50	75 43	580		7A	GOODWIN S. DEFREHN	3 C
LE ROY	4972	BRADFORD	15	41 41	76 43	1040		6P	MRS.DIMMIS M.BAILEY	3
LEWIS RUN 3 SE	4984	MC KEAN	1	41 50	78 39	1740		7A	RUSSELL LINEMAN	3 C
LEWISTOWN	4992	MIFFLIN	6	40 35	77 35	480	7A	7A	AMERICAN VISCOSE CO	2 3 5 7 C
LINESVILLE 5 WNW	5050	CRAWFORD	2	41 41	80 31	1020	7P	8A	MISS RETTA M. CRUMB	2 3 5
LOCK HAVEN	5104	CLINTON	16	41 08	77 27	570	7P	7A	PETER L. STEVENSON	2 3 5
LOCK HAVEN 2	5109	CLINTON	16	41 08	77 27	630		MID	HUGH F. PARKER	C
LONG POND 2 W	5160	MONROE	9	41 03	75 30	1860		7A	THOMAS MECKES	3
LYNCH	5275	FOREST	1	41 36	79 03	1295		7A	CORPS OF ENGINEERS	3
LYNDELL 2 NW	5279	CHESTER	5	40 05	75 46	-		8A	MRS. DOROTHY HARPLE	3
MADERA	5336	CLEARFIELD	16	40 50	78 26	1460	7A	7A	MRS. JULIA J. SHOFF	2 3 5 C
MAHAFFEY	5342	CLEARFIELD	16	40 53	78 44	1280		7A	MISS ELLEN J. MILES	3
MAPLE GLEN	5368	MONTGOMERY	5	40 11	75 11	380		6P	FRANCES E.SCHEIBNER	3
MAPLETON DEPOT	5381	HUNTINGDON	6	40 24	77 56	580		7A	MRS. I. S. BUCHANAN	3
MARCUS HOOK	5390	DELAWARE	5	39 49	75 25	12	MID	MID	SUN OIL CO	2 3 5
MARIENVILLE 1 SW	5400	FOREST	1	41 27	79 09	1700		MID	ROY A. MARKER	C
MARION CENTER 2 SE	5408	INDIANA	1	40 45	79 02	1610		7A	CORPS OF ENGINEERS	3
MARTINSBURG 1 SW	5453	BLAIR	6	40 18	78 20	1360		MID	BLUE MT. CANNERIES	C
MARTINSBURG CAA AP	5454	BLAIR	6	40 18	78 19	1463	MID	MID	CIVIL AERO. ADM.	2 3 5 7
MATAMORAS	5470	PIKE	5	41 22	74 42	439		7A	HARRY BISLAND	3 7
MC CONNELLSBURG	5526	FULTON	12	39 56	78 00	895		7A	MRS. HELEN M. SHIVES	3
MC KEESPORT	5573	ALLEGHENY	10	40 21	79 52	720		8A	NATIONAL TUBE CO	3
MEADOW RUN PONDS	5601	LUZERNE	15	41 13	75 40	1995		MID	GEORGE PEARAGE	C
MEADVILLE 1 S	5606	CRAWFORD	1	41 38	80 10	1065	8A	8A	CITY OF MEADVILLE	2 3 5 7 C
MEDIX RUN	5627	ELK	16	41 17	78 24	1100		7A	MRS.E. M. SNYDER	3 7 C
MERCER 2 NNE	5651	MERCER	2	41 15	80 13	1160	7P	7A	MRS. FRAN. STRUTHERS	2 3 5
MERCER HIWAY SHED	5654	MERCER	2	41 14	80 15	1250		MID	PA DEPT HIGHWAYS	C
MERCERSBURG	5662	FRANKLIN	12	39 50	77 54	605		8A	ROLLIN P. GILBERT	3
MERWINSBURG	5676	MONROE	9	40 58	75 28	970		MID	WILLIAM D. GOULD	C
MEYERSDALE	5684	SOMERSET	17	39 49	79 02	2040		8A	ARTHUR J. POTTER	3
MIDDLETOWN OLMSTED FLD	5703	DAUPHIN	15	40 11	76 46	303	MID	MID	U. S. AIR FORCE	2 3 5
MIDLAND DAM 7	5710	BEAVER	11	40 38	80 28	689	11P	7A	CORPS OF ENGINEERS	2 3 5
MILAN 4 WNW	5732	BRADFORD	15	41 56	76 35	1448		MID	CARL A. MORRIS	C
MILANVILLE	5738	WAYNE	5	41 40	75 04	760		8A	CHARLES W. DAVIS	3
MILLERSBURG 2 E	5775	DAUPHIN	15	40 32	76 56	560		MID	RUSSELL SHEPLEY	C
MILLHEIM	5790	CENTRE	15	40 54	77 29	1090		7A	NEVIN E. BOWERSOX	3
MILLVILLE 2 SW	5817	COLUMBIA	15	41 06	76 34	860		7A	KENNETH LEIGHOW	3 C
MILROY	5825	MIFFLIN	6	40 43	77 35	770		8A	THOMAS C. HARBESON	3
MONTROSE 1 E	5915	SUSQUEHANNA	15	41 50	75 51	1630	7A	7A	WILBER W. HOOPES,JR	2 3 5 7 C
MORGANTOWN	5956	BERKS	15	40 09	75 54	595	MID	MID	PA TURNPIKE COMM	2 3 5
MT GRETNA 2 SE	6028	LANCASTER	15	40 14	76 26	670	MID	MID	PA TURNPIKE COMM	2 3 5
MT POCONO 2 N AP	6055	MONROE	5	41 09	75 22	1915	5P	5P	H. JOHN DAVIS, JR.	2 3 5 C
MOUNT UNION 1 N	6067	MIFFLIN	6	40 24	77 53	820		MID	MT UNION WTR WORKS	C
MUHLENBURG 1 SE	6090	LUZERNE	15	41 13	76 08	1110	6P	6P	THEODORE J. SAMPSON	2 3 5 7
MURRYSVILLE	6111	WESTMORELAND	10	40 26	79 42	903		MID	DAVID C. SHAW	C
MYERSTOWN	6126	LEBANON	14	40 22	76 18	460		8A	MRS.KATHLEEN MANDELL	3
NATRONA LOCK 4	6151	ALLEGHENY	1	40 37	79 43	800		7A	CORPS OF ENGINEERS	3
NEFFS MILLS 3 NE	6174	HUNTINGDON	6	40 40	77 55	900		MID	PA STATE UNIVERSITY	C
NESHAMINY FALLS	6194	BUCKS	5	40 09	74 57	60		MID	PHILA SUB WATER CO	3
NEWBURG 3 W	6225	FRANKLIN	15	40 09	77 37	745	5P	5P	PA TURNPIKE COMM	2 3 5
NEW CASTLE 1 N	6233	LAWRENCE	2	41 01	80 22	825	5P	7A	BAXTER F. JOHNSON	2 3 5 C
NEWELL	6246	FAYETTE	10	40 05	79 54	805	12M	12M	GENERAL CHEMICAL CO	2 3 5
NEW PARK	6289	YORK	15	39 44	76 30	780		6P	CLINTON J. ALLEN	3
NEWPORT	6297	PERRY	6	40 29	77 08	400	7A	7A	MRS. FRANCES K. FRY	2 3 5 7
NEW STANTON	6310	WESTMORELAND	10	40 13	79 36	980	MID	MID	PA TURNPIKE COMM	2 3 5
NEW TRIPOLI	6326	LEHIGH	14	40 41	75 45	570		6P	FRED C. OSWALD	3
NORRISTOWN	6370	MONTGOMERY	14	40 07	75 21	75	MID	8A	GEORGE H. BOONE	2 3 5
NORTH EAST 2 SE	6396	ERIE	8	42 12	79 49	1060		9A	ELLSWORTH WEAVER	3
ORWELL 3 N	6621	BRADFORD	15	41 55	76 16	1620		8A	WILLIAM I. BROWN	3
PALM	6681	MONTGOMERY	14	40 26	75 32	385		8A	FRED C. ESCHBACH	3
#PALMERTON	6689	CARBON	9	40 48	75 37	435	MID	MID	NEW JERSEY ZINC CO	2 3 5 C
PARKER	6721	ARMSTRONG	1	41 05	79 41	1140		7A	LOUIS A. MALARKEY	3
PARKER 1 E	6724	CLARION	1	41 06	79 40	1100		MID	P. M. NEELY	C
PAUPACK 2 WNW	6762	PIKE	5	41 24	75 14	1360		8A	MISS L. VETTERLEIN	3
PECKS POND	6786	PIKE	5	41 17	75 06	1380		9A	MRS. CARRIE NESS	3
#PHIL DREXEL INST OF TEC	6879	PHILADELPHIA	14	39 57	75 11	30	MID	MID	FRANCIS K. DAVIS,JR	2 3 5
PHILADELPHIA WB AP	6889	PHILADELPHIA	5	39 53	75 14	13	MID	MID	U.S. WEATHER BUREAU	2 3 5 7 C
#PHILADELPHIA PT BREEZE	6899	PHILADELPHIA	5	39 55	75 12	32	MID	MID	ATLANTIC REFINING	2 3 5 C
PHILIPSBURG CAA AP	6916	CENTRE	6	40 54	78 05	1918	MID	MID	CIVIL AERO. ADM.	2 3 5 7 C
PHOENIXVILLE 1 E	6927	CHESTER	14	40 07	75 30	105	6P	MID	PHILA SUB WATER CO	2 3 5 C
PIKES CREEK	6939	LUZERNE	15	41 18	76 08	1320		7A	HARRY SHELDON	3 C
PIMPLE HILL	6944	MONROE	9	41 02	75 30	2215	9A	9A	PA DEPT FRST + WTRS	2 3 5 6 7
PINE GROVE 1 NE	6954	SCHUYLKILL	15	40 34	76 22	535		8A	PA POWER + LIGHT CO	3
PITTSBURGH WB AP 2	6993	ALLEGHENY	11	40 30	80 13	1151	MID	MID	U.S. WEATHER BUREAU	2 3 5 7 C
#PITTSBURGH WB CITY	6997	ALLEGHENY	11	40 27	80 00	749	MID	MID	U.S. WEATHER BUREAU	2 3 5 C
PLEASANT MOUNT 1 W	7029	WAYNE	5	41 44	75 27	1800	8A	8A	PA FISH COMM	2 3 5 7 C
PORT CLINTON	7116	SCHUYLKILL	14	40 35	76 02	450	7A	7A	MRS. ADA E. RARICK	2 3 5 C
PORTLAND	7127	NORTHAMPTON	5	40 55	75 06	297		8A	JOINT BRIDGE COMM	INAC 1/56
POTTSVILLE	7161	SCHUYLKILL	14	40 42	76 11	690		8A	LLOYD E. HELLER	3
PUNXSUTAWNEY	7217	JEFFERSON	1	40 57	79 00	1298		MID	JOHN VOLANSKY	C
PUTNEYVILLE 2 SE DAM	7229	ARMSTRONG	1	40 55	79 17	1270	8A	8A	CORPS OF ENGINEERS	2 3 5 C
QUAKERTOWN 1 E	7239	BUCKS	5	40 26	75 20	480	5P	7A	DENNIS K. FLUCK	2 3 5
RAYMOND	7310	POTTER	13	41 52	77 52	2220		7A	MRS. RACHEL LANGAN	3 C
#READING WB CITY	7318	BERKS	14	40 20	75 58	266	MID	MID	U.S. WEATHER BUREAU	2 3 5 7 C
RENOVO	7409	CLINTON	16	41 20	77 46	660		7A	MRS. CAROLINE BAIRD	3
RENOVO 5 S	7410	CLINTON	16	41 14	77 46	2035		MID	C. F. GILLETTE	C
REW	7425	MC KEAN	1	41 54	78 32	2250		8A	HAROLD C. MEALY	3
RICES LANDING L 6	7443	GREENE	10	39 57	80 00	775		7A	CORPS OF ENGINEERS	3
RIDGWAY 3 W	7477	ELK	1	41 25	78 47	1420	7A	7A	BOROUGH OF RIDGWAY	2 3 5
ROCHESTER 1 N	7540	BEAVER	2	40 43	80 18	900		MID	DEQUESNE LIGHT CO	C
RUSH	7694	SUSQUEHANNA	15	41 47	76 03	1000		9A	MISS MAUDE MC CAIN	3
RUSHVILLE	7727	SUSQUEHANNA	15	41 47	76 07	870		7A	CARL KOPATZ	3
SAFE HARBOR	7732	LANCASTER	15	39 55	76 23	270		MID	S.M.WATER POWER CORP	C
SAGAMORE 1 S	7739	INDIANA	1	40 46	79 14	1320		7A	CORPS OF ENGINEERS	3
SALINA 3 W	7782	WESTMORELAND	7	40 31	79 33	1109	6P	6P	MUN AUTH WSTMRLD CO	2 3 5
SAXTON	7846	BEDFORD	6	40 12	78 15	780		8A	MRS.ALVERTA L.HOLMES	3 C
SCANDIA 2 E	7855	WARREN	1	41 55	79 01	2040		MID	DAVID R. ANDERSON	C
SCHENLEY LOCK 5	7863	ARMSTRONG	1	40 41	79 40	783		VAR	CORPS OF ENGINEERS	3
#SCRANTON	7902	LACKAWANNA	15	41 25	75 40	746	7A	7A	U.S. POST OFFICE	2 3 5
SCRANTON WB AIRPORT	7905	LUZERNE	15	41 20	75 44	956	MID	MID	U.S. WEATHER BUREAU	2 3 5 7 C
SELLERSVILLE 2 NW	7938	BUCKS	5	40 23	75 20	530		MID	SELLERSVILLE WTR CO	C

STATION INDEX

CONTINUED

Station	Index No.	County	Drainage ‡	Latitude	Longitude	Elevation	Observation Time Temp.	Observation Time Precip.	Observer	Refer To Tables
SHADE GAP 2 NE	7965	HUNTINGDON	6	40 12	77 52	920		MID	MRS. HELEN M. PYLE	C
SHAMOKIN	7978	NORTHUMBLAND	15	40 48	76 33	770		8A	ROARING CRK WTR CO	3
SHEFFIELD 6 W	8026	WARREN	1	41 41	79 09	1940		MID	L. N. HANSON	C
SHIPPENSBURG	8073	FRANKLIN	15	40 03	77 32	709	4P	4P	KEITH B. ALLEN	2 3 5 7
SHIPPINGPORT WB	8078	BEAVER	11	40 37	80 26	740	MID	MID	U.S. WEATHER BUREAU	2 3 5 7 C
SINNEMAHONING	8145	CAMERON	16	41 19	78 05	790		7A	MRS.FRANCES CALDWELL	3
SLIPPERY ROCK	8184	BUTLER	2	41 04	80 03	1345	7P	7A	WALTER D. ALBERT	2 3 5 7
SMETHPORT HIGHWAY SHED	8190	MC KEAN	1	41 48	78 27	1510		MID	PA DEPT HIGHWAYS	C
SOMERSET FAIRVIEW ST	8244	SOMERSET	17	40 01	79 05	2140		7A	HOWARD G. PECK	3
SOMERSET MAIN ST	8249	SOMERSET	17	40 01	79 05	2150	6P	6P	DAVID L. GROVE	2 3 5
SOUTH CANAAN 1 NE	8275	WAYNE	5	41 31	75 24	1400		MID	EUGENE M. COOK	C
SOUTH MOUNTAIN	8308	FRANKLIN	12	39 51	77 30	1520		7A	PA DEPT OF HEALTH	3
SPRINGBORO	8359	CRAWFORD	8	41 48	80 23	900	8A	8A	SPRINGBORO BOROUGH	2 3 5 C
SPRING GROVE	8379	YORK	15	39 52	76 52	470		4P	P. H. GLATFELTER CO	3 C
SPRINGS 1 SW	8395	SOMERSET	17	39 44	79 10	2500	8P	8P	ALLEN E. YODER	2 3 5 7
#STATE COLLEGE	8449	CENTRE	16	40 48	77 52	1175	7A	7A	PA STATE COLLEGE	2 3 5 6 C6
STRAUSSTOWN	8570	BERKS	14	40 29	76 11	600		8A	JACOB KLAHR	3
STRONGSTOWN	8589	INDIANA	4	40 33	78 55	1880		MID	HARRY F. BENNETT	C
STROUDSBURG	8596	MONROE	5	40 59	75 12	480	11P	11P	WILLIAM MAGERTY	2 3 5 C
STUMP CREEK	8610	JEFFERSON	1	41 01	78 50	1320		7A	CORPS OF ENGINEERS	3
SUNBURY	8668	NORTHUMBLAND	15	40 51	76 48	440	7A	7A	CHARLES W. BAYLER	2 3 5 C
SUSQUEHANNA	8692	SUSQUEHANNA	15	41 57	75 36	1020		7A	MRS. LAURA A.BENSON	3
SUTERSVILLE	8699	ALLEGHENY	17	40 14	79 48	765		7A	FRANK E. MARSH	3
TAMAQUA	8758	SCHUYLKILL	14	40 48	75 58	830		8A	MRS. MARY L.ROBERTS	3
TAMAQUA 4 N DAM	8763	SCHUYLKILL	14	40 51	75 59	1120		7A	PANTHER VLY WTR CO	3 C
TAMARACK 2 S FIRE TWR	8770	CLINTON	16	41 24	77 51	2220	7A	7A	JAMES E. SWARTZ	2 3 5 7
TIONESTA 2 SE DAM	8873	FOREST	1	41 29	79 26	1200	8A	8A	CORPS OF ENGINEERS	2 3 5 7 C
TITUSVILLE	8885	CRAWFORD	1	41 38	79 40	1550		MID	PA ELECTRIC CO	C
TITUSVILLE WATER WORKS	8888	CRAWFORD	1	41 38	79 42	1220	7P	7P	CITY OF TITUSVILLE	2 3 5
TORPEDO 4 W	8901	WARREN	1	41 47	79 32	1735		7A	MRS. LILY B. GARBER	3
TOWANDA	8905	BRADFORD	15	41 46	76 26	760	7P	7A	MRS. M. O. PARKS	2 3 5 7 C
TOWER CITY 5 SW	8910	DAUPHIN	15	40 31	76 37	745		8P	HARRISBURG WTR DEPT	7
TROY	8959	BRADFORD	15	41 47	76 47	1100		7A	JENNIE L. BALLARD	3
TUNNELTON	8989	INDIANA	4	40 27	79 23	890		MID	MRS. MARY E. WEIMER	C
TURTLEPOINT 4 NE	9002	MC KEAN	1	41 54	78 16	1640		7A	ROBERT D. STRAIT	3
TYRONE 4 NE BALD EAGLE	9024	BLAIR	6	40 43	78 12	1020		7A	FREDERICK L. FRIDAY	3 C
UNION CITY	9042	ERIE	1	41 54	79 50	1325		7A	FORREST M. BRALEY	3 C
UNIONTOWN	9050	FAYETTE	10	39 54	79 44	1040	10P	10P	WM. W. MARSTELLER	2 3 5
UPPER DARBY	9074	DELAWARE	5	39 58	75 18	222	7P	7P	PHIL. SUB.TRANS. CO	2 3 5
UTICA	9099	VENANGO	1	41 26	79 57	1030		7A	MRS.FLORENCE MILLER	3
VANDERGRIFT	9128	WESTMORELAND	7	40 36	79 33	800		7A	UNITED ENG+FNDRY CO	3
VANDERGRIFT 2 W	9133	WESTMORELAND	7	40 36	79 36	995		MID	EUGENE R. YOUNG	C
VIRGINVILLE	9196	BERKS	14	40 31	75 52	350		8A	MRS. MARY M. WRIGHT	3
VOWINCKEL	9206	CLARION	1	41 25	79 14	1620		8A	PA DEPT FRST + WTRS	3
VOWINCKEL 1 WSW	9209	CLARION	1	41 24	79 15	1610		8A	PA DEPT FRST + WTRS	3
WARREN	9208	WARREN	1	41 51	79 08	1280	7P	7A	GILBERT H. REIER	2 3 5
WASHINGTON	9312	WASHINGTON	11	40 11	80 14	1200		MID	PA DEPT HIGHWAYS	C
WATSONTOWN	9345	NORTHUMBLAND	16	41 05	76 32	490		8P	WILLIAM BIRD	3
WAYNESBURG 2 W	9362	GREENE	10	39 54	80 13	980	6P	7A	RALPH L. AMOS	2 3 5
WAYNESBURG 1 E	9367	GREENE	10	39 54	80 10	940		MID	SEWAGE DISPOSAL PLT	C
WEBSTER HILLS 3 SW	9380	FULTON	12	39 49	78 05	920		MID	WILLIAM D. COVER	C
WELLSBORO 3 S	9408	TIOGA	16	41 43	77 16	1920	7A	7A	MARION L. SHUMWAY	2 3 5 C
WELLSVILLE	9420	YORK	15	40 03	76 57	500	5P	5P	D. D. HOOVER	2 3 5
WERNERSVILLE 1 W	9430	BERKS	14	40 20	76 06	405		8A	CHARLES A. GRUBER	3
WEST CHESTER	9464	CHESTER	5	39 58	75 36	440	8A	8A	DAILY LOCAL NEWS	2 3 5
WEST GROVE 1 E	9503	CHESTER	5	39 49	75 49	440		8A	CONARD-PYLE CO	3
WEST HICKORY	9507	FOREST	1	41 34	79 25	1090		8A	MRS.HELEN F.KINNEAR	3
WHITESBURG	9655	ARMSTRONG	1	40 45	79 24	1530		7A	CORPS OF ENGINEERS	3
WILKES-BARRE	9702	LAZERNE	15	41 15	75 52	610		7A	MRS. MARY G. NIRMAK	3
WILLIAMSBURG	9714	BLAIR	6	40 28	78 12	860		7A	MYRON K. BIDDLE	3
WILLIAMSPORT WB AP	9728	LYCOMING	16	41 15	76 55	527	MID	MID	U.S. WEATHER BUREAU	2 3 5 7 C
WIND GAP	9781	NORTHAMPTON	5	40 51	75 18	740		MID	W. L. TEMPLETON	C
WOLFSBURG	9823	BEDFORD	6	40 03	78 32	1190		7A	WALTER C. RICE	3
YORK 3 SSW PUMP STA	9933	YORK	15	39 55	76 45	390	5P	5P	YORK WATER COMPANY	2 3 5
YORK 2 S FILTER PLANT	9938	YORK	15	39 56	76 44	640		MID	YORK WATER COMPANY	C
YORK HAVEN	9950	YORK	15	40 07	76 43	310		8A	METROPOL EDISON CO	3
YOUNGSVILLE	9966	WARREN	1	41 51	79 20	1225		MID	HENRY CARLETT	C
ZION GROVE	9990	SCHUYLKILL	15	40 54	76 13	940		7A	JAMES D. TEETER	3
ZIONSVILLE 3 SE	9995	LEHIGH	14	40 27	75 27	660		7A	LESLIE HOWATT	3
CLOSED STATIONS										
#PHILADELPHIA CITY	6909	PHILADELPHIA	5	39 57	75 09	26	9A	9A	USN HYDROGRAPHIC OFF	CLOSED 10/57
WELLSBORO 2 E	9412	TIOGA	16	41 45	77 16	1550		MID	MRS. IDA S. MAYNARD	CLOSED 11/57

‡ 1-ALLEGHENY; 2-BEAVER; 3- 4-CONEMAUGH; 5-DELAWARE; 6-JUNIATA; 7-KISKIMINETAS; 8-LAKE ERIE; 9-LEHIGH; 10-MONONGAHELA; 11-OHIO; 12-POTOMAC; 13-LAKE ONTARIO; 14-SCHUYLKILL; 15-SUSQUEHANNA; 16-WEST BRANCH; 17-YOUGHIOGHENY

REFERENCE NOTES

Additional information regarding the climate of Pennsylvania may be obtained by writing to the State Climatologist at Weather Bureau Airport Station, Harrisburg State Airport, New Cumberland, Pennsylvania, or to any Weather Bureau Office near you.

Figures and letters following the station name, such as 12 SSW, indicate distance in miles and direction from the post office.

Delayed data and corrections will be carried only in the June and December issues of this bulletin.

Monthly and seasonal snowfall and heating degree days for the preceding 12 months will be carried in the June issue of this bulletin.

Stations appearing in the Index, but for which data are not listed in the tables, either are missing or were received too late to be included in this issue.

Divisions, as used in Table 2, became effective with data for September 1956.

Unless otherwise indicated, dimensional units used in this bulletin are: Temperature in °F, precipitation and evaporation in inches, and wind movement in miles. Monthly degree day totals are the sums of the negative departures of average daily temperatures from 65° F.

Evaporation is measured in the standard Weather Bureau type pan of 4 foot diameter unless otherwise shown by footnote following Table 6. Max and Min in Table 6 refer to extremes of temperature of water in pan as recorded during 24 hours ending at time of observation.

Long-term means for full-time stations (those shown in the Station Index as "U. S. Weather Bureau") are based on the period 1921-1950, adjusted to represent observations taken at the present location. Long-term means for all stations except full-time Weather Bureau stations are based on the period 1931-1955.

Water equivalent values published in Table 7 are the water equivalent of snow, sleet or ice on the ground. Samples for obtaining measurements are taken from different points for successive observations; consequently occasional drifting and other causes of local variability in the snowpack result in apparent inconsistencies in the record. Water equivalent of snow on the ground is measured at selected stations when two or more inches of snow are on the ground.

Entries of Snowfall in Tables 2 and 7, and in the seasonal snowfall table, include snow and sleet. Entries of snow on ground include snow, sleet and ice.

Data in Tables 3, 5, and 6 and snowfall in Table 7, when published, are for the 24 hours ending at time of observation. The Station Index lists observation times in the standard of time in local use. During the summer months some observers take the observations on daylight saving time.

Snow on ground in Table 7 is at observation time for all except Weather Bureau and CAA stations. For these stations snow on ground values are at 7:30 a.m., E.S.T.

- \- No record in Tables 3, 6, 7 and the Station Index. No record in Tables 2 and 5, is indicated by no entry. Consult the annual issue of this publication for interpolated monthly precipitation totals.
- \+ And also on a later date or dates.
- ++ Fastest observed one minute wind speed. This station is not equipped with automatic wind instruments.
- * Amount included in following measurement, time distribution unknown.
- // Gage is equipped with a windshield.
- \# Thermometers are generally exposed in a shelter located a few feet above sod-covered ground; however, the reference indicates that the thermometers are exposed in a shelter located on the roof of a building.
- AM Data based on observational day ending before noon.
- B Adjusted to a full month.
- C In the "Refer to Tables" column in the Station Index the letter "C" indicates recorder stations. These stations are processed for special purposes and are published later in "Hourly Precipitation Data".
- D Water equivalent of snowfall wholly or partly estimated, using a ratio of 1 inch water equivalent to every 10 inches of new snowfall.
- G In the "Refer to Tables" column in the Station Index the letter "G" indicates that soil temperatures are published.
- M One or more days of record missing; if average value is entered, less than 10 days record is missing. See Table 3 for detailed daily record. Degree day data, if carried for this station, have been adjusted to represent the value for a full month.
- R Amounts from recording gage (These amounts are essentially accurate but may vary slightly from the amounts to be published later in "Hourly Precipitation Data".)
- SS This entry in time of observation column in Station Index means observation made near sunset.
- T Trace, an amount too small to measure.
- Y Includes total for previous month.
- VAR This entry in time of observation column in Station Index means variable.

Information concerning the history of changes in locations, elevations, exposure etc. of substations through 1955 may be found in the publication "Substation History" for this state, soon to be issued. That publication, when available, may be obtained from the Superintendent of Documents, Government Printing Office, Washington 25, D. C. at a price to be announced. Similar information for regular Weather Bureau stations may be found in the latest issues of Local Climatological Data, Annual for the respective stations, obtained as indicated above, price 15 cents.

Subscription Price: 20 cents per copy, monthly and annual; $2.50 per year. (Yearly subscription includes the Annual Summary). Checks, and money orders should be made payable to the Superintendent of Documents. Remittance and correspondence regarding subscriptions should be sent to the Superintendent of Documents, Government Printing Office, Washington 25, D. C.

USCOMM-WB-Asheville, N. C. --- 1/9/58 --- 1100

See Page 181 for Soil Temperatures

5

U. S. DEPARTMENT OF COMMERCE
SINCLAIR WEEKS, Secretary
WEATHER BUREAU
F. W. REICHELDERFER, Chief

CLIMATOLOGICAL DATA

PENNSYLVANIA

DECEMBER 1957
Volume LXII No. 12

ASHEVILLE: 1958

PENNSYLVANIA - DECEMBER 1957

WEATHER SUMMARY

GENERAL

Bountiful precipitation, much of it in the form of rain that fell on frost-free soil, replenished wells and streams throughout the Keystone State this month to relieve water shortages that had plagued the area since May. Snow storms reversed the usual pattern of snowfall accumulation to give Philadelphia nearly three times the average amount for December while the total at Erie was well under half of the December average.

Precipitation totals were generally 2 to 4 inches above average in the eastern third of the State and 1 to 3 inches above in the Central and Western portions. Erie WB AP was the best approach to a dry spot with a total of 2.20 inches while Pimple Hill was the wet spot with a total of 11.21 inches. The greatest amount for one day was also reported by the Pimple Hill station, 5.00 inches measured on the 21st.

Average temperatures were generally 3 to 5 degrees above the seasonal level as a result of warm weather the latter half of the month that far outweighed brief cold periods during the first half. Extreme temperatures ranged from - 8° on the 5th at Ridgeway 3 W to 68° on the 20th at Franklin.

WEATHER DETAILS

Precipitation was an almost daily feature at most stations the 3rd through the 11th and again the 18th through the 21st. Wet weather also made statewide appearances the 25th-26th and the 31st. The initial precipitation period produced a major snowstorm on the 4th, a less spectacular snowstorm that continued through the greater part of the 10th and 11th, and moderate to heavy rains around the 7th. Heavy rains were widespread on the 20th and again the 26th. Temperatures somewhat below the seasonal average the 1st and the 3rd to the 6th, plus a hard cold snap the 11th-12th represented the extent of cold weather in the Keystone State this month. There was a brief period of quite warm weather around the 7th and beginning with the 15t all full time Weather Bureau stations indi cated above average temperatures every day through the end of the month. Six days of very warm weather the 19th through the 24t produced the high temperature for the mont at all stations, most of them around the 20th.

WEATHER EFFECTS

Mild weather permitted more grazing than usual and a few herds were still on pastur as late as Christmas Day. Considerable plowing for spring crops was accomplished. Nearly all of the rain fell on unfrozen ground and prospects for 1958 crops improv as water soaked through surface soils into the sub-soils. Motor traffic encountered hazardous road conditions as a result of the snowstorms of the 4th and 10th-11th.

DESTRUCTIVE STORMS

A statewide snowstorm on the 4th deposited 3 to 11 inches of snow that drifted to a depth of 6 feet in some places. The heavi est falls occurred in the eastern sections Heart attacks induced by overexertion caus a dozen deaths while auto mishaps added several fatalities and a number of injurie

A second snowstorm the 10th and 11th broug 2 to 4 inches of snow. Numerous auto mishaps were also associated with this storm.

The eastern portion of the State was subjected to a damaging rainstorm on the 20th that poured 4 to 5 inches of water into the Pocono Mountain area in a period of 15 hours. Sections of roads were washed away and considerable property damage resulted from flooding of small streams.

FLOODS

Minor flooding occurred on the Lackawaxen and Lehigh Rivers following the rainstorm of the 20th.

J. T. B. Beard, Climatologist
Weather Records Processing Center
Chattanooga, Tennessee

SPECIAL NOTICE

A survey has indicated that the comprehensive narrative weather story carried in each issue of Climatological Data is of value to only a small number of recipients. This story will be discontinued, therefore, with the January 1958 issue. A table of extremes will be carried each month and a text will be carried whenever unusual and outstanding weather events have occurred. General weather conditions in the U. S. for each month are described in the publications MONTHLY WEATHER REVIEW and the MONTHLY CLIMATOLOGICAL DATA, NATIONAL SUMMARY, either of which may be obtained from the Superintendent of Documents, Government Printing Office, Washington, D. C.

CLIMATOLOGICAL DATA

LE 2

PENNSYLVANIA
DECEMBER 1957

Station		Temperature: Average Maximum	Average Minimum	Average	Departure From Long Term Means	Highest	Date	Lowest	Date	Degree Days	No. of Days: Max 90° or Above	Max 32° or Below	Min 32° or Below	Min 0° or Below	Precipitation: Total	Departure From Long Term Means	Greatest Day	Date	Snow, Sleet: Total	Max. Depth on Ground	Date	No. of Days: .10 or More	.50 or More	1.00 or More
POCONO MOUNTAINS																								
EELAND		40.3M	25.7M	33.0M	5.7	57	21	4	12	988	0	6	28	0	7.90	4.32	2.53	21	11.3	5	4+	12	3	3
WLEY 1 S DAM	AM	40.3	23.4	31.9		60	21+	8	13	1023	0	6	27	0	5.40		2.13	21	5.7	4	4	9	3	2
POCONO 2 N AP		38.3	24.7	31.5	5.8	57	20	4	12	1031	0	9	27	0	010.74	7.18			5.7	3	4+			
HLENBURG 1 SE																								
MPLE HILL	AM	37.4	23.5	30.5		56	21	1	12	1063	0	8	28	0	11.21		5.00	21	9.8	3	4+	12	4	4
EASANT MOUNT 1 W	AM	37.5	21.6	29.6		57	21	5	13	1091	0	8	27	0	6.15	2.88	1.77	21	7.0	3	4+	13	3	2
RANTON	AM	42.8	28.3	35.6	4.7	64	21	11	12+	904	0	3	23	0	4.56	2.30	1.29	21	3.3			11	3	2
RANTON WB AIRPORT		40.7	26.4	33.6	4.0	62	20	8	12	966	0	7	25	0	4.04	1.67	1.46	20	6.0	3	4	6	3	2
ROUDSBURG		41.7	24.1	32.9	2.6	61	20	7	13	984	0	2	26	0	9.89	6.46	5.27	20	9.5	5	4	9	4	2
DIVISION				32.3											7.49				7.3					
EAST CENTRAL MOUNTAINS																								
LLENTOWN WB AP	R	43.5	27.5	35.5	4.4	63	20	12	12	907	0	3	24	0	5.52	2.50	2.19	20	6.9	4	5	9	3	2
LLENTOWN GAS CO	AM	44.2	28.3	36.3	4.2	64	21	12	12+	887	0	3	23	0	6.06	2.83	2.37	21	10.5	4	5	11	2	1
ETHLEHEM LEHIGH UNIV		44.9	29.6	37.3	4.0	61	20	13	11	853	0	1	19	0	5.51	2.24	1.59	20	10.0	7	4	10	4	2
IM THORPE		46.0M	28.0M	37.0M	6.6	62	21	9	12+	857	0	2	22	0	8.09	4.29	2.55	20	3.0	3	4	8	5	3
ALMERTON		42.9	28.3	35.6	4.3	62	20	13	12	905	0	2	23	0	8.09	5.36	3.99	20	2.8	3	5	8	3	3
ORT CLINTON	AM	43.8	25.8	34.8	3.0	62	21	9	13	929	0	3	26	0	D 6.77	3.16	2.47	21	3.0			10	5	1
DIVISION				36.1											6.67				6.0					
SOUTHEASTERN PIEDMONT																								
HESTER	AM	47.1M	32.2M	39.7M		64	21	14	12	773	0	1	17	0	5.59		1.30	12				10	5	1
OATESVILLE 1 SW	AM	45.1	27.3	36.2	3.4	61	21	12	12+	888	0	2	23	0	7.27	3.51	2.29	21		12	5	11	6	2
OLUMBIA		44.1	28.5	36.3		59	20	12	12	881	0	2	23	0	5.19		1.66	20	7.5	7	4	6	4	2
EVAULT 1 W		42.1	28.6	35.4		64	20	8	12	910	0	4	23	0	D 9.14		2.01	20	18.7	14	4	10	5	4
PHRATA		43.5	28.1	35.8	2.9	61	20	10	12	894	0	3	23	0	5.19	2.08	1.52	20		5	4	7	4	2
EORGE SCHOOL	AM	45.2	27.0	36.1	2.7	63	21	7	13	890	0	3	21	0	6.68	3.40	1.79	21	14.5	9	5	9	5	2
RATERFORD	AM	46.3	28.7	37.5		66	21	10	12	851	0	3	23	0	5.53	2.58	1.53	21	11.0	7	5	11	4	2
OLTWOOD		44.5	30.0	37.3	2.7	61	20	6	12	852	0	2	21	0	4.70	2.16	1.48	21	12.0	12	5	10	3	1
ANCASTER 2 NE PUMP STA		44.9	27.0	36.0	2.9	63	20	11	6	893	0	2	23	0					5.5	6	4			
ANDISVILLE 2 NW	AM	43.8	26.8	35.3		63	21	10	6+	911	0	3	25	0	4.30		1.54	21	4.0	4	5	8	3	1
EBANON 3 W	AM	43.5	26.3	34.9	2.9	62	21	11	12+	927	0	2	24	0	6.05	2.71	1.81	21	3.5	4	5	11	5	1
ARCUS HOOK		47.2	34.7	41.0	2.5	62	20+	17	12	739	0	2	11	0	5.23	2.27	1.09	26	9.6	8	4	12	4	1
IDDLETOWN OLMSTED FLD		43.5	30.2	36.9	3.9	62	20	12	12	867	0	3	20	0	5.74	3.03	2.11	26	4.9	4	4+	9	3	2
ORGANTOWN		44.1	27.4	35.8		61	20	9	12	899	0	3	21	0	6.74		2.02	20	2.2	12	4	9	5	3
T GRETNA 2 SE		44.2	28.9	36.6		61	20	11	12	876	0	2	21	0	5.44		1.98	20				7	3	2
ORRISTOWN		46.5	31.5	39.0		64	20	15	12	796	0	2	19	0	6.71		1.60	21	10.4	9	5	13	5	2
HIL DREXEL INST OF TEC		47.5	34.6	41.1		65	20	14	12	736	0	2	10	0	4.63		1.39	26	7.9	6	4+	9	4	1
HILADELPHIA WB AP	R	46.2	32.6	39.4	3.5	64	20	14	12	786	0	3	16	0	4.49	1.82	1.21	26	7.8	7	5	10	4	1
HILADELPHIA PT BREEZE		46.3	35.4	40.9	4.3	65	20	14	12+	741	0	2	9	0	4.98		1.31	26	7.0	6	4	9	4	2
HOENIXVILLE 1 E		46.1	28.4	37.3	3.5	63	20+	10	13	854	0	2	21	0	6.34	3.13	1.21	26	13.0	11	4	10	4	4
UAKERTOWN 1 E																								
EADING WB CITY	R	45.1	32.2	38.7	3.9	63	20	14	12	809	0	2	16	0	5.59	2.79	2.13	20	5.0	4	5	9	4	2
PPER DARBY		46.4	31.4	38.9		63	20	12	12	801	0	2	17	0	4.35		1.20	26	11.4	9	4	9	3	1
EST CHESTER	AM	45.2M	31.6M	38.4M	5.0	63	20	10	12	817	0	2	16	0	6.64	2.88	1.30	21	15.3	13	4			
DIVISION				37.6											5.75				9.0					
LOWER SUSQUEHANNA																								
RENDTSVILLE	AM	43.4	26.5	35.0	2.3	59	21	10	12	925	0	3	24	0	5.70	2.60	1.52	21	4.0	4	5	8	5	3
ARLISLE		45.0	29.1	37.1	5.2	61	20+	13	12	860	0	2	20	0	6.25	3.33	1.92	26	4.5	4	4	8	5	2
HAMBERSBURG 1 ESE		44.8	27.2	36.0	2.9	61	20	11	12	894	0	3	23	0	4.87	2.12	1.57	26	5.0	5	4	9	3	2
ETTYSBURG	AM	44.8	28.8	36.8	4.0	61	21	12	12	869	0	4	23	0	5.66	2.52	1.64	26	4.5	4	5	11	3	2
ANOVER	AM	45.3	28.8	37.1	2.6	61	21	11	12+	861	0	3	20	0	6.02	2.98	2.22	21	6.0	6	5	10	3	2
ARRISBURG WB AP	R	44.2	30.3	37.3	3.4	63	20	13	12	855	0	2	19	0	5.23	2.67	1.98	20	7.0	4	5	7	2	2
EWBURG 3 W		46.4	28.1	37.3		63	20	8	12	855	0	2	20	0			1.95	26						2
HIPPENSBURG		45.3	28.0	36.7	3.8	63	20+	10	12	874	0	3	24	0	5.54	2.42	1.71	26	6.5	6	4	7	5	3
ELLSVILLE		45.4	25.9	35.7		61	20	6	6	905	0	3	26	0	6.12		1.97	26	6.7	6	4	7	5	2
ORK 3 SSW PUMP STA		46.2	28.8	37.5	4.1	62	20+	10	6	845	0	2	21	0	4.30	1.38	1.36	26	9.0	8	4	7	3	1
DIVISION				36.7											5.52				5.9					
MIDDLE SUSQUEHANNA																								
EAVERTOWN		43.8	25.7	34.8		61	20+	10	12	929	0	2	25	0	5.44		1.78	21	9.0			9	4	2
ERWICK		44.5	27.8	36.2		64	21	9	12	886	0	2	23	0	3.94		1.02	26	2.0	2	4+	8	4	1
RATZ 1 N	AM	43.3	27.2	35.3		62	21	10	12	914	0	3	23	0	2.64		.83	27	4.0	4	4+	7	2	0
EWISTOWN	AM	44.7	26.6	35.7		63	21	12	13	903	0	2	25	0	3.96		.90	21	2.0	2	4	9	3	0
EWPORT	AM	44.7	27.1	35.9		61	21	13	12+	893	0	2	24	0	5.78	2.75	1.76	21	1.5	2	4	7	5	2
UNBURY	AM	45.1	27.2	36.2		64	21	13	12	888	0	2	25	0	4.79	1.73	1.65	21	2.0	2	4+	7	4	2
ILLIAMSPORT WB AP		42.4	28.0	35.2	4.3	62	20	12	12	918	0	3	24	0	5.05	2.38	2.40	20	3.0	3	4	6	2	2
DIVISION				35.6											4.51				3.4					
UPPER SUSQUEHANNA																								
ANTON 1 NW	AM	38.7	22.1	30.4		59	21	0	12	1064	0	6	28	1	4.57		1.35	21	6.3	2	4+	7	4	1
IXON	AM	43.7	23.5	33.6		62	21	6	5	966	0	3	26	0	5.47		1.53	27	6.7	3	4	9	3	2
AGLES MERE	AM	37.0	22.7	29.0		61	21	0	12+	1082	0	6	28	2	5.63	1.79	2.04	21	7.0	3	12+	9	3	2
AWRENCEVILLE 2 S	AM	41.8	23.3	32.6	4.4	61	21	2	12	999	0	4	26	0	3.05	1.12	.83	21	4.1	4	10	7	2	0
ONTROSE 1 E	AM	36.6	22.8	29.7	3.6	57	21	4	13	1085	0	10	29	0	4.42	1.78	1.51	21	9.4	3	4+	7	2	2

See Reference Notes Following Station Index

TABLE 2 - CONTINUED

Station	
TOWANDA	
WELLSBORO 3 S	AM
DIVISION	
CENTRAL MOUNTAINS	
BELLEFONTE 4 S	AM
DU BOIS 7 E	
EMPORIUM 2 SSW	AM
LOCK HAVEN	
MADERA	AM
PHILIPSBURG CAA AP	
RIDGWAY 3 W	AM
STATE COLLEGE	AM
TAMARACK 2 S FIRE TWR	AM
DIVISION	
SOUTH CENTRAL MOUNTAINS	
ALTOONA HORSESHOE CURVE	
BURNT CABINS 2 NE	
EBENSBURG	
EVERETT 1 SW	
HUNTINGDON	AM
JOHNSTOWN	AM
KEGG	
MARTINSBURG CAA AP	
DIVISION	
SOUTHWEST PLATEAU	
BAKERSTOWN 3 WNW	
BLAIRSVILLE 6 ENE	
BURGETTSTOWN 2 W	AM
BUTLER	
CLAYSVILLE 3 W	
CONFLUENCE 1 SW DAM	AM
DERRY	
DONEGAL	
DONORA	
FORD CITY 4 S DAM	AM
INDIANA 3 SE	
IRWIN	
MIDLAND DAM 7	
NEW CASTLE 1 N	
NEWELL	AM
NEW STANTON	
PITTSBURGH WB AP 2	//R
PITTSBURGH WB CITY	R
PUTNEYVILLE 2 SE DAM	AM
SALINA 3 W	
SHIPPINGPORT WB	
SLIPPERY ROCK	
SOMERSET MAIN ST	
SPRINGS 1 SW	
UNIONTOWN	
WAYNESBURG 2 W	
DIVISION	
NORTHWEST PLATEAU	
BRADFORD CAA AP	
BRADFORD 4 W RES	
BROOKVILLE CAA AIRPORT	
CLARION 3 SW	
CORRY	
COUDERSPORT 3 NW	
EAST BRADY	
ERIE WB AIRPORT	
FARRELL SHARON	
FRANKLIN	
GREENVILLE	
JAMESTOWN 2 NW	AM
KANE 1 NNE	AM
LINESVILLE 5 WNW	
MEADVILLE 1 S	AM
MERCER 2 NNE	
SPRINGBORO	AM
TIONESTA 2 SE DAM	AM
TITUSVILLE WATER WORKS	
WARREN	
DIVISION	

See Reference Notes Following Station Index

DAILY PRECIPITATION

Total	1	2	3	4	5	6	7	8	9	10	11	12	13	14	15	16	17	18	19	20	21	22	23	24	25	26	27	28	29	30	31
4.01	.03			.16	.12		1.03	.20	.08	T	.01	.01	T	T		.02		.50	.40	.21	1.00	T		.13	T	.80	.20		.01		
5.52			.20	.40		.11	.30	.01	.60	.15	.08			T		.01			.22	2.19	T			.01	T	1.14		.01	T		T
6.06	.33			.27	.29		.19	.36	.29	.43	.06	7				.01			.08	.13	2.37				T	.21	.96		.01		
4.51	.02		.05	.17		.20	.76	.02	.09			8						.17	.57	.25	.38			.05	T	1.68	.02				
5.70				.22	.13			.50	.07	.06									.12	1.12	1.52					1.31	.56				
2.77			T	.07		T	.08	.20	.28	T				.07	T	.10			.30	.19	.60					.38	.17				
-			.01	.02	T	.60	.84					T						-	-	-	-					.27	.18	.06			
5.76	.04		.30	.18			1.01	.65	.05	.01		.05	.07	.05	.03	.09		.19	.80	.41	1.07	.01		.15		.40	.10			T	
-	-						-	-	-	-		-	-	-	-	-	-	-	-	-	-	-	-	-	-	-	-	-	-	-	-
9.52				.23			.47		.22	.03		.05				.02			.77	1.01	1.15					1.45	.12				
3.27	.04			.16	.06		.65	.23	.04	T			T	T		T		.30	.31	.21	.23	T		.11		.74	.15		T		
5.44	.07			.14	.03	.02	.15	.30	.13	.09			T	T		.01		T	.20	.93	1.78					1.03	.56				
3.81				.22			.18						T					.03	.55	.55	.54					1.27	.23				
5.43				.18	.15		.15	.58	.20	.32						T			.10	.38	1.04					.37	.92		T		
3.94				.09				T								T			.52	.79	.83			T		1.02	T				
6.29				.24	.44			.35	.27	.42	.10					T			.04	.18	2.18				T	.20	1.03		.01		
5.51			T	.56				.15	.35	.33	.12								.30	1.59	1.11				.45	.55					
4.71			.10	.40		.34	.51	.03	.22			.14	T			.02		.51	.29	.40	.12			.05	.08	1.20	.04	T	T		
4.58				.24	T	.03	.41	.05	.03			T							.85	1.10	.15					1.72					
5.70				.30	.17								.03					.36	.37	.28	.50			.08		1.50	.45		.02		
4.13	T			.14	.01		.78	.30	.05	.01	.01	.02	T			.03		.38	.33	.20	.71			.06	T	.92	.18				
4.02	.05	.09	.08	.06	T	.13	.69	T	.11	T	.03	.06	.02	.04	.06	.03		.06	.26	1.06	.04		.02	.13	.11	.82	T	.06	T	.01	T
3.95	.06	.12	T	.07			.40	.39	.03	T	T	.05	.02	.03		.22		.02	.31	.26	.76			.24		.78	.12			.05	T
-	.12			.08		.18	.74	.08			.03	.05	.08	.05	.05	.22		.17	.24	.66	-	-	-	-	-	-	-	-	-	-	
▷ 3.87			.01	.36	D.20	.06	.19											.21	.32	.48					.48	1.42					.14
4.79			.23	.05		.59	.62		.14	T	T	.05	T	T	.02	.08		.42	.33	.96	.05			.10	.20	.91	T	.04	T		.02
4.13				.15			*			1.13	.03	.03				.02		.53	.18	.19	.86			.06		.99	T				
4.45	T			.27	.45		.18	.15	.25		T							.22	.43	.35	.20			.01		1.55	.38		.01		
4.63	.01			.29	.07		.81	.36	.03		.01					.01		.68	.26	.28	.43			.15		1.16	.08		T		
▷ 4.66				D.22		.10	.27											.09	.64	.78	.40					2.00					
5.49				.35	.02	.20	1.14	.19	.09				.01	T		.03		.48	.44	.35	.78			.14		1.09	.15				
▷ 6.08				D.43	.30	.03	.62	T	.20							T			.88	2.12						1.50					
-		-	-	-		-	.25	.31	.15					.01	.03				.34	.74	.82					.95	.61				
4.57		.06	T	.16		T	.08	.09	.21						T				.54	.46	1.35					.77	.80				
6.25			T	.42		.05	.84									T		T	.80	1.34	.54				T	1.92					
3.86	.01	T		.05			.95	.15	.13		.04	.02	.02		T	.01		.16	.41	.27	.20			.05	T	1.13	.21		T		
5.22	T	.05	T	.05			.40	.56	.25	T	T	T	T	.03	.06				.50	.60	1.55			T		.90	.27				
▷ 3.34	T		.01	.25			.20	.40	.09	.35	D.10	T	T	.05	.02	.03		T	.45	.65	1.10					1.30	.30		.03		T
6.24	.48			.30			.29	.33	.64	.47	.07	.13								.32	1.02					.47	.61		.16		
4.87			.12	.20		.15	.49											.01	.75	1.15					.26	1.57					.03
4.36				.17	.12		.65		.09	.02	.01	T	.01			T		.45	.28	.18	.80			.06	.03	1.02	.10		T		
5.59				.30	.70		.22		.72	.27		1.30							.4	.03	.95					.38	.58		-	.10	
3.08	T		T	.25			.35	.15	.15	.50		T	.03			T		.10	.45	.45	.15			T		.10	.40	T	T		
4.88	.08			.12	.05		1.06	.52	.09	T	T	.02	T	T		.09		.06	.56	.28	.90	T		.09		.79	.15		.02		
6.41					.23	.10	.22												.06	.26	2.77					.62	.73		.02		
4.90	.01			.32	.13		1.07	.66	.05		.03	.02	T					.38	.24	.29	.38			.07		1.17	.08				
4.57	.04			.17	.05		.36	.47	.12	.02	T	T	.05		T	T		.12	.60	.35	.55			T		1.35	.32				
5.88	.06		.06	.12			.81	.64	.16	.08	T	.03	.06	.03	.10	.15		.07	.38	.51	.70	.05		.06		1.04	.04		T	T	T
7.85	.29			.27			.24	.50	.10	.24		.06							.25	.84	3.14					.45	1.45		.02		
7.27									4	.51	T								.04	.19	2.29				T	.54	1.06		.08		
5.19			T	.60	T		.39	.09	.52										.08	1.66	.34					1.51			T		
4.63	.04			.37	.09		.90	.19	.14	T	.06		T			.03		.34	.20	.13	.24			.01	.02	1.54	.29				
3.17	.01			.48	.16		.96	.21	.12	T	.05	.03	.01			.02		.35	.20	.16	.25			.03	.01	1.74	.38		T		
3.56				.06	.06		.60	.35	.15	.03	.20	.19	.05			.02		.28	.05	.10	.37	.03	.02	.05	.02	.77	.14				
5.07				.47															.05	.28	.40					.32	1.12		.11		
5.27	.09		T	.32	.04		1.03	.58	.10	T	.02	.03	.02	T	.03	.17	.02	.06	.45	.33	.86			.08		.94	.05	.01	.04		
5.67	.10		.02	.29	.05	T	1.06	.54	.07	.02	.01	.03	.03	.01	.03	.12	.02	.10	.50	.38	.82			.11		1.27	.06	T	.03		
4.16				.19			*	1.10			T	T	T			T	.64	.25	.16	*	.61					1.12	.04				
4.62	.07	.11		.04		.16	1.26	.03	.02		.07	.24	.07	.01		.20		.19	.19	.48	.20			.29		.98	T	.01	T	T	
3.93	.03	.11	.10	.18				.48	.18	.01	T		.01	.04	.05	.10		T	.41	.35	.89			.04		.54	.16		.02		T
-		-	-	-			.30	.40			*		*	D.10		.10			.20	.25	.30					.70					
3.98		.09	.11	.12			T	.16	.21	.04	T		T		.01	T			.18	.46	1.05					.80	.75				
3.87				.15			.85	.20	.15									.20	.22	.18	.47			.10		1.15	.15				
4.60	.06			.24			.04	.37	.07				.04					.33	.53	.25	.32					1.25	.33				
5.42	.10		T	.11					.03	.01	.01		.03	.06	.06	.19		.04	.35	.26	.90			.24		.83	.13			.01	.02
4.18				.18			.06	.25	.07	.11		T							.04	.66	1.28					.53	1.00				
-			T	.30		.35	.52	.12	.11		.05	.10					.32	*	.35	-				.08	*	1.15					
▷ 9.14			D.10	D1.30		.05	1.80	.23	.88	.29	D.20	.05							.46	2.01	.04			.06	T	1.52		.09	.06		T
9.47		.03	.08	.31			.09	.05	.06	.15	.08	.14		.03					.16	.63	1.49					.43	1.53				
4.19						.64	.73			.02	.07						T	.44	.20	.45	.03			T	.30	.90	T	T			.05
4.38			.02	.27		.27	.76	.06	.10		.06	.02	T					.47	.16	.47	.48			.07	.01	1.07	.09				
6.91				1.12		.02	.50	.16	.82		.12	.10							.06	.47	1.46			T		1.46			.13		
4.19	.02	T	T	.17		.18	.56	.21	.17		T	.02	T	T		.03		.18	.33	.72	.29			.06		1.24	.01				
4.20	.12	.05	.03	.20				.12	.10	.08	.05	.10	T	T	T	.02	T		.10	.38	2.00					.43	.40				.02
5.63		.07	T	.12						.18				T	T				.31	.75	2.04	.03				.45	1.11		T		.01
5.45	.16		.02	.07	.01	.48	1.49	.08	.02		.01							.54	.18	.79	.45					1.11					
4.31	.10	T		.12	.07		.90	.20	T		T		.07			T		.20	.40	.27	.20			.06		1.27	.35				
4.56	.21	.18		.03			.92						.11	.01	T	.18		.32	.36	.29	.12			T		.87	.10		T		
	RECORD MISSING																														
4.18																			.02	.32	1.10					.71	.93				
▷ 5.13	.03	.03	T	.30			.39	.53	.22	T			T	.07	.05	.10		.04	.59	.55	.78			.01	D.05	1.12	.25				
5.15	.04			.22			.19	.21	.19	.04				.02	.03	.02				.98	1.46					.80	.95				T
5.19				.78		.01	.40	.44	.65	.06		.02							.10	1.52						1.17			.01		
6.09	.32	T	T	.12			.18	.21	.14	.31		.11		1.11		.09			.10	.84	2.84	T			.16		1.10		.06		
2.20	T	T	T	T		.29	.68						T	.03	.07	T		.15	.09	.25	.02		.05	T	.05	.20	T	T		.02	T
▷ 4.89			D.19	D.21			.78	.05										.15	.58	.13					.31	1.57					.92
▷ 3.90			D.10	D.25		.14	1.10	.02				D.18				.02		.50	.05	.37	.04			.12	.11	.90					
4.33	T			.15	.14		1.06	.18	.13		.02	.05	T			.03		.43	.31	.17	.52	T		.11		.90	.13		T		
4.02			.01	.12	T		.88	.56	.03		T	.02	.03			.11		.14	.27	.25	.52			.11		.71	.15	.02	.09		
7.90	.37			.41							.08	.48			.02	T	T		.12	1.35	2.53					.17	1.38	.18			
4.95			.18	.27		.27	.52	.30	.03				.01	.07	.10	.11		T	.40	.45	1.18	T				.83	.23				T
6.65	.29			.28	.70		.22	.55	.45	.40		.06							.04	.23	2.09					.56	.78				
6.68				.45	.73		.08	.29	.51	.62	.03	.42							.02	.26	1.79					.07	1.41				
9.66				.20			.12	.34	.19										.12	.93	1.50					1.84	.23				
4.10	.08	.10	T	.20		.10	.08						T	.05	.10		.04	.46	.28	.92		.20		.70		.40	.14		T	T	T
4.66	.07	.12	.07	.13			.49	.45	.15		.04	.02	.03	.02	.05	.17		.03	.42	.29	.89			.07		.93	.18	T	.03	.01	T
4.28	T			.21			.81	.19	.01		T	.01	T			.03		.61	.38	.27	.44			.14		.97	.12				
7.93	.37			.24			.26	.35	.10	.39	.03	.33							.15	.93	3.08					.42	1.28				
5.53	.53			.12	.48		.16	.38	.29	.54		.11								.21	1.53				.02	.08	1.02		.06		
2.64					T							T			T				T	.27	.23					.38	.83		T		
4.16	.01			.29			.71	.26	.12		.07	T	T			T		.42	.14	.12	.51			.02	.03	1.15	.20		T		
3.71			.02	.20		.37	.78	.02	.16	.02	T							.40	.10	.50	.05				.03	1.01	.05				
4.81	.03		.16	.10		.20	1.48			T	.02	.23	T			.14		.55	.19	.39	T			.21	.04	1.07	T				
6.02	T			.18			.13	.44	.13	.17									.02	.42	2.22					1.02	.83		T		
5.23			.06	.35		.08	.47	T	.20	T				T		T		T	.37	1.98	T				.16	1.54		T			.02
6.18	.01			.15			.24	.44	.15	.07	T					T			.17	1.15	1.86					1.38	.43				
5.74	.34	T	.06	.25			.21	.09	.12	.31	T	.09	T	.08	T	T			.06	.57	1.90				T	.15	1.51	T	T		T
5.40	.22		T	.27			.14	.04	.11	.25	.08			.06					.06	.57	2.13					.10	1.37				
5.89	.27	T	.03	.28			.20	.22	.14	.28	.06	.16	T	T		T			.04	.58	2.27				.03	.22	1.11	T			
4.70	.16			.15					0		T	.03	T						.02	.13	1.48				T	.36	.79		.01		
5.14	.25	T	.03	.23			.12	.08	.15	.20	.02	.05	T	.14	T	.01			.07	.70	2.03			.04		.13	.89				
7.37	.34			.20			.30	.49	.38	.47	.08	.30							.08	.22	2.39				T	.41	.98		.03		
-	-		-	-				T								T		T	.06	*	.85				.46	1.72	.14			T	
3.49	.01		.02	.02	T	T	T	.02			.05	.01	T	T					T	.77	.89					.70	.91				
4.24	.08			.13	.09		.26		9				T			T		T	.43	.46	.37			T	T	1.90	.33				

See Reference Notes Following Station Index

DAILY PRECIPITATION

Table 3—Continued

HUNTSDALE																					
HYNDMAN																					
INDIANA 3 SE																					
IRWIN																					
JAMESTOWN 2 NW																					
JERSEY SHORE																					
JIM THORPE																					
JOHNSTOWN																					
KANE 1 NNE																					
KARTHAUS																					
KEGG																					
KITTANNING LOCK 7																					
KREGAR 4 SE																					
KRESGEVILLE 3 W																					
LAFAYETTE MC KEAN PARK																					
LAKEVILLE 1 NNE																					
LANCASTER 2 NE PUMP STA																					
LANDISVILLE 2 NW																					
LAWRENCEVILLE 2 S																					
LEBANON 3 W																					
LEHIGHTON																					
LE ROY																					
LEWIS RUN 3 SE																					
LEWISTOWN																					
LINESVILLE 5 WNW																					
LOCK HAVEN																					
LONG POND 2 W																					
LYNCH																					
LYNDELL 2 NW																					
MADERA																					
MAHAFFEY																					
MAPLE GLEN																					
MAPLETON DEPOT					.					09											
MARCUS HOOK																					
MARION CENTER 2 SE					.			.01		19											
MARTINSBURG CAA AP								T		22											
MATAMORAS						06															
MC CONNELLSBURG								.01	T	02											
MC KEESPORT					T			.02	.10	42											
MEADVILLE 1 S					.		01	.13		09											
MEDIX RUN					T	01	01	.12		10											
MERCER 2 NNE					-			.20		45											
MERCERSBURG																					
MEYERSDALE										26											
MIDDLETOWN OLMSTED FLD								'													
MIDLAND DAM 7								.02		62											
MILANVILLE					T	10		.02													
MILLHEIM					T																
MILLVILLE 2 SW					T			T													
MILROY					.			.01			.45	.72	.85								
MONTROSE 1 E					T	09		.06			.14	.39	1.51		T						
MORGANTOWN								T			.20	2.02									
MT GRETNA 2 SE											.21	1.98									
MT POCONO 2 N AP											.63	*	5.17		.06						
MUHLENBURG 1 SE																					
MYERSTOWN											.10	.35	1.85								
NATRONA LOCK 4											.37	.19	.69		.15						
NESHAMINY FALLS											.11	1.42	.10								
NEWBURG 3 W										72	.71	1.01	.56								
NEW CASTLE 1 N										44	.29	.46	.20		.05						
NEWELL										53	.09	.13	.58								
NEW PARK											.09	1.50	.46								
NEWPORT											.23	.98	1.76								
NEW STANTON											.12	.55	.02								
NEW TRIPOLI											.87	2.37	.64								
NORRISTOWN											.01	.23	1.60								
NORTH EAST 2 SE											.27	.17	.19		.06						
ORWELL 3 N											.14	.32	1.04								
PALM											.08	.30	2.27								
PALMERTON											.10	3.99	.01		.01						
PARKER					05						.43	.31	.98	T	.02						
PAUPACK 2 WNW											.16	.68	2.72								
PECKS POND						T	T				.38	.75	3.94								
PHIL DREXEL INST OF TEC										T	.06	.92	.03		T						
PHILADELPHIA WB AP R										T	.03	.87	.05		T						
PHILADELPHIA PT BREEZE											.02	1.09	.06								
PHILIPSBURG CAA AP					T	T		T		.28	.84	.98	T		.02						
PHOENIXVILLE 1 E											.25	1.17	.09				1	21			
PIKES CREEK					T	T		T			.20	.83	1.82	T		T		20	1.30		
PIMPLE HILL					.01	.01	.02	.01			.45	1.56	5.00		T	.01	1	04	1.12		
PINE GROVE 1 NE											.36	1.05	2.20				1	17	.79		
PITTSBURGH WB AP 2 //R					T		T	.02	.16	.63	.20	.47	.03		.12	.32		73	T		
PITTSBURGH WB CITY R					T		T	.02	.16	.55	.26	1.01	.03	T	.10	.34		72			
PLEASANT MOUNT 1 W					T	.10	.02	.05			.19	.82	1.77		.02	.03		22	1.40		
PORT CLINTON											.27	.86	2.47				1	65	-		
POTTSVILLE					T						.22	.76	2.82				1	30	.59		
PUTNEYVILLE 2 SE DAM					.02	T		.06		.26	.45	.32	.69		.12		1	15	.15		
QUAKERTOWN 1 E			RECORD MISSING															87	.25		
RAYMOND	5.00	.13	.07	.10	.06	.09	.07	.12			.43	.46	1.18								
READING WB CITY R	5.59					T		T			.18	2.13			T	T	1	18			
RENOVO	4.96	T			T	.02	.02	.03		.03	.60	.58	1.10				1	40	.37		
REW	4.13	.08	.10	.02	.01	.05	.06	.12		T	.38	.27	.92	T	.17			75	.08		
RICES LANDING L 6	4.23	.06								.45	.15	.13	.73		.05	.06		90	.05		
RIDGWAY 3 W	4.50	.05			.02		.07	.13		.05	.51	.29	.77	.02	.06			90	.19		T
RUSH	3.09	.13	.01	-	T	.08		.06			.08	.30	1.10					40	.93		
RUSHVILLE	-.--	...		...		T	.03	.03			.05	.25	1.13	T				05	1.15		
SAGAMORE 1 S	4.56			.20	.10					.20	.55	.20	.35	.10				30	.15	T	
SALINA 3 W	3.51			.12				T		.45	.03	.28	.31		.02	.02	1	03	T		
SAXTON	3.51				T			T		.18	.28	.28	.32		T	T	1	54	.14		
SCHENLEY LOCK 5	5.01				.01	T	T	.04		.51	.34	.25	.78		.12		1	10	.12		
SCRANTON	4.56	.10	.18					.05			.02	.55	1.29			.02		18	1.01		
SCRANTON WB AIRPORT	4.04	.01	T	.10	T	T		T		T	.52	1.46	T		.03	T	1	22	T		
SHAMOKIN	5.03							.02			.08	.98	1.51					73	.80		
SHIPPENSBURG	5.94	T						T		T	1.18	1.09	.22				1	71			
SHIPPINGPORT WB	4.04			.18			.03	T	.16	.63	.27	.44	.03		.16	.35		77		T	
SINNEMAHONING	4.64				T	T	.01	.08		.09	.69	.58	1.20		.01			50	.29		.
SIZERVILLE	-					.07	.03	.15		.17	.51	.47	1.17		.03			98	1.22		
SLIPPERY ROCK	4.36				.05			.05		.15	.43	.34	.40		.07			76	.11		
SOMERSET FAIRVIEW ST					.03			T		.27	.34	.17	.23		.02		1	65	.30		
SOMERSET MAIN ST					.07					.34	.27	.17	.16		.03	.04	1	53	.03		T
SOUTH MOUNTAIN											.03	1.50	.90				1	27	.59		
SPRINGBORO						T	.23	.19		.18	.30	.25	.18		.16				T	T	T
SPRING GROVE	5.13										.17	.78	.84				1	70	T		
SPRINGS 1 SW	4.06	.01		.12	T			.05		.50	.03	.02	.22		.11	.17	1	77	.11	.	
STATE COLLEGE	4.52				.01	T	T	T		.03	.51	.88	.69	T	T	T	1	29	.34		T

See Reference Notes Following Station Index

DAILY PRECIPITATION

Day of month

13	14	15	16	17	18	19	20	21	22	23	24	25	26	27	28	29	30	31
			.01			.17	.77	1.87				T	.97	.76				
T	.01		.01		T	.70	5.27	.02			.05	T	2.00	T	.03	.05	T	T
T					.10	.38	.40	.43			.07		1.86	.21				
		T				.06	.70	1.65					1.03	.60		T		
	.05	T	.08			.07	.37	1.46			.01	T	.16	1.28				
T					.45	.14	.19	.72			.03		.96	.14				
						.23	.91	2.87					.50	1.30				
D.25	D.05	T	T	T		.30	1.01	2.93					.66	1.34				
T	.03	.08	.07		.03	.60	.84	1.09			T		1.20	.38		.04		T
T	T	.02	.16		.09	.46	.35	1.02					.53	.04		.02		
.05	.03		.10		.29	.14	1.13	.10			.29	T	1.08	.04	T	.04		
.05	.01	.06	.15		T	.37	.34	.76					.90	.17		.02	T	T
T	T	.02	T			.10	.29	1.08					.15	.92	T	T		T
						1.63	2.93	.29					2.56					
T		.04	T			.13	.54	.97					.38	.70				
.04	.05	.07	.09		.01	.34	.26	.93			---		.66	.18		.05	.03	.02
.01					.02	.60	.59	.63				T	1.17	.41				
			T	T	.34	.08	.43	.02			.04	.16	.87	.01	T			T
						.19	.35	.50					1.20	.05		.07		
			-		-	-	-	.34					1.02	.15				
			T		.36	.33	.11	.47					.86	.25				
						.06	.20	2.17					.42	.80				
			.16	T	.22	.45	.42	.89					1.21	.06	T	.04		
			.14	.02	.15	.47	.42	.85					1.16	.05	T	.03		
			.22			.44	.27	1.13					[illegible]	.13		[illegible]		.01
			T		.02	.78	2.00	.02										T
					.38	.13	.20	.87										
			.02		T	.28	.45	.80										
						.45	1.50	.80										
						.06	.18	1.96										
						.03	.36	1.30										
							.32	2.03										
			.10		.10	.40	.30	.96										
					.39	.24	.27	.64										
			T			T	.60	1.68										
			.02		.13	.55	.41	.36										
			T		.04	.49	2.40	.02										.02
			T		.23	.35	.30	.27										
						.12	.84	.33										

SUPPLEMENTAL DATA

Station	Wind direction		Wind speed m. p. h.				Relative humidity averages - percent				Number of days with precipitation							Percent of possible sunshine	Average sky cover sunrise to sunset
	Prevailing	Percent of time from prevailing	Average	Fastest mile	Direction of fastest mile	Date of fastest mile	1:00 a EST	7:00 a EST	1:00 p EST	7:00 p EST	Trace	.01–.09	.10–.49	.50–.99	1.00–1.99	2.00 and over	Total		
ENTOWN WB AIRPORT	WNW	13	11.0	-	-	-	81	83	69	76	6	5	6	1	1	1	20	-	7.0
E WB AIRPORT	-	-	15.6	40++	SSE	19	-	-	-	-	12	9	6	1	0	0	28	-	8.3
RISBURG WB AIRPORT	WNW	18	7.8	37	NW	1	71	71	58	62	9	3	5	0	2	0	19	45	7.1
LADELPHIA WB AIRPORT	SW	12	9.3	42	S	20	77	78	63	71	6	4	6	3	1	0	20	48	6.9
TSBURGH WB AIRPORT	WSW	26	12.1	34++	SW	23	78	79	65	73	5	8	7	4	0	0	24	40	7.4
DING WB CITY	-	-	11.8	47	S	20	-	-	-	-	6	3	5	2	1	1	18	40	7.0
ANTON WB AIRPORT	SW	16	10.2	47	SW	20	73	75	64	70	13	5	3	1	2	0	24	31	7.4
PPINGPORT WB	-	-	3.6	30%	WNW	1	-	-	-	-	5	4	7	3	0	0	19	-	-
LIAMSPORT WB AIRPORT	-	-	-	-	-	-	-	75	61	68	6	9	4	0	1	1	21	-	7.6
eak Gust																			

DAILY TEMPERATURES

Table 5

Station		1	2	3	4	5	6	7	8	9	10	11	12	13	14	15	16	17	18	19	20	21	22	23	24	25	26	27	28	29	30	31	Average
ALLENTOWN WB AP	MAX	35	47	35	32	34	35	52	50	40	39	37	21	28	39	45	41	43	42	50	63	57	51	54	50	42	57	42	45	45	44	44	43.5
	MIN	25	27	25	25	17	14	32	35	34	33	19	12	14	25	25	31	28	28	39	55	40	30	25	31	25	35	27	25	28	24	21	27.5
ALLENTOWN GAS CO	MAX	45	38	49	35	32	36	36	51	45	41	39	38	22	30	40	48	42	44	50	60	64	54	50	53	50	47	57	42	45	45	43	44.2
	MIN	27	27	27	28	23	16	22	33	34	33	33	12	12	16	27	29	28	30	30	49	49	39	28	29	26	27	37	28	28	26	23	28.3
ALTOONA HORSESHOE CURVE	MAX	40	42	34	29	32	47	53	52	37	41	36	18	31	48	44	53	43	35	55	58	57	52	63	54	36	38	38	40	39	44	38	42.7
	MIN	16	33	22	24	13	12	41	34	32	25	11	5	- 4	22	26	28	27	30	32	48	39	29	30	35	17	29	28	25	24	28	19	25.2
ARENDTSVILLE	MAX	45	43	48	37	31	34	38	50	42	41	42	33	24	28	52	47	54	42	42	52	59	54	53	52	51	39	42	43	42	42	43	43.4
	MIN	22	24	25	27	22	14	20	36	37	33	32	10	11	16	19	26	25	28	32	41	45	34	26	27	25	26	34	27	30	25	21	26.5
BAKERSTOWN 3 WNW	MAX	40	41	34	30	32	44	53	45	40	34	30	22	38	42	44	51	40	44	61	60	57	54	58	58	42	44	38	48	40	44	40	43.3
	MIN	18	32	26	26	10	24	43	34	30	24	12	10	14	32	26	39	28	36	42	56	42	30	36	37	24	36	32	27	26	32	28	29.4
BEAVERTOWN	MAX	38	45	38	34	35	35	50	49	39	43	39	23	29	46	44	56	49	40	53	61	61	51	52	53	44	39	43	41	43	44	41	43.8
	MIN	22	27	20	25	14	12	31	36	33	29	20	10	14	16	21	30	26	26	38	50	42	29	22	31	17	31	33	24	29	23	16	25.7
BELLEFONTE 4 S	MAX	40	41	40	35	32	33	51	54	45	41	40	21	22	41	40	50	52	40	48	58	62	51	47	60	48	45	39	42	42	39	44	43.5
	MIN	20	20	23	25	9	14	24	28	30	28	23	9	11	15	28	30	30	30	31	47	43	30	25	25	18	20	31	27	27	27	18	24.7
BERWICK	MAX	40	46	38	35	35	37	51	53	40	39	37	23	31	45	43	54	46	40	59	63	64	47	51	50	45	48	43	47	44	40	45	44.5
	MIN	25	27	21	27	12	17	33	39	35	31	23	9	13	22	24	27	33	30	38	57	44	31	24	31	22	31	33	27	31	25	20	27.6
BETHLEHEM LEHIGH UNIV	MAX	46	47	35	33	33	43	50	47	37	37	38	26	40	46	47	43	45	55	60	61	52	49	50	50	54	51	43	44	43	46	40	44.5
	MIN	29	30	26	21	20	22	30	34	33	28	13	15	24	33	35	34	31	37	35	49	39	31	38	26	34	36	28	30	25	30	22	29.6
BLAIRSVILLE 6 ENE	MAX	32	35	30	27	27	45	53	45	35	35	31	14	31	39	39	47	40	35	57	55	51	52	58	50	39	43	34	34	33	45	39	39.
	MIN	12	28	23	21	9	19	41	31	27	20	5	3	5	32	27	32	24	30	33	48	36	27	29	29	22	29	26	26	20	26	28	24.
BRADFORD CAA AP	MAX	32	32	25	28	28	43	50	35	31	34	26	12	28	34	38	40	35	37	53	55	45	46	54	48	35	35	36	39	36	39	35	36.
	MIN	15	19	12	11	5	22	32	30	23	20	2	2	7	27	26	30	27	29	37	45	34	28	40	19	15	29	27	28	22	25	26	23.
BRADFORD 4 W RES	MAX	34	35	29	29	30	41	52	51	35	38	33	15	23	36	36	40	35	35	54	56	56	47	56	56	37	38	38	40	40	40	36	39.
	MIN	16	26	9	20	- 5	20	35	28	27	20	9	- 1	3	19	20	27	26	25	32	38												
BROOKVILLE CAA AIRPORT	MAX	38	37	29	30	33	48	52	39	35	36	31	18	33	39	43	47	40	43	57	57	48	47	58	54	38	40	37	44	38	44	40	41.
	MIN	16	22	21	16	- 1	18	36	33	27	22	7	7	7	30	26	30	28	32	43	47	39	25	26	21	18	32	27	30	25	23	19	24.
BURGETTSTOWN 2 W	MAX	36	39	41	33	31	45	51	53	38	34	38	19	19	37	43	49	51	41	52	61	59	51	55	60	44	46	45	43	45	40	46	43.
	MIN	16	18	19	22	- 1	2	39	32	30	14	14	6	10	13	10	11	13	14	39	47	37	19	19	29	15	19	24	27	16	15	17	19.
BURNT CABINS 2 NE	MAX	48	48			35	44	51	49	40	44	44	22	43		53			43	55	60	61	56	59	60		40	46	46	47	48	44	47.
	MIN	19	30		26	10	12	32	35	35	29	19	7	12		12		27	32	36	49	43	29	24		16	31	33	25	27	22	16	25.
BUTLER	MAX	37	37	37	30	30	41	52	52	40	36	37	18	27	39	46	47	47	49	60	60	55	52	58	60	44	49	48	48	48	46	49	44.
	MIN	15	26	17	24	- 2	20	39	30	30	19	13	8	10	27	32	37	22	33	43	52	40	25	34	38	18	38	31	31	26	24	20	28.
CANTON 1 NW	MAX	45	40	37	28	31	30	41	49	34	36	34	25	13	32	34	38	45	38	40	55	59	45	47	52	46	38	40	37	38	38	38	38.
	MIN	18	20	17	20	14	14	25	32	30	21	19	0	5	10	10	11	23	25	24	39	43	28	30	39	19	20	29	24	28	24	25	22.
CARLISLE	MAX	40	48	43	35	35	33	49	53	41	43	41	24	29	47	48	55	51	40	52	61	61	52	53	52	46	43	43	44	43	44	45	45.
	MIN	25	24	25	28	23	17	31	40	38	33	24	13	18	16	26	26	33	30	38	52	47	36	26	33	26	33	35	28	32	26	20	29.
CHAMBERSBURG 1 ESE	MAX	43	49	38	31	36	33	53	49	41	45	40	23	32	52	47	58	46	39	53	61	55	55	57	51	38	42	44	45	41	46	45	44.
	MIN	22	36	26	22	18	15	33	38	35	33	14	11	15	16	24	26	29	31	38	51	43	30	27	32	19	32	28	27	25	25	21	27.
CHESTER	MAX		38	52	42	35	37	45	54		47	40	40	24	35		47	49	46	51	63	64		55	57		58	57	45		50	46	47.
	MIN		34	31	27	20	18		39	42	34	35	14	14		29	30	31	32	42	48	50		34	41		40	34	29	31		26	32.
CLARION 3 SW	MAX	35	40	34	32	34	43	53	47	39	37	37	21	33	39	39	48	40	42	60	57	55	50	59	56	41	42	39	46	43	45	43	42.
	MIN	14	29	20	24	- 1	18	35	29	28	18	6	6	7	22	18	26	24	21	37	46	39	22	24	31	16	32	28	25	23	22	18	22.
CLAYSVILLE 3 W	MAX	40	43	35	34	35	50	54	40	38	40	36	19	36	46	48	55	40	52	62	61	56	58	62	57	44	49	40	47	40	50	48	45.
	MIN	17	25	20	24	- 1	15	40	35	31	17	19	8	10	30	15	30	15	35	48	49	39	21	25	26	15	26	28	37	16	22	17	24.
COATESVILLE 1 SW	MAX	44	37	51	38	38	35	41	51	44	41	39	36	23	31	46	46	43	44	49	58	61	54	55	55	53	52	54	44	45	45	45	45.
	MIN	26	24	27	29	24	13	20	37	38	33	30	12	12	15	20	26	28	26	33	48	45	36	26	27	27	27	35	25	26	29	21	27.
COLUMBIA	MAX	39	51	41	35	37	35	53	52	39	37	39	23	29	42	47	39	44	42	55	59	54	52	55	50	45	48	45	46	45	45	46	44.
	MIN	25	29	25	23	28	15	31	39	36	31	22	12	16	18	23	29	28	28	42	50	48	31	28	33	23	33	32	28	34	24	21	28.
CONFLUENCE 1 SW DAM	MAX	38	40	42	37	28	42	53	55	39	33	39	19	15	40	46	50	53	46	51	62	61	50	57	60	44	42	46	38	44	39	42	43.
	MIN	17	18	25	26	12	12	39	35	32	27	18	5	6	6	26	29	22	19	35	47	39	31	24	24	18	19	31	27	24	23	19	23.
CORRY	MAX	32	36	30	29	33	44	51	37	34	37	33	16	27	35	38	40	35	37	56	59	54	48	58	54	37	35	34	37	38	38	38	39.
	MIN	16	27	11	22	0	24	35	29	27	21	8	7	9	25	26	31	29	32	37	50	38	23	38	29	17	32	28	29	25	22	26	24.
COUDERSPORT 3 NW	MAX	33	34	25	26	28	41	50	48	31	34	39	13	22	35	33	41	34	34	50	55	49	41	57	53	35	35	36	39	36	35	35	37.
	MIN	16	23	5	17	- 1	19	39	29	25	14	3	1	3	20	18	29	26	27	33	46	37	24	28	25	11	28	21	18	21	21	16	20.
DERRY	MAX	39	42	38	38	33	50	58	52	39	39	36	17	37	44	46	53	42	48	61	61	58	62	54	53	46	50	48	45	41	41	45	46.
	MIN	18	34	32	32	10	22	46	35	33	25	12	7	11	33	24	34	35	33	49	49	37	33	38	19	15	30	28	24	27	33	28	28.
DEVAULT 1 W	MAX	33	46	34	26	31	40	48	47	37	35	33	18	27	40	41	41	41	43	58	64	56	46	51	60	48	54	39	42	44	39	43	42.
	MIN	24	29	25	21	20	22	39	36	32	31	15	8	12	21	28	31	28	26	43	54	42	34	33	32	28	33	29	29	29	28	25	28.
DIXON	MAX	46	40	40	38	33	34	47	53	40	36	34	32	24	31	43	46	55	46	48	60	62	55	49	59	50	44	46	39	45	42	38	43.
	MIN	24	25	17	18	6	7	29	37	35	28	28	10	7	7	21	20	28	21	28	47	45	30	24	31	19	20	34	21	29	18	15	23.
DONEGAL	MAX	33	37		26	27	44	48	34	33	34	27	12	32	40	40	47	42	40	56	53	44	52	56	56	36	40	42	41	32	43	40	39.
	MIN	10	18		12	12	19	30	29	23	18	2	2	3	25	18	22	16	30	40	40	32	20	30	18	15	31	24	23	18	19	18	20.
DONORA	MAX	41	46	43	34	34	46	56	51	40	40	39	21	36	46	47	58	53	47	65	62	58	56	64	61	46	47	42	49	45	50	49	47.
	MIN	41	35	28	28	16	25	42	36	32	24	14	8	13	33	25	39	25	38	44	52	41	29	34	41	24	35	31	33	23	29	27	30.
DU BOIS 7 E	MAX	32	36	31	30	30	45	53	51	35	35	32	17	28	38	38	48	40	35	55	55	56	47	58	55	36	39	36	43	41	43	37	40.
	MIN	14	30	18	24	- 1	16	42	32	31	19	10	3	6	26	26	28	26	30	34	49	38	23	28	34	15	31	28	24	23	25	26	24.
EAGLES MERE	MAX	37	34	36	26	34	30	36	45	34	31	33	26	13	22	36	35	48	33	43	53	61	45	45	46	45	38	40	34	37	36	34	37.
	MIN	19	19	18	19	15	16	22	32	31	23	23	0	0	8	13	21	28	25	29	43	40	28	28	34	20	19	29	26	28	23	25	22.
EAST BRADY	MAX	44	41	36	32	36	46	55	51	42	41	38	26	34	41	47	51	44	42	62	58	55	51	62	57	47	44	43	47	45	48	45	45.
	MIN	22	29	20	28	3	20	30	25	33	22	15	9	12	21	26	22	26	34	40	45	30	25	26	34	20	35	31	30	26	25	21	25.
EBENSBURG	MAX	33	36	39	36	28	45	53	47	35	35	32	14	32	41	40	49	37	35	55	57	56	50	57	52	35	36	34	41	38	40	37	40.
	MIN	13	28	21	15	12	20	43	30	27	22	5	2	5	30	26	30	24	24	34	47	35	26	34	29	16	29	20	27	20	24	21	23.
EMPORIUM 2 SSW	MAX	36	36	36	26	31	30	48	52	36	34	35	20	16	36	33	44	50	37	45	55	58	47	44	57	43	37	36	38	43	37	40	39.
	MIN	16	15	13	18	0	0	21	31	30	15	16	2	2	4	22	24	27	21	23	42	38	23	22	23	12	13	27	20	21	20	13	18.
EPHRATA	MAX	36	50	36	32	37	38	52	43	40	38	36	24	29	40	46	40	44	42	58	61	54	51	54	51	43	53	44	44	45	44	45	43.
	MIN	23	27	26	25	18	14	34	38	34	30	21	10	14	21	27	32	28	29	38	52	45	33	30	32	21	31	33	27	31	25	22	28.
ERIE WB AIRPORT	MAX	41	40	32	33	35	50	53	35	34	38	27	22	37	38	43	43	38	48	61	62	49	51	58	48	43	43	39	44	38	44	45	42.
	MIN	21	32	25	27	15	31	34	32	27	25	13	14	14	33	29	35	32	34	46	48	37	28	44	23	19	36	30	32	29	31	33	29.

See reference notes following Station Index.

DAILY TEMPERATURES

PENNSYLVANIA
DECEMBER 1957

	1	2	3	4	5	6	7	8	9	10	11	12	13	14	15	16	17	18	19	20	21	22	23	24	25	26	27	28	29	30	31	Average
MAX	42	45	36	32	40	44	50	40							50			45	51	58	55	52	52	50	38	39	36	46	40	45	40	42.7
MIN	22	32	28	28	22	16	40	38							26			28	40	50	45	34	32	32	20	34	28	28	32	32	16	29.2
MAX	40	42	35	35			55	39		41	35		35	41		49	40	45	60	60	54	50	62	57	44	48	42	41	43	49	45	44.2
MIN	18	27	25	27			34	29		10	14		13	33		34	25	35	38	43	39	28	37	30	21	35	30	34	24	30	27	27.4
MAX	38	39	40				32		41	35	38		20	39	43	49	52		52	64	60	51	55	60	45	45	45	43	48	40	47	44.0
MIN	17	18	18				37		31	21	16		10	12	19	19	23		35	48	39	25	25	25	16	24	29	27	23	24	20	22.4
MAX	48	40	32	32		45		40		39		20	35		41		41	41	58	68	52	49	60	56	43	42	40	44	43	46	44	43.3
MIN	17	29	21	26		25		33		20		10	12		21		29	34	39	46	41	26	28	23	19	33	30	30	26	26	23	26.1
MAX	35	38	37	27	31	30			38	33	30			40	40	47	47	33	52	56	57	55	55	48	42	47	37	45	38	38		40.3
MIN	18	23	23	21	11	24			30	22	20			20	26	32	28	27	30	52	30	30	30	40		30	32	31	30	22		29.7
MAX		38	50	38				52	42		39	37		29	43	45	42		50	61	63	55	54	55	47	55	58	43	48	46	41	45.2
MIN		28	22	23				40	39		31	11		11	21	25	25		33	50	49	38	35	34	23	26	30	25	28	24	21	27.0
MAX			51		32	37		52		41	42	32	24	30	52	47	49	43	47	56	61	55	55	55	53	40	43	46	43	43	45	44.8
MIN			29		22	16		41		33	31	12	14	18	26	33	30	31	32	45	45	38	29	31	25	29	36	29	31	27	22	28.8
MAX	48					34		42		42	40	30	26	32	48		51	48	64	62	66	58	52	56	44	50	58	43	50	52	48	46.3
MIN	32					16		34		38	24	10	18	20	18		28	26	32	56	52	28	26	36	32	28	36	34	26	24	24	28.7
MAX	42	41	45			33	42	52	41	38	36	33				43	54	43	50	58	62	52	48	55	49	43	40	40	45	45	43	43.3
MIN	24	24	23			12	27	39	36	35	32	10				28	30	28	33	49	44	35	29	32	25	24	34	24	30	25	21	27.2
MAX	38	39	33				53			39	32	20	33	38	41	44	38	42	60	59	53	52	60	56	42	44	40	43	44	48	44	42.6
MIN	17	32	23				37			22	12	10	12	33	18	35	27	34	41	52	41	29	34	33	20	33	30	32	22	27	26	27.2
MAX	41	39	52	38	31	38		53		41	39	36	24	32	52		45	46	51	56	61	56	53	50	53	47	42	45	46	45	46	45.3
MIN	23	28	30	28	15	14		41		32	32	11	11	18	24		27	29	33	45	46	34	35	33	26	33	35	31	31	26	24	28.8
MAX	38	49	38	33		34		51	40	41	40	25	29	45				42	56	63	55	52	52	50	40	46	43	44	43	46	46	44.2
MIN	26	31	28	29		20		40	35	34	16	13	17	20				33	42	53	47	33	30	35	27	34	30	31	32	28	24	30.3
MAX	38	37	36	29	30		43	52	38	35	33			30	41	39	50		43	57	60	49	45	60	48	42	51	35	43	38	35	40.3
MIN	22	22	22	22	15		12	35	31	27	27			12	25	25	32		25	41	46	34	22	22	21	22	31	19	25	22	16	23.4
MAX	41	51	49	39	36	39	50	49	42	40	38		30	42	47	39	42	42	55	61	56	53	54	54	42	50	42	45	41	42	45	44.5
MIN	28	29	29	28	21	20	35	39	37	32	19		18	23	28	28	29	30	41	48	40	36	35	38	31	34	32	30	30	29	27	30.0
MAX	42		47	35			36	52	43	40	43	28	24	31	53	45	58		48	60	62	55	51	62	51	40	41	42	42	42	45	44.5
MIN	23		20	25			17	35	36	27	27	11	11	11	16	17	23		33	46	46	30	20	20	14	15	33	24	29	22	14	22.9
MAX	36	41	35	30	32	47	57	48	38	38				42	43	52		42	61	61	54	53	61	54	43	43	38	47	42	47	44	44.1
MIN	17	26	17	22	-5	10	44	35	32	20				28	20	26		35	40	50	40	24	25	29	17	35	29	27	24	23	21	24.1
MAX			42	40	35	44				41	38		35			55	55	45	64	61			62	50		46	44	51			53	
MIN			24	29	10	21				22	13		12			28	21	36	43	52		27		41			31	29			26	
MAX	37	37	39			42	51		35	33	38		19		38	45	43		50	59	59	50	50	59	40	45	40	39	44	42	46	41.5
MIN	16	20	19			17	39		31	21	12		10		16	16	22		36	48	40	23	24	34	17	28	29	30	21	21	26	23.4
MAX				33	39	35		52						43		53	52	40	55	60	62	54	55	55	49	53	47	46	47	41	44	46.0
MIN				27	20	16		39						24		28	32	30	37	54	44	34	25	32	26	33	34	24	33	25	18	28.0
MAX	41	41	42	37	31	35				36	43		19	42	50	52	55		51	64	62	61	61	64	48	47	42	42	46	46	49	46.7
MIN	19	19	31	29	15	18				29	19		10	12	33	30	32		35	52	40	41	29	29	21	21	29	31	26	26	22	27.1
MAX	35	35		26	29	34	45	51	37	33	34				35		43	35	47	61	55	46	45	55	40	37	37	37	40	36	40	38.3
MIN	16	16		13	-7	-6	33	32	31	20	16				29		28	28	31	44	39	23	23	35	13	13	28	22	23	19	15	20.2
MAX	43	46	29	29	32	45	56		30	35			38		48	48	42	44	48	58	48	50	58	56	40	40	40	40	40	38	40	41.8
MIN	18	30	26	23	10	9	37		30	26			16		22	30	24	24	32	46	41	27	24	24	17	32	27	26	25	23	18	25.0
MAX	41	50	42	35	35	37	52	53		39	39	25	30	39		39	43	43	59	63	62	51	57	50	48	53	43	48	45	42	48	44.9
MIN	25	24	22	26	20	11	31	40		31	24	12	16	17		24	24	24	38	51	45	34	25	30	22	33	34	28	29	22	20	27.0
MAX	43	38	47	37	32	32	40	53	43	41	38	35	29	38	46		39	42	50	58	63	54	49	52	45	49	51	42	45	41	44	43.8
MIN	24	25	23	28	21	10	21	40	37	32	33	12	10	18	24		26	27	32	50	45	35	27	30	22	24	25	27	31	24	21	26.8
MAX	44	39		32	33	36	45	51	35	32	40				42	41	40	37	47	57	61	53	49	60	48	40	41	40	47	40	39	41.8
MIN	23	24		20	8	9	33	35	29	19	19				14	19	32	26	33	47	42	30	28	31	17	17	31	24	29	22	18	23.3
MAX		37	48	37	33	35	38	52		40	40	35	24	30	41		44	40	50	57	62	54	50	52	48	47	48	43	44	42	44	43.5
MIN		23	24	27	19	13	23	39		31	33	11	11	19	19		28	28	32	48	44	34	25	26	22	22	34	27	28	23	19	26.3
MAX	42			36	34	38		50	43	40		32	23	35			58	47	44	58	63	56	51	53	53	41	42	45	43	43	48	44.7
MIN	25			26	16	18		33	37	32		13	12	15			26	30	34	43	45	39	27	25	23	20	32	28	31	28	23	26.6
MAX	36	38	30	33	34	46	53	35	33	37	32		32	67	39	42	36	41	59	59	51	48	58	55	41	44	38	42	42	45	42	41.2
MIN	17	29	18	25	6	25	34	32	29	23	11		12	26	17	28	28	33	40	48	38	22	31	28	17	32	29	32	23	23	22	25.4
MAX	43	42	33	35	37	43	47	47	37	43	32	23	32		42	56	44	42	58	64	53	48	53	53	39	39	44	41	41	43	42	43.0
MIN	24	32	21	27	10	18	32	37	34	29	18	10	15		24	27	32	32	41	53	42	31	24	31	19	33	31	27	29	26	22	27.6
MAX	36	37	39	31	30	30	49	53	39	36	34				44		48	38	45	55	58	46	47	58	43	37	38	34	46	35	38	40.3
MIN	15	15	17	19	-2	-3	15	33	31	21	20				23		26	24	30	43	40	26	22	22	13	12	29	25	24	22	15	19.9
MAX	40	56	40	33	38	42	49	49		41	40	26	32	46	50		48	46	60	62	62	55	56	57	44	57	48	49	50	46	50	47.2
MIN	31	37	32	31	28	26	41	42		37	21	17	19	31	37		35	37	43	53	44	39	36	39	32	39	36	34	36	35	32	34.7
MAX	40	40	32	30	30	45	53	39	35	42			38	47	47	53	41	40	57	58	51	56	62	53	38	36	38	42	38	45	39	42.5
MIN	18	29	25	22	15	20	39	34	30	25			11	35	26	31	29	31	39	47	40	30	35	24	19	32	28	29	25	25	23	26.8
MAX	35	35	39	29	32	41	50	53	35	33	38		20		37		45	39	50	59	58	49	49	59	41	42	42	40	43	42	46	41.3
MIN	15	17	19	23	5	13	38	32	32	23	13		11		21		30	30	35	50	40	23	24	35	19	20	30	30	25	24	23	23.9
MAX	37	40	32	31	33	46	54	40	36	38				38	40	46	34	42	61	58	58	49	59	55	42	44	39	43	41	45	44	42.3
MIN	15	29	24	23	1	22	36	31	28	17				25	14	33	21	30	38	50	38	22	33	28	16	30	27	29	20	26	24	24.2
MAX	37	49	39	32	35	34	54	52	41	40	40	25	29	43	44	41	42	43	55	62	56	49	52	51	40	46	42	44	42	43	45	43.5
MIN	27	31	28	27	22	22	34	40	35	34	18	12	19	20	28	35	31	32	42	54	47	32	30	35	25	34	33	30	30	27	23	30.2
MAX	39	40	34	33	32	49	54	40	35	38	30	19	35	43	41	48	40	47	60	58	50	51	57	55	45	46	38	47	38	43	46	42.9
MIN	21	29	28	26	20	26	38	36	29	24	12	12	16	31	26	31	28	36	46	48	42	31	33	30	26	35	32	34	23	27	28	29.2
MAX	37	34	33	28	28	28	37			32	30				38	38	45	31	39	53	57	48	43	55	46	35	42	31	38	35	33	36.6
MIN	19	19	20	19	14	15	23			23	23				20	24	29	21	27	39	42	31	29	32	19	19	27	22	27	25	23	22.8
MAX	40	48	48	31	35	42	51	51	40	38	36		30	40	44		42	42	58	61	57	48	53	54	42	54	41	44	43	43	45	44.1
MIN	25	31	27	25	16	12	38	38	34	31	16		12	22	27		26	30	39	41	37	32	33	34	22	34	26	27	27	24	22	27.4
MAX	36	49	45	38	36	46	51	50	39	43	38	23	29	38	48	48	42	42	57	61	54	50	52	51	42	48	42	43	42	44	43	44.2
MIN	27	28	28	25	20	25	36	39	33	37	15	11	13	26	28	25	24	24	40	51	38	30	32	41	33	38	28	30	26	24	21	28.9

See reference notes following Station Index.

DAILY TEMPERATURES

Table 5 - Continued

Station		1	2	3	4	5	6	7	8	9	10	11	12	13	14	15	16	17	18	19	20	21	22	23	24	25	26	27	28	29	30	31
MT POCONO 2 N AP	MAX	34	36	31	26	27	30	42	47	35	32	29	20	21	40	38	43	40	30	50	57	56	45	55	47	38	49	38	40	37	35	38
	MIN	19	24	18	22	13	13	29	33	31	27	20	4	7	17	25	27	29	23	30	50	41	31	30	36	20	29	27	19	28	23	20
MUHLENBURG 1 SE	MAX																															
	MIN																															
NEWBURG 3 W	MAX	38	46	40	35	36	33	46	52	42	42	40	22	29	50	50	58	58	46	60	63	62	58	56	55	54	42	42	49	44	48	44
	MIN	24	33	32	26	22	16	34	40	38	29	16	8	14	12	23	28	29	34	44	47	40	35	29	34	19	31	34	25	30	24	20
NEW CASTLE 1 N	MAX	40	41	27	36	36	48	56	41	39	41	38	22	34	41	44	49	39	45	62	60	57	55	61	57	45	46	41	46	44	48	45
	MIN	19	25	19	25	8	26	39	33	32	19	12	10	12	24	15	36	19	34	42	51	41	23	29	34	16	34	31	31	21	25	21
NEWELL	MAX	39	44	45	40	31	47	55	55	41	40	42	21	30	42	46	51	53	42	60	62	56	51	58	62	46	45	42	43	47	42	48
	MIN	22	28	28	31	16	24	43	38	35	27	21	12	14	30	24	35	25	36	42	47	41	28	28	40	25	37	32	31	23	27	24
NEWPORT	MAX	44	43	48	36	34	37	40	53	43	40	42	35	25	30	51	46	57	43	48	57	61	56	50	58	51	42	42	43	43	43	45
	MIN	27	25	25	27	20	17	23	39	38	32	32	13	13	15	18	23	30	30	34	48	46	37	24	25	22	21	36	26	31	24	18
NEW STANTON	MAX	44	42	44	41	40	51	56	45	39	39	38	24	38	46	50	55	52	50	66	64	52	58	63	56	46	54	52	49	40	49	50
	MIN	18	26	20	12	15	18	25	36	28	20	7	7	12	27	17	24	27	35	46	47	40	23	24	21	17	29	28	28	22	21	22
NORRISTOWN	MAX	38	53	39	32	37	43	54	52	42	41	38	23	33	47	48	46	46	46	63	64	58	50	58	53	47	57	45	48	47	45	48
	MIN	29	35	30	28	22	22	40	40	37	35	20	15	16	28	30	33	30	31	44	57	42	33	31	36	30	38	31	32	30	28	25
PALMERTON	MAX	35	47	34	33	36	35	52	51	38	38	37	19	26	41	45	43	42	42	58	62	58	50	52	50	41	55	41	42	44	41	42
	MIN	27	27	23	26	18	15	36	37	35	32	20	13	14	27	26	30	29	29	42	56	40	30	25	33	25	36	28	26	27	24	20
PHIL DREXEL INST OF TEC	MAX	41	53	40	32	38	43	52	51	42	41	40	23	33	46	50	48	47	47	64	65	60	54	58	57	46	58	47	50	49	45	51
	MIN	28	36	30	29	25	26	41	41	40	36	21	14	17	31	36	36	35	36	45	59	48	42	38	37	31	40	38	35	35	33	33
PHILADELPHIA WB AP	MAX	38	52	40	32	36	42	51	51	43	41	39	23	32	45	47	49	45	47	63	64	56	52	58	55	43	58	44	49	46	44	48
	MIN	28	34	30	28	25	22	40	42	39	36	20	14	18	29	31	30	31	35	47	55	43	35	34	37	30	39	35	32	34	30	28
PHILADELPHIA PT BREEZE	MAX	39	52	40	33	35	43	54	51	44	42	40	21	32	42	44	47	44	46	63	65	56	51	58	58	45	58	44	49	47	45	50
	MIN	29	38	32	30	29	28	42	44	40	38	22	14	14	30	35	34	39	37	46	56	46	40	38	40	34	40	36	34	38	38	35
PHILIPSBURG CAA AP	MAX	35	35	30	28	28	48	49	36	33	37	30	15	34	44	39	49	38	37	50	56	47	45	58	53	33	34	35	37	35	40	35
	MIN	14	25	16	17	9	9	36	32	27	22	4	4	6	31	28	30	28	28	37	45	39	27	30	22	13	29	24	29	20	22	22
PHOENIXVILLE 1 E	MAX	48	52	40	38	37	40	50	51	41	42	38	28	30	43	45	45	45	45	62	63	63	49	54	54	46	56	44	46	45	43	46
	MIN	27	26	23	26	21	32	34	39	38	36	26	11	10	20	26	26	25	24	38	53	43	35	24	32	24	35	33	24	30	20	18
PIMPLE HILL	MAX	38	34	38	27	25	27	37	46	35	33	30	28	10	28	38	38	43	34	44	54	56	45	43	55	44	43	48	31	37	37	34
	MIN	18	19	18	20	11	17	22	31	31	25	24	1	3	9	23	27	27	23	25	43	40	30	31	39	18	23	26	24	28	25	27
PITTSBURGH WB AP 2	MAX	40	40	32	29	31	50	53	37	34	37	30	18	39	45	48	51	39	46	60	58	50	55	59	57	43	46	38	46	40	45	45
	MIN	17	28	26	21	14	25	35	34	25	22	9	8	13	31	26	31	26	35	45	47	39	28	41	28	25	34	30	30	21	28	28
PITTSBURGH WB CITY	MAX	43	44	35	32	34	52	57	40	37	42	34	22	39	46	50	55	43	49	62	61	54	56	63	57	48	48	40	50	42	48	49
	MIN	20	34	30	28	22	33	39	37	31	27	12	10	15	38	30	37	30	38	47	51	42	34	36	30	27	37	33	34	26	33	29
PLEASANT MOUNT 1 W	MAX	37	34	34	33	32	28	39	47	37	34	31	29	11	26	38	37	44	33	37	54	57	52	40	54	44	37	44	31	42	35	32
	MIN	19	20	12	13	19	9	25	33	30	24	25	6	5	7	17	16	29	18	26	37	42	32	32	34	18	19	22	17	27	20	18
PORT CLINTON	MAX	42	40	47	35	32	35	36	51	44	40	38	36	22	28	41	47	41	45	49	58	62	55	52	54	52	48	50	45	43	46	44
	MIN	25	22	21	27	19	15	24	34	35	30	31	10	9	15	22	24	21	26	32	47	41	32	28	27	22	32	30	25	33	22	18
PUTNEYVILLE 2 SE DAM	MAX		38	39	32	30	43	50	58	40	40	37	20	20	37	40	47	50	40	50	60	58	49	46	60	43	42	43	40	46	45	45
	MIN	15	15	16	20	-3	0	35	31	29	18	13	4	5	8	17	20	25	25	30	45	36	23	23	26	15	21	25	26	22	22	20
QUAKERTOWN 1 E	MAX																															
	MIN																															
READING WB CITY	MAX	36	49	38	34	37	40	53	53	41	40	38	24	31	42	46	45	45	43	60	63	56	50	56	52	44	58	45	47	44	45	46
	MIN	28	34	30	28	25	23	38	39	35	33	18	14	18	29	34	39	34	32	43	56	46	36	33	36	29	36	32	32	32	29	26
RIDGWAY 3 W	MAX	36	37	36	28	31	36	49	52	39	34	35	19	18	35	38	45	46	40	47	56	57	47	44	56	41	38	39	36	43	36	40
	MIN	19	16	17	19	-8	-8	23	33	32	21	17	-1	5	8	26	27	28	29	33	44	40	23	21	24	12	12	30	23	25	22	15
SALINA 3 W	MAX	38	40	35	30	33	45	55	55	39	38	37	19	34	43	48	51	44	41	60	58	57	54	60	56	47	46	39	47	41	48	49
	MIN	18	31	20	26	9	22	44	35	31	21	11	4	11	32	19	31	22	35	40	50	35	25	31	31		29	26	27	23	25	18
SCRANTON	MAX	43	40	41	32	33	33	40	52	41	38	36	34	18	31	33	45	54	40	49	60	64	51	46	56	51	46	53	39	48	41	39
	MIN	24	28	26	28	18	18	28	38	35	29	29	11	11	13	26	28	33	29	33	47	49	36	30	30	27	29	33	26	30	28	28
SCRANTON WB AIRPORT	MAX	32	40	31	31	30	37	51	45	36	32	33	15	28	40	42	51	38	40	57	62	54	47	54	48	38	50	37	46	40	35	41
	MIN	23	27	22	21	16	17	34	35	27	27	14	8	10	25	28	34	25	27	40	53	40	31	30	29	23	32	26	22	27	25	23
SHIPPENSBURG	MAX	39	47	43	37	33	32	52	51	42	42	40	23	30	51	50	57	53	40	54	63	63	53	53	51	47	42	43	42	42	43	45
	MIN	22	30	29	27	20	15	28	38	38	32	22	10	16	16	28	25	30	30	35	47	45	37	27	33	21	32	32	28	30	27	21
SHIPPINGPORT WB	MAX	40	41	32	32	33	52	55	42	35	38	29	19	38	43	44	50	39	47	61	60	53	56	60	57	45	47	40	43	40	46	47
	MIN	19	25	25	23	16	25	39	35	25	22	10	9	14	29	21	28	23	35	45	48	41	26	31	24	22	34	31	31	21	26	25
SLIPPERY ROCK	MAX	36	40	30	30	35	45	53	42	40	40	38	18	33	39	42	49	51	41	59	57	54	50	60	57	42	43	40	42	41	48	48
	MIN	15	27	24	22	9	22	35	32	28	20	8	7	9	29	22	34	25	33	39	50	38	25	37	29	18	31	27	30	21	26	28
SOMERSET MAIN ST	MAX	35	40	35	31	31	47	53	51	40	38	35	13	33	44	43	52	43	38	59	56	56	55	60	52	38	38	37	43	42	44	40
	MIN	13	31	24	22	11	13	40	32	29	24	8	3	6	29	26	34	23	30	33	48	36	28	26	35	16	29	27	26	20	25	20
SPRINGBORO	MAX	39	40	36	33	34	41	50	53	44	35	37	34	31	36	38	42	40	39	53	59	61	52	49	58	38	40	40	40	43	42	45
	MIN	17	22	18	25	9	23	39	31	31	25	11	8	12	17	18	26	30	32	37	49	35	24	34	36	18	26	30	30	27	23	22
SPRINGS 1 SW	MAX	35	39	32	27	28	47	50	47	35	35	31	10	35	42	51	51	43	35	59	50	52	52	57	53	35	39	37	36	30	41	42
	MIN	13	30	24	22	10	9	45	32	27	22	4	0	0	25	28	28	20	30	34	46	35	29	29	31	21	30	21	20	19	20	19
STATE COLLEGE	MAX	38	41	40	32	32	32	47	51	39	36	40	26	21	40	47	50	53	40	47	56	60	51	46	51	48	39	38	39	42	39	43
	MIN	21	20	26	25	16	17	27	38	33	28	25	8	10	14	28	28	32	30	32	47	44	32	29	30	22	20	32	29	28	26	22
STROUDSBURG	MAX	37	38	35	33	35	33	51	50	37	38	38	17	25	37	44	44	41	38	58	61	54	48	53	50	37	55	39	44	45	39	40
	MIN	24	23	18	23	14	8	31	36	33	30	15	8	7	24	23	24	24	22	38	54	37	25	22	28	21	30	24	21	24	20	17
SUNBURY	MAX	46	46	46	36	38	39	39	50	43	40	42	35	24	31	48	45	58	45	54	60	64	55	50	53	52	45	41	45	44	43	44
	MIN	22	26	23	27	18	18	22	35	35	31	32	13	14	20	23	27	31	29	32	50	45	34	26	27	23	23	35	27	30	25	20
TAMARACK 2 S FIRE TWR	MAX	36	33	33	24	28	29	46	47	32	30	34	22	13	33	35	40	46	34	42	51	54	45	42	47	42	33	33	35	39	35	36
	MIN	17	15	17	18	11	10	23	32	29	20	19	2	3	5	25	24	25	25	25	41	38	27	26	40	18	17	26	25	22	21	25
TIONESTA 2 SE DAM	MAX	36	39	36	28	30	40	50	54	38	34	37	20	20	35	39	46	46	41	49	60	58	49	47	59	40	40	40	40	44	40	45
	MIN	16	17	20	21	1	3	35	33	32	20	15	7	7	11	25	26	29	22	28	45	40	24	24	27	16	18	30	26	25	23	19
TITUSVILLE WATER WORKS	MAX	35	37	30	32	33	45	54	37	34	38	33	19	33	38	38	44	38	40	58	58	53	46	58	55	40	39	37	42	39	44	41
	MIN	15	30	15	20	-2	20	36	32	29	19	9	7	9	29	25	32	29	33	39	39	40	22	25	30	16	32	29	26	25	22	20
TOWANDA	MAX	38	40	32	34	36	38	52	52	35	35	35	21	29	46	46	52	41	39	57	62	63	49	60	54	41	43	40	45	42	36	41
	MIN	23	29	19	24	13	13	34	34	29	24	19	8	9	21	23	28	24	24	36	54	44	30	25	31	18	32	25	22	25	20	20

See reference notes following Station Index.

Table 5 - Continued

DAILY TEMPERATURES

Station		Day Of Month 1	2	3	4	5	6	7	8	9	10	11	12	13	14	15	16	17	18	19	20	21	22	23	24	25	26	27	28	29	30	31	Average
UNIONTOWN	MAX	41	48	41	38	34	49	56	41	39	41	36	18	37	47	50	58	47	46	65	61	53	61	63	55	43	48	42	48	41	52	52	46.7
	415	19	27	26	24	9	18	41	36	31	25	10	7	12	31	22	30	22	39	46	50	41	27	31	27	25	36	30	30	22	25	26	27.3
UPPER DARBY	MAX	42	50	43	36	35	42	48	52	43	40	39	25	30	44	48	48	43	45	61	63	62	56	56	55	49	57	45	47	46	45	46	46.4
	MIN	27	33	34	26	24	16	36	40	38	34	24	12	14	25	30	30	29	30	42	55	46	30	30	40	28	35	34	39	38	30	25	31.4
WARREN	MAX	34	37	30	35	34	44	53	37	37	39	34	18	27	37	40	44	40	38	59	58	57	49	59	55	40	39	40	43	40	44	39	41.2
	MIN	18	29	14	23	3	24	37	31	31	23	12	8	8	27	30	33	30	31	37	51	40	24	31	30	18	33	29	28	27	27	22	26.2
WAYNESBURG 2 W	MAX	41	43	37	34	34	50	56	52	39	41	37	19	38	48	48	55	43	52	64	62	56	59	62	54	46	47	40	49	42	50	50	46.7
	MIN	19	31	22	28	1	11	46	36	31	20	11	7	10	31	17	31	17	35	47	48	40	23	25	32	16	36	31	28	19	23	19	25.5
WELLSBORO 3 S	MAX	42	34	35	26	32	30	41	49	34	31	36	25	14	32	37	38	44	34	43	54	57	48	44	56	44	35	37	36	38	36	35	38.0
	MIN	18	19	17	17	10	11	25	31	28	19	21	1	1	9	22	22	28	26	28	42	41	28	27	35	18	19	28	26	26	24	24	22.3
WELLSVILLE	MAX	40	50	42	35	35	32	50	52	41	40	39	25	30	51	47	45	50	42	54	61	60	52	56	56	55	50	46	43	42	46	41	45.4
	MIN	24	20	21	28	19	6	32	40	36	32	22	11	15	13	19	22	25	26	38	48	44	31	24	30	23	32	30	25	28	20	19	25.9
WEST CHESTER	MAX		33	46	39	30	39	42	50	48	40	37	37	23	33	44	49	46	48	50	63	60	58	54	58	52	40	55	46	48	48	44	45.2
	MIN		24	30	29	23	23	29	42	38	34	34	10	13	21	32	33	32	33	35	50	49	39	36	37	33	26	36	32	35	32	28	31.6
WILLIAMSPORT WB AP	MAX	40	45	32	35	37	35	49	48	37	41	37	22	29	40	41	56	43	40	57	62	53	48	48	52	37	40	43	41	43	42	41	42.4
	MIN	27	27	20	27	19	19	34	37	32	30	17	12	18	26	23	36	30	32	40	52	43	30	26	31	22	33	27	27	27	24	21	28.0
YORK 3 SSW PUMP STA	MAX	41	50	43	36	37	35	52	53	42	39	38	25	30	52	49	46	45	44	57	62	62	54	60	54	48	47	46	47	45	46	47	46.2
	MIN	26	29	24	29	17	10	35	42	38	33	23	13	16	17	23	29	24	28	43	53	43	31	28	38	24	35	39	29	29	24	21	28.0

DAILY SOIL TEMPERATURES

Station And Depth	Time	Day of month 1	2	3	4	5	6	7	8	9	10	11	12	13	14	15	16	17	18	19	20	21	22	23	24	25	26	27	28	29	30	31	Average
STATE COLLEGE																																	
MEASURED UNDER SOD																																	
2 INCHES	8 AM	33	33	33	34	34	33	38	38	36	34	33	30	28	30	31	31	31	32	37	47	43	36	34	41	33	33	33	32	33	32	31	34.1
4 INCHES	8 AM	34	34	34	34	35	34	38	39	37	35	34	32	30	31	32	32	32	32	36	45	44	37	35	41	34	34	34	33	34	33	32	34.9
8 INCHES	8 AM	37	36	36	36	36	35	37	39	38	37	36	34	33	32	33	33	33	33	34	42	44	39	37	40	36	35	35	34	35	34	33	35.9
16 INCHES	8 AM	42	40	40	39	39	38	38	40	40	40	40	38	37	36	36	36	36	36	36	39	42	42	40	40	40	38	38	37	38	37	36	37.2

Ground Cover: Bluegrass Sod.

See reference notes following Station Index.

ALLENTOWN WB AIRPORT

AUSTINBURG 2 W

BRADFORD CAA AIRPORT

BRADFORD 4 W RES

BROOKVILLE CAA AIRPORT

CANTON 1 NW

CARROLLTOWN 2 SSE

COALDALE 2 NW

CORRY

DONEGAL

DU BOIS 7 E

ENGLISH CENTER

ERIE WB AIRPORT

EVERETT 1 SW

FORD CITY 4 S DAM

GALETON

GEORGE SCHOOL

GRATERFORD

GREENSBORO LOCK 7

HANOVER

HARRISBURG WB AIRPORT

HAWLEY 1 S DAM

HOLTWOOD

HOOVERSVILLE

INDIANA 3 SE

KANE 1 NNE

LANCASTER 2 NE PUMP STA

LAWRENCEVILLE 2 S

LEWISTOWN

MARTINSBURG CAA AIRPORT

MATAMORAS

MEADVILLE 1 S

MEDIX RUN

MONTROSE 1 E

NEWPORT

PHILADELPHIA WB AIRPORT

PHILIPSBURG CAA AIRPORT

PIMPLE HILL

See reference notes following Station Index.

Table 7- Continued

SNOWFALL AND SNOW ON GROUND

PENNSYLVANIA
DECEMBER 1957

Station		1	2	3	4	5	6	7	8	9	10	11	12	13	14	15	16	17	18	19	20	21	22	23	24	25	26	27	28	29	30	31
PITTSBURGH WB AIRPORT 2	SNOWFALL	T		1.9	2.0					.5	T	.2	.3	T													T	T				
	SN ON GND	T			3	4	1			T	T	T	T	T																		
	WTR EQUIV				.3	.4																										
PLEASANT MOUNT I W	SNOWFALL	T	1.0		2.5						T	T	2.0	T	1.5	T											T	T				T
	SN ON GND	T	1	T	3	2	2	T			T	T	2	2	3	3	2	T	T								T	T	T	T		T
READING WB CITY	SNOWFALL			.5	3.5							1.0	T													T						
	SN ON GND				2	4	3	2					1	T																		
SCRANTON WB AIRPORT	SNOWFALL	.1	T	2.0	1.0		T			.8		2.1	T	T					T							T	T	T			T	
	SN ON GND	T	T		3	2	1	1			T	T	2	1	1	T	T															
	WTR EQUIV				.2	.1							.1																			
SHIPPENSBURG	SNOWFALL	T			6.5		T						T																			
	SN ON GND				6	4	4																									
SHIPPINGPORT WB	SNOWFALL			1.5	.5							T	T				T										T					T
	SN ON GND			1	2	1							T																			
SLIPPERY ROCK	SNOWFALL	T			3.0	.1				1.0		1.0	1.0	1.0																		
	SN ON GND	T			3	3				1		1	2	3	2																	
SPRINGS 1 SW	SNOWFALL	.2		2.0	6.0					T		1.5	T	T													1.5	T	T			
	SN ON GND	1	T	2	8	7	T			T		2	2	1													2	1	T			
TAMARACK 2 S FIRE TWR	SNOWFALL	T	T	T	3.5	T	T	.5		3.0	.3	T	T	T	1.0	.4	T		.5								.5	T				T
	SN ON GND	T	T	T	3	3	3	T		3	3	3	3	3	3	3	3	T	T	T							1	1	1	T	T	T
TIONESTA 2 SE DAM	SNOWFALL	.5	T	T	3.5	.5						T	.5	T	T													T				
	SN ON GND	1	T	T	4	4	2					T	1	1	1	T												T	T			
TOWANDA	SNOWFALL	.1	T	.2	2.3	T		T		.2	.9	.5	.1	T	T	T				T							T	T	T	T		
	SN ON GND	T		T	2	2	1	T		T	1	1	T	T	T																	
TOWER CITY 5 SW	SNOWFALL	T			4.0							.5	2.0														T					
	SN ON GND	-	-	-	-	-	-	-	-	-	-	-	-	-	-	-	-	-	-	-	-	-	-	-	-	-	-	-	-	-	-	-
WILLIAMSPORT WB AIRPORT	SNOWFALL			2.6	T		T		T	T	T	.2	T	T	T				T							.1	T				.1	
	SN ON GND				3	2	1	T				T																				
	WTR EQUIV				.2	.2																										

Table 3

DAILY PRECIPITATION

PENNSYLVANIA
DELAYED DATA

Station	1	2	3	4	5	6	7	8	9	10	11	12	13	14	15	16	17	18	19	20	21	22	23	24	25	26	27	28	29	30	31	Total
JULY 1957																																
EDINBORO 7 SW					.45				.68			-	.10										.21									-
SEPTEMBER 1957																																
BARTO 4 NW				T			.47		.17	T							.34	.08						.64						T		1.60

CORRECTIONS

MONTH: MAY 1950

Table 3:
Lansford — Total should be 77.29.

MONTH: SEPTEMBER 1957

Table 2:
Johnstown — Correct average temperature as follows: maximum, 79.1; minimum, 49.6; average, 64.4; departure, - .9; total degree days, 110.

Table 5:
Johnstown — Correct as follows: Maximum temperature on 6th, 75; minimum temperature on 9th, 54; 10th, 62; 11th, 54; 22nd, 61; 30th, 45; average maximum, 79.1; average minimum, 49.6.

See reference notes following Station Index.

TOTAL PRECIPITATION

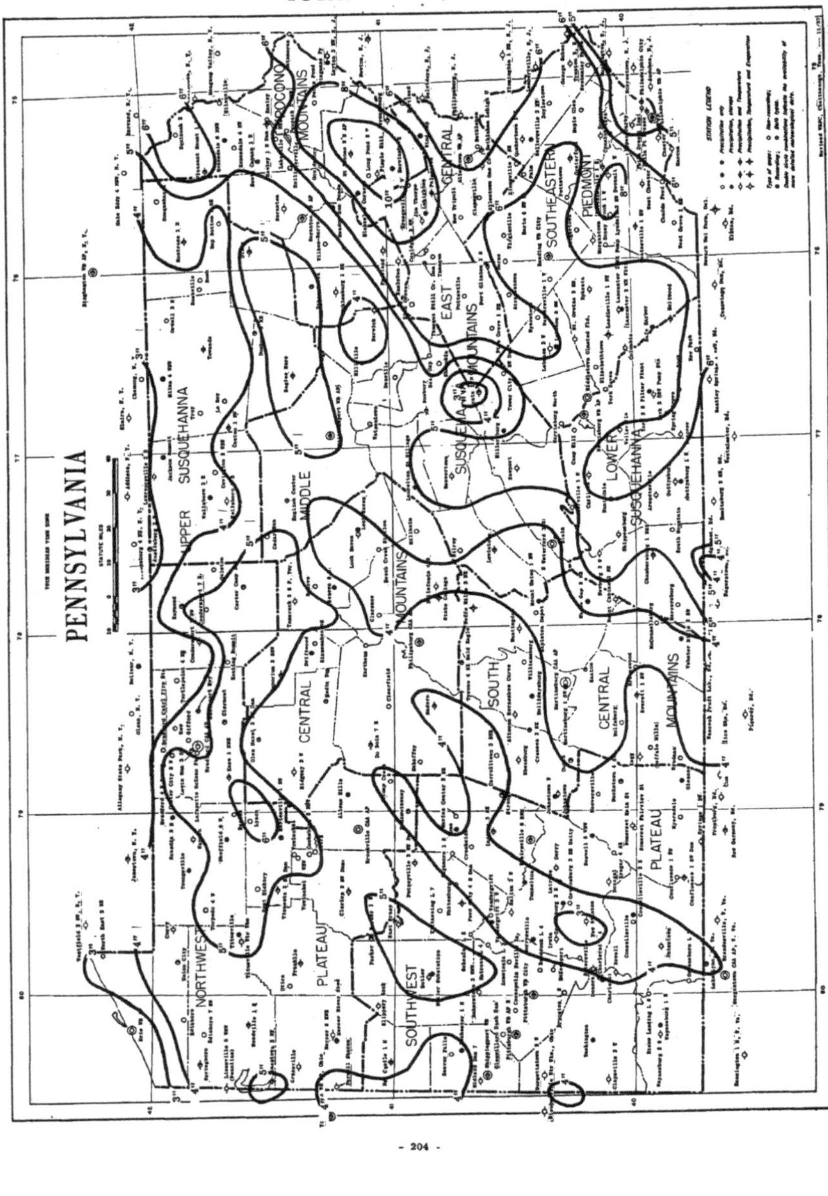

Isolines are drawn through points of approximately equal values. Hourly precipitation data from recorder substations will be available in the publication "Hourly Precipitation Data".

AVERAGE TEMPERATURE

PENNSYLVANIA
DECEMBER 1957

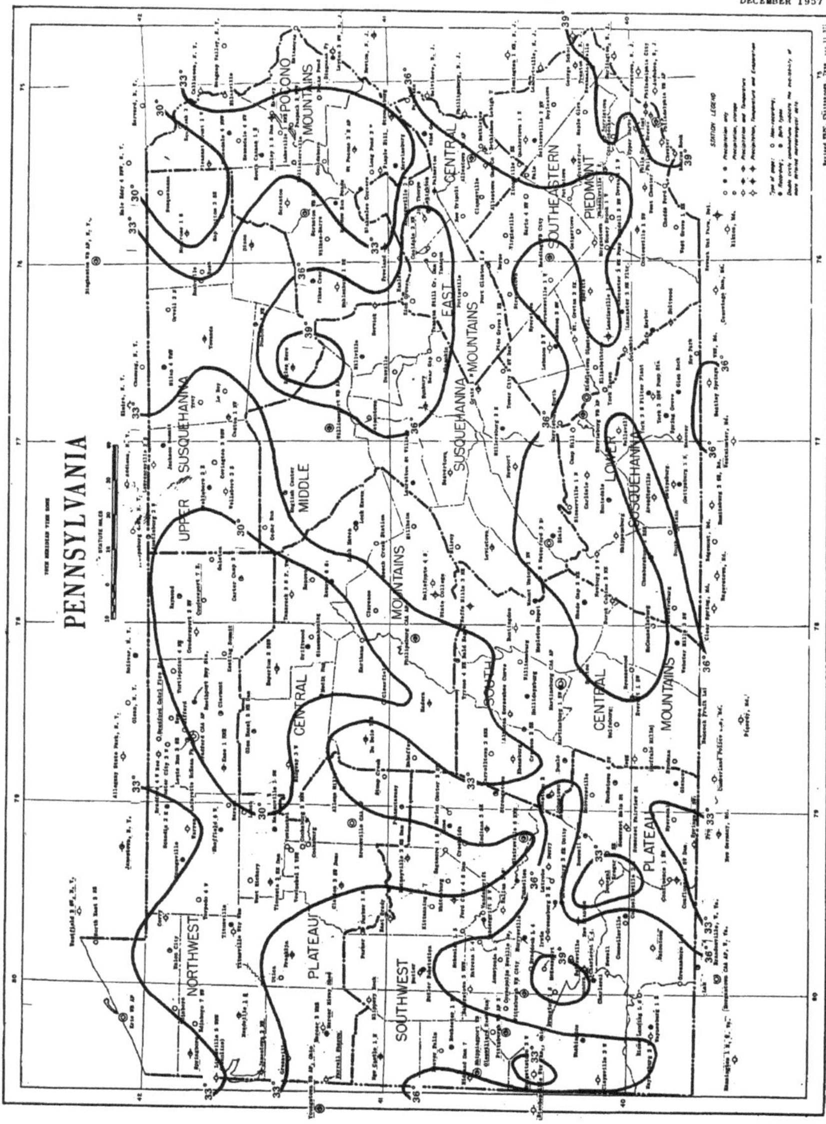

Isolines are drawn through points of approximately equal values. Hourly precipitation data from recorder substations will be available in the publication "Hourly Precipitation Data".

STATION INDEX

Station	Index No.	County	Drainage 1	Latitude	Longitude	Elevation	Observation Time Temp.	Observation Time Precip.	Observer	Refer To Tables
ACMETONIA LOCK 3	0022	ALLEGHENY	1	40 32	79 49	748		7A	CORPS OF ENGINEERS	3
ALLENS MILLS	0099	JEFFERSON	1	41 12	78 55	1600		MID	CHARLES H. ALLEN	C
ALLENTOWN WB AP	0106	LEHIGH	9	40 39	75 26	376	MID	MID	U.S. WEATHER BUREAU	2 3 5 7 C
ALLENTOWN GAS CO	0111	LEHIGH	9	40 36	75 28	254	7A	7A	LEHIGH VLY GAS DIV	2 3 5
ALTOONA HORSESHOE CURVE	0134	BLAIR	6	40 30	78 29	1500	6P	6P	ALTOONA WATER BUR.	2 3 5
ARENDTSVILLE	0229	ADAMS	15	39 55	77 18	710	8A	8A	PA STATE COL EXP	2 3 5
AUSTINBURG 2 W	0313	TIOGA	15	42 00	77 32	1590		7A	OTTO D. BACON	3 7 C
BAKERSTOWN 3 WNW	0355	ALLEGHENY	1	40 39	79 59	1230	7P	7P	PGH CUT FLOWER CO	2 3 5
BARNES	0409	WARREN	1	41 40	79 02	1310		7A	CORPS OF ENGINEERS	3
BARTO 4 NW	0428	BERKS	14	40 26	75 39	312		7A	MARIE B. NICHLAS	3
BEAR GAP	0457	NORTHUMBLAND	15	40 50	76 30	900		3P	ROARING CRK WTR CO	3
BEAVER FALLS	0475	BEAVER	2	40 46	80 19	760		7A	HOWARD R. KEMP	3
BEAVERTOWN	0482	SNYDER	15	40 45	77 10	640	5P	7A	MARLIN R. ETTINGER	2 3 5
BELLEFONTE 4 S	0530	CENTRE	16	40 51	77 47	1110	8A	8A	ROCKVIEW PRISON FARM	2 3 5
BERNE	0590	BERKS	14	40 31	76 00	325		7A	FLOYD W. TRUMP	3
BERWICK	0611	COLUMBIA	15	41 04	76 15	570	6P	6P	AMER CAR + FNDRY CO	2 3 5
BETHLEHEM	0629	NORTHAMPTON	9	40 37	75 22	400		7A	ARTHUR CROPPER	3
#BETHLEHEM LEHIGH UNIV	0634	NORTHAMPTON	9	40 36	75 23	450	MID	MID	LEHIGH UNIVERSITY	2 3 5 C
BLAIN	0725	PERRY	15	40 20	77 31	750		MID	PA DEPT FRST + WTRS	C
BLAIRSVILLE 6 ENE	0736	INDIANA	4	40 27	79 09	2048	8P	8P	U.S. WEATHER BUREAU	2 3 5
BLAKESLEE CORNERS	0743	MONROE	9	41 06	75 36	1650		MID	WALTER WILDRICK	C
BLOSERVILLE 1 N	0763	CUMBERLAND	15	40 16	77 22	650		5P	MRS. B. M. WILLDERS	3
BOSWELL 6 WNW	0820	SOMERSET	1	40 10	79 08	2570		8A	CLARK N. ST. CLAIR	3 C
BRADDOCK LOCK 2	0861	ALLEGHENY	10	40 24	79 52	725		7A	CORPS OF ENGINEERS	3
BRADFORD CAA AIRPORT	0865	MC KEAN	1	41 48	78 38	2150	MID	MID	CIVIL AERO. ADM.	2 3 5 7
BRADFORD CNTRL FIRE STA	0867	MC KEAN	1	41 57	78 39	1500		8A	BRADFORD FIRE DEPT	3
BRADFORD 4 W RES	0868	MC KEAN	1	41 57	78 44	1680	5P	5P	BRADFORD WTR DEPT	2 3 5 7
BREEZEWOOD	0905	BEDFORD	6	40 00	78 14	1352		MID	PA TURNPIKE COMM	3
BROOKVILLE CAA AIRPORT	1002	JEFFERSON	1	41 09	79 06	1417	MID	MID	CIVIL AERO. ADM.	2 3 5 7
BRUCETON 1 S	1033	ALLEGHENY	10	40 18	79 59	1065		7A	AUSTIN R. COOPER	3
BUCKSTOWN 1 SE	1073	SOMERSET	4	40 04	78 50	2460		MID	ALVIN W. MANGES	C
BUFFALO MILLS	1087	BEDFORD	12	39 57	78 39	1318		8A	CLIFFORD C. ADAMS	3
BURGETTSTOWN 2 W	1105	WASHINGTON	11	40 23	80 26	980	7A	7A	SMITH TWP MUN AUTH	2 3 5
BURNT CABINS 2 NE	1115	HUNTINGDON	6	40 05	77 52	900	5P	5P	PA TURNPIKE COMM	2 3 5
#BUTLER	1130	BUTLER	2	40 52	79 54	1100	4P	7A	WILLIAM C. FAUST	2 3 5
BUTLER SUBSTATION	1135	BUTLER	2	40 51	79 53	1140		MID	WEST PENN POWER CO	C
CAMP HILL	1198	CUMBERLAND	15	40 15	76 55	461		6P	JOSEPH N. HOBART	3
CANTON 1 NW	1215	BRADFORD	15	41 40	76 52	1520	7A	7A	MRS.MILDRED SPENCER	2 3 5 7 C
CARLISLE	1234	CUMBERLAND	15	40 12	77 11	460	6P	6P	C. E. MILLER	2 3 5
CARROLLTOWN 2 SSE	1255	CAMBRIA	16	40 35	78 42	2040		8A	ROBERT F. MAURER	3 7
CARTER CAMP 2 W	1262	POTTER	16	41 37	77 45	2030		7A	RICHARD L. MENKEN	3 C
CEDAR RUN	1301	LYCOMING	16	41 31	77 27	800		7A	KATHRYN T.KREIGHBAUM	3
CHADDS FORD	1342	DELAWARE	5	39 52	75 37	170		7A	E. EARL TOUCHTON	3
CHAMBERSBURG 1 ESE	1354	FRANKLIN	12	39 56	77 38	640	9P	9P	CHARLES A. BENDER	2 3 5 C
CHARLEROI	1372	WASHINGTON	10	40 08	79 55	1040		MID	WEST PENN POWER CO	C
CHARLEROI LOCK 4	1377	WESTMORELAND	10	40 09	79 54	749		7A	CORPS OF ENGINEERS	3
#CHESTER	1423	DELAWARE	5	39 51	75 22	86	8A	8A	CHESTER TIMES	2 3 5
CLARENCE	1480	CENTRE	16	41 03	77 56	1410		7A	MISS VELDA SWANCER	3
CLARION 3 SW	1485	CLARION	1	41 12	79 26	1114	8P	7A	PA ELECTRIC CO	2 3 5 C
CLAUSSVILLE	1505	LEHIGH	9	40 37	75 39	670		8A	WILLIAM J. DOTTERER	3
CLAYSVILLE 3 W	1512	WASHINGTON	11	40 07	80 28	1000	7P	7A	MFGRS. L + H CO	2 3 5
CLEARFIELD	1519	CLEARFIELD	16	41 01	78 26	1100		7A	IRA TAYLOR	3
CLERMONT	1529	MC KEAN	1	41 41	78 30	2104		7A	MRS.TILLIE M.SIMONDS	3 C
COALDALE 2 NW	1572	SCHUYLKILL	9	40 50	75 56	1026		7A	PANTHER VLY WTR CO	3 7
COATESVILLE 1 SW	1589	CHESTER	5	39 58	75 50	342	8A	8A	PHILA ELECTRIC CO	2 3 5 C
COLUMBIA	1675	LANCASTER	15	40 02	76 30	300	5S	5S	JAMES H. RUST	2 3 5
CONFLUENCE 1 SW DAM	1705	SOMERSET	17	39 48	79 22	1490	8A	8A	CORPS OF ENGINEERS	2 3 5 6 C
CONFLUENCE 1 NW	1710	FAYETTE	17	39 50	79 22	1331		7A	JOHN L. REID	3
CONNELLSVILLE	1723	FAYETTE	17	40 01	79 36	870		8A	MARSHALL B. MENEFEE	3
CONNELLSVILLE 2 E	1729	FAYETTE	17	40 01	79 33	1300		MID	HARRY C. JOY	C
CONSHOHOCKEN	1737	MONTGOMERY	5	40 04	75 19	70		8A	PHILA ELECTRIC CO	3
COOKSBURG	1749	CLARION	1	41 20	79 13	1180		8A	PA DEPT FRST + WTRS	3
COOKSBURG 2 NNW	1752	CLARION	1	41 21	79 13	1460		8A	PA DEPT FRST + WTRS	3
CORAOPOLIS NEVILLE IS	1773	ALLEGHENY	11	40 30	80 05	720		8A	PGH. COKE + CHEM CO	3
CORRY	1790	ERIE	1	41 55	79 39	1440	6P	6P	RICHARD T. MOUNTAIN	2 3 5 7
COUDERSPORT 3 NW	1806	POTTER	1	41 40	78 03	2020	7P	8A	MISS ELIZABETH NEFF	2 3 5
COUDERSPORT 7 E	1809	POTTER	1	41 46	77 53	2425		7A	DONALD HOUSE	3
COVINGTON 2 WSW	1833	TIOGA	15	41 44	77 07	1745		7A	CALVIN R. PACKARD	3
CREEKSIDE	1881	INDIANA	1	40 41	79 12	1035		7A	CORPS OF ENGINEERS	3
CRESSON 2 SE	1895	CAMBRIA	6	40 27	78 34	2540		7A	MILES M. LINGLE	3 C
CUSTER CITY 2 W	1978	MC KEAN	1	41 55	78 41	2120		8A	M. D. BOOTH AND CO	3
DANVILLE	2013	MONTOUR	15	40 58	76 37	460		7A	MRS.MARIE M. LITTLE	3
DERRY	2108	WESTMORELAND	4	40 20	79 18	1150	6P	6P	MISS M. D. WINEMAN	2 3 5
DEVAULT 1 W	2116	CHESTER	14	40 05	75 33	360	MID	MID	PA TURNPIKE COMM	2 3 5
DINGMANS FERRY	2160	PIKE	5	41 13	74 52	364		MID	CLYDE T. VOORHEES	C
DIXON	2171	WYOMING	15	41 34	75 54	620	7A	7A	HAROLD J. KUSCHEL	2 3 5 C
DONEGAL	2183	WESTMORELAND	17	40 07	79 23	1746	MID	MID	PA TURNPIKE COMM	2 3 5 7
DONORA	2190	WASHINGTON	10	40 10	79 52	900	5P	5P	THEODORE F. MATHUES	2 3 5
DOYLESTOWN	2221	BUCKS	5	40 18	75 08	303		5P	GEORGE HART	3
DRIFTWOOD	2245	CAMERON	16	41 20	78 08	880		MID	SIDNEY KENNEDY	C
DU BOIS 7 E	2265	CLEARFIELD	16	41 06	78 38	1670	5P	5P	CITY OF DU BOIS	2 3 5 7 C
DUNLO	2298	CAMBRIA	4	40 17	78 43	2410		MID	MRS. D. L. WHITE	C
DUSHORE 3 NE	2324	SULLIVAN	16	41 33	76 21	1750		7A	PATRICK F. RYAN	3 C
EAGLES MERE	2343	SULLIVAN	16	41 24	76 35	2020	7A	7A	MRS.ELSIE P. BIGGER	2 3 5 C
EAST BRADY	2363	CLARION	1	40 59	79 37	820	5P	5P	A. B. KEMPEL	2 3 5
EAST WATERFORD 3 E	2458	PERRY	6	40 21	77 33	2125	8A	8A	U.S. WEATHER BUREAU	INAC 5/55
EBENSBURG	2466	CAMBRIA	4	40 29	78 43	2090	7P	7A	ROBERT A. WASSER	2 3 5
EDINBORO	2514	ERIE	1	41 52	80 08	1220		8A	EDINBORO ST TCHR COL	3
EDINBORO 7 SW	2519	CRAWFORD	1	41 47	80 13	1200		8A	THOMAS M. YOUNG	3
ELIZABETHTOWN	2560	LANCASTER	15	40 09	76 37	460		8A	MASONIC HOME	3
EMPORIUM 2 SSW	2634	CAMERON	16	41 28	78 15	1735	7A	7A	JACKSON THOMAS	2 3 5 C
ENGLISH CENTER	2644	LYCOMING	16	41 26	77 17	881		7A	WILLIAM SUDERS	3 7 C
EPHRATA	2662	LANCASTER	15	40 11	76 10	465	6P	6P	STANLEY L.VON NEIDA	2 3 5
EQUINUNK 2	2671	WAYNE	5	41 51	75 13	910		7A	MRS. HENRIETTA MURRY	3
ERIE WB AIRPORT	2682	ERIE	8	42 05	80 12	732	MID	MID	U. S. WEATHER BUREAU	2 3 5 7
EVERETT 1 SW	2721	BEDFORD	6	40 00	78 23	1020	MID	MID	PA TURNPIKE COMM	2 3 5 7 C
FARRELL SHARON	2814	MERCER	2	41 14	80 30	865	7P	7P	SHARON STEEL CORP	2 3 5
FORD CITY 4 S DAM	2942	ARMSTRONG	1	40 43	79 30	950	8A	8A	CORPS OF ENGINEERS	2 3 5 6 7 C
FRANKLIN	3028	VENANGO	1	41 23	79 49	987	7P	7A	ROBERT D. RHOADS	2 3 5 C
FREELAND	3056	LUZERNE	15	41 01	75 54	1900	6P	8A	ANDREW B. EVANSHA	2 3 5
GALETON	3130	POTTER	16	41 44	77 39	1325		7A	W. GALE LUSH	3 7
GEIGERTOWN	3189	BERKS	14	40 13	75 50	400		8A	WALTER C. WOLF	3
GEORGE SCHOOL	3200	BUCKS	5	40 13	74 56	135	8A	8A	GEORGE M. HART	2 3 5 7
#GETTYSBURG	3218	ADAMS	12	39 50	77 14	540	9A	9A	HUGH C. MC ILHENNY	2 3 5
GETTYSBURG 1 S	3223	ADAMS	12	39 48	77 14	560		MID	NAT MILITARY PARK	C
GIFFORD	3237	MC KEAN	1	41 51	78 36	2220		8A	SOUTH PENN OIL CO	3
GLENCOE	3298	SOMERSET	12	39 49	78 51	1620		MID	MRS. MARY M.HARTMAN	C
GLEN HAZEL 2 NE DAM	3311	ELK	1	41 34	78 36	1725		8A	CORPS OF ENGINEERS	3 C
GLEN ROCK	3330	YORK	15	39 48	76 44	620		MID	MRS.E.C.MC WILLIAMS	C
GLENWILLARD DASH DAM	3343	ALLEGHENY	11	40 33	80 13	705		7A	CORPS OF ENGINEERS	3
GOULDSBORO	3394	WAYNE	9	41 15	75 27	1890		7A	L. M. EILENBERGER	3
GRATERFORD	3435	MONTGOMERY	14	40 14	75 27	160	7A	7A	CLAUDE K. KULP	2 3 5 7 C
GRATZ 1 N	3438	DAUPHIN	15	40 38	76 43	760	8A	8A	LEE M. LEITZEL	2 3 5 C
GREENSBORO LOCK 7	3503	GREENE	10	39 47	79 55	808		7A	CORPS OF ENGINEERS	3 7
GREENSBURG 2 E	3515	WESTMORELAND	10	40 18	79 31	1225		MID	PA DEPT HIGHWAYS	C
GREENSBURG 3 SE UNITY	3516	WESTMORELAND	10	40 17	79 30	1245		6P	WESTMORELAND WTR CO	3
GREENVILLE	3526	MERCER	2	41 24	80 23	1026	6P	6P	C. EARL MILLER	2 3 5
HANOVER	3662	YORK	15	39 48	76 59	600	8A	8A	HANOVER EVENING SUN	2 3 5 7
#HARRISBURG WB AP	3699	YORK	15	40 13	76 51	335	MID	MID	U.S. WEATHER BUREAU	2 3 5 7 C
HARRISBURG NORTH	3704	DAUPHIN	15	40 18	76 54	323		9A	GEORGE S. BEAL	3
HAWLEY	3758	WAYNE	5	41 29	75 10	880		7A	MRS. KATHERINE BATES	3
HAWLEY 1 S DAM	3761	WAYNE	5	41 28	75 11	1200	7A	7A	PA POWER + LIGHT CO	2 3 5 6 7 C
HOLLIDAYSBURG	4001	BLAIR	6	40 26	78 24	960		MID	JOHN M. RINGLER	C
HOLLISTERVILLE	4008	WAYNE	5	41 23	75 26	1380		8A	PA POWER + LIGHT CO	3
#HOLTWOOD	4019	LANCASTER	15	39 50	76 20	187	MID	8A	PA POWER + LIGHT CO	2 3 5 7 C
HOME	4027	INDIANA	1	40 45	79 06	1220		MID	MRS. EDNA M. BUSH	C
HONESDALE 4 NW	4043	WAYNE	5	41 37	75 19	1410		9A	GEORGE C. WILLIAMS	3
HONESDALE 6 NNW	4044	WAYNE	5	41 39	75 17	1050		MID	FRIEND E. WALTER	C
HONEY BROOK 1 W	4047	CHESTER	5	40 06	75 56	700		7A	S. M. KURTZ	3
HOOVERSVILLE	4058	SOMERSET	4	40 09	78 55	1670		8A	JAMES A. HAMM	3 7

Station	Index No.	County	Drainage 1	Latitude	Longitude	Elevation	Observation Time Temp.	Observation Time Precip.	Observer	Refer To Tables
HOP BOTTOM 2 SE	4066	SUSQUEHANNA	15	41 43	75 43	900		7A	JOSEPH J. SANAUSKAS	3
HUNTINGDON	4159	HUNTINGDON	6	40 30	78 01	678	7A	7A	DANIEL I. GROVE	2 3 5
HUNTSDALE	4166	CUMBERLAND	15	40 06	77 18	610		8A	METRO P. DOROSH	3 C
HYNDMAN	4190	BEDFORD	12	39 49	78 43	920		8A	MRS.GERTRUDE M.BURTON	3
INDIANA 3 SE	4214	INDIANA	4	40 38	79 07	1102	7P	7A	CLYMER WATER SVC CO	2 3 5 7 C
IRWIN	4276	WESTMORELAND	10	40 20	79 42	1100	5P	5P	WESTMORELAND WTR CO	2 3 5
JACKSON SUMMIT	4304	TIOGA	15	41 57	77 01	1690		MID	ARCHIE LAIN	C
JAMESTOWN 2 NW	4325	CRAWFORD	2	41 30	80 28	1050	8A	8A	PA DEPT FRST + WTRS	2 3 5 6 C
JIM THORPE	4370	CARBON	9	40 52	75 45	830	5P	5P	HENRY S. HAAK	2 3 5
#JOHNSTOWN	4385	CAMBRIA	4	40 20	78 55	1214	9A	9A	JOHNSTOWN TRIBUNE	2 3 5
JOHNSTOWN 2	4390	CAMBRIA	4	40 19	78 55	1275		MID	CITY OF JOHNSTOWN	C
KANE 1 NNE	4432	MC KEAN	1	41 41	78 48	1750	8A	8A	RUDOLPH A. ANDERSON	2 3 5 7 C
KARTHAUS	4450	CLEARFIELD	16	41 07	78 07	950		7A	JEROME S. HOWE	3
KEATING SUMMIT	4466	POTTER	16	41 41	78 11	1840		7A	EUGENE L. KREITNER	INAC 10/57
KEGG	4481	BEDFORD	6	39 59	78 43	1280	MID	MID	PA TURNPIKE COMM	2 3 5
KITTANNING LOCK 7	4611	ARMSTRONG	1	40 49	79 32	790		VAR	CORPS OF ENGINEERS	3
KREGAR 4 SE	4667	WESTMORELAND	17	40 06	79 14	2530		MID	PA TURNPIKE COMM	3
KRESGEVILLE 3 W	4672	CARBON	9	40 54	75 34	720		7A	CITY OF BETHLEHEM	3
LAFAYETTE MC KEAN PARK	4706	MC KEAN	1	41 48	78 40	2130		7A	ORIN A. BUTTERS	3
LAKEVILLE 1 NNE	4733	WAYNE	5	41 27	75 16	1440		8A	MRS. GLADYS REINEKE	3
LANCASTER 2 NE PUMP STA	4758	LANCASTER	15	40 03	76 17	255	6P	6P	LANCASTER WATER BUR	2 3 5 7
LANCASTER 2 NE FILT PL	4763	LANCASTER	15	40 03	76 17	270		MID	LANCASTER WATER BUR	C
LANDISVILLE 2 NW	4778	LANCASTER	15	40 07	76 26	360	8A	8A	PA STATE COLLEGE	2 3 5 6 C
LAURELTON STATE VILLAGE	4853	UNION	15	40 54	77 13	860		MID	PA DEPT OF WELFARE	C
LAWRENCEVILLE 2 S	4873	TIOGA	15	41 50	77 07	1000	7A	7A	HARRY P. HOWLAND	2 3 5 7
LEBANON 3 W	4891	LEBANON	15	40 20	76 29	460	7A	7A	LEON MILLER	2 3 5
LEBANON 3 SW	4896	LEBANON	15	40 19	76 28	490		MID	THOMAS DONNACHIE	C
LEHIGHTON	4934	CARBON	9	40 50	75 43	580		7A	GOODWIN S. DEFREHN	3 C
LE ROY	4972	BRADFORD	15	41 41	76 43	1040		6P	MRS.DIMMIS M.BAILEY	3
LEWIS RUN 3 SE	4984	MC KEAN	1	41 50	78 39	1740		7A	RUSSELL LINEMAN	3 C
LEWISTOWN	4992	MIFFLIN	6	40 35	77 35	480	7A	7A	AMERICAN VISCOSE CO	2 3 5 7 C
LINESVILLE 5 WNW	5050	CRAWFORD	2	41 41	80 31	1020	7P	8A	MISS RETTA M. CRUMB	2 3 5
LOCK HAVEN	5104	CLINTON	16	41 08	77 27	570	7P	7A	PETER L. STEVENSON	2 3 5
LOCK HAVEN 2	5109	CLINTON	16	41 08	77 27	630		MID	HUGH F. PARKER	C
LONG POND 2 W	5160	MONROE	9	41 03	75 30	1860		7A	THOMAS MECKES	3
LYNCH	5275	FOREST	1	41 36	79 03	1295		7A	CORPS OF ENGINEERS	3
LYNDELL 2 NW	5279	CHESTER	5	40 05	75 46	-		8A	MRS. DOROTHY MARPLE	3
MADERA	5336	CLEARFIELD	16	40 50	78 26	1460	7A	7A	MRS. JULIA J. SHOFF	2 3 5 C
MAHAFFEY	5342	CLEARFIELD	16	40 53	78 44	1280		7A	MISS ELLEN J. MILES	3
MAPLE GLEN	5368	MONTGOMERY	5	40 11	75 11	380		6P	FRANCES E.SCHEIBNER	3
MAPLETON DEPOT	5381	HUNTINGDON	6	40 24	77 56	580		7A	MRS. I. S. BUCHANAN	3
MARCUS HOOK	5390	DELAWARE	5	39 49	75 25	12	MID	MID	SUN OIL CO	2 3 5
MARIENVILLE 1 SW	5400	FOREST	1	41 27	79 09	1700		MID	ROY A. MARKER	C
MARION CENTER 2 SE	5408	INDIANA	1	40 45	79 02	1610		7A	CORPS OF ENGINEERS	3
MARTINSBURG 1 SW	5453	BLAIR	6	40 18	78 20	1360		MID	BLUE MT. CANNERIES	C
MARTINSBURG CAA AP	5454	BLAIR	6	40 18	78 19	1463	MID	MID	CIVIL AERO. ADM.	2 3 5 7
MATAMORAS	5470	PIKE	5	41 22	74 42	439		7A	HARRY BISLAND	3 7
MC CONNELLSBURG	5526	FULTON	12	39 56	78 00	895		7A	MRS. HELEN M. SHIVES	3
MC KEESPORT	5573	ALLEGHENY	10	40 21	79 52	720		8A	NATIONAL TUBE CO	3
MEADOW RUN PONDS	5601	LUZERNE	15	41 13	75 40	1995		MID	GEORGE PEARAGE	C
MEADVILLE 1 S	5606	CRAWFORD	1	41 38	80 10	1065	8A	8A	CITY OF MEADVILLE	2 3 5 7 C
MEDIX RUN	5627	ELK	16	41 17	78 24	1100		7A	MRS.E. M. SNYDER	3 7 C
MERCER 2 NNE	5651	MERCER	2	41 15	80 13	1160	7P	7A	MRS. FRAN. STRUTHERS	2 3 5
MERCER HIWAY SHED	5654	MERCER	2	41 14	80 15	1250		MID	PA DEPT HIGHWAYS	C
MERCERSBURG	5662	FRANKLIN	12	39 50	77 54	605		8A	ROLLIN P. GILBERT	3
MERWINSBURG	5676	MONROE	9	40 58	75 28	970		MID	WILLIAM D. GOULD	C
MEYERSDALE	5684	SOMERSET	17	39 49	79 02	2040		8A	ARTHUR J. POTTER	3
MIDDLETOWN OLMSTED FLD	5703	DAUPHIN	15	40 11	76 46	303	MID	MID	U. S. AIR FORCE	2 3 5
MIDLAND DAM 7	5710	BEAVER	11	40 38	80 28	689	11P	7A	CORPS OF ENGINEERS	2 3 5
MILAN 4 WNW	5732	BRADFORD	15	41 56	76 35	1448		MID	CARL A. MORRIS	C
MILANVILLE	5738	WAYNE	5	41 40	75 04	760		8A	CHARLES W. DAVIS	3
MILLERSBURG 2 E	5775	DAUPHIN	15	40 32	76 56	560		MID	RUSSELL SHEPLEY	C
MILLHEIM	5790	CENTRE	15	40 54	77 29	1090		7A	NEVIN E. BOWERSOX	3
MILLVILLE 2 SW	5817	COLUMBIA	15	41 06	76 34	860		7A	KENNETH LEIGHOW	3 C
MILROY	5825	MIFFLIN	6	40 43	77 35	770		8A	THOMAS C. HARBESON	3
MONTROSE 1 E	5915	SUSQUEHANNA	15	41 50	75 51	1630	7A	7A	WILBER W. HOOPES.JR	2 3 5 7 C
MORGANTOWN	5956	BERKS	15	40 09	75 54	595	MID	MID	PA TURNPIKE COMM	2 3 5
MT GRETNA 2 SE	6028	LANCASTER	15	40 14	76 26	670	MID	MID	PA TURNPIKE COMM	2 3 5
MT POCONO 2 N AP	6055	MONROE	5	41 09	75 22	1915	5P	5P	H. JOHN DAVIS, JR.	2 3 5 C
MOUNT UNION 1 N	6067	MIFFLIN	6	40 24	77 53	820		MID	MT UNION WTR WORKS	C
MUHLENBURG 1 SE	6090	LUZERNE	15	41 13	76 08	1110	6P	6P	THEODORE J. SAMPSON	2 3 5 7
MURRYSVILLE	6111	WESTMORELAND	10	40 26	79 42	903		MID	DAVID C. SHAW	C
MYERSTOWN	6126	LEBANON	14	40 22	76 18	480		8A	MRS.KATHLEEN MANDELL	3
NATRONA LOCK 4	6151	ALLEGHENY	1	40 37	79 43	800		7A	CORPS OF ENGINEERS	3
NEFFS MILLS 3 NE	6174	HUNTINGDON	6	40 40	77 55	900		MID	PA STATE UNIVERSITY	C
NESHAMINY FALLS	6194	BUCKS	5	40 09	74 57	60		MID	PHILA SUB WATER CO	3
NEWBURG 3 W	6225	FRANKLIN	15	40 09	77 37	745	5P	5P	PA TURNPIKE COMM	2 3 5
NEW CASTLE 1 N	6233	LAWRENCE	2	41 01	80 22	825	5P	7A	BAXTER F. JOHNSON	2 3 5 C
NEWELL	6246	FAYETTE	10	40 05	79 54	805	12M	12M	GENERAL CHEMICAL CO	2 3 5
NEW PARK	6289	YORK	15	39 44	76 30	780		6P	CLINTON J. ALLEN	3
NEWPORT	6297	PERRY	6	40 29	77 08	400	7A	7A	MRS. FRANCES K. FRY	2 3 5 7
NEW STANTON	6310	WESTMORELAND	10	40 13	79 36	980	MID	MID	PA TURNPIKE COMM	2 3 5
NEW TRIPOLI	6326	LEHIGH	14	40 41	75 45	570		6P	FRED C. OSWALD	3
NORRISTOWN	6370	MONTGOMERY	14	40 07	75 21	75	MID	8A	GEORGE M. BOONE	2 3 5
NORTH EAST 2 SE	6396	ERIE	8	42 12	79 40	1060		9A	ELLSWORTH WEAVER	3
ORWELL 3 N	6621	BRADFORD	15	41 55	76 16	1620		8A	WILLIAM I. BROWN	3
PALM	6681	MONTGOMERY	14	40 26	75 32	385		8A	FRED C. ESCHBACH	3
#PALMERTON	6689	CARBON	9	40 48	75 37	435	MID	MID	NEW JERSEY ZINC CO	2 3 5 C
PARKER	6721	ARMSTRONG	1	41 05	79 41	1140		7A	LOUIS A. MALARKEY	3
PARKER 1 E	6724	CLARION	1	41 06	79 40	1100		MID	P. M. NEELY	C
PAUPACK 2 WNW	6762	PIKE	5	41 24	75 14	1360		8A	MISS L. VETTERLEIN	3
PECKS POND	6786	PIKE	5	41 17	75 06	1380		9A	MRS. CARRIE NESS	3
#PHIL DREXEL INST OF TEC	6879	PHILADELPHIA	14	39 57	75 11	30	MID	MID	FRANCIS K. DAVIS.JR	2 3 5
PHILADELPHIA WB AP	6889	PHILADELPHIA	5	39 53	75 15	13	MID	MID	U.S. WEATHER BUREAU	2 3 5 7 C
#PHILADELPHIA PT BREEZE	6899	PHILADELPHIA	5	39 55	75 12	32	MID	MID	ATLANTIC REFINING	2 3 5 C
PHILIPSBURG CAA AP	6916	CENTRE	6	40 54	78 05	1918	MID	MID	CIVIL AERO. ADM.	2 3 5 7 C
PHOENIXVILLE 1 E	6927	CHESTER	14	40 07	75 30	105	6P	MID	PHILA SUB WATER CO	2 3 5 C
PIKES CREEK	6939	LUZERNE	15	41 18	76 08	1320		7A	HARRY SHELDON	3 C
PIMPLE HILL	6944	MONROE	9	41 02	75 30	2215	9A	9A	PA DEPT FRST + WTRS	2 3 5 6 7
PINE GROVE 1 NE	6954	SCHUYLKILL	15	40 34	76 22	535		8A	PA POWER + LIGHT CO	3
PITTSBURGH WB AP 2	6993	ALLEGHENY	11	40 30	80 13	1151	MID	MID	U.S. WEATHER BUREAU	2 3 5 7 C
#PITTSBURGH WB CITY	6997	ALLEGHENY	11	40 27	80 00	749	MID	MID	U.S. WEATHER BUREAU	2 3 5 C
PLEASANT MOUNT 1 W	7029	WAYNE	5	41 44	75 27	1800	8A	8A	PA FISH COMM	2 3 5 7 C
PORT CLINTON	7116	SCHUYLKILL	14	40 35	76 02	450	7A	7A	MRS. ADA E. RARICK	2 3 5 C
PORTLAND	7127	NORTHAMPTON	5	40 55	75 06	297		8A	JOINT BRIDGE COMM	INAC 1/56
POTTSVILLE	7161	SCHUYLKILL	14	40 42	76 11	690		8A	LLOYD E. WELLER	3
PUNXSUTAWNEY	7217	JEFFERSON	1	40 57	79 00	1298		MID	JOHN VOLANSKY	C
PUTNEYVILLE 2 SE DAM	7229	ARMSTRONG	1	40 55	79 17	1270	8A	8A	CORPS OF ENGINEERS	2 3 5 C
QUAKERTOWN 1 E	7239	BUCKS	5	40 26	75 20	490	5P	7A	DENNIS K. FLUCK	2 3 5
RAYMOND	7310	POTTER	15	41 52	77 52	2220		7A	MRS. RACHEL LANGAN	3 C
#READING WB CITY	7318	BERKS	14	40 20	75 58	266	MID	MID	U.S. WEATHER BUREAU	2 3 5 7 C
RENOVO	7409	CLINTON	16	41 20	77 46	660		7A	MRS. CAROLINE BAIRD	3
RENOVO 5 S	7410	CLINTON	16	41 14	77 46	2035		MID	C. F. BILLETTE	C
REW	7425	MC KEAN	1	41 54	78 32	2250		8A	HAROLD C. MEALY	3
RICES LANDING L 6	7443	GREENE	10	39 57	80 00	775		7A	CORPS OF ENGINEERS	3
RIDGWAY 3 W	7477	ELK	1	41 25	78 47	1420	7A	7A	BOROUGH OF RIDGWAY	2 3 5
ROCHESTER 1 N	7540	BEAVER	2	40 43	80 16	900		MID	DEQUESNE LIGHT CO	C
RUSH	7694	SUSQUEHANNA	15	41 47	76 03	1000		9A	MISS MAUDE MC CAIN	3
RUSHVILLE	7727	SUSQUEHANNA	15	41 47	76 07	870		7A	CARL KOPATZ	3
SAFE HARBOR	7732	LANCASTER	15	39 58	76 23	270		MID	S.W.WATER POWER CORP	C
SAGAMORE 1 S	7739	INDIANA	1	40 46	79 14	1320		7A	CORPS OF ENGINEERS	3
SALINA 3 W	7782	WESTMORELAND	7	40 31	79 33	1109	6P	6P	MUN AUTH WSTMRLD CO	2 3 5
SAXTON	7846	BEDFORD	6	40 12	78 15	780		8A	MRS.ALVERTA L.HOLMES	3 C
SCANDIA 2 E	7855	WARREN	1	41 55	79 01	2040		MID	DAVID R. ANDERSON	C
SCHENLEY LOCK 5	7863	ARMSTRONG	1	40 41	79 40	783		VAR	CORPS OF ENGINEERS	3
#SCRANTON	7902	LACKAWANNA	15	41 25	75 40	746	7A	7A	U.S. POST OFFICE	2 3 5
SCRANTON WB AIRPORT	7905	LUZERNE	15	41 20	75 44	956	MID	MID	U.S. WEATHER BUREAU	2 3 5 7 C
SELLERSVILLE 2 NW	7938	BUCKS	5	40 23	75 20	530		MID	SELLERSVILLE WTR CO	C
SHADE GAP	7965	HUNTINGDON	6	40 11	77 52	920		MID	MRS. HELEN M. PYLE	C

STATION INDEX

Station	Index No.	County	Drainage ‡	Latitude	Longitude	Elevation	Observation Time Temp.	Observation Time Precip.	Observer	Refer To Tables
SHAMOKIN	7979	NORTHUMBLAND	15	40 48	76 33	770		8A	ROARING CRK WTR CO	3
SHEFFIELD 6 W	8026	WARREN	1	41 41	79 09	1940		MID	L. N. HANSON	C
SHIPPENSBURG	8073	FRANKLIN	15	40 03	77 32	709	4P	4P	KEITH B. ALLEN	2 3 5 7
SHIPPINGPORT WB	8078	BEAVER	11	40 37	80 26	740	MID	MID	U.S. WEATHER BUREAU	2 3 5 7 C
SINNEMAHONING	8145	CAMERON	16	41 19	78 05	780		7A	MRS.FRANCES CALDWELL	3
SLIPPERY ROCK	8184	BUTLER	2	41 04	80 03	1345	7P	7A	WALTER D. ALBERT	2 3 5 7
SMETHPORT HIGHWAY SHED	8190	MC KEAN	1	41 48	78 27	1510		MID	PA DEPT HIGHWAYS	C
SOMERSET FAIRVIEW ST	8244	SOMERSET	17	40 01	79 05	2140		7A	HOWARD G. PECK	3
SOMERSET MAIN ST	8249	SOMERSET	17	40 01	79 05	2150	6P	6P	DAVID L. GROVE	2 3 5
SOUTH CANAAN 1 NE	8275	WAYNE	5	41 31	75 24	1400		MID	EUGENE M. COOK	C
SOUTH MOUNTAIN	8308	FRANKLIN	12	39 51	77 30	1520		7A	PA DEPT OF HEALTH	3
SPRINGBORO	8359	CRAWFORD	8	41 48	80 25	900	8A	8A	SPRINGBORO BOROUGH	2 3 5 C
SPRING GROVE	8379	YORK	15	39 52	76 52	470		4P	P. H. GLATFELTER CO	3 C
SPRINGS 1 SW	8395	SOMERSET	17	39 44	79 10	2500	8P	8P	ALLEN E. WOOEA	2 3 5 7
STATE COLLEGE	8449	CENTRE	16	40 48	77 52	1175	7A	7A	PA STATE COLLEGE	2 3 5 6 CG
STRAUSSTOWN	8570	BERKS	14	40 29	76 11	600		8A	JACOB KLAHR	3
STRONGSTOWN	8589	INDIANA	4	40 33	78 55	1880		MID	HARRY F. BENNETT	C
STROUDSBURG	8596	MONROE	5	40 59	75 12	480	11P	11P	WILLIAM MAGERTY	2 3 5 C
STUMP CREEK	8610	JEFFERSON	1	41 01	78 50	1320		7A	CORPS OF ENGINEERS	3
SUNBURY	8668	NORTHUMBLAND	15	40 51	76 48	440	7A	7A	CHARLES W. BAYLER	2 3 5 C
SUSQUEHANNA	8692	SUSQUEHANNA	15	41 57	75 36	1020		7A	MRS. LAURA A.BENSON	3
SUTERSVILLE	8699	ALLEGHENY	17	40 14	79 48	765		7A	FRANK E. MARSH	3
TAMAQUA	8758	SCHUYLKILL	14	40 48	75 58	830		8A	MRS. MARY L.ROBERTS	3
TAMAQUA 4 N DAM	8763	SCHUYLKILL	14	40 51	75 59	1120		7A	PANTHER VLY WTR CO	3 C
TAMARACK 2 S FIRE TWR	8770	CLINTON	16	41 24	77 51	2220	7A	7A	JAMES E. SWARTZ	2 3 5 7
TIONESTA 2 SE DAM	8873	FOREST	1	41 29	79 26	1200	8A	8A	CORPS OF ENGINEERS	2 3 5 7 C
TITUSVILLE	8885	CRAWFORD	1	41 38	79 40	1550			PA ELECTRIC CO	C
TITUSVILLE WATER WORKS	8888				7				CITY OF TITUSVILLE	2 3 5
										3
										2 3 5 7 C
										3
										3
										3
										3
										3
										2 3 5
										2 3 5
										3
										3
										3
										3
										3
										2 3 5

Station	Index No.	County	Drainage ‡	Latitude	Longitude	Elevation	Observation Time Temp.	Observation Time Precip.	Observer	Refer To Tables
WASHINGTON	9312	WASHINGTON	11	40 11	80 14	1200		MID	PA DEPT HIGHWAYS	C
WATSONTOWN	9345	NORTHUMBLAND	16	41 05	76 52	490		VP	WILLIAM BIRD	3
WAYNESBURG 2 W	9362	GREENE	10	39 54	80 13	980	6P	7A	RALPH L. AMOS	2 3 5
WAYNESBURG 1 E	9367	GREENE	10	39 54	80 10	940		MID	SEWAGE DISPOSAL PLT	C
WEBSTER HILLS 3 SW	9380	FULTON	12	39 49	78 05	920		MID	WILLIAM G. COVER	C
WELLSBORO 3 S	9408	TIOGA	16	41 43	77 18	1920	7A	7A	MARION L. SHUMWAY	2 3 5 C
WELLSVILLE	9420	YORK	15	40 03	76 57	500	5P	5P	D. D. HOOVER	2 3 5
WERNERSVILLE 1 W	9430	BERKS	14	40 20	76 06	405		8A	CHARLES A. GRUBER	3
WEST CHESTER	9464	CHESTER	5	39 58	75 36	440	8A	6A	DAILY LOCAL NEWS	2 3 5
WEST GROVE 1 E	9503	CHESTER	5	39 49	75 49	440		8A	CONARD-PYLE CO	3
WEST HICKORY	9507	FOREST	1	41 34	79 25	1090		8P	MRS.HELEN F.KINNEAR	3
WHITESBURG	9655	ARMSTRONG	1	40 45	79 24	1530		7A	CORPS OF ENGINEERS	3
WILKES-BARRE	9702	LAZERNE	15	41 15	75 52	610		7A	MRS. MARY G. MIRMAK	3
WILLIAMSBURG	9714	BLAIR	6	40 28	78 12	860		7A	MYRON K. BIDDLE	3
WILLIAMSPORT WB AP	9728	LYCOMING	16	41 15	76 55	527	MID	MID	U.S. WEATHER BUREAU	2 3 5 7 C
WIND GAP	9781	NORTHAMPTON	5	40 51	75 18	740		MID	W. L. TEMPLETON	C
WOLFSBURG	9823	BEDFORD	6	40 03	78 32	1190		7A	WALTER C. RICE	3
YORK 3 SSW PUMP STA	9933	YORK	15	39 55	76 45	390	5P	5P	YORK WATER COMPANY	2 3 5
YORK 2 S FILTER PLANT	9938	YORK	15	39 56	76 44	640		MID	YORK WATER COMPANY	C
YORK HAVEN	9950	YORK	15	40 07	76 43	310		8A	METROPOL EDISON CO	3
YOUNGSVILLE				1	79 20	1225		MID	HENRY CARLETT	C
ZION GROVE				4	76 13	940		7A	JAMES D. TEETER	3
ZIONSVILLE 3 SE				7	75 27	660		7A	LESLIE HOWATT	3
NEW STATIONS										
CAMP KLINE				5	77 20	590		7A	MRS NETTIE E. TAYLOR	3
JERSEY SHORE				2	77 15	541		7A	GEORGE R. WADDELL	3
SIZERVILLE				5	78 11	1230		7A	MRS AGNES LION	3
CLOSED STATIONS										
BEECH CREEK STATION								7A	HAROLD S. RUPERT	CLOSED 12/57
LATROBE								MID	WEST PENN POWER CO	CLOSED 6/56

‡ 1-ALLEGHENY; 2-BEAVER; 3- 4-CONEMAUGH; 5-DELAWARE; 6-JUNIATA; 7-KISKIMINETAS; 8-LAKE ERIE; 9-LEHIGH; 10-MONONGAHELA; 11-OHIO; 12-POTOMAC; 13-LAKE ONTARIO; 14-SCHUYLKILL; 15-SUSQUEHANNA; 16-WEST BRANCH; 17-YOUGHIOGHENY

REFERENCE NOTES

Additional information regarding the climate of Pennsylvania may be obtained by writing to the State Climatologist at Weather Bureau Airport Station, Harrisburg State Airport, New Cumberland, Pennsylvania, or to any Weather Bureau Office near you.

Figures and letters following the station name, such as 12 SSW, indicate distance in miles and direction from the post office.

Delayed data and corrections will be carried only in the June and December issues of this bulletin.

Monthly and seasonal snowfall and heating degree days for the preceding 12 months will be carried in the June issue of this bulletin.

Stations appearing in the Index, but for which data are not listed in the tables, either are missing or were received too late to be included in this issue.

Divisions, as used in Table 2, became effective with data for September 1956.

Unless otherwise indicated, dimensional units used in this bulletin are: Temperature in °F, precipitation and evaporation in inches, and wind movement in miles. Monthly degree day totals are the sums of the negative departures of average daily temperatures from 65° F.

Evaporation is measured in the standard Weather Bureau type pan of 4 foot diameter unless otherwise shown by footnote following Table 6. Max and Min in Table 6 refer to extremes of temperature of water in pan as recorded during 24 hours ending at time of observation.

Long-term means for full-time stations (those shown in the Station Index as "U. S. Weather Bureau") are based on the period 1921-1950, adjusted to represent observations taken at the present location. Long-term means for all stations except full-time Weather Bureau stations are based on the period 1931-1955.

Water equivalent values published in Table 7 are the water equivalent of snow, sleet or ice on the ground. Samples for obtaining measurements are taken from different points for successive observations; consequently occasional drifting and other causes of local variability in the snowpack result in apparent inconsistencies in the record. Water equivalent of snow on the ground is measured at selected stations when two or more inches of snow are on the ground.

Entries of Snowfall in Tables 2 and 7, and in the seasonal snowfall table, include snow and sleet. Entries of snow on ground include snow, sleet and ice.

Data in Tables 3, 5, and 6 and snowfall in Table 7, when published, are for the 24 hours ending at time of observation. The Station Index lists observation times in the standard of time in local use. During the summer months some observers take the observations on daylight saving time.

Snow on ground in Table 7 is at observation time for all except Weather Bureau and CAA stations. For these stations snow on ground values are at 7:30 a.m., E.S.T.

- − No record in Tables 3, 6, 7 and the Station Index. No record in Tables 2 and 5, is indicated by no entry. Consult the annual issue of this publication for interpolated monthly precipitation totals.
- + And also on a later date or dates.
- ++ Fastest observed one minute wind speed. This station is not equipped with automatic wind instruments.
- * Amount included in following measurement, time distribution unknown.
- // Gage is equipped with a windshield.
- # Thermometers are generally exposed in a shelter located a few feet above sod-covered ground; however, the reference indicates that the thermometers are exposed in a shelter located on the roof of a building.
- AM Data based on observational day ending before noon.
- B Adjusted to a full month.
- C In the "Refer to Tables" column in the Station Index the letter "C" indicates recorder stations. These stations are processed for special purposes and are published later in "Hourly Precipitation Data".
- D Water equivalent of snowfall wholly or partly estimated, using a ratio of 1 inch water equivalent to every 10 inches of new snowfall.
- G In the "Refer to Tables" column in the Station Index the letter "G" indicates that soil temperatures are published.
- M One or more days of record missing; if average value is entered, less than 10 days record is missing. See Table 5 for detailed daily record. Degree day data, if carried for this station, have been adjusted to represent the value for a full month.
- R Amounts from recording gage (These amounts are essentially accurate but may vary slightly from the amounts to be published later in "Hourly Precipitation Data".)
- SS This entry in time of observation column in Station Index means observation made near sunset.
- T Trace, an amount too small to measure.
- Y Includes total for previous month.
- VAR This entry in time of observation column in Station Index means variable.

Information concerning the history of changes in locations, elevations, exposure etc. of substations through 1955 may be found in the publication "Substation History" for this state, soon to be issued. That publication, when available, may be obtained from the Superintendent of Documents, Government Printing Office, Washington 25, D. C. at a price to be announced. Similar information for regular Weather Bureau stations may be found in the latest issues of Local Climatological Data, Annual for the respective stations, obtained as indicated above, price 15 cents.

Subscription Price: 30 cents per copy, monthly and annual; $2.50 per year. (Yearly subscription includes the Annual Summary). Checks, and money orders should be made payable to the Superintendent of Documents. Remittance and correspondence regarding subscriptions should be sent to the Superintendent of Documents, Government Printing Office, Washington 25, D. C.

USCOMM-WB-Asheville, N. C. --- 2/8/58 --- 1100

05

1

U. S. DEPARTMENT OF COMMERCE
SINCLAIR WEEKS, Secretary
WEATHER BUREAU
F. W. REICHELDERFER, Chief

CLIMATOLOGICAL DATA

PENNSYLVANIA

ANNUAL SUMMARY 1957
Volume LXII No. 13

ASHEVILLE: 1958

GENERAL

The year was marked by a poor distribution of precipitation that ranged from fair to generous amounts. Hurricane Audrey rapidly traversed the State on June 28 accompanied by damaging thunderstorms. Unusually cold weather in January was quickly replaced by unseasonably warm weather in February, the latter returning in December. Destructive storms were less frequent and less costly than in the previous year.

WEATHER EFFECTS

Extremely cold weather in mid-January brought outdoor activities to a standstill. Alternate freezing and thawing in February caused some damage to winter grains and grasses. Maple sugar camps opened in February and continued through March, but the flow of sap was hindered by a warm spell in March and the lack of sharply fluctuating temperatures. Good progress was made in March in soil preparation, plowing, and some planting. The mid-March warm spell was beneficial to winter grains and grasses. Cold, rainy weather during the first half of April hindered field work in all areas and delayed planting of oats, peas, and gardens. With a change to warm, drier weather after mid-month, winter grains, grasses, and fruit trees had a sudden surge of growth, and orchards burst into bloom. Oats, potatoes, and peas were planted rapidly. A sudden cold snap early in May brought light freeze damage to fruits, alfalfa, clover, and tobacco. Precipitation remained light in the southeast portion; corn planting was delayed, and the growth of other crops was retarded. Conditions favored field work in southeastern and central areas in June. Harvesting of small grains progressed rapidly; combining of winter wheat began earlier than usual because warm spring weather caused rapid development of the crop. Winds from hurricane Audrey caused some shelling of wheat prior to harvest. Continued lack of moisture in the southeast resulted in small size of early potatoes, and irregular stands of corn. With more favorable rainfall in northern and western sections, legumes and grasses made heavy growth, haying was excellent, and all other crops were in good condition. July saw a turn to significantly drier weather, with adverse effects on crops in all portions of the State. The worst effects were felt in the southeast, where some late season pastures and crops failed. Conditions were excellent for picking of sour cherries and early peaches, however. Water supplies in some localities became so short that irrigation of crops had to be curtailed, and water was hauled for livestock. The dry spell continued through most of August, and all areas were dry by the end of the month. Second and later cuttings of hay were poor, fall planting of alfalfa was delayed in the southeast, and the growth of peaches and apples was retarded in most areas. Much of the corn crop intended for grain was diverted to silage. Potatoes were hard hit in almost all sections. Late tobacco was helped by rains in the southeast toward the end of August, but for many fields they came too late. Moderate rainfall in September improved pastures and alfalfa, and provided necessary soil moisture for planting of fall grains, and germination of grains already planted. Late tobacco and corn improved also. A cold spell near the end of September brought killing frosts to all areas of the State. Damage was most severe to late tobacco in the Lancaster area. Rainfall in October was barely adequate to maintain the growth of grasses and winter grains; subsoils remained dry, and wells and streams remained at low levels. Conditions were favorable for field work and harvesting advanced more rapidly than usual during the month. Corn picking was practically completed by mid-November. Precipitation during the month was sufficient to maintain good growth of winter grains, although mid-month cold weather slowed development. Mild weather in December permitted more grazing than usual, even as

·ecipitation was frequent in January, but mostly ıght. Almost one station in 3 failed to record · much as 0.50 inch on any one day. Amounts were little heavier in the west portion than in the st, as a rule. February was nearly a repeat of e previous month, as very frequent light amounts ve the weather a wet characteristic even though tals were below average at about 75% of the ations. Although the same pattern was repeated March, occurrences of moderate amounts increased frequency. Wet spells tended to a more definite ouping, so that dry periods of as long as 3 days came more common. April was quite wet, particu- rly the first 9 days, and the 17th to the 27th. veral heavy amounts were noted in these wet riods. The precipitation pendulum swung the her way in May; it was a very dry month in the utheast portion, while monthly totals approached e usual values only in the southwest portion. most all of the month's light rainfall occurred the second decade. The end-of-the-month dry riod continued until moderate State-wide rains re noted on June 8. Precipitation during the st of June resulted from thunderstorms, and nsequently was irregularly distributed. Defi- ent precipitation was the major feature of ly's weather; once again, the dryness was more mmon in the southeast portion than elsewhere the State. The dryness spread westward through e State in August, and precipitation totals for e month approached record low values. One ation out of three posted a total precipitation least 3 inches smaller than the long-term mean r the month. Widespread light rains were noted rly in September, and rain was frequent during e week beginning September 10, and, after a ort interruption, during another 3-day wet period. dry spell extended through the last week of ptember and the first 6 days of October, and was ded by a 3-day wet spell. Precipitation resumed ter mid-month, continuing and increasing in fre- ency in November, the east portion of the State eceiving more and heavier amounts than the west ortion. December was quite wet, the heavier mounts being noted in the east portion, particu- arly the northeast.

nnual precipitation totals ranged from 26.54 inches t Gratz 1 N to 51.70 inches at Kregar 4 SE. The reatest daily precipitation amount was 5.27 inches, eported at Stroudsburg on December 20. The rain- est location was Kregar 4 SE, where 116 occurrences f 0.10 or more were noted during the year. The ost frequent heavy precipitation was at Pimple ill and Titusville Water Wks, with 14 days with .00 inch or more.

SNOWFALL

nowfall in 1957 approximated the usual amounts, xcept in the vicinity of Lake Erie, where snow- all was considerably heavier than usual.

ost of January's precipitation occurred as snow, he major exception being the rains that accompa- ied the warm wave on January 22-23. Snowfall in ebruary occurred at the beginning of the month nd during a week at mid-month; monthly totals ere about as usual. March's snowfall came during he first and last decades, and totals were far reater in the extreme north portion than in the outheast. In April, snow occurrences were limited o the first half of the month; once again, snow- all totals in the extreme north portion were far eavier than in the south, and particularly heavy amounts were noted in the Northwest Plateau Divi- sion. Snow on May 4-5 was the last occurrence of the spring. Snowfall returned near the end of October, but appreciable amounts were noted only in the mountain stations. November's snowfall featured heavy amounts on November 9-10, and an extended period of light amounts later in the month. A major snowstorm struck the State on December 4, and another, though lesser, storm occurred on De- cember 10-11. The month closed with light snowfall on several days.

The greatest annual snowfall total was 121.7 inches at Rew. The greatest depth of snow on the ground, however, was noted at Bradford 4 W Res, 22 inches, on January 18.

DESTRUCTIVE STORMS

Severe weather features were not quite as frequent or as costly as they were in the preceding year. Snow and ice storms caused the greatest casualty toll as 13 persons lost their lives in January and December due to overexertion, and several other lives were lost in traffic accidents on slippery pavement in February and December; many persons were seriously injured in these mishaps. Lightning took the lives of 2 persons in April and 6 more in June, while 29 were injured by lightning, most of them in June. Tornadoes injured 5 persons in September.

Three tornadoes in September and 2 more in November each caused considerable damage; a tornado in April, 2 in August, and a possible tornado in July added lesser damages to the list. The most serious pro- perty losses were those due to lightning-set fires in June, mostly associated with thunderstorms that accompanied hurricane Audrey as it raced northward through western Pennsylvania on June 28. Consider- able damage was wrought by lightning strikes in April, May, and August, while lesser damages resulted from several lightning strikes in April, July, and Sep- tember. Localized thunderstorm winds on May 14 and 26, strong winds of nearly state-wide extent in October and November, and winds connected with hurricane Audrey in June each caused considerable damage. Wind damage of lesser severity was noted in each month of the period April-September. Con- siderable damages resulted from snowstorms in Febru- ary, April, and December, and from an ice storm at the end of February. Hailstorms were reported in May and July, but damages were light. A heavy rain- storm on December 20 caused considerable damage, and lighter damage resulted from rain in May.

FLOODS

Flooding was of minor importance this year. Local flooding was noted in January following the thaw on the 22nd-23rd. A minor flood was experienced on the Monongahela River in February, with little damage. The Perkiomen and Lackawaxen Rivers had minor floods in April, and the Lackawaxen and Lehigh Rivers had minor floods in December; damages were not signifi- cant. Heavy local or flash floods were noted in April and June following intense thundershowers; damages were severe in limited areas.

Details of each month's weather may be found in the monthly issues of this publication.

Harold S. Lippmann, Climatologist
Weather Records Processing Center
Chattanooga, Tennessee

SPECIAL NOTICE

A survey has indicated that the comprehensive narrative weather story carried in each issue of Climatological Data is of value to only a small number of recipients. This story will be discontinued, therefore, with the January 1958 issue. A table of extremes will be carried each month and a text will be carried whenever unusual and outstanding weather events have occurred. General weather conditions in the U. S. for each month are described in the publications MONTHLY WEATHER REVIEW and the MONTHLY CLIMATOLOGICAL DATA, NATIONAL SUMMARY, either of which may be obtained from the Superintendent of Documents, Government Printing Office, Washington, D. C.

TURES FROM LONG–TE

ALLENTOWN WB AP									69.9	- 1.9	65.9	1.2	43.9	1.9	35.5	4.4	51.7	
ALLENTOWN GAS CO					73.1	3.4	73.9	- .2	70.5	- 1.5	66.5	1.5	45.1	2.2	36.3	4.2	52.3	
ALTOONA HORSESHOE CURV					69.0	2.3	69.7	- 1.1	67.8	- 1.3	63.3	.3	41.3	.8	34.0	4.1	50.0	
ARENDTSVILLE					72.0	1.6	73.1	- 1.2	71.1	- 1.3	66.5	.6	43.2	.3	35.0	2.3	52.1	-
ARTEMAS 1 WNW																		
BAKERSTOWN 3 WNW					71.4		73.9		72.2		66.3		42.4		36.4		52.8	
BEAVERTOWN					71.6		72.0		70.0		64.4		42.2		34.8		51.4	
BELLEFONTE 4 -					68.9	.7	70.4	- 2.2	67.8	- 2.4	63.1	- .7	40.7	- .3	34.0	3.7		
BERWICK					73.3		73.7		70.2		66.2		43.9		36.2		52.5	
BETHLEHEM LEHIGH UNIV					72.5	1.9	74.5	- .5	70.6	- 2.6	67.6	.8	46.1	1.6	37.3	4.0		
BLAIRSVILLE 6 ENE					68.9		69.6		68.2		63.3		40.1		32.3		49.2	
BRADFORD CAA AIRPORT							63.7		61.4		56.6		36.5		30.0			
BRADFORD 4 W RES					64.6	.3	64.5	- 3.5	61.6	- 4.7	57.7	- 2.2	37.4	- 1.3	M			
BROOKVILLE CAA AIRPORT					67.2	3.1	67.6	- .5	64.8	- 1.2	60.0	- .3	39.2	1.3	32.7	4.7	47.7	
BURGETTSTOWN 2 W					68.7		68.7		65.8		61.6		38.8		31.5		48.6	
BURNT CABINS 2 NE					70.7						65.8		43.8		36.3M			
BUTLER					70.3	1.7	70.3	- 2.0	67.6	- 2.6	62.7	- 1.4	41.5	.1	35.5	4.0	50.6	
CANTON 1 NW					66.3		66.4		63.7		59.4		39.5		30.4		46.0	
CARLISLE					75.5	4.4	76.3	1.3	73.6	.8	69.0	3.5	44.9	3.2	37.1	5.2	55.0	
CHAMBERSBURG 1 ESE					72.3	2.1	73.0	- 1.7	70.6	- 1.8	66.8	.7	43.7	1.2	36.0	2.9	52.7	
CHESTER					74.9		76.3		73.7		69.4		48.6		39.7M		55.3	
CLARION 3 SW					68.2		68.8		66.3		61.8		40.7		32.9		49.0	
CLAYSVILLE 3 W					70.1	1.0	70.2	- 2.5	67.5	- 3.6	64.4	- 1.0	41.5	- .5	35.0	2.6	50.8	-
COATESVILLE 1 SW					72.3	2.0	73.6	- 1.2	70.4	- 2.3	66.5	.4	44.4	1.3	36.2	3.4	52.5	
COLUMBIA					74.3		75.7		72.6		67.9		45.1		36.3		54.2	
CONFLUENCE 1 SW DAM					68.9		68.9		66.4		62.9		41.9		33.7		49.8	
CORRY					M		67.4	- 1.8	64.3	- 2.9	61.3	.2	39.6	.8	32.0	3.4		
COUDERSPORT 3 NW					63.5		64.0		60.9		57.0		38.2		29.0		44.0	
DERRY					M		69.9	- .9	71.6	- 1.0	69.0	- .4	44.3	1.9	37.3	4.9		
DEVAULT 1					M						67.2		42.9		35.4			
DIXON					68.6		68.3		64.1		61.2		40.2		33.6		47.6	
DONEGAL					64.4		66.6		64.1		59.9		36.7		30.1M		49.9	
DONORA					75.1	3.1	75.5	- .3	73.0	- .9	68.5	.6	46.8	1.6	39.0	3.2	55.4	
DU BOIS 7 E					68.2		67.9		65.8		61.4		39.4		32.5		48.1	
EAGLES MERE					65.8		66.6		63.9		59.0		37.8		29.9		45.3	
EAST BRADY					71.9		72.7		70.7		66.1		43.0		35.4		52.4	
EBENSBURG					66.6	1.7	67.1	- 1.1	64.8	- 1.9	60.6	- .4	38.8	.2	32.2	3.8	47.5	
EMPORIUM 2 SSW					64.5		65.1		61.7		57.2		37.2		28.9		44.8	
EPHRATA					72.5	2.5	74.0	- .4	71.1	- 1.5	68.8	.5	44.0	.2	35.8	2.9	52.8	
ERIE WB AIRPORT					67.9	2.4	68.8	- 1.6	66.5	- 2.5	61.8	- 1.4	42.3	1.3	35.8	5.1	48.8	
EVERETT 1 SW					71.6	4.3	72.7	1.2	69.6	.0	66.4	3.8	42.4	1.8	36.0	6.1	52.1	
FARRELL SHARON					71.3	1.5	72.9	- 1.0	69.7	- 1.8	64.2	- 1.2	44.0	2.3	35.8	4.8	51.4	
FORD CITY 4 S DAM					69.3		69.9		67.3		62.5		40.1		33.2		49.4	
FRANKLIN					68.1	1.8	69.2	- 1.4	67.3	- 1.2	61.1	- 1.5	41.2	1.5	34.7	5.2	49.5	
FREELAND					67.7M	2.6	69.7M	.4	67.1	.2	62.7M	2.3	39.9M	2.2	33.0M	5.7	48.5	
GEORGE SCHOOL					72.6	3.1	74.1	- .1	69.9	- 2.3	67.8	1.5	45.3	1.2	36.1	2.7	53.2	
GETTYSBURG					73.7	3.3	74.7	.1	72.0	- .4	68.1	2.1	45.4	2.6	36.8	4.0	53.9	
GRATERFORD					75.2		77.4		71.9		68.7		43.2M		37.5		54.0	
GRATZ 1 N					70.1		71.8		69.2		64.6		42.3		35.3		50.5	
GREENVILLE					69.7	2.4	70.7	- .6	67.8	- 1.2	62.5	- .5	42.1	2.0	34.9	4.1	50.1	
HANOVER					73.0	1.8	74.3	- 1.4	72.0	- 1.6	68.2	.8	45.0	.0	37.1	2.6	53.4	-
HARRISBURG WB AP					73.6	2.5	75.0	- .4	72.3	- .7	67.8	1.7	44.9	.9	37.3	3.4	53.8	
HAWLEY 1 S DAM					66.1		66.2		62.1		59.1		39.9		31.9		45.6	
HOLTWOOD					75.4	2.9	76.3	- .7	73.6	- 1.5	69.5	.6	46.0	.5	37.3	2.7	54.7	
HUNTINGDON					68.6M	.0	70.2M	- 2.2	66.9	- 3.8	63.2	- 1.3	42.6M	.8	33.7	2.1		
INDIANA 3 SE					69.6	1.6	69.5	- 2.4	67.8	- 2.2	63.5	- .9	41.6	.1	34.1	3.1	50.3	-
IRWIN					M		M				M		M		M			
JAMESTOWN 2 NW					67.7		68.7		66.0		61.2		40.1		32.5		48.0	
JIM THORPE					70.3M	2.6	72.0M	.1	68.8	- .9	64.8M	1.1	M		37.0M	6.6		
JOHNSTOWN					70.7	1.3	71.2	- 1.9	68.7	- 2.5	64.4	- .9	42.4	.3	36.9	4.5	50.2	-
KANE 1 NNE					65.4		64.6		61.2		56.0		36.4		29.3		44.4	
KEGG					69.1		70.7		68.8		64.3		41.5		33.4		50.5	
LANCASTER 2NE PUMP STA					72.5	2.3	73.6	- .4	71.0	- 1.2	67.2	1.8	44.4	1.1	36.0	2.9	53.3	
LANDISVILLE 2 NW					72.0		73.2		70.1		66.1		43.1		35.3		51.5	
LAWRENCEVILLE 2 S					67.4	1.1	67.1	- 3.5	63.5	- 4.9	59.3	- 2.5	39.1	.2	32.6	4.4	46.5	-
LEBANON 3 W					71.8	1.9	72.6	- 1.7	70.5	- 1.7	66.0	.3	42.7	.1	34.9	2.9	51.7	
LEWISTOWN					71.4		72.1		70.0		66.4		43.0		35.7		51.9	
LINESVILLE 5 WNW					66.9		68.5		65.8		60.9		40.7		33.3		48.1	
LOCK HAVEN					72.1M	2.5	72.4	- 1.0	69.6	- 1.8	65.2M	.4	42.9	1.2	35.3	4.4	51.8	
MADERA					64.7		64.2		60.6		58.5		37.3		30.1		45.0	
MARCUS HOOK					76.5	1.4	79.2	.2	75.9	- .7	71.2	.7	49.5	1.1	41.0	2.5	57.1	
MARTINSBURG CAA AP					69.4		69.4		68.1		63.5		41.1		34.7		50.0	
MEADVILLE 1 S					67.5	1.7	67.7	- 2.0	65.0	- 2.7	60.6	- 1.4	39.9	.8	32.6	3.6	47.7	
MERCER 2 NNE					67.9		69.3		66.6		61.7		41.2		33.3		49.0	
MIDDLETOWN OLMSTED FLD	54.4	4.3	63.1	1.	74.7	4.0	76.6	1.5	73.3	.4	68.5	2.6	45.1	1.5	36.9	3.9	54.3	
MIDLAND DAM 7	52.8	2.5	62.1	1.	72.7	2.7	75.1	.2	70.4	- 1.7	65.4	.3	43.2	.7	36.1	2.9	52.4	
MONTROSE 1 E	45.0	1.5	52.9	2.	66.6	2.9	66.0	- 2.3	63.4	- 3.4	59.5	- .8	38.0	.6	29.7	3.8	45.2	-
MORGANTOWN	51.6		59.5		70.7M		73.2		70.0		65.9		44.1		35.8		51.8	
MT GRETNA 2 SE	52.9		61.6		72.2		74.5		70.5		67.0		44.2		36.6		52.7	
MT POCONO 2 N AP	46.5	4.1	56.3	2.	66.9M	5.1	67.3M	1.3	64.3	.1	60.5	2.1	39.9	3.4	31.5	5.8	46.9	
MUHLENBURG 1 SE	50.3		58.8		70.0		70.6		67.6		M		M					
NEWBURG 3 W	54.9		64.2		75.1		73.4M		72.6		68.9		45.8M		37.3			
NEW CASTLE 1 N	51.8	3.2	61.0	1.	70.4	1.4	71.1	- 1.4	69.0	- 1.5	64.1	- .2	43.3	2.7	35.3	4.3	51.2	
NEWELL	56.2	5.3	64.8	3.	74.6	5.0	74.8	1.3	72.9	.7	71.4M	4.6	46.4	2.5	37.8	2.8		
NEWPORT	52.6		60.7		72.3		72.7		70.2		65.5		42.6		35.9		51.9	
NEW STANTON	52.5	2.3	60.1	.	70.7	2.0	70.9	- 1.4	69.4	- 1.2	64.7	- .3	43.0	.3	36.0	3.2	51.4	-
NORRISTOWN	54.2		63.3		75.0		76.9		73.0		69.3		47.7		39.0		55.1	
PALMERTON	51.4	3.2	59.2	.	71.0	2.5	71.8	- 1.4	68.1	- 2.5	64.0	.2	42.9	1.1	35.6	4.3	50.9	
PHIL DREXEL INST TECH	59.9		65.3		76.5		79.0		75.8		71.8		50.0		41.1		57.1	
PHILADELPHIA WB AP	54.2	2.6	63.5	.	74.9	2.8	78.6	.3	73.2	- .8	69.2	1.5	47.8	1.9	39.4	3.5	55.1	
PHILADELPHIA PT BREEZE	55.5	2.8	65.1	.7	76.3		79.4	2.0	74.6	- 1.0	71.6	2.1	49.4	1.7	40.9	4.3	57.0	
PHILADELPHIA SHAWMONT	55.2	2.9	64.0	.8	74.8	2.5												
PHILADELPHIA CITY	55.0	2.3	63.8	.1	75.2	2.6	78.5	1.3	74.8	- .4	70.9	1.6						
PHILIPSBURG CAA AP	47.2		55.5		65.2		65.2		62.6		57.8		37.5		31.1		45.8	
PHOENIXVILLE 1 E	55.2	3.3	64.4	2.0	73.6	2.0	75.9	.2	71.7	- 1.8	67.3	.1	45.3	1.1	37.3	3.5	54.3	
PIMPLE HILL	45.6		55.1		66.9		67.4		64.7		60.6		39.0		30.5		46.3	
PITTSBURGH WB AP 2	52.7	3.9	60.9	1.1	70.4	1.8	71.8	- .5	70.0	- .1	64.8	- .1	42.7	1.7	35.3	4.4	51.5	
PITTSBURGH WB CITY	55.1	3.3	63.9	1.3	73.2	1.5	74.9	- .5	72.6	- .5	67.5	- .4	45.8	1.2	38.7	3.5	54.4	
PLEASANT MOUNT 1 W	44.1		52.0		64.4M		M		59.8				37.5		29.6			
PORT CLINTON	50.2	.7	58.4	2.6	70.6	1.4	71.3	- 2.1	68.5	- 2.7	63.7	- 1.5	43.2	1.4	34.8	3.0	50.6	-
PUTNEYVILLE 2 SE DAM	48.9		57.7		68.4		68.2		65.5		60.6		38.9		31.6M		47.9	
QUAKERTOWN 1 E	53.1	4.5	61.6	1.9	72.2	3.8	73.7	1.0	70.5	.1	66.6	2.8	44.6	3.0				
READING WB CITY	54.5	3.2	63.2	.7	74.0	2.7	76.7	1.0	72.9	- .5	68.8	1.7	47.0	1.6	38.7	3.9	54.8	

AVERAGE TEMPERATURES AND DEPARTURES FROM LONG-TERM MEANS

Station	January Temperature	January Departure	February Temperature	February Departure	March Temperature	March Departure	April Temperature	April Departure	May Temperature	May Departure
IDGWAY 3 W	19.4	- 6.1	28.8	3.9						
ALINA 3 W	25.1		35.4							
CRANTON	22.8	- 5.4	32.4	4.1						
CRANTON WB AIRPORT	21.6	- 5.3	31.1	4.0						
ELINSGROVE CAA AP	25.0	- 3.7	32.4	3.8						
HIPPENSBURG	28.8	- 1.9	36.6	5.7						
HIPPINGPORT WB	26.0		34.7							
LIPPERY ROCK	22.6		33.4							
OMERSET MAIN ST	23.7	- 3.2	34.8	7.7						
PRINGBORO	23.1M		30.4M							
PRINGS 1 SW	23.0	- 4.1	33.4M	6.1						
TATE COLLEGE	24.9	- 2.2	33.5	6.3						
TROUDSBURG	20.6	- 6.8	30.9	3.1						
UNBURY										
AMARACK 2 S FIRE TWR										
IONESTA 2 SE DAM										
ITUSVILLE WATER WORKS										
OWANDA										
NIONTOWN										
PPER DARBY										
ARREN										
AYNESBURG 2 W										
ELLSBORO 3 S										
ELLSVILLE										
EST CHESTER										
ILLIANSPORT WB AP										
ORK 3 SSW PUMP STA										

Station	June Temperature	June Departure	July Temperature	July Departure	October Temperature	October Departure	November Temperature	November Departure	December Temperature	December Departure	Annual Temperature	Annual Departure
IDGWAY 3 W	65.3	.8	65.3	- 2.7			30.1	.0	30.0	2.2	45.5	- 1.1
ALINA 3 W	70.6		71.1						35.3M		51.4	
CRANTON	71.3	3.2								7		
CRANTON WB AIRPORT	69.3	1.5	69.6	- 2.6							49.0	-
ELINSGROVE CAA AP	70.7	1.6										
HIPPENSBURG	73.3	2.0	73.8	- .9						9	53.7	1.0
HIPPINGPORT WB	69.9		70.6								51.1	
LIPPERY ROCK	69.6		71.4								50.8	
OMERSET MAIN ST	68.2	3.0	68.4							3	49.3	1.7
PRINGBORO	67.7M		68.1								48.5	
PRINGS 1 SW	65.8	2.1	66.0	- 1.1						7	47.2	.2
TATE COLLEGE	70.3	3.2	70.4	- .6						4	50.4	1.3
TROUDSBURG	69.0	1.4	68.7	- 3.5						5	48.4	- 1.4
UNBURY												
AMARACK 2 S FIRE TWR												
IONESTA 2 SE DAM	67.2		67.6								47.3	
ITUSVILLE WATER WORKS	67.0		67.7								47.7	
OWANDA	69.7	3.7	69.8	- .9							49.1	.8
NIONTOWN	72.4	2.1	73.6	.2							53.7	.6
PPER DARBY	76.1M		77.0M								55.4	
ARREN											48.8	1.1
AYNESBURG 2 W												
ELLSBORO 3 S											45.8	- .5
ELLSVILLE											52.0	
EST CHESTER												
ILLIANSPORT WB AP												.6
ORK 3 SSW PUMP STA												1.6

TOTAL PRECIPITATION AND DEPARTURES FROM LONG–TERM MEANS

TABLE 2

STATION	JANUARY PRECIP.	JANUARY DEPARTURE	FEBRUARY PRECIP.	FEBRUARY DEPARTURE	MARCH PRECIP.	MARCH DEPARTURE	APRIL PRECIP.	APRIL DEPARTURE	MAY PRECIP.	MAY DEPARTURE	JUNE PRECIP.	JUNE DEPARTURE				
ACMETONIA LOCK 3	1.81	-1.59	1.94	- .69	3.32	- .21	6.01	2.57	1.99	-1.79	4.63	.14				
ALLENTOWN WB AP	1.87	-1.34	2.16	- .48	2.31	- .88	6.49	3.10	2.35	-1.62	3.88	- .17				
ALLENTOWN GAS CO	1.54	-1.85	2.11	- .69	2.52	- .88	6.66	3.18	2.40	-1.55	3.60	- .29				
ALTOONA HORSESHOE CURV	2.24	- .73	2.79	.44	2.48	- .74	5.07	1.61	4.04	- .09	7.21	3.03				
ARENDTSVILLE	2.56	- .31	3.04	.54	1.87	-1.09	4.57	.99	1.87	-2.45	4.52	.38				
ARTEMAS 1 WNW	1.71		2.98		-		5.09		-		-					
AUSTINBURG 2 W	1.46	- .11	1.37	- .57	2.90	.57	5.71	3.00	2.76	-1.12	1.93	-1.31				
BAKERSTOWN 3 WNW	1.46		1.33		1.84		6.85		2.20		5.19					
BARNES	2.70		2.00		1.30		5.96		2.27		6.36					
BARTO 4 NW	1.06		-		-		-		-		-					
BEAR GAP	1.89		2.15		3.04		5.71		2.08		4.16					
BEAVER FALLS	1.83	-1.04	1.25	-1.01	2.26	- .69	5.98	2.91	2.65	- .78	3.75	- .27				
BEAVERTOWN	1.91		E 2.47		3.02		6.10		1.78		3.08					
BEECH CREEK STATION	1.22		1.62		2.94		E 5.73		E 1.67		5.44					
BELLEFONTE 4 S	E 1.56	-1.05	1.46	- .68	3.00	- .37	5.03	1.39	2.10	-1.79	4.11	.00				
BERNE	2.03		2.26		2.54		5.99		2.72		3.40					
BERWICK	1.35		1.68		2.49		6.25		3.23		4.08					
BETHLEHEM	1.23		2.10		2.24		6.23		2.08		5.08					
BETHLEHEM LEHIGH UNIV	1.70	-1.71	2.27	- .83	E 2.61	- .82	6.54	3.33	2.08	-1.62	4.48	.44				
BLAIRSVILLE 6 ENE	3.68	.74	3.38	.84	2.52	-1.17	5.36	1.27	2.74	-2.91	6.20	.44				
BLOSERVILLE 1 N	E 1.82	-1.32	E 1.83	- .48	2.23	-1.08	4.20	.42	2.00	-2.55	4.76	.06				
BOSWELL 6 WNW	-		-		-		9.47		2.52		6.69					
BRADDOCK LOCK 2	1.95		1.98		3.77		5.09		2.51		4.81					
BRADFORD CAA AIRPORT	-		-		-		-		-		-					
BRADFORD CNTRL FIRE ST	2.81		1.50		1.90		6.15		2.97		4.48					
BRADFORD 4 W RES	3.40	.21	1.74	- .88	2.08	-1.37	6.09	2.26	3.16	- .86	5.75	1.14				
BREEZEWOOD	1.99		2.51		E 1.62		3.93		1.11		6.69					
BROOKVILLE CAA AIRPORT	2.73	- .47	1.98	- .51	2.04	- .45	5.02	1.84	2.31	-1.45	4.74	.46				
BRUCETON 1 S	1.47	-1.17	1.49	- .90	2.60	-1.10	4.43	.75	2.06	-2.05	5.05	.32				
BUFFALO MILLS	1.84	- .72	2.32	.52	1.88	-1.24	5.31	1.96	2.00	-1.39	4.44	.79				
BURGETTSTOWN 2 W	1.99		1.79		2.78		5.84		3.68		5.10					
BURNT CABINS 2 NE	-		-		-		-		1.24		6.09					
BUTLER	2.04	- .83	1.86	- .53	2.99	- .34	7.18	3.66	1.70	-1.99	4.67	.34				
CAMP HILL	2.18		2.72		3.22		4.04		2.77		4.06					
CAMP KLINE	-		-		-		-		-		-					
CANTON 1 NW	1.08		1.41		E 2.82		5.71		2.18		3.51					
CARLISLE	2.01	-1.14	2.46	- .39	2.40	-1.06	4.62	1.09	1.67	-2.28	4.39	.34				
CARROLLTOWN 2 SSE	3.25		2.72		2.27		9.52		2.44		5.85					
CARTER CAMP 2 W	2.19		1.72		2.90		5.98		3.12		4.36					
CEDAR RUN	2.20	- .41	1.79	- .39	3.37	.30	7.00	3.87	2.17	-1.64	3.26	- .45				
CHADDS FORD	-		-		-		3.79		2.62		1.97					
CHAMBERSBURG 1 ESE	2.04	- .21	2.70	.18	1.76	-1.52	4.08	.91	1.34	-2.46	7.03	3.06				
CHARLEROI LOCK 4	1.76	-1.31	2.04	- .57	2.77	- .85	5.11	1.74	2.44	-1.02	3.18	- .78				
CHESTER	1.80		2.96		3.54		5.00		1.54		3.25					
CLARENCE	2.25		2.00		3.31		5.22		1.71		4.62					
CLARION 3 SW	2.31	-1.19	2.15	- .98	2.71	-1.01	6.64	2.89	2.98	-1.25	4.79	.09				
CLAUSSVILLE	1.97		2.21		2.42		6.12		2.53		4.75					
CLAYSVILLE 3 W	2.03	-1.14	1.30	-1.18	2.38	-1.16	4.77	1.31	1.67	-2.14	2.57	-1.93				
CLEARFIELD	2.61	- .83	2.45	- .16	2.60	-1.10	6.10	2.35	1.88	-2.57	4.57	.05				
CLERMONT	2.63		1.99		1.81		E 6.84		3.02		5.77					
COALDALE 2 NW	1.92	-1.57	2.20	- .74	2.38	-1.40	6.83	2.87	2.04	-2.71	3.70	- .74				
COATESVILLE 1 SW	1.31	-2.56	2.72	- .90	1.77	-2.36	4.69	.96	1.83	-2.07	4.01	.70				
COLUMBIA	2.09		2.30		1.87		4.78		.88		2.72					
CONFLUENCE 1 SW DAM	3.79		3.98		1.87		3.41		3.50		2.26					
CONFLUENCE 1 NW	3.26	- .62	3.81	.62	2.00	-1.85	4.24	.62	2.93	-1.17	3.17	-1.40				
CONNELLSVILLE	2.20		2.17		1.45		3.19		2.42		2.80					
CONSHOHOCKEN	1.41	-1.99	2.66	- .42	2.60	- .73	4.58	1.14	1.14	-2.85	4.08	.38				
COOKSBURG	2.40		2.09		2.88		6.46		2.11		3.56					
COOKSBURG 2 NNW	2.60		2.32		2.76		5.74		2.53		3.77					
CORAOPOLIS NEVILLE IS	1.15	-1.82	1.15	-1.27	2.32	- .88	5.09	1.91	2.47	-1.10	3.25	- .84				
CORRY	2.65	- .75	1.93	-1.10	1.91	-1.71	5.89	2.10	2.11	-1.85	7.11	2.30				
COUDERSPORT 3 NW	1.97		1.53		2.68		5.68		2.47		4.21					
COUDERSPORT 7 E	1.72		2.04		E 2.80		6.02		2.86		4.05					
COVINGTON 2 WSW	1.58		.82		2.46		4.62		2.46		3.37					
CREEKSIDE	2.41		2.81		2.90		6.94		2.38		3.85					
CRESSON 2 SE	E 2.87		2.35		3.03		4.53		2.73		8.18					
CUSTER CITY 2 W	2.94		1.75		1.98		6.09		2.86		5.20					
DANVILLE	1.02		2.11		2.96		5.94		2.05		3.86					
DERRY	2.31	-1.36	2.49	- .48	1.72	-2.34	5.38	1.55	2.17	-1.89	5.98	1.87				
DEVAULT 1 W	2.02		2.59		3.20		6.07		1.50		1.37					
DIXON	1.79		1.36		2.09		5.95		2.77		3.37					
DONEGAL	4.17		3.97		2.59		6.15		2.36		4.87					
DONORA	1.75	- .85	1.77	- .91	2.61	- .94	4.67	1.07	2.60	-1.13	3.88	- .15				
DOYLESTOWN	2.13	-1.27	2.13	-1.13	2.79	- .81	5.25	1.57	1.07	-2.98	1.87	-2.13				
DU BOIS 7 E	1.96	- .96	1.81	-1.09	2.50	- .60	5.20	1.62	2.04	-2.52	4.75	.39				
DUSHORE 3 NE	2.03		1.21		3.17		5.50		2.13		2.56					
EAGLES MERE	E 3.38	- .30	1.95	-1.55	2.23	-2.46	6.67	2.97	1.70	-4.24	7.34	2.83				
EAST BRADY	1.58		1.71		2.44		5.65		2.33		2.96					
EBENSBURG	2.94	- .29	2.99	.16	1.95	-1.54	5.97	2.41	2.82	-1.55	5.23	.39				
EDINBORO	2.97	.45	2.17	- .26	2.01	-1.44	5.77	1.88	2.56	-1.89	8.74	4.53				
EDINBORO 7 SW	-		-		-		-		-		-					
ELIZABETHTOWN	1.87		2.70		2.25		4.85		.66		2.59					
EMPORIUM 2 SSW	2.76		1.99		3.21		5.43		2.40		3.55					
ENGLISH CENTER	1.79		1.85		2.65		6.64		1.40		5.00					
EPHRATA	2.33	- .71	2.09	- .77	3.62	.19	5.72	2.37	1.04	-2.57	2.34	-2.02				
EQUINUNK 2	E 1.92		E 1.78		E 1.91		4.35		3.05		3.26					
ERIE WB AIRPORT	2.93	.50	1.73	- .34	1.97	- .82	6.33	2.82	3.29	.10	7.74	4.87				
EVERETT 1 SW	2.70	- .14	3.30	1.25	E 1.97	-1.17	4.88	1.79	1.66	-2.02	4.62	- .01				
FARRELL SHARON	2.62	.04	.80	-1.16	E 2.22	- .52	6.47	3.33	3.03	- .56	5.40	1.84				
FORD CITY 4 S DAM	1.88		1.92		3.01		5.95		2.35		3.82					
FRANKLIN	2.26	-1.15	1.64	-1.06	2.32	-1.07	6.16	2.94	4.11	.35	6.16	1.86				
FREELAND	1.98	-1.31	E 2.15	- .85	E 2.94	- .99	E 6.64	2.81	3.32	-1.29	8.17	3.46				
GALETON	2.46	- .07	1.52	- .48	2.97	- .42	6.37	3.22	3.52	- .67	3.52	- .06				
GEIGERTOWN	1.32		2.24		1.80		4.79		1.03		1.25					
GEORGE SCHOOL	1.67	-1.70	2.95	.15	2.41	-1.05	5.36	1.88	1.26	-2.52	1.90	-1.86				
GETTYSBURG	2.42	- .67	2.89	.23	1.84	-1.45	4.00	.41	1.36	-2.84	4.36	.40				
GIFFORD	2.81		E 1.95		2.37		6.86		3.28		4.44					
GLEN HAZEL 2 NE DAM	2.57		2.15		2.18		5.13		2.79		E 5.19					
GLENWILLARD DASH DAM	1.62		1.29		2.66		5.74		2.60		5.03					
GOULDSBORO	1.87	-1.23	2.24	- .50	2.29	-1.13	6.16	2.47	3.14	-1.48	3.00	-1.50				
GRATERFORD	1.84	-1.46	2.58	- .20	2.65	- .81	5.86	2.67	1.34	-2.72	1.57	-2.25	3.62	-1.37	1.72	-2.
GRATZ 1 N	1.43		1.84		2.18		3.57		1.41		3.57		1.10		.47	
GREENSBORO LOCK 7	2.42	-1.00	2.79	- .03	2.37	-1.23	3.62	.34	3.41	- .44	2.67	-1.93	3.88	- .71	2.19	-1.
GREENSBURG 3 SE UNITY	1.92	-1.73	2.61	- .28	2.40	-1.42	4.62	.82	2.82	-1.11	5.47	.84	1.95	-2.25	.96	-3.
GREENVILLE	2.22	-1.11	1.54	- .98	1.87	-1.58	6.10	2.84	2.66	-1.10	7.08	3.08	1.51	-2.58	1.07	-2.

See Reference Notes Following Station Index

TOTAL PRECIPITATION AND DEPARTURES FROM LONG-TERM MEANS

JANUARY		FEBRUARY		MARCH		APRIL		MAY		JUNE		JULY		AUGUST		SEPTEMBER		OCTOBER		NOVEMBER		DECEMBER		ANNUAL	
PRECIP	DEPARTURE	PRECIP	DEPARTURE	PRECIP	DEPARTURE	PRECIP	DEPARTURE	PRECIP	DEPARTURE	PRECIP	DEPARTURE	PRECIP	DEPARTURE	PRECIP	DEPARTURE	PRECIP	DEPARTURE	PRECIP	DEPARTURE	PRECIP	DEPARTURE	PRECIP	DEPARTURE	PRECIP	DEPARTURE
2.52	-.64	2.71	.10	2.49	-.83	4.18	.74	2.43	-1.22	3.43	-.50	1.09	-2.39	1.90	-2.26	3.14	-.02	3.62	.47	2.97	.41	6.02	2.96	37.36	-3.14
1.64	-.98	2.64	.40	1.97	-.90	3.89	.92	.84	-2.86	3.38	-.26	1.68	-1.46	.93	-2.41	2.19	-.44	1.78	-1.29	2.81	.06	5.23	2.67	28.98	-7.03
2.05	-.98	2.62	.08	2.27	-1.02	4.34	.70	3.40	-.91	4.50	.42	1.53	-2.65	1.46	-1.95	2.27	-.95	3.18	-.18	2.85	-.19	6.18	3.18	37.15	-4.45
1.57	-1.19	1.42	-1.18	2.19	-.97	4.94	1.61	2.59	-1.39	1.23	-2.63	3.99	-.44	.82	-3.28	2.49	-1.04	3.11	-.12	2.18	-.89	5.74	2.79	32.27	-6.73
1.44		1.17		2.04		E 6.21		2.60		1.36		3.44		1.23		2.47		3.11		1.85		5.40		E32.32	
1.93	-.90	1.60	-1.08	2.66	-.90	6.11	2.36	2.73	-1.46	2.68	-1.69	4.16	-1.02	.79	-2.95	2.05	-1.52	2.52	-.64	2.09	-1.23	5.89	2.90	35.21	-8.13
1.48	-1.52	3.06	.65	2.79	-.19	4.46	1.55	1.58	-1.56	4.64	1.29	1.25	-2.64	1.35	-2.70	5.35	2.72	2.08	-.56	2.91	.43	4.70	2.16	35.65	-.37
1.96		1.69		1.98		5.42		2.77		2.79		3.99		1.82		3.39		2.52		2.26		5.14		35.73	
-		-		-		-		-		-				-		3.27		2.03		2.25		7.37		-	
2.44		2.43		2.38		4.88		2.83		5.00		2.17		1.38		3.32		E 3.65		E 1.39		E 3.89		E35.56	
1.37		.53		1.03		5.13		1.89		2.87		3.04		2.41		1.78		2.49		2.22		3.49		28.25	
-		-		2.51	-.96	5.51	2.07	1.50	-2.66	4.93	.80	1.31	-2.70	.82	-3.09	2.59	-.68	3.01	.08	1.82	-.76	4.24	1.34	-	
1.81		2.00		1.98		4.33		.81		4.09		2.14		3.25		2.34		3.46		2.57		5.71		34.29	
2.41	-.41	2.90	.74	2.17	-.96	4.57	1.22	2.39	-.81	5.33	1.26	1.33	-1.92	.43	-3.46	2.09	-.70	4.62	1.64	1.58	-.58	4.24	1.72	34.06	-2.26
2.69	-.96	2.59	-.32	2.29	-1.63	5.62	1.65	2.14	-2.05	4.97	.06	2.61	-1.99	.83	-3.21	3.03	-.69	2.42	-.97	1.78	-1.15	4.06	.76	35.03	-10.50
2.10	-.86	E 1.62	-.84	2.73	-.74	4.85	1.55	1.18	-2.34	E 4.23	-.22	2.64	-1.34	.39	-3.48	2.28	-.58	2.51	-.27	2.37	-.20	3.05	.13	E29.95	-9.19
1.81	-.74	1.77	-.31	2.16	-.68	5.46	2.16	2.64	-1.33	6.07	2.41	2.60	-1.29	2.69	-1.04	3.05	-.37	2.06	-.79	2.44	-.18	E 5.75	3.50	E38.52	1.34
-		-		-		-		-		-		-		-		-						3.49		-	
2.25	-1.36	2.25	-1.17	2.37	-1.84	6.77	2.93	1.79	-2.55	4.37	-.02	1.48	-3.87	1.47	-3.30	2.54	-1.48	3.71	-.08	E 4.36	.65	8.09	4.29	E41.45	-7.80
3.28	-.80	2.93	-.63	2.03	-2.13	7.03	2.98	2.18	-2.29	4.94	-.09	1.98	-2.47	1.44	-2.93	2.44	-.98	2.45	-.55	1.98	-.99	4.18	.60	36.88	-10.28
2.64	-1.01	2.24	-.71	2.01	-1.81	6.38	2.43	3.31	-1.41	4.98	.33	1.46	-2.95	1.75	-1.88	3.16	-.54	1.88	-1.70	3.57	.03	5.79	2.50	39.17	-6.72
1.92		1.95		2.46		5.11		1.58		4.50		2.76		2.06		2.39		1.97		1.46		4.26		32.42	
2.78		2.03		2.50		6.69		3.37		3.64		2.78		1.80		3.13		-		-		-		-	
1.79		1.98		1.81		3.83		1.92		3.63		1.59		.27		1.94		3.32		1.19		4.31		27.58	
2.12	-1.23	1.93	-.66	2.95	-.67	6.62	3.27	2.33	-1.86	3.59	-.59	2.19	-1.70	2.11	-1.58	4.79	2.16	1.82	-1.52	1.89	-.89	4.59	1.51	38.93	-3.76
5.25		5.14		3.81		6.77		3.16		6.38		1.64		1.29		3.01		4.95		2.32		E 7.98		E51.70	
1.95		2.48		2.24		6.62		2.34		4.01		1.88		1.37		4.02		3.72		4.68		9.01		44.32	
-		2.12		2.03		7.45		-				-		-		-		-				-		-	
1.54	-1.16	1.69	-.90	2.78	-.76	5.31	1.53	3.16	-1.13	2.07	-2.38	3.54	-1.52	1.44	-2.73	3.02	-.59	3.53	.15	2.36	-.92	6.04	3.18	36.48	-7.23
1.71	-1.45	2.21	-.40	2.56	-.89	4.52	1.07	1.00	-2.48	2.90	-1.11	2.13	-2.24	.56	-3.74	3.42	.10	2.67	-.46	2.76	.03	E 4.53	1.41	E31.03	-10.70
1.73		2.51		2.24		4.07		.93		3.56		1.53		.43		1.61		2.45		2.53		4.30		27.89	
1.03	-.84	1.21	-.49	2.14	-.30	5.04	2.19	2.84	-1.09	2.92	-.89	4.62	.54	2.11	-1.70	3.75	.65	1.38	-1.39	1.49	-.79	3.05	1.12	31.58	-2.99
1.85	-1.52	2.82	-.23	3.30	-.29	5.47	2.01	2.10	-1.91	4.97	.84	1.30	-3.25	.55	-3.71	1.58	-1.81	2.86	-.65	3.72	.71	6.05	2.71	38.55	-7.10
1.91	-2.03	2.26	-.29	2.54	-1.51	6.42	3.21	2.43	-2.34	4.90	-.01	1.43	-4.50	1.84	-2.76	4.26	.62	3.15	-.51	4.50	.56	8.09	4.53	43.73	-4.99
.67		.92		1.04		4.91		2.33		2.55		2.95		1.73		3.48		2.02		2.67		E 3.63		E28.90	
2.91		1.05		1.92		6.91		3.52		3.53		2.34		1.57		3.10		2.03		3.48		4.48		37.74	
1.40		1.92		2.49		5.00		1.47		6.34		.90		.53		3.48		4.16		1.64		3.96		E33.29	
2.43	-.22	1.71	-.61	2.04	-1.07	5.83	2.31	2.18	-1.67	7.05	3.27	1.82	-1.93	.91	-2.78	4.38	.54	2.43	-.66	2.95	-.25	4.36	1.71	38.09	-1.38
1.52	-1.41	2.00	-.50	2.57	-.90	6.39	3.02	1.17	-2.94	4.96	.88	3.09	-1.08	1.68	-2.36	3.89	.57	1.98	-1.19	1.80	-.80	3.16	.26	34.21	-6.45
2.31		2.41		2.23		5.89		2.32		3.96		2.01		1.09		4.39		4.43		4.74		9.84		45.62	
-		-		-		-		-		-		-		-		3.30		2.16		3.51		6.47		-	
1.46		2.29		2.45		5.27		1.13		1.62		2.02		2.15		3.90		E 1.89		E 4.26		E 7.68		E36.12	
2.31		2.40		2.31		6.31		3.18		5.81		1.63		1.48		2.25		2.02		1.76		3.61		35.07	
2.86		2.52		3.27		8.09		3.32		4.92		1.40		1.20		3.07		1.95		1.59		5.36		39.55	
1.62		2.34		2.38		4.55		.86		2.43		1.62		1.57		3.77		1.92		3.86		6.29		33.21	
1.35		1.87		2.23		4.13		1.23		4.38		2.13		.86		2.57		2.81		1.75		3.50		28.81	
1.82	-1.63	3.85	.20	2.89	-.77	4.72	1.24	1.68	-2.08	2.55	-1.05	1.13	-3.09	2.05	-3.40	3.56	.45	2.63	.10	3.66	.43	5.23	2.27	35.77	-6.33
3.12		2.50		2.84		6.69		3.32		4.69		3.59		.60		3.46		2.60		2.00		4.37		39.78	
1.49		2.14		1.57		5.01		1.88		6.61		2.77		.90		2.50		2.48		1.38		3.28		32.01	
2.17	-.64	1.65	-.88	2.20	-.05	5.10	1.62	1.95	-1.78	1.58	-2.46	4.18	.19	.97	-2.83	3.37	-.12	3.39	.24	2.33	-.74	6.49	3.44	35.38	-4.91
2.61		1.63		1.72		6.05		3.76		5.97		2.07		-		-		-		-		-		-	
2.11	-.61	2.69	.48	1.96	-.59	3.38	.29	1.03	-4.23	3.92	-.65	2.26	-1.55	.50	-3.74	3.19	.62	3.47	-.17	2.22	-.97	3.90	1.05	30.63	-11.07
2.32	-.17	2.07	-.13	3.16	-.27	4.55	1.39	2.43	-1.04	4.99	1.27	3.07	-.42	.16	-3.49	3.69	.76	1.55	-.75	1.53	-1.04	4.13	1.66	33.65	-2.23
2.25	-.90	1.97	-.70	1.04	-.33	6.60	3.24	3.01	-1.11	8.30	4.19	1.09	-2.23	1.28	-2.34	3.39	-.13	2.22	-1.17	2.70	-.72	4.51	1.50	40.18	-1.70
2.00		1.88		2.70		5.03		2.01		3.57		3.04		1.99		2.68		1.43		1.60		4.38		32.31	
		2.23		E 1.93		E 7.26		2.88		7.35		E 1.88		.62		2.34		1.67		2.98		E 4.99		E38.60	
		3.26		1.73		4.32		1.21		6.18		1.49		.80		2.77		3.02		2.70		4.73		34.91	
-		-		-		-		-		-		-		.67		2.42		4.76		1.45		4.84		-	
3.14		3.22		2.44		3.49		2.12		-		-		-		-		-		-		-		-	
	-1.06	3.02	.67	2.81	-.70	4.37	.99	.82	-3.36	3.08	-.81	1.29	-2.44	.69	-3.35	1.62	-1.67	2.09	-1.29	3.65	.71	5.74	3.03	31.17	-9.28
	-.83	1.32	-.89	2.62	-.98	5.61	2.06	2.86	-1.53	4.55	.55	3.20	-.39	.87	-2.79	2.78	.23	1.81	-1.30	2.93	.39	4.04	1.66	34.43	-3.82
1.62		1.71		1.70		5.50		2.93		2.48		2.97		2.27		3.67		2.64		2.53		5.64		35.66	
1.20		1.91		3.22		5.57		2.14		4.98		2.15		.97		3.79		2.39		2.46		4.88		35.62	
1.43		1.76		2.92		6.02		2.38		2.79		1.44		1.10		2.67		2.94		2.77		4.61		32.83	
1.70		2.13		3.29		5.62		2.00		4.70		1.06		.44		3.55		3.99		2.36		4.81		35.65	
	-1.21	1.68	-.62	2.10	-.78	5.70	2.26	3.40	-.72	4.02	.03	2.99	-1.12	1.34	-2.79	3.10	-.73	2.40	-1.14	2.56	-.31	4.42	1.78	35.13	-5.35
		1.93		1.44		4.28		1.20		2.00		1.03		2.12		2.21		1.85		2.56		6.74		28.78	
1.32		2.70		3.06		5.04		.89		6.18		1.14		.67		1.92		2.04		3.32		5.44		33.72	
2.36	-1.01	E 2.50	-.44	3.13	-.82	6.58	2.64	2.21	-2.14	4.02	-1.06	2.41	-2.85	1.26	-3.18	2.05	-2.14	4.65	.14	E 4.06	1.31	E10.74	7.18	E47.17	-2.32
2.11		2.09		2.56		6.93		2.48		4.04		1.76		1.89		3.19		3.32		E 2.97		E 5.29		E38.63	
1.54		2.74		3.13		6.11		3.46		6.34		.68		.45		1.61		2.74		E 3.58		6.03		E38.41	
1.79	-1.33	1.77	-.84	3.02	-.72	6.49	2.85	2.27	-1.70	4.05	-.49	1.79	-2.35	.33	-3.24	4.91	2.24	1.71	-1.10	1.80	-1.07	4.57	1.81	34.46	-6.03
1.87	-1.39	2.51	-.29	3.19	-.26	4.50	1.05	1.17	-2.62	1.96	-2.19	.91	-3.93	1.59	-3.10	3.39	-.25	1.99	-1.19	3.64	.67	6.21	3.18	32.93	-10.32
1.90		.78		E 2.59		E 6.48		3.93		E 3.84		2.00		.14		3.44		2.72		1.37		E 6.24		E35.43	
2.47	-.47	1.82	-.54	2.10	-.94	5.53	2.44	3.97	.42	4.49	.34	2.93	-1.23	2.35	-.96	4.57	1.52	1.36	-1.35	2.58	.08	4.20	1.62	38.37	.93
2.15	-.65	2.57	.37	2.36	-.69	4.62	1.36	4.02	.73	2.94	-1.18	1.33	-2.30	1.54	-2.03	2.42	-.58	E 2.90	.32	2.23	-.36	3.82	1.39	E32.90	-3.62
2.21	-1.04	3.37	.75	1.46	-1.93	4.76	.99	4.92	.95	4.33	.26	2.11	-2.08	2.25	-2.59	5.30	1.73	3.07	-.37	4.12	.87	6.87	3.93	44.77	1.47
1.63	-1.34	2.25	.06	2.63	-.84	5.15	1.65	1.21	-3.10	5.81	2.20	1.09	-3.42	1.51	-2.72	3.44	.30	2.25	-1.19	3.46	.12	5.78	2.75	36.21	-5.53
2.10	-1.31	2.86	.02	1.81	-1.76	4.19	.44	3.75	-.29	4.00	-.47	2.17	-1.85	1.29	-2.93	3.48	.29	2.80	-.19	1.64	-1.05	2.97	-.15	33.06	-9.25
2.19		2.17		2.65		6.97		2.36		3.05		1.18		1.95		2.38		3.27		4.82		E 7.19		E40.18	
1.19		2.45		2.44		4.43		.87		3.43		1.48		1.43		5.21		2.17		3.35		8.71		35.16	
4.35		2.27		1.98		5.51		3.62		6.67		2.27		2.71		5.70		1.94		2.88		3.38		43.28	
1.32		.77		1.78		4.85		3.39		3.24		2.78		1.72		2.55		2.87		1.71		3.23		30.19	
2.41		2.20		2.59		7.08		2.11		1.89		3.90		1.97		2.12		2.83		3.56		7.35		40.01	
2.18	-.66	2.39	.17	2.11	-.99	6.65	3.58	1.90	-2.04	4.56	.32	1.70	-3.05	1.09	-2.99	4.39	.70	3.62	.45	4.56	1.43	8.09	5.36	43.24	2.30
1.78		2.36		-		-		-		-		-		-		-		-		-		-		-	
1.98	-1.51	1.57	-.33	2.34	-1.32	5.95	2.45	3.40	-.54	5.54	1.32	3.52	-.61	.64	-3.17	3.76	.51	1.53	-1.34	2.65	-.36	5.26	2.06	38.14	-3.84
2.20	-.53	1.61	-.97	2.05	-1.31	5.12	1.56	2.62	-1.42	1.81	-2.26	4.47	-.06	1.43	-2.95	3.17	-.51	3.57	-.01	2.18	-1.11	E 6.58	3.56	E36.81	-6.03
2.08		2.08		2.17		5.17		2.24		1.58		2.90		1.18		3.26		3.92		4.03		8.71		E39.32	
1.63		2.97		2.99		5.26		2.03		2.68		.93		1.19		3.96		2.67		3.56		4.63		34.50	
1.67	-1.70	2.81	-.21	3.24	-.08	4.22	.84	1.21	-2.37	2.41	-1.46	.64	-3.56	3.38	-1.20	3.10	-.36	2.05	-.55	2.98	-.10	4.49	1.82	32.20	-8.93
1.62		2.92		3.19		4.23		1.35		1.43		.77		1.94		3.55		2.23		3.01		4.98		31.22	
2.09	-1.24	3.00	-.06	-		4.39	1.03	1.62	-2.02	-		-		-		-		-		-		-		-	
1.31	-2.08	2.86	-.17	3.39	.02	4.40	1.02	1.27	-2.31	1.83	-2.14	.95	-3.26	1.32	-3.30	2.71	-.72	-		-		-		-	
1.95		2.40		2.89		5.14		1.91		6.04		2.98		1.29		2.95		2.55		2.72		5.39		38.21	
1.45	-2.14	2.78	-.22	2.52	-1.15	6.17	1.79	1.13	-3.10	1.85	-2.02	1.26	-3.56	1.67	-3.05	3.68	.28	1.85	-1.24	3.95	.62	6.34	3.13	33.65	-10.64
1.94		1.89		2.57		7.57		2.60		5.98		2.69		1.51		3.72		4.39		3.32		5.59		43.77	
3.13		3.13		3.08		7.49		2.47		3.13		1.55		1.42		4.80		4.84		5.31		11.21		51.54	
1.85	-1.54	2.25	-.36	3.00	-.65	6.42	2.76	2.49	-1.96	3.53	-1.10	1.11	-3.88	.42	-3.49	2.73	-.97	3.36	-.48	4.09	.26	6.93	3.71	38.18	-7.50
1.65	-1.12	1.35	-.02	2.02	-1.18	4.58	1.39	2.73	-1.04	4.07	.00	3.97	.06	.78	-2.35	4.06	1.09	1.74	-.70	2.50	-.09	4.22	1.71	33.67	-3.25
	-1.33	1.74	-.61	2.56	-.85	4.94	1.86	2.72	-.77	4.75	.92	2.83	-.89	.29	-2.79	3.19	.42	1.42	-1.07	1.80	-.81	4.60	2.03	32.34	-3.89
	-1.78	2.04	-.96	2.15	-1.82	5.82	1.97	2.93	-1.70	E 2.43	-1.89	6.27	1.20	2.16	-1.95	3.49	-.38	2.88	-.98	3.21	-.71	6.15	2.88	E41.37	-6.12
1.05	-2.47	2.86	-.46	2.86	-1.01	6.41	2.27	2.57	-1.57	3.15	-1.31	1.34	-3.56	E 1.07	-4.10	2.81	-1.24	3.50	-.47	3.79	.98	E 6.77	3.16	E38.18	-9.78
1.82		2.21		3.18		6.62		2.07		4.44		1.47		.95		4.06		3.64		4.60		7.03		42.09	
2.31		2.10		2.91		5.95		2.40		4.92		1.70		1.97		4.56		2.16		1.92		4.78		31.68	

See Reference Notes Following Station Index

QUAKERTOWN 1 E
RAYMOND
READING WB CITY
RENOVO
REW

RICES LANDING L
RIDGWAY 3 W
RUSH
RUSHVILLE
SAGAMORE 1 S

SALINA 3 W
SAXTON
SCHENLEY LOCK 5
SCRANTON
SCRANTON WB AIRPORT

SELINSGROVE CAA AP
SHAMOKIN
SHIPPENSBURG
SHIPPINGPORT WB
SINNEMAHONING

SIZERVILLE
SLIPPERY ROCK
SOMERSET FAIRVIEW ST
SOMERSET MAIN ST
SOUTH MOUNTAIN

SPRINGBORO
SPRING GROVE
SPRINGS 1 SW
STATE COLLEGE
STRAUSSTOWN

STROUDSBURG
STUMP CREEK
SUNBURY
SUSQUEHANNA
SUTERSVILLE

TAMAQUA
TAMAQUA 4 N DAM
TAMARACK 2 S FIRE TWR
TIONESTA 2 SE DAM
TITUSVILLE WATER WORKS

TORPEDO 4 W
TOWANDA
TOWER CITY 5 SW
TROY
TURTLEPOINT 4 NE

TYRONE 4 NE BALD EAGL
UNION CITY
UNIONTOWN
UPPER DARBY
UTICA

VANDERGRIFT
VIRGINVILLE
VOWINCKEL
VOWINCKEL 1 SW
WARREN

WATSONTOWN
WAYNESBURG 2 W
WELLSBORO 3 S
WELLSVILLE
WERNERSVILLE 1 W

WEST CHESTER
WEST GROVE 1 E
WEST HICKORY
WHITESBURG
WILKES BARRE

WILLIAMSBURG
WILLIAMSPORT WB AP
WOLFSBURG
YORK 3 SSW PUMP STA
YORK HAVEN

ZION GROVE
ZIONSVILLE 3 SE

TEMPERATURE EXTREMES AND FREEZE DATA

Station	Highest	Date	Lowest	Date	Last spring minimum of 16° or below Date	Temp.	20° or below Date	Temp.	24° or below Date	Temp.	28° or below Date	Temp.	32° or below Date	Temp.	First fall minimum of 32° or below Date	Temp.	28° or below Date	Temp.	24° or below Date	Temp.	20° or below Date	Temp.	16° or below Date	Temp.	Number of days between dates 16° or below	20° or below	24° or below	28° or below	32° or below
ALLENTOWN WB AP	100	7-21+	- 6	1-18	2-12	15	3- 5	19	3-31	24	4-16	28	5- 4	31	10-12	29	11-10	28	11-11	24	12- 5	17	12- 6	14	297	275	225	208	161
ALLENTOWN GAS CO	99	7-22	- 1	1-15+	2-13	15	3- 4	20	3- 6	24	3-31	28	4-16	29	10-12	31	11-10	28	11-13	23	12- 6	16	12- 6	16	296	277	252	224	179
ALTOONA HORSESHOE CURVE	94	9- 2	- 7	1-17	3- 5	13	3-11	20	4-13	22	5- 4	25	5- 4	25	9-27	26	9-27	26	11-10	24	11-11	16	11-11	16	251	245	211	146	146
ARENDTSVILLE	98	7-22	-10	1-18	3- 4	15	3- 5	20	4-15	24	4-15	24	5- 4	29	9-27	32	10-28	28	11-11	20	11-11	20	12- 6	14	277	251	210	196	146
ARTEMAS I WNW	-	-	-	-	3- 4	14	3- 5	20	4-14	22	4-15	25	4-18	32	-		-		-		-		-		-	-	-	-	-
BAKERSTOWN 3 WNW	95	9- 2	- 6	1-17	3- 4	15	3- 4	15	4-15	24	4-15	24	5- 5	31	10-12	32	10-26	26	11-16	24	11-30	18	12- 5	10	276	271	215	194	160
BEAVERTOWN	97	7-21+	- 9	1-18	3- 5	14	3-31	20	4-11	23	5- 4	26	5- 5	32	9-27	27	9-27	27	10-28	23	11-11	16	11-11	16	251	225	200	146	145
BELLEFONTE 4 S	95	6-18+	-13	1-15	3- 5	15	3-11	19	4-11	23	5- 5	28	5- 5	28	9-27	27	9-27	27	11-11	13	11-11	13	11-11	13	251	245	214	145	145
BERWICK	99	7-21	- 7	1-18	3- 5	15	3- 5	15	3-31	21	4-16	27	5- 3	32	9-27	30	10-12	28	11-11	22	11-12	20	12- 5	12	275	252	225	179	147
BETHLEHEM LEHIGH UNIV	101	7-21	-	-	-		-		-		4-16	28	5- 4	32	10-25	32	11-10	27	12- 4	21	12- 5	20	12-11	13	-	-	-	208	174
BLAIRSVILLE 6 ENE	91	8- 3	-12	1-17	3- 4	12	4-15	20	4-15	20	5- 4	26	5- 5	31	9-27	31	10-26	22	10-26	22	11-10	20	12- 1	12	272	209	194	175	145
BRADFORD CAA AP	-	-	-	-	-		-		-		-		-		9- 6	32	9-26	27	9-27	19	9-27	19	11-11	10	-	-	-	-	-
BRADFORD 4 W RES	90	6-17+	-25	1-15	4-15	15	4-15	15	5- 6	24	6- 9	28	6- 9	28	9- 9	27	9- 9	27	9-27	18	9-27	18	11-11	6	210	165	144	92	92
BROOKVILLE CAA AIRPORT	94	6-17	-12	1-17	3- 5	13	4-13	19	4-15	21	5- 5	26	5-17	32	9-26	32	9-27	25	10-12	23	11-11	12	11-12	12	251	212	180	145	132
BRUGETTSTOWN 2 W	94	7-22	-19	1-17	4-15	15	4-15	15	5- 6	23	5- 6	23	5- 7	29	9-27	28	9-27	28	10-12	20	10-12	20	11-11	8	210	180	159	144	143
BURNT CABINS 2 NE	-	-	- 7	1-17	3- 5	14	4-15	19	5- 4	24	5- 5	27	5- 6	32	9-27	25	9-27	25	10-12	23	11-11	15	11-11	15	251	210	161	145	144
BUTLER	93	6-19+	-10	1-15	3- 5	12	4-15	20	4-15	20	4-16	26	5- 7	31	9-27	25	9-27	25	10-12	24	11-10	20	11-11	12	251	209	180	164	143
CANTON 1 NW	91	7-22	-14	1-15	3-11	15	4- 3	20	4-15	24	5- 4	28	5-17	29	9-27	31	10-26	25	11-11	17	11-11	17	11-27	15	261	222	210	175	133
CARLISLE	100	7-21	- 7	1-18	2-12	15	3- 5	19	3- 5	19	4-11	27	4-16	30	10-12	31	11-11	22	11-11	22	11-13	20	12-12	13	303	253	251	214	179
CHAMBERSBURG 1 ESE	98	7-22	- 6	1-17	2-12	15	3- 5	18	4-15	23	5- 4	27	5- 5	30	9-27	30	10-12	28	11-11	19	11-11	19	12- 6	15	297	251	210	161	145
CHESTER	101	7-22	5	1-14+	1-18	13	2-13	20	4-15	24	4-15	24	4-16	32	10-21	32	11-11	26	12- 5	20	12- 5	20	12-12	14	328	295	234	210	188
CLARION 3 SW	94	6-17	-14	1-17	3- 4	6	4-15	19	4-15	19	5- 6	28	5-17	32	9-27	25	9-27	25	10-26	22	11-11	13	11-11	13	252	210	194	144	133
CLAYSVILLE 3 W	96	6-17	-20	1-17	4-15	16	4-15	16	4-16	24	5- 6	26	5- 7	29	9-28	24	9-28	24	9-28	24	10-12	20	11-11	11	210	180	165	145	144
COATESVILLE 1 SW	99	7-22+	- 4	1-18	1-25	14	3- 5	19	4-16	24	4-16	24	5- 4	32	9-28	31	11-11	25	11-12	19	11-12	19	12- 6	13	315	252	210	209	147
COLUMBIA	101	7-21	- 4	1-18	2-12	15	3- 5	20	3-31	24	4-11	27	5- 4	31	9-28	32	10-28	27	11-11	21	12- 6	15	12- 6	15	297	276	225	200	147
CONFLUENCE 1 SW DAM	94	7-22	- 8	1-18	3- 5	13	4-15	20	4-15	20	5- 5	27	5- 7	31	9-27	29	9-28	23	9-28	23	11-11	16	11-11	16	251	210	166	146	143
CORRY	93	6-18	-17	1-15	3-31	16	4-15	20	4-15	20	5-17	28	5-29	32	9- 9	32	9-27	25	10-13	23	11-11	12	11-11	12	225	210	181	133	103
COUDERSPORT 3 NW	90	6-17	-25	1-15	4-15	16	4-15	16	5- 3	24	5-17	26	6- 9	32	9- 6	32	9-27	18	9-27	18	9-27	18	11-11	3	210	165	147	133	89
DERRY	-	-	- 6	1-17	3- 4	11	3-31	20	4-13	23	5- 4	26	5- 5	30	10-12	26	10-12	26	11- 7	24	11-11	17	12- 5	10	276	225	208	161	160
DEVAULT 1 W	-	-	- 5	1-15	3- 5	16	3-30	20	3-31	23	5- 4	26	5-17	32	9-27	32	10-11	28	11-11	21	12- 5	20	12-11	15	281	250	225	160	133
DIXON	95	6-19	-19	1-18	3-31	15	4-11	20	4-16	21	5- 3	28	5-17	30	9-27	25	9-27	25	10-12	24	11- 7	19	11-11	14	225	210	179	147	133
DONEGAL	92	7-21	-16	1-17	4-15	14	4-15	14	5- 5	22	5- 7	27	5-29	32	9-27	24	9-27	24	9-27	24	10-12	19	11-10	14	209	180	145	143	121
DONORA	98	7-22+	- 3	1-17	3- 4	16	3- 4	16	4-15	24	4-15	24	5- 5	32	10-12	31	11- 7	28	11-10	24	11-11	20	12- 5	16	276	252	209	206	160
DUBOIS 7 E	91	6-18+	-17	1-17+	3-31	16	4-15	20	5- 4	23	5- 5	28	5- 7	29	9-27	25	9-27	25	10-12	23	10-26	20	11-11	13	225	194	161	145	143
EAGLES MERE	89	7-22	-12	1-15	3-11	15	4-10	19	5- 4	22	5- 4	22	5- 5	30	None		10-26	24	10-26	24	11-11	16	11-11	16	245	215	175	175	-
EAST BRADY	96	7-21	-17	1-17	3- 5	16	3-31	20	4-15	22	4-16	28	5- 7	32	9-27	30	10-26	28	11- 9	20	11- 9	20	11-10	15	250	223	208	193	143
EBENSBURG	91	6-18	- 9	1-15+	3-11	16	4-13	19	5- 4	24	5- 5	28	5- 7	30	9-27	25	9-27	25	10-12	22	11- 9	16	11- 9	16	243	210	161	145	143
EMPORIUM 2 SSW	90	6-18+	-16	1-17	3-31	15	4-13	17	5- 4	24	5- 5	28	6- 9	32	9-25	30	9-27	19	9-27	19	9-27	19	11-11	10	225	167	146	145	108
EPHRATA	99	7-21+	- 1	1-15+	2-12	14	3- 5	19	3- 5	19	4-15	27	5- 4	30	9-27	31	10-26	28	11-11	22	12- 5	18	12- 6	14	297	275	251	194	146
ERIE WB AIRPORT	92	6-18	- 5	1-17	3- 5	15	3- 6	20	4-15	24	4-15	24	5-17	31	10-12	32	11- 9	27	11-23	23	12- 5	15	12- 5	15	275	274	222	208	148
EVERETT 1 SW	104	7-21	- 4	1-17	3- 4	14	3- 5	20	4-11	24	4-15	28	5- 5	30	9-27	28	9-27	28	10-12	24	11-11	20	11-12	15	253	251	184	165	145
FARRELL SHARON	96	8- 3	- 9	1-15	3- 4	16	3- 4	16	4- 3	24	4-14	27	5- 6	29	9-27	30	9-28	28	11-11	19	11-11	19	12- 5	14	276	252	222	167	144
FORD CITY 4 S DAM	95	8- 4	-15	1-17	3- 5	13	3-31	19	4-15	21	5- 6	28	5- 7	30	9-27	27	9-27	27	10-26	24	11-11	15	11-11	15	251	225	194	144	143
FRANKLIN	92	7-22	-11	11-14	3- 6	15	4- 1	19	4-16	24	4-16	24	5- 8	32	9-27	27	9-27	27	11-11	17	11-11	17	12- 5	4	274	224	209	164	142
FREELAND	91	7-21+	-10	1-15	3- 5	13	3-30	20	4-13	24	5- 4	28	5- 4	28	9-27	29	10-12	27	10-26	23	11-11	17	12- 5	11	275	226	196	161	146
GEORGE SCHOOL	103	7-21	- 8	1-18	2-12	16	3- 4	18	4-15	24	4-16	25	5- 4	30	9-27	31	11-11	22	11-11	22	11-12	20	12- 6	8	297	253	210	209	146
GETTYSBURG	100	7-22	- 7	1-18	1-24	15	3- 4	19	3- 5	21	4-11	28	5- 4	32	10-12	31	11- 7	28	11-11	24	11-12	20	12- 6	16	316	253	251	210	161
GRATERFORD	102	7-21+	- 8	1-17	2-12	16	3- 4	18	3-31	24	4-10	26	4-15	32	9-27	27	9-27	27	11-10	24	12- 6	16	12- 6	16	297	277	224	170	165
GRATZ 1 N	99	7-22	- 7	1-18	3- 5	14	3- 6	19	4-11	24	4-15	26	4-16	29	9-27	29	9-28	28	11-11	21	11-12	20	12- 5	16	275	251	214	166	164
GREENVILLE	95	6-17+	-12	1-15	3- 5	16	3-31	18	4-15	22	5- 6	26	5-17	31	9- 6	32	9-27	25	9-29	21	11-10	20	12- 5	7	275	224	167	144	112
HANOVER	99	7-22	- 1	1-17+	2-13	15	3- 5	18	3-31	24	4-15	26	4-16	30	10-12	31	10-28	28	11-11	22	12- 5	15	12- 5	15	295	275	225	196	179
HARRISBURG WB AP	97	6-18+	- 2	1-18	1-24	15	2-12	17	3- 5	24	4-11	27	4-15	30	10-27	30	11-11	26	11-12	22	12- 5	20	12-11	16	321	296	252	214	195
HAWLEY 1 S DAM	91	6-19	-20	1-19	3-31	16	4-16	20	4-16	20	5-17	26	5-29	32	9-27	26	9-27	26	10-12	23	11-11	20	11-27	12	241	209	179	133	121
HOLTWOOD	98	6-18	3	1-17+	1-20	13	1-20	13	3- 4	23	3- 5	25	4-16	32	11-10	32	11-12	28	12- 5	21	12- 6	20	12-12	6	326	320	276	252	208
HUNTINGDON	96	7-19+	-	-	3- 6	13	3-31	17	4-16	24	5- 4	25	5- 7	30	9-27	24	9-27	24	9-27	24	11- 7	20	11-11	15	250	221	164	146	143
INDIANA 3 SE	94	6-17+	-15	1-17	3- 5	15	5- 3	20	5- 3	20	5- 5	27	5- 7	29	9-27	25	9-27	25	10-12	23	-		-		-	-	162	145	143
IRWIN	-	-	- 7	1-17	3- 4	12	3- 5	19	4-15	24	5- 6	28	5- 6	28	9-27	32	10-14	25	11-12	19	11-12	19	12- 5	10	276	252	211	161	144
JAMESTOWN 2 NW	92	7-22	-14	1-15	3- 5	16	4-15	19	4-15	19	5- 6	25	5-17	29	9-27	27	9-27	27	11-10	23	11-11	16	11-11	16	251	210	209	144	133
JIM THORPE	96	7-21+	-10	1-18	3- 5	16	3- 6	19	4-16	24	4-16	24	4-16	24	9-27	30	10-12	27	11-11	23	11-12	19	12- 6	16	276	251	209	179	164
JOHNSTOWN	98	6-19+	- 7	1-17	3- 6	13	3-31	20	4-14	24	5- 5	27	5- 7	32	9-27	26	9-27	26	10-12	23	11-11	13	11-11	13	250	225	181	145	143
KANE 1 NNE	90	6-18	-22	1-17	4-13	15	4-15	18	5- 4	24	5-28	28	5-28	28	7- 2	32	9-27	17	9-27	17	9-27	17	11-11	4	212	165	146	122	35
KEGG	96	7-21	- 1	1-15	3- 5	14	3- 5	14	4-11	23	5- 4	25	5- 5	30	9-27	28	9-27	28	10-13	24	11-11	17	11-12	15	252	251	185	146	145
LANCASTER 2 NE PUMP STA	98	7-21	- 6	1-18	1-24	15	3- 5	18	3-31	23	4-16	27	5- 4	32	9-27	31	10-12	28	11-11	24	11-12	19	12- 6	11	316	252	225	179	146
LANDISVILLE 2 NW	99	6-19+	- 9	1-18	2-12	15	3- 5	19	4-14	24	5- 4	28	5- 4	28	9-27	28	9-27	28	10-13	24	11-12	20	12- 6	10	297	252	182	146	146
LAWRENCEVILLE 2 S	94	6-19	-23	1-15	3-31	15	4-13	20	4-16	24	5- 6	27	5-17	29	9-27	23	9-27	23	9-27	23	11-11	13	11-11	13	225	212	164	144	133
LEBANON 3 W	99	7-22+	- 3	1-18	3- 4	16	3- 5	20	4-11	24	4-16	27	5- 5	32	9-27	28	9-27	28	11-11	22	11-12	19	12- 6	13	277	252	214	164	145
LEWISTOWN	98	7-22	- 2	1-18+	3- 5	16	3- 5	16	4- 1	24	4-12	26	5- 5	32	9-27	32	11- 8	27	11-11	23	11-12	20	12- 5	16	275	252	224	210	145
LINESVILLE 5 WNW	92	8- 3	-14	1-15	3- 5	12	4- 3	19	4-15	23	5-17	28	5-17	28	9-27	26	9-27	26	10-13	24	11-11	14	11-11	14	251	222	181	133	133
LOCK HAVEN	98	6-18	- 9	1-17+	3- 5	11	3- 5	11	3-11	22	4-16	28	5- 4	29	9-27	30	10-28	27	11-11	21	12- 5	10	12- 5	10	275	275	245	195	146
MADERA	92	7-22+	-16	1-18	4-15	16	5- 5	19	5- 6	24	5- 8	26	5-30	32	9-25	32	9-27	23	9-27	23	10-12	20	11-11	12	210	160	144	142	118
MARCUS HOOK	103	7-21+	4	1-15	1-24	16	1-24	16	2-12	22	3- 5	27	3-11	30	11-10	32	12- 5	28	12-11	21	12-12	17	None		-	322	302	275	244
MARTINSBURG CAA AP	92	6-17+	- 5	1-17	3- 5	16	3- 5	16	4-15	23	5- 4	28	5- 5	32	9-27	29	10-12	27	11-10	23	11-11	19	12- 5	15	275	251	209	161	145
MEADVILLE 1 S	91	6-18+	-10	1-15	3- 5	14	3-31	19	4-15	23	5- 6	28	5-17	30	9-27	27	9-27	27	10-13	24	11-11	14	11-11	14	251	225	181	144	133
MERCER 2 NNE	91	8- 3	-19	1-15	3- 4	16	3- 4	16	3-18	24	4-15	26	5-17	31	9- 6	31	9-27	23	9-27	23	10-13	20	11-23	14	264	223	193	165	112
MIDDLETOWN OLMSTED FLD	100	6-18	1	1-18	1-24	15	3- 4	20	3- 5	23	4-11	27	5- 4	32	10-26	31	11-11	27	11-12	23	12-11	18	12-12	12	322	282	252	214	175
MIDLAND DAM 7	94	6-18	- 2	1-17	1-24	13	3- 4	18	3- 5	23	4-15	26	4-15	26	10-28	31	11-10	26	11-11	22	12- 5	20	12-11	12	321	276	251	209	196
MONTROSE 1 E	90	6-19	-18	1-15	3-12	16	3-26	20	4-14	24	5-17	28	5-17	28	9-27	28	9-27	28	10-26	24	11-11	17	11-27	13	260	230	195	133	133
MORGANTOWN	98	7-21	- 4	1-17+	2-18	16	3- 4	19	3-31	23	4-16	27	5- 4	30	9-27	29	10-12	28	11-11	22	12- 5	16	12- 5	16	290	276	225	179	146
MT GRETNA 2 SE	98	7-21	0	1-16+	2-12	16	2-23	20	4-11	24	4-16	28	5- 3	32	10-11	30	10-26	28	11-26	24	11-27	20	12-11	15	302	277	229	193	161
MT POCONO 2 N AP	91	7-21	-14	1-15	3-11	16	3-31	17	4-15	24	5- 3	26	5-17	30	9-27	25	9-27	25	10-12	22	11-11	16	11-11	16	245	225	180	147	133
MUHLENBURG 1 SE	96	6-18	-14	1-15	3- 5	13	3-11	18	4-15	24	5- 3	28	5-17	31	-		10-12	25	-		-		-		-	-	-	162	-
NEWBURG 3 W	99	7-21	-	-	3- 4	14	3- 5	17	3-31	24	5- 4	28	5- 4	28	9-27	29	10-26	27	11-11	19	11-11	19	12- 6	16	277	251	225	175	146
NEW CASTLE 1 N	93	6-17+	-10	1-17	3- 5	15	4- 3	20	4-15	21	5- 6	28	5- 6	28	9-27	26	9-27	26	10-13	24	11-11	16	11-11	16	251	222	181	144	144
NEWELL	98	6-17+	- 5	1-17	3- 4	11	3- 4	11	4-15	23	4-15	23	5- 5	31	-		11-10	27	11-11	20	11-11	20	12- 5	16	276	252	210	209	-
NEWPORT	100	7-21	- 7	1-18	3- 6	16	3- 6	16	4-11	24	4-16	28	5- 5	32	9-27	30	10-12	28	11-11	19	11-11	19	12-12	13	281	250	214	179	145
NEW STANTON	100	6-17	- 7	1-15+	3- 5	9	4-15	18	5- 4	24	5- 5	26	5- 7	29	9-27	28	9-27	28	10-12	22	11-11	19	11-12	13	252	210	161	145	143
NORRISTOWN	103	7-21	2	1-15	1-20	16	2-12	18	3- 5	23	3-11	28	4-16	32	11-10	31	11-11	28	12- 5	22	12-11	20	12-12	15	325	302	275	245	208
PALMERTON	97	7-21	-10	1-18	3- 5	15	3- 5	15	3-31	23	4-16	25	4-16	25	9-27	31	10-12	28	11-12	22	11-27	20	12- 6	15	276	267	226	179	164
PHIL DREXEL INST OF TEC	102	7-22	4	1-15	1-19	15	2-12	20	3- 4	24	3- 5	27	3-31	31	11-10	32	11-11	28	12-11	21	12-12	14	12-12	14	327	303	282	251	224
PHILADELPHIA WB AP	101	7-21	5	1-15+	1-20	13	2-12	20	3- 4	23	3-11	28	4-15	31	10-28	32	11-11	26	12- 6	22	12-11	20	12-12	14	326	302	277	245	196
PHILADELPHIA PT BREEZE	102	7-21	5	1-15	1-19	13	1-24	19	2-12	24	3- 5	28	3-11	32	10-26	32	12- 6	28	12-11	22	12-12	14	12-12	14	327	322	302	276	229
PHILADELPHIA SHAWMONT	-	-	-	-	1-24	6	3- 4	20	3- 5	22	3-31	27	4-16	29	-		-		-		-		-		-	-	-	-	-
PHILADELPHIA CITY	98	6-17+	8	1-15	1-18	13	1-19	18	2-12	22	3- 5	27	3-11	32	-		-		-		-		-		-	-	-	-	-
PHILIPSBURG CAA AP	92	7-21	-16	1-15+	3-31	12	4-13	19	5- 4	22	5- 5	28	5-29	30	9- 6	32	9-27	19	9-27	19	9-27	19	11-12	15	226	167	146	145	100
PHOENIXVILLE 1 E	105	7-21	- 6	1-18	2-12	16	3- 5	18	4-16	24	4-16	24	5- 4	30	9-27	30	10-13	28	11-11	22	11-12	18	12-12	11	303	252	209	180	146

See reference notes following Station Index.

TEMPERATURE EXTREMES AND FREEZE DATA

Table 3—Continued

Station	Highest	Date	Lowest	Date	Last spring minimum of: 16° or below Date	Temp.	20° or below Date	Temp.	24° or below Date	Temp.	28° or below Date	Temp.	32° or below Date	Temp.	First fall minimum of: 32° or below Date	Temp.	28° or below Date	Temp.	24° or below Date	Temp.	20° or below Date	Temp.	16° or below Date	Temp.	Number of days between dates: 16° or below	20° or below	24° or below	28° or below	32° or below
PIMPLE HILL	91	6-17+	-12	1-15	3-11	15	4-13	19	5- 3	24	5- 4	27	5- 4	27	9-27	27	9-27	27	10-26	23	11-11	16	11-11	16	245	212	176	146	146
PITTSBURGH WB AP 2	93	8- 3	- 6	1-17	3- 4	14	3- 5	20	4-15	24	4-15	24	5- 4	32	10-12	31	10-28	28	11-10	24	12- 1	17	12- 5	14	276	271	209	196	161
PITTSBURGH WB CITY	95	7-21+	- 1	1-17	1-24	13	3- 4	20	3- 5	23	3-10	27	4-15	30	10-26	32	11-10	26	12- 1	20	12- 1	20	12-11	12	321	272	271	245	194
PLEASANT MOUNT 1 W	-	-	-21	1-15	3-11	12	4-15	20	4-16	21	5-17	26	5-17	26	9- 9	32	9-27	26	10-12	23	11-11	15	11-11	15	245	210	179	133	115
PORT CLINTON	100	7-22	- 6	1-19	3- 5	14	3- 6	17	4-16	22	5- 3	28	5-17	31	9-27	25	9-27	25	10-12	23	11-11	19	12- 6	15	276	250	179	147	133
PUTNEYVILLE 2 SE DAM	95	7-22+	-15	1-17	3- 5	10	4-15	19	4-16	24	5- 5	27	5-29	32	9-27	22	9-27	22	9-27	22	10-26	20	11-11	12	251	194	164	145	121
QUAKERTOWN 1 E	99	6-16	- 3	1-15	2-12	14	3- 5	18	4-16	24	4-16	24	5- 4	31	9-27	27	9-27	27	11-11	23	11-12	14	11-12	14	273	252	209	164	146
READING WB CITY	99	7-21	2	1-15	1-24	16	2-12	18	3- 5	24	3- 5	24	4-16	32	11-10	31	11-11	28	12- 6	23	12-11	18	12-12	14	322	302	276	251	208
RIDGWAY 3 W	92	6-18	-18	1-17	4- 3	16	4-15	20	5- 4	23	5- 8	27	5-17	30	9-27	22	9-27	22	9-27	22	10-26	20	11-11	13	222	194	146	142	133
SALINA 3 W	93	7-21+	- 9	1-17	3- 5	15	4-15	20	4-15	20	5- 4	26	5- 7	32	9-27	29	10-12	24	10-12	24	11-11	16	11-11	16	251	210	180	161	143
SCRANTON	-	-	- 6	1-15	3- 5	8	3- 6	18	3-31	22	4-14	27	5- 3	32	9-27	32	11-11	26	11-27	19	11-27	19	12-12	11	282	266	241	211	147
SCRANTON WB AIRPORT	94	7-21	-10	1-15	3- 5	13	3-11	18	3-31	23	5- 3	28	5-17	32	9-27	31	10-12	28	11-10	24	11-27	18	12- 5	16	275	261	224	162	133
SELINSGROVE CAA AP	-	-	- 7	1-18	3- 5	16	3-31	20	4-11	22	4-16	25	5- 5	32	-		-		-		-		-		-	-	-	-	-
SHIPPENSBURG	97	7-21+	- 2	1-17	2-12	14	3- 5	18	3-31	23	4-15	27	5- 4	29	9-27	32	11- 7	28	11-11	22	11-13	20	12- 6	15	297	253	225	206	146
SHIPPINGPORT WB	92	6-18+	- 3	1-17	3- 4	13	3- 5	20	3-31	21	4-15	25	5- 6	31	9-27	31	11- 7	28	11-10	23	11-11	18	12- 5	16	276	251	224	206	144
SLIPPERY ROCK	92	6-17+	- 9	1-17	3- 4	12	3- 5	18	4-16	22	4-16	22	5- 3	29	9-27	30	10-13	27	11-10	23	11-11	16	11-11	16	252	251	208	180	147
SOMERSET MAIN ST	90	7-21	-10	1-17+	3- 5	11	3-31	18	5- 4	24	5- 5	26	5- 9	32	9-27	25	9-27	25	10-12	22	11-10	20	11-11	13	251	224	161	145	141
SPRINGBORO	94	6-18+	-13	1-17	3- 5	12	4- 3	20	4-15	22	5-17	28	6- 3	30	9-27	25	9-27	25	10- 4	24	11-11	20	12- 5	9	275	222	172	133	116
SPRINGS 1 SW	90	7-21	-12	1-17	3- 5	11	4-13	20	5- 5	24	5- 5	24	5- 8	30	9-25	32	9-27	23	9-27	23	10-12	20	11-11	10	251	182	145	145	142
STATE COLLEGE	95	6-17	- 4	1-15+	3- 4	14	3- 5	17	3-11	23	4-15	27	5- 4	30	9-27	30	11-10	27	11-11	22	12- 2	20	12- 5	16	276	272	245	209	146
STROUDSBURG	100	7-21	-22	1-18	3- 6	15	3-30	20	4-16	21	4-16	21	5-29	31	9-27	23	9-27	23	9-27	23	9-28	20	11-11	15	250	182	164	164	121
SUNBURY	-	-	-	-	-		-		-		-		-		9-27	29	9-28	28	11-11	22	11-13	20	12-12	13	-	-	-	-	-
TAMARACK 2 S FIRE TWR	-	-	-12	1-15	3- 6	13	4-13	18	4-16	23	5- 5	28	5- 5	28	9-27	30	10-26	24	10-26	24	11-11	16	11-11	16	250	212	193	174	145
TIONESTA 2 SE DAM	91	6-18	-17	1-17	3- 6	15	4-13	19	4-15	21	4-16	25	5- 7	31	9-27	28	9-27	28	10-14	23	11-11	17	11-23	15	262	212	182	164	143
TITUSVILLE WATER WORKS	93	6-17+	-17	1-17	3-31	15	4-15	18	5- 6	24	5-17	28	5-29	31	9- 9	31	9-27	21	9-27	21	10-13	19	11-11	13	225	181	144	133	103
TOWANDA	96	6-18	-19	1-14	3-11	14	3-31	18	4-16	23	5- 3	28	5-17	30	9-27	25	9-27	25	11-11	18	11-11	18	11-27	13	261	225	209	147	133
UNIONTOWN	96	7-22	- 6	1-17	3- 4	15	3- 4	15	4-15	21	4-15	21	5- 5	30	10-11	31	10-13	27	11- 7	24	11-11	15	11-11	15	252	252	206	181	159
UPPER DARBY	102	7-21	- 2	1-15	1-24	16	2-12	18	3- 5	24	3- 5	24	4-16	31	11-10	30	11-11	27	12- 5	24	12- 6	16	12- 6	16	316	297	275	251	208
WARREN	93	6-17+	-11	1-14+	3- 5	11	3-31	18	4-15	24	4-15	24	5-17	31	9-27	26	9-27	26	10-26	23	11-11	15	11-11	15	251	225	194	165	133
WAYNESBURG 2 W	96	7-20+	-17	1-17	3- 5	15	4-15	17	4-15	17	5- 5	27	5- 7	31	9-27	29	9-28	25	11- 7	19	11- 7	19	11-11	11	251	206	206	146	143
WELLSBORO 3 S	92	7-22	-16	1-15	3- 6	10	4-15	19	4-15	19	5- 4	27	5-17	30	9-27	27	9-27	27	10-28	24	11-11	17	12- 5	10	274	210	196	146	133
WELLSVILLE	99	7-21+	-14	1-18	3- 5	16	4-15	20	4-15	20	5- 4	26	5- 5	31	9-27	26	9-27	26	10-12	24	11-11	15	11-11	15	251	210	180	146	145
WEST CHESTER	104	7-21	1	1-14	-		-		-		-		-		10-26	30	11-10	27	12- 2	24	12-12	10	12-12	10	-	-	-	-	-
WILLIAMSPORT WB AP	97	6-18+	-10	1-18	2-12	12	3- 5	17	4-11	24	4-16	28	4-16	28	10-12	30	11-11	21	11-11	21	12- 3	20	12-12	12	303	273	214	209	179
YORK 3 SSW PUMP STA	100	7-21+	-10	1-18	2-12	12	3- 5	17	4-15	24	5- 4	28	5- 5	31	9-27	30	10-12	28	10-28	24	11-11	20	12- 6	10	297	251	196	161	145

TOTAL EVAPORATION AND WIND MOVEMENT

Table 4

Station		Jan.	Feb.	Mar.	Apr.	May	June	July	Aug.	Sept.	Oct.	Nov.	Dec.	Annual
CONFLUENCE 1 SW DAM	EVAP	-	-	-	-	5.22	5.53	5.75	5.41	3.32	B2.02	-	-	-
	DEP	-	-	-	-	-	-	-	-	-	-	-	-	-
	WIND	-	-	-	-	1742	1482	1458	1265	1389	1596	-	-	-
FORD CITY 4 S DAM	EVAP	-	-	-	-	B5.08	B5.66	6.04	6.07	B4.01	B2.43	-	-	-
	DEP	-	-	-	-	- .42	- .20	- .49	- .42	- .04	- .06	-	-	-
	WIND	-	-	-	-	B1598	1167	1156	1051	1113	1108	-	-	-
HAWLEY 1 S DAM	EVAP	-	-	-	-	5.40	5.60	6.37	4.76	3.41	-	-	-	-
	DEP	-	-	-	-	-	-	-	-	-	-	-	-	-
	WIND	-	-	-	-	2586	1693	1875	1265	1522	-	-	-	-
JAMESTOWN 2 NW	EVAP	-	-	-	-	-	B5.55	5.37	B4.56	3.19	-	-	-	-
	DEP	-	-	-	-	-	- .51	- .45	- .13	- .17	-	-	-	-
	WIND	-	-	-	-	-	645	516	359	681	-	-	-	-
LANDISVILLE 2 NW	EVAP	-	-	-	-	B6.31	7.44	8.29	7.69	5.05	2.85	-	-	-
	DEP	-	-	-	-	-	-	-	-	-	-	-	-	-
	WIND	-	-	-	-	1875	B1252	1449	1622	1434	2023	-	-	-
PIMPLE HILL	EVAP	-	-	-	-	7.12	7.15	B8.16	5.82	3.70	2.45	-	-	-
	DEP	-	-	-	-	-	-	-	-	-	-	-	-	-
	WIND	-	-	-	-	3192	1984	1779	1397	1737	2606	-	-	-
STATE COLLEGE	EVAP	-	-	-	B3.42	5.54	B6.23	-	5.71	3.92	B2.22	-	-	-
	DEP	-	-	-	-	-	-	-	-	-	-	-	-	-
	WIND	-	-	-	1839	1337	960	940	887	798	B1073	-	-	-

See reference notes following Station Index.

SOIL TEMPERATURES

Station and Depth	January		February		March		April		May		June		July		August		September		October		November		December		Annual	
	Average	Extremes	Average	Extremes	Average	Extremes	Average	Extremes	Average	Extremes	Average	Extremes	Average	Extremes	Average	Extremes	Average	Extremes	Average	Extremes	Average	Extremes	Average	Extremes	Average	Extremes
STATE COLLEGE																										
MEASURED UNDER SOD																										
2 INCHES	-	--/--	-	--/--	-	--/--	-	--/--	-	--/--	67.0	74/57	67.7	75/61	65.1	71/61	61.2	70/47	48.0	55 40	40.3	50/33	34.1	47/28	-	75/--
4 INCHES	-	--/--	-	--/--	-	--/--	-	--/--	-	--/--	66.5	74/57	67.6	73/62	65.4	71/60	62.1	70/49	49.1	56/41	40.9	50/34	34.9	45/30	-	74/--
8 INCHES	-	--/--	-	--/--	-	--/--	-	--/--	-	--/--	65.9	73/57	67.5	72/63	66.6	72/61	63.7	70.53	51.0	57/44	41.4	50/36	35.9	44/32	-	73/--
16 INCHES	-	--/--	-	--/--	-	--/--	-	--/-r	-	--/--	65.7	71/60	68.3	72/66	67.9	72/64	65.8	69/59	54.4	59/49	45.5	51/41	37.2	42/36	-	72/--

Monthly averages are obtained by taking the average of single daily observations at 8 a.m. time.

Ground Cover: Bluegrass Sod.

† CHANGES IN STATION NAMES

NEW NAME	OLD NAME	DATE
ERIE WB AP	ERIE CAA AP	February 1957
SHADE GAP 2 NE	SHADE GAP	July 1957
SHADE GAP	SHADE GAP 2 NE	December 1957

RELOCATION AND CHANGES IN EQUIPMENT

ARTEMAS 1 WNW	Recording gage removed	May 17, 1957
AUSTINBURG 2 W	Recording gage moved 0.1 mile W	July 2, 1957
BOSWELL 6 WNW	All equipment moved 1000 feet SE	March 25, 1957
BUFFALO MILLS	All equipment moved 150 feet S	October 15, 1957
CHADDS FORD	All equipment moved 0.1 mile SE	October 20, 1957
CORRY	All equipment moved 1.1 miles SSW	September 18, 1957
DONORA	All equipment moved 1.3 miles SSW	November 1, 1957
EQUINUNK 2	All equipment moved 300 feet ESE	January 1, 1957
EVERETT 1 SW	Temperature equipment and rain gage moved 250 feet E	July 11, 1957
GRATERFORD	Temperature equipment added	January 1, 1957
HANOVER	All equipment moved 50 feet E	March 28, 1957
HONESDALE 6 NNW	Recording gage moved 12 feet S	August 20, 1957
HOOVERSVILLE	All equipment moved 0.7 mile SE	September 12, 1957
HUNTINGDON	All equipment moved 0.7 mile NE	February 25, 1957
MT. POCONO 2 N AP	Rain gage and recording gage moved 75 feet NE	August 20, 1957
SHADE GAP	All equipment moved 0.2 mile NE Station name should not have been changed	July 9, 1957
SUNBURY	Temperature equipment added	August 1, 1957
WIND GAP	All equipment moved 500 feet NW	August 21, 1957

See reference notes following Station Index

TOTAL PRECIPITATION

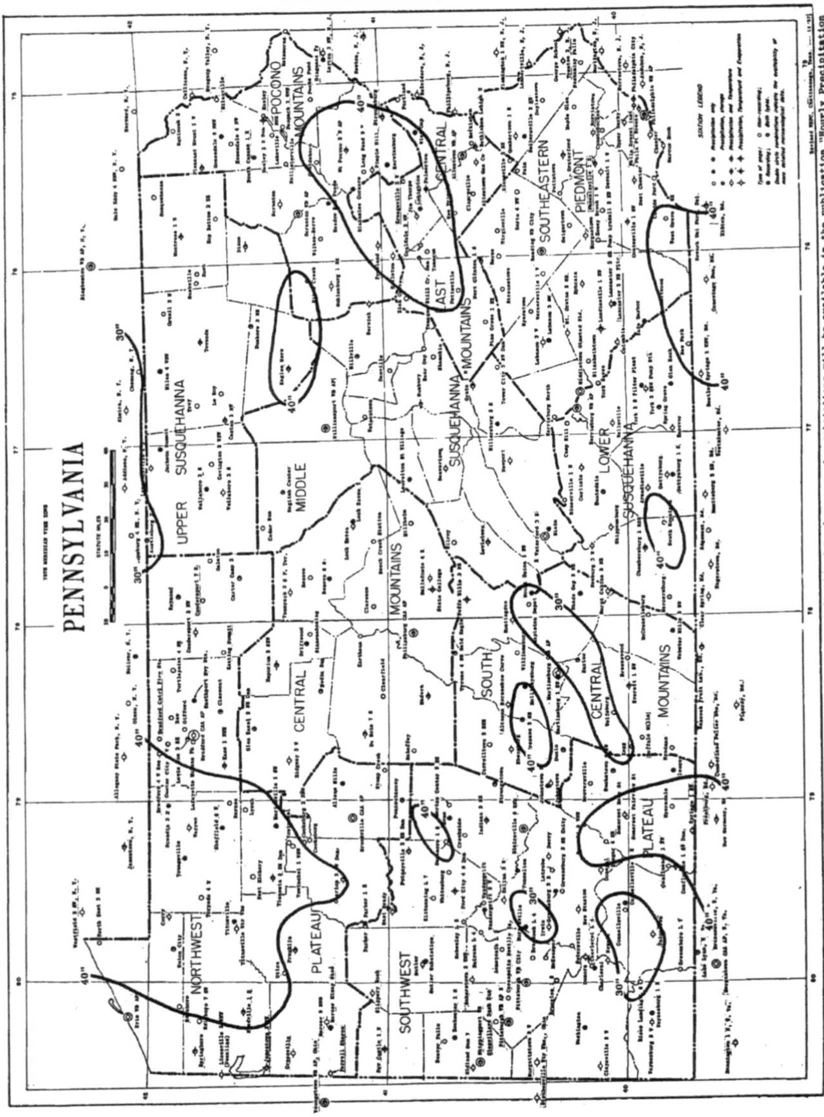

Isolines are drawn through points of approximately equal values. Hourly precipitation data from recorder substations will be available in the publication "Hourly Precipitation Data".

AVERAGE TEMPERATURE

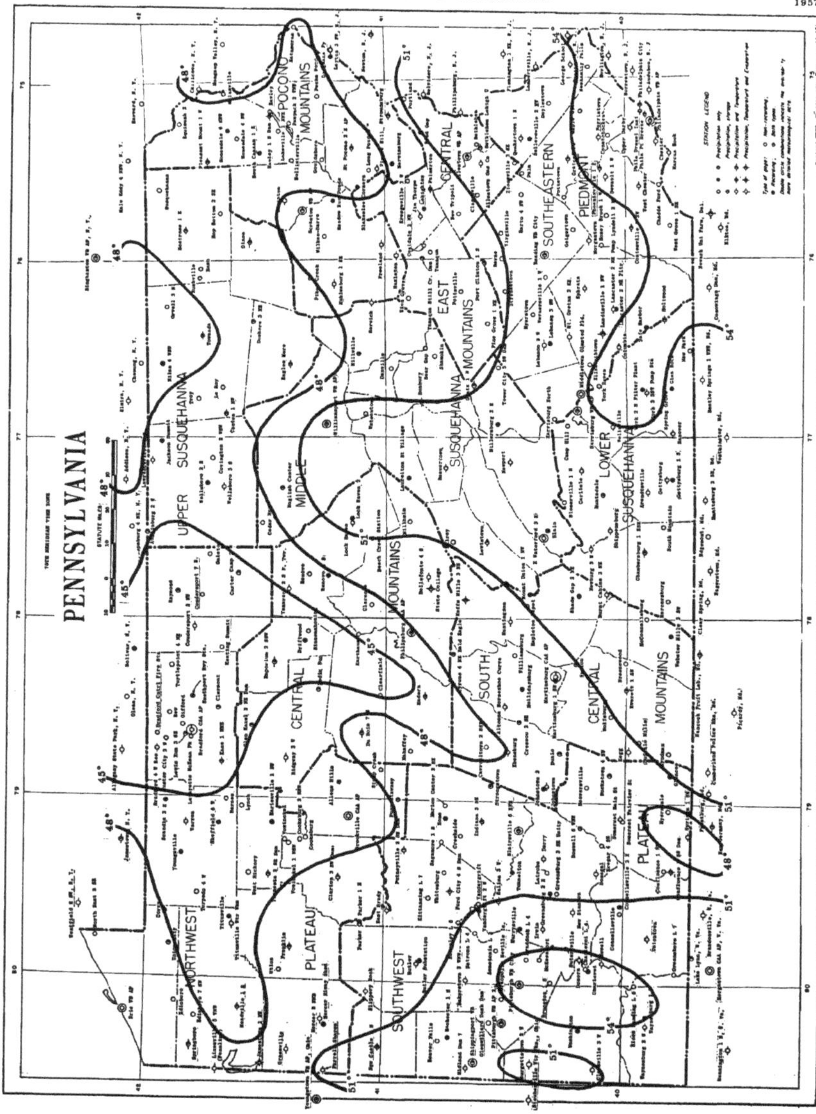

Isolines are drawn through points of approximately equal values. Hourly precipitation data from recorder substations will be available in the publication "Hourly Precipitation Data".

STATION INDEX

Station	Index No.	County	Drainage‡	Latitude	Longitude	Elevation	Years of record: Temp.	Years of record: Precip.	Years of record: Evap.	Opened or closed during yr.: Month opened	Opened or closed during yr.: Month closed	Refer to tables
ACMETONIA LOCK 3	0022	ALLEGHENY	1	40 32	79 49	748		53				2
ALLENS MILLS	0099	JEFFERSON	1	41 12	78 55	1600						C
ALLENTOWN WB AIRPORT	0106	LEHIGH	9	40 39	75 26	376	19	17				1 2 3 C
ALLENTOWN GAS CO	0111	LEHIGH	9	40 36	75 28	254	36	46				1 2 3
ALTOONA HORSESHOE CURVE	0134	BLAIR	6	40 30	78 29	1500	62	73				1 2 3
ARENDTSVILLE	0229	ADAMS	15	39 55	77 18	710	35	35				1 2 3
ARTEMAS 1 WNW	0259	BEDFORD	12	39 45	78 28	1250	5	5			JULY	1 2 3 C
AUSTINBURG 2 W	0313	TIOGA	15	42 00	77 32	1590		21				2 C
BAKERSTOWN 3 WNW	0355	ALLEGHENY	1	40 39	79 59	1230	10	10				1 2 3
BARNES	0409	WARREN	1	41 40	79 02	1310		17				2
BARTO 4 NW	0428	BERKS	14	40 26	75 39	312		1				2
BEAR GAP	0457	NORTH'LAND	15	40 50	76 30	900		12				2
BEAVER FALLS	0475	BEAVER	2	40 46	80 19	760		49				2
BEAVERTOWN	0482	SNYDER	15	40 45	77 10	640	11	11				1 2 3
BEECH CREEK STATION	0499	CENTRE	16	41 04	77 34	620		5			DEC	2
BELLEFONTE A S	0530	CENTRE	16	40 51	77 47	1110	29	41				1 2 3
BERNE	0599	BERKS	14	40 31	76 00	325		1				2
BERWICK	0611	COLUMBIA	15	41 04	76 15	570	12	12				1 2 3
BETHLEHEM	0629	NORTHAMPTON	9	40 37	75 22	400		–				2
#BETHLEHEM LEHIGH UNIVERSITY	0634	NORTHAMPTON	9	40 36	75 23	450	56	73				1 2 3 C
BLAIN	0725	PERRY	15	40 20	77 31	750						C
BLAIRSVILLE 6 ENE	0736	INDIANA	4	40 27	79 09	2048	12	21				1 2 3
BLAKESLEE CORNERS	0743	MONROE	9	41 06	75 36	1650						C
BLOSERVILLE 1 N	0763	CUMBERLAND	15	40 16	77 22	650		45				2
BOSWELL 6 WNW	0820	SOMERSET	1	40 10	79 08	2570		20				2 C
BRADDOCK LOCK 2	0861	ALLEGHENY	10	40 24	79 52	725		23				2
BRADFORD CAA AIRPORT	0865	MC KEAN	1	41 48	78 38	2150	0	0		JULY		1 2 3
BRADFORD CENTRAL FIRE STA	0867	MC KEAN	1	41 57	78 39	1500		10				2
BRADFORD 4 W RESERVOIR	0868	MC KEAN	1	41 57	78 44	1680	31	31				1 2 3
BREEZEWOOD	0905	BEDFORD	6	40 00	78 14	1352	10	16				2
BROOKVILLE CAA AIRPORT	1002	JEFFERSON	1	41 09	79 06	1417	45	66				1 2 3
BRUCETON 1 S	1033	ALLEGHENY	10	40 18	79 59	1065		22				2
BUCKSTOWN 1 SE	1073	SOMERSET	4	40 04	78 50	2460						C
BUFFALO MILLS	1087	BEDFORD	12	39 57	78 39	1318		33				2
BURGETTSTOWN 2 W	1105	WASHINGTON	11	40 23	80 26	980	10	10				1 2 3
BURNT CABINS 2 NE	1115	HUNTINGDON	6	40 05	77 52	990	16	16				1 2 3
#BUTLER	1130	BUTLER	2	40 52	79 54	1100	34	44				1 2 3
BUTLER SUBSTATION	1135	BUTLER	2	40 51	79 53	1140						C
CAMP HILL	1198	CUMBERLAND	15	40 15	76 55	461		12				2
CAMP KLINE	1203	LYCOMING	16	41 16	77 20	590		0		DEC		2
CANTON 1 NW	1215	BRADFORD	15	41 40	76 52	1520	14	18				1 2 3 C
CARLISLE	1234	CUMBERLAND	15	40 12	77 11	460	89	69				1 2 3
CARROLLTOWN 2 SSE	1255	CAMBRIA	16	40 35	78 42	2040		14				2
CARTER CAMP 2 W	1262	POTTER	16	41 37	77 45	2030		19				2 C
CEDAR RUN	1301	LYCOMING	16	41 31	77 27	800		39				2
CHADDS FORD	1342	DELAWARE	5	39 52	75 37	170		17				2
CHAMBERSBURG 1 ESE	1354	FRANKLIN	12	39 56	77 38	640	57	62				1 2 3 C
CHARLEROI	1372	WASHINGTON	10	40 08	79 55	1040						C
CHARLEROI LOCK 4	1377	WESTMORELAND	10	40 09	79 54	749		72				2
#CHESTER	1423	DELAWARE	5	39 51	75 22	86	7	7				1 2 3
CLARENCE	1480	CENTRE	16	41 08	77 56	1410		8				2
CLARION 3 SW	1485	CLARION	1	41 12	79 26	1114	15	50				1 2 3 C
CLAUSSVILLE	1505	LEHIGH	9	40 37	75 39	670		12				2
CLAYSVILLE 3 W	1512	WASHINGTON	11	40 07	80 28	1000	55	55				1 2 3
CLEARFIELD	1519	CLEARFIELD	16	41 01	78 26	1100		49				2
CLERMONT	1529	MC KEAN	1	41 41	78 30	2104		7				2 C
COALDALE 2 NW	1572	SCHUYLKILL	9	40 50	75 56	1026		35				2
COATESVILLE 1 SW	1589	CHESTER	5	39 58	75 50	342	70	70				1 2 3 C
COATESVILLE	1594	CHESTER	5	39 59	75 49	340		9			AUG	2
COLUMBIA	1675	LANCASTER	15	40 02	76 30	300	15	15				1 2 3
CONFLUENCE 1 SW DAM	1705	SOMERSET	17	39 48	79 22	1490	12	12	–			1 2 3 4 C
CONFLUENCE 1 NW	1710	FAYETTE	17	39 50	79 22	1331		83				2
CONNELLSVILLE	1723	FAYETTE	17	40 01	79 36	870		19				2
CONNELLSVILLE 2 E	1729	FAYETTE	17	40 01	79 33	1300						C
CONSHOHOCKEN	1737	MONTGOMERY	5	40 04	75 19	70		34				2
COOKSBURG	1749	CLARION	1	41 20	79 13	1180		3				2
COOKSBURG 2 NNW	1752	CLARION	1	41 21	79 13	1460		3				2
CORAOPOLIS NEVILLE ISLAND	1773	ALLEGHENY	11	40 30	80 05	720		49				2
CORRY	1790	ERIE	1	41 55	79 39	1440	42	42				1 2 3
COUDERSPORT 3 NW	1806	POTTER	1	41 49	78 03	2020	2	2				1 2 3
COUDERSPORT 7 E	1809	POTTER	1	41 46	77 53	2425		11				2
COVINGTON 2 WSW	1833	TIOGA	15	41 44	77 07	1745		1				2
CREEKSIDE	1881	INDIANA	1	40 41	79 12	1035		17				2
CRESSON 2 SE	1895	CAMBRIA	6	40 27	78 34	2540		20				2 C
CUSTER CITY 2 W	1978	MC KEAN	1	41 55	78 41	2120		10				2
DANVILLE	2013	MONTOUR	15	40 58	76 37	460		17				2
DERRY	2108	WESTMORELAND	4	40 20	79 18	1150	60	60				1 2 3
DEVAULT 1 W	2116	CHESTER	14	40 05	75 33	360	7	7				1 2 3
DINGMANS FERRY	2160	PIKE	5	41 13	74 52	364						C
DIXON	2171	WYOMING	15	41 34	75 54	620	9	9				1 2 3 C
DONEGAL	2183	WESTMORELAND	17	40 07	79 23	1746	14	14				1 2 3
DONORA	2190	WASHINGTON	10	40 10	79 52	900	31	31				1 2 3
DOYLESTOWN	2221	BUCKS	5	40 18	75 08	393		67				2
DRIFTWOOD	2245	CAMERON	16	41 20	78 08	880						C
DU BOIS 7 E	2265	CLEARFIELD	16	41 06	78 38	1670	2	20				1 2 3 C
DUNLO	2298	CAMBRIA	4	40 17	78 43	2410		17				C
DUSHORE 3 NE	2324	SULLIVAN	16	41 33	76 21	1750		8				2 C
EAGLES MERE	2343	SULLIVAN	16	41 24	76 35	2020	15	21				1 2 3 C
EAST BRADY	2363	CLARION	1	40 59	79 37	820	9	9				1 2 3
EAST WATERFORD 3 E	2459	PERRY	6	40 21	77 33	2125	11	18			INAC	1 2 3
EBENSBURG	2466	CAMBRIA	4	40 29	78 43	2090	40	40				1 2 3
EDINBORO	2514	ERIE	1	41 52	80 08	1220	10	16				2
†EDINBORO 7 SW	2519	CRAWFORD	1	41 50	80 15	1120		1		APR		2
ELIZABETHTOWN	2560	LANCASTER	15	40 09	76 37	460		12				2
EMPORIUM 2 SSW	2634	CAMERON	16	41 28	78 15	1735	1	1				1 2 3 C
ENGLISH CENTER	2644	LYCOMING	16	41 26	77 17	881		18				2 C
EPHRATA	2662	LANCASTER	15	40 11	76 10	465	55	64				1 2 3
EQUINUNK	2669	WAYNE	5	41 51	75 13	900		11			JAN	2
EQUINUNK 2	2671	WAYNE	5	41 51	75 13	910		12		JAN		2
ERIE CAA AIRPORT	2682	ERIE	8	42 05	80 12	732	13	13				1 2 3
EVERETT 1 SW	2721	BEDFORD	6	40 00	78 23	1020	37	37				1 2 3 C
FARRELL-SHARON	2814	MERCER	2	41 14	80 30	865	45	46				1 2 3
FORD CITY 4 S DAM	2942	ARMSTRONG	1	40 43	79 30	950	14	14	12			1 2 3 4 C
FRANKLIN	3028	VENANGO	1	41 23	79 49	987	63	84				1 2 3 C
FREELAND	3056	LUZERNE	15	41 01	75 54	1900	63	43				1 2 3
GALETON	3130	POTTER	16	41 44	77 39	1325		27				2
GEIGERTOWN	3189	BERKS	14	40 13	75 50	400		12				2
GEORGE SCHOOL	3200	BUCKS	5	40 13	74 56	135	51	51				1 2 3
#GETTYSBURG	3218	ADAMS	12	39 50	77 14	540	81	83				1 2 3
GETTYSBURG 1 S	3223	ADAMS	12	39 48	77 14	560						C
GIFFORD	3237	MC KEAN	1	41 51	78 36	2220		10				2
GLENCOE	3298	SOMERSET	12	39 49	78 51	1620						C
GLEN HAZEL 2 NE DAM	3311	ELK	1	41 34	78 36	1725		6				2 C
GLEN ROCK	3330	YORK	15	39 48	76 44	620						C
GLENWILLARD DASH DAM	3343	ALLEGHENY	11	40 33	80 13	705		13				2
GOULDSBORO	3394	WAYNE	9	41 15	75 27	1890	20	42				2
GRATERFORD	3435	MONTGOMERY	14	40 14	75 27	160	1	42				1 2 3 C
GRATZ 1 N	3438	DAUPHIN	15	40 38	76 43	760	7	7				1 2 3 C
GREENSBORO LOCK 7	3503	GREENE	10	39 47	79 55	808		76				2
GREENSBURG 2 E	3515	WESTMORELAND	10	40 18	79 31	1225						C
GREENSBURG 3 SE UNITY	3516	WESTMORELAND	10	40 17	79 30	1245	37	49				2
GREENVILLE	3526	MERCER	2	41 24	80 23	1026	59	59				1 2 3
HANOVER	3662	YORK	15	39 48	76 59	600	54	54				1 2 3
#HARRISBURG WB AIRPORT	3699	YORK	15	40 13	76 51	335	69	69				1 2 3 C
HARRISBURG NORTH	3704	DAUPHIN	15	40 18	76 54	323		40				2
HAWLEY	3758	WAYNE	5	41 29	75 10	880	34	48				2
HAWLEY 1 S DAM	3761	WAYNE	5	41 28	75 11	1200	22	26	22			1 2 3 4 C
HOLLIDAYSBURG	4001	BLAIR	6	40 26	78 24	960						C
HOLLISTERVILLE	4008	WAYNE	5	41 25	75 26	1360		30				2
#HOLTWOOD	4019	LANCASTER	15	39 50	76 20	187	38	43				1 2 3 C
HOME	4027	INDIANA	1	40 45	79 06	1220						C
HONESDALE 4 NW	4043	WAYNE	5	41 37	75 19	1410		12				2
HONESDALE 6 NNW	4044	WAYNE	5	41 39	75 17	1050						C
HONEY BROOK 1 W	4047	CHESTER	5	40 06	75 56	700		0		AUG		2
HOOVERSVILLE	4058	SOMERSET	4	40 09	78 55	1670		19				2
HOP BOTTOM 2 SE	4086	SUSQUEHANNA	15	41 43	75 43	900		13				2
HUNTINGDON	4159	HUNTINGDON	6	40 30	78 01	678	70	70				1 2 3
HUNTSDALE	4166	CUMBERLAND	15	40 06	77 18	610		17				2 C
HYNDMAN	4190	BEDFORD	12	39 49	78 43	920		45				2
INDIANA 3 SE	4214	INDIANA	4	40 36	79 07	1102	55	56				1 2 3 C
IRWIN	4276	WESTMORELAND	10	40 20	79 42	1100	55	61				1 2 3
JACKSON SUMMIT	4304	TIOGA	15	41 57	77 01	1690						C
JAMESTOWN 2 NW	4325	CRAWFORD	2	41 30	80 28	1050	16	18	16			1 2 3 4 C
JERSEY SHORE	4363	LYCOMING	16	41 12	77 15	541		0		DEC		2
JIM THORPE	4370	CARBON	9	40 52	75 45	830	65	65				1 2 3
#JOHNSTOWN	4385	CAMBRIA	4	40 20	78 55	1214	64	76				1 2 3
JOHNSTOWN 2	4390	CAMBRIA	4	40 19	78 55	1275						C
KANE 1 NNE	4432	MC KEAN	1	41 41	78 48	1750	14	42				1 2 3 C
KARTHAUS	4450	CLEARFIELD	16	41 07	78 07	950		17				2
KEATING SUMMIT	4466	POTTER	16	41 41	78 11	1840		8			DEC	2
KEGG	4481	BEDFORD	6	39 59	78 43	1280	7	7				1 2 3
KITTANNING LOCK 7	4611	ARMSTRONG	1	40 49	79 32	790		7				2
KREGAR 4 SE	4667	WESTMORELAND	17	40 06	79 14	2550		16				2
KRESGEVILLE 3 W	4672	CARBON	9	40 54	75 34	720		15				2
LAFAYETTE MC KEAN PARK	4706	MC KEAN	1	41 48	78 40	2130		10				2
LAKEVILLE 1 NNE	4733	WAYNE	5	41 27	75 16	1440		30				2
LANCASTER 2 NE PUMP STA	4758	LANCASTER	15	40 03	76 17	255	56	70				1 2 3
LANCASTER 2 NE FILTER PLT	4763	LANCASTER	15	40 03	76 17	270						C
LANDISVILLE 2 NW	4778	LANCASTER	15	40 07	76 26	360	12	12	7			1 2 3 4 C
LATROBE	4832	WESTMORELAND	4	40 19	79 23	1000		14			JUNE	2
LAURELTON STATE VILLAGE	4853	UNION	15	40 54	77 13	880						C
LAWRENCEVILLE 2 S	4873	TIOGA	15	41 59	77 07	1000	60	60				1 2 3
LEBANON 3 W	4891	LEBANON	15	40 20	76 29	460	69	74				1 2 3
LEBANON 3 SW	4896	LEBANON	15	40 19	76 28	490						C
LEHIGHTON	4934	CARBON	9	40 50	75 43	580		23				2 C
LE ROY	4972	BRADFORD	15	41 41	76 43	1040		20				2
LEWIS RUN 3 SE	4984	MC KEAN	1	41 50	78 39	1740		10				2 C
LEWISTOWN	4992	MIFFLIN	6	40 35	77 35	480	19	19				1 2 3 C
LINESVILLE 5 WNW	5050	CRAWFORD	2	41 41	80 31	1020	6	40				1 2 3
LOCK HAVEN	5104	CLINTON	16	41 08	77 27	570	66	66				1 2 3
LOCK HAVEN 2	5109	CLINTON	16	41 08	77 27	630						C
LONG POND 2 W	5160	MONROE	9	41 05	75 30	1860		11				2
LYNCH	5275	FOREST	1	41 36	79 09	1295		0		AUG		2
LYNDELL 2 NW	5279	CHESTER	5	40 05	75 46	–		1				2
MADERA	5336	CLEARFIELD	16	40 50	78 26	1460	–	–				1 2 3 C
MAHAFFEY	5342	CLEARFIELD	16	40 53	78 44	1280		8				2
MAPLE GLEN	5368	MONTGOMERY	5	40 11	75 11	380		12				2
MAPLETON DEPOT	5381	HUNTINGDON	6	40 24	77 56	580		19				2
MARCUS HOOK	5390	DELAWARE	5	39 48	75 25	12	31	31				1 2 3
MARIENVILLE 1 SW	5400	FOREST	1	41 27	79 09	1700						C
MARION CENTER 2 SE	5408	INDIANA	1	40 45	79 02	1610		15				2
MARTINSBURG 1 SW	5453	BLAIR	6	40 18	78 20	1360						C
MARTINSBURG CAA AIRPORT	5454	BLAIR	6	40 16	78 19	1463	15	15				1 2 3
MATAMORAS	5470	PIKE	5	41 22	74 42	439		53				2
MAYBURG	5490	FOREST	1	41 36	79 13	1150		12			AUG	2
MC CONNELLSBURG	5526	FULTON	12	39 56	78 00	895		25				2
MC KEESPORT	5573	ALLEGHENY	10	40 21	79 52	720		29				2
MEADOW RUN PONDS	5601	LUZERNE	15	41 13	75 40	1995						C
MEADVILLE 1 S	5606	CRAWFORD	1	41 38	80 10	1065	63	64				1 2 3 C
MEDIX RUN	5627	ELK	16	41 17	78 24	1100		16				2 C
MERCER 2 NNE	5651	MERCER	2	41 15	80 13	1160	6	6				1 2 3
MERCER HIGHWAY SHED	5654	MERCER	2	41 14	80 15	1250						C
MERCERSBURG	5662	FRANKLIN	12	39 50	77 54	605		15				2
MERWINSBURG	5676	MONROE	9	40 58	75 28	970						C
MEYERSDALE	5684	SOMERSET	17	39 49	79 02	2040		18		JULY		2
MEYERSDALE 1 ENE	5685	SOMERSET	17	39 49	79 01	2290		2			JULY	2
MIDDLETOWN OLMSTED FIELD	5705	DAUPHIN	15	40 11	76 46	303	27	27				1 2 3
MIDLAND DAM 7	5710	BEAVER	11	40 38	80 28	689	20	21				1 2 3
MILAN 4 WNW	5732	BRADFORD	15	41 56	76 35	1448						C
MILANVILLE	5738	WAYNE	5	41 40	75 04	760		12				2
MILLERSBURG 2 E	5775	DAUPHIN	15	40 32	76 56	560						C
MILLHEIM	5790	CENTRE	15	40 54	77 29	1090		–				2
MILLVILLE 2 SW	5817	COLUMBIA	15	41 06	76 34	860		8				2 C
MILROY	5825	MIFFLIN	6	40 43	77 35	770		15				2
MONTROSE 1 E	5915	SUSQUEHANNA	15	41 50	75 51	1630	52	52				1 2 3 C
MORGANTOWN	5956	BERKS	15	40 09	75 54	595	7	7				1 2 3
MOUNT GRETNA 2 SE	6028	LANCASTER	15	40 14	76 26	670	7	7				1 2 3
MOUNT POCONO 2 N AIRPORT	6055	MONROE	5	41 09	75 22	1915	–	–				1 2 3 C
MOUNT UNION 1 N	6067	MIFFLIN	6	40 24	77 53	820						C
MUHLENBURG 1 SE	6090	LUZERNE	15	41 13	76 08	1110	5	5				1 2 3
MURRYSVILLE	6111	WESTMORELAND	10	40 26	79 42	880						C
MYERSTOWN	6126	LEBANON	14	40 22	76 18	480		17				2
NATRONA LOCK 4	6151	ALLEGHENY	1	40 37	79 43	800		30				2
NEFFS MILLS 3 NE	6174	HUNTINGDON	6	40 40	77 55	900	15	15	–			C
NESHAMINY FALLS	6194	BUCKS	5	40 09	74 57	60	29	42				2
NEWBURG 3 W	6225	FRANKLIN	15	40 09	77 37	745	16	16				1 2 3
NEW CASTLE 1 N	6233	LAWRENCE	2	41 01	80 22	825	74	71				1 2 3 C
NEWELL	6246	FAYETTE	10	40 05	79 54	805	44	36				1 2 3
NEW PARK	6289	YORK	15	39 44	76 30	780		33				2
NEWPORT	6397	PERRY	6	40 29	77 08	400	10	27				1 2 3
NEW STANTON	6310	WESTMORELAND	10	40 13	79 36	980	6	19				1 2 3
NEW TRIPOLI	6326	LEHIGH	14	40 41	75 45	570		19				2
NORRISTOWN	6370	MONTGOMERY	14	40 07	75 21	75	7	10				1 2 3
NORTH EAST 2 SE	6396	ERIE	8	42 12	79 49	1060		8				2
ORWELL 3 N	6621	BRADFORD	15	41 55	76 16	1620		14				2
PALM	6681	MONTGOMERY	14	40 26	75 32	385		16				2
#PALMERTON	6689	CARBON	9	40 48	75 37	436	40	41				1 2 3 C
PALMYRA	6694	LEBANON	15	40 18	76 35	480		1			MAR	2
PARKER	6721	ARMSTRONG	1	41 05	79 41	1140		7				2
PARKER 1 E	6724	CLARION	1	41 06	79 40	1100						C
PAUPACK 2 WNW	6762	PIKE	5	41 24	75 14	1360		41				2
PECKS POND	6786	PIKE	5	41 17	75 06	1380		12				2
#PHIL DREXEL INST OF TEC	6879	PHILADELPHIA	14	39 57	75 11	30	–	–				1 2 3
PHILADELPHIA WB AIRPORT	6889	PHILADELPHIA	5	39 53	75 15	7	16	16				1 2 3 C
#PHILADELPHIA POINT BREEZE	6899	PHILADELPHIA	5	3955	75 12	32	33	33				1 2 3 C
PHILADELPHIA SHAWMONT	6904	PHILADELPHIA	5	40 02	75 15	70	41	62			JUNE	1 2 3
#PHILADELPHIA CITY	6909	PHILADELPHIA	5	39 57	75 09	26	86	86			OCT	1 2 3 C
PHILIPSBURG CAA AIRPORT	6916	CENTRE	6	40 54	78 05	1918	15	15				1 2 3 C
PHOENIXVILLE 1 E	6927	CHESTER	14	40 07	75 30	105	46	48				1 2 3 C
PIKES CREEK	6959	LUZERNE	15	41 18	76 08	1320		20				2 C

STATION INDEX

Station	Index No.	County	Drainage‡	Latitude	Longitude	Elevation	Years of record: Temp.	Years of record: Precip.	Evap.	Opened or closed during yr.: Month opened	Month closed	Refer to tables
PIMPLE HILL	6944	MONROE	9	41 02	75 30	2215	-	-	7			1 2 3 4
PINE GROVE 1 NE	6954	SCHUYLKILL	15	40 34	76 22	535		33				2
PITTSBURGH WB AIRPORT 2	6993	ALLEGHENY	11	40 30	80 13	1151	6	6				1 2 3 C
#PITTSBURGH WB CITY	6997	ALLEGHENY	11	40 27	80 00	749	87	87				1 2 3 C
PLEASANT MOUNT 1 W	7029	WAYNE	5	41 44	75 27	1800	7	36				1 2 3 C
PORT CLINTON	7116	SCHUYLKILL	14	40 35	76 02	450	19	19				1 2 3 C
PORTLAND	7127	NORTHAMPTON	5	40 55	75 06	297		12			INAC	2
POTTSVILLE	7161	SCHUYLKILL	14	40 42	76 11	690		14				2
PUNXSUTAWNEY	7217	JEFFERSON	1	40 57	79 00	1298		35				C
PUTNEYVILLE 2 SE DAM	7229	ARMSTRONG	1	40 55	79 17	1270	14	14				1 2 3 C
QUAKERTOWN 1 E	7239	BUCKS	5	40 26	75 20	490	71	73				1 2 3
RAYMOND	7310	POTTER	13	41 52	77 52	2220		4				2 C
#READING WB CITY	7318	BERKS	14	40 20	75 58	266	60	88				1 2 3 C
RENOVO	7409	CLINTON	16	41 20	77 46	660		60				2
RENOVO 5 S	7410	CLINTON	16	41 14	77 46	2035						C
REW	7425	MC KEAN	1	41 54	78 32	2250		10				2
RICES LANDING LOCK 6	7443	GREENE	10	39 57	80 00	775		23				2
RIDGWAY 3 W	7477	ELK	1	41 25	78 47	1420	42	51				1 2 3
ROCHESTER 1 N	7540	BEAVER	2	40 43	80 18	900						C
RUSH	7694	SUSQUEHANNA	15	41 47	76 03	1000		13				2
RUSHVILLE	7727	SUSQUEHANNA	15	41 47	76 07	870		-				2
SAFE HARBOR	7732	LANCASTER	15	39 55	76 23	270						C
SAGAMORE 1 S	7739	INDIANA	1	40 46	79 14	1320		17				2
SALINA 3 W	7782	WESTMORELAND	7	40 31	79 33	1109	5	5				1 2 3
SAXTON	7846	BEDFORD	6	40 12	78 15	780		17				2 C
SCANDIA 2 E	7855	WARREN	1	41 55	79 01	2040						C
SCHENLEY LOCK 5	7863	ARMSTRONG	1	40 41	79 40	783		79				2
#SCRANTON	7902	LACKAWANNA	15	41 25	75 40	746	57	57				1 2 3
SCRANTON WB AIRPORT	7905	LUZERNE	15	41 20	75 44	956	10	10				1 2 3 C
SELINSGROVE CAA AIRPORT	7931	SNYDER	15	40 49	76 52	437	67	67			AUG	1 2 3
SELLERSVILLE 2 NW	7938	BUCKS	5	40 23	75 20	530						C
†SHADE GAP	7965	HUNTINGDON	6	40 11	77 52	920						C
SHAMOKIN	7978	NORTH'LAND	15	40 48	76 33	770		53				2
SHEFFIELD 6 W	8026	WARREN	1	41 41	79 09	1940						C
SHIPPENSBURG	8073	FRANKLIN	15	40 03	77 32	709	25	29				1 2 3
SHIPPINGPORT WB	8078	BEAVER	11	40 37	80 26	740	3	3			DEC	1 2 3 C
SINNEMAHONING	8145	CAMERON	16	41 19	78 05	790		7				2
SIZERVILLE	8155	CAMERON	16	41 36	78 11	1230		0		DEC		2
SLIPPERY ROCK	8184	BUTLER	2	41 04	80 03	1345	-	-				1 2 3
SMETHPORT HIGHWAY SHED	8190	MC KEAN	1	41 48	78 27	1510						C
SOMERSET FAIRVIEW STREET	8244	SOMERSET	17	40 01	79 05	2140		-				2
SOMERSET MAIN STREET	8249	SOMERSET	17	40 01	79 05	2150	87	74				1 2 3
SOUTH CANAAN 1 NE	8275	WAYNE	5	41 31	75 24	1400						C
SOUTH MOUNTAIN	8308	FRANKLIN	12	39 51	77 30	1520		18				2
SPRINGBORO	8359	CRAWFORD	8	41 48	80 23	900	3	3				1 2 3 C
SPRING GROVE	8379	YORK	15	39 52	76 52	470		17				2 C
SPRINGS 1 SW	8395	SOMERSET	17	39 44	79 10	2500	38	38				1 2 3
#STATE COLLEGE	8449	CENTRE	16	40 48	77 52	1175	70	73	1			1 2 3 4CG
STRAUSSTOWN	8570	BERKS	14	40 29	76 11	600		12				2
STRONGSTOWN	8589	INDIANA	4	40 33	78 55	1880						C
STROUDSBURG	8596	MONROE	5	40 59	75 12	480	40	40				1 2 3 C
STUMP CREEK	8610	JEFFERSON	1	41 01	78 50	1320		17				2
SUNBURY	8668	NORTH'LAND	15	40 51	76 48	440	67	67				1 2 3 C
SUSQUEHANNA	8692	SUSQUEHANNA	15	41 57	75 36	1020		23				2
SUTERSVILLE	8699	ALLEGHENY	17	40 14	79 48	765		17				2
TAMAQUA	8758	SCHUYLKILL	14	40 48	75 58	830		16				2
TAMAQUA 4 N DAM	8763	SCHUYLKILL	14	40 51	75 59	1120		25				2 C
TAMARACK 2 S FIRE TOWER	8770	CLINTON	16	41 24	77 51	2220	15	16				1 2 3
TIONESTA 2 SE DAM	8873	FOREST	1	41 29	79 26	1200	14	21				1 2 3 C
TITUSVILLE	8885	CRAWFORD	1	41 38	79 40	1550						C
TITUSVILLE WATER WORKS	8888	CRAWFORD	1	41 38	79 42	1220	4	4				1 2 3
TORPEDO 4 W	8901	WARREN	1	41 47	79 32	1735		7				2
TOWANDA	8905	BRADFORD	15	41 46	76 26	760	63	63				1 2 3 C
TOWER CITY 5 SW	8910	DAUPHIN	15	40 31	76 37	745		12				2
TROY	8959	BRADFORD	15	41 47	76 47	1100		7				2
TUNNELTON	8989	INDIANA	4	40 27	79 23	890						C
TURTLEPOINT 4 NE	9002	MC KEAN	1	41 54	78 16	1640		7				2
TYRONE 4 NE BALD EAGLE	9024	BLAIR	6	40 43	78 12	1020		20				2 C
UNION CITY	9042	ERIE	1	41 54	79 50	1325		8				2 C
UNIONTOWN	9050	FAYETTE	10	39 54	79 44	1040	68	69				1 2 3
UPPER DARBY	9074	DELAWARE	5	39 58	75 18	222	8	8				1 2 3
UTICA	9099	VENANGO	1	41 26	79 57	1030		2				2
VANDERGRIFT	9128	WESTMORELAND	7	40 36	79 33	800		18				2
VANDERGRIFT 2 W	9133	WESTMORELAND	7	40 36	79 36	995						C
VIRGINVILLE	9196	BERKS	14	40 31	75 52	350		12				2
VOWINCKEL	9206	CLARION	1	41 25	79 14	1620		3				2
VOWINCKEL 1 WSW	9209	CLARION	1	41 24	79 15	1610		3				2
WARREN	9298	WARREN	1	41 51	79 08	1280	61	69				1 2 3
WASHINGTON	9312	WASHINGTON	11	40 11	80 14	1200						C
WATSONTOWN	9345	NORTH'LAND	16	41 05	76 52	490		10				2
WAYNESBURG 2 W	9362	GREENE	10	39 54	80 13	980	28	30				1 2 3
WAYNESBURG 1 E	9367	GREENE	10	39 54	80 10	940						C
WEBSTER MILLS 3 SW	9380	FULTON	12	39 49	78 05	920						C
WELLSBORO 3 S	9408	TIOGA	16	41 43	77 16	1920	8	8				1 2 3
WELLSBORO 2 E	9412	TIOGA	16	41 45	77 16	1550						C
WELLSVILLE	9420	YORK	15	40 03	76 57	500	11	11				1 2 3
WERNERSVILLE 1 W	9430	BERKS	14	40 20	76 06	405		20				2
WEST CHESTER	9464	CHESTER	5	39 58	75 36	440	102	107				1 2 3
WEST GROVE 1 E	9503	CHESTER	5	39 49	75 49	440		28				2
WEST HICKORY	9507	FOREST	1	41 34	79 25	1090		6				2
WHITESBURG	9655	ARMSTRONG	1	40 45	79 24	1530		17				2
WILKES-BARRE	9702	LUZERNE	15	41 15	75 52	610		72				2
WILLIAMSBURG	9714	BLAIR	6	40 28	78 12	860		-				2
WILLIAMSPORT WB AIRPORT	9728	LYCOMING	16	41 15	76 55	527	17	17				1 2 3 C
WIND GAP	9781	NORTHAMPTON	5	40 51	75 18	740						C
WOLFSBURG	9823	BEDFORD	6	40 03	78 32	1190		8				2
YORK 3 SSW PUMP STATION	9933	YORK	15	39 55	76 45	390	59	70				1 2 3
YORK 2 S FILTER PLANT	9938	YORK	15	39 56	76 44	640						C
YORK HAVEN	9950	YORK	15	40 07	76 43	310		37				2
YOUNGSVILLE	9966	WARREN	1	41 51	79 20	1225						C
ZION GROVE	9990	SCHUYLKILL	15	40 54	76 13	940		7				2
ZIONSVILLE 3 SE	9995	LEHIGH	14	40 27	75 27	660		8				2

‡ 1-ALLEGHENY; 2-BEAVER; 3- 4-CONEMAUGH; 5-DELAWARE; 6-JUNIATA; 7-KISKIMINETAS; 8-LAKE ERIE; 9-LEIGH; 10-MONONGAHELA; 11-OHIO; 12-POTOMAC; 13-ST. LAWRENCE; 14-SCHUYLKILL; 15-SUSQUEHANNA; 16-WEST BRANCH; 17-YOUGHIOGHENY

REFERENCE NOTES

Additional information regarding the climate of Pennsylvania may be obtained by writing to the State Climatologist at Weather Bureau Airport Station, Harrisburg State Airport, New Cumberland, Pennsylvania or to any Weather Bureau Office near you.

Unless otherwise indicated, dimensional units used in this bulletin are: Temperature in °F; precipitation and evaporation in inches, and wind movement in miles.

Evaporation is measured in the standard Weather Bureau type pan of 4 foot diameter unless otherwise shown by footnote following Table 4.

Climatological divisions, outlined on the maps in this bulletin became effective with data for September 1956.

Figures and letters following the station name, such as 12 SSW, indicate distance in miles and direction from the post office.

Delayed data and corrections will be carried in the June and December issues of Climatological Data.

- \- No record.
- \+ Also later date (dates) or months.
- * Amount included in following measurement.
- \# Thermometers are generally exposed in a shelter located a few feet above sod covered ground; however the reference indicates that the thermometers are exposed in a shelter located on the roof of a building.
- B Adjusted to a full month.
- C Data for recorder stations denoted by "C" in the Refer to Tables column of the Station Index are processed for special purposes and published in "Hourly Precipitation Data". Length of record for recorder - only stations may be found in the annual issue of "Hourly Precipitation Data".
- E Amount is wholly or partially estimated.
- G In the "Refer to Tables" column of the Station Index the letter "G" indicates that soil temperatures are published.
- M One or more days record missing; if average value is entered, less than 10 days record is missing. See monthly Climatological Data for detailed daily record.
- T Trace, an amount too small to measure.
- V Includes total for previous month. V in annual column means total is for a two-year period.

Information concerning the history of changes in locations, elevations, exposures, etc., of substations through 1955 may be found in the publication "Substation History" for this state, soon to be issued. That publication, when available, may be obtained from the Superintendent of Documents, Government Printing Office, Washington, D. C. at a price to be announced. Similar information for regular Weather Bureau stations may be found in the latest annual issue of Local Climatological Data, obtained as indicated above, price 15 cents.

Subscription Price: 20 cents per copy, monthly and annual; $2.50 per year. (Yearly subscription includes the Annual Summary.) Checks, and money orders should be made payable to the Superintendent of Documents. Remittances and correspondence regarding subscriptions should be sent to the Superintendent of Documents, Government Printing Office, Washington 25, D. C.

USCOMM-WB-Asheville, N. C. --- 3/7/58 --- 1200

Lightning Source UK Ltd.
Milton Keynes UK
UKHW031416280119
336340UK00010B/781/P